Trapezoid: A four-sided figure with one pair of parallel sides
Area: $A = \frac{1}{2}h(b_1 + b_2)$

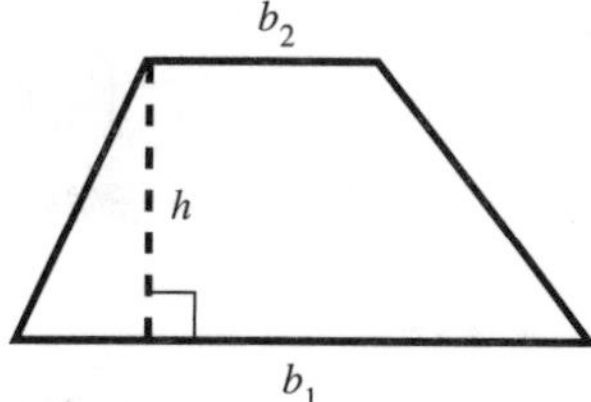

Parallelogram: A four-sided figure with opposite sides parallel
Area: $A = bh$

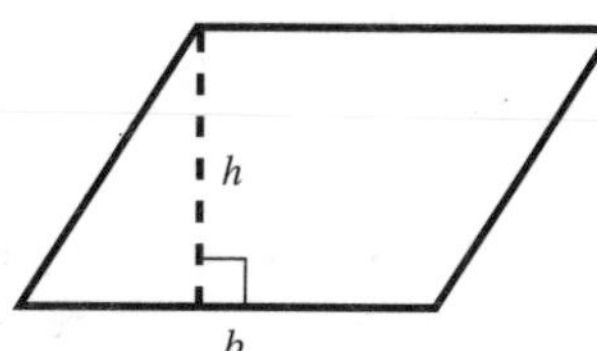

Rectangle: A four-sided figure with four right angles
Area: $A = LW$
Perimeter: $P = 2L + 2W$

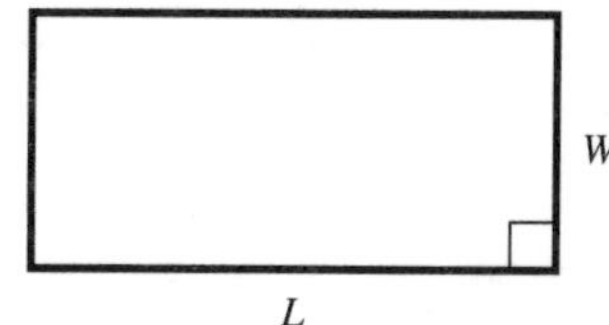

Rhombus: A four-sided figure with four equal sides
Perimeter: $P = 4a$

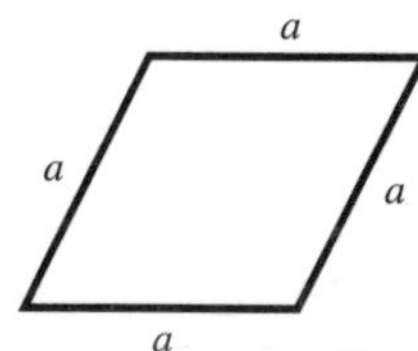

Square: A four-sided figure with four equal sides and four right angles
Area: $A = s^2$
Perimeter: $P = 4s$

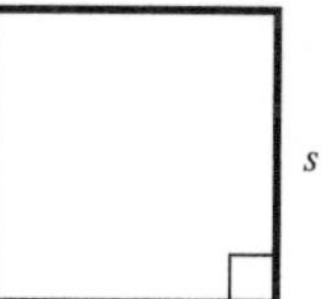

Circle
Area: $A = \pi r^2$
Circumference: $C = 2\pi r$
Diameter: $d = 2r$
Value of pi: $\pi \approx 3.14$

Sphere
Volume: $V = \frac{4}{3}\pi r^3$
Surface Area: $S = 4\pi r^2$

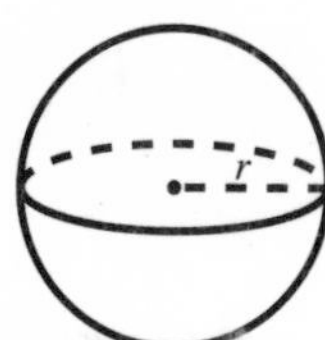

Right Circular Cone
Volume: $V = \frac{1}{3}\pi r^2 h$
Lateral Surface Area: $S = \pi r\sqrt{r^2 + h^2}$

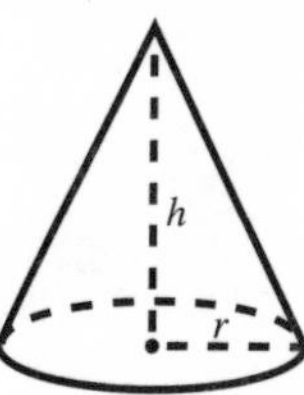

Right Circular Cylinder
Volume: $V = \pi r^2 h$
Lateral Surface Area: $S = 2\pi rh$

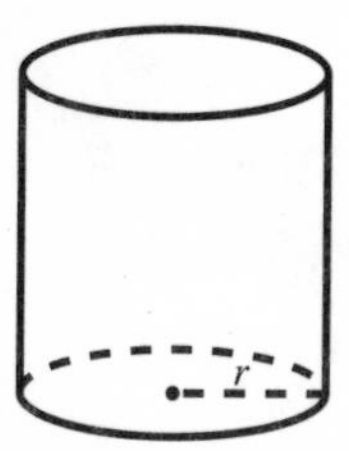

Rectangular Solid
Volume: $V = LWH$
Surface Area:
$A = 2LW + 2WH + 2LH$

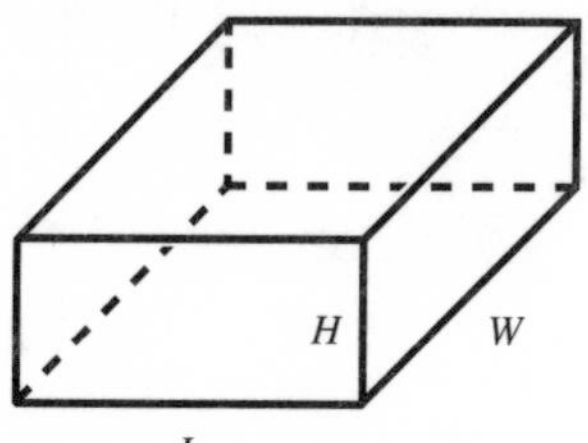

Learn how McGraw-Hill technology can make a difference for you and your students.

A course management site for McGraw-Hill math titles, MathZone™ combines book-specific practice and tutorial content with automatic, online assessment. You can utilize MathZone's algorithmic capabilities to generate multiple versions of assignments and quizzes, edit the problems and exercises we've provided, or create your own. MathZone's automatic gradebook function makes tracking student progress a snap. Learn more about MathZone by visiting www.mathzone.com.

ALEKS® individualizes assessment and learning by recognizing that students learn math in different ways, at different speeds. It is an artificial intelligence system that helps students take "ownership" of their learning process by enabling them to experience success, rather than feeling lost. It's like a tutor who teaches what each student is most ready to learn. To request your FREE 24-hour trial of ALEKS, visit our website at www.highed.aleks.com/guest.html.

NetTutor™ is an online tutoring system where your students can get live, one-on-one help. It requires no special software or downloads on the part of the student. All students need to do is connect to a website. NetTutor™ distinguishes itself from other online tutoring systems in its richness of special mathematical symbols and graphs, which allow the students to use the exact notation presented in their books.

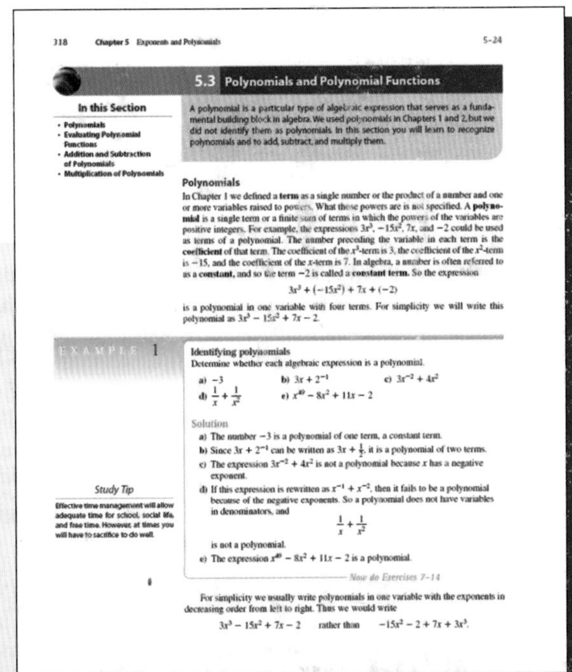

318 Chapter 5 Exponents and Polynomials 5-24

5.3 Polynomials and Polynomial Functions

In this Section

- Polynomials
- Evaluating Polynomial Functions
- Addition and Subtraction of Polynomials
- Multiplication of Polynomials

A polynomial is a particular type of algebraic expression that serves as a fundamental building block in algebra. We used polynomials in Chapters 1 and 2, but we did not identify them as polynomials. In this section you will learn to recognize polynomials and to add, subtract, and multiply them.

Polynomials

In Chapter 1 we defined a **term** as a single number or the product of a number and one or more variables raised to powers. What those powers are is not specified. A **polynomial** is a single term or a finite sum of terms in which the powers of the variables are positive integers. For example, the expressions $3x^3$, $-15x^2$, $7x$, and -2 could be used as terms of a polynomial. The number preceding the variable in each term is the **coefficient** of that term. The coefficient of the x^3-term is 3, the coefficient of the x^2-term is -15, and the coefficient of the x-term is 7. In algebra, a number is often referred to as a **constant**, and so the term -2 is called a **constant term.** So the expression

$$3x^3 + (-15x^2) + 7x + (-2)$$

is a polynomial in one variable with four terms. For simplicity we will write this polynomial as $3x^3 - 15x^2 + 7x - 2$.

EXAMPLE 1 Identifying polynomials

Determine whether each algebraic expression is a polynomial.

a) -3 b) $3x + 2^{-1}$ c) $3x^{-2} + 4x^2$
d) $\frac{1}{x} + \frac{1}{x^2}$ e) $x^{49} - 8x^2 + 11x - 2$

Solution

a) The number -3 is a polynomial of one term, a constant term.
b) Since $3x + 2^{-1}$ can be written as $3x + \frac{1}{2}$, it is a polynomial of two terms.
c) The expression $3x^{-2} + 4x^2$ is not a polynomial because x has a negative exponent.
d) If this expression is rewritten as $x^{-1} + x^{-2}$, then it fails to be a polynomial because of the negative exponents. So a polynomial does not have variables in denominators, and
$$\frac{1}{x} + \frac{1}{x^2}$$
is not a polynomial.
e) The expression $x^{49} - 8x^2 + 11x - 2$ is a polynomial.

Now do Exercises 7–14

Study Tip

Effective time management will allow adequate time for school, social life, and free time. However, at times you will have to sacrifice to do well.

For simplicity we usually write polynomials in one variable with the exponents in decreasing order from left to right. Thus we would write

$$3x^3 - 15x^2 + 7x - 2 \quad \text{rather than} \quad -15x^2 - 2 + 7x + 3x^3.$$

Experience the Difference

Mark Dugopolski's proven approach now has a cleaner, student-friendly design that is more appealing for students and instructors alike. After consulting with a panel of experienced instructors on the optimal page layout to use with their students, the entire textbook was redesigned to be more open, easy to read, and easy for the students to follow.

This new edition combines a strong emphasis on the skills needed to solve real-world applications with time-tested pedagogy that helps students prepare for future math courses. Critical thinking exercises are integrated, encouraging students to think creatively to solve problems that go beyond traditional skillbuilding exercises. Contact your McGraw-Hill sales representative or visit www.mhhe.com to request your complimentary copy.

ALGEBRA FOR COLLEGE STUDENTS with MATHZONE™ CD-ROM, Fourth Edition
by Mark Dugopolski
2006 copyright
Hardcover
ISBN 0-07-301929-1

ELEMENTARY ALGEBRA with MATHZONE™ CD-ROM,
Fifth Edition by Mark Dugopolski
2006 copyright
Hardcover
ISBN 0-07-301928-3

INTERMEDIATE ALGEBRA with MATHZONE™ CD-ROM,
Fifth Edition by Mark Dugopolski
2006 copyright
Hardcover
ISBN 0-07-301927-5

ELEMENTARY AND INTERMEDIATE ALGEBRA with MATHZONE™ CD-ROM,
Second Edition by Mark Dugopolski
2006 copyright
Hardcover
ISBN 0-07-301931-3

McGraw-Hill: Making a Difference in Teaching and Learning
Delivering tools to assist instructors • Making learning easier for students

0-07-319221-X t/a Dugopolski Math Series

Math Zone™ ■ Free ■ Easy ■ Has It All

MathZone's™ powerful feature set includes book-specific, assignable algorithmic content; ADA-compliant videos; and e-Professor animated solutions. MathZone provides students virtually unlimited practice through algorithmic quizzing and testing, and free live tutoring via NetTutor's™ whiteboard technology, and instructors can track their students' progress in the online gradebook.

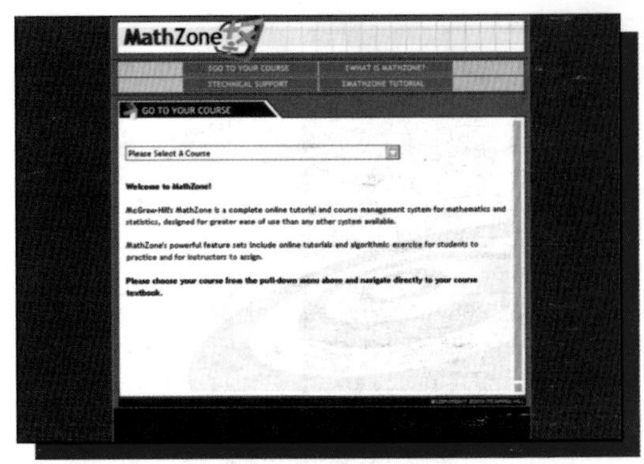

Free to you and your students

MathZone is provided for free with the purchase of a new McGraw-Hill math textbook. Each text is packaged with a registration code for the website at www.mathzone.com and comes with a MathZone CD-ROM.

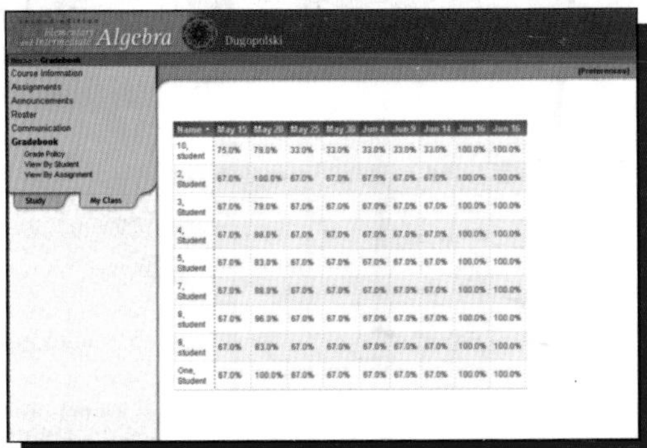

Easy to use

All functions for students and instructors are located within one login. The online course management system offers simple functionality. The gradebook provides detailed feedback on student responses and the problem-solving process that students performed to select those responses. In addition to tracking student performance on problems, the gradebook also tracks students' usage of nonassessed elements such as video lecture or e-Professor. The gradebook can be easily exported to Excel, allowing the instructor the flexibility to use MathZone in a variety of ways.

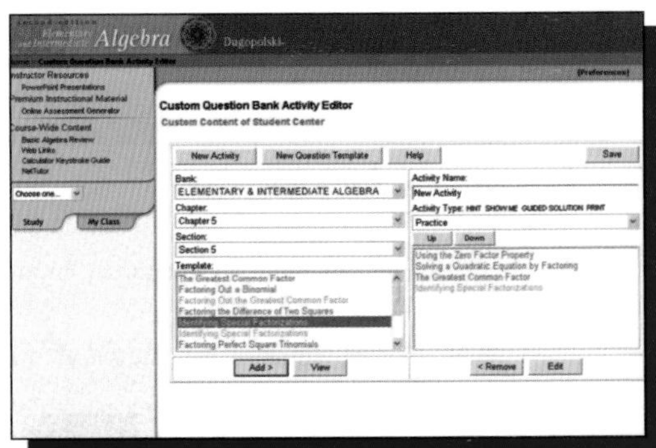

Has it all

MathZone is tailored to a McGraw-Hill textbook, so every assignment, question, e-Professor tutorial, and video-lecture piece is derived directly from text-specific materials. Instructors can modify questions and assignments and create their own from scratch.

With just a few clicks of the mouse, you can share your MathZone course with an unlimited number of colleagues. Instructors can share assignments, algorithmically generated questions, or static questions with simplicity and speed.

Instructor benefits

- Offers complete course management.
- Track students' progress with unprecedented depth.
- Includes 100% algorithmic homework, quizzing, and testing.
- Edit, change, and create algorithmic questions.
- Assign all course resources, including homework, video lectures, and e-Professor.
- Live, book-specific tutoring saves instructors time.
- Provides unmatched ease-of-use in one system.

Student benefits

- Includes video-lectures that are ADA-compliant.
- Provides e-Professor-guided solutions.
- Provides prompted, step-by-step problem solving.
- Includes online algorithmic practice and assessment.
- Students have access to all resources, whether assigned or not.
- The end result is a better understanding and an improved grade.

Elementary and Intermediate Algebra

second edition

Mark Dugopolski
Southeastern Louisiana University

Boston Burr Ridge, IL Dubuque, IA Madison, WI New York San Francisco St. Louis
Bangkok Bogotá Caracas Kuala Lumpur Lisbon London Madrid Mexico City
Milan Montreal New Delhi Santiago Seoul Singapore Sydney Taipei Toronto

The McGraw·Hill Companies

Higher Education

ELEMENTARY AND INTERMEDIATE ALGEBRA, SECOND EDITION

Published by McGraw-Hill, a business unit of The McGraw-Hill Companies, Inc., 1221 Avenue of the Americas, New York, NY 10020. Copyright © 2006, 2002 by The McGraw-Hill Companies, Inc. All rights reserved. No part of this publication may be reproduced or distributed in any form or by any means, or stored in a database or retrieval system, without the prior written consent of The McGraw-Hill Companies, Inc., including, but not limited to, in any network or other electronic storage or transmission, or broadcast for distance learning.

Some ancillaries, including electronic and print components, may not be available to customers outside the United States.

This book is printed on acid-free paper.

1 2 3 4 5 6 7 8 9 0 VNH/VNH 0 9 8 7 6 5 4
1 2 3 4 5 6 7 8 9 0 VNH/VNH 0 9 8 7 6 5 4

ISBN 0–07–253895–3
ISBN 0–07–302224–1 (Annotated Instructor's Edition)

Publisher, Mathematics and Statistics: *William K. Barter*
Publisher, Developmental Mathematics: *Elizabeth J. Haefele*
Director of Development: *David Dietz*
Senior Developmental Editor: *Randy Welch*
Executive Marketing Manager: *Michael Weitz*
Marketing Manager: *Steven R. Stembridge*
Senior Project Manager: *Vicki Krug*
Lead Production Supervisor: *Sandy Ludovissy*
Senior Media Project Manager: *Sandra M. Schnee*
Lead Media Technology Producer: *Jeff Huettman*
Designer: *Rick D. Noel*
Cover/Interior Designer: *Elise Lansdon/Lansdon Design*
(USE) Cover Image: © *Photonica, Pattern with Nonagon by Shigeru Tanaka*
Lead Photo Research Coordinator: *Carrie K. Burger*
Photo Research: *Pam Carley*
Supplement Producer: *Brenda A. Ernzen*
Compositor: *Interactive Composition Corporation*
Typeface: *10.5/12 Times Roman*
Printer: *Von Hoffmann Corporation*

Photo Credits:
Page 69: © Vol. 141/Corbis; p. 76: © Reuters/Corbis; p. 145: © George Disario/Corbis; p. 164: © Vol. 166/Corbis; p. 188 bottom: © Ann M. Job/AP/Wide World Photos; p. 239 top left: © Gary Conner/PhotoEdit; p. 246: © Michael Keller/Corbis; p. 247: © DV169/Digital Vision; p. 447: © Vol. 128/Corbis; p. 549: © Herb Snitzer/Stock Boston; p. 790: © Vol. 168/Corbis; p. 825: © Reuters New Media, Inc./Corbis.

Library of Congress Cataloging-in-Publication Data

Dugopolski, Mark.
Elementary and intermediate algebra / Mark Dugopolski. — 2nd ed.
p. cm.
Includes index.
ISBN 0–07–253895–3 (hard copy : alk. paper)
1. Algebra—Textbooks. I. Title.

QA152.3.D84 2006
512.9—dc22

2004023716
CIP

www.mhhe.com

In loving memory of my parents,
Walter and Anne Dugopolski

MTH 102

Review: 1.8, 2.1–2.3, 3.1–3.4, 5.1–5.6 Topic I

New: 4.5 6.1–6.8 Topic 2

9.1 – 9.5 Topic 3

10.1–10.5 Topic 4

11.1 – 11.7 + supplement Topic 5.

(supplement after 11.2)

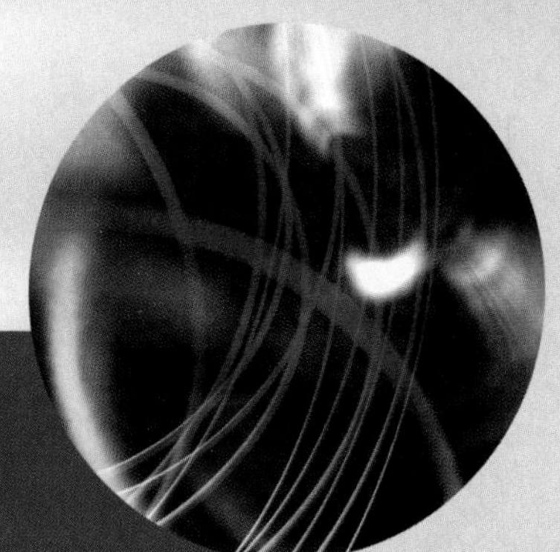

Contents

Linear Equations and Inequalities in Two Variables 165

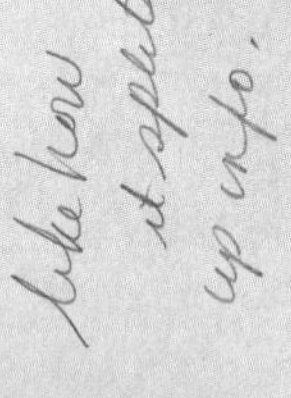

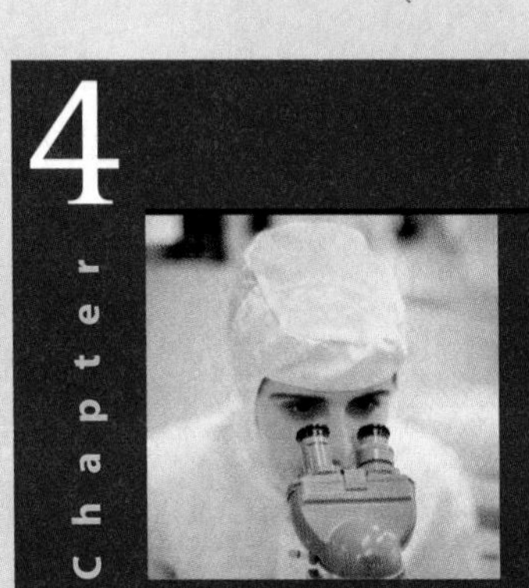

Polynomials and Exponents 247

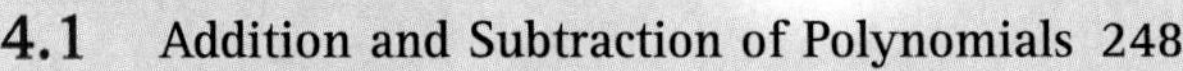

Chapter 8

Chapter 9

Chapter 10

Chapter 11

Chapter 12

Chapter 13

Nonlinear Systems and the Conic Sections 825

Chapter 14

Sequences and Series 887

Appendix A-1

Answers to Selected Exercises A-59

Index I-1

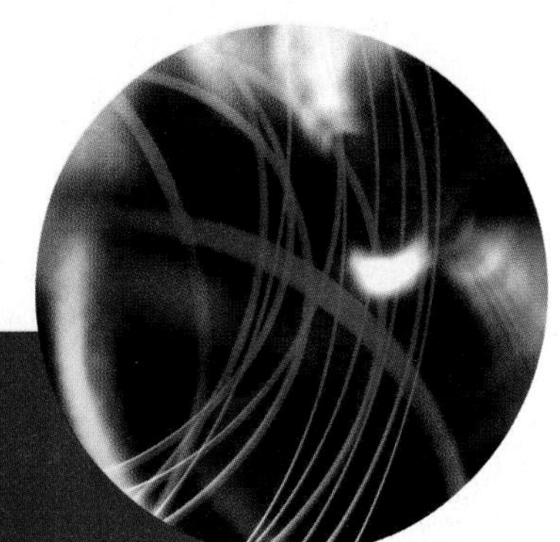

Preface

FROM THE AUTHOR

I would like to thank the many students and faculty who have used my books over the years. You have provided me with excellent feedback that has assisted me in writing a better, more student-focused book in each edition. Your comments are always taken seriously, and I have adjusted my focus on each revision to satisfy your needs.

In this edition in particular, you told me that you wanted a fresh, **new page layout** that was clean and open so that students could read it easily and without distraction. Last fall a group of 15 of you met in Boston to choose this design for my books. I hope that you like our implementation of your feedback, and I will always welcome your feedback on both the content and appearance of the future editions of my texts.

Additionally, you asked me to add **more exercises** that fall on the **easier side of the difficulty spectrum.** I took special time and effort to add the types of exercises you requested in these revisions, and I hope that they will assist your students to succeed in the course through ample practice of the fundamentals before moving on to exercises of medium difficulty.

Understandable Explanations

I originally undertook the task of writing my own book for the Elementary and Intermediate Algebra course so I could explain mathematical concepts to students in language they would understand. Most books claim to do this, but my experience with a variety of texts had proven otherwise. What students and faculty will find in my book are **short, precise explanations** of terms and concepts that are written in **understandable language.**

For example, when I introduce the Commutative Property of Addition, I make the concrete analogy that "the price of a hamburger plus a Coke is the same as the price of a Coke plus a hamburger," a mathematical fact in their daily lives that students can readily grasp. Math doesn't need to remain a mystery to students, and students reading my book will find other analogies like this one that connect abstractions to everyday experiences.

Detailed Examples Keyed to Exercises

My experience as a teacher has taught me two things about examples: they need to be detailed, and they need to help students do their homework. As a result, users of my book will find abundant examples with every step carefully laid out and explained where necessary so that students can follow along in class if the instructor is demonstrating an example on the board. Students will also be able to read them on their own later when they're ready to do the exercise sets.

I have also introduced a **double cross-referencing** system between my examples and exercise sets so that no matter which one students start with, they'll see the connection to the other. All examples in this edition now refer to specific exercises by ending with a phrase such as "Now do Exercises 11–18" so that students will have the opportunity for immediate practice of that concept. If students work an exercise and find they are stumped on how to finish it, they'll see that for that group of exercises they're directed to a specific example to follow as a model. Either way, students will find my book's examples give them the guidance they need to succeed in the course.

Varied Exercises and Applications

A third goal of mine in writing this book was to give students **more variety** in the kinds of exercises they perform than I found in other books. Students won't find an intimidating page of endless drills in my book, but instead will see exercises in manageable groups with specific goals. They will also be able to augment their math proficiency using different formats (true/false, written response, multiple choice) and different methods (discussion, collaboration, calculators). Not only is there an abundance of skill-building exercises, I have also researched a wide variety of **realistic applications** using **real data** so that those "dreaded word problems" will be seen as a useful and practical extension of what students have learned.

Finally, and new to this edition, every chapter ends with **critical thinking exercises** that go beyond numerical computation and call on students to employ their intuitive problem-solving skills to find the answers to mathematical puzzles in **fun and innovative** ways. With all of these resources to choose from, I am sure that instructors will be comfortable adapting my book to fit their course, and that students will appreciate having a text written for their level and to stimulate their interest.

Listening to Student and Instructor Concerns

McGraw-Hill has given me a wonderful resource for making my textbook more responsive to the immediate concerns of students and faculty. In addition to sending my manuscript out for review by instructors at many different colleges, several times a year McGraw-Hill holds symposia and focus groups with math instructors where the emphasis is *not* on selling products but instead on the **publisher listening** to the needs of faculty and their students. These encounters have provided me with a wealth of ideas on how to improve my chapter organization, make the page layout of my books more readable, and fine tune exercises in every chapter. Consequently, students and faculty will feel comfortable using my book because it incorporates their specific suggestions and anticipates their needs. These events have particularly helped me in the shaping of the Second Edition.

Improvements in the Second Edition

- After consulting with a panel of experienced instructors on the **optimal page layout** to use with their students, the entire textbook was redesigned to be more open, easy to read, and easy for students to follow.
- All chapters now end in an exercise section called **"Critical Thinking: For Individual or Group Work,"** which focuses on intuitive problem-solving skills. These exercises go beyond routine algebraic skills to give students the opportunity to think creatively to solve puzzles and challenges.

- **New exercises** have been added or updated throughout the text. Most of the added exercises fall on the easier side of the difficulty spectrum to give students more practice with the fundamentals.
- Every example is now keyed to specific exercises with the advice **"Now do Exercises . . . ,"** so that students will quickly see which exercises they should do to reinforce the concepts presented in the example.
- All the **"Math at Work"** features have been completely rewritten to show how math is used in different professions rather than focus on specific individuals.
- **Teaching Tips** have been added in the margins of the Annotated Instructor's Edition to provide instructors with practical classroom advice on how to present specific topics.
- The **Diagnostic Test on Chapters 1–6,** which previously appeared in the middle of the text, has been moved to an appendix to allow for greater flexibility in assigning this material.
- A new appendix, **Chapters 1–6 Review,** provides students with a brief overview of the first half of the book to better orient them as they study the second half.
- The material on inequalities has been shifted from Chapter 3 to Chapters 2 and 8.
- The previous Chapter 8 has been split into two chapters: Systems of Linear Equations and More on Inequalities.
- Chapter 11 on functions now includes **polynomial and rational functions** and their graphs.
- In Chapter 6, all **answers for rational expressions** have been made consistent so that the denominator is always factored and the numerator is not.
- **Notes on Collaborative Learning** are now included in the Annotated Instructor's Edition.
- A new appendix on **Sets** has been added to give students an optional review of this topic.
- The **index** has been expanded to include more entries based on student and instructor requests.

Acknowledgments

I would like to extend my appreciation to the people at McGraw-Hill for their wholehearted support in producing the new editions of my books. My thanks go to Liz Haefele, Publisher, for being an energetic champion behind her authors and books; to David Dietz, Director of Development, for making the revision process work like a well-oiled machine; to Randy Welch, Senior Developmental Editor, for his advice on shaping the new editions; to Vicki Krug, Senior Project Manager, for expertly overseeing the many details of the production process; to Rick Noel, Designer, for the wonderful new design of my texts; to Carrie Burger, Lead Photo Research Coordinator, for her aid in picking out excellent photos; to Hal Whipple, for checking the accuracy of my texts; to Brenda Ernzen, Supplements Producer, for producing top-notch print supplements; and to Jeff Huettman, Lead Media Technology Producer, and Sandy Schnee, Senior Media Project Manager, for shepherding the development of high-quality media supplements that accompany my textbook. To all of them, my many thanks for their efforts to make my books best-sellers when there are many good books for faculty to choose from.

I sincerely appreciate the efforts of the reviewers who made many helpful suggestions to improve my series of books. I would like to extend special thanks to Mitch Levy for his many detailed and valuable suggestions for improving my exercise sets, and to Richard Maurer for keeping a user diary and alerting me to specific areas that he and his students have identified where I could make things more clear and precise.

Elise Adamson, *Wayland Baptist University*

Ebrahim Ahmadizadeh, *Northampton Community College*

W. Todd Ashby, *Charleston Southern University*

Viola Lee Bean, *Boise State University*

Monika Bender, *Central Texas College*

Mary Kay Best, *Coastal Bend College–Beeville*

Steve Boettcher, *Estrella Mountain Community College*

Annette M. Burden, *Youngstown State University*

Gail Burkett, *Palm Beach Community College*

Linda Clay, *Albuquerque Technical Vocational Institute*

John F. Close, *Salt Lake Community College*

Vivian Dennis-Monzingo, *Eastfield College*

Donna Densmore, *Bossier Parish Community College*

Mark deSaint-Rat, *Miami University–Middletown*

Lenore Desilets, *De Anza College*

William A. Echols, *Houston Community College*

Mike Everett, *Santa Ana College*

Pat Foard, *South Plains College*

Linda Franko, *Cuyahoga Community College*

Joseph Fritzsche, *University of Phoenix*

Corinna Goehring, *Jackson State Community College*

Wael Hassinan, *University of Phoenix*

Steven Hatfield, *Marshall University*

Erin Hines, *College of the Redwoods–Eureka*

Laura L. Hoye, *Trident Technical College*

Matthew Hudock, *St. Philip's College*

Barbara Hughes, *San Jacinto College–Pasadena*

Linda Hurst, *Central Texas College*

Domingo Javier-Litong, *Houston Community College*

Laura Kalbaugh, *Wake Technical Community College*

Krystyna Karminska, *Thomas Nelson Community College*

Joselle D. Kehoe, *DeVry Institute of Technology*

Tor Kwembe, *Chicago State University*

Suzann Kyriazopoulous, *DeVry University–Chicago Campus*

Angela Lawrenz, *Blinn College*

Sheila Ledford, *Coastal Georgia Community College*

Mitchel Levy, *Broward Community College*

Charyl Link, *Kansas City Kansas Community College*

Frederick Lippman, *Shasta College*

Sergio Loch, *Grand View College*

Carol Marinas, *Barry University*

Richard Maurer, *University of Phoenix*

Robert McCoy, *University of Alaska–Anchorage*

David Meredith, *San Francisco State University*

Margaret Michener, *University of Nebraska–Kearney*

Barbara Miller, *Lexington Community College*

Pam Miller, *Phoenix College*

Juan Molina, *Austin Community College*

Joyce Nemeth, *Broward Community College*

Thomas Notermann, *Devry University–Tinley Park*

Kim Nunn, *Northeast State Technical Community College*

Charles Odion, *Houston Community College*

Michele Olsen, *College of the Redwoods*

Frank Pecchioni, *Jefferson Community College*

Joanne Peeples, *El Paso Community College*

Avis Proctor, *Broward Community College*

Togba Sapolucia, *Houston Community College*

E. Jenell Sargent, *Tennessee State University–Nashville*

Paula Schornick, *Seminole State College*

Patty Schovanec, *Texas Tech University*

Mohsen Shirani, *Tennessee State University–Nashville*

Jefferson Shirley, *De Anza College*

Julia Simms, *Southern Illinois University–Edwardsville*

Donald W. Solomon, *University of Wisconsin–Milwaukee*

Sandra L. Spain, *Thomas Nelson Community College*

Brian Stewart, *Tarrant County College–Southeast*

Jo Temple, *Texas Tech University*

Burnette Thompson, *Houston Community College–Northwest*

Timothy Thompson, *Oregon Institute of Technology*

Lourdes Triana, *Humboldt State University*

David Turner, *Faulkner University*

Vivian Turner, *Rochester College*

Emmanuel Ekwere Usen, *Houston Community College*

Nina Verheyn, *Kilgore College*

Paul Visintainer, *Augusta Technical College*

Robert Vogeler, *North Idaho College*

Pam Wahl, *Middlesex Community College*

Brenda Weaver, *Stillman College*

Marjorie Whitmore, *Northwest Arkansas Community College*

Joel D. Williams, *Houston Community College*

Walter Wooden, *Broward Community College*

Kevin Yokoyama, *College of the Redwoods*

Vivian Zabrocki, *Montana State University–Billings*

Jane R. Zegestowsky, *Penn State–Abington*

Limin Zhang, *Columbia Basin College*

Deborah Zopf, *Henry Ford Community College*

I also want to express my sincere appreciation to my wife, Cheryl, for her invaluable patience and support.

Mark Dugopolski
Ponchatoula, Louisiana

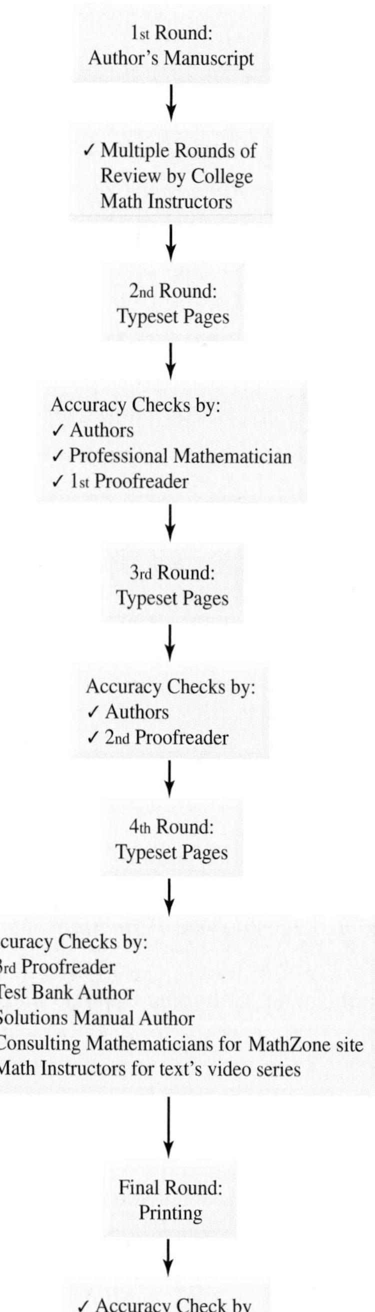

A COMMITMENT TO ACCURACY

You have a right to expect an accurate textbook, and McGraw-Hill invests considerable time and effort to make sure that we deliver one. Listed below are the many steps we take to make sure this happens.

OUR ACCURACY VERIFICATION PROCESS

First Round

Step 1: Numerous **college math instructors** review the manuscript and report on any errors that they may find, and the authors make these corrections in their final manuscript.

Second Round

Step 2: Once the manuscript has been typeset, the **authors** check their manuscript against the first page proofs to ensure that all illustrations, graphs, examples, exercises, solutions, and answers have been correctly laid out on the pages, and that all notation is correctly used.

Step 3: An outside, **professional mathematician** works through every example and exercise in the page proofs to verify the accuracy of the answers.

Step 4: A **proofreader** adds a triple layer of accuracy assurance in the first pages by hunting for errors, then a second, corrected round of page proofs is produced.

Third Round

Step 5: The **author team** reviews the second round of page proofs for two reasons: 1) to make certain that any previous corrections were properly made, and 2) to look for any errors they might have missed on the first round.

Step 6: A **second proofreader** is added to the project to examine the new round of page proofs to double check the author team's work and to lend a fresh, critical eye to the book before the third round of paging.

Fourth Round

Step 7: A **third proofreader** inspects the third round of page proofs to verify that all previous corrections have been properly made and that there are no new or remaining errors.

Step 8: Meanwhile, in partnership with **independent mathematicians,** the text accuracy is verified from a variety of fresh perspectives:

- The **test bank author** checks for consistency and accuracy as they prepare the computerized test item file.
- The **solutions manual author** works every single exercise and verifies their answers, reporting any errors to the publisher.
- A **consulting group of mathematicians,** who write material for the text's MathZone site, notifies the publisher of any errors they encounter in the page proofs.
- A video production company employing **expert math instructors** for the text's videos will alert the publisher of any errors they might find in the page proofs.

Final Round

Step 9: The **project manager,** who has overseen the book from the beginning, performs a **fourth proofread** of the textbook during the printing process, providing a final accuracy review.

⇒ What results is a mathematics textbook that is as accurate and error-free as is humanly possible, and our authors and publishing staff are confident that our many layers of quality assurance have produced textbooks that are the leaders of the industry for their integrity and correctness.

NOTES ON COLLABORATIVE LEARNING

The NCTM Standards

The *Principles and Standards for School Mathematics,* published in 2000 by the National Council of Teachers of Mathematics (NCTM), recommends that students develop collaborative learning skills as well as the ability to analyze problem solutions. The recommendation is the use of group work to give the students a chance to practice collaborative learning skills in the context of mathematical problem solving. The NCTM also recommends the use of open-ended problems so that students get a feel for how to use mathematics in the world outside of the college environment.

About These Collaborative Activities

At the end of each chapter you will find a collaborative activity that incorporates the material presented in the chapter. These activities are designed to be catalysts for creating dialog among students and between students and their instructor. You will need to be actively participating with your students in the group learning process.

Some of the activities will stretch the students' abilities to formulate the mathematics. The students may need some help from you as the instructor. You may want to use something akin to the Socratic method in answering the students' questions; answer with a question that will point their thinking in the direction it should go.

Some of these activities incorporate different learning styles: visual, auditory, kinesthetic, and so on. Students will appreciate the opportunity to use a style that works more naturally for them.

Many of these activities present the mathematical problem in the context of a scenario used to catch the students' attention and help them begin to think creatively. Do not be surprised if some of your students take the scenario further in their answers.

Thus the goal of these activities is to encourage students to think creatively, use other ways of learning from the standard paradigm, and find power in their own abilities to solve mathematical problems.

Implementing Collaborative Activities in the Classroom

Instructor notes that give tips and comments on how to use each activity are provided following these general notes. There is a range of types of activities; some requiring in-class time only and others requiring outside group work. You will want to structure the type and size of the groups in order to best fit the activity assigned. Also, be aware of the group interactions. Students may need help at first learning how to work effectively in groups.

Techniques for Forming Groups

Next is a list of some types of groups you may wish to use and a brief description of each.

- Proximity Pairing—Each student is "paired" with one or two students in his or her immediate vicinity.
- Number Off or Count Off—Students count off, out loud from 1 to n, where n is determined by dividing the number of students in the class by the number of students desired in each group.

- Structured Groups or Teams—Use this type of grouping after two or three weeks of class so that you have an opportunity to become acquainted with the students. Keep groups small, no more than four students per group. You may either mix abilities of students in the group or form groups with "matched" ability. In mixed-ability grouping each group consists of an "A" student, a "B" student, a "C" student, and so on. Matched-ability groups are formed to enable students with the same ability level to learn together.

Assigning Roles

Each group should have a moderator, a quality manager, a recorder, and a messenger. (These are merely suggested roles, and others might also be beneficial.) The moderator keeps the group on task, asks appropriate questions, and encourages everyone to participate. The quality manager makes sure the work and the finished activity is the best the group can produce. The recorder keeps track of ideas and solutions during the group interaction. The messenger interfaces with the instructor by asking questions, or with the rest of the class by reporting results. These roles may be switched or combined during the time that students are working together. Eventually the students will fall into a natural rhythm of working together with the four suggested roles as appropriate, but with flexibility.

Tips for Using Groups

The amount of instructor involvement in helping students work together will depend on the type of activity on which the students are working. For a short, in-class assignment, groups will need less structure. For longer assignments, students will need a structure to help them learn to work together.

Not only will the groups themselves need to work together effectively, but you will need to maintain the proper environment for effective group work. Here are some tips on how to do that:

- Explain the assignment to the whole class, before forming them into groups. This enables the groups to start work quickly.
- Encourage the groups to brainstorm together to solve the problem and not be afraid to ask questions when they are stuck.
- Keep moving about the classroom during an in-class group assignment. This makes you available to the students if they have questions and helps them keep on task.
- Observe progress in an unobtrusive way. You may need to ask leading questions if a group is stuck for some time on one part of the activity.
- Look for students who may be experiencing exceptional difficulty in understanding what is happening in the group.
- Communicate enthusiasm for group work and respect for the students' experience and abilities.

More Help

These are some brief tips on how to get started with collaborative learning in your classroom. For a more extensive discussion on how to use groups effectively, the issues that can come up when using collaborative learning, tips on grading and evaluation, and more collaborative learning activities, refer to the *Collaborative Learning Manual* by Aldrich, Cohen, and Hartsell (Addison-Wesley, 1995).

NOTES ON END OF CHAPTER COLLABORATIVE ACTIVITIES

Chapter 1: Walking the Number Line

Goals: This activity is designed to give students a review of adding and subtracting integers and to provide their first experience with working in groups. It is designed to be most helpful to kinesthetic learners and provides a conceptual basis for the rules we use with integers.

Time: 15 to 20 minutes

Teaching Tips: Emphasize to students that this activity is a fun way to understand what is happening when we add and subtract integers. After they complete the problems in the book, have students make up some of their own. Kinesthetic activities like this one are especially helpful in breaking up long classes. Make sure there is enough room for the students to do this activity.

Answer Key:

1. 1 **2.** -5 **3.** -1 **4.** 5 **5.** 5 **6.** -1 **7.** -5 **8.** 1

Chapter 2: Expression—Equation—Inequality

Goals: In this activity students will practice their skills with simplifying expressions, solving equations, and solving and graphing inequalities. This activity gives students practice in differentiating between the three types of problems.

Time: 20 to 30 minutes

Teaching Tips: This activity uses the following roles: simplifier, solver, and grapher. In the first part of this activity there is a set of problems, each having one expression, one equation, and one inequality not always in this order. The groups need to sort out the problems—give the expression to the simplifier, the equation to the solver, and the inequality to the grapher. Students may need some help in starting this process.

Comments: Learning to look closely at problems before they jump into them is something many developmental education students need to practice.

Answer Key:

1. a. Inequality, $x \le -10$ **b.** Expression, $3x - 18$ **c.** Equation, $x = -6$

2. a. Expression, $4x - 2$ **b.** Equation, $x = -9$ **c.** Inequality, $x < -4$

3. a. Inequality, $x \le \frac{19}{3}$ **b.** Expression, $4x - 6$ **c.** Equation, $x = -4$

4. a. Equation, $x = 7$ **b.** Inequality, $x > \frac{2}{5}$ **c.** Expression, $6x$

Answers will vary for Exercises 5 to 8.

Chapter 3: Inches or Centimeters

Goals: This activity will give students practice in plotting points, finding an equation from data they have generated themselves, and discovering how different points from the same equation will generate the same line.

Time: In-class time 30 minutes

Teaching Tips: This activity can be done anytime after teaching how to plot points. When assigning people to groups, you may want to consider mixing heights as well as abilities. You will need both metric and U.S. tape measures. If these are not available for each group, have students use string to measure each other and then use rulers to measure the strings.

Answer Key: Part I and Part II: Answers will vary. **Part III:** Answers will be close to the conversion formula; $C = 2.54I$, where C is centimeters and I is inches; slope ≈ 2.54; at the origin (0, 0)

Chapter 4: Area as a Model of Binomial Multiplication

Goals: This activity will provide a visual way for students to deal with multiplying binomials. It also leads the students into factoring by asking them to think in reverse for the last two problems.

Time: In-class time 15 minutes

Teaching Tips: Do this activity on the same day that you teach FOIL. After students have finished the activity, have the class discuss the different answers to Problem 7.

Answer Key: 1. $x^2 + 9x + 14$ **2.** $x^2 + 9x + 8$ **3.** $x^2 + 9x + 20$
4. $x^2 + 10x + 21 = (x + 3)(x + 7)$ **5.** $x^2 + 3x + 2 = (x + 2)(x + 1)$

$3x$	21
x^2	$7x$

$2x$	2
x^2	$1x$

6. $(x + 3)(x + 3)$ **7.** $(x + 2)(x + 5)$

Chapter 5: Hannah's Inheritance

Goals: This activity presents a scenario in which students must solve a problem by factoring. The use of hectometers and hectares will make them aware of metric measurement.

Time: 20 to 30 minutes

Teaching Tips: You may want to share the following information about hectares with your students. A hectare is the unit of metric measurement that is similar to an acre. A hectare is a 100 meter by 100 meter square (1 ha = 2.47 acres, 1 acre = 0.4 ha). Students from the United States may not be familiar with this measurement, while foreign students will be familiar with it. Since this problem is solved by factoring, it is important for students to round to the nearest whole number as they work in part two. When solving each quadratic equation students will get two solutions and will need to choose which one is the appropriate answer.

Answer Key: Part I: 15 hm by 15 hm **Part II:** $y = 12$ hm, $z = 3$ hm

Chapter 6: How Do I Get There from Here?

Goals: The goals of this activity are to use the distance formula $D = RT$ to analyze a situation, present information to the other members of the group, and to make a group decision.

Time: In-class time 30 minutes

Teaching Tips: Use this activity after teaching the section on uniform motion. Have students form groups and instruct them to work independently on their part. Then have each student present his or her case to the other members of the group. If the students are handing in this activity, have each of them write about his or her case and then also write a paragraph describing the group choice and why this case was chosen.

Comments: This activity includes both individual and group work, which appeals to some students.

Answer Key: Bike: cost = \$20.00, distance = 2.7 miles, speed = 13.5 mph, time = 12 minutes. Car: cost = \$40.00, distance = 3 miles, speed = 15 mph, time = 12 minutes. Bus: cost = \$16.00, distance = 5 miles, speed = 12 mph, time = 25 minutes. Choices will vary.

Chapter 7: Types of Systems

Goals: Students will attempt to solve systems of equations of the three types (independent, inconsistent, and dependent) and relate these types of solutions to real-to-life situations. The extension asks the students to decide how to fix the inconsistent and dependent systems to make them solvable.

Time: In-class time 30 minutes; assign extension as a group homework assignment

Teaching Tips: Have students assign roles in their groups. Allow them a chance to brainstorm about how to set up the correct equations. Have the messenger in their group show you their equations before they attempt to solve them. You may wish to assign the extension as a homework assignment or have a discussion about what to do with the entire class. Give them some time to brainstorm possible ways to fix the inconsistent and dependent systems as a group before holding the class discussion.

Answer Key:

Part I **1.** $2t + \frac{1}{6}k = 250;\ 1t = 100$ **2.** $k = 300;\ t = 100$

Part II **3.** $\frac{1}{4}m + \frac{1}{2}l = 60;\ 1m + 2l = 240$

4. Both equations become: $m + 2l = 240$ giving a dependent solution (they are the same line). There is not enough information to solve for this system. Karif can make any combination of medium and large kerchiefs that corresponds to points on the $m + 2l = 240$ line.

Part III **5.** $2y + \frac{7}{2}w = 150;\ 2y + \frac{7}{2}w = 200$

6. These lines are parallel. The system is inconsistent. One equation has no relation to the other, that is, the number of cotton mantillas she makes does not depend on the number of lace ones and vice versa. Again, there is not enough information to find a unique solution. She can make any combination of the two sizes that corresponds to points on both lines.

Extension: The systems in Parts II and III are not uniquely solvable as explained above. There would need to be another limiting factor in each, say, for example, if Karif decided to put an appliqué on the large kerchiefs or if Maria decided to trim the cotton mantillas with a lace trim.

Chapter 8: Every-Day Algebra

Goals: The goal of this activity is to give students insight into how algebra is used in "every-day life." It also provides a way for students to practice converting a "word problem" into algebra.

Time: In class time 20 to 30 minutes

Teaching Tips: Make sure each student in each group has an assigned role. It may not be obvious at first how to solve the problem, so encourage the students truly to brainstorm together in their groups: make a list of ideas on a procedure (write down all ideas even if they sound silly), look over the list for the best ideas, implement those ideas, and see if they work. Give the students hints only if they are very stuck. They may find that working together gives them different insights and perspectives. You may also be surprised at the number of different correct ways the students can find to solve the problem. You may wish to have them explain their thought processes on the paper they hand in to you.

Comments: Watch for the students who think they know how to solve the problem immediately and won't listen to other students in their groups.

Answer Key:

1. Variable names may vary. C = wholesale cost, L = buying club price, M = store markup, P = store price before discount, S = store price after discount.

2. Want to find when the buying club price is equal or less than the store price.

(a) Buying Club price: $L = C + 0.08C = 1.08C$
(b) Store price: $P = C + MC = (1 + M)C$;
Discounted price: $S = P - 0.1P = 0.09P = 0.9(1 + M)C$
(c) Inequality: $L \leq S$, or $1.08C \leq 0.9(1 + M)C$

3. Since C is not zero, divide both sides of the inequality by C

(a) $1.08 \leq 0.9(1 + M)$, now divide both sides by 0.9
(b) $1.2 \leq 1 + M$, now subtract 1 from each side
(c) $0.2 \leq M$
(d) The store must have a markup of 20% or more for it to be cheaper to buy through the buying club.

Chapter 9: Laws of Falling Bodies

Goals: This activity enables students to use formulas with radicals to solve problems. Not all of the information needed is supplied in the problem, so students will need to "do some digging" to find the formulas they need.

Time: In-class time 30 minutes. Some out-of-class time may be required to finish.

Teaching Tips: The scenario in this activity appeals to the problem-solving detective in each one of your students. Remind your students to assign roles. Next are some hints (formulas) the students will need to complete the activity. Some of this information is also available to them further on in the book. Allow the students some time to go home and think about what else they need to know to complete the activity before giving them these hints. Write each unit on a piece of paper (one per group) and have the messenger in each group come up and get each hint in sequence from you. You may also wish to have the students present their results in a report.

Hints:

For Problem 1: Use the Pythagorean formula to determine the height of the building.

For Problem 2: For an object with initial velocity of v_0 feet per second at a height of s_0 feet, its altitude S after t seconds is given by $S = -16t^2 + v_0t + s_0$ (from Chapter 6).

For Problem 2: The initial velocity, v_0, is 0 feet per second and the initial height, s_0, is the height of the building.

For Problem 3: Use the formula $D = RT$, where R is how fast the woman is walking and T is the time it takes her to travel D feet.

Answer Key: 1. 59.9 feet **2.** 1.9 seconds **3.** 5 feet/second; answers will vary as to whether Jaki's client could have "done it."

Chapter 10: Completing the Square

Goals: This activity enables students to see a geometric method for completing the square.

Time: 30 minutes

Comments: This may be a good time to assess how well groups are working together. Have them complete a paragraph about how things are going in their groups to hand in with this activity. If there are problems, brainstorm with the class about how to solve them.

Answer Key:

1. Answers will vary.

2. (a) $x = -2 \pm \sqrt{10}$ **(b)** $x = \dfrac{-3 \pm \sqrt{19}}{2}$ **(c)** $x = \dfrac{-2 \pm \sqrt{31}}{3}$

3. $x = \dfrac{-b \pm \sqrt{b^2 + 4ac}}{2a}$

Chapter 11: Life's a Function of What?

Goals: This activity is designed to let students discover functions in their lives and give a real meaning to domain and range.

Time: 20 to 30 minutes

Teaching Tips: Students may need some help in finding something that could be modeled by a function of one variable. There should be a wide variety of functions used and so answers to all questions will vary.

Chapter 12: In How Much Space Could We Live?

Goals: This activity provides a timely situation in which exponential and logarithmic functions enable students to analyze the outcome of population growth.

Time: In-class time 30 minutes to complete problem. If you wish, assign the activity as a group homework assignment and use class time for discussion.

Teaching Tips: After covering exponential growth, pair students by ability, mixing students with different abilities. Rather than having the students turn in written solutions, allow class time for the class as a whole to share their solutions and conclusions. You may wish to assign the work as a group homework assignment and then allow the class time for discussion.

Comments: This activity may elicit lively discussions.

Answer Key:

All answers are found assuming that rounded values are used in the succeeding computations.

1. 2.2% **2.** The surface area computed is 1.1×10^{14} **3.** 230.4 years
4. Answers will vary. **5.** Answers will vary.

Chapter 13: Focus on Comets

Goals: This activity presents applications of conic sections that those who have looked at the night sky will appreciate.

Time: In-class time 15 to 20 minutes in class on the first day and 20 to 30 minutes on the second day; group homework assignment.

Teaching Tips: Pairing students will be especially useful in this activity if you have graphing calculators or computer software available for the students to use. The solution may not be immediately obvious to some of your students. Allow them time outside of class to brainstorm in their groups and dig in their books in order to find what they need. Encourage them to sketch the situation in each problem so that they will know how to begin.

Comments: Students will appreciate the visual and kinesthetic aspects of this activity—drawing the ellipse with a pencil and string. Some students will come away with a better understanding of the equations for conics.

Answer Key:

1. $\frac{x^2}{(17.8)^2} + \frac{y^2}{(4.58)^2} = 1$; See students' models on cardboard.

2. $p = 0.75$; $y = \frac{1}{4(0.75)}x^2 = \frac{1}{3}x^2$. Since the direction of the parabola is not determined by the information in the problem, students may come up with the equation for a parabola opening downward.

3. $\frac{x^2}{(1.5)^2} - \frac{y^2}{(2.6)^2} = 1$

Chapter 14: A Sequence of Investments Can Be Series(ous)

Goals: Many students will identify with the concept of state lotteries and will appreciate the use of series to find out how good (or bad) a deal buying lottery tickets can be.

Time: 20 to 30 minutes

Teaching Tips: Have students assign roles in their groups if needed. Allow the students a chance to come up with the series in the activity by themselves before giving them hints. Have students share their discussions of the results with the rest of the class.

Comments: State lotteries are becoming more and more prevalent. This activity will help students assess the benefits of buying the lottery tickets.

Answer Key:

1. 5, 10, 15, 20, 25, . . . ; an arithmetic sequence; \$3900

2. \$152 per year; $152(1.0375)^{14}$, $152(1.0375)^{13}$, . . . , 152; a geometric sequence; $\sum_{n=1}^{15} 152(1.0375)^{n-1} = \$2987.66$

3. \$65 per quarter; $\sum_{n=1}^{60} 65(1 + 0.0125)^{n-1} = \$5757.34$

4. \$260 per year; $\sum_{n=1}^{15} 260(1 + 0.07375)^{n-1} = \$6725.40$

5. Answers will vary.

Guided Tour: Features and Supplements

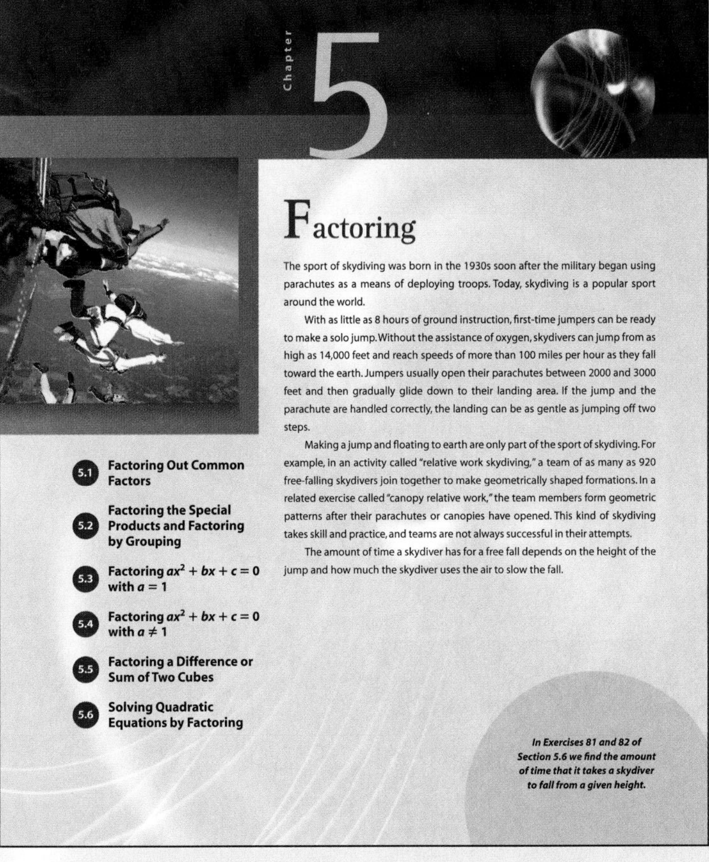

Chapter 5

Factoring

The sport of skydiving was born in the 1930s soon after the military began using parachutes as a means of deploying troops. Today, skydiving is a popular sport around the world.

With as little as 8 hours of ground instruction, first-time jumpers can be ready to make a solo jump. Without the assistance of oxygen, skydivers can jump from as high as 14,000 feet and reach speeds of more than 100 miles per hour as they fall toward the earth. Jumpers usually open their parachutes between 2000 and 3000 feet and then gradually glide down to their landing area. If the jump and the parachute are handled correctly, the landing can be as gentle as jumping off two steps.

Making a jump and floating to earth are only part of the sport of skydiving. For example, in an activity called "relative work skydiving," a team of as many as 920 free-falling skydivers join together to make geometrically shaped formations. In a related exercise called "canopy relative work," the team members form geometric patterns after their parachutes or canopies have opened. This kind of skydiving takes skill and practice, and teams are not always successful in their attempts.

The amount of time a skydiver has for a free fall depends on the height of the jump and how much the skydiver uses the air to slow the fall.

In Exercises 81 and 82 of Section 5.6 we find the amount of time that it takes a skydiver to fall from a given height.

Chapter Opener

Each chapter opener features a real-world situation that can be modeled using mathematics. The application then refers students to a specific exercise in the chapter's exercise sets.

81. ***Skydiving.*** If there were no air resistance, then the height (in feet) above the earth for a skydiver t seconds after jumping from an airplane at 10,000 feet would be given by

$$h(t) = -16t^2 + 10{,}000.$$

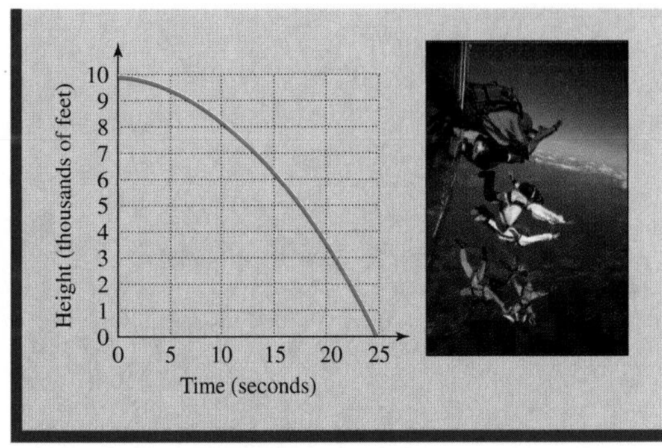

Figure for Exercise 81

EXAMPLE 5

Factoring completely

Factor each polynomial completely.

a) $4x^3 + 14x^2 + 6x$

b) $12x^2y + 6xy + 6y$

Solution

a) $4x^3 + 14x^2 + 6x = 2x(2x^2 + 7x + 3)$ Factor out the GCF, $2x$.

$= 2x(2x + 1)(x + 3)$ Factor $2x^2 + 7x + 3$.

Check by multiplying.

b) $12x^2y + 6xy + 6y = 6y(2x^2 + x + 1)$ Factor out the GCF, $6y$.

To factor $2x^2 + x + 1$ by the *ac* method, we need two numbers with a product of 2 and a sum of 1. Because there are no such numbers, $2x^2 + x + 1$ is prime and the factorization is complete.

Now do Exercises 77–86

Examples

Examples refer directly to exercises, and those exercises in turn refer back to that example. This **double cross-referencing** helps students connect examples to exercises no matter which one they start with.

Factor each polynomial completely. See Examples 5 and 6.

77. $81w^3 - w$
$w(9w - 1)(9w + 1)$

78. $81w^3 - w^2$
$w^2(81w - 1)$

79. $4w^2 + 2w - 30$
$2(2w - 5)(w + 3)$

80. $2x^2 - 28x + 98$
$2(x - 7)^2$

81. $27 + 12x^2 + 36x$
$3(2x + 3)^2$

82. $24y + 12y^2 + 12$
$12(y + 1)^2$

83. $6w^2 - 11w - 35$
$(3w + 5)(2w - 7)$

84. $8y^2 - 14y - 15$
$(2y - 5)(4y + 3)$

85. $3x^2z - 3zx - 18z$
$3z(x - 3)(x + 2)$

86. $a^2b + 2ab - 15b$
$b(a + 5)(a - 3)$

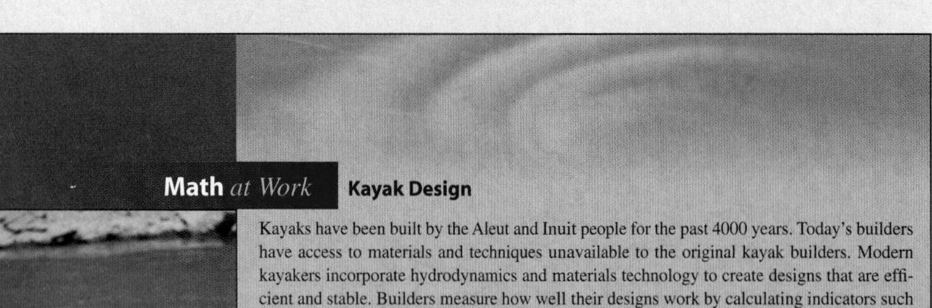

Math *at Work* **Kayak Design**

Kayaks have been built by the Aleut and Inuit people for the past 4000 years. Today's builders have access to materials and techniques unavailable to the original kayak builders. Modern kayakers incorporate hydrodynamics and materials technology to create designs that are efficient and stable. Builders measure how well their designs work by calculating indicators such as prismatic coefficient, block coefficient, and the midship area coefficient, to name a few.

Even the fitting of a kayak to the paddler is done scientifically. For example, the formula

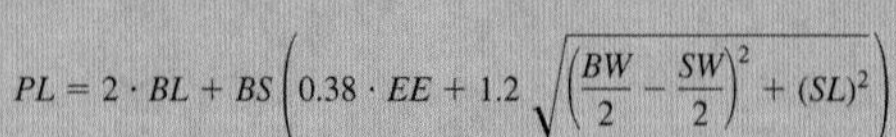

$$PL = 2 \cdot BL + BS\left(0.38 \cdot EE + 1.2\sqrt{\left(\frac{BW}{2} - \frac{SW}{2}\right)^2 + (SL)^2}\right)$$

can be used to calculate the appropriate paddle length. *BL* is the length of the paddle's blade. *BS* is a boating style factor, which is 1.2 for touring, 1.0 for river running, and 0.95 for play boating. *EE* is the elbow to elbow distance with the paddler's arms straight out to the sides. *BW* is the boat width and *SW* is the shoulder width. *SL* is the spine length, which is the distance measured in a sitting position from the chair seat to the top of the paddler's shoulder. All lengths are in centimeters.

The degree of control a kayaker exerts over the kayak depends largely on the body contact with it. A kayaker wears the kayak. So the choice of a kayak should hinge first on the right body fit and comfort and second on the skill level or intended paddling style. So designing, building, and even fitting a kayak is a blend of art and science.

Math at Work

The Math at Work feature appears in each chapter to reinforce the book's theme of real applications in the everyday world of work.

The Factoring Strategy

The following is a summary of the ideas that we use to factor a polynomial completely.

Strategy for Factoring Polynomials Completely

1. If there are any common factors, factor them out first.
2. When factoring a binomial, check to see whether it is a difference of two squares, a difference of two cubes, or a sum of two cubes. *A sum of two squares does not factor.*
3. When factoring a trinomial, check to see whether it is a perfect square trinomial.
4. When factoring a trinomial that is not a perfect square, use the *ac* method or the trial-and-error method.
5. If the polynomial has four terms, try factoring by grouping.
6. Check to see whether any of the factors can be factored again.

Strategy Boxes

The strategy boxes provide a handy reference for students to use when they review key concepts and techniques to prepare for tests and homework.

Margin Notes

Margin notes include **Helpful Hints,** which give advice on the topic they're adjacent to; **Study Tips,** which give more general advice in improving study habits; **Calculator Close-Ups,** which provide advice on using calculators to verify students' work; and **Teaching Tips,** which are especially helpful in programs with new instructors who are looking for alternate ways to explain and reinforce material.

Helpful Hint

We have seen quadratic polynomials that cannot be factored. So not all quadratic equations can be solved by factoring. Methods for solving all quadratic equations are presented in Chapter 10.

Study Tip

A lumber mill turns logs into plywood, adding value to the logs. College is like a lumber mill. If you are not changing, growing, and learning, you may not be increasing in value. Everything that you learn increases your value.

Calculator Close-Up

To evaluate the rational expression in Example 1(a) with a calculator, first use Y= to define the rational expression. Be sure to enclose both numerator and denominator in parentheses.

```
Plot1 Plot2 Plot3
\Y1=(4X-1)/(X+2)
\Y2=
\Y3=
\Y4=
\Y5=
\Y6=
```

Then find $y_1(-3)$.

```
Y1(-3)
                13
```

Teaching Tip Show students how to make up a problem like this example: If $x = 5$, then $(5 - 2)(5 + 7) = 36$. So one of the solutions to $(x - 2)(x + 7) = 36$ is 5. Now solve it to find both solutions.

Exercises
Section exercises are preceded by true/false **Warm-Ups,** which can be used as quizzes or for class discussion.

Warm-Ups

True or false? Explain your answer.

1. $x^2 - 4 = (x - 2)^2$ for any real number x. False
2. The trinomial $4x^2 + 6x + 9$ is a perfect square trinomial. False
3. The polynomial $4y^2 + 25$ is a prime polynomial. True
4. $3y + ay + 3x + ax = (x + y)(3 + a)$ for any values of the variables. True
5. The polynomial $3x^2 + 51$ cannot be factored. False
6. If the GCF is not 1, then you should factor it out first. True
7. $x^2 + 9 = (x + 3)^2$ for any real number x. False
8. The polynomial $x^2 - 3x - 5$ is a prime polynomial. True
9. The polynomial $y^2 - 5y - my + 5m$ can be factored by grouping. True
10. The polynomial $x^2 + ax - 3x + 3a$ can be factored by grouping. False

Next come **Reading and Writing** exercises that can be used for class discussion and to verify students' conceptual understanding. Exercise sets supply a generous and varied amount of drill and realistic **applications** so students can put into practice the skills they have developed.

5.5 Exercises

Boost your GRADE at mathzone.com!

MathZone
- Practice Problems
- Self-Tests
- Videos
- Net Tutor
- e-Professors

Reading and Writing *After reading this section, write out the answers to these questions. Use complete sentences.*

1. What is the relationship between division and factoring?
If there is no remainder, then the dividend factors as the divisor times the quotient.
2. How do we know that $a - b$ is a factor of $a^3 - b^3$?
If you divide $a^3 - b^3$ by $a - b$ there will be no remainder.
3. How do we know that $a + b$ is a factor of $a^3 + b^3$?
If you divide $a^3 + b^3$ by $a + b$ there will be no remainder.
4. How do you recognize if a polynomial is a sum of two cubes?
A sum of two cubes is of the form $a^3 + b^3$.
5. How do you factor a sum of two cubes?
$a^3 + b^3 = (a + b)(a^2 - ab + b^2)$
6. How do you factor a difference of two cubes?
$a^3 - b^3 = (a - b)(a^2 + ab + b^2)$

Factor each polynomial completely, given that the binomial following it is a factor of the polynomial. See Example 1.

7. $x^3 + 3x^2 - 10x - 24$, $x + 4$ $(x + 4)(x - 3)(x + 2)$
8. $x^3 - 7x + 6$, $x - 1$ $(x - 1)(x + 3)(x - 2)$
9. $x^3 + 4x^2 + x - 6$, $x - 1$ $(x - 1)(x + 3)(x + 2)$
10. $x^3 - 5x^2 - 2x + 24$, $x + 2$ $(x + 2)(x - 3)(x - 4)$
11. $x^3 - 8$, $x - 2$ $(x - 2)(x^2 + 2x + 4)$
12. $x^3 + 27$, $x + 3$ $(x + 3)(x^2 - 3x + 9)$

Getting More Involved concludes the exercise set with **Discussion, Writing, Exploration,** and **Cooperative Learning** activities for well-rounded practice in the skills for that section.

Figure for Exercise 109

Getting More Involved

111. *Discussion*

Are there any values for a and b for which $(a + b)^3 = a^3 + b^3$? Find a pair of values for a and b for which $(a + b)^3 \neq a^3 + b^3$. Is $(a + b)^3$ equivalent to $a^3 + b^3$? Explain your answers.
$(-1 + 1)^3 = (-1)^3 + 1^3$, $(1 + 2)^3 \neq 1^3 + 2^3$

112. *Writing*

Explain why $a^2 + ab + b^2$ and $a^2 - ab + b^2$ are prime polynomials.

106. *Exploration*

Find two integers c (positive or negative) for which each polynomial can be factored. Many answers are possible.

a) $x^2 + x + c$ $-2, -6$
b) $x^2 - 2x + c$ $1, -8$
c) $2x^2 - 3x + c$ $1, -9$

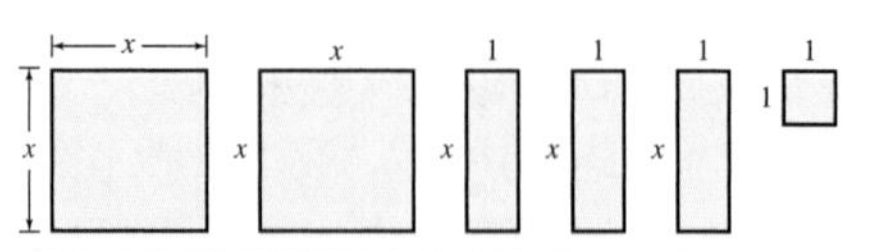

Figure for Exercise 107

107. *Cooperative learning*

Working in groups, cut two large squares, three rectangles, and one small square out of paper that are exactly the same size as shown in the accompanying figure. Then try to place the six figures next to one another so that they form a large rectangle. Do not overlap the pieces or leave any gaps. Explain how factoring $2x^2 + 3x + 1$ can help you solve this puzzle.

108. *Cooperative learning*

Working in groups, cut four squares and eight rectangles out of paper as in the previous exercise to illustrate the trinomial $4x^2 + 7x + 3$. Select one group to demonstrate how to arrange the 12 pieces to form a large rectangle. Have another group explain how factoring the trinomial can help you solve this puzzle.

49. $(5.76x^2 - 3.14x - 7.09) + (3.9x^2 + 1.21x + 5.6)$
$9.66x^2 - 1.93x - 1.49$

50. $(8.5x^2 + 3.27x - 9.33) + (x^2 - 4.39x - 2.32)$
$9.5x^2 - 1.12x - 11.65$

Perform the indicated operation. See Example 5.

51. $(x - 2) - (5x - 8)$
$-4x + 6$

52. $(x - 7) - (3x - 1)$
$-2x - 6$

53. $(m - 2) - (m + 3)$
-5

54. $(m + 5) - (m + 9)$
-4

55. $(2z^2 - 3z) - (3z^2 - 5z)$
$-z^2 + 2z$

56. $(z^2 - 4z) - (5z^2 - 3z)$
$-4z^2 - z$

57. $(w^5 - w^3) - (-w^4 + w^2)$ $w^5 + w^4 - w^3 - w^2$

58. $(w^6 - w^3) - (-w^2 + w)$ $w^6 - w^3 + w^2 - w$

59. $(t^2 - 3t + 4) - (t^2 - 5t - 9)$ $2t + 13$

60. $(t^2 - 6t + 7) - (5t^2 - 3t - 2)$ $-4t^2 - 3t + 9$

61. $(9 - 3y - y^2) - (2 + 5y - y^2)$ $-8y + 7$

62. $(4 - 5y + y^3) - (2 - 3y + y^2)$ $y^3 - y^2 - 2y + 2$

63. $(3.55x - 879) - (26.4x - 455.8)$
$-22.85x - 423.2$

64. $(345.56x - 347.4) - (56.6x + 433)$
$288.96x - 780.4$

Calculator Exercises
Optional calculator exercises provide students with the opportunity to use scientific or graphing calculators to solve various problems.

Collaborative Activities
In addition to the cooperative learning activities in the section exercises, an extensive Collaborative Activity concludes each chapter so that students can solve math problems in a group setting.

Collaborative Activities

Grouping: Three students per group
Topic: Factoring Polynomials

Hannah's Inheritance

Part I: Sally, Kelly, and Hannah inherited property from their father. Sally, who married the neighbor to the east, is given a piece of land adjacent to her husband's property. The land is 5 hectometers wide and the length matches that of her husband's property. Kelly who has married the neighbor to the south is given property that is 4 hectometers wide and its length is the common boundary of her spouse's property. Hannah is to have a square piece that is left after her sister's property is taken out. Hannah wants to find out the dimensions of her land. She knows that her father's land totaled 380 square hectometers. Use the diagram below to find the dimensions of Hannah's land.

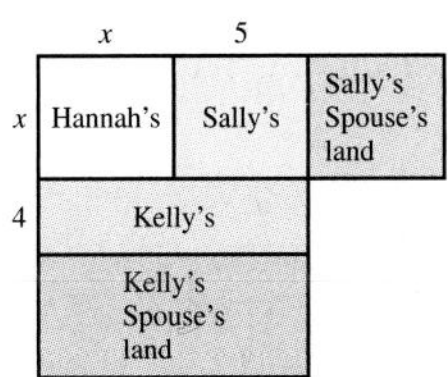

Part II: A few years later Hannah married Harry, a math teacher from town. Now they are getting divorced. As part of the settlement, Harry will get 32% of the land that they now own jointly. However, Harry did not get along with Hannah's sisters and does not want his land to be adjacent to their land. They have agreed that Harry will get a triangular section at the corner as shown in the accompanying figure. Use your answer from Part I to find y and z in the figure.

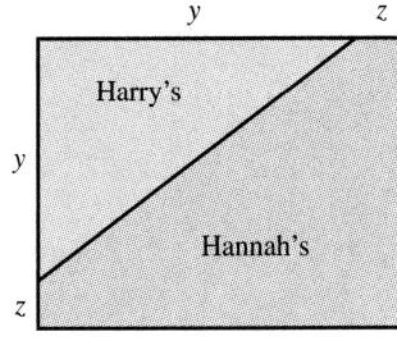

Chapter 5 Wrap-Up

Summary

Factoring		Examples
Prime number	A positive integer larger than 1 that has no integral factors other than 1 and itself	2, 3, 5, 7, 11
Prime polynomial	A polynomial that cannot be factored is prime.	$x^2 + 3$ and $x^2 - x + 5$ are prime.
Strategy for finding the GCF for monomials	1. Find the GCF for the coefficients of the monomials. 2. Form the product of the GCF of the coefficients and each variable that is common to all of the monomials, where the exponent on each variable equals the smallest power of that variable in any of the monomials.	$12x^3yz$, $8x^2y^3$ $\text{GCF} = 4x^2y$

Wrap-Up
The extensive and varied review in the chapter Wrap-Up will help students prepare for tests. First comes the **Summary** with key terms and concepts illustrated by examples, then **Enriching Your Mathematical Word Power** enables students to test their recall of new terminology in a multiple choice format.

Enriching Your Mathematical Word Power

For each mathematical term, choose the correct meaning.

1. factor
a. to write an expression as a product
b. to multiply
c. what two numbers have in common
d. to FOIL a

3. greatest common factor
a. the least common multiple
b. the least common denominator
c. the largest integer that is a factor of two or more integers
d. the largest number in a product c

Review Exercises

5.1 *Find the prime factorization for each integer.*

1. 144 $2^4 \cdot 3^2$

2. 121 11^2

3. 58 $2 \cdot 29$

4. 76 $2^2 \cdot 19$

5. 150 $2 \cdot 3 \cdot 5^2$

6. 200 $2^3 \cdot 5^2$

Find the greatest common factor for each group.

7. 36, 90 18

8. 30, 42, 78 6

18. $a^3b^5 + a^3b^2$ $a^3b^2(b^3 + 1)$

19. $3x^2y - 12xy - 9y^2$ $3y(x^2 - 4x - 3y)$

20. $2a^2 - 4ab^2 - ab$ $a(2a - 4b^2 - b)$

5.2 *Factor each polynomial completely.*

21. $y^2 - 400$ $(y - 20)(y + 20)$

22. $4m^2 - 9$ $(2m - 3)(2m + 3)$

23. $w^2 - 8w + 16$ $(w - 4)^2$

24. $t^2 + 20t + 100$ $(t + 10)^2$

25. $4y^2 + 20y + 25$ $(2y + 5)^2$

26. $2a^2 - 4a - 2$ $2(a^2 - 2a - 1)$

Next come **Review Exercises,** which are first linked back to the section of the chapter that they review, and then the exercises are mixed without section references in the **Miscellaneous** section.

90. $\dfrac{a^{10}}{a^{-4}}$ a^{14}

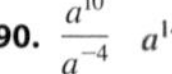

91. $\dfrac{a^3}{a^{-7}}$ a^{10}

92. $\dfrac{b^{-2}}{b^{-6}}$ b^4

Miscellaneous

Perform the indicated operations.

115. $(x + 3)(x + 7)$ $x^2 + 10x + 21$

116. $(k + 5)(k + 4)$ $k^2 + 9k + 20$

117. $(t - 3y)(t - 4y)$ $t^2 - 7ty + 12y^2$

Chapter 5 Test

Give the prime factorization for each integer.

1. 66 $2 \cdot 3 \cdot 11$

2. 336 $2^4 \cdot 3 \cdot 7$

Find the greatest common factor (GCF) for each group.

3. 48, 80 16

4. 42, 66, 78 6

5. $6y^2, 15y^3$ $3y^2$

6. $12a^2b, 18ab^2, 24a^3b^3$ $6ab$

Factor each polynomial completely.

7. $5x^2 - 10x$ $5x(x - 2)$

8. $6x^2y^2 + 12xy^2 + 12y^2$ $6y^2(x^2 + 2x + 2)$

9. $3a^3b - 3ab^3$ $3ab(a - b)(a + b)$

10. $a^2 + 2a - 24$ $(a + 6)(a - 4)$

16. $m^2 + 4mn + 4n^2$ $(m + 2n)^2$

17. $2a^2 - 13a + 15$ $(2a - 3)(a - 5)$

18. $z^3 + 9z^2 + 18z$ $z(z + 3)(z + 6)$

19. $x^3 + 125$ $(x + 5)(x^2 - 5x + 25)$

20. $a^4 - ab^3$ $a(a - b)(a^2 + ab + b^2)$

Factor the polynomial completely, given that $x - 1$ is a factor.

21. $x^3 - 6x^2 + 11x - 6$ $(x - 1)(x - 2)(x - 3)$

Solve each equation.

22. $x^2 + 6x + 9 = 0$ -3

23. $2x^2 + 5x - 12 = 0$ $\frac{3}{2}, -4$

24. $3x^3 = 12x$ $0, -2, 2$

25. $(2x - 1)(3x + 5) = 5$ $-2, \frac{5}{6}$

Chapter Test
The test gives students additional practice to make sure they're ready for the real thing, with **all** answers provided at the back of the book and **all** solutions available in the Student's Solutions Manual.

The **Making Connections** feature following the Chapter Test is a cumulative review of all chapters up to and including the one just finished, helping to tie the course concepts together for students on a regular basis.

Making Connections | A Review of Chapters 1–5

Simplify each expression.

1. $\frac{91 - 17}{17 - 91}$ -1

2. $\frac{4 - 18}{-6 - 1}$ 2

3. $5 - 2(7 - 3)$ -3

4. $3^2 - 4(6)(-2)$ 57

5. $2^5 - 2^4$ 16

6. $0.07(37) + 0.07(63)$ 7

Perform the indicated operations.

7. $x \cdot 2x$ $2x^2$

8. $x + 2x$ $3x$

9. $\frac{6 + 2x}{2}$ $3 + x$

10. $\frac{6 \cdot 2x}{2}$ $6x$

11. $2 \cdot 3y \cdot 4z$ $24yz$

12. $2(3y + 4z)$ $6y + 8z$

13. $2 - (3 - 4z)$ $4z - 1$

14. $t^8 \div t^2$ t^6

15. $t^8 \cdot t^2$ t^{10}

16. $\frac{8t^8}{2t^2}$ $4t^6$

Solve each inequality. State the solution set in interval notation and sketch its graph.

17. $2x - 5 > 3x + 4$ $(-\infty, -9)$

−13 −12 −11 −10 −9 −8 −7

18. $4 - 5x \le -11$ $[3, \infty)$

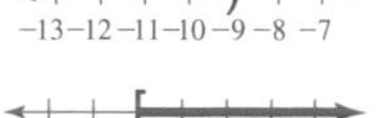

19. $-\frac{2}{3}x + 3 < -5$ $(12, \infty)$

20. $0.05(x - 120) - 24 < 0$ $(-\infty, 600)$

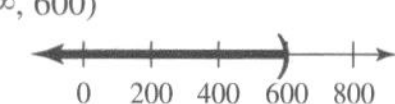

Find the solution set to each equation.

21. $2x - 3 = 0$ $\left\{\frac{3}{2}\right\}$

22. $2x + 1 = 0$ $\left\{-\frac{1}{2}\right\}$

23. $(x - 3)(x + 5) = 0$ $\{3, -5\}$

24. $(2x - 3)(2x + 1) = 0$ $\left\{\frac{3}{2}, -\frac{1}{2}\right\}$

25. $3x(x - 3) = 0$ $\{0, 3\}$

26. $x^2 = x$ $\{0, 1\}$

27. $3x - 3x = 0$ R

28. $3x - 3x = 1$ No solution or $\emptyset$

29. $0.01x - x + 14.9 = 0.5x$ $\{10\}$

30. $0.05x + 0.04(x - 40) = 2$ $\{40\}$

31. $2x^2 = 18$ $\{-3, 3\}$

32. $2x^2 + 7x - 15 = 0$ $\left\{-5, \frac{3}{2}\right\}$

Solve the problem.

33. ***Another ace.*** Professional tennis players can serve a tennis ball at speeds over 120 mph into a rectangular region that has a perimeter of 69 feet and an area of 283.5 square feet. Find the length and width of the service region.
Length 21 ft, width 13.5 ft

Photo for Exercise 33

Critical **Thinking** | For Individual or Group Work | Chapter 5

These exercises can be solved by a variety of techniques, which may or may not require algebra. So be creative and think critically. Explain all answers. Answers are in the Instructor's Edition of this text.

1. ***Counting cubes.*** What is the total number of cubes that are in each of the following diagrams?

a)  

b) 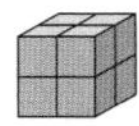

c) 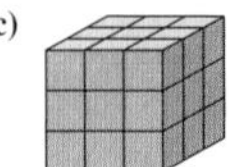

d) 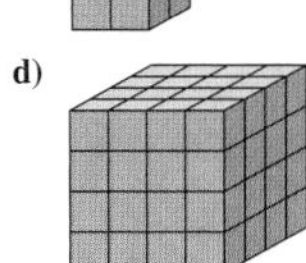

2. ***More cubes.*** Imagine a large cube that is made up of 125 small cubes like those in the previous exercise. What is the total number of cubes that could be found in this arrangement?

3. ***Timely coincidence.*** Starting at 8 A.M. determine the number of times in the next 24 hours for which the hour and minute hands on a clock coincide?

Photo for Exercise 3

4. ***Chess board.*** There are 64 squares on a square chess board. How many squares are neither diagonal squares nor edge squares?

Photo for Exercise 4

5. ***Last digit.*** Find the last digit in 3^{9999}.

6. ***Reconciling remainders.*** Find a positive integer smaller than 500 that has a remainder of 3 when divided by 5, a remainder of 6 when divided by 9, and a remainder of 8 when divided by 11.

7. ***Exact sum.*** Find this sum exactly:

$$\frac{1}{2} + \frac{1}{2^2} + \frac{1}{2^3} + \frac{1}{2^4} + \cdots + \frac{1}{2^{19}}$$

8. ***Ten-digit number.*** Find a 10-digit number whose first digit is the number of 1's in the 10-digit number, whose second digit is the number of 2's in the 10-digit number, whose third digit is the number of 3's in the 10-digit number, and so on. The ninth digit must be the number of nines in the 10-digit number and the tenth digit must be the number of zeros in the 10-digit number.

1. **a)** 1 **b)** 9 **c)** 36 **d)** 100 **2.** 225 **3.** 22 **4.** 24 **5.** 7 **6.** 393 **7.** $\frac{524287}{524288}$ **8.** 2,100,010,006.

Critical Thinking
New to this edition, the Critical Thinking section that concludes every chapter encourages students to think creatively to solve unique and intriguing problems and puzzles.

SUPPLEMENTS FOR INSTRUCTORS

Annotated Instructor's Edition

This version of the student text contains **answers** to all odd- and even-numbered exercises in addition to helpful **teaching tips.** The answers are printed on the same page as the exercises themselves so that there is no need to consult a separate appendix or answer key.

Instructor's Testing and Resource CD

The cross-platform CD-ROM provides a wealth of resources for the instructor. Supplements featured on this CD-ROM include a **computerized test bank** utilizing Brownstone Diploma® **algorithm-based** testing software to quickly create customized exams. This user-friendly program enables instructors to search for questions by topic, format, or difficulty level; edit existing questions or add new ones; and scramble questions and answer keys for multiple versions of the same test.

Instructor's Solutions Manual

This supplement contains detailed solutions to all exercises in the text and is prepared by Mark Dugopolski. The methods used to solve the problems in the manual are the same as those used to solve the examples in the textbook.

www.mathzone.com*

*Web-based product also available on CD-ROM

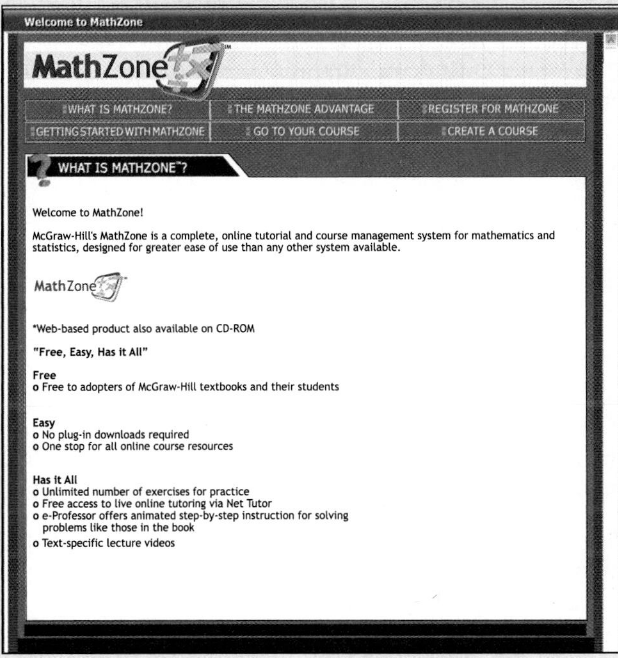

McGraw-Hill's **MathZone** is a complete, online tutorial and course management system for mathematics and statistics, designed for greater ease of use than any other system available. Free on adoption of a McGraw-Hill title, instructors can create and share courses and assignments with colleagues and adjuncts in a matter of a few clicks of the mouse. All assignments, questions, e-Professors, online tutoring, and video lectures are directly tied to text-specific materials in Dugopolski, *Elementary and Intermediate Algebra,* Second Edition. MathZone courses are customized to your textbook, but you can edit questions and algorithms, import your own content, and create announcements and due dates for assignments. MathZone has automatic grading and reporting of easy-to-assign algorithmically generated homework, quizzing, and testing. All student activity within MathZone is automatically recorded and available to you through a fully integrated grade book that can be downloaded to Excel.

ALEKS® (**A**ssessment and **LE**arning in **K**nowledge **S**paces) is an artificial intelligence-based system for individualized math learning, available over the Web. ALEKS delivers precise, qualitative diagnostic assessments of students' math knowledge, guides them in the selection of appropriate new study material, and records their progress toward mastery of curricular goals in a robust classroom management system. See page xxxviii for more details regarding ALEKS.

PageOut

PageOut is McGraw-Hill's unique, intuitive tool enabling instructors to create a full-featured, professional quality course website *without* being a technical expert. With PageOut you can post your syllabus online, assign content from the Dugopolski MathZone site, add links to important off-site resources, and maintain student results in the online grade book. PageOut is free for every McGraw-Hill Higher Education user and, if you're short on time, we even have a team ready to help you create your site. Contact your McGraw-Hill representative for further information.

SUPPLEMENTS FOR STUDENTS

Student's Solutions Manual

This supplement, prepared by Mark Dugopolski, contains complete worked-out solutions to all odd-numbered exercises in the textbook and all odd- and even-numbered problems for the Chapter Tests and Making Connections. Solutions for Critical Thinking are in the Instructor's Solutions Manual only. The methods used to solve the problems in the manual are the same as those used to solve the examples in the textbook. This tool can be an invaluable aid to students who want to check their work and improve their grades by comparing their own solutions to those found in the manual and finding specific areas where they can do better.

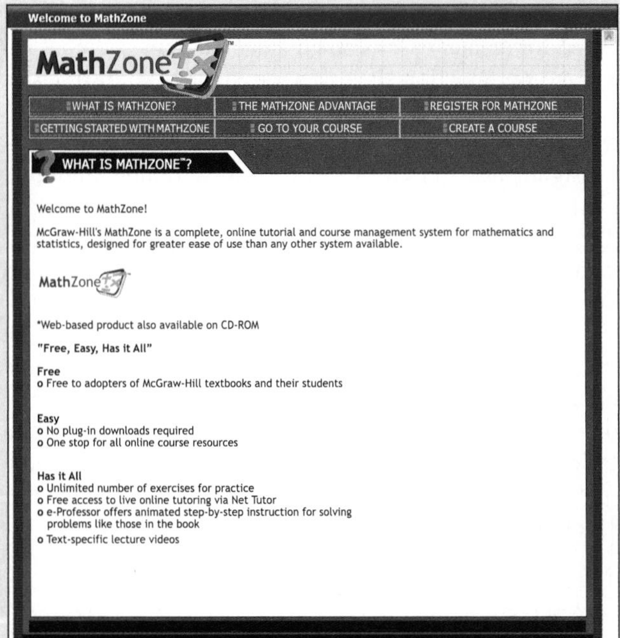

*Web-based product also available on CD-ROM

McGraw-Hill's MathZone is a powerful new online tutorial for homework, quizzing, testing, and interactive applications. MathZone offers:

- **Practice exercises** based on the text and generated in an unlimited number for as much practice as needed to master any topic you study.
- **Videos** of classroom instructors giving lectures and showing you how to solve exercises from the text.

- **e-Professors** to take you through animated, step-by-step instructions (delivered via on-screen text and synchronized audio) for solving problems in the book, enabling you to digest each step at your own pace.
- **NetTutor,** which offers live, personalized tutoring via the Internet.
- Every assignment, question, e-Professor, and video lecture is derived directly from Dugopolski, *Elementary and Intermediate Algebra,* Second Edition.

NetTutor

Also available separately from MathZone, NetTutor is a revolutionary system that enables students to interact with a live tutor over the Web by using NetTutor's Web-based, graphical chat capabilities. Students can also submit questions and receive answers, browse previously answered questions, and view previous live chat sessions. NetTutor can be accessed on the text's MathZone site through the Student Edition.

ALEKS® (**A**ssessment and **LE**arning in **K**nowledge **S**paces) is an artificial intelligence-based system for individualized math learning, available over the Web. ALEKS delivers precise, qualitative diagnostic assessments of students' math knowledge, guides them in the selection of appropriate new study material, and records their progress toward mastery of curricular goals in a robust classroom management system. See page xxxviii for more details regarding ALEKS.

Dugopolski Video Series

The video series is available on DVD and VHS tape and features an instructor introducing topics and working through selected odd-numbered exercises from the text, explaining how to complete them step by step. The DVDs are **closed-captioned** for the hearing-impaired and also **subtitled in Spanish.**

***Math for the Anxious: Building Basic Skills,* by Rosanne Proga**

Math for the Anxious: Building Basic Skills is written to provide a practical approach to the problem of math anxiety. By combining strategies for success with a pain-free introduction to basic math content, students will overcome their anxiety and find greater success in their math courses.

ALEKS is an artificial intelligence-based system for individualized math learning, available for Higher Education from McGraw-Hill over the World Wide Web.

ALEKS delivers precise assessments of math knowledge, guides the student in the selection of appropriate new study material, and records student progress toward mastery of goals.

ALEKS interacts with a student much as a skilled human tutor would, moving between explanation and practice as needed, correcting and analyzing errors, defining terms and changing topics on request. By accurately assessing a student's knowledge, ALEKS can focus clearly on what the student is ready to learn next, helping to master the course content more quickly and easily.

ALEKS is:

- **A comprehensive course management system.** It tells the instructor exactly what students know and don't know.
- **Artificial intelligence.** It totally individualizes assessment and learning.
- **Customizable.** ALEKS can be set to cover the material in your course.
- **Web-based.** It uses a standard browser for easy Internet access.
- **Inexpensive.** There are no setup fees or site license fees.

ALEKS 2.0 adds the following new features:

- **Automatic Textbook Integration**
- **New Instructor Module**
- **Instructor-Created Quizzes**
- **New Message Center**

ALEKS maintains the features that have made it so popular including:

- **Web-Based Delivery** No complicated network or lab setup
- **Immediate Feedback** for students in learning mode
- **Integrated Tracking of Student Progress and Activity**
- **Individualized Instruction** which gives students problems they are ***Ready to Learn***

For more information please contact your McGraw-Hill Sales Representative or visit ALEKS at http://www.highedmath.aleks.com.

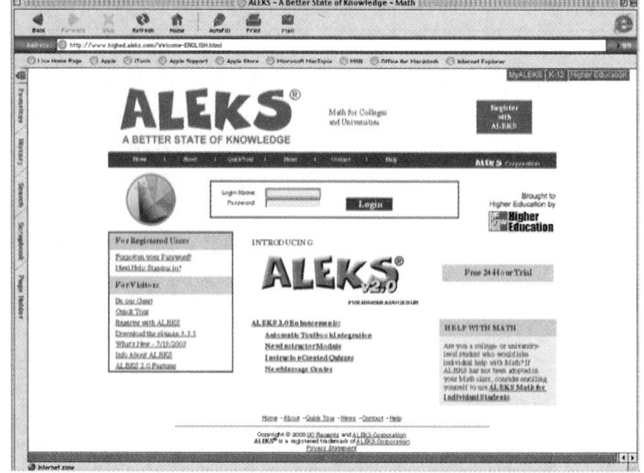

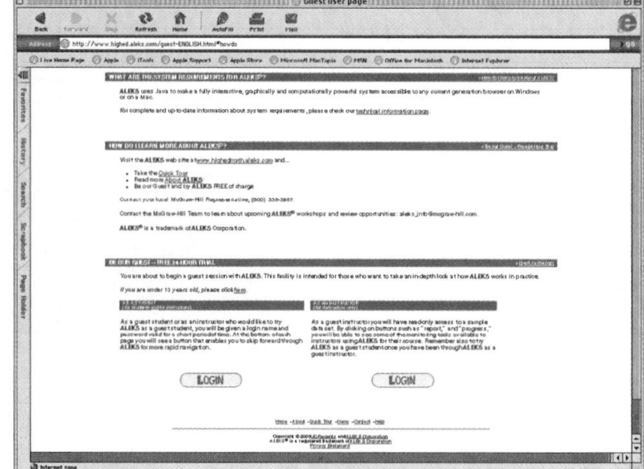

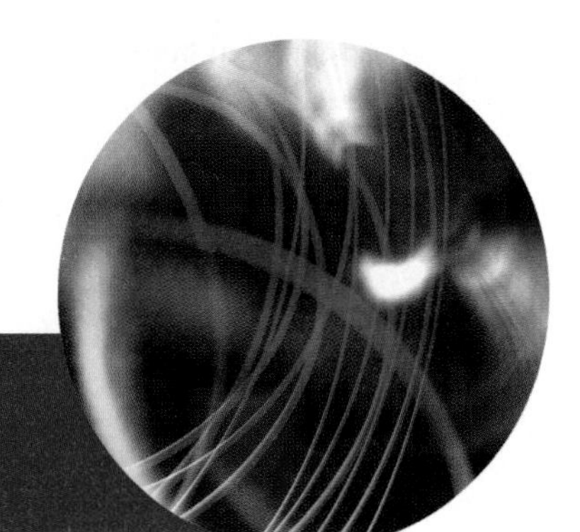

Applications Index

Chemistry

Construction

Consumer Applications

Design

Environment

Geometry

Investment

Puzzles

Science

Sports

Statistics/Demographics

Travel

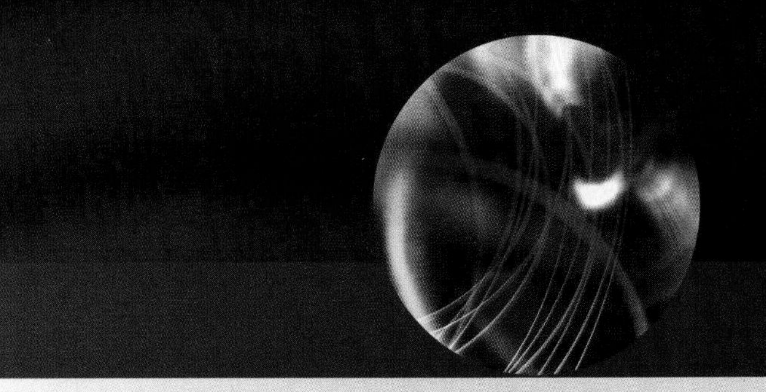

Real Numbers and Their Properties

It has been said that baseball is the "great American pastime." All of us who have played the game or who have only been spectators believe we understand the game. But do we realize that a pitcher must aim for an invisible three-dimensional target that is about 20 inches wide by 23 inches high by 17 inches deep and that a pitcher must throw so that the batter has difficulty hitting the ball? A curve ball may deflect 14 inches to skim over the outside corner of the plate, or a knuckle ball can break 11 inches off center when it is 20 feet from the plate and then curve back over the center of the plate.

The batter is trying to hit a rotating ball that can travel up to 120 miles per hour and must make split-second decisions about shifting his weight, changing his stride, and swinging the bat. The size of the bat each batter uses depends on his strengths, and pitchers in turn try to capitalize on a batter's weaknesses.

Millions of baseball fans enjoy watching this game of strategy and numbers. Many watch their favorite teams at the local ballparks, while others cheer for the home team on television. Of course, baseball fans are always interested in which team is leading the division and the number of games that their favorite team is behind the leader. Finding the number of games behind for each team in the division involves both arithmetic and algebra. Algebra provides the formula for finding games behind, and arithmetic is used to do the computations.

In Exercise 103 of Section 1.6 we will find the number of games behind for each team in the American League East.

1.1 The Real Numbers

In this Section

- The Integers
- The Rational Numbers
- The Number Line
- The Real Numbers
- Intervals of Real Numbers
- Absolute Value

The numbers that we use in algebra are called the real numbers. We start the discussion of the real numbers with some simpler sets of numbers.

The Integers

The most fundamental collection or **set** of numbers is the set of **counting numbers** or **natural numbers.** Of course, these are the numbers that we use for counting. The set of natural numbers is written in symbols as follows.

The Natural Numbers

$$\{1, 2, 3, \ldots\}$$

Braces, { }, are used to indicate a set of numbers. The three dots after 1, 2, and 3, which are read "and so on," mean that the pattern continues without end. There are infinitely many natural numbers.

The natural numbers, together with the number 0, are called the **whole numbers.** The set of whole numbers is written as follows.

The Whole Numbers

$$\{0, 1, 2, 3, \ldots\}$$

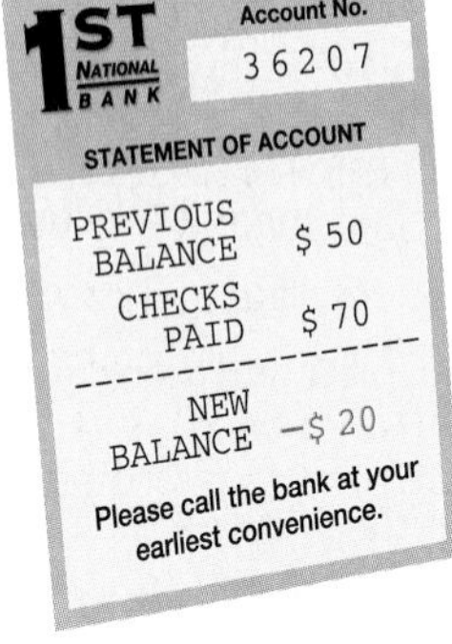

Figure 1.1

Although the whole numbers have many uses, they are not adequate for indicating losses or debts. A debt of \$20 can be expressed by the negative number -20 (negative twenty). See Fig. 1.1. When a thermometer reads 10 degrees below zero on a Fahrenheit scale, we say that the temperature is -10°F. See Fig. 1.2. The whole numbers together with the negatives of the counting numbers form the set of **integers.**

The Integers

$$\{\ldots, -3, -2, -1, 0, 1, 2, 3, \ldots\}$$

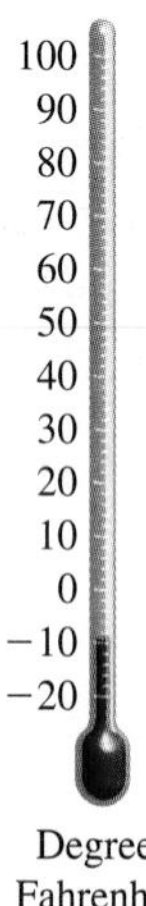

Figure 1.2

The Rational Numbers

A **rational number** is any number that can be expressed as a ratio (or quotient) of two integers. The set of rational numbers includes both the positive and negative fractions. We cannot list the rational numbers as easily as we listed the numbers in the other sets we have been discussing. So we write the set of rational numbers in symbols using **set-builder notation** as follows.

The Rational Numbers

$$\left\{\frac{a}{b} \;\middle|\; a \text{ and } b \text{ are integers, with } b \neq 0\right\}$$

↑ The set of ↑ such that ↑ conditions

Helpful Hint

Rational numbers are used for ratios. For example, if 2 out of 5 students surveyed attend summer school, then the ratio of students who attend summer school to the total number surveyed is 2/5. Note that the ratio 2/5 does not tell how many were surveyed or how many attend summer school.

We read this notation as "the set of numbers of the form $\frac{a}{b}$ such that a and b are integers, with $b \neq 0$." We rule out $b = 0$ because division by zero does not make sense and it is not a defined operation. Note how we use the letters a and b to represent numbers here. A letter used to represent some numbers is called a **variable.**

Examples of rational numbers are

$$\frac{3}{1},\ \frac{5}{4},\ -\frac{7}{10},\ \frac{0}{6},\ \frac{5}{1},\ -\frac{77}{3},\ \text{and}\ \frac{-3}{-6}.$$

Note that we usually use simpler forms for some of these rational numbers. For instance, $\frac{3}{1} = 3$ and $\frac{0}{6} = 0$. The integers are rational numbers because any integer can be written with a denominator of 1.

If you divide the denominator into the numerator, then you can convert a rational number to decimal form. As a decimal, every rational number either repeats indefinitely $\left(\frac{1}{3} = 0.\overline{3} = 0.333\ldots\right)$ or terminates $\left(\frac{1}{8} = 0.125\right)$. The line over the 3 indicates that it repeats forever. The part that repeats can have more digits than the display of your calculator. In this case you will have to divide by hand to do the conversion. For example, try converting $\frac{11}{17}$ to a repeating decimal.

The Number Line

The number line is a diagram that helps us visualize numbers and their relationships to each other. A number line is like the scale on the thermometer in Fig. 1.2. To construct a number line, we draw a straight line and label any convenient point with the number 0. Now we choose any convenient length and use it to locate other points. Points to the right of 0 correspond to the positive numbers, and points to the left of 0 correspond to the negative numbers. Zero is neither positive nor negative. The number line is shown in Fig. 1.3.

Teaching Tip Have students come to the board and locate numbers such as −2/3, −2.25, −3.7, and −5.1 on the number line.

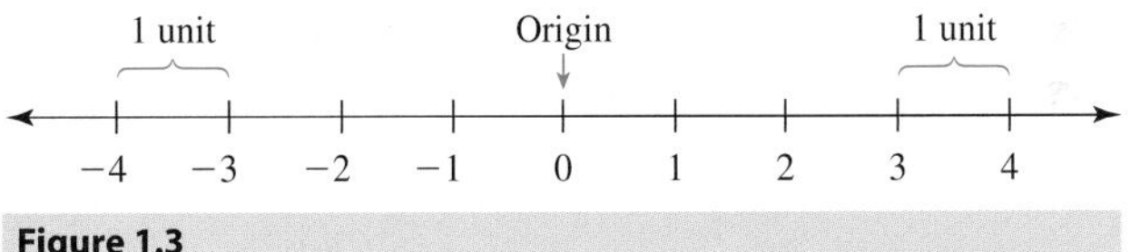

Figure 1.3

The numbers corresponding to the points on the line are called the **coordinates** of the points. The distance between two consecutive integers is called a **unit** and is the same for any two consecutive integers. The point with coordinate 0 is called the **origin.** The numbers on the number line increase in size from left to right. *When we compare the size of any two numbers, the larger number lies to the right of the smaller on the number line.* Zero is larger than any negative number and smaller than any positive number.

EXAMPLE 1

Comparing numbers on a number line

Determine which number is the larger in each given pair of numbers.

a) −3, 2 **b)** 0, −4 **c)** −2, −1

Solution

a) The larger number is 2, because 2 lies to the right of −3 on the number line. In fact, any positive number is larger than any negative number.

b) The larger number is 0, because 0 lies to the right of -4 on the number line.

c) The larger number is -1, because -1 lies to the right of -2 on the number line.

Now do Exercises 7–16

The set of integers is illustrated or *graphed* in Fig. 1.4 by drawing a point for each integer. The three dots to the right and left below the number line and the blue arrows indicate that the numbers go on indefinitely in both directions.

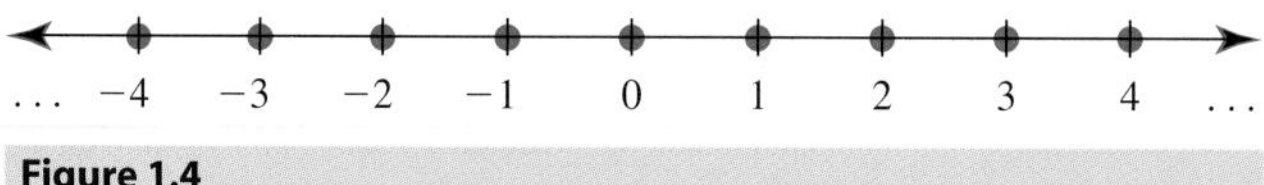

Figure 1.4

EXAMPLE 2

Graphing numbers on a number line

List the numbers described, and graph the numbers on a number line.

a) The whole numbers less than 4

b) The integers between 3 and 9

c) The integers greater than -3

Solution

a) The whole numbers less than 4 are 0, 1, 2, and 3. These numbers are shown in Fig. 1.5.

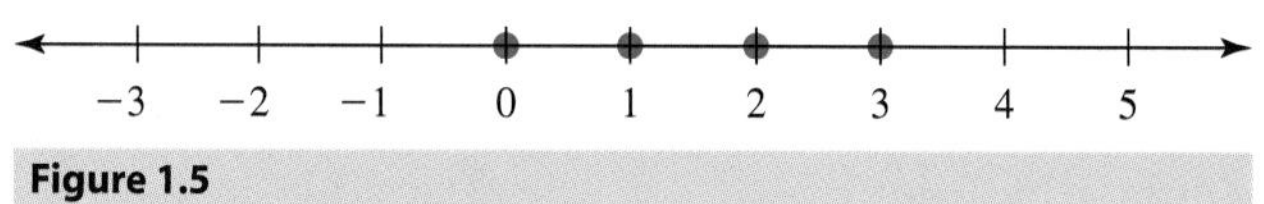

Figure 1.5

b) The integers between 3 and 9 are 4, 5, 6, 7, and 8. Note that 3 and 9 are not considered to be *between* 3 and 9. The graph is shown in Fig. 1.6.

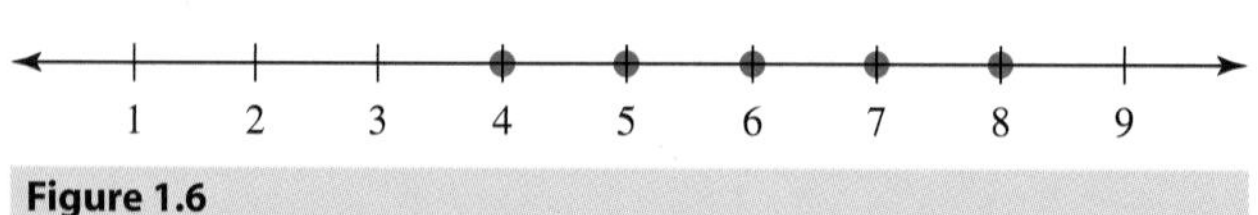

Figure 1.6

c) The integers greater than -3 are -2, -1, 0, 1, and so on. To indicate the continuing pattern, we use three dots on the graph shown in Fig. 1.7.

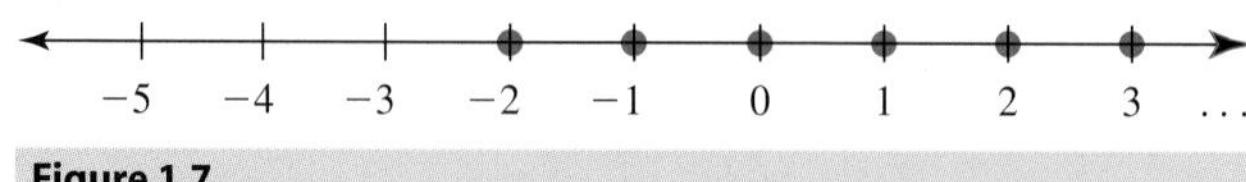

Figure 1.7

Now do Exercises 17–26

Study Tip

Start a personal library. This book as well as other books that you study from should be the basis for your library. You can also add books to your library at garage-sale prices when your bookstore sells its old texts. If you need to reference some material in the future, it is much easier to use a familiar book.

The Real Numbers

For every rational number there is a point on the number line. For example, the number $\frac{1}{2}$ corresponds to a point halfway between 0 and 1 on the number line, and $-\frac{5}{4}$ corresponds to a point one and one-quarter units to the left of 0, as shown in Fig. 1.8. Since there is a correspondence between numbers and points on the number line, the points are often referred to as numbers.

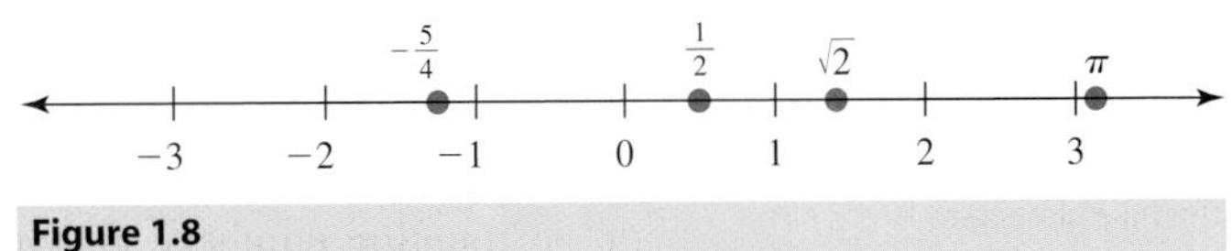

Figure 1.8

Calculator Close-Up

A calculator can give rational approximations for irrational numbers such as $\sqrt{2}$ and π.

```
√(2)
        1.414213562
π
        3.141592654
```

The calculator screens in this text may differ from the screen of the calculator model you use. If so, you may have to consult your manual to get the desired results.

The set of numbers that corresponds to *all* points on a number line is called the set of **real numbers** or R. A graph of the real numbers is shown on a number line by shading all points as in Fig. 1.9. All rational numbers are real numbers, but there are points on the number line that do not correspond to rational numbers. Those real numbers that are not rational are called **irrational.** An irrational number cannot be written as a ratio of integers. It can be shown that numbers such as $\sqrt{2}$ (the square root of 2) and π (Greek letter pi) are irrational. The number $\sqrt{2}$ is a number that can be multiplied by itself to obtain $2(\sqrt{2} \cdot \sqrt{2} = 2)$. The number π is the ratio of the circumference and diameter of any circle. Irrational numbers are not as easy to represent as rational numbers. That is why we use symbols such as $\sqrt{2}$, $\sqrt{3}$, and π for irrational numbers. When we perform computations with irrational numbers, we sometimes use rational approximations for them. For example, $\sqrt{2} \approx 1.414$ and $\pi \approx 3.14$. The symbol $\approx$ means "is approximately equal to." Note that not all square roots are irrational. For example, $\sqrt{9} = 3$, because $3 \cdot 3 = 9$. We will deal with irrational numbers in greater depth when we discuss roots in Chapter 9.

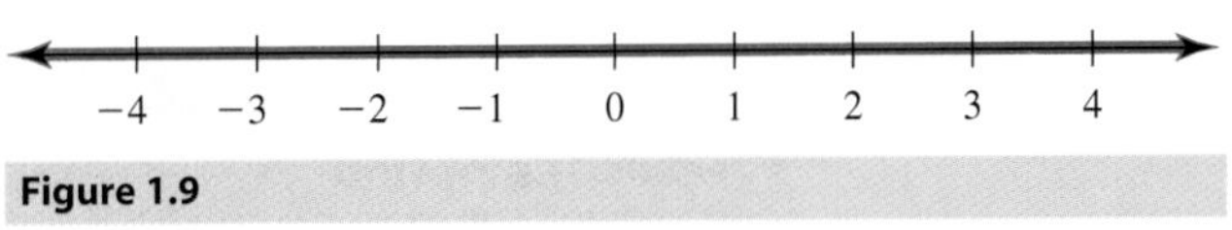

Figure 1.9

Figure 1.10 summarizes the sets of numbers that make up the real numbers, and shows the relationships between them.

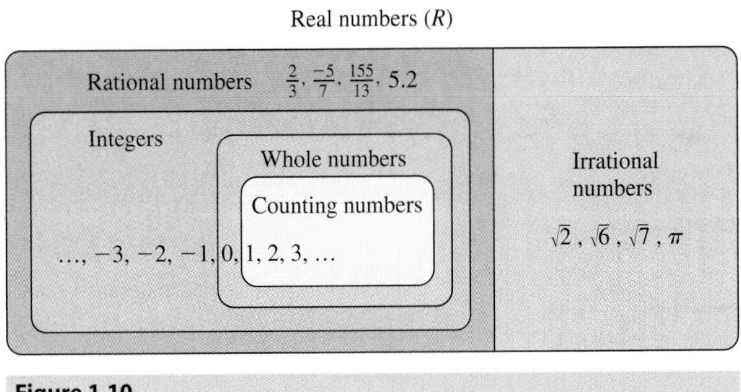

Figure 1.10

EXAMPLE 3

Types of numbers

Determine whether each statement is true or false.

a) Every rational number is an integer.

b) Every counting number is an integer.

c) Every irrational number is a real number.

Teaching Tip Remind students that in math every statement is either true or false. If there is one exception to a statement, then the statement is false. If the exception is noted in the statement, then the statement is true.

Solution

a) False. For example, $\frac{1}{2}$ is a rational number that is not an integer.

b) True, because the integers consist of the counting numbers, the negatives of the counting numbers, and zero.

c) True, because the rational numbers together with the irrational numbers form the real numbers.

Now do Exercises 27–38

Intervals of Real Numbers

Retailers often have a sale for a certain *interval* of time. Between 6 A.M. and 8 A.M. you get a 20% discount. A **bounded** or finite interval of real numbers is the set of real numbers that are between two real numbers, which are called the **endpoints** of the interval. The endpoints may or may not belong to an interval. **Interval notation** is used to represent intervals of real numbers. In interval notation, parentheses are used to indicate that the endpoints do not belong to the interval and brackets indicate that the endpoints do belong to the interval. The following box shows the four types of finite intervals for two real numbers a and b, where a is less than b.

Finite Intervals

Verbal Description	Interval Notation	Graph
The set of real numbers between a and b	(a, b)	
The set of real numbers between a and b inclusive	$[a, b]$	
The set of real numbers greater than a and less than or equal to b	$(a, b]$	
The set of real numbers greater than or equal to a and less than b	$[a, b)$	

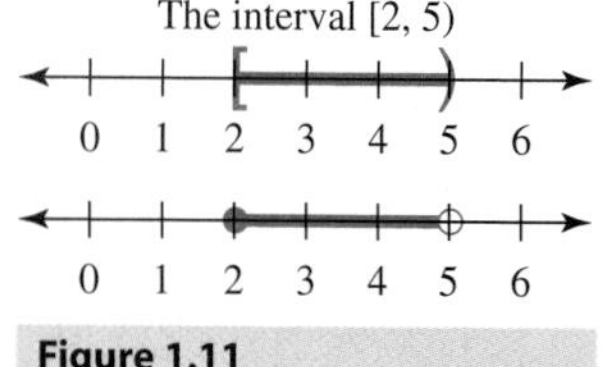

Figure 1.11

Note how the parentheses and brackets are used on the graph and in the interval notation. It is also common to draw the graph of an interval of real numbers using an open circle for an endpoint that does not belong to the interval and a closed circle for an endpoint that belongs to the interval. For example, see the graphs of the interval $[2, 5)$ in Fig. 1.11.

In this text, graphs of intervals will be drawn with parentheses and brackets so that they agree with interval notation.

EXAMPLE 4

Interval notation with finite intervals

Write the interval notation for each interval of real numbers and graph the interval.

a) The set of real numbers greater than 3 and less than or equal to 5

b) The set of real numbers between 0 and 4 inclusive

c) The set of real numbers greater than or equal to -1 and less than 4

d) The set of real numbers between -2 and -1

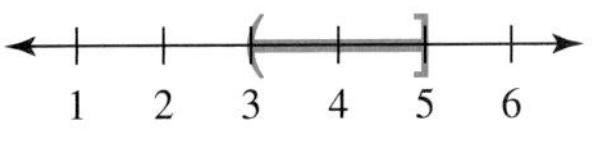

Figure 1.12

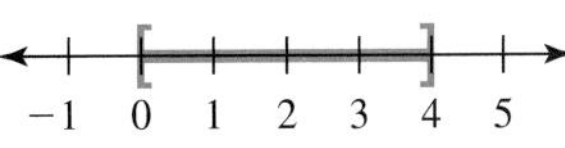

Figure 1.13

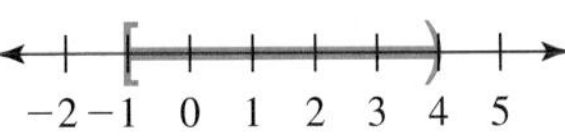

Figure 1.14

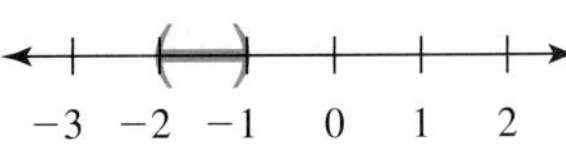

Figure 1.15

Solution

a) The set of real numbers greater than 3 and less than or equal to 5 is written in interval notation as (3, 5] and graphed in Fig. 1.12.

b) The set of real numbers between 0 and 4 inclusive is written in interval notation as [0, 4] and graphed in Fig. 1.13.

c) The set of real numbers greater than or equal to -1 and less than 4 is written in interval notation as $[-1, 4)$ and graphed in Fig. 1.14.

d) The set of real numbers between -2 and -1 is written in interval notation as $(-2, -1)$ and graphed in Fig. 1.15.

Now do Exercises 39–44

Some sales never end. After 8 A.M. all merchandise is 10% off. An **unbounded** or **infinite interval** of real numbers is missing at least one endpoint. It may extend infinitely far to the right or left on the number line. In this case the infinity symbol ∞ is used as an endpoint in the interval notation. Note that parentheses are always used next to ∞ or $-\infty$ in interval notation. The following box shows the five types of infinite intervals for a real number a.

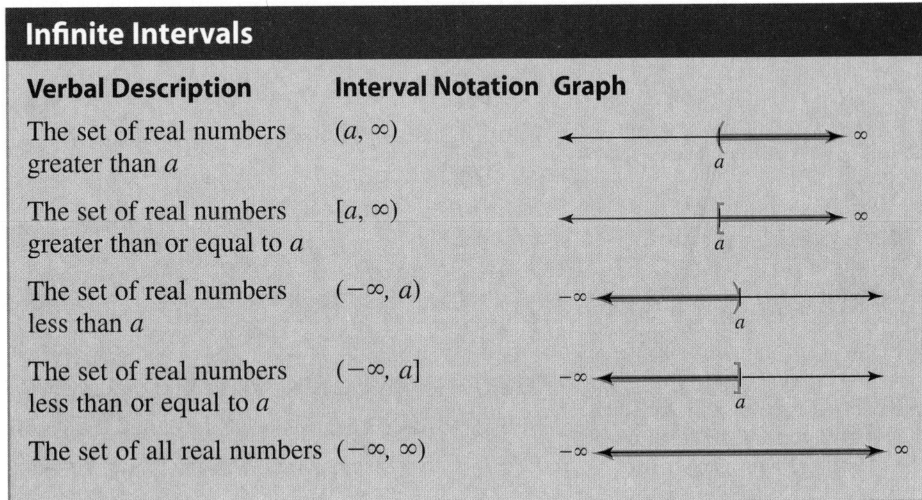

Infinite Intervals

Verbal Description	Interval Notation	Graph
The set of real numbers greater than a	(a, ∞)	
The set of real numbers greater than or equal to a	$[a, \infty)$	
The set of real numbers less than a	$(-\infty, a)$	
The set of real numbers less than or equal to a	$(-\infty, a]$	
The set of all real numbers	$(-\infty, \infty)$	

EXAMPLE 5

Interval notation with infinite intervals

Write each interval of real numbers in interval notation and graph it.

a) The set of real numbers greater than or equal to 3

b) The set of real numbers less than -2

c) The set of real numbers greater than 2.5

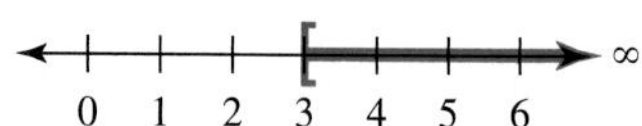

Figure 1.16

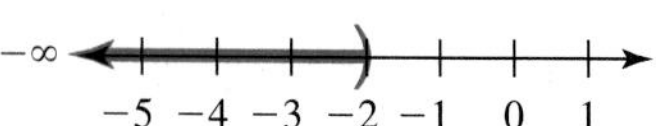

Figure 1.17

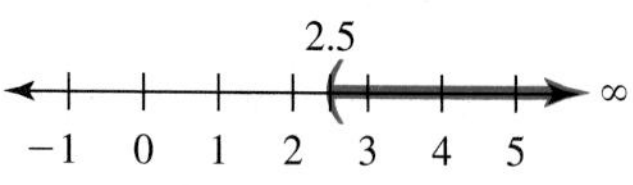

Figure 1.18

Solution

a) The set of real numbers greater than or equal to 3 is written in interval notation as $[3, \infty)$ and graphed in Fig. 1.16.

b) The set of real numbers less than -2 is written in interval notation as $(-\infty, -2)$ and graphed in Fig. 1.17.

c) The set of real numbers greater than 2.5 is written in interval notation as $(2.5, \infty)$ and graphed in Fig. 1.18.

Now do Exercises 45–50

Absolute Value

The concept of absolute value will be used to define the basic operations with real numbers in Section 1.3. The **absolute value** of a number is the number's distance from 0 on the number line. For example, the numbers 5 and -5 are both five units away from 0 on the number line. So the absolute value of each of these numbers is 5. See Fig. 1.19. We write $|a|$ for "the absolute value of a." So

$$|5| = 5 \quad \text{and} \quad |-5| = 5.$$

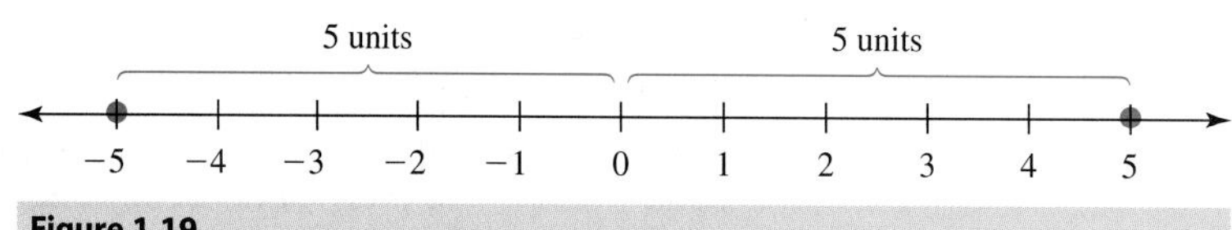

Figure 1.19

The notation $|a|$ represents distance, and distance is never negative. So $|a|$ is greater than or equal to zero for any real number a.

EXAMPLE 6

Finding absolute value

Evaluate.

a) $|3|$ **b)** $|-3|$ **c)** $|0|$

d) $\left|\frac{2}{3}\right|$ **e)** $|-0.39|$

Solution

a) $|3| = 3$ because 3 is three units away from 0.

b) $|-3| = 3$ because -3 is three units away from 0.

c) $|0| = 0$ because 0 is zero units away from 0.

Study Tip

Exercise sets are designed to gradually increase in difficulty. So start from the beginning and work lots of exercises. If you get stuck, go back and study the corresponding examples. If you are still stuck, move ahead to a new type of exercise.

d) $\left|\frac{2}{3}\right| = \frac{2}{3}$

e) $|-0.39| = 0.39$

Now do Exercises 51–58

Two numbers that are located on opposite sides of zero and have the same absolute value are called **opposites** of each other. The numbers 5 and -5 are opposites of each other. We say that the opposite of 5 is -5 and the opposite of -5 is 5. The symbol "$-$" is used to indicate "opposite" as well as "negative." When the negative sign is used before a number, it should be read as "negative." When it is used in front of parentheses or a variable, it should be read as "opposite." For example, $-(5) = -5$ means "the opposite of 5 is negative 5," and $-(-5) = 5$ means "the opposite of negative 5 is 5." Zero does not have an opposite in the same sense as nonzero numbers. Zero is its own opposite. We read $-(0) = 0$ as the "the opposite of zero is zero."

Teaching Tip Ask students whether $-(-(-(-(-(-(-5))))))$ is positive or negative. Ask them to write a rule for deciding.

In general, $-a$ means "the opposite of a." If a is positive, $-a$ is negative. If a is negative, $-a$ is positive. Opposites have the following property.

Opposite of an Opposite

For any real number a,

$$-(-a) = a.$$

Remember that we have defined $|a|$ to be the distance between 0 and a on the number line. Using opposites, we can give a symbolic definition of absolute value.

Absolute Value

$$|a| = \begin{cases} a & \text{if } a \text{ is positive or zero} \\ -a & \text{if } a \text{ is negative} \end{cases}$$

EXAMPLE 7

Using the symbolic definition of absolute value

Evaluate.

a) $|8|$

b) $|0|$

c) $|-8|$

Solution

a) If a is positive, then $|a| = a$. Since 8 is greater than 0, $|8| = 8$.

b) If a is 0, then $|a| = a$. So $|0| = 0$.

c) If a is negative, then $|a| = -a$. So $|-8| = -(-8) = 8$.

Now do Exercises 59–64

Warm-Ups ▼

True or false? Explain your answer.

Teaching Tip The Warm-Ups can be done orally. Ask students to explain their answers.

1. The natural numbers and the counting numbers are the same. True
2. The number 8,134,562,877,565 is a counting number. True
3. Zero is a counting number. False
4. Zero is not a rational number. False
5. The opposite of negative 3 is positive 3. True
6. The absolute value of 4 is -4. False
7. $-(-9) = 9$ True
8. The real number π is in the interval $(3, 4)$. True
9. Negative 6 is greater than negative 3. False
10. Negative 5 is between 4 and 6. False

1.1 Exercises

Boost your GRADE at mathzone.com!

MathZone

▶ Practice Problems ▶ Net Tutor
▶ Self-Tests ▶ e-Professors
▶ Videos

Reading and Writing *After reading this section write out the answers to these questions. Use complete sentences.*

1. What are the integers?
   The integers are the numbers in the set $\{\ldots, -3, -2, -1, 0, 1, 2, 3, \ldots\}$.
2. What are the rational numbers?
   The rational numbers are numbers of the form $\frac{a}{b}$ where a and b are integers and $b \neq 0$.
3. What is the difference between a rational and an irrational number?
   A rational number is a ratio of integers and an irrational number is not.
4. What is a number line?
   A number line is a line on which there is a point corresponding to every real number.
5. How do you know that one number is larger than another?
   The number a is larger than b if a lies to the right of b on the number line.
6. What is the ratio of the circumference and diameter of any circle?
   The ratio of the circumference and diameter of any circle is the number π, which is approximately 3.14.

Determine which number is the larger in each given pair of numbers. See Example 1.

7. $-3, 6$ 6
8. $7, -10$ 7
9. $0, -6$ 0
10. $-8, 0$ 0
11. $-3, -2$ -2
12. $-5, -8$ -5
13. $-12, -15$ -12
14. $-13, -7$ -7
15. $-2.9, -2.1$ -2.1
16. $2.1, 2.9$ 2.9

List the numbers described and graph them on a number line. See Example 2.

17. The counting numbers smaller than 6
    1, 2, 3, 4, 5

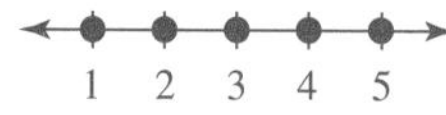

18. The natural numbers larger than 4
    5, 6, 7, 8, 9, . . .

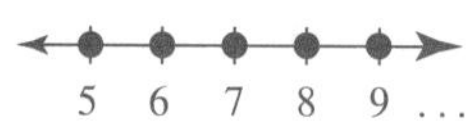

19. The whole numbers smaller than 5
    0, 1, 2, 3, 4

20. The integers between -3 and 3
    $-2, -1, 0, 1, 2$

21. The whole numbers between -5 and 5
    0, 1, 2, 3, 4

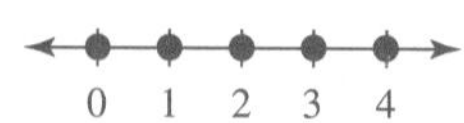

22. The integers smaller than -1
    $-2, -3, -4, -5, \ldots$

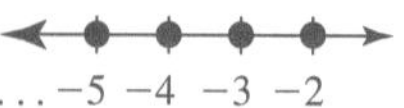

23. The counting numbers larger than -4

1, 2, 3, 4, 5, . . .

24. The natural numbers between -5 and 7

1, 2, 3, 4, 5, 6

25. The integers larger than $\frac{1}{2}$

1, 2, 3, 4, 5, . . .

26. The whole numbers smaller than $\frac{7}{4}$

0, 1

Determine whether each statement is true or false. Explain your answer. See Example 3.

27. Every integer is a rational number. True
28. Every counting number is a whole number. True
29. Zero is a counting number. False
30. Every whole number is a counting number. False
31. The ratio of the circumference and diameter of a circle is an irrational number. True
32. Every rational number can be expressed as a ratio of integers. True
33. Every whole number can be expressed as a ratio of integers. True
34. Some of the rational numbers are integers. True
35. Some of the integers are natural numbers. True
36. There are infinitely many rational numbers. True
37. Zero is an irrational number. False
38. Every irrational number is a real number. True

Write each interval of real numbers in interval notation and graph it. See Example 4.

39. The set of real numbers between 0 and 1

(0, 1)

40. The set of real numbers between 2 and 6

(2, 6)

41. The set of real numbers between -2 and 2 inclusive

$[-2, 2]$

42. The set of real numbers between -3 and 4 inclusive

$[-3, 4]$

43. The set of real numbers greater than 0 and less than or equal to 5

(0, 5]

44. The set of real numbers greater than or equal to -1 and less than 6

$[-1, 6)$

Write each interval of real numbers in interval notation and graph it. See Example 5.

45. The set of real numbers greater than 4

$(4, \infty)$

46. The set of real numbers greater than 2

$(2, \infty)$

47. The set of real numbers less than or equal to -1

$(-\infty, -1]$

48. The set of real numbers less than or equal to -4

$(-\infty, -4]$

49. The set of real numbers greater than or equal to 0

$[0, \infty)$

50. The set of real numbers greater than or equal to 6

$[6, \infty)$

Determine the values of the following. See Examples 6 and 7.

51. $|-6|$ 6
52. $|4|$ 4
53. $|0|$ 0
54. $|2|$ 2
55. $|7|$ 7
56. $|-7|$ 7
57. $|-9|$ 9
58. $|-2|$ 2
59. $|-45|$ 45
60. $|-30|$ 30
61. $\left|\frac{3}{4}\right|$ $\frac{3}{4}$
62. $\left|-\frac{1}{2}\right|$ $\frac{1}{2}$
63. $|-5.09|$ 5.09
64. $|0.00987|$ 0.00987

Select the smaller number in each given pair of numbers.

65. $-16, 9$ -16
66. $-12, -7$ -12
67. $-\frac{5}{2}, -\frac{9}{4}$ $-\frac{5}{2}$
68. $\frac{5}{8}, \frac{6}{7}$ $\frac{5}{8}$
69. $|-3|, 2$ 2
70. $|-6|, 0$ 0
71. $|-4|, 3$ 3
72. $|5|, -4$ -4

Which number in each given pair has the larger absolute value?

73. $-5, -9$ -9
74. $-12, -8$ -12
75. $16, -9$ 16
76. $-12, 7$ -12

Determine which number in each pair is closer to 0 on the number line.

77. $-4, -5$ -4 **78.** $-8.1, 7.9$ 7.9

79. $-2.01, -1.99$ -1.99 **80.** $2.01, 1.99$ 1.99

81. $-75, 74$ 74 **82.** $-75, -74$ -74

What is the distance on the number line between 0 and each of the following numbers?

83. 5.25 5.25 **84.** 4.2 4.2 **85.** -40 40

86. -33 33 **87.** $-\frac{1}{2}$ $\frac{1}{2}$ **88.** $-\frac{1}{3}$ $\frac{1}{3}$

Consider the following nine integers:

$$-4, -3, -2, -1, 0, 1, 2, 3, 4$$

89. Which of these integers has an absolute value equal to 3? -3 and 3

90. Which of these integers has an absolute value equal to 0? 0

91. Which of these integers has an absolute value greater than 2? $-4, -3, 3, 4$

92. Which of these integers has an absolute value greater than 1? $-4, -3, -2, 2, 3, 4$

93. Which of these integers has an absolute value less than 2? $-1, 0, 1$

94. Which of these integers has an absolute value less than 4? $-3, -2, -1, 0, 1, 2, 3$

Write the interval notation for the interval of real numbers shown in each graph.

95. 2 3 4 5 6 7 8 9 $[3, 8]$

96. −6 −4 −2 0 2 4 6 $[-4, 4]$

97. −40 −30 −20 −10 0 10 $(-30, -20]$

98. −50 −40 −30 −20 −10 0 $[-40, -30)$

99. 0 10 20 30 40 50 $[30, \infty)$

100. −10 0 10 20 30 $(-\infty, 20)$

True or false? Explain your answer.

101. If we add the absolute values of -3 and -5, we get 8. True

102. If we multiply the absolute values of -2 and 5, we get 10. True

103. The absolute value of any negative number is greater than 0. True

104. The absolute value of any positive number is less than 0. False

105. The absolute value of -9 is larger than the absolute value of 6. True

106. The absolute value of 12 is larger than the absolute value of -11. True

Getting More Involved

107. ***Writing***

Find a real-life question for which the answer is a rational number that is not an integer.

What is the probability that a tossed coin turns up heads?

108. ***Exploration***

a) Find a rational number between $\frac{1}{3}$ and $\frac{1}{4}$.

b) Find a rational number between -3.205 and -3.114.

c) Find a rational number between $\frac{2}{3}$ and 0.6667.

d) Explain how to find a rational number between any two given rational numbers.

a) $\frac{7}{24}$ **b)** -3.115 **c)** 0.66669

d) Add them and divide the result by 2.

109. ***Discussion***

Suppose that a is a negative real number. Determine whether each of the following is positive or negative, and explain your answer.

a) $-a$ **b)** $|-a|$ **c)** $-|a|$ **d)** $-(-a)$ **e)** $-|-a|$

If a is negative, then $-a$ and $|-a|$ are positive. The rest are negative.

110. ***Discussion***

Determine whether each number listed in the table below is a member of each set listed on the side of the table. For example, $\frac{1}{2}$ is a real number and a rational number. So check marks are placed in those two cells of the table.

	$\frac{1}{2}$	-2	π	$\sqrt{3}$	$\sqrt{9}$	6	0	$-\frac{7}{3}$
Real	✓	✓	✓	✓	✓	✓	✓	✓
Irrational			✓	✓				
Rational	✓	✓			✓	✓	✓	✓
Integer		✓			✓	✓	✓	
Whole					✓	✓	✓	
Counting					✓	✓		

1.2 Fractions

In this Section

- Equivalent Fractions
- Multiplying Fractions
- Dividing Fractions
- Adding and Subtracting Fractions
- Fractions, Decimals, and Percents
- Applications

In this section and Sections 1.3 and 1.4 we will discuss operations performed with real numbers. We begin by reviewing operations with fractions. Note that this section on fractions is not an entire arithmetic course. We are simply reviewing selected fraction topics that will be used in this text.

Equivalent Fractions

If a pizza is cut into 3 equal pieces and you eat 2, you have eaten $\frac{2}{3}$ of the pizza. If the pizza is cut into 6 equal pieces and you eat 4, you have still eaten 2 out of every 3 pieces. So the fraction $\frac{4}{6}$ is considered **equal** or **equivalent** to $\frac{2}{3}$. See Fig. 1.20. Every fraction can be written in infinitely many equivalent forms. Consider the following equivalent forms of $\frac{2}{3}$:

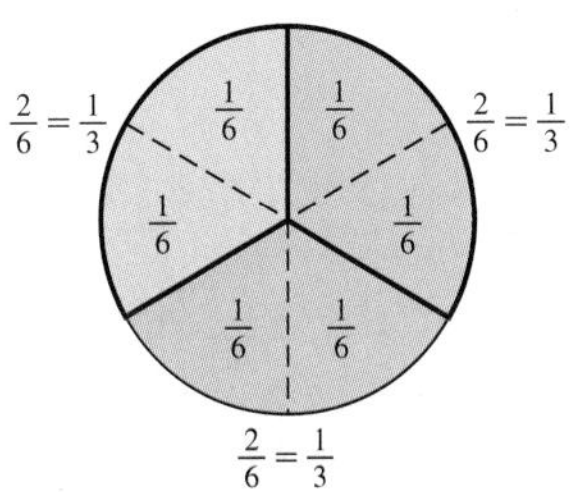

Figure 1.20

$$\frac{2}{3}=\frac{4}{6}=\frac{6}{9}=\frac{8}{12}=\frac{10}{15}=\ldots$$

The three dots mean "and so on."

Notice that each equivalent form of $\frac{2}{3}$ can be obtained by multiplying the numerator (top number) and denominator (bottom number) of $\frac{2}{3}$ by a nonzero number. For example,

$$\frac{2}{3}=\frac{2\cdot 5}{3\cdot 5}=\frac{10}{15}.$$

The raised dot indicates multiplication.

Teaching Tip Insist that students use the methods shown here for building up and reducing fractions. These same methods will be used on rational expressions in Chapter 6.

Converting a fraction into an equivalent fraction with a larger denominator is called **building up** the fraction. A fraction can be built up by multiplying the numerator and denominator by the same number, or by using multiplication of fractions (which will be discussed later in this section). For example, to build up $\frac{2}{3}$ to a denominator of 15 we could multiply $\frac{2}{3}$ by the number 1, using $\frac{5}{5}$ as an equivalent form of 1:

$$\frac{2}{3}=\frac{2}{3}\cdot 1=\frac{2}{3}\cdot\frac{5}{5}=\frac{10}{15}$$

Building Up Fractions

If $b \neq 0$ and $c \neq 0$, then

$$\frac{a}{b}=\frac{a\cdot c}{b\cdot c}.$$

Multiplying the numerator and denominator of a fraction by a nonzero number changes the fraction's appearance but not its value.

EXAMPLE 1

Building up fractions

Build up each fraction so that it is equivalent to the fraction with the indicated denominator.

a) $\frac{3}{4} = \frac{?}{28}$

b) $\frac{5}{3} = \frac{?}{30}$

Solution

a) Because $4 \cdot 7 = 28$, we multiply both the numerator and denominator by 7:

$$\frac{3}{4} = \frac{3 \cdot 7}{4 \cdot 7} = \frac{21}{28}$$

b) Because $3 \cdot 10 = 30$, we multiply both the numerator and denominator by 10:

$$\frac{5}{3} = \frac{5 \cdot 10}{3 \cdot 10} = \frac{50}{30}$$

Now do Exercises 7–18

The method for building up fractions shown in Example 1 will be used again on rational expressions in Chapter 6. So it is good to use this method and show the details. The same goes for the method of reducing fractions that is coming next.

Converting a fraction to an equivalent fraction with a smaller denominator is called **reducing** the fraction. For example, to reduce $\frac{10}{15}$, we *factor* 10 as $2 \cdot 5$ and 15 as $3 \cdot 5$, and then divide out the *common factor* 5:

$$\frac{10}{15} = \frac{2 \cdot \cancel{5}}{3 \cdot \cancel{5}} = \frac{2}{3}$$

The fraction $\frac{2}{3}$ cannot be reduced further because the numerator 2 and the denominator 3 have no factors (other than 1) in common. So we say that $\frac{2}{3}$ is in **lowest terms.**

Reducing Fractions

If $b \neq 0$ and $c \neq 0$, then

$$\frac{a \cdot c}{b \cdot c} = \frac{a}{b}.$$

Dividing the numerator and denominator of a fraction by a nonzero number changes the fraction's appearance but not its value.

EXAMPLE 2

Reducing fractions

Reduce each fraction to lowest terms.

a) $\frac{15}{24}$

b) $\frac{42}{30}$

c) $\frac{13}{26}$

d) $\frac{35}{7}$

Calculator Close-Up

To reduce a fraction to lowest terms using a graphing calculator, display the fraction and use the fraction feature.

```
15/24▸Frac
                5/8
42/30▸Frac
                7/5
123456/222222▸Fr
ac
       .5555525556
```

If the fraction is too complicated, the calculator will return a decimal equivalent instead of reducing it.

Solution

For each fraction, factor the numerator and denominator and then divide by the common factor:

a) $\dfrac{15}{24} = \dfrac{3 \cdot 5}{3 \cdot 8} = \dfrac{5}{8}$

b) $\dfrac{42}{30} = \dfrac{7 \cdot \not{6}}{5 \cdot \not{6}} = \dfrac{7}{5}$

c) $\dfrac{13}{26} = \dfrac{1 \cdot \not{13}}{2 \cdot \not{13}} = \dfrac{1}{2}$ The number 1 in the numerator is essential.

d) $\dfrac{35}{7} = \dfrac{5 \cdot \not{7}}{1 \cdot \not{7}} = \dfrac{5}{1} = 5$

Now do Exercises 19–34

Strategy for Obtaining Equivalent Fractions

Equivalent fractions can be obtained by multiplying or dividing the numerator and denominator by the same nonzero number.

Multiplying Fractions

Suppose a pizza is cut into three equal pieces. If you eat $\frac{1}{2}$ of one piece, you have eaten $\frac{1}{6}$ of the pizza. See Fig. 1.21. You can obtain $\frac{1}{6}$ by multiplying $\frac{1}{2}$ and $\frac{1}{3}$:

$$\frac{1}{2} \cdot \frac{1}{3} = \frac{1 \cdot 1}{2 \cdot 3} = \frac{1}{6}$$

$\frac{1}{6}$ $\frac{1}{6}$ $\frac{1}{6}$ $\frac{1}{6}$ $\frac{1}{6}$ $\frac{1}{6}$

Figure 1.21

This example illustrates the definition of multiplication of fractions. To multiply two fractions, we multiply their numerators and multiply their denominators.

Multiplication of Fractions

If $b \neq 0$ and $d \neq 0$, then

$$\frac{a}{b} \cdot \frac{c}{d} = \frac{a \cdot c}{b \cdot d}.$$

EXAMPLE 3

Multiplying fractions

Find the product, $\frac{2}{3} \cdot \frac{5}{8}$.

Solution

Multiply the numerators and the denominators:

$$\frac{2}{3} \cdot \frac{5}{8} = \frac{10}{24}$$

$= \dfrac{\not{2} \cdot 5}{\not{2} \cdot 12}$ Factor the numerator and denominator.

$= \dfrac{5}{12}$ Divide out the common factor 2.

Now do Exercises 35–40

Teaching Tip Keep on reminding students that canceling works only for multiplication in the numerator and denominator.

It is usually easier to reduce before multiplying, as shown in Example 4.

EXAMPLE 4

Reducing before multiplying

Find the indicated products.

a) $\frac{1}{3} \cdot \frac{3}{4}$ **b)** $\frac{4}{5} \cdot \frac{15}{22}$

Calculator Close-Up

A graphing calculator can multiply fractions and get fractional answers using the fraction feature. Note how a mixed number is written on a graphing calculator.

```
1/3*3/4▸Frac
             1/4
4/5*15/22▸Frac
            6/11
(3+1/4)*8/5▸Frac
            26/5
```

Solution

a) $\frac{1}{3} \cdot \frac{3}{4} = \frac{1}{\not{3}} \cdot \frac{\not{3}}{4} = \frac{1}{4}$

b) Factor the numerators and denominators, and then divide out the common factors before multiplying:

$$\frac{4}{5} \cdot \frac{15}{22} = \frac{2 \cdot \not{2}}{\not{5}} \cdot \frac{3 \cdot \not{5}}{\not{2} \cdot 11} = \frac{6}{11}$$

Now do Exercises 41–46

Dividing Fractions

Suppose that a pizza is cut into three pieces. If one piece is divided between two people $\left(\frac{1}{3} \div 2\right)$, then each of these two people gets $\frac{1}{6}$ of the pizza. Of course $\frac{1}{3}$ times $\frac{1}{2}$ is also $\frac{1}{6}$. So dividing by 2 is equivalent to multiplying by $\frac{1}{2}$. In symbols:

$$\frac{1}{3} \div 2 = \frac{1}{3} \div \frac{2}{1} = \frac{1}{3} \cdot \frac{1}{2} = \frac{1}{6}$$

The pizza example illustrates the general rule for dividing fractions.

Division of Fractions

If $b \neq 0$, $c \neq 0$, and $d \neq 0$, then

$$\frac{a}{b} \div \frac{c}{d} = \frac{a}{b} \cdot \frac{d}{c}.$$

In general if $m \div n = p$, then n is called the **divisor** and p (the result of the division) is called the **quotient** of m and n. We also refer to $m \div n$ and $\frac{m}{n}$ as the quotient of m and n. So in words, *to find the quotient of two fractions we invert the divisor and multiply.*

EXAMPLE 5

Dividing fractions

Find the indicated quotients.

a) $\frac{1}{3} \div \frac{7}{6}$ **b)** $\frac{2}{3} \div 5$

c) $\frac{3}{8} \div \frac{3}{2}$

Calculator Close-Up

When the divisor is a fraction on a graphing calculator, it must be in parentheses. A different result is obtained without using parentheses. Note that when the divisor is a whole number, parentheses are not necessary.

```
1/3/(7/6)▸Frac
            2/7
1/3/7/6▸Frac
          1/126
2/3/5▸Frac
           2/15
```

Try these computations on your calculator.

Solution

In each case we invert the divisor (the number on the right) and multiply.

a) $\frac{1}{3} \div \frac{7}{6} = \frac{1}{3} \cdot \frac{6}{7}$ Invert the divisor.

$= \frac{1}{\cancel{3}} \cdot \frac{2 \cdot \cancel{3}}{7}$ Reduce.

$= \frac{2}{7}$ Multiply.

b) $\frac{2}{3} \div 5 = \frac{2}{3} \div \frac{5}{1} = \frac{2}{3} \cdot \frac{1}{5} = \frac{2}{15}$

c) $\frac{3}{8} \div \frac{3}{2} = \frac{3}{8} \cdot \frac{2}{3} = \frac{\cancel{3} \cdot 1}{4 \cdot \cancel{2}} \cdot \frac{\cancel{2}}{\cancel{3}} = \frac{1}{4}$

Now do Exercises 47–56

Adding and Subtracting Fractions

To understand addition and subtraction of fractions, again consider the pizza that is cut into six equal pieces as shown in Fig. 1.22. If you eat $\frac{3}{6}$ and your friend eats $\frac{2}{6}$, together you have eaten $\frac{5}{6}$ of the pizza. Similarly, if you remove $\frac{1}{6}$ from $\frac{6}{6}$ you have $\frac{5}{6}$ left. To add or subtract fractions with identical denominators, we add or subtract their numerators and write the result over the common denominator.

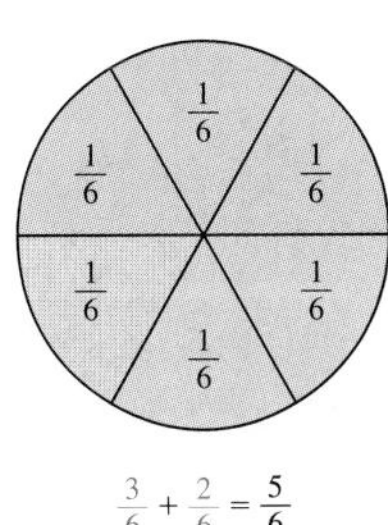

$\frac{3}{6} + \frac{2}{6} = \frac{5}{6}$

Figure 1.22

Addition and Subtraction of Fractions

If $b \neq 0$, then

$$\frac{a}{b} + \frac{c}{b} = \frac{a+c}{b} \quad \text{and} \quad \frac{a}{b} - \frac{c}{b} = \frac{a-c}{b}.$$

An **improper fraction** is a fraction in which the numerator is larger than the denominator. For example, $\frac{7}{6}$ is an improper fraction. A **mixed number** is a natural number plus a fraction, with the plus sign removed. For example, $1\frac{1}{6}$ $\left(\text{or } 1 + \frac{1}{6}\right)$ is a mixed number. Since $1 + \frac{1}{6} = \frac{6}{6} + \frac{1}{6} = \frac{7}{6}$, we have $1\frac{1}{6} = \frac{7}{6}$.

EXAMPLE 6

Adding and subtracting fractions

Perform the indicated operations.

a) $\frac{1}{7} + \frac{2}{7}$

b) $\frac{7}{10} - \frac{3}{10}$

Helpful Hint

A good way to remember that you need common denominators for addition is to think of a simple example. If you own 1/3 share of a car wash and your spouse owns 1/3, then together you own 2/3 of the business.

Solution

a) $\frac{1}{7} + \frac{2}{7} = \frac{3}{7}$

b) $\frac{7}{10} - \frac{3}{10} = \frac{4}{10} = \frac{\cancel{2} \cdot 2}{\cancel{2} \cdot 5} = \frac{2}{5}$

Now do Exercises 57–60

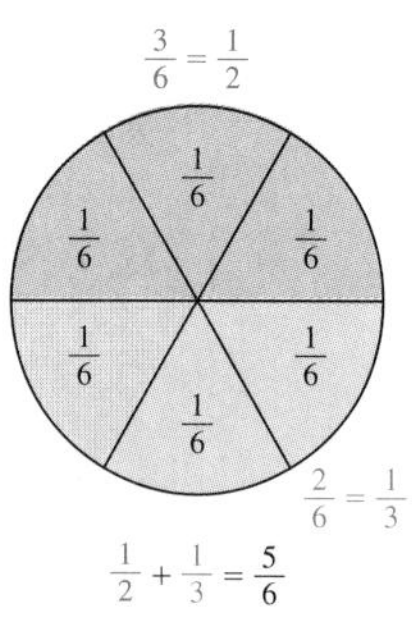

Figure 1.23

To add or subtract fractions with different denominators, we must convert them to equivalent fractions with the same denominator and then add or subtract. For example, to add $\frac{1}{2}$ and $\frac{1}{3}$, we build up each fraction to a denominator of 6. See Fig. 1.23. Since $\frac{1}{2} = \frac{3}{6}$ and $\frac{1}{3} = \frac{2}{6}$, we have

$$\frac{1}{2} + \frac{1}{3} = \frac{3}{6} + \frac{2}{6} = \frac{5}{6}.$$

The smallest number that is a multiple of the denominators of two or more fractions is called the **least common denominator (LCD).** So 6 is the LCD for $\frac{1}{2}$ and $\frac{1}{3}$. Note that we obtained the LCD 6 by examining Fig. 1.23. We must have a more systematic way.

The procedure for finding the LCD is based on factors. For example, to find the LCD for the denominators 6 and 9, factor 6 and 9 as $6 = 2 \cdot 3$ and $9 = 3 \cdot 3$. To obtain a multiple of both 6 and 9 the number must have two 3's as factors and one 2. So the LCD for 6 and 9 is $2 \cdot 3 \cdot 3$ or 18. If any number is omitted from $2 \cdot 3 \cdot 3$, we will not have a multiple of both 6 and 9. So each factor found in either 6 or 9 appears in the LCD the maximum number of times that it appears in either 6 or 9. The general strategy follows.

Helpful Hint

The *least* common denominator is *greater than* or equal to all of the denominators, because they must all divide into the LCD.

Strategy for Finding the LCD

1. Factor each denominator completely.
2. The LCD contains each distinct factor the maximum number of times that it occurs in any of the denominators.

Note that a **prime number** is a number 2 or larger that has no factors other than itself and 1. If a denominator is prime (such as 2, 3, 5, 7, 11) then we do not factor it. A number is **factored completely** when it is written as a product of prime numbers.

EXAMPLE 7

Adding and subtracting fractions

Perform the indicated operations.

a) $\frac{3}{4} + \frac{1}{6}$ **b)** $\frac{1}{3} - \frac{1}{12}$

c) $\frac{7}{12} + \frac{5}{18}$ **d)** $2\frac{1}{3} + \frac{5}{9}$

Solution

a) First factor the denominators as $4 = 2 \cdot 2$ and $6 = 2 \cdot 3$. Since 2 occurs twice in 4 and once in 6, it appears twice in the LCD. Since 3 appears once in 6 and not at all in 4, it appears once in the LCD. So the LCD is $2 \cdot 2 \cdot 3$

Study Tip

Read the material in the text before it is discussed in class, even if you do not totally understand it. The classroom discussion will be the second time you have seen the material and it will be easier to question points that you do not understand.

or 12. Now build up each denominator to 12:

$$\frac{3}{4}+\frac{1}{6}=\frac{3\cdot 3}{4\cdot 3}+\frac{1\cdot 2}{6\cdot 2} \quad \text{Build up each denominator to 12.}$$
$$=\frac{9}{12}+\frac{2}{12} \quad \text{Simplify.}$$
$$=\frac{11}{12} \quad \text{Add.}$$

b) The denominators are 12 and 3. Factor 12 as $12 = 2 \cdot 6 = 2 \cdot 2 \cdot 3$. Since 3 is a prime number we do not factor it. Since 2 occurs twice in 12 and not at all in 3, it appears twice in the LCD. Since 3 occurs once in 3 and once in 12, 3 appears once in the LCD. The LCD is $2 \cdot 2 \cdot 3$ or 12. So we must build up $\frac{1}{3}$ to have a denominator of 12:

$$\frac{1}{3}-\frac{1}{12}=\frac{1\cdot 4}{3\cdot 4}-\frac{1}{12} \quad \text{Build up the first fraction to the LCD.}$$
$$=\frac{4}{12}-\frac{1}{12} \quad \text{Simplify.}$$
$$=\frac{3}{12} \quad \text{Subtract.}$$
$$=\frac{1}{4} \quad \text{Reduce to lowest terms.}$$

c) Since $12 = 2 \cdot 6 = 2 \cdot 2 \cdot 3$ and $18 = 2 \cdot 9 = 2 \cdot 3 \cdot 3$, the factor 2 appears twice in the LCD and the factor 3 appears twice in the LCD. So the LCD is $2 \cdot 2 \cdot 3 \cdot 3$ or 36:

$$\frac{7}{12}+\frac{5}{18}=\frac{7\cdot 3}{12\cdot 3}+\frac{5\cdot 2}{18\cdot 2} \quad \text{Build up each denominator to 36.}$$
$$=\frac{21}{36}+\frac{10}{36} \quad \text{Simplify.}$$
$$=\frac{31}{36} \quad \text{Add.}$$

d) To perform addition with the mixed number $2\frac{1}{3}$, first convert it into an improper fraction: $2\frac{1}{3} = 2 + \frac{1}{3} = \frac{6}{3} + \frac{1}{3} = \frac{7}{3}$.

$$2\frac{1}{3}+\frac{5}{9}=\frac{7}{3}+\frac{5}{9} \quad \text{Write } 2\tfrac{1}{3} \text{ as an improper fraction.}$$
$$=\frac{7\cdot 3}{3\cdot 3}+\frac{5}{9} \quad \text{The LCD is 9.}$$
$$=\frac{21}{9}+\frac{5}{9} \quad \text{Simplify.}$$
$$=\frac{26}{9} \quad \text{Add.}$$

Note that $\frac{1}{3}+\frac{5}{9}=\frac{3}{9}+\frac{5}{9}=\frac{8}{9}$. Then add on the 2 to get $2\frac{8}{9}$, which is the same as $\frac{26}{9}$.

Teaching Tip Emphasize the method for adding and subtracting fractions. Encourage students to write the details as shown in Example 7.

Now do Exercises 61–72

Helpful Hint

Recall the *place value* for decimal numbers:

```
    tenths
    ┌hundredths
    │┌thousandths
    ││┌ten thousandths
0.2635
```

So $0.2635 = \frac{2635}{10{,}000}$.

Fractions, Decimals, and Percents

In the decimal number system, fractions with a denominator of 10, 100, 1000, and so on are written as decimal numbers. For example,

$$\frac{3}{10} = 0.3, \quad \frac{25}{100} = 0.25, \quad \text{and} \quad \frac{5}{1000} = 0.005.$$

Fractions with a denominator of 100 are often written as percents. Think of the percent symbol (%) as representing the denominator of 100. For example,

$$\frac{25}{100} = 25\%, \quad \frac{5}{100} = 5\%, \quad \text{and} \quad \frac{300}{100} = 300\%.$$

Example 8 illustrates further how to convert from any one of the forms (fraction, decimal, percent) to the others.

EXAMPLE 8

Changing forms

Convert each given fraction, decimal, or percent into its other two forms.

a) $\frac{1}{5}$ **b)** 6% **c)** 0.1

Solution

a) $\frac{1}{5} = \frac{1 \cdot 20}{5 \cdot 20} = \frac{20}{100} = 20\%$ and $\frac{1}{5} = \frac{1 \cdot 2}{5 \cdot 2} = \frac{2}{10} = 0.2$

So $\frac{1}{5} = 0.2 = 20\%$. Note that a fraction can also be converted to a decimal by dividing the denominator into the numerator with long division.

b) $6\% = \frac{6}{100} = 0.06$ and $\frac{6}{100} = \frac{\not{2} \cdot 3}{\not{2} \cdot 50} = \frac{3}{50}$

So $6\% = 0.06 = \frac{3}{50}$.

c) $0.1 = \frac{1}{10} = \frac{1 \cdot 10}{10 \cdot 10} = \frac{10}{100} = 10\%$

So $0.1 = \frac{1}{10} = 10\%$.

Now do Exercises 73–84

Teaching Tip Work some examples like $6\frac{3}{4}\%$, $3\frac{1}{3}\%$, and 5.24%.

Calculator Close-Up

A calculator can convert fractions to decimals and decimals to fractions. The calculator shown here converts the terminating decimal 0.333333333333 into 1/3 even though 1/3 is a repeating decimal with infinitely many threes after the decimal point.

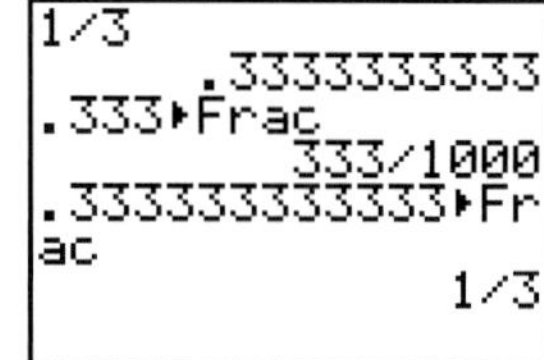

Applications

The dimensions for lumber used in construction are usually given in fractions. For example, a 2 × 4 stud used for framing a wall is actually $1\frac{1}{2}$ in. by $3\frac{1}{2}$ in. by $92\frac{5}{8}$ in. A 2 × 12 floor joist is actually $1\frac{1}{2}$ in. by $11\frac{1}{2}$ in.

Math at Work — Stock Price Analysis

Stock market analysts use mathematics daily to evaluate the potential success of a stock based on its financial statements and its current performance. Each analyst has a philosophy of investing. If an analyst is working for a mutual fund that specializes in retirement investing for clients with a lengthy time horizon, the analyst may recommend higher-risk stocks. If the client base is older and has a shorter time horizon, the analyst may recommend more secure investments.

There are hundreds of ratios and formulas that a stock market analyst uses to estimate the value of a stock. Two popular ones are the capital asset pricing model (CAPM) and the price/earnings ratio (P/E). The CAPM is used to assess the price of a stock in relation to general movements in the stock market whereas the P/E ratio is used to compare the price of one stock to others in the same industry.

Using CAPM a stock's price P is determined by $P = A + BM$, where A is the stock's variance, B is the stock's fluctuation in relation to the market, and M is the market level. For example, a stock trading at \$10.50 on the New York Stock Exchange has a variance of 3.24 and fluctuation of 0.001058 using the Dow Jones Industrial Average. If the Dow is at 9242, then $P = 3.24 + 0.001058(9242) \approx 13.02$. So the stock is worth \$13.02 and is a good buy at \$10.50. If the company has earned \$1.53 per share, then P/E $= 10.50/1.53 \approx 6.9$. If other stocks in the same industry have higher P/E ratios, then this stock is a good buy.

Since there are hundreds of ways to analyze a stock and all analysts have access to the same data, the analysts must decide which data are most important. The analyst must also look beyond data and formulas to determine whether to buy a stock.

EXAMPLE 9

Framing a two-story house

In framing a two-story house, a carpenter uses a 2×4 shoe, a wall stud, two 2×4 plates, then 2×12 floor joists, and a $\frac{3}{4}$-in. plywood floor, before starting the second level. Use the dimensions in Fig. 1.24 to find the total height of the framing shown.

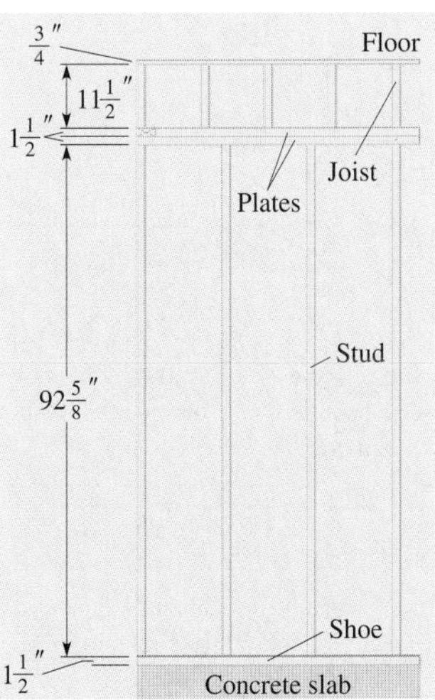

Figure 1.24

Solution

We can find the total height using multiplication and addition:

$$\begin{aligned}3 \cdot 1\frac{1}{2} + 92\frac{5}{8} + 11\frac{1}{2} + \frac{3}{4} &= 4\frac{1}{2} + 92\frac{5}{8} + 11\frac{1}{2} + \frac{3}{4}\\ &= 4\frac{4}{8} + 92\frac{5}{8} + 11\frac{4}{8} + \frac{6}{8}\\ &= 107\frac{19}{8}\\ &= 107 + \frac{16}{8} + \frac{3}{8} = 107 + 2 + \frac{3}{8} = 109\frac{3}{8}\end{aligned}$$

The total height of the framing shown is $109\frac{3}{8}$ in.

Now do Exercises 109–112

Warm-Ups 

True or false? Explain your answer.

1. Every fraction is equal to infinitely many equivalent fractions. True
2. The fraction $\frac{8}{12}$ is equivalent to the fraction $\frac{4}{6}$. True
3. The fraction $\frac{8}{12}$ reduced to lowest terms is $\frac{4}{6}$. False
4. $\frac{1}{2} \cdot \frac{2}{3} = \frac{1}{3}$ True
5. $\frac{1}{2} \cdot \frac{3}{5} = \frac{3}{10}$ True
6. $\frac{1}{2} \cdot \frac{6}{5} = \frac{6}{10}$ True
7. $\frac{1}{2} \div 3 = \frac{1}{6}$ True
8. $5 \div \frac{1}{2} = 10$ True
9. $\frac{1}{2} + \frac{1}{4} = \frac{2}{6}$ False
10. $2 - \frac{1}{2} = \frac{3}{2}$ True

1.2 Exercises

Boost your GRADE at mathzone.com!

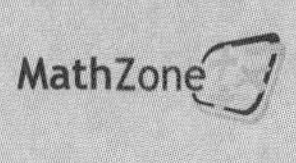

- Practice Problems
- Self-Tests
- Videos
- Net Tutor
- e-Professors

Reading and Writing *After reading this section write out the answers to these questions. Use complete sentences.*

1. What are equivalent fractions?
If two fractions are identical when reduced to lowest terms, then they are equivalent fractions.
2. How can you find all fractions that are equivalent to a given fraction?
Reduce the fraction to lowest terms and then multiply the numerator and denominator by every counting number.
3. What does it mean to reduce a fraction to lowest terms?
To reduce a fraction to lowest terms means to find an equivalent fraction that has no factor common to the numerator and denominator.
4. For which operations with fractions are you required to have common denominators? Why?
Common denominators are required for addition and subtraction, because it makes sense to add $\frac{1}{3}$ of a pie and $\frac{1}{3}$ of a pie and get $\frac{2}{3}$ of a pie.
5. How do you convert a fraction to a decimal?
Convert a fraction to a decimal by dividing the denominator into the numerator.
6. How do you convert a percent to a fraction?
Convert a percent to a fraction by dividing by 100, as in $4\% = \frac{4}{100}$.

Build up each fraction or whole number so that it is equivalent to the fraction with the indicated denominator. See Example 1.

7. $\frac{3}{4} = \frac{?}{8}$ $\frac{6}{8}$
8. $\frac{5}{7} = \frac{?}{21}$ $\frac{15}{21}$
9. $\frac{8}{3} = \frac{?}{12}$ $\frac{32}{12}$
10. $\frac{7}{2} = \frac{?}{8}$ $\frac{28}{8}$
11. $5 = \frac{?}{2}$ $\frac{10}{2}$
12. $9 = \frac{?}{3}$ $\frac{27}{3}$
13. $\frac{3}{4} = \frac{?}{100}$ $\frac{75}{100}$
14. $\frac{1}{2} = \frac{?}{100}$ $\frac{50}{100}$
15. $\frac{3}{10} = \frac{?}{100}$ $\frac{30}{100}$
16. $\frac{2}{5} = \frac{?}{100}$ $\frac{40}{100}$
17. $\frac{5}{3} = \frac{?}{42}$ $\frac{70}{42}$
18. $\frac{5}{7} = \frac{?}{98}$ $\frac{70}{98}$

Reduce each fraction to lowest terms. See Example 2.

19. $\frac{3}{6}$ $\frac{1}{2}$
20. $\frac{2}{10}$ $\frac{1}{5}$
21. $\frac{12}{18}$ $\frac{2}{3}$
22. $\frac{30}{40}$ $\frac{3}{4}$
23. $\frac{15}{5}$ 3
24. $\frac{39}{13}$ 3
25. $\frac{50}{100}$ $\frac{1}{2}$
26. $\frac{5}{1000}$ $\frac{1}{200}$
27. $\frac{200}{100}$ 2
28. $\frac{125}{100}$ $\frac{5}{4}$
29. $\frac{18}{48}$ $\frac{3}{8}$
30. $\frac{34}{102}$ $\frac{1}{3}$
31. $\frac{26}{42}$ $\frac{13}{21}$
32. $\frac{70}{112}$ $\frac{5}{8}$
33. $\frac{84}{91}$ $\frac{12}{13}$
34. $\frac{121}{132}$ $\frac{11}{12}$

Find each product. See Examples 3 and 4.

35. $\frac{2}{3} \cdot \frac{5}{9}$ $\frac{10}{27}$
36. $\frac{1}{8} \cdot \frac{1}{8}$ $\frac{1}{64}$
37. $\frac{1}{3} \cdot 15$ 5
38. $\frac{1}{4} \cdot 16$ 4
39. $\frac{3}{4} \cdot \frac{14}{15}$ $\frac{7}{10}$
40. $\frac{5}{8} \cdot \frac{12}{35}$ $\frac{3}{14}$
41. $\frac{2}{5} \cdot \frac{35}{26}$ $\frac{7}{13}$
42. $\frac{3}{10} \cdot \frac{20}{21}$ $\frac{2}{7}$
43. $\frac{1}{2} \cdot \frac{6}{5}$ $\frac{3}{5}$

44. $\frac{1}{2} \cdot \frac{3}{5}$ $\frac{3}{10}$

45. $\frac{1}{2} \cdot \frac{1}{3}$ $\frac{1}{6}$

46. $\frac{3}{16} \cdot \frac{1}{7}$ $\frac{3}{112}$

Find each quotient. See Example 5.

47. $\frac{3}{4} \div \frac{1}{4}$ 3

48. $\frac{2}{3} \div \frac{1}{2}$ $\frac{4}{3}$

49. $\frac{1}{3} \div 5$ $\frac{1}{15}$

50. $\frac{3}{5} \div 3$ $\frac{1}{5}$

51. $5 \div \frac{5}{4}$ 4

52. $8 \div \frac{2}{3}$ 12

53. $\frac{6}{10} \div \frac{3}{4}$ $\frac{4}{5}$

54. $\frac{2}{3} \div \frac{10}{21}$ $\frac{7}{5}$

55. $\frac{3}{16} \div \frac{5}{2}$ $\frac{3}{40}$

56. $\frac{1}{8} \div \frac{5}{16}$ $\frac{2}{5}$

Find each sum or difference. See Examples 6 and 7.

57. $\frac{1}{4} + \frac{1}{4}$ $\frac{1}{2}$

58. $\frac{1}{10} + \frac{1}{10}$ $\frac{1}{5}$

59. $\frac{5}{12} - \frac{1}{12}$ $\frac{1}{3}$

60. $\frac{17}{14} - \frac{5}{14}$ $\frac{6}{7}$

61. $\frac{1}{2} - \frac{1}{4}$ $\frac{1}{4}$

62. $\frac{1}{3} + \frac{1}{6}$ $\frac{1}{2}$

63. $\frac{1}{3} + \frac{1}{4}$ $\frac{7}{12}$

64. $\frac{1}{2} + \frac{3}{5}$ $\frac{11}{10}$

65. $\frac{3}{4} - \frac{2}{3}$ $\frac{1}{12}$

66. $\frac{4}{5} - \frac{3}{4}$ $\frac{1}{20}$

67. $\frac{1}{6} + \frac{5}{8}$ $\frac{19}{24}$

68. $\frac{3}{4} + \frac{1}{6}$ $\frac{11}{12}$

69. $\frac{5}{24} - \frac{1}{18}$ $\frac{11}{72}$

70. $\frac{3}{16} - \frac{1}{20}$ $\frac{11}{80}$

71. $3\frac{5}{6} + \frac{5}{16}$ $\frac{199}{48}$

72. $5\frac{3}{8} - \frac{15}{16}$ $\frac{71}{16}$

Convert each given fraction, decimal, or percent into its other two forms. See Example 8.

73. $\frac{3}{5}$ 60%, 0.6

74. $\frac{19}{20}$ 95%, 0.95

75. 9% $\frac{9}{100}$, 0.09

76. 60% 0.6, $\frac{3}{5}$

77. 0.08 8%, $\frac{2}{25}$

78. 0.4 40%, $\frac{2}{5}$

79. $\frac{3}{4}$ 0.75, 75%

80. $\frac{5}{8}$ 0.625, 62.5%

81. 2% $\frac{1}{50}$, 0.02

82. 120% $\frac{6}{5}$, 1.20

83. 0.01 $\frac{1}{100}$, 1%

84. 0.005 $\frac{1}{200}$, 0.5%

Perform the indicated operations.

85. $\frac{3}{8} \div \frac{1}{8}$ 3

86. $\frac{7}{8} \div \frac{3}{14}$ $\frac{49}{12}$

87. $\frac{3}{4} \cdot \frac{28}{21}$ 1

88. $\frac{5}{16} \cdot \frac{3}{10}$ $\frac{3}{32}$

89. $\frac{7}{12} + \frac{5}{32}$ $\frac{71}{96}$

90. $\frac{2}{15} + \frac{8}{21}$ $\frac{18}{35}$

91. $\frac{5}{24} - \frac{1}{15}$ $\frac{17}{120}$

92. $\frac{9}{16} - \frac{1}{12}$ $\frac{23}{48}$

93. $3\frac{1}{8} + \frac{15}{16}$ $\frac{65}{16}$

94. $5\frac{1}{4} - \frac{9}{16}$ $\frac{75}{16}$

95. $7\frac{2}{3} \cdot 2\frac{1}{4}$ $\frac{69}{4}$

96. $6\frac{1}{2} \div \frac{7}{2}$ $\frac{13}{7}$

97. $\frac{1}{2} + \frac{1}{3} + \frac{1}{4}$ $\frac{13}{12}$

98. $\frac{1}{2} + \frac{1}{3} - \frac{1}{6}$ $\frac{2}{3}$

99. $\frac{1}{2} \cdot \frac{1}{2} \cdot \frac{1}{2}$ $\frac{1}{8}$

100. $\frac{2}{3} \cdot \frac{2}{3} \cdot \frac{2}{3}$ $\frac{8}{27}$

Fill in the blank so that each equation is correct.

101. $\frac{1}{4} + \frac{3}{\underline{8}} = \frac{5}{8}$

102. $\frac{1}{3} + \frac{1}{\underline{9}} = \frac{4}{9}$

103. $\frac{5}{16} - \frac{3}{\underline{16}} = \frac{1}{8}$

104. $\frac{3}{5} - \frac{1}{\underline{2}} = \frac{1}{10}$

105. $\frac{4}{9} \cdot \frac{2}{\underline{3}} = \frac{8}{27}$

106. $\frac{3}{8} \cdot \underline{2} = \frac{3}{4}$

107. $\frac{2}{3} \div \frac{1}{\underline{2}} = \frac{4}{3}$

108. $\frac{1}{15} \div \frac{1}{\underline{3}} = \frac{1}{5}$

Solve each problem. See Example 9.

109. ***Inheritance.*** Marie is entitled to one-sixth of an estate because of one relationship to the deceased and one-thirty-second of the estate because of another relationship to the deceased. What is the total portion of the estate that she will receive?
$\frac{19}{96}$

110. ***Diversification.*** Helen has $\frac{1}{5}$ of her portfolio in U.S. stocks, $\frac{1}{8}$ of her portfolio in European stocks, and $\frac{1}{10}$ of her portfolio in Japanese stocks. The remainder is invested in municipal bonds. What fraction of her portfolio is invested in municipal bonds? What percent is invested in municipal bonds?
$\frac{23}{40}$, 57.5%

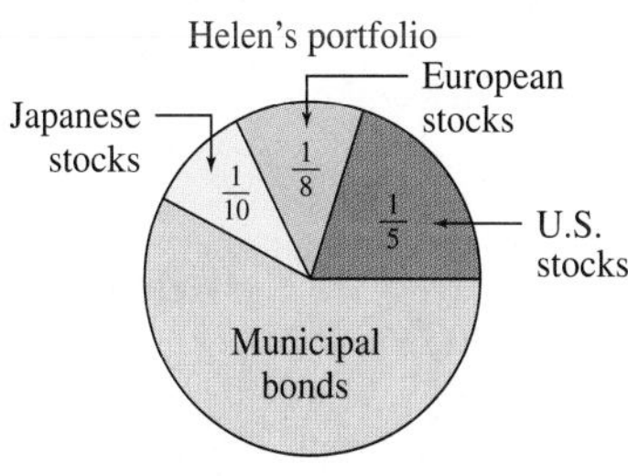

Figure for Exercise 110

111. ***Concrete patio.*** A contractor plans to pour a concrete rectangular patio.

a) Use the table to find the approximate volume of concrete in cubic yards for a 9 ft by 12 ft patio that is 4 inches thick. 1.3 yd^3

b) Find the exact volume of concrete in cubic feet and cubic yards for a patio that is $12\frac{1}{2}$ feet long, $8\frac{3}{4}$ feet wide, and 4 inches thick. $36\frac{11}{24}$ ft^3 or $1\frac{227}{648}$ yd^3

112. ***Bundle of studs.*** A lumber yard receives 2 × 4 studs in a bundle that contains 25 rows (or layers) of studs with 20 studs in each row. A 2 × 4 stud is actually $1\frac{1}{2}$ in. by $3\frac{1}{2}$ in. by $92\frac{5}{8}$ in. Find the cross-sectional area of a bundle in square inches. Find the volume of a bundle in cubic feet. (The formula $V = LWH$ gives the volume of a rectangular solid.) 2625 in.^{2}, 140.7 ft^3

Concrete required for 4 in. thick patio

L (ft)	W (ft)	V (yd^3)
16	14	2.8
14	10	1.7
12	9	1.3
10	8	1.0

Figure for Exercise 111

Getting More Involved

113. ***Writing***

Find an example of a real-life situation in which it is necessary to add two fractions.

114. ***Cooperative learning***

Write a step-by-step procedure for adding two fractions with different denominators. Give your procedure to a classmate to try out on some addition problems. Refine your procedure as necessary.

115. ***Fraction puzzle.*** A wheat farmer in Manitoba left his L-shaped farm (shown in the diagram) to his four daughters. Divide the property into four pieces so that each piece is exactly the same size and shape.

Each daughter gets 3 km^2 ÷ 4 or a $\frac{3}{4}$ km^2 piece of the farm. Divide the farm into 12 equal squares. Give each daughter an L-shaped piece consisting of 3 of those 12 squares.

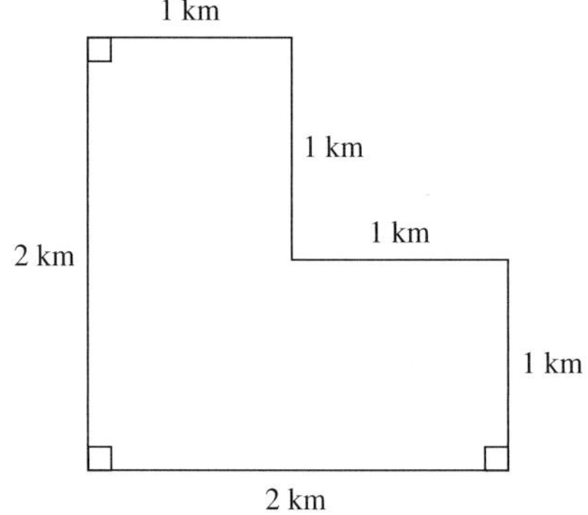

Figure for Exercise 115

1.3 Addition and Subtraction of Real Numbers

In this Section

- **Addition of Two Negative Numbers**
- **Addition of Numbers with Unlike Signs**
- **Subtraction of Signed Numbers**

In arithmetic we add and subtract only positive numbers and zero. In Section 1.1 we introduced the concept of absolute value of a number. Now we will use absolute value to extend the operations of addition and subtraction to the real numbers. We will work only with rational numbers in this chapter. You will learn to perform operations with irrational numbers in Chapter 9.

Addition of Two Negative Numbers

A good way to understand positive and negative numbers is to *think of the positive numbers as assets and the negative numbers as debts.* For this illustration we can think of assets simply as cash. For example, if you have \$3 and \$5 in cash, then your total cash is \$8. You get the total by adding two positive numbers.

Think of debts as unpaid bills such as the electric bill or the phone bill. If you have debts of \$70 and \$80, then your total debt is \$150. You can get the total debt by adding negative numbers:

$$\underset{\text{\$70 debt}}{\underset{\uparrow}{(-70)}} \quad \underset{\text{plus}}{\underset{\uparrow}{+}} \quad \underset{\text{\$80 debt}}{\underset{\uparrow}{(-80)}} \quad = \quad \underset{\text{\$150 debt}}{\underset{\uparrow}{-150}}$$

Teaching Tip Addition of signed numbers can also be illustrated on the number line, but students seem to understand money better. Note how we need absolute value to write a precise rule for addition.

We think of this addition as adding the absolute values of -70 and -80 ($70 + 80 = 150$), and then putting a negative sign on that result to get -150. These examples illustrate the following rule.

Sum of Two Numbers with Like Signs

To find the sum of two numbers with the same sign, add their absolute values. The sum has the same sign as the given numbers.

EXAMPLE 1

Adding numbers with like signs

Perform the indicated operations.

a) $23 + 56$ **b)** $(-12) + (-9)$ **c)** $(-3.5) + (-6.28)$ **d)** $\left(-\frac{1}{2}\right) + \left(-\frac{1}{4}\right)$

Study Tip

Exchange phone numbers, cellular phone numbers, pager numbers, and e-mail addresses with several students in your class. If you miss class and you can't reach your instructor, then you will have someone who can tell you the assignments. If you are stuck on a problem, you can contact a classmate for help.

Solution

a) The sum of two positive numbers is a positive number: $23 + 56 = 79$.

b) The absolute values of -12 and -9 are 12 and 9, and $12 + 9 = 21$. So

$$(-12) + (-9) = -21.$$

c) Add the absolute values of -3.5 and -6.28, and put a negative sign on the sum. Remember to line up the decimal points when adding decimal numbers:

$$\begin{array}{r} 3.50 \\ \underline{6.28} \\ 9.78 \end{array}$$

So $(-3.5) + (-6.28) = -9.78$.

d) $\left(-\frac{1}{2}\right) + \left(-\frac{1}{4}\right) = \left(-\frac{2}{4}\right) + \left(-\frac{1}{4}\right) = -\frac{3}{4}$

Now do Exercises 7–14

Addition of Numbers with Unlike Signs

If you have a debt of \$5 and have only \$5 in cash, then your debts equal your assets (in absolute value), and your net worth is \$0. **Net worth** is the total of debts and assets. Symbolically,

$$\underset{\text{\$5 debt}}{\underset{\uparrow}{-5}} \quad + \quad \underset{\text{\$5 cash}}{\underset{\uparrow}{5}} \quad = \quad \underset{\text{Net worth}}{\underset{\uparrow}{0.}}$$

For any number a, a and its opposite, $-a$, have a sum of zero. For this reason, a and $-a$ are called **additive inverses** of each other. Note that the words "negative," "opposite," and "additive inverse" are often used interchangeably.

Additive Inverse Property

For any number a,

$$a + (-a) = 0 \quad \text{and} \quad (-a) + a = 0.$$

EXAMPLE 2

Finding the sum of additive inverses

Evaluate.

a) $34 + (-34)$ **b)** $-\frac{1}{4} + \frac{1}{4}$ **c)** $2.97 + (-2.97)$

Solution

a) $34 + (-34) = 0$

b) $-\frac{1}{4} + \frac{1}{4} = 0$

c) $2.97 + (-2.97) = 0$

Now do Exercises 15–18

Helpful Hint

We use the illustrations with debts and assets to make the rules for adding signed numbers understandable. However, in the end the carefully written rules tell us exactly how to perform operations with signed numbers, and we must obey the rules.

To understand the sum of a positive and a negative number that are not additive inverses of each other, consider the following situation. If you have a debt of \$6 and \$10 in cash, you may have \$10 in hand, but your net worth is only \$4. Your assets exceed your debts (in absolute value), and you have a positive net worth. In symbols,

$$-6 + 10 = 4.$$

Note that to get 4, we actually subtract 6 from 10.

If you have a debt of \$7 but have only \$5 in cash, then your debts exceed your assets (in absolute value). You have a negative net worth of $-\$2$. In symbols,

$$-7 + 5 = -2.$$

Note that to get the 2 in the answer, we subtract 5 from 7.

As you can see from these examples, the sum of a positive number and a negative number (with different absolute values) may be either positive or negative. These examples help us to understand the rule for adding numbers with unlike signs and different absolute values.

Teaching Tip Note how we need absolute value to state precise rules for adding.

Sum of Two Numbers with Unlike Signs (and Different Absolute Values)

To find the sum of two numbers with unlike signs (and different absolute values), subtract their absolute values.

- The answer is positive if the number with the larger absolute value is positive.
- The answer is negative if the number with the larger absolute value is negative.

EXAMPLE 3 **Adding numbers with unlike signs**

Evaluate.

a) $-5 + 13$ **b)** $6 + (-7)$ **c)** $-6.4 + 2.1$

d) $-5 + 0.09$ **e)** $\left(-\frac{1}{3}\right) + \left(\frac{1}{2}\right)$ **f)** $\frac{3}{8} + \left(-\frac{5}{6}\right)$

Solution

a) The absolute values of -5 and 13 are 5 and 13. Subtract them to get 8. Since the number with the larger absolute value is 13 and it is positive, the result is positive:

$$-5 + 13 = 8$$

b) The absolute values of 6 and -7 are 6 and 7. Subtract them to get 1. Since -7 has the larger absolute value, the result is negative:

$$6 + (-7) = -1$$

c) Line up the decimal points and subtract 2.1 from 6.4.

$$\begin{array}{r} 6.4 \\ -2.1 \\ \hline 4.3 \end{array}$$

Since 6.4 is larger than 2.1, and 6.4 has a negative sign, the sign of the answer is negative. So $-6.4 + 2.1 = -4.3$.

d) Line up the decimal points and subtract 0.09 from 5.00.

$$\begin{array}{r} 5.00 \\ -0.09 \\ \hline 4.91 \end{array}$$

Since 5.00 is larger than 0.09, and 5.00 has the negative sign, the sign of the answer is negative. So $-5 + 0.09 = -4.91$.

e) $\left(-\frac{1}{3}\right) + \left(\frac{1}{2}\right) = \left(-\frac{2}{6}\right) + \left(\frac{3}{6}\right) = \frac{1}{6}$

f) $\frac{3}{8} + \left(-\frac{5}{6}\right) = \frac{9}{24} + \left(-\frac{20}{24}\right) = -\frac{11}{24}$

Now do Exercises 19–28

Calculator Close-Up

Your calculator can add signed numbers. Most calculators have a key for subtraction and a different key for the negative sign.

```
-5+13
                8
-5+.09
            -4.91
3/8+-5/6▸Frac
           -11/24
```

You should do the exercises in this section by hand and then check with a calculator.

Study Tip

The keys to success are desire and discipline. You must want success and you must discipline yourself to do what it takes to get success. There are a lot of things that you can't do anything about, but you can learn to be disciplined. Set your goals, make plans, and schedule your time. Before you know it you will have the discipline that is necessary for success.

Subtraction of Signed Numbers

Each subtraction problem with signed numbers is solved by doing an equivalent addition problem. So before attempting subtraction of signed numbers be sure that you understand addition of signed numbers.

Now think of subtraction as removing debts or assets, and think of addition as receiving debts or assets. If you have \$100 in cash and \$30 is taken from you, your resulting net worth is the same as if you have \$100 cash and a phone bill for \$30 arrives in the mail. In symbols,

$$\underset{\text{Remove}}{100 \quad -} \quad \underset{\text{Cash}}{30} \quad = \quad \underset{\text{Receive}}{100 \quad +} \quad \underset{\text{Debt}}{(-30).}$$

Removing cash is equivalent to receiving a debt.

Teaching Tip Point out that even with whole numbers, we learn addition before subtraction.

Suppose you have \$15 but owe a friend \$5. Your net worth is only \$10. If the debt of \$5 is canceled or forgiven, your net worth will go up to \$15, the same as if you received \$5 in cash. In symbols,

$$\underset{\text{Remove}}{10 \quad -} \quad \underset{\text{Debt}}{(-5)} \quad = \quad \underset{\text{Receive}}{10 \quad +} \quad \underset{\text{Cash}}{5.}$$

Removing a debt is equivalent to receiving cash.

Notice that each subtraction problem is equivalent to an addition problem in which we add the opposite of what we want to subtract. In other words, *subtracting a number is the same as adding its opposite.*

Subtraction of Real Numbers

For any real numbers a and b,

$$a - b = a + (-b).$$

EXAMPLE 4

Subtracting signed numbers

Perform each subtraction.

a) $-5 - 3$

b) $5 - (-3)$

c) $-5 - (-3)$

d) $\frac{1}{2} - \left(-\frac{1}{4}\right)$

e) $-3.6 - (-5)$

f) $0.02 - 8$

Solution

To do *any* subtraction, we can change it to addition of the opposite.

a) $-5 - 3 = -5 + (-3) = -8$

b) $5 - (-3) = 5 + (3) = 8$

c) $-5 - (-3) = -5 + 3 = -2$

d) $\frac{1}{2} - \left(-\frac{1}{4}\right) = \frac{2}{4} + \frac{1}{4} = \frac{3}{4}$

e) $-3.6 - (-5) = -3.6 + 5 = 1.4$

f) $0.02 - 8 = 0.02 + (-8) = -7.98$

Now do Exercises 29–56

Warm-Ups ▼

True or false? Explain your answer.

1. $-9 + 8 = -1$ True
2. $(-2) + (-4) = -6$ True
3. $0 - 7 = -7$ True
4. $5 - (-2) = 3$ False
5. $-5 - (-2) = -7$ False
6. The additive inverse of -3 is 0. False
7. If b is a negative number, then $-b$ is a positive number. True
8. The sum of a positive number and a negative number is a negative number. False
9. The result of a subtracted from b is the same as b plus the opposite of a. True
10. If a and b are negative numbers, then $a - b$ is a negative number. False

1.3 Exercises

Boost your GRADE at mathzone.com!

MathZone
- Practice Problems
- Net Tutor
- Self-Tests
- e-Professors
- Videos

Reading and Writing *After reading this section write out the answers to these questions. Use complete sentences.*

1. What operations did we study in this section?
We studied addition and subtraction of signed numbers.
2. How do you find the sum of two numbers with the same sign?
The sum of two numbers with the same sign is found by adding their absolute values. The sum is negative if the two numbers are negative.
3. When can we say that two numbers are additive inverses of each other?
Two numbers are additive inverses of each other if their sum is zero.
4. What is the sum of two numbers with opposite signs and the same absolute value?
The sum of two numbers with opposite signs and the same absolute value is zero.
5. How do we find the sum of two numbers with unlike signs?
To find the sum of two numbers with unlike signs, subtract their absolute values. The answer is given the sign of the number with the larger absolute value.
6. What is the relationship between subtraction and addition?
Subtraction is defined in terms of addition as $a - b = a + (-b)$.

Perform the indicated operation. See Example 1.

7. $3 + 10$ 13
8. $81 + 19$ 100
9. $(-3) + (-10)$ -13
10. $(-81) + (-19)$ -100
11. $-0.25 + (-0.9)$ -1.15
12. $-0.8 + (-2.35)$ -3.15
13. $\left(-\frac{1}{3}\right) + \left(-\frac{1}{6}\right)$ $-\frac{1}{2}$
14. $\frac{2}{3} + \frac{1}{12}$ $\frac{3}{4}$

Evaluate. See Examples 2 and 3.

15. $-8 + 8$ 0
16. $20 + (-20)$ 0
17. $-\frac{17}{50} + \frac{17}{50}$ 0
18. $\frac{12}{13} + \left(-\frac{12}{13}\right)$ 0
19. $-7 + 9$ 2
20. $10 + (-30)$ -20
21. $7 + (-13)$ -6
22. $-8 + 20$ 12
23. $8.6 + (-3)$ 5.6
24. $-9.5 + 12$ 2.5
25. $3.9 + (-6.8)$ -2.9
26. $-5.24 + 8.19$ 2.95
27. $\frac{1}{4} + \left(-\frac{1}{2}\right)$ $-\frac{1}{4}$
28. $-\frac{2}{3} + 2$ $\frac{4}{3}$

Fill in the parentheses to make each statement correct. See Example 4.

29. $8 - 2 = 8 + (?)$ $8 + (-2)$
30. $3.5 - 1.2 = 3.5 + (?)$ $3.5 + (-1.2)$
31. $4 - 12 = 4 + (?)$ $4 + (-12)$

32. $\frac{1}{2} - \frac{5}{6} = \frac{1}{2} + (?)$ $\frac{1}{2} + \left(-\frac{5}{6}\right)$

33. $-3 - (-8) = -3 + (?)$ $-3 + 8$

34. $-9 - (-2.3) = -9 + (?)$ $-9 + (2.3)$

35. $8.3 - (-1.5) = 8.3 + (?)$ $8.3 + (1.5)$

36. $10 - (-6) = 10 + (?)$ $10 + (6)$

Perform the indicated operation. See Example 4.

37. $6 - 10$ -4

38. $3 - 19$ -16

39. $-3 - 7$ -10

40. $-3 - 12$ -15

41. $5 - (-6)$ 11

42. $5 - (-9)$ 14

43. $-6 - 5$ -11

44. $-3 - 6$ -9

45. $\frac{1}{4} - \frac{1}{2}$ $-\frac{1}{4}$

46. $\frac{2}{5} - \frac{2}{3}$ $-\frac{4}{15}$

47. $\frac{1}{2} - \left(-\frac{1}{4}\right)$ $\frac{3}{4}$

48. $\frac{2}{3} - \left(-\frac{1}{6}\right)$ $\frac{5}{6}$

49. $10 - 3$ 7

50. $13 - 3$ 10

51. $1 - 0.07$ 0.93

52. $0.03 - 1$ -0.97

53. $7.3 - (-2)$ 9.3

54. $-5.1 - 0.15$ -5.25

55. $-0.03 - 5$ -5.03

56. $0.7 - (-0.3)$ 1

Perform the indicated operations. Do not use a calculator.

57. $-5 + 8$ 3

58. $-6 + 10$ 4

59. $-6 + (-3)$ -9

60. $(-13) + (-12)$ -25

61. $-80 - 40$ -120

62. $44 - (-15)$ 59

63. $61 - (-17)$ 78

64. $-19 - 13$ -32

65. $(-12) + (-15)$ -27

66. $-12 + 12$ 0

67. $13 + (-20)$ -7

68. $15 + (-39)$ -24

69. $-102 - 99$ -201

70. $-94 - (-77)$ -17

71. $-161 - 161$ -322

72. $-19 - 88$ -107

73. $-16 + 0.03$ -15.97

74. $0.59 + (-3.4)$ -2.81

75. $0.08 - 3$ -2.92

76. $1.8 - 9$ -7.2

77. $-3.7 + (-0.03)$ -3.73

78. $0.9 + (-1)$ -0.1

79. $-2.3 - (-6)$ 3.7

80. $-7.08 - (-9)$ 1.92

81. $\frac{3}{4} + \left(-\frac{3}{5}\right)$ $\frac{3}{20}$

82. $-\frac{1}{3} + \frac{3}{5}$ $\frac{4}{15}$

83. $-\frac{1}{12} - \left(-\frac{3}{8}\right)$ $\frac{7}{24}$

84. $-\frac{1}{17} - \left(-\frac{1}{17}\right)$ 0

Fill in the parentheses so that each equation is correct.

85. $-5 + (13) = 8$

86. $-9 + (31) = 22$

87. $12 + (-10) = 2$

88. $13 + (-17) = -4$

89. $10 - (14) = -4$

90. $14 - (22) = -8$

91. $6 - (-4) = 10$

92. $3 - (-12) = 15$

93. $-4 - (-3) = -1$

94. $-11 - (-13) = 2$

Use a calculator to perform the indicated operations.

95. $45.87 + (-49.36)$ -3.49

96. $-0.357 + (-3.465)$ -3.822

97. $0.6578 + (-1)$ -0.3422

98. $-2.347 + (-3.5)$ -5.847

99. $-3.45 - 45.39$ -48.84

100. $9.8 - 9.974$ -0.174

101. $-5.79 - 3.06$ -8.85

102. $0 - (-4.537)$ 4.537

Solve each problem.

103. ***Overdrawn.*** Willard opened his checking account with a deposit of \$97.86. He then wrote checks and had other charges as shown in his account register. Find his current balance. $-\$8.85$

Deposit		97.86
Wal-Mart	27.89	
Kmart	42.32	
ATM cash	25.00	
Service charge	3.50	
Check printing	8.00	

Figure for Exercise 103

104. ***Net worth.*** Melanie's house is worth \$125,000, but she still owes \$78,422 on her mortgage. She has \$21,236 in a savings account and has \$9,477 in credit card debt. She owes \$6,131 to the credit union and figures that her cars and other household items are worth a total of \$15,000. What is Melanie's net worth? \$67,206

105. ***Falling temperatures.*** At noon the temperature in Montreal was 5°C. By midnight the mercury had fallen 12°. What was the temperature at midnight? -7°C

106. ***Bitter cold.*** The overnight low temperature in Milwaukee was -13°F for Monday night. The temperature went up 20° during the day on Tuesday and then fell 15° to reach Tuesday night's overnight low temperature.

a) What was the overnight low Tuesday night? -8°F

b) Judging from the accompanying graph, was the average low for the week above or below 0°F? Below zero

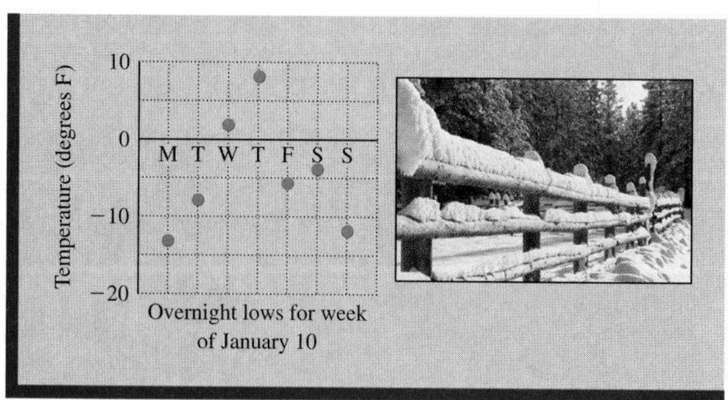

Figure for Exercise 106

Getting More Involved

107. *Writing*

What does absolute value have to do with adding signed numbers? Can you add signed numbers without using absolute value?

When adding signed numbers, we add or subtract only positive numbers which are the absolute values of the original numbers. We then determine the appropriate sign for the answer.

108. *Discussion*

Why do we learn addition of signed numbers before subtraction?

Subtraction is defined as addition of the opposite, $a - b = a + (-b)$.

109. *Discussion*

Aimee and Joni are traveling south in separate cars on Interstate 5 near Stockton. While they are speaking to each other on cellular telephones, Aimee gives her location as mile marker x and Joni gives her location as mile marker y. Which of the following expressions gives the distance between them? Explain your answer.

a) $y - x$ **b)** $x - y$
c) $|x - y|$ **d)** $|y - x|$
e) $|x| + |y|$

The distance between x and y is given by either $|x - y|$ or $|y - x|$.

1.4 Multiplication and Division of Real Numbers

In this Section

- Multiplication of Real Numbers
- Division of Real Numbers
- Division by Zero

In this section we will complete the study of the four basic operations with real numbers.

Multiplication of Real Numbers

The result of multiplying two numbers is referred to as the **product** of the numbers. The numbers multiplied are called **factors.** In algebra we use a raised dot between the factors to indicate multiplication, or we place symbols next to one another to indicate multiplication. Thus $a \cdot b$ or ab are both referred to as the product of a and b. When multiplying numbers, we may enclose them in parentheses to make the meaning clear. To write 5 times 3, we may write it as $5 \cdot 3$, 5(3), (5)3, or (5)(3). In multiplying a number and a variable, no sign is used between them. Thus $5x$ is used to represent the product of 5 and x.

Multiplication is just a short way to do repeated additions. Adding together five 3's gives

$$3 + 3 + 3 + 3 + 3 = 15.$$

So we have the multiplication fact $5 \cdot 3 = 15$. Adding together five -3's gives

$$(-3) + (-3) + (-3) + (-3) + (-3) = -15.$$

So we should have $5(-3) = -15$. We can think of $5(-3) = -15$ as saying that taking on five debts of \$3 each is equivalent to a debt of \$15. Losing five debts of \$3 each is equivalent to gaining \$15, so we should have $(-5)(-3) = 15$.

These examples illustrate the rule for multiplying signed numbers.

Helpful Hint

The product of two numbers with like signs is positive, but the product of three numbers with like signs can be positive or negative. For example,

$$2 \cdot 2 \cdot 2 = 8$$

and

$$(-2)(-2)(-2) = -8.$$

Product of Signed Numbers

To find the product of two nonzero real numbers, multiply their absolute values.

- The product is *positive* if the numbers have *like* signs.
- The product is *negative* if the numbers have *unlike* signs.

EXAMPLE 1

Multiplying signed numbers

Evaluate each product.

a) $(-2)(-3)$ **b)** $3(-6)$ **c)** $-5 \cdot 10$

d) $\left(-\frac{1}{3}\right)\left(-\frac{1}{2}\right)$ **e)** $(-0.02)(0.08)$ **f)** $(-300)(-0.06)$

Calculator Close-Up

Try finding the products in Example 1 with your calculator.

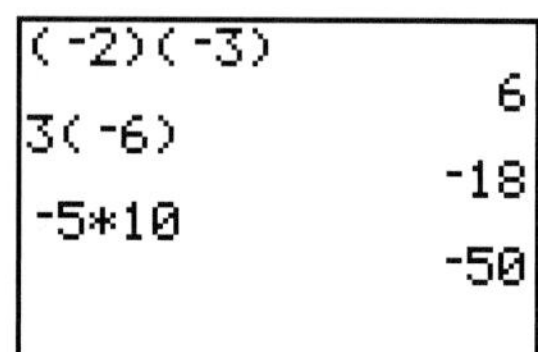

Solution

a) First find the product of the absolute values:

$$|-2| \cdot |-3| = 2 \cdot 3 = 6$$

Because -2 and -3 have the same sign, we get $(-2)(-3) = 6$.

b) First find the product of the absolute values:

$$|3| \cdot |-6| = 3 \cdot 6 = 18$$

Because 3 and -6 have unlike signs, we get $3(-6) = -18$.

c) $-5 \cdot 10 = -50$ Unlike signs, negative result

d) $\left(-\frac{1}{3}\right)\left(-\frac{1}{2}\right) = \frac{1}{6}$ Like signs, positive result

e) When multiplying decimals, we total the number of decimal places in the factors to get the number of decimal places in the product. Thus

$$(-0.02)(0.08) = -0.0016.$$

f) $(-300)(-0.06) = 18$

Now do Exercises 7–18

Teaching Tip Point out to students that you have to learn multiplication before you can divide. Ask them to recall another pair of operations that are related in this manner.

Division of Real Numbers

We say that $10 \div 5 = 2$ because $2 \cdot 5 = 10$. This example illustrates how division is defined in terms of multiplication.

Division of Real Numbers

If a, b, and c are any real numbers with $b \neq 0$, then

$$a \div b = c \quad \text{provided that} \quad c \cdot b = a.$$

Using the definition of division, we get

$$10 \div (-2) = -5$$

because $(-5)(-2) = 10$;

$$-10 \div 2 = -5$$

because $(-5)(2) = -10$; and

$$-10 \div (-2) = 5$$

because $(5)(-2) = -10$. From these examples we see that the rule for dividing signed numbers is similar to that for multiplying signed numbers.

Division of Signed Numbers

To find the quotient of two nonzero real numbers, divide their absolute values.

- The quotient is *positive* if the two numbers have *like* signs.
- The quotient is *negative* if the two numbers have *unlike* signs.

Zero divided by any nonzero real number is zero.

EXAMPLE 2

Dividing signed numbers

Evaluate.

a) $(-8) \div (-4)$ **b)** $(-8) \div 8$ **c)** $8 \div (-4)$

d) $-4 \div \frac{1}{3}$ **e)** $-2.5 \div 0.05$ **f)** $0 \div (-6)$

Solution

a) $(-8) \div (-4) = 2$ Same sign, positive result

b) $(-8) \div 8 = -1$ Unlike signs, negative result

c) $8 \div (-4) = -2$

d) $-4 \div \frac{1}{3} = -4 \cdot \frac{3}{1}$ Invert and multiply.

$= -4 \cdot 3$

$= -12$

e) $-2.5 \div 0.05 = \frac{-2.5}{0.05}$ Write in fraction form.

$= \frac{-2.5 \cdot 100}{0.05 \cdot 100}$ Multiply by 100 to eliminate the decimals.

$= \frac{-250}{5}$ Simplify.

$= -50$ Divide.

f) $0 \div (-6) = 0$

Now do Exercises 19–62

Helpful Hint

Do not use negative numbers in long division. To find $-378 \div 7$, divide 378 by 7:

$$\begin{array}{r} 54 \\ 7\overline{)378} \\ \underline{35} \\ 28 \\ \underline{28} \\ 0 \end{array}$$

Since a negative divided by a positive is negative

$-378 \div 7 = -54.$

Division can also be indicated by a fraction bar. For example,

$$24 \div 6 = \frac{24}{6} = 4.$$

If signed numbers occur in a fraction, we use the rules for dividing signed numbers. For example,

$$\frac{-9}{3} = -3, \quad \frac{9}{-3} = -3, \quad \frac{-1}{2} = \frac{1}{-2} = -\frac{1}{2}, \quad \text{and} \quad \frac{-4}{-2} = 2.$$

Study Tip

If you don't know how to get started on the exercises, go back to the examples. Cover the solution in the text with a piece of paper and see if you can solve the example. After you have mastered the examples, then try the exercises again.

Note that if one negative sign appears in a fraction, the fraction has the same value whether the negative sign is in the numerator, in the denominator, or in front of the fraction. If the numerator and denominator of a fraction are both negative, then the fraction has a positive value.

Division by Zero

Teaching Tip Students often confuse 0/8 and 8/0. Ask them how they will remember the difference.

Why do we exclude division by zero from the definition of division? If we write $10 \div 0 = c$, we need to find a number c such that $c \cdot 0 = 10$. This is impossible. If we write $0 \div 0 = c$, we need to find a number c such that $c \cdot 0 = 0$. In fact, $c \cdot 0 = 0$ is true for any value of c. Having $0 \div 0$ equal to any number would be confusing in doing computations. Thus $a \div b$ is defined only for $b \neq 0$. Quotients such as

$$8 \div 0, \quad 0 \div 0, \quad \frac{8}{0}, \quad \text{and} \quad \frac{0}{0}$$

are said to be **undefined.**

Warm-Ups

True or false? Explain your answer.

1. The product of 7 and y is written as $7y$. True
2. The product of -2 and 5 is 10. False
3. The quotient of x and 3 can be written as $x \div 3$ or $\frac{x}{3}$. True
4. $0 \div 6$ is undefined. False
5. $(-9) \div (-3) = 3$ True
6. $6 \div (-2) = -3$ True
7. $\left(-\frac{1}{2}\right)\left(-\frac{1}{2}\right) = \frac{1}{4}$ True
8. $(-0.2)(0.2) = -0.4$ False
9. $\left(-\frac{1}{2}\right) \div \left(-\frac{1}{2}\right) = 1$ True
10. $\frac{0}{0} = 0$ False

1.4 Exercises

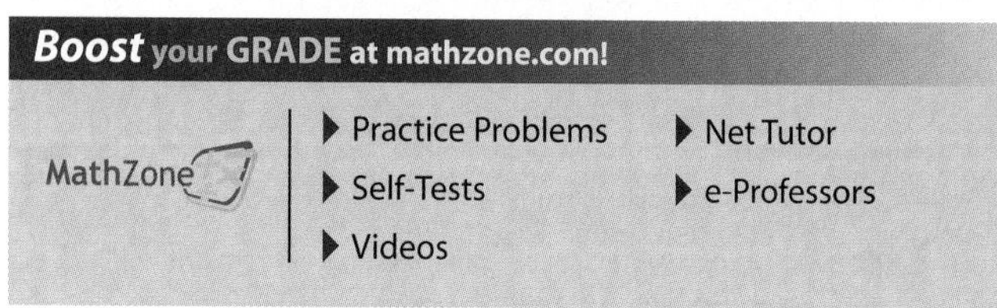

Reading and Writing *After reading this section write out the answers to these questions. Use complete sentences.*

1. What operations did we study in this section?
   We learned to multiply and divide signed numbers.
2. What is a product?
   A product is the result of multiplication. The product of a and b is ab. The product of 2 and 4 is 8.
3. How do you find the product of two signed numbers?
   To find the product of signed numbers, multiply their absolute values and then affix a negative sign if the two original numbers have opposite signs.
4. What is the relationship between division and multiplication?
   Division is defined in terms of multiplication as $a \div b = c$ provided $c \cdot b = a$ and $b \neq 0$.
5. How do you find the quotient of nonzero real numbers?
   To find the quotient of nonzero numbers divide their absolute values and then affix a negative sign if the two original numbers have opposite signs.
6. Why is division by zero undefined?
   Division by zero is undefined because it cannot be made consistent with the definition of division: $a \div b = c$ provided $c \cdot b = a$.

Evaluate. See Example 1.

7. $-3 \cdot 9$ -27
8. $6(-4)$ -24
9. $(-12)(-11)$ 132
10. $(-9)(-15)$ 135
11. $-\frac{3}{4} \cdot \frac{4}{9}$ $-\frac{1}{3}$
12. $\left(-\frac{2}{3}\right)\left(-\frac{6}{7}\right)$ $\frac{4}{7}$
13. $0.5(-0.6)$ -0.3
14. $(-0.3)(0.3)$ -0.09
15. $(-12)(-12)$ 144
16. $(-11)(-11)$ 121
17. $-3 \cdot 0$ 0
18. $0(-7)$ 0

Evaluate. See Example 2.

19. $8 \div (-8)$ -1
20. $-6 \div 2$ -3
21. $(-90) \div (-30)$ 3
22. $(-20) \div (-40)$ $\frac{1}{2}$
23. $\frac{44}{-66}$ $-\frac{2}{3}$
24. $\frac{-33}{-36}$ $\frac{11}{12}$
25. $\left(-\frac{2}{3}\right) \div \left(-\frac{4}{5}\right)$ $\frac{5}{6}$
26. $-\frac{1}{3} \div \frac{4}{9}$ $-\frac{3}{4}$
27. $\frac{-125}{0}$ Undefined
28. $-37 \div 0$ Undefined
29. $0 \div \left(-\frac{1}{3}\right)$ 0
30. $0 \div 43.568$ 0
31. $40 \div (-0.5)$ -80
32. $3 \div (-0.1)$ -30
33. $-0.5 \div (-2)$ 0.25
34. $-0.75 \div (-0.5)$ 1.5

Perform the indicated operations.

35. $(25)(-4)$ -100
36. $(5)(-4)$ -20
37. $(-3)(-9)$ 27
38. $(-51) \div (-3)$ 17
39. $-9 \div 3$ -3
40. $86 \div (-2)$ -43
41. $20 \div (-5)$ -4
42. $(-8)(-6)$ 48
43. $(-6)(5)$ -30
44. $(-18) \div 3$ -6
45. $(-57) \div (-3)$ 19
46. $(-30)(4)$ -120
47. $(0.6)(-0.3)$ -0.18
48. $(-0.2)(-0.5)$ 0.1
49. $(-0.03)(-10)$ 0.3
50. $(0.05)(-1.5)$ -0.075
51. $(-0.6) \div (0.1)$ -6
52. $8 \div (-0.5)$ -16
53. $(-0.6) \div (-0.4)$ 1.5
54. $(-63) \div (-0.9)$ 70
55. $-\frac{12}{5}\left(-\frac{55}{6}\right)$ 22
56. $-\frac{9}{10} \cdot \frac{4}{3}$ $-\frac{6}{5}$
57. $-2\frac{3}{4} \div 8\frac{1}{4}$ $-\frac{1}{3}$
58. $-9\frac{1}{2} \div \left(-3\frac{1}{6}\right)$ 3

Use a calculator to perform the indicated operations. Round approximate answers to two decimal places.

59. $(0.45)(-365)$ -164.25
60. $8.5 \div (-0.15)$ -56.67
61. $(-52) \div (-0.034)$ 1529.41
62. $(-4.8)(5.6)$ -26.88

Fill in the parentheses so that each equation is correct.

63. $-5 \cdot (-12) = 60$
64. $-9 \cdot (-6) = 54$
65. $12 \cdot (-8) = -96$
66. $11 \cdot (-4) = -44$
67. $24 \div (-6) = -4$
68. $51 \div (-3) = -17$
69. $-36 \div (-1) = 36$
70. $-48 \div (-8) = 6$
71. $-40 \div (5) = -8$
72. $-13 \div (13) = -1$

Perform the indicated operations. Use a calculator to check.

73. $(-4)(-4)$ 16
74. $-4 - 4$ -8
75. $-4 + (-4)$ -8
76. $-4 \div (-4)$ 1
77. $-4 + 4$ 0
78. $-4 \cdot 4$ -16
79. $-4 - (-4)$ 0
80. $0 \div (-4)$ 0
81. $0.1 - 4$ -3.9
82. $(0.1)(-4)$ -0.4
83. $(-4) \div (0.1)$ -40
84. $-0.1 - 4$ -4.1
85. $(-0.1)(-4)$ 0.4
86. $-0.1 + 4$ 3.9
87. $|-0.4|$ 0.4
88. $|0.4|$ 0.4
89. $\frac{-0.06}{0.3}$ -0.2
90. $\frac{2}{-0.04}$ -50
91. $\frac{3}{-0.4}$ -7.5
92. $\frac{-1.2}{-0.03}$ 40
93. $-\frac{1}{5} + \frac{1}{6}$ $-\frac{1}{30}$
94. $-\frac{3}{5} - \frac{1}{4}$ $-\frac{17}{20}$
95. $\left(-\frac{3}{4}\right)\left(\frac{2}{15}\right)$ $-\frac{1}{10}$
96. $-1 \div \left(-\frac{1}{4}\right)$ 4

Use a calculator to perform the indicated operations. Round approximate answers to three decimal places.

97. $\frac{45.37}{6}$ 7.562
98. $(-345) \div (28)$ -12.321
99. $(-4.3)(-4.5)$ 19.35
100. $\frac{-12.34}{-3}$ 4.113
101. $\frac{0}{6.345}$ 0
102. $0 \div (34.51)$ 0
103. $199.4 \div 0$ Undefined
104. $\frac{23.44}{0}$ Undefined

Getting More Involved

105. ***Discussion***

If you divide \$0 among five people, how much does each person get? If you divide \$5 among zero people, how much does each person get? What do these questions illustrate?

106. ***Discussion***

What is the difference between the non-negative numbers and the positive numbers?

107. ***Writing***

Why do we learn multiplication of signed numbers before division?

108. ***Writing***

Try to rewrite the rules for multiplying and dividing signed numbers without using the idea of absolute value. Are your rewritten rules clearer than the original rules?

1.5 Exponential Expressions and the Order of Operations

In this Section

- Arithmetic Expressions
- Exponential Expressions
- The Order of Operations

In Sections 1.3 and 1.4 you learned how to perform operations with a pair of real numbers to obtain a third real number. In this section you will learn to evaluate expressions involving several numbers and operations.

Arithmetic Expressions

The result of writing numbers in a meaningful combination with the ordinary operations of arithmetic is called an **arithmetic expression** or simply an **expression.** Consider the expressions

$$(3 + 2) \cdot 5 \qquad \text{and} \qquad 3 + (2 \cdot 5).$$

The parentheses are used as **grouping symbols** and indicate which operation to perform first. Because of the parentheses, these expressions have different values:

$$(3 + 2) \cdot 5 = 5 \cdot 5 = 25$$
$$3 + (2 \cdot 5) = 3 + 10 = 13$$

Absolute value symbols and fraction bars are also used as grouping symbols. The numerator and denominator of a fraction are treated as if each is in parentheses.

EXAMPLE 1

Using grouping symbols

Evaluate each expression.

a) $(3 - 6)(3 + 6)$

b) $|3 - 4| - |5 - 9|$

c) $\dfrac{4 - (-8)}{5 - 9}$

Solution

a) $(3 - 6)(3 + 6) = (-3)(9)$ Evaluate within parentheses first.
$= -27$ Multiply.

b) $|3 - 4| - |5 - 9| = |-1| - |-4|$ Evaluate within absolute value symbols.
$= 1 - 4$ Find the absolute values.
$= -3$ Subtract.

c) $\dfrac{4 - (-8)}{5 - 9} = \dfrac{12}{-4}$ Evaluate the numerator and denominator.
$= -3$ Divide.

Now do Exercises 7–18

Calculator Close-Up

One advantage of a graphing calculator is that you can enter an entire expression on its display and then evaluate it. If your calculator does not allow built-up form for fractions, then you must use parentheses around the numerator and denominator as shown here.

```
(3-6)(3+6)
                -27
abs(3-4)-abs(5-9
)
                 -3
(4--8)/(5-9)
                 -3
```

Exponential Expressions

An arithmetic expression with repeated multiplication can be written by using exponents. For example,

$$2 \cdot 2 \cdot 2 = 2^3 \qquad \text{and} \qquad 5 \cdot 5 = 5^2.$$

Study Tip

If you need help, do not hesitate to get it. Math has a way of building upon the past. What you learn today will be used tomorrow, and what you learn tomorrow will be used the day after. If you don't straighten out problems immediately, then you can get hopelessly lost. If you are having trouble, see your instructor to find out what help is available.

The 3 in 2^3 is the number of times that 2 occurs in the product $2 \cdot 2 \cdot 2$, while the 2 in 5^2 is the number of times that 5 occurs in $5 \cdot 5$. We read 2^3 as "2 cubed" or "2 to the third power." We read 5^2 as "5 squared" or "5 to the second power." In general, an expression of the form a^n is called an **exponential expression** and is defined as follows.

Exponential Expression

For any counting number n,

$$a^n = \underbrace{a \cdot a \cdot a \cdot \ldots \cdot a}_{n \text{ factors}}.$$

We call a the **base** and n the **exponent.**

The expression a^n is read "a to the nth power." If the exponent is 1, it is usually omitted. For example, $9^1 = 9$.

EXAMPLE 2

Using exponential notation

Write each product as an exponential expression.

a) $6 \cdot 6 \cdot 6 \cdot 6 \cdot 6$ **b)** $(-3)(-3)(-3)(-3)$ **c)** $\frac{3}{2} \cdot \frac{3}{2} \cdot \frac{3}{2}$

Solution

a) $6 \cdot 6 \cdot 6 \cdot 6 \cdot 6 = 6^5$

b) $(-3)(-3)(-3)(-3) = (-3)^4$

c) $\frac{3}{2} \cdot \frac{3}{2} \cdot \frac{3}{2} = \left(\frac{3}{2}\right)^3$

Now do Exercises 19–26

EXAMPLE 3

Writing an exponential expression as a product

Write each exponential expression as a product without exponents.

a) y^6 **b)** $(-2)^4$ **c)** $\left(\frac{5}{4}\right)^3$ **d)** $(-0.1)^2$

Solution

a) $y^6 = y \cdot y \cdot y \cdot y \cdot y \cdot y$

b) $(-2)^4 = (-2)(-2)(-2)(-2)$

c) $\left(\frac{5}{4}\right)^3 = \frac{5}{4} \cdot \frac{5}{4} \cdot \frac{5}{4}$

d) $(-0.1)^2 = (-0.1)(-0.1)$

Now do Exercises 27–34

To evaluate an exponential expression, write the base as many times as indicated by the exponent, then multiply the factors from left to right.

EXAMPLE 4

Evaluating exponential expressions

Evaluate.

a) 3^3 **b)** $(-2)^3$ **c)** $\left(\frac{2}{3}\right)^4$ **d)** $(0.4)^2$

Calculator Close-Up

You can use the power key for any power. Most calculators also have an x^2 key that gives the second power. Note that parentheses must be used when raising a fraction to a power.

```
(-2)^3
                -8
(2/3)^4▸Frac
             16/81
.4²
               .16
```

Solution

a) $3^3 = 3 \cdot 3 \cdot 3 = 9 \cdot 3 = 27$

b) $(-2)^3 = (-2)(-2)(-2)$

$= 4(-2)$

$= -8$

c) $\left(\frac{2}{3}\right)^4 = \frac{2}{3} \cdot \frac{2}{3} \cdot \frac{2}{3} \cdot \frac{2}{3}$

$= \frac{4}{9} \cdot \frac{2}{3} \cdot \frac{2}{3}$

$= \frac{8}{27} \cdot \frac{2}{3}$

$= \frac{16}{81}$

d) $(0.4)^2 = (0.4)(0.4) = 0.16$

Now do Exercises 35–50

Teaching Tip Remind students not to multiply by the exponent: $(-2)^4 \neq -2 \cdot 4$.

CAUTION Note that $3^3 \neq 9$. We do not multiply the exponent and the base when evaluating an exponential expression.

Be especially careful with exponential expressions involving negative numbers. An exponential expression with a negative base is written with parentheses around the base as in $(-2)^4$:

$$(-2)^4 = (-2)(-2)(-2)(-2) = 16$$

To evaluate $-(2^4)$, use the base 2 as a factor four times, then find the opposite:

$$-(2^4) = -(2 \cdot 2 \cdot 2 \cdot 2) = -(16) = -16$$

We often omit the parentheses in $-(2^4)$ and simply write -2^4. So

$$-2^4 = -(2^4) = -16.$$

To evaluate $-(-2)^4$, use the base -2 as a factor four times, then find the opposite:

$$-(-2)^4 = -(16) = -16$$

EXAMPLE 5

Evaluating exponential expressions involving negative numbers

Evaluate.

a) $(-10)^4$

b) -10^4

c) $-(-0.5)^2$

d) $-(5 - 8)^2$

Solution

a) $(-10)^4 = (-10)(-10)(-10)(-10)$ Use -10 as a factor four times.

$= 10{,}000$

b) $-10^4 = -(10^4)$ Rewrite using parentheses.

$= -(10{,}000)$ Find 10^4.

$= -10{,}000$ Then find the opposite of 10,000.

c) $-(-0.5)^2 = -(-0.5)(-0.5)$ Use -0.5 as a factor two times.

$= -(0.25)$

$= -0.25$

d) $-(5 - 8)^2 = -(-3)^2$ Evaluate within parentheses first.

$= -(9)$ Square -3 to get 9.

$= -9$ Take the opposite of 9 to get -9.

Now do Exercises 51–58

Helpful Hint

"Please Excuse My Dear Aunt Sally" (PEMDAS) is often used as a memory aid for the order of operations. Do Parentheses, Exponents, Multiplication and Division, then Addition and Subtraction. Multiplication and division have equal priority. The same goes for addition and subtraction.

The Order of Operations

When we evaluate expressions, operations within grouping symbols are always performed first. For example,

$$(3 + 2) \cdot 5 = (5) \cdot 5 = 25 \quad \text{and} \quad (2 \cdot 3)^2 = 6^2 = 36.$$

To make expressions look simpler, we often omit some or all parentheses. In this case, we must agree on the order in which to perform the operations. We agree to do multiplication before addition and exponential expressions before multiplication. So

$$3 + 2 \cdot 5 = 3 + 10 = 13 \quad \text{and} \quad 2 \cdot 3^2 = 2 \cdot 9 = 18.$$

We state the complete **order of operations** in the following box.

Order of Operations

If an expression contains no grouping symbols, evaluate it using the following order. If an expression contains operations within grouping symbols, evaluate the expressions within grouping symbols first, using the following order.

1. Evaluate each exponential expression (in order from left to right).
2. Perform multiplication and division (in order from left to right).
3. Perform addition and subtraction (in order from left to right).

Multiplication and division have equal priority in the order of operations. If both appear in an expression, they are performed in order from left to right. The same holds for addition and subtraction. For example,

$$8 \div 4 \cdot 3 = 2 \cdot 3 = 6 \quad \text{and} \quad 9 - 3 + 5 = 6 + 5 = 11.$$

EXAMPLE 6

Using the order of operations

Evaluate each expression.

a) $2^3 \cdot 3^2$ **b)** $2 \cdot 5 - 3 \cdot 4 + 4^2$ **c)** $2 \cdot 3 \cdot 4 - 3^3 + \frac{8}{2}$

Calculator Close-Up

Most calculators follow the same order of operations shown here. Evaluate these expressions with your calculator.

```
2^3*3²
                72
2*5-3*4+4²
                14
2*3*4-3^3+8/2
                 1
```

Solution

a) $2^3 \cdot 3^2 = 8 \cdot 9$ Evaluate exponential expressions before multiplying.

$= 72$

b) $2 \cdot 5 - 3 \cdot 4 + 4^2 = 2 \cdot 5 - 3 \cdot 4 + 16$ Exponential expressions first

$= 10 - 12 + 16$ Multiplication second

$= 14$ Addition and subtraction from left to right

c) $2 \cdot 3 \cdot 4 - 3^3 + \frac{8}{2} = 2 \cdot 3 \cdot 4 - 27 + \frac{8}{2}$ Exponential expressions first

$= 24 - 27 + 4$ Multiplication and division second

$= 1$ Addition and subtraction from left to right

Now do Exercises 59–70

When grouping symbols are used, we perform operations within grouping symbols first. The order of operations is followed within the grouping symbols.

EXAMPLE 7

Grouping symbols and the order of operations

Evaluate.

a) $3 - 2(7 - 2^3)$ **b)** $3 - |7 - 3 \cdot 4|$ **c)** $\dfrac{9 - 5 + 8}{-5^2 - 3(-7)}$

Teaching Tip Some students think that the first operation to perform is "parentheses." Parentheses are grouping symbols, not an operation. Point out the difference. Absolute value bars, fraction bars, and radicals are used for grouping and an operation.

Solution

a) $3 - 2(7 - 2^3) = 3 - 2(7 - 8)$ Evaluate within parentheses first.

$= 3 - 2(-1)$

$= 3 - (-2)$ Multiply.

$= 5$ Subtract.

b) $3 - |7 - 3 \cdot 4| = 3 - |7 - 12|$ Evaluate within the absolute value symbols first.

$= 3 - |-5|$

$= 3 - 5$ Evaluate the absolute value.

$= -2$ Subtract.

c) $\dfrac{9 - 5 + 8}{-5^2 - 3(-7)} = \dfrac{12}{-25 + 21} = \dfrac{12}{-4} = -3$ Numerator and denominator are treated as if in parentheses.

Now do Exercises 71–84

When grouping symbols occur within grouping symbols, we evaluate within the innermost grouping symbols first and then work outward. In this case, brackets [ ] can be used as grouping symbols along with parentheses to make the grouping clear.

EXAMPLE 8

Grouping within grouping

Evaluate each expression.

a) $6 - 4[5 - (7 - 9)]$ **b)** $-2|3 - (9 - 5)| - |-3|$

Teaching Tip Remind students to be neat and organized. Show steps like the examples.

Solution

a)

$$\begin{aligned} 6 - 4[5 - (7 - 9)] &= 6 - 4[5 - (-2)] && \text{Innermost parentheses first} \\ &= 6 - 4[7] && \text{Next evaluate within the brackets.} \\ &= 6 - 28 && \text{Multiply.} \\ &= -22 && \text{Subtract.} \end{aligned}$$

b)

$$\begin{aligned} -2|3 - (9 - 5)| - |-3| &= -2|3 - 4| - |-3| && \text{Innermost grouping first} \\ &= -2|-1| - |-3| && \text{Evaluate within the first absolute value.} \\ &= -2 \cdot 1 - 3 && \text{Evaluate absolute values.} \\ &= -2 - 3 && \text{Multiply.} \\ &= -5 && \text{Subtract.} \end{aligned}$$

Now do Exercises 85–92

Calculator Close-Up

Graphing calculators can handle grouping symbols within grouping symbols. Since parentheses must occur in pairs, you should have the same number of left parentheses as right parentheses. You might notice other grouping symbols on your calculator, but they may or may not be used for grouping. See your manual.

```
6-4(5-(7-9))
                 -22
-2abs(3-(9-5))-a
bs(-3)
                  -5
```

Warm-Ups ▼

True or false? Explain your answer.

1. $(-3)^2 = -6$ False
2. $5 - 3 \cdot 2 = 4$ False
3. $(5 - 3)2 = 4$ True
4. $|5 - 6| = |5| - |6|$ False
5. $5 + 6 \cdot 2 = (5 + 6) \cdot 2$ False
6. $(2 + 3)^2 = 2^2 + 3^2$ False
7. $5 - 3^3 = 8$ False
8. $(5 - 3)^3 = 8$ True
9. $6 - \frac{6}{2} = \frac{0}{2}$ False
10. $\frac{6 - 6}{2} = 0$ True

1.5 Exercises

Boost your GRADE at mathzone.com!

MathZone

- Practice Problems
- Self-Tests
- Videos
- Net Tutor
- e-Professors

Reading and Writing *After reading this section write out the answers to these questions. Use complete sentences.*

1. What is an arithmetic expression?
   An arithmetic expression is the result of writing numbers in a meaningful combination with the ordinary operations of arithmetic.
2. What is the purpose of grouping symbols?
   The purpose of grouping symbols is to indicate the order in which to perform operations.
3. What is an exponential expression?
   An exponential expression is an expression of the form a^n.
4. What is the difference between -3^6 and $(-3)^6$?
   The value of -3^6 is negative while the value of $(-3)^6$ is positive.
5. What is the purpose of the order of operations?
   The order of operations tells us the order in which to perform operations when grouping symbols are omitted.
6. What were the different types of grouping symbols used in this section?
   Grouping symbols used in this section were parentheses, absolute value bars, and the fraction bar.

Evaluate each expression. See Example 1.

7. $(4 - 3)(5 - 9)$ -4 **8.** $(5 - 7)(-2 - 3)$ 10

9. $|3 + 4| - |-2 - 4|$ 1 **10.** $|-4 + 9| + |-3 - 5|$ 13

11. $\dfrac{7 - (-9)}{3 - 5}$ -8 **12.** $\dfrac{-8 + 2}{-1 - 1}$ 3

13. $(-6 + 5)(7)$ -7 **14.** $-6 + (5 \cdot 7)$ 29

15. $(-3 - 7) - 6$ -16 **16.** $-3 - (7 - 6)$ -4

17. $-16 \div (8 \div 2)$ -4 **18.** $(-16 \div 8) \div 2$ -1

Write each product as an exponential expression. See Example 2.

19. $4 \cdot 4 \cdot 4 \cdot 4$ 4^4 **20.** $1 \cdot 1 \cdot 1 \cdot 1 \cdot 1$ 1^5

21. $(-5)(-5)(-5)(-5)$ $(-5)^4$ **22.** $(-7)(-7)(-7)$ $(-7)^3$

23. $(-y)(-y)(-y)$ $(-y)^3$ **24.** $x \cdot x \cdot x \cdot x \cdot x$ x^5

25. $\dfrac{3}{7} \cdot \dfrac{3}{7} \cdot \dfrac{3}{7} \cdot \dfrac{3}{7} \cdot \dfrac{3}{7}$ $\left(\dfrac{3}{7}\right)^5$ **26.** $\dfrac{y}{2} \cdot \dfrac{y}{2} \cdot \dfrac{y}{2} \cdot \dfrac{y}{2}$ $\left(\dfrac{y}{2}\right)^4$

Write each exponential expression as a product without exponents. See Example 3.

27. 5^3 $5 \cdot 5 \cdot 5$ **28.** $(-8)^4$ $(-8)(-8)(-8)(-8)$

29. b^2 $b \cdot b$ **30.** $(-a)^5$ $(-a)(-a)(-a)(-a)(-a)$

31. $\left(-\dfrac{1}{2}\right)^5$ $\left(-\dfrac{1}{2}\right)\left(-\dfrac{1}{2}\right)\left(-\dfrac{1}{2}\right)\left(-\dfrac{1}{2}\right)\left(-\dfrac{1}{2}\right)$

32. $\left(-\dfrac{13}{12}\right)^3$ $\left(-\dfrac{13}{12}\right)\left(-\dfrac{13}{12}\right)\left(-\dfrac{13}{12}\right)$

33. $(0.22)^4$ $(0.22)(0.22)(0.22)(0.22)$

34. $(1.25)^6$ $(1.25)(1.25)(1.25)(1.25)(1.25)(1.25)$

Evaluate each exponential expression. See Examples 4 and 5.

35. 3^4 81 **36.** 5^3 125 **37.** 0^9 0

38. 0^{12} 0 **39.** $(-5)^4$ 625 **40.** $(-2)^5$ -32

41. $(-6)^3$ -216 **42.** $(-12)^2$ 144 **43.** $(10)^5$ $100{,}000$

44. $(-10)^6$ $1{,}000{,}000$ **45.** $(-0.1)^3$ -0.001 **46.** $(-0.2)^2$ 0.04

47. $\left(\dfrac{1}{2}\right)^3$ $\dfrac{1}{8}$ **48.** $\left(\dfrac{2}{3}\right)^3$ $\dfrac{8}{27}$ **49.** $\left(-\dfrac{1}{2}\right)^2$ $\dfrac{1}{4}$

50. $\left(-\dfrac{2}{3}\right)^2$ $\dfrac{4}{9}$ **51.** -8^2 -64 **52.** -7^2 -49

53. -8^4 -4096 **54.** -7^4 -2401

55. $-(7 - 10)^3$ 27 **56.** $-(6 - 9)^4$ -81

57. $(-2^2) - (3^2)$ -13 **58.** $(-3^4) - (-5^2)$ -56

Evaluate each expression. See Example 6.

59. $3^2 \cdot 2^2$ 36 **60.** $5 \cdot 10^2$ 500

61. $-3 \cdot 2 + 4 \cdot 6$ 18 **62.** $-5 \cdot 4 - 8 \cdot 3$ -44

63. $(-3)^3 + 2^3$ -19 **64.** $3^2 - 5(-1)^3$ 14

65. $-21 + 36 \div 3^2$ -17 **66.** $-18 - 9^2 \div 3^3$ -21

67. $-3 \cdot 2^3 - 5 \cdot 2^2$ -44 **68.** $2 \cdot 5 - 3^2 + 4 \cdot 0$ 1

69. $\dfrac{-8}{2} + 2 \cdot 3 \cdot 5 - 2^3$ 18 **70.** $-4 \cdot 2 \cdot 6 - \dfrac{12}{3} + 3^3$ -25

Evaluate each expression. See Example 7.

71. $(-3 + 4^2)(-6)$ -78 **72.** $-3 \cdot (2^3 + 4) \cdot 5$ -180

73. $(-3 \cdot 2 + 6)^3$ 0 **74.** $5 - 2(-3 + 2)^3$ 7

75. $2 - 5(3 - 4 \cdot 2)$ 27 **76.** $(3 - 7)(4 - 6 \cdot 2)$ 32

77. $3 - 2 \cdot |5 - 6|$ 1 **78.** $3 - |6 - 7 \cdot 3|$ -12

79. $(3^2 - 5) \cdot |3 \cdot 2 - 8|$ 8

80. $|4 - 6 \cdot 3| + |6 - 9|$ 17

81. $\dfrac{3 - 4 \cdot 6}{7 - 10}$ 7 **82.** $\dfrac{6 - (-8)^2}{-3 - (-1)}$ 29

83. $\dfrac{7 - 9 - 3^2}{9 - 7 - 3}$ 11 **84.** $\dfrac{3^2 - 2 \cdot 4}{-30 + 2 \cdot 4^2}$ $\frac{1}{2}$

Evaluate each expression. See Example 8.

85. $3 + 4[9 - 6(2 - 5)]$ 111

86. $9 + 3[5 - (3 - 6)^2]$ −3

87. $6^2 - [(2 + 3)^2 - 10]$ 21

88. $3[(2 - 3)^2 + (6 - 4)^2]$ 15

89. $4 - 5 \cdot |3 - (3^2 - 7)|$ −1

90. $2 + 3 \cdot |4 - (7^2 - 6^2)|$ 29

91. $-2|3 - (7 - 3)| - |-9|$ −11

92. $[3 - (2 - 4)][3 + |2 - 4|]$ 25

Evaluate each expression. Use a calculator to check.

93. $1 + 2^3$ 9 **94.** $(1 + 2)^3$ 27

95. $(-2)^2 - 4(-1)(3)$ 16 **96.** $(-2)^2 - 4(-2)(-3)$ −20

97. $4^2 - 4(1)(-3)$ 28 **98.** $3^2 - 4(-2)(3)$ 33

99. $(-11)^2 - 4(5)(0)$ 121 **100.** $(-12)^2 - 4(3)(0)$ 144

101. $-5^2 - 3 \cdot 4^2$ −73 **102.** $-6^2 - 5(-3)^2$ −81

103. $[3 + 2(-4)]^2$ 25 **104.** $[6 - 2(-3)]^2$ 144

105. $|-1| - |-1|$ 0 **106.** $4 - |1 - 7|$ −2

107. $\dfrac{4 - (-4)}{-2 - 2}$ −2 **108.** $\dfrac{3 - (-7)}{3 - 5}$ −5

109. $3(-1)^2 - 5(-1) + 4$ 12

110. $-2(1)^2 - 5(1) - 6$ −13

111. $5 - 2^2 + 3^4$ 82 **112.** $5 + (-2)^2 - 3^2$ 0

113. $-2 \cdot |9 - 6^2|$ −54 **114.** $8 - 3|5 - 4^2 + 1|$ −22

115. $-3^2 - 5[4 - 2(4 - 9)]$ −79

116. $-2[(3 - 4)^3 - 5] + 7$ 19

117. $1 - 5|5 - (9 + 1)|$ −24

118. $|6 - 3 \cdot 7| + |7 - (5 - 2)|$ 19

Use a calculator to evaluate each expression. Round approximate answers to four decimal places.

119. $3.2^2 - 4(3.6)(-2.2)$ 41.92

120. $(-4.5)^2 - 4(-2.8)(-4.6)$ −31.27

121. $(5.63)^3 - [4.7 - (-3.3)^2]$ 184.643547

122. $9.8^3 - [1.2 - (4.4 - 9.6)^2]$ 967.032

123. $\dfrac{3.44 - (-8.32)}{6.89 - 5.43}$ 8.0548

124. $\dfrac{-4.56 - 3.22}{3.44 - (-6.26)}$ −0.8021

Solve each problem.

125. ***Population of the United States.*** In 2004 the population of the United States was 294.4 million (U.S. Census Bureau, www.census.gov). If the population continues to grow at an annual rate of 1.05%, then the population in the year 2015 will be $294.4(1.0105)^{11}$ million.

a) Evaluate the expression to find the predicted population in 2015 to the nearest tenth of a million people. 330.2 million

b) Use the accompanying graph to estimate the year in which the population will reach 350 million people. 2022

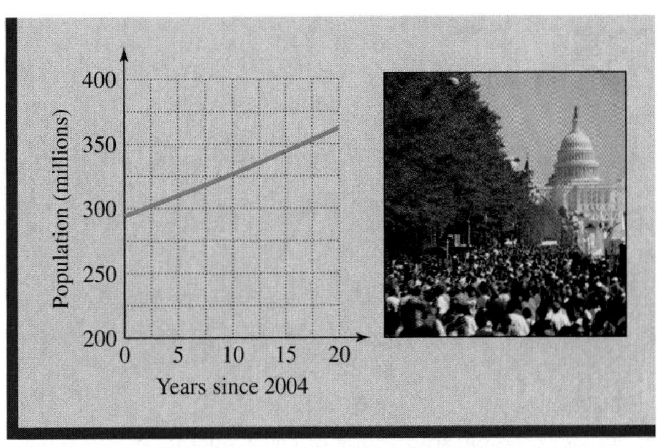

Figure for Exercise 125

126. ***Population of Mexico.*** In 2004 the population of Mexico was 106.5 million. If Mexico's population continues to grow at an annual rate of 1.43%, then the population in 2015 will be $106.5(1.0143)^{11}$ million.

a) Find the predicted population in 2015 to the nearest tenth of a million people. 124.5 million

b) Use the result of Exercise 125 to determine whether United States or Mexico will have the greater increase in population between 2004 and 2015. United States

Getting More Involved

127. ***Discussion***

How do the expressions $(-5)^3$, $-(5^3)$, -5^3, $-(-5)^3$, and $-1 \cdot 5^3$ differ?

$(-5)^3 = -(5^3) = -5^3 = -1 \cdot 5^3$ and $-(-5)^3 = 5^3$

128. ***Discussion***

How do the expressions $(-4)^4$, $-(4^4)$, -4^4, $-(-4)^4$, and $-1 \cdot 4^4$ differ?

$-(4^4) = -4^4 = -(-4)^4 = -1 \cdot 4^4$ and $(-4)^4 = 4^4$

1.6 Algebraic Expressions

In this Section

- **Identifying Algebraic Expressions**
- **Translating Algebraic Expressions**
- **Evaluating Algebraic Expressions**
- **Equations**
- **Applications**

In Section 1.5 you studied arithmetic expressions. In this section you will study expressions that are more general—expressions that involve variables.

Identifying Algebraic Expressions

Since variables (or letters) are used to represent numbers, we can use variables in arithmetic expressions. The result of combining numbers and variables with the ordinary operations of arithmetic (in some meaningful way) is called an **algebraic expression** or simply an **expression.** For example,

$$x + 2, \qquad \pi r^2, \qquad b^2 - 4ac, \qquad \text{and} \qquad \frac{a - b}{c - d}$$

are algebraic expressions.

Teaching Tip Note that we are concentrating on only a few nouns here. We will do more translating of verbal expressions into algebraic expressions in Section 2.5.

Expressions are often named by the last operation to be performed in the expression. For example, the expression $x + 2$ is a **sum** because the only operation in the expression is addition. The expression $a - bc$ is referred to as a **difference** because subtraction is the last operation to be performed. The expression $3(x - 4)$ is a **product,** while $\frac{3}{x - 4}$ is a **quotient.** The expression $(a + b)^2$ is a **square** because the addition is performed before the square is found.

EXAMPLE 1

Naming expressions

Identify each expression as either a sum, difference, product, quotient, or square.

a) $3(x + 2)$

b) $b^2 - 4ac$

c) $\frac{a - b}{c - d}$

d) $(a - b)^2$

Solution

a) In $3(x + 2)$ we add before we multiply. So this expression is a product.

b) By the order of operations the last operation to perform in $b^2 - 4ac$ is subtraction. So this expression is a difference.

c) The last operation to perform in this expression is division. So this expression is a quotient.

d) In $(a - b)^2$ we subtract before we square. This expression is a square.

Now do Exercises 7–18

Helpful Hint

Sum, difference, product, and quotient are nouns. They are used as names for expressions. Add, subtract, multiply, and divide are verbs. They indicate an action to perform.

Translating Algebraic Expressions

Algebra is useful because it can be used to solve problems. Since problems are often communicated verbally, we must be able to translate verbal expressions into algebraic expressions and translate algebraic expressions into verbal expressions. Consider the following examples of verbal expressions and their corresponding algebraic expressions.

Teaching Tip We emphasize the names of the common algebraic expressions now so that phrases like "the sum of two squares" make sense in factoring. You must know the order of operations to name expressions.

Verbal Expressions and Corresponding Algebraic Expressions

Verbal Expression	Algebraic Expression
The sum of $5x$ and 3	$5x + 3$
The product of 5 and $x + 3$	$5(x + 3)$
The sum of 8 and $\frac{x}{3}$	$8 + \frac{x}{3}$
The quotient of $8 + x$ and 3	$\frac{8 + x}{3}$, $(8 + x)/3$, or $(8 + x) \div 3$
The difference of 3 and x^2	$3 - x^2$
The square of $3 - x$	$(3 - x)^2$

Note that the word "difference" must be used carefully. To be consistent, we say that the difference between a and b is $a - b$. So the difference between 10 and 12 is $10 - 12$ or -2. However, outside of a textbook most people would say that the difference in age between a 10-year-old and a 12-year-old is 2, not -2. Users of the English language do not follow precise rules like we follow in mathematics. Of course, in mathematics we must make our mathematics and our English sentences perfectly clear. So we try to avoid using "difference" in an ambiguous or vague manner. (We will study verbal and algebraic expressions further in Section 2.5.)

Example 2 shows how the terms sum, difference, product, quotient, and square are used to describe expressions.

EXAMPLE 2

Algebraic expressions to verbal expressions

Translate each algebraic expression into a verbal expression. Use the word sum, difference, product, quotient, or square.

a) $\frac{3}{x}$ **b)** $2y + 1$ **c)** $3x - 2$ **d)** $(a - b)(a + b)$ **e)** $(a + b)^2$

Solution

a) The quotient of 3 and x

b) The sum of $2y$ and 1

c) The difference of $3x$ and 2

d) The product of $a - b$ and $a + b$

e) The square of the sum $a + b$

Now do Exercises 19–28

EXAMPLE 3

Verbal expressions to algebraic expressions

Translate each verbal expression into an algebraic expression.

a) The quotient of $a + b$ and 5

b) The difference of x^2 and y^2

c) The product of π and r^2

d) The square of the difference $x - y$

Solution

a) $\frac{a+b}{5}$, $(a + b) \div 5$, or $(a + b)/5$

b) $x^2 - y^2$

c) πr^2

d) $(x - y)^2$

Now do Exercises 29–44

Study Tip

Get to class early so that you are relaxed and ready to go when class starts. Collect your thoughts and get your questions ready. If your instructor arrives early, you might be able to get your questions answered before class. Take responsibility for your education. For many come to learn, but not all learn.

Evaluating Algebraic Expressions

The value of an algebraic expression depends on the values given to the variables. For example, the value of $x - 2y$ when $x = -2$ and $y = -3$ is found by replacing x and y by -2 and -3, respectively:

$$x - 2y = -2 - 2(-3) = -2 - (-6) = 4$$

If $x = 1$ and $y = 2$, the value of $x - 2y$ is found by replacing x by 1 and y by 2, respectively:

$$x - 2y = 1 - 2(2) = 1 - 4 = -3$$

Note that we use the order of operations when evaluating an algebraic expression.

EXAMPLE 4

Evaluating algebraic expressions

Evaluate each expression using $a = 3$, $b = -2$, and $c = -4$.

a) $2a + b - c$

b) $(a - b)(a + b)$

c) $b^2 - 4ac$

d) $\frac{-a^2 - b^2}{c - b}$

Solution

a)
$$\begin{aligned} 2a + b - c &= 2(3) + (-2) - (-4) && \text{Replace } a \text{ by 3, } b \text{ by } -2\text{, and } c \text{ by } -4. \\ &= 6 - 2 + 4 && \text{Multiply and remove parentheses.} \\ &= 8 && \text{Addition and subtraction last} \end{aligned}$$

b)
$$\begin{aligned} (a - b)(a + b) &= [3 - (-2)][3 + (-2)] && \text{Replace.} \\ &= [5][1] && \text{Simplify within the brackets.} \\ &= 5 && \text{Multiply.} \end{aligned}$$

c)
$$\begin{aligned} b^2 - 4ac &= (-2)^2 - 4(3)(-4) && \text{Replace.} \\ &= 4 - (-48) && \text{Square } -2\text{, and then multiply before subtracting.} \\ &= 52 && \text{Subtract.} \end{aligned}$$

d)
$$\frac{-a^2 - b^2}{c - b} = \frac{-3^2 - (-2)^2}{-4 - (-2)} = \frac{-9 - 4}{-2} = \frac{13}{2}$$

Now do Exercises 45–68

Teaching Tip Note that the expressions that we are evaluating here are the same kinds of expressions that we will use later in the text.

Mathematical notation is readily available in scientific word processors. However, on Internet pages or in email, multiplication is often written with a star (*), fractions are written with a slash (/), and exponents with a caret (^). For example, $\frac{x+y}{2x^3}$ is written as $(x + y)/(2*x\text{^}3)$. If the numerator or denominator contain more than one symbol it is best to enclose them in parentheses to avoid confusion. An expression such as $1/2x$ is confusing. If your class evaluates it for $x = 4$, some students will probably assume that it is $1/(2x)$ and get $1/8$, and some will assume that it is $(1/2)x$ and get 2.

Equations

An **equation** is a statement of equality of two expressions. For example,

$$11 - 5 = 6, \qquad x + 3 = 9, \qquad 2x + 5 = 13, \qquad \text{and} \qquad \frac{x}{2} - 4 = 1$$

are equations. In an equation involving a variable, any number that gives a true statement when we replace the variable by the number is said to **satisfy** the equation and is called a **solution** or **root** to the equation. For example, 6 is a solution to $x + 3 = 9$ because $6 + 3 = 9$ is true. Because $5 + 3 = 9$ is false, 5 is not a solution to the equation $x + 3 = 9$. We have **solved** an equation when we have found all solutions to the equation. You will learn how to solve certain equations in Chapter 2.

EXAMPLE 5

Satisfying an equation

Determine whether the given number is a solution to the equation following it.

a) $6,\ 3x - 7 = 9$

b) $-3,\ \dfrac{2x - 4}{5} = -2$

c) $-5,\ -x - 2 = 3(x + 6)$

Study Tip

Ask questions in class. If you don't ask questions, then the instructor might believe that you have total understanding. When one student has a question, there are usually several who have the same question but do not speak up. Asking questions not only helps you to learn, but it keeps the classroom more lively and interesting.

Solution

a) Replace x by 6 in the equation $3x - 7 = 9$:

$$3(6) - 7 = 9$$
$$18 - 7 = 9$$
$$11 = 9 \quad \text{False}$$

The number 6 is not a solution to the equation $3x - 7 = 9$.

b) Replace x by -3 in the equation $\dfrac{2x - 4}{5} = -2$:

$$\frac{2(-3) - 4}{5} = -2$$
$$\frac{-10}{5} = -2$$
$$-2 = -2 \quad \text{True}$$

The number -3 is a solution to the equation.

c) Replace x by -5 in $-x - 2 = 3(x + 6)$:

$$-(-5) - 2 = 3(-5 + 6)$$
$$5 - 2 = 3(1)$$
$$3 = 3 \quad \text{True}$$

The number -5 is a solution to the equation $-x - 2 = 3(x + 6)$.

Now do Exercises 69–84

Just as we translated verbal expressions into algebraic expressions, we can translate verbal sentences into algebraic equations. In an algebraic equation we use the equality symbol (=). Equality is indicated in words by phrases such as "is equal to," "is the same as," or simply "is."

EXAMPLE 6

Writing equations

Translate each sentence into an equation.

a) The sum of x and 7 is 12.

b) The product of 4 and x is the same as the sum of y and 5.

c) The quotient of $x + 3$ and 5 is equal to -1.

Teaching Tip Note how important it is to know the meaning of sum, difference, product, and quotient.

Solution

a) $x + 7 = 12$ **b)** $4x = y + 5$ **c)** $\frac{x + 3}{5} = -1$

Now do Exercises 85–92

Applications

Algebraic expressions are used to describe or **model** real-life situations. We can evaluate an algebraic expression for many values of a variable to get a collection of data. A graph (picture) of this data can give us useful information. For example, a forensic scientist can use a graph to estimate the length of a person's femur from the person's height.

EXAMPLE 7

Reading a graph

A forensic scientist uses the expression $69.1 + 2.2F$ as an estimate of the height in centimeters of a male with a femur of length F centimeters (National Space Biomedical Research Institute, www.nsbri.org).

a) If the femur of a male skeleton measures 50.6 cm, then what was the person's height?

b) Use the graph shown in Fig. 1.25 to estimate the length of a femur for a person who is 150 cm tall.

Study Tip

Find a group of students to work with outside of class. Don't just settle for answers. Make sure that everyone in the group understands the solution to a problem. You will find that you really understand a concept when you can explain it to someone else.

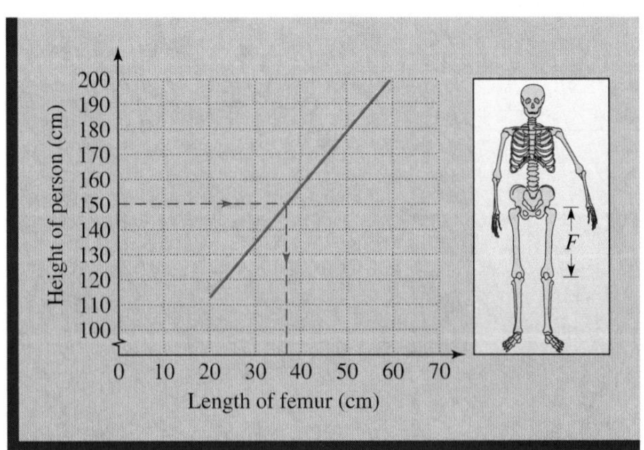

Figure 1.25

Solution

a) To find the height of the person, we use $F = 50.6$ in the expression $69.1 + 2.2F$:

$$69.1 + 2.2(50.6) \approx 180.4$$

So the person was approximately 180.4 cm tall.

b) To find the length of a femur for a person who is 150 cm tall, first locate 150 cm on the height scale of the graph in Fig. 1.25. Now draw a horizontal line to the graph and then a vertical line down to the length scale. So the length of a femur for a person who is 150 cm tall is approximately 36 cm.

Now do Exercises 101–106

Warm-Ups ▼

True or false? Explain your answer.

1. The expression $2x + 3y$ is referred to as a sum. True
2. The expression $5(y - 9)$ is a difference. False
3. The expression $2(x + 3y)$ is a product. True
4. The expression $\frac{x}{2} + \frac{y}{3}$ is a quotient. False
5. The expression $(a - b)(a + b)$ is a product of a sum and a difference. True
6. If x is -2, then the value of $2x + 4$ is 8. False
7. If $a = -3$, then $a^3 - 5 = 22$. False
8. The number 5 is a solution to the equation $2x - 3 = 13$. False
9. The product of $x + 3$ and 5 is $(x + 3)5$. True
10. The expression $2(x + 7)$ should be read as "the sum of 2 times x plus 7." False

1.6 Exercises

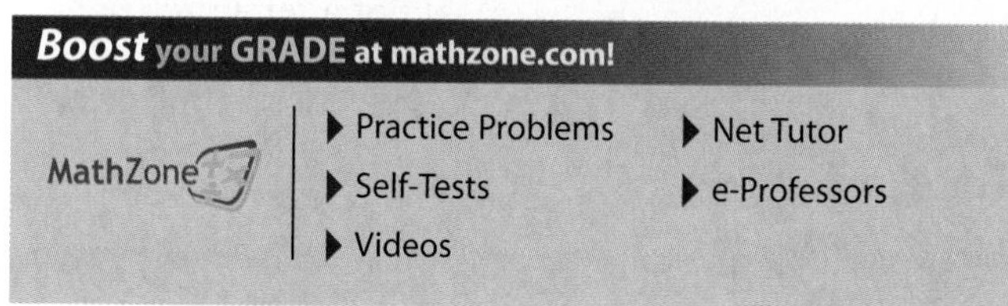

Reading and Writing *After reading this section write out the answers to these questions. Use complete sentences.*

1. What is an algebraic expression?
An algebraic expression is the result of combining numbers and variables with the operations of arithmetic in some meaningful way.

2. What is the difference between an algebraic expression and an arithmetic expression?
An arithmetic expression involves only numbers.

3. How can you tell whether an algebraic expression should be referred to as a sum, difference, product, quotient, or square?
An algebraic expression is named according to the last operation to be performed.

4. How do you evaluate an algebraic expression?
An algebraic expression is evaluated by replacing the variables with numbers and evaluating the resulting arithmetic expression.

5. What is an equation?
An equation is a sentence that expresses equality between two algebraic expressions.

6. What is a solution to an equation?
If an equation is true when the variable is replaced by a number, then that number is a solution to the equation.

Identify each expression as a sum, difference, product, quotient, square, or cube. See Example 1.

7. $a^3 - 1$ Difference **8.** $b(b - 1)$ Product

9. $(w - 1)^3$ Cube **10.** $m^2 + n^2$ Sum

11. $3x + 5y$ Sum **12.** $\frac{a - b}{b - a}$ Quotient

13. $\frac{u}{v} - \frac{v}{u}$ Difference **14.** $(s - t)^2$ Square

15. $3(x + 5y)$ Product **16.** $a - \frac{a}{2}$ Difference

17. $\left(\frac{2}{z}\right)^2$ Square **18.** $(2q - p)^3$ Cube

Use the term sum, difference, product, quotient, square, or cube to translate each algebraic expression into a verbal expression. See Example 2.

19. $x^2 - a^2$ The difference of x^2 and a^2

20. $a^3 + b^3$ The sum of a^3 and b^3

21. $(x - a)^2$ The square of $x - a$

22. $(a + b)^3$ The cube of $a + b$

23. $\frac{x - 4}{2}$ The quotient of $x - 4$ and 2

24. $2(x - 3)$ The product of 2 and $x - 3$

25. $\frac{x}{2} - 4$ The difference of $\frac{x}{2}$ and 4

26. $2x - 3$ The difference of $2x$ and 3

27. $(ab)^3$ The cube of ab

28. a^3b^3 The product of a^3 and b^3

Translate each verbal expression into an algebraic expression. Do not simplify. See Example 3.

29. The sum of 8 and y $8 + y$

30. The sum of $8x$ and $3y$ $8x + 3y$

31. The product of $5x$ and z $5xz$

32. The product of $x + 9$ and $x + 12$ $(x + 9)(x + 12)$

33. The difference of 8 and $7x$ $8 - 7x$

34. The difference of a^3 and b^3 $a^3 - b^3$

35. The quotient of 6 and $x + 4$ $\frac{6}{x + 4}$

36. The quotient of $x - 7$ and $7 - x$ $\frac{x - 7}{7 - x}$

37. The square of $a + b$ $(a + b)^2$

38. The cube of $x - y$ $(x - y)^3$

39. The sum of the cube of x and the square of y $x^3 + y^2$

40. The quotient of the square of a and the cube of b $\frac{a^2}{b^3}$

41. The product of 5 and the square of m $5m^2$

42. The difference of the square of m and the square of n $m^2 - n^2$

43. The square of the sum of s and t $(s + t)^2$

44. The cube of the difference of a and b $(a - b)^3$

Evaluate each expression using $a = -1$, $b = 2$, and $c = -3$. See Example 4.

45. $-(a - b)$ 3 **46.** $b - a$ 3

47. $-b^2 + 7$ 3 **48.** $-c^2 - b^2$ -13

49. $c^2 - 2c + 1$ 16 **50.** $b^2 - 2b + 4$ 4

51. $a^3 - b^3$ -9 **52.** $b^3 - c^3$ 35

53. $(a - b)(a + b)$ -3 **54.** $(a - c)(a + c)$ -8

55. $b^2 - 4ac$ -8 **56.** $a^2 - 4bc$ 25

57. $\frac{a - c}{a - b}$ $-\frac{2}{3}$ **58.** $\frac{b - c}{b + a}$ 5

59. $\frac{2}{a} + \frac{6}{b} - \frac{9}{c}$ 4 **60.** $\frac{c}{a} + \frac{6}{b} - \frac{b}{a}$ 8

61. $a \div |-a|$ -1 **62.** $|a| \div a$ -1

63. $|b| - |a|$ 1 **64.** $|c| + |b|$ 5

65. $-|-a - c|$ -4 **66.** $-|-a - b|$ -1

67. $(3 - |a - b|)^2$ 0 **68.** $(|b + c| - 2)^3$ -1

Determine whether the given number is a solution to the equation following it. See Example 5.

69. 2, $3x + 7 = 13$ Yes

70. -1, $-3x + 7 = 10$ Yes

71. -2, $\frac{3x - 4}{2} = 5$ No

72. -3, $\frac{-2x + 9}{3} = 5$ Yes

73. -2, $-x + 4 = 6$ Yes

74. -9, $-x + 3 = 12$ Yes

75. 4, $3x - 7 = x + 1$ Yes

76. 5, $3x - 7 = 2x + 1$ No

77. 3, $-2(x - 1) = 2 - 2x$ Yes

78. -8, $x - 9 = -(9 - x)$ Yes

79. 1, $x^2 + 3x - 4 = 0$ Yes

80. -1, $x^2 + 5x + 4 = 0$ Yes

81. 8, $\frac{x}{x - 8} = 0$ No **82.** 3, $\frac{x - 3}{x + 3} = 0$ Yes

83. -6, $\frac{x + 6}{x + 6} = 1$ No **84.** 9, $\frac{9}{x - 9} = 0$ No

Translate each sentence into an equation. See Example 6.

85. The sum of $5x$ and $3x$ is $8x$. $5x + 3x = 8x$

86. The sum of $\frac{y}{2}$ and 3 is 7. $\frac{y}{2} + 3 = 7$

87. The product of 3 and $x + 2$ is equal to 12. $3(x + 2) = 12$

88. The product of -6 and $7y$ is equal to 13. $-6(7y) = 13$

89. The quotient of x and 3 is the same as the product of x and 5. $\frac{x}{3} = 5x$

90. The quotient of $x + 3$ and $5y$ is the same as the product of x and y. $\frac{x + 3}{5y} = xy$

91. The square of the sum of a and b is equal to 9. $(a + b)^2 = 9$

92. The sum of the squares of a and b is equal to the square of c. $a^2 + b^2 = c^2$

Fill in the tables with the appropriate values for the given expressions.

93.

x	$2x - 3$
-2	-7
-1	-5
0	-3
1	-1
2	1

94.

x	$-\frac{1}{2}x + 4$
-4	6
-2	5
0	4
2	3
4	2

95.

a	a^2	a^3	a^4
2	4	8	16
$\frac{1}{2}$	$\frac{1}{4}$	$\frac{1}{8}$	$\frac{1}{16}$
10	100	1000	10,000
0.1	0.01	0.001	0.0001

96.

b	$\frac{1}{b}$	$\frac{1}{b^2}$	$\frac{1}{b^3}$
3	$\frac{1}{3}$	$\frac{1}{9}$	$\frac{1}{27}$
$\frac{1}{3}$	3	9	27
10	0.1	0.01	0.001
0.1	10	100	1000

Use a calculator to find the value of $b^2 - 4ac$ for each of the following choices of a, b, and c.

97. $a = 4.2, b = 6.7, c = 1.8$ 14.65

98. $a = -3.5, b = 9.1, c = 3.6$ 133.21

99. $a = -1.2, b = 3.2, c = 5.6$ 37.12

100. $a = 2.4, b = -8.5, c = -5.8$ 127.93

Solve each problem. See Example 7.

101. ***Forensics.*** A forensic scientist uses the expression $81.7 + 2.4T$ to estimate the height in centimeters of a male with a tibia of length T centimeters. If a male skeleton has a tibia of length 36.5 cm, then what was the height of the person? Use the accompanying graph to estimate the length of a tibia for a male with a height of 180 cm. 169.3 cm, 41 cm

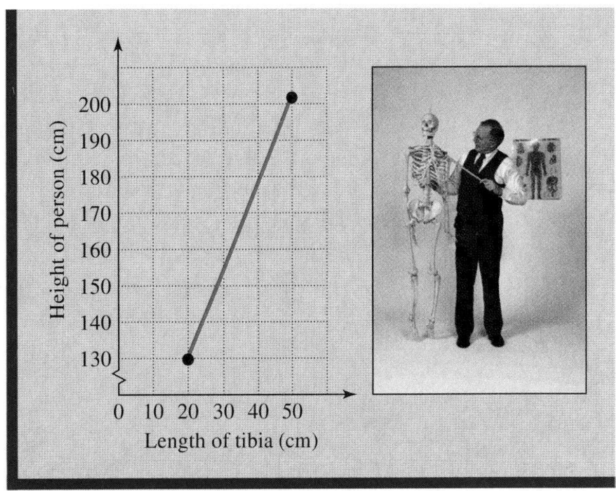

Figure for Exercise 101

102. ***Forensics.*** A forensic scientist uses the expression $72.6 + 2.5T$ to estimate the height in centimeters of a female with a tibia of length T centimeters. If a female skeleton has a tibia of length 32.4 cm, then what was the height of the person? Find the length of your tibia in centimeters, and use the expression from this exercise or the previous exercise to estimate your height. 153.6 cm

103. ***Games behind.*** In baseball a team's standing is measured by its percentage of wins and by the number of games it

	W	L	Pct	GB
NY Yankees	101	61	0.623	–
Boston	95	67	0.586	?
Toronto	86	76	0.531	?
Baltimore	71	91	0.438	?
Tampa Bay	63	99	0.389	?

Table for Exercise 103

is behind the leading team in its division. The expression

$$\frac{(X - x) + (y - Y)}{2}$$

gives the number of games behind for a team with x wins and y losses, where the division leader has X wins and Y losses. The table shown on the previous page gives the won-lost records for the American League East at the end of 2001 (www.espn.com). Fill in the column for the games behind (GB). 6, 15, 30, 38

104. ***Fly ball.*** The approximate distance in feet that a baseball travels when hit at an angle of 45° is given by the expression

$$\frac{(v_0)^2}{32}$$

where v_0 is the initial velocity in feet per second. If Barry Bonds of the Giants hits a ball at a 45° angle with an initial velocity of 120 feet per second, then how far will the ball travel? Use the accompanying graph to estimate the initial velocity for a ball that has traveled 370 feet. 450 feet, 109 feet per second

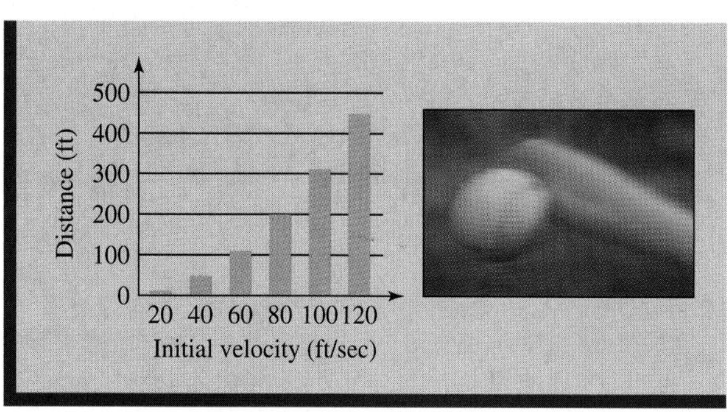

Figure for Exercise 104

105. ***Football field.*** The expression $2L + 2W$ gives the perimeter of a rectangle with length L and width W. What is the perimeter of a football field with length 100 yards and width 160 feet? 920 feet

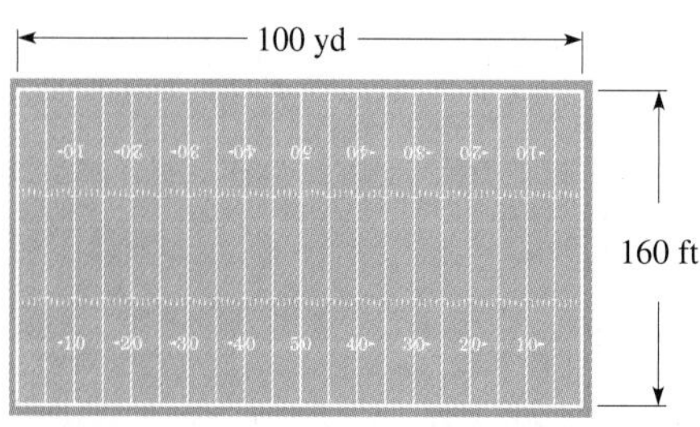

Figure for Exercise 105

106. ***Crop circles.*** The expression πr^2 gives the area of a circle with radius r. How many square meters of wheat were destroyed when an alien ship made a crop circle of diameter 25 meters in the wheat field at the Southwind Ranch? Find π on your calculator. 490.9 m^2

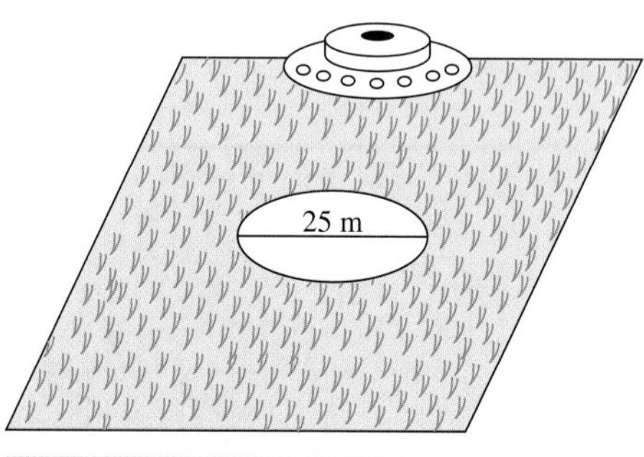

Figure for Exercise 106

Getting More Involved

107. ***Writing***

Explain why the square of the sum of two numbers is different from the sum of the squares of two numbers. For the square of the sum consider $(2 + 3)^2 = 5^2 = 25$. For the sum of the squares consider $2^2 + 3^2 = 4 + 9 = 13$. So $(2 + 3)^2 \neq 2^2 + 3^2$.

108. ***Cooperative learning***

The sum of the integers from 1 through n is $\frac{n(n + 1)}{2}$. The sum of the squares of the integers from 1 through n is $\frac{n(n + 1)(2n + 1)}{6}$. The sum of the cubes of the integers from 1 through n is $\frac{n^2(n + 1)^2}{4}$. Use the appropriate expressions to find the following values.

a) The sum of the integers from 1 through 50 1275

b) The sum of the squares of the integers from 1 through 40 22,140

c) The sum of the cubes of the integers from 1 through 30 216,225

d) The square of the sum of the integers from 1 through 20 44,100

e) The cube of the sum of the integers from 1 through 10 166,375

1.7 Properties of the Real Numbers

In this Section

- The Commutative Properties
- The Associative Properties
- The Distributive Property
- The Identity Properties
- The Inverse Properties
- Multiplication Property of Zero
- Applications

Everyone knows that the price of a hamburger plus the price of a Coke is the same as the price of a Coke plus the price of a hamburger. But do you know that this example illustrates the commutative property of addition? The properties of the real numbers are commonly used by anyone who performs the operations of arithmetic. In algebra we must have a thorough understanding of these properties.

The Commutative Properties

We get the same result whether we evaluate $3 + 5$ or $5 + 3$. This example illustrates the commutative property of addition. The fact that $4 \cdot 6$ and $6 \cdot 4$ are equal illustrates the commutative property of multiplication.

Commutative Property of Addition

For any real numbers a and b,

$$a + b = b + a.$$

Commutative Property of Multiplication

For any real numbers a and b,

$$ab = ba.$$

EXAMPLE 1

The commutative property of addition

Use the commutative property of addition to rewrite each expression.

a) $2 + (-10)$ **b)** $8 + x^2$ **c)** $2y - 4x$

Teaching Tip Ask students to explain each property in their own words.

Solution

a) $2 + (-10) = -10 + 2$

b) $8 + x^2 = x^2 + 8$

c) $2y - 4x = 2y + (-4x) = -4x + 2y$

Now do Exercises 7–12

EXAMPLE 2

The commutative property of multiplication

Use the commutative property of multiplication to rewrite each expression.

a) $n \cdot 3$ **b)** $(x + 2) \cdot 3$ **c)** $5 - yx$

Solution

a) $n \cdot 3 = 3 \cdot n = 3n$ **b)** $(x + 2) \cdot 3 = 3(x + 2)$

c) $5 - yx = 5 - xy$

Now do Exercises 13–18

Addition and multiplication are commutative operations, but what about subtraction and division? Since $5 - 3 = 2$ and $3 - 5 = -2$, subtraction is not commutative. To see that division is not commutative, try dividing \$8 among 4 people and \$4 among 8 people.

The Associative Properties

Consider the computation of $2 + 3 + 6$. Using the order of operations, we add 2 and 3 to get 5 and then add 5 and 6 to get 11. If we add 3 and 6 first to get 9 and then add 2 and 9, we also get 11. So

$$(2 + 3) + 6 = 2 + (3 + 6).$$

We get the same result for either order of addition. This property is called the **associative property of addition.** The commutative and associative properties of addition are the reason that a hamburger, a Coke, and French fries cost the same as French fries, a hamburger, and a Coke.

We also have an **associative property of multiplication.** Consider the following two ways to find the product of 2, 3, and 4:

$$(2 \cdot 3)4 = 6 \cdot 4 = 24$$

$$2(3 \cdot 4) = 2 \cdot 12 = 24$$

We get the same result for either arrangement.

Helpful Hint

In arithmetic we would probably write $(2 + 3) + 7 = 12$ without thinking about the associative property. In algebra, we need the associative property to understand that

$$\begin{aligned}(x + 3) + 7 &= x + (3 + 7)\\ &= x + 10.\end{aligned}$$

Associative Property of Addition

For any real numbers a, b, and c,

$$(a + b) + c = a + (b + c).$$

Associative Property of Multiplication

For any real numbers a, b, and c,

$$(ab)c = a(bc).$$

EXAMPLE 3

Using the properties of multiplication

Use the commutative and associative properties of multiplication and exponential notation to rewrite each product.

a) $(3x)(x)$ **b)** $(xy)(5yx)$

Solution

a) $(3x)(x) = 3(x \cdot x) = 3x^2$

b) The commutative and associative properties of multiplication allow us to rearrange the multiplication in any order. We generally write numbers before variables, and we usually write variables in alphabetical order:

$$(xy)(5yx) = 5xxyy = 5x^2y^2$$

Now do Exercises 19–24

Study Tip

Find out what help is available at your school. Accompanying this text are video tapes, solution manuals, and a computer tutorial. Around most campuses you will find tutors available for hire, but most schools have a math lab where you can get help for free. Some schools even have free one-on-one tutoring available through special programs.

Consider the expression

$$3 - 9 + 7 - 5 - 8 + 4 - 13.$$

According to the accepted order of operations, we could evaluate this by computing from left to right. However, using the definition of subtraction, we can rewrite this expression as addition:

$$3 + (-9) + 7 + (-5) + (-8) + 4 + (-13)$$

The commutative and associative properties of addition allow us to add these numbers in any order we choose. It is usually faster to add the positive numbers, add the negative numbers, and then combine those two totals:

$$3 + 7 + 4 + (-9) + (-5) + (-8) + (-13) = 14 + (-35) = -21$$

Note that by performing the operations in this manner, we must subtract only once. There is no need to rewrite this expression as we have done here. We can sum the positive numbers and the negative numbers from the original expression and then combine their totals.

EXAMPLE 4

Using the properties of addition

Evaluate.

a) $3 - 7 + 9 - 5$ **b)** $4 - 5 - 9 + 6 - 2 + 4 - 8$

Solution

a) First add the positive numbers and the negative numbers:

$$\begin{aligned} 3 - 7 + 9 - 5 &= 12 + (-12) \\ &= 0 \end{aligned}$$

b) $\begin{aligned} 4 - 5 - 9 + 6 - 2 + 4 - 8 &= 14 + (-24) \\ &= -10 \end{aligned}$

Now do Exercises 25–34

Teaching Tip Emphasize that knowing the properties of the real numbers will help students use the real numbers. How many things do you know about your car that help you use it?

It is certainly not essential that we evaluate the expressions of Example 4 as shown. We get the same answer by adding and subtracting from left to right. However, in algebra, just getting the answer is not always the most important point. Learning new methods often increases understanding.

Even though addition is associative, subtraction is not an associative operation. For example, $(8 - 4) - 3 = 1$ and $8 - (4 - 3) = 7$. So

$$(8 - 4) - 3 \neq 8 - (4 - 3).$$

We can also use a numerical example to show that division is not associative. For instance, $(16 \div 4) \div 2 = 2$ and $16 \div (4 \div 2) = 8$. So

$$(16 \div 4) \div 2 \neq 16 \div (4 \div 2).$$

The Distributive Property

If four men and five women pay \$3 each for a movie, there are two ways to find the total amount spent:

$$3(4 + 5) = 3 \cdot 9 = 27$$

$$3 \cdot 4 + 3 \cdot 5 = 12 + 15 = 27$$

Helpful Hint

To visualize the distributive property, we can determine the number of circles shown here in two ways:

o o o o   o o o o o
o o o o   o o o o o
o o o o   o o o o o

There are $3 \cdot 9$ or 27 circles, or there are $3 \cdot 4$ circles in the first group and $3 \cdot 5$ circles in the second group for a total of 27 circles.

Since we get \$27 either way, we can write

$$3(4 + 5) = 3 \cdot 4 + 3 \cdot 5.$$

We say that the multiplication by 3 is *distributed* over the addition. This example illustrates the **distributive property.**

Consider the following expressions involving multiplication and subtraction:

$$5(6 - 4) = 5 \cdot 2 = 10$$

$$5 \cdot 6 - 5 \cdot 4 = 30 - 20 = 10$$

Since both expressions have the same value, we can write

$$5(6 - 4) = 5 \cdot 6 - 5 \cdot 4.$$

Multiplication by 5 is distributed over each number in the parentheses. This example illustrates that multiplication distributes over subtraction.

Teaching Tip Since subtraction is defined in terms of addition, it is not really necessary to state the second distributive property.

Distributive Property

For any real numbers a, b, and c,

$$a(b + c) = ab + ac \quad \text{and} \quad a(b - c) = ab - ac.$$

We can use the distributive property to remove parentheses. If we start with $4(x + 3)$ and write

$$4(x + 3) = 4x + 4 \cdot 3 = 4x + 12,$$

we are using it to multiply 4 and $x + 3$ or to remove the parentheses. We wrote the product $4(x + 3)$ as the sum $4x + 12$.

EXAMPLE 5

Writing a product as a sum or difference

Use the distributive property to remove the parentheses.

a) $a(3 - b)$ **b)** $-3(x - 2)$

Solution

a) $a(3 - b) = a3 - ab$ Distributive property
$= 3a - ab$ $a3 = 3a$

b) $-3(x - 2) = -3x - (-3)(2)$ Distributive property
$= -3x - (-6)$ $(-3)(2) = -6$
$= -3x + 6$ Simplify.

Now do Exercises 35–46

When we write a number or an expression as a product, we are **factoring.** If we start with $3x + 15$ and write

$$3x + 15 = 3x + 3 \cdot 5 = 3(x + 5),$$

we are using the distributive property to factor $3x + 15$. We factored out the common factor 3.

EXAMPLE 6

Writing a sum or difference as a product

Use the distributive property to factor each expression.

a) $7x - 21$ **b)** $5a + 5$

Solution

a) $7x - 21 = 7x - 7 \cdot 3$ Write 21 as $7 \cdot 3$.
$= 7(x - 3)$ Distributive property

b) $5a + 5 = 5a + 5 \cdot 1$ Write 5 as $5 \cdot 1$.
$= 5(a + 1)$ Factor out the common factor 5.

Now do Exercises 47–58

Study Tip

Don't cram for a test. Some students try to cram weeks of work into one "all-nighter." These same students are seen frantically paging through the text up until the moment that the test papers are handed out. These practices create a lot of test anxiety and will only make you sick. Start studying for a test several days in advance, and get a good night's sleep before a test. If you keep up with homework, then there will be no need to cram.

The Identity Properties

The numbers 0 and 1 have special properties. Multiplication of a number by 1 does not change the number, and addition of 0 to a number does not change the number. That is why 1 is called the **multiplicative identity** and 0 is called the **additive identity.**

Additive Identity Property

For any real number a,

$$a + 0 = 0 + a = a.$$

Multiplicative Identity Property

For any real number a,

$$a \cdot 1 = 1 \cdot a = a.$$

Teaching Tip In the identity properties 0 and 1 are used in the operations. In the inverse properties 0 and 1 are the results of the operations.

The Inverse Properties

The idea of additive inverses was introduced in Section 1.3. Every real number a has an **additive inverse** or **opposite,** $-a$, such that $a + (-a) = 0$. Every nonzero real number a also has a **multiplicative inverse** or **reciprocal,** written $\frac{1}{a}$, such that $a \cdot \frac{1}{a} = 1$. Note that the sum of additive inverses is the additive identity and that the product of multiplicative inverses is the multiplicative identity.

Additive Inverse Property

For any real number a, there is a unique number $-a$ such that

$$a + (-a) = 0.$$

Multiplicative Inverse Property

For any nonzero real number a, there is a unique number $\frac{1}{a}$ such that

$$a \cdot \frac{1}{a} = 1.$$

We are already familiar with multiplicative inverses for rational numbers. For example, the multiplicative inverse of $\frac{2}{3}$ is $\frac{3}{2}$ because

$$\frac{2}{3} \cdot \frac{3}{2} = \frac{6}{6} = 1.$$

EXAMPLE 7

Multiplicative inverses

Find the multiplicative inverse of each number.

a) 5 **b)** 0.3

c) $-\frac{3}{4}$ **d)** 1.7

Solution

a) The multiplicative inverse of 5 is $\frac{1}{5}$ because

$$5 \cdot \frac{1}{5} = 1.$$

b) To find the reciprocal of 0.3, we first write 0.3 as a ratio of integers:

$$0.3 = \frac{3}{10}$$

The multiplicative inverse of 0.3 is $\frac{10}{3}$ because

$$\frac{3}{10} \cdot \frac{10}{3} = 1.$$

c) The reciprocal of $-\frac{3}{4}$ is $-\frac{4}{3}$ because

$$\left(-\frac{3}{4}\right)\left(-\frac{4}{3}\right) = 1.$$

d) First convert 1.7 to a ratio of integers:

$$1.7 = 1\frac{7}{10} = \frac{17}{10}$$

The multiplicative inverse is $\frac{10}{17}$.

Now do Exercises 59–70

Calculator Close-Up

You can find multiplicative inverses with a calculator as shown here.

```
1/.3▸Frac
                10/3
1/(-3/4)▸Frac
                -4/3
1/1.7▸Frac
               10/17
```

When the divisor is a fraction, it must be in parentheses.

Study Tip

When you get a test back, do not simply file it in your notebook or the waste basket. While the material is fresh in your mind, rework all problems that you missed. Ask questions about anything that you don't understand and save your test for future reference.

Multiplication Property of Zero

Zero has a property that no other number has. Multiplication involving zero always results in zero.

Multiplication Property of Zero

For any real number a,

$$0 \cdot a = 0 \quad \text{and} \quad a \cdot 0 = 0.$$

EXAMPLE 8

Identifying the properties

Name the property that justifies each equation.

a) $5 \cdot 7 = 7 \cdot 5$

b) $4 \cdot \frac{1}{4} = 1$

c) $1 \cdot 864 = 864$

d) $6 + (5 + x) = (6 + 5) + x$

e) $3x + 5x = (3 + 5)x$

f) $6 + (x + 5) = 6 + (5 + x)$

g) $\pi x^2 + \pi y^2 = \pi(x^2 + y^2)$

h) $325 + 0 = 325$

i) $-3 + 3 = 0$

j) $455 \cdot 0 = 0$

Solution

a) Commutative property of multiplication

b) Multiplicative inverse property

c) Multiplicative identity property

d) Associative property of addition

e) Distributive property

f) Commutative property of addition

g) Distributive property

h) Additive identity property

i) Additive inverse property

j) Multiplication property of 0

Now do Exercises 71–90

Teaching Tip This early introduction to rates will help students with work problems later on.

Applications

Reciprocals are important in problems involving work. For example, if you wax one car in 3 hours, then your rate is $\frac{1}{3}$ of a car per hour. If you can wash one car in 12 minutes $\left(\frac{1}{5} \text{ of an hour}\right)$, then you are washing cars at the rate of 5 cars per hour. In general, if you can complete a task in x hours, then your rate is $\frac{1}{x}$ tasks per hour.

EXAMPLE 9

Washing rates

A car wash has two machines. The old machine washes one car in 0.1 hour, while the new machine washes one car in 0.08 hour. If both machines are operating, then at what rate (in cars per hour) are the cars being washed?

Solution

The old machine is working at the rate of $\frac{1}{0.1}$ cars per hour, and the new machine is working at the rate of $\frac{1}{0.08}$ cars per hour. Their rate working together is the sum of their individual rates:

$$\frac{1}{0.1} + \frac{1}{0.08} = 10 + 12.5 = 22.5$$

So working together, the machines are washing 22.5 cars per hour.

Now do Exercises 105–108

Helpful Hint

When machines or people are working together, we can add their rates provided they do not interfere with each other's work. If operating both car wash machines causes a traffic jam, then the rate together might not be 22.5 cars per hour.

Warm-Ups ▼

True or false? Explain your answer.

1. $24 \div (4 \div 2) = (24 \div 4) \div 2$ False
2. $1 \div 2 = 2 \div 1$ False
3. $6 - 5 = -5 + 6$ True
4. $9 - (4 - 3) = (9 - 4) - 3$ False
5. Multiplication is a commutative operation. True
6. $5x + 5 = 5(x + 1)$ for any value of x. True
7. The multiplicative inverse of 0.02 is 50. True
8. $-3(x - 2) = -3x + 6$ for any value of x. True
9. $3x + 2x = (3 + 2)x$ for any value of x. True
10. The additive inverse of 0 is 0. True

1.7 Exercises

Boost your GRADE at mathzone.com!

MathZone
- Practice Problems
- Self-Tests
- Videos
- Net Tutor
- e-Professors

Reading and Writing *After reading this section write out the answers to these questions. Use complete sentences.*

1. What is the difference between the commutative property of addition and the associative property of addition?
The commutative property says that $a + b = b + a$ and the associative property says that $(a + b) + c = a + (b + c)$.
2. Which property involves two different operations?
The distributive property involves multiplication and addition.
3. What is factoring?
Factoring is the process of writing an expression or number as a product.
4. Which two numbers play a prominent role in the properties studied here?
The number 0 is the additive identity and the number 1 is the multiplicative identity.
5. What is the purpose of studying the properties of real numbers?
The properties help us to understand the operations and how they are related to each other.
6. What is the relationship between rate and time?
If one task is completed in x hours, then the rate is $1/x$ tasks per hour.

Use the commutative property of addition to rewrite each expression. See Example 1.

7. $9 + r$ $\quad r + 9$
8. $t + 6$ $\quad 6 + t$
9. $3(2 + x)$ $\quad 3(x + 2)$
10. $P(1 + rt)$ $\quad P(rt + 1)$
11. $4 - 5x$ $\quad -5x + 4$
12. $b - 2a$ $\quad -2a + b$

Use the commutative property of multiplication to rewrite each expression. See Example 2.

13. $x \cdot 6$ $\quad 6x$
14. $y \cdot (-9)$ $\quad -9y$
15. $(x - 4)(-2)$ $\quad -2(x - 4)$
16. $a(b + c)$ $\quad (b + c)a$
17. $4 - y \cdot 8$ $\quad 4 - 8y$
18. $z \cdot 9 - 2$ $\quad 9z - 2$

Use the commutative and associative properties of multiplication and exponential notation to rewrite each product. See Example 3.

19. $(4w)(w)$ $\quad 4w^2$
20. $(y)(2y)$ $\quad 2y^2$
21. $3a(ba)$ $\quad 3a^2b$
22. $(x \cdot x)(7x)$ $\quad 7x^3$
23. $(x)(9x)(xz)$ $\quad 9x^3z$
24. $y(y \cdot 5)(wy)$ $\quad 5y^3w$

Evaluate by finding first the sum of the positive numbers and then the sum of the negative numbers. See Example 4.

25. $8 - 4 + 3 - 10$ $\quad -3$
26. $-3 + 5 - 12 + 10$ $\quad 0$
27. $8 - 10 + 7 - 8 - 7$ $\quad -10$
28. $6 - 11 + 7 - 9 + 13 - 2$ $\quad 4$
29. $-4 - 11 + 7 - 8 + 15 - 20$ $\quad -21$
30. $-8 + 13 - 9 - 15 + 7 - 22 + 5$ $\quad -29$
31. $-3.2 + 2.4 - 2.8 + 5.8 - 1.6$ $\quad 0.6$

32. $5.4 - 5.1 + 6.6 - 2.3 + 9.1$ 13.7

33. $3.26 - 13.41 + 5.1 - 12.35 - 5$ -22.4

34. $5.89 - 6.1 + 8.58 - 6.06 - 2.34$ -0.03

Use the distributive property to remove the parentheses. See Example 5.

35. $3(x - 5)$ $3x - 15$
36. $4(b - 1)$ $4b - 4$
37. $a(2 + t)$ $2a + at$
38. $b(a + w)$ $ab + bw$
39. $-3(w - 6)$ $-3w + 18$
40. $-3(m - 5)$ $-3m + 15$
41. $-4(5 - y)$ $-20 + 4y$
42. $-3(6 - p)$ $-18 + 3p$
43. $-1(a - 7)$ $-a + 7$
44. $-1(c - 8)$ $-c + 8$
45. $-1(t + 4)$ $-t - 4$
46. $-1(x + 7)$ $-x - 7$

Use the distributive property to factor each expression. See Example 6.

47. $2m + 12$ $2(m + 6)$
48. $3y + 6$ $3(y + 2)$
49. $4x - 4$ $4(x - 1)$
50. $6y + 6$ $6(y + 1)$
51. $4y - 16$ $4(y - 4)$
52. $5x + 15$ $5(x + 3)$
53. $4a + 8$ $4(a + 2)$
54. $7a - 35$ $7(a - 5)$
55. $x + xy$ $x(1 + y)$
56. $a - ab$ $a(1 - b)$
57. $6a - 2b$ $2(3a - b)$
58. $8a + 2c$ $2(4a + c)$

Find the multiplicative inverse (reciprocal) of each number. See Example 7.

59. $\frac{1}{2}$ 2
60. $\frac{1}{3}$ 3
61. -5 $-\frac{1}{5}$
62. -6 $-\frac{1}{6}$
63. 7 $\frac{1}{7}$
64. 8 $\frac{1}{8}$
65. 1 1
66. -1 -1
67. -0.25 -4
68. 0.75 $\frac{4}{3}$
69. 2.5 $\frac{2}{5}$
70. 3.5 $\frac{2}{7}$

Name the property that justifies each equation. See Example 8.

71. $3 \cdot x = x \cdot 3$ Commutative property of multiplication
72. $x + 5 = 5 + x$ Commutative property of addition ✓
73. $2(x - 3) = 2x - 6$ Distributive property
74. $a(bc) = (ab)c$ Associative property of multiplication
75. $-3(xy) = (-3x)y$ Associative property of multiplication
76. $3(x + 1) = 3x + 3$ Distributive property ✓
77. $4 + (-4) = 0$ Additive inverse property
78. $1.3 + 9 = 9 + 1.3$ Commutative property of addition
79. $x^2 \cdot 5 = 5x^2$ Commutative property of multiplication
80. $0 \cdot \pi = 0$ Multiplication property of 0
81. $1 \cdot 3y = 3y$ Multiplicative identity property
82. $(0.1)(10) = 1$ Multiplicative inverse property
83. $2a + 5a = (2 + 5)a$ Distributive property
84. $3 + 0 = 3$ Additive identity property
85. $-7 + 7 = 0$ Additive inverse property
86. $1 \cdot b = b$ Multiplicative identity property
87. $(2346)0 = 0$ Multiplication property of 0
88. $4x + 4 = 4(x + 1)$ Distributive property
89. $ay + y = y(a + 1)$ Distributive property
90. $ab + bc = b(a + c)$ Distributive property

Complete each equation, using the property named.

91. $a + y =$ ____, commutative property of addition $y + a$
92. $6x + 6 =$ ____, distributive property $6(x + 1)$
93. $5(aw) =$ ____, associative property of multiplication $(5a)w$
94. $x + 3 =$ ____, commutative property of addition $3 + x$
95. $\frac{1}{2}x + \frac{1}{2} =$ ____, distributive property $\frac{1}{2}(x + 1)$
96. $-3(x - 7) =$ ____, distributive property $-3x + 21$
97. $6x + 15 =$ ____, distributive property $3(2x + 5)$
98. $(x + 6) + 1 =$ ____, associative property of addition $x + (6 + 1)$
99. $4(0.25) =$ ____, multiplicative inverse property 1
100. $-1(5 - y) =$ ____, distributive property $-5 + y$
101. $0 = 96($____$)$, multiplication property of zero 0
102. $3 \cdot ($____$) = 3$, multiplicative identity property 1
103. $0.33($____$) = 1$, multiplicative inverse property $\frac{100}{33}$
104. $-8(1) =$ ____, multiplicative identity property -8

Solve each problem. See Example 9.

105. ***Laying bricks.*** A bricklayer lays one brick in 0.04 hour, while his apprentice lays one brick in 0.05 hour.

a) If both are working, then at what combined rate (in bricks per hour) are they laying bricks? 45 bricks/hour

b) Which person is working faster? Bricklayer

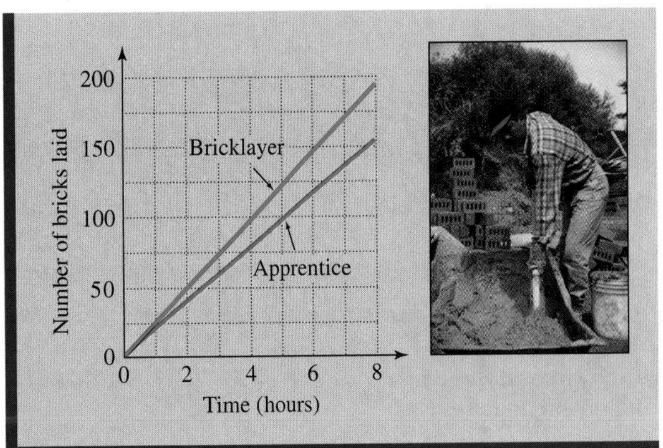

Figure for Exercise 105

106. ***Recovering golf balls.*** Susan and Joan are diving for golf balls in a large water trap. Susan recovers a golf ball every 0.016 hour while Joan recovers a ball every 0.025 hour. If both are working, then at what rate (in golf balls per hour) are they recovering golf balls? 102.5 balls/hour

107. ***Population explosion.*** In 2004 the population of the earth was increasing by one person every 0.4308 second (U.S. Census Bureau, www.census.gov).

a) At what rate in people per second is the population of the earth increasing? 2.3213 people/second

b) At what rate in people per week is the population of the earth increasing? 1,403,900 people/week

108. ***Farmland conversion.*** The amount of farmland in the United States is decreasing by one acre every 0.00876 hours as farmland is being converted to nonfarm use (American Farmland Trust, www.farmland.org). At what rate in acres per day is the farmland decreasing? 2740 acres/day

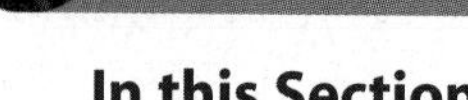
Figure for Exercise 108

Getting More Involved

109. ***Writing***

The perimeter of a rectangle is the sum of twice the length and twice the width. Write in words another way to find the perimeter that illustrates the distributive property. The perimeter is twice the sum of the length and width.

110. ***Discussion***

Eldrid bought a loaf of bread for \$1.69 and a gallon of milk for \$2.29. Using a tax rate of 5%, he correctly figured that the tax on the bread would be 8 cents and the tax on the milk would be 11 cents, for a total of \$4.17. However, at the cash register he was correctly charged \$4.18. How could this happen? Which property of the real numbers is in question in this case?
Due to rounding off, the tax on each item separately does not equal the tax on the total. It looks like the distributive property fails.

111. ***Exploration***

Determine whether each of the following pairs of tasks are "commutative." That is, does the order in which they are performed produce the same result?

a) Put on your coat; put on your hat. Commutative

b) Put on your shirt; put on your coat. Not commutative

Find another pair of "commutative" tasks and another pair of "noncommutative" tasks.

1.8 Using the Properties to Simplify Expressions

In this Section

- **Using the Properties in Computation**
- **Like Terms**
- **Combining Like Terms**
- **Products and Quotients**
- **Removing Parentheses**

The properties of the real numbers can be helpful when we are doing computations. In this section we will see how the properties can be applied in arithmetic and algebra.

Using the Properties in Computation

The properties of the real numbers can often be used to simplify computations. For example, to find the product of 26 and 200, we can write

$$\begin{aligned}(26)(200) &= (26)(2 \cdot 100)\\ &= (26 \cdot 2)(100)\\ &= 52 \cdot 100\\ &= 5200\end{aligned}$$

It is the associative property that allows us to multiply 26 by 2 to get 52, then multiply 52 by 100 to get 5200.

EXAMPLE 1

Using the properties

Use the appropriate property to aid you in evaluating each expression.

a) $347 + 35 + 65$ **b)** $3 \cdot 435 \cdot \frac{1}{3}$ **c)** $6 \cdot 28 + 4 \cdot 28$

Study Tip

Being a full-time student is a full-time job. A successful student spends from two to four hours studying outside of class for every hour spent in the classroom. It is rare to find a person who can handle two full-time jobs and it is just as rare to find a successful full-time student who also works full time.

Solution

a) Notice that the sum of 35 and 65 is 100. So apply the associative property as follows:

$$347 + (35 + 65) = 347 + 100$$
$$= 447$$

b) Use the commutative and associative properties to rearrange this product. We can then do the multiplication quickly:

$$3 \cdot 435 \cdot \frac{1}{3} = 435\left(3 \cdot \frac{1}{3}\right) \quad \text{Commutative and associative properties}$$
$$= 435 \cdot 1 \quad \text{Multiplicative inverse property}$$
$$= 435 \quad \text{Multiplicative identity property}$$

c) Use the distributive property to rewrite this expression.

$$6 \cdot 28 + 4 \cdot 28 = (6 + 4)28$$
$$= 10 \cdot 28$$
$$= 280$$

Now do Exercises 7–22

Like Terms

An expression containing a number or the product of a number and one or more variables raised to powers is called a **term.** For example,

$$-3, \quad 5x, \quad -3x^2y, \quad a, \quad \text{and} \quad -abc$$

are terms. The number preceding the variables in a term is called the **coefficient.** In the term $5x$, the coefficient of x is 5. In the term $-3x^2y$ the coefficient of x^2y is -3. In the term a, the coefficient of a is 1 because $a = 1 \cdot a$. In the term $-abc$ the coefficient of abc is -1 because $-abc = -1 \cdot abc$. If two terms contain the same variables with the same exponents, they are called **like terms.** For example, $3x^2$ and $-5x^2$ are like terms, but $3x^2$ and $-5x^3$ are not like terms.

Combining Like Terms

Using the distributive property on an expression involving the sum of like terms allows us to combine the like terms as shown in Example 2.

EXAMPLE 2

Combining like terms

Use the distributive property to perform the indicated operations.

a) $3x + 5x$ **b)** $-5xy - (-4xy)$

Teaching Tip Having students read the expression $-5xy - (-4xy)$ will help them understand the difference between minus and negative.

Solution

a) $3x + 5x = (3 + 5)x$ Distributive property
$= 8x$ Add the coefficients.

Because the distributive property is valid for any real numbers, we have $3x + 5x = 8x$ no matter what number is used for x.

b) $-5xy - (-4xy) = [-5 - (-4)]xy$ Distributive property
$= -1xy$ $-5 - (-4) = -5 + 4 = -1$
$= -xy$ Multiplying by -1 is the same as taking the opposite.

Now do Exercises 23–28

Of course, we do not want to write out all of the steps shown in Example 2 every time we combine like terms. We can combine like terms as easily as we can add or subtract their coefficients.

EXAMPLE 3

Combining like terms

Perform the indicated operations.

a) $w + 2w$ **b)** $-3a + (-7a)$ **c)** $-9x + 5x$

d) $7xy - (-12xy)$ **e)** $2x^2 + 4x^2$ **f)** $\frac{1}{2}x - \frac{1}{4}x$

Solution

a) $w + 2w = 1w + 2w = 3w$ **b)** $-3a + (-7a) = -10a$

c) $-9x + 5x = -4x$ **d)** $7xy - (-12xy) = 19xy$

e) $2x^2 + 4x^2 = 6x^2$ **f)** $\frac{1}{2}x - \frac{1}{4}x = \left(\frac{1}{2} - \frac{1}{4}\right)x = \frac{1}{4}x$

Now do Exercises 29–42

Study Tip

Note how the exercises are keyed to the examples. This serves two purposes. If you have missed class and are studying on your own, you should study an example and then immediately try to work the corresponding exercises. If you have seen an explanation in class, then you can start the exercises and refer back to the examples as necessary.

CAUTION There are no like terms in expressions such as

$$2 + 5x, \quad 3xy + 5y, \quad 3w + 5a, \quad \text{and} \quad 3z^2 + 5z$$

The terms in these expressions cannot be combined.

Products and Quotients

To **simplify** an expression means to write an equivalent expression that looks simpler, but *simplify* is not a precisely defined term. An expression that uses fewer symbols is usually considered simpler, but we should not be too picky with this idea. So $5x$ is clearly simpler than $2x + 3x$, but we would not say that $\frac{x}{2}$ is simpler that $\frac{1}{2}x$. Since $2ax + 2ay$ and $2a(x + y)$ both have seven symbols, either is an acceptable answer if the directions just read "simplify." If you are asked to write $2a(x + y)$ as a sum or to remove the parentheses rather than to simplify it, then it is clear that the answer should be $2ax + 2ay$. In Example 4 we use the associative property of multiplication to simplify some products.

EXAMPLE 4

Finding products

Simplify.

a) $3(5x)$ **b)** $2\left(\frac{x}{2}\right)$

c) $(4x)(6x)$ **d)** $(-2a)(4b)$

Teaching Tip Emphasize that $\frac{1}{2}x$ and $\frac{x}{2}$ are equivalent.

Solution

a) $3(5x) = (3 \cdot 5)x$ Associative property of multiplication

$= (15)x$ Multiply.

$= 15x$ Remove unnecessary parentheses.

b) $2\left(\frac{x}{2}\right) = 2\left(\frac{1}{2} \cdot x\right)$ Multiplying by $\frac{1}{2}$ is the same as dividing by 2.

$= \left(2 \cdot \frac{1}{2}\right)x$ Associative property of multiplication

$= 1 \cdot x$ Multiplicative inverse property

$= x$ Multiplicative identity property

c) $(4x)(6x) = 4 \cdot 6 \cdot x \cdot x$ Commutative and associative properties

$= 24x^2$ Definition of exponent

d) $(-2a)(4b) = -2 \cdot 4 \cdot a \cdot b = -8ab$

Now do Exercises 43–52

CAUTION Be careful with expressions such as $3(5x)$ and $3(5 + x)$. In $3(5x)$ we multiply 5 by 3 to get $3(5x) = 15x$. In $3(5 + x)$, both 5 and x are multiplied by the 3 to get $3(5 + x) = 15 + 3x$.

In Example 4 we showed how the properties are used to simplify products. However, in practice we usually do not write out any steps for these problems—we can write just the answer.

EXAMPLE 5

Finding products quickly

Find each product.

a) $(-3)(4x)$ **b)** $(-4a)(-7a)$ **c)** $(-3a)\left(\frac{b}{3}\right)$ **d)** $6 \cdot \frac{x}{2}$

Solution

a) $-12x$ **b)** $28a^2$ **c)** $-ab$ **d)** $3x$

Now do Exercises 53–58

In Section 1.1 we found the quotient of two numbers by inverting the divisor and then multiplying. Since $a \div b = a \cdot \frac{1}{b}$, any quotient can be written as a product.

EXAMPLE 6

Simplifying quotients

Simplify.

a) $\frac{10x}{5}$

b) $\frac{4x + 8}{2}$

Solution

a) Since dividing by 5 is equivalent to multiplying by $\frac{1}{5}$, we have

$$\frac{10x}{5} = \frac{1}{5}(10x) = \left(\frac{1}{5} \cdot 10\right)x = (2)x = 2x.$$

Note that you can simply divide 10 by 5 to get 2.

b) Since dividing by 2 is equivalent to multiplying by $\frac{1}{2}$, we have

$$\frac{4x + 8}{2} = \frac{1}{2}(4x + 8) = 2x + 4.$$

Note that both 4 and 8 are divided by 2.

Now do Exercises 59–70

CAUTION It is not correct to divide only one term in the numerator by the denominator. For example,

$$\frac{4 + 7}{2} \neq 2 + 7$$

because $\frac{4 + 7}{2} = \frac{11}{2}$ and $2 + 7 = 9$.

Study Tip

Take notes in class. Write down everything you can. As soon as possible after class, rewrite your notes. Fill in details and make corrections. Make a note of examples and exercises in the text that are similar to examples in your notes. If your instructor takes the time to work an example in class, it is a good bet that your instructor expects you to understand the concepts involved.

Removing Parentheses

Multiplying a number by -1 merely changes the sign of the number. For example,

$$(-1)(7) = -7 \qquad \text{and} \qquad (-1)(-8) = 8.$$

So -1 times a number is the *opposite* of the number. Using variables, we write

$$(-1)x = -x \qquad \text{or} \qquad -1(y + 5) = -(y + 5).$$

When a minus sign appears in front of a sum, we can change the minus sign to -1 and use the distributive property. For example,

$$\begin{aligned} -(w + 4) &= -1(w + 4) \\ &= (-1)w + (-1)4 && \text{Distributive property} \\ &= -w + (-4) && \text{Note: } -1 \cdot w = -w,\ -1 \cdot 4 = -4 \\ &= -w - 4 \end{aligned}$$

Calculator Close-Up

A negative sign in front of parentheses changes the sign of every term inside the parentheses.

```
-(5-3)
                -2
-1(5-3)
                -2
-5+3
                -2
```

Note how the minus sign in front of the parentheses caused all of the signs to change: $-(w + 4) = -w - 4$. As another example, consider the following:

$$\begin{aligned} -(x - 3) &= -1(x - 3) \\ &= (-1)x - (-1)3 \\ &= -x - (-3) \\ &= -x + 3 \end{aligned}$$

CAUTION When removing parentheses preceded by a minus sign, you must change the sign of *every* term within the parentheses.

EXAMPLE 7

Removing parentheses

Simplify each expression.

a) $5 - (x + 3)$ **b)** $3x - 6 - (2x - 4)$ **c)** $-6x - (-x + 2)$

Solution

a) $5 - (x + 3) = 5 - x - 3$ Change the sign of each term in parentheses.

$= 5 - 3 - x$ Commutative property of addition

$= 2 - x$ Combine like terms.

b) $3x - 6 - (2x - 4) = 3x - 6 - 2x + 4$ Remove parentheses and change signs.

$= 3x - 2x - 6 + 4$ Commutative property of addition

$= x - 2$ Combine like terms.

c) $-6x - (-x + 2) = -6x + x - 2$ Remove parentheses and change signs.

$= -5x - 2$ Combine like terms.

Now do Exercises 71–78

Teaching Tip Point out the three ways to read the symbol − in Example 7(c): negative, minus, and opposite.

The commutative and associative properties of addition allow us to rearrange the terms so that we may combine the like terms. However, it is not necessary to actually write down the rearrangement. We can identify the like terms and combine them without rearranging.

EXAMPLE 8

Simplifying algebraic expressions

Simplify.

a) $(-2x + 3) + (5x - 7)$ **b)** $-3x + 6x + 5(4 - 2x)$

c) $-2x(3x - 7) - (x - 6)$ **d)** $x - 0.02(x + 500)$

Solution

a) $(-2x + 3) + (5x - 7) = 3x - 4$ Combine like terms.

b) $-3x + 6x + 5(4 - 2x) = -3x + 6x + 20 - 10x$ Distributive property

$= -7x + 20$ Combine like terms.

c) $-2x(3x - 7) - (x - 6) = -6x^2 + 14x - x + 6$ Distributive property

$= -6x^2 + 13x + 6$ Combine like terms.

d) $x - 0.02(x + 500) = 1x - 0.02x - 10$ Distributive property

$= 0.98x - 10$ Combine like terms.

Now do Exercises 79–96

Warm-Ups ▼

True or false? Explain your answer.

A statement involving variables should be marked true only if it is true for all values of the variable.

1. $3(x + 6) = 3x + 18$ True
2. $-3x + 9 = -3(x + 9)$ False
3. $-1(x - 4) = -x + 4$ True
4. $3a + 4a = 7a$ True
5. $(3a)(4a) = 12a$ False
6. $3(5 \cdot 2) = 15 \cdot 6$ False
7. $x + x = x^2$ False
8. $x \cdot x = 2x$ False
9. $3 + 2x = 5x$ False
10. $-(5x - 2) = -5x + 2$ True

1.8 Exercises

Boost your GRADE at mathzone.com!

MathZone
▶ Practice Problems ▶ Net Tutor
▶ Self-Tests ▶ e-Professors
▶ Videos

Reading and Writing *After reading this section write out the answers to these questions. Use complete sentences.*

1. What are like terms?
Like terms are terms with the same variables and exponents.

2. What is the coefficient of a term?
The coefficient of a term is the number preceding the variable.

3. What can you do to like terms that you cannot do to unlike terms?
We can add or subtract like terms.

4. What operations can you perform with unlike terms?
Unlike terms can be multiplied and divided.

5. What is the difference between a positive sign preceding a set of parentheses and a negative sign preceding a set of parentheses?
If a negative sign precedes a set of parentheses, then signs for all terms in the parentheses are changed when the parentheses are removed.

6. What happens when a number is multiplied by -1?
Multiplying a number by -1 changes the sign of the number.

Use the appropriate properties to evaluate the expressions. See Example 1.

7. $35(200)$ 7000
8. $15(300)$ 4500
9. $\frac{4}{3}(0.75)$ 1
10. $5(0.2)$ 1
11. $256 + 78 + 22$ 356
12. $12 + 88 + 376$ 476
13. $35 \cdot 3 + 35 \cdot 7$ 350
14. $98 \cdot 478 + 2 \cdot 478$ 47,800
15. $18 \cdot 4 \cdot 2 \cdot \frac{1}{4}$ 36
16. $19 \cdot 3 \cdot 2 \cdot \frac{1}{3}$ 38
17. $(120)(300)$ 36,000
18. $150 \cdot 200$ 30,000
19. $12 \cdot 375(-6 + 6)$ 0
20. $354^2(-2 \cdot 4 + 8)$ 0
21. $78 + 6 + 8 + 4 + 2$ 98
22. $-47 + 12 - 6 - 12 + 6$ -47

Combine like terms where possible. See Examples 2 and 3.

23. $5w + 6w$ $11w$
24. $4a + 10a$ $14a$
25. $4x - x$ $3x$
26. $a - 6a$ $-5a$
27. $2x - (-3x)$ $5x$
28. $2b - (-5b)$ $7b$
29. $-3a - (-2a)$ $-a$
30. $-10m - (-6m)$ $-4m$
31. $-a - a$ $-2a$
32. $a - a$ 0
33. $10 - 6t$ $10 - 6t$
34. $9 - 4w$ $9 - 4w$
35. $3x^2 + 5x^2$ $8x^2$
36. $3r^2 + 4r^2$ $7r^2$
37. $-4x + 2x^2$ $-4x + 2x^2$
38. $6w^2 - w$ $6w^2 - w$
39. $5mw^2 - 12mw^2$ $-7mw^2$
40. $4ab^2 - 19ab^2$ $-15ab^2$
41. $\frac{1}{3}a + \frac{1}{2}a$ $\frac{5}{6}a$
42. $\frac{3}{5}b - b$ $-\frac{2}{5}b$

Simplify the following products or quotients. See Examples 4–6.

43. $3(4h)$ $12h$
44. $2(5h)$ $10h$
45. $6b(-3)$ $-18b$
46. $-3m(-1)$ $3m$
47. $(-3m)(3m)$ $-9m^2$
48. $(2x)(-2x)$ $-4x^2$
49. $(-3d)(-4d)$ $12d^2$
50. $(-5t)(-2t)$ $10t^2$
51. $(-y)(-y)$ y^2
52. $y(-y)$ $-y^2$
53. $-3a(5b)$ $-15ab$
54. $-7w(3r)$ $-21rw$
55. $-3a(2 + b)$ $-6a - 3ab$
56. $-2x(3 + y)$ $-6x - 2xy$

57. $-k(1-k)$ $-k+k^2$

58. $-t(t-1)$ $-t^2+t$

59. $\frac{3y}{3}$ y

60. $\frac{-9t}{9}$ $-t$

61. $\frac{-15y}{5}$ $-3y$

62. $\frac{-12b}{2}$ $-6b$

63. $2\left(\frac{y}{2}\right)$ y

64. $6\left(\frac{m}{3}\right)$ $2m$

65. $8y\left(\frac{y}{4}\right)$ $2y^2$

66. $10\left(\frac{2a}{5}\right)$ $4a$

67. $\frac{6a-3}{3}$ $2a-1$

68. $\frac{-8x+6}{2}$ $-4x+3$

69. $\frac{-9x+6}{-3}$ $3x-2$

70. $\frac{10-5x}{-5}$ $-2+x$

Simplify each expression. See Example 7.

71. $x-(3x-1)$ $-2x+1$

72. $4x-(2x-5)$ $2x+5$

73. $5-(y-3)$ $8-y$

74. $8-(m-6)$ $-m+14$

75. $2m+3-(m+9)$ $m-6$

76. $7-8t-(2t+6)$ $-10t+1$

77. $-3-(-w+2)$ $w-5$

78. $-5x-(-2x+9)$ $-3x-9$

Simplify the following expressions by combining like terms. See Example 8.

79. $3x+5x+6+9$ $8x+15$

80. $2x+6x+7+15$ $8x+22$

81. $(-2x+3)+(7x-4)$ $5x-1$

82. $(-3x+12)+(5x-9)$ $2x+3$

83. $3a-7-(5a-6)$ $-2a-1$

84. $4m-5-(m-2)$ $3m-3$

85. $2(a-4)-3(-2-a)$ $5a-2$

86. $2(w+6)-3(-w-5)$ $5w+27$

87. $3x(2x-3)+5(2x-3)$ $6x^2+x-15$

88. $2a(a-5)+4(a-5)$ $2a^2-6a-20$

89. $-b(2b-1)-4(2b-1)$ $-2b^2-7b+4$

90. $-2c(c-8)-3(c-8)$ $-2c^2+13c+24$

91. $-5m+6(m-3)+2m$ $3m-18$

92. $-3a+2(a-5)+7a$ $6a-10$

93. $5-3(x+2)-6$ $-3x-7$

94. $7+2(k-3)-k+6$ $k+7$

95. $x-0.05(x+10)$ $0.95x-0.5$

96. $x-0.02(x+300)$ $0.98x-6$

Simplify each expression.

97. $3x-(4-x)$ $4x-4$

98. $2+8x-11x$ $2-3x$

99. $y-5-(-y-9)$ $2y+4$

100. $a-(b-c-a)$ $2a-b+c$

101. $7-(8-2y-m)$ $2y+m-1$

102. $x-8-(-3-x)$ $2x-5$

103. $\frac{1}{2}(10-2x)+\frac{1}{3}(3x-6)$ 3

104. $\frac{1}{2}(x-20)-\frac{1}{5}(x+15)$ $\frac{3}{10}x-13$

105. $\frac{1}{2}(3a+1)-\frac{1}{3}(a-5)$ $\frac{7}{6}a+\frac{13}{6}$

106. $\frac{1}{4}(6b+2)-\frac{2}{3}(3b-2)$ $-\frac{1}{2}b+\frac{11}{6}$

107. $0.2(x+3)-0.05(x+20)$ $0.15x-0.4$

108. $0.08x+0.12(x+100)$ $0.2x+12$

109. $2k+1-3(5k-6)-k+4$ $-14k+23$

110. $2w-3+3(w-4)-5(w-6)$ 15

111. $-3m-3[2m-3(m+5)]$ 45

112. $6h+4[2h-3(h-9)-(h-1)]$ $-2h+112$

Solve each problem.

113. ***Married filing jointly.*** The value of the expression

$$7820+0.25(x-56{,}800)$$

is the 2003 federal income tax for a married couple filing jointly with a taxable income of x dollars, where x is over \$56,800 but not over \$114,650 (Internal Revenue Service, www.irs.gov).

a) Simplify the expression. $0.25x-6380$

b) Use the expression to find the amount of tax for a couple with a taxable income of \$80,000. \$13,620

c) Use the accompanying graph to estimate the 2003 federal income tax for a couple with a taxable income of \$200,000 \$48,000

d) Use the accompanying graph to estimate the taxable income for a couple who paid \$80,000 in federal income tax. \$300,000

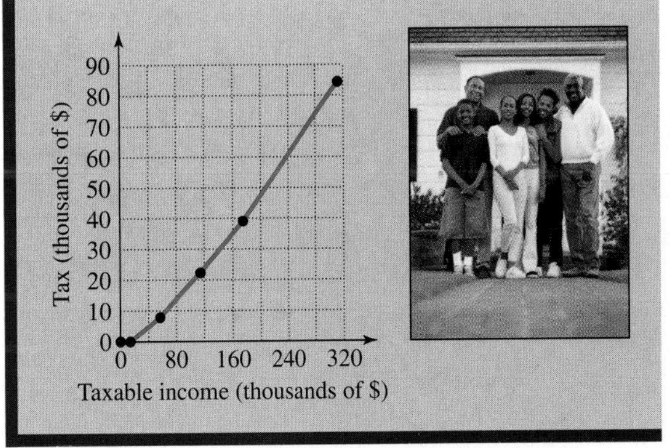

Figure for Exercise 113

114. ***Marriage penalty eliminated.*** The value of the expression

$$3910 + 0.25(x - 28{,}400)$$

is the 2003 federal income tax for a single taxpayer with taxable income of x dollars, where x is over \$28,400 but not over \$68,800.

a) Simplify the expression. $0.25x - 3190$

b) Find the amount of tax for a single taxpayer with taxable income of \$40,000. \$6810

c) Who pays more, a married couple with a joint taxable income of \$80,000 or two single taxpayers with taxable incomes of \$40,000 each? See Exercise 113. Both pay same tax.

115. ***Perimeter of a corral.*** The perimeter of a rectangular corral that has width x feet and length $x + 40$ feet is $2(x) + 2(x + 40)$. Simplify the expression for the perimeter. Find the perimeter if $x = 30$ feet.
$4x + 80$, 200 feet

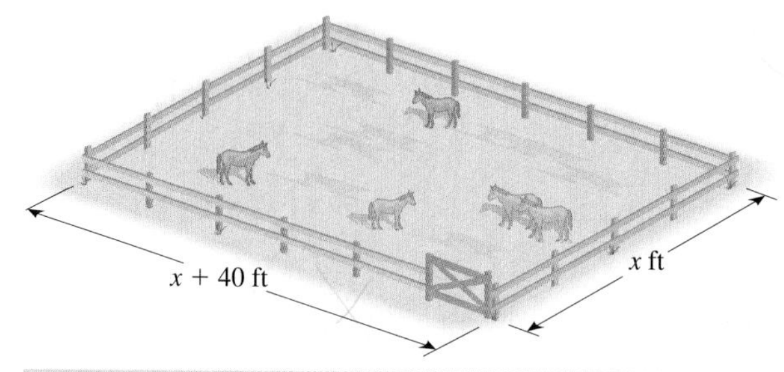

Figure for Exercise 115

Getting More Involved

116. ***Discussion***

What is wrong with the way in which each of the following expressions is simplified?

a) $4(2 + x) = 8 + x$ $\quad 4(2 + x) = 8 + 4x$

b) $4(2x) = 8 \cdot 4x = 32x$ $\quad 4(2x) = (4 \cdot 2)x = 8x$

c) $\dfrac{4 + x}{2} = 2 + x$ $\quad \dfrac{4 + x}{2} = \dfrac{1}{2}(4 + x) = 2 + \dfrac{1}{2}x$

d) $5 - (x - 3) = 5 - x - 3 = 2 - x$
$5 - (x - 3) = 5 - x + 3 = 8 - x$

117. ***Discussion***

An instructor asked his class to evaluate the expression $1/2x$ for $x = 5$. Some students got 0.1; others got 2.5. Which answer is correct and why?
If $x = 5$, then $1/2 \cdot 5 = \frac{1}{2} \cdot 5 = 2.5$ because we do division and multiplication from left to right.

Collaborative Activities

Grouping: Four students per group

Topic: Signed numbers

Walking the Number Line

This activity will help you understand adding and subtracting integers. There are four roles that will be rotated in your group; positive sign holder, negative sign holder, problem reader, and number-line walker.

Preparation. Using 13 note cards or pieces of paper write the integers from -6 to $+6$, one number to a card. Also make a card with a positive sign on it and another card with a negative sign. Place the 13 number cards in order on the floor about a step apart to create a number line.

Assume Your Position. After choosing your roles, have the positive sign holder stand at the positive end of the 13-card number line after $+6$, facing to the center. The negative sign holder will stand at the negative end of the line after -6, facing the center. The walker will be near the line ready to start. The problem reader is close by ready to read the first problem.

Rules. The number line walker will stand on the first number that the problem reader reads. The walker will face the positive sign holder if the second number is positive or face the negative sign holder if the second number is negative. For addition the walker will walk forward the number of spaces of the second number and for subtraction the walker will walk backward the number of spaces of the second number.

Examples. The reader reads $-1 + (-3)$. The walker begins at -1, faces the negative sign holder, then walks forward three steps. The walker should be on -4, which is the correct result for $-1 + (-3)$.

The reader reads $1 - (-4)$. The walker begins at 1, faces the negative sign holder, then walks backward 4 steps. The walker should be on 5, which is the correct result of $1 - (-4)$.

Exercises. Try the following exercises. After each two exercises, rotate the roles. Be sure to check that the walker is on the correct result.

1. $-2 + 3$ **2.** $-2 + (-3)$
3. $2 + (-3)$ **4.** $2 - (-3)$
5. $2 + 3$ **6.** $2 - 3$
7. $-2 + (-3)$ **8.** $-2 - (-3)$

Extension. Make up your own problems using integers between -6 and $+6$ and walk out the results on the number line.

Chapter 1 Wrap-Up

Summary

The Real Numbers		Examples
Counting or natural numbers	$\{1, 2, 3, \ldots\}$	
Whole numbers	$\{0, 1, 2, 3, \ldots\}$	
Integers	$\{\ldots, -3, -2, -1, 0, 1, 2, 3, \ldots\}$	
Rational numbers	$\left\{\frac{a}{b} \middle\vert a \text{ and } b \text{ are integers with } b \neq 0\right\}$	$\frac{3}{2}$, 5, −6, 0
Irrational numbers	$\{x \mid x \text{ is a real number that is not rational}\}$	$\sqrt{2}, \sqrt{3}, \pi$
Real numbers	The set of real numbers consists of all rational numbers together with all irrational numbers.	
Intervals of real numbers	If a is less than b, then the set of real numbers between a and b is written as (a, b). The set of real numbers between a and b inclusive is written as $[a, b]$.	The notation (1, 9) represents the real numbers between 1 and 9. The notation [1, 9] represents the real numbers between 1 and 9 inclusive.

Fractions		Examples
Reducing fractions	$\frac{a \cdot c}{b \cdot c} = \frac{a}{b}$	$\frac{4}{6} = \frac{2 \cdot 2}{2 \cdot 3} = \frac{2}{3}$
Building up fractions	$\frac{a}{b} = \frac{a \cdot c}{b \cdot c}$	$\frac{3}{8} = \frac{3 \cdot 5}{8 \cdot 5} = \frac{15}{40}$
Multiplying fractions	$\frac{a}{b} \cdot \frac{c}{d} = \frac{ac}{bd}$	$\frac{2}{3} \cdot \frac{4}{5} = \frac{8}{15}$
Dividing fractions	$\frac{a}{b} \div \frac{c}{d} = \frac{a}{b} \cdot \frac{d}{c}$	$\frac{2}{3} \div \frac{4}{5} = \frac{2}{3} \cdot \frac{5}{4} = \frac{10}{12} = \frac{5}{6}$

Adding or subtracting fractions	$\frac{a}{b} + \frac{c}{b} = \frac{a+c}{b}$ $\frac{a}{b} - \frac{c}{b} = \frac{a-c}{b}$	$\frac{1}{5} + \frac{2}{5} = \frac{3}{5}$ $\frac{3}{5} - \frac{2}{5} = \frac{1}{5}$
Least common denominator	The smallest number that is a multiple of all denominators.	$\frac{1}{4} + \frac{1}{6} = \frac{3}{12} + \frac{2}{12} = \frac{5}{12}$
Operations with Real Numbers		**Examples**
Absolute value	$\|a\| = \begin{cases} a & \text{if } a \text{ is positive or zero} \\ -a & \text{if } a \text{ is negative} \end{cases}$	$\|3\| = 3, \|0\| = 0$ $\|-3\| = 3$
Sum of two numbers with like signs	Add their absolute values. The sum has the same sign as the given numbers.	$-3 + (-4) = -7$
Sum of two numbers with unlike signs (and different absolute values)	Subtract the absolute values of the numbers. The answer is positive if the number with the larger absolute value is positive. The answer is negative if the number with the larger absolute value is negative.	$-4 + 7 = 3$ $-7 + 4 = -3$
Sum of opposites	The sum of any number and its opposite is 0.	$-6 + 6 = 0$
Subtraction of signed numbers	$a - b = a + (-b)$ Subtract any number by adding its opposite.	$3 - 5 = 3 + (-5) = -2$ $4 - (-3) = 4 + 3 = 7$
Product or quotient	Like signs ↔ Positive result Unlike signs ↔ Negative result	$(-3)(-2) = 6$ $(-8) \div 2 = -4$
Definition of exponents	For any counting number n, $a^n = \underbrace{a \cdot a \cdot a \cdot \ldots \cdot a}_{n \text{ factors}}$.	$2^3 = 2 \cdot 2 \cdot 2 = 8$
Order of operations	No parentheses or absolute value present: 1. Exponential expressions 2. Multiplication and division 3. Addition and subtraction With parentheses or absolute value: First evaluate within each set of parentheses or absolute value, using the order of operations.	 $5 + 2^3 = 13$ $2 + 3 \cdot 5 = 17$ $4 + 5 \cdot 3^2 = 49$ $(2 + 3)(5 - 7) = -10$ $2 + 3\|2 - 5\| = 11$

Properties of the Real Numbers		Examples
	For any real numbers a, b, and c	
Commutative property of Addition Multiplication	 $a + b = b + a$ $a \cdot b = b \cdot a$	 $5 + 7 = 7 + 5$ $6 \cdot 3 = 3 \cdot 6$
Associative property of Addition Multiplication	 $a + (b + c) = (a + b) + c$ $a \cdot (b \cdot c) = (a \cdot b) \cdot c$	 $1 + (2 + 3) = (1 + 2) + 3$ $2(3 \cdot 4) = (2 \cdot 3)4$
Distributive properties	$a(b + c) = ab + ac$ $a(b - c) = ab - ac$	$2(3 + x) = 6 + 2x$ $-2(x - 5) = -2x + 10$
Additive identity property	$a + 0 = a$ and $0 + a = a$ Zero is the additive identity.	$5 + 0 = 0 + 5 = 5$
Multiplicative identity property	$1 \cdot a = a$ and $a \cdot 1 = a$ One is the multiplicative identity.	$7 \cdot 1 = 1 \cdot 7 = 7$
Additive inverse property	For any real number a, there is a number $-a$ (additive inverse or opposite) such that $a + (-a) = 0$ and $-a + a = 0$.	$3 + (-3) = 0$ $-3 + 3 = 0$
Multiplicative inverse property	For any nonzero real number a there is a number $\frac{1}{a}$ (multiplicative inverse or reciprocal) such that $a \cdot \frac{1}{a} = 1$ and $\frac{1}{a} \cdot a = 1$.	$3 \cdot \frac{1}{3} = 1$ $\frac{1}{3} \cdot 3 = 1$
Multiplication property of 0	$a \cdot 0 = 0$ and $0 \cdot a = 0$	$5 \cdot 0 = 0$ $0(-7) = 0$

Enriching Your Mathematical Word Power

For each mathematical term, choose the correct meaning.

1. like terms
a. terms that are identical
b. the terms of a sum
c. terms that have the same variables with the same exponents
d. terms with the same variables c

2. equivalent fractions
a. identical fractions
b. fractions that represent the same number
c. fractions with the same denominator
d. fractions with the same numerator b

3. variable
a. a letter that is used to represent some numbers
b. the letter x
c. an equation with a letter in it
d. not the same a

4. reducing
a. less than
b. losing weight
c. making equivalent
d. dividing out common factors d

5. lowest terms
a. numerator is smaller than the denominator
b. no common factors
c. the best interest rate
d. when the numerator is 1 b

6. additive inverse
a. the number -1
b. the number 0
c. the opposite of addition
d. opposite d

7. order of operations
a. the order in which operations are to be performed in the absence of grouping symbols
b. the order in which the operations were invented
c. the order in which operations are written
d. a list of operations in alphabetical order a

8. least common denominator
a. the smallest divisor of all denominators
b. the denominator that appears the least
c. the smallest identical denominator
d. the least common multiple of the denominators d

9. absolute value
a. definite value
b. positive number
c. distance from 0 on the number line
d. the opposite of a number c

10. natural numbers
a. the counting numbers
b. numbers that are not irrational
c. the nonnegative numbers
d. numbers that we find in nature a

Review Exercises

1.1 *Which of the numbers* $-\sqrt{5}$, -2, 0, 1, 2, 3.14, π, *and* 10 *are*

1. whole numbers? 0, 1, 2, 10

2. natural numbers? 1, 2, 10

3. integers? -2, 0, 1, 2, 10

4. rational numbers? -2, 0, 1, 2, 3.14, 10

5. irrational numbers? $-\sqrt{5}$, π

6. real numbers? All of them

Study Tip

Note how the review exercises are arranged according to the sections in this chapter. If you are having trouble with a certain type of problem, refer back to the appropriate section for examples and explanations.

True or false? Explain your answer.

7. Every whole number is a rational number. True

8. Zero is not a rational number. False

9. The counting numbers between -4 and 4 are -3, -2, -1, 0, 1, 2, and 3. False

10. There are infinitely many integers. True

11. The set of counting numbers smaller than the national debt is infinite. False

12. The decimal number 0.25 is a rational number. True

13. Every integer greater than -1 is a whole number. True

14. Zero is the only number that is neither rational nor irrational. False

Graph each set of numbers.

15. The set of integers between -3 and 3

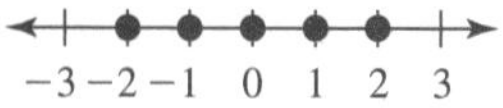

-3 -2 -1 0 1 2 3

16. The set of natural numbers between -3 and 3

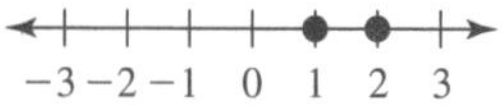

-3 -2 -1 0 1 2 3

17. The set of real numbers between -1 and 4

-2 -1 0 1 2 3 4 5

18. The set of real numbers between -2 and 3 inclusive

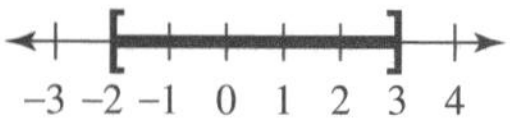

-3 -2 -1 0 1 2 3 4

Write the interval notation for each interval of real numbers.

19. The set of real numbers between 4 and 6 inclusive $[4, 6]$

20. The set of real numbers greater than 2 and less than 5 $(2, 5)$

21. The set of real numbers greater than or equal to -30 $[-30, \infty)$

22. The set of real numbers less than 50 $(-\infty, 50)$

1.2 *Perform the indicated operations.*

23. $\frac{1}{3} + \frac{3}{8}$ $\frac{17}{24}$

24. $\frac{2}{3} - \frac{1}{4}$ $\frac{5}{12}$

25. $\frac{3}{5} \cdot 10$ 6

26. $\frac{3}{5} \div 10$ $\frac{3}{50}$

27. $\frac{2}{5} \cdot \frac{15}{14}$ $\frac{3}{7}$

28. $7 \div \frac{1}{2}$ 14

29. $4 + \frac{2}{3}$ $\frac{14}{3}$

30. $\frac{7}{12} - \frac{1}{4}$ $\frac{1}{3}$

31. $\frac{1}{2} + \frac{1}{3} + \frac{1}{4}$ $\frac{13}{12}$

32. $\frac{3}{4} \div 9$ $\frac{1}{12}$

1.3 *Evaluate.*

33. $-5 + 7$ 2

34. $-9 + (-4)$ -13

35. $35 - 48$ -13

36. $-3 - 9$ -12

37. $-12 + 5$ -7

38. $-12 - 5$ -17

39. $-12 - (-5)$ -7

40. $-9 - (-9)$ 0

41. $-0.05 + 12$ 11.95

42. $-0.03 + (-2)$ -2.03

43. $-0.1 - (-0.05)$ -0.05

44. $-0.3 + 0.3$ 0

45. $\frac{1}{3} - \frac{1}{2}$ $-\frac{1}{6}$

46. $-\frac{2}{3} + \frac{1}{4}$ $-\frac{5}{12}$

47. $-\frac{1}{3} + \left(-\frac{2}{5}\right)$ $-\frac{11}{15}$

48. $\frac{1}{3} - \left(-\frac{1}{4}\right)$ $\frac{7}{12}$

1.4 *Evaluate.*

49. $(-3)(5)$ -15

50. $(-9)(-4)$ 36

51. $(-8) \div (-2)$ 4

52. $50 \div (-5)$ -10

53. $\frac{-20}{-4}$ 5

54. $\frac{30}{-5}$ -6

55. $\left(-\frac{1}{2}\right)\left(-\frac{1}{3}\right)$ $\frac{1}{6}$

56. $8 \div \left(-\frac{1}{3}\right)$ -24

57. $-0.09 \div 0.3$ -0.3

58. $4.2 \div (-0.3)$ -14

59. $(0.3)(-0.8)$ -0.24

60. $0 \div (-0.0538)$ 0

61. $(-5)(-0.2)$ 1

62. $\frac{1}{2}(-12)$ -6

1.5 *Evaluate.*

63. $3 + 7(9)$ 66

64. $(3 + 7)9$ 90

65. $(3 + 4)^2$ 49

66. $3 + 4^2$ 19

67. $3 + 2 \cdot |5 - 6 \cdot 4|$ 41

68. $3 - (8 - 9)$ 4

69. $(3 - 7) - (4 - 9)$ 1

70. $3 - 7 - 4 - 9$ -17

71. $-2 - 4(2 - 3 \cdot 5)$ 50

72. $3^2 - 7 + 5^2$ 27

73. $3^2 - (7 + 5)^2$ -135

74. $|4 - 6 \cdot 3| - |7 - 9|$ 12

75. $\frac{-3 - 5}{2 - (-2)}$ -2

76. $\frac{1 - 9}{4 - 6}$ 4

77. $\frac{6 + 3}{3} - 5 \cdot 4 + 1$ -16

78. $\frac{2 \cdot 4 + 4}{3} - 3(1 - 2)$ 7

1.6 *Let $a = -1$, $b = -2$, and $c = 3$. Find the value of each algebraic expression.*

79. $b^2 - 4ac$ 16

80. $a^2 - 4b$ 9

81. $(c - b)(c + b)$ 5

82. $(a + b)(a - b)$ -3

83. $a^2 + 2ab + b^2$ 9

84. $a^2 - 2ab + b^2$ 1

85. $a^3 - b^3$ 7

86. $a^3 + b^3$ -9

87. $\frac{b + c}{a + b}$ $-\frac{1}{3}$

88. $\frac{b - c}{2b - a}$ $\frac{5}{3}$

89. $|a - b|$ 1

90. $|b - a|$ 1

91. $(a + b)c$ -9

92. $ac + bc$ -9

Determine whether the given number is a solution to the equation following it.

93. 4, $3x - 2 = 10$ Yes

94. 1, $5(x + 3) = 20$ Yes

95. -6, $\frac{3x}{2} = 9$ No

96. -30, $\frac{x}{3} - 4 = 6$ No

97. 15, $\frac{x + 3}{2} = 9$ Yes

98. 1, $\frac{12}{2x + 1} = 4$ Yes

99. 4, $-x - 3 = 1$ No

100. 7, $-x + 1 = 6$ No

1.7 *Name the property that justifies each statement.*

101. $a(x + y) = ax + ay$ Distributive property

102. $3(4y) = (3 \cdot 4)y$ Associative property of multiplication

103. $(0.001)(1000) = 1$ Multiplicative inverse property

104. $xy = yx$ Commutative property of multiplication

105. $0 + y = y$ Additive identity property

106. $325 \cdot 1 = 325$ Multiplicative identity property

107. $3 + (2 + x) = (3 + 2) + x$ Associative property of addition

108. $2x - 6 = 2(x - 3)$ Distributive property

109. $5 \cdot 200 = 200 \cdot 5$ Commutative property of multiplication

110. $3 + (x + 2) = (x + 2) + 3$ Commutative property of addition

111. $-50 + 50 = 0$ Additive inverse property

112. $43 \cdot 59 \cdot 82 \cdot 0 = 0$ Multiplication property of 0

113. $12 \cdot 1 = 12$ Multiplicative identity property

114. $3x + 1 = 1 + 3x$ Commutative property of addition

1.8 *Simplify by combining like terms.*

115. $3a + 7 - (4a - 5)$ $-a + 12$

116. $2m + 6 - (m - 2)$ $m + 8$

117. $2a(3a - 5) + 4a$ $6a^2 - 6a$

118. $3a(a - 5) + 5a(a + 2)$ $8a^2 - 5a$

119. $3(t - 2) - 5(3t - 9)$ $-12t + 39$

120. $2(m + 3) - 3(3 - m)$ $5m - 3$

121. $0.1(a + 0.3) - (a + 0.6)$ $-0.9a - 0.57$

122. $0.1(x + 0.3) - (x - 0.9)$ $-0.9x + 0.93$

123. $0.05(x - 20) - 0.1(x + 30)$ $-0.05x - 4$

124. $0.02(x - 100) + 0.2(x - 50)$ $0.22x - 12$

125. $5 - 3x(-5x - 2) + 12x^2$ $27x^2 + 6x + 5$

126. $7 - 2x(3x - 7) - x^2$ $-7x^2 + 14x + 7$

127. $-(a - 2) - 2 - a$ $-2a$

128. $-(w - y) - 3(y - w)$ $-2y + 2w$

129. $x(x + 1) + 3(x - 1)$ $x^2 + 4x - 3$

130. $y(y - 2) + 3(y + 1)$ $y^2 + y + 3$

Miscellaneous

Evaluate each expression. Use a calculator to check.

131. $752(-13) + 752(13)$ 0

132. $75 - (-13)$ 88

133. $|15 - 23|$ 8

134. $4^2 - 6^2$ -20

135. $-6^2 + 3(5)$ -21

136. $(0.03)(-200)$ -6

137. $\frac{2}{5} + \frac{1}{10}$ $\frac{1}{2}$

138. $\frac{2 + 1}{5 + 10}$ $\frac{1}{5}$

139. $(0.05) \div (-0.1)$ -0.5

140. $(4 - 9)^2 + (2 \cdot 3 - 1)^2$ 50

141. $2\left(-\frac{1}{2}\right)^2 + \left(-\frac{1}{2}\right) - 1$ -1

142. $\left(-\frac{6}{7}\right)\left(\frac{21}{26}\right)$ $-\frac{9}{13}$

Simplify each expression if possible.

143. $\frac{2x + 4}{2}$ $x + 2$

144. $4(2x)$ $8x$

145. $4 + 2x$ $4 + 2x$

146. $4(2 + x)$ $8 + 4x$

147. $4 \cdot \frac{x}{2}$ $2x$

148. $4 - (x - 2)$ $-x + 6$

149. $-4(x - 2)$ $-4x + 8$

150. $(4x)(2x)$ $8x^2$

151. $4x + 2x$ $6x$

152. $2 + (x + 4)$ $x + 6$

153. $4 \cdot \frac{x}{4}$ x

154. $4 \cdot \frac{3x}{2}$ $6x$

155. $2 \cdot x \cdot 4$ $8x$

156. $4 - 2(2 - x)$ $2x$

157. $2(x - 4) - x(x - 4)$ $-x^2 + 6x - 8$

158. $-x(2 - x) - 2(2 - x)$ $x^2 - 4$

159. $\frac{1}{2}(x - 4) - \frac{1}{4}(x - 2)$ $\frac{1}{4}x - \frac{3}{2}$

160. $\frac{1}{4}(x + 2) - \frac{1}{2}(x - 4)$ $-\frac{1}{4}x + \frac{5}{2}$

Fill in the tables with the appropriate values for the given expressions.

161.

x	$-\frac{1}{3}x + 1$
-6	3
-3	2
0	1
3	0
6	-1

162.

x	$\frac{1}{2}x + 3$
-4	1
-2	2
0	3
2	4
4	5

163.

a	a^2	a^3	a^4
5	25	125	625
-4	16	-64	256

164.

b	$\frac{1}{b}$	$\frac{1}{b^2}$	$\frac{1}{b^3}$
-3	$-\frac{1}{3}$	$\frac{1}{9}$	$-\frac{1}{27}$
$-\frac{1}{2}$	-2	4	-8

Solve each problem.

165. ***Telemarketing.*** Brenda and Nicki sell memberships in an automobile club over the telephone. Brenda sells one membership every 0.125 hour, and Nicki sells one membership every 0.1 hour. At what rate (in memberships per hour) are the memberships being sold when both are working? 18 memberships per hour

166. ***High-income bracket.*** The expression

$$90{,}514.5 + 0.35(x - 311{,}950)$$

represents the amount for the 2003 federal income tax in dollars for a single taxpayer with x dollars of taxable income, where x is over \$311,950 (www.irs.gov).

a) Simplify the expression. $0.35x - 18{,}668$

Tax (thousands of \$): 0, 40, 80, 120, 160, 200
Taxable income (thousands of \$): 0, 100, 200, 300, 400, 500, 600

Figure for Exercise 166

b) Use the graph in the accompanying figure to estimate the amount of tax for a single taxpayer with a taxable income of \$450,000. \$140,000.

c) Find the amount of tax for MLB player Alex Rodriguez for 2003. At \$22 million he was the highest paid baseball player that year (www.usatoday.com). \$7,681,332

Chapter 1 Test

Which of the numbers -3, $-\sqrt{3}$, $-\frac{1}{4}$, 0, $\sqrt{5}$, π, *and* 8 *are*

1. Whole numbers? 0, 8

2. Integers? $-3, 0, 8$

3. Rational numbers? $-3, -\frac{1}{4}, 0, 8$

4. Irrational numbers? $-\sqrt{3}, \sqrt{5}, \pi$

Evaluate each expression.

5. $6 + 3(-9)$ -21

6. $(-2)^2 - 4(-2)(-1)$ -4

7. $\dfrac{-3^2 - 9}{3 - 5}$ 9

8. $-5 + 6 - 12 + 4$ -7

9. $0.05 - 1$ -0.95

10. $(5 - 9)(5 + 9)$ -56

11. $(878 + 89) + 11$ 978

12. $6 + |3 - 5(2)|$ 13

13. $8 - 3|7 - 10|$ -1

14. $(839 + 974)[3(-4) + 12]$ 0

15. $974(7) + 974(3)$ 9740

16. $-\frac{2}{3} + \frac{3}{8}$ $-\frac{7}{24}$

17. $(-0.05)(400)$ -20

18. $\left(-\frac{3}{4}\right)\left(\frac{2}{9}\right)$ $-\frac{1}{6}$

19. $13 \div \left(-\frac{1}{3}\right)$ -39

Study Tip

Before you take an in-class exam on this chapter, work the sample test given here. Set aside one hour to work this test and use the answers in the back of this book to grade yourself. Even though your instructor might not ask exactly the same questions, you will get a good idea of your test readiness.

Graph each set of numbers.

20. The set of whole numbers less than 5

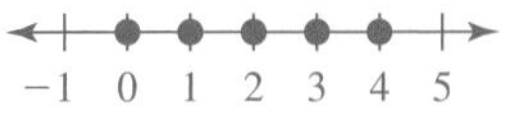

21. The set of real numbers less than or equal to 4

Write the interval notation for each interval of real numbers.

22. The real numbers greater than 2 $(2, \infty)$

23. The real numbers greater than or equal to 3 and less than 9 $[3, 9)$

Identify the property that justifies each equation.

24. $2(x + 7) = 2x + 14$ Distributive property

25. $48 \cdot 1000 = 1000 \cdot 48$ Commutative property of multiplication

26. $2 + (6 + x) = (2 + 6) + x$ Associative property of addition

27. $-348 + 348 = 0$ Additive inverse property

28. $1 \cdot (-6) = -6$ Multiplicative identity property

29. $0 \cdot 388 = 0$ Multiplication property of 0

Use the distributive property to write each sum or difference as a product.

30. $3x + 30$ $3(x + 10)$

31. $7w - 7$ $7(w - 1)$

Simplify each expression.

32. $6 + 4x + 2x$ $6x + 6$

33. $6 + 4(x - 2)$ $4x - 2$

34. $5x - (3 - 2x)$ $7x - 3$

35. $x + 10 - 0.1(x + 25)$ $0.9x + 7.5$

36. $2a(4a - 5) - 3a(-2a - 5)$ $14a^2 + 5a$

37. $\dfrac{6x + 12}{6}$ $x + 2$

38. $8 \cdot \frac{t}{2}$ $4t$

39. $(-9xy)(-6xy)$ $54x^2y^2$

40. $\frac{1}{2}(3x + 2) - \frac{1}{4}(3x - 2)$ $\frac{3}{4}x + \frac{3}{2}$

Evaluate each expression if $a = -2$, $b = 3$, *and* $c = 4$.

41. $b^2 - 4ac$ 41

42. $\dfrac{a - b}{b - c}$ 5

43. $(a - c)(a + c)$ -12

Determine whether the given number is a solution to the equation following it.

44. -2, $3x - 4 = 2$ No

45. 13, $\dfrac{x + 3}{8} = 2$ Yes

46. -3, $-x + 5 = 8$ Yes

Solve each problem.

47. Burke and Nora deliver pizzas for Godmother's Pizza. Burke averages one delivery every 0.25 hour, and Nora averages one delivery every 0.2 hour. At what rate (in deliveries per hour) are the deliveries made when both are working? 9 deliveries per hour

48. A forensic scientist uses the expression $80.405 + 3.660R - 0.06(A - 30)$ to estimate the height in centimeters for a male with a radius (bone in the forearm) of length R centimeters and age A in years, where A is over 30. Simplify the expression. Use the expression to estimate the height of an 80-year-old male with a radius of length 25 cm. $3.66R - 0.06A + 82.205$, 168.905 cm

Critical Thinking | For Individual or Group Work | Chapter 1

These exercises can be solved by a variety of techniques, which may or may not require algebra. So be creative and think critically. Explain all answers. Answers are in the Instructor's Edition of this text.

1. ***Dividing evenly.*** Suppose that you have a three-ounce glass, a five-ounce glass, and an eight-ounce glass, as shown in the accompanying figure. The two smaller glasses are empty, but the largest glass contains eight ounces of milk. How can you divide the milk into two equal parts by using only these three glasses as measuring devices?

Figure for Exercise 1

2. ***Totaling one hundred.*** Start with the sequence of digits 123456789. Place any number of plus or minus signs between the digits in the sequence so that the value of the resulting expression is 100. For example, we could write

$$123 - 45 + 6 + 78 - 9,$$

but the value is not 100.

3. ***More hundreds.*** We can easily find an expression whose value is 6 using only 2's. For example, $2^2 + 2 = 6$. Find an expression whose value is 100 using only 3's. Only 4's, and so on.

4. ***Forming triangles.*** It is possible to draw three straight lines through a capital M to form nine nonoverlapping triangles. Try it.

5. ***The right time.*** Starting at 12 noon determine the number of times in the next 24 hours for which the hour and minute hands on a clock form a right angle?

Photo for Exercise 5

6. ***Perfect power.*** One is the smallest positive integer that is a perfect square, a perfect cube, and a perfect fifth power. What is the next larger positive integer that is a perfect square, a perfect cube, and a perfect fifth power?

7. ***Summing the digits.*** The sum of all of the digits that are used in writing the integers from 29 through 32 is

$$2 + 9 + 3 + 0 + 3 + 1 + 3 + 2$$

or 23. Find the sum of all of the digits that are used in writing the integers from 1 through 1000 without using a calculator.

8. ***Integral rectangles.*** Find all rectangles whose sides are integers and the numerical value for the area is equal to the numerical value for the perimeter.

1. If (0, 0, 8) is the original amount of milk in the 3, 5, and 8 ounce glasses, then pour as follows: (0, 0, 8), (3, 0, 5), (3, 3, 2), (1, 5, 2), (1, 0, 7), (0, 1, 7), (3, 1, 4), (0, 4, 4) **2.** $12 + 3 - 4 + 5 + 67 + 8 + 9 = 100$ or $123 + 4 - 5 + 67 - 89 = 100$ **3.** $3 \cdot 33 + 3/3 = 100$, $4 \cdot 4 \cdot 4 + 4 \cdot 4 + 4 \cdot 4 + 4 = 100$, $5 \cdot 5 \cdot 5 - 5 \cdot 5 = 100$ **4.**  **5.** 44 **6.** 2^{30} or 1,073,741,824 **7.** 13,501 **8.** 3 by 6 and 4 by 4

Chapter 2

Linear Equations and Inequalities in One Variable

Some ancient peoples chewed on leaves to cure their headaches. Thousands of years ago, the Egyptians used honey, salt, cedar oil, and sycamore bark to cure illnesses. Currently, some of the indigenous people of North America use black birch as a pain reliever.

Today, we are grateful for modern medicine and the seemingly simple cures for illnesses. From our own experiences we know that just the right amount of a drug can work wonders but too much of a drug can do great harm. Even though physicians often prescribe the same drug for children and adults, the amount given must be tailored to the individual. The portion of a drug given to children is usually reduced on the basis of factors such as the weight and height of the child. Likewise, older adults frequently need a lower dosage of medication than what would be prescribed for a younger, more active person.

Various algebraic formulas have been developed for determining the proper dosage for a child and an older adult.

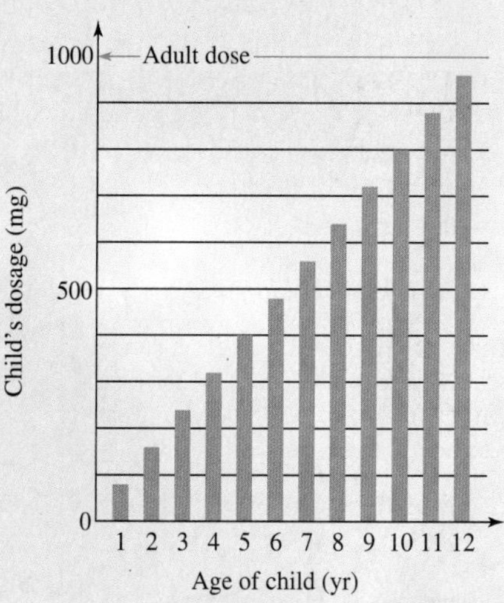

In Exercises 97 and 98 of Section 2.4 you will see two formulas that are used to determine a child's dosage by using the adult dosage and the child's age.

2.1 The Addition and Multiplication Properties of Equality

In this Section

- The Addition Property of Equality
- The Multiplication Property of Equality
- Variables on Both Sides
- Applications

In Section 1.6, an **equation** was defined as a statement that two expressions are equal. A **solution** to an equation is a number that can be used in place of the variable to make the equation a true statement. The **solution set** is the set of all solutions to an equation. Equations with the same solution set are **equivalent equations.** To **solve** an equation means to find all solutions to the equation. In this section you will learn systematic procedures for solving equations.

The Addition Property of Equality

If two workers have equal salaries and each gets a $1000 raise, then they will have equal salaries after the raise. If two people are the same age now, then in 5 years they will still be the same age. If you add the same number to two equal quantities, the results will be equal. This idea is called the *addition property of equality:*

The Addition Property of Equality

Adding the same number to both sides of an equation does not change the solution to the equation. In symbols, if $a = b$, then

$$a + c = b + c.$$

EXAMPLE 1

Adding the same number to both sides

Solve $x - 3 = -7$.

Solution

We can remove the 3 from the left side of the equation by adding 3 to each side of the equation:

$$x - 3 = -7$$

$$x - 3 + 3 = -7 + 3 \quad \text{Add 3 to each side.}$$

$$x + 0 = -4 \quad \text{Simplify each side.}$$

$$x = -4 \quad \text{Zero is the additive identity.}$$

Since -4 satisfies the last equation, it should also satisfy the original equation because all of the previous equations are equivalent. Check that -4 satisfies the original equation by replacing x by -4:

$$x - 3 = -7 \quad \text{Original equation}$$

$$-4 - 3 = -7 \quad \text{Replace } x \text{ by } -4.$$

$$-7 = -7 \quad \text{Simplify.}$$

Since $-4 - 3 = -7$ is correct, $\{-4\}$ is the solution set to the equation.

Now do Exercises 7–16

Helpful Hint

Think of an equation like a balance scale. To keep the scale in balance, what you add to one side you must also add to the other side.

Note that enclosing the solutions to an equation in braces is not absolutely necessary. It is simply a formal way of saying "This is my final answer."

The equations that we work with in this section and Sections 2.2 and 2.3 are called linear equations.

Linear Equation

A **linear equation in one variable** x is an equation that can be written in the form

$$ax + b = 0,$$

where a and b are real numbers and $a \neq 0$.

An equation such as $2x + 3 = 0$ is a linear equation. We also refer to equations such as

$$x + 8 = 0, \quad 3x = 7, \quad 2x + 5 = 9 - 5x, \quad \text{and} \quad 3 + 5(x - 1) = -7 + x$$

as linear equations, because these equations could be written in the form $ax + b = 0$ using the properties of equality.

In Example 1, we used addition to isolate the variable on the left-hand side of the equation. Once the variable is isolated, we can determine the solution to the equation. Because subtraction is defined in terms of addition, we can also use subtraction to isolate the variable.

EXAMPLE 2

Subtracting the same number from both sides

Solve $9 + x = -2$.

Solution

We can remove the 9 from the left side by adding -9 to each side or by subtracting 9 from each side of the equation:

$$\begin{aligned} 9 + x &= -2 \\ 9 + x - 9 &= -2 - 9 && \text{Subtract 9 from each side.} \\ x &= -11 && \text{Simplify each side.} \end{aligned}$$

Check that -11 satisfies the original equation by replacing x by -11:

$$\begin{aligned} 9 + x &= -2 && \text{Original equation} \\ 9 + (-11) &= -2 && \text{Replace } x \text{ by } -11. \end{aligned}$$

Since $9 + (-11) = -2$ is correct, $\{-11\}$ is the solution set to the equation.

Now do Exercises 17–26

Teaching Tip Remind students that -9 is the additive inverse of 9 and that we will be using the properties from Chapter 1 in this chapter.

Our goal in solving equations is to isolate the variable. In Examples 1 and 2, the variable was isolated on the left side of the equation. In Example 3, we isolate the variable on the right side of the equation.

EXAMPLE 3

Isolating the variable on the right side

Solve $\frac{1}{2} = -\frac{1}{4} + y$.

Solution

We can remove $-\frac{1}{4}$ from the right side by adding $\frac{1}{4}$ to both sides of the equation:

$$\frac{1}{2} = -\frac{1}{4} + y$$

$$\frac{1}{2} + \frac{1}{4} = -\frac{1}{4} + y + \frac{1}{4} \quad \text{Add } \tfrac{1}{4} \text{ to each side.}$$

$$\frac{3}{4} = y \quad \text{Simplify each side.}$$

Check that $\frac{3}{4}$ satisfies the original equation by replacing y by $\frac{3}{4}$:

$$\frac{1}{2} = -\frac{1}{4} + y \quad \text{Original equation}$$

$$\frac{1}{2} = -\frac{1}{4} + \frac{3}{4} \quad \text{Replace } y \text{ by } \tfrac{3}{4}.$$

$$\frac{1}{2} = \frac{2}{4} \quad \text{Simplify.}$$

Since $\frac{1}{2} = \frac{2}{4}$ is correct, $\left\{\frac{3}{4}\right\}$ is the solution set to the equation.

Now do Exercises 27–34

Study Tip

Don't simply work exercises to get answers. Keep reminding yourself of what it is that you are doing. Look for the big picture. What properties are you using? What does a solution mean? Is it reasonable? Does it check?

The Multiplication Property of Equality

To isolate a variable that is involved in a product or a quotient, we need the multiplication property of equality.

The Multiplication Property of Equality

Multiplying both sides of an equation by the same nonzero number does not change the solution to the equation. In symbols, if $a = b$ and $c \neq 0$, then

$$ac = bc.$$

We specified that $c \neq 0$ in the multiplication property of equality because multiplying by 0 can change the solution to an equation. For example, $x = 4$ is satisfied only by 4, but $0 \cdot x = 0 \cdot 4$ is true for any real number x.

In Example 4 we use the multiplication property of equality to solve an equation.

EXAMPLE 4

Multiplying both sides by the same number

Solve $\frac{z}{2} = 6$.

Teaching Tip Point out how we are using the multiplicative inverse and multiplicative identity properties here.

Solution

We isolate the variable z by multiplying each side of the equation by 2.

$$\frac{z}{2} = 6 \quad \text{Original equation}$$

$$2 \cdot \frac{z}{2} = 2 \cdot 6 \quad \text{Multiply each side by 2.}$$

$$1z = 12 \quad \text{Because } 2 \cdot \tfrac{z}{2} = 2 \cdot \tfrac{1}{2}z = 1z$$

$$z = 12 \quad \text{Multiplicative identity}$$

Because $\frac{12}{2} = 6$, $\{12\}$ is the solution set to the equation.

Now do Exercises 35–42

Because dividing by a number is the same as multiplying by its reciprocal, the multiplication property of equality allows us to divide each side of the equation by any nonzero number.

EXAMPLE 5

Dividing both sides by the same number

Solve $-5w = 30$.

Teaching Tip Ask the students to solve this equation by multiplying each side by $-\frac{1}{5}$.

Solution

Since w is multiplied by -5, we can isolate w by multiplying by $-\frac{1}{5}$ or by dividing each side by -5:

$$-5w = 30 \quad \text{Original equation}$$

$$\frac{-5w}{-5} = \frac{30}{-5} \quad \text{Divide each side by } -5.$$

$$1 \cdot w = -6 \quad \text{Because } \tfrac{-5}{-5} = 1$$

$$w = -6 \quad \text{Multiplicative identity}$$

Because $-5(-6) = 30$, $\{-6\}$ is the solution set to the equation.

Now do Exercises 43–52

In Example 6, the coefficient of the variable is a fraction. We could divide each side by the coefficient as we did in Example 5, but it is easier to multiply each side by the reciprocal of the coefficient.

EXAMPLE 6

Multiplying by the reciprocal

Solve $\frac{4}{5}p = 40$.

Solution

Multiply each side by $\frac{5}{4}$, the reciprocal of $\frac{4}{5}$, to isolate p on the left side.

$$\frac{4}{5}p = 40$$

$$\frac{5}{4} \cdot \frac{4}{5}p = \frac{5}{4} \cdot 40 \quad \text{Multiply each side by } \tfrac{5}{4}.$$

$$1 \cdot p = 50 \quad \text{Multiplicative inverses}$$

$$p = 50 \quad \text{Multiplicative identity}$$

Because $\frac{4}{5} \cdot 50 = 40$, we can be sure that the solution set is $\{50\}$.

Now do Exercises 53–60

Helpful Hint

You could solve this equation by multiplying each side by 5 to get $4p = 200$, and then dividing each side by 4 to get $p = 50$.

If the coefficient of the variable is an integer, we usually divide each side by that integer, as we did in solving $-5w = 30$ in Example 5. Of course we could also solve that equation by multiplying each side by $-\frac{1}{5}$. If the coefficient of the variable is a fraction, we usually multiply each side by the reciprocal of the fraction as we did in solving $\frac{4}{5}p = 40$ in Example 6. Of course we could also solve that equation by dividing each side by $\frac{4}{5}$. If $-x$ appears in an equation, we can multiply by -1 to get x or divide by -1 to get x, because $-1(-x) = x$ and $\frac{-x}{-1} = x$.

EXAMPLE 7

Multiplying by −1

Solve $-h = 12$.

Solution

Multiply each side by -1 to get h on the left side.

$$-h = 12$$

$$-1(-h) = -1 \cdot 12$$

$$h = -12$$

Since $-(-12) = 12$, the solution set is $\{-12\}$.

Now do Exercises 61–68

Variables on Both Sides

In Example 8, the variable occurs on both sides of the equation. Because the variable represents a real number, we can still isolate the variable by using the addition property of equality. Note that it does not matter whether the variable ends up on the right side or the left side.

EXAMPLE 8

Subtracting an algebraic expression from both sides

Solve $-9 + 6y = 7y$.

Helpful Hint

It does not matter whether the variable ends up on the left or right side of the equation. Whether we get $y = -9$ or $-9 = y$ we can still conclude that the solution is -9.

Solution

The expression $6y$ can be removed from the left side of the equation by subtracting $6y$ from both sides.

$$-9 + 6y = 7y$$
$$-9 + 6y - 6y = 7y - 6y \quad \text{Subtract } 6y \text{ from each side.}$$
$$-9 = y \quad \text{Simplify each side.}$$

Check by replacing y by -9 in the original equation:

$$-9 + 6(-9) = 7(-9)$$
$$-63 = -63$$

The solution set to the equation is $\{-9\}$.

Now do Exercises 69–76

Applications

In Example 9, we use the multiplication property of equality in an applied situation.

EXAMPLE 9

Comparing populations

In the 2000 census, Georgia had $\frac{2}{3}$ as many people as Illinois (U.S. Bureau of Census, www.census.gov). If the population of Georgia was 8 million, then what was the population of Illinois?

Teaching Tip We are doing a few simple word problems here to build student confidence with word problems.

Solution

If p represents the population of Illinois, then $\frac{2}{3}p$ represents the population of Georgia. Since the population of Georgia was 8 million we can write the equation $\frac{2}{3}p = 8$. To find p, solve the equation:

$$\frac{2}{3}p = 8$$
$$\frac{3}{2} \cdot \frac{2}{3}p = \frac{3}{2} \cdot 8 \quad \text{Multiply each side by } \tfrac{3}{2}.$$
$$p = 12 \quad \text{Simplify.}$$

So the population of Illinois was 12 million in 2000.

Now do Exercises 97–100

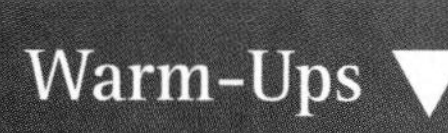

Warm-Ups ▼

True or false? Explain your answer.

1. The solution to $x - 5 = 5$ is 10. True
2. The equation $\frac{x}{2} = 4$ is equivalent to the equation $x = 8$. True
3. To solve $\frac{3}{4}y = 12$, we should multiply each side by $\frac{3}{4}$. False
4. The equation $\frac{x}{7} = 4$ is equivalent to $\frac{1}{7}x = 4$. True
5. Multiplying each side of an equation by any real number will result in an equation that is equivalent to the original equation. False
6. To isolate t in $2t = 7 + t$, subtract t from each side. True
7. To solve $\frac{2r}{3} = 30$, we should multiply each side by $\frac{3}{2}$. True
8. Adding any real number to both sides of an equation will result in an equation that is equivalent to the original equation. True
9. The equation $5x = 0$ is equivalent to $x = 0$. True
10. The solution to $2x - 3 = x + 1$ is 4. True

2.1 Exercises

Boost your GRADE at mathzone.com!

MathZone
- Practice Problems
- Net Tutor
- Self-Tests
- e-Professors
- Videos

Reading and Writing *After reading this section, write out the answers to these questions. Use complete sentences.*

1. What does the addition property of equality say?
The addition property of equality says that adding the same number to each side of an equation does not change the solution to the equation.

2. What are equivalent equations?
Equivalent equations are equations that have the same solution set.

3. What is the multiplication property of equality?
The multiplication property of equality says that multiplying both sides of an equation by the same nonzero number does not change the solution to the equation.

4. What is a linear equation in one variable?
A linear equation in one variable is an equation of the form $ax + b = 0$ where $a \neq 0$.

5. How can you tell if your solution to an equation is correct?
Replace the variable in the equation with your solution. If the resulting statement is correct, then the solution is correct.

6. To obtain an equivalent equation, what are you not allowed to do to both sides of the equation?
In solving equations, you are not allowed to multiply or divide both sides by 0.

Solve each equation. Show your work and check your answer. See Example 1.

7. $x - 6 = -5$ $\{1\}$

8. $x - 7 = -2$ $\{5\}$

9. $-13 + x = -4$ $\{9\}$

10. $-8 + x = -12$ $\{-4\}$

11. $y - \frac{1}{2} = \frac{1}{2}$ $\{1\}$

12. $y - \frac{1}{4} = \frac{1}{2}$ $\left\{\frac{3}{4}\right\}$

13. $w - \frac{1}{3} = \frac{1}{3}$ $\left\{\frac{2}{3}\right\}$

14. $w - \frac{1}{3} = \frac{1}{2}$ $\left\{\frac{5}{6}\right\}$

15. $a - 0.2 = -0.08$ $\{0.12\}$

16. $b - 1 = -0.03$ $\{0.97\}$

Solve each equation. Show your work and check your answer. See Example 2.

17. $x + 3 = -6$ $\{-9\}$

18. $x + 4 = -3$ $\{-7\}$

19. $12 + x = -7$ $\{-19\}$

20. $19 + x = -11$ $\{-30\}$

21. $t + \frac{1}{2} = \frac{3}{4}$ $\left\{\frac{1}{4}\right\}$

22. $t + \frac{1}{3} = 1$ $\left\{\frac{2}{3}\right\}$

23. $\frac{1}{19} + m = \frac{1}{19}$ $\{0\}$

24. $\frac{1}{3} + n = \frac{1}{2}$ $\left\{\frac{1}{6}\right\}$

25. $a + 0.05 = 6$ $\{5.95\}$

26. $b + 4 = -0.7$ $\{-4.7\}$

Solve each equation. Show your work and check your answer. See Example 3.

27. $2 = x + 7$ $\{-5\}$
28. $3 = x + 5$ $\{-2\}$
29. $-13 = y - 9$ $\{-4\}$
30. $-14 = z - 12$ $\{-2\}$
31. $0.5 = -2.5 + x$ $\{3\}$
32. $0.6 = -1.2 + x$ $\{1.8\}$
33. $\frac{1}{8} = -\frac{1}{8} + r$ $\left\{\frac{1}{4}\right\}$
34. $\frac{1}{6} = -\frac{1}{6} + h$ $\left\{\frac{1}{3}\right\}$

Solve each equation. Show your work and check your answer. See Example 4.

35. $\frac{x}{2} = -4$ $\{-8\}$
36. $\frac{x}{3} = -6$ $\{-18\}$
37. $0.03 = \frac{y}{60}$ $\{1.8\}$
38. $0.05 = \frac{y}{80}$ $\{4\}$
39. $\frac{a}{2} = \frac{1}{3}$ $\left\{\frac{2}{3}\right\}$
40. $\frac{b}{2} = \frac{1}{5}$ $\left\{\frac{2}{5}\right\}$
41. $\frac{1}{6} = \frac{c}{3}$ $\left\{\frac{1}{2}\right\}$
42. $\frac{1}{12} = \frac{d}{3}$ $\left\{\frac{1}{4}\right\}$

Solve each equation. Show your work and check your answer. See Example 5.

43. $-3x = 15$ $\{-5\}$
44. $-5x = -20$ $\{4\}$
45. $20 = 4y$ $\{5\}$
46. $18 = -3a$ $\{-6\}$
47. $2w = 2.5$ $\{1.25\}$
48. $-2x = -5.6$ $\{2.8\}$
49. $5 = 20x$ $\left\{\frac{1}{4}\right\}$
50. $-3 = 27d$ $\left\{-\frac{1}{9}\right\}$
51. $5x = \frac{3}{4}$ $\left\{\frac{3}{20}\right\}$
52. $3x = -\frac{2}{3}$ $\left\{-\frac{2}{9}\right\}$

Solve each equation. Show your work and check your answer. See Example 6.

53. $\frac{3}{2}x = -3$ $\{-2\}$
54. $\frac{2}{3}x = -8$ $\{-12\}$
55. $90 = \frac{3y}{4}$ $\{120\}$
56. $14 = \frac{7y}{8}$ $\{16\}$
57. $-\frac{3}{5}w = -\frac{1}{3}$ $\left\{\frac{5}{9}\right\}$
58. $-\frac{5}{2}t = -\frac{3}{5}$ $\left\{\frac{6}{25}\right\}$
59. $\frac{2}{3} = -\frac{4x}{3}$ $\left\{-\frac{1}{2}\right\}$
60. $\frac{1}{14} = -\frac{6p}{7}$ $\left\{-\frac{1}{12}\right\}$

Solve each equation. Show your work and check your answer. See Example 7.

61. $-x = 8$ $\{-8\}$
62. $-x = 4$ $\{-4\}$
63. $-y = -\frac{1}{3}$ $\left\{\frac{1}{3}\right\}$
64. $-y = -\frac{7}{8}$ $\left\{\frac{7}{8}\right\}$
65. $3.4 = -z$ $\{-3.4\}$
66. $4.9 = -t$ $\{-4.9\}$
67. $-k = -99$ $\{99\}$
68. $-m = -17$ $\{17\}$

Solve each equation. Show your work and check your answer. See Example 8.

69. $4x = 3x - 7$ $\{-7\}$
70. $3x = 2x + 9$ $\{9\}$
71. $9 - 6y = -5y$ $\{9\}$
72. $12 - 18w = -17w$ $\{12\}$
73. $-6x = 8 - 7x$ $\{8\}$
74. $-3x = -6 - 4x$ $\{-6\}$
75. $\frac{1}{2}c = 5 - \frac{1}{2}c$ $\{5\}$
76. $-\frac{1}{2}h = 13 - \frac{3}{2}h$ $\{13\}$

Use the appropriate property of equality to solve each equation.

77. $12 = x + 17$ $\{-5\}$
78. $-3 = x + 6$ $\{-9\}$
79. $\frac{3}{4}y = -6$ $\{-8\}$
80. $\frac{5}{9}z = -10$ $\{-18\}$
81. $-3.2 + x = -1.2$ $\{2\}$
82. $t - 3.8 = -2.9$ $\{0.9\}$
83. $2a = \frac{1}{3}$ $\left\{\frac{1}{6}\right\}$
84. $-3w = \frac{1}{2}$ $\left\{-\frac{1}{6}\right\}$
85. $-9m = 3$ $\left\{-\frac{1}{3}\right\}$
86. $-4h = -2$ $\left\{\frac{1}{2}\right\}$
87. $-b = -44$ $\{44\}$
88. $-r = 55$ $\{-55\}$
89. $\frac{2}{3}x = \frac{1}{2}$ $\left\{\frac{3}{4}\right\}$
90. $\frac{3}{4}x = \frac{1}{3}$ $\left\{\frac{4}{9}\right\}$
91. $-5x = 7 - 6x$ $\{7\}$
92. $-\frac{1}{2} + 3y = 4y$ $\left\{-\frac{1}{2}\right\}$
93. $\frac{5a}{7} = -10$ $\{-14\}$
94. $\frac{7r}{12} = -14$ $\{-24\}$
95. $\frac{1}{2}v = -\frac{1}{2}v + \frac{3}{8}$ $\left\{\frac{3}{8}\right\}$
96. $\frac{1}{3}s + \frac{7}{9} = \frac{4}{3}s$ $\left\{\frac{7}{9}\right\}$

Solve each problem by writing and solving an equation. See Example 9.

97. ***Births to teenagers.*** In 2000 there were 48.5 births per 1000 females 15 to 19 years of age (National Center for Health Statistics, www.cdc.gov/nchs). This birth rate is $\frac{4}{5}$ of the birth rate for teenagers in 1991.

a) Write an equation and solve it to find the birth rate for teenagers in 1991.
$\frac{4}{5}x = 48.5$, 60.6 births per 1000 females

b) Use the accompanying graph to estimate the birth rate to teenagers in 1996. 54 births per 1000 females

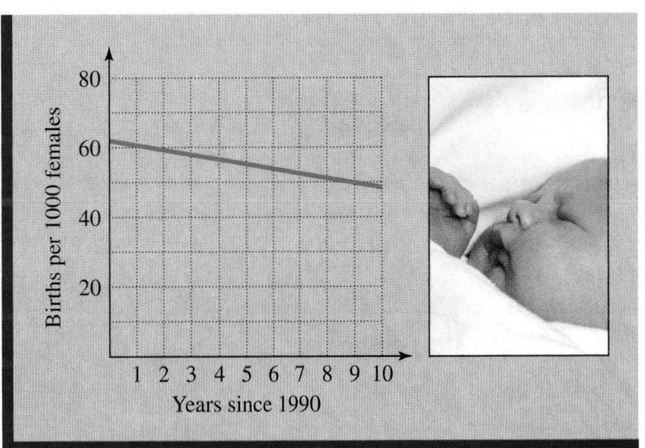

Figure for Exercise 97

98. ***World grain demand.*** Freeport McMoRan projects that in 2010 world grain supply will be 1.8 trillion metric tons and the supply will be only $\frac{3}{4}$ of world grain demand. What will world grain demand be in 2010? 2.4 trillion metric tons

99. ***Advancers and decliners.*** On Thursday, $\frac{2}{3}$ of the stocks traded on the New York Stock Exchange advanced in price. If 1918 stocks advanced, then how many stocks were traded on that day? 2877 stocks

100. ***Births in the United States.*** In 2000, one-third of all births in the United States were to unmarried women (National Center for Health Statistics, www.cdc.gov/nchs). If there were 1,352,938 births to unmarried women, then how many births were there in 2000? 4,058,814

Photo for Exercise 98

2.2 Solving General Linear Equations

In this Section

- **Equations of the Form $ax + b = 0$**
- **Equations of the Form $ax + b = cx + d$**
- **Equations with Parentheses**
- **Applications**

All of the equations that we solved in Section 2.1 required only a single application of a property of equality. In this section you will solve equations that require more than one application of a property of equality.

Equations of the Form $ax + b = 0$

To solve an equation of the form $ax + b = 0$ we might need to apply both the addition property of equality and the multiplication property of equality.

EXAMPLE 1

Using the addition and multiplication properties of equality

Solve $3r - 5 = 0$.

Solution

To isolate r, first add 5 to each side, then divide each side by 3.

$$3r - 5 = 0 \quad \text{Original equation}$$
$$3r - 5 + 5 = 0 + 5 \quad \text{Add 5 to each side.}$$
$$3r = 5 \quad \text{Combine like terms.}$$
$$\frac{3r}{3} = \frac{5}{3} \quad \text{Divide each side by 3.}$$
$$r = \frac{5}{3} \quad \text{Simplify.}$$

Checking $\frac{5}{3}$ in the original equation gives

$$3 \cdot \frac{5}{3} - 5 = 5 - 5 = 0.$$

So $\left\{\frac{5}{3}\right\}$ is the solution set to the equation.

Now do Exercises 5–12

Helpful Hint

If we divide each side by 3 first, we must divide each term on the left side by 3 to get $r - \frac{5}{3} = 0$. Then add $\frac{5}{3}$ to each side to get $r = \frac{5}{3}$. Although we get the correct answer, we usually save division to the last step so that fractions do not appear until necessary.

CAUTION In solving $ax + b = 0$ we usually use the addition property of equality first and the multiplication property last. Note that this is the reverse of the order of operations (multiplication before addition), because we are undoing the operations that are done in the expression $ax + b$.

EXAMPLE 2

Using the addition and multiplication properties of equality

Solve $-\frac{2}{3}x + 8 = 0$.

Teaching Tip Remind students that being neat and organized will help eliminate errors.

Solution

To isolate x, first subtract 8 from each side, then multiply each side by $-\frac{3}{2}$.

$$-\frac{2}{3}x + 8 = 0 \quad \text{Original equation}$$

$$-\frac{2}{3}x + 8 - 8 = 0 - 8 \quad \text{Subtract 8 from each side.}$$

$$-\frac{2}{3}x = -8 \quad \text{Combine like terms.}$$

$$-\frac{3}{2}\left(-\frac{2}{3}x\right) = -\frac{3}{2}(-8) \quad \text{Multiply each side by } -\tfrac{3}{2}.$$

$$x = 12 \quad \text{Simplify.}$$

Checking 12 in the original equation gives

$$-\frac{2}{3}(12) + 8 = -8 + 8 = 0.$$

So $\{12\}$ is the solution set to the equation.

Now do Exercises 13–20

Equations of the Form $ax + b = cx + d$

In solving equations our goal is to isolate the variable. We use the addition property of equality to eliminate unwanted terms. Note that it does not matter whether the variable ends up on the right or left side. For some equations we will perform fewer steps if we isolate the variable on the right side.

EXAMPLE 3

Isolating the variable on the right side

Solve $3w - 8 = 7w$.

Study Tip

Talk to your classmates. Discuss new terms and ideas. How does this lesson fit in with the last lesson? Form a study group. Does your college have a learning lab where you can study together?

Solution

To eliminate the $3w$ from the left side, we can subtract $3w$ from both sides.

$$3w - 8 = 7w \quad \text{Original equation}$$

$$3w - 8 - 3w = 7w - 3w \quad \text{Subtract } 3w \text{ from each side.}$$

$$-8 = 4w \quad \text{Simplify each side.}$$

$$-\frac{8}{4} = \frac{4w}{4} \quad \text{Divide each side by 4.}$$

$$-2 = w \quad \text{Simplify.}$$

To check, replace w with -2 in the original equation:

$$3w - 8 = 7w \quad \text{Original equation}$$
$$3(-2) - 8 = 7(-2)$$
$$-14 = -14$$

Since -2 satisfies the original equation, the solution set is $\{-2\}$.

Now do Exercises 21–28

You should solve the equation in Example 3 by isolating the variable on the left side to see that it takes more steps. In Example 4, it is simplest to isolate the variable on the left side.

EXAMPLE 4

Teaching Tip Point out that to isolate b we undo the operations on the left side in reverse of the order of operations. You put on your shirt and coat, but you take off your coat and then your shirt.

Isolating the variable on the left side

Solve $\frac{1}{2}b - 8 = 12$.

Solution

To eliminate the 8 from the left side, we add 8 to each side.

$$\frac{1}{2}b - 8 = 12 \quad \text{Original equation}$$
$$\frac{1}{2}b - 8 + 8 = 12 + 8 \quad \text{Add 8 to each side.}$$
$$\frac{1}{2}b = 20 \quad \text{Simplify each side.}$$
$$2 \cdot \frac{1}{2}b = 2 \cdot 20 \quad \text{Multiply each side by 2.}$$
$$b = 40 \quad \text{Simplify.}$$

To check, replace b with 40 in the original equation:

$$\frac{1}{2}b - 8 = 12 \quad \text{Original equation}$$
$$\frac{1}{2}(40) - 8 = 12$$
$$12 = 12$$

Since 40 satisfies the original equation, the solution set is $\{40\}$.

Now do Exercises 29–36

In Example 5 both sides of the equation contain two terms.

EXAMPLE 5

Solving $ax + b = cx + d$

Solve $2m - 4 = 4m - 10$.

Solution

First, we decide to isolate the variable on the left side. So we must eliminate the 4 from the left side and eliminate $4m$ from the right side:

$$
\begin{aligned}
2m - 4 &= 4m - 10 && \\
2m - 4 + 4 &= 4m - 10 + 4 && \text{Add 4 to each side.} \\
2m &= 4m - 6 && \text{Simplify each side.} \\
2m - 4m &= 4m - 6 - 4m && \text{Subtract } 4m \text{ from each side.} \\
-2m &= -6 && \text{Simplify each side.} \\
\frac{-2m}{-2} &= \frac{-6}{-2} && \text{Divide each side by } -2. \\
m &= 3 && \text{Simplify.}
\end{aligned}
$$

To check, replace m by 3 in the original equation:

$$
\begin{aligned}
2m - 4 &= 4m - 10 && \text{Original equation} \\
2 \cdot 3 - 4 &= 4 \cdot 3 - 10 && \\
2 &= 2 &&
\end{aligned}
$$

Since 3 satisfies the original equation, the solution set is $\{3\}$.

Now do Exercises 37–44

Study Tip

Take good notes. Note taking helps you to concentrate in class and provides a source for review. Rewrite your notes after class and fill in anything that is missing. Practice solving the problems that were demonstrated in class.

Equations with Parentheses

Equations that contain parentheses or like terms on the same side should be simplified as much as possible before applying any properties of equality.

EXAMPLE 6

Simplifying before using properties of equality

Solve $2(q - 3) + 5q = 8(q - 1)$.

Solution

First remove parentheses and combine like terms on each side of the equation.

$$
\begin{aligned}
2(q - 3) + 5q &= 8(q - 1) && \text{Original equation} \\
2q - 6 + 5q &= 8q - 8 && \text{Distributive property} \\
7q - 6 &= 8q - 8 && \text{Combine like terms.} \\
7q - 6 + 6 &= 8q - 8 + 6 && \text{Add 6 to each side.} \\
7q &= 8q - 2 && \text{Combine like terms.} \\
7q - 8q &= 8q - 2 - 8q && \text{Subtract } 8q \text{ from each side.} \\
-q &= -2 && \\
-1(-q) &= -1(-2) && \text{Multiply each side by } -1. \\
q &= 2 && \text{Simplify.}
\end{aligned}
$$

Calculator Close-Up

You can check an equation by entering the equation on the home screen as shown here. The equal sign is in the TEST menu.

When you press ENTER, the calculator returns the number 1 if the equation is true or 0 if the equation is false. Since the calculator shows a 1, we can be sure that 2 is the solution.

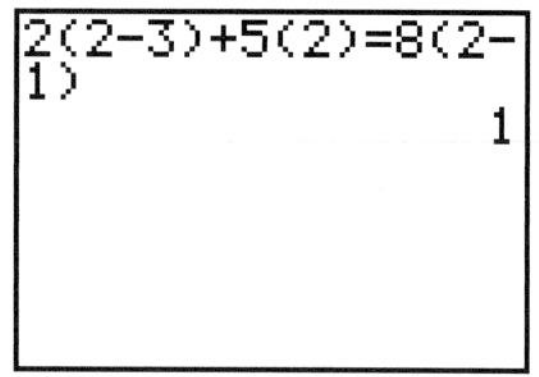

To check, we replace q by 2 in the original equation and simplify:

$$2(q - 3) + 5q = 8(q - 1) \quad \text{Original equation}$$
$$2(2 - 3) + 5(2) = 8(2 - 1) \quad \text{Replace } q \text{ by 2.}$$
$$2(-1) + 10 = 8(1)$$
$$8 = 8$$

Because both sides have the same value, the solution set is $\{2\}$.

Now do Exercises 45–52

Linear equations can vary greatly in appearance, but there is a strategy that you can use for solving any of them. The following strategy summarizes the techniques that we have been using in the examples. Keep it in mind when you are solving linear equations.

Strategy for Solving Equations

1. Remove parentheses by using the distributive property and then combine like terms to simplify each side as much as possible.
2. Use the addition property of equality to get like terms from opposite sides onto the same side so that they may be combined.
3. The multiplication property of equality is generally used last.
4. Check that the solution satisfies the original equation.

Applications

Linear equations occur in business situations where there is a fixed cost and a per item cost. A mail order company might charge \$3 plus \$2 per CD for shipping and handling. A lawyer might charge \$300 plus \$65 per hour for handling your lawsuit. AT&T might charge 5 cents per minute plus \$2.95 for long distance calls. Example 7 illustrates the kind of problem that can be solved in this situation.

EXAMPLE 7

Long distance charges

With AT&T's One Rate plan you are charged 5 cents per minute plus \$2.95 for long distance service for one month. If a long distance bill is \$4.80, then what is the number of minutes used?

Teaching Tip We are again doing a few simple word problems to build student confidence.

Solution

Let x represent the number of minutes of calls in the month. At \$0.05 per minute, the cost for x minutes is the product $0.05x$ dollars. Since there is a fixed cost of \$2.95, an expression for the total cost is $0.05x + 2.95$ dollars. Since the total cost is \$4.80, we have $0.05x + 2.95 = 4.80$. Solve this equation to find x.

$$
\begin{aligned}
0.05x + 2.95 &= 4.80 \\
0.05x + 2.95 - 2.95 &= 4.80 - 2.95 && \text{Subtract 2.95 from each side.} \\
0.05x &= 1.85 && \text{Simplify.} \\
\frac{0.05x}{0.05} &= \frac{1.85}{0.05} && \text{Divide each side by 0.05.} \\
x &= 37 && \text{Simplify.}
\end{aligned}
$$

So the bill is for 37 minutes.

Now do Exercises 93–100

Warm-Ups ▼

True or false? Explain your answer.

1. The solution to $4x - 3 = 3x$ is 3. True
2. The equation $2x + 7 = 8$ is equivalent to $2x = 1$. True
3. To solve $3x - 5 = 8x + 7$, you should add 5 to each side and subtract $8x$ from each side. True
4. To solve $5 - 4x = 9 + 7x$, you should subtract 9 from each side and then subtract $7x$ from each side. False
5. Multiplying each side of an equation by the same nonzero real number will result in an equation that is equivalent to the original equation. True
6. To isolate y in $3y - 7 = 6$, divide each side by 3 and then add 7 to each side. False
7. To solve $\frac{3w}{4} = 300$, we should multiply each side by $\frac{4}{3}$. True
8. The equation $-n = 9$ is equivalent to $n = -9$. True
9. The equation $-y = -7$ is equivalent to $y = 7$. True
10. The solution to $7x = 5x$ is 0. True

2.2 Exercises

Boost your GRADE at mathzone.com!

MathZone

▶ Practice Problems ▶ Net Tutor
▶ Self-Tests ▶ e-Professors
▶ Videos

Reading and Writing *After reading this section, write out the answers to these questions. Use complete sentences.*

1. What properties of equality do you apply to solve $ax + b = 0$?
   We can solve $ax + b = 0$ with the addition property and the multiplication property of equality.
2. Which property of equality is usually applied last?
   The multiplication property of equality is usually applied last.
3. What property of equality is used to solve $-x = 8$?
   Use the multiplication property of equality to solve $-x = 8$.
4. What is usually the first step in solving a linear equation involving parentheses?
   If an equation involves parentheses, then we first remove the parentheses.

Solve each equation. Show your work and check your answer. See Examples 1 and 2.

5. $5a - 10 = 0$ $\{2\}$
6. $8y + 24 = 0$ $\{-3\}$
7. $-3y - 6 = 0$ $\{-2\}$
8. $-9w - 54 = 0$ $\{-6\}$

9. $3x - 2 = 0$ $\left\{\frac{2}{3}\right\}$

10. $5y + 1 = 0$ $\left\{-\frac{1}{5}\right\}$

11. $2p + 5 = 0$ $\left\{-\frac{5}{2}\right\}$

12. $9z - 8 = 0$ $\left\{\frac{8}{9}\right\}$

13. $\frac{1}{2}w - 3 = 0$ $\{6\}$

14. $\frac{3}{8}t + 6 = 0$ $\{-16\}$

15. $-\frac{2}{3}x + 8 = 0$ $\{12\}$

16. $-\frac{1}{7}z - 5 = 0$ $\{-35\}$

17. $-m + \frac{1}{2} = 0$ $\left\{\frac{1}{2}\right\}$

18. $-y - \frac{3}{4} = 0$ $\left\{-\frac{3}{4}\right\}$

19. $3p + \frac{1}{2} = 0$ $\left\{-\frac{1}{6}\right\}$

20. $9z - \frac{1}{4} = 0$ $\left\{\frac{1}{36}\right\}$

Solve each equation. See Examples 3 and 4.

21. $6x - 8 = 4x$ $\{4\}$

22. $9y + 14 = 2y$ $\{-2\}$

23. $4z = 5 - 2z$ $\left\{\frac{5}{6}\right\}$

24. $3t = t - 3$ $\left\{-\frac{3}{2}\right\}$

25. $4a - 9 = 7$ $\{4\}$

26. $7r + 5 = 47$ $\{6\}$

27. $9 = -6 - 3b$ $\{-5\}$

28. $13 = 3 - 10s$ $\{-1\}$

29. $\frac{1}{2}w - 4 = 13$ $\{34\}$

30. $\frac{1}{3}q + 13 = -5$ $\{-54\}$

31. $6 - \frac{1}{3}d = \frac{1}{3}d$ $\{9\}$

32. $9 - \frac{1}{2}a = \frac{1}{4}a$ $\{12\}$

33. $2w - 0.4 = 2$ $\{1.2\}$

34. $10h - 1.3 = 6$ $\{0.73\}$

35. $x = 3.3 - 0.1x$ $\{3\}$

36. $y = 2.4 - 0.2y$ $\{2\}$

Solve each equation. See Example 5.

37. $3x - 3 = x + 5$ $\{4\}$

38. $9y - 1 = 6y + 5$ $\{2\}$

39. $4 - 7d = 13 - 4d$ $\{-3\}$

40. $y - 9 = 12 - 6y$ $\{3\}$

41. $c + \frac{1}{2} = 3c - \frac{1}{2}$ $\left\{\frac{1}{2}\right\}$

42. $x - \frac{1}{4} = \frac{1}{2} - x$ $\left\{\frac{3}{8}\right\}$

43. $\frac{2}{3}a - 5 = \frac{1}{3}a + 5$ $\{30\}$

44. $\frac{1}{2}t - 3 = \frac{1}{4}t - 9$ $\{-24\}$

Solve each equation. See Example 6.

45. $5(a - 1) + 3 = 28$ $\{6\}$

46. $2(w + 4) - 1 = 1$ $\{-3\}$

47. $2 - 3(q - 1) = 10 - (q + 1)$ $\{-2\}$

48. $-2(y - 6) = 3(7 - y) - 5$ $\{4\}$

49. $2(x - 1) + 3x = 6x - 20$ $\{18\}$

50. $3 - (r - 1) = 2(r + 1) - r$ $\{1\}$

51. $2\left(y - \frac{1}{2}\right) = 4\left(y - \frac{1}{4}\right) + y$ $\{0\}$

52. $\frac{1}{2}(4m - 6) = \frac{2}{3}(6m - 9) + 3$ $\{0\}$

Solve each linear equation. Show your work and check your answer.

53. $2x = \frac{1}{3}$ $\left\{\frac{1}{6}\right\}$

54. $3x = \frac{6}{11}$ $\left\{\frac{2}{11}\right\}$

55. $5t = -2 + 4t$ $\{-2\}$

56. $8y = 6 + 7y$ $\{6\}$

57. $3x - 7 = 0$ $\left\{\frac{7}{3}\right\}$

58. $5x + 4 = 0$ $\left\{-\frac{4}{5}\right\}$

59. $-x + 6 = 5$ $\{1\}$

60. $-x - 2 = 9$ $\{-11\}$

61. $-9 - a = -3$ $\{-6\}$

62. $4 - r = 6$ $\{-2\}$

63. $2q + 5 = q - 7$ $\{-12\}$

64. $3z - 6 = 2z - 7$ $\{-1\}$

65. $-3x + 1 = 5 - 2x$ $\{-4\}$

66. $5 - 2x = 6 - x$ $\{-1\}$

67. $-12 - 5x = -4x + 1$ $\{-13\}$

68. $-3x - 4 = -2x + 8$ $\{-12\}$

69. $3x + 0.3 = 2 + 2x$ $\{1.7\}$

70. $2y - 0.05 = y + 1$ $\{1.05\}$

71. $k - 0.6 = 0.2k + 1$ $\{2\}$

72. $2.3h + 6 = 1.8h - 1$ $\{-14\}$

73. $0.2x - 4 = 0.6 - 0.8x$ $\{4.6\}$

74. $0.3x = 1 - 0.7x$ $\{1\}$

75. $-3(k - 6) = 2 - k$ $\{8\}$

76. $-2(h - 5) = 3 - h$ $\{7\}$

77. $2(p + 1) - p = 36$ $\{34\}$

78. $3(q + 1) - q = 23$ $\{10\}$

79. $7 - 3(5 - u) = 5(u - 4)$ $\{6\}$

80. $v - 4(4 - v) = -2(2v - 1)$ $\{2\}$

81. $4(x + 3) = 12$ $\{0\}$

82. $5(x - 3) = -15$ $\{0\}$

83. $\frac{w}{5} - 4 = -6$ $\{-10\}$

84. $\frac{q}{2} + 13 = -22$ $\{-70\}$

85. $\frac{2}{3}y - 5 = 7$ $\{18\}$

86. $\frac{3}{4}u - 9 = -6$ $\{4\}$

87. $4 - \frac{2n}{5} = 12$ $\{-20\}$

88. $9 - \frac{2m}{7} = 19$ $\{-35\}$

89. $-\frac{1}{3}p - \frac{1}{2} = \frac{1}{2}$ $\{-3\}$

90. $-\frac{3}{4}z - \frac{2}{3} = \frac{1}{3}$ $\left\{-\frac{4}{3}\right\}$

91. $3.5x - 23.7 = -38.75$ $\{-4.3\}$

92. $3(x - 0.87) - 2x = 4.98$ $\{7.59\}$

Solve each problem. See Example 7.

93. ***The practice.*** A lawyer charges \$300 plus \$65 per hour for a divorce. If the total charge for Bill's divorce was \$1405, then for what number of hours did the lawyer work on the case? 17 hr

94. ***The plumber.*** Tamika paid \$165 to her plumber for a service call. If her plumber charges \$45 plus \$40 per hour for a service call, then for how many hours did the plumber work? 3 hr

95. ***Celsius temperature.*** If the air temperature in Quebec is 68° Fahrenheit, then the solution to the equation $\frac{9}{5}C + 32 = 68$ gives the Celsius temperature of the air. Find the Celsius temperature. 20°C

96. ***Fahrenheit temperature.*** Water boils at 212°F.

a) Use the accompanying graph to determine the Celsius temperature at which water boils. 100°C

b) Find the Fahrenheit temperature of hot tap water at 70°C by solving the equation

$$70 = \frac{5}{9}(F - 32).\quad 158°\text{F}$$

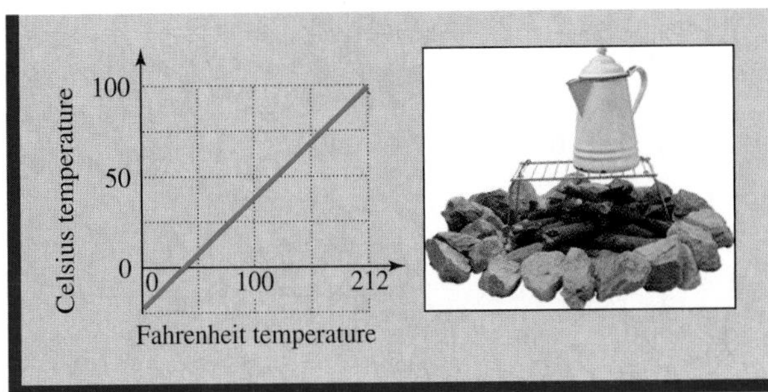

Figure for Exercise 96

97. ***Rectangular patio.*** If a rectangular patio has a length that is 3 feet longer than its width and a perimeter of 42 feet, then the width can be found by solving the equation $2x + 2(x + 3) = 42$. What is the width? 9 ft

98. ***Perimeter of a triangle.*** The perimeter of the triangle shown in the accompanying figure is 12 meters. Determine the values of x, $x + 1$, and $x + 2$ by solving the equation

$$x + (x + 1) + (x + 2) = 12.$$

3 m, 4 m, 5 m

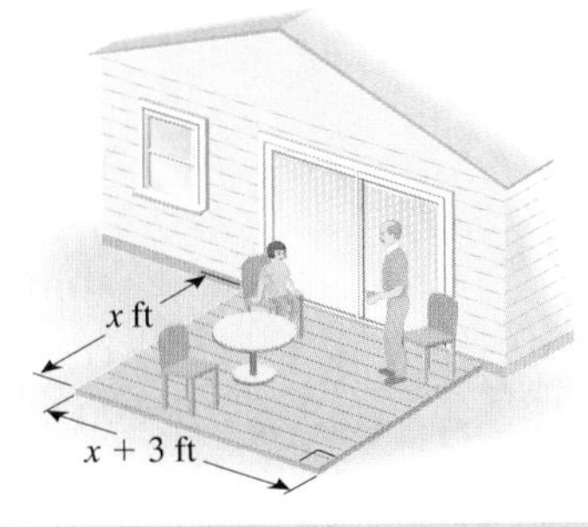

Figure for Exercise 97

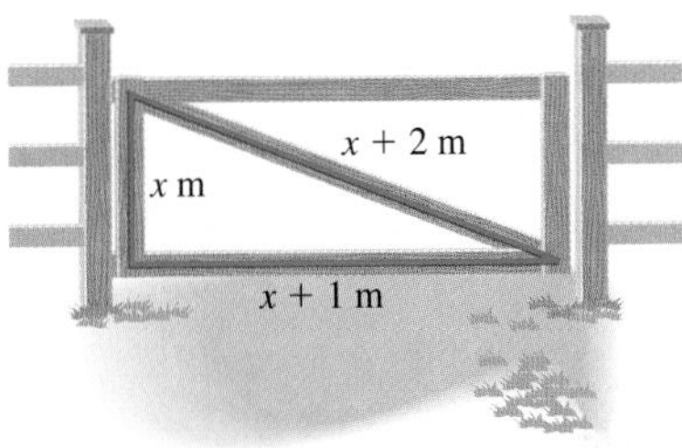

Figure for Exercise 98

99. ***Cost of a car.*** Jane paid 9% sales tax and a $150 title and license fee when she bought her new Saturn for a total of $16,009.50. If x represents the price of the car, then x satisfies $x + 0.09x + 150 = 16{,}009.50$. Find the price of the car by solving the equation. $14,550

100. ***Cost of labor.*** An electrician charged Eunice $29.96 for a service call plus $39.96 per hour for a total of $169.82 for installing her electric dryer. If n represents the number of hours for labor, then n satisfies

$$39.96n + 29.96 = 169.82.$$

Find n by solving this equation. 3.5 hrs

2.3 More Equations

In this Section

- Equations Involving Fractions
- Equations Involving Decimals
- Simplifying the Process
- Identities
- Conditional Equations
- Inconsistent Equations

In this section we will solve more equations of the type that we solved in Sections 2.1 and 2.2. However, some equations in this section will contain fractions or decimal numbers. Some equations will have infinitely many solutions and some will have no solution.

Equations Involving Fractions

We solved some equations involving fractions in Sections 2.1 and 2.2. Here, we will solve equations with fractions by eliminating all fractions in the first step. All of the fractions will be eliminated if we multiply each side by the least common denominator.

EXAMPLE 1

Multiplying by the least common denominator

Solve $\frac{y}{2} - 1 = \frac{y}{3} + 1$.

Solution

The least common denominator (LCD) for the denominators 2 and 3 is 6. Since both 2 and 3 divide into 6 evenly, multiplying each side by 6 will eliminate the fractions:

$$6\left(\frac{y}{2} - 1\right) = 6\left(\frac{y}{3} + 1\right) \quad \text{Multiply each side by 6.}$$

$$6 \cdot \frac{y}{2} - 6 \cdot 1 = 6 \cdot \frac{y}{3} + 6 \cdot 1 \quad \text{Distributive property}$$

$$3y - 6 = 2y + 6 \quad \text{Simplify: } 6 \cdot \tfrac{y}{2} = 3y$$

$$3y = 2y + 12 \quad \text{Add 6 to each side.}$$

$$y = 12 \quad \text{Subtract } 2y \text{ from each side.}$$

Check 12 in the original equation:

$$\frac{12}{2} - 1 = \frac{12}{3} + 1$$

$$5 = 5$$

Since 12 satisfies the original equation, the solution set is {12}.

Now do Exercises 7–22

Helpful Hint

Note that the fractions in Example 1 will be eliminated if you multiply each side of the equation by any number divisible by both 2 and 3. For example, multiplying by 24 yields

$$12y - 24 = 8y + 24$$
$$4y = 48$$
$$y = 12.$$

Equations Involving Decimals

When an equation involves decimal numbers, we can work with the decimal numbers or we can eliminate all of the decimal numbers by multiplying both sides by 10, or 100, or 1000, and so on. Multiplying a decimal number by 10 moves the decimal point one place to the right. Multiplying by 100 moves the decimal point two places to the right, and so on.

EXAMPLE 2

An equation involving decimals

Solve $0.3p + 8.04 = 12.6$.

Solution

The largest number of decimal places appearing in the decimal numbers of the equation is two (in the number 8.04). Therefore we multiply each side of the

Helpful Hint

After you have used one of the properties of equality on each side of an equation, be sure to simplify all expressions as much as possible before using another property of equality. This step is like making sure that all of the injured football players are removed from the field before proceeding to the next play.

equation by 100 because multiplying by 100 moves decimal points two places to the right:

$$
\begin{aligned}
0.3p + 8.04 &= 12.6 && \text{Original equation} \\
100(0.3p + 8.04) &= 100(12.6) && \text{Multiplication property of equality} \\
100(0.3p) + 100(8.04) &= 100(12.6) && \text{Distributive property} \\
30p + 804 &= 1260 \\
30p + 804 - 804 &= 1260 - 804 && \text{Subtract 804 from each side.} \\
30p &= 456 \\
\frac{30p}{30} &= \frac{456}{30} && \text{Divide each side by 30.} \\
p &= 15.2
\end{aligned}
$$

You can use a calculator to check that

$$0.3(15.2) + 8.04 = 12.6.$$

The solution set is $\{15.2\}$.

Now do Exercises 23–32

EXAMPLE 3

Another equation with decimals

Solve $0.5x + 0.4(x + 20) = 13.4$.

Solution

First use the distributive property to remove the parentheses:

$$
\begin{aligned}
0.5x + 0.4(x + 20) &= 13.4 && \text{Original equation} \\
0.5x + 0.4x + 8 &= 13.4 && \text{Distributive property} \\
10(0.5x + 0.4x + 8) &= 10(13.4) && \text{Multiply each side by 10.} \\
5x + 4x + 80 &= 134 && \text{Simplify.} \\
9x + 80 &= 134 && \text{Combine like terms.} \\
9x + 80 - 80 &= 134 - 80 && \text{Subtract 80 from each side.} \\
9x &= 54 && \text{Simplify.} \\
x &= 6 && \text{Divide each side by 9.}
\end{aligned}
$$

Check 6 in the original equation:

$$
\begin{aligned}
0.5(6) + 0.4(6 + 20) &= 13.4 && \text{Replace } x \text{ by 6.} \\
3 + 0.4(26) &= 13.4 \\
3 + 10.4 &= 13.4
\end{aligned}
$$

Since both sides of the equation have the same value, the solution set is $\{6\}$.

Now do Exercises 33–36

Teaching Tip Ask students to solve this equation without multiplying by 10 to eliminate the decimals.

CAUTION If you multiply each side by 10 in Example 3 before using the distributive property, be careful how you handle the terms in parentheses:

$$10 \cdot 0.5x + 10 \cdot 0.4(x + 20) = 10 \cdot 13.4$$
$$5x + 4(x + 20) = 134$$

It is not correct to multiply 0.4 by 10 *and also* to multiply $x + 20$ by 10.

Simplifying the Process

It is very important to develop the skill of solving equations in a systematic way, writing down every step as we have been doing. As you become more skilled at solving equations, you will probably want to simplify the process a bit. One way to simplify the process is by writing only the result of performing an operation on each side. Another way is to isolate the variable on the side where the variable has the larger coefficient, when the variable occurs on both sides. We use these ideas in Example 4 and in future examples in this text.

EXAMPLE 4

Simplifying the process

Solve each equation.

a) $2a - 3 = 0$ **b)** $2k + 5 = 3k + 1$

Study Tip

I hear and I forget; I see and I remember; I do and I understand. There is no substitute for doing exercises, lots of exercises.

Solution

a) Add 3 to each side, then divide each side by 2:

$$2a - 3 = 0$$
$$2a = 3 \quad \text{Add 3 to each side.}$$
$$a = \frac{3}{2} \quad \text{Divide each side by 2.}$$

Check that $\frac{3}{2}$ satisfies the original equation. The solution set is $\left\{\frac{3}{2}\right\}$.

b) For this equation we can get a single k on the right by subtracting $2k$ from each side. (If we subtract $3k$ from each side, we get $-k$, and then we need another step.)

$$2k + 5 = 3k + 1$$
$$5 = k + 1 \quad \text{Subtract } 2k \text{ from each side.}$$
$$4 = k \quad \text{Subtract 1 from each side.}$$

Check that 4 satisfies the original equation. The solution set is $\{4\}$.

Now do Exercises 37–52

Identities

Teaching Tip Ask students to give some examples of identities.

It is easy to find equations that are satisfied by any real number that we choose as a replacement for the variable. For example, the equations

$$x \div 2 = \frac{1}{2}x, \qquad x + x = 2x, \qquad \text{and} \qquad x + 1 = x + 1$$

are satisfied by all real numbers. The equation

$$\frac{5}{x} = \frac{5}{x}$$

is satisfied by any real number except 0 because division by 0 is undefined.

Identity

An equation that is satisfied by every real number for which both sides are defined is called an **identity.**

We cannot recognize that the equation in Example 5 is an identity until we have simplified each side.

EXAMPLE 5

Solving an identity

Solve $7 - 5(x - 6) + 4 = 3 - 2(x - 5) - 3x + 28$.

Solution

We first use the distributive property to remove the parentheses:

$$7 - 5(x - 6) + 4 = 3 - 2(x - 5) - 3x + 28$$
$$7 - 5x + 30 + 4 = 3 - 2x + 10 - 3x + 28$$
$$41 - 5x = 41 - 5x \quad \text{Combine like terms.}$$

This last equation is true for any value of x because the two sides are identical. So the solution set to the original equation is the set of all real numbers or R.

Now do Exercises 53–54

CAUTION If you get an equation in which both sides are identical, as in Example 5, there is no need to continue to simplify the equation. If you do continue, you will eventually get $0 = 0$, from which you can still conclude that the equation is an identity.

Study Tip

Life is a game that holds many rewards for those who compete. Winning is never an accident. To win you must know the rules and have a game plan.

Conditional Equations

The statement $2x + 4 = 10$ is true only on condition that we choose $x = 3$. The equation $x^2 = 4$ is satisfied only if we choose $x = 2$ or $x = -2$. These equations are called conditional equations.

Conditional Equation

A **conditional equation** is an equation that is satisfied by at least one real number but is not an identity.

Every equation that we solved in Sections 2.1 and 2.2 is a conditional equation.

Teaching Tip Ask students for some examples of inconsistent equations.

Inconsistent Equations

It is easy to find equations that are false no matter what number we use to replace the variable. Consider the equation

$$x = x + 1.$$

If we replace x by 3, we get $3 = 3 + 1$, which is false. If we replace x by 4, we get $4 = 4 + 1$, which is also false. Clearly, there is no number that will satisfy $x = x + 1$. Other examples of equations with no solutions include

$$x = x - 2, \qquad x - x = 5, \qquad \text{and} \qquad 0 \cdot x + 6 = 7.$$

Inconsistent Equation

An equation that has no solution is called an **inconsistent equation.**

The solution set to an inconsistent equation has no members. The set with no members is called the **empty set** and it is denoted by the symbol $\emptyset$.

EXAMPLE 6

Solving an inconsistent equation

Solve $2 - 3(x - 4) = 4(x - 7) - 7x$.

Solution

Use the distributive property to remove the parentheses:

$2 - 3(x - 4) = 4(x - 7) - 7x$	The original equation
$2 - 3x + 12 = 4x - 28 - 7x$	Distributive property
$14 - 3x = -28 - 3x$	Combine like terms on each side.
$14 - 3x + 3x = -28 - 3x + 3x$	Add $3x$ to each side.
$14 = -28$	Simplify.

The last equation is not true for any x. So the solution set to the original equation is the empty set, $\emptyset$. The equation is inconsistent.

Now do Exercises 55–72

Keep the following points in mind in solving equations.

Summary: Identities and Inconsistent Equations

1. An equation that is equivalent to an equation in which both sides are identical is an identity. The equation is satisfied by all real numbers for which both sides are defined.
2. An equation that is equivalent to an equation that is always false is inconsistent. The equation has no solution. The solution set is the empty set, $\emptyset$.

Warm-Ups ▼

True or false? Explain your answer.

1. To solve $\frac{1}{2}x - \frac{1}{3} = x + \frac{1}{6}$ multiply each side by 6. True
2. The equation $\frac{1}{2}x - \frac{1}{3} = x + \frac{1}{6}$ is equivalent to $3x - 2 = 6x + 1$. True
3. The equation $0.2x + 0.03x = 8$ is equivalent to $20x + 3x = 8$. False
4. The solution set to $3h + 8 = 0$ is $\left\{\frac{8}{3}\right\}$. False
5. The equation $5a + 3 = 0$ is an inconsistent equation. False
6. The equation $2t = t$ is a conditional equation. True
7. The equation $w - 0.1w = 0.9w$ is an identity. True
8. All real numbers satisfy the equation $1 \div x = \frac{1}{x}$. False
9. The equation $\frac{x}{x} = 1$ is an identity. True
10. The equation $x - x = 99$ has no solution. True

2.3 Exercises

Boost your GRADE at mathzone.com!

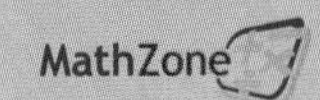

- Practice Problems
- Self-Tests
- Videos
- Net Tutor
- e-Professors

Reading and Writing *After reading this section, write out the answers to these questions. Use complete sentences.*

1. What is the usual first step when solving an equation involving fractions?
   If an equation involves fractions we usually multiply each side by the LCD of all of the fractions.
2. What is a good first step for solving an equation involving decimals?
   If an equation involves decimals we usually multiply each side by a power of 10 to eliminate all decimals.
3. What is an identity?
   An identity is an equation that is satisfied by all numbers for which both sides are defined.
4. What is a conditional equation?
   A conditional equation has at least one solution but is not an identity.
5. What is an inconsistent equation?
   An inconsistent equation has no solutions.
6. What is the solution set to an inconsistent equation?
   The solution set to an inconsistent equation is the empty set, $\varnothing$.

Solve each equation by first eliminating the fractions. See Example 1.

7. $\frac{x}{4} - \frac{3}{10} = 0$ $\left\{\frac{6}{5}\right\}$
8. $\frac{x}{15} + \frac{1}{6} = 0$ $\left\{-\frac{5}{2}\right\}$
9. $3x - \frac{1}{6} = \frac{1}{2}$ $\left\{\frac{2}{9}\right\}$
10. $5x + \frac{1}{2} = \frac{3}{4}$ $\left\{\frac{1}{20}\right\}$
11. $\frac{x}{2} + 3 = x - \frac{1}{2}$ $\{7\}$
12. $13 - \frac{x}{2} = x - \frac{1}{2}$ $\{9\}$
13. $\frac{x}{2} + \frac{x}{3} = 20$ $\{24\}$
14. $\frac{x}{2} - \frac{x}{3} = 5$ $\{30\}$
15. $\frac{w}{2} + \frac{w}{4} = 12$ $\{16\}$
16. $\frac{a}{4} - \frac{a}{2} = -5$ $\{20\}$
17. $\frac{3z}{2} - \frac{2z}{3} = -10$ $\{-12\}$
18. $\frac{3m}{4} + \frac{m}{2} = -5$ $\{-4\}$
19. $\frac{1}{3}p - 5 = \frac{1}{4}p$ $\{60\}$
20. $\frac{1}{2}q - 6 = \frac{1}{5}q$ $\{20\}$
21. $\frac{1}{6}v + 1 = \frac{1}{4}v - 1$ $\{24\}$
22. $\frac{1}{15}k + 5 = \frac{1}{6}k - 10$ $\{150\}$

Solve each equation by first eliminating the decimal numbers. See Examples 2 and 3.

23. $x - 0.2x = 72$ $\{90\}$
24. $x - 0.1x = 63$ $\{70\}$
25. $0.3x + 1.2 = 0.5x$ $\{6\}$
26. $0.4x - 1.6 = 0.6x$ $\{-8\}$
27. $0.02x - 1.56 = 0.8x$ $\{-2\}$
28. $0.6x + 10.4 = 0.08x$ $\{-20\}$
29. $0.1a - 0.3 = 0.2a - 8.3$ $\{80\}$
30. $0.5b + 3.4 = 0.2b + 12.4$ $\{30\}$
31. $0.05r + 0.4r = 27$ $\{60\}$
32. $0.08t + 28.3 = 0.5t - 9.5$ $\{90\}$
33. $0.05y + 0.03(y + 50) = 17.5$ $\{200\}$
34. $0.07y + 0.08(y - 100) = 44.5$ $\{350\}$
35. $0.1x + 0.05(x - 300) = 105$ $\{800\}$
36. $0.2x - 0.05(x - 100) = 35$ $\{200\}$

Solve each equation. If you feel proficient enough, try simplifying the process, as described in Example 4.

37. $2x - 9 = 0$ $\left\{\frac{9}{2}\right\}$
38. $3x + 7 = 0$ $\left\{-\frac{7}{3}\right\}$
39. $-2x + 6 = 0$ $\{3\}$
40. $-3x - 12 = 0$ $\{-4\}$
41. $\frac{z}{5} + 1 = 6$ $\{25\}$
42. $\frac{s}{2} + 2 = 5$ $\{6\}$
43. $\frac{c}{2} - 3 = -4$ $\{-2\}$
44. $\frac{b}{3} - 4 = -7$ $\{-9\}$
45. $3 = t + 6$ $\{-3\}$
46. $-5 = y - 9$ $\{4\}$
47. $5 + 2q = 3q$ $\{5\}$
48. $-4 - 5p = -4p$ $\{-4\}$
49. $8x - 1 = 9 + 9x$ $\{-10\}$
50. $4x - 2 = -8 + 5x$ $\{6\}$
51. $-3x + 1 = -1 - 2x$ $\{2\}$
52. $-6x + 3 = -7 - 5x$ $\{10\}$

Solve each equation. Identify each as a conditional equation, an inconsistent equation, or an identity. See Examples 5 and 6.

53. $x + x = 2x$ All real numbers, identity
54. $2x - x = x$ All real numbers, identity
55. $a - 1 = a + 1$ $\varnothing$, inconsistent
56. $r + 7 = r$ $\varnothing$, inconsistent
57. $3y + 4y = 12y$ $\{0\}$, conditional
58. $9t - 8t = 7$ $\{7\}$, conditional
59. $-4 + 3(w - 1) = w + 2(w - 2) - 1$ $\varnothing$, inconsistent
60. $4 - 5(w + 2) = 2(w - 1) - 7w - 4$ All real numbers, identity
61. $3(m + 1) = 3(m + 3)$ $\varnothing$, inconsistent
62. $5(m - 1) - 6(m + 3) = 4 - m$ $\varnothing$, inconsistent
63. $x + x = 2$ $\{1\}$, conditional
64. $3x - 5 = 0$ $\left\{\frac{5}{3}\right\}$, conditional
65. $2 - 3(5 - x) = 3x$ $\varnothing$, inconsistent
66. $3 - 3(5 - x) = 0$ $\{4\}$, conditional
67. $(3 - 3)(5 - z) = 0$ All real numbers, identity
68. $(2 \cdot 4 - 8)p = 0$ All real numbers, identity
69. $\frac{0}{x} = 0$ All nonzero real numbers, identity
70. $\frac{2x}{2} = x$ All real numbers, identity
71. $x \cdot x = x^2$ All real numbers, identity
72. $\frac{2x}{2x} = 1$ All nonzero real numbers, identity

Solve each equation.

73. $3x - 5 = 2x - 9$ $\{-4\}$
74. $5x - 9 = x - 4$ $\left\{\frac{5}{4}\right\}$
75. $x + 2(x + 4) = 3(x + 3) - 1$ R
76. $u + 3(u - 4) = 4(u - 5)$ $\varnothing$
77. $23 - 5(3 - n) = -4(n - 2) + 9n$ R
78. $-3 - 4(t - 5) = -2(t + 3) + 11$ $\{6\}$
79. $0.05x + 30 = 0.4x - 5$ $\{100\}$
80. $x - 0.08x = 460$ $\{500\}$
81. $-\frac{2}{3}a + 1 = 2$ $\left\{-\frac{3}{2}\right\}$
82. $-\frac{3}{4}t = \frac{1}{2}$ $\left\{-\frac{2}{3}\right\}$
83. $\frac{y}{2} + \frac{y}{6} = 20$ $\{30\}$
84. $\frac{3w}{5} - 1 = \frac{w}{2} + 1$ $\{20\}$
85. $0.09x - 0.2(x + 4) = -1.46$ $\{6\}$
86. $0.08x + 0.5(x + 100) = 73.2$ $\{40\}$
87. $436x - 789 = -571$ $\{0.5\}$
88. $0.08x + 4533 = 10x + 69$ $\{450\}$
89. $\frac{x}{344} + 235 = 292$ $\{19{,}608\}$
90. $34(x - 98) = \frac{x}{2} + 475$ $\{113.642\}$

Solve each problem.

91. ***Sales commission.*** Danielle sold her house through an agent who charged 8% of the selling price. After the commission was paid, Danielle received \$117,760. If x is the selling price, then x satisfies

$$x - 0.08x = 117{,}760.$$

Solve this equation to find the selling price. \$128,000

92. ***Raising rabbits.*** Before Roland sold two female rabbits, half of his rabbits were female. After the sale, only one-third of his rabbits were female. If x represents his original number of rabbits, then

$$\frac{1}{2}x - 2 = \frac{1}{3}(x - 2).$$

Solve this equation to find the number of rabbits that he had before the sale. 8 rabbits

93. ***Eavesdropping.*** Reginald overheard his boss complaining that his federal income tax for 2003 was \$60,531.

a) Use the accompanying graph to estimate his boss's taxable income for 2003. \$240,000

b) Find his boss's exact taxable income for 2003 by solving the equation

$$39{,}096.50 + 0.33(x - 174{,}700) = 60{,}531.$$

\$239,653

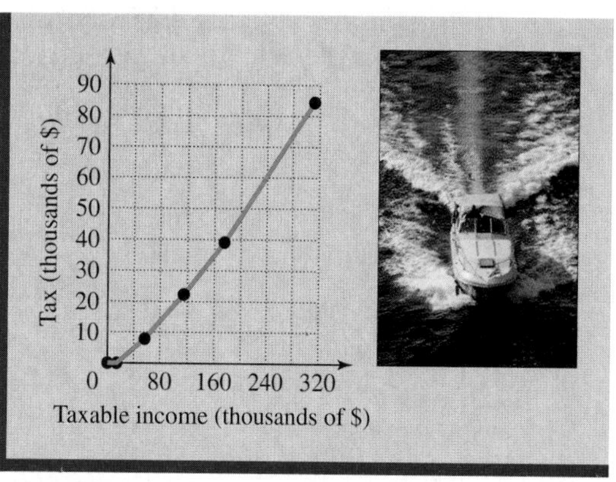

Figure for Exercise 93

94. ***Federal taxes.*** According to Bruce Harrell, CPA, the federal income tax for a class C corporation is found by solving a linear equation. The reason for the equation is that the amount x of federal tax is deducted before the state tax is figured, and the amount of state tax is deducted before the federal tax is figured. To find the amount of federal tax for a corporation with a taxable income of \$200,000, for which the federal tax rate is 25% and the state tax rate is 10%, Bruce must solve

$$x = 0.25[200{,}000 - 0.10(200{,}000 - x)].$$

Solve the equation for Bruce. \$46,153.85

2.4 Formulas

In this Section

- **Solving for a Variable**
- **Finding the Value of a Variable**

In this section, you will learn to rewrite formulas using the same properties of equality that we used to solve equations. You will also learn how to find the value of one of the variables in a formula when we know the value of all of the others.

Solving for a Variable

Most drivers know the relationship between distance, rate, and time. For example, if you drive 70 mph for 3 hours, then you will travel 210 miles. At 60 mph a 300-mile trip will take 5 hours. If a 400-mile trip took 8 hours, then you averaged 50 mph. The relationship between distance D, rate R, and time T is expressed by the formula

$$D = R \cdot T.$$

A **formula** or **literal equation** is an equation involving two or more variables.

To find the time for a 300-mile trip at 60 mph, you are using the formula in the form $T = \frac{D}{R}$. The process of rewriting a formula for one variable in terms of the others is called **solving for a certain variable.** To solve for a certain variable, we use the same techniques that we use in solving equations.

EXAMPLE 1

Solving for a certain variable

Solve the formula $D = RT$ for T.

Solution

Since T is multiplied by R, dividing each side of the equation by R will isolate T:

$$D = RT \quad \text{Original formula}$$

$$\frac{D}{R} = \frac{R \cdot T}{R} \quad \text{Divide each side by } R.$$

$$\frac{D}{R} = T \quad \text{Divide out (or cancel) the common factor } R.$$

$$T = \frac{D}{R} \quad \text{It is customary to write the single variable on the left.}$$

Now do Exercises 7–18

The formula $C = \frac{5}{9}(F - 32)$ is used to find the Celsius temperature for a given Fahrenheit temperature. If we solve this formula for F, then we have a formula for finding Fahrenheit temperature for a given Celsius temperature.

EXAMPLE 2

Solving for a certain variable

Solve the formula $C = \frac{5}{9}(F - 32)$ for F.

Teaching Tip Ask students to solve this equation by using the distributive property first.

Solution

We could apply the distributive property to the right side of the equation, but it is simpler to proceed as follows:

$$C = \frac{5}{9}(F - 32)$$

$$\frac{9}{5}C = \frac{9}{5} \cdot \frac{5}{9}(F - 32) \quad \text{Multiply each side by } \tfrac{9}{5}\text{, the reciprocal of } \tfrac{5}{9}.$$

$$\frac{9}{5}C = F - 32 \quad \text{Simplify.}$$

$$\frac{9}{5}C + 32 = F - 32 + 32 \quad \text{Add 32 to each side.}$$

$$\frac{9}{5}C + 32 = F \quad \text{Simplify.}$$

The formula is usually written as $F = \frac{9}{5}C + 32$.

Now do Exercises 19–24

When solving for a variable that appears more than once in the equation, we must combine the terms to obtain a single occurrence of the variable. *When a formula has been solved for a certain variable, that variable will not occur on both sides of the equation.*

EXAMPLE 3

Solving for a variable that appears on both sides

Solve $5x - b = 3x + d$ for x.

Solution

First get all terms involving x onto one side and all other terms onto the other side:

$$5x - b = 3x + d \quad \text{Original formula}$$

$$5x - 3x - b = d \quad \text{Subtract } 3x \text{ from each side.}$$

$$5x - 3x = b + d \quad \text{Add } b \text{ to each side.}$$

$$2x = b + d \quad \text{Combine like terms.}$$

$$x = \frac{b + d}{2} \quad \text{Divide each side by 2.}$$

The formula solved for x is $x = \frac{b + d}{2}$.

Now do Exercises 25–32

In Chapter 3, it will be necessary to solve an equation involving x and y for y.

EXAMPLE 4

Solving for y

Solve $x + 2y = 6$ for y. Write the answer in the form $y = mx + b$, where m and b are fixed real numbers.

Solution

$$x + 2y = 6 \quad \text{Original equation}$$

$$2y = 6 - x \quad \text{Subtract } x \text{ from each side.}$$

$$\frac{1}{2} \cdot 2y = \frac{1}{2}(6 - x) \quad \text{Multiply each side by } \tfrac{1}{2}.$$

$$y = 3 - \frac{1}{2}x \quad \text{Distributive property}$$

$$y = -\frac{1}{2}x + 3 \quad \text{Rearrange to get } y = mx + b \text{ form.}$$

Now do Exercises 33–42

Helpful Hint

If we simply wanted to solve $x + 2y = 6$ for y, we could have written

$$y = \frac{6 - x}{2} \text{ or } y = \frac{-x + 6}{2}.$$

However, in Example 4 we requested the form $y = mx + b$. This form is a popular form that we will study in detail in Chapter 3.

Notice that in Example 4 we multiplied each side of the equation by $\frac{1}{2}$, and so we multiplied each term on the right-hand side by $\frac{1}{2}$. Instead of multiplying by $\frac{1}{2}$, we could have divided each side of the equation by 2. We would then divide each term on the right side by 2. This idea is illustrated in Example 5.

EXAMPLE 5

Solving for y

Solve $2x - 3y = 9$ for y. Write the answer in the form $y = mx + b$, where m and b are real numbers. (When we study lines in Chapter 3 you will see that $y = mx + b$ is the slope-intercept form of the equation of a line.)

Teaching Tip Remind students that if plus is written in a general form such as $y = mx + b$, then we also allow minus, and vice versa.

Solution

$$
\begin{aligned}
2x - 3y &= 9 && \text{Original equation} \\
-3y &= -2x + 9 && \text{Subtract } 2x \text{ from each side.} \\
\frac{-3y}{-3} &= \frac{-2x + 9}{-3} && \text{Divide each side by } -3. \\
y &= \frac{-2x}{-3} + \frac{9}{-3} && \text{By the distributive property, each term is divided by } -3. \\
y &= \frac{2}{3}x - 3 && \text{Simplify.}
\end{aligned}
$$

Now do Exercises 43–54

Even though we wrote $y = \frac{2}{3}x - 3$ in Example 5, the equation is still considered to be in the form $y = mx + b$ because we could have written $y = \frac{2}{3}x + (-3)$.

Finding the Value of a Variable

In many situations we know the values of all variables in a formula except one. We use the formula to determine the unknown value.

EXAMPLE 6

Finding the value of a variable in a formula

If $2x - 3y = 9$, find y when $x = 6$.

Solution

Method 1: First solve the equation for y. Because we have already solved this equation for y in Example 5 we will not repeat that process in this example. We have

$$y = \frac{2}{3}x - 3.$$

Now replace x by 6 in this equation:

$$
\begin{aligned}
y &= \frac{2}{3}(6) - 3 \\
&= 4 - 3 = 1
\end{aligned}
$$

So when $x = 6$, we have $y = 1$.

Method 2: First replace x by 6 in the original equation, then solve for y:

$$
\begin{aligned}
2x - 3y &= 9 && \text{Original equation} \\
2 \cdot 6 - 3y &= 9 && \text{Replace } x \text{ by 6.} \\
12 - 3y &= 9 && \text{Simplify.} \\
-3y &= -3 && \text{Subtract 12 from each side.} \\
y &= 1 && \text{Divide each side by } -3.
\end{aligned}
$$

So when $x = 6$, we have $y = 1$.

Now do Exercises 63–72

If we had to find the value of y for many different values of x, it would be best to solve the equation for y, then insert the various values of x. Method 1 of Example 6 would be the better method. If we must find only one value of y, it does not matter which method we use. When doing the exercises corresponding to this example, you should try both methods.

The next example involves the simple interest formula $I = Prt$, where I is the amount of interest, P is the principal or the amount invested, r is the annual interest rate, and t is the time in years. The interest rate is generally expressed as a percent. When using a rate in computations, you must convert it to a decimal.

EXAMPLE 7

Helpful Hint

All interest computation is based on simple interest. However, depositors do not like to wait two years to get interest as in Example 7. More often the time is $\frac{1}{12}$ year or $\frac{1}{365}$ year. Simple interest computed every month is said to be compounded monthly. Simple interest computed every day is said to be compounded daily.

Using the simple interest formula

If the simple interest is \$120, the principal is \$400, and the time is 2 years, find the rate.

Solution

First, solve the formula $I = Prt$ for r, then insert values of P, I, and t:

$$Prt = I \qquad \text{Simple interest formula}$$
$$\frac{Prt}{Pt} = \frac{I}{Pt} \qquad \text{Divide each side by } Pt.$$
$$r = \frac{I}{Pt} \qquad \text{Simplify.}$$
$$r = \frac{120}{400 \cdot 2} \qquad \text{Substitute the values of } I, P, \text{ and } t.$$
$$r = 0.15 \qquad \text{Simplify.}$$
$$r = 15\% \qquad \text{Move the decimal point two places to the right.}$$

Now do Exercises 73–76

In solving a geometric problem, it is always helpful to draw a diagram, as we do in Example 8.

EXAMPLE 8

Teaching Tip Many students confuse area and perimeter. It is also very useful to know that length plus width is half the perimeter.

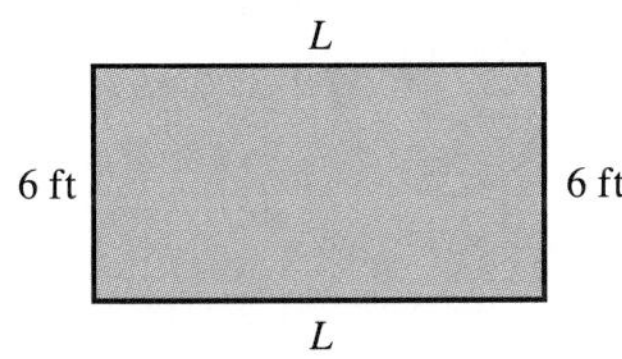

Figure 2.1

Using a geometric formula

The perimeter of a rectangle is 36 feet. If the width is 6 feet, then what is the length?

Solution

First, put the given information on a diagram as shown in Fig. 2.1. Substitute the given values into the formula for the perimeter of a rectangle found inside the front cover of this book, and then solve for L. (We could solve for L first and then insert the given values.)

$$P = 2L + 2W \qquad \text{Perimeter of a rectangle}$$
$$36 = 2L + 2 \cdot 6 \qquad \text{Substitute 36 for } P \text{ and 6 for } W.$$
$$36 = 2L + 12 \qquad \text{Simplify.}$$
$$24 = 2L \qquad \text{Subtract 12 from each side.}$$
$$12 = L \qquad \text{Divide each side by 2.}$$

Check: If $L = 12$ and $W = 6$, then $P = 2(12) + 2(6) = 36$ feet. So we can be certain that the length is 12 feet.

Now do Exercises 77–80

If L is the list price or original price of an item and r is the rate of discount, then the amount of discount is rL, the product of the rate and the list price. The sale price S is the list price minus the amount of discount. So $S = L - rL$. The rate of discount is generally expressed as a percent. In computations, rates must be written as decimals or fractions.

EXAMPLE 9

Finding the original price

What was the original price of a stereo that sold for \$560 after a 20% discount?

Solution

Express 20% as the decimal 0.20 or 0.2 and use the formula $S = L - rL$:

$$\text{Selling price} = \text{list price} - \text{amount of discount}$$

$$560 = L - 0.2L$$

$$10(560) = 10(L - 0.2L) \quad \text{Multiply each side by 10.}$$

$$5600 = 10L - 2L \quad \text{Remove the parentheses.}$$

$$5600 = 8L \quad \text{Combine like terms.}$$

$$\frac{5600}{8} = \frac{8L}{8} \quad \text{Divide each side by 8.}$$

$$700 = L$$

Since 20% of \$700 is \$140 and \$700 − \$140 = \$560, we can be sure that the original price was \$700. Note that if the discount is 20%, then the selling price is 80% of the list price. So we could have started with the equation $560 = 0.80L$.

Now do Exercises 81–86

Study Tip

Don't wait for inspiration to strike, it probably won't. Algebra is learned one tiny step at a time. So do lots of exercises and keep taking those tiny steps.

Warm-Ups ▼

True or false? Explain your answer.

1. If we solve $D = R \cdot T$ for T, we get $T \cdot R = D$. False
2. If we solve $a - b = 3a - m$ for a, we get $a = 3a - m + b$. False
3. Solving $A = LW$ for L, we get $L = \frac{W}{A}$. False
4. Solving $D = RT$ for R, we get $R = \frac{d}{t}$. False
5. The perimeter of a rectangle is the product of its length and width. False
6. The volume of a shoe box is the product of its length, width, and height. True
7. The sum of the length and width of a rectangle is one-half of its perimeter. True
8. Solving $y - x = 5$ for y gives us $y = x + 5$. True
9. If $x = -1$ and $y = -3x + 6$, then $y = 3$. False
10. The circumference of a circle is the product of its diameter and the number π. True

2.4 Exercises

Boost your GRADE at mathzone.com!

MathZone

- Practice Problems
- Net Tutor
- Self-Tests
- e-Professors
- Videos

Reading and Writing *After reading this section, write out the answers to these questions. Use complete sentences.*

1. What is a formula?
A formula is an equation with two or more variables.

2. What is a literal equation?
A literal equation is a formula.

3. What does it mean to solve a formula for a certain variable?
To solve for a variable means to find an equivalent equation in which the variable is isolated.

4. How do you solve a formula for a variable that appears on both sides?
If the variable appears on both sides, then get all terms with the variable onto the same side. Then combine like terms to get one occurrence of the variable.

5. What are the two methods shown for finding the value of a variable in a formula?
To find the value of a variable in a formula, we can solve for the variable and then insert values for the other variables, or insert values for the other variables and then solve for the variable.

6. What formula expresses the perimeter of a rectangle in terms of its length and width?
The formula for the perimeter of a rectangle is $P = 2L + 2W$.

Solve each formula for the specified variable. See Examples 1 and 2.

7. $D = RT$ for R $\quad R = \dfrac{D}{T}$

8. $A = LW$ for W $\quad W = \dfrac{A}{L}$

9. $C = \pi D$ for D $\quad D = \dfrac{C}{\pi}$

10. $F = ma$ for a $\quad a = \dfrac{F}{m}$

11. $I = Prt$ for P $\quad P = \dfrac{I}{rt}$

12. $I = Prt$ for t $\quad t = \dfrac{I}{Pr}$

13. $F = \dfrac{9}{5}C + 32$ for C $\quad C = \dfrac{5}{9}(F - 32)$

14. $y = \dfrac{3}{4}x - 7$ for x $\quad x = \dfrac{4y + 28}{3}$

15. $A = \dfrac{1}{2}bh$ for h $\quad h = \dfrac{2A}{b}$

16. $A = \dfrac{1}{2}bh$ for b $\quad b = \dfrac{2A}{h}$

17. $P = 2L + 2W$ for L $\quad L = \dfrac{P - 2W}{2}$

18. $P = 2L + 2W$ for W $\quad W = \dfrac{P - 2L}{2}$

19. $A = \dfrac{1}{2}(a + b)$ for a $\quad a = 2A - b$

20. $A = \dfrac{1}{2}(a + b)$ for b $\quad b = 2A - a$

21. $S = P + Prt$ for r $\quad r = \dfrac{S - P}{Pt}$

22. $S = P + Prt$ for t $\quad t = \dfrac{S - P}{Pr}$

23. $A = \dfrac{1}{2}h(a + b)$ for a $\quad a = \dfrac{2A - bh}{h}$

24. $A = \dfrac{1}{2}h(a + b)$ for b $\quad b = \dfrac{2A - ah}{h}$

Solve each equation for x. See Example 3.

25. $5x + a = 3x + b$ $\quad x = \dfrac{b - a}{2}$

26. $2c - x = 4x + c - 5b$ $\quad x = \dfrac{c + 5b}{5}$

27. $4(a + x) - 3(x - a) = 0$ $\quad x = -7a$

28. $-2(x - b) - (5a - x) = a + b$ $\quad x = b - 6a$

29. $3x - 2(a - 3) = 4x - 6 - a$ $\quad x = 12 - a$

30. $2(x - 3w) = -3(x + w)$ $\quad x = \dfrac{3w}{5}$

31. $3x + 2ab = 4x - 5ab$ $\quad x = 7ab$

32. $x - a = -x + a + 4b$ $\quad x = a + 2b$

Solve each equation for y. See Examples 4 and 5.

33. $x + y = -9$ $\quad y = -x - 9$

34. $3x + y = -5$ $\quad y = -3x - 5$

35. $x + y - 6 = 0$ $\quad y = -x + 6$

36. $4x + y - 2 = 0$ $\quad y = -4x + 2$

37. $2x - y = 2$ $\quad y = 2x - 2$

38. $x - y = -3$ $\quad y = x + 3$

39. $3x - y + 4 = 0$ $\quad y = 3x + 4$

40. $-2x - y + 5 = 0$ $\quad y = -2x + 5$

41. $x + 2y = 4$ $\quad y = -\dfrac{1}{2}x + 2$

42. $3x + 2y = 6$ $\quad y = -\dfrac{3}{2}x + 3$

43. $2x - 2y = 1$ $y = x - \frac{1}{2}$

44. $3x - 2y = -6$ $y = \frac{3}{2}x + 3$

45. $y + 2 = 3(x - 4)$ $y = 3x - 14$

46. $y - 3 = -3(x - 1)$ $y = -3x + 6$

47. $y - 1 = \frac{1}{2}(x - 2)$ $y = \frac{1}{2}x$

48. $y - 4 = -\frac{2}{3}(x - 9)$ $y = -\frac{2}{3}x + 10$

49. $\frac{1}{2}x - \frac{1}{3}y = -2$ $y = \frac{3}{2}x + 6$

50. $\frac{x}{2} + \frac{y}{4} = \frac{1}{2}$ $y = -2x + 2$

51. $y - 2 = \frac{3}{2}(x + 3)$ $y = \frac{3}{2}x + \frac{13}{2}$

52. $y + 4 = \frac{2}{3}(x - 2)$ $y = \frac{2}{3}x - \frac{16}{3}$

53. $y - \frac{1}{2} = -\frac{1}{4}\left(x - \frac{1}{2}\right)$ $y = -\frac{1}{4}x + \frac{5}{8}$

54. $y + \frac{1}{2} = -\frac{1}{3}\left(x + \frac{1}{2}\right)$ $y = -\frac{1}{3}x - \frac{2}{3}$

Fill in the tables using the given formulas.

55. $y = -3x + 30$

x	y
−10	60
0	30
10	0
20	−30
30	−60

56. $y = 4x - 20$

x	y
−10	−60
−5	−40
0	−20
5	0
10	20

57. $F = \frac{9}{5}C + 32$

C	F
−10	14
−5	23
0	32
40	104
100	212

58. $C = \frac{5}{9}(F - 32)$

F	C
−40	−40
14	−10
32	0
59	15
86	30

59. $T = \frac{400}{R}$

R (mph)	T (hr)
10	40
20	20
40	10
80	5
100	4

60. $R = \frac{100}{T}$

T (hr)	R (mph)
1	100
5	20
20	5
50	2
100	1

61. $S = \frac{n(n+1)}{2}$

n	S
1	1
2	3
3	6
4	10
5	15

62. $S = \frac{n(n+1)(2n+1)}{6}$

n	S
1	1
2	5
3	14
4	30
5	55

For each equation that follows, find y given that x = 2. See Example 6.

63. $y = 3x - 4$ 2

64. $y = -2x + 5$ 1

65. $3x - 2y = -8$ 7

66. $4x + 6y = 8$ 0

67. $\frac{3x}{2} - \frac{5y}{3} = 6$ $-\frac{9}{5}$

68. $\frac{2y}{5} - \frac{3x}{4} = \frac{1}{2}$ 5

69. $y - 3 = \frac{1}{2}(x - 6)$ 1

70. $y - 6 = -\frac{3}{4}(x - 2)$ 6

71. $y - 4.3 = 0.45(x - 8.6)$ 1.33

72. $y + 33.7 = 0.78(x - 45.6)$ −67.708

Solve each of the following problems. Some geometric formulas that may be helpful can be found inside the front cover of this text. See Examples 7–9.

73. ***Finding the rate.*** If the simple interest on \$5000 for 3 years is \$600, then what is the rate? 4%

74. ***Finding the rate.*** Wayne paid \$420 in simple interest on a loan of \$1000 for 7 years. What was the rate? 6%

75. ***Finding the time.*** Kathy paid \$500 in simple interest on a loan of \$2500. If the annual interest rate was 5%, then what was the time? 4 years

76. ***Finding the time.*** Robert paid \$240 in simple interest on a loan of \$1000. If the annual interest rate was 8%, then what was the time? 3 years

77. ***Finding the length.*** The area of a rectangle is 28 square yards. The width is 4 yards. Find the length. 7 yards

78. ***Finding the width.*** The area of a rectangle is 60 square feet. The length is 4 feet. Find the width. 15 feet

79. ***Finding the length.*** If it takes 600 feet of wire fencing to fence a rectangular feed lot that has a width of 75 feet, then what is the length of the lot? 225 feet

80. ***Finding the depth.*** If it takes 500 feet of fencing to enclose a rectangular lot that is 104 feet wide, then how deep is the lot? 146 feet

81. ***Finding MSRP.*** What was the manufacturer's suggested retail price (MSRP) for a Lexus SC 430 that sold for \$54,450 after a 10% discount? \$60,500

82. ***Finding MSRP.*** What was the MSRP for a Hummer H1 that sold for $107,272 after an 8% discount? $116,600

83. ***Finding the original price.*** Find the original price if there is a 15% discount and the sale price is $255. $300

84. ***Finding the list price.*** Find the list price if there is a 12% discount and the sale price is $4400. $5000

85. ***Rate of discount.*** Find the rate of discount if the discount is $40 and the original price is $200. 20%

86. ***Rate of discount.*** Find the rate of discount if the discount is $20 and the original price is $250. 8%

87. ***Width of a football field.*** The perimeter of a football field in the NFL, excluding the end zones, is 920 feet. How wide is the field? 160 feet

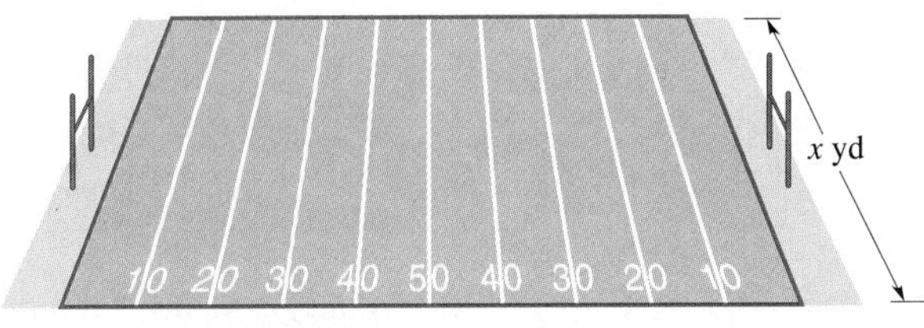

Figure for Exercise 87

88. ***Perimeter of a frame.*** If a picture frame is 16 inches by 20 inches, then what is its perimeter? 72 inches

89. ***Volume of a box.*** A rectangular box measures 2 feet wide, 3 feet long, and 4 feet deep. What is its volume? 24 cubic feet

90. ***Volume of a refrigerator.*** The volume of a rectangular refrigerator is 20 cubic feet. If the top measures 2 feet by 2.5 feet, then what is the height? 4 feet

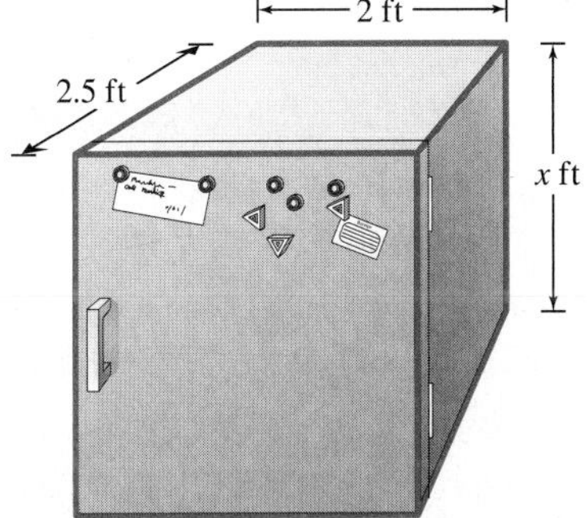

Figure for Exercise 90

91. ***Radius of a pizza.*** If the circumference of a pizza is 8π inches, then what is the radius? 4 inches

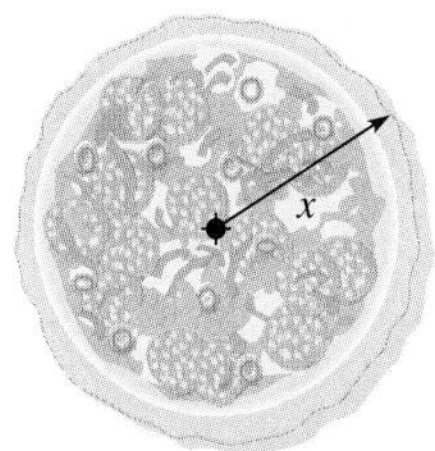

Figure for Exercise 91

92. ***Diameter of a circle.*** If the circumference of a circle is 4π meters, then what is the diameter? 4 meters

93. ***Height of a banner.*** If a banner in the shape of a triangle has an area of 16 square feet with a base of 4 feet, then what is the height of the banner? 8 feet

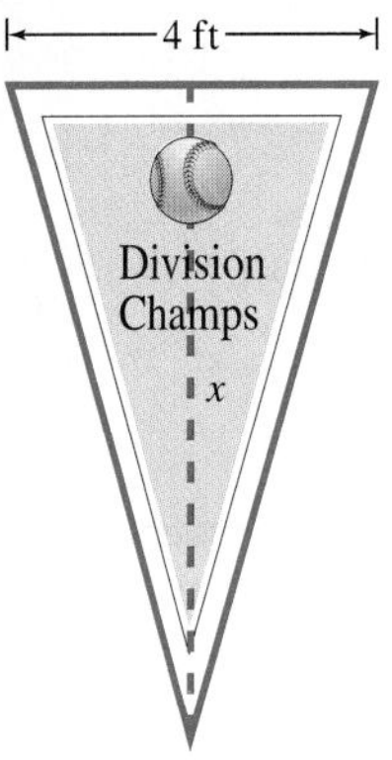

Figure for Exercise 93

94. ***Length of a leg.*** If a right triangle has an area of 14 square meters and one leg is 4 meters in length, then what is the length of the other leg? 7 meters

95. ***Length of the base.*** A trapezoid with height 20 inches and lower base 8 inches has an area of 200 square inches. What is the length of its upper base? 12 inches

96. ***Height of a trapezoid.*** The end of a flower box forms the shape of a trapezoid. The area of the trapezoid is 300 square

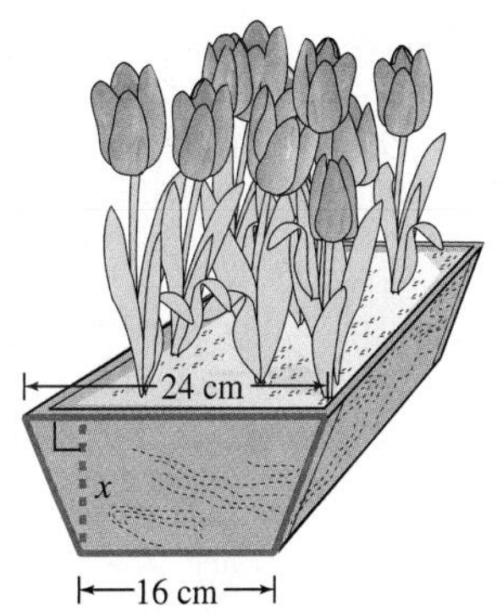

Figure for Exercise 96

centimeters. The bases are 16 centimeters and 24 centimeters in length. Find the height. 15 centimeters

97. ***Fried's rule.*** Doctors often prescribe the same drugs for children as they do for adults. The formula $d = 0.08aD$ (Fried's rule) is used to calculate the child's dosage d, where a is the child's age and D is the adult dosage. If a doctor prescribes 1000 milligrams of acetaminophen for an adult, then how many milligrams would the doctor prescribe for an eight-year-old child? Use the bar graph to determine the age at which a child would get the same dosage as an adult. 640 milligrams, age 13

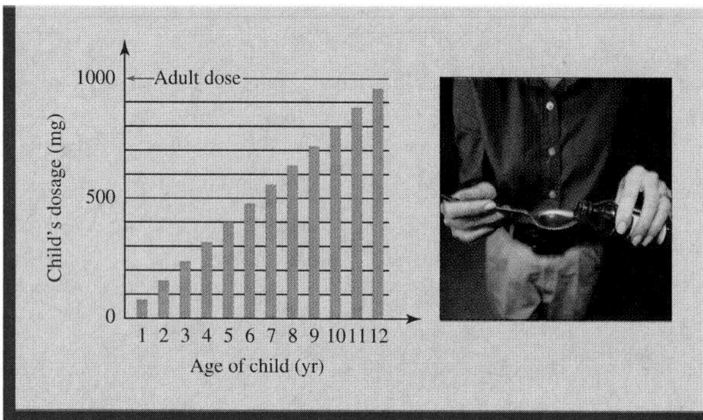

Figure for Exercise 97

98. ***Cowling's rule.*** Cowling's rule is another method for determining the dosage of a drug to prescribe to a child. For this rule, the formula

$$d = \frac{D(a + 1)}{24}$$

gives the child's dosage d, where D is the adult dosage and a is the age of the child in years. If the adult dosage of a drug is 600 milligrams and a doctor uses this formula to determine that a child's dosage is 200 milligrams, then how old is the child? Age 7

99. ***Administering Vancomycin.*** A patient is to receive 750 mg of the antibiotic Vancomycin. However, Vancomycin comes in a solution containing 1 gram (available dose) of Vancomycin per 5 milliliters (quantity) of solution. Use the formula

$$\text{Amount} = \frac{\text{desired dose}}{\text{available dose}} \times \text{quantity}$$

to find the amount of this solution that should be administered to the patient. 3.75 milliliters

100. ***International communications.*** The global investment in telecom infrastructure since 1990 can be modeled by the formula

$$I = 7.5T + 115,$$

where I is in billions of dollars and t is the number of years since 1990 (*Fortune,* www.fortune.com).

a) Use the formula to find the global investment in 2000. \$190 billion

b) Use the accompanying graph to estimate the year in which the global investment will reach \$250 billion. 2008

c) Use the formula to find the year in which the global investment will reach \$250 billion. 2008

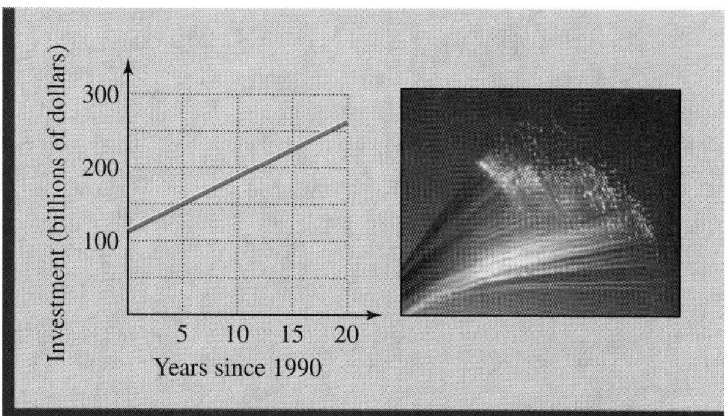

Figure for Exercise 100

101. ***The 2.4-meter rule.*** A 2.4-meter sailboat is a one-person boat that is about 13 feet in length, has a displacement of about 550 pounds, and a sail area of about 81 square feet. To compete in the 2.4-meter class, a boat must satisfy the formula

$$2.4 = \frac{L + 2D - F\sqrt{S}}{2.37},$$

where L = length, F = freeboard, D = girth, and S = sail area. Solve the formula for L. $L = F\sqrt{S} - 2D + 5.688$

Photo for Exercise 101

2.5 Translating Verbal Expressions into Algebraic Expressions

In this Section

- Writing Algebraic Expressions
- Pairs of Numbers
- Consecutive Integers
- Using Formulas
- Writing Equations

You translated some verbal expressions into algebraic expressions in Section 1.6; in this section you will study translating in more detail.

Writing Algebraic Expressions

The following box contains a list of some frequently occurring verbal expressions and their equivalent algebraic expressions.

Teaching Tip Note that, in common usage, difference can mean subtract in either order. A difference in ages is always given as a positive number no matter who is mentioned first.

Translating Words into Algebra

	Verbal Phrase	Algebraic Expression
Addition:	The sum of a number and 8	$x + 8$
	Five is added to a number	$x + 5$
	Two more than a number	$x + 2$
	A number increased by 3	$x + 3$
Subtraction:	Four is subtracted from a number	$x - 4$
	Three less than a number	$x - 3$
	The difference between 7 and a number	$7 - x$
	A number decreased by 2	$x - 2$
Multiplication:	The product of 5 and a number	$5x$
	Twice a number	$2x$
	One-half of a number	$\frac{1}{2}x$
	Five percent of a number	$0.05x$
Division:	The ratio of a number to 6	$\frac{x}{6}$
	The quotient of 5 and a number	$\frac{5}{x}$
	Three divided by some number	$\frac{3}{x}$

EXAMPLE 1

Writing algebraic expressions

Translate each verbal expression into an algebraic expression.

a) The sum of a number and 9

b) Eighty percent of a number

c) A number divided by 4

d) The result of a number subtracted from 5

e) Three less than a number

Solution

a) If x is the number, then the sum of x and 9 is $x + 9$.

b) If w is the number, then eighty percent of the number is $0.80w$.

c) If y is the number, then the number divided by 4 is $\frac{y}{4}$.

d) If z is the number, then the result of subtracting z from 5 is $5 - z$.

e) If a is the number, then 3 less than a is $a - 3$.

Now do Exercises 7–18

Helpful Hint

We know that x and $10 - x$ have a sum of 10 for any value of x. We can easily check that fact by adding:

$$x + 10 - x = 10$$

In general it is not true that x and $x - 10$ have a sum of 10, because

$$x + x - 10 = 2x - 10.$$

For what value of x is the sum of x and $x - 10$ equal to 10?

Pairs of Numbers

There is often more than one unknown quantity in a problem, but a relationship between the unknown quantities is given. For example, if one unknown number is 5 more than another unknown number, we can use

$$x \quad \text{and} \quad x + 5,$$

to represent them. Note that x and $x + 5$ can also be used to represent two unknown numbers that differ by 5, for if two numbers differ by 5, one of the numbers is 5 more than the other.

How would you represent two numbers that have a sum of 10? If one of the numbers is 2, the other is certainly $10 - 2$, or 8. Thus if x is one of the numbers, then $10 - x$ is the other. The expressions

$$x \quad \text{and} \quad 10 - x$$

have a sum of 10 for any value of x.

EXAMPLE 2

Algebraic expressions for pairs of numbers

Write algebraic expressions for each pair of numbers.

a) Two numbers that differ by 12 **b)** Two numbers with a sum of -8

Solution

a) The expressions x and $x - 12$ represent two numbers that differ by 12. We can check by subtracting:

$$x - (x - 12) = x - x + 12 = 12$$

Of course, x and $x + 12$ also differ by 12 because $x + 12 - x = 12$.

b) The expressions x and $-8 - x$ have a sum of -8. We can check by addition:

$$x + (-8 - x) = x - 8 - x = -8$$

Now do Exercises 19–30

Pairs of numbers occur in geometry in discussing measures of angles. You will need the following facts about degree measures of angles.

Teaching Tip Some students might not be familiar with degree measures. You might have to review this topic.

Degree Measures of Angles

Two angles are called **complementary** if the sum of their degree measures is 90°.

Two angles are called **supplementary** if the sum of their degree measures is 180°.

The sum of the degree measures of the three angles of any triangle is 180°.

For complementary angles, we use x and $90 - x$ for their degree measures. For supplementary angles, we use x and $180 - x$. Complementary angles that share a common side form a right angle. Supplementary angles that share a common side form a straight angle or straight line.

EXAMPLE 3

Degree measures

Write algebraic expressions for each pair of angles shown.

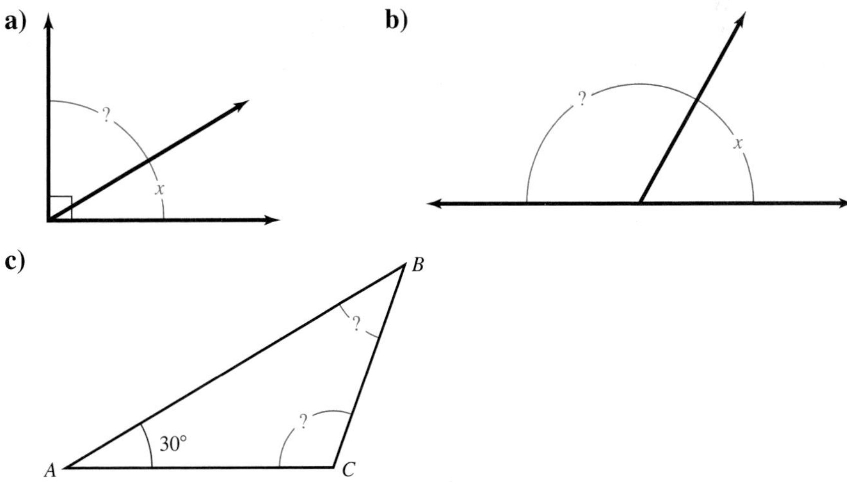

Solution

a) Since the angles shown are complementary, we can use x to represent the degree measure of the smaller angle and $90 - x$ to represent the degree measure of the larger angle.

b) Since the angles shown are supplementary, we can use x to represent the degree measure of the smaller angle and $180 - x$ to represent the degree measure of the larger angle.

c) If we let x represent the degree measure of angle B, then $180 - x - 30$, or $150 - x$, represents the degree measure of angle C.

Now do Exercises 31–34

Consecutive Integers

Note that each integer is one larger than the previous integer. For example, if $x = 5$, then $x + 1 = 6$ and $x + 2 = 7$. So if x is an integer, then x, $x + 1$, and $x + 2$ represent three consecutive integers. Each even (or odd) integer is two larger than the previous even (or odd) integer. For example, if $x = 6$, then $x + 2 = 8$, and $x + 4 = 10$. If $x = 7$, then $x + 2 = 9$, and $x + 4 = 11$. So x, $x + 2$, and $x + 4$ represent three consecutive even integers if x is even and three consecutive odd integers if x is odd.

CAUTION The expressions x, $x + 1$, and $x + 3$ do not represent three consecutive odd integers no matter what x represents.

EXAMPLE 4

Expressions for integers

Write algebraic expressions for the following unknown integers.

a) Two consecutive integers, the smallest of which is w.

b) Three consecutive even integers, the smallest of which is z.

c) Four consecutive odd integers, the smallest of which is y.

Teaching Tip Integer problems are relatively easy and should build student confidence.

Solution

a) Each integer is 1 larger than the preceding integer. So if w represents the smallest of two consecutive integers, then w and $w + 1$ represent the integers.

b) Each even integer is 2 larger than the preceding even integer. So if z represents the smallest of three consecutive even integers, then z, $z + 2$, and $z + 4$ represent the three consecutive even integers.

c) Each odd integer is 2 larger than the preceding odd integer. So if y represents the smallest of four consecutive odd integers, then y, $y + 2$, $y + 4$, and $y + 6$ represent the four consecutive odd integers.

Now do Exercises 35–42

Using Formulas

In writing expressions for unknown quantities, we often use standard formulas such as those given inside the front cover of this book.

EXAMPLE 5

Writing algebraic expressions using standard formulas

Find an algebraic expression for

a) the distance if the rate is 30 miles per hour and the time is T hours.

b) the discount if the rate is 40% and the original price is p dollars.

Solution

a) Using the formula $D = RT$, we have $D = 30T$. So $30T$ is an expression that represents the distance in miles.

b) Since the discount is the rate times the original price, an algebraic expression for the discount is $0.40p$ dollars.

Now do Exercises 43–66

Writing Equations

To solve a problem using algebra, we describe or **model** the problem with an equation. In this section we write the equations only, and in Section 2.6 we write and solve them. Sometimes we must write an equation from the information given in the problem and sometimes we use a standard model to get the equation. Some standard models are shown in the following box.

Study Tip

It is a good idea to work with others, but don't be misled. Working a problem with help is not the same as working a problem on your own. In the end, mathematics is personal. Make sure that you can do it. Give yourself a weekly quiz by working 10 exercises randomly selected from the material covered since the last test.

Uniform Motion Model

Distance = Rate · Time $D = R \cdot T$

Percentage Models

What number is 5% of 40? $x = 0.05 \cdot 40$
Ten is what percent of 80? $10 = x \cdot 80$
Twenty is 4% of what number? $20 = 0.04 \cdot x$

Selling Price and Discount Model

Discount = Rate of discount · Original price
Selling Price = Original price − Discount

Real Estate Commission Model

Commission = Rate of commission · Selling price
Amount for owner = Selling price − Commission

Geometric Models for Perimeter

Perimeter of any figure = the sum of the lengths of the sides
Rectangle: $P = 2L + 2W$ Square: $P = 4s$

Geometric Models for Area

Rectangle: $A = LW$ Square: $A = s^2$
Parallelogram: $A = bh$ Triangle: $A = \frac{1}{2}bh$
More geometric formulas can be found inside the front cover of this text.

EXAMPLE 6

Writing equations

Identify the variable and write an equation that describes each situation.

a) Find two numbers that have a sum of 14 and a product of 45.

b) A coat is on sale for 25% off the list price. If the sale price is \$87, then what is the list price?

c) What percent of 8 is 2?

d) The value of x dimes and $x - 3$ quarters is \$2.05.

Helpful Hint

At this point we are simply learning to write equations that model certain situations. Don't worry about solving these equations now. In Section 2.6 we will solve problems by writing an equation and solving it.

Solution

a) Let x = one of the numbers and $14 - x$ = the other number. Since their product is 45, we have

$$x(14 - x) = 45.$$

b) Let $x =$ the list price and $0.25x =$ the amount of discount. We can write an equation expressing the fact that the selling price is the list price minus the discount:

$$\text{List price} - \text{discount} = \text{selling price}$$
$$x - 0.25x = 87$$

c) If we let x represent the percentage, then the equation is $x \cdot 8 = 2$, or $8x = 2$.

d) The value of x dimes at 10 cents each is $10x$ cents. The value of $x - 3$ quarters at 25 cents each is $25(x - 3)$ cents. We can write an equation expressing the fact that the total value of the coins is 205 cents:

$$\text{Value of dimes} + \text{value of quarters} = \text{total value}$$
$$10x + 25(x - 3) = 205$$

Now do Exercises 67–92

CAUTION The value of the coins in Example 6(d) is either 205 cents or 2.05 dollars. If the total value is expressed in dollars, then all of the values must be expressed in dollars. So we could also write the equation as

$$0.10x + 0.25(x - 3) = 2.05.$$

Warm-Ups ▼

True or false? Explain your answer.

1. For any value of x, the numbers x and $x + 6$ differ by 6. True
2. For any value of a, a and $10 - a$ have a sum of 10. True
3. If Jack ran at x miles per hour for 3 hours, he ran $3x$ miles. True
4. If Jill ran at x miles per hour for 10 miles, she ran for $10x$ hours. False
5. If the realtor gets 6% of the selling price and the house sells for x dollars, the owner gets $x - 0.06x$ dollars. True
6. If the owner got \$50,000 and the realtor got 10% of the selling price, the house sold for \$55,000. False
7. Three consecutive odd integers can be represented by x, $x + 1$, and $x + 3$. False
8. The value in cents of n nickels and d dimes is $0.05n + 0.10d$. False
9. If the sales tax rate is 5% and x represents the price of the goods purchased, then the total bill is $1.05x$. True
10. If the length of a rectangle is 4 feet more than the width w, then the perimeter is $w + (w + 4)$ feet. False

2.5 Exercises

Boost your GRADE at mathzone.com!

MathZone

- Practice Problems
- Self-Tests
- Videos
- Net Tutor
- e-Professors

Reading and Writing *After reading this section, write out the answers to these questions. Use complete sentences.*

1. What are the different ways of verbally expressing the operation of addition?
To express addition we use words such as plus, sum, increased by, and more than.

2. How can you algebraically express two numbers using only one variable?
We can algebraically express two numbers using one variable provided the numbers are related in some known way.

3. What are complementary angles?
Complementary angles have degree measures with a sum of 90°.

4. What are supplementary angles?
Supplementary angles have degree measures with a sum of 180°.

5. What is the relationship between distance, rate, and time?
Distance is the product of rate and time.

6. What is the difference between expressing consecutive even integers and consecutive odd integers algebraically?
If x is an even integer, then x and $x + 2$ represent consecutive even integers. If x is an odd integer, then x and $x + 2$ represent consecutive odd integers.

Translate each verbal expression into an algebraic expression. See Example 1.

7. The sum of a number and 3 $x + 3$

8. Two more than a number $x + 2$

9. Three less than a number $x - 3$

10. Four subtracted from a number $x - 4$

11. The product of a number and 5 $5x$

12. Five divided by some number $\frac{5}{x}$

13. Ten percent of a number $0.1x$

14. Eight percent of a number $0.08x$

15. The ratio of a number and 3 $\frac{x}{3}$

16. The quotient of 12 and a number $\frac{12}{x}$

17. One-third of a number $\frac{1}{3}x$

18. Three-fourths of a number $\frac{3}{4}x$

Write algebraic expressions for each pair of numbers. See Example 2.

19. Two numbers with a difference of 15 x and $x + 15$

20. Two numbers that differ by 9 x and $x + 9$

21. Two numbers with a sum of 6 x and $6 - x$

22. Two numbers with a sum of 5 x and $5 - x$

23. Two numbers with a sum of -4 x and $-4 - x$

24. Two numbers with a sum of -8 x and $-8 - x$

25. Two numbers such that one is 3 larger than the other
x and $x + 3$

26. Two numbers such that one is 8 smaller than the other
x and $x + 8$

27. Two numbers such that one is 5% of the other
x and $0.05x$

28. Two numbers such that one is 40% of the other
x and $0.4x$

29. Two numbers such that one is 30% more than the other
x and $1.30x$

30. Two numbers such that one is 20% smaller than the other
x and $0.80x$

Each of the following figures shows a pair of angles. Write algebraic expressions for the degree measures of each pair of angles. See Example 3.

31.

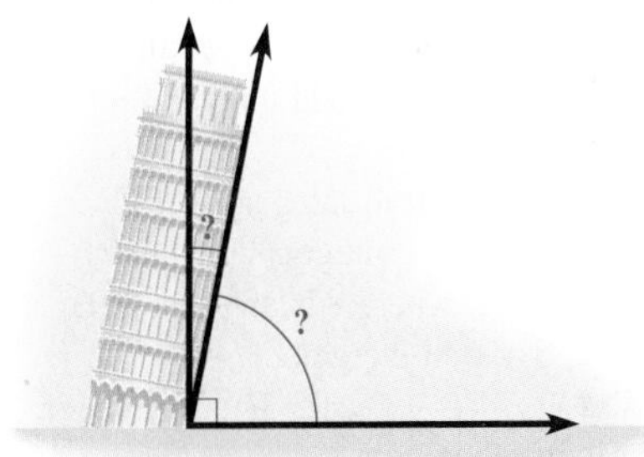

Figure for Exercise 31

x and $90 - x$

32.

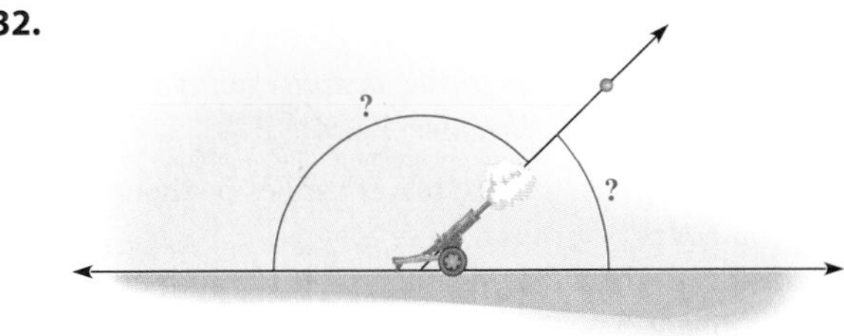

Figure for Exercise 32

x and $180 - x$

33.

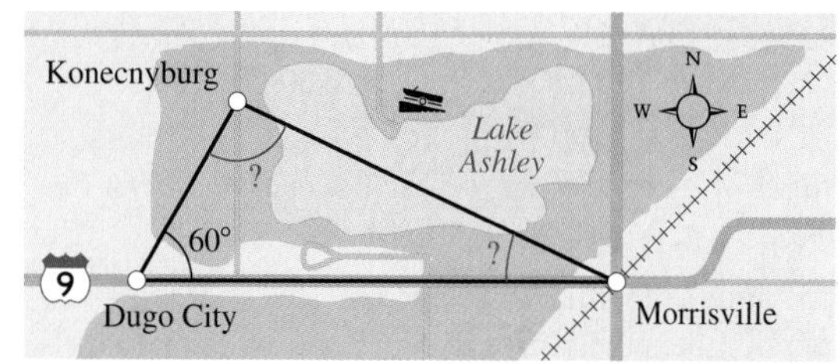

Figure for Exercise 33

x and $120 - x$

34.

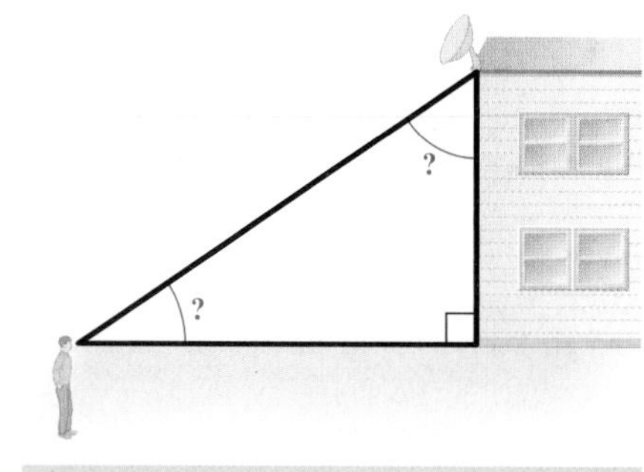

Figure for Exercise 34

x and $90 - x$

Write algebraic expressions for the following unknown integers. See Example 4.

35. Two consecutive even integers, the smallest of which is n
n and $n + 2$, where n is an even integer

36. Two consecutive odd integers, the smallest of which is x
x and $x + 2$, where x is an odd integer

37. Two consecutive integers
x and $x + 1$, where x is an integer

38. Three consecutive even integers
x, $x + 2$, and $x + 4$, where x is an even integer

39. Three consecutive odd integers
x, $x + 2$, and $x + 4$, where x is an odd integer

40. Three consecutive integers
x, $x + 1$, and $x + 2$, where x is an integer

41. Four consecutive even integers
x, $x + 2$, $x + 4$, and $x + 6$, where x is an even integer

42. Four consecutive odd integers
x, $x + 2$, $x + 4$, and $x + 6$, where x is an odd integer

Find an algebraic expression for the quantity in italics using the given information. See Example 5.

43. The *distance,* given that the rate is x miles per hour and the time is 3 hours $3x$ miles

44. The *distance,* given that the rate is $x + 10$ miles per hour and the time is 5 hours $5x + 50$ miles

45. The *discount,* given that the rate is 25% and the original price is q dollars $0.25q$ dollars

46. The *discount,* given that the rate is 10% and the original price is t yen $0.10t$ yen

47. The *time,* given that the distance is x miles and the rate is 20 miles per hour $\frac{x}{20}$ hour

48. The *time,* given that the distance is 300 kilometers and the rate is $x + 30$ kilometers per hour
$\frac{300}{x + 30}$ hour

49. The *rate,* given that the distance is $x - 100$ meters and the time is 12 seconds $\frac{x - 100}{12}$ meters per second

50. The *rate,* given that the distance is 200 feet and the time is $x + 3$ seconds $\frac{200}{x + 3}$ feet per second

51. The *area* of a rectangle with length x meters and width 5 meters $5x$ square meters

52. The *area* of a rectangle with sides b yards and $b - 6$ yards
$b(b - 6)$ square yards

53. The *perimeter* of a rectangle with length $w + 3$ inches and width w inches $2w + 2(w + 3)$ inches

54. The *perimeter* of a rectangle with length r centimeters and width $r - 1$ centimeters
$2r + 2(r - 1)$ centimeters

55. The *width* of a rectangle with perimeter 300 feet and length x feet $150 - x$ feet

56. The *length* of a rectangle with area 200 square feet and width w feet $\frac{200}{w}$ feet

57. The *length* of a rectangle, given that its width is x feet and its length is 1 foot longer than twice the width
$2x + 1$ feet

58. The *length* of a rectangle, given that its width is w feet and its length is 3 feet shorter than twice the width
$2w - 3$ feet

59. The *area* of a rectangle, given that the width is x meters and the length is 5 meters longer than the width
$x(x + 5)$ square meters

60. The *perimeter* of a rectangle, given that the length is x yards and the width is 10 yards shorter
$2(x) + 2(x - 10)$ yards

61. The *simple interest,* given that the principal is $x + 1000$, the rate is 18%, and the time is 1 year
$0.18(x + 1000)$

62. The *simple interest,* given that the principal is $3x$, the rate is 6%, and the time is 1 year $0.06(3x)$

63. The *price per pound* of peaches, given that x pounds sold for \$16.50 $\frac{16.50}{x}$ dollars per pound

64. The *rate per hour* of a mechanic who gets \$480 for working x hours $\frac{480}{x}$ dollars per hour

65. The *degree measure* of an angle, given that its complementary angle has measure x degrees $90 - x$ degrees

66. The *degree measure* of an angle, given that its supplementary angle has measure x degrees $180 - x$ degrees

Identify the variable and write an equation that describes each situation. Do not solve the equation. See Example 6.

67. Two numbers differ by 5 and have a product of 8.
x is the smaller number, $x(x + 5) = 8$

68. Two numbers differ by 6 and have a product of -9.
x is the smaller number, $x(x + 6) = -9$

69. Herman's house sold for x dollars. The real estate agent received 7% of the selling price and Herman received \$84,532.
x is the selling price, $x - 0.07x = 84{,}532$

70. Gwen sold her car on consignment for x dollars. The saleswoman's commission was 10% of the selling price and Gwen received \$6570.
x is the selling price, $x - 0.10x = 6570$

71. What percent of 500 is 100?
x is the percent, $500x = 100$

72. What percent of 40 is 120?
x is the percent, $40x = 120$

73. The value of x nickels and $x + 2$ dimes is \$3.80.
x is the number of nickels, $0.05x + 0.10(x + 2) = 3.80$

74. The value of d dimes and $d - 3$ quarters is \$6.75.
d is the number of dimes, $0.10d + 0.25(d - 3) = 6.75$

75. The sum of a number and 5 is 13.
x is the number, $x + 5 = 13$

76. Twelve subtracted from a number is -6.
x is the number, $x - 12 = -6$

77. The sum of three consecutive integers is 42.
x is the smallest integer, $x + (x + 1) + (x + 2) = 42$

78. The sum of three consecutive odd integers is 27.
x is the smallest odd integer, $x + x + 2 + x + 4 = 27$

79. The product of two consecutive integers is 182.
x is the smaller integer, $x(x + 1) = 182$

80. The product of two consecutive even integers is 168.
x is the smaller even integer, $x(x + 2) = 168$

81. Twelve percent of Harriet's income is \$3000.
x is Harriet's income, $0.12x = 3000$

82. If 9% of the members buy tickets, then we will sell 252 tickets to this group.
x is the number of members, $0.09x = 252$

83. Thirteen is 5% of what number?
x is the number, $0.05x = 13$

84. Three hundred is 8% of what number?
x is the number, $0.08x = 300$

85. The length of a rectangle is 5 feet longer than the width, and the area is 126 square feet.
x is the width, $x(x + 5) = 126$

86. The length of a rectangle is 1 yard shorter than twice the width, and the perimeter is 298 yards.
x is the width, $2x + 2(2x - 1) = 298$

87. The value of n nickels and $n - 1$ dimes is 95 cents.
n is the number of nickels, $5n + 10(n - 1) = 95$

88. The value of q quarters, $q + 1$ dimes, and $2q$ nickels is 90 cents.
q is the number of quarters, $25q + 10(q + 1) + 5(2q) = 90$

89. The measure of an angle is 38° smaller than the measure of its supplementary angle.
x is the measure of the larger angle, $x + x - 38 = 180$

90. The measure of an angle is 16° larger than the measure of its complementary angle.
x is the measure of the smaller angle, $x + x + 16 = 90$

91. ***Target heart rate.*** For a cardiovascular workout, fitness experts recommend that you reach your target heart rate and stay at that rate for at least 20 minutes (HealthStatus, www.healthstatus.com). To find your target heart rate, find the sum of your age and your resting heart rate, then subtract that sum from 220. Find 60% of that result and add it to your resting heart rate.

a) Write an equation with variable r expressing the fact that the target heart rate for 30-year-old Bob is 144.

b) Judging from the accompanying graph, does the target heart rate for a 30-year-old increase or decrease as the resting heart rate increases.

a) $r + 0.6(220 - (30 + r)) = 144$, where r is the resting heart rate

b) Target heart rate increases as resting heart rate increases.

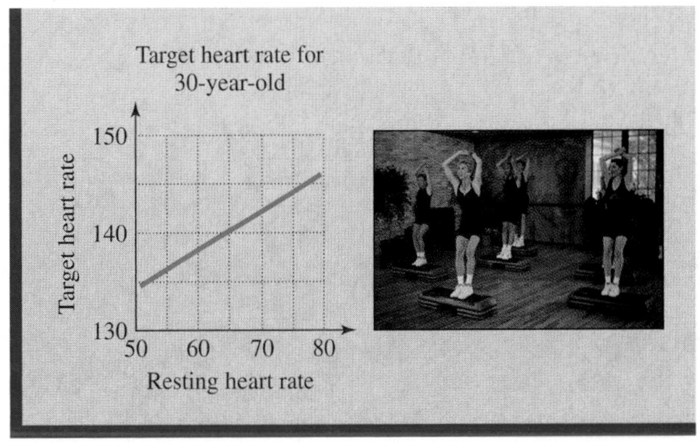

Figure for Exercise 91

92. ***Adjusting the saddle.*** The saddle height on a bicycle should be 109% of the rider's inside leg measurement L (www.harriscyclery.com). See the figure on the next page. Write an equation expressing the fact that the saddle height for Brenda is 36 in.
$1.09L = 36$, where L is the inside leg measurement

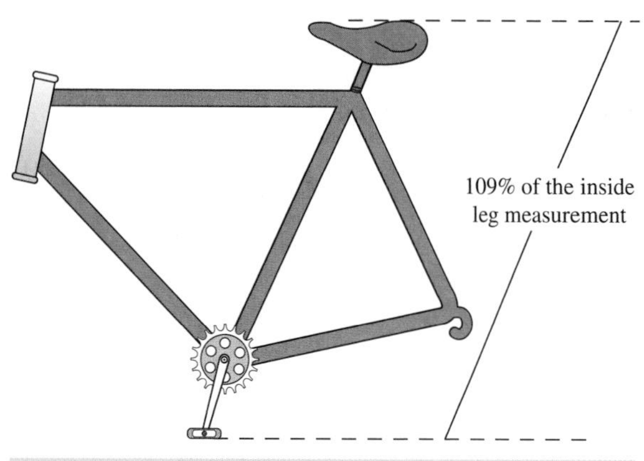

Figure for Exercise 92

Translate each verbal expression into an algebraic expression. Do not simplify.

93. The sum of 6 and x $6 + x$

94. w less than 12 $12 - w$

95. m increased by 9 $m + 9$

96. q decreased by 5 $q - 5$

97. t multiplied by 11 $11t$

98. 10 less than the square of y $y^2 - 10$

99. 5 times the difference between x and 2 $5(x - 2)$

100. The sum of two-thirds of k and 1 $\frac{2}{3}k + 1$

101. m decreased by the product of 3 and m $m - 3m$

102. 7 increased by the quotient of x and 2 $7 + \frac{x}{2}$

103. The ratio of 8 more than h and h $\frac{h + 8}{h}$

104. The product of 5 and the total of r and 3 $5(r + 3)$

105. 5 divided by the difference between y and 9 $\frac{5}{y - 9}$

106. The product of n and the sum of n and 6 $n(n + 6)$

107. The quotient of 8 less than w and twice w $\frac{w - 8}{2w}$

108. 3 more than one-third of the square of b $\frac{1}{3}b^2 + 3$

109. 9 less than the product of v and -3 $-3v - 9$

110. The total of 4 times the cube of t and the square of b $4t^3 + b^2$

111. x decreased by the quotient of x and 7 $x - \frac{x}{7}$

112. Five-eighths of the sum of y and 3 $\frac{5}{8}(y + 3)$

113. The difference between the square of m and the total of m and 7 $m^2 - (m + 7)$

114. The product of 13 and the total of t and 6 $13(t + 6)$

115. x increased by the difference between 9 times x and 8 $x + (9x - 8)$

116. The quotient of twice y and 8 $\frac{2y}{8}$

117. 9 less than the product of 13 and n $13n - 9$

118. The product of s and 5 more than s $s(s + 5)$

119. 6 increased by one-third of the sum of x and 2 $6 + \frac{1}{3}(x + 2)$

120. x decreased by the difference between $5x$ and 9 $x - (5x - 9)$

121. The sum of x divided by 2 and x $\frac{x}{2} + x$

122. Twice the sum of 6 times n and 5 $2(6n + 5)$

Given that the area of each figure is 24 square feet, use the dimensions shown to write an equation expressing this fact. Do not solve the equation.

123.

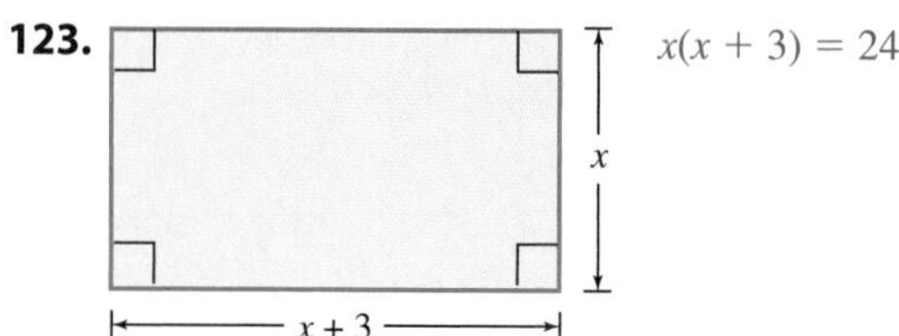

$x(x + 3) = 24$

124.

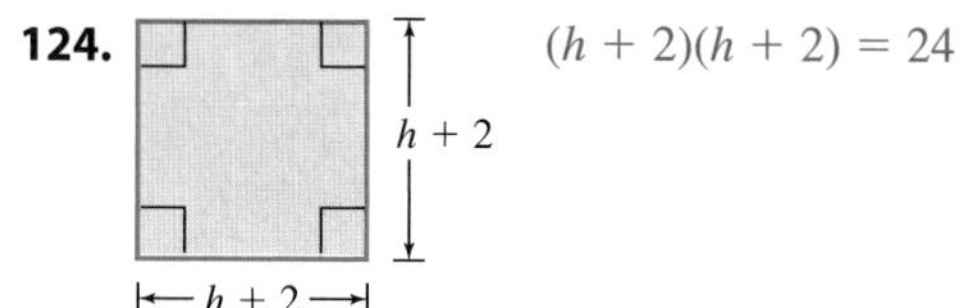

$(h + 2)(h + 2) = 24$

125.

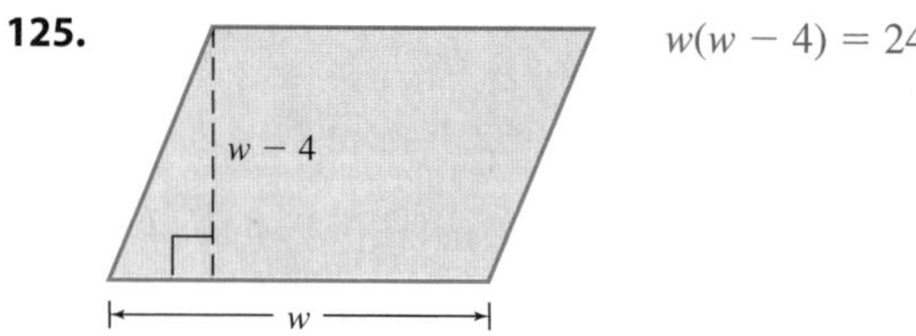

$w(w - 4) = 24$

126.

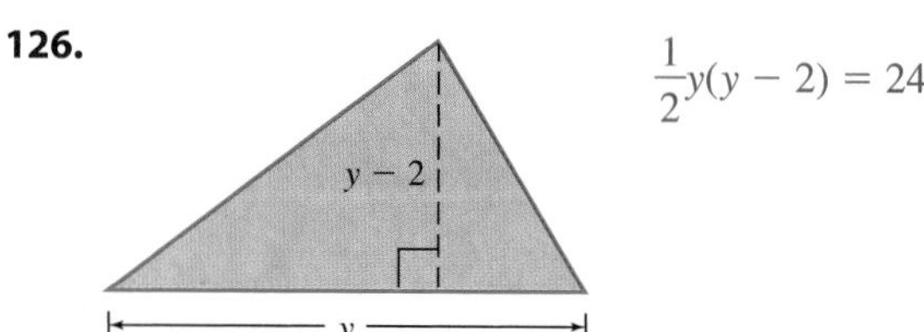

$\frac{1}{2}y(y - 2) = 24$

2.6 Number, Geometric, and Uniform Motion Applications

In this Section

- **Number Problems**
- **General Strategy for Solving Verbal Problems**
- **Geometric Problems**
- **Unit Conversion**
- **Uniform Motion Problems**

In this section, we apply the ideas of Section 2.5 to solving problems. Many of the problems can be solved by using arithmetic only and not algebra. However, remember that we are not just trying to find the answer, we are trying to learn how to apply algebra. So even if the answer is obvious to you, set the problem up and solve it by using algebra as shown in the examples.

Number Problems

Algebra is often applied to problems involving time, rate, distance, interest, or discount. **Number problems** do not involve any physical situation. In number problems we simply find some numbers that satisfy some given conditions. Number problems can provide good practice for solving more complex problems.

EXAMPLE 1

A consecutive integer problem

The sum of three consecutive integers is 48. Find the integers.

Solution

If x represents the smallest of the three consecutive integers, then x, $x + 1$, and $x + 2$ represent the three consecutive integers. Since the sum of x, $x + 1$, and $x + 2$ is 48, we write that fact as an equation and solve it:

$$x + (x + 1) + (x + 2) = 48$$
$$3x + 3 = 48 \quad \text{Combine like terms.}$$
$$3x = 45 \quad \text{Subtract 3 from each side.}$$
$$x = 15 \quad \text{Divide each side by 3.}$$
$$x + 1 = 16 \quad \text{If } x \text{ is 15, then } x + 1 \text{ is 16 and } x + 2 \text{ is 17.}$$
$$x + 2 = 17$$

Because $15 + 16 + 17 = 48$, the three consecutive integers that have a sum of 48 are 15, 16, and 17.

Now do Exercises 7–12

Helpful Hint

Making a guess can be a good way to get familiar with the problem. For example, let's guess that the answers to Example 1 are 20, 21, and 22. Since $20 + 21 + 22 = 63$, these are not the correct numbers. But now we realize that we should use x, $x + 1$, and $x + 2$ and that the equation should be

$$x + x + 1 + x + 2 = 48.$$

General Strategy for Solving Verbal Problems

You should use the following steps as a guide for solving problems.

Strategy for Solving Problems

1. Read the problem as many times as necessary. Guessing the answer and checking it will help you understand the problem.
2. If possible, draw a diagram to illustrate the problem.
3. Choose a variable and *write* what it represents.

Teaching Tip Use guessing to familiarize only when students are having a lot of trouble getting started. To make a guess and check it you must understand the problem.

4. Write algebraic expressions for any other unknowns in terms of that variable.
5. Write an equation that describes the situation.
6. Solve the equation.
7. Answer the original question.
8. Check your answer in the original problem (not the equation).

Geometric Problems

Geometric problems involve geometric figures. For these problems you should always draw the figure and label it.

EXAMPLE 2

A perimeter problem

The length of a rectangular piece of property is 1 foot less than twice the width. If the perimeter is 748 feet, find the length and width.

Solution

Let x = the width. Since the length is 1 foot less than twice the width, $2x - 1$ = the length. Draw a diagram as in Fig. 2.2. We know that $2L + 2W = P$ is the formula for perimeter of a rectangle. Substituting $2x - 1$ for L and x for W in this formula yields an equation in x:

$$2L + 2W = P$$
$$2(2x - 1) + 2(x) = 748 \quad \text{Replace } L \text{ by } 2x - 1 \text{ and } W \text{ by } x.$$
$$4x - 2 + 2x = 748 \quad \text{Remove the parentheses.}$$
$$6x - 2 = 748 \quad \text{Combine like terms.}$$
$$6x = 750 \quad \text{Add 2 to each side.}$$
$$x = 125 \quad \text{Divide each side by 6.}$$
$$2x - 1 = 249 \quad \text{If } x = 125, \text{ then } 2x - 1 = 2(125) - 1 = 249.$$

Check these answers by computing $2L + 2W$:

$$2(249) + 2(125) = 748$$

So the width is 125 feet, and the length is 249 feet.

Now do Exercises 13-18

Helpful Hint

To get familiar with the problem, guess that the width is 50 ft. Then the length is $2 \cdot 50 - 1$ or 99. The perimeter would be

$$2(50) + 2(99) = 298,$$

which is too small. But now we realize that we should let x be the width, $2x - 1$ be the length, and we should solve

$$2x + 2(2x - 1) = 748.$$

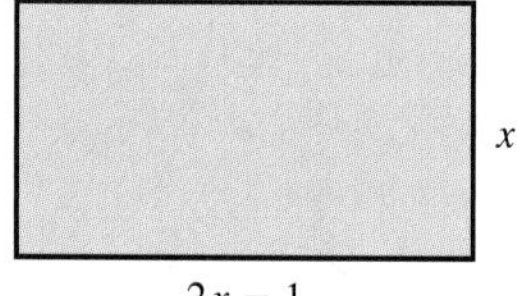

Figure 2.2

Example 3 involves the degree measures of angles. For this problem, the figure is given.

EXAMPLE 3

Complementary angles

In Fig. 2.3 the angle formed by the guy wire and the ground is 3.5 times as large as the angle formed by the guy wire and the antenna. Find the degree measure of each of these angles.

Solution

Let x = the degree measure of the smaller angle, and let $3.5x$ = the degree measure of the larger angle. Since the antenna meets the ground at a 90° angle, the sum of the degree measures of the other two angles of the right triangle is 90°.

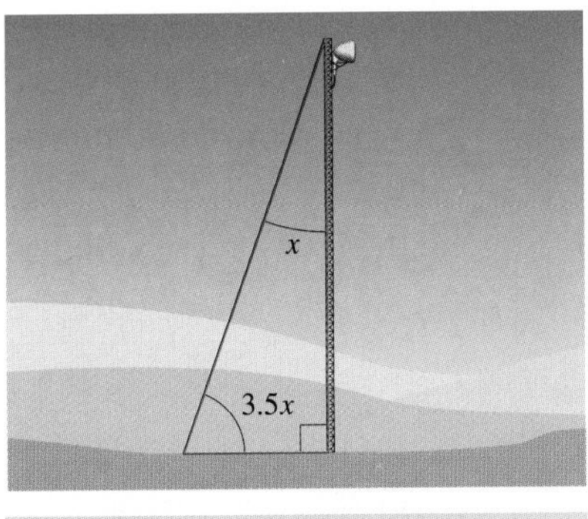

Figure 2.3

(They are complementary angles.) So we have the following equation:

$$x + 3.5x = 90$$
$$4.5x = 90 \quad \text{Combine like terms.}$$
$$x = 20 \quad \text{Divide each side by 4.5.}$$
$$3.5x = 70 \quad \text{Find the other angle.}$$

Check: 70° is 3.5 · 20° and 20° + 70° = 90°. So the smaller angle is 20°, and the larger angle is 70°.

Now do Exercises 19–20

Unit Conversion

Most measurements can be expressed in a variety of units. For example, distance could be in miles or kilometers. Converting from one unit of measurement to another can always be done by multiplying by a conversion factor expressed as a fraction. (Some common conversion factors can be found on the inside back cover of this text.) This method is called **cancellation of units,** because the units cancel just like the common factors cancel in multiplication of fractions.

EXAMPLE 4

Unit conversion

a) Convert 6 yards to feet.

b) Convert 12 miles to kilometers.

c) Convert 60 miles per hour to feet per second.

Solution

a) Because 3 feet = 1 yard, multiplying by $\frac{3 \text{ feet}}{1 \text{ yard}}$ is equivalent to multiplying by 1. Notice how yards cancels and the result is feet.

$$6 \text{ yd} = 6 \cancel{\text{yd}} \cdot \frac{3 \text{ ft}}{1 \cancel{\text{yd}}} = 18 \text{ ft}$$

b) There are two ways to convert 12 miles to kilometers using the conversion factors given on the inside back cover:

$$12 \text{ mi} = 12 \cancel{\text{mi}} \cdot \frac{1.609 \text{ km}}{1 \cancel{\text{mi}}} \approx 19.31 \text{ km}$$

$$12 \text{ mi} = 12 \cancel{\text{mi}} \cdot \frac{1 \text{ km}}{0.6215 \cancel{\text{mi}}} \approx 19.31 \text{ km}$$

Teaching Tip Emphasize that the cancellation of units method is generally taught and used in the sciences and can be used on any conversions.

Notice that in the second method we are also multiplying by a fraction that is equivalent to 1, but we actually divide 12 by 0.6215.

c) Convert 60 miles per hour to feet per second as follows:

$$60 \text{ mi/hr} = \frac{60 \text{ mi}}{1 \text{ hr}} \cdot \frac{5280 \text{ ft}}{1 \text{ mi}} \cdot \frac{1 \text{ hr}}{60 \text{ min}} \cdot \frac{1 \text{ min}}{60 \text{ sec}} = 88 \text{ ft/sec}$$

Now do Exercises 21–32

Uniform Motion Problems

Problems involving motion at a constant rate are called **uniform motion problems.** In uniform motion problems we often use an average rate when the actual rate is not constant. For example, you can drive all day and average 50 miles per hour, but you are not driving at a constant 50 miles per hour.

EXAMPLE 5

Finding the rate

Bridgette drove her car for 2 hours on an icy road. When the road cleared up, she increased her speed by 35 miles per hour and drove 3 more hours, completing her 255-mile trip. How fast did she travel on the icy road?

Helpful Hint

To get familiar with the problem, guess that she traveled 20 mph on the icy road and 55 mph (20 + 35) on the clear road. Her total distance would be

$$20 \cdot 2 + 55 \cdot 3 = 205 \text{ mi.}$$

Of course this is not correct, but now you are familiar with the problem.

Solution

It is helpful to draw a diagram and then make a table to classify the given information. Remember that $D = RT$.

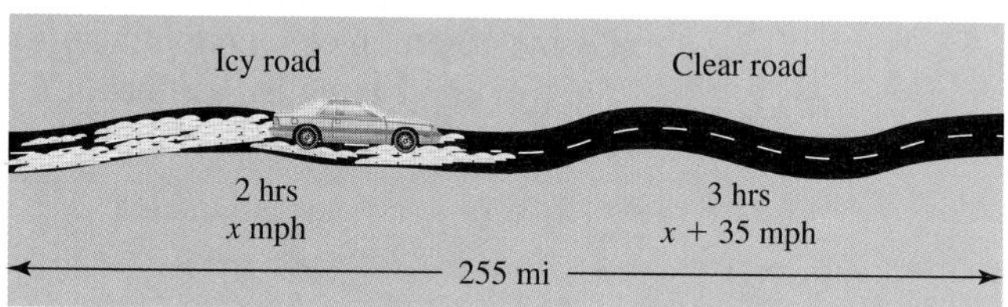

	Rate	Time	Distance
Icy road	$x \frac{\text{mi}}{\text{hr}}$	2 hr	$2x$ mi
Clear road	$x + 35 \frac{\text{mi}}{\text{hr}}$	3 hr	$3(x + 35)$ mi

The equation expresses the fact that her total distance traveled was 255 miles:

$$\text{Icy road distance} + \text{clear road distance} = \text{total distance}$$

$$\begin{aligned} 2x + 3(x + 35) &= 255 \\ 2x + 3x + 105 &= 255 \\ 5x + 105 &= 255 \\ 5x &= 150 \\ x &= 30 \\ x + 35 &= 65 \end{aligned}$$

If she drove at 30 miles per hour for 2 hours on the icy road, she went 60 miles. If she drove at 65 miles per hour for 3 hours on the clear road, she went 195 miles. Since $60 + 195 = 255$, we can be sure that her speed on the icy road was 30 mph.

Now do Exercises 33–36

In the next uniform motion problem we find the time.

EXAMPLE 6

Finding the time

Pierce drove from Allentown to Baker, averaging 55 miles per hour. His journey back to Allentown using the same route took 3 hours longer because he averaged only 40 miles per hour. How long did it take him to drive from Allentown to Baker? What is the distance between Allentown and Baker?

Study Tip

When taking a test, put a check mark beside every question that you have answered and checked. When you have finished the test, then you can go back and spend the remaining time on the problems that are not yet checked. You won't waste time reworking problems that you know are correct.

Solution

Draw a diagram and then make a table to classify the given information. Remember that $D = RT$.

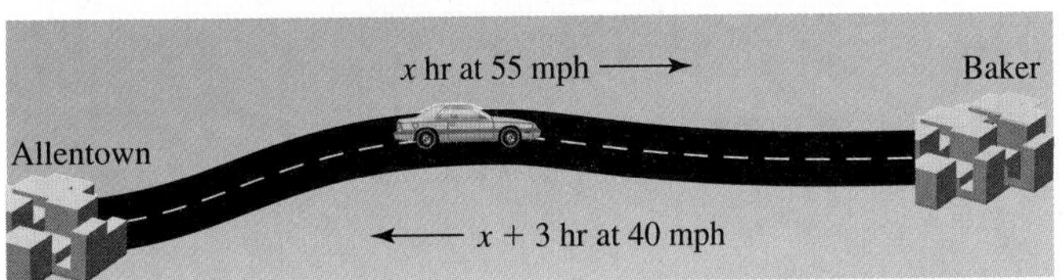

	Rate	Time	Distance
Going	$55 \frac{\text{mi}}{\text{hr}}$	x hr	$55x$ mi
Returning	$40 \frac{\text{mi}}{\text{hr}}$	$x + 3$ hr	$40(x + 3)$ mi

We can write an equation expressing the fact that the distance either way is the same:

$$\text{Distance going} = \text{distance returning}$$
$$55x = 40(x + 3)$$
$$55x = 40x + 120$$
$$15x = 120$$
$$x = 8$$

The trip from Allentown to Baker took 8 hours. The distance between Allentown and Baker is $55 \cdot 8$, or 440 miles.

Now do Exercises 37–38

Warm-Ups

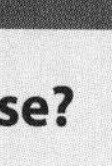

True or false? Explain your answer.

1. The first step in solving a word problem is to write the equation. False
2. You should always write down what the variable represents. True
3. Diagrams and tables are used as aids in solving problems. True
4. To represent two consecutive odd integers, we use x and $x + 1$. False
5. If $5x$ is 2 miles more than $3(x + 20)$, then $5x + 2 = 3(x + 20)$. False
6. We can represent two numbers with a sum of 6 by x and $6 - x$. True
7. Two numbers that differ by 7 can be represented by x and $x + 7$. True
8. The degree measures of two complementary angles can be represented by x and $90 - x$. True
9. The degree measures of two supplementary angles can be represented by x and $x + 180$. False
10. If x is half as large as $x + 50$, then $2x = x + 50$. True

2.6 Exercises

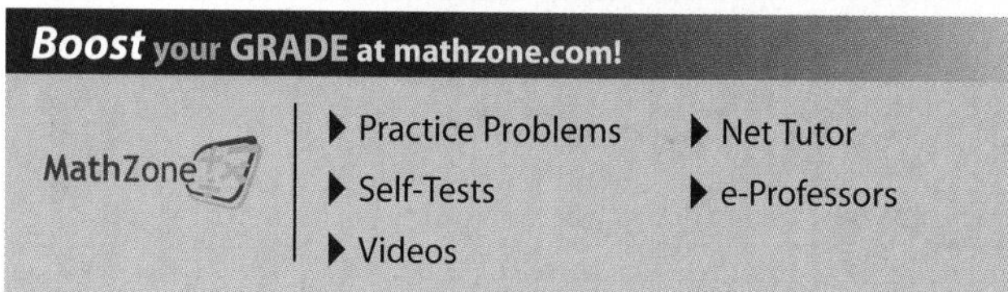

Boost your GRADE at mathzone.com!

MathZone

- Practice Problems
- Self-Tests
- Videos
- Net Tutor
- e-Professors

Reading and Writing *After reading this section, write out the answers to these questions. Use complete sentences.*

1. What types of problems are discussed in this section?
In this section we studied number, geometric, and uniform motion problems.
2. Why do we solve number problems?
We solve number problems to gain experience at problem solving.
3. What is uniform motion?
Uniform motion is motion at a constant rate of speed.
4. What are supplementary angles?
Supplementary angles are angles whose degree measures have a sum of 180°.
5. What are complementary angles?
Complementary angles are angles whose degree measures have a sum of 90°.
6. What should you always do when solving a geometric problem?
When solving a geometric problem draw a figure and label the sides.

Show a complete solution to each problem. See Example 1.

7. ***Consecutive integers.*** Find three consecutive integers whose sum is 141. 46, 47, 48
8. ***Consecutive even integers.*** Find three consecutive even integers whose sum is 114. 36, 38, 40
9. ***Consecutive odd integers.*** Two consecutive odd integers have a sum of 152. What are the integers? 75, 77
10. ***Consecutive odd integers.*** Four consecutive odd integers have a sum of 120. What are the integers? 27, 29, 31, 33
11. ***Consecutive integers.*** Find four consecutive integers whose sum is 194. 47, 48, 49, 50
12. ***Consecutive even integers.*** Find four consecutive even integers whose sum is 340. 82, 84, 86, 88

Show a complete solution to each problem. See Examples 2 and 3.

13. ***Olympic swimming.*** If an Olympic swimming pool is twice as long as it is wide and the perimeter is 150 meters, then what are the length and width?
Length 50 meters, width 25 meters

Study Tip

Don't spend too much time on a single problem. If you get stuck on a problem, look at some examples in the text, move on to the next problem, or get help. It is often helpful to work some other problems and then come back to that one pesky problem.

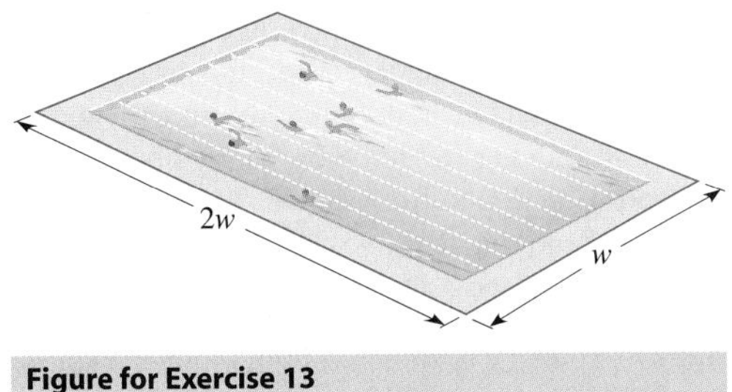

Figure for Exercise 13

14. ***Wimbledon tennis.*** If the perimeter of a tennis court is 228 feet and the length is 6 feet longer than twice the width, then what are the length and width?
Length 78 feet, width 36 feet

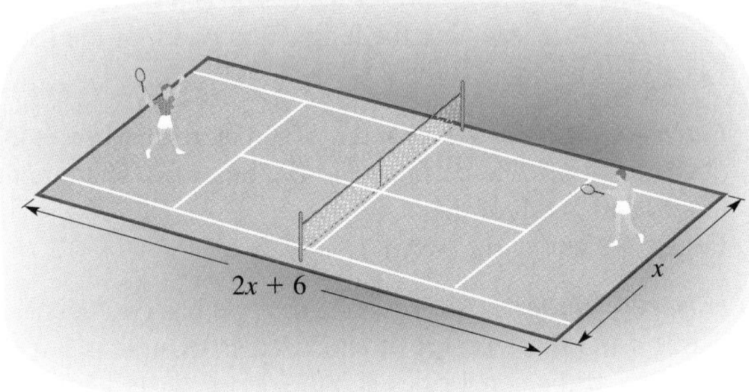

Figure for Exercise 14

15. ***Framed.*** Julia framed an oil painting that her uncle gave her. The painting was 4 inches longer than it was wide, and it took 176 inches of frame molding. What were the dimensions of the picture?
Width 42 inches, length 46 inches

16. ***Industrial triangle.*** Geraldo drove his truck from Indianapolis to Chicago, then to St. Louis, and then back to Indianapolis. He observed that the second side of his triangular route was 81 miles short of being twice as long as the first side and that the third side was 61 miles longer than the first side. If he traveled a total of 720 miles, then how long is each side of this triangular route?
185 miles, 289 miles, 246 miles

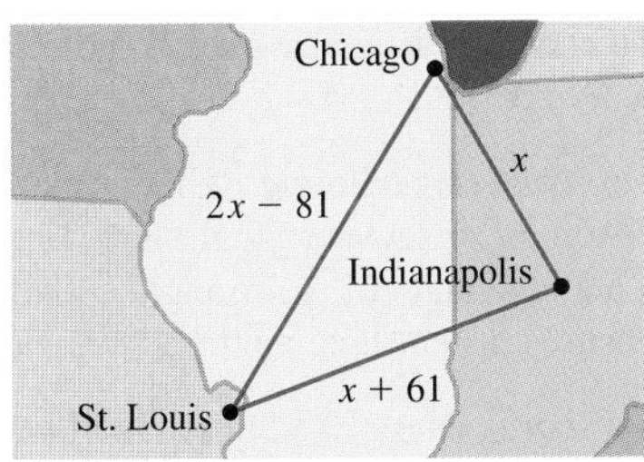

Figure for Exercise 16

17. ***Triangular banner.*** A banner in the shape of an isosceles triangle has a base that is 5 inches shorter than either of the equal sides. If the perimeter of the banner is 34 inches, then what is the length of the equal sides? 13 inches

18. ***Border paper.*** Dr. Good's waiting room is 8 feet longer than it is wide. When Vincent wallpapered Dr. Good's waiting room, he used 88 feet of border paper. What are the dimensions of Dr. Good's waiting room?
18 feet by 26 feet

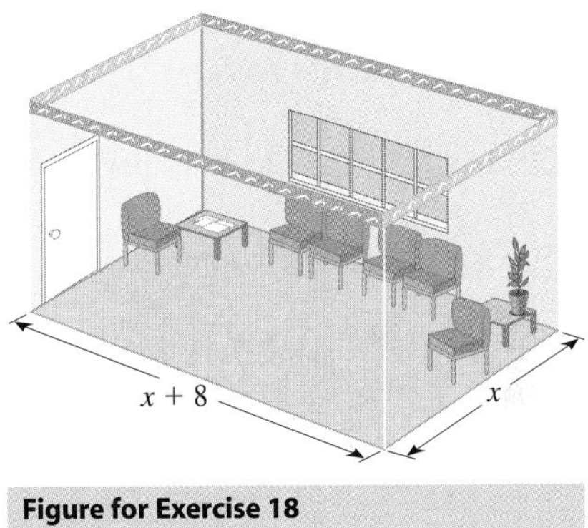

Figure for Exercise 18

19. ***Ramping up.*** A civil engineer is planning a highway overpass as shown in the figure. Find the degree measure of the angle marked w. 35°

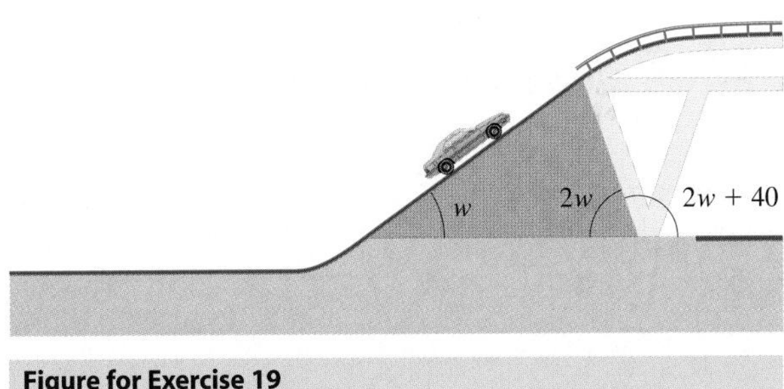

Figure for Exercise 19

20. ***Ramping down.*** For the other side of the overpass, the engineer has drawn the plans shown in the figure. Find the degree measure of the angle marked z. 24°

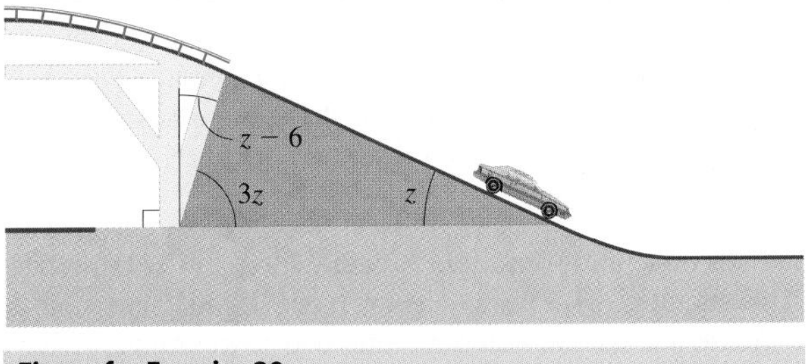

Figure for Exercise 20

Perform the indicated unit conversions. See Example 4. Round approximate answers to the nearest hundredth. Answers can vary slightly depending on the conversion factors used.

21. Convert 96 feet to inches. 1152 in.

22. Convert 33 yards to feet. 99 ft

23. Convert 14.22 miles to kilometers. 22.88 km

24. Convert 33.6 kilometers to miles 20.88 mi

25. Convert 13.5 centimeters to inches. 5.31 in.

26. Convert 42.1 inches to centimeters. 106.93 cm

27. Convert 14.2 ounces to grams. 402.57 g

28. Convert 233 grams to ounces. 8.22 oz

29. Convert 40 miles per hour to feet per second. 58.67 ft/sec

30. Convert 200 feet per second to miles per hour. 136.36 mi/hr

31. Convert 500 feet per second to kilometers per hour. 548.53 km/hr

32. Convert 230 yards per second to miles per minute. 7.84 mi/min

Show a complete solution to each problem. See Examples 5 and 6.

33. ***Highway miles.*** Bret drove for 4 hours on the freeway, then decreased his speed by 20 miles per hour and drove for 5 more hours on a country road. If his total trip was 485 miles, then what was his speed on the freeway? 65 miles per hour

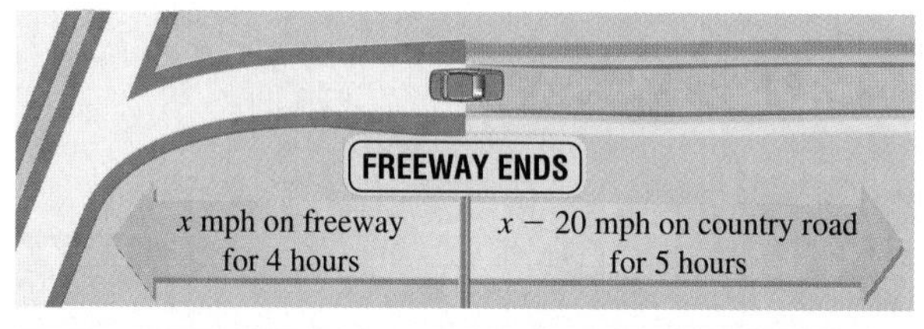

Figure for Exercise 33

34. ***Walking and running.*** On Saturday morning, Lynn walked for 2 hours and then ran for 30 minutes. If she ran twice as fast as she walked and she covered 12 miles altogether, then how fast did she walk? 4 miles per hour

35. ***Driving all night.*** Kathryn drove her rig 5 hours before dawn and 6 hours after dawn. If her average speed was 5 miles per hour more in the dark and she covered 630 miles altogether, then what was her speed after dawn? 55 miles per hour

36. ***Commuting to work.*** On Monday, Roger drove to work in 45 minutes. On Tuesday he averaged 12 miles per hour more, and it took him 9 minutes less to get to work. How far does he travel to work? 36 miles

37. ***Head winds.*** A jet flew at an average speed of 640 mph from Los Angeles to Chicago. Because of head winds the jet averaged only 512 mph on the return trip, and the return trip took 48 minutes longer. How many hours was the flight from Chicago to Los Angeles? How far is it from Chicago to Los Angeles? 4 hours, 2048 miles

38. ***Ride the Peaks.*** Penny's bicycle trip from Colorado Springs to Pikes Peak took 1.5 hours longer than the return trip to Colorado Springs. If she averaged 6 mph on the way to Pikes Peak and 15 mph for the return trip, then how long was the ride from Colorado Springs to Pikes Peak? 2.5 hours

Solve each problem.

39. ***Perimeter of a frame.*** The perimeter of a rectangular frame is 64 in. If the width of the frame is 8 in. less than the length, then what are the length and width of the frame? Length 20 inches, width 12 inches

40. ***Perimeter of a box.*** The width of a rectangular box is 20% of the length. If the perimeter is 192 cm, then what are the length and width of the box? Length 80 cm, width 16 cm

41. ***Isosceles triangle.*** An isosceles triangle has two equal sides. If the shortest side of an isosceles triangle is 2 ft less than one of the equal sides and the perimeter is 13 ft, then what are the lengths of the sides? 5 ft, 5 ft, 3 ft

42. ***Scalene triangle.*** A scalene triangle has three unequal sides. The perimeter of a scalene triangle is 144 m. If the first side is twice as long as the second side and the third side is 24 m longer than the second side, then what are the measures of the sides? 60 m, 30 m, 54 m

43. ***Angles of a scalene triangle.*** The largest angle in a scalene triangle is six times as large as the smallest. If the middle angle is twice the smallest, then what are the degree measures of the three angles? 20°, 40°, 120°

44. ***Angles of a right triangle.*** If one of the acute angles in a right triangle is 38°, then what are the degree measures of all three angles? 38°, 52°, 90°

45. ***Angles of an isosceles triangle.*** One of the equal angles in an isosceles triangle is four times as large as the smallest angle in the triangle. What are the degree measures of the three angles? 20°, 80°, 80°

46. ***Angles of an isosceles triangle.*** The measure of one of the equal angles in an isosceles triangle is 10° larger than twice the smallest angle in the triangle. What are the degree measures of the three angles? 32°, 74°, 74°

47. ***Super Bowl score.*** The 1977 Super Bowl was played in the Rose Bowl in Pasadena. In that football game the Oakland Raiders scored 18 more points than the Minnesota

Vikings. If the total number of points scored was 46, then what was the final score for the game?
Raiders 32, Vikings 14

48. ***Top payrolls.*** Payrolls for the three highest paid baseball teams (the Yankees, Mets, and Braves) for 2003 totaled \$376 million (www.usatoday.com). If the team payroll for the Yankees was \$36 million greater than the payroll for the Mets and the payroll for the Mets was \$11 million greater than the payroll for the Braves, then what was the 2003 payroll for each team?
Yankees \$153 million, Mets \$117 million, Braves \$106 million

49. ***Idabel to Lawton.*** Before lunch, Sally drove from Idabel to Ardmore, averaging 50 mph. After lunch she continued on to Lawton, averaging 53 mph. If her driving time after lunch was 1 hour less than her driving time before lunch and the total trip was 256 miles, then how many hours did she drive before lunch? How far is it from Ardmore to Lawton? 3 hours, 106 miles

50. ***Norfolk to Chadron.*** On Monday, Chuck drove from Norfolk to Valentine, averaging 47 mph. On Tuesday, he continued on to Chadron, averaging 69 mph. His driving time on Monday was 2 hours longer than his driving time on Tuesday. If the total distance from Norfolk to Chadron is 326 miles, then how many hours did he drive on Monday? How far is it from Valentine to Chadron?
4 hours, 138 miles

51. ***Golden oldies.*** Joan Crawford, John Wayne, and James Stewart were born in consecutive years (*Doubleday Almanac*). Joan Crawford was the oldest of the three, and James Stewart was the youngest. In 1950, after all three had their birthdays, the sum of their ages was 129. In what years were they born?
Crawford 1906, Wayne 1907, Stewart 1908

52. ***Leading men.*** Bob Hope was born 2 years after Clark Gable and 2 years before Henry Fonda (*Doubleday Almanac*). In 1951, after all three of them had their birthdays, the sum of their ages was 144. In what years were they born? Hope 1903, Gable 1901, Fonda 1905

53. ***Trimming a garage door.*** A carpenter used 30 ft of molding in three pieces to trim a garage door. If the long piece was 2 ft longer than twice the length of each shorter piece, then how long was each piece? 7 ft, 7 ft, 16 ft

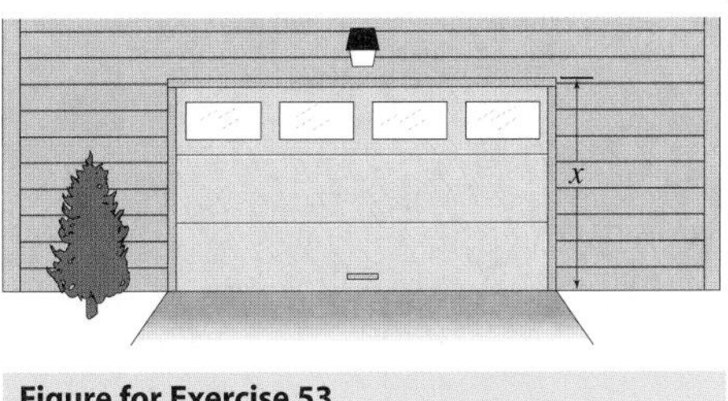

Figure for Exercise 53

54. ***Fencing dog pens.*** Clint is constructing two adjacent rectangular dog pens. Each pen will be three times as long as it is wide, and the pens will share a common long side. If Clint has 65 ft of fencing, what are the dimensions of each pen? 5 ft by 15 ft

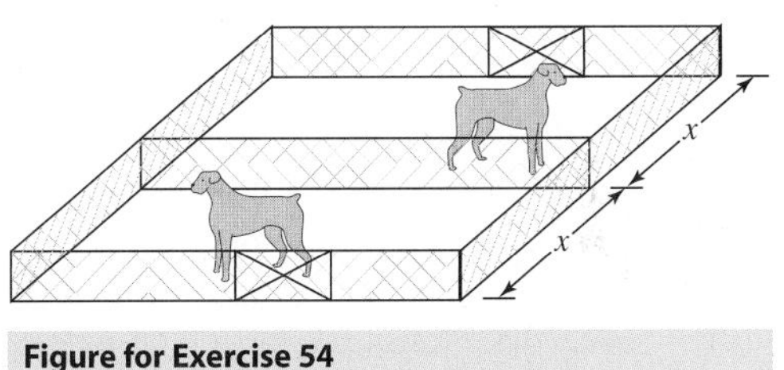

Figure for Exercise 54

2.7 Discount, Investment, and Mixture Applications

In this Section

- Discount Problems
- Commission Problems
- Investment Problems
- Mixture Problems

In this section, we continue our study of applications of algebra. The problems in this section involve percents.

Discount Problems

When an item is sold at a discount, the amount of the discount is usually described as being a percentage of the original price. The percentage is called the **rate of discount.** Multiplying the rate of discount and the original price gives the amount of the discount.

EXAMPLE 1

Finding the original price

Ralph got a 12% discount when he bought his new 2002 Corvette Coupe. If the amount of his discount was \$6606, then what was the original price of the Corvette?

Solution

Let x represent the original price. The discount is found by multiplying the 12% rate of discount and the original price:

$$\text{Rate of discount} \cdot \text{original price} = \text{amount of discount}$$

$$0.12x = 6606$$

$$x = \frac{6606}{0.12} \quad \text{Divide each side by 0.12.}$$

$$x = 55{,}050$$

To check, find 12% of \$55,050. Since $0.12 \cdot 55{,}050 = 6606$, the original price of the Corvette was \$55,050.

Now do Exercises 7–8

EXAMPLE 2

Finding the original price

When Susan bought her new car, she also got a discount of 12%. She paid \$17,600 for her car. What was the original price of Susan's car?

Helpful Hint

To get familiar with the problem, guess that the original price was \$30,000. Then her discount is 0.12(30,000) or \$3600. The price she paid would be 30,000 − 3600 or \$26,400, which is incorrect.

Solution

Let x represent the original price for Susan's car. The amount of discount is 12% of x, or $0.12x$. We can write an equation expressing the fact that the original price minus the discount is the price Susan paid.

$$\text{Original price} - \text{discount} = \text{sale price}$$

$$x - 0.12x = 17{,}600$$

$$0.88x = 17{,}600 \quad 1.00x - 0.12x = 0.88x$$

$$x = \frac{17{,}600}{0.88} \quad \text{Divide each side by 0.88.}$$

$$x = 20{,}000$$

Check: 12% of \$20,000 is \$2400, and \$20,000 − \$2400 = \$17,600. The original price of Susan's car was \$20,000.

Now do Exercises 9–10

Commission Problems

A salesperson's commission for making a sale is often a percentage of the selling price. **Commission problems** are very similar to other problems involving percents. The commission is found by multiplying the rate of commission and the selling price.

EXAMPLE 3

Real estate commission

Sarah is selling her house through a real estate agent whose commission rate is 7%. What should the selling price be so that Sarah can get the $83,700 she needs to pay off the mortgage?

Teaching Tip Students often have trouble with $x - 0.07x$. You might need to do more examples of this idea.

Solution

Let x be the selling price. The commission is 7% of x (not 7% of $83,700). Sarah receives the selling price less the sales commission:

$$\text{Selling price} - \text{commission} = \text{Sarah's share}$$

$$x - 0.07x = 83{,}700$$

$$0.93x = 83{,}700 \quad 1.00x - 0.07x = 0.93x$$

$$x = \frac{83{,}700}{0.93}$$

$$x = 90{,}000$$

Check: 7% of $90,000 is $6300, and $90,000 − $6300 = $83,700. So the house should sell for $90,000.

Now do Exercises 11–14

Investment Problems

The interest on an investment is a percentage of the investment, just as the sales commission is a percentage of the sale amount. However, in **investment problems** we must often account for more than one investment at different rates. So it is a good idea to make a table, as in Example 4.

EXAMPLE 4

Diversified investing

Ruth Ann invested some money in a certificate of deposit with an annual yield of 9%. She invested twice as much in a mutual fund with an annual yield of 10%. Her interest from the two investments at the end of the year was $232. How much was invested at each rate?

Helpful Hint

To get familiar with the problem, guess that she invested $1000 at 9% and $2000 at 10%. Then her interest in one year would be

$$0.09(1000) + 0.10(2000)$$

or $290, which is close but incorrect.

Solution

When there are many unknown quantities, it is often helpful to identify them in a table. Since the time is 1 year, the amount of interest is the product of the interest rate and the amount invested.

	Interest rate	**Amount invested**	**Interest for 1 year**
CD	9%	x	$0.09x$
Mutual fund	10%	$2x$	$0.10(2x)$

Since the total interest from the investments was \$232, we can write the following equation:

$$\text{CD interest} + \text{mutual fund interest} = \text{total interest}$$

$$0.09x + 0.10(2x) = 232$$

$$0.09x + 0.20x = 232$$

$$0.29x = 232$$

$$x = \frac{232}{0.29}$$

$$x = 800$$

$$2x = 1600$$

To check, we find the total interest:

$$0.09(800) + 0.10(1600) = 72 + 160$$

$$= 232$$

So Ruth Ann invested \$800 at 9% and \$1600 at 10%.

Now do Exercises 15–18

Study Tip

Finding out what happened in class and attending class are not the same. Attend every class and use class as a learning time. Take notes, ask questions, and make sure that you are learning in the classroom.

Mixture Problems

Mixture problems are concerned with the result of mixing two quantities, each of which contains another substance. Notice how similar the following mixture problem is to the last investment problem.

EXAMPLE 5

Mixing milk

How many gallons of milk containing 4% butterfat must be mixed with 80 gallons of 1% milk to obtain 2% milk?

Helpful Hint

To get familiar with the problem, guess that we need 100 gal of 4% milk. Mixing that with 80 gal of 1% milk would produce 180 gal of 2% milk. Now the two milks separately have

$$0.04(100) + 0.01(80)$$

or 4.8 gal of fat. Together the amount of fat is 0.02(180) or 3.6 gal. Since these amounts are not equal, our guess is incorrect.

Solution

It is helpful to draw a diagram and then make a table to classify the given information.

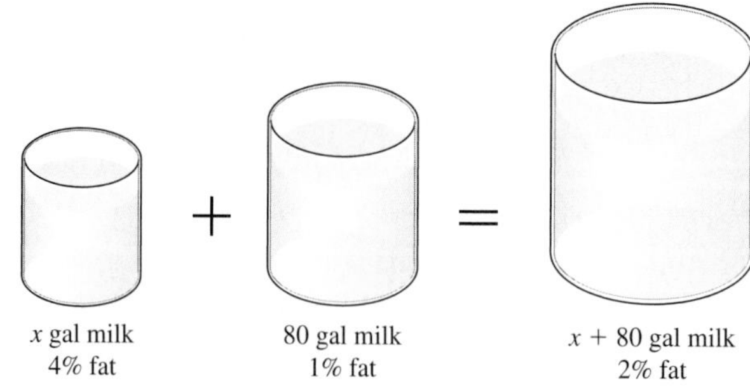

	Percentage of fat	Amount of milk	Amount of fat
4% milk	4%	x	$0.04x$
1% milk	1%	80	0.01(80)
2% milk	2%	$x + 80$	$0.02(x + 80)$

The equation expresses the fact that the total fat from the first two types of milk is the same as the fat in the mixture:

$$\begin{aligned} \text{Fat in 4\% milk} + \text{fat in 1\% milk} &= \text{fat in 2\% milk} \\ 0.04x + 0.01(80) &= 0.02(x + 80) \\ 0.04x + 0.8 &= 0.02x + 1.6 && \text{Simplify.} \\ 100(0.04x + 0.8) &= 100(0.02x + 1.6) && \text{Multiply each side by 100.} \\ 4x + 80 &= 2x + 160 && \text{Distributive property.} \\ 2x + 80 &= 160 && \text{Subtract } 2x \text{ from each side.} \\ 2x &= 80 && \text{Subtract 80 from each side.} \\ x &= 40 && \text{Divide each side by 2.} \end{aligned}$$

To check, calculate the total fat:

$$2\% \text{ of 120 gallons} = 0.02(120) = 2.4 \text{ gallons of fat}$$
$$0.04(40) + 0.01(80) = 1.6 + 0.8 = 2.4 \text{ gallons of fat}$$

So we mix 40 gallons of 4% milk with 80 gallons of 1% milk to get 120 gallons of 2% milk.

Now do Exercises 19–22

Study Tip

Don't expect to understand a new topic the first time that you see it. Learning mathematics takes time, patience, and repetition. Keep reading the text, asking questions, and working problems. Someone once said, "All mathematics is easy once you understand it."

In mixture problems, the solutions might contain fat, alcohol, salt, or some other substance. We always assume that the substance neither appears nor disappears in the process. For example, if there are 3 grams of salt in one glass of water and 2 grams in another, then there are exactly 5 grams in a mixture of the two.

Warm-Ups ▼

True or false? Explain your answer.

1. If Jim gets a 12% commission for selling a $1000 Wonder Vac, then his commission is $120. True
2. If Bob earns a 5% commission on an $80,000 motorhome sale, then Bob earns $400. False
3. If Sue gets a 20% discount on a TV with a list price of x dollars, then Sue pays $0.8x$ dollars. True
4. If you get a 6% discount on a car that has an MSRP of x dollars, then your discount is $0.6x$ dollars. False
5. If the original price is w and the discount is 8%, then the selling price is $w - 0.08w$. True
6. If x is the selling price and the commission is 8% of the selling price, then the commission is $0.08x$. True
7. If you need $40,000 for your house and the agent gets 10% of the selling price, then the agent gets $4000, and the house sells for $44,000. False
8. If you mix 10 liters of a 20% acid solution with x liters of a 30% acid solution, then the total amount of acid is $2 + 0.3x$ liters. True
9. A 10% acid solution mixed with a 14% acid solution results in a 24% acid solution. False
10. If a TV costs x dollars and sales tax is 5%, then the total bill is $1.05x$ dollars. True

2.7 Exercises

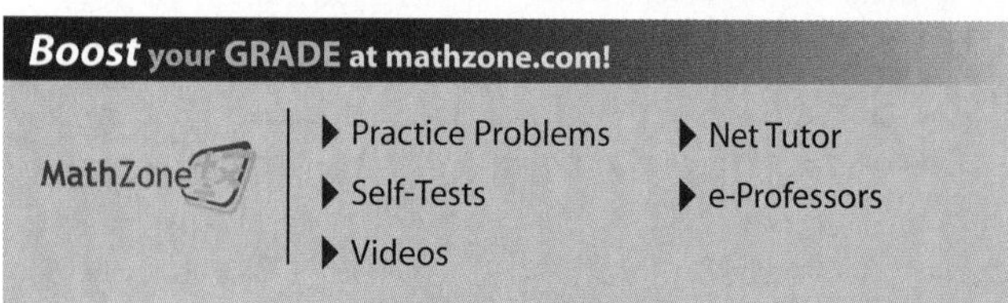

Reading and Writing *After reading this section, write out the answers to these questions. Use complete sentences.*

1. What types of problems are discussed in this section?
We studied discount, investment, and mixture problems in this section.
2. What is the difference between discount and rate of discount?
The rate of discount is a percentage and the discount is the actual amount that the price is reduced.
3. What is the relationship between discount, original price, rate of discount, and sale price?
The product of the rate and the original price gives the amount of discount. The original price minus the discount is the sale price.
4. What do mixture problems and investment problems have in common?
Both mixture problems and investment problems involve rates.
5. Why do we make a table when solving certain problems.
A table helps us to organize the information given in a problem.
6. What is the relationship between amount of interest, amount invested, and interest rate?
The product of the interest rate and the amount invested gives the amount of interest.

Show a complete solution to each problem. See Examples 1 and 2.

7. ***Close-out sale.*** At a 25% off sale, Jose saved $80 on a 19-inch Panasonic TV. What was the original price of the television. $320
8. ***Nice tent.*** A 12% discount on a Walrus tent saved Melanie $75. What was the original price of the tent? $625
9. ***Circuit city.*** After getting a 20% discount, Robert paid $320 for a Pioneer CD player for his car. What was the original price of the CD player? $400
10. ***Chrysler Sebring.*** After getting a 15% discount on the price of a new Chrysler Sebring convertible, Helen paid $27,000. What was the original price of the convertible? $31,765

Show a complete solution to each problem. See Example 3.

11. ***Selling price of a home.*** Kirk wants to get $115,000 for his house. The real estate agent gets a commission equal to 8% of the selling price for selling the house. What should the selling price be? $125,000

Photo for Exercise 11

12. ***Horse trading.*** Gene is selling his palomino at an auction. The auctioneer's commission is 10% of the selling price. If Gene still owes $810 on the horse, then what must the horse sell for so that Gene can pay off his loan? $900
13. ***Sales tax collection.*** Merilee sells tomatoes at a roadside stand. Her total receipts including the 7% sales tax were $462.24. What amount of sales tax did she collect? $30.24
14. ***Toyota Corolla.*** Gwen bought a new Toyota Corolla. The selling price plus the 8% state sales tax was $15,714. What was the selling price? $14,550

Show a complete solution to each problem. See Example 4.

15. ***Wise investments.*** Wiley invested some money in the Berger 100 Fund and $3000 more than that amount in the Berger 101 Fund. For the year he was in the fund, the 100 Fund paid 18% simple interest and the 101 Fund paid 15% simple interest. If the income from the two investments totaled $3750 for one year, then how much did he invest in each fund? 100 Fund $10,000, 101 Fund $13,000
16. ***Loan shark.*** Becky lent her brother some money at 8% simple interest, and she lent her sister twice as much at twice the interest rate. If she received a total of 20 cents interest, then how much did she lend to each of them?
Brother $0.50, sister $1.00
17. ***Investing in bonds.*** David split his $25,000 inheritance between Fidelity Short-Term Bond Fund with an annual yield of 5% and T. Rowe Price Tax-Free Short-Intermediate Fund with an annual yield of 4%. If his total income for one year on the two investments was $1140, then how much did he invest in each fund?
Fidelity $14,000, Price $11,000

18. ***High-risk funds.*** Of the \$50,000 that Natasha pocketed on her last real estate deal, \$20,000 went to charity. She invested part of the remainder in Dreyfus New Leaders Fund with an annual yield of 16% and the rest in Templeton Growth Fund with an annual yield of 25%. If she made \$6060 on these investments in one year, then how much did she invest in each fund?
Dreyfus \$16,000, Templeton \$14,000

Show a complete solution to each problem. See Example 5.

19. ***Mixing milk.*** How many gallons of milk containing 1% butterfat must be mixed with 30 gallons of milk containing 3% butterfat to obtain a mixture containing 2% butterfat? 30 gallons

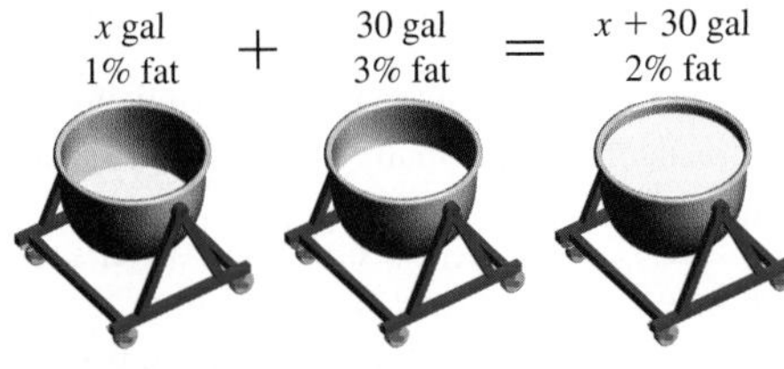

Figure for Exercise 19

20. ***Acid solutions.*** How many gallons of a 5% acid solution should be mixed with 30 gallons of a 10% acid solution to obtain a mixture that is 8% acid? 20 gallons

21. ***Alcohol solutions.*** Gus has on hand a 5% alcohol solution and a 20% alcohol solution. He needs 30 liters of a 10% alcohol solution. How many liters of each solution should he mix together to obtain the 30 liters?
20 liters of 5% alcohol, 10 liters of 20% alcohol

22. ***Adjusting antifreeze.*** Angela needs 20 quarts of 50% antifreeze solution in her radiator. She plans to obtain this by mixing some pure antifreeze with an appropriate amount of a 40% antifreeze solution. How many quarts of each should she use?
$\frac{10}{3}$ quarts of pure antifreeze, $\frac{50}{3}$ quarts of 40% solution

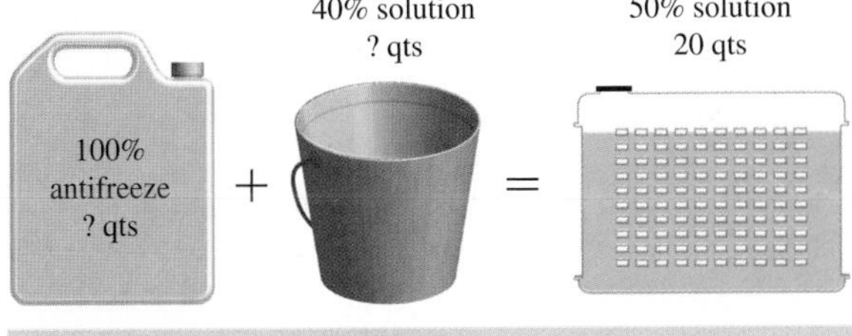

Figure for Exercise 22

Solve each problem.

23. ***Registered voters.*** If 60% of the registered voters of Lancaster County voted in the November election and 33,420 votes were cast, then how many registered voters are there in Lancaster County? 55,700

Photo for Exercise 23

24. ***Tough on crime.*** In a random sample of voters, 594 respondents said that they favored passage of a \$33 billion crime bill. If the number in favor of the crime bill was 45% of the number of voters in the sample, then how many voters were in the sample? 1320

25. ***Ford Taurus.*** At an 8% sales tax rate, the sales tax on Peter's new Ford Taurus was \$1200. What was the price of the car? \$15,000

26. ***Taxpayer blues.*** Last year, Faye paid 24% of her income to taxes. If she paid \$9600 in taxes, then what was her income? \$40,000

27. ***Making a profit.*** A retail store buys shirts for \$8 and sells them for \$14. What percent increase is this? 75%

28. ***Monitoring AIDS.*** If 28 new AIDS cases were reported in Landon County this year and 35 new cases were reported last year, then what percent decrease in new cases is this?
20%

29. ***High school integration.*** Wilson High School has 400 students, of whom 20% are African American. The school board plans to merge Wilson High with Jefferson High. This one school will then have a student population that is 44% African American. If Jefferson currently has a student population that is 60% African American, then how many students are at Jefferson? 600

30. ***Junior high integration.*** The school board plans to merge two junior high schools into one school of 800 students in which 40% of the students will be Caucasian. One of the schools currently has 58% Caucasian students; the other has only 10% Caucasian students. How many students are in each of the two schools? 500 students in the 58% school, 300 students in the 10% school

31. ***Hospital capacity.*** When Memorial Hospital is filled to capacity, it has 18 more people in semiprivate rooms (two patients to a room) than in private rooms. The room rates are \$200 per day for a private room and \$150 per day for a semiprivate room. If the total receipts for rooms is

$17,400 per day when all are full, then how many rooms of each type does the hospital have?
42 private rooms, 30 semiprivate rooms

32. ***Public relations.*** Memorial Hospital is planning an advertising campaign. It costs the hospital $3000 each time a television ad is aired and $2000 each time a radio ad is aired. The administrator wants to air 60 more television ads than radio ads. If the total cost of airing the ads is $580,000, then how many ads of each type will be aired?
140 TV ads, 80 radio ads

33. ***Mixed nuts.*** Cashews sell for $4.80 per pound, and pistachios sell for $6.40 per pound. How many pounds of pistachios should be mixed with 20 pounds of cashews to get a mixture that sells for $5.40 per pound? 12 pounds

34. ***Premium blend.*** Premium coffee sells for $6.00 per pound, and regular coffee sells for $4.00 per pound. How many pounds of each type of coffee should be blended to obtain 100 pounds of a blend that sells for $4.64 per pound?
32 pounds of premium, 68 pounds of regular

35. ***Nickels and dimes.*** Candice paid her library fine with 10 coins consisting of nickels and dimes. If the fine was $0.80, then how many of each type of coin did she use?
4 nickels, 6 dimes

36. ***Dimes and quarters.*** Jeremy paid for his breakfast with 36 coins consisting of dimes and quarters. If the bill was $4.50, then how many of each type of coin did he use? 30 dimes, 6 quarters

37. ***Cooking oil.*** Crisco Canola Oil is 7% saturated fat. Crisco blends corn oil that is 14% saturated fat with Crisco Canola Oil to get Crisco Canola and Corn Oil, which is 11% saturated fat. How many gallons of corn oil must Crisco mix with 600 gallons of Crisco Canola Oil to get Crisco Canola and Corn Oil? 800 gallons

38. ***Chocolate ripple.*** The Delicious Chocolate Shop makes a dark chocolate that is 35% fat and a white chocolate that is 48% fat. How many kilograms of dark chocolate should be mixed with 50 kilograms of white chocolate to make a ripple blend that is 40% fat? 80 kilograms

39. ***Hawaiian Punch.*** Hawaiian Punch is 10% fruit juice. How much water would you have to add to one gallon of Hawaiian Punch to get a drink that is 6% fruit juice? $\frac{2}{3}$ gal

40. ***Diluting wine.*** A restaurant manager has 2 liters of white wine that is 12% alcohol. How many liters of white grape juice should he add to get a drink that is 10% alcohol? $\frac{2}{5}$ liter

41. ***Bargain hunting.*** A smart shopper bought 5 pairs of shorts and 8 tops for a total of $108. If the price of a pair of shorts was twice the price of a top, then what was the price of each type of clothing? Shorts $12, tops $6

42. ***VCRs and CDs.*** The manager of a stereo shop placed an order for $10,710 worth of VCRs at $120 each and CD players at $150 each. If the number of VCRs she ordered was three times the number of CD players, then how many of each did she order? 21 CD players, 63 VCRs

2.8 Inequalities

In this Section

- Basic Ideas
- Graphing Inequalities
- Graphing Compound Inequalities
- Checking Inequalities
- Writing Inequalities

In Chapter 1, we defined inequality in terms of the number line. One number is greater than another number if it lies to the right of the other number on the number line. In this section you will study inequality in greater depth.

Helpful Hint

A good way to learn inequality symbols is to notice that the inequality symbol always points at the smaller number. This observation will help you read an inequality such as $-2 < x$. Reading right to left, we say that x is greater than -2. It is usually easier to understand an inequality if you read the variable first.

Basic Ideas

The symbols used to express inequality and their meanings are given in the following box.

Inequality Symbols

Symbol	Meaning
$<$	Is less than
$\le$	Is less than or equal to
$>$	Is greater than
$\ge$	Is greater than or equal to

The statement $a < b$ means that a is to the left of b on the number line as shown in Fig. 2.4. The statement $c > d$ means that c is to the right of d on the number line, as shown in Fig. 2.5. Of course, $a < b$ has the same meaning as $b > a$. The statement $a \leq b$ means that either a is to the left of b or a corresponds to the same point as b on the number line. The statement $a \leq b$ has the same meaning as the statement $b \geq a$.

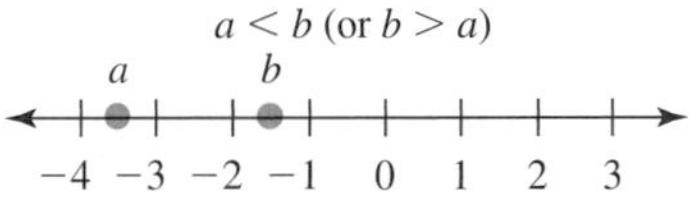

Figure 2.4

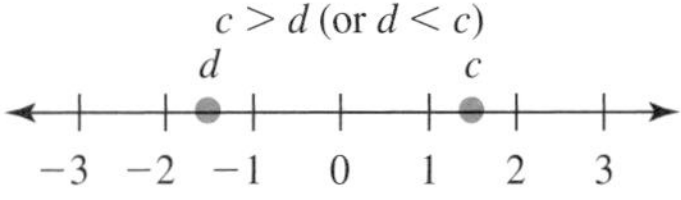

Figure 2.5

EXAMPLE 1

Verifying inequalities

Determine whether each of the following statements is correct.

a) $3 < 4$ **b)** $-1 < -2$ **c)** $-2 \leq 0$

d) $0 \geq 0$ **e)** $2(-3) + 8 > 9$ **f)** $(-2)(-5) \leq 10$

Calculator Close-Up

A graphing calculator can determine whether an inequality is correct. Use the inequality symbols from the TEST menu to enter the inequality.

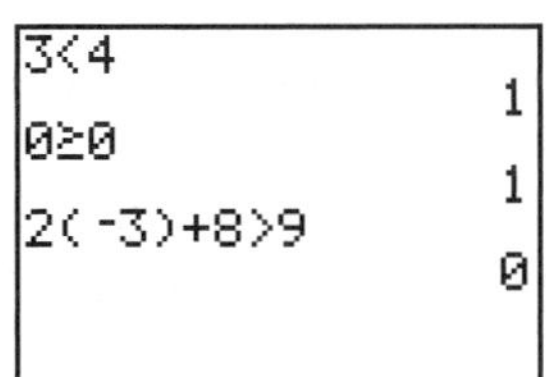

When ENTER is pressed, the calculator returns a 1 if the inequality is correct or a 0 if the inequality is incorrect.

Solution

a) Locate 3 and 4 on the number line shown in Fig. 2.6. Because 3 is to the left of 4 on the number line, $3 < 4$ is correct.

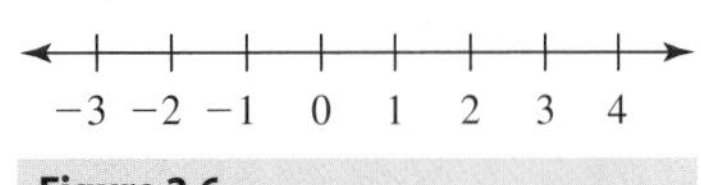

Figure 2.6

b) Locate -1 and -2 on the number line shown in Fig. 2.6. Because -1 is to the right of -2, on the number line, $-1 < -2$ is not correct.

c) Because -2 is to the left of 0 on the number line, $-2 \leq 0$ is correct.

d) Because 0 is equal to 0, $0 \geq 0$ is correct.

e) Simplify the left side of the inequality to get $2 > 9$, which is not correct.

f) Simplify the left side of the inequality to get $10 \leq 10$, which is correct.

Now do Exercises 7–20

Graphing Inequalities

If a is a fixed real number, then any real number x located to the right of a on the number line satisfies $x > a$. The set of real numbers located to the right of a on the number line is the solution set to $x > a$. This solution set is written in set-builder notation as $\{x \mid x > a\}$, or more simply in interval notation as (a, ∞). We **graph the inequality** by graphing the solution set (a, ∞). Recall from Chapter 1 that a bracket means that an endpoint is included in an interval and a parenthesis means that an endpoint is not included in an interval.

EXAMPLE 2

Graphing inequalities

State the solution set to each inequality in interval notation and sketch its graph.

a) $x < 5$ **b)** $-2 < x$ **c)** $x \geq 10$

Solution

a) All real numbers less than 5 satisfy $x < 5$. The solution set is the interval $(-\infty, 5)$ and the graph of the solution set is shown in Fig. 2.7.

b) The inequality $-2 < x$ indicates that x is greater than -2. The solution set is the interval $(-2, \infty)$ and the graph of the inequality is shown in Fig. 2.8.

c) All real numbers greater than or equal to 10 satisfy $x \geq 10$. The solution set is the interval $[10, \infty)$ and the graph is shown in Fig. 2.9.

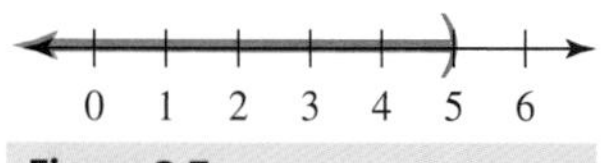

Figure 2.7

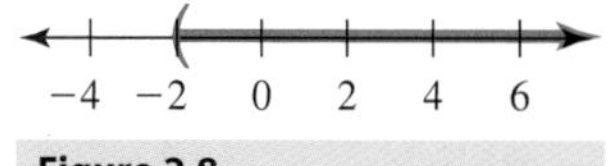

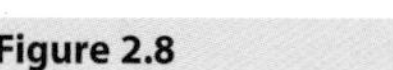

Figure 2.8

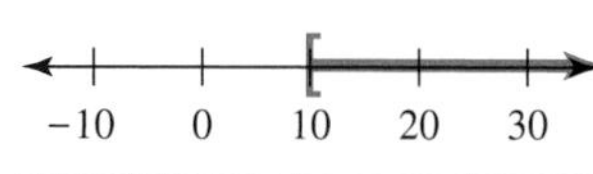

Figure 2.9

Now do Exercises 21–32

Helpful Hint

A person in debt has a negative net worth. If Bob's net worth is $-\$8000$ and Mary's net worth is $-\$3000$, then Bob certainly has the greater debt, but we write

$$-8000 < -3000$$

because -8000 lies to the left of -3000 on the number line.

Teaching Tip The obvious inequality symbol $\neq$ is not mentioned here because we do not want to solve inequalities using it at this time.

Graphing Compound Inequalities

A statement involving more than one inequality is a **compound inequality.** We will study one type of compound inequality here and see other types in Section 8.1.

If a and b are real numbers and $a < b$, then the compound inequality

$$a < x < b$$

means that $a < x$ *and* $x < b$. Reading x first makes $a < x < b$ clearer:

"x is greater than a *and* x is less than b."

If x is greater than a and less than b, then x is between a and b. So the solution set to $a < x < b$ is the interval (a, b).

EXAMPLE 3

Graphing compound inequalities

State the solution set to each inequality in interval notation and sketch its graph.

a) $2 < x < 3$ **b)** $-2 \leq x < 1$

Solution

a) All real numbers between 2 and 3 satisfy $2 < x < 3$. The solution set is the interval $(2, 3)$ and the graph of the solution set is shown in Fig. 2.10.

b) The real numbers that satisfy $-2 \leq x < 1$ are between -2 and 1, including -2 but not including 1. So the solution set is the interval $[-2, 1)$ and the graph of this compound inequality is shown in Fig. 2.11.

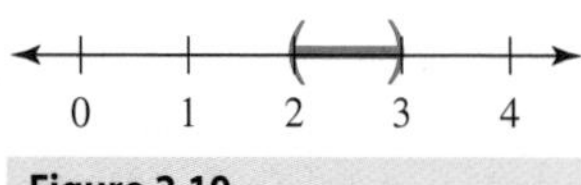

Figure 2.10

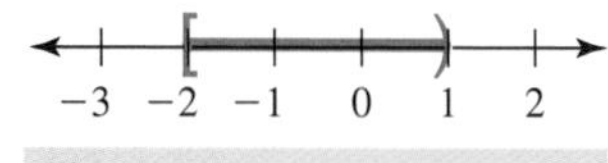

Figure 2.11

Now do Exercises 33–40

Study Tip

No two students learn in the same way or at the same speed. No one can tell you exactly how to study and learn. Learning is personal. You must discover what it takes for you to learn mathematics and then do whatever it takes.

CAUTION We write $a < x < b$ only if $a < b$, and we write $a > x > b$ only if $a > b$. Similar rules hold for $\leq$ and $\geq$. So $4 < x < 9$ and $-6 \geq x \geq -8$ are correct uses of this notation, but $5 < x < 2$ is not correct. Also, the inequalities should *not* point in opposite directions as in $5 < x > 7$.

Checking Inequalities

In Examples 2 and 3 we determined the solution sets to some inequalities. In Section 2.9 more complicated inequalities will be solved by using steps similar to those used for solving equations. In Example 4, we determine whether a given number satisfies an inequality of the type that we will be solving in Section 2.9.

EXAMPLE 4

Checking inequalities

Determine whether the given number satisfies the inequality following it.

a) $0,\ 2x - 3 \leq -5$ **b)** $-4,\ x - 5 > 2x + 1$ **c)** $\frac{13}{3},\ 6 < 3x - 5 < 14$

Solution

a) Replace x by 0 in the inequality and simplify:

$$2x - 3 \leq -5$$
$$2 \cdot 0 - 3 \leq -5$$
$$-3 \leq -5 \quad \text{Incorrect}$$

Since this last inequality is incorrect, 0 is not a solution to the inequality.

b) Replace x by -4 and simplify:

$$x - 5 > 2x + 1$$
$$-4 - 5 > 2(-4) + 1$$
$$-9 > -7 \quad \text{Incorrect}$$

Since this last inequality is incorrect, -4 is not a solution to the inequality.

c) Replace x by $\frac{13}{3}$ and simplify:

$$6 < 3x - 5 < 14$$
$$6 < 3 \cdot \frac{13}{3} - 5 < 14$$
$$6 < 13 - 5 < 14$$
$$6 < 8 < 14 \quad \text{Correct}$$

Since 8 is greater than 6 and less than 14, this inequality is correct. So $\frac{13}{3}$ satisfies the original inequality.

Now do Exercises 51–68

Calculator Close-Up

To check 13/3 in

$$6 < 3x - 5 < 14$$

we check each part of the compound inequality separately.

```
6<3(13/3)-5
                  1
3(13/3)-5<14
                  1
```

Because both parts of the compound inequality are correct, 13/3 satisfies the compound inequality.

Writing Inequalities

Inequalities occur in applications, just as equations do. Certain verbal phrases indicate inequalities. For example, if you must be at least 18 years old to vote, then you can vote if you are 18 or older. The phrase "at least" means "greater than or equal to." If an elevator has a capacity of at most 20 people, then it can hold 20 people or fewer. The phrase "at most" means "less than or equal to."

Math *at Work* Body Mass Index

Medical professionals say that two-thirds of all Americans are overweight and excess weight has about the same effect on life expectancy as smoking. How can you tell if you are overweight or normal? Body mass index (BMI) can help you decide. To determine BMI divide your weight in kilograms by the square of your height in meters. Don't know your weight and height in the metric system? Then use the formula $\text{BMI} = 703W/H^2$, where W is your weight in pounds and H is your height in inches.

If $23 < \text{BMI} < 25$, then you are probably not overweight. If $\text{BMI} \geq 26$, then you are probably overweight and are statistically likely to have a lower life expectancy. According to the National Heart, Lung, and Blood Institute, you are overweight if $25 < \text{BMI} < 29.9$ and obese if $\text{BMI} \geq 30$. If your BMI is between 17 and 22, your life span might be longer than average. Men are usually happy with a BMI between 23 and 25 and women like to see their BMI between 20 and 22. However, BMI does not distinguish between muscle and fat and can wrongly suggest that a person with a short muscular build is overweight. Also, the BMI does not work well for children, because normal varies with age.

If you want to learn more about body mass index or don't want to do the calculations yourself, then check out any of the numerous websites that discuss BMI and even have online BMI calculators. Just do a search for body mass index.

EXAMPLE 5

Writing inequalities

Write an inequality that describes each situation.

a) Lois plans to spend at most \$500 on a washing machine including the 9% sales tax.

b) The length of a certain rectangle must be 4 meters longer than the width, and the perimeter must be at least 120 meters.

c) Fred made a 76 on the midterm exam. To get a B, the average of his midterm and his final exam must be between 80 and 90.

Solution

a) If x is the price of the washing machine, then $0.09x$ is the amount of sales tax. Since the total must be less than or equal to \$500, the inequality is

$$x + 0.09x \leq 500.$$

b) If W represents the width of the rectangle, then $W + 4$ represents the length. Since the perimeter $(2W + 2L)$ must be greater than or equal to 120, the inequality is

$$2(W) + 2(W + 4) \geq 120.$$

c) If we let x represent Fred's final exam score, then his average is $\frac{x + 76}{2}$. To indicate that the average is between 80 and 90, we use the compound inequality

$$80 < \frac{x + 76}{2} < 90.$$

Now do Exercises 77–89

Teaching Tip Students often have trouble with "at least" and "at most." Ask them to write a few sentences using these phrases and analyze them.

In Example 4(b) you are given that L is 4 meters longer than W. So $L = W + 4$, and you can use $W + 4$ in place of L. If you knew only that L was longer than W, then you would know only that $L > W$.

Warm-Ups ▼

True or false? Explain your answer.

1. $-2 \leq -2$ True
2. $-5 < 4 < 6$ True
3. $-3 < 0 < -1$ False
4. The inequalities $7 < x$ and $x > 7$ have the same graph. True
5. The graph of $x < -3$ includes the point at -3. False
6. The number 5 satisfies the inequality $x > 2$. True
7. The number -3 is a solution to $-2 < x$. False
8. The number 4 satisfies the inequality $2x - 1 < 4$. False
9. The number 0 is a solution to the inequality $2x - 3 \leq 5x - 3$. True
10. The inequalities $2x - 1 < x$ and $x < 2x - 1$ have the same solutions. False

2.8 Exercises

Boost your GRADE at mathzone.com!

MathZone

- Practice Problems
- Self-Tests
- Videos
- Net Tutor
- e-Professors

Reading and Writing *After reading this section, write out the answers to these questions. Use complete sentences.*

1. What are the inequality symbols used in this section?
   The inequality symbols are $<$, $\leq$, $>$, and $\geq$.
2. What different looking inequality means the same as $a < b$?
   The inequalities $a < b$ and $b > a$ have the same meaning.
3. How do you know when to use a bracket and when to use a parenthesis when graphing an inequality on a number line?
   For $\leq$ and $\geq$ use a bracket and for $<$ and $>$ use a parenthesis.
4. What is a compound inequality?
   A compound inequality is a statement involving more than one inequality.
5. What is the meaning of the compound inequality $a < b < c$?
   The compound inequality $a < b < c$ means $b > a$ and $b < c$, or b is between a and c.
6. What is the difference between "at most" and "at least?"
   "At most" means less than or equal to and "at least" means greater than or equal to.

Determine whether each of the following statements is correct. See Example 1.

7. $-3 < 5$ True
8. $-6 < 0$ True
9. $4 \leq 4$ True
10. $-3 \geq -3$ True
11. $-6 > -5$ False
12. $-2 < -9$ False
13. $-4 \leq -3$ True
14. $-5 \geq -10$ True
15. $(-3)(4) - 1 < 0 - 3$ True
16. $2(4) - 6 \leq -3(5) + 1$ False
17. $-4(5) - 6 \geq 5(-6)$ True
18. $4(8) - 30 > 7(5) - 2(17)$ True
19. $7(4) - 12 \leq 3(9) - 2$ True
20. $-3(4) + 12 \leq 2(3) - 6$ True

State the solution set to each inequality in interval notation and sketch its graph. See Examples 2 and 3.

21. $x \leq 3$
    $(-\infty, 3]$

22. $x \leq -7$
    $(-\infty, -7]$

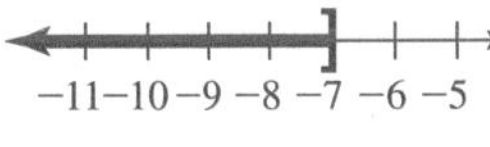

23. $x > -2$
    $(-2, \infty)$

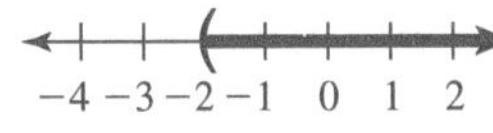

24. $x > 4$
$(4, \infty)$

25. $-1 > x$
$(-\infty, -1)$

26. $0 > x$
$(-\infty, 0)$

27. $-2 \le x$
$[-2, \infty)$

28. $-5 \ge x$
$(-\infty, -5]$

29. $x \ge \frac{1}{2}$
$\left[\frac{1}{2}, \infty\right)$

30. $x \ge -\frac{2}{3}$
$\left[-\frac{2}{3}, \infty\right)$

31. $x \le 5.3$
$(-\infty, 5.3]$

32. $x \le -3.4$
$(-\infty, -3.4]$

33. $-3 < x < 1$
$(-3, 1)$

34. $0 < x < 5$
$(0, 5)$

35. $3 \le x \le 7$
$[3, 7]$

36. $-3 \le x \le -1$
$[-3, -1]$

37. $-5 \le x < 0$
$[-5, 0)$

38. $-2 < x \le 2$
$(-2, 2]$

39. $40 < x \le 100$
$(40, 100]$

40. $0 \le x < 600$
$[0, 600)$

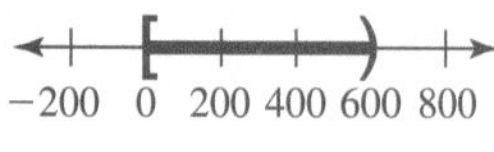

For each graph, write the corresponding inequality and the solution set to the inequality using interval notation.

41. $x > 3$ $(3, \infty)$

42. $x \le 4$ $(-\infty, 4]$

43. $x \le 2$ $(-\infty, 2]$

44. $0 < x \le 3$ $(0, 3]$

45. $0 < x < 2$ $(0, 2)$

46. $-1 \le x < 3$ $[-1, 3)$

47. $-5 < x \le 7$ $(-5, 7]$

48. $x < 4$ $(-\infty, 4)$

49. $x > -4$ $(-4, \infty)$

50. $0 < x \le 2$ $(0, 2]$

Determine whether the given number satisfies the inequality following it. See Example 4.

51. $-9, -x > 3$ Yes
52. $5, -3 < -x$ No
53. $-2, 5 \le x$ No
54. $4, 4 \ge x$ Yes
55. $-6, 2x - 3 > -11$ No
56. $4, 3x - 5 < 7$ No
57. $3, -3x + 4 > -7$ Yes
58. $-4, -5x + 1 > -5$ Yes
59. $0, 3x - 7 \le 5x - 7$ Yes
60. $0, 2x + 6 \ge 4x - 9$ Yes
61. $2.5, -10x + 9 \le 3(x + 3)$ Yes
62. $1.5, 2x - 3 \le 4(x - 1)$ Yes
63. $-7, -5 < x < 9$ No
64. $-9, -6 \le x \le 40$ No
65. $-2, -3 \le 2x + 5 \le 9$ Yes
66. $-5, -3 < -3x - 7 \le 8$ Yes

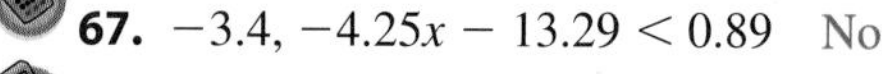

67. $-3.4, -4.25x - 13.29 < 0.89$ No

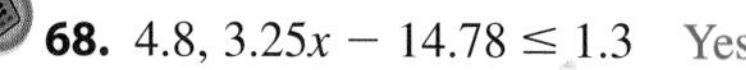

68. $4.8, 3.25x - 14.78 \le 1.3$ Yes

For each inequality, determine which of the numbers -5.1, 0, *and* 5.1 *satisfies the inequality.*

69. $x > -5$ 0, 5.1

70. $x \leq 0$ -5.1, 0

71. $5 < x$ 5.1

72. $-5 > x$ -5.1

73. $5 < x < 7$ 5.1

74. $5 < -x < 7$ -5.1

75. $-6 < -x < 6$ -5.1, 0, 5.1

76. $-5 \leq x - 0.1 \leq 5$ 5.1, 0

Write an inequality to describe each situation. See Example 5.

77. ***Sales tax.*** At an 8% sales tax rate, Susan paid more than \$1500 sales tax when she purchased her new Camaro. Let p represent the price of the Camaro. $0.08p > 1500$

78. ***Internet shopping.*** Carlos paid less than \$1000 including \$40 for shipping and 9% sales tax when he bought his new computer. Let p represent the price of the computer.
$p + 0.09p + 40 < 1000$

79. ***Fine dining.*** At Burger Brothers the price of a hamburger is twice the price of an order of French fries, and the price of a Coke is \$0.25 more than the price of the fries. Burger Brothers advertises that you can get a complete meal (burger, fries, and Coke) for under \$2.00. Let p represent the price of an order of fries. $p + 2p + p + 0.25 < 2.00$

80. ***Cats and dogs.*** Willow Creek Kennel boards only cats and dogs. One Friday night there were twice as many dogs as cats in the kennel and at least 30 animals spent the night there. Let d represent the number of dogs.
$d + \frac{1}{2}d \geq 30$

81. ***Barely passing.*** Travis made 44 and 72 on the first two tests in algebra and has one test remaining. The average on the three tests must be at least 60 for Travis to pass the course. Let s represent his score on the last test.
$\frac{44 + 72 + s}{3} \geq 60$

82. ***Ace the course.*** Florence made 87 on her midterm exam in psychology. The average of her midterm and her final must be at least 90 to get an A in the course. Let s represent her score on the final. $\frac{87 + s}{2} \geq 90$

83. ***Coast to coast.*** On Howard's recent trip from Bangor to San Diego, he drove for 8 hours each day and traveled between 396 and 453 miles each day. Let R represent his average speed for each day. $396 < 8R < 453$

84. ***Mother's Day present.*** Bart and Betty are looking at color televisions that range in price from \$399.99 to \$579.99. Bart can afford more than Betty and has agreed to spend \$100 more than Betty when they purchase this gift for their mother. Let b represent Betty's portion of the gift.
$399.99 < b + b + 100 < 579.99$

85. ***Positioning a ladder.*** Write an inequality in the variable x for the degree measure of the angle at the base of the ladder shown in the figure, given that the angle at the base must be between 60° and 70°. $60 < 90 - x < 70$

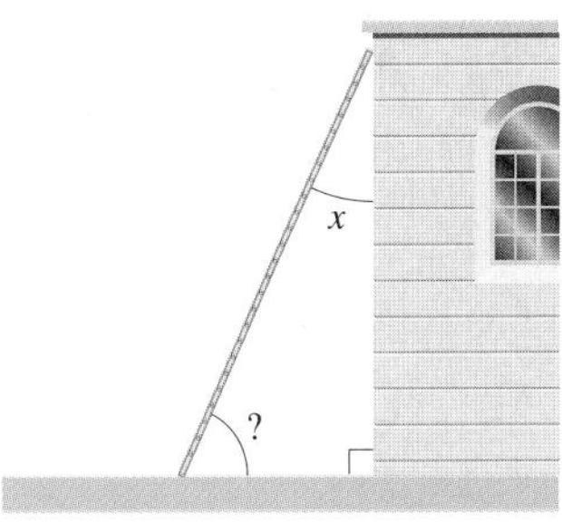

Figure for Exercise 85

86. ***Building a ski ramp.*** Write an inequality in the variable x for the degree measure of the smallest angle of the triangle shown in the figure, given that the degree measure of the smallest angle is at most 30°. $180 - x - (x + 8) \leq 30$

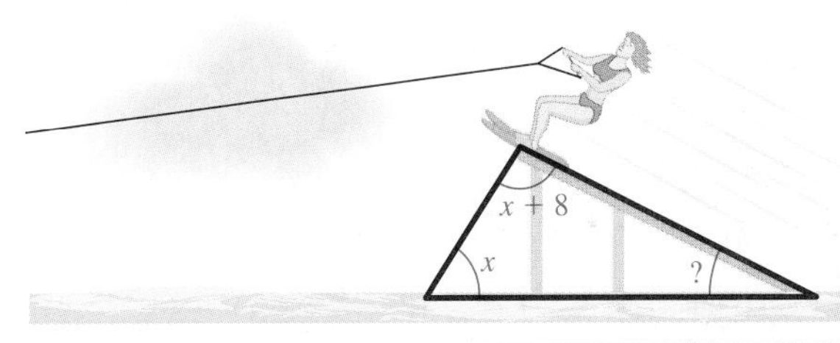

Figure for Exercise 86

87. ***Maximum girth.*** United Parcel Service defines the girth of a box as the sum of the length, twice the width, and twice the height. The maximum girth that UPS will ship is 130 in.

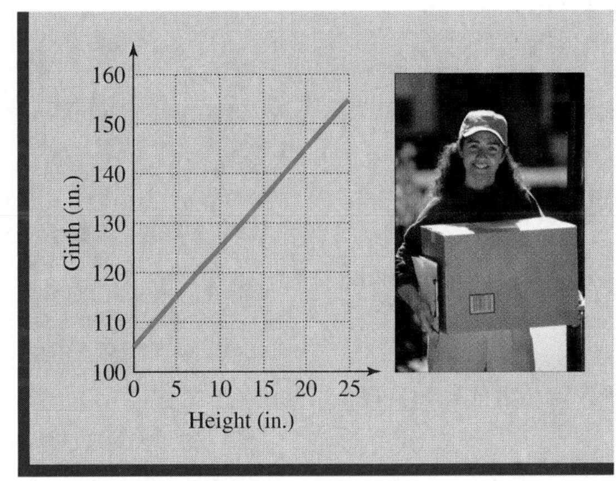

Figure for Exercise 87

a) If a box has a length of 45 in. and a width of 30 in., then what inequality must be satisfied by the height? $45 + 2(30) + 2h \leq 130$

b) The accompanying graph shows the girth of a box with a length of 45 in., a width of 30 in., and height of h in. Use the graph to estimate the maximum height that is allowed for this box. Approximately 12 in.

88. ***Batting average.*** Near the end of the season a professional baseball player has 93 hits in 317 times at bat for an average of 93/317 or 0.293. He gets a $1 million bonus if his season average is over 0.300. He estimates that he will bat 20 more times before the season ends. Let x represent the number of hits in the last 20 at bats of the season.

a) Write an inequality that must be satisfied for him to get the bonus. $\frac{93 + x}{337} > 0.300$

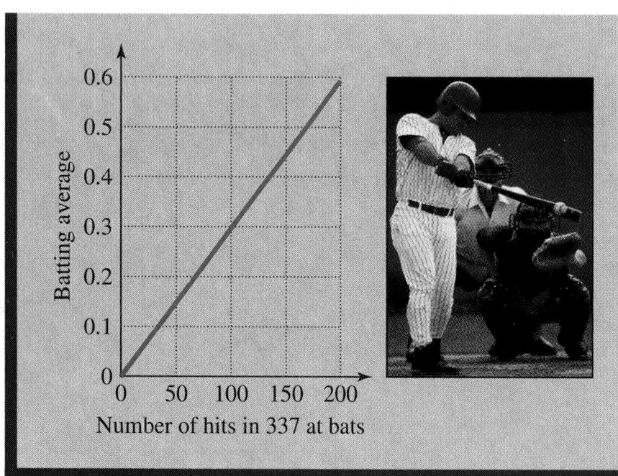

Figure for Exercise 88

b) Use the accompanying graph to estimate the number of hits in 337 at bats that will put his average over 0.300. More than 100 hits

Solve.

89. ***Bicycle gear ratios.*** The gear ratio r for a bicycle is defined by the formula

$$r = \frac{Nw}{n},$$

where N is the number of teeth on the chainring (by the pedal), n is the number of teeth on the cog (by the wheel), and w is the wheel diameter in inches (*Cycling,* Burkett and Darst). The following chart gives uses for the various gear ratios.

Ratio	Use
$r > 90$	hard pedaling on level ground
$70 < r \leq 90$	moderate effort on level ground
$50 < r \leq 70$	mild hill climbing
$35 < r \leq 50$	long hill climbing with load

A bicycle with a 27-inch diameter wheel has 50 teeth on the chainring and 17 teeth on the cog. Find the gear ratio and indicate what this gear ratio is good for.
79, moderate effort on level ground

2.9 Solving Inequalities and Applications

In this Section

- Rules for Inequalities
- Solving Inequalities
- Applications of Inequalities

To solve equations, we write a sequence of equivalent equations that ends in a very simple equation whose solution is obvious. In this section you will learn that the procedure for solving inequalities is the same. However, the rules for performing operations on each side of an inequality are slightly different from the rules for equations.

Rules for Inequalities

Equivalent inequalities are inequalities that have exactly the same solutions. Inequalities such as $x > 3$ and $x + 2 > 5$ are equivalent because any number that is larger than 3 certainly satisfies $x + 2 > 5$ and any number that satisfies $x + 2 > 5$ must certainly be larger than 3.

We can get equivalent inequalities by performing operations on each side of an inequality just as we do for solving equations. If we start with the inequality $6 < 10$ and add 2 to each side, we get the true statement $8 < 12$. Examine the results of performing the same operation on each side of $6 < 10$.

Helpful Hint

You can think of an inequality like a seesaw that is out of balance.

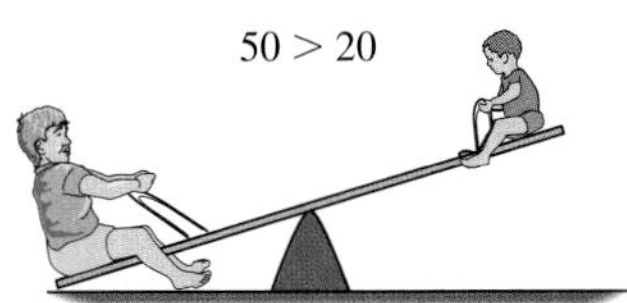

If the same weight is added to or subtracted from each side, it will remain in the same state of imbalance.

Perform these operations on each side:

	Add 2	Subtract 2	Multiply by 2	Divide by 2
Start with $6 < 10$	$8 < 12$	$4 < 8$	$12 < 20$	$3 < 5$

All of the resulting inequalities are correct. Now if we repeat these operations using -2, we get the following results.

Perform these operations on each side:

	Add -2	Subtract -2	Multiply by -2	Divide by -2
Start with $6 < 10$	$4 < 8$	$8 < 12$	$-12 > -20$	$-3 > -5$

Notice that the direction of the inequality symbol is the same for all of the results except the last two. When we multiplied each side by -2 and when we divided each side by -2, we had to reverse the inequality symbol to get a correct result. These tables illustrate the rules for solving inequalities.

Study Tip

Get in the habit of checking your work and having confidence in your answers. The answers to the odd-numbered exercises are in the back of this book, but you should look in the answer section only after you have checked on your own. You will not always have an answer section available.

Addition Property of Inequality

If we add the same number to each side of an inequality we get an equivalent inequality. If $a < b$, then $a + c < b + c$.

The addition property of inequality also allows us to subtract the same number from each side of an inequality because subtraction is defined in terms of addition.

Helpful Hint

Changing the signs of numbers, changes their relative position on the number line. For example, 3 lies to the left of 5 on the number line, but -3 lies to the right of -5. So $3 < 5$, but $-3 > -5$. Since multiplying and dividing by a negative cause sign changes, these operations reverse the inequality.

Multiplication Property of Inequality

If we multiply each side of an inequality by the same *positive* number, we get an equivalent inequality. If $a < b$ and $c > 0$, then $ac < bc$. If we multiply each side of an inequality by the same *negative* number and *reverse the inequality symbol,* we get an equivalent inequality. If $a < b$ and $c < 0$, then $ac > bc$.

The multiplication property of inequality also enables us to divide each side of an inequality by a nonzero number because division is defined in terms of multiplication. So if we multiply or divide each side by a negative number, the inequality symbol is reversed.

EXAMPLE 1

Writing equivalent inequalities

Write the appropriate inequality symbol in the blank so that the two inequalities are equivalent.

a) $x + 3 > 9$, x _____ 6 **b)** $-2x \le 6$, x _____ -3

Solution

a) If we subtract 3 from each side of $x + 3 > 9$, we get the equivalent inequality $x > 6$.

b) If we divide each side of $-2x \leq 6$ by -2, we get the equivalent inequality $x \geq -3$.

Now do Exercises 7–14

CAUTION We use the properties of inequality just as we use the properties of equality. However, when we multiply or divide each side by a negative number, we must reverse the inequality symbol.

Solving Inequalities

To solve inequalities, we use the properties of inequality to isolate x on one side.

EXAMPLE 2

Isolating the variable on the left side

Solve the inequality $4x - 5 > 19$. State the solution set using interval notation and sketch its graph.

Solution

$$
\begin{aligned}
4x - 5 &> 19 && \text{Original inequality} \\
4x - 5 + 5 &> 19 + 5 && \text{Add 5 to each side.} \\
4x &> 24 && \text{Simplify.} \\
x &> 6 && \text{Divide each side by 4.}
\end{aligned}
$$

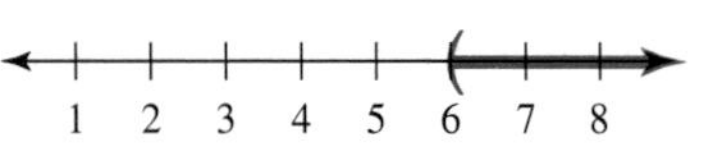

Figure 2.12

Since the last inequality is equivalent to the first, it has the same solution set as the first. So the solution set to $4x - 5 > 19$ is $(6, \infty)$. The graph is shown in Fig. 2.12.

Now do Exercises 15–16

Calculator Close-Up

You can use the TABLE feature of a graphing calculator to numerically support the solution to the inequality $4x - 5 > 19$ in Example 2. Use the Y = key to enter the equation $y_1 = 4x - 5$.

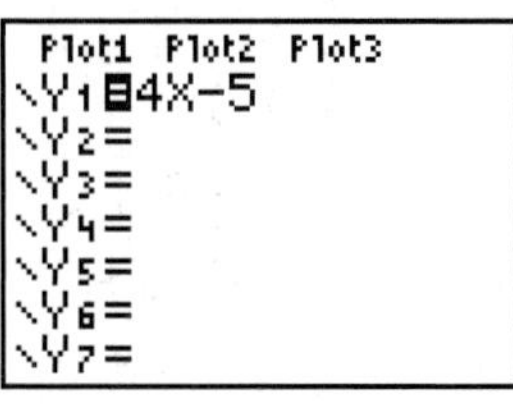

Next, use TBLSET to set the table so that the values of x start at 4.5 and the change in x is 0.5.

Finally, press TABLE to see lists of x-values and the corresponding y-values.

Notice that when x is larger than 6, y_1 (or $4x - 5$) is larger than 19. The table verifies or supports the algebraic solution, but it should not replace the algebraic method.

X	Y1
4.5	13
5	15
5.5	17
6	19
6.5	21
7	23
7.5	25

X=6

Remember that $5 < x$ is equivalent to $x > 5$. So the variable can be isolated on the right side of an inequality as shown in Example 3.

EXAMPLE 3

Isolating the variable on the right side

Solve the inequality $5x - 2 \le 7x - 5$. State the solution set using interval notation and sketch its graph.

Solution

$$\begin{aligned} 5x - 2 &\le 7x - 5 && \text{Original inequality} \\ 5x - 2 - 5x &\le 7x - 5 - 5x && \text{Subtract } 5x \text{ from each side.} \\ -2 &\le 2x - 5 && \text{Simplify.} \\ 3 &\le 2x && \text{Add 5 to each side.} \\ \frac{3}{2} &\le x && \text{Divide each side by 2.} \end{aligned}$$

Note that $\frac{3}{2} \le x$ is equivalent to $x \ge \frac{3}{2}$. The solution set is the interval $\left[\frac{3}{2}, \infty\right)$ and the graph is shown in Fig. 2.13. Notice that $\frac{3}{2}$ is half way between 1 and 2 on the number line.

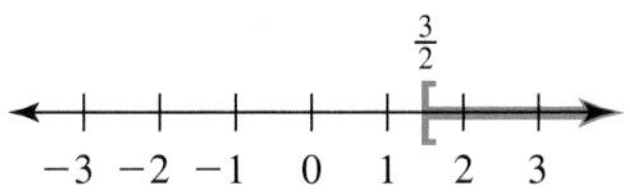

$\frac{3}{2}$

−3 −2 −1 0 1 2 3

Figure 2.13

Now do Exercises 17–20

Rewriting $\frac{3}{2} \le x$ as $x \ge \frac{3}{2}$ in Example 3 is not "reversing the inequality." Multiplying or dividing each side of $\frac{3}{2} \le x$ by a negative number would reverse the inequality. For example, multiplying by -1 yields $-\frac{3}{2} \ge -x$. In Example 4, we divide each side of an inequality by a negative number and reverse the inequality symbol.

EXAMPLE 4

Reversing the inequality symbol

Solve $5 - 5x \le 1 + 2(5 - x)$. State the solution set in interval notation and sketch its graph.

Solution

$$\begin{aligned} 5 - 5x &\le 1 + 2(5 - x) && \text{Original inequality} \\ 5 - 5x &\le 11 - 2x && \text{Simplify the right side.} \\ 5 - 3x &\le 11 && \text{Add 2x to each side.} \\ -3x &\le 6 && \text{Subtract 5 from each side.} \\ x &\ge -2 && \text{Divide each side by } -3 \text{, and reverse the inequality.} \end{aligned}$$

The solution set is the interval $[-2, \infty)$ and the graph is shown in Fig. 2.14.

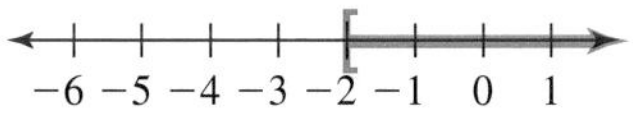

−6 −5 −4 −3 −2 −1 0 1

Figure 2.14

Now do Exercises 21–42

We can use the rules for solving inequalities on the compound inequalities that we studied in Section 2.8.

EXAMPLE 5

Solving a compound inequality

Solve $-9 \le \frac{2x}{3} - 7 < 5$. State the solution set in interval notation and sketch its graph.

Solution

$$-9 \le \frac{2x}{3} - 7 < 5 \quad \text{Original inequality}$$

$$-9 + 7 \le \frac{2x}{3} - 7 + 7 < 5 + 7 \quad \text{Add 7 to each part.}$$

$$-2 \le \frac{2x}{3} < 12 \quad \text{Simplify.}$$

$$\frac{3}{2}(-2) \le \frac{3}{2} \cdot \frac{2x}{3} < \frac{3}{2} \cdot 12 \quad \text{Multiply each part by } \frac{3}{2}.$$

$$-3 \le x < 18 \quad \text{Simplify.}$$

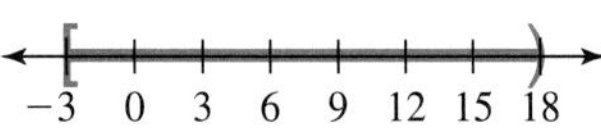

Figure 2.15

Since the last compound inequality is equivalent to the first, the solution set is $[-3, 18)$. The graph is shown in Fig. 2.15.

Now do Exercises 43–46

CAUTION There are many negative numbers in Example 5, but the inequality was not reversed, since we did not multiply or divide by a negative number. An inequality is reversed only if you multiply or divide by a negative number.

EXAMPLE 6

Reversing inequality symbols in a compound inequality

Solve $-3 \le 5 - x \le 5$. State the solution set in interval notation and sketch its graph.

Solution

$$-3 \le 5 - x \le 5 \quad \text{Original inequality}$$

$$-3 - 5 \le 5 - x - 5 \le 5 - 5 \quad \text{Subtract 5 from each part.}$$

$$-8 \le -x \le 0 \quad \text{Simplify.}$$

$$(-1)(-8) \ge (-1)(-x) \ge (-1)(0) \quad \text{Multiply each part by } -1\text{, reversing the inequality symbols.}$$

$$8 \ge x \ge 0$$

It is customary to write $8 \ge x \ge 0$ with the smallest number on the left:

$$0 \le x \le 8$$

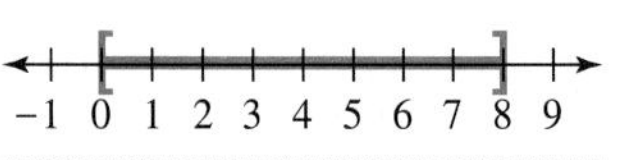

Figure 2.16

Since the last compound inequality is equivalent to the first, the solution set is $[0, 8]$. The graph is shown in Fig. 2.16.

Now do Exercises 47–56

Applications of Inequalities

Example 7 shows how inequalities can be used in applications.

EXAMPLE 7

Averaging test scores

Mei Lin made a 76 on the midterm exam in history. To get a B, the average of her midterm and her final exam must be between 80 and 90. For what range of scores on the final exam will she get a B?

Solution

Let x represent the final exam score. Her average is then $\frac{x + 76}{2}$. The inequality expresses the fact that the average must be between 80 and 90:

$$80 < \frac{x + 76}{2} < 90$$

$$2(80) < 2\left(\frac{x + 76}{2}\right) < 2(90) \quad \text{Multiply each part by 2.}$$

$$160 < x + 76 < 180 \quad \text{Simplify.}$$

$$160 - 76 < x + 76 - 76 < 180 - 76 \quad \text{Subtract 76 from each part.}$$

$$84 < x < 104 \quad \text{Simplify.}$$

The last inequality indicates that Mei Lin's final exam score must be between 84 and 104.

Now do Exercises 63–78

Helpful Hint

Remember that all inequality symbols in a compound inequality must point in the same direction. We usually have them all point to the left so that the numbers are increasing in size as you go from left to right in the inequality.

Warm-Ups ▼

True or false? Explain your answer.

1. The inequality $2x > 18$ is equivalent to $x > 9$. True
2. The inequality $x - 5 > 0$ is equivalent to $x < 5$. False
3. We can divide each side of an inequality by any real number. False
4. The inequality $-2x \le 6$ is equivalent to $-x \le 3$. True
5. The statement "x is at most 7" is written as $x < 7$. False
6. "The sum of x and $0.05x$ is at least 76" is written as $x + 0.05x \ge 76$. True
7. The statement "x is not more than 85" is written as $x < 85$. False
8. The inequality $-3 > x > -9$ is equivalent to $-9 < x < -3$. True
9. If x is the sale price of Glen's truck, the sales tax rate is 8%, and the title fee is \$50, then the total that he pays is $1.08x + 50$ dollars. True
10. If the selling price of the house, x, less the sales commission of 6% must be at least \$60,000, then $x - 0.06x \le 60{,}000$. False

2.9 Exercises

Boost your GRADE at mathzone.com!

MathZone

- Practice Problems
- Self-Tests
- Videos
- Net Tutor
- e-Professors

Reading and Writing *After reading this section, write out the answers to these questions. Use complete sentences.*

1. What are equivalent inequalities?
Equivalent inequalities are inequalities that have the same solutions.

2. What is the addition property of inequality?
The addition property of inequality says that adding any real number to each side of an inequality produces an equivalent inequality.

3. What is the multiplication property of inequality?
According to the multiplication property of inequality, the inequality symbol is reversed when multiplying (or dividing) by a negative number and not reversed when multiplying (or dividing) by a positive number.

4. What similarities are there between solving equations and solving inequalities?
For equations or inequalities we try to isolate the variable. The properties of equality and inequality are similar.

5. How do we solve compound inequalities?
We solve compound inequalities using the properties of inequality as we do for simple inequalities.

6. How do you know when to reverse the direction of an inequality symbol?
The direction of the inequality symbol is reversed when we multiply or divide by a negative number.

Write the appropriate inequality symbol in the blank so that the two inequalities are equivalent. See Example 1.

7. $x + 7 > 0$
$x \geq -7$

8. $x - 6 < 0$
$x \leq 6$

9. $9 \leq 3w$
$w \geq 3$

10. $10 \geq 5z$
$z \leq 2$

11. $-4k < -4$
$k \geq 1$

12. $-9t > 27$
$t \leq -3$

13. $-\frac{1}{2}y \geq 4$
$y \leq -8$

14. $-\frac{1}{3}x \leq 4$
$x \geq -12$

Solve each inequality. State the solution set in interval notation and sketch its graph. See Examples 2–4.

15. $x + 3 > 0$ $(-3, \infty)$

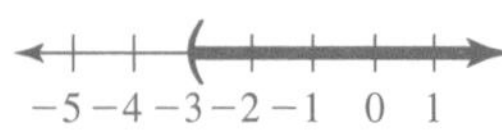

16. $x + 9 \leq -8$ $(-\infty, -17]$

17. $-3 < w - 1$ $(-2, \infty)$

18. $9 > w - 12$ $(-\infty, 21)$

19. $8 > 2b$ $(-\infty, 4)$

20. $35 < 7b$ $(5, \infty)$

21. $-8z \leq 4$ $\left[-\frac{1}{2}, \infty\right)$

22. $-4y \geq -10$ $\left(-\infty, \frac{5}{2}\right]$

23. $3y - 2 < 7$ $(-\infty, 3)$

24. $2y - 5 > -9$ $(-2, \infty)$

25. $3 - 9z \leq 6$ $\left[-\frac{1}{3}, \infty\right)$

26. $5 - 6z \geq 13$ $\left(-\infty, -\frac{4}{3}\right]$

27. $6 > -r + 3$ $(-3, \infty)$

28. $6 \leq 12 - r$ $(-\infty, 6]$

29. $5 - 4p > -8 - 3p$ $(-\infty, 13)$

30. $7 - 9p > 11 - 8p$ $(-\infty, -4)$

31. $-\frac{5}{6}q \geq -20$ $(-\infty, 24]$

32. $-\frac{2}{3}q \geq -4$ $(-\infty, 6]$

33. $1 - \frac{1}{4}t \geq \frac{1}{8}$ $\left(-\infty, \frac{7}{2}\right]$

34. $\frac{1}{6} - \frac{1}{3}t > 0$ $\left(-\infty, \frac{1}{2}\right)$

35. $0.1x + 0.35 > 0.2$
$(-1.5, \infty)$

36. $1 - 0.02x \leq 0.6$ $[20, \infty)$

37. $2x + 5 < x - 6$ $(-\infty, -11)$

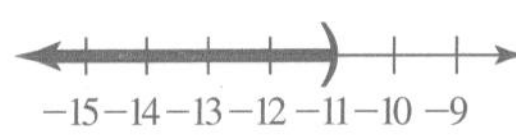

38. $3x - 4 < 2x + 9$ $(-\infty, 13)$

39. $x - 4 < 2(x + 3)$ $(-10, \infty)$

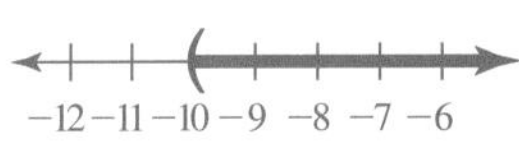

40. $2x + 3 < 3(x - 5)$ $(18, \infty)$

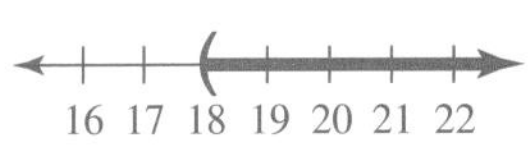

41. $0.52x - 35 < 0.45x + 8$
$(-\infty, 614.3)$

42. $8455(x - 3.4) > 4320$
$(3.91, \infty)$

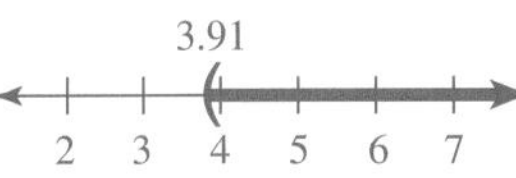

Solve each compound inequality. State the solution set in interval notation and sketch its graph. See Examples 5 and 6.

43. $5 < x - 3 < 7$ $(8, 10)$

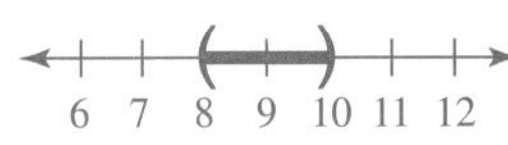

44. $2 < x - 5 < 6$ $(7, 11)$

45. $3 < 2v + 1 < 10$ $\left(1, \frac{9}{2}\right)$

46. $-3 < 3v + 4 < 7$ $\left(-\frac{7}{3}, 1\right)$

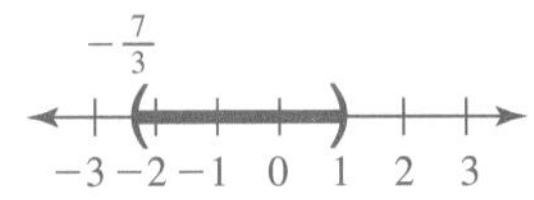

47. $-4 \leq 5 - k \leq 7$ $[-2, 9]$

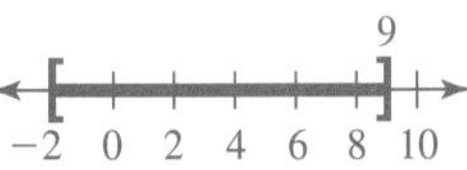

48. $2 \leq 3 - k \leq 8$ $[-5, 1]$

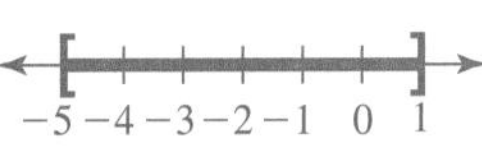

49. $-2 < 7 - 3y \leq 22$ $[-5, 3)$

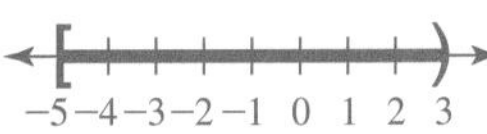

50. $-1 \leq 1 - 2y < 3$ $(-1, 1]$

51. $5 < \frac{2u}{3} - 3 < 17$ $(12, 30)$

52. $-4 < \frac{3u}{4} - 1 < 11$ $(-4, 16)$

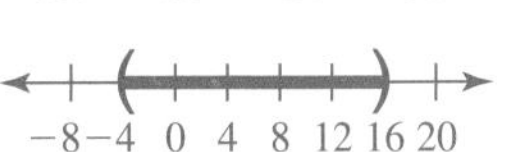

53. $-2 < \frac{4m - 4}{3} \leq \frac{2}{3}$ $\left(-\frac{1}{2}, \frac{3}{2}\right]$

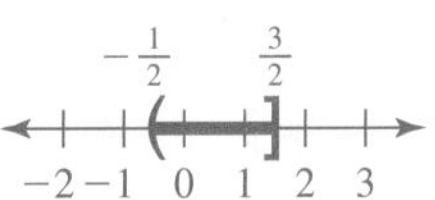

54. $0 \leq \frac{3 - 2m}{2} < 9$ $\left(-\frac{15}{2}, \frac{3}{2}\right]$

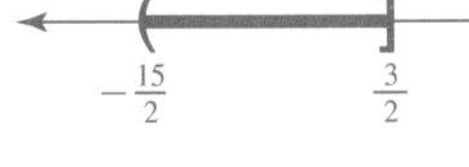

55. $0.02 < 0.54 - 0.0048x < 0.05$
$(102.1, 108.3)$

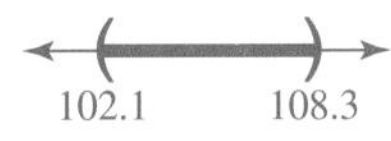

56. $0.44 < \frac{34.55 - 22.3x}{124.5} < 0.76$
$(-2.69, -0.91)$

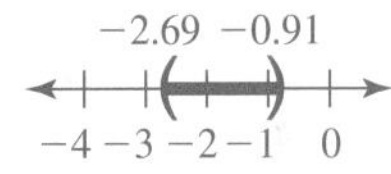

Solve each inequality. State the solution set in interval notation and sketch its graph.

57. $\frac{1}{2}x - 1 \leq 4 - \frac{1}{3}x$ $(-\infty, 6]$

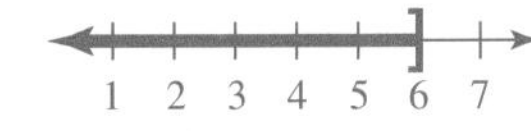

58. $\frac{y}{4} - \frac{5}{12} \geq \frac{y}{3} + \frac{1}{4}$ $(-\infty, -8]$

59. $\frac{1}{2}\left(x - \frac{1}{4}\right) > \frac{1}{4}\left(6x - \frac{1}{2}\right)$
$(-\infty, 0)$

60. $-\frac{1}{2}\left(z - \frac{2}{5}\right) < \frac{2}{3}\left(\frac{3}{4}z - \frac{6}{5}\right)$
$(1, \infty)$

61. $\frac{1}{3} < \frac{1}{4}x - \frac{1}{6} < \frac{7}{12}$
$(2, 3)$

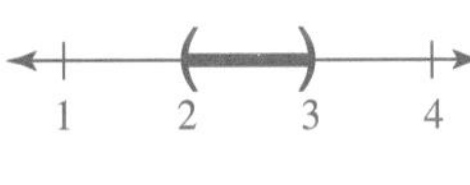

62. $-\frac{3}{5} < \frac{1}{5} - \frac{2}{15}w < -\frac{1}{3}$
$(4, 6)$

Solve each of the following problems by using an inequality. See Example 7.

63. ***Boat storage.*** The length of a rectangular boat storage shed must be 4 meters more than the width, and the perimeter must be at least 120 meters. What is the range of values for the width? At least 28 meters

64. ***Fencing a garden.*** Elka is planning a rectangular garden that is to be twice as long as it is wide. If she can afford to buy at most 180 feet of fencing, then what are the possible values for the width? At most 30 feet

Photo for Exercise 64

65. ***Car shopping.*** Harold Ivan is shopping for a new car. In addition to the price of the car, there is a 5% sales tax and a $144 title and license fee. If Harold Ivan decides that he will spend less than $9970 total, then what is the price range for the car? Less than $9358

66. ***Car selling.*** Ronald wants to sell his car through a broker who charges a commission of 10% of the selling price. Ronald still owes $11,025 on the car. Ronald must get enough to at least pay off the loan. What is the range of the selling price? At least $12,250

67. ***Microwave oven.*** Sherie is going to buy a microwave in a city with an 8% sales tax. She has at most $594 to spend. In what price range should she look? At most $550

68. ***Dining out.*** At Burger Brothers the price of a hamburger is twice the price of an order of French fries, and the price of a Coke is $0.40 more than the price of the fries. Burger Brothers advertises that you can get a complete meal (burger, fries, and Coke) for under $4.00. What is the price range of an order of fries? Less than 90 cents

69. ***Averaging test scores.*** Tilak made 44 and 72 on the first two tests in algebra and has one test remaining. For Tilak to pass the course, the average on the three tests must be at least 60. For what range of scores on his last test will Tilak pass the course? At least 64

70. ***Averaging income.*** Helen earned $400 in January, $450 in February, and $380 in March. To pay all of her bills, she must average at least $430 per month. For what income in April would her average for the four months be at least $430? At least $490

71. ***Going for a C.*** Professor Williams gives only a midterm exam and a final exam. The semester average is computed by taking $\frac{1}{3}$ of the midterm exam score plus $\frac{2}{3}$ of the final exam score. To get a C, Stacy must have a semester average between 70 and 79 inclusive. If Stacy scored only 48 on the midterm, then for what range of scores on the final exam will Stacy get a C? Between 81 and 94.5 inclusive

72. ***Different weights.*** Professor Williamson counts his midterm as $\frac{2}{3}$ of the grade and his final as $\frac{1}{3}$ of the grade. Wendy scored only 48 on the midterm. What range of scores on the final exam would put Wendy's average between 70 and 79 inclusive? Compare to the previous exercise. Between 114 and 141 inclusive

73. ***Average driving speed.*** On Halley's recent trip from Bangor to San Diego, she drove for 8 hours each day and traveled between 396 and 453 miles each day. In what range was her average speed for each day of the trip? Between 49.5 and 56.625 miles per hour

74. ***Driving time.*** On Halley's trip back to Bangor, she drove at an average speed of 55 mph every day and traveled between 330 and 495 miles per day. In what range was her daily driving time? Between 6 and 9 hours

75. ***Sailboat navigation.*** As the sloop sailed north along the coast, the captain sighted the lighthouse at points A and B as shown in the figure. If the degree measure of the angle at the lighthouse is less than 30°, then what are the possible values for x? Between 55° and 85°

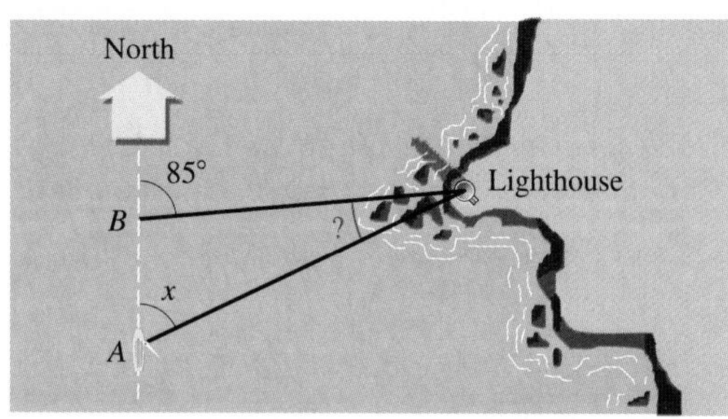

Figure for Exercise 75

76. ***Flight plan.*** A pilot started at point A and flew in the direction shown in the diagram for some time. At point B she made a 110° turn to end up at point C, due east of where she started. If the measure of angle C is less than 85°, then what are the possible values for x? Between 0° and 65°

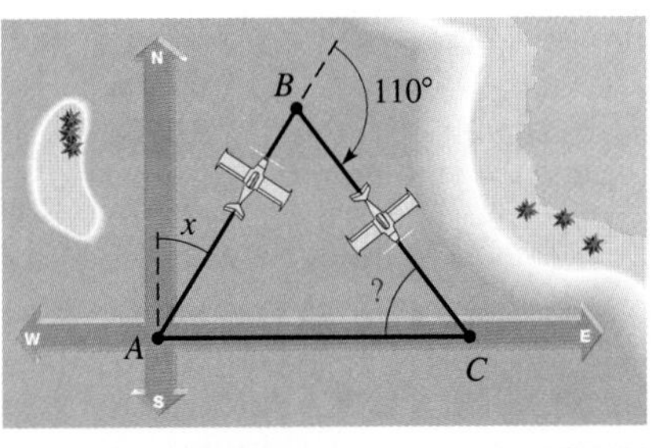

Figure for Exercise 76

77. ***Bicycle gear ratios.*** The gear ratio r for a bicycle is defined by the formula

$$r = \frac{Nw}{n},$$

where N is the number of teeth on the chainring (by the pedal), n is the number of teeth on the cog (by the wheel), and w is the wheel diameter in inches (www.sheldonbrown.com/gears).

a) If the wheel has a diameter of 27 in. and there are 12 teeth on the cog, then for what number of teeth on the chainring is the gear ratio between 60 and 80?
Between 27 and 35 teeth inclusive

b) If a bicycle has 48 teeth on the chainring and 17 teeth on the cog, then for what diameter wheel is the gear ratio between 65 and 70?
Between 23.02 in. and 24.79 in.

c) If a bicycle has a 26-in. diameter wheel and 40 teeth on the chainring, then for what number of teeth on the cog is the gear ratio less than 75?
At least 14 teeth

78. ***Virtual demand.*** The weekly demand (the number bought by consumers) for the Acme Virtual Pet is given by the formula

$$d = 9000 - 60p$$

where p is the price each in dollars.

a) What is the demand when the price is \$30 each?
7200

b) In what price range will the demand be above 6000?
Less than \$50

Collaborative Activities

Grouping: Three students per group

Topic: Expressions, Equations, and Inequalities

Expression-Equation-Inequality

In this activity you will practice your skills with simplifying expressions, solving equations, and solving and graphing inequalities. The roles are simplifier, solver, and grapher. The simplifier will simplify all expressions, the solver will solve all equations, and the grapher will first solve and then graph all inequalities.

Sorting Out the Work. Each of the following exercises contains one expression to be simplified, one equation to be solved, and one inequality to be graphed, not necessarily in that order. For each exercise your group will first sort out the three parts: give the expression to the simplifier, the equation to the solver, and the inequality to the grapher. After each person has completed his or her assigned task, pass the paper to the left for checking. Take on the role of the paper that you now have and proceed to the next exercise.

1. **a)** $-2x \geq 20$
b) $2(x - 4) + x - 10$
c) $3x - 5 = 4x + 1$

2. **a)** $\frac{1}{2}x + 3 + \frac{7}{2}x - 5$
b) $4(x + 3) = 3(1 + x)$
c) $5x - 7 > 8x + 5$

3. **a)** $4(2x - 5) \leq 5x - 1$
b) $3(x + 2) - (12 - x)$
c) $\frac{5}{3}x + 4 = \frac{2}{3}x$

4. **a)** $5x - 6 + x = 9 + 4x - 1$
b) $\frac{2(5x + 1)}{3} > 2$
c) $5x - x + 2x$

Creating Your Own. Each student now creates and solves the type of problem he or she worked last, using the terms given here. For example, given the terms $4y$, $2y$, and -4 you could make up the expression $4y - 2y + (-4)$, the equation $4y - 2y = -4$, and the inequality $4y + 2y < -4$. Pass your work to the person on your left to check. Then proceed to the next exercise as before.

5. $6x, 2x, 3$

6. $-10x, 5x, 20, -15$

7. $3y, -7y, 5, -4$

8. $-4w, 7, -6w, 22$

Chapter 2 Wrap-Up

Summary

Equations		**Examples**
Linear equation	An equation of the form $ax + b = 0$ with $a \neq 0$	$3x + 7 = 0$
Identity	An equation that is satisfied by every number for which both sides are defined	$x + x = 2x$
Conditional equation	An equation that has at least one solution but is not an identity	$5x - 10 = 0$
Inconsistent equation	An equation that has no solution	$x = x + 1$
Equivalent equations	Equations that have exactly the same solutions	$2x + 1 = 5$ $2x = 4$
Properties of equality	If the same number is added to or subtracted from each side of an equation, the resulting equation is equivalent to the original equation.	$x - 5 = -9$ $x = -4$
	If each side of an equation is multiplied or divided by the same nonzero number, the resulting equation is equivalent to the original equation.	$9x = 27$ $x = 3$
Solving equations	**1.** Remove parentheses by using the distributive property and then combine like terms to simplify each side as much as possible. **2.** Use the addition property of equality to get like terms from opposite sides onto the same side so that they may be combined. **3.** The multiplication property of equality is generally used last. **4.** Check that the solution satisfies the original equation.	$2(x - 3) = -7 + 3(x - 1)$ $2x - 6 = -10 + 3x$ $-x - 6 = -10$ $-x = -4$ $x = 4$ *Check:* $2(4 - 3) = -7 + 3(4 - 1)$ $2 = 2$
Applications		
Steps in solving applied problems	**1.** Read the problem. **2.** If possible, draw a diagram to illustrate the problem. **3.** Choose a variable and write down what it represents.	

4. Represent any other unknowns in terms of that variable.
5. Write an equation that describes the situation.
6. Solve the equation.
7. Answer the original question.
8. Check your answer by using it to solve the original problem (not the equation).

Inequalities		**Examples**
Properties of inequality	Addition, subtraction, multiplication, and division may be performed on each side of an inequality, just as we do in solving equations, with one exception. When multiplying or dividing by a negative number, the inequality symbol is reversed.	$-3x + 1 > 7$ $-3x > 6$ $x < -2$

Enriching Your Mathematical Word Power

For each mathematical term, choose the correct meaning.

1. linear equation
a. an equation in which the terms are in line
b. an equation of the form $ax + b = 0$ where $a \neq 0$
c. the equation $a = b$
d. an equation of the form $a^2 + b^2 = c^2$ b

2. identity
a. an equation that is satisfied by all real numbers
b. an equation that is satisfied by every real number
c. an equation that is identical
d. an equation that is satisfied by every real number for which both sides are defined d

3. conditional equation
a. an equation that has at least one real solution
b. an equation that is correct
c. an equation that is satisfied by at least one real number but is not an identity
d. an equation that we are not sure how to solve c

4. inconsistent equation
a. an equation that is wrong
b. an equation that is only sometimes consistent
c. an equation that has no solution
d. an equation with two variables c

5. equivalent equations
a. equations that are identical
b. equations that are correct
c. equations that are equal
d. equations that have the same solution d

6. formula
a. an equation
b. a type of race car
c. a process
d. an equation involving two or more variables d

7. literal equation
a. a formula
b. an equation with words
c. a false equation
d. a fact a

8. complementary angles
a. angles that compliment each other
b. angles whose degree measures total 90°
c. angles whose degree measures total 180°
d. angles with the same vertex b

9. supplementary angles
a. angles with soft flexible sides
b. angles whose degree measures total 90°
c. angles whose degree measures total 180°
d. angles that form a square c

10. uniform motion
a. movement of an army
b. movement in a straight line
c. consistent motion
d. motion at a constant rate d

Review Exercises

2.1 *Solve each equation and check your answer.*

1. $x - 23 = 12$ $\{35\}$

2. $14 = 18 + y$ $\{-4\}$

3. $\frac{2}{3}u = -4$ $\{-6\}$

4. $-\frac{3}{8}r = 15$ $\{-40\}$

5. $-5y = 35$ $\{-7\}$

6. $-12 = 6h$ $\{-2\}$

7. $6m = 13 + 5m$ $\{13\}$

8. $19 - 3n = -2n$ $\{19\}$

Study Tip

Note how the review exercises are arranged according to the sections in this chapter. If you are having trouble with a certain type of problem, refer back to the appropriate section for examples and explanations.

2.2 *Solve each equation and check your answer.*

9. $2x - 5 = 9$ $\{7\}$

10. $5x - 8 = 38$ $\left\{\frac{46}{5}\right\}$

11. $3p - 14 = -4p$ $\{2\}$

12. $36 - 9y = 3y$ $\{3\}$

13. $2z + 12 = 5z - 9$ $\{7\}$

14. $15 - 4w = 7 - 2w$ $\{4\}$

15. $2(h - 7) = -14$ $\{0\}$

16. $2(t - 7) = 0$ $\{7\}$

17. $3(w - 5) = 6(w + 2) - 3$ $\{-8\}$

18. $2(a - 4) + 4 = 5(9 - a)$ $\{7\}$

2.3 *Solve each equation. Identify each equation as a conditional equation, an inconsistent equation, or an identity.*

19. $2(x - 7) - 5 = 5 - (3 - 2x)$ $\varnothing$, inconsistent

20. $2(x - 7) + 5 = -(9 - 2x)$ All real numbers, identity

21. $2(w - w) = 0$ All real numbers, identity

22. $2y - y = 0$ $\{0\}$, conditional

23. $\frac{3r}{3r} = 1$ All nonzero real numbers, identity

24. $\frac{3t}{3} = 1$ $\{1\}$, conditional

25. $\frac{1}{2}a - 5 = \frac{1}{3}a - 1$ $\{24\}$, conditional

26. $\frac{1}{2}b - \frac{1}{2} = \frac{1}{4}b$ $\{2\}$, conditional

27. $0.06q + 14 = 0.3q - 5.2$ $\{80\}$, conditional

28. $0.05(z + 20) = 0.1z - 0.5$ $\{30\}$, conditional

29. $0.05(x + 100) + 0.06x = 115$ $\{1000\}$, conditional

30. $0.06x + 0.08(x + 1) = 0.41$ $\left\{\frac{33}{14}\right\}$, conditional

Solve each equation.

31. $2x + \frac{1}{2} = 3x + \frac{1}{4}$ $\left\{\frac{1}{4}\right\}$

32. $5x - \frac{1}{3} = 6x - \frac{1}{2}$ $\left\{\frac{1}{6}\right\}$

33. $\frac{x}{2} - \frac{3}{4} = \frac{x}{6} + \frac{1}{8}$ $\left\{\frac{21}{8}\right\}$

34. $\frac{1}{3} - \frac{x}{5} = \frac{1}{2} - \frac{x}{10}$ $\left\{-\frac{5}{3}\right\}$

35. $\frac{5}{6}x = -\frac{2}{3}$ $\left\{-\frac{4}{5}\right\}$

36. $-\frac{2}{3}x = \frac{3}{4}$ $\left\{-\frac{9}{8}\right\}$

37. $-\frac{1}{2}(x - 10) = \frac{3}{4}x$ $\{4\}$

38. $-\frac{1}{3}(6x - 9) = 23$ $\{-10\}$

39. $3 - 4(x - 1) + 6 = -3(x + 2) - 5$ $\{24\}$

40. $6 - 5(1 - 2x) + 3 = -3(1 - 2x) - 1$ $\{-2\}$

41. $5 - 0.1(x - 30) = 18 + 0.05(x + 100)$ $\{-100\}$

42. $0.6(x - 50) = 18 - 0.3(40 - 10x)$ $\{-15\}$

2.4 *Solve each equation for x.*

43. $ax + b = 0$

$x = -\frac{b}{a}$

44. $mx + e = t$

$x = \frac{t - e}{m}$

45. $ax - 2 = b$

$x = \frac{b + 2}{a}$

46. $b = 5 - x$

$x = 5 - b$

47. $LWx = V$

$x = \frac{V}{LW}$

48. $3xy = 6$

$x = \frac{2}{y}$

49. $2x - b = 5x$

$x = -\frac{b}{3}$

50. $t - 5x = 4x$

$x = \frac{t}{9}$

Solve each equation for y. Write the answer in the form $y = mx + b$, where m and b are real numbers.

51. $5x + 2y = 6$

$y = -\frac{5}{2}x + 3$

52. $5x - 3y + 9 = 0$

$y = \frac{5}{3}x + 3$

53. $y - 1 = -\frac{1}{2}(x - 6)$

$y = -\frac{1}{2}x + 4$

54. $y + 6 = \frac{1}{2}(x + 8)$

$y = \frac{1}{2}x - 2$

55. $\frac{1}{2}x + \frac{1}{4}y = 4$

$y = -2x + 16$

56. $-\frac{x}{3} + \frac{y}{2} = 1$

$y = \frac{2}{3}x + 2$

Find the value of y in each formula if $x = -3$.

57. $y = 3x - 4$ -13

58. $2x - 3y = -7$ $\frac{1}{3}$

59. $5xy = 6$ $-\frac{2}{5}$

60. $3xy - 2x = -12$ 2

61. $y - 3 = -2(x - 4)$ 17

62. $y + 1 = 2(x - 5)$ -17

Fill in the tables using the given formulas.

63. $y = -5x + 10$

x	y
−1	15
0	10
1	5
2	0
3	−5

64. $y = 2x - 4$

x	y
0	−4
1	−2
2	0
3	2
4	4

65. $y = \frac{2}{3}x - 1$

x	y
−3	−3
0	−1
3	1
6	3

66. $y = 10x + 100$

x	y
−20	−100
−10	0
0	100
10	200

2.5 *Translate each verbal expression into an algebraic expression.*

67. The sum of a number and 9

$x + 9$, where x is the number

68. The product of a number and 7

$7x$, where x is the number

69. Two numbers that differ by 8

x and $x + 8$, where x is the smaller number

70. Two numbers with a sum of 12

x and $12 - x$, where x is one number

71. Sixty-five percent of a number

$0.65x$, where x is the number

72. One half of a number

$\frac{1}{2}x$, where x is the number

Identify the variable, and write an equation that describes each situation. Do not solve the equation.

73. One side of a rectangle is 5 feet longer than the other, and the area is 98 square feet.

$x(x + 5) = 98$, where x is the width

74. One side of a rectangle is one foot longer than twice the other side, and the perimeter is 56 feet.
$2x + 2(2x + 1) = 56$, where x is the width

75. By driving 10 miles per hour slower than Jim, Barbara travels the same distance in 3 hours as Jim does in 2 hours.
$2x = 3(x - 10)$, where x is Jim's rate

76. Gladys and Ned drove 840 miles altogether, with Gladys averaging 5 miles per hour more in her 6 hours at the wheel than Ned did in his 5 hours at the wheel.
$6(x + 5) + 5x = 840$, where x is Ned's rate

77. The sum of three consecutive even integers is 90.
$x + x + 2 + x + 4 = 90$, where x is the smallest of the three even integers

78. The sum of two consecutive odd integers is 40.
$x + x + 2 = 40$, where x is the smaller of the two odd integers

79. The three angles of a triangle have degree measures of t, $2t$, and $t - 10$.
$t + 2t + t - 10 = 180$, where t is the degree measure of an angle

80. Two complementary angles have degree measures p and $3p - 6$.
$p + 3p - 6 = 90$, where p is the degree measure of an angle

2.6–7 *Solve each problem.*

81. ***Odd integers.*** If the sum of three consecutive odd integers is 237, then what are the integers?
77, 79, 81

82. ***Even integers.*** Find two consecutive even integers that have a sum of 450.
224, 226

83. ***Driving to the shore.*** Lawanda and Betty both drive the same distance to the shore. By driving 15 miles per hour faster than Betty, Lawanda can get there in 3 hours while Betty takes 4 hours. How fast does each of them drive?
Betty 45 mph, Lawanda 60 mph

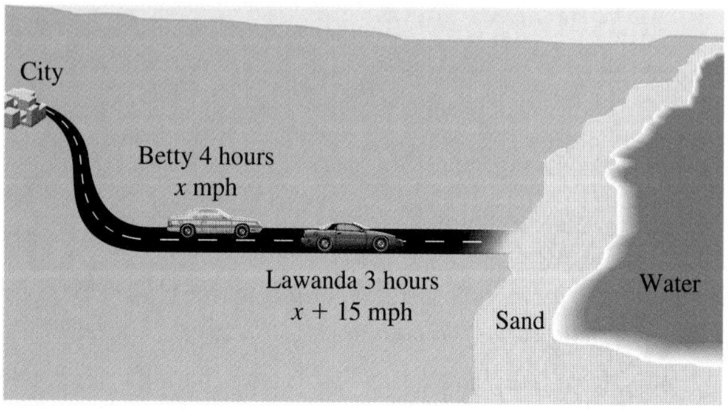

Figure for Exercise 83

84. ***Rectangular lot.*** The length of a rectangular lot is 50 feet more than the width. If the perimeter is 500 feet, then what are the length and width?
Length 150 feet, width 100 feet

85. ***Combined savings.*** Wanda makes \$6000 more per year than her husband does. Wanda saves 10% of her income for retirement, and her husband saves 6%. If together they save \$5400 per year, then how much does each of them make per year?
Wanda \$36,000, husband \$30,000

86. ***Layoffs looming.*** American Products plans to lay off 10% of its employees in its aerospace division and 15% of its employees in its agricultural division. If altogether 12% of the 3000 employees in these two divisions will be laid off, then how many employees are in each division?
Aerospace 1800, agriculture 1200

2.8 *Determine whether the given number is a solution to the inequality following it.*

87. $3, -2x + 5 \le x - 6$ No

88. $-2, 5 - x > 4x + 3$ Yes

89. $-1, -2 \le 6 + 4x < 0$ No

90. $0, 4x + 9 \ge 5(x - 3)$ Yes

For each graph write the corresponding inequality and the solution set to the inequality using interval notation.

91. 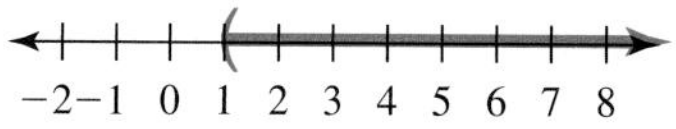

$x > 1, (1, \infty)$

92. 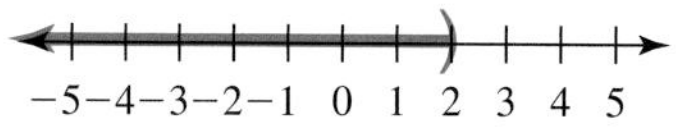

$x < 2, (-\infty, 2)$

93. 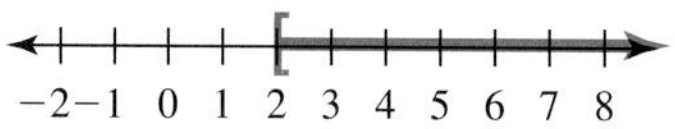

$x \ge 2, [2, \infty)$

94. 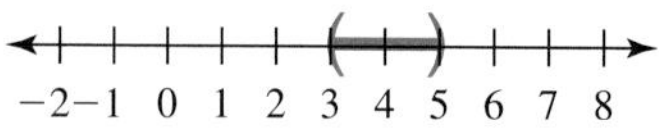

$3 < x < 5, (3, 5)$

95. 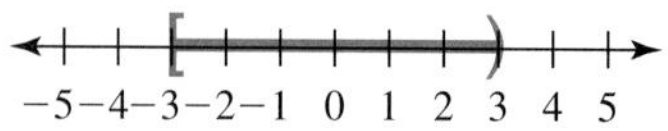

$-3 \le x < 3, [-3, 3)$

96. 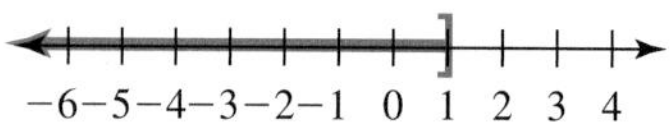

$x \le 1, (-\infty, 1]$

97. 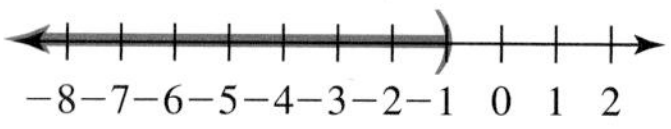

$x < -1, (-\infty, -1)$

98. 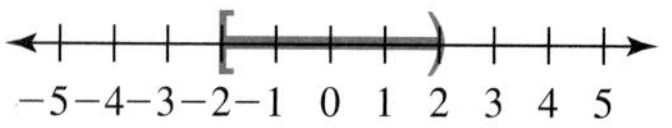

$-2 \le x < 2, [-2, 2)$

2.9 *Solve each inequality. State the solution set in interval notation and sketch its graph.*

99. $x + 2 > 1$ $(-1, \infty)$

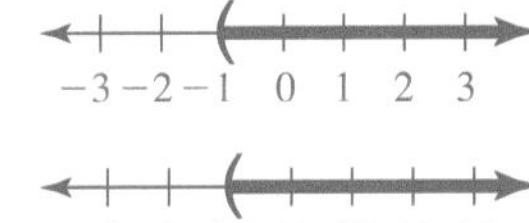

100. $x - 3 > 7$ $(10, \infty)$

101. $3x - 5 < x + 1$ $(-\infty, 3)$

102. $5x - 5 > 9 - 2x$ $(2, \infty)$

103. $-\frac{3}{4}x \geq 3$ $(-\infty, -4]$

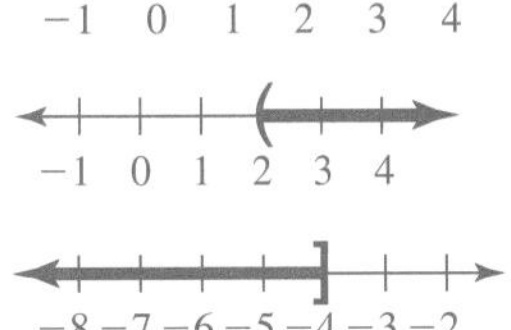

104. $-\frac{2}{3}x \leq 10$ $[-15, \infty)$

105. $3 - 2x < 11$ $(-4, \infty)$

106. $5 - 3x > 35$ $(-\infty, -10)$

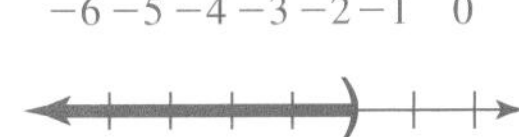

107. $-3 < 2x - 1 < 9$ $(-1, 5)$

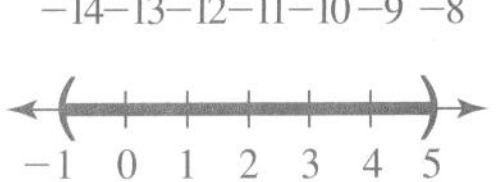

108. $2 \leq 3x + 2 < 8$ $[0, 2)$

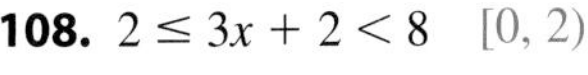

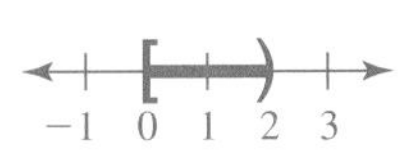

109. $0 \leq 1 - 2x < 5$ $\left(-2, \frac{1}{2}\right]$

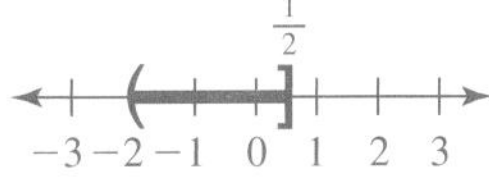

110. $-5 < 3 - 4x \leq 7$ $[-1, 2)$

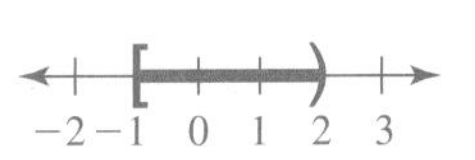

111. $-1 \leq \frac{2x - 3}{3} \leq 1$ $[0, 3]$

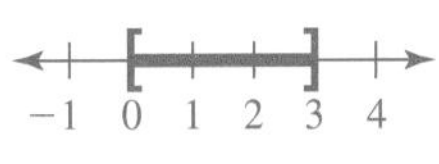

112. $-3 < \frac{4 - x}{2} < 2$ $(0, 10)$

113. $\frac{1}{3} < \frac{1}{3} + \frac{x}{2} < \frac{5}{6}$ $(0, 1)$

114. $-\frac{3}{8} \leq -\frac{1}{4}x + \frac{1}{8} < \frac{5}{8}$ $(-2, 2]$

Miscellaneous

Use an equation, inequality, or formula to solve each problem.

115. ***Long-term yields.*** The accompanying graph shows the *yield curve* for U.S. Treasury Bonds on February 20, 2002 (Bloomberg, www.bloomberg.com). The annual yield on a 30-year treasury bond was 5.375%. Use the simple interest formula to find the amount of interest earned during the first year on a 30-year bond of \$10,000. \$537.50

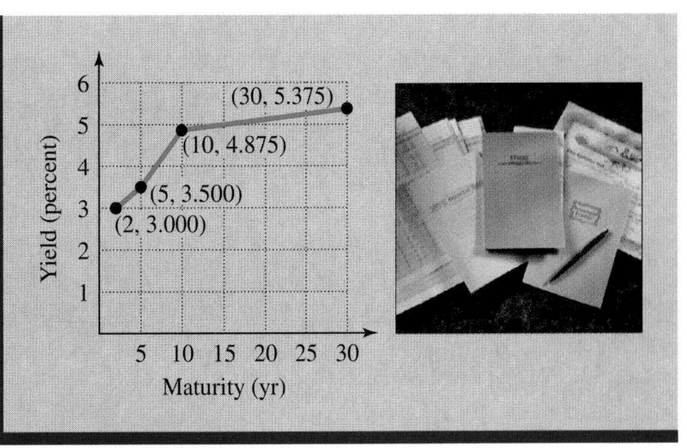

Figure for Exercise 115

116. ***Short-term yields.*** On February 20, 2002 the annual yield on a two-year treasury bond was 3.000%. Use the simple interest formula to find the amount of interest earned during the first year on a two-year treasury bond of \$10,000. \$300

117. ***Combined videos.*** The owners of ABC Video discovered that they had no movies in common with XYZ Video and bought XYZ's entire stock. Although XYZ had 200 titles, they had no children's movies, while 60% of ABC's titles were children's movies. If 40% of the movies in the combined stock are children's movies, then how many movies did ABC have before the merger? 400

118. ***Living comfortably.*** Gary has figured that he needs to take home \$30,400 a year to live comfortably. If the government gets 24% of Gary's income, then what must his income be for him to live comfortably? \$40,000

119. ***Bracing a gate.*** The diagonal brace on a rectangular gate forms an angle with the horizontal side with degree measure x and an angle with the vertical side with degree measure $2x - 3$. Find x. $31°$

120. ***Digging up the street.*** A contractor wants to install a pipeline connecting point A with point C on opposite sides of a road as shown in the figure. To save money, the contractor has decided to lay the pipe to point B and then under the road to point C. Find the measure of the angle marked x in the figure. $70°$

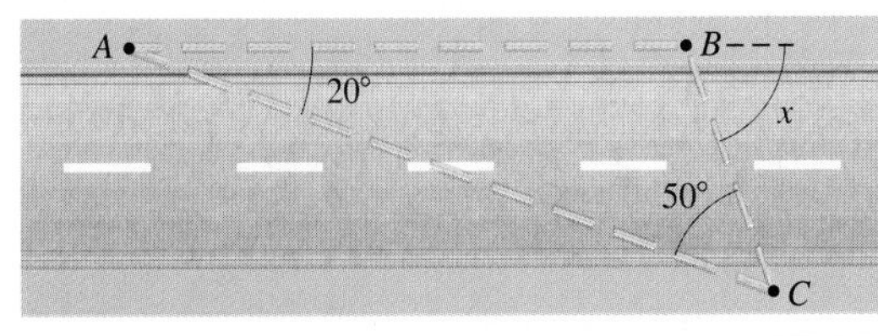

Figure for Exercise 120

121. ***Perimeter of a triangle.*** One side of a triangle is 1 foot longer than the shortest side, and the third side is twice as long as the shortest side. If the perimeter is less than 25 feet, then what is the range of the length of the shortest side?
Less than 6 feet

122. ***Restricted hours.*** Alana makes \$5.80 per hour working in the library. To keep her job, she must make at least \$116 per week; but to keep her scholarship, she must not earn more than \$145 per week. What is the range of the number of hours per week that she may work?
Between 20 and 25 hours per week inclusive

Chapter 2 Test

Solve each equation.

1. $-10x - 6 + 4x = -4x + 8$ $\{-7\}$

2. $5(2x - 3) = x + 3$ $\{2\}$

3. $-\frac{2}{3}x + 1 = 7$ $\{-9\}$

4. $x + 0.06x = 742$ $\{700\}$

5. $x - 0.03x = 0.97$ $\{1\}$

6. $6x - 7 = 0$ $\left\{\frac{7}{6}\right\}$

7. $\frac{1}{2}x - \frac{1}{3} = \frac{1}{4}x + \frac{1}{6}$ $\{2\}$

8. $2(x + 6) = 2x - 5$ $\varnothing$

9. $x + 7x = 8x$ All real numbers

Study Tip

Determine your readiness for an in-class test by working this sample test without looking at examples or notes. Give yourself one hour and grade your paper using the answers in the back of this book.

Solve for the indicated variable.

10. $2x - 3y = 9$ for y

$y = \frac{2}{3}x - 3$

11. $m = aP - w$ for a

$a = \frac{m + w}{P}$

For each graph write the corresponding inequality and the solution set to the inequality using interval notation.

12. 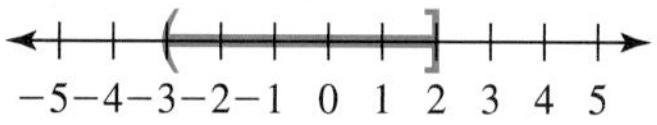

$-3 < x \leq 2$, $(-3, 2]$

13. 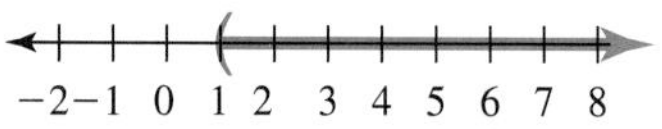

$x > 1$, $(1, \infty)$

Solve each inequality. State the solution set in interval notation and sketch its graph.

14. $4 - 3(w - 5) < -2w$ $(19, \infty)$

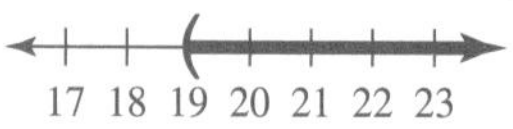

15. $1 < \frac{1 - 2x}{3} < 5$ $(-7, -1)$

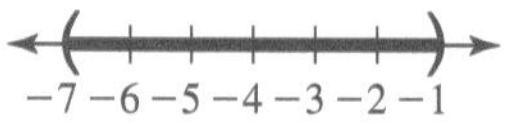

16. $1 < 3x - 2 < 7$ $(1, 3)$

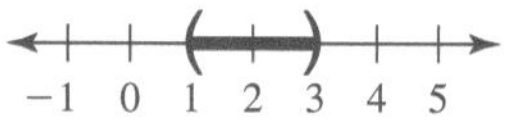

17. $-\frac{2}{3}y < 4$ $(-6, \infty)$

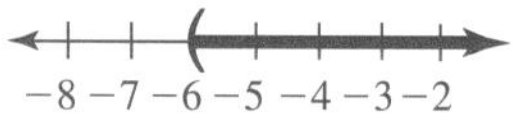

Write a complete solution to each problem.

18. The perimeter of a rectangle is 72 meters. If the width is 8 meters less than the length, then what is the width of the rectangle? 14 meters

19. If the area of a triangle is 54 square inches and the base is 12 inches, then what is the height? 9 in.

20. How many liters of a 20% alcohol solution should Maria mix with 50 liters of a 60% alcohol solution to obtain a 30% solution? 150 liters

21. Brandon gets a 40% discount on loose diamonds where he works. The cost of the setting is \$250. If he plans to spend at most \$1450, then what is the price range (list price) of the diamonds that he can afford? At most \$2000

22. If the degree measure of the smallest angle of a triangle is one-half of the degree measure of the second largest angle and one-third of the degree measure of the largest angle, then what is the degree measure of each angle?
30°, 60°, 90°

Making Connections | A Review of Chapters 1–2

Simplify each expression.

1. $3x + 5x$ $8x$

2. $3x \cdot 5x$ $15x^2$

3. $\dfrac{4x + 2}{2}$ $2x + 1$

4. $5 - 4(3 - x)$ $4x - 7$

5. $3x + 8 - 5(x - 1)$ $-2x + 13$

6. $(-6)^2 - 4(-3)2$ 60

7. $3^2 \cdot 2^3$ 72

8. $4(-7) - (-6)(3)$ -10

9. $-2x \cdot x \cdot x$ $-2x^3$

10. $(-1)(-1)(-1)(-1)(-1)$ -1

Perform the following operations.

11. $\frac{1}{2} + \frac{1}{6}$ $\frac{2}{3}$

12. $\frac{1}{2} - \frac{1}{3}$ $\frac{1}{6}$

13. $\frac{5}{3} \cdot \frac{1}{15}$ $\frac{1}{9}$

14. $\frac{2}{3} \cdot \frac{5}{6}$ $\frac{5}{9}$

15. $6 \cdot \left(\frac{5}{3} + \frac{1}{2}\right)$ 13

16. $15\left(\frac{2}{3} - \frac{2}{15}\right)$ 8

17. $4 \cdot \left(\frac{x}{2} + \frac{1}{4}\right)$ $2x + 1$

18. $12\left(\frac{5}{6}x - \frac{3}{4}\right)$ $10x - 9$

Find the solution set to each equation or inequality.

19. $x - \frac{1}{2} = \frac{1}{6}$ $\left\{\frac{2}{3}\right\}$

20. $x + \frac{1}{3} = \frac{1}{2}$ $\left\{\frac{1}{6}\right\}$

21. $x - \frac{1}{2} > \frac{1}{6}$ $\left(\frac{2}{3}, \infty\right)$

22. $x + \frac{1}{3} \le \frac{1}{2}$ $\left(-\infty, \frac{1}{6}\right]$

23. $\frac{3}{5}x = \frac{1}{15}$ $\left\{\frac{1}{9}\right\}$

24. $\frac{3}{2}x = \frac{5}{6}$ $\left\{\frac{5}{9}\right\}$

25. $-\frac{3}{5}x \le \frac{1}{15}$ $\left[-\frac{1}{9}, \infty\right)$

26. $-\frac{3}{2}x > \frac{5}{6}$ $\left(-\infty, -\frac{5}{9}\right)$

27. $\frac{5}{3}x + \frac{1}{2} = 1$ $\left\{\frac{3}{10}\right\}$

28. $\frac{2}{3}x - \frac{2}{15} = 2$ $\left\{\frac{16}{5}\right\}$

29. $\frac{x}{2} + \frac{1}{4} = \frac{1}{2}$ $\left\{\frac{1}{2}\right\}$

30. $\frac{5}{6}x - \frac{3}{4} = \frac{5}{12}$ $\left\{\frac{7}{5}\right\}$

31. $3x + 5x = 8$
$\{1\}$

32. $3x + 5x = 8x$
All real numbers

33. $3x + 5x = 7x$
$\{0\}$

34. $3x + 5 = 8$
$\{1\}$

35. $3x + 5x > 7x$
$(0, \infty)$

36. $3x + 5x > 8x$
$\varnothing$

37. $3x + 1 = 7$
$\{2\}$

38. $5 - 4(3 - x) = 1$
$\{2\}$

39. $3x + 8 = 5(x - 1)$
$\left\{\frac{13}{2}\right\}$

40. $x - 0.05x = 190$
$\{200\}$

Solve the problem.

41. ***Linear Depreciation.*** In computing income taxes, a company is allowed to depreciate a \$20,000 computer system over five years. Using *linear depreciation,* the value V of the computer system at any year t from 0 through 5 is given by

$$V = C - \frac{(C - S)}{5}t,$$

where C is the initial cost of the system and S is the scrap value of the system.

a) What is the value of the computer system after two years if its scrap value is \$4000?
\$13,600

b) If the value of the system after three years is claimed to be \$14,000, then what is the scrap value of the company's system?
\$10,000

c) If the accompanying graph models the depreciation of the system, then what is the scrap value of the system?
\$12,000

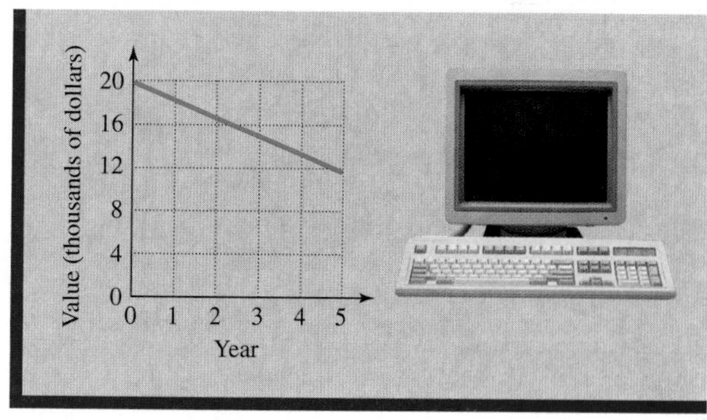

Figure for Exercise 41

Study Tip

Don't wait until the final exam to review material. Do some review on a regular basis. The Making Connections exercises on this page can be used to review, compare, and contrast different concepts that you have studied. A good time to work these exercises is between a test and the start of new material.

*Critical***Thinking** | For Individual or Group Work | Chapter 2

These exercises can be solved by a variety of techniques, which may or may not require algebra. So be creative and think critically. Explain all answers. Answers are in the Instructor's Edition of this text.

1. ***Visible squares.*** How many squares are visible in each of the following diagrams?

a) 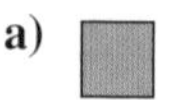

b) 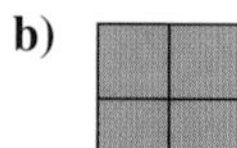

c) 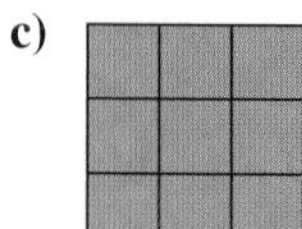

d) 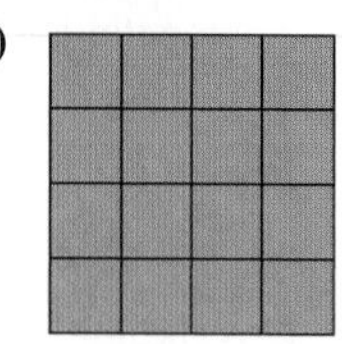

2. ***Baker's dilemma.*** A baker needs 8 cups of flour. He sends his apprentice to the flour bin with a scoop that holds 6 cups and a scoop that holds 11 cups. How can the apprentice measure 8 cups of flour with these scoops?

Photo for Exercise 2

3. ***Totaling one hundred.*** Start with the sequence of digits 987654321. Place any number of plus or minus signs between the digits in the sequence so that the value of the resulting expression is 100. For example,

$$98 + 7 - 6 - 5 + 4 + 3 - 2 + 1 = 100.$$

4. ***Four threes.*** Check out these equations:

$$\frac{3 \cdot 3}{3 \cdot 3} = 1, \frac{3}{3} + \frac{3}{3} = 2, (3 - 3)3 + 3 = 3.$$

Using exactly four 3's write arithmetic expressions whose values are 4, 5, 6, and so on. How far can you go?

5. ***Palindrome time.*** A palindrome is a sequence of words or numbers the reads the same forward or backward. For example, "A TOYOTA" is a palindrome and 14341 is a palindromic number. How many times per day does a digital clock display a palindromic number? Of course the answer depends on the format in which the digital clock displays the time. First, state precisely the type of digital clock display you are using, then count the palindromic numbers for that type of display.

6. ***Reversible products.*** Find the product of 32 and 46. Now reverse the digits and find the product of 23 and 64. The products are the same. Does this happen with any pair of two-digit numbers? Find two other pairs of two-digit numbers (with different digits) that have this property.

7. ***Running late.*** Alice, Bea, Carl, and Don all have an 8 o'clock class. Alice's watch is 8 minutes fast, but she thinks it is 4 minutes slow. Bea's watch is 8 minutes slow, but she thinks it is 8 minutes fast. Carl's watch is 4 minutes slow, but he thinks it is 8 minutes fast. Don's watch is 4 minutes fast, but he thinks it is 8 minutes slow. Each student leaves so they will get to class at exactly 8 o'clock. Each student assumes the correct time is what they think it is by their watch. Who is late to class and by how much?

8. ***Automorphic numbers.*** Automorphic numbers are integers whose squares end in the given integer. Since $1^2 = 1$ and $6^2 = 36$, both 1 and 6 are automorphic. Find the next four automorphic numbers.

1. a) 1 **b)** 5 **c)** 14 **d)** 30 **2.** The apprentice can fill a scoop, pour from one scoop to the other, or empty a scoop into the bin. Use the following sequence of amounts in the scoops: (0, 11), (6, 5), (0, 5), (5, 0), (5, 11), (6, 10), (0, 10), (6, 4), (0, 4), (4, 0), (4, 11), (6, 9), (0, 9), (6, 3), (0, 3), (3, 0), (3, 11), (6, 8), (0, 8). **3.** $9 + 8 + 76 + 5 - 4 + 3 + 2 + 1 = 100$ or $98 - 76 + 54 + 3 + 21 = 100$ **4.** $3 + 3^{3-3} = 4$, $3 + 3 - 3/3 = 5$, $3 + 3 + 3 - 3 = 6$ **5.** With hours from 1–12 (no leading zeros) and minutes from 00–59 (no seconds), there are 57 palindromic displays. **6.** 39 and 62, 64 and 69. **7.** Bea 16 minutes late, Carl 12 minutes late. **8.** 25, 76, 376, 625.

Chapter 3

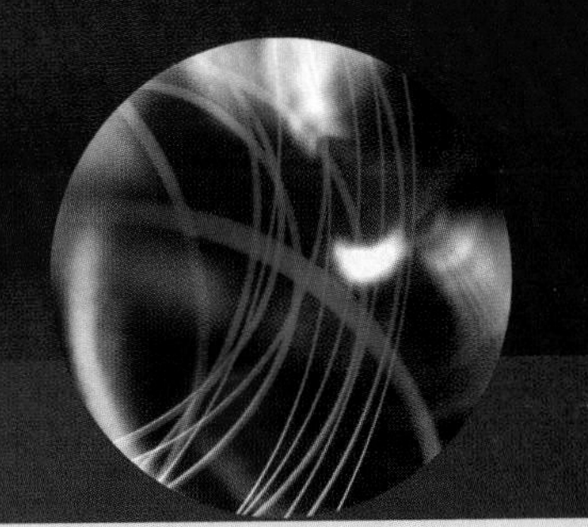

Linear Equations and Inequalities in Two Variables

If you pick up any package of food and read the label, you will find a long list that usually ends with some mysterious looking names. Many of these strange elements are food additives. A food additive is a substance or a mixture of substances other than basic foodstuffs that is present in food as a result of production, processing, storage, or packaging. They can be natural or synthetic and are categorized in many ways: preservatives, coloring agents, processing aids, and nutritional supplements, to name a few.

Food additives have been around since prehistoric humans discovered that salt would help to preserve meat. Today, food additives can include simple ingredients such as red color from Concord grape skins, calcium, or an enzyme. Throughout the centuries there have been lively discussions on what is healthy to eat. At the present time the food industry is working to develop foods that have less cholesterol, fats, and other unhealthy ingredients.

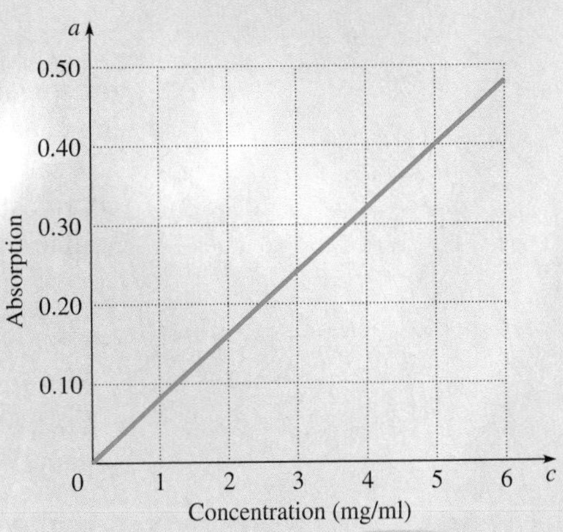

Although they frequently have different viewpoints, the food industry and the Food and Drug Administration (FDA) are working to provide consumers with information on a healthier diet. Recent developments such as the synthetically engineered tomato stirred great controversy, even though the FDA declared the tomato safe to eat.

In Exercise 91 of Section 3.4 you will see how a food chemist uses a linear equation in testing the concentration of an enzyme in a fruit juice.

3.1 Graphing Lines in the Coordinate Plane

In this Section

- Ordered Pairs
- The Rectangular Coordinate System
- Plotting Points
- Graphing a Linear Equation
- Graphing a Line Using Intercepts
- Applications

In Chapter 1 you learned to graph numbers on a number line. We also used number lines to illustrate the solution to inequalities in Chapter 2. In this section you will learn to graph pairs of numbers in a coordinate system made up of a pair of number lines. We will use this coordinate system to illustrate the solution to equations and inequalities in two variables.

Ordered Pairs

The equation $y = 2x - 1$ is an equation in two variables. This equation is satisfied if we choose a value for x and a value for y that make it true. If we choose $x = 2$ and $y = 3$, then $y = 2x - 1$ becomes

$$\overset{y}{\downarrow}\quad\ \overset{x}{\downarrow}$$
$$3 = 2(2) - 1.$$
$$3 = 3$$

Helpful Hint

In this chapter you will be doing a lot of graphing. Using graph paper will help you understand the concepts and help you recognize errors. For your convenience, a page of graph paper can be found on page 243 of this text. Make as many copies of it as you wish.

Because the last statement is true, we say that the pair of numbers 2 and 3 **satisfies the equation** or is a **solution to the equation.** We use the **ordered pair** (2, 3) to represent $x = 2$ and $y = 3$. The format is to always write the value for x first and the value for y second. The numbers in an ordered pair are called **coordinates.** In the pair (2, 3) the first coordinate or x-coordinate is 2 and the second coordinate or y-coordinate is 3. Note that the ordered pair (3, 2) does not satisfy the equation $y = 2x - 1$, because for $x = 3$ and $y = 2$ we have

$$2 \neq 2(3) - 1.$$

The variable corresponding to the first coordinate of an ordered pair is called the **independent variable** and the variable corresponding to the second coordinate is called the **dependent variable.** We think of the value for the first coordinate as being selected arbitrarily and the value for the second coordinate as being determined from the first coordinate by a rule such as $y = 2x - 1$. Of course, if the ordered pair must satisfy a simple equation, then we can find either coordinate when given the other coordinate.

EXAMPLE 1

Finding solutions to an equation

Each of the ordered pairs below is missing one coordinate. Complete each ordered pair so that it satisfies the equation $y = -3x + 4$.

a) (2,) **b)** (, −5) **c)** (0,)

Solution

a) The x-coordinate of (2,) is 2. Let $x = 2$ in the equation $y = -3x + 4$:

$$\begin{aligned} y &= -3 \cdot 2 + 4 \\ &= -6 + 4 \\ &= -2 \end{aligned}$$

The ordered pair (2, −2) satisfies the equation.

Teaching Tip Point out the connection between the x-coordinate and the solution to a linear equation. The skills learned in Chapter 2 will be needed here.

b) The y-coordinate of (, −5) is −5. Let $y = -5$ in the equation $y = -3x + 4$:

$$-5 = -3x + 4$$
$$-9 = -3x$$
$$3 = x$$

The ordered pair (3, −5) satisfies the equation.

c) Replace x by 0 in the equation $y = -3x + 4$:

$$y = -3 \cdot 0 + 4 = 4$$

So (0, 4) satisfies the equation.

Now do Exercises 7–16

The Rectangular Coordinate System

We use the **rectangular** (or **Cartesian**) **coordinate system** to get a visual image of ordered pairs of real numbers. The rectangular coordinate system consists of two number lines drawn at a right angle to one another, intersecting at zero on each number line, as shown in Fig. 3.1. The plane containing these number lines is called the **coordinate plane.** On the horizontal number line the positive numbers are to the right of zero, and on the vertical number line the positive numbers are above zero.

Teaching Tip Students do much better with graphing when they use graph paper. A page of blank grids that can be copied is provided on page 243 of this text. You will also find pages of graph paper in the Instructor's Solutions Manual and Student's Solutions Manual.

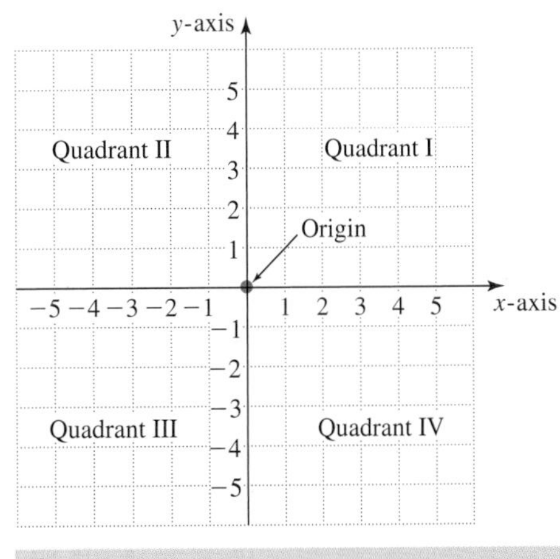

Figure 3.1

The horizontal number line is called the ***x*-axis,** and the vertical number line is called the ***y*-axis.** The point at which they intersect is called the **origin.** The two number lines divide the plane into four regions called **quadrants.** They are numbered as shown in Fig. 3.1. The quadrants do not include any points on the axes.

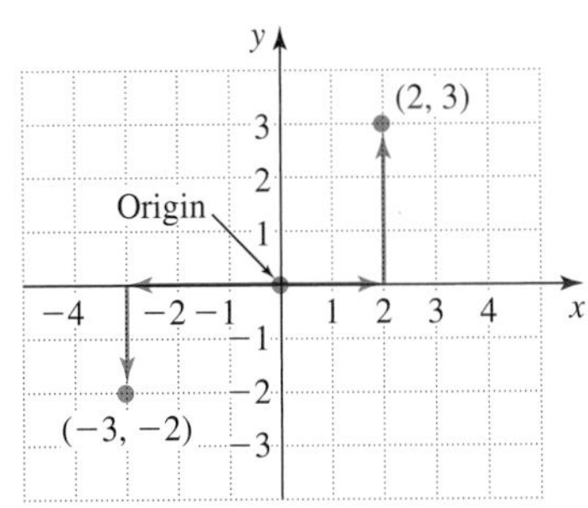

Figure 3.2

Plotting Points

Just as every real number corresponds to a point on the number line, *every pair of real numbers corresponds to a point in the rectangular coordinate system.* For example, the point corresponding to the pair (2, 3) is found by starting at the origin and moving two units to the right and then three units up. The point corresponding to the pair (−3, −2) is found by starting at the origin and moving three units to the left and then two units down. Both of these points are shown in Fig. 3.2.

When we locate a point in the rectangular coordinate system, we are **plotting** or **graphing** the point. Because ordered pairs of numbers correspond to points in the coordinate plane, we frequently refer to an ordered pair as a point.

EXAMPLE 2

Plotting points

Plot the points (2, 5), (−1, 4), (−3, −4), and (3, −2).

Solution

To locate (2, 5), start at the origin, move two units to the right, and then move up five units. To locate (−1, 4), start at the origin, move one unit to the left, and then move up four units. All four points are shown in Fig. 3.3.

Now do Exercises 17–32

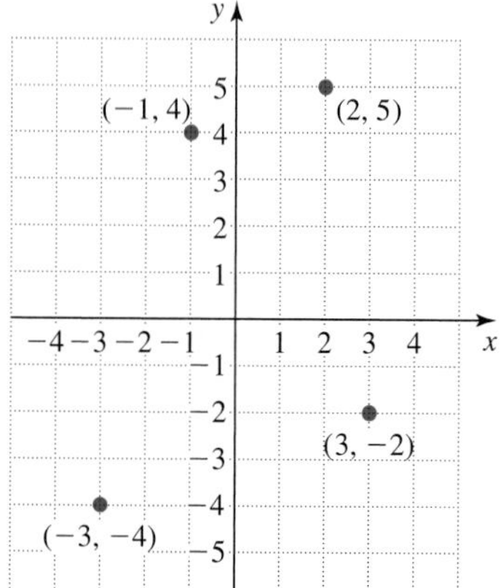

Figure 3.3

Graphing a Linear Equation

The **graph** of an equation in two variables is an illustration in the coordinate plane that shows all of the ordered pairs that satisfy the equation. When we draw the graph, we are *graphing the equation.* Since an equation in two variables is usually satisfied by infinitely many ordered pairs, we cannot possibly find or plot all of them. Instead, we find and plot some ordered pairs and then try to determine what the entire graph looks like from the few ordered pairs that we have plotted.

EXAMPLE 3

Graphing an equation

Graph the equation $y = 2x - 1$ in the coordinate plane.

Solution

To find ordered pairs that satisfy $y = 2x - 1$, we arbitrarily select some x-coordinates and calculate the corresponding y-coordinates:

$$
\begin{aligned}
&\text{If } x = -3, && \text{then } y = 2(-3) - 1 = -7.\\
&\text{If } x = -2, && \text{then } y = 2(-2) - 1 = -5.\\
&\text{If } x = -1, && \text{then } y = 2(-1) - 1 = -3.\\
&\text{If } x = 0, && \text{then } y = 2(0) - 1 = -1.\\
&\text{If } x = 1, && \text{then } y = 2(1) - 1 = 1.\\
&\text{If } x = 2, && \text{then } y = 2(2) - 1 = 3.\\
&\text{If } x = 3, && \text{then } y = 2(3) - 1 = 5.
\end{aligned}
$$

We can make a table for these results as follows:

x	−3	−2	−1	0	1	2	3
$y = 2x - 1$	−7	−5	−3	−1	1	3	5

Calculator Close-Up

You can make a table of values for x and y with a graphing calculator. Enter the equation $y = 2x - 1$ using Y= and then press TABLE.

X	Y1
-3	-7
-2	-5
-1	-3
0	-1
1	1
2	3
3	5

X=0

The ordered pairs $(-3, -7)$, $(-2, -5)$, $(-1, -3)$, $(0, -1)$, $(1, 1)$, $(2, 3)$, and $(3, 5)$ are graphed in Fig. 3.4. Notice that the points lie in a straight line. If we choose any real number for x and find the point that satisfies $y = 2x - 1$, we get another point on this line. Likewise, any point on this line satisfies the equation. So the graph of $y = 2x - 1$ is the straight line in Fig. 3.5. The arrows on the ends of the line indicate that it goes indefinitely in both directions.

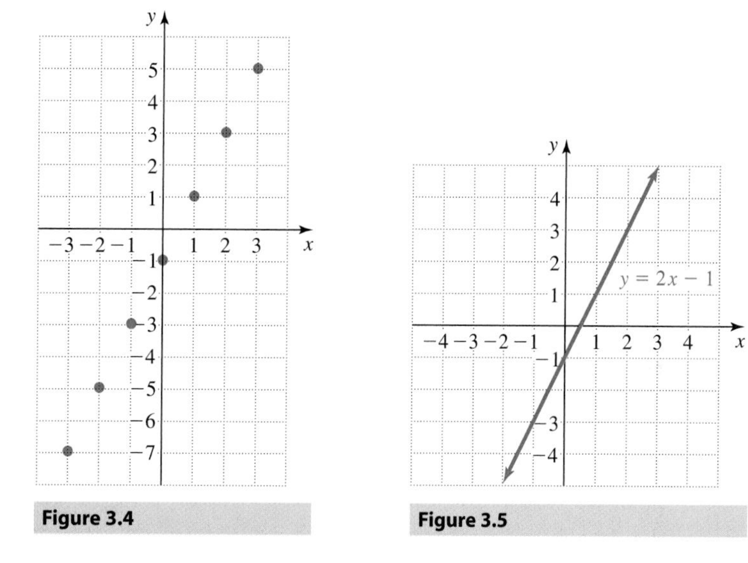

Figure 3.4

Figure 3.5

Now do Exercises 39–46

Because its graph is a straight line, the equation $y = 2x - 1$ in Example 3 is called a *linear equation in two variables.*

Linear Equation in Two Variables

A **linear equation in two variables** is an equation that can be written in the form

$$Ax + By = C,$$

where A, B, and C are real numbers, with A and B not both equal to zero.

Equations such as

$$x - y = 5, \quad y = 2x + 3, \quad 2x - 5y - 9 = 0, \quad \text{and} \quad x = 8$$

are linear equations because they could all be rewritten in the form $Ax + By = C$. The graph of any linear equation is a straight line.

EXAMPLE 4

Graphing an equation

Graph the equation $3x + y = 2$. Plot at least five points.

Solution

It is easier to make a table of ordered pairs if the equation is solved for y. So subtract $3x$ from each side to get $y = -3x + 2$. Now select some values for x and then calculate the corresponding y-coordinates:

If $x = -2$, then $y = -3(-2) + 2 = 8$.
If $x = -1$, then $y = -3(-1) + 2 = 5$.
If $x = 0$, then $y = -3(0) + 2 = 2$.
If $x = 1$, then $y = -3(1) + 2 = -1$.
If $x = 2$, then $y = -3(2) + 2 = -4$.

The following table shows these five ordered pairs:

x	-2	-1	0	1	2
$y = -3x + 2$	8	5	2	-1	-4

The graph of the line through these points is shown in Fig. 3.6.

Now do Exercises 47–50

Teaching Tip Ask students to identify the pattern in the table. Does the equation $y = -3x + 2$ have anything to do with this?

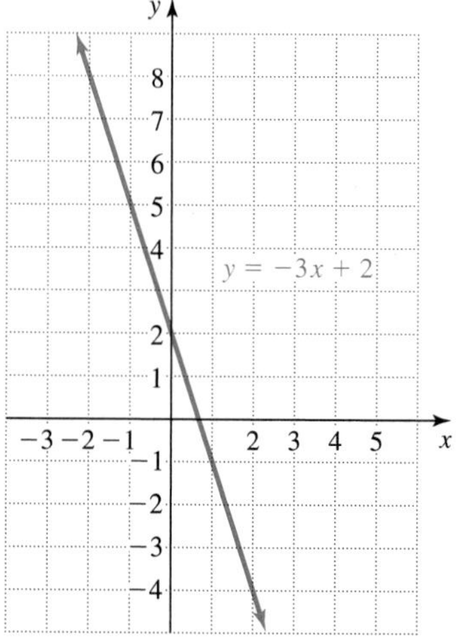

Figure 3.6

Calculator Close-Up

To graph $y = -3x + 2$, enter the equation using the Y= key:

Plot1 Plot2 Plot3
\Y1 ■ -3X+2
\Y2=
\Y3=
\Y4=
\Y5=
\Y6=
\Y7=

Next, set the viewing window (WINDOW) to get the desired view of the graph. Xmin and Xmax indicate the minimum and maximum x-values used for the graph; likewise for Ymin and Ymax. Xscl and Yscl (scale) give the distance between tick marks on the respective axes.

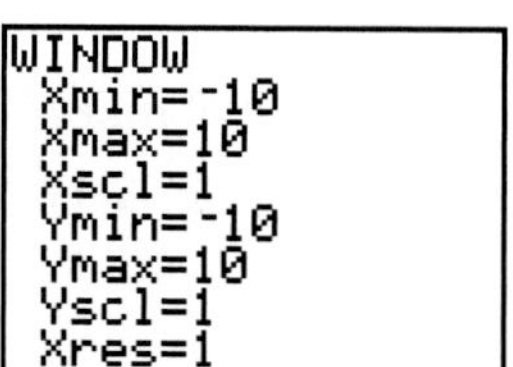
WINDOW
Xmin=-10
Xmax=10
Xscl=1
Ymin=-10
Ymax=10
Yscl=1
Xres=1

Press GRAPH to get the graph:

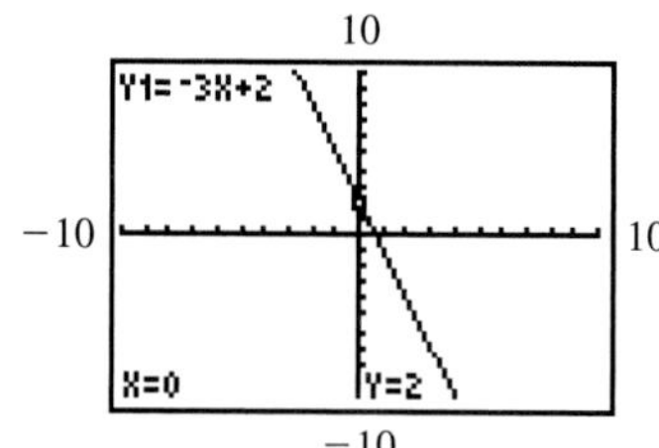

Even though the graph is not really "straight," it is consistent with the graph of $y = -3x + 2$ in Fig. 3.6.

In the linear equation $Ax + By = C$ either A or B could be zero. For example, $0 \cdot x + y = 4$ is a linear equation. Since x is multiplied by 0 this equation is usually written simply as $y = 4$. To graph $y = 4$ in the coordinate plane, we must understand that it comes from $0 \cdot x + y = 4$.

EXAMPLE 5

Horizontal and vertical lines

Graph each linear equation.

a) $y = 4$ **b)** $x = 3$

Solution

a) The equation $y = 4$ is a simplification of $0 \cdot x + y = 4$. So if y is replaced with 4, then we can use any real number for x. For example, $(-1, 4)$ satisfies $0 \cdot x + y = 4$ because $0(-1) + 4 = 4$ is correct. The following table shows five ordered pairs that satisfy $y = 4$.

x	-2	-1	0	1	2
$y = 4$	4	4	4	4	4

Figure 3.7 shows a horizontal line through these points.

b) The equation $x = 3$ is a simplification of $x + 0 \cdot y = 3$. So if x is replaced with 3, then we can use any real number for y. For example, $(3, -2)$ satisfies $x + 0 \cdot y = 3$ because $3 + 0(-2) = 3$ is correct. The following table shows five ordered pairs that satisfy $x = 3$.

$x = 3$	3	3	3	3	3
y	-2	-1	0	1	2

Figure 3.8 shows a vertical line through these points.

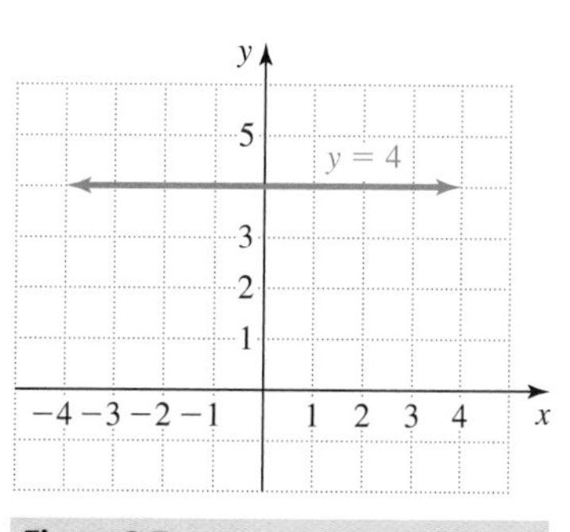

Figure 3.7

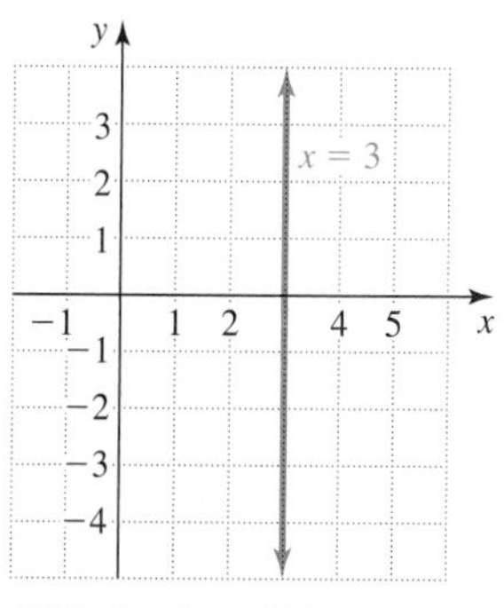

Figure 3.8

Now do Exercises 51–62

Calculator Close-Up

You cannot graph the vertical line $x = 3$ on most graphing calculators. The only equations that can be graphed are ones in which y is written in terms of x.

CAUTION If an equation such as $x = 3$ is discussed in the context of equations in two variables, then we assume that it is a simplified form of $x + 0 \cdot y = 3$, and there are infinitely many ordered pairs that satisfy the equation. If the equation $x = 3$ is discussed in the context of equations in a single variable, then $x = 3$ has only one solution, 3.

All of the equations we have considered so far have involved single-digit numbers. If an equation involves large numbers, then we must change the scale on the x-axis, the y-axis, or both to accommodate the numbers involved. The change of scale is arbitrary, and the graph will look different for different scales.

EXAMPLE 6

Adjusting the scale

Graph the equation $y = 20x + 500$. Plot at least five points.

Teaching Tip Students often have trouble picking a scale other than 1, 2, 3. Remind them that they can find the intercepts first and then select a scale to accommodate the intercepts.

Solution

The following table shows five ordered pairs that satisfy the equation.

x	-20	-10	0	10	20
$y = 20x + 500$	100	300	500	700	900

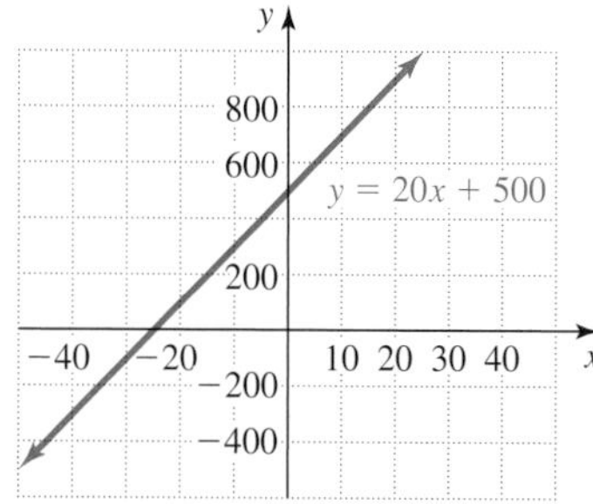

Figure 3.9

To fit these points onto a graph, we change the scale on the x-axis to let each division represent 10 units and change the scale on the y-axis to let each division represent 200 units. The graph is shown in Fig. 3.9.

Now do Exercises 75–80

Graphing a Line Using Intercepts

We know that the graph of a linear equation is a straight line. Because it takes only two points to determine a line, we can graph a linear equation using only two points. The two points that are the easiest to locate are usually the points where the line crosses the axes. The point where the graph crosses the x-axis is the ***x*-intercept.** The y-coordinate of the x-intercept is zero. The point where the graph crosses the y-axis is the ***y*-intercept.** The x-coordinate of the y-intercept is zero.

EXAMPLE 7

Graphing a line using intercepts

Graph the equation $2x - 3y = 6$ by using the x- and y-intercepts.

Helpful Hint

You can find the intercepts for $2x - 3y = 6$ using the *cover-up method.* Cover up $-3y$ with your pencil, then solve $2x = 6$ mentally to get $x = 3$ and an x-intercept of $(3, 0)$. Now cover up $2x$ and solve $-3y = 6$ to get $y = -2$ and a y-intercept of $(0, -2)$.

Solution

To find the x-intercept, let $y = 0$ in the equation $2x - 3y = 6$:

$$\begin{aligned} 2x - 3 \cdot 0 &= 6 \\ 2x &= 6 \\ x &= 3 \end{aligned}$$

The x-intercept is $(3, 0)$. To find the y-intercept, let $x = 0$ in $2x - 3y = 6$:

$$\begin{aligned} 2 \cdot 0 - 3y &= 6 \\ -3y &= 6 \\ y &= -2 \end{aligned}$$

The y-intercept is $(0, -2)$. Locate the intercepts and draw a line through them as shown in Fig. 3.10. To check, find one additional point that satisfies the equation, say $(6, 2)$, and see whether the line goes through that point.

Calculator Close-Up

To check the result in Example 6, graph $y = (2/3)x - 2$:

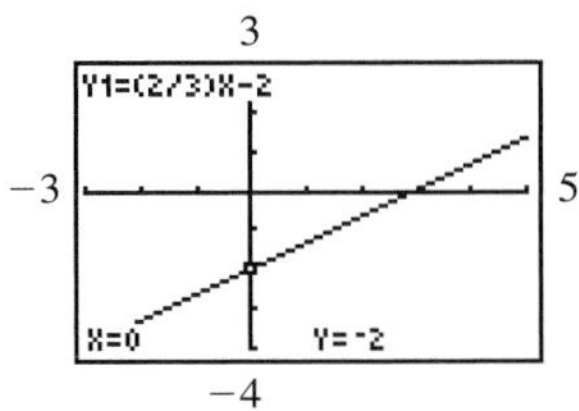

Since the calculator graph appears to be the same as the graph in Fig. 3.10, it supports the conclusion that Fig. 3.10 is correct.

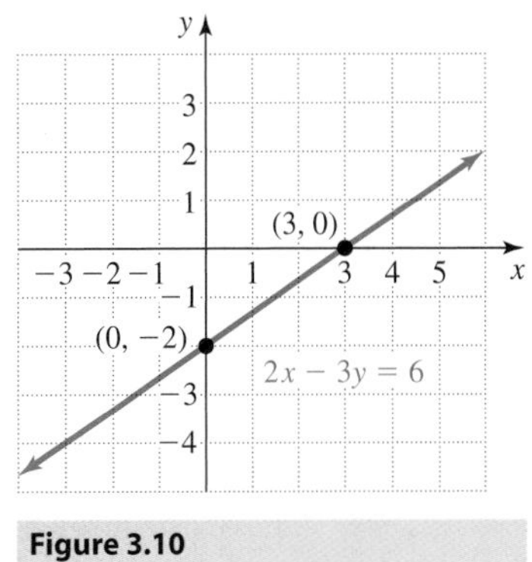

Figure 3.10

Now do Exercises 81–88

Applications

Linear equations occur in many real-life situations. If the cost of plans for a house is \$475 for one copy plus \$30 for each additional copy, then $C = 475 + 30x$, where x is the number of additional copies. If you have \$1000 budgeted for landscaping with trees at \$50 each and bushes at \$20 each, then $50t + 20b = 1000$, where t is the number of trees and b is the number of bushes. In the next example we see a linear equation that models ticket demand.

EXAMPLE 8

Ticket demand

The demand for tickets to see the Ice Gators play hockey can be modeled by the equation $d = 8000 - 100p$, where d is the number of tickets sold and p is the price per ticket in dollars.

a) How many tickets will be sold at \$20 per ticket?

b) Find the intercepts and interpret them.

c) Graph the linear equation.

d) What happens to the demand as the price increases?

Solution

a) If tickets are \$20 each, then $d = 8000 - 100 \cdot 20 = 6000$. So at \$20 per ticket, the demand will be 6000 tickets.

b) Replace d with 0 in the equation $d = 8000 - 100p$ and solve for p:

$$0 = 8000 - 100p$$

$$100p = 8000 \quad \text{Add } 100p \text{ to each side.}$$

$$p = 80 \quad \text{Divide each side by 100.}$$

If $p = 0$, then $d = 8000 - 100 \cdot 0 = 8000$. So the intercepts are (0, 8000) and (80, 0). If the tickets are free, the demand will be 8000 tickets. At \$80 per ticket, no tickets will be sold.

c) Graph the line using the intercepts (0, 8000) and (80, 0) as shown in Fig. 3.11. The line is graphed in the first quadrant only, because negative values for demand or price are meaningless.

d) When the tickets are free, the demand is high. As the price increases, the demand goes down. At \$80 per ticket, there will be no demand.

Now do Exercises 89–96

Teaching Tip Point out how knowing the intercepts helps you determine the scale to use on the graph.

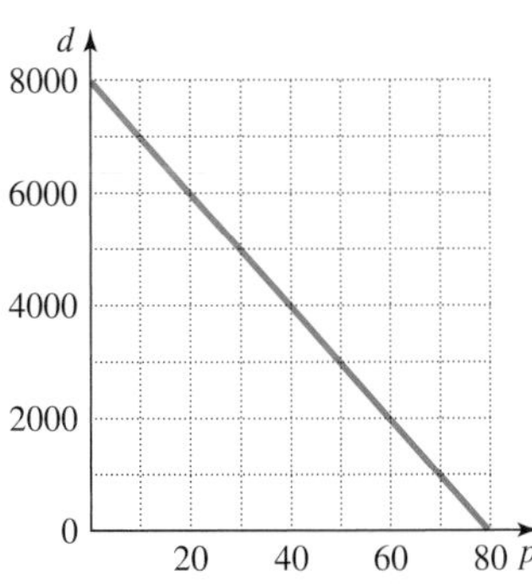

Figure 3.11

Math *at Work* Predicting the Future

No one knows what the future may bring, but everyone plans for and tries to predict the future. Stock market analysts predict the profits of companies, pollsters predict the outcomes of elections, and urban planners predict sizes of cities. These predictions of the future are often based on the trends of the past.

Consider the accompanying table, which shows the population of the United States in millions for each census year from 1950 through 2000. It certainly appears that the population is going up and it would be a safe bet to predict that the population in 2010 will be somewhat larger than 279 million. We get a different perspective if we look at the accompanying graph of the population data. Not only does the graph show an increasing population, it shows the population increasing in a linear manner. Now we can make a prediction based on the line that appears to fit the data. The equation of this line, the *regression line,* is $y = 2.47x - 4666$, where x is the year and y is the population. The equation of the regression line can be found with a computer or graphing calculator. Now if $x = 2010$, then $y = 2.47(2010) - 4666 \approx 299$. So we can predict 299 million people in 2010.

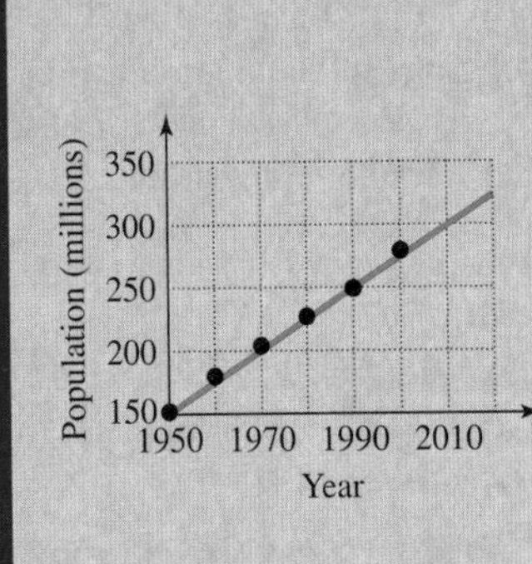

Year	Population (millions)
1950	152
1960	180
1970	204
1980	227
1990	249
2000	279

Warm-Ups ▼

True or false? Explain your answer.

1. The point (2, 4) satisfies the equation $2y - 3x = -8$. False
2. If (1, 5) satisfies an equation, then (5, 1) also satisfies the equation. False
3. The origin is in quadrant I. False
4. The point (4, 0) is on the y-axis. False
5. The graph of $x + 0 \cdot y = 9$ is the same as the graph of $x = 9$. True
6. The graph of $x = -5$ is a vertical line. True
7. The graph of $0 \cdot x + y = 6$ is a horizontal line. True
8. The y-intercept for the line $x + 2y = 5$ is (5, 0). False
9. The point (5, −3) is in quadrant II. False
10. The point (−349, 0) is on the x-axis. True

3.1 Exercises

Boost your GRADE at mathzone.com!

MathZone

- Practice Problems
- Self-Tests
- Videos
- Net Tutor
- e-Professors

Reading and Writing *After reading this section, write out the answers to these questions. Use complete sentences.*

1. What is an ordered pair?
An ordered pair is a pair of numbers in which there is a first number and a second number, usually written as (a, b).

2. What is the rectangular coordinate system?
The rectangular coordinate system is a means of dividing up the plane with two number lines in order to picture all ordered pairs of real numbers.

3. What name is given to the point of intersection of the x-axis and the y-axis?
The origin is the point of intersection of the x-axis and y-axis.

4. What is the graph of an equation?
The graph of an equation is a picture of all ordered pairs that satisfy the equation drawn in the rectangular coordinate system.

5. What is a linear equation in two variables?
A linear equation in two variables is an equation of the form $Ax + By = C$, where A and B are not both zero.

6. What are intercepts?
Intercepts are the points at which a graph crosses the axes.

Complete each ordered pair so that it satisfies the given equation. See Example 1.

7. $y = 3x + 9$: $(0,\ \ )$, $(\ \ , 24)$, $(2,\ \ )$
$(0, 9)$, $(5, 24)$, $(2, 15)$

8. $y = 2x + 5$: $(8,\ \ )$, $(-1,\ \ )$, $(\ \ , -1)$
$(8, 21)$, $(-1, 3)$, $(-3, -1)$

9. $y = -3x - 7$: $(0,\ \ )$, $\left(\frac{1}{3},\ \ \right)$, $(\ \ , -5)$
$(0, -7)$, $\left(\frac{1}{3}, -8\right)$, $\left(-\frac{2}{3}, -5\right)$

10. $y = -5x - 3$: $(-1,\ \ )$, $\left(-\frac{1}{2},\ \ \right)$, $(\ \ , -2)$
$(-1, 2)$, $\left(-\frac{1}{2}, -\frac{1}{2}\right)$, $\left(-\frac{1}{5}, -2\right)$

11. $y = 1.2x + 54.3$: $(0,\ \ )$, $(10,\ \ )$, $(\ \ , 54.9)$
$(0, 54.3)$, $(10, 66.3)$, $(0.5, 54.9)$

12. $y = 1.8x + 22.6$: $(1,\ \ )$, $(-10,\ \ )$, $(\ \ , 22.6)$
$(1, 24.4)$, $(-10, 4.6)$, $(0, 22.6)$

13. $2x - 3y = 6$: $(3,\ \ )$, $(\ \ , -2)$, $(12,\ \ )$
$(3, 0)$, $(0, -2)$, $(12, 6)$

14. $3x + 5y = 0$: $(-5,\ \ )$, $(\ \ , -3)$, $(10,\ \ )$
$(-5, 3)$, $(5, -3)$, $(10, -6)$

15. $0 \cdot y + x = 5$: $(\ \ , -3)$, $(\ \ , 5)$, $(\ \ , 0)$
$(5, -3)$, $(5, 5)$, $(5, 0)$

16. $0 \cdot x + y = -6$: $(3,\ \ )$, $(-1,\ \ )$, $(4,\ \ )$
$(3, -6)$, $(-1, -6)$, $(4, -6)$

Plot the points on a rectangular coordinate system. See Example 2.

17. $(1, 5)$
18. $(4, 3)$
19. $(-2, 1)$
20. $(-3, 5)$
21. $\left(3, -\frac{1}{2}\right)$
22. $\left(2, -\frac{1}{3}\right)$
23. $(-2, -4)$
24. $(-3, -5)$
25. $(0, 3)$
26. $(0, -2)$
27. $(-3, 0)$
28. $(5, 0)$
29. $(\pi, 1)$
30. $(-2, \pi)$
31. $(1.4, 4)$
32. $(-3, 0.4)$

17–31 odd

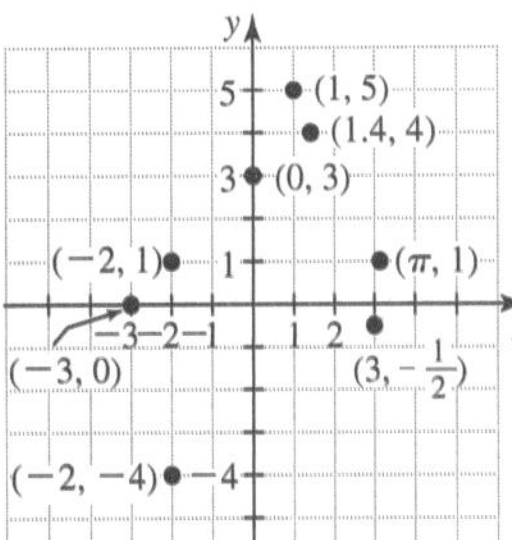

18–32 even

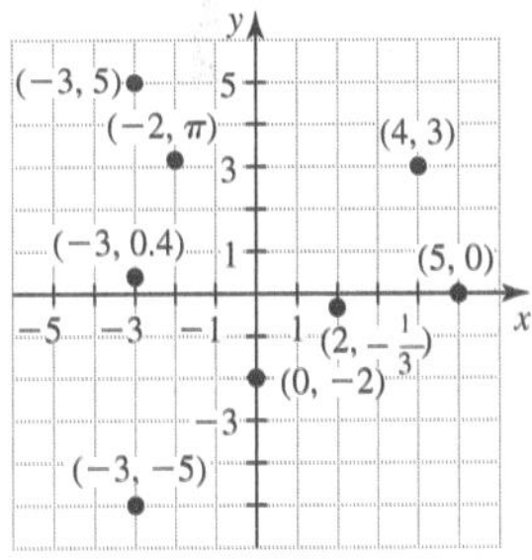

Use the given equations to find the missing coordinates in the following tables.

33. $y = -2x + 5$

x	y
−2	9
0	5
2	1
4	−3
6	−7

34. $y = -x + 4$

x	y
−2	6
0	4
2	2
4	0
6	−2

35. $y = \frac{1}{3}x + 2$

x	y
−6	0
−3	1
0	2
3	3

36. $y = -\frac{1}{2}x + 1$

x	y
−2	2
−1	$\frac{3}{2}$
0	1
1	$\frac{1}{2}$

37. $y - 20x = 400$

x	y
−30	−200
−20	0
−10	200
0	400
10	600

38. $200x + y = 50$

x	y
$-\frac{1}{2}$	−150
$-\frac{1}{4}$	100
0	50
$\frac{1}{4}$	0
$\frac{1}{2}$	−50

Graph each equation. Plot at least five points for each equation. Use graph paper. See Examples 3–5. If you have a graphing calculator, use it to check your graphs when possible.

39. $y = x + 1$

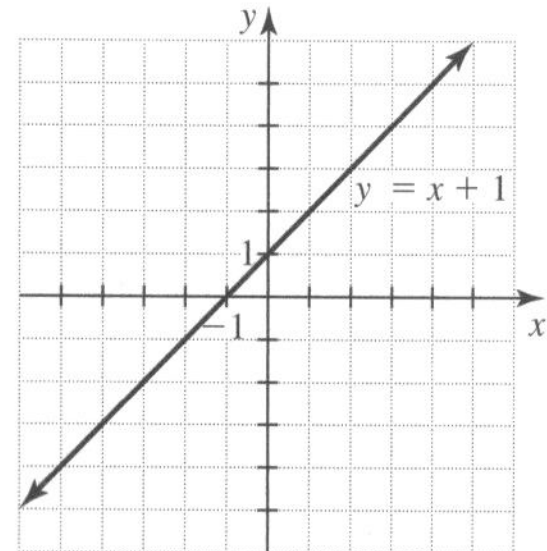

40. $y = x - 1$

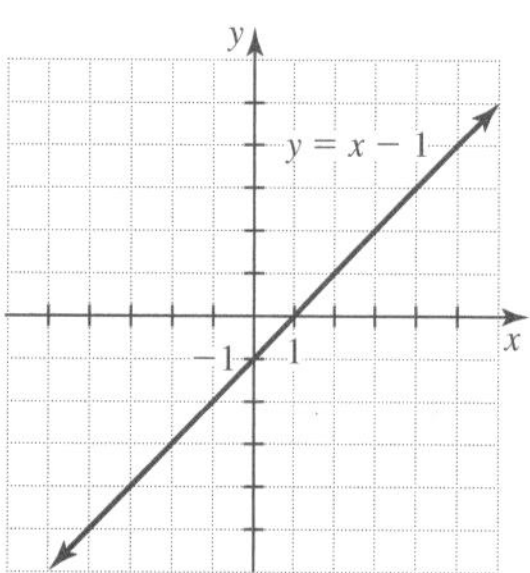

41. $y = 2x + 1$

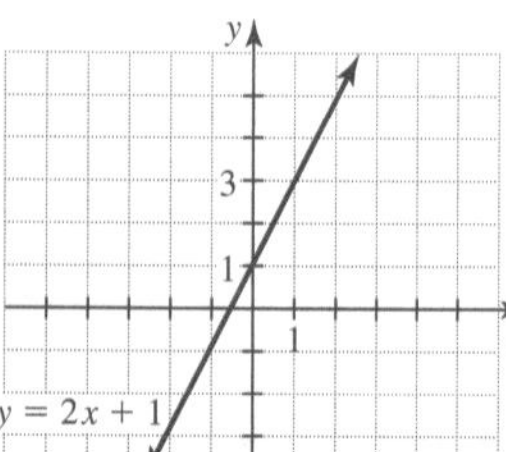

42. $y = 3x - 1$

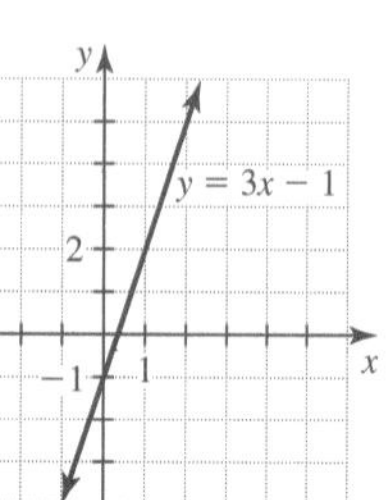

43. $y = 3x - 2$

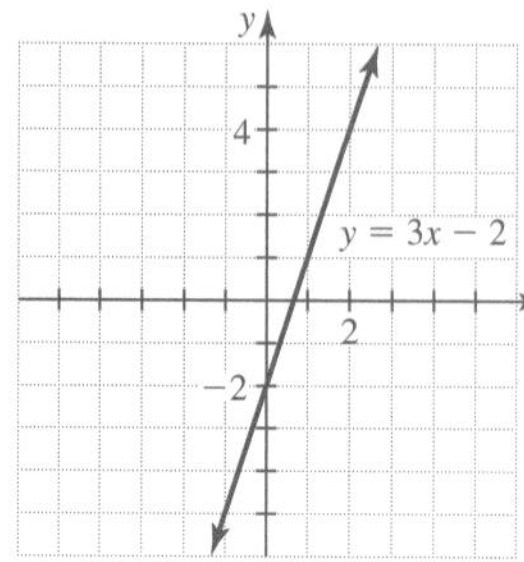

44. $y = 2x + 3$

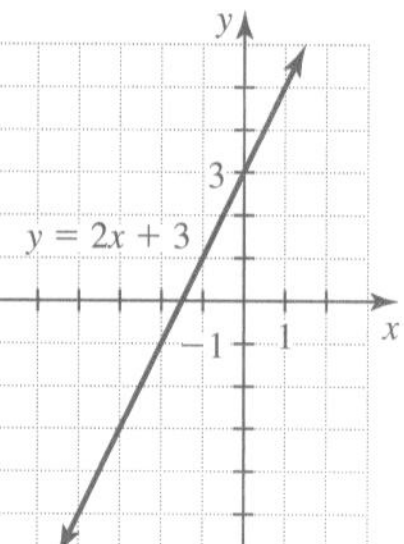

45. $y = x$

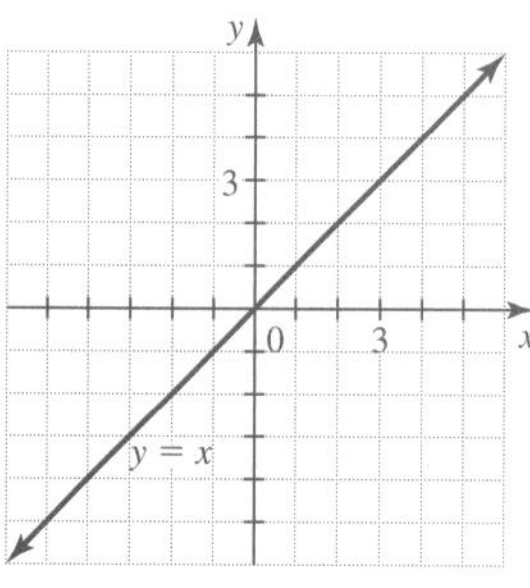

46. $y = -x$

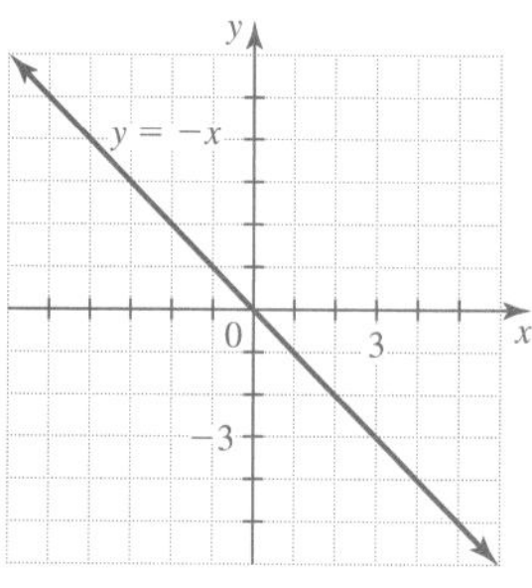

47. $y = 1 - x$

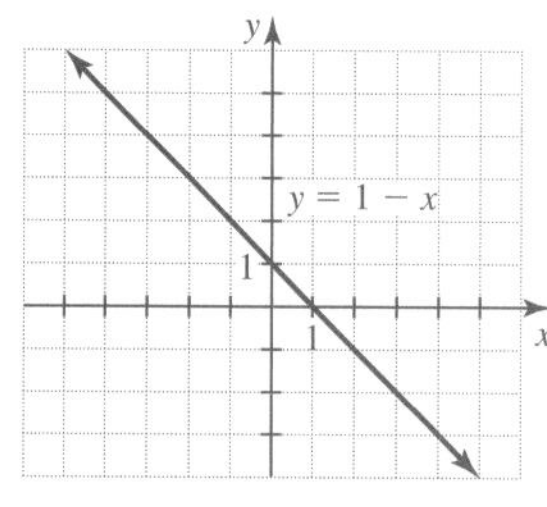

48. $y = 2 - x$

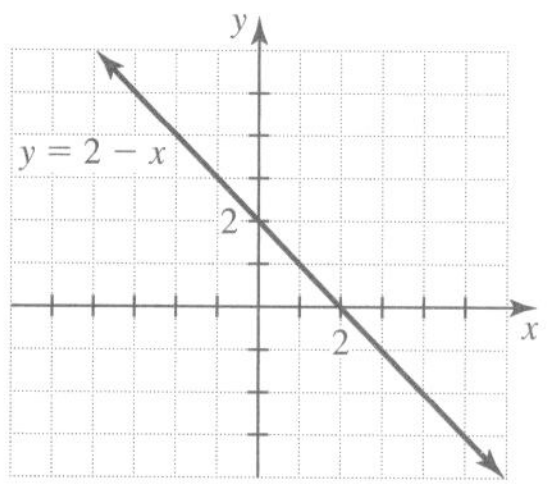

49. $y = -2x + 3$

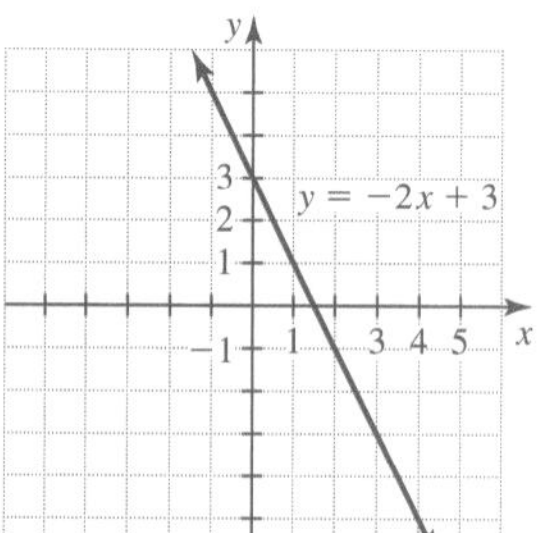

50. $y = -3x + 2$

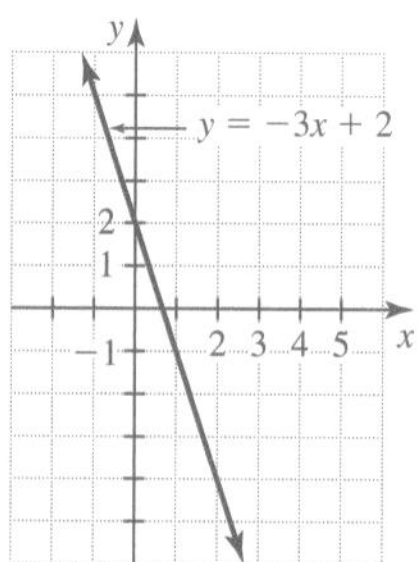

51. $y = -3$

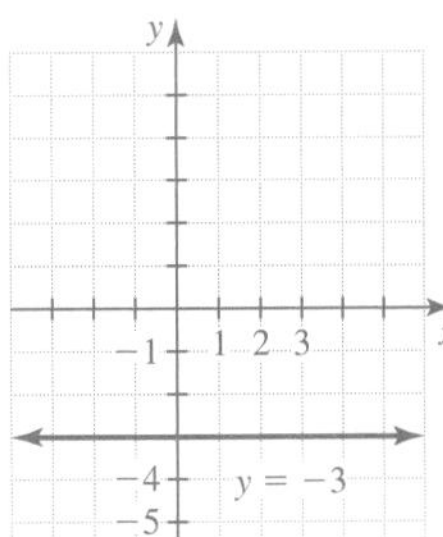

52. $y = 2$

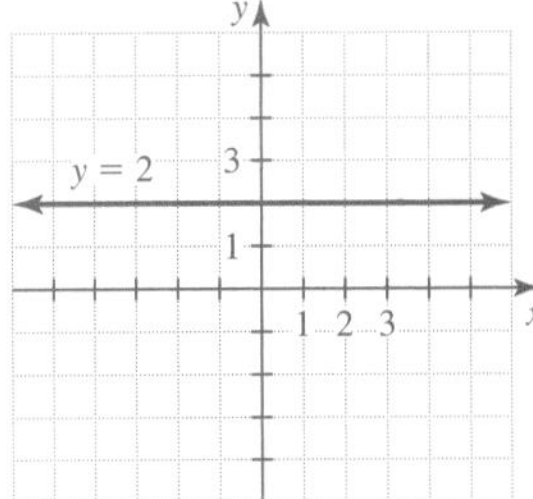

53. $x = 2$

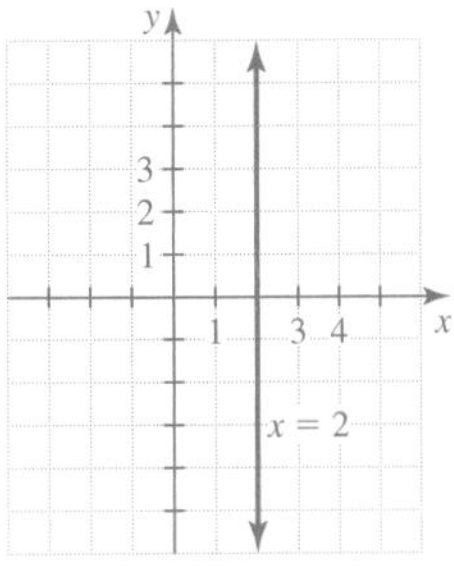

54. $x = -4$

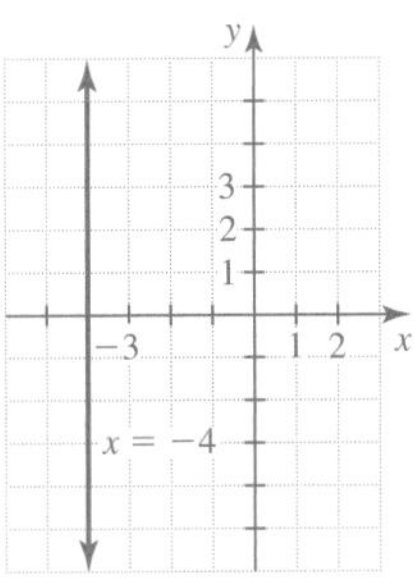

55. $2x + y = 5$

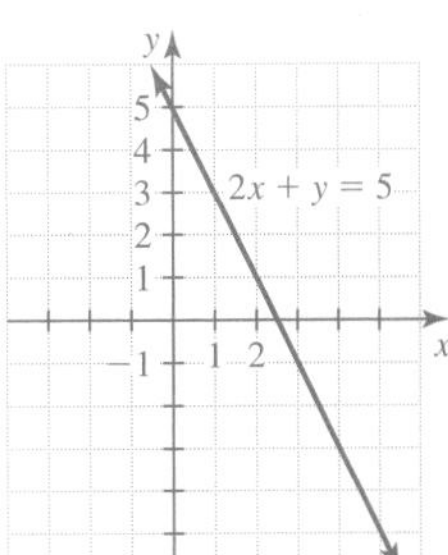

56. $3x + y = 5$

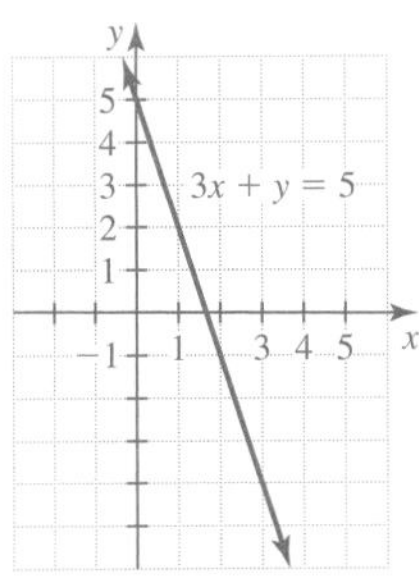

57. $x + 2y = 4$

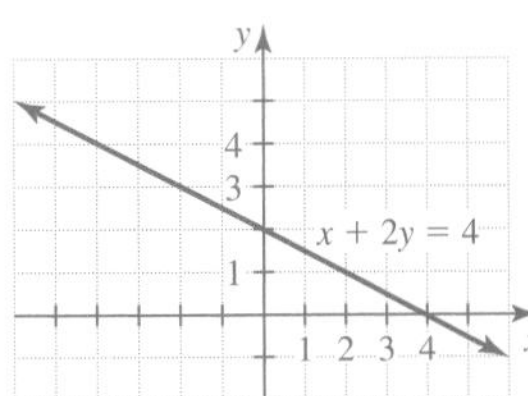

58. $x - 2y = 6$

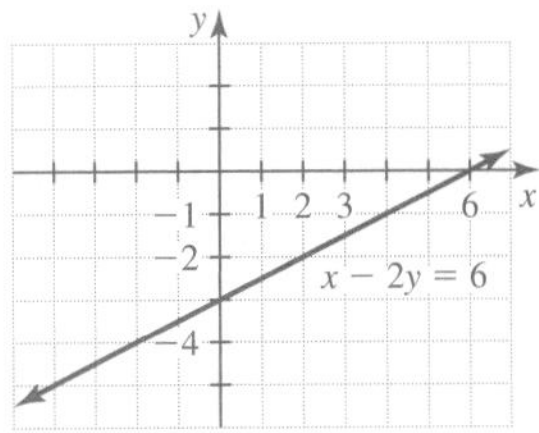

59. $x - 3y = 6$

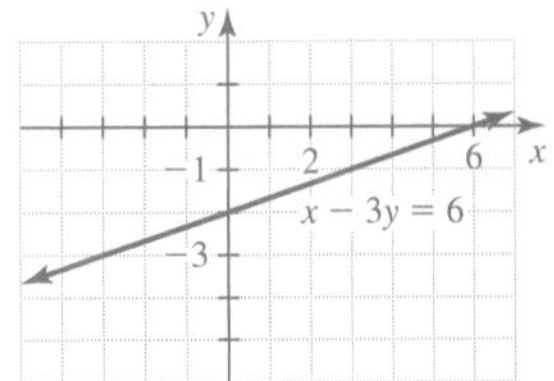

60. $x + 4y = 5$

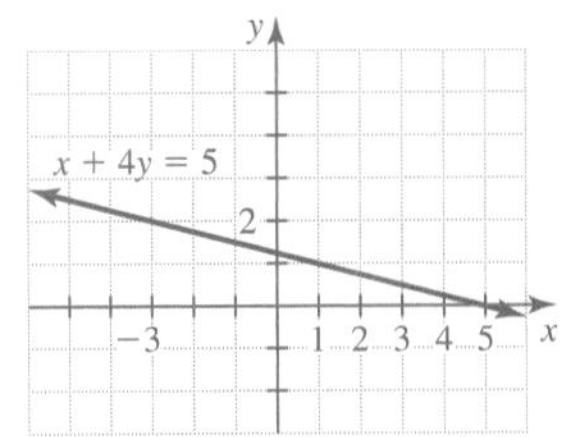

61. $y = 0.36x + 0.4$

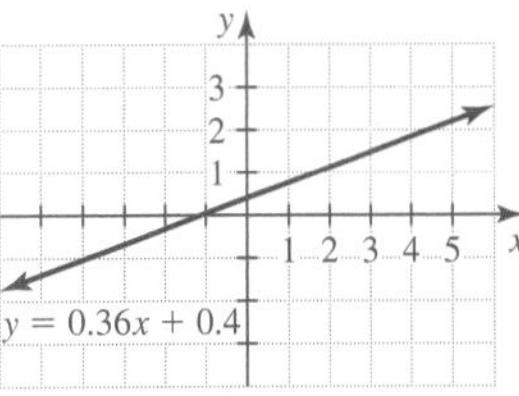

62. $y = 0.27x - 0.42$

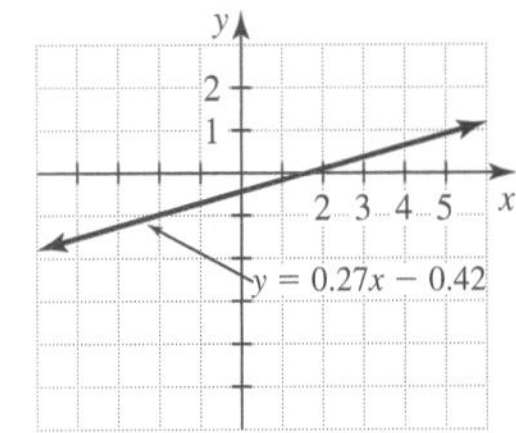

For each point, name the quadrant in which it lies or the axis on which it lies.

63. $(-3, 45)$
Quadrant II

64. $(-33, 47)$
Quadrant II

65. $(-3, 0)$
x-axis

66. $(0, -9)$
y-axis

67. $(-2.36, -5)$
Quadrant III

68. $(89.6, 0)$
x-axis

69. $(3.4, 8.8)$
Quadrant I

70. $(4.1, 44)$
Quadrant I

71. $\left(-\frac{1}{2}, 50\right)$
Quadrant II

72. $\left(-6, -\frac{1}{2}\right)$
Quadrant III

73. $(0, -99)$
y-axis

74. $(\pi, 0)$
x-axis

Graph each equation. Plot at least five points for each equation. Use graph paper. See Example 6. If you have a graphing calculator, use it to check your graphs.

75. $y = x + 1200$

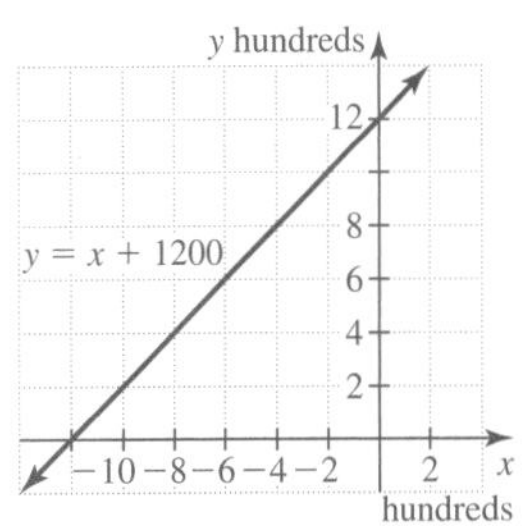

76. $y = 2x - 3000$

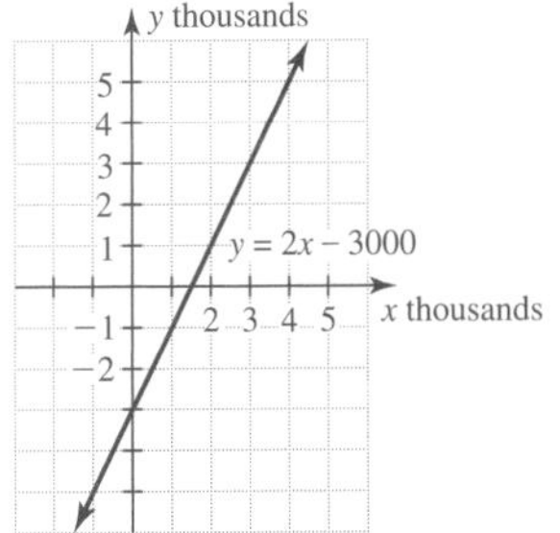

77. $y = 50x - 2000$

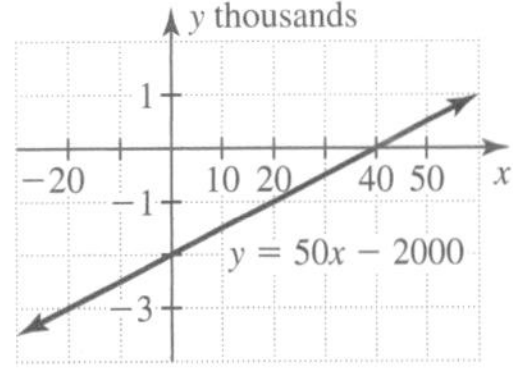

78. $y = -300x + 4500$

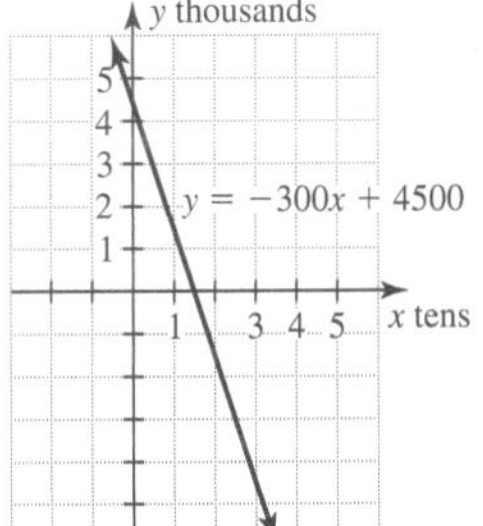

79. $y = -400x + 2000$

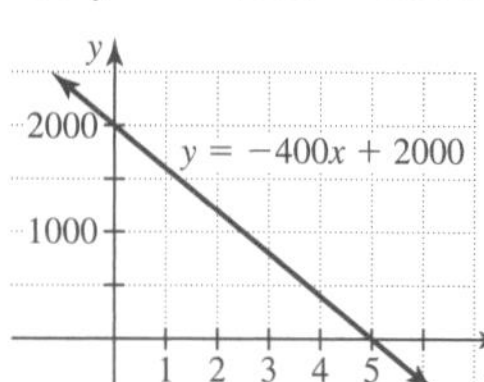

80. $y = 500x + 3$

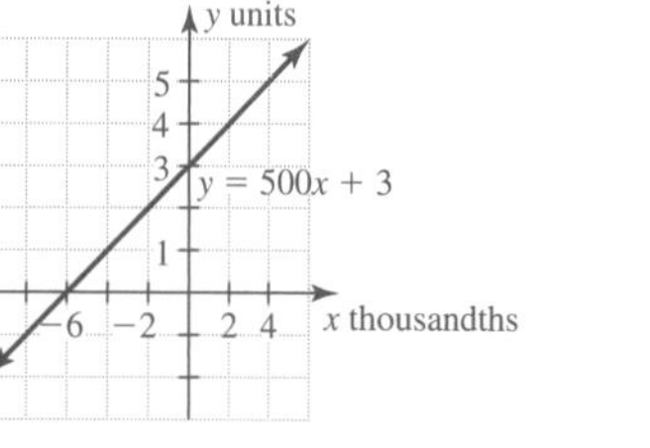

For each equation, state the x-intercept and y-intercept. Then graph the equation using the intercepts and a third point. See Example 7.

81. $3x + 2y = 6$
(2, 0), (0, 3)

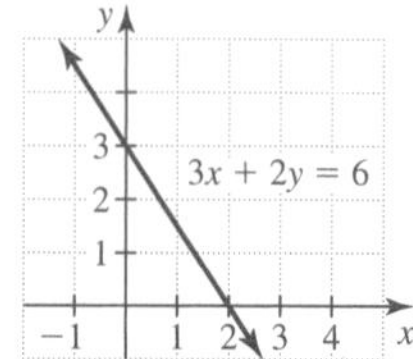

82. $2x + y = 6$
(3, 0), (0, 6)

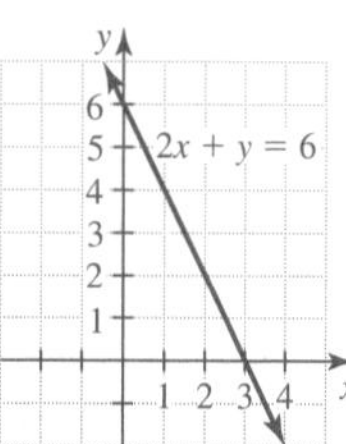

83. $x - 4y = 4$
(4, 0), (0, −1)

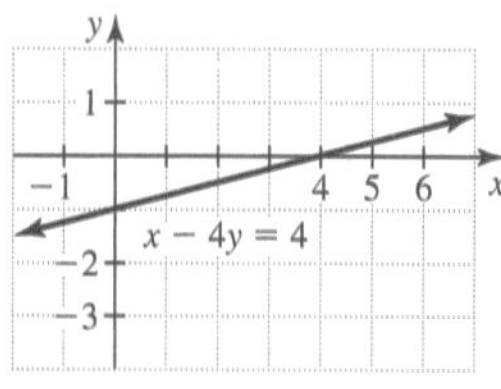

84. $-2x + y = 4$
(−2, 0), (0, 4)

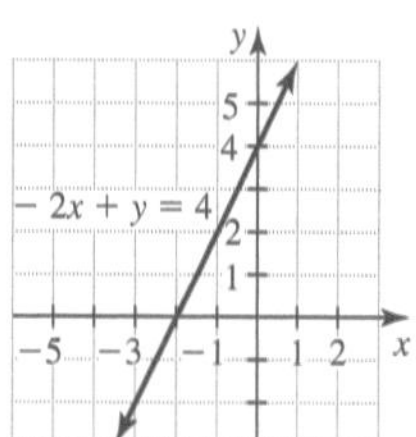

85. $y = \frac{3}{4}x - 9$
(12, 0), (0, −9)

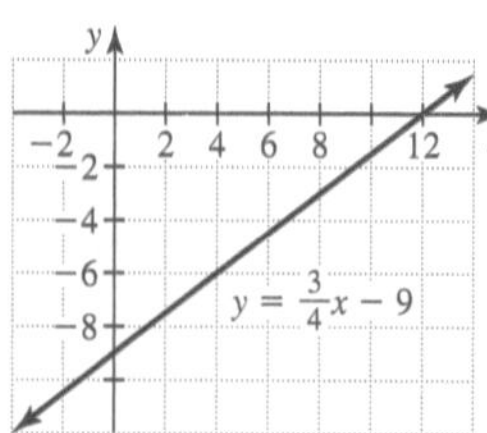

86. $y = -\frac{1}{2}x + 5$
(10, 0), (0, 5)

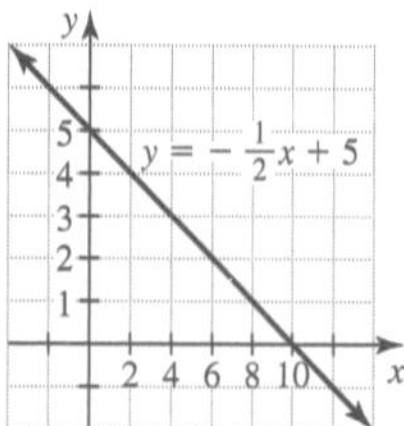

87. $\frac{1}{2}x + \frac{1}{4}y = 1$
(2, 0), (0, 4)

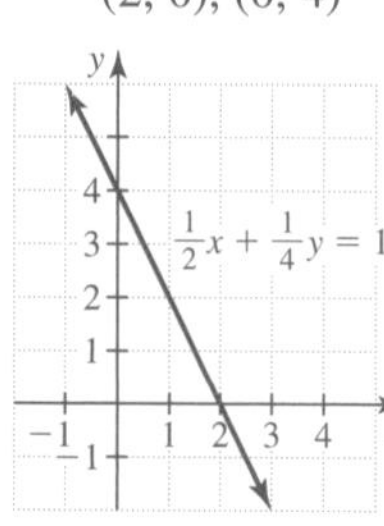

88. $\frac{1}{3}x - \frac{1}{2}y = 3$
(9, 0), (0, −6)

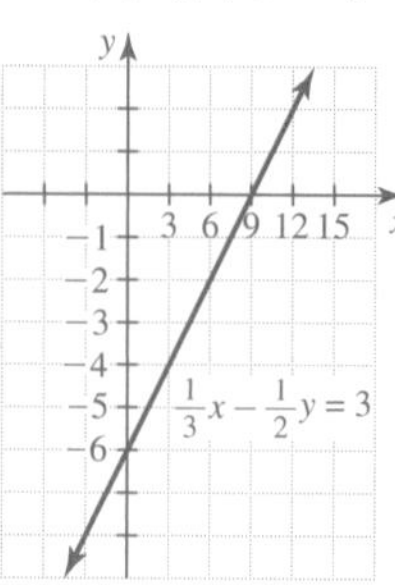

Solve each problem. See Example 8.

89. ***Percentage of full benefit.*** The age at which you retire affects your Social Security benefits. The accompanying graph gives the percentage of full benefit for each age from 62 through 70, based on current legislation and retirement after the year 2005 (Source: Social Security Administration). What percentage of full benefit does a person receive if that person retires at age 63? At what age will a retiree receive the full benefit? For what ages do you receive more than the full benefit? 75%, 67, 68 and up

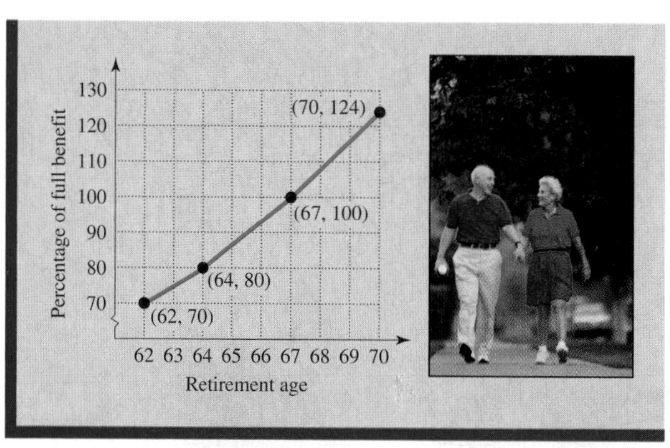

Figure for Exercise 89

90. ***Heel motion.*** When designing running shoes, Chris Edington studies the motion of a runner's foot. The following data gives the coordinates of the heel (in centimeters) at intervals of 0.05 millisecond during one cycle of level treadmill running at 3.8 meters per second (*Sagittal Plane Kinematics, Milliron and Cavanagh*):

(31.7, 5.7), (48.0, 5.7), (68.3, 5.8), (88.9, 6.9), (107.2, 13.3), (119.4, 24.7), (127.2, 37.8), (125.7, 52.0), (116.1, 60.2), (102.2, 59.5), (88.7, 50.2), (73.9, 35.8), (52.6, 20.6), (29.6, 10.7), (22.4, 5.9)

Graph these ordered pairs to see the heel motion.

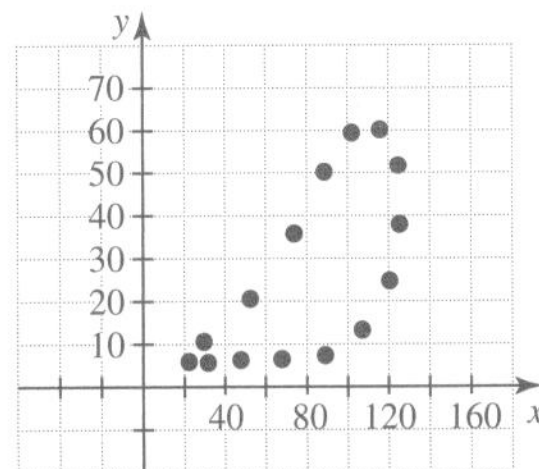

91. ***Medicaid spending.*** The cost in billions of dollars for federal Medicaid (health care for the poor) can be modeled by the equation

$$C = 3.2n + 65.3,$$

where n is the number of years since 1990 (Health Care Financing Administration, www.hcfa.gov).

a) What was the cost of federal Medicaid in 2000?
b) In what year will the cost reach \$150 billion?
c) Graph the equation for n ranging from 0 through 20.

a) \$97.3 billion **b)** 2016
c)

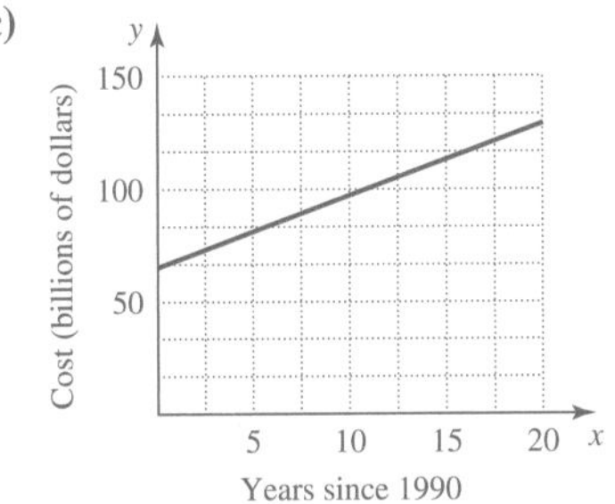

92. ***Dental services.*** The national cost C in billions of dollars for dental services can be modeled by the linear equation

$$C = 2.85n + 30.52,$$

where n is the number of years since 1990 (Health Care Financing Administration, www.hcfa.gov).

a) Find and interpret the C-intercept for the line.
b) Find and interpret the n-intercept for the line.
c) Graph the line for n ranging from 0 through 20.
d) If this trend continues, then in what year will the cost of dental services reach 100 billion?

a) (0, 30.52); The cost was \$30.52 billion in 1990.
b) (−10.71, 0); The cost was zero dollars in 1979.
c) **d)** 2014

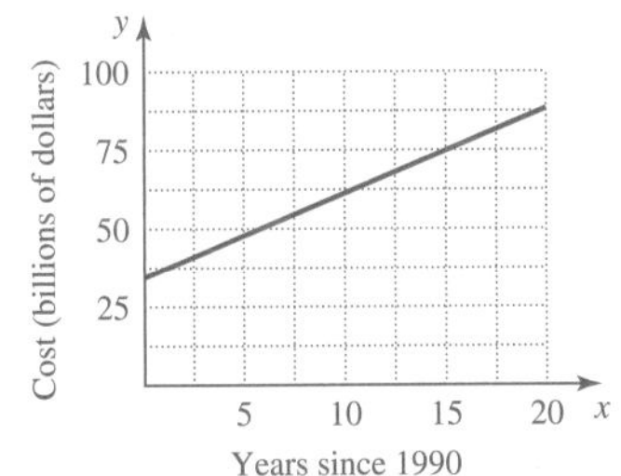

93. ***Hazards of depth.*** The accompanying table shows the depth below sea level and atmospheric pressure (*Encyclopedia of Sports Science,* 1997). The equation

$$A = 0.03d + 1$$

expresses the atmospheric pressure in terms of the depth d.

a) Find the atmospheric pressure at the depth where nitrogen narcosis begins. 4 atm
b) Find the maximum depth for intermediate divers. 130 ft
c) Graph the equation for d ranging from 0 to 250 feet.

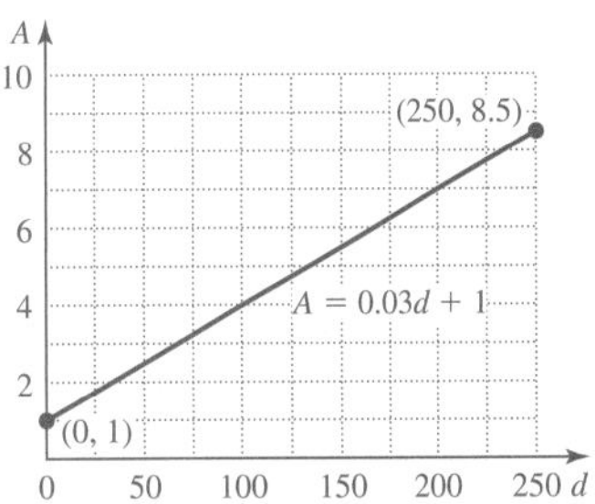

Depth (ft)	Atmospheric Pressure (atm)	Comments
21	1.63	Bends are a danger
60	2.8	Maximum for beginners
100		Nitrogen narcosis begins
	4.9	Maximum for intermediate
200	7.0	Severe nitrogen narcosis
250	8.5	Extremely dangerous depth

Figure for Exercise 93

94. ***Demand equation.*** Helen's Health Foods usually sells 400 cans of ProPac Muscle Punch per week when the price is \$5 per can. After experimenting with prices for some time, Helen has determined that the weekly demand can be found by using the equation

$$d = 600 - 40p,$$

where d is the number of cans and p is the price per can.

a) Will Helen sell more or less Muscle Punch if she raises her price from \$5? Less
b) What happens to her sales every time she raises her price by \$1? Goes down by 40 cans

c) Graph the equation.

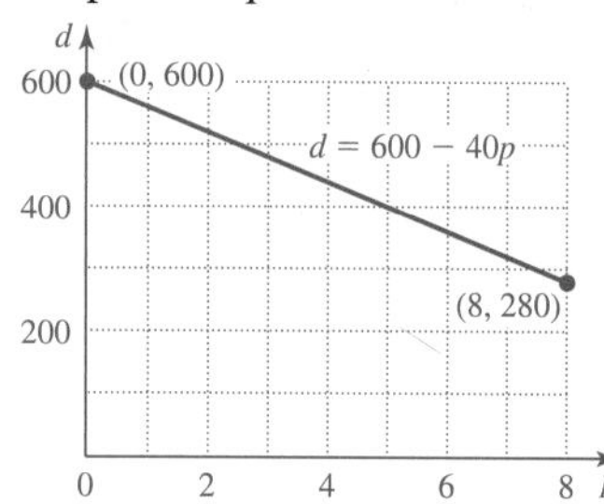

d) What is the maximum price that she can charge and still sell at least one can? $14.97

95. ***Advertising blitz.*** Furniture City in Toronto had $24,000 to spend on advertising a year-end clearance sale. A 30-second radio ad costs $300, and a 30-second local television ad costs $400. To model this situation, the advertising manager wrote the equation $300x + 400y = 24{,}000$. What do x and y represent? Graph the equation. How many solutions are there to the equation, given that the number of ads of each type must be a whole number?
$x =$ the number of radio ads,
$y =$ the number of TV ads, 21 solutions

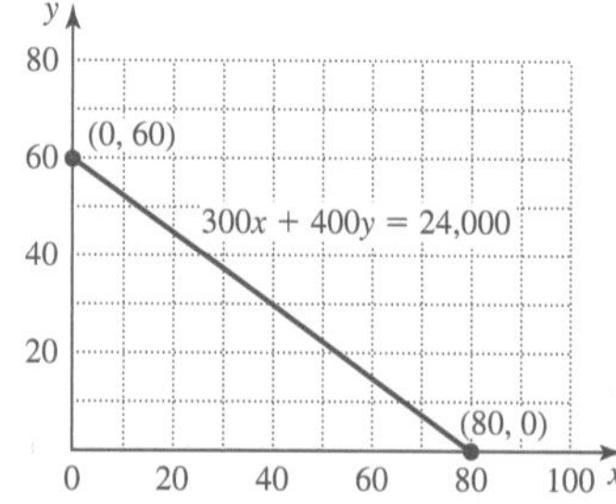

96. ***Material allocation.*** A tent maker had 4500 square yards of nylon tent material available. It takes 45 square yards of nylon to make an 8×10 tent and 50 square yards to make a 9×12 tent. To model this situation, the manager wrote the equation $45x + 50y = 4500$. What do x and y represent? Graph the equation. How many solutions are there to the equation, given that the number of tents of each type must be a whole number?
$x =$ the number of 8×10 tents,
$y =$ the number of 9×12 tents, 11 solutions

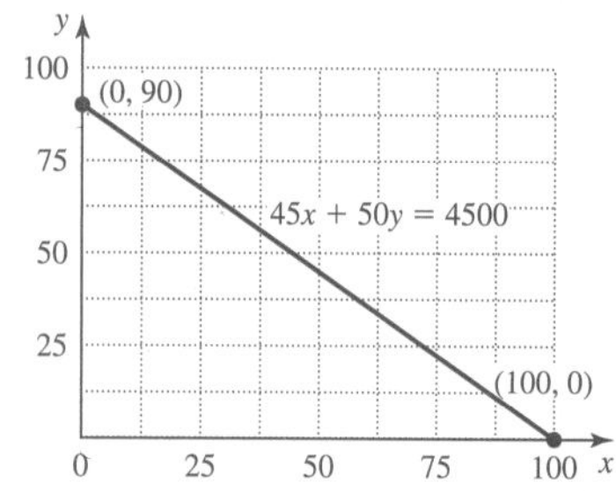

Graphing Calculator Exercises

Graph each straight line on your graphing calculator using a viewing window that shows both intercepts. Answers may vary.

97. $2x + 3y = 1200$

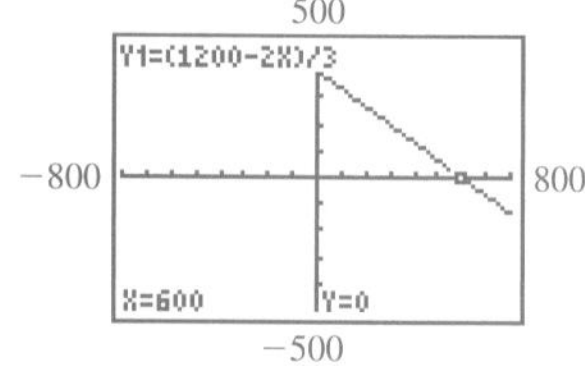

98. $3x - 700y = 2100$

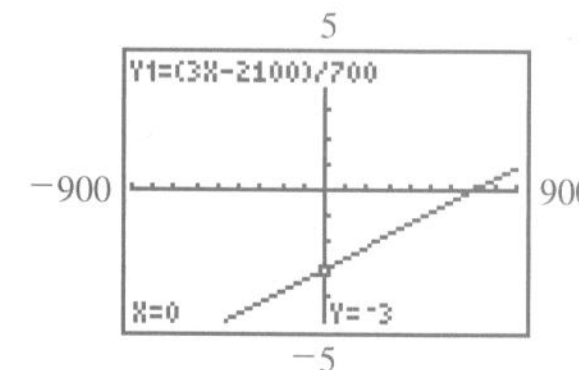

99. $200x - 300y = 6$

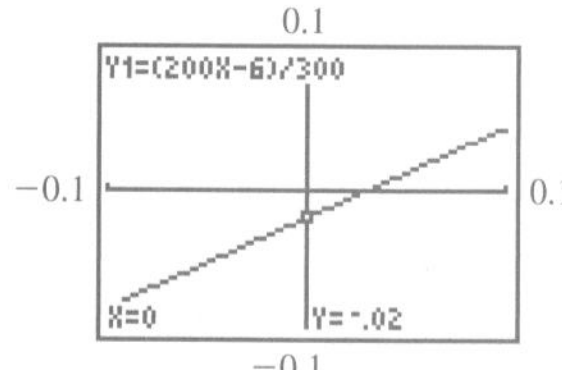

100. $300x + 5y = 20$

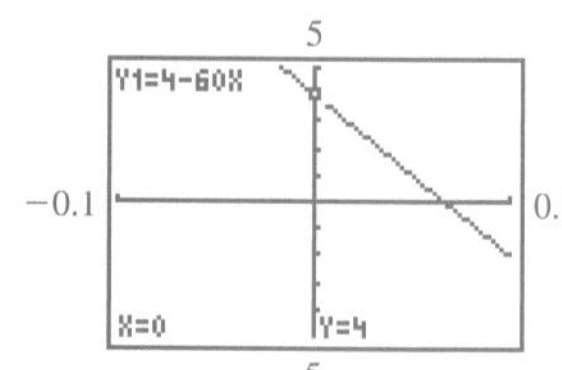

101. $y = 300x - 1$

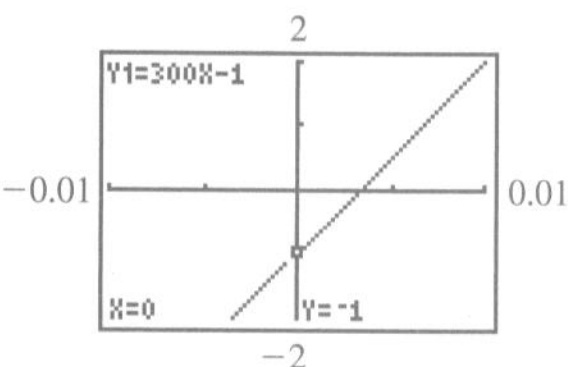

102. $y = 300x - 6000$

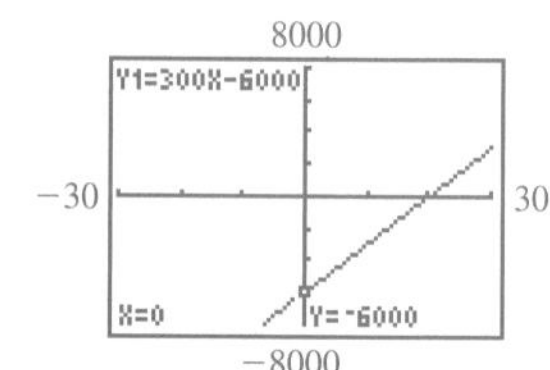

3.2 Slope

In this Section

- Slope Concepts
- Slope Using Coordinates
- Graphing a Line Given a Point and Its Slope
- Parallel Lines
- Perpendicular Lines
- Interpreting Slope

In Section 3.1 you learned that the graph of a linear equation is a straight line. In this section, we will continue our study of lines in the coordinate plane.

Slope Concepts

If a highway rises 6 feet in a horizontal run of 100 feet, then the grade is $\frac{6}{100}$ or 6%. See Fig. 3.12. The grade of a road is a measurement of the steepness of the road. It is the rate at which the road is going upward.

Figure 3.12

The steepness of a line is called the **slope** of the line and it is measured like the grade of a road. As you move from (1, 1) to (4, 3) in Fig. 3.13 the x-coordinate increases by 3 and the y-coordinate increases by 2. The line rises 2 units in a horizontal run of 3 units. So the slope of the line is $\frac{2}{3}$. The slope is the rate at which the y-coordinate is increasing. It increases 2 units for every 3-unit increase in x or it increases $\frac{2}{3}$ of a unit for every 1-unit increase in x. In general, we have the following definition of slope.

> **Slope**
>
> $$\text{Slope} = \frac{\text{change in } y\text{-coordinate}}{\text{change in } x\text{-coordinate}}$$

Teaching Tip Another example of slope is the pitch of a roof. A 5 - 12 pitch means a roof rises 5 feet in a run of 12 feet. Ask students to determine the pitch of the roof in the house in which they live.

If we move from the point (4, 3) to the point (1, 1), there is a change of -2 in the y-coordinate and a change of -3 in the x-coordinate. See Fig. 3.14. In this case we get

$$\text{Slope} = \frac{-2}{-3} = \frac{2}{3}.$$

Note that going from (4, 3) to (1, 1) gives the same slope as going from (1, 1) to (4, 3).

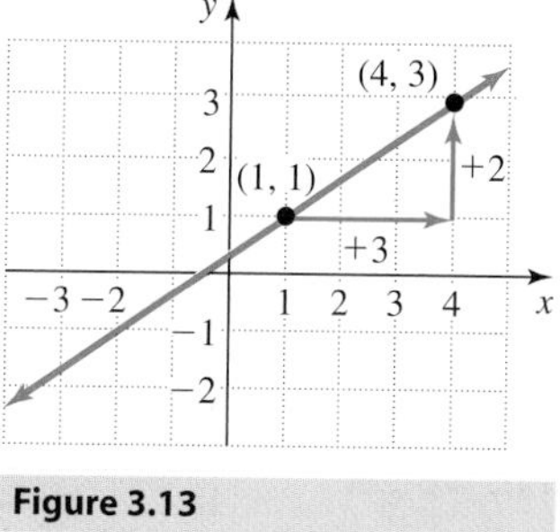

Figure 3.13

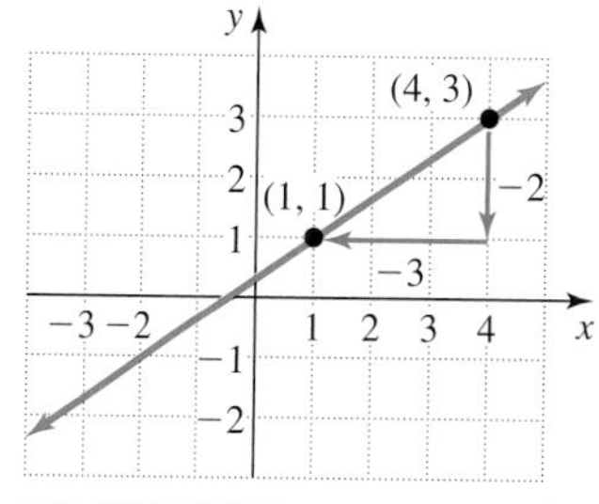

Figure 3.14

We call the change in y-coordinate the **rise** and the change in x-coordinate the **run.** Moving up is a positive rise, and moving down is a negative rise. Moving to the right is a positive run, and moving to the left is a negative run. We usually use the letter m to stand for slope. So we have

$$m = \frac{\text{change in } y}{\text{change in } x} = \frac{\text{rise}}{\text{run}}.$$

EXAMPLE 1

Finding the slope of a line

Find the slopes of the given lines by going from point A to point B.

a) 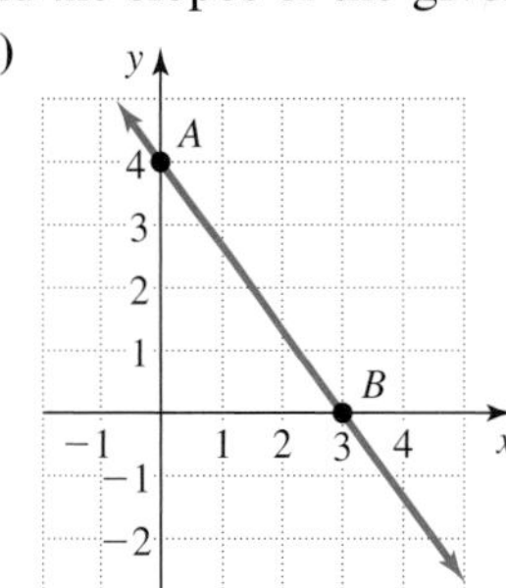

b) 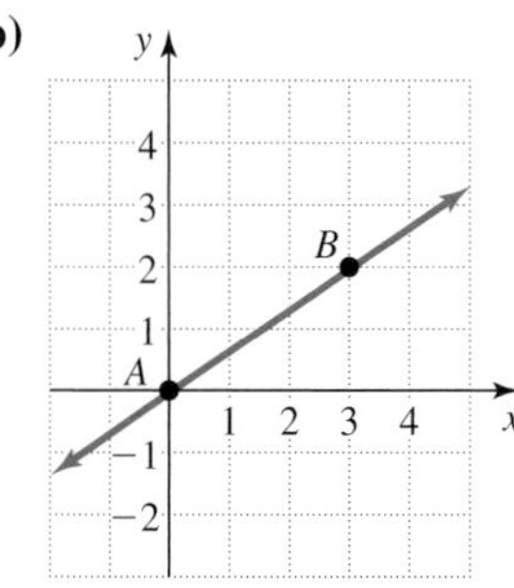

c) 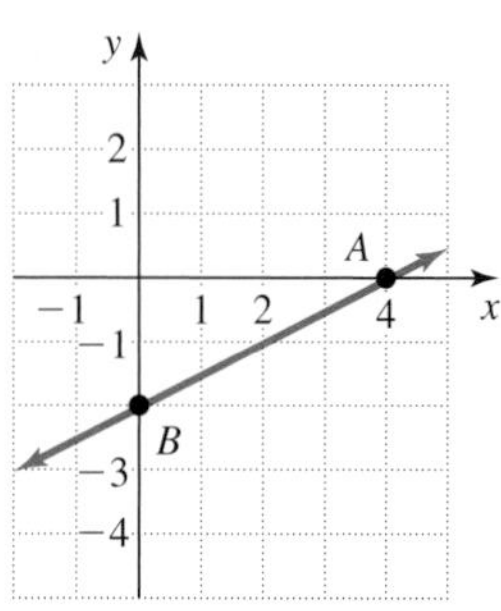

Solution

a) The coordinates of point A are (0, 4), and the coordinates of point B are (3, 0). Going from A to B, the change in y is -4, and the change in x is $+3$. So

$$m = \frac{-4}{3} = -\frac{4}{3}.$$

b) Going from A to B, the rise is 2, and the run is 3. So

$$m = \frac{2}{3}.$$

c) Going from A to B, the rise is -2, and the run is -4. So

$$m = \frac{-2}{-4} = \frac{1}{2}.$$

Now do Exercises 7–10

Study Tip

Working problems 1 hour per day every day of the week is better than working problems for 7 hours on one day of the week. It is usually better to spread out your study time than to try and learn everything in one big session.

CAUTION The change in y is always in the numerator, and the change in x is always in the denominator.

The ratio of rise to run is the ratio of the lengths of the two legs of any right triangle whose hypotenuse is on the line. As long as one leg is vertical and the other is horizontal, all such triangles for a certain line have the same shape. These triangles are similar triangles. The ratio of the length of the vertical side to the length of the horizontal side for any two such triangles is the same number. So we get the same value for the slope no matter which two points of the line are used to calculate it or in which order the points are used.

EXAMPLE 2

Finding slope

Find the slope of the line shown here using points A and B, points A and C, and points B and C.

Solution

Using A and B, we get

$$m = \frac{\text{rise}}{\text{run}} = \frac{1}{4}.$$

Using A and C, we get

$$m = \frac{\text{rise}}{\text{run}} = \frac{2}{8} = \frac{1}{4}.$$

Using B and C, we get

$$m = \frac{\text{rise}}{\text{run}} = \frac{1}{4}.$$

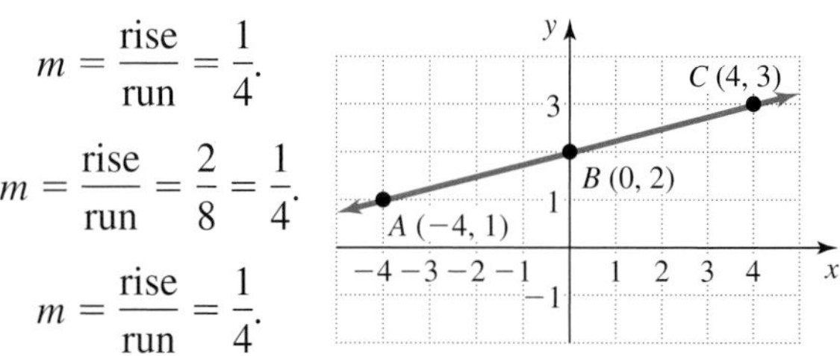

Now do Exercises 11–18

Helpful Hint

It is good to think of what the slope represents when x and y are measured quantities rather than just numbers. For example, if the change in y is 50 miles and the change in x is 2 hours, then the slope is 25 mph (or 25 miles per 1 hour). So the slope is the amount of change in y for a change of one in x.

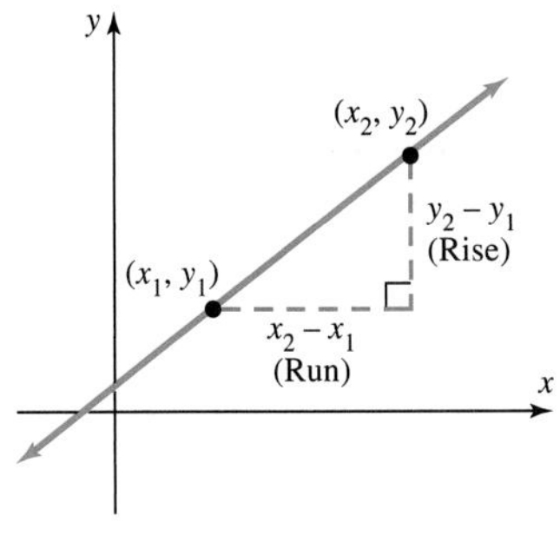

Figure 3.15

Slope Using Coordinates

One way to obtain the rise and run is from a graph. The rise and run can also be found by using the coordinates of two points on the line as shown in Fig. 3.15.

Coordinate Formula for Slope

The slope of the line containing the points (x_1, y_1) and (x_2, y_2) is given by

$$m = \frac{y_2 - y_1}{x_2 - x_1},$$

provided that $x_2 - x_1 \neq 0$.

EXAMPLE 3

Using coordinates to find slope

Find the slope of each of the following lines.

a) The line through (0, 5) and (6, 3)

b) The line through (−3, 4) and (−5, −2)

c) The line through (−4, 2) and the origin

Solution

a) If $(x_1, y_1) = (0, 5)$ and $(x_2, y_2) = (6, 3)$ then

$$m = \frac{y_2 - y_1}{x_2 - x_1} = \frac{3 - 5}{6 - 0} = \frac{-2}{6} = -\frac{1}{3}.$$

If $(x_1, y_1) = (6, 3)$ and $(x_2, y_2) = (0, 5)$ then

$$m = \frac{y_2 - y_1}{x_2 - x_1} = \frac{5 - 3}{0 - 6} = \frac{2}{-6} = -\frac{1}{3}.$$

Note that it does not matter which point is called (x_1, y_1) and which is called (x_2, y_2). In either case the slope is $-\frac{1}{3}$.

b) Let $(x_1, y_1) = (-3, 4)$ and $(x_2, y_2) = (-5, -2)$:

$$m = \frac{y_2 - y_1}{x_2 - x_1} = \frac{-2 - 4}{-5 - (-3)} = \frac{-6}{-2} = 3$$

c) Let $(x_1, y_1) = (0, 0)$ and $(x_2, y_2) = (-4, 2)$:

$$m = \frac{2 - 0}{-4 - 0} = \frac{2}{-4} = -\frac{1}{2}$$

Now do Exercises 19–30

Study Tip

Students who have difficulty with algebra often schedule it in a class that meets one day per week so they do not have to see it as often. However, many students do better in classes that meet more often for shorter time periods. So schedule your classes to maximize your chances of success.

Teaching Tip To get the numbers in the right positions in the slope formula, observe that the coordinates of each point are lined up vertically.

CAUTION It does not matter which point is called (x_1, y_1) and which is called (x_2, y_2), but if you divide $y_2 - y_1$ by $x_1 - x_2$, the slope will have the wrong sign.

Because division by zero is undefined, slope is undefined if $x_2 - x_1 = 0$ or $x_2 = x_1$. The x-coordinates of two distinct points on a line are equal only if the points are on a vertical line. *So slope is undefined for vertical lines.* The concept of slope does not exist for a vertical line.

Any two points on a horizontal line have equal y-coordinates. So for points on a horizontal line we have $y_2 - y_1 = 0$. Since $y_2 - y_1$ is in the numerator of the slope formula, *the slope for any horizontal line is zero.* We never refer to a line as having "no slope" because in English no can mean zero or does not exist.

EXAMPLE 4

Slope for vertical and horizontal lines

Find the slope of the line through each pair of points.

a) (2, 1) and (2, −3)

b) (−2, 2) and (4, 2)

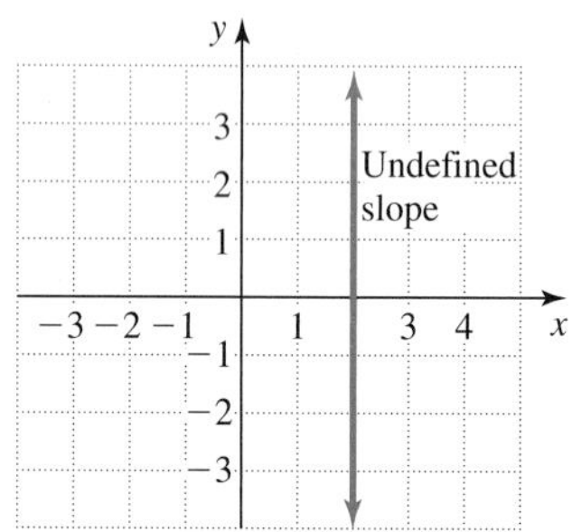

Vertical line

Figure 3.16

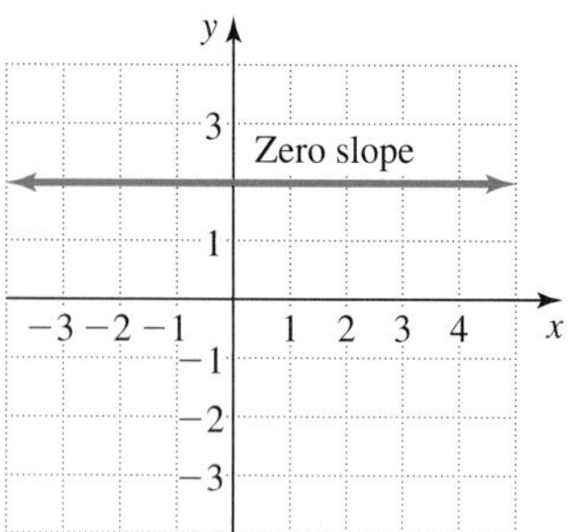

Horizontal line

Figure 3.17

Solution

a) The points (2, 1) and (2, −3) are on the vertical line shown in Fig. 3.16. Since slope is undefined for vertical lines, this line does not have a slope. Using the slope formula we get

$$m = \frac{-3 - 1}{2 - 2} = \frac{-4}{0}.$$

Since division by zero is undefined, we can again conclude that slope is undefined for the vertical line through the given points.

b) The points (−2, 2) and (4, 2) are on the horizontal line shown in Fig. 3.17. Using the slope formula we get

$$m = \frac{2 - 2}{-2 - 4} = \frac{0}{-6} = 0.$$

So the slope of the horizontal line through these points is 0.

Now do Exercises 31–34

Teaching Tip Emphasize that slope is the amount of change in y for a unit change in x. Slope is the rate at which y is changing with respect to x.

Note that for a line with *positive slope,* the y-values increase as the x-values increase. For a line with *negative slope,* the y-values decrease as the x-values increase. See Fig. 3.18.

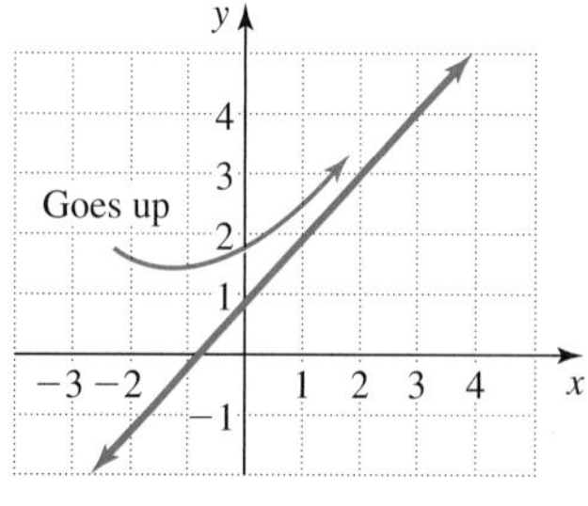

Positive slope

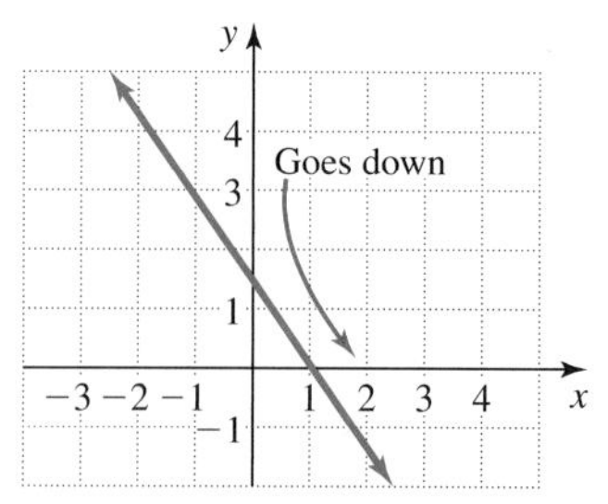

Negative slope

Figure 3.18

Graphing a Line Given a Point and Its Slope

To graph a line from its equation we usually make a table of ordered pairs and then draw a line through the points or we use the intercepts. In Example 5 we will graph a line using one point and the slope. From the slope we find additional points by using the rise and the run.

EXAMPLE 5

Graphing a line given a point and its slope

Graph each line.

a) The line through (2, 1) with slope $\frac{3}{4}$

b) The line through (−2, 4) with slope −3

Solution

a) First locate the point (2, 1). Because the slope is $\frac{3}{4}$, we can find another point on the line by going up three units and to the right four units to get the point (6, 4), as shown in Fig. 3.19. Now draw a line through (2, 1) and (6, 4). Since $\frac{3}{4} = \frac{-3}{-4}$ we could have obtained the second point by starting at (1, 2) and going down 3 units and to the left 4 units.

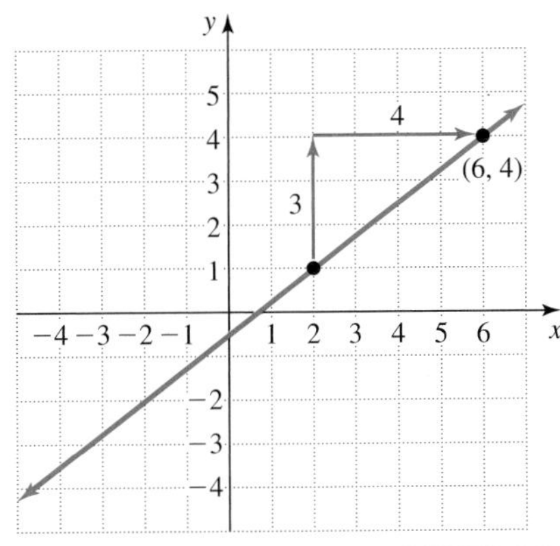

Figure 3.19

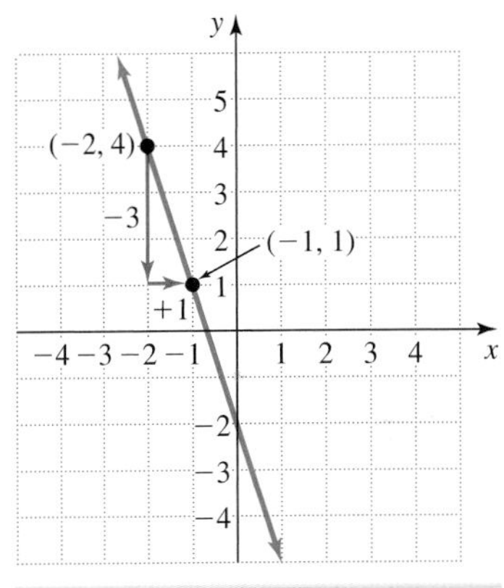

Figure 3.20

b) First locate the point (−2, 4). Because the slope is −3, or $\frac{-3}{1}$, we can locate another point on the line by starting at (−2, 4) and moving down three units and then one unit to the right to get the point (−1, 1). Now draw a line through (−2, 4) and (−1, 1) as shown in Fig. 3.20. Since $\frac{-3}{1} = \frac{3}{-1}$ we could have obtained the second point by starting at (−2, 4) and going up 3 units and to the left 1 unit.

Now do Exercises 37–42

Teaching Tip Remind students that a slope of −3/1 can be stepped off on the graph as a rise of −3 and a run of 1 or a run of −1 and a rise of 3, whichever is more convenient.

Calculator Close-Up

When we graph a line we usually draw a graph that shows both intercepts, because they are important features of the graph. If the intercepts are not between −10 and 10, you will have to adjust the window to get a good graph. The viewing window that has *x*- and *y*-values ranging from a minimum of −10 to a maximum of 10 is called the *standard viewing window.*

Parallel Lines

Every nonvertical line has a unique slope, but there are infinitely many lines with a given slope. All lines that have a given slope are parallel.

Parallel Lines

Nonvertical lines are parallel if and only if they have equal slopes. Any two vertical lines are parallel to each other.

EXAMPLE 6

Graphing parallel lines

Draw a line through the point $(-2, 1)$ with slope $\frac{1}{2}$ and a line through $(3, 0)$ with slope $\frac{1}{2}$.

Solution

Because slope is the ratio of rise to run, a slope of $\frac{1}{2}$ means that we can locate a second point of the line by starting at $(-2, 1)$ and going up one unit and to the right two units. For the line through $(3, 0)$ we start at $(3, 0)$ and go up one unit and to the right two units. See Fig. 3.21.

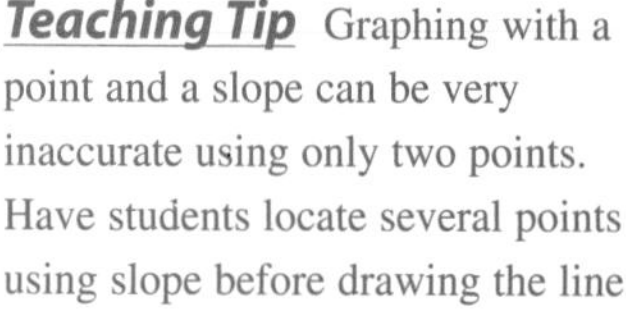

Teaching Tip Graphing with a point and a slope can be very inaccurate using only two points. Have students locate several points using slope before drawing the line.

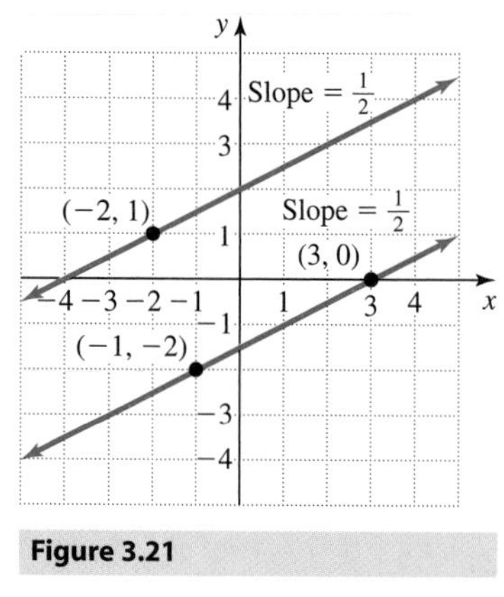

Figure 3.21

Now do Exercises 43–44

Perpendicular Lines

Figure 3.22 shows two right triangles with acute angles of 20° and 70° and legs with lengths a and b $(a > 0, b > 0)$ positioned along a vertical line. The angle between lines l_1 and l_2 in Fig. 3.22 must be 90° because that angle along with 20° and 70° together form the vertical line. Now the slope of l_1 is $\frac{a}{b}$ and the slope of l_2 is $\frac{-b}{a}$. That is, the slope of one line is the opposite of the reciprocal of the slope of the other.

Teaching Tip Using graph paper have students graph $y = -\frac{1}{2}x$ and then visually draw a perpendicular to $y = -\frac{1}{2}x$ through $(0, 0)$. Now determine the slope of the perpendicular. The class average should be 2.

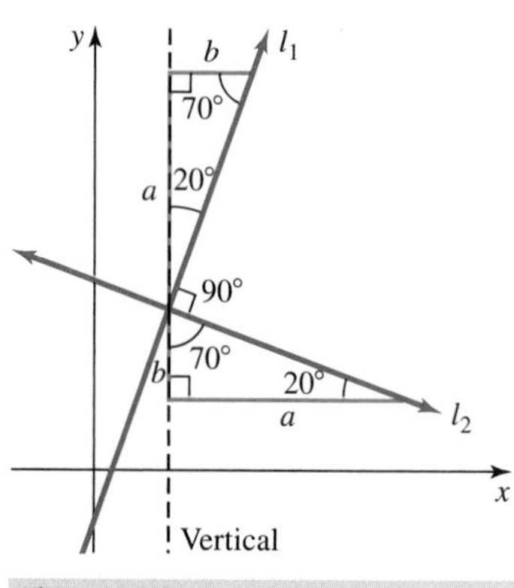

Figure 3.22

This example illustrates the following rule.

Perpendicular Lines

Two lines with slopes m_1 and m_2 are perpendicular if and only if

$$m_1 = -\frac{1}{m_2}.$$

Any vertical line is perpendicular to any horizontal line.

Notice that we cannot compare slopes of horizontal and vertical lines to see if they are perpendicular because slope is not defined for vertical lines.

EXAMPLE 7

Graphing perpendicular lines

Draw two lines through the point $(-1, 2)$, one with slope $-\frac{1}{3}$ and the other with slope 3.

Solution

Because slope is the ratio of rise to run, a slope of $-\frac{1}{3}$ means that we can locate a second point on the line by starting at $(-1, 2)$ and going down one unit and to the right three units. For the line with slope 3, we start at $(-1, 2)$ and go up three units and to the right one unit. See Fig. 3.23.

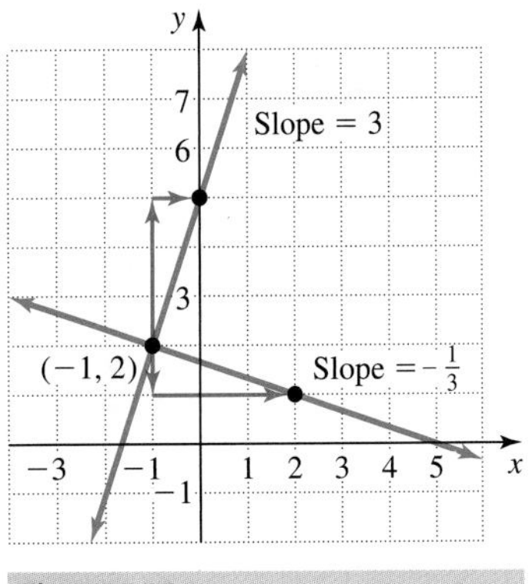

Figure 3.23

Now do Exercises 45–52

Helpful Hint

The relationship between the slopes of perpendicular lines can also be remembered as

$$m_1 \cdot m_2 = -1.$$

For example, lines with slopes -3 and $\frac{1}{3}$ are perpendicular because $-3 \cdot \frac{1}{3} = -1$.

Interpreting Slope

Slope of a line is the ratio of the rise and the run. If the rise is measured in dollars and the run in days, then the slope is measured in dollars per day or dollars/day. The slope of a line is the rate at which the dependent variable is increasing or decreasing.

EXAMPLE 8

Interpreting slope

A car goes from 60 mph to 0 mph in 120 feet after applying the brakes.

a) Find and interpret the slope of the line shown here.

b) What is the velocity at a distance of 80 feet?

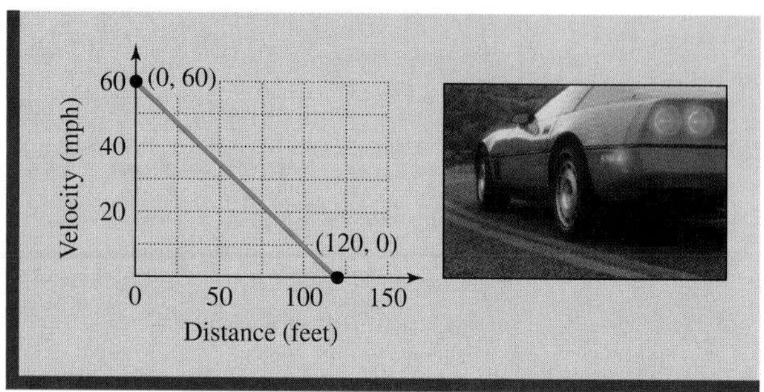

Solution

a) Find the slope of the line through (0, 60) and (120, 0):

$$m = \frac{60 - 0}{0 - 120} = -0.5$$

Because the vertical axis is miles per hour and the horizontal axis is feet, the slope is -0.5 mph/ft, which means the car is losing 0.5 mph of velocity for every foot it travels after the brakes are applied.

b) If the velocity is decreasing 0.5 mph for every foot the car travels, then in 80 feet the velocity goes down 0.5(80) or 40 mph. So the velocity at 80 feet is $60 - 40$ or 20 mph.

Now do Exercises 61–64

EXAMPLE 9

Finding points when given the slope

Assume that the base price of a new Jeep Wrangler is increasing $300 per year. Find the data that is missing from the table.

Year	Price (dollars)
2001	15,600
2002	
2003	
	18,300
	20,100

Solution

The price in 2002 is $15,900 and in 2003 it is $16,200 because the slope is $300 per year. The rise in price from $16,200 to $18,300 is $2100, which takes 7 years at $300 per year. So in 2010 the price is $18,300. The rise from $18,300 to $20,100 is $1800, which takes 6 years at $300 per year. So in 2016 the price is $20,100.

Now do Exercises 65–66

Warm-Ups ▼

True or false? Explain your answer.

1. Slope is a measurement of the steepness of a line. True
2. Slope is rise divided by run. True
3. Every line in the coordinate plane has a slope. False
4. The line through the point (1, 1) and the origin has slope 1. True
5. Slope can never be negative. False
6. A line with slope 2 is perpendicular to any line with slope -2. False
7. The slope of the line through (0, 3) and (4, 0) is $\frac{3}{4}$. False
8. Two different lines cannot have the same slope. False
9. The line through (1, 3) and $(-5, 3)$ has zero slope. True
10. Slope can have units such as feet per second. True

3.2 Exercises

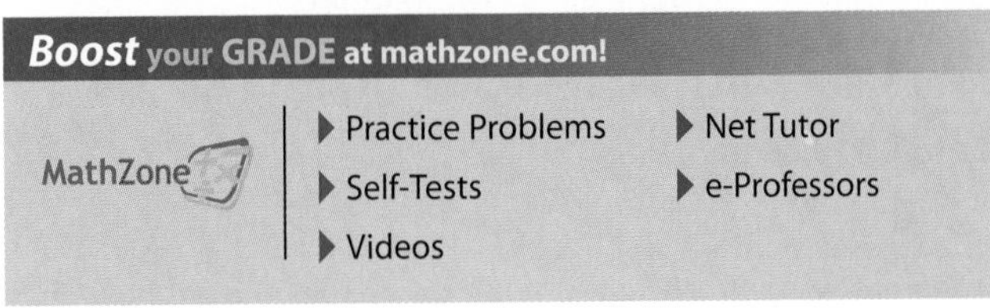

Reading and Writing *After reading this section, write out the answers to these questions. Use complete sentences.*

1. What is the slope of a line?
   The slope of a line is the ratio of its rise and run.
2. What is the difference between rise and run?
   Rise is the amount of vertical change and run is the amount of horizontal change.
3. For which lines is slope undefined?
   Slope is undefined for vertical lines.
4. Which lines have zero slope?
   Horizontal lines have zero slope.
5. What is the difference between lines with positive slope and lines with negative slope?
   Lines with positive slope are rising as you go from left to right, while lines with negative slope are falling as you go from left to right.
6. What is the relationship between the slopes of perpendicular lines?
   If m_1 and m_2 are slopes of perpendicular lines, then $m_1 = -\frac{1}{m_2}$.

In Exercises 7–18, find the slope of each line. See Examples 1 and 2.

7. **8.**

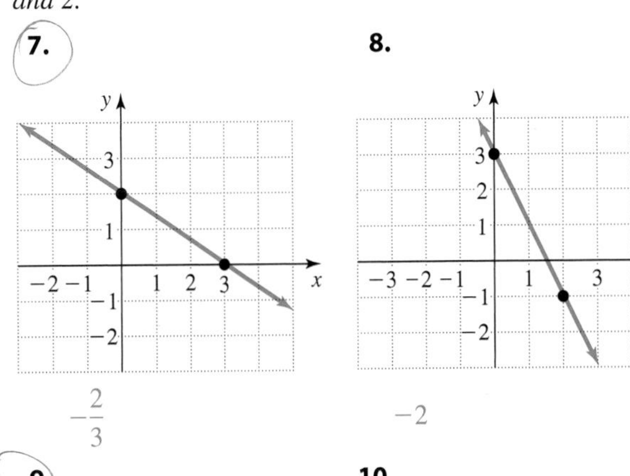

$-\frac{2}{3}$ -2

9. **10.**

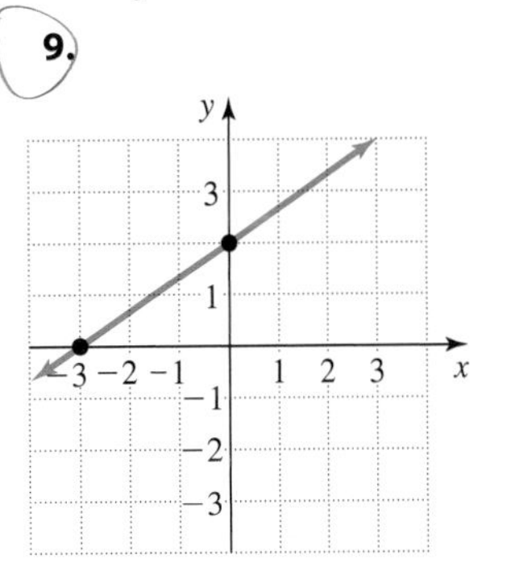

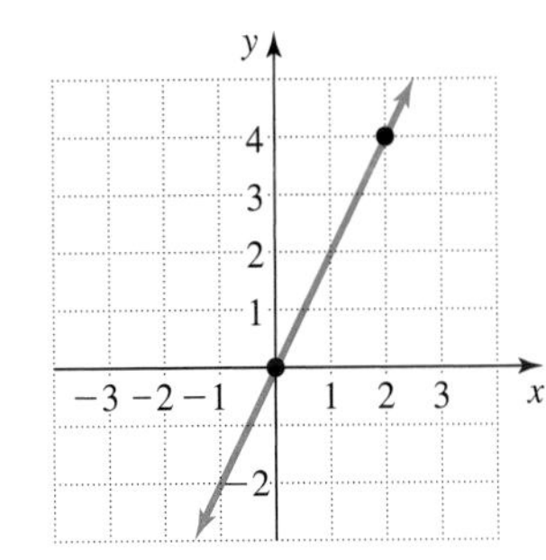

$\frac{2}{3}$ 2

11.

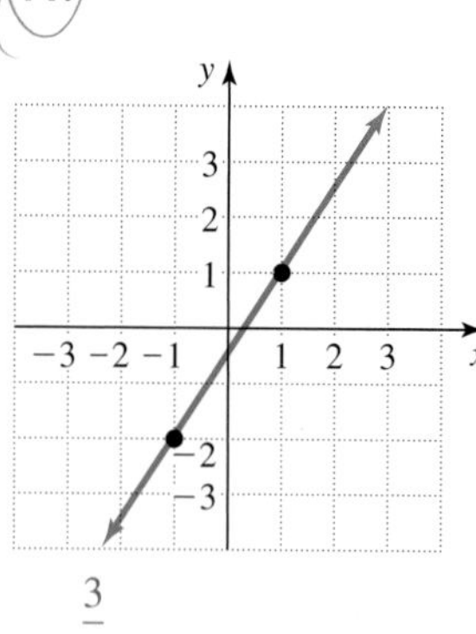

$\frac{3}{2}$

12.

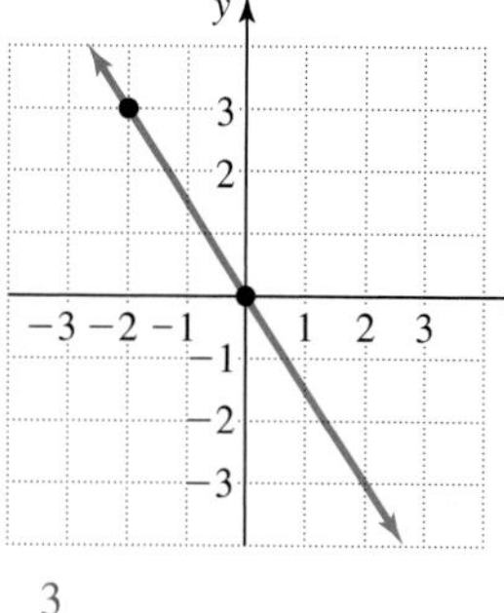

$-\frac{3}{2}$

13.

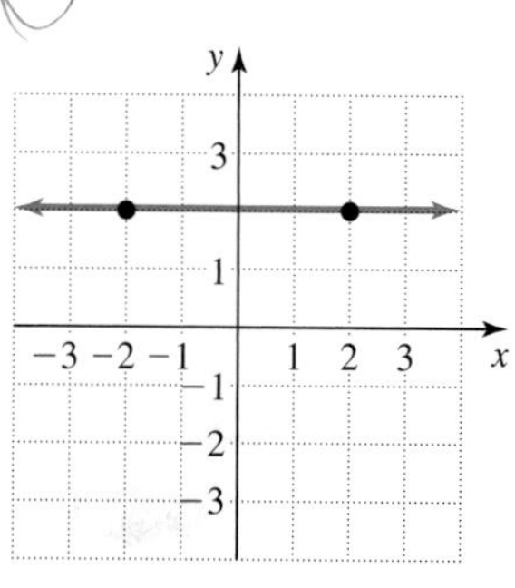

0

14.

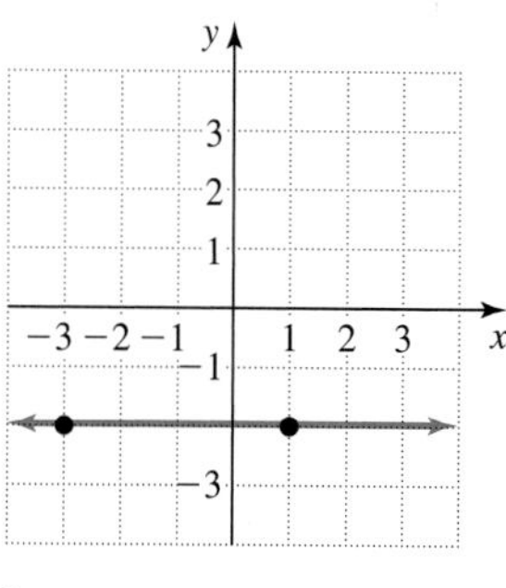

0

15.

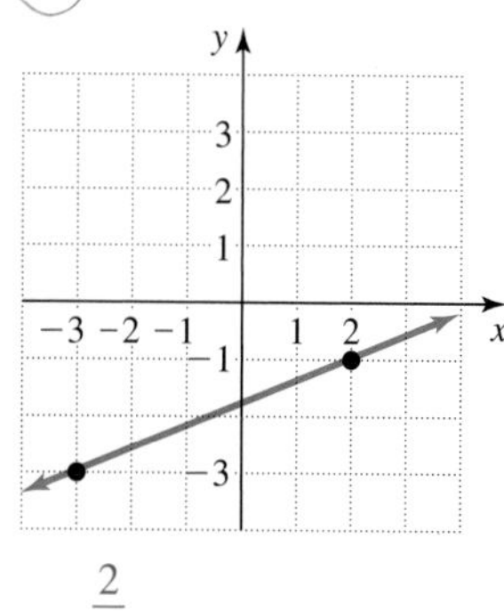

$\frac{2}{5}$

16.

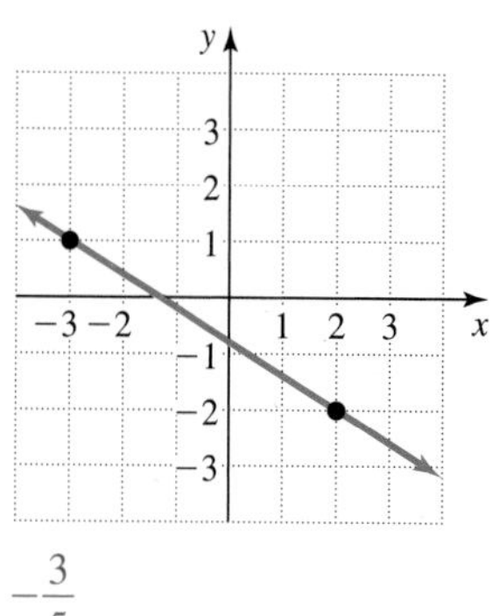

$-\frac{3}{5}$

17.

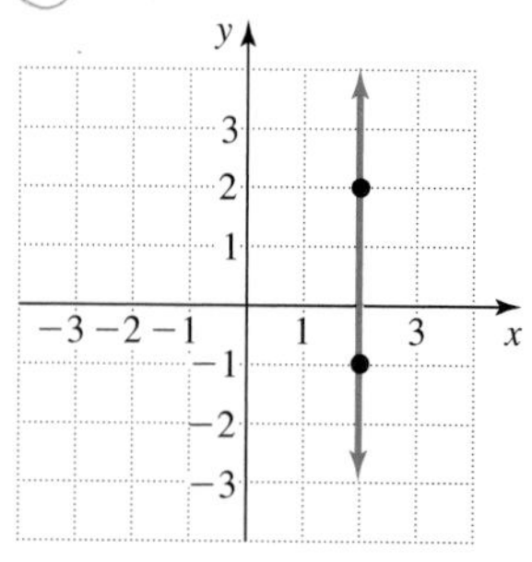

Undefined

18.

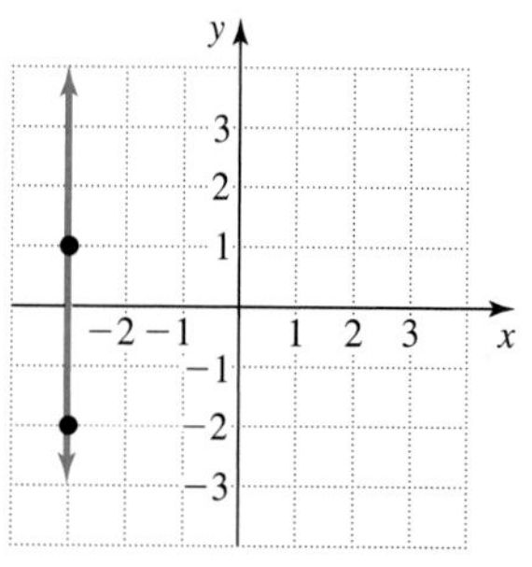

Undefined

Find the slope of the line that goes through each pair of points. See Examples 3 and 4.

19. (1, 2), (3, 6) 2

20. (2, 5), (6, 10) $\frac{5}{4}$

21. (2, 4), (5, −1) $-\frac{5}{3}$

22. (3, 1), (6, −2) −1

23. (−2, 4), (5, 9) $\frac{5}{7}$

24. (−1, 3), (3, 5) $\frac{1}{2}$

25. (−2, −3), (−5, 1) $-\frac{4}{3}$

26. (−6, −3), (−1, 1) $\frac{4}{5}$

27. (−3, 4), (3, −2) −1

28. (−1, 3), (5, −2) $-\frac{5}{6}$

29. $\left(\frac{1}{2}, 2\right), \left(-1, \frac{1}{2}\right)$ 1

30. $\left(\frac{1}{3}, 2\right), \left(-\frac{1}{3}, 1\right)$ $\frac{3}{2}$

31. (2, 3), (2, −9) Undefined

32. (−3, 6), (8, 6) 0

33. (−2, −5), (9, −5) 0

34. (4, −9), (4, 6) Undefined

35. (0.3, 0.9), (−0.1, −0.3) 3

36. (−0.1, 0.2), (0.5, 0.8) 1

Graph the line with the given point and slope. See Example 5.

37. The line through (1, 1) with slope $\frac{2}{3}$

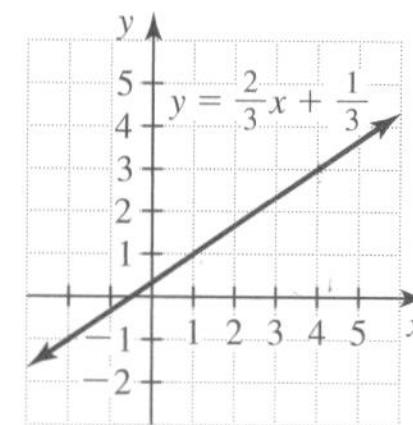

38. The line through (2, 3) with slope $\frac{1}{2}$

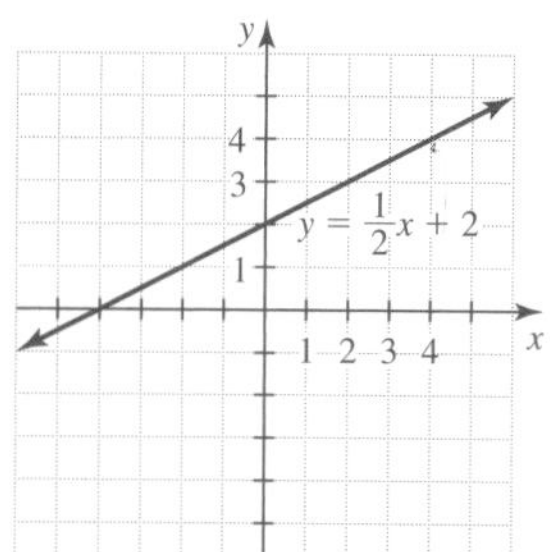

39. The line through $(-2, 3)$ with slope -2

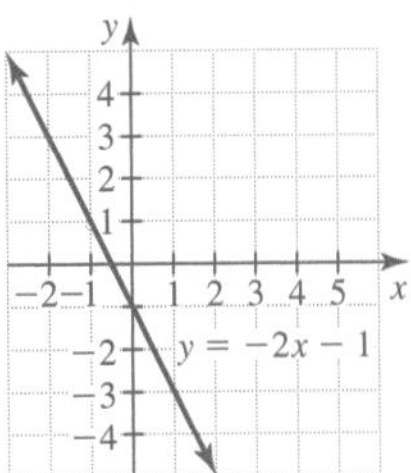

40. The line through $(-2, 5)$ with slope -1

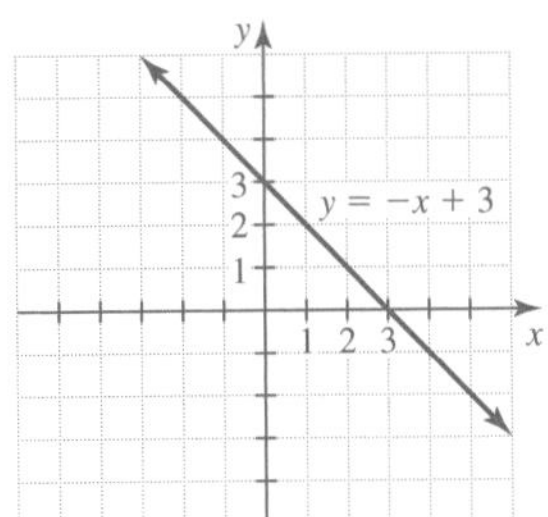

41. The line through $(0, 0)$ with slope $-\frac{2}{5}$

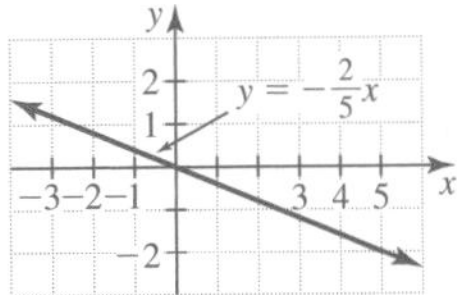

42. The line through $(-1, 4)$ with slope $-\frac{2}{3}$

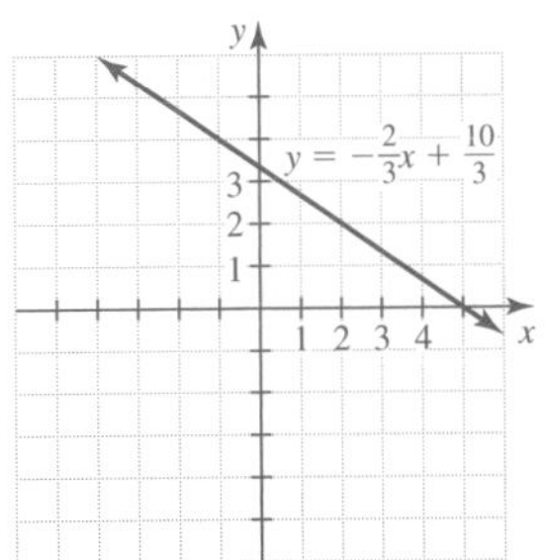

Solve each problem. See Examples 6 and 7.

43. Draw line l_1 through $(1, -2)$ with slope $\frac{1}{2}$ and line l_2 through $(-1, 1)$ with slope $\frac{1}{2}$.

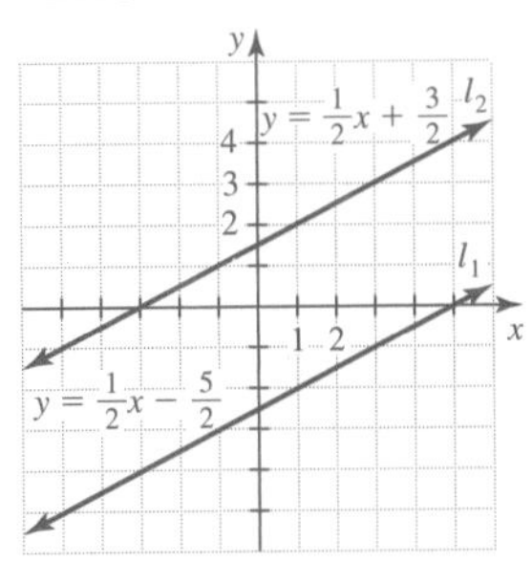

44. Draw line l_1 through $(0, 3)$ with slope 1 and line l_2 through $(0, 0)$ with slope 1.

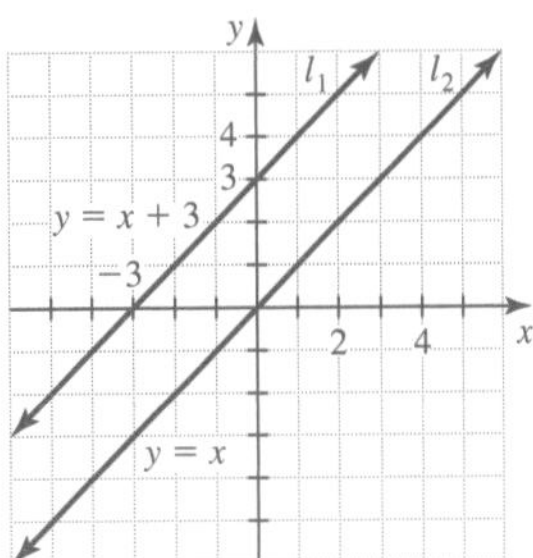

45. Draw l_1 through $(1, 2)$ with slope $\frac{1}{2}$, and draw l_2 through $(1, 2)$ with slope -2.

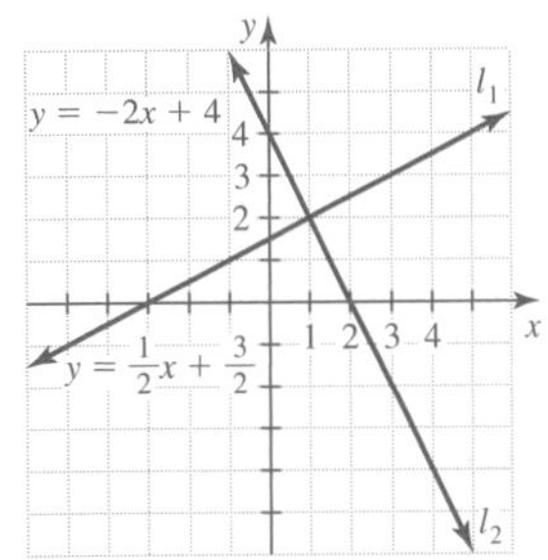

46. Draw l_1 through $(-2, 1)$ with slope $\frac{2}{3}$, and draw l_2 through $(-2, 1)$ with slope $-\frac{3}{2}$.

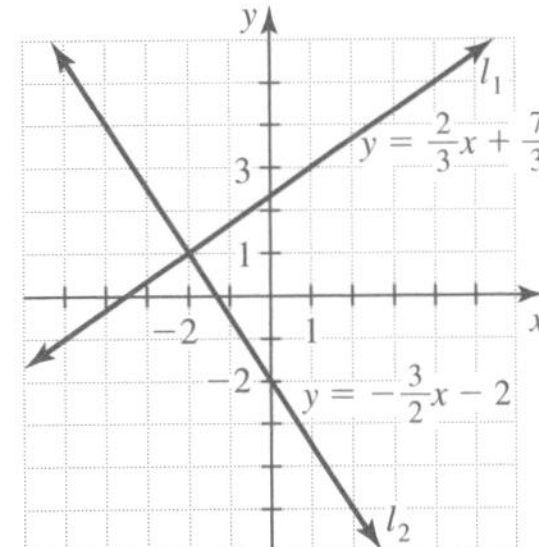

47. Draw any line l_1 with slope $\frac{3}{4}$. What is the slope of any line perpendicular to l_1? Draw any line l_2 perpendicular to l_1.

$-\frac{4}{3}$

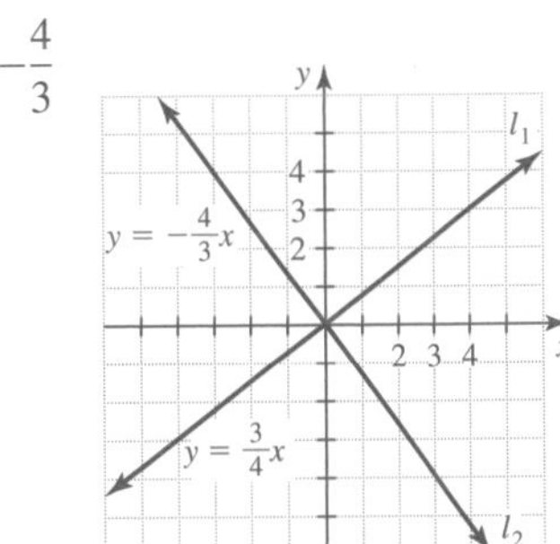

48. Draw any line l_1 with slope -1. What is the slope of any line perpendicular to l_1? Draw any line l_2 perpendicular to l_1.

1

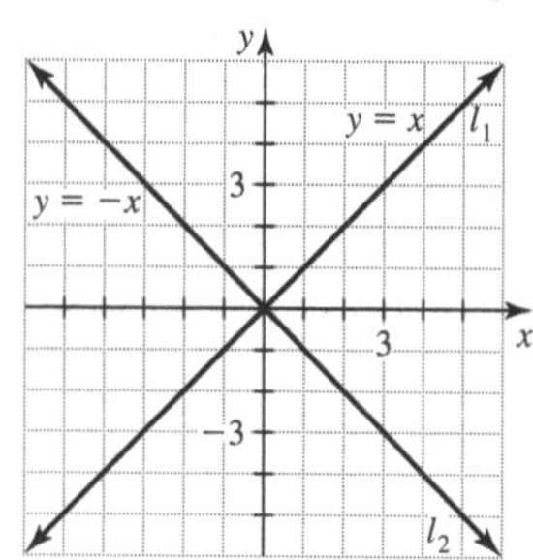

49. Draw l_1 through $(-2, -3)$ and $(4, 0)$. What is the slope of any line parallel to l_1? Draw l_2 through $(1, 2)$ so that it is parallel to l_1.

$\frac{1}{2}$

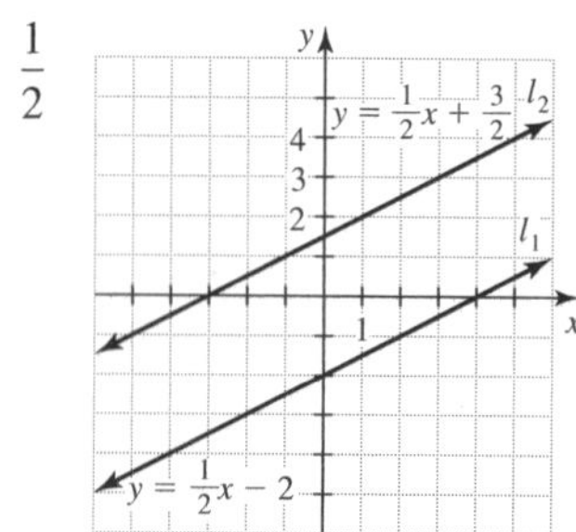

50. Draw l_1 through $(-4, 0)$ and $(0, 6)$. What is the slope of any line parallel to l_1? Draw l_2 through the origin and parallel to l_1.

$\frac{3}{2}$

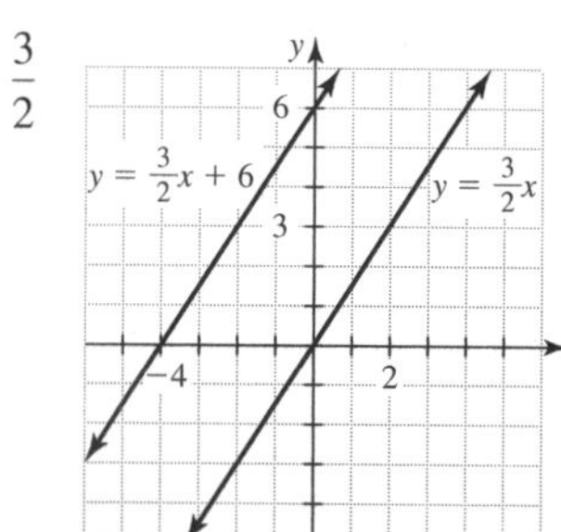

51. Draw l_1 through $(-2, 4)$ and $(3, -1)$. What is the slope of any line perpendicular to l_1? Draw l_2 through $(1, 3)$ so that it is perpendicular to l_1.

1

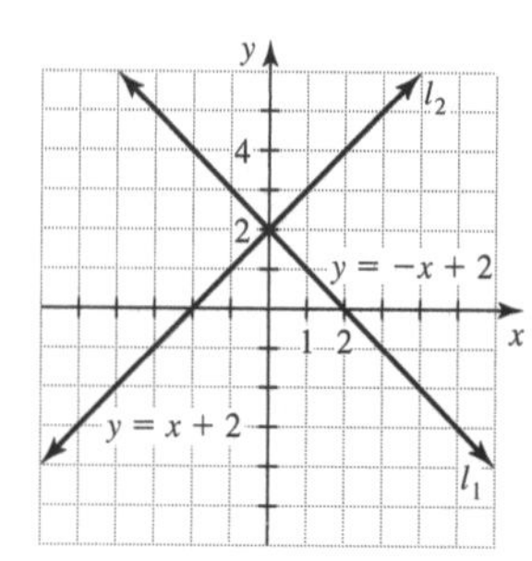

52. Draw l_1 through $(0, -3)$ and $(3, 0)$. What is the slope of any line perpendicular to l_1? Draw l_2 through the origin so that it is perpendicular to l_1.

-1

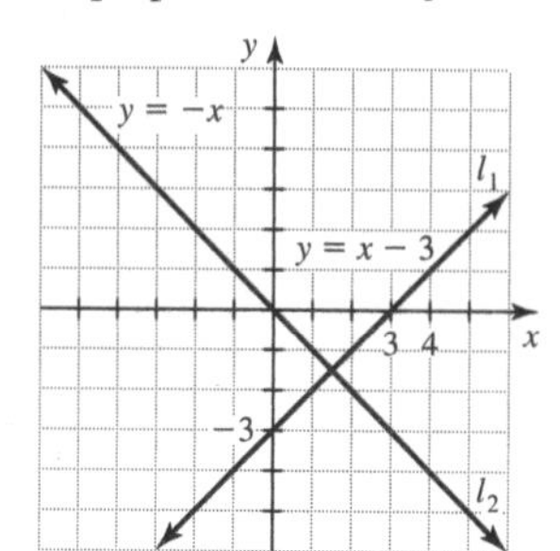

In each case, determine whether the lines l_1 and l_2 are parallel, perpendicular, or neither.

53. Line l_1 goes through $(3, 5)$ and $(4, 7)$. Line l_2 goes through $(11, 7)$ and $(12, 9)$.
Parallel

54. Line l_1 goes through $(-2, -2)$ and $(2, 0)$. Line l_2 goes through $(-2, 5)$ and $(-1, 3)$.
Perpendicular

55. Line l_1 goes through $(-1, 4)$ and $(2, 6)$. Line l_2 goes through $(2, -2)$ and $(4, 1)$.
Neither

56. Line l_1 goes through $(-2, 5)$ and $(4, 7)$. Line l_2 goes through $(2, 4)$ and $(3, 1)$.
Perpendicular

57. Line l_1 goes through $(-1, 4)$ and $(4, 6)$. Line l_2 goes through $(-7, 0)$ and $(3, 4)$.
Parallel

58. Line l_1 goes through $(1, 2)$ and $(1, -1)$. Line l_2 goes through $(4, 4)$ and $(3, 3)$.
Neither

59. Line l_1 goes through $(3, 5)$ and $(3, 6)$. Line l_2 goes through $(-2, 4)$ and $(-3, 4)$.
Perpendicular

60. Line l_1 goes through $(-3, 7)$ and $(4, 7)$. Line l_2 goes through $(-5, 1)$ and $(-3, 1)$.
Parallel

Solve each problem. See Examples 8 and 9.

61. ***Super cost.*** The average cost of 30-second ad during the 1998 Super Bowl was \$1.3 million, and in 2004 it was \$2.4 million (www.adage.com).

a) Find the slope of the line through (1998, 1.3) and (2004, 2.4) and interpret your result.
Approximately 0.183 slope; Cost is increasing about \$183,000 per year.

b) Use the slope to estimate the average cost of an ad in 2002. Is your estimate consistent with the accompanying graph? $2.03 million; yes

c) Use the slope to predict the average cost in 2008? $3.13 million

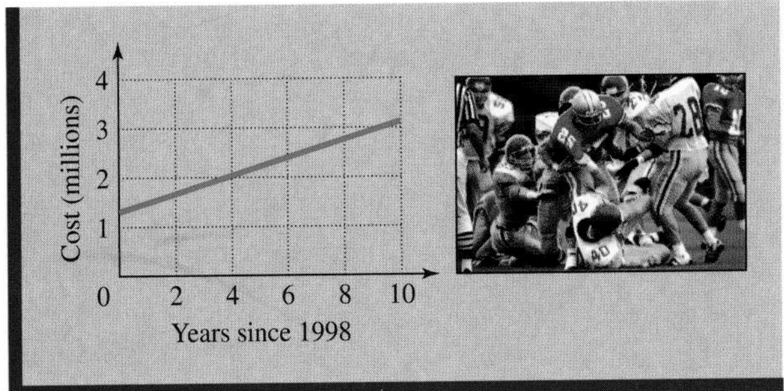

Figure for Exercise 61

62. ***Retirement pay.*** The annual Social Security benefit of a retiree depends on the age at the time of retirement. The accompanying graph gives the annual benefit for persons retiring at ages 62 through 70 in the year 2005 or later (Social Security Administration, www.ssa.gov). What is the annual benefit for a person who retires at age 64? At what retirement age does a person receive an annual benefit of $11,600? Find the slope of each line segment on the graph, and interpret your results. Why do people who postpone retirement until 70 years of age get the highest benefit? $8000, 69, 500, 666.66, 800; The slopes are the yearly increases for each segment.

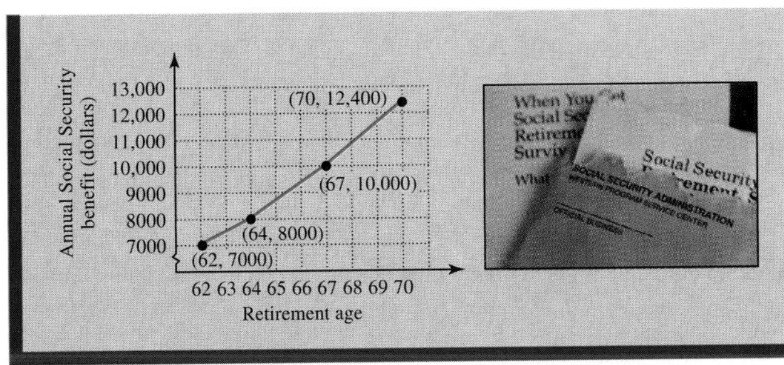

Figure for Exercise 62

63. ***Increasing training.*** The accompanying graph shows the percentage of U.S. workers receiving training by their employers. The percentage went from 5% in 1982 to 25% in 2002 (Department of Labor, www.dol.gov). Find the slope of this line. Interpret your result. 1 slope; The percentage increases 1% per year.

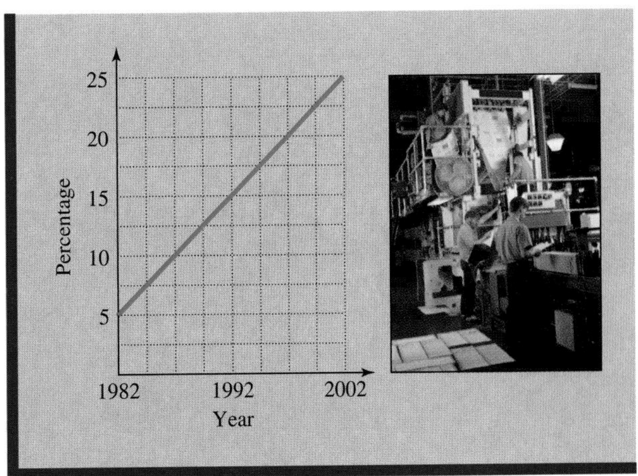

Figure for Exercise 63

64. ***Saving for retirement.*** Financial advisors at Fidelity Investments, Boston, use the accompanying table as a measure of whether a client is on the road to a comfortable retirement.

a) Graph these points and draw a line through them.

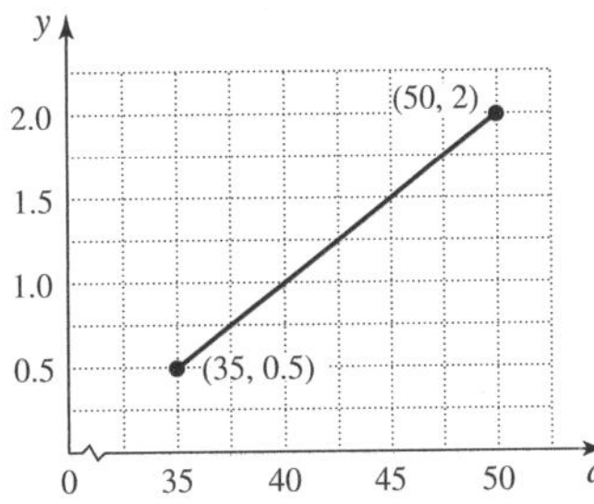

b) What is the slope of the line? 0.1

c) By what percentage of your salary should you be increasing your savings every year? 10%

Age (a)	Years of Salary Saved (y)
35	0.5
40	1.0
45	1.5
50	2.0

Figure for Exercise 64

65. ***Increasing salary.*** An elementary school teacher gets a raise of $400 per year. Find the data that is missing from the table on the next page.

Year	Salary (dollars)
2000	28,100
2002	28,900
2003	29,300
2012	32,900
2015	34,100

66. ***Declining population.*** The population of Springfield is decreasing at a rate of 250 people per year. Find the data that is missing from the table.

Year	Population
2001	8400
2002	8150
2008	6650
2011	5900
2015	4900

Determine whether the points in each table lie on a straight line.

67.

x	y
4	10
7	19
11	31
17	49

Yes

68.

x	y
2	−4
4	−14
8	−34
13	−59

Yes

69.

x	y
−2	7
0	3
3	−3
9	−16

No

70.

x	y
−3	−12
0	2
2	10
6	26

No

3.3 Equations of Lines in Slope-Intercept Form

In this Section

- Slope-Intercept Form
- Standard Form
- Using Slope-Intercept Form for Graphing
- Writing the Equation for a Line
- Applications

In Section 3.1 you learned that the graph of all solutions to a linear equation in two variables is a straight line. In this section we start with a line or a description of a line and write an equation for the line. The equation of a line in any form is called a **linear equation in two variables.**

Slope-Intercept Form

Consider the line through (0, 1) with slope $\frac{2}{3}$ shown in Fig. 3.24. If we use the points (x, y) and (0, 1) in the slope formula, we get an equation that is satisfied by every point on the line:

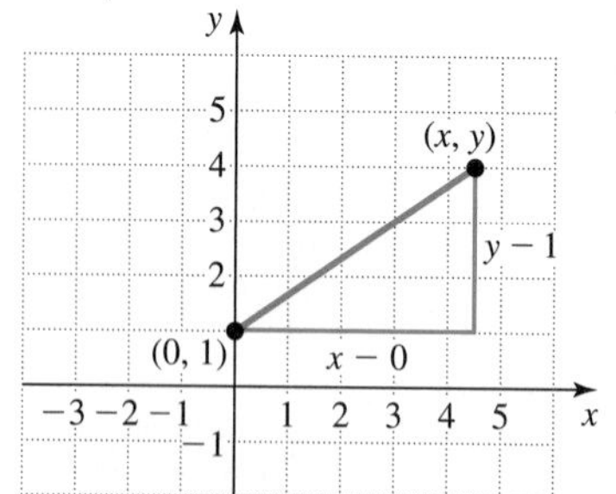

Figure 3.24

$$\frac{y_2 - y_1}{x_2 - x_1} = m \quad \text{Slope formula}$$

$$\frac{y - 1}{x - 0} = \frac{2}{3} \quad \text{Let } (x_1, y_1) = (0, 1) \text{ and } (x_2, y_2) = (x, y).$$

$$\frac{y - 1}{x} = \frac{2}{3}$$

Now solve the equation for y:

$$x \cdot \frac{y - 1}{x} = \frac{2}{3} \cdot x \quad \text{Multiply each side by } x.$$

$$y - 1 = \frac{2}{3}x$$

$$y = \frac{2}{3}x + 1 \quad \text{Add 1 to each side.}$$

Teaching Tip Remind students that $y = 3x - 2$ is in slope-intercept form even though the form is

$$y = mx + b.$$

Because (0, 1) is on the y-axis, it is called the **y-intercept** of the line. Note how the slope $\frac{2}{3}$ and the y-coordinate of the y-intercept (0, 1) appear in $y = \frac{2}{3}x + 1$. For this reason it is called the **slope-intercept form** of the equation of the line.

Slope-Intercept Form

The equation of the line with y-intercept $(0, b)$ and slope m is

$$y = mx + b.$$

EXAMPLE 1

Using slope-intercept form

Write the equation of each line in slope-intercept form.

a)

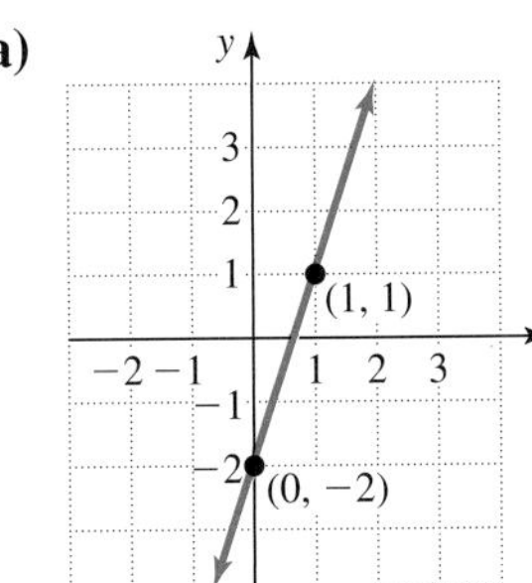

b)

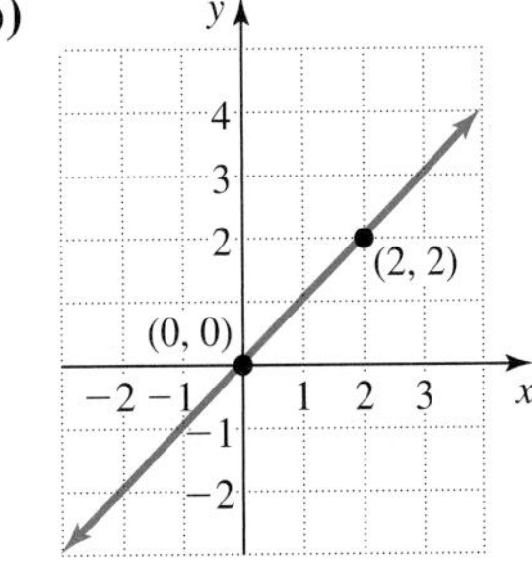

c)

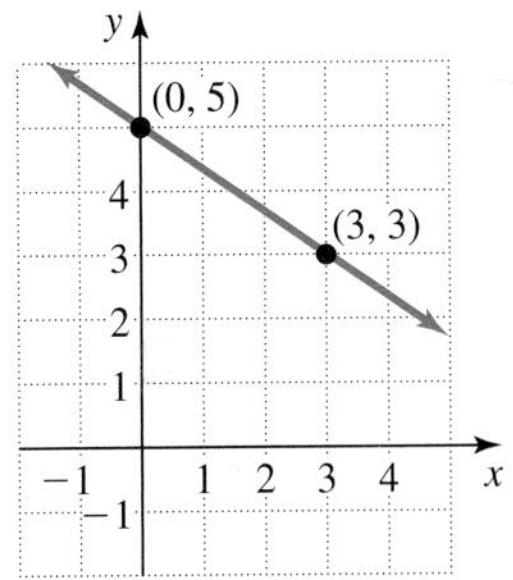

Solution

a) The y-intercept is $(0, -2)$, and the slope is 3. Use the form $y = mx + b$ with $b = -2$ and $m = 3$. The equation in slope-intercept form is

$$y = 3x - 2.$$

b) The y-intercept is (0, 0), and the slope is 1. So the equation is

$$y = x.$$

c) The y-intercept is (0, 5), and the slope is $-\frac{2}{3}$. So the equation is

$$y = -\frac{2}{3}x + 5.$$

Now do Exercises 7–18

Calculator Close-Up

Since a graphing calculator screen has a finite number of pixels, a graphing calculator plots only a finite number of ordered pairs that satisfy an equation. A graph is supposed to be a picture of all of the ordered pairs that satisfy an equation. In spite of this limitation, the speed and accuracy of a graphing calculator make it a very useful tool.

The equation of a line may take many different forms. The easiest way to find the slope and y-intercept for a line is to rewrite the equation in slope-intercept form.

EXAMPLE 2

Finding slope and y-intercept

Determine the slope and y-intercept of the line $3x - 2y = 6$.

Solution

Solve for y to get slope-intercept form:

$$3x - 2y = 6$$
$$-2y = -3x + 6$$
$$y = \frac{3}{2}x - 3$$

The slope is $\frac{3}{2}$, and the y-intercept is $(0, -3)$.

Now do Exercises 19–36

Teaching Tip Remind students to use built-up fractions and write them clearly. Writing $y = 3/2x - 3$ can be confusing and $y = \frac{3}{2x} - 3$ is wrong.

Standard Form

The graph of the equation $x = 3$ is a vertical line. Because slope is not defined for vertical lines, this line does not have an equation in slope-intercept form. Only nonvertical lines have equations in slope-intercept form. However, there is a form that includes all lines. It is called **standard form.**

Helpful Hint

In geometry we learn that two points determine a line. However, if you locate two points that are close together and draw a line through them, your line can have a lot of error in it at locations far from the two chosen points. Locating five points on the graph will improve your accuracy. If you use only two points to sketch a line, then they should be chosen as far apart as possible.

Standard Form

Every line has an equation in the form

$$Ax + By = C$$

where A, B, and C are real numbers with A and B not both zero.

To write the equation $x = 3$ in this form, let $A = 1$, $B = 0$, and $C = 3$. We get

$$1 \cdot x + 0 \cdot y = 3,$$

which is equivalent to

$$x = 3.$$

In Example 2 we converted an equation in standard form to slope-intercept form. Any linear equation in standard form with $B \neq 0$ can be written in slope-intercept form by solving for y. In Example 3 we convert an equation in slope-intercept form to standard form.

EXAMPLE 3

Converting to standard form

Write the equation of the line $y = \frac{2}{5}x + 3$ in standard form using only integers.

Solution

To get standard form, first subtract $\frac{2}{5}x$ from each side:

$$y = \frac{2}{5}x + 3$$

$$-\frac{2}{5}x + y = 3$$

$$-5\left(-\frac{2}{5}x + y\right) = -5 \cdot 3 \quad \text{Multiply each side by } -5 \text{ to eliminate the fraction and get positive } 2x.$$

$$2x - 5y = -15$$

Now do Exercises 37–52

Teaching Tip Point out that slope-intercept form is unique, but standard form is not.

The answer $2x - 5y = -15$ in Example 3 is not the only answer using only integers. Equations such as $-2x + 5y = 15$ and $4x - 10y = -30$ are equivalent equations in standard form. We prefer to write $2x - 5y = -15$ because the greatest common factor of 2, 5, and 15 is 1 and the coefficient of x is positive.

Using Slope-Intercept Form for Graphing

One way to graph a linear equation is to find several points that satisfy the equation and then draw a straight line through them. We can also graph a linear equation by using the y-intercept and the slope.

Strategy for Graphing a Line Using *y*-Intercept and Slope

1. Write the equation in slope-intercept form if necessary.
2. Plot the *y*-intercept.
3. Starting from the *y*-intercept, use the rise and run to locate a second point.
4. Draw a line through the two points.

EXAMPLE 4

Calculator Close-Up

To check Example 4, graph $y = (2/3)x - 1$ on a graphing calculator as follows:

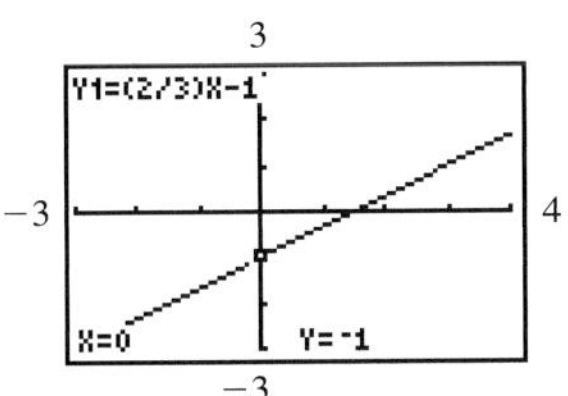

The calculator graph is consistent with the graph in Fig. 3.25.

Graphing a line using *y*-intercept and slope

Graph the line $2x - 3y = 3$.

Solution

First write the equation in slope-intercept form:

$$2x - 3y = 3$$
$$-3y = -2x + 3 \quad \text{Subtract } 2x \text{ from each side.}$$
$$y = \frac{2}{3}x - 1 \quad \text{Divide each side by } -3.$$

The slope is $\frac{2}{3}$, and the *y*-intercept is $(0, -1)$. A slope of $\frac{2}{3}$ means a rise of 2 and a run of 3. Start at $(0, -1)$ and go up two units and to the right three units to locate a second point on the line. Now draw a line through the two points. See Fig. 3.25 for the graph of $2x - 3y = 3$.

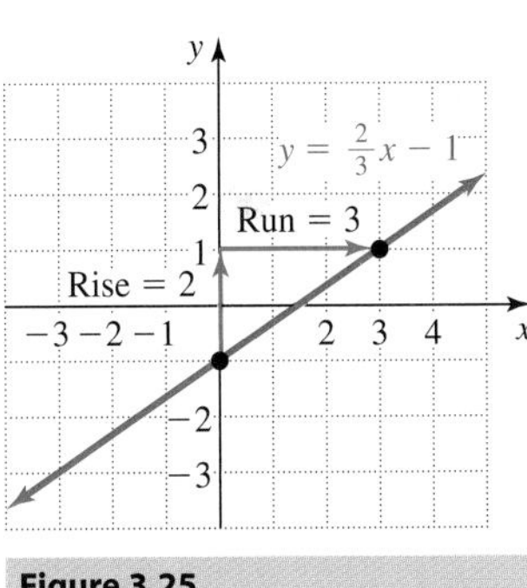

Figure 3.25

Now do Exercises 53–54

CAUTION When using the slope to find a second point on the line, be sure to start at the *y*-intercept, not at the origin.

EXAMPLE 5

Graphing lines with *y*-intercept and slope

Graph each line.

a) $y = -3x + 4$ **b)** $2y - 5x = 0$

Solution

a) For $y = -3x + 4$ the slope is -3 and the *y*-intercept is $(0, 4)$. Because $-3 = \frac{-3}{1}$, the rise is -3 and the run is 1. First plot the *y*-intercept $(0, 4)$. To locate a second point on the line start at $(0, 4)$ and go down three units and to the right one unit. Draw a line through $(0, 4)$ and $(1, 1)$. See Fig. 3.26 on the next page.

b) First solve the equation for *y*:

$$2y - 5x = 0$$
$$2y = 5x$$
$$y = \frac{5}{2}x$$

The slope is $\frac{5}{2}$ and the *y*-intercept is $(0, 0)$. Using a rise of five and a run of two from the origin yields the point $(2, 5)$. Draw a line through $(0, 0)$ and $(2, 5)$ as shown in Fig. 3.27 on the next page.

Teaching Tip Students often count off the slope from (0, 0) rather than from the *y*-intercept.

Study Tip

Keep reviewing. After doing your current assignment, go back a section or two and try a few problems. You will be amazed at how you will improve with a regular review.

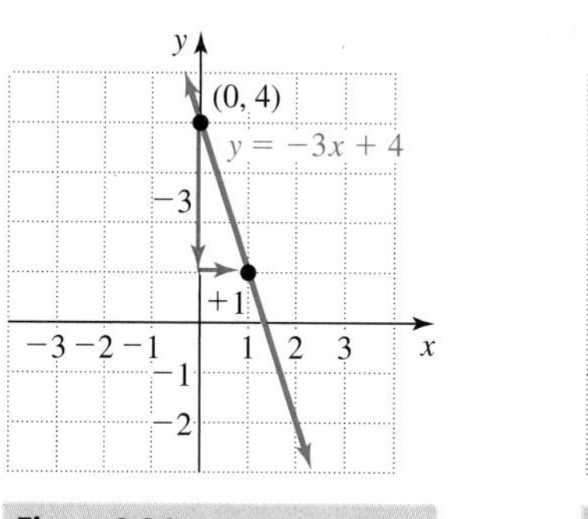

Figure 3.26

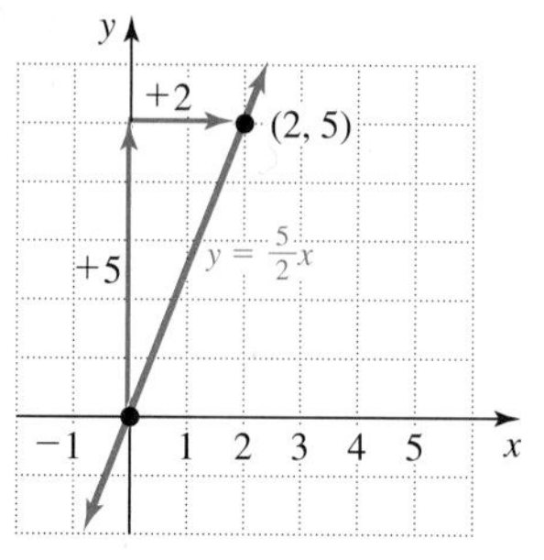

Figure 3.27

Now do Exercises 55–66

Writing the Equation for a Line

In Example 1 we wrote the equation of a line by finding its slope and y-intercept from a graph. In Example 6 we write the equation of a line from a description of the line.

EXAMPLE 6

Writing an equation

Write the equation in slope-intercept form for each line:

a) The line through (0, 3) that is parallel to the line $y = 2x - 1$

b) The line through (0, 4) that is perpendicular to the line $2x - 4y = 1$

Solution

a) The line $y = 2x - 1$ has slope 2 and any line parallel to it has slope 2. So the equation of the line with y-intercept (0, 3) and slope 2 is $y = 2x + 3$.

b) First find the slope of $2x - 4y = 1$:

$$2x - 4y = 1$$
$$-4y = -2x + 1$$
$$y = \frac{1}{2}x - \frac{1}{4}$$

So $2x - 4y = 1$ has slope $\frac{1}{2}$ and the slope of any line perpendicular to $2x - 4y = 1$ is the opposite of the reciprocal of $\frac{1}{2}$ or -2. The equation of the line through the y-intercept (0, 4) with slope -2 is $y = -2x + 4$.

Now do Exercises 75–88

Calculator Close-Up

If you use the same minimum and maximum window values for x and y, then the length of one unit on the x-axis is larger than on the y-axis because the screen is longer in the x-direction. In this case, perpendicular lines will not look perpendicular. The viewing window chosen here for the lines in Example 6 makes them look perpendicular. Any viewing window proportional to this one will also produce approximately the same unit length on each axis. Some calculators have a square feature that automatically makes the unit length the same on both axes.

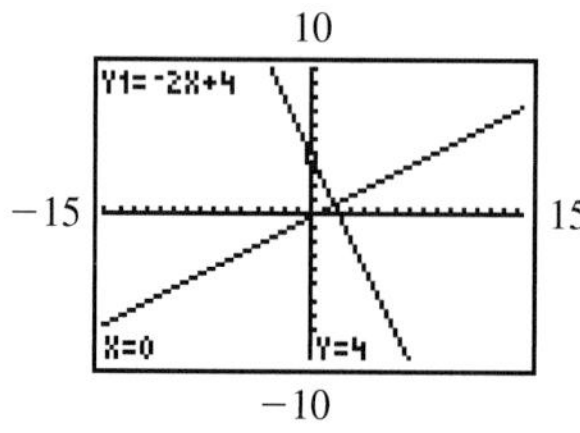

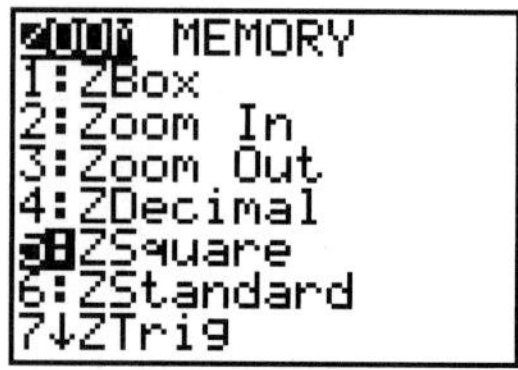

Applications

In Example 7 we see that the slope-intercept and standard forms are both important in applications.

EXAMPLE 7

Teaching Tip This is a good example to show the importance of standard and slope-intercept form.

Changing forms

A landscaper has a total of \$800 to spend on bushes at \$20 each and trees at \$50 each. So if x is the number of bushes and y is the number of trees he can buy, then $20x + 50y = 800$. Write this equation in slope-intercept form. Find and interpret the y-intercept and the slope.

Solution

Write in slope-intercept form:

$$20x + 50y = 800$$
$$50y = -20x + 800$$
$$y = -\frac{2}{5}x + 16$$

The slope is $-\frac{2}{5}$ and the intercept is $(0, 16)$. So he can get 16 trees if he buys no bushes and he loses $\frac{2}{5}$ of a tree for each additional bush that he purchases.

Now do Exercises 89–94

Warm-Ups

True or false? Explain your answer.

1. There is only one line with y-intercept $(0, 3)$ and slope $-\frac{4}{3}$. True
2. The equation of the line through $(1, 2)$ with slope 3 is $y = 3x + 2$. False
3. The vertical line $x = -2$ has no y-intercept. True
4. The equation $x = 5$ has a graph that is a vertical line. True
5. The line $y = x - 3$ is perpendicular to the line $y = 5 - x$. True
6. The line $y = 2x - 3$ is parallel to the line $y = 4x - 3$. False
7. The line $2y = 3x - 8$ has a slope of 3. False
8. Every straight line in the coordinate plane has an equation in standard form. True
9. The line $x = 2$ is perpendicular to the line $y = 5$. True
10. The line $y = x$ has no y-intercept. False

3.3 Exercises

Boost your GRADE at mathzone.com!

MathZone

- Practice Problems
- Net Tutor
- Self-Tests
- e-Professors
- Videos

Reading and Writing *After reading this section, write out the answers to these questions. Use complete sentences.*

1. What is the slope-intercept form for the equation of a line?
   Slope-intercept form is $y = mx + b$.

2. How can you determine the slope and y-intercept from the slope-intercept form.
The slope is m and the y-intercept is $(0, b)$.

3. What is the standard form for the equation of a line?
The standard form is $Ax + By = C$.

4. How can you graph a line when the equation is in slope-intercept form?
From slope-intercept form, locate the intercept and a second point by counting the rise and run from the y-intercept.

5. What form is used in this section to write an equation of a line from a description of the line?
The slope-intercept form allows us to write the equation from the y-intercept and the slope.

6. What makes lines look perpendicular on a graph?
Lines with slopes m and $\frac{-1}{m}$ look perpendicular only if the same unit distance is used on both axes.

Write an equation for each line. Use slope-intercept form if possible. See Example 1.

7.

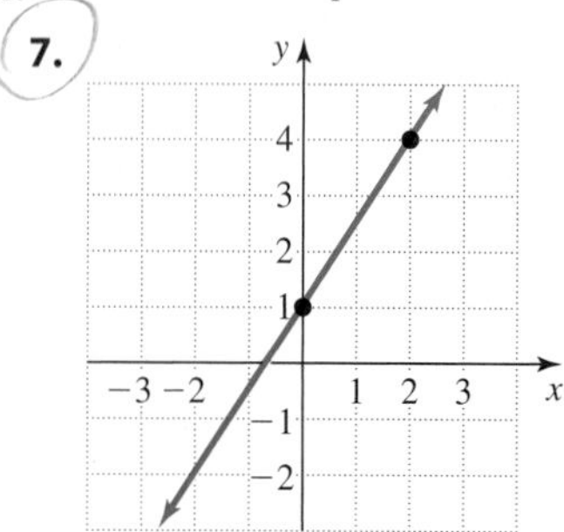

$y = \frac{3}{2}x + 1$

8.

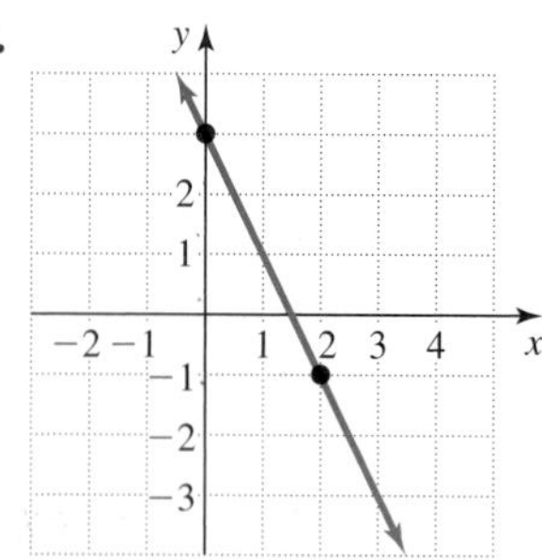

$y = -2x + 3$

9.

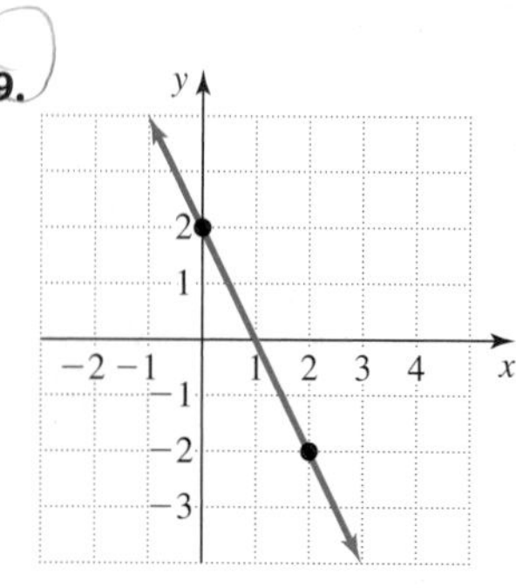

$y = -2x + 2$

10.

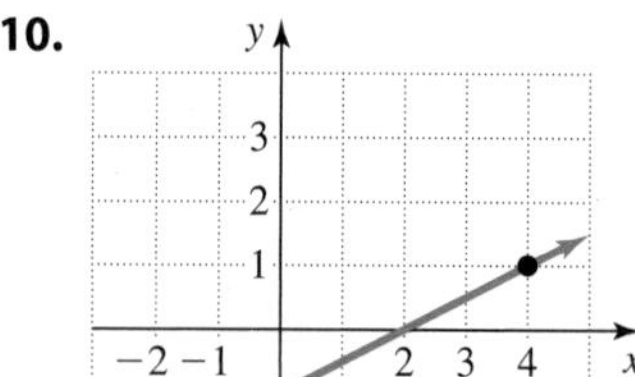

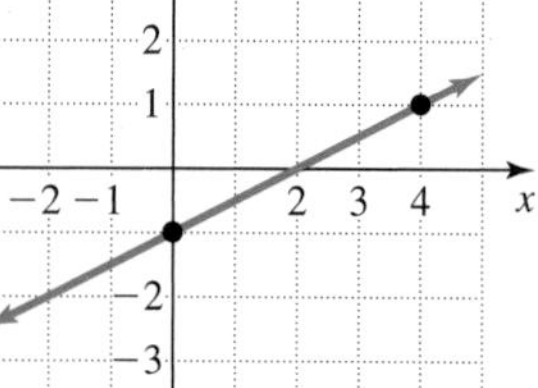

$y = \frac{1}{2}x - 1$

11.

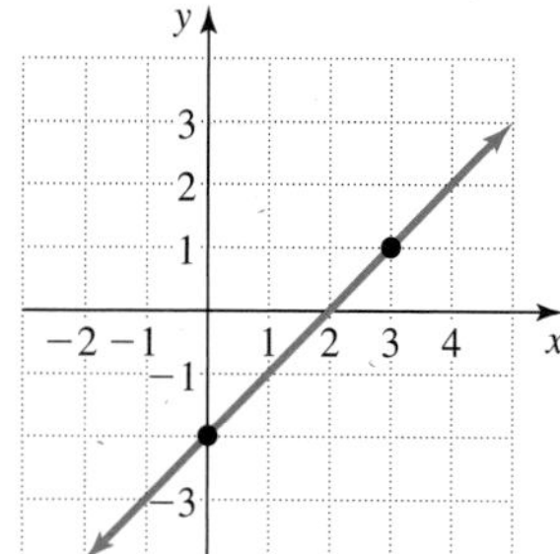

$y = x - 2$

12.

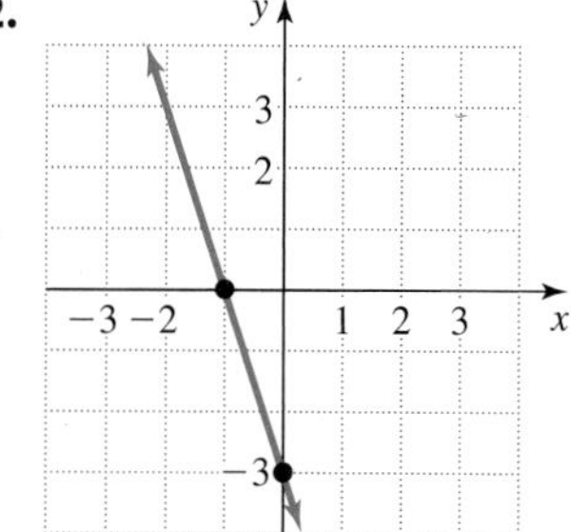

$y = -3x - 3$

13.

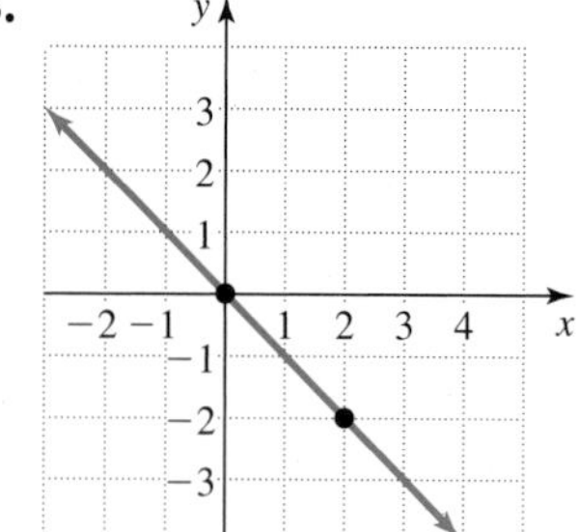

$y = -x$

14.

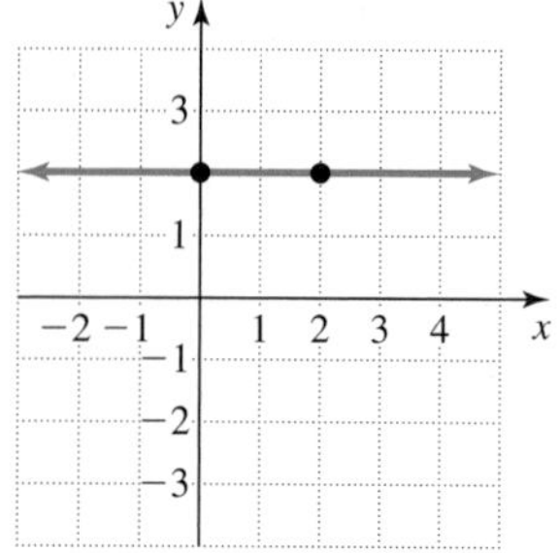

$y = 2$

15.

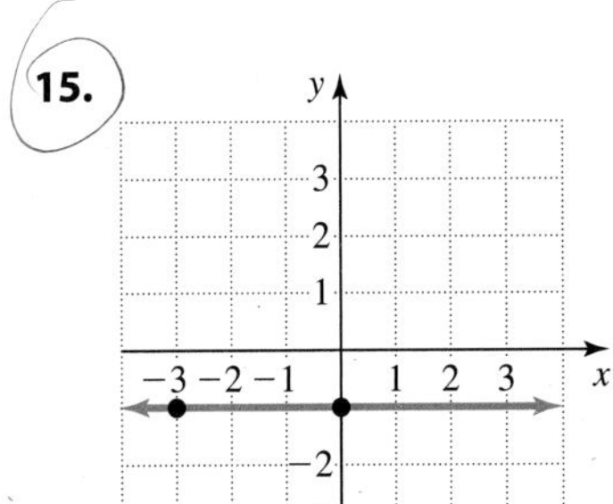

$y = -1$

16.

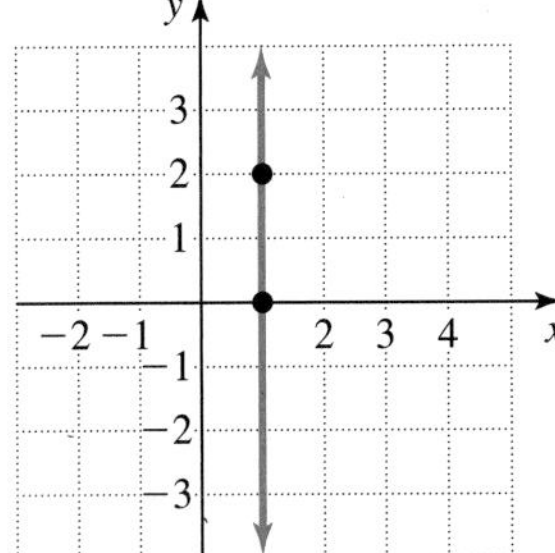

$x = 1$

17.

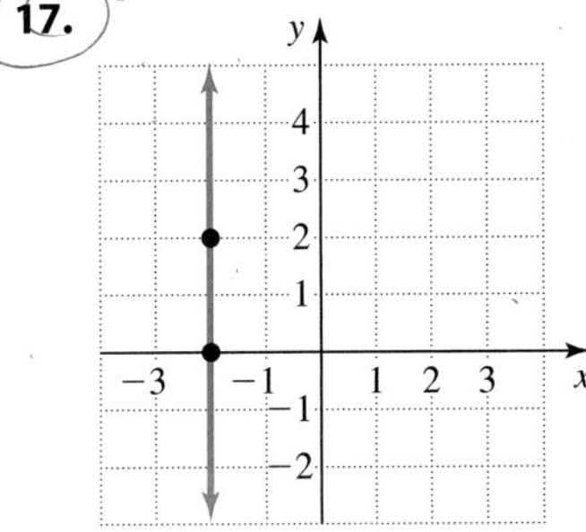

$x = -2$

18.

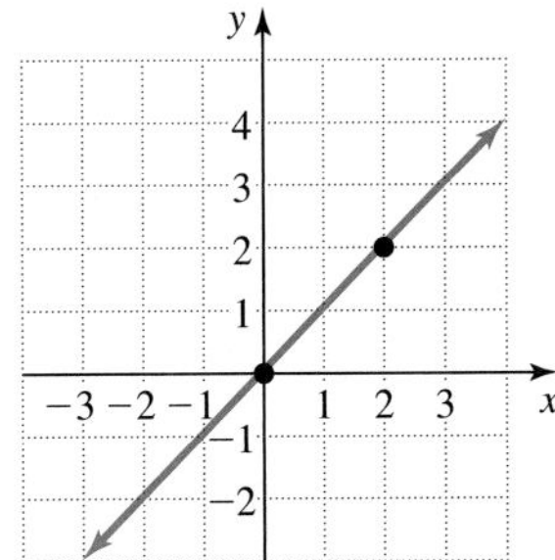

$y = x$

Find the slope and y-intercept for each line that has a slope and y-intercept. See Example 2.

19. $y = 3x - 9$
$3, (0, -9)$

20. $y = -5x + 4$
$-5, (0, 4)$

21. $y = -\frac{1}{2}x + 3$
$-\frac{1}{2}, (0, 3)$

22. $y = \frac{1}{4}x + 2$
$\frac{1}{4}, (0, 2)$

23. $y = 4$
$0, (0, 4)$

24. $y = -5$
$0, (0, -5)$

25. $y = -3x$
$-3, (0, 0)$

26. $y = 2x$
$2, (0, 0)$

27. $x + y = 5$
$-1, (0, 5)$

28. $x - y = 4$
$1, (0, -4)$

29. $x - 2y = 4$
$\frac{1}{2}, (0, -2)$

30. $x + 2y = 3$
$-\frac{1}{2}, \left(0, \frac{3}{2}\right)$

31. $2x - 5y = 10$
$\frac{2}{5}, (0, -2)$

32. $2x + 3y = 9$
$-\frac{2}{3}, (0, 3)$

33. $2x - y + 3 = 0$
$2, (0, 3)$

34. $3x - 4y - 8 = 0$
$\frac{3}{4}, (0, -2)$

35. $x = -3$ Undefined slope, no *y*-intercept

36. $\frac{2}{3}x = 4$ Undefined slope, no *y*-intercept

Write each equation in standard form using only integers. See Example 3.

37. $y = -x + 2$
$x + y = 2$

38. $y = 3x - 5$
$3x - y = 5$

39. $y = \frac{1}{2}x + 3$
$x - 2y = -6$

40. $y = \frac{2}{3}x - 4$
$2x - 3y = 12$

41. $y = \frac{3}{2}x - \frac{1}{3}$
$9x - 6y = 2$

42. $y = \frac{4}{5}x + \frac{2}{3}$
$12x - 15y = -10$

43. $y = -\frac{3}{5}x + \frac{7}{10}$
$6x + 10y = 7$

44. $y = -\frac{2}{3}x - \frac{5}{6}$
$4x + 6y = -5$

45. $\frac{3}{5}x + 6 = 0$
$x = -10$

46. $\frac{1}{2}x - 9 = 0$
$x = 18$

47. $\frac{3}{4}y = \frac{5}{2}$
$3y = 10$

48. $\frac{2}{3}y = \frac{1}{9}$
$6y = 1$

49. $\frac{x}{2} = \frac{3y}{5}$
$5x - 6y = 0$

50. $\frac{x}{8} = -\frac{4y}{5}$
$5x + 32y = 0$

51. $y = 0.02x + 0.5$
$x - 50y = -25$

52. $0.2x = 0.03y - 0.1$
$20x - 3y = -10$

Draw the graph of each line using its y-intercept and its slope. See Examples 4 and 5.

53. $y = 2x - 1$

54. $y = 3x - 2$

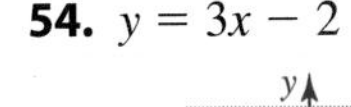

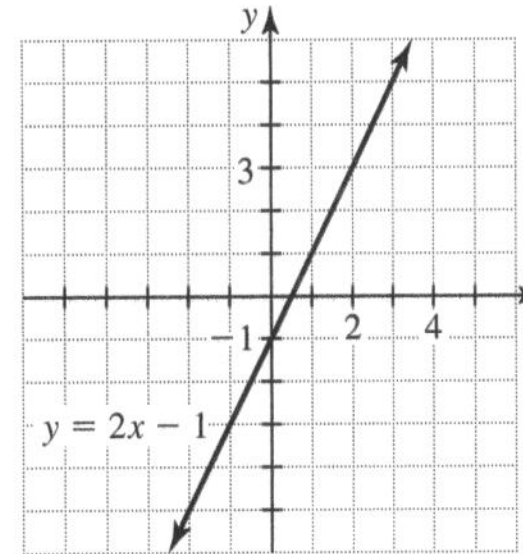

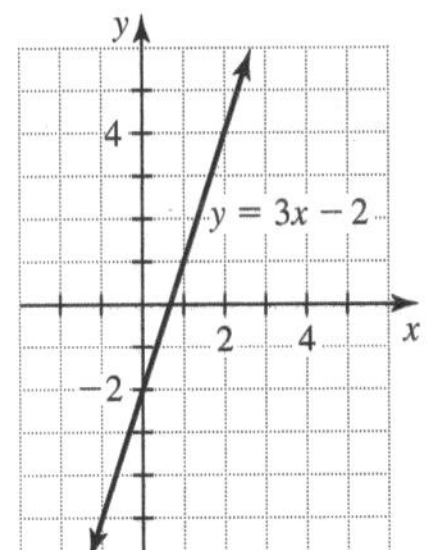

55. $y = -3x + 5$

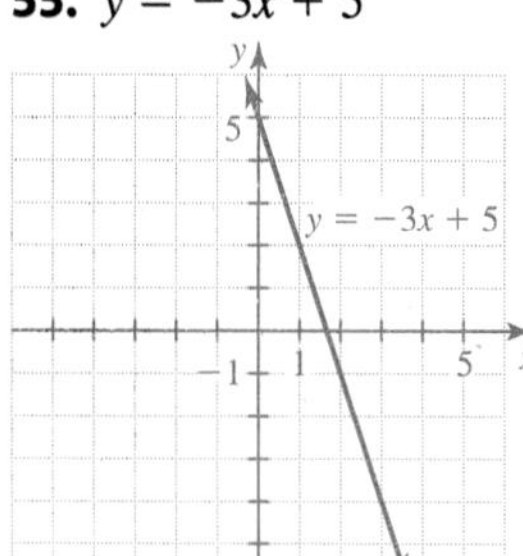

56. $y = -4x + 1$

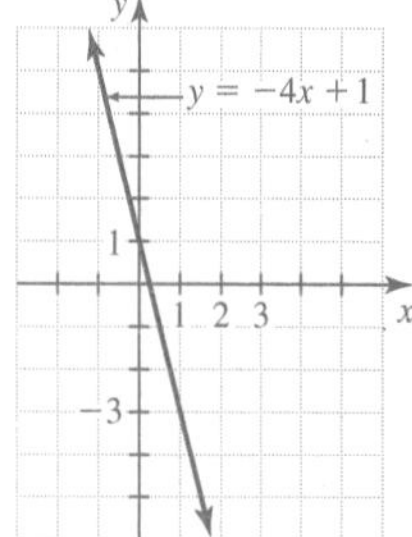

57. $y = \frac{3}{4}x - 2$

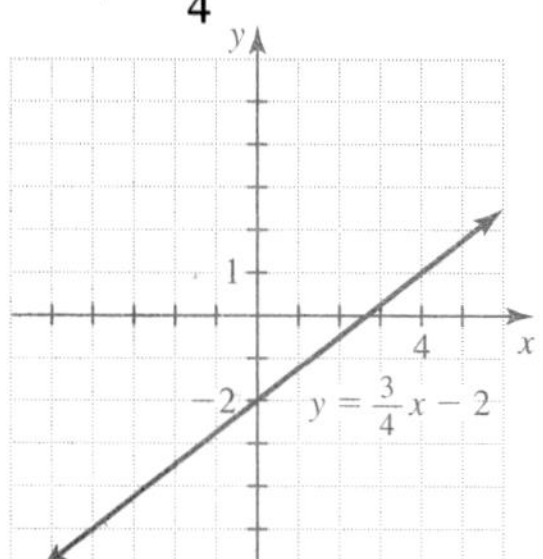

58. $y = \frac{3}{2}x - 4$

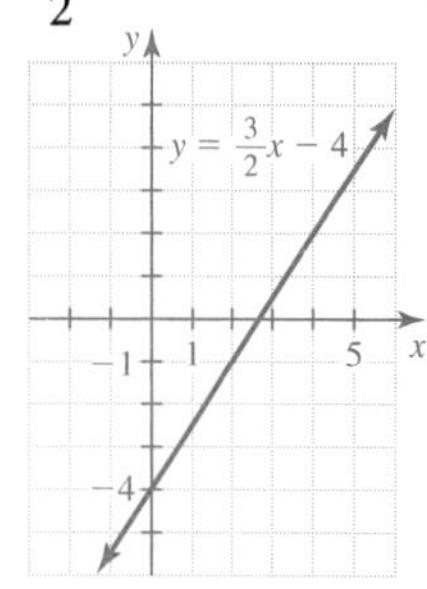

59. $2y + x = 0$

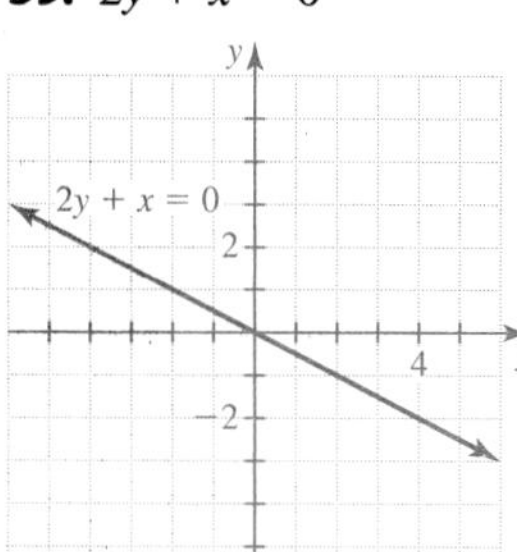

60. $2x + y = 0$

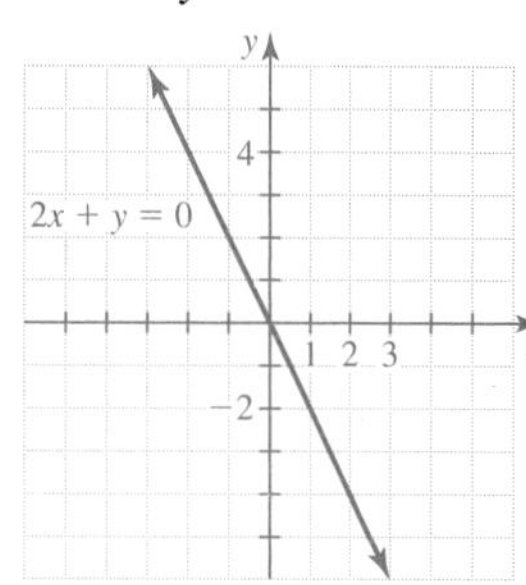

61. $3x - 2y = 10$

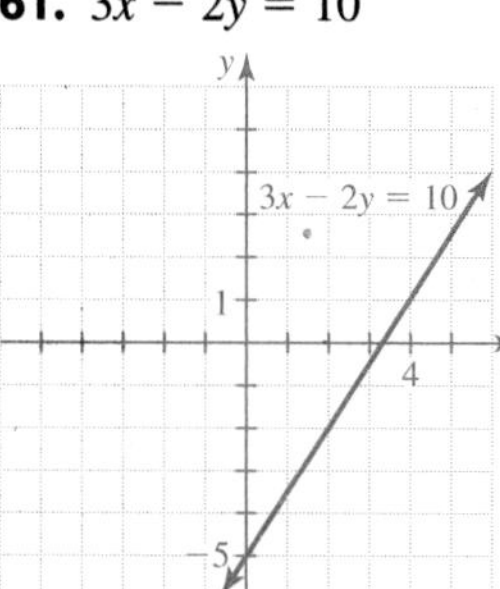

62. $4x + 3y = 9$

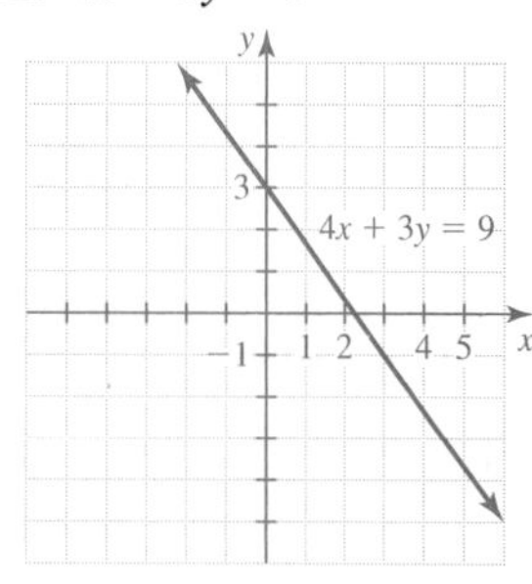

63. $4y + x = 8$

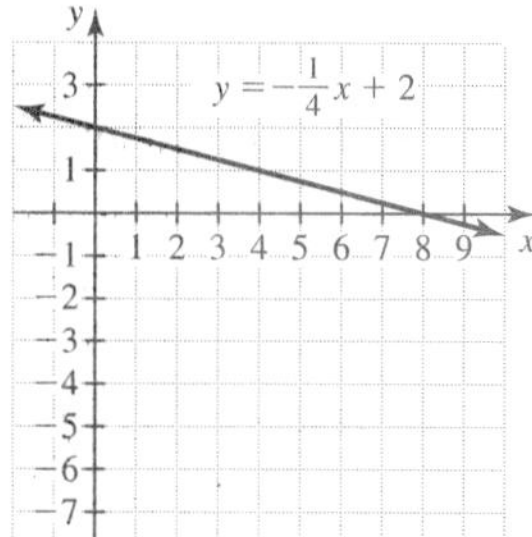

64. $y + 4x = 8$

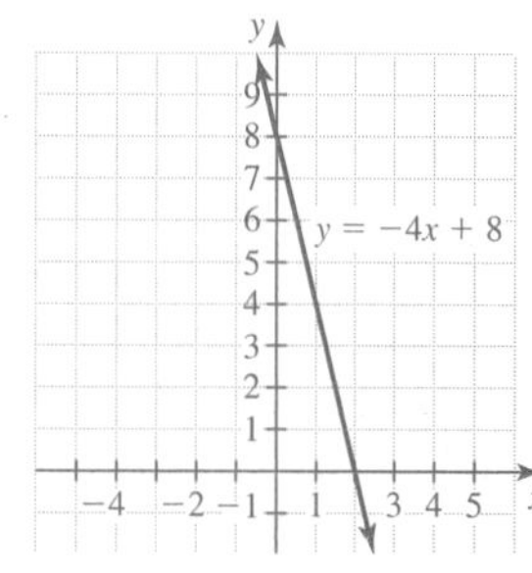

65. $y - 2 = 0$

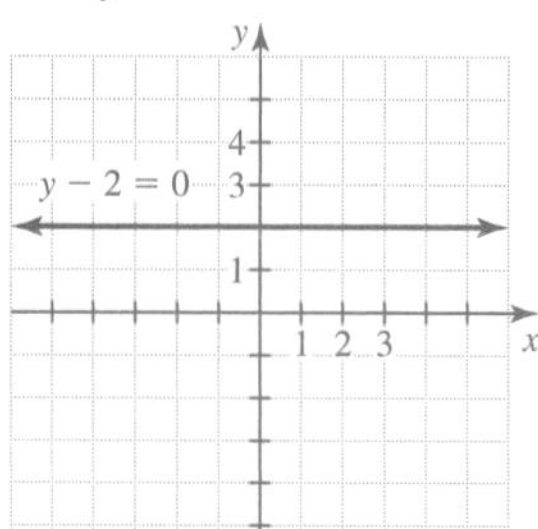

66. $y + 5 = 0$

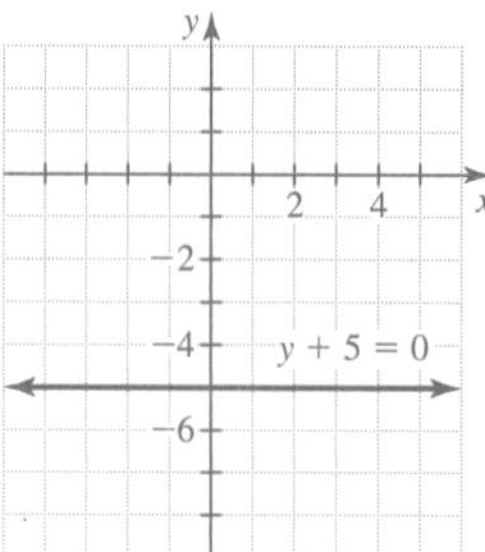

In each case determine whether the lines are parallel, perpendicular, or neither.

67. $y = 3x - 4$
$y = 3x - 9$
Parallel

68. $y = -5x + 7$
$y = \frac{1}{5}x - 6$
Perpendicular

69. $y = 2x - 1$
$y = -2x + 1$
Neither

70. $y = x + 7$
$y = -x + 2$
Perpendicular

71. $y = 3$
$y = -\frac{1}{3}$
Parallel

72. $y = 3x + 2$
$y = \frac{1}{3}x - 4$
Neither

73. $y = -4x + 1$
$y = \frac{1}{4}x - 5$
Perpendicular

74. $y = \frac{1}{3}x + \frac{1}{2}$
$y = \frac{1}{3}x - 2$
Parallel

Write an equation in slope-intercept form, if possible, for each line. See Example 6.

75. The line through $(0, -4)$ with slope $\frac{1}{2}$ $y = \frac{1}{2}x - 4$

76. The line through $(0, 4)$ with slope $-\frac{1}{2}$ $y = -\frac{1}{2}x + 4$

77. The line through $(0, 3)$ that is parallel to the line $y = 2x - 1$ $y = 2x + 3$

78. The line through $(0, -2)$ that is parallel to the line $y = -\frac{1}{3}x + 6$ $y = -\frac{1}{3}x - 2$

79. The line through $(0, 6)$ that is perpendicular to the line $y = 3x - 5$ $y = -\frac{1}{3}x + 6$

80. The line through $(0, -1)$ that is perpendicular to the line $y = x$ $y = -x - 1$

81. The line with y-intercept $(0, 3)$ that is parallel to the line $2x + y = 5$ $y = -2x + 3$

82. The line through the origin that is parallel to the line $y - 3x = -3$ $y = 3x$

83. The line through $(2, 3)$ that runs parallel to the x-axis $y = 3$

84. The line through $(-3, 5)$ that runs parallel to the y-axis $x = -3$

85. The line through (0, 4) that is perpendicular to $2x - 3y = 6$ $y = -\frac{3}{2}x + 4$

86. The line through (0, -1) that is perpendicular to $2x - 5y = 10$ $y = -\frac{5}{2}x - 1$

87. The line through (0, 4) and (5, 0) $y = -\frac{4}{5}x + 4$

88. The line through (0, -3) and (4, 0) $y = \frac{3}{4}x - 3$

Solve each problem. See Example 7.

89. ***Marginal cost.*** A manufacturer plans to spend \$150,000 on research and development for a new lawn mower and then \$200 to manufacture each mower. The formula $C = 200n + 150{,}000$ gives the cost in dollars of n mowers. What is the cost of 5000 mowers? What is the cost of 5001 mowers? By how much did the one extra lawn mower increase the cost? (The increase in cost is called the *marginal cost* of the 5001st lawn mower.)
\$1,150,000, \$1,150,200, \$200

90. ***Marginal revenue.*** A defense attorney charges her client \$4000 plus \$120 per hour. The formula $R = 120n + 4000$ gives her revenue in dollars for n hours of work. What is her revenue for 100 hours of work? What is her revenue for 101 hours of work? By how much did the one extra hour of work increase the revenue? (The increase in revenue is called the *marginal revenue* for the 101st hour.)
\$16,000, \$16,120, \$120

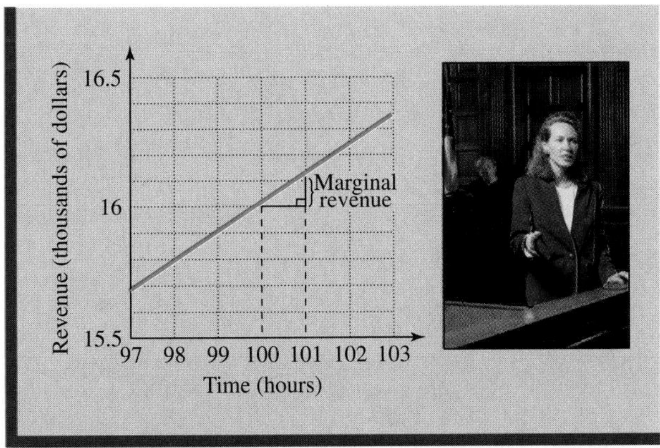

Figure for Exercise 90

91. ***In-house training.*** The accompanying graph shows the percentage of U.S. workers receiving training by their employers (Department of Labor, www.dol.gov). The percentage went from 5% in 1982 to 25% in 2002.

a) Find and interpret the slope of the line.
b) Write the equation of the line in slope-intercept form.
c) What is the meaning of the y-intercept?

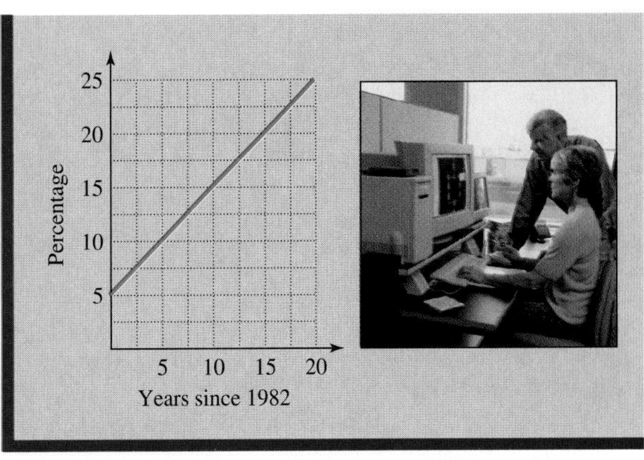

Figure for Exercise 91

d) Use your equation to predict the percentage that will be receiving training in 2010.

a) A slope of 1 means that the percentage of workers receiving training is going up 1% per year.
b) $y = x + 5$ where x is the number of years since 1982
c) The y-intercept (0, 5) means that 5% of the workers received training in 1982.
d) 33%

92. ***Single women.*** The percentage of women in the 20–24 age group who have never married went from 55% in 1970 to 73% in 2000 (Census Bureau, www.census.gov). Let 1970 be year 0 and 2000 be year 30.

a) Find and interpret the slope of the line through the points (0, 55) and (30, 73).
b) Find the equation of the line in part (a).
c) What is the meaning of the y-intercept?
d) Use the equation to predict the percentage in 2010.
e) If this trend continues, then in what year will the percentage of women in the 20–24 age group who have never married reach 100%?

a) A slope of 0.6 means that the percentage is increasing by 0.6% per year.
b) $y = 0.6x + 55$
c) The y-intercept (0, 55) means that in 1970 55% of the women between 20 and 24 had never been married.
d) 79%
e) 2045

93. ***Pansies and snapdragons.*** A nursery manager plans to spend \$100 on 6-packs of pansies at 50 cents per pack and snapdragons at 25 cents per pack. The equation $0.50x + 0.25y = 100$ can be used to model this situation.

a) What do x and y represent?
$x =$ the number of packs of pansies, $y =$ the number of packs of snapdragons

b) Graph the equation.

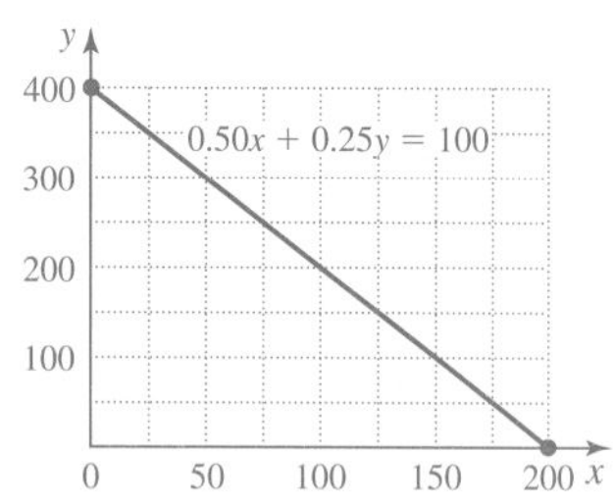

c) Write the equation in slope-intercept form.
$y = -2x + 400$

d) What is the slope of the line? -2

e) What does the slope tell you?
If the number of packs of pansies goes up by 1, then the number of packs of snapdragons goes down by 2.

94. ***Pens and pencils.*** A bookstore manager plans to spend \$60 on pens at 30 cents each and pencils at 10 cents each. The equation $0.10x + 0.30y = 60$ can be used to model this situation.

a) What do x and y represent?
x = the number of pencils, y = the number of pens

b) Graph the equation.

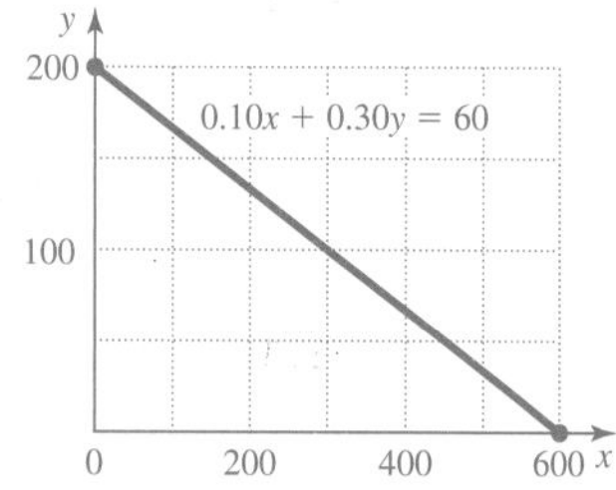

c) Write the equation in slope-intercept form.
$y = -\frac{1}{3}x + 200$

d) What is the slope of the line?
$-\frac{1}{3}$

e) What does the slope tell you?
If the number of pencils increases by 3, then the number of pens goes down by 1.

Graphing Calculator Exercises

Graph each pair of straight lines on your graphing calculator using a viewing window that makes the lines look perpendicular. Answers may vary.

95. $y = 12x - 100,\ y = -\frac{1}{12}x + 50$

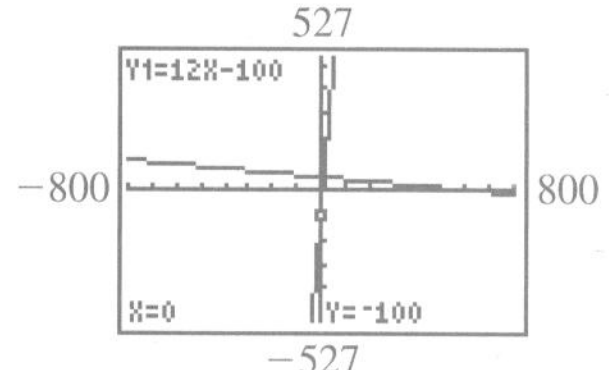

96. $2x - 3y = 300,\ 3x + 2y = -60$

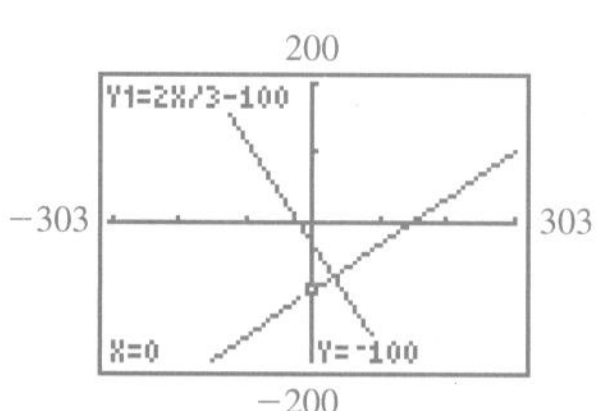

3.4 The Point-Slope Form

In this Section

- **Point-Slope Form**
- **Parallel Lines**
- **Perpendicular Lines**
- **Applications**

In Section 3.3 we wrote the equation of a line given its slope and *y*-intercept. In this section you will learn to write the equation of a line given the slope and *any* other point on the line.

Point-Slope Form

Consider a line through the point (4, 1) with slope $\frac{2}{3}$ as shown in Fig. 3.28. Because the slope can be found by using any two points on the line, we use (4, 1) and an arbitrary

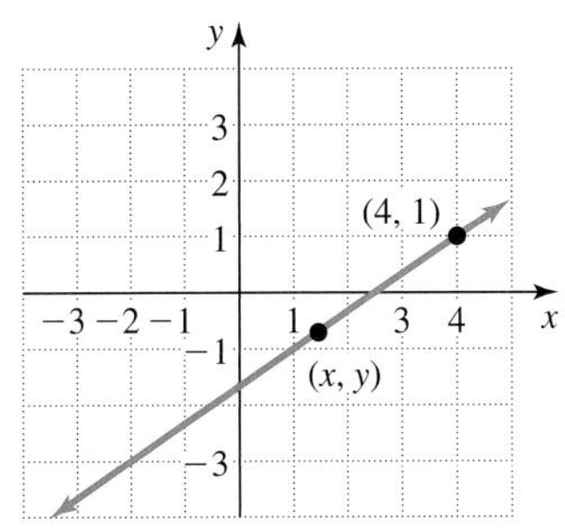

Figure 3.28

Helpful Hint

If a point (x, y) is on a line with slope m through (x_1, y_1), then

$$\frac{y - y_1}{x - x_1} = m.$$

Multiplying each side of this equation by $x - x_1$ gives us the point-slope form.

point (x, y) in the formula for slope:

$$\frac{y_2 - y_1}{x_2 - x_1} = m \quad \text{Slope formula}$$

$$\frac{y - 1}{x - 4} = \frac{2}{3} \quad \text{Let } m = \tfrac{2}{3}, (x_1, y_1) = (4, 1), \text{ and } (x_2, y_2) = (x, y).$$

$$y - 1 = \frac{2}{3}(x - 4) \quad \text{Multiply each side by } x - 4.$$

Note how the coordinates of the point (4, 1) and the slope $\frac{2}{3}$ appear in the above equation. We can use the same procedure to get the equation of any line given one point on the line and the slope. The resulting equation is called the **point-slope form** of the equation of the line.

Point-Slope Form

The equation of the line through the point (x_1, y_1) with slope m is

$$y - y_1 = m(x - x_1).$$

EXAMPLE 1

Writing an equation given a point and a slope

Find the equation of the line through $(-2, 3)$ with slope $\frac{1}{2}$, and write it in slope-intercept form.

Solution

Because we know a point and the slope, we can use the point-slope form:

$$y - y_1 = m(x - x_1) \quad \text{Point-slope form}$$

$$y - 3 = \frac{1}{2}[x - (-2)] \quad \text{Substitute } m = \tfrac{1}{2} \text{ and } (x_1, y_1) = (-2, 3).$$

$$y - 3 = \frac{1}{2}(x + 2) \quad \text{Simplify.}$$

$$y - 3 = \frac{1}{2}x + 1 \quad \text{Distributive property}$$

$$y = \frac{1}{2}x + 4 \quad \text{Slope-intercept form}$$

Alternate Solution

Replace m by $\frac{1}{2}$, x by -2, and y by 3 in the slope-intercept form:

$$y = mx + b \quad \text{Slope-intercept form}$$

$$3 = \frac{1}{2}(-2) + b \quad \text{Substitute } m = \tfrac{1}{2} \text{ and } (x, y) = (-2, 3).$$

$$3 = -1 + b \quad \text{Simplify.}$$

$$4 = b$$

Since $b = 4$, we can write $y = \frac{1}{2}x + 4$.

Now do Exercises 7–22

Teaching Tip Have students practice some problems in class using both methods. Students usually resist knowing two methods.

The alternate solution to Example 1 is shown because many students have seen that method in the past. This does not mean that you should ignore the point-slope form. It is always good to know more than one method to accomplish a task. The good thing about using the point-slope form is that you immediately write down the equation and then you simplify it. In the alternate solution, the last thing you do is to write the equation.

The point-slope form can be used to find the equation of a line for *any* given point and slope. However, if the given point is the y-intercept, then it is simpler to use the slope-intercept form. Note that it is not necessary that the slope be given, because the slope can be found from any two points. So if we know two points on a line, then we can find the slope and use the slope with either one of the points in the point-slope form.

EXAMPLE 2

Writing an equation given two points

Find the equation of the line that contains the points $(-3, -2)$ and $(4, -1)$, and write it in standard form.

Solution

First find the slope using the two given points:

$$m = \frac{-2 - (-1)}{-3 - 4} = \frac{-1}{-7} = \frac{1}{7}$$

Now use one of the points, say $(-3, -2)$, and slope $\frac{1}{7}$ in the point-slope form:

$$y - y_1 = m(x - x_1) \qquad \text{Point-slope form}$$
$$y - (-2) = \frac{1}{7}[x - (-3)] \qquad \text{Substitute.}$$
$$y + 2 = \frac{1}{7}(x + 3) \qquad \text{Simplify.}$$
$$7(y + 2) = 7 \cdot \frac{1}{7}(x + 3) \qquad \text{Multiply each side by 7.}$$
$$7y + 14 = x + 3$$
$$7y = x - 11 \qquad \text{Subtract 14 from each side.}$$
$$-x + 7y = -11 \qquad \text{Subtract } x \text{ from each side.}$$
$$x - 7y = 11 \qquad \text{Multiply each side by } -1.$$

The equation in standard form is $x - 7y = 11$. Using the other given point, $(4, -1)$, would give the same final equation in standard form. Try it.

Now do Exercises 23-42

Calculator Close-Up

Graph $y = (x + 3)/7 - 2$ to see that the line goes through $(-3, -2)$ and $(4, -1)$.

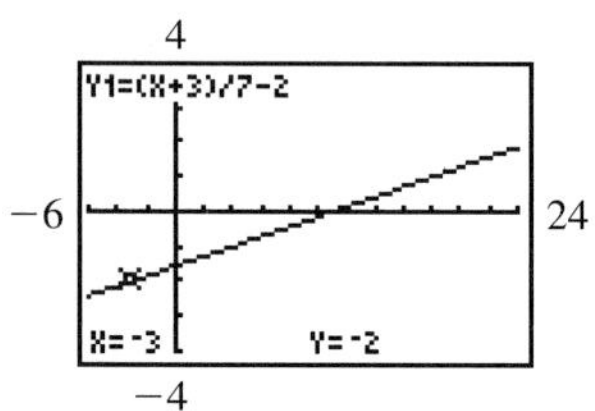

Note that the form of the equation does not matter on the calculator as long as it is solved for y.

Parallel Lines

In Section 3.2 you learned that parallel lines have the same slope. We will use this fact in Example 3.

EXAMPLE 3

Using point-slope form with parallel lines

Find the equation of each line. Write the answer in slope-intercept form.

a) The line through $(2, -1)$ that is parallel to $y = -3x + 9$

b) The line through $(3, 4)$ that is parallel to $2x - 3y = 6$

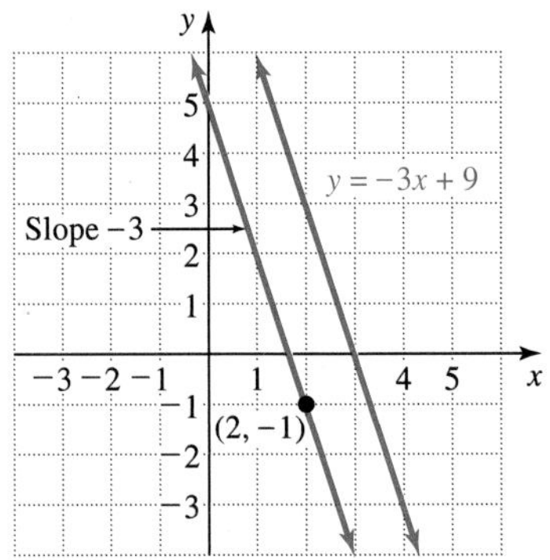

Figure 3.29

Solution

a) The slope of $y = -3x + 9$ and any line parallel to it is -3. See Fig. 3.29. Now use the point $(2, -1)$ and slope -3 in point-slope form:

$$\begin{aligned} y - y_1 &= m(x - x_1) && \text{Point-slope form} \\ y - (-1) &= -3(x - 2) && \text{Substitute.} \\ y + 1 &= -3x + 6 && \text{Simplify.} \\ y &= -3x + 5 && \text{Slope-intercept form} \end{aligned}$$

Since $-1 = -3(2) + 5$ is correct, the line $y = -3x + 5$ goes through $(2, -1)$. It is certainly parallel to $y = -3x + 9$. So $y = -3x + 5$ is the desired equation.

b) Solve $2x - 3y = 6$ for y to determine its slope:

$$\begin{aligned} 2x - 3y &= 6 \\ -3y &= -2x + 6 \\ y &= \frac{2}{3}x - 2 \end{aligned}$$

So the slope of $2x - 3y = 6$ and any line parallel to it is $\frac{2}{3}$. Now use the point $(3, 4)$ and slope $\frac{2}{3}$ in the point-slope form:

$$\begin{aligned} y - y_1 &= m(x - x_1) && \text{Point-slope form} \\ y - 4 &= \frac{2}{3}(x - 3) && \text{Substitute.} \\ y - 4 &= \frac{2}{3}x - 2 && \text{Simplify.} \\ y &= \frac{2}{3}x + 2 && \text{Slope-intercept form} \end{aligned}$$

Since $4 = \frac{2}{3}(3) + 2$ is correct, the line $y = \frac{2}{3}x + 2$ contains the point $(3, 4)$. Since $y = \frac{2}{3}x + 2$ and $y = \frac{2}{3}x - 2$ have the same slope, they are parallel. So the equation is $y = \frac{2}{3}x + 2$.

Now do Exercises 49–50

Teaching Tip Even though a graph is not required to solve this problem, it is a good idea for students to draw a graph showing both lines.

Perpendicular Lines

In Section 3.2 you learned that lines with slopes m and $-\frac{1}{m}$ (for $m \neq 0$) are perpendicular to each other. For example, the lines

$$y = -2x + 7 \qquad \text{and} \qquad y = \frac{1}{2}x - 8$$

are perpendicular to each other. In the next example we will write the equation of a line that is perpendicular to a given line and contains a given point.

EXAMPLE 4

Writing an equation given a point and a perpendicular line

Write the equation of the line that is perpendicular to $3x + 2y = 8$ and contains the point $(1, -3)$. Write the answer in slope-intercept form.

Solution

First graph $3x + 2y = 8$ and a line through $(1, -3)$ that is perpendicular to $3x + 2y = 8$ as shown in Fig. 3.30. The right angle symbol is used in the figure to indicate that the lines are perpendicular. Now write $3x + 2y = 8$ in slope-intercept form to determine its slope:

$$3x + 2y = 8$$
$$2y = -3x + 8$$
$$y = -\frac{3}{2}x + 4 \quad \text{Slope-intercept form}$$

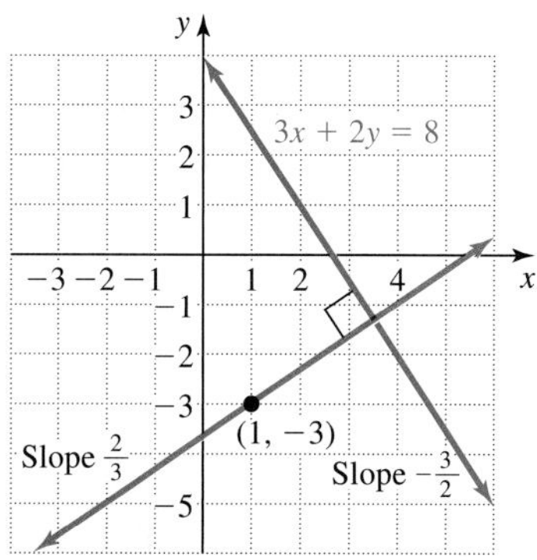

Figure 3.30

The slope of the given line is $-\frac{3}{2}$. The slope of any line perpendicular to it is $\frac{2}{3}$. Now we use the point-slope form with the point $(1, -3)$ and the slope $\frac{2}{3}$:

$$y - y_1 = m(x - x_1) \quad \text{Point-slope form}$$
$$y - (-3) = \frac{2}{3}(x - 1)$$
$$y + 3 = \frac{2}{3}x - \frac{2}{3}$$
$$y = \frac{2}{3}x - \frac{2}{3} - 3 \quad \text{Subtract 3 from each side.}$$
$$y = \frac{2}{3}x - \frac{11}{3} \quad \text{Slope-intercept form}$$

So $y = \frac{2}{3}x - \frac{11}{3}$ is the equation of the line that contains $(1, -3)$ and is perpendicular to $3x + 2y = 8$. Check that $(1, -3)$ satisfies $y = \frac{2}{3}x - \frac{11}{3}$.

Now do Exercises 47–48

Calculator Close-Up

Graph $y_1 = (2/3)x - 11/3$ and $y_2 = (-3/2)x + 4$ as shown:

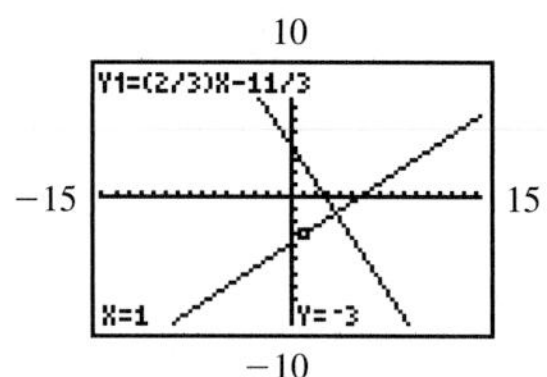

Because the lines look perpendicular and y_1 goes through $(1, -3)$, the graph supports the answer to Example 4.

Applications

We use the point-slope form to find the equation of a line given two points on the line. In Example 5 we use that same procedure to find a linear equation that relates two variables in an applied situation.

EXAMPLE 5

Writing a formula given two points

A contractor charges \$30 for installing 100 feet of pipe and \$120 for installing 500 feet of pipe. To determine the charge he uses a linear equation that gives the charge C in terms of the length L. Find the equation and find the charge for installing 240 feet of pipe.

Teaching Tip Students have trouble getting the right numbers on top in the slope formula here. Deciding what comes first and writing the ordered pairs (100, 30) and (500, 120) will clear this up. Of course reversing everything will also give the correct answer.

Solution

Because C is determined from L, we let C take the place of the dependent variable y and let L take the place of the independent variable x. So the ordered pairs are in the form (L, C). We can use the slope formula to find the slope of the line through the two points (100, 30) and (500, 120) shown in Fig. 3.31.

$$m = \frac{120 - 30}{500 - 100} = \frac{90}{400} = \frac{9}{40}$$

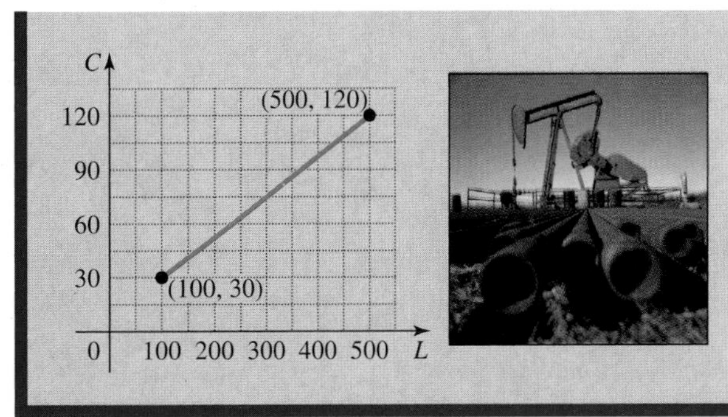

Figure 3.31

Now we use the point-slope form with the point (100, 30) and slope $\frac{9}{40}$:

$$y - y_1 = m(x - x_1)$$

$$C - 30 = \frac{9}{40}(L - 100)$$

$$C - 30 = \frac{9}{40}L - \frac{45}{2}$$

$$C = \frac{9}{40}L - \frac{45}{2} + 30$$

$$C = \frac{9}{40}L + \frac{15}{2}$$

Note that $C = \frac{9}{40}L + \frac{15}{2}$ means that the charge is $\frac{9}{40}$ dollars/foot plus a fixed charge of $\frac{15}{2}$ dollars (or \$7.50). We can now find C when $L = 240$:

$$C = \frac{9}{40} \cdot 240 + \frac{15}{2}$$

$$C = 54 + 7.5$$

$$C = 61.5$$

The charge for installing 240 feet of pipe is \$61.50.

Now do Exercises 77–92

Study Tip

When working a test, scan the problems and pick out the ones that are the easiest for you. Do them first. Save the harder problems till last.

Warm-Ups

True or false? Explain your answer.

1. The formula $y = m(x - x_1)$ is the point-slope form for a line. False
2. It is impossible to find the equation of a line through (2, 5) and (−3, 1). False
3. The point-slope form will not work for the line through (3, 4) and (3, 6). True
4. The equation of the line through the origin with slope 1 is $y = x$. True
5. The slope of the line $5x + y = 4$ is 5. False
6. The slope of any line perpendicular to the line $y = 4x - 3$ is $-\frac{1}{4}$. True
7. The slope of any line parallel to the line $x + y = 1$ is −1. True
8. The line $2x - y = -1$ goes through the point (−2, −3). True
9. The lines $2x + y = 4$ and $y = -2x + 7$ are parallel. True
10. The equation of the line through (0, 0) perpendicular to $y = x$ is $y = -x$. True

3.4 Exercises

Boost your GRADE at mathzone.com!

MathZone

- Practice Problems
- Self-Tests
- Videos
- Net Tutor
- e-Professors

Reading and Writing *After reading this section, write out the answers to these questions. Use complete sentences.*

1. What is the point-slope form for the equation of a line?
   Point-slope form is $y - y_1 = m(x - x_1)$.
2. For what is the point-slope form used?
   If we know any point and the slope of a line we can use point-slope form to write the equation.
3. What is the procedure for finding the equation of a line when given two points on the line?
   If you know two points on a line, find the slope. Then use it along with either point in point-slope form to write the equation of the line.
4. How can you find the slope of a line when given the equation of the line?
   Rewrite any equation in slope-intercept form to find the slope of the line.
5. What is the relationship between the slopes of parallel lines?
   Nonvertical parallel lines have equal slopes.
6. What is the relationship between the slopes of perpendicular lines?
   If lines with slopes m_1 and m_2 are perpendicular, then $m_1 = -\frac{1}{m_2}$.

Write each equation in slope-intercept form. See Example 1.

7. $y - 1 = 5(x + 2)$ $\quad y = 5x + 11$
8. $y + 3 = -3(x - 6)$ $\quad y = -3x + 15$
9. $3x - 4y = 80$ $\quad y = \frac{3}{4}x - 20$
10. $2x + 3y = 90$ $\quad y = -\frac{2}{3}x + 30$
11. $y - \frac{1}{2} = \frac{2}{3}\left(x - \frac{1}{4}\right)$ $\quad y = \frac{2}{3}x + \frac{1}{3}$
12. $y + \frac{2}{3} = -\frac{1}{2}\left(x - \frac{2}{5}\right)$ $\quad y = -\frac{1}{2}x - \frac{7}{15}$

Find the equation of the line that goes through the given point and has the given slope. Write the answer in slope-intercept form. See Example 1.

13. (1, 2), 3
$y = 3x - 1$

14. (2, 5), 4
$y = 4x - 3$

15. (2, 4), $\frac{1}{2}$
$y = \frac{1}{2}x + 3$

16. (4, 6), $\frac{1}{2}$
$y = \frac{1}{2}x + 4$

17. (2, 3), $\frac{1}{3}$
$y = \frac{1}{3}x + \frac{7}{3}$

18. (1, 4), $\frac{1}{4}$
$y = \frac{1}{4}x + \frac{15}{4}$

19. (−2, 5), $-\frac{1}{2}$
$y = -\frac{1}{2}x + 4$

20. (−3, 1), $-\frac{1}{3}$
$y = -\frac{1}{3}x$

21. (−1, −7), −6
$y = -6x - 13$

22. (−1, −5), −8
$y = -8x - 13$

Write each equation in standard form using only integers. See Example 2.

23. $y - 3 = 2(x - 5)$
$2x - y = 7$

24. $y + 2 = -3(x - 1)$
$3x + y = 1$

25. $y = \frac{1}{2}x - 3$
$x - 2y = 6$

26. $y = \frac{1}{3}x + 5$
$x - 3y = -15$

27. $y - 2 = \frac{2}{3}(x - 4)$
$2x - 3y = 2$

28. $y + 1 = \frac{3}{2}(x + 4)$
$3x - 2y = -10$

Find the equation of the line through each given pair of points. Write the answer in standard form using only integers. See Example 2.

29. (1, 3), (2, 5)
$2x - y = -1$

30. (2, 5), (3, 9)
$4x - y = 3$

31. (1, 1), (2, 2)
$x - y = 0$

32. (−1, 1), (1, −1)
$x + y = 0$

33. (1, 2), (5, 8)
$3x - 2y = -1$

34. (3, 5), (8, 15)
$2x - y = 1$

35. (−2, −1), (3, −4)
$3x + 5y = -11$

36. (−1, −3), (2, −1)
$2x - 3y = 7$

37. (−2, 0), (0, 2)
$x - y = -2$

38. (0, 3), (5, 0)
$3x + 5y = 15$

39. (2, 4), (2, 6)
$x = 2$

40. (−3, 5), (−3, −1)
$x = -3$

41. (−3, 9), (3, 9)
$y = 9$

42. (2, 5), (4, 5)
$y = 5$

The lines in each figure are perpendicular. Find the equation (in slope-intercept form) for the solid line.

43.
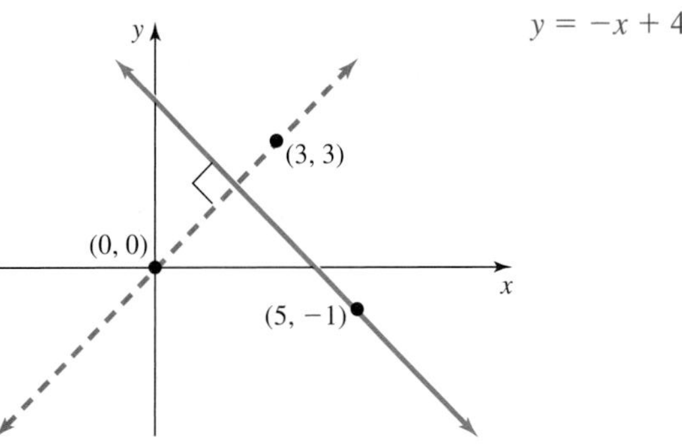

$y = -x + 4$

44.
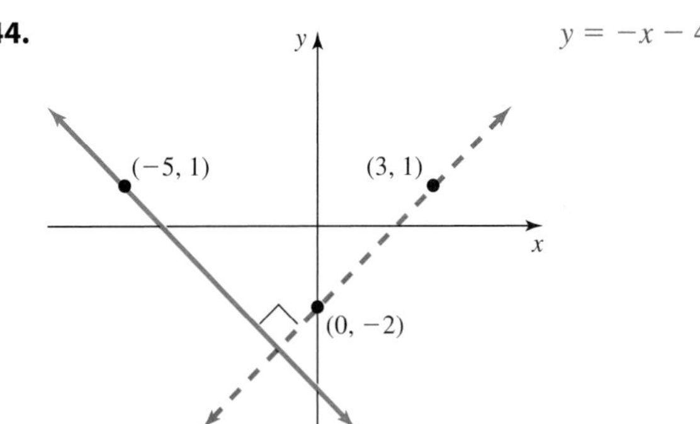

$y = -x - 4$

45.
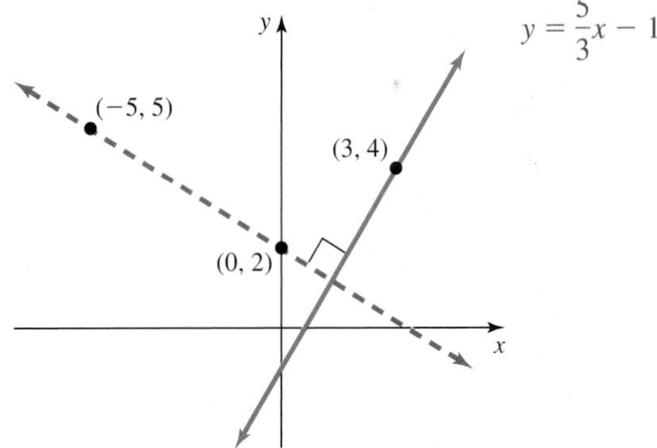

$y = \frac{5}{3}x - 1$

46.
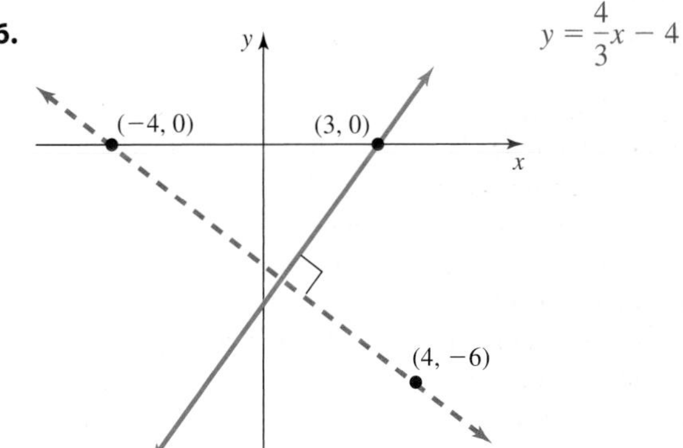

$y = \frac{4}{3}x - 4$

Find the equation of each line. Write each answer in slope-intercept form. See Examples 3 and 4.

47. The line contains the point (3, 4) and is perpendicular to $y = 3x - 1$. $y = -\frac{1}{3}x + 5$

48. The line contains the point (−2, 3) and is perpendicular to $y = 2x + 7$. $y = -\frac{1}{2}x + 2$

49. The line is parallel to $y = x - 9$ and goes through the point (7, 10). $y = x + 3$

50. The line is parallel to $y = -x + 5$ and goes through the point (−3, 6). $y = -x + 3$

51. The line is perpendicular to $3x - 2y = 10$ and passes through the point (1, 1). $y = -\frac{2}{3}x + \frac{5}{3}$

52. The line is perpendicular to $x - 5y = 4$ and passes through the point (−1, 1). $y = -5x - 4$

53. The line is parallel to $2x + y = 8$ and contains the point (−1, −3). $y = -2x - 5$

54. The line is parallel to $-3x + 2y = 9$ and contains the point (−2, 1). $y = \frac{3}{2}x + 4$

55. The line goes through (−1, 2) and is perpendicular to $3x + y = 5$. $y = \frac{1}{3}x + \frac{7}{3}$

56. The line goes through (1, 2) and is perpendicular to $y = \frac{1}{2}x - 3$. $y = -2x + 4$

57. The line goes through (2, 3) and is parallel to $-2x + y = 6$. $y = 2x - 1$

58. The line goes through (1, 4) and is parallel to $x - 2y = 6$. $y = \frac{1}{2}x + \frac{7}{2}$

Find the equation of each line in the form $y = mx + b$ if possible.

59. The line through (3, 2) with slope 0 $y = 2$

60. The line through (3, 2) with undefined slope $x = 3$

61. The line through (3, 2) and the origin $y = \frac{2}{3}x$

62. The line through the origin that is perpendicular to $y = \frac{2}{3}x$ $y = -\frac{3}{2}x$

63. The line through the origin that is parallel to the line through (5, 0) and (0, 5) $y = -x$

64. The line through the origin that is perpendicular to the line through (−3, 0) and (0, −3) $y = x$

65. The line through (−30, 50) that is perpendicular to the line $x = 400$ $y = 50$

66. The line through (20, −40) that is parallel to the line $y = 6000$ $y = -40$

67. The line through (−5, −1) that is perpendicular to the line through (0, 0) and (3, 5) $y = -\frac{3}{5}x - 4$

68. The line through (3, 1) that is parallel to the line through (−3, −2) and (0, 0) $y = \frac{2}{3}x - 1$

For each line described here choose the correct equation from (a) through (h).

69. The line through (1, 3) and (2, 5) e

70. The line through (1, 3) and (5, 2) a

71. The line through (1, 3) with no x-intercept f

72. The line through (1, 3) with no y-intercept b

73. The line through (1, 3) with x-intercept (5, 0) h

74. The line through (1, 3) with y-intercept (0, −5) d

75. The line through (1, 3) with slope −2 g

76. The line through (1, 3) with slope $\frac{1}{2}$ c

a) $x + 4y = 13$ **b)** $x = 1$
c) $x - 2y = -5$ **d)** $y = 8x - 5$
e) $y = 2x + 1$ **f)** $y = 3$
g) $2x + y = 5$ **h)** $3x + 4y = 15$

Solve each problem. See Example 5.

77. ***Automated tellers.*** ATM volume reached 10.6 billion transactions in 1996 and 14.2 billion transactions in 2000 as shown in the accompanying graph. If 1996 is year 0 and 2000 is year 4, then the line goes through the points (0, 10.6) and (4, 14.2).

a) Find and interpret the slope of the line.
b) Write the equation of the line in slope-intercept form.
c) Use your equation from part (b) to predict the number of transactions at automated teller machines in 2010.

a) Slope 0.9 means that the number of ATM transactions is increasing by 0.9 billion per year.
b) $y = 0.9x + 10.6$ **c)** 23.2 billion

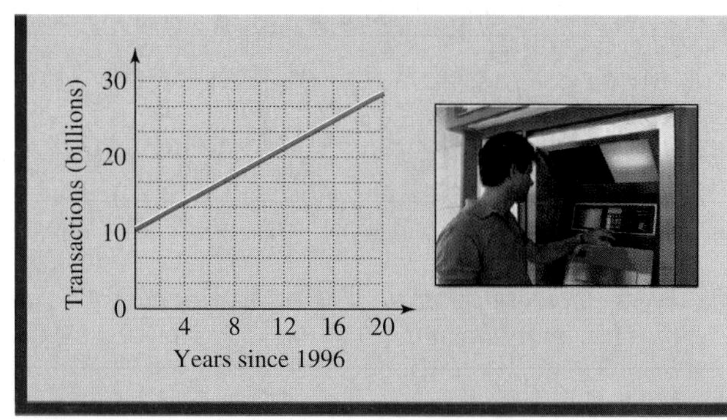

Figure for Exercise 77

78. ***Direct deposit.*** The percentage of workers receiving direct deposit of their paychecks went from 32% in 1994 to 60% in 2004 (www.directdeposit.com). Let 1994 be year 0 and 2004 be year 10.

a) Write the equation of the line through (0, 32) and (10, 60) to model the growth of direct deposit. $y = 2.8x + 32$
b) Use the graph on the next page to predict the year in which 100% of all workers will receive direct deposit of their paychecks. About 2018
c) Use the equation from part (a) to predict the year in which 100% of all workers will receive direct deposit. 2018

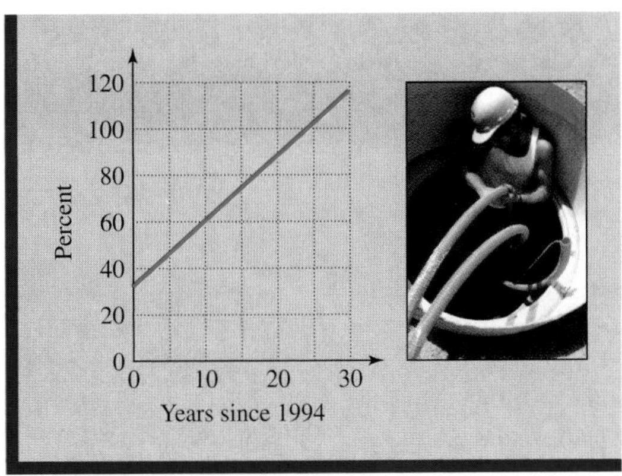

Figure for Exercise 78

79. ***Gross domestic product.*** The U.S. gross domestic product (GDP) per employed person increased from \$62.7 thousand in 1996 to \$71.6 thousand in 2002 (Bureau of Labor Statistics, www.bls.gov). Let 1996 be year 6 and 2002 be year 12.

a) Find the equation of the line through (6, 62.7) and (12, 71.6) to model the gross domestic product.
$y = 1.5x + 53.8$

b) What do x and y represent in your equation?
x = years since 1990, y = GDP in thousands of dollars

c) Use the equation to predict the GDP per employed person in 2010. \$83,800

d) Graph the equation.

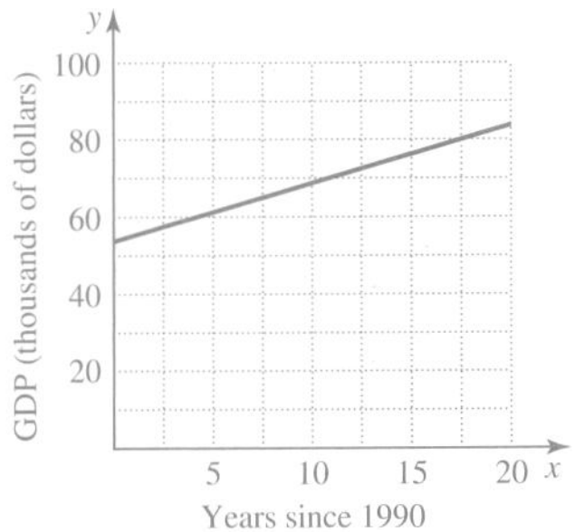

80. ***Age at first marriage.*** The median age at first marriage for females increased from 24.5 years in 1995 to 25.1 years in 2000 (U.S. Census Bureau, www.census.gov). Let 1995 be year 5 and 2000 be year 10.

a) Find the equation of the line through (5, 24.5) and (10, 25.1). $y = 0.12x + 23.9$

b) What do x and y represent in your equation?
x = the number of years since 1990, y = median age at first marriage

c) Interpret the slope of this line.
Median age increases 0.12 year each year or approximately 1 year in 8 years.

d) In what year will the median age be 30. 2041

e) Graph the equation.

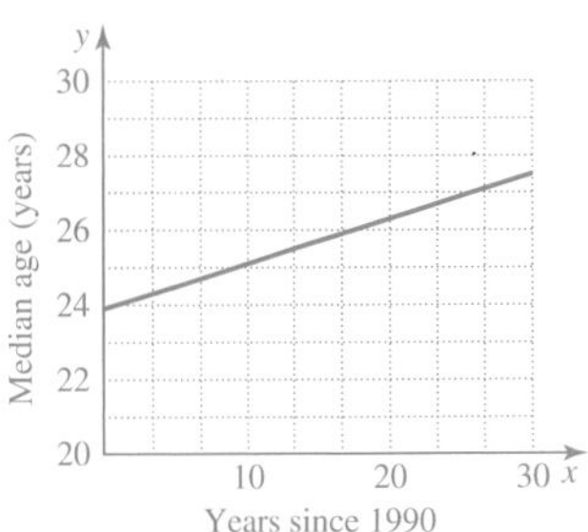

81. ***Plumbing charges.*** Pete the plumber worked 2 hours at Millie's house and charged her \$70. He then worked 4 hours at Rosalee's house and charged her \$110. To determine the amount he charges Pete uses a linear equation that gives the charge C in terms of the number of hours worked n. Find the equation and find the charge for 7 hours at Fred's house. $C = 20n + 30$, \$170

82. ***Interior angles.*** The sum of the measures of the interior angles of a triangle is 180°. The sum of the measures of the interior angles of a square is 360°. Let S represent the sum of the measures of the interior angles of a polygon and n represent the number of sides of the polygon. There is a linear equation that gives S in terms of n. Find the equation and find the sum of the measures of the interior angles of the stop sign shown in the accompanying figure.
$S = 180n - 360$, 1080°

STOP

Figure for Exercise 82

83. ***Shoe sizes.*** If a child's foot is 7.75 inches long, then the child wears a size 13 shoe. If a child's foot is 5.75 inches long, then the child wears a size 7 shoe. Let S represent the shoe size and L represent the length of the foot in inches. There is a linear equation that gives S in terms of L. Find the equation and find the shoe size for a child with a 6.25-inch foot. See the figure on the next page.
$S = 3L - \frac{41}{4}$, 8.5

84. ***Celsius to Fahrenheit.*** Water freezes at 0°C or 32°F and boils at 100°C or 212°F. There is a linear equation that expresses the number of degrees Fahrenheit (F) in terms

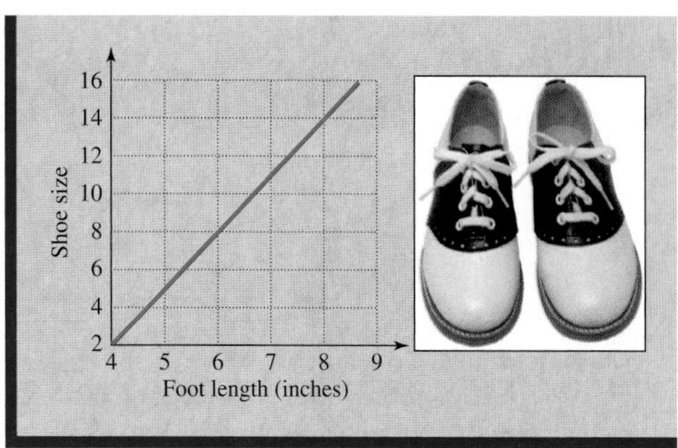

Figure for Exercise 83

of the number of degrees Celsius (C). Find the equation and find the Fahrenheit temperature when the Celsius temperature is 45°.
$F = \frac{9}{5}C + 32$, 113°F

85. ***Velocity of a projectile.*** A ball is thrown downward from the top of a tall building. Its velocity is 42 feet per second after 1 second and 74 feet per second after 2 seconds. There is a linear equation that expresses the velocity v in terms of the time t. Find the equation and find the velocity after 3.5 seconds.
$v = 32t + 10$, 122 ft/sec

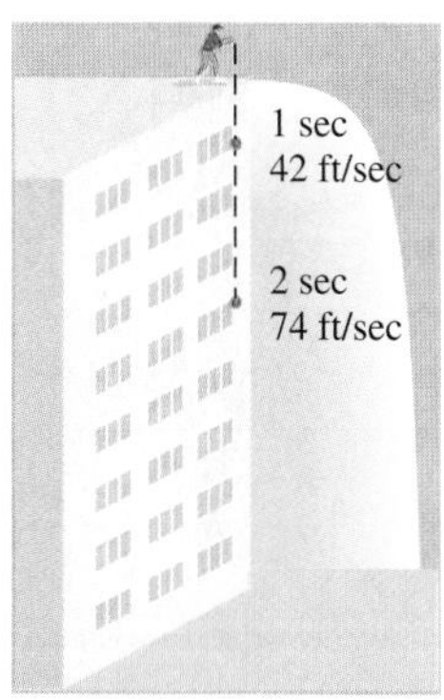

Figure for Exercise 85

86. ***Natural gas.*** The cost of 1000 cubic feet of natural gas is \$39 and the cost of 3000 cubic feet is \$99. There is a linear equation that expresses the cost C in terms of the number of cubic feet n. Find the equation and find the cost of 2400 cubic feet of natural gas.
$C = 0.03n + 9$, \$81

87. ***Expansion joint.*** When the temperature is 90°F the width of an expansion joint on a bridge is 0.75 inch. When the temperature is 30°F the width is 1.25 inches. There is a linear equation that expresses the width w in terms of the temperature t.

a) Find the equation.
b) What is the width when the temperature is 80°F?
c) What is the temperature when the width is 1 inch?

a) $w = -\frac{1}{120}t + \frac{3}{2}$ b) $\frac{5}{6}$ inch c) 60°F

88. ***Perimeter of a rectangle.*** A rectangle has a fixed width and a variable length. Let P represent the perimeter and L represent the length. $P = 28$ inches when $L = 6.5$ inches and $P = 36$ inches when $L = 10.5$ inches. There is a linear equation that expresses P in terms of L.

a) Find the equation.
b) What is the perimeter when the $L = 40$ inches?
c) What is the length when $P = 215$ inches?
d) What is the width of the rectangle?

a) $P = 2L + 15$ b) 95 in. c) 100 in. d) 7.5 in.

89. ***Stretching a spring.*** A weight of 3 pounds stretches a spring 1.8 inches beyond its natural length and weight of 5 pounds stretches the same spring 3 inches beyond its natural length. Let A represent the amount of stretch and w the weight. There is a linear equation that expresses A in terms of w. Find the equation and find the amount that the spring will stretch with a weight of 6 pounds.
$A = 0.6w$, 3.6 in.

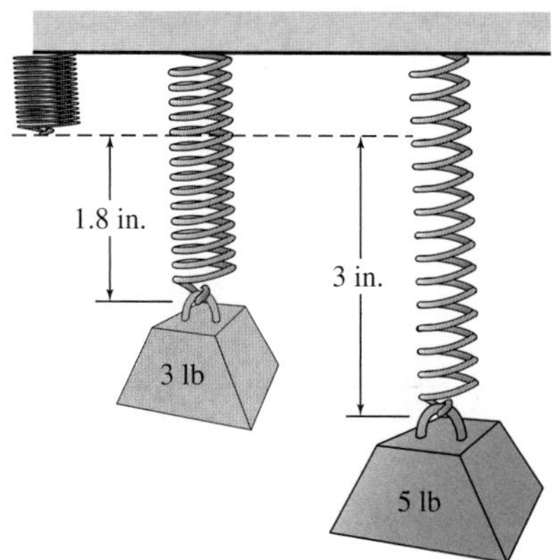

Figure for Exercise 89

90. ***Velocity of a bullet.*** A gun is fired straight upward. The bullet leaves the gun at 100 feet per second (time $t = 0$). After 2 seconds the velocity of the bullet is 36 feet per second. There is a linear equation that gives the velocity v in terms of the time t. Find the equation and find the velocity after 3 seconds.
$v = -32t + 100$, 4 ft/sec

91. ***Enzyme concentration.*** The amount of light absorbed by a certain liquid depends on the concentration of an enzyme in the liquid. A concentration of 2 milligrams

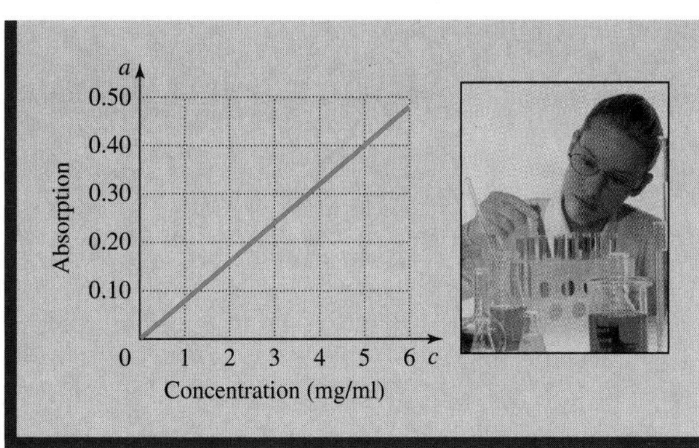

Figure for Exercise 91

per milliliter (mg/ml) produces an absorption of 0.16 and a concentration of 5 mg/ml produces an absorption of 0.40. There is a linear equation that expresses the absorption a in terms of the concentration c.

a) Find the equation.
b) What is the absorption when the concentration is 3 mg/ml?
c) Use the graph above to estimate the concentration when the absorption is 0.50.

a) $a = 0.08c$ **b)** 0.24 **c)** 6.25 mg/ml

92. ***Basal energy requirement.*** The basal energy requirement B is the number of calories that a person needs to maintain the life process. For a 28-year-old female with a height of 160 centimeters and a weight of 45 kilograms (kg), B is 1300 calories. If her weight increases to 50 kg, then B is 1365 calories. There is a linear equation that expresses B in terms of her weight w. Find the equation and find the basal energy requirement if her weight is 53.2 kg.
$B = 13w + 715$, 1406.6 calories

Getting More Involved

93. ***Exploration***

Each linear equation in the following table is given in standard form $Ax + By = C$. In each case identify A, B, and the slope of the line.

Equation	A	B	Slope
$2x + 3y = 9$	2	3	$-\frac{2}{3}$
$4x - 5y = 6$	4	-5	$\frac{4}{5}$
$\frac{1}{2}x + 3y = 1$	$\frac{1}{2}$	3	$-\frac{1}{6}$
$2x - \frac{1}{3}y = 7$	2	$-\frac{1}{3}$	6

94. ***Exploration***

Find a pattern in the table of Exercise 93 and write a formula for the slope of $Ax + By = C$, where $B \neq 0$.
$m = -\frac{A}{B}$

Graphing Calculator Exercises

95. Graph each equation on a graphing calculator. Choose a viewing window that includes both the x- and y-intercepts. Use the calculator output to help you draw the graph on paper.

a) $y = 20x - 300$
b) $y = -30x + 500$
c) $2x - 3y = 6000$

a)

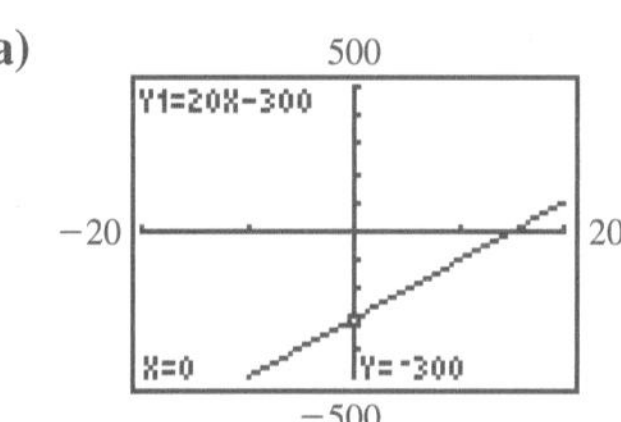

b)

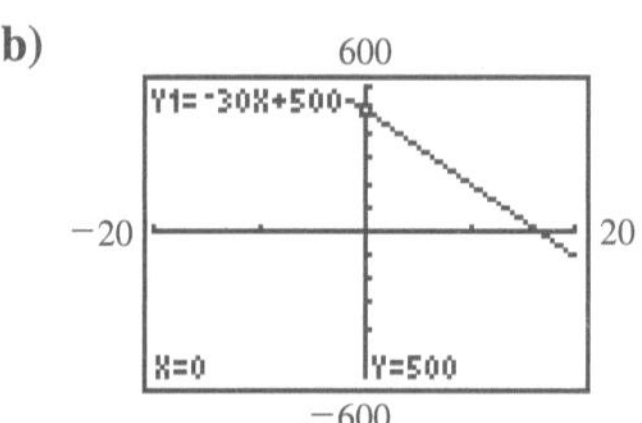

c)

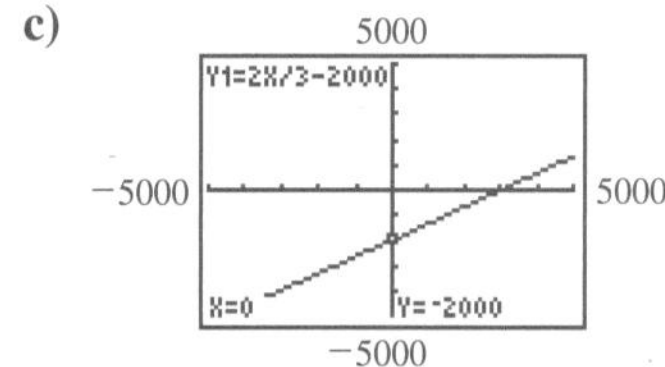

96. Graph $y = 2x + 1$ and $y = 1.99x - 1$ on a graphing calculator. Are these lines parallel? Explain your answer.
They look parallel, but they are not.

97. Graph $y = 0.5x + 0.8$ and $y = 0.5x + 0.7$ on a graphing calculator. Find a viewing window in which the two lines are separate.
$-1 \leq x \leq 1, -1 \leq y \leq 1$

98. Graph $y = 3x + 1$ and $y = -\frac{1}{3}x + 2$ on a graphing calculator. Do the lines look perpendicular? Explain.
They will look perpendicular in the right window.

3.5 Variation

In this Section

- **Direct Variation**
- **Finding the Constant**
- **Inverse Variation**
- **Joint Variation**

If $y = 5x$, then the value of y depends on the value of x. As x varies, so does y. Simple relationships like $y = 5x$ are customarily expressed in terms of variation. In this section you will learn the language of variation and learn to write formulas from verbal descriptions.

Direct Variation

Suppose you average 60 miles per hour on the freeway. The distance D that you travel depends on the amount of time T that you travel. Using the formula $D = R \cdot T$, we can write

$$D = 60T.$$

Consider the possible values for T and D given in the following table.

T (hours)	1	2	3	4	5	6
D (miles)	60	120	180	240	300	360

The graph of $D = 60T$ is shown in Fig. 3.32. Note that as T gets larger, so does D. In this situation we say that *D varies directly with T*, or D is *directly proportional* to T. The constant rate of 60 miles per hour is called the **variation constant** or **proportionality constant.** Notice that $D = 60T$ is simply a linear equation. We are just introducing some new terms to express an old idea.

Teaching Tip Note that in $y = 3x + 5$ there is something besides x (the constant 5) that is used to determine y, and so y does not vary directly with x.

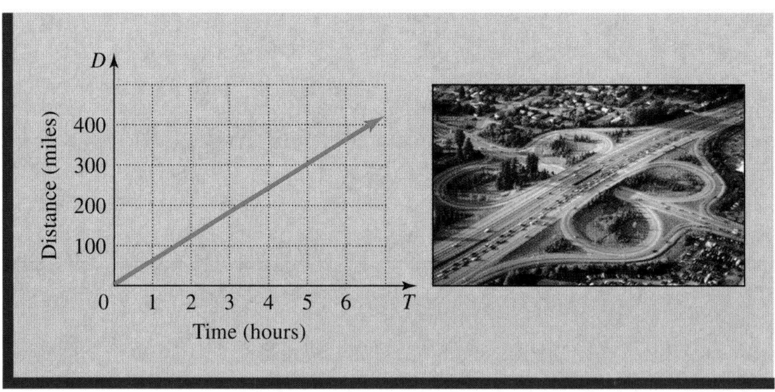

Figure 3.32

Teaching Tip Ask students for examples of direct variation.

Direct Variation

The statement **"y varies directly as x"** or **"y is directly proportional to x"** means that

$$y = kx$$

for some constant k. The constant of variation k is a fixed nonzero real number.

CAUTION Direct variation refers only to equations of the form $y = kx$ (lines through the origin). We do *not* refer to $y = 3x + 5$ as a direct variation.

Finding the Constant

If we know one ordered pair in a direct variation, then we can find the constant of variation.

EXAMPLE 1

Finding a constant of variation

Natasha is traveling by car, and the distance D that she travels varies directly as the rate R at which she drives. At 45 miles per hour, Natasha travels 135 miles. Find the constant of variation, and write a formula for D in terms of R.

Helpful Hint

In any variation problem you must first determine the general form of the relationship. Because this problem involves direct variation, the general form is $y = kx$.

Solution

Because D varies directly as R, there is a constant k such that

$$D = kR.$$

Because $D = 135$ when $R = 45$, we can write

$$135 = k \cdot 45$$

or

$$3 = k.$$

So $D = 3R$.

Now do Exercises 15–16

In Example 2 we find the constant of variation and use it to solve a variation problem.

EXAMPLE 2

A direct variation problem

Your electric bill at Middle States Electric Co-op varies directly with the amount of electricity that you use. If the bill for 2800 kilowatts of electricity is \$196, then what is the bill for 4000 kilowatts of electricity?

Study Tip

If your grades are not what you would like and you are doing all of your work, then see your teacher for advice. Your grade varies directly with the amount of effort that you put forth.

Solution

Because the amount A of the electric bill varies directly as the amount E of electricity used, we have

$$A = kE$$

for some constant k. Because 2800 kilowatts cost \$196, we have

$$196 = k \cdot 2800$$

or

$$0.07 = k.$$

So $A = 0.07E$. Now if $E = 4000$ we get

$$A = 0.07(4000) = 280.$$

The bill for 4000 kilowatts would be \$280.

Now do Exercises 25–26

Inverse Variation

If you plan to make a 400-mile trip by car, the time it will take depends on your rate of speed. Using the formula $D = RT$, we can write

$$T = \frac{400}{R}.$$

Consider the possible values for R and T given in the following table:

Teaching Tip Having the students make some tables like this will improve their understanding of these concepts.

R (mph)	10	20	40	50	80	100
T (hours)	40	20	10	8	5	4

The graph of $T = \frac{400}{R}$ is shown in Fig. 3.33. As your rate increases, the time for the trip decreases. In this situation we say that the time is *inversely proportional* to the speed. Note that the graph of $T = \frac{400}{R}$ is not a straight line because $T = \frac{400}{R}$ is not a linear equation.

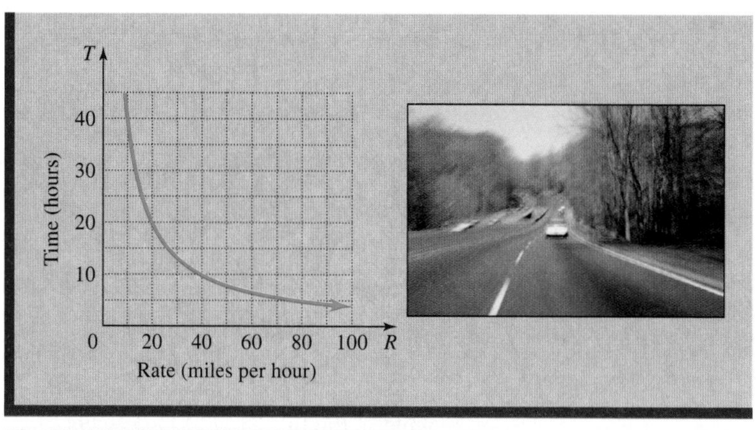

Figure 3.33

Teaching Tip Ask students for examples of inverse variation.

> **Inverse Variation**
>
> The statement **"*y* varies inversely as *x*"** or **"*y* is inversely proportional to *x*"** means that
>
> $$y = \frac{k}{x}$$
>
> for some nonzero constant of variation k.

CAUTION The constant of variation is usually positive because most physical examples involve positive quantities. However, the definitions of direct and inverse variation do not rule out a negative constant.

EXAMPLE 3

An inverse variation problem

The volume of a gas in a cylinder is inversely proportional to the pressure on the gas. If the volume is 12 cubic centimeters when the pressure on the gas is 200 kilograms per square centimeter, then what is the volume when the pressure is 150 kilograms per square centimeter? See Fig. 3.34.

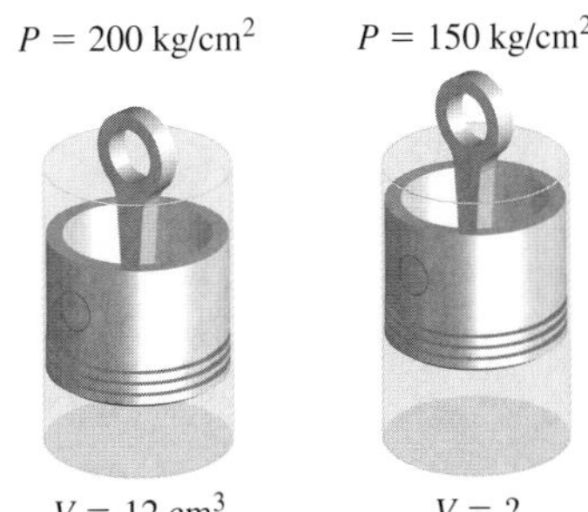

Figure 3.34

Solution

Because the volume V is inversely proportional to the pressure P, we have

$$V = \frac{k}{P}$$

for some constant k. Because $V = 12$ when $P = 200$, we can find k:

$$12 = \frac{k}{200}$$

$$200 \cdot 12 = 200 \cdot \frac{k}{200} \quad \text{Multiply each side by 200.}$$

$$2400 = k$$

Now to find V when $P = 150$, we can use the formula $V = \frac{2400}{P}$:

$$V = \frac{2400}{150} = 16$$

So the volume is 16 cubic centimeters when the pressure is 150 kilograms per square centimeter.

Now do Exercises 27–28

Joint Variation

If the price of carpet is \$30 per square yard, then the cost C of carpeting a rectangular room depends on the width W (in yards) and the length L (in yards). As the width or length of the room increases, so does the cost. We can write the cost in terms of the two variables L and W:

$$C = 30LW$$

We say that C *varies jointly* as L and W.

Joint Variation

The statement **"y varies jointly as x and z"** or **"y is jointly proportional to x and z"** means that

$$y = kxz$$

for some nonzero constant of variation k.

EXAMPLE 4

A joint variation problem

The cost of shipping a piece of machinery by truck varies jointly with the weight of the machinery and the distance that it is shipped. It costs \$3000 to ship a 2500-lb milling machine a distance of 600 miles. Find the cost for shipping a 1500-lb lathe a distance of 800 miles.

Solution

Because the cost C varies jointly with the weight w and the distance d, we have

$$C = kwd$$

where k is the constant of variation. To find k, we use $C = 3000$, $w = 2500$, and $d = 600$:

$$3000 = k \cdot 2500 \cdot 600$$

$$\frac{3000}{2500 \cdot 600} = k \quad \text{Divide each side by } 2500 \cdot 600.$$

$$0.002 = k$$

Now use $w = 1500$ and $d = 800$ in the formula $C = 0.002wd$:

$$C = 0.002 \cdot 1500 \cdot 800$$

$$= 2400$$

So the cost of shipping the lathe is \$2400.

Now do Exercises 29–30

Helpful Hint

Because the variation in this problem is joint, we know the general form is $y = kxz$, where k is the constant of variation.

Teaching Tip Ask students for another example of joint variation in real life. Does the cost of a fill-up vary jointly with the size of the tank and the price per gallon? Do UPS shipping costs vary jointly with weight and distance?

CAUTION The variation words (directly, inversely, or jointly) are never used to indicate addition or subtraction. We use multiplication in the formula unless we see the word "inversely." We use division for inverse variation.

Warm-Ups ▼

True or false? Explain your answer.

1. If y varies directly as z, then $y = kz$ for some constant k. True
2. If a varies inversely as b, then $a = \frac{b}{k}$ for some constant k. False
3. If y varies directly as x and $y = 8$ when $x = 2$, then the variation constant is 4. True
4. If y varies inversely as x and $y = 8$ when $x = 2$, then the variation constant is $\frac{1}{4}$. False
5. If C varies jointly as h and t, then $C = ht$. False
6. The amount of sales tax on a new car varies directly with the purchase price of the car. True
7. If z varies inversely as w and $z = 10$ when $w = 2$, then $z = \frac{20}{w}$. True
8. The time that it takes to travel a fixed distance varies inversely with the rate. True
9. If m varies directly as w, then $m = w + k$ for some constant k. False
10. If y varies jointly as x and z, then $y = k(x + z)$ for some constant k. False

3.5 Exercises

Boost your GRADE at mathzone.com!

MathZone

- Practice Problems
- Self-Tests
- Videos
- Net Tutor
- e-Professors

Reading and Writing *After reading this section, write out the answers to these questions. Use complete sentences.*

1. What does it mean to say that y varies directly as x?
If y varies directly as x, then there is a constant k such that $y = kx$.

2. What is a variation constant?
A variation constant is the constant k in the formulas $y = kx$ or $y = \frac{k}{x}$.

3. What does it mean to say that y is inversely proportional to x?
If y is inversely proportional to x, then there is a constant k such that $y = \frac{k}{x}$.

4. What does it mean to say that y varies jointly as x and z?
If y varies jointly as x and z, then there is a constant k such that $y = kxz$.

Write a formula that expresses the relationship described by each statement. Use k for the constant in each case. See Examples 1–4.

5. T varies directly as h. $T = kh$

6. m varies directly as p. $m = kp$

7. y varies inversely as r. $y = \frac{k}{r}$

8. u varies inversely as n. $u = \frac{k}{n}$

9. R is jointly proportional to t and s. $R = kts$

10. W varies jointly as u and v. $W = kuv$

11. i is directly proportional to b. $i = kb$

12. p is directly proportional to x. $p = kx$

13. A is jointly proportional to y and m. $A = kym$

14. t is inversely proportional to e. $t = \frac{k}{e}$

Find the variation constant, and write a formula that expresses the indicated variation. See Example 1.

15. y varies directly as x, and $y = 5$ when $x = 3$. $y = \frac{5}{3}x$

16. m varies directly as w, and $m = \frac{1}{2}$ when $w = \frac{1}{4}$. $m = 2w$

17. A varies inversely as B, and $A = 3$ when $B = 2$. $A = \frac{6}{B}$

18. c varies inversely as d, and $c = 5$ when $d = 2$. $c = \frac{10}{d}$

19. m varies inversely as p, and $m = 22$ when $p = 9$. $m = \frac{198}{p}$

20. s varies inversely as v, and $s = 3$ when $v = 4$. $s = \frac{12}{v}$

21. A varies jointly as t and u, and $A = 24$ when $t = 6$ and $u = 2$. $A = 2tu$

22. N varies jointly as p and q, and $N = 720$ when $p = 3$ and $q = 2$. $N = 120pq$

23. T varies directly as u, and $T = 9$ when $u = 2$. $T = \frac{9}{2}u$

24. R varies directly as p, and $R = 30$ when $p = 6$. $R = 5p$

Solve each variation problem. See Examples 2–4.

25. Y varies directly as x, and $Y = 100$ when $x = 20$. Find Y when $x = 5$. 25

26. n varies directly as q, and $n = 39$ when $q = 3$. Find n when $q = 8$. 104

27. a varies inversely as b, and $a = 3$, when $b = 4$. Find a when $b = 12$. 1

28. y varies inversely as w, and $y = 9$ when $w = 2$. Find y when $w = 6$. 3

29. P varies jointly as s and t, and $P = 56$ when $s = 2$ and $t = 4$. Find P when $s = 5$ and $t = 3$. 105

30. B varies jointly as u and v, and $B = 12$ when $u = 4$ and $v = 6$. Find B when $u = 5$ and $v = 8$. 20

Use the given formula to fill in the missing entries in each table and determine whether b varies directly or inversely as a.

31. $b = \frac{300}{a}$

a	**b**
$\frac{1}{2}$	600
1	300
30	10
900	$\frac{1}{3}$

Inversely

32. $b = \frac{500}{a}$

a	**b**
$\frac{1}{5}$	2500
1	500
50	10
1500	$\frac{1}{3}$

Inversely

33. $b = \frac{3}{4}a$

a	**b**
$\frac{1}{3}$	$\frac{1}{4}$
8	6
12	9
20	15

Directly

34. $b = \frac{2}{3}a$

a	**b**
$\frac{1}{2}$	$\frac{1}{3}$
3	2
9	6
21	14

Directly

For each table, determine whether y varies directly or inversely as x and find a formula for y in terms of x.

35.

x	y
2	7
3	10.5
4	14
5	17.5

Directly, $y = 3.5x$

36.

x	y
10	5
15	7.5
20	10
25	12.5

Directly, $y = 0.5x$

37.

x	y
2	10
4	5
10	2
20	1

Inversely, $y = \frac{20}{x}$

38.

x	y
5	100
10	50
50	10
250	2

Inversely, $y = \frac{500}{x}$

Solve each problem.

39. *Distance.* With the cruise control set at 65 mph, the distance traveled varies directly with the time spent traveling. Fill in the missing entries in the following table.

Time (hours)	1	2	3	4
Distance (miles)	65	130	195	260

40. *Cost.* With gas selling for $1.60 per gallon, the cost of filling your tank varies directly with the amount of gas that you pump. Fill in the missing entries in the following table.

Amount (gallons)	5	10	15	20
Cost (dollars)	8	16	24	32

41. *Time.* The time that it takes to complete a 400-mile trip varies inversely with your average speed. Fill in the missing entries in the following table.

Speed (mph)	20	40	50	200
Time (hours)	20	10	8	2

42. *Amount.* The amount of gasoline that you can buy for $20 varies inversely with the price per gallon. Fill in the missing entries in the following table.

Price per gallon (dollars)	1	2	4	10
Amount (gallons)	20	10	5	2

43. *Carpeting.* The cost C of carpeting a rectangular living room with $20 per square yard carpet varies jointly with the length L and the width W. Fill in the missing entries in the following table.

Length (yd)	Width (yd)	Cost ($)
8	10	1600
10	12	2400
12	14	3360

44. *Waterfront property.* At $50 per square foot, the price of a rectangular waterfront lot varies jointly with the length and width. Fill in the missing entries in the following table.

Length (ft)	Width (ft)	Cost ($)
60	100	300,000
80	90	360,000
100	150	750,000

45. *Aluminum flatboat.* The weight of an aluminum flatboat varies directly with the length of the boat. If a 12-foot boat weighs 86 pounds, then what is the weight of a 14-foot boat? 100.3 pounds

46. *Christmas tree.* The price of a Christmas tree varies directly with the height. If a 5-foot tree costs $20, then what is the price of a 6-foot tree? $24

47. *Sharing the work.* The time it takes to erect the big circus tent varies inversely as the number of elephants working on the job. If it takes four elephants 75 minutes, then how long would it take six elephants? 50 minutes

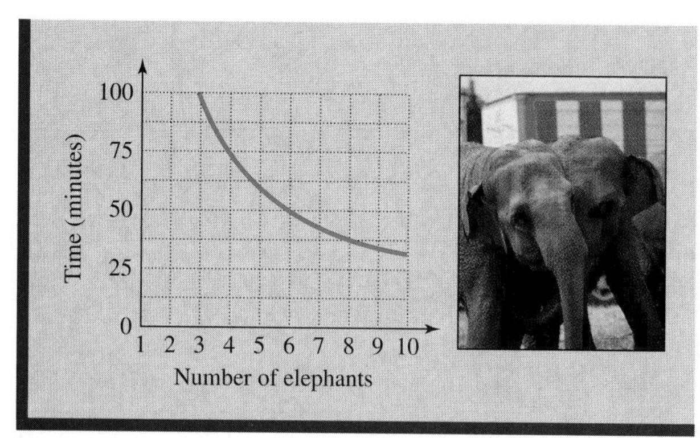

Figure for Exercise 47

48. *Gas laws.* The volume of a gas is inversely proportional to the pressure on the gas. If the volume is 6 cubic centimeters when the pressure on the gas is 8 kilograms per square centimeter, then what is the volume when the pressure is 12 kilograms per square centimeter? 4 cm^3

49. ***Steel tubing.*** The cost of steel tubing is jointly proportional to its length and diameter. If a 10-foot tube with a 1-inch diameter costs \$5.80, then what is the cost of a 15-foot tube with a 2-inch diameter?
\$17.40

50. ***Sales tax.*** The amount of sales tax varies jointly with the number of Cokes purchased and the price per Coke. If the sales tax on eight Cokes at 65 cents each is 26 cents, then what is the sales tax on six Cokes at 90 cents each?
27 cents

51. ***Approach speed.*** The approach speed of an airplane is directly proportional to its landing speed. If the approach speed for a Piper Cheyenne is 90 mph with a landing speed of 75 mph, then what is the landing speed for an airplane with an approach speed of 96 mph?
80 mph

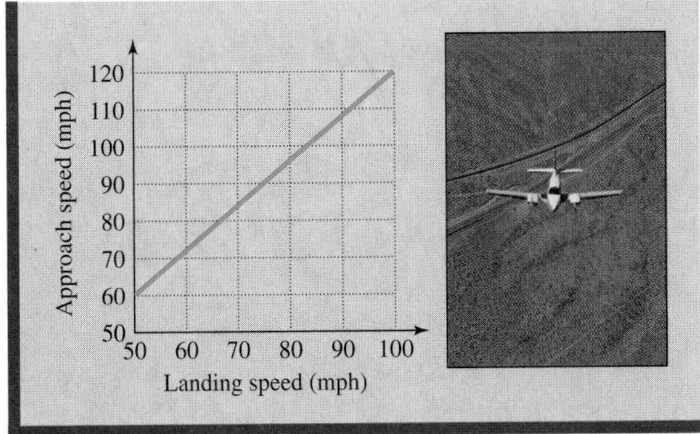

Figure for Exercise 51

52. ***Ideal waist size.*** According to Dr. Aaron R. Folsom of the University of Minnesota School of Public Health, your maximum ideal waist size is directly proportional to your hip size. For a woman with 40-inch hips, the maximum ideal waist size is 32 inches. What is the maximum ideal waist size for a woman with 35-inch hips?
28 inches

53. ***Sugar Pops.*** The number of days that it takes to eat a large box of Sugar Pops varies inversely with the size of the family. If a family of three eats a box in 7 days, then how many days does it take a family of seven?
3 days

54. ***Cost of CDs.*** The cost for manufacturing a CD varies inversely with the number of CDs made. If the cost is \$2.50 per CD when 10,000 are made, then what is the cost per CD when 100,000 are made.
\$0.25 per CD

Getting More Involved

55. ***Discussion*** 

If y varies directly as x, then the graph of the equation is a straight line. What is its slope? What is the y-intercept? If $y = 3x + 2$, then does y vary directly as x? Which straight lines correspond to direct variations?
k, (0, 0), no, $y = kx$

56. ***Writing*** 

Write a summary of the three types of variation. Include an example of each type that is not found in this text.

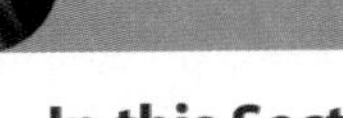

3.6 Graphing Linear Inequalities in Two Variables

In this Section

- **Definition**
- **Graphing a Linear Inequality**
- **Using a Test Point to Graph an Inequality**
- **Applications**

You studied linear equations and inequalities in one variable in Chapter 2. In this section we extend the ideas of linear equations in two variables to study linear inequalities in two variables.

Definition

Linear inequalities in two variables have the same form as linear equations in two variables. An inequality symbol is used in place of the equal sign.

Linear Inequality in Two Variables

If A, B, and C are real numbers with A and B not both zero, then

$$Ax + By < C$$

is called a **linear inequality in two variables.** In place of $<$, we can also use $\leq$, $>$, or $\geq$.

The inequalities

$$3x - 4y \leq 8, \qquad y > 2x - 3, \qquad \text{and} \qquad x - y + 9 < 0$$

are linear inequalities. Not all of these are in the form of the definition, but they could all be rewritten in that form.

An ordered pair is a solution to an inequality in two variables if the ordered pair satisfies the inequality.

EXAMPLE 1

Satisfying a linear inequality

Determine whether each point satisfies the inequality $2x - 3y \geq 6$.

a) $(4, 1)$ **b)** $(3, 0)$ **c)** $(3, -2)$

Solution

a) To determine whether $(4, 1)$ is a solution to the inequality, we replace x by 4 and y by 1 in the inequality $2x - 3y \geq 6$:

$$2(4) - 3(1) \geq 6$$
$$8 - 3 \geq 6$$
$$5 \geq 6 \quad \text{Incorrect}$$

So $(4, 1)$ does not satisfy the inequality $2x - 3y \geq 6$.

b) Replace x by 3 and y by 0:

$$2(3) - 3(0) \geq 6$$
$$6 \geq 6 \quad \text{Correct}$$

So the point $(3, 0)$ satisfies the inequality $2x - 3y \geq 6$.

c) Replace x by 3 and y by -2:

$$2(3) - 3(-2) \geq 6$$
$$6 + 6 \geq 6$$
$$12 \geq 6 \quad \text{Correct}$$

So the point $(3, -2)$ satisfies the inequality $2x - 3y \geq 6$.

Now do Exercises 7–12

Study Tip

Write about what you read in the text. Sum things up in your own words. Write out important facts on note cards. When you have a few spare minutes in between classes review your note cards. Try to get the information on the cards into your memory.

Teaching Tip Remind students to write down the equation for the boundary line. Students sometimes find two points that satisfy the inequality and then draw the boundary line through them.

Graphing a Linear Inequality

The graph of a linear inequality in two variables consists of all points in the rectangular coordinate system that satisfy the inequality. For example, the graph of the inequality

$$y > x + 2$$

consists of all points where the y-coordinate is larger than the x-coordinate plus 2. Consider the point (3, 5) on the line

$$y = x + 2.$$

The y-coordinate of (3, 5) is equal to the x-coordinate plus 2. If we choose a point with a larger y-coordinate, such as (3, 6), it satisfies the inequality and it is above the line $y = x + 2$. In fact, any point above the line $y = x + 2$ satisfies $y > x + 2$. Likewise, all points below the line $y = x + 2$ satisfy the inequality $y < x + 2$. See Fig. 3.35.

Helpful Hint

Why do we keep drawing graphs? When we solve $2x + 1 = 7$, we don't bother to draw a graph showing 3, because the solution set is so simple. However, the solution set to a linear inequality is a very large set of ordered pairs. Graphing gives us a way to visualize the solution set.

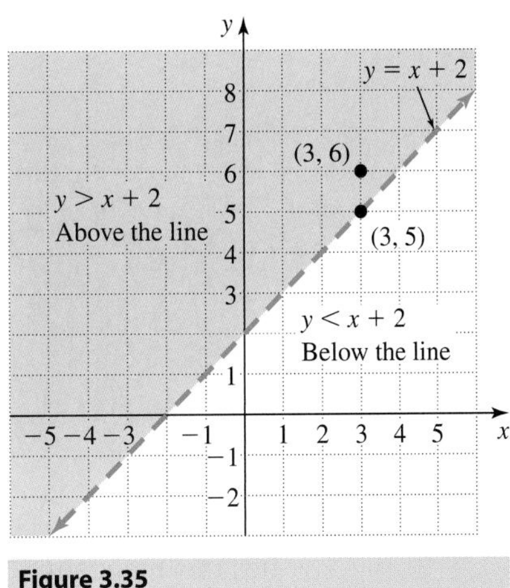

Figure 3.35

To graph the inequality, we shade all points above the line $y = x + 2$. To indicate that the line is not included in the graph of $y > x + 2$, we use a dashed line.

The procedure for graphing linear inequalities is summarized as follows.

Teaching Tip The test-point method will work for an inequality in any form. However, it is convenient to know that values of y are larger above the line and smaller below the line.

Strategy for Graphing a Linear Inequality in Two Variables

1. Solve the inequality for y, then graph $y = mx + b$.

$y > mx + b$ is the region above the line.

$y = mx + b$ is the line itself.

$y < mx + b$ is the region below the line.

2. If the inequality involves only x, then graph the vertical line $x = k$.

$x > k$ is the region to the right of the line.

$x = k$ is the line itself.

$x < k$ is the region to the left of the line.

EXAMPLE 2

Graphing a linear inequality

Graph each inequality.

a) $y < \frac{1}{3}x + 1$ **b)** $y \geq -2x + 3$

c) $2x - 3y < 6$

Teaching Tip It is a good idea to review graphing using slope and y-intercept and graphing using both intercepts at this time.

Solution

a) The set of points satisfying this inequality is the region below the line

$$y = \frac{1}{3}x + 1.$$

To show this region, we first graph the boundary line. The slope of the line is $\frac{1}{3}$, and the y-intercept is (0, 1). We draw the line dashed because it is not part of the graph of $y < \frac{1}{3}x + 1$. In Fig. 3.36 the graph is the shaded region.

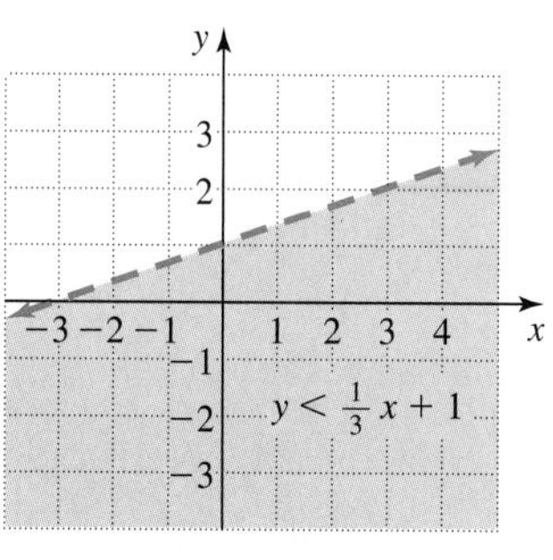

Figure 3.36

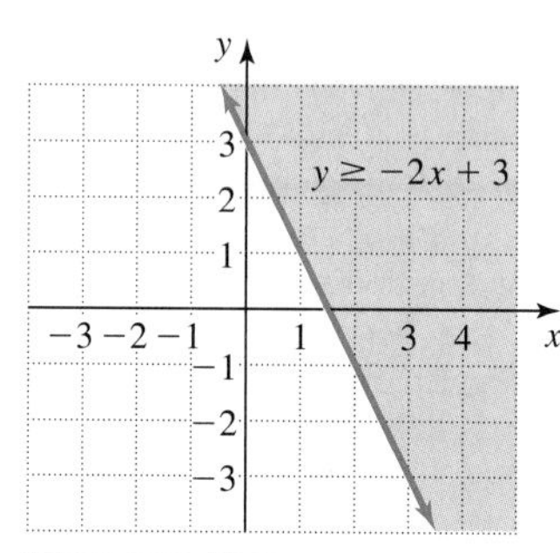

Figure 3.37

b) Because the inequality symbol is $\geq$, every point on or above the line satisfies this inequality. We use the fact that the slope of this line is -2 and the y-intercept is (0, 3) to draw the graph of the line. To show that the line $y = -2x + 3$ is included in the graph, we make it a solid line and shade the region above. See Fig. 3.37.

c) First solve for y:

$$2x - 3y < 6$$

$$-3y < -2x + 6$$

$$y > \frac{2}{3}x - 2 \quad \text{Divide by } -3 \text{ and reverse the inequality.}$$

To graph this inequality, we first graph the line with slope $\frac{2}{3}$ and y-intercept (0, −2). We use a dashed line for the boundary because it is not included, and we shade the region above the line. Remember, "less than" means below the line and "greater than" means above the line only when the inequality is solved for y. See Fig. 3.38 for the graph.

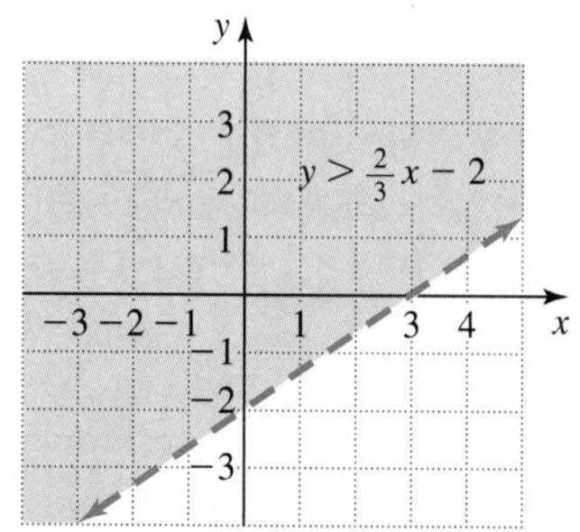

Figure 3.38

Now do Exercises 13–26

EXAMPLE 3

Teaching Tip Point out that $x > 3$ is an interval of real numbers if the context is inequalities in one variable. The context is important.

Horizontal and vertical boundary lines

Graph each inequality.

a) $y \leq 4$ **b)** $x > 3$

Solution

a) The line $y = 4$ is the horizontal line with y-intercept (0, 4). We draw a solid horizontal line and shade below it as in Fig. 3.39.

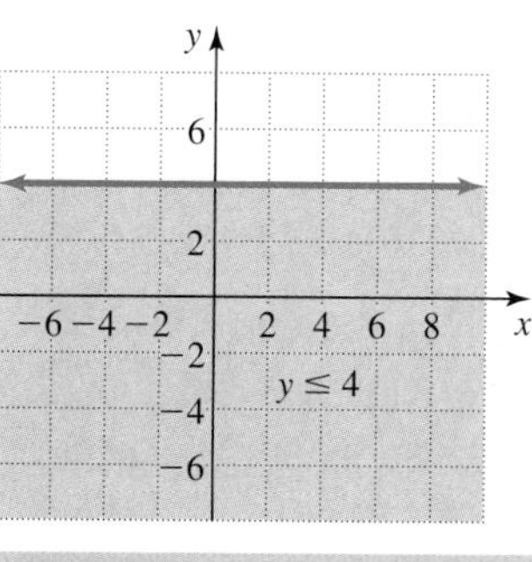

Figure 3.39

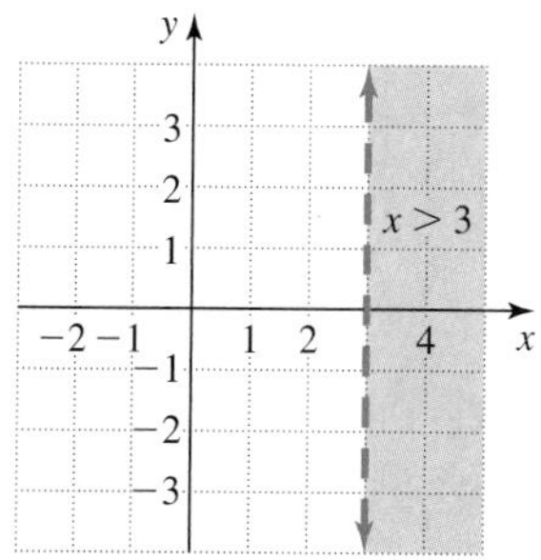

Figure 3.40

b) The line $x = 3$ is a vertical line through (3, 0). Any point to the right of this line has an x-coordinate larger than 3. The graph is shown in Fig. 3.40.

Now do Exercises 27–30

Using a Test Point to Graph an Inequality

The graph of a linear equation such as $2x - 3y = 6$ separates the coordinate plane into two regions. One region satisfies the inequality $2x - 3y > 6$, and the other region satisfies the inequality $2x - 3y < 6$. We can tell which region satisfies which inequality by testing a point in one region. With this method it is not necessary to solve the inequality for y.

EXAMPLE 4

Helpful Hint

Some people always like to choose (0, 0) as the test point for lines that do not go through (0, 0). The arithmetic for testing (0, 0) is generally easier than for any other point.

Using a test point

Graph the inequality $2x - 3y > 6$.

Solution

First graph the equation $2x - 3y = 6$ using the x-intercept (3, 0) and the y-intercept (0, −2) as shown in Fig. 3.41. Select a point on one side of the line, say (0, 1), to test in the inequality. Because

$$2(0) - 3(1) > 6$$

is false, the region on the other side of the line satisfies the inequality. The graph of $2x - 3y > 6$ is shown in Fig. 3.42.

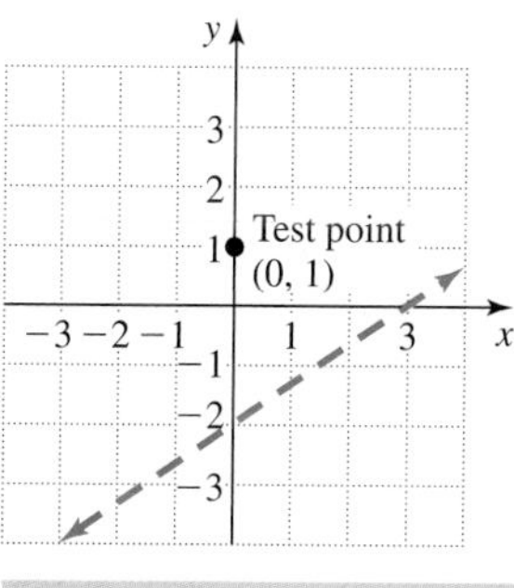

Figure 3.41

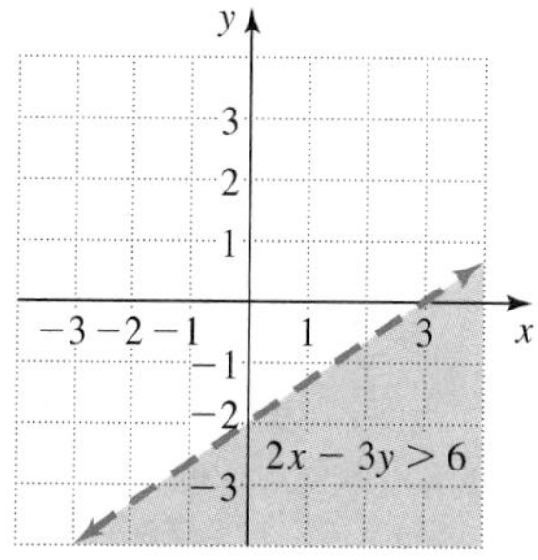

Figure 3.42

Now do Exercises 37–48

Applications

The values of variables used in applications are often restricted to nonnegative numbers. So solutions to inequalities in these applications are graphed in the first quadrant only.

EXAMPLE 5

Manufacturing tables

The Ozark Furniture Company can obtain at most 8000 board feet of oak lumber for making two types of tables. It takes 50 board feet to make a round table and 80 board feet to make a rectangular table. Write an inequality that limits the possible number of tables of each type that can be made. Draw a graph showing all possibilities for the number of tables that can be made.

Solution

If x is the number of round tables and y is the number of rectangular tables, then x and y satisfy the inequality

$$50x + 80y \le 8000.$$

Now find the intercepts for the line $50x + 80y = 8000$:

$$\begin{aligned} 50 \cdot 0 + 80y &= 8000 \\ 80y &= 8000 \\ y &= 100 \end{aligned} \qquad \begin{aligned} 50x + 80 \cdot 0 &= 8000 \\ 50x &= 8000 \\ x &= 160 \end{aligned}$$

Draw the line through (0, 100) and (160, 0). Because (0, 0) satisfies the inequality, the number of tables must be below the line. Since the number of tables cannot be negative, the number of tables made must be below the line and in the first quadrant as shown in Fig. 3.43. Assuming that Ozark will not make a fraction of a table, only points in Fig. 3.43 with whole-number coordinates are practical.

Teaching Tip This is a good time to discuss the domain of a variable. In Example 5, the variables are understood to represent nonnegative integers.

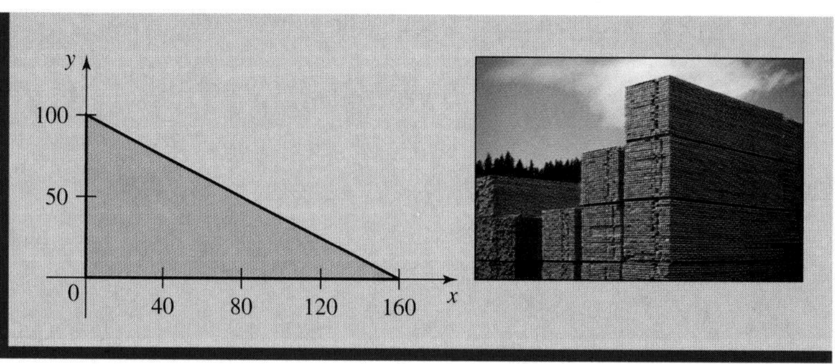

Figure 3.43

Now do Exercises 49–52

Warm-Ups ▼

True or false? Explain your answer.

1. The point $(-1, 4)$ satisfies the inequality $y > 3x + 1$. True

2. The point $(2, -3)$ satisfies the inequality $3x - 2y \geq 12$. True

3. The graph of the inequality $y > x + 9$ is the region above the line $y = x + 9$. True

4. The graph of the inequality $x < y + 2$ is the region below the line $x = y + 2$. False

5. The graph of $x = 3$ is a single point on the x-axis. False

6. The graph of $y \leq 5$ is the region below the horizontal line $y = 5$. False

7. The graph of $x < 3$ is the region to the left of the vertical line $x = 3$. True

8. In graphing the inequality $y \geq x$ we use a dashed boundary line. False

9. The point $(0, 0)$ is on the graph of the inequality $y \geq x$. True

10. The point $(0, 0)$ lies above the line $y = 2x + 1$. False

3.6 Exercises

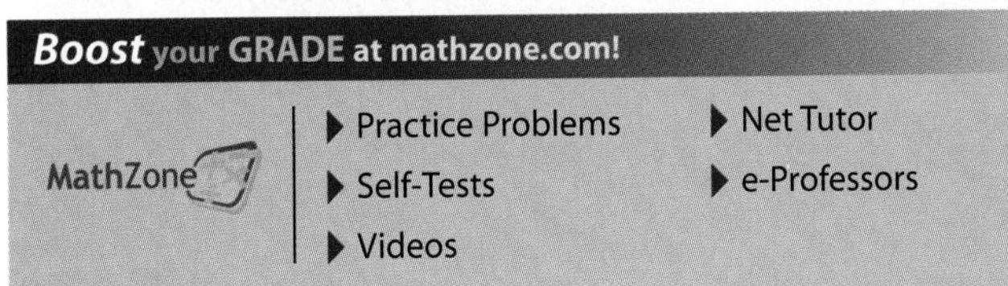

Reading and Writing *After reading this section, write out the answers to these questions. Use complete sentences.*

1. What is a linear inequality in two variables?
A linear inequality has the same form as a linear equation except that an inequality symbol is used.

2. How can you tell if an ordered pair satisfies a linear inequality in two variables?
An ordered pair satisfies a linear inequality if the inequality is correct when the variables are replaced by the coordinates of the ordered pair.

3. How do you determine whether to draw the boundary line of the graph of a linear inequality dashed or solid?
If the inequality symbol includes equality, then the boundary line is solid; otherwise it is dashed.

4. How do you decide which side of the boundary line to shade?
We shade the side that satisfies the inequality.

5. What is the test point method?
In the test point method we test a point to see which side of the boundary line satisfies the inequality.

6. What is the advantage of the test point method?
With the test point method you can use the inequality in any form.

Determine which of the points following each inequality satisfy that inequality. See Example 1.

7. $x - y > 5$ $(2, 3), (-3, -9), (8, 3)$ $(-3, -9)$

8. $2x + y < 3$ $(-2, 6), (0, 3), (3, 0)$ $(-2, 6)$

9. $y \geq -2x + 5$ $(3, 0), (1, 3), (-2, 5)$ $(3, 0), (1, 3)$

10. $y \leq -x + 6$ $(2, 0), (-3, 9), (-4, 12)$ $(2, 0), (-3, 9)$

11. $x > -3y + 4$ $(2, 3), (7, -1), (0, 5)$ $(2, 3), (0, 5)$

12. $x < -y - 3$ $(1, 2), (-3, -4), (0, -3)$ $(-3, -4)$

Graph each inequality. See Examples 2 and 3.

13. $y < x + 4$

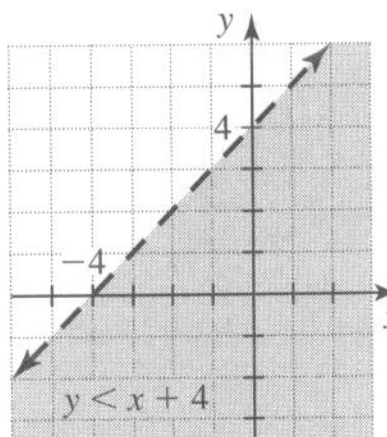

14. $y < 2x + 2$

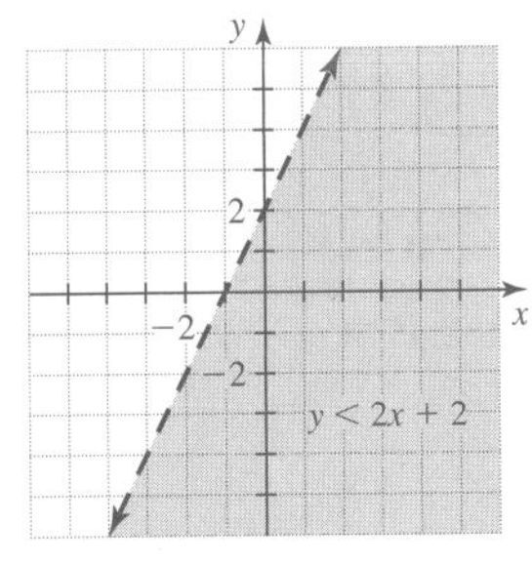

15. $y > -x + 3$

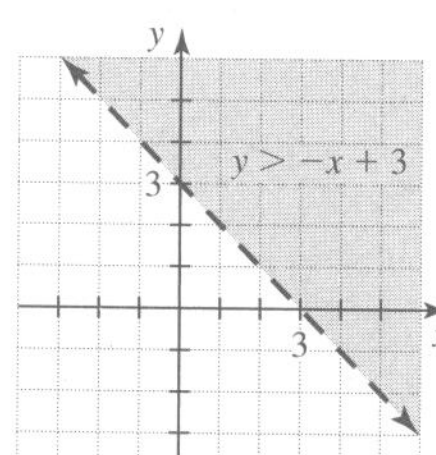

16. $y < -2x + 1$

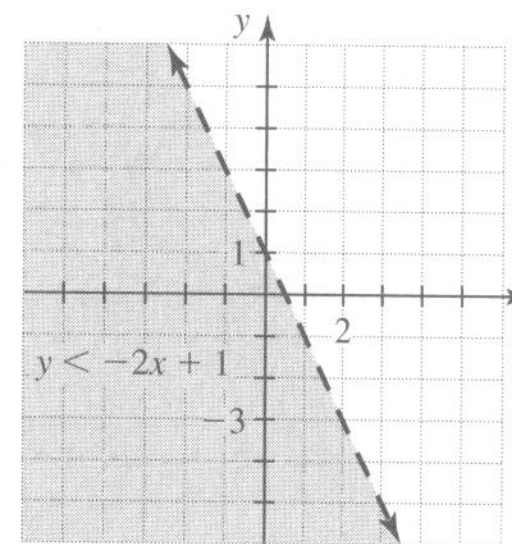

17. $y > \frac{2}{3}x - 3$

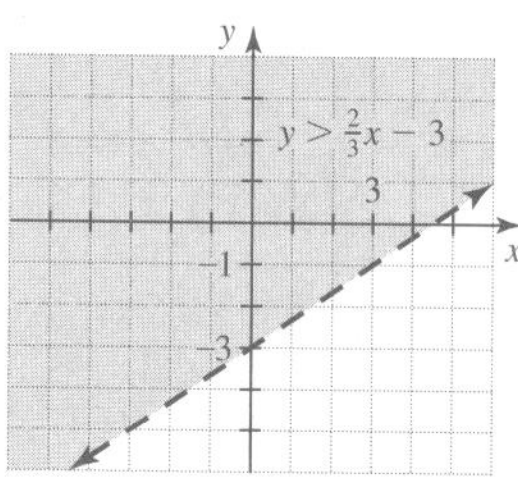

18. $y < \frac{1}{2}x + 1$

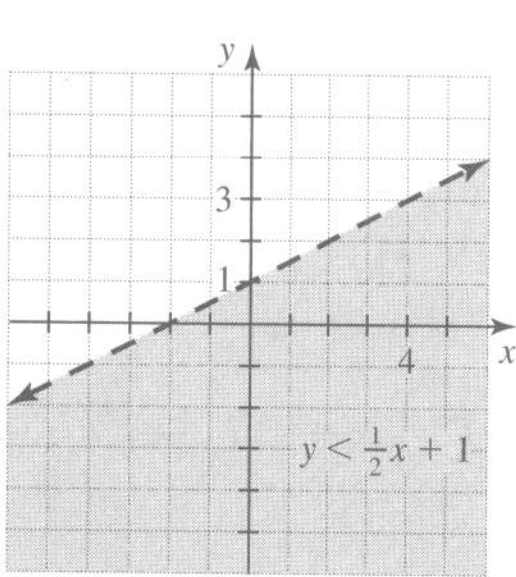

19. $y \leq -\frac{2}{5}x + 2$

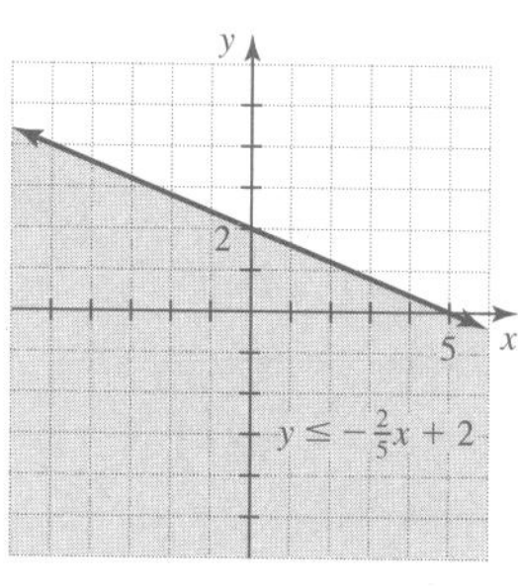
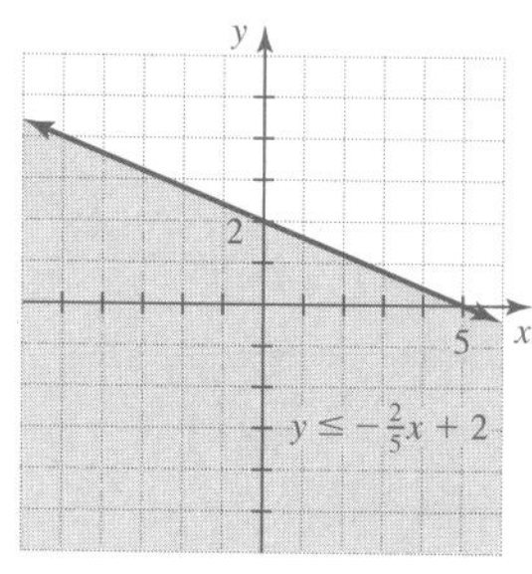

20. $y \geq -\frac{1}{2}x + 3$

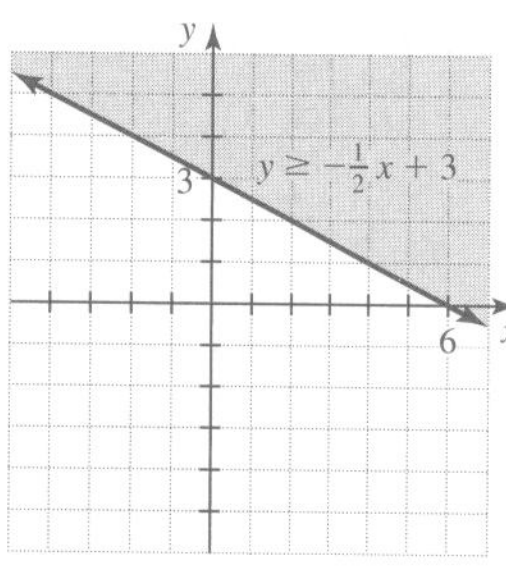
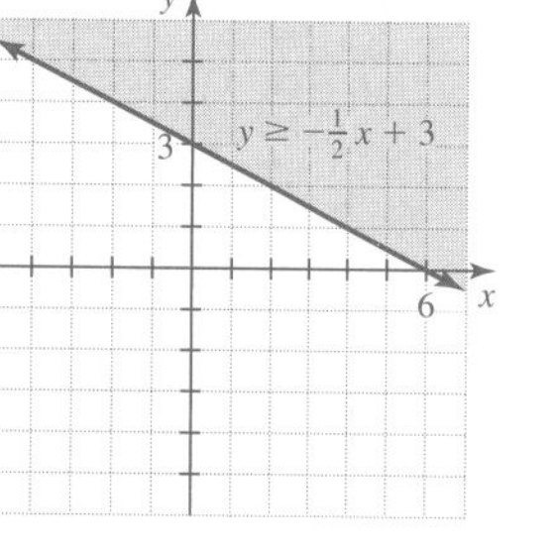

21. $y - x \geq 0$

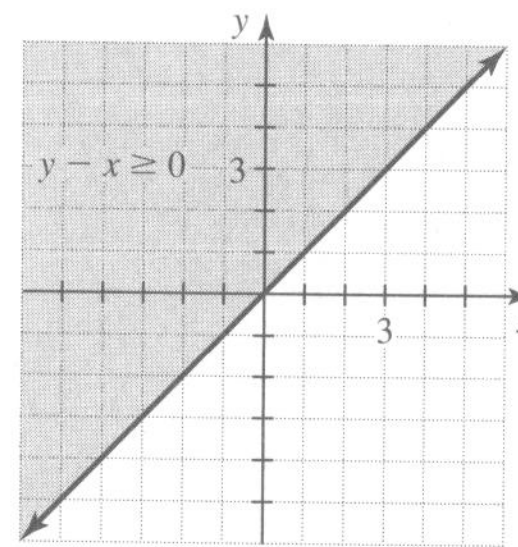

22. $x - 2y \leq 0$

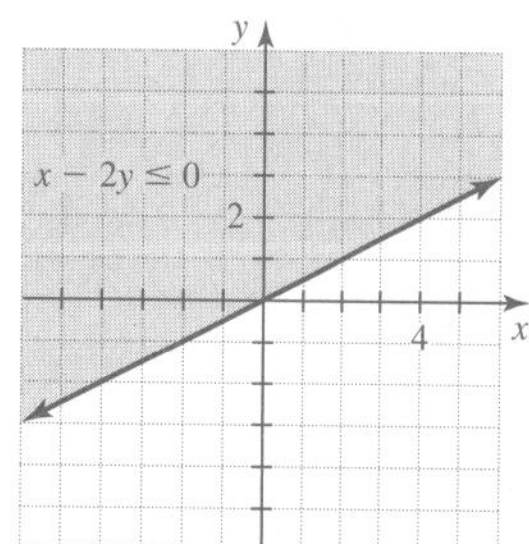

23. $x > y - 5$

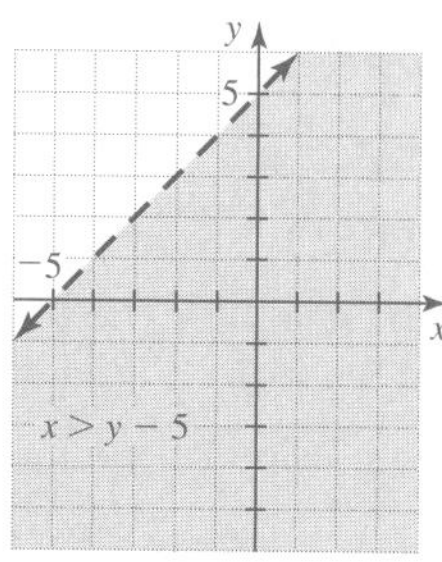

24. $2x < 3y + 6$

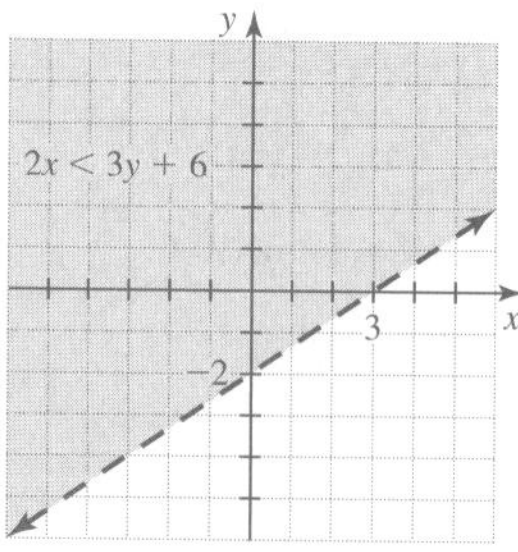

25. $x - 2y + 4 \leq 0$

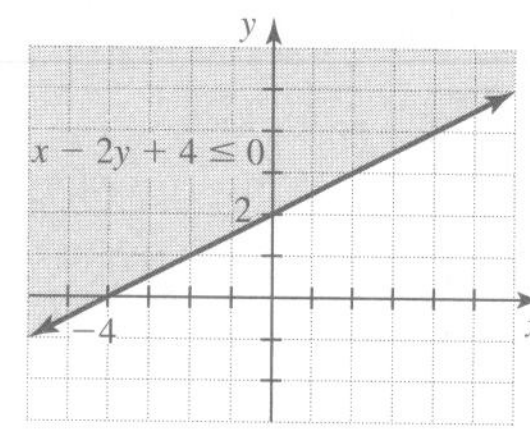

26. $2x - y + 3 \geq 0$

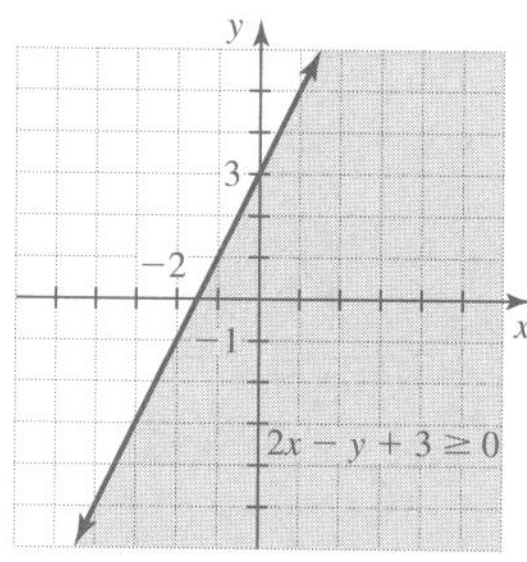

27. $y \geq 2$

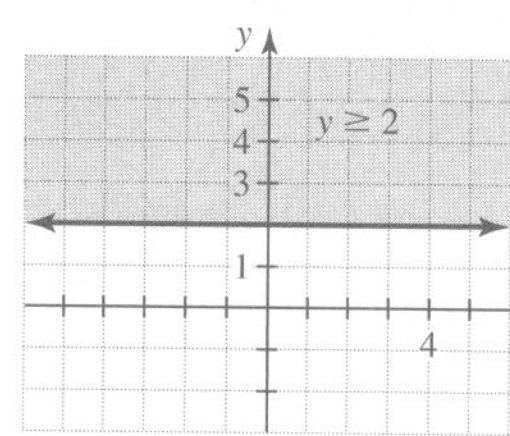

28. $y < 7$

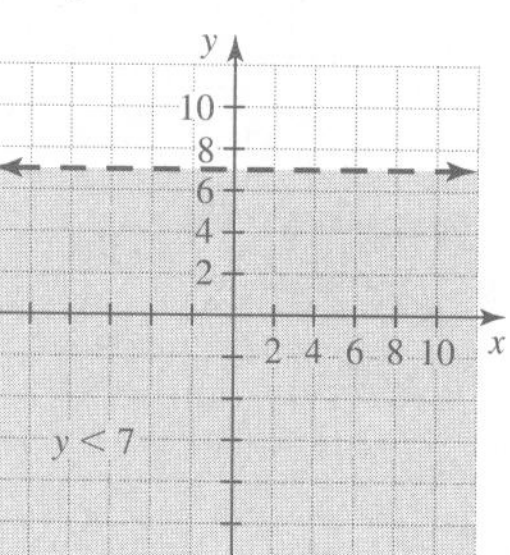

29. $x > 9$

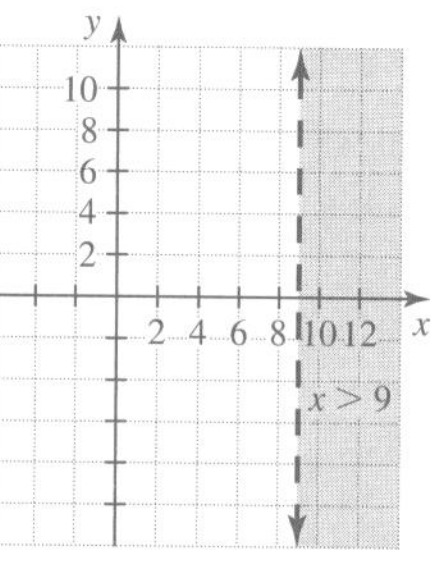

30. $x \leq 1$

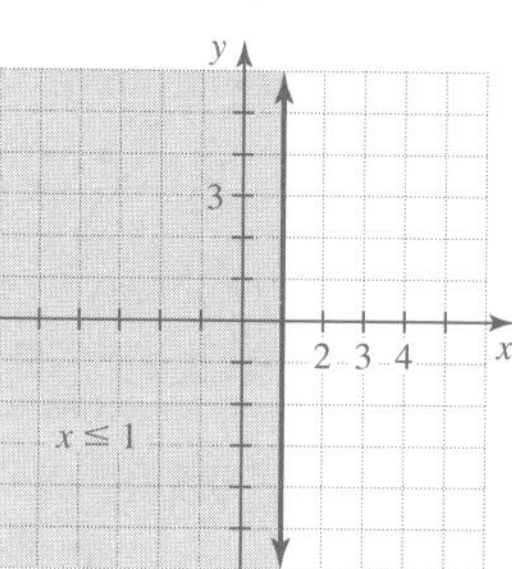

31. $x + y \leq 60$

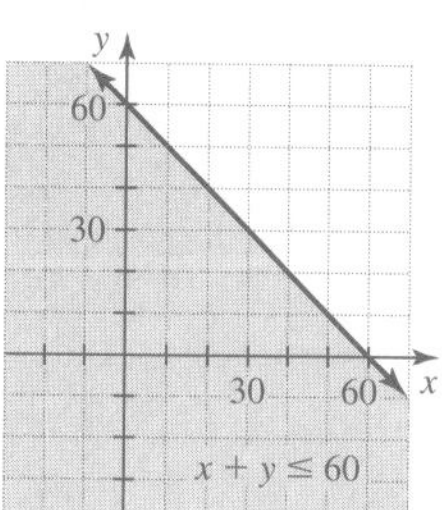

32. $x - y \leq 90$

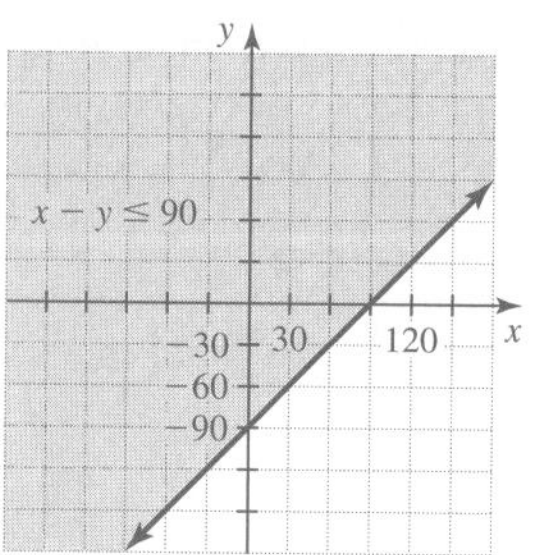

33. $x \le 100y$

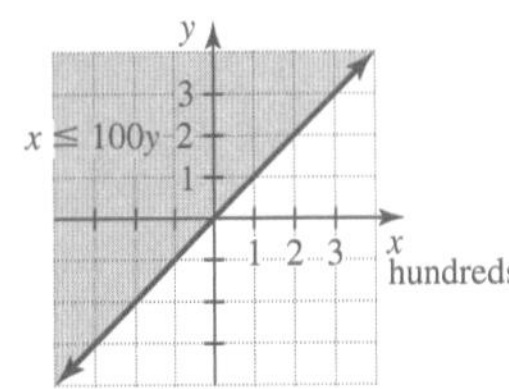

34. $y \ge 600x$

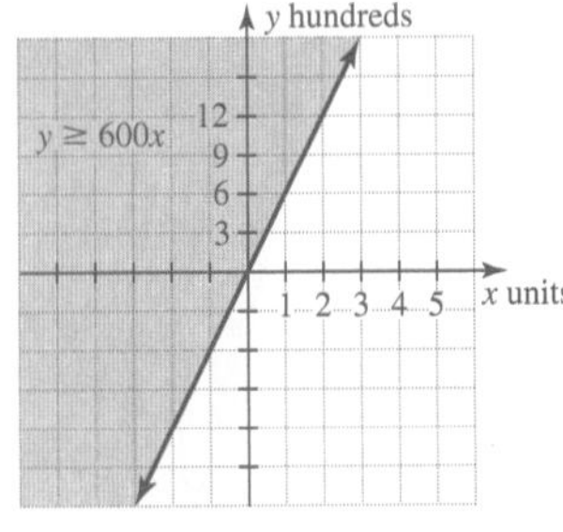

35. $3x - 4y \le 8$

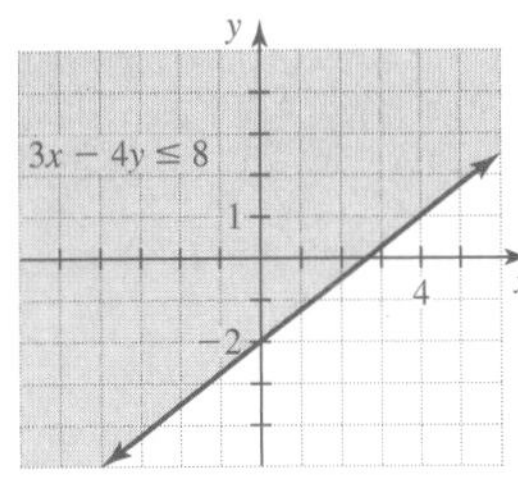

36. $2x + 5y \ge 10$

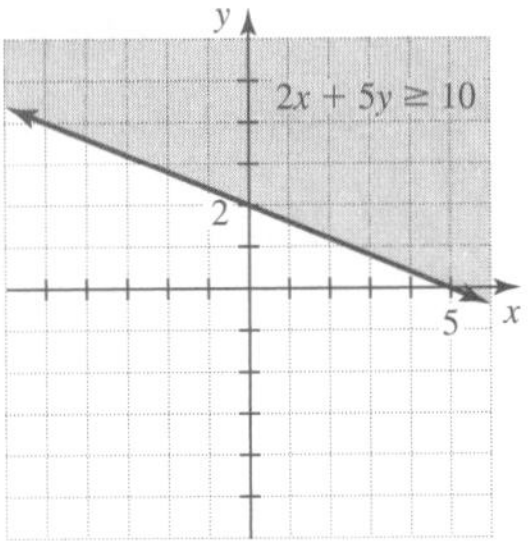

Graph each inequality. Use the test point method of Example 4.

37. $2x - 3y < 6$

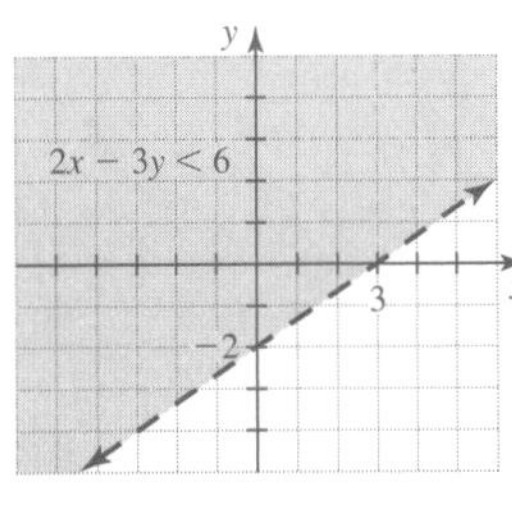

38. $x - 4y > 4$

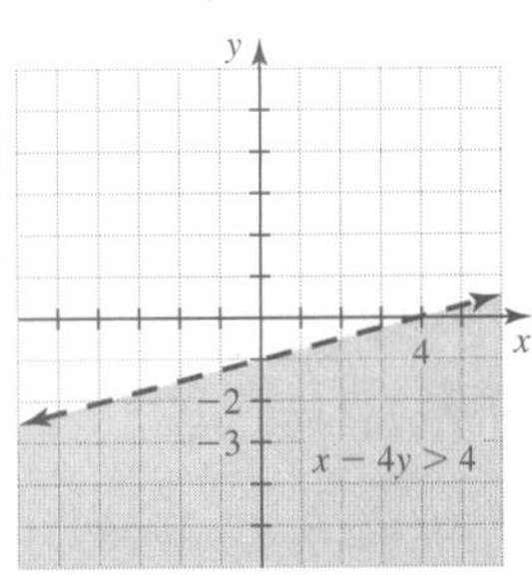

39. $x - 4y \le 8$

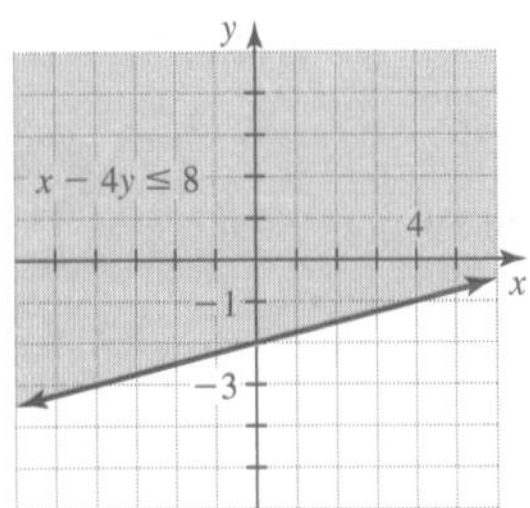

40. $3y - 5x \ge 15$

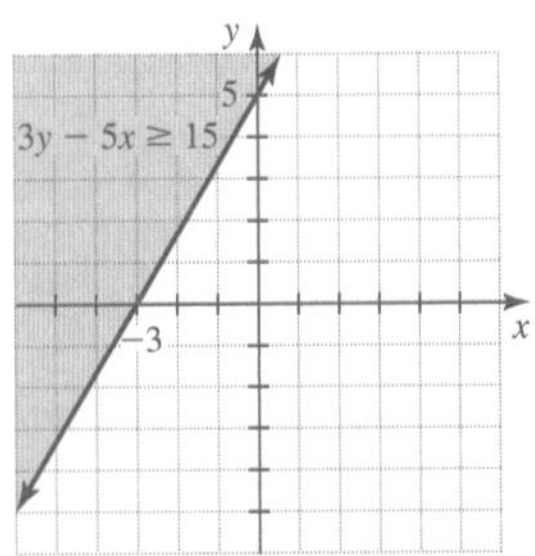

41. $y - \frac{7}{2}x \le 7$

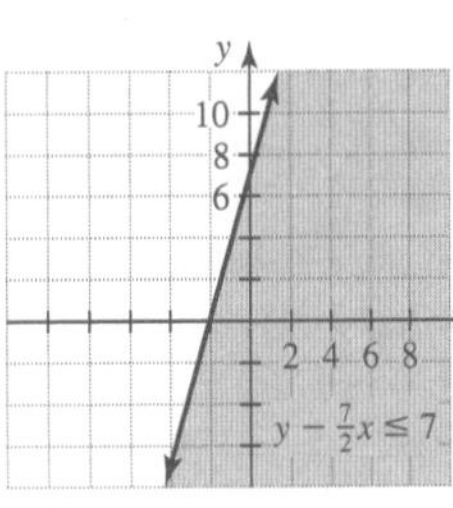

42. $\frac{2}{3}x + 3y \le 12$

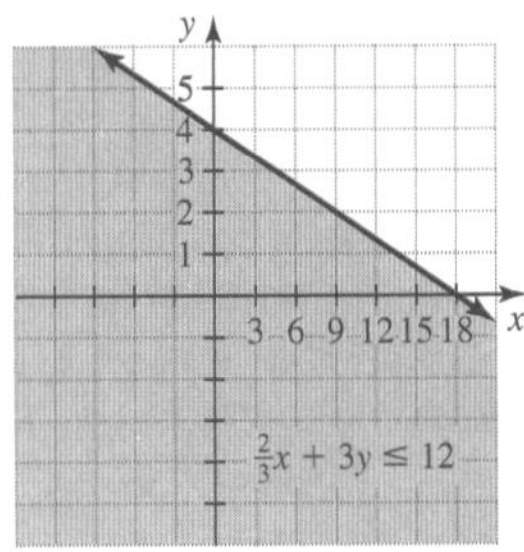

43. $x - y < 5$

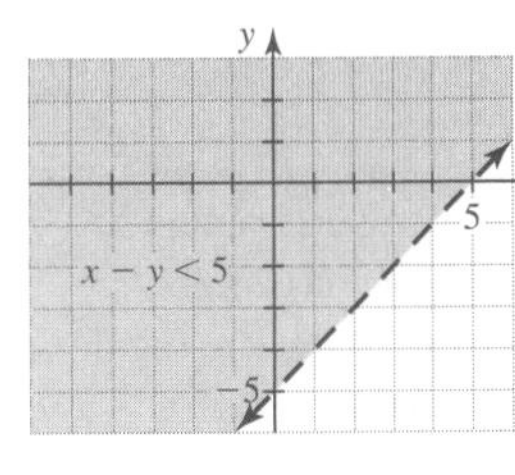

44. $y - x > -3$

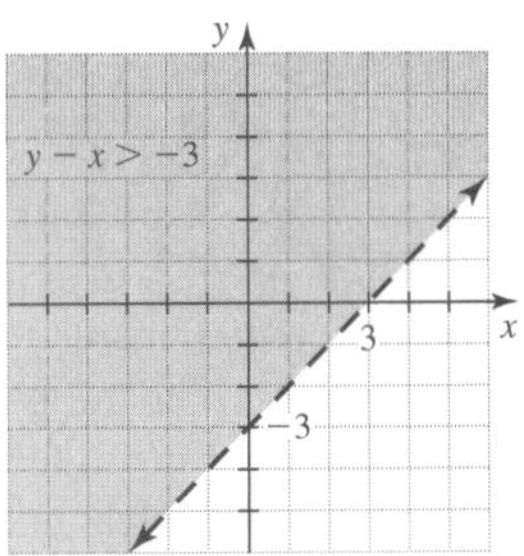

45. $3x - 4y < -12$

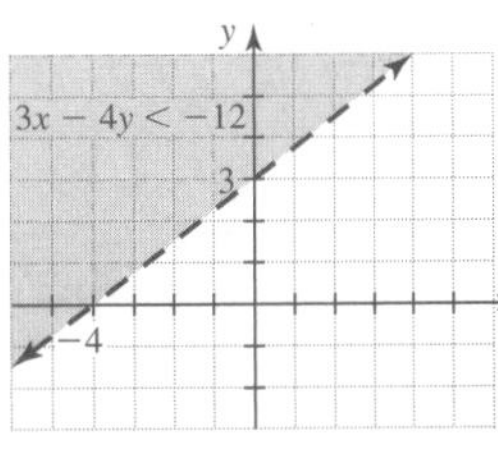

46. $4x + 3y > 24$

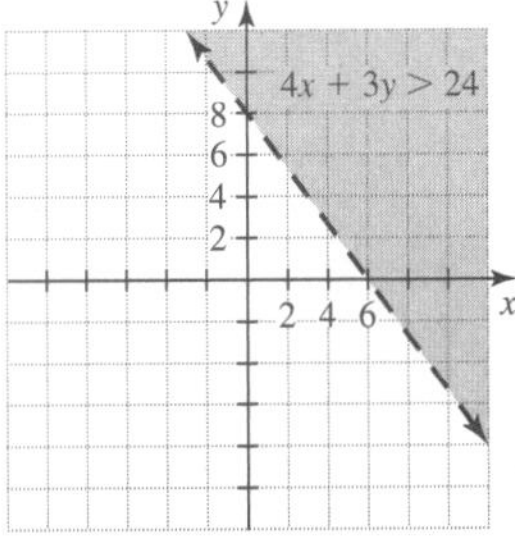

47. $x < 5y - 100$

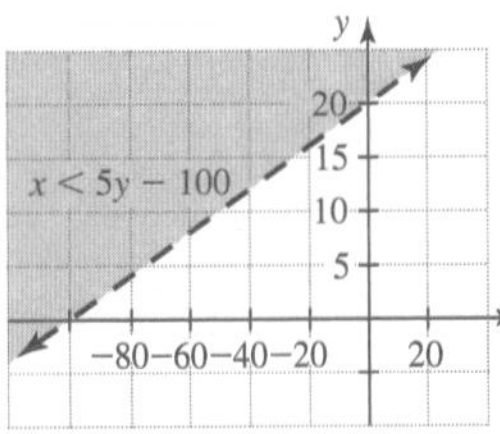

48. $-x > 70 - y$

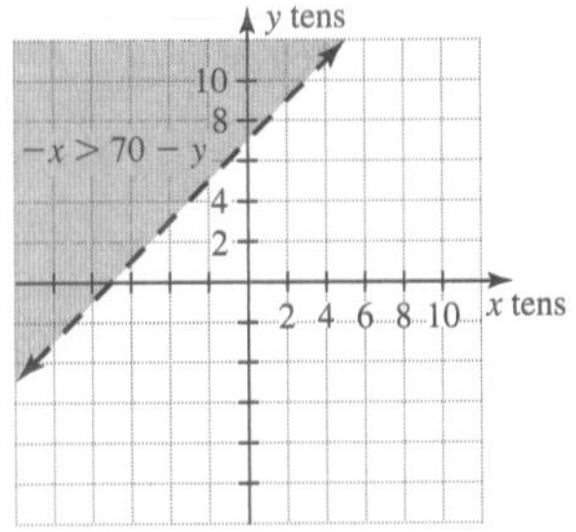

Solve each problem. See Example 5.

49. ***Storing the tables.*** Ozark Furniture Company must store its oak tables before shipping. A round table is packaged in a carton with a volume of 25 cubic feet (ft^3), and a rectangular table is packaged in a carton with a volume of 35 ft^3. The warehouse has at most 3850 ft^3 of space available for these tables. Write an inequality that limits the possible number of tables of each type that can be stored, and graph the inequality in the first quadrant. $5x + 7y \le 770$

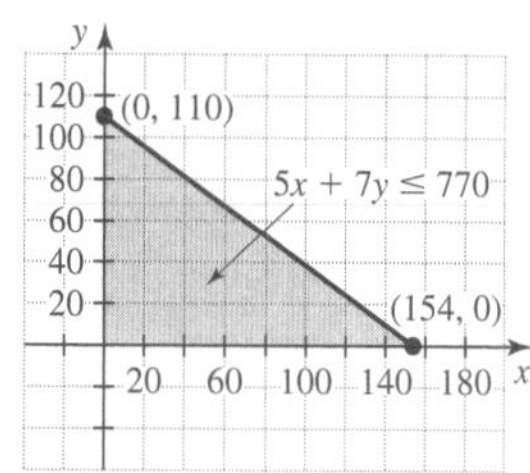

Photo for Exercise 50

50. ***Maple rockers.*** Ozark Furniture Company can obtain at most 3000 board feet of maple lumber for making its classic and modern maple rocking chairs. A classic maple rocker requires 15 board feet of maple, and a modern rocker requires 12 board feet of maple. Write an inequality that limits the possible number of maple rockers of each type that can be made, and graph the inequality in the first quadrant. $5x + 4y \le 1000$

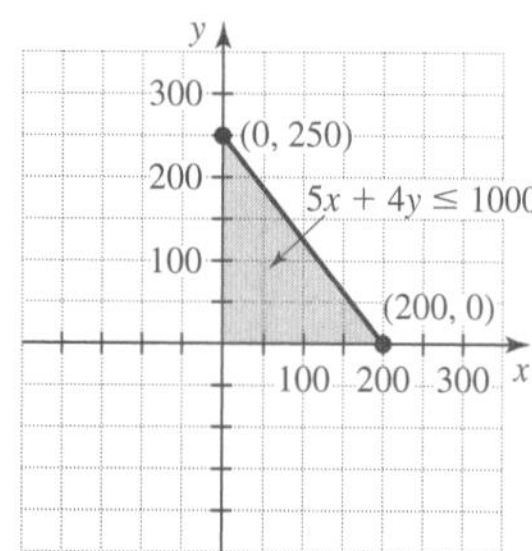

51. ***Pens and notebooks.*** A student has at most \$4 to spend on pens at \$0.25 each and notebooks at \$0.40 each. Write an inequality that limits the possibilities for the number of pens (x) and the number of notebooks (y) that can be purchased. Graph the inequality in the first quadrant.
$5x + 8y \le 80$

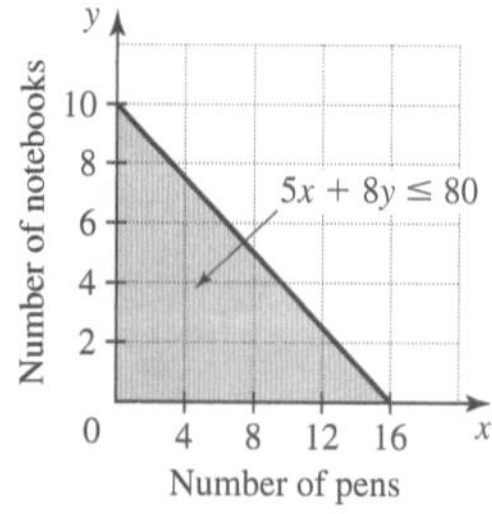

52. ***Enzyme concentration.*** A food chemist tests enzymes for their ability to break down pectin in fruit juices (Dennis Callas, *Snapshots of Applications in Mathematics*). Excess pectin makes juice cloudy. In one test, the chemist measures the concentration of the enzyme, c, in milligrams per milliliter and the fraction of light absorbed by the liquid, a. If $a > 0.07c + 0.02$, then the enzyme is working as it should. Graph the inequality in the first quadrant.

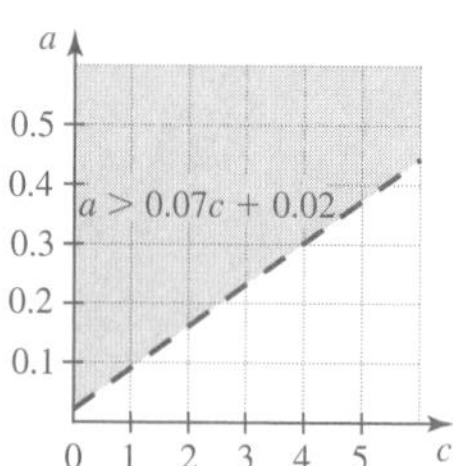

Getting More Involved

53. ***Discussion***

When asked to graph the inequality $x + 2y < 12$, a student found that (0, 5) and (8, 0) both satisfied $x + 2y < 12$. The student then drew a dashed line through these two points and shaded the region below the line. What is wrong with this method? Do all of the points graphed by this student satisfy the inequality?

54. ***Writing***

Compare and contrast the two methods presented in this section for graphing linear inequalities. What are the advantages and disadvantages of each method? How do you choose which method to use?

Collaborative Activities

Grouping: Three to four students

Topic: Plotting points, graphing lines

Inches or Centimeters?

In this activity you will generate data by measuring in both inches and centimeters the height of each member of your group. Then you will plot the points on a graph and use any two of your points to find the conversion formula for converting inches to centimeters.

Part I: Measure the height of each person in your group and fill out a table like the one shown here:

Name	Height in Inches	Height in Centimeters

Part II: The numbers for inches and centimeters from the table will give you three or four ordered pairs to graph. Plot these points on a graph. Let inches be the horizontal x-axis and centimeters be the vertical y-axis. Let each mark on the axes represent 10 units. When graphing, you will need to estimate the place to plot fractional values.

Part III: Use any two of your points to find an equation of the line you have graphed. What is the slope of your line? Where does it cross the horizontal axis?

Extension: Look up the conversion formula for converting inches to centimeters. Is it the same as the one you found by measuring? If it is different, what could account for the difference?

Chapter 3 Wrap-Up

Summary

Slope of a Line		**Examples**
Slope	The slope of the line through (x_1, y_1) and (x_2, y_2) is given by $$m = \frac{y_2 - y_1}{x_2 - x_1}, \text{ provided that } x_2 - x_1 \neq 0.$$	(0, 1), (3, 5) $$m = \frac{5-1}{3-0} = \frac{4}{3}$$
	Slope is the ratio of the rise to the run for any two points on the line: $$m = \frac{\text{change in } y}{\text{change in } x} = \frac{\text{rise}}{\text{run}}$$	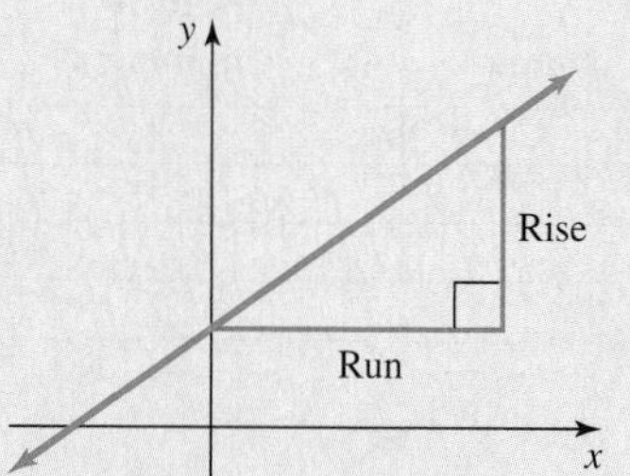
Types of slope	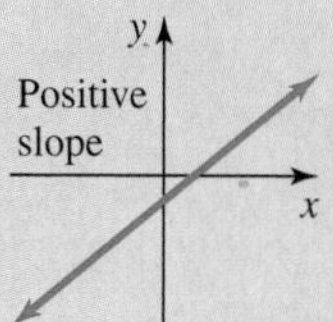 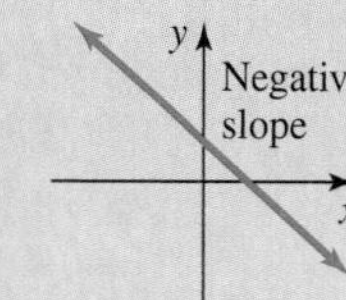 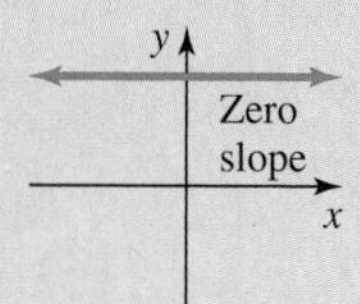	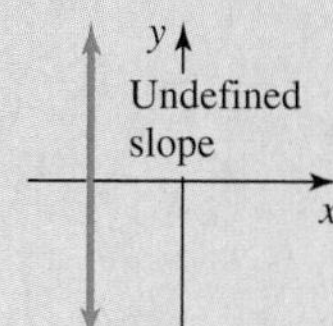
Parallel lines	Nonvertical parallel lines have equal slopes. Two vertical lines are parallel.	The lines $y = 3x - 9$ and $y = 3x + 7$ are parallel lines.
Perpendicular lines	Lines with slopes m and $-\frac{1}{m}$ are perpendicular. Any vertical line is perpendicular to any horizontal line.	The lines $y = -5x + 7$ and $y = \frac{1}{5}x$ are perpendicular.
Equations of Lines		**Examples**
Slope-intercept form	The equation of the line with y-intercept $(0, b)$ and slope m is $y = mx + b$.	$y = 3x - 1$ has slope 3 and y-intercept $(0, -1)$.
Point-slope form	The equation of the line with slope m that contains the point (x_1, y_1) is $y - y_1 = m(x - x_1)$.	The line through $(2, -1)$ with slope -5 is $y + 1 = -5(x - 2)$.
Standard form	Every line has an equation of the form $Ax + By = C$, where A, B, and C are real numbers with A and B not both equal to zero.	$4x - 9y = 15$ $x = 5$ (vertical line) $y = -7$ (horizontal line)

Graphing a line using y-intercept and slope	1. Write the equation in slope-intercept form. 2. Plot the y-intercept. 3. Use the rise and run to locate a second point. 4. Draw a line through the two points.	
Variation		**Examples**
Direct	If $y = kx$, then y varies directly as x.	$D = 50T$
Inverse	If $y = \frac{k}{x}$, then y varies inversely as x.	$R = \frac{400}{T}$
Joint	If $y = kxz$, then y varies jointly as x and z.	$V = 6LW$
Linear Inequalities in Two Variables		**Examples**
Graphing the solution to an inequality in two variables	1. Solve the inequality for y, then graph $y = mx + b$. $y > mx + b$ is the region above the line. $y = mx + b$ is the line itself. $y < mx + b$ is the region below the line.	$y > x + 3$ $y = x + 3$ $y < x + 3$
	Remember that "less than" means below the line and "greater than" means above the line only when the inequality is solved for y.	
	2. If the inequality involves only x, then graph the vertical line $x = k$. $x > k$ is the region to the right of the line. $x = k$ is the line itself. $x < k$ is the region to the left of the line.	$x > 5$ Region to right of vertical line $x = 5$
Test points	A linear inequality may also be graphed by graphing the equation and then testing a point to determine which region satisfies the inequality.	$x + y > 4$ (0, 6) satisfies the inequality.

Enriching Your Mathematical Word Power

For each mathematical term, choose the correct meaning.

1. graph of an equation
a. the Cartesian coordinate system
b. two number lines that intersect at a right angle
c. the x-axis and y-axis
d. an illustration in the coordinate plane that shows all ordered pairs that satisfy an equation d

2. x-coordinate
a. the first number in an ordered pair
b. the second number in an ordered pair
c. a point on the x-axis
d. a point where a graph crosses the x-axis a

3. y-intercept
a. the second number in an ordered pair
b. a point at which a graph intersects the y-axis
c. any point on the y-axis
d. the point where the y-axis intersects the x-axis b

4. coordinate plane
a. a matching plane
b. when the x-axis is coordinated with the y-axis
c. a plane with a rectangular coordinate system
d. a coordinated system for graphs c

5. **slope**
   a. the change in x divided by the change in y
   b. a measure of the steepness of a line
   c. the run divided by the rise
   d. the slope of a line b
6. **slope-intercept form**
   a. $y = mx + b$
   b. rise over run
   c. the point at which a line crosses the y-axis
   d. $y - y_1 = m(x - x_1)$ a
7. **point-slope form**
   a. $Ax + By = C$
   b. rise over run
   c. $y - y_1 = m(x - x_1)$
   d. the slope of a line at a single point c
8. **independent variable**
   a. a rational constant
   b. an irrational constant
   c. the first variable of an ordered pair
   d. the second variable of an ordered pair c
9. **dependent variable**
   a. an irrational variable
   b. a rational variable
   c. the first variable of an ordered pair
   d. the second variable of an ordered pair d
10. **direct variation**
   a. $y = \pi$
   b. $y = kx$
   c. $y = k/x$
   d. $y = kxz$ b
11. **inverse variation**
   a. $y = \pi$
   b. $y = kx$
   c. $y = k/x$
   d. $y = kxz$ c
12. **joint variation**
   a. $y = \pi$
   b. $y = kx$
   c. $y = k/x$
   d. $y = kxz$ d
13. **linear inequality in two variables**
   a. when two lines are not equal
   b. line segments that are unequal in length
   c. an inequality of the form $Ax + By \geq C$ or with another symbol of inequality
   d. an inequality of the form $Ax^2 + By^2 < C^2$ c

Review Exercises

3.1 *For each point, name the quadrant in which it lies or the axis on which it lies.*

1. $(-2, 5)$
   Quadrant II
2. $(-3, -5)$
   Quadrant III
3. $(3, 0)$
   x-axis
4. $(9, 10)$
   Quadrant I
5. $(0, -6)$
   y-axis
6. $(0, \pi)$
   y-axis
7. $(1.414, -3)$
   Quadrant IV
8. $(-4, 1.732)$
   Quadrant II

Study Tip

Note how the review exercises are arranged according to the sections in this chapter. If you are having trouble with a certain type of problem, refer back to the appropriate section for examples and explanations.

Complete the given ordered pairs so that each ordered pair satisfies the given equation.

9. $y = 3x - 5$: $(0,\ \ )$, $(-3,\ \ )$, $(4,\ \ )$
   $(0, -5)$, $(-3, -14)$, $(4, 7)$
10. $y = -2x + 1$: $(9,\ \ )$, $(3,\ \ )$, $(-1,\ \ )$
   $(9, -17)$, $(3, -5)$, $(-1, 3)$
11. $2x - 3y = 8$: $(0,\ \ )$, $(3,\ \ )$, $(-6,\ \ )$
   $\left(0, -\frac{8}{3}\right)$, $\left(3, -\frac{2}{3}\right)$, $\left(-6, -\frac{20}{3}\right)$
12. $x + 2y = 1$: $(0,\ \ )$, $(-2,\ \ )$, $(2,\ \ )$
   $\left(0, \frac{1}{2}\right)$, $\left(-2, \frac{3}{2}\right)$, $\left(2, -\frac{1}{2}\right)$

Sketch the graph of each equation by finding three ordered pairs that satisfy each equation.

13. $y = -3x + 4$

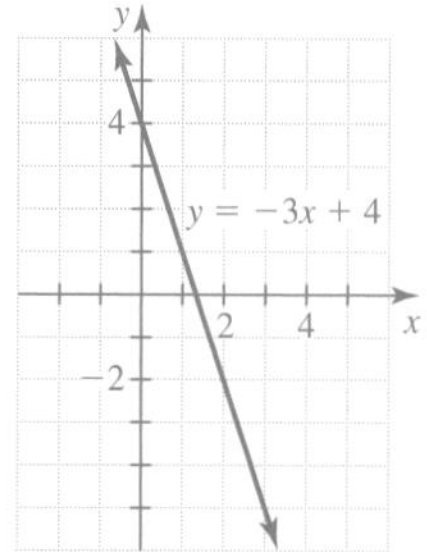

14. $y = 2x - 6$

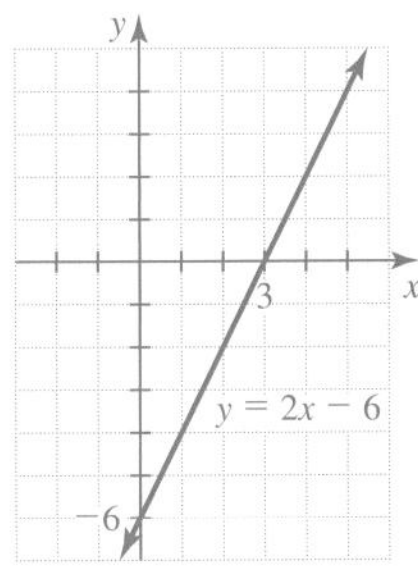

15. $x + y = 7$

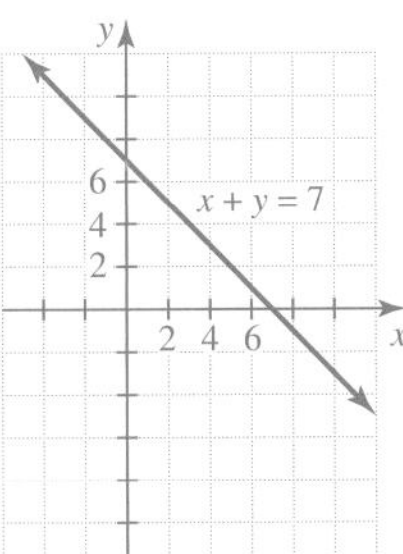

16. $x - y = 4$

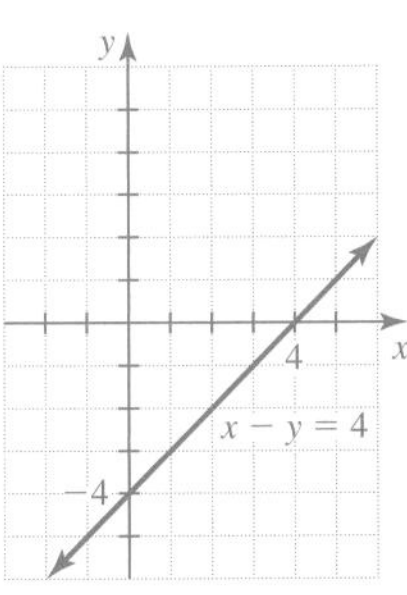

3.2 *Determine the slope of the line that goes through each pair of points.*

17. (0, 0) and (1, 1) 1

18. (−1, 1) and (2, −2) −1

19. (−2, −3) and (0, 0) $\frac{3}{2}$

20. (−1, −2) and (4, −1) $\frac{1}{5}$

21. (−4, −2) and (3, 1) $\frac{3}{7}$

22. (0, 4) and (5, 0) $-\frac{4}{5}$

3.3 *Find the slope and y-intercept for each line.*

23. $y = 3x - 18$ 3, (0, −18)

24. $y = -x + 5$ −1, (0, 5)

25. $2x - y = 3$ 2, (0, −3)

26. $x - 2y = 1$ $\frac{1}{2}, \left(0, -\frac{1}{2}\right)$

27. $4x - 2y - 8 = 0$ 2, (0, −4)

28. $3x + 5y + 10 = 0$ $-\frac{3}{5}$, (0, −2)

Sketch the graph of each equation.

29. $y = \frac{2}{3}x - 5$

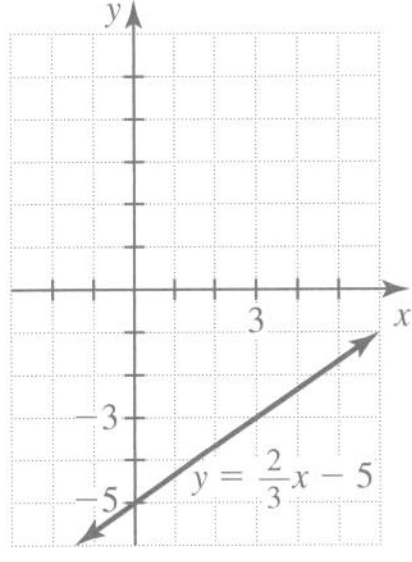

30. $y = \frac{3}{2}x + 1$

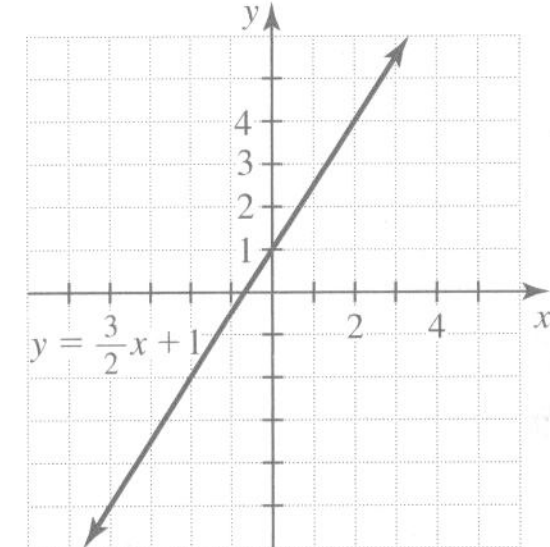

31. $2x + y = -6$

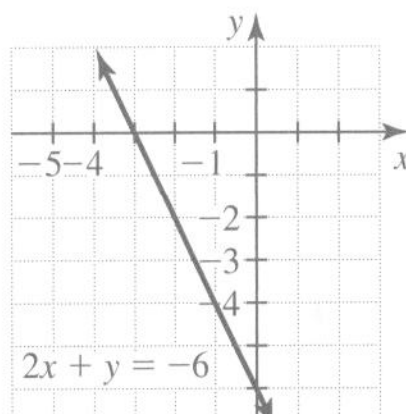

32. $-3x - y = 2$

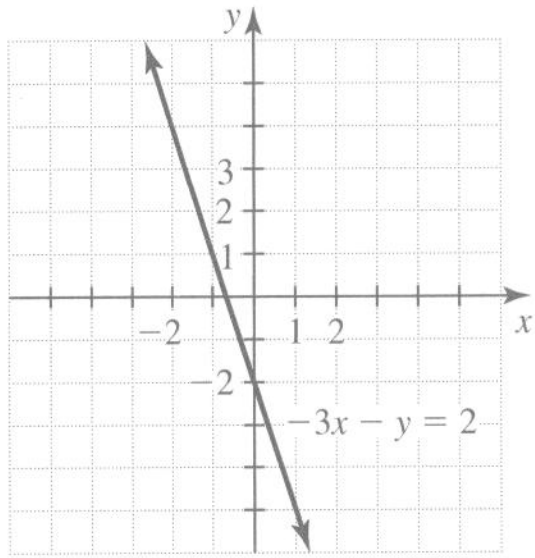

33. $y = -4$

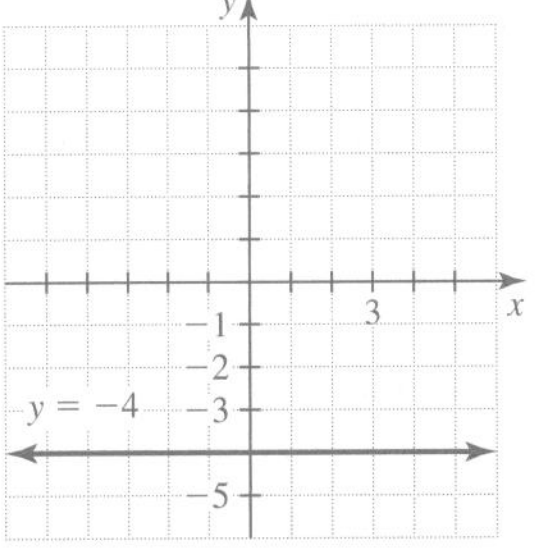

34. $x = 9$

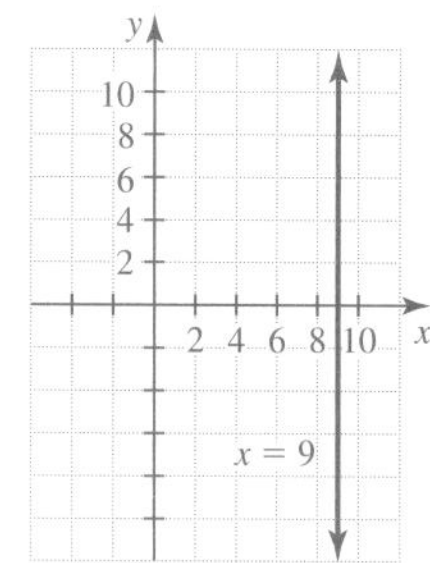

Determine the equation of each line. Write the answer in standard form using only integers as the coefficients.

35. The line through (0, 4) with slope $\frac{1}{3}$ $x - 3y = -12$

36. The line through $(-2, 0)$ with slope $-\frac{3}{4}$ $3x + 4y = -6$

37. The line through the origin that is perpendicular to the line $y = 2x - 1$ $x + 2y = 0$

38. The line through (0, 9) that is parallel to the line $3x + 5y = 15$ $3x + 5y = 45$

39. The line through (3, 5) that is parallel to the x-axis $y = 5$

40. The line through $(-2, 4)$ that is perpendicular to the x-axis $x = -2$

3.4 *Write each equation in slope-intercept form.*

41. $y - 3 = \frac{2}{3}(x + 6)$ $y = \frac{2}{3}x + 7$

42. $y + 2 = -6(x - 1)$ $y = -6x + 4$

43. $3x - 7y - 14 = 0$ $y = \frac{3}{7}x - 2$

44. $1 - x - y = 0$ $y = -x + 1$

45. $y - 5 = -\frac{3}{4}(x + 1)$ $y = -\frac{3}{4}x + \frac{17}{4}$

46. $y + 8 = -\frac{2}{5}(x - 2)$ $y = -\frac{2}{5}x - \frac{36}{5}$

Determine the equation of each line. Write the answer in slope-intercept form.

47. The line through $(-4, 7)$ with slope -2 $y = -2x - 1$

48. The line through (9, 0) with slope $\frac{1}{2}$ $y = \frac{1}{2}x - \frac{9}{2}$

49. The line through the two points $(-2, 1)$ and $(3, 7)$ $y = \frac{6}{5}x + \frac{17}{5}$

50. The line through the two points (4, 0) and $(-3, -5)$ $y = \frac{5}{7}x - \frac{20}{7}$

51. The line through $(3, -5)$ that is parallel to the line $y = 3x - 1$ $y = 3x - 14$

52. The line through (4, 0) that is perpendicular to the line $x + y = 3$ $y = x - 4$

Solve each problem.

53. ***Rental charge.*** The charge for renting an air hammer for two days is \$113 and the charge for five days is \$209. The charge C is determined by the number of days n using a linear equation. Find the equation and find the charge for a four-day rental.
$C = 32n + 49$, \$177

54. ***Time on a treadmill.*** After 2 minutes on a treadmill, Jenny has a heart rate of 82. After 3 minutes she has a heart rate of 86. Assume that there is a linear equation that gives her heart rate h in terms of time on the treadmill t. Find the equation and use it to predict her heart rate after 10 minutes on the treadmill.
$h = 4t + 74$, 114

55. ***Probability of rain.*** If the probability p of rain is 90%, the probability q that it does not rain is 10%. If the probability of rain is 80%, then the probability that it does not rain is 20%. There is a linear equation that gives q in terms of p.

a) Find the equation.
b) Use the accompanying graph to determine the probability of rain if the probability that it does not rain is 0.

a) $q = 1 - p$
b) 1

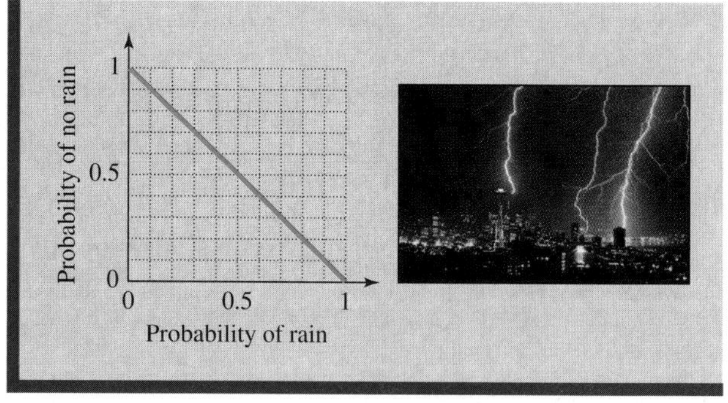

Figure for Exercise 55

56. ***Social Security benefits.*** If you earned an average of \$25,000 over your working life and you retire after 2005 at age 62, 63, or 64, then your annual Social Security benefit will be \$7000, \$7500, or \$8000, respectively (Social Security Administration, www.ssa.gov). There is a linear equation that gives the annual benefit b in terms of age a for these three years. Find the equation.
$b = 500a - 24{,}000$

57. ***Predicting freshman GPA.*** A researcher who is studying the relationship between ACT score and grade point average for freshman gathered the data shown in the accompanying table. Find the equation of the line in slope-intercept form that goes through these points.
$y = 0.1x + 0.6$

ACT Score (*x*)	GPA (*y*)
4	1.0
14	2.0
24	3.0
34	4.0

Table for Exercise 57

58. ***Interest rates.*** A credit manager rates each applicant for a car loan on a scale of 1 through 5 and then determines the interest rate from the accompanying table. Find the equation of the line in slope-intercept form that goes through these points.
$y = -4x + 28$

Credit Rating	Interest Rate (%)
1	24
2	20
3	16
4	12
5	8

Table for Exercise 58

3.5 *Solve each variation problem.*

59. Suppose y varies directly as w. If $y = 48$ when $w = 4$, then what is y when $w = 11$?
132

60. Suppose m varies directly as t. If $m = 13$ when $t = 2$, then what is m when $t = 6$?
39

61. If y varies inversely as v and $y = 8$ when $v = 6$, then what is y when $v = 24$?
2

62. If y varies inversely as r and $y = 9$ when $r = 3$, then what is y when $r = 9$?
3

63. Suppose y varies jointly as u and v, and $y = 72$ when $u = 3$ and $v = 4$. Find y when $u = 5$ and $v = 2$.
60

64. Suppose q varies jointly as s and t, and $q = 10$ when $s = 4$ and $t = 3$. Find q when $s = 25$ and $t = 6$.
125

65. ***Taxi fare.*** The cost of a taxi ride varies directly with the length of the ride in minutes. A 12-minute ride costs \$9.00.

a) Write the cost in terms of the length of the ride.
b) What is the cost of a 20-minute ride?
c) Is the cost increasing or decreasing as the length of the ride increases?

a) $C = 0.75T$ **b)** \$15 **c)** Increasing

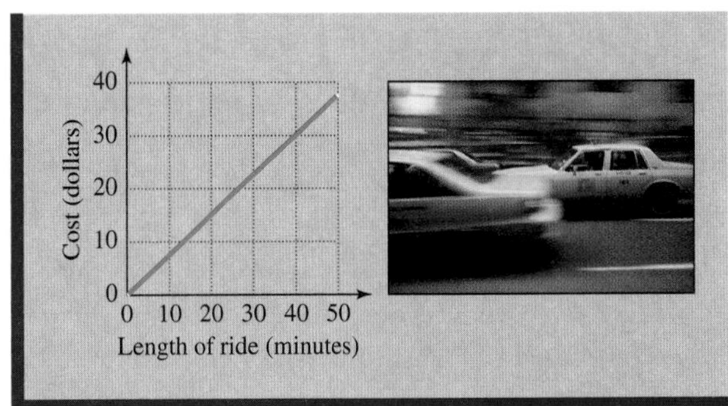

Figure for Exercise 65

66. ***Applying shingles.*** The number of hours that it takes to apply 296 bundles of shingles varies inversely with the number of roofers working on the job. Three workers can complete the job in 40 hours.

a) Write the number of hours in terms of the number of roofers on the job.

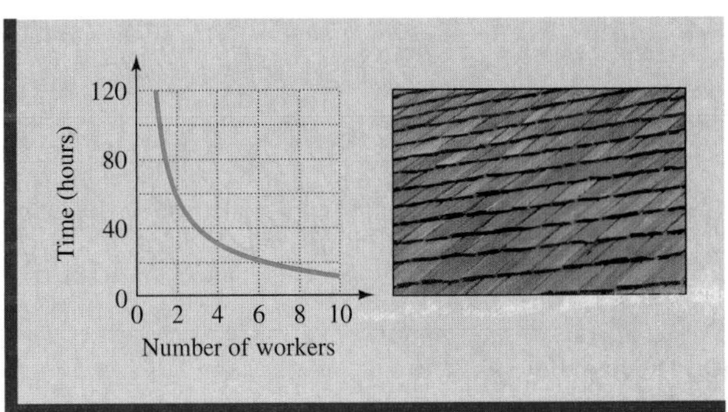

Figure for Exercise 66

b) How long would it take five roofers to complete the job?

c) Is the time to complete the job increasing or decreasing as the number of workers increases?

a) $h = \frac{120}{n}$ b) 24 hours c) Decreasing

3.6 *Graph each inequality.*

67. $y > \frac{1}{3}x - 5$

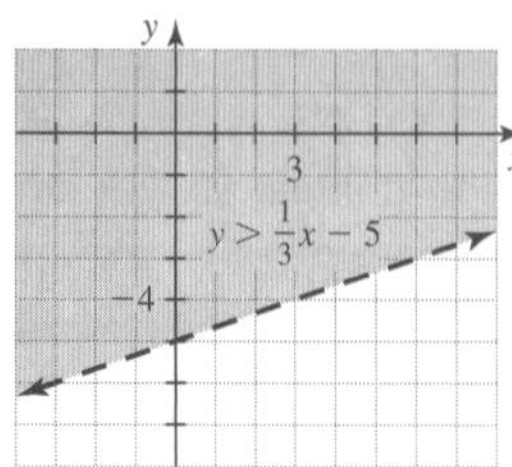

68. $y < \frac{1}{2}x + 2$

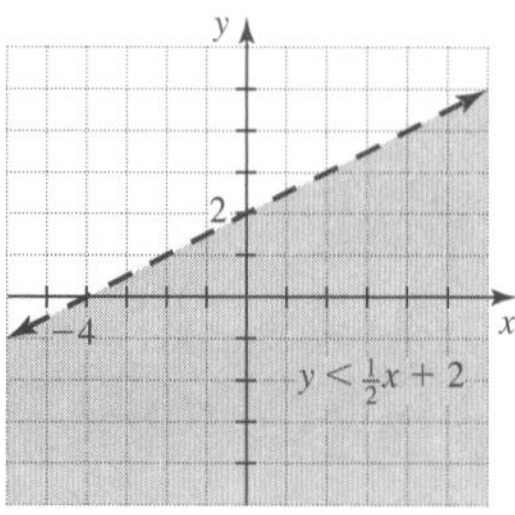

69. $y \le -2x + 7$

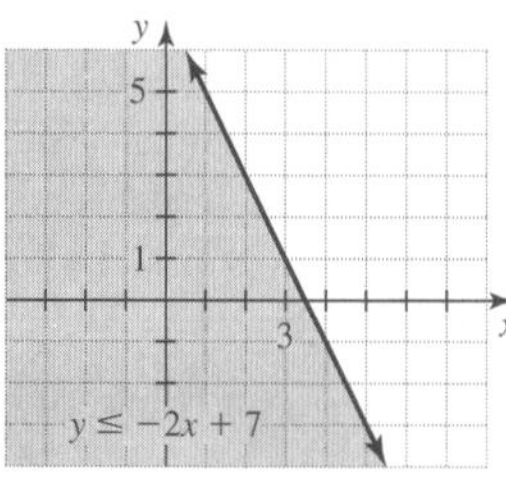

70. $y \ge x - 6$

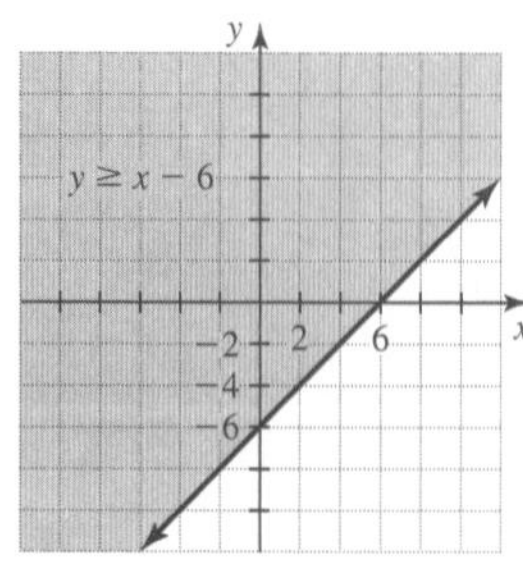

71. $y \le 8$

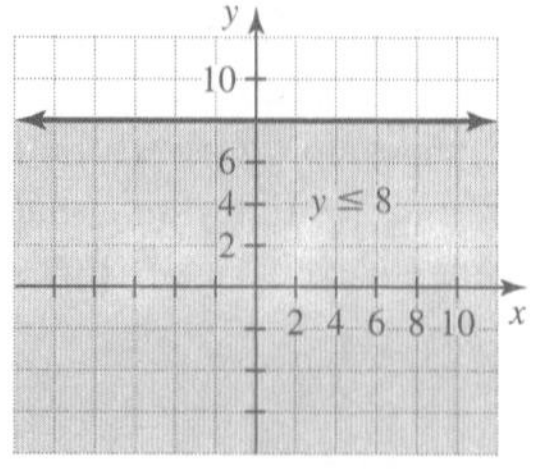

72. $x \ge -6$

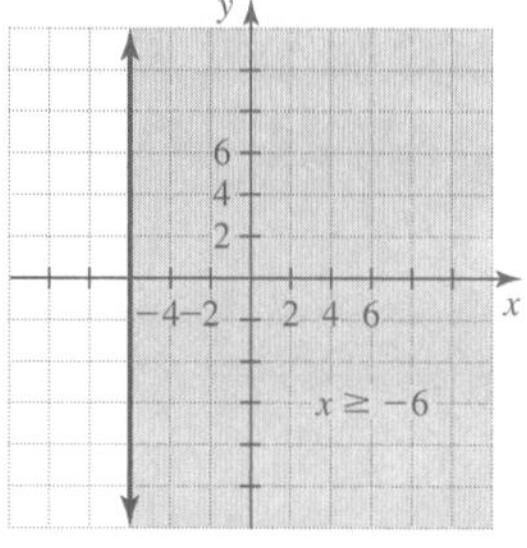

73. $2x + 3y \le -12$

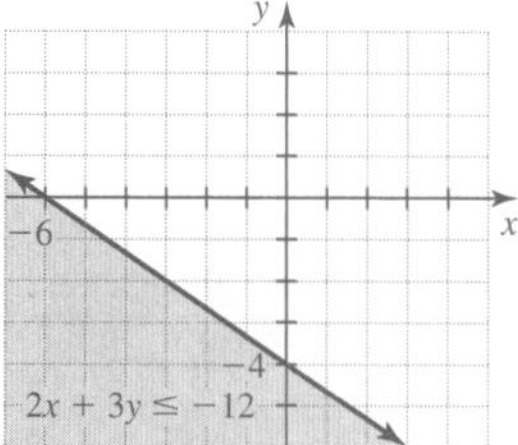

74. $x - 3y < 9$

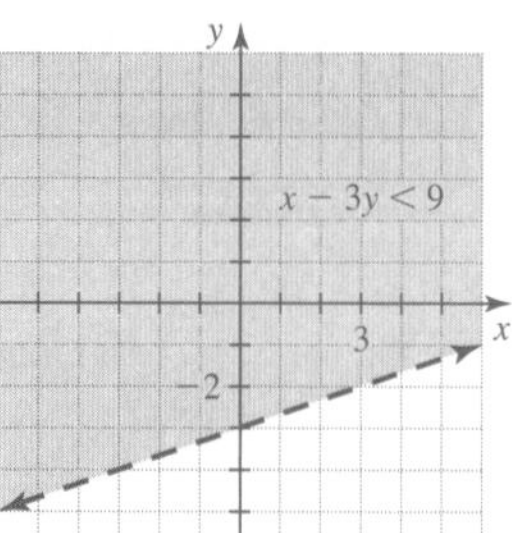

Chapter 3 Test

For each point, name the quadrant in which it lies or the axis on which it lies.

1. $(-2, 7)$ Quadrant II
2. $(-\pi, 0)$ x-axis
3. $(3, -6)$ Quadrant IV
4. $(0, 1785)$ y-axis

Find the slope of the line through each pair of points.

5. $(3, 3)$ and $(4, 4)$ 1
6. $(-2, -3)$ and $(4, -8)$ $-\frac{5}{6}$

Find the slope of each line.

7. The line $y = 3x - 5$ 3
8. The line $y = 3$ 0
9. The line $x = 5$ Undefined
10. The line $2x - 3y = 4$ $\frac{2}{3}$

Write the equation of each line. Give the answer in slope-intercept form.

11. The line through $(0, 3)$ with slope $-\frac{1}{2}$ $y = -\frac{1}{2}x + 3$
12. The line through $(-1, -2)$ with slope $\frac{3}{7}$ $y = \frac{3}{7}x - \frac{11}{7}$

Write the equation of each line. Give the answer in standard form using only integers as the coefficients.

13. The line through $(2, -3)$ that is perpendicular to the line $y = -3x + 12$ $x - 3y = 11$
14. The line through $(3, 4)$ that is parallel to the line $5x + 3y = 9$ $5x + 3y = 27$

Study Tip

Before you take an in-class exam on this chapter, work the sample test given here. Set aside one hour to work this test and use the answers in the back of this book to grade yourself. Even though your instructor might not ask exactly the same questions, you will get a good idea of your test readiness.

Sketch the graph of each equation.

15. $y = \frac{1}{2}x - 3$

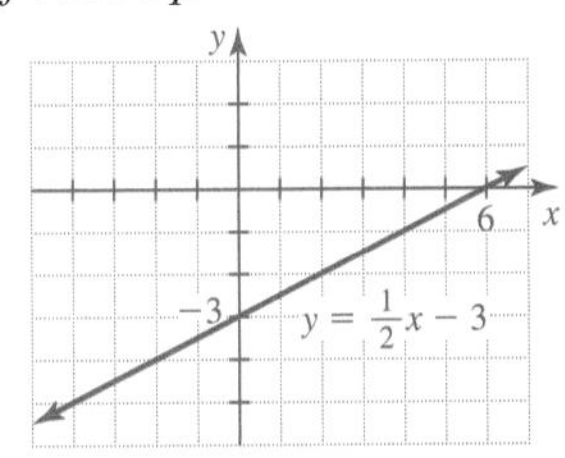

16. $2x - 3y = 6$

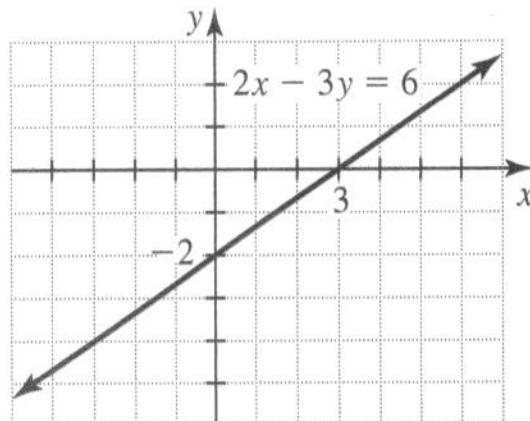

17. $y = 4$

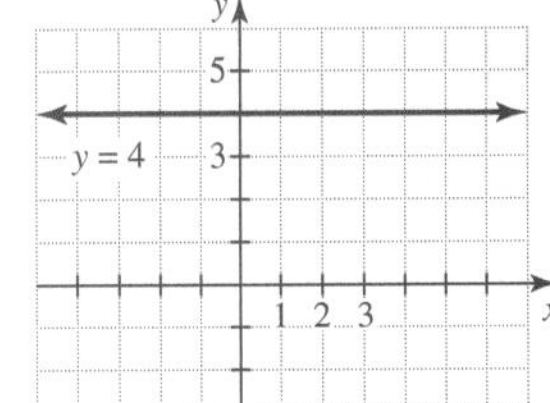

18. $x = -2$

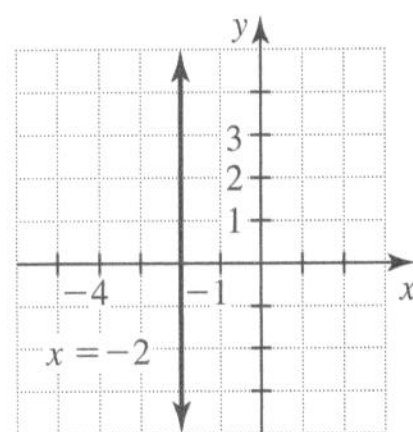

Graph each inequality.

19. $y > 3x - 5$

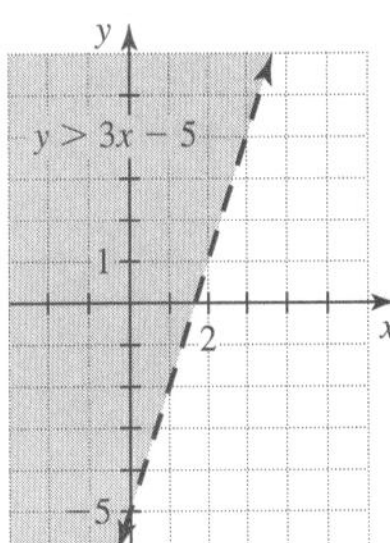

20. $x - y < 3$

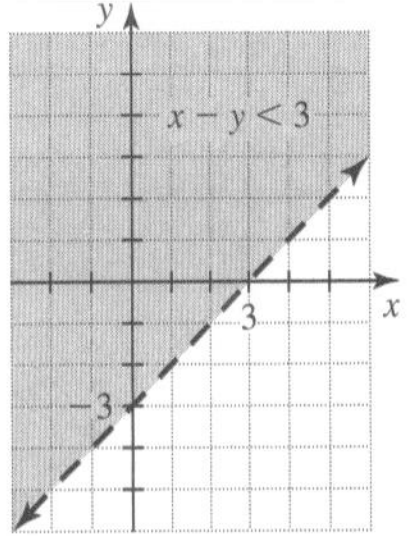

21. $x - 2y \geq 4$

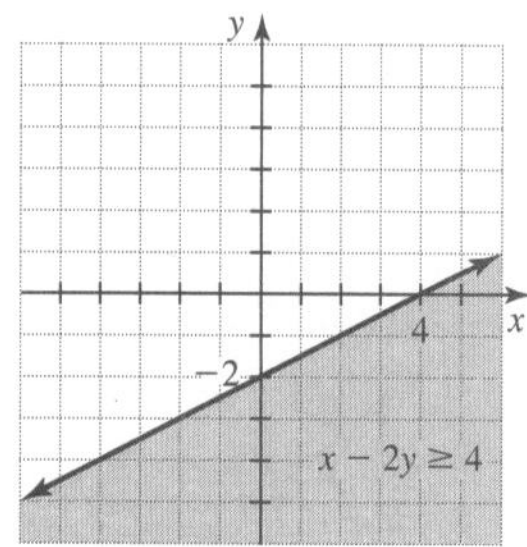

Solve each problem.

22. Julie's mail-order CD club charges a shipping and handling fee of \$2.50 plus \$0.75 per CD for each order shipped. Write the shipping and handling fee S in terms of the number n of CDs in the order. $S = 0.75n + 2.50$

23. A 10-ounce soft drink sells for 50 cents, and a 16-ounce soft drink sells for 68 cents. The price P is determined from the volume of the cup v by a linear equation. Find the equation and find the price for a 20-ounce soft drink.
$P = 3v + 20$, 80 cents

24. The price of a watermelon varies directly with its weight. If the price of a 30-pound watermelon is \$4.20, then what is the price of a 20-pound watermelon?
\$2.80

25. The number of days that Jerry spends on the road is inversely proportional to his sales for the previous month. If Jerry spent 15 days on the road when his previous month's sales were \$75,000, then how many days would he spend on the road when his previous month's sales were \$60,000? Does his road time increase or decrease as his sales increase?
18.75 days, decreases

26. The labor cost for installing ceramic floor tile in a rectangular room varies jointly with the length and width. For a room that is 8 feet by 10 feet the cost is \$400. For a room that is 9 feet by 12 feet the cost is \$540. What is the cost for a room that is 11 feet by 14 feet?
\$770

Graph Paper

Use these grids for graphing. Make as many copies of this page as you need.

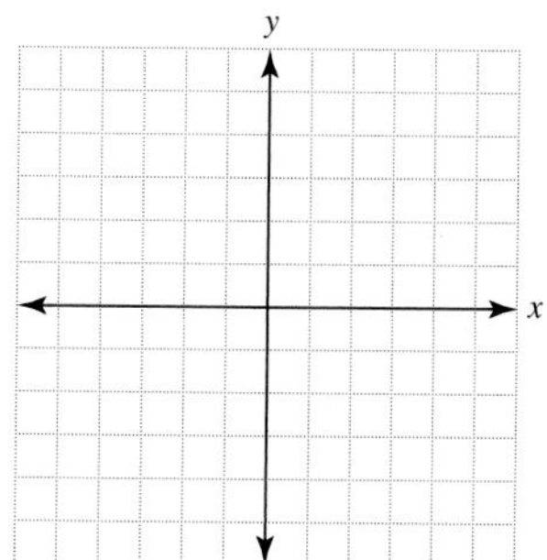

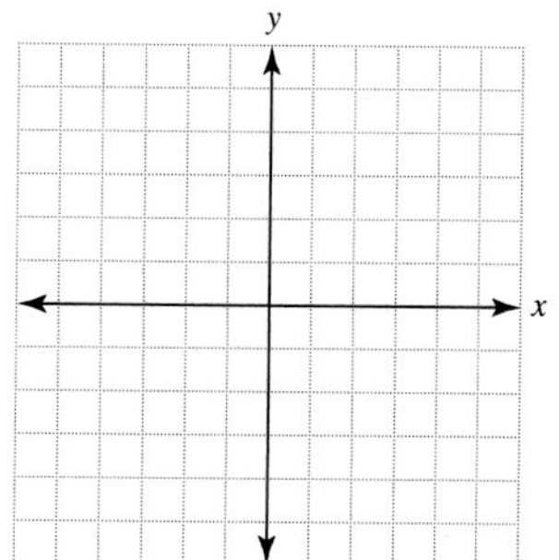

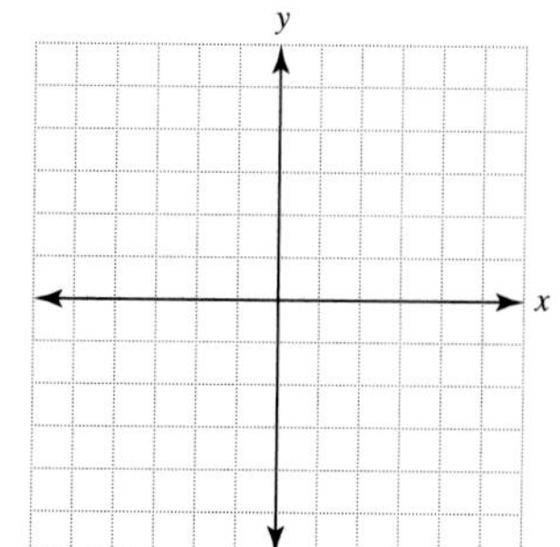

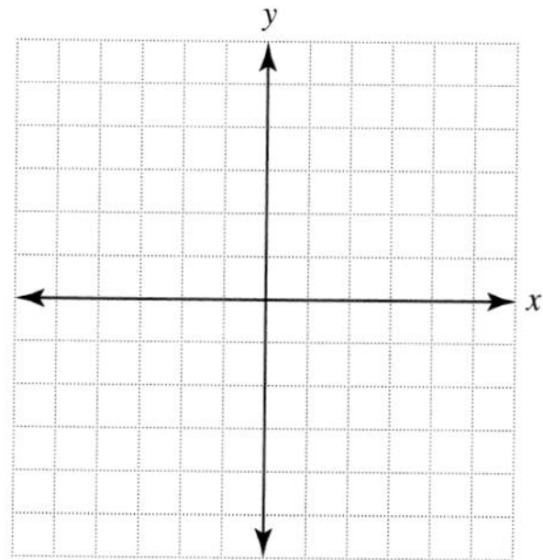

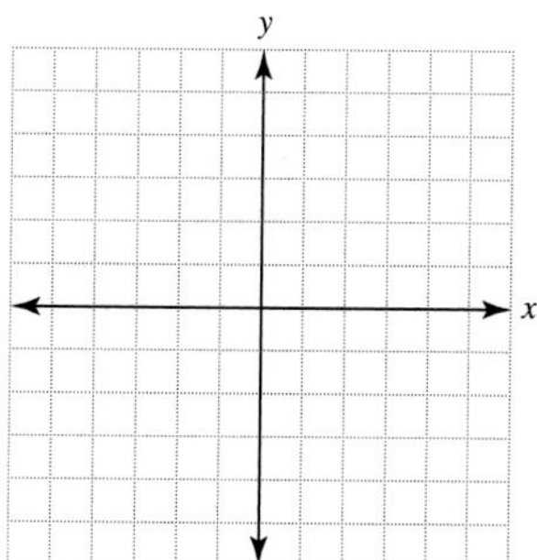

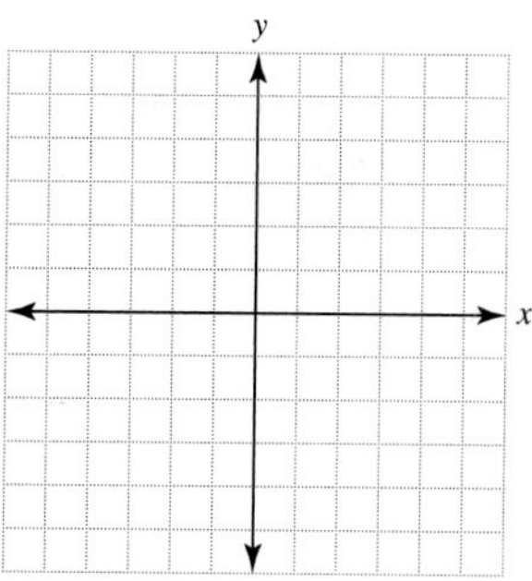

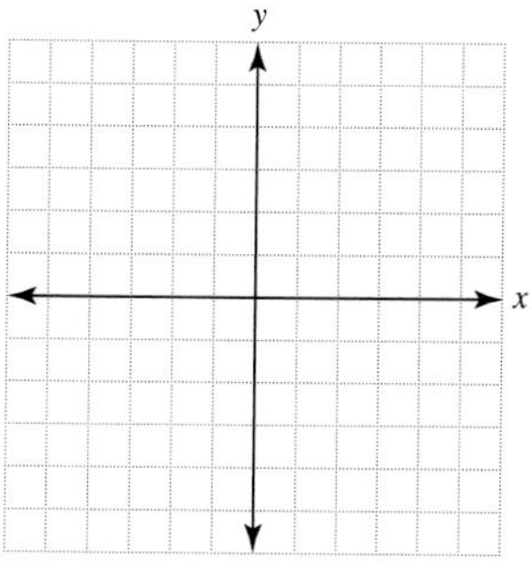

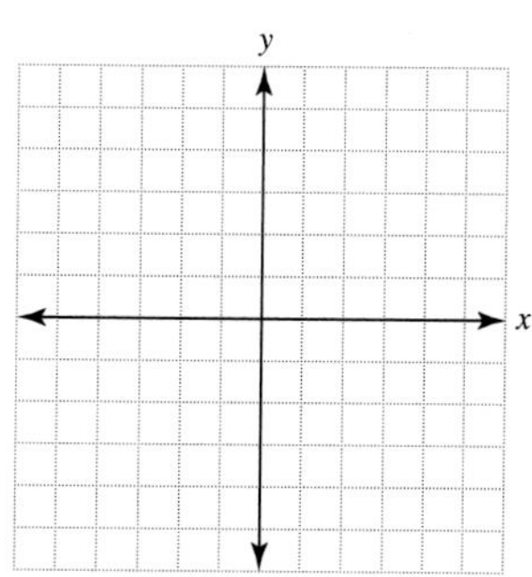

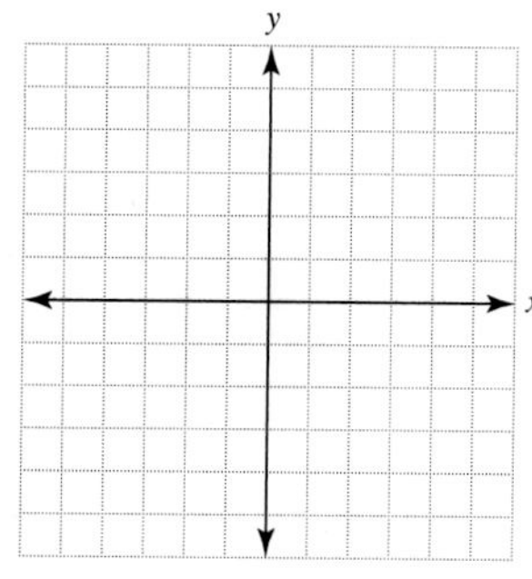

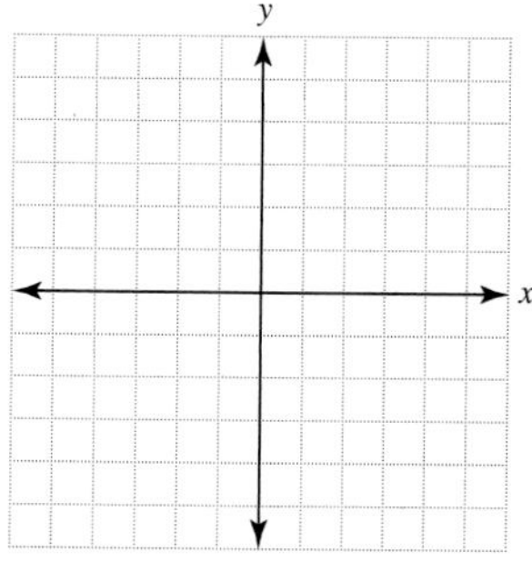

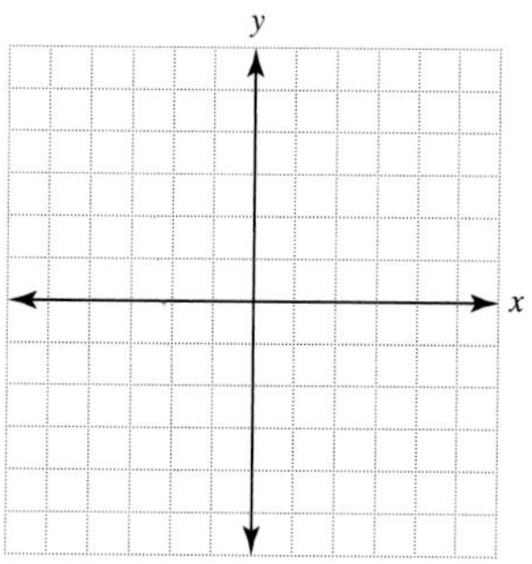

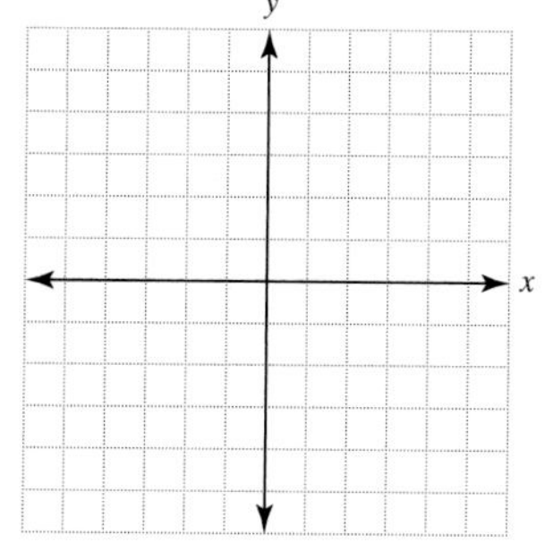

*Making*Connections | A Review of Chapters 1–3

Simplify each arithmetic expression.

1. $9 - 5 \cdot 2$ -1

2. $-4 \cdot 5 - 7 \cdot 2$ -34

3. $3^2 - 2^3$ 1

4. $3^2 \cdot 2^3$ 72

5. $(-4)^2 - 4(1)(5)$ -4

6. $-4^2 - 4 \cdot 3$ -28

7. $\dfrac{-5 - 9}{2 - (-2)}$ $-\dfrac{7}{2}$

8. $\dfrac{6 - 3.6}{6}$ 0.4

9. $\dfrac{1 - \frac{1}{2}}{4 - (-1)}$ $\dfrac{1}{10}$

10. $\dfrac{4 - (-6)}{1 - \frac{1}{3}}$ 15

Simplify the given expression or solve the given equation, whichever is appropriate.

11. $4x - (-9x)$ $13x$

12. $4(x - 9) - x$ $3x - 36$

13. $5(x - 3) + x = 0$ $\left\{\dfrac{5}{2}\right\}$

14. $5 - 2(x - 1) = x$ $\left\{\dfrac{7}{3}\right\}$

15. $\dfrac{1}{2} - \dfrac{1}{3}$ $\dfrac{1}{6}$

16. $\dfrac{1}{4} + \dfrac{1}{6}$ $\dfrac{5}{12}$

17. $\dfrac{1}{2}x - \dfrac{1}{3} = \dfrac{1}{4}x + \dfrac{1}{6}$ $\{2\}$

18. $\dfrac{2}{3}x + \dfrac{1}{5} = \dfrac{3}{5}x - \dfrac{1}{15}$ $\{-4\}$

19. $\dfrac{4x - 8}{2}$ $2x - 4$

20. $\dfrac{-5x - 10}{-5}$ $x + 2$

21. $\dfrac{6 - 2(x - 3)}{2} = 1$ $\{5\}$

22. $\dfrac{20 - 5(x - 5)}{5} = 6$ $\{3\}$

23. $-4(x - 9) - 4 = -4x$ $\varnothing$

24. $4(x - 6) = -4(6 - x)$ All real numbers

Study Tip

Don't wait until the final exam to review material. Do some review on a regular basis. The Making Connections exercises on this page can be used to review, compare, and contrast different concepts that you have studied. A good time to work these exercises is between a test and the start of new material.

Solve each inequality. State the solution set using interval notation.

25. $2x - 3 > 6$ $(4.5, \infty)$

26. $5 - 3x < 7$ $\left(-\dfrac{2}{3}, \infty\right)$

27. $51 - 2x \le 3x + 1$ $[10, \infty)$

28. $4x - 80 \ge 60 - 3x$ $[20, \infty)$

29. $-1 < 4 - 2x \le 5$ $\left[-\dfrac{1}{2}, \dfrac{5}{2}\right)$

30. $1 - 2x \le x + 1 < 3 - 2x$ $\left[0, \dfrac{2}{3}\right)$

Solve each equation for y.

31. $3\pi y + 2 = t$ $y = \dfrac{t - 2}{3\pi}$

32. $x = \dfrac{y - b}{m}$ $y = mx + b$

33. $3x - 3y - 12 = 0$ $y = x - 4$

34. $2y - 3 = 9$ $y = 6$

35. $\dfrac{y}{2} - \dfrac{y}{4} = \dfrac{1}{5}$ $y = \dfrac{4}{5}$

36. $0.6y - 0.06y = 108$ $y = 200$

Solve.

37. ***Financial planning.*** Financial advisors at Fidelity Investments use the information in the accompanying graph as a guide for retirement investing.

a) What is the slope of the line segment for ages 35 through 50?

b) What is the slope of the line segment for ages 50 through 65?

c) If a 38-year-old man is making \$40,000 per year, then what percent of his income should he be saving?

d) If a 58-year-old woman has an annual salary of \$60,000, then how much should she have saved and how much should she be saving per year?

a) $\frac{2}{15}$ **b)** $\frac{1}{5}$ **c)** About 13% per year
d) \$276,000 saved, \$12,000 per year

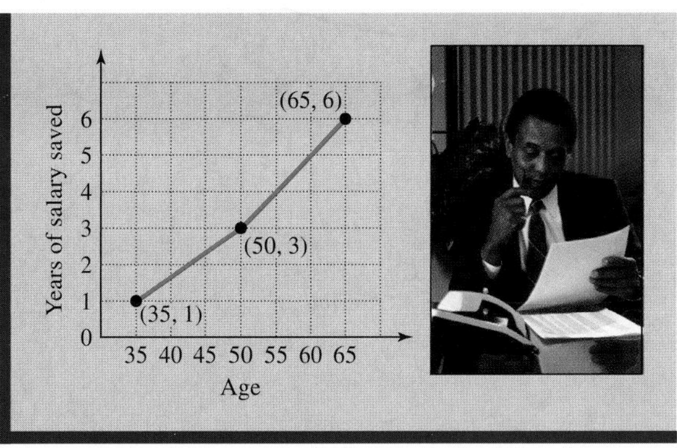

Figure for Exercise 37

Critical **Thinking** | For Individual or Group Work | Chapter 3

These exercises can be solved by a variety of techniques, which may or may not require algebra. So be creative and think critically. Explain all answers. Answers are in the Instructor's Edition of this text.

1. ***Share and share alike.*** A chocolate bar consists of two rows of small squares with four squares in each row as shown in (a) of the accompanying figure. You want to share it with your friends.

a) How many times must you break it to get it divided into 8 small squares?

b) If the bar has 3 rows of 5 squares in each row as shown in (b) of the accompanying figure, then how many breaks does it take to separate it into 15 small squares?

c) If the bar is divided into m rows with n small squares in each row, then how many breaks does it take to separate it into mn small squares?

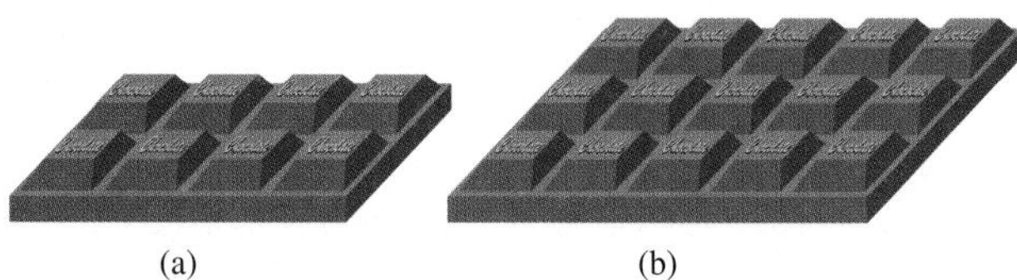

(a) (b)

Figure for Exercise 1

2. ***Straight time.*** Starting at 8 A.M. determine the number of times in the next 24 hours for which the hour and minute hands on a clock form a 180° angle.

3. ***Dividing days by months.*** For how many days of the year do you get a whole number when you divide the day number by the month number? For example, for December 24, the result of 24 divided by 12 is 2.

4. ***Crossword fanatic.*** Ms. Smith loves to work the crossword puzzle in her daily newspaper. To keep track of her efforts, she gives herself 2 points for every crossword puzzle that she completes correctly and deducts 3 points for every crossword puzzle that she fails to complete or completes incorrectly. For the month of June her total score was zero. How many puzzles did she solve correctly in June?

Photo for Exercise 4

5. ***Counting ones.*** If you write down the integers between 1 and 100 inclusive, then how many times will you write the number one?

6. ***Smallest sum.*** What is the smallest possible sum that can be obtained by adding five positive integers that have a product of 48?

7. ***Mind control.*** Each student in your class should think of an integer between 2 and 9 inclusive. Multiply your integer by 9. Think of the sum of the digits in your answer. Subtract 5 from your answer. Think of the letter in the alphabet that corresponds to the last answer. Think of a state that begins with that letter. Think of the second letter in the name of the state. Think of a large mammal that begins with that letter. Think of the color of that animal. What is the color that is on everyone's mind? Explain.

8. ***Four-digit numbers.*** How many four-digit whole numbers are there such that the thousands digit is odd, the hundreds digit is even, and all four digits are different? How many four-digit whole numbers are there such that the thousands digit is even, hundreds digit is odd, and all four digits are different?

1. a) 7 **b)** 14 **c)** $mn - 1$ **2.** 22 **3.** 90 **4.** 18 **5.** 21 **6.** 11 **7.** Fourth letter, Delaware, elephant, gray **8.** 1400, 1120

Chapter 4

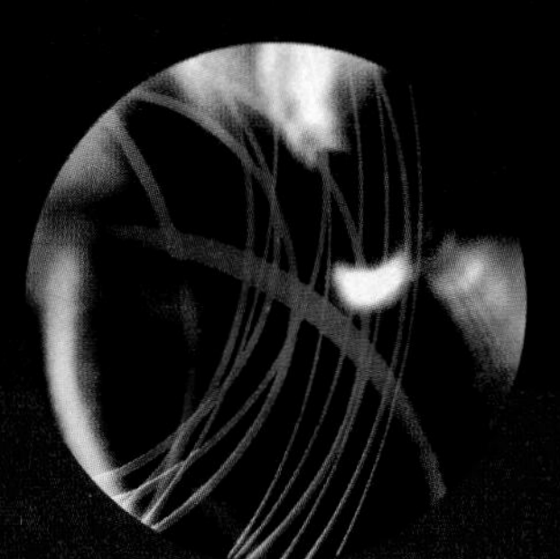

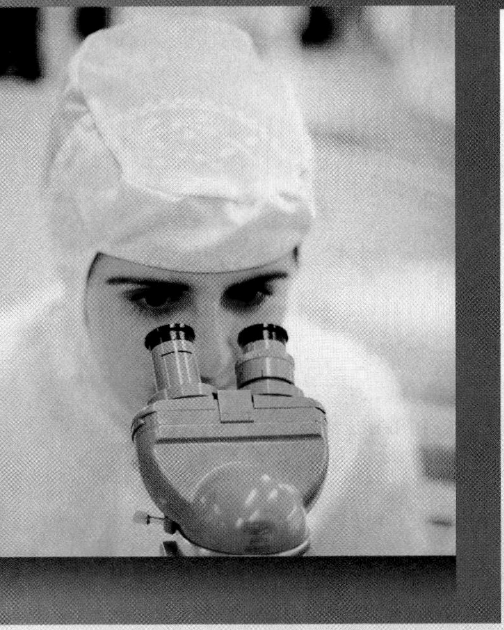

Polynomials and Exponents

The nineteenth-century physician and physicist Jean Louis Marie Poiseuille (1799–1869) is given credit for discovering a formula associated with the circulation of blood through arteries. Poiseuille's law, as it is known, can be used to determine the velocity of blood in an artery at a given distance from the center of the artery. The formula states that the flow of blood in an artery is faster toward the center of the blood vessel and is slower toward the outside. Blood flow can also be affected by a person's blood pressure, the length of the blood vessel, and the viscosity of the blood itself.

In later years, Poiseuille's continued interest in blood circulation led him to experiments to show that blood pressure rises and falls when a person exhales and inhales. In modern medicine, physicians can use Poiseuille's law to determine how much the radius of a blocked blood vessel must be widened to create a healthy flow of blood.

In this chapter you will study polynomials, the fundamental expressions of algebra. Polynomials are to algebra what integers are to arithmetic. We use polynomials to represent quantities in general, such as perimeter, area, revenue, and the volume of blood flowing through an artery.

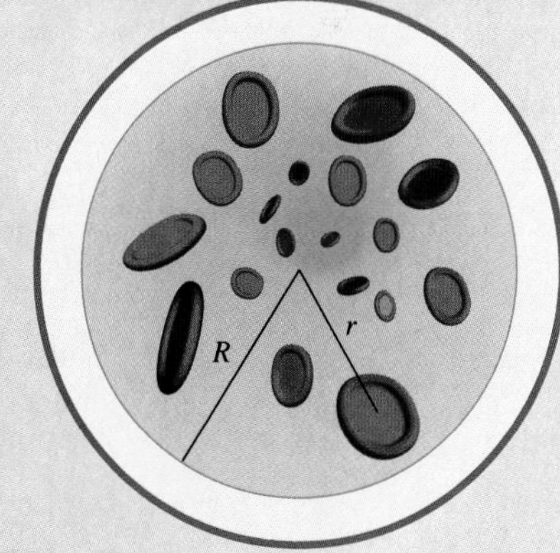

In Exercise 89 of Section 4.4, you will see Poiseuille's law represented by a polynomial.

4.1 Addition and Subtraction of Polynomials

In this Section

- Polynomials
- Using Function Notation with Polynomials
- Addition of Polynomials
- Subtraction of Polynomials
- Applications

We first used polynomials in Chapter 1 but did not identify them as polynomials. Polynomials also occurred in the equations and inequalities of Chapter 2. In this section we will define polynomials and begin a thorough study of polynomials.

Polynomials

In Chapter 1 we defined a **term** as an expression containing a number or the product of a number and one or more variables raised to powers. Some examples of terms are

$$4x^3,\ -x^2y^3,\ 6ab, \text{ and } -2.$$

A **polynomial** is a single term or a finite sum of terms in which the powers of the variables are positive integers. Later in this text you will see that negative integers and fractions can be used as exponents, but in a polynomial the exponents must be positive integers. For example,

$$4x^3 + (-15x^2) + x^1 + (-2)$$

is a polynomial. Because it is simpler to write addition of a negative as subtraction and $x^1 = x$, this polynomial is usually written as

$$4x^3 - 15x^2 + x - 2.$$

Study Tip

Many commuting students find it difficult to get help. Students are often stuck on a minor point that can be easily resolved over the telephone. So ask your instructor if he or she will answer questions over the telephone and during what hours.

The **degree of a polynomial** in one variable is the highest power of the variable in the polynomial. So $4x^3 - 15x^2 + x - 2$ has degree 3 and $7w - w^2$ has degree 2. The **degree of a term** is the power of the variable in the term. Because the last term has no variable, its degree is 0. The degree of x is 1 because $x = x^1$.

$$4x^3 - 15x^2 + x - 2$$

Third-degree term — Second-degree term — First-degree term — Zero-degree term

A single number is called a **constant** and so the last term is the **constant term.** The degree of a polynomial consisting of a single number such as 8 is 0.

The number preceding the variable in each term is called the **coefficient** of that variable or the coefficient of that term. In $4x^3 - 15x^2 + x - 2$ the coefficient of x^3 is 4, the coefficient of x^2 is -15, and the coefficient of x is 1 because $x = 1 \cdot x$.

EXAMPLE 1

Identifying coefficients

Determine the coefficients of x^3 and x^2 in each polynomial:

a) $x^3 + 5x^2 - 6$ **b)** $4x^6 - x^3 + x$

Solution

a) Write the polynomial as $1 \cdot x^3 + 5x^2 - 6$ to see that the coefficient of x^3 is 1 and the coefficient of x^2 is 5.

b) The x^2-term is missing in $4x^6 - x^3 + x$. Because $4x^6 - x^3 + x$ can be written as

$$4x^6 - 1 \cdot x^3 + 0 \cdot x^2 + x,$$

the coefficient of x^3 is -1 and the coefficient of x^2 is 0.

Now do Exercises 7–12

For simplicity we generally write polynomials in one variable with the exponents decreasing from left to right and the constant term last. So we write

$$x^3 - 4x^2 + 5x + 1 \qquad \text{rather than} \qquad -4x^2 + 1 + 5x + x^3.$$

When a polynomial is written with decreasing exponents, the coefficient of the first term is called the **leading coefficient.**

Certain polynomials are given special names. A **monomial** is a polynomial that has one term, a **binomial** is a polynomial that has two terms, and a **trinomial** is a polynomial that has three terms. For example, $3x^5$ is a monomial, $2x - 1$ is a binomial, and $4x^6 - 3x + 2$ is a trinomial.

EXAMPLE 2

Types of polynomials

Identify each polynomial as a monomial, binomial, or trinomial and state its degree.

a) $5x^2 - 7x^3 + 2$ **b)** $x^{43} - x^2$ **c)** $5x$ **d)** -12

Study Tip

Be active in class. Don't be embarrassed to ask questions or answer questions. You can often learn more from a wrong answer than a right one. Your instructor knows that you are not yet an expert in algebra. Instructors love active classrooms and they will not think less of you for speaking out.

Solution

a) The polynomial $5x^2 - 7x^3 + 2$ is a third-degree trinomial.

b) The polynomial $x^{43} - x^2$ is a binomial with degree 43.

c) Because $5x = 5x^1$, this polynomial is a monomial with degree 1.

d) The polynomial -12 is a monomial with degree 0.

Now do Exercises 13–24

Using Function Notation with Polynomials

A polynomial such as $x^2 - x + 3$ has a value if x is replaced by a real number. For example, if $x = 2$, then replacing x with 2 yields

$$x^2 - x + 3 = 2^2 - 2 + 3 = 5.$$

So the value of the polynomial is 5 when $x = 2$. Putting 2 into the polynomial gives an output of 5. To make it easier to discuss polynomials and their values, polynomials are often named with letters. For example, if $P = x^2 - x + 3$, then $P = 5$ when $x = 2$.

Teaching Tip Using function notation for polynomials will get students familiar with the notation before they study functions in detail.

Another notation that is commonly used in mathematics, computer science, and on graphing calculators is to follow the letter that names the polynomial with the number used for x and write the result as a single equation. So $P = 5$ when $x = 2$ is written as $P(2) = 5$ and read as "P evaluated at 2 is 5" or simply "P of 2 is 5." Think of $P(2) = 5$ as P being applied to the input number 2 and yielding an output of 5. This notation is called **function notation.** (See Section 11.1 for more information on functions.) Using function notation we write the polynomial as $P(x) = x^2 - x + 3$ rather than $P = x^2 - x + 3$. [Read $P(x)$ as "P of x."]

Function notation is very useful when we are evaluating a polynomial at several values of x. For example, if $P(x) = x^2 - x + 3$, then $P(0) = 3$, $P(1) = 3$, and $P(2) = 5$. Note that in function notation $P(x)$ does *not* mean P times x.

EXAMPLE 3

Evaluating polynomials

a) Find the value of $-3x^4 - x^3 + 20x + 3$ when $x = 1$.

b) Find the value of $-3x^4 - x^3 + 20x + 3$ when $x = -2$.

c) If $P(x) = -3x^4 - x^3 + 20x + 3$, find $P(1)$.

Calculator Close-Up

To evaluate the polynomial in Example 3 with a calculator, first use Y= to define the polynomial.

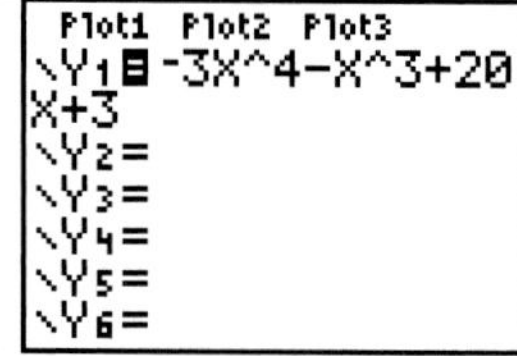

Then find $y_1(-2)$ and $y_1(1)$.

Y1(-2)
-77
Y1(1)
19

Solution

a) Replace x by 1 in the polynomial:

$$\begin{aligned} -3x^4 - x^3 + 20x + 3 &= -3(1)^4 - (1)^3 + 20(1) + 3 \\ &= -3 - 1 + 20 + 3 \\ &= 19 \end{aligned}$$

So the value of the polynomial is 19 when $x = 1$.

b) Replace x by -2 in the polynomial:

$$\begin{aligned} -3x^4 - x^3 + 20x + 3 &= -3(-2)^4 - (-2)^3 + 20(-2) + 3 \\ &= -3(16) - (-8) - 40 + 3 \\ &= -48 + 8 - 40 + 3 \\ &= -77 \end{aligned}$$

So the value of the polynomial is -77 when $x = -2$.

c) To find $P(1)$, replace x by 1 in the formula for $P(x)$:

$$\begin{aligned} P(x) &= -3x^4 - x^3 + 20x + 3 \\ P(1) &= -3(1)^4 - (1)^3 + 20(1) + 3 \\ &= 19 \end{aligned}$$

So $P(1) = 19$. The value of the polynomial when $x = 1$ is 19.

Now do Exercises 25–36

Addition of Polynomials

You learned how to combine like terms in Chapter 1. Also, you combined like terms when solving equations in Chapter 2. Addition of polynomials is done simply by adding the like terms.

Addition of Polynomials

To add two polynomials, add the like terms.

Polynomials can be added horizontally or vertically, as shown in Example 4.

EXAMPLE 4

Adding polynomials

Perform the indicated operation.

a) $(x^2 - 6x + 5) + (-3x^2 + 5x - 9)$

b) $(-5a^3 + 3a - 7) + (4a^2 - 3a + 7)$

Helpful Hint

When we perform operations with polynomials and write the results as equations, those equations are identities. For example,

$$(x + 1) + (3x + 5) = 4x + 6$$

is an identity. This equation is satisfied by every real number.

Solution

a) We can use the commutative and associative properties to get the like terms next to each other and then combine them:

$$(x^2 - 6x + 5) + (-3x^2 + 5x - 9) = x^2 - 3x^2 - 6x + 5x + 5 - 9$$
$$= -2x^2 - x - 4$$

b) When adding vertically, we line up the like terms:

$$\begin{array}{rrrr} -5a^3 & & +\ 3a & -\ 7 \\ & 4a^2 & -\ 3a & +\ 7 \\ \hline -5a^3 & +\ 4a^2 & & \end{array} \quad \text{Add.}$$

Now do Exercises 37–50

Subtraction of Polynomials

When we subtract polynomials, we subtract the like terms. Because $a - b = a + (-b)$, we can subtract by adding the opposite of the second polynomial to the first polynomial. Remember that a negative sign in front of parentheses changes the sign of each term in the parentheses. For example,

$$-(x^2 - 2x + 8) = -x^2 + 2x - 8.$$

Polynomials can be subtracted horizontally or vertically, as shown in Example 5.

EXAMPLE 5

Subtracting polynomials

Perform the indicated operation.

a) $(x^2 - 5x - 3) - (4x^2 + 8x - 9)$ **b)** $(4y^3 - 3y + 2) - (5y^2 - 7y - 6)$

Helpful Hint

For subtraction, write the original problem and then rewrite it as addition with the signs changed. Many students have trouble when they write the original problem and then overwrite the signs. Vertical subtraction is essential for performing long division of polynomials in Section 4.5.

Solution

a) $(x^2 - 5x - 3) - (4x^2 + 8x - 9) = x^2 - 5x - 3 - 4x^2 - 8x + 9$ Change signs.

$= -3x^2 - 13x + 6$ Add.

b) To subtract $5y^2 - 7y - 6$ from $4y^3 - 3y + 2$ vertically, we line up the like terms as we do for addition:

$$\begin{array}{rrrr} 4y^3 & & -\ 3y & +\ 2 \\ - & (5y^2 & -\ 7y & -\ 6) \\ \hline \end{array}$$

Now change the signs of $5y^2 - 7y - 6$ and add the like terms:

$$\begin{array}{rrrr} 4y^3 & & -\ 3y & +\ 2 \\ & -5y^2 & +\ 7y & +\ 6 \\ \hline 4y^3 & -\ 5y^2 & +\ 4y & +\ 8 \end{array}$$

Now do Exercises 51–64

CAUTION When adding or subtracting polynomials vertically, be sure to line up the like terms.

In Example 6 we combine addition and subtraction of polynomials.

EXAMPLE 6

Adding and subtracting

Perform the indicated operations:

$$(2x^2 - 3x) + (x^3 + 6) - (x^4 - 6x^2 - 9)$$

Solution

Remove the parentheses and combine the like terms:

$$\begin{aligned}(2x^2 - 3x) + (x^3 + 6) - (x^4 - 6x^2 - 9) &= 2x^2 - 3x + x^3 + 6 - x^4 + 6x^2 + 9\\ &= -x^4 + x^3 + 8x^2 - 3x + 15\end{aligned}$$

Now do Exercises 81–88

Teaching Tip Ask students to identify the values of x for which the equation is true. What is the equation called?

Applications

Polynomials are often used to represent unknown quantities. In certain situations it is necessary to add or subtract such polynomials.

EXAMPLE 7

Profit from prints

Trey pays \$60 per day for a permit to sell famous art prints in the Student Union Mall. Each print costs him \$4, so the polynomial $C(x) = 4x + 60$ represents his daily cost in dollars for x prints sold. He sells the prints for \$10 each. So the polynomial $R(x) = 10x$ represents his daily revenue for x prints sold. Find a polynomial $P(x)$ that represents his daily profit from selling x prints. Evaluate the profit polynomial for $x = 30$.

Solution

Because profit is revenue minus cost, we can subtract the corresponding polynomials to get a polynomial that represents the daily profit:

$$\begin{aligned}P(x) &= R(x) - C(x)\\ &= 10x - (4x + 60)\\ &= 10x - 4x - 60\\ &= 6x - 60\end{aligned}$$

So the daily profit polynomial is $P(x) = 6x - 60$. Now evaluate this profit polynomial for $x = 30$:

$$\begin{aligned}P(30) &= 6(30) - 60\\ &= 120\end{aligned}$$

So if Trey sells 30 prints, his profit is \$120.

Now do Exercises 89–100

Teaching Tip Point out how function notation makes it easy to indicate in symbols that the profit for 30 prints is \$120: $P(30) = 120$.

Warm-Ups

True or false? Explain your answer.

1. In the polynomial $2x^2 - 4x + 7$ the coefficient of x is 4. False
2. The degree of the polynomial $x^2 + 5x - 9x^3 + 6$ is 2. False
3. In the polynomial $x^2 - x$ the coefficient of x is -1. True
4. The degree of the polynomial $x^2 - x$ is 2. True
5. A binomial always has a degree of 2. False

6. If $P(x) = 3x - 1$, then $P(5) = 14$. True
7. Every trinomial has degree 2. False
8. $x^2 - 7x^2 = -6x^2$ for any value of x. True
9. $(3x^2 - 8x + 6) + (x^2 + 4x - 9) = 4x^2 - 4x - 3$ for any value of x. True
10. $(x^2 - 4x) - (x^2 - 3x) = -7x$ for any value of x. False

4.1 Exercises

Boost your GRADE at mathzone.com!

MathZone
- Practice Problems
- Self-Tests
- Videos
- Net Tutor
- e-Professors

Reading and Writing *After reading this section, write out the answers to these questions. Use complete sentences.*

1. What is a term?
   A term is a single number or the product of a number and one or more variables raised to powers.
2. What is a polynomial?
   A polynomial is a single term or a finite sum of terms.
3. What is the degree of a polynomial?
   The degree of a polynomial in one variable is the highest power of the variable in the polynomial.
4. What is the value of a polynomial?
   The value of a polynomial is the number obtained when the variable is replaced by a number.
5. How do we add polynomials?
   Polynomials are added by adding the like terms.
6. How do we subtract polynomials?
   Polynomials are subtracted by subtracting like terms.

Determine the coefficients of x^3 and x^2 in each polynomial. See Example 1.

7. $-3x^3 + 7x^2$ $-3, 7$
8. $10x^3 - x^2$ $10, -1$
9. $x^4 + 6x^2 - 9$ $0, 6$
10. $x^5 - x^3 + 3$ $-1, 0$
11. $\frac{x^3}{3} + \frac{7x^2}{2} - 4$ $\frac{1}{3}, \frac{7}{2}$
12. $\frac{x^3}{2} - \frac{x^2}{4} + 2x + 1$ $\frac{1}{2}, -\frac{1}{4}$

Identify each polynomial as a monomial, binomial, or trinomial and state its degree. See Example 2.

13. -1 Monomial, 0
14. 5 Monomial, 0
15. m^3 Monomial, 3
16. $3a^8$ Monomial, 8
17. $4x + 7$ Binomial, 1
18. $a + 6$ Binomial, 1
19. $x^{10} - 3x^2 + 2$ Trinomial, 10
20. $y^6 - 6y^3 + 9$ Trinomial, 6
21. $x^6 + 1$ Binomial, 6
22. $b^2 - 4$ Binomial, 2
23. $a^3 - a^2 + 5$ Trinomial, 3
24. $-x^2 + 4x - 9$ Trinomial, 2

Evaluate each polynomial as indicated. See Example 3.

25. Evaluate $2x^2 - 3x + 1$ for $x = -1$. 6
26. Evaluate $3x^2 - x + 2$ for $x = -2$. 16
27. Evaluate $\frac{1}{2}x^2 - x + 1$ for $x = \frac{1}{2}$. $\frac{5}{8}$
28. Evaluate $3x^2 + \frac{1}{2}x - 1$ for $x = \frac{1}{3}$. $-\frac{1}{2}$
29. Evaluate $-3x^3 - x^2 + 3x - 4$ for $x = 3$. -85
30. Evaluate $-2x^4 - 3x^2 + 5x - 9$ for $x = 2$. -43
31. If $P(x) = x^2 - 4$, find $P(3)$. 5
32. If $P(x) = x^3 + 1$, find $P(2)$. 9
33. If $P(x) = 3x^4 - 2x^3 + 7$, find $P(-2)$. 71
34. If $P(x) = -2x^3 + 5x^2 - 12$, find $P(5)$. -137
35. If $P(x) = 1.2x^3 - 4.3x - 2.4$, find $P(1.45)$. -4.97665
36. If $P(x) = -3.5x^4 - 4.6x^3 + 5.5$, find $P(-2.36)$. -42.608

Perform the indicated operation. See Example 4.

37. $(x - 3) + (3x - 5)$ $4x - 8$
38. $(x - 2) + (x + 3)$ $2x + 1$
39. $(q - 3) + (q + 3)$ $2q$
40. $(q + 4) + (q + 6)$ $2q + 10$
41. $(3x + 2) + (x^2 - 4)$ $x^2 + 3x - 2$
42. $(5x^2 - 2) + (-3x^2 - 1)$ $2x^2 - 3$
43. $(4x - 1) + (x^3 + 5x - 6)$ $x^3 + 9x - 7$
44. $(3x - 7) + (x^2 - 4x + 6)$ $x^2 - x - 1$
45. $(a^2 - 3a + 1) + (2a^2 - 4a - 5)$ $3a^2 - 7a - 4$
46. $(w^2 - 2w + 1) + (2w - 5 + w^2)$ $2w^2 - 4$
47. $(w^2 - 9w - 3) + (w - 4w^2 + 8)$ $-3w^2 - 8w + 5$
48. $(a^3 - a^2 - 5a) + (6 - a - 3a^2)$ $a^3 - 4a^2 - 6a + 6$

49. $(5.76x^2 - 3.14x - 7.09) + (3.9x^2 + 1.21x + 5.6)$
$9.66x^2 - 1.93x - 1.49$

50. $(8.5x^2 + 3.27x - 9.33) + (x^2 - 4.39x - 2.32)$
$9.5x^2 - 1.12x - 11.65$

Perform the indicated operation. See Example 5.

51. $(x - 2) - (5x - 8)$
$-4x + 6$

52. $(x - 7) - (3x - 1)$
$-2x - 6$

53. $(m - 2) - (m + 3)$
-5

54. $(m + 5) - (m + 9)$
-4

55. $(2z^2 - 3z) - (3z^2 - 5z)$
$-z^2 + 2z$

56. $(z^2 - 4z) - (5z^2 - 3z)$
$-4z^2 - z$

57. $(w^5 - w^3) - (-w^4 + w^2)$ $w^5 + w^4 - w^3 - w^2$

58. $(w^6 - w^3) - (-w^2 + w)$ $w^6 - w^3 + w^2 - w$

59. $(t^2 - 3t + 4) - (t^2 - 5t - 9)$ $2t + 13$

60. $(t^2 - 6t + 7) - (5t^2 - 3t - 2)$ $-4t^2 - 3t + 9$

61. $(9 - 3y - y^2) - (2 + 5y - y^2)$ $-8y + 7$

62. $(4 - 5y + y^3) - (2 - 3y + y^2)$ $y^3 - y^2 - 2y + 2$

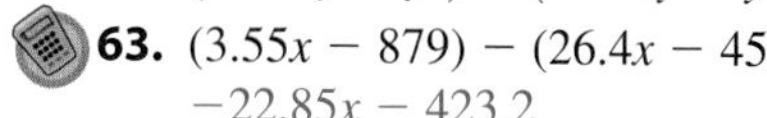

63. $(3.55x - 879) - (26.4x - 455.8)$
$-22.85x - 423.2$

64. $(345.56x - 347.4) - (56.6x + 433)$
$288.96x - 780.4$

Add or subtract the polynomials as indicated. See Examples 4 and 5.

65. Add:
$$\begin{array}{r} 3a - 4 \\ a + 6 \\ \hline 4a + 2 \end{array}$$

66. Add:
$$\begin{array}{r} 2w - 8 \\ w + 3 \\ \hline 3w - 5 \end{array}$$

67. Subtract:
$$\begin{array}{r} 3x + 11 \\ 5x + 7 \\ \hline -2x + 4 \end{array}$$

68. Subtract:
$$\begin{array}{r} 4x + 3 \\ 2x + 9 \\ \hline 2x - 6 \end{array}$$

69. Add:
$$\begin{array}{r} a - b \\ a + b \\ \hline 2a \end{array}$$

70. Add:
$$\begin{array}{r} s - 6 \\ s - 1 \\ \hline 2s - 7 \end{array}$$

71. Subtract:
$$\begin{array}{r} -3m + 1 \\ 2m - 6 \\ \hline -5m + 7 \end{array}$$

72. Subtract:
$$\begin{array}{r} -5n + 2 \\ 3n - 4 \\ \hline -8n + 6 \end{array}$$

73. Add:
$$\begin{array}{r} 2x^2 - x - 3 \\ 2x^2 + x + 4 \\ \hline 4x^2 + 1 \end{array}$$

74. Add:
$$\begin{array}{r} -x^2 + 4x - 6 \\ 3x^2 - x - 5 \\ \hline 2x^2 + 3x - 11 \end{array}$$

75. Subtract:
$$\begin{array}{r} 3a^3 - 5a^2 \qquad + 7 \\ 2a^3 + 4a^2 - 2a \qquad \\ \hline a^3 - 9a^2 + 2a + 7 \end{array}$$

76. Subtract:
$$\begin{array}{r} -2b^3 + 7b^2 \qquad - 9 \\ b^3 \qquad - 4b - 2 \\ \hline -3b^3 + 7b^2 + 4b - 7 \end{array}$$

77. Subtract:
$$\begin{array}{r} x^2 - 3x + 6 \\ x^2 \qquad - 3 \\ \hline -3x + 9 \end{array}$$

78. Subtract:
$$\begin{array}{r} x^4 - 3x^2 + 2 \\ 3x^4 - 2x^2 \qquad \\ \hline -2x^4 - x^2 + 2 \end{array}$$

79. Add:
$$\begin{array}{r} y^3 + 4y^2 - 6y - 5 \\ y^3 + 3y^2 + 2y - 9 \\ \hline 2y^3 + 7y^2 - 4y - 14 \end{array}$$

80. Add:
$$\begin{array}{r} q^2 - 4q + 9 \\ -3q^2 - 7q + 5 \\ \hline -2q^2 - 11q + 14 \end{array}$$

Perform the indicated operations. See Example 6.

81. $(4m - 2) + (2m + 4) - (9m - 1)$ $-3m + 3$

82. $(-5m - 6) + (8m - 3) - (-5m + 3)$ $8m - 12$

83. $(6y - 2) - (8y + 3) - (9y - 2)$ $-11y - 3$

84. $(-5y - 1) - (8y - 4) - (y + 3)$ $-14y$

85. $(-x^2 - 5x + 4) + (6x^2 - 8x + 9) - (3x^2 - 7x + 1)$
$2x^2 - 6x + 12$

86. $(-8x^2 + 5x - 12) + (-3x^2 - 9x + 18)$
$- (-3x^2 + 9x - 4)$ $-8x^2 - 13x + 10$

87. $(-6z^4 - 3z^3 + 7z^2) - (5z^3 + 3z^2 - 2)$
$+ (z^4 - z^2 + 5)$ $-5z^4 - 8z^3 + 3z^2 + 7$

88. $(-v^3 - v^2 - 1) - (v^4 - v^2 - v - 1) + (v^3 - 3v^2 + 6)$
$-v^4 - 3v^2 + v + 6$

Solve each problem. See Example 7.

89. ***Profitable pumps.*** Walter Waterman, of Walter's Water Pumps in Winnipeg has found that when he produces x water pumps per month, his revenue is $R(x) = x^2 + 400x + 300$ dollars. His cost for producing x water pumps per month is $C(x) = x^2 + 300x - 200$ dollars. Write a polynomial that represents his monthly profit $P(x)$ for x water pumps. Evaluate this profit polynomial for $x = 50$. $P(x) = 100x + 500$ dollars, \$5500

90. ***Manufacturing costs.*** Ace manufacturing has determined that the cost of labor for producing x transmissions is $L(x) = 0.3x^2 + 400x + 550$ dollars, while the cost of materials is $M(x) = 0.1x^2 + 50x + 800$ dollars.

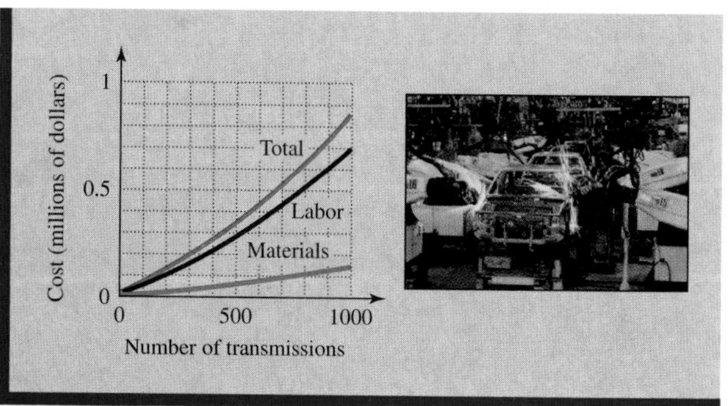

Figure for Exercise 90

a) Write a polynomial $T(x)$ that represents the total cost of materials and labor for producing x transmissions.

b) Evaluate the total cost polynomial for $x = 500$.

c) Find the cost of labor for 500 transmissions and the cost of materials for 500 transmissions.

a) $T(x) = 0.4x^2 + 450x + 1350$ b) \$326,350
c) \$275,550, \$50,800

91. ***Perimeter of a triangle.*** The shortest side of a triangle is x meters, and the other two sides are $3x - 1$ and $2x + 4$ meters. Write a polynomial $P(x)$ that represents the perimeter and then evaluate the perimeter polynomial if x is 4 meters.
$P(x) = 6x + 3$, $P(4) = 27$ meters

92. ***Perimeter of a rectangle.*** The width of a rectangular playground is $2x - 5$ feet, and the length is $3x + 9$ feet. Write a polynomial $P(x)$ that represents the perimeter and then evaluate this perimeter polynomial if x is 4 feet.
$P(x) = 10x + 8$, $P(4) = 48$ feet

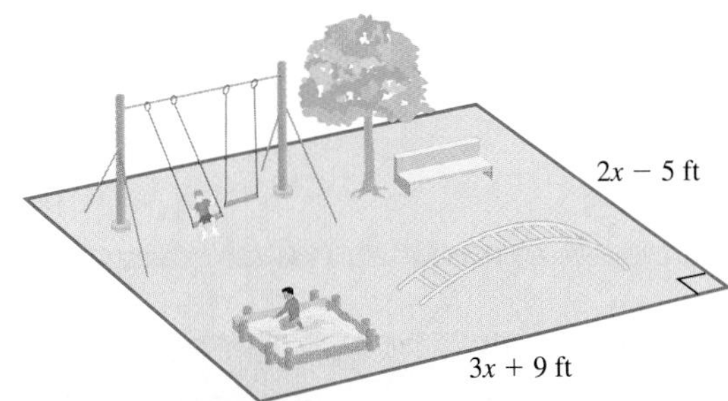

Figure for Exercise 92

93. ***Before and after.*** Jessica traveled $2x + 50$ miles in the morning and $3x - 10$ miles in the afternoon. Write a polynomial that represents the total distance that she traveled. Find the total distance if $x = 20$.
$5x + 40$ miles, 140 miles

94. ***Total distance.*** Hanson drove his rig at x mph for 3 hours, then increased his speed to $x + 15$ mph and drove for 2 more hours. Write a polynomial that represents the total distance that he traveled. Find the total distance if $x =$ 45 mph. $5x + 30$ miles, 255 miles

95. ***Sky divers.*** Bob and Betty simultaneously jump from two airplanes at different altitudes. Bob's altitude t seconds after leaving the plane is $-16t^2 + 6600$ feet. Betty's altitude t seconds after leaving the plane is $-16t^2 + 7400$ feet. Write a polynomial that represents the difference between their altitudes t seconds after leaving the planes. What is the difference between their altitudes 3 seconds after leaving the planes? 800 feet, 800 feet

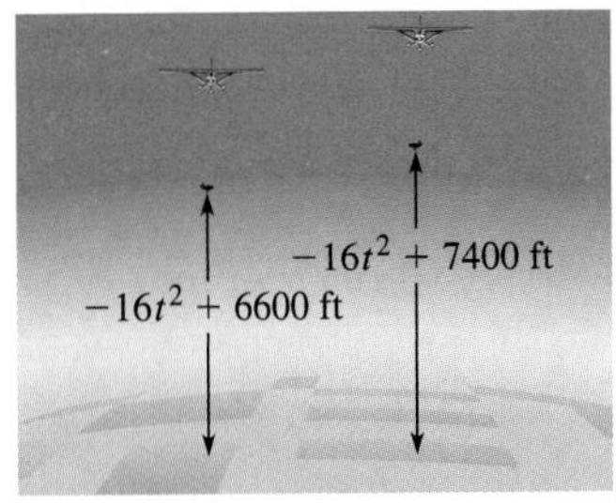

Figure for Exercise 95

96. ***Height difference.*** A red ball and a green ball are simultaneously tossed into the air. The red ball is given an initial velocity of 96 feet per second, and its height t seconds after it is tossed is $-16t^2 + 96t$ feet. The green ball is given an initial velocity of 80 feet per second, and its height t seconds after it is tossed is $-16t^2 + 80t$ feet.

a) Find a polynomial that represents the difference in the heights of the two balls. $16t$ feet

b) How much higher is the red ball 2 seconds after the balls are tossed? 32 feet

c) In reality, when does the difference in the heights stop increasing? when green ball hits ground

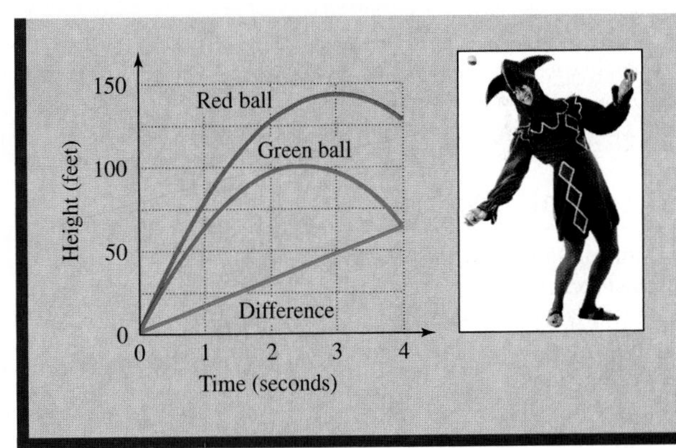

Figure for Exercise 96

97. ***Total interest.*** Donald received $0.08(x + 554)$ dollars interest on one investment and $0.09(x + 335)$ interest on another investment. Write a polynomial that represents the total interest he received. What is the total interest if $x = 1000$?
$0.17x + 74.47$ dollars, \$244.47

98. ***Total acid.*** Deborah figured that the amount of acid in one bottle of solution is $0.12x$ milliliters and the amount of acid in another bottle of solution is $0.22(75 - x)$ milliliters.

Find a polynomial that represents the total amount of acid? What is the total amount of acid if $x = 50$?
$-0.1x + 16.5$ milliliters, 11.5 milliliters

99. ***Harris-Benedict for females.*** The Harris-Benedict polynomial

$$655.1 + 9.56w + 1.85h - 4.68a$$

represents the number of calories needed to maintain a female at rest for 24 hours, where w is her weight in kilograms, h is her height in centimeters, and a is her age in years. Find the number of calories needed by a 30-year-old 54-kilogram female who is 157 centimeters tall. 1321.39 calories

100. ***Harris-Benedict for males.*** The Harris-Benedict polynomial

$$66.5 + 13.75w + 5.0h - 6.78a$$

represents the number of calories needed to maintain a male at rest for 24 hours, where w is his weight in kilograms, h is his height in centimeters, and a is his age in years. Find the number of calories needed by a 40-year-old 90-kilogram male who is 185 centimeters tall.
1957.8 calories

Getting More Involved

101. ***Discussion***

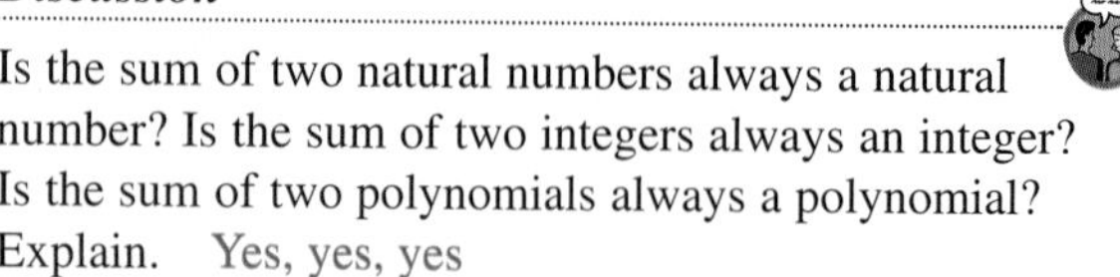

Is the sum of two natural numbers always a natural number? Is the sum of two integers always an integer? Is the sum of two polynomials always a polynomial? Explain. Yes, yes, yes

102. ***Discussion***

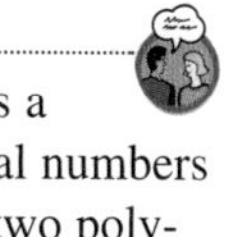

Is the difference of two natural numbers always a natural number? Is the difference of two rational numbers always a rational number? Is the difference of two polynomials always a polynomial? Explain. No, yes, yes

103. ***Writing***

Explain why the polynomial $2^4 - 7x^3 + 5x^2 - x$ has degree 3 and not degree 4.
The highest power of x is 3.

104. ***Discussion***

Which of the following polynomials does not have degree 2? Explain.

a) πr^2 **b)** $\pi^2 - 4$
c) $y^2 - 4$ **d)** $x^2 - x^4$
e) $a^2 - 3a + 9$
b and d

4.2 Multiplication of Polynomials

In this Section

- **Multiplying Monomials with the Product Rule**
- **Multiplying Polynomials**
- **The Opposite of a Polynomial**
- **Applications**

You learned to multiply some polynomials in Chapter 1. In this section you will learn how to multiply any two polynomials.

Multiplying Monomials with the Product Rule

To multiply two monomials, such as x^3 and x^5, recall that

$$x^3 = x \cdot x \cdot x \quad \text{and} \quad x^5 = x \cdot x \cdot x \cdot x \cdot x.$$

So

$$x^3 \cdot x^5 = \underbrace{\overbrace{(x \cdot x \cdot x)}^{\text{3 factors}}\overbrace{(x \cdot x \cdot x \cdot x \cdot x)}^{\text{5 factors}}}_{\text{8 factors}} = x^8.$$

Teaching Tip Emphasize that $2^3 \cdot 2^2 \neq 4^5$. The bases are not multiplied in the product rule.

The exponent of the product of x^3 and x^5 is the sum of the exponents 3 and 5. This example illustrates the **product rule** for multiplying exponential expressions.

Product Rule

If a is any real number and m and n are any positive integers, then

$$a^m \cdot a^n = a^{m+n}.$$

EXAMPLE 1

Multiplying monomials

Find the indicated products.

a) $x^2 \cdot x^4 \cdot x$ **b)** $(-2ab)(-3ab)$ **c)** $-4x^2y^2 \cdot 3xy^5$ **d)** $(3a)^2$

Solution

a) $x^2 \cdot x^4 \cdot x = x^2 \cdot x^4 \cdot x^1$

$= x^7$ Product rule

b) $(-2ab)(-3ab) = (-2)(-3) \cdot a \cdot a \cdot b \cdot b$

$= 6a^2b^2$ Product rule

c) $(-4x^2y^2)(3xy^5) = (-4)(3)x^2 \cdot x \cdot y^2 \cdot y^5$

$= -12x^3y^7$ Product rule

d) $(3a)^2 = 3a \cdot 3a$

$= 9a^2$

Now do Exercises 7–22

CAUTION Be sure to distinguish between adding and multiplying monomials. You can add like terms to get $3x^4 + 2x^4 = 5x^4$, but you cannot combine the terms in $3w^5 + 6w^2$. However, you can multiply any two monomials: $3x^4 \cdot 2x^4 = 6x^8$ and $3w^5 \cdot 6w^2 = 18w^7$.

Multiplying Polynomials

To multiply a monomial and a polynomial, we use the distributive property.

EXAMPLE 2

Multiplying monomials and polynomials

Find each product.

a) $3x^2(x^3 - 4x)$ **b)** $(y^2 - 3y + 4)(-2y)$ **c)** $-a(b - c)$

Solution

a) $3x^2(x^3 - 4x) = 3x^2 \cdot x^3 - 3x^2 \cdot 4x$ Distributive property

$= 3x^5 - 12x^3$

b) $(y^2 - 3y + 4)(-2y) = y^2(-2y) - 3y(-2y) + 4(-2y)$ Distributive property

$= -2y^3 - (-6y^2) + (-8y)$

$= -2y^3 + 6y^2 - 8y$

c) $-a(b - c) = (-a)b - (-a)c$ Distributive property

$= -ab + ac$

$= ac - ab$

Note in part (c) that either of the last two binomials is the correct answer. The last one is just a little simpler to read.

Now do Exercises 23–36

Study Tip

When doing homework or taking notes, use a pencil with an eraser. Everyone makes mistakes. If you get a problem wrong, don't start over. Check your work for errors and use the eraser. It is better to find out where you went wrong than to simply get the right answer.

Just as we use the distributive property to find the product of a monomial and a polynomial, we can use the distributive property to find the product of two binomials and the product of a binomial and a trinomial.

EXAMPLE 3

Multiplying polynomials

Use the distributive property to find each product.

a) $(x + 2)(x + 5)$ **b)** $(x + 3)(x^2 + 2x - 7)$

Solution

Teaching Tip Make sure students practice both horizontal multiplication and the vertical multiplication in Example 4.

a) First multiply each term of $x + 5$ by $x + 2$:

$$\begin{aligned} (x + 2)(x + 5) &= (x + 2)x + (x + 2)5 && \text{Distributive property} \\ &= x^2 + 2x + 5x + 10 && \text{Distributive property} \\ &= x^2 + 7x + 10 && \text{Combine like terms.} \end{aligned}$$

b) First multiply each term of the trinomial by $x + 3$:

$$\begin{aligned} (x + 3)(x^2 + 2x - 7) &= (x + 3)x^2 + (x + 3)2x + (x + 3)(-7) && \text{Distributive property} \\ &= x^3 + 3x^2 + 2x^2 + 6x - 7x - 21 && \text{Distributive property} \\ &= x^3 + 5x^2 - x - 21 && \text{Combine like terms.} \end{aligned}$$

Now do Exercises 37–48

Products of polynomials can also be found by arranging the multiplication vertically like multiplication of whole numbers.

EXAMPLE 4

Multiplying vertically

Find each product.

a) $(x - 2)(3x + 7)$ **b)** $(x + y)(a + 3)$

Solution

Helpful Hint

Many students find vertical multiplication easier than applying the distributive property twice horizontally. However, you should learn both methods because horizontal multiplication will help you with factoring by grouping in Section 5.2.

a)

$$\begin{array}{rrl} & 3x + 7 & \\ & x - 2 & \\ \hline & -6x - 14 & \leftarrow -2 \text{ times } 3x + 7 \\ 3x^2 + 7x & & \leftarrow x \text{ times } 3x + 7 \\ \hline 3x^2 + & x - 14 & \text{Add.} \end{array}$$

b)

$$\begin{array}{rr} & x + y \\ & a + 3 \\ \hline & 3x + 3y \\ ax + ay & \\ \hline ax + ay + & 3x + 3y \end{array}$$

Now do Exercises 49–64

Examples 2 to 4 illustrate the following rule.

Multiplication of Polynomials

To multiply polynomials, multiply each term of one polynomial by every term of the other polynomial, then combine like terms.

Teaching Tip Knowing that $a - b = -1(b - a)$ will help with rational expressions in Chapter 6.

The Opposite of a Polynomial

Note the result of multiplying the difference $a - b$ by -1:

$$-1(a - b) = -a + b = b - a$$

Because multiplying by -1 is the same as taking the opposite, we can write

$$-(a - b) = b - a.$$

So $a - b$ and $b - a$ are opposites or additive inverses of each other. If a and b are replaced by numbers, the values of $a - b$ and $b - a$ are additive inverses. For example, $3 - 7 = -4$ and $7 - 3 = 4$.

CAUTION The opposite of $a + b$ is $-a - b$, *not* $a - b$.

EXAMPLE 5

Opposite of a polynomial

Find the opposite of each polynomial.

a) $x - 2$

b) $9 - y^2$

c) $a + 4$

d) $-x^2 + 6x - 3$

Solution

a) $-(x - 2) = 2 - x$

b) $-(9 - y^2) = y^2 - 9$

c) $-(a + 4) = -a - 4$

d) $-(-x^2 + 6x - 3) = x^2 - 6x + 3$

Now do Exercises 65–72

Applications

EXAMPLE 6

Multiplying polynomials

A parking lot is 20 yards wide and 30 yards long. If the college increases the length and width by the same amount to handle an increasing number of cars, then what polynomial represents the area of the new lot? What is the new area if the increase is 15 yards?

Solution

If x is the amount of increase, then the new lot will be $x + 20$ yards wide and $x + 30$ yards long as shown in Fig. 4.1. Multiply the length and width to get the area:

$$\begin{aligned}(x + 20)(x + 30) &= (x + 20)x + (x + 20)30 \\ &= x^2 + 20x + 30x + 600 \\ &= x^2 + 50x + 600\end{aligned}$$

The polynomial $x^2 + 50x + 600$ represents the area of the new lot. If $x = 15$, then

$$x^2 + 50x + 600 = (15)^2 + 50(15) + 600 = 1575.$$

If the increase is 15 yards, then the area of the lot will be 1575 square yards.

Now do Exercises 93–104

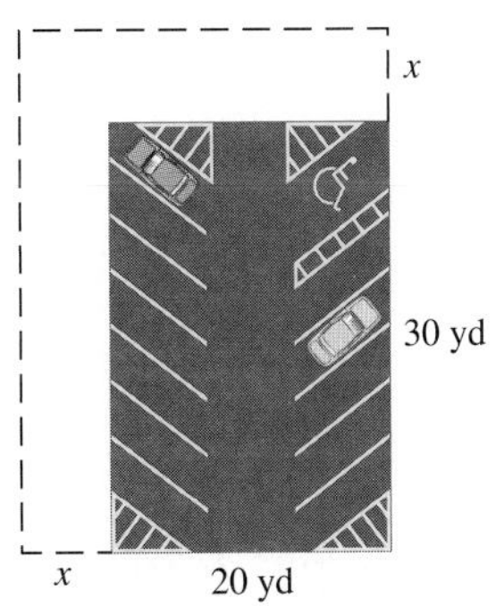

Figure 4.1

Warm-Ups ▼

True or false? Explain your answer.

1. $3x^3 \cdot 5x^4 = 15x^{12}$ for any value of x. False
2. $3x^2 \cdot 2x^7 = 5x^9$ for any value of x. False
3. $(3y^3)^2 = 9y^6$ for any value of y. True
4. $-3x(5x - 7x^2) = -15x^3 + 21x^2$ for any value of x. False
5. $2x(x^2 - 3x + 4) = 2x^3 - 6x^2 + 8x$ for any number x. True
6. $-2(3 - x) = 2x - 6$ for any number x. True
7. $(a + b)(c + d) = ac + ad + bc + bd$ for any values of a, b, c, and d. True
8. $-(x - 7) = 7 - x$ for any value of x. True
9. $83 - 37 = -(37 - 83)$ True
10. The opposite of $x + 3$ is $x - 3$ for any number x. False

4.2 Exercises

Boost your GRADE at mathzone.com!

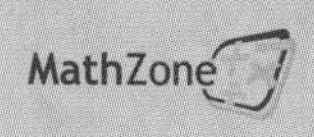

MathZone

- Practice Problems
- Self-Tests
- Videos
- Net Tutor
- e-Professors

Reading and Writing *After reading this section, write out the answers to these questions. Use complete sentences.*

1. What is the product rule for exponents?
   The product rule for exponents says that $a^m \cdot a^n = a^{m+n}$.
2. Why is the sum of two monomials not necessarily a monomial?
   The sum of two monomials can be a binomial if the terms are not like terms.
3. What property of the real numbers is used when multiplying a monomial and a polynomial?
   To multiply a monomial and a polynomial we use the distributive property.
4. What property of the real numbers is used when multiplying two binomials?
   To multiply two binomials we use the distributive property twice.
5. How do we multiply any two polynomials?
   To multiply any two polynomials we multiply each term of the first polynomial by every term of the second polynomial.
6. How do we find the opposite of a polynomial?
   To find the opposite of a polynomial, change the sign of each term in the polynomial.

Find each product. See Example 1.

7. $3x^2 \cdot 9x^3$ $27x^5$
8. $5x^7 \cdot 3x^5$ $15x^{12}$
9. $2a^3 \cdot 7a^8$ $14a^{11}$
10. $3y^{12} \cdot 5y^{15}$ $15y^{27}$
11. $-6x^2 \cdot 5x^2$ $-30x^4$
12. $-2x^2 \cdot 8x^5$ $-16x^7$
13. $(-9x^{10})(-3x^7)$ $27x^{17}$
14. $(-2x^2)(-8x^9)$ $16x^{11}$
15. $-6st \cdot 9st$ $-54s^2t^2$
16. $-12sq \cdot 3s$ $-36qs^2$
17. $3wt \cdot 8w^7t^6$ $24t^7w^8$
18. $h^8k^3 \cdot 5h$ $5h^9k^3$
19. $(5y)^2$ $25y^2$
20. $(6x)^2$ $36x^2$
21. $(2x^3)^2$ $4x^6$
22. $(3y^5)^2$ $9y^{10}$

Find each product. See Example 2.

23. $x(x + y^2)$ $x^2 + xy^2$
24. $x^2(x - y)$ $x^3 - x^2y$
25. $4y^2(y^5 - 2y)$ $4y^7 - 8y^3$
26. $6t^3(t^5 + 3t^2)$ $6t^8 + 18t^5$
27. $-3y(6y - 4)$ $-18y^2 + 12y$
28. $-9y(y^2 - 1)$ $-9y^3 + 9y$
29. $(y^2 - 5y + 6)(-3y)$ $-3y^3 + 15y^2 - 18y$

30. $(x^3 - 5x^2 - 1)7x^2$ $7x^5 - 35x^4 - 7x^2$

31. $-x(y^2 - x^2)$ $-xy^2 + x^3$

32. $-ab(a^2 - b^2)$ $ab^3 - a^3b$

33. $(3ab^3 - a^2b^2 - 2a^3b)5a^3$ $15a^4b^3 - 5a^5b^2 - 10a^6b$

34. $(3c^2d - d^3 + 1)8cd^2$ $24c^3d^3 - 8cd^5 + 8cd^2$

35. $-\frac{1}{2}t^2v(4t^3v^2 - 6tv - 4v)$ $-2t^5v^3 + 3t^3v^2 + 2t^2v^2$

36. $-\frac{1}{3}m^2n^3(-6mn^2 + 3mn - 12)$
$2m^3n^5 - m^3n^4 + 4m^2n^3$

Use the distributive property to find each product. See Example 3.

37. $(x + 1)(x + 2)$
$x^2 + 3x + 2$

38. $(x + 6)(x + 3)$
$x^2 + 9x + 18$

39. $(x - 3)(x + 5)$
$x^2 + 2x - 15$

40. $(y - 2)(y + 4)$
$y^2 + 2y - 8$

41. $(t - 4)(t - 9)$
$t^2 - 13t + 36$

42. $(w - 3)(w - 5)$
$w^2 - 8w + 15$

43. $(x + 1)(x^2 + 2x + 2)$
$x^3 + 3x^2 + 4x + 2$

44. $(x - 1)(x^2 + x + 1)$
$x^3 - 1$

45. $(3y + 2)(2y^2 - y + 3)$
$6y^3 + y^2 + 7y + 6$

46. $(4y + 3)(y^2 + 3y + 1)$
$4y^3 + 15y^2 + 13y + 3$

47. $(y^2z - 2y^4)(y^2z + 3z^2 - y^4)$
$2y^8 - 3y^6z - 5y^4z^2 + 3y^2z^3$

48. $(m^3 - 4mn^2)(6m^4n^2 - 3m^6 + m^2n^4)$
$18m^7n^2 - 23m^5n^4 - 3m^9 - 4m^3n^6$

Find each product vertically. See Example 4.

49. $\begin{array}{r} 2a - 3 \\ a + 5 \\ \hline \end{array}$
$2a^2 + 7a - 15$

50. $\begin{array}{r} 2w - 6 \\ w + 5 \\ \hline \end{array}$
$2w^2 + 4w - 30$

51. $\begin{array}{r} 7x + 30 \\ 2x + 5 \\ \hline \end{array}$
$14x^2 + 95x + 150$

52. $\begin{array}{r} 5x + 7 \\ 3x + 6 \\ \hline \end{array}$
$15x^2 + 51x + 42$

53. $\begin{array}{r} 5x + 2 \\ 4x - 3 \\ \hline \end{array}$
$20x^2 - 7x - 6$

54. $\begin{array}{r} 4x + 3 \\ 2x - 6 \\ \hline \end{array}$
$8x^2 - 18x - 18$

55. $\begin{array}{r} m - 3n \\ 2a + b \\ \hline \end{array}$
$2am - 6an + bm - 3bn$

56. $\begin{array}{r} 3x + 7 \\ a - 2b \\ \hline \end{array}$
$3ax + 7a - 6bx - 14b$

57. $\begin{array}{r} x^2 + 3x - 2 \\ x + 6 \\ \hline \end{array}$
$x^3 + 9x^2 + 16x - 12$

58. $\begin{array}{r} -x^2 + 3x - 5 \\ x - 7 \\ \hline \end{array}$
$-x^3 + 10x^2 - 26x + 35$

59. $\begin{array}{r} 2a^3 - 3a^2 + 4 \\ -2a - 3 \\ \hline \end{array}$
$-4a^4 + 9a^2 - 8a - 12$

60. $\begin{array}{r} -3x^2 + 5x - 2 \\ -5x - 6 \\ \hline \end{array}$
$15x^3 - 7x^2 - 20x + 12$

61. $\begin{array}{r} x - y \\ x + y \\ \hline \end{array}$
$x^2 - y^2$

62. $\begin{array}{r} a^2 + b^2 \\ a^2 - b^2 \\ \hline \end{array}$
$a^4 - b^4$

63. $\begin{array}{r} x^2 - xy + y^2 \\ x + y \\ \hline \end{array}$
$x^3 + y^3$

64. $\begin{array}{r} 4w^2 + 2wv + v^2 \\ 2w - v \\ \hline \end{array}$
$8w^3 - v^3$

Find the opposite of each polynomial. See Example 5.

65. $3t - u$ $u - 3t$

66. $-3t - u$ $3t + u$

67. $3x + y$ $-3x - y$

68. $x - 3y$ $3y - x$

69. $-3a^2 - a + 6$ $3a^2 + a - 6$

70. $3b^2 - b - 6$ $-3b^2 + b + 6$

71. $3v^2 + v - 6$ $-3v^2 - v + 6$

72. $-3t^2 + t - 6$ $3t^2 - t + 6$

Perform the indicated operation.

73. $-3x(2x - 9)$
$-6x^2 + 27x$

74. $-1(2 - 3x)$
$3x - 2$

75. $2 - 3x(2x - 9)$
$-6x^2 + 27x + 2$

76. $6 - 3(4x - 8)$
$-12x + 30$

77. $(2 - 3x) + (2x - 9)$
$-x - 7$

78. $(2 - 3x) - (2x - 9)$
$-5x + 11$

79. $(6x^6)^2$ $36x^{12}$

80. $(-3a^3b)^2$ $9a^6b^2$

81. $3ab^3(-2a^2b^7)$
$-6a^3b^{10}$

82. $-4xst \cdot 8xs$
$-32s^2tx^2$

83. $(5x + 6)(5x + 6)$
$25x^2 + 60x + 36$

84. $(5x - 6)(5x - 6)$
$25x^2 - 60x + 36$

85. $(5x - 6)(5x + 6)$
$25x^2 - 36$

86. $(2x - 9)(2x + 9)$
$4x^2 - 81$

87. $2x^2(3x^5 - 4x^2)$
$6x^7 - 8x^4$

88. $4a^3(3ab^3 - 2ab^3)$
$4a^4b^3$

89. $(m - 1)(m^2 + m + 1)$
$m^3 - 1$

90. $(a + b)(a^2 - ab + b^2)$
$a^3 + b^3$

91. $(3x - 2)(x^2 - x - 9)$ $3x^3 - 5x^2 - 25x + 18$

92. $(5 - 6y)(3y^2 - y - 7)$ $-18y^3 + 21y^2 + 37y - 35$

Solve each problem. See Example 6.

93. ***Office space.*** The length of a professor's office is x feet, and the width is $x + 4$ feet. Write a polynomial that represents the area. Find the area if $x = 10$ ft.
$x^2 + 4x$ square feet, 140 square feet

94. ***Swimming space.*** The length of a rectangular swimming pool is $2x - 1$ meters, and the width is $x + 2$ meters. Write a polynomial that represents the area. Find the area if x is 5 meters. $2x^2 + 3x - 2$ square meters, 63 square meters

95. ***Area.*** A roof truss is in the shape of a triangle with height of x feet and a base of $2x + 1$ feet. Write a polynomial $A(x)$ that represents the area of the triangle. Find $A(5)$. See the figure on the next page.
$A(x) = x^2 + \frac{1}{2}x$, $A(5) = 27.5$ square feet

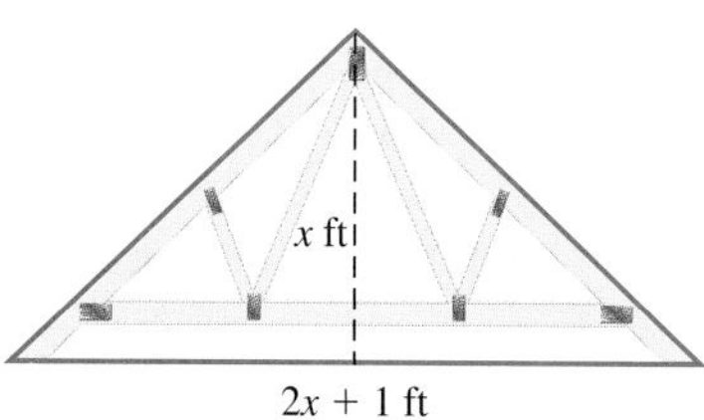

Figure for Exercise 95

96. ***Volume.*** The length, width, and height of a box are x, $2x$, and $3x - 5$ inches, respectively. Write a polynomial $V(x)$ that represents its volume. Find $V(3)$.
$V(x) = 6x^3 - 10x^2$, $V(3) = 72$ cubic inches

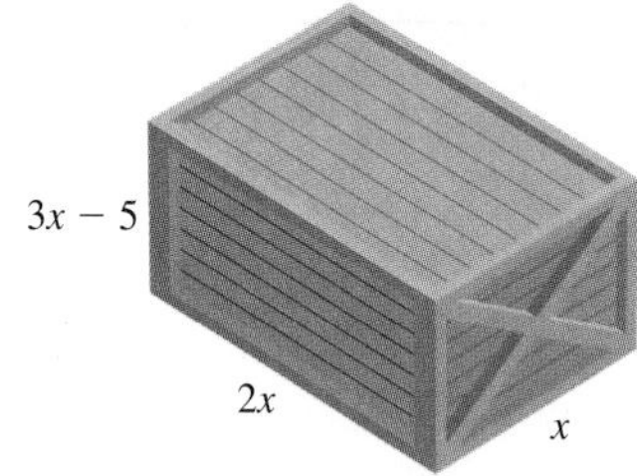

Figure for Exercise 96

97. ***Number pairs.*** If two numbers differ by 5, then what polynomial represents their product? $x^2 + 5x$

98. ***Number pairs.*** If two numbers have a sum of 9, then what polynomial represents their product? $9x - x^2$

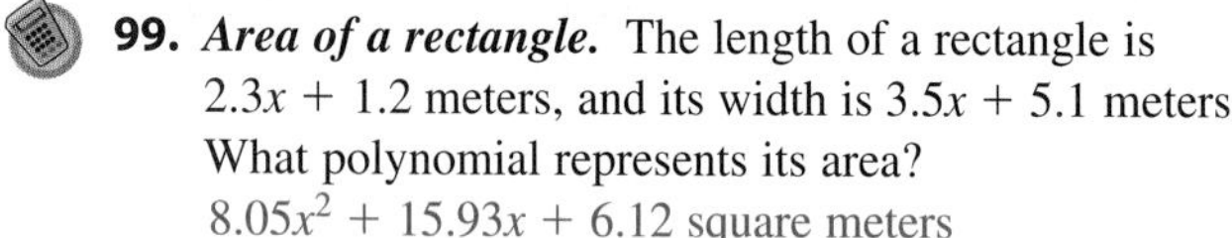

99. ***Area of a rectangle.*** The length of a rectangle is $2.3x + 1.2$ meters, and its width is $3.5x + 5.1$ meters. What polynomial represents its area?
$8.05x^2 + 15.93x + 6.12$ square meters

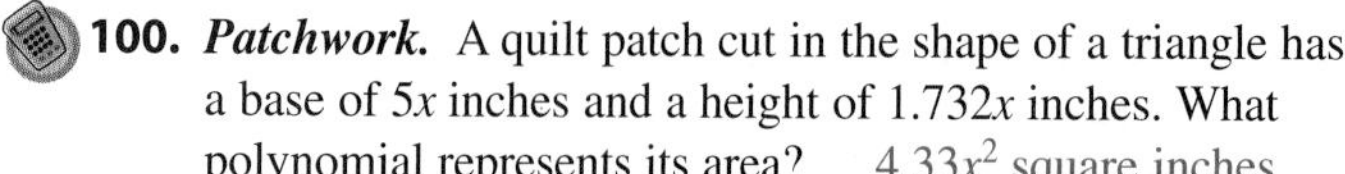

100. ***Patchwork.*** A quilt patch cut in the shape of a triangle has a base of $5x$ inches and a height of $1.732x$ inches. What polynomial represents its area? $4.33x^2$ square inches

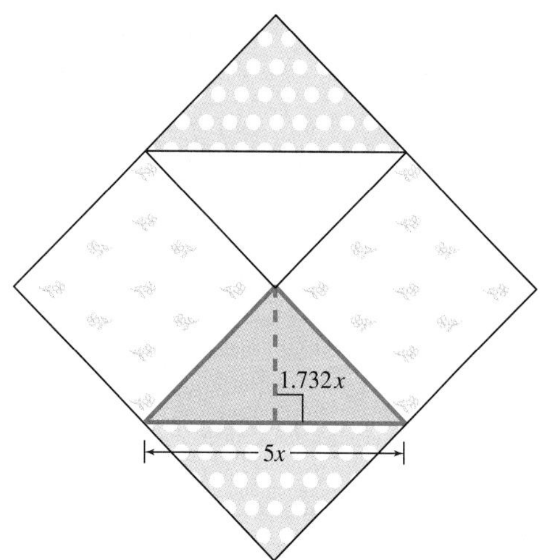

Figure for Exercise 100

101. ***Total revenue.*** If a promoter charges p dollars per ticket for a concert in Tulsa, then she expects to sell $40{,}000 - 1000p$ tickets to the concert. How many tickets will she sell if the tickets are \$10 each? Find the total revenue when the tickets are \$10 each. What polynomial represents the total revenue expected for the concert when the tickets are p dollars each?
30,000, \$300,000, $40{,}000p - 1000p^2$

102. ***Manufacturing shirts.*** If a manufacturer charges p dollars each for rugby shirts, then he expects to sell $2000 - 100p$ shirts per week. What polynomial represents the total revenue expected for a week? How many shirts will be sold if the manufacturer charges \$20 each for the shirts? Find the total revenue when the shirts are sold for \$20 each. Use the bar graph to determine the price that will give the maximum total revenue.
$2000p - 100p^2$, 0, \$0, \$10

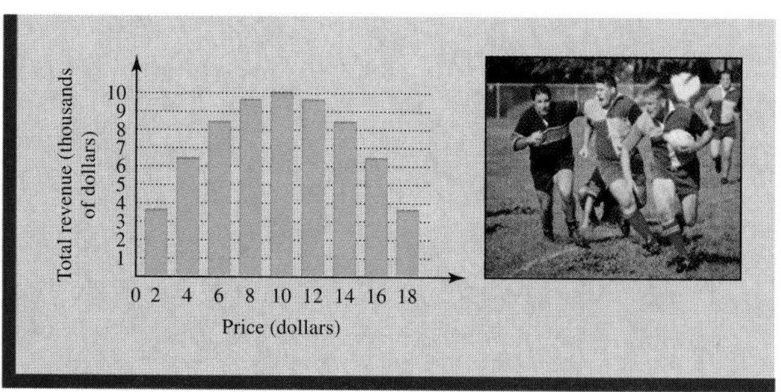

Figure for Exercise 102

103. ***Periodic deposits.*** At the beginning of each year for 5 years, an investor invests \$10 in a mutual fund with an average annual return of r. If we let $x = 1 + r$, then at the end of the first year (just before the next investment) the value is $10x$ dollars. Because \$10 is then added to the $10x$ dollars, the amount at the end of the second year is $(10x + 10)x$ dollars. Find a polynomial that represents the value of the investment at the end of the fifth year. Evaluate this polynomial if $r = 10\%$.
$10x^5 + 10x^4 + 10x^3 + 10x^2 + 10x$, \$67.16

104. ***Increasing deposits.*** At the beginning of each year for 5 years, an investor invests in a mutual fund with an average annual return of r. The first year, she invests \$10; the second year, she invests \$20; the third year, she invests \$30; the fourth year, she invests \$40; the fifth year, she invests \$50. Let $x = 1 + r$ as in Exercise 103 and write a polynomial in x that represents the value of the investment at the end of the fifth year. Evaluate this polynomial for $r = 8\%$.
$10x^5 + 20x^4 + 30x^3 + 40x^2 + 50x$, \$180.35

Getting More Involved

105. ***Discussion***

Name all properties of the real numbers that are used in finding the following products:

a) $-2ab^3c^2 \cdot 5a^2bc$ **b)** $(x^2 + 3)(x^2 - 8x - 6)$

106. ***Discussion***

Find the product of 27 and 436 without using a calculator. Then use the distributive property to find the product $(20 + 7)(400 + 30 + 6)$ as you would find the product of a binomial and a trinomial. Explain how the two methods are related.

4.3 Multiplication of Binomials

In this Section

- **The FOIL Method**
- **Multiplying Binomials Quickly**

In Section 4.2 you learned to multiply polynomials. In this section you will learn a rule that makes multiplication of binomials simpler.

The FOIL Method

We can use the distributive property to find the product of two binomials. For example,

$$\begin{aligned}(x + 2)(x + 3) &= (x + 2)x + (x + 2)3 && \text{Distributive property}\\ &= x^2 + 2x + 3x + 6 && \text{Distributive property}\\ &= x^2 + 5x + 6 && \text{Combine like terms.}\end{aligned}$$

There are four terms in $x^2 + 2x + 3x + 6$. The term x^2 is the product of the *first* terms of each binomial, x and x. The term $3x$ is the product of the two *outer* terms, 3 and x. The term $2x$ is the product of the two *inner* terms, 2 and x. The term 6 is the product of the last terms of each binomial, 2 and 3. We can connect the terms multiplied by lines as follows:

$$(x + 2)(x + 3)$$

(F and L lines above; I and O lines below)

F = First terms
O = Outer terms
I = Inner terms
L = Last terms

Teaching Tip Have students actually draw lines connecting the first, inner, outer, and last terms of the binomials when they first learn FOIL.

If you remember the word FOIL, you can get the product of the two binomials much faster than writing out all of the steps above. This method is called the **FOIL method.** The name should make it easier to remember.

EXAMPLE 1

Using the FOIL method

Find each product.

a) $(x + 2)(x - 4)$ **b)** $(2x + 5)(3x - 4)$

c) $(a - b)(2a - b)$ **d)** $(x + 3)(y + 5)$

Solution

$$\begin{aligned}\textbf{a)}\ (x + 2)(x - 4) &= \overset{F}{x^2} \overset{O}{- 4x} \overset{I}{+ 2x} \overset{L}{- 8}\\ &= x^2 - 2x - 8 && \text{Combine the like terms.}\end{aligned}$$

Helpful Hint

You may have to practice FOIL a while to get good at it. However, the better you are at FOIL, the easier you will find factoring in Chapter 5.

b) $(2x + 5)(3x - 4) = 6x^2 - 8x + 15x - 20$
$= 6x^2 + 7x - 20$ Combine the like terms.

c) $(a - b)(2a - b) = 2a^2 - ab - 2ab + b^2$
$= 2a^2 - 3ab + b^2$

d) $(x + 3)(y + 5) = xy + 5x + 3y + 15$ There are no like terms to combine.

Now do Exercises 5–28

FOIL can be used to multiply any two binomials. The binomials in Example 2 have higher powers than those of Example 1.

EXAMPLE 2

Using the FOIL method

Find each product.

a) $(x^3 - 3)(x^3 + 6)$ **b)** $(2a^2 + 1)(a^2 + 5)$

Solution

a) $(x^3 - 3)(x^3 + 6) = x^6 + 6x^3 - 3x^3 - 18$
$= x^6 + 3x^3 - 18$

b) $(2a^2 + 1)(a^2 + 5) = 2a^4 + 10a^2 + a^2 + 5$
$= 2a^4 + 11a^2 + 5$

Now do Exercises 29-40

Teaching Tip If students cannot do FOIL quickly, they will have a lot of trouble with factoring trinomials.

Multiplying Binomials Quickly

The outer and inner products in the FOIL method are often like terms, and we can combine them without writing them down. Once you become proficient at using FOIL, you can find the product of two binomials without writing anything except the answer.

EXAMPLE 3

Using FOIL to find a product quickly

Find each product. Write down only the answer.

a) $(x + 3)(x + 4)$ **b)** $(2x - 1)(x + 5)$ **c)** $(a - 6)(a + 6)$

Solution

a) $(x + 3)(x + 4) = x^2 + 7x + 12$ Combine like terms: $3x + 4x = 7x$.

b) $(2x - 1)(x + 5) = 2x^2 + 9x - 5$ Combine like terms: $10x - x = 9x$.

c) $(a - 6)(a + 6) = a^2 - 36$ Combine like terms: $6a - 6a = 0$.

Now do Exercises 41–64

EXAMPLE 4

Products of three binomials

Find each product.

a) $(b - 1)(b + 2)(b - 3)$

b) $\left(\frac{1}{2}x + 3\right)\left(\frac{1}{2}x - 3\right)(2x + 5)$

Solution

a) Use FOIL to find $(b - 1)(b + 2) = b^2 + b - 2$. Then use the distributive property to multiply $b^2 + b - 2$ and $b - 3$:

$$\begin{aligned}(b - 1)(b + 2)(b - 3) &= (b^2 + b - 2)(b - 3) && \text{FOIL}\\ &= (b^2 + b - 2)b + (b^2 + b - 2)(-3) && \text{Distributive property}\\ &= b^3 + b^2 - 2b - 3b^2 - 3b + 6 && \text{Distributive property}\\ &= b^3 - 2b^2 - 5b + 6 && \text{Combine like terms.}\end{aligned}$$

b)
$$\begin{aligned}\left(\frac{1}{2}x + 3\right)\left(\frac{1}{2}x - 3\right)(2x + 5) &= \left(\frac{1}{4}x^2 - 9\right)(2x + 5) && \text{FOIL}\\ &= \frac{1}{2}x^3 + \frac{5}{4}x^2 - 18x - 45 && \text{FOIL}\end{aligned}$$

Now do Exercises 65–72

EXAMPLE 5

Area of a garden

Sheila has a square garden with sides of length x feet. If she increases the length by 7 feet and decreases the width by 2 feet, then what trinomial represents the area of the new rectangular garden?

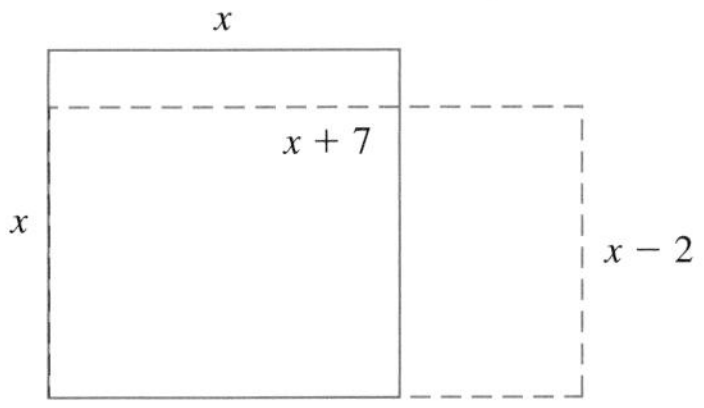

Figure 4.2

Solution

The length of the new garden is $x + 7$ and the width is $x - 2$ as shown in Fig. 4.2. The area is $(x + 7)(x - 2)$ or $x^2 + 5x - 14$ square feet.

Now do Exercises 95–98

Warm-Ups ▼

True or false? Explain your answer.

1. $(x + 3)(x + 2) = x^2 + 6$ False
2. $(x + 2)(y + 1) = xy + x + 2y + 2$ True
3. $(3a - 5)(2a + 1) = 6a^2 + 3a - 10a - 5$ True
4. $(y + 3)(y - 2) = y^2 + y - 6$ True
5. $(x^2 + 2)(x^2 + 3) = x^4 + 5x^2 + 6$ True
6. $(3a^2 - 2)(3a^2 + 2) = 9a^2 - 4$ False
7. $(t + 3)(t + 5) = t^2 + 8t + 15$ True
8. $(y - 9)(y - 2) = y^2 - 11y - 18$ False
9. $(x + 4)(x - 7) = x^2 + 4x - 28$ False
10. It is not necessary to learn FOIL as long as you can get the answer. False

4.3 Exercises

Boost your GRADE at mathzone.com!

MathZone

- Practice Problems
- Self-Tests
- Videos
- Net Tutor
- e-Professors

Reading and Writing *After reading this section, write out the answers to these questions. Use complete sentences.*

1. What property of the real numbers do we usually use to find the product of two binomials?
   We use the distributive property to find the product of two binomials.
2. What does FOIL stand for?
   FOIL stands for first, outer, inner, and last.
3. What is the purpose of FOIL?
   The purpose of FOIL is to provide a faster method for finding the product of two binomials.
4. What is the maximum number of terms that can be obtained when two binomials are multiplied?
   The maximum number of terms obtained in multiplying binomials is four.

Use FOIL to find each product. See Example 1.

5. $(x + 2)(x + 4)$ $x^2 + 6x + 8$
6. $(x + 3)(x + 5)$ $x^2 + 8x + 15$
7. $(a + 1)(a + 4)$ $a^2 + 5a + 4$
8. $(w + 3)(w + 6)$ $w^2 + 9w + 18$
9. $(x + 9)(x + 10)$ $x^2 + 19x + 90$
10. $(x + 5)(x + 7)$ $x^2 + 12x + 35$
11. $(2x + 1)(x + 3)$ $2x^2 + 7x + 3$
12. $(3x + 2)(2x + 1)$ $6x^2 + 7x + 2$
13. $(a - 3)(a + 2)$ $a^2 - a - 6$
14. $(b - 1)(b + 2)$ $b^2 + b - 2$
15. $(2x - 1)(x - 2)$ $2x^2 - 5x + 2$
16. $(2y - 5)(y - 2)$ $2y^2 - 9y + 10$
17. $(2a - 3)(a + 1)$ $2a^2 - a - 3$
18. $(3x - 5)(x + 4)$ $3x^2 + 7x - 20$
19. $(w - 50)(w - 10)$ $w^2 - 60w + 500$
20. $(w - 30)(w - 20)$ $w^2 - 50w + 600$
21. $(y - a)(y + 5)$ $y^2 + 5y - ay - 5a$
22. $(a + t)(3 - y)$ $3a - ay + 3t - ty$
23. $(5 - w)(w + m)$ $5w + 5m - w^2 - mw$
24. $(a - h)(b + t)$ $ab + at - bh - ht$
25. $(2m - 3t)(5m + 3t)$ $10m^2 - 9mt - 9t^2$
26. $(2x - 5y)(x + y)$ $2x^2 - 3xy - 5y^2$
27. $(5a + 2b)(9a + 7b)$ $45a^2 + 53ab + 14b^2$
28. $(11x + 3y)(x + 4y)$ $11x^2 + 47xy + 12y^2$

Use FOIL to find each product. See Example 2.

29. $(x^2 - 5)(x^2 + 2)$ $x^4 - 3x^2 - 10$
30. $(y^2 + 1)(y^2 - 2)$ $y^4 - y^2 - 2$
31. $(h^3 + 5)(h^3 + 5)$ $h^6 + 10h^3 + 25$
32. $(y^6 + 1)(y^6 - 4)$ $y^{12} - 3y^6 - 4$
33. $(3b^3 + 2)(b^3 + 4)$ $3b^6 + 14b^3 + 8$
34. $(5n^4 - 1)(n^4 + 3)$ $5n^8 + 14n^4 - 3$
35. $(y^2 - 3)(y - 2)$ $y^3 - 2y^2 - 3y + 6$
36. $(x - 1)(x^2 - 1)$ $x^3 - x^2 - x + 1$
37. $(3m^3 - n^2)(2m^3 + 3n^2)$ $6m^6 + 7m^3n^2 - 3n^4$
38. $(6y^4 - 2z^2)(6y^4 - 3z^2)$ $36y^8 - 30y^4z^2 + 6z^4$
39. $(3u^2v - 2)(4u^2v + 6)$ $12u^4v^2 + 10u^2v - 12$
40. $(5y^3w^2 + z)(2y^3w^2 + 3z)$ $10y^6w^4 + 17y^3w^2z + 3z^2$

Find each product. Try to write only the answer. See Example 3.

41. $(b + 4)(b + 5)$ $b^2 + 9b + 20$
42. $(y + 8)(y + 4)$ $y^2 + 12y + 32$
43. $(x - 3)(x + 9)$ $x^2 + 6x - 27$
44. $(m + 7)(m - 8)$ $m^2 - m - 56$
45. $(a + 5)(a + 5)$ $a^2 + 10a + 25$
46. $(t - 4)(t - 4)$ $t^2 - 8t + 16$
47. $(2x - 1)(2x - 1)$ $4x^2 - 4x + 1$
48. $(3y + 4)(3y + 4)$ $9y^2 + 24y + 16$
49. $(z - 10)(z + 10)$ $z^2 - 100$
50. $(3h - 5)(3h + 5)$ $9h^2 - 25$
51. $(a + b)(a + b)$ $a^2 + 2ab + b^2$
52. $(x - y)(x - y)$ $x^2 - 2xy + y^2$
53. $(a - 1)(a - 2)$ $a^2 - 3a + 2$
54. $(b - 8)(b - 1)$ $b^2 - 9b + 8$
55. $(2x - 1)(x + 3)$ $2x^2 + 5x - 3$
56. $(3y + 5)(y - 3)$ $3y^2 - 4y - 15$
57. $(5t - 2)(t - 1)$ $5t^2 - 7t + 2$
58. $(2t - 3)(2t - 1)$ $4t^2 - 8t + 3$
59. $(h - 7)(h - 9)$ $h^2 - 16h + 63$
60. $(h - 7w)(h - 7w)$ $h^2 - 14hw + 49w^2$
61. $(h + 7w)(h + 7w)$ $h^2 + 14hw + 49w^2$
62. $(h - 7q)(h + 7q)$ $h^2 - 49q^2$
63. $(2h^2 - 1)(2h^2 - 1)$ $4h^4 - 4h^2 + 1$
64. $(3h^2 + 1)(3h^2 + 1)$ $9h^4 + 6h^2 + 1$

Find each product. See Example 4.

65. $(a + 1)(a - 2)(a + 5)$ $a^3 + 4a^2 - 7a - 10$
66. $(y - 1)(y + 3)(y - 4)$ $y^3 - 2y^2 - 11y + 12$
67. $(h + 2)(h + 3)(h + 4)$ $h^3 + 9h^2 + 26h + 24$
68. $(m - 1)(m - 3)(m - 5)$ $m^3 - 9m^2 + 23m - 15$
69. $\left(\frac{1}{2}x + 4\right)\left(\frac{1}{2}x - 4\right)(4x - 8)$ $x^3 - 2x^2 - 64x + 128$

70. $\left(\frac{1}{3}w - 3\right)\left(\frac{1}{3}w + 3\right)(w - 6)$ $\frac{1}{9}w^3 - \frac{2}{3}w^2 - 9w + 54$

71. $\left(x + \frac{1}{2}\right)\left(x - \frac{1}{2}\right)(x + 8)$ $x^3 + 8x^2 - \frac{1}{4}x - 2$

72. $\left(x + \frac{1}{3}\right)\left(x - \frac{1}{3}\right)(x + 9)$ $x^3 + 9x^2 - \frac{1}{9}x - 1$

Perform the indicated operations.

73. $(x + 10)(x + 5)$ $x^2 + 15x + 50$

74. $(x + 4)(x + 8)$ $x^2 + 12x + 32$

75. $\left(x + \frac{1}{2}\right)\left(x + \frac{1}{2}\right)$ $x^2 + x + \frac{1}{4}$

76. $\left(x + \frac{1}{3}\right)\left(x + \frac{1}{6}\right)$ $x^2 + \frac{1}{2}x + \frac{1}{18}$

77. $\left(4x + \frac{1}{2}\right)\left(2x + \frac{1}{4}\right)$ $8x^2 + 2x + \frac{1}{8}$

78. $\left(3x + \frac{1}{6}\right)\left(6x + \frac{1}{3}\right)$ $18x^2 + 2x + \frac{1}{18}$

79. $\left(2a + \frac{1}{2}\right)\left(4a - \frac{1}{2}\right)$ $8a^2 + a - \frac{1}{4}$

80. $\left(3b + \frac{2}{3}\right)\left(6b - \frac{1}{3}\right)$ $18b^2 + 3b - \frac{2}{9}$

81. $\left(\frac{1}{2}x - \frac{1}{3}\right)\left(\frac{1}{4}x + \frac{1}{2}\right)$ $\frac{1}{8}x^2 + \frac{1}{6}x - \frac{1}{6}$

82. $\left(\frac{2}{3}t - \frac{1}{4}\right)\left(\frac{1}{2}t - \frac{1}{2}\right)$ $\frac{1}{3}t^2 - \frac{11}{24}t + \frac{1}{8}$

83. $a(a + 3)(a + 4)$ $a^3 + 7a^2 + 12a$

84. $w(w + 5)(w + 9)$ $w^3 + 14w^2 + 45w$

85. $x^3(x + 6)(x + 7)$ $x^5 + 13x^4 + 42x^3$

86. $x^2(x^2 + 1)(x^2 + 8)$ $x^6 + 9x^4 + 8x^2$

87. $-2x^4(3x - 1)(2x + 5)$ $-12x^6 - 26x^5 + 10x^4$

88. $4xy^3(2x - y)(3x + y)$ $24x^3y^3 - 4x^2y^4 - 4xy^5$

89. $(x - 1)(x + 1)(x + 3)$ $x^3 + 3x^2 - x - 3$

90. $(a - 3)(a + 4)(a - 5)$ $a^3 - 4a^2 - 17a + 60$

91. $(3x - 2)(3x + 2)(x + 5)$ $9x^3 + 45x^2 - 4x - 20$

92. $(x - 6)(9x + 4)(9x - 4)$ $81x^3 - 486x^2 - 16x + 96$

93. $(x - 1)(x + 2) - (x + 3)(x - 4)$ $2x + 10$

94. $(k - 4)(k + 9) - (k - 3)(k + 7)$ $k - 15$

Solve each problem.

95. ***Area of a rug.*** Find a trinomial that represents the area of a rectangular rug whose sides are $x + 3$ feet and $2x - 1$ feet. $2x^2 + 5x - 3$ square feet

96. ***Area of a parallelogram.*** Find a trinomial that represents the area of a parallelogram whose base is $3x + 2$ meters and whose height is $2x + 3$ meters. $6x^2 + 13x + 6$ square meters

97. ***Area of a sail.*** The sail of a tall ship is triangular in shape with a base of $4.57x + 3$ meters and a height of $2.3x -$ 1.33 meters. Find a polynomial that represents the area of the triangle. $5.2555x^2 + 0.41095x - 1.995$ square meters

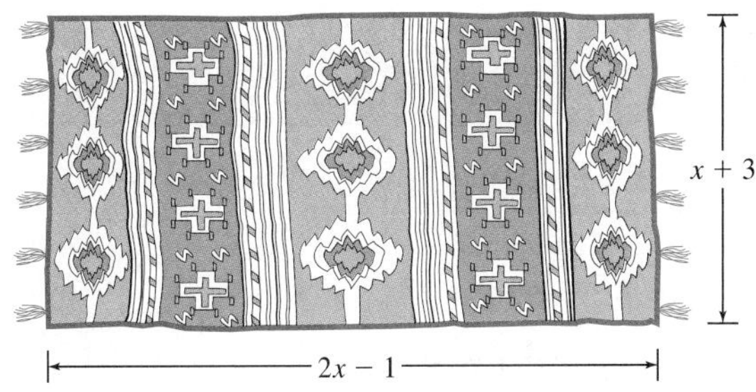

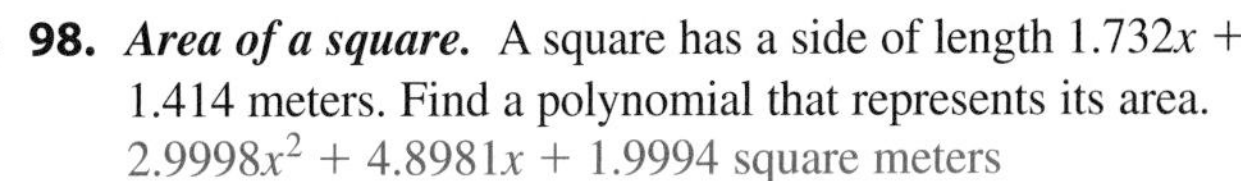

Figure for Exercise 95

98. ***Area of a square.*** A square has a side of length $1.732x +$ 1.414 meters. Find a polynomial that represents its area. $2.9998x^2 + 4.8981x + 1.9994$ square meters

Getting More Involved

99. ***Exploration***

Find the area of each of the four regions shown in the figure. What is the total area of the four regions? What does this exercise illustrate? 12 ft^2, $3h$ ft^2, $4h$ ft^2, h^2 ft^2, $h^2 + 7h + 12$ ft^2, $(h + 3)(h + 4) = h^2 + 7h + 12$

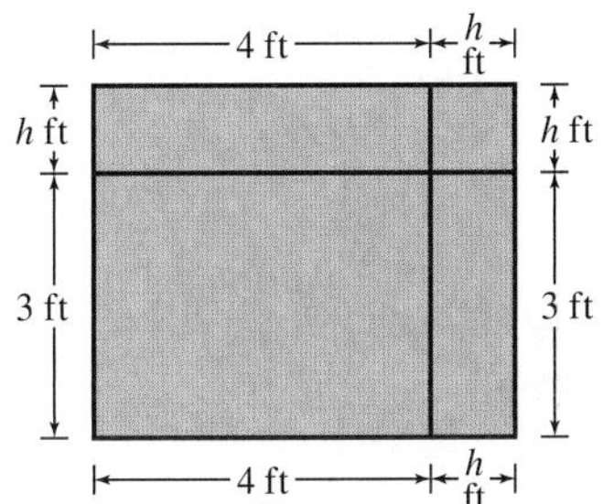

Figure for Exercise 99

100. ***Exploration***

Find the area of each of the four regions shown in the figure. What is the total area of the four regions? What does this exercise illustrate? a^2, ab, ab, b^2, $a^2 + 2ab + b^2$, $(a + b)(a + b) = a^2 + 2ab + b^2$

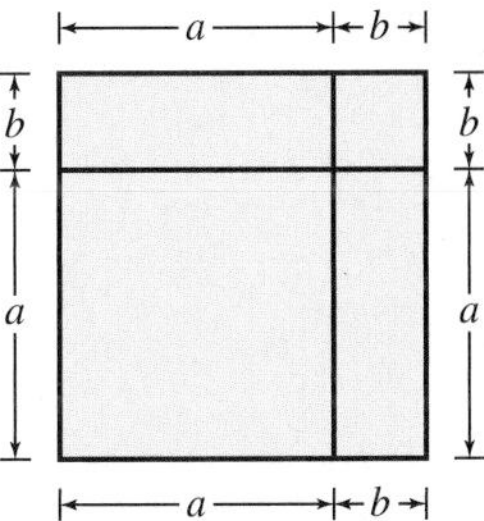

Figure for Exercise 100

4.4 Special Products

In this Section

- The Square of a Binomial
- Product of a Sum and a Difference
- Higher Powers of Binomials
- Applications to Area

In Section 4.3 you learned the FOIL method to make multiplying binomials simpler. In this section you will learn rules for squaring binomials and for finding the product of a sum and a difference. These products are called **special products.**

Helpful Hint

To visualize the square of a sum, draw a square with sides of length $a + b$ as shown.

	a	b
a	a^2	ab
b	ab	b^2

The area of the large square is $(a + b)^2$. It comes from four terms as stated in the rule for the square of a sum.

The Square of a Binomial

To compute $(a + b)^2$, the square of a binomial, we can write it as $(a + b)(a + b)$ and use FOIL:

$$\begin{aligned}(a + b)^2 &= (a + b)(a + b)\\ &= a^2 + ab + ab + b^2\\ &= a^2 + 2ab + b^2\end{aligned}$$

So to square $a + b$, *we square the first term* (a^2), *add twice the product of the two terms* ($2ab$), *then add the square of the last term* (b^2). The square of a binomial occurs so frequently that it is helpful to learn this new rule to find it. The rule for squaring a sum is given symbolically as follows.

The Square of a Sum

$$(a + b)^2 = a^2 + 2ab + b^2$$

EXAMPLE 1

Using the rule for squaring a sum

Find the square of each sum.

a) $(x + 3)^2$ **b)** $(2a + 5)^2$

Solution

a) $(x + 3)^2 = x^2 + 2(x)(3) + 3^2 = x^2 + 6x + 9$

(Square of first: x^2; Twice the product: $2(x)(3)$; Square of last: 3^2)

b) $(2a + 5)^2 = (2a)^2 + 2(2a)(5) + 5^2$
$= 4a^2 + 20a + 25$

Now do Exercises 7–20

CAUTION Do not forget the middle term when squaring a sum. The equation $(x + 3)^2 = x^2 + 6x + 9$ is an identity, but $(x + 3)^2 = x^2 + 9$ is not an identity. For example, if $x = 1$ in $(x + 3)^2 = x^2 + 9$, then we get $4^2 = 1^2 + 9$, which is false.

When we use FOIL to find $(a - b)^2$, we see that

$$\begin{aligned}(a - b)^2 &= (a - b)(a - b)\\ &= a^2 - ab - ab + b^2\\ &= a^2 - 2ab + b^2.\end{aligned}$$

So to square $a - b$, *we square the first term* (a^2), *subtract twice the product of the two terms* $(-2ab)$, *and add the square of the last term* (b^2). The rule for squaring a difference is given symbolically as follows.

The Square of a Difference

$$(a - b)^2 = a^2 - 2ab + b^2$$

EXAMPLE 2

Using the rule for squaring a difference

Find the square of each difference.

a) $(x - 4)^2$ **b)** $(4b - 5y)^2$

Solution

a) $(x - 4)^2 = x^2 - 2(x)(4) + 4^2$
$= x^2 - 8x + 16$

b) $(4b - 5y)^2 = (4b)^2 - 2(4b)(5y) + (5y)^2$
$= 16b^2 - 40by + 25y^2$

Now do Exercises 21–34

Helpful Hint

Many students keep using FOIL to find the square of a sum or difference. However, learning the new rules for these special cases will pay off in the future.

Product of a Sum and a Difference

If we multiply the sum $a + b$ and the difference $a - b$ by using FOIL, we get

$$\begin{aligned}(a + b)(a - b) &= a^2 - ab + ab - b^2\\ &= a^2 - b^2.\end{aligned}$$

The inner and outer products have a sum of 0. So *the product of a sum and a difference of the same two terms is equal to the difference of two squares.*

The Product of a Sum and a Difference

$$(a + b)(a - b) = a^2 - b^2$$

EXAMPLE 3

Product of a sum and a difference

Find each product.

a) $(x + 2)(x - 2)$ **b)** $(b + 7)(b - 7)$ **c)** $(3x - 5)(3x + 5)$

Solution

a) $(x + 2)(x - 2) = x^2 - 4$

b) $(b + 7)(b - 7) = b^2 - 49$

c) $(3x - 5)(3x + 5) = 9x^2 - 25$

Now do Exercises 35–46

Helpful Hint

You can use

$$(a + b)(a - b) = a^2 - b^2$$

to perform mental arithmetic tricks like

$$\begin{aligned}19 \cdot 21 &= (20 - 1)(20 + 1)\\ &= 400 - 1\\ &= 399.\end{aligned}$$

What is $29 \cdot 31$? $28 \cdot 32$?

Higher Powers of Binomials

To find a power of a binomial that is higher than 2, we can use the rule for squaring a binomial along with the method of multiplying binomials using the distributive property. Finding the second or higher power of a binomial is called **expanding the binomial** because the result has more terms than the original.

EXAMPLE 4

Higher powers of a binomial

Expand each binomial.

a) $(x + 4)^3$ **b)** $(y - 2)^4$

Study Tip

Correct answers often have more than one form. If your answer to an exercise doesn't agree with the one in the back of this text, try to determine if it is simply a different form of the answer. For example, $\frac{1}{2}x$ and $\frac{x}{2}$ look different but they are equivalent expressions.

Solution

a)
$$\begin{aligned}(x + 4)^3 &= (x + 4)^2(x + 4)\\ &= (x^2 + 8x + 16)(x + 4)\\ &= (x^2 + 8x + 16)x + (x^2 + 8x + 16)4\\ &= x^3 + 8x^2 + 16x + 4x^2 + 32x + 64\\ &= x^3 + 12x^2 + 48x + 64\end{aligned}$$

b)
$$\begin{aligned}(y - 2)^4 &= (y - 2)^2(y - 2)^2\\ &= (y^2 - 4y + 4)(y^2 - 4y + 4)\\ &= (y^2 - 4y + 4)(y^2) + (y^2 - 4y + 4)(-4y) + (y^2 - 4y + 4)(4)\\ &= y^4 - 4y^3 + 4y^2 - 4y^3 + 16y^2 - 16y + 4y^2 - 16y + 16\\ &= y^4 - 8y^3 + 24y^2 - 32y + 16\end{aligned}$$

Now do Exercises 47–54

Applications to Area

EXAMPLE 5

Area of a pizza

A pizza parlor saves money by making all of its round pizzas one inch smaller in radius than advertised. Write a trinomial for the actual area of a pizza with an advertised radius of r inches.

Teaching Tip A good outside exercise is to ask students to price their favorite pizza in two sizes and determine which is the better value. Does the pizza maker size the pizzas by radius or diameter?

Solution

A pizza advertised as r inches has an actual radius of $r - 1$ inches. The actual area is $\pi(r - 1)^2$:

$$\pi(r - 1)^2 = \pi(r^2 - 2r + 1) = \pi r^2 - 2\pi r + \pi.$$

So $\pi r^2 - 2\pi r + \pi$ is a trinomial representing the actual area.

Now do Exercises 85–94

Warm-Ups

True or false? Explain your answer.

1. $(2 + 3)^2 = 2^2 + 3^2$ False
2. $(x + 3)^2 = x^2 + 6x + 9$ for any value of x. True
3. $(3 + 5)^2 = 9 + 30 + 25$ True
4. $(2x + 7)^2 = 4x^2 + 28x + 49$ for any value of x. True
5. $(y + 8)^2 = y^2 + 64$ for any value of y. False
6. The product of a sum and a difference of the same two terms is equal to the difference of two squares. True
7. $(40 - 1)(40 + 1) = 1599$ True
8. $49 \cdot 51 = 2499$ True
9. $(x - 3)^2 = x^2 - 3x + 9$ for any value of x. False
10. The square of a sum is equal to a sum of two squares. False

4.4 Exercises

Boost your GRADE at mathzone.com!

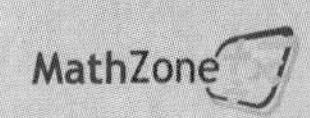

- Practice Problems
- Net Tutor
- Self-Tests
- e-Professors
- Videos

Reading and Writing *After reading this section, write out the answers to these questions. Use complete sentences.*

1. What are the special products?
   The special products are $(a + b)^2$, $(a - b)^2$, and $(a + b)(a - b)$.
2. What is the rule for squaring a sum?
   $(a + b)^2 = a^2 + 2ab + b^2$
3. Why do we need a new rule to find the square of a sum when we already have FOIL?
   It is faster to do by the new rule than with FOIL.
4. What happens to the inner and outer products in the product of a sum and a difference?
   In $(a + b)(a - b)$ the inner and outer products have a sum of zero.
5. What is the rule for finding the product of a sum and a difference?
   $(a + b)(a - b) = a^2 - b^2$
6. How can you find higher powers of binomials?
   Higher powers of binomials are found by using the distributive property.

Square each binomial. See Example 1.

7. $(x + 1)^2$
   $x^2 + 2x + 1$
8. $(y + 2)^2$
   $y^2 + 4y + 4$
9. $(y + 4)^2$
   $y^2 + 8y + 16$
10. $(z + 3)^2$
    $z^2 + 6z + 9$
11. $(m + 6)^2$
    $m^2 + 12m + 36$
12. $(w + 7)^2$
    $w^2 + 14w + 49$
13. $(3x + 8)^2$
    $9x^2 + 48x + 64$
14. $(2m + 7)^2$
    $4m^2 + 28m + 49$
15. $(s + t)^2$
    $s^2 + 2st + t^2$
16. $(x + z)^2$
    $x^2 + 2xz + z^2$
17. $(2x + y)^2$
    $4x^2 + 4xy + y^2$
18. $(3t + v)^2$
    $9t^2 + 6tv + v^2$
19. $(2t + 3h)^2$
    $4t^2 + 12ht + 9h^2$
20. $(3z + 5k)^2$
    $9z^2 + 30kz + 25k^2$

Square each binomial. See Example 2.

21. $(p - 2)^2$
    $p^2 - 4p + 4$
22. $(b - 5)^2$
    $b^2 - 10b + 25$
23. $(a - 3)^2$
    $a^2 - 6a + 9$
24. $(w - 4)^2$
    $w^2 - 8w + 16$
25. $(t - 1)^2$
    $t^2 - 2t + 1$
26. $(t - 6)^2$
    $t^2 - 12t + 36$
27. $(3t - 2)^2$
    $9t^2 - 12t + 4$
28. $(5a - 6)^2$
    $25a^2 - 60a + 36$

29. $(s - t)^2$
$s^2 - 2st + t^2$

30. $(r - w)^2$
$r^2 - 2rw + w^2$

31. $(3a - b)^2$
$9a^2 - 6ab + b^2$

32. $(4w - 7)^2$
$16w^2 - 56w + 49$

33. $(3z - 5y)^2$
$9z^2 - 30yz + 25y^2$

34. $(2z - 3w)^2$
$4z^2 - 12wz + 9w^2$

Find each product. See Example 3.

35. $(a - 5)(a + 5)$
$a^2 - 25$

36. $(x - 6)(x + 6)$
$x^2 - 36$

37. $(y - 1)(y + 1)$
$y^2 - 1$

38. $(p + 2)(p - 2)$
$p^2 - 4$

39. $(3x - 8)(3x + 8)$
$9x^2 - 64$

40. $(6x + 1)(6x - 1)$
$36x^2 - 1$

41. $(r + s)(r - s)$
$r^2 - s^2$

42. $(b - y)(b + y)$
$b^2 - y^2$

43. $(8y - 3a)(8y + 3a)$
$64y^2 - 9a^2$

44. $(4u - 9v)(4u + 9v)$
$16u^2 - 81v^2$

45. $(5x^2 - 2)(5x^2 + 2)$
$25x^4 - 4$

46. $(3y^2 + 1)(3y^2 - 1)$
$9y^4 - 1$

Expand each binomial. See Example 4.

47. $(x + 1)^3$ $x^3 + 3x^2 + 3x + 1$

48. $(y - 1)^3$ $y^3 - 3y^2 + 3y - 1$

49. $(2a - 3)^3$ $8a^3 - 36a^2 + 54a - 27$

50. $(3w - 1)^3$ $27w^3 - 27w^2 + 9w - 1$

51. $(a - 3)^4$ $a^4 - 12a^3 + 54a^2 - 108a + 81$

52. $(2b + 1)^4$ $16b^4 + 32b^3 + 24b^2 + 8b + 1$

53. $(a + b)^4$ $a^4 + 4a^3b + 6a^2b^2 + 4ab^3 + b^4$

54. $(2a - 3b)^4$ $16a^4 - 96a^3b + 216a^2b^2 - 216ab^3 + 81b^4$

Find each product.

55. $(a - 20)(a + 20)$
$a^2 - 400$

56. $(1 - x)(1 + x)$
$1 - x^2$

57. $(x + 8)(x + 7)$
$x^2 + 15x + 56$

58. $(x - 9)(x + 5)$
$x^2 - 4x - 45$

59. $(4x - 1)(4x + 1)$
$16x^2 - 1$

60. $(9y - 1)(9y + 1)$
$81y^2 - 1$

61. $(9y - 1)^2$
$81y^2 - 18y + 1$

62. $(4x - 1)^2$
$16x^2 - 8x + 1$

63. $(2t - 5)(3t + 4)$
$6t^2 - 7t - 20$

64. $(2t + 5)(3t - 4)$
$6t^2 + 7t - 20$

65. $(2t - 5)^2$
$4t^2 - 20t + 25$

66. $(2t + 5)^2$
$4t^2 + 20t + 25$

67. $(2t + 5)(2t - 5)$
$4t^2 - 25$

68. $(3t - 4)(3t + 4)$
$9t^2 - 16$

69. $(x^2 - 1)(x^2 + 1)$
$x^4 - 1$

70. $(y^3 - 1)(y^3 + 1)$
$y^6 - 1$

71. $(2y^3 - 9)^2$
$4y^6 - 36y^3 + 81$

72. $(3z^4 - 8)^2$
$9z^8 - 48z^4 + 64$

73. $(2x^3 + 3y^2)^2$
$4x^6 + 12x^3y^2 + 9y^4$

74. $(4y^5 + 2w^3)^2$
$16y^{10} + 16y^5w^3 + 4w^6$

75. $\left(\frac{1}{2}x + \frac{1}{3}\right)^2$
$\frac{1}{4}x^2 + \frac{1}{3}x + \frac{1}{9}$

76. $\left(\frac{2}{3}y - \frac{1}{2}\right)^2$
$\frac{4}{9}y^2 - \frac{2}{3}y + \frac{1}{4}$

77. $(0.2x - 0.1)^2$ $0.04x^2 - 0.04x + 0.01$

78. $(0.1y + 0.5)^2$ $0.01y^2 + 0.1y + 0.25$

79. $(a + b)^3$ $a^3 + 3a^2b + 3ab^2 + b^3$

80. $(2a - 3b)^3$ $8a^3 - 36a^2b + 54ab^2 - 27b^3$

81. $(1.5x + 3.8)^2$ $2.25x^2 + 11.4x + 14.44$

82. $(3.45a - 2.3)^2$ $11.9025a^2 - 15.87a + 5.29$

83. $(3.5t - 2.5)(3.5t + 2.5)$ $12.25t^2 - 6.25$

84. $(4.5h + 5.7)(4.5h - 5.7)$ $20.25h^2 - 32.49$

Solve each problem. See Example 5.

85. ***Shrinking garden.*** Rose's garden is a square with sides of length x feet. Next spring she plans to make it rectangular by lengthening one side 5 feet and shortening the other side by 5 feet. What polynomial represents the new area? By how much will the area of the new garden differ from that of the old garden? $x^2 - 25$ square feet, 25 square feet smaller

86. ***Square lot.*** Sam lives on a lot that he thought was a square, 157 feet by 157 feet. When he had it surveyed, he discovered that one side was actually 2 feet longer than he thought and the other was actually 2 feet shorter than he thought. How much less area does he have than he thought he had? 4 square feet

87. ***Area of a circle.*** Find a polynomial that represents the area of a circle whose radius is $b + 1$ meters. Use the value 3.14 for π. $3.14b^2 + 6.28b + 3.14$ square meters

88. ***Comparing dart boards.*** A toy store sells two sizes of circular dartboards. The larger of the two has a radius that is 3 inches greater than that of the other. The radius of the smaller dartboard is t inches. Find a polynomial that represents the difference in area between the two dartboards. $6\pi t + 9\pi$ square centimeters

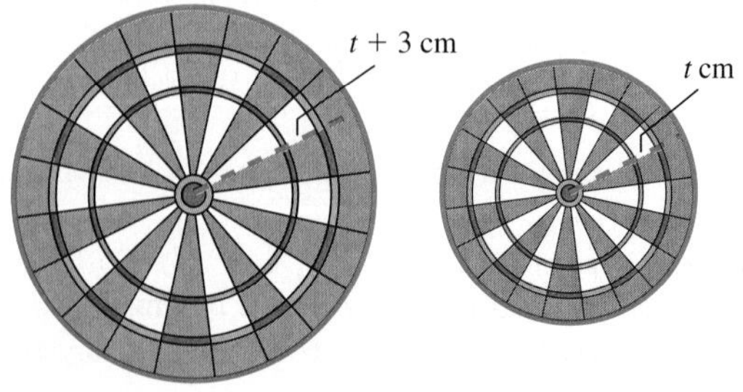

Figure for Exercise 88

89. ***Poiseuille's law.*** According to the nineteenth-century physician Poiseuille, the velocity (in centimeters per second) of blood r centimeters from the center of an artery of radius R centimeters is given by

$$v = k(R - r)(R + r),$$

where k is a constant. Rewrite the formula using a special product rule. $v = k(R^2 - r^2)$

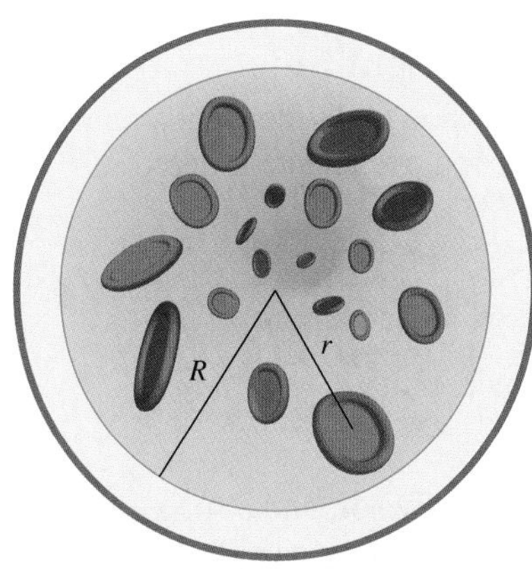

Figure for Exercise 89

90. ***Going in circles.*** A promoter is planning a circular race track with an inside radius of r feet and a width of w feet. The cost in dollars for paving the track is given by the formula

$$C = 1.2\pi[(r + w)^2 - r^2].$$

Use a special product rule to simplify this formula. What is the cost of paving the track if the inside radius is 1000 feet and the width of the track is 40 feet?
$C = 1.2\pi(2rw + w^2)$, \$307,624.75

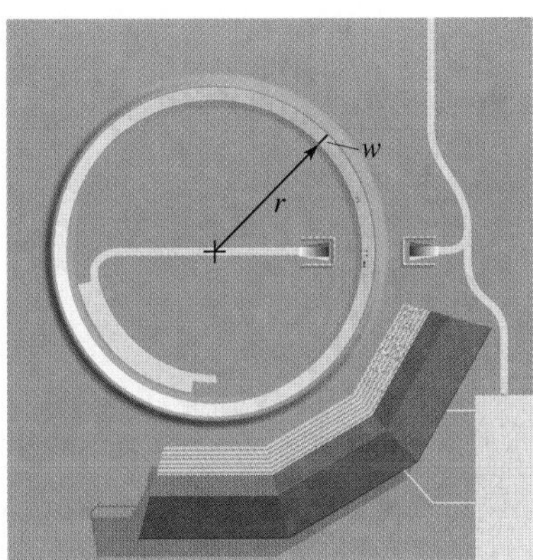

Figure for Exercise 90

91. ***Compounded annually.*** P dollars is invested at annual interest rate r for 2 years. If the interest is compounded annually, then the polynomial $P(1 + r)^2$ represents the value of the investment after 2 years. Rewrite this expression without parentheses. Evaluate the polynomial if $P = \$200$ and $r = 10\%$.
$P + 2Pr + Pr^2$, \$242

92. ***Compounded semiannually.*** P dollars is invested at annual interest rate r for 1 year. If the interest is compounded semiannually, then the polynomial $P\left(1 + \frac{r}{2}\right)^2$ represents the value of the investment after 1 year. Rewrite this expression without parentheses. Evaluate the polynomial if $P = \$200$ and $r = 10\%$.
$P + Pr + \frac{Pr^2}{4}$, \$220.50

93. ***Investing in treasury bills.*** An investment advisor uses the polynomial $P(1 + r)^{10}$ to predict the value in 10 years of a client's investment of P dollars with an average annual return r. The accompanying graph shows historic average annual returns for the last 20 years for various asset classes (T. Rowe Price, www.troweprice.com). Use the historical average return to predict the value in 10 years of an investment of \$10,000 in U.S. treasury bills. \$20,230.06

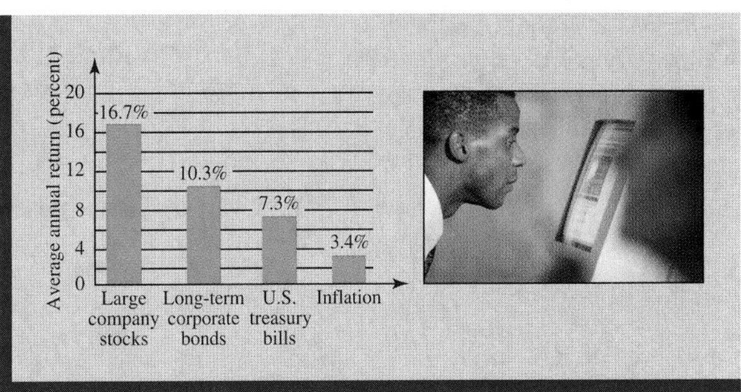

Figure for Exercises 93 and 94

94. ***Comparing investments.*** How much more would the investment in Exercise 93 be worth in 10 years if the client invests in large company stocks rather than U.S. treasury bills? \$26,619.83

Getting More Involved

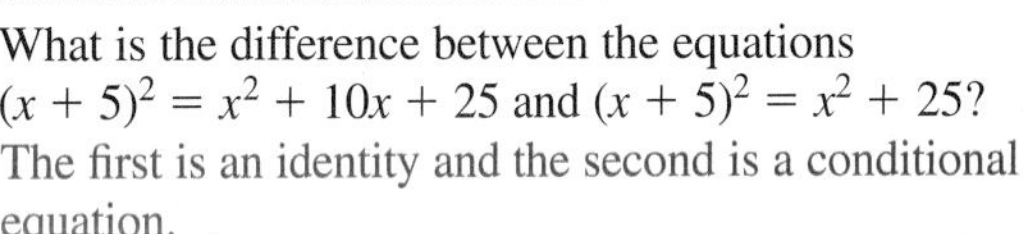

95. ***Writing***

What is the difference between the equations $(x + 5)^2 = x^2 + 10x + 25$ and $(x + 5)^2 = x^2 + 25$?
The first is an identity and the second is a conditional equation.

96. ***Writing***

Is it possible to square a sum or a difference without using the rules presented in this section? Why should you learn the rules given in this section?
A sum or difference can be squared with the distributive property, FOIL, or the special product rules. It is easier with the special product rules.

4.5 Division of Polynomials

In this Section

- **Dividing Monomials Using the Quotient Rule**
- **Dividing a Polynomial by a Monomial**
- **Dividing a Polynomial by a Binomial**

You multiplied polynomials in Section 4.2. In this section you will learn to divide polynomials.

Dividing Monomials Using the Quotient Rule

In Chapter 1 we used the definition of division to divide signed numbers. Because the definition of division applies to any division, we restate it here.

Division of Real Numbers

If a, b, and c are any numbers with $b \neq 0$, then

$$a \div b = c \qquad \text{provided that} \qquad c \cdot b = a.$$

Study Tip

Establish a regular routine of eating, sleeping, and exercise. The ability to concentrate depends on adequate sleep, decent nutrition, and the physical well-being that comes with exercise.

If $a \div b = c$, we call a the **dividend,** b the **divisor,** and c (or $a \div b$) the **quotient.**

You can find the quotient of two monomials by writing the quotient as a fraction and then reducing the fraction. For example,

$$x^5 \div x^2 = \frac{x^5}{x^2} = \frac{x \cdot x \cdot x \cdot \cancel{x} \cdot \cancel{x}}{\cancel{x} \cdot \cancel{x}} = x^3.$$

You can be sure that x^3 is correct by checking that $x^3 \cdot x^2 = x^5$. You can also divide x^2 by x^5, but the result is not a monomial:

$$x^2 \div x^5 = \frac{x^2}{x^5} = \frac{1 \cdot \cancel{x} \cdot \cancel{x}}{x \cdot x \cdot x \cdot \cancel{x} \cdot \cancel{x}} = \frac{1}{x^3}$$

Note that the exponent 3 can be obtained in either case by subtracting 5 and 2. These examples illustrate the quotient rule for exponents.

Quotient Rule

Suppose $a \neq 0$, and m and n are positive integers.

$$\text{If } m \geq n, \text{ then } \frac{a^m}{a^n} = a^{m-n}.$$

$$\text{If } n > m, \text{ then } \frac{a^m}{a^n} = \frac{1}{a^{n-m}}.$$

Teaching Tip Remind students that there are a few expressions that are undefined because any definition of them would cause inconsistencies with other rules and definitions.

Note that if you use the quotient rule to subtract the exponents in $x^4 \div x^4$, you get the expression x^{4-4}, or x^0, which has not been defined yet. Because we must have $x^4 \div x^4 = 1$ if $x \neq 0$, we define the zero power of a nonzero real number to be 1. We do not define the expression 0^0.

Zero Exponent

For any nonzero real number a,

$$a^0 = 1.$$

EXAMPLE 1

Using the definition of zero exponent

Simplify each expression. Assume that all variables are nonzero real numbers.

a) 5^0 **b)** $(3xy)^0$ **c)** $a^0 + b^0$

Solution

a) $5^0 = 1$ **b)** $(3xy)^0 = 1$ **c)** $a^0 + b^0 = 1 + 1 = 2$

Now do Exercises 7–14

With the definition of zero exponent the quotient rule is valid for all positive integers as stated.

EXAMPLE 2

Using the quotient rule in dividing monomials

Find each quotient.

a) $\dfrac{y^9}{y^5}$ **b)** $\dfrac{12b^2}{3b^7}$

c) $-6x^3 \div (2x^9)$ **d)** $\dfrac{x^8y^2}{x^2y^2}$

Solution

a) $\dfrac{y^9}{y^5} = y^{9-5} = y^4$

Use the definition of division to check that $y^4 \cdot y^5 = y^9$.

b) $\dfrac{12b^2}{3b^7} = \dfrac{12}{3} \cdot \dfrac{b^2}{b^7} = 4 \cdot \dfrac{1}{b^{7-2}} = \dfrac{4}{b^5}$

Use the definition of division to check that

$$\frac{4}{b^5} \cdot 3b^7 = \frac{12b^7}{b^5} = 12b^2.$$

c) $-6x^3 \div (2x^9) = \dfrac{-6x^3}{2x^9} = \dfrac{-3}{x^6}$

Use the definition of division to check that

$$\frac{-3}{x^6} \cdot 2x^9 = \frac{-6x^9}{x^6} = -6x^3.$$

d) $\dfrac{x^8y^2}{x^2y^2} = \dfrac{x^8}{x^2} \cdot \dfrac{y^2}{y^2} = x^6 \cdot y^0 = x^6$

Use the definition of division to check that $x^6 \cdot x^2y^2 = x^8y^2$.

Now do Exercises 15–30

Study Tip

As soon as possible after class, find a quiet place and work on your homework. The longer you wait the harder it is to remember what happened in class.

Teaching Tip Remind students that these equations are identities. For which real numbers are they not true?

Note that the parentheses in Example 2(c) are important. According to the order of operations, multiplication and division are performed from left to right in the absence of parentheses. So without parentheses, $-6x^3 \div 2x^9 = \frac{-6x^3}{2} \cdot x^9$.

Teaching Tip Emphasize that both terms in the numerator are divided by the denominator.

Dividing a Polynomial by a Monomial

We divided some simple polynomials by monomials in Chapter 1. For example,

$$\frac{6x + 8}{2} = \frac{1}{2}(6x + 8) = 3x + 4.$$

We use the distributive property to take one-half of $6x$ and one-half of 8 to get $3x + 4$. So both $6x$ and 8 are divided by 2. To divide any polynomial by a monomial, we divide each term of the polynomial by the monomial.

EXAMPLE 3

Dividing a polynomial by a monomial

Find the quotient for $(-8x^6 + 12x^4 - 4x^2) \div (4x^2)$.

Solution

$$\frac{-8x^6 + 12x^4 - 4x^2}{4x^2} = \frac{-8x^6}{4x^2} + \frac{12x^4}{4x^2} - \frac{4x^2}{4x^2}$$
$$= -2x^4 + 3x^2 - 1$$

The quotient is $-2x^4 + 3x^2 - 1$. We can check by multiplying.

$$4x^2(-2x^4 + 3x^2 - 1) = -8x^6 + 12x^4 - 4x^2.$$

Now do Exercises 31–38

Study Tip

Play offensive math, not defensive math. A student who says, "Give me a question and I'll see if I can answer it," is playing defensive math. The student is taking a passive approach to learning. A student who takes an active approach and knows the usual questions and answers for each topic is playing offensive math.

Because division by zero is undefined, we will always assume that the divisor is nonzero in any quotient involving variables. For example, the division in Example 3 is valid only if $4x^2 \neq 0$, or $x \neq 0$.

Dividing a Polynomial by a Binomial

Division of whole numbers is often done with a procedure called **long division.** For example, 253 is divided by 7 as follows:

```
               36   ← Quotient
Divisor →   7)253   ← Dividend
              21
               43
               42
                1   ← Remainder
```

Note that $36 \cdot 7 + 1 = 253$. It is always true that

$$(\text{quotient})(\text{divisor}) + (\text{remainder}) = \text{dividend}.$$

To divide a polynomial by a binomial, we perform the division like long division of whole numbers. For example, to divide $x^2 - 3x - 10$ by $x + 2$, we get the first term of the quotient by dividing the first term of $x + 2$ into the first term of $x^2 - 3x - 10$.

So divide x^2 by x to get x, then multiply and subtract as follows:

1	Divide:	x	$x^2 \div x = x$
2	Multiply:	$x + 2\overline{)x^2 - 3x - 10}$	
		$x^2 + 2x$	$x \cdot (x + 2) = x^2 + 2x$
3	Subtract:	$-5x$	$-3x - 2x = -5x$

Now bring down -10 and continue the process. We get the second term of the quotient (below) by dividing the first term of $x + 2$ into the first term of $-5x - 10$. So divide $-5x$ by x to get -5:

Teaching Tip Students often have trouble with the subtraction part of the division process.

1	Divide:	$x - 5$	$-5x \div x = -5$
2	Multiply:	$x + 2\overline{)x^2 - 3x - 10}$	
		$x^2 + 2x \quad \downarrow$	Bring down -10.
		$-5x - 10$	
		$-5x - 10$	$-5(x + 2) = -5x - 10$
3	Subtract:	0	$-10 - (-10) = 0$

So the quotient is $x - 5$, and the remainder is 0.

In Example 4 there is a term missing in the dividend. To account for the missing term we insert a term with a zero coefficient.

EXAMPLE 4

Dividing a polynomial by a binomial

Determine the quotient and remainder when $x^3 - 5x - 1$ is divided by $x - 4$.

Solution

Because the x^2-term in the dividend $x^3 - 5x - 1$ is missing, we write $0 \cdot x^2$ for it:

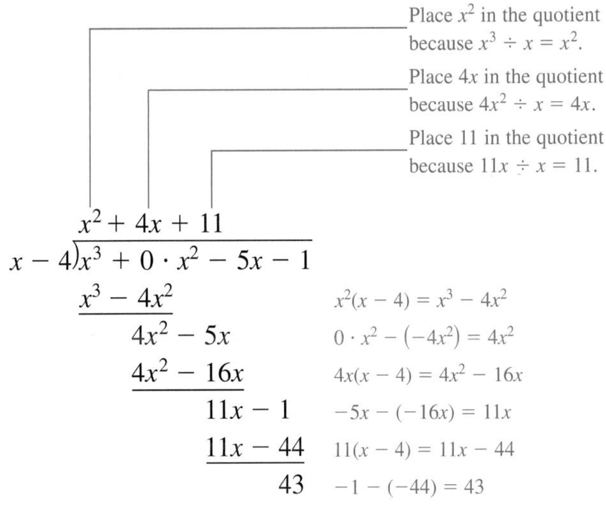

The quotient is $x^2 + 4x + 11$ and the remainder is 43.

Now do Exercises 39–42

In Example 5 the terms of the dividend are not in order of decreasing exponents and there is a missing term.

EXAMPLE 5

Dividing a polynomial by a binomial

Divide $2x^3 - 4 - 7x^2$ by $2x - 3$, and identify the quotient and the remainder.

Helpful Hint

Students usually have the most difficulty with the subtraction part of long division. So pay particular attention to that step and double check your work.

Solution

Rearrange the dividend as $2x^3 - 7x^2 - 4$. Because the x-term in the dividend is missing, we write $0 \cdot x$ for it:

$$\begin{array}{rll}
 & x^2 - 2x - 3 & 2x^3 \div (2x) = x^2 \\
2x - 3 \,\big) & 2x^3 - 7x^2 + 0 \cdot x - 4 & \\
 & \underline{2x^3 - 3x^2} & x^2(2x - 3) = 2x^3 - 3x^2 \\
 & -4x^2 + 0 \cdot x & -7x^2 - (-3x^2) = -4x^2 \\
 & \underline{-4x^2 + 6x} & -2x(2x - 3) = -4x^2 + 6x \\
 & -6x - 4 & 0 \cdot x - 6x = -6x \\
 & \underline{-6x + 9} & -3(2x - 3) = -6x + 9 \\
 & -13 & -4 - (9) = -13
\end{array}$$

The quotient is $x^2 - 2x - 3$, and the remainder is -13. Note that the degree of the remainder is 0 and the degree of the divisor is 1. To check, we must verify that

$$(2x - 3)(x^2 - 2x - 3) - 13 = 2x^3 - 7x^2 - 4.$$

Now do Exercises 43–56

CAUTION To avoid errors, always write the terms of the divisor and the dividend in descending order of the exponents and insert a zero for any term that is missing.

If we divide both sides of the equation

$$\text{dividend} = (\text{quotient})(\text{divisor}) + (\text{remainder})$$

by the divisor, we get the equation

$$\frac{\text{dividend}}{\text{divisor}} = \text{quotient} + \frac{\text{remainder}}{\text{divisor}}.$$

This fact is used in expressing improper fractions as mixed numbers. For example, if 19 is divided by 5, the quotient is 3 and the remainder is 4. So

$$\frac{19}{5} = 3 + \frac{4}{5} = 3\frac{4}{5}.$$

We can also use this form to rewrite algebraic fractions.

EXAMPLE 6

Rewriting algebraic fractions

Express $\frac{-3x}{x-2}$ in the form

$$\text{quotient} + \frac{\text{remainder}}{\text{divisor}}.$$

Teaching Tip Note that the form of the result is specified here so that students don't simply list the quotient and remainder.

Solution

Use long division to get the quotient and remainder:

$$\begin{array}{r} -3 \\ x-2\overline{)-3x+0} \\ \underline{-3x+6} \\ -6 \end{array}$$

Because the quotient is -3 and the remainder is -6, we can write

$$\frac{-3x}{x-2} = -3 + \frac{-6}{x-2}.$$

To check, we must verify that $-3(x-2) - 6 = -3x$.

Now do Exercises 57–72

CAUTION When dividing polynomials by long division, we do not stop until the remainder is 0 or the degree of the remainder is smaller than the degree of the divisor. For example, we stop dividing in Example 6 because the degree of the remainder -6 is 0 and the degree of the divisor $x - 2$ is 1.

Warm-Ups

True or false? Explain your answer.

1. $y^{10} \div y^2 = y^5$ for any nonzero value of y. False
2. $\frac{7x+2}{7} = x + 2$ for any value of x. False
3. $\frac{7x^2}{7} = x^2$ for any value of x. True
4. If $3x^2 + 6$ is divided by 3, the quotient is $x^2 + 6$. False
5. If $4y^2 - 6y$ is divided by $2y$, the quotient is $2y - 3$. True
6. The quotient times the remainder plus the dividend equals the divisor. False
7. $(x + 2)(x + 1) + 3 = x^2 + 3x + 5$ for any value of x. True
8. If $x^2 + 3x + 5$ is divided by $x + 2$, then the quotient is $x + 1$. True
9. If $x^2 + 3x + 5$ is divided by $x + 2$, the remainder is 3. True
10. If the remainder is zero, then (divisor)(quotient) = dividend. True

4.5 Exercises

Boost your GRADE at mathzone.com!

MathZone

- Practice Problems
- Self-Tests
- Videos
- Net Tutor
- e-Professors

Reading and Writing *After reading this section, write out the answers to these questions. Use complete sentences.*

1. What rule is important for dividing monomials?
The quotient rule is used for dividing monomials.
2. What is the meaning of a zero exponent?
The zero power of a nonzero real number is 1.
3. How many terms should you get when dividing a polynomial by a monomial?
When dividing a polynomial by a monomial the quotient should have the same number of terms as the polynomial.
4. How should the terms of the polynomials be written when dividing with long division?
The terms of a polynomial should be written in descending order of the exponents.
5. How do you know when to stop the process in long division of polynomials?
The long division process stops when the degree of the remainder is less than the degree of the divisor.
6. How do you handle missing terms in the dividend polynomial when doing long division?
Insert a term with zero coefficient for each missing term when doing long division.

Simplify each expression. See Example 1.

7. 9^0 1 **8.** m^0 1 **9.** $(-2x^3)^0$ 1

10. $(5a^3b)^0$ 1 **11.** $2 \cdot 5^0 - 3^0$ 1 **12.** $-4^0 - 8^0$ -2

13. $(2x - y)^0$ 1 **14.** $(a^2 + b^2)^0$ 1

Find each quotient. Try to write only the answer. See Example 2.

15. $\dfrac{x^8}{x^2}$ x^6 **16.** $\dfrac{y^9}{y^3}$ y^6

17. $\dfrac{a^5}{a^{14}}$ $\dfrac{1}{a^9}$ **18.** $\dfrac{b^{12}}{b^{19}}$ $\dfrac{1}{b^7}$

19. $\dfrac{6a^7}{2a^{12}}$ $\dfrac{3}{a^5}$ **20.** $\dfrac{30b^2}{3b^6}$ $\dfrac{10}{b^4}$

21. $a^9 \div a^3$ a^6 **22.** $b^{12} \div b^4$ b^8

23. $-12x^5 \div (3x^9)$ $\dfrac{-4}{x^4}$ **24.** $-6y^5 \div (-3y^{10})$ $\dfrac{2}{y^5}$

25. $-6y^2 \div (6y)$ $-y$ **26.** $-3a^2b \div (3ab)$ $-a$

27. $\dfrac{-6x^3y^2}{2x^2y^2}$ $-3x$ **28.** $\dfrac{-4h^2k^4}{-2hk^3}$ $2hk$

29. $\dfrac{-9x^2y^2}{3x^5y^2}$ $\dfrac{-3}{x^3}$ **30.** $\dfrac{-12z^4y^2}{-2z^{10}y^2}$ $\dfrac{6}{z^6}$

Find the quotients. See Example 3.

31. $\dfrac{3x - 6}{3}$ $x - 2$

32. $\dfrac{5y - 10}{-5}$ $-y + 2$

33. $\dfrac{x^5 + 3x^4 - x^3}{x^2}$ $x^3 + 3x^2 - x$

34. $\dfrac{6y^6 - 9y^4 + 12y^2}{3y^2}$ $2y^4 - 3y^2 + 4$

35. $\dfrac{-8x^2y^2 + 4x^2y - 2xy^2}{-2xy}$ $4xy - 2x + y$

36. $\dfrac{-9ab^2 - 6a^3b^3}{-3ab^2}$ $3 + 2a^2b$

37. $(x^2y^3 - 3x^3y^2) \div (x^2y)$ $y^2 - 3xy$

38. $(4h^5k - 6h^2k^2) \div (-2h^2k)$ $-2h^3 + 3k$

Complete each division and identify the quotient and remainder. See Example 4.

39. $x - 1\overline{)2x - 3}$ with quotient 2; $\underline{2x - 2}$
2, -1

40. $x + 2\overline{)-3x + 4}$ with quotient -3; $\underline{-3x - 6}$
-3, 10

41. $x - 3\overline{)x^2 + 2x + 1}$ with quotient x; $\underline{x^2 - 3x}$
$x + 5$, 16

42. $x + 4\overline{)x^2 - 3x + 2}$ with quotient x; $\underline{x^2 + 4x}$
$x - 7$, 30

Find the quotient and remainder for each division. Check by using the fact that dividend = (divisor)(quotient) + remainder. See Example 5.

43. $(x^2 + 5x + 13) \div (x + 3)$ $x + 2, 7$
44. $(x^2 + 3x + 6) \div (x + 3)$ $x, 6$
45. $(2x) \div (x + 5)$ $2, -10$
46. $(5x) \div (x - 1)$ $5, 5$
47. $(a^3 + 4a - 3) \div (a - 2)$ $a^2 + 2a + 8, 13$
48. $(w^3 + 2w^2 - 3) \div (w - 2)$ $w^2 + 4w + 8, 13$
49. $(x^2 - 3x) \div (x + 1)$ $x - 4, 4$
50. $(3x^2) \div (x + 1)$ $3x - 3, 3$
51. $(h^3 - 27) \div (h - 3)$ $h^2 + 3h + 9, 0$
52. $(w^3 + 1) \div (w + 1)$ $w^2 - w + 1, 0$
53. $(6x^2 - 13x + 7) \div (3x - 2)$ $2x - 3, 1$
54. $(4b^2 + 25b - 3) \div (4b + 1)$ $b + 6, -9$

55. $(x^3 - x^2 + x - 2) \div (x - 1)$ $x^2 + 1, -1$

56. $(a^3 - 3a^2 + 4a - 4) \div (a - 2)$ $a^2 - a + 2, 0$

Write each expression in the form

$$quotient + \frac{remainder}{divisor}.$$

See Example 6.

57. $\frac{3x}{x-5}$ $3 + \frac{15}{x-5}$

58. $\frac{2x}{x-1}$ $2 + \frac{2}{x-1}$

59. $\frac{-x}{x+3}$ $-1 + \frac{3}{x+3}$

60. $\frac{-3x}{x+1}$ $-3 + \frac{3}{x+1}$

61. $\frac{x-1}{x}$ $1 - \frac{1}{x}$

62. $\frac{a-5}{a}$ $1 - \frac{5}{a}$

63. $\frac{3x+1}{x}$ $3 + \frac{1}{x}$

64. $\frac{2y+1}{y}$ $2 + \frac{1}{y}$

65. $\frac{x^2}{x+1}$ $x - 1 + \frac{1}{x+1}$

66. $\frac{x^2}{x-1}$ $x + 1 + \frac{1}{x-1}$

67. $\frac{x^2+4}{x+2}$ $x - 2 + \frac{8}{x+2}$

68. $\frac{x^2+1}{x-1}$ $x + 1 + \frac{2}{x-1}$

69. $\frac{x^3}{x-2}$ $x^2 + 2x + 4 + \frac{8}{x-2}$

70. $\frac{x^3-1}{x+1}$ $x^2 - x + 1 + \frac{-2}{x+1}$

71. $\frac{x^3+3}{x}$ $x^2 + \frac{3}{x}$

72. $\frac{2x^2+4}{2x}$ $x + \frac{2}{x}$

Find each quotient.

73. $-6a^3b \div (2a^2b)$ $-3a$

74. $-14x^7 \div (-7x^2)$ $2x^5$

75. $-8w^4t^7 \div (-2w^9t^3)$ $\frac{4t^4}{w^5}$

76. $-9y^7z^4 \div (3y^3z^{11})$ $\frac{-3y^4}{z^7}$

77. $(3a - 12) \div (-3)$ $-a + 4$

78. $(-6z + 3z^2) \div (-3z)$ $2 - z$

79. $(3x^2 - 9x) \div (3x)$ $x - 3$

80. $(5x^3 + 15x^2 - 25x) \div (5x)$ $x^2 + 3x - 5$

81. $(12x^4 - 4x^3 + 6x^2) \div (-2x^2)$ $-6x^2 + 2x - 3$

82. $(-9x^3 + 3x^2 - 15x) \div (-3x)$ $3x^2 - x + 5$

83. $(t^2 - 5t - 36) \div (t - 9)$ $t + 4$

84. $(b^2 + 2b - 35) \div (b - 5)$ $b + 7$

85. $(6w^2 - 7w - 5) \div (3w - 5)$ $2w + 1$

86. $(4z^2 + 23z - 6) \div (4z - 1)$ $z + 6$

87. $(8x^3 + 27) \div (2x + 3)$ $4x^2 - 6x + 9$

88. $(8y^3 - 1) \div (2y - 1)$ $4y^2 + 2y + 1$

89. $(t^3 - 3t^2 + 5t - 6) \div (t - 2)$ $t^2 - t + 3$

90. $(2u^3 - 13u^2 - 8u + 7) \div (u - 7)$ $2u^2 + u - 1$

91. $(-6v^2 - 4 + 9v + v^3) \div (v - 4)$ $v^2 - 2v + 1$

92. $(14y + 8y^2 + y^3 + 12) \div (6 + y)$ $y^2 + 2y + 2$

Solve each problem.

93. ***Area of a rectangle.*** The area of a rectangular billboard is $x^2 + x - 30$ square meters. If the length is $x + 6$ meters, find a binomial that represents the width. $x - 5$ meters

Figure for Exercise 93

94. ***Perimeter of a rectangle.*** The perimeter of a rectangular backyard is $6x + 6$ yards. If the width is x yards, find a binomial that represents the length. $2x + 3$ yards

Figure for Exercise 94

Getting More Involved

95. ***Exploration***

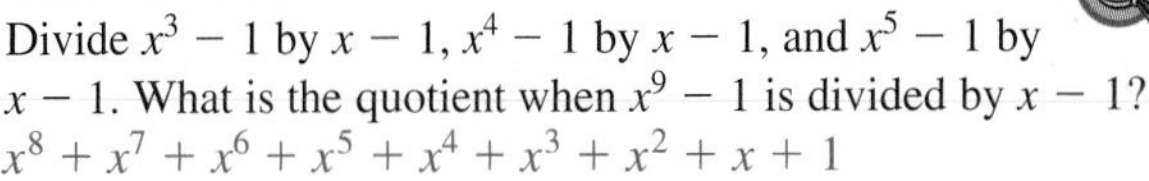

Divide $x^3 - 1$ by $x - 1$, $x^4 - 1$ by $x - 1$, and $x^5 - 1$ by $x - 1$. What is the quotient when $x^9 - 1$ is divided by $x - 1$? $x^8 + x^7 + x^6 + x^5 + x^4 + x^3 + x^2 + x + 1$

96. ***Exploration***

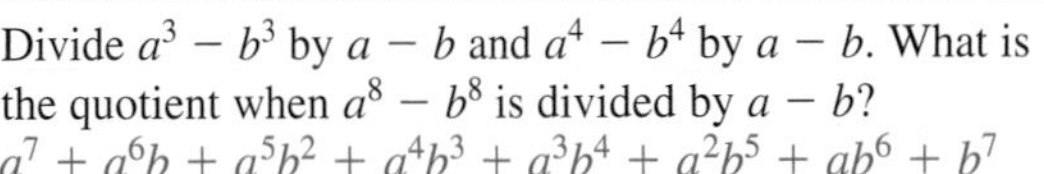

Divide $a^3 - b^3$ by $a - b$ and $a^4 - b^4$ by $a - b$. What is the quotient when $a^8 - b^8$ is divided by $a - b$? $a^7 + a^6b + a^5b^2 + a^4b^3 + a^3b^4 + a^2b^5 + ab^6 + b^7$

97. ***Discussion***

Are the expressions $\frac{10x}{5x}$, $10x \div 5x$, and $(10x) \div (5x)$ equivalent? Before you answer, review the order of operations in Section 1.5 and evaluate each expression for $x = 3$. $10x \div 5x$ is not equivalent to the other two.

4.6 Nonnegative Integral Exponents

In this Section

- The Product and Quotient Rules
- Raising an Exponential Expression to a Power
- Power of a Product
- Power of a Quotient
- Summary of Rules

The product rule for positive integral exponents was presented in Section 4.2, and the quotient rule was presented in Section 4.5. In this section we review those rules and then further investigate the properties of exponents.

The Product and Quotient Rules

The rules that we have already discussed are summarized below.

The following rules hold for nonnegative integers m and n and $a \neq 0$.

$$a^m \cdot a^n = a^{m+n} \quad \text{Product rule}$$

$$\frac{a^m}{a^n} = a^{m-n} \quad \text{if } m \geq n \quad \text{Quotient rule}$$

$$\frac{a^m}{a^n} = \frac{1}{a^{n-m}} \quad \text{if } n > m$$

$$a^0 = 1 \quad \text{Zero exponent}$$

CAUTION The product and quotient rules apply only if the bases of the expressions are identical. For example, $3^2 \cdot 3^4 = 3^6$, but the product rule cannot be applied to $5^2 \cdot 3^4$. Note also that the bases are not multiplied: $3^2 \cdot 3^4 \neq 9^6$.

Note that in the quotient rule the exponents are always subtracted, as in

$$\frac{x^7}{x^3} = x^4 \quad \text{and} \quad \frac{y^5}{y^8} = \frac{1}{y^3}.$$

If the larger exponent is in the denominator, then the result is placed in the denominator.

EXAMPLE 1

Using the product and quotient rules

Use the rules of exponents to simplify each expression. Assume that all variables represent nonzero real numbers.

a) $2^3 \cdot 2^2$ **b)** $(3x)^0(5x^2)(4x)$ **c)** $\dfrac{8x^2}{-2x^5}$ **d)** $\dfrac{(3a^2b)b^9}{(6a^5)a^3b^2}$

Solution

a) Because the bases are both 2, we can use the product rule:

$$\begin{aligned} 2^3 \cdot 2^2 &= 2^5 && \text{Product rule} \\ &= 32 && \text{Simplify.} \end{aligned}$$

b)

$$\begin{aligned} (3x)^0(5x^2)(4x) &= 1 \cdot 5x^2 \cdot 4x && \text{Definition of zero exponent} \\ &= 20x^3 && \text{Product rule} \end{aligned}$$

Study Tip

Keep track of your time for one entire week. Account for how you spend every half hour. Add up your totals for sleep, study, work, and recreation. You should be sleeping 50–60 hours per week and studying 1–2 hours for every hour you spend in the classroom.

c) $\dfrac{8x^2}{-2x^5} = -\dfrac{4}{x^3}$ Quotient rule

d) First use the product rule to simplify the numerator and denominator:

$$\frac{(3a^2b)b^9}{(6a^5)a^3b^2} = \frac{3a^2b^{10}}{6a^8b^2} \quad \text{Product rule}$$

$$= \frac{b^8}{2a^6} \quad \text{Quotient rule}$$

Now do Exercises 7–18

Raising an Exponential Expression to a Power

When we raise an exponential expression to a power, we can use the product rule to find the result, as shown in the following example:

$$(w^4)^3 = w^4 \cdot w^4 \cdot w^4 \quad \text{Three factors of } w^4 \text{ because of the exponent 3}$$

$$= w^{12} \quad \text{Product rule}$$

By the product rule we add the three 4's to get 12, but 12 is also the product of 4 and 3. This example illustrates the **power rule** for exponents.

Power Rule

If m and n are nonnegative integers and $a \neq 0$, then

$$(a^m)^n = a^{mn}.$$

In Example 2 we use the new rule along with the other rules.

EXAMPLE 2

Using the power rule

Use the rules of exponents to simplify each expression. Assume that all variables represent nonzero real numbers.

a) $3x^2(x^3)^5$ **b)** $\dfrac{(2^3)^4 \cdot 2^7}{2^5 \cdot 2^9}$ **c)** $\dfrac{3(x^5)^4}{15x^{22}}$

Teaching Tip Remind students that the rules of exponents work so nicely here because these expressions do not involve addition or subtraction.

Solution

a) $3x^2(x^3)^5 = 3x^2x^{15}$ Power rule

$= 3x^{17}$ Product rule

b) $\dfrac{(2^3)^4 \cdot 2^7}{2^5 \cdot 2^9} = \dfrac{2^{12} \cdot 2^7}{2^{14}}$ Power rule and product rule

$= \dfrac{2^{19}}{2^{14}}$ Product rule

$= 2^5$ Quotient rule

$= 32$ Evaluate 2^5.

c) $\dfrac{3(x^5)^4}{15x^{22}} = \dfrac{3x^{20}}{15x^{22}} = \dfrac{1}{5x^2}$

Now do Exercises 19–26

Teaching Tip This is a good place to remind students that a power of a sum or difference is not as simple as a power of a product:

$$(a + b)^2 = a^2 + 2ab + b^2$$

Power of a Product

Consider an example of raising a monomial to a power. We will use known rules to rewrite the expression.

$$\begin{aligned}(2x)^3 &= 2x \cdot 2x \cdot 2x && \text{Definition of exponent 3}\\ &= 2 \cdot 2 \cdot 2 \cdot x \cdot x \cdot x && \text{Commutative and associative properties}\\ &= 2^3x^3 && \text{Definition of exponents}\end{aligned}$$

Note that the power 3 is applied to each factor of the product. This example illustrates the **power of a product rule.**

Power of a Product Rule

If a and b are real numbers and n is a positive integer, then

$$(ab)^n = a^nb^n.$$

EXAMPLE 3

Using the power of a product rule

Simplify. Assume that the variables are nonzero.

a) $(xy^3)^5$ **b)** $(-3m)^3$ **c)** $(2x^3y^2z^7)^3$

Solution

a) $$\begin{aligned}(xy^3)^5 &= x^5(y^3)^5 && \text{Power of a product rule}\\ &= x^5y^{15} && \text{Power rule}\end{aligned}$$

b) $$\begin{aligned}(-3m)^3 &= (-3)^3m^3 && \text{Power of a product rule}\\ &= -27m^3 && (-3)(-3)(-3) = -27\end{aligned}$$

c) $(2x^3y^2z^7)^3 = 2^3(x^3)^3(y^2)^3(z^7)^3 = 8x^9y^6z^{21}$

Now do Exercises 27–34

Helpful Hint

Note that these rules of exponents are not absolutely necessary. We could simplify every expression here by using only the definition of exponent. However, these rules make it a lot simpler.

Power of a Quotient

Raising a quotient to a power is similar to raising a product to a power:

$$\begin{aligned}\left(\frac{x}{5}\right)^3 &= \frac{x}{5} \cdot \frac{x}{5} \cdot \frac{x}{5} && \text{Definition of exponent 3}\\ &= \frac{x \cdot x \cdot x}{5 \cdot 5 \cdot 5} && \text{Definition of multiplication of fractions}\\ &= \frac{x^3}{5^3} && \text{Definition of exponents}\end{aligned}$$

The power is applied to both the numerator and denominator. This example illustrates the **power of a quotient rule.**

Power of a Quotient Rule

If a and b are real numbers, $b \neq 0$, and n is a positive integer, then

$$\left(\frac{a}{b}\right)^n = \frac{a^n}{b^n}.$$

EXAMPLE 4

Using the power of a quotient rule

Simplify. Assume that the variables are nonzero.

a) $\left(\frac{2}{5x^3}\right)^2$ **b)** $\left(\frac{3x^4}{2y^3}\right)^3$ **c)** $\left(\frac{-12a^5b}{4a^2b^7}\right)^3$

Solution

a) $\left(\frac{2}{5x^3}\right)^2 = \frac{2^2}{(5x^3)^2}$ Power of a quotient rule

$= \frac{4}{25x^6}$ $(5x^3)^2 = 5^2(x^3)^2 = 25x^6$

b) $\left(\frac{3x^4}{2y^3}\right)^3 = \frac{3^3x^{12}}{2^3y^9}$ Power of a quotient and power of a product rules

$= \frac{27x^{12}}{8y^9}$ Simplify.

c) Use the quotient rule to simplify the expression inside the parentheses before using the power of a quotient rule.

$\left(\frac{-12a^5b}{4a^2b^7}\right)^3 = \left(\frac{-3a^3}{b^6}\right)^3$ Use the quotient rule first.

$= \frac{-27a^9}{b^{18}}$ Power of a quotient rule

Now do Exercises 35–42

Teaching Tip Emphasize the importance of doing one step at a time, having a reason for each step, and writing neatly.

Summary of Rules

The rules for exponents are summarized in the following box.

Helpful Hint

Note that the rules of exponents show how exponents behave with respect to multiplication and division only. We studied the more complicated problem of using exponents with addition and subtraction in Section 4.4 when we learned rules for $(a + b)^2$ and $(a - b)^2$.

Rules for Nonnegative Integral Exponents

The following rules hold for nonzero real numbers a and b and nonnegative integers m and n.

1. $a^0 = 1$ Definition of zero exponent
2. $a^m \cdot a^n = a^{m+n}$ Product rule
3. $\frac{a^m}{a^n} = a^{m-n}$ for $m \geq n$,

   $\frac{a^m}{a^n} = \frac{1}{a^{n-m}}$ for $n > m$ Quotient rule
4. $(a^m)^n = a^{mn}$ Power rule
5. $(ab)^n = a^n \cdot b^n$ Power of a product rule
6. $\left(\frac{a}{b}\right)^n = \frac{a^n}{b^n}$ Power of a quotient rule

Warm-Ups 

True or false? Explain your answer.

1. $-3^0 = 1$ False
2. $2^5 \cdot 2^8 = 4^{13}$ False
3. $2^3 \cdot 3^2 = 6^5$ False
4. $(2x)^4 = 2x^4$ False
5. $(q^3)^5 = q^8$ False
6. $(-3x^2)^3 = 27x^6$ False
7. $(ab^3)^4 = a^4b^{12}$ True
8. $\frac{a^{12}}{a^4} = a^3$ False
9. $\frac{6w^4}{3w^9} = 2w^5$ False
10. $\left(\frac{2y^3}{9}\right)^2 = \frac{4y^6}{81}$ True

4.6 Exercises

Boost your GRADE at mathzone.com!

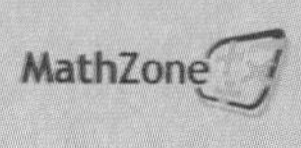

- Practice Problems
- Self-Tests
- Videos
- Net Tutor
- e-Professors

Reading and Writing *After reading this section, write out the answers to these questions. Use complete sentences.*

1. What is the product rule for exponents?
   The product rule says that $a^m a^n = a^{m+n}$.
2. What is the quotient rule for exponents?
   The quotient rule says that $a^m/a^n = a^{m-n}$ if $m \ge n$ and $a^m/a^n = 1/a^{n-m}$ if $n > m$.
3. Why must the bases be the same in these rules?
   These rules do not make sense without identical bases.
4. What is the power rule for exponents?
   The power rule for exponents says that $(a^m)^n = a^{mn}$.
5. What is the power of a product rule?
   The power of a product rule says that $(ab)^n = a^n b^n$.
6. What is the power of a quotient rule?
   The power of a quotient rule says that $\left(\frac{a}{b}\right)^n = \frac{a^n}{b^n}$.

For all exercises in this section, assume that the variables represent nonzero real numbers.

Simplify the exponential expressions. See Example 1.

7. $2^2 \cdot 2^5$ 128
8. $x^6 \cdot x^7$ x^{13}
9. $(-3u^8)(-2u^2)$ $6u^{10}$
10. $(3r^4)(-6r^2)$ $-18r^6$
11. $a^3b^4 \cdot ab^6(ab)^0$ a^4b^{10}
12. $x^2y \cdot x^3y^6(x + y)^0$ x^5y^7
13. $\frac{-2a^3}{4a^7}$ $\frac{-1}{2a^4}$
14. $\frac{-3t^9}{6t^{18}}$ $\frac{-1}{2t^9}$
15. $\frac{2a^5b \cdot 3a^7b^3}{15a^6b^8}$ $\frac{2a^6}{5b^4}$
16. $\frac{3xy^8 \cdot 5xy^9}{20x^3y^{14}}$ $\frac{3y^3}{4x}$
17. $2^3 \cdot 5^2$ 200
18. $2^2 \cdot 10^3$ 4000

Simplify. See Example 2.

19. $(x^2)^3$ x^6
20. $(y^2)^4$ y^8
21. $2x^2 \cdot (x^2)^5$ $2x^{12}$
22. $(y^2)^6 \cdot 3y^5$ $3y^{17}$
23. $\frac{(t^2)^5}{(t^3)^4}$ $\frac{1}{t^2}$
24. $\frac{(r^4)^2}{(r^5)^3}$ $\frac{1}{r^7}$
25. $\frac{3x(x^5)^2}{6x^3(x^2)^4}$ $\frac{1}{2}$
26. $\frac{5y^3(y^5)^2}{10y^5(y^2)^6}$ $\frac{1}{2y^4}$

Simplify. See Example 3.

27. $(xy^2)^3$ x^3y^6
28. $(wy^2)^6$ w^6y^{12}
29. $(-2t^5)^3$ $-8t^{15}$
30. $(-3r^3)^3$ $-27r^9$
31. $(-2x^2y^5)^3$ $-8x^6y^{15}$
32. $(-3y^2z^3)^3$ $-27y^6z^9$
33. $\frac{(a^4b^2c^5)^3}{a^3b^4c}$ $a^9b^2c^{14}$
34. $\frac{(2ab^2c^3)^5}{(2a^3bc)^4}$ $\frac{2b^6c^{11}}{a^7}$

Simplify. See Example 4.

35. $\left(\frac{x^4}{4}\right)^3$ $\frac{x^{12}}{64}$
36. $\left(\frac{y^2}{2}\right)^3$ $\frac{y^6}{8}$
37. $\left(\frac{-2a^2}{b^3}\right)^4$ $\frac{16a^8}{b^{12}}$
38. $\left(\frac{-9r^3}{t^5}\right)^2$ $\frac{81r^6}{t^{10}}$
39. $\left(\frac{2x^2y}{-4y^2}\right)^3$ $-\frac{x^6}{8y^3}$
40. $\left(\frac{3y^8}{2zy^2}\right)^4$ $\frac{81y^{24}}{16z^4}$
41. $\left(\frac{-6x^2y^4z^9}{3x^6y^4z^3}\right)^2$ $\frac{4z^{12}}{x^8}$
42. $\left(\frac{-10rs^9t^4}{2rs^2t^7}\right)^3$ $\frac{-125s^{21}}{t^9}$

Simplify each expression. Your answer should be an integer or a fraction. Do not use a calculator.

43. $3^2 + 6^2$ 45

44. $(5 - 3)^2$ 4

45. $(3 + 6)^2$ 81

46. $5^2 - 3^2$ 16

47. $2^3 - 3^3$ -19

48. $3^3 + 4^3$ 91

49. $(2 - 3)^3$ -1

50. $(3 + 4)^3$ 343

51. $\left(\frac{2}{5}\right)^3$ $\frac{8}{125}$

52. $\left(\frac{3}{4}\right)^3$ $\frac{27}{64}$

53. $5^2 \cdot 2^3$ 200

54. $10^3 \cdot 3^3$ 27,000

55. $2^3 \cdot 2^4$ 128

56. $10^2 \cdot 10^4$ 1,000,000

57. $\left(\frac{2^3}{2^5}\right)^2$ $\frac{1}{16}$

58. $\left(\frac{3}{3^3}\right)^2$ $\frac{1}{81}$

Simplify each expression.

59. $x^4 \cdot x^3$ x^7

60. $x^5 \cdot x^8$ x^{13}

61. $(a^8)^4$ a^{32}

62. $(b^5)^8$ b^{40}

63. $(a^4b^2)^3$ $a^{12}b^6$

64. $(x^2t^4)^6$ $x^{12}t^{24}$

65. $\frac{x^4}{x^7}$ $\frac{1}{x^3}$

66. $\frac{m^8}{m^{10}}$ $\frac{1}{m^2}$

67. $\frac{a^{13}}{a^9}$ a^4

68. $\frac{t^9}{t^6}$ t^3

69. $\left(\frac{a^3}{b^4}\right)^3$ $\frac{a^9}{b^{12}}$

70. $\left(\frac{t}{m^2}\right)^4$ $\frac{t^4}{m^8}$

71. $\left(\frac{x^3}{x^4}\right)^5$ $\frac{1}{x^5}$

72. $\left(\frac{w^5}{w^2}\right)^8$ w^{24}

73. $3x^4 \cdot 5x^7$ $15x^{11}$

74. $-2y^3(3y)$ $-6y^4$

75. $(-5x^4)^3$ $-125x^{12}$

76. $(4z^3)^3$ $64z^9$

77. $-3y^5z^{12} \cdot 9yz^7$ $-27y^6z^{19}$

78. $2a^4b^5 \cdot 2a^9b^2$ $4a^{13}b^7$

79. $\frac{-9u^4v^9}{-3u^5v^8}$ $\frac{3v}{u}$

80. $\frac{-20a^5b^{13}}{5a^4b^{13}}$ $-4a$

81. $(-xt^2)(-2x^2t)^4$ $-16x^9t^6$

82. $(-ab)^3(-3ba^2)^4$ $-81a^{11}b^7$

83. $\left(\frac{2x^2}{x^4}\right)^3$ $\frac{8}{x^6}$

84. $\left(\frac{3y^8}{y^5}\right)^2$ $9y^6$

85. $\left(\frac{-8a^3b^4}{4c^5}\right)^5$ $\frac{-32a^{15}b^{20}}{c^{25}}$

86. $\left(\frac{-10a^5c}{5a^5b^4}\right)^5$ $\frac{-32c^5}{b^{20}}$

87. $\left(\frac{-8x^4y^7}{-16x^5y^6}\right)^5$ $\frac{y^5}{32x^5}$

88. $\left(\frac{-5x^2yz^3}{-5x^2yz}\right)^5$ z^{10}

Solve each problem.

89. ***Long-term investing.*** Sheila invested P dollars at annual rate r for 10 years. At the end of 10 years her investment was worth $P(1 + r)^{10}$ dollars. She then reinvested this money for another 5 years at annual rate r. At the end of the second time period her investment was worth $P(1 + r)^{10}(1 + r)^5$ dollars. Which law of exponents can be used to simplify the last expression? Simplify it. Product rule, $P(1 + r)^{15}$

90. ***CD rollover.*** Ronnie invested P dollars in a 2-year CD with an annual rate of return of r. After the CD rolled over three times, its value was $P((1 + r)^2)^3$. Which law of exponents can be used to simplify the expression? Simplify it. Power rule, $P(1 + r)^6$

Getting More Involved

91. ***Writing*** 

When we square a product, we square each factor in the product. For example, $(3b)^2 = 9b^2$. Explain why we cannot square a sum by simply squaring each term of the sum.

92. ***Writing***

Explain why we define 2^0 to be 1. Explain why $-2^0 \neq 1$.

4.7 Negative Exponents and Scientific Notation

In this Section

- Negative Integral Exponents
- Rules for Integral Exponents
- Converting from Scientific Notation
- Converting to Scientific Notation
- Computations with Scientific Notation

We defined exponential expressions with positive integral exponents in Chapter 1 and learned the rules for positive integral exponents in Section 4.6. In this section you will first study negative exponents and then see how positive and negative integral exponents are used in scientific notation.

Negative Integral Exponents

If x is nonzero, the reciprocal of x is written as $\frac{1}{x}$. For example, the reciprocal of 2^3 is written as $\frac{1}{2^3}$. To write the reciprocal of an exponential expression in a simpler way, we use a negative exponent. So $2^{-3} = \frac{1}{2^3}$. In general we have the following definition.

Negative Integral Exponents

If a is a nonzero real number and n is a positive integer, then

$$a^{-n} = \frac{1}{a^n}. \quad \text{(If } n \text{ is positive, } -n \text{ is negative.)}$$

EXAMPLE 1

Simplifying expressions with negative exponents

Simplify.

a) 2^{-5} **b)** $(-2)^{-5}$ **c)** $\frac{2^{-3}}{3^{-2}}$

Solution

a) $2^{-5} = \frac{1}{2^5} = \frac{1}{32}$

b) $(-2)^{-5} = \frac{1}{(-2)^5}$ Definition of negative exponent

$= \frac{1}{-32} = -\frac{1}{32}$

c) $\frac{2^{-3}}{3^{-2}} = 2^{-3} \div 3^{-2}$

$= \frac{1}{2^3} \div \frac{1}{3^2}$

$= \frac{1}{8} \div \frac{1}{9} = \frac{1}{8} \cdot \frac{9}{1} = \frac{9}{8}$

Now do Exercises 7–14

Calculator Close-Up

You can evaluate expressions with negative exponents on a calculator as shown here.

```
2^-5▸Frac
                1/32
(-2)^-5▸Frac
               -1/32
2^-3/3^-2▸Frac
                 9/8
```

CAUTION In simplifying -5^{-2}, the negative sign preceding the 5 is used after 5 is squared and the reciprocal is found. So $-5^{-2} = -(5^{-2}) = -\frac{1}{25}$.

To evaluate a^{-n}, you can first find the nth power of a and then find the reciprocal. However, the result is the same if you first find the reciprocal of a and then find the nth power of the reciprocal. For example,

$$3^{-2} = \frac{1}{3^2} = \frac{1}{9} \quad \text{or} \quad 3^{-2} = \left(\frac{1}{3}\right)^2 = \frac{1}{3} \cdot \frac{1}{3} = \frac{1}{9}.$$

So the power and the reciprocal can be found in either order. If the exponent is -1, we simply find the reciprocal. For example,

$$5^{-1} = \frac{1}{5}, \quad \left(\frac{1}{4}\right)^{-1} = 4, \quad \text{and} \quad \left(-\frac{3}{5}\right)^{-1} = -\frac{5}{3}.$$

Because $3^{-2} \cdot 3^2 = 1$, the reciprocal of 3^{-2} is 3^2, and we have

$$\frac{1}{3^{-2}} = 3^2.$$

These examples illustrate the following rules.

Helpful Hint

Just because the exponent is negative, it doesn't mean the expression is negative. Note that $(-2)^{-3} = -\frac{1}{8}$ while $(-2)^{-4} = \frac{1}{16}$.

Teaching Tip Ask students why we specify that $a \neq 0$. Why do we specify that n is a positive integer? What are the positive integers?

Rules for Negative Exponents

If a is a nonzero real number and n is a positive integer, then

$$a^{-n} = \left(\frac{1}{a}\right)^n, \quad a^{-1} = \frac{1}{a}, \quad \frac{1}{a^{-n}} = a^n, \quad \text{and} \quad \left(\frac{a}{b}\right)^{-n} = \left(\frac{b}{a}\right)^n.$$

EXAMPLE 2

Using the rules for negative exponents

Simplify

a) $\left(\frac{3}{4}\right)^{-3}$ **b)** $10^{-1} + 10^{-1}$ **c)** $\frac{2}{10^{-3}}$

Solution

a) We can find the third power and the reciprocal in either order:

$$\left(\frac{3}{4}\right)^{-3} = \left(\frac{4}{3}\right)^{3} = \frac{64}{27} \qquad \left(\frac{3}{4}\right)^{-3} = \left(\frac{27}{64}\right)^{-1} = \frac{64}{27}$$

b) $10^{-1} + 10^{-1} = \frac{1}{10} + \frac{1}{10} = \frac{2}{10} = \frac{1}{5}$

c) $\frac{2}{10^{-3}} = 2 \cdot \frac{1}{10^{-3}} = 2 \cdot 10^3 = 2 \cdot 1000 = 2000$

Now do Exercises 15–22

Calculator Close-Up

You can use a calculator to demonstrate that the product rule for exponents holds when the exponents are negative numbers.

```
2^-3*2^-5
          .00390625
2^(-3+-5)
          .00390625
```

Rules for Integral Exponents

Negative exponents are used to make expressions involving reciprocals simpler looking and easier to write. Negative exponents have the added benefit of working in conjunction with all of the rules of exponents that you learned in Section 4.6. For example, we can use the product rule to get

$$x^{-2} \cdot x^{-3} = x^{-2+(-3)} = x^{-5}$$

and the quotient rule to get

$$\frac{y^3}{y^5} = y^{3-5} = y^{-2}.$$

With negative exponents there is no need to state the quotient rule in two parts as we did in Section 4.6. It can be stated simply as

$$\frac{a^m}{a^n} = a^{m-n}$$

for any integers m and n. We list the rules of exponents here for easy reference.

Helpful Hint

The definitions of the different types of exponents are a really clever mathematical invention. The fact that we have rules for performing arithmetic with those exponents makes the notation of exponents even more amazing.

Rules for Integral Exponents

The following rules hold for nonzero real numbers a and b and any integers m and n.

1. $a^0 = 1$	Definition of zero exponent
2. $a^m \cdot a^n = a^{m+n}$	Product rule
3. $\frac{a^m}{a^n} = a^{m-n}$	Quotient rule
4. $(a^m)^n = a^{mn}$	Power rule
5. $(ab)^n = a^n \cdot b^n$	Power of a product rule
6. $\left(\frac{a}{b}\right)^n = \frac{a^n}{b^n}$	Power of a quotient rule

EXAMPLE 3

The product and quotient rules for integral exponents

Simplify. Write your answers without negative exponents. Assume that the variables represent nonzero real numbers.

a) $b^{-3}b^5$ **b)** $-3x^{-3} \cdot 5x^2$ **c)** $\dfrac{m^{-6}}{m^{-2}}$ **d)** $\dfrac{4y^5}{-12y^{-3}}$

Solution

a) $b^{-3}b^5 = b^{-3+5}$ Product rule
$= b^2$ Simplify.

b) $-3x^{-3} \cdot 5x^2 = -15x^{-1}$ Product rule
$= -\dfrac{15}{x}$ Definition of negative exponent

c) $\dfrac{m^{-6}}{m^{-2}} = m^{-6-(-2)}$ Quotient rule
$= m^{-4}$ Simplify.
$= \dfrac{1}{m^4}$ Definition of negative exponent

Note that we could use the rules for negative exponents and the old quotient rule:

$$\frac{m^{-6}}{m^{-2}} = \frac{m^2}{m^6} = \frac{1}{m^4}$$

d) $\dfrac{4y^5}{-12y^{-3}} = \dfrac{y^{5-(-3)}}{-3} = \dfrac{-y^8}{3}$

Now do Exercises 23–34

Teaching Tip At this time, there are many different ways to proceed to the correct answer. This is both good and bad. Some students want there to be only one way.

In Example 4 we use the power rules with negative exponents.

EXAMPLE 4

The power rules for integral exponents

Simplify each expression. Write your answers with positive exponents only. Assume that all variables represent nonzero real numbers.

a) $(a^{-3})^2$ **b)** $(10x^{-3})^{-2}$ **c)** $\left(\dfrac{4x^{-5}}{y^2}\right)^{-2}$

Solution

a) $(a^{-3})^2 = a^{-3 \cdot 2}$ Power rule
$= a^{-6}$
$= \dfrac{1}{a^6}$ Definition of negative exponent

b) $(10x^{-3})^{-2} = 10^{-2}(x^{-3})^{-2}$ Power of a product rule
$= 10^{-2}x^{(-3)(-2)}$ Power rule
$= \dfrac{x^6}{10^2}$ Definition of negative exponent
$= \dfrac{x^6}{100}$

Calculator Close-Up

You can use a calculator to demonstrate that the power rule for exponents holds when the exponents are negative integers.

```
(3^-2)^-5
                59049
3^(-2*-5)
                59049
```

Helpful Hint

The exponent rules in this section apply to expressions that involve only multiplication and division. This is not too surprising since exponents, multiplication, and division are closely related. Recall that $a^3 = a \cdot a \cdot a$ and $a \div b = a \cdot b^{-1}$.

c) $\left(\frac{4x^{-5}}{y^2}\right)^{-2} = \frac{(4x^{-5})^{-2}}{(y^2)^{-2}}$ Power of a quotient rule

$= \frac{4^{-2}x^{10}}{y^{-4}}$ Power of a product rule and power rule

$= 4^{-2} \cdot x^{10} \cdot \frac{1}{y^{-4}}$ Because $\frac{a}{b} = a \cdot \frac{1}{b}$.

$= \frac{1}{4^2} \cdot x^{10} \cdot y^4$ Definition of negative exponent

$= \frac{x^{10}y^4}{16}$ Simplify.

Now do Exercises 35–46

Converting from Scientific Notation

Many of the numbers occurring in science are either very large or very small. The speed of light is 983,569,000 feet per second. One millimeter is equal to 0.000001 kilometer. In scientific notation, numbers larger than 10 or smaller than 1 are written by using positive or negative exponents.

Scientific notation is based on multiplication by integral powers of 10. Multiplying a number by a positive power of 10 moves the decimal point to the right:

$$10(5.32) = 53.2$$
$$10^2(5.32) = 100(5.32) = 532$$
$$10^3(5.32) = 1000(5.32) = 5320$$

Multiplying by a negative power of 10 moves the decimal point to the left:

$$10^{-1}(5.32) = \frac{1}{10}(5.32) = 0.532$$
$$10^{-2}(5.32) = \frac{1}{100}(5.32) = 0.0532$$
$$10^{-3}(5.32) = \frac{1}{1000}(5.32) = 0.00532$$

So if n is a positive integer, multiplying by 10^n moves the decimal point n places to the right and multiplying by 10^{-n} moves it n places to the left.

A number in scientific notation is written as a product of a number between 1 and 10 and a power of 10. The times symbol $\times$ indicates multiplication. For example, 3.27×10^9 and 2.5×10^{-4} are numbers in scientific notation. In scientific notation, there is one digit to the left of the decimal point.

To convert 3.27×10^9 to standard notation, move the decimal point nine places to the right:

$$3.27 \times 10^9 = 3,270,000,000$$

9 places to the right

Of course, it is not necessary to put the decimal point in when writing a whole number.

To convert 2.5×10^{-4} to standard notation, the decimal point is moved four places to the left:

$$2.5 \times 10^{-4} = 0.00025$$

4 places to the left

Calculator Close-Up

On a graphing calculator you can write scientific notation by actually using the power of 10 or press EE to get the letter E, which indicates that the following number is the power of 10.

```
3.27*10^9
          3270000000
3.27E9
          3270000000
```

Note that if the exponent is not too large, scientific notation is converted to standard notation when you press ENTER.

In general, we use the following strategy to convert from scientific notation to standard notation.

Strategy for Converting from Scientific Notation to Standard Notation

1. Determine the number of places to move the decimal point by examining the exponent on the 10.
2. Move to the right for a positive exponent and to the left for a negative exponent.

EXAMPLE 5

Converting scientific notation to standard notation

Write in standard notation.

a) 7.02×10^6 **b)** 8.13×10^{-5}

Solution

a) Because the exponent is positive, move the decimal point six places to the right:

$$7.02 \times 10^6 = 7020000. = 7{,}020{,}000$$

b) Because the exponent is negative, move the decimal point five places to the left:

$$8.13 \times 10^{-5} = 0.0000813$$

Now do Exercises 67–74

Study Tip

Remember that everything we do in solving problems is based on principles (which are also called rules, theorems, and definitions). These principles justify the steps we take. Be sure that you understand the reasons. If you just memorize procedures without understanding, you will soon forget the procedures.

Converting to Scientific Notation

To convert a positive number to scientific notation, we just reverse the strategy for converting from scientific notation.

Strategy for Converting to Scientific Notation

1. Count the number of places (n) that the decimal must be moved so that it will follow the first nonzero digit of the number.
2. If the original number was larger than 10, use 10^n.
3. If the original number was smaller than 1, use 10^{-n}.

Remember that the scientific notation for a number larger than 10 will have a positive power of 10 and the scientific notation for a number between 0 and 1 will have a negative power of 10.

Math *at Work* Aerospace Engineering

Aircraft design is a delicate balance between weight and strength. Saving 1 pound of weight could save the plane's operators \$5000 over 20 years. Mathematics is used to calculate the strength of each of a plane's parts and to predict when the material making up a part will fail. If calculations show that one kind of metal isn't strong enough, designers usually have to choose another material or change the design.

As an example, consider an aluminum stringer with a circular cross section. The stringer is used inside the wing of an air plane as shown in the accompanying figure. The aluminum rod has a diameter of 20 mm and will support a load of 5×10^4 Newtons (N). The maximum stress on aluminum is 1×10^8 Pascals (Pa), where 1 Pa = 1 N/m^2. To calculate the stress S on the rod we use S = (load)/(cross sectional area). Note that we must divide the diameter by 2 to get the radius and convert square millimeters to square meters:

$$S = \frac{L}{\pi r^2} = \frac{5 \times 10^4 \text{ N}}{\pi(10 \text{ mm})^2} \cdot \left(\frac{1000 \text{ mm}}{1 \text{ m}}\right)^2 \approx 1.6 \times 10^8 \text{ Pa}$$

Since the stress is 1.6×10^8 Pa and the maximum stress on aluminum is 1×10^8 Pa, the aluminum rod is not strong enough. The design must be changed. The diameter of the aluminum rod could be increased or stronger/lighter metal such as titanium could be used.

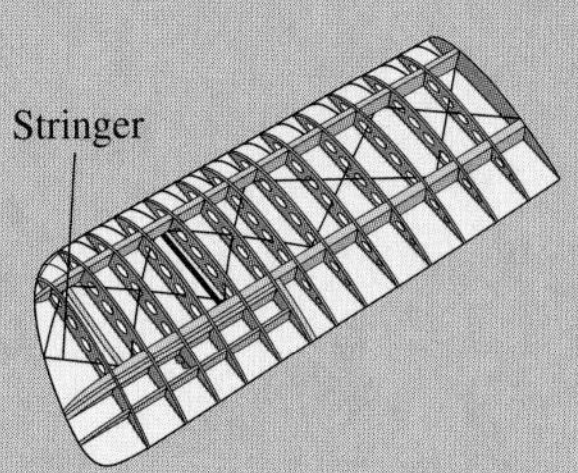

EXAMPLE 6

Converting numbers to scientific notation

Write in scientific notation.

a) 7,346,200 **b)** 0.0000348 **c)** 135×10^{-12}

Solution

a) Because 7,346,200 is larger than 10, the exponent on the 10 will be positive:

$$7{,}346{,}200 = 7.3462 \times 10^6$$

b) Because 0.0000348 is smaller than 1, the exponent on the 10 will be negative:

$$0.0000348 = 3.48 \times 10^{-5}$$

c) There should be only one nonzero digit to the left of the decimal point:

$$135 \times 10^{-12} = 1.35 \times 10^2 \times 10^{-12} \quad \text{Convert 135 to scientific notation.}$$
$$= 1.35 \times 10^{-10} \quad \text{Product rule}$$

Now do Exercises 75–82

Calculator Close-Up

To convert to scientific notation, set the mode to scientific. In scientific mode all results are given in scientific notation.

```
7346200
           7.3462E6
.0000348
             3.48E-5
135E-12
            1.35E-10
```

Computations with Scientific Notation

An important feature of scientific notation is its use in computations. Numbers in scientific notation are nothing more than exponential expressions, and you have already studied operations with exponential expressions in this section. We use the same rules of exponents on numbers in scientific notation that we use on any other exponential expressions.

EXAMPLE 7

Using the rules of exponents with scientific notation

Perform the indicated computations. Write the answers in scientific notation.

a) $(3 \times 10^6)(2 \times 10^8)$ **b)** $\dfrac{4 \times 10^5}{8 \times 10^{-2}}$ **c)** $(5 \times 10^{-7})^3$

Solution

a) $(3 \times 10^6)(2 \times 10^8) = 3 \cdot 2 \cdot 10^6 \cdot 10^8 = 6 \times 10^{14}$

b)
$$\frac{4 \times 10^5}{8 \times 10^{-2}} = \frac{4}{8} \cdot \frac{10^5}{10^{-2}} = \frac{1}{2} \cdot 10^{5-(-2)} \quad \text{Quotient rule}$$
$$= (0.5)10^7 \quad \frac{1}{2} = 0.5$$
$$= 5 \times 10^{-1} \cdot 10^7 \quad \text{Write 0.5 in scientific notation.}$$
$$= 5 \times 10^6 \quad \text{Product rule}$$

c)
$$(5 \times 10^{-7})^3 = 5^3(10^{-7})^3 \quad \text{Power of a product rule}$$
$$= 125 \cdot 10^{-21} \quad \text{Power rule}$$
$$= 1.25 \times 10^2 \times 10^{-21} \quad 125 = 1.25 \times 10^2$$
$$= 1.25 \times 10^{-19} \quad \text{Product rule}$$

Now do Exercises 83–94

Calculator Close-Up

With a calculator's built-in scientific notation, some parentheses can be omitted as shown below. Writing out the powers of 10 can lead to errors.

```
4E5/8E-2
                5E6
4*10^5/8*10^-2
                5E2
```

Try these computations with your calculator.

EXAMPLE 8

Converting to scientific notation for computations

Perform these computations by first converting each number into scientific notation. Give your answer in scientific notation.

a) (3,000,000)(0.0002) **b)** $(20{,}000{,}000)^3(0.0000003)$

Solution

a)
$$(3{,}000{,}000)(0.0002) = 3 \times 10^6 \cdot 2 \times 10^{-4} \quad \text{Scientific notation}$$
$$= 6 \times 10^2 \quad \text{Product rule}$$

b)
$$(20{,}000{,}000)^3(0.0000003) = (2 \times 10^7)^3(3 \times 10^{-7}) \quad \text{Scientific notation}$$
$$= 8 \times 10^{21} \cdot 3 \times 10^{-7} \quad \text{Power of a product rule}$$
$$= 24 \times 10^{14}$$
$$= 2.4 \times 10^1 \times 10^{14} \quad 24 = 2.4 \times 10^1$$
$$= 2.4 \times 10^{15} \quad \text{Product rule}$$

Now do Exercises 95–102

Teaching Tip Many students have trouble converting 24×10^{14} to scientific notation. Be sure they write $2.4 \times 10^1 \times 10^{14}$ and then add exponents.

Warm-Ups ▼

True or false? Explain your answer.

1. $10^{-2} = \frac{1}{100}$ True

2. $\left(-\frac{1}{5}\right)^{-1} = 5$ False

3. $3^{-2} \cdot 2^{-1} = 6^{-3}$ False

4. $\frac{3^{-2}}{3^{-1}} = \frac{1}{3}$ True

5. $23.7 = 2.37 \times 10^{-1}$ False

6. $0.000036 = 3.6 \times 10^{-5}$ True

7. $25 \cdot 10^7 = 2.5 \times 10^8$ True

8. $0.442 \times 10^{-3} = 4.42 \times 10^{-4}$ True

9. $(3 \times 10^{-9})^2 = 9 \times 10^{-18}$ True

10. $(2 \times 10^{-5})(4 \times 10^4) = 8 \times 10^{-20}$ False

4.7 Exercises

Boost your GRADE at mathzone.com!

MathZone

▶ Practice Problems ▶ Net Tutor
▶ Self-Tests ▶ e-Professors
▶ Videos

Reading and Writing *After reading this section, write out the answers to these questions. Use complete sentences.*

1. What does a negative exponent mean?
A negative exponent means "reciprocal," as in $a^{-n} = \frac{1}{a^n}$.

2. What is the correct order for evaluating the operations indicated by a negative exponent?
The operations can be evaluated in any order.

3. What is the new quotient rule for exponents?
The new quotient rule is $a^m/a^n = a^{m-n}$ for any integers m and n.

4. How do you convert a number from scientific notation to standard notation?
Convert from scientific notation by multiplying by the appropriate power of 10.

5. How do you convert a number from standard notation to scientific notation?
Convert from standard notation by counting the number of places the decimal must move so that there is one nonzero digit to the left of the decimal point.

6. Which numbers are not usually written in scientific notation?
Numbers between 1 and 10 are not written in scientific notation.

Variables in all exercises represent positive real numbers. Evaluate each expression. See Example 1.

7. 3^{-1} $\frac{1}{3}$

8. 3^{-3} $\frac{1}{27}$

9. $(-2)^{-4}$ $\frac{1}{16}$

10. $(-3)^{-4}$ $\frac{1}{81}$

11. -4^{-2} $-\frac{1}{16}$

12. -2^{-4} $-\frac{1}{16}$

13. $\frac{5^{-2}}{10^{-2}}$ 4

14. $\frac{3^{-4}}{6^{-2}}$ $\frac{4}{9}$

Simplify. See Example 2.

15. $\left(\frac{5}{2}\right)^{-3}$ $\frac{8}{125}$

16. $\left(\frac{4}{3}\right)^{-2}$ $\frac{9}{16}$

17. $6^{-1} + 6^{-1}$ $\frac{1}{3}$

18. $2^{-1} + 4^{-1}$ $\frac{3}{4}$

19. $\frac{10}{5^{-3}}$ 1250

20. $\frac{1}{25 \cdot 10^{-4}}$ 400

21. $\frac{1}{4^{-3}} + \frac{3^2}{2^{-1}}$ 82

22. $\frac{2^3}{10^{-2}} - \frac{2}{7^{-2}}$ 702

Simplify. Write answers without negative exponents. See Example 3.

23. $x^{-1}x^2$ x

24. $y^{-3}y^5$ y^2

25. $-2x^2 \cdot 8x^{-6}$ $-\frac{16}{x^4}$

26. $5y^5(-6y^{-7})$ $-\frac{30}{y^2}$

27. $-3a^{-2}(-2a^{-3})$ $\frac{6}{a^5}$

28. $(-b^{-3})(-b^{-5})$ $\frac{1}{b^8}$

29. $\frac{u^{-5}}{u^3}$ $\frac{1}{u^8}$

30. $\frac{w^{-4}}{w^6}$ $\frac{1}{w^{10}}$

31. $\dfrac{8t^{-3}}{-2t^{-5}}$ $-4t^2$

32. $\dfrac{-22w^{-4}}{-11w^{-3}}$ $\dfrac{2}{w}$

33. $\dfrac{-6x^5}{-3x^{-6}}$ $2x^{11}$

34. $\dfrac{-51y^6}{17y^{-9}}$ $-3y^{15}$

Simplify each expression. Write answers without negative exponents. See Example 4.

35. $(x^2)^{-5}$ $\dfrac{1}{x^{10}}$

36. $(y^{-2})^4$ $\dfrac{1}{y^8}$

37. $(a^{-3})^{-3}$ a^9

38. $(b^{-5})^{-2}$ b^{10}

39. $(2x^{-3})^{-4}$ $\dfrac{x^{12}}{16}$

40. $(3y^{-1})^{-2}$ $\dfrac{y^2}{9}$

41. $(4x^2y^{-3})^{-2}$ $\dfrac{y^6}{16x^4}$

42. $(6s^{-2}t^4)^{-1}$ $\dfrac{s^2}{6t^4}$

43. $\left(\dfrac{2x^{-1}}{y^{-3}}\right)^{-2}$ $\dfrac{x^2}{4y^6}$

44. $\left(\dfrac{a^{-2}}{3b^3}\right)^{-3}$ $27a^6b^9$

45. $\left(\dfrac{2a^{-3}}{ac^{-2}}\right)^{-4}$ $\dfrac{a^{16}}{16c^8}$

46. $\left(\dfrac{3w^2}{w^4x^3}\right)^{-2}$ $\dfrac{w^4x^6}{9}$

Simplify. Write answers without negative exponents.

47. $2 \cdot 3w^{-5}$ $\dfrac{6}{w^5}$

48. $4 \cdot 3m^{-6}$ $\dfrac{12}{m^6}$

49. $(2h)^{-3}$ $\dfrac{1}{8h^3}$

50. $(3t)^{-4}$ $\dfrac{1}{81t^4}$

51. $(x^{-4})^{-3}(x^{-5})^6$ $\dfrac{1}{x^{18}}$

52. $(y^{-5})^{-6}(y^{-6})^7$ $\dfrac{1}{y^{12}}$

53. $\dfrac{(b^3)^{-5}}{(b^{-7})^4}$ b^{13}

54. $\dfrac{(a^9)^{-3}}{(a^{-4})^7}$ a

55. $\dfrac{(v^{-3})^6(v^{-5})^{-4}}{(v^{-7})^3}$ v^{23}

56. $\dfrac{(k^{-3})^4(k^5)^{-5}}{(k^{-5})^4}$ $\dfrac{1}{k^{17}}$

57. $\dfrac{(c^{-1})^{-12}(c^{-5})^6}{(c^{-4})^0(c^3)^{-3}}$ $\dfrac{1}{c^9}$

58. $\dfrac{(p^{-5})^{-9}(p^{-6})^4}{(p^{-8})^0(p^4)^{-5}}$ p^{41}

59. $2^{-1} \cdot 3^{-1}$ $\dfrac{1}{6}$

60. $2^{-1} + 3^{-1}$ $\dfrac{5}{6}$

61. $(2 \cdot 3^{-1})^{-1}$ $\dfrac{3}{2}$

62. $(2^{-1} + 3)^{-1}$ $\dfrac{2}{7}$

63. $(x^{-2})^{-3} + 3x^7(-5x^{-1})$ $-14x^6$

64. $(ab^{-1})^2 - ab(-ab^{-3})$ $\dfrac{2a^2}{b^2}$

65. $\dfrac{a^3b^{-2}}{a^{-1}} + \left(\dfrac{b^6a^{-2}}{b^5}\right)^{-2}$ $\dfrac{2a^4}{b^2}$

66. $\left(\dfrac{x^{-3}y^{-1}}{2x}\right)^{-3} + \dfrac{6x^9y^3}{-3x^{-3}}$ $6x^{12}y^3$

Write each number in standard notation. See Example 5.

67. 9.86×10^9 9,860,000,000

68. 4.007×10^4 40,070

69. 1.37×10^{-3} 0.00137

70. 9.3×10^{-5} 0.000093

71. 1×10^{-6} 0.000001

72. 3×10^{-1} 0.3

73. 6×10^5 600,000

74. 8×10^6 8,000,000

Write each number in scientific notation. See Example 6.

75. 9000 9×10^3

76. 5,298,000 5.298×10^6

77. 0.00078 7.8×10^{-4}

78. 0.000214 2.14×10^{-4}

79. 0.0000085 8.5×10^{-6}

80. 5,670,000,000 5.67×10^9

81. 525×10^9 5.25×10^{11}

82. 0.0034×10^{-8} 3.4×10^{-11}

Perform the computations. Write answers in scientific notation. See Example 7.

83. $(3 \times 10^5)(2 \times 10^{-15})$ 6×10^{-10}

84. $(2 \times 10^{-9})(4 \times 10^{23})$ 8×10^{14}

85. $\dfrac{4 \times 10^{-8}}{2 \times 10^{30}}$ 2×10^{-38}

86. $\dfrac{9 \times 10^{-4}}{3 \times 10^{-6}}$ 3×10^2

87. $\dfrac{3 \times 10^{20}}{6 \times 10^{-8}}$ 5×10^{27}

88. $\dfrac{1 \times 10^{-8}}{4 \times 10^7}$ 2.5×10^{-16}

89. $(3 \times 10^{12})^2$ 9×10^{24}

90. $(2 \times 10^{-5})^3$ 8×10^{-15}

91. $(5 \times 10^4)^3$ 1.25×10^{14}

92. $(5 \times 10^{14})^{-1}$ 2×10^{-15}

93. $(4 \times 10^{32})^{-1}$ 2.5×10^{-33}

94. $(6 \times 10^{11})^2$ 3.6×10^{23}

Perform the following computations by first converting each number into scientific notation. Write answers in scientific notation. See Example 8.

95. (4300)(2,000,000) 8.6×10^9

96. (40,000)(4,000,000,000) 1.6×10^{14}

97. (4,200,000)(0.00005) 2.1×10^2

98. (0.00075)(4,000,000) 3×10^3

99. $(300)^3(0.000001)^5$ 2.7×10^{-23}

100. $(200)^4(0.0005)^3$ 2×10^{-1}

101. $\dfrac{(4000)(90{,}000)}{0.00000012}$ 3×10^{15}

102. $\dfrac{(30{,}000)(80{,}000)}{(0.000006)(0.002)}$ 2×10^{17}

Perform the following computations with the aid of a calculator. Write answers in scientific notation. Round to three decimal places.

103. $(6.3 \times 10^6)(1.45 \times 10^{-4})$ 9.135×10^2

104. $(8.35 \times 10^9)(4.5 \times 10^3)$ 3.758×10^{13}

105. $(5.36 \times 10^{-4}) + (3.55 \times 10^{-5})$ 5.715×10^{-4}

106. $(8.79 \times 10^8) + (6.48 \times 10^9)$ 7.359×10^9

107. $\dfrac{(3.5 \times 10^5)(4.3 \times 10^{-6})}{3.4 \times 10^{-8}}$ 4.426×10^7

108. $\dfrac{(3.5 \times 10^{-8})(4.4 \times 10^{-4})}{2.43 \times 10^{45}}$ 6.337×10^{-57}

109. $(3.56 \times 10^{85})(4.43 \times 10^{96})$ 1.577×10^{182}

110. $(8 \times 10^{99}) + (3 \times 10^{99})$ 1.1×10^{100}

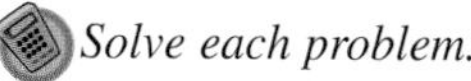

Solve each problem.

111. ***Distance to the sun.*** The distance from the earth to the sun is 93 million miles. Express this distance in feet. (1 mile = 5280 feet.) 4.910×10^{11} feet

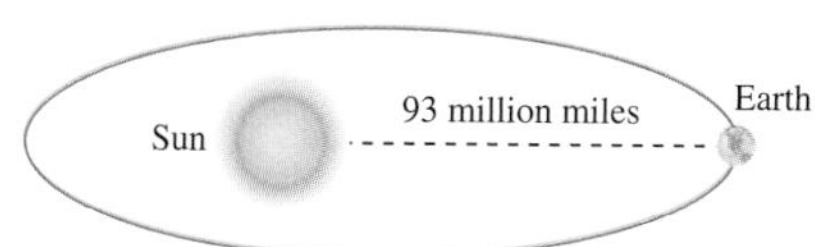

Figure for Exercise 111

112. ***Speed of light.*** The speed of light is 9.83569×10^8 feet per second. How long does it take light to travel from the sun to the earth? See Exercise 111.
8.3 minutes

113. ***Warp drive, Scotty.*** How long does it take a spacecraft traveling at 2×10^{35} miles per hour (warp factor 4) to travel 93 million miles?
4.65×10^{-28} hours

114. ***Area of a dot.*** If the radius of a very small circle is 2.35×10^{-8} centimeters, then what is the circle's area?
1.735×10^{-15} cm^2

115. ***Circumference of a circle.*** If the circumference of a circle is 5.68×10^9 feet, then what is its radius?
9.040×10^8 feet

116. ***Diameter of a circle.*** If the diameter of a circle is 1.3×10^{-12} meters, then what is its radius?
6.5×10^{-13} meters

117. ***Present value.*** The present value P that will amount to A dollars in n years with interest compounded annually at annual interest rate r, is given by

$$P = A(1 + r)^{-n}.$$

Find the present value that will amount to \$50,000 in 20 years at 8% compounded annually.
\$10,727.41

118. ***Investing in stocks.*** U.S. small company stocks have returned an average of 14.9% annually for the last 50 years (T. Rowe Price, www.troweprice.com). Use the present value formula from the previous exercise to find the amount invested today in small company stocks that would be worth \$1 million in 50 years, assuming that small company stocks continue to return 14.9% annually for the next 50 years.
\$963.83

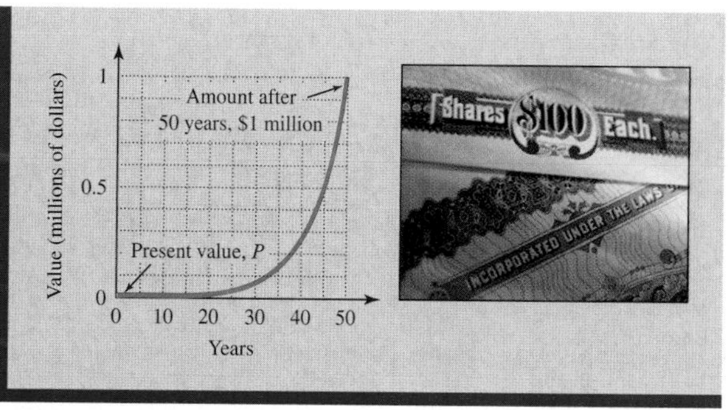

Figure for Exercise 118

Getting More Involved

119. *Exploration*

a) If $w^{-3} < 0$, then what can you say about w?

b) If $(-5)^m < 0$, then what can you say about m?

c) What restriction must be placed on w and m so that $w^m < 0$?

a) $w < 0$

b) m is odd

c) $w < 0$ and m odd

120. *Discussion*

Which of the following expressions is not equal to -1? Explain your answer.

a) -1^{-1}

b) -1^{-2}

c) $(-1^{-1})^{-1}$

d) $(-1)^{-1}$

e) $(-1)^{-2}$ e

Collaborative Activities

Grouping: Two students per group

Topic: Multiplying Polynomials

Area as a Model of Binomial Multiplication

Drawings and diagrams are often used to illustrate mathematical ideas. In this activity we use areas of rectangles to illustrate multiplication of binomials.

Example. The product $15 \cdot 13$ is the area of a 15 by 13 rectangle. Rewrite the product as $(10 + 5)(10 + 3)$ and make the following drawing.

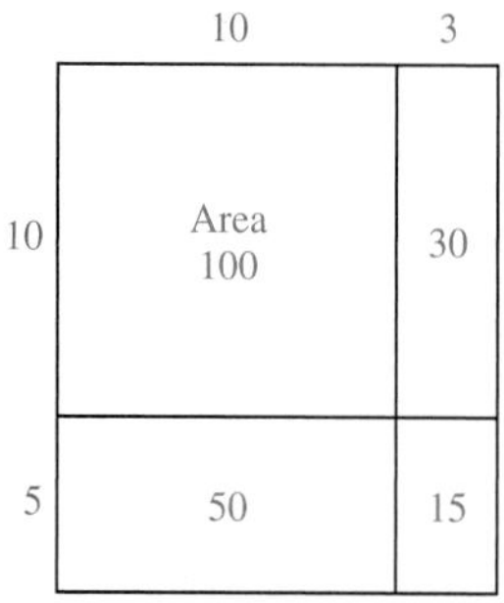

Note that the areas of the four regions are the four parts of FOIL:

$$\begin{aligned}(10 + 5)(10 + 3) &= \overset{\text{First}}{10^2} + \overset{\text{Outer}}{10 \cdot 3} + \overset{\text{Inner}}{5 \cdot 10} + \overset{\text{Last}}{5 \cdot 3} \\ &= 100 + 30 + 50 + 15 \\ &= 195\end{aligned}$$

Exercises

1. Make a drawing using graph paper to illustrate the product $12 \cdot 13$ as the product of two binomials $(10 + 2)(10 + 3)$. Have each square of your graph paper represent one unit. One partner should draw the rectangle and find the total of the areas of the four regions that correspond to FOIL while the other should find $12 \cdot 13$ in the "usual" way. Check your answers.

2. We have been using 10 for the first term of our binomials, but now we will use x. Choose any positive integer for x and draw an $x + 2$ by $x + 4$ rectangle on your graph paper. Have one partner draw the rectangle and find the total of the areas of the four regions that correspond to FOIL while the other will find $(x + 2)(x + 4)$ in the "usual" way. Check your answers.

3. Suppose that the area of the $x + 2$ by $x + 4$ rectangle drawn in the last exercise is actually 120. Does your rectangle have an area of 120? If not, then draw an $x + 2$ by $x + 4$ rectangle with an area of 120. What is x? Is x an integer?

4. Is there an $x + 3$ by $x + 6$ rectangle for which the area is 120 and x is a positive integer?

5. Is there an $x + 7$ by $x + 14$ rectangle for which the area is 120 and x is a positive integer?

6. How many ways are there to partition a 10 by 12 rectangle into four regions using sides $x + a$ and $x + b$, where x, a, and b are positive integers?

Chapter 4 Wrap-Up

Summary

Polynomials		**Examples**
Term	A number or the product of a number and one or more variables raised to powers	$5x^3$, $-4x$, 7
Polynomial	A single term or a finite sum of terms	$2x^5 - 9x^2 + 11$
Degree of a polynomial	The highest degree of any of the terms	Degree of $2x - 9$ is 1. Degree of $5x^3 - x^2$ is 3.
Naming a Polynomial	A polynomial can be named with a letter such as P or $P(x)$ (function notation).	$P = x^2 - 1$ $P(x) = x^2 - 1$
Evaluating a polynomial	The value of a polynomial is the real number that is obtained when the variable (x) is replaced with a real number.	If $x = 3$ then $P = 8$, or $P(3) = 8$.

Adding, Subtracting, and Multiplying Polynomials		**Examples**
Add or subtract polynomials	Add or subtract the like terms.	$(x + 1) + (x - 4) = 2x - 3$ $(x^2 - 3x) - (4x^2 - x)$ $= -3x^2 - 2x$
Multiply monomials	Use the product rule for exponents.	$-2x^5 \cdot 6x^8 = -12x^{13}$
Multiply polynomials	Multiply each term of one polynomial by every term of the other polynomial, then combine like terms.	$\begin{array}{r} x^2 + 2x + 5 \\ x - 1 \\ \hline -x^2 - 2x - 5 \\ x^3 + 2x^2 + 5x \\ \hline x^3 + x^2 + 3x - 5 \end{array}$

Binomials		**Examples**
FOIL	A method for multiplying two binomials quickly	$(x - 2)(x + 3) = x^2 + x - 6$
Square of a sum	$(a + b)^2 = a^2 + 2ab + b^2$	$(x + 3)^2 = x^2 + 6x + 9$
Square of a difference	$(a - b)^2 = a^2 - 2ab + b^2$	$(m - 5)^2 = m^2 - 10m + 25$
Product of a sum and a difference	$(a - b)(a + b) = a^2 - b^2$	$(x + 2)(x - 2) = x^2 - 4$

Dividing Polynomials		**Examples**
Dividing monomials	Use the quotient rule for exponents	$8x^5 \div (2x^2) = 4x^3$
Divide a polynomial by a monomial	Divide each term of the polynomial by the monomial.	$\dfrac{3x^5 + 9x}{3x} = x^4 + 3$
Divide a polynomial by a binomial	If the divisor is a binomial, use long division. (divisor)(quotient) + (remainder) = dividend	$\begin{array}{r l} & x - 7 \leftarrow \text{Quotient} \\ \text{Divisor} \rightarrow x + 2 \overline{)x^2 - 5x - 4} & \leftarrow \text{Dividend} \\ \underline{x^2 + 2x} & \\ -7x - 4 & \\ \underline{-7x - 14} & \\ 10 & \leftarrow \text{Remainder} \end{array}$

Rules of Exponents		**Examples**
The following rules hold for any integers m and n, and nonzero real numbers a and b.		
Zero exponent	$a^0 = 1$	$2^0 = 1$, $(-34)^0 = 1$
Product rule	$a^m \cdot a^n = a^{m+n}$	$a^2 \cdot a^3 = a^5$ $3x^6 \cdot 4x^9 = 12x^{15}$
Quotient rule	$\dfrac{a^m}{a^n} = a^{m-n}$	$x^8 \div x^2 = x^6$, $\dfrac{y^3}{y^3} = y^0 = 1$ $\dfrac{c^7}{c^9} = c^{-2} = \dfrac{1}{c^2}$
Power rule	$(a^m)^n = a^{mn}$	$(2^2)^3 = 2^6$, $(w^5)^3 = w^{15}$
Power of a product rule	$(ab)^n = a^n b^n$	$(2t)^3 = 8t^3$
Power of a quotient rule	$\left(\dfrac{a}{b}\right)^n = \dfrac{a^n}{b^n}$	$\left(\dfrac{x}{3}\right)^3 = \dfrac{x^3}{27}$

Negative Exponents		**Examples**
Negative integral exponents	If n is a positive integer and a is a nonzero real number, then $a^{-n} = \dfrac{1}{a^n}$	$3^{-2} = \dfrac{1}{3^2}$, $x^{-5} = \dfrac{1}{x^5}$
Rules for negative exponents	If a is a nonzero real number and n is a positive integer, then $a^{-n} = \left(\dfrac{1}{a}\right)^n$, $a^{-1} = \dfrac{1}{a}$, and $\dfrac{1}{a^{-n}} = a^n$.	$\left(\dfrac{2}{3}\right)^{-3} = \left(\dfrac{3}{2}\right)^3$, $5^{-1} = \dfrac{1}{5}$ $\dfrac{1}{w^{-8}} = w^8$

Scientific Notation		Examples
Converting from scientific notation	1. Find the number of places to move the decimal point by examining the exponent on the 10. 2. Move to the right for a positive exponent and to the left for a negative exponent.	$5.6 \times 10^3 = 5600$ $9 \times 10^{-4} = 0.0009$
Converting into scientific notation (positive numbers)	1. Count the number of places (n) that the decimal point must be moved so that it will follow the first nonzero digit of the number. 2. If the original number was larger than 10, use 10^n. 3. If the original number was smaller than 1, use 10^{-n}.	$304.6 = 3.046 \times 10^2$ $0.0035 = 3.5 \times 10^{-3}$

Enriching Your Mathematical Word Power

For each mathematical term, choose the correct meaning.

1. term
a. an expression containing a number or the product of a number and one or more variables
b. the amount of time spent in this course
c. a word that describes a number
d. a variable a

2. polynomial
a. four or more terms
b. many numbers
c. a sum of four or more numbers
d. a single term or a finite sum of terms d

3. degree of a polynomial
a. the number of terms in a polynomial
b. the highest degree of any of the terms of a polynomial
c. the value of a polynomial when $x = 0$
d. the largest coefficient of any of the terms of a polynomial b

4. leading coefficient
a. the first coefficient
b. the largest coefficient
c. the coefficient of the first term when a polynomial is written with decreasing exponents
d. the most important coefficient c

5. monomial
a. a single polynomial
b. one number
c. an equation that has only one solution
d. a polynomial that has one term d

6. FOIL
a. a method for adding polynomials
b. first, outer, inner, last
c. an equation with no solution
d. a polynomial with five terms b

7. dividend
a. a in a/b
b. b in a/b
c. the result of a/b
d. what a bank pays on deposits a

8. divisor
a. a in a/b
b. b in a/b
c. the result of a/b
d. two visors b

9. quotient
a. a in a/b
b. b in a/b
c. a/b
d. the divisor plus the remainder c

10. binomial
a. a polynomial with two terms
b. any two numbers
c. the two coordinates in an ordered pair
d. an equation with two variables a

11. integral exponent
a. an exponent that is an integer
b. a positive exponent
c. a rational exponent
d. a fractional exponent a

12. scientific notation
a. the notation of rational exponents
b. the notation of algebra
c. a notation for expressing large or small numbers with powers of 10
d. radical notation c

Review Exercises

4.1 *Perform the indicated operations.*

1. $(2w - 6) + (3w + 4)$ $5w - 2$

2. $(1 - 3y) + (4y - 6)$ $y - 5$

3. $(x^2 - 2x - 5) - (x^2 + 4x - 9)$ $-6x + 4$

4. $(3 - 5x - x^2) - (x^2 - 7x + 8)$ $-2x^2 + 2x - 5$

5. $(5 - 3w + w^2) + (w^2 - 4w - 9)$ $2w^2 - 7w - 4$

6. $(-2t^2 + 3t - 4) + (t^2 - 7t + 2)$ $-t^2 - 4t - 2$

7. $(4 - 3m - m^2) - (m^2 - 6m + 5)$ $-2m^2 + 3m - 1$

8. $(n^3 - n^2 + 9) - (n^4 - n^3 + 5)$ $-n^4 + 2n^3 - n^2 + 4$

4.2 *Perform the indicated operations.*

9. $5x^2 \cdot (-10x^9)$ $-50x^{11}$

10. $3h^3t^2 \cdot 2h^2t^5$ $6h^5t^7$

11. $(-11a^7)^2$ $121a^{14}$

12. $(12b^3)^2$ $144b^6$

13. $x - 5(x - 3)$
$-4x + 15$

14. $x - 4(x - 9)$
$-3x + 36$

15. $5x + 3(x^2 - 5x + 4)$
$3x^2 - 10x + 12$

16. $5 + 4x^2(x - 5)$
$4x^3 - 20x^2 + 5$

17. $3m^2(5m^3 - m + 2)$
$15m^5 - 3m^3 + 6m^2$

18. $-4a^4(a^2 + 2a + 4)$
$-4a^6 - 8a^5 - 16a^4$

19. $(x - 5)(x^2 - 2x + 10)$
$x^3 - 7x^2 + 20x - 50$

20. $(x + 2)(x^2 - 2x + 4)$
$x^3 + 8$

21. $(x^2 - 2x + 4)(3x - 2)$
$3x^3 - 8x^2 + 16x - 8$

22. $(5x + 3)(x^2 - 5x + 4)$
$5x^3 - 22x^2 + 5x + 12$

4.3 *Perform the indicated operations.*

23. $(q - 6)(q + 8)$
$q^2 + 2q - 48$

24. $(w + 5)(w + 12)$
$w^2 + 17w + 60$

25. $(2t - 3)(t - 9)$
$2t^2 - 21t + 27$

26. $(5r + 1)(5r + 2)$
$25r^2 + 15r + 2$

27. $(4y - 3)(5y + 2)$
$20y^2 - 7y - 6$

28. $(11y + 1)(y + 2)$
$11y^2 + 23y + 2$

29. $(3x^2 + 5)(2x^2 + 1)$
$6x^4 + 13x^2 + 5$

30. $(x^3 - 7)(2x^3 + 7)$
$2x^6 - 7x^3 - 49$

4.4 *Perform the indicated operations. Try to write only the answers.*

31. $(z - 7)(z + 7)$
$z^2 - 49$

32. $(a - 4)(a + 4)$
$a^2 - 16$

33. $(y + 7)^2$
$y^2 + 14y + 49$

34. $(a + 5)^2$
$a^2 + 10a + 25$

35. $(w - 3)^2$
$w^2 - 6w + 9$

36. $(a - 6)^2$
$a^2 - 12a + 36$

37. $(x^2 - 3)(x^2 + 3)$
$x^4 - 9$

38. $(2b^2 - 1)(2b^2 + 1)$
$4b^4 - 1$

39. $(3a + 1)^2$
$9a^2 + 6a + 1$

40. $(1 - 3c)^2$
$1 - 6c + 9c^2$

41. $(4 - y)^2$
$16 - 8y + y^2$

42. $(9 - t)^2$
$81 - 18t + t^2$

Study Tip

Note how the review exercises are arranged according to the sections in this chapter. If you are having trouble with a certain type of problem, refer back to the appropriate section for examples and explanations.

4.5 *Find each quotient.*

43. $-10x^5 \div (2x^3)$ $-5x^2$

44. $-6x^4y^2 \div (-2x^2y^2)$ $3x^2$

45. $\dfrac{6a^5b^7c^6}{-3a^3b^9c^6}$ $\dfrac{-2a^2}{b^2}$

46. $\dfrac{-9h^5t^9r^2}{3h^7t^6r^2}$ $\dfrac{-3t^3}{h^2}$

47. $\dfrac{3x - 9}{-3}$ $-x + 3$

48. $\dfrac{7 - y}{-1}$ $y - 7$

49. $\dfrac{9x^3 - 6x^2 + 3x}{-3x}$ $-3x^2 + 2x - 1$

50. $\dfrac{-8x^3y^5 + 4x^2y^4 - 2xy^3}{2xy^2}$ $-4x^2y^3 + 2xy^2 - y$

51. $(a - 1) \div (1 - a)$ -1

52. $(t - 3) \div (3 - t)$ -1

53. $(m^4 - 16) \div (m - 2)$ $m^3 + 2m^2 + 4m + 8$

54. $(x^4 - 1) \div (x - 1)$ $x^3 + x^2 + x + 1$

Find the quotient and remainder.

55. $(3m^3 - 9m^2 + 18m) \div (3m)$
$m^2 - 3m + 6, 0$

56. $(8x^3 - 4x^2 - 18x) \div (2x)$
$4x^2 - 2x - 9, 0$

57. $(b^2 - 3b + 5) \div (b + 2)$
$b - 5, 15$

58. $(r^2 - 5r + 9) \div (r - 3)$
$r - 2, 3$

59. $(4x^2 - 9) \div (2x + 1)$
$2x - 1, -8$

60. $(9y^3 + 2y) \div (3y + 2)$
$3y^2 - 2y + 2, -4$

61. $(x^3 + x^2 - 11x + 10) \div (x - 1)$
$x^2 + 2x - 9, 1$

62. $(y^3 - 9y^2 + 3y - 6) \div (y + 1)$
$y^2 - 10y + 13, -19$

Write each expression in the form

$$\textit{quotient} + \frac{\textit{remainder}}{\textit{divisor}}.$$

63. $\dfrac{2x}{x - 3}$ $2 + \dfrac{6}{x - 3}$

64. $\dfrac{3x}{x - 4}$ $3 + \dfrac{12}{x - 4}$

65. $\dfrac{2x}{1 - x}$ $-2 + \dfrac{2}{1 - x}$

66. $\dfrac{3x}{5 - x}$ $-3 + \dfrac{15}{5 - x}$

67. $\dfrac{x^2 - 3}{x + 1}$ $x - 1 - \dfrac{2}{x + 1}$

68. $\dfrac{x^2 + 3x + 1}{x - 3}$ $x + 6 + \dfrac{19}{x - 3}$

69. $\dfrac{x^2}{x + 1}$ $x - 1 + \dfrac{1}{x + 1}$

70. $\dfrac{-2x^2}{x - 3}$ $-2x - 6 + \dfrac{-18}{x - 3}$

4.6 *Simplify each expression.*

71. $2y^{10} \cdot 3y^{20}$ $6y^{30}$

72. $(-3a^5)(5a^3)$ $-15a^8$

73. $\dfrac{-10b^5c^3}{2b^5c^9}$ $\dfrac{-5}{c^6}$

74. $\dfrac{-30k^3y^9}{15k^3y^2}$ $-2y^7$

75. $(b^5)^6$ b^{30}

76. $(y^5)^8$ y^{40}

77. $(-2x^3y^2)^3$ $-8x^9y^6$

78. $(-3a^4b^6)^4$ $81a^{16}b^{24}$

79. $\left(\dfrac{2a}{b}\right)^3$ $\dfrac{8a^3}{b^3}$

80. $\left(\dfrac{3y}{2}\right)^3$ $\dfrac{27y^3}{8}$

81. $\left(\dfrac{-6x^2y^5}{-3z^6}\right)^3$ $\dfrac{8x^6y^{15}}{z^{18}}$

82. $\left(\dfrac{-3a^4b^8}{6a^3b^{12}}\right)^4$ $\dfrac{a^4}{16b^{16}}$

For the following exercises, assume that all of the variables represent positive real numbers.

4.7 *Simplify each expression. Use only positive exponents in answers.*

83. 2^{-5} $\dfrac{1}{32}$

84. -2^{-4} $-\dfrac{1}{16}$

85. 10^{-3} $\dfrac{1}{1000}$

86. $5^{-1} \cdot 5^0$ $\dfrac{1}{5}$

87. x^5x^{-8} $\dfrac{1}{x^3}$

88. $a^{-3}a^{-9}$ $\dfrac{1}{a^{12}}$

89. $\dfrac{a^{-8}}{a^{-12}}$ a^4

90. $\dfrac{a^{10}}{a^{-4}}$ a^{14}

91. $\dfrac{a^3}{a^{-7}}$ a^{10}

92. $\dfrac{b^{-2}}{b^{-6}}$ b^4

93. $(x^{-3})^4$ $\dfrac{1}{x^{12}}$

94. $(x^5)^{-10}$ $\dfrac{1}{x^{50}}$

95. $(2x^{-3})^{-3}$ $\dfrac{x^9}{8}$

96. $(3y^{-5})^2$ $\dfrac{9}{y^{10}}$

97. $\left(\dfrac{a}{3b^{-3}}\right)^{-2}$ $\dfrac{9}{a^2b^6}$

98. $\left(\dfrac{a^{-2}}{5b}\right)^{-3}$ $125a^6b^3$

Convert each number in scientific notation to a number in standard notation, and convert each number in standard notation to a number in scientific notation.

99. 5000 5×10^3

100. 0.00009 9×10^{-5}

101. 3.4×10^5 340,000

102. 5.7×10^{-8} 0.000000057

103. 0.0000461 4.61×10^{-5}

104. 44,000 4.4×10^4

105. 5.69×10^{-6} 0.00000569

106. 5.5×10^9 5,500,000,000

Perform each computation without using a calculator. Write answers in scientific notation.

107. $(3.5 \times 10^8)(2.0 \times 10^{-12})$ 7×10^{-4}

108. $(9 \times 10^{12})(2 \times 10^{17})$ 1.8×10^{30}

109. $(2 \times 10^{-4})^4$ 1.6×10^{-15}

110. $(-3 \times 10^5)^3$ -2.7×10^{16}

111. (0.00000004)(2,000,000,000) 8×10^1

112. (3,000,000,000) ÷ (0.000002) 1.5×10^{15}

113. $(0.0000002)^5$ 3.2×10^{-34}

114. $(50{,}000{,}000{,}000)^3$ 1.25×10^{32}

Miscellaneous

Perform the indicated operations.

115. $(x + 3)(x + 7)$ $x^2 + 10x + 21$

116. $(k + 5)(k + 4)$ $k^2 + 9k + 20$

117. $(t - 3y)(t - 4y)$ $t^2 - 7ty + 12y^2$

118. $(t + 7z)(t + 6z)$ $t^2 + 13tz + 42z^2$

119. $(2x^3)^0 + (2y)^0$ 2

120. $(4y^2 - 9)^0$ 1

121. $(-3ht^6)^3$ $-27h^3t^{18}$

122. $(-9y^3c^4)^2$ $81y^6c^8$

123. $(2w + 3)(w - 6)$ $2w^2 - 9w - 18$

124. $(3x + 5)(2x - 6)$ $6x^2 - 8x - 30$

125. $(3u - 5v)(3u + 5v)$ $9u^2 - 25v^2$

126. $(9x^2 - 2)(9x^2 + 2)$ $81x^4 - 4$

127. $(3h + 5)^2$ $9h^2 + 30h + 25$

128. $(4v - 3)^2$ $16v^2 - 24v + 9$

129. $(x + 3)^3$ $x^3 + 9x^2 + 27x + 27$

130. $(k - 10)^3$ $k^3 - 30k^2 + 300k - 1000$

131. $(-7s^2t)(-2s^3t^5)$ $14s^5t^6$

132. $-5w^3r^2 \cdot 2w^4r^8$ $-10w^7r^{10}$

133. $\left(\frac{k^4m^2}{2k^2m^2}\right)^4$ $\frac{k^8}{16}$

134. $\left(\frac{-6h^3y^5}{2h^7y^2}\right)^4$ $\frac{81y^{12}}{h^{16}}$

135. $(5x^2 - 8x - 8) - (4x^2 + x - 3)$
$x^2 - 9x - 5$

136. $(4x^2 - 6x - 8) - (9x^2 - 5x + 7)$
$-5x^2 - x - 15$

137. $(2x^2 - 2x - 3) + (3x^2 + x - 9)$
$5x^2 - x - 12$

138. $(x^2 - 3x - 1) + (x^2 - 2x + 1)$
$2x^2 - 5x$

139. $(x + 4)(x^2 - 5x + 1)$
$x^3 - x^2 - 19x + 4$

140. $(2x^2 - 7x + 4)(x + 3)$
$2x^3 - x^2 - 17x + 12$

141. $(x^2 + 4x - 12) \div (x - 2)$
$x + 6$

142. $(a^2 - 3a - 10) \div (a - 5)$
$a + 2$

Solve each problem.

143. ***Roundball court.*** The length of a basketball court is 44 feet more than its width w. Find polynomials $P(w)$ and $A(w)$ that represent its perimeter and area. Find $P(50)$ and $A(50)$. $P(w) = 4w + 88, A(w) = w^2 + 44w,$ $P(50) = 288$ ft, $A(50) = 4700$ ft^2

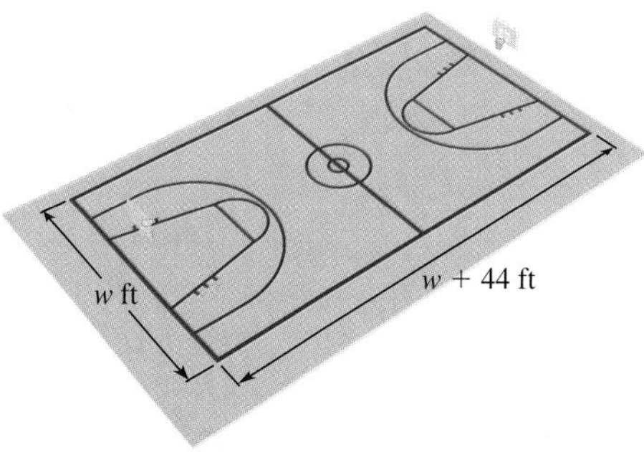

Figure for Exercise 143

144. ***Badminton court.*** The width of a badminton court is 24 feet less than its length x. Find polynomials $P(x)$ and $A(x)$ that represent its perimeter and area. Find $P(44)$ and $A(44)$.
$P(x) = 4x - 48, A(x) = x^2 - 24x, P(44) = 128$ ft, $A(44) = 880$ ft^2

145. ***Smoke alert.*** A retailer of smoke alarms knows that at a price of p dollars each, she can sell $600 - 15p$ smoke alarms per week. Find a polynomial that represents the weekly revenue for the smoke alarms. Find the revenue for a week in which the price is \$12 per smoke alarm. Use the bar graph to find the price per smoke alarm that gives the maximum weekly revenue.
$R = -15p^2 + 600p$, \$5040, \$20

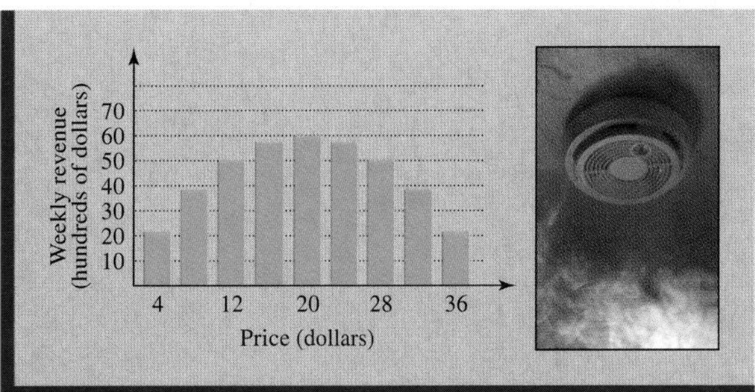

Figure for Exercise 145

146. ***Boom box sales.*** A retailer of boom boxes knows that at a price of q dollars each, he can sell $900 - 3q$ boom boxes per month. Find a polynomial that represents the monthly revenue for the boom boxes. How many boom boxes will he sell if the price is \$300 each?
$R = -3q^2 + 900q$, 0

Chapter 4 Test

Perform the indicated operations.

1. $(7x^3 - x^2 - 6) + (5x^2 + 2x - 5)$ $7x^3 + 4x^2 + 2x - 11$

2. $(x^2 - 3x - 5) - (2x^2 + 6x - 7)$ $-x^2 - 9x + 2$

3. $\dfrac{6y^3 - 9y^2}{-3y}$ $-2y^2 + 3y$

4. $(x - 2) \div (2 - x)$ -1

5. $(x^3 - 2x^2 - 4x + 3) \div (x - 3)$ $x^2 + x - 1$

6. $3x^2(5x^3 - 7x^2 + 4x - 1)$ $15x^5 - 21x^4 + 12x^3 - 3x^2$

Find the products.

7. $(x + 5)(x - 2)$ $x^2 + 3x - 10$

8. $(3a - 7)(2a + 5)$ $6a^2 + a - 35$

9. $(a - 7)^2$ $a^2 - 14a + 49$

10. $(4x + 3y)^2$ $16x^2 + 24xy + 9y^2$

11. $(b - 3)(b + 3)$ $b^2 - 9$

12. $(3t^2 - 7)(3t^2 + 7)$ $9t^4 - 49$

13. $(4x^2 - 3)(x^2 + 2)$ $4x^4 + 5x^2 - 6$

14. $(x - 2)(x + 3)(x - 4)$ $x^3 - 3x^2 - 10x + 24$

Write each expression in the form

$$quotient + \frac{remainder}{divisor}.$$

15. $\dfrac{2x}{x - 3}$ $2 + \dfrac{6}{x - 3}$

16. $\dfrac{x^2 - 3x + 5}{x + 2}$ $x - 5 + \dfrac{15}{x + 2}$

Use the rules of exponents to simplify each expression. Write answers without negative exponents.

17. $-5x^3 \cdot 7x^5$ $-35x^8$

18. $3x^3y \cdot (2xy^4)^2$ $12x^5y^9$

19. $-4a^6b^5 \div (2a^5b)$ $-2ab^4$

20. $3x^{-2} \cdot 5x^7$ $15x^5$

21. $\left(\dfrac{-2a}{b^2}\right)^5$ $\dfrac{-32a^5}{b^{10}}$

22. $\dfrac{-6a^7b^6c^2}{-2a^3b^8c^2}$ $\dfrac{3a^4}{b^2}$

23. $\dfrac{6t^{-7}}{2t^9}$ $\dfrac{3}{t^{16}}$

24. $\dfrac{w^{-6}}{w^{-4}}$ $\dfrac{1}{w^2}$

25. $(-3s^{-3}t^2)^{-2}$ $\dfrac{s^6}{9t^4}$

26. $(-2x^{-6}y)^3$ $\dfrac{-8y^3}{x^{18}}$

Study Tip

Before you take an in-class exam on this chapter, work the sample test given here. Set aside one hour to work this test and use the answers in the back of this book to grade yourself. Even though your instructor might not ask exactly the same questions, you will get a good idea of your test readiness.

Convert to scientific notation.

27. 5,433,000 5.433×10^6

28. 0.0000065 6.5×10^{-6}

Perform each computation by converting to scientific notation. Give answers in scientific notation.

29. (80,000)(0.000006) 4.8×10^{-1}

30. $(0.0000003)^4$ 8.1×10^{-27}

Solve each problem.

31. Find the quotient and remainder when $x^2 - 5x + 9$ is divided by $x - 3$.
$x - 2$, 3

32. Subtract $3x^2 - 4x - 9$ from $x^2 - 3x + 6$.
$-2x^2 + x + 15$

33. The width of a pool table is x feet, and the length is 4 feet longer than the width. Find polynomials $A(x)$ and $P(x)$ that represent the area and perimeter of the pool table. Find $A(4)$ and $P(4)$.
$A(x) = x^2 + 4x$, $P(x) = 4x + 8$, $A(4) = 32$ ft^2, $P(4) = 24$ ft

34. If a manufacturer charges q dollars each for footballs, then he can sell $3000 - 150q$ footballs per week. Find a polynomial that represents the revenue for one week. Find the weekly revenue if the price is \$8 for each football.
$R = -150q^2 + 3000q$, \$14,400

Making **Connections** | A Review of Chapters 1–4

Evaluate each arithmetic expression.

1. $-16 \div (-2)$ 8

2. $-16 \div \left(-\frac{1}{2}\right)$ 32

3. $(-5)^2 - 3(-5) + 1$ 41

4. $-5^2 - 4(-5) + 3$ -2

5. $2^{15} \div 2^{10}$ 32

6. $2^6 - 2^5$ 32

7. $-3^2 \cdot 4^2$ -144

8. $(-3 \cdot 4)^2$ 144

9. $\left(\frac{1}{2}\right)^3 + \frac{1}{2}$ $\frac{5}{8}$

10. $\left(\frac{2}{3}\right)^2 - \frac{1}{3}$ $\frac{1}{9}$

11. $(5 + 3)^2$ 64

12. $5^2 + 3^2$ 34

13. $3^{-1} + 2^{-1}$ $\frac{5}{6}$

14. $2^{-2} - 3^{-2}$ $\frac{5}{36}$

15. $(30 - 1)(30 + 1)$ 899

16. $(30 - 1) \div (1 - 30)$ -1

Perform the indicated operations.

17. $(x + 3)(x + 5)$
$x^2 + 8x + 15$

18. $x + 3(x + 5)$
$4x + 15$

19. $-5t^3v \cdot 3t^2v^6$
$-15t^5v^7$

20. $(-10t^3v^2) \div (-2t^2v)$
$5tv$

21. $(x^2 + 8x + 15) + (x + 5)$ $x^2 + 9x + 20$

22. $(x^2 + 8x + 15) - (x + 5)$ $x^2 + 7x + 10$

23. $(x^2 + 8x + 15) \div (x + 5)$ $x + 3$

24. $(x^2 + 8x + 15)(x + 5)$ $x^3 + 13x^2 + 55x + 75$

25. $(-6y^3 + 8y^2) \div (-2y^2)$ $3y - 4$

26. $(18y^4 - 12y^3 + 3y^2) \div (3y^2)$ $6y^2 - 4y + 1$

Solve each equation.

27. $2x + 1 = 0$ $\left\{-\frac{1}{2}\right\}$

28. $x - 7 = 0$ $\{7\}$

29. $\frac{3}{4}x - 3 = \frac{1}{2}$ $\left\{\frac{14}{3}\right\}$

30. $\frac{x}{2} - \frac{3}{4} = \frac{1}{8}$ $\left\{\frac{7}{4}\right\}$

31. $2(x - 3) = 3(x - 2)$ $\{0\}$

32. $2(3x - 3) = 3(2x - 2)$ All real numbers

Solve.

33. Find the x-intercept for the line $y = 2x + 1$. $\left(-\frac{1}{2}, 0\right)$

34. Find the y-intercept for the line $y = x - 7$. $(0, -7)$

35. Find the slope of the line $y = 2x + 1$. 2

36. Find the slope of the line that goes through $(0, 0)$ and $\left(\frac{1}{2}, \frac{1}{3}\right)$. $\frac{2}{3}$

37. If $y = \frac{3}{4}x - 3$ and y is $\frac{1}{2}$, then what is x? $\frac{14}{3}$

38. Find y if $y = \frac{x}{2} - \frac{3}{4}$ and x is $\frac{1}{2}$. $-\frac{1}{2}$

Solve the problem.

39. ***Average cost.*** Pineapple Recording plans to spend \$100,000 to record a new CD by the Woozies and \$2.25 per CD to manufacture the disks. The polynomial $2.25n + 100{,}000$ represents the total cost in dollars for recording and manufacturing n disks. Find an expression that represents the average cost per disk by dividing the total cost by n. Find the average cost per disk for $n = 1000$, 100,000, and 1,000,000. What happens to the large initial investment of \$100,000 if the company sells one million CDs?
$\frac{2.25n + 100{,}000}{n}$, \$102.25, \$3.25, \$2.35, It averages out to 10 cents per disk.

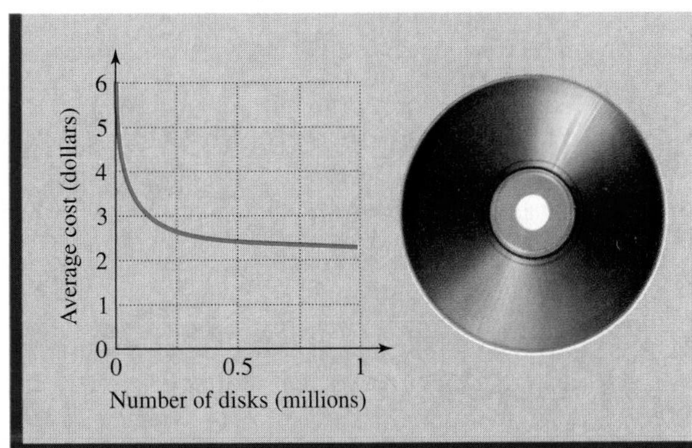

Figure for Exercise 39

Critical **Thinking** | For Individual or Group Work | Chapter 4

These exercises can be solved by a variety of techniques, which may or may not require algebra. So be creative and think critically. Explain all answers. Answers are in the Instructor's Edition of this text.

1. ***Throwing darts.*** A dart board contains a region worth 9 points and a region worth 4 points as shown in the accompanying figure. If you are allowed to throw as many darts as you wish, then what is the largest possible total score that you *cannot* get?

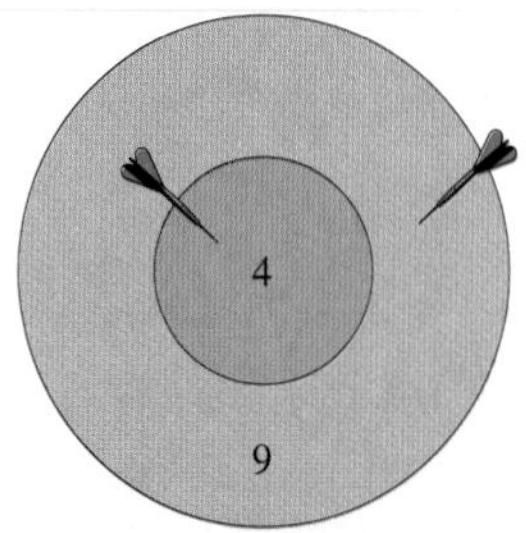

Figure for Exercise 1

2. ***Counting squares.*** A square checkerboard is made up of 36 alternately colored 1 inch by 1 inch squares.

a) What is the total number of squares that are visible on this checkerboard? (*Hint:* Count the 6 by 6 squares, then the 5 by 5 squares, and so on.)

b) How many are visible on a checkerboard that has 64 alternately colored 1 inch by 1 inch squares?

3. ***Four fours.*** Check out these equations:

$$\frac{4+4}{4+4} = 1, \quad \frac{4}{4} + \frac{4}{4} = 2, \quad 4 - 4^{4-4} = 3.$$

a) Using exactly four 4's write arithmetic expressions whose values are 4, 5, 6, and so on. How far can you go?

b) Repeat this exercise using four 5's, three 4's, and three 5's.

4. ***Four coins.*** Place four coins on a table with heads facing downward. On each move you must turn over exactly three coins. Count the number of moves it takes to get all four coins with heads facing upward. What is the minimum number of moves necessary to get all four heads facing upward?

5. ***Snakes and iguanas.*** A woman has a collection of snakes and iguanas. Her young son observed that the reptiles have a total of 50 eyes and 56 feet. How many reptiles of each type does the woman have?

Photo for Exercise 5

6. ***Hungry bugs.*** If it takes a colony of termites one day to devour a block of wood that is 2 inches wide, 2 inches long, and 2 inches high, then how long will it take them to devour a block of wood that is 4 inches wide, 4 inches long, and 4 inches high. Assume that they keep eating at the same rate.

7. ***Ancient history.*** This problem is from the second century. Four numbers have a sum of 9900. The second exceeds the first by one-seventh of the first. The third exceeds the sum of the first two by 300. The fourth exceeds the sum of the first three by 300. Find the four numbers.

8. ***Related digits.*** What is the largest four-digit number such that the second digit is one-fourth of the third digit, the third digit is twice the first digit, and the last digit is the same as the first digit?

1. 23 **2. a)** 91 **b)** 204 **3.** $4^{4-4} \cdot 4 = 4$, $4^{4-4} + 4 = 5$, $(4!)/4 + 4 - 4 = 6$ **4.** 4 **5.** 11 snakes and 14 iguanas **6.** 8 days **7.** 1050, 1200, 2550, 5100 **8.** 4284

Chapter 5

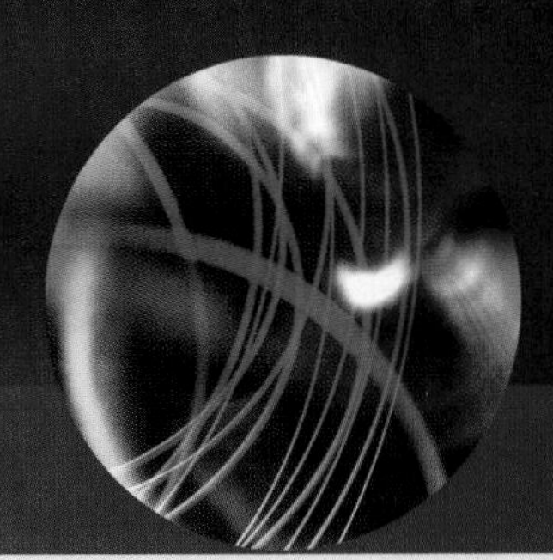

Factoring

The sport of skydiving was born in the 1930s soon after the military began using parachutes as a means of deploying troops. Today, skydiving is a popular sport around the world.

With as little as 8 hours of ground instruction, first-time jumpers can be ready to make a solo jump. Without the assistance of oxygen, skydivers can jump from as high as 14,000 feet and reach speeds of more than 100 miles per hour as they fall toward the earth. Jumpers usually open their parachutes between 2000 and 3000 feet and then gradually glide down to their landing area. If the jump and the parachute are handled correctly, the landing can be as gentle as jumping off two steps.

Making a jump and floating to earth are only part of the sport of skydiving. For example, in an activity called "relative work skydiving," a team of as many as 920 free-falling skydivers join together to make geometrically shaped formations. In a related exercise called "canopy relative work," the team members form geometric patterns after their parachutes or canopies have opened. This kind of skydiving takes skill and practice, and teams are not always successful in their attempts.

The amount of time a skydiver has for a free fall depends on the height of the jump and how much the skydiver uses the air to slow the fall.

In Exercises 81 and 82 of Section 5.6 we find the amount of time that it takes a skydiver to fall from a given height.

5.1 Factoring Out Common Factors

In this Section

- **Prime Factorization of Integers**
- **Greatest Common Factor**
- **Finding the Greatest Common Factor for Monomials**
- **Factoring Out the Greatest Common Factor**
- **Factoring Out the Opposite of the GCF**

In Chapter 4 you learned how to multiply a monomial and a polynomial. In this section you will learn how to reverse that multiplication by finding the greatest common factor for the terms of a polynomial and then factoring the polynomial.

Prime Factorization of Integers

To **factor** an expression means to write the expression as a product. For example, if we start with 12 and write $12 = 4 \cdot 3$, we have factored 12. Both 4 and 3 are **factors** or **divisors** of 12. There are other factorizations of 12:

$$12 = 2 \cdot 6 \qquad 12 = 1 \cdot 12 \qquad 12 = 2 \cdot 2 \cdot 3 = 2^2 \cdot 3$$

The one that is most useful to us is $12 = 2^2 \cdot 3$, because it expresses 12 as a product of *prime numbers.*

Teaching Tip If 1 was allowed to be prime, then there would be more than one way to factor a composite number using primes. For example, $6 = 2 \cdot 3$ and $6 = 1 \cdot 2 \cdot 3$.

Prime Number

A positive integer larger than 1 that has no integral factors other than itself and 1 is called a **prime number.**

The numbers 2, 3, 5, 7, 11, 13, 17, 19, and 23 are the first nine prime numbers. A positive integer larger than 1 that is not a prime is a **composite number.** The numbers 4, 6, 8, 9, 10, and 12 are the first six composite numbers. Every composite number is a product of prime numbers. The **prime factorization** for 12 is $2^2 \cdot 3$.

EXAMPLE 1

Prime factorization

Find the prime factorization for 36.

Solution

We start by writing 36 as a product of two integers:

$$\begin{aligned} 36 &= 2 \cdot 18 && \text{Write 36 as } 2 \cdot 18. \\ &= 2 \cdot 2 \cdot 9 && \text{Replace 18 by } 2 \cdot 9. \\ &= 2 \cdot 2 \cdot 3 \cdot 3 && \text{Replace 9 by } 3 \cdot 3. \\ &= 2^2 \cdot 3^2 && \text{Use exponential notation.} \end{aligned}$$

The prime factorization for 36 is $2^2 \cdot 3^2$.

Now do Exercises 7–12

Helpful Hint

The prime factorization of 36 can be found also with a *factoring tree:*

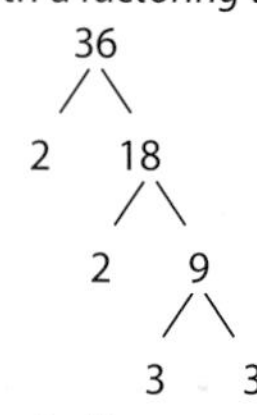

So $36 = 2 \cdot 2 \cdot 3 \cdot 3$.

For larger integers, it is better to use the method shown in Example 2 and to recall some divisibility rules. Even numbers are divisible by 2. If the sum of the digits of a number is divisible by 3, then the number is divisible by 3. Numbers that end in 0 or 5 are divisible by 5. Two-digit numbers with repeated digits (11, 22, 33, . . .) are divisible by 11.

EXAMPLE 2

Factoring a large number

Find the prime factorization for 420.

Helpful Hint

The fact that every composite number has a unique prime factorization is known as the fundamental theorem of arithmetic.

Solution

Start by dividing 420 by the smallest prime number that will divide into it evenly (without remainder). The smallest prime divisor of 420 is 2.

$$2\overline{)420}\quad 210$$

Now find the smallest prime that will divide evenly into the quotient, 210. The smallest prime divisor of 210 is 2. Continue this procedure, as follows, until the quotient is a prime number:

$$\begin{array}{rl} 7 & 35 \div 5 = 7 \\ 5\overline{)35} & 105 \div 3 = 35 \\ 3\overline{)105} & 210 \div 2 = 105 \\ 2\overline{)210} & \\ \text{Start here} \rightarrow\ 2\overline{)420} & \end{array}$$

The prime factorization for 420 is $2 \cdot 2 \cdot 3 \cdot 5 \cdot 7$, or $2^2 \cdot 3 \cdot 5 \cdot 7$. Note that it is really not necessary to divide by the smallest prime divisor at each step. We obtain the same factorization if we divide by any prime divisor at each step.

Now do Exercises 13–16

Greatest Common Factor

The largest integer that is a factor of two or more integers is called the **greatest common factor (GCF)** of the integers. For example, 1, 2, 3, and 6 are common factors of 18 and 24. Because 6 is the largest, 6 is the GCF of 18 and 24. We can use prime factorizations to find the GCF. For example, to find the GCF of 8 and 12, we first factor 8 and 12:

$$8 = 2 \cdot 2 \cdot 2 = 2^3 \qquad 12 = 2 \cdot 2 \cdot 3 = 2^2 \cdot 3$$

We see that the factor 2 appears twice in both 8 and 12. So 2^2, or 4, is the GCF of 8 and 12. Notice that 2 is a factor in both 2^3 and $2^2 \cdot 3$ and that 2^2 is the smallest power of 2 in these factorizations. In general, we can use the following strategy to find the GCF.

Strategy for Finding the GCF for Positive Integers

1. Find the prime factorization for each integer.
2. The GCF is the product of the common prime factors using the smallest exponent that appears on each of them.

If two integers have no common prime factors, then their greatest common factor is 1, because 1 is a factor of every integer. For example, 6 and 35 have no common prime factors because $6 = 2 \cdot 3$ and $35 = 5 \cdot 7$. However, because $6 = 1 \cdot 6$ and $35 = 1 \cdot 35$, the GCF for 6 and 35 is 1.

EXAMPLE 3

Greatest common factor

Find the GCF for each group of numbers.

a) 150, 225 **b)** 216, 360, 504 **c)** 55, 168

Teaching Tip Students often find the GCF for small numbers without factoring. With larger numbers factoring is essential.

Solution

a) First find the prime factorization for each number:

$$\begin{array}{r} 5 \\ 5\overline{)25} \\ 3\overline{)75} \\ 2\overline{)150} \end{array} \qquad \begin{array}{r} 5 \\ 5\overline{)25} \\ 3\overline{)75} \\ 3\overline{)225} \end{array}$$

$$150 = 2 \cdot 3 \cdot 5^2 \qquad 225 = 3^2 \cdot 5^2$$

Because 2 is not a factor of 225, it is not a common factor of 150 and 225. Only 3 and 5 appear in both factorizations. Looking at both $2 \cdot 3 \cdot 5^2$ and $3^2 \cdot 5^2$, we see that the smallest power of 5 is 2 and the smallest power of 3 is 1. So the GCF for 150 and 225 is $3 \cdot 5^2$, or 75.

b) First find the prime factorization for each number:

$$216 = 2^3 \cdot 3^3 \qquad 360 = 2^3 \cdot 3^2 \cdot 5 \qquad 504 = 2^3 \cdot 3^2 \cdot 7$$

The only common prime factors are 2 and 3. The smallest power of 2 in the factorizations is 3, and the smallest power of 3 is 2. So the GCF is $2^3 \cdot 3^2$, or 72.

c) First find the prime factorization for each number:

$$55 = 5 \cdot 11 \qquad 168 = 2^3 \cdot 3 \cdot 7$$

Because there are no common factors other than 1, the GCF is 1.

Now do Exercises 17–26

Finding the Greatest Common Factor for Monomials

To find the GCF for a group of monomials, we use the same procedure as that used for integers.

Strategy for Finding the GCF for Monomials

1. Find the GCF for the coefficients of the monomials.
2. Form the product of the GCF for the coefficients and each variable that is common to all of the monomials, where the exponent on each variable is the smallest power of that variable in any of the monomials.

Math *at Work* Kayak Design

Kayaks have been built by the Aleut and Inuit people for the past 4000 years. Today's builders have access to materials and techniques unavailable to the original kayak builders. Modern kayakers incorporate hydrodynamics and materials technology to create designs that are efficient and stable. Builders measure how well their designs work by calculating indicators such as prismatic coefficient, block coefficient, and the midship area coefficient, to name a few.

Even the fitting of a kayak to the paddler is done scientifically. For example, the formula

$$PL = 2 \cdot BL + BS\left(0.38 \cdot EE + 1.2\sqrt{\left(\frac{BW}{2} - \frac{SW}{2}\right)^2 + (SL)^2}\right)$$

can be used to calculate the appropriate paddle length. BL is the length of the paddle's blade. BS is a boating style factor, which is 1.2 for touring, 1.0 for river running, and 0.95 for play boating. EE is the elbow to elbow distance with the paddler's arms straight out to the sides. BW is the boat width and SW is the shoulder width. SL is the spine length, which is the distance measured in a sitting position from the chair seat to the top of the paddler's shoulder. All lengths are in centimeters.

The degree of control a kayaker exerts over the kayak depends largely on the body contact with it. A kayaker wears the kayak. So the choice of a kayak should hinge first on the right body fit and comfort and second on the skill level or intended paddling style. So designing, building, and even fitting a kayak is a blend of art and science.

EXAMPLE 4

Greatest common factor for monomials

Find the greatest common factor for each group of monomials.

a) $15x^2, 9x^3$ **b)** $12x^2y^2, 30x^2yz, 42x^3y$

Solution

a) The GCF for 15 and 9 is 3, and the smallest power of x is 2. So the GCF for the monomials is $3x^2$. If we write these monomials as

$$15x^2 = 5 \cdot 3 \cdot x \cdot x \quad \text{and} \quad 9x^3 = 3 \cdot 3 \cdot x \cdot x \cdot x,$$

we can see that $3x^2$ is the GCF.

b) The GCF for 12, 30, and 42 is 6. For the common variables x and y, 2 is the smallest power of x and 1 is the smallest power of y. So the GCF for the monomials is $6x^2y$.

Now do Exercises 27–38

Study Tip

Success in school depends on effective time management, and effective time management is all about goals. Write down your long-term, short-term, and daily goals. Assess them, develop methods for meeting them, and reward yourself when you do.

Factoring Out the Greatest Common Factor

In Chapter 4 we used the distributive property to multiply monomials and polynomials. For example,

$$6(5x - 3) = 30x - 18.$$

If we start with $30x - 18$ and write

$$30x - 18 = 6(5x - 3),$$

we have factored $30x - 18$. Because multiplication is the last operation to be performed in $6(5x - 3)$, the expression $6(5x - 3)$ is a product. Because 6 is the GCF for 30 and 18, we have **factored out** the GCF.

EXAMPLE 5

Factoring out the greatest common factor

Factor the following polynomials by factoring out the GCF.

a) $25a^2 + 40a$ **b)** $6x^4 - 12x^3 + 3x^2$ **c)** $x^2y^5 + x^6y^3$

Solution

a) The GCF for the coefficients 25 and 40 is 5. Because the smallest power of the common factor a is 1, we can factor $5a$ out of each term:

$$\begin{aligned} 25a^2 + 40a &= 5a \cdot 5a + 5a \cdot 8 \\ &= 5a(5a + 8) \end{aligned}$$

b) The GCF for 6, 12, and 3 is 3. We can factor x^2 out of each term, since the smallest power of x in the three terms is 2. So factor $3x^2$ out of each term as follows:

$$\begin{aligned} 6x^4 - 12x^3 + 3x^2 &= 3x^2 \cdot 2x^2 - 3x^2 \cdot 4x + 3x^2 \cdot 1 \\ &= 3x^2(2x^2 - 4x + 1) \end{aligned}$$

Check by multiplying: $3x^2(2x^2 - 4x + 1) = 6x^4 - 12x^3 + 3x^2$.

c) The GCF for the numerical coefficients is 1. Both x and y are common to each term. Using the lowest powers of x and y, we get

$$\begin{aligned} x^2y^5 + x^6y^3 &= x^2y^3 \cdot y^2 + x^2y^3 \cdot x^4 \\ &= x^2y^3(y^2 + x^4). \end{aligned}$$

Check by multiplying.

Now do Exercises 51–66

Study Tip

The keys to college success are motivation and time management. Anyone who tells you that they are making great grades without studying is probably not telling the truth. Success in college takes effort.

Because of the commutative property of multiplication, the common factor can be placed on either side of the other factor. So in Example 5, the answers could be written as $(5a + 8)5a$, $(2x^2 - 4x + 1)3x^2$, and $(y^2 + x^4)x^2y^3$.

Teaching Tip Emphasize the 1 here. Students often write $ab + b = a(b)$.

CAUTION If the GCF is one of the terms of the polynomial, then you must remember to leave a 1 in place of that term when the GCF is factored out. For example,

$$ab + b = a \cdot b + 1 \cdot b = b(a + 1).$$

You should always check your answer by multiplying the factors.

In Example 6 the greatest common factor is a binomial. This type of factoring will be used in factoring trinomials in Section 5.2.

EXAMPLE 6

A binomial factor

Factor out the greatest common factor.

a) $(a + b)w + (a + b)6$ **b)** $x(x + 2) + 3(x + 2)$

c) $y(y - 3) - (y - 3)$

Teaching Tip Remind students that the commutative property enables us to place the GCF on the left or right when it is factored out.

Solution

a) The greatest common factor is $a + b$:

$$(a + b)w + (a + b)6 = (a + b)(w + 6)$$

b) The greatest common factor is $x + 2$:

$$x(x + 2) + 3(x + 2) = (x + 3)(x + 2)$$

c) The greatest common factor is $y - 3$:

$$y(y - 3) - (y - 3) = y(y - 3) - 1(y - 3)$$
$$= (y - 1)(y - 3)$$

Now do Exercises 67–74

Teaching Tip Ask students why we say opposite of the GCF rather than negative GCF.

Factoring Out the Opposite of the GCF

The greatest common factor for $-4x + 2xy$ is $2x$. Note that you can factor out the GCF ($2x$) or the opposite of the GCF ($-2x$):

$$-4x + 2xy = 2x(-2 + y) \qquad -4x + 2xy = -2x(2 - y)$$

It is useful to know both of these factorizations. For example, if we wanted to show that $2 - y$ is a factor of $-4x + 2xy$, then the second factorization shows it. Factoring out the opposite of the GCF will be used in factoring by grouping in Section 5.2 and in factoring trinomials with negative leading coefficients in Section 5.4. Remember to check all factoring by multiplying the factors to see if you get the original polynomial.

EXAMPLE 7

Factoring out the opposite of the GCF

Factor each polynomial twice. First factor out the greatest common factor, and then factor out the opposite of the GCF.

a) $3x - 3y$ **b)** $a - b$

c) $-x^3 + 2x^2 - 8x$

Solution

a) $3x - 3y = 3(x - y)$ Factor out 3.

$= -3(-x + y)$ Factor out -3.

Note that the signs of the terms in parentheses change when -3 is factored out. Check the answers by multiplying.

b) $a - b = 1(a - b)$ Factor out 1, the GCF of a and b.

$= -1(-a + b)$ Factor out -1.

We can also write $a - b = -1(b - a)$.

c) $-x^3 + 2x^2 - 8x = x(-x^2 + 2x - 8)$ Factor out x.

$= -x(x^2 - 2x + 8)$ Factor out $-x$.

Now do Exercises 75–90

CAUTION Be sure to change the sign of each term in parentheses when you factor out the opposite of the greatest common factor.

Warm-Ups

True or false? Explain your answer.

1. There are only nine prime numbers. False
2. The prime factorization of 32 is $2^3 \cdot 3$. False
3. The integer 51 is a prime number. False
4. The GCF for the integers 12 and 16 is 4. True
5. The GCF for the integers 10 and 21 is 1. True
6. The GCF for the polynomial $x^5y^3 - x^4y^7$ is x^4y^3. True
7. For the polynomial $2x^2y - 6xy^2$ we can factor out either $2xy$ or $-2xy$. True
8. The greatest common factor for the polynomial $8a^3b - 12a^2b$ is $4ab$. False
9. $x - 7 = 7 - x$ for any real number x. False
10. $-3x^2 + 6x = -3x(x - 2)$ for any real number x. True

5.1 Exercises

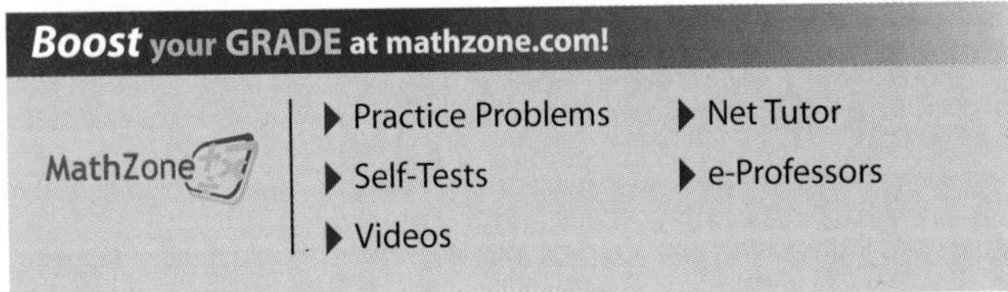

Reading and Writing *After reading this section, write out the answers to these questions. Use complete sentences.*

1. What does it mean to factor an expression?
To factor means to write as a product.
2. What is a prime number?
A prime number is an integer greater than 1 that has no factors besides itself and 1.
3. How do you find the prime factorization for a number?
You can find the prime factorization by dividing by prime factors until the result is prime.
4. What is the greatest common factor for two numbers?
The GCF for two numbers is the largest number that is a factor of both.
5. What is the greatest common factor for two monomials?
The GCF for two monomials consists of the GCF of their coefficients and every variable that they have in common raised to the lowest power that appears on the variable.
6. How can you check if you have factored an expression correctly?
You can check all factoring by multiplying the factors.

Find the prime factorization of each integer. See Examples 1 and 2.

7. 18 $2 \cdot 3^2$
8. 20 $2^2 \cdot 5$
9. 52 $2^2 \cdot 13$
10. 76 $2^2 \cdot 19$
11. 98 $2 \cdot 7^2$
12. 100 $2^2 \cdot 5^2$
13. 460 $2^2 \cdot 5 \cdot 23$
14. 345 $3 \cdot 5 \cdot 23$
15. 924 $2^2 \cdot 3 \cdot 7 \cdot 11$
16. 585 $3^2 \cdot 5 \cdot 13$

Find the greatest common factor (GCF) for each group of integers. See Example 3.

17. 8, 20 4
18. 18, 42 6
19. 36, 60 12
20. 42, 70 14
21. 40, 48, 88 8
22. 15, 35, 45 5
23. 76, 84, 100 4
24. 66, 72, 120 6
25. 39, 68, 77 1
26. 81, 200, 539 1

Find the greatest common factor (GCF) for each group of monomials. See Example 4.

27. $6x, 8x^3$ $2x$
28. $12x^2, 4x^3$ $4x^2$
29. $12x^3, 4x^2, 6x$ $2x$
30. $3y^5, 9y^4, 15y^3$ $3y^3$
31. $3x^2y, 2xy^2$ xy
32. $7a^2x^3, 5a^3x$ a^2x
33. $24a^2bc, 60ab^2$ $12ab$
34. $30x^2yz^3, 75x^3yz^6$ $15x^2yz^3$
35. $12u^3v^2, 25s^2t^4$ 1
36. $45m^2n^5, 56a^4b^8$ 1
37. $18a^3b, 30a^2b^2, 54ab^3$ $6ab$
38. $16x^2z, 40xz^2, 72z^3$ $8z$

Complete the factoring of each monomial.

39. $27x = 9(3x)$
40. $51y = 3y(17)$
41. $24t^2 = 8t(3t)$
42. $18u^2 = 3u(6u)$
43. $36y^5 = 4y^2(9y^3)$
44. $42z^4 = 3z^2(14z^2)$
45. $u^4v^3 = uv(u^3v^2)$
46. $x^5y^3 = x^2y(x^3y^2)$
47. $-14m^4n^3 = 2m^4(-7n^3)$
48. $-8y^3z^4 = 4z^3(-2y^3z)$
49. $-33x^4y^3z^2 = -3x^3yz(11xy^2z)$
50. $-96a^3b^4c^5 = -12ab^3c^3(8a^2bc^2)$

Factor out the GCF in each expression. See Example 5.

51. $2w + 4t$ $2(w + 2t)$
52. $6y + 3$ $3(2y + 1)$
53. $12x - 18y$ $6(2x - 3y)$
54. $24a - 36b$ $12(2a - 3b)$
55. $x^3 - 6x$ $x(x^2 - 6)$
56. $10y^4 - 30y^2$ $10y^2(y^2 - 3)$
57. $5ax + 5ay$ $5a(x + y)$
58. $6wz + 15wa$ $3w(2z + 5a)$
59. $h^5 + h^3$ $h^3(h^2 + 1)$
60. $y^6 + y^5$ $y^5(y + 1)$
61. $-2k^7m^4 + 4k^3m^6$ $2k^3m^4(-k^4 + 2m^2)$
62. $-6h^5t^2 + 3h^3t^6$ $3h^3t^2(-2h^2 + t^4)$
63. $2x^3 - 6x^2 + 8x$ $2x(x^2 - 3x + 4)$
64. $6x^3 + 18x^2 + 24x$ $6x(x^2 + 3x + 4)$
65. $12x^4t + 30x^3t - 24x^2t^2$ $6x^2t(2x^2 + 5x - 4t)$
66. $15x^2y^2 - 9xy^2 + 6x^2y$ $3xy(5xy - 3y + 2x)$

Factor out the GCF in each expression. See Example 6.

67. $(x - 3)a + (x - 3)b$ $(x - 3)(a + b)$
68. $(y + 4)3 + (y + 4)z$ $(y + 4)(3 + z)$
69. $x(x - 1) - 5(x - 1)$ $(x - 5)(x - 1)$
70. $a(a + 1) - 3(a + 1)$ $(a - 3)(a + 1)$
71. $m(m + 9) + (m + 9)$ $(m + 1)(m + 9)$
72. $(x - 2)x - (x - 2)$ $(x - 2)(x - 1)$
73. $a(y + 1)^2 + b(y + 1)^2$ $(a + b)(y + 1)^2$
74. $w(w + 2)^2 + 8(w + 2)^2$ $(w + 8)(w + 2)^2$

First factor out the GCF, and then factor out the opposite of the GCF. See Example 7.

75. $8x - 8y$ $8(x - y), -8(-x + y)$
76. $2a - 6b$ $2(a - 3b), -2(-a + 3b)$
77. $-4x + 8x^2$ $4x(-1 + 2x), -4x(1 - 2x)$
78. $-5x^2 + 10x$ $5x(-x + 2), -5x(x - 2)$
79. $x - 5$ $1(x - 5), -1(-x + 5)$
80. $a - 6$ $1(a - 6), -1(-a + 6)$
81. $4 - 7a$ $1(4 - 7a), -1(-4 + 7a)$
82. $7 - 5b$ $1(7 - 5b), -1(-7 + 5b)$
83. $-24a^3 + 16a^2$ $8a^2(-3a + 2), -8a^2(3a - 2)$
84. $-30b^4 + 75b^3$ $15b^3(-2b + 5), -15b^3(2b - 5)$
85. $-12x^2 - 18x$ $6x(-2x - 3), -6x(2x + 3)$
86. $-20b^2 - 8b$ $4b(-5b - 2), -4b(5b + 2)$
87. $-2x^3 - 6x^2 + 14x$
$2x(-x^2 - 3x + 7), -2x(x^2 + 3x - 7)$
88. $-8x^4 + 6x^3 - 2x^2$
$2x^2(-4x^2 + 3x - 1), -2x^2(4x^2 - 3x + 1)$
89. $4a^3b - 6a^2b^2 - 4ab^3$
$2ab(2a^2 - 3ab - 2b^2), -2ab(-2a^2 + 3ab + 2b^2)$
90. $12u^5v^6 + 18u^2v^3 - 15u^4v^5$
$3u^2v^3(4u^3v^3 + 6 - 5u^2v^2), -3u^2v^3(-4u^3v^3 - 6 + 5u^2v^2)$

Solve each problem by factoring.

91. ***Uniform motion.*** Helen traveled a distance of $20x + 40$ miles at 20 miles per hour on the Yellowhead Highway. Find a binomial that represents the time that she traveled. $x + 2$ hours

92. ***Area of a painting.*** A rectangular painting with a width of x centimeters has an area of $x^2 + 50x$ square centimeters. Find a binomial that represents the length. See the figure on the next page. $x + 50$ cm

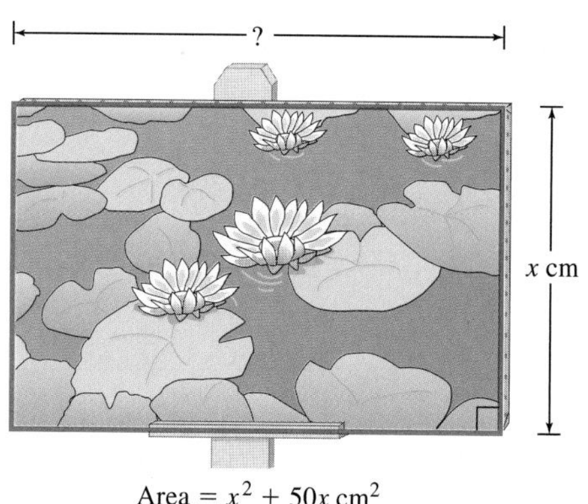

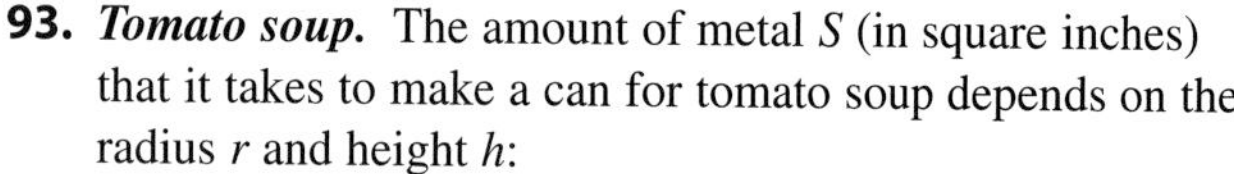

Figure for Exercise 92

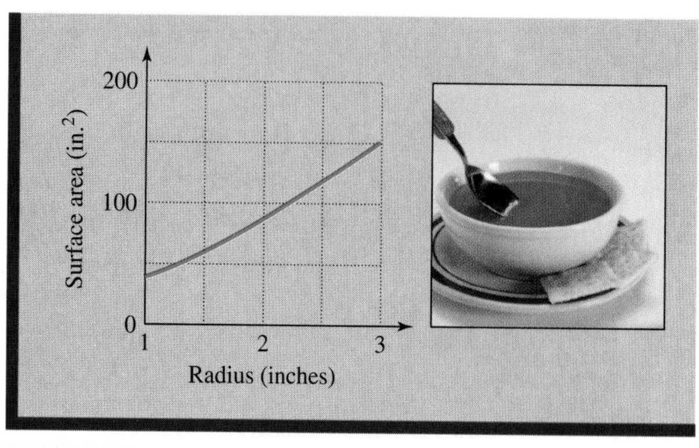

Figure for Exercise 93

93. ***Tomato soup.*** The amount of metal S (in square inches) that it takes to make a can for tomato soup depends on the radius r and height h:

$$S = 2\pi r^2 + 2\pi rh$$

a) Rewrite this formula by factoring out the greatest common factor on the right-hand side. $S = 2\pi r(r + h)$

b) Let $h = 5$ in. and write a formula that expresses S in terms of r. $S = 2\pi r^2 + 10\pi r$

c) The accompanying graph shows S for r between 1 in. and 3 in. (with $h = 5$ in.). Which of these r-values gives the maximum surface area? 3 in.

94. ***Amount of an investment.*** The amount of an investment of P dollars for t years at simple interest rate r is given by $A = P + Prt$.

a) Rewrite this formula by factoring out the greatest common factor on the right-hand side. $A = P(1 + rt)$

b) Find A if \$8300 is invested for 3 years at a simple interest rate of 15%. \$12,035

Getting More Involved

95. ***Discussion***

Is the greatest common factor of $-6x^2 + 3x$ positive or negative? Explain.
The GCF is an algebraic expression.

96. ***Writing***

Explain in your own words why you use the smallest power of each common prime factor when finding the GCF of two or more integers.

5.2 Factoring the Special Products and Factoring by Grouping

In this Section

- Factoring a Difference of Two Squares
- Factoring a Perfect Square Trinomial
- Factoring Completely
- Factoring by Grouping

In Section 4.4 you learned how to find the special products: the square of a sum, the square of a difference, and the product of a sum and a difference. In this section you will learn how to reverse those operations.

Factoring a Difference of Two Squares

In Section 4.4 you learned that the product of a sum and a difference is a difference of two squares:

$$(a + b)(a - b) = a^2 - ab + ab - b^2 = a^2 - b^2$$

So a difference of two squares can be factored as a product of a sum and a difference, using the following rule.

Factoring a Difference of Two Squares

For any real numbers a and b,

$$a^2 - b^2 = (a + b)(a - b).$$

Note that the square of an integer is a perfect square. For example, 64 is a perfect square because $64 = 8^2$. The square of a monomial in which the coefficient is an integer is also called a **perfect square** or simply a **square.** For example, $9m^2$ is a perfect square because $9m^2 = (3m)^2$.

EXAMPLE 1

Factoring a difference of two squares

Factor each polynomial.

a) $y^2 - 81$ **b)** $9m^2 - 16$ **c)** $4x^2 - 9y^2$

Solution

a) Because $81 = 9^2$, the binomial $y^2 - 81$ is a difference of two squares:

$$\begin{aligned} y^2 - 81 &= y^2 - 9^2 && \text{Rewrite as a difference of two squares.} \\ &= (y + 9)(y - 9) && \text{Factor.} \end{aligned}$$

Check by multiplying.

b) Because $9m^2 = (3m)^2$ and $16 = 4^2$, the binomial $9m^2 - 16$ is a difference of two squares:

$$\begin{aligned} 9m^2 - 16 &= (3m)^2 - 4^2 && \text{Rewrite as a difference of two squares.} \\ &= (3m + 4)(3m - 4) && \text{Factor.} \end{aligned}$$

Check by multiplying.

c) Because $4x^2 = (2x)^2$ and $9y^2 = (3y)^2$, the binomial $4x^2 - 9y^2$ is a difference of two squares:

$$4x^2 - 9y^2 = (2x + 3y)(2x - 3y)$$

Now do Exercises 7–18

Factoring a Perfect Square Trinomial

In Section 4.4 you learned how to square a binomial using the rule

$$(a + b)^2 = a^2 + 2ab + b^2.$$

You can reverse this rule to factor a trinomial such as $x^2 + 6x + 9$. Notice that

$$x^2 + 6x + 9 = \underset{\uparrow\atop a^2}{x^2} + \underbrace{2 \cdot x \cdot 3}_{2ab} + \underset{\uparrow\atop b^2}{3^2}.$$

Teaching Tip Emphasize that learning the special cases now will pay off later. The special cases are presented prior to general trinomial factoring, because students do not see the need to learn them after learning the general methods.

So if $a = x$ and $b = 3$, then $x^2 + 6x + 9$ fits the form $a^2 + 2ab + b^2$, and

$$x^2 + 6x + 9 = (x + 3)^2.$$

A trinomial that is of the form $a^2 + 2ab + b^2$ or $a^2 - 2ab + b^2$ is called a **perfect square trinomial.** A perfect square trinomial is the square of a binomial. Perfect square trinomials can be identified by using the following strategy.

Strategy for Identifying a Perfect Square Trinomial

A trinomial is a perfect square trinomial if

1. the first and last terms are of the form a^2 and b^2 (perfect squares).

2. the middle term is $2ab$ or $-2ab$.

EXAMPLE 2

Identifying the special products

Determine whether each binomial is a difference of two squares and whether each trinomial is a perfect square trinomial.

a) $x^2 - 14x + 49$ **b)** $4x^2 - 81$

c) $4a^2 + 24a + 25$ **d)** $9y^2 - 24y - 16$

Study Tip

A lumber mill turns logs into plywood, adding value to the logs. College is like a lumber mill. If you are not changing, growing, and learning, you may not be increasing in value. Everything that you learn increases your value.

Solution

a) The first term is x^2, and the last term is 7^2. The middle term, $-14x$, is $-2 \cdot x \cdot 7$. So this trinomial is a perfect square trinomial.

b) Both terms of $4x^2 - 81$ are perfect squares, $(2x)^2$ and 9^2. So $4x^2 - 81$ is a difference of two squares.

c) The first term of $4a^2 + 24a + 25$ is $(2a)^2$ and the last term is 5^2. However, $2 \cdot 2a \cdot 5$ is $20a$. Because the middle term is $24a$, this trinomial is not a perfect square trinomial.

d) The first and last terms in a perfect square trinomial are both positive. Because the last term in $9y^2 - 24y - 16$ is negative, the trinomial is not a perfect square trinomial.

Now do Exercises 19–30

Note that the middle term in a perfect square trinomial may have a positive or a negative coefficient, while the first and last terms must be positive. Any perfect square trinomial can be factored as the square of a binomial by using the following rule.

Factoring Perfect Square Trinomials

For any real numbers a and b,

$$a^2 + 2ab + b^2 = (a + b)^2$$

$$a^2 - 2ab + b^2 = (a - b)^2.$$

EXAMPLE 3

Factoring perfect square trinomials

Factor.

a) $x^2 - 4x + 4$ **b)** $a^2 + 16a + 64$ **c)** $4x^2 - 12x + 9$

Solution

a) The first term is x^2, and the last term is 2^2. Because the middle term is $-2 \cdot 2 \cdot x$, or $-4x$, this polynomial is a perfect square trinomial:

$$x^2 - 4x + 4 = (x - 2)^2$$

Check by expanding $(x - 2)^2$.

b) $a^2 + 16a + 64 = (a + 8)^2$

Check by expanding $(a + 8)^2$.

c) The first term is $(2x)^2$, and the last term is 3^2. Because $-2 \cdot 2x \cdot 3 = -12x$, the polynomial is a perfect square trinomial. So

$$4x^2 - 12x + 9 = (2x - 3)^2.$$

Check by expanding $(2x - 3)^2$.

Now do Exercises 31–48

Factoring Completely

To factor a polynomial means to write it as a product of simpler polynomials. A polynomial that cannot be factored is called a **prime** or **irreducible polynomial.** The polynomials $3x$, $w + 1$, and $4m - 5$ are prime polynomials. A polynomial is **factored completely** when it is written as a product of prime polynomials. So $(y - 8)(y + 1)$ is a complete factorization. When factoring polynomials, we usually do not factor integers that occur as common factors. So $6x(x - 7)$ is considered to be factored completely even though 6 could be factored.

Some polynomials have a factor common to all terms. To factor such polynomials completely, it is simpler to factor out the greatest common factor (GCF) and then factor the remaining polynomial. Example 4 illustrates factoring completely.

EXAMPLE 4

Factoring completely

Factor each polynomial completely.

a) $2x^3 - 50x$ **b)** $8x^2y - 32xy + 32y$

Solution

a) The greatest common factor of $2x^3$ and $50x$ is $2x$:

$$2x^3 - 50x = 2x(x^2 - 25) \quad \text{Check this step by multiplying.}$$
$$= 2x(x + 5)(x - 5) \quad \text{Difference of two squares}$$

b) $8x^2y - 32xy + 32y = 8y(x^2 - 4x + 4)$ Check this step by multiplying.

$= 8y(x - 2)^2$ Perfect square trinomial

Now do Exercises 49–68

Study Tip

When you take notes, leave space. Go back later and fill in more details, make corrections, or work another problem of the same type.

Remember that factoring reverses multiplication and *every step of factoring can be checked by multiplication.*

Factoring by Grouping

The product of two binomials may be a polynomial with four terms. For example,

$$(x + a)(x + 3) = (x + a)x + (x + a)3$$
$$= x^2 + ax + 3x + 3a.$$

We can factor a polynomial of this type by simply reversing the steps we used to find the product. To reverse these steps, we factor out common factors from the first two terms and from the last two terms. This procedure is called **factoring by grouping.**

EXAMPLE 5

Factoring by grouping

Use grouping to factor each polynomial completely.

a) $xy + 2y + 3x + 6$ **b)** $2x^3 - 3x^2 - 2x + 3$ **c)** $ax + 3y - 3x - ay$

Solution

a) Notice that the first two terms have a common factor of y and the last two terms have a common factor of 3:

$$xy + 2y + 3x + 6 = (xy + 2y) + (3x + 6) \quad \text{Use the associative property to group the terms.}$$
$$= y(x + 2) + 3(x + 2) \quad \text{Factor out the common factors in each group.}$$
$$= (y + 3)(x + 2) \quad \text{Factor out } x + 2.$$

Teaching Tip Some students always put the common factor on the left. So they might write $(x + 2)(y + 3)$, which of course is correct also.

b) We can factor x^2 out of the first two terms and 1 out of the last two terms:

$$2x^3 - 3x^2 - 2x + 3 = (2x^3 - 3x^2) + (-2x + 3) \quad \text{Group the terms.}$$
$$= x^2(2x - 3) + 1(-2x + 3)$$

However, we cannot proceed any further because $2x - 3$ and $-2x + 3$ are not the same. To get $2x - 3$ as a common factor, we must factor out -1 from the last two terms:

$$2x^3 - 3x^2 - 2x + 3 = x^2(2x - 3) - 1(2x - 3) \quad \text{Factor out the common factors.}$$
$$= (x^2 - 1)(2x - 3) \quad \text{Factor out } 2x - 3.$$
$$= (x - 1)(x + 1)(2x - 3) \quad \text{Difference of two squares}$$

c) In $ax + 3y - 3x - ay$ there are no common factors in the first two or the last two terms. However, if we use the commutative property to rewrite the polynomial as $ax - 3x - ay + 3y$, then we can factor by grouping:

$$ax + 3y - 3x - ay = ax - 3x - ay + 3y \quad \text{Rearrange the terms.}$$
$$= x(a - 3) - y(a - 3) \quad \text{Factor out } x \text{ and } -y.$$
$$= (x - y)(a - 3) \quad \text{Factor out } a - 3.$$

Now do Exercises 69–84

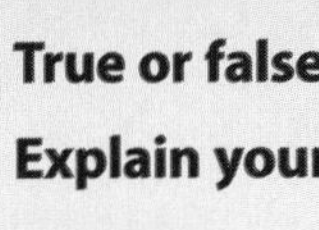

Warm-Ups ▼

True or false? Explain your answer.

1. The polynomial $x^2 + 16$ is a difference of two squares. False
2. The polynomial $x^2 - 8x + 16$ is a perfect square trinomial. True
3. The polynomial $9x^2 + 21x + 49$ is a perfect square trinomial. False
4. $4x^2 + 4 = (2x + 2)^2$ for any real number x. False
5. A difference of two squares is equal to a product of a sum and a difference. True
6. The polynomial $16y + 1$ is a prime polynomial. True
7. The polynomial $x^2 + 9$ can be factored as $(x + 3)(x + 3)$. False
8. The polynomial $4x^2 - 4$ is factored completely as $4(x^2 - 1)$. False
9. $y^2 - 2y + 1 = (y - 1)^2$ for any real number y. True
10. $2x^2 - 18 = 2(x - 3)(x + 3)$ for any real number x. True

5.2 Exercises

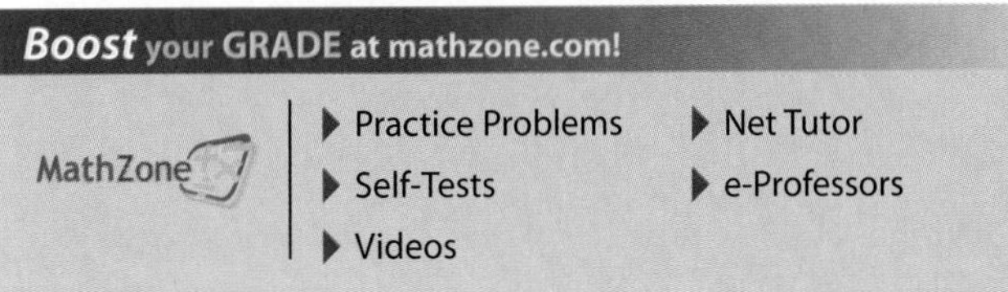

Reading and Writing *After reading this section, write out the answers to these questions. Use complete sentences.*

1. What is a perfect square?
   A perfect square is a square of an integer or an algebraic expression.
2. How do we factor a difference of two squares?
   $a^2 - b^2 = (a + b)(a - b)$
3. How can you recognize if a trinomial is a perfect square?
   A perfect square trinomial is of the form $a^2 + 2ab + b^2$ or $a^2 - 2ab + b^2$.
4. What is a prime polynomial?
   A prime polynomial is a polynomial that cannot be factored.
5. When is a polynomial factored completely?
   A polynomial is factored completely when it is a product of prime polynomials.
6. What should you always look for first when attempting to factor a polynomial completely?
   Always factor out the GCF first.

Factor each polynomial. See Example 1.

7. $a^2 - 4$ $(a - 2)(a + 2)$
8. $h^2 - 9$ $(h - 3)(h + 3)$
9. $x^2 - 49$ $(x - 7)(x + 7)$
10. $y^2 - 36$ $(y - 6)(y + 6)$
11. $y^2 - 9x^2$ $(y + 3x)(y - 3x)$
12. $16x^2 - y^2$ $(4x - y)(4x + y)$
13. $25a^2 - 49b^2$ $(5a + 7b)(5a - 7b)$
14. $9a^2 - 64b^2$ $(3a - 8b)(3a + 8b)$
15. $121m^2 - 1$ $(11m + 1)(11m - 1)$
16. $144n^2 - 1$ $(12n - 1)(12n + 1)$
17. $9w^2 - 25c^2$ $(3w - 5c)(3w + 5c)$
18. $144w^2 - 121a^2$ $(12w - 11a)(12w + 11a)$

Determine whether each polynomial is a difference of two squares, a perfect square trinomial, or neither of these. See Example 2.

19. $x^2 - 20x + 100$ Perfect square trinomial
20. $x^2 - 10x - 25$ Neither
21. $y^2 - 40$ Neither
22. $a^2 - 49$ Difference of two squares
23. $4y^2 + 12y + 9$ Perfect square trinomial
24. $9a^2 - 30a - 25$ Neither

25. $x^2 - 8x + 64$ Neither
26. $x^2 + 4x + 4$ Perfect square trinomial
27. $9y^2 - 25c^2$ Difference of two squares
28. $9x^2 + 4$ Neither
29. $9a^2 + 6ab + b^2$ Perfect square trinomial
30. $4x^2 - 4xy + y^2$ Perfect square trinomial

Factor each perfect square trinomial. See Example 3.

31. $x^2 + 2x + 1$ $(x + 1)^2$
32. $y^2 + 4y + 4$ $(y + 2)^2$
33. $a^2 + 6a + 9$ $(a + 3)^2$
34. $w^2 + 10w + 25$ $(w + 5)^2$
35. $x^2 + 12x + 36$ $(x + 6)^2$
36. $y^2 + 14y + 49$ $(y + 7)^2$
37. $a^2 - 4a + 4$ $(a - 2)^2$
38. $b^2 - 6b + 9$ $(b - 3)^2$
39. $4w^2 + 4w + 1$ $(2w + 1)^2$
40. $9m^2 + 6m + 1$ $(3m + 1)^2$
41. $16x^2 - 8x + 1$ $(4x - 1)^2$
42. $25y^2 - 10y + 1$ $(5y - 1)^2$
43. $4t^2 + 20t + 25$ $(2t + 5)^2$
44. $9y^2 - 12y + 4$ $(3y - 2)^2$
45. $9w^2 + 42w + 49$ $(3w + 7)^2$
46. $144x^2 + 24x + 1$ $(12x + 1)^2$
47. $n^2 + 2nt + t^2$ $(n + t)^2$
48. $x^2 - 2xy + y^2$ $(x - y)^2$

Factor each polynomial completely. See Example 4.

49. $5x^2 - 125$ $5(x - 5)(x + 5)$
50. $3y^2 - 27$ $3(y - 3)(y + 3)$
51. $-2x^2 + 18$ $-2(x - 3)(x + 3)$
52. $-5y^2 + 20$ $-5(y - 2)(y + 2)$
53. $a^3 - ab^2$ $a(a - b)(a + b)$
54. $x^2y - y$ $y(x - 1)(x + 1)$
55. $3x^2 + 6x + 3$ $3(x + 1)^2$
56. $12a^2 + 36a + 27$ $3(2a + 3)^2$
57. $-5y^2 + 50y - 125$ $-5(y - 5)^2$
58. $-2a^2 - 16a - 32$ $-2(a + 4)^2$
59. $x^3 - 2x^2y + xy^2$ $x(x - y)^2$
60. $x^3y + 2x^2y^2 + xy^3$ $xy(x + y)^2$
61. $-3x^2 + 3y^2$ $-3(x - y)(x + y)$
62. $-8a^2 + 8b^2$ $-8(a - b)(a + b)$
63. $2ax^2 - 98a$ $2a(x - 7)(x + 7)$
64. $32x^2y - 2y^3$ $2y(4x - y)(4x + y)$
65. $3ab^2 - 18ab + 27a$ $3a(b - 3)^2$
66. $-2a^2b + 8ab - 8b$ $-2b(a - 2)^2$
67. $-4m^3 + 24m^2n - 36mn^2$ $-4m(m - 3n)^2$
68. $10a^3 - 20a^2b + 10ab^2$ $10a(a - b)^2$

Use grouping to factor each polynomial completely. See Example 5.

69. $bx + by + cx + cy$ $(b + c)(x + y)$
70. $3x + 3z + ax + az$ $(3 + a)(x + z)$
71. $x^3 + x^2 - 4x - 4$ $(x - 2)(x + 2)(x + 1)$
72. $x^3 + x^2 - x - 1$ $(x - 1)(x + 1)^2$
73. $3a - 3b - xa + xb$ $(3 - x)(a - b)$
74. $ax - bx - 4a + 4b$ $(x - 4)(a - b)$
75. $a^3 + 3a^2 + a + 3$ $(a^2 + 1)(a + 3)$
76. $y^3 - 5y^2 + 8y - 40$ $(y^2 + 8)(y - 5)$
77. $xa + ay + 3y + 3x$ $(a + 3)(x + y)$
78. $x^3 + ax + 3a + 3x^2$ $(x + 3)(x^2 + a)$
79. $abc - 3 + c - 3ab$ $(c - 3)(ab + 1)$
80. $xa + tb + ba + tx$ $(a + t)(x + b)$
81. $x^2a - b + bx^2 - a$ $(a + b)(x - 1)(x + 1)$
82. $a^2m - b^2n + a^2n - b^2m$ $(m + n)(a - b)(a + b)$
83. $y^2 + y + by + b$ $(y + b)(y + 1)$
84. $ac + mc + aw^2 + mw^2$ $(c + w^2)(a + m)$

Factor each polynomial completely.

85. $6a^3y + 24a^2y^2 + 24ay^3$ $6ay(a + 2y)^2$
86. $8b^5c - 8b^4c^2 + 2b^3c^3$ $2b^3c(2b - c)^2$
87. $24a^3y - 6ay^3$ $6ay(2a - y)(2a + y)$
88. $27b^3c - 12bc^3$ $3bc(3b - 2c)(3b + 2c)$
89. $2a^3y^2 - 6a^2y$ $2a^2y(ay - 3)$
90. $9x^3y - 18x^2y^2$ $9x^2y(x - 2y)$
91. $ab + 2bw - 4aw - 8w^2$ $(b - 4w)(a + 2w)$
92. $3am - 6n - an + 18m$ $(3m - n)(a + 6)$

Use factoring to solve each problem.

93. ***Skydiving.*** The height (in feet) above the earth for a skydiver t seconds after jumping from an airplane at 6400 ft is approximated by the formula $h = -16t^2 + 6400$, provided that $t < 5$. Rewrite the formula with the right-hand side factored completely. Use your revised formula to find h when $t = 2$. $h = -16(t - 20)(t + 20)$, 6336 feet

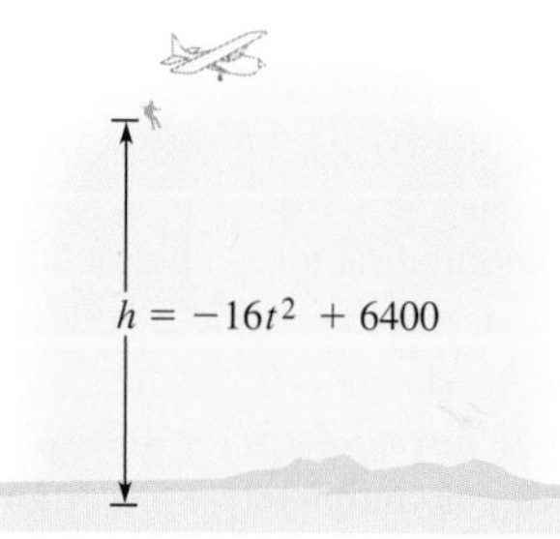

Figure for Exercise 93

94. ***Demand for pools.*** Tropical Pools sells an aboveground model for p dollars each. The monthly revenue from the sale of this model is given by

$$R = -0.08p^2 + 300p.$$

Revenue is the product of the price p and the demand (quantity sold).

a) Factor out the price on the right-hand side of the formula. $R = p(-0.08p + 300)$

b) What is an expression for the monthly demand? $-0.08p + 300$

c) What is the monthly demand for this pool when the price is \$3000? 60 pools

d) Use the graph to estimate the price at which the revenue is maximized. Approximately how many pools will be sold monthly at this price? \$2000, 140 pools

e) What is the approximate maximum revenue? \$280,000

Figure for Exercise 94

f) Use the accompanying graph to estimate the price at which the revenue is zero. \$0 or \$3800

95. ***Volume of a tank.*** The volume of a fish tank with a square base and height y is $y^3 - 6y^2 + 9y$ cubic inches. Find the length of a side of the square base. $y - 3$ inches

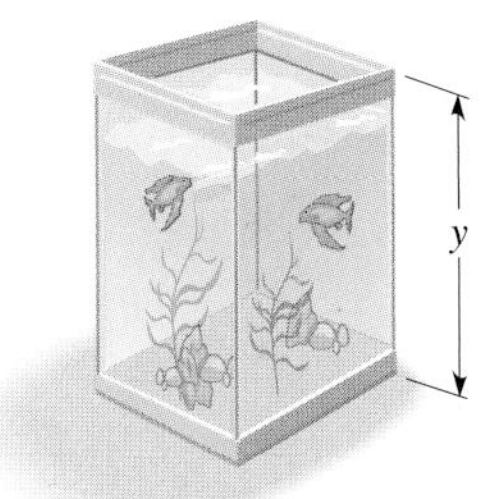

Figure for Exercise 95

Getting More Involved

96. ***Discussion***

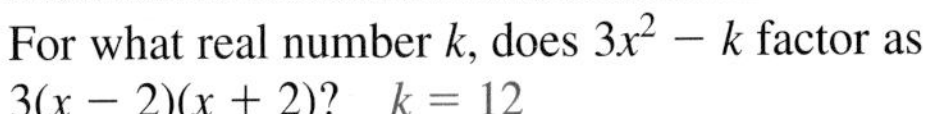

For what real number k, does $3x^2 - k$ factor as $3(x - 2)(x + 2)$? $k = 12$

97. ***Writing***

Explain in your own words how to factor a four-term polynomial by grouping.

98. ***Writing***

Explain how you know that $x^2 + 1$ is a prime polynomial.

5.3 Factoring $ax^2 + bx + c$ with $a = 1$

In this Section

- Factoring $ax^2 + bx + c$ with $a = 1$
- Prime Polynomials
- Factoring with Two Variables
- Factoring Completely

In this section we will factor the type of trinomials that result from multiplying two different binomials. We will do this only for trinomials in which the coefficient of x^2, the leading coefficient, is 1. Factoring trinomials with leading coefficient not equal to 1 will be done in Section 5.4.

Factoring $ax^2 + bx + c$ with $a = 1$

Let's look closely at an example of finding the product of two binomials using the distributive property:

$$\begin{aligned}(x + 2)(x + 3) &= (x + 2)x + (x + 2)3 && \text{Distributive property}\\ &= x^2 + 2x + 3x + 6 && \text{Distributive property}\\ &= x^2 + 5x + 6 && \text{Combine like terms.}\end{aligned}$$

To factor $x^2 + 5x + 6$, we reverse these steps as shown in Example 1.

EXAMPLE 1

Factoring a trinomial

Factor.

a) $x^2 + 5x + 6$ **b)** $x^2 + 8x + 12$ **c)** $a^2 - 9a + 20$

Solution

a) The coefficient 5 is the sum of two numbers that have a product of 6. The only integers that have a product of 6 and a sum of 5 are 2 and 3. So write $5x$ as $2x + 3x$, then factor by grouping:

$$\begin{aligned} x^2 + 5x + 6 &= x^2 + 2x + 3x + 6 && \text{Replace } 5x \text{ by } 2x + 3x. \\ &= (x^2 + 2x) + (3x + 6) && \text{Group terms together.} \\ &= x(x + 2) + 3(x + 2) && \text{Factor out common factors.} \\ &= (x + 2)(x + 3) && \text{Factor out } x + 2. \end{aligned}$$

b) To factor $x^2 + 8x + 12$, we must find two integers that have a product of 12 and a sum of 8. The pairs of integers with a product of 12 are 1 and 12, 2 and 6, and 3 and 4. Only 2 and 6 have a sum of 8. So write $8x$ as $2x + 6x$ and factor by grouping:

$$\begin{aligned} x^2 + 8x + 12 &= x^2 + 2x + 6x + 12 \\ &= (x + 2)x + (x + 2)6 && \text{Factor out the common factors.} \\ &= (x + 2)(x + 6) && \text{Factor out } x + 2. \end{aligned}$$

Check by using FOIL: $(x + 2)(x + 6) = x^2 + 8x + 12$.

c) To factor $a^2 - 9a + 20$, we need two integers that have a product of 20 and a sum of -9. The integers are -4 and -5. Now replace $-9a$ by $-4a - 5a$ and factor by grouping:

$$\begin{aligned} a^2 - 9a + 20 &= a^2 - 4a - 5a + 20 && \text{Replace } -9a \text{ by } -4a - 5a. \\ &= a(a - 4) - 5(a - 4) && \text{Factor by grouping.} \\ &= (a - 5)(a - 4) && \text{Factor out } a - 4. \end{aligned}$$

Now do Exercises 7–18

Teaching Tip Note that in Example 1 the common factor is factored out sometimes to the left and sometimes to the right to show that it can be done either way.

Study Tip

Effective time management will allow adequate time for school, social life, and free time. However, at times you will have to sacrifice to do well.

After sufficient practice factoring trinomials, you may be able to skip most of the steps shown in these examples. For example, to factor $x^2 + x - 6$, simply find a pair of integers with a product of -6 and a sum of 1. The integers are 3 and -2, so we can write

$$x^2 + x - 6 = (x + 3)(x - 2)$$

and check by using FOIL.

EXAMPLE 2

Factoring trinomials

Factor.

a) $x^2 + 5x + 4$

b) $y^2 + 6y - 16$

c) $w^2 - 5w - 24$

Solution

a) To get a product of 4 and a sum of 5, use 1 and 4:

$$x^2 + 5x + 4 = (x + 1)(x + 4)$$

Check by using FOIL on $(x + 1)(x + 4)$.

b) To get a product of -16 we need a positive number and a negative number. To also get a sum of 6, use 8 and -2:

$$y^2 + 6y - 16 = (y + 8)(y - 2)$$

Check by using FOIL on $(y + 8)(y - 2)$.

c) To get a product of -24 and a sum of -5, use -8 and 3:

$$w^2 - 5w - 24 = (w - 8)(w + 3)$$

Check by using FOIL.

Now do Exercises 19–26

Polynomials are easiest to factor when they are in the form $ax^2 + bx + c$. So if a polynomial can be rewritten into that form, rewrite it before attempting to factor it. In Example 3 we factor polynomials that need to be rewritten.

EXAMPLE 3

Factoring trinomials

Factor.

a) $2x - 8 + x^2$ **b)** $-36 + t^2 - 9t$

Solution

a) Before factoring, write the trinomial as $x^2 + 2x - 8$. Now, to get a product of -8 and a sum of 2, use -2 and 4:

$$\begin{aligned} 2x - 8 + x^2 &= x^2 + 2x - 8 && \text{Write in } ax^2 + bx + c \text{ form.} \\ &= (x + 4)(x - 2) && \text{Factor and check by multiplying.} \end{aligned}$$

b) Before factoring, write the trinomial as $t^2 - 9t - 36$. Now, to get a product of -36 and a sum of -9, use -12 and 3:

$$\begin{aligned} -36 + t^2 - 9t &= t^2 - 9t - 36 && \text{Write in } ax^2 + bx + c \text{ form.} \\ &= (t - 12)(t + 3) && \text{Factor and check by multiplying.} \end{aligned}$$

Now do Exercises 27–28

Study Tip

Stay alert for the entire class period. The first 20 minutes is the easiest and the last 20 minutes the hardest. Some students put down their pencils, fold up their notebooks, and daydream for those last 20 minutes. Don't give in. Recognize when you are losing it and force yourself to stay alert. Think of how much time you will have to spend outside of class figuring out what happened during those last 20 minutes.

Prime Polynomials

To factor $x^2 + bx + c$, we try pairs of integers that have a product of c until we find a pair that has a sum of b. If there is no such pair of integers, then the polynomial cannot be factored and it is a prime polynomial. Before you can conclude that a polynomial is prime, you must try *all* possibilities.

EXAMPLE 4

Prime polynomials

Factor.

a) $x^2 + 7x - 6$ **b)** $x^2 + 9$

Solution

a) Because the last term is -6, we want a positive integer and a negative integer that have a product of -6 and a sum of 7. Check all possible pairs of integers:

Product	Sum
$-6 = (-1)(6)$	$-1 + 6 = 5$
$-6 = (1)(-6)$	$1 + (-6) = -5$
$-6 = (2)(-3)$	$2 + (-3) = -1$
$-6 = (-2)(3)$	$-2 + 3 = 1$

None of these possible factors of -6 have a sum of 7, so we can be certain that $x^2 + 7x - 6$ cannot be factored. It is a prime polynomial.

b) Because the x-term is missing in $x^2 + 9$, its coefficient is 0. That is, $x^2 + 9 = x^2 + 0x + 9$. So we seek two positive integers or two negative integers that have a product of 9 and a sum of 0. Check all possibilities:

Product	Sum
$9 = (3)(3)$	$3 + 3 = 6$
$9 = (-3)(-3)$	$-3 + (-3) = -6$
$9 = (9)(1)$	$9 + 1 = 10$
$9 = (-9)(-1)$	$-9 + (-1) = -10$

None of these pairs of integers have a sum of 0, so we can conclude that $x^2 + 9$ is a prime polynomial. Note that $x^2 + 9$ does not factor as $(x + 3)^2$ because $(x + 3)^2$ has a middle term: $(x + 3)^2 = x^2 + 6x + 9$.

Now do Exercises 29–56

Helpful Hint

Don't confuse $a^2 + b^2$ with the difference of two squares $a^2 - b^2$ which is not a prime polynomial:

$$a^2 - b^2 = (a + b)(a - b).$$

Teaching Tip Note that a sum of two squares of the type $(a^3)^2 + (b^3)^2$ is not prime because it is also a sum of two cubes, $(a^2)^3 + (b^2)^3$.

The prime polynomial $x^2 + 9$ in Example 4(b) is a sum of two squares. It can be shown that any sum of two squares (in which there are no common factors) is a prime polynomial.

Sum of Two Squares

If a sum of two squares, $a^2 + b^2$, has no common factor other than 1, then it is a prime polynomial.

Factoring with Two Variables

In Example 5 we factor polynomials that have two variables using the same technique that we used for one variable.

EXAMPLE 5

Polynomials with two variables

Factor.

a) $x^2 + 2xy - 8y^2$ **b)** $a^2 - 7ab + 10b^2$

Solution

a) To get a product of -8 and a sum of 2, use 4 and -2. To get a product of $-8y^2$ use $4y$ and $-2y$:

$$x^2 + 2xy - 8y^2 = (x + 4y)(x - 2y)$$

Check by multiplying $(x + 4y)(x - 2y)$.

b) To get a product of 10 and a sum of -7, use -5 and -2. To get a product of $10b^2$, we use $-5b$ and $-2b$:

$$a^2 - 7ab + 10b^2 = (a - 5b)(a - 2b)$$

Check by multiplying.

Now do Exercises 57–64

Factoring Completely

In Section 5.2 you learned that binomials such as $3x - 5$ (with no common factor) are prime polynomials. In Example 4 of this section we saw a trinomial that is a prime polynomial. There are infinitely many prime trinomials. When factoring a polynomial completely, we could have a factor that is a prime trinomial.

EXAMPLE 6

Factoring completely

Factor each polynomial completely.

a) $x^3 - 6x^2 - 16x$

b) $4x^3 + 4x^2 + 4x$

Solution

a) $x^3 - 6x^2 - 16x = x(x^2 - 6x - 16)$ Factor out the GCF.

$= x(x - 8)(x + 2)$ Factor $x^2 - 6x - 16$.

b) First factor out $4x$, the greatest common factor:

$$4x^3 + 4x^2 + 4x = 4x(x^2 + x + 1)$$

To factor $x^2 + x + 1$, we would need two integers with a product of 1 and a sum of 1. Because there are no such integers, $x^2 + x + 1$ is prime, and the factorization is complete.

Now do Exercises 65–106

Warm-Ups ▼

True or false? Explain your answer.

1. $x^2 - 6x + 9 = (x - 3)^2$ True
2. $x^2 + 6x + 9 = (x + 3)^2$ True
3. $x^2 + 10x + 9 = (x - 9)(x - 1)$ False
4. $x^2 - 8x - 9 = (x - 8)(x - 9)$ False
5. $x^2 + 8x - 9 = (x + 9)(x - 1)$ True
6. $x^2 + 8x + 9 = (x + 3)^2$ False
7. $x^2 - 10xy + 9y^2 = (x - y)(x - 9y)$ True
8. $x^2 + x + 1 = (x + 1)(x + 1)$ False
9. $x^2 + xy + 20y^2 = (x + 5y)(x - 4y)$ False
10. $x^2 + 1 = (x + 1)(x + 1)$ False

5.3 Exercises

Boost your GRADE at mathzone.com!

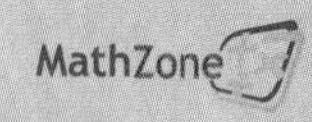

MathZone

- Practice Problems
- Self-Tests
- Videos
- Net Tutor
- e-Professors

Reading and Writing *After reading this section, write out the answers to these questions. Use complete sentences.*

1. What types of polynomials did we factor in this section?
   We factored $ax^2 + bx + c$ with $a = 1$.
2. How can you check if you have factored a trinomial correctly?
   You can check all factoring by multiplying the factors.
3. How can you determine if $x^2 + bx + c$ is prime?
   If there are no two integers that have a product of c and a sum of b, then $x^2 + bx + c$ is prime.
4. How do you factor a sum of two squares?
   A sum of two squares with no common factor is prime.
5. When is a polynomial factored completely?
   A polynomial is factored completely when all of the factors are prime polynomials.
6. What should you always look for first when attempting to factor a polynomial completely?
   Always look for the GCF first.

Factor each trinomial. Write out all of the steps as shown in Example 1.

7. $x^2 + 4x + 3$
   $(x + 3)(x + 1)$
8. $y^2 + 6y + 5$
   $(y + 5)(y + 1)$
9. $x^2 + 9x + 18$
   $(x + 3)(x + 6)$
10. $w^2 + 6w + 8$
    $(w + 2)(w + 4)$
11. $a^2 + 7a + 10$
    $(a + 2)(a + 5)$
12. $b^2 + 7b + 12$
    $(b + 3)(b + 4)$
13. $a^2 - 7a + 12$
    $(a - 3)(a - 4)$
14. $m^2 - 9m + 14$
    $(m - 2)(m - 7)$
15. $b^2 - 5b - 6$
    $(b - 6)(b + 1)$
16. $a^2 + 5a - 6$
    $(a + 6)(a - 1)$
17. $x^2 + 3x - 10$
    $(x - 2)(x + 5)$
18. $x^2 - x - 12$
    $(x + 3)(x - 4)$

Factor each polynomial. If the polynomial is prime, say so. See Examples 2–4.

19. $y^2 + 7y + 10$ $(y + 2)(y + 5)$
20. $x^2 + 8x + 15$ $(x + 3)(x + 5)$
21. $a^2 - 6a + 8$ $(a - 2)(a - 4)$
22. $b^2 - 8b + 15$ $(b - 3)(b - 5)$
23. $m^2 - 10m + 16$ $(m - 8)(m - 2)$
24. $m^2 - 17m + 16$ $(m - 16)(m - 1)$
25. $w^2 + 9w - 10$ $(w + 10)(w - 1)$
26. $m^2 + 6m - 16$ $(m + 8)(m - 2)$

27. $w^2 - 8 - 2w$ $(w - 4)(w + 2)$

28. $-16 + m^2 - 6m$ $(m - 8)(m + 2)$

29. $a^2 - 2a - 12$ Prime

30. $x^2 + 3x + 3$ Prime

31. $15m - 16 + m^2$ $(m + 16)(m - 1)$

32. $3y + y^2 - 10$ $(y + 5)(y - 2)$

33. $a^2 - 4a + 12$ Prime

34. $y^2 - 6y - 8$ Prime

35. $z^2 - 25$ $(z - 5)(z + 5)$

36. $p^2 - 1$ $(p - 1)(p + 1)$

37. $h^2 + 49$ Prime

38. $q^2 + 4$ Prime

39. $m^2 + 12m + 20$ $(m + 2)(m + 10)$

40. $m^2 + 21m + 20$ $(m + 1)(m + 20)$

41. $t^2 - 3t + 10$ Prime

42. $x^2 - 5x - 3$ Prime

43. $m^2 - 18 - 17m$ $(m - 18)(m + 1)$

44. $h^2 - 36 + 5h$ $(h + 9)(h - 4)$

45. $m^2 - 23m + 24$ Prime

46. $m^2 + 23m + 24$ Prime

47. $5t - 24 + t^2$ $(t + 8)(t - 3)$

48. $t^2 - 24 - 10t$ $(t - 12)(t + 2)$

49. $t^2 - 2t - 24$ $(t - 6)(t + 4)$

50. $t^2 + 14t + 24$ $(t + 12)(t + 2)$

51. $t^2 - 10t - 200$ $(t - 20)(t + 10)$

52. $t^2 + 30t + 200$ $(t + 20)(t + 10)$

53. $x^2 - 5x - 150$ $(x - 15)(x + 10)$

54. $x^2 - 25x + 150$ $(x - 15)(x - 10)$

55. $13y + 30 + y^2$ $(y + 3)(y + 10)$

56. $18z + 45 + z^2$ $(z + 3)(z + 15)$

Factor each polynomial. See Example 5.

57. $x^2 + 5ax + 6a^2$ $(x + 3a)(x + 2a)$

58. $a^2 + 7ab + 10b^2$ $(a + 2b)(a + 5b)$

59. $x^2 - 4xy - 12y^2$ $(x - 6y)(x + 2y)$

60. $y^2 + yt - 12t^2$ $(y + 4t)(y - 3t)$

61. $x^2 - 13xy + 12y^2$ $(x - 12y)(x - y)$

62. $h^2 - 9hs + 9s^2$ Prime

63. $x^2 + 4xz - 33z^2$ Prime

64. $x^2 - 5xs - 24s^2$ $(x - 8s)(x + 3s)$

Factor each polynomial completely. Use the methods discussed in Sections 5.1 through 5.3. If the polynomial is prime say so. See Example 6.

65. $5x^3 + 5x$ $5x(x^2 + 1)$

66. $b^3 + 49b$ $b(b^2 + 49)$

67. $w^2 - 8w$ $w(w - 8)$

68. $x^4 - x^3$ $x^3(x - 1)$

69. $2w^2 - 162$ $2(w - 9)(w + 9)$

70. $6w^4 - 54w^2$ $6w^2(w - 3)(w + 3)$

71. $-2b^2 - 98$ $-2(b^2 + 49)$

72. $-a^3 - 100a$ $-a(a^2 + 100)$

73. $x^3 - 2x^2 - 9x + 18$ $(x + 3)(x - 3)(x - 2)$

74. $x^3 + 7x^2 - x - 7$ $(x + 7)(x + 1)(x - 1)$

75. $4r^2 + 9$ Prime

76. $t^2 + 4z^2$ Prime

77. $x^2w^2 + 9x^2$ $x^2(w^2 + 9)$

78. $a^4b + a^2b^3$ $a^2b(a^2 + b^2)$

79. $w^2 - 18w + 81$ $(w - 9)^2$

80. $w^2 + 30w + 81$ $(w + 3)(w + 27)$

81. $6w^2 - 12w - 18$ $6(w - 3)(w + 1)$

82. $9w - w^3$ $w(3 - w)(3 + w)$

83. $3y^2 + 75$ $3(y^2 + 25)$

84. $5x^2 + 500$ $5(x^2 + 100)$

85. $ax + ay + cx + cy$ $(a + c)(x + y)$

86. $y^3 + y^2 - 4y - 4$ $(y - 2)(y + 2)(y + 1)$

87. $-2x^2 - 10x - 12$ $-2(x + 2)(x + 3)$

88. $-a^3 - 2a^2 - a$ $-a(a + 1)^2$

89. $32x^2 - 2x^4$ $2x^2(4 - x)(4 + x)$

90. $20w^2 + 100w + 40$ $20(w^2 + 5w + 2)$

91. $3w^2 + 27w + 54$ $3(w + 3)(w + 6)$

92. $w^3 - 3w^2 - 18w$ $w(w - 6)(w + 3)$

93. $18w^2 + w^3 + 36w$ $w(w^2 + 18w + 36)$

94. $18a^2 + 3a^3 + 36a$ $3a(a^2 + 6a + 12)$

95. $9y^2 + 1 + 6y$ $(3y + 1)^2$

96. $2a^2 + 1 + 3a$ $(2a + 1)(a + 1)$

97. $8vw^2 + 32vw + 32v$ $8v(w + 2)^2$

98. $3h^2t + 6ht + 3t$ $3t(h + 1)^2$

99. $6x^3y + 30x^2y^2 + 36xy^3$ $6xy(x + 3y)(x + 2y)$

100. $3x^3y^2 - 3x^2y^2 + 3xy^2$ $3xy^2(x^2 - x + 1)$

101. $5 + 8w + 3w^2$ $(3w + 5)(w + 1)$

102. $-3 + 2y + 21y^2$ $(3y - 1)(7y + 3)$

103. $-3y^3 + 6y^2 - 3y$ $-3y(y - 1)^2$

104. $-4w^3 - 16w^2 + 20w$ $-4w(w - 1)(w + 5)$

105. $a^3 + ab + 3b + 3a^2$ $(a + 3)(a^2 + b)$

106. $ac + xc + aw^2 + xw^2$ $(a + x)(c + w^2)$

Use factoring to solve each problem.

107. ***Area of a deck.*** A rectangular deck has an area of $x^2 + 6x + 8$ square feet and a width of $x + 2$ feet. Find the length of the deck. See the figure on the next page. $x + 4$ feet

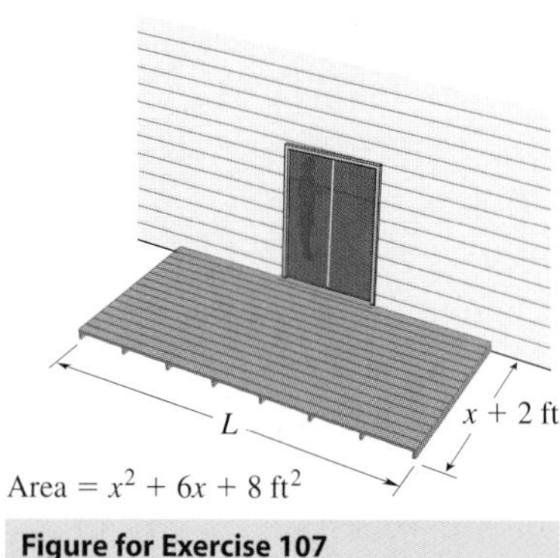

Figure for Exercise 107

108. ***Area of a sail.*** A triangular sail has an area of $x^2 + 5x + 6$ square meters and a height of $x + 3$ meters. Find the length of the sail's base. $2x + 4$ meters

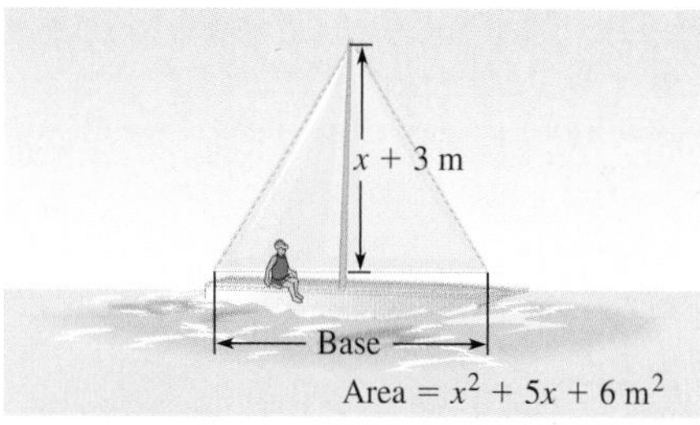

Figure for Exercise 108

109. ***Volume of a cube.*** Hector designed a cubic box with volume x^3 cubic feet. After increasing the dimensions of the bottom, the box has a volume of $x^3 + 8x^2 + 15x$ cubic feet. If each of the dimensions of the bottom was increased by a whole number of feet, then how much was each increase? 3 feet and 5 feet

110. ***Volume of a container.*** A cubic shipping container had a volume of a^3 cubic meters. The height was decreased by a whole number of meters and the width was increased by a whole number of meters so that the volume of the container is now $a^3 + 2a^2 - 3a$ cubic meters. By how many meters were the height and width changed? Height 1 foot smaller, width 3 feet larger

Getting More Involved

111. ***Discussion***

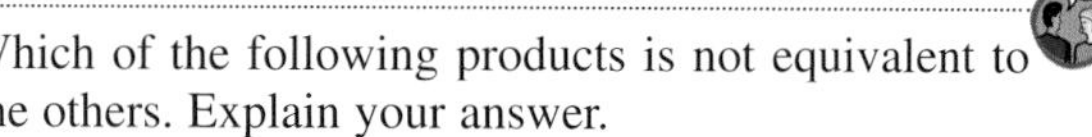

Which of the following products is not equivalent to the others. Explain your answer.

a) $(2x - 4)(x + 3)$ **b)** $(x - 2)(2x + 6)$
c) $2(x - 2)(x + 3)$ **d)** $(2x - 4)(2x + 6)$ d

112. ***Discussion***

When asked to factor completely a certain polynomial, four students gave the following answers. Only one student gave the correct answer. Which one must it be? Explain your answer.

a) $3(x^2 - 2x - 15)$ **b)** $(3x - 5)(5x - 15)$
c) $3(x - 5)(x - 3)$ **d)** $(3x - 15)(x - 3)$ c

5.4 Factoring $ax^2 + bx + c$ with $a \neq 1$

In this Section

- The *ac* Method
- Trial and Error
- Factoring Completely

In Section 5.3 we used grouping to factor trinomials with a leading coefficient of 1. In this section we will also use grouping to factor trinomials with a leading coefficient that is not equal to 1.

The *ac* Method

The first step in factoring $ax^2 + bx + c$ with $a = 1$ is to find two numbers with a product of c and a sum of b. If $a \neq 1$, then the first step is to find two numbers with a product of ac and a sum of b. This method is called the ***ac* method.** The strategy for factoring by the ac method follows. Note that this strategy works whether or not the leading coefficient is 1.

Strategy for Factoring $ax^2 + bx + c$ by the *ac* Method

To factor the trinomial $ax^2 + bx + c$:

1. Find two numbers that have a product equal to ac and a sum equal to b.
2. Replace bx by two terms using the two new numbers as coefficients.
3. Factor the resulting four-term polynomial by grouping.

EXAMPLE 1

The *ac* method

Factor each trinomial.

a) $2x^2 + 7x + 6$ **b)** $2x^2 + x - 6$ **c)** $10x^2 + 13x - 3$

Solution

a) In $2x^2 + 7x + 6$ we have $a = 2$, $b = 7$, and $c = 6$. So

$$ac = 2 \cdot 6 = 12.$$

Now we need two integers with a product of 12 and a sum of 7. The pairs of integers with a product of 12 are 1 and 12, 2 and 6, and 3 and 4. Only 3 and 4 have a sum of 7. Replace $7x$ by $3x + 4x$ and factor by grouping:

$$2x^2 + 7x + 6 = 2x^2 + 3x + 4x + 6 \quad \text{Replace } 7x \text{ by } 3x + 4x.$$
$$= (2x + 3)x + (2x + 3)2 \quad \text{Factor out the common factors.}$$
$$= (2x + 3)(x + 2) \quad \text{Factor out } 2x + 3.$$

Check by FOIL.

b) In $2x^2 + x - 6$ we have $a = 2$, $b = 1$, and $c = -6$. So

$$ac = 2(-6) = -12.$$

Now we need two integers with a product of -12 and a sum of 1. We can list the possible pairs of integers with a product of -12 as follows:

1 and -12	2 and -6	3 and -4
-1 and 12	-2 and 6	-3 and 4

Only -3 and 4 have a sum of 1. Replace x by $-3x + 4x$ and factor by grouping:

$$2x^2 + x - 6 = 2x^2 - 3x + 4x - 6 \quad \text{Replace } x \text{ by } -3x + 4x.$$
$$= (2x - 3)x + (2x - 3)2 \quad \text{Factor out the common factors.}$$
$$= (2x - 3)(x + 2) \quad \text{Factor out } 2x - 3.$$

Check by FOIL.

c) Because $ac = 10(-3) = -30$, we need two integers with a product of -30 and a sum of 13. The product is negative, so the integers must have opposite signs. We can list all pairs of factors of -30 as follows:

1 and -30	2 and -15	3 and -10	5 and -6
-1 and 30	-2 and 15	-3 and 10	-5 and 6

Teaching Tip Many students like the *ac* method because it is systematic. However, when factoring appears in a later course, students generally remember only trial and error.

The only pair that has a sum of 13 is -2 and 15:

$$10x^2 + 13x - 3 = 10x^2 - 2x + 15x - 3 \quad \text{Replace } 13x \text{ by } -2x + 15x.$$
$$= (5x - 1)2x + (5x - 1)3 \quad \text{Factor out the common factors.}$$
$$= (5x - 1)(2x + 3) \quad \text{Factor out } 5x - 1.$$

Check by FOIL.

Now do Exercises 5–40

EXAMPLE 2

Factoring a trinomial in two variables by the *ac* method

Factor $8x^2 - 14xy + 3y^2$

Solution

Since $a = 8$, $b = -14$, and $c = 3$, we have $ac = 24$. Two numbers with a product of 24 and a sum of -14 must both be negative. The possible pairs with a product of 24 follow:

-1 and -24 $\qquad$ -3 and -8

-2 and -12 $\qquad$ -4 and -6

Only -2 and -12 have a sum of -14. Replace $-14xy$ by $-2xy - 12xy$ and factor by grouping:

$$8x^2 - 14xy + 3y^2 = 8x^2 - 2xy - 12xy + 3y^2$$
$$= (4x - y)2x + (4x - y)(-3y)$$
$$= (4x - y)(2x - 3y)$$

Check by FOIL.

Now do Exercises 41–46

Trial and Error

After you have gained some experience at factoring by the *ac* method, you can often find the factors without going through the steps of grouping. For example, consider the polynomial

$$3x^2 + 7x - 6.$$

The factors of $3x^2$ can only be $3x$ and x. The factors of 6 could be 2 and 3 or 1 and 6. We can list all of the possibilities that give the correct first and last terms, without regard to the signs:

$$(3x \quad 3)(x \quad 2) \qquad (3x \quad 2)(x \quad 3) \qquad (3x \quad 6)(x \quad 1) \qquad (3x \quad 1)(x \quad 6)$$

Because the factors of -6 have unlike signs, one binomial factor is a sum and the other binomial is a difference. Now we try some products to see if we get a middle term of $7x$:

$$(3x + 3)(x - 2) = 3x^2 - 3x - 6 \quad \text{Incorrect}$$
$$(3x - 3)(x + 2) = 3x^2 + 3x - 6 \quad \text{Incorrect}$$

Helpful Hint

The *ac* method is more systematic than trial and error. However, trial and error can be faster and easier, especially if your first or second trial is correct.

Actually, there is no need to try $(3x \quad 3)(x \quad 2)$ or $(3x \quad 6)(x \quad 1)$ because each contains a binomial with a common factor. A common factor in the binomial causes a common factor in the product. But $3x^2 + 7x - 6$ has no common factor. So the factors must come from either $(3x \quad 2)(x \quad 3)$ or $(3x \quad 1)(x \quad 6)$. So we try again:

$$(3x + 2)(x - 3) = 3x^2 - 7x - 6 \quad \text{Incorrect}$$
$$(3x - 2)(x + 3) = 3x^2 + 7x - 6 \quad \text{Correct}$$

Even though there may be many possibilities in some factoring problems, it is often possible to find the correct factors without writing down every possibility. We can use a bit of guesswork in factoring trinomials. *Try* whichever possibility you think might work. *Check* it by multiplying. If it is not right, then *try again.* That is why this method is called **trial and error.**

EXAMPLE 3

Trial and error

Factor each trinomial using trial and error.

a) $2x^2 + 5x - 3$ **b)** $3x^2 - 11x + 6$

Solution

a) Because $2x^2$ factors only as $2x \cdot x$ and 3 factors only as $1 \cdot 3$, there are only two possible ways to get the correct first and last terms, without regard to the signs:

$$(2x \quad 1)(x \quad 3) \qquad \text{and} \qquad (2x \quad 3)(x \quad 1)$$

Because the last term of the trinomial is negative, one of the missing signs must be $+$, and the other must be $-$. The trinomial is factored correctly as

$$2x^2 + 5x - 3 = (2x - 1)(x + 3).$$

Check by using FOIL.

b) There are four possible ways to factor $3x^2 - 11x + 6$:

$$(3x \quad 1)(x \quad 6) \qquad (3x \quad 2)(x \quad 3)$$
$$(3x \quad 6)(x \quad 1) \qquad (3x \quad 3)(x \quad 2)$$

Because the last term in $3x^2 - 11x + 6$ is positive and the middle term is negative, both signs in the factors must be negative. Because $3x^2 - 11x + 6$ has no common factor, we can rule out $(3x \quad 6)(x \quad 1)$ and $(3x \quad 3)(x \quad 2)$. So the only possibilities left are $(3x - 1)(x - 6)$ and $(3x - 2)(x - 3)$. The trinomial is factored correctly as

$$3x^2 - 11x + 6 = (3x - 2)(x - 3).$$

Check by using FOIL.

Now do Exercises 47–66

Study Tip

Have you ever used excuses to avoid studying? ("Before I can study, I have to do my laundry and go to the bank.") Since the average attention span for one task is approximately 20 minutes, it is better to take breaks from studying to run errands and do laundry than to get everything done before you start studying.

Factoring by trial and error is not just guessing. In fact, if the trinomial has a positive leading coefficient, we can determine in advance whether its factors are sums or differences.

Using Signs in Trial and Error

1. If the signs of the terms of a trinomial are + + + then both factors are sums: $x^2 + 5x + 6 = (x + 2)(x + 3)$.
2. If the signs are + − + then both factors are differences: $x^2 - 5x + 6 = (x - 2)(x - 3)$.
3. If the signs are + + − or + − − then one factor is a sum and the other is a difference: $x^2 + x - 6 = (x + 3)(x - 2)$ and $x^2 - x - 6 = (x - 3)(x + 2)$.

In Example 4 we factor a trinomial that has two variables.

EXAMPLE 4

Factoring a trinomial with two variables by trial and error

Factor $6x^2 - 7xy + 2y^2$.

Solution

We list the possible ways to factor the trinomial:

$(3x \quad 2y)(2x \quad y) \qquad (3x \quad y)(2x \quad 2y) \qquad (6x \quad 2y)(x \quad y) \qquad (6x \quad y)(x \quad 2y)$

Because the last term of the trinomial is positive and the middle term is negative, both factors must contain subtraction symbols. To get the middle term of $-7xy$, we use the first possibility listed:

$$6x^2 - 7xy + 2y^2 = (3x - 2y)(2x - y)$$

Now do Exercises 67–70

Factoring Completely

You can use the latest factoring technique along with the techniques that you learned earlier to factor polynomials completely. Remember always to first factor out the greatest common factor (if it is not 1).

EXAMPLE 5

Factoring completely

Factor each polynomial completely.

a) $4x^3 + 14x^2 + 6x$ **b)** $12x^2y + 6xy + 6y$

Solution

a) $4x^3 + 14x^2 + 6x = 2x(2x^2 + 7x + 3)$ Factor out the GCF, $2x$.

$= 2x(2x + 1)(x + 3)$ Factor $2x^2 + 7x + 3$.

Check by multiplying.

b) $12x^2y + 6xy + 6y = 6y(2x^2 + x + 1)$ Factor out the GCF, $6y$.

To factor $2x^2 + x + 1$ by the *ac* method, we need two numbers with a product of 2 and a sum of 1. Because there are no such numbers, $2x^2 + x + 1$ is prime and the factorization is complete.

Now do Exercises 77–86

Our first step in factoring is to factor out the greatest common factor (if it is not 1). If the first term of a polynomial has a negative coefficient, then it is better to factor out the opposite of the GCF so that the resulting polynomial will have a positive leading coefficient.

EXAMPLE 6

Factoring out the opposite of the GCF

Factor each polynomial completely.

a) $-18x^3 + 51x^2 - 15x$

b) $-3a^2 + 2a + 21$

Teaching Tip If the leading coefficient is negative, both ac and trial and error will work, but students find it easier to have a positive leading coefficient.

Solution

a) The GCF is $3x$. Because the first term has a negative coefficient, we factor out $-3x$:

$$-18x^3 + 51x^2 - 15x = -3x(6x^2 - 17x + 5) \quad \text{Factor out } -3x.$$
$$= -3x(3x - 1)(2x - 5) \quad \text{Factor } 6x^2 - 17x + 5.$$

b) The GCF for $-3a^2 + 2a + 21$ is 1. Because the first term has a negative coefficient, factor out -1:

$$-3a^2 + 2a + 21 = -1(3a^2 - 2a - 21) \quad \text{Factor out } -1.$$
$$= -1(3a + 7)(a - 3) \quad \text{Factor } 3a^2 - 2a - 21.$$

Now do Exercises 87–102

Warm-Ups ▼

True or false? Explain your answer.

1. $2x^2 + 3x + 1 = (2x + 1)(x + 1)$ True
2. $2x^2 + 5x + 3 = (2x + 1)(x + 3)$ False
3. $3x^2 + 10x + 3 = (3x + 1)(x + 3)$ True
4. $15x^2 + 31x + 14 = (3x + 7)(5x + 2)$ False
5. $2x^2 - 7x - 9 = (2x - 9)(x + 1)$ True
6. $2x^2 + 3x - 9 = (2x + 3)(x - 3)$ False
7. $2x^2 - 16x - 9 = (2x - 9)(2x + 1)$ False
8. $8x^2 - 22x - 5 = (4x - 1)(2x + 5)$ False
9. $9x^2 + x - 1 = (5x - 1)(4x + 1)$ False
10. $12x^2 - 13x + 3 = (3x - 1)(4x - 3)$ True

5.4 Exercises

Boost your GRADE at mathzone.com!

MathZone

- Practice Problems
- Self-Tests
- Videos
- Net Tutor
- e-Professors

Reading and Writing *After reading this section, write out the answers to these questions. Use complete sentences.*

1. What types of polynomials did we factor in this section?
We factored $ax^2 + bx + c$ with $a \neq 1$.

2. What is the *ac* method of factoring?
In the *ac* method we find two integers whose product is equal to *ac* and whose sum is *b*, and then we use factoring by grouping.

3. How can you determine if $ax^2 + bx + c$ is prime?
If there are no two integers whose product is *ac* and whose sum is *b*, then $ax^2 + bx + c$ is prime.

4. What is the trial-and-error method of factoring?
In trial and error, we make an educated guess at the factors and then check by FOIL.

Find the following. See Example 1.

5. Two integers that have a product of 20 and a sum of 12
2 and 10

6. Two integers that have a product of 36 and a sum of -20
-2 and -18

7. Two integers that have a product of -12 and a sum of -4
-6 and 2

8. Two integers that have a product of -8 and a sum of 7
8 and -1

Each of the following trinomials is in the form $ax^2 + bx + c$. For each trinomial, find two integers that have a product of ac and a sum of b. Do not factor the trinomials. See Example 1.

9. $6x^2 + 7x + 2$
3 and 4

10. $5x^2 + 17x + 6$
2 and 15

11. $6y^2 - 11y + 3$
-2 and -9

12. $6z^2 - 19z + 10$
-4 and -15

13. $12w^2 + w - 1$
-3 and 4

14. $15t^2 - 17t - 4$
-20 and 3

Factor each trinomial using the ac method. See Example 1.

15. $2x^2 + 3x + 1$
$(2x + 1)(x + 1)$

16. $2x^2 + 11x + 5$
$(2x + 1)(x + 5)$

17. $2x^2 + 9x + 4$
$(2x + 1)(x + 4)$

18. $2h^2 + 7h + 3$
$(2h + 1)(h + 3)$

19. $3t^2 + 7t + 2$
$(3t + 1)(t + 2)$

20. $3t^2 + 8t + 5$
$(3t + 5)(t + 1)$

21. $2x^2 + 5x - 3$
$(2x - 1)(x + 3)$

22. $3x^2 - x - 2$
$(3x + 2)(x - 1)$

23. $6x^2 + 7x - 3$
$(3x - 1)(2x + 3)$

24. $21x^2 + 2x - 3$
$(3x - 1)(7x + 3)$

25. $3x^2 - 5x + 4$ Prime

26. $6x^2 - 5x + 3$ Prime

27. $2x^2 - 7x + 6$
$(2x - 3)(x - 2)$

28. $3a^2 - 14a + 15$
$(3a - 5)(a - 3)$

29. $5b^2 - 13b + 6$
$(5b - 3)(b - 2)$

30. $7y^2 + 16y - 15$
$(7y - 5)(y + 3)$

31. $4y^2 - 11y - 3$
$(4y + 1)(y - 3)$

32. $35x^2 - 2x - 1$
$(7x + 1)(5x - 1)$

33. $3x^2 + 2x + 1$ Prime

34. $6x^2 - 4x - 5$ Prime

35. $8x^2 - 2x - 1$
$(4x + 1)(2x - 1)$

36. $8x^2 - 10x - 3$
$(4x + 1)(2x - 3)$

37. $9t^2 - 9t + 2$
$(3t - 1)(3t - 2)$

38. $9t^2 + 5t - 4$
$(9t - 4)(t + 1)$

39. $15x^2 + 13x + 2$
$(5x + 1)(3x + 2)$

40. $15x^2 - 7x - 2$
$(5x + 1)(3x - 2)$

Use the ac method to factor each trinomial. See Example 2.

41. $4a^2 + 16ab + 15b^2$
$(2a + 3b)(2a + 5b)$

42. $10x^2 + 17xy + 3y^2$
$(5x + y)(2x + 3y)$

43. $6m^2 - 7mn - 5n^2$
$(3m - 5n)(2m + n)$

44. $3a^2 + 2ab - 21b^2$
$(3a - 7b)(a + 3b)$

45. $3x^2 - 8xy + 5y^2$
$(x - y)(3x - 5y)$

46. $3m^2 - 13mn + 12n^2$
$(m - 3n)(3m - 4n)$

Factor each trinomial using trial and error. See Examples 3 and 4.

47. $5a^2 + 6a + 1$
$(5a + 1)(a + 1)$

48. $7b^2 + 8b + 1$
$(7b + 1)(b + 1)$

49. $6x^2 + 5x + 1$
$(2x + 1)(3x + 1)$

50. $15y^2 + 8y + 1$
$(3y + 1)(5y + 1)$

51. $5a^2 + 11a + 2$
$(5a + 1)(a + 2)$

52. $3y^2 + 10y + 7$
$(3y + 7)(y + 1)$

53. $4w^2 + 8w + 3$
$(2w + 3)(2w + 1)$

54. $6z^2 + 13z + 5$
$(2z + 1)(3z + 5)$

55. $15x^2 - x - 2$
$(5x - 2)(3x + 1)$

56. $15x^2 + 13x - 2$
$(15x - 2)(x + 1)$

57. $8x^2 - 6x + 1$
$(4x - 1)(2x - 1)$

58. $8x^2 - 22x + 5$
$(4x - 1)(2x - 5)$

59. $15x^2 - 31x + 2$
$(15x - 1)(x - 2)$

60. $15x^2 + 31x + 2$
$(15x + 1)(x + 2)$

61. $4x^2 - 4x + 3$ Prime

62. $4x^2 + 12x - 5$ Prime

63. $2x^2 + 18x - 90$
$2(x^2 + 9x - 45)$

64. $3x^2 + 11x + 10$
$(x + 2)(3x + 5)$

65. $3x^2 + x - 10$
$(3x - 5)(x + 2)$

66. $3x^2 - 17x + 10$
$(3x - 2)(x - 5)$

67. $10x^2 - 3xy - y^2$ $(5x + y)(2x - y)$

68. $8x^2 - 2xy - y^2$ $(4x + y)(2x - y)$

69. $42a^2 - 13ab + b^2$ $(6a - b)(7a - b)$

70. $10a^2 - 27ab + 5b^2$ $(5a - b)(2a - 5b)$

Complete the factoring.

71. $3x^2 + 7x + 2 = (x + 2)(3x + 1)$

72. $2x^2 - x - 15 = (x - 3)(2x + 5)$

73. $5x^2 + 11x + 2 = (5x + 1)(x + 2)$

74. $4x^2 - 19x - 5 = (4x + 1)(x - 5)$

75. $6a^2 - 17a + 5 = (3a - 1)(2a - 5)$

76. $4b^2 - 16b + 15 = (2b - 5)(2b - 3)$

Factor each polynomial completely. See Examples 5 and 6.

77. $81w^3 - w$ $w(9w - 1)(9w + 1)$

78. $81w^3 - w^2$ $w^2(81w - 1)$

79. $4w^2 + 2w - 30$ $2(2w - 5)(w + 3)$

80. $2x^2 - 28x + 98$ $2(x - 7)^2$

81. $27 + 12x^2 + 36x$ $3(2x + 3)^2$

82. $24y + 12y^2 + 12$ $12(y + 1)^2$

83. $6w^2 - 11w - 35$ $(3w + 5)(2w - 7)$

84. $8y^2 - 14y - 15$ $(2y - 5)(4y + 3)$

85. $3x^2z - 3zx - 18z$ $3z(x - 3)(x + 2)$

86. $a^2b + 2ab - 15b$ $b(a + 5)(a - 3)$

87. $9x^3 - 21x^2 + 18x$ $3x(3x^2 - 7x + 6)$

88. $-8x^3 + 4x^2 - 2x$ $-2x(4x^2 - 2x + 1)$

89. $a^2 + 2ab - 15b^2$ $(a + 5b)(a - 3b)$

90. $a^2b^2 - 2a^2b - 15a^2$ $a^2(b - 5)(b + 3)$

91. $2x^2y^2 + xy^2 + 3y^2$ $y^2(2x^2 + x + 3)$

92. $18x^2 - 6x + 6$ $6(3x^2 - x + 1)$

93. $-6t^3 - t^2 + 2t$ $-t(3t + 2)(2t - 1)$

94. $-36t^2 - 6t + 12$ $-6(3t + 2)(2t - 1)$

95. $12t^4 - 2t^3 - 4t^2$ $2t^2(3t - 2)(2t + 1)$

96. $12t^3 + 14t^2 + 4t$ $2t(3t + 2)(2t + 1)$

97. $4x^2y - 8xy^2 + 3y^3$ $y(2x - y)(2x - 3y)$

98. $9x^2 + 24xy - 9y^2$ $3(3x - y)(x + 3y)$

99. $-4w^2 + 7w - 3$ $-1(w - 1)(4w - 3)$

100. $-30w^2 + w + 1$ $-1(5w - 1)(6w + 1)$

101. $-12a^3 + 22a^2b - 6ab^2$ $-2a(2a - 3b)(3a - b)$

102. $-36a^2b + 21ab^2 - 3b^3$ $-3b(3a - b)(4a - b)$

Solve each problem.

103. ***Height of a ball.*** If a ball is thrown upward at 40 feet per second from a rooftop 24 feet above the ground, then its height above the ground t seconds after it is thrown is given by $h = -16t^2 + 40t + 24$. Rewrite this formula with the polynomial on the right-hand side factored completely. Use the factored version of the formula to find h when $t = 3$.
$h = -8(2t + 1)(t - 3)$, 0 feet

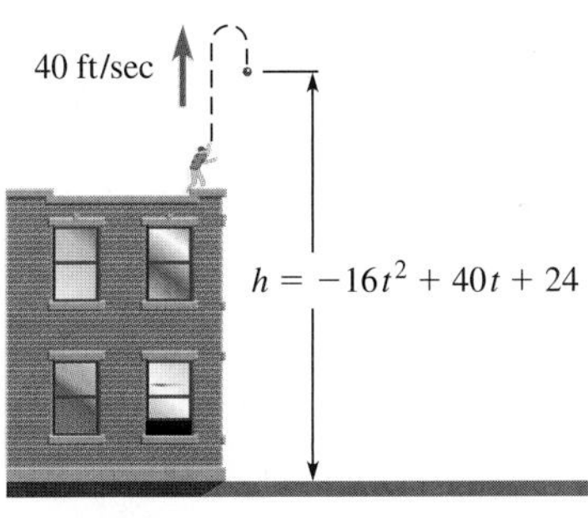

Figure for Exercise 103

104. ***Worker efficiency.*** In a study of worker efficiency at Wong Laboratories it was found that the number of components assembled per hour by the average worker t hours after starting work could be modeled by the formula

$$N(t) = -3t^3 + 23t^2 + 8t.$$

a) Rewrite the formula by factoring the right-hand side completely. $N(t) = -t(3t + 1)(t - 8)$

b) Use the factored version of the formula to find $N(3)$. 150 components

c) Use the accompanying graph to estimate the time at which the workers are most efficient. 5 hr

d) Use the accompanying graph to estimate the maximum number of components assembled per hour during an 8-hour shift. 250 components

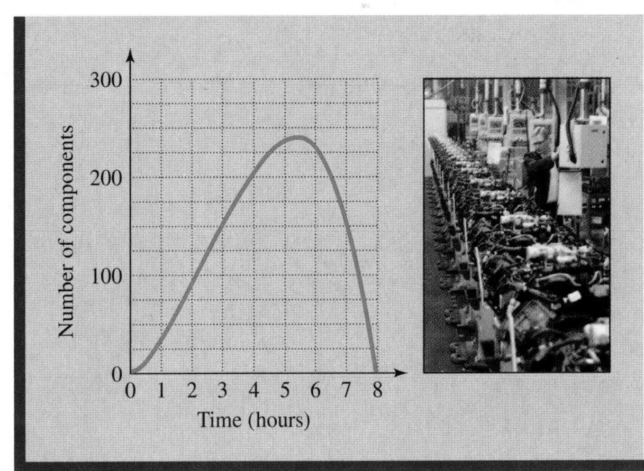

Figure for Exercise 104

Getting More Involved

105. ***Exploration*** 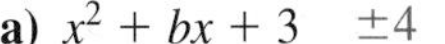

Find all positive and negative integers b for which each polynomial can be factored.

a) $x^2 + bx + 3$ ± 4

b) $3x^2 + bx + 5$ $\pm 8, \pm 16$

c) $2x^2 + bx - 15$ $\pm 1, \pm 7, \pm 13, \pm 29$

106. ***Exploration***

Find two integers c (positive or negative) for which each polynomial can be factored. Many answers are possible.

a) $x^2 + x + c$ $-2, -6$

b) $x^2 - 2x + c$ $1, -8$

c) $2x^2 - 3x + c$ $1, -9$

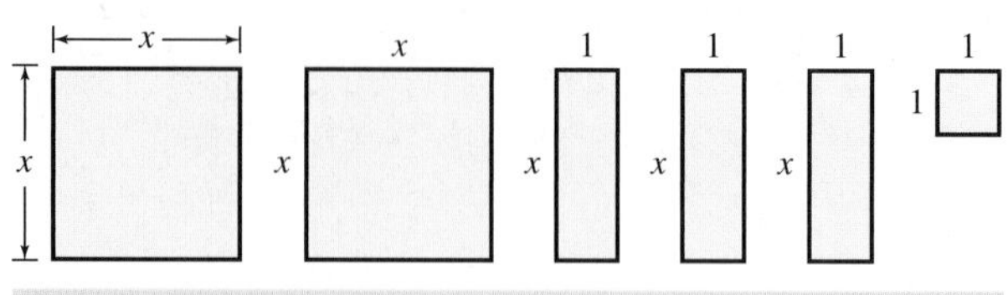

Figure for Exercise 107

107. ***Cooperative learning***

Working in groups, cut two large squares, three rectangles, and one small square out of paper that are exactly the same size as shown in the accompanying figure. Then try to place the six figures next to one another so that they form a large rectangle. Do not overlap the pieces or leave any gaps. Explain how factoring $2x^2 + 3x + 1$ can help you solve this puzzle.

108. ***Cooperative learning***

Working in groups, cut four squares and eight rectangles out of paper as in the previous exercise to illustrate the trinomial $4x^2 + 7x + 3$. Select one group to demonstrate how to arrange the 12 pieces to form a large rectangle. Have another group explain how factoring the trinomial can help you solve this puzzle.

5.5 Factoring a Difference or Sum of Two Cubes

In this Section

- Using Division in Factoring
- Factoring a Difference or Sum of Two Cubes
- Factoring a Difference of Two Fourth Powers
- The Factoring Strategy

In Sections 5.1 to 5.4 we established the general idea of factoring and some special cases. In this section we will see how division relates to factoring and see two more special cases. We will then summarize all of the factoring that we have done with a factoring strategy.

Using Division in Factoring

To find the prime factorization for a large integer such as 1001, you could divide possible factors (prime numbers) into 1001 until you find one that leaves no remainder. If you are told that 13 is a factor (or make a lucky guess), then you could divide 1001 by 13 to get the quotient 77. With this information you can factor 1001:

$$1001 = 77 \cdot 13$$

Now you can factor 77 to get the prime factorization of 1001:

$$1001 = 7 \cdot 11 \cdot 13$$

We can use this same idea with polynomials that are of higher degree than the ones we have been factoring. If we can guess a factor or if we are given a factor, we can use division to find the other factor and then proceed to factor the polynomial completely. Of course, it is harder to guess a factor of a polynomial than it is to guess a factor of an integer. In Example 1 we will factor a third-degree polynomial completely, given one factor.

EXAMPLE 1

Using division in factoring

Factor the polynomial $x^3 + 2x^2 - 5x - 6$ completely, given that the binomial $x + 1$ is a factor of the polynomial.

Solution

Divide the polynomial by the binomial:

$$
\begin{array}{r}
x^2 + x - 6 \\
x + 1 \overline{)x^3 + 2x^2 - 5x - 6} \\
\underline{x^3 + x^2} \qquad\qquad \\
x^2 - 5x \qquad \\
\underline{x^2 + x} \qquad \\
-6x - 6 \quad -5x - x = -6x \\
\underline{-6x - 6} \\
0 \quad -6 - (-6) = 0
\end{array}
$$

Because the remainder is 0, the dividend is the divisor times the quotient:

$$x^3 + 2x^2 - 5x - 6 = (x + 1)(x^2 + x - 6)$$

Now we factor the remaining trinomial to get the complete factorization:

$$x^3 + 2x^2 - 5x - 6 = (x + 1)(x + 3)(x - 2)$$

Now do Exercises 7–16

Study Tip

Everyone has a different attention span. Start by studying 10–15 minutes at a time and then build up to longer periods over time. In your senior year, you should be able to concentrate on one task for 30–45 minutes without a break. Be realistic. When you can't remember what you have read and can no longer concentrate, take a break.

Factoring a Difference or Sum of Two Cubes

We can use division to discover that $a - b$ is a factor of $a^3 - b^3$ (a difference of two cubes) and $a + b$ is a factor of $a^3 + b^3$ (a sum of two cubes):

$$
\begin{array}{r}
a^2 + ab + b^2 \\
a - b \overline{)a^3 + 0a^2b + 0ab^2 - b^3} \\
\underline{a^3 - a^2b} \qquad\qquad\qquad \\
a^2b + 0ab^2 \qquad \\
\underline{a^2b - ab^2} \qquad \\
ab^2 - b^3 \\
\underline{ab^2 - b^3} \\
0
\end{array}
\qquad
\begin{array}{r}
a^2 - ab + b^2 \\
a + b \overline{)a^3 + 0a^2b + 0ab^2 + b^3} \\
\underline{a^3 + a^2b} \qquad\qquad\qquad \\
-a^2b + 0ab^2 \qquad \\
\underline{-a^2b - ab^2} \qquad \\
ab^2 + b^3 \\
\underline{ab^2 + b^3} \\
0
\end{array}
$$

Teaching Tip It is a good exercise to have the students actually perform these two divisions and discover the rules for themselves.

So $a - b$ is a factor of $a^3 - b^3$, and $a + b$ is a factor of $a^3 + b^3$. These results give us two more factoring rules.

Factoring a Difference or Sum of Two Cubes

$$a^3 - b^3 = (a - b)(a^2 + ab + b^2)$$
$$a^3 + b^3 = (a + b)(a^2 - ab + b^2)$$

Note that $a^2 + ab + b^2$ and $a^2 - ab + b^2$ are prime. Do not confuse them with $a^2 + 2ab + b^2$ and $a^2 - 2ab + b^2$, which are not prime because

$$a^2 + 2ab + b^2 = (a + b)^2 \quad \text{and} \quad a^2 - 2ab + b^2 = (a - b)^2.$$

These similarities can help you remember the rules for factoring $a^3 - b^3$ and $a^3 + b^3$. Note also how $a^3 - b^3$ compares with $a^2 - b^2$:

$$a^2 - b^2 = (a - b)(a + b)$$
$$a^3 - b^3 = (a - b)(a^2 + ab + b^2)$$

EXAMPLE 2

Factoring a difference or sum of two cubes

Factor each polynomial.

a) $w^3 - 8$ **b)** $x^3 + 1$ **c)** $8y^3 - 27$

Solution

a) Because $8 = 2^3$, $w^3 - 8$ is a difference of two cubes. To factor $w^3 - 8$, let $a = w$ and $b = 2$ in the formula $a^3 - b^3 = (a - b)(a^2 + ab + b^2)$:

$$w^3 - 8 = (w - 2)(w^2 + 2w + 4)$$

b) Because $1 = 1^3$, the binomial $x^3 + 1$ is a sum of two cubes. Let $a = x$ and $b = 1$ in the formula $a^3 + b^3 = (a + b)(a^2 - ab + b^2)$:

$$x^3 + 1 = (x + 1)(x^2 - x + 1)$$

c) $8y^3 - 27 = (2y)^3 - 3^3$ This is a difference of two cubes.

$= (2y - 3)(4y^2 + 6y + 9)$ Let $a = 2y$ and $b = 3$ in the formula.

Now do Exercises 17–32

Teaching Tip This is a good opportunity to discuss the differences between $(a + b)^3$, $a^3 + b^3$, and $(ab)^3$.

In Example 2, we used the first three perfect cubes, 1, 8, and 27. You should verify that 1, 8, 27, 64, 125, 216, 343, 512, 729, and 1000 are the first 10 perfect cubes.

CAUTION The polynomial $(a - b)^3$ is not equivalent to $a^3 - b^3$ because if $a = 2$ and $b = 1$, then

$$(a - b)^3 = (2 - 1)^3 = 1^3 = 1$$

and

$$a^3 - b^3 = 2^3 - 1^3 = 8 - 1 = 7.$$

Likewise, $(a + b)^3$ is not equivalent to $a^3 + b^3$.

Factoring a Difference of Two Fourth Powers

A difference of two fourth powers of the form $a^4 - b^4$ is also a difference of two squares, $(a^2)^2 - (b^2)^2$. It can be factored by the rule for factoring a difference of two squares:

$a^4 - b^4 = (a^2)^2 - (b^2)^2$ Write as a difference of two squares.

$= (a^2 - b^2)(a^2 + b^2)$ Difference of two squares

$= (a - b)(a + b)(a^2 + b^2)$ Factor completely.

Note that the sum of two squares $a^2 + b^2$ is prime and cannot be factored.

EXAMPLE 3

Factoring a difference of two fourth powers

Factor each polynomial completely.

a) $x^4 - 16$ **b)** $81m^4 - n^4$

Solution

a) $x^4 - 16 = (x^2)^2 - 4^2$ Write as a difference of two squares.

$= (x^2 - 4)(x^2 + 4)$ Difference of two squares

$= (x - 2)(x + 2)(x^2 + 4)$ Factor completely.

b) $81m^4 - n^4 = (9m^2)^2 - (n^2)^2$ Write as a difference of two squares.

$= (9m^2 - n^2)(9m^2 + n^2)$ Factor.

$= (3m - n)(3m + n)(9m^2 + n^2)$ Factor completely.

Now do Exercises 33–40

The Factoring Strategy

The following is a summary of the ideas that we use to factor a polynomial completely.

Study Tip

Many schools have study skills centers that offer courses, workshops, and individual help on how to study. A search for "study skills" on the World Wide Web will turn up more information than you could possibly read. If you are not having the success in school that you would like, do something about it. What you do now will affect you the rest of your life.

Strategy for Factoring Polynomials Completely

1. If there are any common factors, factor them out first.
2. When factoring a binomial, check to see whether it is a difference of two squares, a difference of two cubes, or a sum of two cubes. *A sum of two squares does not factor.*
3. When factoring a trinomial, check to see whether it is a perfect square trinomial.
4. When factoring a trinomial that is not a perfect square, use the *ac* method or the trial-and-error method.
5. If the polynomial has four terms, try factoring by grouping.
6. Check to see whether any of the factors can be factored again.

We will use the factoring strategy in Example 3.

EXAMPLE 4

Factoring polynomials

Factor each polynomial completely.

a) $2a^2b - 24ab + 72b$

b) $3x^3 + 6x^2 - 75x - 150$

Solution

a) $2a^2b - 24ab + 72b = 2b(a^2 - 12a + 36)$ First factor out the GCF, $2b$.
$= 2b(a - 6)^2$ Factor the perfect square trinomial.

b) $3x^3 + 6x^2 - 75x - 150 = 3[x^3 + 2x^2 - 25x - 50]$ Factor out the GCF, 3.
$= 3[x^2(x + 2) - 25(x + 2)]$ Factor out common factors.
$= 3(x^2 - 25)(x + 2)$ Factor by grouping.
$= 3(x + 5)(x - 5)(x + 2)$ Factor the difference of two squares.

Now do Exercises 41–108

Warm-Ups ▼

True or false? Explain your answer.

1. $x^2 - 4 = (x - 2)^2$ for any real number x. False
2. The trinomial $4x^2 + 6x + 9$ is a perfect square trinomial. False
3. The polynomial $4y^2 + 25$ is a prime polynomial. True
4. $3y + ay + 3x + ax = (x + y)(3 + a)$ for any values of the variables. True
5. The polynomial $3x^2 + 51$ cannot be factored. False
6. If the GCF is not 1, then you should factor it out first. True
7. $x^2 + 9 = (x + 3)^2$ for any real number x. False
8. The polynomial $x^2 - 3x - 5$ is a prime polynomial. True
9. The polynomial $y^2 - 5y - my + 5m$ can be factored by grouping. True
10. The polynomial $x^2 + ax - 3x + 3a$ can be factored by grouping. False

5.5 Exercises

Boost your GRADE at mathzone.com!

MathZone
- ▶ Practice Problems
- ▶ Self-Tests
- ▶ Videos
- ▶ Net Tutor
- ▶ e-Professors

Reading and Writing *After reading this section, write out the answers to these questions. Use complete sentences.*

1. What is the relationship between division and factoring?
   If there is no remainder, then the dividend factors as the divisor times the quotient.
2. How do we know that $a - b$ is a factor of $a^3 - b^3$?
   If you divide $a^3 - b^3$ by $a - b$ there will be no remainder.
3. How do we know that $a + b$ is a factor of $a^3 + b^3$?
   If you divide $a^3 + b^3$ by $a + b$ there will be no remainder.
4. How do you recognize if a polynomial is a sum of two cubes?
   A sum of two cubes is of the form $a^3 + b^3$.
5. How do you factor a sum of two cubes?
   $a^3 + b^3 = (a + b)(a^2 - ab + b^2)$
6. How do you factor a difference of two cubes?
   $a^3 - b^3 = (a - b)(a^2 + ab + b^2)$

Factor each polynomial completely, given that the binomial following it is a factor of the polynomial. See Example 1.

7. $x^3 + 3x^2 - 10x - 24$, $x + 4$ $(x + 4)(x - 3)(x + 2)$
8. $x^3 - 7x + 6$, $x - 1$ $(x - 1)(x + 3)(x - 2)$
9. $x^3 + 4x^2 + x - 6$, $x - 1$ $(x - 1)(x + 3)(x + 2)$
10. $x^3 - 5x^2 - 2x + 24$, $x + 2$ $(x + 2)(x - 3)(x - 4)$
11. $x^3 - 8$, $x - 2$ $(x - 2)(x^2 + 2x + 4)$
12. $x^3 + 27$, $x + 3$ $(x + 3)(x^2 - 3x + 9)$

13. $x^3 + 4x^2 - 3x + 10, x + 5$ $(x + 5)(x^2 - x + 2)$
14. $2x^3 - 5x^2 - x - 6, x - 3$ $(x - 3)(2x^2 + x + 2)$
15. $x^3 + 2x^2 + 2x + 1, x + 1$ $(x + 1)(x^2 + x + 1)$
16. $x^3 + 2x^2 - 5x - 6, x + 3$ $(x + 3)(x - 2)(x + 1)$

Factor each difference or sum of cubes. See Example 2.

17. $m^3 - 1$ $(m - 1)(m^2 + m + 1)$
18. $z^3 - 27$ $(z - 3)(z^2 + 3z + 9)$
19. $x^3 + 8$ $(x + 2)(x^2 - 2x + 4)$
20. $y^3 + 27$ $(y + 3)(y^2 - 3y + 9)$
21. $a^3 + 125$ $(a + 5)(a^2 - 5a + 25)$
22. $b^3 - 216$ $(b - 6)(b^2 + 6b + 36)$
23. $c^3 - 343$ $(c - 7)(c^2 + 7c + 49)$
24. $d^3 + 1000$ $(d + 10)(d^2 - 10d + 100)$
25. $8w^3 + 1$ $(2w + 1)(4w^2 - 2w + 1)$
26. $125m^3 + 1$ $(5m + 1)(25m^2 - 5m + 1)$
27. $8t^3 - 27$ $(2t - 3)(4t^2 + 6t + 9)$
28. $125n^3 - 8$ $(5n - 2)(25n^2 + 10n + 4)$
29. $x^3 - y^3$ $(x - y)(x^2 + xy + y^2)$
30. $m^3 + n^3$ $(m + n)(m^2 - mn + n^2)$
31. $8t^3 + y^3$ $(2t + y)(4t^2 - 2ty + y^2)$
32. $u^3 - 125v^3$ $(u - 5v)(u^2 + 5uv + 25v^2)$

Factor each polynomial completely. See Example 3.

33. $x^4 - y^4$ $(x - y)(x + y)(x^2 + y^2)$
34. $m^4 - n^4$ $(m - n)(m + n)(m^2 + n^2)$
35. $x^4 - 1$ $(x - 1)(x + 1)(x^2 + 1)$
36. $a^4 - 81$ $(a - 3)(a + 3)(a^2 + 9)$
37. $16b^4 - 1$ $(2b - 1)(2b + 1)(4b^2 + 1)$
38. $625b^4 - 1$ $(5b - 1)(5b + 1)(25b^2 + 1)$
39. $a^4 - 81b^4$ $(a - 3b)(a + 3b)(a^2 + 9b^2)$
40. $16a^4 - m^4$ $(2a - m)(2a + m)(4a^2 + m^2)$

Factor each polynomial completely. If a polynomial is prime, say so. See Example 4.

41. $2x^2 - 18$ $2(x - 3)(x + 3)$
42. $3x^3 - 12x$ $3x(x - 2)(x + 2)$
43. $a^2 + 4$ Prime
44. $x^2 + y^2$ Prime
45. $4x^2 + 8x - 60$ $4(x + 5)(x - 3)$
46. $3x^2 + 18x + 27$ $3(x + 3)^2$
47. $x^3 + 4x^2 + 4x$ $x(x + 2)^2$
48. $a^3 - 5a^2 + 6a$ $a(a - 2)(a - 3)$
49. $5max^2 + 20ma$ $5am(x^2 + 4)$
50. $3bmw^2 - 12bm$ $3bm(w - 2)(w + 2)$
51. $2x^2 - 3x - 1$ Prime
52. $3x^2 - 8x - 5$ Prime
53. $9x^2 + 6x + 1$ $(3x + 1)^2$
54. $9x^2 + 6x + 3$ $3(3x^2 + 2x + 1)$
55. $9m^2 + 1$ Prime
56. $4b^2 + 25$ Prime
57. $w^4 - z^4$ $(w - z)(w + z)(w^2 + z^2)$
58. $y^4 - 1$ $(y - 1)(y + 1)(y^2 + 1)$
59. $6x^2y + xy - 2y$ $y(3x + 2)(2x - 1)$
60. $5x^2y^2 - xy^2 - 6y^2$ $y^2(5x - 6)(x + 1)$
61. $y^2 + 10y - 25$ Prime
62. $x^2 - 20x + 25$ Prime
63. $48a^2 - 24a + 3$ $3(4a - 1)^2$
64. $8b^2 + 24b + 18$ $2(2b + 3)^2$
65. $16m^2 - 4m - 2$ $2(4m + 1)(2m - 1)$
66. $32a^2 + 4a - 6$ $2(2a + 1)(8a - 3)$
67. $s^4 - 16t^4$ $(s - 2t)(s + 2t)(s^2 + 4t^2)$
68. $81 - q^4$ $(3 - q)(3 + q)(9 + q^2)$
69. $9a^2 + 24a + 16$ $(3a + 4)^2$
70. $3x^2 - 18x - 48$ $3(x - 8)(x + 2)$
71. $24x^2 - 26x + 6$ $2(3x - 1)(4x - 3)$
72. $4x^2 - 6x - 12$ $2(2x^2 - 3x - 6)$
73. $3m^2 + 27$ $3(m^2 + 9)$
74. $5a^2 + 20b^2$ $5(a^2 + 4b^2)$
75. $3a^2 - 27a$ $3a(a - 9)$
76. $a^2 - 25a$ $a(a - 25)$
77. $8 - 2x^2$ $2(2 - x)(2 + x)$
78. $x^3 + 6x^2 + 9x$ $x(x + 3)^2$
79. $w^2 + 4t^2$ Prime
80. $9x^2 + 4y^2$ Prime
81. $6x^3 - 5x^2 + 12x$ $x(6x^2 - 5x + 12)$
82. $x^3 + 2x^2 - x - 2$ $(x - 1)(x + 1)(x + 2)$
83. $a^3b - 4ab$ $ab(a - 2)(a + 2)$
84. $2m^2 - 1800$ $2(m - 30)(m + 30)$
85. $x^3 + 2x^2 - 4x - 8$ $(x - 2)(x + 2)^2$
86. $-2x^3 - 50x$ $-2x(x^2 + 25)$
87. $-7m^3n - 28mn^3$ $-7mn(m^2 + 4n^2)$
88. $x^3 - x^2 - x + 1$ $(x + 1)(x - 1)^2$
89. $2x^3 + 16$ $2(x + 2)(x^2 - 2x + 4)$
90. $m^2a + 2ma^2 + a^3$ $a(m + a)^2$
91. $2w^4 - 16w$ $2w(w - 2)(w^2 + 2w + 4)$
92. $m^4n + mn^4$ $mn(m + n)(m^2 - mn + n^2)$
93. $3a^2w - 18aw + 27w$ $3w(a - 3)^2$
94. $8a^3 + 4a$ $4a(2a^2 + 1)$
95. $5x^2 - 500$ $5(x - 10)(x + 10)$
96. $25x^2 - 16y^2$ $(5x - 4y)(5x + 4y)$
97. $2m + 2n - wm - wn$ $(2 - w)(m + n)$
98. $aw - 5b - bw + 5a$ $(w + 5)(a - b)$
99. $3x^4 + 3x$ $3x(x + 1)(x^2 - x + 1)$
100. $3a^5 - 81a^2$ $3a^2(a - 3)(a^2 + 3a + 9)$
101. $4w^2 + 4w - 4$ $4(w^2 + w - 1)$
102. $4w^2 + 8w - 5$ $(2w + 5)(2w - 1)$
103. $a^4 + 7a^3 - 30a^2$ $a^2(a + 10)(a - 3)$
104. $2y^5 + 3y^4 - 20y^3$ $y^3(2y - 5)(y + 4)$
105. $4aw^3 - 12aw^2 + 9aw$ $aw(2w - 3)^2$
106. $9bn^3 + 15bn^2 - 14bn$ $bn(3n - 2)(3n + 7)$
107. $t^2 + 6t + 9$ $(t + 3)^2$
108. $t^3 + 12t^2 + 36t$ $t(t + 6)^2$

Solve each problem.

109. ***Increasing cube.*** Each of the three dimensions of a cube with a volume of x^3 cubic centimeters is increased by a whole number of centimeters. If the new volume is $x^3 + 10x^2 + 31x + 30$ cubic centimeters and the new height is $x + 2$ centimeters, then what are the new length and width?
Length $x + 5$ cm, width $x + 3$ cm

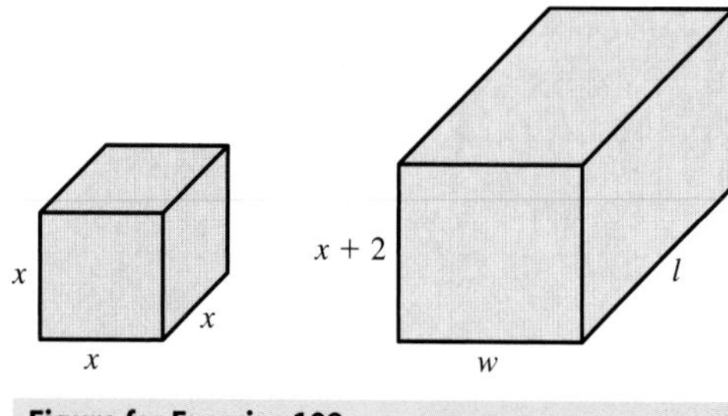

Figure for Exercise 109

110. ***Decreasing cube.*** Each of the three dimensions of a cube with a volume of y^3 cubic centimeters is decreased by a whole number of centimeters. If the new volume is $y^3 - 13y^2 + 54y - 72$ cubic centimeters and the new width is $y - 6$ centimeters, then what are the new length and height? Length $y - 3$ cm, height $y - 4$ cm

Getting More Involved

111. ***Discussion***

Are there any values for a and b for which $(a + b)^3 = a^3 + b^3$? Find a pair of values for a and b for which $(a + b)^3 \neq a^3 + b^3$. Is $(a + b)^3$ equivalent to $a^3 + b^3$? Explain your answers.
$(-1 + 1)^3 = (-1)^3 + 1^3$, $(1 + 2)^3 \neq 1^3 + 2^3$

112. ***Writing***

Explain why $a^2 + ab + b^2$ and $a^2 - ab + b^2$ are prime polynomials.

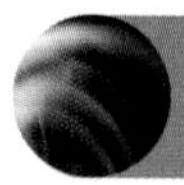

5.6 Solving Quadratic Equations by Factoring

In this Section

- **The Zero Factor Property**
- **Applications**

The techniques of factoring can be used to solve equations involving polynomials. These equations cannot be solved by the other methods that you have learned. After you learn to solve equations by factoring, you will use this technique to solve some new types of problems.

The Zero Factor Property

In this chapter you learned to factor polynomials such as $x^2 + x - 6$. The equation $x^2 + x - 6 = 0$ is called a *quadratic equation.*

Quadratic Equation

If a, b, and c are real numbers with $a \neq 0$, then

$$ax^2 + bx + c = 0$$

is called a **quadratic equation.**

A quadratic equation always has a second-degree term because it is specified in the definition that a is not zero. The main idea used to solve quadratic equations, the **zero factor property,** is simply a fact about multiplication by zero.

The Zero Factor Property

The equation $a \cdot b = 0$ is equivalent to

$$a = 0 \quad \text{or} \quad b = 0.$$

So if a product is zero, then one or the other of the factors is zero. In Example 1 we combine the zero factor property with factoring to solve a quadratic equation.

EXAMPLE 1

Helpful Hint

Some students grow up believing that the only way to solve an equation is to "do the same thing to each side." Then along come quadratic equations and the zero factor property. For a quadratic equation, we write an equivalent compound equation that is not obtained by "doing the same thing to each side."

Using the zero factor property

Solve $x^2 + x - 6 = 0$.

Solution

First factor the polynomial on the left-hand side:

$$x^2 + x - 6 = 0$$

$$(x + 3)(x - 2) = 0 \quad \text{Factor the left-hand side.}$$

$$x + 3 = 0 \quad \text{or} \quad x - 2 = 0 \quad \text{Zero factor property}$$

$$x = -3 \quad \text{or} \quad x = 2 \quad \text{Solve each equation.}$$

We now check that -3 and 2 satisfy the original equation.

For $x = -3$:

$$x^2 + x - 6 = (-3)^2 + (-3) - 6 = 9 - 3 - 6 = 0$$

For $x = 2$:

$$x^2 + x - 6 = (2)^2 + (2) - 6 = 4 + 2 - 6 = 0$$

The solutions to $x^2 + x - 6 = 0$ are -3 and 2.

Now do Exercises 7–18

A sentence such as $x = -3$ or $x = 2$, which is made up of two or more equations connected with the word "or" is called a **compound equation.** In Example 2 we again solve a quadratic equation by using the zero factor property to write a compound equation.

EXAMPLE 2

Teaching Tip Another good example to work at this point is to solve $x^2 = x$.

Using the zero factor property

Solve the equation $3x^2 = -3x$.

Solution

First rewrite the equation with 0 on the right-hand side:

$$3x^2 = -3x$$

$$3x^2 + 3x = 0 \quad \text{Add } 3x \text{ to each side.}$$

$$3x(x + 1) = 0 \quad \text{Factor the left-hand side.}$$

$$3x = 0 \quad \text{or} \quad x + 1 = 0 \quad \text{Zero factor property}$$

$$x = 0 \quad \text{or} \quad x = -1 \quad \text{Solve each equation.}$$

Check 0 and -1 in the original equation $3x^2 = -3x$.

For $x = 0$: $3(0)^2 = -3(0)$, $0 = 0$

For $x = -1$: $3(-1)^2 = -3(-1)$, $3 = 3$

There are two solutions to the original equation, 0 and -1.

Now do Exercises 19–26

CAUTION If in Example 2 you divide each side of $3x^2 = -3x$ by $3x$, you would get $x = -1$ but not the solution $x = 0$. For this reason we usually do not divide each side of an equation by a variable.

The basic strategy for solving an equation by factoring follows.

Helpful Hint

We have seen quadratic polynomials that cannot be factored. So not all quadratic equations can be solved by factoring. Methods for solving all quadratic equations are presented in Chapter 10.

Strategy for Solving an Equation by Factoring

1. Rewrite the equation with 0 on one side.
2. Factor the other side completely.
3. Use the zero factor property to get simple linear equations.
4. Solve the linear equations.
5. Check the answer in the original equation.
6. State the solution(s) to the original equation.

EXAMPLE 3

Using the zero factor property

Solve $(2x + 1)(x - 1) = 14$.

Study Tip

Set short-term goals and reward yourself for accomplishing them. When you have solved 10 problems, take a short break and listen to your favorite music.

Solution

To write the equation with 0 on the right-hand side, multiply the binomials on the left and then subtract 14 from each side:

$$(2x + 1)(x - 1) = 14 \quad \text{Original equation}$$
$$2x^2 - x - 1 = 14 \quad \text{Multiply the binomials.}$$
$$2x^2 - x - 15 = 0 \quad \text{Subtract 14 from each side.}$$
$$(2x + 5)(x - 3) = 0 \quad \text{Factor.}$$
$$2x + 5 = 0 \quad \text{or} \quad x - 3 = 0 \quad \text{Zero factor property}$$
$$2x = -5 \quad \text{or} \quad x = 3$$
$$x = -\frac{5}{2} \quad \text{or} \quad x = 3$$

Teaching Tip Show students how to make up a problem like this example: If $x = 5$, then $(5 - 2)(5 + 7) = 36$. So one of the solutions to $(x - 2)(x + 7) = 36$ is 5. Now solve it to find both solutions.

Check $-\frac{5}{2}$ and 3 in the original equation:

$$\left(2 \cdot -\frac{5}{2} + 1\right)\left(-\frac{5}{2} - 1\right) = (-5 + 1)\left(-\frac{5}{2} - \frac{2}{2}\right)$$
$$= (-4)\left(-\frac{7}{2}\right)$$
$$= 14$$
$$(2 \cdot 3 + 1)(3 - 1) = (7)(2)$$
$$= 14$$

So the solutions are $-\frac{5}{2}$ and 3.

Now do Exercises 27–32

CAUTION In Example 3 we started with a product of two factors equal to 14. Because there are many pairs of factors that have a product of 14, we *cannot make any conclusion about the factors.* If the product of two factors is 0, then we can conclude that one or the other factor is 0.

If a perfect square trinomial occurs in a quadratic equation, then there are two identical factors of the trinomial. In this case it is not necessary to set both factors equal to zero. The solution can be found from one factor.

EXAMPLE 4

An equation with a repeated factor

Solve $5x^2 - 30x + 45 = 0$.

Solution

Notice that the trinomial on the left-hand side has a common factor:

$$5x^2 - 30x + 45 = 0$$
$$5(x^2 - 6x + 9) = 0 \quad \text{Factor out the GCF.}$$
$$5(x - 3)^2 = 0 \quad \text{Factor the perfect square trinomial.}$$
$$(x - 3)^2 = 0 \quad \text{Divide each side by 5.}$$
$$x - 3 = 0 \quad \text{Zero factor property}$$
$$x = 3$$

Even though $x - 3$ occurs twice as a factor, it is not necessary to write $x - 3 = 0$ or $x - 3 = 0$. If $x = 3$ in $5x^2 - 30x + 45 = 0$, we get

$$5 \cdot 3^2 - 30 \cdot 3 + 45 = 0,$$

which is correct. So the only solution to the equation is 3.

Now do Exercises 33–36

Teaching Tip There are two trouble spots here, the constant factor and the repeated factor. You might need to work another example: $-12x^2 - 36x - 27 = 0$.

CAUTION To simplify $5(x - 3)^2 = 0$ in Example 4, we divided each side by 5. If we had used the zero factor property, we would have gotten $5 = 0$ or $(x - 3)^2 = 0$. Since $5 = 0$ has no solution, we can ignore it and continue to solve $(x - 3)^2 = 0$.

If the left-hand side of the equation has more than two factors, we can write an equivalent equation by setting each factor equal to zero.

EXAMPLE 5

An equation with three solutions

Solve $2x^3 - x^2 - 8x + 4 = 0$.

Solution

We can factor the four-term polynomial by grouping:

$$2x^3 - x^2 - 8x + 4 = 0$$

$$x^2(2x - 1) - 4(2x - 1) = 0 \quad \text{Factor out the common factors.}$$

$$(x^2 - 4)(2x - 1) = 0 \quad \text{Factor out } 2x - 1.$$

$$(x - 2)(x + 2)(2x - 1) = 0 \quad \text{Difference of two squares}$$

$$x - 2 = 0 \quad \text{or} \quad x + 2 = 0 \quad \text{or} \quad 2x - 1 = 0 \quad \text{Zero factor property}$$

$$x = 2 \quad \text{or} \quad x = -2 \quad \text{or} \quad x = \frac{1}{2} \quad \text{Solve each equation.}$$

To check let $x = -2, \frac{1}{2}$, and 2 in $2x^3 - x^2 - 8x + 4 = 0$:

$$2(-2)^3 - (-2)^2 - 8(-2) + 4 = 0$$

$$2\left(\frac{1}{2}\right)^3 - \left(\frac{1}{2}\right)^2 - 8\left(\frac{1}{2}\right) + 4 = 0$$

$$2(2)^3 - 2^2 - 8(2) + 4 = 0$$

Since all of these equations are correct, the solutions are $-2, \frac{1}{2}$, and 2.

Now do Exercises 37–44

Helpful Hint

Compare the number of solutions in Examples 1 through 5 to the degree of the polynomial. The number of real solutions to any polynomial equation is less than or equal to the degree of the polynomial. This fact is known as the fundamental theorem of algebra.

Note that all of the equations in this section can be solved by factoring. However, we can write equations involving prime polynomials. Such equations cannot be solved by factoring but can be solved by the methods in Chapter 10.

Applications

There are many problems that can be solved by equations like those we have just discussed.

EXAMPLE 6

Area of a garden

Merida's garden has a rectangular shape with a length that is 1 foot longer than twice the width. If the area of the garden is 55 square feet, then what are the dimensions of the garden?

Solution

If x represents the width of the garden, then $2x + 1$ represents the length. See Fig. 5.1. Because the area of a rectangle is the length times the width, we can write the equation

$$x(2x + 1) = 55.$$

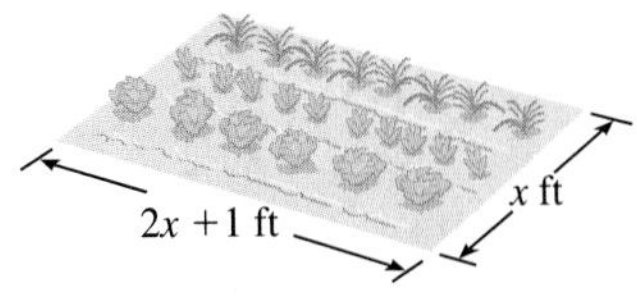

Figure 5.1

We must have zero on the right-hand side of the equation to use the zero factor property. So we rewrite the equation and then factor:

$$2x^2 + x - 55 = 0$$

$$(2x + 11)(x - 5) = 0 \quad \text{Factor.}$$

$$2x + 11 = 0 \quad \text{or} \quad x - 5 = 0 \quad \text{Zero factor property}$$

$$x = -\frac{11}{2} \quad \text{or} \quad x = 5$$

The width is certainly not $-\frac{11}{2}$. So we use $x = 5$ to get the length:

$$2x + 1 = 2(5) + 1 = 11$$

We check by multiplying 11 feet and 5 feet to get the area of 55 square feet. So the width is 5 ft, and the length is 11 ft.

Now do Exercises 63–64

Helpful Hint

To prove the Pythagorean theorem, draw two squares with sides of length $a + b$, and partition them as shown.

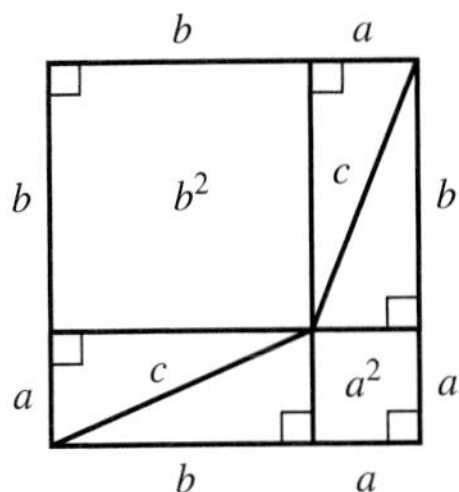

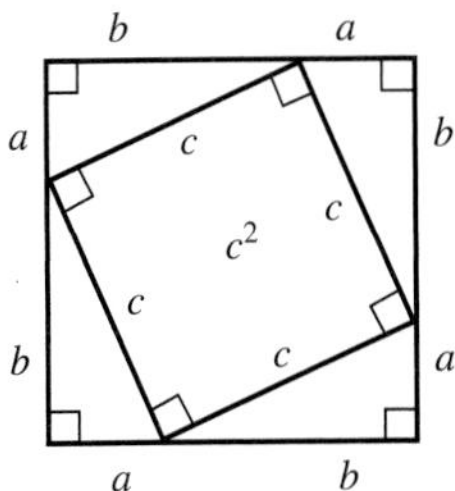

Erasing the four identical triangles from each picture will subtract the same amount of area from each original square. Since we started with equal areas, we will have equal areas after erasing the triangles:

$$a^2 + b^2 = c^2$$

The next application involves a theorem from geometry called the **Pythagorean theorem.** This theorem says that in any right triangle the sum of the squares of the lengths of the legs is equal to the square of the length of the hypotenuse.

The Pythagorean Theorem

The triangle shown in Fig. 5.2 is a right triangle if and only if

$$a^2 + b^2 = c^2.$$

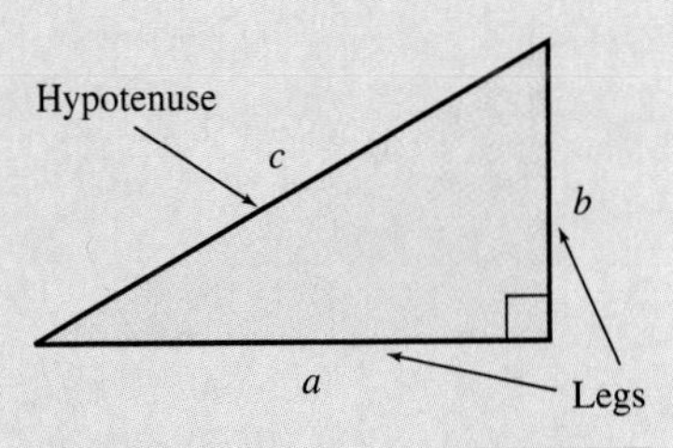

Figure 5.2

EXAMPLE 7

Using the Pythagorean theorem

The length of a rectangle is 1 meter longer than the width, and the diagonal measures 5 meters. What are the length and width?

Solution

If x represents the width of the rectangle, then $x + 1$ represents the length. Because the two sides are the legs of a right triangle, we can use the Pythagorean theorem to get a relationship between the length, width, and diagonal. See Fig. 5.3.

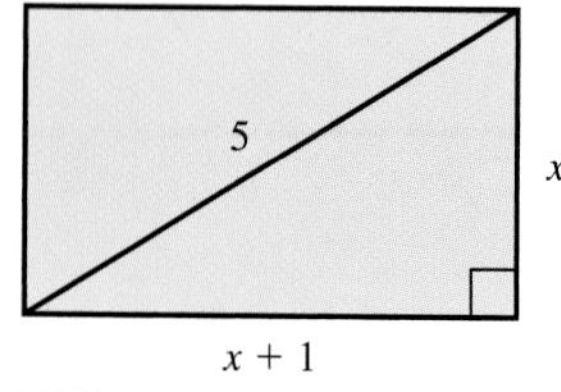

Figure 5.3

$$x^2 + (x + 1)^2 = 5^2 \quad \text{Pythagorean theorem}$$
$$x^2 + x^2 + 2x + 1 = 25 \quad \text{Simplify.}$$
$$2x^2 + 2x - 24 = 0$$
$$x^2 + x - 12 = 0 \quad \text{Divide each side by 2.}$$
$$(x - 3)(x + 4) = 0$$
$$x - 3 = 0 \quad \text{or} \quad x + 4 = 0 \quad \text{Zero factor property}$$
$$x = 3 \quad \text{or} \quad x = -4 \quad \text{The length cannot be negative.}$$
$$x + 1 = 4$$

To check this answer, we compute $3^2 + 4^2 = 5^2$, or $9 + 16 = 25$. So the rectangle is 3 meters by 4 meters.

Now do Exercises 65–66

CAUTION The hypotenuse is the longest side of a right triangle. So if the lengths of the sides of a right triangle are 5 meters, 12 meters, and 13 meters, then the length of the hypotenuse is 13 meters, and $5^2 + 12^2 = 13^2$.

Warm-Ups ▼

True or false? Explain your answer.

1. The equation $x(x + 2) = 3$ is equivalent to $x = 3$ or $x + 2 = 3$. False
2. Equations solved by factoring always have two different solutions. False
3. The equation $a \cdot d = 0$ is equivalent to $a = 0$ or $d = 0$. True
4. If x is the width in feet of a rectangular room and the length is 5 feet longer than the width, then the area is $x^2 + 5x$ square feet. True
5. Both 1 and -4 are solutions to the equation $(x - 1)(x + 4) = 0$. True
6. If a, b, and c are the sides of any triangle, then $a^2 + b^2 = c^2$. False
7. If the perimeter of a rectangular room is 50 feet, then the sum of the length and width is 25 feet. True
8. Equations solved by factoring may have more than two solutions. True
9. Both 0 and 2 are solutions to the equation $x(x - 2) = 0$. True
10. The solutions to $3(x - 2)(x + 5) = 0$ are 3, 2, and -5. False

5.6 Exercises

Boost your GRADE at mathzone.com!

MathZone

- Practice Problems
- Self-Tests
- Videos
- Net Tutor
- e-Professors

Reading and Writing *After reading this section, write out the answers to these questions. Use complete sentences.*

1. What is a quadratic equation?
A quadratic equation has the form $ax^2 + bx + c = 0$ with $a \neq 0$.

2. What is a compound equation?
A compound equation is two equations connected with the word "or."

3. What is the zero factor property?
The zero factor property says that if $ab = 0$ then $a = 0$ or $b = 0$.

4. What method is used to solve quadratic equations in this section?
Quadratic equations are solved by factoring in this section.

5. Why don't we usually divide each side of an equation by a variable?
Dividing each side by a variable is not usually done because the variable might have a value of zero.

6. What is the Pythagorean theorem?
A triangle is a right triangle if and only if the sum of the squares of the legs is equal to the square of the hypotenuse.

Solve each equation. See Example 1.

7. $(x + 5)(x + 4) = 0$ $-4, -5$
8. $(a + 6)(a + 5) = 0$ $-6, -5$
9. $(2x + 5)(3x - 4) = 0$ $-\frac{5}{2}, \frac{4}{3}$
10. $(3k - 8)(4k + 3) = 0$ $\frac{8}{3}, -\frac{3}{4}$
11. $x^2 + 3x + 2 = 0$ $-2, -1$
12. $x^2 + 7x + 12 = 0$ $-4, -3$
13. $w^2 - 9w + 14 = 0$ $2, 7$
14. $t^2 + 6t - 27 = 0$ $-9, 3$
15. $y^2 - 2y - 24 = 0$ $-4, 6$
16. $q^2 + 3q - 18 = 0$ $-6, 3$
17. $2m^2 + m - 1 = 0$ $-1, \frac{1}{2}$
18. $2h^2 - h - 3 = 0$ $-1, \frac{3}{2}$

Solve each equation. See Examples 2 and 3.

19. $x^2 = x$ $0, 1$
20. $w^2 = 2w$ $0, 2$
21. $m^2 = -7m$ $0, -7$
22. $h^2 = -5h$ $0, -5$
23. $a^2 + a = 20$ $-5, 4$
24. $p^2 + p = 42$ $-7, 6$
25. $2x^2 + 5x = 3$ $\frac{1}{2}, -3$
26. $3x^2 - 10x = -7$ $1, \frac{7}{3}$
27. $(x + 2)(x + 6) = 12$ $0, -8$
28. $(x + 2)(x - 6) = 20$ $-4, 8$
29. $(a + 3)(2a - 1) = 15$ $-\frac{9}{2}, 2$
30. $(b - 3)(3b + 4) = 10$ $\frac{11}{3}, -2$
31. $2(4 - 5h) = 3h^2$ $\frac{2}{3}, -4$
32. $2w(4w + 1) = 1$ $-\frac{1}{2}, \frac{1}{4}$

Solve each equation. See Examples 4 and 5.

33. $2x^2 + 50 = 20x$ 5
34. $3x^2 + 48 = 24x$ 4
35. $4m^2 - 12m + 9 = 0$ $\frac{3}{2}$
36. $25y^2 + 20y + 4 = 0$ $-\frac{2}{5}$
37. $x^3 - 9x = 0$ $0, -3, 3$
38. $25x - x^3 = 0$ $-5, 0, 5$
39. $w^3 + 4w^2 - 4w = 16$ $-4, -2, 2$
40. $a^3 + 2a^2 - a = 2$ $-2, -1, 1$
41. $n^3 - 3n^2 + 3 = n$ $-1, 1, 3$
42. $w^3 + w^2 - 25w = 25$ $-5, -1, 5$
43. $y^3 - 9y^2 + 20y = 0$ $0, 4, 5$
44. $m^3 + 2m^2 - 3m = 0$ $-3, 0, 1$

Solve each equation.

45. $x^2 - 16 = 0$ $-4, 4$
46. $x^2 - 36 = 0$ $-6, 6$
47. $x^2 = 9$ $-3, 3$
48. $x^2 = 25$ $-5, 5$
49. $a^3 = a$ $0, -1, 1$
50. $x^3 = 4x$ $-2, 0, 2$
51. $3x^2 + 15x + 18 = 0$ $-3, -2$
52. $-2x^2 - 2x + 24 = 0$ $-4, 3$
53. $z^2 + \frac{11}{2}z = -6$ $-\frac{3}{2}, -4$
54. $m^2 + \frac{8}{3}m = 1$ $-3, \frac{1}{3}$
55. $(t - 3)(t + 5) = 9$ $-6, 4$
56. $3x(2x + 1) = 18$ $-2, \frac{3}{2}$
57. $(x - 2)^2 + x^2 = 10$ $-1, 3$
58. $(x - 3)^2 + (x + 2)^2 = 17$ $-1, 2$
59. $\frac{1}{16}x^2 + \frac{1}{8}x = \frac{1}{2}$ $-4, 2$
60. $\frac{1}{18}h^2 - \frac{1}{2}h + 1 = 0$ $3, 6$

61. $a^3 + 3a^2 - 25a = 75$ $-5, -3, 5$

62. $m^4 + m^3 = 100m^2 + 100m$ $-10, -1, 0, 10$

Solve each problem. See Examples 6 and 7.

63. ***Dimensions of a rectangle.*** The perimeter of a rectangle is 34 feet, and the diagonal is 13 feet long. What are the length and width of the rectangle? Length 12 ft, width 5 ft

64. ***Address book.*** The perimeter of the cover of an address book is 14 inches, and the diagonal measures 5 inches. What are the length and width of the cover? Width 3 in., length 4 in.

Figure for Exercise 64

65. ***Violla's bathroom.*** The length of Violla's bathroom is 2 feet longer than twice the width. If the diagonal measures 13 feet, then what are the length and width? Width 5 ft, length 12 ft

66. ***Rectangular stage.*** One side of a rectangular stage is 2 meters longer than the other. If the diagonal is 10 meters, then what are the lengths of the sides? 6 m and 8 m

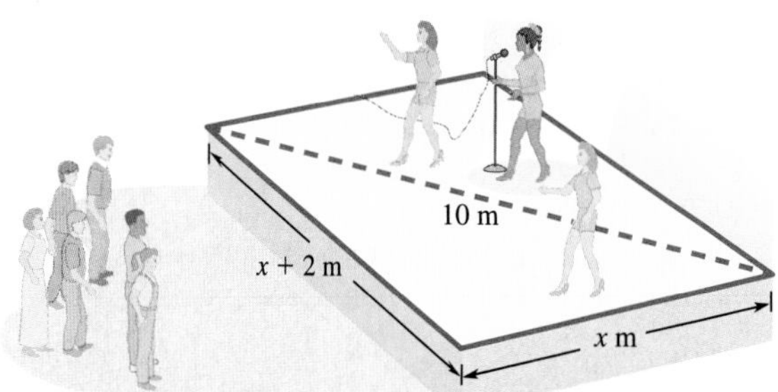

Figure for Exercise 66

67. ***Consecutive integers.*** The sum of the squares of two consecutive integers is 13. Find the integers.
2 and 3, or -3 and -2

68. ***Consecutive integers.*** The sum of the squares of two consecutive even integers is 52. Find the integers.
-6 and -4, or 4 and 6

69. ***Two numbers.*** The sum of two numbers is 11, and their product is 30. Find the numbers. 5 and 6

70. ***Missing ages.*** Molly's age is twice Anita's. If the sum of the squares of their ages is 80, then what are their ages?
Anita 4, Molly 8

71. ***Three even integers.*** The sum of the squares of three consecutive even integers is 116. Find the integers.
$-8, -6, -4$, or 4, 6, 8

72. ***Two odd integers.*** The product of two consecutive odd integers is 63. Find the integers. -9 and -7, or 7 and 9

73. ***Consecutive integers.*** The product of two consecutive integers is 5 more than their sum. Find the integers.
-2 and -1, or 3 and 4

74. ***Consecutive even integers.*** If the product of two consecutive even integers is 34 larger than their sum, then what are the integers? -6 and -4, or 6 and 8

75. ***Two integers.*** Two integers differ by 5. If the sum of their squares is 53, then what are the integers?
-7 and -2, or 2 and 7

76. ***Two negative integers.*** Two negative integers have a sum of -10. If the sum of their squares is 68, then what are the integers? -8 and -2

77. ***Area of a rectangle.*** The area of a rectangle is 72 square feet. If the length is 6 feet longer than the width, then what are the length and the width? Length 12 feet, width 6 feet

78. ***Area of a triangle.*** The base of a triangle is 4 inches longer than the height. If its area is 70 square inches, then what are the base and the height?
Base 14 inches, height 10 inches

79. ***Legs of a right triangle.*** The hypotenuse of a right triangle is 15 meters. If one leg is 3 meters longer than the other, then what are the lengths of the legs?
9 meters and 12 meters

80. ***Legs of a right triangle.*** If the longer leg of a right triangle is 1 cm longer than the shorter leg and the hypotenuse is 5 cm, then what are the lengths of the legs? 3 cm and 4 cm

81. ***Skydiving.*** If there were no air resistance, then the height (in feet) above the earth for a skydiver t seconds after

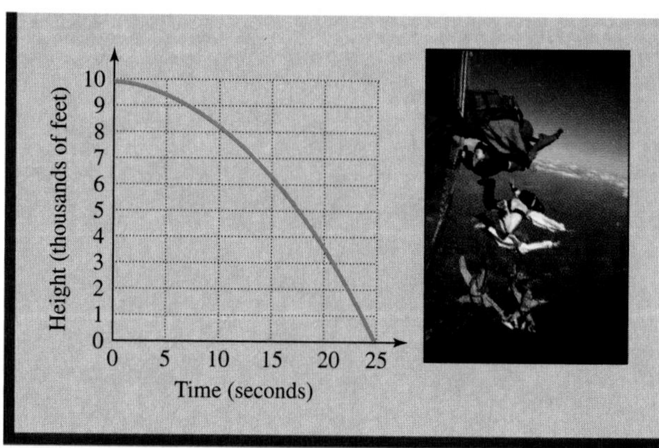

Figure for Exercise 81

jumping from an airplane at 10,000 feet would be given by

$$h(t) = -16t^2 + 10{,}000.$$

a) Find the time that it would take to fall to earth with no air resistance; that is, find t for which $h(t) = 0$. A skydiver actually gets about twice as much free fall time due to air resistance.
25 sec

b) Use the accompanying graph to determine whether the skydiver (with no air resistance) falls farther in the first 5 seconds or the last 5 seconds of the fall.
last 5 sec

c) Is the skydiver's velocity increasing or decreasing as she falls? increasing

82. ***Skydiving.*** If a skydiver jumps from an airplane at a height of 8256 feet, then for the first five seconds, her height above the earth is approximated by the formula $h = -16t^2 + 8256$. How many seconds does it take her to reach 8000 feet? 4 sec

83. ***Throwing a sandbag.*** If a balloonist throws a sandbag downward at 24 feet per second from an altitude of 720 feet, then its height (in feet) above the ground after t seconds is given by $S = -16t^2 - 24t + 720$. How long does it take for the sandbag to reach the earth? (On the ground, $S = 0$.) 6 sec

84. ***Throwing a sandbag.*** If the balloonist of Exercise 83 throws his sandbag downward from an altitude of 128 feet with an initial velocity of 32 feet per second, then its altitude after t seconds is given by the formula $S = -16t^2 - 32t + 128$. How long does it take for the sandbag to reach the earth? 2 sec

85. ***Glass prism.*** One end of a glass prism is in the shape of a triangle with a height that is 1 inch longer than twice the base. If the area of the triangle is 39 square inches, then how long are the base and height?
Base 6 in., height 13 in.

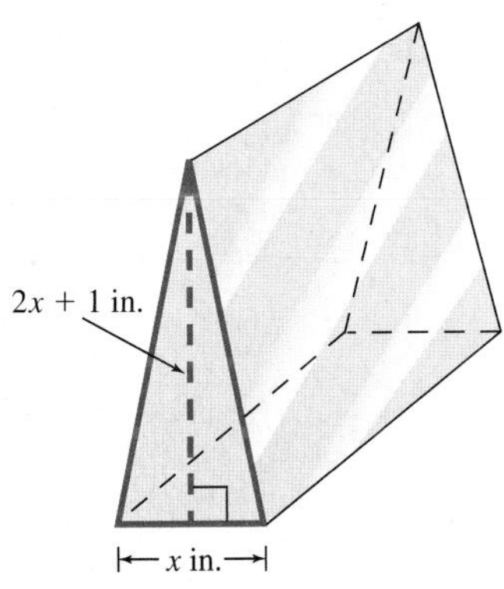

Figure for Exercise 85

86. ***Areas of two circles.*** The radius of a circle is 1 meter longer than the radius of another circle. If their areas differ by 5π square meters, then what is the radius of each?
2 m and 3 m

87. ***Changing area.*** Last year Otto's garden was square. This year he plans to make it smaller by shortening one side 5 feet and the other 8 feet. If the area of the smaller garden will be 180 square feet, then what was the size of Otto's garden last year? 20 ft by 20 ft

88. ***Dimensions of a box.*** Rosita's Christmas present from Carlos is in a box that has a width that is 3 inches shorter than the height. The length of the base is 5 inches longer than the height. If the area of the base is 84 square inches, then what is the height of the package? 9 in.

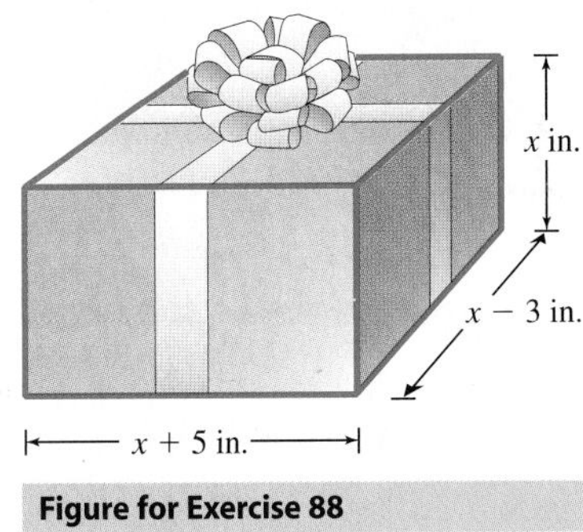

Figure for Exercise 88

89. ***Flying a kite.*** Imelda and Gordon have designed a new kite. While Imelda is flying the kite, Gordon is standing directly below it. The kite is designed so that its altitude is always 20 feet larger than the distance between Imelda and Gordon. What is the altitude of the kite when it is 100 feet from Imelda? 80 ft

90. ***Avoiding a collision.*** A car is traveling on a road that is perpendicular to a railroad track. When the car is 30 meters from the crossing, the car's new collision detector warns the driver that there is a train 50 meters from the car and heading toward the same crossing. How far is the train from the crossing? 40 m

91. ***Carpeting two rooms.*** Virginia is buying carpet for two square rooms. One room is 3 yards wider than the other. If she needs 45 square yards of carpet, then what are the dimensions of each room? 3 yd by 3 yd, 6 yd by 6 yd

92. ***Winter wheat.*** While finding the amount of seed needed to plant his three square wheat fields, Hank observed that the side of one field was 1 kilometer longer than the side of the smallest field and that the side of the largest field was 3 kilometers longer than the side of the smallest field. If the total area of the three fields is 38 square kilometers, then what is the area of each field?
4 km^2, 9 km^2, 25 km^2

93. ***Sailing to Miami.*** At point A the captain of a ship determined that the distance to Miami was 13 miles. If she sailed north to point B and then west to Miami, the distance would be 17 miles. If the distance from point A to point B is greater than the distance from point B to Miami, then how far is it from point A to point B? 12 mi

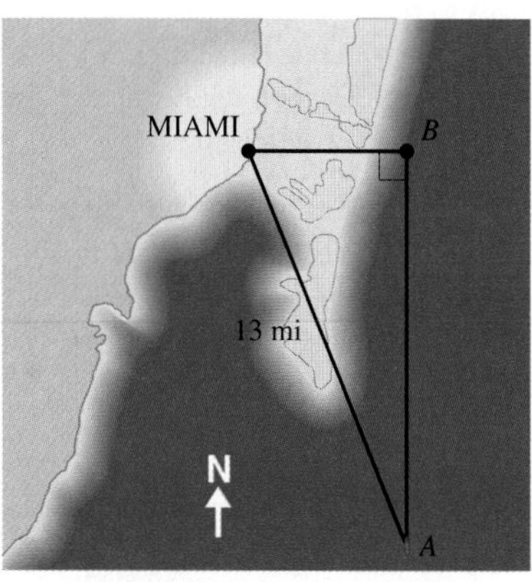

Figure for Exercise 93

94. ***Buried treasure.*** Ahmed has half of a treasure map, which indicates that the treasure is buried in the desert $2x + 6$ paces from Castle Rock. Vanessa has the other half of the map. Her half indicates that to find the treasure, one must get to Castle Rock, walk x paces to the north, and then walk $2x + 4$ paces to the east. If they share their information, then they can find x and save a lot of digging. What is x? 10 paces

95. ***Emerging markets.*** Catarina's investment of $16,000 in an emerging market fund grew to $25,000 in two years. Find the average annual rate of return by solving the equation $16{,}000(1 + r)^2 = 25{,}000$. 25%

96. ***Venture capital.*** Henry invested $12,000 in a new restaurant. When the restaurant was sold two years later, he received $27,000. Find his average annual return by solving the equation $12{,}000(1 + r)^2 = 27{,}000$. 50%

Collaborative Activities

Grouping: Three students per group

Topic: Factoring Polynomials

Hannah's Inheritance

Part I: Sally, Kelly, and Hannah inherited property from their father. Sally, who married the neighbor to the east, is given a piece of land adjacent to her husband's property. The land is 5 hectometers wide and the length matches that of her husband's property. Kelly who has married the neighbor to the south is given property that is 4 hectometers wide and its length is the common boundary of her spouse's property. Hannah is to have a square piece that is left after her sister's property is taken out. Hannah wants to find out the dimensions of her land. She knows that her father's land totaled 380 square hectometers. Use the diagram below to find the dimensions of Hannah's land.

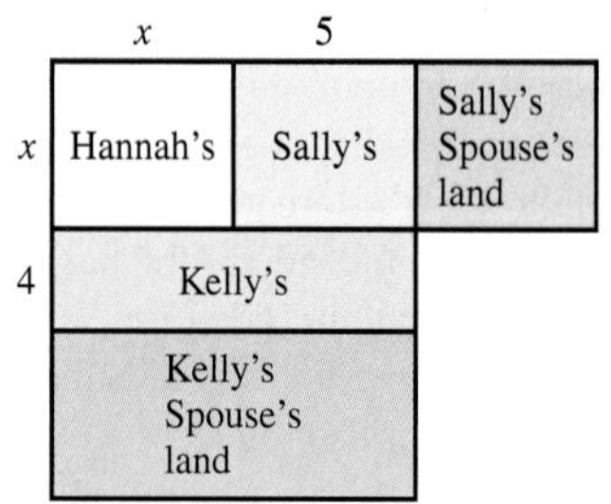

Part II: A few years later Hannah married Harry, a math teacher from town. Now they are getting divorced. As part of the settlement, Harry will get 32% of the land that they now own jointly. However, Harry did not get along with Hannah's sisters and does not want his land to be adjacent to their land. They have agreed that Harry will get a triangular section at the corner as shown in the accompanying figure. Use your answer from Part I to find y and z in the figure.

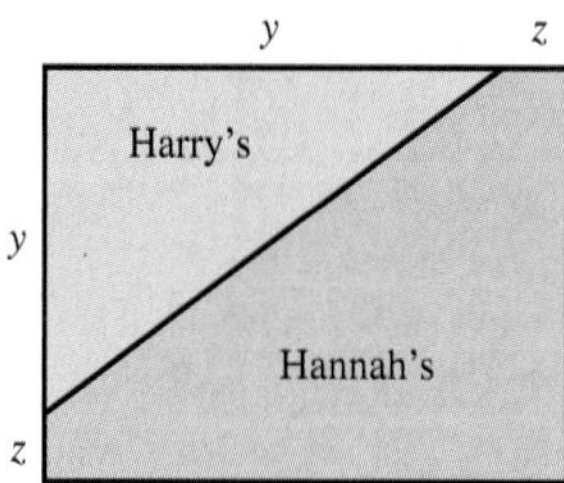

Chapter 5 Wrap-Up

Summary

Factoring		**Examples**
Prime number	A positive integer larger than 1 that has no integral factors other than 1 and itself	2, 3, 5, 7, 11
Prime polynomial	A polynomial that cannot be factored is prime.	$x^2 + 3$ and $x^2 - x + 5$ are prime.
Strategy for finding the GCF for monomials	1. Find the GCF for the coefficients of the monomials. 2. Form the product of the GCF of the coefficients and each variable that is common to all of the monomials, where the exponent on each variable equals the smallest power of that variable in any of the monomials.	$12x^3yz$, $8x^2y^3$ GCF $= 4x^2y$
Factoring out the GCF	Use the distributive property to factor out the GCF from all terms of a polynomial.	$2x^3 - 4x = 2x(x^2 - 2)$

Special Cases		**Examples**
Difference of two squares	$a^2 - b^2 = (a + b)(a - b)$	$m^2 - 9 = (m - 3)(m + 3)$
Perfect square trinomial	$a^2 + 2ab + b^2 = (a + b)^2$ $a^2 - 2ab + b^2 = (a - b)^2$	$x^2 + 6x + 9 = (x + 3)^2$ $4h^2 - 12h + 9 = (2h - 3)^2$
Difference or sum of two cubes	$a^3 - b^3 = (a - b)(a^2 + ab + b^2)$ $a^3 + b^3 = (a + b)(a^2 - ab + b^2)$	$t^3 - 8 = (t - 2)(t^2 + 2t + 4)$ $p^3 + 1 = (p + 1)(p^2 - p + 1)$

Factoring Polynomials		**Examples**
Factoring by grouping	Factor out common factors from groups of terms.	$6x + 6w + ax + aw$ $= 6(x + w) + a(x + w)$ $= (6 + a)(x + w)$
Strategy for factoring $ax^2 + bx + c$ by the *ac* method	1. Find two numbers that have a product equal to *ac* and a sum equal to *b*. 2. Replace *bx* by two terms using the two new numbers as coefficients. 3. Factor the resulting four-term polynomial by grouping.	$6x^2 + 17x + 12$ $= 6x^2 + 9x + 8x + 12$ $= (2x + 3)3x + (2x + 3)4$ $= (2x + 3)(3x + 4)$

Factoring by trial and error	Try possible factors of the trinomial and check by using FOIL. If incorrect, try again.	$2x^2 + 5x - 12 = (2x - 3)(x + 4)$
Strategy for factoring polynomials completely	1. First factor out any common factors. 2. When factoring a binomial, check to see whether it is a difference of two squares, a difference of two cubes, or a sum of two cubes. Remember that a sum of two squares (with no common factor) is prime. 3. When factoring a trinomial, check to see whether it is a perfect square trinomial. 4. When factoring a trinomial that is not a perfect square, use the *ac* method or trial and error. 5. If the polynomial has four terms, try factoring by grouping. 6. Check to see whether any factors can be factored again.	
Solving Equations		**Examples**
Zero factor property	The equation $a \cdot b = 0$ is equivalent to $a = 0$ or $b = 0$.	$x(x - 1) = 0$ $x = 0$ or $x - 1 = 0$
Strategy for solving an equation by factoring	1. Rewrite the equation with 0 on the right-hand side. 2. Factor the left-hand side completely. 3. Set each factor equal to zero to get linear equations. 4. Solve the linear equations. 5. Check the answers in the original equation. 6. State the solution(s) to the original equation.	$x^2 + 3x = 18$ $x^2 + 3x - 18 = 0$ $(x + 6)(x - 3) = 0$ $x + 6 = 0$ or $x - 3 = 0$ $x = -6$ or $x = 3$

Enriching Your Mathematical Word Power

For each mathematical term, choose the correct meaning.

1. factor
a. to write an expression as a product
b. to multiply
c. what two numbers have in common
d. to FOIL a

2. prime number
a. a polynomial that cannot be factored
b. a number with no divisors
c. an integer between 1 and 10
d. an integer larger than 1 that has no integral factors other than itself and 1 d

3. greatest common factor
a. the least common multiple
b. the least common denominator
c. the largest integer that is a factor of two or more integers
d. the largest number in a product c

4. prime polynomial
a. a polynomial that has no factors
b. a product of prime numbers
c. a first-degree polynomial
d. a monomial a

5. **factor completely**
   a. to factor by grouping
   b. to factor out a prime number
   c. to write as a product of primes
   d. to factor by trial and error c

6. **sum of two cubes**
   a. $(a + b)^3$
   b. $a^3 + b^3$
   c. $a^3 - b^3$
   d. a^3b^3 b

7. **quadratic equation**
   a. $ax + b = 0$ where $a \neq 0$
   b. $ax + b = cx + d$
   c. $ax^2 + bx + c = 0$ where $a \neq 0$
   d. any equation with four terms c

8. **zero factor property**
   a. If $ab = 0$ then $a = 0$ or $b = 0$
   b. $a \cdot 0 = 0$ for any a
   c. $a = a + 0$ for any real number a
   d. $a + (-a) = 0$ for any real number a a

9. **Pythagorean theorem**
   a. $a^2 + b^2 = (a + b)^2$
   b. a triangle is a right triangle if and only if it has one right angle
   c. the legs of a right triangle meet at a 90° angle
   d. a theorem that gives a relationship between the two legs and the hypotenuse of a right triangle d

10. **difference of two squares**
   a. $a^3 - b^3$
   b. $2a - 2b$
   c. $a^2 - b^2$
   d. $(a - b)^2$ c

Review Exercises

5.1 *Find the prime factorization for each integer.*

1. 144 $2^4 \cdot 3^2$

2. 121 11^2

3. 58 $2 \cdot 29$

4. 76 $2^2 \cdot 19$

5. 150 $2 \cdot 3 \cdot 5^2$

6. 200 $2^3 \cdot 5^2$

Find the greatest common factor for each group.

7. 36, 90 18

8. 30, 42, 78 6

9. $8x, 12x^2$ $4x$

10. $6a^2b, 9ab^2, 15a^2b^2$ $3ab$

Complete the factorization of each binomial.

11. $3x + 6 = 3(x + 2)$

12. $7x^2 + x = x(7x + 1)$

13. $2a - 20 = -2(-a + 10)$

14. $a^2 - a = -a(-a + 1)$

Factor each polynomial by factoring out the GCF.

15. $2a - a^2$ $a(2 - a)$

16. $9 - 3b$ $3(3 - b)$

17. $6x^2y^2 - 9x^5y$ $3x^2y(2y - 3x^3)$

18. $a^3b^5 + a^3b^2$ $a^3b^2(b^3 + 1)$

19. $3x^2y - 12xy - 9y^2$ $3y(x^2 - 4x - 3y)$

20. $2a^2 - 4ab^2 - ab$ $a(2a - 4b^2 - b)$

5.2 *Factor each polynomial completely.*

21. $y^2 - 400$ $(y - 20)(y + 20)$

22. $4m^2 - 9$ $(2m - 3)(2m + 3)$

23. $w^2 - 8w + 16$ $(w - 4)^2$

24. $t^2 + 20t + 100$ $(t + 10)^2$

25. $4y^2 + 20y + 25$ $(2y + 5)^2$

26. $2a^2 - 4a - 2$ $2(a^2 - 2a - 1)$

27. $r^2 - 4r + 4$ $(r - 2)^2$

28. $3m^2 - 75$ $3(m - 5)(m + 5)$

29. $8t^3 - 24t^2 + 18t$ $2t(2t - 3)^2$

30. $t^2 - 9w^2$ $(t - 3w)(t + 3w)$

31. $x^2 + 12xy + 36y^2$ $(x + 6y)^2$

32. $9y^2 - 12xy + 4x^2$ $(3y - 2x)^2$

33. $x^2 + 5x - xy - 5y$ $(x - y)(x + 5)$

34. $x^2 + xy + ax + ay$ $(x + a)(x + y)$

5.3 *Factor each polynomial.*

35. $b^2 + 5b - 24$ $(b + 8)(b - 3)$

36. $a^2 - 2a - 35$ $(a - 7)(a + 5)$

37. $r^2 - 4r - 60$
$(r - 10)(r + 6)$

38. $x^2 + 13x + 40$
$(x + 8)(x + 5)$

39. $y^2 - 6y - 55$
$(y - 11)(y + 5)$

40. $a^2 + 6a - 40$
$(a + 10)(a - 4)$

41. $u^2 + 26u + 120$
$(u + 20)(u + 6)$

42. $v^2 - 22v - 75$
$(v - 25)(v + 3)$

Factor completely.

43. $3t^3 + 12t^2$
$3t^2(t + 4)$

44. $-4m^4 - 36m^2$
$-4m^2(m^2 + 9)$

45. $5w^3 + 25w^2 + 25w$
$5w(w^2 + 5w + 5)$

46. $-3t^3 + 3t^2 - 6t$
$-3t(t^2 - t + 2)$

47. $2a^3b + 3a^2b^2 + ab^3$
$ab(2a + b)(a + b)$

48. $6x^2y^2 - xy^3 - y^4$
$y^2(2x - y)(3x + y)$

49. $9x^3 - xy^2$
$x(3x - y)(3x + y)$

50. $h^4 - 100h^2$
$h^2(h - 10)(h + 10)$

5.4 *Factor each polynomial completely.*

51. $14t^2 + t - 3$
$(7t - 3)(2t + 1)$

52. $15x^2 - 22x - 5$
$(5x + 1)(3x - 5)$

53. $6x^2 - 19x - 7$
$(3x + 1)(2x - 7)$

54. $2x^2 - x - 10$
$(x + 2)(2x - 5)$

55. $6p^2 + 5p - 4$
$(3p + 4)(2p - 1)$

56. $3p^2 + 2p - 5$
$(p - 1)(3p + 5)$

57. $-30p^3 + 8p^2 + 8p$
$-2p(5p + 2)(3p - 2)$

58. $-6q^2 - 40q - 50$
$-2(3q + 5)(q + 5)$

59. $6x^2 - 29xy - 5y^2$
$(6x + y)(x - 5y)$

60. $10a^2 + ab - 2b^2$
$(5a - 2b)(2a + b)$

61. $32x^2 + 16xy + 2y^2$
$2(4x + y)^2$

62. $8a^2 + 40ab + 50b^2$
$2(2a + 5b)^2$

5.5 *Factor completely.*

63. $5x^3 + 40x$ $\quad 5x(x^2 + 8)$

64. $w^2 + 6w + 9$ $\quad (w + 3)^2$

65. $9x^2 + 3x - 2$ $\quad (3x - 1)(3x + 2)$

66. $ax^3 + ax$ $\quad ax(x^2 + 1)$

67. $n^2 + 64$ Prime

68. $4t^2 + h^2$ Prime

69. $x^3 + 2x^2 - x - 2$ $\quad (x + 2)(x - 1)(x + 1)$

70. $16x^2 - 2x - 3$ $\quad (8x + 3)(2x - 1)$

71. $x^2y - 16xy^2$ $\quad xy(x - 16y)$

72. $-3x^2 + 27$ $\quad -3(x - 3)(x + 3)$

73. $w^2 + 4w + 5$ Prime

74. $2n^2 + 3n - 1$ Prime

75. $a^2 + 2a + 1$ $\quad (a + 1)^2$

76. $-2w^2 - 12w - 18$ $\quad -2(w + 3)^2$

77. $x^3 - x^2 + x - 1$ $\quad (x^2 + 1)(x - 1)$

78. $9x^2y^2 - 9y^2$ $\quad 9y^2(x - 1)(x + 1)$

79. $a^2 + ab + 2a + 2b$ $\quad (a + 2)(a + b)$

80. $4m^2 + 20m + 25$ $\quad (2m + 5)^2$

81. $-2x^2 + 16x - 24$ $\quad -2(x - 6)(x - 2)$

82. $6x^2 + 21x - 45$ $\quad 3(2x - 3)(x + 5)$

83. $m^3 - 1000$ $\quad (m - 10)(m^2 + 10m + 100)$

84. $8p^3 + 1$ $\quad (2p + 1)(4p^2 - 2p + 1)$

85. $p^4 - q^4$ $\quad (p - q)(p + q)(p^2 + q^2)$

86. $z^4 - 81$ $\quad (z - 3)(z + 3)(z^2 + 9)$

Factor each polynomial completely, given that the binomial following it is a factor of the polynomial.

87. $x^3 + x + 10, x + 2$ $(x + 2)(x^2 - 2x + 5)$

88. $x^3 - 5x - 12, x - 3$ $(x - 3)(x^2 + 3x + 4)$

89. $x^3 + 6x^2 - 7x - 60, x + 4$ $(x + 4)(x + 5)(x - 3)$

90. $x^3 - 4x^2 - 3x - 10, x - 5$ $(x - 5)(x^2 + x + 2)$

5.6 *Solve each equation.*

91. $x^3 = 5x^2$ 0, 5

92. $2m^2 + 10m = -12$ $-3, -2$

93. $(a - 2)(a - 3) = 6$ 0, 5

94. $(w - 2)(w + 3) = 50$ $-8, 7$

95. $2m^2 - 9m - 5 = 0$ $-\frac{1}{2}, 5$

96. $12x^2 + 5x - 3 = 0$ $-\frac{3}{4}, \frac{1}{3}$

97. $m^3 + 4m^2 - 9m = 36$ $-4, -3, 3$

98. $w^3 + 5w^2 - w = 5$ $-5, -1, 1$

99. $(x + 3)^2 + x^2 = 5$ $-2, -1$

100. $(h - 2)^2 + (h + 1)^2 = 9$ $-1, 2$

101. $p^2 + \frac{1}{4}p - \frac{1}{8} = 0$ $-\frac{1}{2}, \frac{1}{4}$

102. $t^2 + 1 = \frac{13}{6}t$ $\frac{2}{3}, \frac{3}{2}$

Solve each problem.

103. ***Positive numbers.*** Two positive numbers differ by 6, and their squares differ by 96. Find the numbers. 5, 11

104. ***Consecutive integers.*** Find three consecutive integers such that the sum of their squares is 77.
$-6, -5, -4$ or 4, 5, 6

105. ***Dimensions of a notebook.*** The perimeter of a notebook is 28 inches, and the diagonal measures 10 inches. What are the length and width of the notebook?
6 in. by 8 in.

106. ***Two numbers.*** The sum of two numbers is 8.5, and their product is 18. Find the numbers.
4 and 4.5

107. ***Poiseuille's law.*** According to the nineteenth-century physician Poiseuille, the velocity (in centimeters per second) of blood r centimeters from the center of an artery of radius R centimeters is given by $v = kR^2 - kr^2$, where k is a constant. Rewrite the formula by factoring the right-hand side completely.
$v = k(R - r)(R + r)$

108. ***Racquetball.*** The volume of rubber (in cubic centimeters) in a hollow rubber ball used in racquetball is given by

$$V = \frac{4}{3}\pi R^3 - \frac{4}{3}\pi r^3,$$

where the inside radius is r centimeters and the outside radius is R centimeters.

a) Rewrite the formula by factoring the right-hand side completely. $V = \frac{4}{3}\pi(R - r)(R^2 + Rr + r^2)$

b) The accompanying graph shows the relationship between r and V when $R = 3$. Use the graph to estimate the value of r for which $V = 100$ cm^3.
1.5 cm

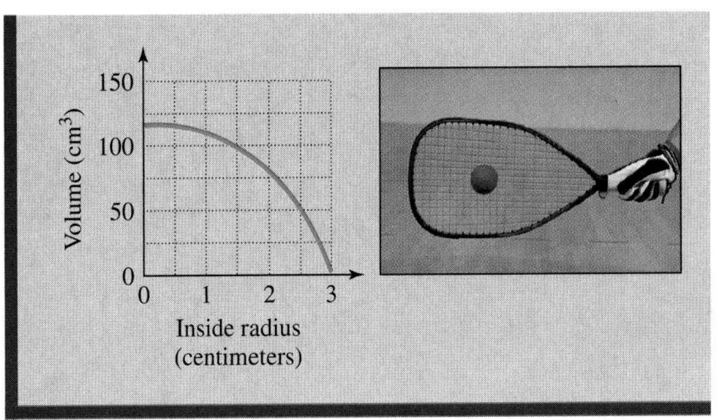

Figure for Exercise 108

109. ***Leaning ladder.*** A 10-foot ladder is placed against a building so that the distance from the bottom of the ladder to the building is 2 feet less than the distance from the top of the ladder to the ground. What is the distance from the bottom of the ladder to the building? 6 ft

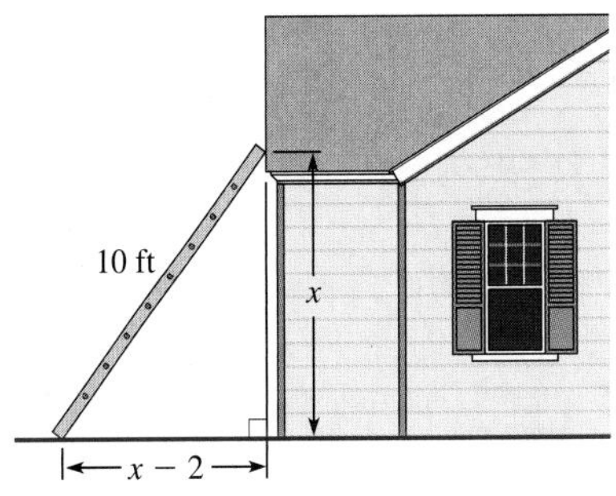

Figure for Exercise 109

110. ***Towering antenna.*** A guy wire of length 50 feet is attached to the ground and to the top of an antenna. The height of the antenna is 10 feet larger than the distance from the base of the antenna to the point where the guy wire is attached to the ground. What is the height of the antenna? 40 ft

Chapter 5 Test

Give the prime factorization for each integer.

1. 66 $2 \cdot 3 \cdot 11$

2. 336 $2^4 \cdot 3 \cdot 7$

Find the greatest common factor (GCF) for each group.

3. 48, 80 16

4. 42, 66, 78 6

5. $6y^2$, $15y^3$ $3y^2$

6. $12a^2b$, $18ab^2$, $24a^3b^3$ $6ab$

Factor each polynomial completely.

7. $5x^2 - 10x$ $5x(x - 2)$

8. $6x^2y^2 + 12xy^2 + 12y^2$ $6y^2(x^2 + 2x + 2)$

9. $3a^3b - 3ab^3$ $3ab(a - b)(a + b)$

10. $a^2 + 2a - 24$ $(a + 6)(a - 4)$

11. $4b^2 - 28b + 49$ $(2b - 7)^2$

12. $3m^3 + 27m$ $3m(m^2 + 9)$

13. $ax - ay + bx - by$ $(a + b)(x - y)$

14. $ax - 2a - 5x + 10$ $(a - 5)(x - 2)$

15. $6b^2 - 7b - 5$ $(3b - 5)(2b + 1)$

16. $m^2 + 4mn + 4n^2$ $(m + 2n)^2$

17. $2a^2 - 13a + 15$ $(2a - 3)(a - 5)$

18. $z^3 + 9z^2 + 18z$ $z(z + 3)(z + 6)$

19. $x^3 + 125$ $(x + 5)(x^2 - 5x + 25)$

20. $a^4 - ab^3$ $a(a - b)(a^2 + ab + b^2)$

Factor the polynomial completely, given that $x - 1$ is a factor.

21. $x^3 - 6x^2 + 11x - 6$ $(x - 1)(x - 2)(x - 3)$

Solve each equation.

22. $x^2 + 6x + 9 = 0$ -3

23. $2x^2 + 5x - 12 = 0$ $\frac{3}{2}, -4$

24. $3x^3 = 12x$ $0, -2, 2$

25. $(2x - 1)(3x + 5) = 5$ $-2, \frac{5}{6}$

Write a complete solution to each problem.

26. If the length of a rectangle is 3 feet longer than the width and the diagonal is 15 feet, then what are the length and width?
Length 12 ft, width 9 ft

27. The sum of two numbers is 4, and their product is -32. Find the numbers.
-4 and 8

Making Connections | A Review of Chapters 1–5

Simplify each expression.

1. $\dfrac{91 - 17}{17 - 91}$ -1
2. $\dfrac{4 - 18}{-6 - 1}$ 2
3. $5 - 2(7 - 3)$ -3
4. $3^2 - 4(6)(-2)$ 57
5. $2^5 - 2^4$ 16
6. $0.07(37) + 0.07(63)$ 7

Perform the indicated operations.

7. $x \cdot 2x$ $2x^2$
8. $x + 2x$ $3x$
9. $\dfrac{6 + 2x}{2}$ $3 + x$
10. $\dfrac{6 \cdot 2x}{2}$ $6x$
11. $2 \cdot 3y \cdot 4z$ $24yz$
12. $2(3y + 4z)$ $6y + 8z$
13. $2 - (3 - 4z)$ $4z - 1$
14. $t^8 \div t^2$ t^6
15. $t^8 \cdot t^2$ t^{10}
16. $\dfrac{8t^8}{2t^2}$ $4t^6$

Solve each inequality. State the solution set in interval notation and sketch its graph.

17. $2x - 5 > 3x + 4$ $(-\infty, -9)$

−13 −12 −11 −10 −9 −8 −7

18. $4 - 5x \le -11$ $[3, \infty)$

1 2 3 4 5 6 7

19. $-\dfrac{2}{3}x + 3 < -5$ $(12, \infty)$

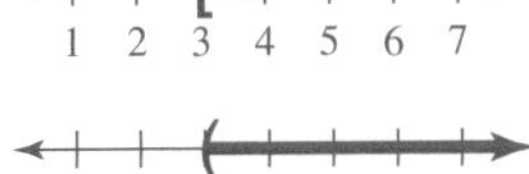

20. $0.05(x - 120) - 24 < 0$ $(-\infty, 600)$

0 200 400 600 800

Find the solution set to each equation.

21. $2x - 3 = 0$ $\left\{\dfrac{3}{2}\right\}$
22. $2x + 1 = 0$ $\left\{-\dfrac{1}{2}\right\}$
23. $(x - 3)(x + 5) = 0$ $\{3, -5\}$
24. $(2x - 3)(2x + 1) = 0$ $\left\{\dfrac{3}{2}, -\dfrac{1}{2}\right\}$
25. $3x(x - 3) = 0$ $\{0, 3\}$
26. $x^2 = x$ $\{0, 1\}$
27. $3x - 3x = 0$ R
28. $3x - 3x = 1$ No solution or $\varnothing$
29. $0.01x - x + 14.9 = 0.5x$ $\{10\}$
30. $0.05x + 0.04(x - 40) = 2$ $\{40\}$
31. $2x^2 = 18$ $\{-3, 3\}$
32. $2x^2 + 7x - 15 = 0$ $\left\{-5, \dfrac{3}{2}\right\}$

Solve the problem.

33. ***Another ace.*** Professional tennis players can serve a tennis ball at speeds over 120 mph into a rectangular region that has a perimeter of 69 feet and an area of 283.5 square feet. Find the length and width of the service region.
Length 21 ft, width 13.5 ft

Photo for Exercise 33

Critical **Thinking** | For Individual or Group Work | Chapter 5

These exercises can be solved by a variety of techniques, which may or may not require algebra. So be creative and think critically. Explain all answers. Answers are in the Instructor's Edition of this text.

1. ***Counting cubes.*** What is the total number of cubes that are in each of the following diagrams?

a) 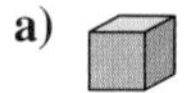

b) 

c) 

d) 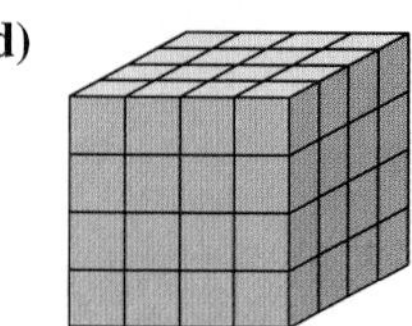

2. ***More cubes.*** Imagine a large cube that is made up of 125 small cubes like those in the previous exercise. What is the total number of cubes that could be found in this arrangement?

3. ***Timely coincidence.*** Starting at 8 A.M. determine the number of times in the next 24 hours for which the hour and minute hands on a clock coincide?

Photo for Exercise 3

4. ***Chess board.*** There are 64 squares on a square chess board. How many squares are neither diagonal squares nor edge squares?

Photo for Exercise 4

5. ***Last digit.*** Find the last digit in 3^{9999}.

6. ***Reconciling remainders.*** Find a positive integer smaller than 500 that has a remainder of 3 when divided by 5, a remainder of 6 when divided by 9, and a remainder of 8 when divided by 11.

7. ***Exact sum.*** Find this sum exactly:

$$\frac{1}{2} + \frac{1}{2^2} + \frac{1}{2^3} + \frac{1}{2^4} + \cdots + \frac{1}{2^{19}}$$

8. ***Ten-digit number.*** Find a 10-digit number whose first digit is the number of 1's in the 10-digit number, whose second digit is the number of 2's in the 10-digit number, whose third digit is the number of 3's in the 10-digit number, and so on. The ninth digit must be the number of nines in the 10-digit number and the tenth digit must be the number of zeros in the 10-digit number.

1. a) 1 **b)** 9 **c)** 36 **d)** 100 **2.** 225 **3.** 22 **4.** 24 **5.** 7 **6.** 393 **7.** $\frac{524287}{524288}$ **8.** 2,100,010,006

Chapter 6

Rational Expressions

Advanced technical developments have made sports equipment faster, lighter, and more responsive to the human body. Behind the more flexible skis, lighter bats, and comfortable athletic shoes lies the science of biomechanics, which is the study of human movement and the factors that influence it.

Designing and testing an athletic shoe go hand in hand. While a shoe is being designed, it is tested in a multitude of ways, including long-term wear, rear foot stability, and strength of materials. Testing basketball shoes usually includes an evaluation of the force applied to the ground by the foot during running, jumping, and landing. Many biomechanics laboratories have a special platform that can measure the force exerted when a player cuts from side to side as well as the force against the bottom of the shoe. Force exerted in landing from a lay-up shot can be as high as 14 times the weight of the body. Side-to-side force is usually about 1 to 2 body weights in a cutting movement.

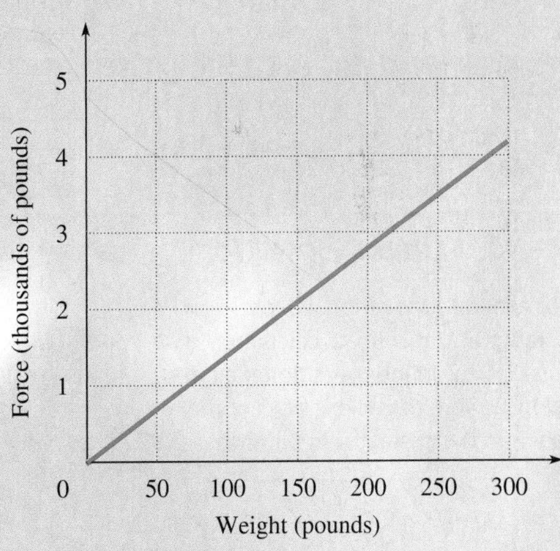

In Exercises 57 and 58 of Section 6.7 you will see how designers of athletic shoes use proportions to find the amount of force on the foot and soles of shoes for activities such as running and jumping.

6.1 Reducing Rational Expressions

In this Section

- Rational Expressions
- Reducing to Lowest Terms
- Reducing with the Quotient Rule
- Dividing $a - b$ by $b - a$
- Factoring Out the Opposite of a Common Factor
- Writing Rational Expressions

Rational expressions in algebra are similar to the rational numbers in arithmetic. In this section you will learn the basic ideas of rational expressions.

Rational Expressions

A rational number is the ratio of two integers with the denominator not equal to 0. For example,

$$\frac{3}{4}, \quad \frac{-9}{-6}, \quad 7, \quad \text{and} \quad 0$$

are rational numbers. A **rational expression** is the ratio of two polynomials with the denominator not equal to 0. Because an integer is a monomial, a rational number is a rational expression. The following expressions are rational expressions:

$$\frac{x^2 - 1}{x + 8}, \quad \frac{3a^2 + 5a - 3}{a - 9}, \quad \frac{3}{7}, \quad w$$

We say that w is a rational expression because w can be written as $\frac{w}{1}$.

A rational expression involving a variable has no value unless we assign a value to the variable. Once the variable is given a value we can evaluate the expression. We can discuss the value of a rational expression using the notation that we used for evaluating polynomials in Chapter 4.

EXAMPLE 1 Evaluating a rational expression

a) Find the value of $\frac{4x - 1}{x + 2}$ for $x = -3$.

b) If $R(x) = \frac{3x + 2}{2x - 1}$, find $R(4)$.

Solution

a) To find the value of $\frac{4x - 1}{x + 2}$ for $x = -3$, replace x by -3 in the rational expression:

$$\frac{4(-3) - 1}{-3 + 2} = \frac{-13}{-1} = 13$$

So the value of the rational expression is 13.

b) $R(4)$ is the value of the rational expression when $x = 4$. To find $R(4)$ replace x by 4 in $R(x) = \frac{3x + 2}{2x - 1}$:

$$R(4) = \frac{3(4) + 2}{2(4) - 1}$$

$$R(4) = \frac{14}{7} = 2$$

So the value of the rational expression is 2 when $x = 4$, or $R(4) = 2$ (read "R of 4 is 2").

Now do Exercises 7–12

Calculator Close-Up

To evaluate the rational expression in Example 1(a) with a calculator, first use Y= to define the rational expression. Be sure to enclose both numerator and denominator in parentheses.

```
Plot1 Plot2 Plot3
\Y1■(4X-1)/(X+2)
\Y2=
\Y3=
\Y4=
\Y5=
\Y6=
```

Then find $y_1(-3)$.

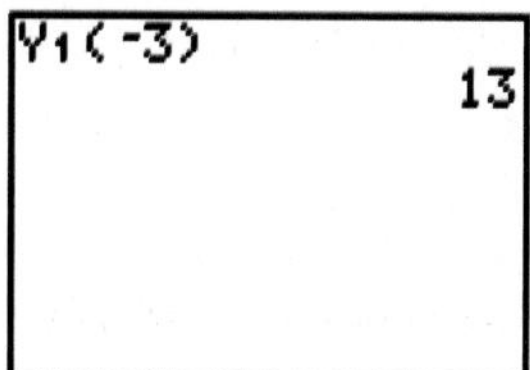

Because the denominator cannot be zero, any number can be used in place of the variable *except* numbers that cause the denominator to be zero.

EXAMPLE 2

Ruling out values for x

Which numbers cannot be used in place of x in each rational expression?

a) $\dfrac{x^2 - 1}{x + 8}$ **b)** $\dfrac{x + 2}{2x + 1}$ **c)** $\dfrac{x + 5}{x^2 - 4}$

Solution

a) The denominator is 0 if $x + 8 = 0$, or $x = -8$. So -8 cannot be used in place of x.

b) The denominator is zero if $2x + 1 = 0$, or $x = -\frac{1}{2}$. So we cannot use $-\frac{1}{2}$ in place of x.

c) The denominator is zero if $x^2 - 4 = 0$. Solve this equation:

$$
\begin{aligned}
x^2 - 4 &= 0 \\
(x - 2)(x + 2) &= 0 \quad \text{Factor.} \\
x - 2 = 0 \quad \text{or} \quad x + 2 &= 0 \quad \text{Zero factor property} \\
x = 2 \quad \text{or} \quad x &= -2
\end{aligned}
$$

So 2 and -2 cannot be used in place of x.

Now do Exercises 13–20

Teaching Tip It is more difficult for students to state which numbers can be used for x rather than which numbers cannot be used for x.

When dealing with rational expressions in this book, we will generally assume that the variables represent numbers for which the denominator is not zero.

Reducing to Lowest Terms

Rational expressions are a generalization of rational numbers. The operations that we perform on rational numbers can be performed on rational expressions in exactly the same manner.

Each rational number can be written in infinitely many equivalent forms. For example,

$$\frac{3}{5} = \frac{6}{10} = \frac{9}{15} = \frac{12}{20} = \frac{15}{25} = \cdots.$$

Each equivalent form of $\frac{3}{5}$ is obtained from $\frac{3}{5}$ by multiplying both numerator and denominator by the same nonzero number. This is equivalent to multiplying the fraction by 1, which does not change its value. For example,

$$\frac{3}{5} = \frac{3}{5} \cdot 1 = \frac{3}{5} \cdot \frac{2}{2} = \frac{6}{10} \quad \text{and} \quad \frac{3}{5} = \frac{3 \cdot 3}{5 \cdot 3} = \frac{9}{15}.$$

Helpful Hint

Most students learn to convert 3/5 into 6/10 by dividing 5 into 10 to get 2 and then multiply 2 by 3 to get 6. In algebra it is better to do this conversion by multiplying the numerator and denominator of 3/5 by 2 as shown here.

If we start with $\frac{6}{10}$ and convert it into $\frac{3}{5}$, we say that we are **reducing $\frac{6}{10}$ to lowest terms.** We reduce by dividing the numerator and denominator by the common factor 2:

$$\frac{6}{10} = \frac{\cancel{2} \cdot 3}{\cancel{2} \cdot 5} = \frac{3}{5}$$

A rational number is expressed in lowest terms when the numerator and the denominator have no common factors other than 1.

CAUTION We can reduce fractions only by dividing the numerator and the denominator by a common factor. Although it is true that

$$\frac{6}{10} = \frac{2 + 4}{2 + 8},$$

we cannot eliminate the 2's, because they are not factors. Removing them from the sums in the numerator and denominator would not result in $\frac{3}{5}$.

Reducing Fractions

If $a \neq 0$ and $c \neq 0$, then

$$\frac{ab}{ac} = \frac{b}{c}.$$

To reduce rational expressions to lowest terms, we use exactly the same procedure as with fractions:

Reducing Rational Expressions

1. Factor the numerator and denominator completely.
2. Divide the numerator and denominator by the greatest common factor.

Dividing the numerator and denominator by the GCF is often referred to as **dividing out the GCF.**

EXAMPLE 3

Reducing

Reduce to lowest terms.

a) $\frac{30}{42}$ **b)** $\frac{x^2 - 9}{6x + 18}$ **c)** $\frac{3x^2 + 9x + 6}{2x^2 - 8}$

Solution

a) $\frac{30}{42} = \frac{2 \cdot 3 \cdot 5}{2 \cdot 3 \cdot 7}$ Factor.

$= \frac{5}{7}$ Divide out the GCF: $2 \cdot 3$ or 6.

b) $\frac{x^2 - 9}{6x + 18} = \frac{(x - 3)(x + 3)}{6(x + 3)}$ Factor.

$= \frac{x - 3}{6}$ Divide out the GCF: $x + 3$.

c) $\frac{3x^2 + 9x + 6}{2x^2 - 8} = \frac{3(x + 2)(x + 1)}{2(x + 2)(x - 2)}$ Factor completely.

$= \frac{3x + 3}{2(x - 2)}$ Divide out the GCF: $x + 2$.

Now do Exercises 21–40

Note that in Example 3(c) the answer was given with the denominator factored and the numerator not factored. If the form of the denominator is not specified, then that is how answers will be given in this text. The reason for this practice is that common denominators for addition or subtraction are determined from factored form in the denominators. Note that

$$\frac{3x + 3}{2(x - 2)} = \frac{3(x + 1)}{2(x - 2)} = \frac{3(x + 1)}{2x - 4} = \frac{3x + 3}{2x - 4}$$

and any of these other three rational expressions is also the correct answer to Example 3(c).

If two rational expressions are equivalent, then they have the same numerical value for any replacement of the variables. Of course, the replacement must not give us an undefined expression (0 in the denominator). So in Example 3(b) the equation

$$\frac{x^2 - 9}{6x + 18} = \frac{x - 3}{6}$$

is satisfied by all real numbers except $x = -3$. The equation is an identity.

Study Tip

Find a clean, comfortable, well-lit place to study. But don't get too comfortable. Sitting at a desk is preferable to lying in bed. Where you study can influence your concentration and your study habits.

Reducing with the Quotient Rule

To reduce rational expressions involving exponential expressions, we use the quotient rule for exponents from Chapter 4. We restate it here for reference.

Quotient Rule

Suppose $a \neq 0$, and m and n are positive integers.

$$\text{If } m \geq n, \text{ then } \frac{a^m}{a^n} = a^{m-n}.$$

$$\text{If } m < n, \text{ then } \frac{a^m}{a^n} = \frac{1}{a^{n-m}}.$$

EXAMPLE 4

Using the quotient rule in reducing

Reduce to lowest terms.

a) $\dfrac{3a^{15}}{6a^7}$ **b)** $\dfrac{6x^4y^2}{4xy^5}$

Teaching Tip We did problems like this in Chapter 4 when we introduced the quotient rule. We repeat them here because they are also problems in reducing rational expressions.

Solution

a)

$$\frac{3a^{15}}{6a^7} = \frac{\cancel{3}a^{15}}{\cancel{3} \cdot 2a^7} \quad \text{Factor.}$$

$$= \frac{a^{15-7}}{2} \quad \text{Quotient rule}$$

$$= \frac{a^8}{2}$$

b) $\dfrac{6x^4y^2}{4xy^5} = \dfrac{\not{2} \cdot 3x^4y^2}{\not{2} \cdot 2xy^5}$ Factor.

$= \dfrac{3x^{4-1}}{2y^{5-2}}$ Quotient rule

$= \dfrac{3x^3}{2y^3}$

Now do Exercises 41–52

The essential part of reducing is getting a complete factorization for the numerator and denominator. To get a complete factorization, you must use the techniques for factoring from Chapter 5. If there are large integers in the numerator and denominator, you can use the technique shown in Section 5.1 to get a prime factorization of each integer.

EXAMPLE 5

Reducing expressions involving large integers

Reduce $\frac{420}{616}$ to lowest terms.

Solution

Use the method of Section 5.1 to get a prime factorization of 420 and 616:

$$\begin{array}{rr} 7 & 11 \\ 5\overline{)35} & 7\overline{)77} \\ 3\overline{)105} & 2\overline{)154} \\ 2\overline{)210} & 2\overline{)308} \\ \text{Start here} \rightarrow 2\overline{)420} & 2\overline{)616} \end{array}$$

The complete factorization for 420 is $2^2 \cdot 3 \cdot 5 \cdot 7$, and the complete factorization for 616 is $2^3 \cdot 7 \cdot 11$. To reduce the fraction, we divide out the common factors:

$$\frac{420}{616} = \frac{2^2 \cdot 3 \cdot 5 \cdot 7}{2^3 \cdot 7 \cdot 11}$$

$$= \frac{3 \cdot 5}{2 \cdot 11}$$

$$= \frac{15}{22}$$

Now do Exercises 53–60

Dividing *a* − *b* by *b* − *a*

In Section 4.2 you learned that $a - b = -(b - a) = -1(b - a)$. So if $a - b$ is divided by $b - a$, the quotient is -1:

$$\frac{a - b}{b - a} = \frac{-1(b - a)}{b - a}$$

$$= -1$$

We will use this fact in Example 6.

EXAMPLE 6

Expressions with $a - b$ and $b - a$

Reduce to lowest terms.

a) $\dfrac{5x - 5y}{4y - 4x}$ b) $\dfrac{m^2 - n^2}{n - m}$

Solution

a) $\dfrac{5x - 5y}{4y - 4x} = \dfrac{5(x - y)}{4(y - x)}$ Factor.

$= \dfrac{5}{4} \cdot (-1)$ $\dfrac{x - y}{y - x} = -1$

$= -\dfrac{5}{4}$

b) $\dfrac{m^2 - n^2}{n - m} = \dfrac{\overset{-1}{(m - n)}(m + n)}{n - m}$ Factor.

$= -1(m + n)$ $\dfrac{m - n}{n - m} = -1$

$= -m - n$

Now do Exercises 61–68

Teaching Tip Some students might prefer to factor $y - x$ as $-1(x - y)$ and then divide out or cancel identical factors.

CAUTION We can reduce $\frac{a - b}{b - a}$ to -1, but we cannot reduce $\frac{a - b}{a + b}$. There is no factor that is common to the numerator and denominator of $\frac{a - b}{a + b}$ or $\frac{a + b}{a - b}$.

Factoring Out the Opposite of a Common Factor

If we can factor out a common factor, we can also factor out the opposite of that common factor. For example, from $-3x - 6y$ we can factor out the common factor 3 or the common factor -3:

$$-3x - 6y = 3(-x - 2y) \quad \text{or} \quad -3x - 6y = -3(x + 2y)$$

To reduce an expression, it is sometimes necessary to factor out the opposite of a common factor.

EXAMPLE 7

Factoring out the opposite of a common factor

Reduce $\frac{-3w - 3w^2}{w^2 - 1}$ to lowest terms.

Solution

We can factor $3w$ or $-3w$ from the numerator. If we factor out $-3w$, we get a common factor in the numerator and denominator:

$\dfrac{-3w - 3w^2}{w^2 - 1} = \dfrac{-3w(1 + w)}{(w - 1)(w + 1)}$ Factor.

$= \dfrac{-3w}{w - 1}$ Since $1 + w = w + 1$, we divide out $w + 1$.

$= \dfrac{3w}{1 - w}$ Multiply numerator and denominator by -1.

The last step in this reduction is not absolutely necessary, but we usually perform it to make the answer look a little simpler.

Now do Exercises 69–76

The main points to remember for reducing rational expressions are summarized in the following reducing strategy.

Strategy for Reducing Rational Expressions

1. Reducing is done by dividing out all common factors.
2. Factor the numerator and denominator completely to see the common factors.
3. Use the quotient rule to reduce a ratio of two monomials.
4. You may have to factor out a common factor with a negative sign to get identical factors in the numerator and denominator.
5. The quotient of $a - b$ and $b - a$ is -1.

Writing Rational Expressions

Rational expressions occur naturally in applications involving rates.

EXAMPLE 8

Writing rational expressions

Answer each question with a rational expression.

a) If a trucker drives 500 miles in $x + 1$ hours, then what is his average speed?

b) If a wholesaler buys 100 pounds of shrimp for x dollars, then what is the price per pound?

c) If a painter completes an entire house in $2x$ hours, then at what rate is she painting?

Teaching Tip These are good exercises to get students ready for word problems involving rational expressions.

Solution

a) Because $R = \frac{D}{T}$, he is averaging $\frac{500}{x + 1}$ mph.

b) At x dollars for 100 pounds, the wholesaler is paying $\frac{x}{100}$ dollars per pound or $\frac{x}{100}$ dollars/pound.

c) By completing 1 house in $2x$ hours, her rate is $\frac{1}{2x}$ house/hour.

Now do Exercises 97–102

Warm-Ups ▼

True or false? Explain your answer.

1. A complete factorization of 3003 is $2 \cdot 3 \cdot 7 \cdot 11 \cdot 13$. False
2. A complete factorization of 120 is $2^3 \cdot 3 \cdot 5$. True
3. Any number can be used in place of x in the expression $\frac{x - 2}{5}$. True
4. We cannot replace x by -1 or 3 in the expression $\frac{x + 1}{x - 3}$. False
5. The rational expression $\frac{x + 2}{2}$ reduces to x. False
6. $\frac{2x}{2} = x$ for any real number x. True

7. $\frac{x^{13}}{x^{20}} = \frac{1}{x^7}$ for any nonzero value of x. True

8. $\frac{a^2 + b^2}{a + b}$ reduced to lowest terms is $a + b$. False

9. If $a \neq b$, then $\frac{a - b}{b - a} = 1$. False

10. The expression $\frac{-3x - 6}{x + 2}$ reduces to -3. True

6.1 Exercises

Boost your GRADE at mathzone.com!

MathZone
- Practice Problems
- Self-Tests
- Videos
- Net Tutor
- e-Professors

Reading and Writing *After reading this section, write out the answers to these questions. Use complete sentences.*

1. What is a rational number?
A rational number is a ratio of two integers with the denominator not 0.

2. What is a rational expression?
A rational expression is a ratio of two polynomials with the denominator not 0.

3. How do you reduce a rational number to lowest terms?
A rational number is reduced to lowest terms by dividing the numerator and denominator by the GCF.

4. How do you reduce a rational expression to lowest terms?
A rational expression is reduced to lowest terms by dividing the numerator and denominator by the GCF.

5. How is the quotient rule used in reducing rational expressions?
The quotient rule is used in reducing ratios of monomials.

6. What is the relationship between $a - b$ and $b - a$?
The expressions $a - b$ and $b - a$ are opposites.

Evaluate each rational expression. See Example 1.

7. Evaluate $\frac{3x - 3}{x + 5}$ for $x = -2$. -3

8. Evaluate $\frac{3x + 1}{4x - 4}$ for $x = 5$. 1

9. If $R(x) = \frac{2x + 9}{x}$, find $R(3)$. 5

10. If $R(x) = \frac{-20x - 2}{x - 8}$, find $R(-1)$. -2

11. If $R(x) = \frac{x - 5}{x + 3}$, find $R(2)$, $R(-4)$, $R(-3.02)$, and $R(-2.96)$.
$-0.6, 9, 401, -199$

12. If $R(x) = \frac{x^2 - 2x - 3}{x - 2}$, find $R(3)$, $R(5)$, $R(2.05)$, and $R(1.999)$.
$0, 4, -57.95, 3001.999$

Which numbers cannot be used in place of the variable in each rational expression? See Example 2.

13. $\frac{x}{x + 1}$ -1

14. $\frac{3x}{x - 7}$ 7

15. $\frac{7a}{3a - 5}$ $\frac{5}{3}$

16. $\frac{84}{3 - 2a}$ $\frac{3}{2}$

17. $\frac{2x + 3}{x^2 - 16}$ $4, -4$

18. $\frac{2y + 1}{y^2 - y - 6}$ $-2, 3$

19. $\frac{p - 1}{2}$
Any number can be used.

20. $\frac{m + 31}{5}$
Any number can be used.

Reduce each rational expression to lowest terms. Assume that the variables represent only numbers for which the denominators are nonzero. See Example 3.

21. $\frac{6}{27}$ $\frac{2}{9}$

22. $\frac{14}{21}$ $\frac{2}{3}$

23. $\frac{42}{90}$ $\frac{7}{15}$

24. $\frac{42}{54}$ $\frac{7}{9}$

25. $\frac{36a}{90}$ $\frac{2a}{5}$

26. $\frac{56y}{40}$ $\frac{7y}{5}$

27. $\frac{78}{30w}$ $\frac{13}{5w}$

28. $\frac{68}{44y}$ $\frac{17}{11y}$

29. $\frac{6x + 2}{6}$ $\frac{3x + 1}{3}$

30. $\frac{2w + 2}{2w}$ $\frac{w + 1}{w}$

31. $\frac{2x + 4y}{6y + 3x}$ $\frac{2}{3}$

32. $\frac{3m + 9w}{3m - 6w}$ $\frac{m + 3w}{m - 2w}$

33. $\frac{w^2 - 49}{w + 7}$ $w - 7$

34. $\frac{a^2 - b^2}{a - b}$ $a + b$

35. $\frac{a^2 - 1}{a^2 + 2a + 1}$ $\frac{a - 1}{a + 1}$

36. $\frac{x^2 - y^2}{x^2 + 2xy + y^2}$ $\frac{x - y}{x + y}$

37. $\frac{2x^2 + 4x + 2}{4x^2 - 4}$ $\frac{x + 1}{2(x - 1)}$

38. $\frac{2x^2 + 10x + 12}{3x^2 - 27}$ $\frac{2x + 4}{3(x - 3)}$

39. $\frac{3x^2 + 18x + 27}{21x + 63}$ $\frac{x + 3}{7}$

40. $\frac{x^3 - 3x^2 - 4x}{x^2 - 4x}$ $x + 1$

Reduce each expression to lowest terms. Assume that all denominators are nonzero. See Example 4.

41. $\frac{x^{10}}{x^7}$ x^3

42. $\frac{y^8}{y^5}$ y^3

43. $\frac{z^3}{z^8}$ $\frac{1}{z^5}$

44. $\frac{w^9}{w^{12}}$ $\frac{1}{w^3}$

45. $\frac{4x^7}{-2x^5}$ $-2x^2$

46. $\frac{-6y^3}{3y^9}$ $\frac{-2}{y^6}$

47. $\frac{-12m^9n^{18}}{8m^6n^{16}}$ $\frac{-3m^3n^2}{2}$

48. $\frac{-9u^9v^{19}}{6u^9v^{14}}$ $\frac{-3v^5}{2}$

49. $\frac{6b^{10}c^4}{-8b^{10}c^7}$ $\frac{-3}{4c^3}$

50. $\frac{9x^{20}y}{-6x^{25}y^3}$ $\frac{-3}{2x^5y^2}$

51. $\frac{30a^3bc}{18a^7b^{17}}$ $\frac{5c}{3a^4b^{16}}$

52. $\frac{15m^{10}n^3}{24m^{12}np}$ $\frac{5n^2}{8m^2p}$

Reduce each expression to lowest terms. See Example 5.

53. $\frac{210}{264}$ $\frac{35}{44}$

54. $\frac{616}{660}$ $\frac{14}{15}$

55. $\frac{231}{168}$ $\frac{11}{8}$

56. $\frac{936}{624}$ $\frac{3}{2}$

57. $\frac{630x^5}{300x^9}$ $\frac{21}{10x^4}$

58. $\frac{96y^2}{108y^5}$ $\frac{8}{9y^3}$

59. $\frac{924a^{23}}{448a^{19}}$ $\frac{33a^4}{16}$

60. $\frac{270b^{75}}{165b^{12}}$ $\frac{18b^{63}}{11}$

Reduce each expression to lowest terms. See Example 6.

61. $\frac{3a - 2b}{2b - 3a}$ -1

62. $\frac{5m - 6n}{6n - 5m}$ -1

63. $\frac{h^2 - t^2}{t - h}$ $-h - t$

64. $\frac{r^2 - s^2}{s - r}$ $-r - s$

65. $\frac{2g - 6h}{9h^2 - g^2}$ $\frac{-2}{3h + g}$

66. $\frac{5a - 10b}{4b^2 - a^2}$ $\frac{-5}{2b + a}$

67. $\frac{x^2 - x - 6}{9 - x^2}$ $\frac{-x - 2}{x + 3}$

68. $\frac{1 - a^2}{a^2 + a - 2}$ $-\frac{a + 1}{a + 2}$

Reduce each expression to lowest terms. See Example 7.

69. $\frac{-x - 6}{x + 6}$ -1

70. $\frac{-5x - 20}{3x + 12}$ $-\frac{5}{3}$

71. $\frac{-2y - 6y^2}{3 + 9y}$ $\frac{-2y}{3}$

72. $\frac{y^2 - 16}{-8 - 2y}$ $\frac{4 - y}{2}$

73. $\frac{-3x - 6}{3x - 6}$ $\frac{x + 2}{2 - x}$

74. $\frac{8 - 4x}{-8x - 16}$ $\frac{x - 2}{2(x + 2)}$

75. $\frac{-12a - 6}{2a^2 + 7a + 3}$ $\frac{-6}{a + 3}$

76. $\frac{-2b^2 - 6b - 4}{b^2 - 1}$ $\frac{-2b - 4}{b - 1}$

Reduce each expression to lowest terms.

77. $\frac{2x^{12}}{4x^8}$ $\frac{x^4}{2}$

78. $\frac{4x^2}{2x^9}$ $\frac{2}{x^7}$

79. $\frac{2x + 4}{4x}$

$\frac{x+2}{2x}$

80. $\frac{2x + 4x^2}{4x}$

$\frac{1+2x}{2}$

81. $\frac{a - 4}{4 - a}$

-1

82. $\frac{2b - 4}{2b + 4}$

$\frac{b-2}{b+2}$

83. $\frac{2c - 4}{4 - c^2}$

$\frac{-2}{c+2}$

84. $\frac{-2t - 4}{4 - t^2}$

$\frac{2}{t-2}$

85. $\frac{x^2 + 4x + 4}{x^2 - 4}$

$\frac{x+2}{x-2}$

86. $\frac{3x - 6}{x^2 - 4x + 4}$

$\frac{3}{x-2}$

87. $\frac{-2x - 4}{x^2 + 5x + 6}$

$\frac{-2}{x+3}$

88. $\frac{-2x - 8}{x^2 + 2x - 8}$

$\frac{-2}{x-2}$

89. $\frac{2q^8 + q^7}{2q^6 + q^5}$

q^2

90. $\frac{8s^{12}}{12s^6 - 16s^5}$

$\frac{2s^7}{3s-4}$

91. $\frac{u^2 - 6u - 16}{u^2 - 16u + 64}$

$\frac{u+2}{u-8}$

92. $\frac{v^2 + 3v - 18}{v^2 + 12v + 36}$

$\frac{v-3}{v+6}$

93. $\frac{a^3 - 8}{2a - 4}$

$\frac{a^2+2a+4}{2}$

94. $\frac{4w^2 - 12w + 36}{2w^3 + 54}$

$\frac{2}{w+3}$

95. $\frac{y^3 - 2y^2 - 4y + 8}{y^2 - 4y + 4}$

$y + 2$

96. $\frac{mx + 3x + my + 3y}{m^2 - 3m - 18}$

$\frac{x+y}{m-6}$

Answer each question with a rational expression. Be sure to include the units. See Example 8.

97. If Sergio drove 300 miles at $x + 10$ miles per hour, then how many hours did he drive?

$\frac{300}{x+10}$ hr

98. If Carrie walked 40 miles in x hours, then how fast did she walk?

$\frac{40}{x}$ mph

99. If $x + 4$ pounds of peaches cost \$4.50, then what is the cost per pound?

$\frac{4.50}{x+4}$ dollars/lb

100. If nine pounds of pears cost x dollars, then what is the price per pound?

$\frac{x}{9}$ dollars/lb

101. If Ayesha can clean the entire swimming pool in x hours, then how much of the pool does she clean per hour?

$\frac{1}{x}$ pool/hr

102. If Ramon can mow the entire lawn in $x - 3$ hours, then how much of the lawn does he mow per hour?

$\frac{1}{x-3}$ lawn/hr

Solve each problem.

103. ***Annual reports.*** The Crest Meat Company found that the cost per report for printing x annual reports at Peppy Printing is given by the formula

$$C(x) = \frac{150 + 0.60x}{x},$$

where $C(x)$ is in dollars.

a) Use the accompanying graph to estimate the cost per report for printing 1000 reports.

b) Use the formula to find the cost per report for printing 1000, 5000, and 10,000 reports.

c) What happens to the cost per report as the number of reports gets very large?

a) \$0.75
b) \$0.75, \$0.63, \$0.615
c) Approaches \$0.60

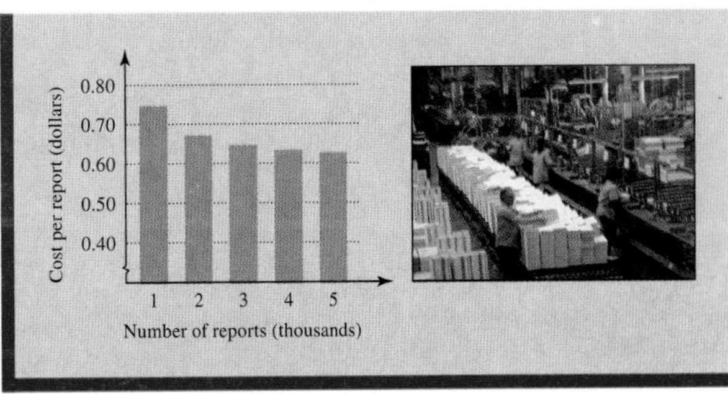

Figure for Exercise 103

104. ***Toxic pollutants.*** The annual cost in dollars for removing $p\%$ of the toxic chemicals from a town's water supply is given by the formula

$$C(p) = \frac{500{,}000}{100 - p}.$$

a) Use the accompanying graph to estimate the cost for removing 90% and 95% of the toxic chemicals.

b) Use the formula to determine the cost for removing 99.5% of the toxic chemicals.

c) What happens to the cost as the percentage of pollutants removed approaches 100%?

a) \$50,000, \$100,000 **b)** \$1,000,000
c) Gets larger and larger without bound

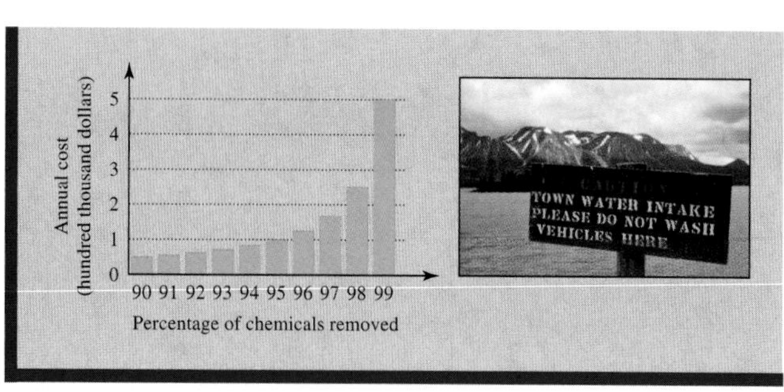

Figure for Exercise 104

6.2 Multiplication and Division

In this Section

In Section 6.1 you learned to reduce rational expressions in the same way that we reduce rational numbers. In this section we will multiply and divide rational expressions using the same procedures that we use for rational numbers.

Multiplication of Rational Numbers

Two rational numbers are multiplied by multiplying their numerators and multiplying their denominators.

Multiplication of Rational Numbers

If $b \neq 0$ and $d \neq 0$, then

$$\frac{a}{b} \cdot \frac{c}{d} = \frac{ac}{bd}.$$

EXAMPLE 1

Helpful Hint

Did you know that the line separating the numerator and denominator in a fraction is called the *vinculum?*

Multiplying rational numbers

Find the product $\frac{6}{7} \cdot \frac{14}{15}$.

Solution

The product is found by multiplying the numerators and multiplying the denominators:

$$\frac{6}{7} \cdot \frac{14}{15} = \frac{84}{105}$$

$$= \frac{21 \cdot 4}{21 \cdot 5} \quad \text{Factor the numerator and denominator.}$$

$$= \frac{4}{5} \quad \text{Divide out the GCF 21.}$$

The reducing that we did after multiplying is easier to do before multiplying. First factor all terms, reduce, and then multiply:

$$\frac{6}{7} \cdot \frac{14}{15} = \frac{2 \cdot \cancel{3}}{\cancel{7}} \cdot \frac{2 \cdot \cancel{7}}{\cancel{3} \cdot 5}$$
$$= \frac{4}{5}$$

Now do Exercises 5–12

Multiplication of Rational Expressions

We multiply rational expressions in the same way we multiply rational numbers. As with rational numbers, we can factor, reduce, and then multiply.

EXAMPLE 2

Multiplying rational expressions

Find the indicated products.

a) $\frac{9x}{5y} \cdot \frac{10y}{3xy}$

b) $\frac{-8xy^4}{3z^3} \cdot \frac{15z}{2x^5y^3}$

Teaching Tip Since students find multiplication and division easier than addition and subtraction we study them first.

Solution

a) $\frac{9x}{5y} \cdot \frac{10y}{3xy} = \frac{3 \cdot \cancel{3}\cancel{x}}{\cancel{5}\cancel{y}} \cdot \frac{2 \cdot \cancel{5}\cancel{y}}{\cancel{3}\cancel{x}y}$ Factor.

$= \frac{6}{y}$

b) $\frac{-8xy^4}{3z^3} \cdot \frac{15z}{2x^5y^3} = \frac{-2 \cdot 2 \cdot \cancel{2}xy^4}{\cancel{3}z^3} \cdot \frac{\cancel{3} \cdot 5z}{\cancel{2}x^5y^3}$ Factor.

$= \frac{-20xy^4z}{z^3x^5y^3}$ Reduce.

$= \frac{-20y}{z^2x^4}$ Quotient rule

Now do Exercises 13–20

EXAMPLE 3

Multiplying rational expressions

Find the indicated products.

a) $\frac{2x - 2y}{4} \cdot \frac{2x}{x^2 - y^2}$

b) $\frac{x^2 + 7x + 12}{2x + 6} \cdot \frac{x}{x^2 - 16}$

c) $\frac{a + b}{6a} \cdot \frac{8a^2}{a^2 + 2ab + b^2}$

Study Tip

We are all creatures of habit. When you find a place in which you study successfully, stick with it. Using the same place for studying will help you to concentrate and associate the place with good studying.

Solution

a) $\dfrac{2x - 2y}{4} \cdot \dfrac{2x}{x^2 - y^2} = \dfrac{2(x - y)}{2 \cdot 2} \cdot \dfrac{2 \cdot x}{(x - y)(x + y)}$ Factor.

$= \dfrac{x}{x + y}$ Reduce.

b) $\dfrac{x^2 + 7x + 12}{2x + 6} \cdot \dfrac{x}{x^2 - 16} = \dfrac{(x + 3)(x + 4)}{2(x + 3)} \cdot \dfrac{x}{(x - 4)(x + 4)}$ Factor.

$= \dfrac{x}{2(x - 4)}$ Reduce.

c) $\dfrac{a + b}{6a} \cdot \dfrac{8a^2}{a^2 + 2ab + b^2} = \dfrac{a + b}{2 \cdot 3a} \cdot \dfrac{2 \cdot 4a^2}{(a + b)^2}$ Factor.

$= \dfrac{4a}{3(a + b)}$ Reduce.

Now do Exercises 21–28

Division of Rational Numbers

Division of rational numbers can be accomplished by multiplying by the reciprocal of the divisor.

Division of Rational Numbers

If $b \neq 0$, $c \neq 0$, and $d \neq 0$, then

$$\frac{a}{b} \div \frac{c}{d} = \frac{a}{b} \cdot \frac{d}{c}.$$

EXAMPLE 4 **Dividing rational numbers**

Find each quotient.

a) $5 \div \dfrac{1}{2}$

b) $\dfrac{6}{7} \div \dfrac{3}{14}$

Solution

a) $5 \div \dfrac{1}{2} = 5 \cdot 2 = 10$

b) $\dfrac{6}{7} \div \dfrac{3}{14} = \dfrac{6}{7} \cdot \dfrac{14}{3} = \dfrac{2 \cdot 3}{7} \cdot \dfrac{2 \cdot 7}{3} = 4$

Now do Exercises 29–36

Division of Rational Expressions

We divide rational expressions in the same way we divide rational numbers: Invert the divisor and multiply.

EXAMPLE 5

Dividing rational expressions

Find each quotient.

a) $\frac{5}{3x} \div \frac{5}{6x}$

b) $\frac{x^7}{2} \div (2x^2)$

c) $\frac{4 - x^2}{x^2 + x} \div \frac{x - 2}{x^2 - 1}$

Solution

a) $\frac{5}{3x} \div \frac{5}{6x} = \frac{5}{3x} \cdot \frac{6x}{5}$ Invert the divisor and multiply.

$= \frac{\cancel{5}}{\cancel{3x}} \cdot \frac{2 \cdot \cancel{3x}}{\cancel{5}}$ Factor.

$= 2$ Divide out the common factors.

b) $\frac{x^7}{2} \div (2x^2) = \frac{x^7}{2} \cdot \frac{1}{2x^2}$ Invert and multiply.

$= \frac{x^5}{4}$ Quotient rule

c) $\frac{4 - x^2}{x^2 + x} \div \frac{x - 2}{x^2 - 1} = \frac{4 - x^2}{x^2 + x} \cdot \frac{x^2 - 1}{x - 2}$ Invert and multiply.

$= \frac{\overset{-1}{\cancel{(2 - x)}}(2 + x)}{x\cancel{(x + 1)}} \cdot \frac{\cancel{(x + 1)}(x - 1)}{\cancel{x - 2}}$ Factor.

$= \frac{-1(2 + x)(x - 1)}{x}$ $\frac{2 - x}{x - 2} = -1$

$= \frac{-1(x^2 + x - 2)}{x}$ Simplify.

$= \frac{-x^2 - x + 2}{x}$

Now do Exercises 37–50

Helpful Hint

A doctor told a nurse to give a patient half of the usual dose of a certain medicine. The nurse figured, "dividing in half means dividing by 1/2 which means multiply by 2." So the patient got four times the prescribed amount and died (true story). There is a big difference between dividing a quantity in half and dividing by one-half.

We sometimes write division of rational expressions using the fraction bar. For example, we can write

$$\frac{a + b}{3} \div \frac{1}{6} \quad \text{as} \quad \frac{\frac{a + b}{3}}{\frac{1}{6}}.$$

No matter how division is expressed, we invert the divisor and multiply.

EXAMPLE 6

Division expressed with a fraction bar

Find each quotient.

a) $\dfrac{\frac{a + b}{3}}{\frac{1}{6}}$ **b)** $\dfrac{\frac{x^2 - 1}{2}}{\frac{x - 1}{3}}$ **c)** $\dfrac{\frac{a^2 + 5}{3}}{2}$

Solution

a)

$$\frac{\frac{a + b}{3}}{\frac{1}{6}} = \frac{a + b}{3} \div \frac{1}{6} \quad \text{Rewrite as division.}$$

$$= \frac{a + b}{3} \cdot \frac{6}{1} \quad \text{Invert and multiply.}$$

$$= \frac{a + b}{\cancel{3}} \cdot \frac{2 \cdot \cancel{3}}{1} \quad \text{Factor.}$$

$$= (a + b)2 \quad \text{Reduce.}$$

$$= 2a + 2b$$

b)

$$\frac{\frac{x^2 - 1}{2}}{\frac{x - 1}{3}} = \frac{x^2 - 1}{2} \div \frac{x - 1}{3} \quad \text{Rewrite as division.}$$

$$= \frac{x^2 - 1}{2} \cdot \frac{3}{x - 1} \quad \text{Invert and multiply.}$$

$$= \frac{\cancel{(x - 1)}(x + 1)}{2} \cdot \frac{3}{\cancel{x - 1}} \quad \text{Factor.}$$

$$= \frac{3x + 3}{2} \quad \text{Reduce.}$$

c)

$$\frac{\frac{a^2 + 5}{3}}{2} = \frac{a^2 + 5}{3} \div 2 \quad \text{Rewrite as division.}$$

$$= \frac{a^2 + 5}{3} \cdot \frac{1}{2}$$

$$= \frac{a^2 + 5}{6}$$

Now do Exercises 51–58

Teaching Tip Another example that is good to work here is

$$\frac{\frac{2x + 6}{5}}{2} = \frac{x + 3}{5}.$$

Applications

We saw in Section 6.1 that rational expressions can be used to represent rates. Note that there are several ways to write rates. For example, miles per hour is written mph, mi/hr, or $\frac{\text{mi}}{\text{hr}}$. The last way is best when doing operations with rates because it helps us reconcile our answers. Notice how hours "cancels" when we multiply miles per hour and hours in Example 7, giving an answer in miles, as it should be.

EXAMPLE 7

Writing rational expressions

Answer each question with a rational expression.

a) Shasta averaged $\frac{200}{x}$ mph for x hours before she had lunch. How many miles did she drive in the first 3 hours after lunch assuming that she continued to average $\frac{200}{x}$ mph?

b) If a bathtub can be filled in x minutes, then the rate at which it is filling is $\frac{1}{x}$ tub/min. How much of the tub is filled in 10 minutes?

Solution

a) Because $R \cdot T = D$, the distance she traveled after lunch is the product of the rate and time:

$$\frac{200}{x}\frac{\text{mi}}{\cancel{\text{hr}}} \cdot 3\,\cancel{\text{hr}} = \frac{600}{x}\text{ mi}$$

b) Because $R \cdot T = W$, the work completed is the product of the rate and time:

$$\frac{1}{x}\frac{\text{tub}}{\cancel{\text{min}}} \cdot 10\,\cancel{\text{min}} = \frac{10}{x}\text{ tub}$$

Now do Exercises 79–82

Teaching Tip These exercises are designed to get students ready for word problems. Note the cancellation of units here.

Warm-Ups ▼

True or false? Explain your answer.

1. $\frac{2}{3} \cdot \frac{5}{3} = \frac{10}{9}$. True
2. The product of $\frac{x-7}{3}$ and $\frac{6}{7-x}$ is -2. True
3. Dividing by 2 is equivalent to multiplying by $\frac{1}{2}$. True
4. $3 \div x = \frac{1}{3} \cdot x$ for any nonzero number x. False
5. Factoring polynomials is essential in multiplying rational expressions. True
6. One-half of one-fourth is one-sixth. False
7. One-half divided by three is three-halves. False
8. The quotient of $(839 - 487)$ and $(487 - 839)$ is -1. True
9. $\frac{a}{3} \div 3 = \frac{a}{9}$ for any value of a. True
10. $\frac{a}{b} \cdot \frac{b}{a} = 1$ for any nonzero values of a and b. True

6.2 Exercises

Boost your GRADE at mathzone.com!

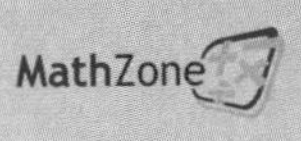

MathZone

- Practice Problems
- Self-Tests
- Videos
- Net Tutor
- e-Professors

Reading and Writing *After reading this section, write out the answers to these questions. Use complete sentences.*

1. How do you multiply rational numbers?
   Rational numbers are multiplied by multiplying their numerators and their denominators.

2. How do you multiply rational expressions?
Rational expressions are multiplied by multiplying their numerators and their denominators.

3. What can be done to simplify the process of multiplying rational numbers or rational expressions?
Reducing can be done before multiplying rational numbers or expressions.

4. How do you divide rational numbers or rational expressions?
To divide rational expressions, invert the divisor and multiply.

Perform the indicated operation. See Example 1.

5. $\frac{2}{3} \cdot \frac{5}{6}$ $\frac{5}{9}$

6. $\frac{3}{4} \cdot \frac{2}{5}$ $\frac{3}{10}$

7. $\frac{8}{15} \cdot \frac{35}{24}$ $\frac{7}{9}$

8. $\frac{3}{4} \cdot \frac{8}{21}$ $\frac{2}{7}$

9. $\frac{12}{17} \cdot \frac{51}{10}$ $\frac{18}{5}$

10. $\frac{25}{48} \cdot \frac{56}{35}$ $\frac{5}{6}$

11. $24 \cdot \frac{7}{20}$ $\frac{42}{5}$

12. $\frac{3}{10} \cdot 35$ $\frac{21}{2}$

Perform the indicated operation. See Example 2.

13. $\frac{2x}{3} \cdot \frac{5}{4x}$ $\frac{5}{6}$

14. $\frac{3y}{7} \cdot \frac{21}{2y}$ $\frac{9}{2}$

15. $\frac{5a}{12b} \cdot \frac{3ab}{55a}$ $\frac{a}{44}$

16. $\frac{3m}{7p} \cdot \frac{35p}{6mp}$ $\frac{5}{2p}$

17. $\frac{-2x^6}{7a^5} \cdot \frac{21a^2}{6x}$ $\frac{-x^5}{a^3}$

18. $\frac{5z^3w}{-9y^3} \cdot \frac{-6y^5}{20z^9}$ $\frac{wy^2}{6z^6}$

19. $\frac{15t^3y^5}{20w^7} \cdot 24t^5w^3y^2$ $\frac{18t^8y^7}{w^4}$

20. $22x^2y^3z \cdot \frac{6x^5}{33y^3z^4}$ $\frac{4x^7}{z^3}$

Perform the indicated operation. See Example 3.

21. $\frac{2x + 2y}{7} \cdot \frac{15}{6x + 6y}$ $\frac{5}{7}$

22. $\frac{3}{a^2 + a} \cdot \frac{2a + 2}{6}$ $\frac{1}{a}$

23. $\frac{3a + 3b}{15} \cdot \frac{10a}{a^2 - b^2}$ $\frac{2a}{a - b}$

24. $\frac{b^3 + b}{5} \cdot \frac{10}{b^2 + b}$ $\frac{2b^2 + 2}{b + 1}$

25. $(x^2 - 6x + 9) \cdot \frac{3}{x - 3}$ $3x - 9$

26. $\frac{12}{4x + 10} \cdot (4x^2 + 20x + 25)$ $12x + 30$

27. $\frac{16a + 8}{5a^2 + 5} \cdot \frac{2a^2 + a - 1}{4a^2 - 1}$ $\frac{8a + 8}{5(a^2 + 1)}$

28. $\frac{6x - 18}{2x^2 - 5x - 3} \cdot \frac{4x^2 + 4x + 1}{6x + 3}$ 2

Perform the indicated operation. See Example 4.

29. $\frac{1}{4} \div \frac{1}{2}$ $\frac{1}{2}$

30. $\frac{1}{6} \div \frac{1}{2}$ $\frac{1}{3}$

31. $12 \div \frac{2}{5}$ 30

32. $32 \div \frac{1}{4}$ 128

33. $\frac{5}{7} \div \frac{15}{14}$ $\frac{2}{3}$

34. $\frac{3}{4} \div \frac{15}{2}$ $\frac{1}{10}$

35. $\frac{40}{3} \div 12$ $\frac{10}{9}$

36. $\frac{22}{9} \div 9$ $\frac{22}{81}$

Perform the indicated operation. See Example 5.

37. $\frac{x^2}{4} \div \frac{x}{2}$ $\frac{x}{2}$

38. $\frac{3}{2a^2} \div \frac{6}{2a}$ $\frac{1}{2a}$

39. $\frac{5x^2}{3} \div \frac{10x}{21}$ $\frac{7x}{2}$

40. $\frac{4u^2}{3v} \div \frac{14u}{15v^6}$ $\frac{10uv^5}{7}$

41. $\frac{8m^3}{n^4} \div (12mn^2)$ $\frac{2m^2}{3n^6}$

42. $\frac{2p^4}{3q^3} \div (4pq^5)$ $\frac{p^3}{6q^8}$

43. $\frac{y - 6}{2} \div \frac{6 - y}{6}$ -3

44. $\frac{4 - a}{5} \div \frac{a^2 - 16}{3}$ $\frac{-3}{5(a + 4)}$

45. $\frac{x^2 + 4x + 4}{8} \div \frac{(x + 2)^3}{16}$ $\frac{2}{x + 2}$

46. $\frac{a^2 + 2a + 1}{3} \div \frac{a^2 - 1}{a}$ $\frac{a^2 + a}{3(a - 1)}$

47. $\frac{t^2 + 3t - 10}{t^2 - 25} \div (4t - 8)$ $\frac{1}{4(t - 5)}$

48. $\frac{w^2 - 7w + 12}{w^2 - 4w} \div (w^2 - 9)$ $\frac{1}{w(w + 3)}$

49. $(2x^2 - 3x - 5) \div \frac{2x - 5}{x - 1}$ $x^2 - 1$

50. $(6y^2 - y - 2) \div \frac{2y + 1}{3y - 2}$ $9y^2 - 12y + 4$

Perform the indicated operation. See Example 6.

51. $\frac{\frac{x - 2y}{5}}{\frac{1}{10}}$ $2x - 4y$

52. $\frac{\frac{3m + 6n}{8}}{\frac{3}{4}}$ $\frac{m + 2n}{2}$

53. $\frac{\frac{x^2 - 4}{12}}{\frac{x - 2}{6}}$ $\frac{x + 2}{2}$

54. $\frac{\frac{6a^2 + 6}{5}}{\frac{6a + 6}{5}}$ $\frac{a^2 + 1}{a + 1}$

55. $\frac{\frac{x^2 + 9}{3}}{5}$ $\frac{x^2 + 9}{15}$

56. $\frac{\frac{1}{a - 3}}{4}$ $\frac{1}{4(a - 3)}$

57. $\dfrac{x^2 - y^2}{\dfrac{x - y}{9}}$ $9x + 9y$

58. $\dfrac{x^2 + 6x + 8}{\dfrac{x + 2}{x + 1}}$ $x^2 + 5x + 4$

Perform the indicated operation.

59. $\dfrac{x - 1}{3} \cdot \dfrac{9}{1 - x}$ -3

60. $\dfrac{2x - 2y}{3} \cdot \dfrac{1}{y - x}$ $-\dfrac{2}{3}$

61. $\dfrac{3a + 3b}{a} \cdot \dfrac{1}{3}$ $\dfrac{a + b}{a}$

62. $\dfrac{a - b}{2b - 2a} \cdot \dfrac{2}{5}$ $-\dfrac{1}{5}$

63. $\dfrac{\frac{b}{a}}{\frac{1}{2}}$ $\dfrac{2b}{a}$

64. $\dfrac{\frac{2g}{3h}}{\frac{1}{h}}$ $\dfrac{2g}{3}$

65. $\dfrac{6y}{3} \div (2x)$ $\dfrac{y}{x}$

66. $\dfrac{8x}{9} \div (18x)$ $\dfrac{4}{81}$

67. $\dfrac{a^3b^4}{-2ab^2} \cdot \dfrac{a^5b^7}{ab}$ $\dfrac{-a^6b^8}{2}$

68. $\dfrac{-2a^2}{3a^2} \cdot \dfrac{20a}{15a^3}$ $\dfrac{-8}{9a^2}$

69. $\dfrac{2mn^4}{6mn^2} \div \dfrac{3m^5n^7}{m^2n^4}$ $\dfrac{1}{9m^3n}$

70. $\dfrac{rt^2}{rt^2} \div \dfrac{rt^2}{r^3t^2}$ r^2

71. $\dfrac{3x^2 + 16x + 5}{x} \cdot \dfrac{x^2}{9x^2 - 1}$ $\dfrac{x^2 + 5x}{3x - 1}$

72. $\dfrac{x^2 + 6x + 5}{x} \cdot \dfrac{x^4}{3x + 3}$ $\dfrac{x^4 + 5x^3}{3}$

73. $\dfrac{a^2 - 2a + 4}{a^2 - 4} \cdot \dfrac{(a + 2)^3}{2a + 4}$ $\dfrac{a^3 + 8}{2(a - 2)}$

74. $\dfrac{w^2 - 1}{(w - 1)^2} \cdot \dfrac{w - 1}{w^2 + 2w + 1}$ $\dfrac{1}{w + 1}$

75. $\dfrac{2x^2 + 19x - 10}{x^2 - 100} \div \dfrac{4x^2 - 1}{2x^2 - 19x - 10}$ 1

76. $\dfrac{x^3 - 1}{x^2 + 1} \div \dfrac{9x^2 + 9x + 9}{x^2 - x}$ $\dfrac{x^3 - 2x^2 + x}{9(x^2 + 1)}$

77. $\dfrac{9 + 6m + m^2}{9 - 6m + m^2} \cdot \dfrac{m^2 - 9}{m^2 + mk + 3m + 3k}$

$\dfrac{m^2 + 6m + 9}{(m - 3)(m + k)}$

78. $\dfrac{3x + 3w + bx + bw}{x^2 - w^2} \cdot \dfrac{6 - 2b}{9 - b^2}$ $\dfrac{2}{x - w}$

Solve each problem. Answers could be rational expressions. Be sure to give your answer with appropriate units. See Example 7.

79. ***Distance.*** Florence averaged $\frac{26.2}{x}$ mph for the x hours in which she ran the Boston Marathon. If she ran at that same rate for $\frac{1}{2}$ hour in the Manchac Fun Run, then how many miles did she run at Manchac?
$\dfrac{13.1}{x}$ mi

80. ***Work.*** Henry sold 120 magazine subscriptions in $x + 2$ days. If he sold at the same rate for another week, then how many magazines did he sell in the extra week?
$\dfrac{840}{x + 2}$ magazines

81. ***Area of a rectangle.*** If the length of a rectangular flag is x meters and its width is $\frac{5}{x}$ meters, then what is the area of the rectangle? 5 square meters

Figure for Exercise 81

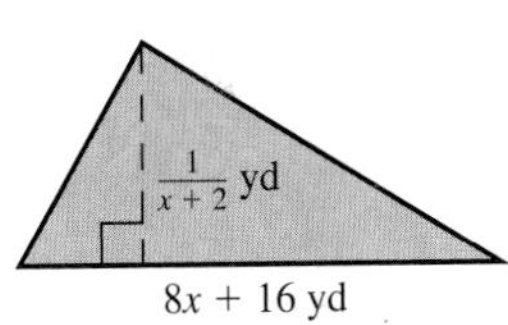

Figure for Exercise 82

82. ***Area of a triangle.*** If the base of a triangle is $8x + 16$ yards and its height is $\frac{1}{x + 2}$ yards, then what is the area of the triangle? 4 yd^2

Getting More Involved

83. ***Discussion***

Evaluate each expression.

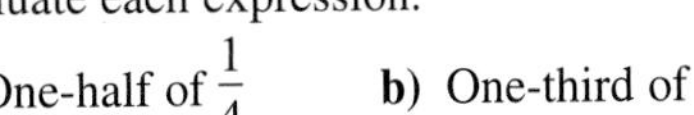

a) One-half of $\dfrac{1}{4}$ **b)** One-third of 4

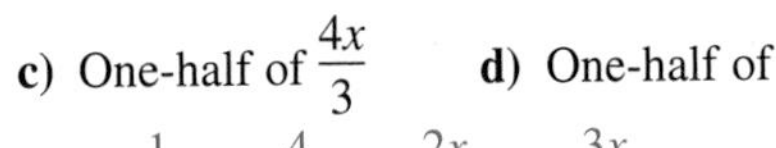

c) One-half of $\dfrac{4x}{3}$ **d)** One-half of $\dfrac{3x}{2}$

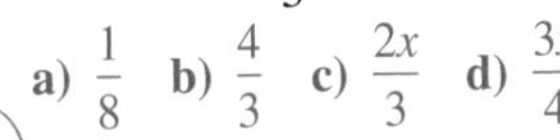

a) $\dfrac{1}{8}$ **b)** $\dfrac{4}{3}$ **c)** $\dfrac{2x}{3}$ **d)** $\dfrac{3x}{4}$

84. ***Exploration***

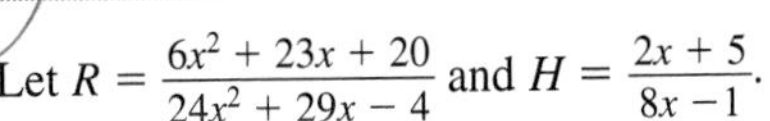

Let $R = \dfrac{6x^2 + 23x + 20}{24x^2 + 29x - 4}$ and $H = \dfrac{2x + 5}{8x - 1}$.

a) Find R when $x = 2$ and $x = 3$. Find H when $x = 2$ and $x = 3$.

b) How are these values of R and H related and why?

a) $R = \dfrac{3}{5}$, $R = \dfrac{11}{23}$, $H = \dfrac{3}{5}$, $H = \dfrac{11}{23}$

b) The values of R and H are the same since R reduces to H.

6.3 Finding the Least Common Denominator

In this Section

- **Building Up the Denominator**
- **Finding the Least Common Denominator**
- **Converting to the LCD**

Every rational expression can be written in infinitely many equivalent forms. Because we can add or subtract only fractions with identical denominators, we must be able to change the denominator of a fraction. You have already learned how to change the denominator of a fraction by reducing. In this section you will learn the opposite of reducing, which is called **building up the denominator.**

Building Up the Denominator

To convert the fraction $\frac{2}{3}$ into an equivalent fraction with a denominator of 21, we factor 21 as $21 = 3 \cdot 7$. Because $\frac{2}{3}$ already has a 3 in the denominator, multiply the numerator and denominator of $\frac{2}{3}$ by the missing factor 7 to get a denominator of 21:

$$\frac{2}{3} = \frac{2}{3} \cdot \frac{7}{7} = \frac{14}{21}$$

For rational expressions the process is the same. To convert the rational expression

$$\frac{5}{x + 3}$$

into an equivalent rational expression with a denominator of $x^2 - x - 12$, first factor $x^2 - x - 12$:

$$x^2 - x - 12 = (x + 3)(x - 4)$$

From the factorization we can see that the denominator $x + 3$ needs only a factor of $x - 4$ to have the required denominator. So multiply the numerator and denominator by the missing factor $x - 4$:

$$\frac{5}{x + 3} = \frac{5(x - 4)}{(x + 3)(x - 4)} = \frac{5x - 20}{x^2 - x - 12}$$

EXAMPLE 1

Building up the denominator

Build each rational expression into an equivalent rational expression with the indicated denominator.

a) $3 = \frac{?}{12}$ **b)** $\frac{3}{w} = \frac{?}{wx}$ **c)** $\frac{2}{3y^3} = \frac{?}{12y^8}$

Solution

a) Because $3 = \frac{3}{1}$, we get a denominator of 12 by multiplying the numerator and denominator by 12:

$$3 = \frac{3}{1} = \frac{3 \cdot 12}{1 \cdot 12} = \frac{36}{12}$$

b) Multiply the numerator and denominator by x:

$$\frac{3}{w} = \frac{3 \cdot x}{w \cdot x} = \frac{3x}{wx}$$

c) To build the denominator $3y^3$ up to $12y^8$, multiply by $4y^5$:

$$\frac{2}{3y^3} = \frac{2 \cdot 4y^5}{3y^3 \cdot 4y^5} = \frac{8y^5}{12y^8}$$

Now do Exercises 5–22

In Example 2 we must factor the original denominator before building up the denominator.

EXAMPLE 2

Building up the denominator

Build each rational expression into an equivalent rational expression with the indicated denominator.

a) $\dfrac{7}{3x - 3y} = \dfrac{?}{6y - 6x}$ **b)** $\dfrac{x - 2}{x + 2} = \dfrac{?}{x^2 + 8x + 12}$

Helpful Hint

Notice that reducing and building up are exactly the opposite of each other. In reducing you remove a factor that is common to the numerator and denominator, and in building up you put a common factor into the numerator and denominator.

Solution

a) Because $3x - 3y = 3(x - y)$, we factor -6 out of $6y - 6x$. This will give a factor of $x - y$ in each denominator:

$$3x - 3y = 3(x - y)$$
$$6y - 6x = -6(x - y) = -2 \cdot 3(x - y)$$

To get the required denominator, we multiply the numerator and denominator by -2 only:

$$\frac{7}{3x - 3y} = \frac{7(-2)}{(3x - 3y)(-2)}$$
$$= \frac{-14}{6y - 6x}$$

b) Because $x^2 + 8x + 12 = (x + 2)(x + 6)$, we multiply the numerator and denominator by $x + 6$, the missing factor:

$$\frac{x - 2}{x + 2} = \frac{(x - 2)(x + 6)}{(x + 2)(x + 6)}$$
$$= \frac{x^2 + 4x - 12}{x^2 + 8x + 12}$$

Now do Exercises 23–34

CAUTION When building up a denominator, *both* the numerator and the denominator must be multiplied by the appropriate expression, because that is how we build up fractions.

Finding the Least Common Denominator

We can use the idea of building up the denominator to convert two fractions with different denominators into fractions with identical denominators. For example,

$$\frac{5}{6} \quad \text{and} \quad \frac{1}{4}$$

can both be converted into fractions with a denominator of 12, since $12 = 2 \cdot 6$ and $12 = 3 \cdot 4$:

$$\frac{5}{6} = \frac{5 \cdot 2}{6 \cdot 2} = \frac{10}{12} \qquad \frac{1}{4} = \frac{1 \cdot 3}{4 \cdot 3} = \frac{3}{12}$$

The smallest number that is a multiple of all of the denominators is called the **least common denominator (LCD).** The LCD for the denominators 6 and 4 is 12.

To find the LCD in a systematic way, we look at a complete factorization of each denominator. Consider the denominators 24 and 30:

$$24 = 2 \cdot 2 \cdot 2 \cdot 3 = 2^3 \cdot 3$$
$$30 = 2 \cdot 3 \cdot 5$$

Study Tip

Studying in a quiet place is better than studying in a noisy place. There are very few people who can listen to music or a conversation and study at the same time.

Any multiple of 24 must have three 2's in its factorization, and any multiple of 30 must have one 2 as a factor. So a number with three 2's in its factorization will have enough to be a multiple of both 24 and 30. The LCD must also have one 3 and one 5 in its factorization. *We use each factor the maximum number of times it appears in either factorization.* So the LCD is $2^3 \cdot 3 \cdot 5$:

$$2^3 \cdot 3 \cdot 5 = \overbrace{2 \cdot 2 \cdot 2 \cdot 3}^{24} \cdot 5 = 120 \quad (\text{with } \underbrace{2 \cdot 3 \cdot 5}_{30})$$

If we omitted any one of the factors in $2 \cdot 2 \cdot 2 \cdot 3 \cdot 5$, we would not have a multiple of both 24 and 30. That is what makes 120 the *least* common denominator. To find the LCD for two polynomials, we use the same strategy.

Strategy for Finding the LCD for Polynomials

1. Factor each denominator completely. Use exponent notation for repeated factors.
2. Write the product of all of the different factors that appear in the denominators.
3. On each factor, use the highest power that appears on that factor in any of the denominators.

EXAMPLE 3

Finding the LCD

If the given expressions were used as denominators of rational expressions, then what would be the LCD for each group of denominators?

a) 20, 50

b) x^3yz^2, x^5y^2z, xyz^5

c) $a^2 + 5a + 6, a^2 + 4a + 4$

Solution

a) First factor each number completely:

$$20 = 2^2 \cdot 5 \qquad 50 = 2 \cdot 5^2$$

The highest power of 2 is 2, and the highest power of 5 is 2. So the LCD of 20 and 50 is $2^2 \cdot 5^2$, or 100.

b) The expressions x^3yz^2, x^5y^2z, and xyz^5 are already factored. For the LCD, use the highest power of each variable. So the LCD is $x^5y^2z^5$.

c) First factor each polynomial.

$$a^2 + 5a + 6 = (a + 2)(a + 3) \qquad a^2 + 4a + 4 = (a + 2)^2$$

The highest power of $(a + 3)$ is 1, and the highest power of $(a + 2)$ is 2. So the LCD is $(a + 3)(a + 2)^2$.

Now do Exercises 35–48

Converting to the LCD

When adding or subtracting rational expressions, we must convert the expressions into expressions with identical denominators. To keep the computations as simple as possible, we use the least common denominator.

EXAMPLE 4

Converting to the LCD

Find the LCD for the rational expressions, and convert each expression into an equivalent rational expression with the LCD as the denominator.

a) $\dfrac{4}{9xy}, \dfrac{2}{15xz}$ **b)** $\dfrac{5}{6x^2}, \dfrac{1}{8x^3y}, \dfrac{3}{4y^2}$

Helpful Hint

What is the difference between LCD, GCF, CBS, and NBC? The LCD for the denominators 4 and 6 is 12. The *least* common denominator is *greater than* or equal to both numbers. The GCF for 4 and 6 is 2. The *greatest* common factor is *less than* or equal to both numbers. CBS and NBC are TV networks.

Solution

a) Factor each denominator completely:

$$9xy = 3^2xy \qquad 15xz = 3 \cdot 5xz$$

The LCD is $3^2 \cdot 5xyz$. Now convert each expression into an expression with this denominator. We must multiply the numerator and denominator of the first rational expression by $5z$ and the second by $3y$:

$$\left.\begin{aligned} \frac{4}{9xy} &= \frac{4 \cdot 5z}{9xy \cdot 5z} = \frac{20z}{45xyz} \\ \frac{2}{15xz} &= \frac{2 \cdot 3y}{15xz \cdot 3y} = \frac{6y}{45xyz} \end{aligned}\right\} \text{Same denominator}$$

b) Factor each denominator completely:

$$6x^2 = 2 \cdot 3x^2 \qquad 8x^3y = 2^3x^3y \qquad 4y^2 = 2^2y^2$$

The LCD is $2^3 \cdot 3 \cdot x^3y^2$ or $24x^3y^2$. Now convert each expression into an expression with this denominator:

$$\frac{5}{6x^2} = \frac{5}{6x^2} \cdot \frac{4xy^2}{4xy^2} = \frac{20xy^2}{24x^3y^2}$$

$$\frac{1}{8x^3y} = \frac{1}{8x^3y} \cdot \frac{3y}{3y} = \frac{3y}{24x^3y^2}$$

$$\frac{3}{4y^2} = \frac{3}{4y^2} \cdot \frac{6x^3}{6x^3} = \frac{18x^3}{24x^3y^2}$$

Now do Exercises 49–60

EXAMPLE 5

Converting to the LCD

Find the LCD for the rational expressions

$$\frac{5x}{x^2 - 4} \quad \text{and} \quad \frac{3}{x^2 + x - 6}$$

and convert each into an equivalent rational expression with that denominator.

Solution

First factor the denominators:

$$x^2 - 4 = (x - 2)(x + 2)$$
$$x^2 + x - 6 = (x - 2)(x + 3)$$

Teaching Tip Point out that the LCD is what you get when you make the denominators the same with the least amount of multiplying.

The LCD is $(x - 2)(x + 2)(x + 3)$. Now we multiply the numerator and denominator of the first rational expression by $(x + 3)$ and those of the second rational expression by $(x + 2)$. Because each denominator already has one factor of $(x - 2)$, there is no reason to multiply by $(x - 2)$. We multiply each denominator by the factors in the LCD that are missing from that denominator:

$$\frac{5x}{x^2 - 4} = \frac{5x(x + 3)}{(x - 2)(x + 2)(x + 3)} = \frac{5x^2 + 15x}{(x - 2)(x + 2)(x + 3)}$$

$$\frac{3}{x^2 + x - 6} = \frac{3(x + 2)}{(x - 2)(x + 3)(x + 2)} = \frac{3x + 6}{(x - 2)(x + 2)(x + 3)}$$

Same denominator

Now do Exercises 61–72

Note that in Example 5 we multiplied the expressions in the numerators but left the denominators in factored form. The numerators are simplified because it is the numerators that must be added when we add rational expressions in Section 6.4. Because we can add rational expressions with identical denominators, there is no need to multiply the denominators.

Warm-Ups ▼

True or false? Explain your answer.

1. To convert $\frac{2}{3}$ into an equivalent fraction with a denominator of 18, we would multiply only the denominator of $\frac{2}{3}$ by 6. False
2. Factoring has nothing to do with finding the least common denominator. False
3. $\dfrac{3}{2ab^2} = \dfrac{15a^2b^2}{10a^3b^4}$ for any nonzero values of a and b. True
4. The LCD for the denominators $2^5 \cdot 3$ and $2^4 \cdot 3^2$ is $2^5 \cdot 3^2$. True
5. The LCD for the fractions $\frac{1}{6}$ and $\frac{1}{10}$ is 60. False
6. The LCD for the denominators $6a^2b$ and $4ab^3$ is $2ab$. False
7. The LCD for the denominators $a^2 + 1$ and $a + 1$ is $a^2 + 1$. False
8. $\dfrac{x}{2} = \dfrac{x+7}{2+7}$ for any real number x. False
9. The LCD for the rational expressions $\dfrac{1}{x-2}$ and $\dfrac{3}{x+2}$ is $x^2 - 4$. True
10. $x = \dfrac{3x}{3}$ for any real number x. True

6.3 Exercises

Boost your GRADE at mathzone.com!

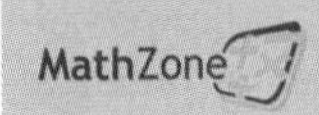

- Practice Problems
- Self-Tests
- Videos
- Net Tutor
- e-Professors

Reading and Writing *After reading this section, write out the answers to these questions. Use complete sentences.*

1. What is building up the denominator?
   We can build up a denominator by multiplying the numerator and denominator of a fraction by the same nonzero number.
2. How do we build up the denominator of a rational expression?
   To build up the denominator of a rational expression, we can multiply the numerator and denominator by the same polynomial.
3. What is the least common denominator for fractions?
   For fractions, the LCD is the smallest number that is a multiple of all of the denominators.
4. How do you find the LCD for two polynomial denominators?
   For polynomial denominators, the LCD consists of every factor that appears, raised to the highest power that appears on the factor.

Build each rational expression into an equivalent rational expression with the indicated denominator. See Example 1.

5. $\dfrac{1}{3} = \dfrac{?}{27}$ $\dfrac{9}{27}$
6. $\dfrac{2}{5} = \dfrac{?}{35}$ $\dfrac{14}{35}$
7. $\dfrac{3}{4} = \dfrac{?}{16}$ $\dfrac{12}{16}$
8. $\dfrac{3}{7} = \dfrac{?}{28}$ $\dfrac{12}{28}$
9. $2 = \dfrac{?}{6}$ $\dfrac{12}{6}$
10. $5 = \dfrac{?}{12}$ $\dfrac{60}{12}$
11. $\dfrac{5}{x} = \dfrac{?}{ax}$ $\dfrac{5a}{ax}$
12. $\dfrac{x}{3} = \dfrac{?}{3x}$ $\dfrac{x^2}{3x}$
13. $7 = \dfrac{?}{2x}$ $\dfrac{14x}{2x}$
14. $6 = \dfrac{?}{4y}$ $\dfrac{24y}{4y}$
15. $\dfrac{5}{b} = \dfrac{?}{3bt}$ $\dfrac{15t}{3bt}$
16. $\dfrac{7}{2ay} = \dfrac{?}{2ayz}$ $\dfrac{7z}{2ayz}$
17. $\dfrac{-9z}{2aw} = \dfrac{?}{8awz}$ $\dfrac{-36z^2}{8awz}$
18. $\dfrac{-7yt}{3x} = \dfrac{?}{18xyt}$ $\dfrac{-42y^2t^2}{18xyt}$
19. $\dfrac{2}{3a} = \dfrac{?}{15a^3}$ $\dfrac{10a^2}{15a^3}$
20. $\dfrac{7b}{12c^5} = \dfrac{?}{36c^8}$ $\dfrac{21bc^3}{36c^8}$
21. $\dfrac{4}{5xy^2} = \dfrac{?}{10x^2y^5}$ $\dfrac{8xy^3}{10x^2y^5}$
22. $\dfrac{5y^2}{8x^3z} = \dfrac{?}{24x^5z^3}$ $\dfrac{15x^2y^2z^2}{24x^5z^3}$

Build each rational expression into an equivalent rational expression with the indicated denominator. See Example 2.

23. $\frac{5}{x+3} = \frac{?}{2x+6}$ $\frac{10}{2x+6}$

24. $\frac{4}{a-5} = \frac{?}{3a-15}$ $\frac{12}{3a-15}$

25. $\frac{5}{2x+2} = \frac{?}{-8x-8}$ $\frac{-20}{-8x-8}$

26. $\frac{3}{m-n} = \frac{?}{2n-2m}$ $\frac{-6}{2n-2m}$

27. $\frac{8a}{5b^2-5b} = \frac{?}{20b^2-20b^3}$ $\frac{-32ab}{20b^2-20b^3}$

28. $\frac{5x}{-6x-9} = \frac{?}{18x^2+27x}$ $\frac{-15x^2}{18x^2+27x}$

29. $\frac{3}{x+2} = \frac{?}{x^2-4}$ $\frac{3x-6}{x^2-4}$

30. $\frac{a}{a+3} = \frac{?}{a^2-9}$ $\frac{a^2-3a}{a^2-9}$

31. $\frac{3x}{x+1} = \frac{?}{x^2+2x+1}$ $\frac{3x^2+3x}{x^2+2x+1}$

32. $\frac{-7x}{2x-3} = \frac{?}{4x^2-12x+9}$ $\frac{-14x^2+21x}{4x^2-12x+9}$

33. $\frac{y-6}{y-4} = \frac{?}{y^2+y-20}$ $\frac{y^2-y-30}{y^2+y-20}$

34. $\frac{z-6}{z+3} = \frac{?}{z^2-2z-15}$ $\frac{z^2-11z+30}{z^2-2z-15}$

If the given expressions were used as denominators of rational expressions, then what would be the LCD for each group of denominators? See Example 3.

35. 12, 16 48

36. 28, 42 84

37. 12, 18, 20 180

38. 24, 40, 48 240

39. $6a^2, 15a$ $30a^2$

40. $18x^2, 20xy$ $180x^2y$

41. $2a^4b, 3ab^6, 4a^3b^2$ $12a^4b^6$

42. $4m^3nw, 6mn^5w^8, 9m^6nw$ $36m^6n^5w^8$

43. $x^2-16, x^2+8x+16$ $(x-4)(x+4)^2$

44. x^2-9, x^2+6x+9 $(x-3)(x+3)^2$

45. $x, x+2, x-2$ $x(x+2)(x-2)$

46. $y, y-5, y+2$ $y(y-5)(y+2)$

47. $x^2-4x, x^2-16, 2x$ $2x(x-4)(x+4)$

48. $y, y^2-3y, 3y$ $3y(y-3)$

Find the LCD for the given rational expressions, and convert each rational expression into an equivalent rational expression with the LCD as the denominator. See Example 4.

49. $\frac{1}{6}, \frac{3}{8}$ $\frac{4}{24}, \frac{9}{24}$

50. $\frac{5}{12}, \frac{3}{20}$ $\frac{25}{60}, \frac{9}{60}$

51. $\frac{1}{2x}, \frac{5}{6x}$ $\frac{3}{6x}, \frac{5}{6x}$

52. $\frac{3}{5x}, \frac{1}{10x}$ $\frac{6}{10x}, \frac{1}{10x}$

53. $\frac{2}{3a}, \frac{1}{2b}$ $\frac{4b}{6ab}, \frac{3a}{6ab}$

54. $\frac{y}{4x}, \frac{x}{6y}$ $\frac{3y^2}{12xy}, \frac{2x^2}{12xy}$

55. $\frac{3}{84a}, \frac{5}{63b}$ $\frac{9b}{252ab}, \frac{20a}{252ab}$

56. $\frac{4b}{75a}, \frac{6}{105ab}$ $\frac{28b^2}{525ab}, \frac{30}{525ab}$

57. $\frac{1}{3x^2}, \frac{3}{2x^5}$ $\frac{2x^3}{6x^5}, \frac{9}{6x^5}$

58. $\frac{3}{8a^3b^9}, \frac{5}{6a^2c}$ $\frac{9c}{24a^3b^9c}, \frac{20ab^9}{24a^3b^9c}$

59. $\frac{x}{9y^5z}, \frac{y}{12x^3}, \frac{1}{6x^2y}$ $\frac{4x^4}{36x^3y^5z}, \frac{3y^6z}{36x^3y^5z}, \frac{6xy^4z}{36x^3y^5z}$

60. $\frac{5}{12a^6b}, \frac{3b}{14a^3}, \frac{1}{2ab^3}$ $\frac{35b^2}{84a^6b^3}, \frac{18a^3b^4}{84a^6b^3}, \frac{42a^5}{84a^6b^3}$

Find the LCD for the given rational expressions, and convert each rational expression into an equivalent rational expression with the LCD as the denominator. See Example 5.

61. $\frac{2x}{x-3}, \frac{5x}{x+2}$ $\frac{2x^2+4x}{(x-3)(x+2)}, \frac{5x^2-15x}{(x-3)(x+2)}$

62. $\frac{2a}{a-5}, \frac{3a}{a+2}$ $\frac{2a^2+4a}{(a-5)(a+2)}, \frac{3a^2-15a}{(a-5)(a+2)}$

63. $\frac{4}{a-6}, \frac{5}{6-a}$ $\frac{4}{a-6}, \frac{-5}{a-6}$

64. $\frac{4}{x-y}, \frac{5x}{2y-2x}$ $\frac{8}{2(x-y)}, \frac{-5x}{2(x-y)}$

65. $\frac{x}{x^2-9}, \frac{5x}{x^2-6x+9}$
$\frac{x^2-3x}{(x-3)^2(x+3)}, \frac{5x^2+15x}{(x-3)^2(x+3)}$

66. $\frac{5x}{x^2-1}, \frac{-4}{x^2-2x+1}$
$\frac{5x^2-5x}{(x+1)(x-1)^2}, \frac{-4x-4}{(x+1)(x-1)^2}$

67. $\dfrac{w+2}{w^2-2w-15}, \dfrac{-2w}{w^2-4w-5}$

$\dfrac{w^2+3w+2}{(w-5)(w+3)(w+1)}, \dfrac{-2w^2-6w}{(w-5)(w+3)(w+1)}$

68. $\dfrac{z-1}{z^2+6z+8}, \dfrac{z+1}{z^2+5z+6}$

$\dfrac{z^2+2z-3}{(z+2)(z+4)(z+3)}, \dfrac{z^2+5z+4}{(z+2)(z+4)(z+3)}$

69. $\dfrac{-5}{6x-12}, \dfrac{x}{x^2-4}, \dfrac{3}{2x+4}$

$\dfrac{-5x-10}{6(x-2)(x+2)}, \dfrac{6x}{6(x-2)(x+2)}, \dfrac{9x-18}{6(x-2)(x+2)}$

70. $\dfrac{3}{4b^2-9}, \dfrac{2b}{2b+3}, \dfrac{-5}{2b^2-3b}$

$\dfrac{3b}{b(2b-3)(2b+3)}, \dfrac{4b^3-6b^2}{b(2b-3)(2b+3)}, \dfrac{-10b-15}{b(2b-3)(2b+3)}$

71. $\dfrac{2}{2q^2-5q-3}, \dfrac{3}{2q^2+9q+4}, \dfrac{4}{q^2+q-12}$

$\dfrac{2q+8}{(2q+1)(q-3)(q+4)}, \dfrac{3q-9}{(2q+1)(q-3)(q+4)}, \dfrac{8q+4}{(2q+1)(q-3)(q+4)}$

72. $\dfrac{-3}{2p^2+7p-15}, \dfrac{p}{2p^2-11p+12}, \dfrac{2}{p^2+p-20}$

$\dfrac{-3p+12}{(2p-3)(p+5)(p-4)}, \dfrac{p^2+5p}{(2p-3)(p+5)(p-4)}, \dfrac{4p-6}{(2p-3)(p+5)(p-4)}$

Getting More Involved

73. *Discussion*

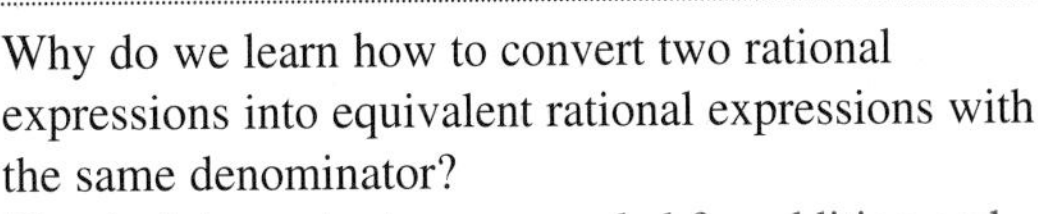

Why do we learn how to convert two rational expressions into equivalent rational expressions with the same denominator?
Identical denominators are needed for addition and subtraction.

74. *Discussion*

Which expression is the LCD for

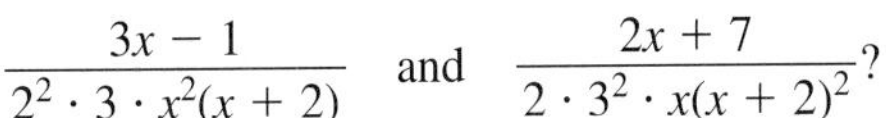

$$\frac{3x-1}{2^2 \cdot 3 \cdot x^2(x+2)} \quad \text{and} \quad \frac{2x+7}{2 \cdot 3^2 \cdot x(x+2)^2}?$$

a) $2 \cdot 3 \cdot x(x+2)$
b) $36x(x+2)$
c) $36x^2(x+2)^2$
d) $2^3 \cdot 3^3x^3(x+2)^2$ c

6.4 Addition and Subtraction

In this Section

- Addition and Subtraction of Rational Numbers
- Addition and Subtraction of Rational Expressions
- Applications

In Section 6.3 you learned how to find the LCD and build up the denominators of rational expressions. In this section we will use that knowledge to add and subtract rational expressions with different denominators.

Addition and Subtraction of Rational Numbers

We can add or subtract rational numbers (or fractions) only with identical denominators according to the following definition.

Addition and Subtraction of Rational Numbers

If $b \neq 0$, then

$$\frac{a}{b} + \frac{c}{b} = \frac{a+c}{b} \quad \text{and} \quad \frac{a}{b} - \frac{c}{b} = \frac{a-c}{b}.$$

EXAMPLE 1

Adding or subtracting fractions with the same denominator

Perform the indicated operations. Reduce answers to lowest terms.

a) $\frac{1}{12} + \frac{7}{12}$

b) $\frac{1}{4} - \frac{3}{4}$

Solution

a) $\frac{1}{12} + \frac{7}{12} = \frac{8}{12} = \frac{\cancel{4} \cdot 2}{\cancel{4} \cdot 3} = \frac{2}{3}$

b) $\frac{1}{4} - \frac{3}{4} = \frac{-2}{4} = -\frac{1}{2}$

Now do Exercises 5–12

If the rational numbers have different denominators, we must convert them to equivalent rational numbers that have identical denominators and then add or subtract. Of course, it is most efficient to use the least common denominator (LCD), as in the following example.

EXAMPLE 2

Adding or subtracting fractions with different denominators

Find each sum or difference.

a) $\frac{3}{20} + \frac{7}{12}$

b) $\frac{1}{6} - \frac{4}{15}$

Solution

a) Because $20 = 2^2 \cdot 5$ and $12 = 2^2 \cdot 3$, the LCD is $2^2 \cdot 3 \cdot 5$, or 60. Convert each fraction to an equivalent fraction with a denominator of 60:

$$\frac{3}{20} + \frac{7}{12} = \frac{3 \cdot 3}{20 \cdot 3} + \frac{7 \cdot 5}{12 \cdot 5}$$ Build up the denominators.

$$= \frac{9}{60} + \frac{35}{60}$$ Simplify numerators and denominators.

$$= \frac{44}{60}$$ Add the fractions.

$$= \frac{4 \cdot 11}{4 \cdot 15}$$ Factor.

$$= \frac{11}{15}$$ Reduce.

Helpful Hint

Note how all of the operations with rational expressions are performed according to the rules for fractions. So keep thinking of how you perform operations with fractions and you will improve your skills with fractions and with rational expressions.

b) Because $6 = 2 \cdot 3$ and $15 = 3 \cdot 5$, the LCD is $2 \cdot 3 \cdot 5$ or 30:

$$\frac{1}{6} - \frac{4}{15} = \frac{1}{2 \cdot 3} - \frac{4}{3 \cdot 5}$$ Factor the denominators.

$$= \frac{1 \cdot 5}{2 \cdot 3 \cdot 5} - \frac{4 \cdot 2}{3 \cdot 5 \cdot 2}$$ Build up the denominators.

$$= \frac{5}{30} - \frac{8}{30}$$ Simplify the numerators and denominators.

$$= \frac{-3}{30}$$ Subtract.

$$= \frac{-1 \cdot 3}{10 \cdot 3}$$ Factor.

$$= -\frac{1}{10}$$ Reduce.

Now do Exercises 13–20

Addition and Subtraction of Rational Expressions

Rational expressions are added or subtracted just like rational numbers. We can add or subtract only rational expressions that have identical denominators.

EXAMPLE 3

Rational expressions with the same denominator

Perform the indicated operations and reduce answers to lowest terms.

a) $\frac{2}{3y} + \frac{4}{3y}$

b) $\frac{2x}{x + 2} + \frac{4}{x + 2}$

c) $\frac{x^2 + 2x}{(x - 1)(x + 3)} - \frac{2x + 1}{(x - 1)(x + 3)}$

Study Tip

Eliminate the obvious distractions when you study. Disconnect the telephone and put away newspapers, magazines, and unfinished projects. Even the sight of a textbook from another class might keep reminding you of how far behind you are in that class.

Solution

a) $$\frac{2}{3y} + \frac{4}{3y} = \frac{6}{3y}$$ Add the fractions.

$$= \frac{2}{y}$$ Reduce.

b) $$\frac{2x}{x + 2} + \frac{4}{x + 2} = \frac{2x + 4}{x + 2}$$ Add the fractions.

$$= \frac{2(x + 2)}{x + 2}$$ Factor the numerator.

$$= 2$$ Reduce.

c) $\frac{x^2 + 2x}{(x - 1)(x + 3)} - \frac{2x + 1}{(x - 1)(x + 3)} = \frac{x^2 + 2x - (2x + 1)}{(x - 1)(x + 3)}$ Subtract the fractions.

$= \frac{x^2 + 2x - 2x - 1}{(x - 1)(x + 3)}$ Remove parentheses.

$= \frac{x^2 - 1}{(x - 1)(x + 3)}$ Combine like terms.

$= \frac{(x - 1)(x + 1)}{(x - 1)(x + 3)}$ Factor.

$= \frac{x + 1}{x + 3}$ Reduce.

Now do Exercises 21–32

CAUTION When subtracting a numerator containing more than one term, be sure to enclose it in parentheses, as in Example 3(c). Because that numerator is a binomial, the sign of each of its terms must be changed for the subtraction.

In Example 4 the rational expressions have different denominators.

EXAMPLE 4

Rational expressions with different denominators

Perform the indicated operations.

a) $\frac{5}{2x} + \frac{2}{3}$

b) $\frac{4}{x^3y} + \frac{2}{xy^3}$

c) $\frac{a + 1}{6} - \frac{a - 2}{8}$

Helpful Hint

You can remind yourself of the difference between addition and multiplication of fractions with a simple example: If you and your spouse each own 1/7 of Microsoft, then together you own 2/7 of Microsoft. If you own 1/7 of Microsoft, and give 1/7 of your stock to your child, then your child owns 1/49 of Microsoft.

Solution

a) The LCD for $2x$ and 3 is $6x$:

$\frac{5}{2x} + \frac{2}{3} = \frac{5 \cdot 3}{2x \cdot 3} + \frac{2 \cdot 2x}{3 \cdot 2x}$ Build up both denominators to $6x$.

$= \frac{15}{6x} + \frac{4x}{6x}$ Simplify numerators and denominators.

$= \frac{15 + 4x}{6x}$ Add the rational expressions.

b) The LCD is x^3y^3.

$\frac{4}{x^3y} + \frac{2}{xy^3} = \frac{4 \cdot y^2}{x^3y \cdot y^2} + \frac{2 \cdot x^2}{xy^3 \cdot x^2}$ Build up both denominators to the LCD.

$= \frac{4y^2}{x^3y^3} + \frac{2x^2}{x^3y^3}$ Simplify numerators and denominators.

$= \frac{4y^2 + 2x^2}{x^3y^3}$ Add the rational expressions.

c) Because $6 = 2 \cdot 3$ and $8 = 2^3$, the LCD is $2^3 \cdot 3$, or 24:

$$\frac{a+1}{6} - \frac{a-2}{8} = \frac{(a+1)4}{6 \cdot 4} - \frac{(a-2)3}{8 \cdot 3}$$ Build up both denominators to the LCD 24.

$$= \frac{4a+4}{24} - \frac{3a-6}{24}$$ Simplify numerators and denominators.

$$= \frac{4a+4-(3a-6)}{24}$$ Subtract the rational expressions.

$$= \frac{4a+4-3a+6}{24}$$ Remove the parentheses.

$$= \frac{a+10}{24}$$ Combine like terms.

Now do Exercises 33–48

EXAMPLE 5

Rational expressions with different denominators

Perform the indicated operations:

a) $\frac{1}{x^2-9} + \frac{2}{x^2+3x}$ **b)** $\frac{4}{5-a} - \frac{2}{a-5}$

Helpful Hint

Once the denominators are factored as in Example 5(a), you can simply look at each denominator and ask, "What factor does the other denominator(s) have that is missing from this one?" Then use the missing factor to build up the denominator. Repeat until all denominators are identical and you will have the LCD.

Solution

a) $$\frac{1}{x^2-9} + \frac{2}{x^2+3x} = \underbrace{\frac{1}{(x-3)(x+3)}}_{\text{Needs } x} + \underbrace{\frac{2}{x(x+3)}}_{\text{Needs } x-3}$$ The LCD is $x(x-3)(x+3)$.

$$= \frac{1 \cdot x}{(x-3)(x+3)x} + \frac{2(x-3)}{x(x+3)(x-3)}$$

$$= \frac{x}{x(x-3)(x+3)} + \frac{2x-6}{x(x-3)(x+3)}$$

$$= \frac{3x-6}{x(x-3)(x+3)}$$ We usually leave the denominator in factored form.

b) Because $-1(5-a) = a-5$, we can get identical denominators by multiplying only the first expression by -1 in the numerator and denominator:

$$\frac{4}{5-a} - \frac{2}{a-5} = \frac{4(-1)}{(5-a)(-1)} - \frac{2}{a-5}$$

$$= \frac{-4}{a-5} - \frac{2}{a-5}$$

$$= \frac{-6}{a-5}$$ $-4 - 2 = -6$

$$= -\frac{6}{a-5}$$

Now do Exercises 49–66

In Example 6 we combine three rational expressions by addition and subtraction.

EXAMPLE 6

Rational expressions with different denominators

Perform the indicated operations.

$$\frac{x + 1}{x^2 + 2x} + \frac{2x + 1}{6x + 12} - \frac{1}{6}$$

Solution

The LCD for $x(x + 2)$, $6(x + 2)$, and 6 is $6x(x + 2)$.

$$\frac{x + 1}{x^2 + 2x} + \frac{2x + 1}{6x + 12} - \frac{1}{6} = \frac{x + 1}{x(x + 2)} + \frac{2x + 1}{6(x + 2)} - \frac{1}{6} \quad \text{Factor denominators.}$$

$$= \frac{6(x + 1)}{6x(x + 2)} + \frac{x(2x + 1)}{6x(x + 2)} - \frac{1x(x + 2)}{6x(x + 2)} \quad \text{Build up to the LCD.}$$

$$= \frac{6x + 6}{6x(x + 2)} + \frac{2x^2 + x}{6x(x + 2)} - \frac{x^2 + 2x}{6x(x + 2)} \quad \text{Simplify numerators.}$$

$$= \frac{6x + 6 + 2x^2 + x - x^2 - 2x}{6x(x + 2)} \quad \text{Combine the numerators.}$$

$$= \frac{x^2 + 5x + 6}{6x(x + 2)} \quad \text{Combine like terms.}$$

$$= \frac{(x + 3)(x + 2)}{6x(x + 2)} \quad \text{Factor.}$$

$$= \frac{x + 3}{6x} \quad \text{Reduce.}$$

Now do Exercises 67–72

Applications

We have seen how rational expressions can occur in problems involving rates. In Example 7 we see an applied situation in which we add rational expressions.

EXAMPLE 7

Adding work

Harry takes twice as long as Lucy to proofread a manuscript. Write a rational expression for the amount of work they do in 3 hours working together on a manuscript.

Teaching Tip Emphasize the importance of tables for keeping all of the information organized. Note that in work problems the product of rate and time is work. In motion problems $RT = D$.

Solution

Let $x =$ the number of hours it would take Lucy to complete the manuscript alone and $2x =$ the number of hours it would take Harry to complete the manuscript alone. Make a table showing rate, time, and work completed:

	Rate	Time	Work
Lucy	$\frac{1}{x}\frac{\text{msp}}{\text{hr}}$	3 hr	$\frac{3}{x}$ msp
Harry	$\frac{1}{2x}\frac{\text{msp}}{\text{hr}}$	3 hr	$\frac{3}{2x}$ msp

Math *at Work* Gravity on the Moon

Hundreds of years before humans even considered traveling beyond the earth, Isaac Newton established the laws of gravity. So when Neil Armstrong made the first human step onto the moon in 1969 he knew what amount of gravitational force to expect. Let's see how he knew.

Newton's equation for the force of gravity between two objects is $F = G\frac{m_1 m_2}{d^2}$, where m_1 and m_2 are the masses of the objects (in kilograms), d is the distance (in meters) between the centers of the two objects, and G is the gravitational constant 6.67×10^{-11}. To find the force of gravity for Armstrong on earth use 5.98×10^{24} kg for the mass of the earth, 6.378×10^6 m for the radius of the earth, 80 kg for Armstrong's mass. We get

$$F = 6.67 \times 10^{-11} \cdot \frac{5.98 \times 10^{24}\text{ kg} \cdot 80\text{ kg}}{(6.378 \times 10^6\text{ m})^2} \approx 784\text{ Newtons.}$$

To find the force of gravity for Armstrong on the moon use 7.34×10^{22} kg for the mass of the moon and 1.737×10^6 m for the radius of the moon. We get

$$F = 6.67 \times 10^{-11} \cdot \frac{7.34 \times 10^{22}\text{ kg} \cdot 80\text{ kg}}{(1.737 \times 10^6\text{ m})^2} \approx 130\text{ Newtons.}$$

So the force of gravity for Armstrong on the moon was about one-sixth of the force of gravity for Armstrong on earth. Fortunately, the moon is smaller than the earth. Walking on a planet much larger than the earth would present a real problem in terms of gravitational force.

Now find the sum of each person's work.

$$\frac{3}{x} + \frac{3}{2x} = \frac{2 \cdot 3}{2 \cdot x} + \frac{3}{2x}$$
$$= \frac{6}{2x} + \frac{3}{2x}$$
$$= \frac{9}{2x}$$

So in 3 hours working together they will complete $\frac{9}{2x}$ of the manuscript.

Now do Exercises 83–88

Warm-Ups ▼

True or false? Explain your answer.

1. $\frac{1}{2} + \frac{1}{3} = \frac{2}{5}$ False

2. $\frac{7}{12} - \frac{1}{12} = \frac{1}{2}$ True

3. $\frac{3}{5} + \frac{4}{3} = \frac{29}{15}$ True

4. $\frac{4}{5} - \frac{5}{7} = \frac{3}{35}$ True

5. $\frac{5}{20} + \frac{3}{4} = 1$ True

6. $\frac{2}{x} + 1 = \frac{3}{x}$ for any nonzero value of x. False

7. $1 + \frac{1}{a} = \frac{a+1}{a}$ for any nonzero value of a. True

8. $a - \frac{1}{4} = \frac{3}{4}a$ for any value of a. False

9. $\frac{a}{2} + \frac{b}{3} = \frac{3a+2b}{6}$ for any values of a and b. True

10. The LCD for the rational expressions $\frac{1}{x}$ and $\frac{3x}{x-1}$ is $x^2 - 1$. False

6.4 Exercises

Boost your GRADE at mathzone.com!

MathZone
- Practice Problems
- Self-Tests
- Videos
- Net Tutor
- e-Professors

Reading and Writing *After reading this section, write out the answers to these questions. Use complete sentences.*

1. How do you add or subtract rational numbers?
We can add rational numbers with identical denominators as follows: $\frac{a}{c} + \frac{b}{c} = \frac{a+b}{c}$.
2. How do you add or subtract rational expressions?
Rational expressions with identical denominators are added in the same manner as rational numbers.
3. What is the least common denominator?
The LCD is the smallest number that is a multiple of all denominators.
4. Why do we use the *least* common denominator when adding rational expressions?
We use the least common denominator to keep the addition process as simple as possible.

Perform the indicated operation. Reduce each answer to lowest terms. See Example 1.

5. $\frac{1}{10} + \frac{1}{10}$ $\frac{1}{5}$
6. $\frac{1}{8} + \frac{3}{8}$ $\frac{1}{2}$
7. $\frac{7}{8} - \frac{1}{8}$ $\frac{3}{4}$
8. $\frac{4}{9} - \frac{1}{9}$ $\frac{1}{3}$
9. $\frac{1}{6} - \frac{5}{6}$ $-\frac{2}{3}$
10. $-\frac{3}{8} - \frac{7}{8}$ $-\frac{5}{4}$
11. $-\frac{7}{8} + \frac{1}{8}$ $-\frac{3}{4}$
12. $-\frac{9}{20} + \left(-\frac{3}{20}\right)$ $-\frac{3}{5}$

Perform the indicated operation. Reduce each answer to lowest terms. See Example 2.

13. $\frac{1}{3} + \frac{2}{9}$ $\frac{5}{9}$
14. $\frac{1}{4} + \frac{5}{6}$ $\frac{13}{12}$
15. $\frac{7}{16} + \frac{5}{18}$ $\frac{103}{144}$
16. $\frac{7}{6} + \frac{4}{15}$ $\frac{43}{30}$
17. $\frac{1}{8} - \frac{9}{10}$ $-\frac{31}{40}$
18. $\frac{2}{15} - \frac{5}{12}$ $-\frac{17}{60}$
19. $-\frac{1}{6} - \left(-\frac{3}{8}\right)$ $\frac{5}{24}$
20. $-\frac{1}{5} - \left(-\frac{1}{7}\right)$ $-\frac{2}{35}$

Perform the indicated operation. Reduce each answer to lowest terms. See Example 3.

21. $\frac{1}{2x} + \frac{1}{2x}$ $\frac{1}{x}$

22. $\frac{1}{3y} + \frac{2}{3y}$ $\frac{1}{y}$

23. $\frac{3}{2w} + \frac{7}{2w}$ $\frac{5}{w}$

24. $\frac{5x}{3y} + \frac{7x}{3y}$ $\frac{4x}{y}$

25. $\frac{3a}{a+5} + \frac{15}{a+5}$ 3

26. $\frac{a+7}{a-4} + \frac{9-5a}{a-4}$ -4

27. $\frac{q-1}{q-4} - \frac{3q-9}{q-4}$ -2

28. $\frac{3-a}{3} - \frac{a-5}{3}$ $\frac{8-2a}{3}$

29. $\frac{4h-3}{h(h+1)} - \frac{h-6}{h(h+1)}$ $\frac{3}{h}$

30. $\frac{2t-9}{t(t-3)} - \frac{t-9}{t(t-3)}$ $\frac{1}{t-3}$

31. $\frac{x^2-x-5}{(x+1)(x+2)} + \frac{1-2x}{(x+1)(x+2)}$ $\frac{x-4}{x+2}$

32. $\frac{2x-5}{(x-2)(x+6)} + \frac{x^2-2x+1}{(x-2)(x+6)}$ $\frac{x+2}{x+6}$

Perform the indicated operation. Reduce each answer to lowest terms. See Example 4.

33. $\frac{1}{a} + \frac{1}{2a}$ $\frac{3}{2a}$

34. $\frac{1}{3w} + \frac{2}{w}$ $\frac{7}{3w}$

35. $\frac{x}{3} + \frac{x}{2}$ $\frac{5x}{6}$

36. $\frac{y}{4} + \frac{y}{2}$ $\frac{3y}{4}$

37. $\frac{m}{5} + m$ $\frac{6m}{5}$

38. $\frac{y}{4} + 2y$ $\frac{9y}{4}$

39. $\frac{1}{x} + \frac{2}{y}$ $\frac{2x+y}{xy}$

40. $\frac{2}{a} + \frac{3}{b}$ $\frac{3a+2b}{ab}$

41. $\frac{3}{2a} + \frac{1}{5a}$ $\frac{17}{10a}$

42. $\frac{5}{6y} - \frac{3}{8y}$ $\frac{11}{24y}$

43. $\frac{w-3}{9} - \frac{w-4}{12}$ $\frac{w}{36}$

44. $\frac{y+4}{10} - \frac{y-2}{14}$ $\frac{y+19}{35}$

45. $\frac{b^2}{4a} - c$ $\frac{b^2-4ac}{4a}$

46. $y + \frac{3}{7b}$ $\frac{7by+3}{7b}$

47. $\frac{2}{wz^2} + \frac{3}{w^2z}$ $\frac{2w+3z}{w^2z^2}$

48. $\frac{1}{a^5b} - \frac{5}{ab^3}$ $\frac{b^2-5a^4}{a^5b^3}$

Perform the indicated operation. Reduce each answer to lowest terms. See Examples 5 and 6.

49. $\frac{1}{x} + \frac{1}{x+2}$ $\frac{2x+2}{x(x+2)}$

50. $\frac{1}{y} + \frac{2}{y+1}$ $\frac{3y+1}{y(y+1)}$

51. $\frac{2}{x+1} - \frac{3}{x}$ $\frac{-x-3}{x(x+1)}$

52. $\frac{1}{a-1} - \frac{2}{a}$ $\frac{2-a}{a(a-1)}$

53. $\frac{2}{a-b} + \frac{1}{a+b}$ $\frac{3a+b}{(a-b)(a+b)}$

54. $\frac{3}{x+1} + \frac{2}{x-1}$ $\frac{5x-1}{(x+1)(x-1)}$

55. $\frac{3}{x^2+x} - \frac{4}{5x+5}$ $\frac{15-4x}{5x(x+1)}$

56. $\frac{3}{a^2+3a} - \frac{2}{5a+15}$ $\frac{15-2a}{5a(a+3)}$

57. $\frac{2a}{a^2-9} + \frac{a}{a-3}$ $\frac{a^2+5a}{(a-3)(a+3)}$

58. $\frac{x}{x^2-1} + \frac{3}{x-1}$ $\frac{4x+3}{(x-1)(x+1)}$

59. $\frac{4}{a-b} + \frac{4}{b-a}$ 0

60. $\frac{2}{x-3} + \frac{3}{3-x}$ $\frac{1}{3-x}$

61. $\frac{3}{2a-2} - \frac{2}{1-a}$ $\frac{7}{2(a-1)}$

62. $\frac{5}{2x-4} - \frac{3}{2-x}$ $\frac{11}{2(x-2)}$

63. $\frac{1}{x^2-4} - \frac{3}{x^2-3x-10}$ $\frac{-2x+1}{(x-5)(x+2)(x-2)}$

64. $\frac{2x}{x^2-9} + \frac{3x}{x^2+4x+3}$ $\frac{5x^2-7x}{(x-3)(x+3)(x+1)}$

65. $\frac{3}{x^2+x-2} + \frac{4}{x^2+2x-3}$ $\frac{7x+17}{(x+2)(x-1)(x+3)}$

66. $\frac{x-1}{x^2-x-12} + \frac{x+4}{x^2+5x+6}$

$\frac{2x^2+x-18}{(x+2)(x+3)(x-4)}$

67. $\frac{1}{a} + \frac{1}{b} + \frac{1}{c}$ $\frac{bc+ac+ab}{abc}$

68. $\frac{1}{x} + \frac{1}{x^2} + \frac{1}{x^3}$ $\quad \frac{x^2 + x + 1}{x^3}$

69. $\frac{2}{x} - \frac{1}{x - 1} + \frac{1}{x + 2}$ $\quad \frac{2x^2 - x - 4}{x(x - 1)(x + 2)}$

70. $\frac{1}{a} - \frac{2}{a + 1} + \frac{3}{a - 1}$ $\quad \frac{2a^2 + 5a - 1}{a(a - 1)(a + 1)}$

71. $\frac{5}{3a - 9} - \frac{3}{2a} + \frac{4}{a^2 - 3a}$ $\quad \frac{a + 51}{6a(a - 3)}$

72. $\frac{3}{4c + 2} - \frac{c - 4}{2c^2 + c} - \frac{5}{6c}$ $\quad \frac{-7c + 19}{6c(2c + 1)}$

Match each expression in (a)–(f) with the equivalent expression in (A)–(F).

73. **a)** $\frac{1}{y} + 2$ F **b)** $\frac{1}{y} + \frac{2}{y}$ A **c)** $\frac{1}{y} + \frac{1}{2}$ E

d) $\frac{1}{y} + \frac{1}{2y}$ B **e)** $\frac{2}{y} + 1$ D **f)** $\frac{y}{2} + 1$ C

A) $\frac{3}{y}$ **B)** $\frac{3}{2y}$ **C)** $\frac{y + 2}{2}$

D) $\frac{y + 2}{y}$ **E)** $\frac{y + 2}{2y}$ **F)** $\frac{2y + 1}{y}$

74. **a)** $\frac{1}{x} - x$ C **b)** $\frac{1}{x} - \frac{1}{x^2}$ F **c)** $\frac{1}{x} - 1$ B

d) $\frac{1}{x^2} - x$ A **e)** $x - \frac{1}{x}$ E **f)** $\frac{1}{x^2} - \frac{1}{x}$ D

A) $\frac{1 - x^3}{x^2}$ **B)** $\frac{1 - x}{x}$ **C)** $\frac{1 - x^2}{x}$

D) $\frac{1 - x}{x^2}$ **E)** $\frac{x^2 - 1}{x}$ **F)** $\frac{x - 1}{x^2}$

Perform the indicated operation. Reduce each answer to lowest terms.

75. $\frac{3}{2p} - \frac{1}{2p + 8}$ $\quad \frac{p + 6}{p(p + 4)}$

76. $\frac{3}{2y} - \frac{3}{2y + 4}$ $\quad \frac{3}{y(y + 2)}$

77. $\frac{3}{a^2 + 3a + 2} + \frac{3}{a^2 + 5a + 6}$ $\quad \frac{6}{(a + 1)(a + 3)}$

78. $\frac{4}{w^2 + w} + \frac{12}{w^2 - 3w}$ $\quad \frac{16}{(w + 1)(w - 3)}$

79. $\frac{2}{b^2 + 4b + 3} - \frac{1}{b^2 + 5b + 6}$ $\quad \frac{1}{(b + 1)(b + 2)}$

80. $\frac{9}{m^2 - m - 2} - \frac{6}{m^2 - 1}$ $\quad \frac{3}{(m - 1)(m - 2)}$

81. $\frac{3}{2t} - \frac{2}{t + 2} - \frac{3}{t^2 + 2t}$ $\quad \frac{-1}{2(t + 2)}$

82. $\frac{4}{3n} + \frac{2}{n + 1} + \frac{2}{n^2 + n}$ $\quad \frac{10}{3n}$

Solve each problem. See Example 7.

83. ***Perimeter of a rectangle.*** Suppose that the length of a rectangle is $\frac{3}{x}$ feet and its width is $\frac{5}{2x}$ feet. Find a rational expression for the perimeter of the rectangle.
$\frac{11}{x}$ feet

84. ***Perimeter of a triangle.*** The lengths of the sides of a triangle are $\frac{1}{x}$, $\frac{1}{2x}$, and $\frac{2}{3x}$ meters. Find a rational expression for the perimeter of the triangle.
$\frac{13}{6x}$ meters

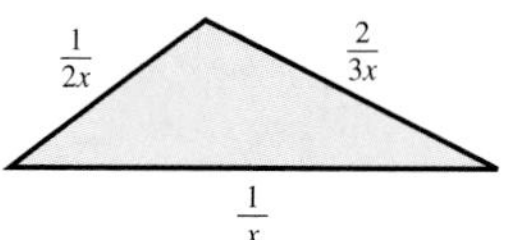

Figure for Exercise 84

85. ***Traveling time.*** Janet drove 120 miles at x mph before 6:00 A.M. After 6:00 A.M., she increased her speed by 5 mph and drove 195 additional miles. Use the fact that $T = \frac{D}{R}$ to complete the following table.

	Rate	Time	Distance
Before	$x \frac{\text{mi}}{\text{hr}}$	$\frac{120}{x}$ hr	120 mi
After	$x + 5 \frac{\text{mi}}{\text{hr}}$	$\frac{195}{x + 5}$ hr	195 mi

Write a rational expression for her total traveling time. Evaluate the expression for $x = 60$.
$\frac{315x + 600}{x(x + 5)}$ hours, 5 hours

86. ***Traveling time.*** After leaving Moose Jaw, Hanson drove 200 kilometers at x km/hr and then decreased his speed by 20 km/hr and drove 240 additional kilometers. Make a table like the one in Exercise 85. Write a rational expression for his total traveling time. Evaluate the expression for $x = 100$.
$\frac{440x - 4000}{x(x - 20)}$ hours, 5 hours

87. ***House painting.*** Kent can paint a certain house by himself in x days. His helper Keith can paint the same house by himself in $x + 3$ days. Suppose that they work together on the job for 2 days. To complete the table, use the fact that the work completed is the product of the rate and the time.

	Rate	Time	Work
Kent	$\frac{1}{x}\frac{\text{job}}{\text{day}}$	2 days	$\frac{2}{x}$ job
Keith	$\frac{1}{x+3}\frac{\text{job}}{\text{day}}$	2 days	$\frac{2}{x+3}$ job

Write a rational expression for the fraction of the house that they complete by working together for 2 days. Evaluate the expression for $x = 6$.

$\frac{4x+6}{x(x+3)}$ job, $\frac{5}{9}$ job

88. ***Barn painting.*** Melanie can paint a certain barn by herself in x days. Her helper Melissa can paint the same barn by herself in $2x$ days. Write a rational expression for the fraction of the barn that they complete in one day by working together. Evaluate the expression for $x = 5$.

$\frac{3}{2x}$ barn, $\frac{3}{10}$ barn

Photo for Exercise 88

Getting More Involved

89. *Writing*

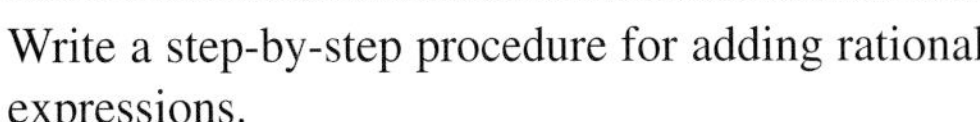

Write a step-by-step procedure for adding rational expressions.

90. *Writing*

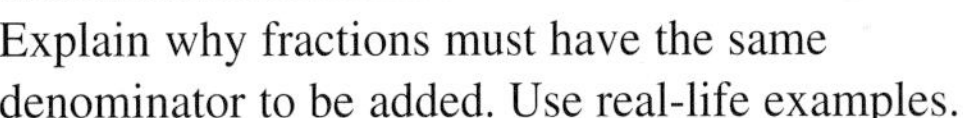

Explain why fractions must have the same denominator to be added. Use real-life examples.

6.5 Complex Fractions

In this Section

- Complex Fractions
- Using the LCD to Simplify Complex Fractions
- Applications

In this section we will use the idea of least common denominator to simplify complex fractions. Also we will see how complex fractions can arise in applications.

Complex Fractions

A **complex fraction** is a fraction having rational expressions in the numerator, denominator, or both. Consider the following complex fraction:

$$\frac{\frac{1}{2}+\frac{2}{3}}{\frac{1}{4}-\frac{5}{8}} \quad \begin{matrix} \leftarrow \text{Numerator of complex fraction} \\ \\ \leftarrow \text{Denominator of complex fraction} \end{matrix}$$

To simplify it, we can combine the fractions in the numerator as follows:

$$\frac{1}{2}+\frac{2}{3}=\frac{1\cdot 3}{2\cdot 3}+\frac{2\cdot 2}{3\cdot 2}=\frac{3}{6}+\frac{4}{6}=\frac{7}{6}$$

We can combine the fractions in the denominator as follows:

$$\frac{1}{4}-\frac{5}{8}=\frac{1\cdot 2}{4\cdot 2}-\frac{5}{8}=\frac{2}{8}-\frac{5}{8}=-\frac{3}{8}$$

Teaching Tip It is good to know both methods for simplifying complex fractions, but in most cases multiplying by the LCD is simpler and it shows another use of the LCD.

Now divide the numerator by the denominator:

$$\frac{\frac{1}{2}+\frac{2}{3}}{\frac{1}{4}-\frac{5}{8}} = \frac{\frac{7}{6}}{-\frac{3}{8}} = \frac{7}{6} \div \left(-\frac{3}{8}\right)$$

$$= \frac{7}{6} \cdot \left(-\frac{8}{3}\right)$$

$$= -\frac{56}{18} = -\frac{28}{9}$$

Using the LCD to Simplify Complex Fractions

A complex fraction can be simplified by writing the numerator and denominator as single fractions and then dividing, as we just did. However, there is a better method. Example 1 shows how to simplify a complex fraction by using the LCD of all of the single fractions in the complex fraction.

EXAMPLE 1

Using the LCD to simplify a complex fraction

Use the LCD to simplify

$$\frac{\frac{1}{2}+\frac{2}{3}}{\frac{1}{4}-\frac{5}{8}}.$$

Calculator Close-Up

You can check Example 1 with a calculator as shown here.

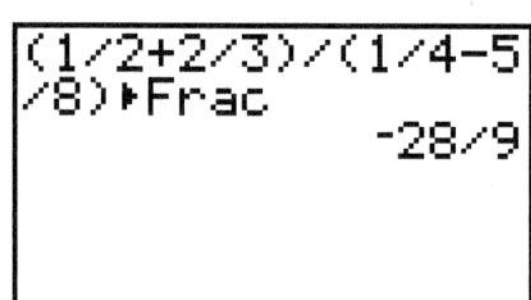

Solution

The LCD of 2, 3, 4, and 8 is 24. Now multiply the numerator and denominator of the complex fraction by the LCD:

$$\frac{\frac{1}{2}+\frac{2}{3}}{\frac{1}{4}-\frac{5}{8}} = \frac{\left(\frac{1}{2}+\frac{2}{3}\right)24}{\left(\frac{1}{4}-\frac{5}{8}\right)24} \quad \text{Multiply the numerator and denominator by the LCD.}$$

$$= \frac{\frac{1}{2}\cdot 24 + \frac{2}{3}\cdot 24}{\frac{1}{4}\cdot 24 - \frac{5}{8}\cdot 24} \quad \text{Distributive property}$$

$$= \frac{12+16}{6-15} \quad \text{Simplify.}$$

$$= \frac{28}{-9}$$

$$= -\frac{28}{9}$$

Now do Exercises 3–14

CAUTION We simplify a complex fraction by multiplying the numerator and denominator of the *complex fraction* by the LCD. Do not multiply the numerator and denominator of each fraction in the complex fraction by the LCD.

In Example 2 we simplify a complex fraction involving variables.

EXAMPLE 2

A complex fraction with variables

Simplify

$$\frac{2 - \frac{1}{x}}{\frac{1}{x^2} - \frac{1}{2}}.$$

Solution

The LCD of the denominators x, x^2, and 2 is $2x^2$:

$$\frac{2 - \frac{1}{x}}{\frac{1}{x^2} - \frac{1}{2}} = \frac{\left(2 - \frac{1}{x}\right)(2x^2)}{\left(\frac{1}{x^2} - \frac{1}{2}\right)(2x^2)} \quad \text{Multiply the numerator and denominator by } 2x^2.$$

$$= \frac{2 \cdot 2x^2 - \frac{1}{x} \cdot 2x^2}{\frac{1}{x^2} \cdot 2x^2 - \frac{1}{2} \cdot 2x^2} \quad \text{Distributive property}$$

$$= \frac{4x^2 - 2x}{2 - x^2} \quad \text{Simplify.}$$

The numerator of this answer can be factored, but the rational expression cannot be reduced.

Now do Exercises 15–24

Helpful Hint

When students see addition or subtraction in a complex fraction, they often convert all fractions to the same denominator. This is not wrong, but it is not necessary. Simply multiplying every fraction by the LCD eliminates the denominators of the original fractions.

The general strategy for simplifying a complex fraction is stated as follows.

Strategy for Simplifying a Complex Fraction

1. Find the LCD for all the denominators in the complex fraction.
2. Multiply both the numerator and the denominator of the complex fraction by the LCD. Use the distributive property if necessary.
3. Combine like terms if possible.
4. Reduce to lowest terms when possible.

EXAMPLE 3

Simplifying a complex fraction

Simplify

$$\frac{\dfrac{1}{x-2}-\dfrac{2}{x+2}}{\dfrac{3}{2-x}+\dfrac{4}{x+2}}.$$

Solution

Because $x - 2$ and $2 - x$ are opposites, we can use $(x - 2)(x + 2)$ as the LCD. Multiply the numerator and denominator by $(x - 2)(x + 2)$:

Teaching Tip If desired you can rewrite $\frac{3}{2-x}$ as $\frac{-3}{x-2}$.

$$\frac{\dfrac{1}{x-2}-\dfrac{2}{x+2}}{\dfrac{3}{2-x}+\dfrac{4}{x+2}} = \frac{\dfrac{1}{x-2}(x-2)(x+2)-\dfrac{2}{x+2}(x-2)(x+2)}{\dfrac{3}{2-x}(x-2)(x+2)+\dfrac{4}{x+2}(x-2)(x+2)}$$

$$= \frac{x+2-2(x-2)}{3(-1)(x+2)+4(x-2)} \quad \frac{x-2}{2-x}=-1$$

$$= \frac{x+2-2x+4}{-3x-6+4x-8} \quad \text{Distributive property}$$

$$= \frac{-x+6}{x-14} \quad \text{Combine like terms.}$$

Now do Exercises 25–40

Applications

As their name suggests, complex fractions arise in some fairly complex situations.

EXAMPLE 4

Fast-food workers

A survey of college students found that $\frac{1}{2}$ of the female students had jobs and $\frac{2}{3}$ of the male students had jobs. It was also found that $\frac{1}{4}$ of the female students worked in fast-food restaurants and $\frac{1}{6}$ of the male students worked in fast-food restaurants. If equal numbers of male and female students were surveyed, then what fraction of the working students worked in fast-food restaurants?

Solution

Let x represent the number of males surveyed. The number of females surveyed is also x. The total number of students working in fast-food restaurants is

$$\frac{1}{4}x + \frac{1}{6}x.$$

The total number of working students in the survey is

$$\frac{1}{2}x + \frac{2}{3}x.$$

So the fraction of working students who work in fast-food restaurants is

$$\frac{\frac{1}{4}x + \frac{1}{6}x}{\frac{1}{2}x + \frac{2}{3}x}.$$

The LCD of the denominators 2, 3, 4, and 6 is 12. Multiply the numerator and denominator by 12 to eliminate the fractions as follows:

$$\frac{\frac{1}{4}x + \frac{1}{6}x}{\frac{1}{2}x + \frac{2}{3}x} = \frac{\left(\frac{1}{4}x + \frac{1}{6}x\right)12}{\left(\frac{1}{2}x + \frac{2}{3}x\right)12} \quad \text{Multiply numerator and denominator by 12.}$$

$$= \frac{3x + 2x}{6x + 8x} \quad \text{Distributive property}$$

$$= \frac{5x}{14x} \quad \text{Combine like terms.}$$

$$= \frac{5}{14} \quad \text{Reduce.}$$

So $\frac{5}{14}$ (or about 36%) of the working students work in fast-food restaurants.

Now do Exercises 55–56

Warm-Ups ▼

True or false? Explain your answer.

1. The LCD for the denominators 4, x, 6, and x^2 is $12x^3$. False
2. The LCD for the denominators $a - b$, $2b - 2a$, and 6 is $6a - 6b$. True
3. The fraction $\frac{4117}{7983}$ is a complex fraction. False
4. The LCD for the denominators $a - 3$ and $3 - a$ is $a^2 - 9$. False
5. The largest common denominator for the fractions $\frac{1}{2}$, $\frac{1}{3}$, and $\frac{1}{4}$ is 24. False

Questions 6–10 refer to the following complex fractions:

a) $\dfrac{\frac{1}{2} + \frac{x}{3}}{\frac{1}{4} + \frac{1}{5}}$ b) $\dfrac{1 + \frac{2}{b}}{\frac{2}{a} + 5}$ c) $\dfrac{x - \frac{1}{2}}{x + \frac{3}{2}}$ d) $\dfrac{\frac{1}{2} + \frac{1}{3}}{1 + \frac{1}{2}}$

6. To simplify (a), we multiply the numerator and denominator by $60x$. False
7. To simplify (b), we multiply the numerator and denominator by $\frac{ab}{ab}$. False

8. The complex fraction (c) is equivalent to $\frac{2x-1}{2x+3}$. True

9. If $x \neq -\frac{3}{2}$, then (c) represents a real number. True

10. The complex fraction (d) can be written as $\frac{5}{6} \div \frac{3}{2}$. True

6.5 Exercises

Boost your GRADE at mathzone.com!

MathZone

- Practice Problems
- Self-Tests
- Videos
- Net Tutor
- e-Professors

Reading and Writing *After reading this section, write out the answers to these questions. Use complete sentences.*

1. What is a complex fraction?
A complex fraction is a fraction that has fractions in its numerator, denominator, or both.
2. What are the two ways to simplify a complex fraction?
You can multiply the numerator and denominator by the LCD or you can simplify the numerator and denominator, and then divide.

Simplify each complex fraction. See Example 1.

3. $\dfrac{\frac{1}{2}+\frac{1}{4}}{\frac{1}{2}+\frac{3}{4}}$ $\frac{3}{5}$

4. $\dfrac{\frac{1}{3}+\frac{5}{6}}{\frac{2}{3}+\frac{1}{6}}$ $\frac{7}{5}$

5. $\dfrac{\frac{1}{2}+\frac{1}{3}}{\frac{1}{4}-\frac{1}{2}}$ $-\frac{10}{3}$

6. $\dfrac{\frac{1}{3}-\frac{1}{4}}{\frac{1}{3}+\frac{1}{6}}$ $\frac{1}{6}$

7. $\dfrac{\frac{2}{5}+\frac{5}{6}-\frac{1}{2}}{\frac{1}{2}-\frac{1}{3}+\frac{1}{15}}$ $\frac{22}{7}$

8. $\dfrac{\frac{2}{5}-\frac{2}{9}-\frac{1}{3}}{\frac{1}{3}+\frac{1}{5}+\frac{2}{15}}$ $-\frac{7}{30}$

9. $\dfrac{1+\frac{1}{2}}{2+\frac{1}{4}}$ $\frac{2}{3}$

10. $\dfrac{\frac{1}{3}+1}{\frac{1}{6}+2}$ $\frac{8}{13}$

11. $\dfrac{3+\frac{1}{2}}{5-\frac{3}{4}}$ $\frac{14}{17}$

12. $\dfrac{1+\frac{1}{12}}{1-\frac{1}{12}}$ $\frac{13}{11}$

13. $\dfrac{1-\frac{1}{6}+\frac{2}{3}}{1+\frac{1}{15}-\frac{3}{10}}$ $\frac{45}{23}$

14. $\dfrac{3-\frac{2}{9}-\frac{1}{6}}{\frac{5}{18}-\frac{1}{3}-2}$ $-\frac{47}{37}$

Simplify each complex fraction. See Example 2.

15. $\dfrac{\frac{1}{a}+\frac{1}{b}}{\frac{2}{a}+\frac{2}{b}}$ $\frac{1}{2}$

16. $\dfrac{\frac{1}{x}+\frac{1}{y}}{\frac{3}{x}+\frac{3}{y}}$ $\frac{1}{3}$

17. $\dfrac{\frac{1}{a}+\frac{3}{b}}{\frac{1}{b}-\frac{3}{a}}$ $\frac{3a+b}{a-3b}$

18. $\dfrac{\frac{1}{x}-\frac{3}{2}}{\frac{3}{4}+\frac{1}{x}}$ $\frac{4-6x}{3x+4}$

19. $\dfrac{5-\frac{3}{a}}{3+\frac{1}{a}}$ $\frac{5a-3}{3a+1}$

20. $\dfrac{4+\frac{3}{y}}{1-\frac{2}{y}}$ $\frac{4y+3}{y-2}$

21. $\dfrac{\frac{1}{2}-\frac{2}{x}}{3-\frac{1}{x^2}}$ $\frac{x^2-4x}{2(3x^2-1)}$

22. $\dfrac{\frac{2}{a}+\frac{5}{3}}{\frac{3}{a}-\frac{3}{a^2}}$ $\frac{6a+5a^2}{9(a-1)}$

23. $\dfrac{\frac{3}{2b}+\frac{1}{b}}{\frac{3}{4}-\frac{1}{b^2}}$ $\frac{10b}{3b^2-4}$

24. $\dfrac{\frac{3}{2w}+\frac{4}{3w}}{\frac{1}{4w}-\frac{5}{9w}}$ $-\frac{102}{11}$

Simplify each complex fraction. See Example 3.

25. $\dfrac{\frac{1}{x+1}+1}{\frac{3}{x+1}+3}$ $\frac{1}{3}$

26. $\dfrac{\frac{2}{x+3}+1}{\frac{4}{x+3}+2}$ $\frac{1}{2}$

27. $\dfrac{1-\frac{3}{y+1}}{3+\frac{1}{y+1}}$ $\frac{y-2}{3y+4}$

28. $\dfrac{2-\frac{1}{a-3}}{3-\frac{1}{a-3}}$ $\frac{2a-7}{3a-10}$

29. $\dfrac{x+\frac{4}{x-2}}{x-\frac{x+1}{x-2}}$ $\frac{x^2-2x+4}{x^2-3x-1}$

30. $\dfrac{x-\frac{x-6}{x-1}}{x-\frac{x+15}{x-1}}$ $\frac{x^2-2x+6}{(x-5)(x+3)}$

31. $\dfrac{\frac{1}{3-x}-5}{\frac{1}{x-3}-2}$ $\quad\dfrac{5x-14}{2x-7}$

32. $\dfrac{\frac{2}{x-5}-x}{\frac{3x}{5-x}-1}$ $\quad\dfrac{x^2-5x-2}{4x-5}$

33. $\dfrac{1-\frac{5}{a-1}}{3-\frac{2}{1-a}}$ $\quad\dfrac{a-6}{3a-1}$

34. $\dfrac{\frac{1}{3}-\frac{2}{9-x}}{\frac{1}{6}-\frac{1}{x-9}}$ $\quad\dfrac{2x-6}{x-15}$

35. $\dfrac{\frac{1}{m-3}-\frac{4}{m}}{\frac{3}{m-3}+\frac{1}{m}}$ $\quad\dfrac{-3m+12}{4m-3}$

36. $\dfrac{\frac{1}{y+3}-\frac{4}{y}}{\frac{1}{y}-\frac{2}{y+3}}$ $\quad\dfrac{3y+12}{y-3}$

37. $\dfrac{\frac{2}{w-1}-\frac{3}{w+1}}{\frac{4}{w+1}+\frac{5}{w-1}}$ $\quad\dfrac{-w+5}{9w+1}$

38. $\dfrac{\frac{1}{x+2}-\frac{3}{x+3}}{\frac{2}{x+3}+\frac{3}{x+2}}$ $\quad\dfrac{-2x-3}{5x+13}$

39. $\dfrac{\frac{1}{a-b}-\frac{1}{a+b}}{\frac{1}{b-a}+\frac{1}{b+a}}$ $\quad -1$

40. $\dfrac{\frac{1}{2+x}-\frac{1}{2-x}}{\frac{1}{x+2}-\frac{1}{x-2}}$ $\quad -\dfrac{x}{2}$

Simplify each complex fraction. Reduce each answer to lowest terms.

41. $\dfrac{1-\frac{4}{a^2}}{1+\frac{2}{a}-\frac{8}{a^2}}$ $\quad\dfrac{a+2}{a+4}$

42. $\dfrac{\frac{1}{3}+\frac{1}{y}}{\frac{y}{3}-\frac{3}{y}}$ $\quad\dfrac{1}{y-3}$

43. $\dfrac{\frac{1}{2}+\frac{1}{4x}}{\frac{x}{3}-\frac{1}{12x}}$ $\quad\dfrac{3}{2x-1}$

44. $\dfrac{\frac{1}{9}+\frac{1}{3x}}{\frac{x}{9}-\frac{1}{x}}$ $\quad\dfrac{1}{x-3}$

45. $\dfrac{\frac{1}{3}-\frac{5}{3x}+\frac{2}{x^2}}{\frac{1}{3}-\frac{3}{x^2}}$ $\quad\dfrac{x-2}{x+3}$

46. $\dfrac{\frac{1}{2}-\frac{3}{2x}+\frac{1}{x^2}}{\frac{1}{2}-\frac{1}{2x^2}}$ $\quad\dfrac{x-2}{x+1}$

47. $\dfrac{\frac{2x-9}{6}}{\frac{2x-3}{9}}$ $\quad\dfrac{6x-27}{2(2x-3)}$

48. $\dfrac{\frac{a-5}{12}}{\frac{a+2}{15}}$ $\quad\dfrac{5a-25}{4(a+2)}$

49. $\dfrac{\frac{2x-4y}{xy^2}}{\frac{3x-6y}{x^3y}}$ $\quad\dfrac{2x^2}{3y}$

50. $\dfrac{\frac{ab+b^2}{4ab^5}}{\frac{a+b}{6a^2b^4}}$ $\quad\dfrac{3a}{2}$

51. $\dfrac{\frac{a^2+2a-24}{a+1}}{\frac{a^2-a-12}{(a+1)^2}}$ $\quad\dfrac{a^2+7a+6}{a+3}$

52. $\dfrac{\frac{y^2-3y-18}{y^2-4}}{\frac{y^2+5y+6}{y-2}}$ $\quad\dfrac{y-6}{(y+2)^2}$

53. $\dfrac{\frac{x}{x+1}}{\frac{1}{x^2-1}-\frac{1}{x-1}}$ $\quad 1-x$

54. $\dfrac{\frac{a}{a^2-b^2}}{\frac{1}{a+b}+\frac{1}{a-b}}$ $\quad\dfrac{1}{2}$

Solve each problem. See Example 4.

55. ***Sophomore math.*** A survey of college sophomores showed that $\frac{5}{6}$ of the males were taking a mathematics class and $\frac{3}{4}$ of the females were taking a mathematics class. One-third of the males were enrolled in calculus, and $\frac{1}{5}$ of the females were enrolled in calculus. If just as many males as females were surveyed, then what fraction of the surveyed students taking mathematics were enrolled in calculus? Rework this problem assuming that the number of females in the survey was twice the number of males. $\frac{32}{95}, \frac{11}{35}$

56. ***Commuting students.*** At a well-known university, $\frac{1}{4}$ of the undergraduate students commute, and $\frac{1}{3}$ of the graduate students commute. One-tenth of the undergraduate students drive more than 40 miles daily, and $\frac{1}{6}$ of the graduate students drive more than 40 miles daily. If there are twice as many undergraduate students as there are graduate students, then what fraction of the commuters drive more than 40 miles daily? $\frac{11}{25}$

Photo for Exercise 56

Getting More Involved

57. ***Exploration***

Simplify

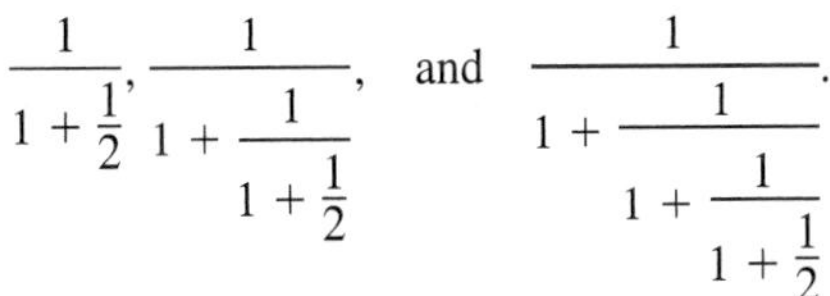

$$\frac{1}{1+\frac{1}{2}},\quad \frac{1}{1+\frac{1}{1+\frac{1}{2}}},\quad\text{and}\quad \frac{1}{1+\frac{1}{1+\frac{1}{1+\frac{1}{2}}}}.$$

a) Are these fractions getting larger or smaller as the fractions become more complex? Neither

b) Continuing the pattern, find the next two complex fractions and simplify them. $\frac{8}{13}, \frac{13}{21}$

c) Now what can you say about the values of all five complex fractions? Converging to 0.61803

58. ***Discussion***

A complex fraction can be simplified by writing the numerator and denominator as single fractions and then dividing them or by multiplying the numerator and denominator by the LCD. Simplify the complex fraction

$$\frac{\frac{4}{xy^2} - \frac{6}{xy}}{\frac{2}{x^2} + \frac{4}{x^2y}}$$

by using each of these methods. Compare the number of steps used in each method, and determine which method requires fewer steps.

6.6 Solving Equations with Rational Expressions

In this Section

- Equations with Rational Expressions
- Extraneous Solutions

Many problems in algebra can be solved by using equations involving rational expressions. In this section you will learn how to solve equations that involve rational expressions, and in Sections 6.7 and 6.8 you will solve problems using these equations.

Equations with Rational Expressions

We solved some equations involving fractions in Section 2.3. In that section the equations had only integers in the denominators. Our first step in solving those equations was to multiply by the LCD to eliminate all of the denominators.

EXAMPLE 1 **Integers in the denominators**

Solve $\frac{1}{2} - \frac{x-2}{3} = \frac{1}{6}$.

Solution

The LCD for 2, 3, and 6 is 6. Multiply each side of the equation by 6:

$\frac{1}{2} - \frac{x-2}{3} = \frac{1}{6}$	Original equation
$6\left(\frac{1}{2} - \frac{x-2}{3}\right) = 6 \cdot \frac{1}{6}$	Multiply each side by 6.
$6 \cdot \frac{1}{2} - \overset{2}{\cancel{6}} \cdot \frac{x-2}{\cancel{3}} = \cancel{6} \cdot \frac{1}{\cancel{6}}$	Distributive property
$3 - 2(x - 2) = 1$	Simplify.
$3 - 2x + 4 = 1$	Distributive property
$-2x = -6$	Subtract 7 from each side.
$x = 3$	Divide each side by -2.

Helpful Hint

Note that it is not necessary to convert each fraction into an equivalent fraction with a common denominator here. Since we can multiply both sides of an equation by any expression we choose, we choose to multiply by the LCD. This tactic eliminates the fractions in one step.

Check $x = 3$ in the original equation:

$$\frac{1}{2} - \frac{3-2}{3} = \frac{1}{2} - \frac{1}{3} = \frac{3}{6} - \frac{2}{6} = \frac{1}{6}$$

The solution to the equation is 3.

Now do Exercises 5–14

CAUTION When a numerator contains a binomial, as in Example 1, the numerator must be enclosed in parentheses when the denominator is eliminated.

To solve an equation involving rational expressions, we usually multiply each side of the equation by the LCD for all the denominators involved, just as we do for an equation with fractions.

EXAMPLE 2

Variables in the denominators

Solve $\frac{1}{x} + \frac{1}{6} = \frac{1}{4}$.

Teaching Tip Students often confuse solving equations containing rational expressions with adding or subtracting rational expressions. To solve this problem be sure to assign Exercises 99–118 in the Review Exercises.

Solution

We multiply each side of the equation by $12x$, the LCD for 4, 6, and x:

$$\frac{1}{x} + \frac{1}{6} = \frac{1}{4} \quad \text{Original equation}$$

$$12x\left(\frac{1}{x} + \frac{1}{6}\right) = 12x\left(\frac{1}{4}\right) \quad \text{Multiply each side by } 12x.$$

$$12\cancel{x} \cdot \frac{1}{\cancel{x}} + \overset{2}{\cancel{12}}x \cdot \frac{1}{\cancel{6}} = \overset{3}{\cancel{12}}x \cdot \frac{1}{\cancel{4}} \quad \text{Distributive property}$$

$$12 + 2x = 3x \quad \text{Simplify.}$$

$$12 = x \quad \text{Subtract } 2x \text{ from each side.}$$

Check that 12 satisfies the original equation:

$$\frac{1}{12} + \frac{1}{6} = \frac{1}{12} + \frac{2}{12} = \frac{3}{12} = \frac{1}{4}$$

The solution to the equation is 12.

Now do Exercises 15–26

EXAMPLE 3

An equation with two solutions

Solve the equation $\frac{100}{x} + \frac{100}{x + 5} = 9$.

Solution

The LCD for the denominators x and $x + 5$ is $x(x + 5)$:

$$\frac{100}{x} + \frac{100}{x + 5} = 9 \quad \text{Original equation}$$

$$x(x + 5)\frac{100}{x} + x(x + 5)\frac{100}{x + 5} = x(x + 5)9 \quad \text{Multiply each side by } x(x + 5).$$

$$(x + 5)100 + x(100) = (x^2 + 5x)9 \quad \text{All denominators are eliminated.}$$

$$100x + 500 + 100x = 9x^2 + 45x \quad \text{Simplify.}$$

$$500 + 200x = 9x^2 + 45x$$

$$0 = 9x^2 - 155x - 500 \quad \text{Get 0 on one side.}$$

$$0 = (9x + 25)(x - 20) \quad \text{Factor.}$$

$$9x + 25 = 0 \quad \text{or} \quad x - 20 = 0 \quad \text{Zero factor property}$$

$$x = -\frac{25}{9} \quad \text{or} \quad x = 20$$

A check will show that both $-\frac{25}{9}$ and 20 satisfy the original equation.

Now do Exercises 27–34

Study Tip

Your mood for studying should match the mood in which you are tested. Being too relaxed during studying will not match the increased level of activation you attain during a test. Likewise, if you get too tensed-up during a test, you will not do well because your test-taking mood will not match your studying mood.

Extraneous Solutions

In a rational expression we can replace the variable only by real numbers that do not cause the denominator to be 0. When solving equations involving rational expressions, we must check every solution to see whether it causes 0 to appear in a denominator. If a number causes the denominator to be 0, then it cannot be a solution to the equation. A number that appears to be a solution but causes 0 in a denominator is called an **extraneous solution.**

EXAMPLE 4

An equation with an extraneous solution

Solve the equation $\frac{1}{x - 2} = \frac{x}{2x - 4} + 1$.

Solution

Because the denominator $2x - 4$ factors as $2(x - 2)$, the LCD is $2(x - 2)$.

$$2(x - 2)\frac{1}{x - 2} = 2(x - 2)\frac{x}{2(x - 2)} + 2(x - 2) \cdot 1 \quad \text{Multiply each side of the original equation by } 2(x - 2).$$

$$2 = x + 2x - 4 \quad \text{Simplify.}$$

$$2 = 3x - 4$$

$$6 = 3x$$

$$2 = x$$

Check 2 in the original equation:

$$\frac{1}{2-2} = \frac{2}{2 \cdot 2 - 4} + 1$$

The denominator $2 - 2$ is 0. So 2 does not satisfy the equation, and it is an extraneous solution. The equation has no solutions.

Now do Exercises 35–38

EXAMPLE 5

Another extraneous solution

Solve the equation $\frac{1}{x} + \frac{1}{x-3} = \frac{x-2}{x-3}$.

Solution

The LCD for the denominators x and $x - 3$ is $x(x - 3)$:

$$\frac{1}{x} + \frac{1}{x-3} = \frac{x-2}{x-3} \quad \text{Original equation}$$

$$x(x-3) \cdot \frac{1}{x} + x(x-3) \cdot \frac{1}{x-3} = x(x-3) \cdot \frac{x-2}{x-3} \quad \text{Multiply each side by } x(x-3).$$

$$x - 3 + x = x(x - 2)$$

$$2x - 3 = x^2 - 2x$$

$$0 = x^2 - 4x + 3$$

$$0 = (x - 3)(x - 1)$$

$$x - 3 = 0 \quad \text{or} \quad x - 1 = 0$$

$$x = 3 \quad \text{or} \quad x = 1$$

If $x = 3$, then the denominator $x - 3$ has a value of 0. If $x = 1$, the original equation is satisfied. The only solution to the equation is 1.

Now do Exercises 39–42

Study Tip

Studying in an environment similar to the one in which you will be tested can increase your chances of recalling information. When possible, review for a test in the classroom in which you will take the test.

CAUTION Always be sure to check your answers in the original equation to determine whether they are extraneous solutions.

Warm-Ups ▼

True or false? Explain your answers.

1. The LCD is not used in solving equations with rational expressions. False
2. To solve the equation $x^2 = 8x$, we divide each side by x. False
3. An extraneous solution is an irrational number. False

Use the following equations for Questions 4–10.

a) $\frac{3}{x} + \frac{5}{x-2} = \frac{2}{3}$ **b)** $\frac{1}{x} + \frac{1}{2} = \frac{3}{4}$ **c)** $\frac{1}{x-1} + 2 = \frac{1}{x+1}$

4. To solve Eq. (a), we must add the expressions on the left-hand side. False
5. Both 0 and 2 satisfy Eq. (a). False

6. To solve Eq. (a), we multiply each side by $3x^2 - 6x$. True
7. The only solution to Eq. (b) is 4. True
8. Equation (b) is equivalent to $4 + 2x = 3x$. True
9. To solve Eq. (c), we multiply each side by $x^2 - 1$. True
10. The numbers 1 and -1 do not satisfy Eq. (c). True

6.6 Exercises

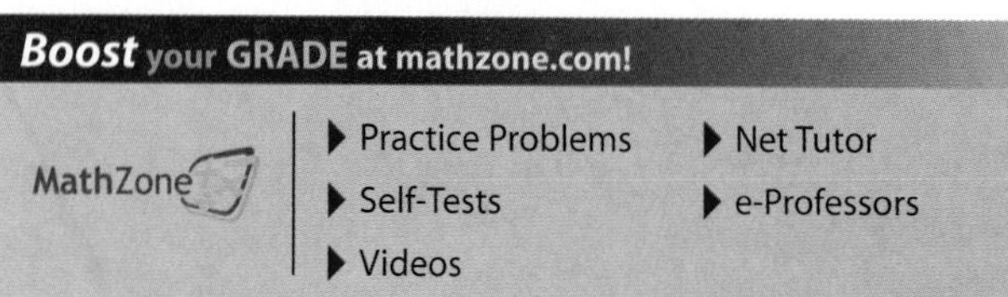

Reading and Writing *After reading this section, write out the answers to these questions. Use complete sentences.*

1. What is the typical first step for solving an equation involving rational expressions?
The first step is usually to multiply each side by the LCD.

2. What is the difference in procedure for solving an equation involving rational expressions and adding rational expressions?
In adding rational expressions we build up each expression to get the LCD as the common denominator.

3. What is an extraneous solution?
An extraneous solution is a number that appears to be a solution when we solve an equation, but it does not check in the original equation.

4. Why do extraneous solutions sometimes occur for equations with rational expressions?
Extraneous solutions occur because we multiply by an expression involving a variable and that variable expression might have a value of zero.

Solve each equation. See Example 1.

5. $\frac{x}{2} + 1 = \frac{x}{4}$ -4

6. $\frac{x}{3} + 2 = \frac{x}{6}$ -12

7. $\frac{x}{3} - 5 = \frac{x}{2} - 7$ 12

8. $\frac{x}{3} - \frac{x}{2} = \frac{x}{5} - 11$ 30

9. $\frac{y}{5} - \frac{2}{3} = \frac{y}{6} + \frac{1}{3}$ 30

10. $\frac{z}{6} + \frac{5}{4} = \frac{z}{2} - \frac{3}{4}$ 6

11. $\frac{3}{4} - \frac{t-4}{3} = \frac{t}{12}$ 5

12. $\frac{4}{5} - \frac{v-1}{10} = \frac{v-5}{30}$ 8

13. $\frac{1}{5} - \frac{w+10}{15} = \frac{1}{10} - \frac{w+1}{6}$ 4

14. $\frac{q}{5} - \frac{q-1}{2} = \frac{13}{20} - \frac{q+1}{4}$ 2

Solve each equation. See Example 2.

15. $\frac{1}{x} + \frac{1}{2} = 3$ $\frac{2}{5}$

16. $\frac{2}{x} + \frac{3}{4} = 5$ $\frac{8}{17}$

17. $\frac{1}{x} + \frac{2}{x} = 7$ $\frac{3}{7}$

18. $\frac{5}{x} + \frac{6}{x} = 12$ $\frac{11}{12}$

19. $\frac{1}{x} + \frac{1}{2} = \frac{3}{4}$ 4

20. $\frac{3}{x} + \frac{1}{4} = \frac{5}{8}$ 8

21. $\frac{2}{3x} + \frac{1}{2x} = \frac{7}{24}$ 4

22. $\frac{1}{6x} - \frac{1}{8x} = \frac{1}{72}$ 3

23. $\frac{1}{2} + \frac{a-2}{a} = \frac{a+2}{2a}$ 3

24. $\frac{1}{b} + \frac{1}{5} = \frac{b-1}{5b} + \frac{3}{10}$ 4

25. $\frac{1}{3} - \frac{k+3}{6k} = \frac{1}{3k} - \frac{k-1}{2k}$ 2

26. $\frac{3}{p} - \frac{p+3}{3p} = \frac{2p-1}{2p} - \frac{5}{6}$ 5

Solve each equation. See Example 3.

27. $\frac{x}{2} = \frac{5}{x+3}$ $-5, 2$

28. $\frac{x}{3} = \frac{4}{x+1}$ $-4, 3$

29. $\frac{x}{x+1} = \frac{6}{x+7}$ $-3, 2$

30. $\frac{x}{x+3} = \frac{2}{x-3}$ $-1, 6$

31. $\frac{2}{x+1} = \frac{1}{x} + \frac{1}{6}$ 2, 3

32. $\frac{1}{w+1} - \frac{1}{2w} = \frac{3}{40}$ $\frac{5}{3}, 4$

33. $\frac{a-1}{a^2-4} + \frac{1}{a-2} = \frac{a+4}{a+2}$ $-3, 3$

34. $\frac{b+17}{b^2-1} - \frac{1}{b+1} = \frac{b-2}{b-1}$ $-4, 5$

Solve each equation. Watch for extraneous solutions. See Examples 4 and 5.

35. $\frac{1}{x-1}+\frac{2}{x}=\frac{x}{x-1}$ 2

36. $\frac{4}{x}+\frac{3}{x-3}=\frac{x}{x-3}-\frac{1}{3}$ 6

37. $\frac{5}{x+2}+\frac{2}{x-3}=\frac{x-1}{x-3}$ No solution

38. $\frac{6}{y-2}+\frac{7}{y-8}=\frac{y-1}{y-8}$ No solution

39. $1+\frac{3y}{y-2}=\frac{6}{y-2}$ No solution

40. $\frac{5}{y-3}=\frac{y+7}{2y-6}+1$ No solution

41. $\frac{z}{z+1}-\frac{1}{z+2}=\frac{2z+5}{z^2+3z+2}$ 3

42. $\frac{z}{z-2}-\frac{1}{z+5}=\frac{7}{z^2+3z-10}$ 1

Solve each equation.

43. $\frac{a}{4}=\frac{5}{2}$ 10

44. $\frac{y}{3}=\frac{6}{5}$ $\frac{18}{5}$

45. $\frac{w}{6}=\frac{3w}{11}$ 0

46. $\frac{2m}{3}=\frac{3m}{2}$ 0

47. $\frac{5}{x}=\frac{x}{5}$ $-5, 5$

48. $\frac{-3}{x}=\frac{x}{-3}$ $-3, 3$

49. $\frac{x-3}{5}=\frac{x-3}{x}$ 3, 5

50. $\frac{a+4}{2}=\frac{a+4}{a}$ $-4, 2$

51. $\frac{1}{x+2}=\frac{x}{x+2}$ 1

52. $\frac{-3}{w+2}=\frac{w}{w+2}$ -3

53. $\frac{1}{2x-4}+\frac{1}{x-2}=\frac{3}{2}$ 3

54. $\frac{7}{3x-9}-\frac{1}{x-3}=\frac{4}{3}$ 4

55. $\frac{3}{a^2-a-6}=\frac{2}{a^2-4}$ 0

56. $\frac{8}{a^2+a-6}=\frac{6}{a^2-9}$ 6

57. $\frac{4}{c-2}-\frac{1}{2-c}=\frac{25}{c+6}$ 4

58. $\frac{3}{x+1}-\frac{1}{1-x}=\frac{10}{x^2-1}$ 3

59. $\frac{1}{x^2-9}+\frac{3}{x+3}=\frac{4}{x-3}$ -20

60. $\frac{3}{x-2}-\frac{5}{x+3}=\frac{1}{x^2+x-6}$ 9

61. $\frac{3}{2x+4}-\frac{1}{x+2}=\frac{1}{3x+1}$ 3

62. $\frac{5}{2m+6}-\frac{1}{m+1}=\frac{1}{m+3}$ 3

63. $\frac{2t-1}{3t+3}+\frac{3t-1}{6t+6}=\frac{t}{t+1}$ 3

64. $\frac{4w-1}{3w+6}-\frac{w-1}{3}=\frac{w-1}{w+2}$ 2

Solve each problem.

65. ***Lens equation.*** The focal length f for a camera lens is related to the object distance o and the image distance i by the formula

$$\frac{1}{f}=\frac{1}{o}+\frac{1}{i}.$$

See the accompanying figure. The image is in focus at distance i from the lens. For an object that is 600 mm from a 50-mm lens, use $f = 50$ mm and $o = 600$ mm to find i.

$54\frac{6}{11}$ mm

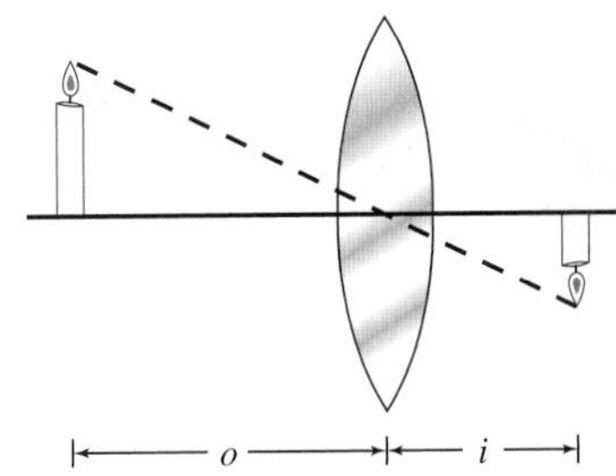

Figure for Exercise 65

66. ***Telephoto lens.*** Use the formula from Exercise 65 to find the image distance i for an object that is 2,000,000 mm from a 250-mm telephoto lens. 250.03 mm

Photo for Exercise 66

6.7 Applications of Ratios and Proportions

In this Section

- **Ratios**
- **Proportions**

In this section we will use the ideas of rational expressions in ratio and proportion problems. We will solve proportions in the same way we solved equations in Section 6.6.

Ratios

In Chapter 1 we defined a rational number as the *ratio of two integers*. We will now give a more general definition of ratio. If a and b are any real numbers (not just integers), with $b \neq 0$, then the expression $\frac{a}{b}$ is called the **ratio of a and b** or the **ratio of a to b.** The ratio of a to b is also written as $a:b$. A ratio is a comparison of two numbers. Some examples of ratios are

$$\frac{3}{4}, \quad \frac{4.2}{2.1}, \quad \frac{\frac{1}{4}}{\frac{1}{2}}, \quad \frac{3.6}{5}, \quad \text{and} \quad \frac{100}{1}.$$

Ratios are treated just like fractions. We can reduce ratios, and we can build them up. We generally express ratios as ratios of integers. When possible, we will convert a ratio into an equivalent ratio of integers in lowest terms.

EXAMPLE 1

Finding equivalent ratios

Find an equivalent ratio of integers in lowest terms for each ratio.

a) $\frac{4.2}{2.1}$ **b)** $\frac{\frac{1}{4}}{\frac{1}{2}}$ **c)** $\frac{3.6}{5}$

Solution

a) Because both the numerator and the denominator have one decimal place, we will multiply the numerator and denominator by 10 to eliminate the decimals:

$$\frac{4.2}{2.1} = \frac{4.2(10)}{2.1(10)} = \frac{42}{21} = \frac{21 \cdot 2}{21 \cdot 1} = \frac{2}{1}$$ Do not omit the 1 in a ratio.

So the ratio of 4.2 to 2.1 is equivalent to the ratio 2 to 1.

b) This ratio is a complex fraction. We can simplify this expression using the LCD method as shown in Section 6.5. Multiply the numerator and denominator of this ratio by 4:

$$\frac{\frac{1}{4}}{\frac{1}{2}} = \frac{\frac{1}{4} \cdot 4}{\frac{1}{2} \cdot 4} = \frac{1}{2}$$

Study Tip

To get the "big picture," survey the chapter that you are studying. Read the headings to get the general idea of the chapter content. Read the chapter summary to see what is important in the chapter. Repeat this survey procedure several times while you are working in a chapter.

c) We can get a ratio of integers if we multiply the numerator and denominator by 10.

$$\frac{3.6}{5} = \frac{3.6(10)}{5(10)} = \frac{36}{50}$$

$$= \frac{18}{25} \qquad \text{Reduce to lowest terms.}$$

Now do Exercises 7–22

In Example 2 a ratio is used to compare quantities.

EXAMPLE 2

Nitrogen to potash

In a 50-pound bag of lawn fertilizer there are 8 pounds of nitrogen and 12 pounds of potash. What is the ratio of nitrogen to potash?

Solution

The nitrogen and potash occur in this fertilizer in the ratio of 8 pounds to 12 pounds:

$$\frac{8}{12} = \frac{2 \cdot \cancel{4}}{3 \cdot \cancel{4}} = \frac{2}{3}$$

So the ratio of nitrogen to potash is 2 to 3.

Now do Exercises 23–24

EXAMPLE 3

Males to females

In a class of 50 students, there were exactly 20 male students. What was the ratio of males to females in this class?

Solution

Because there were 20 males in the class of 50, there were 30 females. The ratio of males to females was 20 to 30, or 2 to 3.

Now do Exercises 25–26

Teaching Tip You can write a ratio of males to females because they are both people. You should not write a ratio of inches to feet, because they are not the same unit.

Ratios give us a means of comparing the size of two quantities. For this reason *the numbers compared in a ratio should be expressed in the same units.* For example, if one dog is 24 inches high and another is 1 foot high, then the ratio of their heights is 2 to 1, not 24 to 1.

EXAMPLE 4

Quantities with different units

What is the ratio of length to width for a poster with a length of 30 inches and a width of 2 feet?

Solution

Because the width is 2 feet, or 24 inches, the ratio of length to width is 30 to 24. Reduce as follows:

$$\frac{30}{24} = \frac{5 \cdot 6}{4 \cdot 6} = \frac{5}{4}$$

So the ratio of length to width is 5 to 4.

Now do Exercises 27–30

Proportions

A **proportion** is any statement expressing the equality of two ratios. The statement

$$\frac{a}{b} = \frac{c}{d} \quad \text{or} \quad a:b = c:d$$

is a proportion. In any proportion the numbers in the positions of a and d shown here are called the **extremes.** The numbers in the positions of b and c as shown are called the **means.** In the proportion

$$\frac{30}{24} = \frac{5}{4},$$

the means are 24 and 5, and the extremes are 30 and 4.

If we multiply each side of the proportion

$$\frac{a}{b} = \frac{c}{d}$$

by the LCD, bd, we get

$$\frac{a}{b} \cdot bd = \frac{c}{d} \cdot bd$$

or

$$a \cdot d = b \cdot c.$$

We can express this result by saying *that the product of the extremes is equal to the product of the means*. We call this fact the **extremes-means property** or **cross-multiplying.**

Helpful Hint

The extremes-means property or cross-multiplying is nothing new. You can accomplish the same thing by multiplying each side of the equation by the LCD.

Extremes-Means Property (Cross-Multiplying)

Suppose a, b, c, and d are real numbers with $b \neq 0$ and $d \neq 0$. If

$$\frac{a}{b} = \frac{c}{d}, \quad \text{then} \quad ad = bc.$$

We use the extremes-means property to solve proportions.

EXAMPLE 5

Teaching Tip Remind students that the extremes-means property works on proportions and not on an equation like $\frac{3}{x} = \frac{8}{x+1} - 1$.

Using the extremes-means property

Solve the proportion $\frac{3}{x} = \frac{5}{x+5}$ for x.

Solution

Instead of multiplying each side by the LCD, we use the extremes-means property:

$$\frac{3}{x} = \frac{5}{x+5} \quad \text{Original proportion}$$

$$3(x+5) = 5x \quad \text{Extremes-means property}$$

$$3x + 15 = 5x \quad \text{Distributive property}$$

$$15 = 2x$$

$$\frac{15}{2} = x$$

Check:

$$\frac{3}{\frac{15}{2}} = 3 \cdot \frac{2}{15} = \frac{2}{5}$$

$$\frac{5}{\frac{15}{2} + 5} = \frac{5}{\frac{25}{2}} = 5 \cdot \frac{2}{25} = \frac{2}{5}$$

So $\frac{15}{2}$ is the solution to the equation or the solution to the proportion.

Now do Exercises 31–42

EXAMPLE 6

Solving a proportion

The ratio of men to women at Brighton City College is 2 to 3. If there are 894 men, then how many women are there?

Solution

Because the ratio of men to women is 2 to 3, we have

$$\frac{\text{Number of men}}{\text{Number of women}} = \frac{2}{3}.$$

If x represents the number of women, then we have the following proportion:

$$\frac{894}{x} = \frac{2}{3}$$

$$2x = 2682 \quad \text{Extremes-means property}$$

$$x = 1341$$

The number of women is 1341.

Now do Exercises 43–46

Note that any proportion can be solved by multiplying each side by the LCD as we did when we solved other equations involving rational expressions. The extremes-means property gives us a shortcut for solving proportions.

EXAMPLE 7

Solving a proportion

In a conservative portfolio the ratio of the amount invested in bonds to the amount invested in stocks should be 3 to 1. A conservative investor invested $2850 more in bonds than she did in stocks. How much did she invest in each category?

Solution

Because the ratio of the amount invested in bonds to the amount invested in stocks is 3 to 1, we have

$$\frac{\text{Amount invested in bonds}}{\text{Amount invested in stocks}} = \frac{3}{1}.$$

If x represents the amount invested in stocks and $x + 2850$ represents the amount invested in bonds, then we can write and solve the following proportion:

$$\frac{x + 2850}{x} = \frac{3}{1}$$

$$3x = x + 2850 \quad \text{Extremes-means property}$$

$$2x = 2850$$

$$x = 1425$$

$$x + 2850 = 4275$$

So she invested $4275 in bonds and $1425 in stocks. Note that these amounts are in the ratio of 3 to 1.

Now do Exercises 47–50

Example 8 shows how conversions from one unit of measurement to another can be done by using proportions.

EXAMPLE 8

Converting measurements

There are 3 feet in 1 yard. How many feet are there in 12 yards?

Teaching Tip Note that in doing conversions the units can be mixed in a proportion. Note that the ratio of 3 feet to 1 yard is 1.

Solution

Let x represent the number of feet in 12 yards. There are two proportions that we can write to solve the problem:

$$\frac{3 \text{ feet}}{x \text{ feet}} = \frac{1 \text{ yard}}{12 \text{ yards}} \qquad \frac{3 \text{ feet}}{1 \text{ yard}} = \frac{x \text{ feet}}{12 \text{ yards}}$$

The ratios in the second proportion violate the rule of comparing only measurements that are expressed in the same units. Note that each side of the second proportion is actually the ratio 1 to 1, since 3 feet = 1 yard and x feet = 12 yards. For doing conversions we can use ratios like this to compare measurements in different units. Applying the extremes-means property to either proportion gives

$$3 \cdot 12 = x \cdot 1,$$

or

$$x = 36.$$

So there are 36 feet in 12 yards.

Now do Exercises 51–54

Warm-Ups

True or false? Explain your answer.

1. The ratio of 40 men to 30 women can be expressed as the ratio 4 to 3. True
2. The ratio of 3 feet to 2 yards can be expressed as the ratio 3 to 2. False
3. If the ratio of men to women in the Chamber of Commerce is 3 to 2 and there are 20 men, then there must be 30 women. False
4. The ratio of 1.5 to 2 is equivalent to the ratio of 3 to 4. True
5. A statement that two ratios are equal is called a proportion. True
6. The product of the extremes is equal to the product of the means. True
7. If $\frac{2}{x} = \frac{3}{5}$, then $5x = 6$. False
8. The ratio of the height of a 12-inch cactus to the height of a 3-foot cactus is 4 to 1. False
9. If 30 out of 100 lawyers preferred aspirin and the rest did not, then the ratio of lawyers that preferred aspirin to those who did not is 30 to 100. False
10. If $\frac{x+5}{x} = \frac{2}{3}$, then $3x + 15 = 2x$. True

6.7 Exercises

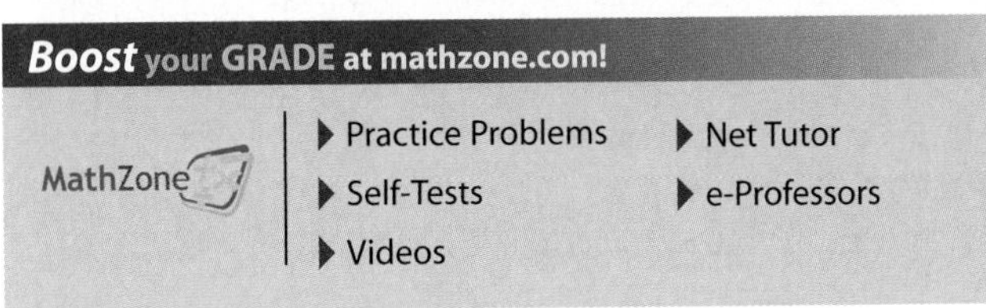

Reading and Writing *After reading this section, write out the answers to these questions. Use complete sentences.*

1. What is a ratio?
   A ratio is a comparison of two numbers.
2. What are the different ways of expressing a ratio?
   The ratio of a to b is also written as $\frac{a}{b}$ or $a : b$.
3. What are equivalent ratios?
   Equivalent ratios are ratios that are equivalent as fractions.
4. What is a proportion?
   A proportion is an equation that expresses equality of two ratios.
5. What are the means and what are the extremes?
   In the proportion $\frac{a}{b} = \frac{c}{d}$ the means are b and c and the extremes are a and d.
6. What is the extremes-means property?
   The extremes-means property says that if $\frac{a}{b} = \frac{c}{d}$ then $ad = bc$.

For each ratio, find an equivalent ratio of integers in lowest terms. See Example 1.

7. $\frac{4}{6}$ $\frac{2}{3}$

8. $\frac{10}{20}$ $\frac{1}{2}$

9. $\frac{200}{150}$ $\frac{4}{3}$

10. $\frac{1000}{200}$ $\frac{5}{1}$ **11.** $\frac{2.5}{3.5}$ $\frac{5}{7}$ **12.** $\frac{4.8}{1.2}$ $\frac{4}{1}$

13. $\frac{0.32}{0.6}$ $\frac{8}{15}$ **14.** $\frac{0.05}{0.8}$ $\frac{1}{16}$ **15.** $\frac{35}{10}$ $\frac{7}{2}$

16. $\frac{88}{33}$ $\frac{8}{3}$ **17.** $\frac{4.5}{7}$ $\frac{9}{14}$ **18.** $\frac{3}{2.5}$ $\frac{6}{5}$

19. $\frac{\frac{1}{2}}{\frac{1}{5}}$ $\frac{5}{2}$ **20.** $\frac{\frac{2}{3}}{\frac{3}{4}}$ $\frac{8}{9}$ **21.** $\frac{5}{\frac{1}{3}}$ $\frac{15}{1}$

22. $\frac{4}{\frac{1}{4}}$ $\frac{16}{1}$

Find a ratio for each of the following, and write it as a ratio of integers in lowest terms. See Examples 2–4.

23. ***Men and women.*** Find the ratio of men to women in a bowling league containing 12 men and 8 women. 3 to 2

24. ***Coffee drinkers.*** Among 100 coffee drinkers, 36 said that they preferred their coffee black and the rest did not prefer their coffee black. Find the ratio of those who prefer black coffee to those who prefer nonblack coffee. 9 to 16

Photo for Exercise 24

25. ***Smokers.*** A life insurance company found that among its last 200 claims, there were six dozen smokers. What is the ratio of smokers to nonsmokers in this group of claimants? 9 to 16

26. ***Hits and misses.*** A woman threw 60 darts and hit the target a dozen times. What is her ratio of hits to misses? 1 to 4

27. ***Violence and kindness.*** While watching television for one week, a consumer group counted 1240 acts of violence and 40 acts of kindness. What is the violence to kindness ratio for television, according to this group? 31 to 1

28. ***Length to width.*** What is the ratio of length to width for the rectangle shown? 8 to 5

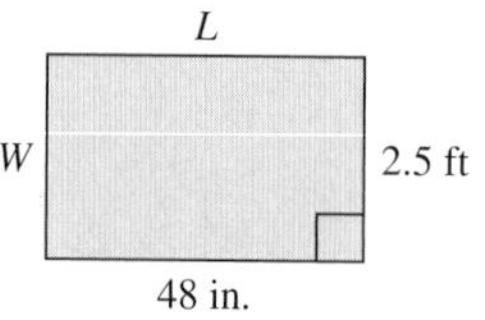

Figure for Exercise 28

29. ***Rise to run.*** What is the ratio of rise to run for the stairway shown in the accompanying figure? 2 to 3

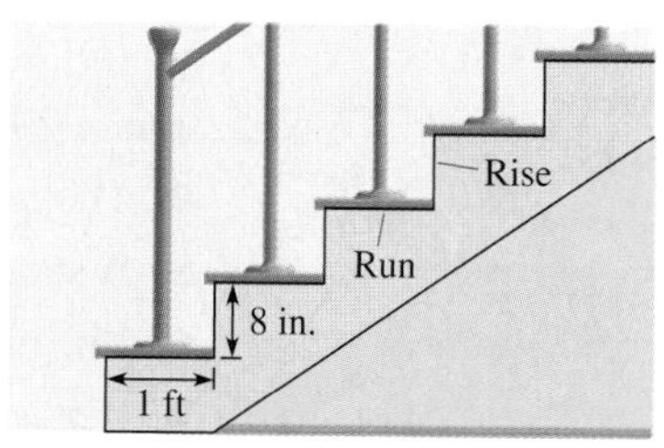

Figure for Exercise 29

30. ***Rise and run.*** If the rise is $\frac{3}{2}$ and the run is 5, then what is the ratio of the rise to the run? 3 to 10

Solve each proportion. See Example 5.

31. $\frac{4}{x} = \frac{2}{3}$ 6 **32.** $\frac{9}{x} = \frac{3}{2}$ 6

33. $\frac{a}{2} = \frac{-1}{5}$ $-\frac{2}{5}$ **34.** $\frac{b}{3} = \frac{-3}{4}$ $-\frac{9}{4}$

35. $-\frac{5}{9} = \frac{3}{x}$ $-\frac{27}{5}$ **36.** $-\frac{3}{4} = \frac{5}{x}$ $-\frac{20}{3}$

37. $\frac{10}{x} = \frac{34}{x + 12}$ 5 **38.** $\frac{x}{3} = \frac{x + 1}{2}$ -3

39. $\frac{a}{a + 1} = \frac{a + 3}{a}$ $-\frac{3}{4}$ **40.** $\frac{c + 3}{c - 1} = \frac{c + 2}{c - 3}$ -7

41. $\frac{m - 1}{m - 2} = \frac{m - 3}{m + 4}$ $\frac{5}{4}$ **42.** $\frac{h}{h - 3} = \frac{h}{h - 9}$ 0

Use a proportion to solve each problem. See Examples 6–8.

43. ***New shows and reruns.*** The ratio of new shows to reruns on cable TV is 2 to 27. If Frank counted only eight new shows one evening, then how many reruns were there? 108

44. ***Fast food.*** If four out of five doctors prefer fast food, then at a convention of 445 doctors, how many prefer fast food? 356

45. ***Voting.*** If 220 out of 500 voters surveyed said that they would vote for the incumbent, then how many votes could the incumbent expect out of the 400,000 voters in the state? 176,000

Figure for Exercise 45

46. ***New product.*** A taste test with 200 randomly selected people found that only three of them said that they would buy a box of new Sweet Wheats cereal. How many boxes could the manufacturer expect to sell in a country of 280 million people? 4.2 million

47. ***Basketball blowout.*** As the final buzzer signaled the end of the basketball game, the Lions were 34 points ahead of the Tigers. If the Lions scored 5 points for every 3 scored by the Tigers, then what was the final score? Lions 85, Tigers 51

48. ***The golden ratio.*** The ancient Greeks thought that the most pleasing shape for a rectangle was one for which the ratio of the length to the width was 8 to 5, the golden ratio. If the length of a rectangular painting is 2 ft longer than its width, then for what dimensions would the length and width have the golden ratio? Length $\frac{16}{3}$ ft, width $\frac{10}{3}$ ft

49. ***Automobile sales.*** The ratio of sports cars to luxury cars sold in Wentworth one month was 3 to 2. If 20 more sports cars were sold than luxury cars, then how many of each were sold that month? 40 luxury cars, 60 sports cars

50. ***Foxes and rabbits.*** The ratio of foxes to rabbits in the Deerfield Forest Preserve is 2 to 9. If there are 35 fewer foxes than rabbits, then how many of each are there? 45 rabbits, 10 foxes

51. ***Inches and feet.*** If there are 12 inches in 1 foot, then how many inches are there in 7 feet? 84 in.

52. ***Feet and yards.*** If there are 3 feet in 1 yard, then how many yards are there in 28 feet? $\frac{28}{3}$ yd

53. ***Minutes and hours.*** If there are 60 minutes in 1 hour, then how many minutes are there in 0.25 hour? 15 min

54. ***Meters and kilometers.*** If there are 1000 meters in 1 kilometer, then how many meters are there in 2.33 kilometers? 2330 m

55. ***Miles and hours.*** If Alonzo travels 230 miles in 3 hours, then how many miles does he travel in 7 hours? $\frac{1610}{3}$ or 536.7 mi

56. ***Hiking time.*** If Evangelica can hike 19 miles in 2 days on the Appalachian Trail, then how many days will it take her to hike 63 miles? $\frac{126}{19}$ days

57. ***Force on basketball shoes.*** The force exerted on shoe soles in a jump shot is proportional to the weight of the person jumping. If a 70-pound boy exerts a force of 980 pounds on his shoe soles when he returns to the court after a jump, then what force does a 6 ft 8 in. professional ball player weighing 280 pounds exert on the soles of his shoes when he returns to the court after a jump? Use the accompanying graph to estimate the force for a 150-pound player. 3920 lbs, 2000 lbs

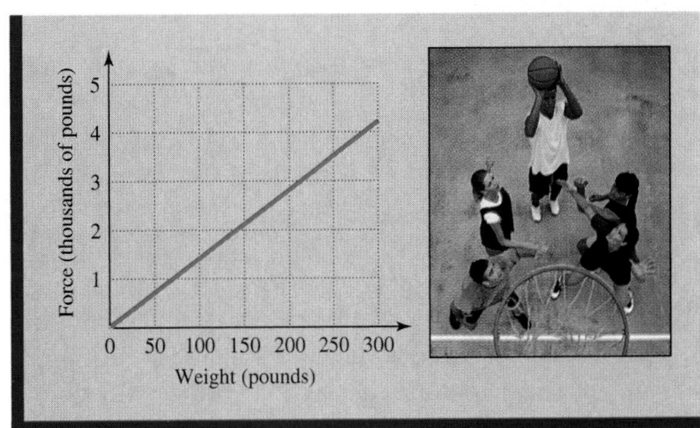

Figure for Exercise 57

58. ***Force on running shoes.*** The ratio of the force on the shoe soles to the weight of a runner is 3 to 1. What force does a 130-pound jogger exert on the soles of her shoes? 390 lbs

59. ***Capture-recapture.*** To estimate the number of trout in Trout Lake, rangers used the capture-recapture method. They caught, tagged, and released 200 trout. One week later, they caught a sample of 150 trout and found that 5 of them were tagged. Assuming that the ratio of tagged trout to the total number of trout in the lake is the same as the ratio of tagged trout in the sample to the number of trout in the sample, find the number of trout in the lake. 6000

60. ***Bear population.*** To estimate the size of the bear population on the Keweenaw Peninsula, conservationists captured, tagged, and released 50 bears. One year later, a random sample of 100 bears included only 2 tagged bears. What is the conservationist's estimate of the size of the bear population? 2500

61. ***Fast-food waste.*** The accompanying figure shows the typical distribution of waste at a fast-food restaurant (U.S. Environmental Protection Agency, www.epa.gov).

a) What is the ratio of customer waste to food waste? 3 to 17

b) If a typical McDonald's generates 67 more pounds of food waste than customer waste per day, then how many pounds of customer waste does it generate? $\frac{201}{14}$ or 14.4 lbs

WASTE GENERATION AT A FAST-FOOD RESTAURANT

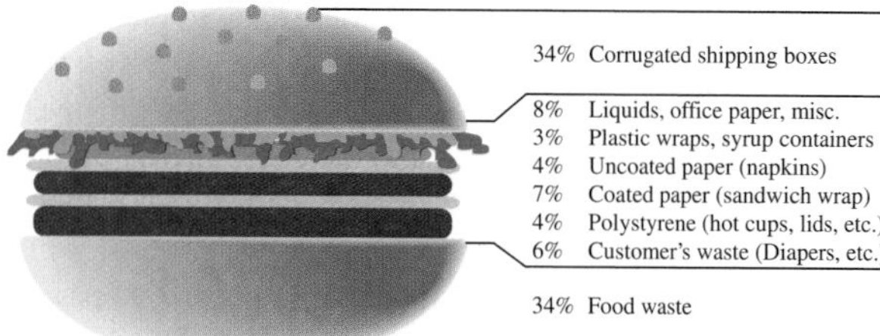

Figure for Exercises 61 and 62

62. ***Corrugated waste.*** Use the accompanying figure to find the ratio of waste from corrugated shipping boxes to waste not from corrugated shipping boxes. If a typical McDonald's generates 81 pounds of waste per day from corrugated shipping boxes, then how many pounds of waste per day does it generate that is not from corrugated shipping boxes?
17 to 33, $\frac{2673}{17}$ or 157.2 lbs

63. ***Mascara needs.*** In determining warehouse needs for a particular mascara for a chain of 2000 stores, Mike Pittman first determines a need B based on sales figures for the past 52 weeks. He then determines the actual need A from the equation $\frac{A}{B} = k$, where

$$k = 1 + V + C + X - D.$$

He uses $V = 0.22$ if there is a national TV ad and $V = 0$ if not, $C = 0.26$ if there is a national coupon and $C = 0$ if not, $X = 0.36$ if there is a chain-specific ad and $X = 0$ if not, and $D = 0.29$ if there is a special display in the chain and $D = 0$ if not. (D is subtracted because less product is needed in the warehouse when more is on display in the store.) If $B = 4200$ units and there is a special display and a national coupon but no national TV ad and no chain-specific ad, then what is the value of A? 4074

Getting More Involved

64. ***Discussion***

Which of the following equations is not a proportion? Explain.

a) $\frac{1}{2} = \frac{1}{2}$ **b)** $\frac{x}{x+2} = \frac{4}{5}$

c) $\frac{x}{4} = \frac{9}{x}$ **d)** $\frac{8}{x+2} - 1 = \frac{5}{x+2}$

d

65. ***Discussion***

Find all of the errors in the following solution to an equation.

$$\frac{7}{x} = \frac{8}{x+3} + 1$$
$$7(x + 3) = 8x + 1$$
$$7x + 3 = 8x$$
$$-x = -3$$
$$x = 3$$

6.8 Applications of Rational Expressions

In this Section

- **Formulas**
- **Uniform Motion Problems**
- **Work Problems**
- **Purchasing Problems**

In this section we will study additional applications of rational expressions.

Formulas

Many formulas involve rational expressions. When solving a formula of this type for a certain variable, we usually multiply each side by the LCD to eliminate the denominators.

EXAMPLE 1

Teaching Tip Note that the left side of this equation is slope of the line through (x, y) and $(-2, 4)$.

An equation of a line

The equation for the line through $(-2, 4)$ with slope $\frac{3}{2}$ can be written as

$$\frac{y - 4}{x + 2} = \frac{3}{2}.$$

We studied equations of this type in Chapter 3. Solve this equation for y.

Solution

To isolate y on the left-hand side of the equation, we multiply each side by $x + 2$:

$$\frac{y - 4}{x + 2} = \frac{3}{2} \quad \text{Original equation}$$

$$(x + 2) \cdot \frac{y - 4}{x + 2} = (x + 2) \cdot \frac{3}{2} \quad \text{Multiply by } x + 2.$$

$$y - 4 = \frac{3}{2}x + 3 \quad \text{Simplify.}$$

$$y = \frac{3}{2}x + 7 \quad \text{Add 4 to each side.}$$

Because the original equation is a proportion, we could have used the extremes-means property to solve it for y.

Now do Exercises 1–8

EXAMPLE 2

Distance, rate, and time

Solve the formula $\frac{D}{T} = R$ for T.

Solution

Because the only denominator is T, we multiply each side by T:

$$\frac{D}{T} = R \quad \text{Original formula}$$

$$T \cdot \frac{D}{T} = T \cdot R \quad \text{Multiply each side by } T.$$

$$D = TR$$

$$\frac{D}{R} = \frac{TR}{R} \quad \text{Divide each side by } R.$$

$$\frac{D}{R} = T \quad \text{Simplify.}$$

The formula solved for T is $T = \frac{D}{R}$.

Now do Exercises 9–14

Study Tip

As you study from the text, think about the material. Ask yourself questions. If you were the professor, what questions would you ask on the test?

In Example 3, different subscripts are used on a variable to indicate that they are different variables. Think of R_1 as the first resistance, R_2 as the second resistance, and R as a combined resistance.

EXAMPLE 3

Total resistance

The formula

$$\frac{1}{R} = \frac{1}{R_1} + \frac{1}{R_2}$$

(from physics) expresses the relationship between different amounts of resistance in a parallel circuit. Solve it for R_2.

Solution

The LCD for R, R_1, and R_2 is RR_1R_2:

$$\frac{1}{R} = \frac{1}{R_1} + \frac{1}{R_2} \quad \text{Original formula}$$

$$RR_1R_2 \cdot \frac{1}{R} = RR_1R_2 \cdot \frac{1}{R_1} + RR_1R_2 \cdot \frac{1}{R_2} \quad \text{Multiply each side by the LCD, } RR_1R_2.$$

$$R_1R_2 = RR_2 + RR_1 \quad \text{All denominators are eliminated.}$$

$$R_1R_2 - RR_2 = RR_1 \quad \text{Get all terms involving } R_2 \text{ onto the left side.}$$

$$R_2(R_1 - R) = RR_1 \quad \text{Factor out } R_2.$$

$$R_2 = \frac{RR_1}{R_1 - R} \quad \text{Divide each side by } R_1 - R.$$

Now do Exercises 15–22

EXAMPLE 4

Finding the value of a variable

In the formula of Example 1, find x if $y = -3$.

Solution

Substitute $y = -3$ into the formula, then solve for x:

$$\frac{y - 4}{x + 2} = \frac{3}{2} \quad \text{Original formula}$$

$$\frac{-3 - 4}{x + 2} = \frac{3}{2} \quad \text{Replace } y \text{ by } -3.$$

$$\frac{-7}{x + 2} = \frac{3}{2} \quad \text{Simplify.}$$

$$3x + 6 = -14 \quad \text{Extremes-means property}$$

$$3x = -20$$

$$x = -\frac{20}{3}$$

Now do Exercises 23–32

Uniform Motion Problems

In uniform motion problems we use the formula $D = RT$. In some problems in which the time is unknown, we can use the formula $T = \frac{D}{R}$ to get an equation involving rational expressions.

EXAMPLE 5

Driving to Florida

Susan drove 1500 miles to Daytona Beach for spring break. On the way back she averaged 10 miles per hour less, and the drive back took her 5 hours longer. Find Susan's average speed on the way to Daytona Beach.

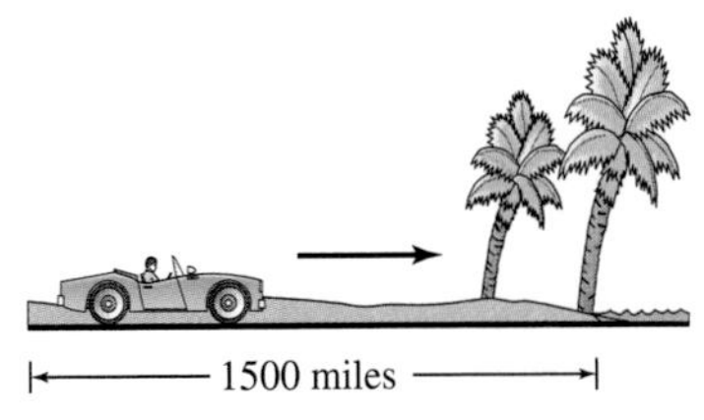

Figure 6.1

Solution

If x represents her average speed going there, then $x - 10$ is her average speed for the return trip. See Fig. 6.1. We use the formula $T = \frac{D}{R}$ to make the following table.

	D	*R*	*T*	
Going	1500	x	$\frac{1500}{x}$	← Shorter time
Returning	1500	$x - 10$	$\frac{1500}{x - 10}$	← Longer time

Because the difference between the two times is 5 hours, we have

$$\text{longer time} - \text{shorter time} = 5.$$

Using the time expressions from the table, we get the following equation:

$$\frac{1500}{x - 10} - \frac{1500}{x} = 5$$

$$x(x - 10)\frac{1500}{x - 10} - x(x - 10)\frac{1500}{x} = x(x - 10)5 \quad \text{Multiply by } x(x - 10).$$

$$1500x - 1500(x - 10) = 5x^2 - 50x$$

$$15{,}000 = 5x^2 - 50x \quad \text{Simplify.}$$

$$3000 = x^2 - 10x \quad \text{Divide each side by 5.}$$

$$0 = x^2 - 10x - 3000$$

$$(x + 50)(x - 60) = 0 \quad \text{Factor.}$$

$$x + 50 = 0 \quad \text{or} \quad x - 60 = 0$$

$$x = -50 \quad \text{or} \quad x = 60$$

The answer $x = -50$ is a solution to the equation, but it cannot indicate the average speed of the car. Her average speed going to Daytona Beach was 60 mph.

Now do Exercises 33–38

Work Problems

If you can complete a job in 3 hours, then you are working at the rate of $\frac{1}{3}$ of the job per hour. If you work for 2 hours at the rate of $\frac{1}{3}$ of the job per hour, then you will complete $\frac{2}{3}$ of the job. The product of the rate and time is the amount of work completed. For problems involving work, we will always assume that the work is done at a constant rate. So if a job takes x hours to complete, then the rate is $\frac{1}{x}$ of the job per hour.

Helpful Hint

Notice that a work rate is the same as a slope from Chapter 3. The only difference is that the work rates here can contain a variable.

EXAMPLE 6

Shoveling snow

After a heavy snowfall, Brian can shovel all of the driveway in 30 minutes. If his younger brother Allen helps, the job takes only 20 minutes. How long would it take Allen to do the job by himself?

Solution

Let x represent the number of minutes it would take Allen to do the job by himself. Brian's rate for shoveling is $\frac{1}{30}$ of the driveway per minute, and Allen's rate for shoveling is $\frac{1}{x}$ of the driveway per minute. We organize all of the information in a table like the table in Example 5.

	Rate	Time	Work
Brian	$\frac{1 \text{ job}}{30 \text{ min}}$	20 min	$\frac{2}{3}$ job
Allen	$\frac{1 \text{ job}}{x \text{ min}}$	20 min	$\frac{20}{x}$ job

If Brian works for 20 min at the rate $\frac{1}{30}$ of the job per minute, then he does $\frac{20}{30}$ or $\frac{2}{3}$ of the job, as shown in Fig. 6.2. The amount of work that each boy does is a fraction of the whole job. So the expressions for work in the last column of the table have a sum of 1:

$$\frac{2}{3} + \frac{20}{x} = 1$$

$$3x \cdot \frac{2}{3} + 3x \cdot \frac{20}{x} = 3x \cdot 1 \quad \text{Multiply each side by } 3x.$$

$$2x + 60 = 3x$$

$$60 = x$$

If it takes Allen 60 min to do the job by himself, then he works at the rate of $\frac{1}{60}$ of the job per minute. In 20 minutes he does $\frac{1}{3}$ of the job while Brian does $\frac{2}{3}$. So it would take Allen 60 minutes to shovel the driveway by himself.

Now do Exercises 39–44

Helpful Hint

The secret to work problems is remembering that the individual rates or the amounts of work can be added when people work together. If your painting rate is 1/10 of the house per day and your helper's rate is 1/5 of the house per day, then your rate together will be 3/10 of the house per day. In 2 days you will paint 2/10 of the house and your helper will paint 2/5 of the house for a total of 3/5 of the house completed.

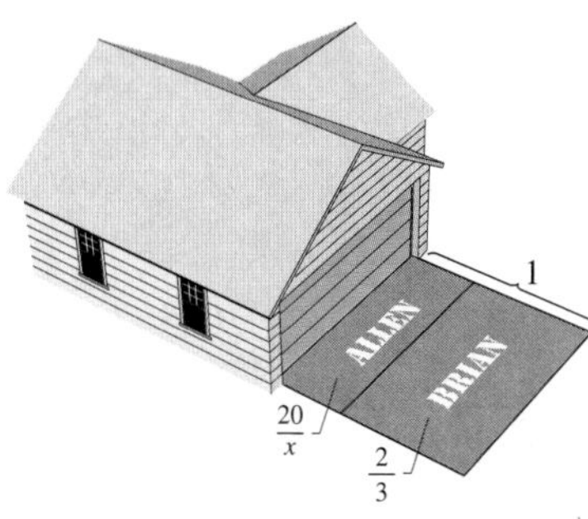

Figure 6.2

Notice the similarities between the uniform motion problem in Example 5 and the work problem in Example 6. In both cases, it is beneficial to make a table. We use $D = R \cdot T$ in uniform motion problems and $W = R \cdot T$ in work problems. The main points to remember when solving work problems are summarized in the following strategy.

Teaching Tip Note how the tables in Examples 5, 6, and 7 tie them together. Making tables will help students solve these problems.

Strategy for Solving Work Problems

1. If a job is completed in x hours, then the rate is $\frac{1}{x}$ job/hr.
2. Make a table showing rate, time, and work completed ($W = R \cdot T$) for each person or machine.
3. The total work completed is the sum of the individual amounts of work completed.
4. If the job is completed, then the total work done is 1 job.

Purchasing Problems

Rates are used in uniform motion and work problems. But rates also occur in purchasing problems. If gasoline is 149.9 cents/gallon, then that is the rate at which your bill is increasing as you pump the gallons into your tank. In purchasing problems the product of the rate and the quantity purchased is the total cost.

EXAMPLE 7

Oranges and grapefruit

Tamara bought 50 pounds of fruit consisting of Florida oranges and Texas grapefruit. She paid twice as much per pound for the grapefruit as she did for the oranges. If Tamara bought \$12 worth of oranges and \$16 worth of grapefruit, then how many pounds of each did she buy?

Solution

Let x represent the number of pounds of oranges and $50 - x$ represent the number of pounds of grapefruit. See Fig. 6.3. Make a table.

x lb

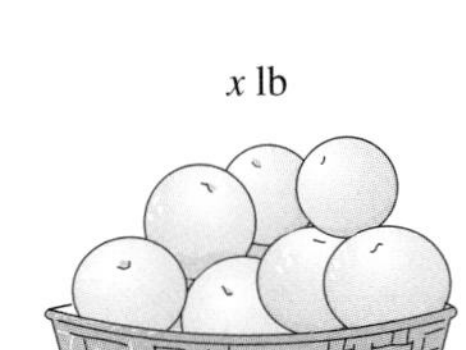

Oranges

50 − x lb

Grapefruit

Figure 6.3

	Rate	Quantity	Total Cost
Oranges	$\frac{12}{x}$ dollars/pound	x pounds	12 dollars
Grapefruit	$\frac{16}{50-x}$ dollars/pound	$50 - x$ pounds	16 dollars

Since the price per pound for the grapefruit is twice that for the oranges, we have:

$$2(\text{price per pound for oranges}) = \text{price per pound for grapefruit}$$

$$2\left(\frac{12}{x}\right) = \frac{16}{50 - x}$$

$$\frac{24}{x} = \frac{16}{50 - x}$$

$$16x = 1200 - 24x \quad \text{Extremes-means property}$$

$$40x = 1200$$

$$x = 30$$

$$50 - x = 20$$

If Tamara purchased 20 pounds of grapefruit for \$16, then she paid \$0.80 per pound. If she purchased 30 pounds of oranges for \$12, then she paid \$0.40 per pound. Because \$0.80 is twice \$0.40, we can be sure that she purchased 20 pounds of grapefruit and 30 pounds of oranges.

Now do Exercises 45–48

Warm-Ups ▼

True or false? Explain your answer.

1. The formula $t = \frac{1-t}{m}$, solved for m, is $m = \frac{1-t}{t}$. True
2. To solve $\frac{1}{m} + \frac{1}{n} = \frac{1}{2}$ for m, we multiply each side by $2mn$. True
3. If Fiona drives 300 miles in x hours, then her average speed is $\frac{x}{300}$ mph. False
4. If Miguel drives 20 hard bargains in x hours, then he is driving $\frac{20}{x}$ hard bargains per hour. True
5. If Fred can paint a house in y days, then he paints $\frac{1}{y}$ of the house per day. True
6. If $\frac{1}{x}$ is 1 less than $\frac{2}{x+3}$, then $\frac{1}{x} - 1 = \frac{2}{x+3}$. False
7. If a and b are nonzero and $a = \frac{m}{b}$, then $b = am$. False
8. If $D = RT$, then $T = \frac{D}{R}$. True
9. Solving $P + Prt = I$ for P gives $P = I - Prt$. False
10. To solve $3R + yR = m$ for R, we must first factor the left-hand side. True

6.8 Exercises

Boost your GRADE at mathzone.com!

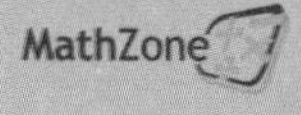

- Practice Problems
- Self-Tests
- Videos
- Net Tutor
- e-Professors

Solve each equation for y. See Example 1.

1. $\frac{y-1}{x-3} = 2$
   $y = 2x - 5$

2. $\frac{y-2}{x-4} = -2$
   $y = -2x + 10$

3. $\frac{y-1}{x+6} = -\frac{1}{2}$
   $y = -\frac{1}{2}x - 2$

4. $\frac{y+5}{x-2} = -\frac{1}{2}$
   $y = -\frac{1}{2}x - 4$

5. $\frac{y+a}{x-b} = m$
   $y = mx - mb - a$

6. $\frac{y-h}{x+k} = a$
   $y = ax + ak + h$

7. $\frac{y-1}{x+4} = -\frac{1}{3}$
   $y = -\frac{1}{3}x - \frac{1}{3}$

8. $\frac{y-1}{x+3} = -\frac{3}{4}$
   $y = -\frac{3}{4}x - \frac{5}{4}$

Solve each formula for the indicated variable. See Examples 2 and 3.

9. $A = \frac{B}{C}$ for C
   $C = \frac{B}{A}$

10. $P = \frac{A}{C+D}$ for A
    $A = PC + PD$

11. $\frac{1}{a} + m = \frac{1}{p}$ for p
    $p = \frac{a}{1 + am}$

12. $\frac{2}{f} + t = \frac{3}{m}$ for m
    $m = \frac{3f}{2 + ft}$

13. $F = k\dfrac{m_1m_2}{r^2}$ for m_1

$m_1 = \dfrac{r^2F}{km_2}$

14. $F = \dfrac{mv^2}{r}$ for r

$r = \dfrac{mv^2}{F}$

15. $\dfrac{1}{a} + \dfrac{1}{b} = \dfrac{1}{f}$ for a

$a = \dfrac{bf}{b - f}$

16. $\dfrac{1}{R} = \dfrac{1}{R_1} + \dfrac{1}{R_2}$ for R

$R = \dfrac{R_1R_2}{R_1 + R_2}$

17. $S = \dfrac{a}{1 - r}$ for r

$r = \dfrac{S - a}{S}$

18. $I = \dfrac{E}{R + r}$ for R

$R = \dfrac{E - Ir}{I}$

19. $\dfrac{P_1V_1}{T_1} = \dfrac{P_2V_2}{T_2}$ for P_2

$P_2 = \dfrac{P_1V_1T_2}{T_1V_2}$

20. $\dfrac{P_1V_1}{T_1} = \dfrac{P_2V_2}{T_2}$ for T_1

$T_1 = \dfrac{P_1V_1T_2}{P_2V_2}$

21. $V = \dfrac{4}{3}\pi r^2h$ for h

$h = \dfrac{3V}{4\pi r^2}$

22. $h = \dfrac{S - 2\pi r^2}{2\pi r}$ for S

$S = 2\pi rh + 2\pi r^2$

Find the value of the indicated variable. See Example 4.

23. In the formula of Exercise 9, if $A = 12$ and $B = 5$, find C. $\dfrac{5}{12}$

24. In the formula of Exercise 10, if $A = 500$, $P = 100$, and $C = 2$, find D. 3

25. In the formula of Exercise 11, if $p = 6$ and $m = 4$, find a. $-\dfrac{6}{23}$

26. In the formula of Exercise 12, if $m = 4$ and $t = 3$, find f. $-\dfrac{8}{9}$

27. In the formula of Exercise 13, if $F = 32$, $r = 4$, $m_1 = 2$, and $m_2 = 6$, find k. $\dfrac{128}{3}$

28. In the formula of Exercise 14, if $F = 10$, $v = 8$, and $r = 6$, find m. $\dfrac{15}{16}$

29. In the formula of Exercise 15, if $f = 3$ and $a = 2$, find b. -6

30. In the formula of Exercise 16, if $R = 3$ and $R_1 = 5$, find R_2. $\dfrac{15}{2}$

31. In the formula of Exercise 17, if $S = \dfrac{3}{2}$ and $r = \dfrac{1}{5}$, find a. $\dfrac{6}{5}$

32. In the formula of Exercise 18, if $I = 15$, $E = 3$, and $R = 2$, find r. $-\dfrac{9}{5}$

Show a complete solution to each problem. See Example 5.

33. ***Fast walking.*** Marcie can walk 8 miles in the same time as Frank walks 6 miles. If Marcie walks 1 mile per hour faster than Frank, then how fast does each person walk? Marcie 4 mph, Frank 3 mph

34. ***Upstream, downstream.*** Junior's boat will go 15 miles per hour in still water. If he can go 12 miles downstream in the same amount of time as it takes to go 9 miles upstream, then what is the speed of the current? $\dfrac{15}{7}$ mph

35. ***Delivery routes.*** Pat travels 70 miles on her milk route, and Bob travels 75 miles on his route. Pat travels 5 miles per hour slower than Bob, and her route takes her one-half hour longer than Bob's. How fast is each one traveling? Bob 25 mph, Pat 20 mph

36. ***Ride the peaks.*** Smith bicycled 45 miles going east from Durango, and Jones bicycled 70 miles. Jones averaged 5 miles per hour more than Smith, and his trip took one-half hour longer than Smith's. How fast was each one traveling? Smith 15 mph and Jones 20 mph, or Smith 30 mph and Jones 35 mph

Photo for Exercise 36

37. ***Walking and running.*** Raffaele ran 8 miles and then walked 6 miles. If he ran 5 miles per hour faster than he walked and the total time was 2 hours, then how fast did he walk? 5 mph

38. ***Triathlon.*** Luisa participated in a triathlon in which she swam 3 miles, ran 5 miles, and then bicycled 10 miles. Luisa ran twice as fast as she swam, and she cycled three times as fast as she swam. If her total time for the triathlon was 1 hour and 46 minutes, then how fast did she swim? 5 mph

Show a complete solution to each problem. See Example 6.

39. ***Fence painting.*** Kiyoshi can paint a certain fence in 3 hours by himself. If Red helps, the job takes only 2 hours. How long would it take Red to paint the fence by himself? 6 hours

40. ***Envelope stuffing.*** Every week, Linda must stuff 1000 envelopes. She can do the job by herself in 6 hours. If

Laura helps, they get the job done in $5\frac{1}{2}$ hours. How long would it take Laura to do the job by herself? 66 hours

41. ***Garden destroying.*** Mr. McGregor has discovered that a large dog can destroy his entire garden in 2 hours and that a small boy can do the same job in 1 hour. How long would it take the large dog and the small boy working together to destroy Mr. McGregor's garden? 40 minutes

42. ***Draining the vat.*** With only the small valve open, all of the liquid can be drained from a large vat in 4 hours. With only the large valve open, all of the liquid can be drained from the same vat in 2 hours. How long would it take to drain the vat with both valves open? 1 hour 20 minutes

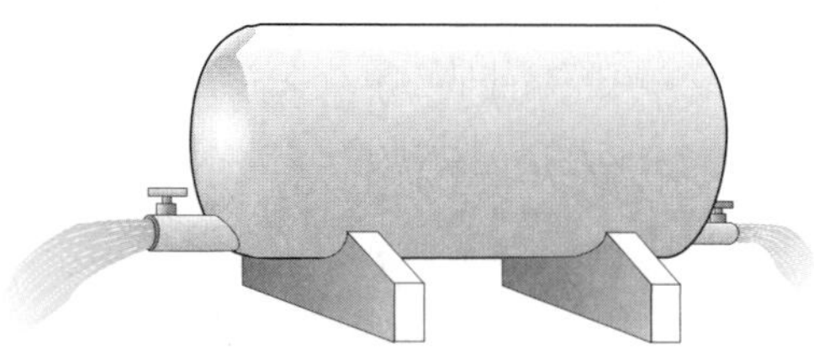

Figure for Exercise 42

43. ***Cleaning sidewalks.*** Edgar can blow the leaves off the sidewalks around the capitol building in 2 hours using a gasoline-powered blower. Ellen can do the same job in 8 hours using a broom. How long would it take them working together? 1 hour 36 minutes

44. ***Computer time.*** It takes a computer 8 days to print all of the personalized letters for a national sweepstakes. A new computer is purchased that can do the same job in 5 days. How long would it take to do the job with both computers working on it? $\frac{40}{13}$ days

Show a complete solution to each problem. See Example 7.

45. ***Apples and bananas.*** Bertha bought 18 pounds of fruit consisting of apples and bananas. She paid \$9 for the apples and \$2.40 for the bananas. If the price per pound of the apples was 3 times that of the bananas, then how many pounds of each type of fruit did she buy?
Bananas 8 pounds, apples 10 pounds

46. ***Running backs.*** In the playoff game the ball was carried by either Anderson or Brown on 21 plays. Anderson gained 36 yards, and Brown gained 54 yards. If Brown averaged twice as many yards per carry as Anderson, then on how many plays did Anderson carry the ball? 12

Photo for Exercise 46

47. ***Fuel efficiency.*** Last week, Joe's Electric Service used 110 gallons of gasoline in its two trucks. The large truck was driven 800 miles, and the small truck was driven 600 miles. If the small truck gets twice as many miles per gallon as the large truck, then how many gallons of gasoline did the large truck use? 80 gallons

48. ***Repair work.*** Sally received a bill for a total of 8 hours labor on the repair of her bulldozer. She paid \$50 to the master mechanic and \$90 to his apprentice. If the master mechanic gets \$10 more per hour than his apprentice, then how many hours did each work on the bulldozer?
Master 2 hours, apprentice 6 hours

Show a complete solution to each problem.

49. ***Small plane.*** It took a small plane 1 hour longer to fly 480 miles against the wind than it took the plane to fly the same distance with the wind. If the wind speed was 20 mph, then what is the speed of the plane in calm air?
140 mph

50. ***Fast boat.*** A motorboat at full throttle takes two hours longer to travel 75 miles against the current than it takes to travel the same distance with the current. If the rate of the current is 5 mph, then what is the speed of the boat at full throttle in still water? 20 mph

51. ***Light plane.*** At full throttle a light plane flies 275 miles against the wind in the same time as it flies 325 miles with the wind. If the plane flies at 120 mph at full throttle in still air, then what is the wind speed? 10 mph

52. ***Big plane.*** A six-passenger plane cruises at 180 mph in calm air. If the plane flies 7 miles with the wind in the same amount of time as it flies 5 miles against the wind, then what is the wind speed? 30 mph

53. ***Two cyclists.*** Ben and Jerry start from the same point and ride their bicycles in opposite directions. If Ben rides twice as fast as Jerry and they are 90 miles apart after four hours, then what is the speed of each rider?
Ben 15 mph, Jerry 7.5 mph

54. ***Catching up.*** A sailboat leaves port and travels due south at an average speed of 9 mph. Four hours later a motorboat leaves the same port and travels due south at an average speed of 21 mph. How long will it take the motorboat to catch the sailboat? 3 hours

55. ***Road trip.*** The Griswalds averaged 45 mph on their way to Las Vegas and 60 mph on the way back home using the same route. Find the distance from their home to Las Vegas if the total driving time was 70 hours. 1800 miles

56. ***Meeting cyclists.*** Tanya and Lebron start at the same time from opposite ends of a bicycle trail that is 81 miles long. Tanya averages 12 mph and Lebron averages 15 mph. How long does it take for them to meet? 3 hours

57. ***Filling a fountain.*** Pete's fountain can be filled using a pipe or a hose. The fountain can be filled using the pipe in 6 hours or the hose in 12 hours. How long will it take to fill the fountain using both the pipe and the hose? 4 hours

58. ***Mowing a lawn.*** Albert can mow a lawn in 40 minutes, while his cousin Vinnie can mow the same lawn in one hour. How long would it take to mow the lawn if Albert and Vinnie work together? 24 minutes

59. ***Printing a report.*** Debra plans to use two computers to print all of the copies of the annual report that are needed for the year-end meeting. The new computer can do the whole job in 2 hours while the old computer can do the whole job in 3 hours. How long will it take to get the job done using both computers simultaneously? 1.2 hours or 1 hour 12 minutes

60. ***Installing a dishwasher.*** A plumber can install a dishwasher in 50 min. If the plumber brings his apprentice to help, the job takes 40 minutes. How long would it take the apprentice working alone to install the dishwasher? 200 minutes

61. ***Filling a tub.*** Using the hot and cold water faucets together, a bathtub fills in 8 minutes. Using the hot water faucet alone, the tub fills in 12 minutes. How long does it take to fill the tub using only the cold water faucet? 24 minutes

62. ***Filling a tank.*** A water tank has an inlet pipe and a drain pipe. A full tank can be emptied in 30 minutes if the drain is opened and an empty tank can be filled in 45 minutes with the inlet pipe opened. If both pipes are accidentally opened when the tank is full, then how long will it take to empty the tank? 90 minutes

Collaborative Activities

Grouping: Three students per group

Topic: Distance formula

How Do I Get There from Here?

Suppose that you want to decide whether to ride your bicycle, drive your car, or take the bus to school this year. The best thing to do is to analyze each of your options. Read all the information given here and then have each person in your group pick one mode of transportation. Working individually, answer the questions using the given information, the accompanying map, and the distance formula $D = RT$. Present a case to your group for your type of transportation. Compute costs for one entire 32-week school year (two 16-week semesters).

If you travel by car, you will need to pay for a parking permit, which costs \$150/year. Traffic has increased, so it takes 12 minutes to get to school. What is your average speed? Determine the cost (use current gas prices) of your gasoline for a full 32-week academic year assuming your car will get 30 mpg. Are there any other costs associated with using a car?

If you travel by bicycle, then you will need to buy a new bike lock for \$25 and two new tubes at \$5.00 apiece. As well as cost, determine how fast you would have to bike to beat the car.

If you travel by bus, then it will cost \$7.50 per month for a student bus pass. The bus stops at the end of your block. It leaves at 8:30 A.M. and will get to the college at 8:55 A.M. On Mondays and Wednesdays you have a 9:00 A.M. class, four blocks from the bus stop. As well as cost find the average speed of the bus and figure the cost for the full 32-week school year.

When you present your case, include the time needed to get there, speed, total cost, convenience, and any other expenses. Have at least three reasons why this would be the best way to travel. Consider unique features of your area such as traffic, weather, and terrain.

After each of you has presented your case, decide as a group which type of transportation to choose.

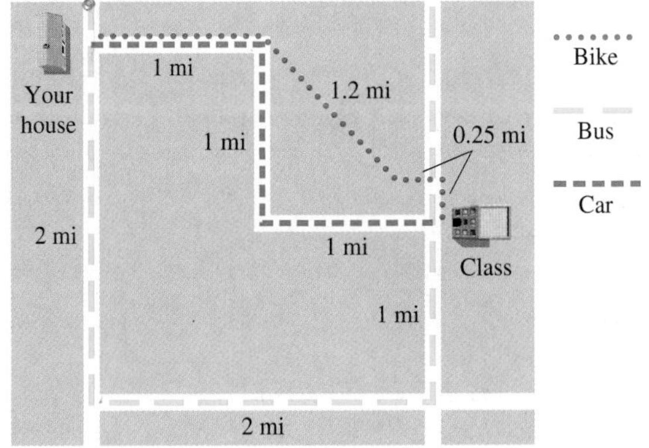

Chapter 6 Wrap-Up

Summary

Rational Expressions		**Examples**
Rational expression	The ratio of two polynomials with the denominator not equal to 0	$\frac{x-1}{x-3} (x \neq 3)$
Rule for reducing rational expressions	If $a \neq 0$ and $c \neq 0$, then $\frac{ab}{ac} = \frac{b}{c}$. (Divide out the common factors.)	$\frac{8x+2}{4x} = \frac{2(4x+1)}{2(2x)} = \frac{4x+1}{2x}$
Quotient rule for exponents	Suppose $a \neq 0$ and m and n are positive integers. If $m \geq n$, then $\frac{a^m}{a^n} = a^{m-n}$. If $m < n$, then $\frac{a^m}{a^n} = \frac{1}{a^{n-m}}$.	$\frac{x^7}{x^5} = x^2$ $\frac{x^2}{x^5} = \frac{1}{x^3}$

Multiplication and Division of Rational Expressions		**Examples**
Multiplication	If $b \neq 0$ and $d \neq 0$, then $\frac{a}{b} \cdot \frac{c}{d} = \frac{ac}{bd}$.	$\frac{3}{x^3} \cdot \frac{6}{x^5} = \frac{18}{x^8}$
Division	If $b \neq 0$, $c \neq 0$, and $d \neq 0$, then $\frac{a}{b} \div \frac{c}{d} = \frac{a}{b} \cdot \frac{d}{c}$. (Invert the divisor and multiply.)	$\frac{a}{x^3} \div \frac{5}{x^9} = \frac{a}{x^3} \cdot \frac{x^9}{5} = \frac{ax^6}{5}$

Addition and Subtraction of Rational Expressions		**Examples**
Least common denominator	The LCD of a group of denominators is the smallest number that is a multiple of all of them.	8, 12 LCD = 24
Finding the least common denominator	1. Factor each denominator completely. Use exponent notation for repeated factors. 2. Write the product of all of the different factors that appear in the denominators. 3. On each factor, use the highest power that appears on that factor in any of the denominators.	$4ab^3$, $6a^2b$ $4ab^3 = 2^2ab^3$ $6a^2b = 2 \cdot 3a^2b$ $\text{LCD} = 2^2 \cdot 3a^2b^3 = 12a^2b^3$

Addition and subtraction of rational expressions	If $b \neq 0$, then $\frac{a}{b} + \frac{c}{b} = \frac{a + c}{b}$ and $\frac{a}{b} - \frac{c}{b} = \frac{a - c}{b}$. If the denominators are not identical, change each fraction to an equivalent fraction so that all denominators are identical.	$\frac{2x}{x - 3} + \frac{7x}{x - 3} = \frac{9x}{x - 3}$ $\frac{2}{x} + \frac{1}{3x} = \frac{6}{3x} + \frac{1}{3x} = \frac{7}{3x}$
Complex fraction	A rational expression that has fractions in the numerator and/or the denominator	$\dfrac{\frac{1}{2} + \frac{1}{3}}{\frac{1}{3} - \frac{3}{4}}$
Simplifying complex fractions	Multiply the numerator and denominator by the LCD.	$\dfrac{\left(\frac{1}{2} + \frac{1}{3}\right)12}{\left(\frac{1}{3} - \frac{3}{4}\right)12} = \frac{6 + 4}{4 - 9} = -2$
Equations with Rational Expressions		**Examples**
Solving equations	Multiply each side by the LCD.	$\frac{1}{x} - \frac{1}{3} = \frac{1}{2x} - \frac{1}{6}$ $6x\left(\frac{1}{x} - \frac{1}{3}\right) = 6x\left(\frac{1}{2x} - \frac{1}{6}\right)$ $6 - 2x = 3 - x$
Proportion	An equation expressing the equality of two ratios	$\frac{a}{b} = \frac{c}{d}$
Extremes-means property (Cross-multiply)	If $b \neq 0$ and $d \neq 0$, then $\frac{a}{b} = \frac{c}{d}$ is equivalent to $ad = bc$. Cross-multiplying is a quick way to eliminate the fractions in a proportion.	$\frac{2}{x - 3} = \frac{5}{6}$ $2 \cdot 6 = (x - 3)5$ $12 = 5x - 15$

Enriching Your Mathematical Word Power

For each mathematical term, choose the correct meaning.

1. rational expression
a. a fraction
b. a ratio of two polynomials with denominator not equal to 0
c. an expression involving fractions
d. a fraction in which the numerator and denominator contain fractions b

2. complex fraction
a. a fraction having rational expressions in the numerator, denominator, or both
b. a fraction with a large denominator
c. the sum of two fractions
d. a fraction with a variable in the denominator a

3. building up the denominator
a. the opposite of reducing a fraction
b. finding the least common denominator
c. adding the same number to the numerator and denominator
d. writing a fraction larger a

4. least common denominator
a. the largest number that is a multiple of all denominators
b. the sum of the denominators
c. the product of the denominators
d. the smallest number that is a multiple of all denominators d

5. extraneous solution
a. a number that appears to be a solution to an equation but does not satisfy the equation
b. an extra solution to an equation
c. the second solution
d. a nonreal solution a

6. ratio of *a* to *b*
a. b/a
b. a/b
c. $a/(a + b)$
d. ab b

7. proportion
a. a ratio
b. two ratios
c. the product of the means equals the product of the extremes
d. a statement expressing the equality of two ratios d

8. extremes
a. a and d in $a/b = c/d$
b. b and c in $a/b = c/d$
c. the extremes-means property
d. if $a/b = c/d$ then $ad = bc$ a

9. means
a. the average of a, b, c, and d
b. a and d in $a/b = c/d$
c. b and c in $a/b = c/d$
d. if $a/b = c/d$, then $(a + b)/2 = (c + d)/2$ c

10. cross-multiplying
a. $ab = ba$ for any real numbers a and b
b. $(a - b)^2 = (b - a)^2$ for any real numbers a and b
c. if $a/b = c/d$, then $ab = cd$
d. if $a/b = c/d$, then $ad = bc$ d

Review Exercises

6.1 *Reduce each rational expression to lowest terms.*

1. $\frac{24}{28}$ $\frac{6}{7}$

2. $\frac{42}{18}$ $\frac{7}{3}$

3. $\frac{2a^3c^3}{8a^5c}$ $\frac{c^2}{4a^2}$

4. $\frac{39x^6}{15x}$ $\frac{13x^5}{5}$

5. $\frac{6w - 9}{9w - 12}$ $\frac{2w - 3}{3w - 4}$

6. $\frac{3t - 6}{8 - 4t}$ $-\frac{3}{4}$

7. $\frac{x^2 - 1}{3 - 3x}$ $-\frac{x + 1}{3}$

8. $\frac{3x^2 - 9x + 6}{10 - 5x}$ $\frac{3 - 3x}{5}$

6.2 *Perform the indicated operation.*

9. $\frac{1}{6k} \cdot 3k^2$ $\frac{1}{2}k$

10. $\frac{1}{15abc} \cdot 5a^3b^5c^2$ $\frac{1}{3}a^2b^4c$

11. $\frac{2xy}{3} \div y^2$ $\frac{2x}{3y}$

12. $4ab \div \frac{1}{2a^4}$ $8a^5b$

13. $\frac{a^2 - 9}{a - 2} \cdot \frac{a^2 - 4}{a + 3}$ $a^2 - a - 6$

14. $\frac{x^2 - 1}{3x} \cdot \frac{6x}{2x - 2}$ $x + 1$

15. $\frac{w - 2}{3w} \div \frac{4w - 8}{6w}$ $\frac{1}{2}$

16. $\frac{2y + 2x}{x - xy} \div \frac{x^2 + 2xy + y^2}{y^2 - y}$ $\frac{-2y}{x(x + y)}$

6.3 *Find the least common denominator for each group of denominators.*

17. 36, 54 108

18. 10, 15, 35 210

19. $6ab^3$, $8a^7b^2$ $24a^7b^3$

20. $20u^4v$, $18uv^5$, $12u^2v^3$ $180u^4v^5$

21. $4x$, $6x - 6$ $12x(x - 1)$

22. $8a$, $6a$, $2a^2 + 2a$ $24a(a + 1)$

23. $x^2 - 4$, $x^2 - x - 2$ $(x + 1)(x - 2)(x + 2)$

24. $x^2 - 9$, $x^2 + 6x + 9$ $(x - 3)(x + 3)^2$

Convert each rational expression into an equivalent rational expression with the indicated denominator.

25. $\frac{5}{12} = \frac{?}{36}$ $\frac{15}{36}$

26. $\frac{2a}{15} = \frac{?}{45}$ $\frac{6a}{45}$

27. $\frac{2}{3xy} = \frac{?}{15x^2y}$ $\frac{10x}{15x^2y}$

28. $\frac{3z}{7x^2y} = \frac{?}{42x^3y^8}$ $\frac{18xy^7z}{42x^3y^8}$

29. $\frac{5}{y - 6} = \frac{?}{12 - 2y}$ $\frac{-10}{12 - 2y}$

30. $\dfrac{-3}{2-t} = \dfrac{?}{2t-4}$ $\dfrac{6}{2t-4}$

31. $\dfrac{x}{x-1} = \dfrac{?}{x^2-1}$ $\dfrac{x^2+x}{x^2-1}$

32. $\dfrac{t}{t-3} = \dfrac{?}{t^2+2t-15}$ $\dfrac{t^2+5t}{t^2+2t-15}$

6.4 *Perform the indicated operation.*

33. $\dfrac{5}{36} + \dfrac{9}{28}$ $\dfrac{29}{63}$

34. $\dfrac{7}{30} - \dfrac{11}{42}$ $-\dfrac{1}{35}$

35. $3 - \dfrac{4}{x}$ $\dfrac{3x-4}{x}$

36. $1 + \dfrac{3a}{2b}$ $\dfrac{2b+3a}{2b}$

37. $\dfrac{2}{ab^2} - \dfrac{1}{a^2b}$ $\dfrac{2a-b}{a^2b^2}$

38. $\dfrac{3}{4x^3} + \dfrac{5}{6x^2}$ $\dfrac{10x+9}{12x^3}$

39. $\dfrac{9a}{2a-3} + \dfrac{5}{3a-2}$ $\dfrac{27a^2-8a-15}{(2a-3)(3a-2)}$

40. $\dfrac{3}{x-2} - \dfrac{5}{x+3}$ $\dfrac{-2x+19}{(x-2)(x+3)}$

41. $\dfrac{1}{a-8} - \dfrac{2}{8-a}$ $\dfrac{3}{a-8}$

42. $\dfrac{5}{x-14} + \dfrac{4}{14-x}$ $\dfrac{1}{x-14}$

43. $\dfrac{3}{2x-4} + \dfrac{1}{x^2-4}$ $\dfrac{3x+8}{2(x+2)(x-2)}$

44. $\dfrac{x}{x^2-2x-3} - \dfrac{3x}{x^2-9}$ $\dfrac{-2x^2}{(x-3)(x+3)(x+1)}$

6.5 *Simplify each complex fraction.*

45. $\dfrac{\frac{1}{2}-\frac{3}{4}}{\frac{2}{3}+\frac{1}{2}}$ $-\dfrac{3}{14}$

46. $\dfrac{\frac{2}{3}+\frac{5}{8}}{\frac{1}{2}-\frac{3}{8}}$ $\dfrac{31}{3}$

47. $\dfrac{\frac{1}{a}+\frac{2}{3b}}{\frac{1}{2b}-\frac{3}{a}}$ $\dfrac{6b+4a}{3(a-6b)}$

48. $\dfrac{\frac{3}{xy}-\frac{1}{3y}}{\frac{1}{6x}-\frac{3}{5y}}$ $\dfrac{90-10x}{5y-18x}$

49. $\dfrac{\frac{1}{x-2}-\frac{3}{x+3}}{\frac{2}{x+3}+\frac{1}{x-2}}$ $\dfrac{-2x+9}{3x-1}$

50. $\dfrac{\frac{4}{a+1}+\frac{5}{a^2-1}}{\frac{1}{a^2-1}-\frac{3}{a-1}}$ $\dfrac{4a+1}{-3a-2}$

51. $\dfrac{\frac{x-1}{x-3}}{\frac{1}{x^2-x-6}-\frac{4}{x+2}}$ $\dfrac{x^2+x-2}{-4x+13}$

52. $\dfrac{\frac{6}{a^2+5a+6}-\frac{8}{a+2}}{\frac{2}{a+3}-\frac{4}{a+2}}$ $\dfrac{4a+9}{a+4}$

6.6 *Solve each equation.*

53. $\dfrac{-2}{5} = \dfrac{3}{x}$ $-\dfrac{15}{2}$

54. $\dfrac{3}{x} + \dfrac{5}{3x} = 1$ $\dfrac{14}{3}$

55. $\dfrac{14}{a^2-1} + \dfrac{1}{a-1} = \dfrac{3}{a+1}$ 9

56. $2 + \dfrac{3}{y-5} = \dfrac{2y}{y-5}$ No solution

57. $z - \dfrac{3z}{2-z} = \dfrac{6}{z-2}$ -3

58. $\dfrac{1}{x} + \dfrac{1}{3} = \dfrac{1}{2}$ 6

6.7 *Solve each proportion.*

59. $\dfrac{3}{x} = \dfrac{2}{7}$ $\dfrac{21}{2}$

60. $\dfrac{4}{x} = \dfrac{x}{4}$ $-4, 4$

61. $\dfrac{2}{w-3} = \dfrac{5}{w}$ 5

62. $\dfrac{3}{t-3} = \dfrac{5}{t+4}$ $\dfrac{27}{2}$

Solve each problem by using a proportion.

63. ***Taxis in Times Square.*** The ratio of taxis to private automobiles in Times Square at 6:00 P.M. on New Year's Eve was estimated to be 15 to 2. If there were 60 taxis, then how many private automobiles were there? 8

Photo for Exercise 63

64. ***Student-teacher ratio.*** The student-teacher ratio for Washington High was reported to be 27.5 to 1. If there are 42 teachers, then how many students are there? 1155

65. ***Water and rice.*** At Wong's Chinese Restaurant the secret recipe for white rice calls for a 2 to 1 ratio of water to rice. In one batch the chef used 28 more cups of water than rice. How many cups of each did he use? 56 cups water, 28 cups rice

Photo for Exercise 65

66. ***Oil and gas.*** An outboard motor calls for a fuel mixture that has a gasoline-to-oil ratio of 50 to 1. How many pints of oil should be added to 6 gallons of gasoline? $\frac{24}{25}$ pints

6.8 *Solve each formula for the indicated variable.*

67. $\frac{y - b}{m} = x$ for y $\quad y = mx + b$

68. $\frac{A}{h} = \frac{a + b}{2}$ for a $\quad a = \frac{2A - hb}{h}$

69. $F = \frac{mv + 1}{m}$ for m $\quad m = \frac{1}{F - v}$

70. $m = \frac{r}{1 + rt}$ for r $\quad r = \frac{m}{1 - mt}$

71. $\frac{y + 1}{x - 3} = 4$ for y $\quad y = 4x - 13$

72. $\frac{y - 3}{x + 2} = \frac{-1}{3}$ for y $\quad y = -\frac{1}{3}x + \frac{7}{3}$

Solve each problem.

73. ***Making a puzzle.*** Tracy, Stacy, and Fred assembled a very large puzzle together in 40 hours. If Stacy worked twice as fast as Fred and Tracy worked just as fast as Stacy, then how long would it have taken Fred to assemble the puzzle alone? 200 hours

74. ***Going skiing.*** Leon drove 270 miles to the lodge in the same time as Pat drove 330 miles to the lodge. If Pat drove 10 miles per hour faster than Leon, then how fast did each of them drive? Leon 45 mph, Pat 55 mph

Photo for Exercise 74

75. ***Merging automobiles.*** When Bert and Ernie merged their automobile dealerships, Bert had 10 more cars than Ernie. While 36% of Ernie's stock consisted of new cars, only 25% of Bert's stock consisted of new cars. If they had 33 new cars on the lot after the merger, then how many cars did each one have before the merger? Bert 60 cars, Ernie 50 cars

76. ***Magazine sales.*** A company specializing in magazine sales over the telephone found that in 2500 phone calls, 360 resulted in sales and were made by male callers, and 480 resulted in sales and were made by female callers. If the company gets twice as many sales per call with a woman's voice than with a man's voice, then how many of the 2500 calls were made by females? 1000

77. ***Distribution of waste.*** The accompanying figure shows the distribution of the total municipal solid waste into various categories in 2000 (U.S. Environmental Protection Agency, www.epa.gov). If the paper waste was 59.8 million tons greater than the yard waste, then what was the amount of yard waste generated? 27.83 million tons

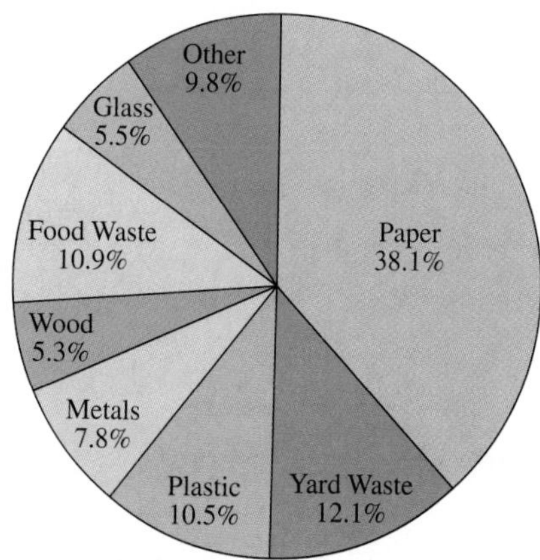

Figure for Exercises 77 and 78

78. ***Total waste.*** Use the information given in Exercise 77 to find the total waste generated in 2000 and the amount of food waste. 230 million tons, 25.07 million tons

Miscellaneous

In place of each question mark, put an expression that makes each equation an identity.

79. $\frac{5}{x} = \frac{?}{2x}$ $\frac{10}{2x}$

80. $\frac{?}{a} = \frac{6}{3a}$ $\frac{2}{a}$

81. $\frac{2}{a-5} = \frac{?}{5-a}$ $\frac{-2}{5-a}$

82. $\frac{-1}{a-7} = \frac{1}{?}$ $\frac{1}{7-a}$

83. $3 = \frac{?}{x}$ $\frac{3x}{x}$

84. $2a = \frac{?}{b}$ $\frac{2ab}{b}$

85. $m \div \frac{1}{2} = ?$ $2m$

86. $5x \div \frac{1}{x} = ?$ $5x^2$

87. $2a \div ? = 12a$ $\frac{1}{6}$

88. $10x \div ? = 20x^2$ $\frac{1}{2x}$

89. $\frac{a-1}{a^2-1} = \frac{1}{?}$ $\frac{1}{a+1}$

90. $\frac{?}{x^2-9} = \frac{1}{x-3}$ $\frac{x+3}{x^2-9}$

91. $\frac{1}{a} - \frac{1}{5} = ?$ $\frac{5-a}{5a}$

92. $\frac{3}{7} - \frac{2}{b} = ?$ $\frac{3b-14}{7b}$

93. $\frac{a}{2} - 1 = \frac{?}{2}$ $\frac{a-2}{2}$

94. $\frac{1}{a} - 1 = \frac{?}{a}$ $\frac{1-a}{a}$

95. $(a-b) \div (-1) = ?$ $b-a$

96. $(a-7) \div (7-a) = ?$ -1

97. $\frac{\frac{1}{5a}}{2} = ?$ $\frac{1}{10a}$

98. $\frac{3a}{\frac{1}{2}} = ?$ $6a$

For each expression in Exercises 99–118, either perform the indicated operation or solve the equation, whichever is appropriate.

99. $\frac{1}{x} + \frac{1}{2x}$ $\frac{3}{2x}$

100. $\frac{1}{y} + \frac{1}{3y} = 2$ $\frac{2}{3}$

101. $\frac{2}{3xy} + \frac{1}{6x}$ $\frac{4+y}{6xy}$

102. $\frac{3}{x-1} - \frac{3}{x}$ $\frac{3}{x(x-1)}$

103. $\frac{5}{a-5} - \frac{3}{5-a}$ $\frac{8}{a-5}$

104. $\frac{2}{x-2} - \frac{3}{x} = \frac{-1}{x}$ No solution

105. $\frac{2}{x-1} - \frac{2}{x} = 1$ $-1, 2$

106. $\frac{2}{x-2} \cdot \frac{6x-12}{14}$ $\frac{6}{7}$

107. $\frac{-3}{x+2} \cdot \frac{5x+10}{9}$ $-\frac{5}{3}$

108. $\frac{3}{10} = \frac{5}{x}$ $\frac{50}{3}$

109. $\frac{1}{-3} = \frac{-2}{x}$ 6

110. $\frac{x^2 - 4}{x} \div \frac{4x - 8}{x}$ $\frac{x + 2}{4}$

111. $\frac{ax + am + 3x + 3m}{a^2 - 9} \div \frac{2x + 2m}{a - 3}$ $\frac{1}{2}$

112. $\frac{-2}{x} = \frac{3}{x + 2}$ $-\frac{4}{5}$

113. $\frac{2}{x^2 - 25} + \frac{1}{x^2 - 4x - 5}$ $\frac{3x + 7}{(x - 5)(x + 5)(x + 1)}$

114. $\frac{4}{a^2 - 1} + \frac{1}{2a + 2}$ $\frac{a + 7}{2(a + 1)(a - 1)}$

115. $\frac{-3}{a^2 - 9} - \frac{2}{a^2 + 5a + 6}$ $\frac{-5a}{(a - 3)(a + 3)(a + 2)}$

116. $\frac{-5}{a^2 - 4} - \frac{2}{a^2 - 3a + 2}$ $\frac{-7a + 1}{(a + 2)(a - 2)(a - 1)}$

117. $\frac{1}{a^2 - 1} + \frac{2}{1 - a} = \frac{3}{a + 1}$ $\frac{2}{5}$

118. $3 + \frac{1}{x - 2} = \frac{2x - 3}{x - 2}$ No solution

Chapter 6 Test

What numbers cannot be used for x in each rational expression?

1. $\frac{2x - 1}{x^2 - 1}$ $-1, 1$

2. $\frac{5}{2 - 3x}$ $\frac{2}{3}$

3. $\frac{1}{x}$ 0

Perform the indicated operation. Write each answer in lowest terms.

4. $\frac{2}{15} - \frac{4}{9}$ $-\frac{14}{45}$

5. $\frac{1}{y} + 3$ $\frac{1 + 3y}{y}$

6. $\frac{3}{a - 2} - \frac{1}{2 - a}$ $\frac{4}{a - 2}$

7. $\frac{2}{x^2 - 4} - \frac{3}{x^2 + x - 2}$ $\frac{-x + 4}{(x + 2)(x - 2)(x - 1)}$

8. $\frac{m^2 - 1}{(m - 1)^2} \cdot \frac{2m - 2}{3m + 3}$ $\frac{2}{3}$

9. $\frac{a - b}{3} \div \frac{b^2 - a^2}{6}$ $\frac{-2}{a + b}$

10. $\frac{5a^2b}{12a} \cdot \frac{2a^3b}{15ab^6}$ $\frac{a^3}{18b^4}$

Simplify each complex fraction.

11. $\dfrac{\frac{2}{3} + \frac{4}{5}}{\frac{2}{5} - \frac{3}{2}}$ $-\frac{4}{3}$

12. $\dfrac{\frac{2}{x} + \frac{1}{x - 2}}{\frac{1}{x - 2} - \frac{3}{x}}$ $\frac{-3x + 4}{2(x - 3)}$

Solve each equation.

13. $\frac{3}{x} = \frac{7}{5}$ $\frac{15}{7}$

14. $\frac{x}{x - 1} - \frac{3}{x} = \frac{1}{2}$ $2, 3$

15. $\frac{1}{x} + \frac{1}{6} = \frac{1}{4}$ 12

Solve each formula for the indicated variable.

16. $\frac{y - 3}{x + 2} = \frac{-1}{5}$ for y $y = -\frac{1}{5}x + \frac{13}{5}$

17. $M = \frac{1}{3}b(c + d)$ for c $c = \frac{3M - bd}{b}$

Solve each problem.

18. If $R(x) = \frac{x + 2}{1 - x}$, then what is $R(0.9)$? 29

19. When all of the grocery carts escape from the supermarket, it takes Reginald 12 minutes to round them up and bring them back. Because Norman doesn't make as much per hour as Reginald, it takes Norman 18 minutes to do the same job. How long would it take them working together to complete the roundup? 7.2 minutes

20. Brenda and her husband Randy bicycled cross-country together. One morning, Brenda rode 30 miles. By traveling only 5 miles per hour faster and putting in one more hour, Randy covered twice the distance Brenda covered. What was the speed of each cyclist?
Brenda 15 mph and Randy 20 mph, or Brenda 10 mph and Randy 15 mph

21. For a certain time period the ratio of the dollar value of exports to the dollar value of imports for the United States was 2 to 3. If the value of exports during that time period was 48 billion dollars, then what was the value of imports?
\$72 billion

*Making*Connections | A Review of Chapters 1–6

Solve each equation.

1. $3x - 2 = 5$
$\frac{7}{3}$

2. $\frac{3}{5}x = -2$
$-\frac{10}{3}$

3. $2(x - 2) = 4x$
-2

4. $2(x - 2) = 2x$
No solution

5. $2(x + 3) = 6x + 6$
0

6. $2(3x + 4) + x^2 = 0$
$-4, -2$

7. $4x - 4x^3 = 0$
$-1, 0, 1$

8. $\frac{3}{x} = \frac{-2}{5}$
$-\frac{15}{2}$

9. $\frac{3}{x} = \frac{x}{12}$
$-6, 6$

10. $\frac{x}{2} = \frac{4}{x - 2}$
$-2, 4$

11. $\frac{w}{18} - \frac{w - 1}{9} = \frac{4 - w}{6}$
5

12. $\frac{x}{x + 1} + \frac{1}{2x + 2} = \frac{7}{8}$
3

Solve each equation for y.

13. $2x + 3y = c$
$y = \frac{c - 2x}{3}$

14. $\frac{y - 3}{x - 5} = \frac{1}{2}$
$y = \frac{1}{2}x + \frac{1}{2}$

15. $2y = ay + c$
$y = \frac{c}{2 - a}$

16. $\frac{A}{y} = \frac{C}{B}$
$y = \frac{AB}{C}$

17. $\frac{A}{y} + \frac{1}{3} = \frac{B}{y}$
$y = 3B - 3A$

18. $\frac{A}{y} - \frac{1}{2} = \frac{1}{3}$
$y = \frac{6A}{5}$

19. $3y - 5ay = 8$
$y = \frac{8}{3 - 5a}$

20. $y^2 - By = 0$
$y = 0$ or $y = B$

21. $A = \frac{1}{2}h(b + y)$
$y = \frac{2A - hb}{h}$

22. $2(b + y) = b$
$y = -\frac{b}{2}$

Calculate the value of $b^2 - 4ac$ for each choice of a, b, and c.

23. $a = 1, b = 2, c = -15$
64

24. $a = 1, b = 8, c = 12$
16

25. $a = 2, b = 5, c = -3$
49

26. $a = 6, b = 7, c = -3$
121

Perform each indicated operation.

27. $(3x - 5) - (5x - 3)$
$-2x - 2$

28. $(2a - 5)(a - 3)$
$2a^2 - 11a + 15$

29. $x^7 \div x^3$
x^4

30. $\frac{x - 3}{5} + \frac{x + 4}{5}$
$\frac{2x + 1}{5}$

31. $\frac{1}{2} \cdot \frac{1}{x}$
$\frac{1}{2x}$

32. $\frac{1}{2} + \frac{1}{x}$
$\frac{x + 2}{2x}$

33. $\frac{1}{2} \div \frac{1}{x}$
$\frac{x}{2}$

34. $\frac{1}{2} - \frac{1}{x}$
$\frac{x - 2}{2x}$

35. $\frac{x - 3}{5} - \frac{x + 4}{5}$
$-\frac{7}{5}$

36. $\frac{3a}{2} \div 2$
$\frac{3a}{4}$

37. $(x - 8)(x + 8)$
$x^2 - 64$

38. $3x(x^2 - 7)$
$3x^3 - 21x$

39. $2a^5 \cdot 5a^9$
$10a^{14}$

40. $x^2 \cdot x^8$
x^{10}

41. $(k - 6)^2$
$k^2 - 12k + 36$

42. $(j + 5)^2$
$j^2 + 10j + 25$

43. $(g - 3) \div (3 - g)$
-1

44. $(6x^3 - 8x^2) \div (2x)$
$3x^2 - 4x$

Solve.

45. ***Present value.*** An investor is interested in the amount or present value that she would have to invest today to receive periodic payments in the future. The present value of \$1 in one year and \$1 in 2 years with interest rate r compounded annually is given by the formula

$$P = \frac{1}{1 + r} + \frac{1}{(1 + r)^2}.$$

a) Rewrite the formula so that the right-hand side is a single rational expression.

b) Find P if $r = 7\%$.

c) The present value of \$1 per year for the next 10 years is given by the formula

$$P = \frac{1}{1 + r} + \frac{1}{(1 + r)^2} + \frac{1}{(1 + r)^3} + \cdots + \frac{1}{(1 + r)^{10}}.$$

Use this formula to find P if $r = 5\%$.

$P = \frac{r + 2}{(1 + r)^2}$, \$1.81, \$7.72

Critical **Thinking** | For Individual or Group Work | Chapter 6

These exercises can be solved by a variety of techniques, which may or may not require algebra. So be creative and think critically. Explain all answers. Answers are in the Instructor's Edition of this text.

1. ***Equilateral triangles.*** Consider the sequence of three equilateral triangles shown in the accompanying figure.

a) How many equilateral triangles are there in (a) of the accompanying figure?

b) How many equilateral triangles congruent to the one in (a) can be found in (b) of the accompanying figure? How many are found in (c)?

c) Suppose the sequence of equilateral triangles shown in (a), (b), and (c) is continued. How many equilateral triangles [congruent to the one in (a)] could be found in the nth such figure?

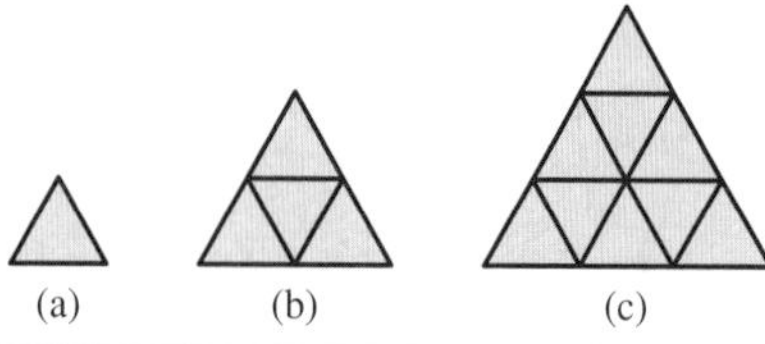

Figure for Exercise 1

2. ***The amazing Amber.*** Amber has been amazing her friends with a math trick. Amber has a friend select a three-digit number and reverse the digits. The friend then finds the difference of the two numbers and reads the first two digits of the difference (from left to right). Amber can always tell the last digit of the difference. Explain how Amber does this.

3. ***Missing proceeds.*** Ruth and Betty sell apples at a farmers market. Ruth's apples sell at 2 for \$1 while Betty's slightly smaller apples sell at 3 for \$1. When Betty leaves to pick up her kids they each have 30 apples and Ruth takes charge of both businesses. To simplify things, Ruth puts all 60 of the apples together and sells them at 5 for \$2. When Betty returns, all of the apples have been sold, but they begin arguing over how to divide up the proceeds. What is the problem? Explain what went wrong.

4. ***Eyes and feet.*** A rancher has some sheep and ostriches. His young daughter observed that the animals have a total of 60 eyes and 86 feet. How many animals of each type does the rancher have?

Photo for Exercise 4

5. ***Evaluation nightmare.*** Evaluate:

$$\frac{9876543210}{9876543211^2 - 9876543210 \cdot 9876543212}$$

6. ***Perfect squares.*** Find a positive integer such that the integer increased by 1 is a perfect square and one-half of the integer increased by 1 is a perfect square. Also find the next two larger positive integers that have this same property.

7. ***Multiplying primes.*** Find the units digit of the product of the first 500 prime numbers.

8. ***Ones and zeros.*** Find the sum of all seven-digit numbers that can be written using only ones or zeros.

1. a) 1 **b)** 4, 9 **c)** n^2 **2.** The difference is a multiple of 99 and the last digit is the difference between the first two. **3.** If they had sold separately they would have \$15 and \$10, but together have only \$24. The average price of an apple before combining is $\left(50 + 33\frac{1}{3}\right)/2$, or $41\frac{2}{3}$ cents, but Ruth sold them for an average of 40 cents each. **4.** 17 ostriches, 13 sheep **5.** 9876543210 **6.** 48, 1680, 57,120 **7.** 0 **8.** 67,555,552

Chapter 7

Systems of Linear Equations

In his letter to M. Leroy in 1789 Benjamin Franklin said, "In this world nothing is certain but death and taxes." Since that time taxes have become not only inevitable, but also intricate and complex.

Each year the U.S. Congress revises parts of the Federal Income Tax Code. To help clarify these revisions, the Internal Revenue Service issues frequent revenue rulings. In addition, there are seven tax courts that further interpret changes and revisions, sometimes in entirely different ways. Is it any wonder that tax preparation has become complicated and few individuals actually prepare their own taxes? Both corporate and individual tax preparation is a growing business, and there are over 500,000 tax counselors helping more than 60 million taxpayers to file their returns correctly.

Everyone knows that doing taxes involves a lot of arithmetic, but not everyone knows that computing taxes can also involve algebra. In fact, to find state and federal taxes for certain corporations, you must solve a system of equations.

You will see an example of using algebra to find amounts of income taxes in Exercises 83 and 84 of Section 7.1.

7.1 Solving Systems by Graphing and Substitution

In this Section

- **Solving a System by Graphing**
- **Independent, Inconsistent, and Dependent Equations**
- **Solving by Substitution**
- **Applications**

In Chapter 3 we studied linear equations in two variables, but we have usually considered only one equation at a time. In this chapter we will see problems that involve more than one equation. Any collection of two or more equations is called a **system** of equations. If the equations of a system involve two variables, then the set of ordered pairs that satisfy all of the equations is the **solution set of the system.** In this section we solve systems of linear equations in two variables and use systems to solve problems.

Solving a System by Graphing

Because the graph of each linear equation is a line, points that satisfy both equations lie on both lines. For some systems these points can be found by graphing.

EXAMPLE 1

A system with only one solution

Solve the system by graphing:

$$y = x + 2$$
$$x + y = 4$$

Solution

First write the equations in slope-intercept form:

$$y = x + 2$$
$$y = -x + 4$$

Use the y-intercept and the slope to graph each line. The graph of the system is shown in Fig. 7.1. From the graph it appears that these lines intersect at (1, 3). To be certain, we can check that (1, 3) satisfies both equations. Let $x = 1$ and $y = 3$ in $y = x + 2$ to get

$$3 = 1 + 2.$$

Let $x = 1$ and $y = 3$ in $x + y = 4$ to get

$$1 + 3 = 4.$$

Because (1, 3) satisfies both equations, the solution set to the system is $\{(1, 3)\}$.

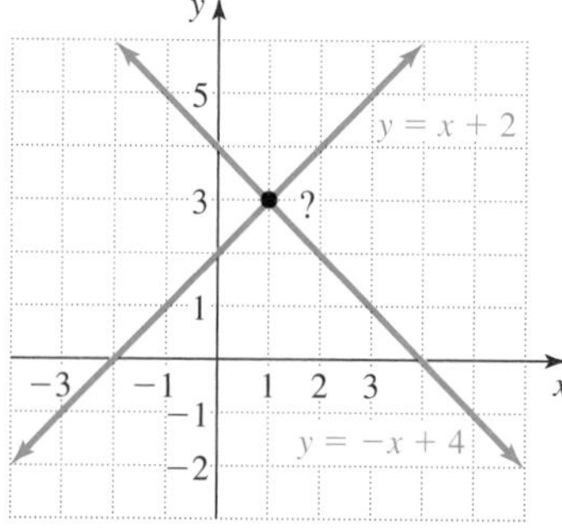

Figure 7.1

Now do Exercises 7–12

Calculator Close-Up

To check Example 1, graph

$$y_1 = x + 2$$

and

$$y_2 = -x + 4.$$

From the CALC menu, choose intersect to have the calculator locate the point of intersection of the two lines. After choosing intersect, you must indicate which two lines you want to intersect and then guess the point of intersection.

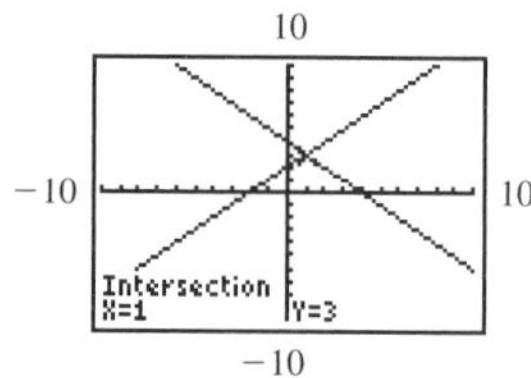

Teaching Tip Encourage students to use graph paper. There is a page of graph paper on page 243 of this text. The Instructor's and Student's Solutions Manuals also contain pages of graph paper.

The graphs of the equations in Example 2 are parallel lines, and there is no point of intersection.

EXAMPLE 2

A system with no solution

Solve the system by graphing:

$$2x - 3y = 6$$
$$3y - 2x = 3$$

Teaching Tip Ask students if they can determine that the solution set is empty when they see both equations in slope-intercept form.

Solution

First write each equation in slope-intercept form:

$$\begin{aligned} 2x - 3y &= 6 \\ -3y &= -2x + 6 \\ y &= \frac{2}{3}x - 2 \end{aligned} \qquad \begin{aligned} 3y - 2x &= 3 \\ 3y &= 2x + 3 \\ y &= \frac{2}{3}x + 1 \end{aligned}$$

The graph of the system is shown in Fig. 7.2. Because the two lines in Fig. 7.2 are parallel, there is no ordered pair that satisfies both equations. The solution set to the system is the empty set, ∅.

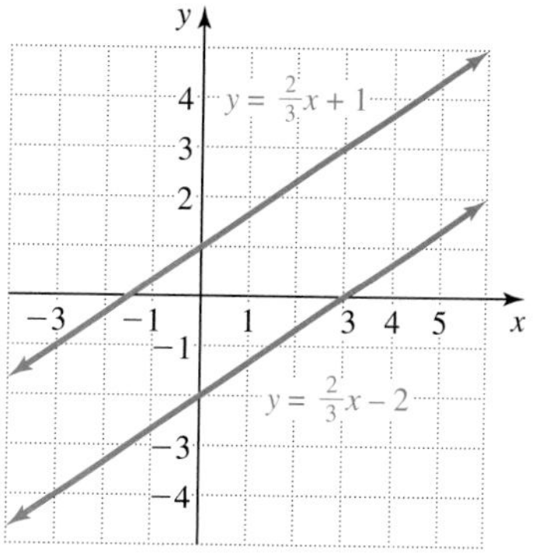

Figure 7.2

Now do Exercises 13–14

The equations in Example 3 are two different equations for the same straight line.

EXAMPLE 3

A system with infinitely many solutions

Solve the system by graphing:

$$2(y + 2) = x$$
$$x - 2y = 4$$

Solution

Write each equation in slope-intercept form:

$$\begin{aligned} 2(y + 2) &= x \\ 2y + 4 &= x \\ y &= \frac{1}{2}x - 2 \end{aligned} \qquad \begin{aligned} x - 2y &= 4 \\ -2y &= -x + 4 \\ y &= \frac{1}{2}x - 2 \end{aligned}$$

Because the equations have the same slope-intercept form, the original equations are equivalent. Their graphs are the same straight line as shown in Fig. 7.3. Every point on the line satisfies both equations of the system. There are infinitely many points in the solution set. The solution set is $\{(x, y) \mid x - 2y = 4\}$.

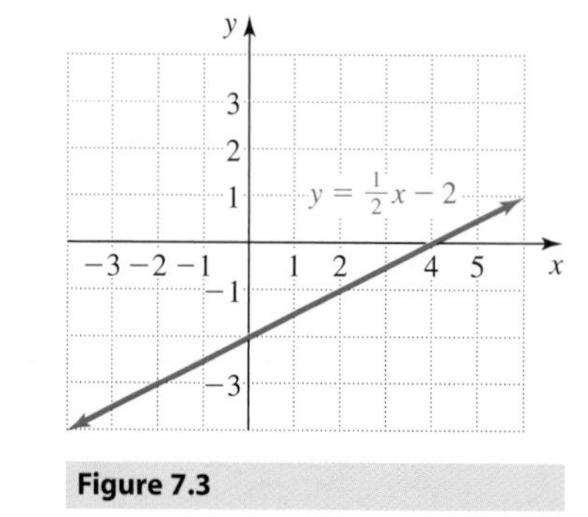

Figure 7.3

Now do Exercises 15–20

Independent, Inconsistent, and Dependent Equations

Our first three examples illustrate the three possible ways in which two lines can be positioned in a plane. In Example 1 the lines intersect in a single point. In this case we say that the equations are **independent** or the system is independent. If the two lines are parallel, as in Example 2, then there is no solution to the system, and the equations are **inconsistent** or the system is inconsistent. If the two equations of a system are equivalent, as in Example 3, the equations are **dependent** or the system is dependent. Figure 7.4 shows the types of graphs that correspond to independent, inconsistent, and dependent systems.

Teaching Tip Actually, all systems can be classified as consistent or inconsistent, and dependent or independent. We use only three words here to simplify the situation.

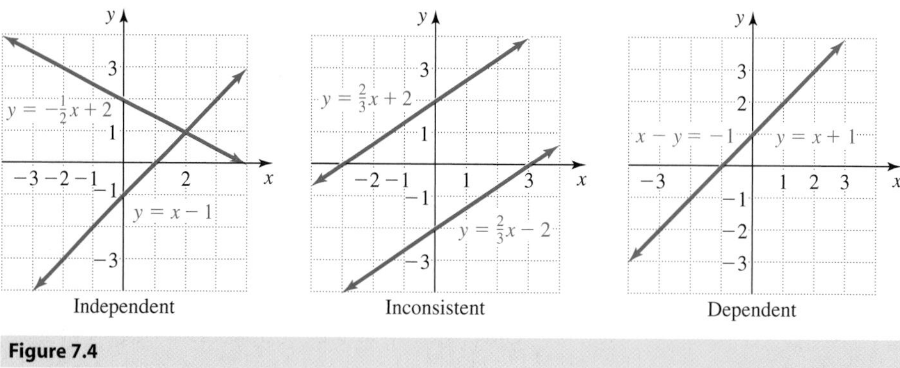

Figure 7.4

Solving by Substitution

Solving a system by graphing is certainly limited by the accuracy of the graph. If the lines intersect at a point whose coordinates are not integers, then it is difficult to determine those coordinates from the graph. The method of solving a system by **substitution** does not depend on a graph and is totally accurate. For substitution we replace a variable in one equation with an equivalent expression obtained from the other equation. Our intention in this substitution step is to eliminate a variable and to give us an equation involving only one variable.

EXAMPLE 4

An independent system solved by substitution

Solve the system by substitution:

$$2x + 3y = 8$$
$$y + 2x = 6$$

Teaching Tip To illustrate independence ask each student to secretly write down an equation in standard form. Collect them and see if the graphs of any two are parallel or coincident lines.

Solution

We can easily solve $y + 2x = 6$ for y to get $y = -2x + 6$. Now replace y in the first equation by $-2x + 6$:

$$\begin{aligned} 2x + 3y &= 8 \\ 2x + 3(-2x + 6) &= 8 \quad \text{Substitute } -2x + 6 \text{ for } y. \\ 2x - 6x + 18 &= 8 \\ -4x &= -10 \\ x &= \frac{5}{2} \end{aligned}$$

To find y, we let $x = \frac{5}{2}$ in the equation $y = -2x + 6$:

$$y = -2\left(\frac{5}{2}\right) + 6 = -5 + 6 = 1$$

The next step is to check $x = \frac{5}{2}$ and $y = 1$ in each equation. If $x = \frac{5}{2}$ and $y = 1$ in $2x + 3y = 8$, we get

$$2\left(\frac{5}{2}\right) + 3(1) = 8.$$

If $x = \frac{5}{2}$ and $y = 1$ in $y + 2x = 6$, we get

$$1 + 2\left(\frac{5}{2}\right) = 6.$$

Because both of these equations are true, the solution set to the system is $\left\{\left(\frac{5}{2}, 1\right)\right\}$. The equations of this system are independent.

Now do Exercises 25–30

Calculator Close-Up

To check Example 4, graph

$$y_1 = (8 - 2x)/3$$

and

$$y_2 = -2x + 6.$$

From the CALC menu, choose intersect to have the calculator locate the point of intersection of the two lines.

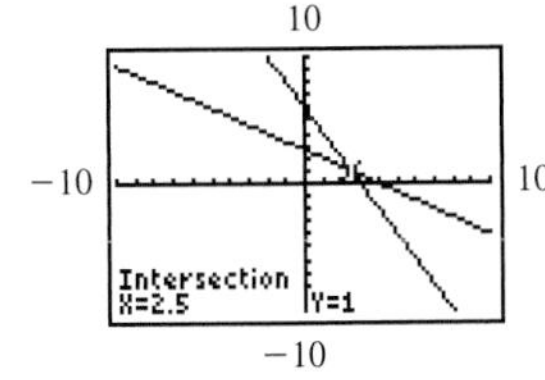

EXAMPLE 5

An inconsistent system solved by substitution

Solve by substitution:

$$x - 2y = 3$$
$$2x - 4y = 7$$

Solution

Solve the first equation for x to get $x = 2y + 3$. Substitute $2y + 3$ for x in the second equation:

$$\begin{aligned} 2x - 4y &= 7 \\ 2(2y + 3) - 4y &= 7 \\ 4y + 6 - 4y &= 7 \\ 6 &= 7 \end{aligned}$$

Helpful Hint

The purpose of Example 5 is to show what happens when you try to solve an inconsistent system by substitution. If we had first written the equations in slope-intercept form, we would have known that the lines are parallel and the solution set is the empty set.

Because $6 = 7$ is incorrect no matter what values are chosen for x and y, there is no solution to this system of equations. The equations are inconsistent. To check, we write each equation in slope-intercept form:

$$\begin{aligned} x - 2y &= 3 \\ -2y &= -x + 3 \\ y &= \frac{1}{2}x - \frac{3}{2} \end{aligned} \qquad \begin{aligned} 2x - 4y &= 7 \\ -4y &= -2x + 7 \\ y &= \frac{1}{2}x - \frac{7}{4} \end{aligned}$$

The graphs of these equations are parallel lines with different y-intercepts. The solution set to the system is the empty set, $\varnothing$.

Now do Exercises 31–32

EXAMPLE 6

A dependent system solved by substitution

Solve by substitution:

$$\begin{aligned} 2x + 3y &= 5 + x + 4y \\ y &= x - 5 \end{aligned}$$

Helpful Hint

The purpose of Example 6 is to show what happens when a dependent system is solved by substitution. If we had first written the first equation in slope-intercept form, we would have known that the equations are dependent and would not have done substitution.

Solution

Substitute $y = x - 5$ into the first equation:

$$\begin{aligned} 2x + 3(x - 5) &= 5 + x + 4(x - 5) \\ 2x + 3x - 15 &= 5 + x + 4x - 20 \\ 5x - 15 &= 5x - 15 \end{aligned}$$

Because the last equation is an identity, any ordered pair that satisfies $y = x - 5$ will also satisfy $2x + 3y = 5 + x + 4y$. The equations of this system are dependent. The solution set to the system is the set of all points that satisfy $y = x - 5$. We write the solution set in set notation as

$$\{(x, y) \mid y = x - 5\}.$$

We can verify this result by writing $2x + 3y = 5 + x + 4y$ in slope-intercept form:

$$\begin{aligned} 2x + 3y &= 5 + x + 4y \\ 3y &= -x + 5 + 4y \\ -y &= -x + 5 \\ y &= x - 5 \end{aligned}$$

Because this slope-intercept form is identical to the slope-intercept form of the other equation, they are two different equations for the same straight line.

Now do Exercises 33–46

If a system is dependent, then an identity will result after the substitution. If the system is inconsistent, then an inconsistent equation will result after the substitution.

Math *at Work* Circuit Breakers

Electricity is the flow of electrons through a circuit. It is measured in volts, amps, and watts. Volts measure the force that causes the electricity or electrons to flow. Amps measure the amount of electric current. Watts measure the amount of work done by a certain amount of current at a certain force or voltage. The basic relationship in watts = amps · volts or $W = A \cdot V$.

A circuit breaker is used as a safety device in a circuit. If the amperage exceeds a certain level, the breaker trips and prevents damage to the system. For example, suppose that 8 strings of Christmas lights each containing 25 bulbs that are 7 watts each are all plugged into one 120-volt circuit containing a 15-amp breaker. Will the breaker trip? The total wattage is $8 \cdot 25 \cdot 7$ or 1400 watts. Use $A = W/V$ to get $A = 1400/120 \approx 11.7$. So the lights will not blow a 15-amp fuse. See the accompanying figure.

While houses use standard single-phase electricity, electrical power companies may supply power for large users to transformers through three-phase lines. The power in a three-phase system is measured in volt-amps. The formula used here is volt-amps $= \sqrt{3} \cdot A \cdot V$. For example, suppose a large shopping mall has a 1,000,000 volt-amp transformer and the power company provides 25,000 volts to the mall's transformer. Will this power trip a 20-amp breaker? Because $A = \text{volt-amps}/(\sqrt{3} \cdot V)$, we have $A = 1{,}000{,}000/(\sqrt{3} \cdot 25{,}000) \approx$ 23.1 amps. So the 20-amp breaker will blow.

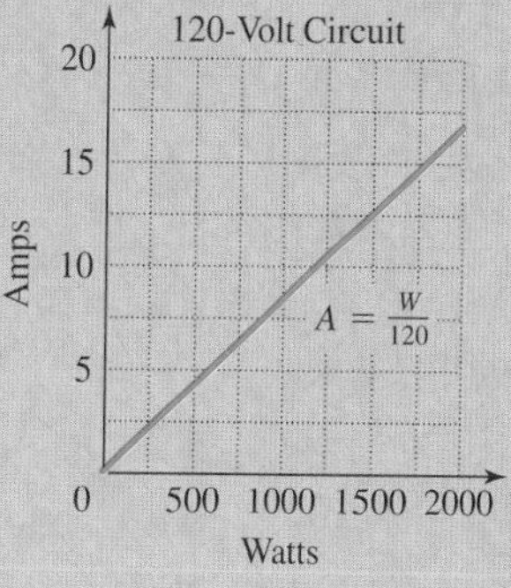

The strategy for solving an independent system by substitution can be summarized as follows.

Study Tip

When working a test, scan the problems and pick out the ones that are the easiest for you. Do them first. Save the harder problems until the last.

The Substitution Method

1. Solve one of the equations for one variable in terms of the other. Choose the equation that is easiest to solve for x or y.
2. Substitute into the other equation to get an equation in one variable.
3. Solve for the remaining variable (if possible).
4. Insert the value just found into one of the original equations to find the value of the other variable.
5. Check the two values in both equations.

Applications

Many of the problems that we solved in previous chapters involved more than one unknown quantity. To solve them, we wrote expressions for all of the unknowns in terms of one variable. Now we can solve problems involving two unknowns by using two variables and writing a system of equations.

EXAMPLE 7

Perimeter of a rectangle

The length of a rectangular swimming pool is twice the width. If the perimeter is 120 feet, then what are the length and width?

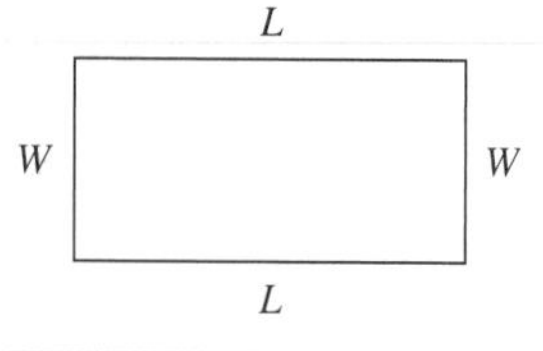

Figure 7.5

Solution

Draw a diagram as shown in Fig. 7.5. If L represents the length and W represents the width, then we can write the following system.

$$L = 2W$$
$$2L + 2W = 120$$

Since $L = 2W$, we can replace L in $2L + 2W = 120$ with $2W$:

$$2(2W) + 2W = 120$$
$$4W + 2W = 120$$
$$6W = 120$$
$$W = 20$$

So the width is 20 feet and the length is 2(20) or 40 feet.

Now do Exercises 63–74

EXAMPLE 8

Tale of two investments

Belinda had \$20,000 to invest. She invested part of it at 10% and the remainder at 12%. If her income from the two investments was \$2160, then how much did she invest at each rate?

Helpful Hint

In Chapter 2 we would have done Example 8 with one variable by letting x represent the amount invested at 10% and $20{,}000 - x$ represent the amount invested at 12%.

Solution

Let x be the amount invested at 10% and y be the amount invested at 12%. We can summarize all of the given information in a table:

	Amount	Rate	Interest
First investment	x	10%	$0.10x$
Second investment	y	12%	$0.12y$

Teaching Tip Note that the decimals could be eliminated by multiplying by 100.

We can write one equation about the amounts invested and another about the interest from the investments:

$$x + y = 20{,}000 \quad \text{Total amount invested}$$
$$0.10x + 0.12y = 2160 \quad \text{Total interest}$$

Calculator Close-Up

To check Example 8, graph

$$y_1 = 20{,}000 - x$$

and

$$y_2 = (2160 - 0.1x)/0.12.$$

The viewing window needs to be large enough to contain the point of intersection. Use the intersection feature to find the point of intersection.

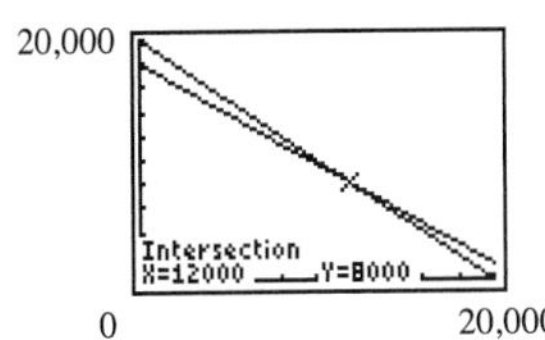

Solve the first equation for x to get $x = 20{,}000 - y$. Substitute $20{,}000 - y$ for x in the second equation:

$$0.10x + 0.12y = 2160$$
$$0.10(20{,}000 - y) + 0.12y = 2160 \quad \text{Replace } x \text{ by } 20{,}000 - y.$$
$$2000 - 0.10y + 0.12y = 2160 \quad \text{Solve for } y.$$
$$0.02y = 160$$
$$y = 8000$$
$$x = 12{,}000 \quad \text{Because } x = 20{,}000 - y$$

To check this answer, find 10% of \$12,000 and 12% of \$8000:

$$0.10(12{,}000) = 1200$$
$$0.12(8000) = 960$$

Because \$1200 + \$960 = \$2160 and \$8000 + \$12,000 = \$20,000, we can be certain that Belinda invested \$12,000 at 10% and \$8000 at 12%.

Now do Exercises 75–88

Warm-Ups 

True or false? Explain your answer.

1. The ordered pair (1, 2) is in the solution set to the equation $2x + y = 4$. True
2. The ordered pair (1, 2) satisfies $2x + y = 4$ and $3x - y = 6$. False
3. The ordered pair (2, 3) satisfies $4x - y = 5$ and $4x - y = -5$. False
4. If two distinct straight lines in the coordinate plane are not parallel, then they intersect in exactly one point. True
5. The substitution method is used to eliminate a variable. True
6. No ordered pair satisfies $y = 3x - 5$ and $y = 3x + 1$. True
7. The equations $y = 3x - 6$ and $y = 2x + 4$ are independent. True
8. The equations $y = 2x + 7$ and $y = 2x + 8$ are inconsistent. True
9. The graphs of dependent equations are the same. True
10. The graphs of independent linear equations intersect at exactly one point. True

7.1 Exercises

Boost your GRADE at mathzone.com!

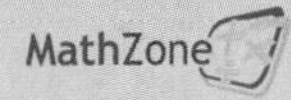

- Practice Problems
- Self-Tests
- Videos
- Net Tutor
- e-Professors

Reading and Writing *After reading this section, write out the answers to these questions. Use complete sentences.*

1. How do we solve a system of linear equations by graphing?
   The intersection point of the graphs is the solution to an independent system.

2. How can you determine whether a system has no solution by graphing?
The lines do not intersect if the system has no solution.
3. What is the major disadvantage to solving a system by graphing?
The graphing method can be very inaccurate.
4. How do we solve systems by substitution?
For substitution we eliminate a variable by substituting one equation into the other.
5. How can you identify an inconsistent system when solving by substitution?
If the equation you get after substituting turns out to be incorrect, such as $0 = 9$, then the system has no solution.
6. How can you identify a dependent system when solving by substitution?
If the substitution results in an identity, then the system is dependent.

Solve each system by graphing. See Examples 1–3.

7. $y = 2x$
$y = -x + 3$
$\{(1, 2)\}$

8. $y = x - 3$
$y = -x + 1$
$\{(2, -1)\}$

9. $y = 2x - 1$
$2y = x - 2$
$\{(0, -1)\}$

10. $y = 2x + 1$
$x + y = -2$
$\{(-1, -1)\}$

11. $y = x - 3$
$x - 2y = 4$
$\{(2, -1)\}$

12. $y = -3x$
$x + y = 2$
$\{(-1, 3)\}$

13. $2y - 2x = 2$
$2y - 2x = 6$
$\varnothing$

14. $3y - 3x = 9$
$x - y = 1$
$\varnothing$

15. $y = -\frac{1}{2}x + 4$
$x + 2y = 8$
$\{(x, y) \mid x + 2y = 8\}$

16. $2x - 3y = 6$
$y = \frac{2}{3}x - 2$
$\{(x, y) \mid 2x - 3y = 6\}$

17. $y = 2x + 4$
$3x + y = -1$
$\{(-1, 2)\}$

18. $3x - 2y = 6$
$3x + 2y = 6$
$\{(2, 0)\}$

19. $y = -\frac{1}{4}x$
$x + 4y = 8$
$\varnothing$

20. $y = -\frac{2}{3}x$
$2x + 3y = 5$
$\varnothing$

The graphs of the following systems are given in (a) through (d). Match each system with the correct graph.

21. $5x + 4y = 7$
$x - 3y = 9$
c

22. $3x - 5y = -9$
$5x - 6y = -8$
d

23. $4x - 5y = -2$
$3y - x = -3$
b

24. $4x + 5y = -2$
$4y - x = 11$
a

a)

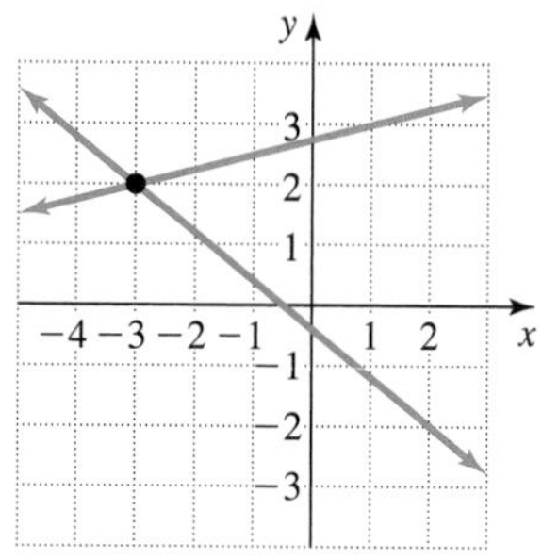

b)

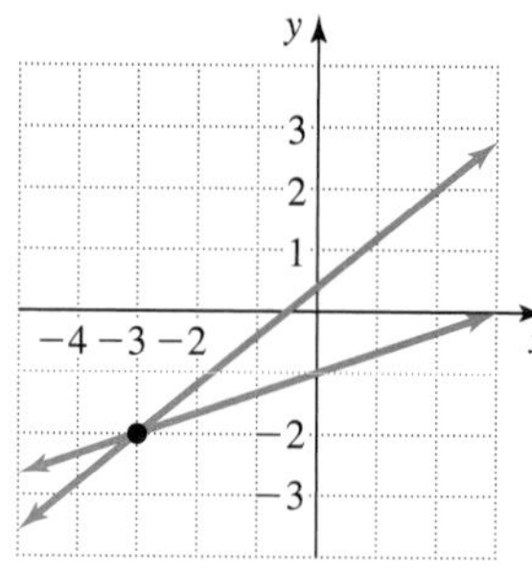

c)

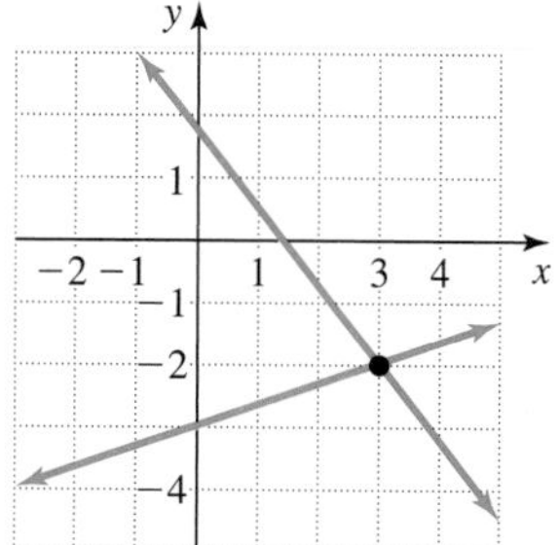

d)

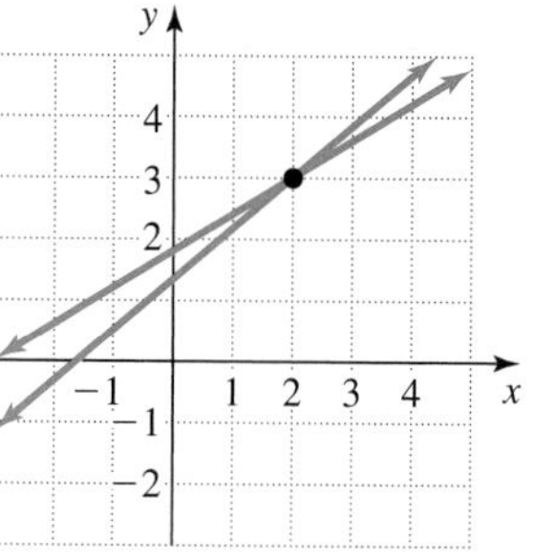

Solve each system by the substitution method. Determine whether the equations are independent, dependent, or inconsistent. See Examples 4–6.

25. $y = x - 5$
$2x - 5y = 1$
$\{(8, 3)\}$, independent

26. $y = x + 4$
$3y - 5x = 6$
$\{(3, 7)\}$, independent

27. $x = 2y - 7$
$3x + 2y = -5$
$\{(-3, 2)\}$, independent

28. $x = y + 3$
$3x - 2y = 4$
$\{(-2, -5)\}$, independent

29. $y = 2x - 30$
$\frac{1}{5}x - \frac{1}{2}y = -1$
$\{(20, 10)\}$, independent

30. $3x - 5y = 4$
$y = \frac{3}{4}x - 2$
$\{(8, 4)\}$, independent

31. $x - y = 5$
$2x = 2y + 14$
$\varnothing$, inconsistent

32. $2x - y = 4$
$2x - y = 3$
$\varnothing$, inconsistent

33. $y = 2x - 5$
$y + 1 = 2(x - 2)$
$\{(x, y) \mid y = 2x - 5\}$, dependent

34. $2x - y = 3$
$2y = 4x - 6$
$\{(x, y) \mid 2x - y = 3\}$, dependent

35. $2x + y = 9$
$2x - 5y = 15$
$\{(5, -1)\}$, independent

36. $3y - x = 0$
$x - 4y = -2$
$\{(6, 2)\}$, independent

37. $x - y = 0$
$2x + 3y = 35$
$\{(7, 7)\}$, independent

38. $2y = x + 6$
$-3x + 2y = -2$
$\{(4, 5)\}$, independent

39. $x + y = 40$
$0.2x + 0.8y = 23$
$\{(15, 25)\}$, independent

40. $x - y = 10$
$0.1x + 0.5y = 13$
$\{(30, 20)\}$, independent

41. $y = \frac{5}{7}x$
$x = -\frac{2}{3}y$
$\{(0, 0)\}$, independent

42. $7y = 9x$
$-3x = 4y$
$\{(0, 0)\}$, independent

43. $3(y - 1) = 2(x - 3)$
$3y - 2x = -3$
$\{(x, y) \mid 3y - 2x = -3\}$, dependent

44. $y = 3(x - 4)$
$3x - y = 12$
$\{(x, y) \mid 3x - y = 12\}$, dependent

45. $y = 3x$
$y = 3x + 1$
$\emptyset$, inconsistent

46. $y = 3x - 4$
$y = 3x + 4$
$\emptyset$, inconsistent

Solve each system by the substitution method.

47. $y = \frac{5}{2}x$
$x + 3y = 3$
$\left\{\left(\frac{6}{17}, \frac{15}{17}\right)\right\}$

48. $6x - 3y = 3$
$10x = y + 7$
$\left\{\left(\frac{3}{4}, \frac{1}{2}\right)\right\}$

49. $x + y = 4$
$x - y = 5$
$\left\{\left(\frac{9}{2}, -\frac{1}{2}\right)\right\}$

50. $3x - 6y = 5$
$2y = 4x - 6$
$\left\{\left(\frac{13}{9}, -\frac{1}{9}\right)\right\}$

51. $2x - 4y = 0$
$6x + 8y = 5$
$\left\{\left(\frac{1}{2}, \frac{1}{4}\right)\right\}$

52. $-3x + 10y = 4$
$6x - 5y = 1$
$\left\{\left(\frac{2}{3}, \frac{3}{5}\right)\right\}$

53. $3x + y = 2$
$-x - 3y = 6$
$\left\{\left(\frac{3}{2}, -\frac{5}{2}\right)\right\}$

54. $x + 3y = 2$
$-x + y = 1$
$\left\{\left(-\frac{1}{4}, \frac{3}{4}\right)\right\}$

55. $-9x + 6y = 3$
$18x + 30y = 1$
$\left\{\left(-\frac{2}{9}, \frac{1}{6}\right)\right\}$

56. $x + 6y = -2$
$5x - 20y = 5$
$\left\{\left(-\frac{1}{5}, -\frac{3}{10}\right)\right\}$

57. $y = -2x$
$3y - x = 1$
$\left\{\left(-\frac{1}{7}, \frac{2}{7}\right)\right\}$

58. $y = 2x$
$15x - 10y = -2$
$\left\{\left(\frac{2}{5}, \frac{4}{5}\right)\right\}$

59. $x = -6y + 1$
$2y = -5x$
$\left\{\left(-\frac{1}{14}, \frac{5}{28}\right)\right\}$

60. $x = -3y + 2$
$7y = 3x$
$\left\{\left(\frac{7}{8}, \frac{3}{8}\right)\right\}$

61. $x - y = 0.1$
$2x - 3y = -0.5$
$\{(0.8, 0.7)\}$

62. $y - 2x = -7.5$
$3x - 5y = 3.2$
$\{(4.9, 2.3)\}$

Write a system of two equations in two unknowns for each problem. Solve each system by substitution. See Examples 7 and 8.

63. ***Rectangular patio.*** The length of a rectangular patio is 12 feet greater than the width. If the perimeter is 84 feet, then what are the length and width? Length 27 ft, width 15 ft

64. ***Rectangular notepad.*** The length of a rectangular notepad is 2 cm longer than twice the width. If the perimeter is 34 cm, then what are the length and width? Length 12 cm, width 5 cm

65. ***Rectangular table.*** The width of a rectangular table is 1 ft less than half of the length. If the perimeter is 28 ft, then what are the length and width? Length 10 ft, width 4 ft

66. ***Rectangular painting.*** The width of a rectangular painting is two-thirds of its length. If the perimeter is 60 in., then what are the length and width? Length 18 in., width 12 in.

67. ***Sum and difference.*** The sum of two numbers is 10 and their difference is 3. Find the numbers. 3.5 and 6.5

68. ***Sum and difference.*** The sum of two numbers is 51 and their difference is 26. Find the numbers. 12.5 and 38.5

69. ***Sum and difference.*** The sum of two numbers is 1 and their difference is 20. Find the numbers. −9.5 and 10.5

70. ***Sum and difference.*** The sum of two numbers is 5 and their difference is 30. Find the numbers. 17.5 and −12.5

71. ***Flying to Vegas.*** Two hundred people were on a charter flight to Las Vegas. Some paid $200 for their tickets and some paid $250. If the total revenue for the flight was $44,000 then how many tickets of each type were sold? 120 tickets for $200, 80 tickets for $250

72. ***Annual concert.*** A total of 150 tickets were sold for the annual concert to students and nonstudents. Student tickets were $5 and nonstudent tickets were $8. If the total revenue for the concert was $930, then how many tickets of each type were sold? 90 tickets for $5, 60 tickets for $8

73. ***Annual play.*** There were twice as many tickets sold to nonstudents than to students for the annual play. Student tickets were $6 and nonstudent tickets were $11. If the total revenue for the play was $1540, then how many tickets of each type were sold? 55 tickets for $6, 110 tickets for $11

74. ***Soccer game.*** There were 1000 more students at the soccer game than nonstudents. Student tickets were $8.50 and nonstudent tickets were $13.25. If the total revenue for the game was $75,925, then how many tickets of each type were sold? 4100 tickets for $8.50, 3100 tickets for $13.25

75. ***Mixing investments.*** Helen invested $40,000 and received a total of $2300 in interest after one year. If part of the money returned 5% and the remainder 8%, then how much did she invest at each rate? $30,000 at 5%, $10,000 at 8%

76. ***Investing her bonus.*** Donna invested her $33,000 bonus and received a total of $970 in interest after one year. If part of the money returned 4% and the remainder 2.25%, then how much did she invest at each rate? $13,000 at 4%, $20,000 at 2.25%

77. ***Different interest rates.*** Mrs. Brighton invested \$30,000 and received a total of \$2300 in interest. If she invested part of the money at 10% and the remainder at 5%, then how much did she invest at each rate?
\$14,000 at 5%, \$16,000 at 10%

78. ***Different growth rates.*** The combined population of Marysville and Springfield was 25,000 in 1990. By 1995 the population of Marysville had increased by 10%, while Springfield had increased by 9%. If the total population increased by 2380 people, then what was the population of each city in 1990? Marysville 13,000, Springfield 12,000

79. ***Finding numbers.*** The sum of two numbers is 2, and their difference is 26. Find the numbers. -12 and 14

80. ***Finding more numbers.*** The sum of two numbers is -16, and their difference is 8. Find the numbers. -4 and -12

81. ***Toasters and vacations.*** During one week a land developer gave away Florida vacation coupons or toasters to 100 potential customers who listened to a sales presentation. It costs the developer \$6 for a toaster and \$24 for a Florida vacation coupon. If his bill for prizes that week was \$708, then how many of each prize did he give away?
94 toasters, 6 vacation coupons

82. ***Ticket sales.*** Tickets for a concert were sold to adults for \$3 and to students for \$2. If the total receipts were \$824 and twice as many adult tickets as student tickets were sold, then how many of each were sold?
103 student tickets, 206 adult tickets

83. ***Corporate taxes.*** According to Bruce Harrell, CPA, the amount of federal income tax for a class C corporation is deductible on the Louisiana state tax return, and the amount of state income tax for a class C corporation is deductible on the federal tax return. So for a state tax rate of 5% and a federal tax rate of 30%, we have

$$\text{state tax} = 0.05(\text{taxable income} - \text{federal tax})$$

and

$$\text{federal tax} = 0.30(\text{taxable income} - \text{state tax}).$$

Find the amounts of state and federal income taxes for a class C corporation that has a taxable income of \$100,000.
State tax \$3553, federal tax \$28,934

84. ***More taxes.*** Use the information given in Exercise 83 to find the amounts of state and federal income taxes for a class C corporation that has a taxable income of \$300,000. Use a state tax rate of 6% and a federal tax rate of 40%.
State tax \$11,066, federal tax \$115,574

85. ***Cost accounting.*** The problems presented in this exercise and the next are encountered in cost accounting. A company has agreed to distribute 20% of its net income N to its employees as a bonus; $B = 0.20N$. If the company has income of \$120,000 before the bonus, the bonus B is deducted from the \$120,000 as an expense to determine net income; $N = 120{,}000 - B$. Solve the system of two equations in N and B to find the amount of the bonus.
\$20,000

86. ***Bonus and taxes.*** A company has an income of \$100,000 before paying taxes and a bonus. The bonus B is to be 20% of the income after deducting income taxes T but before deducting the bonus. So

$$B = 0.20(100{,}000 - T).$$

Because the bonus is a deductible expense, the amount of income tax T at a 40% rate is 40% of the income after deducting the bonus. So

$$T = 0.40(100{,}000 - B).$$

a) Use the accompanying graph to estimate the values of T and B that satisfy both equations. (35,000, 15,000)

b) Solve the system algebraically to find the bonus and the amount of tax. Bonus \$13,043, taxes \$34,783

Figure for Exercise 86

87. ***Textbook case.*** The accompanying graph shows the cost of producing textbooks and the revenue from the sale of those textbooks.

a) What is the cost of producing 10,000 textbooks?

b) What is the revenue when 10,000 textbooks are sold?

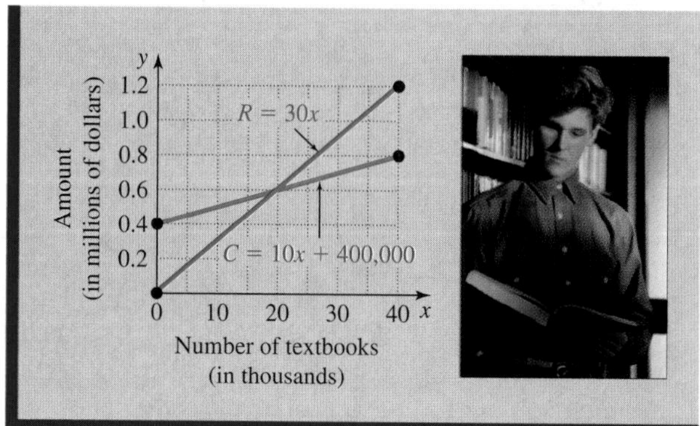

Figure for Exercise 87

c) For what number of textbooks is the cost equal to the revenue?

d) The cost of producing zero textbooks is called the *fixed cost*. Find the fixed cost.

a) \$500,000 b) \$300,000 c) 20,000 d) \$400,000

88. ***Free market.*** The function $S = 5000 + 200x$ and $D = 9500 - 100x$ express the supply S and the demand D, respectively, for a popular compact disc brand as a function of its price x (in dollars).

a) Graph the functions on the same coordinate system.

b) What happens to the supply as the price increases?

c) What happens to the demand as the price increases?

d) The price at which supply and demand are equal is called the *equilibrium price*. What is the equilibrium price?

a)

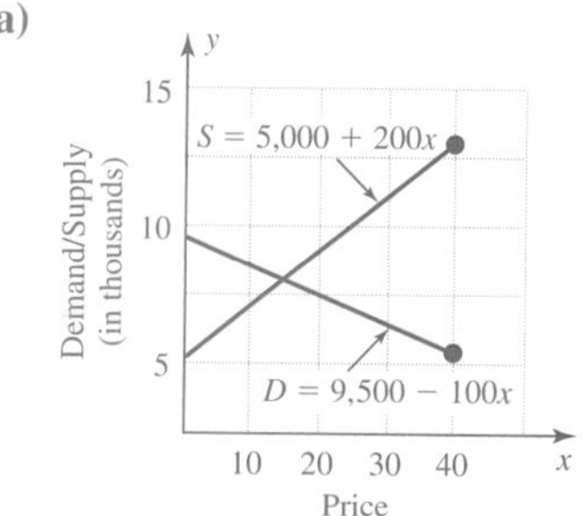

b) The supply increases.
c) The demand decreases.
d) Equilibrium price is \$15.

Getting More Involved

89. ***Discussion***

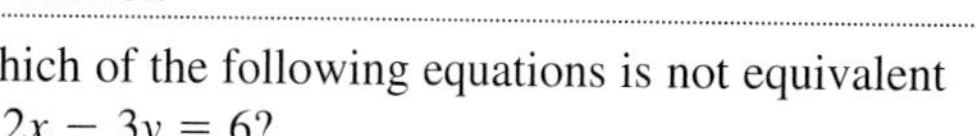

Which of the following equations is not equivalent to $2x - 3y = 6$?

a) $3y - 2x = 6$

b) $y = \frac{2}{3}x - 2$

c) $x = \frac{3}{2}y + 3$

d) $2(x - 5) = 3y - 4$ a

90. ***Discussion***

Which of the following equations is inconsistent with the equation $3x + 4y = 8$?

a) $y = \frac{3}{4}x + 2$

b) $6x + 8y = 16$

c) $y = -\frac{3}{4}x + 8$

d) $3x - 4y = 8$ c

Graphing Calculator Exercises

91. Solve each system by graphing each pair of equations on a graphing calculator and using the trace feature or intersect feature to estimate the point of intersection. Find the coordinates of the intersection to the nearest tenth.

a) $y = 3.5x - 7.2$
$y = -2.3x + 9.1$
(2.8, 2.6)

b) $2.3x - 4.1y = 3.3$
$3.4x + 9.2y = 1.3$
(1.0, −0.2)

7.2 The Addition Method

In this Section

- The Addition Method
- Equations Involving Fractions or Decimals
- Applications

In Section 7.1 you used substitution to eliminate a variable in a system of equations. In this section we see another method for eliminating a variable in a system of equations.

The Addition Method

In the **addition method** we eliminate a variable by adding the equations.

EXAMPLE 1

An independent system solved by addition

Solve the system by the addition method:

$$3x - 5y = -9$$
$$4x + 5y = 23$$

Calculator Close-Up

To check Example 1, graph

$$y_1 = (-9 - 3x)/-5$$

and

$$y_2 = (23 - 4x)/5.$$

Use the intersect feature to find the point of intersection of the two lines.

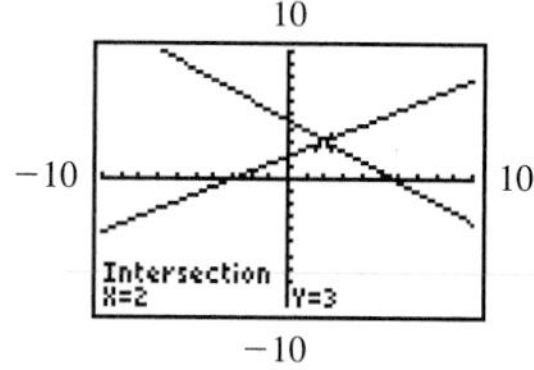

Solution

The addition property of equality allows us to add the same number to each side of an equation. We can also use the addition property of equality to add the two left sides and add the two right sides:

$$\begin{aligned} 3x - 5y &= -9 \\ 4x + 5y &= 23 \\ \hline 7x \qquad &= 14 \quad \text{Add.} \\ x &= 2 \end{aligned}$$

The y-term was eliminated when we added the equations because the coefficients of the y-terms were opposites. Now use $x = 2$ in one of the original equations to find y. It does not matter which original equation we use. In this example we will use both equations to see that we get the same y in either case.

$$\begin{aligned} 3x - 5y &= -9 \\ 3(2) - 5y &= -9 \quad \text{Replace } x \text{ by 2.} \\ 6 - 5y &= -9 \quad \text{Solve for } y. \\ -5y &= -15 \\ y &= 3 \end{aligned} \qquad \begin{aligned} 4x + 5y &= 23 \\ 4(2) + 5y &= 23 \\ 8 + 5y &= 23 \\ 5y &= 15 \\ y &= 3 \end{aligned}$$

Because $3(2) - 5(3) = -9$ and $4(2) + 5(3) = 23$ are both true, (2, 3) satisfies both equations. The solution set is $\{(2, 3)\}$.

Now do Exercises 7–12

Teaching Tip Have students practice writing dependent, inconsistent, and independent systems in slope-intercept form. Then do it in standard form.

Actually the addition method can be used to eliminate any variable whose coefficients are opposites. If neither variable has coefficients that are opposites, then we use the multiplication property of equality to change the coefficients of the variables, as shown in Examples 2 and 3.

EXAMPLE 2

Using multiplication and addition

Solve the system by the addition method:

$$\begin{aligned} 2x - 3y &= -13 \\ 5x - 12y &= -46 \end{aligned}$$

Solution

If we multiply both sides of the first equation by -4, the coefficients of y will be 12 and -12, and y will be eliminated by addition.

$$\begin{aligned} (-4)(2x - 3y) &= (-4)(-13) \quad \text{Multiply each side by } -4. \\ 5x - 12y &= -46 \end{aligned}$$

$$\begin{aligned} -8x + 12y &= 52 \\ 5x - 12y &= -46 \quad \text{Add.} \\ \hline -3x \qquad &= 6 \\ x &= -2 \end{aligned}$$

Study Tip

Keep on reviewing. After you have done your current assignment, go back a section or two and try a few problems. You will be amazed at how much your knowledge will improve with a regular review.

Replace x by -2 in one of the original equations to find y:

$$\begin{aligned} 2x - 3y &= -13 \\ 2(-2) - 3y &= -13 \\ -4 - 3y &= -13 \\ -3y &= -9 \\ y &= 3 \end{aligned}$$

Because $2(-2) - 3(3) = -13$ and $5(-2) - 12(3) = -46$ are both true, the solution set is $\{(-2, 3)\}$.

Now do Exercises 13–16

EXAMPLE 3

Multiplying both equations before adding

Solve the system by the addition method:

$$\begin{aligned} -2x + 3y &= 6 \\ 3x - 5y &= -11 \end{aligned}$$

Solution

To eliminate x, we multiply the first equation by 3 and the second by 2:

$$\begin{aligned} 3(-2x + 3y) &= 3(6) && \text{Multiply each side by 3.} \\ 2(3x - 5y) &= 2(-11) && \text{Multiply each side by 2.} \end{aligned}$$

$$\begin{aligned} -6x + 9y &= 18 \\ 6x - 10y &= -22 && \text{Add.} \\ \hline -y &= -4 \\ y &= 4 \end{aligned}$$

Note that we could have eliminated y by multiplying by 5 and 3. Now insert $y = 4$ into one of the original equations to find x:

$$\begin{aligned} -2x + 3(4) &= 6 && \text{Let } y = 4 \text{ in } -2x + 3y = 6. \\ -2x + 12 &= 6 \\ -2x &= -6 \\ x &= 3 \end{aligned}$$

Check that (3, 4) satisfies both equations. The solution set is $\{(3, 4)\}$.

Now do Exercises 17–22

Teaching Tip Emphasize the importance of writing every step and checking every step before proceeding to the next step. It is best to avoid early errors.

We can always use the addition method as long as the equations in a system are in the same form.

EXAMPLE 4

Using the addition method for an inconsistent system

Solve the system:

$$\begin{aligned} -4y &= 5x + 7 \\ 4y &= -5x + 12 \end{aligned}$$

Calculator Close-Up

To check Example 4, graph

$$y_1 = (5x + 7)/-4$$

and

$$y_2 = (-5x + 12)/4.$$

Since the lines appear to be parallel, the graph supports the conclusion that the system is inconsistent.

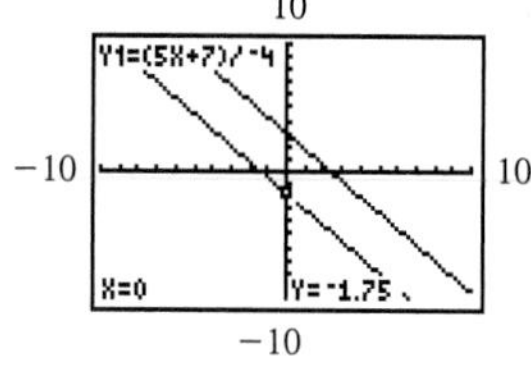

Solution

If these equations are added, both variables are eliminated:

$$\begin{aligned} -4y &= 5x + 7 \\ 4y &= -5x + 12 \\ \hline 0 &= 19 \end{aligned}$$

Because this equation is inconsistent, the original equations are inconsistent. The solution set to the system is the empty set, $\varnothing$.

Now do Exercises 23–28

Equations Involving Fractions or Decimals

When a system of equations involves fractions or decimals, we can use the multiplication property of equality to eliminate the fractions or decimals.

EXAMPLE 5

A system with fractions

Solve the system:

$$\frac{1}{2}x - \frac{2}{3}y = 7$$

$$\frac{2}{3}x - \frac{3}{4}y = 11$$

Calculator Close-Up

To check Example 5, graph

$$y_1 = (7 - (1/2)x)/(-2/3)$$

and

$$y_2 = (11 - (2/3)x)/(-3/4).$$

The lines appear to intersect at (30, 12).

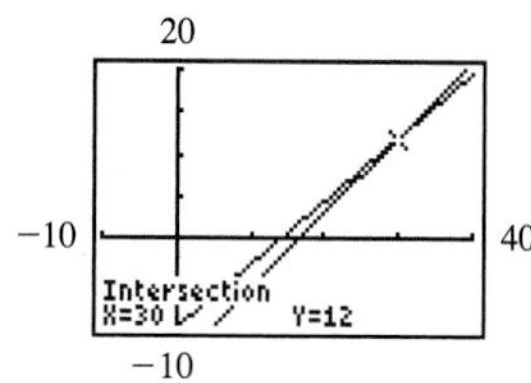

Solution

Multiply the first equation by 6 and the second equation by 12:

$$6\left(\frac{1}{2}x - \frac{2}{3}y\right) = 6(7) \quad \rightarrow \quad 3x - 4y = 42$$

$$12\left(\frac{2}{3}x - \frac{3}{4}y\right) = 12(11) \quad \rightarrow \quad 8x - 9y = 132$$

To eliminate x, multiply the first equation by -8 and the second by 3:

$$-8(3x - 4y) = -8(42) \quad \rightarrow \quad -24x + 32y = -336$$

$$3(8x - 9y) = 3(132) \quad \rightarrow \quad 24x - 27y = 396$$

$$\begin{aligned} 5y &= 60 \\ y &= 12 \end{aligned}$$

Substitute $y = 12$ into the first of the original equations:

$$\begin{aligned} \frac{1}{2}x - \frac{2}{3}(12) &= 7 \\ \frac{1}{2}x - 8 &= 7 \\ \frac{1}{2}x &= 15 \\ x &= 30 \end{aligned}$$

Check (30, 12) in the original system. The solution set is $\{(30, 12)\}$.

Now do Exercises 29–36

EXAMPLE 6

A system with decimals

Solve the system:

$$0.05x + 0.7y = 40$$
$$x + 0.4y = 120$$

Solution

Multiply the first equation by 100 and the second by 10 to eliminate the decimals:

$$100(0.05x + 0.7y) = 100(40) \quad \rightarrow \quad 5x + 70y = 4000$$
$$10(x + 0.4y) = 10(120) \quad \rightarrow \quad 10x + 4y = 1200$$

To eliminate x by addition, multiply the first equation by -2:

$$-2(5x + 70y) = -2(4000) \quad \rightarrow \quad -10x - 140y = -8000$$
$$10x + 4y = 1200 \quad \rightarrow \quad 10x + 4y = 1200$$
$$-136y = -6800$$
$$y = 50$$

Use $y = 50$ in $x + 0.4y = 120$ to find x:

$$x + 0.4(50) = 120$$
$$x + 20 = 120$$
$$x = 100$$

Check (100, 50) in the original system. The solution set is $\{(100, 50)\}$.

Now do Exercises 37–44

Teaching Tip Of course it is not necessary to eliminate decimals. Try multiplying the second equation by -0.05 and adding.

The strategy for solving an independent system by addition is summarized as follows.

The Addition Method

1. Write both equations in the same form (usually $Ax + By = C$).
2. Multiply one or both of the equations by appropriate numbers (if necessary) so that one of the variables will be eliminated by addition.
3. Add the equations to get an equation in one variable.
4. Solve the equation in one variable.
5. Substitute the value obtained for one variable into one of the original equations to obtain the value of the other variable.
6. Check the two values in both of the original equations.

Applications

Any system of two linear equations in two variables can be solved by either the addition method or substitution. In applications we use whichever method appears to be the simpler for the problem at hand.

EXAMPLE 7

Fajitas and burritos

At the Cactus Cafe the total price for four fajita dinners and three burrito dinners is \$48, and the total price for three fajita dinners and two burrito dinners is \$34. What is the price of each type of dinner?

Helpful Hint

You can see from Example 7 that the standard form $Ax + By = C$ occurs naturally in accounting. This form will occur whenever we have the price of each item and a quantity of two items and want to express the total cost.

Solution

Let x represent the price (in dollars) of a fajita dinner, and let y represent the price (in dollars) of a burrito dinner. We can write two equations to describe the given information:

$$4x + 3y = 48$$
$$3x + 2y = 34$$

Because 12 is the least common multiple of 4 and 3 (the coefficients of x), we multiply the first equation by -3 and the second by 4:

$$-3(4x + 3y) = -3(48) \quad \text{Multiply each side by } -3.$$
$$4(3x + 2y) = 4(34) \quad \text{Multiply each side by } 4.$$

$$-12x - 9y = -144$$
$$12x + 8y = 136 \quad \text{Add.}$$
$$-y = -8$$
$$y = 8$$

To find x, use $y = 8$ in the first equation $4x + 3y = 48$:

$$4x + 3(8) = 48$$
$$4x + 24 = 48$$
$$4x = 24$$
$$x = 6$$

So the fajita dinners are \$6 each, and the burrito dinners are \$8 each. Check this solution in the original problem.

Now do Exercises 63–68

EXAMPLE 8

Mixing cooking oil

Canola oil is 7% saturated fat, and corn oil is 14% saturated fat. Crisco sells a blend, Crisco Canola and Corn Oil, which is 11% saturated fat. How many gallons of each type of oil must be mixed to get 280 gallons of this blend?

Teaching Tip The word problems here are not really new. This is a good time to revisit some old ideas and situations and solve the equations by a new method.

Solution

Let x represent the number of gallons of canola oil, and let y represent the number of gallons of corn oil. Make a table to summarize all facts:

	Amount (gallons)	% fat	Amount of Fat (gallons)
Canola oil	x	7	$0.07x$
Corn oil	y	14	$0.14y$
Canola and Corn Oil	280	11	0.11(280) or 30.8

Teaching Tip Note that multiplying by 100 to eliminate all decimals might make this solution look rather complicated.

We can write two equations to express the following facts: (1) the total amount of oil is 280 gallons and (2) the total amount of fat is 30.8 gallons. Then we can use multiplication and addition to solve the system.

$$(1)\qquad x + y = 280 \qquad \text{Multiply by } -0.07.$$

$$(2)\qquad 0.07x + 0.14y = 30.80$$

$$\begin{aligned} -0.07x - 0.07y &= -19.6 \\ 0.07x + 0.14y &= 30.8 \\ \hline 0.07y &= 11.2 \\ y &= \frac{11.2}{0.07} = 160 \end{aligned}$$

If $y = 160$ and $x + y = 280$, then $x = 120$. Check that $0.07(120) + 0.14(160) = 30.8$. So it takes 120 gallons of canola oil and 160 gallons of corn oil to make 280 gallons of Crisco Canola and Corn Oil.

Now do Exercises 69–76

Study Tip

Play offensive math, not defensive math. A student who says, "Give me a question and I'll see if I can answer it," is playing defensive math. The student is taking a passive approach to learning. A student who takes an active approach and knows the usual questions and answers for each topic is playing offensive math.

Warm-Ups

True or false? Explain your answer.

Exercises 1–6 refer to the following systems.

a) $3x - y = 9$
$2x + y = 6$

b) $4x - 2y = 20$
$-2x + y = -10$

c) $x - y = 6$
$x - y = 7$

1. To solve system (a) by addition, we simply add the equations. True
2. To solve system (a) by addition, we can multiply the first equation by 2 and the second by 3 and then add. False
3. To solve system (b) by addition, we can multiply the second equation by 2 and then add. True
4. Both $(0, -10)$ and $(5, 0)$ are in the solution set to system (b). True
5. The solution set to system (b) is the set of all real numbers. False
6. System (c) has no solution. True
7. Both the addition method and substitution method are used to eliminate a variable from a system of two linear equations in two variables. True
8. For the addition method, both equations must be in standard form. False
9. To eliminate fractions in an equation, we multiply each side by the least common denominator of all fractions involved. True
10. We can eliminate either variable by using the addition method. True

7.2 Exercises

Boost your GRADE at mathzone.com!

MathZone
- Practice Problems
- Net Tutor
- Self-Tests
- e-Professors
- Videos

Reading and Writing *After reading this section, write out the answers to these questions. Use complete sentences.*

1. What method is presented in this section for solving a system of linear equations?
In this section we learned the addition method.

2. What are we trying to accomplish by adding the equations?
We try to eliminate a variable by adding the equations.

3. What must we sometimes do before we add the equations?
In some cases we multiply one or both of the equations on each side to change the coefficients of the variable that we are trying to eliminate.

4. How can you recognize an inconsistent system when solving by addition?
If a false equation, such as $3 = 4$, results from addition of the equations, then the equations are inconsistent.

5. How can you recognize a dependent system when solving by addition?
If an identity, such as $0 = 0$, results from addition of the equations, then the equations are dependent.

6. For which systems is the addition method easier to use than substitution?
Addition is usually easier to use when the equations are in the same form.

Solve each system by the addition method. See Examples 1–3.

7. $x + y = 7$
$x - y = 9$
$\{(8, -1)\}$

8. $3x - 4y = 11$
$-3x + 2y = -7$
$\{(1, -2)\}$

9. $x - y = 12$
$2x + y = 3$
$\{(5, -7)\}$

10. $x - 2y = -1$
$-x + 5y = 4$
$\{(1, 1)\}$

11. $3x - y = 5$
$5x + y = -2$
$\left\{\left(\frac{3}{8}, -\frac{31}{8}\right)\right\}$

12. $-x + 2y = 4$
$x - 5y = 1$
$\left\{\left(-\frac{22}{3}, -\frac{5}{3}\right)\right\}$

13. $2x - y = -5$
$3x + 2y = 3$
$\{(-1, 3)\}$

14. $3x + 5y = -11$
$x - 2y = 11$
$\{(3, -4)\}$

15. $-3x + 5y = 1$
$9x - 3y = 5$
$\left\{\left(\frac{7}{9}, \frac{2}{3}\right)\right\}$

16. $7x - 4y = -3$
$x + 2y = 3$
$\left\{\left(\frac{1}{3}, \frac{4}{3}\right)\right\}$

17. $2x - 5y = 13$
$3x + 4y = -15$
$\{(-1, -3)\}$

18. $3x + 4y = -5$
$5x + 6y = -7$
$\{(1, -2)\}$

19. $2x = 3y + 11$
$7x - 4y = 6$
$\{(-2, -5)\}$

20. $2x = 2 - y$
$3x + y = -1$
$\{(-3, 8)\}$

21. $x + y = 48$
$12x + 14y = 628$
$\{(22, 26)\}$

22. $x + y = 13$
$22x + 36y = 356$
$\{(8, 5)\}$

Solve each system by the addition method. Determine whether the equations are independent, dependent, or inconsistent. See Example 4.

23. $3x - 4y = 9$
$-3x + 4y = 12$
$\emptyset$, inconsistent

24. $x - y = 3$
$-6x + 6y = 17$
$\emptyset$, inconsistent

25. $5x - y = 1$
$10x - 2y = 2$
$\{(x, y) \mid 5x - y = 1\}$, dependent

26. $4x + 3y = 2$
$-12x - 9y = -6$
$\{(x, y) \mid 4x + 3y = 2\}$, dependent

27. $2x - y = 5$
$2x + y = 5$
$\left\{\left(\frac{5}{2}, 0\right)\right\}$, independent

28. $-3x + 2y = 8$
$3x + 2y = 8$
$\{(0, 4)\}$, independent

Solve each system by the addition method. See Examples 5 and 6.

29. $\frac{1}{4}x + \frac{1}{3}y = 5$
$x - y = 6$
$\{(12, 6)\}$

30. $\frac{3x}{2} - \frac{2y}{3} = 10$
$\frac{1}{2}x + \frac{1}{2}y = -1$
$\{(4, -6)\}$

31. $\frac{x}{4} - \frac{y}{3} = -4$
$\frac{x}{8} + \frac{y}{6} = 0$
$\{(-8, 6)\}$

32. $\frac{x}{3} - \frac{y}{2} = -\frac{5}{6}$
$\frac{x}{5} - \frac{y}{3} = -\frac{3}{5}$
$\{(2, 3)\}$

33. $\frac{1}{8}x + \frac{1}{4}y = 5$
$\frac{1}{16}x + \frac{1}{2}y = 7$
$\{(16, 12)\}$

34. $\frac{3}{7}x + \frac{5}{9}y = 27$
$\frac{1}{9}x + \frac{2}{7}y = 7$
$\{(63, 0)\}$

35. $\frac{1}{3}x + \frac{1}{2}y = \frac{1}{3}$
$\frac{5}{6}x - \frac{3}{4}y = \frac{1}{6}$
$\left\{\left(\frac{1}{2}, \frac{1}{3}\right)\right\}$

36. $\frac{2}{3}x + \frac{5}{6}y = \frac{1}{4}$
$\frac{1}{5}x - \frac{1}{10}y = -\frac{1}{10}$
$\left\{\left(-\frac{1}{4}, \frac{1}{2}\right)\right\}$

37. $0.05x + 0.10y = 1.30$
$x + y = 19$
$\{(12, 7)\}$

38. $0.1x + 0.06y = 9$
$0.09x + 0.5y = 52.7$
$\{(30, 100)\}$

39. $x + y = 1200$
$0.12x + 0.09y = 120$
$\{(400, 800)\}$

40. $x - y = 100$
$0.20x + 0.06y = 150$
$\{(600, 500)\}$

41. $1.5x - 2y = -0.25$
$3x + 1.5y = 6.375$
$\{(1.5, 1.25)\}$

42. $3x - 2.5y = 7.125$
$2.5x - 3y = 7.3125$
$\{(1.125, -1.5)\}$

43. $0.24x + 0.6y = 0.58$
$0.8x - 0.12y = 0.52$
$\left\{\left(\frac{3}{4}, \frac{2}{3}\right)\right\}$

44. $0.18x + 0.27y = 0.09$
$0.06x - 0.54y = -0.04$
$\left\{\left(\frac{1}{3}, \frac{1}{9}\right)\right\}$

Solve each system by substitution or addition, whichever is easier.

45. $y = x + 1$
$2x - 5y = -20$
$\{(5, 6)\}$

46. $y = 3x - 4$
$x + y = 32$
$\{(9, 23)\}$

47. $x - y = 19$
$2x + y = -13$
$\{(2, -17)\}$

48. $x + y = 3$
$7x - y = 29$
$\{(4, -1)\}$

49. $2y = x + 2$
$x = y - 1$
$\{(0, 1)\}$

50. $2y - x = 3$
$x = 3y - 5$
$\{(1, 2)\}$

51. $2y - 3x = -1$
$5y + 3x = 29$
$\{(3, 4)\}$

52. $y - 5 = 2x$
$y - 9 = -2x$
$\{(1, 7)\}$

53. $6x + 3y = 4$
$y = \frac{2}{3}x$
$\left\{\left(\frac{1}{2}, \frac{1}{3}\right)\right\}$

54. $3x - 2y = 2$
$x = \frac{2}{9}y$
$\left\{\left(-\frac{1}{3}, -\frac{3}{2}\right)\right\}$

55. $y = 3x + 1$
$x = \frac{1}{3}y + 5$
$\varnothing$

56. $y = -\frac{2}{3}x - 3$
$x = -\frac{3}{2}y + 9$
$\varnothing$

57. $x - y = 0$
$x + y = 2x$
$\{(x, y) \mid y = x\}$

58. $5x - 4y = 9$
$8y - 10x = -18$
$\{(x, y) \mid 5x - 4y = 9\}$

For each system find the value of a so that the solution set to the system is $\{(2, 3)\}$.

59. $x + y = 5$
$x - y = a$
$a = -1$

60. $2x - y = 1$
$ax + y = 13$
$a = 5$

For each system find the values of a and b so that the solution set to the system is $\{(5, 12)\}$.

61. $y = ax + 2$
$y = bx + 17$
$a = 2, b = -1$

62. $y = 3x + a$
$y = -2x + b$
$a = -3, b = 22$

Write a system of two equations in two unknowns for each problem. Solve each system by the method of your choice. See Examples 7 and 8.

63. ***Coffee and doughnuts.*** On Monday, Archie paid \$3.40 for three doughnuts and two coffees. On Tuesday he paid \$3.60 for two doughnuts and three coffees. On Wednesday he was tired of paying the tab and went out for coffee by himself. What was his bill for one doughnut and one coffee?
\$1.40

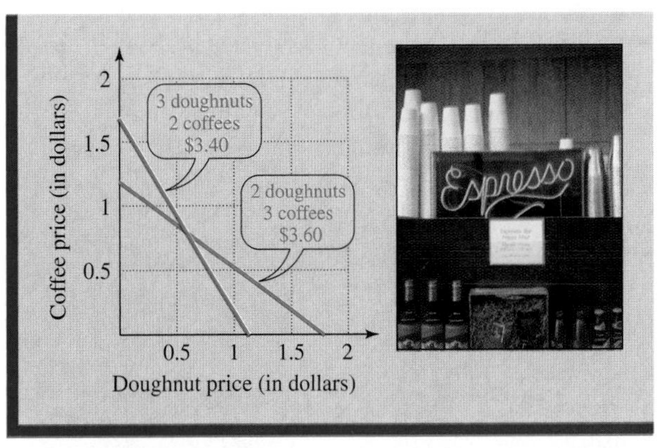

Figure for Exercise 63

64. ***Books and magazines.*** At Gwen's garage sale, all books were one price, and all magazines were another price. Harriet bought four books and three magazines for \$1.45, and June bought two books and five magazines for \$1.25. What was the price of a book and what was the price of a magazine?
Books \$0.25 each, magazines \$0.15 each

65. ***Boys and girls.*** One-half of the boys and one-third of the girls of Freemont High attended the homecoming game, whereas one-third of the boys and one-half of the girls attended the homecoming dance. If there were 570 students at the game and 580 at the dance, then how many students are there at Freemont High?
1380 students

66. ***Girls and boys.*** There are 385 surfers in Surf City. Two-thirds of the boys are surfers and one-twelfth of the girls are surfers. If there are two girls for every boy, then how many boys and how many girls are there in Surf City?
462 boys, 924 girls

67. ***Nickels and dimes.*** Winborne has 35 coins consisting of dimes and nickels. If the value of his coins is \$3.30, then how many of each type does he have?
31 dimes, 4 nickels

68. ***Pennies and nickels.*** Wendy has 52 coins consisting of nickels and pennies. If the value of the coins is \$1.20, then how many of each type does she have?
17 nickels, 35 pennies

69. ***Blending fudge.*** The Chocolate Factory in Vancouver blends its double-dark-chocolate fudge, which is 35% fat, with its peanut butter fudge, which is 25% fat, to obtain double-dark-peanut fudge, which is 29% fat.

a) Use the accompanying graph to estimate the number of pounds of each type that must be mixed to obtain 50 pounds of double-dark-peanut fudge.

b) Write a system of equations and solve it algebraically to find the exact amount of each type that should be used to obtain 50 pounds of double-dark-peanut fudge.

a) 20 pounds chocolate, 30 pounds peanut butter
b) 20 pounds chocolate, 30 pounds peanut butter

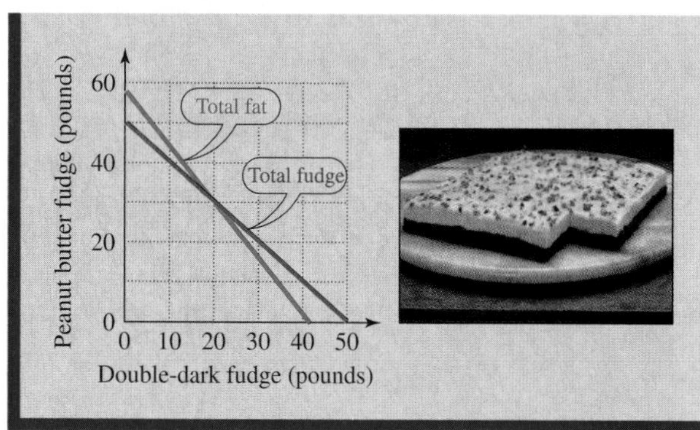

Figure for Exercise 69

70. ***Low-fat yogurt.*** Ziggy's Famous Yogurt blends regular yogurt that is 3% fat with its no-fat yogurt to obtain low-fat yogurt that is 1% fat. How many pounds of regular yogurt and how many pounds of no-fat yogurt should be mixed to obtain 60 pounds of low-fat yogurt?
20 pounds regular, 40 pounds no-fat

71. ***Keystone state.*** Judy averaged 42 miles per hour (mph) driving from Allentown to Harrisburg and 51 mph driving from Harrisburg to Pittsburgh. See the accompanying figure. If she drove a total of 288 miles in 6 hours, then how long did it take her to drive from Harrisburg to Pittsburgh? 4 hours

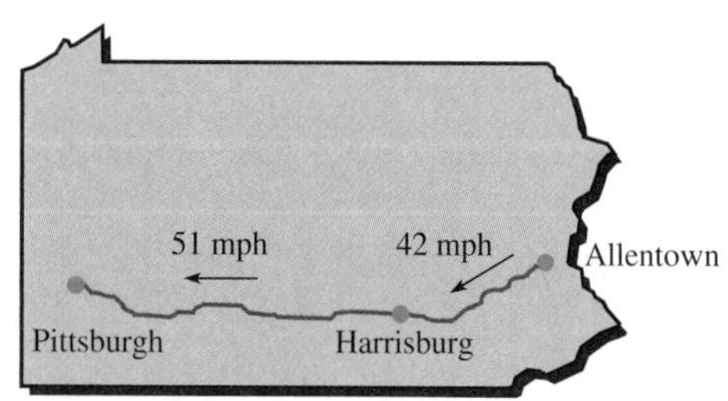

Figure for Exercise 71

72. ***Empire state.*** Spike averaged 45 mph driving from Rochester to Syracuse and 49 mph driving from Syracuse to Albany. If he drove a total of 237 miles in 5 hours, then how far is it from Syracuse to Albany? 147 miles

73. ***Probability of rain.*** The probability of rain tomorrow is four times the probability that it does not rain tomorrow. The probability that it rains plus the probability that it does not rain is 1. What is the probability that it rains tomorrow? 80%

74. ***Super Bowl contender.*** The probability that San Francisco plays in the next Super Bowl is nine times the probability that they do not play in the next Super Bowl. The probability that San Francisco plays in the next Super Bowl plus the probability that they do not play is 1. What is the probability that San Francisco plays in the next Super Bowl? 90%

75. ***Rectangular lot.*** The width of a rectangular lot is 75% of its length. If the perimeter is 700 meters, then what are the length and width? Width 150 meters, length 200 meters

76. ***Fence painting.*** Darren and Douglas must paint the 792-foot fence that encircles their family home. Because Darren is older, he has agreed to paint 20% more than Douglas. How much of the fence will each boy paint?
Darren 432 feet, Douglas 360 feet

Getting More Involved

77. ***Discussion***

Explain how you decide whether it is easier to solve a system by substitution or addition.

78. ***Exploration***

a) Write a linear equation in two variables that is satisfied by $(-3, 5)$.

b) Write another linear equation in two variables that is satisfied by $(-3, 5)$.

c) Are your equations independent or dependent?

d) Explain how to select the second equation so that it will be independent of the first.

79. ***Exploration***

a) Make up a system of two linear equations in two variables such that both $(-1, 2)$ and $(4, 5)$ are in the solution set.

b) Are your equations independent or dependent?

c) Is it possible to find an independent system that is satisfied by both ordered pairs? Explain.

7.3 Systems of Linear Equations in Three Variables

In this Section

- Definition
- Solving a System by Elimination
- Graphs of Equations in Three Variables
- Applications

The techniques that you learned in Section 7.2 can be extended to systems of equations in more than two variables. In this section we use elimination of variables to solve systems of equations in three variables.

Definition

The equation $5x - 4y = 7$ is called a linear equation in two variables because its graph is a straight line. The equation $2x + 3y - 4z = 12$ is similar in form, and so it is a linear equation in three variables. An equation in three variables is graphed in a three-dimensional coordinate system. The graph of a linear equation in three variables is a plane, not a line. We will not graph equations in three variables in this text, but we can solve systems without graphing. In general, we make the following definition.

Study Tip

Everyone knows that you must practice to be successful with musical instruments, foreign languages, and sports. Success in algebra also requires regular practice. Thus budget your time so that you have a regular practice period for algebra.

Linear Equation in Three Variables

If A, B, C, and D are real numbers, with A, B, and C not all zero, then

$$Ax + By + Cz = D$$

is called a **linear equation in three variables.**

Solving a System by Elimination

A solution to an equation in three variables is an **ordered triple** such as $(-2, 1, 5)$, where the first coordinate is the value of x, the second coordinate is the value of y, and the third coordinate is the value of z. There are infinitely many solutions to a linear equation in three variables.

The solution to a system of equations in three variables is the set of all ordered triples that satisfy all of the equations of the system. The techniques for solving a system of linear equations in three variables are similar to those used on systems of linear equations in two variables. We eliminate variables by either substitution or addition.

EXAMPLE 1

A linear system with a single solution

Solve the system:

$$\begin{aligned} (1) &\quad x + y - z = -1 \\ (2) &\quad 2x - 2y + 3z = 8 \\ (3) &\quad 2x - y + 2z = 9 \end{aligned}$$

Solution

We can eliminate y from Eqs. (1) and (2) by multiplying Eq. (1) by 2 and adding it to Eq. (2):

$$\begin{aligned} 2x + 2y - 2z &= -2 \quad \text{Eq. (1) multiplied by 2} \\ 2x - 2y + 3z &= 8 \quad \text{Eq. (2)} \\ (4) \quad 4x \qquad + z &= 6 \end{aligned}$$

Teaching Tip Students often have trouble checking their work in three variables. Encourage them to write notes about what they are doing as is done in the examples.

Now we must eliminate the same variable, y, from another pair of equations. Eliminate y from Eqs. (1) and (3) by simply adding them:

$$\begin{array}{rl} x + y - z = -1 & \text{Eq. (1)} \\ 2x - y + 2z = 9 & \text{Eq. (3)} \\ \hline (5) \quad 3x + z = 8 & \end{array}$$

Equations (4) and (5) give us a system with two variables. We now solve this system. Eliminate z by multiplying Eq. (4) by -1 and adding the equations:

$$\begin{array}{rl} -4x - z = -6 & \text{Eq. (4) multiplied by } -1 \\ 3x + z = 8 & \text{Eq. (5)} \\ \hline -x = 2 & \\ x = -2 & \end{array}$$

Calculator Close-Up

You can use a calculator to check that $(-2, 15, 14)$ satisfies all three equations of the original system.

```
-2+15-14
                 -1
2*-2-2*15+3*14
                  8
2*-2-15+2*14
                  9
```

Now that we have x, we can replace x by -2 in Eq. (5) to find y:

$$\begin{aligned} 3x + z &= 8 \quad \text{Eq. (5)} \\ 3(-2) + z &= 8 \\ -6 + z &= 8 \\ z &= 14 \end{aligned}$$

Now replace x by -2 and z by 14 in Eq. (1) to find y:

$$\begin{aligned} x + y - z &= -1 \quad \text{Eq. (1)} \\ -2 + y - 14 &= -1 \quad x = -2, z = 14 \\ y - 16 &= -1 \\ y &= 15 \end{aligned}$$

Check that $(-2, 15, 14)$ satisfies all three of the original equations. The solution set is $\{(-2, 15, 14)\}$.

Now do Exercises 7–10

Note that we could have eliminated any one of the three variables in Example 1 to get a system of two equations in two variables. We chose to eliminate y first because it was the easiest to eliminate. The strategy that we follow for solving a system of three linear equations in three variables is stated as follows:

Solving a System in Three Variables

1. Use substitution or addition to eliminate any one of the variables from a pair of equations of the system. Look for the easiest variable to eliminate.
2. Eliminate the same variable from another pair of equations of the system.
3. Solve the resulting system of two equations in two unknowns.
4. After you have found the values of two of the variables, substitute into one of the original equations to find the value of the third variable.
5. Check the three values in all of the original equations.

In Example 2 we use a combination of addition and substitution.

EXAMPLE 2

Using addition and substitution

Solve the system:

$$\begin{aligned}
(1)\quad & x + y \phantom{{}- 3z} = 4 \\
(2)\quad & 2x \phantom{{}+ y} - 3z = 14 \\
(3)\quad & \phantom{x+{}} 2y + z = 2
\end{aligned}$$

Helpful Hint

In Example 2 we chose to eliminate y first. Try solving Example 2 by first eliminating z. Write $z = 2 - 2y$ and then substitute $2 - 2y$ for z in Eqs. (1) and (2).

Solution

From Eq. (1) we get $y = 4 - x$. If we substitute $y = 4 - x$ into Eq. (3), then Eqs. (2) and (3) will be equations involving x and z only.

$$\begin{aligned}
(3)\qquad 2y + z &= 2 \\
2(4 - x) + z &= 2 && \text{Replace } y \text{ by } 4 - x. \\
8 - 2x + z &= 2 && \text{Simplify.} \\
(4)\qquad -2x + z &= -6
\end{aligned}$$

Now solve the system consisting of Eqs. (2) and (4) by addition:

$$\begin{aligned}
2x - 3z &= 14 && \text{Eq. (2)} \\
-2x + z &= -6 && \text{Eq. (4)} \\
\hline
-2z &= 8 \\
z &= -4
\end{aligned}$$

Use Eq. (3) to find y:

$$\begin{aligned}
2y + z &= 2 && \text{Eq. (3)} \\
2y + (-4) &= 2 && \text{Let } z = -4. \\
2y &= 6 \\
y &= 3
\end{aligned}$$

Use Eq. (1) to find x:

$$\begin{aligned}
x + y &= 4 && \text{Eq. (1)} \\
x + 3 &= 4 && \text{Let } y = 3. \\
x &= 1
\end{aligned}$$

Check that $(1, 3, -4)$ satisfies all three of the original equations. The solution set is $\{(1, 3, -4)\}$.

Now do Exercises 11–26

CAUTION In solving a system in three variables it is essential to keep your work organized and neat. Writing short notes that explain your steps (as was done in the examples) will allow you to go back and check your work.

Graphs of Equations in Three Variables

The graph of any equation in three variables can be drawn on a three-dimensional coordinate system. The graph of a linear equation in three variables is a plane. To solve a system of three linear equations in three variables by graphing, we would have to draw the three planes and then identify the points that lie on all three of them. This method would be difficult even when the points have simple coordinates. So we will not attempt to solve these systems by graphing.

Teaching Tip We have included some graphs here to show that there is some geometry behind these systems. Students are not asked to draw these graphs.

By considering how three planes might intersect, we can better understand the different types of solutions to a system of three equations in three variables. Figure 7.6 shows some of the possibilities for the positioning of three planes in three-dimensional space. In most of the problems that we will solve the planes intersect at a single point as in Fig. 7.6(a). The solution set consists of one ordered triple. However, the system may include two equations corresponding to parallel planes that have no intersection. In this case the equations are said to be **inconsistent.** If the system has at least two inconsistent equations, then the solution set is the empty set [see Figs. 7.6(b) and 7.6(c)].

There are two ways in which the intersection of three planes can consist of infinitely many points. The intersection could be a line or a plane. To get a line, we can have either three different planes intersecting along a line, as in Fig. 7.6(d) or two equations for the same plane, with the third plane intersecting that plane. If all three equations are equations of the same plane, we get that plane for the intersection. We will not solve systems corresponding to all of the possible configurations described. The following examples illustrate two of these cases.

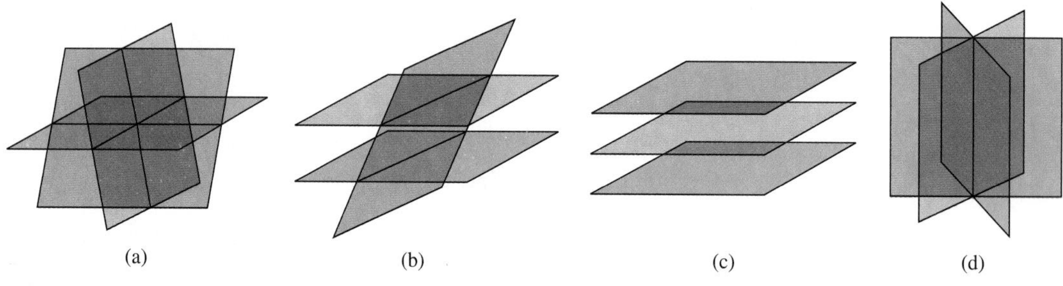

Figure 7.6

EXAMPLE 3

An inconsistent system of three linear equations

Solve the system:

$$\begin{aligned} (1)\quad & x + y - z = 5 \\ (2)\quad & 3x - 2y + z = 8 \\ (3)\quad & 2x + 2y - 2z = 7 \end{aligned}$$

Solution

We can eliminate the variable z from Eqs. (1) and (2) by adding them:

$$\begin{array}{rl} x + y - z = 5 & \text{Eq. (1)} \\ 3x - 2y + z = 8 & \text{Eq. (2)} \\ \hline 4x - y \quad = 13 & \end{array}$$

To eliminate z from Eqs. (1) and (3), multiply Eq. (1) by -2 and add the resulting equation to Eq. (3):

$$\begin{array}{rl} -2x - 2y + 2z = -10 & \text{Eq. (1) multiplied by } -2 \\ 2x + 2y - 2z = 7 & \text{Eq. (3)} \\ \hline 0 = -3 & \end{array}$$

Because the last equation is false, there are two inconsistent equations in the system. Therefore the solution set is the empty set.

Now do Exercises 27–28

EXAMPLE 4

A dependent system of three equations

Solve the system:

$$\begin{aligned} (1)\quad 2x - 3y - z &= 4 \\ (2)\quad -6x + 9y + 3z &= -12 \\ (3)\quad 4x - 6y - 2z &= 8 \end{aligned}$$

Helpful Hint

If you recognize that multiplying Eq. (1) by −3 will produce Eq. (2), and multiplying Eq. (1) by 2 will produce Eq. (3), then you can conclude that all three equations are equivalent and there is no need to add the equations.

Solution

We will first eliminate x from Eqs. (1) and (2). Multiply Eq. (1) by 3 and add the resulting equation to Eq. (2):

$$\begin{aligned} 6x - 9y - 3z &= 12 \quad \text{Eq. (1) multiplied by 3} \\ -6x + 9y + 3z &= -12 \quad \text{Eq. (2)} \\ \hline 0 &= 0 \end{aligned}$$

The last statement is an identity. The identity occurred because Eq. (2) is a multiple of Eq. (1). In fact, Eq. (3) is also a multiple of Eq. (1). These equations are dependent. They are all equations for the same plane. The solution set is the set of all points on that plane,

$$\{(x, y, z) \mid 2x - 3y - z = 4\}.$$

Now do Exercises 29–38

Applications

Problems involving three unknown quantities can often be solved by using a system of three equations in three variables.

EXAMPLE 5

Finding three unknown rents

Theresa took in a total of \$1240 last week from the rental of three condominiums. She had to pay 10% of the rent from the one-bedroom condo for repairs, 20% of the rent from the two-bedroom condo for repairs, and 30% of the rent from the three-bedroom condo for repairs. If the three-bedroom condo rents for twice as much as the one-bedroom condo and her total repair bill was \$276, then what is the rent for each condo?

Helpful Hint

A problem involving two unknowns can often be solved with one variable as in Chapter 2. Likewise, you can often solve a problem with three unknowns using only two variables. Solve Example 5 by letting a, b, and $2a$ be the rent for a one-bedroom, two-bedroom, and a three-bedroom condo.

Solution

Let x, y, and z represent the rent on the one-bedroom, two-bedroom, and three-bedroom condos, respectively. We can write one equation for the total rent, another equation for the total repairs, and a third equation expressing the fact that the rent for the three-bedroom condo is twice that for the one-bedroom condo:

$$\begin{aligned} x + y + z &= 1240 \\ 0.1x + 0.2y + 0.3z &= 276 \\ z &= 2x \end{aligned}$$

Substitute $z = 2x$ into both of the other equations to eliminate z:

$$x + y + 2x = 1240$$
$$0.1x + 0.2y + 0.3(2x) = 276$$

$$3x + y = 1240$$
$$0.7x + 0.2y = 276$$

$$-2(3x + y) = -2(1240) \quad \text{Multiply each side by } -2.$$
$$10(0.7x + 0.2y) = 10(276) \quad \text{Multiply each side by 10.}$$

$$-6x - 2y = -2480$$
$$7x + 2y = 2760 \quad \text{Add.}$$
$$x = 280$$

$$z = 2(280) = 560 \quad \text{Because } z = 2x$$
$$280 + y + 560 = 1240 \quad \text{Because } x + y + z = 1240$$
$$y = 400$$

Check that (280, 400, 560) satisfies all three of the original equations. The condos rent for \$280, \$400, and \$560 per week.

Now do Exercises 41–54

Warm-Ups 

True or false? Explain your answer.

1. The point $(1, -2, 3)$ is in the solution set to the equation $x + y - z = 4$. False
2. The point $(4, 1, 1)$ is the only solution to the equation $x + y - z = 4$. False
3. The ordered triple $(1, -1, 2)$ satisfies $x + y + z = 2$, $x - y - z = 0$, and $2x + y - z = -1$. True
4. Substitution cannot be used on three equations in three variables. False
5. Two distinct planes are either parallel or intersect in a single point. False
6. The equations $x - y + 2z = 6$ and $x - y + 2z = 4$ are inconsistent. True
7. The equations $3x + 2y - 6z = 4$ and $-6x - 4y + 12z = -8$ are dependent. True
8. The graph of $y = 2x - 3z + 4$ is a straight line. False
9. The value of x nickels, y dimes, and z quarters is $0.05x + 0.10y + 0.25z$ cents. False
10. If $x = -2$, $z = 3$, and $x + y + z = 6$, then $y = 7$. False

7.3 Exercises

Boost your GRADE at mathzone.com!

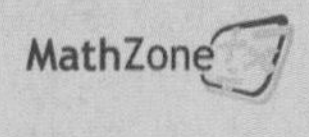

- Practice Problems
- Self-Tests
- Videos
- Net Tutor
- e-Professors

Reading and Writing *After reading this section, write out the answers to these questions. Use complete sentences.*

1. What is a linear equation in three variables?
   A linear equation in three variables is an equation of the form $Ax + By + Cz = D$ where A, B, and C cannot all be zero.

2. What is an ordered triple?
An ordered triple is a collection of three numbers [written as (a, b, c)] in which the order of the numbers is important.

3. What is a solution to a system of linear equations in three variables?
A solution to a system of linear equations in three variables is an ordered triple that satisfies all of the equations in the system.

4. How do we solve systems of linear equations in three variables?
We solve systems in three variables by using addition or substitution to eliminate variables.

5. What does the graph of a linear equation in three variables look like?
The graph of a linear equation in three variables is a plane in a three-dimensional coordinate system.

6. How are the planes positioned when a system of linear equations in three variables is inconsistent?
For an inconsistent system at least two of the planes are parallel.

Solve each system of equations. See Examples 1 and 2.

7. $x + y + z = 9$, $y + z = 7$, $z = 4$
$\{(2, 3, 4)\}$

8. $x + y - z = 4$, $y = 6$, $y + z = 13$
$\{(5, 6, 7)\}$

9. $x + y + z = 10$, $x - y = -1$, $x + y = 5$
$\{(2, 3, 5)\}$

10. $x + y - z = 6$, $y + z = 11$, $y - z = 3$
$\{(3, 7, 4)\}$

11. $x + y + z = 6$, $x - y + z = 2$, $x - y - z = -4$
$\{(1, 2, 3)\}$

12. $x + y + z = 0$, $x + y - z = 2$, $x - y + z = 0$
$\{(1, 0, -1)\}$

13. $x + y + z = 2$, $x + 2y - z = 6$, $2x + y - z = 5$
$\{(1, 2, -1)\}$

14. $2x - y + 3z = 14$, $x + y - 2z = -5$, $3x + y - z = 2$
$\{(2, -1, 3)\}$

15. $x - 2y + 4z = 3$, $x + 3y - 2z = 6$, $x - 4y + 3z = -5$
$\{(1, 3, 2)\}$

16. $2x + 3y + z = 13$, $-3x + 2y + z = -4$, $4x - 4y + z = 5$
$\{(3, 2, 1)\}$

17. $2x - y + z = 10$, $3x - 2y - 2z = 7$, $x - 3y - 2z = 10$
$\{(1, -5, 3)\}$

18. $x - 3y + 2z = -11$, $2x - 4y + 3z = -15$, $3x - 5y - 4z = 5$
$\{(1, 2, -3)\}$

19. $2x - 3y + z = -9$, $-2x + y - 3z = 7$, $x - y + 2z = -5$
$\{(-1, 2, -1)\}$

20. $3x - 4y + z = 19$, $2x + 4y + z = 0$, $x - 2y + 5z = 17$
$\{(3, -2, 2)\}$

21. $2x - 5y + 2z = 16$, $3x + 2y - 3z = -19$, $4x - 3y + 4z = 18$
$\{(-1, -2, 4)\}$

22. $-2x + 3y - 4z = 3$, $3x - 5y + 2z = 4$, $-4x + 2y - 3z = 0$
$\{(1, -1, -2)\}$

23. $x + y = 4$, $y - z = -2$, $x + y + z = 9$
$\{(1, 3, 5)\}$

24. $x + y - z = 0$, $x - y = -2$, $y + z = 10$
$\{(2, 4, 6)\}$

25. $x + y = 7$, $y - z = -1$, $x + 3z = 18$
$\{(3, 4, 5)\}$

26. $2x - y = -8$, $y + 3z = 22$, $x - z = -8$
$\{(-2, 4, 6)\}$

Solve each system. See Examples 3 and 4.

27. $x + y + z = 9$, $x + y = 5$, $z = 1$
$\varnothing$

28. $x - y + z = 2$, $y - z = 3$, $x = 4$
$\varnothing$

29. $x + y - z = 2$, $-x - y + z = -2$, $2x + 2y - 2z = 4$
$\{(x, y, z) \mid x + y - z = 2\}$

30. $x + y + z = 1$, $2x + 2y + 2z = 2$, $4x + 4y + 4z = 4$
$\{(x, y, x) \mid x + y + z = 1\}$

31. $x - y + 2z = 3$, $2x + y - z = 5$, $3x - 3y + 6z = 4$ $\varnothing$

32. $4x - 2y - 2z = 5$, $2x - y - z = 7$, $-4x + 2y + 2z = 6$ $\varnothing$

33. $2x - 4y + 6z = 12$, $6x - 12y + 18z = 36$, $-x + 2y - 3z = -6$
$\{(x, y, z) \mid -x + 2y - 3z = -6\}$

34. $3x - y + z = 5$, $9x - 3y + 3z = 15$, $-12x + 4y - 4z = -20$
$\{(x, y, z) \mid 3x - y + z = 5\}$

35. $x - y = 3$, $y + z = 8$, $2x + 2z = 7$ $\varnothing$

36. $2x - y = 6$, $2y + z = -4$, $8x + 2z = 3$ $\varnothing$

37. $0.10x + 0.08y - 0.04z = 3$, $5x + 4y - 2z = 150$, $0.3x + 0.24y - 0.12z = 9$
$\{(x, y, z) \mid 5x + 4y - 2z = 150\}$

38. $0.06x - 0.04y + z = 6$, $3x - 2y + 50z = 300$, $0.03x - 0.02y + 0.5z = 3$
$\{(x, y, z) \mid 3x - 2y + 50z = 300\}$

Use a calculator to solve each system.

39. $3x + 2y - 0.4z = 0.1$
$3.7x - 0.2y + 0.05z = 0.41$
$-2x + 3.8y - 2.1z = -3.26$ $\{(0.1, 0.3, 2)\}$

40. $3x - 0.4y + 9z = 1.668$
$0.3x + 5y - 8z = -0.972$
$5x - 4y - 8z = 1.8$ $\{(0.36, -0.12, 0.06)\}$

Solve each problem by using a system of three equations in three unknowns. See Example 5.

41. ***Three cars.*** The town of Springfield purchased a Chevrolet, a Ford, and a Toyota for a total of \$66,000. The Ford was \$2,000 more than the Chevrolet and the Toyota was \$2,000 more than the Ford. What was the price of each car? Chevrolet \$20,000, Ford \$22,000, Toyota \$24,000

42. ***Buying texts.*** Melissa purchased an English text, a math text, and a chemistry text for a total of \$276. The English text was \$20 more than the math text and the chemistry text was twice the price of the math text. What was the price of each text?
English \$84, math \$64, chemistry \$128

43. ***Three-day drive.*** In three days, Carter drove 2196 miles in 36 hours behind the wheel. The first day he averaged 64 mph, the second day 62 mph, and the third day 58 mph. If he drove 4 more hours on the third day than on the first day, then how many hours did he drive each day?
First 10 hr, second 12 hr, third 14 hr

44. ***Three-day trip.*** In three days, Katy traveled 146 miles down the Mississippi River in her kayak with 30 hours of paddling. The first day she averaged 6 mph, the second day 5 mph, and the third day 4 mph. If her distance on the third day was equal to her distance on the first day, then for how many hours did she paddle each day?
First 8 hr, second 10 hr, third 12 hr

45. ***Diversification.*** Ann invested a total of \$12,000 in stocks, bonds, and a mutual fund. She received a 10% return on her stock investment, an 8% return on her bond investment, and a 12% return on her mutual fund. Her total return was \$1,230. If the total investment in stocks and bonds equaled her mutual fund investment, then how much did she invest in each?
\$1500 stocks, \$4500 bonds, \$6000 mutual fund

46. ***Paranoia.*** Fearful of a bank failure, Norman split his life savings of \$60,000 among three banks. He received 5%, 6%, and 7% on the three deposits. In the account earning 7% interest, he deposited twice as much as in the account earning 5% interest. If his total earnings were \$3,760, then how much did he deposit in each account?
\$16,000 at 5%, \$12,000 at 6%, \$32,000 at 7%

47. ***Weighing in.*** Anna, Bob, and Chris will not disclose their weights but agree to be weighed in pairs. Anna and Bob together weigh 226 pounds. Bob and Chris together weigh 210 pounds. Anna and Chris together weigh 200 pounds. How much does each student weigh?
Anna 108 pounds, Bob 118 pounds, Chris 92 pounds

Figure for exercise 47

48. ***Big tipper.*** On Monday Headley paid \$1.70 for two cups of coffee and one doughnut, including the tip. On Tuesday he paid \$1.65 for two doughnuts and a cup of coffee, including the tip. On Wednesday he paid \$1.30 for one coffee and one doughnut, including the tip. If he always tips the same amount, then what is the amount of each item? Coffee \$0.40, doughnut \$0.35, tip \$0.55

49. ***Three coins.*** Nelson paid \$1.75 for his lunch with 13 coins, consisting of nickels, dimes, and quarters. If the number of dimes was twice the number of nickels, then how many of each type of coin did he use?
3 nickels, 6 dimes, 4 quarters

50. ***Pocket change.*** Harry has \$2.25 in nickels, dimes, and quarters. If he had twice as many nickels, half as many dimes, and the same number of quarters, he would have \$2.50. If he has 27 coins altogether, then how many of each does he have? 15 nickels, 10 dimes, 2 quarters

51. ***Working overtime.*** To make ends meet, Ms. Farnsby works three jobs. Her total income last year was \$48,000. Her income from teaching was just \$6000 more than her income from house painting. Royalties from her textbook sales were one-seventh of the total money she received from teaching and house painting. How much did she make from each source last year?
\$24,000 teaching, \$18,000 painting, \$6000 royalties

52. ***Lunch-box special.*** Salvador's Fruit Mart sells variety packs. The small pack contains three bananas, two apples, and one orange for \$1.80. The medium pack contains four bananas, three apples, and three oranges for \$3.05. The family size contains six bananas, five apples, and four oranges for \$4.65. What price should Salvador charge for his lunch-box special that consists of one banana, one apple, and one orange? \$0.95

53. ***Three generations.*** Edwin, his father, and his grandfather have an average age of 53. One-half of his grandfather's age, plus one-third of his father's age, plus one-fourth of Edwin's age is 65. If 4 years ago, Edwin's grandfather was four times as old as Edwin, then how old are they all now? Edwin 24, father 51, grandfather 84

54. ***Three-digit number.*** The sum of the digits of a three-digit number is 11. If the digits are reversed, the new number is 46 more than five times the old number. If the hundreds digit plus twice the tens digit is equal to the units digit, then what is the number? 137

Getting More Involved

55. ***Exploration***

Draw diagrams showing the possible ways to position three planes in three-dimensional space.

56. ***Discussion***

Make up a system of three linear equations in three variables for which the solution set is $\{(0, 0, 0)\}$. A system with this solution set is called a *homogeneous* system. Why do you think it is given that name?

7.4 Solving Linear Systems Using Matrices

In this Section

- Matrices
- The Augmented Matrix
- The Gauss-Jordan Elimination Method
- Inconsistent and Dependent Equations

You solved linear systems in two variables by substitution and addition in Sections 7.1 and 7.2. Those methods are done differently on each system. In this section you will learn the Gauss-Jordan elimination method, which is related to the addition method. The Gauss-Jordan elimination method is performed in the same way on every system. We first need to introduce some new terminology.

Matrices

A **matrix** is a rectangular array of numbers enclosed in brackets. The **rows** of a matrix run horizontally, and the **columns** of a matrix run vertically. A matrix with m rows and n columns has **size** $m \times n$ (read "m by n"). Each number in a matrix is called an **element** or **entry** of the matrix.

EXAMPLE 1

Size of a matrix

Determine the size of each matrix.

a) $\begin{bmatrix} -1 & 2 \\ 5 & \sqrt{2} \\ 0 & 3 \end{bmatrix}$ **b)** $\begin{bmatrix} 2 & 3 \\ -1 & 5 \end{bmatrix}$

c) $\begin{bmatrix} 1 & 2 & 3 \\ 4 & 5 & 6 \\ -1 & 0 & 2 \end{bmatrix}$ **d)** $\begin{bmatrix} 1 & 3 & 6 \end{bmatrix}$

Solution

Because matrix (a) has 3 rows and 2 columns, its size is 3×2. Matrix (b) is a 2×2 matrix, matrix (c) is a 3×3 matrix, and matrix (d) is a 1×3 matrix.

Now do Exercises 7–12

Study Tip

As soon as possible after class, find a quiet place and work on your homework. The longer you wait, the harder it is to remember what happened in class.

The Augmented Matrix

The solution to a system of linear equations such as

$$\begin{aligned} x - 2y &= -5 \\ 3x + y &= 6 \end{aligned}$$

depends on the coefficients of x and y and the constants on the right-hand side of the equation. The matrix of coefficients for this system is the 2×2 matrix

$$\begin{bmatrix} 1 & -2 \\ 3 & 1 \end{bmatrix}.$$

If we insert the constants from the right-hand side of the system into the matrix of coefficients, we get the 2×3 matrix

$$\left[\begin{array}{cc|c} 1 & -2 & -5 \\ 3 & 1 & 6 \end{array}\right].$$

We use a vertical line between the coefficients and the constants to represent the equal signs. This matrix is the **augmented matrix** of the system. Two systems of linear equations are **equivalent** if they have the same solution set. Two augmented matrices are **equivalent** if the systems they represent are equivalent.

EXAMPLE 2

Writing the augmented matrix

Write the augmented matrix for each system of equations.

a) $\begin{aligned} 3x - 5y &= 7 \\ x + y &= 4 \end{aligned}$

b) $\begin{aligned} x + y - z &= 5 \\ 2x + z &= 3 \\ 2x - y + 4z &= 0 \end{aligned}$

c) $\begin{aligned} x + y &= 1 \\ y + z &= 6 \\ z &= -5 \end{aligned}$

Solution

a) $\left[\begin{array}{cc|c} 3 & -5 & 7 \\ 1 & 1 & 4 \end{array}\right]$

b) $\left[\begin{array}{ccc|c} 1 & 1 & -1 & 5 \\ 2 & 0 & 1 & 3 \\ 2 & -1 & 4 & 0 \end{array}\right]$

c) $\left[\begin{array}{ccc|c} 1 & 1 & 0 & 1 \\ 0 & 1 & 1 & 6 \\ 0 & 0 & 1 & -5 \end{array}\right]$

Now do Exercises 13–16

EXAMPLE 3

Writing the system

Write the system of equations represented by each augmented matrix.

a) $\left[\begin{array}{cc|c} 1 & 4 & -2 \\ 1 & -1 & 3 \end{array}\right]$

b) $\left[\begin{array}{cc|c} 1 & 0 & 5 \\ 0 & 1 & 1 \end{array}\right]$

c) $\left[\begin{array}{ccc|c} 2 & 3 & 4 & 6 \\ -1 & 0 & 5 & -2 \\ 1 & -2 & 3 & 1 \end{array}\right]$

Solution

a) Use the first two numbers in each row as the coefficients of x and y and the last number as the constant to get the following system:

$$\begin{aligned} x + 4y &= -2 \\ x - y &= 3 \end{aligned}$$

Study Tip

Relax and don't worry about grades. If you are doing everything you can and should be doing, then there is no reason to worry. If you are neglecting your homework and skipping class, then you should be worried.

b) Use the first two numbers in each row as the coefficients of x and y and the last number as the constant to get the following system:

$$x = 5$$
$$y = 1$$

c) Use the first three numbers in each row as the coefficients of x, y, and z and the last number as the constant to get the following system:

$$\begin{aligned} 2x + 3y + 4z &= 6 \\ -x \qquad + 5z &= -2 \\ x - 2y + 3z &= 1 \end{aligned}$$

Now do Exercises 17–20

The Gauss-Jordan Elimination Method

When we solve a single equation, we write simpler and simpler equivalent equations to get an equation whose solution is obvious. In the **Gauss-Jordan elimination method** we write simpler and simpler equivalent augmented matrices until we get an augmented matrix [like the one in Example 3(b)] in which the solution to the corresponding system is obvious.

Because each row of an augmented matrix represents an equation, we can perform the operations on the rows of the augmented matrix. These **row operations,** which follow, correspond to the usual operations with equations used in the addition method.

Row Operations

The following row operations on an augmented matrix give an equivalent augmented matrix:

1. Interchange two rows of the matrix.
2. Multiply every element in a row by a nonzero real number.
3. Add to a row a multiple of another row.

In the Gauss-Jordan elimination method our goal is to use row operations to obtain an augmented matrix that has ones on the **diagonal** in its matrix of coefficients and zeros elsewhere:

$$\left[\begin{array}{cc|c} 1 & 0 & a \\ 0 & 1 & b \end{array}\right]$$

The system corresponding to this augmented matrix is $x = a$ and $y = b$. So the solution set to the system is $\{(a, b)\}$.

EXAMPLE 4

Gauss-Jordan elimination with two equations in two variables

Use the Gauss-Jordan elimination method to solve the system:

$$\begin{aligned} x - 3y &= 11 \\ 2x + y &= 1 \end{aligned}$$

Study Tip

Be active in class. Don't be embarrassed to ask questions or answer questions. You can often learn more from a wrong answer than from a right one. Your instructor knows that you are not yet an expert in algebra. Instructors love active classrooms and will not think less of you for speaking out.

Solution

Start with the augmented matrix:

$$\left[\begin{array}{rr|r} 1 & -3 & 11 \\ 2 & 1 & 1 \end{array}\right]$$

To get a 0 in the first position of the second row (R_2), multiply the first row (R_1) by -2 and add the result to R_2. In symbols, $-2R_1 + R_2 \rightarrow R_2$, where the arrow is read as "replaces." Because $-2R_1 = [-2, 6, -22]$ and $R_2 = [2, 1, 1]$, we add corresponding entries to get $-2R_1 + R_2 = [0, 7, -21]$. Note that with this operation the coefficient of x in the second equation is 0 and we get the following matrix:

$$\left[\begin{array}{rr|r} 1 & -3 & 11 \\ 0 & 7 & -21 \end{array}\right] \quad -2R_1 + R_2 \rightarrow R_2$$

Multiply each element of row 2 by $\frac{1}{7}$ (in symbols, $\frac{1}{7}R_2 \rightarrow R_2$):

$$\left[\begin{array}{rr|r} 1 & -3 & 11 \\ 0 & 1 & -3 \end{array}\right] \quad \tfrac{1}{7}R_2 \rightarrow R_2$$

Multiply row 2 by 3 and add the result to row 1. Because $3R_2 = [0, 3, -9]$ and $R_1 = [1, -3, 11]$, $3R_2 + R_1 = [1, 0, 2]$. Note that the coefficient of y in the first equation is now 0. We get the following matrix:

$$\left[\begin{array}{rr|r} 1 & 0 & 2 \\ 0 & 1 & -3 \end{array}\right] \quad 3R_2 + R_1 \rightarrow R_1$$

This augmented matrix represents the system $x = 2$ and $y = -3$. So the solution set to the system is $\{(2, -3)\}$. Check in the original system.

Now do Exercises 21–46

In Example 5 we use the row operations on the augmented matrix of a system of three linear equations in three variables.

EXAMPLE 5

Gauss-Jordan elimination with three equations in three variables

Use the Gauss-Jordan elimination method to solve the following system:

$$\begin{aligned} 2x - y + z &= -3 \\ x + y - z &= 6 \\ 3x - y - z &= 4 \end{aligned}$$

Helpful Hint

It is not necessary to perform the row operations in exactly the same order as is shown in Example 5. As long as you use the legitimate row operations and get to the final form, you will get the solution to the system. Of course, you must double check your arithmetic at every step if you want to be successful at Gauss-Jordan elimination.

Solution

Start with the augmented matrix and interchange the first and second rows to get a 1 in the upper left position in the matrix:

$$\left[\begin{array}{rrr|r} 2 & -1 & 1 & -3 \\ 1 & 1 & -1 & 6 \\ 3 & -1 & -1 & 4 \end{array}\right] \quad \text{The augmented matrix}$$

$$\left[\begin{array}{rrr|r} 1 & 1 & -1 & 6 \\ 2 & -1 & 1 & -3 \\ 3 & -1 & -1 & 4 \end{array}\right] \quad R_1 \leftrightarrow R_2$$

Now multiply the first row by -2 and add the result to the second row. Multiply the first row by -3 and add the result to the third row. These two steps eliminate the variable x from the second and third rows:

$$\left[\begin{array}{rrr|r} 1 & 1 & -1 & 6 \\ 0 & -3 & 3 & -15 \\ 0 & -4 & 2 & -14 \end{array}\right] \quad \begin{array}{l} -2R_1 + R_2 \rightarrow R_2 \\ -3R_1 + R_3 \rightarrow R_3 \end{array}$$

Teaching Tip Encourage students to make notes at each step as is done in the examples. This will make checking a lot easier.

Multiply the second row by $-\frac{1}{3}$ to get 1 in the second position on the diagonal:

$$\left[\begin{array}{rrr|r} 1 & 1 & -1 & 6 \\ 0 & 1 & -1 & 5 \\ 0 & -4 & 2 & -14 \end{array}\right] \quad -\tfrac{1}{3}R_2 \rightarrow R_2$$

Use the second row to eliminate the variable y from the first and third rows:

$$\left[\begin{array}{rrr|r} 1 & 0 & 0 & 1 \\ 0 & 1 & -1 & 5 \\ 0 & 0 & -2 & 6 \end{array}\right] \quad \begin{array}{l} -1R_2 + R_1 \rightarrow R_1 \\ \\ 4R_2 + R_3 \rightarrow R_3 \end{array}$$

Multiply the third row by $-\frac{1}{2}$ to get a 1 in the third position on the diagonal:

$$\left[\begin{array}{rrr|r} 1 & 0 & 0 & 1 \\ 0 & 1 & -1 & 5 \\ 0 & 0 & 1 & -3 \end{array}\right] \quad -\tfrac{1}{2}R_3 \rightarrow R_3$$

Use the third row to eliminate the variable z from the second row:

$$\left[\begin{array}{rrr|r} 1 & 0 & 0 & 1 \\ 0 & 1 & 0 & 2 \\ 0 & 0 & 1 & -3 \end{array}\right] \quad R_3 + R_2 \rightarrow R_2$$

This last augmented matrix represents the system $x = 1$, $y = 2$, and $z = -3$. So the solution set to the system is $\{(1, 2, -3)\}$.

Now do Exercises 51–64

Inconsistent and Dependent Equations

Inconsistent and dependent equations are easily recognized in using the Gauss-Jordan elimination method.

EXAMPLE 6

Gauss-Jordan elimination with an inconsistent system

Solve the system:

$$\begin{aligned} x - y &= 1 \\ -3x + 3y &= 4 \end{aligned}$$

Solution

Start with the augmented matrix:

$$\left[\begin{array}{rr|r} 1 & -1 & 1 \\ -3 & 3 & 4 \end{array}\right]$$

Multiply row 1 by 3 and add the result to row 2. We get the following matrix:

$$\left[\begin{array}{rr|r} 1 & -1 & 1 \\ 0 & 0 & 7 \end{array}\right] \quad 3R_1 + R_2 \to R_2$$

The second row of the augmented matrix corresponds to the equation $0 = 7$. So the equations are inconsistent, and there is no solution to the system.

Now do Exercises 47–48

Helpful Hint

The point of Example 6 is to recognize an inconsistent system with Gauss-Jordan elimination. We could also observe that -3 times the first equation yields

$$-3x + 3y = -3,$$

which is inconsistent with

$$-3x + 3y = 4.$$

EXAMPLE 7

Gauss-Jordan elimination with a dependent system

Solve the system:

$$\begin{aligned} 3x + y &= 1 \\ 6x + 2y &= 2 \end{aligned}$$

Solution

Start with the augmented matrix:

$$\left[\begin{array}{rr|r} 3 & 1 & 1 \\ 6 & 2 & 2 \end{array}\right]$$

Multiply row 1 by -2 and add the result to row 2. We get the following matrix:

$$\left[\begin{array}{rr|r} 3 & 1 & 1 \\ 0 & 0 & 0 \end{array}\right] \quad -2R_1 + R_2 \to R_2$$

In the second row of the augmented matrix we have the equation $0 = 0$. So the equations are dependent. Every ordered pair that satisfies the first equation satisfies both equations. The solution set is $\{(x, y) \mid 3x + y = 1\}$.

Now do Exercises 49–50

The Gauss-Jordan elimination method may be applied to a system of n linear equations in n unknowns, where $n \geq 2$. However, it is a rather tedious method to perform when n is greater than 2, especially when fractions are involved. Computers are programmed to work with matrices, and the Gauss-Jordan elimination method is a popular method for computers.

Warm-Ups

True or false? Explain your answer.

Statements 1–7 refer to the following matrices:

a) $\left[\begin{array}{rr|r} 1 & 3 & 5 \\ -1 & -3 & 2 \end{array}\right]$ b) $\left[\begin{array}{rr|r} 1 & 3 & 5 \\ 0 & 0 & 7 \end{array}\right]$

c) $\left[\begin{array}{rr|r} -1 & 2 & -3 \\ 2 & -4 & 3 \end{array}\right]$ d) $\left[\begin{array}{rr|r} 1 & 3 & 5 \\ 0 & 0 & 0 \end{array}\right]$

1. The augmented matrix for $x + 3y = 5$ and $-x - 3y = 2$ is matrix (a). True
2. The augmented matrix for $2y - x = -3$ and $2x - 4y = 3$ is matrix (c). True
3. Matrix (a) is equivalent to matrix (b). True
4. Matrix (c) is equivalent to matrix (d). False
5. The system corresponding to matrix (b) is inconsistent. True
6. The system corresponding to matrix (c) is dependent. False
7. The system corresponding to matrix (d) is independent. False
8. The augmented matrix for a system of two linear equations in two unknowns is a 2×2 matrix. False
9. The notation $2R_1 + R_3 \to R_3$ means to replace R_3 by $2R_1 + R_3$. True
10. The notation $R_1 \leftrightarrow R_2$ means to replace R_2 by R_1. False

7.4 Exercises

Boost your GRADE at mathzone.com!

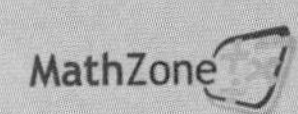

MathZone

- Practice Problems
- Self-Tests
- Videos
- Net Tutor
- e-Professors

Reading and Writing *After reading this section, write out the answers to these questions. Use complete sentences.*

1. What is a matrix?
   A matrix is a rectangular array of numbers.
2. What is the difference between a row and a column of a matrix?
   A row runs horizontally and a column runs vertically.
3. What is the size of a matrix?
   The size of a matrix is the number of rows and columns.
4. What is an element of a matrix?
   An element of a matrix is a number that occupies a position in the matrix.
5. What is an augmented matrix?
   An augmented matrix is a matrix where the entries in the first column are the coefficients of x, the entries in the second column are the coefficients of y, and the entries in the third column are the constants from a system of two linear equations in two unknowns.
6. What is the goal of Gauss-Jordan elimination?
   The goal of Gauss-Jordan elimination is to get ones on the diagonal.

Determine the size of each matrix. See Example 1.

7. $\begin{bmatrix} 5 & 0 \\ -2 & 3 \end{bmatrix}$
   2×2
8. $\begin{bmatrix} 1 & 3 & 6 \\ -7 & 0 & 2 \end{bmatrix}$
   2×3
9. $\begin{bmatrix} a & c \\ 0 & d \\ 3 & w \end{bmatrix}$
   3×2
10. $\begin{bmatrix} 0 & a & b \\ 5 & 7 & -8 \\ a & b & 2 \end{bmatrix}$
    3×3

11. $\begin{bmatrix} -\sqrt{3} \\ \pi \\ \frac{1}{2} \end{bmatrix}$ 3×1

12. $[3 \quad 0 \quad 4]$ 1×3

Write the augmented matrix for each system of equations. See Example 2.

13. $2x - 3y = 9$
$-3x + y = -1$
$\left[\begin{array}{rr|r} 2 & -3 & 9 \\ -3 & 1 & -1 \end{array}\right]$

14. $x - y = 4$
$2x + y = 3$
$\left[\begin{array}{rr|r} 1 & -1 & 4 \\ 2 & 1 & 3 \end{array}\right]$

15. $x - y + z = 1$
$x + y - 2z = 3$
$y - 3z = 4$
$\left[\begin{array}{rrr|r} 1 & -1 & 1 & 1 \\ 1 & 1 & -2 & 3 \\ 0 & 1 & -3 & 4 \end{array}\right]$

16. $x + y = 2$
$y - 3z = 5$
$-3x + 2z = 8$
$\left[\begin{array}{rrr|r} 1 & 1 & 0 & 2 \\ 0 & 1 & -3 & 5 \\ -3 & 0 & 2 & 8 \end{array}\right]$

Write the system of equations represented by each augmented matrix. See Example 3.

17. $\left[\begin{array}{rr|r} 5 & 1 & -1 \\ 2 & -3 & 0 \end{array}\right]$
$5x + y = -1$
$2x - 3y = 0$

18. $\left[\begin{array}{rr|r} 1 & 0 & 4 \\ 0 & 1 & -3 \end{array}\right]$
$x = 4$
$y = -3$

19. $\left[\begin{array}{rrr|r} 1 & 0 & 0 & 6 \\ -1 & 0 & 1 & -3 \\ 1 & 1 & 0 & 1 \end{array}\right]$
$x = 6$
$-x + z = -3$
$x + y = 1$

20. $\left[\begin{array}{rrr|r} 1 & 0 & 4 & 3 \\ 0 & 2 & 1 & -1 \\ 1 & 1 & 1 & 1 \end{array}\right]$
$x + 4z = 3$
$2y + z = -1$
$x + y + z = 1$

Fill in the blanks in the augmented matrices using the indicated row operations. See Example 4.

21. $\left[\begin{array}{rr|r} 0 & 2 & 4 \\ 1 & 0 & 6 \end{array}\right]$

$\left[\begin{array}{rr|r} 1 & 0 & 6 \\ 0 & 2 & 4 \end{array}\right]$ $R_1 \leftrightarrow R_2$

22. $\left[\begin{array}{rr|r} 0 & 3 & 6 \\ 1 & 2 & 5 \end{array}\right]$

$\left[\begin{array}{rr|r} 1 & 2 & 5 \\ 0 & 3 & 6 \end{array}\right]$ $R_1 \leftrightarrow R_2$

23. $\left[\begin{array}{rr|r} 4 & 12 & 16 \\ 2 & -4 & 3 \end{array}\right]$

$\left[\begin{array}{rr|r} 1 & 3 & 4 \\ 2 & -4 & 3 \end{array}\right]$ $\frac{1}{4}R_1 \rightarrow R_1$

24. $\left[\begin{array}{rr|r} 1 & 0 & -9 \\ 0 & -3 & 6 \end{array}\right]$

$\left[\begin{array}{rr|r} 1 & 0 & -9 \\ 0 & 1 & -2 \end{array}\right]$ $-\frac{1}{3}R_2 \rightarrow R_2$

25. $\left[\begin{array}{rr|r} 1 & 0 & -3 \\ -1 & 2 & 4 \end{array}\right]$

$\left[\begin{array}{rr|r} 1 & 0 & -3 \\ 0 & 2 & 1 \end{array}\right]$ $R_1 + R_2 \rightarrow R_2$

26. $\left[\begin{array}{rr|r} 1 & 2 & 7 \\ 0 & -2 & 6 \end{array}\right]$

$\left[\begin{array}{rr|r} 1 & 0 & 13 \\ 0 & -2 & 6 \end{array}\right]$ $R_2 + R_1 \rightarrow R_1$

27. $\left[\begin{array}{rr|r} 1 & 2 & 3 \\ -2 & 3 & 5 \end{array}\right]$

$\left[\begin{array}{rr|r} 1 & 2 & 3 \\ 0 & 7 & 11 \end{array}\right]$ $2R_1 + R_2 \rightarrow R_2$

28. $\left[\begin{array}{rr|r} 1 & 3 & 7 \\ 0 & 1 & 4 \end{array}\right]$

$\left[\begin{array}{rr|r} 1 & 0 & -5 \\ 0 & 1 & 4 \end{array}\right]$ $-3R_2 + R_1 \rightarrow R_1$

Determine the row operation that was used to convert each given augmented matrix into the equivalent augmented matrix that follows it. See Example 4.

29. $\left[\begin{array}{rr|r} 3 & 2 & 12 \\ 1 & -1 & -1 \end{array}\right], \left[\begin{array}{rr|r} 1 & -1 & -1 \\ 3 & 2 & 12 \end{array}\right]$ $R_1 \leftrightarrow R_2$

30. $\left[\begin{array}{rr|r} 1 & -1 & -1 \\ 3 & 2 & 12 \end{array}\right], \left[\begin{array}{rr|r} 1 & -1 & -1 \\ 0 & 5 & 15 \end{array}\right]$ $-3R_1 + R_2 \rightarrow R_2$

31. $\left[\begin{array}{rr|r} 1 & -1 & -1 \\ 0 & 5 & 15 \end{array}\right], \left[\begin{array}{rr|r} 1 & -1 & -1 \\ 0 & 1 & 3 \end{array}\right]$ $\frac{1}{5}R_2 \rightarrow R_2$

32. $\left[\begin{array}{rr|r} 1 & -1 & -1 \\ 0 & 1 & 3 \end{array}\right], \left[\begin{array}{rr|r} 1 & 0 & 2 \\ 0 & 1 & 3 \end{array}\right]$ $R_2 + R_1 \rightarrow R_1$

Solve each system using the Gauss-Jordan elimination method. See Examples 4–7.

33. $x - y = -3$
$y = 4$
$\{(1, 4)\}$

34. $x + y = 3$
$y = 6$
$\{(-9, 6)\}$

35. $x + y = -6$
$3y = 6$
$\{(-8, 2)\}$

36. $x - y = -7$
$4y = 12$
$\{(-4, 3)\}$

37. $x - y = 7$
$-x - y = -3$
$\{(5, -2)\}$

38. $x + y = 6$
$-x + y = 8$
$\{(-1, 7)\}$

39. $x + y = 3$
$-3x + y = -1$
$\{(1, 2)\}$

40. $x - y = -1$
$2x - y = 2$
$\{(3, 4)\}$

41. $2x - y = 3$
$x + y = 9$
$\{(4, 5)\}$

42. $3x - 4y = -1$
$x - y = 0$
$\{(1, 1)\}$

43. $3x - y = 4$
$2x + y = 1$
$\{(1, -1)\}$

44. $2x - y = -3$
$3x + y = -2$
$\{(-1, 1)\}$

45. $6x - 7y = 0$
$2x + y = 20$
$\{(7, 6)\}$

46. $2x + y = 11$
$2x - y = 1$
$\{(3, 5)\}$

47. $2x - 3y = 4$
$-2x + 3y = 5$
$\varnothing$

48. $x - 3y = 8$
$2x - 6y = 1$
$\varnothing$

49. $x + 2y = 1$
$3x + 6y = 3$
$\{(x, y) \mid x + 2y = 1\}$

50. $2x - 3y = 1$
$-6x + 9y = -3$
$\{(x, y) \mid 2x - 3y = 1\}$

51. $x + y - z = 4$
$y + z = 6$
$z = 2$
$\{(2, 4, 2)\}$

52. $x - y + z = 5$
$y + z = 8$
$z = 3$
$\{(7, 5, 3)\}$

53. $x + y + z = 6$
$x - y + z = 2$
$2y - z = 1$
$\{(1, 2, 3)\}$

54. $x - y - z = 0$
$-x - y + z = -4$
$-x + y - z = -2$
$\{(3, 2, 1)\}$

55. $2x + y + z = 4$
$x + y - z = 1$
$x - y + 2z = 2$
$\{(1, 1, 1)\}$

56. $3x - y = 1$
$x + y + z = 4$
$x + 2z = 3$
$\{(1, 2, 1)\}$

57. $2x - y + z = 0$
$x + y - 3z = 3$
$x - y + z = -1$
$\{(1, 2, 0)\}$

58. $x - y - z = 0$
$-x - y + 2z = -1$
$-x + y - 2z = -3$
$\{(2, 1, 1)\}$

59. $-x + 3y + z = 0$
$x - y - 4z = -3$
$x + y + 2z = 3$
$\{(1, 0, 1)\}$

60. $-x + z = -2$
$2x - y = 5$
$y + 3z = 9$
$\{(4, 3, 2)\}$

61. $x - y + z = 1$
$2x - 2y + 2z = 2$
$-3x + 3y - 3z = -3$
$\{(x, y, z) \mid x - y + z = 1\}$

62. $4x - 2y + 2z = 2$
$2x - y + z = 1$
$-2x + y - z = -1$
$\{(x, y, z) \mid 2x - y + z = 1\}$

63. $x + y - z = 2$
$2x - y + z = 1$
$3x + 3y - 3z = 8$
$\varnothing$

64. $x + y + z = 5$
$x - y - z = 8$
$-x + y + z = 2$
$\varnothing$

Solve each problem using a system of linear equations and the Gauss-Jordan elimination method.

65. ***Two numbers.*** The sum of two numbers is 12 and their difference is 2. Find the numbers. 5 and 7

66. ***Two more numbers.*** The sum of two numbers is 11 and their difference is 6. Find the numbers. 2.5 and 8.5

67. ***Paper size.*** The length of a rectangular piece of paper is 2.5 inches greater than the width. The perimeter is 39 inches. Find the length and width.
Length 11 in., width 8.5 in.

68. ***Photo size.*** The length of a rectangular photo is 2 inches greater than the width. The perimeter is 20 inches. Find the length and width.
Length 6 in., width 4 in.

69. ***Buy and sell.*** Cory buys and sells baseball cards on ebay. He always buys at the same price and then sells the cards for \$2 more than he buys them. One month he broke even after buying 56 cards and selling 49. Find his buying price and selling price.
Buys for \$14, sells for \$16

70. ***Jay Leno's garage.*** Jay Leno's collection of cars and motorcycles totals 187. When he checks the air in the tires he has 588 tires to check. How many cars and how many motorcycles does he own? Assume that the cars all have four tires and the motorcycles have two.
107 cars, 80 motorcycles

71. ***Parking lot boredom.*** A late-night parking lot attendant counted 50 vehicles on the lot consisting of four-wheel cars, three-wheel cars, and two-wheel motorcycles. She then counted 192 tires touching the ground and observed that the number of four-wheel cars was nine times the total of the other vehicles on the lot. How many of each type of vehicle were on the lot?
45 four-wheel cars, 2 three-wheel cars, and 3 two-wheel motorcycles

72. ***Happy meals.*** The total price of a hamburger, an order of fries, and Coke at a fast food restaurant is \$3.00. The price of a hamburger minus the price of an order of fries is \$0.20 and the price of an order of fries minus the price of a Coke is also \$0.20. Find the price of each item.
Hamburger \$1.20, fries, \$1.00, Coke \$0.80

Getting More Involved

73. ***Cooperative learning***

Write a step-by-step procedure for solving any system of two linear equations in two variables by the Gauss-Jordan elimination method. Have a classmate evaluate your procedure by using it to solve a system.

74. ***Cooperative learning***

Repeat Exercise 73 for a system of three linear equations in three variables.

7.5 Determinants and Cramer's Rule

In this Section

- Determinants
- Cramer's Rule (2 × 2)
- Minors
- Evaluating a 3 × 3 Determinant
- Cramer's Rule (3 × 3)

The Gauss-Jordan elimination method of Section 7.4 can be performed the same way on every system. Another method that is applied the same way for every system is Cramer's rule, which we study in this section. Before you learn Cramer's rule, we need to introduce a new number associated with a matrix, called a *determinant*.

Determinants

The determinant of a square matrix is a real number corresponding to the matrix. For a 2 × 2 matrix the determinant is defined as follows.

Determinant of a 2 × 2 Matrix

The **determinant** of the matrix $\begin{bmatrix} a & b \\ c & d \end{bmatrix}$ is defined to be the real number $ad - bc$. We write

$$\begin{vmatrix} a & b \\ c & d \end{vmatrix} = ad - bc.$$

Note that the symbol for the determinant is a pair of vertical lines similar to the absolute value symbol, while a matrix is enclosed in brackets.

EXAMPLE 1

Using the definition of determinant

Find the determinant of each matrix.

a) $\begin{bmatrix} 1 & 3 \\ -2 & 5 \end{bmatrix}$ **b)** $\begin{bmatrix} 2 & 4 \\ 6 & 12 \end{bmatrix}$

Solution

a) $\begin{vmatrix} 1 & 3 \\ -2 & 5 \end{vmatrix} = 1 \cdot 5 - 3(-2)$
$= 5 + 6$
$= 11$

b) $\begin{vmatrix} 2 & 4 \\ 6 & 12 \end{vmatrix} = 2 \cdot 12 - 4 \cdot 6$
$= 24 - 24$
$= 0$

Now do Exercises 7–14

Cramer's Rule (2 × 2)

To understand Cramer's rule, we first solve a general system of two linear equations in two variables. Consider the system

$$(1) \quad a_1x + b_1y = c_1$$
$$(2) \quad a_2x + b_2y = c_2$$

Calculator Close-Up

With a graphing calculator you can define matrix *A* using MATRX EDIT.

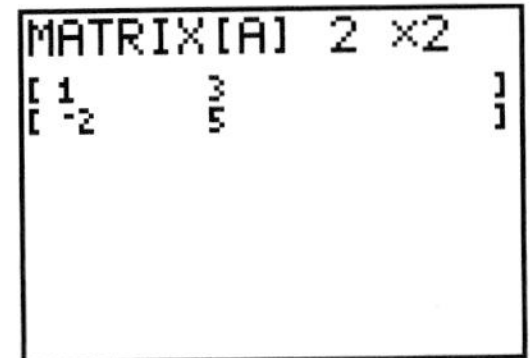

Then use the determinant function (det) found in MATRX MATH and the *A* from MATRX NAMES to find its determinant.

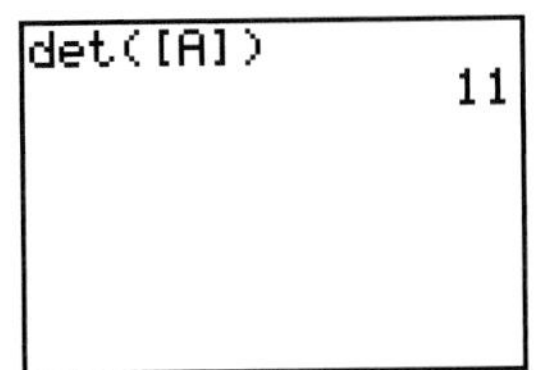

Helpful Hint

Notice that Cramer's rule gives us a precise formula for finding the solution to an independent system. The addition and substitution methods are more like guidelines under which we choose the best way to proceed.

where a_1, b_1, c_1, a_2, b_2, and c_2 represent real numbers. To eliminate y, we multiply Eq. (1) by b_2 and Eq. (2) by $-b_1$:

$$\begin{aligned} a_1b_2x + b_1b_2y &= c_1b_2 && \text{Eq. (1) multiplied by } b_2 \\ -a_2b_1x - b_1b_2y &= -c_2b_1 && \text{Eq. (2) multiplied by } -b_1 \\ \hline a_1b_2x - a_2b_1x &= c_1b_2 - c_2b_1 && \text{Add.} \\ (a_1b_2 - a_2b_1)x &= c_1b_2 - c_2b_1 \\ x &= \frac{c_1b_2 - c_2b_1}{a_1b_2 - a_2b_1} && \text{Provided that } a_1b_2 - a_2b_1 \neq 0 \end{aligned}$$

Using similar steps to eliminate x from the system, we get

$$y = \frac{a_1c_2 - a_2c_1}{a_1b_2 - a_2b_1},$$

provided that $a_1b_2 - a_2b_1 \neq 0$. These formulas for x and y can be written by using determinants. In the determinant form they are known as **Cramer's rule.**

Cramer's Rule

The solution to the system

$$\begin{aligned} a_1x + b_1y &= c_1 \\ a_2x + b_2y &= c_2 \end{aligned}$$

is given by $x = \frac{D_x}{D}$ and $y = \frac{D_y}{D}$, where

$$D = \begin{vmatrix} a_1 & b_1 \\ a_2 & b_2 \end{vmatrix}, \quad D_x = \begin{vmatrix} c_1 & b_1 \\ c_2 & b_2 \end{vmatrix}, \quad \text{and} \quad D_y = \begin{vmatrix} a_1 & c_1 \\ a_2 & c_2 \end{vmatrix},$$

provided that $D \neq 0$.

Note that D is the determinant made up of the original coefficients of x and y. D is used in the denominator for both x and y. D_x is obtained by replacing the first (or x) column of D by the constants c_1 and c_2. D_y is found by replacing the second (or y) column of D by the constants c_1 and c_2.

EXAMPLE 2

Solving an independent system with Cramer's rule

Use Cramer's rule to solve the system:

$$\begin{aligned} 3x - 2y &= 4 \\ 2x + y &= -3 \end{aligned}$$

Calculator Close-Up

Use MATRX EDIT to define D, D_x, and D_y as A, B, and C. Now use Cramer's rule on the home screen to find x and y.

```
det([B])/det([A]
)▸Frac
                -2/7
det([C])/det([A]
)▸Frac
               -17/7
```

Solution

First find the determinants D, D_x, and D_y:

$$D = \begin{vmatrix} 3 & -2 \\ 2 & 1 \end{vmatrix} = 3 - (-4) = 7$$

$$D_x = \begin{vmatrix} 4 & -2 \\ -3 & 1 \end{vmatrix} = 4 - 6 = -2, \qquad D_y = \begin{vmatrix} 3 & 4 \\ 2 & -3 \end{vmatrix} = -9 - 8 = -17$$

By Cramer's rule, we have

$$x = \frac{D_x}{D} = -\frac{2}{7} \quad \text{and} \quad y = \frac{D_y}{D} = -\frac{17}{7}.$$

Check in the original equations. The solution set is $\left\{\left(-\frac{2}{7}, -\frac{17}{7}\right)\right\}$.

Now do Exercises 15–28

CAUTION Cramer's rule works *only* when the determinant D is *not* equal to zero. Cramer's rule solves only those systems that have a single point in their solution set. If $D = 0$, we use elimination to determine whether the solution set is empty or contains all points of a line.

Minors

To each element of a 3×3 matrix there corresponds a 2×2 matrix that is obtained by deleting the row and column of that element. The determinant of the 2×2 matrix is called the **minor** of that element.

EXAMPLE 3 Finding minors

Find the minors for the elements 2, 3, and -6 of the 3×3 matrix

$$\begin{bmatrix} 2 & -1 & -8 \\ 0 & -2 & 3 \\ 4 & -6 & 7 \end{bmatrix}.$$

Solution

To find the minor for 2, delete the first row and first column of the matrix:

$$\begin{bmatrix} 2 & -1 & -8 \\ 0 & -2 & 3 \\ 4 & -6 & 7 \end{bmatrix}$$

Now find the determinant of $\begin{bmatrix} -2 & 3 \\ -6 & 7 \end{bmatrix}$:

$$\begin{vmatrix} -2 & 3 \\ -6 & 7 \end{vmatrix} = (-2)(7) - (-6)(3) = 4$$

The minor for 2 is 4. To find the minor for 3, delete the second row and third column of the matrix:

$$\begin{bmatrix} 2 & -1 & -8 \\ 0 & -2 & 3 \\ 4 & -6 & 7 \end{bmatrix}$$

Now find the determinant of $\begin{bmatrix} 2 & -1 \\ 4 & -6 \end{bmatrix}$:

$$\begin{vmatrix} 2 & -1 \\ 4 & -6 \end{vmatrix} = (2)(-6) - (4)(-1) = -8$$

The minor for 3 is -8. To find the minor for -6, delete the third row and the second column of the matrix:

$$\begin{bmatrix} 2 & -1 & -8 \\ 0 & -2 & 3 \\ 4 & -6 & 7 \end{bmatrix}$$

Now find the determinant of $\begin{bmatrix} 2 & -8 \\ 0 & 3 \end{bmatrix}$:

$$\begin{vmatrix} 2 & -8 \\ 0 & 3 \end{vmatrix} = (2)(3) - (0)(-8) = 6$$

The minor for -6 is 6.

Now do Exercises 29–36

Evaluating a 3 × 3 Determinant

The determinant of a 3 × 3 matrix is defined in terms of the determinants of minors.

Study Tip

Remember that everything we do in solving problems is based on principles (which are also called rules, theorems, and definitions). These principles justify the steps we take. Be sure that you understand the reasons. If you just memorize procedures without understanding, you will soon forget the procedures.

Determinant of a 3 × 3 Matrix

The determinant of a 3 × 3 matrix is defined as follows:

$$\begin{vmatrix} a_1 & b_1 & c_1 \\ a_2 & b_2 & c_2 \\ a_3 & b_3 & c_3 \end{vmatrix} = a_1 \cdot \begin{vmatrix} b_2 & c_2 \\ b_3 & c_3 \end{vmatrix} - a_2 \cdot \begin{vmatrix} b_1 & c_1 \\ b_3 & c_3 \end{vmatrix} + a_3 \cdot \begin{vmatrix} b_1 & c_1 \\ b_2 & c_2 \end{vmatrix}$$

Note that the determinants following a_1, a_2, and a_3 are the minors for a_1, a_2, and a_3, respectively. Writing the determinant of a 3 × 3 matrix in terms of minors is called **expansion by minors.** In the definition we expanded by minors about the first column. Later we will see how to expand by minors using any row or column and get the same value for the determinant.

EXAMPLE 4

Determinant of a 3 × 3 matrix

Find the determinant of the matrix by expansion by minors about the first column.

$$\begin{bmatrix} 1 & 3 & -5 \\ -2 & 4 & 6 \\ 0 & -7 & 9 \end{bmatrix}$$

Solution

$$\begin{vmatrix} 1 & 3 & -5 \\ -2 & 4 & 6 \\ 0 & -7 & 9 \end{vmatrix} = 1 \cdot \begin{vmatrix} 4 & 6 \\ -7 & 9 \end{vmatrix} - (-2) \cdot \begin{vmatrix} 3 & -5 \\ -7 & 9 \end{vmatrix} + 0 \cdot \begin{vmatrix} 3 & -5 \\ 4 & 6 \end{vmatrix}$$

$$= 1 \cdot [36 - (-42)] + 2 \cdot (27 - 35) + 0 \cdot [18 - (-20)]$$

$$= 1 \cdot 78 + 2 \cdot (-8) + 0$$

$$= 78 - 16$$

$$= 62$$

Now do Exercises 37–44

In Example 5 we evaluate a determinant using expansion by minors about the second row. In expanding about any row or column, the signs of the coefficients of the minors alternate according to the **sign array** that follows:

$$\begin{bmatrix} + & - & + \\ - & + & - \\ + & - & + \end{bmatrix}$$

The sign array is easily remembered by observing that there is a "+" sign in the upper left position and then alternating signs for all of the remaining positions.

EXAMPLE 5

Determinant of a 3 × 3 matrix

Evaluate the determinant of the matrix by expanding by minors about the second row.

$$\begin{bmatrix} 1 & 3 & -5 \\ -2 & 4 & 6 \\ 0 & -7 & 9 \end{bmatrix}$$

Solution

For expansion using the second row we prefix the signs "− + −" from the second row of the sign array to the corresponding numbers in the second row of the matrix, −2, 4, and 6. Note that the signs from the sign array are used in addition to any signs that occur on the numbers in the second row.

From the sign array, second row

$$\begin{vmatrix} 1 & 3 & -5 \\ -2 & 4 & 6 \\ 0 & -7 & 9 \end{vmatrix} = -(-2) \cdot \begin{vmatrix} 3 & -5 \\ -7 & 9 \end{vmatrix} + 4 \cdot \begin{vmatrix} 1 & -5 \\ 0 & 9 \end{vmatrix} - 6 \cdot \begin{vmatrix} 1 & 3 \\ 0 & -7 \end{vmatrix}$$

$$= 2(27 - 35) + 4(9 - 0) - 6(-7 - 0)$$

$$= 2(-8) + 4(9) - 6(-7)$$

$$= -16 + 36 + 42$$

$$= 62$$

Teaching Tip Have students find the same determinant by expanding about different rows or columns.

Note that 62 is the same value that was obtained for this determinant in Example 4.

Now do Exercises 45–48

It can be shown that expanding by minors using any row or column prefixed by the corresponding signs from the sign array yields the same value for the determinant. Because we can use any row or column to evaluate a determinant of a 3×3 matrix, we can choose a row or column that makes the work easier. We can shorten the work considerably by picking a row or column with zeros in it.

Calculator Close-Up

A calculator is very useful for finding the determinant of a 3×3 matrix. Define *A* using MATRX EDIT.

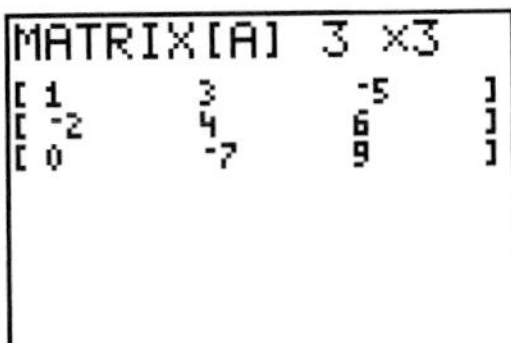

Now use the determinant function from MATRX MATH and the *A* from MATRX NAMES to find the determinant.

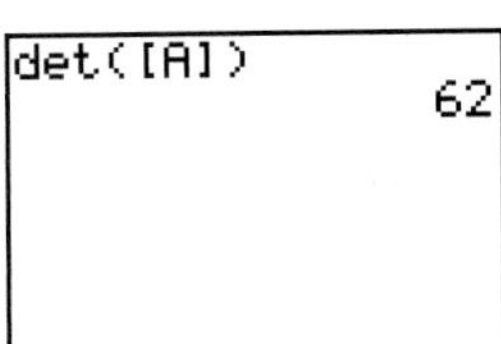

EXAMPLE 6

Choosing the simplest row or column

Find the determinant of the matrix

$$\begin{bmatrix} 3 & -5 & 0 \\ 4 & -6 & 0 \\ 7 & 9 & 2 \end{bmatrix}.$$

Solution

We choose to expand by minors about the third column of the matrix because the third column contains two zeros. Prefix the third-column entries 0, 0, 2 by the signs "+ – +" from the third column of the sign array:

$$\begin{vmatrix} 3 & -5 & 0 \\ 4 & -6 & 0 \\ 7 & 9 & 2 \end{vmatrix} = 0 \cdot \begin{vmatrix} 4 & -6 \\ 7 & 9 \end{vmatrix} - 0 \cdot \begin{vmatrix} 3 & -5 \\ 7 & 9 \end{vmatrix} + 2 \cdot \begin{vmatrix} 3 & -5 \\ 4 & -6 \end{vmatrix}$$

$$= 0 - 0 + 2[-18 - (-20)]$$

$$= 4$$

Now do Exercises 49–52

Cramer's Rule (3 × 3)

A system of three linear equations in three variables can be solved by using determinants and Cramer's rule.

Teaching Tip Point out that Cramer's rule is important because it is a rule that solves every independent system and it is easy to apply it with a calculator.

Cramer's Rule for Three Equations in Three Unknowns

The solution to the system

$$a_1x + b_1y + c_1z = d_1$$
$$a_2x + b_2y + c_2z = d_2$$
$$a_3x + b_3y + c_3z = d_3$$

is given by $x = \frac{D_x}{D}$, $y = \frac{D_y}{D}$, and $z = \frac{D_z}{D}$, where

$$D = \begin{vmatrix} a_1 & b_1 & c_1 \\ a_2 & b_2 & c_2 \\ a_3 & b_3 & c_3 \end{vmatrix}, \qquad D_x = \begin{vmatrix} d_1 & b_1 & c_1 \\ d_2 & b_2 & c_2 \\ d_3 & b_3 & c_3 \end{vmatrix},$$

$$D_y = \begin{vmatrix} a_1 & d_1 & c_1 \\ a_2 & d_2 & c_2 \\ a_3 & d_3 & c_3 \end{vmatrix}, \qquad D_z = \begin{vmatrix} a_1 & b_1 & d_1 \\ a_2 & b_2 & d_2 \\ a_3 & b_3 & d_3 \end{vmatrix},$$

provided that $D \neq 0$.

Note that D_x, D_y, and D_z are obtained from D by replacing the x-, y-, or z-column with the constants d_1, d_2, and d_3.

EXAMPLE 7

Solving an independent system with Cramer's rule

Use Cramer's rule to solve the system:

$$\begin{aligned} x + y + z &= 4 \\ x - y \quad &= -3 \\ x + 2y - z &= 0 \end{aligned}$$

Calculator Close-Up

When you see the amount of arithmetic required to solve the system in Example 7 by Cramer's rule, you can understand why computers and calculators have been programmed to perform this method. Some calculators can find determinants for matrices as large as 10×10. Try to solve Example 7 with a graphing calculator that has determinants.

Solution

We first calculate D, D_x, D_y, and D_z. To calculate D, expand by minors about the third column because the third column has a zero in it:

$$D = \begin{vmatrix} 1 & 1 & 1 \\ 1 & -1 & 0 \\ 1 & 2 & -1 \end{vmatrix} = 1 \cdot \begin{vmatrix} 1 & -1 \\ 1 & 2 \end{vmatrix} - 0 \cdot \begin{vmatrix} 1 & 1 \\ 1 & 2 \end{vmatrix} + (-1) \cdot \begin{vmatrix} 1 & 1 \\ 1 & -1 \end{vmatrix}$$

$$= 1 \cdot [2 - (-1)] - 0 + (-1)[-1 - 1]$$
$$= 3 - 0 + 2$$
$$= 5$$

For D_x, expand by minors about the first column:

$$D_x = \begin{vmatrix} 4 & 1 & 1 \\ -3 & -1 & 0 \\ 0 & 2 & -1 \end{vmatrix} = 4 \cdot \begin{vmatrix} -1 & 0 \\ 2 & -1 \end{vmatrix} - (-3) \cdot \begin{vmatrix} 1 & 1 \\ 2 & -1 \end{vmatrix} + 0 \cdot \begin{vmatrix} 1 & 1 \\ -1 & 0 \end{vmatrix}$$

$$= 4 \cdot (1 - 0) + 3 \cdot (-1 - 2) + 0$$
$$= 4 - 9 + 0 = -5$$

For D_y, expand by minors about the third row:

$$D_y = \begin{vmatrix} 1 & 4 & 1 \\ 1 & -3 & 0 \\ 1 & 0 & -1 \end{vmatrix} = 1 \cdot \begin{vmatrix} 4 & 1 \\ -3 & 0 \end{vmatrix} - 0 \cdot \begin{vmatrix} 1 & 1 \\ 1 & 0 \end{vmatrix} + (-1) \cdot \begin{vmatrix} 1 & 4 \\ 1 & -3 \end{vmatrix}$$

$$= 1 \cdot 3 - 0 + (-1)(-7) = 10$$

To get D_z, expand by minors about the third row:

$$D_z = \begin{vmatrix} 1 & 1 & 4 \\ 1 & -1 & -3 \\ 1 & 2 & 0 \end{vmatrix} = 1 \cdot \begin{vmatrix} 1 & 4 \\ -1 & -3 \end{vmatrix} - 2 \cdot \begin{vmatrix} 1 & 4 \\ 1 & -3 \end{vmatrix} + 0 \cdot \begin{vmatrix} 1 & 1 \\ 1 & -1 \end{vmatrix}$$

$$= 1 \cdot 1 - 2(-7) + 0 = 15$$

Now, by Cramer's rule,

$$x = \frac{D_x}{D} = \frac{-5}{5} = -1, \qquad y = \frac{D_y}{D} = \frac{10}{5} = 2, \qquad \text{and} \qquad z = \frac{D_z}{D} = \frac{15}{5} = 3.$$

Check $(-1, 2, 3)$ in the original equations. The solution set is $\{(-1, 2, 3)\}$.

Now do Exercises 53–62

If $D = 0$, Cramer's rule does not apply. Cramer's rule provides the solution only to a system of three equations with three variables that has a single point in the solution set. If $D = 0$, then the solution set either is empty or consists of infinitely many points, and we can use the methods discussed in Sections 7.3 or 7.4 to find the solution.

Warm-Ups ▼

True or false? Explain your answer.

1. $\begin{vmatrix} -1 & 2 \\ 3 & -5 \end{vmatrix} = -1$ True **2.** $\begin{vmatrix} 2 & 4 \\ -4 & 8 \end{vmatrix} = 0$ False

3. Cramer's rule solves any system of two linear equations in two variables. False

4. The determinant of a 2×2 matrix is a real number. True

5. If $D = 0$, then there might be no solution to the system. True

6. Cramer's rule is used to solve systems of linear equations only. True

7. If the graphs of a pair of linear equations intersect at exactly one point, then this point can be found by using Cramer's rule. True

8. The determinant of a 3×3 matrix is found by using minors. True

9. Expansion by minors about any row or any column gives the same value for the determinant of a 3×3 matrix. True

10. The sign array is used in evaluating the determinant of a 3×3 matrix. True

7.5 Exercises

Boost your GRADE at mathzone.com!

MathZone

- Practice Problems
- Net Tutor
- Self-Tests
- e-Professors
- Videos

Reading and Writing *After reading this section, write out the answers to these questions. Use complete sentences.*

1. What is a determinant?
   A determinant is a real number associated with a square matrix.
2. What is Cramer's rule used for?
   Cramer's rule can be used to solve systems of linear equations.
3. Which systems can be solved using Cramer's rule?
   Cramer's rule works on systems that have exactly one solution.
4. What is a minor?
   A minor for an element in a 3×3 matrix is the determinant of a 2×2 matrix.
5. How do you find the minor for an element of a 3×3 matrix?
   A minor for an element is obtained by deleting the row and column of the element and finding the determinant of the 2×2 matrix that remains.
6. What is the purpose of the sign array?
   The sign array tells what signs to use in the expansion by minors.

Find the value of each determinant. See Example 1.

7. $\begin{vmatrix} 2 & 5 \\ 3 & 7 \end{vmatrix}$ -1

8. $\begin{vmatrix} -1 & 0 \\ 1 & 1 \end{vmatrix}$ -1

9. $\begin{vmatrix} 0 & 3 \\ 1 & 5 \end{vmatrix}$ -3

10. $\begin{vmatrix} 2 & 4 \\ 6 & 12 \end{vmatrix}$ 0

11. $\begin{vmatrix} -3 & -2 \\ -4 & 2 \end{vmatrix}$ -14

12. $\begin{vmatrix} -2 & 2 \\ -3 & -5 \end{vmatrix}$ 16

13. $\begin{vmatrix} 0.05 & 0.06 \\ 10 & 20 \end{vmatrix}$ 0.4

14. $\begin{vmatrix} 0.02 & -0.5 \\ 30 & 50 \end{vmatrix}$ 16

Solve each system using Cramer's rule. See Example 2.

15. $x - y = -4$
$2y = 12$
$\{(2, 6)\}$

16. $x + y = -2$
$3y = 3$
$\{(-3, 1)\}$

17. $x + y = 0$
$2x = -16$
$\{(-8, 8)\}$

18. $x - y = 0$
$3x = -3$
$\{(-1, -1)\}$

19. $2x - y = 5$
$3x + 2y = -3$
$\{(1, -3)\}$

20. $3x + y = -1$
$x + 2y = 8$
$\{(-2, 5)\}$

21. $3x - 5y = -2$
$2x + 3y = 5$
$\{(1, 1)\}$

22. $x - y = 1$
$3x - 2y = 0$
$\{(-2, -3)\}$

23. $4x - 3y = 5$
$2x + 5y = 7$
$\left\{\left(\frac{23}{13}, \frac{9}{13}\right)\right\}$

24. $2x - y = 2$
$3x - 2y = 1$
$\{(3, 4)\}$

25. $0.5x + 0.2y = 8$
$0.4x - 0.6y = -5$
$\{(10, 15)\}$

26. $0.6x + 0.5y = 18$
$0.5x - 0.25y = 7$
$\{(20, 12)\}$

27. $\frac{1}{2}x + \frac{1}{4}y = 5$
$\frac{1}{3}x - \frac{1}{2}y = -1$
$\left\{\left(\frac{27}{4}, \frac{13}{2}\right)\right\}$

28. $\frac{1}{2}x + \frac{2}{3}y = 4$
$\frac{3}{4}x + \frac{1}{3}y = -2$
$\{(-8, 12)\}$

Find the indicated minors using the following matrix. See Example 3.

$$\begin{bmatrix} 3 & -2 & 5 \\ 4 & -3 & 7 \\ 0 & 1 & -6 \end{bmatrix}$$

29. Minor for 3 11

30. Minor for -2 -24

31. Minor for 5 4

32. Minor for -3 -18

33. Minor for 7 3

34. Minor for 0 1

35. Minor for 1 1

36. Minor for -6 -1

Find the determinant of each 3×3 matrix by using expansion by minors about the first column. See Example 4.

37. $\begin{bmatrix} 1 & 1 & 2 \\ 2 & 3 & 1 \\ 3 & 1 & 5 \end{bmatrix}$ -7

38. $\begin{bmatrix} 2 & 1 & 3 \\ 1 & 1 & 2 \\ 3 & 4 & 6 \end{bmatrix}$ -1

39. $\begin{bmatrix} 2 & 1 & 0 \\ 1 & 0 & 1 \\ 3 & 1 & 2 \end{bmatrix}$ -1

40. $\begin{bmatrix} 1 & 0 & 2 \\ 2 & 1 & 3 \\ 4 & 3 & 0 \end{bmatrix}$ -5

41. $\begin{bmatrix} -2 & 1 & 2 \\ -3 & 3 & 1 \\ -5 & 4 & 0 \end{bmatrix}$ 9

42. $\begin{bmatrix} -2 & 1 & 3 \\ -1 & 4 & 2 \\ 2 & 1 & 1 \end{bmatrix}$ -26

43. $\begin{bmatrix} 1 & 1 & 5 \\ 0 & 3 & 2 \\ 0 & 2 & 3 \end{bmatrix}$ 5

44. $\begin{bmatrix} 1 & 0 & 6 \\ 0 & 1 & 4 \\ 0 & 0 & 9 \end{bmatrix}$ 9

Evaluate the determinant of each 3 × 3 matrix using expansion by minors about the row or column of your choice. See Examples 5 and 6.

45. $\begin{bmatrix} 3 & 1 & 5 \\ 2 & 0 & 6 \\ 4 & 0 & 1 \end{bmatrix}$ 22

46. $\begin{bmatrix} 2 & 1 & 2 \\ 1 & 2 & 5 \\ 3 & 0 & 0 \end{bmatrix}$ 3

47. $\begin{bmatrix} -2 & 1 & 3 \\ 0 & 1 & -1 \\ 2 & -4 & -3 \end{bmatrix}$ 6

48. $\begin{bmatrix} -2 & 0 & 1 \\ -3 & 2 & -5 \\ 4 & -2 & 6 \end{bmatrix}$ −6

49. $\begin{bmatrix} -2 & -3 & 0 \\ 4 & -1 & 0 \\ 0 & 3 & 5 \end{bmatrix}$ 70

50. $\begin{bmatrix} -2 & 6 & 3 \\ 0 & 4 & 0 \\ -1 & -4 & 5 \end{bmatrix}$ −28

51. $\begin{bmatrix} 2 & 1 & 1 \\ 0 & 0 & 5 \\ 5 & 0 & 4 \end{bmatrix}$ 25

52. $\begin{bmatrix} 2 & 3 & 0 \\ 6 & 4 & 1 \\ 1 & 2 & 0 \end{bmatrix}$ −1

Use Cramer's rule to solve each system. See Example 7.

53. $x + y + z = 6$
$x - y + z = 2$
$2x + y + z = 7$
$\{(1, 2, 3)\}$

54. $x + y + z = 2$
$x - y - 2z = -3$
$2x - y + z = 7$
$\{(1, -2, 3)\}$

55. $x - 3y + 2z = 0$
$x + y + z = 2$
$x - y + z = 0$
$\{(-1, 1, 2)\}$

56. $3x + 2y + 2z = 0$
$x - y + z = 1$
$x + y - z = 3$
$\{(2, -1, -2)\}$

57. $x + y = -1$
$2y - z = 3$
$x + y + z = 0$
$\{(-3, 2, 1)\}$

58 $x - y = 8$
$x - 2z = 0$
$x + y - z = 1$
$\{(6, -2, 3)\}$

59. $x + y - z = 0$
$2x + 2y + z = 6$
$x - 3y = 0$
$\left\{\left(\frac{3}{2}, \frac{1}{2}, 2\right)\right\}$

60. $x + y + z = 1$
$5x - y = 0$
$3x + y + 2z = 0$
$\left\{\left(\frac{1}{2}, \frac{5}{2}, -2\right)\right\}$

61. $x + y + z = 0$
$2y + 2z = 0$
$3x - y = -1$
$\{(0, 1, -1)\}$

62. $x + z = 0$
$x - 3y = 1$
$4y - 3z = 3$
$\{(1, 0, -1)\}$

Solve each problem by using two equations in two variables and Cramer's rule.

63. ***Peas and beets.*** One serving of canned peas contains 3 grams of protein and 11 grams of carbohydrates. One serving of canned beets contains 1 gram of protein and 8 grams of carbohydrates. A dietitian wants to determine the number of servings of each that would provide 38 grams of protein and 187 grams of carbohydrates.

a) Use the accompanying graph to estimate the number of servings of each.

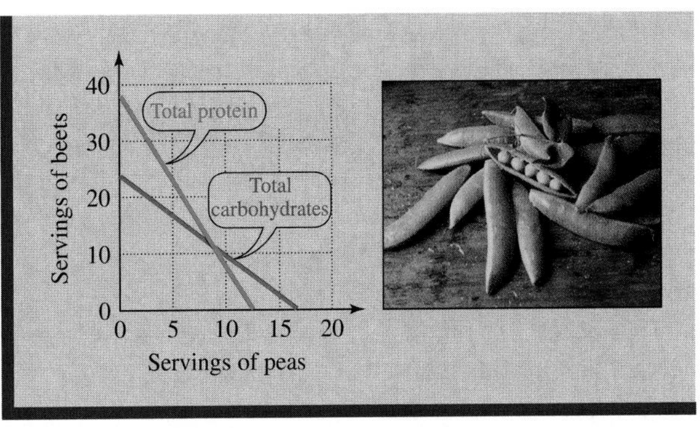

Figure for Exercise 63

b) Use Cramer's rule to find the number of servings of each.

a) 9 servings peas, 11 servings beets
b) 9 servings peas, 11 servings beets

64. ***Protein and carbohydrates.*** One serving of Cornies breakfast cereal contains 2 grams of protein and 25 grams of carbohydrates. One serving of Oaties breakfast cereal contains 4 grams of protein and 20 grams of carbohydrates. How many servings of each would provide exactly 24 grams of protein and 210 grams of carbohydrates?
Cornies 6 servings, Oaties 3 servings

65. ***Milk and a magazine.*** Althia bought a gallon of milk and a magazine for a total of $4.65, excluding tax. Including the tax, the bill was $4.95. If there is a 5% sales tax on milk and an 8% sales tax on magazines, then what was the price of each item?
Milk $2.40, magazine $2.25

66. ***Washing machines and refrigerators.*** A truck carrying 3600 cubic feet of cargo consisting of washing machines and refrigerators was hijacked. The washing machines are worth $300 each and are shipped in 36-cubic-foot cartons. The refrigerators are worth $900 each and are shipped in 45-cubic-foot cartons. If the total value of the cargo was $51,000, then how many of each were there on the truck?
50 washing machines, 40 refrigerators

67. ***Singles and doubles.*** Windy's Hamburger Palace sells singles and doubles. Toward the end of the evening, Windy himself noticed that he had on hand only 32 patties and 34 slices of tomatoes. If a single takes 1 patty and 2 slices, and a double takes 2 patties and 1 slice, then how many more singles and doubles must Windy sell to use up all of his patties and tomato slices?
12 singles, 10 doubles

68. ***Valuable wrenches.*** Carmen has a total of 28 wrenches, all of which are either box wrenches or open-end wrenches. For insurance purposes she values the box wrenches at \$3.00 each and the open-end wrenches at \$2.50 each. If the value of her wrench collection is \$78, then how many of each type does she have?
16 box wrenches, 12 open-end wrenches

69. ***Gary and Harry.*** Gary is 5 years older than Harry. Twenty-nine years ago, Gary was twice as old as Harry. How old are they now?
Gary 39, Harry 34

70. ***Acute angles.*** One acute angle of a right triangle is 3° more than twice the other acute angle. What are the sizes of the acute angles?
29° and 61°

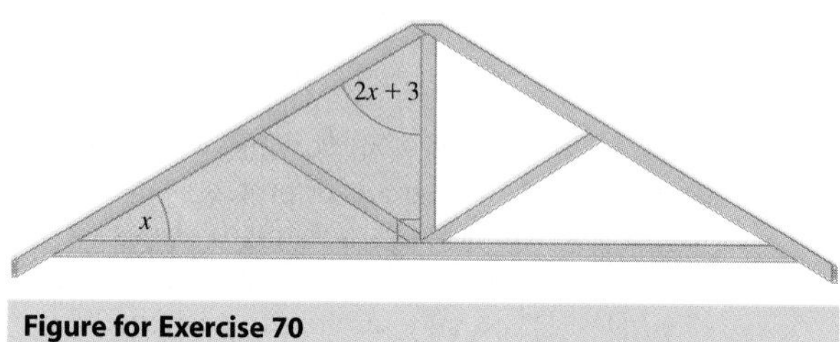

Figure for Exercise 70

71. ***Equal perimeters.*** A rope of length 80 feet is to be cut into two pieces. One piece will be used to form a square, and the other will be used to form an equilateral triangle. If the figures are to have equal perimeters, then what should be the length of a side of each?
Square 10 feet, triangle $\frac{40}{3}$ feet

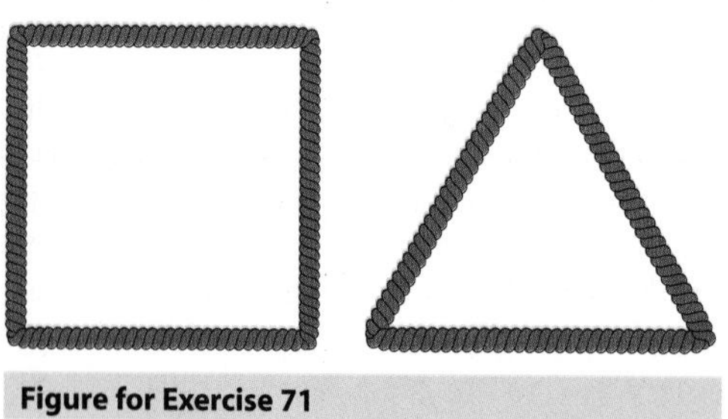
Figure for Exercise 71

72. ***Coffee and doughnuts.*** For a cup of coffee and a doughnut, Thurrel spent \$2.25, including a tip. Later he spent \$4.00 for two coffees and three doughnuts, including a tip. If he always tips \$1.00, then what is the price of a cup of coffee? \$0.75

73. ***Chlorine mixture.*** A 10% chlorine solution is to be mixed with a 25% chlorine solution to obtain 30 gallons of 20% solution. How many gallons of each must be used?
10 gallons of 10% solution, 20 gallons of 25% solution

74. ***Safe drivers.*** Emily and Camille started from the same city and drove in opposite directions on the freeway. After 3 hours they were 354 miles apart. If they had gone in the same direction, Emily would have been 18 miles ahead of Camille. How fast did each woman drive?
Emily 62 mph, Camille 56 mph

Write a system of three equations in three variables for each word problem. Use Cramer's rule to solve each system.

75. ***Weighing dogs.*** Cassandra wants to determine the weights of her two dogs, Mimi and Mitzi. However, neither dog will sit on the scale by herself. Cassandra, Mimi, and Mitzi altogether weigh 175 pounds. Cassandra and Mimi together weigh 143 pounds. Cassandra and Mitzi together weigh 139 pounds. How much does each weigh individually?
Mimi 36 pounds, Mitzi 32 pounds, Cassandra 107 pounds

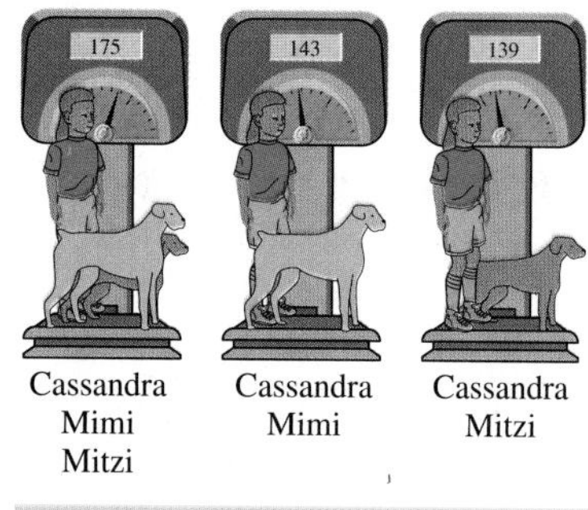

Figure for Exercise 75

76. ***Nickels, dimes, and quarters.*** Bernard has 41 coins consisting of nickels, dimes, and quarters, and they are worth a total of \$4.00. If the number of dimes plus the number of quarters is one more than the number of nickels, then how many of each does he have?
20 nickels, 15 dimes, 6 quarters

77. ***Finding three angles.*** If the two acute angles of a right triangle differ by 12°, then what are the measures of the three angles of this triangle?
39°, 51°, 90°

78. ***Two acute and one obtuse.*** The obtuse angle of a triangle is twice as large as the sum of the two acute angles. If the smallest angle is only one-eighth as large as the sum of the other two, then what is the measure of each angle?
20°, 40°, 120°

Getting More Involved

79. *Writing*

Explain what to do when you are trying to use Cramer's rule and $D = 0$. Use another method.

80. *Exploration*

For what value of a does the system

$$ax - y = 3$$
$$x + 2y = 1$$

have a single solution? $a \neq -\frac{1}{2}$

81. *Exploration*

Can Cramer's rule be used to solve this system? Explain.

$$2x^2 - y = 3$$
$$3x^2 + 2y = 22$$

No. These are nonlinear equations.

82. *Writing*

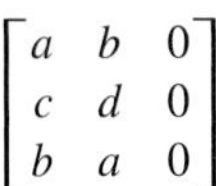

For what values of a, b, c, and d is the determinant of the matrix

$$\begin{bmatrix} a & b & 0 \\ c & d & 0 \\ b & a & 0 \end{bmatrix}$$

equal to zero? Explain your answer.
The determinant is zero for any a, b, c, and d.

Graphing Calculator Exercises

83. Use the determinant feature on your graphing calculator to find the determinants in Exercises 7–14 and 37–44 of this section.

84. Solve the systems in Exercises 15–28 and 53–62 of this section by using your graphing calculator to find the necessary determinants.

Collaborative Activities

Grouping: Two to four students per group

Topic: Types of solutions to systems of equations

Types of Systems

Assign roles in your groups. Set up the system of equations for each scenario that follows and attempt to solve it. Analyze your results.

Part I: Talia's Tallitot. Talia plans to make tallitot (prayer shawls) and matching kipot (prayer hats) from a bolt of material. The fabric she plans to use is 250 yards long. She will need 2 yards of material for each tallit (prayer shawl) and $\frac{1}{6}$ of a yard for each kipah (prayer hat). She also plans to put tzitzit (fringes) on the tallit and will need 1 yard of cord for each tallit. The kipot will not have any fringes. She has 100 yards of cord to use for the tzitzit.

1. Write two equations to use to solve for how many kipot and tallitot she can make from the supplies on hand. Let t equal the number of tallitot made and k equal the number of kipot made.

2. Try to solve this system of equations. If you get a solution, state what it is. If not, describe what your result means.

Part II: Karif's Kerchiefs. Karif plans to make red and green kerchiefs in two sizes, medium and large. He has 60 yards of each color of material. He will need $\frac{1}{4}$ of a yard of the appropriate colored fabric for each medium kerchief and $\frac{1}{2}$ of a yard for each large kerchief. He also plans to trim each kerchief with the alternate color of ribbon. He has 240 yards of each color of ribbon. He will need 1 yard of ribbon for each medium kerchief and 2 yards for each large kerchief.

3. Let m equal the number of medium kerchiefs and l equal the number of large kerchiefs. Set up two equations to use to solve for the number of each color of kerchiefs Karif can make from the supplies on hand.

4. Try to solve this system of equations. If you get a solution, state what it is. If not, describe what your result means.

Part III: Maria's Mantillas. Maria plans to make two different kinds of mantillas (veils), some out of lace and some out of a sheer cotton fabric. She also plans to make two sizes of mantillas, one size for women and one size for young girls. She has 150 yards of the lace fabric and 200 yards of the cotton fabric. She will need 2 yards of either fabric for the smaller mantillas and $3\frac{1}{2}$ yards of either fabric for the larger mantillas.

5. Let w equal the number of mantillas for the women and y equal the number of mantillas for the young girls. Set up two equations to use to solve for the number of each mantilla Maria can make from each type of fabric.

6. Try to solve this system of equations. If you get a solution, state what it is. If not, describe what your result means.

Extension: Explain what you would need to do for the systems of equations you could not solve to make them solvable.

Chapter 7 Wrap-Up

Summary

Systems of Linear Equations		**Examples**
Methods for solving systems in two variables	Graphing: Sketch the graphs to see the solution.	The graphs of $y = x - 1$ and $x + y = 3$ intersect at (2, 1).
	Substitution: Solve one equation for one variable in terms of the other, then substitute into the other equation.	Substitution: $x + (x - 1) = 3$
	Addition: Multiply each equation as necessary to eliminate a variable upon addition of the equations.	$\begin{array}{r} -x + y = -1 \\ x + y = 3 \\ \hline 2y = 2 \end{array}$
Types of linear systems in two variables	Independent: One point in solution set The lines intersect at one point.	$y = x - 5$ $y = 2x + 3$
	Inconsistent: Empty solution set The lines are parallel.	$2x + y = 1$ $2x + y = 5$
	Dependent: Infinite solution set The lines are the same.	$2x + 3y = 4$ $4x + 6y = 8$
Linear equation in three variables	$Ax + By + Cz = D$ In a three-dimensional coordinate system the graph is a plane.	$2x - y + 3z = 5$
Linear systems in three variables	Use substitution or addition to eliminate variables in the system. The solution set may be a single point, the empty set, or an infinite set of points.	$x + y - z = 3$ $2x - 3y + z = 2$ $x - y - 4z = 14$

Matrices and Determinants		**Examples**
Matrix	A rectangular array of real numbers An $n \times m$ matrix has n rows and m columns.	$\begin{bmatrix} 1 & -3 \\ 2 & 5 \end{bmatrix}, \begin{bmatrix} 1 & 0 & 1 \\ 2 & 1 & 4 \end{bmatrix}$
Augmented matrix	The matrix of coefficients and constants from a system of linear equations	$x - 3y = -7$ $2x + 5y = 19$ Augmented matrix: $\left[\begin{array}{rr|r} 1 & -3 & -7 \\ 2 & 5 & 19 \end{array}\right]$

Gauss-Jordan elimination method	Use the row operations to get ones on the diagonal and zeros elsewhere for the coefficients in the augmented matrix.	$\left[\begin{array}{cc\|c} 1 & 0 & 2 \\ 0 & 1 & 3 \end{array}\right]$ $x = 2$ and $y = 3$
Determinant	A real number corresponding to a square matrix	
Determinant of a 2×2 matrix	$\begin{vmatrix} a_1 & b_1 \\ a_2 & b_2 \end{vmatrix} = a_1b_2 - a_2b_1$	$\begin{vmatrix} 1 & -3 \\ 2 & 5 \end{vmatrix} = 5 - (-6)$ $= 11$
Determinant of a 3×3 matrix	Expand by minors about any row or column, using signs from the sign array. $\begin{vmatrix} a_1 & b_1 & c_1 \\ a_2 & b_2 & c_2 \\ a_3 & b_3 & c_3 \end{vmatrix} = a_1 \cdot \begin{vmatrix} b_2 & c_2 \\ b_3 & c_3 \end{vmatrix} - a_2 \cdot \begin{vmatrix} b_1 & c_1 \\ b_3 & c_3 \end{vmatrix} + a_3 \cdot \begin{vmatrix} b_1 & c_1 \\ b_2 & c_2 \end{vmatrix}$	Sign array: $\begin{bmatrix} + & - & + \\ - & + & - \\ + & - & + \end{bmatrix}$

Cramer's Rules

Two linear equations in two variables	The solution to the system $a_1x + b_1y = c_1$ $a_2x + b_2y = c_2$ is given by $x = \frac{D_x}{D}$ and $y = \frac{D_y}{D}$, where $D = \begin{vmatrix} a_1 & b_1 \\ a_2 & b_2 \end{vmatrix}$, $D_x = \begin{vmatrix} c_1 & b_1 \\ c_2 & b_2 \end{vmatrix}$, and $D_y = \begin{vmatrix} a_1 & c_1 \\ a_2 & c_2 \end{vmatrix}$ provided that $D \neq 0$.
Three linear equations in three variables	The solution to the system $a_1x + b_1y + c_1z = d_1$ $a_2x + b_2y + c_2z = d_2$ $a_3x + b_3y + c_3z = d_3$ is given by $x = \frac{D_x}{D}$, $y = \frac{D_y}{D}$, and $z = \frac{D_z}{D}$, where $D = \begin{vmatrix} a_1 & b_1 & c_1 \\ a_2 & b_2 & c_2 \\ a_3 & b_3 & c_3 \end{vmatrix}$, $D_x = \begin{vmatrix} d_1 & b_1 & c_1 \\ d_2 & b_2 & c_2 \\ d_3 & b_3 & c_3 \end{vmatrix}$, $D_y = \begin{vmatrix} a_1 & d_1 & c_1 \\ a_2 & d_2 & c_2 \\ a_3 & d_3 & c_3 \end{vmatrix}$, and $D_z = \begin{vmatrix} a_1 & b_1 & d_1 \\ a_2 & b_2 & d_2 \\ a_3 & b_3 & d_3 \end{vmatrix}$, provided that $D \neq 0$.

Enriching Your Mathematical Word Power

For each mathematical term, choose the correct meaning.

1. system of equations
a. a systematic method for classifying equations
b. a method for solving an equation
c. two or more equations
d. the properties of equality c

2. independent linear system
a. a system with exactly one solution
b. an equation that is satisfied by every real number
c. equations that are identical
d. a system of lines a

3. inconsistent system
a. a system with no solution
b. a system of inconsistent equations
c. a system that is incorrect
d. a system that we are not sure how to solve a

4. dependent system
a. a system that is independent
b. a system that depends on a variable
c. a system that has no solution
d. a system for which the graphs coincide d

5. substitution method
a. replacing the variables by the correct answer
b. a method of eliminating a variable by substituting one equation into the other
c. the replacement method
d. any method of solving a system b

6. addition method
a. adding the same number to each side of an equation
b. adding fractions
c. eliminating a variable by adding two equations
d. the sum of a number and its additive inverse is zero c

7. linear equation in three variables
a. $Ax + By + Cz = D$ with A, B, and C not all zero
b. $Ax + By = C$ with A and B not both zero
c. the equation of a line
d. $A/x + B/y = C$ with A and B not both zero a

8. matrix
a. a movie
b. a maze
c. a rectangular array of numbers
d. coordinates in four dimensions c

9. augmented matrix
a. a matrix with a power booster
b. a matrix with no solution
c. a square matrix
d. a matrix containing the coefficients and constants of a system of equations d

10. size of a matrix
a. the length of a matrix
b. the number of rows and columns in a matrix
c. the highest power of a matrix
d. the lowest power of a matrix b

11. determinant
a. a number corresponding to a square matrix
b. a number that is determined by any matrix
c. the first entry of a matrix
d. a number that determines whether a matrix has a solution a

12. sign array
a. the signs of the entries of a matrix
b. the sign of the determinant
c. the signs of the answers
d. a matrix of + and − signs used in computing a determinant d

Review Exercises

7.1 *Solve by graphing. Indicate whether each system is independent, inconsistent, or dependent.*

1. $y = 2x - 1$
$x + y = 2$ $\{(1, 1)\}$, independent

2. $y = 3x - 4$
$y = -2x + 1$ $\{(1, -1)\}$, independent

3. $x + 2y = 4$
$y = -\frac{1}{2}x + 2$ $\{(x, y) \mid x + 2y = 4\}$, dependent

4. $2x - 3y = 12$
$3y - 2x = -12$
$\{(x, y) \mid 2x - 3y = 12\}$, dependent

5. $y = -x$
$y = -x + 3$
$\varnothing$, inconsistent

6. $3x - y = 4$
$3x - y = 0$
$\varnothing$, inconsistent

Solve each system by the substitution method. Indicate whether each system is independent, inconsistent, or dependent.

7. $y = 3x + 11$
$2x + 3y = 0$
$\{(-3, 2)\}$, independent

8. $x - y = 3$
$3x - 2y = 3$
$\{(-3, -6)\}$, independent

9. $x = y + 5$
$2x - 2y = 12$
$\varnothing$, inconsistent

10. $3y = x + 5$
$3x - 9y = -10$
$\varnothing$, inconsistent

11. $2x - y = 3$
$6x - 9 = 3y$
$\{(x, y) \mid 2x - y = 3\}$, dependent

12. $y = \frac{1}{2}x - 9$
$3x - 6y = 54$
$\left\{(x, y) \mid y = \frac{1}{2}x - 9\right\}$, dependent

13. $y = \frac{1}{2}x - 3$
$y = \frac{1}{3}x + 2$
$\{(30, 12)\}$, independent

14. $x = \frac{1}{8}y - 1$
$y = \frac{1}{4}x + 39$
$\{(4, 40)\}$, independent

15. $x + 2y = 1$
$8x + 6y = 4$
$\left\{\left(\frac{1}{5}, \frac{2}{5}\right)\right\}$, independent

16. $x - 5y = 4$
$4x + 8y = -5$
$\left\{\left(\frac{1}{4}, -\frac{3}{4}\right)\right\}$, independent

7.2 *Solve each system by the addition method. Indicate whether each system is independent, inconsistent, or dependent.*

17. $5x - 3y = -20$
$3x + 2y = 7$
$\{(-1, 5)\}$, independent

18. $-3x + y = 3$
$2x - 3y = 5$
$\{(-2, -3)\}$, independent

19. $2(y - 5) + 4 = 3(x - 6)$
$3x - 2y = 12$
$\{(x, y) \mid 3x - 2y = 12\}$, dependent

20. $x + 3(y - 1) = 11$
$2(x - y) + 8y = 28$
$\{(x, y) \mid x + 3y = 14\}$, dependent

Study Tip

Note how the review exercises are arranged according to the sections in this chapter. If you are having trouble with a certain type of problem, refer back to the appropriate section for examples and explanations.

21. $3x - 4(y - 5) = x + 2$
$2y - x = 7$
$\varnothing$, inconsistent

22. $4(1 - x) + y = 3$
$3(1 - y) - 4x = -4y$
$\varnothing$, inconsistent

23. $\frac{1}{4}x + \frac{3}{8}y = \frac{3}{8}$
$\frac{5}{2}x - 6y = 7$
$\left\{\left(2, -\frac{1}{3}\right)\right\}$, independent

24. $\frac{1}{3}x - \frac{1}{6}y = \frac{1}{3}$
$\frac{1}{6}x + \frac{1}{4}y = 0$
$\left\{\left(\frac{3}{4}, -\frac{1}{2}\right)\right\}$, independent

25. $0.4x + 0.06y = 11.6$
$0.8x - 0.05y = 13$
$\{(20, 60)\}$, independent

26. $0.08x + 0.7y = 37.4$
$0.06x - 0.05y = -0.7$
$\{(30, 50)\}$, independent

7.3 *Solve each system by elimination of variables.*

27. $x - y + z = 4$
$-x + 2y - z = 0$
$-x + y - 3z = -16$
$\{(2, 4, 6)\}$

28. $2x - y + z = 5$
$x + y - 2z = -4$
$3x - y + 3z = 10$
$\{(1, -1, 2)\}$

29. $2x - y - z = 3$
$3x + y + 2z = 4$
$4x + 2y - z = -4$
$\{(1, -3, 2)\}$

30. $2x + 3y - 2z = -11$
$3x - 2y + 3z = 7$
$x - 4y + 4z = 14$
$\{(-2, 1, 5)\}$

31. $x + y - z = 4$
$y + z = 6$
$x + 2y = 8$
$\varnothing$

32. $x - 3y + z = 5$
$2x - 4y - z = 7$
$2x - 6y + 2z = 6$
$\varnothing$

33. $x - 2y + z = 8$
$-x + 2y - z = -8$
$2x - 4y + 2z = 16$
$\{(x, y, z) \mid x - 2y + z = 8\}$

34. $x - y + z = 1$
$2x - 2y + 2z = 2$
$-3x + 3y - 3z = -3$
$\{(x, y, z) \mid x - y + z = 1\}$

7.4 *Solve each system by the Gauss-Jordan elimination method.*

35. $x + y = 7$
$-x + 2y = 5$
$\{(3, 4)\}$

36. $-x + y = 1$
$2x - 3y = -7$
$\{(4, 5)\}$

37. $2x + y = 0$
$x - 3y = 14$
$\{(2, -4)\}$

38. $2x - y = 8$
$3x + 2y = -2$
$\{(2, -4)\}$

39. $x + y - z = 0$
$x - y + 2z = 4$
$2x + y - z = 1$
$\{(1, 1, 2)\}$

40. $2x - y + 2z = 9$
$x + 3y = 5$
$3x + z = 9$
$\{(2, 1, 3)\}$

7.5 *Evaluate each determinant.*

41. $\begin{vmatrix} 1 & 3 \\ 0 & 2 \end{vmatrix}$ 2

42. $\begin{vmatrix} -1 & 2 \\ -3 & 5 \end{vmatrix}$ 1

43. $\begin{vmatrix} 0.01 & 0.02 \\ 50 & 80 \end{vmatrix}$ -0.2

44. $\begin{vmatrix} \frac{1}{2} & \frac{1}{3} \\ \frac{1}{4} & \frac{1}{5} \end{vmatrix}$ $\frac{1}{60}$

Solve each system. Use Cramer's rule.

45. $2x - y = 0$
$3x + y = -5$
$\{(-1, -2)\}$

46. $3x - 2y = 14$
$2x + 3y = -8$
$\{(2, -4)\}$

47. $y = 2x - 3$
$3x - 2y = 4$
$\{(2, 1)\}$

48. $y = 2x - 5$
$y = 3x - 3y$
$\{(4, 3)\}$

Evaluate each determinant.

49. $\begin{vmatrix} 2 & 3 & 1 \\ -1 & 2 & 4 \\ 6 & 1 & 1 \end{vmatrix}$ 58

50. $\begin{vmatrix} 1 & -1 & 0 \\ -2 & 0 & 0 \\ 3 & 1 & 5 \end{vmatrix}$ -10

51. $\begin{vmatrix} 2 & 3 & -2 \\ 2 & 0 & 4 \\ -1 & 0 & 3 \end{vmatrix}$ -30

52. $\begin{vmatrix} 3 & -1 & 4 \\ 2 & -1 & 1 \\ -2 & 0 & 1 \end{vmatrix}$ -7

Solve each system. Use Cramer's rule.

53. $x + y = 3$
$x + y + z = 0$
$x - y - z = 2$
$\{(1, 2, -3)\}$

54. $2x - y + z = 0$
$4x + 6y - 2z = 0$
$x - 2y - z = -9$
$\{(-1, 2, 4)\}$

Miscellaneous

Use a system of equations in two or three variables to solve each problem. Solve by the method of your choice.

55. ***Perimeter of a rectangle.*** The length of a rectangular swimming pool is 15 feet longer than the width. If the perimeter is 82 feet, then what are the length and width?
Width 13 feet, length 28 feet

56. ***Household income.*** Alkena and Hsu together earn \$84,326 per year. If Alkena earns \$12,468 more per year than Hsu, then how much does each of them earn per year?
Hsu \$35,929, Alkena \$48,397

57. ***Two-digit number.*** The sum of the digits in a two-digit number is 15. When the digits are reversed, the new number is 9 more than the original number. What is the original number?
78

58. ***Two-digit number.*** The sum of the digits in a two-digit number is 8. When the digits are reversed, the new number is 18 less than the original number. What is the original number?
53

59. ***Traveling by boat.*** Alonzo can travel from his camp downstream to the mouth of the river in 30 minutes. If it takes him 45 minutes to come back, then how long would it take him to go that same distance in the lake with no current?
36 minutes

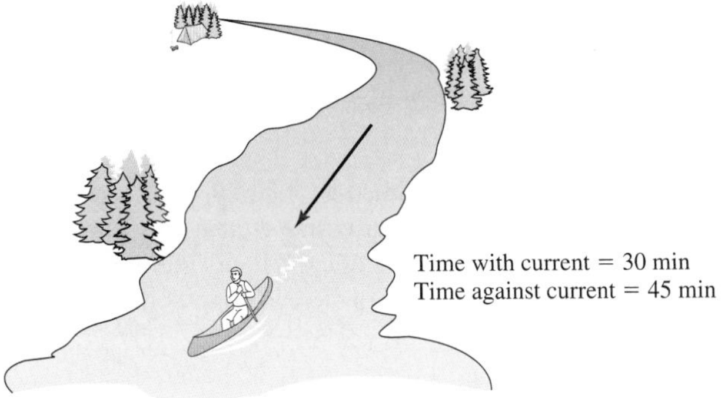

Figure for Exercise 59

60. ***Driving and dating.*** In 4 years Gasper will be old enough to drive. His parents said that he must have a driver's license for 2 years before he can date. Three years ago, Gasper's age was only one-half of the age necessary to date. How old must Gasper be to drive, and how old is he now?
16 years old to drive, 12 years old at present

61. ***Three solutions.*** A chemist has three solutions of acid that must be mixed to obtain 20 liters of a solution that is 38% acid. Solution A is 30% acid, solution B is 20% acid, and solution C is 60% acid. Because of another chemical in these solutions, the chemist must keep the ratio of solution C to solution A at 2 to 1. How many liters of each should she mix together?
4 liters of A, 8 liters of B, 8 liters of C

62. ***Mixing investments.*** Darlene invested a total of \$20,000. The part that she invested in Dell Computer stock returned 70% and the part that she invested in U.S. Treasury bonds returned 5%. Her total return on these two investments was \$9,580.

a) Use the accompanying graph to estimate the amount that she put into each investment.
\$13,000 in Dell, \$7000 in bonds

b) Solve a system of equations to find the exact amount that she put into each investment.
\$13,200 in Dell, \$6800 in bonds

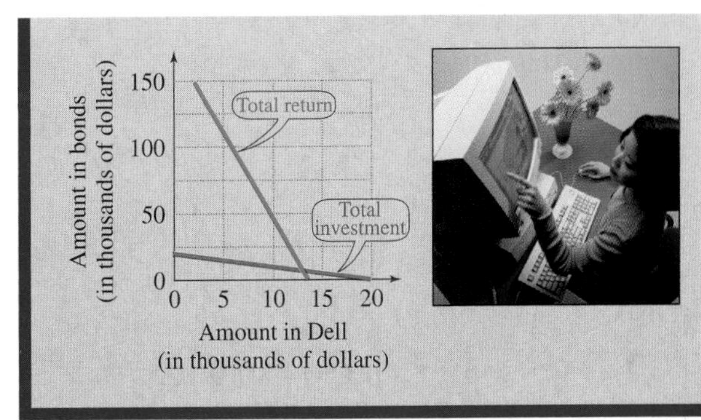

Figure for Exercise 62

63. ***Beets and beans.*** One serving of canned beets contains 1 gram of protein and 6 grams of carbohydrates. One serving of canned red beans contains 6 grams of protein and 20 grams of carbohydrates. How many servings of each would it take to get exactly 21 grams of protein and 78 grams of carbohydrates?
Three servings of each

Chapter 7 Test

Solve the system by graphing.

1. $x + y = 4$
$y = 2x + 1$
$\{(1, 3)\}$

Solve each system by substitution.

2. $y = 2x - 8$
$4x + 3y = 1$
$\left\{\left(\frac{5}{2}, -3\right)\right\}$

3. $y = x - 5$
$3x - 4(y - 2) = 28 - x$
$\{(x, y) \mid y = x - 5\}$

Solve each system by the addition method.

4. $3x + 2y = 3$
$4x - 3y = -13$
$\{(-1, 3)\}$

5. $3x - y = 5$
$-6x + 2y = 1$
$\emptyset$

Determine whether each system is independent, inconsistent, or dependent.

6. $y = 3x - 5$
$y = 3x + 2$
Inconsistent

7. $2x + 2y = 8$
$x + y = 4$
Dependent

8. $y = 2x - 3$
$y = 5x - 14$
Independent

Solve the following system by elimination of variables.

9. $x + y - z = 2$
$2x - y + 3z = -5$
$x - 3y + z = 4$
$\{(1, -2, -3)\}$

Solve by the Gauss-Jordan elimination method.

10. $3x - y = 1$
$x + 2y = 12$
$\{(2, 5)\}$

11. $x - y - z = 1$
$-x - y + 2z = -2$
$-x - 3y + z = -5$
$\{(3, 1, 1)\}$

Evaluate each determinant.

12. $\begin{vmatrix} 2 & 3 \\ 4 & -3 \end{vmatrix}$ -18

13. $\begin{vmatrix} 1 & -2 & -1 \\ 2 & 3 & 1 \\ 1 & 1 & 0 \end{vmatrix}$ -2

Solve each system by using Cramer's rule.

14. $2x - y = -4$
$3x + y = -1$
$\{(-1, 2)\}$

15. $x + y = 0$
$x - y + 2z = 6$
$2x + y - z = 1$
$\{(2, -2, 1)\}$

Study Tip

Before you take an in-class exam on this chapter, work the sample test given here. Set aside one hour to work this test and use the answers in the back of this book to grade yourself. Even though your instructor might not ask exactly the same questions, you will get a good idea of your test readiness.

For each problem, write a system of equations in two or three variables. Use the method of your choice to solve each system.

16. One night the manager of the Sea Breeze Motel rented 5 singles and 12 doubles for a total of \$390. The next night he rented 9 singles and 10 doubles for a total of \$412. What is the rental charge for each type of room?
Singles \$18, doubles \$25

17. Jill, Karen, and Betsy studied a total of 93 hours last week. Jill's and Karen's study time totaled only one-half as much as Betsy's. If Jill studied 3 hours more than Karen, then how many hours did each one of the girls spend studying?
Jill 17 hours, Karen 14 hours, Betsy 62 hours

Making Connections | A Review of Chapters 1–7

Simplify each expression.

1. -3^4 -81

2. $\frac{1}{3}(3) + 6$ 7

3. $(-5)^2 - 4(-2)(6)$ 73

4. $6 - (0.2)(0.3)$ 5.94

5. $5(t - 3) - 6(t - 2)$ $-t - 3$

6. $0.1(x - 1) - (x - 1)$ $-0.9x + 0.9$

7. $\frac{-9x^2 - 6x + 3}{-3}$ $3x^2 + 2x - 1$

8. $\frac{4y - 6}{2} - \frac{3y - 9}{3}$ y

Solve each equation for y.

9. $3x - 5y = 7$ $y = \frac{3}{5}x - \frac{7}{5}$

10. $Cx - Dy = W$ $y = \frac{C}{D}x - \frac{W}{D}$

11. $Cy = Wy - K$ $y = \frac{K}{W - C}$

12. $A = \frac{1}{2}b(w - y)$ $y = \frac{bw - 2A}{b}$

Solve each system.

13. $y = x - 5$
$2x + 3y = 5$
$\{(4, -1)\}$

14. $0.05x + 0.06y = 67$
$x + y = 1200$
$\{(500, 700)\}$

15. $3x - 15y = -51$
$x + 17 = 5y$
$\{(x, y) \mid x + 17 = 5y\}$

16. $0.07a + 0.3b = 6.70$
$7a + 30b = 67$
$\emptyset$

Find the equation of each line.

17. The line through $(0, 55)$ and $(-99, 0)$
$y = \frac{5}{9}x + 55$

18. The line through $(2, -3)$ and $(-4, 8)$
$y = -\frac{11}{6}x + \frac{2}{3}$

19. The line through $(-4, 6)$ that is parallel to $y = 5x$
$y = 5x + 26$

20. The line through $(4, 7)$ that is perpendicular to $y = -2x + 1$
$y = \frac{1}{2}x + 5$

21. The line through $(3, 5)$ that is parallel to the x-axis
$y = 5$

22. The line through $(-7, 0)$ that is perpendicular to the x-axis
$x = -7$

Study Tip

Don't wait until the final exam to review material. Do some review on a regular basis. The Making Connections exercises on this page can be used to review, compare, and contrast different concepts that you have studied. A good time to work these exercises is between a test and the start of new material.

Solve.

23. ***Comparing copiers.*** A self-employed consultant has prepared the accompanying graph to compare the total cost of purchasing and using two different copy machines.

a) Which machine has the larger purchase price?
b) What is the per copy cost for operating each machine, not including the purchase price?
c) Find the slope of each line and interpret your findings.
d) Find the equation of each line.
e) Find the number of copies for which the total cost is the same for both machines.

a) Machine A
b) Machine B \$0.04 per copy, machine A \$0.03 per copy
c) The slopes 0.04 and 0.03 are the per copy cost for each machine.
d) B: $y = 0.04x + 2000$, A: $y = 0.03x + 4000$
e) 200,000

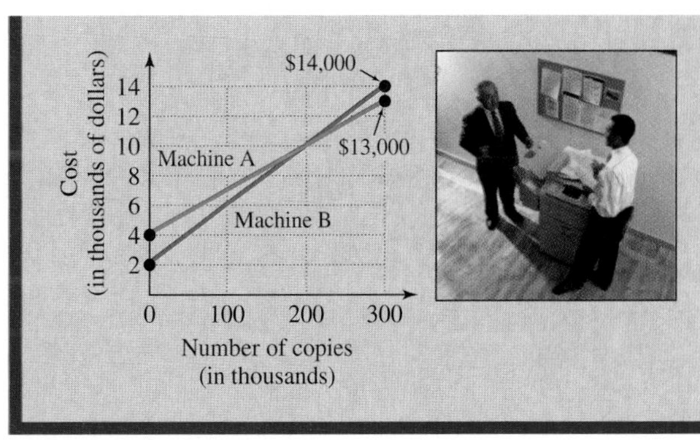

Figure for Exercise 23

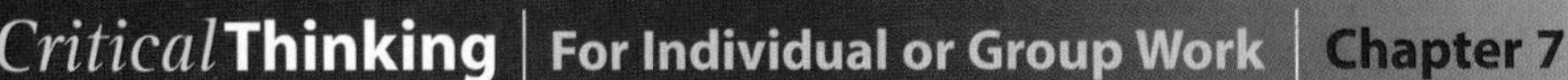

Critical **Thinking** | For Individual or Group Work | Chapter 7

These exercises can be solved by a variety of techniques, which may or may not require algebra. So be creative and think critically. Explain all answers. Answers are in the Instructor's Edition of this text.

1. ***Tricky square.*** Start with a square and write any integer at each vertex. (a) At the midpoint of each side write the absolute value of the difference between the numbers at the endpoints of that side. (b) Connect the midpoints to obtain another square. Repeat (a) and (b) to obtain a sequence of nested squares as shown in the accompanying figure. What numbers will you always end up with?

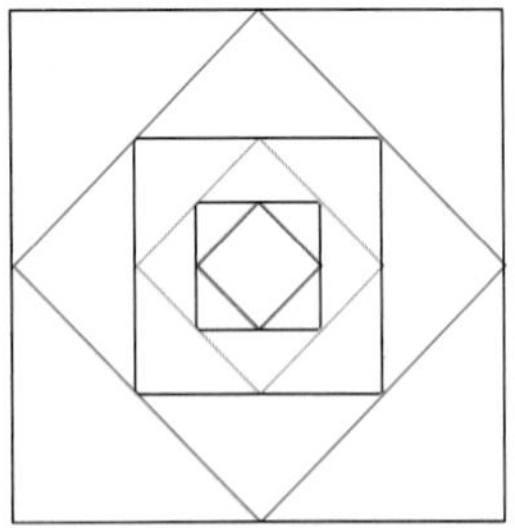

Figure for Exercise 1

2. ***Planning ahead.*** Thaddeus takes one month to build a kayak (K) and two months to build a canoe (C).

Photo for Exercise 2

While planning ahead for one month, he notes that there is only one thing to do that will not result in any partially finished boats. That is, build one kayak. For planning two months ahead there are two possibilities, KK or C. For a three-month plan there are three possibilities, KKK or KC or CK.

a) Find the number of possibilities for a four-month plan, a five-month plan, and a six-month plan by listing the possibilities. Look for a pattern.

b) Find the number of possibilities for a seven-month plan and an eight-month plan without making a list.

3. ***Five coins.*** Place five coins on a table with heads facing downward. On each move you must turn over exactly three coins. What is the minimum number of moves necessary to get all five heads facing upward?

4. ***Rotating tires.*** Helen bought a new car with four tires and a full-size spare. If she rotated the tires so that each tire would have the same amount of wear, then how many miles were on each tire when her odometer showed 40,000 miles?

5. ***Cutting pizza.*** What is the largest number of pieces of pizza you can get if you cut a circular pizza with five straight cuts? What is the largest number of pieces of pizza you can get if you cut a circular pizza with seven straight cuts?

6. ***Mysterious rectangle.*** The length of a rectangle is a two-digit number with identical digits (aa). The width of the rectangle is one-tenth of the length ($a.a$). The perimeter is numerically twice as large as the area. Find the length, width, perimeter, and area.

7. ***Finding squares.*** Evaluate the expression

$$100^2 - 99^2 + 98^2 - 97^2 + 96^2 \cdots - 3^2 + 2^2 - 1^2$$

without using a calculator.

8. ***Five-digit sum.*** Find the sum of all five-digit numbers that are formed by using the digits 1, 2, 3, 4, and 5 once and only once.

1. 0 **2. a)** 5, 8, 13 **b)** 21, 34 **3.** 5 **4.** 32,000 miles **5.** 15, 26 **6.** 11, 1.1, 24.2, 12.1 **7.** 5050 **8.** 399,960

Chapter 8

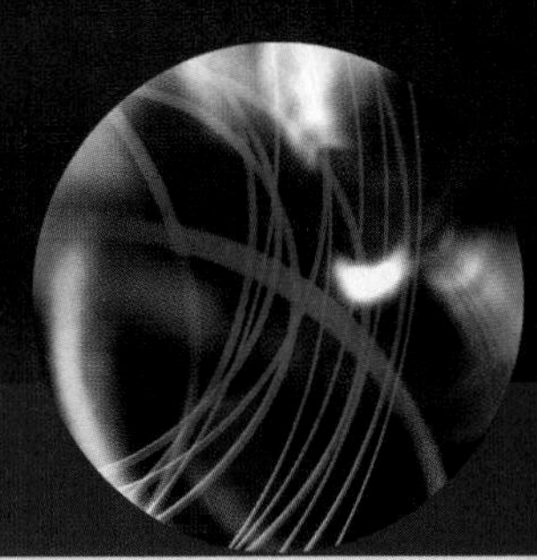

More on Inequalities

The practice of awarding degrees originated in the universities of medieval Europe. The first known degree, a degree in civil law, was awarded in Italy at the University of Bologna in the twelfth century. The University of Paris awarded its first bachelor's degree in the thirteenth century. By the time the first colleges were opened in the American colonies, the process of awarding degrees was firmly established. At first, American schools offered only a few types of degrees. The colleges established in the colonies were primarily to train young men for the ministry. Notable were Harvard (1636; Puritan), William and Mary (1693; Anglican), Yale (1701; Congregationalist), Princeton (1746; New Lights Presbyterian), Brown (1765; Baptist), and Rutgers (1766; Dutch Reformed).

The industrial revolution sparked a demand for training in many areas. Today, approximately 1500 types of degrees are granted by academic institutions in the United States. Over 1 million Bachelor of Arts (B.A.) or of Science (B.S.) degrees are granted annually. Over one-quarter of a million Master of Arts (M.A.) or Science (M.S.) degrees are awarded annually.

The growth of bachelor's and master's degrees is modeled with linear equations in Exercise 91 of Section 8.1. In that exercise we also use inequalities and compound inequalities to discuss the growth of these degrees.

8.1 Compound Inequalities in One Variable

In this Section

- Basics
- Graphing the Solution Set
- Applications

The inequality $a < x < b$, from Section 2.9, is one type of compound inequality in one variable. This inequality indicates that x is both greater than a and less than b. That is, x is between a and b. In this section we will study other types of compound inequalities in one variable.

Basics

Inequalities involving a single inequality symbol are **simple inequalities.** If we join two simple inequalities with the connective "and" or the connective "or," we get a **compound inequality.** A compound inequality using the connective "and" is true if and only if *both* simple inequalities are true.

EXAMPLE 1

Compound inequalities using the connective "and"

Determine whether each compound inequality is true.

a) $3 > 2$ and $3 < 5$ **b)** $6 > 2$ and $6 < 5$

Solution

a) The compound inequality is true because $3 > 2$ is true and $3 < 5$ is true.

b) The compound inequality is false because $6 < 5$ is false.

Now do Exercises 7–10

A compound inequality using the connective "or" is true if one or the other or both of the simple inequalities are true. It is false only if both simple inequalities are false.

EXAMPLE 2

Compound inequalities using the connective "or"

Determine whether each compound inequality is true.

a) $2 < 3$ or $2 > 7$ **b)** $4 < 3$ or $4 \geq 7$

Solution

a) The compound inequality is true because $2 < 3$ is true.

b) The compound inequality is false because both $4 < 3$ and $4 \geq 7$ are false.

Now do Exercises 11–12

Helpful Hint

There is a big difference between "and" and "or." To get money from an automatic teller you must have a bank card *and* know a secret number (PIN). There would be a lot of problems if you could get money by having a bank card *or* knowing a PIN.

If a compound inequality involves a variable, then we are interested in the solution set to the inequality. The solution set to an "and" inequality consists of all numbers that satisfy both simple inequalities, whereas the solution set to an "or" inequality consists of all numbers that satisfy at least one of the simple inequalities.

EXAMPLE 3

Solutions of compound inequalities

Determine whether 5 satisfies each compound inequality.

a) $x < 6$ and $x < 9$ **b)** $2x - 9 \leq 5$ or $-4x \geq -12$

Solution

a) Because $5 < 6$ and $5 < 9$ are both true, 5 satisfies the compound inequality.

b) Because $2 \cdot 5 - 9 \leq 5$ is true, it does not matter that $-4 \cdot 5 \geq -12$ is false. So 5 satisfies the compound inequality.

Now do Exercises 13–18

Graphing the Solution Set

If A and B are sets of numbers, then the **intersection** of A and B is the set of all numbers that are in both A and B. The intersection of A and B is denoted as $A \cap B$ (read "A intersect B"). For example, if $A = \{1, 2, 3\}$ and $B = \{2, 3, 4, 5\}$, then $A \cap B = \{2, 3\}$ because only 2 and 3 are in both A and B. If you are not familiar with the general ideas of intersections and unions of sets, see Appendix B for more details and exercises.

The solution set to a compound inequality using the connective "and" is the intersection of the solution sets to each of the simple inequalities. Using graphs, as shown in the next example, will help you understand compound inequalities.

EXAMPLE 4

Graphing compound inequalities

Graph the solution set to the compound inequality $x > 2$ and $x < 5$.

Solution

First sketch the graph of $x > 2$ and then the graph of $x < 5$, as shown in the top two number lines in Fig. 8.1. The intersection of these two solution sets is the portion of the number line that is shaded on both graphs, just the part between 2 and 5, not including the endpoints. In symbols, $(2, \infty) \cap (-\infty, 5) = (2, 5)$. So the solution set is the interval $(2, 5)$ and its graph is shown at the bottom of Fig. 8.1. Recall from Section 2.9 that $x > 2$ and $x < 5$ is also written as $2 < x < 5$.

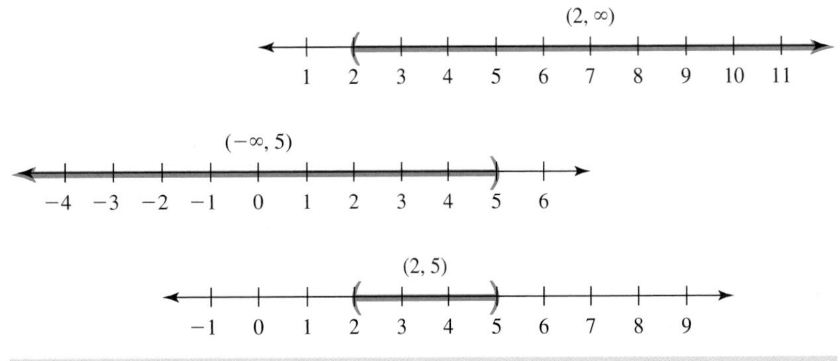

Figure 8.1

Now do Exercises 19–22

Study Tip

Never leave an exam early. Most papers turned in early contain careless errors that could be found and corrected. Every point counts. Reread the questions to be sure that you don't have a nice solution to a question that wasn't asked. Check all arithmetic. You can check many problems by using a different method. Some problems can be checked with a calculator. Make sure that you did not forget to answer a question.

If A and B are sets of numbers, then the **union** of A and B is the set of all numbers that are in either A or B. The union of A and B is denoted as $A \cup B$ (read "A union B"). For example, if $A = \{1, 2, 3\}$ and $B = \{2, 3, 4, 5\}$, then $A \cup B = \{1, 2, 3, 4, 5\}$ because all of these numbers are in A or B. Notice that the numbers in A and B are in $A \cup B$.

The solution set to a compound inequality using the connective "or" is the union of the solution sets to each of the simple inequalities.

EXAMPLE 5

Graphing compound inequalities

Graph the solution set to the compound inequality $x > 4$ or $x < -1$.

Solution

First graph the solution sets to the simple inequalities as shown in Fig. 8.2. The union of these two intervals is shown at the bottom of Fig. 8.2. Since the union does not simplify to a single interval, the solution set is written using the symbol for union as $(-\infty, -1) \cup (4, \infty)$.

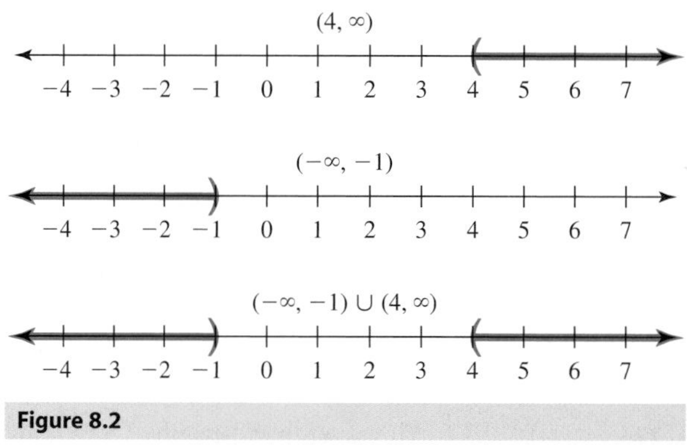

Figure 8.2

Now do Exercises 23–24

CAUTION When graphing the intersection of two simple inequalities, do not draw too much. For the intersection, graph only numbers that satisfy *both* inequalities. Omit numbers that satisfy one but not the other inequality. Graphing a union is usually easier because we can simply draw both solution sets on the same number line.

It is not always necessary to graph the solution set to each simple inequality before graphing the solution set to the compound inequality. We can save time and work if we learn to think of the two preliminary graphs but draw only the final one.

EXAMPLE 6

Overlapping intervals

Sketch the graph and write the solution set in interval notation to each compound inequality.

a) $x < 3$ and $x < 5$

b) $x > 4$ or $x > 0$

Teaching Tip Remind students that "or" includes both.

Solution

a) To graph $x < 3$ and $x < 5$, we shade only the numbers that are both less than 3 and less than 5. So numbers between 3 and 5 are not shaded in Fig. 8.3. The compound inequality $x < 3$ and $x < 5$ is equivalent to the simple inequality $x < 3$. The solution set can be written as $(-\infty, 3)$. In symbols, $(-\infty, 3) \cap (-\infty, 5) = (-\infty, 3)$.

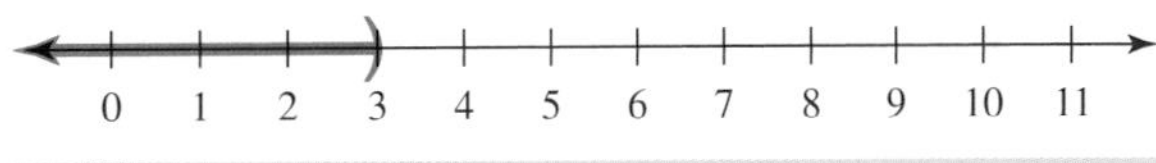

Figure 8.3

b) To graph $x > 4$ or $x > 0$, we shade both regions on the same number line as shown in Fig. 8.4. The compound inequality $x > 4$ or $x > 0$ is equivalent to the simple inequality $x > 0$. The solution set is $(0, \infty)$. In symbols, $(4, \infty) \cup (0, \infty) = (0, \infty)$.

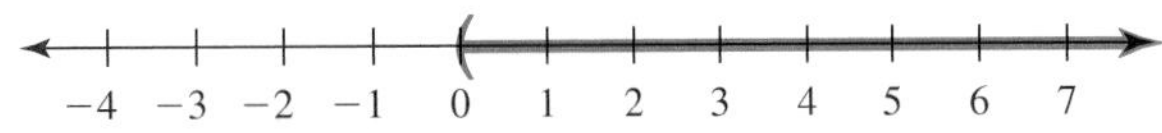

Figure 8.4

Now do Exercises 25–26

Example 7 shows a compound inequality that has no solution and one that is satisfied by every real number.

EXAMPLE 7

All or nothing

Sketch the graph and write the solution set in interval notation to each compound inequality.

a) $x < 2$ and $x > 6$

b) $x < 3$ or $x > 1$

Study Tip

Make sure you know exactly how your grade in this course is determined. You should know how much weight is given to tests, quizzes, projects, homework, and the final exam. You should know the policy for making up work in case of illness. Record all scores and compute your final grade.

Solution

a) A number satisfies $x < 2$ and $x > 6$ if it is both less than 2 *and* greater than 6. There are no such numbers. The solution set is the empty set, $\emptyset$. In symbols, $(-\infty, 2) \cap (6, \infty) = \emptyset$.

b) To graph $x < 3$ or $x > 1$, we shade both regions on the same number line as shown in Fig. 8.5. Since the two regions cover the entire line, the solution set is the set of all real numbers $(-\infty, \infty)$. In symbols, $(-\infty, 3) \cup (1, \infty) = (-\infty, \infty)$.

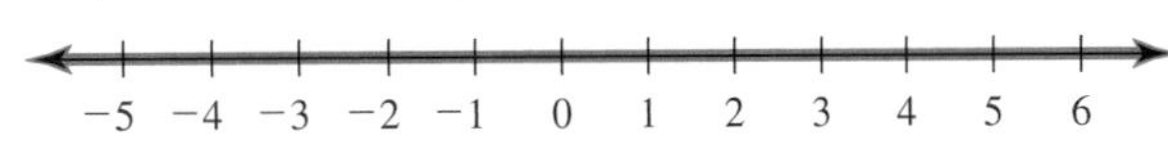

Figure 8.5

Now do Exercises 27–32

If we start with a more complicated compound inequality, we first simplify each part of the compound inequality and then find the union or intersection.

EXAMPLE 8

Calculator Close-Up

To check Example 8, press Y= and let $y_1 = x + 2$ and $y_2 = x - 6$. Now scroll through a table of values for y_1 and y_2. From the table you can see that y_1 is greater than 3 and y_2 is less than 7 precisely when x is between 1 and 13.

X	Y1	Y2
1	3	-5
3	5	-3
5	7	-1
7	9	1
9	11	3
11	13	5
13	15	7

Y1=X+2

Intersection

Solve $x + 2 > 3$ and $x - 6 < 7$. Graph the solution set.

Solution

First simplify each simple inequality:

$$x + 2 - 2 > 3 - 2 \quad \text{and} \quad x - 6 + 6 < 7 + 6$$
$$x > 1 \quad \text{and} \quad x < 13$$

The intersection of these two solution sets is the set of numbers between (but not including) 1 and 13. Its graph is shown in Fig. 8.6. The solution set is written in interval notation as (1, 13). Recall from Section 2.9 that $x > 1$ and $x < 13$ is also written as $1 < x < 13$.

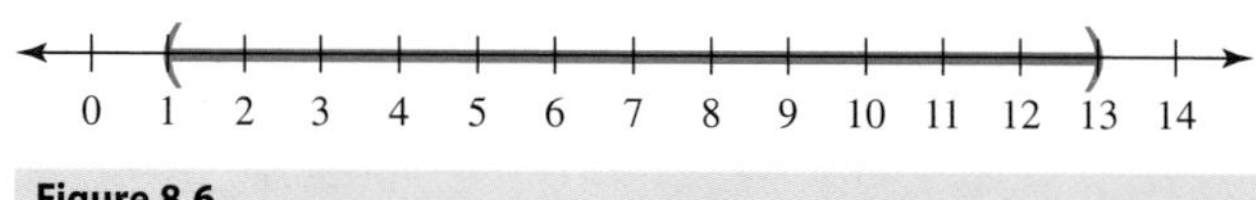

Figure 8.6

Now do Exercises 33–36

EXAMPLE 9

Calculator Close-Up

To check Example 9, press Y= and let $y_1 = 5 - 7x$ and $y_2 = 3x - 2$. Now scroll through a table of values for y_1 and y_2. From the table you can see that either $y_1 \ge 12$ or $y_2 < 7$ is true for $x < 3$. Note also that for $x \ge 3$ both $y_1 \ge 12$ and $y_2 < 7$ are incorrect. The table supports the conclusion of Example 9.

X	Y1	Y2
1	-2	1
2	-9	4
3	-16	7
4	-23	10
5	-30	13
6	-37	16
7	-44	19

Y1=5-7X

Union

Graph the solution set to the inequality

$$5 - 7x \ge 12 \quad \text{or} \quad 3x - 2 < 7.$$

Solution

First solve each of the simple inequalities:

$$5 - 7x - 5 \ge 12 - 5 \quad \text{or} \quad 3x - 2 + 2 < 7 + 2$$
$$-7x \ge 7 \quad \text{or} \quad 3x < 9$$
$$x \le -1 \quad \text{or} \quad x < 3$$

The union of the two solution intervals is $(-\infty, 3)$. The graph is shown in Fig. 8.7.

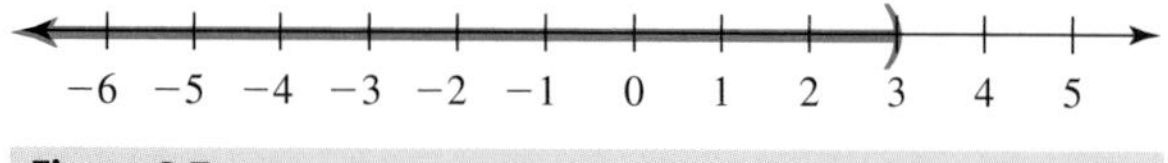

Figure 8.7

Now do Exercises 37–44

If x is between a and b and $a < b$, then we can use the "between" notation, $a < x < b$ rather than writing $x > a$ and $x < b$. We solved compound inequalities of this type in Section 2.9. For completeness, we review that method in Examples 10 and 11.

EXAMPLE 10

Calculator Close-Up

Do not use a table on your calculator as a method of solving an inequality. Use a table to check your algebraic solution and you will get a better understanding of inequalities.

Using "between" notation

Solve the inequality and graph the solution set:

$$-2 \le 2x - 3 < 7$$

Solution

This inequality could be written as the compound inequality

$$2x - 3 \ge -2 \quad \text{and} \quad 2x - 3 < 7.$$

However, there is no need to rewrite the inequality because we can solve it in its original form.

$$-2 + 3 \le 2x - 3 + 3 < 7 + 3 \qquad \text{Add 3 to each part.}$$
$$1 \le 2x < 10$$
$$\frac{1}{2} \le \frac{2x}{2} < \frac{10}{2} \qquad \text{Divide each part by 2.}$$
$$\frac{1}{2} \le x < 5$$

The solution set is $\left[\frac{1}{2}, 5\right)$, and its graph is shown in Fig. 8.8.

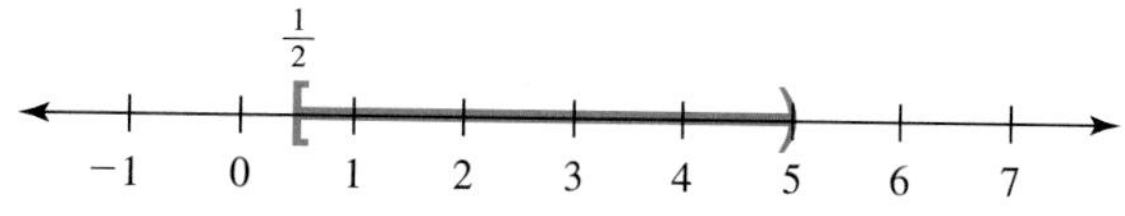

Figure 8.8

Now do Exercises 45–48

EXAMPLE 11

Calculator Close-Up

Let $y_1 = 3 - 2x$ and make a table. Scroll through the table to see that y_1 is between -1 and 9 when x is between -3 and 2. The table supports the conclusion of Example 11.

X	Y1
-3	9
-2	7
-1	5
0	3
1	1
2	-1
3	-3

Y1=3−2X

Solving a compound inequality

Solve the inequality $-1 < 3 - 2x < 9$ and graph the solution set.

Solution

$$-1 - 3 < 3 - 2x - 3 < 9 - 3 \qquad \text{Subtract 3 from each part of the inequality.}$$
$$-4 < -2x < 6$$
$$2 > x > -3 \qquad \text{Divide each part by } -2 \text{ and reverse both inequality symbols.}$$
$$-3 < x < 2 \qquad \text{Rewrite the inequality with the smallest number on the left.}$$

The solution set is $(-3, 2)$, and its graph is shown in Fig. 8.9.

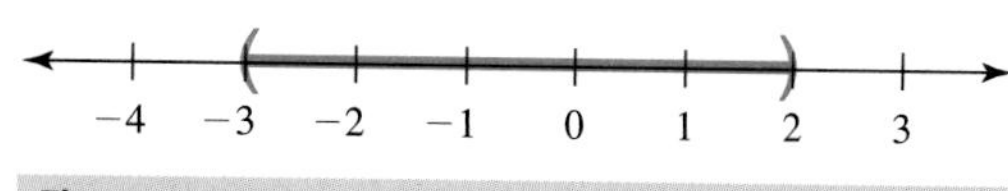

Figure 8.9

Now do Exercises 49–56

Applications

When final exams are approaching, students are often interested in finding the final exam score that would give them a certain grade for a course.

Math *at Work* Pediatric Dosing Rules

A drug is generally tested on adults and an appropriate adult dose (AD) of the drug is determined. When a drug is given to a child, a doctor determines an appropriate child's dose (CD) using pediatric dosing rules. However, no single rule works for all children. Determining a child's dose also involves common sense and experience.

Clark's rule is based on the ratio of the child's body weight to the mean weight of an adult, 150 pounds. By Clark's rule, $CD = \frac{\text{child's weight in lbs}}{\text{150 lbs}} \cdot AD$. A dose determined by body weight alone might be too little to be effective in a small child.

Young's rule is based on the assumption that age approximates body weight for patients over 2 years old. Of course there is a great variability of bodyweight of children of any give age. By Young's rule, $CD = \frac{\text{age in years}}{\text{age in years} + 12} \cdot AD$.

The area rule is often used for drugs required in radioactive imaging. It is based on the idea that (body mass)$^{2/3}$ is approximately the body surface area. For radioactive imaging the adult's body mass (MA) often determines AD. By the area rule, $CD = \frac{(MC)^{2/3}}{(MA)^{2/3}} \cdot AD$, where MC is the child's body mass.

Webster's rule uses age to approximate the ratio in the area rule and agrees well with the area rule until age 11 or 12. By Webster's rule $CD = \frac{\text{age} + 1}{\text{age} + 7} \cdot AD$.

Fried's rule is generally used for patients less than one year old. By Fried's rule $CD = \frac{\text{age in months}}{150} \cdot AD$.

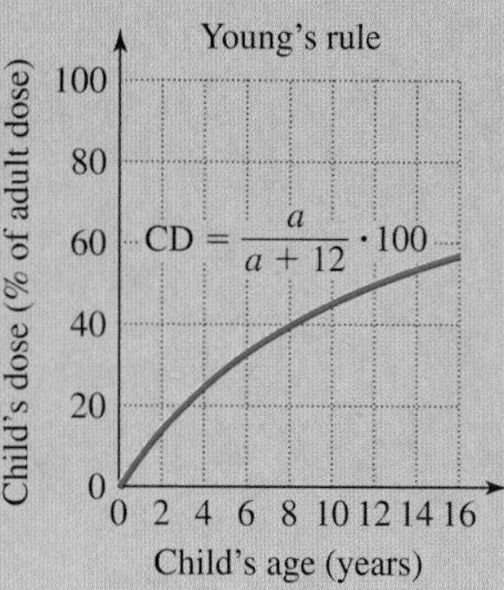

EXAMPLE 12

Final exam scores

Fiana made a score of 76 on her midterm exam. For her to get a B in the course, the average of her midterm exam and final exam must be between 80 and 89 inclusive. What possible scores on the final exam would give Fiana a B in the course?

Solution

Let x represent her final exam score. Between 80 and 89 inclusive means that an average between 80 and 89 as well as an average of exactly 80 or 89 will get a B.

Helpful Hint

When you use two inequality symbols as in Example 12, they must both point in the same direction. In fact, we usually have them both point to the left so that the numbers increase in size from left to right.

So the average of the two scores must be greater than or equal to 80 and less than or equal to 89.

$$80 \le \frac{x + 76}{2} \le 89$$

$$160 \le x + 76 \le 178 \quad \text{Multiply by 2.}$$

$$160 - 76 \le x \le 178 - 76 \quad \text{Subtract 76.}$$

$$84 \le x \le 102$$

If Fiana scores between 84 and 102 inclusive, she will get a B in the course.

Now do Exercises 81–92

Warm-Ups ▼

True or false? Explain your answer.

1. $3 < 5$ and $3 \le 10$ True
2. $3 < 5$ or $3 < 10$ True
3. $3 > 5$ and $3 < 10$ False
4. $3 \ge 5$ or $3 \le 10$ True
5. $4 < 8$ and $4 > 2$ True
6. $4 < 8$ or $4 > 2$ True
7. $-3 < 0 < -2$ False
8. $(3, \infty) \cap (8, \infty) = (8, \infty)$ True
9. $(3, \infty) \cup [8, \infty) = [8, \infty)$ False
10. $(-2, \infty) \cap (-\infty, 9) = (-2, 9)$ True

8.1 Exercises

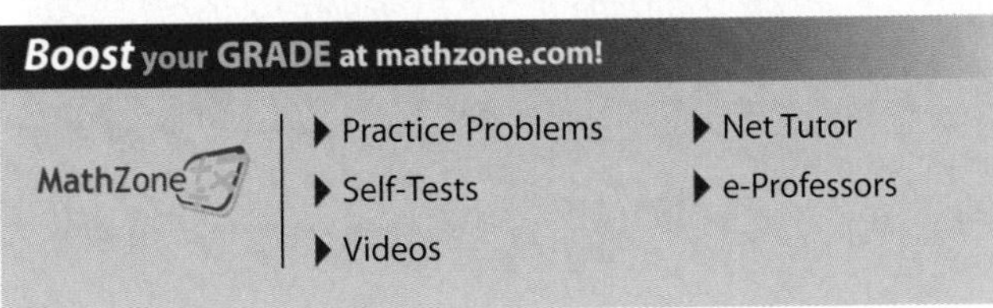

Reading and Writing *After reading this section, write out the answers to these questions. Use complete sentences.*

1. What is a compound inequality?
   A compound inequality consists of two inequalities joined with the words "and" or "or."
2. When is a compound inequality using "and" true?
   A compound inequality using "and" is true only when both simple inequalities are true.
3. When is a compound inequality using "or" true?
   A compound inequality using "or" is true when either one or the other or both inequalities is true.
4. How do we solve compound inequalities?
   Solve each simple inequality and then find either the union or intersection of the solution sets.
5. What is the meaning of $a < b < c$?
   The inequality $a < b < c$ means that $a < b$ and $b < c$.
6. What is the meaning of $5 < x > 7$?
   The inequality $5 < x > 7$ has no meaning. All inequality symbols must point in the same direction in this notation.

Determine whether each compound inequality is true. See Examples 1 and 2.

7. $-6 < 5$ and $-6 > -3$ No
8. $3 < 5$ or $0 < -3$ Yes
9. $4 \le 4$ and $-4 \le 0$ Yes
10. $1 < 5$ and $1 > -3$ Yes
11. $6 < 5$ or $-4 > -3$ No
12. $4 \le -4$ or $0 \le 0$ Yes

Determine whether −4 satisfies each compound inequality. See Example 3.

13. $x < 5$ and $x > -3$ No

14. $x < 5$ or $x > -3$ Yes

15. $x - 3 \geq -7$ or $x + 1 > 1$ Yes

16. $2x \leq -8$ and $5x \leq 0$ Yes

17. $2x - 1 < -7$ or $-2x > 18$ Yes

18. $-3x > 0$ and $3x - 4 < 11$ Yes

Graph the solution set to each compound inequality. See Examples 4–7.

19. $x > -1$ and $x < 4$

20. $x \leq 5$ and $x \geq 4$

21. $x \leq 3$ and $x \leq 0$

22. $x > 2$ and $x > 0$

23. $x \geq 2$ or $x \geq 5$

24. $x < -1$ or $x < 3$

25. $x \leq 6$ or $x > -2$

26. $x > -2$ and $x \leq 4$

27. $x \leq 6$ and $x > 9$ $\varnothing$

28. $x < 7$ or $x > 0$

29. $x \leq 6$ or $x > 9$

30. $x \geq 4$ and $x \leq -4$ $\varnothing$

31. $x \geq 6$ and $x \leq 1$ $\varnothing$

32. $x > 3$ or $x < -3$

Solve each compound inequality. Write the solution set using interval notation and graph it. See Examples 8 and 9.

33. $x - 3 > 7$ or $3 - x > 2$ $(-\infty, 1) \cup (10, \infty)$

34. $x - 5 > 6$ or $2 - x > 4$ $(-\infty, -2) \cup (11, \infty)$

35. $3 < x$ and $1 + x > 10$ $(9, \infty)$

36. $-0.3x < 9$ and $0.2x > 2$ $(10, \infty)$

37. $\frac{1}{2}x > 5$ or $-\frac{1}{3}x < 2$ $(-6, \infty)$

38. $5 < x$ or $3 - \frac{1}{2}x < 7$ $(-8, \infty)$

39. $2x - 3 \leq 5$ and $x - 1 > 0$ $(1, 4]$

40. $\frac{3}{4}x < 9$ and $-\frac{1}{3}x \leq -15$ $\varnothing$

41. $\frac{1}{2}x - \frac{1}{3} \geq -\frac{1}{6}$ or $\frac{2}{7}x \leq \frac{1}{10}$ $(-\infty, \infty)$

42. $\frac{1}{4}x - \frac{1}{3} > -\frac{1}{5}$ and $\frac{1}{2}x < 2$ $\left(\frac{8}{15}, 4\right)$

43. $0.5x < 2$ and $-0.6x < -3$ $\varnothing$

44. $0.3x < 0.6$ or $0.05x > -4$ $(-\infty, \infty)$

Solve each compound inequality. Write the solution set in interval notation and graph it. See Examples 10 and 11.

45. $-3 < x + 1 < 3$ $(-4, 2)$

46. $-4 \leq x - 4 \leq 1$ $[0, 5]$

47. $5 < 2x - 3 < 11$ $(4, 7)$

48. $-2 < 3x + 1 < 10$ $(-1, 3)$

49. $-1 < 5 - 3x \leq 14$ $[-3, 2)$

50. $-1 \leq 3 - 2x < 11$ $(-4, 2]$

51. $-3 < \frac{3m + 1}{2} \leq 5$ $\left(-\frac{7}{3}, 3\right]$

52. $0 \le \frac{3-2x}{2} < 5$ $\left(-\frac{7}{2}, \frac{3}{2}\right]$

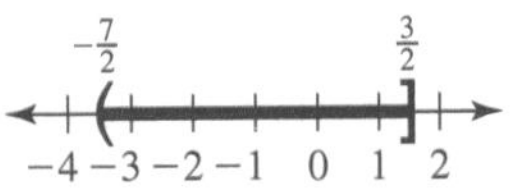

53. $-2 < \frac{1-3x}{-2} < 7$ $(-1, 5)$

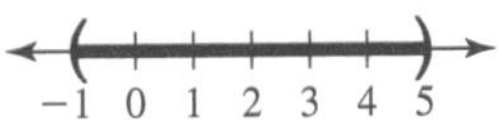

54. $-3 < \frac{2x-1}{3} < 7$ $(-4, 11)$

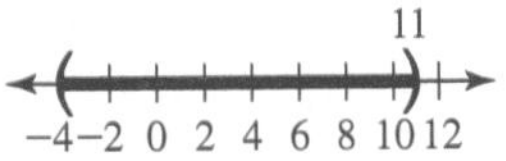

55. $3 \le 3 - 5(x-3) \le 8$ $[2, 3]$

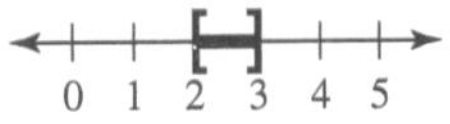

56. $2 \le 4 - \frac{1}{2}(x-8) \le 10$ 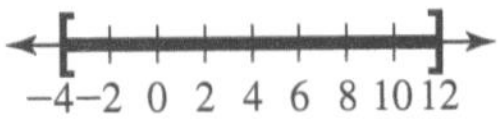 $[-4, 12]$

Write each union or intersection of intervals as a single interval if possible.

57. $(2, \infty) \cup (4, \infty)$ $(2, \infty)$

58. $(-3, \infty) \cup (-6, \infty)$ $(-6, \infty)$

59. $(-\infty, 5) \cap (-\infty, 9)$ $(-\infty, 5)$

60. $(-\infty, -2) \cap (-\infty, 1)$ $(-\infty, -2)$

61. $(-\infty, 4] \cap [2, \infty)$ $[2, 4]$

62. $(-\infty, 8) \cap [3, \infty)$ $[3, 8)$

63. $(-\infty, 5) \cup [-3, \infty)$ $(-\infty, \infty)$

64. $(-\infty, -2] \cup (2, \infty)$ $(-\infty, -2] \cup (2, \infty)$

65. $(3, \infty) \cap (-\infty, 3]$ $\varnothing$

66. $[-4, \infty) \cap (-\infty, -6]$ $\varnothing$

67. $(3, 5) \cap [4, 8)$ $[4, 5)$

68. $[-2, 4] \cap (0, 9]$ $(0, 4]$

69. $[1, 4) \cup (2, 6]$ $[1, 6]$

70. $[1, 3) \cup (0, 5)$ $(0, 5)$

Write either a simple or a compound inequality that has the given graph as its solution set.

71. $x > 2$

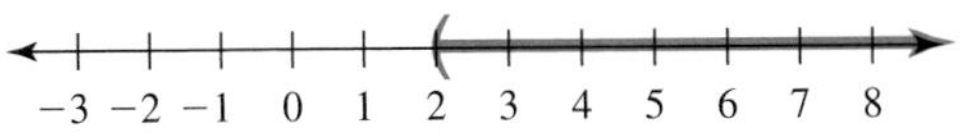

72. $x \le 5$

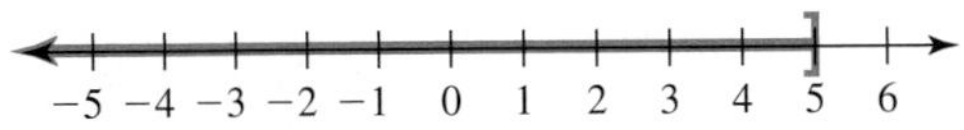

73. $x < 3$

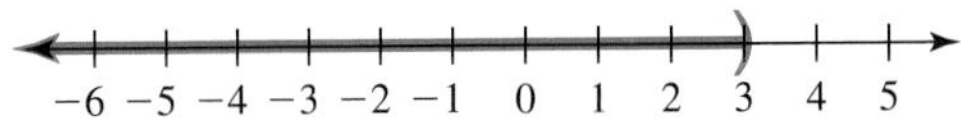

74. $x < -4$ or $x > 3$

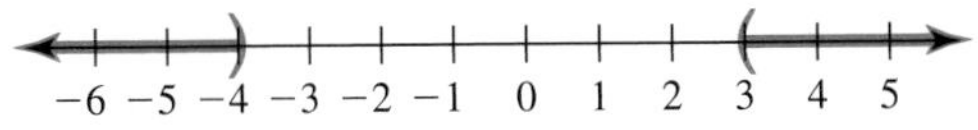

75. $x > 2$ or $x \le -1$

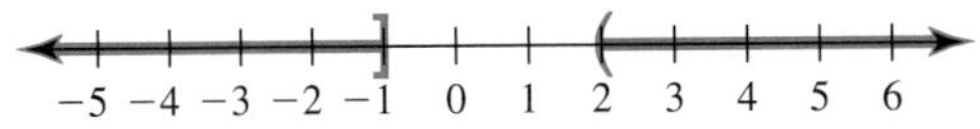

76. $-1 < x < 2$

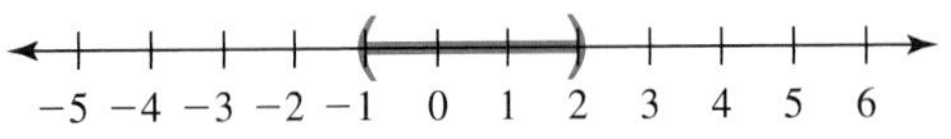

77. $-2 \le x < 3$

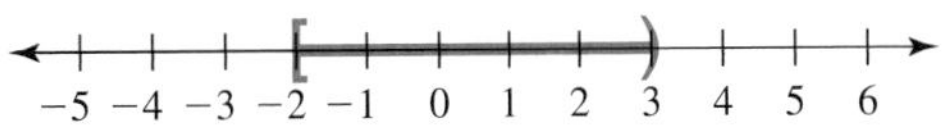

78. $x < 2$

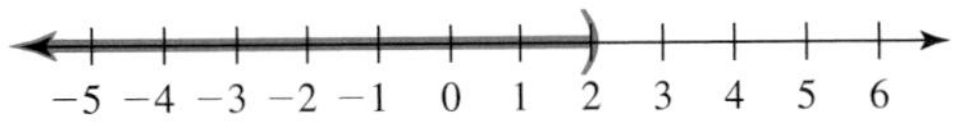

79. $x \ge -3$

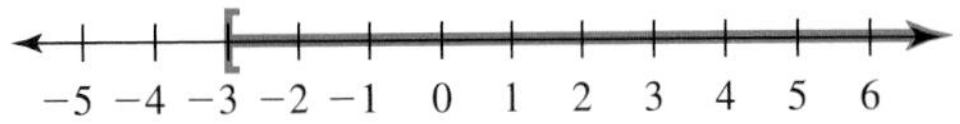

80. $x \le 0$ or $x > 1$

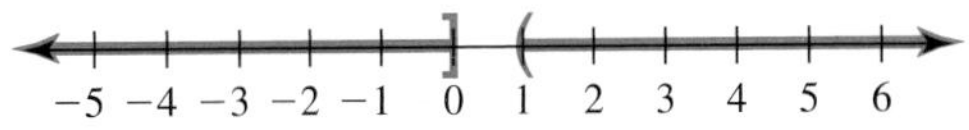

Solve each problem by using a compound inequality. See Example 12.

81. ***Car costs.*** A company uses the expression $0.0004x + 20$ to estimate the cost in cents per mile for operating a company car and the expression $20{,}000 - 0.2x$ to estimate the value of the car in dollars, where x is the number of miles on the odometer. If the company plans to replace any car for which the operating cost is greater than 40 cents per mile *and* the value is less than \$12,000, then for what values of x is a car replaced? Use interval notation. $(50{,}000, \infty)$

82. ***Changing plans.*** The company in Exercise 81 has changed its policy and has decided to replace any car for which the operating cost is greater than 40 cents per mile *or* the value is less than \$12,000. For what values of x is a car replaced? Use interval notation. $(40{,}000, \infty)$

83. ***Supply and demand.*** An energy minister in a small country uses the expression $20 + 0.1x$ to estimate the amount of oil in millions of barrels per day that will be supplied to his country and the expression $30 - 0.5x$ to estimate the demand for oil in millions of barrels per day, where x is the price of oil in dollars per barrel. The government must get involved if the supply is less than 22 million barrels per day *or* if the demand is less than 15 million barrels per day. For what values of x must the government get involved? Use interval notation. $(-\infty, 20) \cup (30, \infty)$

84. ***Predicting recession.*** The country of Exercise 83 will be in recession if the supply of oil is greater than 23 million barrels per day *and* the demand is less than 14 million barrels per day. For what values of x will the country be in recession? Use interval notation. $(32, \infty)$

85. ***Aiming for a C.*** Professor Johnson gives only a midterm exam and a final exam. The semester average is computed by taking $\frac{1}{3}$ of the midterm exam score plus $\frac{2}{3}$ of the final exam score. To get a C, Beth must have a semester average between 70 and 79 inclusive. If Beth scored only 64 on the midterm, then for what range of scores on the final exam would Beth get a C? x = final exam score, $73 \le x \le 86.5$

86. ***Two tests only.*** Professor Davis counts his midterm as $\frac{2}{3}$ of the grade, and his final as $\frac{1}{3}$ of the grade. Jason scored only 64 on the midterm. What range of scores on the final exam would put Jason's average between 70 and 79 inclusive? x = final exam score, $82 \le x \le 109$

87. ***Keep on truckin'.*** Abdul is shopping for a new truck in a city with an 8% sales tax. There is also an $84 title and license fee to pay. He wants to get a good truck and plans to spend at least $12,000 but no more than $15,000. What is the price range for the truck?
x = price of truck, $\$11{,}033 \le x \le \$13{,}811$

88. ***Selling-price range.*** Renee wants to sell her car through a broker who charges a commission of 10% of the selling price. The book value of the car is $14,900, but Renee still owes $13,104 on it. Although the car is in only fair condition and will not sell for more than the book value, Renee must get enough to at least pay off the loan. What is the range of the selling price?
x = selling price, $\$14{,}560 \le x \le \$14{,}900$

89. ***Hazardous to her health.*** Trying to break her smoking habit, Jane calculates that she smokes only three full cigarettes a day, one after each meal. The rest of the time she smokes on the run and smokes only half of the cigarette. She estimates that she smokes the equivalent of 5 to 12 cigarettes per day. How many times a day does she light up on the run?
x = number of cigarettes on the run, $4 \le x \le 18$

90. ***Possible width.*** The length of a rectangle is 20 meters longer than the width. The perimeter must be between 80 and 100 meters. What are the possible values for the width of the rectangle? w = width, $10 < w < 15$

91. ***Higher education.*** The formulas

$$B = 16.45n + 1062.45$$

and

$$M = 7.79n + 326.82$$

can be used to approximate the number of bachelor's and master's degrees in thousands, respectively, awarded per year, n years after 1990 (National Center for Educational Statistics, www.nces.ed.gov).

a) How many bachelor's degrees were awarded in 2000?
1,226,950

b) In what year will the number of bachelor's degrees that are awarded reach 1.4 million? 2011

c) What is the first year in which both B is greater than 1.4 million and M is greater than 0.55 million? 2019

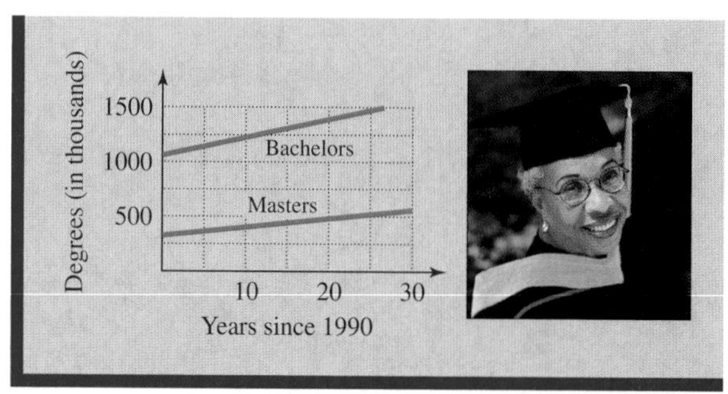

Figure for Exercise 91

d) What is the first year in which either B is greater than 1.4 million or M is greater than 0.55 million?
2011

92. ***Senior citizens.*** The number of senior citizens (65 and over) in the United States in millions n years after 1990 can be estimated by using the formula

$$s = 0.38n + 31.2$$

(U.S. Bureau of the Census, www.census.gov). The percentage of senior citizens living below the poverty level n years after 1990 can be estimated by using the formula

$$p = -0.25n + 12.2.$$

a) How many senior citizens were there in 2000?
35 million

b) In what year will the percentage of seniors living below the poverty level reach 7%?
2011

c) What is the first year in which we can expect both the number of seniors to be greater than 40 million and fewer than 7% living below the poverty level?
2013

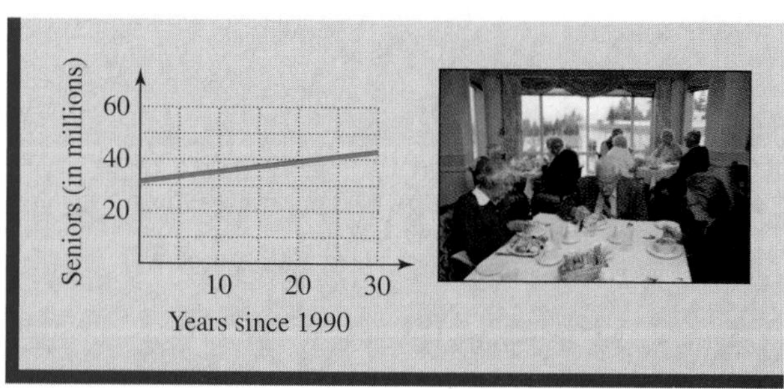

Figure for Exercise 92

Getting More Involved

93. ***Discussion***

If $-x$ is between a and b, then what can you say about x? $-b < x < -a$ provided $a < b$

94. ***Discussion***

For which of the inequalities is the notation used correctly?

a) $-2 \le x < 3$ **b)** $-4 \ge x < 7$ **c)** $-1 \le x > 0$
d) $6 < x \le -8$ **e)** $5 \ge x \ge -9$
Notation is used correctly in **(a)** and **(e)**.

95. ***Discussion***

In each case, write the resulting set of numbers in interval notation. Explain your answers.

a) Every number in $(3, 8)$ is multiplied by 4. $(12, 32)$
b) Every number in $[-2, 4)$ is multiplied by -5. $(-20, 10]$
c) Three is added to every number in $(-3, 6)$. $(0, 9)$
d) Every number in $[3, 9]$ is divided by -3. $[-3, -1]$

96. ***Discussion***

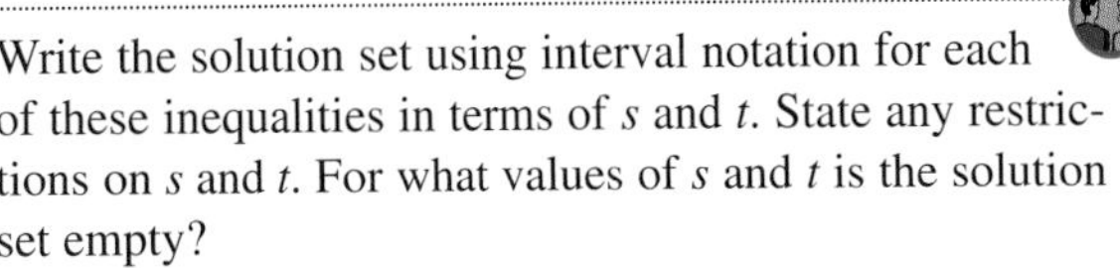

Write the solution set using interval notation for each of these inequalities in terms of s and t. State any restrictions on s and t. For what values of s and t is the solution set empty?

a) $x > s$ and $x < t$ (s, t) if $s < t$, no solution if $t \le s$
b) $x > s$ and $x > t$ (s, ∞) if $s \ge t$, (t, ∞) if $t \ge s$

8.2 Absolute Value Equations and Inequalities

In this Section

- **Absolute Value Equations**
- **Absolute Value Inequalities**
- **All or Nothing**
- **Applications**

In Chapter 1 we learned that absolute value measures the distance of a number from 0 on the number line. In this section we will learn to solve equations and inequalities involving absolute value.

Absolute Value Equations

Solving equations involving absolute value requires some techniques that are different from those studied in previous sections. For example, the solution set to the equation

$$|x| = 5$$

is $\{-5, 5\}$ because both 5 and -5 are five units from 0 on the number line, as shown in Fig. 8.10. So $|x| = 5$ is equivalent to the compound equation

$$x = 5 \text{ or } x = -5.$$

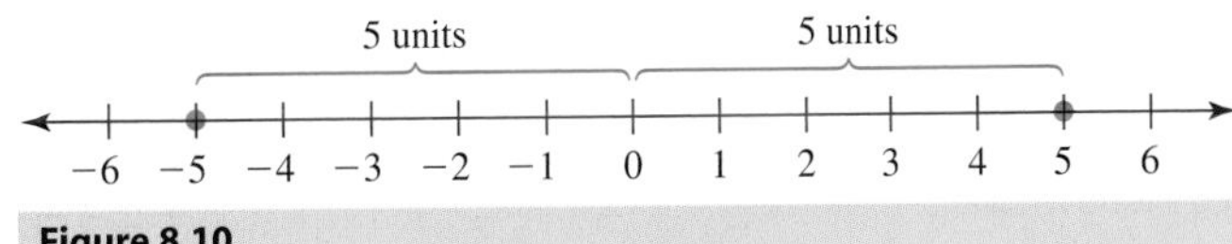

Figure 8.10

The equation $|x| = 0$ is equivalent to the equation $x = 0$ because 0 is the only number whose distance from 0 is zero. The solution set to $|x| = 0$ is $\{0\}$.

The equation $|x| = -7$ is inconsistent because absolute value measures distance, and distance is never negative. So the solution set is empty. These ideas are summarized as follows.

Helpful Hint

Some students grow up believing that the only way to solve an equation is to "do the same thing to each side." Then along comes absolute value equations. For an absolute value equation we write an equivalent compound equation that is not obtained by "doing the same thing to each side."

Basic Absolute Value Equations

Absolute Value Equation	Equivalent Equation	Solution Set
$\|x\| = k \ (k > 0)$	$x = k$ or $x = -k$	$\{k, -k\}$
$\|x\| = 0$	$x = 0$	$\{0\}$
$\|x\| = k \ (k < 0)$		$\varnothing$

We can use these ideas to solve more complicated absolute value equations.

EXAMPLE 1

Calculator Close-Up

Use Y= to set $y_1 = \text{abs}(x - 7)$. Make a table to see that y_1 has value 2 when $x = 5$ or $x = 9$. The table supports the conclusion of Example 1(a).

X	Y1	
5	2	
6	1	
7	0	
8	1	
9	2	
10	3	
11	4	

Y1=abs(X−7)

Absolute value equal to a positive number

Solve each equation.

a) $|x - 7| = 2$ **b)** $|3x - 5| = 7$

Solution

a) First rewrite $|x - 7| = 2$ without absolute value:

$$x - 7 = 2 \quad \text{or} \quad x - 7 = -2 \quad \text{Equivalent equation}$$
$$x = 9 \quad \text{or} \quad x = 5$$

The solution set is $\{5, 9\}$. The distance from 5 to 7 or from 9 to 7 is 2 units.

b) First rewrite $|3x - 5| = 7$ without absolute value:

$$3x - 5 = 7 \quad \text{or} \quad 3x - 5 = -7 \quad \text{Equivalent equation}$$
$$3x = 12 \quad \text{or} \quad 3x = -2$$
$$x = 4 \quad \text{or} \quad x = -\frac{2}{3}$$

The solution set is $\left\{-\frac{2}{3}, 4\right\}$.

Now do Exercises 7–12

EXAMPLE 2

Helpful Hint

Examples 1, 2, and 3 show the three basic types of absolute value equations—absolute value equal to a positive number, zero, or a negative number. These equations have 2, 1, and no solutions, respectively.

Absolute value equal to zero

Solve $|2(x - 6) + 7| = 0$.

Solution

Since 0 is the only number whose absolute value is 0, the expression within the absolute value bars must be 0.

$$2(x - 6) + 7 = 0 \quad \text{Equivalent equation}$$
$$2x - 12 + 7 = 0$$
$$2x - 5 = 0$$
$$2x = 5$$
$$x = \frac{5}{2}$$

The solution set is $\left\{\frac{5}{2}\right\}$.

Now do Exercises 13–18

EXAMPLE 3

Absolute value equal to a negative number

Solve each equation.

a) $|x - 9| = -6$ **b)** $-5|3x - 7| + 4 = 14$

Teaching Tip Emphasize that when you see absolute value equal to a number you must stop and think. What you do next depends on whether the number is positive, negative, or zero.

Solution

a) The equation indicates that $|x - 9| = -6$. However, the absolute value of any quantity is greater than or equal to zero. So there is no solution to the equation.

b) First subtract 4 from each side to isolate the absolute value expression:

$$-5|3x - 7| + 4 = 14 \quad \text{Original equation}$$
$$-5|3x - 7| = 10 \quad \text{Subtract 4 from each side.}$$
$$|3x - 7| = -2 \quad \text{Divide each side by } -5.$$

There is no solution because no quantity has a negative absolute value.

Now do Exercises 19–30

The equation in Example 4 has an absolute value on both sides.

EXAMPLE 4

Absolute value on both sides

Solve $|2x - 1| = |x + 3|$.

Solution

Two quantities have the same absolute value only if they are equal or opposites. So we can write an equivalent compound equation:

$$2x - 1 = x + 3 \quad \text{or} \quad 2x - 1 = -(x + 3)$$
$$x - 1 = 3 \quad \text{or} \quad 2x - 1 = -x - 3$$
$$x = 4 \quad \text{or} \quad 3x = -2$$
$$x = 4 \quad \text{or} \quad x = -\frac{2}{3}$$

Check 4 and $-\frac{2}{3}$ in the original equation. The solution set is $\left\{-\frac{2}{3}, 4\right\}$.

Now do Exercises 31–36

Absolute Value Inequalities

Since absolute value measures distance from 0 on the number line, $|x| > 5$ indicates that x is more than five units from 0. Any number on the number line to the right of 5 or to the left of -5 is more than five units from 0. So $|x| > 5$ is equivalent to

$$x > 5 \quad \text{or} \quad x < -5.$$

The solution set to this inequality is the union of the solution sets to the two simple inequalities. The solution set is $(-\infty, -5) \cup (5, \infty)$. The graph of $|x| > 5$ is shown in Fig. 8.11 on the next page.

Study Tip

Many commuting students find it difficult to get help. Students are often stuck on a minor point that can be easily resolved over the telephone. So ask your instructor if he or she will answer questions over the telephone and during what hours.

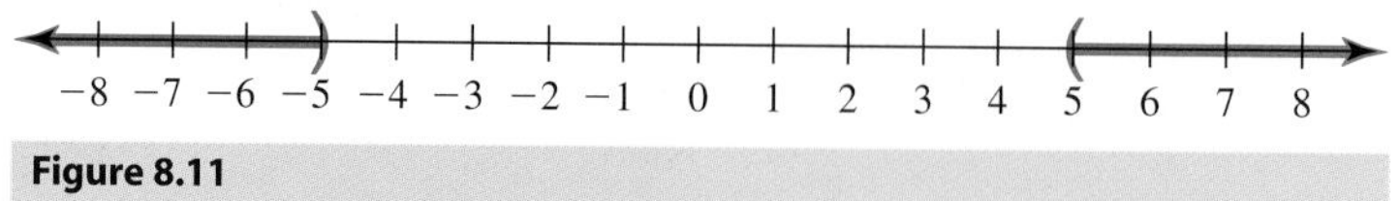

Figure 8.11

The inequality $|x| \leq 3$ indicates that x is less than or equal to three units from 0. Any number between -3 and 3 inclusive satisfies that condition. So $|x| \leq 3$ is equivalent to

$$-3 \leq x \leq 3.$$

The graph of $|x| \leq 3$ is shown in Fig. 8.12. These examples illustrate the basic types of absolute value inequalities.

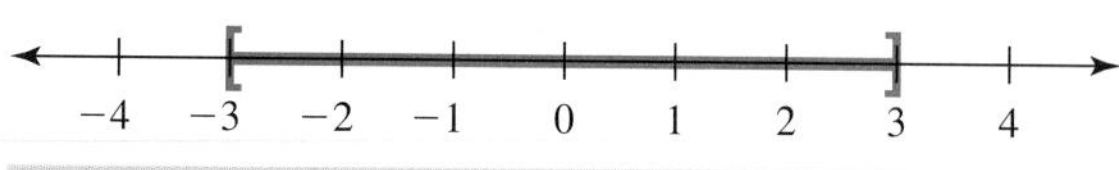

Figure 8.12

Teaching Tip Have students make a table like this for a few values of k.

Basic Absolute Value Inequalities ($k > 0$)

Absolute Value Inequality	Equivalent Inequality	Solution Set	Graph of Solution Set
$\lvert x \rvert > k$	$x > k$ or $x < -k$	$(-\infty, -k) \cup (k, \infty)$	$-k$ k
$\lvert x \rvert \geq k$	$x \geq k$ or $x \leq -k$	$(-\infty, -k] \cup [k, \infty)$	$-k$ k
$\lvert x \rvert < k$	$-k < x < k$	$(-k, k)$	$-k$ k
$\lvert x \rvert \leq k$	$-k \leq x \leq k$	$[-k, k]$	$-k$ k

We can solve more complicated inequalities in the same manner as simple ones.

EXAMPLE 5

Absolute value inequality

Solve $|x - 9| < 2$ and graph the solution set.

Solution

Because $|x| < k$ is equivalent to $-k < x < k$, we can rewrite $|x - 9| < 2$ as follows:

$$-2 < x - 9 < 2$$

$$-2 + 9 < x - 9 + 9 < 2 + 9 \quad \text{Add 9 to each part of the inequality.}$$

$$7 < x < 11$$

The graph of the solution set (7, 11) is shown in Fig. 8.13. Note that the graph consists of all real numbers that are within two units of 9.

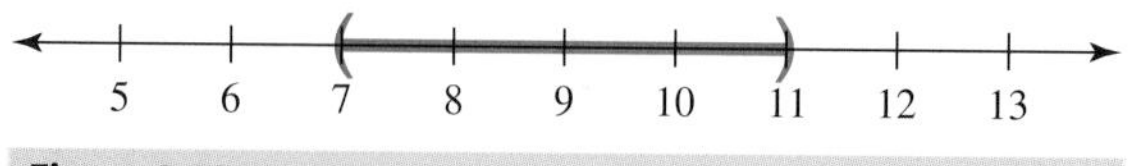

Figure 8.13

Now do Exercises 37–38

Calculator Close-Up

Use Y= to set y_1 = abs(x − 9). Make a table to see that $y_1 < 2$ when x is between 7 and 11.

X	Y1
6	3
7	2
8	1
9	0
10	1
11	2
12	3

Y1=abs(X−9)

EXAMPLE 6

Absolute value inequality

Solve $|3x + 5| > 2$ and graph the solution set.

Solution

$$3x + 5 > 2 \quad \text{or} \quad 3x + 5 < -2 \qquad \text{Equivalent compound inequality}$$

$$3x > -3 \quad \text{or} \quad 3x < -7$$

$$x > -1 \quad \text{or} \quad x < -\frac{7}{3}$$

The solution set is $\left(-\infty, -\frac{7}{3}\right) \cup (-1, \infty)$, and its graph is shown in Fig. 8.14.

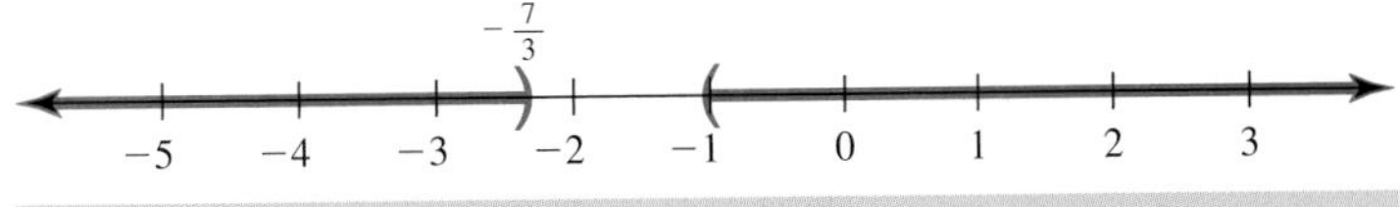

Figure 8.14

Now do Exercises 39–40

EXAMPLE 7

Absolute value inequality

Solve $|5 - 3x| \le 6$ and graph the solution set.

Solution

$$-6 \le 5 - 3x \le 6 \qquad \text{Equivalent inequality}$$

$$-11 \le -3x \le 1 \qquad \text{Subtract 5 from each part.}$$

$$\frac{11}{3} \ge x \ge -\frac{1}{3} \qquad \text{Divide by } -3 \text{ and reverse each inequality symbol.}$$

$$-\frac{1}{3} \le x \le \frac{11}{3} \qquad \text{Write } -\frac{1}{3} \text{ on the left because it is smaller than } \frac{11}{3}.$$

The solution set is $\left[-\frac{1}{3}, \frac{11}{3}\right]$ and its graph is shown in Fig. 8.15.

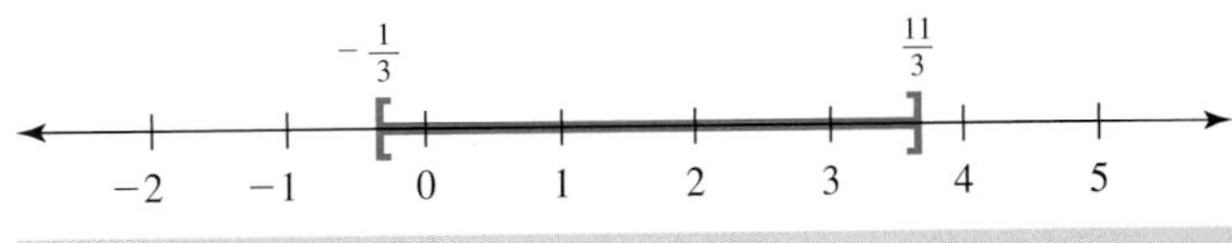

Figure 8.15

Now do Exercises 41–44

Calculator Close-Up

Use Y= to set $y_1 = \text{abs}(5 - 3x)$. The table supports the conclusion that $y \le 6$ when x is between $-\frac{1}{3}$ and $\frac{11}{3}$ even though $-\frac{1}{3}$ and $\frac{11}{3}$ do not appear in the table. For more accuracy, make a table in which the change in x is $\frac{1}{3}$.

X	Y1
-1	8
0	5
1	2
2	1
3	4
4	7
5	10

Y1≡abs(5-3X)

All or Nothing

The solution to an absolute value inequality can be all real numbers or no real numbers. To solve such inequalities you must remember that the absolute value of any real number or is greater than or equal to zero.

EXAMPLE 8

All real numbers

Solve $3 + |7 - 2x| \geq 3$.

Solution

Subtract 3 from each side to isolate the absolute value expression.

$$|7 - 2x| \geq 0$$

Because the absolute value of any real number is greater than or equal to 0, the solution set is R, the set of all real numbers.

Now do Exercises 67–72

EXAMPLE 9

No real numbers

Solve $|5x - 12| < -2$.

Solution

We write an equivalent inequality only when the value of k is positive. With -2 on the right-hand side, we do not write an equivalent inequality. Since the absolute value of any quantity is greater than or equal to 0, no value for x can make this absolute value less than -2. The solution set is $\emptyset$, the empty set.

Now do Exercises 73–76

Teaching Tip Students have trouble with absolute value inequalities because there are so many different cases. They must truly understand the meaning of absolute value to be successful here.

Applications

A simple example will show how absolute value inequalities can be used in applications.

EXAMPLE 10

Controlling water temperature

The water temperature in a certain manufacturing process must be kept at 143°F. The computer is programmed to shut down the process if the water temperature is more than 7° away from what it is supposed to be. For what temperature readings is the process shut down?

Solution

If we let x represent the water temperature, then $x - 143$ represents the difference between the actual temperature and the desired temperature. The quantity $x - 143$ could be positive or negative. The process is shut down if the absolute value of $x - 143$ is greater than 7.

$$|x - 143| > 7$$

$$x - 143 > 7 \quad \text{or} \quad x - 143 < -7$$

$$x > 150 \quad \text{or} \quad x < 136$$

The process is shut down for temperatures greater than 150°F or less than 136°F.

Now do Exercises 85–90

Study Tip

When taking a test, try not to spend too much time on a single problem. If a problem is taking a long time, then you might be approaching it incorrectly. Move on to another problem and make sure that you get finished with the test.

Warm-Ups ▼

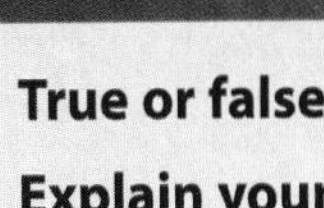

True or false? Explain your answer.

1. The equation $|x| = 2$ is equivalent to $x = 2$ or $x = -2$. True
2. All absolute value equations have two solutions. False
3. The equation $|2x - 3| = 7$ is equivalent to $2x - 3 = 7$ or $2x + 3 = 7$. False
4. The inequality $|x| > 5$ is equivalent to $x > 5$ or $x < -5$. True
5. The equation $|x| = -5$ is equivalent to $x = 5$ or $x = -5$. False
6. There is only one solution to the equation $|3 - x| = 0$. True
7. We should write the inequality $x > 3$ or $x < -3$ as $3 < x < -3$. False
8. The inequality $|x| < 7$ is equivalent to $-7 \le x \le 7$. False
9. The equation $|x| + 2 = 5$ is equivalent to $|x| = 3$. True
10. If x is any real number, then the absolute value of x is positive. False

8.2 Exercises

Boost your GRADE at mathzone.com!

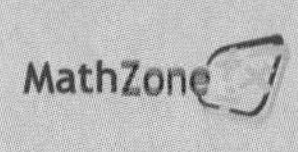

- Practice Problems
- Self-Tests
- Videos
- Net Tutor
- e-Professors

Reading and Writing *After reading this section, write out the answers to these questions. Use complete sentences.*

1. What does absolute value measure?
   Absolute value of a number is the number's distance from 0 on the number line.
2. Why does $|x| = 0$ have only one solution?
   Only 0 is 0 units from 0 on the number line.
3. Why does $|x| = 4$ have two solutions?
   Since both 4 and -4 are four units from 0, $|x| = 4$ has two solutions.
4. Why is $|x| = -3$ inconsistent?
   Since $|x| \ge 0$ for every real number x, $|x| = -3$ is impossible.
5. Why do all real numbers satisfy $|x| \ge 0$?
   Since the distance from 0 for every number on the number line is greater than or equal to 0, $|x| \ge 0$.
6. Why do no real numbers satisfy $|x| < -3$?
   Since $|x| \ge 0$ for all x, $|x| < -3$ is impossible.

Solve each absolute value equation. See Examples 1–3.

7. $|a| = 5$ $\{-5, 5\}$
8. $|x| = 2$ $\{-2, 2\}$
9. $|x - 3| = 1$ $\{2, 4\}$
10. $|x - 5| = 2$ $\{3, 7\}$
11. $|3 - x| = 6$ $\{-3, 9\}$
12. $|7 - x| = 6$ $\{1, 13\}$
13. $|3x - 4| = 12$ $\left\{-\frac{8}{3}, \frac{16}{3}\right\}$
14. $|5x + 2| = -3$ $\varnothing$
15. $\left|\frac{2}{3}x - 8\right| = 0$ $\{12\}$
16. $\left|3 - \frac{3}{4}x\right| = \frac{1}{4}$ $\left\{\frac{11}{3}, \frac{13}{3}\right\}$
17. $|6 - 0.2x| = 10$ $\{-20, 80\}$
18. $|5 - 0.1x| = 0$ $\{50\}$
19. $|7(x - 6)| = -3$ $\varnothing$
20. $|2(a + 3)| = 15$ $\left\{-\frac{21}{2}, \frac{9}{2}\right\}$
21. $|2(x - 4) + 3| = 5$ $\{0, 5\}$
22. $|3(x - 2) + 7| = 6$ $\left\{\frac{5}{3}, -\frac{7}{3}\right\}$
23. $|7.3x - 5.26| = 4.215$ $\{0.143, 1.298\}$
24. $|5.74 - 2.17x| = 10.28$ $\{-2.092, 7.382\}$

Solve each absolute value equation. See Examples 3 and 4.

25. $3 + |x| = 5$ $\{-2, 2\}$
26. $|x| - 10 = -3$ $\{-7, 7\}$
27. $2 - |x + 3| = -6$ $\{-11, 5\}$
28. $4 - 3|x - 2| = -8$ $\{-2, 6\}$
29. $5 - \frac{|3 - 2x|}{3} = 4$ $\{0, 3\}$
30. $3 - \frac{1}{2}\left|\frac{1}{2}x - 4\right| = 2$ $\{4, 12\}$

31. $|x - 5| = |2x + 1|$ $\left\{-6, \frac{4}{3}\right\}$

32. $|w - 6| = |3 - 2w|$ $\{-3, 3\}$

33. $\left|\frac{5}{2} - x\right| = \left|2 - \frac{x}{2}\right|$ $\{1, 3\}$

34. $\left|x - \frac{1}{4}\right| = \left|\frac{1}{2}x - \frac{3}{4}\right|$ $\left\{-1, \frac{2}{3}\right\}$

35. $|x - 3| = |3 - x|$ $(-\infty, \infty)$

36. $|a - 6| = |6 - a|$ $(-\infty, \infty)$

Write an absolute value inequality whose solution set is shown by the graph. See Examples 5–7.

37.
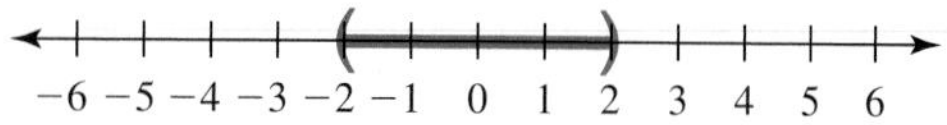

$|x| < 2$

38.
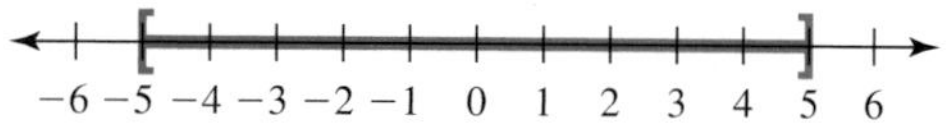

$|x| \le 5$

39.
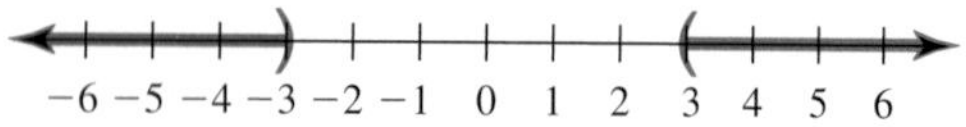

$|x| > 3$

40.
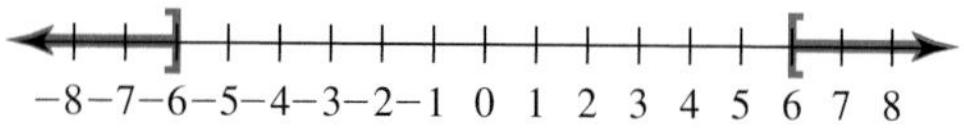

$|x| \ge 6$

41.
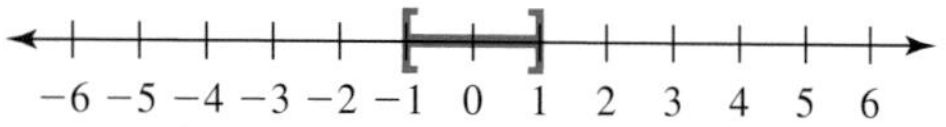

$|x| \le 1$

42.
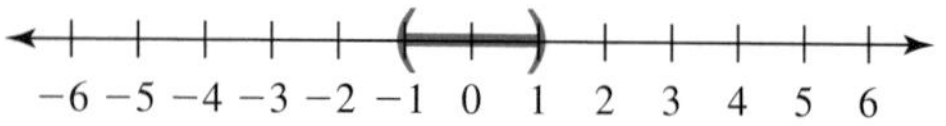

$|x| < 1$

43.
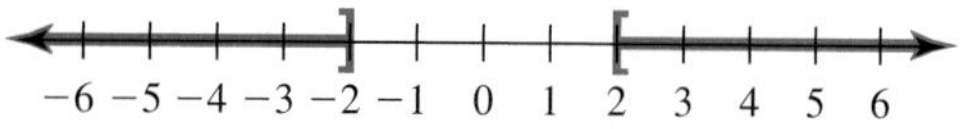

$|x| \ge 2$

44.
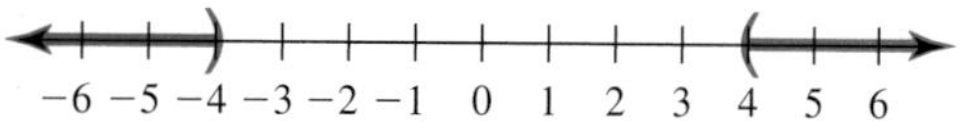

$|x| > 4$

Determine whether each absolute value inequality is equivalent to the inequality following it. See Examples 5–7.

45. $|x| < 3, x < 3$ No **46.** $|x| > 3, x > 3$ No

47. $|x - 3| > 1, x - 3 > 1$ or $x - 3 < -1$ Yes

48. $|x - 3| \le 1, -1 \le x - 3 \le 1$ Yes

49. $|x - 3| \ge 1, x - 3 \ge 1$ or $x - 3 \le 1$ No

50. $|x - 3| > 0, x - 3 > 0$ No

51. $|4 - x| < 1, 4 - x < 1$ and $-(4 - x) < 1$ Yes

52. $|4 - x| > 1, 4 - x > 1$ or $-(4 - x) > 1$ Yes

Solve each absolute value inequality and graph the solution set. See Examples 5–7.

53. $|x| > 6$
$(-\infty, -6) \cup (6, \infty)$

54. $|w| \ge 3$
$(-\infty, -3] \cup [3, \infty)$

55. $|t| \le 2$
$[-2, 2]$

56. $|b| < 4$
$(-4, 4)$
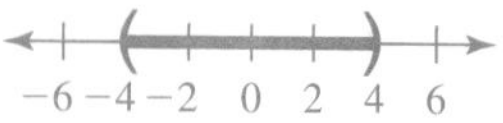

57. $|2a| < 6$
$(-3, 3)$
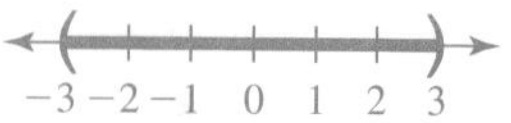

58. $|3x| < 21$
$(-7, 7)$

59. $|x - 2| \ge 3$
$(-\infty, -1] \cup [5, \infty)$

60. $|x - 5| \ge 1$
$(-\infty, 4] \cup [6, \infty)$

61. $\frac{1}{5}|2x - 4| < 1$
$\left(-\frac{1}{2}, \frac{9}{2}\right)$
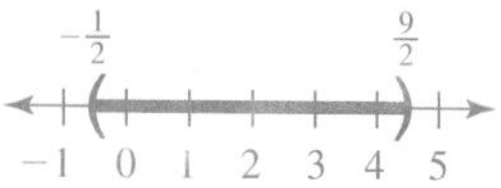

62. $\frac{1}{3}|2x - 1| < 1$
$(-1, 2)$
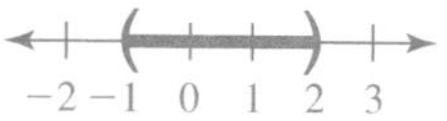

63. $-2|5 - x| \ge -14$
$[-2, 12]$

64. $-3|6 - x| \ge -3$
$[5, 7]$
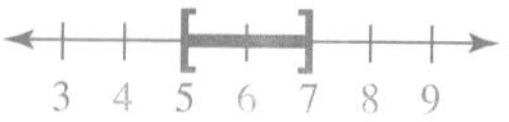

65. $2|3 - 2x| - 6 \ge 18$
$\left(-\infty, -\frac{9}{2}\right] \cup \left[\frac{15}{2}, \infty\right)$

66. $2|5 - 2x| - 15 \ge 5$
$\left(-\infty, -\frac{5}{2}\right] \cup \left[\frac{15}{2}, \infty\right)$
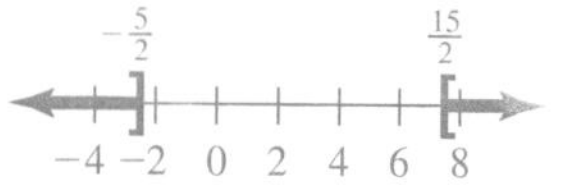

Solve each absolute value inequality and graph the solution set. See Examples 8 and 9.

67. $|x| > 0$
$(-\infty, 0) \cup (0, \infty)$

68. $|x - 2| > 0$
$(-\infty, 2) \cup (2, \infty)$
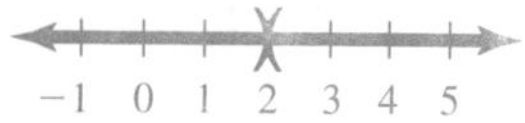

69. $|x| \le 0$
$\{0\}$

70. $|x| < 0$ $\varnothing$

71. $|x - 5| \geq 0$

$(-\infty, \infty)$

−3 −2 −1 0 1 2 3

72. $|3x - 7| \geq -3$

$(-\infty, \infty)$

−3 −2 −1 0 1 2 3

73. $-2|3x - 7| > 6$ $\varnothing$

74. $-3|7x - 42| > 18$ $\varnothing$

75. $|2x + 3| + 6 > 0$

$(-\infty, \infty)$

−3 −2 −1 0 1 2 3

76. $|5 - x| + 5 > 5$

$(-\infty, 5) \cup (5, \infty)$

2 3 4 5 6 7 8

Solve each inequality. Write the solution set using interval notation.

77. $1 < |x + 2|$ $(-\infty, -3) \cup (-1, \infty)$

78. $5 \geq |x - 4|$ $[-1, 9]$

79. $5 > |x| + 1$ $(-4, 4)$

80. $4 \leq |x| - 6$ $(-\infty, -10] \cup [10, \infty)$

81. $3 - 5|x| > -2$ $(-1, 1)$

82. $1 - 2|x| < -7$ $(-\infty, -4) \cup (4, \infty)$

83. $|5.67x - 3.124| < 1.68$ $(0.255, 0.847)$

84. $|4.67 - 3.2x| \geq 1.43$ $(-\infty, 1.0125] \cup [1.90625, \infty)$

Solve each problem by using an absolute value equation or inequality. See Example 10.

85. ***Famous battles.*** In the Hundred Years' War, Henry V defeated a French army in the battle of Agincourt and Joan of Arc defeated an English army in the battle of Orleans (*The Doubleday Almanac*). Suppose you know only that these two famous battles were 14 years apart and that the battle of Agincourt occurred in 1415. Use an absolute value equation to find the possibilities for the year in which the battle of Orleans occurred. 1401 or 1429

86. ***World records.*** In July 1985 Steve Cram of Great Britain set a world record of 3 minutes 29.67 seconds for the 1500-meter race and a world record of 3 minutes 46.31 seconds for the 1-mile race (*The Doubleday Almanac*). Suppose you know only that these two events occurred 11 days apart and that the 1500-meter record was set on July 16. Use an absolute value equation to find the possible dates for the 1-mile record run. July 5 or July 27

87. ***Weight difference.*** Research at a major university has shown that identical twins generally differ by less than 6 pounds in body weight. If Kim weighs 127 pounds, then in what range is the weight of her identical twin sister Kathy? Between 121 and 133 pounds

88. ***Intelligence quotient.*** Jude's IQ score is more than 15 points away from Sherry's. If Sherry scored 110, then in what range is Jude's score?
Greater than 125 or less than 95

89. ***Unidentified flying objects.*** The formula

$$S = -16t^2 + v_0t + s_0$$

gives height in feet above the earth at time t seconds for an object projected into the air with an initial velocity of v_0 feet per second (ft/sec) from an initial height of s_0 feet. Two balls are tossed into the air simultaneously, one from the ground at 50 ft/sec and one from a height of 10 feet at 40 ft/sec. See the accompanying graph.

a) Use the graph to estimate the time at which the balls are at the same height.

b) Find the time from part (a) algebraically.

c) For what values of t will their heights above the ground differ by less than 5 feet (while they are both in the air)?

a) 1 second **b)** 1 second **c)** $0.5 < t < 1.5$

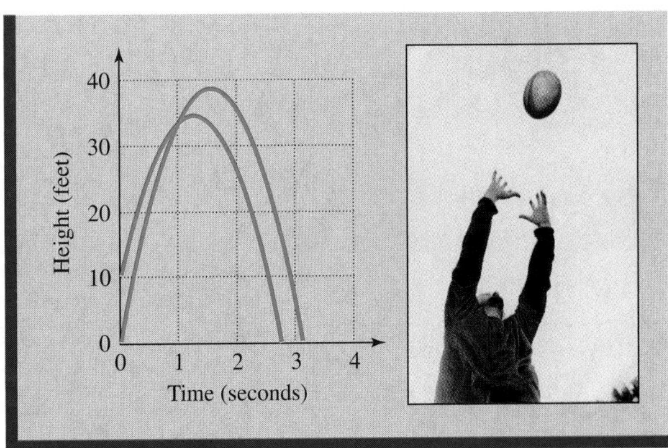

Figure for Exercise 89

90. ***Playing catch.*** A circus clown at the top of a 60-foot platform is playing catch with another clown on the ground. The clown on the platform drops a ball at the same time as the one on the ground tosses a ball upward at 80 ft/sec. For what length of time is the distance between the balls less than or equal to 10 feet? (*Hint:* Use the formula given in Exercise 89. The initial velocity of a ball that is dropped is 0 ft/sec.) See the figure on the next page. 0.25 second

Getting More Involved

91. ***Discussion***

For which real numbers m and n is each equation satisfied?

a) $|m - n| = |n - m|$

$(-\infty, \infty)$

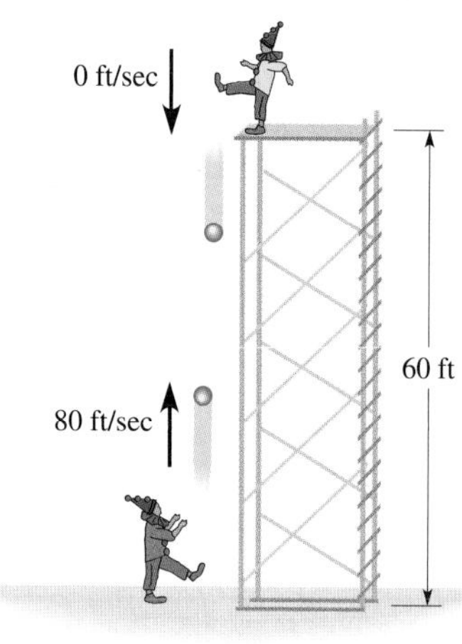

Figure for Exercise 90

b) $|mn| = |m| \cdot |n|$
$(-\infty, \infty)$

c) $\left|\frac{m}{n}\right| = \frac{|m|}{|n|}$
all reals except $n = 0$

92. ***Exploration***

a) Evaluate $|m + n|$ and $|m| + |n|$ for

i) $m = 3$ and $n = 5$

ii) $m = -3$ and $n = 5$ $|m + n| = 8$ or 2,

iii) $m = 3$ and $n = -5$ $|m| + |n| = 8$

iv) $m = -3$ and $n = -5$

b) What can you conclude about the relationship between $|m + n|$ and $|m| + |n|$?
$|m + n| \le |m| + |n|$

8.3 Compound Inequalities in Two Variables

In this Section

- Satisfying a Compound Inequality
- Graphing Compound Inequalities
- Absolute Value Inequalities
- Inequalities with No Solution
- Applications

A **simple inequality** in two variables involves only one inequality symbol. For example, $y > x - 3$ is a simple inequality in two variables. We graphed simple inequalities in two variables in Section 3.6. In this section we study compound inequalities in two variables.

Satisfying a Compound Inequality

A **compound inequality in two variables** consists of two simple inequalities joined with "and" or "or." For example, $y > x - 3$ and $y < 2 - x$ is a compound inequality in two variables. An ordered pair (or point) satisfies an "and" inequality only if it satisfies both of the simple inequalities. An ordered pair satisfies an "or" inequality if it satisfies one or the other or both inequalities.

EXAMPLE 1

Satisfying compound inequalities

Determine whether $(-2, 3)$ satisfies each compound inequality.

a) $y > x$ and $x - y < -4$

b) $y > x$ and $x - y > -4$

c) $y > x$ or $x - y > -4$

Solution

a) Replacing x with -2 and y with 3 in $y > x$ and $x - y < -4$ yields $3 > -2$ and $-2 - 3 < -4$. Since both inequalities are correct, $(-2, 3)$ satisfies the compound inequality.

b) Replacing x with -2 and y with 3 in $y > x$ and $x - y > -4$ yields $3 > -2$ and $-2 - 3 > -4$. Since the second inequality is not correct, $(-2, 3)$ does not satisfy the compound inequality.

c) Replacing x with -2 and y with 3 in $y > x$ or $x - y > -4$ yields $3 > -2$ and $-2 - 3 > -4$. Since the first inequality is correct and the connecting word is "or," $(-2, 3)$ satisfies the compound inequality.

Now do Exercises 7–12

Graphing Compound Inequalities

To graph the solution set to a compound inequality in two variables use the following strategy.

Graphing Compound Inequalities in Two Variables

1. Graph the boundary lines, which are found by replacing the inequality symbols with equal signs.
2. Select an arbitrary test point in each of the regions determined by the boundary lines and check whether it satisfies the compound inequality.
3. Shade all regions that satisfy the compound inequality.
4. Use solid boundary lines for $\leq$ or $\geq$. Use dashed boundary lines for $<$ or $>$.

Example 1 illustrates this **test point method.** Note that if the word connecting the two inequalities is "and," then the solution set is the intersection of the solution sets to the individual inequalities.

EXAMPLE 2

Graphing a compound inequality with *and*

Graph the compound inequality $y > x - 3$ and $y < -\frac{1}{2}x + 2$.

Solution

We first graph the equations $y = x - 3$ and $y = -\frac{1}{2}x + 2$. These lines divide the plane into four regions as shown in Fig. 8.16(a). Now test one point of each region to determine which region satisfies the compound inequality. Test the points (3, 3), (0, 0), $(4, -5)$, and (5, 0):

$3 > 3 - 3$	and	$3 < -\frac{1}{2} \cdot 3 + 2$	Second inequality is incorrect.
$0 > 0 - 3$	and	$0 < -\frac{1}{2} \cdot 0 + 2$	Both inequalities are correct.
$-5 > 4 - 3$	and	$-5 < -\frac{1}{2} \cdot 4 + 2$	First inequality is incorrect.
$0 > 5 - 3$	and	$5 < -\frac{1}{2} \cdot 0 + 2$	Both inequalities are incorrect.

Teaching Tip Point out that the shaded region is above $y = x - 3$ and below $y = -\frac{1}{2}x + 2$.

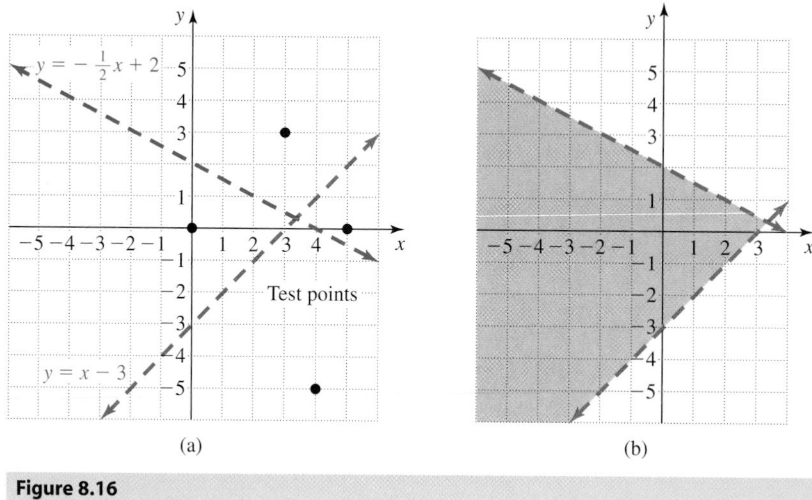

Figure 8.16

The only point that satisfies both inequalities is (0, 0). So the solution set to the compound inequality consists of all points in the region containing (0, 0). The graph of the compound inequality is shown in Fig. 8.16(b).

Now do Exercises 13–14

In Example 3, we graph a compound inequality using "or." Note that in this case the graph is the union of the solution sets to the individual inequalities.

EXAMPLE 3

Graphing a compound inequality with *or*

Graph the compound inequality

$$2x - 3y \le -6 \quad \text{or} \quad x + 2y \ge 4.$$

Helpful Hint

When graphing a compound inequality connected with "or," shade the region that satisfies the first inequality and then shade the region that satisfies the second inequality. If the inequalities are connected with "and," then you must be careful not to shade too much.

Solution

First graph the lines $2x - 3y = -6$ and $x + 2y = 4$. If we graph the lines using x- and y-intercepts, then we do not have to solve the equations for y. The lines are shown in Fig. 8.17(a). The graph of the compound inequality is the set of all

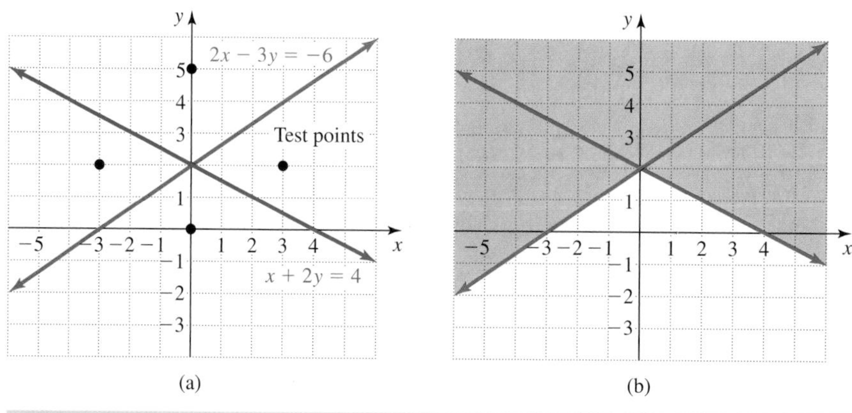

Figure 8.17

points that satisfy either one inequality or the other (or both). Test the points (0, 0), (3, 2), (0, 5), and (−3, 2). You should verify that only (0, 0) fails to satisfy at least one of the inequalities. So only the region containing the origin is left unshaded. The graph of the compound inequality is shown in Fig. 8.17(b).

Now do Exercises 15–34

Absolute Value Inequalities

In Section 8.2 we learned that the absolute value inequality $|x| > 2$ is equivalent to the compound inequality $x < -2$ or $x > 2$. The absolute value inequality $|x| < 2$ is equivalent to the compound inequality $x > -2$ and $x < 2$. We can also write $|x| < 2$ as $-2 < x < 2$. We use these ideas with inequalities in two variables in Example 4.

EXAMPLE 4

Graphing absolute value inequalities

Graph each absolute value inequality.

a) $|y - 2x| \le 3$ **b)** $|x - y| > 1$

Helpful Hint

Remember that absolute value of a quantity is its distance from 0 (Section 1.1). If $|w| < 3$, then w is less than 3 units from 0:

$$-3 < w < 3$$

If $|w| > 1$, then w is more than 1 unit away from 0:

$$w > 1 \quad \text{or} \quad w < -1$$

In Example 4 we are using an expression in place of w.

Solution

a) The inequality $|y - 2x| \le 3$ is equivalent to $-3 \le y - 2x \le 3$, which is equivalent to the compound inequality

$$y - 2x \le 3 \quad \text{and} \quad y - 2x \ge -3.$$

First graph the lines $y - 2x = 3$ and $y - 2x = -3$ as shown in Fig. 8.18(a). These lines divide the plane into three regions. Test a point from each region in the original inequality, say (−5, 0), (0, 1), and (5, 0):

$$|0 - 2(-5)| \le 3 \qquad |1 - 2 \cdot 0| \le 3 \qquad |0 - 2 \cdot 5| \le 3$$
$$10 \le 3 \qquad\qquad 1 \le 3 \qquad\qquad 10 \le 3$$

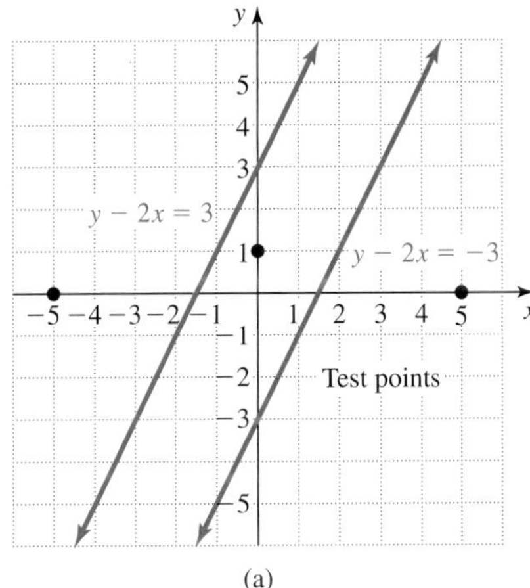

(a)

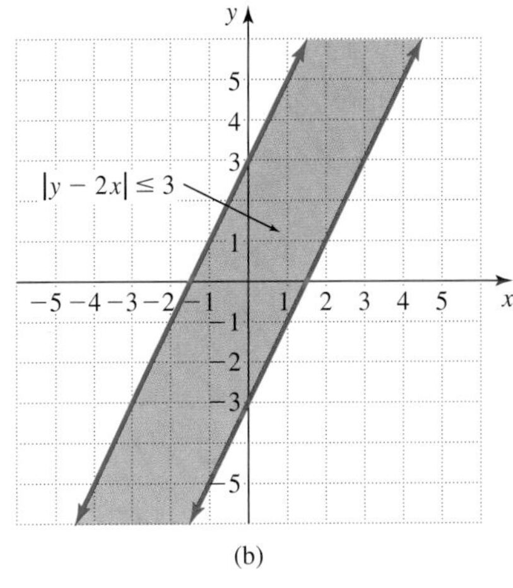

(b)

Figure 8.18

Only (0, 1) satisfies the original inequality. So the region satisfying the absolute value inequality is the shaded region containing (0, 1) as shown in Fig. 8.18(b). The boundary lines are solid because of the $\le$ symbol.

b) The inequality $|x - y| > 1$ is equivalent to

$$x - y > 1 \quad \text{or} \quad x - y < -1.$$

First graph the lines $x - y = 1$ and $x - y = -1$ as shown in Fig. 8.19(a). Test a point from each region in the original inequality, say $(-4, 0)$, $(0, 0)$, and $(4, 0)$:

$$|-4 - 0| > 1 \qquad |0 - 0| > 1 \qquad |4 - 0| > 1$$
$$4 > 1 \qquad 0 > 1 \qquad 4 > 1$$

Because $(-4, 0)$ and $(4, 0)$ satisfy the inequality, we shade those regions as shown in Fig. 8.19(b). The boundary lines are dashed because of the $>$ symbol.

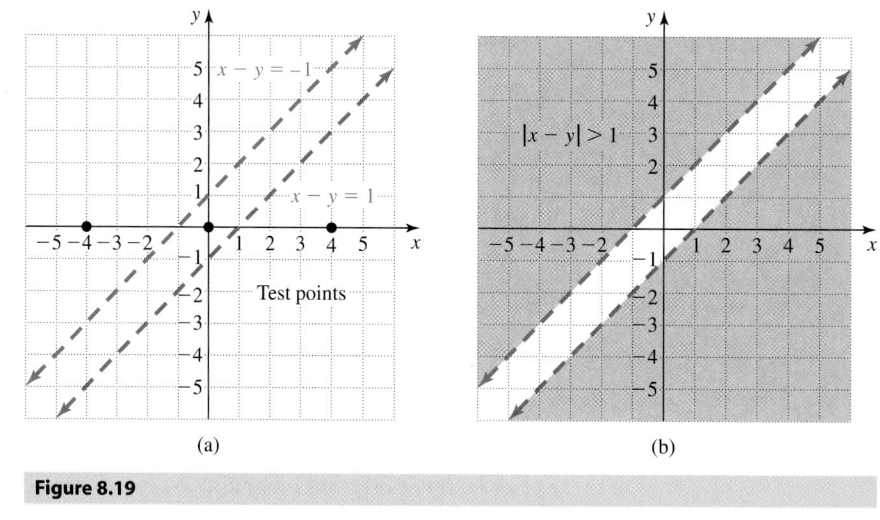

Figure 8.19

Now do Exercises 35–50

Inequalities with No Solution

The solution set to a compound inequality using "or" is the union of the individual solution sets. So the solution set to an "or" inequality is not empty unless all of the individual inequalities are inconsistent. However, the solution set to an "and" inequality can be empty even when the solution sets to the individual inequalities are not empty.

EXAMPLE 5

Compound inequalities with no solution

Solve each inequality.

a) $y > x + 1$ and $y < x - 2$ **b)** $x \ge 1$ and $x \le 0$ **c)** $|x - y| \le -3$

Solution

a) Note that the lines $y = x + 1$ and $y = x - 2$ are parallel lines and $y = x + 1$ lies above $y = x - 2$. There are no points in the coordinate plane that lie above $y = x + 1$ and below $y = x - 2$. So there are no ordered pairs that satisfy $y > x + 1$ and $y < x - 2$. The solution set is the empty set, $\varnothing$.

b) Note that $x = 1$ and $x = 0$ are vertical parallel lines and $x = 1$ lies to the right of $x = 0$. There are no points in the coordinate plane that lie to the right of $x = 1$ and to the left of $x = 0$. So there are no ordered pairs that satisfy $x \geq 1$ and $x \leq 0$. The solution set is the empty set, $\varnothing$.

c) Since the absolute value of any real number is nonnegative, there are no ordered pairs that satisfy $|x - y| \leq -3$. The solution set is the empty set, $\varnothing$.

Now do Exercises 51–66

Applications

In real situations x and y often represent quantities or amounts, which cannot be negative. In this case our graphs are restricted to the first quadrant, where x and y are both nonnegative.

EXAMPLE 6

Inequalities in business

The manager of a furniture store can spend a maximum of \$3000 on advertising per week. It costs \$50 to run a 30-second ad on an AM radio station and \$75 to run the ad on an FM station. Graph the region that shows the possible numbers of AM and FM ads that can be purchased and identify some possibilities.

Solution

If x represents the number of AM ads and y represents the number of FM ads, then x and y must satisfy the inequality $50x + 75y \leq 3000$. Because the number of ads cannot be negative, we also have $x \geq 0$ and $y \geq 0$. So we graph only points in the first quadrant that satisfy $50x + 75y \leq 3000$. The line $50x + 75y = 3000$ goes through (0, 40) and (60, 0). The inequality is satisfied below this line. The region showing the possible numbers of AM ads and FM ads is shown in Fig. 8.20. We shade the entire region in Fig. 8.20, but only points in the shaded region in which both coordinates are whole numbers actually satisfy the given condition. For example, 40 AM ads and 10 FM ads could be purchased. Other possibilities are 30 AM ads and 20 FM ads, or 10 AM ads and 10 FM ads.

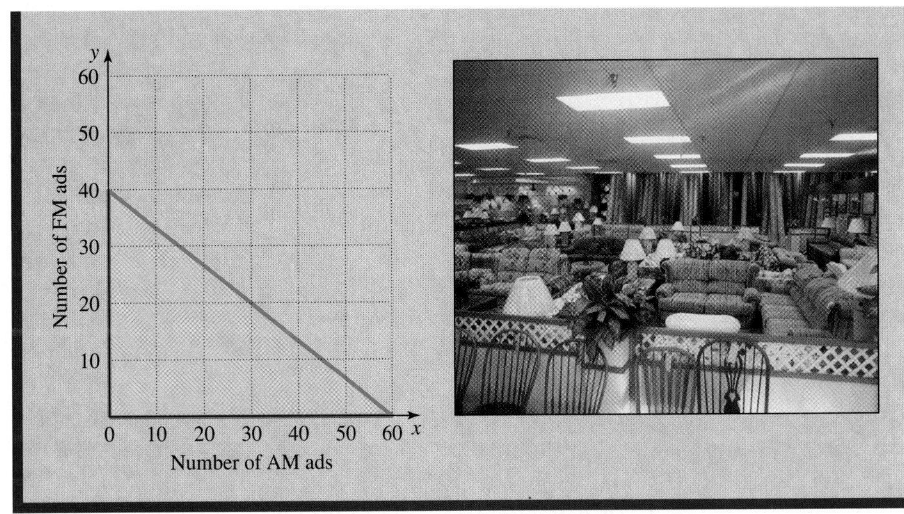

Figure 8.20

Now do Exercises 67–74

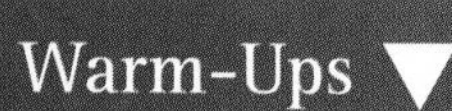

Warm-Ups

True or false? Explain your answer.

1. The point $(2, -3)$ satisfies the inequality $y > -3x + 2$. True
2. The graph of $3x - y > 2$ is the region above the line $3x - y = 2$. False
3. The graph of $3x + y < 5$ is the region below the line $y = -3x + 5$. True
4. The graph of $x < -3$ is the region to the left of the vertical line $x = 3$. False
5. The graph of $y > x + 3$ and $y < 2x - 6$ is the intersection of two regions. True
6. The graph of $y \le 2x - 3$ or $y \ge 3x + 5$ is the union of two regions. True
7. The ordered pair $(2, -5)$ satisfies $y > -3x + 5$ and $y < 2x - 3$. False
8. The ordered pair $(-3, 2)$ satisfies $y \le 3x - 6$ or $y \le x + 5$. True
9. The inequality $|2x - y| \le 4$ is equivalent to $2x - y \le 4$ and $2x + y \le 4$. False
10. The inequality $|x - y| > 3$ is equivalent to $x - y > 3$ or $x - y < -3$. True

8.3 Exercises

Boost your GRADE at mathzone.com!

MathZone
- Practice Problems
- Self-Tests
- Videos
- Net Tutor
- e-Professors

Reading and Writing *After reading this section, write out the answers to these questions. Use complete sentences.*

1. What is a compound inequality in two variables?
   A compound inequality in two variables is formed by connecting two simple inequalities with "and" or "or."
2. When does a point satisfy an "or" inequality?
   A point satisfies an "or" inequality if it satisfies one or the other or both inequalities.
3. When does a point satisfy an "and" inequality?
   A point satisfies an "and" inequality only if it satisfies both inequalities.
4. How do you know whether to use the union or intersection of the solution sets to the individual inequalities?
   For "or" we use the union of the solution sets and for "and" we use the intersection.
5. What is a test point use for?
   A test point is used to check whether all points in the region of the test point satisfy the compound inequality.
6. When are solid boundary lines used?
   Solid boundaries are used if the inequality symbols include equality.

Determine which of the ordered pairs $(1, 3)$, $(-2, 5)$, $(-6, -4)$, and $(7, -8)$ satisfy each compound or absolute value inequality. See Example 1.

7. $y > 5x$ and $y < -x$
   $(-6, -4)$
8. $y > 5x$ and $y > -x$
   $(-2, 5)$
9. $y > -x + 1$ or $y > 4x$
   $(1, 3), (-2, 5), (-6, -4)$
10. $y > -x + 1$ or $y < 4x$
   $(1, 3), (-2, 5), (7, -8)$
11. $|x + y| < 3$
   $(7, -8)$
12. $|x - y| > 2$
   $(-2, 5), (7, -8)$

Graph each compound inequality. See Examples 2 and 3.

13. $y > x$ and
    $y > -2x + 3$

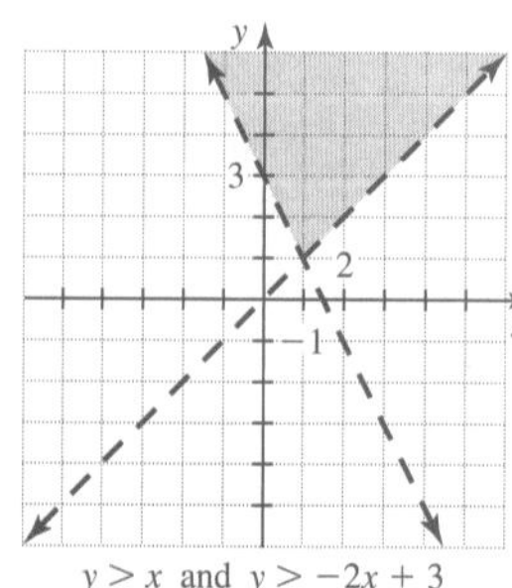

$y > x$ and $y > -2x + 3$

14. $y < x$ and
    $y < -3x + 2$

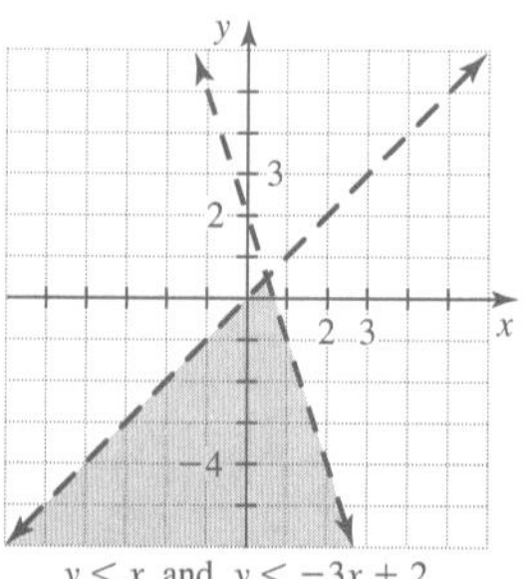

$y < x$ and $y < -3x + 2$

15. $y < x + 3$ or $y > -x + 2$

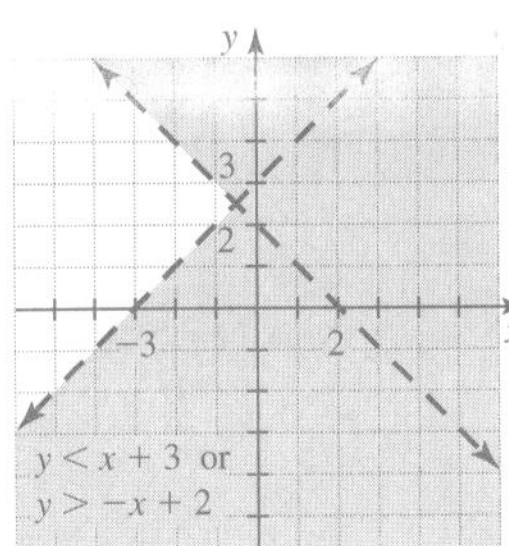

16. $y \geq x - 5$ or $y \leq -2x + 1$

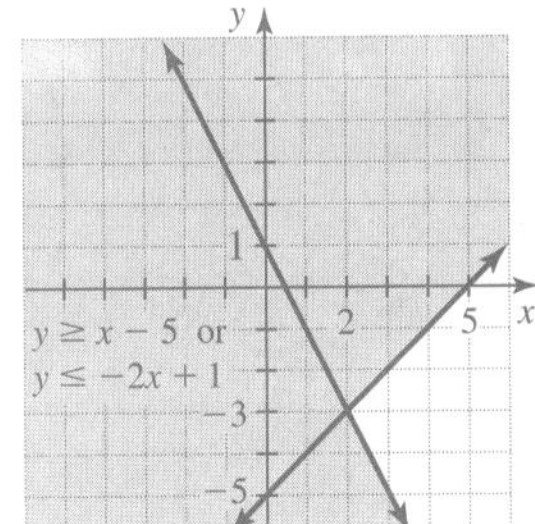

17. $x - 4y < 0$ and $3x + 2y \geq 6$

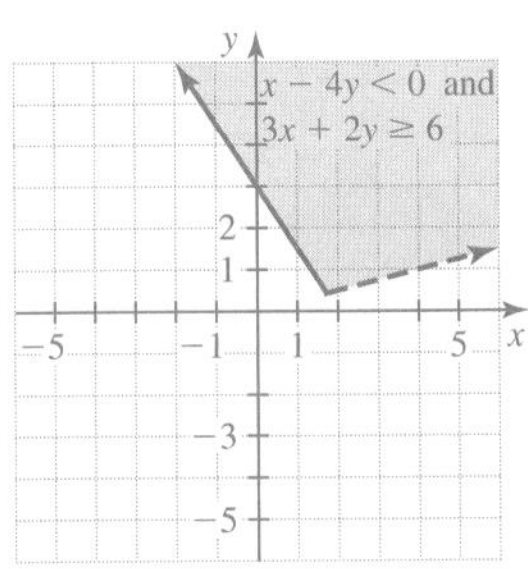

18. $x \geq -2y$ and $x - 3y < 6$

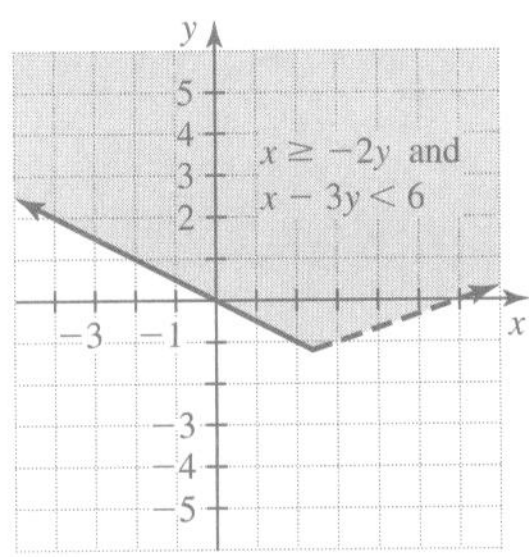

19. $x + y \leq 5$ and $x - y \leq 3$

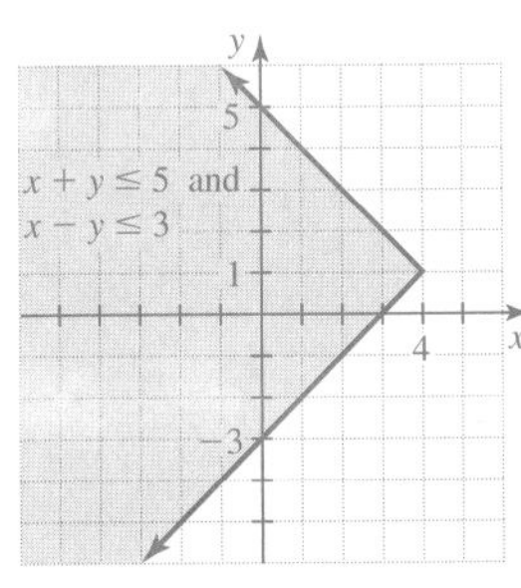

20. $2x - y < 3$ and $3x - y > 0$

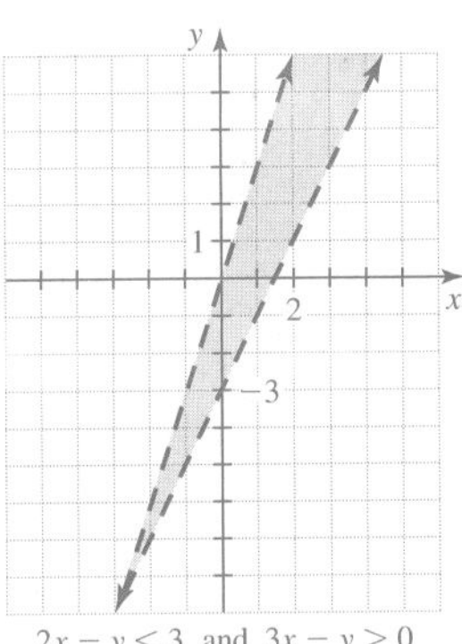

21. $x - 2y \leq 4$ or $2x - 3y \leq 6$

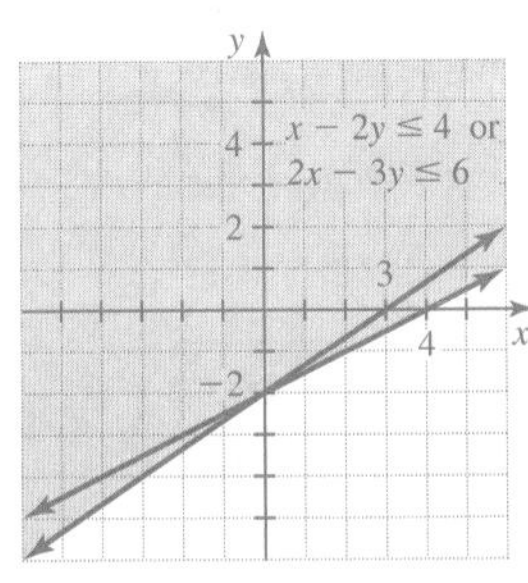

22. $4x - 3y \leq 3$ or $2x + y \geq 2$

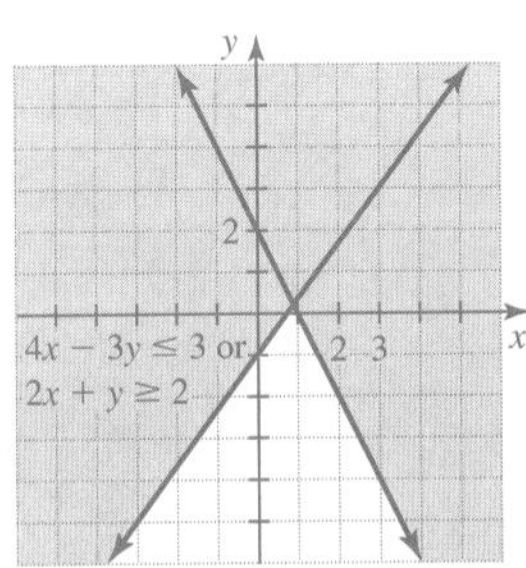

23. $y > 2$ and $x < 3$

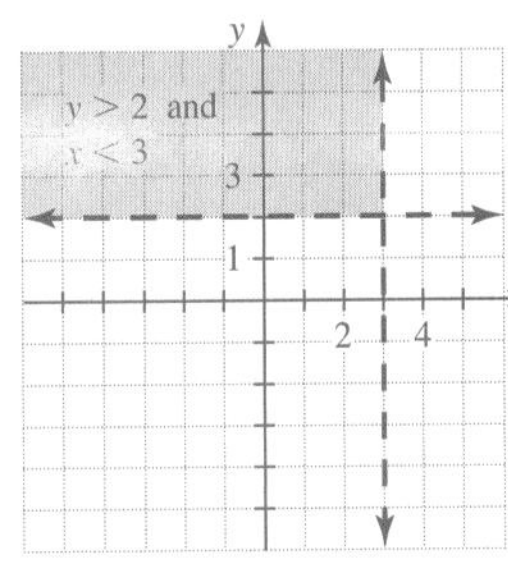

24. $x \leq 5$ and $y \geq -1$

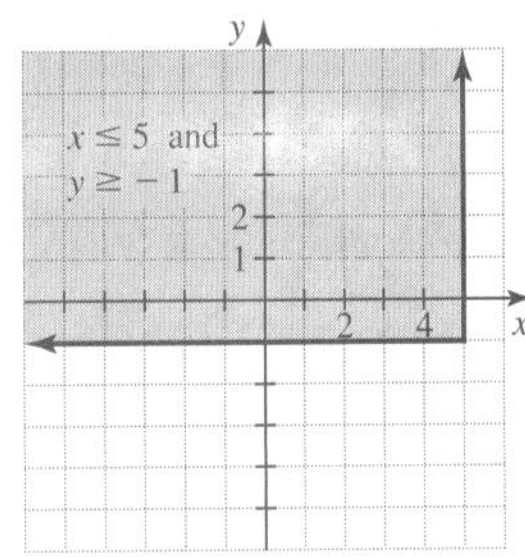

25. $y \geq x$ and $x \leq 2$

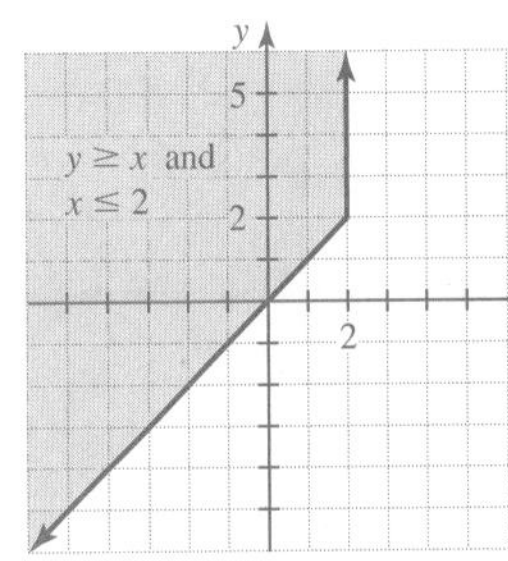

26. $y < x$ and $y > 0$

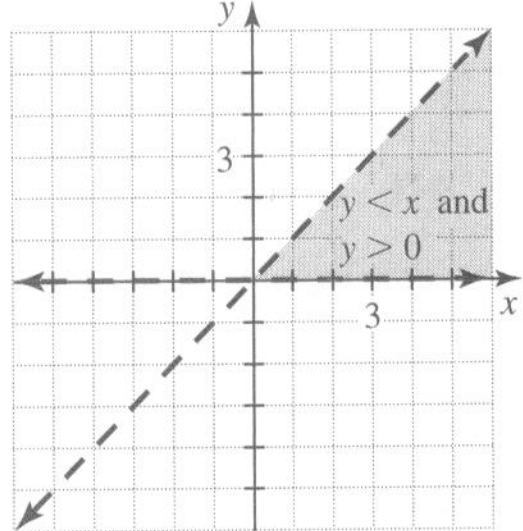

27. $2x < y + 3$ or $y > 2 - x$

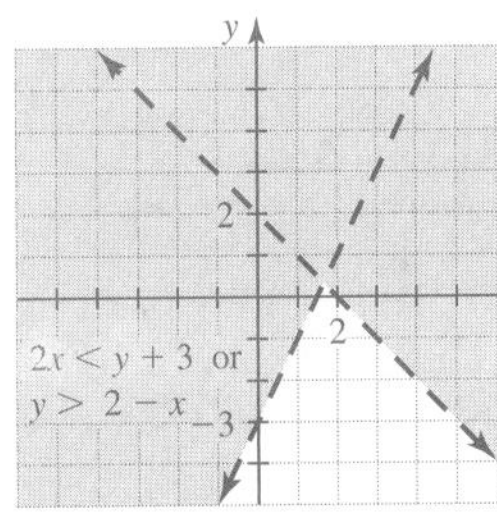

28. $3 - x < y + 2$ or $x > y + 5$

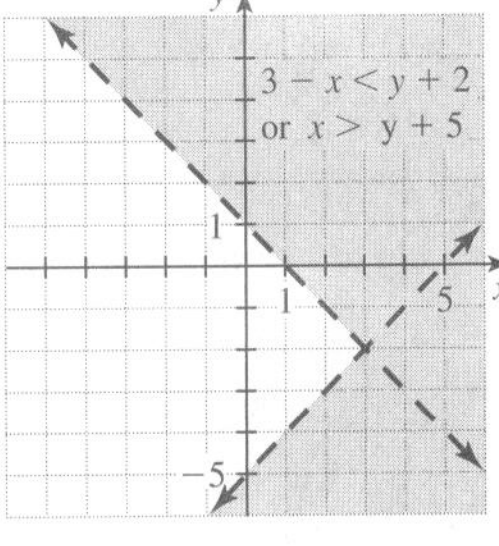

29. $y > x - 1$ and $y < x + 3$

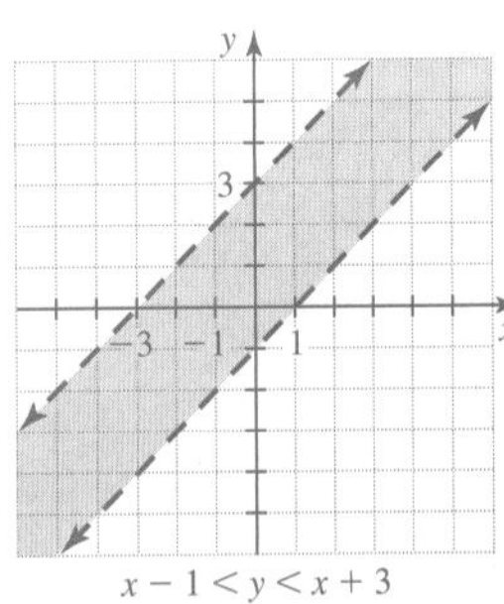

30. $y > x - 1$ and $y < 2x + 5$

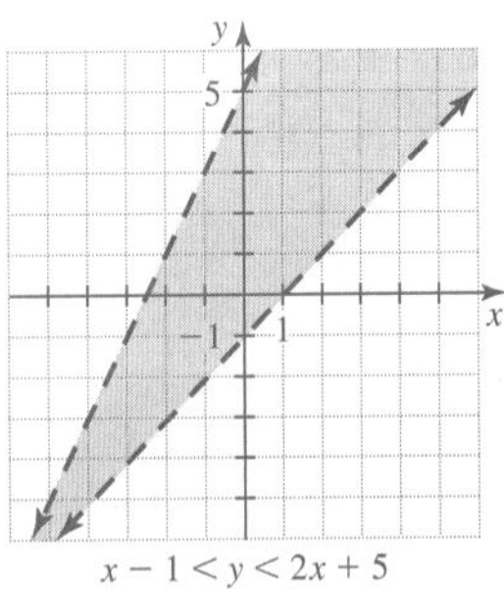

31. $0 \le y \le x$ and $x \le 1$

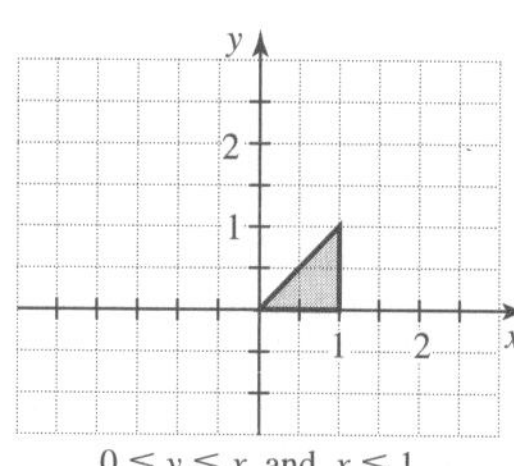
$0 \le y \le x$ and $x \le 1$

32. $x \le y \le 1$ and $x \ge 0$

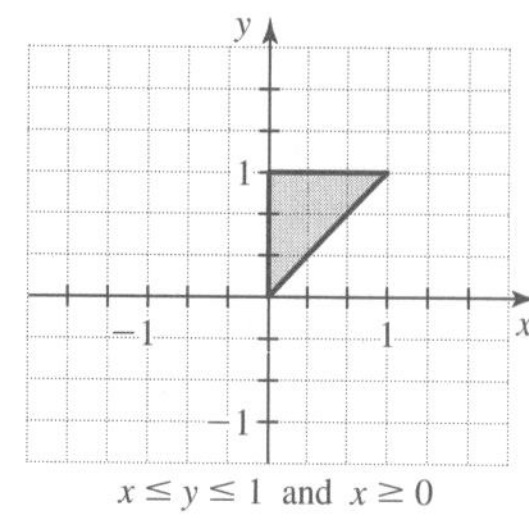
$x \le y \le 1$ and $x \ge 0$

33. $1 \le x \le 3$ and $2 \le y \le 5$

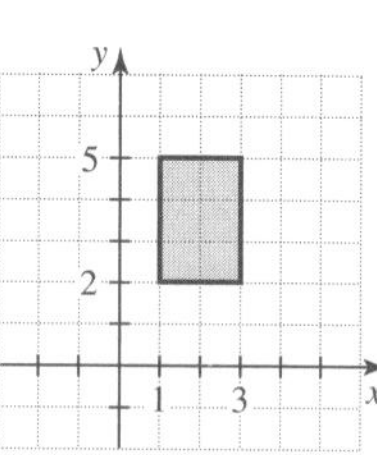
$1 \le x \le 3$ and $2 \le y \le 5$

34. $-1 < x < 1$ and $-1 < y < 1$

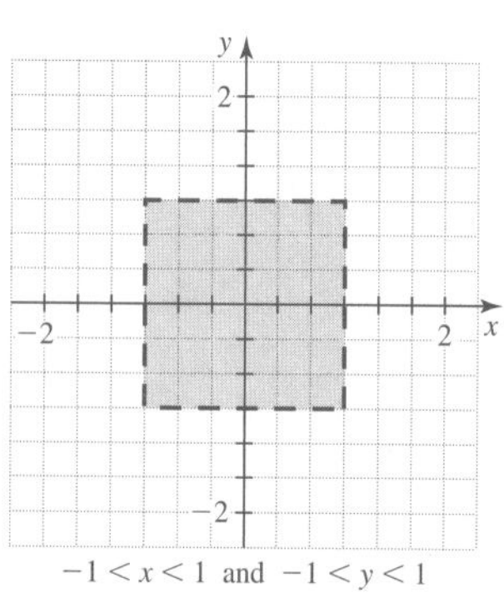
$-1 < x < 1$ and $-1 < y < 1$

Graph the absolute value inequalities. See Example 4.

35. $|x + y| < 2$

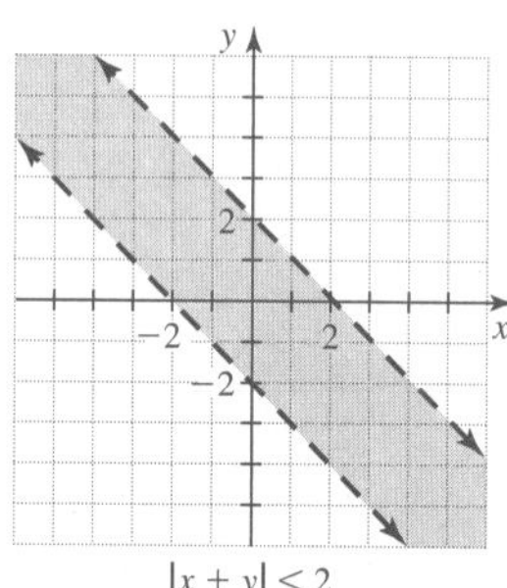
$|x + y| < 2$

36. $|2x + y| < 1$

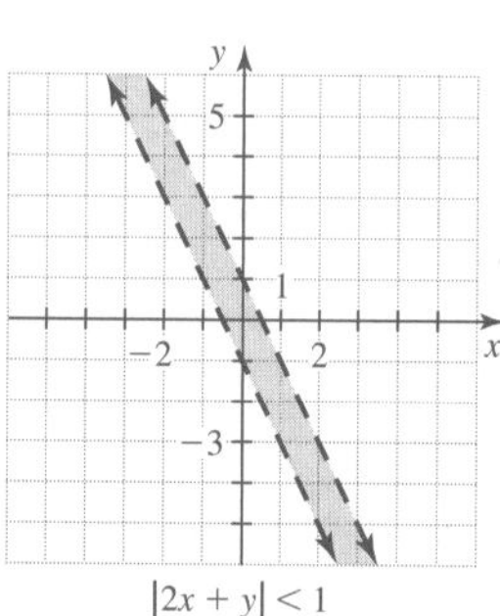
$|2x + y| < 1$

37. $|2x + y| \ge 1$

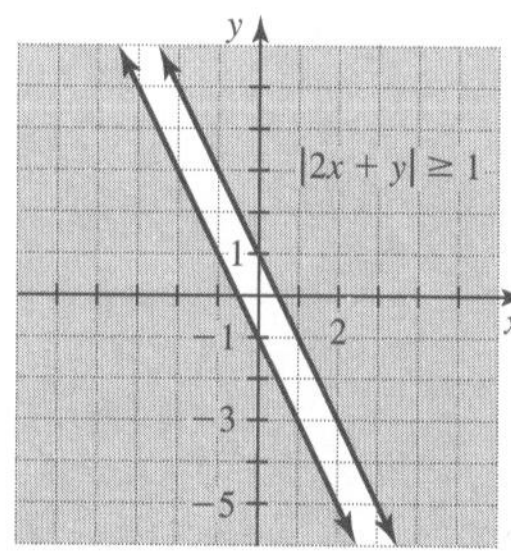

38. $|x + 2y| \ge 6$

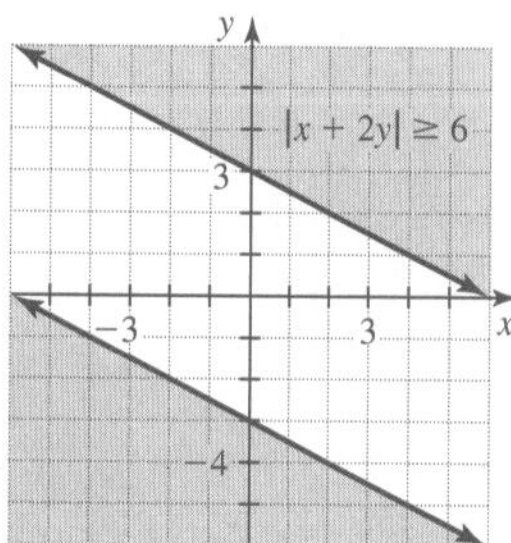

39. $|y - x| > 2$

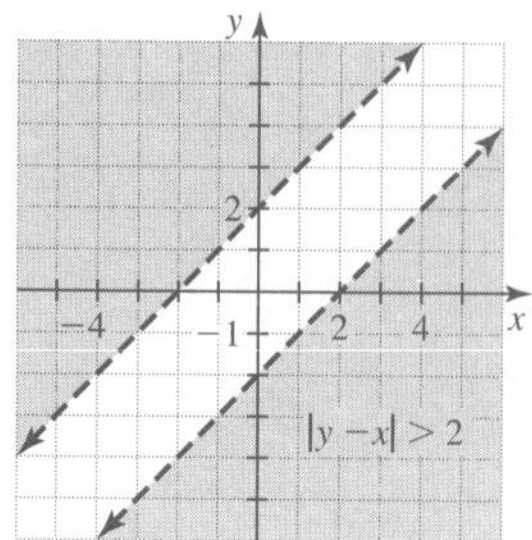

40. $|2y - x| > 6$

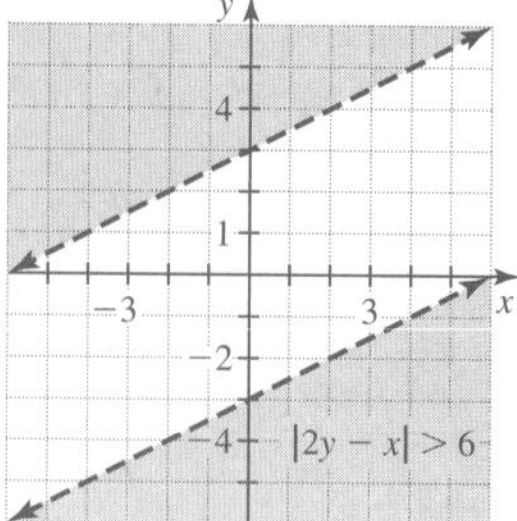

41. $|x - 2y| \le 4$

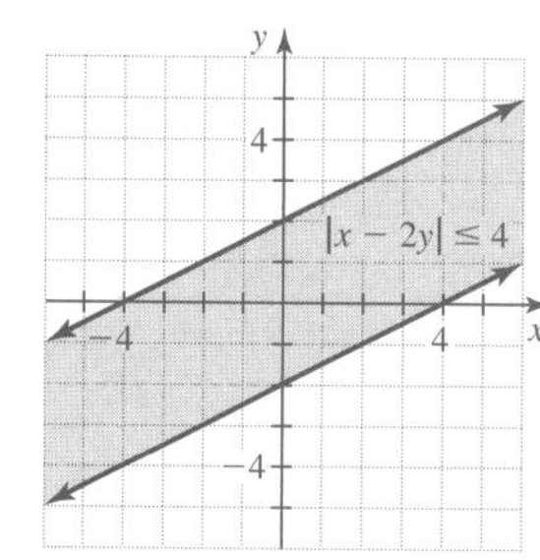

42. $|x - 3y| \le 6$

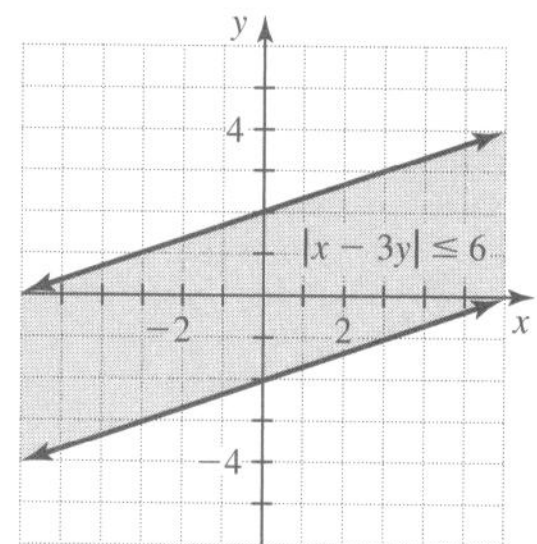

43. $|x| > 2$

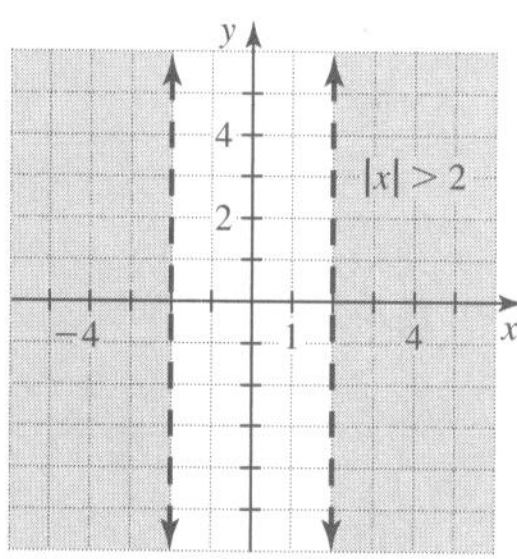

44. $|x| \le 3$

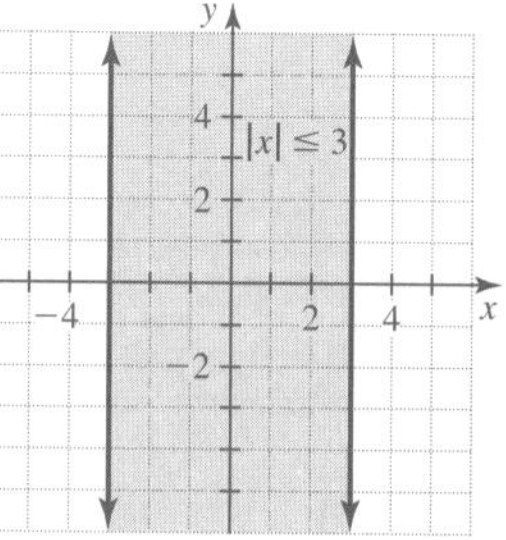

45. $|y| < 1$

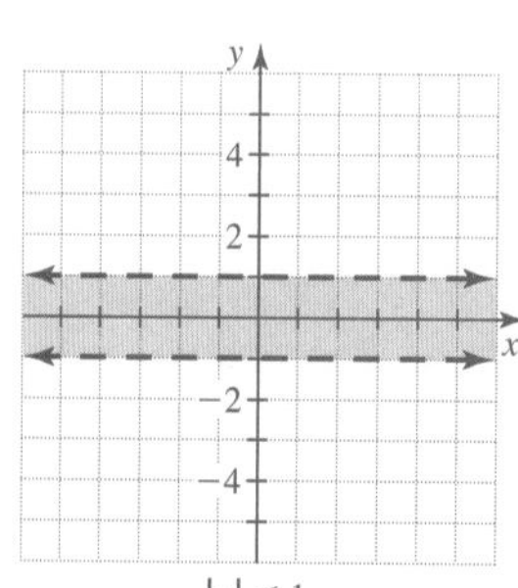
$|y| < 1$

46. $|y| \ge 2$

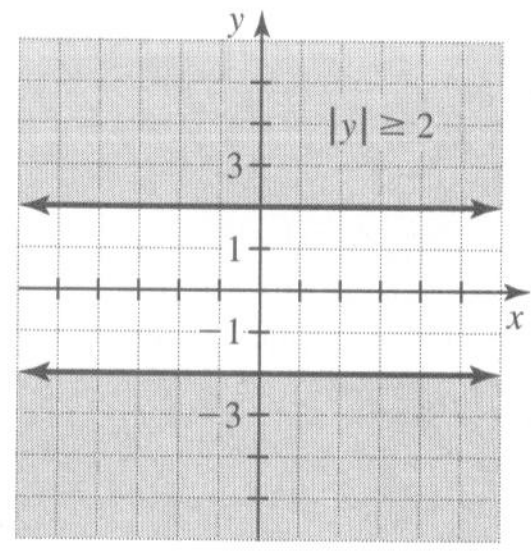

47. $|x| < 2$ and $|y| < 3$

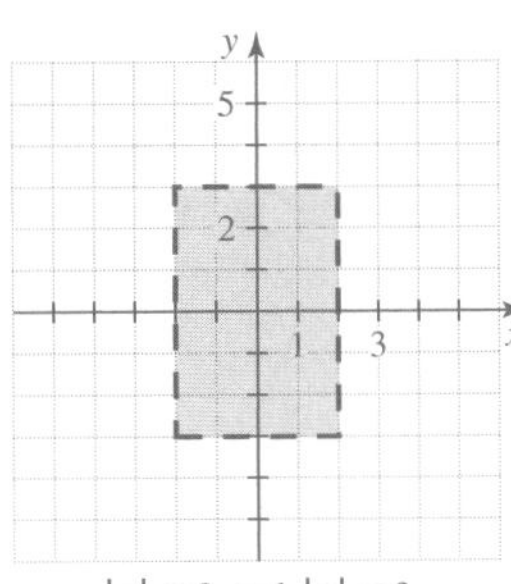

48. $|x| \geq 3$ or $|y| \geq 1$

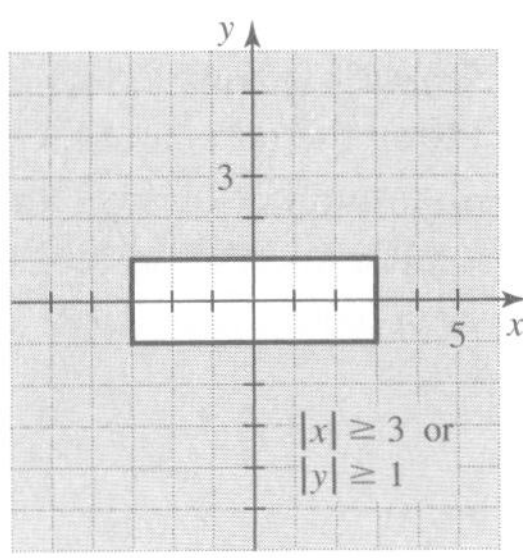

49. $|x - 3| < 1$ and $|y - 2| < 1$

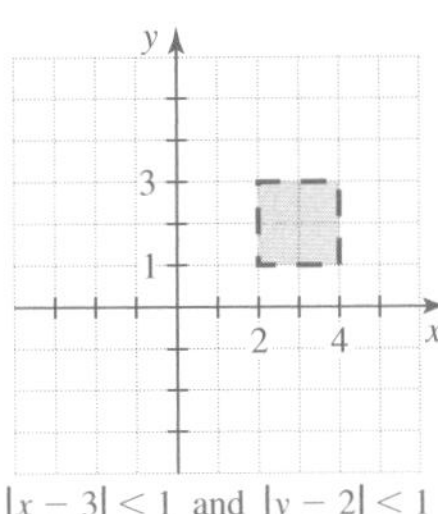

50. $|x - 2| \geq 3$ or $|y - 5| \geq 2$

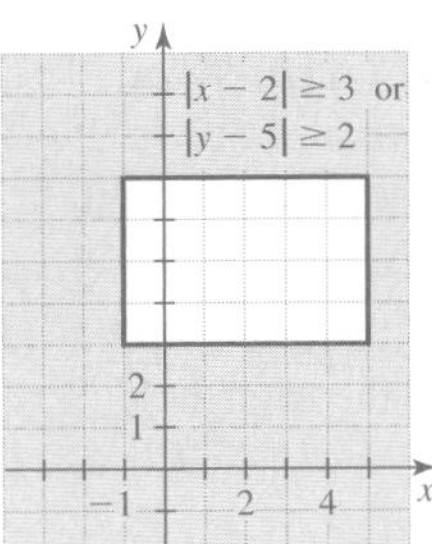

Determine whether the solution set to each compound or absolute value inequality is the empty set or not. See Example 5.

51. $y > x$ and $x < 1$
Not the empty set

52. $y > x$ and $x > 1$
Not the empty set

53. $y < 2x - 5$ and $y > 2x + 5$
$\varnothing$

54. $y \geq 3x$ and $y \leq 3x - 1$
$\varnothing$

55. $y < 2x - 5$ or $y > 2x + 5$
Not the empty set

56. $y \geq 3x$ or $y \leq 3x - 1$
Not the empty set

57. $y < 2x$ and $y > 3x$
Not the empty set

58. $y < 2x$ or $y > 3x$
Not the empty set

59. $y < x$ and $x < y$
$\varnothing$

60. $y > 3$ and $y < 1$
$\varnothing$

61. $|y + 2x| < 0$
$\varnothing$

62. $|x - 2y| < 0$
$\varnothing$

63. $|3x + 2y| \leq -4$
$\varnothing$

64. $|x - 2y| < -9$
$\varnothing$

65. $|x + y| > -4$
Not the empty set

66. $|2x + 3y| < 4$
Not the empty set

Solve each problem. See Example 6.

67. ***Budget planning.*** The Highway Patrol can spend a maximum of \$120,000 on new vehicles this year. They can get a fully equipped compact car for \$15,000 or a fully equipped full-size car for \$20,000. Graph the region that shows the number of cars of each type that could be purchased.

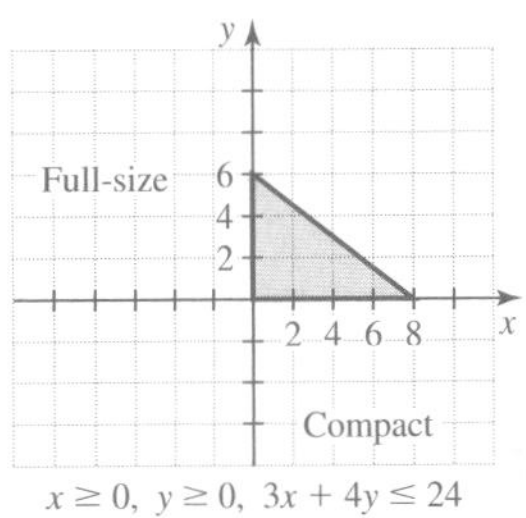

68. ***Allocating resources.*** A furniture maker has a shop that can employ 12 workers for 40 hours per week at its maximum capacity. The shop makes tables and chairs. It takes 16 hours of labor to make a table and 8 hours of labor to make a chair. Graph the region that shows the possibilities for the number of tables and chairs that could be made in one week.

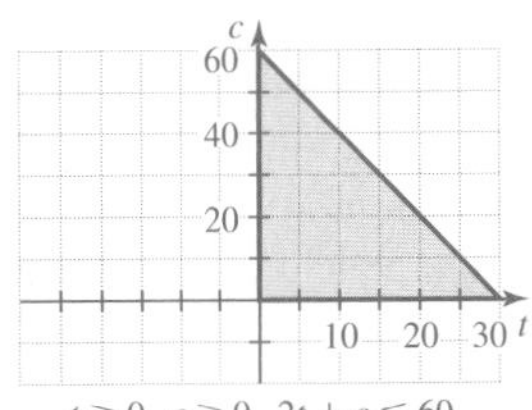

69. ***More restrictions.*** In Exercise 67, add the condition that the number of full-size cars must be greater than or equal to the number of compact cars. Graph the region showing the possibilities for the number of cars of each type that could be purchased.

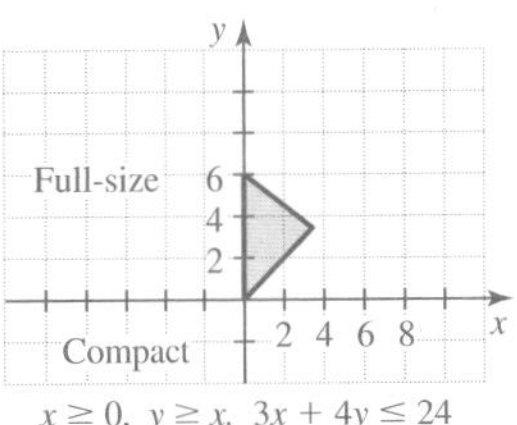

70. ***Chairs per table.*** In Exercise 68, add the condition that the number of chairs must be at least four times the number of

tables and at most six times the number of tables. Graph the region showing the possibilities for the number of tables and chairs that could be made in one week.

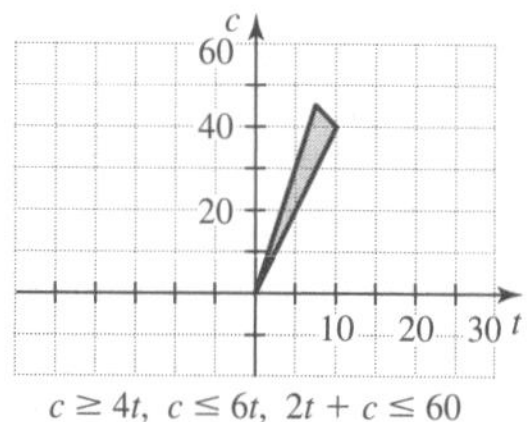

$c \geq 4t,\ c \leq 6t,\ 2t + c \leq 60$

71. ***Building fitness.*** To achieve cardiovascular fitness, you should exercise so that your target heart rate is between 70% and 85% of its maximum rate. Your target heart rate h depends on your age a. For building fitness, you should have $h \leq 187 - 0.85a$ and $h \geq 154 - 0.70a$ (NordicTrack brochure). Graph this compound inequality for $20 \leq a \leq 75$ to see the heart rate target zone for building fitness.

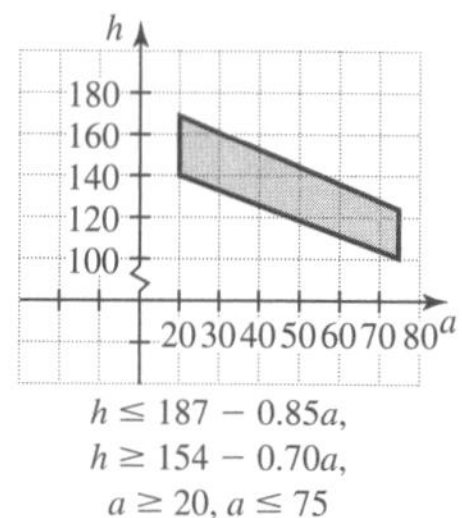

$h \leq 187 - 0.85a,$
$h \geq 154 - 0.70a,$
$a \geq 20,\ a \leq 75$

72. ***Waist-to-hip ratio.*** A study by Dr. Aaron R. Folsom concluded that waist-to-hip ratios are a better predictor of 5-year survival than more traditional height-to-weight ratios. Dr. Folsom concluded that for good health the waist size of a woman aged 50 to 69 should be less than or equal to 80% of her hip size, $w \leq 0.80h$. Make a graph showing possible waist and hip sizes for good health for women in this age group for which hip size is no more than 50 inches.

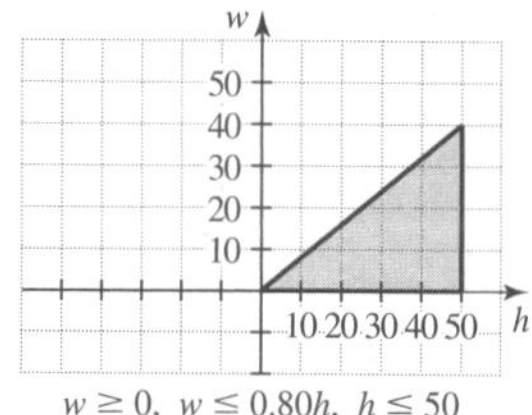

$w \geq 0,\ w \leq 0.80h,\ h \leq 50$

73. ***Advertising dollars.*** A restaurant manager can spend at most \$9000 on advertising per month and has two choices for advertising. The manager can purchase an ad in the *Daily Chronicle* (a 7-day-per-week newspaper) for \$300 per day or a 30-second ad on WBTU television for \$1000 each time the ad is aired. Graph the region that shows the possible number of days that an ad can be run in the newspaper and the possible number of times that an ad can be aired on television.

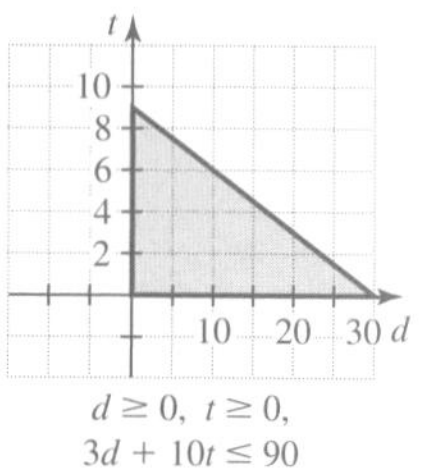

$d \geq 0,\ t \geq 0,$
$3d + 10t \leq 90$

74. ***Shipping restrictions.*** The accompanying graph shows all of the possibilities for the number of refrigerators and the number of TVs that will fit into an 18-wheeler.

a) Write an inequality to describe this region.
b) Will the truck hold 71 refrigerators and 118 TVs?
c) Will the truck hold 51 refrigerators and 176 TVs?
a) $3r + t \leq 330$ **b)** no **c)** yes

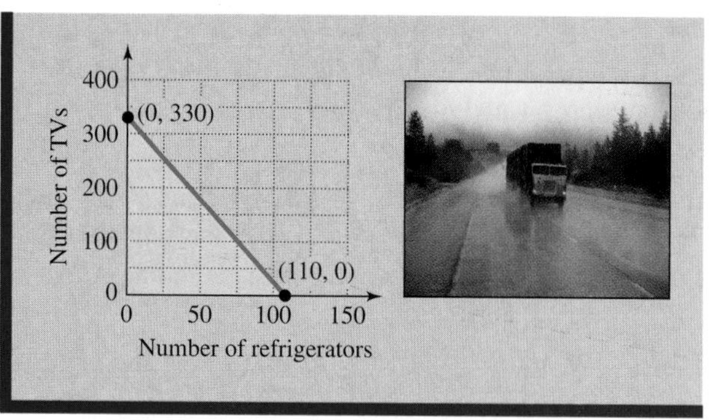

Figure for Exercise 74

Getting More Involved

75. ***Writing***

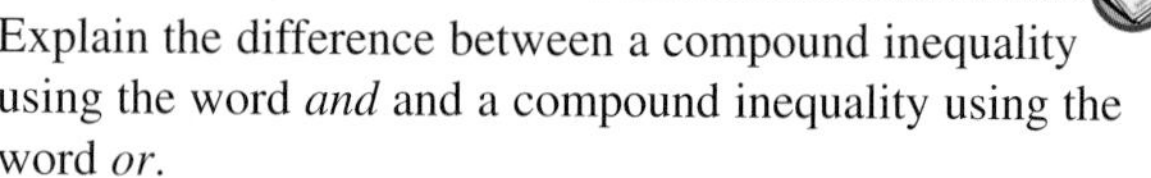

Explain the difference between a compound inequality using the word *and* and a compound inequality using the word *or*.

76. ***Discussion***

Explain how to write an absolute value inequality as a compound inequality.

8.4 Linear Programming

In this Section

- Graphing the Constraints
- Maximizing or Minimizing a Linear Function

In this section we graph the solution set to a system of several linear inequalities in two variables as in Section 8.3. We then use the solution set to the inequalities to determine the maximum or minimum value of another variable. The method that we use is called **linear programming.**

Graphing the Constraints

In linear programming we have two variables that must satisfy several linear inequalities. These inequalities are called the **constraints** because they restrict the variables to only certain values. A graph in the coordinate plane is used to indicate the points that satisfy all of the constraints.

EXAMPLE 1

Graphing the constraints

Graph the solution set to the system of inequalities and identify each vertex of the region:

$$x \geq 0, \quad y \geq 0$$
$$3x + 2y \leq 12$$
$$x + 2y \leq 8$$

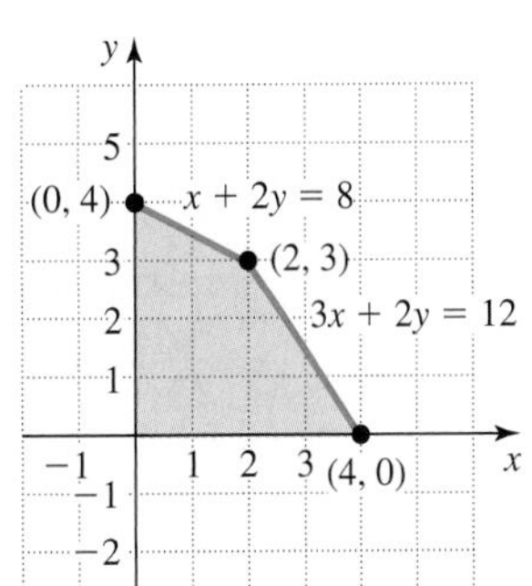

Figure 8.21

Solution

The points on or to the right of the y-axis satisfy $x \geq 0$. The points on or above the x-axis satisfy $y \geq 0$. The points on or below the line $3x + 2y = 12$ satisfy $3x + 2y \leq 12$. The points on or below the line $x + 2y = 8$ satisfy $x + 2y \leq 8$. Graph each straight line and shade the region that satisfies all four inequalities as shown in Fig. 8.21. Three of the vertices are easily identified as (0, 0), (0, 4), and (4, 0). The fourth vertex is found by solving the system $3x + 2y = 12$ and $x + 2y = 8$. The fourth vertex is (2, 3).

Now do Exercises 7–16

In linear programming the constraints usually come from physical limitations in some problem. In Example 2 we write the constraints and then graph the points in the coordinate plane that satisfy all of the constraints.

EXAMPLE 2

Teaching Tip Remind students to read the problem several times before writing constraints about different materials.

Writing the constraints

Jules is in the business of constructing dog houses. A small dog house requires 8 square feet (ft^2) of plywood and 6 ft^2 of insulation. A large dog house requires 16 ft^2 of plywood and 3 ft^2 of insulation. Jules has available only 48 ft^2 of plywood and 18 ft^2 of insulation. Write the constraints on the number of small and large dog houses that he can build with the available supplies and graph the solution set to the system of constraints.

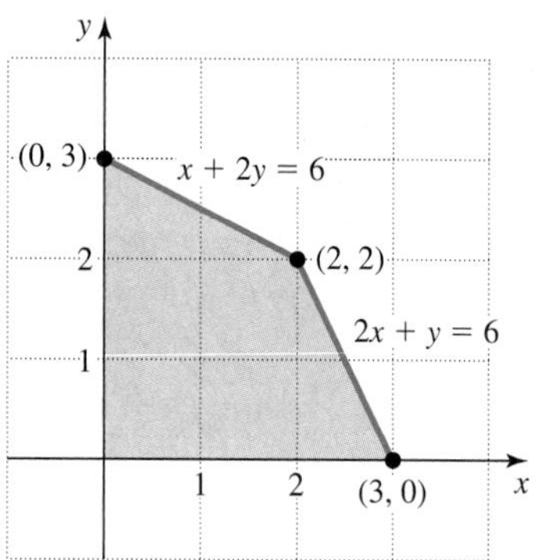

Figure 8.22

Solution

Let x represent the number of small dog houses and y represent the number of large dog houses. We have two natural constraints $x \geq 0$ and $y \geq 0$ since he cannot build a negative number of dog houses. Since the total plywood available for use is at most 48 ft^2, $8x + 16y \leq 48$. Since the total insulation available is at most 18 ft^2, $6x + 3y \leq 18$. Simplify the inequalities to get the following constraints:

$$x \geq 0, \quad y \geq 0$$
$$x + 2y \leq 6$$
$$2x + y \leq 6$$

The graph of the solution set to the system of inequalities is shown in Fig. 8.22.

Now do Exercises 23–24

Maximizing or Minimizing

If a small dog house sells for \$15 and a large sells for \$20, then the total revenue in dollars from the sale of x small and y large dog houses is given by $R = 15x + 20y$. Since R is determined by or *is a function of* x and y, we use the function notation that was introduced in Section 4.1 and write $R(x, y)$ in place of R. The equation $R(x, y) = 15x + 20y$ is called a *linear function* of x and y. Any ordered pair within the region shown in Fig. 8.22 is a possibility for the number of dog houses of each type that could be built and so it is the *domain* of the function R. (We will study functions in general in Chapter 12.)

Linear Function of Two Variables

An equation of the form $f(x, y) = Ax + By + C$, where A, B, and C are fixed real numbers, is called a **linear function of two variables** (x and y).

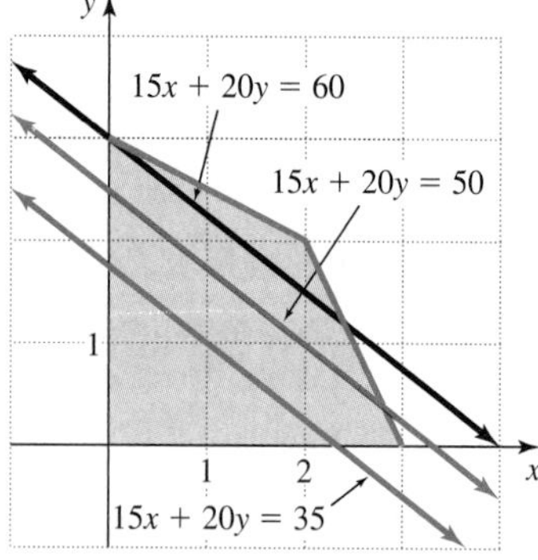

Figure 8.23

Naturally, we are interested in the maximum revenue subject to the constraints on x and y. To investigate some possible revenues, replace R in $R = 15x + 20y$ with, say 35, 50, and 60. The graphs of the parallel lines $15x + 20y = 35$, $15x + 20y = 50$, and $15x + 20y = 60$ are shown in Fig. 8.23. The revenue at any point on the line $15x + 20y = 35$ is \$35. We get a larger revenue on a higher revenue line (and lower revenue on a lower line). The maximum revenue possible will be on the highest revenue line that still intersects the region. Because the sides of the region are straight-line segments, the intersection of the highest (or lowest) revenue line with the region must include a vertex of the region. This is the fundamental principle behind linear programming.

Teaching Tip The lines in Fig. 8.23 are like level lines on a topographic map. To go up in altitude you must travel northeast.

The Principle of Linear Programming

The maximum or minimum value of a linear function subject to linear constraints occurs at a vertex of the region determined by the constraints.

EXAMPLE 3

Maximizing a linear function with linear constraints

A small dog house requires 8 ft^2 of plywood and 6 ft^2 of insulation. A large dog house requires 16 ft^2 of plywood and 3 ft^2 of insulation. Only 48 ft^2 of plywood and 18 ft^2 of insulation are available. If a small dog house sells for \$15 and a large dog house sells for \$20, then how many dog houses of each type should be built to maximize the revenue and to satisfy the constraints?

Solution

Let x be the number of small dog houses and y be the number of large dog houses. We wrote and graphed the constraints for this problem in Example 2, so we will not repeat that here. The graph in Fig. 8.23 has four vertices: (0, 0), (0, 3), (3, 0), and (2, 2). The revenue function is $R(x, y) = 15x + 20y$. Since the maximum value of this function must occur at a vertex, we evaluate the function at each vertex:

$$R(0, 0) = 15(0) + 20(0) = \$0$$
$$R(0, 3) = 15(0) + 20(3) = \$60$$
$$R(3, 0) = 15(3) + 20(0) = \$45$$
$$R(2, 2) = 15(2) + 20(2) = \$70$$

From this list we can see that the maximum revenue is \$70 when two small and two large dog houses are built. We also see that the minimum revenue is \$0 when no dog houses of either type are built.

Now do Exercises 25–26

We can summarize the procedure for solving linear programming problems with the following strategy.

Strategy for Linear Programming

Use the following steps to find the maximum or minimum value of a linear function subject to linear constraints.

1. Graph the region that satisfies all of the constraints.
2. Determine the coordinates of each vertex of the region.
3. Evaluate the function at each vertex of the region.
4. Identify which vertex gives the maximum or minimum value of the function.

In Example 4 we solve another linear programming problem.

EXAMPLE 4

Minimizing a linear function with linear constraints

One serving of food A contains 2 grams of protein and 6 grams of carbohydrates. One serving of food B contains 4 grams of protein and 3 grams of carbohydrates. A dietitian wants a meal that contains at least 12 grams of protein and at least 18 grams of carbohydrates. If the cost of food A is 9 cents per serving and the cost of food B is 20 cents per serving, then how many servings of each food would minimize the cost and satisfy the constraints?

Solution

Let x equal the number of servings of food A and y equal the number of servings of food B. If the meal is to contain at least 12 grams of protein, then $2x + 4y \geq 12$. If the meal is to contain at least 18 grams of carbohydrates, then $6x + 3y \geq 18$. Simplify each inequality and use the two natural constraints to get the following system:

$$x \geq 0, \quad y \geq 0$$
$$x + 2y \geq 6$$
$$2x + y \geq 6$$

The graph of the constraints is shown in Fig. 8.24. The vertices are (0, 6), (6, 0), and (2, 2). The cost in cents for x servings of A and y servings of B is $C(x, y) = 9x + 20y$. Evaluate the cost at each vertex:

$$C(0, 6) = 9(0) + 20(6) = 120 \text{ cents}$$
$$C(6, 0) = 9(6) + 20(0) = 54 \text{ cents}$$
$$C(2, 2) = 9(2) + 20(2) = 58 \text{ cents}$$

The minimum cost of 54 cents is attained by using six servings of food A and no servings of food B.

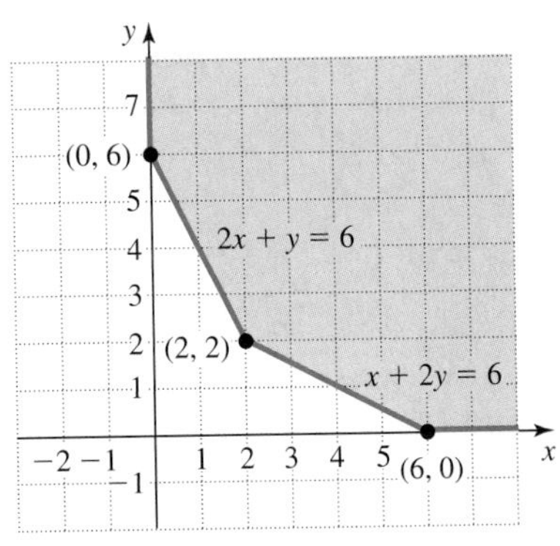

Figure 8.24

Now do Exercises 27–34

Warm-Ups ▼

True or false? Explain your answer.

1. The graph of $x \geq 0$ in the coordinate plane consists of the points on or above the x-axis. False
2. The graph of $y \geq 0$ in the coordinate plane consists of the points on or to the right of the y-axis. False
3. The graph of $x + y \leq 6$ consists of the points below the line $x + y = 6$. False
4. The graph of $2x + 3y = 30$ has x-intercept (0, 10) and y-intercept (15, 0). False
5. The graph of a system of inequalities is a union of their individual solution sets. False
6. In linear programming, constraints are inequalities that restrict the possible values that the variables can assume. True
7. The function $F(x, y) = Ax^2 + By^2 + C$ is a linear function of x and y. False
8. The value of $R(x, y) = 3x + 5y$ at the point (2, 4) is 26. True
9. If $C(x, y) = 12x + 10y$, then $C(0, 5) = 62$. False
10. In solving a linear programming problem, we must determine the vertices of the region defined by the constraints. True

8.4 Exercises

Boost your GRADE at mathzone.com!

MathZone

- Practice Problems
- Self-Tests
- Videos
- Net Tutor
- e-Professors

Reading and Writing *After reading this section, write out the answers to these questions. Use complete sentences.*

1. What is a constraint?
A constraint is an inequality that restricts the values of the variables.

2. What is linear programming?
Linear programming is the process used to maximize or minimize a linear function subject to linear constraints.

3. Where do the constraints come from in a linear programming problem?
Constraints may be limitations on the amount of available supplies, money, or other resources.

4. What is a linear function of two variables?
A linear function of two variables is a function of the form $f(x, y) = Ax + By + C$.

5. Where does the maximum or minimum value of a linear function subject to linear constraints occur?
The maximum or minimum of a linear function subject to linear constraints occurs at a vertex of the region determined by the constraints.

6. What is the strategy for solving a linear programming problem?
Write the constraints, graph the region that they determine, locate each vertex, then evaluate the function at each vertex, and identify the maximum or minimum.

Graph the solution set to each system of inequalities and identify each vertex of the region. See Example 1.

7. $x \geq 0, y \geq 0$
$x + y \leq 5$

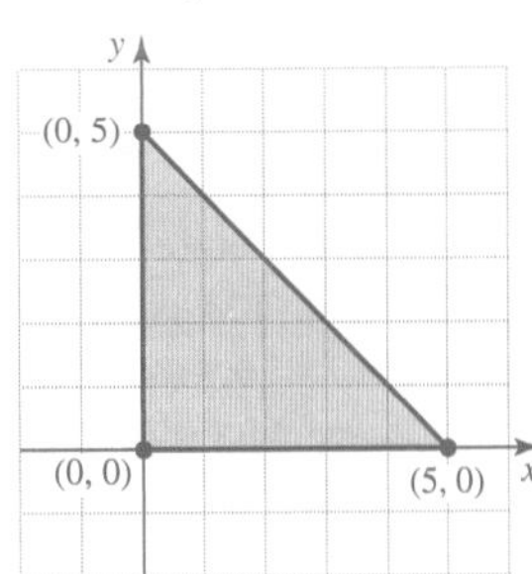

8. $x \geq 0, y \geq 0$
$y \leq 5, y \geq x$

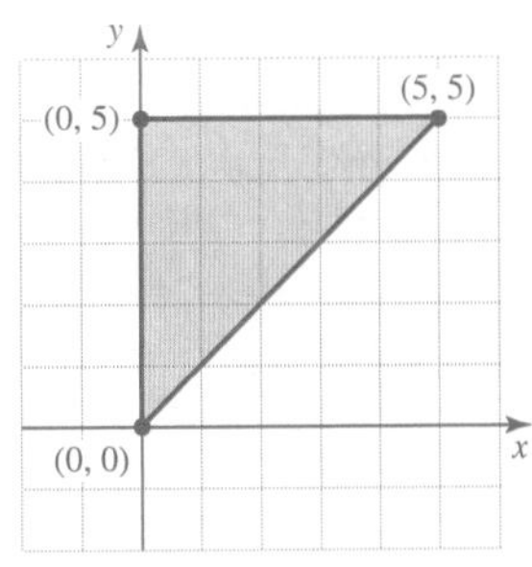

9. $x \geq 0, y \geq 0$
$2x + y \leq 4$
$x + y \leq 3$

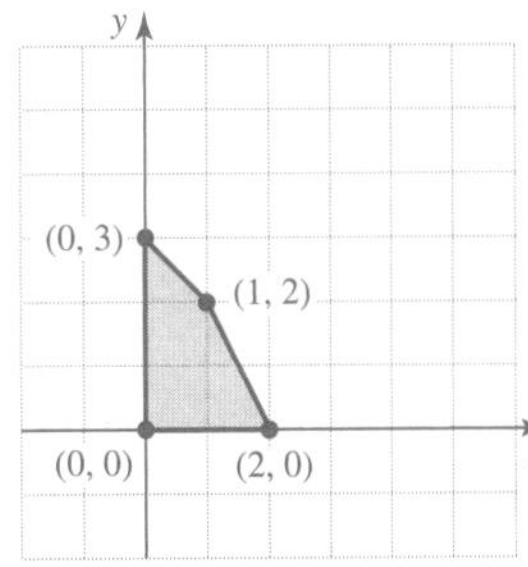

10. $x \geq 0, y \geq 0$
$x + y \leq 4$
$x + 2y \leq 6$

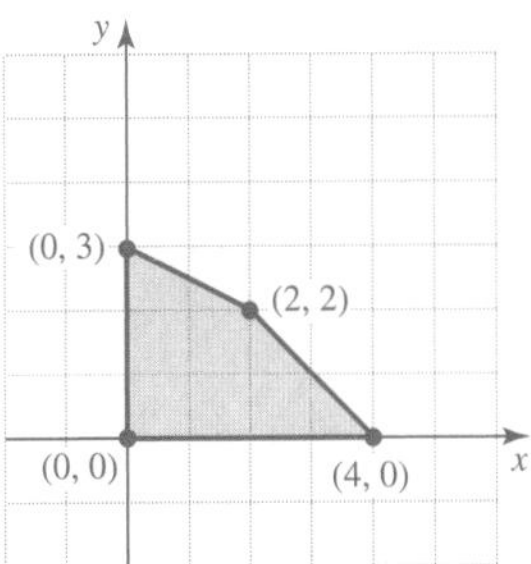

11. $x \geq 0, y \geq 0$

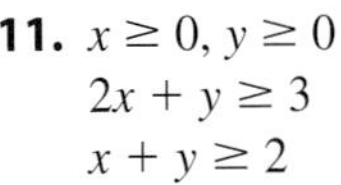

$2x + y \geq 3$
$x + y \geq 2$

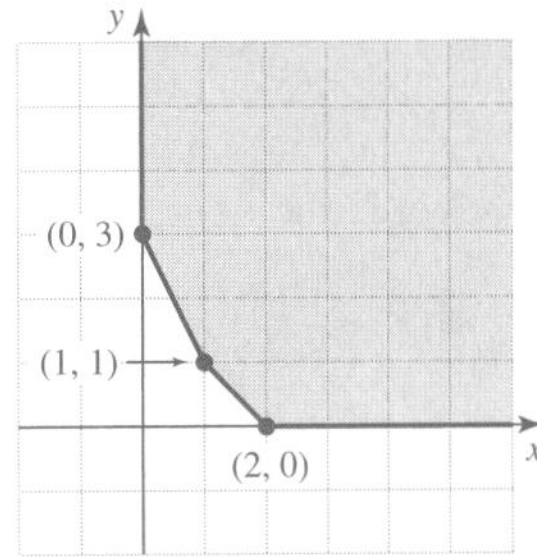

12. $x \geq 0, y \geq 0$
$3x + 2y \geq 12$
$2x + y \geq 7$

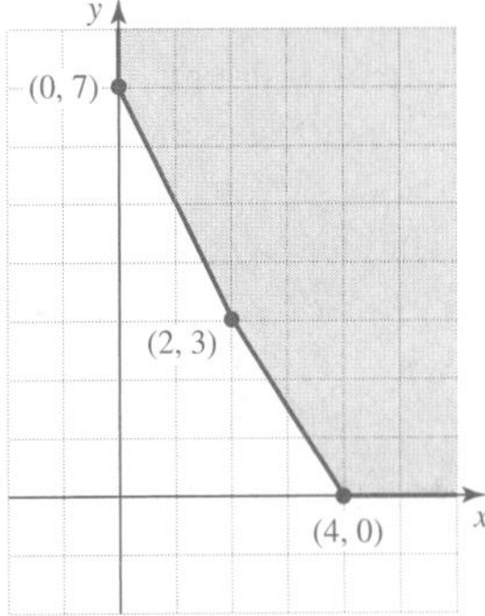

13. $x \geq 0, y \geq 0$
$x + 3y \leq 15$
$2x + y \leq 10$

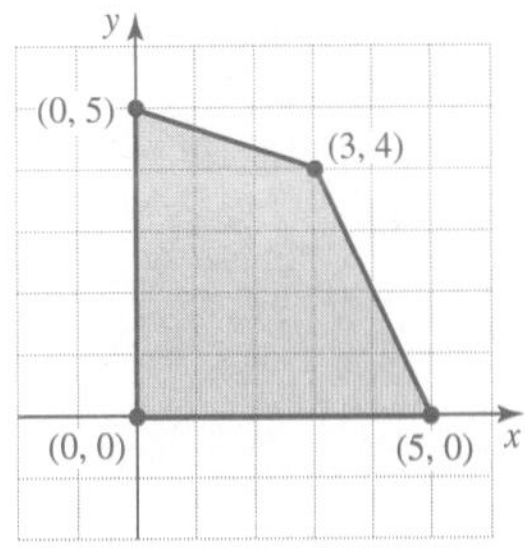

14. $x \geq 0, y \geq 0$
$2x + 3y \leq 15$
$x + y \leq 7$

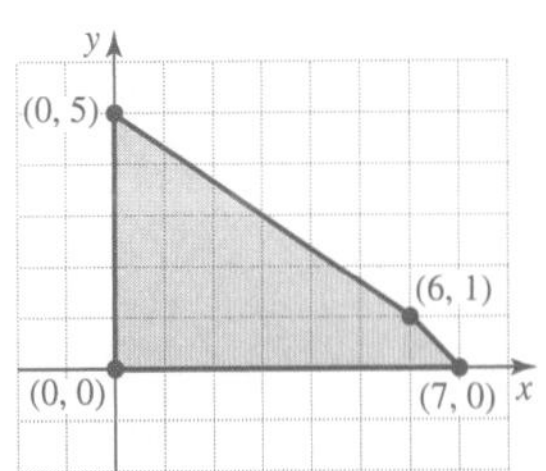

15. $x \geq 0, y \geq 0$
$x + y \geq 4$
$3x + y \geq 6$

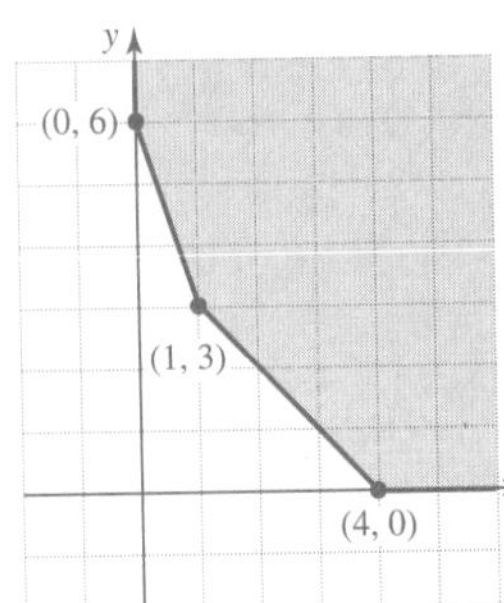

16. $x \geq 0, y \geq 0$
$x + 3y \geq 6$
$2x + y \geq 7$

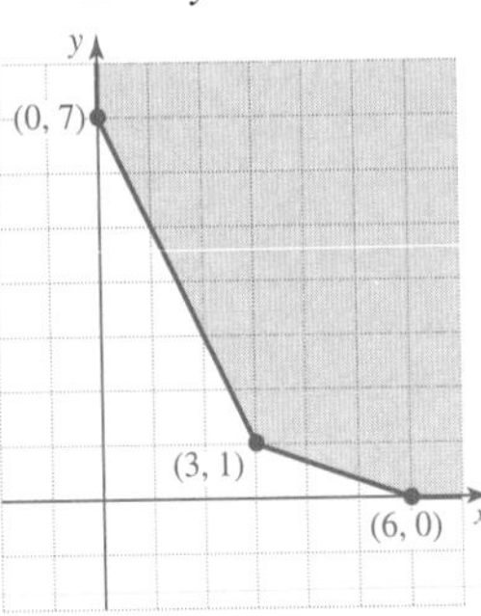

Let $P(x, y) = 6x + 8y$, $R(x, y) = 11x + 20y$, *and* $C(x, y) = 5x + 12y$. *Evaluate each expression.*

17. $P(1, 5)$ 46
18. $P(3, 8)$ 82
19. $R(8, 0)$ 88
20. $R(5, 10)$ 255
21. $C(4, 9)$ 128
22. $C(0, 6)$ 72

Solve each problem. See Examples 2–4.

23. ***Phase I advertising.*** The publicity director for Mercy Hospital is planning to bolster the hospital's image by running a TV ad and a radio ad. Due to budgetary and other constraints, the number of times that she can run the TV ad, x, and the number of times that she can run the radio ad, y, must be in the region shown in the figure. The function

$$A = 9000x + 4000y$$

gives the total number of people reached by the ads.

a) Find the total number of people reached by the ads at each vertex of the region.
b) What mix of TV and radio ads maximizes the number of people reached?
a) 0, 320,000, 510,000, 450,000
b) 30 TV ads and 60 radio ads

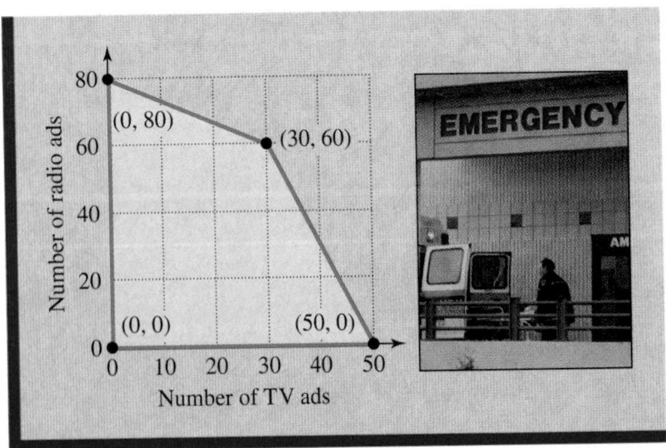

Figure for Exercises 23 and 24

24. ***Phase II advertising.*** Suppose the radio station in Exercise 23 starts playing country music and the function for the total number of people changes to

$$A = 9000x + 2000y.$$

a) Find A at each vertex of the region using this function.
b) What mix of TV and radio ads maximizes the number of people reached?
a) 0, 160,000, 390,000, 450,000
b) 50 TV ads and 0 radio ads

25. At Burger Heaven a double contains 2 meat patties and 6 pickles, whereas a triple contains 3 meat patties and 3 pickles. Near closing time one day, only 24 meat patties and 48 pickles are available. If a double burger sells for \$1.20 and a triple burger sells for \$1.50, then how many of each should be made to maximize the total revenue?
6 doubles, 4 triples

26. Sam and Doris manufacture rocking chairs and porch swings in the Ozarks. Each rocker requires 3 hours of work from Sam and 2 hours from Doris. Each swing requires 2 hours of work from Sam and 2 hours from Doris. Sam cannot work more than 48 hours per week, and Doris cannot work more than 40 hours per week. If a rocker sells for \$160 and a swing sells for \$100, then how many of each should be made per week to maximize the revenue?
16 chairs, 0 swings

27. If a double burger sells for \$1.00 and a triple burger sells for \$2.00, then how many of each should be made to maximize the total revenue subject to the constraints of Exercise 25? 0 doubles, 8 triples

28. If a rocker sells for \$120 and a swing sells for \$100, then how many of each should be made to maximize the total revenue subject to the constraints of Exercise 26?
8 chairs, 12 swings

29. One cup of Doggie Dinner contains 20 grams of protein and 40 grams of carbohydrates. One cup of Puppy Power contains 30 grams of protein and 20 grams of carbohydrates. Susan wants her dog to get at least 200 grams of protein and 180 grams of carbohydrates per day. If Doggie Dinner costs 16 cents per cup and Puppy Power costs 20 cents per cup, then how many cups of each would satisfy the constraints and minimize the total cost?
1.75 cups Doggie Dinner, 5.5 cups Puppy Power

30. Mammoth Muffler employs supervisors and helpers. According to the union contract, a supervisor does 2 brake jobs and 3 mufflers per day, whereas a helper does 6 brake jobs and 3 mufflers per day. The home office requires enough staff for at least 24 brake jobs and for at least 18 mufflers per day. If a supervisor makes \$90 per day and a helper makes \$100 per day, then how many of each should be employed to satisfy the constraints and to minimize the daily labor cost?
3 supervisors, 3 helpers

31. Suppose in Exercise 29 Doggie Dinner costs 4 cents per cup and Puppy Power costs 10 cents per cup. How many cups of each would satisfy the constraints and minimize the total cost? 10 cups Doggie Dinner, 0 cups Puppy Power

32. Suppose in Exercise 30 the supervisor makes \$110 per day and the helper makes \$100 per day. How many of each should be employed to satisfy the constraints and to minimize the daily labor cost? 0 supervisors, 6 helpers

33. Anita has at most \$24,000 to invest in her brother-in-law's laundromat and her nephew's car wash. Her brother-in-law has high blood pressure and heart disease but he will pay 18%, whereas her nephew is healthier but will pay only 12%. So the amount she will invest in the car wash will be at least twice the amount that she will invest in the laundromat but not more than three times as much. How much should she invest in each to maximize her total income from the two investments? Laundromat \$8000, car wash \$16,000

34. Herbert assembles computers in his shop. The parts for each economy model are shipped to him in a carton with a volume of 2 cubic feet (ft^3) and the parts for each deluxe model are shipped to him in a carton with a volume of 3 ft^3. After assembly, each economy model is shipped out in a carton with a volume of 4 ft^3, and each deluxe model is shipped out in a carton with a volume of 4 ft^3. The truck that delivers the parts has a maximum capacity of 180 ft^3, and the truck that takes out the completed computers has a maximum capacity of 280 ft^3. He can receive only one shipment of parts and send out one shipment of computers per week. If his profit on an economy model is \$60 and his profit on a deluxe model is \$100, then how many of each should he order per week to maximize his profit? 0 economy models, 60 deluxe models

Collaborative Activities

Grouping: 2 to 4 students per group

Topic: Use of algebra in common occurrences

Everyday Algebra

Every day, people use algebra without even knowing it. Any time you solve for an unknown quantity, you are using algebra. Here is an example of a simple problem that you could solve without even thinking of algebra.

- While shopping Joe notices a store brand that is available at a lower price than the name brand. If the name brand product costs \$3.79 and Joe has a coupon for 50 cents, what would the store brand price need to be for Joe to save money with the coupon?

This is a problem you could solve mentally by subtracting the two quantities and finding that if the store brand costs \$3.29 or more, Joe would save money with the coupon. If the store brand is less than \$3.29, then Joe would save money by buying it instead. The beauty of algebra is not apparent in cases like this because you already know what operation to perform to find the unknown quantity. Algebra becomes useful when it is not clear what to do.

We will consider another situation in which we want to find the best price of an item. For this situation we will use the following formulas.

The formula for markup of an item is

$$P = C + rC,$$

where P is the price of the item, C is the wholesale cost of the item, and r is the percent of markup.

The formula for discounting an item is

$$S = P - dP,$$

where S is the discounted price and d is the percent discount.

- Lane belongs to a wholesale buying club. She can order items through the club with a markup of 8% above the wholesale cost. She also can buy the same items in a store where she can get a 10% discount off the shelf price. Lane wants to know what the store markup on any particular item must be for it to be cheaper to order through the club.

Form groups of two to four people. Assign a role to each person: **Recorder, Moderator, Messenger, or Quality Manager** (roles may be combined if there are fewer than four people in a group). In your groups:

1. Decide how to rewrite Lane's problem using algebra. Decide what the unknown quantities are and assign them variable names.
2. Write the equations or inequalities on your paper using the variables that you just defined.
3. Solve the problem and state the group's decision on what Lane should do.

Extension: Pick a similar problem from your own lives to use algebra to solve.

Chapter 8 Wrap-Up

Summary

Compound Inequalities

Examples

In one variable

Two simple inequalities in one variable connected with the word "and" or "or"

The solution set for an "and" inequality is the intersection of the solution sets.

$x > 1$ and $x < 5$

0 1 2 3 4 5 6

The solution set for an "or" inequality is the union of the solution sets.

$x > 3$ or $x < 1$

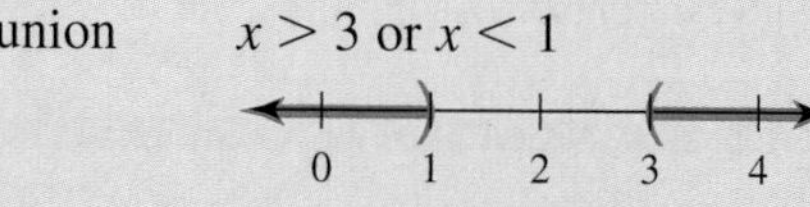

In two variables

Two simple inequalities in two variables connected with the word "and" or "or"

The solution set for an "and" inequality is the intersection of the solution sets.

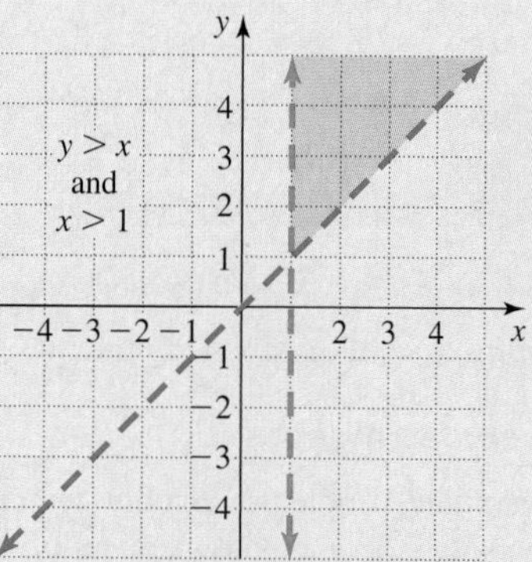

The solution set for an "or" inequality is the union of the solution sets.

Note that the graph of $x > 1$ (an inequality containing only one variable) in the rectangular coordinate system is the region to the right of the vertical line $x = 1$.

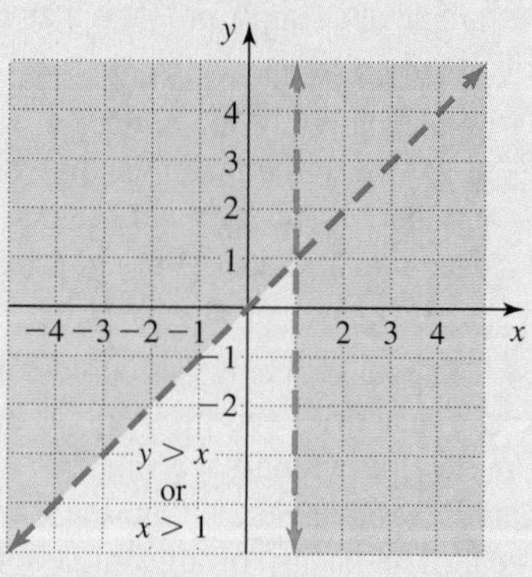

Absolute Value

	Absolute Value Equation	Equivalent Equation	Solution Set
Basic absolute value equations	$\lvert x \rvert = k \quad (k > 0)$	$x = k$ or $x = -k$	$\{k, -k\}$
	$\lvert x \rvert = 0$	$x = 0$	$\{0\}$
	$\lvert x \rvert = k \quad (k < 0)$		$\varnothing$

	Absolute Value Inequality	Equivalent Inequality	Solution Set	Graph of Solution Set
Basic absolute value inequalities ($k > 0$)	$\|x\| > k$	$x > k$ or $x < -k$	$(-\infty, -k) \cup (k, \infty)$	$-k$ k
	$\|x\| \geq k$	$x \geq k$ or $x \leq -k$	$(-\infty, -k] \cup [k, \infty)$	$-k$ k
	$\|x\| < k$	$-k < x < k$	$(-k, k)$	$-k$ k
	$\|x\| \leq k$	$-k \leq x \leq k$	$[-k, k]$	$-k$ k

Linear Programming

Use the following steps to find the maximum or minimum value of a linear function subject to linear constraints.

1. Graph the region that satisfies all of the constraints.
2. Determine the coordinates of each vertex of the region.
3. Evaluate the function at each vertex of the region.
4. Identify which vertex gives the maximum or minimum value of the function.

Enriching Your Mathematical Word Power

For each mathematical term, choose the correct meaning.

1. simple inequality
a. an easy inequality
b. an inequality with no solution
c. an inequality involving only one inequality symbol
d. an inequality that anyone can solve c

2. compound inequality
a. a hard inequality
b. an inequality that reverses when divided by a negative number
c. an inequality involving fractions
d. two simple inequalities joined with "and" or "or" d

3. intersection of sets A and B
a. the set of elements in both A and B
b. the set of elements in either A or B
c. the set of elements in neither A nor B
d. the empty set a

4. union of sets A and B
a. the set of elements in both A and B
b. the set of elements in either A or B
c. the set of elements in neither A nor B
d. the empty set b

5. absolute value equation
a. an equation involving absolute value
b. an equation with an absolute solution
c. an equation with a definite value
d. an equation with a positive solution a

6. absolute value inequality
a. an equation involving only positive numbers
b. an inequality with no solution
c. an inequality that is always positive
d. an inequality involving absolute value d

7. $a < x < b$
a. $a < x$ and $a < b$
b. $x > a$ or $x < b$
c. $x > a$ and $x < b$
d. $a < b < x$ c

8. $|x| = k$ for $k > 0$
a. $x = k$ or $x = -k$
b. $x = k$ and $x = -k$
c. $x = k$
d. $x = -k$ a

9. $|x| > k$ **for** $k > 0$

a. $x > k$ or $x > -k$
b. $x > k$ and $x > -k$
c. $x > k$ or $x < -k$
d. $x > k$ and $x < -k$ c

10. constraints

a. inequalities in a linear programming problem
b. variables in a word problem
c. variables with a constant value
d. equations with only one solution a

11. linear programming

a. programming in a straight line
b. a method for maximizing or minimizing a linear function of two variables subject to linear constraints
c. a list of television shows
d. solving systems of linear equations b

Review Exercises

8.1 *Solve each compound inequality. State the solution set using interval notation and graph it.*

1. $x + 2 > 3$ or $x - 6 < -10$

$(-\infty, -4) \cup (1, \infty)$

2. $x - 2 > 5$ or $x - 2 < -1$

$(-\infty, 1) \cup (7, \infty)$

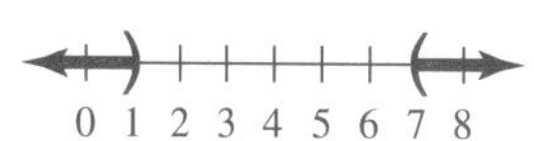

3. $x > 0$ and $x - 6 < 3$

$(0, 9)$

4. $x \leq 0$ and $x + 6 > 3$

$(-3, 0]$

5. $6 - x < 3$ or $-x < 0$

$(0, \infty)$

6. $-x > 0$ or $x + 2 < 7$

$(-\infty, 5)$

7. $2x < 8$ and $2(x - 3) < 6$

$(-\infty, 4)$

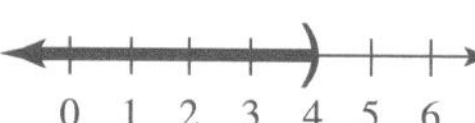

8. $\frac{1}{3}x > 2$ and $\frac{1}{4}x > 2$

$(8, \infty)$

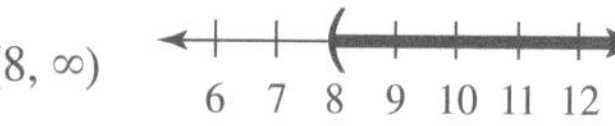

9. $x - 6 > 2$ and $6 - x > 0$ $\varnothing$

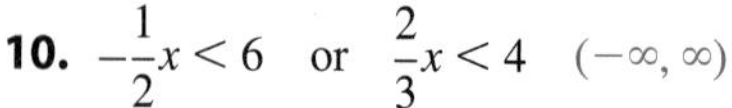

10. $-\frac{1}{2}x < 6$ or $\frac{2}{3}x < 4$ $(-\infty, \infty)$

11. $0.5x > 10$ or $0.1x < 3$ $(-\infty, \infty)$

12. $0.02x > 4$ and $0.2x < 3$ $\varnothing$

13. $-2 \leq \frac{2x - 3}{10} \leq 1$

$\left[-\frac{17}{2}, \frac{13}{2}\right]$

14. $-3 < \frac{4 - 3x}{5} < 2$

$\left(-2, \frac{19}{3}\right)$

Write each union or intersection of intervals as a single interval.

15. $[1, 4) \cup (2, \infty)$ $[1, \infty)$

16. $(2, 5) \cup (-1, \infty)$ $(-1, \infty)$

17. $(3, 6) \cap [2, 8]$ $(3, 6)$

18. $[-1, 3] \cap [0, 8]$ $[0, 3]$

19. $(-\infty, 5) \cup [5, \infty)$ $(-\infty, \infty)$

20. $(-\infty, 1) \cup (0, \infty)$ $(-\infty, \infty)$

21. $(-3, -1] \cap [-2, 5]$ $[-2, -1]$

22. $[-2, 4] \cap (4, 7]$ $\varnothing$

8.2 *Solve each absolute value equation and graph the solution set.*

23. $|x| + 2 = 16$ $\{-14, 14\}$

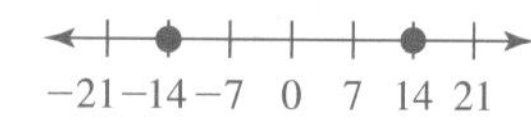

24. $\left|\frac{x}{2}\right| - 5 = -1$ $\{-8, 8\}$

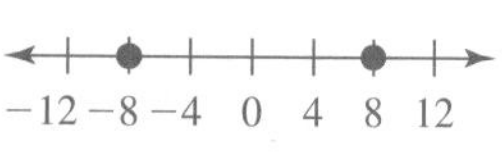

25. $|4x - 12| = 0$ $\{3\}$

26. $|2x - 8| = 0$ $\{4\}$

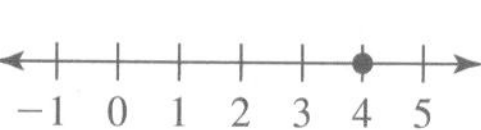

27. $|x| = -5$ $\varnothing$

28. $\left|\frac{x}{2} - 5\right| = -1$ $\varnothing$

29. $|2x - 1| - 3 = 0$ $\{-1, 2\}$

30. $|5 - x| - 2 = 0$ $\{3, 7\}$

Solve each absolute value inequality and graph the solution set.

31. $|2x| \ge 8$
$(-\infty, -4] \cup [4, \infty)$

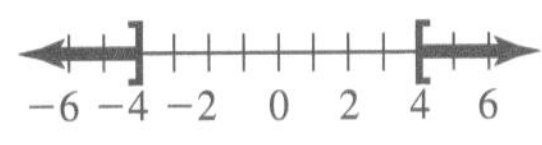

32. $|5x - 1| \le 14$
$\left[-\frac{13}{5}, 3\right]$

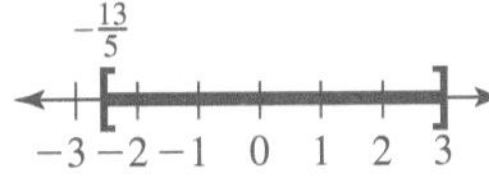

33. $\left|1 - \frac{x}{5}\right| > \frac{9}{5}$
$(-\infty, -4) \cup (14, \infty)$

34. $\left|1 - \frac{1}{6}x\right| < \frac{1}{2}$ $(3, 9)$

35. $|x - 3| < -3$ $\varnothing$

36. $|x - 7| \le -4$ $\varnothing$

37. $|x + 4| \ge -1$ $(-\infty, \infty)$

38. $|6x - 1| \ge 0$ $(-\infty, \infty)$

39. $1 - \frac{3}{2}|x - 2| < -\frac{1}{2}$
$(-\infty, 1) \cup (3, \infty)$

40. $1 > \frac{1}{2}|6 - x| - \frac{3}{4}$ $\left(\frac{5}{2}, \frac{19}{2}\right)$

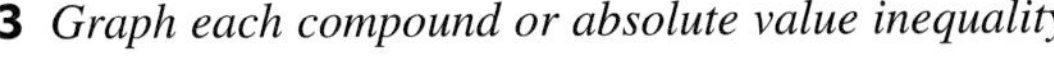

8.3 *Graph each compound or absolute value inequality.*

41. $y > 3$ and
$y - x < 5$

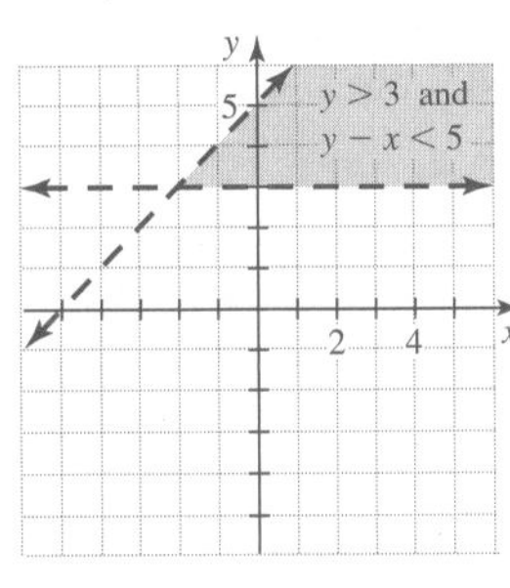

42. $x + y \le 1$ or
$y \le 4$

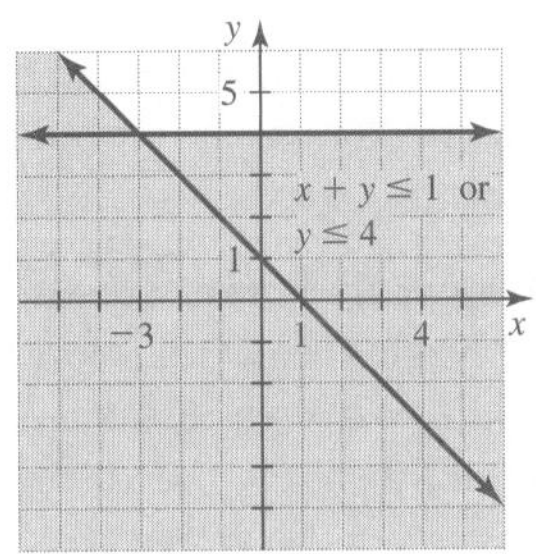

43. $3x + 2y \ge 8$ or
$3x - 2y \le 6$

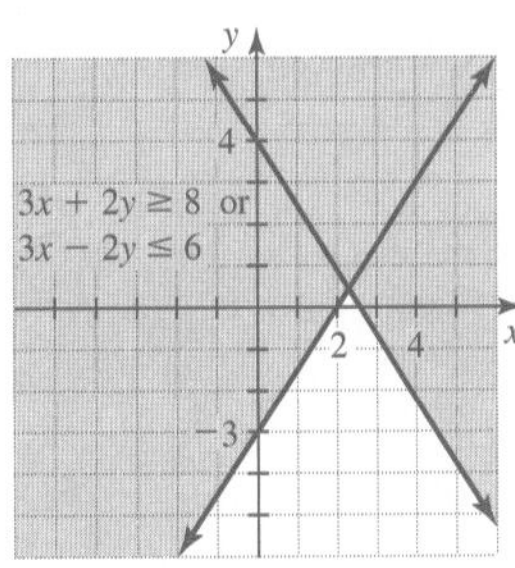

44. $x + 8y > 8$ and
$x - 2y < 10$

45. $|x + 2y| < 10$

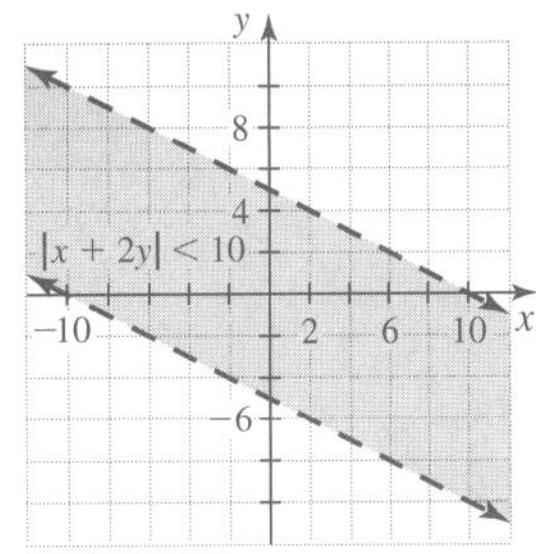
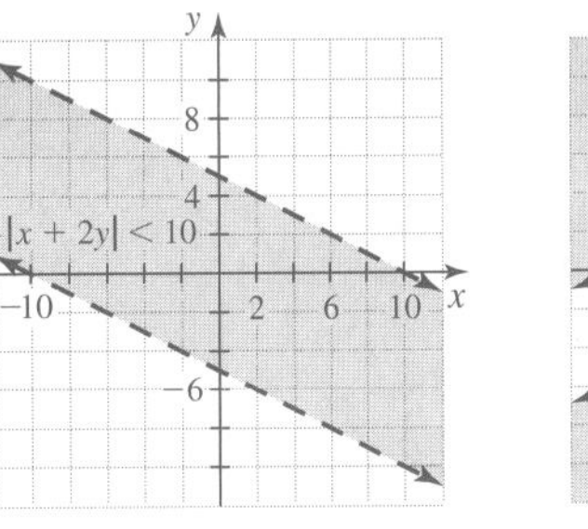

46. $|x - 3y| \ge 9$

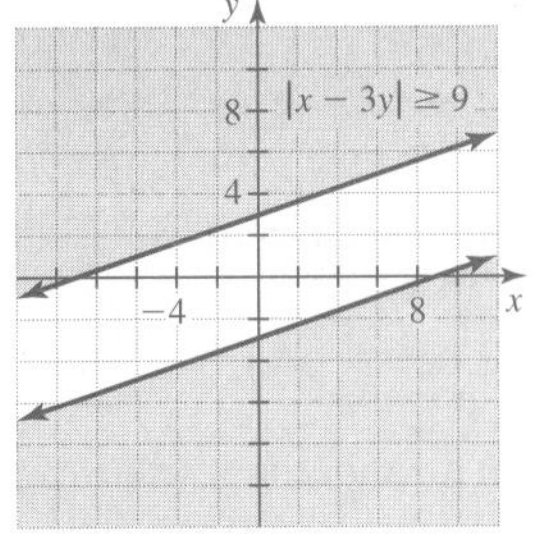

47. $|x| \le 5$

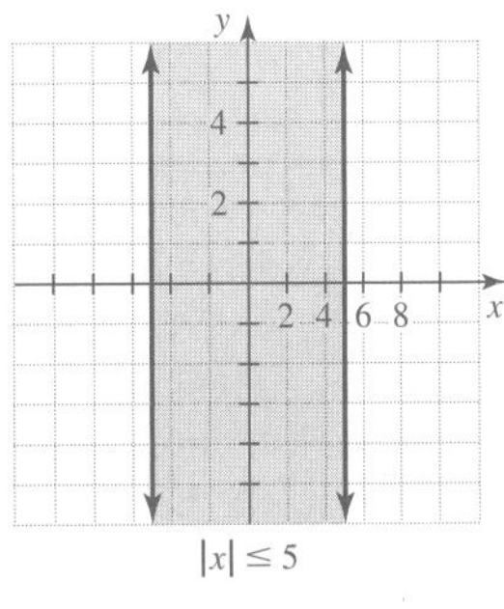
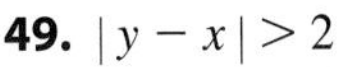

48. $|y| > 6$

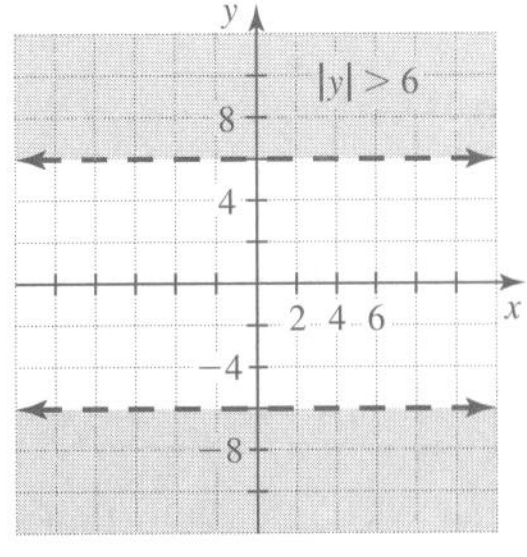

49. $|y - x| > 2$

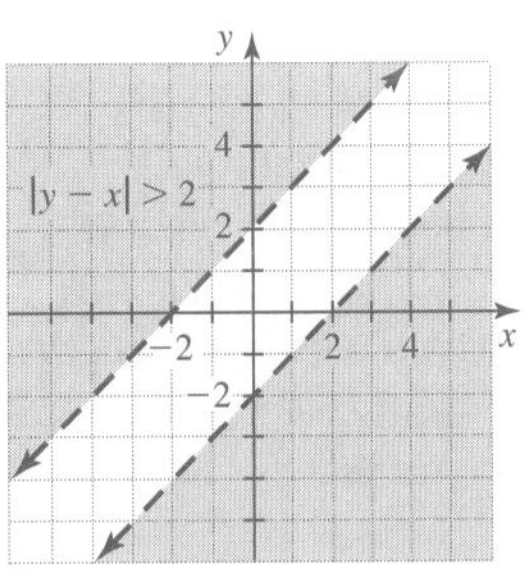

50. $|x - y| \le 1$

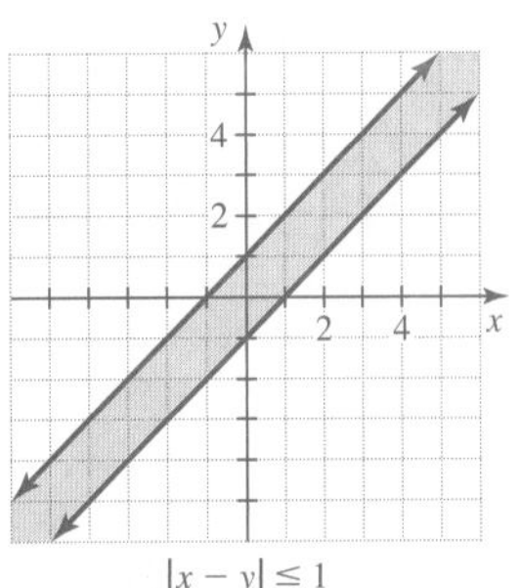

8.4 *Graph each system of inequalities and identify each vertex of the region.*

51. $x \geq 0, y \geq 0$
$x + 2y \leq 6$
$x + y \leq 5$

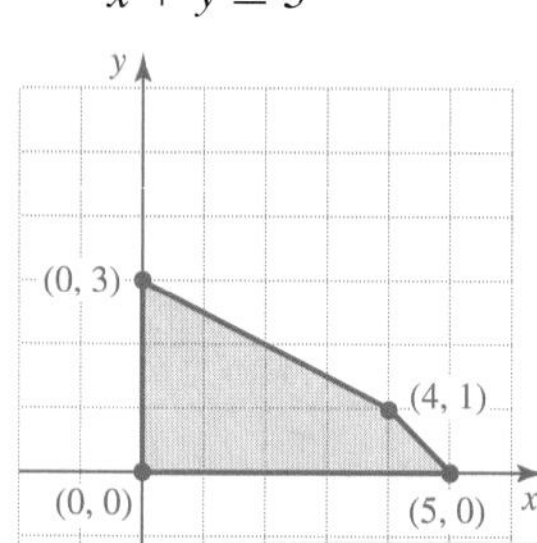

52. $x \geq 0, y \geq 0$
$3x + 2y \geq 12$
$x + 2y \geq 8$

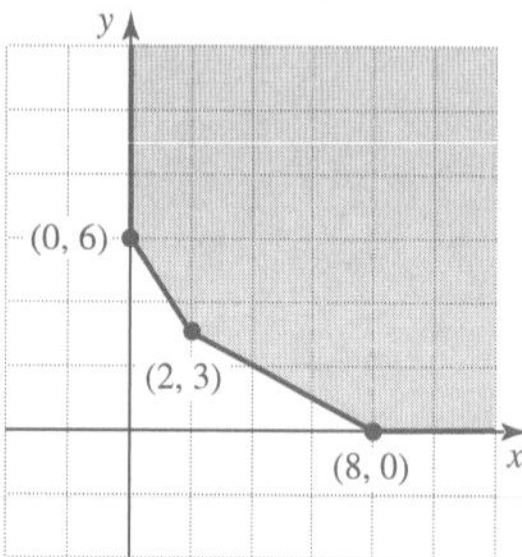

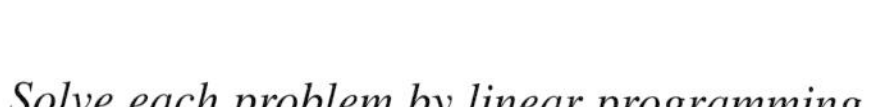

Solve each problem by linear programming.

53. Find the maximum value of the function $R(x, y) = 6x + 9y$ subject to the following constraints:

$$x \geq 0, y \geq 0$$
$$2x + y \leq 6$$
$$x + 2y \leq 6$$

30

54. Find the minimum value of the function $C(x, y) = 9x + 10y$ subject to the following constraints:

$$x \geq 0, y \geq 0$$
$$x + y \geq 4$$
$$3x + y \geq 6$$

36

Miscellaneous

Solve each problem.

55. ***Rockbuster video.*** Stephen plans to open a video rental store in Edmonton. Industry statistics show that 45% of the rental price goes for overhead. If the maximum that anyone will pay to rent a tape is \$5 and Stephen wants a profit of at least \$1.65 per tape, then in what range should the rental price be?
x = rental price, $\$3 \leq x \leq \$5$

56. ***Working girl.*** Regina makes \$6.80 per hour working in the snack bar. To keep her grant, she may not earn more than \$51 per week. What is the range of the number of hours per week that she may work? [0, 7.5]

57. ***Skeletal remains.*** Forensic scientists use the formula $h = 60.089 + 2.238F$ to predict the height h (in centimeters) for a male whose femur measures F centimeters. (See the accompanying figure.) In what range is the length of the femur for males between 150 centimeters and 180 centimeters in height? Round to the nearest tenth of a centimeter. (40.2, 53.6)

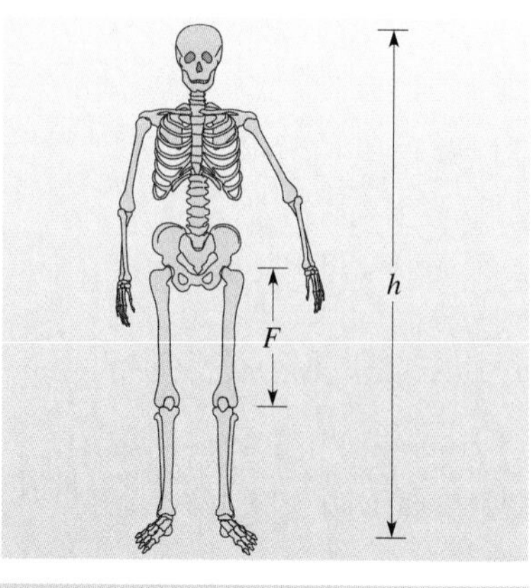

Figure for Exercise 57

58. ***Female femurs.*** Forensic scientists use the formula $h = 61.412 + 2.317F$ to predict the height h in centimeters for a female whose femur measures F centimeters.

a) Use the accompanying graph to estimate the femur length for a female with height of 160 centimeters.

b) In what range is the length of the femur for females who are over 170 centimeters tall?

a) 43 centimeters
b) $F > 46.9$

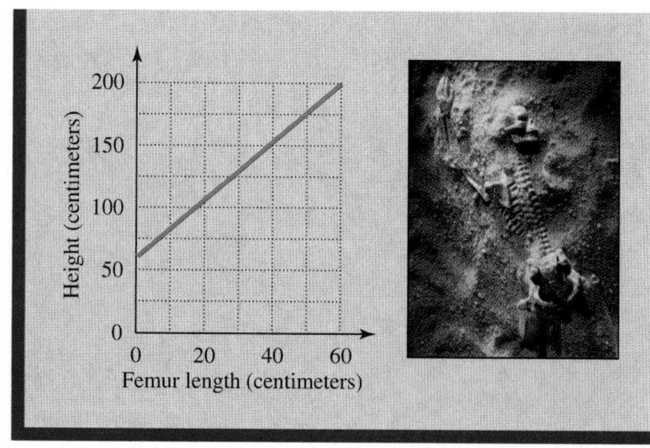

Figure for Exercise 58

59. ***Car trouble.*** Dane's car was found abandoned at mile marker 86 on the interstate. If Dane was picked up by the police on the interstate exactly 5 miles away, then at what mile marker was he picked up?
81 or 91

60. ***Comparing scores.*** Scott scored 72 points on the midterm, and Katie's score was more than 16 points away from Scott's. What was Katie's score?
Greater than 88 or less than 56

For each graph in Exercises 61–78, write an equation or inequality that has the solution set shown by the graph. Use absolute value when possible.

61. 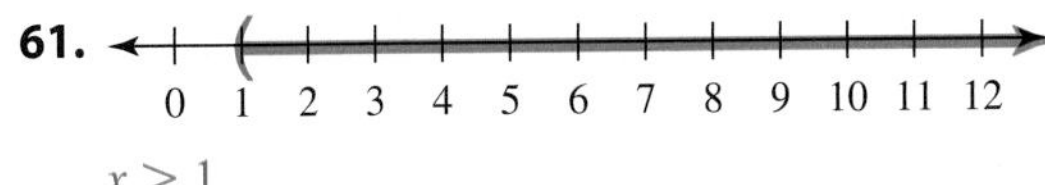
0 1 2 3 4 5 6 7 8 9 10 11 12

$x > 1$

62. 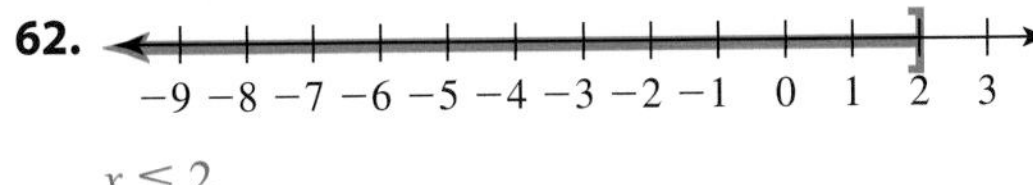
−9 −8 −7 −6 −5 −4 −3 −2 −1 0 1 2 3

$x \le 2$

63. −6 −5 −4 −3 −2 −1 0 1 2 3 4 5 6

$|x - 2| = 0$

64. −2 −1 0 1 2 3 4 5 6 7 8 9 10

$3 \le x < 5$

65. −6 −5 −4 −3 −2 −1 0 1 2 3 4 5 6

$|x| = 3$

66. −2 −1 0 1 2 3 4 5 6 7 8 9 10

$|x - 1| = 0$

67. −6 −5 −4 −3 −2 −1 0 1 2 3 4 5 6

$x \le -1$

68. −6 −5 −4 −3 −2 −1 0 1 2 3 4 5 6

$|x| > 2$

69. −6 −5 −4 −3 −2 −1 0 1 2 3 4 5 6

$|x| \le 2$

70. −6 −5 −4 −3 −2 −1 0 1 2 3 4 5 6

$|x| = 5$

71. −1 0 1 2 3 4 5 6 7 8 9 10 11

$x \le 2$ or $x \ge 7$

72. −6 −5 −4 −3 −2 −1 0 1 2 3 4 5 6

$|x| \le 1$

73. −6 −5 −4 −3 −2 −1 0 1 2 3 4 5 6

$|x| > 3$

74. −5 −4 −3 −2 −1 0 1 2 3 4 5 6 7

$x > 3$ or $x < -1$

75. 0 1 2 3 4 5 6 7 8 9 10 11 12

$5 < x < 7$ or $|x - 6| < 1$

76. −6 −5 −4 −3 −2 −1 0 1 2 3 4 5 6

$|x| > 4$

77. −6 −5 −4 −3 −2 −1 0 1 2 3 4 5 6

$|x| > 0$

78. −6 −5 −4 −3 −2 −1 0 1 2 3 4 5 6

$-6 \le x < 6$

Chapter 8 Test

Write an inequality that describes the graph.

1. −5 −4 −3 −2 −1 0 1 2 3 4 5 $-3 < x \le 2$

2. −2 −1 0 1 2 3 4 5 6 7 8 $x > 1$

Write the solution set to each inequality using interval notation.

3. $x \ge 3$ $[3, \infty)$

4. $x > 1$ and $x \le 6$ $(1, 6]$

5. $x < 5$ or $x > 9$ $(-\infty, 5) \cup (9, \infty)$

6. $|x| < 3$ $(-3, 3)$

7. $|x| \ge 2$ $(-\infty, -2] \cup [2, \infty)$

Solve each inequality. State the solution set using interval notation and graph the solution set.

8. $2x + 3 > 1$ $(-1, \infty)$ 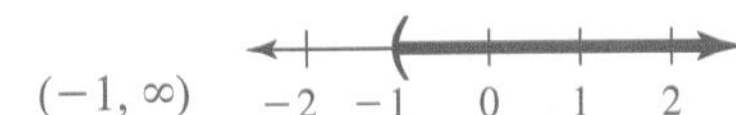
−2 −1 0 1 2

9. $|m - 6| \leq 2$ $[4, 8]$

10. $2|x - 3| - 5 > 15$ $(-\infty, -7) \cup (13, \infty)$

11. $2 - 3(w - 1) < -2w$ $(5, \infty)$

12. $3x - 2 < 7$ and $-3x \leq 15$ $[-5, 3)$

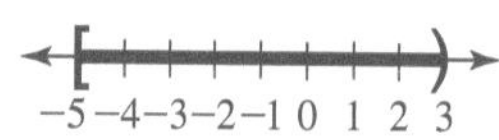

13. $\frac{2}{3}y < 4$ or $y - 3 < 12$ $(-\infty, 15)$

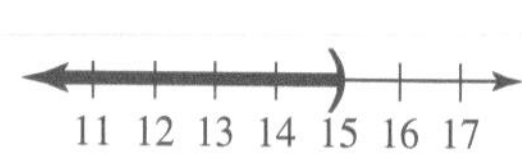

Solve each equation or inequality.

14. $|2x - 7| = -3$ $\varnothing$

15. $x - 4 > 1$ or $x < 12$ $(-\infty, \infty)$

16. $3x < 0$ and $x - 5 > 2$ $\varnothing$

17. $|2x - 5| \leq 0$ $\{2.5\}$

18. $|x - 3| < 0$ $\varnothing$

19. $|x - 6| > -6$ $(-\infty, \infty)$

Sketch the graph of each inequality.

20. $x > 2$ and $x + y > 0$

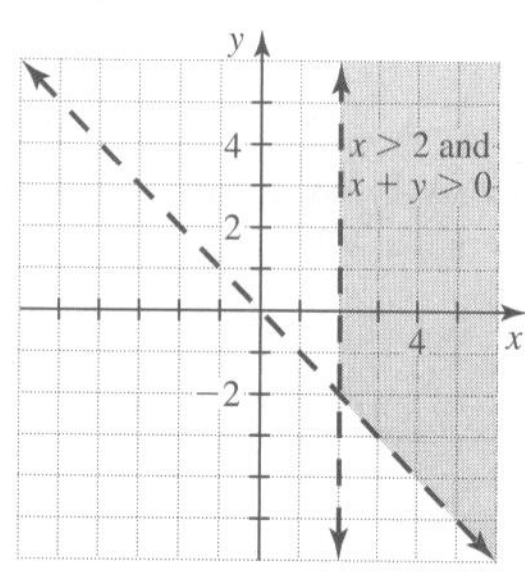

21. $|2x + y| \geq 3$

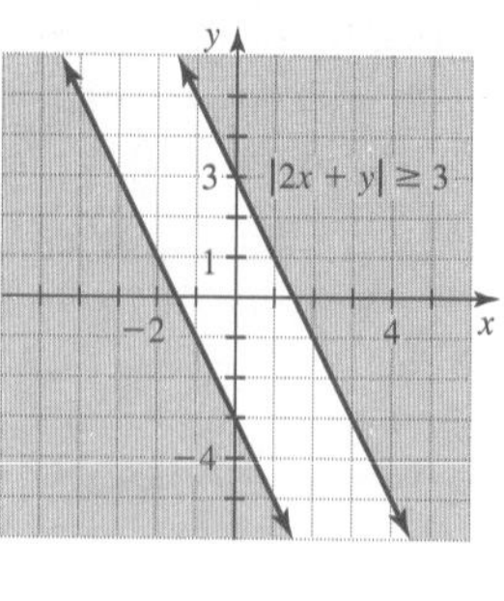

22. $x + y > 1$ or $x - y < 2$

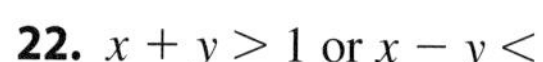

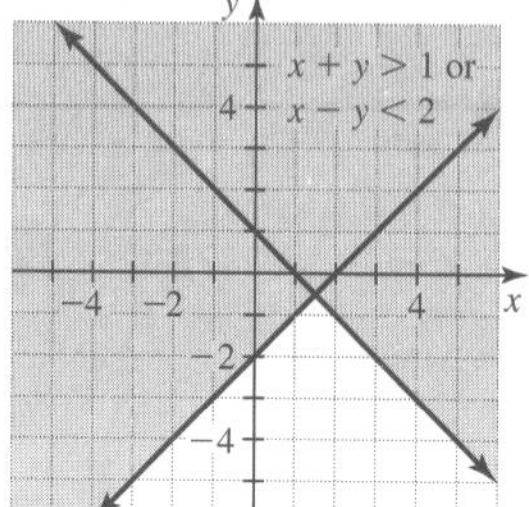

Solve the inequality problem.

23. Al and Brenda do the same job, but their annual salaries differ by more than \$3,000. Assume, Al makes \$28,000 per year and write an absolute value inequality to describe this situation. What are the possibilities for Brenda's salary? $|x - 28{,}000| > 3{,}000$ where x is Brenda's salary, Brenda makes more than \$31,000 or less than \$25,000.

Solve the following problem by linear programming.

24. Find the maximum value of the function

$$P(x, y) = 8x + 10y$$

subject to the following constraints:

$$x \geq 0,\ y \geq 0$$
$$2x + 3y \leq 12$$
$$x + y \leq 5$$

44

*Making*Connections | A Review of Chapters 1–8

Simplify each expression.

1. $5x + 6x$
$11x$

2. $5x \cdot 6x$
$30x^2$

3. $\dfrac{6x + 2}{2}$
$3x + 1$

4. $5 - 4(2 - x)$
$4x - 3$

5. $(30 - 1)(30 + 1)$
899

6. $(30 + 1)^2$
961

7. $(30 - 1)^2$
841

8. $(2 + 3)^2$
25

9. $2^2 + 3^2$
13

10. $(8 - 3)(3 - 8)$
-25

11. $(-1)(3 - 8)$
5

12. -2^2
-4

13. $3x + 8 - 5(x - 1)$
$-2x + 13$

14. $(-6)^2 - 4(-3)2$
60

15. $3^2 \cdot 2^3$
72

16. $4(-6) - (-5)(3)$
-9

Solve each equation.

17. $5x + 6x = 8x$ $\{0\}$

18. $5x + 6x = 11x$ R or $(-\infty, \infty)$

19. $5x + 6x = 0$ $\{0\}$

20. $5x + 6 = 11x$ $\{1\}$

21. $3x + 1 = 0$ $\left\{-\dfrac{1}{3}\right\}$

22. $5 - 4(2 - x) = 1$ $\{1\}$

23. $x - 0.01x = 990$
$\{1000\}$

24. $|5x + 6| = 11$
$\left\{-\dfrac{17}{5}, 1\right\}$

Solve each system of equations.

25. $2x + y = 5$
$x - y = 7$
$\{(4, -3)\}$

26. $3x - y = 5$
$y - 3x = -5$
$\{(x, y) \mid 3x - y = 5\}$

27. $2x + 5y = 16$
$3x - 4y = -22$
$\{(-2, 4)\}$

28. $\dfrac{1}{2}x - \dfrac{2}{3}y = -6$
$\dfrac{3}{4}x + \dfrac{2}{5}y = 12$ $\{(8, 15)\}$

Study Tip

Don't wait until the final exam to review material. Do some review on a regular basis. The Making Connections exercises on this page can be used to review, compare, and contrast different concepts that you have studied. A good time to work these exercises is between a test and the start of new material.

Match each inequality in 29–38 with an equivalent inequality in A–J.

29. $2 - x < 5$ E

30. $x + 1 > x - 2$ F

31. $x > 2$ and $x > 5$ G

32. $x < -5$ or $x < -3$ D

33. $x < -9$ and $x > -3$ H

34. $x < -3$ or $x > 3$ C

35. $x > -3$ and $x < 3$ B

36. $|x + 3| > 0$ I

37. $y < x + 3$ and $y < x$ A

38. $y > x - 3$ or $y > x$ J

A. $y < x$
B. $|x| < 3$
C. $|x| > 3$
D. $x < -3$
E. $x > -3$
F. $x + 1 > x$
G. $x > 5$
H. $x + 1 < x$
I. $x \neq -3$
J. $y > x - 3$

Solve the problem.

39. ***Cost analysis.*** Diller Electronics can rent a copy machine for 5 years from American Business Supply for \$75 per month plus 6 cents per copy. The same copier can be purchased for \$8000, but then it costs only 2 cents per copy for supplies and maintenance. The purchased copier has no value after 5 years.

a) Use the accompanying graph to estimate the number of copies for 5 years for which the cost of renting would equal the cost of buying.
b) Write a formula for the 5-year cost under each plan.
c) Algebraically find the number of copies for which the 5-year costs would be equal.
d) If Diller makes 120,000 copies in 5 years, which plan is cheaper and by how much?
e) For what range of copies do the two plans differ by less than \$500?

a) 87,500 **b)** $C_r = 4500 + 0.06x$, $C_b = 8000 + 0.02x$
c) 87,500 **d)** Buying is \$1300 cheaper
e) (75,000, 100,000)

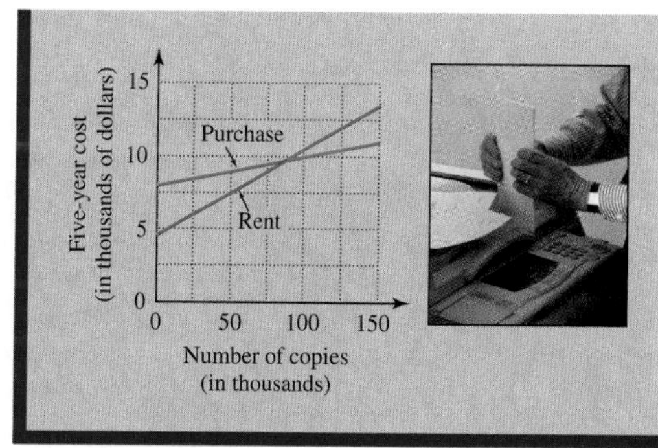

Figure for Exercise 39

Critical Thinking | For Individual or Group Work | Chapter 8

These exercises can be solved by a variety of techniques, which may or may not require algebra. So be creative and think critically. Explain all answers. Answers are in the Instructor's Edition of this text.

1. ***Tennis Time.*** Tennis balls are sold in a cylindrical container that contains three balls. Assume that the balls just fit into the container as shown in the accompanying figure. What is the ratio of the amount of space in the container that is occupied by the balls to the amount of space that is not occupied by the balls?

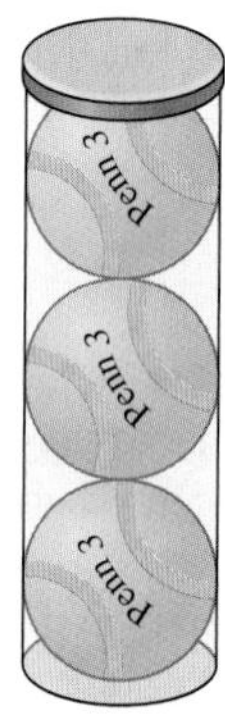

Figure for Exercise 1

2. ***Planting Trees.*** A landscaper planted 7 trees so that they were arranged in 6 rows with 3 trees in each row. How did she do this?

3. ***Division Problem.*** Start with any three-digit number and write the number twice to form a six-digit number. Divide the six-digit number by 7. Divide the answer by 11. Finally, divide the last answer by 13. What do you notice? Explain why this works.

4. ***Totaling 25.*** How many ways are there to add three different positive integers and get a sum of 25? Do not count rearrangements of the integers. For example, count 1, 2, and 22 as one possibility, but do not count 2, 22, and 1 as another.

5. ***Temple of Gloom.*** The famous explorer Indiana Smith wants to cross a desert on foot. He plans to hire some men to help him carry supplies on the journey. However, the journey takes six days, but Smith and his helpers can each carry only a four-day supply of food and water. Of course every day, each man must consume a one-day supply of food and water or he will die. Devise a plan for getting Smith across the desert without anyone dying and using the minimum number of helpers.

Photo for Exercise 5

6. ***Counting Zeros.*** How many zeros are at the end of the number $(5^5)!$?

7. ***Perfect Computers.*** Of 6000 computers coming off a manufacturer's assembly line, every third computer had a hardware problem, every fourth computer had a software problem, and every tenth computer had a cosmetic defect. The remaining computers were perfect and were shipped to Wal-Mart. How many were shipped to Wal-Mart?

8. ***Leap Frog.*** In Martha's garden is a circular pond with a diameter of 100 feet. A frog with an average leap of two and a quarter feet is sitting on a lily pad in the exact center of the pond. If the lily pads are all in the right places, then what is the minimum number of leaps required for the frog to jump out of the pond.

1. 2 to 1 **2.** Draw an equilateral triangle and place one tree at each vertex and one at the midpoint of each side. Connect vertex A with the opposite midpoint. Connect vertex B with the opposite midpoint. Place the last tree at the intersection of these lines. There is at least one other possible arrangement. **3.** The product of 7, 11, and 13 is 1001. The product of a three-digit number and 1001 is a six-digit number in which the first three digits and the last three digits are your original three-digit number. So dividing that type of number by 7, 11, and 13 gives back your original number. **4.** 38 **5.** If he uses three helpers, then one turns back after day one, the other two turn back after day two, leaving Smith with a four-day supply of food and water to finish the trip. **6.** 781 **7.** 2800 **8.** 23

Chapter 9

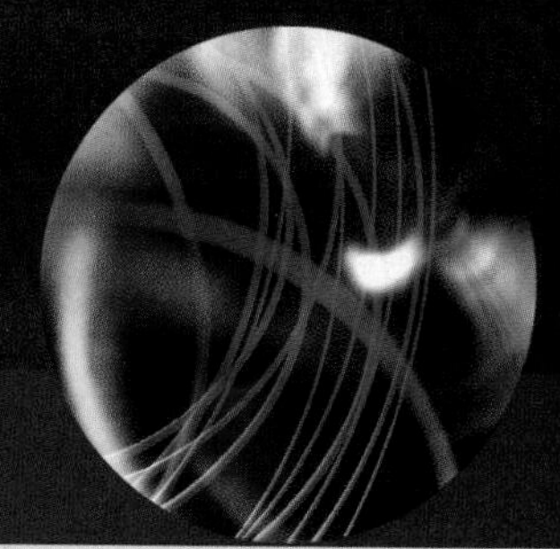

Radicals and Rational Exponents

Just how cold is it in Fargo, North Dakota, in winter? According to local meteorologists, the mercury hit a low of −33°F on January 18, 1994. But air temperature alone is not always a reliable indicator of how cold you feel. On the same date the average wind velocity was 13.8 miles per hour. This dramatically affected how cold people felt when they stepped outside. High winds along with cold temperatures make exposed skin feel colder because the wind significantly speeds up the loss of body heat. Meteorologists use the terms "wind chill factor," "wind chill index," and "wind chill temperature" to take into account both air temperature and wind velocity.

Through experimentation in Antarctica, Paul A. Siple developed a formula in the 1940s that measures the wind chill from the velocity of the wind and the air temperature. His complex formula involving the square root of the velocity of the wind is still used today to calculate wind chill temperatures. Siple's formula is unlike most scientific formulas in that it is not based on theory. Siple experimented with various formulas involving wind velocity and temperature until he found a formula that seemed to predict how cold the air felt.

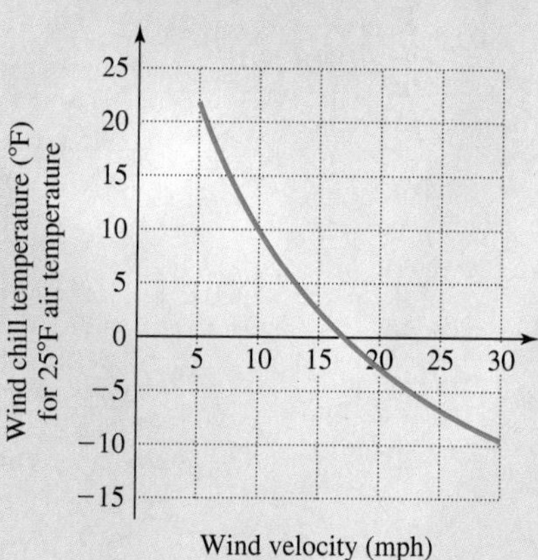

Siple's formula is stated and used in Exercises 109 and 110 of Section 9.1.

9.1 Radicals

In this Section

- Roots
- Roots and Variables
- Product Rule for Radicals
- Quotient Rule for Radicals
- Domain of a Radical Expression

In Section 4.1 you learned the basic facts about powers. In this section you will study roots and see how powers and roots are related.

Roots

We use the idea of roots to reverse powers. Because $3^2 = 9$ and $(-3)^2 = 9$, both 3 and -3 are square roots of 9. Because $2^4 = 16$ and $(-2)^4 = 16$, both 2 and -2 are fourth roots of 16. Because $2^3 = 8$ and $(-2)^3 = -8$, there is only one real cube root of 8 and only one real cube root of -8. The cube root of 8 is 2 and the cube root of -8 is -2.

*n*th Roots

If $a = b^n$ for a positive integer n, then b is an ***n*th root of *a*.** If $a = b^2$, then b is a **square root** of a. If $a = b^3$, then b is the **cube root** of a.

If n is a positive even integer and a is positive, then there are two real nth roots of a. We call these roots **even roots.** The positive even root of a positive number is called the **principal root.** The principal square root of 9 is 3 and the principal fourth root of 16 is 2 and these roots are even roots.

If n is a positive odd integer and a is any real number, there is only one real nth root of a. We call that root an **odd root.** Because $2^5 = 32$, the fifth root of 32 is 2 and 2 is an odd root.

We use the **radical symbol** $\sqrt{\ }$ to signify roots.

Helpful Hint

The parts of a radical:

Index → $\sqrt[n]{a}$ ← Radical symbol; Radicand ↑ a

$\sqrt[n]{a}$

If n is a positive *even* integer and a is positive, then $\sqrt[n]{a}$ denotes the *principal nth root of a.*

If n is a positive *odd* integer, then $\sqrt[n]{a}$ denotes the nth root of a.

If n is any positive integer, then $\sqrt[n]{0} = 0$.

We read $\sqrt[n]{a}$ as "the nth root of a." In the notation $\sqrt[n]{a}$, n is the **index of the radical** and a is the **radicand.** For square roots the index is omitted, and we simply write $\sqrt{a}$.

EXAMPLE 1

Evaluating radical expressions

Find the following roots:

a) $\sqrt{25}$

b) $\sqrt[3]{-27}$

c) $\sqrt[6]{64}$

d) $-\sqrt{4}$

Teaching Tip Have students make lists of perfect squares, perfect cubes, etc. This will help them in evaluating roots.

Solution

a) Because $5^2 = 25$, $\sqrt{25} = 5$.

b) Because $(-3)^3 = -27$, $\sqrt[3]{-27} = -3$.

c) Because $2^6 = 64$, $\sqrt[6]{64} = 2$.

d) Because $\sqrt{4} = 2$, $-\sqrt{4} = -(\sqrt{4}) = -2$.

Now do Exercises 7–24

CAUTION In radical notation, $\sqrt{4}$ represents the *principal square root of* 4, so $\sqrt{4} = 2$. Note that -2 is also a square root of 4, but $\sqrt{4} \neq -2$.

Calculator Close-Up

We can use the radical symbol to find a square root on a graphing calculator, but for other roots we use the xth root symbol as shown. The xth root symbol is in the MATH menu.

```
√(25)
                 5
3 ×√ -27
                -3
6 ×√64
                 2
```

Note that even roots of negative numbers are omitted from the definition of nth roots because even powers of real numbers are never negative. So no real number can be an even root of a negative number. Expressions such as

$$\sqrt{-9}, \quad \sqrt[4]{-81}, \quad \text{and} \quad \sqrt[6]{-64}$$

are not real numbers. Square roots of negative numbers will be discussed in Section 9.6 when we discuss the imaginary numbers.

Roots and Variables

Consider the result of squaring a power of x:

$$(x^1)^2 = x^2, \quad (x^2)^2 = x^4, \quad (x^3)^2 = x^6, \quad \text{and} \quad (x^4)^2 = x^8$$

When a power of x is squared, the exponent is multiplied by 2. So any even power of x is a perfect square.

Perfect Squares

The following expressions are perfect squares:

$$x^2, \quad x^4, \quad x^6, \quad x^8, \quad x^{10}, \quad x^{12}, \quad \ldots$$

Since taking a square root reverses the operation of squaring, the square root of an even power of x is found by dividing the exponent by 2. Provided x is nonnegative (see the next Caution), we have

$$\sqrt{x^2} = x^1 = x, \quad \sqrt{x^4} = x^2, \quad \sqrt{x^6} = x^3, \quad \text{and} \quad \sqrt{x^8} = x^4.$$

CAUTION If x is negative, equations like $\sqrt{x^2} = x$ and $\sqrt{x^6} = x^3$ are not correct because the radical represents the nonnegative square root but x and x^3 are negative. That is why we assume x is nonnegative.

If a power of x is cubed, the exponent is multiplied by 3:

$$(x^1)^3 = x^3, \quad (x^2)^3 = x^6, \quad (x^3)^3 = x^9, \quad \text{and} \quad (x^4)^3 = x^{12}$$

So if the exponent is a multiple of 3, we have a perfect cube.

Perfect Cubes

The following expressions are perfect cubes:

$$x^3, \quad x^6, \quad x^9, \quad x^{12}, \quad x^{15}, \quad \ldots$$

Since the cube root reverses the operation of cubing, the cube root of any of these perfect cubes is found by dividing the exponent by 3:

$$\sqrt[3]{x^3} = x^1 = x, \quad \sqrt[3]{x^6} = x^2, \quad \sqrt[3]{x^9} = x^3, \quad \text{and} \quad \sqrt[3]{x^{12}} = x^4$$

If the exponent is divisible by 4, we have a perfect fourth power, and so on.

EXAMPLE 2

Roots of exponential expressions

Find each root. Assume that all variables represent nonnegative real numbers.

a) $\sqrt{x^{22}}$ **b)** $\sqrt[3]{t^{18}}$ **c)** $\sqrt[5]{s^{30}}$

Solution

a) $\sqrt{x^{22}} = x^{11}$ because $(x^{11})^2 = x^{22}$.

b) $\sqrt[3]{t^{18}} = t^6$ because $(t^6)^3 = t^{18}$.

c) $\sqrt[5]{s^{30}} = s^6$ because one-fifth of 30 is 6.

Now do Exercises 25–36

Calculator Close-Up

You can illustrate the product rule for radicals with a calculator.

```
√(2)*√(3)
          2.449489743
√(6)
          2.449489743
```

Product Rule for Radicals

Consider the expression $\sqrt{2} \cdot \sqrt{3}$. If we square this product, we get

$$\begin{aligned} (\sqrt{2} \cdot \sqrt{3})^2 &= (\sqrt{2})^2(\sqrt{3})^2 && \text{Power of a product rule} \\ &= 2 \cdot 3 && (\sqrt{2})^2 = 2 \text{ and } (\sqrt{3})^2 = 3 \\ &= 6. \end{aligned}$$

The number $\sqrt{6}$ is the unique positive number whose square is 6. Because we squared $\sqrt{2} \cdot \sqrt{3}$ and obtained 6, we must have $\sqrt{6} = \sqrt{2} \cdot \sqrt{3}$. This example illustrates the product rule for radicals.

Product Rule for Radicals

The nth root of a product is equal to the product of the nth roots. In symbols,

$$\sqrt[n]{ab} = \sqrt[n]{a} \cdot \sqrt[n]{b},$$

provided all of these roots are real numbers.

EXAMPLE 3

Using the product rule for radicals to simplify

Simplify each radical. Assume that all variables represent nonnegative real numbers.

a) $\sqrt{4y}$ **b)** $\sqrt{3y^8}$ **c)** $\sqrt[3]{125w^2}$

Solution

a) $\sqrt{4y} = \sqrt{4} \cdot \sqrt{y}$ Product rule for radicals

$= 2\sqrt{y}$ Simplify.

b) $\sqrt{3y^8} = \sqrt{3} \cdot \sqrt{y^8}$ Product rule for radicals

$= \sqrt{3} \cdot y^4$ Simplify.

$= y^4\sqrt{3}$ A radical is usually written last in a product.

c) $\sqrt[3]{125w^2} = \sqrt[3]{125} \cdot \sqrt[3]{w^2} = 5\sqrt[3]{w^2}$

Now do Exercises 37–48

In Example 4 we simplify by factoring the radicand before applying the product rule.

EXAMPLE 4

Using the product rule to simplify

Simplify each radical.

a) $\sqrt{12}$ **b)** $\sqrt[3]{54}$ **c)** $\sqrt[4]{80}$ **d)** $\sqrt[5]{64}$

Solution

a) Since $12 = 4 \cdot 3$ and 4 is a perfect square, we can factor and then apply the product rule:

$$\sqrt{12} = \sqrt{4 \cdot 3} = \sqrt{4} \cdot \sqrt{3} = 2\sqrt{3}$$

b) Since $54 = 27 \cdot 2$ and 27 is a perfect cube, we can factor and then apply the product rule:

$$\sqrt[3]{54} = \sqrt[3]{27 \cdot 2} = \sqrt[3]{27} \cdot \sqrt[3]{2} = 3\sqrt[3]{2}$$

c) Since $80 = 16 \cdot 5$ and 16 is a perfect fourth power, we can factor and then apply the product rule:

$$\sqrt[4]{80} = \sqrt[4]{16 \cdot 5} = \sqrt[4]{16} \cdot \sqrt[4]{5} = 2\sqrt[4]{5}$$

d) $\sqrt[5]{64} = \sqrt[5]{32 \cdot 2} = \sqrt[5]{32} \cdot \sqrt[5]{2} = 2\sqrt[5]{2}$

Now do Exercises 49–62

Teaching Tip To find $\sqrt{17} \cdot \sqrt{17}$ students often use the product rule to get $\sqrt{289}$ and then get out a calculator. Keep reminding them that $\sqrt{a} \cdot \sqrt{a} = a$ for $a \geq 0$.

In general, we simplify radical expressions of index n by using the product rule to remove any perfect nth powers from the radicand. In Example 5 we use the product rule to simplify more radicals involving variables. Remember x^n is a perfect square if n is divisible by 2, a perfect cube if n is divisible by 3, and so on.

EXAMPLE 5

Using the product rule to simplify

Simplify each radical. Assume that all variables represent nonnegative real numbers.

a) $\sqrt{20x^3}$ **b)** $\sqrt[3]{40a^8}$ **c)** $\sqrt[4]{48a^4b^{11}}$ **d)** $\sqrt[5]{w^7}$

Solution

a) Factor $20x^3$ so that all possible perfect squares are inside one radical:

$$\begin{aligned}\sqrt{20x^3} &= \sqrt{4x^2 \cdot 5x} && \text{Factor out perfect squares.}\\ &= \sqrt{4x^2} \cdot \sqrt{5x} && \text{Product rule}\\ &= 2x\sqrt{5x} && \text{Simplify.}\end{aligned}$$

b) Factor $40a^8$ so that all possible perfect cubes are inside one radical:

$$\begin{aligned}\sqrt[3]{40a^8} &= \sqrt[3]{8a^6 \cdot 5a^2} && \text{Factor out perfect cubes.}\\ &= \sqrt[3]{8a^6} \cdot \sqrt[3]{5a^2} && \text{Product rule}\\ &= 2a^2\sqrt[3]{5a^2} && \text{Simplify.}\end{aligned}$$

c) Factor $48a^4b^{11}$ so that all possible perfect fourth powers are inside one radical:

$$\begin{aligned}\sqrt[4]{48a^4b^{11}} &= \sqrt[4]{16a^4b^8 \cdot 3b^3} && \text{Factor out perfect fourth powers.}\\ &= \sqrt[4]{16a^4b^8} \cdot \sqrt[4]{3b^3} && \text{Product rule}\\ &= 2ab^2\sqrt[4]{3b^3} && \text{Simplify.}\end{aligned}$$

d) $\sqrt[5]{w^7} = \sqrt[5]{w^5 \cdot w^2} = \sqrt[5]{w^5} \cdot \sqrt[5]{w^2} = w\sqrt[5]{w^2}$

Now do Exercises 63–76

Quotient Rule for Radicals

Because $\sqrt{2} \cdot \sqrt{3} = \sqrt{6}$, we have $\sqrt{6} \div \sqrt{3} = \sqrt{2}$, or

$$\sqrt{2} = \sqrt{\frac{6}{3}} = \frac{\sqrt{6}}{\sqrt{3}}.$$

This example illustrates the quotient rule for radicals.

Quotient Rule for Radicals

The nth root of a quotient is equal to the quotient of the nth roots. In symbols,

$$\sqrt[n]{\frac{a}{b}} = \frac{\sqrt[n]{a}}{\sqrt[n]{b}},$$

provided that all of these roots are real numbers and $b \neq 0$.

Calculator Close-Up

You can illustrate the quotient rule for radicals with a calculator.

```
√(6)/√(3)
         1.414213562
√(6/3)
         1.414213562
```

EXAMPLE 6

Using the quotient rule for radicals

Simplify each radical. Assume that all variables represent positive real numbers.

a) $\sqrt{\frac{25}{9}}$ **b)** $\frac{\sqrt{15}}{\sqrt{3}}$ **c)** $\sqrt[3]{\frac{b}{125}}$ **d)** $\sqrt[3]{\frac{x^{21}}{y^6}}$

Teaching Tip Even though we have some radicals in denominators here, they will all disappear without rationalizing the denominator. That topic is discussed in Section 9.4

Solution

a) $\sqrt{\frac{25}{9}} = \frac{\sqrt{25}}{\sqrt{9}}$ Quotient rule for radicals

$= \frac{5}{3}$ Simplify.

b) $\frac{\sqrt{15}}{\sqrt{3}} = \sqrt{\frac{15}{3}}$ Quotient rule for radicals

$= \sqrt{5}$ Simplify.

c) $\sqrt[3]{\frac{b}{125}} = \frac{\sqrt[3]{b}}{\sqrt[3]{125}} = \frac{\sqrt[3]{b}}{5}$

d) $\sqrt[3]{\frac{x^{21}}{y^6}} = \frac{\sqrt[3]{x^{21}}}{\sqrt[3]{y^6}} = \frac{x^7}{y^2}$

Now do Exercises 77–88

In Example 7 we use the product and quotient rule to simplify radical expressions.

EXAMPLE 7

Using the product and quotient rules for radicals

Simplify each radical. Assume that all variables represent positive real numbers.

a) $\sqrt{\frac{50}{49}}$ **b)** $\sqrt[3]{\frac{x^5}{8}}$ **c)** $\sqrt[4]{\frac{a^5}{b^8}}$

Solution

a) $\sqrt{\frac{50}{49}} = \frac{\sqrt{25} \cdot \sqrt{2}}{\sqrt{49}}$ Product and quotient rules for radicals

$= \frac{5\sqrt{2}}{7}$ Simplify.

b) $\sqrt[3]{\frac{x^5}{8}} = \frac{\sqrt[3]{x^3} \cdot \sqrt[3]{x^2}}{\sqrt[3]{8}} = \frac{x\sqrt[3]{x^2}}{2}$

c) $\sqrt[4]{\frac{a^5}{b^8}} = \frac{\sqrt[4]{a^4} \cdot \sqrt[4]{a}}{\sqrt[4]{b^8}} = \frac{a\sqrt[4]{a}}{b^2}$

Now do Exercises 89–100

Math *at Work* Deficit and Debt

Have you ever heard politicians talk about budget surpluses and lowering the deficit, while the national debt keeps increasing? The national debt has increased every year since 1967 and stood at \$6.6 trillion in 2003. Confusing? Not if you know the definitions of these words. If the federal government spends more than it collects in taxes in a particular year, then it has a *deficit*. The amount that is overspent must be borrowed and that adds to the *national debt*, which is the total amount that the federal government owes. Interest alone on the national debt was \$333 billion in 2002 and is the second largest expense in the federal budget.

To get an idea of the size of the national debt, divide the \$6.6 trillion debt in 2003 by the U.S. population of 291 million to get about \$23,000 per person. The national debt went from \$2.4 trillion in 1987 to \$6.6 trillion in 2003. We can calculate the average annual percentage increase in the debt for these 16 years using the formula $i = \sqrt[n]{A/P} - 1$, which yields $i = \sqrt[16]{6.6/2.4} - 1 \approx 6.5\%$. With the U.S. population increasing an average of 1% per year and the debt increasing 6.5% per year, in 25 years the debt will be $6.6(1 + 0.065)^{25}$ or about \$31.9 trillion while the population will increase to $291(1 + 0.01)^{25}$ or about 373 million. So in 25 years the debt will be about \$86,000 per person. Since only one person in three is a wage earner, the debt will be about one-quarter of a million dollars per wage earner!

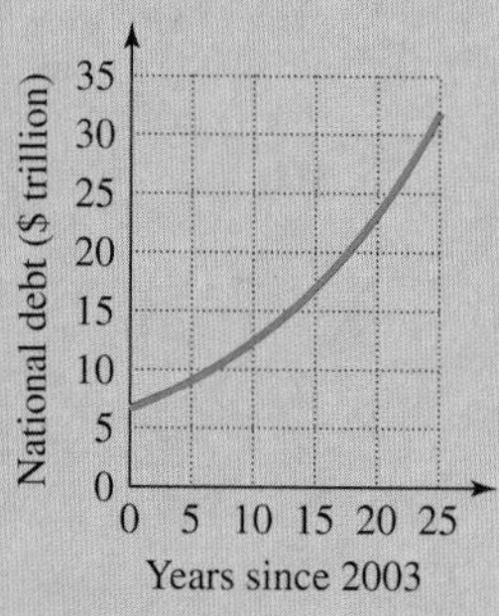

Domain of a Radical Expression

The **domain** of any expression involving one variable is the set of all real numbers that can be used in place of the variable. For many expressions the domain of the expression is the set of all real numbers. For example, any real number can be used in place of x in the expression $2x + 3$ and its domain is the set of all real numbers, $(-\infty, \infty)$.

For a radical expression the domain depends on the radicand and whether the root is even or odd. Since every real number has an odd root, the domain of $\sqrt[3]{x}$ is $(-\infty, \infty)$. Since there are no real even roots of negative numbers, the domain of $\sqrt{x}$ is the set of nonnegative real numbers or $[0, \infty)$.

EXAMPLE 8

Domain of a radical expression

Find the domain of each expression. Express the answer in interval notation.

a) $\sqrt{x - 5}$ **b)** $\sqrt[3]{x + 7}$ **c)** $\sqrt[4]{2x + 6}$

Solution

a) Since the radicand in a square root must be nonnegative, $x - 5$ must be nonnegative:

$$x - 5 \geq 0$$
$$x \geq 5$$

Teaching Tip This example combines the ideas of radicals, domains, linear inequalities, and interval notation.

So only values of x that are 5 or larger can be used for x. The domain is $[5, \infty)$.

b) Since every real number has a cube root, any real number can be used in place of x in $\sqrt[3]{x + 7}$. So the domain is $(-\infty, \infty)$.

c) Since the radicand in a fourth root must be nonnegative, $2x + 6$ must be nonnegative:

$$2x + 6 \geq 0$$
$$2x \geq -6$$
$$x \geq -3$$

So the domain of $\sqrt[4]{2x + 6}$ is $[-3, \infty)$.

Now do Exercises 101–108

Warm-Ups ▼

True or false? Explain your answer.

1. $\sqrt{2} \cdot \sqrt{2} = 2$ True
2. $\sqrt[3]{2} \cdot \sqrt[3]{2} = 2$ False
3. $\sqrt[3]{-27} = -3$ True
4. $\sqrt{-25} = -5$ False
5. $\sqrt[4]{16} = 2$ True
6. $\sqrt{9} = \pm 3$ False
7. $\sqrt{2^9} = 2^3$ False
8. $\dfrac{\sqrt{10}}{2} = \sqrt{5}$ False
9. $\sqrt{\dfrac{1}{4}} = \dfrac{1}{2}$ True
10. $\dfrac{\sqrt{6}}{\sqrt{3}} = \sqrt{2}$ True

9.1 Exercises

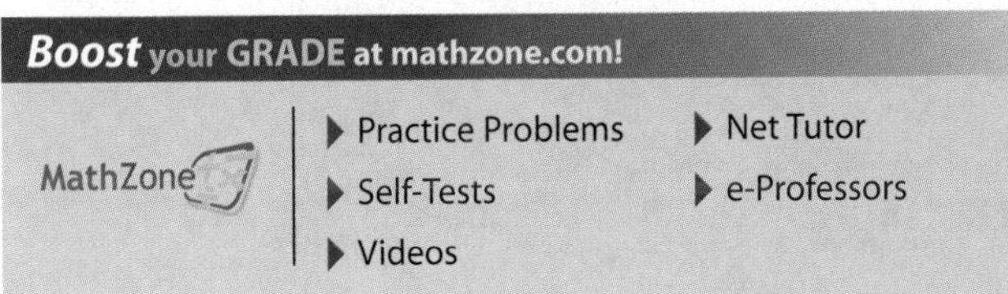

Reading and Writing *After reading this section, write out the answers to these questions. Use complete sentences.*

1. How do you know if b is an nth root of a?
   If $b^n = a$, then b is an nth root of a.
2. What is a principal root?
   The principal root is the positive even root of a positive number.
3. What is the difference between an even root and an odd root?
   If $b^n = a$, then b is an even root of a provided n is even or an odd root of a provided n is odd.
4. What symbol is used to indicate an nth root?
   The nth root of a is written as $\sqrt[n]{a}$.
5. What is the product rule for radicals?
   The product rule for radicals says that $\sqrt[n]{a} \cdot \sqrt[n]{b} = \sqrt[n]{ab}$ provided all of these roots are real.
6. What is the quotient rule for radicals?
   The quotient rule for radicals says that $\sqrt[n]{a}/\sqrt[n]{b} = \sqrt[n]{a/b}$ provided all of these roots are real.

Find each root. See Example 1.

7. $\sqrt{36}$ 6
8. $\sqrt{49}$ 7
9. $\sqrt{100}$ 10
10. $\sqrt{81}$ 9
11. $-\sqrt{9}$ -3
12. $-\sqrt{25}$ -5
13. $\sqrt[3]{8}$ 2
14. $\sqrt[3]{27}$ 3
15. $\sqrt[3]{-8}$ -2
16. $\sqrt[3]{-1}$ -1
17. $\sqrt[5]{32}$ 2
18. $\sqrt[4]{81}$ 3
19. $\sqrt[3]{1000}$ 10
20. $\sqrt[4]{16}$ 2
21. $\sqrt[4]{-16}$ Not a real number
22. $\sqrt{-1}$ Not a real number
23. $\sqrt[5]{-32}$ -2
24. $\sqrt[3]{-125}$ -5

Find each root. See Example 2. All variables represent nonnegative real numbers.

25. $\sqrt{m^2}$ m
26. $\sqrt{m^6}$ m^3
27. $\sqrt{x^{16}}$ x^8
28. $\sqrt{y^{36}}$ y^{18}
29. $\sqrt[5]{y^{15}}$ y^3
30. $\sqrt[4]{m^8}$ m^2
31. $\sqrt[3]{y^{15}}$ y^5
32. $\sqrt{m^8}$ m^4
33. $\sqrt[3]{m^3}$ m
34. $\sqrt[4]{x^4}$ x
35. $\sqrt[4]{w^{12}}$ w^3
36. $\sqrt[5]{a^{30}}$ a^6

Use the product rule for radicals to simplify each expression. See Example 3. All variables represent nonnegative real numbers.

37. $\sqrt{9y}$ $3\sqrt{y}$
38. $\sqrt{16n}$ $4\sqrt{n}$
39. $\sqrt{4a^2}$ $2a$
40. $\sqrt{36n^2}$ $6n$
41. $\sqrt{x^4y^2}$ x^2y
42. $\sqrt{w^6t^2}$ w^3t
43. $\sqrt{5m^{12}}$ $m^6\sqrt{5}$
44. $\sqrt{7z^{16}}$ $z^8\sqrt{7}$
45. $\sqrt[3]{8y}$ $2\sqrt[3]{y}$
46. $\sqrt[3]{27z^2}$ $3\sqrt[3]{z^2}$
47. $\sqrt[3]{3a^6}$ $a^2\sqrt[3]{3}$
48. $\sqrt[3]{5b^9}$ $b^3\sqrt[3]{5}$

Use the product rule to simplify. See Example 4.

49. $\sqrt{20}$ $2\sqrt{5}$
50. $\sqrt{18}$ $3\sqrt{2}$
51. $\sqrt{50}$ $5\sqrt{2}$
52. $\sqrt{45}$ $3\sqrt{5}$
53. $\sqrt{72}$ $6\sqrt{2}$
54. $\sqrt{98}$ $7\sqrt{2}$
55. $\sqrt[3]{40}$ $2\sqrt[3]{5}$
56. $\sqrt[3]{24}$ $2\sqrt[3]{3}$
57. $\sqrt[3]{81}$ $3\sqrt[3]{3}$
58. $\sqrt[3]{250}$ $5\sqrt[3]{2}$
59. $\sqrt[4]{48}$ $2\sqrt[4]{3}$
60. $\sqrt[4]{32}$ $2\sqrt[4]{2}$
61. $\sqrt[5]{96}$ $2\sqrt[5]{3}$
62. $\sqrt[5]{2430}$ $3\sqrt[5]{10}$

Use the product rule to simplify. See Example 5. All variables represent nonnegative real numbers.

63. $\sqrt{a^3}$ $a\sqrt{a}$
64. $\sqrt{b^5}$ $b^2\sqrt{b}$
65. $\sqrt{18a^6}$ $3a^3\sqrt{2}$
66. $\sqrt{12x^8}$ $2x^4\sqrt{3}$
67. $\sqrt{20x^5y}$ $2x^2\sqrt{5xy}$
68. $\sqrt{8w^3y^3}$ $2wy\sqrt{2wy}$
69. $\sqrt[3]{24m^4}$ $2m\sqrt[3]{3m}$
70. $\sqrt[3]{54ab^5}$ $3b\sqrt[3]{2ab^2}$
71. $\sqrt[4]{32a^5}$ $2a\sqrt[4]{2a}$
72. $\sqrt[4]{162b^4}$ $3b\sqrt[4]{2}$
73. $\sqrt[5]{64x^6}$ $2x\sqrt[5]{2x}$
74. $\sqrt[5]{96a^8}$ $2a\sqrt[5]{3a^3}$
75. $\sqrt{48x^3y^8z^7}$ $4xy^4z^3\sqrt{3xz}$
76. $\sqrt[3]{48x^3y^8z^7}$ $2xy^2z^2\sqrt[3]{6y^2z}$

Simplify each radical. See Example 6. All variables represent positive real numbers.

77. $\sqrt{\dfrac{t}{4}}$ $\dfrac{\sqrt{t}}{2}$
78. $\sqrt{\dfrac{w}{36}}$ $\dfrac{\sqrt{w}}{6}$
79. $\sqrt{\dfrac{625}{16}}$ $\dfrac{25}{4}$
80. $\sqrt{\dfrac{9}{144}}$ $\dfrac{1}{4}$
81. $\dfrac{\sqrt{30}}{\sqrt{3}}$ $\sqrt{10}$
82. $\dfrac{\sqrt{50}}{\sqrt{2}}$ 5
83. $\sqrt[3]{\dfrac{t}{8}}$ $\dfrac{\sqrt[3]{t}}{2}$
84. $\sqrt[3]{\dfrac{a}{27}}$ $\dfrac{\sqrt[3]{a}}{3}$
85. $\sqrt[3]{\dfrac{-8x^6}{y^3}}$ $\dfrac{-2x^2}{y}$
86. $\sqrt[3]{\dfrac{-27y^{36}}{1000}}$ $\dfrac{-3y^{12}}{10}$
87. $\sqrt{\dfrac{4a^6}{9}}$ $\dfrac{2a^3}{3}$
88. $\sqrt{\dfrac{9a^2}{49b^4}}$ $\dfrac{3a}{7b^2}$

Use the product and quotient rules to simplify. See Example 7. All variables represent positive real numbers.

89. $\sqrt{\dfrac{12}{25}}$ $\dfrac{2\sqrt{3}}{5}$
90. $\sqrt{\dfrac{8}{81}}$ $\dfrac{2\sqrt{2}}{9}$
91. $\sqrt{\dfrac{27}{16}}$ $\dfrac{3\sqrt{3}}{4}$
92. $\sqrt{\dfrac{98}{9}}$ $\dfrac{7\sqrt{2}}{3}$
93. $\sqrt[3]{\dfrac{a^4}{125}}$ $\dfrac{a\sqrt[3]{a}}{5}$
94. $\sqrt[3]{\dfrac{b^7}{1000}}$ $\dfrac{b^2\sqrt[3]{b}}{10}$
95. $\sqrt[3]{\dfrac{81}{8b^3}}$ $\dfrac{3\sqrt[3]{3}}{2b}$
96. $\sqrt[3]{\dfrac{a^3b^4}{125}}$ $\dfrac{ab\sqrt[3]{b}}{5}$
97. $\sqrt[4]{\dfrac{x^7}{y^8}}$ $\dfrac{x\sqrt[4]{x^3}}{y^2}$
98. $\sqrt[4]{\dfrac{x^5y^4}{z^{12}}}$ $\dfrac{xy\sqrt[4]{x}}{z^3}$
99. $\sqrt[4]{\dfrac{a^5}{16b^{12}}}$ $\dfrac{a\sqrt[4]{a}}{2b^3}$
100. $\sqrt[4]{\dfrac{a^7b}{81c^{16}}}$ $\dfrac{a\sqrt[4]{a^3b}}{3c^4}$

Find the domain of each radical expression. See Example 8.

101. $\sqrt{x-2}$ $[2, \infty)$
102. $\sqrt{2-x}$ $(-\infty, 2]$
103. $\sqrt[3]{3x-7}$ $(-\infty, \infty)$
104. $\sqrt[3]{5-4x}$ $(-\infty, \infty)$
105. $\sqrt[4]{9-3x}$ $(-\infty, 3]$

106. $\sqrt[4]{4x - 8}$ $[2, \infty)$

107. $\sqrt{2x + 1}$ $\left[-\frac{1}{2}, \infty\right)$

108. $\sqrt{4x - 1}$ $\left[\frac{1}{4}, \infty\right)$

Solve each problem.

109. ***Factoring in the wind.*** Through experimentation in Antarctica, Paul Siple developed the formula

$$W = 91.4 - \frac{(10.5 + 6.7\sqrt{v} - 0.45v)(457 - 5t)}{110}$$

to calculate the wind chill temperature W (in degrees Fahrenheit) from the wind velocity v [in miles per hour (mph)] and the air temperature t (in degrees Fahrenheit). Find the wind chill temperature to the nearest whole degree when the air temperature is 25°F and the wind velocity is 20 mph. Use the accompanying graph to estimate the wind chill temperature when the air temperature is 25°F and the wind velocity is 30 mph. −4°F, −10°F

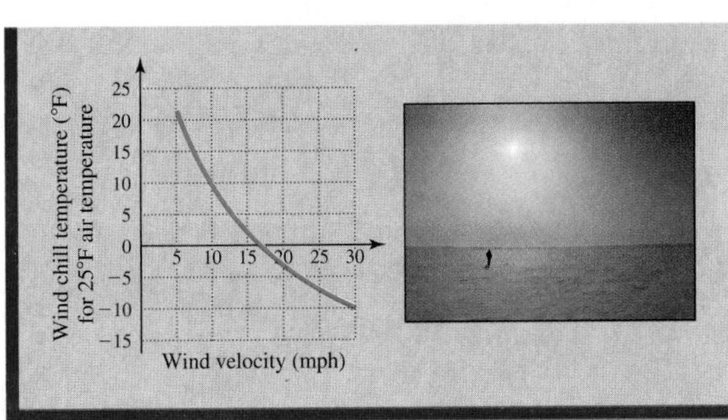

Figure for Exercise 109

110. ***Comparing wind chills.*** Use the formula from Exercise 109 to determine who will feel colder: a person in Minneapolis at 10°F with a 15-mph wind or a person in Chicago at 20°F with a 25-mph wind. Minneapolis

111. ***Diving time.*** The time t (in seconds) that it takes for a cliff diver to reach the water is determined by the height h (in feet) from which he dives:

$$t = \sqrt{\frac{h}{16}}$$

a) Use the properties of radicals to simplify this formula.

b) Find the exact time (according to the formula) that it takes for a diver to hit the water when diving from a height of 40 feet.

c) Use the graph to estimate the height if a diver takes 2.5 seconds to reach the water.

a) $t = \frac{\sqrt{h}}{4}$ **b)** $\frac{\sqrt{10}}{2}$ sec **c)** 100 ft

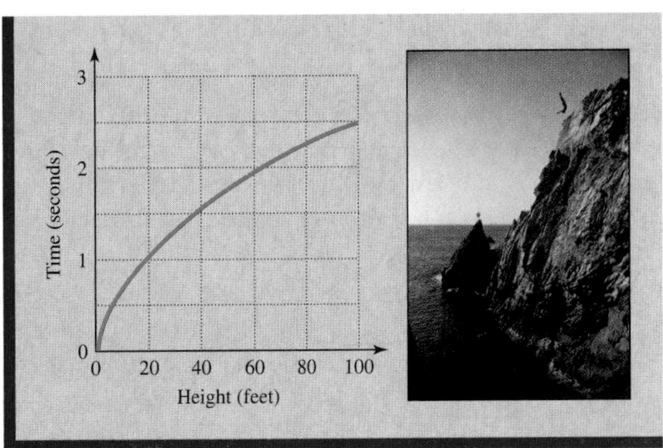

Figure for Exercise 111

112. ***Sky diving.*** The formula in Exercise 111 accounts for the effect of gravity only on a falling object. According to that formula, how long would it take a sky diver to reach the earth when jumping from 17,000 feet? (A sky diver can actually get about twice as much falling time by spreading out and using the air to slow the fall.) 32.6 seconds

113. ***Maximum sailing speed.*** To find the maximum possible speed in knots (nautical miles per hour) for a sailboat, sailors use the formula $M = 1.3\sqrt{w}$, where w is the length of the waterline in feet. If the waterline for the sloop *Golden Eye* is 20 feet, then what is the maximum speed of the *Golden Eye?* 5.8 knots

114. ***America's Cup.*** Since 1988 basic yacht dimensions for the America's Cup competition have satisfied the inequality

$$L + 1.25\sqrt{S} - 9.8\sqrt[3]{D} \le 16.296,$$

where L is the boat's length in meters (m), S is the sail area in square meters, and D is the displacement in cubic meters (www.sailing.com). A team of naval architects is planning to build a boat with a displacement of 21.44 cubic meters (m^3), a sail area of 320.13 square meters (m^2), and a length of 21.22 m. Does this boat satisfy the inequality? If the length and displacement of this boat cannot be changed, then how many square meters of sail area must be removed so that the boat satisfies the inequality? No, 1.84 m^2

115. ***Landing a Piper Cheyenne.*** Aircraft design engineers determine the proper landing speed V [in feet per second (ft/sec)] for an airplane from the formula

$$V = \sqrt{\frac{841L}{CS}},$$

where L is the gross weight of the aircraft in pounds (lb), C is the coefficient of lift, and S is the wing surface area in square feet. According to Piper Aircraft of Vero Beach, Florida, the Piper Cheyenne has a gross weight of 8700 lb, a coefficient of lift of 2.81, and a wing surface area of 200 ft^2. Find the proper landing speed for this plane. What is the landing speed in miles per hour (mph)? 114.1 ft/sec, 77.8 mph

116. ***Landing speed and weight.*** Because the gross weight of the Piper Cheyenne depends on how much fuel and cargo are on board, the proper landing speed (from Exercise 115) is not always the same. The formula $V = \sqrt{1.496L}$ gives the landing speed in terms of the gross weight only.

a) Find the landing speed if the gross weight is 7000 lb.
b) What gross weight corresponds to a landing speed of 115 ft/sec? **a)** 102.3 ft/sec **b)** 8840 lb

Getting More Involved

117. *Cooperative learning*

Work in a group to determine whether each equation is an identity. Explain your answers.

a) $\sqrt{x^2} = |x|$ **b)** $\sqrt[3]{x^3} = |x|$
c) $\sqrt{x^4} = x^2$ **d)** $\sqrt[4]{x^4} = |x|$
a) Yes **b)** No **c)** Yes **d)** Yes

For which values of n is $\sqrt[n]{x^n} = x$ an identity?

118. *Cooperative learning*

Work in a group to determine whether each inequality is correct.

a) $\sqrt{0.9} > 0.9$
b) $\sqrt{1.01} > 1.01$
c) $\sqrt[3]{0.99} > 0.99$
d) $\sqrt[3]{1.001} > 1.001$
a) Correct **b)** Incorrect
c) Correct **d)** Incorrect

For which values of x and n is $\sqrt[n]{x} > x$?

119. *Discussion*

If your test scores are 80 and 100, then the arithmetic mean of your scores is 90. The geometric mean of the scores is a number h such that

$$\frac{80}{h} = \frac{h}{100}.$$

Are you better off with the arithmetic mean or the geometric mean? Arithmetic mean

9.2 Rational Exponents

In this Section

- Rational Exponents
- Using the Rules of Exponents
- Simplifying Expressions Involving Variables

You have learned how to use exponents to express powers of numbers and radicals to express roots. In this section you will see that roots can be expressed with exponents also. The advantage of using exponents to express roots is that the rules of exponents can be applied to the expressions.

Calculator Close-Up

You can find the fifth root of 2 using radical notation or exponent notation. Note that the fractional exponent 1/5 must be in parentheses.

```
5ˣ√(2)
          1.148698355
2^(1/5)
          1.148698355
2^.2
          1.148698355
```

Rational Exponents

The nth root of a number can be expressed by using radical notation or the exponent $1/n$. For example, $8^{1/3}$ and $\sqrt[3]{8}$ both represent the cube root of 8, and we have

$$8^{1/3} = \sqrt[3]{8} = 2.$$

Definition of $a^{1/n}$

If n is any positive integer, then

$$a^{1/n} = \sqrt[n]{a},$$

provided that $\sqrt[n]{a}$ is a real number.

Later in this section we will see that using exponent $1/n$ for nth root is compatible with the rules for integral exponents that we already know.

EXAMPLE 1

Radicals or exponents

Write each radical expression using exponent notation and each exponential expression using radical notation.

a) $\sqrt[3]{35}$ **b)** $\sqrt[4]{xy}$ **c)** $5^{1/2}$ **d)** $a^{1/5}$

Solution

a) $\sqrt[3]{35} = 35^{1/3}$

b) $\sqrt[4]{xy} = (xy)^{1/4}$

c) $5^{1/2} = \sqrt{5}$

d) $a^{1/5} = \sqrt[5]{a}$

Now do Exercises 7–14

In the next example we evaluate some exponential expressions.

EXAMPLE 2

Finding roots

Evaluate each expression.

a) $4^{1/2}$ **b)** $(-8)^{1/3}$ **c)** $81^{1/4}$

d) $(-9)^{1/2}$ **e)** $-9^{1/2}$

Solution

a) $4^{1/2} = \sqrt{4} = 2$

b) $(-8)^{1/3} = \sqrt[3]{-8} = -2$

c) $81^{1/4} = \sqrt[4]{81} = 3$

d) Because $(-9)^{1/2}$ or $\sqrt{-9}$ is an even root of a negative number, it is not a real number.

e) Because the exponent in $-a^n$ is applied only to the base a (Section 1.4), we have $-9^{1/2} = -\sqrt{9} = -3$.

Now do Exercises 15–22

We now extend the definition of exponent $1/n$ to include any rational number as an exponent. The numerator of the rational number indicates the power, and the denominator indicates the root. For example, the expression

$$8^{2/3}$$

(Power: 2; Root: 3)

represents the square of the cube root of 8. So we have

$$8^{2/3} = (8^{1/3})^2 = (2)^2 = 4.$$

Definition of $a^{m/n}$

If m and n are positive integers and $a^{1/n}$ is a real number, then

$$a^{m/n} = (a^{1/n})^m.$$

Using radical notation, $a^{m/n} = (\sqrt[n]{a})^m$.

Helpful Hint

Note that in $a^{m/n}$ we do not require m/n to be reduced. As long as the nth root of a is real, then the value of $a^{m/n}$ is the same whether or not m/n is in lowest terms.

By definition $a^{m/n}$ is the mth power of the nth root of a. However, $a^{m/n}$ is also equal to the nth root of the mth power of a. For example,

$$8^{2/3} = (8^2)^{1/3} = 64^{1/3} = 4.$$

Evaluating $a^{m/n}$ in Either Order

If m and n are positive integers and $a^{1/n}$ is a real number, then

$$a^{m/n} = (a^{1/n})^m = (a^m)^{1/n}.$$

Using radical notation, $a^{m/n} = (\sqrt[n]{a})^m = \sqrt[n]{a^m}$.

A negative rational exponent indicates a reciprocal:

Definition of $a^{-m/n}$

If m and n are positive integers, $a \neq 0$, and $a^{1/n}$ is a real number, then

$$a^{-m/n} = \frac{1}{a^{m/n}}.$$

Using radical notation, $a^{-m/n} = \dfrac{1}{(\sqrt[n]{a})^m}$.

EXAMPLE 3

Radicals or exponents

Write each radical expression using exponent notation and each exponential expression using radical notation.

a) $\sqrt[3]{x^2}$ **b)** $\dfrac{1}{\sqrt[4]{m^3}}$ **c)** $5^{2/3}$ **d)** $a^{-2/5}$

Solution

a) $\sqrt[3]{x^2} = x^{2/3}$

b) $\dfrac{1}{\sqrt[4]{m^3}} = \dfrac{1}{m^{3/4}} = m^{-3/4}$

c) $5^{2/3} = \sqrt[3]{5^2}$

d) $a^{-2/5} = \dfrac{1}{\sqrt[5]{a^2}}$

Now do Exercises 23–30

To evaluate an expression with a negative rational exponent, remember that the denominator indicates root, the numerator indicates power, and the negative sign indicates reciprocal:

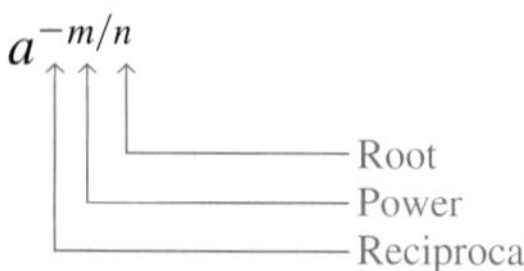

The root, power, and reciprocal can be evaluated in any order. However, to evaluate $a^{-m/n}$ mentally it is usually simplest to use the following strategy.

Strategy for Evaluating $a^{-m/n}$ Mentally

1. Find the nth root of a.
2. Raise your result to the mth power.
3. Find the reciprocal.

For example, to evaluate $8^{-2/3}$ mentally, we find the cube root of 8 (which is 2), square 2 to get 4, then find the reciprocal of 4 to get $\frac{1}{4}$. In print $8^{-2/3}$ could be written for evaluation as $((8^{1/3})^2)^{-1}$ or $\frac{1}{(8^{1/3})^2}$.

EXAMPLE 4

Rational exponents

Evaluate each expression.

a) $27^{2/3}$ **b)** $4^{-3/2}$ **c)** $81^{-3/4}$ **d)** $(-8)^{-5/3}$

Solution

a) Because the exponent is 2/3, we find the cube root of 27 and then square it:

$$27^{2/3} = (27^{1/3})^2 = 3^2 = 9$$

b) Because the exponent is $-3/2$, we find the square root of 4, cube it, and find the reciprocal:

$$4^{-3/2} = \frac{1}{(4^{1/2})^3} = \frac{1}{2^3} = \frac{1}{8}$$

c) Because the exponent is $-3/4$, we find the fourth root of 81, cube it, and find the reciprocal:

$$81^{-3/4} = \frac{1}{(81^{1/4})^3} = \frac{1}{3^3} = \frac{1}{27} \quad \text{Definition of negative exponent}$$

d) $(-8)^{-5/3} = \frac{1}{((-8)^{1/3})^5} = \frac{1}{(-2)^5} = \frac{1}{-32} = -\frac{1}{32}$

Now do Exercises 31–42

Calculator Close-Up

A negative fractional exponent indicates a reciprocal, a root, and a power. To find $4^{-3/2}$ you can find the reciprocal first, the square root first, or the third power first as shown here.

```
(1/4)^(3/2)
                .125
(√(4))^-3
                .125
(4³)^(-1/2)
                .125
```

CAUTION An expression with a negative base and a negative exponent can have a positive or a negative value. For example,

$$(-8)^{-5/3} = -\frac{1}{32} \quad \text{and} \quad (-8)^{-2/3} = \frac{1}{4}.$$

Using the Rules of Exponents

All of the rules for exponents hold for rational exponents as well as integral exponents. Of course, we cannot apply the rules of exponents to expressions that are not real numbers.

Rules for Rational Exponents

The following rules hold for any nonzero real numbers a and b and rational numbers r and s for which the expressions represent real numbers.

1. $a^r a^s = a^{r+s}$ Product rule
2. $\frac{a^r}{a^s} = a^{r-s}$ Quotient rule
3. $(a^r)^s = a^{rs}$ Power of a power rule
4. $(ab)^r = a^r b^r$ Power of a product rule
5. $\left(\frac{a}{b}\right)^r = \frac{a^r}{b^r}$ Power of a quotient rule

Teaching Tip If $a^{m/n}$ is defined only when m/n is in lowest terms (as is often done), then we cannot write $(a^{1/4})^2 = a^{2/4} = a^{1/2}$.

We can use the product rule to add rational exponents. For example,

$$16^{1/4} \cdot 16^{1/4} = 16^{2/4}.$$

The fourth root of 16 is 2, and 2 squared is 4. So $16^{2/4} = 4$. Because we also have $16^{1/2} = 4$, we see that a rational exponent can be reduced to its lowest terms. If an exponent can be reduced, it is usually simpler to reduce the exponent before we evaluate the expression. We can simplify $16^{1/4} \cdot 16^{1/4}$ as follows:

$$16^{1/4} \cdot 16^{1/4} = 16^{2/4} = 16^{1/2} = 4$$

EXAMPLE 5

Using the product and quotient rules with rational exponents

Simplify each expression.

a) $27^{1/6} \cdot 27^{1/2}$ **b)** $\frac{5^{3/4}}{5^{1/4}}$

Teaching Tip This is a good time to refresh student's memories of the operations with fractions.

Solution

a) $27^{1/6} \cdot 27^{1/2} = 27^{1/6+1/2}$ Product rule for exponents

$= 27^{2/3}$

$= 9$

b) $\frac{5^{3/4}}{5^{1/4}} = 5^{3/4-1/4} = 5^{2/4} = 5^{1/2} = \sqrt{5}$ We used the quotient rule to subtract the exponents.

Now do Exercises 43-50

EXAMPLE 6

Using the power rules with rational exponents

Simplify each expression.

a) $3^{1/2} \cdot 12^{1/2}$ **b)** $(3^{10})^{1/2}$ **c)** $\left(\frac{2^6}{3^9}\right)^{-1/3}$

Solution

a) Because the bases 3 and 12 are different, we cannot use the product rule to add the exponents. Instead, we use the power of a product rule to place the 1/2 power outside the parentheses:

$$3^{1/2} \cdot 12^{1/2} = (3 \cdot 12)^{1/2} = 36^{1/2} = 6$$

b) Use the power of a power rule to multiply the exponents:

$$(3^{10})^{1/2} = 3^5$$

c)
$$\left(\frac{2^6}{3^9}\right)^{-1/3} = \frac{(2^6)^{-1/3}}{(3^9)^{-1/3}} \quad \text{Power of a quotient rule}$$
$$= \frac{2^{-2}}{3^{-3}} \quad \text{Power of a power rule}$$
$$= \frac{3^3}{2^2} \quad \text{Definition of negative exponent}$$
$$= \frac{27}{4}$$

Now do Exercises 51–60

Helpful Hint

We usually think of squaring and taking a square root as inverse operations, which they are as long as we stick to positive numbers. We can square 3 to get 9, and then find the square root of 9 to get 3—what we started with. We don't get back to where we began if we start with -3.

Simplifying Expressions Involving Variables

When simplifying expressions involving rational exponents and variables, we must be careful to write equivalent expressions. For example, in the equation

$$(x^2)^{1/2} = x$$

it looks as if we are correctly applying the power of a power rule. However, this statement is false if x is negative because the $1/2$ power on the left-hand side indicates the positive square root of x^2. For example, if $x = -3$, we get

$$[(-3)^2]^{1/2} = 9^{1/2} = 3,$$

which is not equal to -3. To write a simpler equivalent expression for $(x^2)^{1/2}$, we use absolute value as follows.

Square Root of x^2

$$(x^2)^{1/2} = |x| \text{ for any real number } x.$$

Note that $(x^2)^{1/2} = |x|$ is also written as $\sqrt{x^2} = |x|$. Both of these equations are identities.

It is also necessary to use absolute value when writing identities for other even roots of expressions involving variables.

EXAMPLE 7

Using absolute value symbols with roots

Simplify each expression. Assume the variables represent any real numbers and use absolute value symbols as necessary.

a) $(x^8y^4)^{1/4}$ **b)** $\left(\frac{x^9}{8}\right)^{1/3}$

Solution

a) Apply the power of a product rule to get the equation $(x^8y^4)^{1/4} = x^2y$. The left-hand side is nonnegative for any choices of x and y, but the right-hand side is negative when y is negative. So for any real values of x and y we have

$$(x^8y^4)^{1/4} = x^2|y|.$$

Note that the absolute value symbols could also be placed around the entire expression: $(x^8y^4)^{1/4} = |x^2y|$.

b) Using the power of a quotient rule, we get

$$\left(\frac{x^9}{8}\right)^{1/3} = \frac{x^3}{2}.$$

This equation is valid for every real number x, so no absolute value signs are used.

Now do Exercises 61–70

Because there are no real even roots of negative numbers, the expressions

$$a^{1/2}, \quad x^{-3/4}, \quad \text{and} \quad y^{1/6}$$

are not real numbers if the variables have negative values. To simplify matters, we sometimes assume the variables represent only positive numbers when we are working with expressions involving variables with rational exponents. That way we do not have to be concerned with undefined expressions and absolute value.

EXAMPLE 8

Expressions involving variables with rational exponents

Use the rules of exponents to simplify the following. Write your answers with positive exponents. Assume all variables represent *positive* real numbers.

a) $x^{2/3}x^{4/3}$ **b)** $\dfrac{a^{1/2}}{a^{1/4}}$ **c)** $(x^{1/2}y^{-3})^{1/2}$ **d)** $\left(\dfrac{x^2}{y^{1/3}}\right)^{-1/2}$

Solution

a) $x^{2/3}x^{4/3} = x^{6/3}$ Use the product rule to add the exponents.

$= x^2$ Reduce the exponent.

b) $\dfrac{a^{1/2}}{a^{1/4}} = a^{1/2-1/4}$ Use the quotient rule to subtract the exponents.

$= a^{1/4}$ Simplify.

c) $(x^{1/2}y^{-3})^{1/2} = (x^{1/2})^{1/2}(y^{-3})^{1/2}$ Power of a product rule

$= x^{1/4}y^{-3/2}$ Power of a power rule

$= \dfrac{x^{1/4}}{y^{3/2}}$ Definition of negative exponent

d) Because this expression is a negative power of a quotient, we can first find the reciprocal of the quotient, then apply the power of a power rule:

$$\left(\frac{x^2}{y^{1/3}}\right)^{-1/2} = \left(\frac{y^{1/3}}{x^2}\right)^{1/2} = \frac{y^{1/6}}{x} \qquad \frac{1}{3}\cdot\frac{1}{2} = \frac{1}{6}$$

Now do Exercises 71–84

Warm-Ups ▼

True or false? Explain your answer.

1. $9^{1/3} = \sqrt[3]{9}$ True
2. $8^{5/3} = \sqrt[5]{8^3}$ False
3. $(-16)^{1/2} = -16^{1/2}$ False
4. $9^{-3/2} = \frac{1}{27}$ True
5. $6^{-1/2} = \frac{\sqrt{6}}{6}$ True
6. $\frac{2}{2^{1/2}} = 2^{1/2}$ True
7. $2^{1/2} \cdot 2^{1/2} = 4^{1/2}$ True
8. $16^{-1/4} = -2$ False
9. $6^{1/6} \cdot 6^{1/6} = 6^{1/3}$ True
10. $(2^8)^{3/4} = 2^6$ True

9.2 Exercises

Boost your GRADE at mathzone.com!

MathZone

- Practice Problems
- Self-Tests
- Videos
- Net Tutor
- e-Professors

Reading and Writing *After reading this section, write out the answers to these questions. Use complete sentences.*

1. How do we indicate an nth root using exponents?
   The nth root of a is $a^{1/n}$.
2. How do we indicate the mth power of the nth root using exponents?
   The mth power of the nth root of a is $a^{m/n}$.
3. What is the meaning of a negative rational exponent?
   The expression $a^{-m/n}$ means $\frac{1}{a^{m/n}}$.
4. Which rules of exponents hold for rational exponents?
   All of the rules of exponents hold for rational exponents.
5. In what order must you perform the operations indicated by a negative rational exponent?
   The operations can be performed in any order, but the easiest is usually root, power, and then reciprocal.
6. When is $a^{-m/n}$ a real number?
   The expression $a^{-m/n}$ is a real number except when n is even and a is negative, or when $a = 0$.

Write each radical expression using exponent notation. See Example 1.

7. $\sqrt[4]{7}$ $7^{1/4}$
8. $\sqrt[3]{cbs}$ $(cbs)^{1/3}$
9. $\sqrt{5x}$ $(5x)^{1/2}$
10. $\sqrt{3y}$ $(3y)^{1/2}$

Write each exponential expression using radical notation. See Example 1.

11. $9^{1/5}$ $\sqrt[5]{9}$
12. $3^{1/2}$ $\sqrt{3}$
13. $a^{1/2}$ $\sqrt{a}$
14. $(-b)^{1/5}$ $\sqrt[5]{-b}$

Evaluate each expression. See Example 2.

15. $25^{1/2}$ 5
16. $16^{1/2}$ 4
17. $(-125)^{1/3}$ -5
18. $(-32)^{1/5}$ -2
19. $16^{1/4}$ 2
20. $8^{1/3}$ 2
21. $(-4)^{1/2}$ Not a real number
22. $(-16)^{1/4}$ Not a real number

Write each radical expression using exponent notation and each exponential expression using radical notation. See Example 3.

23. $\sqrt[3]{w^7}$ $w^{7/3}$
24. $\sqrt{a^5}$ $a^{5/2}$
25. $\frac{1}{\sqrt[3]{2^{10}}}$ $2^{-10/3}$
26. $\sqrt[3]{\frac{1}{a^2}}$ $a^{-2/3}$
27. $w^{-3/4}$ $\sqrt[4]{\frac{1}{w^3}}$
28. $6^{-5/3}$ $\sqrt[3]{\frac{1}{6^5}}$
29. $(ab)^{3/2}$ $\sqrt{(ab)^3}$
30. $(3m)^{-1/5}$ $\sqrt[5]{\frac{1}{3m}}$

Evaluate each expression. See Example 4.

31. $125^{2/3}$ 25
32. $1000^{2/3}$ 100
33. $25^{3/2}$ 125
34. $16^{3/2}$ 64
35. $27^{-4/3}$ $\frac{1}{81}$
36. $16^{-3/4}$ $\frac{1}{8}$
37. $16^{-3/2}$ $\frac{1}{64}$
38. $25^{-3/2}$ $\frac{1}{125}$
39. $(-27)^{-1/3}$ $-\frac{1}{3}$
40. $(-8)^{-4/3}$ $\frac{1}{16}$
41. $(-16)^{-1/4}$ Not a real number
42. $(-100)^{-3/2}$ Not a real number

Use the rules of exponents to simplify each expression. See Examples 5 and 6.

43. $3^{1/3}3^{1/4}$ $3^{7/12}$
44. $2^{1/2}2^{1/3}$ $2^{5/6}$
45. $3^{1/3}3^{-1/3}$ 1
46. $5^{1/4}5^{-1/4}$ 1

47. $\frac{8^{1/3}}{8^{2/3}}$ $\frac{1}{2}$

48. $\frac{27^{-2/3}}{27^{-1/3}}$ $\frac{1}{3}$

49. $4^{3/4} \div 4^{1/4}$ 2

50. $9^{1/4} \div 9^{3/4}$ $\frac{1}{3}$

51. $18^{1/2}2^{1/2}$ 6

52. $8^{1/2}2^{1/2}$ 4

53. $(2^6)^{1/3}$ 4

54. $(3^{10})^{1/5}$ 9

55. $(3^8)^{1/2}$ 81

56. $(3^{-6})^{1/3}$ $\frac{1}{9}$

57. $(2^{-4})^{1/2}$ $\frac{1}{4}$

58. $(5^4)^{1/2}$ 25

59. $\left(\frac{3^4}{2^6}\right)^{1/2}$ $\frac{9}{8}$

60. $\left(\frac{5^4}{3^6}\right)^{1/2}$ $\frac{25}{27}$

Simplify each expression. Assume the variables represent any real numbers and use absolute value as necessary. See Example 7.

61. $(x^4)^{1/4}$ $|x|$

62. $(y^6)^{1/6}$ $|y|$

63. $(a^8)^{1/2}$ a^4

64. $(b^{10})^{1/2}$ $|b^5|$

65. $(y^3)^{1/3}$ y

66. $(w^9)^{1/3}$ w^3

67. $(9x^6y^2)^{1/2}$ $|3x^3y|$

68. $(16a^8b^4)^{1/4}$ $|2a^2b|$

69. $\left(\frac{81x^{12}}{y^{20}}\right)^{1/4}$ $\left|\frac{3x^3}{y^5}\right|$

70. $\left(\frac{144a^8}{9y^{18}}\right)^{1/2}$ $\frac{4a^4}{|y^9|}$

Simplify. Assume all variables represent positive numbers. Write answers with positive exponents only. See Example 8.

71. $x^{1/2}x^{1/4}$ $x^{3/4}$

72. $y^{1/3}y^{1/3}$ $y^{2/3}$

73. $(x^{1/2}y)(x^{-3/4}y^{1/2})$ $\frac{y^{3/2}}{x^{1/4}}$

74. $(a^{1/2}b^{-1/3})(ab)$ $a^{3/2}b^{2/3}$

75. $\frac{w^{1/3}}{w^3}$ $\frac{1}{w^{8/3}}$

76. $\frac{a^{1/2}}{a^2}$ $\frac{1}{a^{3/2}}$

77. $(144x^{16})^{1/2}$ $12x^8$

78. $(125a^8)^{1/3}$ $5a^{8/3}$

79. $\left(\frac{a^{-1/2}}{b^{-1/4}}\right)^{-4}$ $\frac{a^2}{b}$

80. $\left(\frac{2a^{1/2}}{b^{1/3}}\right)^6$ $\frac{64a^3}{b^2}$

81. $\left(\frac{2w^{1/3}}{w^{-3/4}}\right)^3$ $8w^{13/4}$

82. $\left(\frac{a^{-1/2}}{3a^{2/3}}\right)^{-3}$ $27a^{7/2}$

83. $\frac{9^{1/4}h^{1/2}k^{3/2}}{9^{3/4}h^{1/3}k^2}$ $\frac{h^{1/6}}{3k^{1/2}}$

84. $\frac{4^{1/4}s^{1/3}t^{-1/2}}{(4s^2t^{-3})^{-1/4}}$ $\frac{2s^{5/6}}{t^{5/4}}$

Simplify each expression. Write your answers with positive exponents. Assume that all variables represent positive real numbers.

85. $(9^2)^{1/2}$ 9

86. $(4^{16})^{1/2}$ 4^8

87. $-16^{-3/4}$ $-\frac{1}{8}$

88. $-25^{-3/2}$ $-\frac{1}{125}$

89. $125^{-4/3}$ $\frac{1}{625}$

90. $27^{-2/3}$ $\frac{1}{9}$

91. $2^{1/2}2^{-1/4}$ $2^{1/4}$

92. $9^{-1}9^{1/2}$ $\frac{1}{3}$

93. $3^{0.26}3^{0.74}$ 3

94. $2^{1.5}2^{0.5}$ 4

95. $3^{1/4}27^{1/4}$ 3

96. $3^{2/3}9^{2/3}$ 9

97. $\left(-\frac{8}{27}\right)^{2/3}$ $\frac{4}{9}$

98. $\left(-\frac{8}{27}\right)^{-1/3}$ $-\frac{3}{2}$

99. $\left(-\frac{1}{16}\right)^{-3/4}$ Not a real number

100. $\left(-\frac{5}{9}\right)^{-7/2}$ Not a real number

101. $\left(\frac{9}{16}\right)^{-1/2}$ $\frac{4}{3}$

102. $\left(\frac{16}{81}\right)^{-1/4}$ $\frac{3}{2}$

103. $-\left(\frac{25}{36}\right)^{-3/2}$ $-\frac{216}{125}$

104. $\left(-\frac{27}{8}\right)^{-4/3}$ $\frac{16}{81}$

105. $(9x^9)^{1/2}$ $3x^{9/2}$

106. $(-27x^9)^{1/3}$ $-3x^3$

107. $(3a^{-2/3})^{-3}$ $\frac{a^2}{27}$

108. $(5x^{-1/2})^{-2}$ $\frac{x}{25}$

109. $(a^{1/2}b)^{1/2}(ab^{1/2})$ $a^{5/4}b$

110. $(m^{1/4}n^{1/2})^2(m^2n^3)^{1/2}$ $m^{3/2}n^{5/2}$

111. $(km^{1/2})^3(k^3m^5)^{1/2}$ $k^{9/2}m^4$

112. $(tv^{1/3})^2(t^2v^{-3})^{-1/2}$ $tv^{13/6}$

Use a scientific calculator with a power key (x^y) to find the decimal value of each expression. Round approximate answers to four decimal places.

113. $2^{1/3}$ 1.2599

114. $5^{1/2}$ 2.2361

115. $-2^{1/2}$ -1.4142

116. $(-3)^{1/3}$ -1.4422

117. $1024^{1/10}$ 2

118. $7776^{0.2}$ 6

119. $\left(\frac{64}{15{,}625}\right)^{-1/6}$ 2.5

120. $\left(\frac{32}{243}\right)^{-3/5}$ 3.375

Simplify each expression. Assume a and b are positive real numbers and m and n are rational numbers.

121. $a^{m/2} \cdot a^{m/4}$ $a^{3m/4}$

122. $b^{n/2} \cdot b^{-n/3}$ $b^{n/6}$

123. $\frac{a^{-m/5}}{a^{-m/3}}$ $a^{2m/15}$

124. $\frac{b^{-n/4}}{b^{-n/3}}$ $b^{n/12}$

125. $(a^{-1/m}b^{-1/n})^{-mn}$ a^nb^m

126. $(a^{-m/2}b^{-n/3})^{-6}$ $a^{3m}b^{2n}$

127. $\left(\frac{a^{-3m}b^{-6n}}{a^{9m}}\right)^{-1/3}$ $a^{4m}b^{2n}$

128. $\left(\frac{a^{-3/m}b^{6/n}}{a^{-6/m}b^{9/n}}\right)^{-1/3}$ $\frac{b^{1/n}}{a^{1/m}}$

In Exercises 129–136, solve each problem. Round answers to two decimal places when necessary.

129. ***Diagonal of a box.*** The length of the diagonal of a box can be found from the formula

$$D = (L^2 + W^2 + H^2)^{1/2},$$

where L, W, and H represent the length, width, and height of the box, respectively. If the box is 12 inches long, 4 inches wide, and 3 inches high, then what is the length of the diagonal? 13 inches

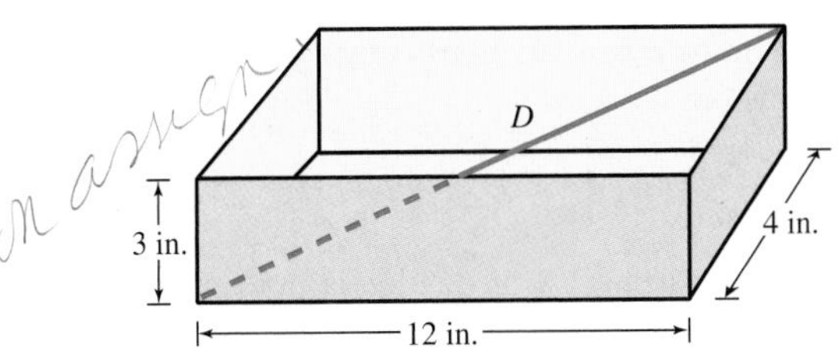

Figure for Exercise 129

130. ***Radius of a sphere.*** The radius of a sphere is given by the formula

$$r = \left(\frac{0.75V}{\pi}\right)^{1/3},$$

where V is its volume. Find the radius of a spherical tank that has a volume of $\frac{32\pi}{3}$ cubic meters. 2 meters

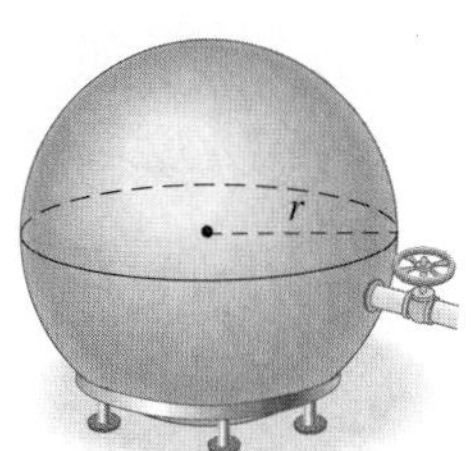

Figure for Exercise 130

131. ***Maximum sail area.*** According to the new International America's Cup Class Rules, the maximum sail area in square meters for a yacht in the America's Cup race is given by

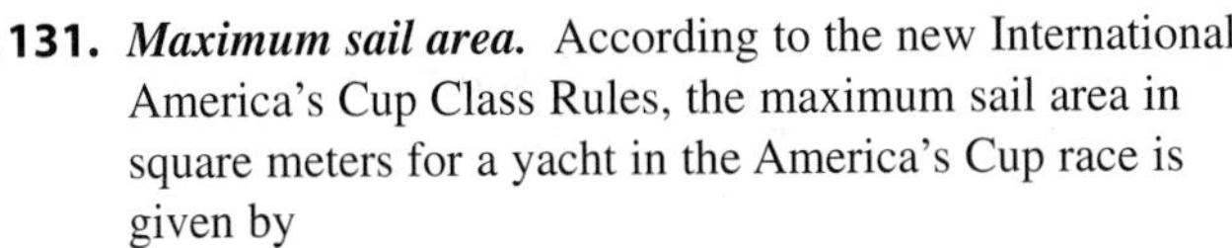

$$S = (13.0368 + 7.84D^{1/3} - 0.8L)^2,$$

where D is the displacement in cubic meters (m^3), and L is the length in meters (m). (www.sailing.com). Find the maximum sail area for a boat that has a displacement of 18.42 m^3 and a length of 21.45 m. 274.96 m^2

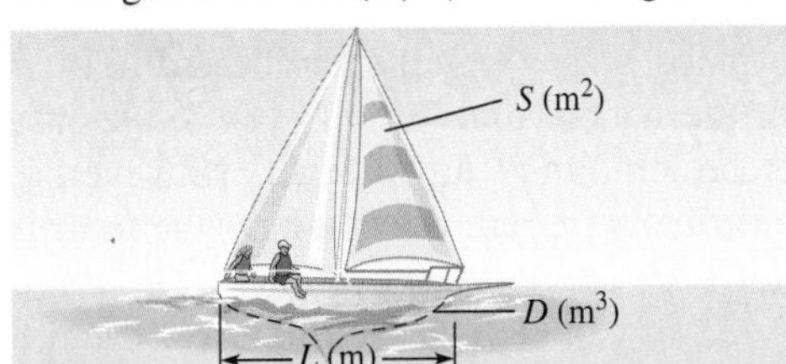

Figure for Exercise 131

132. ***Orbits of the planets.*** According to Kepler's third law of planetary motion, the average radius R of the orbit of a planet around the sun is determined by $R = T^{2/3}$, where T is the number of years for one orbit and R is measured in astronomical units or AUs (Windows to the Universe, www.windows.umich.edu).

a) It takes Mars 1.881 years to make one orbit of the sun. What is the average radius (in AUs) of the orbit of Mars?

b) The average radius of the orbit of Saturn is 9.05 AU. Use the accompanying graph to estimate the number of years it takes Saturn to make one orbit of the sun.

a) 1.52 AU **b)** 27 years

Figure for Exercise 132

133. ***Top stock fund.*** The average annual return r for an investment is given by the formula

$$r = \left(\frac{S}{P}\right)^{1/n} - 1,$$

where P is the initial investment and S is the amount it is worth after n years. An investment of \$10,000 in 1999 in the Shroeder Ultra Investors Fund was worth \$20,130 in 2002 (www.money.com). Find the 3-year average annual return. 26.26%

134. ***Top bond fund.*** An investment of \$10,000 in 1997 in the Spartan Investment Grade Bond Fund grew to \$14,309.61 in 2002 (www.fidelity.com). Use the formula from the previous exercise to find the 5-year average annual return. 7.43%

135. ***Overdue loan payment.*** In 1777 a wealthy Pennsylvania merchant, Jacob DeHaven, lent \$450,000 to the Continental Congress to rescue the troops at Valley Forge. The loan was not repaid. In 1990 DeHaven's descendants filed suit for \$141.6 billion (*New York Times*, May 27, 1990). What average annual rate of return were they using to calculate the value of the debt after 213 years? (See Exercise 133.) 6.12%

136. ***California growin'.*** The population of California grew from 19.9 million in 1970 to 32.5 million in 2000 (U.S. Census Bureau, www.census.gov). Find the average annual rate of growth for that time period. (Use the formula from Exercise 133 with P being the initial population and S being the population n years later.) 1.65%

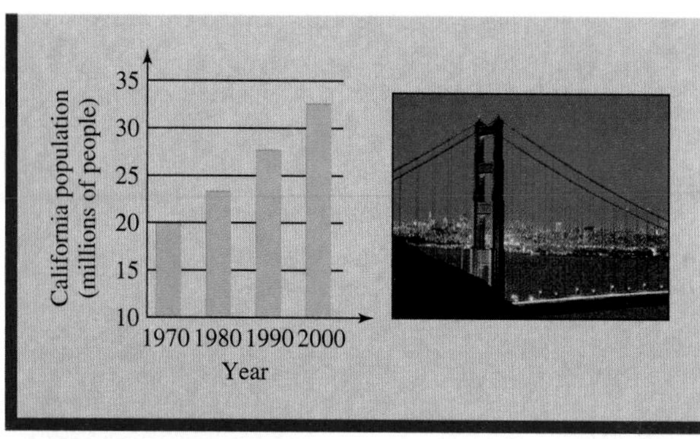

Figure for Exercise 136

Getting More Involved

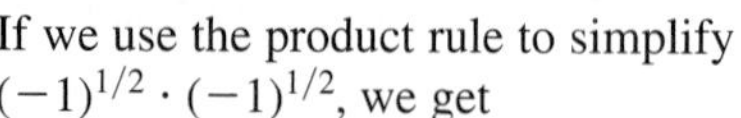

137. ***Discussion***

If we use the product rule to simplify $(-1)^{1/2} \cdot (-1)^{1/2}$, we get

$$(-1)^{1/2} \cdot (-1)^{1/2} = (-1)^1 = -1.$$

If we use the power of a product rule, we get

$$(-1)^{1/2} \cdot (-1)^{1/2} = (-1 \cdot -1)^{1/2} = 1^{1/2} = 1.$$

Which of these computations is incorrect? Explain your answer.
Second is incorrect.

138. ***Discussion***

Determine whether each equation is an identity. Explain.

a) $(w^2x^2)^{1/2} = |w| \cdot |x|$ Identity

b) $(w^2x^2)^{1/2} = |wx|$ Identity

c) $(w^2x^2)^{1/2} = w|x|$ Not an identity

9.3 Operations with Radicals

In this Section

- **Adding and Subtracting Radicals**
- **Multiplying Radicals**
- **Conjugates**

In this section we will use the ideas of Section 9.1 in performing arithmetic operations with radical expressions.

Adding and Subtracting Radicals

To find the sum of $\sqrt{2}$ and $\sqrt{3}$, we can use a calculator to get $\sqrt{2} \approx 1.414$ and $\sqrt{3} \approx 1.732$. (The symbol $\approx$ means "is approximately equal to.") We can then add the decimal numbers and get

$$\sqrt{2} + \sqrt{3} \approx 1.414 + 1.732 = 3.146.$$

We cannot write an exact decimal form for $\sqrt{2} + \sqrt{3}$; the number 3.146 is an approximation of $\sqrt{2} + \sqrt{3}$. To represent the exact value of $\sqrt{2} + \sqrt{3}$, we just use the form $\sqrt{2} + \sqrt{3}$. This form cannot be simplified any further. However, a sum of like radicals can be simplified. **Like radicals** are radicals that have the same index and the same radicand.

To simplify the sum $3\sqrt{2} + 5\sqrt{2}$, we can use the fact that $3x + 5x = 8x$ is true for any value of x. Substituting $\sqrt{2}$ for x gives us $3\sqrt{2} + 5\sqrt{2} = 8\sqrt{2}$. So like radicals can be combined just as like terms are combined.

EXAMPLE 1

Adding and subtracting like radicals

Simplify the following expressions. Assume the variables represent positive numbers.

a) $3\sqrt{5} + 4\sqrt{5}$ **b)** $\sqrt[4]{w} - 6\sqrt[4]{w}$

c) $\sqrt{3} + \sqrt{5} - 4\sqrt{3} + 6\sqrt{5}$ **d)** $3\sqrt[3]{6x} + 2\sqrt[3]{x} + \sqrt[3]{6x} + \sqrt[3]{x}$

Solution

a) $3\sqrt{5} + 4\sqrt{5} = 7\sqrt{5}$ **b)** $\sqrt[4]{w} - 6\sqrt[4]{w} = -5\sqrt[4]{w}$

c) $\sqrt{3} + \sqrt{5} - 4\sqrt{3} + 6\sqrt{5} = -3\sqrt{3} + 7\sqrt{5}$ Only like radicals are combined.

d) $3\sqrt[3]{6x} + 2\sqrt[3]{x} + \sqrt[3]{6x} + \sqrt[3]{x} = 4\sqrt[3]{6x} + 3\sqrt[3]{x}$

Now do Exercises 5–16

Remember that *only radicals with the same index and same radicand can be combined by addition or subtraction.* If the radicals are not in simplified form, then they must be simplified before you can determine whether they can be combined.

EXAMPLE 2

Simplifying radicals before combining

Perform the indicated operations. Assume the variables represent positive numbers.

a) $\sqrt{8} + \sqrt{18}$ **b)** $\sqrt{2x^3} - \sqrt{4x^2} + 5\sqrt{18x^3}$

c) $\sqrt[3]{16x^4y^3} - \sqrt[3]{54x^4y^3}$

Calculator Close-Up

Check that

$\sqrt{8} + \sqrt{18} = 5\sqrt{2}.$

```
√(8)+√(18)
         7.071067812
5√(2)
         7.071067812
```

Solution

a) $\sqrt{8} + \sqrt{18} = \sqrt{4} \cdot \sqrt{2} + \sqrt{9} \cdot \sqrt{2}$

$= 2\sqrt{2} + 3\sqrt{2}$ Simplify each radical.

$= 5\sqrt{2}$ Add like radicals.

Note that $\sqrt{8} + \sqrt{18} \neq \sqrt{26}$.

b) $\sqrt{2x^3} - \sqrt{4x^2} + 5\sqrt{18x^3} = \sqrt{x^2} \cdot \sqrt{2x} - 2x + 5 \cdot \sqrt{9x^2} \cdot \sqrt{2x}$

$= x\sqrt{2x} - 2x + 15x\sqrt{2x}$ Simplify each radical.

$= 16x\sqrt{2x} - 2x$ Add like radicals only.

c) $\sqrt[3]{16x^4y^3} - \sqrt[3]{54x^4y^3} = \sqrt[3]{8x^3y^3} \cdot \sqrt[3]{2x} - \sqrt[3]{27x^3y^3} \cdot \sqrt[3]{2x}$

$= 2xy\sqrt[3]{2x} - 3xy\sqrt[3]{2x}$ Simplify each radical.

$= -xy\sqrt[3]{2x}$

Now do Exercises 17–32

Multiplying Radicals

The product rule for radicals, $\sqrt[n]{a} \cdot \sqrt[n]{b} = \sqrt[n]{ab}$, allows multiplication of radicals with the same index, such as

$$\sqrt{5} \cdot \sqrt{3} = \sqrt{15}, \quad \sqrt[3]{2} \cdot \sqrt[3]{5} = \sqrt[3]{10}, \quad \text{and} \quad \sqrt[5]{x^2} \cdot \sqrt[5]{x} = \sqrt[5]{x^3}.$$

CAUTION The product rule does not allow multiplication of radicals that have different indices. We cannot use the product rule to multiply $\sqrt{2}$ and $\sqrt[3]{5}$.

EXAMPLE 3

Multiplying radicals with the same index

Multiply and simplify the following expressions. Assume the variables represent positive numbers.

a) $5\sqrt{6} \cdot 4\sqrt{3}$ **b)** $\sqrt{3a^2} \cdot \sqrt{6a}$

c) $\sqrt[3]{4} \cdot \sqrt[3]{4}$ **d)** $\sqrt[4]{\dfrac{x^3}{2}} \cdot \sqrt[4]{\dfrac{x^2}{8}}$

Helpful Hint

Students often write

$$\sqrt{15} \cdot \sqrt{15} = \sqrt{225} = 15.$$

Although this is correct, you should get used to the idea that

$$\sqrt{15} \cdot \sqrt{15} = 15.$$

Because of the definition of a square root, $\sqrt{a} \cdot \sqrt{a} = a$ for any positive number a.

Solution

a) $5\sqrt{6} \cdot 4\sqrt{3} = 5 \cdot 4 \cdot \sqrt{6} \cdot \sqrt{3}$

$= 20\sqrt{18}$ Product rule for radicals

$= 20 \cdot 3\sqrt{2}$ $\sqrt{18} = \sqrt{9} \cdot \sqrt{2} = 3\sqrt{2}$

$= 60\sqrt{2}$

b) $\sqrt{3a^2} \cdot \sqrt{6a} = \sqrt{18a^3}$ Product rule for radicals

$= \sqrt{9a^2} \cdot \sqrt{2a}$

$= 3a\sqrt{2a}$ Simplify.

c) $\sqrt[3]{4} \cdot \sqrt[3]{4} = \sqrt[3]{16}$

$= \sqrt[3]{8} \cdot \sqrt[3]{2}$ Simplify.

$= 2\sqrt[3]{2}$

d) $\sqrt[4]{\dfrac{x^3}{2}} \cdot \sqrt[4]{\dfrac{x^2}{8}} = \sqrt[4]{\dfrac{x^5}{16}}$ Product rule for radicals

$= \dfrac{\sqrt[4]{x^4} \cdot \sqrt[4]{x}}{\sqrt[4]{16}}$ Product and quotient rules for radicals

$= \dfrac{x\sqrt[4]{x}}{2}$ Simplify.

Now do Exercises 33–42

We find a product such as $3\sqrt{2}(4\sqrt{2} - \sqrt{3})$ by using the distributive property as we do when multiplying a monomial and a binomial. A product such as $(2\sqrt{3} + \sqrt{5})(3\sqrt{3} - 2\sqrt{5})$ can be found by using FOIL as we do for the product of two binomials.

EXAMPLE 4

Multiplying radicals

Multiply and simplify.

a) $3\sqrt{2}(4\sqrt{2} - \sqrt{3})$ **b)** $\sqrt[3]{a}(\sqrt[3]{a} - \sqrt[3]{a^2})$

c) $(2\sqrt{3} + \sqrt{5})(3\sqrt{3} - 2\sqrt{5})$ **d)** $(3 + \sqrt{x - 9})^2$

Solution

a) $3\sqrt{2}(4\sqrt{2} - \sqrt{3}) = 3\sqrt{2} \cdot 4\sqrt{2} - 3\sqrt{2} \cdot \sqrt{3}$ Distributive property

$= 12 \cdot 2 - 3\sqrt{6}$ Because $\sqrt{2} \cdot \sqrt{2} = 2$ and $\sqrt{2} \cdot \sqrt{3} = \sqrt{6}$

$= 24 - 3\sqrt{6}$

b) $\sqrt[3]{a}(\sqrt[3]{a} - \sqrt[3]{a^2}) = \sqrt[3]{a^2} - \sqrt[3]{a^3}$ Distributive property

$= \sqrt[3]{a^2} - a$

c) $(2\sqrt{3} + \sqrt{5})(3\sqrt{3} - 2\sqrt{5})$

$$= \overbrace{2\sqrt{3} \cdot 3\sqrt{3}}^{F} - \overbrace{2\sqrt{3} \cdot 2\sqrt{5}}^{O} + \overbrace{\sqrt{5} \cdot 3\sqrt{3}}^{I} - \overbrace{\sqrt{5} \cdot 2\sqrt{5}}^{L}$$

$= 18 - 4\sqrt{15} + 3\sqrt{15} - 10$

$= 8 - \sqrt{15}$ Combine like radicals.

d) To square a sum, we use $(a + b)^2 = a^2 + 2ab + b^2$:

$$(3 + \sqrt{x - 9})^2 = 3^2 + 2 \cdot 3\sqrt{x - 9} + (\sqrt{x - 9})^2$$
$$= 9 + 6\sqrt{x - 9} + x - 9$$
$$= x + 6\sqrt{x - 9}$$

Now do Exercises 43–56

In Example 5 we multiply radicals that have different indices.

EXAMPLE 5

Multiplying radicals with different indices

Write each product as a single radical expression.

a) $\sqrt[3]{2} \cdot \sqrt[4]{2}$ **b)** $\sqrt[3]{2} \cdot \sqrt{3}$

Solution

a) $\sqrt[3]{2} \cdot \sqrt[4]{2} = 2^{1/3} \cdot 2^{1/4}$ Write in exponential notation.

$= 2^{7/12}$ Product rule for exponents: $\frac{1}{3} + \frac{1}{4} = \frac{7}{12}$

$= \sqrt[12]{2^7}$ Write in radical notation.

$= \sqrt[12]{128}$

b) $\sqrt[3]{2} \cdot \sqrt{3} = 2^{1/3} \cdot 3^{1/2}$ Write in exponential notation.

$= 2^{2/6} \cdot 3^{3/6}$ Write the exponents with the LCD of 6.

$= \sqrt[6]{2^2} \cdot \sqrt[6]{3^3}$ Write in radical notation.

$= \sqrt[6]{2^2 \cdot 3^3}$ Product rule for radicals

$= \sqrt[6]{108}$ $2^2 \cdot 3^3 = 4 \cdot 27 = 108$

Now do Exercises 57–64

Calculator Close-Up

Check that

$\sqrt[3]{2} \cdot \sqrt[4]{2} = \sqrt[12]{128}.$

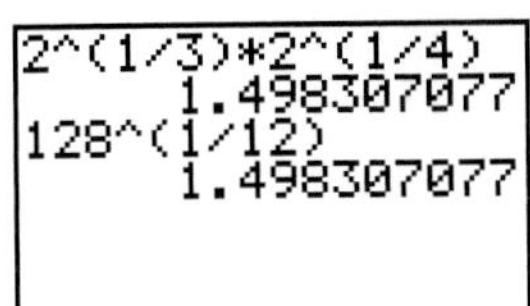

CAUTION Because the bases in $2^{1/3} \cdot 2^{1/4}$ are identical, we can add the exponents [Example 5(a)]. Because the bases in $2^{2/6} \cdot 3^{3/6}$ are not the same, we cannot add the exponents [Example 5(b)]. Instead, we write each factor as a sixth root and use the product rule for radicals.

Teaching Tip You might need to compare and contrast more examples with same bases and different bases. Try $3^{1/2} \cdot 3^{1/4}$ and $3^{1/2} \cdot 5^{1/4}$

Conjugates

Recall the special product rule $(a + b)(a - b) = a^2 - b^2$. The product of the sum $4 + \sqrt{3}$ and the difference $4 - \sqrt{3}$ can be found by using this rule:

$$(4 + \sqrt{3})(4 - \sqrt{3}) = 4^2 - (\sqrt{3})^2 = 16 - 3 = 13$$

The product of the irrational number $4 + \sqrt{3}$ and the irrational number $4 - \sqrt{3}$ is the rational number 13. For this reason the expressions $4 + \sqrt{3}$ and $4 - \sqrt{3}$ are called **conjugates** of one another. We will use conjugates in Section 9.4 to rationalize some denominators.

EXAMPLE 6

Multiplying conjugates

Find the products. Assume the variables represent positive real numbers.

a) $(2 + 3\sqrt{5})(2 - 3\sqrt{5})$

b) $(\sqrt{3} - \sqrt{2})(\sqrt{3} + \sqrt{2})$

c) $(\sqrt{2x} - \sqrt{y})(\sqrt{2x} + \sqrt{y})$

Solution

a) $(2 + 3\sqrt{5})(2 - 3\sqrt{5}) = 2^2 - (3\sqrt{5})^2$ $\quad (a + b)(a - b) = a^2 - b^2$

$= 4 - 45$ $\quad (3\sqrt{5})^2 = 9 \cdot 5 = 45$

$= -41$

b) $(\sqrt{3} - \sqrt{2})(\sqrt{3} + \sqrt{2}) = 3 - 2$

$= 1$

c) $(\sqrt{2x} - \sqrt{y})(\sqrt{2x} + \sqrt{y}) = 2x - y$

Now do Exercises 65–74

Warm-Ups

True or false? Explain your answer.

1. $\sqrt{3} + \sqrt{3} = \sqrt{6}$ False

2. $\sqrt{8} + \sqrt{2} = 3\sqrt{2}$ True

3. $2\sqrt{3} \cdot 3\sqrt{3} = 6\sqrt{3}$ False

4. $\sqrt[3]{2} \cdot \sqrt[3]{2} = 2$ False

5. $2\sqrt{5} \cdot 3\sqrt{2} = 6\sqrt{10}$ True

6. $2\sqrt{5} + 3\sqrt{5} = 5\sqrt{10}$ False

7. $\sqrt{2}(\sqrt{3} - \sqrt{2}) = \sqrt{6} - 2$ True

8. $\sqrt{12} = 2\sqrt{6}$ False

9. $(\sqrt{2} + \sqrt{3})^2 = 2 + 3$ False

10. $(\sqrt{3} - \sqrt{2})(\sqrt{3} + \sqrt{2}) = 1$ True

9.3 Exercises

Boost your GRADE at mathzone.com!

MathZone
- Practice Problems
- Self-Tests
- Videos
- Net Tutor
- e-Professors

Reading and Writing *After reading this section, write out the answers to these questions. Use complete sentences.*

1. What are like radicals?
Like radicals are radicals with the same index and the same radicand.

2. How do we combine like radicals?
Like radicals are combined using the distributive property just as we combine like terms.

3. Does the product rule allow multiplication of unlike radicals?
In the product rule the radicals must have the same index but do not have to have the same radicand.

4. How do we multiply radicals of different indices?
To multiply radicals of different indices, we convert them to equivalent radicals with the same index.

All variables in the following exercises represent positive numbers.

Simplify the sums and differences. Give exact answers. See Example 1.

5. $\sqrt{3} - 2\sqrt{3}$ $\quad -\sqrt{3}$

6. $\sqrt{5} - 3\sqrt{5}$ $\quad -2\sqrt{5}$

7. $5\sqrt{7x} + 4\sqrt{7x}$ $\quad 9\sqrt{7x}$

8. $3\sqrt{6a} + 7\sqrt{6a}$ $\quad 10\sqrt{6a}$

9. $2\sqrt[3]{2} + 3\sqrt[3]{2}$ $\quad 5\sqrt[3]{2}$

10. $\sqrt[3]{4} + 4\sqrt[3]{4}$ $\quad 5\sqrt[3]{4}$

11. $\sqrt{3} - \sqrt{5} + 3\sqrt{3} - \sqrt{5}$ $\quad 4\sqrt{3} - 2\sqrt{5}$

12. $\sqrt{2} - 5\sqrt{3} - 7\sqrt{2} + 9\sqrt{3}$ $\quad -6\sqrt{2} + 4\sqrt{3}$

13. $\sqrt[3]{2} + \sqrt[3]{x} - \sqrt[3]{2} + 4\sqrt[3]{x}$ $\quad 5\sqrt[3]{x}$

14. $\sqrt[3]{5y} - 4\sqrt[3]{5y} + \sqrt[3]{x} + \sqrt[3]{x}$ $\quad -3\sqrt[3]{5y} + 2\sqrt[3]{x}$

15. $\sqrt[3]{x} - \sqrt{2x} + \sqrt[3]{x}$ $\quad 2\sqrt[3]{x} - \sqrt{2x}$

16. $\sqrt[3]{ab} + \sqrt{a} + 5\sqrt{a} + \sqrt[3]{ab}$ $\quad 2\sqrt[3]{ab} + 6\sqrt{a}$

Simplify each expression. Give exact answers. See Example 2.

17. $\sqrt{8} + \sqrt{28}$ $\quad 2\sqrt{2} + 2\sqrt{7}$

18. $\sqrt{12} + \sqrt{24}$ $\quad 2\sqrt{3} + 2\sqrt{6}$

19. $\sqrt{8} + \sqrt{18}$ $\quad 5\sqrt{2}$

20. $\sqrt{12} + \sqrt{27}$ $\quad 5\sqrt{3}$

21. $2\sqrt{45} - 3\sqrt{20}$ $\quad 0$

22. $3\sqrt{50} - 2\sqrt{32}$ $\quad 7\sqrt{2}$

23. $\sqrt{2} - \sqrt{8}$ $\quad -\sqrt{2}$

24. $\sqrt{20} - \sqrt{125}$ $\quad -3\sqrt{5}$

25. $\sqrt{45x^3} - \sqrt{18x^2} + \sqrt{50x^2} - \sqrt{20x^3}$ $\quad x\sqrt{5x} + 2x\sqrt{2}$

26. $\sqrt{12x^5} - \sqrt{18x} - \sqrt{300x^5} + \sqrt{98x}$ $\quad 4\sqrt{2x} - 8x^2\sqrt{3x}$

27. $2\sqrt[3]{24} + \sqrt[3]{81}$ $\quad 7\sqrt[3]{3}$

28. $5\sqrt[3]{24} + 2\sqrt[3]{375}$ $\quad 20\sqrt[3]{3}$

29. $\sqrt[4]{48} - 2\sqrt[4]{243}$ $\quad -4\sqrt[4]{3}$

30. $\sqrt[5]{64} + 7\sqrt[5]{2}$ $\quad 9\sqrt[5]{2}$

31. $\sqrt[3]{54t^4y^3} - \sqrt[3]{16t^4y^3}$ $\quad ty\sqrt[3]{2t}$

32. $\sqrt[3]{2000w^2z^5} - \sqrt[3]{16w^2z^5}$ $\quad 8z\sqrt[3]{2w^2z^2}$

Simplify the products. Give exact answers. See Examples 3 and 4.

33. $\sqrt{3} \cdot \sqrt{5}$ $\quad \sqrt{15}$

34. $\sqrt{5} \cdot \sqrt{7}$ $\quad \sqrt{35}$

35. $2\sqrt{5} \cdot 3\sqrt{10}$ $\quad 30\sqrt{2}$

36. $(3\sqrt{2})(-4\sqrt{10})$ $\quad -24\sqrt{5}$

37. $2\sqrt{7a} \cdot 3\sqrt{2a}$ $\quad 6a\sqrt{14}$

38. $2\sqrt{5c} \cdot 5\sqrt{5}$ $\quad 50\sqrt{c}$

39. $\sqrt[4]{9} \cdot \sqrt[4]{27}$ $\quad 3\sqrt[4]{3}$

40. $\sqrt[3]{5} \cdot \sqrt[3]{100}$ $\quad 5\sqrt[3]{4}$

41. $(2\sqrt{3})^2$ $\quad 12$

42. $(-4\sqrt{2})^2$ $\quad 32$

43. $2\sqrt{3}(\sqrt{6} + 3\sqrt{3})$ $\quad 6\sqrt{2} + 18$

44. $2\sqrt{5}(\sqrt{3} + 3\sqrt{5})$ $\quad 2\sqrt{15} + 30$

45. $\sqrt{5}(\sqrt{10} - 2)$ $\quad 5\sqrt{2} - 2\sqrt{5}$

46. $\sqrt{6}(\sqrt{15} - 1)$ $\quad 3\sqrt{10} - \sqrt{6}$

47. $\sqrt[3]{3t}(\sqrt[3]{9t} - \sqrt[3]{t^2})$ $\quad 3\sqrt[3]{t^2} - t\sqrt[3]{3}$

48. $\sqrt[3]{2}(\sqrt[3]{12x} - \sqrt[3]{2x})$ $\quad 2\sqrt[3]{3x} - \sqrt[3]{4x}$

49. $(\sqrt{3} + 2)(\sqrt{3} - 5)$ $\quad -7 - 3\sqrt{3}$

50. $(\sqrt{5} + 2)(\sqrt{5} - 6)$ $\quad -7 - 4\sqrt{5}$

51. $(\sqrt{11} - 3)(\sqrt{11} + 3)$ $\quad 2$

52. $(\sqrt{2} + 5)(\sqrt{2} + 5)$ $\quad 27 + 10\sqrt{2}$

53. $(2\sqrt{5} - 7)(2\sqrt{5} + 4)$ $\quad -8 - 6\sqrt{5}$

54. $(2\sqrt{6} - 3)(2\sqrt{6} + 4)$ $\quad 12 + 2\sqrt{6}$

55. $(2\sqrt{3} - \sqrt{6})(\sqrt{3} + 2\sqrt{6})$ $\quad -6 + 9\sqrt{2}$

56. $(3\sqrt{3} - \sqrt{2})(\sqrt{2} + \sqrt{3})$ $\quad 7 + 2\sqrt{6}$

Write each product as a single radical expression. See Example 5.

57. $\sqrt[3]{3} \cdot \sqrt{3}$ $\quad \sqrt[6]{3^5}$

58. $\sqrt{3} \cdot \sqrt[4]{3}$ $\quad \sqrt[4]{27}$

59. $\sqrt[3]{5} \cdot \sqrt[4]{5}$ $\quad \sqrt[12]{5^7}$

60. $\sqrt[3]{2} \cdot \sqrt[5]{2}$ $\quad \sqrt[15]{2^8}$

61. $\sqrt[3]{2} \cdot \sqrt{5}$ $\quad \sqrt[6]{500}$

62. $\sqrt{6} \cdot \sqrt[3]{2}$ $\quad \sqrt[6]{864}$

63. $\sqrt[3]{2} \cdot \sqrt[4]{3}$ $\quad \sqrt[12]{432}$

64. $\sqrt[3]{3} \cdot \sqrt[4]{2}$ $\quad \sqrt[12]{648}$

Find the product of each pair of conjugates. See Example 6.

65. $(\sqrt{3} - 2)(\sqrt{3} + 2)$ $\quad -1$

66. $(7 - \sqrt{3})(7 + \sqrt{3})$ $\quad 46$

67. $(\sqrt{5} + \sqrt{2})(\sqrt{5} - \sqrt{2})$ $\quad 3$

68. $(\sqrt{6} + \sqrt{5})(\sqrt{6} - \sqrt{5})$ $\quad 1$

69. $(2\sqrt{5} + 1)(2\sqrt{5} - 1)$ $\quad 19$

70. $(3\sqrt{2} - 4)(3\sqrt{2} + 4)$ $\quad 2$

71. $(3\sqrt{2} + \sqrt{5})(3\sqrt{2} - \sqrt{5})$ 13

72. $(2\sqrt{3} - \sqrt{7})(2\sqrt{3} + \sqrt{7})$ 5

73. $(5 - 3\sqrt{x})(5 + 3\sqrt{x})$ $25 - 9x$

74. $(4\sqrt{y} + 3\sqrt{z})(4\sqrt{y} - 3\sqrt{z})$ $16y - 9z$

Simplify each expression.

75. $\sqrt{300} + \sqrt{3}$ $11\sqrt{3}$

76. $\sqrt{50} + \sqrt{2}$ $6\sqrt{2}$

77. $2\sqrt{5} \cdot 5\sqrt{6}$ $10\sqrt{30}$

78. $3\sqrt{6} \cdot 5\sqrt{10}$ $30\sqrt{15}$

79. $(3 + 2\sqrt{7})(\sqrt{7} - 2)$ $8 - \sqrt{7}$

80. $(2 + \sqrt{7})(\sqrt{7} - 2)$ 3

81. $4\sqrt{w} \cdot 4\sqrt{w}$ $16w$

82. $3\sqrt{m} \cdot 5\sqrt{m}$ $15m$

83. $\sqrt{3x^3} \cdot \sqrt{6x^2}$ $3x^2\sqrt{2x}$

84. $\sqrt{2t^5} \cdot \sqrt{10t^4}$ $2t^4\sqrt{5t}$

85. $(2\sqrt{5} + \sqrt{2})(3\sqrt{5} - \sqrt{2})$ $28 + \sqrt{10}$

86. $(3\sqrt{2} - \sqrt{3})(2\sqrt{2} + 3\sqrt{3})$ $3 + 7\sqrt{6}$

87. $\frac{\sqrt{2}}{3} + \frac{\sqrt{2}}{5}$ $\frac{8\sqrt{2}}{15}$

88. $\frac{\sqrt{2}}{4} + \frac{\sqrt{3}}{5}$ $\frac{5\sqrt{2} + 4\sqrt{3}}{20}$

89. $(5 + 2\sqrt{2})(5 - 2\sqrt{2})$ 17

90. $(3 - 2\sqrt{7})(3 + 2\sqrt{7})$ -19

91. $(3 + \sqrt{x})^2$ $9 + 6\sqrt{x} + x$

92. $(1 - \sqrt{x})^2$ $1 - 2\sqrt{x} + x$

93. $(5\sqrt{x} - 3)^2$ $25x - 30\sqrt{x} + 9$

94. $(3\sqrt{a} + 2)^2$ $9a + 12\sqrt{a} + 4$

95. $(1 + \sqrt{x + 2})^2$ $x + 3 + 2\sqrt{x + 2}$

96. $(\sqrt{x - 1} + 1)^2$ $x + 2\sqrt{x - 1}$

97. $\sqrt{4w} - \sqrt{9w}$ $-\sqrt{w}$

98. $10\sqrt{m} - \sqrt{16m}$ $6\sqrt{m}$

99. $2\sqrt{a^3} + 3\sqrt{a^3} - 2a\sqrt{4a}$ $a\sqrt{a}$

100. $5\sqrt{w^2y} - 7\sqrt{w^2y} + 6\sqrt{w^2y}$ $4w\sqrt{y}$

101. $\sqrt{x^5} + 2x\sqrt{x^3}$ $3x^2\sqrt{x}$

102. $\sqrt{8x^3} + \sqrt{50x^3} - x\sqrt{2x}$ $6x\sqrt{2x}$

103. $\sqrt[3]{-16x^4} + 5x\sqrt[3]{54x}$ $13x\sqrt[3]{2x}$

104. $\sqrt[3]{3x^5y^7} - \sqrt[3]{24x^5y^7}$ $-xy^2\sqrt[3]{3x^2y}$

105. $\sqrt[3]{2x} \cdot \sqrt{2x}$ $\sqrt[6]{32x^5}$

106. $\sqrt[3]{2m} \cdot \sqrt[4]{2n}$ $\sqrt[12]{128m^4n^3}$

In Exercises 107–110, solve each problem.

107. ***Area of a rectangle.*** Find the exact area of a rectangle that has a length of $\sqrt{6}$ feet and a width of $\sqrt{3}$ feet. $3\sqrt{2}$ square feet (ft^2)

108. ***Volume of a cube.*** Find the exact volume of a cube with sides of length $\sqrt{3}$ meters. $3\sqrt{3}$ cubic meters (m^3)

109. ***Area of a trapezoid.*** Find the exact area of a trapezoid with a height of $\sqrt{6}$ feet and bases of $\sqrt{3}$ feet and $\sqrt{12}$ feet. $\frac{9\sqrt{2}}{2}$ ft^2

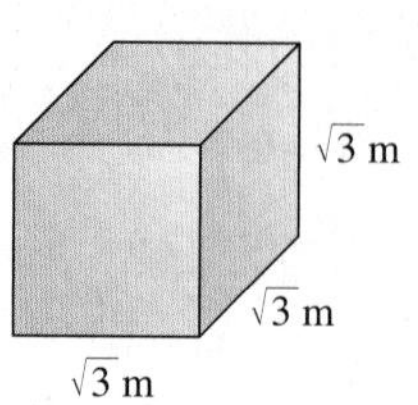

Figure for Exercise 108

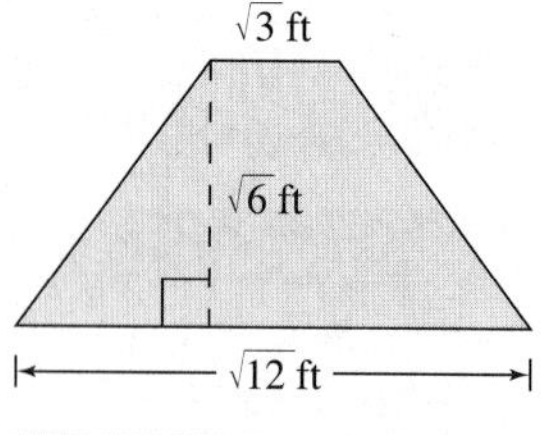

Figure for Exercise 109

110. ***Area of a triangle.*** Find the exact area of a triangle with a base of $\sqrt{30}$ meters and a height of $\sqrt{6}$ meters. $3\sqrt{5}$ square meters (m^2)

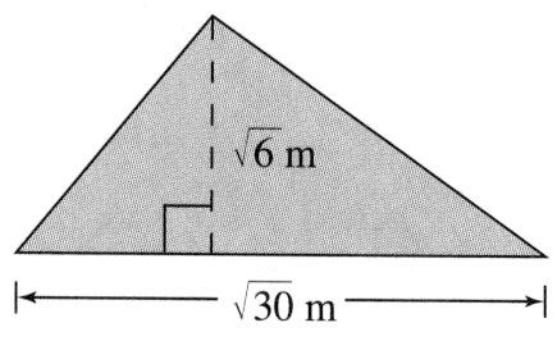

Figure for Exercise 110

Getting More Involved

111. ***Discussion***

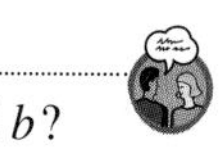

Is $\sqrt{a} + \sqrt{b} = \sqrt{a + b}$ for all values of a and b? No

112. ***Discussion***

Which of the following equations are identities? Explain your answers.

a) $\sqrt{9x} = 3\sqrt{x}$

b) $\sqrt{9 + x} = 3 + \sqrt{x}$

c) $\sqrt{x - 4} = \sqrt{x} - 2$

d) $\sqrt{\frac{x}{4}} = \frac{\sqrt{x}}{2}$ a and d

113. ***Exploration***

Because 3 is the square of $\sqrt{3}$, a binomial such as $y^2 - 3$ is a difference of two squares.

a) Factor $y^2 - 3$ and $2a^2 - 7$ using radicals.

b) Use factoring with radicals to solve the equation $x^2 - 8 = 0$.

c) Assuming a is a positive real number, solve the equation $x^2 - a = 0$.

a) $(y - \sqrt{3})(y + \sqrt{3})$, $(\sqrt{2}a - \sqrt{7})(\sqrt{2}a + \sqrt{7})$

b) $\{\pm 2\sqrt{2}\}$

c) $\{\pm\sqrt{a}\}$

9.4 Quotients, Powers, and Rationalizing Denominators

In this Section

In this section we will continue studying operations with radicals. We will first learn how to rationalize denominators, then we will find quotients and powers with radicals.

Rationalizing the Denominator

Square roots such as $\sqrt{2}$, $\sqrt{3}$, and $\sqrt{5}$ are irrational numbers. If roots of this type appear in the denominator of a fraction, it is customary to rewrite the fraction with a rational number in the denominator, or **rationalize** it. We rationalize a denominator by multiplying both the numerator and denominator by another radical that makes the denominator rational.

You can find products of radicals in two ways. By definition, $\sqrt{2}$ is the positive number that you multiply by itself to get 2. So

$$\sqrt{2} \cdot \sqrt{2} = 2.$$

By the product rule, $\sqrt{2} \cdot \sqrt{2} = \sqrt{4} = 2$. Note that $\sqrt[3]{2} \cdot \sqrt[3]{2} = \sqrt[3]{4}$ by the product rule, but $\sqrt[3]{4} \neq 2$. By definition of a cube root,

$$\sqrt[3]{2} \cdot \sqrt[3]{2} \cdot \sqrt[3]{2} = 2.$$

EXAMPLE 1

Rationalizing the denominator

Rewrite each expression with a rational denominator.

a) $\dfrac{\sqrt{3}}{\sqrt{5}}$ **b)** $\dfrac{3}{\sqrt[3]{2}}$

Helpful Hint

If you are going to compute the value of a radical expression with a calculator, it does not matter if the denominator is rational. However, rationalizing the denominator provides another opportunity to practice building up the denominator of a fraction and multiplying radicals.

Solution

a) Because $\sqrt{5} \cdot \sqrt{5} = 5$, multiplying both the numerator and denominator by $\sqrt{5}$ will rationalize the denominator:

$$\frac{\sqrt{3}}{\sqrt{5}} = \frac{\sqrt{3}}{\sqrt{5}} \cdot \frac{\sqrt{5}}{\sqrt{5}} = \frac{\sqrt{15}}{5} \quad \text{By the product rule, } \sqrt{3} \cdot \sqrt{5} = \sqrt{15}.$$

b) We must build up the denominator to be the cube root of a perfect cube. So we multiply by $\sqrt[3]{4}$ to get $\sqrt[3]{4} \cdot \sqrt[3]{2} = \sqrt[3]{8}$:

$$\frac{3}{\sqrt[3]{2}} = \frac{3}{\sqrt[3]{2}} \cdot \frac{\sqrt[3]{4}}{\sqrt[3]{4}} = \frac{3\sqrt[3]{4}}{\sqrt[3]{8}} = \frac{3\sqrt[3]{4}}{2}$$

Now do Exercises 1–8

CAUTION To rationalize a denominator with a single square root, you simply multiply by that square root. If the denominator has a cube root, you build the denominator to a cube root of a perfect cube, as in Example 1(b). For a fourth root you build to a fourth root of a perfect fourth power, and so on.

Simplifying Radicals

When simplifying a radical expression, we have three specific conditions to satisfy. First, we use the product rule to factor out perfect nth powers from the radicand in nth roots. That is, we factor out perfect squares in square roots, perfect cubes in cube roots, and so on. For example,

$$\sqrt{72} = \sqrt{36} \cdot \sqrt{2} = 6\sqrt{2} \qquad \text{and} \qquad \sqrt[3]{24} = \sqrt[3]{8} \cdot \sqrt[3]{3} = 2\sqrt[3]{3}.$$

Second, we use the quotient rule to remove all fractions from inside a radical. For example,

$$\sqrt{\frac{2}{3}} = \frac{\sqrt{2}}{\sqrt{3}}.$$

Teaching Tip Some teachers feel that rationalizing the denominator is not essential. However, it does reinforce many other rules. Some students learn for the first time here that $\sqrt{2} \cdot \sqrt{2} = 2$ and skip the $\sqrt{4}$ step.

Third, we remove radicals from denominators by rationalizing the denominator:

$$\sqrt{\frac{2}{3}} = \frac{\sqrt{2} \cdot \sqrt{3}}{\sqrt{3} \cdot \sqrt{3}} = \frac{\sqrt{6}}{3}$$

A radical expression that satisfies the three conditions is in *simplified radical form.*

Simplified Radical Form for Radicals of Index *n*

A radical expression of index n is in **simplified radical form** if it has

1. *no* perfect nth powers as factors of the radicand,
2. *no* fractions inside the radical, and
3. *no* radicals in the denominator.

EXAMPLE 2

Writing radical expressions in simplified radical form

Simplify.

a) $\dfrac{\sqrt{10}}{\sqrt{6}}$ **b)** $\sqrt[3]{\dfrac{5}{9}}$

Solution

a) To rationalize the denominator, multiply the numerator and denominator by $\sqrt{6}$:

$$\frac{\sqrt{10}}{\sqrt{6}} = \frac{\sqrt{10}}{\sqrt{6}} \cdot \frac{\sqrt{6}}{\sqrt{6}} \qquad \text{Rationalize the denominator.}$$

$$= \frac{\sqrt{60}}{6}$$

$$= \frac{\sqrt{4}\sqrt{15}}{6} \qquad \text{Remove the perfect square from } \sqrt{60}.$$

$$= \frac{2\sqrt{15}}{6}$$

$$= \frac{\sqrt{15}}{3} \qquad \text{Reduce } \tfrac{2}{6} \text{ to } \tfrac{1}{3}. \text{ Note that } \sqrt{15} \div 3 \neq \sqrt{5}.$$

b) To rationalize the denominator, build up the denominator to a cube root of a perfect cube. Because $\sqrt[3]{9} \cdot \sqrt[3]{3} = \sqrt[3]{27} = 3$, we multiply by $\sqrt[3]{3}$:

$$\sqrt[3]{\frac{5}{9}} = \frac{\sqrt[3]{5}}{\sqrt[3]{9}} \quad \text{Quotient rule for radicals}$$

$$= \frac{\sqrt[3]{5}}{\sqrt[3]{9}} \cdot \frac{\sqrt[3]{3}}{\sqrt[3]{3}} \quad \text{Rationalize the denominator.}$$

$$= \frac{\sqrt[3]{15}}{\sqrt[3]{27}}$$

$$= \frac{\sqrt[3]{15}}{3}$$

Now do Exercises 9–18

EXAMPLE 3

Rationalizing the denominator with variables

Simplify each expression. Assume all variables represent positive real numbers.

a) $\sqrt{\frac{a}{b}}$ **b)** $\sqrt{\frac{x^3}{y^5}}$ **c)** $\sqrt[3]{\frac{x}{y}}$

Study Tip

Write about what you read in the text. Sum things up in your own words. Write out important facts on note cards. When you have a few spare minutes in between classes review your note cards. Try to memorize all the information on the cards.

Solution

a) $$\sqrt{\frac{a}{b}} = \frac{\sqrt{a}}{\sqrt{b}} \quad \text{Quotient rule for radicals}$$

$$= \frac{\sqrt{a} \cdot \sqrt{b}}{\sqrt{b} \cdot \sqrt{b}} \quad \text{Rationalize the denominator.}$$

$$= \frac{\sqrt{ab}}{b}$$

b) $$\sqrt{\frac{x^3}{y^5}} = \frac{\sqrt{x^3}}{\sqrt{y^5}} \quad \text{Quotient rule for radicals}$$

$$= \frac{\sqrt{x^2} \cdot \sqrt{x}}{\sqrt{y^4} \cdot \sqrt{y}} \quad \text{Product rule for radicals}$$

$$= \frac{x\sqrt{x}}{y^2\sqrt{y}} \quad \text{Simplify.}$$

$$= \frac{x\sqrt{x} \cdot \sqrt{y}}{y^2\sqrt{y} \cdot \sqrt{y}} \quad \text{Rationalize the denominator.}$$

$$= \frac{x\sqrt{xy}}{y^2 \cdot y} = \frac{x\sqrt{xy}}{y^3}$$

c) Multiply by $\sqrt[3]{y^2}$ to rationalize the denominator:

$$\sqrt[3]{\frac{x}{y}} = \frac{\sqrt[3]{x}}{\sqrt[3]{y}} = \frac{\sqrt[3]{x}}{\sqrt[3]{y}} \cdot \frac{\sqrt[3]{y^2}}{\sqrt[3]{y^2}} = \frac{\sqrt[3]{xy^2}}{\sqrt[3]{y^3}} = \frac{\sqrt[3]{xy^2}}{y}$$

Now do Exercises 19–28

Dividing Radicals

In Section 9.3 you learned how to add, subtract, and multiply radical expressions. To divide two radical expressions, simply write the quotient as a ratio and then simplify. In general, we have

$$\sqrt[n]{a} \div \sqrt[n]{b} = \frac{\sqrt[n]{a}}{\sqrt[n]{b}} = \sqrt[n]{\frac{a}{b}},$$

provided that all expressions represent real numbers. Note that the quotient rule is applied only to radicals that have the same index.

EXAMPLE 4

Dividing radicals with the same index

Divide and simplify. Assume the variables represent positive numbers.

a) $\sqrt{10} \div \sqrt{5}$ **b)** $(3\sqrt{2}) \div (2\sqrt{3})$ **c)** $\sqrt[3]{10x^2} \div \sqrt[3]{5x}$

Solution

a) $\sqrt{10} \div \sqrt{5} = \frac{\sqrt{10}}{\sqrt{5}}$ $\quad a \div b = \frac{a}{b}$, provided that $b \neq 0$.

$= \sqrt{\frac{10}{5}}$ Quotient rule for radicals

$= \sqrt{2}$ Reduce.

b) $(3\sqrt{2}) \div (2\sqrt{3}) = \frac{3\sqrt{2}}{2\sqrt{3}}$

$= \frac{3\sqrt{2}}{2\sqrt{3}} \cdot \frac{\sqrt{3}}{\sqrt{3}}$ Rationalize the denominator.

$= \frac{3\sqrt{6}}{2 \cdot 3}$

$= \frac{\sqrt{6}}{2}$ Note that $\sqrt{6} \div 2 \neq \sqrt{3}$.

c) $\sqrt[3]{10x^2} \div \sqrt[3]{5x} = \frac{\sqrt[3]{10x^2}}{\sqrt[3]{5x}}$

$= \sqrt[3]{\frac{10x^2}{5x}}$ Quotient rule for radicals

$= \sqrt[3]{2x}$ Reduce.

Now do Exercises 29–36

Note that in Example 4(a) we applied the quotient rule to get $\sqrt{10} \div \sqrt{5} = \sqrt{2}$. In Example 4(b) we did not use the quotient rule because 2 is not evenly divisible by 3. Instead, we rationalized the denominator to get the result in simplified form.

When working with radicals it is usually best to write them in simplified radical form before doing any operations with the radicals.

EXAMPLE 5

Simplifying before dividing

Divide and simplify. Assume the variables represent positive numbers.

a) $\sqrt{12} \div \sqrt{72x}$ **b)** $\sqrt[4]{16a} \div \sqrt[4]{a^5}$

Solution

a) $\sqrt{12} \div \sqrt{72x} = \dfrac{\sqrt{4} \cdot \sqrt{3}}{\sqrt{36} \cdot \sqrt{2x}}$ Factor out perfect squares.

$= \dfrac{2\sqrt{3}}{6\sqrt{2x}}$ Simplify.

$= \dfrac{\sqrt{3} \cdot \sqrt{2x}}{3\sqrt{2x} \cdot \sqrt{2x}}$ Reduce $\frac{2}{6}$ to $\frac{1}{3}$ and rationalize.

$= \dfrac{\sqrt{6x}}{6x}$ Multiply the radicals.

b) $\sqrt[4]{16a} \div \sqrt[4]{a^5} = \dfrac{\sqrt[4]{16} \cdot \sqrt[4]{a}}{\sqrt[4]{a^4} \cdot \sqrt[4]{a}}$ Factor out perfect fourth powers.

$= \dfrac{\sqrt[4]{16}}{\sqrt[4]{a^4}}$ Reduce.

$= \dfrac{2}{a}$ Simplify the radicals.

Now do Exercises 37–44

Teaching Tip These problems can be solved in many ways. It is good to try other methods.

In Chapter 10 it will be necessary to simplify expressions of the type found in Example 6.

EXAMPLE 6

Simplifying radical expressions

Simplify.

a) $\dfrac{4 - \sqrt{12}}{4}$ **b)** $\dfrac{-6 + \sqrt{20}}{-2}$

Solution

a) First write $\sqrt{12}$ in simplified form. Then simplify the expression.

$\dfrac{4 - \sqrt{12}}{4} = \dfrac{4 - 2\sqrt{3}}{4}$ Simplify $\sqrt{12}$.

$= \dfrac{2(2 - \sqrt{3})}{2 \cdot 2}$ Factor.

$= \dfrac{2 - \sqrt{3}}{2}$ Divide out the common factor.

b) $\dfrac{-6 + \sqrt{20}}{-2} = \dfrac{-6 + 2\sqrt{5}}{-2}$

$= \dfrac{-2(3 - \sqrt{5})}{-2}$

$= 3 - \sqrt{5}$

Now do Exercises 45–48

Helpful Hint

The expressions in Example 6 are the types of expressions that you must simplify when learning the quadratic formula in Chapter 10.

CAUTION To simplify the expressions in Example 6, you must simplify the radical, factor the numerator, and then divide out the common factors. You cannot simply "cancel" the 4's in $\frac{4 - \sqrt{12}}{4}$ or the 2's in $\frac{2 - \sqrt{3}}{2}$ because they are not common factors.

Rationalizing Denominators Using Conjugates

A simplified expression involving radicals does not have radicals in the denominator. If an expression such as $4 - \sqrt{3}$ appears in a denominator, we can multiply both the numerator and denominator by its conjugate $4 + \sqrt{3}$ to get a rational number in the denominator.

EXAMPLE 7

Rationalizing the denominator using conjugates

Write in simplified form.

a) $\dfrac{2 + \sqrt{3}}{4 - \sqrt{3}}$ **b)** $\dfrac{\sqrt{5}}{\sqrt{6} + \sqrt{2}}$

Solution

a) $\dfrac{2 + \sqrt{3}}{4 - \sqrt{3}} = \dfrac{(2 + \sqrt{3})(4 + \sqrt{3})}{(4 - \sqrt{3})(4 + \sqrt{3})}$ Multiply the numerator and denominator by $4 + \sqrt{3}$.

$= \dfrac{8 + 6\sqrt{3} + 3}{13}$ $(4 - \sqrt{3})(4 + \sqrt{3}) = 16 - 3 = 13$

$= \dfrac{11 + 6\sqrt{3}}{13}$ Simplify.

b) $\dfrac{\sqrt{5}}{\sqrt{6} + \sqrt{2}} = \dfrac{\sqrt{5}(\sqrt{6} - \sqrt{2})}{(\sqrt{6} + \sqrt{2})(\sqrt{6} - \sqrt{2})}$ Multiply the numerator and denominator by $\sqrt{6} - \sqrt{2}$.

$= \dfrac{\sqrt{30} - \sqrt{10}}{4}$ $(\sqrt{6} + \sqrt{2})(\sqrt{6} - \sqrt{2}) = 6 - 2 = 4$

Now do Exercises 49–58

Study Tip

Read the text and recite to yourself what you have read. Ask questions and answer them out loud. Listen to your answers to see if they are complete and correct. Would other students understand your answers?

Powers of Radical Expressions

In Example 8 we use the power of a product rule $[(ab)^n = a^n b^n]$ and the power of a power rule $[(a^m)^n = a^{mn}]$ with radical expressions. We also use the fact that a root and a power can be found in either order. That is, $(\sqrt[n]{a})^m = \sqrt[n]{a^m}$.

EXAMPLE 8

Finding powers of rational expressions

Simplify. Assume the variables represent positive numbers.

a) $(5\sqrt{2})^3$ **b)** $(2\sqrt{x^3})^4$ **c)** $(3w\sqrt[3]{2w})^3$ **d)** $(2t\sqrt[4]{3t})^3$

Solution

a) $(5\sqrt{2})^3 = 5^3(\sqrt{2})^3$ Power of a product rule

$= 125\sqrt{8}$ $(\sqrt{2})^3 = \sqrt{2^3} = \sqrt{8}$

$= 125 \cdot 2\sqrt{2}$ $\sqrt{8} = \sqrt{4}\sqrt{2} = 2\sqrt{2}$

$= 250\sqrt{2}$

b) $(2\sqrt{x^3})^4 = 2^4(\sqrt{x^3})^4$ Power of a product rule

$= 2^4\sqrt{(x^3)^4}$ $(\sqrt[n]{a})^m = \sqrt[n]{a^m}$

$= 16\sqrt{x^{12}}$ $(a^m)^n = a^{mn}$

$= 16x^6$

c) $(3w\sqrt[3]{2w})^3 = 3^3w^3(\sqrt[3]{2w})^3$

$= 27w^3(2w)$

$= 54w^4$

d) $(2t\sqrt[4]{3t})^3 = 2^3t^3(\sqrt[4]{3t})^3 = 8t^3\sqrt[4]{27t^3}$

Now do Exercises 59–70

Warm-Ups ▼

True or false? Explain your answer.

1. $\frac{\sqrt{6}}{\sqrt{2}} = \sqrt{3}$ True

2. $\frac{2}{\sqrt{2}} = \sqrt{2}$ True

3. $\frac{4 - \sqrt{10}}{2} = 2 - \sqrt{10}$ False

4. $\frac{1}{\sqrt{3}} = \frac{\sqrt{3}}{3}$ True

5. $\frac{8\sqrt{7}}{2\sqrt{7}} = 4\sqrt{7}$ False

6. $\frac{2(2 + \sqrt{3})}{(2 - \sqrt{3})(2 + \sqrt{3})} = 4 + 2\sqrt{3}$ True

7. $\frac{\sqrt{12}}{3} = \sqrt{4}$ False

8. $\frac{\sqrt{20}}{\sqrt{5}} = 2$ True

9. $(2\sqrt{4})^2 = 16$ True

10. $(3\sqrt{5})^3 = 27\sqrt{125}$ True

9.4 Exercises

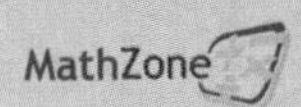

Boost your GRADE at mathzone.com!

MathZone

- Practice Problems
- Self-Tests
- Videos
- Net Tutor
- e-Professors

All variables in the following exercises represent positive numbers.

Rewrite each expression with a rational denominator. See Example 1.

1. $\frac{2}{\sqrt{5}}$ $\frac{2\sqrt{5}}{5}$

2. $\frac{5}{\sqrt{3}}$ $\frac{5\sqrt{3}}{3}$

3. $\frac{\sqrt{3}}{\sqrt{7}}$ $\frac{\sqrt{21}}{7}$

4. $\frac{\sqrt{6}}{\sqrt{5}}$ $\frac{\sqrt{30}}{5}$

5. $\frac{1}{\sqrt[3]{4}}$ $\frac{\sqrt[3]{2}}{2}$

6. $\frac{7}{\sqrt[3]{3}}$ $\frac{7\sqrt[3]{9}}{3}$

7. $\frac{\sqrt[3]{6}}{\sqrt[3]{5}}$ $\frac{\sqrt[3]{150}}{5}$

8. $\frac{\sqrt[4]{2}}{\sqrt[4]{27}}$ $\frac{\sqrt[4]{6}}{3}$

Write each radical expression in simplified radical form. See Example 2.

9. $\frac{\sqrt{5}}{\sqrt{12}}$ $\frac{\sqrt{15}}{6}$

10. $\frac{\sqrt{7}}{\sqrt{18}}$ $\frac{\sqrt{14}}{6}$

11. $\frac{\sqrt{3}}{\sqrt{12}}$ $\frac{1}{2}$

12. $\frac{\sqrt{2}}{\sqrt{18}}$ $\frac{1}{3}$

13. $\sqrt{\frac{1}{2}}$ $\frac{\sqrt{2}}{2}$

14. $\sqrt{\frac{3}{8}}$ $\frac{\sqrt{6}}{4}$

15. $\sqrt[3]{\frac{2}{3}}$ $\frac{\sqrt[3]{18}}{3}$

16. $\sqrt[3]{\frac{3}{5}}$ $\frac{\sqrt[3]{75}}{5}$

17. $\sqrt[3]{\frac{7}{4}}$ $\frac{\sqrt[3]{14}}{2}$

18. $\sqrt[4]{\frac{1}{5}}$ $\frac{\sqrt[4]{125}}{5}$

Simplify. See Example 3.

19. $\sqrt{\frac{x}{y}}$ $\frac{\sqrt{xy}}{y}$

20. $\sqrt{\frac{x^2}{a}}$ $\frac{x\sqrt{a}}{a}$

21. $\sqrt{\frac{a^3}{b^7}}$ $\frac{a\sqrt{ab}}{b^4}$

22. $\sqrt{\frac{w^5}{y^3}}$ $\frac{w^2\sqrt{wy}}{y^2}$

23. $\sqrt{\frac{a}{3b}}$ $\frac{\sqrt{3ab}}{3b}$

24. $\sqrt{\frac{5x}{2y}}$ $\frac{\sqrt{10xy}}{2y}$

25. $\sqrt[3]{\frac{a}{b}}$ $\frac{\sqrt[3]{ab^2}}{b}$

26. $\sqrt[3]{\frac{4a}{b}}$ $\frac{\sqrt[3]{4ab^2}}{b}$

27. $\sqrt[3]{\frac{5}{2b^2}}$ $\frac{\sqrt[3]{20b}}{2b}$

28. $\sqrt[3]{\frac{3}{4a^2}}$ $\frac{\sqrt[3]{6a}}{2a}$

Divide and simplify. See Examples 4 and 5.

29. $\sqrt{15} \div \sqrt{5}$ $\sqrt{3}$

30. $\sqrt{14} \div \sqrt{7}$ $\sqrt{2}$

31. $\sqrt{3} \div \sqrt{5}$ $\frac{\sqrt{15}}{5}$

32. $\sqrt{5} \div \sqrt{7}$ $\frac{\sqrt{35}}{7}$

33. $(3\sqrt{3}) \div (5\sqrt{6})$ $\frac{3\sqrt{2}}{10}$

34. $(2\sqrt{2}) \div (4\sqrt{10})$ $\frac{\sqrt{5}}{10}$

35. $(2\sqrt{3}) \div (3\sqrt{6})$ $\frac{\sqrt{2}}{3}$

36. $(5\sqrt{12}) \div (4\sqrt{6})$ $\frac{5\sqrt{2}}{4}$

37. $\sqrt{24a^2} \div \sqrt{72a}$ $\frac{\sqrt{3a}}{3}$

38. $\sqrt{32x^3} \div \sqrt{48x^2}$ $\frac{\sqrt{6x}}{3}$

39. $\sqrt[3]{20} \div \sqrt[3]{2}$ $\sqrt[3]{10}$

40. $\sqrt[3]{8x^7} \div \sqrt[3]{2x}$ $x^2\sqrt[3]{4}$

41. $\sqrt[4]{48} \div \sqrt[4]{3}$ 2

42. $\sqrt[4]{4a^{10}} \div \sqrt[4]{2a^2}$ $a^2\sqrt[4]{2}$

43. $\sqrt[4]{16w} \div \sqrt[4]{w^5}$ $\frac{2}{w}$

44. $\sqrt[4]{81b^5} \div \sqrt[4]{b}$ $3b$

Simplify. See Example 6.

45. $\frac{6 + \sqrt{45}}{3}$ $2 + \sqrt{5}$

46. $\frac{10 + \sqrt{50}}{5}$ $2 + \sqrt{2}$

47. $\frac{-2 + \sqrt{12}}{-2}$ $1 - \sqrt{3}$

48. $\frac{-6 + \sqrt{72}}{-6}$ $1 - \sqrt{2}$

Simplify each expression by rationalizing the denominator. See Example 7.

49. $\frac{4}{2 + \sqrt{8}}$ $2\sqrt{2} - 2$

50. $\frac{6}{3 - \sqrt{18}}$ $-2 - 2\sqrt{2}$

51. $\frac{3}{\sqrt{11} - \sqrt{5}}$ $\frac{\sqrt{11} + \sqrt{5}}{2}$

52. $\frac{6}{\sqrt{5} - \sqrt{14}}$ $\frac{-2\sqrt{5} - 2\sqrt{14}}{3}$

53. $\frac{1 + \sqrt{2}}{\sqrt{3} - 1}$ $\frac{1 + \sqrt{6} + \sqrt{2} + \sqrt{3}}{2}$

54. $\frac{2 - \sqrt{3}}{\sqrt{2} + \sqrt{6}}$ $\frac{3\sqrt{6} - 5\sqrt{2}}{4}$

55. $\frac{\sqrt{2}}{\sqrt{6} + \sqrt{3}}$ $\frac{2\sqrt{3} - \sqrt{6}}{3}$

56. $\frac{5}{\sqrt{7} - \sqrt{5}}$ $\frac{5\sqrt{7} + 5\sqrt{5}}{2}$

57. $\frac{2\sqrt{3}}{3\sqrt{2} - \sqrt{5}}$ $\frac{6\sqrt{6} + 2\sqrt{15}}{13}$

58. $\frac{3\sqrt{5}}{5\sqrt{2} + \sqrt{6}}$ $\frac{15\sqrt{10} - 3\sqrt{30}}{44}$

Simplify. See Example 8.

59. $(2\sqrt{2})^5$ $128\sqrt{2}$

60. $(3\sqrt{3})^4$ 729

61. $(\sqrt{x})^5$ $x^2\sqrt{x}$

62. $(2\sqrt{y})^3$ $8y\sqrt{y}$

63. $(-3\sqrt{x^3})^3$ $-27x^4\sqrt{x}$

64. $(-2\sqrt{x^3})^4$ $16x^6$

65. $(2x\sqrt[3]{x^2})^3$ $8x^5$

66. $(2y\sqrt[3]{4y})^3$ $32y^4$

67. $(-2\sqrt[3]{5})^2$ $4\sqrt[3]{25}$

68. $(-3\sqrt[3]{4})^2$ $18\sqrt[3]{2}$

69. $(\sqrt[3]{x^2})^6$ x^4

70. $(2\sqrt[4]{y^3})^3$ $8y^2\sqrt[4]{y}$

Simplify.

71. $\frac{\sqrt{3}}{\sqrt{2}} + \frac{2}{\sqrt{2}}$ $\frac{\sqrt{6} + 2\sqrt{2}}{2}$

72. $\frac{2}{\sqrt{7}} + \frac{5}{\sqrt{7}}$ $\sqrt{7}$

73. $\dfrac{\sqrt{3}}{\sqrt{2}} + \dfrac{3\sqrt{6}}{2}$

$2\sqrt{6}$

74. $\dfrac{\sqrt{3}}{2\sqrt{2}} + \dfrac{\sqrt{5}}{3\sqrt{2}}$

$\dfrac{3\sqrt{6} + 2\sqrt{10}}{12}$

75. $\dfrac{\sqrt{6}}{2} \cdot \dfrac{1}{\sqrt{3}}$

$\dfrac{\sqrt{2}}{2}$

76. $\dfrac{\sqrt{6}}{\sqrt{7}} \cdot \dfrac{\sqrt{14}}{\sqrt{3}}$

2

77. $(2\sqrt{w}) \div (3\sqrt{w})$

$\dfrac{2}{3}$

78. $2 \div (3\sqrt{a})$

$\dfrac{2\sqrt{a}}{3a}$

79. $\dfrac{8 - \sqrt{32}}{20}$

$\dfrac{2 - \sqrt{2}}{5}$

80. $\dfrac{4 - \sqrt{28}}{6}$

$\dfrac{2 - \sqrt{7}}{3}$

81. $\dfrac{5 + \sqrt{75}}{10}$

$\dfrac{1 + \sqrt{3}}{2}$

82. $\dfrac{3 + \sqrt{18}}{6}$

$\dfrac{1 + \sqrt{2}}{2}$

83. $\sqrt{a}(\sqrt{a} - 3)$

$a - 3\sqrt{a}$

84. $3\sqrt{m}(2\sqrt{m} - 6)$

$6m - 18\sqrt{m}$

85. $4\sqrt{a}(a + \sqrt{a})$

$4a\sqrt{a} + 4a$

86. $\sqrt{3ab}(\sqrt{3a} + \sqrt{3})$

$3a\sqrt{b} + 3\sqrt{ab}$

87. $(2\sqrt{3m})^2$

$12m$

88. $(-3\sqrt{4y})^2$

$36y$

89. $(-2\sqrt{xy^2z})^2$

$4xy^2z$

90. $(5a\sqrt{ab})^2$

$25a^3b$

91. $\sqrt[3]{m}(\sqrt[3]{m^2} - \sqrt[3]{m^5})$

$m - m^2$

92. $\sqrt[4]{w}(\sqrt[4]{w^3} - \sqrt[4]{w^7})$

$w - w^2$

93. $\sqrt[3]{8x^4} + \sqrt[3]{27x^4}$

$5x\sqrt[3]{x}$

94. $\sqrt[3]{16a^4} + a\sqrt[3]{2a}$

$3a\sqrt[3]{2a}$

95. $(2m\sqrt[4]{2m^2})^3$

$8m^4\sqrt[4]{8m^2}$

96. $(-2t\sqrt[6]{2t^2})^5$

$-32t^6\sqrt[6]{32t^4}$

97. $\dfrac{x - 9}{\sqrt{x} - 3}$ $\quad\sqrt{x} + 3$

98. $\dfrac{x - y}{\sqrt{x} - \sqrt{y}}$ $\quad\sqrt{x} + \sqrt{y}$

99. $\dfrac{3\sqrt{k}}{\sqrt{k} + \sqrt{7}}$ $\quad\dfrac{3k - 3\sqrt{7k}}{k - 7}$

100. $\dfrac{\sqrt{hk}}{\sqrt{h} + 3\sqrt{k}}$ $\quad\dfrac{h\sqrt{k} - 3k\sqrt{h}}{h - 9k}$

101. $\dfrac{5}{\sqrt{2} - 1} + \dfrac{3}{\sqrt{2} + 1}$ $\quad 2 + 8\sqrt{2}$

102. $\dfrac{\sqrt{3}}{\sqrt{6} - 1} - \dfrac{\sqrt{3}}{\sqrt{6} + 1}$ $\quad\dfrac{2\sqrt{3}}{5}$

103. $\dfrac{1}{\sqrt{2}} + \dfrac{1}{\sqrt{3}}$ $\quad\dfrac{3\sqrt{2} + 2\sqrt{3}}{6}$

104. $\dfrac{4}{2\sqrt{3}} + \dfrac{1}{\sqrt{5}}$ $\quad\dfrac{10\sqrt{3} + 3\sqrt{5}}{15}$

105. $\dfrac{3}{\sqrt{2} - 1} + \dfrac{4}{\sqrt{2} + 1}$ $\quad 7\sqrt{2} - 1$

106. $\dfrac{3}{\sqrt{5} - \sqrt{3}} - \dfrac{2}{\sqrt{5} + \sqrt{3}}$ $\quad\dfrac{\sqrt{5} + 5\sqrt{3}}{2}$

107. $\dfrac{\sqrt{x}}{\sqrt{x} + 2} + \dfrac{3\sqrt{x}}{\sqrt{x} - 2}$ $\quad\dfrac{4x + 4\sqrt{x}}{x - 4}$

108. $\dfrac{\sqrt{5}}{3 - \sqrt{y}} - \dfrac{\sqrt{5y}}{3 + \sqrt{y}}$ $\quad\dfrac{3\sqrt{5} + y\sqrt{5} - 2\sqrt{5y}}{9 - y}$

109. $\dfrac{1}{\sqrt{x}} + \dfrac{1}{1 - \sqrt{x}}$ $\quad\dfrac{x + \sqrt{x}}{x(1 - x)}$

110. $\dfrac{\sqrt{x}}{\sqrt{x} - 3} + \dfrac{5}{\sqrt{x}}$ $\quad\dfrac{x^2 + 8x\sqrt{x} - 45\sqrt{x}}{x(x - 9)}$

Getting More Involved

111. ***Exploration***

A polynomial is prime if it cannot be factored by using integers, but many prime polynomials can be factored if we use radicals.

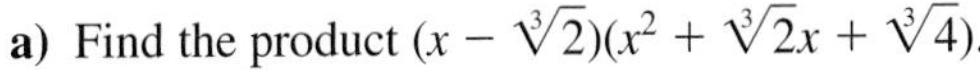

a) Find the product $(x - \sqrt[3]{2})(x^2 + \sqrt[3]{2}x + \sqrt[3]{4})$.

b) Factor $x^3 + 5$ using radicals.

c) Find the product

$$(\sqrt[3]{5} - \sqrt[3]{2})(\sqrt[3]{25} + \sqrt[3]{10} + \sqrt[3]{4}).$$

d) Use radicals to factor $a + b$ as a sum of two cubes and $a - b$ as a difference of two cubes.

a) $x^3 - 2$
b) $(x + \sqrt[3]{5})(x^2 - \sqrt[3]{5}x + \sqrt[3]{25})$
c) 3
d) $(\sqrt[3]{a} + \sqrt[3]{b})(\sqrt[3]{a^2} - \sqrt[3]{ab} + \sqrt[3]{b^2})$, $(\sqrt[3]{a} - \sqrt[3]{b})(\sqrt[3]{a^2} + \sqrt[3]{ab} + \sqrt[3]{b^2})$

112. ***Discussion***

Which one of the following expressions is not equivalent to the others?

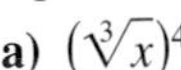

a) $(\sqrt[3]{x})^4$ **b)** $\sqrt[4]{x^3}$ **c)** $\sqrt[3]{x^4}$

d) $x^{4/3}$ **e)** $(x^{1/3})^4$

b

9.5 Solving Equations with Radicals and Exponents

In this Section

- **The Odd-Root Property**
- **The Even-Root Property**
- **Equations Involving Radicals**
- **Equations Involving Rational Exponents**
- **Summary of Methods**
- **Applications**

One of our goals in algebra is to keep increasing our knowledge of solving equations because the solutions to equations can give us the answers to various applied questions. In this section we will apply our knowledge of radicals and exponents to solving some new types of equations.

The Odd-Root Property

Because $(-2)^3 = -8$ and $2^3 = 8$, the equation $x^3 = 8$ is equivalent to $x = 2$. The equation $x^3 = -8$ is equivalent to $x = -2$. Because there is only one real odd root of each real number, there is a simple rule for writing an equivalent equation in this situation.

Odd-Root Property

If n is an odd positive integer,

$$x^n = k \quad \text{is equivalent to} \quad x = \sqrt[n]{k}$$

for any real number k.

EXAMPLE 1

Using the odd-root property

Solve each equation.

a) $x^3 = 27$ **b)** $x^5 + 32 = 0$ **c)** $(x - 2)^3 = 24$

Solution

a) $x^3 = 27$

$x = \sqrt[3]{27}$ Odd-root property

$x = 3$

Check 3 in the original equation. The solution set is $\{3\}$.

b) $x^5 + 32 = 0$

$x^5 = -32$ Isolate the variable.

$x = \sqrt[5]{-32}$ Odd-root property

$x = -2$

Check -2 in the original equation. The solution set is $\{-2\}$.

c) $(x - 2)^3 = 24$

$x - 2 = \sqrt[3]{24}$ Odd-root property

$x = 2 + 2\sqrt[3]{3}$ $\sqrt[3]{24} = \sqrt[3]{8} \cdot \sqrt[3]{3} = 2\sqrt[3]{3}$

Check. The solution set is $\{2 + 2\sqrt[3]{3}\}$.

Now do Exercises 5–12

The Even-Root Property

In solving the equation $x^2 = 4$, you might be tempted to write $x = 2$ as an equivalent equation. But $x = 2$ is not equivalent to $x^2 = 4$ because $2^2 = 4$ and $(-2)^2 = 4$. So the solution set to $x^2 = 4$ is $\{-2, 2\}$. The equation $x^2 = 4$ is equivalent to the compound sentence $x = 2$ or $x = -2$, which we can abbreviate as $x = \pm 2$. The equation $x = \pm 2$ is read "x equals positive or negative 2."

Teaching Tip Have students solve $x^2 - 4 = 0$ by factoring and observe the two solutions. Then show the square root property. Students often forget that there are two solutions to $x^2 = 4$.

Equations involving other even powers are handled like the squares. Because $2^4 = 16$ and $(-2)^4 = 16$, the equation $x^4 = 16$ is equivalent to $x = \pm 2$. So $x^4 = 16$ has two real solutions. Note that $x^4 = -16$ has no real solutions. The equation $x^6 = 5$ is equivalent to $x = \pm\sqrt[6]{5}$. We can now state a general rule.

Even-Root Property

Suppose n is a positive even integer.

If $k > 0$, then $x^n = k$ is equivalent to $x = \pm\sqrt[n]{k}$.
If $k = 0$, then $x^n = k$ is equivalent to $x = 0$.
If $k < 0$, then $x^n = k$ has no real solution.

EXAMPLE 2 **Using the even-root property**

Solve each equation.

a) $x^2 = 10$ **b)** $w^8 = 0$ **c)** $x^4 = -4$

Solution

a) $x^2 = 10$
$x = \pm\sqrt{10}$ Even-root property
The solution set is $\{-\sqrt{10}, \sqrt{10}\}$, or $\{\pm\sqrt{10}\}$.

b) $w^8 = 0$
$w = 0$ Even-root property
The solution set is $\{0\}$.

c) By the even-root property, $x^4 = -4$ has no real solution. (The fourth power of any real number is nonnegative.)

Now do Exercises 13–18

Helpful Hint

We do not say, "take the square root of each side." We are not doing the same thing to each side of $x^2 = 9$ when we write $x = \pm 3$. This is the third time that we have seen a rule for obtaining an equivalent equation without "doing the same thing to each side." (What were the other two?) Because there is only one odd root of every real number, you can actually take an odd root of each side.

Whether an equation has a solution depends on the domain of the variable. For example, $2x = 5$ has no solution in the set of integers and $x^2 = -9$ has no solution in the set of real numbers. We can say that the solution set to both of these equations is the empty set, $\varnothing$, as long as the domain of the variable is clear. In the next section we introduce a new set of numbers, the *imaginary numbers,* in which $x^2 = -9$ will have two solutions. So in this section it is best to say that $x^2 = -9$ has no real solution, because in the next section its solution set will *not* be $\varnothing$. An equation such as $x = x + 1$ never has a solution and so saying that its solution set is $\varnothing$ is clear.

In Example 3 the even-root property is used to solve some equations that are a bit more complicated than those of Example 2.

EXAMPLE 3

Using the even-root property

Solve each equation.

a) $(x - 3)^2 = 4$ **b)** $2(x - 5)^2 - 7 = 0$ **c)** $x^4 - 1 = 80$

Teaching Tip Note that parts (a) and (b) of Example 3 are getting students ready for completing the square.

Solution

a) $(x - 3)^2 = 4$

$x - 3 = 2$ or $x - 3 = -2$ Even-root property

$x = 5$ or $x = 1$ Add 3 to each side.

The solution set is $\{1, 5\}$.

b) $2(x - 5)^2 - 7 = 0$

$2(x - 5)^2 = 7$ Add 7 to each side.

$(x - 5)^2 = \frac{7}{2}$ Divide each side by 2.

$x - 5 = \sqrt{\frac{7}{2}}$ or $x - 5 = -\sqrt{\frac{7}{2}}$ Even-root property

$x = 5 + \frac{\sqrt{14}}{2}$ or $x = 5 - \frac{\sqrt{14}}{2}$ $\sqrt{\frac{7}{2}} = \frac{\sqrt{7} \cdot \sqrt{2}}{\sqrt{2} \cdot \sqrt{2}} = \frac{\sqrt{14}}{2}$

$x = \frac{10 + \sqrt{14}}{2}$ or $x = \frac{10 - \sqrt{14}}{2}$

The solution set is $\left\{\frac{10 + \sqrt{14}}{2}, \frac{10 - \sqrt{14}}{2}\right\}$.

c) $x^4 - 1 = 80$

$x^4 = 81$

$x = \pm\sqrt[4]{81} = \pm 3$

The solution set is $\{-3, 3\}$.

Study Tip

Review, review, review! Don't wait until the end of a chapter to review. Do a little review every time you study for this course.

Now do Exercises 19–28

In Chapter 5 we solved quadratic equations by factoring. The quadratic equations that we encounter in this chapter can be solved by using the even-root property as in parts (a) and (b) of Example 3. In Chapter 10 you will learn general methods for solving any quadratic equation.

Equations Involving Radicals

If we start with the equation $x = 3$ and square both sides, we get $x^2 = 9$. The solution set to $x^2 = 9$ is $\{-3, 3\}$; the solution set to the original equation is $\{3\}$. Squaring both sides of an equation might produce a *nonequivalent* equation that has more solutions than the original equation. We call these additional solutions **extraneous solutions.** However, any solution of the original must be among the solutions to the new equation.

CAUTION When you solve an equation by raising each side to a power, you must check your answers. Raising each side to an odd power will always give an equivalent equation; raising each side to an even power might not.

EXAMPLE 4

Raising each side to a power to eliminate radicals

Solve each equation.

a) $\sqrt{2x - 3} - 5 = 0$ **b)** $\sqrt[3]{3x + 5} = \sqrt[3]{x - 1}$ **c)** $\sqrt{3x + 18} = x$

Solution

a) Eliminate the square root by raising each side to the power 2:

$$\begin{aligned} \sqrt{2x - 3} - 5 &= 0 && \text{Original equation} \\ \sqrt{2x - 3} &= 5 && \text{Isolate the radical.} \\ (\sqrt{2x - 3})^2 &= 5^2 && \text{Square both sides.} \\ 2x - 3 &= 25 \\ 2x &= 28 \\ x &= 14 \end{aligned}$$

Check by evaluating $x = 14$ in the original equation:

$$\begin{aligned} \sqrt{2(14) - 3} - 5 &= 0 \\ \sqrt{28 - 3} - 5 &= 0 \\ \sqrt{25} - 5 &= 0 \\ 0 &= 0 \end{aligned}$$

The solution set is $\{14\}$.

b)

$$\begin{aligned} \sqrt[3]{3x + 5} &= \sqrt[3]{x - 1} && \text{Original equation} \\ (\sqrt[3]{3x + 5})^3 &= (\sqrt[3]{x - 1})^3 && \text{Cube each side.} \\ 3x + 5 &= x - 1 \\ 2x &= -6 \\ x &= -3 \end{aligned}$$

Check $x = -3$ in the original equation:

$$\begin{aligned} \sqrt[3]{3(-3) + 5} &= \sqrt[3]{-3 - 1} \\ \sqrt[3]{-4} &= \sqrt[3]{-4} \end{aligned}$$

Note that $\sqrt[3]{-4}$ is a real number. The solution set is $\{-3\}$. In this example we checked for arithmetic mistakes. There was no possibility of extraneous solutions here because we raised each side to an odd power.

c)

$$\begin{aligned} \sqrt{3x + 18} &= x && \text{Original equation} \\ (\sqrt{3x + 18})^2 &= x^2 && \text{Square both sides.} \\ 3x + 18 &= x^2 && \text{Simplify.} \\ -x^2 + 3x + 18 &= 0 && \text{Subtract } x^2 \text{ from each side to get zero on one side.} \\ x^2 - 3x - 18 &= 0 && \text{Multiply each side by } -1 \text{ for easier factoring.} \\ (x - 6)(x + 3) &= 0 && \text{Factor.} \end{aligned}$$

$$\begin{aligned} x - 6 &= 0 \quad \text{or} \quad x + 3 = 0 && \text{Zero factor property} \\ x &= 6 \quad \text{or} \quad x = -3 \end{aligned}$$

Calculator Close-Up

If 14 satisfies the equation

$$\sqrt{2x - 3} - 5 = 0,$$

then (14, 0) is an x-intercept for the graph of

$$y = \sqrt{2x - 3} - 5.$$

So the calculator graph shown here provides visual support for the conclusion that 14 is the only solution to the equation.

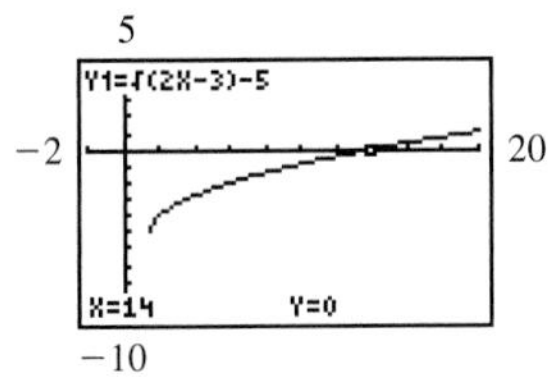

Calculator Close-Up

The graphs of

$$y_1 = \sqrt{3x + 18}$$

and $y_2 = x$ provide visual support that 6 is the only value of x for which x and $\sqrt{3x + 18}$ are equal.

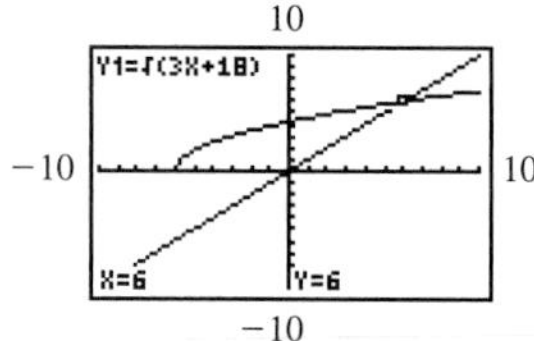

Because we squared both sides, we must check for extraneous solutions. If $x = -3$ in the original equation $\sqrt{3x + 18} = x$, we get

$$\sqrt{3(-3) + 18} = -3$$
$$\sqrt{9} = -3$$
$$3 = -3,$$

which is not correct. If $x = 6$ in the original equation, we get

$$\sqrt{3(6) + 18} = 6,$$

which is correct. The solution set is $\{6\}$.

Now do Exercises 29–44

In Example 5 the radicals are not eliminated after squaring both sides of the equation. In this case we must square both sides a second time. Note that we square the side with two terms the same way we square a binomial.

EXAMPLE 5

Teaching Tip Point out that the binomial on one side is squared but the binomial on the other side is inside a radical and is not squared.

Squaring both sides twice

Solve $\sqrt{5x - 1} - \sqrt{x + 2} = 1$.

Solution

It is easier to square both sides if the two radicals are not on the same side.

$\sqrt{5x - 1} - \sqrt{x + 2} = 1$	Original equation
$\sqrt{5x - 1} = 1 + \sqrt{x + 2}$	Add $\sqrt{x + 2}$ to each side.
$(\sqrt{5x - 1})^2 = (1 + \sqrt{x + 2})^2$	Square both sides.
$5x - 1 = 1 + 2\sqrt{x + 2} + x + 2$	Square the right side like a binomial.
$5x - 1 = 3 + x + 2\sqrt{x + 2}$	Combine like terms on the right side.
$4x - 4 = 2\sqrt{x + 2}$	Isolate the square root.
$2x - 2 = \sqrt{x + 2}$	Divide each side by 2.
$(2x - 2)^2 = (\sqrt{x + 2})^2$	Square both sides.
$4x^2 - 8x + 4 = x + 2$	Square the binomial on the left side.

$$4x^2 - 9x + 2 = 0$$
$$(4x - 1)(x - 2) = 0$$
$$4x - 1 = 0 \quad \text{or} \quad x - 2 = 0$$
$$x = \frac{1}{4} \quad \text{or} \quad x = 2$$

Check to see whether $\sqrt{5x - 1} - \sqrt{x + 2} = 1$ for $x = \frac{1}{4}$ and for $x = 2$:

$$\sqrt{5 \cdot \frac{1}{4} - 1} - \sqrt{\frac{1}{4} + 2} = \sqrt{\frac{1}{4}} - \sqrt{\frac{9}{4}} = \frac{1}{2} - \frac{3}{2} = -1$$
$$\sqrt{5 \cdot 2 - 1} - \sqrt{2 + 2} = \sqrt{9} - \sqrt{4} = 3 - 2 = 1$$

So the original equation is not satisfied for $x = \frac{1}{4}$ but is satisfied for $x = 2$. Since 2 is the only solution to the equation, the solution set is $\{2\}$.

Now do Exercises 45–58

Equations Involving Rational Exponents

Equations involving rational exponents can be solved by combining the methods that you just learned for eliminating radicals and integral exponents. For equations involving rational exponents, always eliminate the root first and the power second.

EXAMPLE 6

Eliminating the root, then the power

Solve each equation.

a) $x^{2/3} = 4$

b) $(w - 1)^{-2/5} = 4$

Solution

a) Because the exponent 2/3 indicates a cube root, raise each side to the power 3:

$$x^{2/3} = 4 \qquad \text{Original equation}$$
$$(x^{2/3})^3 = 4^3 \qquad \text{Cube each side.}$$
$$x^2 = 64 \qquad \text{Multiply the exponents: } \frac{2}{3} \cdot 3 = 2.$$
$$x = 8 \quad \text{or} \quad x = -8 \qquad \text{Even-root property}$$

All of the equations are equivalent. Check 8 and -8 in the original equation. The solution set is $\{-8, 8\}$.

b)
$$(w - 1)^{-2/5} = 4 \qquad \text{Original equation}$$
$$[(w - 1)^{-2/5}]^{-5} = 4^{-5} \qquad \text{Raise each side to the power } -5 \text{ to eliminate the negative exponent.}$$
$$(w - 1)^2 = \frac{1}{1024} \qquad \text{Multiply the exponents: } -\frac{2}{5}(-5) = 2.$$
$$w - 1 = \pm\sqrt{\frac{1}{1024}} \qquad \text{Even-root property}$$
$$w - 1 = \frac{1}{32} \quad \text{or} \quad w - 1 = -\frac{1}{32}$$
$$w = \frac{33}{32} \quad \text{or} \quad w = \frac{31}{32}$$

Check the values in the original equation. The solution set is $\left\{\frac{31}{32}, \frac{33}{32}\right\}$.

Now do Exercises 59–70

Helpful Hint

Note how we eliminate the root first by raising each side to an integer power, and then apply the even-root property to get two solutions in Example 6(a). A common mistake is to raise each side to the 3/2 power and get $x = 4^{3/2} = 8$. If you do not use the even-root property you can easily miss the solution -8.

Teaching Tip Note that raising each side to the power $-5/2$ is a common approach, but then the negative square root is usually lost.

Calculator Close-Up

Check that 31/32 and 33/32 satisfy the original equation.

```
(31/32-1)^(-2/5)
                4
(33/32-1)^(-2/5)
                4
```

An equation with a rational exponent might not have a real solution because all even powers of real numbers are nonnegative.

EXAMPLE 7

An equation with no solution

Solve $(2t - 3)^{-2/3} = -1$.

Solution

Raise each side to the power -3 to eliminate the root and the negative sign in the exponent:

$$(2t - 3)^{-2/3} = -1 \quad \text{Original equation}$$

$$[(2t - 3)^{-2/3}]^{-3} = (-1)^{-3} \quad \text{Raise each side to the } -3 \text{ power.}$$

$$(2t - 3)^{2} = -1 \quad \text{Multiply the exponents: } -\frac{2}{3}(-3) = 2.$$

By the even-root property this equation has no real solution. The square of every real number is nonnegative.

Now do Exercises 71–72

Summary of Methods

The three most important rules for solving equations with exponents and radicals are restated here.

Strategy for Solving Equations with Exponents and Radicals

1. In raising each side of an equation to an even power, we can create an equation that gives extraneous solutions. We must check all possible solutions in the original equation.
2. When applying the even-root property, remember that there is a positive and a negative even root for any positive real number.
3. For equations with rational exponents, raise each side to a positive or negative integral power first, then apply the even- or odd-root property. (Positive fraction—raise to a positive power; negative fraction—raise to a negative power.)

Applications

The square of the hypotenuse of any right triangle is equal to the sum of the squares of the legs (the Pythagorean theorem). In Example 8 we use this fact and the even-root property to find a distance on a baseball diamond.

EXAMPLE 8

Diagonal of a baseball diamond

A baseball diamond is actually a square, 90 feet on each side. What is the distance from third base to first base?

Solution

First make a sketch as in Fig. 9.1. The distance x from third base to first base is the length of the diagonal of the square shown in Fig. 9.1. The Pythagorean theorem

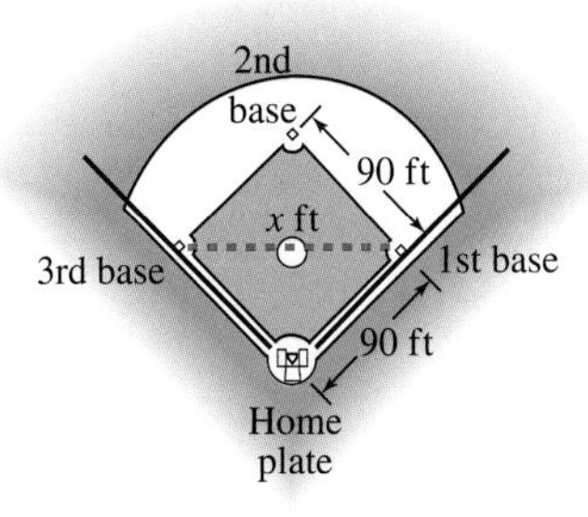

Figure 9.1

can be applied to the right triangle formed from the diagonal and two sides of the square. The sum of the squares of the sides is equal to the diagonal squared:

$$x^2 = 90^2 + 90^2$$
$$x^2 = 8100 + 8100$$
$$x^2 = 16{,}200$$
$$x = \pm\sqrt{16{,}200} = \pm 90\sqrt{2}$$

The length of the diagonal of a square must be positive, so we disregard the negative solution. Checking the answer in the original equation verifies that the *exact* length of the diagonal is $90\sqrt{2}$ feet.

Now do Exercises 93–108

Warm-Ups ▼

True or false? Explain your answer.

1. The equations $x^2 = 4$ and $x = 2$ are equivalent. False
2. The equation $x^2 = -25$ has no real solution. True
3. There is no solution to the equation $x^2 = 0$. False
4. The equation $x^3 = 8$ is equivalent to $x = \pm 2$. False
5. The equation $-\sqrt{x} = 16$ has no real solution. True
6. To solve $\sqrt{x - 3} = \sqrt{2x + 5}$, first apply the even-root property. False
7. Extraneous solutions are solutions that cannot be found. False
8. Squaring both sides of $\sqrt{x} = -7$ yields an equation with an extraneous solution. True
9. The equations $x^2 - 6 = 0$ and $x = \pm\sqrt{6}$ are equivalent. True
10. Cubing each side of an equation will not produce an extraneous solution. True

9.5 Exercises

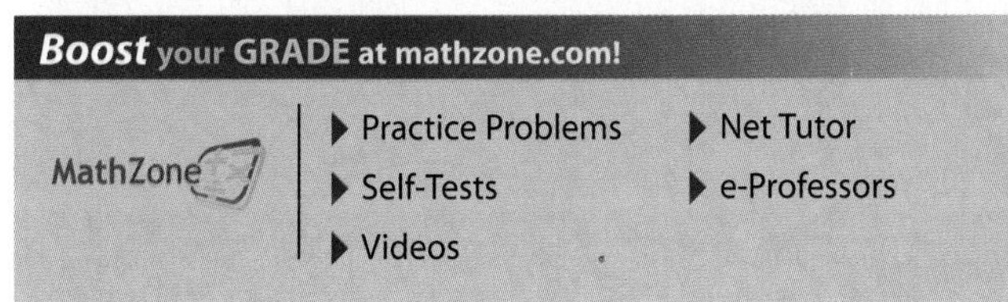

Reading and Writing *After reading this section, write out the answers to these questions. Use complete sentences.*

1. What is the odd-root property?
The odd-root property says that if n is an odd positive integer, then $x^n = k$ is equivalent to $x = \sqrt[n]{k}$ for any real number k.

2. What is the even-root property?
The even-root property says that if n is a positive even integer, then $x^n = k$ is equivalent to $x = \pm\sqrt[n]{k}$ for $k > 0$, $x = 0$ for $k = 0$, and has no real solution for $k < 0$.

3. What is an extraneous solution?
An extraneous solution is a solution that appears when solving an equation but does not satisfy the original equation.

4. Why can raising each side to a power produce an extraneous solution?
Raising each side to an even power can produce an extraneous root because the even powers of both negative and positive numbers are positive. For example, if $\sqrt{x} = -2$, then squaring each side produces an extraneous root.

Solve each equation. See Example 1.

5. $x^3 = -1000$ $\{-10\}$

6. $y^3 = 125$ $\{5\}$

7. $32m^5 - 1 = 0$ $\left\{\frac{1}{2}\right\}$

8. $243a^5 + 1 = 0$ $\left\{-\frac{1}{3}\right\}$

9. $(y - 3)^3 = -8$ $\{1\}$

10. $(x - 1)^3 = -1$ $\{0\}$

11. $\frac{1}{2}x^3 + 4 = 0$ $\{-2\}$

12. $3(x - 9)^7 = 0$ $\{9\}$

Find all real solutions to each equation. See Examples 2 and 3.

13. $x^2 = 25$ $\{-5, 5\}$

14. $x^2 = 36$ $\{-6, 6\}$

15. $x^2 - 20 = 0$ $\{-2\sqrt{5}, 2\sqrt{5}\}$

16. $a^2 - 40 = 0$ $\{-2\sqrt{10}, 2\sqrt{10}\}$

17. $x^2 + 9 = 0$ No real solution

18. $w^2 + 49 = 0$ No real solution

19. $(x - 3)^2 = 16$ $\{-1, 7\}$

20. $(a - 2)^2 = 25$ $\{-3, 7\}$

21. $(x + 1)^2 - 8 = 0$ $\{-1 - 2\sqrt{2}, -1 + 2\sqrt{2}\}$

22. $(w + 3)^2 - 12 = 0$ $\{-3 - 2\sqrt{3}, -3 + 2\sqrt{3}\}$

23. $\frac{1}{2}x^2 = 5$ $\{-\sqrt{10}, \sqrt{10}\}$

24. $\frac{1}{3}x^2 = 6$ $\{\pm 3\sqrt{2}\}$

25. $(y - 3)^4 = 0$ $\{3\}$

26. $(2x - 3)^6 = 0$ $\left\{\frac{3}{2}\right\}$

27. $2x^6 = 128$ $\{-2, 2\}$

28. $3y^4 = 48$ $\{-2, 2\}$

Solve each equation and check for extraneous solutions. See Example 4.

29. $\sqrt{x - 3} - 3 = 4$ $\{52\}$

30. $\sqrt{a - 1} - 5 = 1$ $\{37\}$

31. $2\sqrt{w + 4} = 5$ $\left\{\frac{9}{4}\right\}$

32. $3\sqrt{w + 1} = 6$ $\{3\}$

33. $\sqrt[3]{2x + 3} = \sqrt[3]{x + 12}$ $\{9\}$

34. $\sqrt[3]{a + 3} = \sqrt[3]{2a - 7}$ $\{10\}$

35. $\sqrt{2t - 4} = \sqrt{t - 1}$ $\{3\}$

36. $\sqrt{w - 3} = \sqrt{4w - 15}$ $\{4\}$

37. $\sqrt{4x^2 + x - 3} = 2x$ $\{3\}$

38. $\sqrt{x^2 - 5x + 2} = x$ $\left\{\frac{2}{5}\right\}$

39. $\sqrt{x^2 + 2x - 6} = 3$ $\{-5, 3\}$

40. $\sqrt{x^2 - x - 4} = 4$ $\{-4, 5\}$

41. $\sqrt{2x^2 - 1} = x$ $\{1\}$

42. $\sqrt{2x^2 - 3x - 10} = x$ $\{5\}$

43. $\sqrt{2x^2 + 5x + 6} = x$ $\varnothing$

44. $\sqrt{2x^2 + 6x + 9} = x$ $\varnothing$

Solve each equation and check for extraneous solutions. See Example 5.

45. $\sqrt{x} + \sqrt{x - 3} = 3$ $\{4\}$

46. $\sqrt{x} + \sqrt{x + 3} = 3$ $\{1\}$

47. $\sqrt{x + 2} + \sqrt{x - 1} = 3$ $\{2\}$

48. $\sqrt{x} + \sqrt{x - 5} = 5$ $\{9\}$

49. $\sqrt{x + 3} - \sqrt{x - 2} = 1$ $\{6\}$

50. $\sqrt{2x + 1} - \sqrt{x} = 1$ $\{0, 4\}$

51. $\sqrt{2x + 2} - \sqrt{x - 3} = 2$ $\{7\}$

52. $\sqrt{3x} - \sqrt{x - 2} = 4$ $\{27\}$

53. $\sqrt{4 - x} - \sqrt{x + 6} = 2$ $\{-5\}$

54. $\sqrt{6 - x} - \sqrt{x - 2} = 2$ $\{2\}$

55. $\sqrt{x - 5} - \sqrt{x} = 3$ $\varnothing$

56. $\sqrt{2x} - \sqrt{2x - 12} = 6$ $\varnothing$

57. $\sqrt{3x + 1} + \sqrt{2x + 4} = 3$ $\{0\}$

58. $\sqrt{2x + 5} + \sqrt{x + 2} = 1$ $\{-2\}$

Solve each equation. See Examples 6 and 7.

59. $x^{2/3} = 3$ $\{-3\sqrt{3}, 3\sqrt{3}\}$

60. $a^{2/3} = 2$ $\{-2\sqrt{2}, 2\sqrt{2}\}$

61. $y^{-2/3} = 9$ $\left\{-\frac{1}{27}, \frac{1}{27}\right\}$

62. $w^{-2/3} = 4$ $\left\{-\frac{1}{8}, \frac{1}{8}\right\}$

63. $w^{1/3} = 8$ $\{512\}$

64. $a^{1/3} = 27$ $\{19{,}683\}$

65. $t^{-1/2} = 9$ $\left\{\frac{1}{81}\right\}$

66. $w^{-1/4} = \frac{1}{2}$ $\{16\}$

67. $(3a - 1)^{-2/5} = 1$ $\left\{0, \frac{2}{3}\right\}$

68. $(r - 1)^{-2/3} = 1$ $\{0, 2\}$

69. $(t - 1)^{-2/3} = 2$ $\left\{\frac{4 - \sqrt{2}}{4}, \frac{4 + \sqrt{2}}{4}\right\}$

70. $(w + 3)^{-1/3} = \frac{1}{3}$ $\{24\}$

71. $(x - 3)^{2/3} = -4$ No real solution

72. $(x + 2)^{3/2} = -1$ No real solution

Solve each equation.

73. $2x^2 + 3 = 7$ $\{-\sqrt{2}, \sqrt{2}\}$

74. $3x^2 - 5 = 16$ $\{-\sqrt{7}, \sqrt{7}\}$

75. $\sqrt[3]{2w + 3} = \sqrt[3]{w - 2}$ $\{-5\}$

76. $\sqrt[3]{2 - w} = \sqrt[3]{2w - 28}$ $\{10\}$

77. $(w + 1)^{2/3} = -3$ No real solution

78. $(x - 2)^{4/3} = -2$ No real solution

79. $(a + 1)^{1/3} = -2$ $\{-9\}$

80. $(a - 1)^{1/3} = -3$ $\{-26\}$

81. $(4y - 5)^7 = 0$ $\left\{\frac{5}{4}\right\}$

82. $(5x)^9 = 0$ $\{0\}$

83. $\sqrt{5x^2 + 4x + 1} - x = 0$ $\varnothing$

84. $3 + \sqrt{x^2 - 8x} = 0$ $\varnothing$

85. $\sqrt{4x^2} = x + 2$ $\left\{-\frac{2}{3}, 2\right\}$

86. $\sqrt{9x^2} = x + 6$ $\left\{-\frac{3}{2}, 3\right\}$

87. $(t + 2)^4 = 32$ $\{-2 - 2\sqrt[4]{2}, -2 + 2\sqrt[4]{2}\}$

88. $(w + 1)^4 = 48$ $\{-1 - 2\sqrt[4]{3}, -1 + 2\sqrt[4]{3}\}$

89. $\sqrt{x^2 - 3x} = x$ $\{0\}$

90. $\sqrt[4]{4x^4 - 48} = -x$ $\{-2\}$

91. $x^{-3} = 8$ $\left\{\frac{1}{2}\right\}$

92. $x^{-2} = 4$ $\left\{\pm\frac{1}{2}\right\}$

Solve each problem by writing an equation and solving it. Find the exact answer and simplify it using the rules for radicals. See Example 8.

93. ***Side of a square.*** Find the length of the side of a square whose diagonal is 8 feet. $4\sqrt{2}$ feet

94. ***Diagonal of a patio.*** Find the length of the diagonal of a square patio with an area of 40 square meters. $4\sqrt{5}$ meters

95. ***Side of a sign.*** Find the length of the side of a square sign whose area is 50 square feet. $5\sqrt{2}$ feet

96. ***Side of a cube.*** Find the length of the side of a cubic box whose volume is 80 cubic feet. $2\sqrt[3]{10}$ feet

97. ***Diagonal of a rectangle.*** If the sides of a rectangle are 30 feet and 40 feet in length, find the length of the diagonal of the rectangle. 50 feet

98. ***Diagonal of a sign.*** What is the length of the diagonal of a rectangular billboard whose sides are 5 meters and 12 meters? 13 meters

99. ***Sailboat stability.*** To be considered safe for ocean sailing, the capsize screening value C should be less than 2 (www.sailing.com). For a boat with a beam (or width) b in feet and displacement d in pounds, C is determined by the formula

$$C = 4d^{-1/3}b.$$

a) Find the capsize screening value for the Tartan 4100, which has a displacement of 23,245 pounds and a beam of 13.5 feet. 1.89

b) Solve this formula for d. $d = \frac{64b^3}{C^3}$

c) The accompanying graph shows C as a function of d for the Tartan 4100 ($b = 13.5$). For what displacement is the Tartan 4100 safe for ocean sailing? $d > 19{,}683$ pounds

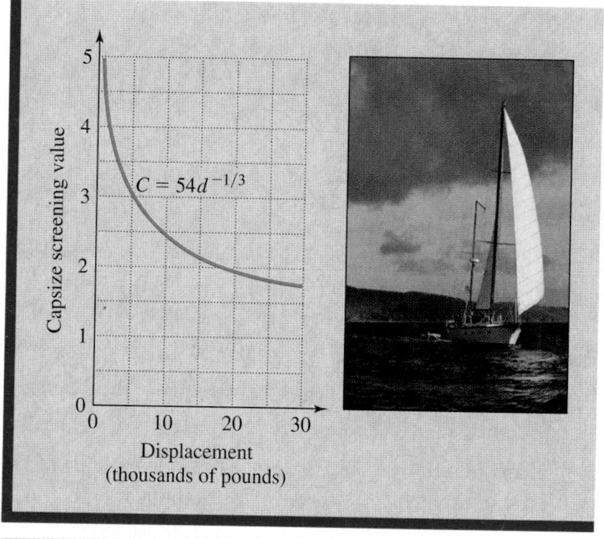

Figure for Exercise 99

100. ***Sailboat speed.*** The sail area-displacement ratio S provides a measure of the sail power available to drive a boat. For a boat with a displacement of d pounds and a sail area of A square feet

$$S = 16Ad^{-2/3}.$$

a) Find S to the nearest tenth for the Tartan 4100, which has a sail area of 810 square feet and a displacement of 23,245 pounds. 15.9

b) Solve the formula for d. $d = \left(\frac{16A}{S}\right)^{3/2}$ or $d = 64\left(\frac{A}{S}\right)^{3/2}$

101. ***Diagonal of a side.*** Find the length of the diagonal of a side of a cubic packing crate whose volume is 2 cubic meters. $\sqrt[6]{32}$ meters

102. ***Volume of a cube.*** Find the volume of a cube on which the diagonal of a side measures 2 feet. $2\sqrt{2}$ cubic feet (ft^3)

103. ***Length of a road.*** An architect designs a public park in the shape of a trapezoid. Find the length of the diagonal road marked a in the figure. $\sqrt{73}$ kilometers (km)

104. ***Length of a boundary.*** Find the length of the border of the park marked b in the trapezoid shown in the figure. $\sqrt{13}$ km

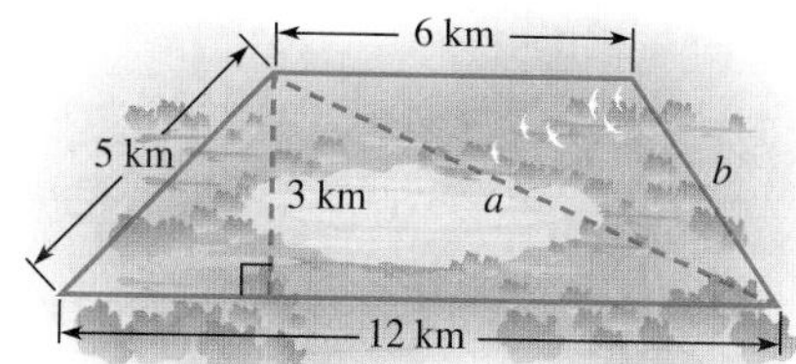

Figure for Exercises 103 and 104

105. ***Average annual return.*** The formula

$$r = \left(\frac{S}{P}\right)^{1/n} - 1$$

was used to find the average annual return on an investment in Exercise 133 in Section 7.2. Solve the formula for S (the amount). Solve it for P (the original principal). $S = P(1 + r)^n$, $P = S(1 + r)^{-n}$

106. ***Surface area of a cube.*** The formula $A = 6V^{2/3}$ gives the surface area of a cube in terms of its volume V. What is the volume of a cube with surface area 12 square feet? $2\sqrt{2}$ ft^3

107. ***Kepler's third law.*** According to Kepler's third law of planetary motion, the ratio $\frac{T^2}{R^3}$ has the same value for every planet in our solar system. R is the average radius of the orbit of the planet measured in astronomical units (AU), and T is the number of years it takes for one complete orbit of the sun. Jupiter orbits the sun in 11.86 years with an average radius of 5.2 AU, whereas Saturn orbits the sun in 29.46 years. Find the average radius of the orbit of Saturn. (One AU is the distance from the earth to the sun.) 9.5 AU

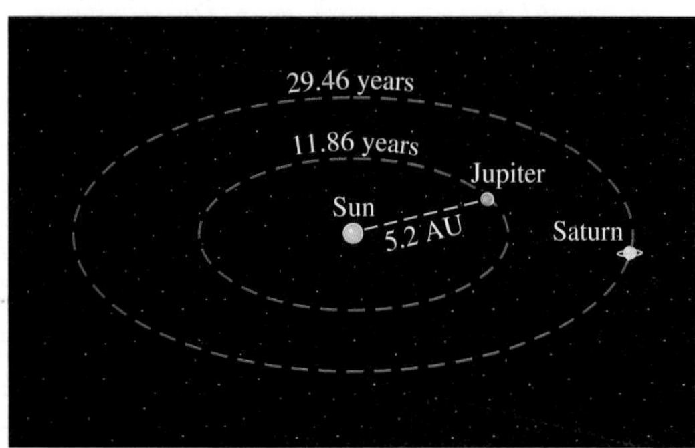

Figure for Exercise 107

108. ***Orbit of Venus.*** If the average radius of the orbit of Venus is 0.723 AU, then how many years does it take for Venus to complete one orbit of the sun? Use the information in Exercise 107. 0.61 year

Use a calculator to find approximate solutions to the following equations. Round your answers to three decimal places.

109. $x^2 = 3.24$ $\{-1.8, 1.8\}$

110. $(x + 4)^3 = 7.51$ $\{-2.042\}$

111. $\sqrt{x - 2} = 1.73$ $\{4.993\}$

112. $\sqrt[3]{x - 5} = 3.7$ $\{55.653\}$

113. $x^{2/3} = 8.86$ $\{-26.372, 26.372\}$

114. $(x - 1)^{-3/4} = 7.065$ $\{1.074\}$

Getting More Involved

115. ***Cooperative learning*** 

Work in a small group to write a formula that gives the side of a cube in terms of the volume of the cube and explain the formula to the other groups.

116. ***Cooperative learning*** 

Work in a small group to write a formula that gives the side of a square in terms of the diagonal of the square and explain the formula to the other groups.

9.6 Complex Numbers

In this Section

- **Definition**
- **Addition, Subtraction, and Multiplication**
- **Division of Complex Numbers**
- **Square Roots of Negative Numbers**
- **Imaginary Solutions to Equations**

In Chapter 1 we discussed the real numbers and the various subsets of the real numbers. In this section we define a set of numbers that has the real numbers as a subset.

Definition

The equation $2x = 1$ has no solution in the set of integers, but in the set of rational numbers, $2x = 1$ has a solution. The situation is similar for the equation $x^2 = -4$. It has no solution in the set of real numbers because the square of every real number is nonnegative. However, in the set of complex numbers $x^2 = -4$ has two solutions. The complex numbers were developed so that equations such as $x^2 = -4$ would have solutions.

Teaching Tip A number of the form bi, where $b \neq 0$ is called pure imaginary. That term is not used here to keep the situation as simple as possible.

The complex numbers are based on the symbol $\sqrt{-1}$. In the real number system this symbol has no meaning. In the set of complex numbers this symbol is given meaning. We call it i. We make the definition that

$$i = \sqrt{-1} \quad \text{and} \quad i^2 = -1.$$

Complex Numbers

The set of **complex numbers** is the set of all numbers of the form

$$a + bi,$$

where a and b are real numbers, $i = \sqrt{-1}$, and $i^2 = -1$.

In the complex number $a + bi$, a is called the **real part** and b is called the **imaginary part.** If $b \neq 0$, the number $a + bi$ is called an **imaginary number.**

In dealing with complex numbers, we treat $a + bi$ as if it were a binomial, with i being a variable. Thus we would write $2 + (-3)i$ as $2 - 3i$. We agree that $2 + i3$, $3i + 2$, and $i3 + 2$ are just different ways of writing $2 + 3i$ (the standard form). Some examples of complex numbers are

$$-3 - 5i, \quad \frac{2}{3} - \frac{3}{4}i, \quad 1 + i\sqrt{2}, \quad 9 + 0i, \quad \text{and} \quad 0 + 7i.$$

For simplicity we write only $7i$ for $0 + 7i$. The complex number $9 + 0i$ is the real number 9, and $0 + 0i$ is the real number 0. Any complex number with $b = 0$ is a real number. For any real number a,

$$a + 0i = a.$$

Study Tip

Make sure that you know what your instructor expects from you. You can determine what your instructor feels is important by looking at the examples that your instructor works in class and the homework assignments. When in doubt, ask your instructor what you will be responsible for and write down the answer.

The set of real numbers is a subset of the set of complex numbers. See Fig. 9.2.

Complex numbers

Real numbers	Imaginary numbers
$3, \pi, \frac{5}{2}, 0, -9, \sqrt{2}$	$i, 2 + 3i, \sqrt{-5}, -3 - 8i$

Figure 9.2

Addition, Subtraction, and Multiplication

Addition and subtraction of complex numbers are performed as if the complex numbers were algebraic expressions with i being a variable.

EXAMPLE 1

Addition and subtraction of complex numbers

Find the sums and differences.

a) $(2 + 3i) + (6 + i)$

b) $(-2 + 3i) + (-2 - 5i)$

c) $(3 + 5i) - (1 + 2i)$

d) $(-2 - 3i) - (1 - i)$

Solution

a) $(2 + 3i) + (6 + i) = 8 + 4i$

b) $(-2 + 3i) + (-2 - 5i) = -4 - 2i$

c) $(3 + 5i) - (1 + 2i) = 2 + 3i$

d) $(-2 - 3i) - (1 - i) = -3 - 2i$

Now do Exercises 7–14

Teaching Tip Remind students that it is not necessary to memorize these rules. All operations are performed like binomial operations where $i^2 = -1$.

We can give a symbolic definition of addition and subtraction as follows.

Addition and Subtraction of Complex Numbers

The sum and difference of $a + bi$ and $c + di$ are defined as follows:

$$(a + bi) + (c + di) = (a + c) + (b + d)i$$
$$(a + bi) - (c + di) = (a - c) + (b - d)i$$

Complex numbers are multiplied as if they were algebraic expressions. Whenever i^2 appears, we replace it by -1.

EXAMPLE 2

Products of complex numbers

Find each product.

a) $2i(1 + i)$ **b)** $(2 + 3i)(4 + 5i)$ **c)** $(3 + i)(3 - i)$

Calculator Close-Up

Many graphing calculators can perform operations with complex numbers.

```
2i(1+i)
              -2+2i
(2+3i)(4+5i)
              -7+22i
(3+i)(3-i)
                 10
```

Solution

a) $2i(1 + i) = 2i + 2i^2$ Distributive property

$= 2i + 2(-1)$ $i^2 = -1$

$= -2 + 2i$

b) Use the FOIL method to find the product:

$$(2 + 3i)(4 + 5i) = 8 + 10i + 12i + 15i^2$$
$$= 8 + 22i + 15(-1) \quad \text{Replace } i^2 \text{ by } -1.$$
$$= 8 + 22i - 15$$
$$= -7 + 22i$$

c) This product is the product of a sum and a difference.

$$(3 + i)(3 - i) = 9 - 3i + 3i - i^2$$
$$= 9 - (-1) \quad i^2 = -1$$
$$= 10$$

Now do Exercises 15–32

We can find powers of i using the fact that $i^2 = -1$. For example,

$$i^3 = i^2 \cdot i = -1 \cdot i = -i.$$

The value of i^4 is found from the value of i^3:

$$i^4 = i^3 \cdot i = -i \cdot i = -i^2 = 1$$

In Example 3 we find more powers of imaginary numbers.

EXAMPLE 3

Powers of imaginary numbers

Write each expression in the form $a + bi$.

a) $(2i)^2$ **b)** $(-2i)^2$ **c)** i^6

Solution

a) $(2i)^2 = 2^2 \cdot i^2 = 4(-1) = -4$

b) $(-2i)^2 = (-2)^2 \cdot i^2 = 4i^2 = 4(-1) = -4$

c) $i^6 = i^2 \cdot i^4 = -1 \cdot 1 = -1$

Now do Exercises 33–40

For completeness we give the following symbolic definition of multiplication of complex numbers. However, it is simpler to find products as we did in Examples 2 and 3 than to use this definition.

Multiplication of Complex Numbers

The complex numbers $a + bi$ and $c + di$ are multiplied as follows:

$$(a + bi)(c + di) = (ac - bd) + (ad + bc)i$$

Division of Complex Numbers

To divide a complex number by a real number, divide each term by the real number, just as we would divide a binomial by a number. For example,

$$\frac{4 + 6i}{2} = \frac{2(2 + 3i)}{2}$$

$$= 2 + 3i.$$

Helpful Hint

Here is that word "conjugate" again. It is generally used to refer to two things that go together in some way.

To understand division by a complex number, we first look at imaginary numbers that have a real product. The product of the two imaginary numbers in Example 2(c) is a real number:

$$(3 + i)(3 - i) = 10$$

We say that $3 + i$ and $3 - i$ are complex conjugates of each other.

Complex Conjugates

The complex numbers $a + bi$ and $a - bi$ are called **complex conjugates** of one another. Their product is the real number $a^2 + b^2$.

EXAMPLE 4

Products of conjugates

Find the product of the given complex number and its conjugate.

a) $2 + 3i$ **b)** $5 - 4i$

Solution

a) The conjugate of $2 + 3i$ is $2 - 3i$.

$$\begin{aligned}(2 + 3i)(2 - 3i) &= 4 - 9i^2 \\ &= 4 + 9 \\ &= 13\end{aligned}$$

b) The conjugate of $5 - 4i$ is $5 + 4i$.

$$\begin{aligned}(5 - 4i)(5 + 4i) &= 25 + 16 \\ &= 41\end{aligned}$$

Now do Exercises 41–58

We use the idea of complex conjugates to divide complex numbers. The process is similar to rationalizing the denominator. Multiply the numerator and denominator of the quotient by the complex conjugate of the denominator.

EXAMPLE 5

Dividing complex numbers

Find each quotient. Write the answer in the form $a + bi$.

a) $\dfrac{5}{3 - 4i}$ **b)** $\dfrac{3 - i}{2 + i}$

c) $\dfrac{3 + 2i}{i}$

Solution

a) Multiply the numerator and denominator by $3 + 4i$, the conjugate of $3 - 4i$:

$$\begin{aligned}\frac{5}{3 - 4i} &= \frac{5(3 + 4i)}{(3 - 4i)(3 + 4i)} \\ &= \frac{15 + 20i}{9 - 16i^2} \\ &= \frac{15 + 20i}{25} \qquad 9 - 16i^2 = 9 - 16(-1) = 25 \\ &= \frac{15}{25} + \frac{20}{25}i \\ &= \frac{3}{5} + \frac{4}{5}i\end{aligned}$$

b) Multiply the numerator and denominator by $2 - i$, the conjugate of $2 + i$:

$$\begin{aligned}\frac{3-i}{2+i} &= \frac{(3-i)(2-i)}{(2+i)(2-i)}\\ &= \frac{6-5i+i^2}{4-i^2}\\ &= \frac{6-5i-1}{4-(-1)}\\ &= \frac{5-5i}{5}\\ &= 1-i\end{aligned}$$

c) Multiply the numerator and denominator by $-i$, the conjugate of i:

$$\begin{aligned}\frac{3+2i}{i} &= \frac{(3+2i)(-i)}{i(-i)}\\ &= \frac{-3i-2i^2}{-i^2}\\ &= \frac{-3i+2}{1}\\ &= 2-3i\end{aligned}$$

Now do Exercises 49–60

The symbolic definition of division of complex numbers follows.

Division of Complex Numbers

We divide the complex number $a + bi$ by the complex number $c + di$ as follows:

$$\frac{a+bi}{c+di} = \frac{(a+bi)(c-di)}{(c+di)(c-di)}$$

Square Roots of Negative Numbers

In Examples 3(a) and 3(b) we saw that both

$$(2i)^2 = -4 \quad \text{and} \quad (-2i)^2 = -4.$$

Because the square of each of these complex numbers is -4, both $2i$ and $-2i$ are square roots of -4. We write $\sqrt{-4} = 2i$. In the complex number system the square root of any negative number is an imaginary number.

Square Root of a Negative Number

For any positive real number b,

$$\sqrt{-b} = i\sqrt{b}.$$

For example, $\sqrt{-9} = i\sqrt{9} = 3i$ and $\sqrt{-7} = i\sqrt{7}$. Note that the expression $\sqrt{7}i$ could easily be mistaken for the expression $\sqrt{7i}$, where i is under the radical. For this reason, when the coefficient of i is a radical, we write i preceding the radical.

Note that the product rule ($\sqrt{a} \cdot \sqrt{b} = \sqrt{ab}$) does not apply to negative numbers. For example $\sqrt{-2} \cdot \sqrt{-3} \neq \sqrt{6}$:

$$\sqrt{-2} \cdot \sqrt{-3} = i\sqrt{2} \cdot i\sqrt{3} = i^2\sqrt{6} = -\sqrt{6}$$

Square roots of negative numbers must written in terms of i before operations are performed.

EXAMPLE 6

Square roots of negative numbers

Write each expression in the form $a + bi$, where a and b are real numbers.

a) $3 + \sqrt{-9}$ **b)** $\sqrt{-12} + \sqrt{-27}$

c) $\dfrac{-1 - \sqrt{-18}}{3}$ **d)** $\sqrt{-4} \cdot \sqrt{-9}$

Solution

a) $3 + \sqrt{-9} = 3 + i\sqrt{9}$

$= 3 + 3i$

b) $\sqrt{-12} + \sqrt{-27} = i\sqrt{12} + i\sqrt{27}$

$= 2i\sqrt{3} + 3i\sqrt{3}$ $\quad \sqrt{12} = \sqrt{4}\sqrt{3} = 2\sqrt{3}$, $\sqrt{27} = \sqrt{9}\sqrt{3} = 3\sqrt{3}$

$= 5i\sqrt{3}$

c) $\dfrac{-1 - \sqrt{-18}}{3} = \dfrac{-1 - i\sqrt{18}}{3}$

$= \dfrac{-1 - 3i\sqrt{2}}{3}$

$= -\dfrac{1}{3} - i\sqrt{2}$

d) $\sqrt{-4} \cdot \sqrt{-9} = i\sqrt{4} \cdot i\sqrt{9} = 2i \cdot 3i = 6i^2 = -6$

Now do Exercises 61–78

Imaginary Solutions to Equations

In the complex number system the even-root property can be restated so that $x^2 = k$ is equivalent to $x = \pm\sqrt{k}$ for any $k \neq 0$. So an equation such as $x^2 = -9$ that has no real solutions has two imaginary solutions in the complex numbers.

EXAMPLE 7

Complex solutions to equations

Find the complex solutions to each equation.

a) $x^2 = -9$ **b)** $3x^2 + 2 = 0$

Solution

a) First apply the even-root property:

$x^2 = -9$

$x = \pm\sqrt{-9}$ $\quad$ Even-root property

$= \pm i\sqrt{9}$

$= \pm 3i$

Check these solutions in the original equation:

$$(3i)^2 = 9i^2 = 9(-1) = -9$$
$$(-3i)^2 = 9i^2 = -9$$

The solution set is $\{\pm 3i\}$.

b) First solve the equation for x^2:

$$3x^2 + 2 = 0$$
$$x^2 = -\frac{2}{3}$$
$$x = \pm\sqrt{-\frac{2}{3}} = \pm i\sqrt{\frac{2}{3}} = \pm i\frac{\sqrt{6}}{3}$$

Check these solutions in the original equation. The solution set is $\left\{\pm i\frac{\sqrt{6}}{3}\right\}$.

Now do Exercises 79–86

The basic facts about complex numbers are listed in the following box.

Complex Numbers

1. Definition of i: $i = \sqrt{-1}$, and $i^2 = -1$.
2. A complex number has the form $a + bi$, where a and b are real numbers.
3. The complex number $a + 0i$ is the real number a.
4. If b is a positive real number, then $\sqrt{-b} = i\sqrt{b}$.
5. The numbers $a + bi$ and $a - bi$ are called complex conjugates of each other. Their product is the real number $a^2 + b^2$.
6. Add, subtract, and multiply complex numbers as if they were algebraic expressions with i being the variable, and replace i^2 by -1.
7. Divide complex numbers by multiplying the numerator and denominator by the conjugate of the denominator.
8. In the complex number system $x^2 = k$ for any real number k is equivalent to $x = \pm\sqrt{k}$.

Warm-Ups ▼

True or false? Explain your answer.

1. The set of real numbers is a subset of the set of complex numbers. True
2. $2 - \sqrt{-6} = 2 - 6i$ False
3. $\sqrt{-9} = \pm 3i$ False
4. The solution set to the equation $x^2 = -9$ is $\{\pm 3i\}$. True
5. $2 - 3i - (4 - 2i) = -2 - i$ True
6. $i^4 = 1$ True
7. $(2 - i)(2 + i) = 5$ True
8. $i^3 = i$ False
9. $i^{48} = 1$ True
10. The equation $x^2 = k$ has two complex solutions for any real number k. False

9.6 Exercises

Boost your GRADE at mathzone.com!

MathZone

- Practice Problems
- Self-Tests
- Videos
- Net Tutor
- e-Professors

Reading and Writing *After reading this section, write out the answers to these questions. Use complete sentences.*

1. What are complex numbers?
   A complex number is a number of the form $a + bi$, where a and b are real numbers.
2. What is an imaginary number?
   An imaginary number is a complex number in which $b \neq 0$.
3. What is the relationship among the real numbers, the imaginary numbers, and the complex numbers?
   The union of the real numbers and the imaginary numbers is the set of complex numbers.
4. How do we add, subtract, and multiply complex numbers?
   Addition, subtraction, and multiplication of complex numbers are done as if the complex numbers were binomials with i being a variable. When i^2 occurs, we replace it with -1.
5. What is the conjugate of a complex number?
   The conjugate of $a + bi$ is $a - bi$.
6. How do we divide complex numbers?
   To divide complex numbers, write the quotient as a fraction and multiply the numerator and denominator by the conjugate of the denominator.

Find the indicated sums and differences of complex numbers. See Example 1.

7. $(2 + 3i) + (-4 + 5i)$ $-2 + 8i$

8. $(-1 + 6i) + (5 - 4i)$ $4 + 2i$

9. $(2 - 3i) - (6 - 7i)$ $-4 + 4i$

10. $(2 - 3i) - (6 - 2i)$ $-4 - i$

11. $(-1 + i) + (-1 - i)$ -2

12. $(-5 + i) + (-5 - i)$ -10

13. $(-2 - 3i) - (6 - i)$ $-8 - 2i$

14. $(-6 + 4i) - (2 - i)$ $-8 + 5i$

Find each product. Express each answer in the form $a + bi$. See Example 2.

15. $3(2 + 5i)$ $6 + 15i$

16. $4(1 - 3i)$ $4 - 12i$

17. $2i(i - 5)$ $-2 - 10i$

18. $3i(2 - 6i)$ $18 + 6i$

19. $-4i(3 - i)$ $-4 - 12i$

20. $-5i(2 + 3i)$ $15 - 10i$

21. $(2 + 3i)(4 + 6i)$ $-10 + 24i$

22. $(2 + i)(3 + 4i)$ $2 + 11i$

23. $(-1 + i)(2 - i)$ $-1 + 3i$

24. $(3 - 2i)(2 - 5i)$ $-4 - 19i$

25. $(-1 - 2i)(2 + i)$ $-5i$

26. $(1 - 3i)(1 + 3i)$ 10

27. $(5 - 2i)(5 + 2i)$ 29

28. $(4 + 3i)(4 + 3i)$ $7 + 24i$

29. $(1 - i)(1 + i)$ 2

30. $(2 + 6i)(2 - 6i)$ 40

31. $(4 + 2i)(4 - 2i)$ 20

32. $(4 - i)(4 + i)$ 17

Find the indicated powers of complex numbers. See Example 3.

33. $(3i)^2$ -9

34. $(5i)^2$ -25

35. $(-5i)^2$ -25

36. $(-9i)^2$ -81

37. $(2i)^4$ 16

38. $(-2i)^3$ $8i$

39. i^9 i

40. i^{12} 1

Find the product of the given complex number and its conjugate. See Example 4.

41. $3 + 5i$ 34

42. $3 + i$ 10

43. $1 - 2i$ 5

44. $4 - 6i$ 52

45. $-2 + i$ 5

46. $-3 - 2i$ 13

47. $2 - i\sqrt{3}$ 7

48. $\sqrt{5} - 4i$ 21

Find each quotient. Express each answer in the form $a + bi$. See Example 5.

49. $\frac{3}{4 + i}$ $\frac{12}{17} - \frac{3}{17}i$

50. $\frac{6}{7 - 2i}$ $\frac{42}{53} + \frac{12}{53}i$

51. $\frac{2 + i}{3 - 2i}$ $\frac{4}{13} + \frac{7}{13}i$

52. $\frac{3 + 5i}{2 - i}$ $\frac{1}{5} + \frac{13}{5}i$

53. $\frac{4 + 3i}{i}$ $3 - 4i$

54. $\frac{5 - 6i}{3i}$ $-2 - \frac{5}{3}i$

55. $\frac{2 + 6i}{2}$ $1 + 3i$

56. $\frac{9 - 3i}{-6}$ $-\frac{3}{2} + \frac{1}{2}i$

57. $\frac{1 + i}{3i - 2}$ $\frac{1}{13} - \frac{5}{13}i$

58. $\frac{2 + i}{i + 5}$ $\frac{11}{26} + \frac{3}{26}i$

59. $\frac{6}{3i}$ $-2i$

60. $\frac{8}{-2i}$ $4i$

Write each expression in the form a + bi, where a and b are real numbers. See Example 6.

61. $2 + \sqrt{-4}$
$2 + 2i$

62. $3 + \sqrt{-9}$
$3 + 3i$

63. $2\sqrt{-9} + 5$
$5 + 6i$

64. $3\sqrt{-16} + 2$
$2 + 12i$

65. $7 - \sqrt{-6}$
$7 - i\sqrt{6}$

66. $\sqrt{-5} + 3$
$3 + i\sqrt{5}$

67. $\sqrt{-8} + \sqrt{-18}$
$5i\sqrt{2}$

68. $2\sqrt{-20} - \sqrt{-45}$
$i\sqrt{5}$

69. $\frac{2 + \sqrt{-12}}{2}$
$1 + i\sqrt{3}$

70. $\frac{-6 - \sqrt{-18}}{3}$
$-2 - i\sqrt{2}$

71. $\frac{-4 - \sqrt{-24}}{4}$
$-1 - \frac{1}{2}i\sqrt{6}$

72. $\frac{8 + \sqrt{-20}}{-4}$
$-2 - \frac{1}{2}i\sqrt{5}$

73. $\sqrt{-2} \cdot \sqrt{-6}$
$-2\sqrt{3}$

74. $\sqrt{-3} \cdot \sqrt{-15}$
$-3\sqrt{5}$

75. $\sqrt{-3} \cdot \sqrt{-27}$ -9

76. $\sqrt{-3} \cdot \sqrt{-7}$ $-\sqrt{21}$

77. $\frac{\sqrt{8}}{\sqrt{-4}}$ $-i\sqrt{2}$

78. $\frac{\sqrt{6}}{\sqrt{-2}}$ $-i\sqrt{3}$

Find the complex solutions to each equation. See Example 7.

79. $x^2 = -36$
$\{\pm 6i\}$

80. $x^2 + 4 = 0$
$\{\pm 2i\}$

81. $x^2 = -12$
$\{\pm 2i\sqrt{3}\}$

82. $x^2 = -25$
$\{\pm 5i\}$

83. $2x^2 + 5 = 0$
$\left\{\pm\frac{i\sqrt{10}}{2}\right\}$

84. $3x^2 + 4 = 0$
$\left\{\pm\frac{2i\sqrt{3}}{3}\right\}$

85. $3x^2 + 6 = 0$
$\{\pm i\sqrt{2}\}$

86. $x^2 + 1 = 0$
$\{\pm i\}$

Write each expression in the form a + bi, where a and b are real numbers.

87. $(2 - 3i)(3 + 4i)$
$18 - i$

88. $(2 - 3i)(2 + 3i)$
13

89. $(2 - 3i) + (3 + 4i)$
$5 + i$

90. $(3 - 5i) - (2 - 7i)$
$1 + 2i$

91. $\frac{2 - 3i}{3 + 4i}$
$-\frac{6}{25} - \frac{17}{25}i$

92. $\frac{-3i}{3 - 6i}$
$\frac{2}{5} - \frac{1}{5}i$

93. $i(2 - 3i)$
$3 + 2i$

94. $-3i(4i - 1)$
$12 + 3i$

95. $(-3i)^2$
-9

96. $(-2i)^6$
-64

97. $\sqrt{-12} + \sqrt{-3}$
$3i\sqrt{3}$

98. $\sqrt{-49} - \sqrt{-25}$
$2i$

99. $(2 - 3i)^2$
$-5 - 12i$

100. $(5 + 3i)^2$
$16 + 30i$

101. $\frac{-4 + \sqrt{-32}}{2}$
$-2 + 2i\sqrt{2}$

102. $\frac{-2 - \sqrt{-27}}{-6}$
$\frac{1}{3} + \frac{1}{2}i\sqrt{3}$

Getting More Involved

103. ***Writing***

Explain why $2 - i$ is a solution to

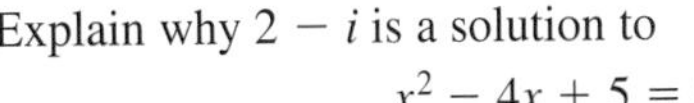

$$x^2 - 4x + 5 = 0.$$

104. ***Cooperative learning***

Work with a group to verify that $-1 + i\sqrt{3}$ and $-1 - i\sqrt{3}$ satisfy the equation

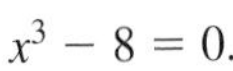

$$x^3 - 8 = 0.$$

In the complex number system there are three cube roots of 8. What are they?

105. ***Discussion***

What is wrong with using the product rule for radicals to get

$$\sqrt{-4} \cdot \sqrt{-4} = \sqrt{(-4)(-4)} = \sqrt{16} = 4?$$

What is the correct product?

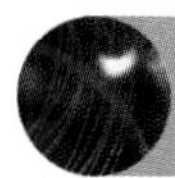

Collaborative Activities

Grouping: 2 to 4 students per group

Topic: Applications of formulas with square roots

Laws of Falling Bodies

Jaki Sena is a private investigator working on a case. Her client is accused of killing a woman who had lived in the same apartment building as he did. She pulls over the file of notes from across her desk and looks through it yet again.

"Okay, so my client said he was on the roof of the building just before 4:00 A.M., dropping blocks over into the alleyway. He dropped the last block just as the clock tower began striking the hour. I wonder how high the building is," Jaki says to herself.

During her initial investigation of the crime scene Jaki had asked the building manager whether he knew the height of the five-story building. He had been very condescending and had told her nothing. Another tenant of the building, some sort of math instructor at the city college, had told her about an experiment he had done with shadows and a climbing rope. He had given her a drawing.

Jaki looked through the file until she found the following drawing.

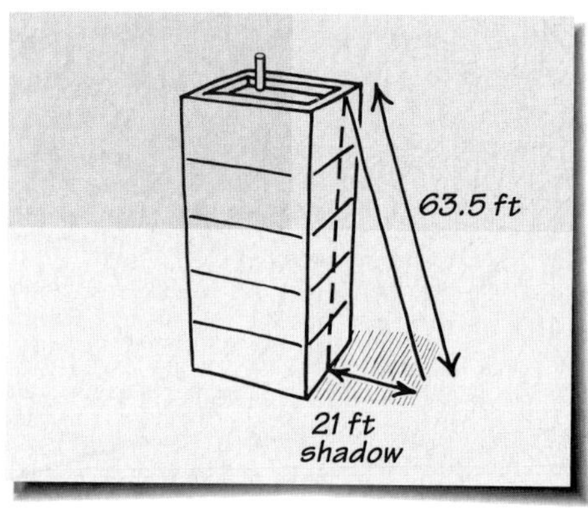

She pulled out a blank piece of paper, and using a calculator, she soon had a number.

"Now I can find out how long it took the block to fall!" Jaki exclaimed. "Okay, now the witness who saw my client on the top of the building also swears he saw the woman walking past the steps next door as the clock tower started to chime 4:00," Jaki said out loud as she got up from her desk and looked out the window. "I have no idea how fast the woman was walking. That may be a hard one to answer. But I do know the steps begin about $9\frac{1}{2}$ feet from where the block fell." Jaki turned back to the file of notes on her desk. She soon found another piece of paper with measurements on it.

"And I do know the woman was 5 feet tall!" Jaki exclaimed, taking out her calculator again.

1. Working in your groups, find the height of the building from the information on Jaki's paper. Round your answer to the nearest tenth of a foot.
2. Find out how many seconds it would take the block to fall from the top of the building to hit the woman on the head. Round your answer to the nearest tenth of a second. (*Hint:* You may need to look in other chapters of the book to find the formulas you need here.)
3. How fast would the woman have to walk to have been hit on the head by the block? Round your answer to the nearest tenth of a foot per second.
4. Could Jaki's client have "done it"? Give a reason for your answer.

Chapter 9 Wrap-Up

Summary

Powers and Roots		**Examples**
nth roots	If $a = b^n$ for a positive integer n, then b is an nth root of a.	2 and -2 are fourth roots of 16.
Principal root	The positive even root of a positive number.	The principal fourth root of 16 is 2.
Radical notation	If n is a positive even integer and a is positive, then the symbol $\sqrt[n]{a}$ denotes the principal nth root of a.	$\sqrt[4]{16} = 2$ $\sqrt[4]{16} \neq -2$
	If n is a positive odd integer, then the symbol $\sqrt[n]{a}$ denotes the nth root of a.	$\sqrt[3]{-8} = -2$, $\sqrt[3]{8} = 2$
	If n is any positive integer, then $\sqrt[n]{0} = 0$.	$\sqrt[5]{0} = 0$, $\sqrt[6]{0} = 0$
Domain of a radical expression	The set of all real numbers that can be used in place of the variable in a radical expression	$\sqrt{x}$, domain $[0, \infty)$ $\sqrt[3]{x-1}$, domain $(-\infty, \infty)$ $\sqrt[4]{x-5}$, domain $[5, \infty)$
Definition of $a^{1/n}$	If n is any positive integer, then $a^{1/n} = \sqrt[n]{a}$, provided that $\sqrt[n]{a}$ is a real number.	$8^{1/3} = \sqrt[3]{8} = 2$ $(-4)^{1/2}$ is not real.
Definition of $a^{m/n}$	If m and n are positive integers, then $a^{m/n} = (a^{1/n})^m$, provided that $a^{1/n}$ is a real number.	$8^{2/3} = (8^{1/3})^2 = 2^2 = 4$ $(-16)^{3/4}$ is not real.
Definition of $a^{-m/n}$	If m and n are positive integers and $a \neq 0$, then $a^{-m/n} = \frac{1}{a^{m/n}}$, provided that $a^{1/n}$ is a real number.	$8^{-2/3} = \frac{1}{8^{2/3}} = \frac{1}{4}$

Rules for Radicals		**Examples**
Product rule for radicals	Provided that all roots are real, $\sqrt[n]{ab} = \sqrt[n]{a} \cdot \sqrt[n]{b}$.	$\sqrt{2} \cdot \sqrt{3} = \sqrt{6}$ $\sqrt{4x} = 2\sqrt{x}$
Quotient rule for radicals	Provided that all roots are real and $b \neq 0$, $\sqrt[n]{\frac{a}{b}} = \frac{\sqrt[n]{a}}{\sqrt[n]{b}}$.	$\sqrt{\frac{5}{9}} = \frac{\sqrt{5}}{3}$ $\sqrt{10} \div \sqrt{5} = \sqrt{2}$

Simplified radical form for radicals of index n	A simplified radical of index n has 1. *no* perfect nth powers as factors of the radicand, 2. *no* fractions inside the radical, and 3. *no* radicals in the denominator.	$\sqrt{20} = \sqrt{4 \cdot 5} = 2\sqrt{5}$ $\sqrt{\frac{3}{2}} = \frac{\sqrt{3}}{\sqrt{2}}$ $\frac{\sqrt{3}}{\sqrt{2}} = \frac{\sqrt{3}}{\sqrt{2}} \cdot \frac{\sqrt{2}}{\sqrt{2}} = \frac{\sqrt{6}}{2}$

Rules for Rational Exponents		Examples
If a and b are nonzero real numbers and r and s are rational numbers, then the following rules hold, provided all expressions represent real numbers.		
Product rule	$a^r \cdot a^s = a^{r+s}$	$3^{1/4} \cdot 3^{1/2} = 3^{3/4}$
Quotient rule	$\frac{a^r}{a^s} = a^{r-s}$	$\frac{x^{3/4}}{x^{1/4}} = x^{1/2}$
Power of a power rule	$(a^r)^s = a^{rs}$	$(2^{1/2})^{-1/2} = 2^{-1/4}$ $(x^{3/4})^4 = x^3$
Power of a product rule	$(ab)^r = a^r b^r$	$(a^2b^6)^{1/2} = ab^3$
Power of a quotient rule	$\left(\frac{a}{b}\right)^r = \frac{a^r}{b^r}$	$\left(\frac{8}{x^6}\right)^{2/3} = \frac{4}{x^4}$

Equations		Examples
Equations with radicals and exponents	1. In raising each side of an equation to an even power, we can create an equation that gives extraneous solutions. We must check.	$\sqrt{x} = -3$ $x = 9$
	2. When applying the even-root property, remember that there is a positive and a negative root.	$x^2 = 36$ $x = \pm 6$
	3. For equations with rational exponents, raise each side to a positive or a negative power first, then apply the even- or odd-root property.	$x^{-2/3} = 4$ $(x^{-2/3})^{-3} = 4^{-3}$ $x^2 = \frac{1}{64}$ $x = \pm\frac{1}{8}$

Complex Numbers		Examples
Complex numbers	Numbers of form $a + bi$, where a and b are real numbers: $i = \sqrt{-1}$, $i^2 = -1$	$2 + 3i$ $-6i$ $\sqrt{2} + i$

Complex conjugates	Complex numbers of the form $a + bi$ and $a - bi$: Their product is the real number $a^2 + b^2$.	$(2 + 3i)(2 - 3i) = 2^2 + 3^2$ $= 13$
Complex number operations	Add, subtract, and multiply as algebraic expressions with i being the variable. Simplify using $i^2 = -1$. Divide complex numbers by multiplying numerator and denominator by the conjugate of the denominator.	$(2 + 5i) + (4 - 2i) = 6 + 3i$ $(2 + 5i) - (4 - 2i) = -2 + 7i$ $(2 + 5i)(4 - 2i) = 18 + 16i$ $(2 + 5i) \div (4 - 2i)$ $= \frac{(2 + 5i)(4 + 2i)}{(4 - 2i)(4 + 2i)}$ $= \frac{-2 + 24i}{20} = -\frac{1}{10} + \frac{6}{5}i$
Square root of a negative number	For any positive real number b, $\sqrt{-b} = i\sqrt{b}$.	$\sqrt{-9} = i\sqrt{9} = 3i$
Imaginary solutions to equations	In the complex number system, $x^2 = k$ for any real k is equivalent to $x = \pm\sqrt{k}$.	$x^2 = -25$ $x = \pm\sqrt{-25} = \pm 5i$

Enriching Your Mathematical Word Power

For each mathematical term, choose the correct meaning.

1. nth root of a
a. a square root
b. the root of a^n
c. a number b such that $a^n = b$
d. a number b such that $b^n = a$ d

2. square of a
a. a number b such that $b^2 = a$
b. a^2
c. $|a|$
d. $\sqrt{a}$ b

3. cube root of a
a. a^3
b. a number b such that $b^3 = a$
c. $a/3$
d. a number b such that $b = a^3$ b

4. principal root
a. the main root
b. the positive even root of a positive number
c. the positive odd root of a negative number
d. the negative odd root of a negative number b

5. odd root of a
a. the number b such that $b^n = a$, where a is an odd number
b. the opposite of the even root of a
c. the nth root of a
d. the number b such that $b^n = a$, where n is an odd number d

6. index of a radical
a. the number n in $n\sqrt{a}$
b. the number n in $\sqrt[n]{a}$
c. the number n in a^n
d. the number n in $\sqrt{a^n}$ b

7. like radicals
a. radicals with the same index
b. radicals with the same radicand
c. radicals with the same radicand and the same index
d. radicals with even indices c

8. domain of an expression
a. the real numbers that can be used in place of the variable in an expression
b. a combination of mathematical symbols
c. all real numbers
d. the variable(s) in an expression a

9. integral exponent
a. an exponent that is an integer
b. a positive exponent
c. a rational exponent
d. a fractional exponent a

10. rational exponent
a. an exponent that produces a rational number
b. an integral exponent
c. an exponent that is a real number
d. an exponent that is a rational number d

11. radicand
a. the expression $\sqrt[n]{a}$
b. the expression $\sqrt{a}$
c. the number a in $\sqrt[n]{a}$
d. the number n in $\sqrt[n]{a}$ c

12. complex numbers
a. $a + bi$, where a and b are real
b. irrational numbers
c. imaginary numbers
d. $\sqrt{-1}$ a

13. imaginary unit
a. 1
b. -1
c. i
d. $\sqrt{1}$ c

14. imaginary number
a. $a + bi$, where a and b are real
b. i
c. a complex number
d. a complex number in which $b \neq 0$ d

15. complex conjugates
a. i and $\sqrt{-1}$
b. $a + bi$ and $a - bi$
c. $(a + b)(a - b)$
d. i and -1 b

Review Exercises

9.1 *Simplify each radical expression. Assume all variables represent positive real numbers.*

1. $\sqrt[5]{32}$ 2
2. $\sqrt[3]{-27}$ -3
3. $\sqrt[3]{1000}$ 10
4. $\sqrt{100}$ 10
5. $\sqrt{72}$ $6\sqrt{2}$
6. $\sqrt{48}$ $4\sqrt{3}$
7. $\sqrt{x^{12}}$ x^6
8. $\sqrt{a^{10}}$ a^5
9. $\sqrt[3]{x^6}$ x^2
10. $\sqrt[3]{a^9}$ a^3
11. $\sqrt{2x^9}$ $x^4\sqrt{2x}$
12. $\sqrt{3a^7}$ $a^3\sqrt{3a}$
13. $\sqrt{8w^5}$ $2w^2\sqrt{2w}$
14. $\sqrt{20n^{25}}$ $2n^{12}\sqrt{5n}$
15. $\sqrt[3]{16x^4}$ $2x\sqrt[3]{2x}$
16. $\sqrt[3]{54b^5}$ $3b\sqrt[3]{2b^2}$
17. $\sqrt[4]{a^9b^5}$ $a^2b\sqrt[4]{ab}$
18. $\sqrt[4]{32m^{11}}$ $2m^2\sqrt[4]{2m^3}$
19. $\sqrt{\dfrac{x^3}{16}}$ $\dfrac{x\sqrt{x}}{4}$
20. $\sqrt{\dfrac{12a^3}{25}}$ $\dfrac{2a\sqrt{3a}}{5}$

Find the domain of each radical expression. Use interval notation.

21. $\sqrt{2x-5}$ $[2.5, \infty)$
22. $\sqrt{3x+12}$ $[-4, \infty)$
23. $\sqrt[3]{7x-1}$ $(-\infty, \infty)$
24. $\sqrt[3]{9-2x}$ $(-\infty, \infty)$
25. $\sqrt[4]{-3x+1}$ $\left(-\infty, \dfrac{1}{3}\right]$
26. $\sqrt[4]{-5x-1}$ $\left(-\infty, -\dfrac{1}{5}\right]$
27. $\sqrt{\dfrac{1}{2}x+1}$ $[-2, \infty)$
28. $\sqrt{\dfrac{2}{3}x-2}$ $[3, \infty)$

9.2 *Simplify the expressions involving rational exponents. Assume all variables represent positive real numbers. Write your answers with positive exponents.*

29. $(-27)^{-2/3}$ $\dfrac{1}{9}$
30. $-25^{3/2}$ -125
31. $(2^6)^{1/3}$ 4
32. $(5^2)^{1/2}$ 5
33. $100^{-3/2}$ $\dfrac{1}{1000}$
34. $1000^{-2/3}$ $\dfrac{1}{100}$
35. $\dfrac{3x^{-1/2}}{3^{-2}x^{-1}}$ $27x^{1/2}$
36. $\dfrac{(x^2y^{-3}z)^{1/2}}{x^{1/2}yz^{-1/2}}$ $\dfrac{x^{1/2}z}{y^{5/2}}$
37. $(a^{1/2}b)^3(ab^{1/4})^2$ $a^{7/2}b^{7/2}$
38. $(t^{-1/2})^{-2}(t^{-2}v^2)$ $\dfrac{v^2}{t}$
39. $(x^{1/2}y^{1/4})(x^{1/4}y)$ $x^{3/4}y^{5/4}$
40. $(a^{1/3}b^{1/6})^2(a^{1/3}b^{2/3})$ ab

9.3 *Perform the operations and simplify. Assume the variables represent positive real numbers.*

41. $\sqrt{13} \cdot \sqrt{13}$ 13
42. $\sqrt[3]{14} \cdot \sqrt[3]{14} \cdot \sqrt[3]{14}$ 14
43. $\sqrt{27} + \sqrt{45} - \sqrt{75}$ $3\sqrt{5} - 2\sqrt{3}$
44. $\sqrt{12} - \sqrt{50} + \sqrt{72}$ $2\sqrt{3} + \sqrt{2}$
45. $3\sqrt{2}(5\sqrt{2} - 7\sqrt{3})$ $30 - 21\sqrt{6}$
46. $-2\sqrt{a}(\sqrt{a} - \sqrt{ab^6})$ $-2a + 2ab^3$
47. $(2 - \sqrt{3})(3 + \sqrt{2})$ $6 - 3\sqrt{3} + 2\sqrt{2} - \sqrt{6}$
48. $(2\sqrt{x} - \sqrt{y})(\sqrt{x} + \sqrt{y})$ $2x + \sqrt{xy} - y$

9.4 *Perform the operations and simplify.*

49. $5 \div \sqrt{2}$ $\dfrac{5\sqrt{2}}{2}$
50. $(10\sqrt{6}) \div (2\sqrt{2})$ $5\sqrt{3}$
51. $\sqrt{\dfrac{2}{5}}$ $\dfrac{\sqrt{10}}{5}$
52. $\sqrt{\dfrac{1}{6}}$ $\dfrac{\sqrt{6}}{6}$

53. $\sqrt[3]{\frac{2}{3}}$ $\frac{\sqrt[3]{18}}{3}$

54. $\sqrt[3]{\frac{1}{9}}$ $\frac{\sqrt[3]{3}}{3}$

55. $\frac{2}{\sqrt{3x}}$ $\frac{2\sqrt{3x}}{3x}$

56. $\frac{3}{\sqrt{2y}}$ $\frac{3\sqrt{2y}}{2y}$

57. $\frac{\sqrt{10y^3}}{\sqrt{6}}$ $\frac{y\sqrt{15y}}{3}$

58. $\frac{\sqrt{5x^5}}{\sqrt{8}}$ $\frac{x^2\sqrt{10x}}{4}$

59. $\frac{3}{\sqrt[3]{2a}}$ $\frac{3\sqrt[3]{4a^2}}{2a}$

60. $\frac{a}{\sqrt[3]{a^2}}$ $\sqrt[3]{a}$

61. $\frac{5}{\sqrt[4]{3x^2}}$ $\frac{5\sqrt[4]{27x^2}}{3x}$

62. $\frac{b}{\sqrt[4]{a^2b^3}}$ $\frac{\sqrt[4]{a^2b}}{a}$

63. $(\sqrt{3})^4$ 9

64. $(-2\sqrt{x})^9$ $-512x^4\sqrt{x}$

65. $\frac{2-\sqrt{8}}{2}$ $1-\sqrt{2}$

66. $\frac{-3-\sqrt{18}}{-6}$ $\frac{1+\sqrt{2}}{2}$

67. $\frac{\sqrt{6}}{1-\sqrt{3}}$ $\frac{-\sqrt{6}-3\sqrt{2}}{2}$

68. $\frac{\sqrt{15}}{2+\sqrt{5}}$ $-2\sqrt{15}+5\sqrt{3}$

69. $\frac{2\sqrt{3}}{3\sqrt{6}-\sqrt{12}}$ $\frac{3\sqrt{2}+2}{7}$

70. $\frac{-\sqrt{xy}}{3\sqrt{x}+\sqrt{xy}}$ $\frac{-3\sqrt{y}+y}{9-y}$

71. $(2w\sqrt[3]{2w^2})^6$ $256w^{10}$

72. $(m\sqrt[4]{m^3})^8$ m^{14}

9.5 *Find all real solutions to each equation.*

73. $x^2 = 16$ $\{-4, 4\}$

74. $w^2 = 100$ $\{-10, 10\}$

75. $(a-5)^2 = 4$ $\{3, 7\}$

76. $(m-7)^2 = 25$ $\{2, 12\}$

77. $(a+1)^2 = 5$ $\{-1-\sqrt{5}, -1+\sqrt{5}\}$

78. $(x+5)^2 = 3$ $\{-5-\sqrt{3}, -5+\sqrt{3}\}$

79. $(m+1)^2 = -8$ No real solution

80. $(w+4)^2 = 16$ $\{-8, 0\}$

81. $\sqrt{m-1} = 3$ $\{10\}$

82. $3\sqrt{x+5} = 12$ $\{11\}$

83. $\sqrt[3]{2x+9} = 3$ $\{9\}$

84. $\sqrt[4]{2x-1} = 2$ $\left\{\frac{17}{2}\right\}$

85. $w^{2/3} = 4$ $\{-8, 8\}$

86. $m^{-4/3} = 16$ $\left\{-\frac{1}{8}, \frac{1}{8}\right\}$

87. $(m+1)^{1/3} = 5$ $\{124\}$

88. $(w-3)^{-2/3} = 4$ $\left\{\frac{23}{8}, \frac{25}{8}\right\}$

89. $\sqrt{x-3} = \sqrt{x+2} - 1$ $\{7\}$

90. $\sqrt{x^2+3x+6} = 4$ $\{-5, 2\}$

91. $\sqrt{5x-x^2} = \sqrt{6}$ $\{2, 3\}$

92. $\sqrt{x+4} - 2\sqrt{x-1} = -1$ $\{5\}$

93. $\sqrt{x+7} - 2\sqrt{x} = -2$ $\{9\}$

94. $\sqrt{x} - \sqrt{x-1} = 1$ $\{1\}$

95. $2\sqrt{x} - \sqrt{x-3} = 3$ $\{4\}$

96. $1 + \sqrt{x+7} = \sqrt{2x+7}$ $\{9\}$

9.6 *Perform the indicated operations. Write answers in the form a + bi.*

97. $(2-3i)(-5+5i)$ $5+25i$

98. $(2+i)(5-2i)$ $12+i$

99. $(2+i)+(5-4i)$ $7-3i$

100. $(2+i)+(3-6i)$ $5-5i$

101. $(1-i)-(2-3i)$ $-1+2i$

102. $(3-2i)-(1-i)$ $2-i$

103. $\frac{6+3i}{3}$ $2+i$

104. $\frac{8+12i}{4}$ $2+3i$

105. $\frac{4-\sqrt{-12}}{2}$ $2-i\sqrt{3}$

106. $\frac{6+\sqrt{-18}}{3}$ $2+i\sqrt{2}$

107. $\frac{2-3i}{4+i}$ $\frac{5}{17}-\frac{14}{17}i$

108. $\frac{3+i}{2-3i}$ $\frac{3}{13}+\frac{11}{13}i$

Find the imaginary solutions to each equation.

109. $x^2 + 100 = 0$ $\{\pm 10i\}$

110. $25a^2 + 3 = 0$ $\left\{\pm\frac{i\sqrt{3}}{5}\right\}$

111. $2b^2 + 9 = 0$ $\left\{\pm\frac{3i\sqrt{2}}{2}\right\}$

112. $3y^2 + 8 = 0$ $\left\{\pm\frac{2i\sqrt{6}}{3}\right\}$

Miscellaneous

Determine whether each equation is true or false and explain your answer. An equation involving variables should be marked true only if it is an identity. Do not use a calculator.

113. $2^3 \cdot 3^2 = 6^5$ False

114. $16^{1/4} = 4^{1/2}$ True

115. $(\sqrt{2})^3 = 2\sqrt{2}$ True

116. $\sqrt[3]{9} = 3$ False

117. $8^{200} \cdot 8^{200} = 64^{200}$ True

118. $\sqrt{295} \cdot \sqrt{295} = 295$ True

119. $4^{1/2} = \sqrt{2}$ False

120. $\sqrt{a^2} = |a|$ True

121. $5^2 \cdot 5^2 = 25^4$ False

122. $\sqrt{6} \div \sqrt{2} = \sqrt{3}$ True

123. $\sqrt{w^{10}} = w^5$ False

124. $\sqrt{a^{16}} = a^4$ False

125. $\sqrt{x^6} = x^3$ False

126. $\sqrt[6]{16} = \sqrt[3]{4}$ True

127. $\sqrt{x^8} = x^4$ True

128. $\sqrt[9]{2^6} = 2^{2/3}$ True

129. $\sqrt{16} = 2$ False

130. $2^{1/2} \cdot 2^{1/4} = 2^{3/4}$ True

131. $2^{600} = 4^{300}$ True

132. $\sqrt{2} \cdot \sqrt[4]{2} = \sqrt[6]{2}$ False

133. $\dfrac{2 + \sqrt{6}}{2} = 1 + \sqrt{6}$ False

134. $\dfrac{4 + 2\sqrt{3}}{2} = 2 + \sqrt{3}$ True

135. $\sqrt{\dfrac{4}{6}} = \dfrac{2}{3}$ False

136. $8^{200} \cdot 8^{200} = 8^{400}$ True

137. $81^{2/4} = 81^{1/2}$ True

138. $(-64)^{2/6} = (-64)^{1/3}$ False

139. $(a^4b^2)^{1/2} = |a^2b|$ True

140. $\left(\dfrac{a^2}{b^6}\right)^{1/2} = \dfrac{|a|}{b^3}$ False

Solve each problem.

141. ***Falling objects.*** If we neglect air resistance, the number of feet s that an object falls from rest during t seconds is given by the equation $s = 16t^2$. How long would it take the landing gear of an airplane to reach the earth if it fell off the airplane at 12,000 feet? $5\sqrt{30}$ seconds

142. ***Timber.*** Anne is pulling on a 60-foot rope attached to the top of a 48-foot tree while Walter is cutting the tree at its base. How far from the base of the tree is Anne standing? 36 feet

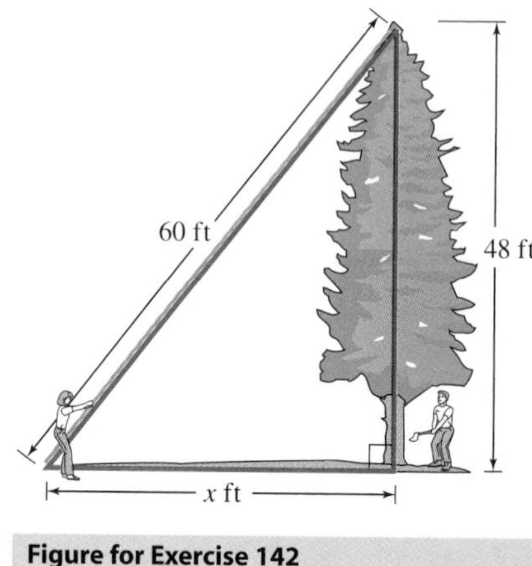

Figure for Exercise 142

143. ***Guy wire.*** If a guy wire of length 40 feet is attached to an antenna at a height of 30 feet, then how far from the base of the antenna is the wire attached to the ground? $10\sqrt{7}$ feet

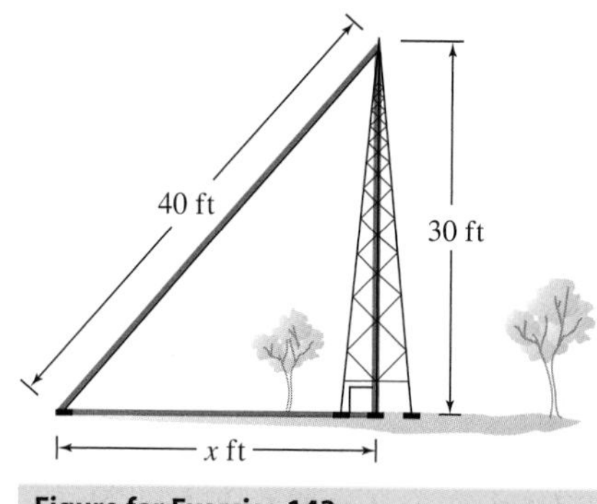

Figure for Exercise 143

144. ***Touchdown.*** Suppose at the kickoff of a football game, the receiver catches the football at the left side of the goal line and runs for a touchdown diagonally across the field. How many yards would he run? (A football field is 100 yards long and 160 feet wide.)

$113\frac{1}{3}$ yards

145. ***Long guy wires.*** The manufacturer of an antenna recommends that guy wires from the top of the antenna to the ground be attached to the ground at a distance from the base equal to the height of the antenna. How long would the guy wires be for a 200-foot antenna? $200\sqrt{2}$ feet

146. ***Height of a post.*** Betty observed that the lamp post in front of her house casts a shadow of length 8 feet when the angle of inclination of the sun is 60 degrees. How tall is the lamp post? (In a 30-60-90 right triangle, the side opposite 30 is one-half the length of the hypotenuse.) $8\sqrt{3}$ feet

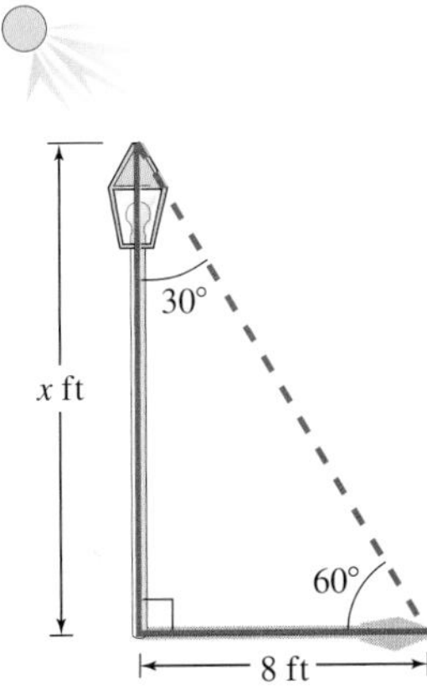

Figure for Exercise 146

147. ***Manufacturing a box.*** A cubic box has a volume of 40 cubic feet. The amount of recycled cardboard that it takes to make the six-sided box is 10% larger than the surface area of the box. Find the exact amount of recycled cardboard used in manufacturing the box. $26.4\sqrt[3]{25}$ ft^2

148. ***Shipping parts.*** A cubic box with a volume of 32 cubic feet is to be used to ship some machine parts. All of the parts are small except for a long, straight steel connecting rod. What is the maximum length of a connecting rod that will fit into this box? $2\sqrt[6]{432}$ ft

149. ***Health care costs.*** Total annual cost of health care in the United States grew from \$993.3 billion in 1995 to \$1630.3 billion in 2004 (Statistical Abstract of the United States, www.census.gov).

a) Find the average annual rate of growth r for that period by solving $1630.3 = 993.3(1 + r)^9$. 5.7%

b) Estimate the total annual cost of health care in 2010 by reading the accompanying graph. Approximately \$2300 billion

150. ***Population growth rate.*** The formula $P = P_0(1 + r)^n$ gives the population P at the end of an n-year time period, where P_0 is the initial population and r is the average annual growth rate. The U.S. population grew from 248.7 million in 1990 to 294.4 million in 2004 (U.S. Census Bureau). Find the average annual rate of growth for the U.S. population for that period. 1.2%

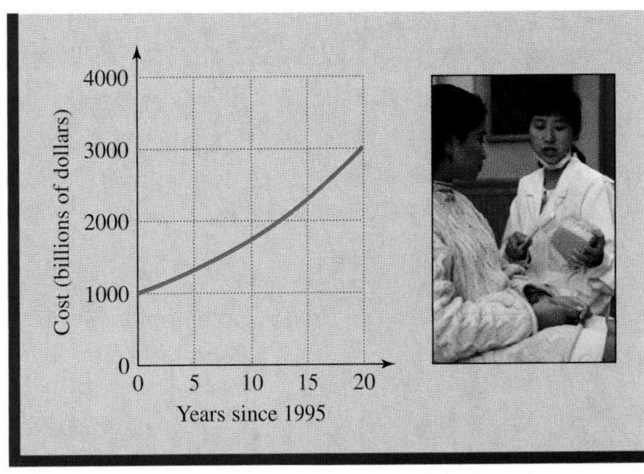

Figure for Exercise 149

151. ***Landing speed.*** Aircraft engineers determine the proper landing speed V (in feet per second) for an airplane from the formula

$$V = \sqrt{\frac{841L}{CS}},$$

where L is the gross weight of the aircraft in pounds, C is the coefficient of lift, and S is the wing surface area in square feet. Rewrite the formula so that the expression on the right-hand side is in simplified radical form.
$V = \frac{29\sqrt{LCS}}{CS}$

152. ***Spillway capacity.*** Civil engineers use the formula

$$Q = 3.32LH^{3/2}$$

to find the maximum discharge that the dam (a broad-crested weir) shown in the figure can pass before the water breaches its abutments (*Standard Handbook for Civil Engineers,* 1968). In the formula Q is the discharge in cubic feet per second, L is the length of the spillway in feet, and H is the depth of the spillway. Find Q given that $L = 60$ feet and $H = 5$ feet. Find H given that $Q = 3000$ cubic feet per second and $L = 70$ feet.
2227 ft^3/sec, 5.5 ft

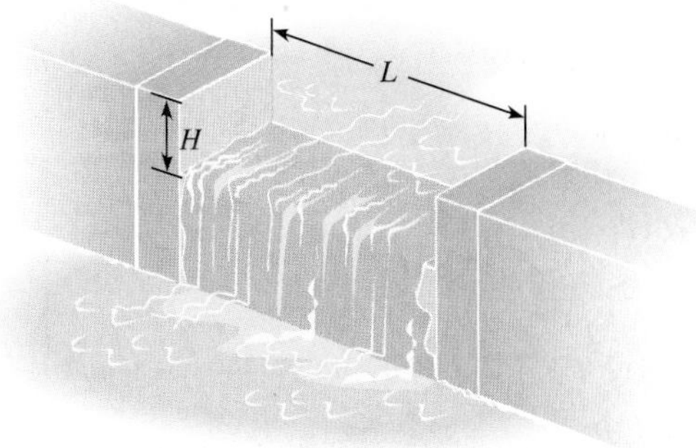

Figure for Exercise 152

Chapter 9 Test

Simplify each expression. Assume all variables represent positive numbers.

1. $8^{2/3}$ 4

2. $4^{-3/2}$ $\frac{1}{8}$

3. $\sqrt{21} \div \sqrt{7}$ $\sqrt{3}$

4. $2\sqrt{5} \cdot 3\sqrt{5}$ 30

5. $\sqrt{20} + \sqrt{5}$ $3\sqrt{5}$

6. $\sqrt{5} + \frac{1}{\sqrt{5}}$ $\frac{6\sqrt{5}}{5}$

7. $2^{1/2} \cdot 2^{1/2}$ 2

8. $\sqrt{72}$ $6\sqrt{2}$

9. $\sqrt{\frac{5}{12}}$ $\frac{\sqrt{15}}{6}$

10. $\frac{6 + \sqrt{18}}{6}$ $\frac{2 + \sqrt{2}}{2}$

11. $(2\sqrt{3} + 1)(\sqrt{3} - 2)$ $4 - 3\sqrt{3}$

12. $\sqrt[4]{32a^5y^8}$ $2ay^2\sqrt[4]{2a}$

13. $\frac{1}{\sqrt[3]{2x^2}}$ $\frac{\sqrt[3]{4x}}{2x}$

14. $\sqrt{\frac{8a^9}{b^3}}$ $\frac{2a^4\sqrt{2ab}}{b^2}$

15. $\sqrt[3]{-27x^9}$ $-3x^3$

16. $\sqrt{20m^3}$ $2m\sqrt{5m}$

17. $x^{1/2} \cdot x^{1/4}$ $x^{3/4}$

18. $(9y^4x^{1/2})^{1/2}$ $3y^2x^{1/4}$

19. $\sqrt[3]{40x^7}$ $2x^2\sqrt[3]{5x}$

20. $(4 + \sqrt{3})^2$ $19 + 8\sqrt{3}$

Find the domain of each radical expression. Use interval notation.

21. $\sqrt{4 - x}$ $(-\infty, 4]$

22. $\sqrt[3]{5x - 3}$ $(-\infty, \infty)$

Rationalize the denominator and simplify.

23. $\frac{2}{5 - \sqrt{3}}$ $\frac{5 + \sqrt{3}}{11}$

24. $\frac{\sqrt{6}}{4\sqrt{3} + \sqrt{2}}$ $\frac{6\sqrt{2} - \sqrt{3}}{23}$

Write each expression in the form $a + bi$.

25. $(3 - 2i)(4 + 5i)$ $22 + 7i$

26. $i^4 - i^5$ $1 - i$

27. $\frac{3 - i}{1 + 2i}$ $\frac{1}{5} - \frac{7}{5}i$

28. $\frac{-6 + \sqrt{-12}}{8}$ $-\frac{3}{4} + \frac{1}{4}i\sqrt{3}$

Find all real or imaginary solutions to each equation.

29. $(x - 2)^2 = 49$ $\{-5, 9\}$

30. $2\sqrt{x + 4} = 3$ $\left\{-\frac{7}{4}\right\}$

31. $w^{2/3} = 4$ $\{-8, 8\}$

32. $9y^2 + 16 = 0$ $\left\{\pm\frac{4}{3}i\right\}$

33. $\sqrt{2x^2 + x - 12} = x$ $\{3\}$

34. $\sqrt{x - 1} + \sqrt{x + 4} = 5$ $\{5\}$

Show a complete solution to each problem.

35. Find the exact length of the side of a square whose diagonal is 3 feet. $\frac{3\sqrt{2}}{2}$ feet

36. Two positive numbers differ by 11, and their square roots differ by 1. Find the numbers.
25 and 36

37. If the perimeter of a rectangle is 20 feet and the diagonal is $2\sqrt{13}$ feet, then what are the length and width?
Length 6 ft, width 4 ft

38. The average radius R of the orbit of a planet around the sun is determined by $R = T^{2/3}$, where T is the number of years for one orbit and R is measured in astronomical units (AU). If it takes Pluto 248.530 years to make one orbit of the sun, then what is the average radius of the orbit of Pluto? If the average radius of the orbit of Neptune is 30.08 AU, then how many years does it take Neptune to complete one orbit of the sun?
39.53 AU, 164.97 years

Making **Connections** | A Review of Chapters 1–9

Find all real solutions to each equation or inequality. For the inequalities, also sketch the graph of the solution set.

1. $3(x - 2) + 5 = 7 - 4(x + 3)$ $\left\{-\frac{4}{7}\right\}$

2. $\sqrt{6x + 7} = 4$ $\left\{\frac{3}{2}\right\}$

3. $|2x + 5| > 1$ $(-\infty, -3) \cup (-2, \infty)$

−5 −4 −3 −2 −1 0

4. $8x^3 - 27 = 0$ $\left\{\frac{3}{2}\right\}$

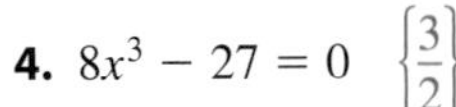

5. $2x - 3 > 3x - 4$ $(-\infty, 1)$

−3 −2 −1 0 1 2 3

6. $\sqrt{2x - 3} - \sqrt{3x + 4} = 0$ $\emptyset$

7. $\frac{w}{3} + \frac{w - 4}{2} = \frac{11}{2}$ $\{9\}$

8. $2(x + 7) - 4 = x - (10 - x)$ $\emptyset$

9. $(x + 7)^2 = 25$ $\{-12, -2\}$

10. $a^{-1/2} = 4$ $\left\{\frac{1}{16}\right\}$

11. $x - 3 > 2$ or $x < 2x + 6$

$(-6, \infty)$ −8 −7 −6 −5 −4 −3 −2

12. $a^{-2/3} = 16$ $\left\{-\frac{1}{64}, \frac{1}{64}\right\}$

13. $3x^2 - 1 = 0$ $\left\{-\frac{\sqrt{3}}{3}, \frac{\sqrt{3}}{3}\right\}$

14. $5 - 2(x - 2) = 3x - 5(x - 2) - 1$ R

15. $|3x - 4| < 5$

$\left(-\frac{1}{3}, 3\right)$ $-\frac{1}{3}$ −2 −1 0 1 2 3 4

16. $3x - 1 = 0$ $\left\{\frac{1}{3}\right\}$

17. $\sqrt{y - 1} = 9$ $\{82\}$

18. $|5(x - 2) + 1| = 3$ $\left\{\frac{6}{5}, \frac{12}{5}\right\}$

19. $0.06x - 0.04(x - 20) = 2.8$ $\{100\}$

20. $|3x - 1| > -2$ R

21. $\frac{3\sqrt{2}}{x} = \frac{\sqrt{3}}{4\sqrt{5}}$ $\{4\sqrt{30}\}$

22. $\frac{\sqrt{x} - 4}{x} = \frac{1}{\sqrt{x} + 5}$ $\{400\}$

23. $\frac{3\sqrt{2} + 4}{\sqrt{2}} = \frac{x\sqrt{18}}{3\sqrt{2} + 2}$ $\left\{\frac{13 + 9\sqrt{2}}{3}\right\}$

24. $\frac{x}{2\sqrt{5} - \sqrt{2}} = \frac{2\sqrt{5} + \sqrt{2}}{x}$ $\{-3\sqrt{2}, 3\sqrt{2}\}$

25. $\frac{\sqrt{2x} - 5}{x} = \frac{-3}{\sqrt{2x} + 5}$ $\{5\}$

26. $\frac{\sqrt{6} + 2}{x} = \frac{2}{\sqrt{6} + 4}$ $\{7 + 3\sqrt{6}\}$

27. $\frac{x - 1}{\sqrt{6}} = \frac{\sqrt{6}}{x}$ $\{-2, 3\}$

28. $\frac{x + 3}{\sqrt{10}} = \frac{\sqrt{10}}{x}$ $\{-5, 2\}$

29. $\frac{1}{x} - \frac{1}{x - 1} = -\frac{1}{6}$ $\{-2, 3\}$

30. $\frac{1}{x^2 - 2x} + \frac{1}{x} = \frac{2}{3}$ $\left\{\frac{1}{2}, 3\right\}$

The expression $\frac{-b + \sqrt{b^2 - 4ac}}{2a}$ *will be used in Chapter 10 to solve quadratic equations. Evaluate it for the given values of a, b, and c.*

31. $a = 1, b = 2, c = -15$ 3

32. $a = 1, b = 8, c = 12$ -2

33. $a = 2, b = 5, c = -3$ $\frac{1}{2}$

34. $a = 6, b = 7, c = -3$ $\frac{1}{3}$

Solve each problem.

35. ***Popping corn.*** If 1 gram of popcorn with moisture content $x\%$ is popped in a hot-air popper, then the volume of popped corn v (in cubic centimeters) that results is modeled by the formula

$$v = -94.8 + 21.4x - 0.761x^2.$$

a) Use the formula to find the volume that results when 1 gram of popcorn with moisture content 11% is popped. 48.5 cm^3

b) Use the accompanying graph to estimate the moisture content that will produce the maximum volume of popped corn. 14%

c) Use the graph to estimate the maximum possible volume for popping 1 gram of popcorn in a hot-air popper. 56 cm^3

Figure for Exercise 35

Critical **Thinking** | For Individual or Group Work | Chapter 9

These exercises can be solved by a variety of techniques, which may or may not require algebra. So be creative and think critically. Explain all answers. Answers are in the Instructor's Edition of this text.

1. ***Wagon wheel.*** A wagon wheel is placed against a wall as shown in the accompanying figure. One point on the edge of the wheel is 5 inches from the ground and 10 inches from the wall. What is the radius of the wheel?

Figure for Exercise 1

2. ***Comparing jobs.*** Bob has two job offers with a starting salary of \$100,000 per year and monthly paychecks. The Atlanta employer will raise his annual salary by \$2000 at the end of every year, while the Chicago employer will raise his annual salary by \$1000 at the end of every six months.

a) Which job is the better deal?

b) How much more will Bob have made at the end of 10 years with the better deal?

3. ***Floor tiles.*** A square floor is tiled using 121 square floor tiles. Only whole tiles are used. How many tiles are neither diagonal tiles nor edge tiles?

4. ***Counting days.*** If the first day of this century was January 1, 2000, then how many days are there in this century? (A year is a leap year if it is divisible by 4, unless it's divisible by 100, in which case it isn't, unless it's divisible by 400 in which case it is.)

5. ***Planting trees.*** How can you plant ten trees in five rows with four trees in each row?

6. ***Counting rectangles.*** How many rectangles of any size are there on an 8 by 8 checker board?

7. ***Chime time.*** The clock in the bell tower at Webster College chimes every hour on the hour: once at 1 o'clock, twice at 2 o'clock, and so on. The clock takes 5 seconds to chime at 4 o'clock and 15 seconds to chime at 10 o'clock. The time needed to chime 1 o'clock is negligible. What is the total number of seconds needed for the clock to do all of its chiming in a 24-hour period starting at 1 P.M.?

Photo for Exercise 7

8. ***Arranging digits.*** In how many ways can you arrange the digits 8, 7, 6, and 3 to form a four-digit number divisible by 9, using each digit once and only once?

1. 5 in. or 25 in. **2. a)** Chicago **b)** \$5,000 **3.** 39 **4.** 36,525 **5.** Draw equilateral triangle ABC. Place a tree at A, B, and C and at the midpoint of each side. Connect A and B with the midpoints of their opposite sides. Place the last tree at the intersection of these lines. There is at least one other possible arrangement. **6.** Draw a star with five points and put a tree at the intersection of every pair of lines. **7.** 220 seconds **8.** None

Quadratic Equations and Inequalities

Is it possible to measure beauty? For thousands of years artists and philosophers have been challenged to answer this question. The seventeenth-century philosopher John Locke said, "Beauty consists of a certain composition of color and figure causing delight in the beholder." Over the centuries many architects, sculptors, and painters have searched for beauty in their work by exploring numerical patterns in various art forms.

Today many artists and architects still use the concepts of beauty given to us by the ancient Greeks. One principle, called the Golden Rectangle, concerns the most pleasing proportions of a rectangle. The Golden Rectangle appears in nature as well as in many cultures. Examples of it can be seen in Leonardo da Vinci's *Proportions of the Human Figure* as well as in Indonesian temples and Chinese pagodas. Perhaps one of the best-known examples of the Golden Rectangle is in the façade and floor plan of the Parthenon, built in Athens in the fifth century B.C.

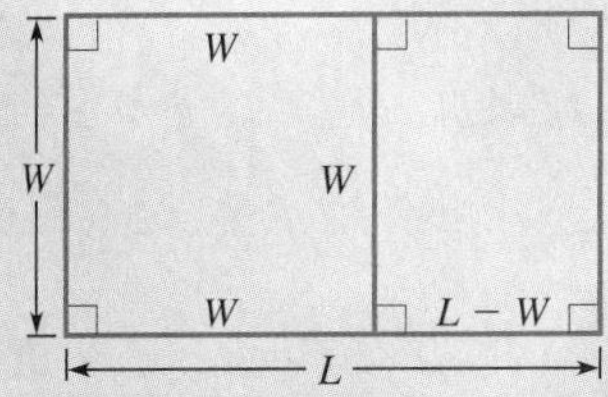

In Exercise 91 of Section 10.4 we will see that the principle of the Golden Rectangle is based on a proportion that we can solve using the quadratic formula.

10.1 Factoring and Completing the Square

In this Section

- Review of Factoring
- Review of the Even-Root Property
- Completing the Square
- Miscellaneous Equations
- Imaginary Solutions

Factoring and the even-root property were used to solve quadratic equations in Chapters 5, 6, and 9. In this section we first review those methods. Then you will learn the method of completing the square, which can be used to solve any quadratic equation.

Review of Factoring

A quadratic equation has the form $ax^2 + bx + c = 0$, where a, b, and c are real numbers with $a \neq 0$. In Section 5.6 we solved quadratic equations by factoring and then applying the zero factor property.

Zero Factor Property

The equation $ab = 0$ is equivalent to the compound equation

$$a = 0 \quad \text{or} \quad b = 0.$$

Teaching Tip We are reviewing factoring and the even-root property so that all of the methods for solving quadratics will be in one location.

Of course we can only use the factoring method when we can factor the quadratic polynomial. To solve a quadratic equation by factoring we use the following strategy.

Strategy for Solving Quadratic Equations by Factoring

1. Write the equation with 0 on one side.
2. Factor the other side.
3. Use the zero factor property to set each factor equal to zero.
4. Solve the simpler equations.
5. Check the answers in the original equation.

EXAMPLE 1

Solving a quadratic equation by factoring

Solve $3x^2 - 4x = 15$ by factoring.

Helpful Hint

After you have factored the quadratic polynomial, use FOIL to check that you have factored correctly before proceeding to the next step.

Solution

Subtract 15 from each side to get 0 on the right-hand side:

$$3x^2 - 4x - 15 = 0$$

$$(3x + 5)(x - 3) = 0 \quad \text{Factor the left-hand side.}$$

$$3x + 5 = 0 \quad \text{or} \quad x - 3 = 0 \quad \text{Zero factor property}$$

$$3x = -5 \quad \text{or} \quad x = 3$$

$$x = -\frac{5}{3}$$

The solution set is $\left\{-\frac{5}{3}, 3\right\}$. Check the solutions in the original equation.

Now do Exercises 5–14

Review of the Even-Root Property

In Chapter 9 we solved some simple quadratic equations by using the even-root property, which we restate as follows:

Even-Root Property

Suppose n is a positive even integer.

If $k > 0$, then $x^n = k$ is equivalent to $x = \pm\sqrt[n]{k}$.
If $k = 0$, then $x^n = k$ is equivalent to $x = 0$.
If $k < 0$, then $x^n = k$ has no real solution.

By the even-root property $x^2 = 4$ is equivalent to $x = \pm 2$, $x^2 = 0$ is equivalent to $x = 0$, and $x^2 = -4$ has no real solutions.

EXAMPLE 2

Solving a quadratic equation by the even-root property

Solve $(a - 1)^2 = 9$.

Teaching Tip Solving this type of quadratic equation by the even-root property prepares students for completing the square.

Solution

By the even-root property $x^2 = k$ is equivalent to $x = \pm\sqrt{k}$.

$$(a - 1)^2 = 9$$
$$a - 1 = \pm\sqrt{9} \quad \text{Even-root property}$$
$$a - 1 = 3 \quad \text{or} \quad a - 1 = -3$$
$$a = 4 \quad \text{or} \quad a = -2$$

Check these solutions in the original equation. The solution set is $\{-2, 4\}$.

Now do Exercises 15–24

Completing the Square

We cannot solve every quadratic by factoring because not all quadratic polynomials can be factored. However, we can write any quadratic equation in the form of Example 2 and then apply the even-root property to solve it. This method is called **completing the square.**

The essential part of completing the square is to recognize a perfect square trinomial when given its first two terms. For example, if we are given $x^2 + 6x$, how do we recognize that these are the first two terms of the perfect square trinomial $x^2 + 6x + 9$? To answer this question, recall that $x^2 + 6x + 9$ is a perfect square trinomial because it is the square of the binomial $x + 3$:

$$(x + 3)^2 = x^2 + 2 \cdot 3x + 3^2 = x^2 + 6x + 9$$

Notice that the 6 comes from multiplying 3 by 2 and the 9 comes from squaring the 3. So to find the missing 9 in $x^2 + 6x$, divide 6 by 2 to get 3, then square 3 to get 9. This procedure can be used to find the last term in any perfect square trinomial in which the coefficient of x^2 is 1.

Helpful Hint

The area of an x by x square and two x by 3 rectangles is $x^2 + 6x$. The area needed to "complete the square" in this figure is 9:

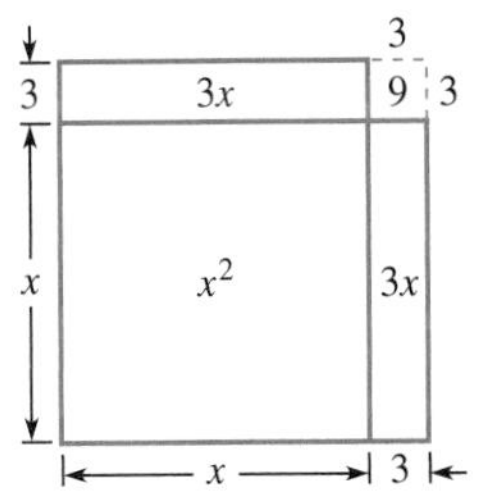

Rule for Finding the Last Term

The last term of a perfect square trinomial is the square of one-half of the coefficient of the middle term. In symbols, the perfect square trinomial whose first two terms are $x^2 + bx$ is $x^2 + bx + \left(\frac{b}{2}\right)^2$.

EXAMPLE 3

Finding the last term

Find the perfect square trinomial whose first two terms are given.

a) $x^2 + 8x$ **b)** $x^2 - 5x$ **c)** $x^2 + \frac{4}{7}x$ **d)** $x^2 - \frac{3}{2}x$

Solution

a) One-half of 8 is 4, and 4 squared is 16. So the perfect square trinomial is

$$x^2 + 8x + 16.$$

b) One-half of -5 is $-\frac{5}{2}$, and $-\frac{5}{2}$ squared is $\frac{25}{4}$. So the perfect square trinomial is

$$x^2 - 5x + \frac{25}{4}.$$

c) Since $\frac{1}{2} \cdot \frac{4}{7} = \frac{2}{7}$ and $\frac{2}{7}$ squared is $\frac{4}{49}$, the perfect square trinomial is

$$x^2 + \frac{4}{7}x + \frac{4}{49}.$$

d) Since $\frac{1}{2}\left(-\frac{3}{2}\right) = -\frac{3}{4}$ and $\left(-\frac{3}{4}\right)^2 = \frac{9}{16}$, the perfect square trinomial is

$$x^2 - \frac{3}{2}x + \frac{9}{16}.$$

Teaching Tip Note how Examples 2, 3, and 4 are setting the stage for completing the square.

Now do Exercises 25–32

Another essential step in completing the square is to write the perfect square trinomial as the square of a binomial. Recall that

$$a^2 + 2ab + b^2 = (a + b)^2$$

and

$$a^2 - 2ab + b^2 = (a - b)^2.$$

EXAMPLE 4

Factoring perfect square trinomials

Factor each trinomial.

a) $x^2 + 12x + 36$ **b)** $y^2 - 7y + \frac{49}{4}$

c) $z^2 - \frac{4}{3}z + \frac{4}{9}$

Helpful Hint

To square a binomial use the following rule (not FOIL):

- Square the first term.
- Add twice the product of the terms.
- Add the square of the last term.

Solution

a) The trinomial $x^2 + 12x + 36$ is of the form $a^2 + 2ab + b^2$ with $a = x$ and $b = 6$. So

$$x^2 + 12x + 36 = (x + 6)^2.$$

Check by squaring $x + 6$.

b) The trinomial $y^2 - 7y + \frac{49}{4}$ is of the form $a^2 - 2ab + b^2$ with $a = y$ and $b = \frac{7}{2}$. So

$$y^2 - 7y + \frac{49}{4} = \left(y - \frac{7}{2}\right)^2.$$

Check by squaring $y - \frac{7}{2}$.

c) The trinomial $z^2 - \frac{4}{3}z + \frac{4}{9}$ is of the form $a^2 - 2ab + b^2$ with $a = z$ and $b = -\frac{2}{3}$. So

$$z^2 - \frac{4}{3}z + \frac{4}{9} = \left(z - \frac{2}{3}\right)^2.$$

Now do Exercises 33–40

In Example 5 we use the skills that we practiced in Examples 2, 3, and 4 to solve the quadratic equation $ax^2 + bx + c = 0$ with $a = 1$ by the method of completing the square.

EXAMPLE 5

Completing the square with $a = 1$

Solve $x^2 + 6x + 5 = 0$ by completing the square.

Solution

The perfect square trinomial whose first two terms are $x^2 + 6x$ is

$$x^2 + 6x + 9.$$

So we move 5 to the right-hand side of the equation, then add 9 to each side to create a perfect square on the left side:

$$x^2 + 6x = -5 \quad \text{Subtract 5 from each side.}$$

$$x^2 + 6x + 9 = -5 + 9 \quad \text{Add 9 to each side to get a perfect square trinomial.}$$

$$(x + 3)^2 = 4 \quad \text{Factor the left-hand side.}$$

$$x + 3 = \pm\sqrt{4} \quad \text{Even-root property}$$

$$x + 3 = 2 \quad \text{or} \quad x + 3 = -2$$

$$x = -1 \quad \text{or} \quad x = -5$$

Check in the original equation:

$$(-1)^2 + 6(-1) + 5 = 0$$

and

$$(-5)^2 + 6(-5) + 5 = 0$$

The solution set is $\{-1, -5\}$.

Now do Exercises 41–48

Calculator Close-Up

The solutions to

$$x^2 + 6x + 5 = 0$$

correspond to the x-intercepts for the graph of

$$y = x^2 + 6x + 5.$$

So we can check our solutions by graphing and using the TRACE feature as shown here.

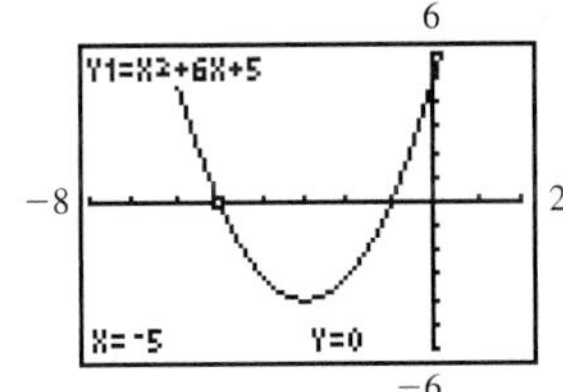

CAUTION All of the perfect square trinomials that we have used so far had a leading coefficient of 1. If $a \neq 1$, then we must divide each side of the equation by a to get an equation with a leading coefficient of 1.

The strategy for solving a quadratic equation by completing the square is stated in the following box.

Study Tip

Most instructors believe that what they do in class is important. If you miss class, then you miss what is important to your instructor and what is most likely to appear on the test.

Strategy for Solving Quadratic Equations by Completing the Square

1. If $a \neq 1$, then divide each side of the equation by a.
2. Get only the x^2 and the x terms on the left-hand side.
3. Add to each side the square of $\frac{1}{2}$ the coefficient of x.
4. Factor the left-hand side as the square of a binomial.
5. Apply the even-root property.
6. Solve for x.
7. Simplify.

EXAMPLE 6

Completing the square with $a \neq 1$

Solve $2x^2 + 3x - 2 = 0$ by completing the square.

Solution

For completing the square, the coefficient of x^2 must be 1. So we first divide each side of the equation by 2:

$$\frac{2x^2 + 3x - 2}{2} = \frac{0}{2} \quad \text{Divide each side by 2.}$$

$$x^2 + \frac{3}{2}x - 1 = 0 \quad \text{Simplify.}$$

$$x^2 + \frac{3}{2}x = 1 \quad \text{Get only } x^2 \text{ and } x \text{ terms on the left-hand side.}$$

$$x^2 + \frac{3}{2}x + \frac{9}{16} = 1 + \frac{9}{16} \quad \text{One-half of } \tfrac{3}{2} \text{ is } \tfrac{3}{4}, \text{ and } \left(\tfrac{3}{4}\right)^2 = \tfrac{9}{16}.$$

$$\left(x + \frac{3}{4}\right)^2 = \frac{25}{16} \quad \text{Factor the left-hand side.}$$

$$x + \frac{3}{4} = \pm\sqrt{\frac{25}{16}} \quad \text{Even-root property}$$

$$x + \frac{3}{4} = \frac{5}{4} \quad \text{or} \quad x + \frac{3}{4} = -\frac{5}{4}$$

$$x = \frac{2}{4} = \frac{1}{2} \quad \text{or} \quad x = -\frac{8}{4} = -2$$

Check these values in the original equation. The solution set is $\left\{-2, \frac{1}{2}\right\}$.

Now do Exercises 49–50

Calculator Close-Up

Note that the x-intercepts for the graph of the function

$$y = 2x^2 + 3x - 2$$

are $(-2, 0)$ and $\left(\frac{1}{2}, 0\right)$:

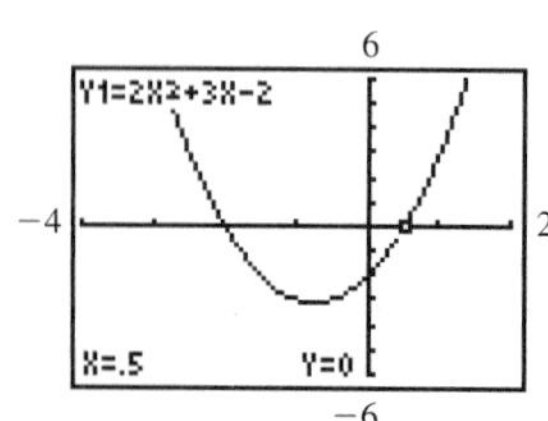

Math *at Work* Financial Matters

In the United States over 1 million new homes are sold annually, with a median price of about \$200,000. Over 17 million new cars are sold each year with a median price over \$20,000. Americans are constantly saving and borrowing. Nearly everyone will need to know a monthly payment or what their savings will total over time. The answers to these questions are in the following table.

What \$*P* Left at Compound Interest Will Grow to	What \$*R* Deposited Periodically Will Grow to	Periodic Payment That Will Pay off a Loan of \$*P*
$P(1 + i)^{nt}$	$R\dfrac{(1 + i)^{nt} - 1}{i}$	$P\dfrac{i}{1 - (1 + i)^{-nt}}$

In each case n is the number of periods per year, r is the annual percentage rate (APR), t is the number of years, and i is the interest rate per period $\left(i = \frac{r}{n}\right)$. For periodic payments or deposits these expressions apply only if the compounding period equals the payment period. So let's see what these expressions do.

A person inherits \$10,000 and lets it grow at 4% APR compounded daily for 20 years. Use the first expression with $n = 365$, $i = \frac{0.04}{365}$, and $t = 20$ to get $10{,}000\left(1 + \frac{0.04}{365}\right)^{365\cdot 20}$ or \$22,254.43, which is the amount after 20 years.

More often, people save money with periodic deposits. Suppose you deposit \$100 per month at 4% compounded monthly for 20 years. Use the second expression with $R = 100$, $i = \frac{0.04}{12}$, $n = 12$, and $t = 20$ to get $100\frac{(1 + 0.04/12)^{12\cdot 20} - 1}{0.04/12}$ or \$36,677.46, which is the amount after 20 years.

Suppose that you get a 20-year \$200,000 mortgage at 7% APR compounded monthly to buy an average house. Try using the third expression to calculate the monthly payment of \$1550.60. See the accompanying figure.

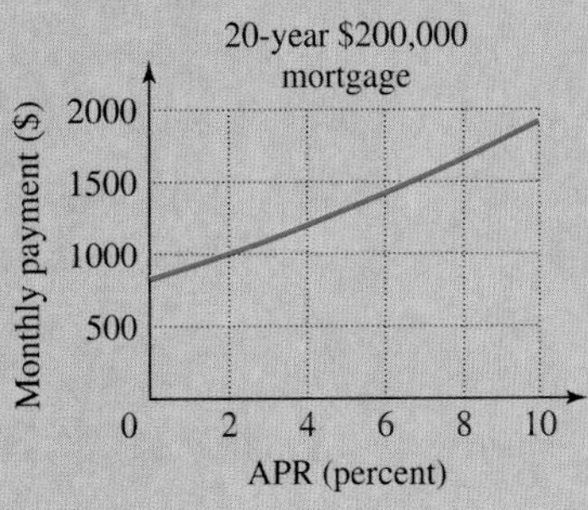

In Examples 5 and 6 the solutions were rational numbers, and the equations could have been solved by factoring. In Example 7 the solutions are irrational numbers, and factoring will not work.

EXAMPLE 7

A quadratic equation with irrational solutions

Solve $x^2 - 3x - 6 = 0$ by completing the square.

Solution

Because $a = 1$, we first get the x^2 and x terms on the left-hand side:

$$x^2 - 3x - 6 = 0$$

$$x^2 - 3x \quad = 6 \qquad \text{Add 6 to each side.}$$

$$x^2 - 3x + \frac{9}{4} = 6 + \frac{9}{4} \qquad \text{One-half of } -3 \text{ is } -\tfrac{3}{2}, \text{ and } \left(-\tfrac{3}{2}\right)^2 = \tfrac{9}{4}.$$

$$\left(x - \frac{3}{2}\right)^2 = \frac{33}{4} \qquad 6 + \tfrac{9}{4} = \tfrac{24}{4} + \tfrac{9}{4} = \tfrac{33}{4}$$

$$x - \frac{3}{2} = \pm\sqrt{\frac{33}{4}} \qquad \text{Even-root property}$$

$$x = \frac{3}{2} \pm \frac{\sqrt{33}}{2} \qquad \text{Add } \tfrac{3}{2} \text{ to each side.}$$

$$x = \frac{3 \pm \sqrt{33}}{2}$$

The solution set is $\left\{\frac{3 + \sqrt{33}}{2}, \frac{3 - \sqrt{33}}{2}\right\}$.

Now do Exercises 51–58

Teaching Tip Point out that completing the square is needed to find the irrational solutions to this equation.

Miscellaneous Equations

Examples 8 and 9 show equations that are not originally in the form of quadratic equations. However, after simplifying these equations, we get quadratic equations. Even though completing the square can be used on any quadratic equation, factoring and the square root property are usually easier and we can use them when applicable. In Examples 8 and 9 we will use the most appropriate method.

EXAMPLE 8

An equation containing a radical

Solve $x + 3 = \sqrt{153 - x}$.

Solution

Square both sides of the equation to eliminate the radical:

$$x + 3 = \sqrt{153 - x} \qquad \text{The original equation}$$

$$(x + 3)^2 = \left(\sqrt{153 - x}\right)^2 \qquad \text{Square each side.}$$

$$x^2 + 6x + 9 = 153 - x \qquad \text{Simplify.}$$

$$x^2 + 7x - 144 = 0$$

$$(x - 9)(x + 16) = 0 \qquad \text{Factor.}$$

$$x - 9 = 0 \quad \text{or} \quad x + 16 = 0 \qquad \text{Zero factor property}$$

$$x = 9 \quad \text{or} \quad x = -16$$

Calculator Close-Up

You can provide graphical support for the solution to Example 8 by graphing

$$y_1 = x + 3$$

and

$$y_2 = \sqrt{153 - x}.$$

It appears that the only point of intersection occurs when $x = 9$.

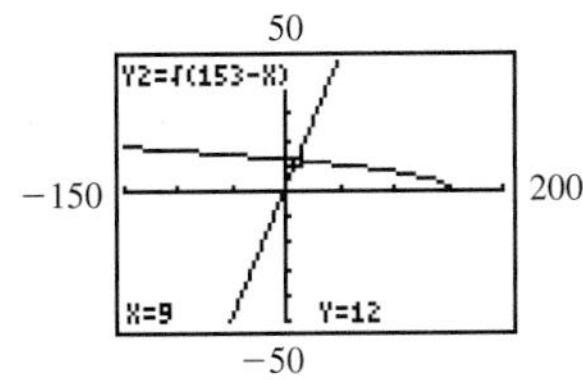

Because we squared each side of the original equation, we must check for extraneous roots. Let $x = 9$ in the original equation:

$$9 + 3 = \sqrt{153 - 9}$$
$$12 = \sqrt{144} \quad \text{Correct}$$

Let $x = -16$ in the original equation:

$$-16 + 3 = \sqrt{153 - (-16)}$$
$$-13 = \sqrt{169} \quad \text{Incorrect because } \sqrt{169} = 13$$

Because -16 is an extraneous root, the solution set is $\{9\}$.

Now do Exercises 59–62

EXAMPLE 9

An equation containing rational expressions

Solve $\frac{1}{x} + \frac{3}{x-2} = \frac{5}{8}$.

Solution

The least common denominator (LCD) for x, $x - 2$, and 8 is $8x(x - 2)$.

$$\frac{1}{x} + \frac{3}{x-2} = \frac{5}{8}$$

$$8x(x-2)\frac{1}{x} + 8x(x-2)\frac{3}{x-2} = 8x(x-2)\frac{5}{8} \quad \text{Multiply each side by the LCD.}$$

$$8x - 16 + 24x = 5x^2 - 10x$$

$$32x - 16 = 5x^2 - 10x$$

$$-5x^2 + 42x - 16 = 0$$

$$5x^2 - 42x + 16 = 0 \quad \text{Multiply each side by } -1 \text{ for easier factoring.}$$

$$(5x - 2)(x - 8) = 0 \quad \text{Factor.}$$

$$5x - 2 = 0 \quad \text{or} \quad x - 8 = 0$$

$$x = \frac{2}{5} \quad \text{or} \quad x = 8$$

Check these values in the original equation. The solution set is $\left\{\frac{2}{5}, 8\right\}$.

Now do Exercises 63–66

Imaginary Solutions

In Chapter 9 we found imaginary solutions to quadratic equations using the even-root property. We can get imaginary solutions also by completing the square.

EXAMPLE 10

An equation with imaginary solutions

Find the complex solutions to $x^2 - 4x + 12 = 0$.

Solution

Because the quadratic polynomial cannot be factored, we solve the equation by completing the square.

$$x^2 - 4x + 12 = 0 \quad \text{The original equation}$$

$$x^2 - 4x = -12 \quad \text{Subtract 12 from each side.}$$

$$x^2 - 4x + 4 = -12 + 4 \quad \text{One-half of } -4 \text{ is } -2\text{, and } (-2)^2 = 4.$$

$$(x - 2)^2 = -8$$

$$x - 2 = \pm\sqrt{-8} \quad \text{Even-root property}$$

$$x = 2 \pm i\sqrt{8}$$

$$= 2 \pm 2i\sqrt{2}$$

Check these values in the original equation. The solution set is $\{2 \pm 2i\sqrt{2}\}$.

Now do Exercises 67–76

Calculator Close-Up

The answer key (ANS) can be used to check imaginary answers as shown here.

```
2+2i√(2)
      2+2.828427125i
Ans²-4Ans+12
                   0
```

Warm-Ups ▼

True or false? Explain your answer.

1. Completing the square means drawing the fourth side. False
2. The equation $(x - 3)^2 = 12$ is equivalent to $x - 3 = 2\sqrt{3}$. False
3. Every quadratic equation can be solved by factoring. False
4. The trinomial $x^2 + \frac{4}{3}x + \frac{16}{9}$ is a perfect square trinomial. False
5. Every quadratic equation can be solved by completing the square. True
6. To complete the square for $2x^2 + 6x = 4$, add 9 to each side. False
7. $(2x - 3)(3x + 5) = 0$ is equivalent to $x = \frac{3}{2}$ or $x = \frac{5}{3}$. False
8. In completing the square for $x^2 - 3x = 4$, add $\frac{9}{4}$ to each side. True
9. The equation $x^2 = -8$ is equivalent to $x = \pm 2\sqrt{2}$. False
10. All quadratic equations have two distinct complex solutions. False

10.1 Exercises

Boost your GRADE at mathzone.com!

▶ Practice Problems ▶ Net Tutor
▶ Self-Tests ▶ e-Professors
▶ Videos

Reading and Writing *After reading this section, write out the answers to these questions. Use complete sentences.*

1. What are the three methods discussed in this section for solving a quadratic equation?
In this section quadratic equations are solved by factoring, the even-root property, and completing the square.

2. Which quadratic equations can be solved by the even-root property?
If $b = 0$ in $ax^2 + bx + c = 0$, then the equation can be solved by the even-root property.

3. How do you find the last term for a perfect square trinomial when completing the square?
The last term is the square of one-half the coefficient of the middle term.

4. How do you complete the square when the leading coefficient is not 1?
If the leading coefficient is not 1, then the first step is to divide each side by the leading coefficient.

Solve by factoring. See Example 1.

5. $x^2 - x - 6 = 0$ $\{-2, 3\}$

6. $x^2 + 6x + 8 = 0$ $\{-4, -2\}$

7. $a^2 + 2a = 15$ $\{-5, 3\}$

8. $w^2 - 2w = 15$ $\{-3, 5\}$

9. $2x^2 - x - 3 = 0$ $\left\{-1, \frac{3}{2}\right\}$

10. $6x^2 - x - 15 = 0$ $\left\{-\frac{3}{2}, \frac{5}{3}\right\}$

11. $y^2 + 14y + 49 = 0$ $\{-7\}$

12. $a^2 - 6a + 9 = 0$ $\{3\}$

13. $a^2 - 16 = 0$ $\{-4, 4\}$

14. $4w^2 - 25 = 0$ $\left\{-\frac{5}{2}, \frac{5}{2}\right\}$

Use the even-root property to solve each equation. See Example 2.

15. $x^2 = 81$ $\{-9, 9\}$

16. $x^2 = \frac{9}{4}$ $\left\{-\frac{3}{2}, \frac{3}{2}\right\}$

17. $x^2 = \frac{16}{9}$ $\left\{-\frac{4}{3}, \frac{4}{3}\right\}$

18. $a^2 = 32$ $\{-4\sqrt{2}, 4\sqrt{2}\}$

19. $(x - 3)^2 = 16$ $\{-1, 7\}$

20. $(x + 5)^2 = 4$ $\{-7, -3\}$

21. $(z + 1)^2 = 5$ $\{-1 - \sqrt{5}, -1 + \sqrt{5}\}$

22. $(a - 2)^2 = 8$ $\{2 - 2\sqrt{2}, 2 + 2\sqrt{2}\}$

23. $\left(w - \frac{3}{2}\right)^2 = \frac{7}{4}$ $\left\{\frac{3 - \sqrt{7}}{2}, \frac{3 + \sqrt{7}}{2}\right\}$

24. $\left(w + \frac{2}{3}\right)^2 = \frac{5}{9}$ $\left\{\frac{-2 - \sqrt{5}}{3}, \frac{-2 + \sqrt{5}}{3}\right\}$

Find the perfect square trinomial whose first two terms are given. See Example 3.

25. $x^2 + 2x$ $x^2 + 2x + 1$

26. $m^2 + 14m$ $m^2 + 14m + 49$

27. $x^2 - 3x$ $x^2 - 3x + \frac{9}{4}$

28. $w^2 - 5w$ $w^2 - 5w + \frac{25}{4}$

29. $y^2 + \frac{1}{4}y$ $y^2 + \frac{1}{4}y + \frac{1}{64}$

30. $z^2 + \frac{3}{2}z$ $z^2 + \frac{3}{2}z + \frac{9}{16}$

31. $x^2 + \frac{2}{3}x$ $x^2 + \frac{2}{3}x + \frac{1}{9}$

32. $p^2 + \frac{6}{5}p$ $p^2 + \frac{6}{5}p + \frac{9}{25}$

Factor each perfect square trinomial. See Example 4.

33. $x^2 + 8x + 16$ $(x + 4)^2$

34. $x^2 - 10x + 25$ $(x - 5)^2$

35. $y^2 - 5y + \frac{25}{4}$ $\left(y - \frac{5}{2}\right)^2$

36. $w^2 + w + \frac{1}{4}$ $\left(w + \frac{1}{2}\right)^2$

37. $z^2 - \frac{4}{7}z + \frac{4}{49}$ $\left(z - \frac{2}{7}\right)^2$

38. $m^2 - \frac{6}{5}m + \frac{9}{25}$ $\left(m - \frac{3}{5}\right)^2$

39. $t^2 + \frac{3}{5}t + \frac{9}{100}$ $\left(t + \frac{3}{10}\right)^2$

40. $h^2 + \frac{3}{2}h + \frac{9}{16}$ $\left(h + \frac{3}{4}\right)^2$

Solve by completing the square. See Examples 5–7. Use your calculator to check.

41. $x^2 - 2x - 15 = 0$ $\{-3, 5\}$

42. $x^2 - 6x - 7 = 0$ $\{-1, 7\}$

43. $2x^2 - 4x = 70$ $\{-5, 7\}$

44. $3x^2 - 6x = 24$ $\{-2, 4\}$

45. $w^2 - w - 20 = 0$ $\{-4, 5\}$

46. $y^2 - 3y - 10 = 0$ $\{-2, 5\}$

47. $q^2 + 5q = 14$ $\{-7, 2\}$

48. $z^2 + z = 2$ $\{-2, 1\}$

49. $2h^2 - h - 3 = 0$ $\left\{-1, \frac{3}{2}\right\}$

50. $2m^2 - m - 15 = 0$ $\left\{-\frac{5}{2}, 3\right\}$

51. $x^2 + 4x = 6$ $\{-2 - \sqrt{10}, -2 + \sqrt{10}\}$

52. $x^2 + 6x - 8 = 0$ $\{-3 - \sqrt{17}, -3 + \sqrt{17}\}$

53. $x^2 + 8x - 4 = 0$ $\{-4 - 2\sqrt{5}, -4 + 2\sqrt{5}\}$

54. $x^2 + 10x - 3 = 0$ $\{-5 - 2\sqrt{7}, -5 + 2\sqrt{7}\}$

55. $4x^2 - 4x - 1 = 0$ $\left\{\frac{1 - \sqrt{2}}{2}, \frac{1 + \sqrt{2}}{2}\right\}$

56. $4x^2 + 4x - 2 = 0$ $\left\{\frac{-1-\sqrt{3}}{2}, \frac{-1+\sqrt{3}}{2}\right\}$

57. $2x^2 + 3x - 4 = 0$ $\left\{\frac{-3-\sqrt{41}}{4}, \frac{-3+\sqrt{41}}{4}\right\}$

58. $2x^2 + 5x - 1 = 0$ $\left\{\frac{-5-\sqrt{33}}{4}, \frac{-5+\sqrt{33}}{4}\right\}$

Solve each equation by an appropriate method. See Examples 8 and 9.

59. $\sqrt{2x+1} = x - 1$ $\{4\}$

60. $\sqrt{2x-4} = x - 14$ $\{20\}$

61. $w = \frac{\sqrt{w+1}}{2}$ $\left\{\frac{1+\sqrt{17}}{8}\right\}$

62. $y - 1 = \frac{\sqrt{y+1}}{2}$ $\left\{\frac{9+\sqrt{33}}{8}\right\}$

63. $\frac{t}{t-2} = \frac{2t-3}{t}$ $\{1, 6\}$

64. $\frac{z}{z+3} = \frac{3z}{5z-1}$ $\{0, 5\}$

65. $\frac{2}{x^2} + \frac{4}{x} + 1 = 0$ $\{-2-\sqrt{2}, -2+\sqrt{2}\}$

66. $\frac{1}{x^2} + \frac{3}{x} + 1 = 0$ $\left\{\frac{-3-\sqrt{5}}{2}, \frac{-3+\sqrt{5}}{2}\right\}$

Use completing the square to find the imaginary solutions to each equation. See Example 10.

67. $x^2 + 2x + 5 = 0$ $\{-1-2i, -1+2i\}$

68. $x^2 + 4x + 5 = 0$ $\{-2-i, -2+i\}$

69. $x^2 - 6x + 11 = 0$ $\{3+i\sqrt{2}, 3-i\sqrt{2}\}$

70. $x^2 - 8x + 19 = 0$ $\{4+i\sqrt{3}, 4-i\sqrt{3}\}$

71. $x^2 = -\frac{1}{2}$ $\left\{\pm\frac{i\sqrt{2}}{2}\right\}$

72. $x^2 = -\frac{1}{8}$ $\left\{\pm\frac{i\sqrt{2}}{4}\right\}$

73. $x^2 + 12 = 0$ $\{-2i\sqrt{3}, 2i\sqrt{3}\}$

74. $-3x^2 - 21 = 0$ $\{-i\sqrt{7}, i\sqrt{7}\}$

75. $5z^2 - 4z + 1 = 0$ $\left\{\frac{2 \pm i}{5}\right\}$

76. $2w^2 - 3w + 2 = 0$ $\left\{\frac{3 \pm i\sqrt{7}}{4}\right\}$

Find all real or imaginary solutions to each equation. Use the method of your choice.

77. $x^2 = -121$ $\{\pm 11i\}$

78. $w^2 = -225$ $\{\pm 15i\}$

79. $4x^2 + 25 = 0$ $\left\{-\frac{5}{2}i, \frac{5}{2}i\right\}$

80. $5w^2 - 3 = 0$ $\left\{-\frac{\sqrt{15}}{5}, \frac{\sqrt{15}}{5}\right\}$

81. $\left(p + \frac{1}{2}\right)^2 = \frac{9}{4}$ $\{-2, 1\}$

82. $\left(y - \frac{2}{3}\right)^2 = \frac{4}{9}$ $\left\{0, \frac{4}{3}\right\}$

83. $5t^2 + 4t - 3 = 0$ $\left\{\frac{-2-\sqrt{19}}{5}, \frac{-2+\sqrt{19}}{5}\right\}$

84. $3v^2 + 4v - 1 = 0$ $\left\{\frac{-2-\sqrt{7}}{3}, \frac{-2+\sqrt{7}}{3}\right\}$

85. $m^2 + 2m - 24 = 0$ $\{-6, 4\}$

86. $q^2 + 6q - 7 = 0$ $\{-7, 1\}$

87. $(x - 2)^2 = -9$ $\{2 \pm 3i\}$

88. $(2x - 1)^2 = -4$ $\left\{\frac{1 \pm 2i}{2}\right\}$

89. $-x^2 + x + 6 = 0$ $\{-2, 3\}$

90. $-x^2 + x + 12 = 0$ $\{-3, 4\}$

91. $x^2 - 6x + 10 = 0$ $\{3-i, 3+i\}$

92. $x^2 - 8x + 17 = 0$ $\{4-i, 4+i\}$

93. $2x - 5 = \sqrt{7x+7}$ $\{6\}$

94. $\sqrt{7x+29} = x + 3$ $\{5\}$

95. $\frac{1}{x} + \frac{1}{x-1} = \frac{1}{4}$ $\left\{\frac{9-\sqrt{65}}{2}, \frac{9+\sqrt{65}}{2}\right\}$

96. $\frac{1}{x} - \frac{2}{1-x} = \frac{1}{2}$ $\left\{\frac{7-\sqrt{41}}{2}, \frac{7+\sqrt{41}}{2}\right\}$

If the solution to an equation is imaginary or irrational, it takes a bit more effort to check. Replace x by each given number to verify each statement.

97. Both $2 + \sqrt{3}$ and $2 - \sqrt{3}$ satisfy $x^2 - 4x + 1 = 0$.

98. Both $1 + \sqrt{2}$ and $1 - \sqrt{2}$ satisfy $x^2 - 2x - 1 = 0$.

99. Both $1 + i$ and $1 - i$ satisfy $x^2 - 2x + 2 = 0$.

100. Both $2 + 3i$ and $2 - 3i$ satisfy $x^2 - 4x + 13 = 0$.

Solve each problem.

101. ***Approach speed.*** The formula $1211.1L = CA^2S$ is used to determine the approach speed for landing an aircraft, where L is the gross weight of the aircraft in pounds, C is the coefficient of lift, S is the surface area of the wings in square feet (ft^2), and A is approach speed in feet per second. Find A for the Piper Cheyenne, which has a gross weight of 8700 lb, a coefficient of lift of 2.81, and wing surface area of 200 ft^2. 136.9 ft/sec

102. ***Time to swing.*** The period T (time in seconds for one complete cycle) of a simple pendulum is related to the length L (in feet) of the pendulum by the formula $8T^2 = \pi^2 L$. If a child is on a swing with a 10-foot chain, then how long does it take to complete one cycle of the swing? 3.5 sec

103. ***Time for a swim.*** Tropical Pools figures that its monthly revenue in dollars on the sale of x aboveground pools is given by $R = 1500x - 3x^2$, where x is less than 25. What number of pools sold would provide a revenue of \$17,568? 12

104. ***Pole vaulting.*** In 1981 Vladimir Poliakov (USSR) set a world record of 19 ft $\frac{3}{4}$ in. for the pole vault (www.polevault.com). To reach that height, Poliakov obtained a speed of approximately 36 feet per second on the runway. The formula $h = -16t^2 + 36t$ gives his height t seconds after leaving the ground.

a) Use the formula to find the exact values of t for which his height was 18 feet.

b) Use the accompanying graph to estimate the value of t for which he was at his maximum height.

c) Approximately how long was he in the air?

a) 0.75 sec and 1.5 sec **b)** 1.125 sec **c)** 2.25 sec

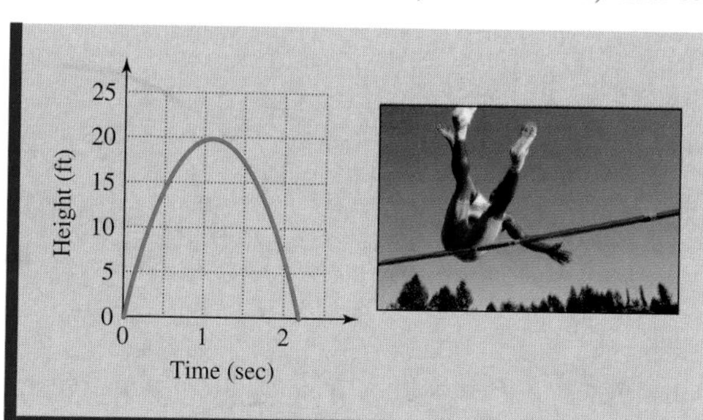

Figure for Exercise 104

Getting More Involved

105. *Discussion*

Which of the following equations is not a quadratic equation? Explain your answer.

a) $\pi x^2 - \sqrt{5}x - 1 = 0$ **b)** $3x^2 - 1 = 0$

c) $4x + 5 = 0$ **d)** $0.009x^2 = 0$ c

106. *Exploration*

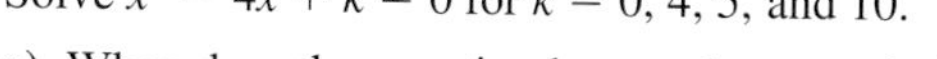

Solve $x^2 - 4x + k = 0$ for $k = 0, 4, 5,$ and 10.

a) When does the equation have only one solution?

b) For what values of k are the solutions real?

c) For what values of k are the solutions imaginary?

a) $k = 4$ **b)** $k \le 4$ **c)** $k > 4$

107. *Cooperative learning*

Write a quadratic equation of each of the following types, then trade your equations with those of a classmate. Solve the equations and verify that they are of the required types.

a) a single rational solution **b)** two rational solutions

c) two irrational solutions **d)** two imaginary solutions

108. *Exploration*

In the next section we will solve $ax^2 + bx + c = 0$ for x by completing the square. Try it now without looking ahead.

Graphing Calculator Exercises

For each equation, find approximate solutions rounded to two decimal places.

109. $x^2 - 7.3x + 12.5 = 0$ $\{4.56, 2.74\}$

110. $1.2x^2 - \pi x + \sqrt{2} = 0$ $\{2.04, 0.58\}$

111. $2x - 3 = \sqrt{20 - x}$ $\{3.53\}$

112. $x^2 - 1.3x = 22.3 - x^2$ $\{-3.03, 3.68\}$

10.2 The Quadratic Formula

In this Section

- Developing the Formula
- Using the Formula
- Number of Solutions
- Applications

Completing the square from Section 10.1 can be used to solve any quadratic equation. Here we apply this method to the general quadratic equation to get a formula for the solutions to any quadratic equation.

Developing the Formula

Start with the general form of the quadratic equation,

$$ax^2 + bx + c = 0.$$

Assume a is positive for now, and divide each side by a:

$$\frac{ax^2 + bx + c}{a} = \frac{0}{a}$$

$$x^2 + \frac{b}{a}x + \frac{c}{a} = 0$$

$$x^2 + \frac{b}{a}x = -\frac{c}{a} \qquad \text{Subtract } \frac{c}{a} \text{ from each side.}$$

One-half of $\frac{b}{a}$ is $\frac{b}{2a}$, and $\frac{b}{2a}$ squared is $\frac{b^2}{4a^2}$:

$$x^2 + \frac{b}{a}x + \frac{b^2}{4a^2} = -\frac{c}{a} + \frac{b^2}{4a^2}$$

Factor the left-hand side and get a common denominator for the right-hand side:

$$\left(x + \frac{b}{2a}\right)^2 = \frac{b^2}{4a^2} - \frac{4ac}{4a^2} \qquad \frac{c(4a)}{a(4a)} = \frac{4ac}{4a^2}$$

$$\left(x + \frac{b}{2a}\right)^2 = \frac{b^2 - 4ac}{4a^2}$$

$$x + \frac{b}{2a} = \pm\sqrt{\frac{b^2 - 4ac}{4a^2}} \qquad \text{Even-root property}$$

$$x = \frac{-b}{2a} \pm \frac{\sqrt{b^2 - 4ac}}{2a} \qquad \text{Because } a > 0, \sqrt{4a^2} = 2a.$$

$$x = \frac{-b \pm \sqrt{b^2 - 4ac}}{2a}$$

Teaching Tip Don't expect students to reproduce this proof of the quadratic formula. At this point they should see that it is simply completing the square in a general case.

We assumed a was positive so that $\sqrt{4a^2} = 2a$ would be correct. If a is negative, then $\sqrt{4a^2} = -2a$, and we get

$$x = \frac{-b}{2a} \pm \frac{\sqrt{b^2 - 4ac}}{-2a}.$$

However, the negative sign can be omitted in $-2a$ because of the $\pm$ symbol preceding it. For example, the results of $5 \pm (-3)$ and 5 ± 3 are the same. So when a is negative, we get the same formula as when a is positive. It is called the **quadratic formula.**

The Quadratic Formula

The solution to $ax^2 + bx + c = 0$, with $a \neq 0$, is given by the formula

$$x = \frac{-b \pm \sqrt{b^2 - 4ac}}{2a}.$$

Using the Formula

The quadratic formula solves any quadratic equation. Simply identify a, b, and c and insert those numbers into the formula. Note that if b is positive then $-b$ (the opposite of b) is a negative number. If b is negative, then $-b$ is a *positive* number.

EXAMPLE 1

Two rational solutions

Solve $x^2 + 2x - 15 = 0$ using the quadratic formula.

Solution

To use the formula, we first identify the values of a, b, and c:

$$\underset{\substack{\uparrow \\ a}}{1}x^2 + \underset{\substack{\uparrow \\ b}}{2}x - \underset{\substack{\uparrow \\ c}}{15} = 0$$

The coefficient of x^2 is 1, so $a = 1$. The coefficient of $2x$ is 2, so $b = 2$. The constant term is -15, so $c = -15$. Substitute these values into the quadratic formula:

$$x = \frac{-2 \pm \sqrt{2^2 - 4(1)(-15)}}{2(1)}$$

$$= \frac{-2 \pm \sqrt{4 + 60}}{2}$$

$$= \frac{-2 \pm \sqrt{64}}{2}$$

$$= \frac{-2 \pm 8}{2}$$

$$x = \frac{-2 + 8}{2} = 3 \quad \text{or} \quad x = \frac{-2 - 8}{2} = -5$$

Check 3 and -5 in the original equation. The solution set is $\{-5, 3\}$.

Now do Exercises 7–12

Calculator Close-Up

Note that the two solutions to

$$x^2 + 2x - 15 = 0$$

correspond to the two x-intercepts for the graph of

$$y = x^2 + 2x - 15.$$

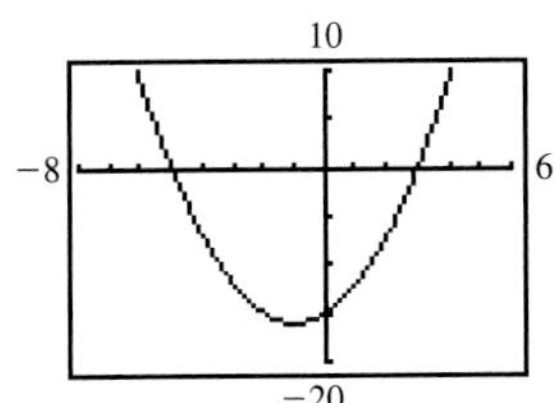

CAUTION To identify a, b, and c for the quadratic formula, the equation must be in the standard form $ax^2 + bx + c = 0$. If it is not in that form, then you must first rewrite the equation.

EXAMPLE 2

One rational solution

Solve $4x^2 = 12x - 9$ by using the quadratic formula.

Solution

Rewrite the equation in the form $ax^2 + bx + c = 0$ before identifying a, b, and c:

$$4x^2 - 12x + 9 = 0$$

Calculator Close-Up

Note that the single solution to

$$4x^2 - 12x + 9 = 0$$

corresponds to the single x-intercept for the graph of

$$y = 4x^2 - 12x + 9.$$

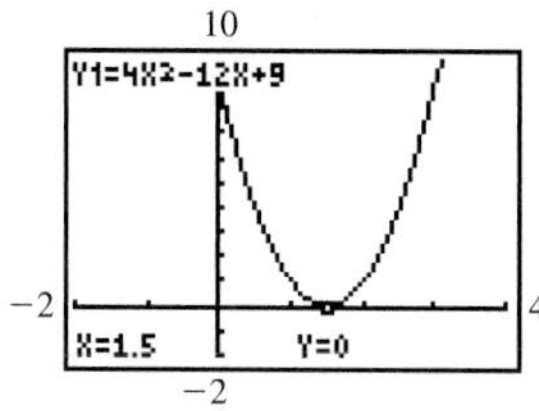

In this form we get $a = 4$, $b = -12$, and $c = 9$.

$$x = \frac{12 \pm \sqrt{(-12)^2 - 4(4)(9)}}{2(4)} \quad \text{Because } b = -12, -b = 12.$$

$$= \frac{12 \pm \sqrt{144 - 144}}{8}$$

$$= \frac{12 \pm 0}{8}$$

$$= \frac{12}{8}$$

$$= \frac{3}{2}$$

Check $\frac{3}{2}$ in the original equation. The solution set is $\left\{\frac{3}{2}\right\}$.

Now do Exercises 13–18

Because the solutions to the equations in Examples 1 and 2 were rational numbers, these equations could have been solved by factoring. In Example 3 the solutions are irrational.

EXAMPLE 3

Two irrational solutions

Solve $2x^2 + 6x + 3 = 0$.

Solution

Let $a = 2$, $b = 6$, and $c = 3$ in the quadratic formula:

$$x = \frac{-6 \pm \sqrt{(6)^2 - 4(2)(3)}}{2(2)}$$

$$= \frac{-6 \pm \sqrt{36 - 24}}{4}$$

$$= \frac{-6 \pm \sqrt{12}}{4}$$

$$= \frac{-6 \pm 2\sqrt{3}}{4}$$

$$= \frac{2(-3 \pm \sqrt{3})}{2 \cdot 2}$$

$$= \frac{-3 \pm \sqrt{3}}{2}$$

Check these values in the original equation. The solution set is $\left\{\frac{-3 \pm \sqrt{3}}{2}\right\}$.

Now do Exercises 19–24

Calculator Close-Up

The two irrational solutions to

$$2x^2 + 6x + 3 = 0$$

correspond to the two x-intercepts for the graph of

$$y = 2x^2 + 6x + 3.$$

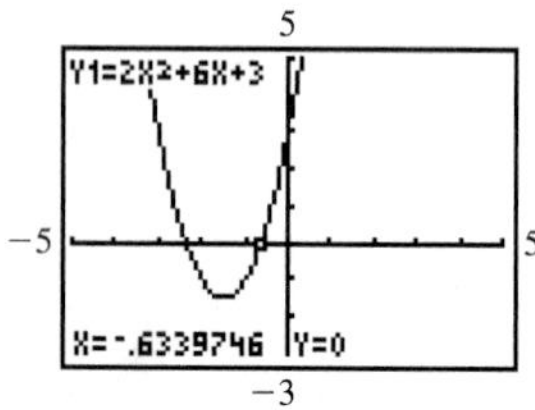

EXAMPLE 4

Two imaginary solutions, no real solutions

Find the complex solutions to $x^2 + x + 5 = 0$.

Solution

Let $a = 1$, $b = 1$, and $c = 5$ in the quadratic formula:

$$x = \frac{-1 \pm \sqrt{(1)^2 - 4(1)(5)}}{2(1)}$$

$$= \frac{-1 \pm \sqrt{-19}}{2}$$

$$= \frac{-1 \pm i\sqrt{19}}{2}$$

Check these values in the original equation. The solution set is $\left\{\frac{-1 \pm i\sqrt{19}}{2}\right\}$. There are no real solutions to the equation.

Now do Exercises 25–30

Calculator Close-Up

Because $x^2 + x + 5 = 0$ has no real solutions, the graph of

$$y = x^2 + x + 5$$

has no x-intercepts.

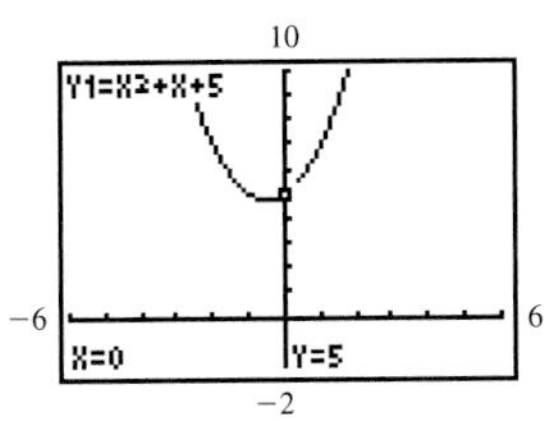

You have learned to solve quadratic equations by four different methods: the even-root property, factoring, completing the square, and the quadratic formula. The even-root property and factoring are limited to certain special equations, but you should use those methods when possible. Any quadratic equation can be solved by completing the square or using the quadratic formula. Because the quadratic formula is usually faster, it is used more often than completing the square. However, completing the square is an important skill to learn. It will be used in the study of conic sections later in this text.

Teaching Tip It is good practice to have students solve the same equation by as many different methods as they can.

Methods for Solving $ax^2 + bx + c = 0$

Method	Comments	Examples
Even-root property	Use when $b = 0$.	$(x - 2)^2 = 8$ $x - 2 = \pm\sqrt{8}$
Factoring	Use when the polynomial can be factored.	$x^2 + 5x + 6 = 0$ $(x + 2)(x + 3) = 0$
Quadratic formula	Solves any quadratic equation	$x^2 + 5x + 3 = 0$ $x = \frac{-5 \pm \sqrt{25 - 4(3)}}{2}$
Completing the square	Solves any quadratic equation, but quadratic formula is faster	$x^2 - 6x + 7 = 0$ $x^2 - 6x + 9 = -7 + 9$ $(x - 3)^2 = 2$

Number of Solutions

The quadratic equations in Examples 1 and 3 had two real solutions each. In each of those examples the value of $b^2 - 4ac$ was positive. In Example 2 the quadratic equation had only one solution because the value of $b^2 - 4ac$ was zero. In Example 4 the quadratic equation had no real solutions because $b^2 - 4ac$ was negative. Because $b^2 - 4ac$ determines the kind and number of solutions to a quadratic equation, it is called the **discriminant.**

Number of Solutions to a Quadratic Equation

The quadratic equation $ax^2 + bx + c = 0$ with $a \neq 0$ has
two real solutions if $b^2 - 4ac > 0$,
one real solution if $b^2 - 4ac = 0$, and
no real solutions (two imaginary solutions) if $b^2 - 4ac < 0$.

EXAMPLE 5

Using the discriminant

Use the discriminant to determine the number of real solutions to each quadratic equation.

a) $x^2 - 3x - 5 = 0$

b) $x^2 = 3x - 9$

c) $4x^2 - 12x + 9 = 0$

Teaching Tip Remind students that $(-3)^2$ and -3^2 have different values. If $b = -3$, then $b^2 = (-3)^2 = 9$.

Solution

a) For $x^2 - 3x - 5 = 0$, use $a = 1$, $b = -3$, and $c = -5$ in $b^2 - 4ac$:

$$b^2 - 4ac = (-3)^2 - 4(1)(-5) = 9 + 20 = 29$$

Because the discriminant is positive, there are two real solutions to this quadratic equation.

b) Rewrite $x^2 = 3x - 9$ as $x^2 - 3x + 9 = 0$. Then use $a = 1$, $b = -3$, and $c = 9$ in $b^2 - 4ac$:

$$b^2 - 4ac = (-3)^2 - 4(1)(9) = 9 - 36 = -27$$

Because the discriminant is negative, the equation has no real solutions. It has two imaginary solutions.

c) For $4x^2 - 12x + 9 = 0$, use $a = 4$, $b = -12$, and $c = 9$ in $b^2 - 4ac$:

$$b^2 - 4ac = (-12)^2 - 4(4)(9) = 144 - 144 = 0$$

Because the discriminant is zero, there is only one real solution to this quadratic equation.

Now do Exercises 31–46

Applications

With the quadratic formula we can easily solve problems whose solutions are irrational numbers. When the solutions are irrational numbers, we usually use a calculator to find rational approximations and to check.

EXAMPLE 6

Area of a tabletop

The area of a rectangular tabletop is 6 square feet. If the width is 2 feet shorter than the length, then what are the dimensions?

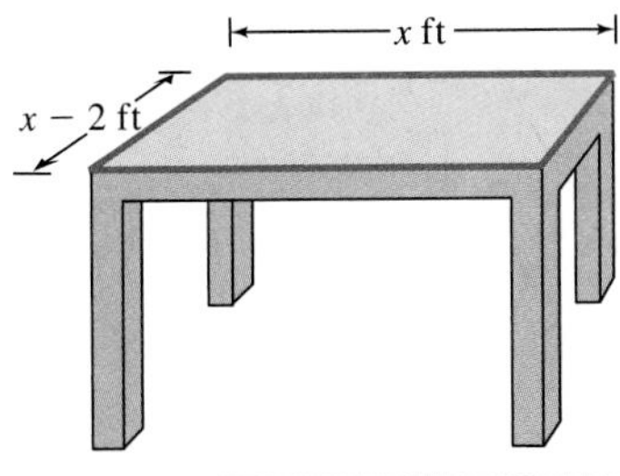

Figure 10.1

Solution

Let x be the length and $x - 2$ be the width, as shown in Fig. 10.1. Because the area is 6 square feet and $A = LW$, we can write the equation

$$x(x - 2) = 6$$

or

$$x^2 - 2x - 6 = 0.$$

Because this equation cannot be factored, we use the quadratic formula with $a = 1$, $b = -2$, and $c = -6$:

$$x = \frac{2 \pm \sqrt{(-2)^2 - 4(1)(-6)}}{2(1)}$$

$$= \frac{2 \pm \sqrt{28}}{2} = \frac{2 \pm 2\sqrt{7}}{2} = 1 \pm \sqrt{7}$$

Because $1 - \sqrt{7}$ is a negative number, it cannot be the length of a tabletop. If $x = 1 + \sqrt{7}$, then $x - 2 = 1 + \sqrt{7} - 2 = \sqrt{7} - 1$. Checking the product of $\sqrt{7} + 1$ and $\sqrt{7} - 1$, we get

$$(\sqrt{7} + 1)(\sqrt{7} - 1) = 7 - 1 = 6.$$

The exact length is $\sqrt{7} + 1$ feet, and the width is $\sqrt{7} - 1$ feet. Using a calculator, we find that the approximate length is 3.65 feet and the approximate width is 1.65 feet.

Now do Exercises 75–94

Teaching Tip These applied problems may seem a bit complicated, but that is unavoidable if we want to illustrate the need for the quadratic formula.

Warm-Ups ▼

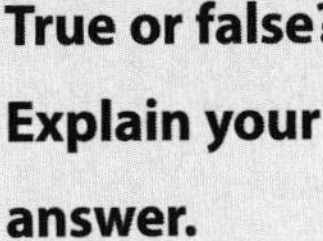

True or false? Explain your answer.

1. Completing the square is used to develop the quadratic formula. True
2. For the equation $3x^2 = 4x - 7$, we have $a = 3$, $b = 4$, and $c = -7$. False
3. If $dx^2 + ex + f = 0$ and $d \neq 0$, then $x = \frac{-e \pm \sqrt{e^2 - 4df}}{2d}$. True
4. The quadratic formula will not work on the equation $x^2 - 3 = 0$. False
5. If $a = 2$, $b = -3$, and $c = -4$, then $b^2 - 4ac = 41$. True
6. If the discriminant is zero, then there are no imaginary solutions. True
7. If $b^2 - 4ac > 0$, then $ax^2 + bx + c = 0$ has two real solutions. True
8. To solve $2x - x^2 = 0$ by the quadratic formula, let $a = -1$, $b = 2$, and $c = 0$. True
9. Two numbers that have a sum of 6 can be represented by x and $x + 6$. False
10. Some quadratic equations have one real and one imaginary solution. False

10.2 Exercises

Boost your GRADE at mathzone.com!

MathZone

- Practice Problems
- Self-Tests
- Videos
- Net Tutor
- e-Professors

Reading and Writing *After reading this section, write out the answers to these questions. Use complete sentences.*

1. What is the quadratic formula used for?
The quadratic formula can be used to solve any quadratic equation.

2. When do you use the even-root property to solve a quadratic equation?
The even-root property is used when $b = 0$.

3. When do you use factoring to solve a quadratic equation?
Factoring is used when the quadratic polynomial is simple enough to factor.

4. When do you use the quadratic formula to solve a quadratic equation?
The quadratic formula can be used on any quadratic equation, but generally we use factoring or the even-root property when applicable.

5. What is the discriminant?
The discriminant is $b^2 - 4ac$.

6. How many solutions are there to any quadratic equation in the complex number system?
In the complex number system any quadratic equation has either one or two solutions.

Solve each equation by using the quadratic formula. See Example 1.

7. $x^2 + 5x + 6 = 0$ $\{-3, -2\}$

8. $x^2 - 7x + 12 = 0$ $\{3, 4\}$

9. $y^2 + y = 6$ $\{-3, 2\}$

10. $m^2 + 2m = 8$ $\{-4, 2\}$

11. $-6z^2 + 7z + 3 = 0$ $\left\{-\frac{1}{3}, \frac{3}{2}\right\}$

12. $-8q^2 - 2q + 1 = 0$ $\left\{-\frac{1}{2}, \frac{1}{4}\right\}$

Solve each equation by using the quadratic formula. See Example 2.

13. $4x^2 - 4x + 1 = 0$ $\left\{\frac{1}{2}\right\}$

14. $4x^2 - 12x + 9 = 0$ $\left\{\frac{3}{2}\right\}$

15. $-9x^2 + 6x - 1 = 0$ $\left\{\frac{1}{3}\right\}$

16. $-9x^2 + 24x - 16 = 0$ $\left\{\frac{4}{3}\right\}$

17. $9 + 24x + 16x^2 = 0$ $\left\{-\frac{3}{4}\right\}$

18. $4 + 20x = -25x^2$ $\left\{-\frac{2}{5}\right\}$

Solve each equation by using the quadratic formula. See Example 3.

19. $v^2 + 8v + 6 = 0$ $\{-4 \pm \sqrt{10}\}$

20. $p^2 + 6p + 4 = 0$ $\{-3 \pm \sqrt{5}\}$

21. $-x^2 - 5x + 1 = 0$ $\left\{\frac{-5 \pm \sqrt{29}}{2}\right\}$

22. $-x^2 - 3x + 5 = 0$ $\left\{\frac{-3 \pm \sqrt{29}}{2}\right\}$

23. $2t^2 - 6t + 1 = 0$ $\left\{\frac{3 \pm \sqrt{7}}{2}\right\}$

24. $3z^2 - 8z + 2 = 0$ $\left\{\frac{4 \pm \sqrt{10}}{3}\right\}$

Solve each equation by using the quadratic formula. See Example 4.

25. $2t^2 - 6t + 5 = 0$ $\left\{\frac{3 \pm i}{2}\right\}$

26. $2y^2 + 1 = 2y$ $\left\{\frac{1 \pm i}{2}\right\}$

27. $-2x^2 + 3x = 6$ $\left\{\frac{3 \pm i\sqrt{39}}{4}\right\}$

28. $-3x^2 - 2x - 5 = 0$ $\left\{\frac{-1 \pm i\sqrt{14}}{3}\right\}$

29. $\frac{1}{2}x^2 + 13 = 5x$ $\{5 \pm i\}$

30. $\frac{1}{4}x^2 + \frac{17}{4} = 2x$ $\{4 \pm i\}$

Find $b^2 - 4ac$ and the number of real solutions to each equation. See Example 5.

31. $x^2 - 6x + 2 = 0$ 28, 2

32. $x^2 + 6x + 9 = 0$ 0, 1

33. $-2x^2 + 5x - 6 = 0$ -23, 0

34. $-x^2 + 3x - 4 = 0$ -7, 0

35. $4m^2 + 25 = 20m$ 0, 1

36. $y^2 = 3y + 5$ 29, 2

37. $y^2 - \frac{1}{2}y + \frac{1}{4} = 0$ $-\frac{3}{4}$, 0

38. $\frac{1}{2}w^2 - \frac{1}{3}w + \frac{1}{4} = 0$ $-\frac{7}{18}$, 0

39. $-3t^2 + 5t + 6 = 0$ 97, 2

40. $9m^2 + 16 = 24m$ 0, 1

41. $9 - 24z + 16z^2 = 0$ 0, 1

42. $12 - 7x + x^2 = 0$ 1, 2

43. $5x^2 - 7 = 0$ 140, 2

44. $-6x^2 - 5 = 0$ -120, 0

45. $x^2 = x$ 1, 2

46. $-3x^2 + 7x = 0$ 49, 2

Solve each equation by the method of your choice.

47. $\frac{1}{4}y^2 + y = 1$ $\{-2 \pm 2\sqrt{2}\}$

48. $\frac{1}{2}x^2 + x = 1$ $\{-1 \pm \sqrt{3}\}$

49. $\frac{1}{3}x^2 + \frac{1}{2}x = \frac{1}{3}$ $\left\{-2, \frac{1}{2}\right\}$

50. $\frac{4}{9}w^2 + 1 = \frac{5}{3}w$ $\left\{3, \frac{3}{4}\right\}$

51. $3y^2 + 2y - 4 = 0$
$\left\{\frac{-1 \pm \sqrt{13}}{3}\right\}$

52. $2y^2 - 3y - 6 = 0$
$\left\{\frac{3 \pm \sqrt{57}}{4}\right\}$

53. $\frac{w}{w - 2} = \frac{w}{w - 3}$
$\{0\}$

54. $\frac{y}{3y - 4} = \frac{2}{y + 4}$
$\{1 \pm i\sqrt{7}\}$

55. $\frac{9(3x - 5)^2}{4} = 1$ $\left\{\frac{13}{9}, \frac{17}{9}\right\}$

56. $\frac{25(2x + 1)^2}{9} = 0$ $\left\{-\frac{1}{2}\right\}$

57. $25 - \frac{1}{3}x^2 = 0$
$\{\pm 5\sqrt{3}\}$

58. $\frac{49}{2} - \frac{1}{4}x^2 = 0$
$\{\pm 7\sqrt{2}\}$

59. $1 + \frac{20}{x^2} = \frac{8}{x}$ $\{4 \pm 2i\}$

60. $\frac{34}{x^2} = \frac{6}{x} - 1$ $\{3 \pm 5i\}$

61. $(x - 8)(x + 4) = -42$
$\{2 \pm i\sqrt{6}\}$

62. $(x - 10)(x - 2) = -20$
$\{6 \pm 2i\}$

63. $y = \frac{3(2y + 5)}{8(y - 1)}$ $\left\{-\frac{3}{4}, \frac{5}{2}\right\}$

64. $z = \frac{7z - 4}{12(z - 1)}$ $\left\{\frac{1}{4}, \frac{4}{3}\right\}$

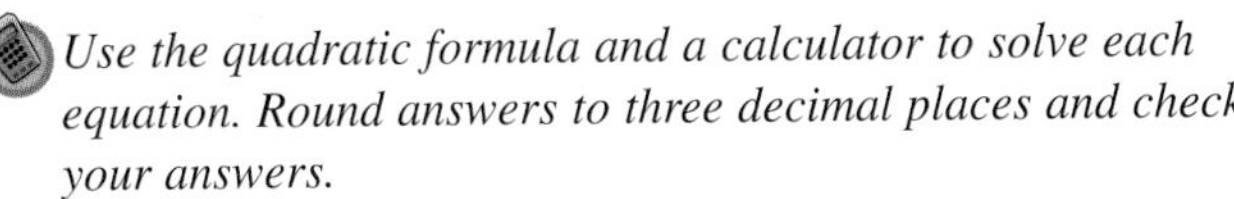

Use the quadratic formula and a calculator to solve each equation. Round answers to three decimal places and check your answers.

65. $x^2 + 3.2x - 5.7 = 0$ $\{-4.474, 1.274\}$

66. $x^2 + 7.15x + 3.24 = 0$ $\{-6.664, -0.486\}$

67. $x^2 - 7.4x + 13.69 = 0$ $\{3.7\}$

68. $1.44x^2 + 5.52x + 5.29 = 0$ $\{-1.917\}$

69. $1.85x^2 + 6.72x + 3.6 = 0$ $\{-2.979, -0.653\}$

70. $3.67x^2 + 4.35x - 2.13 = 0$ $\{-1.558, 0.373\}$

71. $3x^2 + 14{,}379x + 243 = 0$ $\{-4792.983, -0.017\}$

72. $x^2 + 12{,}347x + 6741 = 0$ $\{-12{,}346.454, -0.546\}$

73. $x^2 + 0.00075x - 0.0062 = 0$ $\{-0.079, 0.078\}$

74. $4.3x^2 - 9.86x - 3.75 = 0$ $\{-0.332, 2.625\}$

Find the exact solution(s) to each problem. If the solution(s) are irrational, then also find approximate solution(s) to the nearest tenth. See Example 6.

75. ***Missing numbers.*** Find two positive real numbers that differ by 1 and have a product of 16.
$\frac{1 + \sqrt{65}}{2}$ and $\frac{-1 + \sqrt{65}}{2}$, or 4.5 and 3.5

76. ***Missing numbers.*** Find two positive real numbers that differ by 2 and have a product of 10.
$1 + \sqrt{11}$ and $-1 + \sqrt{11}$, or 4.3 and 2.3

77. ***More missing numbers.*** Find two real numbers that have a sum of 6 and a product of 4.
$3 + \sqrt{5}$ and $3 - \sqrt{5}$, or 5.2 and 0.8

78. ***More missing numbers.*** Find two real numbers that have a sum of 8 and a product of 2.
$4 - \sqrt{14}$ and $4 + \sqrt{14}$, or 0.3 and 7.7

79. ***Bulletin board.*** The length of a bulletin board is one foot more than the width. The diagonal has a length of $\sqrt{3}$ feet (ft). Find the length and width of the bulletin board.
$W = \frac{-1 + \sqrt{5}}{2} \approx 0.6$ ft, $L = \frac{1 + \sqrt{5}}{2} \approx 1.6$ ft

80. ***Diagonal brace.*** The width of a rectangular gate is 2 meters (m) larger than its height. The diagonal brace measures $\sqrt{6}$ m. Find the width and height.
$W = -1 + \sqrt{2} \approx 0.4$ m, $L = 1 + \sqrt{2} \approx 2.4$ m

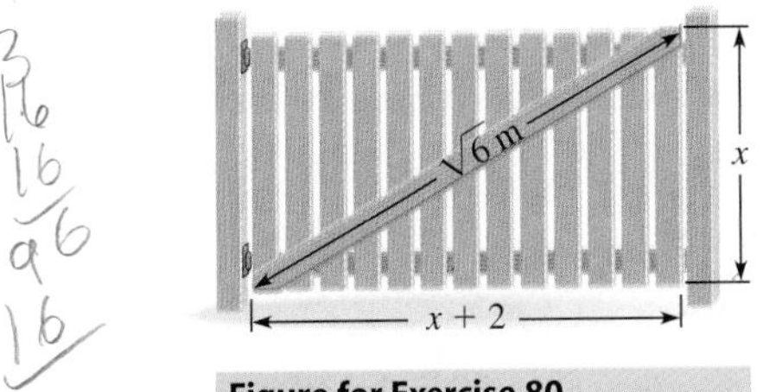

Figure for Exercise 80

81. ***Area of a rectangle.*** The length of a rectangle is 4 ft longer than the width, and its area is 10 square feet (ft^2). Find the length and width.
$W = -2 + \sqrt{14} \approx 1.7$ ft, $L = 2 + \sqrt{14} \approx 5.7$ ft

82. ***Diagonal of a square.*** The diagonal of a square is 2 m longer than a side. Find the length of a side. $2 + 2\sqrt{2} \approx 4.8$ m

If an object is given an initial velocity of v_0 feet per second from a height of s_0 feet, then its height S after t seconds is given by the formula $S = -16t^2 + v_0t + s_0$.

83. ***Projected pine cone.*** If a pine cone is projected upward at a velocity of 16 ft/sec from the top of a 96-foot pine tree, then how long does it take to reach the earth? 3 sec

84. ***Falling pine cone.*** If a pine cone falls from the top of a 96-foot pine tree, then how long does it take to reach the earth? $\sqrt{6}$ or 2.4 sec

85. ***Tossing a ball.*** A ball is tossed into the air at 10 ft/sec from a height of 5 feet. How long does it take to reach the earth?
$\frac{5 + \sqrt{105}}{16}$ or 1.0 sec

86. ***Time in the air.*** A ball is tossed into the air from a height of 12 feet at 16 ft/sec. How long does it take to reach the earth? 1.5 sec

87. ***Penny tossing.*** If a penny is thrown downward at 30 ft/sec from the bridge at Royal Gorge, Colorado, how long does it take to reach the Arkansas River 1000 ft below? 7.0 sec

88. ***Foul ball.*** Suppose Charlie O'Brian hits a baseball straight upward at 150 ft/sec from a height of 5 ft.

a) Use the formula to determine how long it takes the ball to return to the earth. 9.4 sec

b) Use the graph on the next page to estimate the maximum height reached by the ball. 350 ft

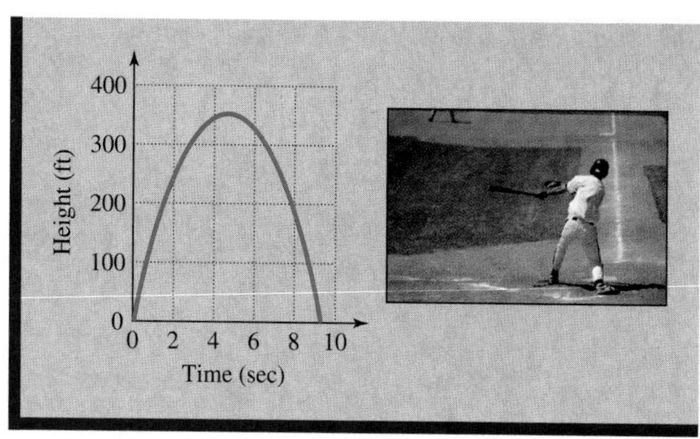

Figure for Exercise 88

Solve each problem.

89. ***Kitchen countertop.*** A 30 in. by 40 in. countertop for a work island is to be covered with green ceramic tiles, except for a border of uniform width as shown in the figure. If the area covered by the green tiles is 704 square inches (in.^{2}), then how wide is the border? 4 in.

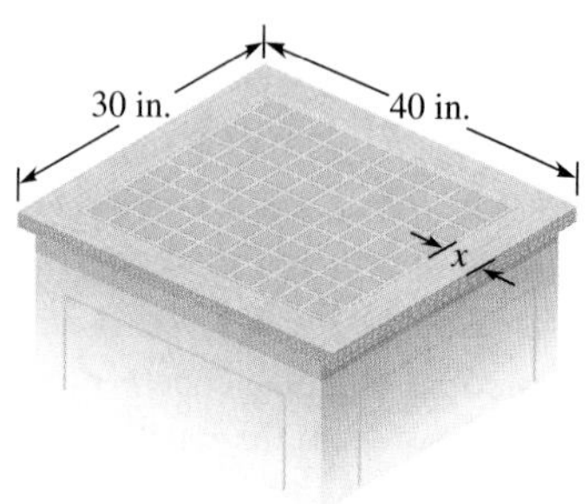

Figure for Exercise 89

90. ***Recovering an investment.*** The manager at Cream of the Crop bought a load of watermelons for \$200. She priced the melons so that she would make \$1.50 profit on each melon. When all but 30 had been sold, the manager had recovered her initial investment. How many did she buy originally? 80

91. ***Baby shower.*** A group of office workers plans to share equally the \$100 cost of giving a baby shower for a coworker. If they can get six more people to share the cost then the cost per person will decrease by \$15. How many people are in the original group? 4

92. ***Sharing cost.*** The members of a flying club plan to share equally the cost of a \$200,000 airplane. The members want to find five more people to join the club so that the cost per person will decrease by \$2000. How many members are currently in the club? 20

93. ***Farmer's Delight.*** The manager of Farmer's Delight bought a load of watermelons for \$750 and priced the watermelons so that he would make a profit of \$2 on each melon. When all but 100 of the melons had been sold, he broke even. How many did he buy originally?
250 melons

94. ***Traveling club.*** The members of a traveling club plan to share equally the cost of a \$150,000 motorhome. If they can find 10 more people to join and share the cost, then the cost per person will decrease by \$1250. How many members are there originally in the club? 30 members

Getting More Involved

95. ***Discussion***

Find the solutions to $6x^2 + 5x - 4 = 0$. Is the sum of your solutions equal to $-\frac{b}{a}$? Explain why the sum of the solutions to any quadratic equation is $-\frac{b}{a}$. (*Hint:* Use the quadratic formula.)

96. ***Discussion***

Use the result of Exercise 95 to check whether $\left\{\frac{2}{3}, \frac{1}{3}\right\}$ is the solution set to $9x^2 - 3x - 2 = 0$. If this solution set is not correct, then what is the correct solution set?

97. ***Discussion***

What is the product of the two solutions to $6x^2 + 5x - 4 = 0$? Explain why the product of the solutions to any quadratic equation is $\frac{c}{a}$.

98. ***Discussion***

Use the result of the previous exercise to check whether $\left\{\frac{9}{2}, -2\right\}$ is the solution set to $2x^2 - 13x + 18 = 0$. If this solution set is not correct, then what is the correct solution set?

Graphing Calculator Exercises

Determine the number of real solutions to each equation by examining the calculator graph of $y = ax^2 + bx + c$. Use the discriminant to check your conclusions.

99. $x^2 - 6.33x + 3.7 = 0$ 2

100. $1.8x^2 + 2.4x - 895 = 0$ 2

101. $4x^2 - 67.1x + 344 = 0$ 0

102. $-2x^2 - 403 = 0$ 0

103. $-x^2 + 30x - 226 = 0$ 0

104. $16x^2 - 648x + 6562 = 0$ 0

10.3 Graphing Parabolas

In this Section

- Finding Ordered Pairs
- Graphing Parabolas
- The Vertex and Intercepts
- Applications

The graph of any equation of the form $y = mx + b$ is a straight line. In this section we will see that all equations of the form $y = ax^2 + bx + c$ (with $a \neq 0$) have graphs that are in the shape of a *parabola.*

Finding Ordered Pairs

It is straightforward to calculate y when given x for an equation of the form $y = ax^2 + bx + c$. However, if we are given y and want to find x, then we must use methods for solving quadratic equations.

EXAMPLE 1

Finding ordered pairs

Complete each ordered pair so that it satisfies the given equation.

a) (2,), (, 0), $y = x^2 - x - 6$

b) (0,), (, 20), $y = -16x^2 + 48x + 84$

Solution

a) If $x = 2$, then $y = 2^2 - 2 - 6 = -4$. So the ordered pair is $(2, -4)$. To find x when $y = 0$, replace y by 0 and solve the resulting quadratic equation:

$$x^2 - x - 6 = 0$$
$$(x - 3)(x + 2) = 0$$
$$x - 3 = 0 \quad \text{or} \quad x + 2 = 0$$
$$x = 3 \quad \text{or} \quad x = -2$$

The ordered pairs are $(-2, 0)$ and $(3, 0)$.

b) If $x = 0$, then $y = -16 \cdot 0^2 + 48 \cdot 0 + 84 = 84$. The ordered pair is $(0, 84)$. To find x when $y = 20$, replace y by 20 and solve the equation for x:

$$-16x^2 + 48x + 84 = 20$$
$$-16x^2 + 48x + 64 = 0 \quad \text{Subtract 20 from each side.}$$
$$x^2 - 3x - 4 = 0 \quad \text{Divide each side by } -16.$$
$$(x - 4)(x + 1) = 0 \quad \text{Factor.}$$
$$x - 4 = 0 \quad \text{or} \quad x + 1 = 0 \quad \text{Zero factor property}$$
$$x = 4 \quad \text{or} \quad x = -1$$

The ordered pairs are $(-1, 20)$ and $(4, 20)$.

Now do Exercises 7–10

Graphing Parabolas

All equations of the form $y = ax^2 + bx + c$ with $a \neq 0$ have graphs that are similar in shape. The graph of any equation of this form is called a **parabola.** Note that any real number can be used in place of x.

EXAMPLE 2

The simplest parabola

Make a table of ordered pairs that satisfy $y = x^2$ and then sketch the graph of $y = x^2$.

Solution

Make a table of values for x and y:

x	-2	-1	0	1	2
$y = x^2$	4	1	0	1	4

Plot the ordered pairs from the table and draw a parabola through the points as shown in Fig. 10.2.

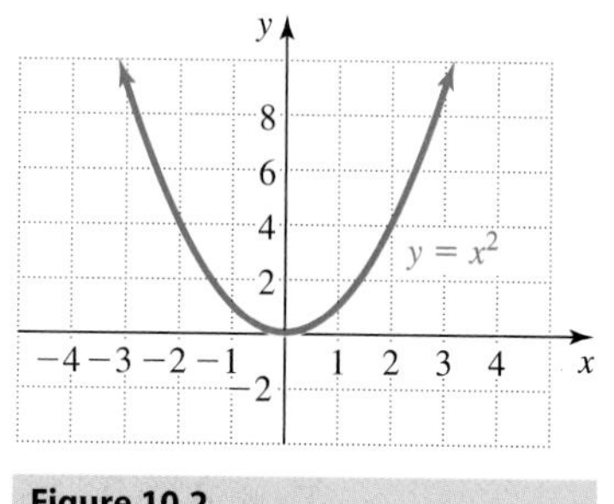

Figure 10.2

Now do Exercises 17–20

Calculator Close-Up

This close-up view of $y = x^2$ shows how rounded the curve is at the bottom. When drawing a parabola by hand, be sure to draw it smoothly.

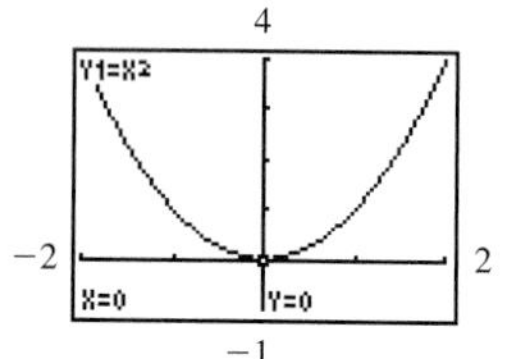

The parabola in Fig. 10.2 is said to **open upward.** In the next example we see a parabola that **opens downward.** If $a > 0$ in the equation $y = ax^2 + bx + c$, then the parabola opens upward. If $a < 0$, then the parabola opens downward.

EXAMPLE 3

A parabola opening downward

Graph $y = 4 - x^2$.

Solution

We plot enough points to get the correct shape of the graph:

x	-2	-1	0	1	2
$y = 4 - x^2$	0	3	4	3	0

See Fig. 10.3 for the graph.

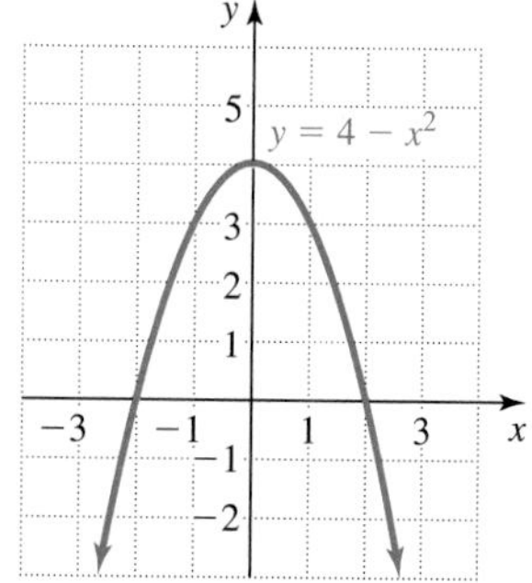

Figure 10.3

Now do Exercises 21–26

The Vertex and Intercepts

The lowest point on a parabola that opens upward or the highest point on a parabola that opens downward is called the **vertex.** The y-coordinate of the vertex is the **minimum value** of y if the parabola opens upward, and it is the **maximum value** of y if the parabola opens downward. For $y = x^2$ the vertex is (0, 0), and 0 is the minimum value of y. For $y = 4 - x^2$ the vertex is (0, 4), and 4 is the maximum value of y.

If $y = ax^2 + bx + c$ has x-intercepts, they can be found by solving $ax^2 + bx + c = 0$ by the quadratic formula. The vertex is midway between the x-intercepts as shown in Fig. 10.4. Note that in the quadratic formula

$$x = \frac{-b \pm \sqrt{b^2 - 4ac}}{2a},$$

$\sqrt{b^2 - 4ac}$ is added and subtracted from the numerator of $\frac{-b}{2a}$. So $\left(\frac{-b}{2a}, 0\right)$ is the point midway between the x-intercepts and the vertex has the same x-coordinate. Even if the parabola has no x-intercepts, the x-coordinate of the vertex is still $\frac{-b}{2a}$.

Study Tip

Although you should avoid cramming, there are times when you have no other choice. In this case concentrate on what is in your class notes and the homework assignments. Try to work one or two problems of each type. Instructors often ask some relatively easy questions on a test to see if you have understood the major ideas.

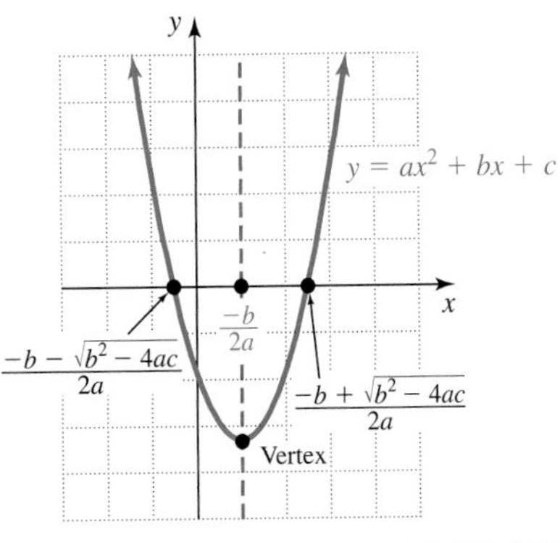

Figure 10.4

Vertex of a Parabola

The x-coordinate of the vertex of $y = ax^2 + bx + c$ is $\frac{-b}{2a}$, provided that $a \neq 0$.

When you graph a parabola, you should always locate the vertex because it is the point at which the graph "turns around." With the vertex and several nearby points you can see the correct shape of the parabola.

Recall from Section 4.1 how we used function notation for naming and evaluating polynomials. So instead of $y = x^2$ we can write $f(x) = x^2$, where we read $f(x)$ as "f of x." Note that $f(x)$ is simply used as the second coordinate in place of y. So instead of writing $y = 4$ when $x = 2$, we simply write $f(2) = 4$. We will use this function notation in Example 4.

EXAMPLE 4

Using the vertex in graphing a parabola

Find the vertex and graph $f(x) = -x^2 - x + 2$.

Teaching Tip Students have trouble selecting appropriate values for x. Stress the importance of finding the vertex first, then a couple of values on either side of the vertex are appropriate.

Solution

First find the x-coordinate of the vertex:

$$x = \frac{-b}{2a} = \frac{-(-1)}{2(-1)} = \frac{1}{-2} = -\frac{1}{2}$$

Now find $f\left(-\frac{1}{2}\right)$:

$$f\left(-\frac{1}{2}\right) = -\left(-\frac{1}{2}\right)^2 - \left(-\frac{1}{2}\right) + 2 = -\frac{1}{4} + \frac{1}{2} + 2 = \frac{9}{4}$$

The vertex is $\left(-\frac{1}{2}, \frac{9}{4}\right)$. Now find a few points on either side of the vertex:

x	-2	-1	$-\frac{1}{2}$	0	1
$f(x) = -x^2 - x + 2$	0	2	$\frac{9}{4}$	2	0

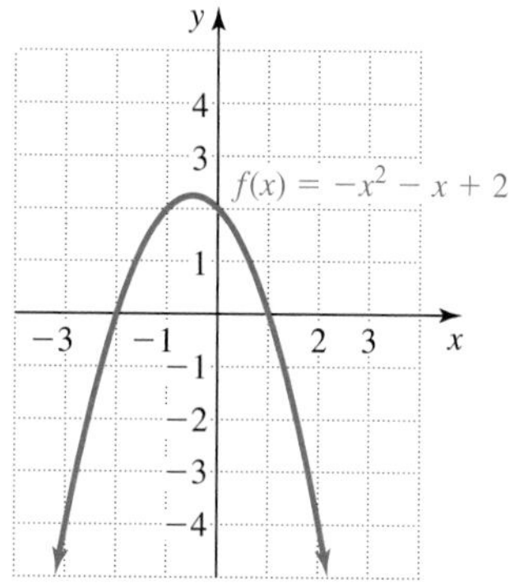

Figure 10.5

Sketch a parabola through these points as in Fig. 10.5.

Now do Exercises 27–34

The y-intercept of a parabola is the point that has 0 as the first coordinate. The x-intercepts are the points that have 0 as their second coordinates.

EXAMPLE 5

Using the intercepts in graphing a parabola

Find the vertex and intercepts, and sketch the graph of each parabola.

a) $f(x) = x^2 - 2x - 8$

b) $s = -16t^2 + 64t$

Solution

a) Use $x = \frac{-b}{2a}$ to get $x = 1$ as the x-coordinate of the vertex. If $x = 1$, then

$$\begin{aligned} f(1) &= 1^2 - 2 \cdot 1 - 8 \\ &= -9. \end{aligned}$$

So the vertex is $(1, -9)$. If $x = 0$, then

$$\begin{aligned} f(0) &= 0^2 - 2 \cdot 0 - 8 \\ &= -8. \end{aligned}$$

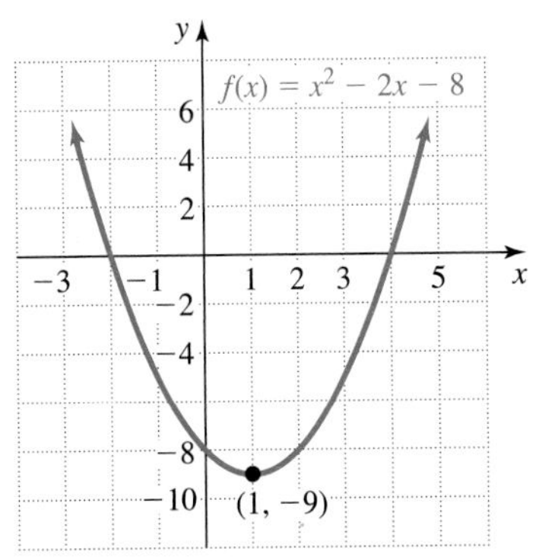

Figure 10.6

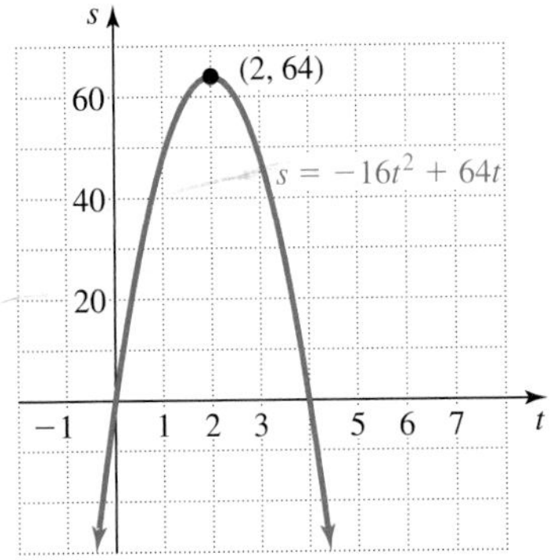

Figure 10.7

The y-intercept is $(0, -8)$. To find the x-intercepts, replace $f(x)$ by 0:

$$x^2 - 2x - 8 = 0$$
$$(x - 4)(x + 2) = 0$$
$$x - 4 = 0 \quad \text{or} \quad x + 2 = 0$$
$$x = 4 \quad \text{or} \quad x = -2$$

The x-intercepts are $(-2, 0)$ and $(4, 0)$. The graph is shown in Fig. 10.6.

b) Because s is expressed in terms of t in the equation $s = -16t^2 + 64t$, the independent variable is t and the dependent variable is s. Since we always put the independent variable first in an ordered pair, the ordered pairs are written in the form (t, s). To find the vertex use $t = -\frac{b}{2a}$ to get

$$t = \frac{-64}{2(-16)} = 2.$$

If $t = 2$, then

$$s = -16 \cdot 2^2 + 64 \cdot 2$$
$$= 64.$$

So the vertex is $(2, 64)$. If $t = 0$, then

$$s = -16 \cdot 0^2 + 64 \cdot 0$$
$$= 0.$$

So the s-intercept is $(0, 0)$. To find the t-intercepts, replace s by 0:

$$-16t^2 + 64t = 0$$
$$-16t(t - 4) = 0$$
$$-16t = 0 \quad \text{or} \quad t - 4 = 0$$
$$t = 0 \quad \text{or} \quad t = 4$$

The t-intercepts are $(0, 0)$ and $(4, 0)$. The graph is shown in Fig. 10.7.

Now do Exercises 35–50

Calculator Close-Up

You can find the vertex of a parabola with a calculator by using either the maximum or minimum feature. First graph the parabola as shown.

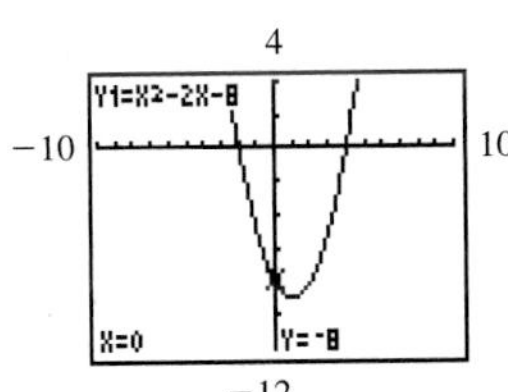

Because this parabola opens upward, the y-coordinate of the vertex is the minimum y-coordinate on the graph. Press CALC and choose minimum.

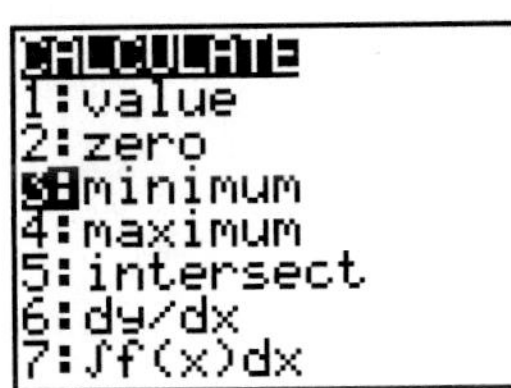

The calculator will ask for a left bound, a right bound, and a guess. For the left bound choose a point to the left of the vertex by moving the cursor to the point and pressing ENTER. For the right bound choose a point to the right of the vertex. For the guess choose a point close to the vertex.

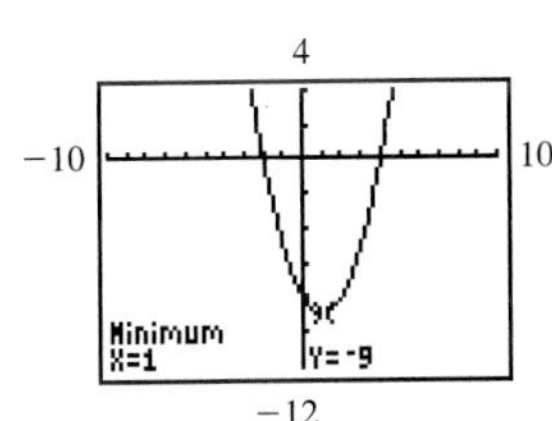

Applications

In applications we are often interested in finding the maximum or minimum value of a variable. If the graph of a parabola opens downward, then the maximum value of the dependent variable is the second coordinate of the vertex. If the parabola opens upward, then the minimum value of the dependent variable is the second coordinate of the vertex.

EXAMPLE 6

Finding the maximum height

If a projectile is launched with an initial velocity of v_0 feet per second from an initial height of s_0 feet, then its height $s(t)$ in feet is determined by $s(t) = -16t^2 + v_0t + s_0$, where t is the time in seconds. If a ball is tossed upward with velocity 64 feet per second from a height of 5 feet, then what is the maximum height reached by the ball?

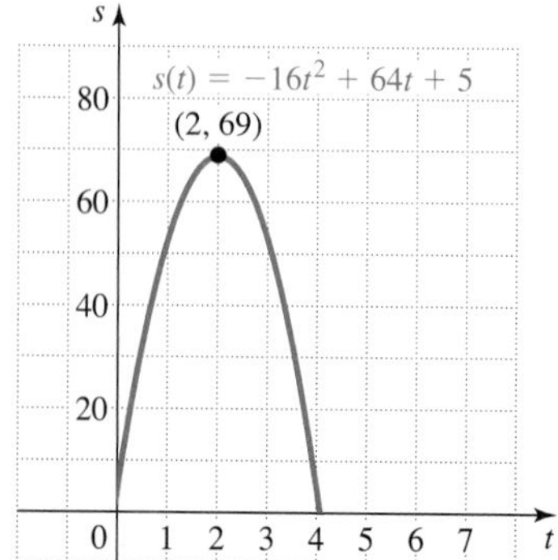

Figure 10.8

Solution

The height $s(t)$ of the ball for any time t is given by $s(t) = -16t^2 + 64t + 5$. Because the maximum height occurs at the vertex of the parabola, we use $t = \frac{-b}{2a}$ to find the vertex:

$$t = \frac{-64}{2(-16)} = 2$$

Now use $t = 2$ to find the second coordinate of the vertex:

$$s(2) = -16(2)^2 + 64(2) + 5 = 69$$

The maximum height reached by the ball is 69 feet. See Fig. 10.8.

Now do Exercises 59–67

Warm-Ups ▼

True or false? Explain your answer.

1. The ordered pair $(-2, -1)$ satisfies $f(x) = x^2 - 5$. True
2. The y-intercept for $g(x) = x^2 - 3x + 9$ is $(9, 0)$. False
3. The x-intercepts for $y = x^2 - 5$ are $(\sqrt{5}, 0)$ and $(-\sqrt{5}, 0)$. True
4. The graph of $f(x) = x^2 - 12$ opens upward. True
5. The graph of $y = 4 + x^2$ opens downward. False
6. The vertex of $y = x^2 + 2x$ is $(-1, -1)$. True
7. The parabola $y = x^2 + 1$ has no x-intercepts. True
8. The y-intercept for $g(x) = ax^2 + bx + c$ is $(0, c)$. True
9. If $w = -2v^2 + 9$, then the maximum value of w is 9. True
10. If $y = 3x^2 - 7x + 9$, then the maximum value of y occurs when $x = \frac{7}{6}$. False

10.3 Exercises

Boost your GRADE at mathzone.com!

MathZone

- Practice Problems
- Self-Tests
- Videos
- Net Tutor
- e-Professors

Reading and Writing *After reading this section, write out the answers to these questions. Use complete sentences.*

1. What equation has a graph called a parabola?
   The graph of $y = ax^2 + bx + c$ with $a \neq 0$ is a parabola.
2. When does a parabola open upward and when does a parabola open downward?
   If $a > 0$ then the parabola opens upward. If $a < 0$ then the parabola opens downward.
3. How can you find the x-intercepts for a parabola?
   To find the x-intercepts solve $ax^2 + bx + c = 0$.
4. How can you find the y-intercept?
   To find the y-intercept let $x = 0$ in $y = ax^2 + bx + c$.
5. What is the x-coordinate of the vertex of a parabola?
   The x-coordinate of the vertex is $-b/(2a)$.
6. How do you find the y-coordinate of the vertex?
   To find the y-coordinate evaluate $y = ax^2 + bx + c$ with $x = -b/(2a)$.

Complete each ordered pair so that it satisfies the given equation. See Example 1.

7. $y = x^2 - x - 12$ $(3,\quad), (\quad, 0)$
   $(3, -6), (4, 0), (-3, 0)$
8. $y = -\frac{1}{2}x^2 - x + 1$ $(0,\quad), (\quad, -3)$
   $(0, 1), (-4, -3), (2, -3)$
9. $y = -16x^2 + 32x$ $(4,\quad), (\quad, 0)$
   $(4, -128), (0, 0), (2, 0)$
10. $y = x^2 + 4x + 5$ $(-2,\quad), (\quad, 2)$
    $(-2, 1), (-1, 2), (-3, 2)$

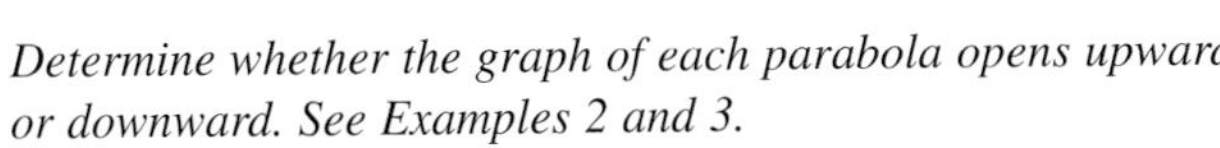

Determine whether the graph of each parabola opens upward or downward. See Examples 2 and 3.

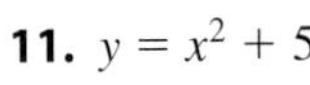

11. $y = x^2 + 5$
    Upward
12. $y = 2x^2 + x - 1$
    Upward
13. $y = -3x^2 + 4x + 2$
    Downward
14. $y = -x^2 + 3$
    Downward
15. $y = (-2x + 3)^2$
    Upward
16. $y = (5 - x)^2$
    Upward

Graph each parabola. See Examples 2 and 3.

17. $y = x^2 + 2$

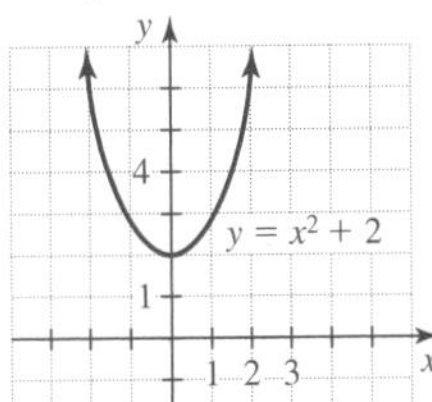

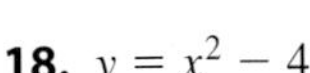

18. $y = x^2 - 4$

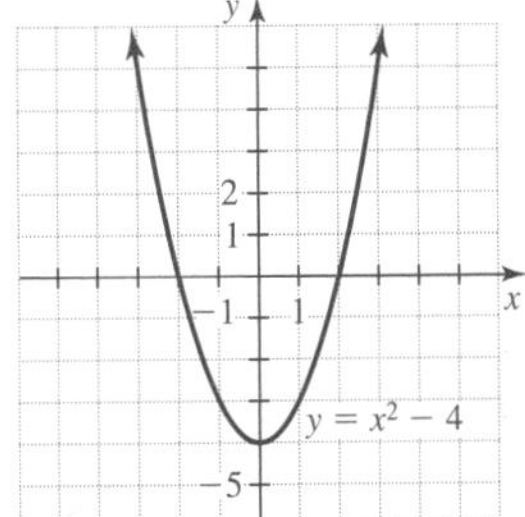

19. $y = \frac{1}{2}x^2 - 4$

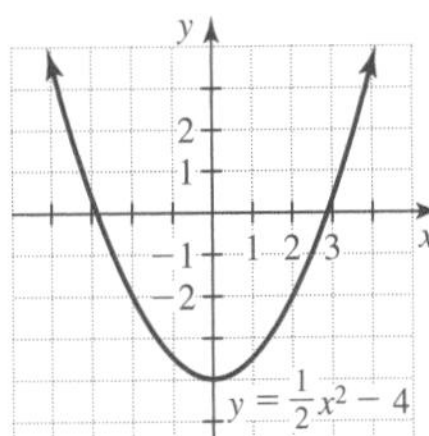

20. $y = \frac{1}{3}x^2 - 6$

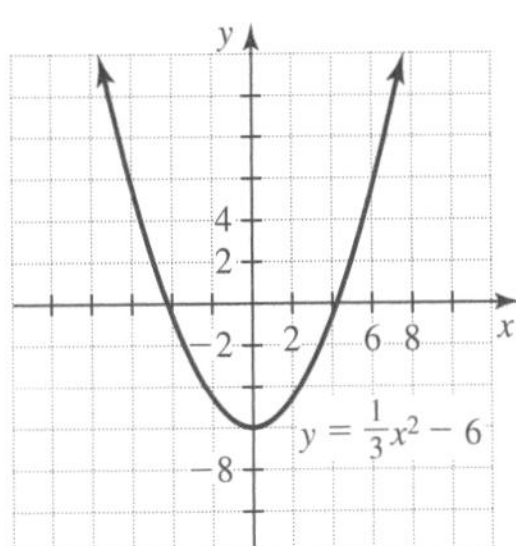

21. $y = -2x^2 + 5$

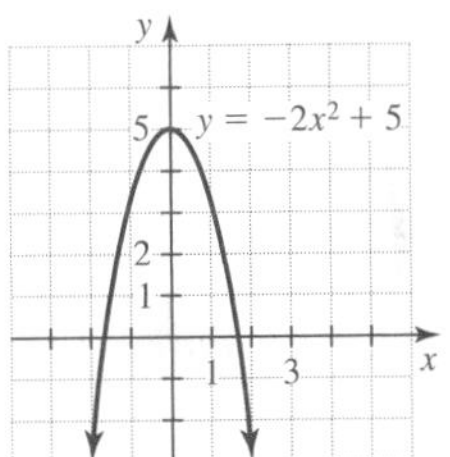

22. $y = -x^2 - 1$

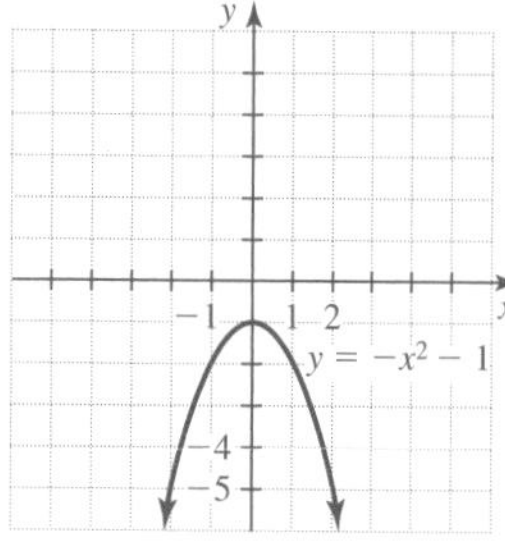

23. $y = -\frac{1}{3}x^2 + 5$

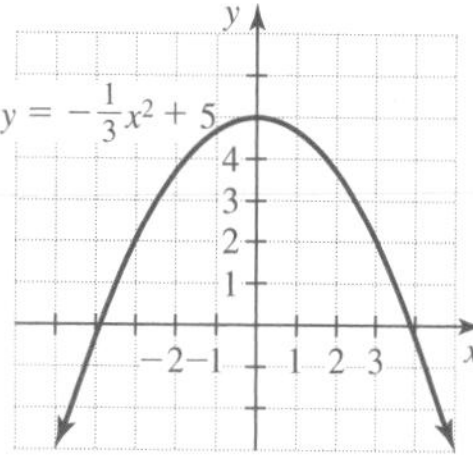

24. $y = -\frac{1}{2}x^2 + 3$

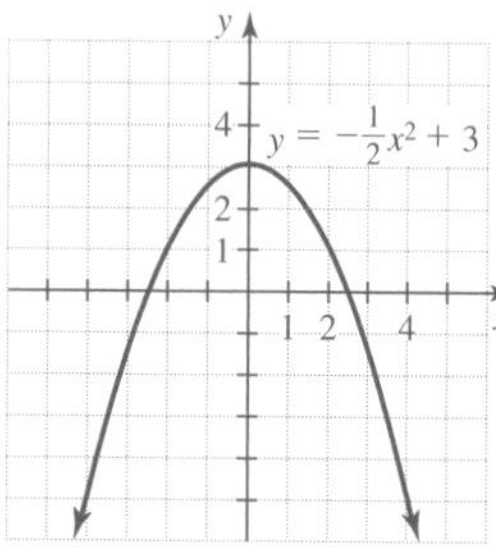

25. $y = (x - 2)^2$

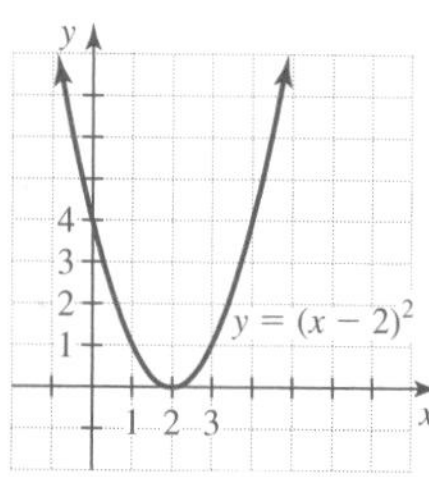

26. $y = (x + 3)^2$

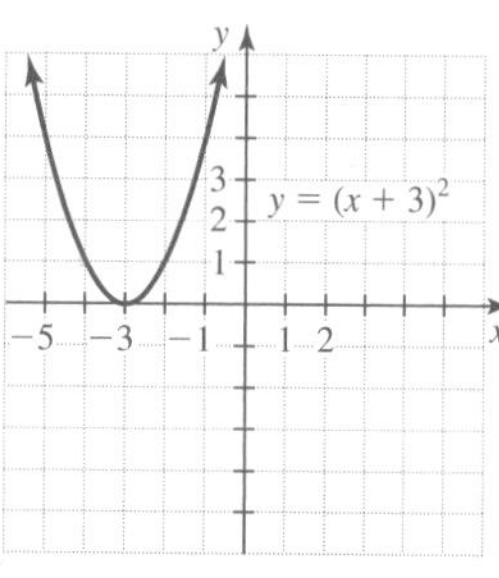

Find the vertex for the graph of each parabola. See Example 4.

27. $f(x) = x^2 - 9$ $(0, -9)$

28. $f(x) = x^2 + 12$ $(0, 12)$

29. $y = x^2 - 4x + 1$ $(2, -3)$

30. $y = x^2 + 8x - 3$ $(-4, -19)$

31. $f(x) = -2x^2 + 20x + 1$ $(5, 51)$

32. $f(x) = -3x^2 + 18x - 7$ $(3, 20)$

33. $y = x^2 - x + 1$ $\left(\frac{1}{2}, \frac{3}{4}\right)$

34. $y = 3x^2 - 2x + 1$ $\left(\frac{1}{3}, \frac{2}{3}\right)$

Find all intercepts for the graph of each parabola. See Example 5.

35. $f(x) = 16 - x^2$ $(0, 16), (-4, 0), (4, 0)$

36. $f(x) = x^2 - 9$ $(0, -9), (-3, 0), (3, 0)$

37. $y = x^2 - 2x - 8$ $(0, -8), (-2, 0), (4, 0)$

38. $y = x^2 - x - 6$ $(0, -6), (-2, 0), (3, 0)$

39. $f(x) = -4x^2 + 12x - 9$ $(0, -9), \left(\frac{3}{2}, 0\right)$

40. $f(x) = -2x^2 - x + 3$ $(0, 3), \left(-\frac{3}{2}, 0\right), (1, 0)$

Find the vertex and intercepts for each parabola. Sketch the graph. See Examples 4 and 5.

41. $f(x) = x^2 - x - 2$

Vertex $\left(\frac{1}{2}, -\frac{9}{4}\right)$, intercepts $(0, -2), (-1, 0), (2, 0)$

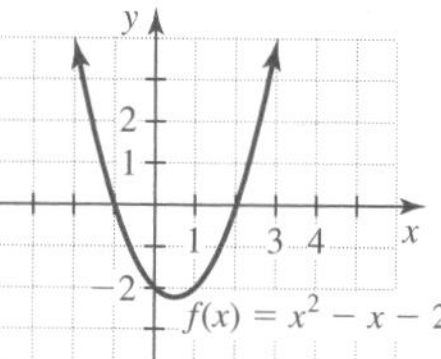

42. $f(x) = x^2 + 2x - 3$

Vertex $(-1, -4)$, intercepts $(0, -3)$, $(-3, 0), (1, 0)$

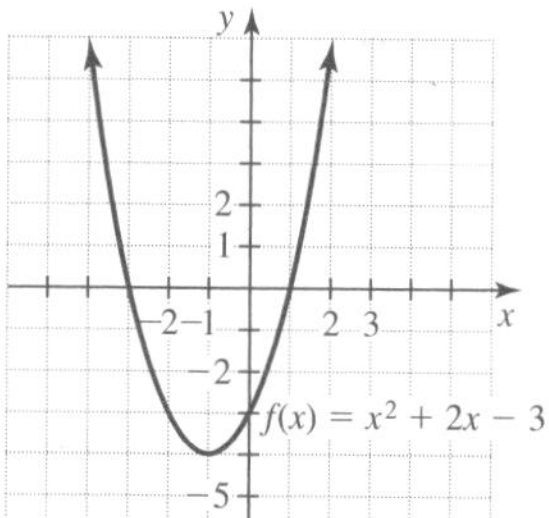

43. $g(x) = x^2 + 2x - 8$

Vertex $(-1, -9)$, intercepts $(0, -8), (-4, 0), (2, 0)$

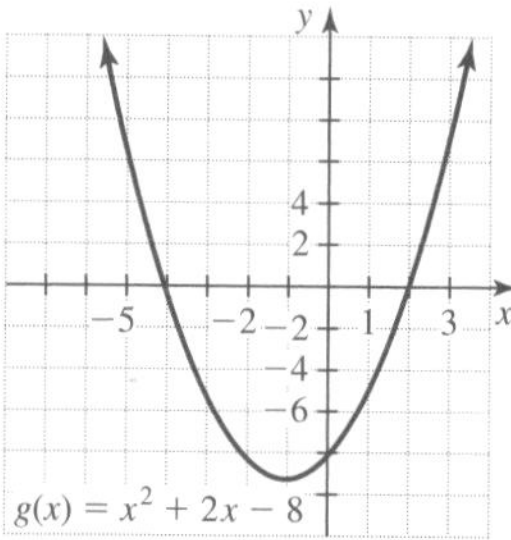

44. $g(x) = x^2 + x - 6$

Vertex $\left(-\frac{1}{2}, -\frac{25}{4}\right)$, intercepts $(0, -6)$, $(-3, 0), (2, 0)$

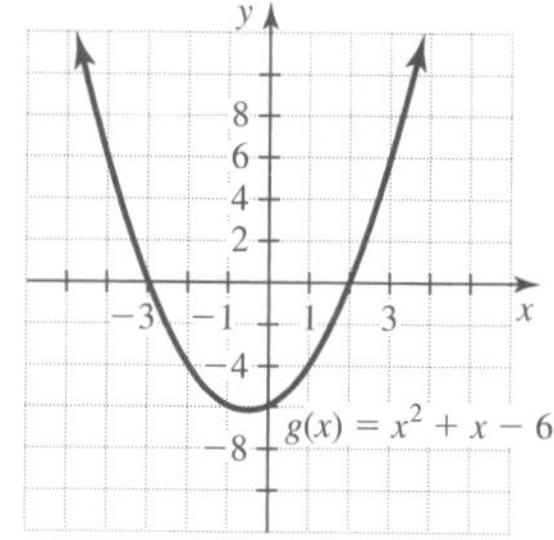

45. $y = -x^2 - 4x - 3$
Vertex $(-2, 1)$, intercepts $(0, -3)$, $(-1, 0)$, $(-3, 0)$

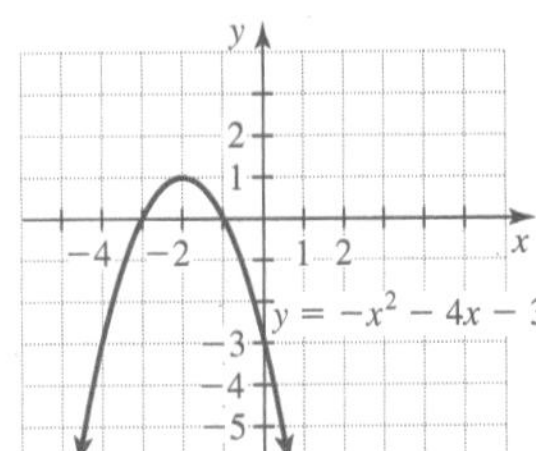

46. $y = -x^2 - 5x - 4$
Vertex $\left(-\frac{5}{2}, \frac{9}{4}\right)$, intercepts $(0, -4)$, $(-1, 0)$, $(-4, 0)$

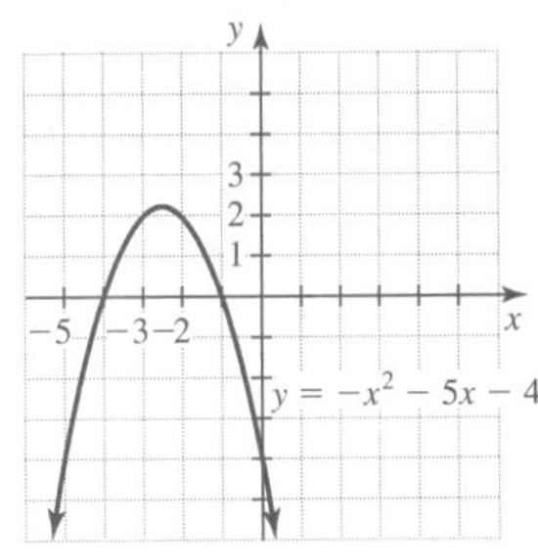

47. $h(x) = -x^2 + 3x + 4$
Vertex $\left(\frac{3}{2}, \frac{25}{4}\right)$, intercepts $(0, 4)$, $(4, 0)$, $(-1, 0)$

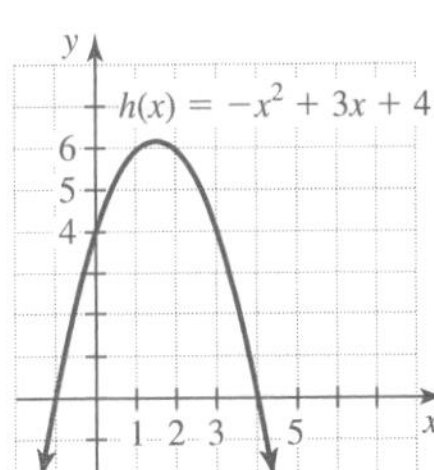

48. $h(x) = -x^2 - 2x + 8$
Vertex $(-1, 9)$, intercepts $(0, 8)$, $(-4, 0)$, $(2, 0)$

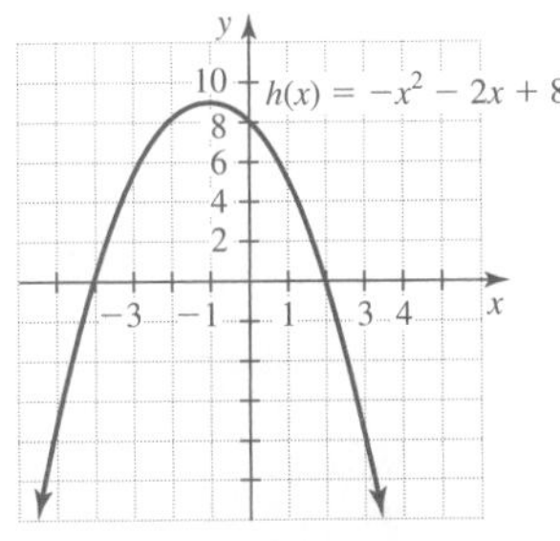

49. $a = b^2 - 6b - 16$
Vertex $(3, -25)$, intercepts $(0, -16)$, $(8, 0)$, $(-2, 0)$

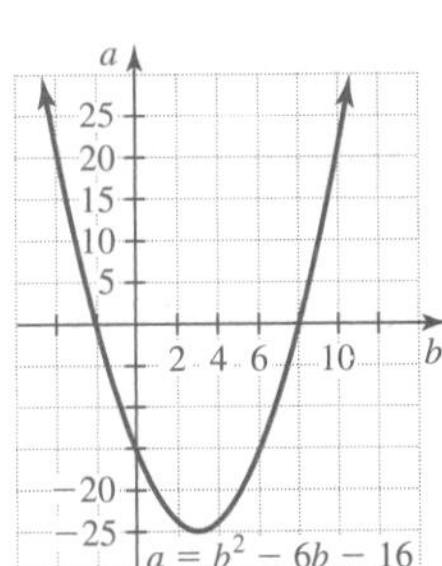

50. $v = -u^2 - 8u + 9$
Vertex $(-4, 25)$, intercepts $(0, 9)$, $(-9, 0)$, $(1, 0)$

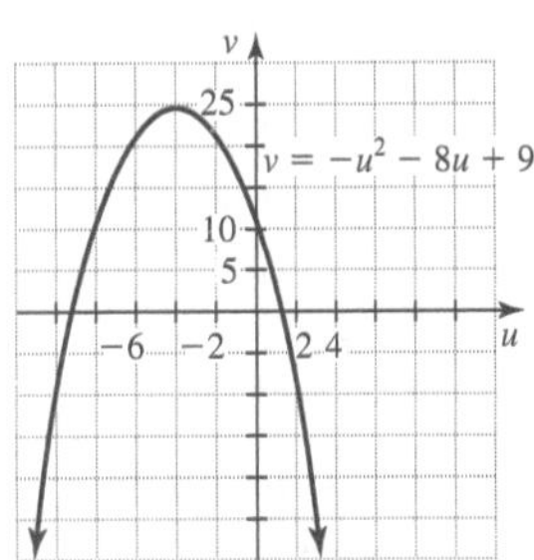

Find the maximum or minimum value of y.

51. $y = x^2 - 8$
Minimum -8

52. $y = 33 - x^2$
Maximum 33

53. $y = -3x^2 + 14$
Maximum 14

54. $y = 6 + 5x^2$
Minimum 6

55. $y = x^2 + 2x + 3$
Minimum 2

56. $y = x^2 - 2x + 5$
Minimum 4

57. $y = -2x^2 - 4x$
Maximum 2

58. $y = -3x^2 + 24x$
Maximum 48

Solve each problem. See Example 6.

59. ***Maximum height.*** If a baseball is projected upward from ground level with an initial velocity of 64 feet per second, then its height in feet is given by

$$s(t) = -16t^2 + 64t$$

where t is time in seconds. Graph this parabola for $0 \le t \le 4$. What is the maximum height reached by the ball?
Maximum 64 feet

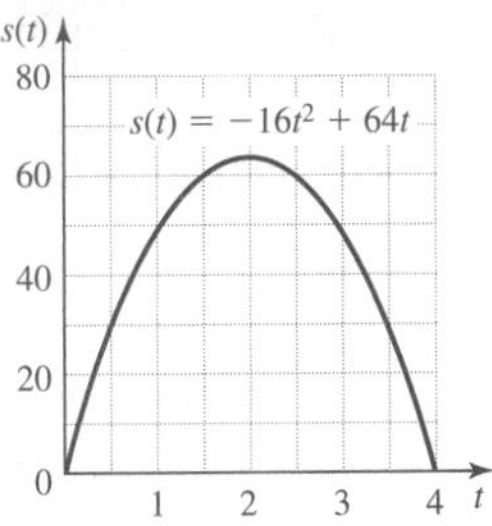

60. ***Maximum height.*** If a soccer ball is kicked straight up from the ground with an initial velocity of 32 feet per second, then its height above the earth in feet is given by $s(t) = -16t^2 + 32t$ where t is time in seconds. Graph this parabola for $0 \le t \le 2$. What is the maximum height reached by the ball?
Maximum 16 feet

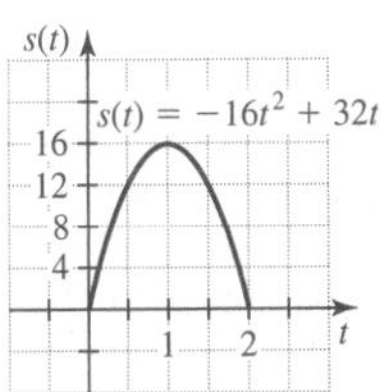

61. ***Minimum cost.*** It costs Acme Manufacturing C dollars per hour to operate its golf ball division. An analyst has determined that C is related to the number of golf balls produced per hour, x, by the equation $C = 0.009x^2 - 1.8x + 100$. What number of balls per hour should Acme produce to minimize the cost per hour of manufacturing these golf balls? 100

62. ***Maximum profit.*** A chain store manager has been told by the main office that daily profit, P, is related to the number of clerks working that day, x, according to the equation $P = -25x^2 + 300x$. What number of clerks will maximize the profit, and what is the maximum possible profit? 6 clerks, \$900

63. ***Maximum area.*** Jason plans to fence a rectangular area with 100 meters of fencing. He has written the formula $A = w(50 - w)$ to express the area in terms of the width w. What is the maximum possible area that he can enclose with his fencing? 625 square meters

Photo for Exercise 63

64. ***Minimizing cost.*** A company uses the formula $C(x) = 0.02x^2 - 3.4x + 150$ to model the unit cost in dollars for producing x stabilizer bars. For what number of bars is the unit cost at its minimum? What is the unit cost at that level of production? 85, \$5.50

65. ***Air pollution.*** The amount of nitrogen dioxide A in parts per million (ppm) that was present in the air in the city of Homer on a certain day in June is modeled by the formula

$$A(t) = -2t^2 + 32t + 12,$$

where t is the number of hours after 6:00 A.M. Use this formula to find the time at which the nitrogen dioxide level was at its maximum. 2 P.M.

66. ***Stabilization ratio.*** The stabilization ratio (births/deaths) for South and Central America can be modeled by the formula

$$y = -0.0012x^2 + 0.074x + 2.69$$

where y is the number of births divided by the number of deaths in the year $1950 + x$ (World Resources Institute, www.wri.org).

a) Use the graph to estimate the year in which the stabilization ratio was at its maximum.

b) Use the formula to find the year in which the stabilization ratio was at its maximum.

c) What was the maximum stabilization ratio from part (b)?

d) What is the significance of a stabilization ratio of 1?

a) 1980 b) 1981 c) 3.83 d) Stable population

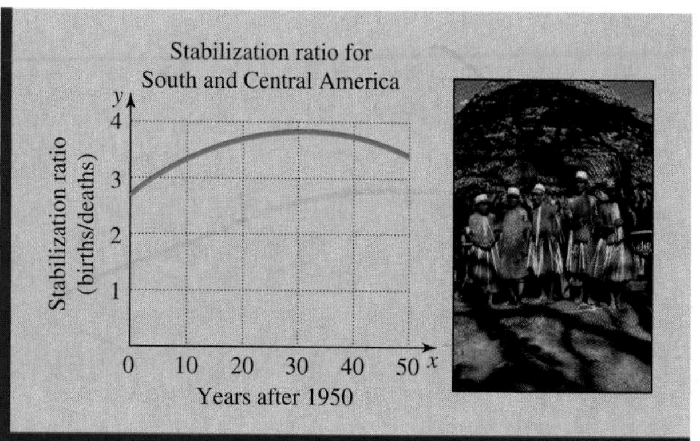

Figure for Exercise 66

67. ***Suspension bridge.*** The cable of the suspension bridge shown in the figure hangs in the shape of a parabola with equation $y = 0.0375x^2$, where x and y are in meters. What is the height of each tower above the roadway? What is the length z for the cable bracing the tower? 15 meters, 25 meters

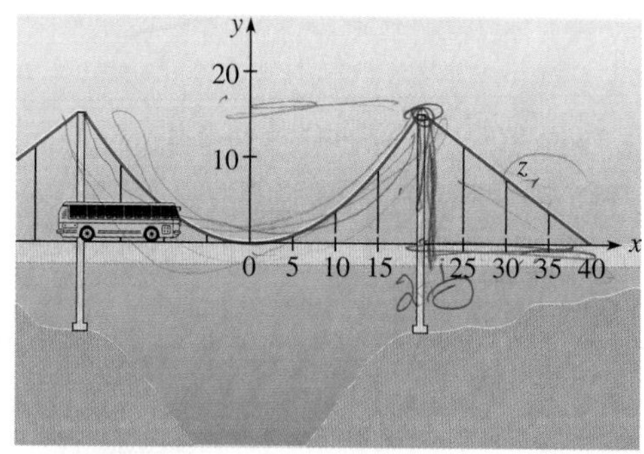

Figure for Exercise 67

Getting More Involved

68. ***Exploration***

a) Write the equation $y = 3(x - 2)^2 + 6$ in the form $y = ax^2 + bx + c$, and find the vertex of the parabola using the formula $x = \frac{-b}{2a}$.

b) Repeat part (a) with the equations $y = -4(x - 5)^2 - 9$ and $y = 3(x + 2)^2 - 6$.

c) What is the vertex for a parabola that is written in the form $y = a(x - h)^2 + k$? Explain your answer.

a) $y = 3x^2 - 12x + 18$, $(2, 6)$
b) $y = -4x^2 + 40x - 109$, $(5, -9)$, $y = 3x^2 + 12x + 6$, $(-2, -6)$ **c)** (h, k)

Graphing Calculator Exercises

69. Graph $y = x^2$, $y = \frac{1}{2}x^2$, and $y = 2x^2$ on the same coordinate system. What can you say about the graph of $y = ax^2$ for $a > 0$? The graph of $y = ax^2$ gets narrower as a gets larger.

70. Graph $y = x^2$, $y = (x - 3)^2$, and $y = (x + 3)^2$ on the same coordinate system. How does the graph of $y = (x - h)^2$ compare to the graph of $y = x^2$?
The graph of $y = (x - h)^2$ lies h units to the right of $y = x^2$ if $h > 0$ and $-h$ units to the left of $y = x^2$ if $h < 0$.

71. The equation $x = y^2$ is equivalent to $y = \pm\sqrt{x}$. Graph both $y = \sqrt{x}$ and $y = -\sqrt{x}$ on a graphing calculator. How does the graph of $x = y^2$ compare to the graph of $y = x^2$?
The graph of $y = x^2$ has the same shape as $x = y^2$.

72. Graph each of the following equations by solving for y.

a) $x = y^2 - 1$ $y = \pm\sqrt{x + 1}$

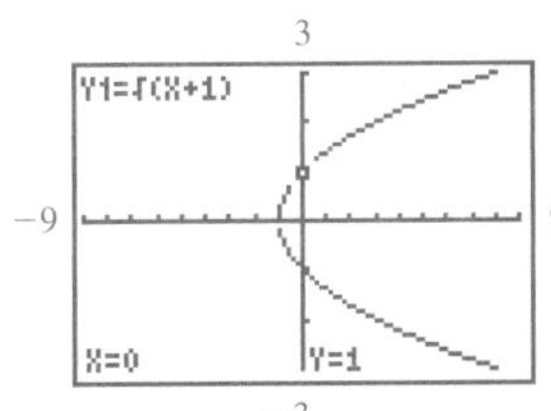

b) $x = -y^2$ $y = \pm\sqrt{-x}$

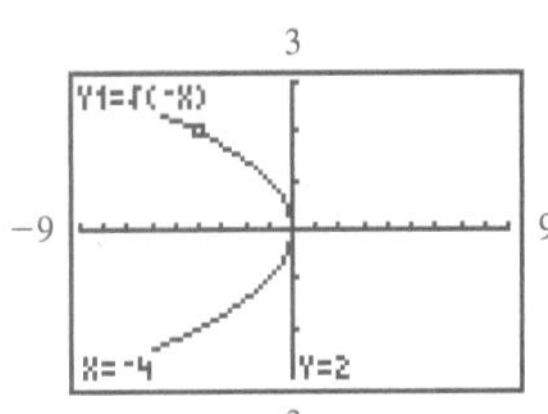

c) $x^2 + y^2 = 4$ $y = \pm\sqrt{4 - x^2}$

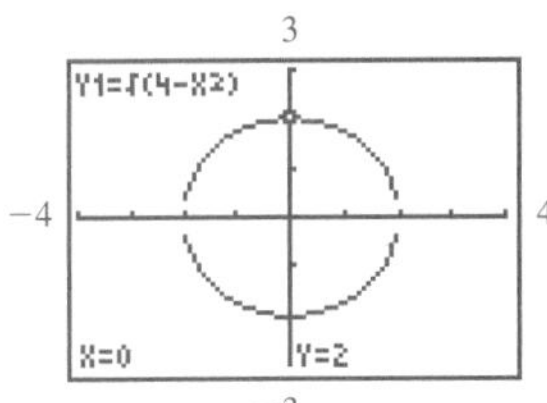

73. Determine the approximate vertex and x-intercepts for each parabola.

a) $y = 3.2x^2 - 5.4x + 1.6$
b) $y = -1.09x^2 + 13x + 7.5$

a) Vertex $(0.84, -0.68)$, x-intercepts $(1.30, 0)$, $(0.38, 0)$
b) Vertex $(5.96, 46.26)$, x-intercepts $(12.48, 0)$, $(-0.55, 0)$

10.4 More on Quadratic Equations

In this Section

- Writing a Quadratic Equation with Given Solutions
- Using the Discriminant in Factoring
- Equations Quadratic in Form
- Applications

In this section we use the ideas and methods of the previous sections to explore additional topics involving quadratic equations.

Writing a Quadratic Equation with Given Solutions

Not every quadratic equation can be solved by factoring, but the factoring method can be used (in reverse) to write a quadratic equation with given solutions.

EXAMPLE 1

Writing a quadratic given the solutions

Write a quadratic equation that has each given pair of solutions.

a) $4, -6$ **b)** $-\sqrt{2}, \sqrt{2}$ **c)** $-3i, 3i$

Solution

a) Reverse the factoring method using solutions 4 and -6:

$$x = 4 \quad \text{or} \quad x = -6$$
$$x - 4 = 0 \quad \text{or} \quad x + 6 = 0$$
$$(x - 4)(x + 6) = 0 \quad \text{Zero factor property}$$
$$x^2 + 2x - 24 = 0 \quad \text{Multiply the factors.}$$

b) Reverse the factoring method using solutions $-\sqrt{2}$ and $\sqrt{2}$:

$$x = -\sqrt{2} \quad \text{or} \quad x = \sqrt{2}$$
$$x + \sqrt{2} = 0 \quad \text{or} \quad x - \sqrt{2} = 0$$
$$(x + \sqrt{2})(x - \sqrt{2}) = 0 \quad \text{Zero factor property}$$
$$x^2 - 2 = 0 \quad \text{Multiply the factors.}$$

c) Reverse the factoring method using solutions $-3i$ and $3i$:

$$x = -3i \quad \text{or} \quad x = 3i$$
$$x + 3i = 0 \quad \text{or} \quad x - 3i = 0$$
$$(x + 3i)(x - 3i) = 0 \quad \text{Zero factor property}$$
$$x^2 - 9i^2 = 0 \quad \text{Multiply the factors.}$$
$$x^2 + 9 = 0 \quad \text{Note: } i^2 = -1$$

Now do Exercises 5–16

Calculator Close-Up

The graph of $y = x^2 + 2x - 24$ supports the conclusion in Example 2(a) because the graph crosses the x-axis at (4, 0) and $(-6, 0)$.

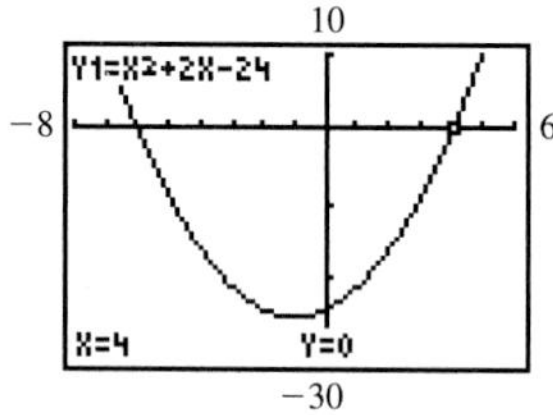

The process in Example 1 can be shortened somewhat if we observe the correspondence between the solutions to the equation and the factors.

Teaching Tip Writing equations with given solutions illustrates the correspondence between the solutions and the factors.

Correspondence Between Solutions and Factors

If a and b are solutions to a quadratic equation, then the equation is equivalent to

$$(x - a)(x - b) = 0.$$

So if 2 and -3 are solutions to a quadratic equation, then the equation is $(x - 2)(x + 3) = 0$ or $x^2 + x - 6 = 0$. If the solutions are fractions, it is not necessary to use fractions in the factors. For example, if $-\frac{1}{5}$ and $\frac{2}{3}$ are solutions to a quadratic equation, then the equation is $(5x + 1)(3x - 2) = 0$ or $15x^2 - 7x - 2 = 0$.

Using the Discriminant in Factoring

The quadratic formula $x = \frac{-b \pm \sqrt{b^2 - 4ac}}{2a}$ gives the solutions to the quadratic equation $ax^2 + bx + c = 0$. If a, b, and c are integers and $b^2 - 4ac$ is a perfect square, then $\sqrt{b^2 - 4ac}$ is a whole number and the quadratic formula produces solutions that are rational. The quadratic equations with rational solutions are precisely the ones that we solve by factoring. So we can use the discriminant $b^2 - 4ac$ to determine whether a quadratic polynomial is prime.

Identifying Prime Quadratic Polynomials Using $b^2 - 4ac$

Let $ax^2 + bx + c$ be a quadratic polynomial with integral coefficients having a greatest common factor of 1. The quadratic polynomial is prime if and only if the discriminant $b^2 - 4ac$ is *not* a perfect square.

EXAMPLE 2

Using the discriminant

Use the discriminant to determine whether each polynomial can be factored.

a) $6x^2 + x - 15$ **b)** $5x^2 - 3x + 2$

Solution

a) Use $a = 6$, $b = 1$, and $c = -15$ to find $b^2 - 4ac$:

$$b^2 - 4ac = 1^2 - 4(6)(-15) = 361$$

Because $\sqrt{361} = 19$, $6x^2 + x - 15$ can be factored. Using the *ac* method, we get

$$6x^2 + x - 15 = (2x - 3)(3x + 5).$$

b) Use $a = 5$, $b = -3$, and $c = 2$ to find $b^2 - 4ac$:

$$b^2 - 4ac = (-3)^2 - 4(5)(2) = -31$$

Because the discriminant is not a perfect square, $5x^2 - 3x + 2$ is prime.

Now do Exercises 17–26

Equations Quadratic in Form

In a quadratic equation we have a variable and its square (x and x^2). An equation that contains an expression and the square of that expression is **quadratic in form** if substituting a single variable for that expression results in a quadratic equation. Equations that are quadratic in form can be solved by using methods for quadratic equations.

EXAMPLE 3

Teaching Tip Point out the connection between the degree of the polynomial and the number of roots to the equation.

An equation quadratic in form

Solve $(x + 15)^2 - 3(x + 15) - 18 = 0$.

Solution

Note that $x + 15$ and $(x + 15)^2$ both appear in the equation. Let $a = x + 15$ and substitute a for $x + 15$ in the equation:

$$(x + 15)^2 - 3(x + 15) - 18 = 0$$
$$a^2 - 3a - 18 = 0$$
$$(a - 6)(a + 3) = 0 \quad \text{Factor.}$$
$$a - 6 = 0 \quad \text{or} \quad a + 3 = 0$$
$$a = 6 \quad \text{or} \quad a = -3$$
$$x + 15 = 6 \quad \text{or} \quad x + 15 = -3 \quad \text{Replace } a \text{ by } x + 15.$$
$$x = -9 \quad \text{or} \quad x = -18$$

Check in the original equation. The solution set is $\{-18, -9\}$.

Now do Exercises 27–32

In Example 4 we have a fourth-degree equation that is quadratic in form. Note that the fourth-degree equation has four solutions.

EXAMPLE 4

Helpful Hint

The fundamental theorem of algebra says that the number of solutions to a polynomial equation is less than or equal to the degree of the polynomial. This famous theorem was proved by Carl Friedrich Gauss when he was a young man.

A fourth-degree equation

Solve $x^4 - 6x^2 + 8 = 0$.

Solution

Note that x^4 is the square of x^2. If we let $w = x^2$, then $w^2 = x^4$. Substitute these expressions into the original equation.

$$x^4 - 6x^2 + 8 = 0$$

$$w^2 - 6w + 8 = 0 \quad \text{Replace } x^4 \text{ by } w^2 \text{ and } x^2 \text{ by } w.$$

$$(w - 2)(w - 4) = 0 \quad \text{Factor.}$$

$$w - 2 = 0 \quad \text{or} \quad w - 4 = 0$$

$$w = 2 \quad \text{or} \quad w = 4$$

$$x^2 = 2 \quad \text{or} \quad x^2 = 4 \quad \text{Substitute } x^2 \text{ for } w.$$

$$x = \pm\sqrt{2} \quad \text{or} \quad x = \pm 2 \quad \text{Even-root property}$$

Check. The solution set is $\{-2, -\sqrt{2}, \sqrt{2}, 2\}$.

Now do Exercises 33–40

CAUTION If you replace x^2 by w, do not quit when you find the values of w. If the variable in the original equation is x, then you must solve for x.

EXAMPLE 5

Calculator Close-Up

The four x-intercepts on the graph of
$y = (x^2 + 2x)^2 - 11(x^2 + 2x) + 24$
support the conclusion in Example 5.

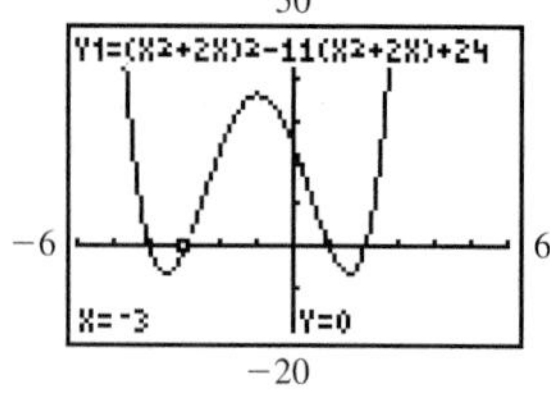

Teaching Tip Note that we have fourth degree, four intercepts, four factors, and four solutions.

A quadratic within a quadratic

Solve $(x^2 + 2x)^2 - 11(x^2 + 2x) + 24 = 0$.

Solution

Note that $x^2 + 2x$ and $(x^2 + 2x)^2$ appear in the equation. Let $a = x^2 + 2x$ and substitute.

$$a^2 - 11a + 24 = 0$$

$$(a - 8)(a - 3) = 0 \quad \text{Factor.}$$

$$a - 8 = 0 \quad \text{or} \quad a - 3 = 0$$

$$a = 8 \quad \text{or} \quad a = 3$$

$$x^2 + 2x = 8 \quad \text{or} \quad x^2 + 2x = 3 \quad \text{Replace } a \text{ by } x^2 + 2x.$$

$$x^2 + 2x - 8 = 0 \quad \text{or} \quad x^2 + 2x - 3 = 0$$

$$(x - 2)(x + 4) = 0 \quad \text{or} \quad (x + 3)(x - 1) = 0$$

$$x - 2 = 0 \quad \text{or} \quad x + 4 = 0 \quad \text{or} \quad x + 3 = 0 \quad \text{or} \quad x - 1 = 0$$

$$x = 2 \quad \text{or} \quad x = -4 \quad \text{or} \quad x = -3 \quad \text{or} \quad x = 1$$

Check. The solution set is $\{-4, -3, 1, 2\}$.

Now do Exercises 41–46

Example 6 involves a fractional exponent. To identify this type of equation as quadratic in form, recall how to square an expression with a fractional exponent. For example, $(x^{1/2})^2 = x$, $(x^{1/4})^2 = x^{1/2}$, and $(x^{1/3})^2 = x^{2/3}$.

EXAMPLE 6

A fractional exponent

Solve $x - 9x^{1/2} + 14 = 0$.

Solution

Note that the square of $x^{1/2}$ is x. Let $w = x^{1/2}$; then $w^2 = (x^{1/2})^2 = x$. Now substitute w and w^2 into the original equation:

$$w^2 - 9w + 14 = 0$$
$$(w - 7)(w - 2) = 0$$
$$w - 7 = 0 \quad \text{or} \quad w - 2 = 0$$
$$w = 7 \quad \text{or} \quad w = 2$$
$$x^{1/2} = 7 \quad \text{or} \quad x^{1/2} = 2 \quad \text{Replace } w \text{ by } x^{1/2}.$$
$$x = 49 \quad \text{or} \quad x = 4 \quad \text{Square each side.}$$

Because we squared each side, we must check for extraneous roots. First evaluate $x - 9x^{1/2} + 14$ for $x = 49$:

$$49 - 9 \cdot 49^{1/2} + 14 = 49 - 9 \cdot 7 + 14 = 0$$

Now evaluate $x - 9x^{1/2} + 14$ for $x = 4$:

$$4 - 9 \cdot 4^{1/2} + 14 = 4 - 9 \cdot 2 + 14 = 0$$

Because each solution checks, the solution set is $\{4, 49\}$.

Now do Exercises 47–54

CAUTION An equation of quadratic form must have a term that is the square of another. Equations such as $x^4 - 5x^3 + 6 = 0$ or $x^{1/2} - 3x^{1/3} - 18 = 0$ are not quadratic in form and cannot be solved by substitution.

Applications

Applied problems often result in quadratic equations that cannot be factored. For such equations we use the quadratic formula to find exact solutions and a calculator to find decimal approximations for the exact solutions.

EXAMPLE 7

Changing area

Marvin's flower bed is rectangular in shape with a length of 10 feet and a width of 5 feet (ft). He wants to increase the length and width by the same amount to obtain a flower bed with an area of 75 square feet (ft^2). What should the amount of increase be?

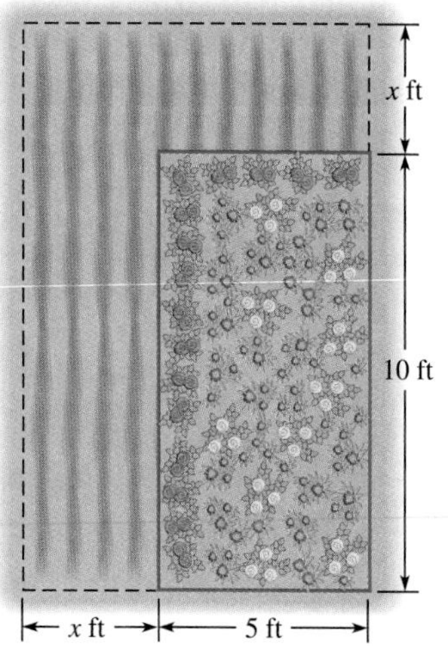

Figure 10.9

Solution

Let x be the amount of increase. The length and width of the new flower bed are $x + 10$ ft and $x + 5$ ft, as shown in Fig. 10.9. Because the area is to be 75 ft^2, we have

$$(x + 10)(x + 5) = 75.$$

Write this equation in the form $ax^2 + bx + c = 0$:

$$x^2 + 15x + 50 = 75$$

$$x^2 + 15x - 25 = 0 \quad \text{Get 0 on the right.}$$

$$x = \frac{-15 \pm \sqrt{225 - 4(1)(-25)}}{2(1)}$$

$$= \frac{-15 \pm \sqrt{325}}{2} = \frac{-15 \pm 5\sqrt{13}}{2}$$

Because the value of x must be positive, the exact increase is

$$\frac{-15 + 5\sqrt{13}}{2} \text{ feet.}$$

Using a calculator, we can find that x is approximately 1.51 ft. If $x = 1.51$ ft, then the new length is 11.51 ft, and the new width is 6.51 ft. The area of a rectangle with these dimensions is 74.93 ft^2. Of course, the approximate dimensions do not give an area of exactly 75 ft^2.

Now do Exercises 81–88

EXAMPLE 8

Mowing the lawn

It takes Carla 1 hour longer to mow the lawn than it takes Sharon to mow the lawn. If they can mow the lawn in 5 hours working together, then how long would it take each girl by herself?

Solution

If Sharon can mow the lawn by herself in x hours, then she works at the rate of $\frac{1}{x}$ of the lawn per hour. If Carla can mow the lawn by herself in $x + 1$ hours, then she works at the rate of $\frac{1}{x+1}$ of the lawn per hour. We can use a table to list all of the important quantities.

	Rate	Time	Work
Sharon	$\frac{1}{x} \frac{\text{lawn}}{\text{hr}}$	5 hr	$\frac{5}{x}$ lawn
Carla	$\frac{1}{x+1} \frac{\text{lawn}}{\text{hr}}$	5 hr	$\frac{5}{x+1}$ lawn

Helpful Hint

Note that the equation concerns the portion of the job done by each girl. We could have written an equation about the rates at which the two girls work. Because they can finish the lawn together in 5 hours, they are mowing together at the rate of $\frac{1}{5}$ lawn per hour. So

$$\frac{1}{x} + \frac{1}{x+1} = \frac{1}{5}.$$

Because they complete the lawn in 5 hours, the portion of the lawn done by Sharon and the portion done by Carla have a sum of 1:

$$\frac{5}{x} + \frac{5}{x+1} = 1$$

$$x(x+1)\frac{5}{x} + x(x+1)\frac{5}{x+1} = x(x+1)1 \quad \text{Multiply by the LCD.}$$

$$5x + 5 + 5x = x^2 + x$$

$$10x + 5 = x^2 + x$$

$$-x^2 + 9x + 5 = 0$$

$$x^2 - 9x - 5 = 0$$

$$x = \frac{9 \pm \sqrt{(-9)^2 - 4(1)(-5)}}{2(1)}$$

$$= \frac{9 \pm \sqrt{101}}{2}$$

Using a calculator, we find that $\frac{9 - \sqrt{101}}{2}$ is negative. So Sharon's time alone is

$$\frac{9 + \sqrt{101}}{2} \text{ hours.}$$

To find Carla's time alone, we add one hour to Sharon's time:

$$\frac{9 + \sqrt{101}}{2} + 1 = \frac{9 + \sqrt{101}}{2} + \frac{2}{2} = \frac{11 + \sqrt{101}}{2} \text{ hours}$$

Sharon's time alone is approximately 9.525 hours, and Carla's time alone is approximately 10.525 hours.

Now do Exercises 89–92

Warm-Ups ▼

True or false? Explain your answer.

1. To solve $x^4 - 5x^2 + 6 = 0$ by substitution, we can let $w = x^2$. True
2. We can solve $x^5 - 3x^3 - 10 = 0$ by substitution if we let $w = x^3$. False
3. We always use the quadratic formula on equations of quadratic form. False
4. If $w = x^{1/6}$, then $w^2 = x^{1/3}$. True
5. To solve $x - 7\sqrt{x} + 10 = 0$ by substitution, we let $\sqrt{w} = x$. False
6. If $y = 2^{1/2}$, then $y^2 = 2^{1/4}$. False
7. If John paints a 100-foot fence in x hours, then his rate is $\frac{100}{x}$ of the fence per hour. False
8. If Elvia drives 300 miles in x hours, then her rate is $\frac{300}{x}$ miles per hour (mph). True
9. If Ann's boat goes 10 mph in still water, then against a 5-mph current, it will go 2 mph. False
10. If squares with sides of length x inches are cut from the corners of an 11-inch by 14-inch rectangular piece of sheet metal and the sides are folded up to form a box, then the dimensions of the bottom will be $11 - x$ by $14 - x$. False

10.4 Exercises

Boost your GRADE at mathzone.com!

MathZone

- Practice Problems
- Self-Tests
- Videos
- Net Tutor
- e-Professors

Reading and Writing *After reading this section, write out the answers to these questions. Use complete sentences.*

1. How can you use the discriminant to determine if a quadratic polynomial can be factored?
If the coefficients are integers and the discriminant is a perfect square, then the quadratic polynomial can be factored.

2. What is the relationship between solutions to a quadratic equation and factors of a quadratic polynomial?
The number k is a solution to a quadratic equation if and only if $x - k$ is a factor of the quadratic polynomial.

3. How do we write a quadratic equation with given solutions?
If the solutions are a and b, then the quadratic equation $(x - a)(x - b) = 0$ has those solutions.

4. What is an equation quadratic in form?
An equation of quadratic form is one that can be converted to a quadratic equation by making a substitution.

For each given pair of numbers find a quadratic equation with integral coefficients that has the numbers as its solutions. See Example 1.

5. $3, -7$ $x^2 + 4x - 21 = 0$

6. $-8, 2$ $x^2 + 6x - 16 = 0$

7. $4, 1$ $x^2 - 5x + 4 = 0$

8. $3, 2$ $x^2 - 5x + 6 = 0$

9. $\sqrt{5}, -\sqrt{5}$ $x^2 - 5 = 0$

10. $-\sqrt{7}, \sqrt{7}$ $x^2 - 7 = 0$

11. $4i, -4i$ $x^2 + 16 = 0$

12. $-3i, 3i$ $x^2 + 9 = 0$

13. $i\sqrt{2}, -i\sqrt{2}$ $x^2 + 2 = 0$

14. $3i\sqrt{2}, -3i\sqrt{2}$ $x^2 + 18 = 0$

15. $\frac{1}{2}, \frac{1}{3}$
$6x^2 - 5x + 1 = 0$

16. $-\frac{1}{5}, -\frac{1}{2}$
$10x^2 + 7x + 1 = 0$

Use the discriminant to determine whether each quadratic polynomial can be factored, then factor the ones that are not prime. See Example 2.

17. $2x^2 - x + 4$
Prime

18. $2x^2 + 3x - 5$
$(2x + 5)(x - 1)$

19. $2x^2 + 6x - 5$ Prime

20. $3x^2 + 5x - 1$ Prime

21. $6x^2 + 19x - 36$
$(3x - 4)(2x + 9)$

22. $8x^2 + 6x - 27$
$(2x - 3)(4x + 9)$

23. $4x^2 - 5x - 12$
Prime

24. $4x^2 - 27x + 45$
$(4x - 15)(x - 3)$

25. $8x^2 - 18x - 45$
$(4x - 15)(2x + 3)$

26. $6x^2 + 9x - 16$
Prime

Find all real solutions to each equation. See Example 3.

27. $(x - 1)^2 - 2(x - 1) - 8 = 0$ $\{-1, 5\}$

28. $(m + 3)^2 + 5(m + 3) - 14 = 0$ $\{-10, -1\}$

29. $(2a - 1)^2 + 2(2a - 1) - 8 = 0$ $\left\{-\frac{3}{2}, \frac{3}{2}\right\}$

30. $(3a + 2)^2 - 3(3a + 2) = 10$ $\left\{-\frac{4}{3}, 1\right\}$

31. $(w - 1)^2 + 5(w - 1) + 5 = 0$ $\left\{\frac{-3 \pm \sqrt{5}}{2}\right\}$

32. $(2x - 1)^2 - 4(2x - 1) + 2 = 0$ $\left\{\frac{3 \pm \sqrt{2}}{2}\right\}$

Find all real solutions to each equation. See Example 4.

33. $x^4 - 13x^2 + 36 = 0$ $\{\pm 2, \pm 3\}$

34. $x^4 - 20x^2 + 64 = 0$ $\{\pm 2, \pm 4\}$

35. $x^6 - 28x^3 + 27 = 0$ $\{1, 3\}$

36. $x^6 - 3x^3 - 4 = 0$ $\{-1, \sqrt[3]{4}\}$

37. $x^4 - 14x^2 + 45 = 0$ $\{\pm\sqrt{5}, \pm 3\}$

38. $x^4 + 2x^2 = 15$ $\{\pm\sqrt{3}\}$

39. $x^6 + 7x^3 = 8$ $\{-2, 1\}$

40. $a^6 + 6a^3 = 16$ $\{-2, \sqrt[3]{2}\}$

Find all real solutions to each equation. See Example 5.

41. $(x^2 + 1)^2 - 11(x^2 + 1) = -10$ $\{0, \pm 3\}$

42. $(x^2 + 2)^2 - 11(x^2 + 2) = -30$ $\{\pm\sqrt{3}, \pm 2\}$

43. $(x^2 + 2x)^2 - 7(x^2 + 2x) + 12 = 0$ $\{-1 \pm \sqrt{5}, -3, 1\}$

44. $(x^2 + 3x)^2 + (x^2 + 3x) - 20 = 0$ $\{-4, 1\}$

45. $(y^2 + y)^2 - 8(y^2 + y) + 12 = 0$ $\{-3, -2, 1, 2\}$

46. $(w^2 - 2w)^2 + 24 = 11(w^2 - 2w)$ $\{-2, -1, 3, 4\}$

Find all real solutions to each equation. See Example 6.

47. $x - 3x^{1/2} + 2 = 0$ $\{1, 4\}$

48. $x^{1/2} - 3x^{1/4} + 2 = 0$ $\{1, 16\}$

49. $x^{2/3} + 4x^{1/3} + 3 = 0$ $\{-27, -1\}$

50. $x^{2/3} - 3x^{1/3} - 10 = 0$ $\{-8, 125\}$

51. $x^{1/2} - 5x^{1/4} + 6 = 0$ $\{16, 81\}$

52. $2x - 5\sqrt{x} + 2 = 0$ $\left\{\frac{1}{4}, 4\right\}$

53. $2x - 5x^{1/2} - 3 = 0$ $\{9\}$

54. $x^{1/4} + 2 = x^{1/2}$ $\{16\}$

Find all real solutions to each equation.

55. $x^{-2} + x^{-1} - 6 = 0$ $\left\{-\frac{1}{3}, \frac{1}{2}\right\}$

56. $x^{-2} - 2x^{-1} = 8$ $\left\{-\frac{1}{2}, \frac{1}{4}\right\}$

57. $x^{1/6} - x^{1/3} + 2 = 0$
$\{64\}$

58. $x^{2/3} - x^{1/3} - 20 = 0$
$\{-64, 125\}$

59. $\left(\frac{1}{y-1}\right)^2 + \left(\frac{1}{y-1}\right) = 6$ $\left\{\frac{2}{3}, \frac{3}{2}\right\}$

60. $\left(\frac{1}{w+1}\right)^2 - 2\left(\frac{1}{w+1}\right) - 24 = 0$ $\left\{-\frac{5}{6}, -\frac{5}{4}\right\}$

61. $2x^2 - 3 - 6\sqrt{2x^2 - 3} + 8 = 0$ $\left\{\pm\frac{\sqrt{14}}{2}, \pm\frac{\sqrt{38}}{2}\right\}$

62. $x^2 + x + \sqrt{x^2 + x} - 2 = 0$ $\left\{\frac{-1 \pm \sqrt{5}}{2}\right\}$

63. $x^{-2} - 2x^{-1} - 1 = 0$ $\{-1 + \sqrt{2}, -1 - \sqrt{2}\}$

64. $x^{-2} - 6x^{-1} + 6 = 0$ $\left\{\frac{3 + \sqrt{3}}{6}, \frac{3 - \sqrt{3}}{6}\right\}$

Find all real and imaginary solutions to each equation.

65. $w^2 + 4 = 0$ $\{\pm 2i\}$

66. $w^2 + 9 = 0$ $\{\pm 3i\}$

67. $a^4 + 6a^2 + 8 = 0$ $\{\pm i\sqrt{2}, \pm 2i\}$

68. $b^4 + 13b^2 + 36 = 0$ $\{\pm 2i, \pm 3i\}$

69. $m^4 - 16 = 0$ $\{\pm 2, \pm 2i\}$

70. $t^4 - 4 = 0$ $\{\pm\sqrt{2}, \pm i\sqrt{2}\}$

71. $16b^4 - 1 = 0$ $\left\{\pm\frac{1}{2}, \pm\frac{i}{2}\right\}$

72. $b^4 - 81 = 0$ $\{\pm 3, \pm 3i\}$

73. $x^3 + 1 = 0$ $\left\{\frac{1 \pm i\sqrt{3}}{2}, -1\right\}$

74. $x^3 - 1 = 0$ $\left\{\frac{-1 \pm i\sqrt{3}}{2}, 1\right\}$

75. $x^3 + 8 = 0$ $\{1 \pm i\sqrt{3}, -2\}$

76. $x^3 - 27 = 0$ $\left\{\frac{-3 \pm 3i\sqrt{3}}{2}, 3\right\}$

77. $a^{-2} - 2a^{-1} + 5 = 0$ $\left\{\frac{1 \pm 2i}{5}\right\}$

78. $b^{-2} - 4b^{-1} + 6 = 0$ $\left\{\frac{2 \pm i\sqrt{2}}{6}\right\}$

79. $(2x - 1)^2 - 2(2x - 1) + 5 = 0$ $\{1 \pm i\}$

80. $(4x - 1)^2 - 6(4x - 1) + 25 = 0$ $\{1 \pm i\}$

Find the exact solution to each problem. If the exact solution is an irrational number, then also find an approximate decimal solution. See Examples 7 and 8.

81. ***Country singers.*** Harry and Gary are traveling to Nashville to make their fortunes. Harry leaves on the train at 8:00 A.M. and Gary travels by car, starting at 9:00 A.M. To complete the 300-mile trip and arrive at the same time as Harry, Gary travels 10 miles per hour (mph) faster than the train. At what time will they both arrive in Nashville? 2:00 P.M.

82. ***Gone fishing.*** Debbie traveled by boat 5 miles upstream to fish in her favorite spot. Because of the 4-mph current, it took her 20 minutes longer to get there than to return. How fast will her boat go in still water? $2\sqrt{34}$ or 11.662 mph

83. ***Cross-country cycling.*** Erin was traveling across the desert on her bicycle. Before lunch she traveled 60 miles (mi); after lunch she traveled 46 mi. She put in one hour more after lunch than before lunch, but her speed was 4 mph slower than before. What was her speed before lunch and after lunch? Before $-5 + \sqrt{265}$ or 11.3 mph, after $-9 + \sqrt{265}$ or 7.3 mph

Photo for Exercise 83

84. ***Extreme hardship.*** Kim starts to walk 3 mi to school at 7:30 A.M. with a temperature of 0°F. Her brother Bryan starts at 7:45 A.M. on his bicycle, traveling 10 mph faster than Kim. If they get to school at the same time, then how fast is each one traveling? Kim $-5 + \sqrt{145}$ or 7.042 mph, Bryan $5 + \sqrt{145}$ or 17.042 mph

85. ***American pie.*** John takes 3 hours longer than Andrew to peel 500 pounds (lb) of apples. If together they can peel 500 lb of apples in 8 hours, then how long would it take each one working alone?
Andrew $\frac{13 + \sqrt{265}}{2}$ or 14.6 hours, John $\frac{19 + \sqrt{265}}{2}$ or 17.6 hours

86. ***On the half shell.*** It takes Brent one hour longer than Calvin to shuck a sack of oysters. If together they shuck a sack of oysters in 45 minutes, then how long would it take each one working alone?
Brent $\frac{5 + \sqrt{13}}{4}$ or 2.151 hours, Calvin $\frac{1 + \sqrt{13}}{4}$ or 1.151 hours

87. ***The growing garden.*** Eric's garden is 20 ft by 30 ft. He wants to increase the length and width by the same amount to have a 1000-ft^2 garden. What should be the new dimensions of the garden? Length $5 + 5\sqrt{41}$ or 37.02 ft, width $-5 + 5\sqrt{41}$ or 27.02 ft

88. ***Open-top box.*** Thomas is going to make an open-top box by cutting equal squares from the four corners of an

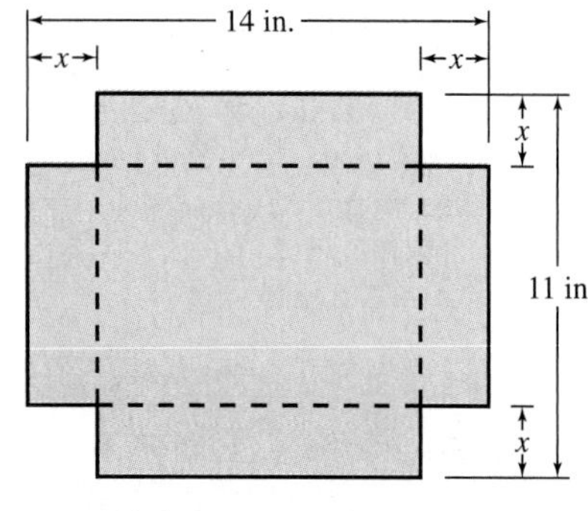

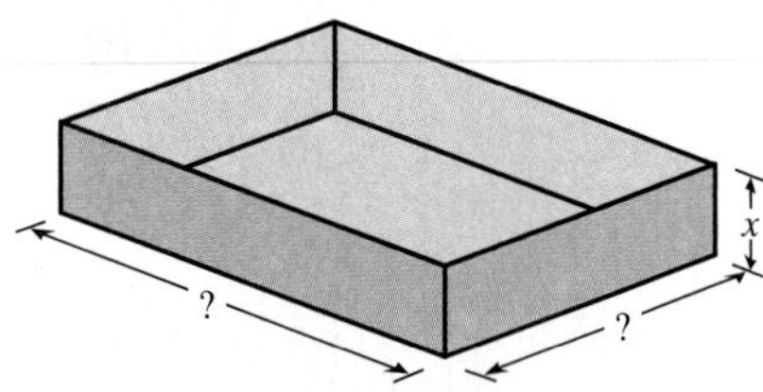

Figure for Exercise 88

11 inch by 14 inch sheet of cardboard and folding up the sides. If the area of the base is to be 80 square inches, then what size square should be cut from each corner?

$\frac{25 - \sqrt{329}}{4}$ or 1.715 inches

89. ***Pumping the pool.*** It takes pump A 2 hours less time than pump B to empty a certain swimming pool. Pump A is started at 8:00 A.M., and pump B is started at 11:00 A.M. If the pool is still half full at 5:00 P.M., then how long would it take pump A working alone? $14 + 2\sqrt{58}$ or 29.2 hours

90. ***Time off for lunch.*** It usually takes Eva 3 hours longer to do the monthly payroll than it takes Cicely. They start working on it together at 9:00 A.M. and at 5:00 P.M. they have 90% of it done. If Eva took a 2-hour lunch break while Cicely had none, then how much longer will it take for them to finish the payroll working together? 0.788 hour or 47 minutes

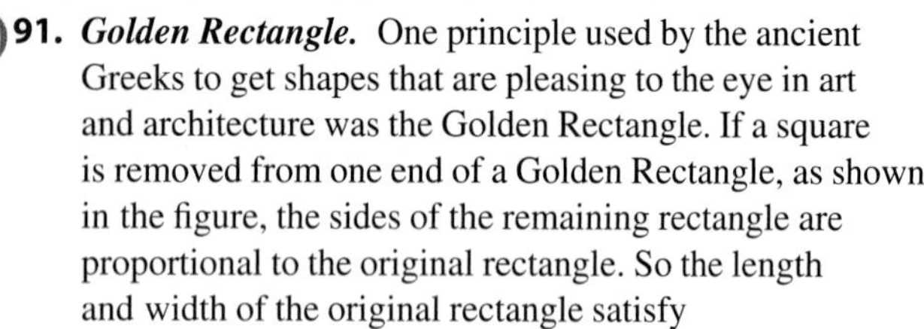

91. ***Golden Rectangle.*** One principle used by the ancient Greeks to get shapes that are pleasing to the eye in art and architecture was the Golden Rectangle. If a square is removed from one end of a Golden Rectangle, as shown in the figure, the sides of the remaining rectangle are proportional to the original rectangle. So the length and width of the original rectangle satisfy

$$\frac{L}{W} = \frac{W}{L - W}.$$

If the length of a Golden Rectangle is 10 meters, then what is its width? $-5 + 5\sqrt{5}$ or 6.2 meters

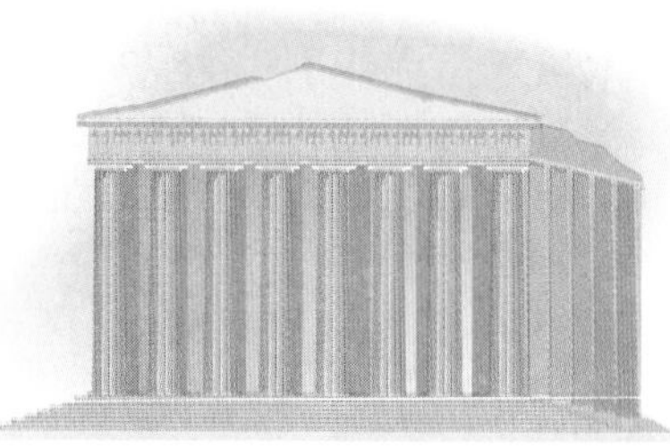

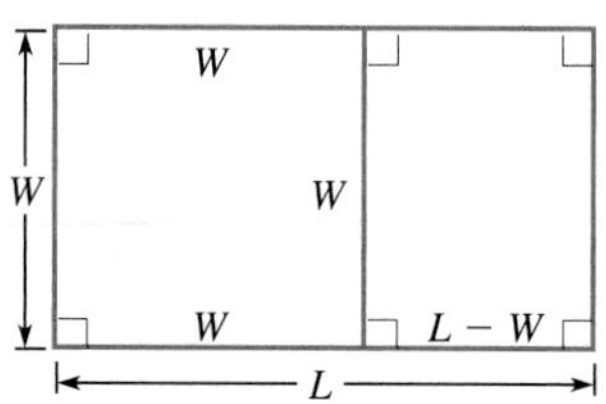

Figure for Exercise 91

92. ***Golden painting.*** An artist wants her painting to be in the shape of a golden rectangle. If the length of the painting is 36 inches, then what should be the width? See the previous exercise.
$-18 + 18\sqrt{5}$ or approximately 22.2 in.

Getting More Involved

93. ***Exploration***

a) Given that $P(x) = x^4 + 6x^2 - 27$, find $P(3i)$, $P(-3i)$, $P(\sqrt{3})$, and $P(-\sqrt{3})$.

b) What can you conclude about the values $3i$, $-3i$, $\sqrt{3}$, and $-\sqrt{3}$ and their relationship to each other?

94. ***Cooperative learning***

Work with a group to write a quadratic equation that has each given pair of solutions.

a) $3 + \sqrt{5}, 3 - \sqrt{5}$

b) $4 - 2i, 4 + 2i$

c) $\frac{1 + i\sqrt{3}}{2}, \frac{1 - i\sqrt{3}}{2}$

Graphing Calculator Exercises

Solve each equation by locating the x-intercepts on a calculator graph. Round approximate answers to two decimal places.

95. $(5x - 7)^2 - (5x - 7) - 6 = 0$ $\{1, 2\}$

96. $x^4 - 116x^2 + 1600 = 0$
$\{-10, -4, 4, 10\}$

97. $(x^2 + 3x)^2 - 7(x^2 + 3x) + 9 = 0$
$\{-4.25, -3.49, 0.49, 1.25\}$

98. $x^2 - 3x^{1/2} - 12 = 0$ $\{4.27\}$

10.5 Quadratic and Rational Inequalities

In this Section

In this section we solve inequalities involving quadratic polynomials. We use a new technique based on the rules for multiplying real numbers.

Solving Quadratic Inequalities with a Sign Graph

An inequality involving a quadratic polynomial is called a **quadratic** inequality.

Quadratic Inequality

A quadratic inequality is an inequality of the form

$$ax^2 + bx + c > 0,$$

where a, b, and c are real numbers with $a \neq 0$. The inequality symbols $<$, $\leq$, and $\geq$ may also be used.

If we can factor a quadratic inequality, then the inequality can be solved with a **sign graph,** which shows where each factor is positive, negative, or zero.

EXAMPLE 1

Solving a quadratic inequality

Use a sign graph to solve the inequality $x^2 + 3x - 10 > 0$.

Solution

Because the left-hand side can be factored, we can write the inequality as

$$(x + 5)(x - 2) > 0.$$

This inequality says that the product of $x + 5$ and $x - 2$ is positive. If both factors are negative or both are positive, the product is positive. To analyze the signs of each factor, we make a sign graph as follows. First consider the possible values of the factor $x + 5$:

Value	Where	On the Number Line
$x + 5 = 0$	if $x = -5$	Put a 0 above -5.
$x + 5 > 0$	if $x > -5$	Put + signs to the right of -5.
$x + 5 < 0$	if $x < -5$	Put − signs to the left of -5.

The sign graph shown in Fig. 10.10 for the factor $x + 5$ is made from the information in the preceding table.

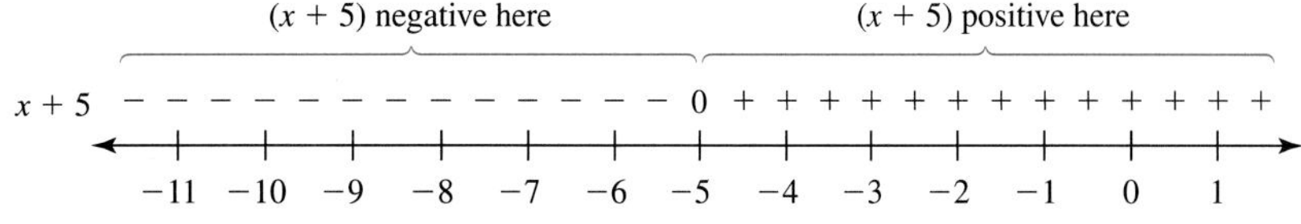

Figure 10.10

Calculator Close-Up

Use Y= to set $y_1 = x + 5$ and $y_2 = x - 2$. Now make a table and scroll through the table. The table numerically supports the sign graph in Fig. 10.11.

X	Y1	Y2
-7	-2	-9
-5	0	-7
-3	2	-5
-1	4	-3
1	6	-1
3	8	1
5	10	3

Y1=X+5

Note that the graph of $y = x^2 + 3x - 10$ is above the x-axis when $x < -5$ or when $x > 2$.

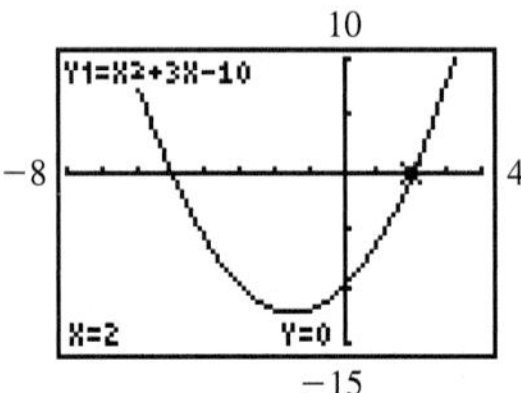

Now consider the possible values of the factor $x - 2$:

Value	Where	On the Number Line
$x - 2 = 0$	if $x = 2$	Put a 0 above 2.
$x - 2 > 0$	if $x > 2$	Put + signs to the right of 2.
$x - 2 < 0$	if $x < 2$	Put − signs to the left of 2.

We put the information for the factor $x - 2$ on the sign graph for the factor $x + 5$ as shown in Fig. 10.11. We can see from Fig. 10.11 that the product is positive if $x < -5$ and the product is positive if $x > 2$. The solution set for the quadratic inequality is shown in Fig. 10.12. Note that -5 and 2 are not included in the graph because for those values of x the product is zero. The solution set is $(-\infty, -5) \cup (2, \infty)$.

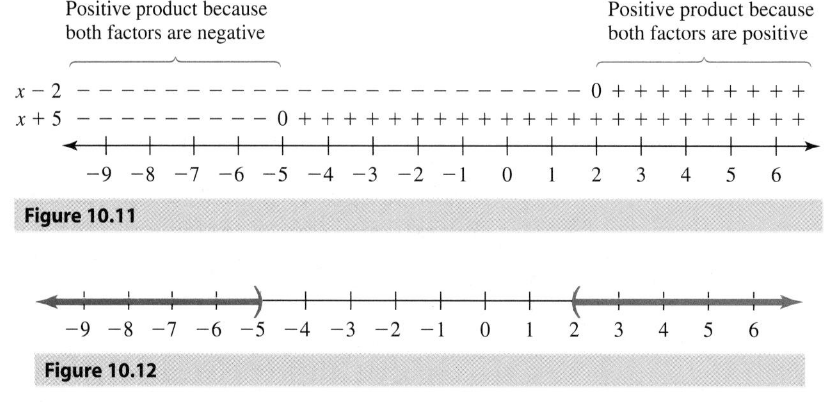

Figure 10.11

Figure 10.12

Now do Exercises 5–8

In Example 2 we will make the procedure from Example 1 a bit more efficient.

EXAMPLE 2

Solving a quadratic inequality

Solve $2x^2 + 5x \leq 3$ and graph the solution set.

Solution

Rewrite the inequality with 0 on one side:

$$2x^2 + 5x - 3 \leq 0$$

$$(2x - 1)(x + 3) \leq 0 \quad \text{Factor.}$$

Examine the signs of each factor:

$$2x - 1 = 0 \quad \text{if} \quad x = \frac{1}{2} \qquad x + 3 = 0 \quad \text{if} \quad x = -3$$

$$2x - 1 > 0 \quad \text{if} \quad x > \frac{1}{2} \qquad x + 3 > 0 \quad \text{if} \quad x > -3$$

$$2x - 1 < 0 \quad \text{if} \quad x < \frac{1}{2} \qquad x + 3 < 0 \quad \text{if} \quad x < -3$$

Calculator Close-Up

Use Y= to set $y_1 = 2x - 1$ and $y_2 = x + 3$. The table of values for y_1 and y_2 supports the sign graph in Fig. 10.13.

X	Y1	Y2
-4	-9	-1
-3	-7	0
-2	-5	1
-1	-3	2
0	-1	3
1	1	4
2	3	5

Y1=2X-1

Note that the graph of $y = 2x^2 + 5x - 3$ is below the x-axis when x is between -3 and $\frac{1}{2}$.

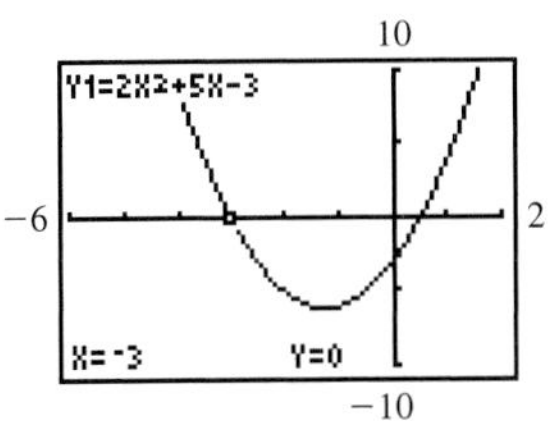

Make a sign graph as shown in Fig. 10.13. The product of the factors is negative between -3 and $\frac{1}{2}$, when one factor is negative and the other is positive. The product is 0 at -3 and at $\frac{1}{2}$. So the solution set is the interval $\left[-3, \frac{1}{2}\right]$. The graph of the solution set is shown in Fig. 10.14.

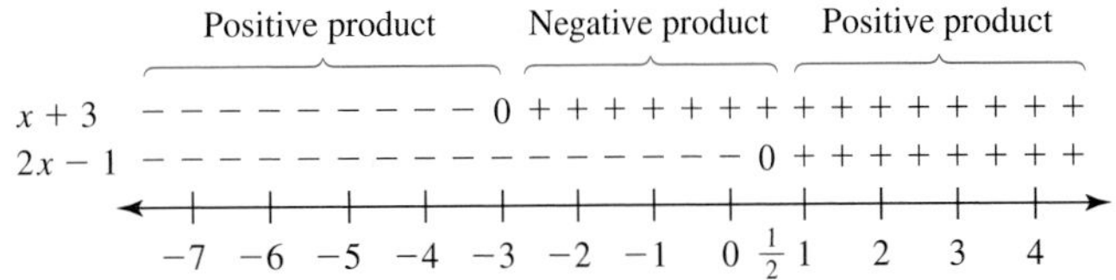

Figure 10.13

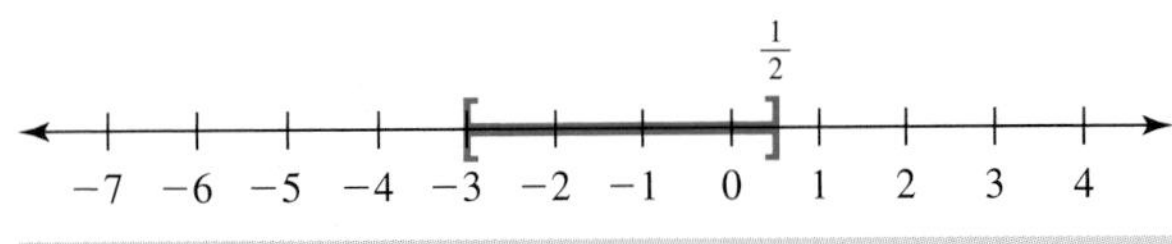

Figure 10.14

Now do Exercises 9–16

We summarize the strategy used for solving a quadratic inequality as follows.

Strategy for Solving a Quadratic Inequality with a Sign Graph

1. Write the inequality with 0 on the right.
2. Factor the quadratic polynomial on the left.
3. Make a sign graph showing where each factor is positive, negative, or zero.
4. Use the rules for multiplying signed numbers to determine which intervals satisfy the original inequality.
5. Write the solution set using interval notation.

Perfect Square Inequalities

In Examples 1 and 2 the quadratic inequalities have two different factors. If the quadratic polynomial is a perfect square, the factors are identical and it is not necessary to make a sign graph. Such inequalities can be solved using the fact that the square of every nonzero real number is greater than zero and the square of zero is zero.

EXAMPLE 3

Perfect square inequalities

Solve each inequality. State the solution set using interval notation and graph it if possible.

a) $x^2 + 6x + 9 > 0$ **b)** $x^2 - 10x + 25 \geq 0$

c) $4x^2 - 20x + 25 < 0$ **d)** $9x^2 - 6x + 1 \leq 0$

Solution

a) Factor $x^2 + 6x + 9 > 0$ as $(x + 3)^2 > 0$. Since the square of every nonzero real number is greater than zero, there is only one number that

Calculator Close-Up

The graph of $y = x^2 + 6x + 9$ is above the x-axis for all x except -3, which supports the conclusion in Example 3(a).

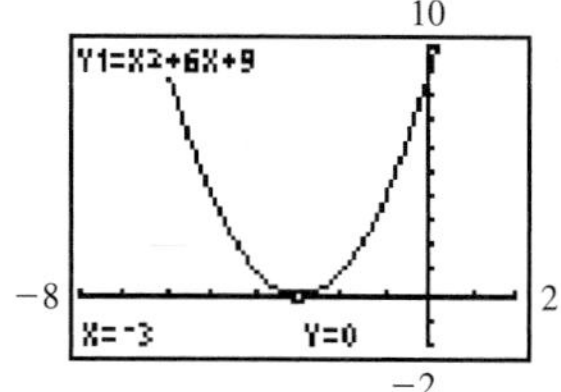

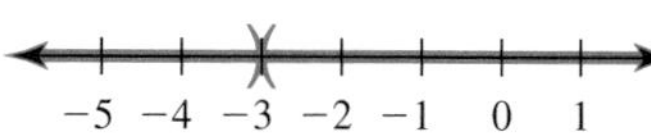

Figure 10.15

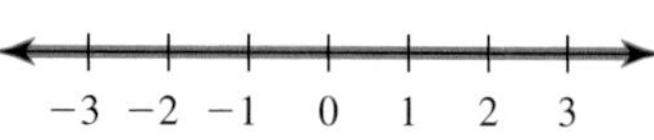

Figure 10.16

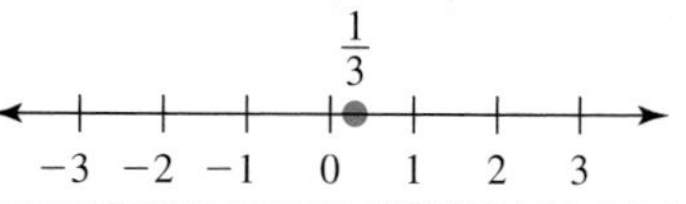

Figure 10.17

fails to satisfy this inequality and that number is the solution to $x + 3 = 0$. So the solution set is all real numbers except -3, which is written in interval notation as $(-\infty, -3) \cup (-3, \infty)$. The graph is shown in Fig. 10.15.

b) Factor $x^2 - 10x + 25 \geq 0$ as $(x - 5)^2 \geq 0$. Since the square of every real number is greater than or equal to zero, all real numbers satisfy the inequality. The solution set is $(-\infty, \infty)$. The graph is shown in Fig. 10.16.

c) Factor $4x^2 - 20x + 25 < 0$ as $(2x - 5)^2 < 0$. Since no real number has a negative square, there are no solutions to this equation. The solution set is the empty set, $\varnothing$.

d) Factor $9x^2 - 6x + 1 \leq 0$ as $(3x - 1)^2 \leq 0$. Since no real number has a negative square there are no solutions to $(3x - 1)^2 < 0$. But $(3x - 1)^2 = 0$ does have one solution and that is $\frac{1}{3}$. So the solution set is $\left\{\frac{1}{3}\right\}$. The graph is shown in Fig. 10.17.

Now do Exercises 17–24

Solving Rational Inequalities with a Sign Graph

The inequalities

$$\frac{x+2}{x-3} \leq 2, \quad \frac{2x-3}{x+5} \leq 0 \quad \text{and} \quad \frac{2}{x+4} \geq \frac{1}{x+1}$$

are called **rational inequalities.** When we solve *equations* that involve rational expressions, we usually multiply each side by the LCD. However, if we multiply each side of any inequality by a negative number, we must reverse the inequality, and when we multiply by a positive number, we do not reverse the inequality. For this reason we generally *do not multiply inequalities by expressions involving variables.* The values of the expressions might be positive or negative. Examples 4 and 5 show how to use a sign graph to solve rational inequalities that have variables in the denominator.

EXAMPLE 4

Solving a rational inequality

Solve $\frac{x+2}{x-3} \leq 2$ and graph the solution set.

Helpful Hint

By getting 0 on one side of the inequality, we can use the rules for dividing signed numbers. The only way to obtain a negative result is to divide numbers with opposite signs.

Solution

We *do not* multiply each side by $x - 3$. Instead, subtract 2 from each side to get 0 on the right:

$$\frac{x+2}{x-3} - 2 \leq 0$$

$$\frac{x+2}{x-3} - \frac{2(x-3)}{x-3} \leq 0 \quad \text{Get a common denominator.}$$

$$\frac{x+2}{x-3} - \frac{2x-6}{x-3} \leq 0 \quad \text{Simplify.}$$

$$\frac{x+2-2x+6}{x-3} \leq 0 \quad \text{Subtract the rational expressions.}$$

$$\frac{-x+8}{x-3} \leq 0 \quad \text{The quotient of } -x+8 \text{ and } x-3 \text{ is less than or equal to 0.}$$

Calculator Close-Up

Graph $y = \frac{-x+8}{x-3}$ to support the conclusion that $y \le 0$ when $x < 3$ or $x \ge 8$.

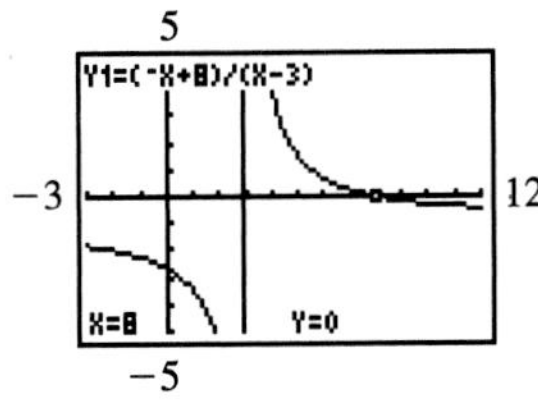

Examine the signs of the numerator and denominator:

$$x - 3 = 0 \quad \text{if} \quad x = 3 \qquad -x + 8 = 0 \quad \text{if} \quad x = 8$$
$$x - 3 > 0 \quad \text{if} \quad x > 3 \qquad -x + 8 > 0 \quad \text{if} \quad x < 8$$
$$x - 3 < 0 \quad \text{if} \quad x < 3 \qquad -x + 8 < 0 \quad \text{if} \quad x > 8$$

Make a sign graph as shown in Fig. 10.18. Using the rule for dividing signed numbers and the sign graph, we can identify where the quotient is negative or zero. The solution set is $(-\infty, 3) \cup [8, \infty)$. Note that 3 is not in the solution set because the quotient is undefined if $x = 3$. The graph of the solution set is shown in Fig. 10.19.

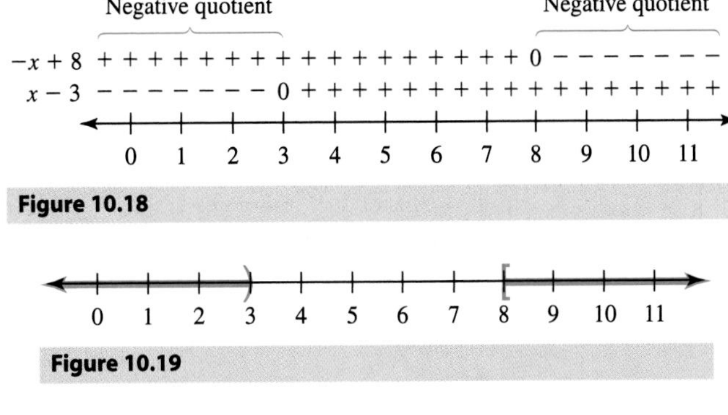

Figure 10.18

0 1 2 3 4 5 6 7 8 9 10 11

Figure 10.19

Now do Exercises 25–34

CAUTION Remember to reverse the inequality sign when multiplying or dividing by a negative number. For example, $x - 3 > 0$ is equivalent to $x > 3$. But $-x + 8 > 0$ is equivalent to $-x > -8$, or $x < 8$.

EXAMPLE 5

Solving a rational inequality

Solve $\frac{2}{x+4} \ge \frac{1}{x+1}$ and graph the solution set.

Teaching Tip Note that if you did multiply each side by the LCD, you would simply get $x - 2 \ge 0$, which does not give the correct solution set.

Solution

We do not multiply by the LCD as we do in solving equations. Instead, subtract $\frac{1}{x+1}$ from each side:

$$\frac{2}{x+4} - \frac{1}{x+1} \ge 0$$

$$\frac{2(x+1)}{(x+4)(x+1)} - \frac{1(x+4)}{(x+1)(x+4)} \ge 0 \quad \text{Get a common denominator.}$$

$$\frac{2x + 2 - x - 4}{(x+1)(x+4)} \ge 0 \quad \text{Simplify.}$$

$$\frac{x-2}{(x+1)(x+4)} \ge 0$$

Make a sign graph as shown in Fig. 10.20.

```
x + 1   - - - - - - - - - 0 + + + + + + + + + + + + +
x + 4   - - - 0 + + + + + + + + + + + + + + + + + + +
x - 2   - - - - - - - - - - - - - - - 0 + + + + + + +
      <--+----+----+----+----+----+----+----+----+----+----+-->
        -5   -4   -3   -2   -1    0    1    2    3    4    5
```

Figure 10.20

Calculator Close-Up

Graph $y = \frac{x - 2}{(x + 1)(x + 4)}$ to support the conclusion that $y \geq 0$ when x is between -4 and -1 or when $x \geq 2$.

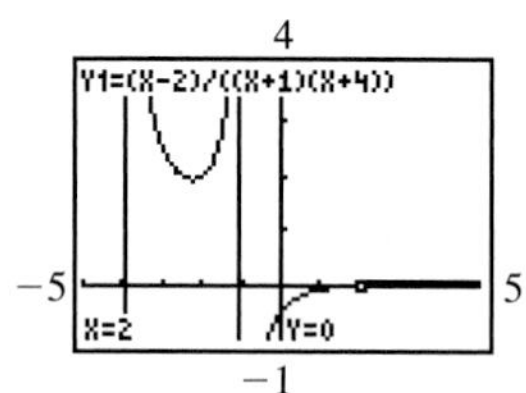

The computation of

$$\frac{x - 2}{(x + 1)(x + 4)}$$

involves multiplication and division. The result of this computation is positive if all of the three binomials are positive or if only one is positive and the other two are negative. The sign graph shows that this rational expression will have a positive value when x is between -4 and -1 and again when x is larger than 2. The solution set is $(-4, -1) \cup [2, \infty)$. Note that -1 and -4 are not in the solution set because they make the denominator zero. The graph of the solution set is shown in Fig. 10.21.

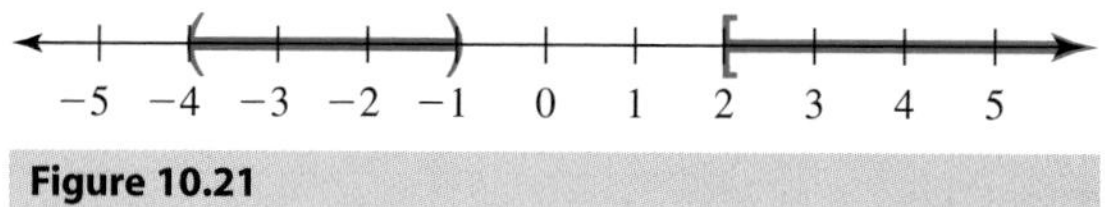

Figure 10.21

Now do Exercises 35–40

Solving rational inequalities with a sign graph is summarized next.

Strategy for Solving a Rational Inequality with a Sign Graph

1. Rewrite the inequality with 0 on the right-hand side.
2. Use only addition and subtraction to get an equivalent inequality.
3. Factor the numerator and denominator if possible.
4. Make a sign graph showing where each factor is positive, negative, or zero.
5. Use the rules for multiplying and dividing signed numbers to determine the intervals that satisfy the original inequality.
6. Write the solution set using interval notation.

Another method for solving quadratic and rational inequalities will be shown in Example 6. This method, called the **test point method,** can be used instead of the sign graph to solve the inequalities of Examples 1–5.

Quadratic Inequalities That Cannot Be Factored

Example 6 shows how to solve a quadratic inequality that involves a prime polynomial.

EXAMPLE 6

Solving a quadratic inequality using the quadratic formula

Solve $x^2 - 4x - 6 > 0$ and graph the solution set.

Solution

The quadratic polynomial is prime, but we can solve $x^2 - 4x - 6 = 0$ by the quadratic formula:

$$x = \frac{4 \pm \sqrt{16 - 4(1)(-6)}}{2(1)} = \frac{4 \pm \sqrt{40}}{2} = \frac{4 \pm 2\sqrt{10}}{2} = 2 \pm \sqrt{10}$$

As in the previous examples, the solutions to the equation divide the number line into the intervals $(-\infty, 2 - \sqrt{10})$, $(2 - \sqrt{10}, 2 + \sqrt{10})$, and $(2 + \sqrt{10}, \infty)$ on which the quadratic polynomial has either a positive or negative value. To determine which, we select an arbitrary **test point** in each interval. Because $2 + \sqrt{10} \approx 5.2$ and $2 - \sqrt{10} \approx -1.2$, we choose a test point that is less than -1.2, one between -1.2 and 5.2, and one that is greater than 5.2. We have selected -2, 0, and 7 for test points, as shown in Fig. 10.22. Now evaluate $x^2 - 4x - 6$ at each test point.

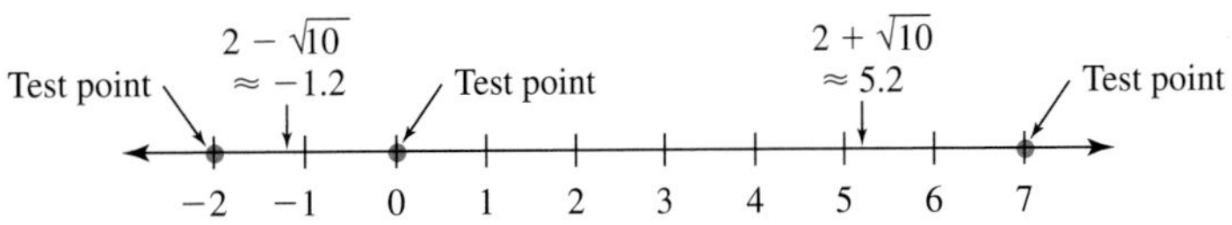

Figure 10.22

Test Point	Value of $x^2 - 4x - 6$ at the Test Point	Sign of $x^2 - 4x - 6$ in Interval of Test Point
-2	6	Positive
0	-6	Negative
7	15	Positive

Because $x^2 - 4x - 6$ is positive at the test points -2 and 7, it is positive at every point in the intervals containing those test points. So the solution set to the inequality $x^2 - 4x - 6 > 0$ is

$$(-\infty, 2 - \sqrt{10}) \cup (2 + \sqrt{10}, \infty),$$

and its graph is shown in Fig. 10.23.

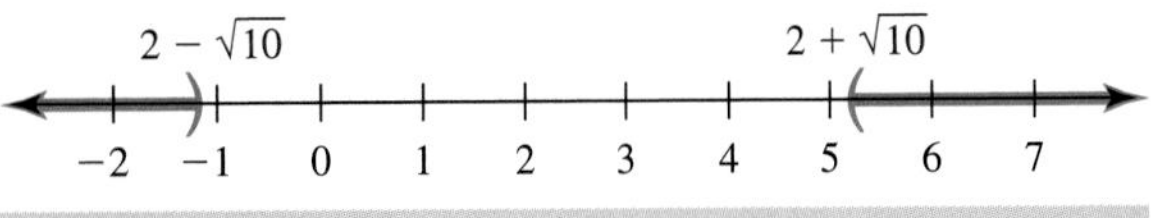

Figure 10.23

Now do Exercises 41–48

Study Tip

If you must miss class, let your instructor know. Be sure to get notes from a reliable classmate. Take good notes yourself in case a classmate comes to you for notes.

Calculator Close-Up

Notice that the graph of

$$y = x^2 - 4x - 6$$

lies above the x-axis when

$$x < 2 - \sqrt{10}$$

or

$$x > 2 + \sqrt{10}.$$

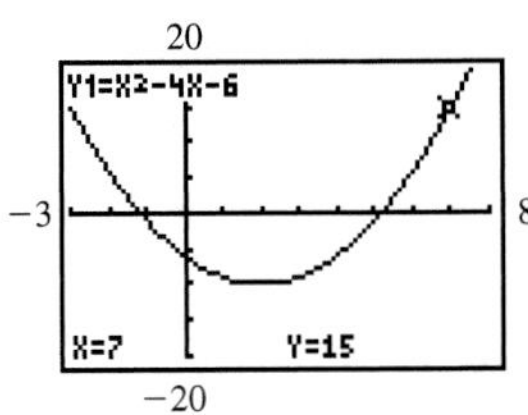

The test point method used in Example 6 can be used also on inequalities that do factor. We summarize the strategy for solving inequalities using test points in the following box.

Strategy for Solving Quadratic Inequalities Using Test Points

1. Rewrite the inequality with 0 on the right.
2. Solve the quadratic equation that results from replacing the inequality symbol with the equals symbol.
3. Locate the solutions to the quadratic equation on a number line.
4. Select a test point in each interval determined by the solutions to the quadratic equation.
5. Test each point in the original quadratic inequality to determine which intervals satisfy the inequality.
6. Write the solution set using interval notation.

In Example 6 the quadratic equation had two irrational solutions. These numbers correspond to points on the number line at which the value of the quadratic polynomial changes its sign. If the quadratic equation has no real solutions then there is no point on the number line at which the value of the quadratic polynomial can change signs. So the value of the quadratic polynomial is either always positive or always negative. The inequality is satisfied by all real numbers or none, depending on the inequality symbol used. A single test point will decide the issue.

EXAMPLE 7

All or nothing

Solve each inequality. State the solution set using interval notation if possible.

a) $x^2 + 5x + 8 > 0$ **b)** $-x^2 + 3x - 5 \geq 0$

Solution

a) For $x^2 + 5x + 8 = 0$ we have $b^2 - 4ac = 5^2 - 4(1)(8) = -7$. So the equation has no real solutions and $x^2 + 5x + 8$ does not change sign. So $x^2 + 5x + 8 > 0$ is either correct for all real numbers or incorrect for all real numbers. Select a test point, say 0, to get $0^2 + 5(0) + 8 > 0$, which is correct. So the inequality is satisfied by 0 and all other real numbers. The solution set is $(-\infty, \infty)$.

b) For $-x^2 + 3x - 5 = 0$ we have $b^2 - 4ac = 3^2 - 4(-1)(-5) = -11$. So the quadratic equation has no real solutions and $-x^2 + 3x - 5 \geq 0$ is satisfied by all real numbers or none. Select a test point, say 0, to get $-0^2 + 3(0) - 5 \geq 0$, which is false. So no real numbers satisfy the inequality and the solution set is the empty set, $\emptyset$.

Now do Exercises 49–54

Calculator Close-Up

The graph of $y = x^2 + 5x + 8$ is above the x-axis and the graph of $y = -x^2 + 3x - 5$ is below the x-axis for all values of x. These graphs support the conclusions in Example 7.

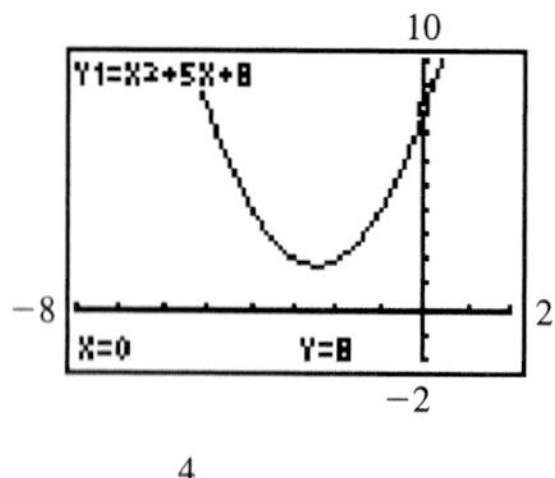

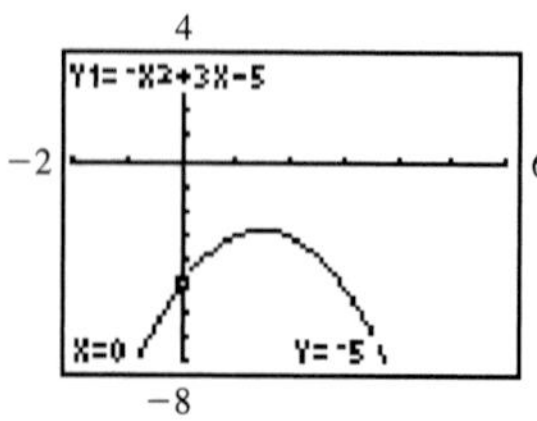

Applications

Example 8 shows how a quadratic inequality can be used to solve a problem.

EXAMPLE 8

Making a profit

Charlene's daily profit P (in dollars) for selling x magazine subscriptions is determined by the formula

$$P = -x^2 + 80x - 1500.$$

For what values of x is her profit positive?

Solution

We can find the values of x for which $P > 0$ by solving a quadratic inequality:

$$-x^2 + 80x - 1500 > 0$$

$$x^2 - 80x + 1500 < 0 \quad \text{Multiply each side by } -1.$$

$$(x - 30)(x - 50) < 0 \quad \text{Factor.}$$

Make a sign graph as shown in Fig. 10.24. The product of the two factors is negative for x between 30 and 50. Because the last inequality is equivalent to the first, the profit is positive when the number of magazine subscriptions sold is greater than 30 and less than 50.

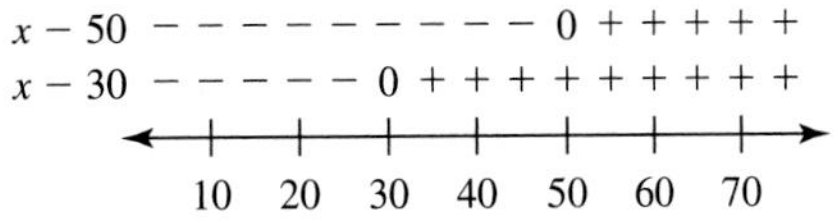

x − 50 − − − − − − − − − − 0 + + + + +
x − 30 − − − − − 0 + + + + + + + + + +
10 20 30 40 50 60 70

Figure 10.24

Now do Exercises 85–90

Warm-Ups

True or false? Explain your answer.

1. The solution set to $x^2 > 4$ is $(2, \infty)$. False
2. The inequality $\frac{x}{x-3} > 2$ is equivalent to $x > 2x - 6$. False
3. The inequality $(x - 1)(x + 2) < 0$ is equivalent to $x - 1 < 0$ or $x + 2 < 0$. False
4. We cannot solve quadratic inequalities that do not factor. False
5. One technique for solving quadratic inequalities is based on the rules for multiplying signed numbers. True
6. Multiplying each side of an inequality by a variable should be avoided. True
7. In solving quadratic or rational inequalities, we always get 0 on one side. True
8. The inequality $\frac{x}{2} > 3$ is equivalent to $x > 6$. True
9. The inequality $\frac{x-3}{x+2} < 1$ is equivalent to $\frac{x-3}{x+2} - 1 < 0$. True
10. The solution set to $\frac{x+2}{x-4} \geq 0$ is $(-\infty, -2] \cup [4, \infty)$. False

10.5 Exercises

Boost your GRADE at mathzone.com!

MathZone
- Practice Problems
- Self-Tests
- Videos
- Net Tutor
- e-Professors

Reading and Writing *After reading this section, write out the answers to these questions. Use complete sentences.*

1. What is a quadratic inequality?
   A quadratic inequality has the form $ax^2 + bx + c > 0$. In place of $>$ we can also use $<$, $\le$, or $\ge$.
2. What is a sign graph?
   A sign graph shows signs of the factors for all possible values of x.
3. What is a rational inequality?
   A rational inequality is an inequality involving a rational expression.
4. Why don't we usually multiply each side of an inequality by an expression involving a variable?
   Multiplying each side by a positive number does not change the direction of the inequality, but multiplying by a negative number does. So if we multiply by a variable, it is difficult to know which way the inequality goes.

Solve each inequality. Graph the solution set and state the solution set using interval notation. See Examples 1 and 2.

5. $x^2 + x - 6 < 0$
   $(-3, 2)$

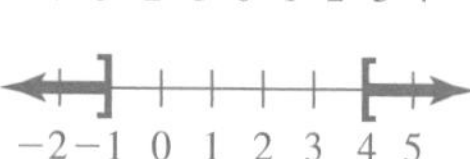

6. $z^2 - 16 < 0$
   $(-4, 4)$

7. $x^2 - 3x - 4 \ge 0$
   $(-\infty, -1] \cup [4, \infty)$

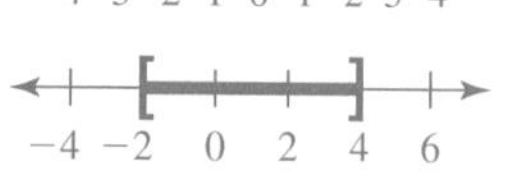

8. $y^2 - 4 > 0$
   $(-\infty, -2) \cup (2, \infty)$

9. $x^2 - 2x - 8 \le 0$
   $[-2, 4]$

10. $x^2 + x - 12 \le 0$
    $[-4, 3]$

11. $2u^2 + 5u \ge 12$
    $(-\infty, -4] \cup \left[\frac{3}{2}, \infty\right)$

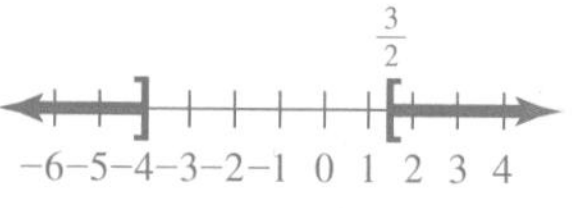

12. $2v^2 + 7v < 4$
    $\left(-4, \frac{1}{2}\right)$

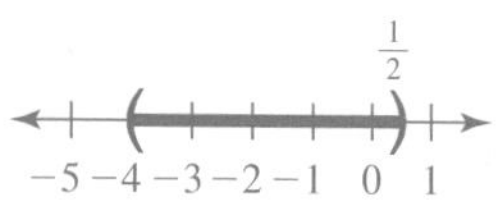

13. $4x^2 - 8x \ge 0$
    $(-\infty, 0] \cup [2, \infty)$

14. $x^2 + x > 0$
    $(-\infty, -1) \cup (0, \infty)$

15. $5x - 10x^2 < 0$
    $(-\infty, 0) \cup \left(\frac{1}{2}, \infty\right)$

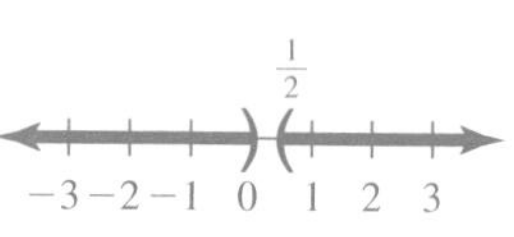

16. $3x - x^2 > 0$
    $(0, 3)$

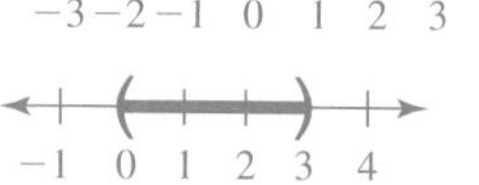

Solve each quadratic inequality. State the solution set using interval notation and sketch its graph if possible. See Example 3.

17. $x^2 + 6x + 9 \ge 0$
    $(-\infty, \infty)$

18. $x^2 + 10x + 25 \ge 0$
    $(-\infty, \infty)$

19. $x^2 + 4 < 4x$ $\emptyset$
20. $x^2 < 8x - 16$ $\emptyset$
21. $4x^2 - 20x + 25 \le 0$
    $\left\{\frac{5}{2}\right\}$

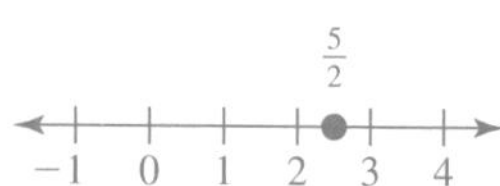

22. $9x^2 + 12x + 4 \le 0$
    $\left\{-\frac{2}{3}\right\}$

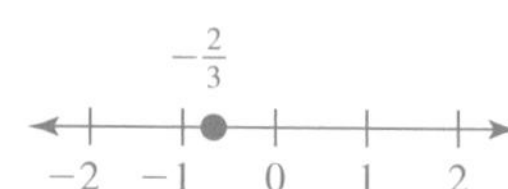

23. $25x^2 + 10x + 1 > 0$
    $\left(-\infty, -\frac{1}{5}\right) \cup \left(-\frac{1}{5}, \infty\right)$

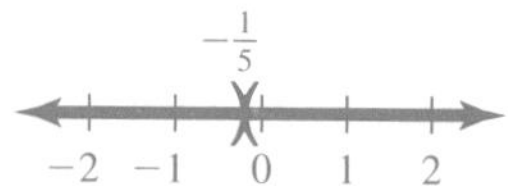

24. $16x^2 - 16x + 4 > 0$
    $\left(-\infty, \frac{1}{2}\right) \cup \left(\frac{1}{2}, \infty\right)$

Solve each rational inequality. State and graph the solution set. See Examples 4 and 5.

25. $\frac{1}{x} > 0$
    $(0, \infty)$

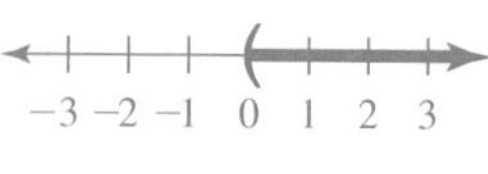

26. $\frac{1}{x} \le 0$
    $(-\infty, 0)$

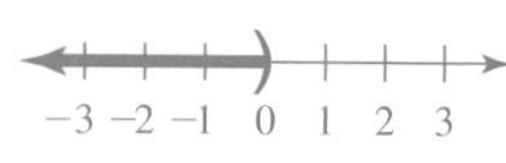

27. $\frac{x}{x-3} > 0$ $(-\infty, 0) \cup (3, \infty)$

28. $\frac{a}{a+2} > 0$ $(-\infty, -2) \cup (0, \infty)$

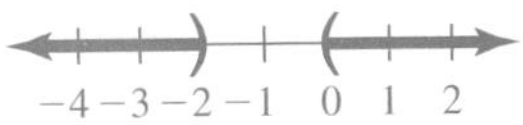

29. $\frac{x+2}{x} \le 0$ $[-2, 0)$

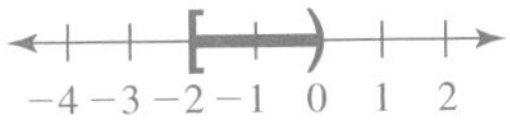

30. $\frac{w-6}{w} \le 0$ $(0, 6]$

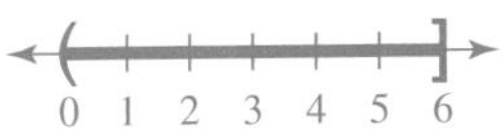

31. $\frac{t-3}{t+6} > 0$ $(-\infty, -6) \cup (3, \infty)$

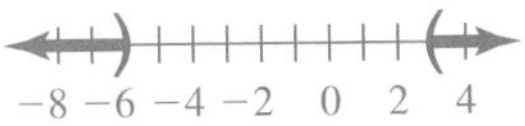

32. $\frac{x-2}{2x+5} < 0$ $\left(-\frac{5}{2}, 2\right)$

33. $\frac{x}{x+2} > -1$ $(-\infty, -2) \cup (-1, \infty)$

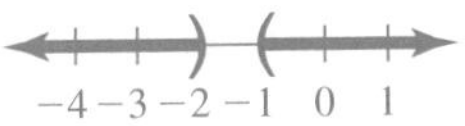

34. $\frac{x+3}{x} \le -2$ $[-1, 0)$

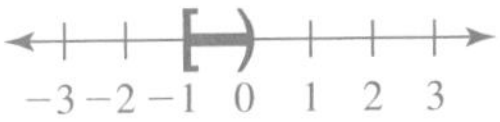

35. $\frac{2}{x-5} > \frac{1}{x+4}$ $(-13, -4) \cup (5, \infty)$

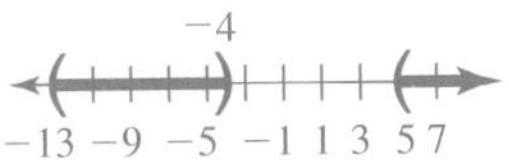

36. $\frac{3}{x+2} > \frac{2}{x-1}$ $(-2, 1) \cup (7, \infty)$

37. $\frac{m}{m-5} + \frac{3}{m-1} > 0$ $(-\infty, -5) \cup (1, 3) \cup (5, \infty)$

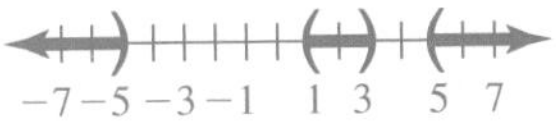

38. $\frac{p}{p-16} + \frac{2}{p-6} \le 0$ $[-4, 6) \cup [8, 16)$

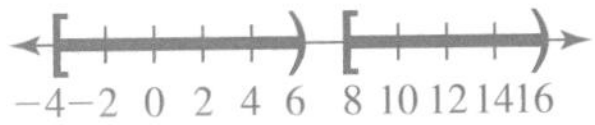

39. $\frac{x}{x-3} \le \frac{-8}{x-6}$ $[-6, 3) \cup [4, 6)$

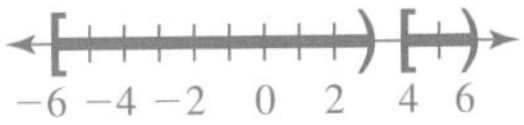

40. $\frac{x}{x+20} > \frac{2}{x+8}$ $(-\infty, -20) \cup (-10, -8) \cup (4, \infty)$

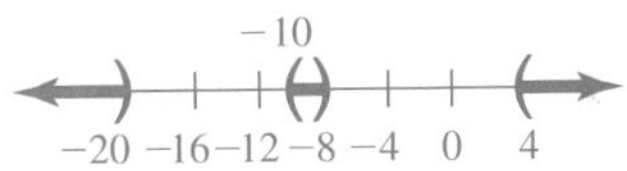

Solve each inequality. State and graph the solution set. See Example 6.

41. $x^2 - 5 > 0$ $(-\infty, -\sqrt{5}) \cup (\sqrt{5}, \infty)$

42. $x^2 - 3 < 0$ $(-\sqrt{3}, \sqrt{3})$

43. $x^2 - 2x - 5 \le 0$ $[1 - \sqrt{6}, 1 + \sqrt{6}]$

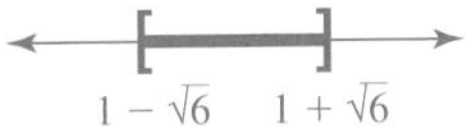

44. $x^2 - 2x - 4 > 0$ $(-\infty, 1 - \sqrt{5}) \cup (1 + \sqrt{5}, \infty)$

45. $2x^2 - 6x + 3 \ge 0$ $\left(-\infty, \frac{3-\sqrt{3}}{2}\right] \cup \left[\frac{3+\sqrt{3}}{2}, \infty\right)$

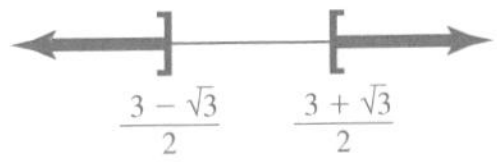

46. $2x^2 - 8x + 3 < 0$ $\left(\frac{4-\sqrt{10}}{2}, \frac{4+\sqrt{10}}{2}\right)$

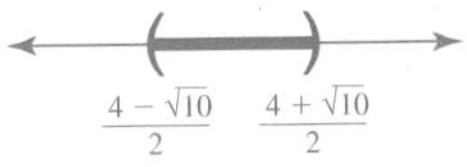

47. $y^2 - 3y - 9 \le 0$ $\left[\frac{3-3\sqrt{5}}{2}, \frac{3+3\sqrt{5}}{2}\right]$

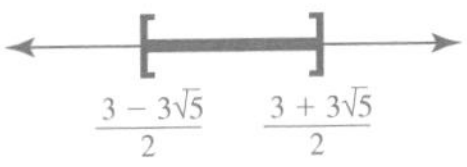

48. $z^2 - 5z - 7 < 0$ $\left(\frac{5-\sqrt{53}}{2}, \frac{5+\sqrt{53}}{2}\right)$

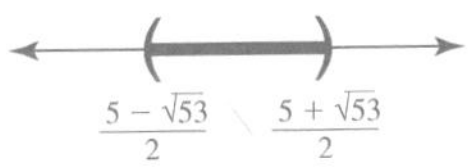

Solve each quadratic inequality. State the solution set using interval notation if possible. See Example 7.

49. $x^2 + 5x + 12 \ge 0$ $(-\infty, \infty)$

50. $x^2 + 3x + 9 > 0$ $(-\infty, \infty)$

51. $2x^2 + 5x + 5 < 0$ $\varnothing$

52. $-3x^2 + x - 6 \geq 0$ $\varnothing$

53. $-5x^2 + 2x \leq 4$ $(-\infty, \infty)$

54. $3x - 5 \leq 3x^2$ $(-\infty, \infty)$

Solve each inequality. State the solution set using interval notation when possible.

55. $x^2 > 0$ $(-\infty, 0) \cup (0, \infty)$

56. $x^2 \geq 0$ $(-\infty, \infty)$

57. $x^2 + 4 \geq 0$ $(-\infty, \infty)$

58. $x^2 + 1 \leq 0$ $\varnothing$

59. $\frac{1}{x} < 0$ $(-\infty, 0)$

60. $\frac{1}{x^2} \geq 0$ $(-\infty, 0) \cup (0, \infty)$

61. $x^2 \leq 9$ $[-3, 3]$

62. $x^2 \geq 36$ $(-\infty, -6] \cup [6, \infty)$

63. $16 - x^2 > 0$ $(-4, 4)$

64. $9 - x^2 < 0$ $(-\infty, -3) \cup (3, \infty)$

65. $x^2 - 4x \geq 0$ $(-\infty, 0] \cup [4, \infty)$

66. $4x^2 - 9 > 0$ $\left(-\infty, -\frac{3}{2}\right) \cup \left(\frac{3}{2}, \infty\right)$

67. $3(2w^2 - 5) < w$ $\left(-\frac{3}{2}, \frac{5}{3}\right)$

68. $6(y^2 - 2) + y < 0$ $\left(-\frac{3}{2}, \frac{4}{3}\right)$

69. $z^2 \geq 4(z + 3)$ $(-\infty, -2] \cup [6, \infty)$

70. $t^2 < 3(2t - 3)$ $\varnothing$

71. $(q + 4)^2 > 10q + 31$ $(-\infty, -3) \cup (5, \infty)$

72. $(2p + 4)(p - 1) < (p + 2)^2$ $(-2, 4)$

73. $\frac{1}{2}x^2 \geq 4 - x$ $(-\infty, -4] \cup [2, \infty)$

74. $\frac{1}{2}x^2 \leq x + 12$ $[-4, 6]$

75. $\frac{x - 4}{x + 3} \leq 0$ $(-3, 4]$

76. $\frac{2x - 1}{x + 5} \geq 0$ $(-\infty, -5) \cup \left[\frac{1}{2}, \infty\right)$

77. $(x - 2)(x + 1)(x - 5) \geq 0$
$[-1, 2] \cup [5, \infty)$

78. $(x - 1)(x + 2)(2x - 5) < 0$
$(-\infty, -2) \cup (1, 2.5)$

79. $x^3 + 3x^2 - x - 3 < 0$
$(-\infty, -3) \cup (-1, 1)$

80. $x^3 + 5x^2 - 4x - 20 \geq 0$
$[-5, -2] \cup [2, \infty)$

81. $0.23x^2 + 6.5x + 4.3 < 0$
$(-27.58, -0.68)$

82. $0.65x^2 + 3.2x + 5.1 > 0$
$(-\infty, \infty)$

83. $\frac{x}{x - 2} > \frac{-1}{x + 3}$
$(-\infty, -2 - \sqrt{6}) \cup (-3, -2 + \sqrt{6}) \cup (2, \infty)$

84. $\frac{x}{3 - x} > \frac{2}{x + 5}$
$\left(\frac{-7 - \sqrt{73}}{2}, -5\right) \cup \left(\frac{-7 + \sqrt{73}}{2}, 3\right)$

Solve each problem by using a quadratic inequality. See Example 8.

85. ***Positive profit.*** The monthly profit P (in dollars) that Big Jim makes on the sale of x mobile homes is determined by the formula $P = x^2 + 5x - 50$. For what values of x is his profit positive?
Greater than 5, or 6, 7, 8, . . .

86. ***Profitable fruitcakes.*** Sharon's revenue R (in dollars) on the sale of x fruitcakes is determined by the formula $R = 50x - x^2$. Her cost C (in dollars) for producing x fruitcakes is given by the formula $C = 2x + 40$. For what values of x is Sharon's profit positive? (Profit = revenue − cost.)
Between 0 and 48, or 1, 2, 3, . . . , 47

If an object is given an initial velocity straight upward of v_0 feet per second from a height of s_0 feet, then its altitude S after t seconds is given by the formula

$$S = -16t^2 + v_0 t + s_0.$$

87. ***Flying high.*** An arrow is shot straight upward with a velocity of 96 feet per second (ft/sec) from an altitude of 6 feet. For how many seconds is this arrow more than 86 feet high?
4 seconds

88. ***Putting the shot.*** In 1978 Udo Beyer (East Germany) set a world record in the shot-put of 72 ft 8 in. If Beyer had projected the shot straight upward with a velocity of 30 ft/sec from a height of 5 ft, then for what values of t would the shot be under 15 ft high?
$t < 0.43$ second or $t > 1.44$ seconds

If a projectile is fired at a 45° angle from a height of s_0 feet with initial velocity v_0 ft/sec, then its altitude S in feet after t seconds is given by

$$S = -16t^2 + \frac{v_0}{\sqrt{2}}t + s_0.$$

89. *Siege and garrison artillery.* An 8-inch mortar used in the Civil War fired a 44.5-lb projectile from ground level a distance of 3600 ft when aimed at a 45° angle (Harold R. Peterson, *Notes on Ordinance of the American Civil War*). The accompanying graph shows the altitude of the projectile when it is fired with a velocity of $240\sqrt{2}$ ft/sec.

a) Use the graph to estimate the maximum altitude reached by the projectile.
900 ft

b) Use the graph to estimate approximately how long the altitude of the projectile was greater than 864 ft.
3 seconds

c) Use the formula to determine the length of time for which the projectile had an altitude of more than 864 ft.
3 seconds

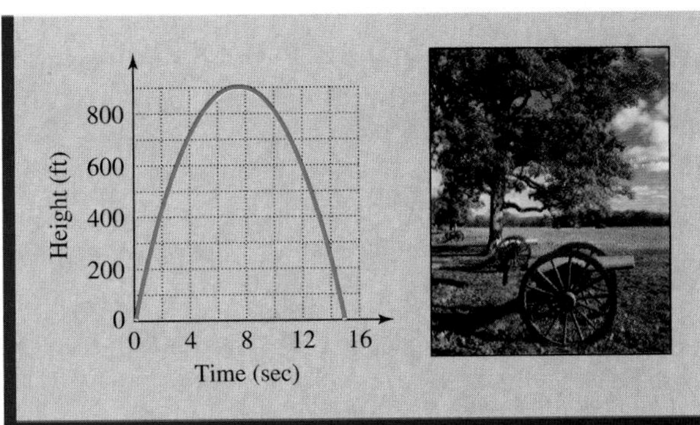

Figure for Exercise 89

90. *Seacoast artillery.* The 13-inch mortar used in the Civil War fired a 220-lb projectile a distance of 12,975 ft when aimed at a 45° angle. If the 13-inch mortar was fired from a hill 100 ft above sea level with an initial velocity of 644 ft/sec, then for how long was the projectile more than 800 ft above sea level?
25.2 seconds

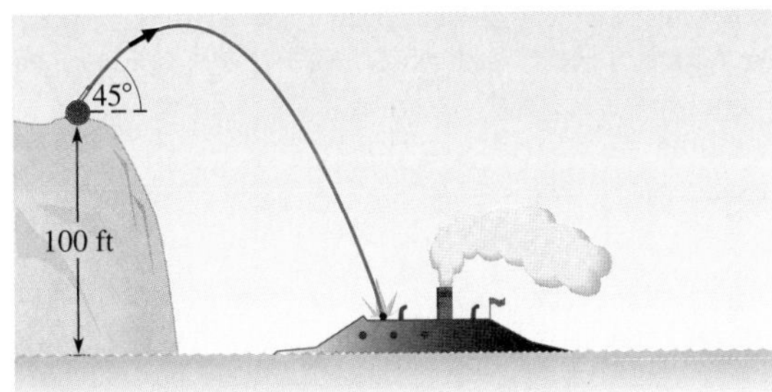

Figure for Exercise 90

Getting More Involved

91. *Cooperative learning*

Work in a small group to solve each inequality for x, given that h and k are real numbers with $h < k$.

a) $(x - h)(x - k) < 0$
(h, k)

b) $(x - h)(x - k) > 0$
$(-\infty, h) \cup (k, \infty)$

c) $(x + h)(x + k) < 0$
$(-k, -h)$

d) $(x + h)(x + k) \geq 0$
$(-\infty, -k] \cup [-h, \infty)$

e) $\dfrac{x - h}{x - k} \geq 0$
$(-\infty, h] \cup (k, \infty)$

f) $\dfrac{x + h}{x + k} \leq 0$
$(-k, -h]$

92. *Cooperative learning*

Work in a small group to solve $ax^2 + bx + c > 0$ for x in each case.

a) $b^2 - 4ac = 0$ and $a > 0$
$(-\infty, -b/(2a)) \cup (-b/(2a), \infty)$

b) $b^2 - 4ac = 0$ and $a < 0$ $\varnothing$

c) $b^2 - 4ac < 0$ and $a > 0$ $(-\infty, \infty)$

d) $b^2 - 4ac < 0$ and $a < 0$ $\varnothing$

e) $b^2 - 4ac > 0$ and $a > 0$
$$\left(-\infty, \frac{-b - \sqrt{b^2 - 4ac}}{2a}\right) \cup \left(\frac{-b + \sqrt{b^2 - 4ac}}{2a}, \infty\right)$$

f) $b^2 - 4ac > 0$ and $a < 0$
$$\left(\frac{-b - \sqrt{b^2 - 4ac}}{2a}, \frac{-b + \sqrt{b^2 - 4ac}}{2a}\right)$$

Graphing Calculator Exercises

Match the given inequalities with their solution sets (a through d) by examining a table or a graph.

93. $x^2 - 2x - 8 < 0$ c

94. $x^2 - 3x > 54$ d

95. $\dfrac{x}{x - 2} > 2$ b

96. $\dfrac{3}{x - 2} < \dfrac{5}{x + 2}$ a

a. $(-2, 2) \cup (8, \infty)$

b. $(2, 4)$

c. $(-2, 4)$

d. $(-\infty, -6) \cup (9, \infty)$

Collaborative Activities

Grouping: 3 students per group

Topic: A geometric solution to a quadratic

Completing the Square

Al-Khwarizmi, an Arab mathematician who lived in Baghdad in the mid-800s, wrote the first book on algebra that is more analytic than geometric. It looks like our algebra books today. The word "algebra" comes from his book called *The Book of Algebra and Almucabola.* His book describes methods of solving quadratic equations that are based on a geometric understanding of what the equations represent. In this activity you will explore how to derive the quadratic formula geometrically and learn why the method is called "completing the square."

Consider the equation $2x^2 + 4x = 8$. To solve it geometrically, we first divide by the leading coefficient, 2, to get

$$x^2 + 2x = 4.$$

Now this equation can be viewed geometrically as an x by x square and an x by 2 rectangle having a total area of 4:

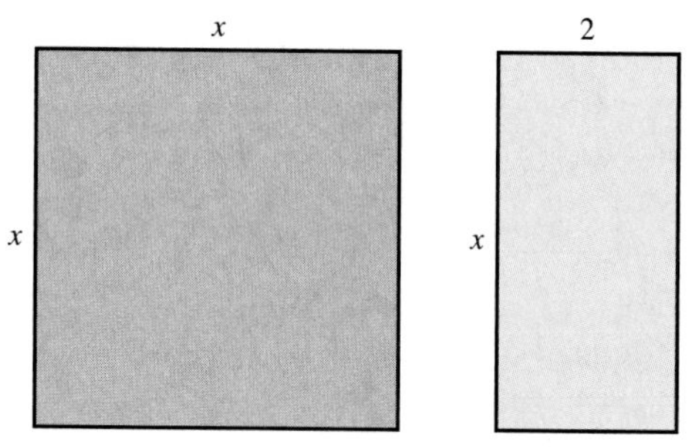

To complete the square, divide the x by 2 rectangle into four x by $\frac{1}{2}$ rectangles and add them to the sides of the x by x square:

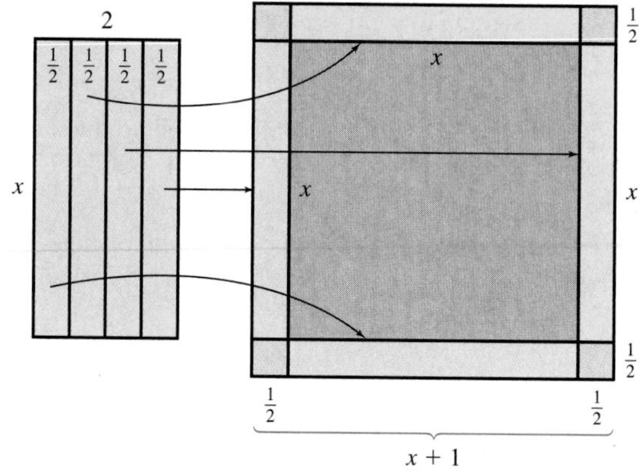

The square is complete except for the four $\frac{1}{2}$ by $\frac{1}{2}$ squares in the corners, each of which has area $\frac{1}{4}$. Filling those in will add 1 square unit of area to the 4 we had already for a total of 5. Since the sides of the completed square are $x + 1$, we have

$$(x + 1)^2 = 5.$$

Solve for x to get $x + 1 = \pm\sqrt{5}$ or $x = -1 \pm \sqrt{5}$.

Complete the following in your groups:

1. Verify and write down the steps for the geometric method of completing the square.
2. Use the geometric method of completing the square to solve each equation for x:

   a) $3x^2 + 12x = 18$ **b)** $2x^2 + 6x = 5$ **c)** $3x^2 + 4x = 9$
3. Solve $ax^2 + bx = c$ by the geometric method. Explain why the formula found in this general case is not quite the quadratic formula.

Chapter 10 Wrap-Up

Summary

Quadratic Equations		Examples
Quadratic equation	An equation of the form $ax^2 + bx + c = 0$, where a, b, and c are real numbers, with $a \neq 0$	$x^2 = 11$ $(x - 5)^2 = 99$ $x^2 + 3x - 20 = 0$
Methods for solving quadratic equations	Factoring: Factor the quadratic polynomial, then set each factor equal to 0.	$x^2 + x - 6 = 0$ $(x + 3)(x - 2) = 0$ $x + 3 = 0$ or $x - 2 = 0$
	The even-root property: If $x^2 = k$ $(k > 0)$, then $x = \pm\sqrt{k}$. If $x^2 = 0$, then $x = 0$. There are no real solutions to $x^2 = k$ for $k < 0$.	$(x - 5)^2 = 10$ $x - 5 = \pm\sqrt{10}$
	Completing the square: Take one-half of middle term, square it, then add it to each side.	$x^2 + 6x = -4$ $x^2 + 6x + 9 = -4 + 9$ $(x + 3)^2 = 5$
	Quadratic formula: Solves $ax^2 + bx + c = 0$ with $a \neq 0$: $x = \dfrac{-b \pm \sqrt{b^2 - 4ac}}{2a}$	$2x^2 + 3x - 5 = 0$ $x = \dfrac{-3 \pm \sqrt{3^2 - 4(2)(-5)}}{2(2)}$
Number of solutions	Determined by the discriminant $b^2 - 4ac$: $b^2 - 4ac > 0$ 2 real solutions	$x^2 + 6x - 12 = 0$ $6^2 - 4(1)(-12) > 0$
	$b^2 - 4ac = 0$ 1 real solution	$x^2 + 10x + 25 = 0$ $10^2 - 4(1)(25) = 0$
	$b^2 - 4ac < 0$ no real solutions, 2 imaginary solutions	$x^2 + 2x + 20 = 0$ $2^2 - 4(1)(20) < 0$
Writing equations	To write an equation with given solutions, reverse the steps in solving an equation by factoring.	$x = 2$ or $x = -3$ $(x - 2)(x + 3) = 0$ $x^2 + x - 6 = 0$
Factoring	The quadratic polynomial $ax^2 + bx + c$ (with integral coefficients) can be factored if and only if $b^2 - 4ac$ is a perfect square.	$2x^2 - 11x + 12$ $b^2 - 4ac = 25$ $(2x - 3)(x - 4)$
Equations quadratic in form	Use substitution to convert to a quadratic.	$x^4 + 3x^2 - 10 = 0$ Let $a = x^2$ $a^2 + 3a - 10 = 0$

Graphing Parabolas		**Examples**
Parabola	The graph of $y = ax^2 + bx + c$ with $a \neq 0$ is a parabola.	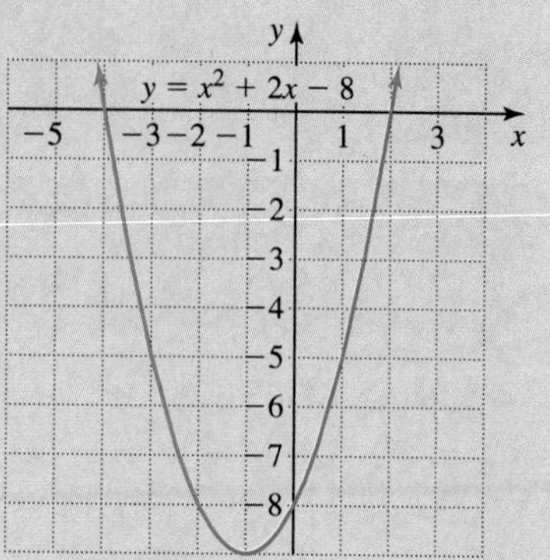
Properties of parabolas	If $a > 0$, then the parabola opens upward. If $a < 0$, then the parabola opens downward. The first coordinate of the vertex is $\frac{-b}{2a}$.	$y = x^2 + 2x - 8$ Opens upward $x = \frac{-b}{2a} = \frac{-2}{2(1)} = -1$
	The second coordinate of the vertex is the minimum y-value if $a > 0$ or the maximum y-value if $a < 0$.	Vertex: $(-1, -9)$ Minimum y-value: -9
	The x-intercepts are found by solving $ax^2 + bx + c = 0$. Let $x = 0$ to find the y-intercept.	x-intercepts: $(-4, 0)$, $(2, 0)$ y-intercept: $(0, -8)$

Quadratic and Rational Inequalities		**Examples**
Quadratic inequality	An inequality involving a quadratic polynomial	$2x^2 - 7x + 6 \geq 0$ $x^2 - 4x - 5 < 0$
Rational inequality	An inequality involving a rational expression	$\frac{1}{x-1} < \frac{3}{x-2}$
Solving quadratic and rational inequalities	Get 0 on one side and express the other side as a product and/or quotient of linear factors. Make a sign graph showing the signs of the factors. Use test points if the quadratic polynomial is prime.	$(x - 5)(x + 1) < 0$ $x + 1$: − − 0 + + + + + + + + $x - 5$: − − − − − − − − 0 + + −3 −2 −1 0 1 2 3 4 5 6 7

Enriching Your Mathematical Word Power

For each mathematical term, choose the correct meaning.

1. quadratic equation
a. $ax + b = c$ with $a \neq 0$
b. $ax^2 + bx + c = 0$ with $a \neq 0$
c. $ax + b = 0$ with $a \neq 0$
d. $a/x^2 + b/x = c$ with $x \neq 0$ b

2. perfect square trinomial
a. a trinomial of the form $a^2 + 2ab + b^2$
b. a trinomial of the form $a^2 + b^2$
c. a trinomial of the form $a^2 + ab + b^2$
d. a trinomial of the form $a^2 - 2ab - b^2$
a

3. **completing the square**
   a. drawing a perfect square
   b. evaluating $(a + b)^2$
   c. drawing the fourth side when given three sides of a square
   d. finding the third term of a perfect square trinomial d

4. **quadratic formula**
   a. $x = \dfrac{-b \pm \sqrt{b^2 - 4ac}}{2}$
   b. $x = -b \pm \dfrac{\sqrt{b^2 - 4ac}}{2a}$
   c. $x = \dfrac{-b \pm \sqrt{b^2 - 4ac}}{2a}$
   d. $x = \dfrac{b \pm \sqrt{b^2 - 4ac}}{2a}$ c

5. **discriminant**
   a. the vertex of a parabola
   b. the radicand in the quadratic formula
   c. the leading coefficient in $ax^2 + bx + c$
   d. to treat unfairly b

6. **parabola**
   a. the graph of $y = mx + b$ with $m \neq 0$
   b. the graph of $y = ax^2 + bx + c$ with $a \neq 0$
   c. the solution set to $ax^2 + bx + c = 0$ with $a \neq 0$
   d. the solution set to $(x - a)(x - b) = 0$ b

7. **quadratic in form**
   a. $ax^2 + bx + c = 0$
   b. a parabola
   c. an equation that is quadratic after a substitution
   d. having four equal sides c

8. **quadratic inequality**
   a. $ax^2 + bx + c > 0$ with $a \neq 0$ or with $\geq$, $<$, or $\leq$
   b. $ax + b > 0$ with $a \neq 0$ or with $\geq$, $<$, or $\leq$
   c. completing the square
   d. the Pythagorean theorem a

9. **sign graph**
   a. a graph showing the sign of x
   b. a sign on which a graph is drawn
   c. a number line showing the signs of factors
   d. to graph in sign language c

10. **rational inequality**
   a. an inequality involving a rational expression(s)
   b. a quadratic inequality
   c. an inequality with rational exponents
   d. an inequality that compares two fractions a

11. **test point**
   a. the end of a chapter
   b. to check if a point is in the right location
   c. a number that is used to check if an inequality is satisfied
   d. a positive integer c

Review Exercises

10.1 *Solve by factoring.*

1. $x^2 - 2x - 15 = 0$ $\{-3, 5\}$
2. $x^2 - 2x - 24 = 0$ $\{-4, 6\}$
3. $2x^2 + x = 15$ $\left\{-3, \dfrac{5}{2}\right\}$
4. $2x^2 + 7x = 4$ $\left\{-4, \dfrac{1}{2}\right\}$
5. $w^2 - 25 = 0$ $\{-5, 5\}$
6. $a^2 - 121 = 0$ $\{-11, 11\}$
7. $4x^2 - 12x + 9 = 0$ $\left\{\dfrac{3}{2}\right\}$
8. $x^2 - 12x + 36 = 0$ $\{6\}$

Solve by using the even-root property.

9. $x^2 = 12$ $\{\pm 2\sqrt{3}\}$
10. $x^2 = 20$ $\{\pm 2\sqrt{5}\}$
11. $(x - 1)^2 = 9$ $\{-2, 4\}$
12. $(x + 4)^2 = 4$ $\{-6, -2\}$
13. $(x - 2)^2 = \dfrac{3}{4}$ $\left\{\dfrac{4 \pm \sqrt{3}}{2}\right\}$
14. $(x - 3)^2 = \dfrac{1}{4}$ $\left\{\dfrac{5}{2}, \dfrac{7}{2}\right\}$
15. $4x^2 = 9$ $\left\{\pm\dfrac{3}{2}\right\}$
16. $2x^2 = 3$ $\left\{\pm\dfrac{\sqrt{6}}{2}\right\}$

Solve by completing the square.

17. $x^2 - 6x + 8 = 0$ $\{2, 4\}$
18. $x^2 + 4x + 3 = 0$ $\{-3, -1\}$
19. $x^2 - 5x + 6 = 0$ $\{2, 3\}$
20. $x^2 - x - 6 = 0$ $\{-2, 3\}$

21. $2x^2 - 7x + 3 = 0$ $\left\{\frac{1}{2}, 3\right\}$

22. $2x^2 - x = 6$ $\left\{-\frac{3}{2}, 2\right\}$

23. $x^2 + 4x + 1 = 0$ $\{-2 \pm \sqrt{3}\}$

24. $x^2 + 2x - 2 = 0$ $\{-1 \pm \sqrt{3}\}$

10.2 *Solve by the quadratic formula.*

25. $x^2 - 3x - 10 = 0$ $\{-2, 5\}$

26. $x^2 - 5x - 6 = 0$ $\{-1, 6\}$

27. $6x^2 - 7x = 3$ $\left\{-\frac{1}{3}, \frac{3}{2}\right\}$

28. $6x^2 = x + 2$ $\left\{-\frac{1}{2}, \frac{2}{3}\right\}$

29. $x^2 + 4x + 2 = 0$ $\{-2 \pm \sqrt{2}\}$

30. $x^2 + 6x = 2$ $\{-3 \pm \sqrt{11}\}$

31. $3x^2 + 1 = 5x$ $\left\{\frac{5 \pm \sqrt{13}}{6}\right\}$

32. $2x^2 + 3x - 1 = 0$ $\left\{\frac{-3 \pm \sqrt{17}}{4}\right\}$

Find the value of the discriminant and the number of real solutions to each equation.

33. $25x^2 - 20x + 4 = 0$ 0, 1

34. $16x^2 + 1 = 8x$ 0, 1

35. $x^2 - 3x + 7 = 0$ -19, 0

36. $3x^2 - x + 8 = 0$ -95, 0

37. $2x^2 + 1 = 5x$ 17, 2

38. $-3x^2 + 6x - 2 = 0$ 12, 2

Find the complex solutions to the quadratic equations.

39. $2x^2 - 4x + 3 = 0$ $\left\{\frac{2 \pm i\sqrt{2}}{2}\right\}$

40. $2x^2 - 6x + 5 = 0$ $\left\{\frac{3 \pm i}{2}\right\}$

41. $2x^2 + 3 = 3x$ $\left\{\frac{3 \pm i\sqrt{15}}{4}\right\}$

42. $x^2 + x + 1 = 0$ $\left\{\frac{-1 \pm i\sqrt{3}}{2}\right\}$

43. $3x^2 + 2x + 2 = 0$ $\left\{\frac{-1 \pm i\sqrt{5}}{3}\right\}$

44. $x^2 + 2 = 2x$ $\{1 \pm i\}$

45. $\frac{1}{2}x^2 + 3x + 8 = 0$ $\{-3 \pm i\sqrt{7}\}$

46. $\frac{1}{2}x^2 - 5x + 13 = 0$ $\{5 \pm i\}$

10.3 *Find the vertex and intercepts for each parabola, and sketch its graph.*

47. $f(x) = x^2 - 6x$
Vertex $(3, -9)$,
intercepts $(0, 0)$, $(6, 0)$

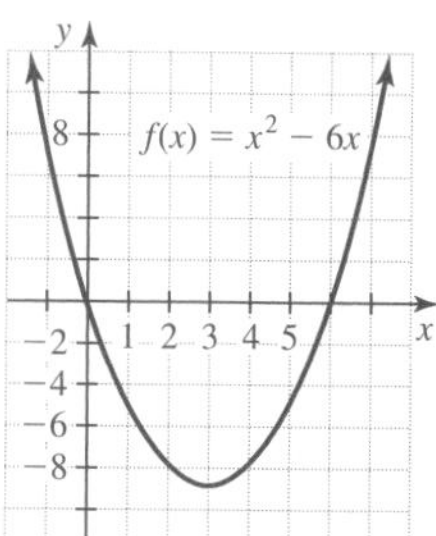

48. $f(x) = x^2 + 4x$
Vertex $(-2, -4)$,
intercepts $(0, 0)$, $(-4, 0)$

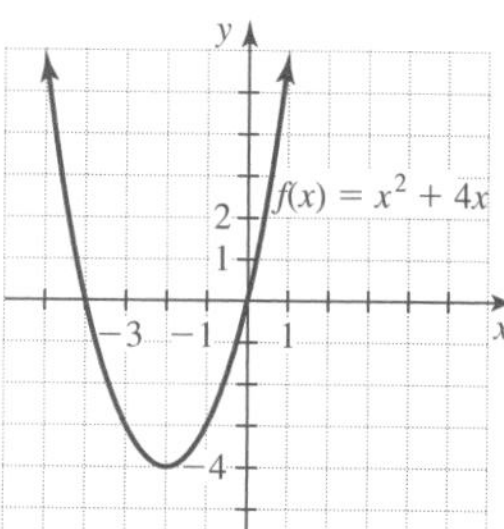

49. $g(x) = x^2 - 4x - 12$
Vertex $(2, -16)$,
intercepts $(0, -12)$,
$(-2, 0)$, and $(6, 0)$

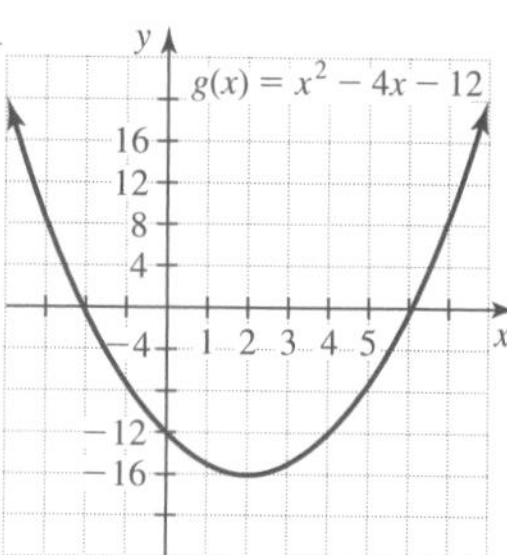

50. $g(x) = x^2 + 2x - 24$
Vertex $(-1, -25)$,
intercepts $(0, -24)$,
$(-6, 0)$, $(4, 0)$

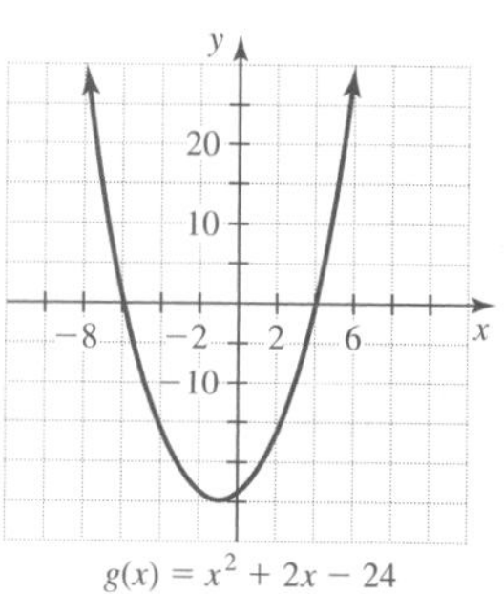

$g(x) = x^2 + 2x - 24$

51. $h(x) = -2x^2 + 8x$
Vertex (2, 8),
intercepts (0, 0), (4, 0)

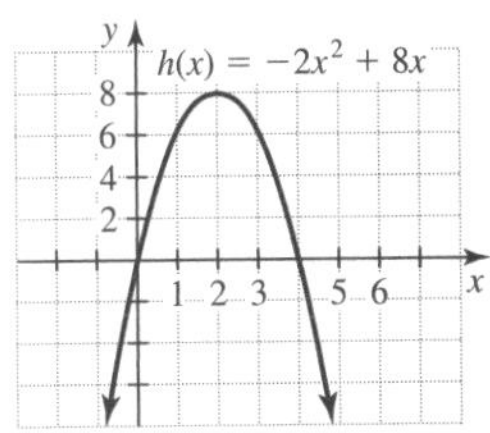

52. $h(x) = -3x^2 + 6x$
Vertex (1, 3),
intercepts (0, 0), (2, 0)

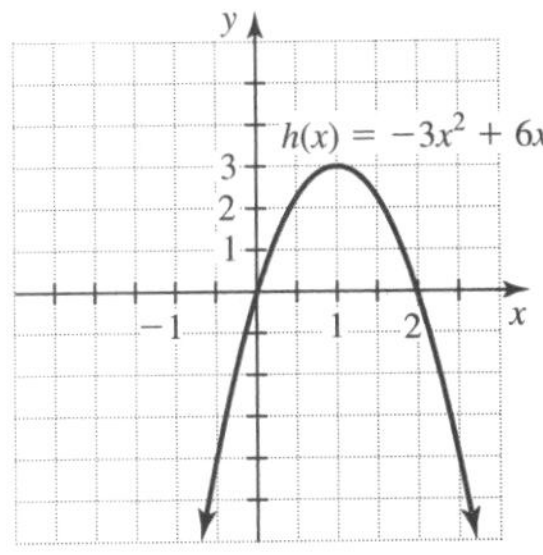

53. $y = -x^2 + 2x + 3$
Vertex (1, 4),
intercepts (0, 3), (−1, 0),
(3, 0)

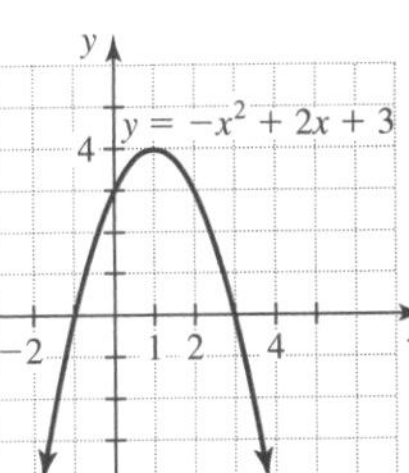

54. $y = -x^2 - 3x - 2$
Vertex $\left(-\frac{3}{2}, \frac{1}{4}\right)$,
intercepts (0, −2),
(−2, 0), (−1, 0)

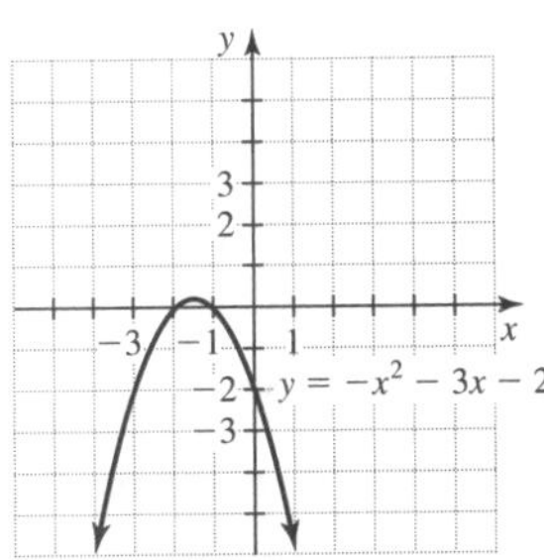

Determine whether each equation has a maximum or minimum y-value and find it.

55. $f(x) = x^2 + 4x + 1$ Minimum, −3

56. $f(x) = x^2 - 6x + 2$ Minimum, −7

57. $y = -2x^2 - x + 4$ Maximum, 4.125

58. $y = -3x^2 + 2x + 7$ Maximum, $\frac{22}{3}$

10.4 *Use the discriminant to determine whether each quadratic polynomial can be factored, then factor the ones that are not prime.*

59. $8x^2 - 10x - 3$ $(4x + 1)(2x - 3)$

60. $18x^2 + 9x - 2$ $(6x - 1)(3x + 2)$

61. $4x^2 - 5x + 2$ Prime

62. $6x^2 - 7x - 4$ Prime

63. $8y^2 + 10y - 25$ $(4y - 5)(2y + 5)$

64. $25z^2 - 15z - 18$ $(5z + 3)(5z - 6)$

Write a quadratic equation that has each given pair of solutions.

65. $-3, -6$ $x^2 + 9x + 18 = 0$

66. $4, -9$ $x^2 + 5x - 36 = 0$

67. $-5\sqrt{2}, 5\sqrt{2}$ $x^2 - 50 = 0$

68. $-2i\sqrt{3}, 2i\sqrt{3}$ $x^2 + 12 = 0$

Find all real solutions to each equation.

69. $x^6 + 7x^3 - 8 = 0$ $\{-2, 1\}$

70. $8x^6 + 63x^3 - 8 = 0$ $\left\{-2, \frac{1}{2}\right\}$

71. $x^4 - 13x^2 + 36 = 0$ $\{\pm 2, \pm 3\}$

72. $x^4 + 7x^2 + 12 = 0$ $\varnothing$

73. $(x^2 + 3x)^2 - 28(x^2 + 3x) + 180 = 0$ $\{-6, -5, 2, 3\}$

74. $(x^2 + 1)^2 - 8(x^2 + 1) + 15 = 0$ $\{\pm 2, \pm\sqrt{2}\}$

75. $x^2 - 6x + 6\sqrt{x^2 - 6x} - 40 = 0$ $\{-2, 8\}$

76. $x^2 - 3x - 3\sqrt{x^2 - 3x} + 2 = 0$ $\left\{-1, 4, \frac{3 \pm \sqrt{13}}{2}\right\}$

77. $t^{-2} + 5t^{-1} - 36 = 0$ $\left\{-\frac{1}{9}, \frac{1}{4}\right\}$

78. $a^{-2} + a^{-1} - 6 = 0$ $\left\{-\frac{1}{3}, \frac{1}{2}\right\}$

79. $w - 13\sqrt{w} + 36 = 0$ $\{16, 81\}$

80. $4a - 5\sqrt{a} + 1 = 0$ $\left\{\frac{1}{16}, 1\right\}$

10.5 *Solve each inequality. State the solution set using interval notation and graph it.*

81. $a^2 + a > 6$ $(-\infty, -3) \cup (2, \infty)$

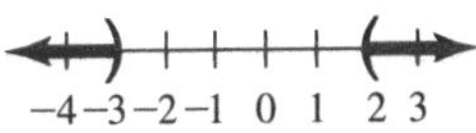

82. $x^2 - 5x + 6 > 0$ $(-\infty, 2) \cup (3, \infty)$

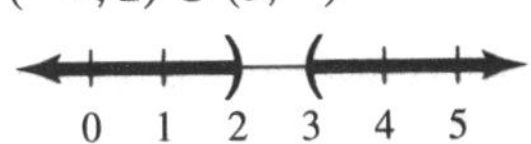

83. $x^2 - x - 20 \le 0$ $[-4, 5]$

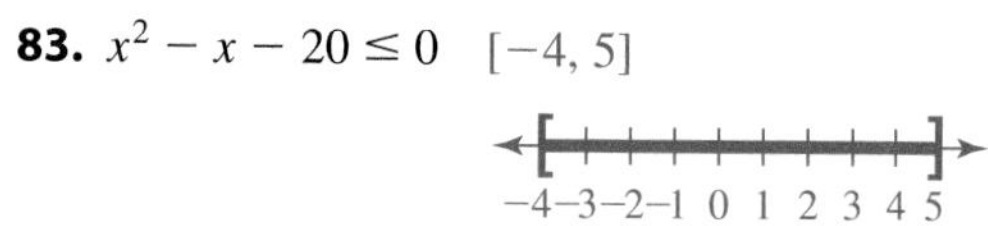

84. $a^2 + 2a \le 15$ $[-5, 3]$

85. $w^2 - w < 0$ $(0, 1)$

86. $x - x^2 \le 0$ $(-\infty, 0] \cup [1, \infty)$

87. $\dfrac{x-4}{x+2} \ge 0$ $(-\infty, -2) \cup [4, \infty)$

88. $\dfrac{x-3}{x+5} < 0$ $(-5, 3)$

89. $\dfrac{x-2}{x+3} < 1$ $(-3, \infty)$

90. $\dfrac{x-3}{x+4} > 2$ $(-11, -4)$

91. $\dfrac{3}{x+2} > \dfrac{1}{x+1}$ $(-2, -1) \cup \left(-\dfrac{1}{2}, \infty\right)$

92. $\dfrac{1}{x+1} < \dfrac{1}{x-1}$ $(-\infty, -1) \cup (1, \infty)$

Miscellaneous

In Exercises 93–104, find all real or imaginary solutions to each equation.

93. $144x^2 - 120x + 25 = 0$ $\left\{\dfrac{5}{12}\right\}$

94. $49x^2 + 9 = 42x$ $\left\{\dfrac{3}{7}\right\}$

95. $(2x + 3)^2 + 7 = 12$ $\left\{\dfrac{-3 \pm \sqrt{5}}{2}\right\}$

96. $6x = -\dfrac{19x + 25}{x + 1}$ $\left\{-\dfrac{5}{3}, -\dfrac{5}{2}\right\}$

97. $1 + \dfrac{20}{9x^2} = \dfrac{8}{3x}$ $\left\{\dfrac{4 \pm 2i}{3}\right\}$

98. $\dfrac{x-1}{x+2} = \dfrac{2x-3}{x+4}$ $\{1 \pm \sqrt{3}\}$

99. $\sqrt{3x^2 + 7x - 30} = x$ $\left\{\dfrac{5}{2}\right\}$

100. $\dfrac{x^4}{3} = x^2 + 6$ $\{\pm\sqrt{6}, \pm i\sqrt{3}\}$

101. $2(2x + 1)^2 + 5(2x + 1) = 3$ $\left\{-2, -\dfrac{1}{4}\right\}$

102. $(w^2 - 1)^2 + 2(w^2 - 1) = 15$ $\{\pm 2i, \pm 2\}$

103. $x^{1/2} - 15x^{1/4} + 50 = 0$ $\{625, 10{,}000\}$

104. $x^{-2} - 9x^{-1} + 18 = 0$ $\left\{\dfrac{1}{6}, \dfrac{1}{3}\right\}$

Find exact and approximate solutions to each problem.

105. ***Missing numbers.*** Find two positive real numbers that differ by 4 and have a product of 4.
$-2 + 2\sqrt{2}$ and $2 + 2\sqrt{2}$, or 0.83 and 4.83

106. ***One on one.*** Find two positive real numbers that differ by 1 and have a product of 1.
$\dfrac{-1 + \sqrt{5}}{2}$ and $\dfrac{1 + \sqrt{5}}{2}$, or 0.62 and 1.62

107. ***Big screen TV.*** On a 19-inch diagonal measure television picture screen, the height is 4 inches less than the width. Find the height and width.
Width $\dfrac{4 + \sqrt{706}}{2}$ or 15.3 inches, height $\dfrac{-4 + \sqrt{706}}{2}$ or 11.3 inches

108. ***Boxing match.*** A boxing ring is in the shape of a square, 20 ft on each side. How far apart are the fighters when they are in opposite corners of the ring? $20\sqrt{2}$ or 28.284 ft

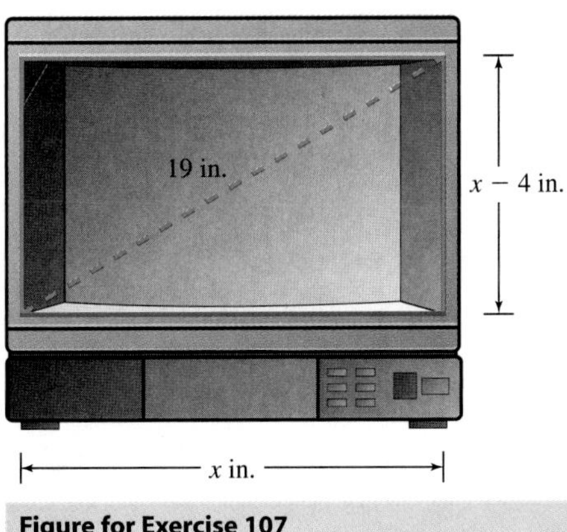

Figure for Exercise 107

Figure for Exercise 111

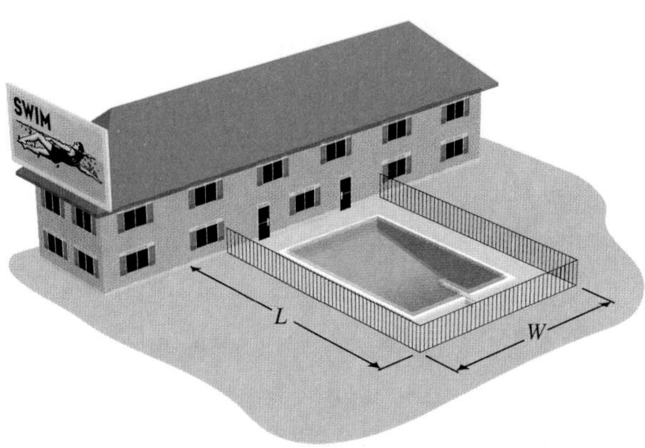

Figure for Exercise 112

109. ***Students for a Clean Environment.*** A group of environmentalists plans to print a message on an 8 inch by 10 inch paper. If the typed message requires 24 square inches of paper and the group wants an equal border on all sides, then how wide should the border be? 2 inches

Figure for Exercise 109

110. ***Winston works faster.*** Winston can mow his dad's lawn in 1 hour less than it takes his brother Willie. If they take 2 hours to mow it when working together, then how long would it take Winston working alone?
$\frac{3 + \sqrt{17}}{2}$ or 3.562 hours

111. ***Ping Pong.*** The table used for table tennis is 4 ft longer than it is wide and has an area of 45 ft^2. What are the dimensions of the table? Width 5 ft, length 9 ft

112. ***Swimming pool design.*** An architect has designed a motel pool within a rectangular area that is fenced on three sides as shown in the figure. If she uses 60 yards of fencing to enclose an area of 352 square yards, then what are the dimensions marked L and W in the figure? Assume L is greater than W.
$L = 22$ yards and $W = 16$ yards

113. ***Minimizing cost.*** The unit cost in dollars for manufacturing n starters is given by $C(n) = 0.004n^2 - 3.2n + 660$. What is the unit cost when 390 starters are manufactured? For what number of starters is the unit cost at a minimum?
$20.40, 400

114. ***Maximizing profit.*** The total profit (in dollars) for sales of x rowing machines is given by $P(x) = -0.2x^2 + 300x - 200$. What is the profit if 500 are sold? For what value of x will the profit be at a maximum? $99,800, 750

115. ***Decathlon champion.*** For 1989 and 1990 Dave Johnson had the highest decathlon score in the world. When Johnson reached a speed of 32 ft/sec on the pole vault runway, his height above the ground t seconds after leaving the ground was given by $h = -16t^2 + 32t$. (The elasticity of the pole converts the horizontal speed into vertical speed.) Find the value of t for which his height was 12 ft. 0.5 second and 1.5 seconds

116. ***Time of flight.*** Use the information from Exercise 115 to determine how long Johnson was in the air. For how long was he more than 14 ft in the air?
2 seconds, $0.5\sqrt{2}$ or 0.707 seconds

Chapter 10 Test

Calculate the value of $b^2 - 4ac$, and state how many real solutions each equation has.

1. $2x^2 - 3x + 2 = 0$ $-7, 0$

2. $-3x^2 + 5x - 1 = 0$ $13, 2$

3. $4x^2 - 4x + 1 = 0$ $0, 1$

Solve by using the quadratic formula.

4. $2x^2 + 5x - 3 = 0$ $\left\{-3, \frac{1}{2}\right\}$

5. $x^2 + 6x + 6 = 0$ $\{-3 \pm \sqrt{3}\}$

Solve by completing the square.

6. $x^2 + 10x + 25 = 0$ $\{-5\}$

7. $2x^2 + x - 6 = 0$ $\left\{-2, \frac{3}{2}\right\}$

Solve by any method.

8. $x(x + 1) = 12$ $\{-4, 3\}$

9. $a^4 - 5a^2 + 4 = 0$ $\{\pm 1, \pm 2\}$

10. $x - 2 - 8\sqrt{x - 2} + 15 = 0$ $\{11, 27\}$

Find the complex solutions to the quadratic equations.

11. $x^2 + 36 = 0$ $\{\pm 6i\}$

12. $x^2 + 6x + 10 = 0$ $\{-3 \pm i\}$

13. $3x^2 - x + 1 = 0$ $\left\{\frac{1 \pm i\sqrt{11}}{6}\right\}$

Graph each parabola. Identify the vertex, intercepts, and the maximum or minimum y-value.

14. $f(x) = 16 - x^2$
Vertex (0, 16),
intercepts (0, 16), (−4, 0), (4, 0),
maximum y-value 16

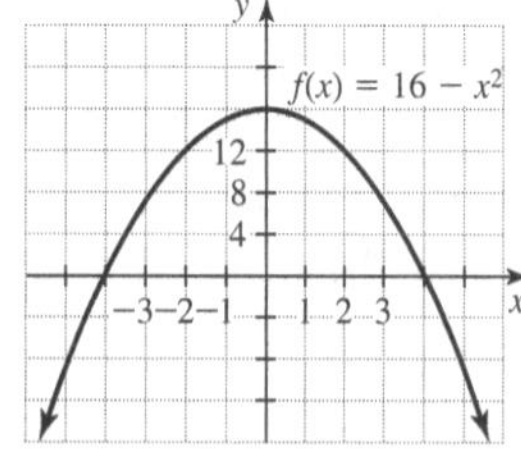

15. $y = x^2 - 3x$

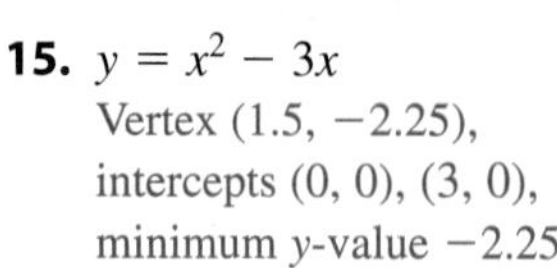

Vertex (1.5, −2.25),
intercepts (0, 0), (3, 0),
minimum y-value −2.25

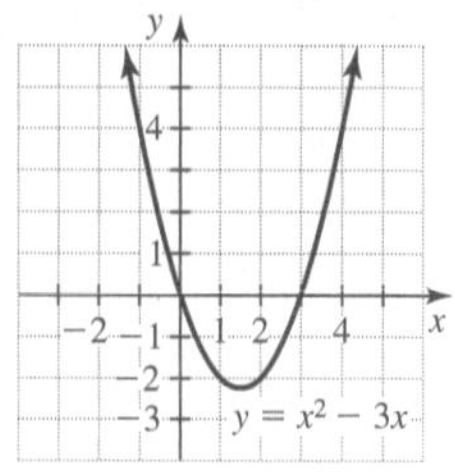

Write a quadratic equation that has each given pair of solutions.

16. $-4, 6$ $x^2 - 2x - 24 = 0$

17. $-5i, 5i$ $x^2 + 25 = 0$

Solve each inequality. State and graph the solution set.

18. $w^2 + 3w < 18$ $(-6, 3)$

−6 −5 −4 −3 −2 −1 0 1 2 3

19. $\frac{2}{x - 2} < \frac{3}{x + 1}$ $(-1, 2) \cup (8, \infty)$

−1 0 1 2 3 4 5 6 7 8 9 10

Find the exact solution to each problem.

20. The length of a rectangle is 2 ft longer than the width. If the area is 16 ft², then what are the length and width?
Width $-1 + \sqrt{17}$ ft, length $1 + \sqrt{17}$ ft

21. A new computer can process a company's monthly payroll in 1 hour less time than the old computer. To really save time, the manager used both computers and finished the payroll in 3 hours. How long would it take the new computer to do the payroll by itself?
$\frac{5 + \sqrt{37}}{2}$ or 5.5 hours

22. The height in feet for a ball thrown upward at 48 feet per second is given by $s(t) = -16t^2 + 48t$, where t is the time in seconds after the ball is tossed. What is the maximum height that the ball will reach?
36 feet

Making **Connections** | A Review of Chapters 1–10

Solve each equation.

1. $2x - 15 = 0$ $\left\{\frac{15}{2}\right\}$

2. $2x^2 - 15 = 0$ $\left\{\pm\frac{\sqrt{30}}{2}\right\}$

3. $2x^2 + x - 15 = 0$ $\left\{-3, \frac{5}{2}\right\}$

4. $2x^2 + 4x - 15 = 0$ $\left\{\frac{-2 \pm \sqrt{34}}{2}\right\}$

5. $|4x + 11| = 3$ $\left\{-\frac{7}{2}, -2\right\}$

6. $|4x^2 + 11x| = 3$ $\left\{-3, \frac{1}{4}, \frac{-11 \pm \sqrt{73}}{8}\right\}$

7. $\sqrt{x} = x - 6$ $\{9\}$

8. $(2x - 5)^{2/3} = 4$ $\left\{-\frac{3}{2}, \frac{13}{2}\right\}$

Solve each inequality. State the solution set using interval notation.

9. $1 - 2x < 5 - x$ $(-4, \infty)$

10. $(1 - 2x)(5 - x) \le 0$ $\left[\frac{1}{2}, 5\right]$

11. $\frac{1 - 2x}{5 - x} \le 0$ $\left[\frac{1}{2}, 5\right)$

12. $|5 - x| < 3$ $(2, 8)$

13. $3x - 1 < 5$ and $-3 \le x$ $[-3, 2)$

14. $x - 3 < 1$ or $2x \ge 8$ $(-\infty, \infty)$

Solve each equation for y.

15. $2x - 3y = 9$ $y = \frac{2}{3}x - 3$

16. $\frac{y - 3}{x + 2} = -\frac{1}{2}$ $y = -\frac{1}{2}x + 2$

17. $3y^2 + cy + d = 0$ $y = \frac{-c \pm \sqrt{c^2 - 12d}}{6}$

18. $my^2 - ny = w$ $y = \frac{n \pm \sqrt{n^2 + 4mw}}{2m}$

19. $\frac{1}{3}x - \frac{2}{5}y = \frac{5}{6}$ $y = \frac{5}{6}x - \frac{25}{12}$

20. $y - 3 = -\frac{2}{3}(x - 4)$ $y = -\frac{2}{3}x + \frac{17}{3}$

Let $m = \frac{y_2 - y_1}{x_2 - x_1}$. *Find the value of m for each of the following choices of* x_1, x_2, y_1, *and* y_2.

21. $x_1 = 2, x_2 = 5, y_1 = 3, y_2 = 7$ $\frac{4}{3}$

22. $x_1 = -3, x_2 = 4, y_1 = 5, y_2 = -6$ $-\frac{11}{7}$

23. $x_1 = 0.3, x_2 = 0.5, y_1 = 0.8, y_2 = 0.4$ -2

24. $x_1 = \frac{1}{2}, x_2 = \frac{1}{3}, y_1 = \frac{3}{5}, y_2 = -\frac{4}{3}$ $\frac{58}{5}$

Solve each problem.

25. ***Ticket prices.*** If the price of a concert ticket goes up, then the number sold will go down, as shown in the figure. If you use the formula $n = 48{,}000 - 400p$ to predict the number sold depending on the price p, then how many will be sold at \$20 per ticket? How many will be sold at \$25 per ticket? Use the bar graph to estimate the price if 35,000 tickets were sold. 40,000, 38,000, \$32.50

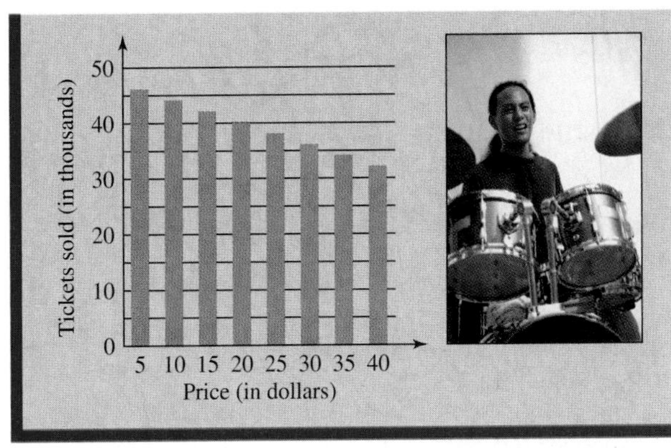

Figure for Exercise 25

26. ***Increasing revenue.*** Even though the number of tickets sold for a concert decreases with increasing price, the revenue generated does not necessarily decrease. Use the formula $R = p(48{,}000 - 400p)$ to determine the revenue when the price is \$20 and when the price is \$25. What price would produce a revenue of \$1.28 million? Use the graph to find the price that determines the maximum revenue. \$800,000, \$950,000, \$40 or \$80, \$60

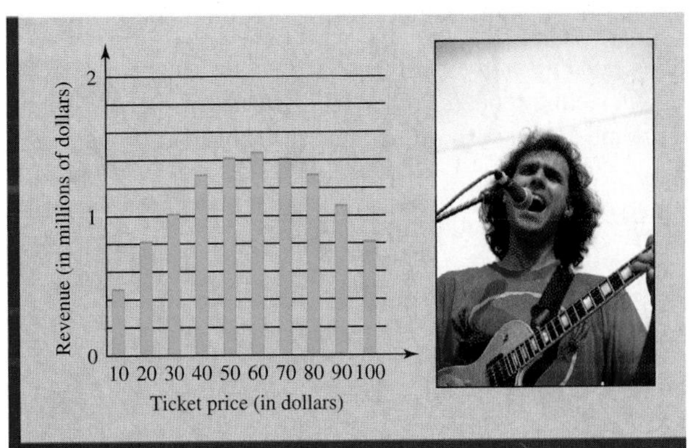

Figure for Exercise 26

Critical Thinking | For Individual or Group Work | Chapter 10

These exercises can be solved by a variety of techniques, which may or may not require algebra. So be creative and think critically. Explain all answers. Answers are in the Instructor's Edition of this text.

1. ***Ant parade.*** An ant marches from point A to point B on the cylindrical garbage can shown in the accompanying figure. The can is 1 foot in diameter and 2 feet high. If the ant makes two complete revolutions of the can in a perfect spiral, then exactly how far did he travel?

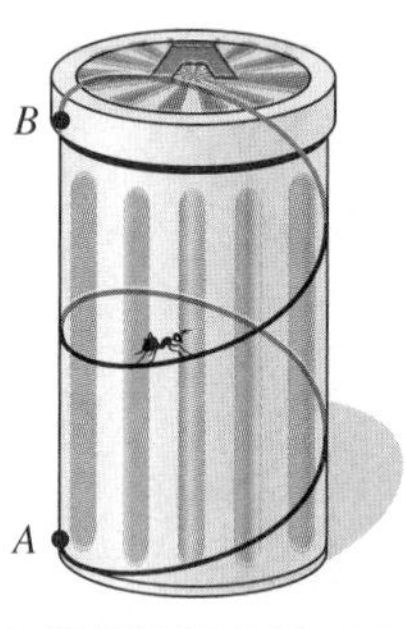

Figure for Exercise 1

2. ***Connecting points.*** Draw a circle and pick any three points on the circle.

a) How many line segments can be drawn connecting these points?

b) How many line segments can be drawn connecting four points on a circle? Five points? Six points?

c) How many line segments can be drawn connecting n points on a circle?

3. ***Summing the digits.*** Find the sum of the digits in the standard form of the number $2^{2005} \cdot 5^{2007}$.

4. ***Consecutive odd numbers.*** Find three consecutive odd whole numbers such that the sum of their squares is a four-digit whole number whose digits are all the same.

5. ***Reversible prime numbers.*** The prime number 13 has an interesting property, when its digits are reversed, the new number 31 is also prime. Find the sum of all prime numbers greater than 10 yet less than 125 that have this property.

6. ***Circles and squares.*** Start with a square piece of paper. Draw the largest possible circle inside the square. Cut out the circle and keep it. Now draw the largest possible square inside the circle. Cut out the square and keep it. What is the ratio of the area of the original square to the area of the final square? If you repeat this process six more times, then what is the ratio of the area of the original square to the area of the final square?

7. ***Perpendicular hands.*** What are the first two times (to the nearest second) after 12 noon for which the minute hand and hour hand of a clock are perpendicular to each other?

Photo for Exercise 7

8. ***Going broke.*** Albert and Zelda agreed to play a game. If heads appeared on the toss of an ordinary coin, Zelda had to double the amount of money that Albert had. If the result was tails, then Albert had to pay Zelda \$24. As it turned out, the coin came up heads, tails, heads, tails, heads, tails. Then Albert was broke. How much money did Albert start with?

1. $2\sqrt{\pi^2 + 1}$ feet **2. a)** 3 **b)** 6, 10, 15 **c)** $\dfrac{n(n-1)}{2}$ **3.** 7 **4.** 41, 43, 45 **5.** 750 **6.** 2 to 1, 128 to 1 **7.** 12:16:22 and 12:49:05 **8.** \$21

Functions

Working in a world of numbers, designers of racing boats blend art with science to design attractive boats that are also fast and safe. If the sail area is increased, the boat will go faster but will be less stable in open seas. If the displacement is increased, the boat will be more stable but slower. Increasing length increases speed but reduces stability. To make yacht racing both competitive and safe, racing boats must satisfy complex systems of rules, many of which involve mathematical formulas.

After the 1988 mismatch between Dennis Conner's catamaran and New Zealander Michael Fay's 133-foot monohull, an international group of yacht designers rewrote the America's Cup rules to ensure the fairness of the race. In addition to hundreds of pages of other rules, every yacht must satisfy the basic inequality

$$\frac{L + 1.25\sqrt{S} - 9.8\sqrt[3]{D}}{0.679} \le 24.000,$$

which balances the length L, the sail area S, and the displacement D.

In the 1979 Fastnet Race 15 sailors lost their lives. After *Exide Challenger*'s carbon-fiber keel snapped off, Tony Bullimore spent 4 days inside the overturned hull before being rescued by the Australian navy. Yacht racing is a dangerous sport. To determine the general performance and safety of a yacht, designers calculate the displacement-length ratio, the sail area-displacement ratio, the ballast-displacement ratio, and the capsize screening value.

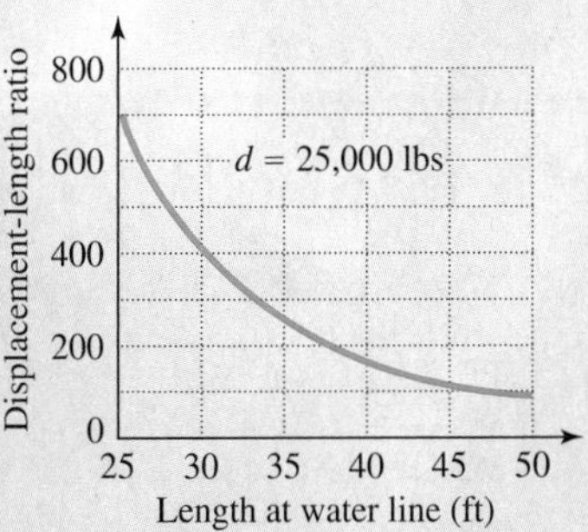

In Exercises 85 and 86 of Section 11.6 we will see how composition of functions is used to define the displacement-length ratio and the sail area-displacement ratio.

11.1 Functions and Relations

In this Section

- The Concept of a Function
- Functions Expressed by Formulas
- Functions Expressed by Tables
- Functions Expressed by Ordered Pairs
- The Vertical-Line Test
- Domain and Range
- Function Notation

You have seen functions and relations throughout this text, but we have not identified them as functions or relations. In this section we will study the function concept.

The Concept of a Function

If the value of the variable y is determined by the value of the variable x, then y **is a function of** $\boldsymbol{x}$. So "is a function of" means "is uniquely determined by." But what does uniquely determined mean? According to the dictionary "determine" means "to settle conclusively." There can be no ambiguity. There is only one y for any x.

The x-value is thought of as *input* and the y-value as *output*. If y is a function of x, then there is only one output for any input. For example, after a shopper places an order on the Internet, the shopper is asked to *input* a ZIP code so that the shipping cost (*output*) can be determined. For that order the shipping cost is a function of ZIP code. Note that many different ZIP codes can correspond to the same output. If any ZIP code caused the computer to output more than one shipping cost, then shipping cost is not a function of ZIP code. The shopper is confused and probably cancels the order. See Fig. 11.1.

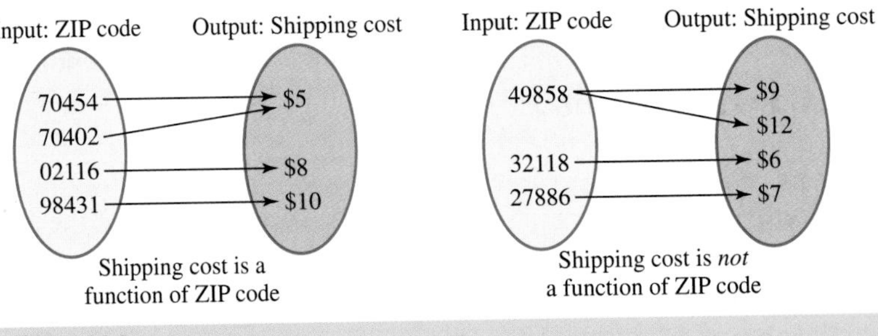

Figure 11.1

EXAMPLE 1 Deciding if y is a function of x

In each case determine whether y is a function of x.

a) Consider all possible circles. Let y represent the area of a circle and x represent its radius.

b) Consider all possible first-class letters mailed today in the United States. Let y represent the weight of a letter and x represent the amount of postage on the letter.

c) Consider all students at Pasadena City College. Let y represent the weight of a student to the nearest pound and x represent the height of the same student to the nearest inch.

d) Consider all possible rectangles. Let y represent the area of a rectangle and x represent the width.

e) Consider all cars sold at Bill Hood Ford this year where the sales tax rate is 9%. Let y represent the amount of sales tax and x represent the selling price of the car.

Solution

Teaching Tip Ask students for more examples of functions and relations that are not functions in real life.

a) Can the area of a circle be determined from its radius? The well-known formula $A = \pi r^2$ (or in this case $y = \pi x^2$) indicates exactly how to determine the area if the radius is known. So there is only one area for any given radius and y is a function of x.

b) Can the weight of a letter be determined if the amount of postage on the letter is known? There are certainly letters that have the same amount of postage and different weights. Since the weight cannot be determined conclusively from the postage, the weight is *not* a function of the postage and y is *not* a function of x.

c) Can the weight of a student be determined from the height of the student? Imagine that we have a list containing the weights and heights for all students. There will certainly be two 5 ft 9 in. students with different weights. So weight cannot be determined from the height and y is *not* a function of x.

d) Can the area of a rectangle be determined from the width? Among all possible rectangles there are infinitely many rectangles with width 1 ft and different areas. So the area is not determined by the width and y is *not* a function of x.

e) Can the amount of sales tax be determined from the price of the car? The formula $y = 0.09x$ is used to determine the amount of tax. For example, the tax on every \$20,000 car is \$1800. So y is a function of x.

Now do Exercises 7–14

Functions Expressed by Formulas

If you get a speeding ticket in St. John's Parish, Louisiana there is a rule that is used to determine your fine. You can mail to the judge \$153 plus \$1 for every mile per hour over 80 miles per hour, but if your speed is over 90 miles per hour you must appear before the judge. Since there is no ambiguity, the amount of the fine is a function of your speed.

Function (as a Rule)

A function is a rule by which any allowable value of one variable (the **independent variable**) determines a *unique* value of a second variable (the **dependent variable**).

There are many ways to express a rule. A rule can be expressed verbally (as in the speeding ticket), with a formula, a table, or a graph. Of course, in mathematics we prefer the preciseness that formulas or equations provide. Since a formula such as $A = \pi r^2$ gives us a rule for obtaining the value of the dependent variable A from the value of the independent variable r, we say that this formula is a function. Formulas are used to describe or **model** relationships between variables.

EXAMPLE 2

Writing a formula for a function

A carpet layer charges \$25 plus \$4 per square yard for installing carpet. Write the total charge C as a function of the number n of square yards of carpet installed.

Solution

At \$4 per square yard, n square yards installed cost $4n$ dollars. If we include the \$25 charge, then the total cost is $4n + 25$ dollars. Thus the equation

$$C = 4n + 25$$

expresses C as a function of n.

Now do Exercises 15–18

Any formula that has the form $y = mx + b$ with $m \neq 0$ is a **linear function.** If $m = 0$ then the formula has the form $y = b$ and is called a **constant function.** So in Example 2, the charge is a linear function of the number of square yards installed and $C = 4n + 25$ is a linear function.

EXAMPLE 3

A function in geometry

Express the area of a circle as a function of its diameter.

Solution

The area of a circle is given by $A = \pi r^2$. Because the radius of a circle is one-half of the diameter, we have $r = \frac{d}{2}$. Now replace r by $\frac{d}{2}$ in the formula $A = \pi r^2$:

$$A = \pi\left(\frac{d}{2}\right)^2$$

$$= \frac{\pi d^2}{4}$$

So $A = \frac{\pi}{4}d^2$ expresses the area of a circle as a function of its diameter.

Now do Exercises 19–24

Functions Expressed by Tables

Tables are often used to provide a rule for pairing the value of one variable with the value of another. For a table to define a function, each value of the independent variable must correspond to only one value of the dependent variable.

EXAMPLE 4

Functions defined by tables

Determine whether each table expresses y as a function of x.

a)

Weight (lbs) x	Cost (\$) y
0 to 10	4.60
11 to 30	12.75
31 to 79	32.90
80 to 99	55.82

b)

Weight (lbs) x	Cost (\$) y
0 to 15	4.60
10 to 30	12.75
31 to 79	32.90
80 to 99	55.82

c)

x	y
1	1
−1	1
2	2
−2	2
3	3

Study Tip

When one student asks another for help, it is often the one who does the explaining that learns the most. When you work together, don't let one person do all of the talking. If you must work alone, then try explaining things to yourself. You might even try talking to yourself.

Solution

a) For each allowable weight, this table gives a unique cost. So the cost is a function of the weight and y is a function of x.

b) Using this table a weight of say 12 pounds would correspond to a cost of \$4.60 and also to \$12.75. Either the table has an error or perhaps there is some other factor that is being used to determine cost. In any case the weight does not determine a unique cost and y is *not* a function of x.

c) In this table every allowable value for x corresponds to a unique y-value so y is a function of x. Note that different values of x corresponding to the same y-value are permitted in a function.

Now do Exercises 25–32

Helpful Hint

In a function, every value for the independent variable determines conclusively a corresponding value for the dependent variable. If there is more than one possible value for the dependent variable, then the set of ordered pairs is not a function.

Functions Expressed by Ordered Pairs

A computer at your grocery store determines the price of each item by searching a long list of ordered pairs in which the first coordinate is the universal product code and the second coordinate is the price of the item with that code. For each product code there is a unique price. This process certainly satisfies the rule definition of a function. Since the set of ordered pairs is the essential part of this rule we say that the set of ordered pairs is a function.

Function (as a Set of Ordered Pairs)

A function is a set of ordered pairs of real numbers such that no two ordered pairs have the same first coordinates and different second coordinates.

Note the importance of the phrase "no two ordered pairs have the same first coordinates and different second coordinates." Imagine the problems at the grocery store if the computer gave two different prices for the same universal product code. Note also that the product code is an identification number and it cannot be used in calculations. So the computer can use a function defined by a formula to determine the amount of tax, but it cannot use a formula to determine the price from the product code.

Any set of ordered pairs is called a **relation.** A function is a special relation.

EXAMPLE 5

Relations given as lists of ordered pairs

Determine whether each relation is a function.

a) $\{(1, 2), (1, 5), (3, 7)\}$ **b)** $\{(4, 5), (3, 5), (2, 6), (1, 7)\}$

Teaching Tip Remind students that no matter how a function is described, the underlying concept is ordered pairs.

Solution

a) This relation is not a function because $(1, 2)$ and $(1, 5)$ have the same first coordinate but different second coordinates.

b) This relation is a function. Note that the same second coordinate with different first coordinates is permitted in a function.

Now do Exercises 33–40

The solution set to any equation in x and y is the set of ordered pairs that satisfy the equation. For example, the solution set to $x = y^2$ is expressed in set-builder notation as $\{(x, y) \mid x = y^2\}$. Since any set of ordered pairs is a relation, this solution set is a relation. We can use the definition of a function to determine whether the solution set is a function. For simplicity we often refer to an equation in x and y as a relation or a function.

EXAMPLE 6

Relations given as equations

Determine whether each relation is a function.

a) $x = y^2$

b) $y = 2x$

c) $x = |y|$

Helpful Hint

To determine whether an equation expresses y as a function of x, always select a number for x (the independent variable) and then see if there is more than one corresponding value for y (the dependent variable). If there is more than one corresponding y-value, then y is not a function of x.

Solution

a) Is it possible to find two ordered pairs with the same first coordinate and different second coordinates that satisfy $x = y^2$? Since (1, 1) and (1, −1) both satisfy $x = y^2$, this relation is not a function.

b) The equation $y = 2x$ indicates that the y-coordinate is always twice the x-coordinate. Ordered pairs such as (0, 0), (2, 4), and (3, 6) satisfy $y = 2x$. It is not possible to find two ordered pairs with the same first coordinate and different second coordinates. So $y = 2x$ is a function.

c) The equation $x = |y|$ is satisfied by ordered pairs such as (2, 2) and (2, −2) because $2 = |2|$ and $2 = |-2|$ are both correct. So this relation is not a function.

Now do Exercises 41–68

The Vertical-Line Test

Since every graph illustrates a set of ordered pairs, every graph is a relation. To determine whether a graph is a function, we must see whether there are two (or more) ordered pairs on the graph that have the same first coordinate and different second coordinates. Two points with the same first coordinate lie on a vertical line that crosses the graph.

The Vertical-Line Test

A graph is the graph of a function if and only if there is no vertical line that crosses the graph more than once.

If there is a vertical line that crosses a graph twice (or more), then we have two points with the same x-coordinate and different y-coordinates, and the graph is not the graph of a function. If you mentally consider every possible vertical line and none of them crosses the graph more than once, then you can conclude that the graph is the graph of a function.

EXAMPLE 7

Using the vertical-line test

Which of these graphs are graphs of functions?

a)

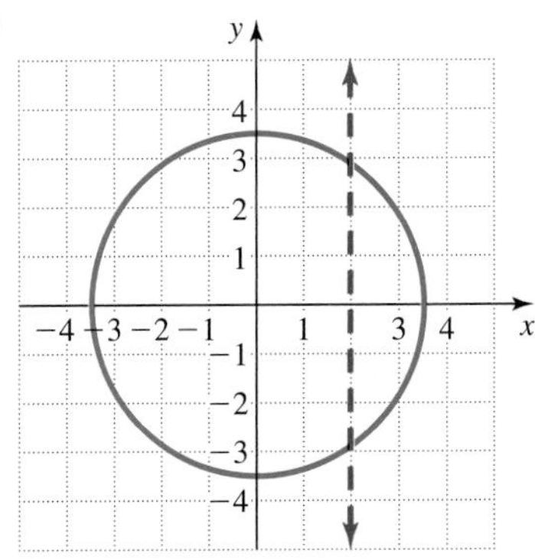

b)

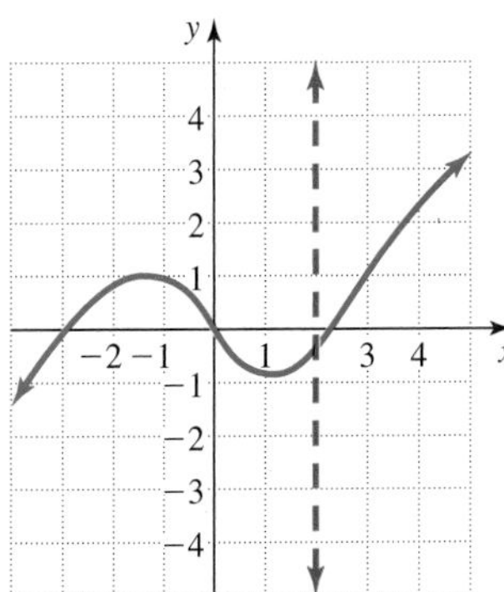

c)

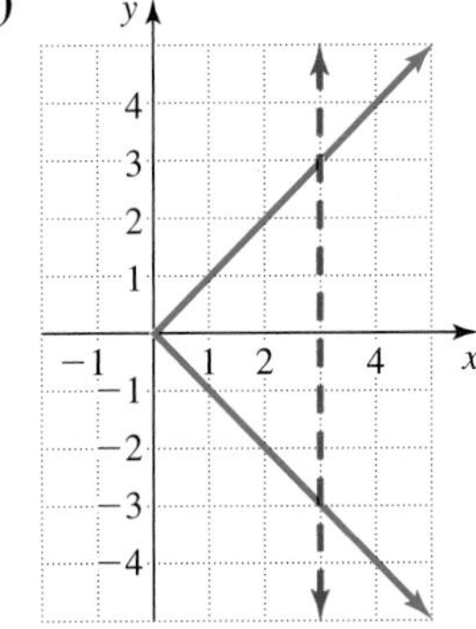

Solution

Neither (a) nor (c) is the graph of a function, since we can draw vertical lines that cross these graphs twice. The graph (b) is the graph of a function, since no vertical line crosses it more than once.

Now do Exercises 69–74

Teaching Tip Emphasize that the vertical-line test is not dependable. Using equations is better.

The vertical-line test illustrates the visual difference between a set of ordered pairs that is a function and one that is not. Because graphs are not precise and not always complete, the vertical-line test might be inconclusive.

Domain and Range

A relation (or function) is a set of ordered pairs. The set of all first coordinates of the ordered pairs is the **domain** of the relation (or function). The set of all second coordinates of the ordered pairs is the **range** of the relation (or function). A function is a rule that pairs each member of the domain (the inputs) with a unique member of the range (the outputs). See Fig. 11.2. If a function is given as a table or a list of ordered pairs, then the domain and range are determined by simply reading them from the table or list. More often, a relation or function is given by an equation, with no domain stated. In this case, *the domain consists of all real numbers that, when substituted for the independent variable, produce real numbers for the dependent variable.*

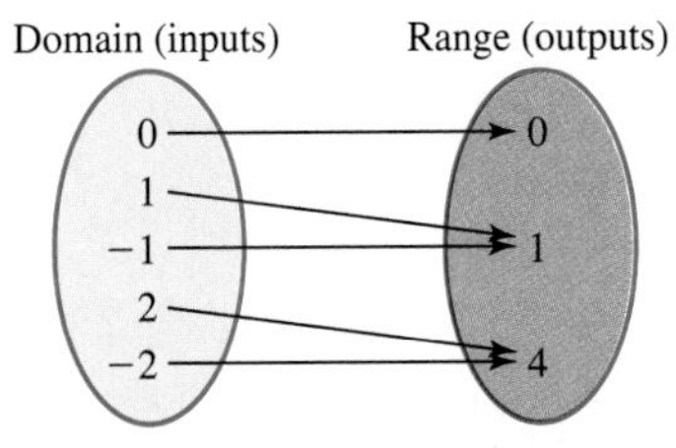

Figure 11.2

EXAMPLE 8

Identifying the domain and range

Determine the domain and range of each relation.

a) $\{(2, 5), (2, 7), (4, 3)\}$ b) $y = 2x$ c) $y = \sqrt{x - 1}$

Solution

a) The domain is the set of first coordinates, $\{2, 4\}$. The range is the set of second coordinates, $\{3, 5, 7\}$.

b) Since any real number can be used in place of x in $y = 2x$, the domain is $(-\infty, \infty)$. Since any real number can be used in place of y in $y = 2x$, the range is also $(-\infty, \infty)$.

c) Since the square root of a negative number is not a real number, we must have $x - 1 \geq 0$ or $x \geq 1$. So the domain is the interval $[1, \infty)$. Since the square root of a nonnegative real number is a nonnegative real number, we must have $y \geq 0$. So the range is the interval $[0, \infty)$.

Now do Exercises 75–86

Function Notation

If y is a function of x, we can use the notation $f(x)$ to represent y. The expression $f(x)$ is read as "f of x." The notation $f(x)$ is called **function notation.** So if x is the independent variable, then either y or $f(x)$ is the dependent variable. For example, the function $y = 2x + 3$ can be written as

$$f(x) = 2x + 3.$$

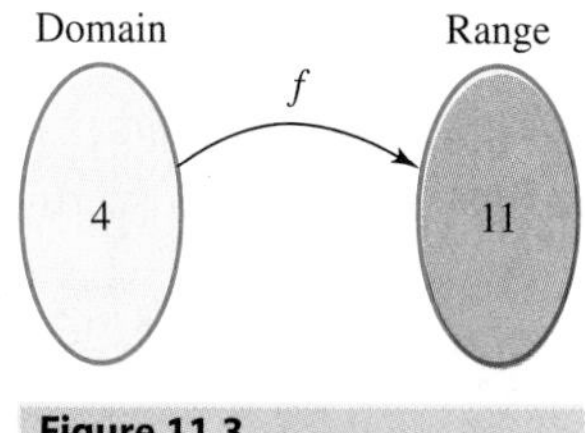

Figure 11.3

We use y and $f(x)$ interchangeably. We can think of f as the name of the function. We may use letters other than f. For example $g(x) = 2x + 3$ is the same function as $f(x) = 2x + 3$. The ordered pairs for each function are identical. Note that $f(x)$ does not mean f times x. The expression $f(x)$ represents the second coordinate when the first coordinate is x.

If $f(x) = 2x + 3$, then $f(4) = 2(4) + 3 = 11$. So the second coordinate is 11 if the first coordinate is 4. The ordered pair (4, 11) is an ordered pair in the function f. Figure 11.3 illustrates this situation.

EXAMPLE 9

Using function notation

Let $f(x) = 3x - 2$ and $g(x) = x^2 - x$. Evaluate each expression.

a) $f(-5)$ b) $g(-5)$ c) $f(0) + g(3)$

Solution

a) Replace x by -5 in the equation defining the function f:

$$\begin{aligned} f(x) &= 3x - 2 \\ f(-5) &= 3(-5) - 2 \\ &= -17 \end{aligned}$$

So $f(-5) = -17$.

b) Replace x by -5 in the equation defining the function g:

$$g(x) = x^2 - x$$
$$g(-5) = (-5)^2 - (-5) = 30$$

So $g(-5) = 30$.

c) Since $f(0) = 3(0) - 2 = -2$ and $g(3) = 3^2 - 3 = 6$, we have $f(0) + g(3) = -2 + 6 = 4$.

Now do Exercises 87–102

EXAMPLE 10

An application of function notation

To determine the cost of an in-home repair, a computer technician uses the linear function $C(n) = 40n + 30$, where n is the time in hours and $C(n)$ is the cost in dollars. Find $C(2)$ and $C(4)$.

Solution

Replace n with 2 to get

$$C(2) = 40(2) + 30 = 110.$$

Replace n with 4 to get

$$C(4) = 40(4) + 30 = 190.$$

So for 2 hours the cost is \$110 and for 4 hours the cost is \$190.

Now do Exercises 103–110

Calculator Close-Up

A graphing calculator has function notation built in. To find $C(2)$ and $C(4)$ with a graphing calculator, enter $y_1 = 40x + 30$ as shown here:

```
Plot1 Plot2 Plot3
\Y1■40X+30
\Y2=
\Y3=
\Y4=
\Y5=
\Y6=
\Y7=
```

To find $C(2)$ and $C(4)$, enter $y_1(2)$ and $y_1(4)$ as shown here:

```
Y1(2)
                110
Y1(4)
                190
```

In this section we studied functions of one variable. However, a variable can be a function of another variable or a function of many other variables. For example, your grade on the next test is not a function of the number of hours that you study for it. Your grade is a function of many variables: study time, sleep time, work time, your mother's IQ, and so on. Even though study time alone does not determine your grade, it is the variable that has the most influence on your grade.

Warm-Ups ▼

True or false? Explain your answer.

1. Any set of ordered pairs is a function. False
2. The circumference of a circle is a function of the diameter. True
3. The set $\{(1, 2), (3, 2), (5, 2)\}$ is a function. True
4. The set $\{(1, 5), (3, 6), (1, 7)\}$ is a function. False
5. The equation $y = x^2$ is a function. True
6. Every relation is a function. False

7. The domain of a relation is the set of first coordinates. True
8. The domain of a function is the set of second coordinates. False
9. The domain of $f(x) = \sqrt{x}$ is $[0, \infty)$. True
10. If $h(x) = x^2 - 3$, then $h(-2) = 1$. True

11.1 Exercises

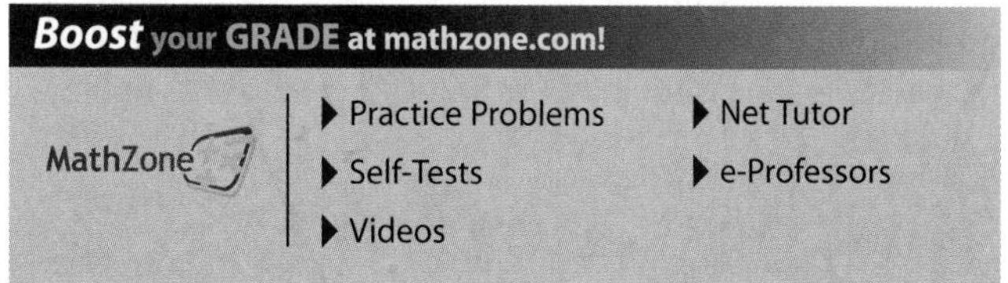

Reading and Writing *After reading this section, write out the answers to these questions. Use complete sentences.*

1. What does it mean to say that b is a function of a?
   It means that b is uniquely determined by a.
2. What is a function?
   A function is a set of ordered pairs in which no two pairs have the same first coordinate and different second coordinates.
3. What is a relation?
   A relation is any set of ordered pairs.
4. What is the domain of a relation?
   The domain of a relation is the set of all first coordinates.
5. What is the range of a relation?
   The range of a relation is the set of all second coordinates.
6. What is function notation?
   Function notation is the notation in which $f(x)$ is used in place of y for the dependent variable.

In each situation determine whether y is a function of x. Explain your answer. See Example 1.

7. Consider all gas stations in your area. Let x represent the price per gallon of regular unleaded gasoline and y represent the number of gallons that you can get for $10. Yes
8. Consider all items at Sears. Let x represent the universal product code for an item and y represent the price of that item. Yes
9. Consider all students taking algebra at your school. Let x represent the number of hours (to the nearest hour) a student spent studying for the first test and y represent the student's score on the test. No
10. Consider all students taking algebra at your school. Let x represent a student's height to the nearest inch and y represent the student's IQ. No
11. Consider the air temperature at noon today in every town in the United States. Let x represent the Celsius temperature for a town and y represent the Fahrenheit temperature. Yes
12. Consider all first-class letters mailed within the United States today. Let x represent the weight of a letter and y represent the amount of postage on the letter. Yes
13. Consider all items for sale at the nearest Wal-Mart. Let x represent the cost of an item and y represent the universal product code for the item. No
14. Consider all packages shipped by UPS. Let x represent the weight of a package and y represent the cost of shipping that package. No

Write a formula that describes the function. See Examples 2 and 3.

15. A small pizza costs $5.00 plus 50 cents for each topping. Express the total cost C as a function of the number of toppings t. $C = 0.50t + 5$
16. A developer prices condominiums in Florida at $20,000 plus $40 per square foot of living area. Express the cost C as a function of the number of square feet of living area s. $C = 40s + 20{,}000$
17. The sales tax rate on groceries in Mayberry is 9%. Express the total cost T (including tax) as a function of the total price of the groceries S. $T = 1.09S$
18. With a GM MasterCard, 5% of the amount charged is credited toward a rebate on the purchase of a new car. Express the rebate R as a function of the amount charged A. $R = 0.05A$
19. Express the circumference of a circle as a function of its radius. $C = 2\pi r$
20. Express the circumference of a circle as a function of its diameter. $C = \pi d$
21. Express the perimeter P of a square as a function of the length s of a side. $P = 4s$
22. Express the perimeter P of a rectangle with width 10 ft as a function of its length L. $P = 2L + 20$

23. Express the area A of a triangle with a base of 10 m as a function of its height h. $A = 5h$

24. Express the area A of a trapezoid with bases 12 cm and 10 cm as a function of its height h. $A = 11h$

Determine whether each table expresses the second variable as a function of the first variable. See Example 4.

25. Yes

x	y
1	1
4	2
9	3
16	4
25	5
36	6
49	8

26. Yes

x	y
2	4
3	9
4	16
5	25
8	36
9	49
10	100

27. Yes

t	v
2	2
−2	2
3	3
−3	3
4	4
−4	4
5	5

28. Yes

s	W
5	17
6	17
−1	17
−2	17
−3	17
7	17
8	17

29. No

a	P
2	2
2	−2
3	3
3	−3
4	4
4	−4
5	5

30. No

n	r
17	5
17	6
17	−1
17	−2
17	−3
17	−4
17	−5

31. Yes

b	q
1970	0.14
1972	0.18
1974	0.18
1976	0.22
1978	0.25
1980	0.28

32. Yes

c	h
345	0.3
350	0.4
355	0.5
360	0.6
365	0.7
370	0.8
380	0.9

Determine whether each relation is a function. See Example 5.

33. $\{(2, 4), (3, 4), (4, 5)\}$ Yes

34. $\{(2, -5), (2, 5), (3, 10)\}$ No

35. $\{(-2, 4), (-2, 6), (3, 6)\}$ No

36. $\{(3, 6), (6, 3)\}$ Yes

37. $\{(\pi, -1), (\pi, 1)\}$ No

38. $\{(-0.3, -0.3), (-0.2, 0), (-0.3, 1)\}$ No

39. $\left\{\left(\frac{1}{2}, \frac{1}{2}\right)\right\}$ Yes

40. $\left\{\left(\frac{1}{3}, 7\right), \left(-\frac{1}{3}, 7\right), \left(\frac{1}{6}, 7\right)\right\}$ Yes

Find two ordered pairs that satisfy each equation and have the same x-coordinate but different y-coordinates. Answers may vary. See Example 6.

41. $x = 2y^2$ $(2, 1), (2, -1)$

42. $x^2 = y^2$ $(3, 3), (3, -3)$

43. $x = |2y|$ $(8, 4), (8, -4)$

44. $|x| = |y|$ $(1, 1), (1, -1)$

45. $x^2 + y^2 = 1$ $(0, 1), (0, -1)$

46. $x^2 + y^2 = 4$ $(0, 2), (0, -2)$

47. $x = y^4$ $(16, 2), (16, -2)$

48. $x^4 = y^4$ $(1, 1), (1, -1)$

49. $x - 2 = |y|$ $(3, 1), (3, -1)$

50. $x + 5 = |y|$ $(-4, 1), (-4, -1)$

Determine whether each relation is a function. See Example 6.

51. $y = x^2$ Yes

52. $y = x^2 + 3$ Yes

53. $x = |y| + 1$ No

54. $|x| = |y + 1|$ No

55. $y = x$ Yes

56. $x = y + 4$ Yes

57. $x = y^4 + 1$ No

58. $x^4 = y^2$ No

59. $y = \sqrt{x}$ Yes

60. $x = \sqrt{y}$ Yes

61. $|x| = |2y|$ No

62. $|4x| = |2y|$ No

63. $x^2 + y^2 = 9$ No

64. $x^2 + y^4 = 1$ No

65. $x = 2\sqrt{y}$ Yes

66. $y = \sqrt{x - 5}$ Yes

67. $x + 5 = |y|$ No

68. $x - 2 = |y|$ No

Use the vertical-line test to determine which of the graphs are graphs of functions. See Example 7.

69.

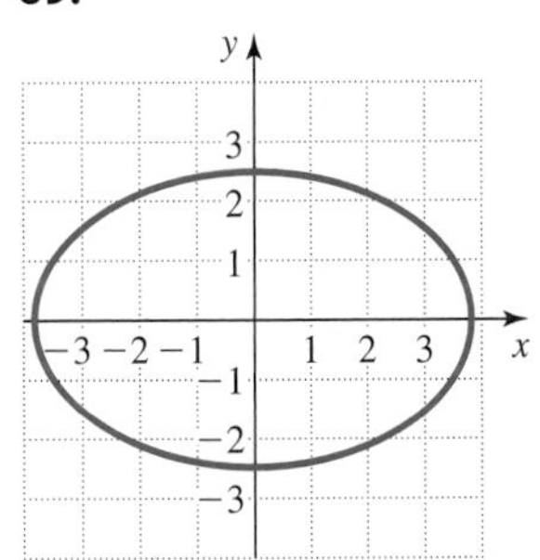

No

70.

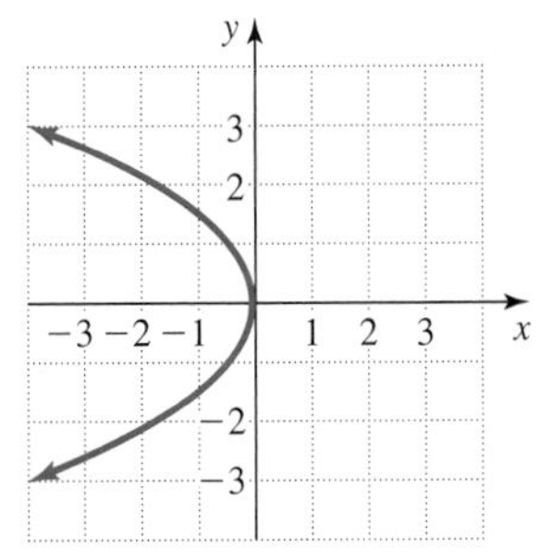

No

71.

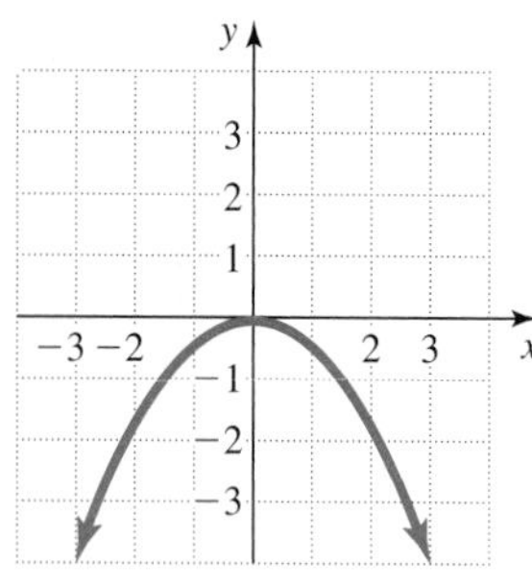

Yes

72.

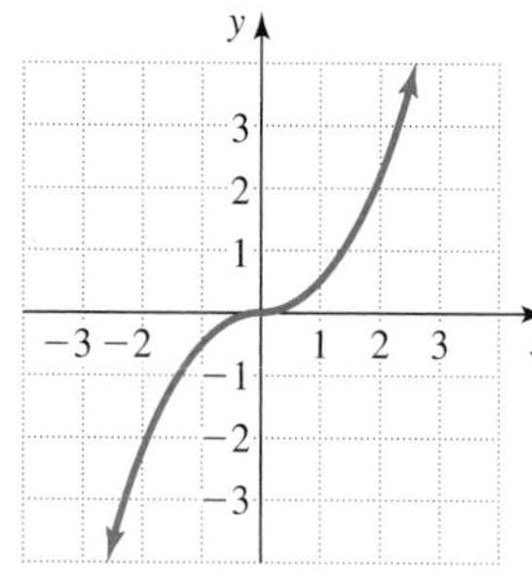

Yes

73.

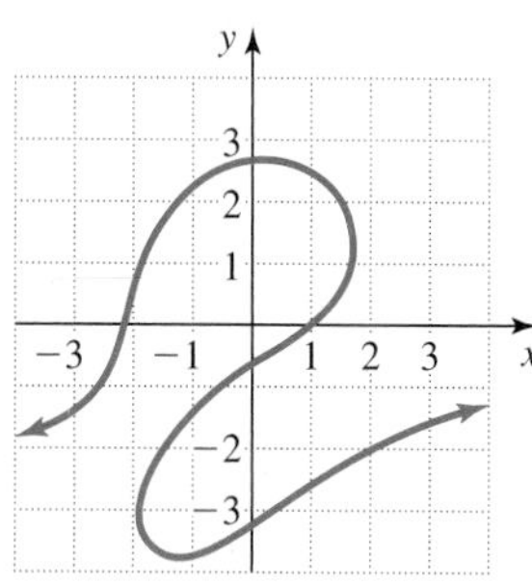

No

74.

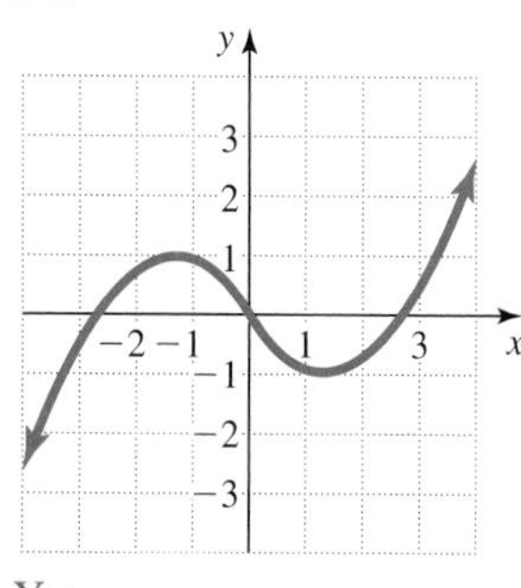

Yes

Determine the domain and range of each relation. See Example 8.

75. $\{(4, 1), (7, 1)\}$ $\{4, 7\}, \{1\}$
76. $\{(0, 2), (3, 5)\}$ $\{0, 3\}, \{2, 5\}$
77. $\{(2, 3), (2, 5), (2, 7)\}$ $\{2\}, \{3, 5, 7\}$
78. $\{(3, 1), (5, 1), (4, 1)\}$ $\{3, 4, 5\}, \{1\}$
79. $y = x + 1$ $(-\infty, \infty), (-\infty, \infty)$
80. $y = 3x + 1$ $(-\infty, \infty), (-\infty, \infty)$
81. $y = 5 - x$ $(-\infty, \infty), (-\infty, \infty)$
82. $y = -2x + 1$ $(-\infty, \infty), (-\infty, \infty)$
83. $y = \sqrt{x - 2}$ $[2, \infty), [0, \infty)$
84. $y = \sqrt{x + 4}$ $[-4, \infty), [0, \infty)$
85. $y = \sqrt{2x}$ $[0, \infty), [0, \infty)$
86. $y = \sqrt{2x - 4}$ $[2, \infty), [0, \infty)$

Let $f(x) = 3x - 2$, $g(x) = -x^2 + 3x - 2$, and $h(x) = |x + 2|$. Evaluate each expression. See Example 9.

87. $f(0)$ -2
88. $f(1)$ 1
89. $f(4)$ 10
90. $f(100)$ 298
91. $g(-2)$ -12
92. $g(-3)$ -20
93. $h(-3)$ 1
94. $h(-19)$ 17
95. $h(-4.236)$ 2.236
96. $h(-1.99)$ 0.01
97. $f(2) + g(3)$ 2
98. $f(1) - g(0)$ 3
99. $\dfrac{g(2)}{h(-3)}$ 0
100. $\dfrac{h(-10)}{f(2)}$ 2
101. $f(-1) \cdot h(-4)$ -10
102. $h(0) \cdot g(0)$ -4

Solve each problem. See Example 10.

103. ***Height.*** If a ball is dropped from the top of a 256 ft building, then the formula

$$h(t) = 256 - 16t^2$$

expresses its height $h(t)$ in feet as a function of the time t in seconds.

a) Find $h(2)$, the height of the ball 2 seconds after it is dropped. 192 ft
b) Find $h(4)$. 0 ft

104. ***Velocity.*** If a ball is dropped from a height of 256 ft, then the formula

$$v(t) = -32t$$

expresses its velocity $v(t)$ in feet per second as a function of time t in seconds.

a) Find $v(0)$, the velocity of the ball at time $t = 0$. 0 ft/sec
b) Find $v(4)$. -128 ft/sec

105. ***Area of a square.*** Find a formula that expresses the area of a square A as a function of the length of its side s. $A = s^2$ or $A(s) = s^2$

106. ***Perimeter of a square.*** Find a formula that expresses the perimeter of a square P as a function of the length of its side s. $P = 4s$ or $P(s) = 4s$

107. ***Cost of fabric.*** If a certain fabric is priced at \$3.98 per yard, express the cost $C(x)$ as a function of the number of yards x. Find $C(3)$. $C(x) = 3.98x$, \$11.94

108. ***Earned income.*** If Mildred earns \$14.50 per hour, express her total pay $P(h)$ as a function of the number of hours worked h. Find $P(40)$. $P(h) = 14.50h$, \$580

109. ***Cost of pizza.*** A pizza parlor charges \$14.95 for a pizza plus \$0.50 for each topping. Express the total cost of a pizza $C(n)$ in dollars as a function of the number of toppings n. Find $C(6)$. $C(n) = 14.95 + 0.50n$, \$17.95

110. ***Cost of gravel.*** A gravel dealer charges \$50 plus \$30 per cubic yard for delivering a truckload of gravel. Express the total cost $C(n)$ in dollars as a function of the number of cubic yards delivered n. Find $C(12)$. $C(n) = 30n + 50$, \$410

Getting More Involved

111. ***Writing***

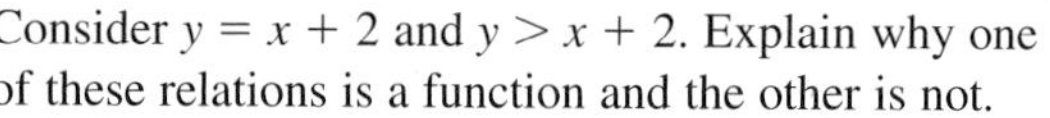

Consider $y = x + 2$ and $y > x + 2$. Explain why one of these relations is a function and the other is not.

112. ***Writing***

Consider the graphs of $y = 2$ and $x = 3$ in the rectangular coordinate system. Explain why one of these relations is a function and the other is not.

11.2 Graphs of Functions and Relations

In this Section

- Linear and Constant Functions
- Absolute Value Functions
- Quadratic Functions
- Square-Root Functions
- Graphing Relations

Functions were introduced in Section 11.1. In this section we will study the graphs of several types of functions. We graphed linear functions in Chapter 3 and quadratic functions in Chapter 10, but for completeness we will review them here.

Linear and Constant Functions

Linear functions get their name from the fact that their graphs are straight lines.

Linear Function

A **linear function** is a function of the form

$$f(x) = mx + b,$$

where m and b are real numbers with $m \neq 0$.

The graph of the linear function $f(x) = mx + b$ is exactly the same as the graph of the linear equation $y = mx + b$. If $m = 0$, then we get $f(x) = b$, which is called a **constant function.** If $m = 1$ and $b = 0$, then we get the function $f(x) = x$, which is called the **identity function.** When we graph a function given in function notation, we usually label the vertical axis as $f(x)$ rather than y.

EXAMPLE 1

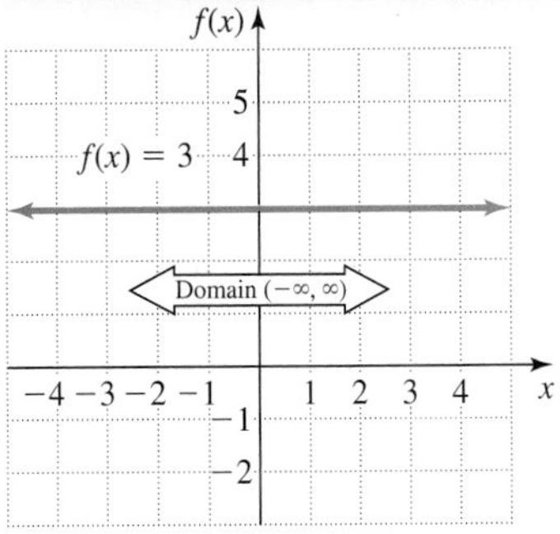

Graphing a constant function

Graph $f(x) = 3$ and state the domain and range.

Solution

The graph of $f(x) = 3$ is the same as the graph of $y = 3$, which is the horizontal line in Fig. 11.4. Since any real number can be used for x in $f(x) = 3$ and since the line in Fig. 11.4 extends without bounds to the left and right, the domain is the set of all real numbers, $(-\infty, \infty)$. Since the only y-coordinate for $f(x) = 3$ is 3, the range is $\{3\}$.

Figure 11.4

Now do Exercises 7–8

The domain and range of a function can be determined from the formula or the graph. However, the graph is usually very helpful for understanding domain and range.

EXAMPLE 2

Graphing a linear function

Graph the function $f(x) = 3x - 4$ and state the domain and range.

Solution

The y-intercept is $(0, -4)$ and the slope of the line is 3. We can use the y-intercept and the slope to draw the graph in Fig. 11.5. Since any real number can be used for x in $f(x) = 3x - 4$, and since the line in Fig. 11.5 extends without bounds to the left and right, the domain is the set of all real numbers, $(-\infty, \infty)$. Since the graph extends without bounds upward and downward, the range is the set of all real numbers, $(-\infty, \infty)$.

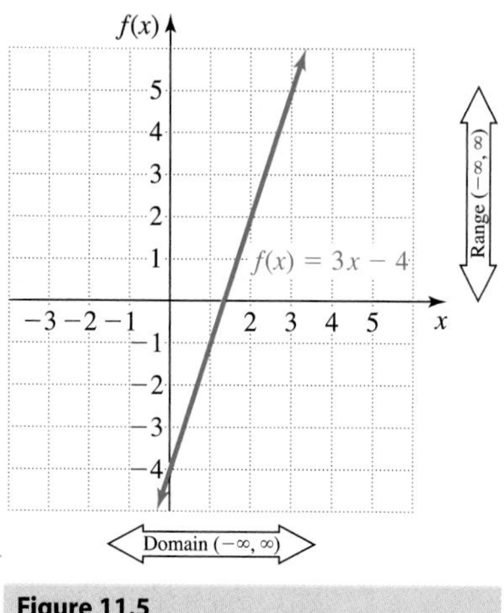

Figure 11.5

Now do Exercises 9–16

Teaching Tip In this section students should be graphing by simply plotting points. In the next section we will discuss transformations and make generalizations.

Absolute Value Functions

The equation $y = |x|$ defines a function because every value of x determines a unique value of y. We call this function the absolute value function.

Absolute Value Function

The **absolute value function** is the function defined by

$$f(x) = |x|.$$

To graph the absolute value function, we simply plot enough ordered pairs of the function to see what the graph looks like.

EXAMPLE 3

The absolute value function

Graph $f(x) = |x|$ and state the domain and range.

Solution

To graph this function, we find points that satisfy the equation $f(x) = |x|$.

x	-2	-1	0	1	2
$f(x) = \|x\|$	2	1	0	1	2

Plotting these points, we see that they lie along the V-shaped graph shown in Fig. 11.6 on the next page. Since any real number can be used for x in $f(x) = |x|$ and since the graph extends without bounds to the left and right, the domain is $(-\infty, \infty)$.

Helpful Hint

The most important feature of an absolute value function is its V-shape. If we had plotted only points in the first quadrant, we would not have seen the V-shape. So for an absolute value function we always plot enough points to see the V-shape.

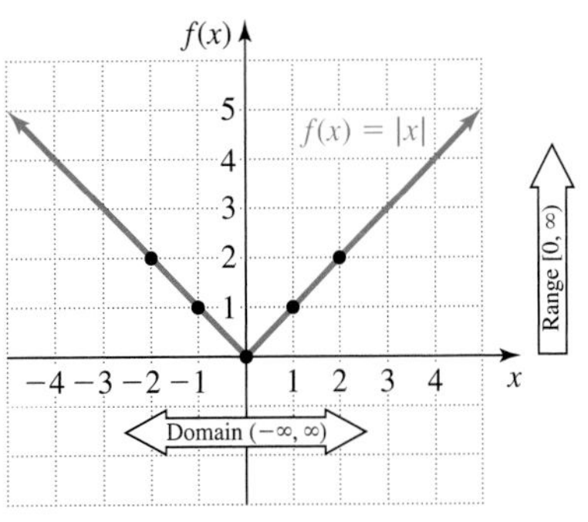

Figure 11.6

Because the graph does not go below the x-axis and because $|x|$ is never negative, the range is the set of nonnegative real numbers, $[0, \infty)$.

Now do Exercises 17–18

Many functions involving absolute value have graphs that are V-shaped, as in Fig. 11.6. To graph functions involving absolute value, we must choose points that determine the correct shape and location of the V-shaped graph.

EXAMPLE 4

Other functions involving absolute value

Graph each function and state the domain and range.

a) $f(x) = |x| - 2$ **b)** $g(x) = |2x - 6|$

Solution

a) Choose values for x and find $f(x)$.

x	-2	-1	0	1	2
$f(x) = \lvert x \rvert - 2$	0	-1	-2	-1	0

Plot these points and draw a V-shaped graph through them as shown in Fig. 11.7. The domain is $(-\infty, \infty)$, and the range is $[-2, \infty)$.

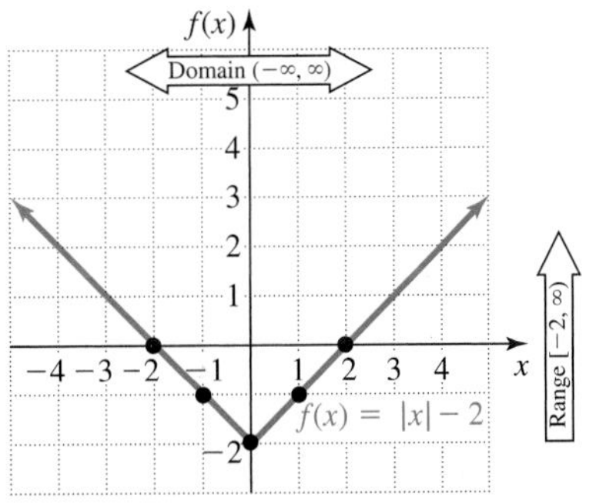

Figure 11.7

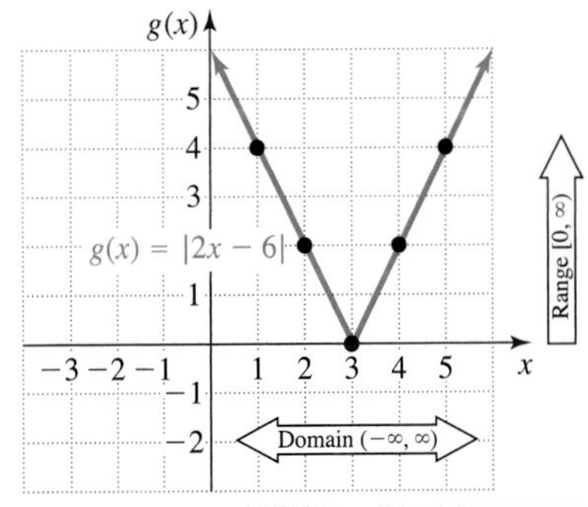

Figure 11.8

Calculator Close-Up

To check Example 4(a) set

$$y_1 = \text{abs}(x) - 2$$

and then press GRAPH.

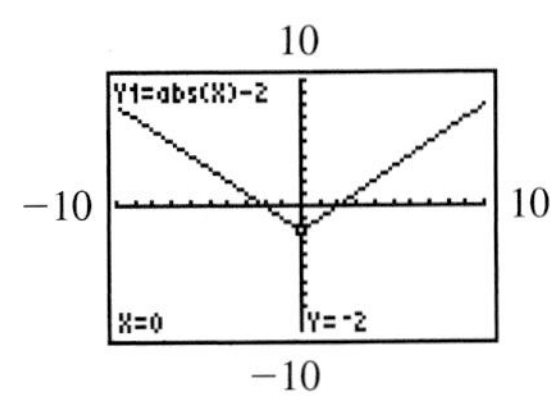

To check Example 4(b) set

$$y_2 = \text{abs}(2x - 6)$$

and then press GRAPH.

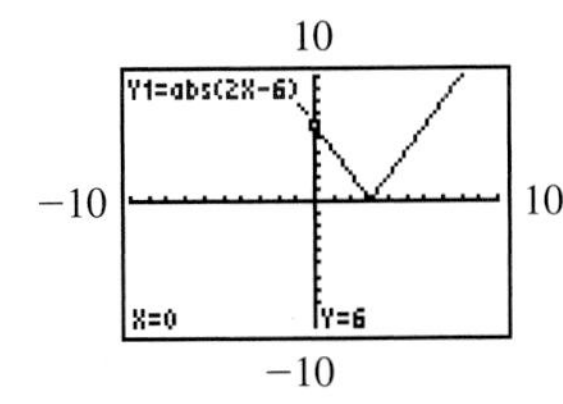

b) Make a table of values for x and $g(x)$.

x	1	2	3	4	5
$g(x) = \|2x - 6\|$	4	2	0	2	4

Draw the graph as shown in Fig. 11.8. The domain is $(-\infty, \infty)$, and the range is $[0, \infty)$.

Now do Exercises 19–26

Quadratic Functions

A function defined by a second-degree polynomial is a *quadratic function.*

Quadratic Function

A **quadratic function** is a function of the form

$$f(x) = ax^2 + bx + c,$$

where a, b, and c are real numbers, with $a \neq 0$.

In Chapter 10 we learned that the graph of any quadratic function is a parabola, which opens upward or downward. The vertex of a parabola is the lowest point on a parabola that opens upward or the highest point on a parabola that opens downward. Parabolas will be discussed again when we study conic sections later in this text.

EXAMPLE 5

A quadratic function

Graph the function $g(x) = 4 - x^2$ and state the domain and range.

Solution

We plot enough points to get the correct shape of the graph.

x	−2	−1	0	1	2
$g(x) = 4 - x^2$	0	3	4	3	0

See Fig. 11.9 for the graph. The domain is $(-\infty, \infty)$. From the graph we see that the largest y-coordinate is 4. So the range is $(-\infty, 4]$.

Figure 11.9

Now do Exercises 27–34

Calculator Close-Up

You can find the vertex of a parabola with a calculator. For example, graph

$$y = -x^2 - x + 2.$$

Then use the maximum feature, which is found in the CALC menu. For the left bound pick a point to the left of the vertex; for the right bound pick a point to the right of the vertex; and for the guess pick a point near the vertex.

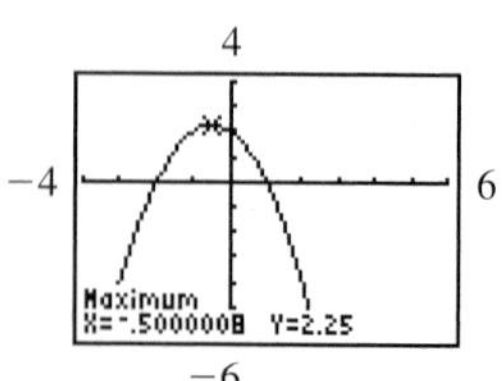

Square-Root Functions

Functions involving square roots typically have graphs that look like half a parabola.

Square-Root Function

The **square-root function** is the function defined by

$$f(x) = \sqrt{x}.$$

EXAMPLE 6

Square-root functions

Graph each equation and state the domain and range.

a) $y = \sqrt{x}$ **b)** $y = \sqrt{x + 3}$

Solution

a) The graph of the equation $y = \sqrt{x}$ and the graph of the function $f(x) = \sqrt{x}$ are the same. Because $\sqrt{x}$ is a real number only if $x \geq 0$, the domain of this function is the set of nonnegative real numbers. The following ordered pairs are on the graph:

x	0	1	4	9
$y = \sqrt{x}$	0	1	2	3

The graph goes through these ordered pairs as shown in Fig. 11.10. Note that x is chosen from the nonnegative numbers. The domain is $[0, \infty)$ and the range is $[0, \infty)$.

b) Note that $\sqrt{x + 3}$ is a real number only if $x + 3 \geq 0$, or $x \geq -3$. So we make a table of ordered pairs in which $x \geq -3$:

x	-3	-2	1	6
$y = \sqrt{x + 3}$	0	1	2	3

The graph goes through these ordered pairs as shown in Fig. 11.11. The domain is $[-3, \infty)$ and the range is $[0, \infty)$.

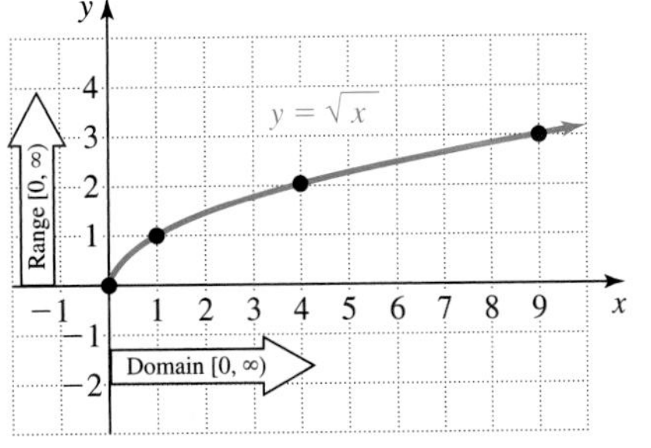

Figure 11.10

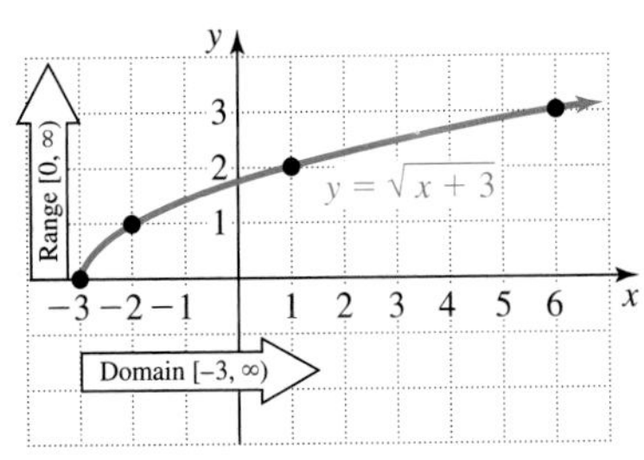

Figure 11.11

Now do Exercises 35–42

Graphing Relations

A function is a set of ordered pairs in which no two have the same first coordinate and different second coordinates. A relation is any set of ordered pairs. The domain of a relation is the set of x-coordinates of the ordered pairs and the range of a relation is the set of y-coordinates of the ordered pairs. In Example 7 we graph the relation $x = y^2$. Note that this relation is not a function because ordered pairs such as (4, 2) and (4, −2) satisfy $x = y^2$.

EXAMPLE 7

Graphing relations that are not functions

Graph each relation and state the domain and range.

a) $x = y^2$

b) $x = |y - 3|$

Solution

a) Because the equation $x = y^2$ expresses x in terms of y, it is easier to choose the y-coordinate first and then find the x-coordinate:

$x = y^2$	4	1	0	1	4
y	−2	−1	0	1	2

Figure 11.12 shows the graph. The domain is $[0, \infty)$ and the range is $(-\infty, \infty)$.

b) Again we select values for y first and find the corresponding x-coordinates:

$x = \|y - 3\|$	2	1	0	1	2
y	1	2	3	4	5

Plot these points as shown in Fig. 11.13. The domain is $[0, \infty)$ and the range is $(-\infty, \infty)$.

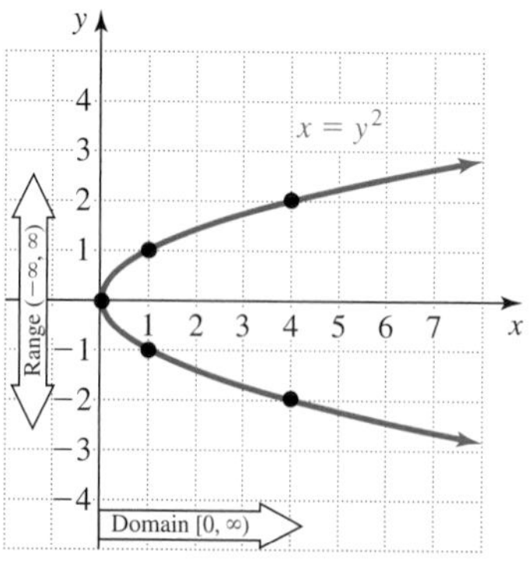

Figure 11.12

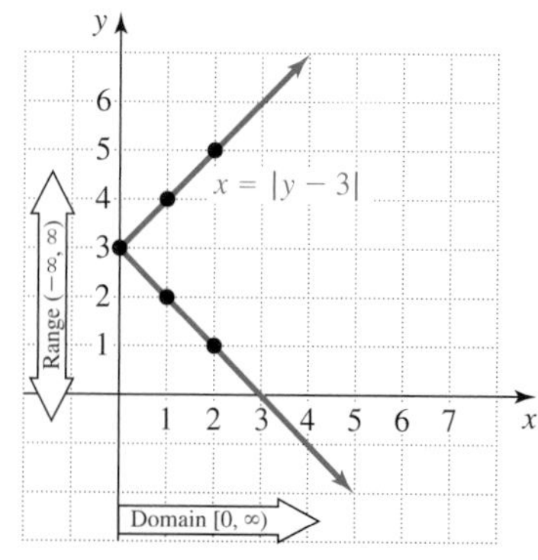

Figure 11.13

Now do Exercises 43–54

Warm-Ups ▼

True or false? Explain your answer.

1. The graph of a function is a picture of all ordered pairs of the function. True
2. The graph of every linear function is a straight line. True
3. The absolute value function has a V-shaped graph. True
4. The domain of $f(x) = 3$ is $(-\infty, \infty)$. True
5. The graph of a quadratic function is a parabola. True
6. The range of any quadratic function is $(-\infty, \infty)$. False
7. The y-axis and the $f(x)$-axis are the same. True
8. The domain of $x = y^2$ is $[0, \infty)$. True
9. The domain of $f(x) = \sqrt{x - 1}$ is $(1, \infty)$. False
10. The domain of any quadratic function is $(-\infty, \infty)$. True

11.2 Exercises

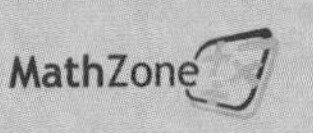

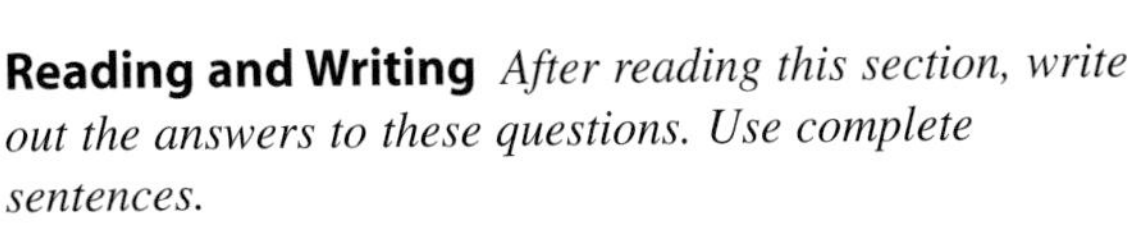

Reading and Writing *After reading this section, write out the answers to these questions. Use complete sentences.*

1. What is a linear function?
   A linear function is a function of the form $f(x) = mx + b$, where m and b are real numbers with $m \neq 0$.
2. What is a constant function?
   A constant function is a function of the form $f(x) = k$, where k is a real number.
3. What is the graph of a constant function?
   The graph of a constant function is a horizontal line.
4. What shape is the graph of an absolute value function?
   The absolute value function has a V-shaped graph.
5. What is the graph of quadratic function called?
   The graph of a quadratic function is a parabola.
6. What is the identity function?
   The identity function is $f(x) = x$.

Graph each function and state its domain and range. See Examples 1 and 2.

7. $h(x) = -2$
   $(-\infty, \infty)$, $\{-2\}$

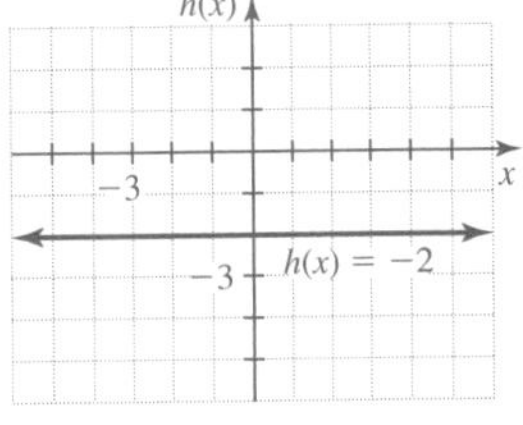

8. $f(x) = 4$
   $(-\infty, \infty)$, $\{4\}$

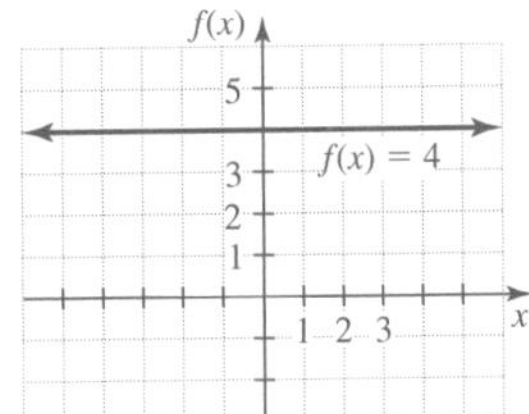

9. $f(x) = 2x - 1$
   $(-\infty, \infty)$, $(-\infty, \infty)$

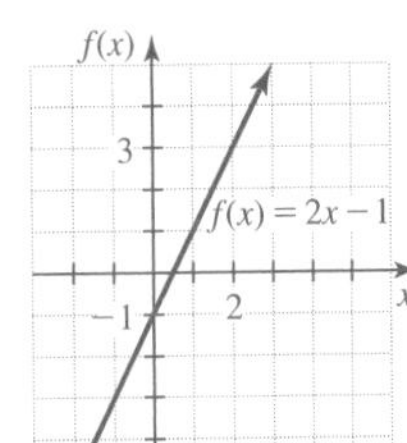

10. $g(x) = x + 2$
    $(-\infty, \infty)$, $(-\infty, \infty)$

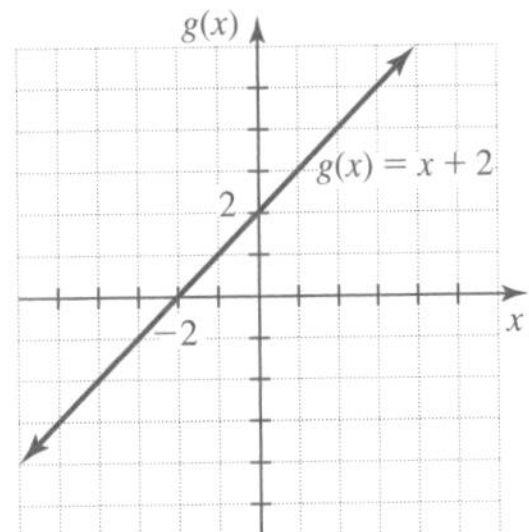

11. $g(x) = \frac{1}{2}x + 2$

$(-\infty, \infty), (-\infty, \infty)$

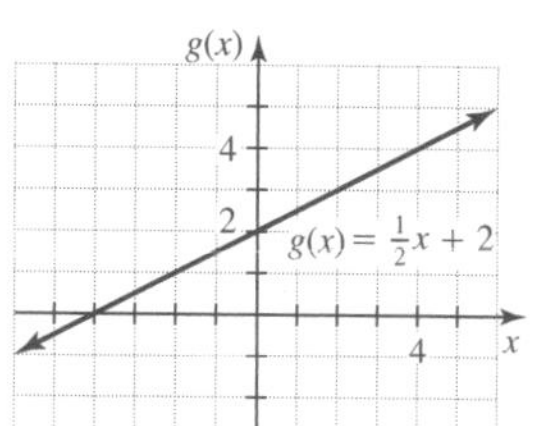

12. $h(x) = \frac{2}{3}x - 4$

$(-\infty, \infty), (-\infty, \infty)$

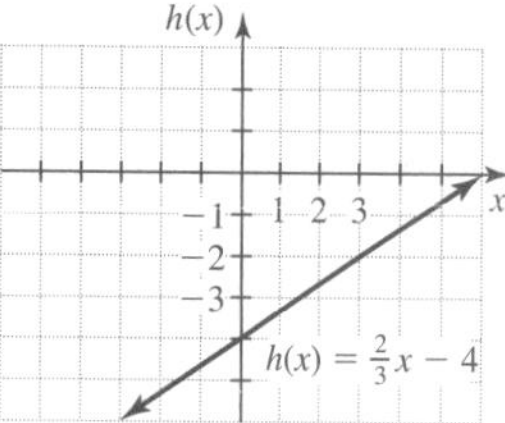

19. $h(x) = |x + 1|$

$(-\infty, \infty), [0, \infty)$

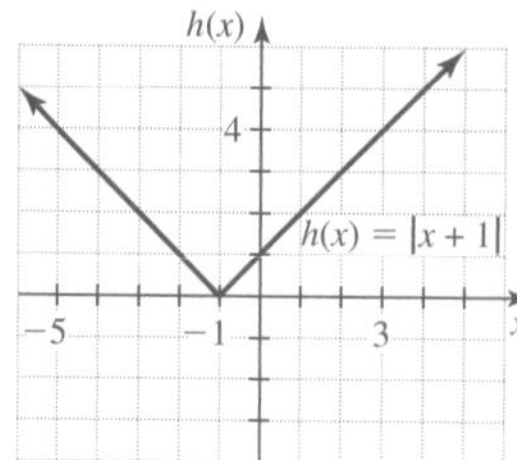

20. $f(x) = |x - 2|$

$(-\infty, \infty), [0, \infty)$

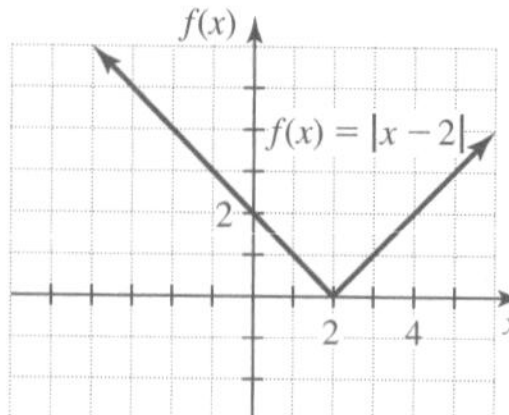

13. $y = -\frac{2}{3}x + 3$

$(-\infty, \infty), (-\infty, \infty)$

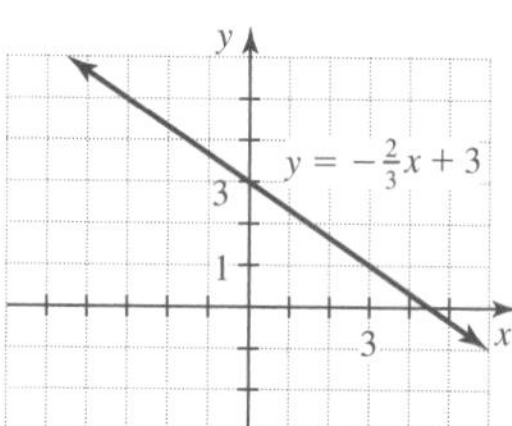

14. $y = -\frac{3}{4}x + 4$

$(-\infty, \infty), (-\infty, \infty)$

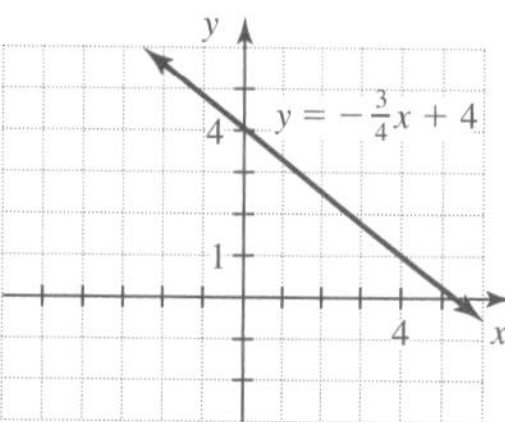

21. $g(x) = |3x|$

$(-\infty, \infty), [0, \infty)$

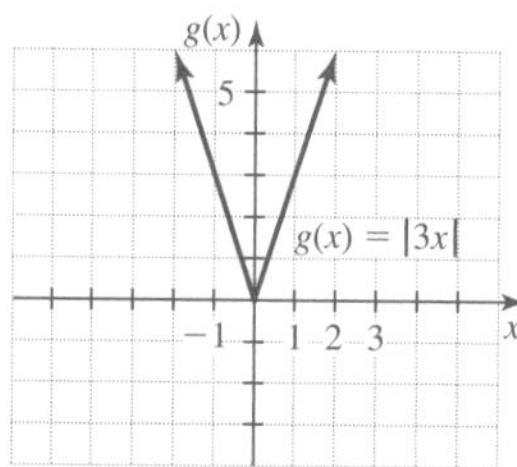

22. $h(x) = |-2x|$

$(-\infty, \infty), [0, \infty)$

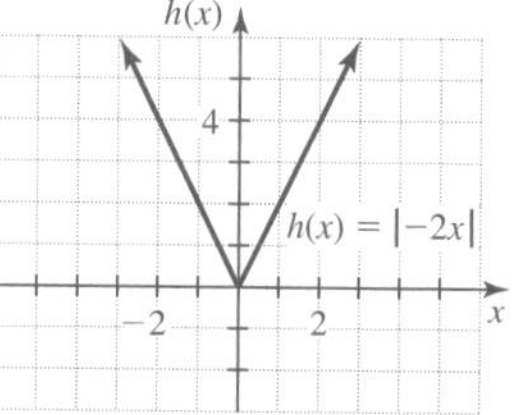

15. $y = -0.3x + 6.5$

$(-\infty, \infty), (-\infty, \infty)$

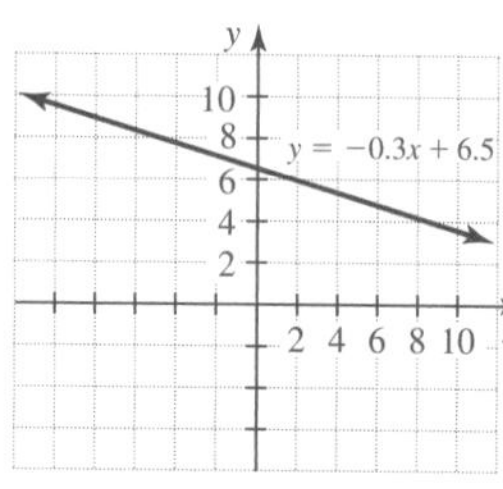

16. $y = 0.25x - 0.5$

$(-\infty, \infty), (-\infty, \infty)$

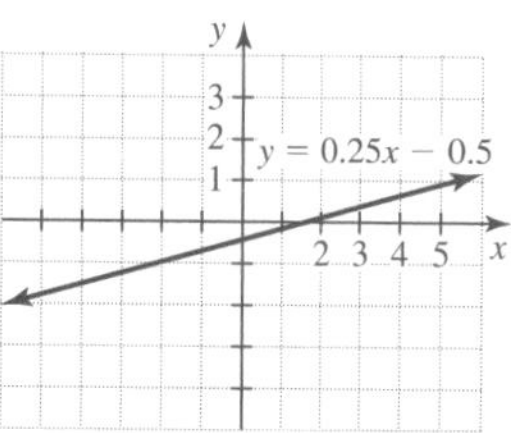

23. $f(x) = |2x - 1|$

$(-\infty, \infty), [0, \infty)$

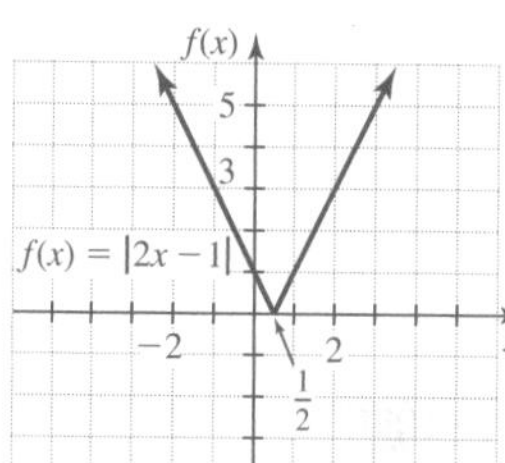

24. $y = |2x - 3|$

$(-\infty, \infty), [0, \infty)$

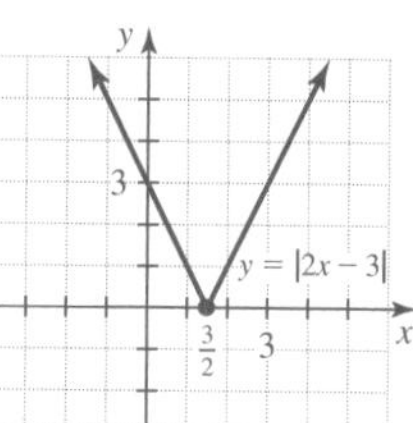

Graph each absolute value function and state its domain and range. See Examples 3 and 4.

17. $f(x) = |x| + 1$

$(-\infty, \infty), [1, \infty)$

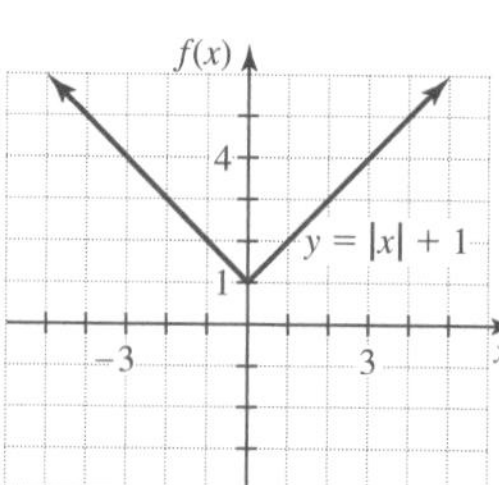

18. $g(x) = |x| - 3$

$(-\infty, \infty), [-3, \infty)$

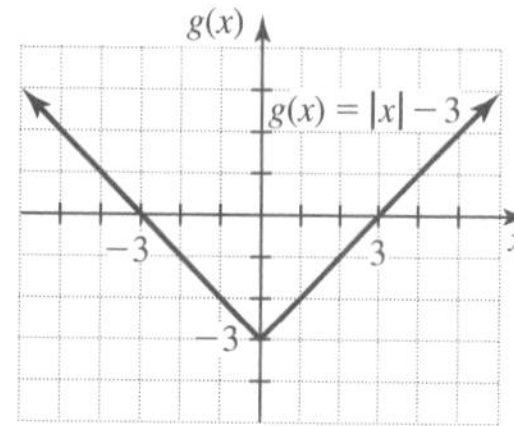

25. $f(x) = |x - 2| + 1$

$(-\infty, \infty), [1, \infty)$

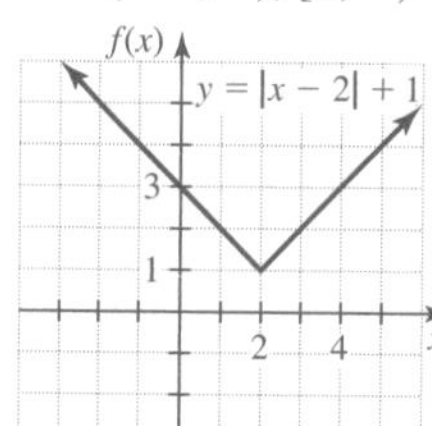

26. $y = |x - 1| + 2$

$(-\infty, \infty), [2, \infty)$

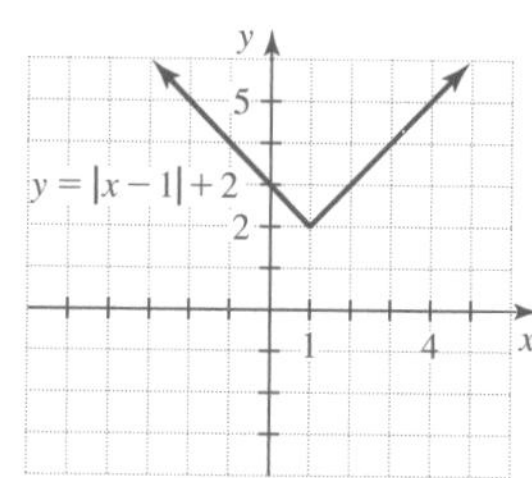

Graph each quadratic function and state its domain and range. See Example 5.

27. $y = x^2$

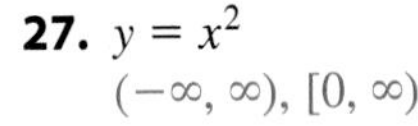

$(-\infty, \infty)$, $[0, \infty)$

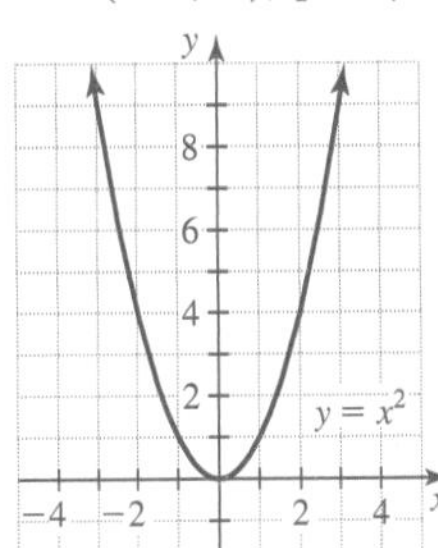

28. $y = -x^2$

$(-\infty, \infty)$, $(-\infty, 0]$

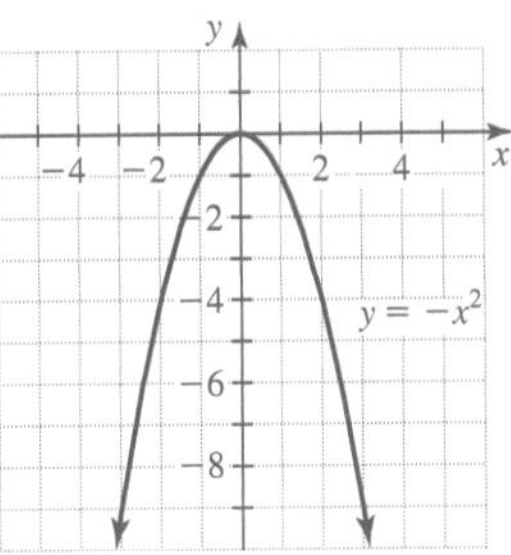

29. $g(x) = x^2 + 2$

$(-\infty, \infty)$, $[2, \infty)$

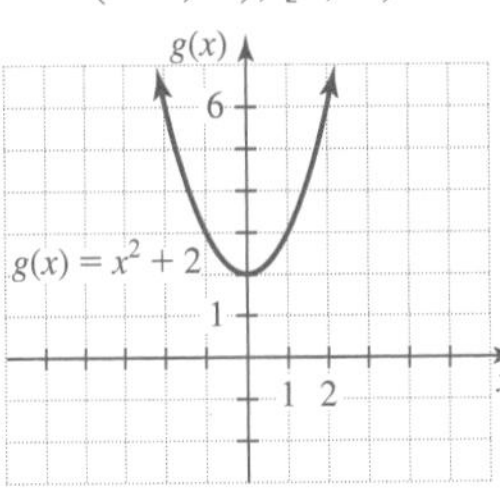

30. $f(x) = x^2 - 4$

$(-\infty, \infty)$, $[-4, \infty)$

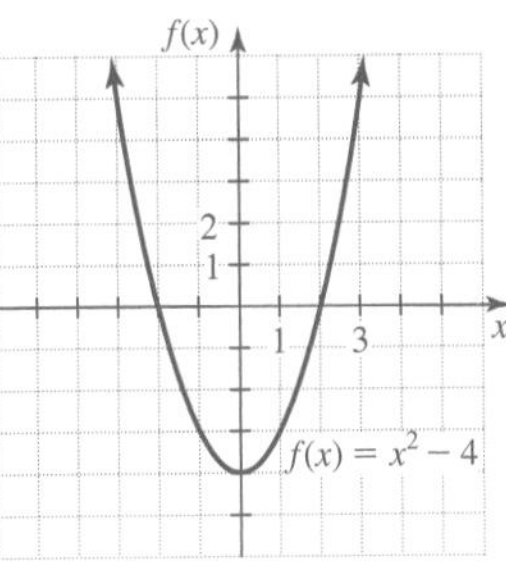

31. $f(x) = 2x^2$

$(-\infty, \infty)$, $[0, \infty)$

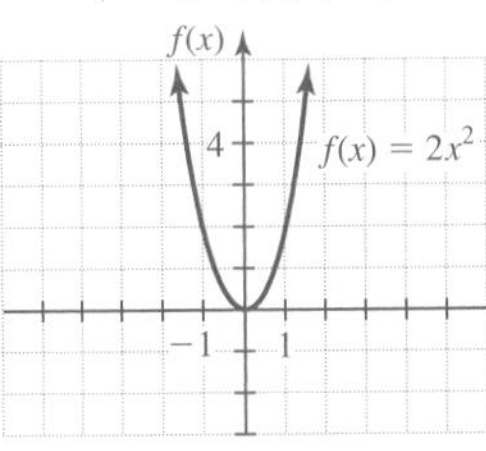

32. $h(x) = -3x^2$

$(-\infty, \infty)$, $(-\infty, 0]$

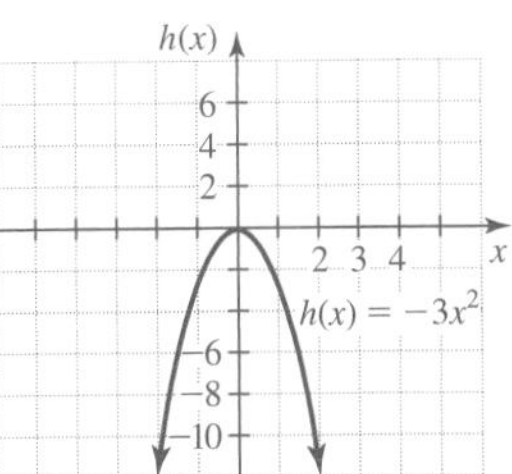

33. $y = 6 - x^2$

$(-\infty, \infty)$, $(-\infty, 6]$

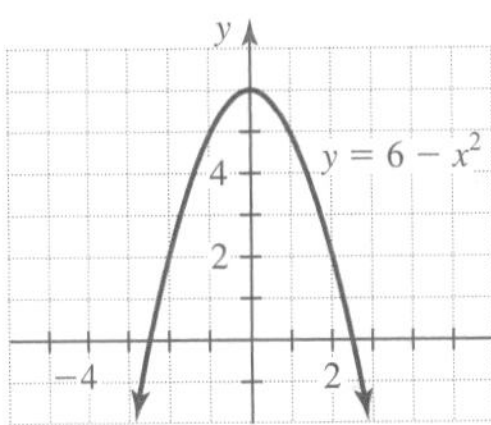

34. $y = -2x^2 + 3$

$(-\infty, \infty)$, $(-\infty, 3]$

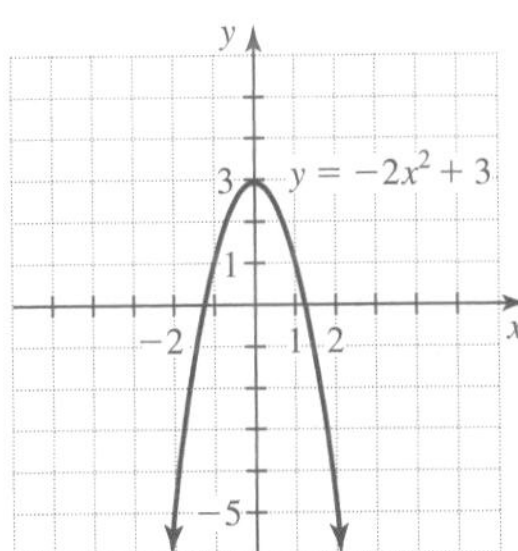

Graph each square-root function and state its domain and range. See Example 6.

35. $g(x) = 2\sqrt{x}$

$[0, \infty)$, $[0, \infty)$

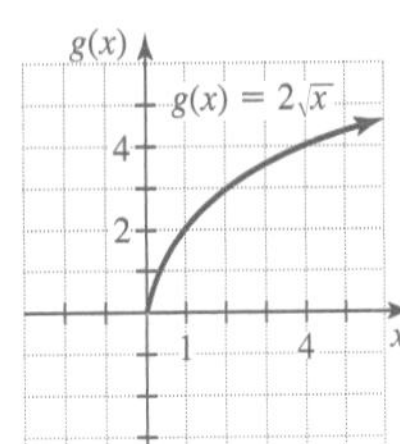

36. $g(x) = \sqrt{x} - 1$

$[0, \infty)$, $[-1, \infty)$

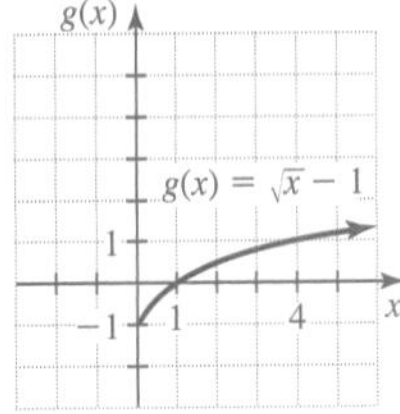

37. $f(x) = \sqrt{x - 1}$

$[1, \infty)$, $[0, \infty)$

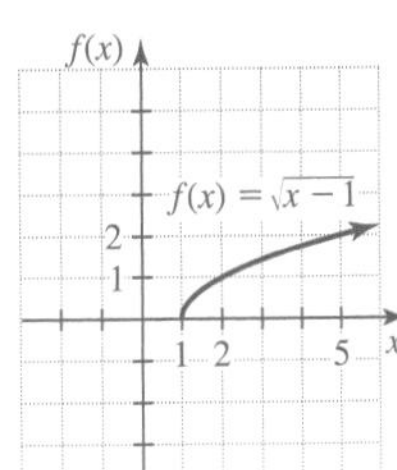

38. $f(x) = \sqrt{x + 1}$

$[-1, \infty)$, $[0, \infty)$

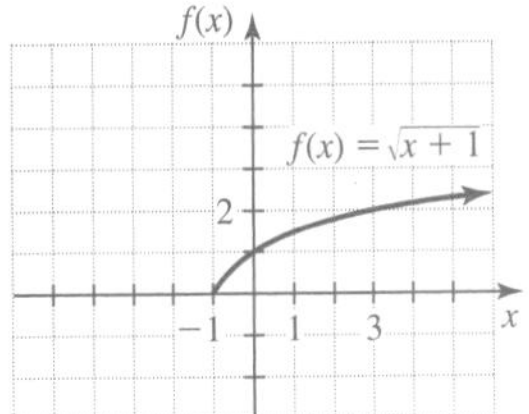

39. $h(x) = -\sqrt{x}$

$[0, \infty)$, $(-\infty, 0]$

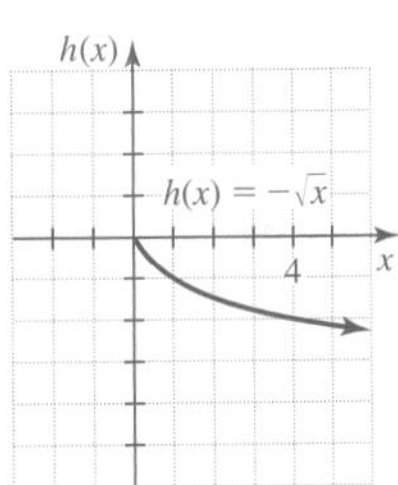

40. $h(x) = -\sqrt{x - 1}$

$[1, \infty)$, $(-\infty, 0]$

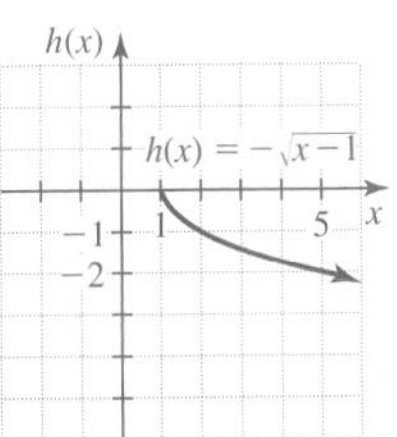

41. $y = \sqrt{x} + 2$

$[0, \infty)$, $[2, \infty)$

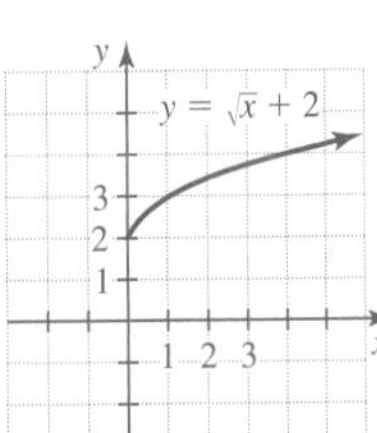

42. $y = 2\sqrt{x} + 1$

$[0, \infty)$, $[1, \infty)$

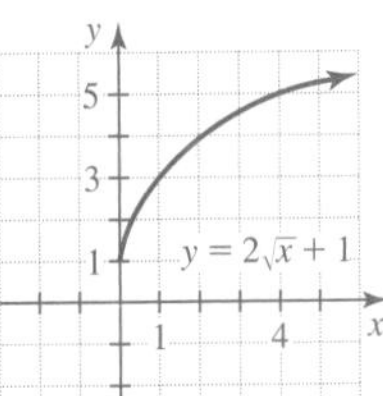

Graph each relation and state its domain and range. See Example 7.

43. $x = |y|$
$[0, \infty), (-\infty, \infty)$

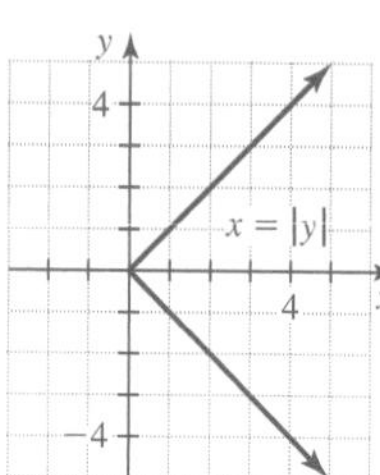

44. $x = -|y|$
$(-\infty, 0], (-\infty, \infty)$

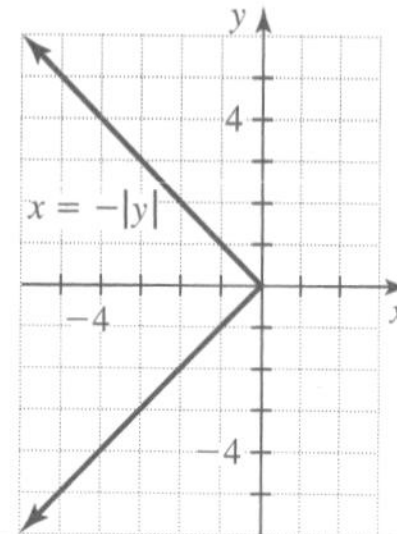

45. $x = -y^2$
$(-\infty, 0], (-\infty, \infty)$

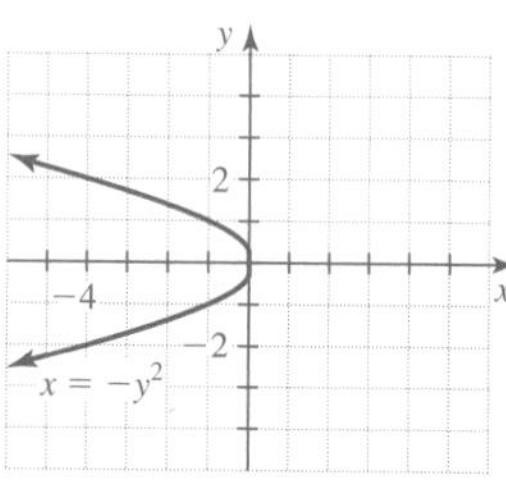

46. $x = 1 - y^2$
$(-\infty, 1], (-\infty, \infty)$

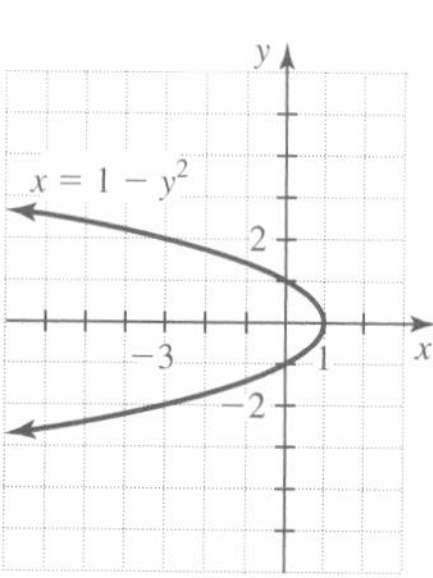

47. $x = 5$
$\{5\}, (-\infty, \infty)$

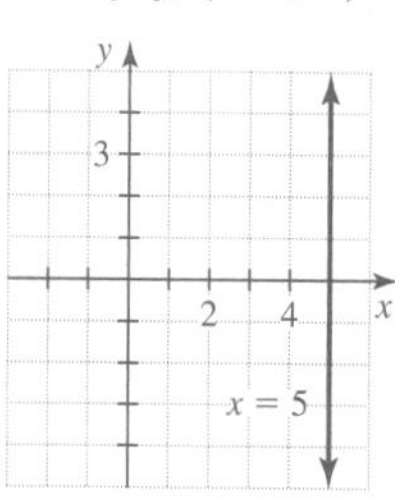

48. $x = -3$
$\{-3\}, (-\infty, \infty)$

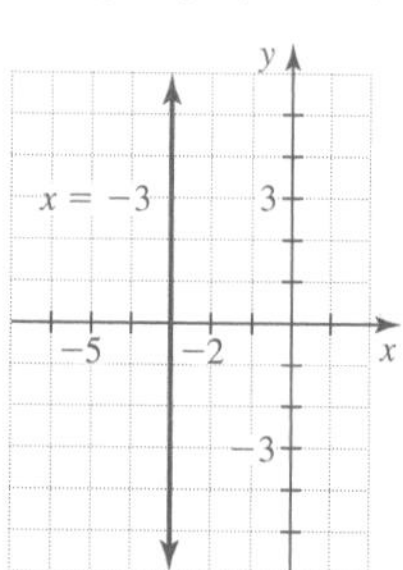

49. $x + 9 = y^2$
$[-9, \infty), (-\infty, \infty)$

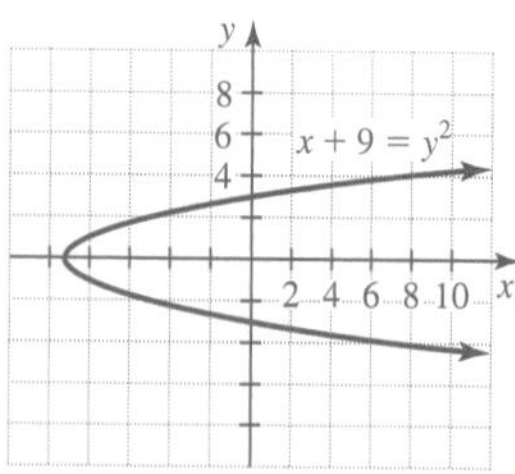

50. $x + 3 = |y|$
$[-3, \infty), (-\infty, \infty)$

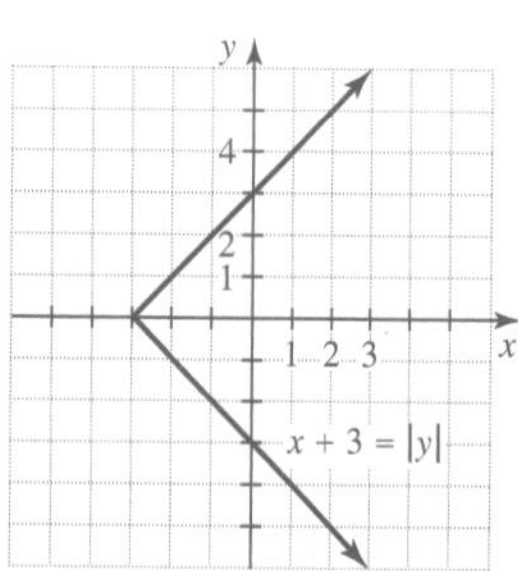

51. $x = \sqrt{y}$
$[0, \infty), [0, \infty)$

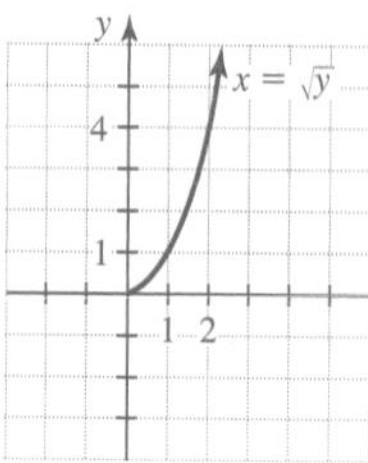

52. $x = -\sqrt{y}$
$(-\infty, 0], [0, \infty)$

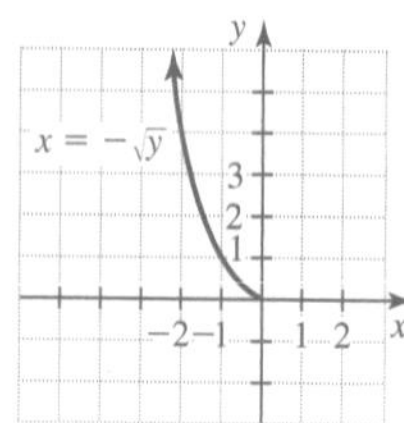

53. $x = (y - 1)^2$
$[0, \infty), (-\infty, \infty)$

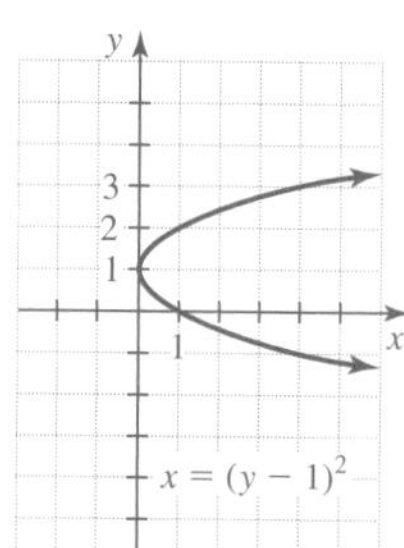

54. $x = (y + 2)^2$
$[0, \infty), (-\infty, \infty)$

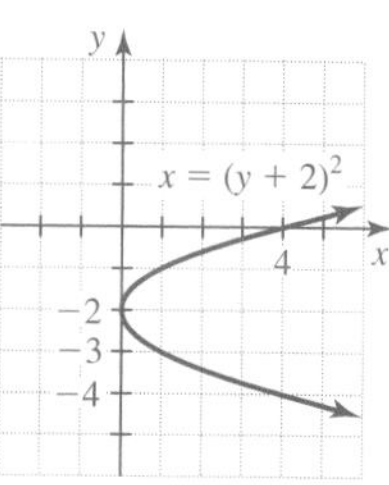

Graph each function and state the domain and range.

55. $f(x) = 1 - |x|$
$(-\infty, \infty), (-\infty, 1]$

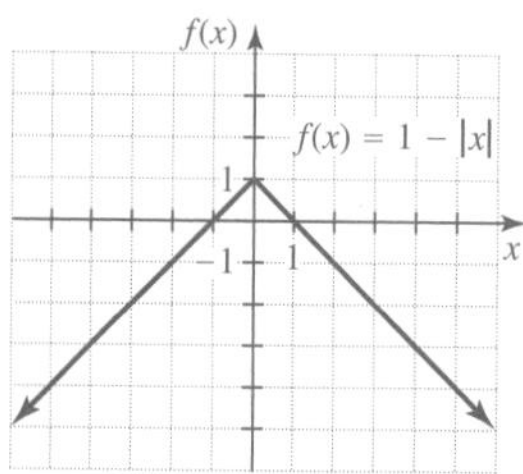

56. $h(x) = \sqrt{x - 3}$
$[3, \infty), [0, \infty)$

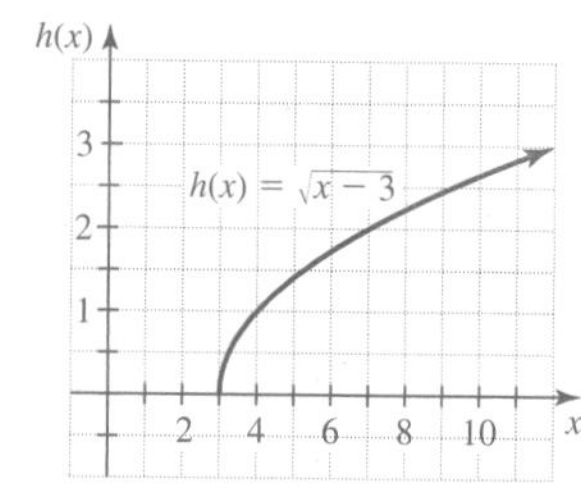

57. $y = (x - 3)^2 - 1$
$(-\infty, \infty), [-1, \infty)$

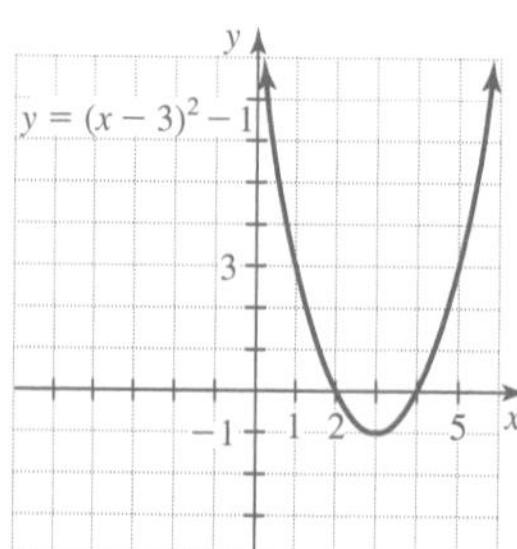

58. $y = x^2 - 2x - 3$
$(-\infty, \infty), [-4, \infty)$

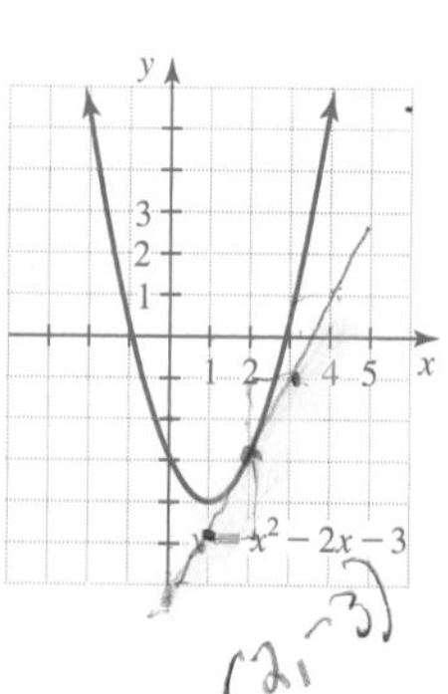

59. $y = |x + 3| + 1$
$(-\infty, \infty), [1, \infty)$

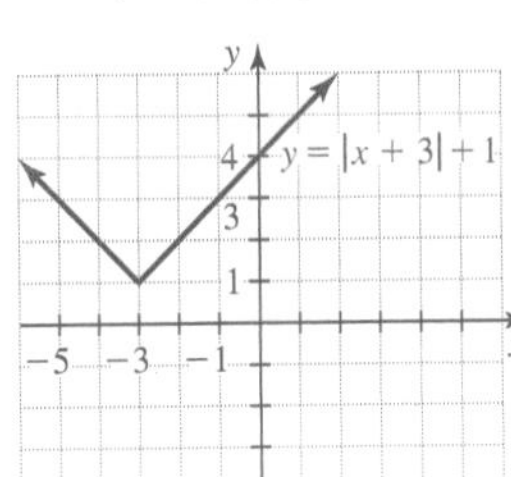

60. $f(x) = -2x + 4$
$(-\infty, \infty), (-\infty, \infty)$

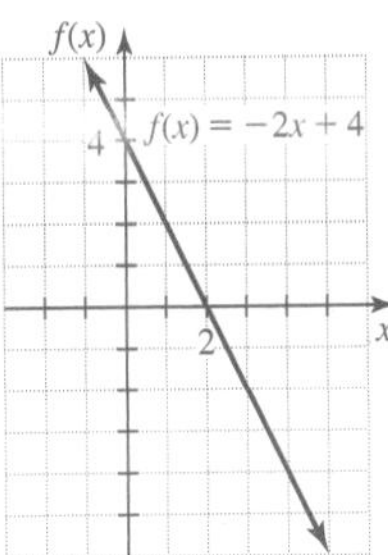

61. $y = \sqrt{x} - 3$
$[0, \infty), [-3, \infty)$

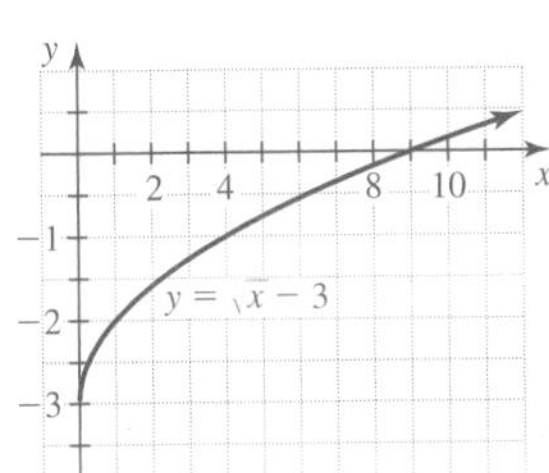

62. $y = 2|x|$
$(-\infty, \infty), [0, \infty)$

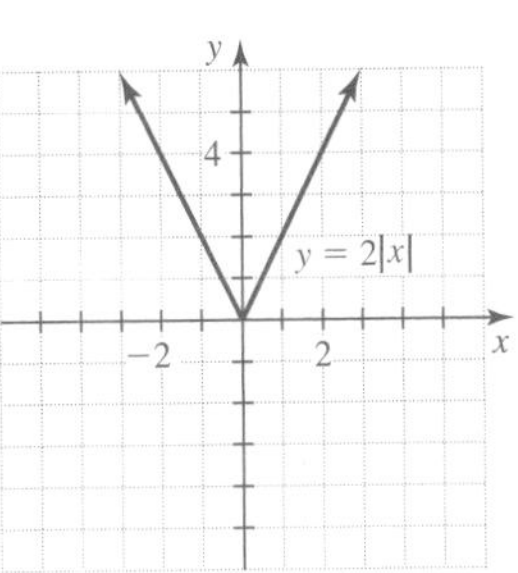

63. $y = 3x - 5$ $(-\infty, \infty), (-\infty, \infty)$

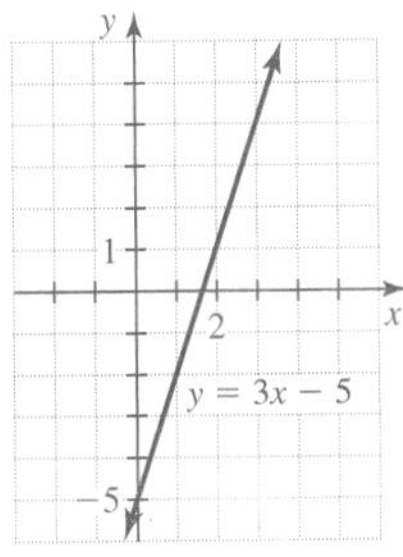

64. $g(x) = (x + 2)^2$ $(-\infty, \infty), [0, \infty)$

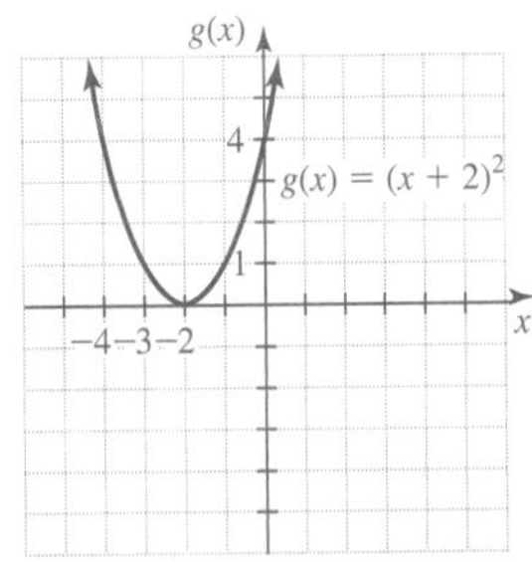

65. $y = -x^2 + 4x - 4$ $(-\infty, \infty), (-\infty, 0]$

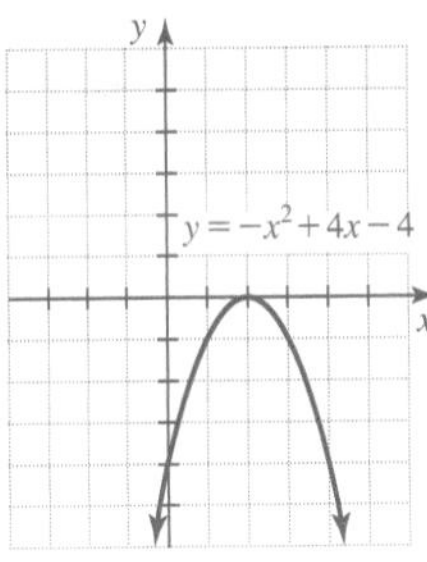

66. $y = -2|x - 1| + 4$ $(-\infty, \infty), (-\infty, 4]$

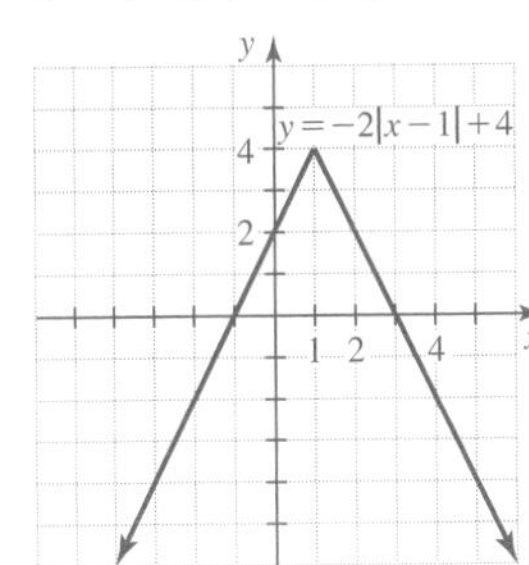

Graphing Calculator Exercises

67. Graph the function $f(x) = \sqrt{x^2}$ and explain what this graph illustrates.
The graph of $f(x) = \sqrt{x^2}$ is the same as the graph of $f(x) = |x|$.

68. Graph the function $f(x) = \frac{1}{x}$ and state the domain and range.
$(-\infty, 0) \cup (0, \infty), (-\infty, 0) \cup (0, \infty)$

69. Graph $y = x^2$, $y = \frac{1}{2}x^2$, and $y = 2x^2$ on the same coordinate system. What can you say about the graph of $y = ax^2$ for $a > 0$? For large values of a the graph gets narrower and for smaller values of a the graph gets broader.

70. Graph $y = x^2$, $y = x^2 + 2$, and $y = x^2 - 3$ on the same screen. What can you say about the position of $y = x^2 + k$ relative to $y = x^2$.
The graph of $y = x^2 + k$ moves upward for $k > 0$ and downward for $k < 0$.

71. Graph $y = x^2$, $y = (x + 5)^2$, and $y = (x - 2)^2$ on the same screen. What can you say about the position of $y = (x - h)^2$ relative to $y = x^2$.
The graph of $y = (x - h)^2$ moves to the right for $h > 0$ and to the left for $h < 0$.

72. You can graph the relation $x = y^2$ by graphing the two functions $y = \sqrt{x}$ and $y = -\sqrt{x}$. Try it and explain why this works.
The equation $x = y^2$ is equivalent to $y = \sqrt{x}$ or $y = -\sqrt{x}$.

73. Graph $y = (x - 3)^2$, $y = |x - 3|$, and $y = \sqrt{x - 3}$ on the same coordinate system. How does the graph of $y = f(x - h)$ compare to the graph of $y = f(x)$?
The graph of $y = f(x - h)$ lies to the right of the graph of $y = f(x)$ when $h > 0$.

11.3 Transformations of Graphs

In this Section

- **Reflecting**
- **Translating**
- **Stretching and Shrinking**
- **Multiple Transformations**

We can discover what the graph of almost any function looks like if we plot enough points. However, it is helpful to know something about a graph so that we do not have to plot very many points. In this section we will learn how one graph can be transformed into another by modifying the formula that defines the function.

Calculator Close-Up

With a graphing calculator, you can quickly see the result of modifying the formula for a function. If you have a graphing calculator, use it to graph the functions in the examples. Experimenting with it will help you to understand the ideas in this section.

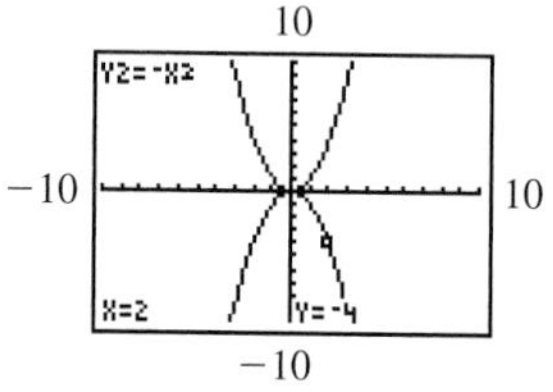

Reflecting

Consider the graphs of $f(x) = x^2$ and $g(x) = -x^2$ shown in Fig. 11.14. Notice that the graph of g is a mirror image of the graph of f. For any value of x we compute the y-coordinate of an ordered pair of f by squaring x. For an ordered pair of g we square first and then find the opposite because of the order of operations. This gives a correspondence between the ordered pairs of f and the ordered pairs of g. For every ordered pair on the graph of f there is a corresponding ordered pair directly below it on the graph of g, and these ordered pairs are the same distance from the x-axis. We say that the graph of g is obtained by reflecting the graph of f in the x-axis or that g is a reflection of the graph of f.

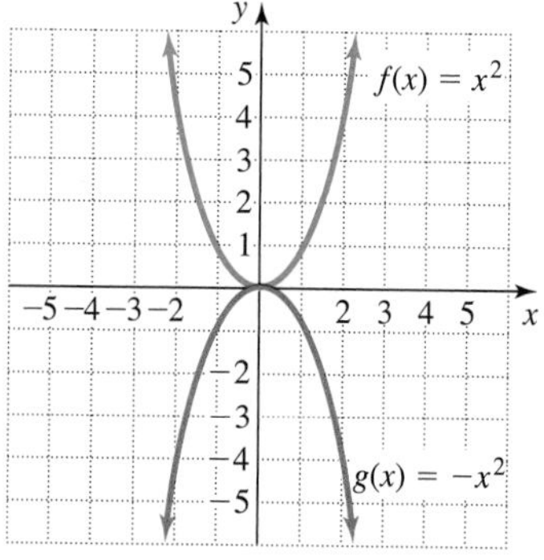

Figure 11.14

Reflection

The graph of $y = -f(x)$ is a **reflection** in the x-axis of the graph of $y = f(x)$.

EXAMPLE 1

Reflection

Sketch the graphs of each pair of functions on the same coordinate system.

a) $f(x) = \sqrt{x}$, $g(x) = -\sqrt{x}$ **b)** $f(x) = |x|$, $g(x) = -|x|$

Solution

In each case the graph of g is a reflection in the x-axis of the graph of f. Recall that we graphed the square root function and the absolute value function in the last section. Figures 11.15 and 11.16 show the graphs for these functions.

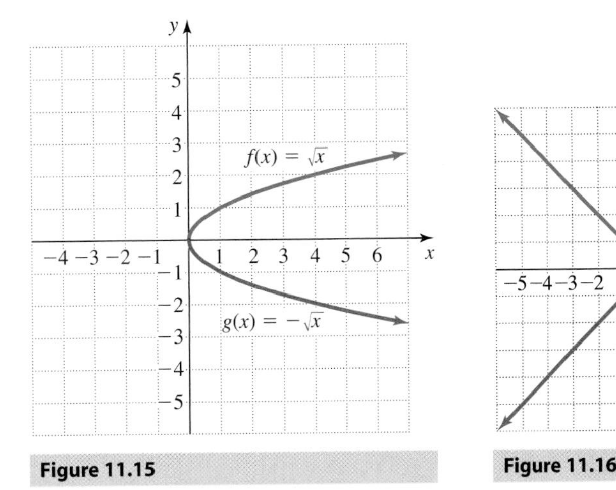

Figure 11.15

Figure 11.16

Now do Exercises 7–14

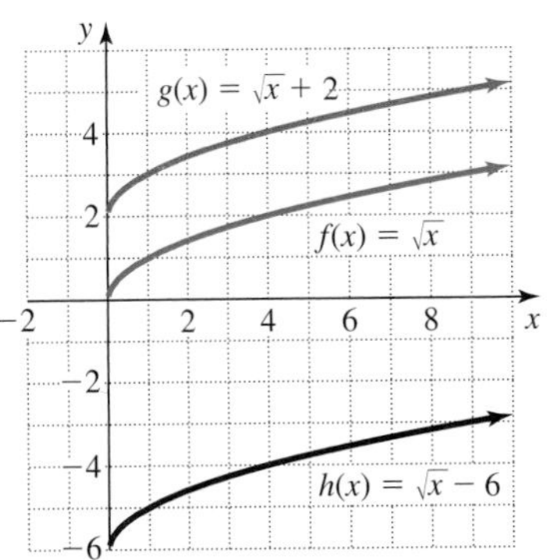

Figure 11.17

Teaching Tip Point out the reflecting and translating are rigid transformations because the shape of the graph does not change.

Translating

Consider the graphs of the functions $f(x) = \sqrt{x}$, $g(x) = \sqrt{x} + 2$, and $h(x) = \sqrt{x} - 6$ shown in Fig. 11.17. In the expression $\sqrt{x} + 2$, adding 2 is the last operation to perform. So every point on the graph of g is exactly two units above a corresponding point on the graph of f, and g has the same shape as the graph of f. Every point on the graph of h is exactly six units below a corresponding point on the graph of f. The graph of g is an upward translation of the graph of f, and the graph of h is a downward translation of the graph of f.

Translating Upward or Downward

If $k > 0$, then the graph of $y = f(x) + k$ is an **upward translation** of the graph of $y = f(x)$.

If $k < 0$, then the graph of $y = f(x) + k$ is a **downward translation** of the graph of $y = f(x)$.

Consider the graphs of $f(x) = \sqrt{x}$, $g(x) = \sqrt{x - 2}$, and $h(x) = \sqrt{x + 6}$ shown in Fig. 11.18. In the expression $\sqrt{x - 2}$ subtracting 2 is the first operation to perform. So every point on the graph of g is exactly two units to the right of a corresponding point on the graph of f. (We must start with a larger value of x to get the same y-coordinate because we first subtract 2.) Every point on the graph of h is exactly six units to the left of a corresponding point on the graph of f.

Calculator Close-Up

Note that for a translation of six units to the left, $x + 6$ must be written in parentheses on a graphing calculator.

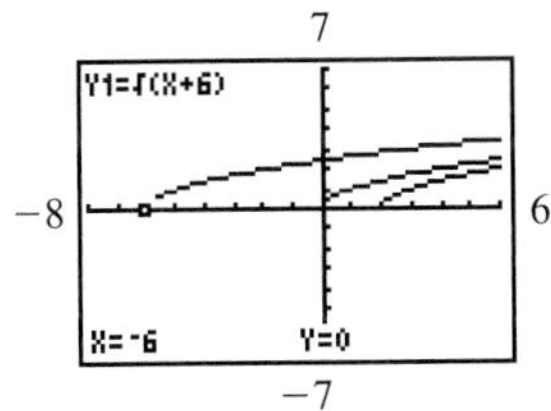

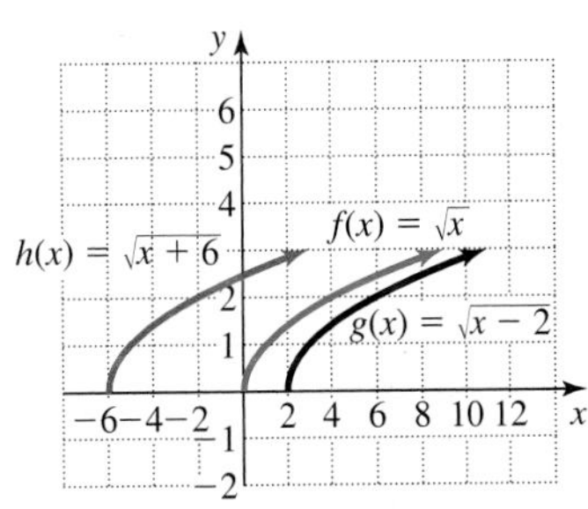

Figure 11.18

Translating to the Right or Left

If $h > 0$, then the graph of $y = f(x - h)$ is a **translation to the right** of the graph of $y = f(x)$.

If $h < 0$, then the graph of $y = f(x - h)$ is a **translation to the left** of the graph of $y = f(x)$.

EXAMPLE 2

Translation

Sketch the graph of each function and state the domain and range.

a) $f(x) = |x| - 6$ **b)** $f(x) = (x - 2)^2$ **c)** $f(x) = |x + 3|$

Solution

a) The graph of $f(x) = |x| - 6$ is a translation six units downward of the familiar graph of $f(x) = |x|$. Calculate a few ordered pairs for accuracy. The ordered pairs $(0, -6)$, $(1, -5)$, and $(-1, -5)$ are on the graph in Fig. 11.19. Since any real number can be used in place of x in $|x| - 6$, the domain is $(-\infty, \infty)$. Since the graph extends upward from $(0, -6)$ the range is $[-6, \infty)$.

b) The graph of $f(x) = (x - 2)^2$ is a translation two units to the right of the familiar graph of $f(x) = x^2$. Calculate a few ordered pairs for accuracy. The points $(2, 0)$, $(0, 4)$, and $(4, 4)$ are on the graph in Fig. 11.20. Since any real number can be used in place of x in $(x - 2)^2$, the domain is $(-\infty, \infty)$. Since the graph extends upward from $(2, 0)$ the range is $[0, \infty)$.

c) The graph of $f(x) = |x + 3|$ is a translation three units to the left of the familiar graph of $f(x) = |x|$. The points $(0, 3)$, $(-3, 0)$, and $(-6, 3)$ are on the graph in Fig. 11.21. Since any real number can be used in place of x in $|x + 3|$, the domain is $(-\infty, \infty)$. Since the graph extends upward from $(-3, 0)$ the range is $[0, \infty)$.

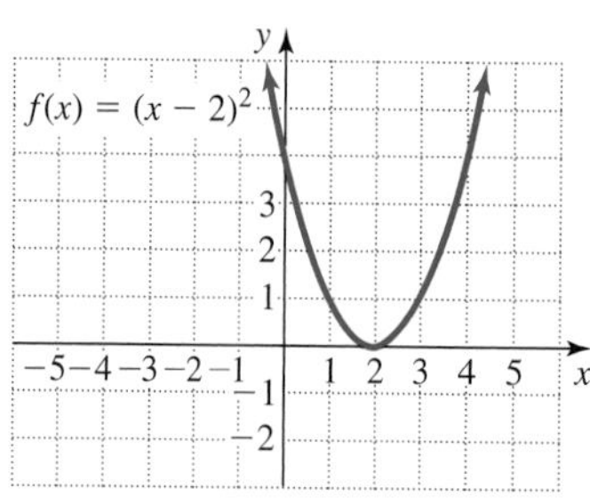

Figure 11.20

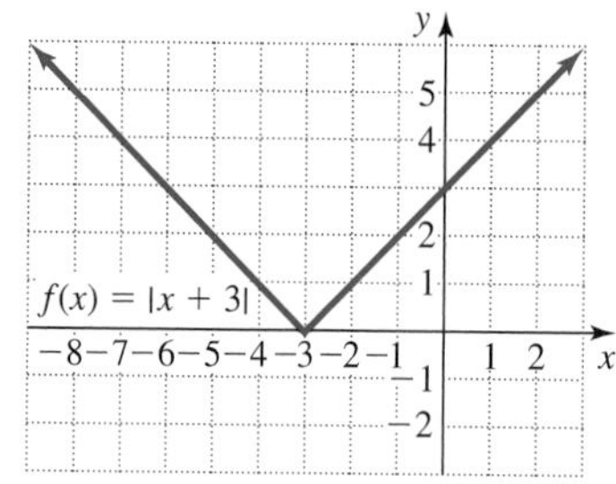

Figure 11.21

Now do Exercises 15–28

Teaching Tip Knowing about translations tells us what to expect. We do not actually draw a graph and then slide it over to obtain a new one.

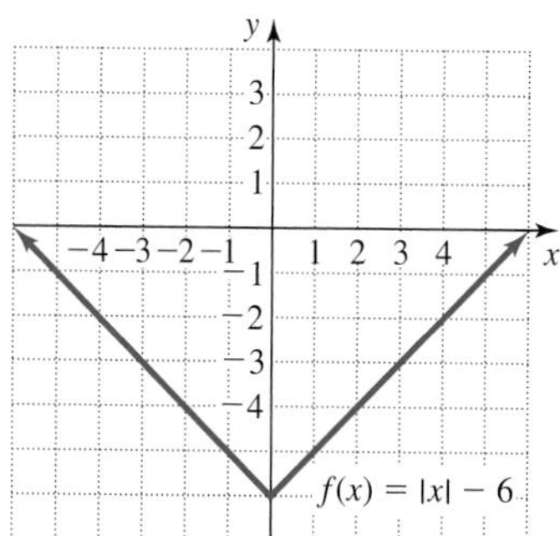

Figure 11.19

Calculator Close-Up

A typical graphing calculator can draw 10 curves on the same screen. On this screen there are the curves $y = 0.1x^2$, $y = 0.2x^2$, and so on, through $y = x^2$.

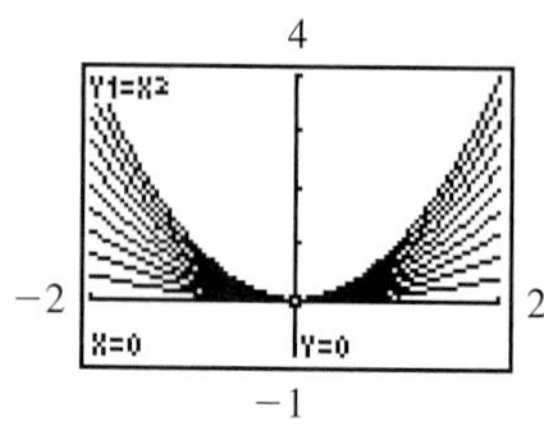

Stretching and Shrinking

Consider the graphs of $f(x) = x^2$, $g(x) = 2x^2$, and $h(x) = \frac{1}{2}x^2$ shown in Fig. 11.22. Every point on $g(x) = 2x^2$ corresponds to a point directly below on the graph of $f(x) = x^2$. The y-coordinate on g is exactly twice as large as the corresponding y-coordinate on f. This situation occurs because in the expression $2x^2$, multiplying by

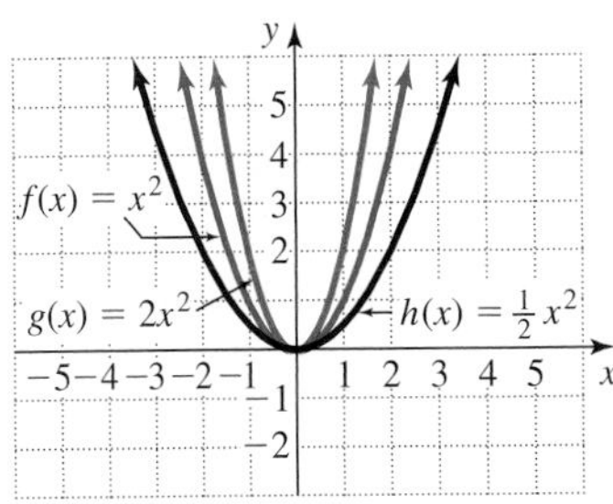

Figure 11.22

2 is the last operation performed. Every point on h corresponds to a point directly above on f, where the y-coordinate on h is half as large as the y-coordinate on f. The factor 2 has stretched the graph of f to form the graph of g, and the factor $\frac{1}{2}$ has shrunk the graph of f to form the graph of h.

Stretching and Shrinking

If $a > 1$, then the graph of $y = af(x)$ is obtained by **stretching** the graph of $y = f(x)$. If $0 < a < 1$, then the graph of $y = af(x)$ is obtained by **shrinking** the graph of $y = f(x)$.

Teaching Tip Point out that stretching and shrinking are nonrigid transformations because they change the shape. Changing the shape can also be accomplished by changing the scales on the axes.

Note that the last operation to be performed in stretching or shrinking is multiplication by a. Whereas the function $g(x) = 2\sqrt{x}$ is obtained by stretching $f(x) = \sqrt{x}$ by a factor of 2, $h(x) = \sqrt{2x}$ is not.

EXAMPLE 3

Stretching and shrinking

Graph the functions $f(x) = \sqrt{x}$, $g(x) = 2\sqrt{x}$, and $h(x) = \frac{1}{2}\sqrt{x}$ on the same coordinate system.

Solution

The graph of g is obtained by stretching the graph of f, and the graph of h is obtained by shrinking the graph of f. The graph of f includes the points (0, 0), (1, 1), and (4, 2). The graph of g includes the points (0, 0), (1, 2), and (4, 4). The graph of h includes the points (0, 0), (1, 0.5), and (4, 1). The graphs are shown in Fig. 11.23.

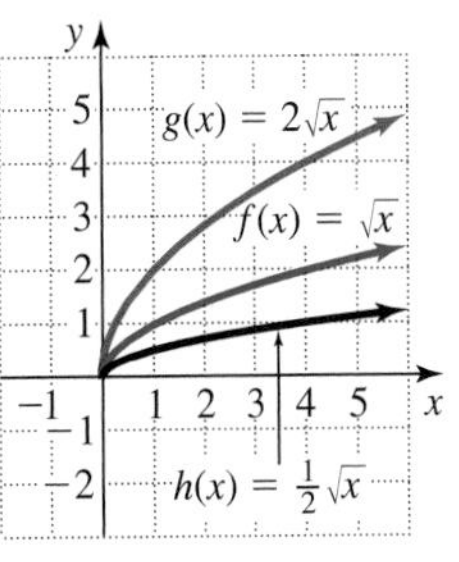

Figure 11.23

Now do Exercises 29–36

Calculator Close-Up

The following calculator screen shows the curves $y = \sqrt{x}, y = 2\sqrt{x}$, $y = 3\sqrt{x}$, and so on, through $y = 10\sqrt{x}$.

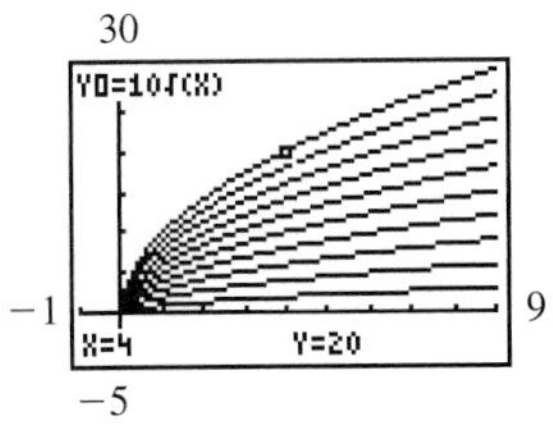

Teaching Tip Stress the importance of the order here. The order comes from the order of operations.

Multiple Transformations

When graphing a function containing more than one transformation perform the transformations in the following order:

1. Left or right translation
2. Stretching or shrinking
3. Reflection in the x-axis
4. Upward or downward translation

Math *at Work* Sailboat Design

Mention sailing and your mind drifts to exotic locations, azure seas with soothing tropical breezes, crystal-clear waters, and dazzling white sand. But sailboat designers live in a world of computers, numbers, and formulas. Some of the measurements and formulas used to describe the sailing characteristics and stability of sailboats are the maximum hull speed formula, the sail area-displacement ratio, and the motion-comfort ratio.

To estimate the theoretical maximum hull speed (M) in knots, designers use the formula $M = 1.34\sqrt{LWL}$, where LWL is the load waterline length (the length of the hull at the waterline). See the accompanying figure.

Sail area-displacement ratio r indicates how fast the boat is in light wind. It is given by $r = \frac{A}{D^{2/3}}$, where A is the sail area in square feet and D is the displacement in cubic feet. Values of r range from 10 to 15 for cruisers and above 24 for high-performance racers.

The motion-comfort ratio MCR, created by boat designer Ted Brewer, predicts the speed of the upward and downward motion of the boat as it encounters waves. The faster the motion the more uncomfortable the passengers. If D is the displacement in pounds, LWL the loaded waterline length in feet, LOA the length overall, and B is the beam (width) in feet, then

$$MCR = \frac{D}{\frac{2}{3}B^{3/4}\left(\frac{7}{10}LWL + \frac{1}{3}LOA\right)}.$$

As the displacement increases, MCR increases. As the length and beam increases, MCR decreases. MCR should be in the low 30's for a boat with an LOA of 42 feet.

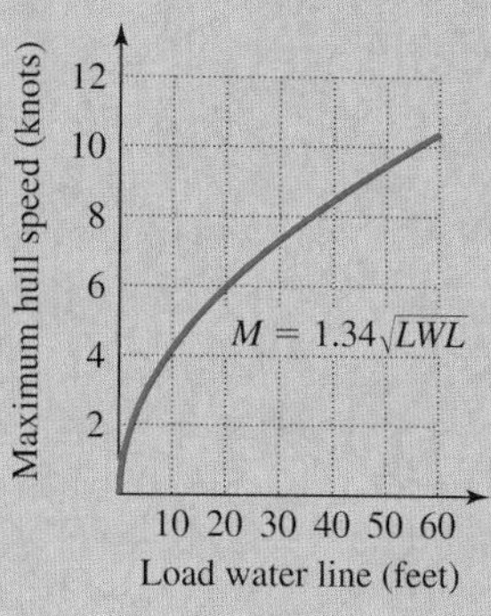

For example, the graph of $y = -2|x + 3| + 5$ is obtained by translating $y = |x|$ to the left 3 units, then stretching by a factor of 2, reflecting in the x-axis, and finally translating 5 units upward.

EXAMPLE 4

A multiple transformation of $y = \sqrt{x}$

Graph the function $f(x) = -2\sqrt{x - 3}$ and state the domain and range.

Solution

Start with the graph of $y = \sqrt{x}$ through (0, 0), (1, 1), and (4, 2), as shown in Fig. 11.24 on the next page. Translate it three units to the right to get the graph of $y = \sqrt{x - 3}$. Stretch this graph by a factor of two to get the graph of $y = 2\sqrt{x - 3}$ shown in Fig. 11.24. Now reflect in the x-axis to get the graph of $y = -2\sqrt{x - 3}$.

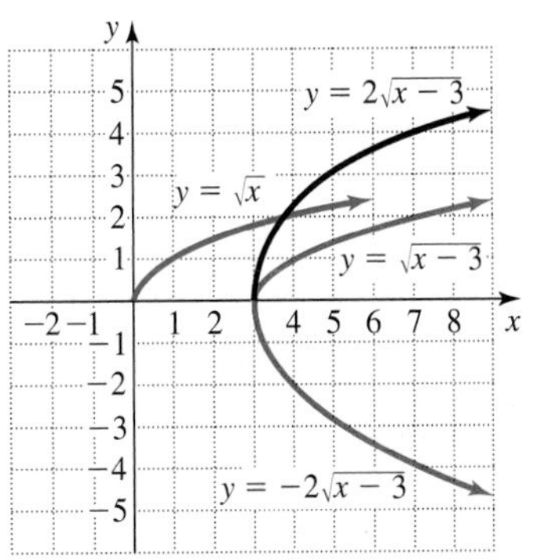

Figure 11.24

To get an accurate graph calculate a few points on the final graph as follows:

x	3	4	7
$y = -2\sqrt{x-3}$	0	-2	-4

Since $x - 3$ must be nonnegative in the expression $-2\sqrt{x-3}$, we must have $x - 3 \geq 0$ and $x \geq 3$. So the domain is $[3, \infty)$. Since the graph extends downward from the point $(3, 0)$ the range is $(-\infty, 0]$.

Now do Exercises 37–38

Calculator Close-Up

You can check Example 4 by graphing $y = -2\sqrt{x-3}$ with a graphing calculator.

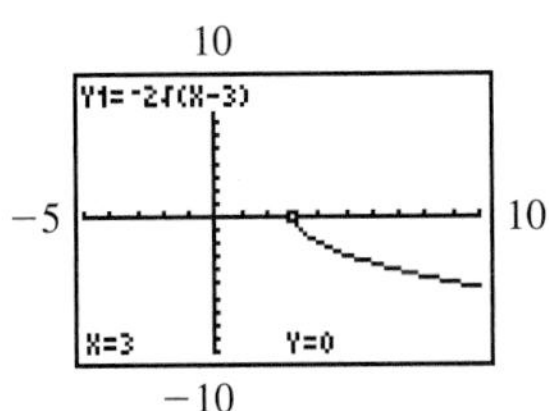

The graph of $y = x^2$ is a parabola opening upward with vertex $(0, 0)$. The graph of a function of the form $y = a(x - h)^2 + k$ is a transformation of $y = x^2$ and is also a parabola. It opens upward if $a > 0$ and downward if $a < 0$. Its vertex is (h, k). In Example 5 we graph a transformation of $y = x^2$.

EXAMPLE 5

A multiple transformation of the parabola $y = x^2$

Graph the function $y = -2(x + 3)^2 + 4$ and state the domain and range.

Solution

Think of the parabola $y = x^2$ through $(-1, 1)$, $(0, 0)$, and $(1, 1)$. To get the graph of $y = -2(x + 3)^2 + 4$, translate it three units to the left, stretch by a factor of two, reflect in the x-axis, and finally translate upward four units. The graph is a stretched parabola opening downward from the vertex $(-3, 4)$ as shown in Fig. 11.25. To get

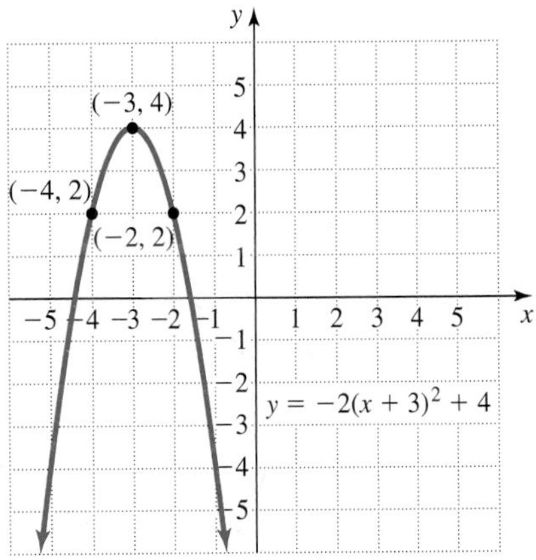

Figure 11.25

an accurate graph calculate a few points around the vertex as follows:

x	-5	-4	-3	-2	-1
$y = -2(x + 3)^2 + 4$	-4	2	4	2	-4

Since any real number can be used for x in $-2(x + 3)^2 + 4$, the domain is $(-\infty, \infty)$. Since the graph extends downward from $(-3, 4)$ the range is $(-\infty, 4]$.

Now do Exercises 39–40

Understanding transformations helps us to see the location of the graph of a function. To get an accurate graph we must still calculate ordered pairs that satisfy the equation. However, if we know where to expect the graph it is easier to choose appropriate ordered pairs.

EXAMPLE 6

A multiple transformation of the absolute value function $y = |x|$

Graph the function $y = \frac{1}{2}|x - 4| - 1$ and state the domain and range.

Solution

Think of the V-shaped graph of $y = |x|$ through $(-1, 1)$, $(0, 0)$, and $(1, 1)$. To get the graph of $y = \frac{1}{2}|x - 4| - 1$, translate $y = |x|$ to the right four units, shrink by a factor of $\frac{1}{2}$, and finally translate downward one unit. The graph is shown in Fig. 11.26. To get an accurate graph calculate a few points around the lowest point on the V-shaped graph as follows:

x	2	4	6
$y = \frac{1}{2}\|x - 4\| - 1$	0	-1	0

Since any real number can be used for x in $\frac{1}{2}|x - 4| - 1$, the domain is $(-\infty, \infty)$. Since the graph extends upward from $(4, -1)$ the range is $[-1, \infty)$.

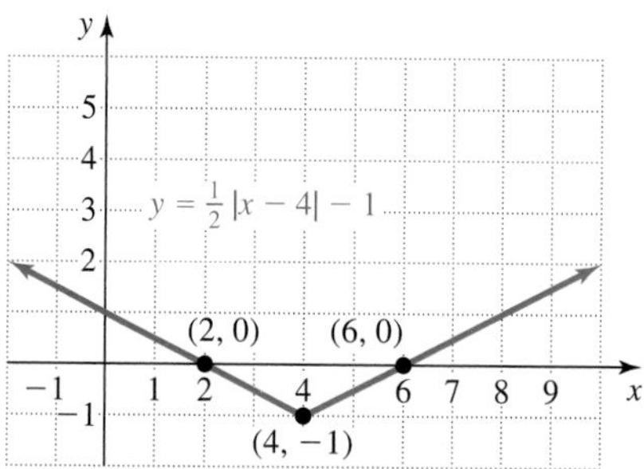

Figure 11.26

Now do Exercises 41–42

Warm-Ups ▼

True or false? Explain your answer.

1. The graph of $f(x) = (-x)^2$ is a reflection in the x-axis of the graph of $g(x) = x^2$. False
2. The graph of $f(x) = -2$ is a reflection in the x-axis of the graph of $f(x) = 2$. True
3. The graph of $f(x) = x + 3$ lies three units to the left of the graph of $f(x) = x$. True
4. The graph of $y = |x - 3|$ lies three units to the left of the graph of $y = |x|$. False
5. The graph of $y = |x| - 3$ lies three units below the graph of $y = |x|$. True
6. The graph of $y = -2x^2$ can be obtained by stretching and reflecting the graph of $y = x^2$. True
7. The graph of $f(x) = (x - 2)^2$ is symmetric about the y-axis. False
8. For each point on the graph of $y = \sqrt{x/9}$ there is a corresponding point on $y = \sqrt{x}$ that has a y-coordinate three times as large. True
9. The graph of $y = \sqrt{x - 3} + 5$ has the same shape as the graph of $y = \sqrt{x}$. True
10. The graph of $y = -(x + 2)^2 - 7$ can be obtained by moving $y = x^2$ two units to the left and down seven units and then reflecting in the x-axis. False

11.3 Exercises

Boost your GRADE at mathzone.com!

MathZone

▶ Practice Problems ▶ Net Tutor
▶ Self-Tests ▶ e-Professors
▶ Videos

Reading and Writing *After reading this section, write out the answers to these questions. Use complete sentences.*

1. What is a reflection in the x-axis of a graph?
   The graph of $y = -f(x)$ is a reflection in the x-axis of the graph of $y = f(x)$.
2. What is an upward translation of a graph?
   The graph of $y = f(x) + k$ for $k > 0$ is an upward translation of the graph of $y = f(x)$.
3. What is a downward translation of a graph?
   The graph of $y = f(x) + k$ for $k < 0$ is a downward translation of $y = f(x)$.
4. What is a translation to the right of a graph?
   The graph of $y = f(x - h)$ for $h > 0$ is a translation to the right of $y = f(x)$.
5. What is a translation to the left of a graph?
   The graph of $y = f(x - h)$ for $h < 0$ is a translation to the left of $y = f(x)$.
6. What is stretching and shrinking of a graph?
   The graph of $y = af(x)$ is a stretching of $y = f(x)$ if $a > 1$ and a shrinking of $y = f(x)$ if $0 < a < 1$.

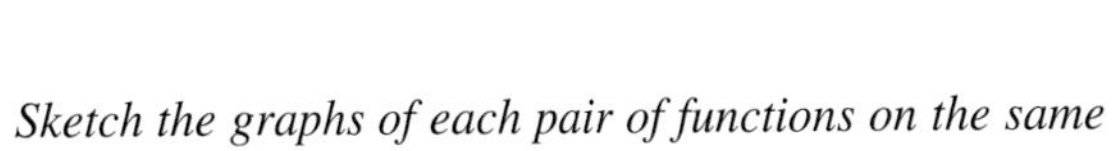

Sketch the graphs of each pair of functions on the same coordinate system. See Example 1.

7. $f(x) = \sqrt{2x}$, $g(x) = -\sqrt{2x}$

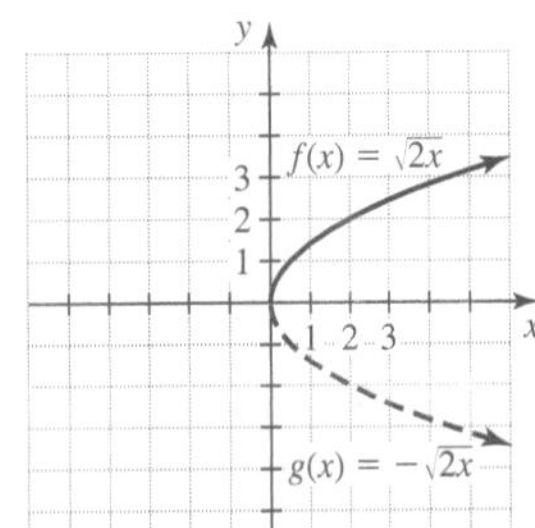

8. $y = x$, $y = -x$

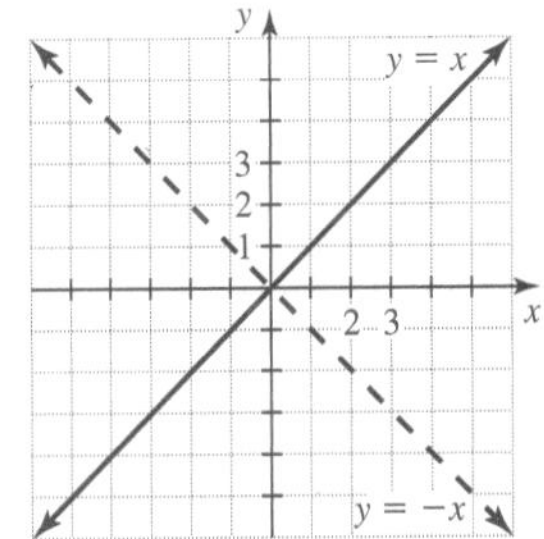

9. $f(x) = x^2 + 1,$
$g(x) = -(x^2 + 1)$

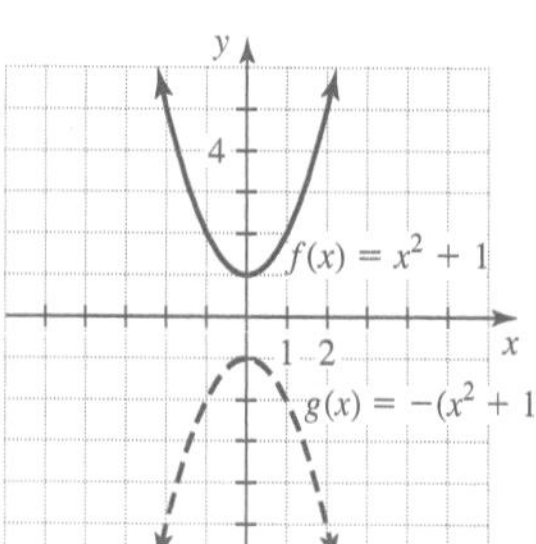

10. $f(x) = |x| + 1,$
$g(x) = -|x| - 1$

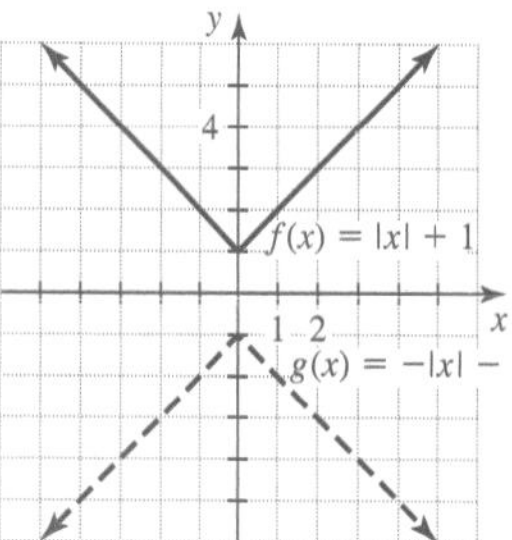

11. $y = \sqrt{x - 2},$
$y = -\sqrt{x - 2}$

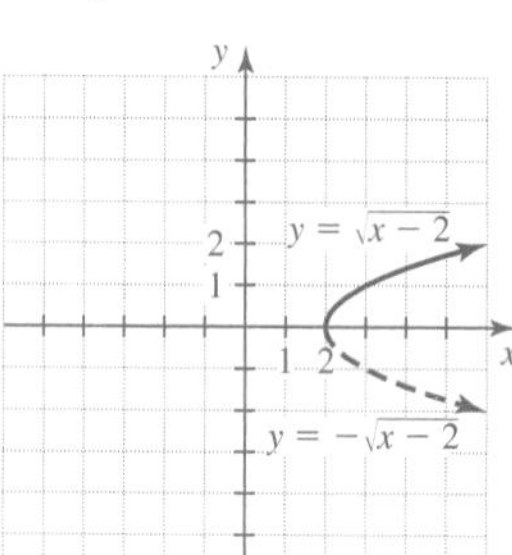

12. $y = |x - 1|,$
$y = -|x - 1|$

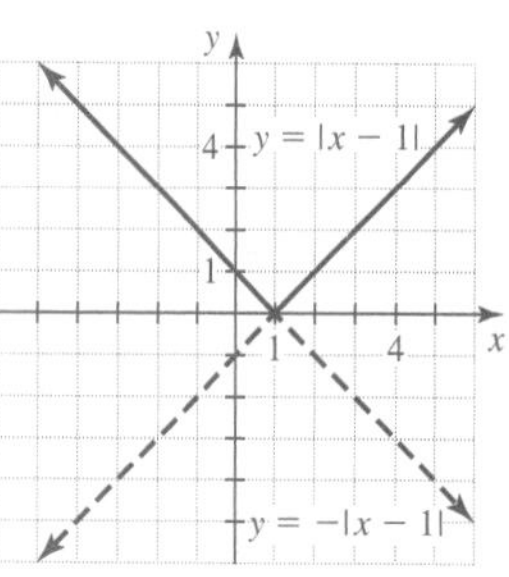

13. $f(x) = x - 3,$
$g(x) = 3 - x$

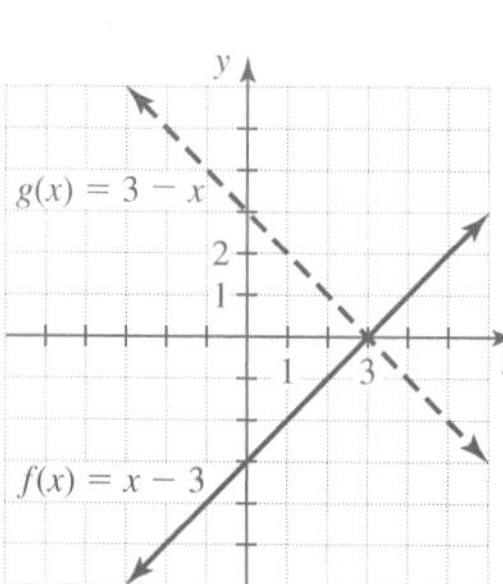

14. $f(x) = x^2 - 2,$
$g(x) = 2 - x^2$

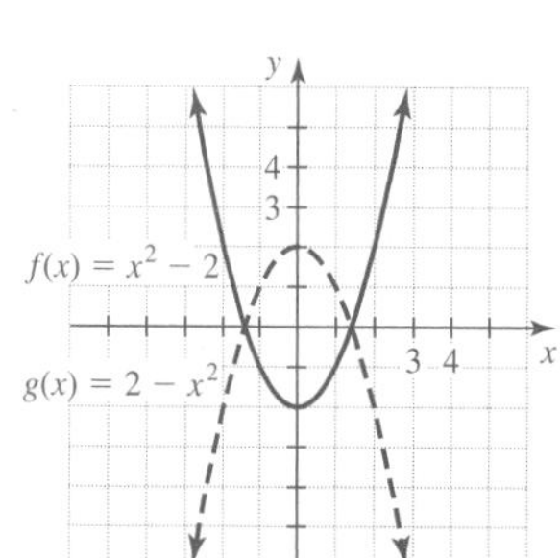

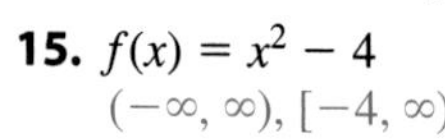
Use translation to graph each function and state the domain and range. See Example 2.

15. $f(x) = x^2 - 4$
$(-\infty, \infty), [-4, \infty)$

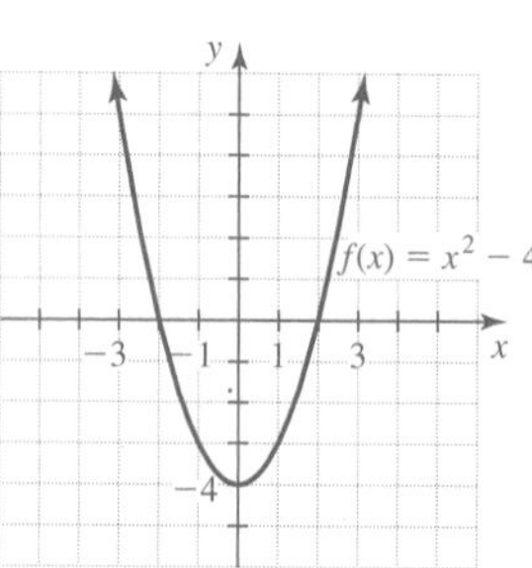

16. $f(x) = x^2 + 2$
$(-\infty, \infty), [2, \infty)$

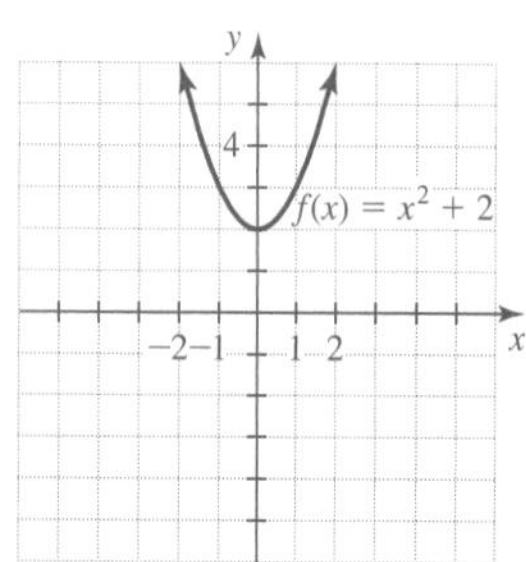

17. $y = x + 3$
$(-\infty, \infty), (-\infty, \infty)$

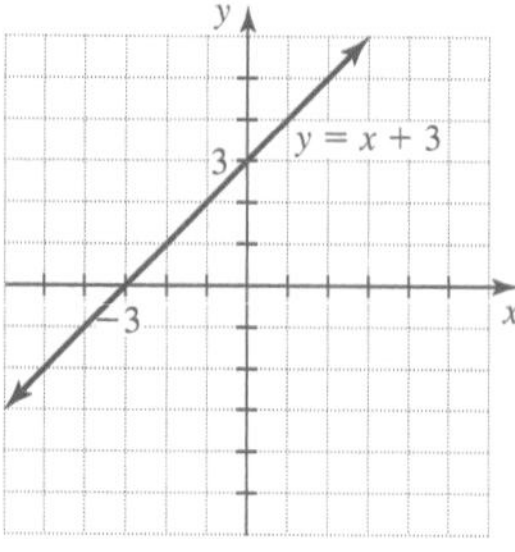

18. $y = x - 1$
$(-\infty, \infty), (-\infty, \infty)$

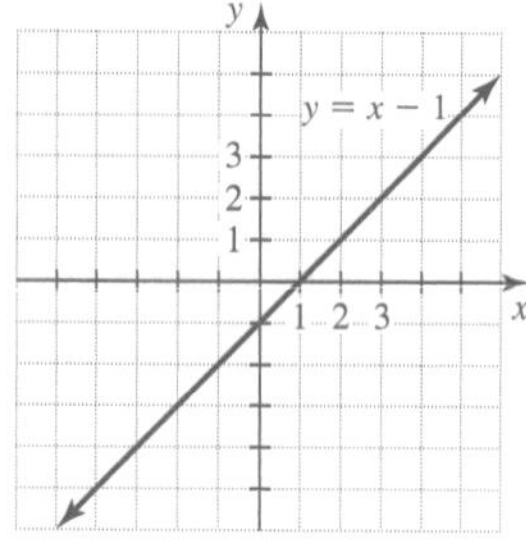

19. $f(x) = (x - 3)^2$
$(-\infty, \infty), [0, \infty)$

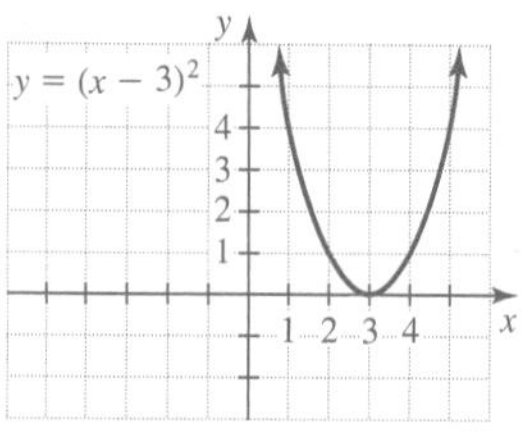

20. $f(x) = (x + 1)^2$
$(-\infty, \infty), [0, \infty)$

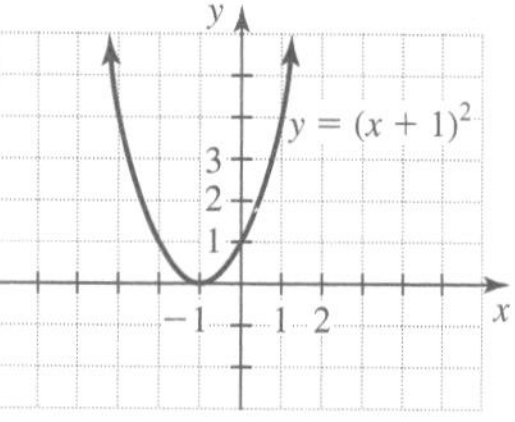

21. $y = \sqrt{x} + 1$
$[0, \infty), [1, \infty)$

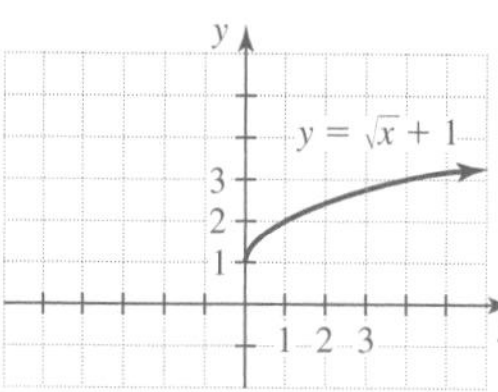

22. $y = \sqrt{x} - 3$
$[0, \infty), [-3, \infty)$

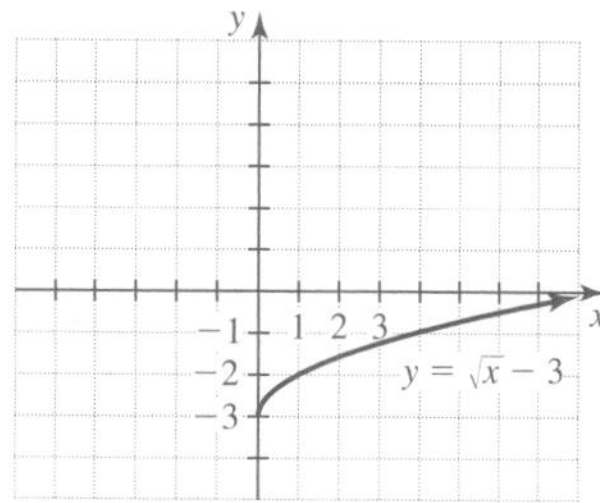

23. $f(x) = |x + 2|$
$(-\infty, \infty), [0, \infty)$

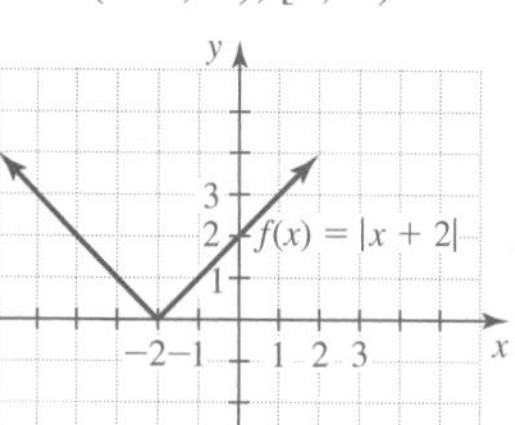

24. $f(x) = |x - 4|$
$(-\infty, \infty), [0, \infty)$

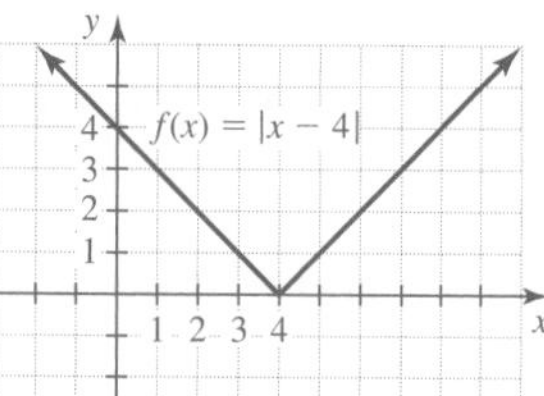

25. $y = |x| + 2$
$(-\infty, \infty), [2, \infty)$

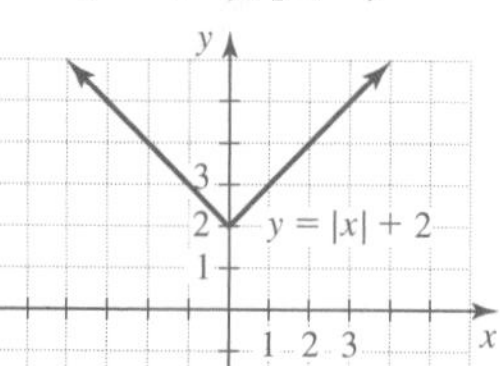

26. $y = |x| - 4$
$(-\infty, \infty), [-4, \infty)$

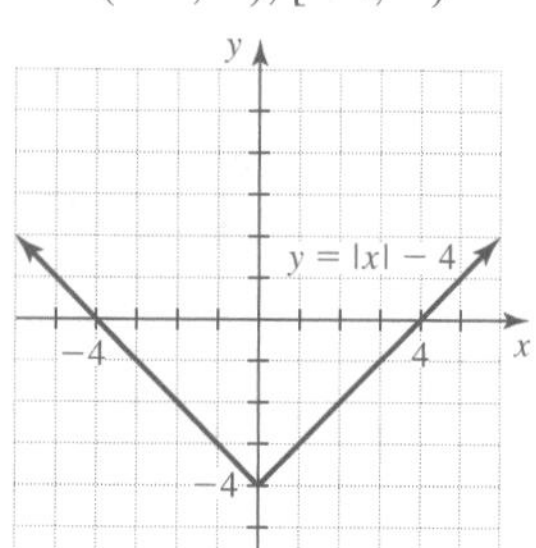

27. $f(x) = \sqrt{x - 1}$
$[1, \infty), [0, \infty)$

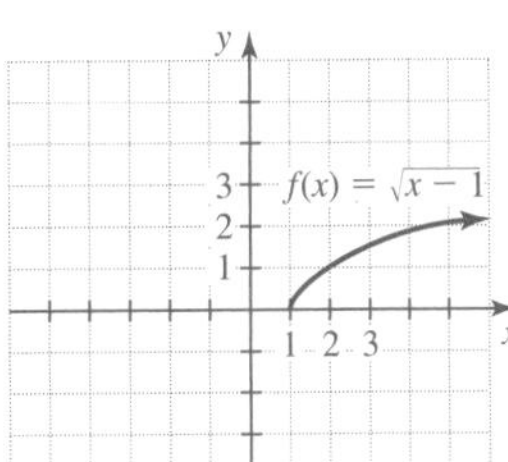

28. $f(x) = \sqrt{x + 6}$
$[-6, \infty), [0, \infty)$

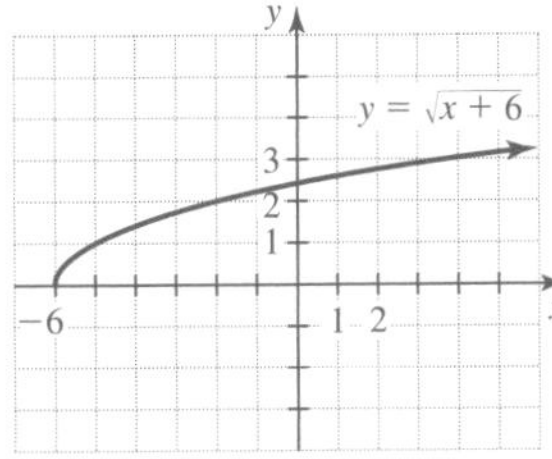

Use stretching and shrinking to graph each function and state the domain and range. See Example 3.

29. $f(x) = 3x^2$
$(-\infty, \infty), [0, \infty)$

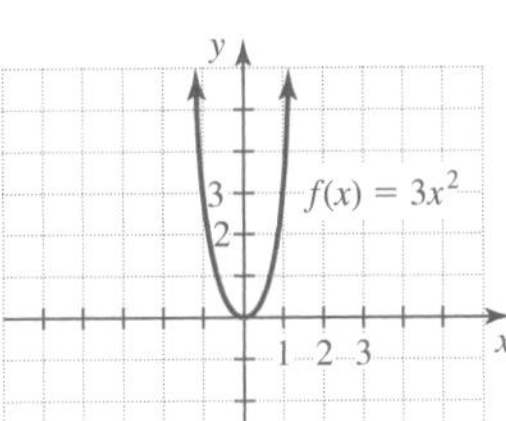

30. $f(x) = \frac{1}{3}x^2$
$(-\infty, \infty), [0, \infty)$

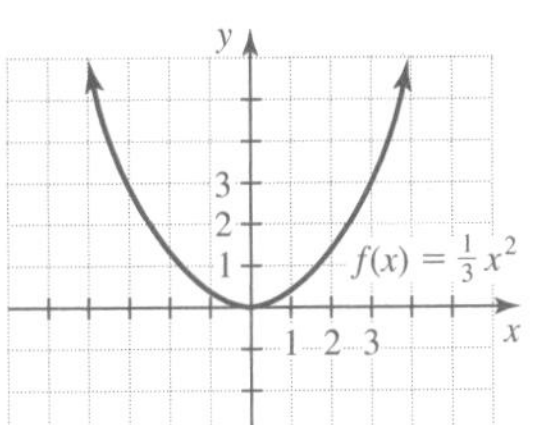

31. $y = \frac{1}{5}x$
$(-\infty, \infty), (-\infty, \infty)$

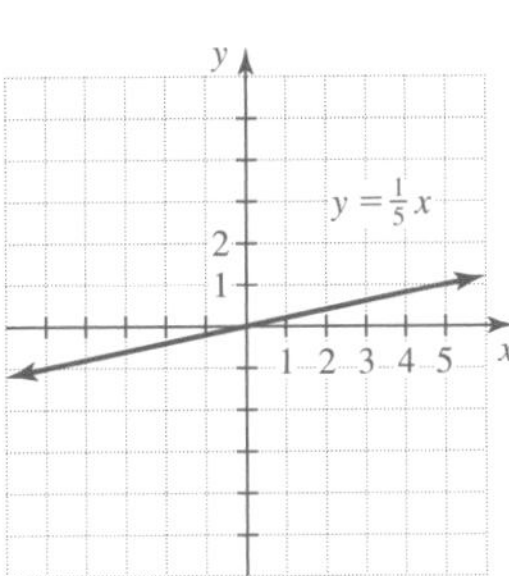

32. $y = 5x$
$(-\infty, \infty), (-\infty, \infty)$

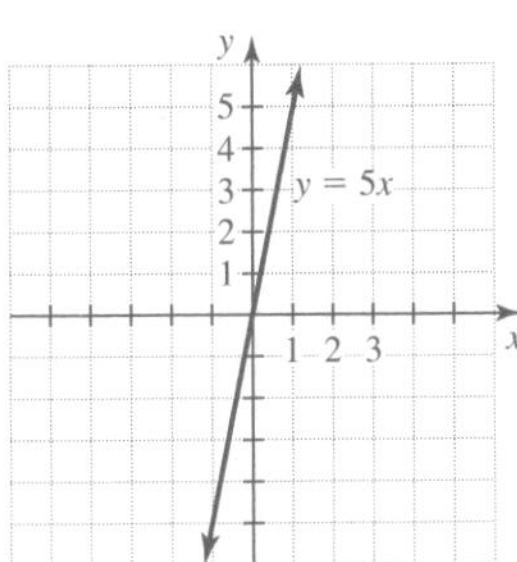

33. $f(x) = 3\sqrt{x}$
$[0, \infty), [0, \infty)$

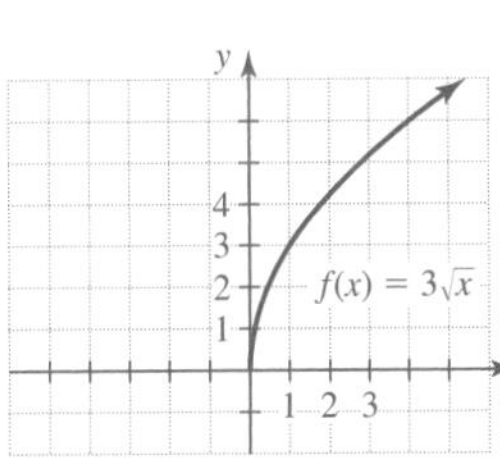

34. $f(x) = \frac{1}{3}\sqrt{x}$
$[0, \infty), [0, \infty)$

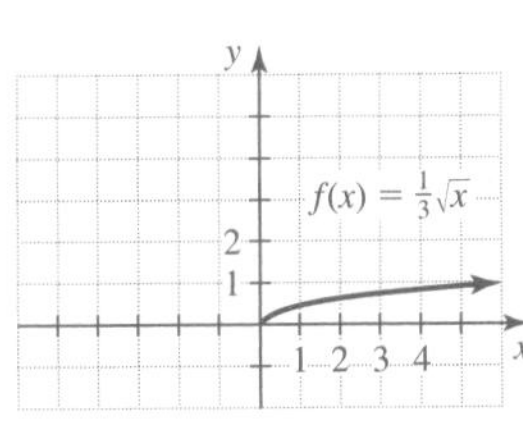

35. $y = \frac{1}{4}|x|$
$(-\infty, \infty), [0, \infty)$

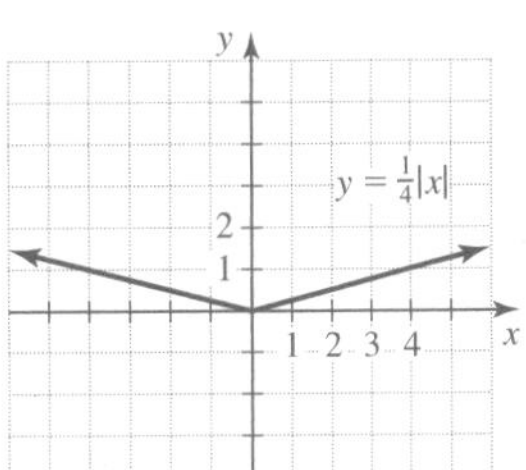

36. $y = 4|x|$
$(-\infty, \infty), [0, \infty)$

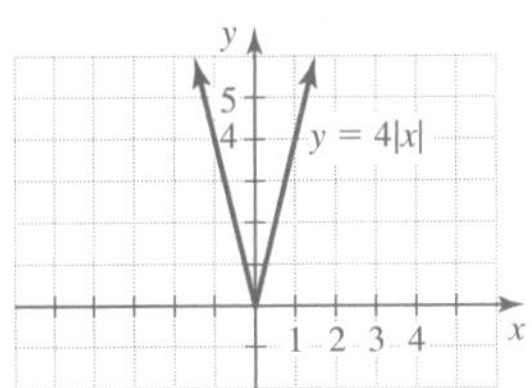

Sketch the graph of each function and state the domain and range. See Examples 4–6.

37. $y = \sqrt{x - 2} + 1$
$[2, \infty), [1, \infty)$

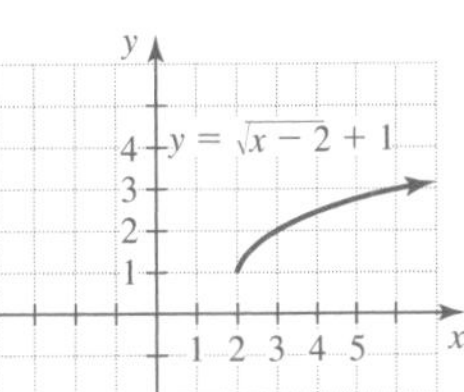

38. $y = -\sqrt{x + 3}$
$[-3, \infty), (-\infty, 0]$

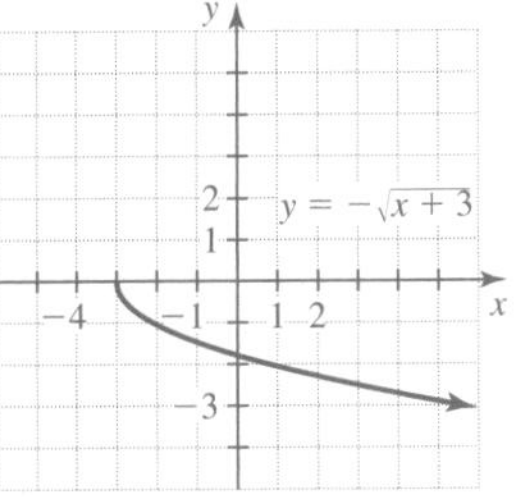

39. $f(x) = (x + 3)^2 - 5$
$(-\infty, \infty), [-5, \infty)$

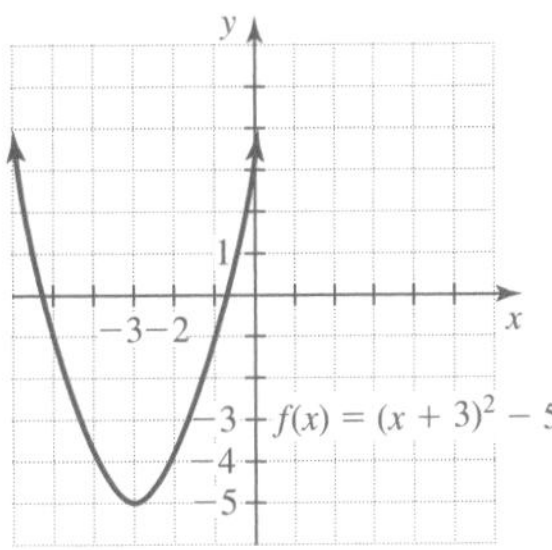

40. $f(x) = -2x^2$
$(-\infty, \infty), (-\infty, 0]$

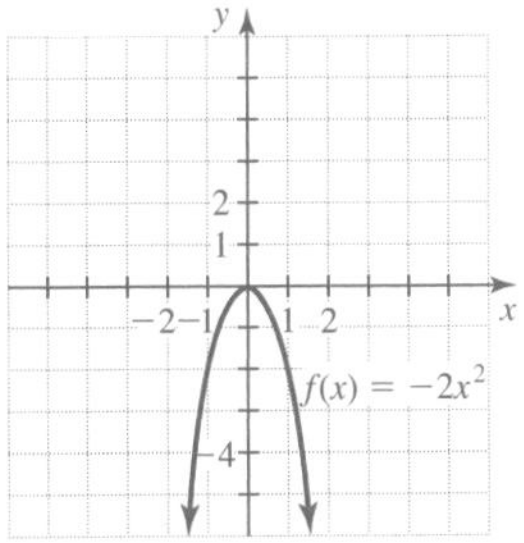

41. $y = -|x + 3|$
$(-\infty, \infty), (-\infty, 0]$

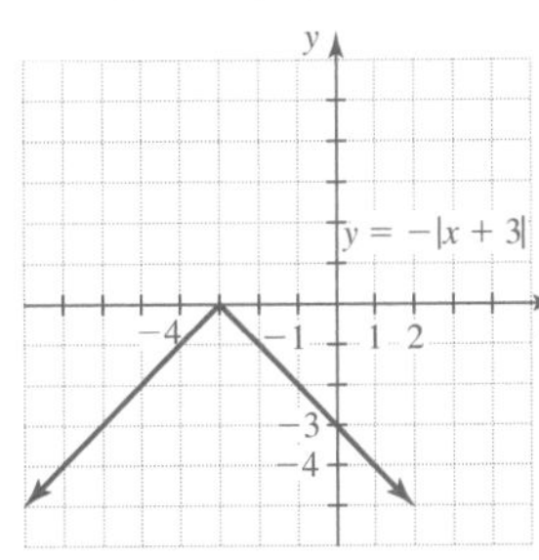

42. $y = |x - 2| + 1$
$(-\infty, \infty), [1, \infty)$

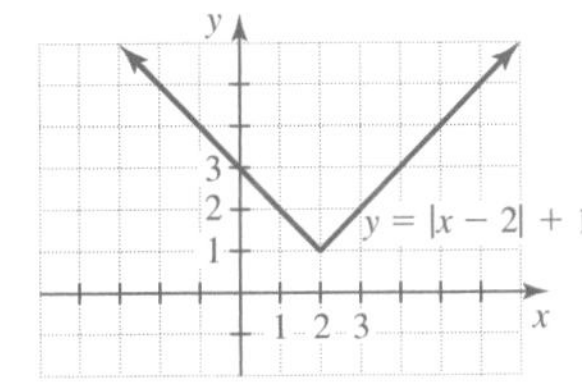

43. $y = -\sqrt{x + 1} - 2$
$[-1, \infty), (-\infty, -2]$

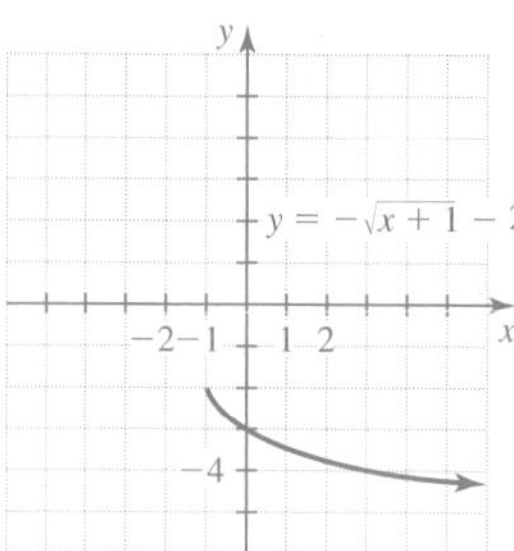

44. $y = -3\sqrt{x + 4} + 6$
$[-4, \infty), (-\infty, 6]$

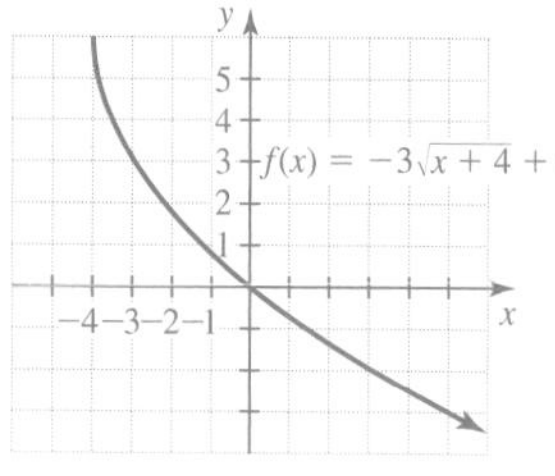

45. $y = -2|x - 3| + 4$
$(-\infty, \infty), (-\infty, 4]$

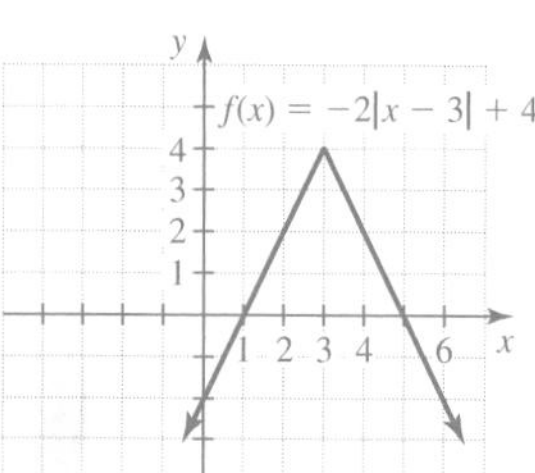

46. $y = 3|x - 1| + 2$
$(-\infty, \infty), [2, \infty)$

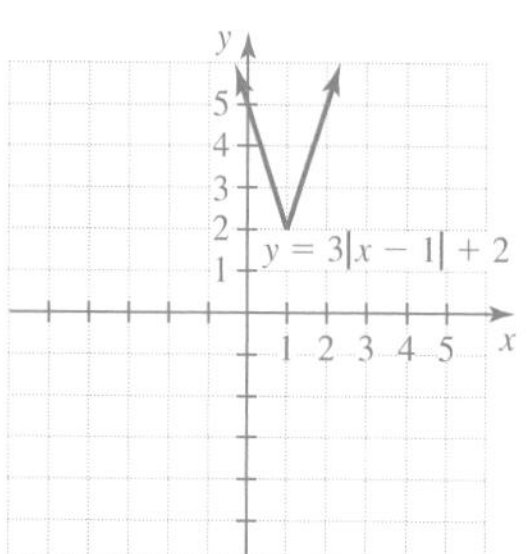

47. $y = -2x + 3$
$(-\infty, \infty), (-\infty, \infty)$

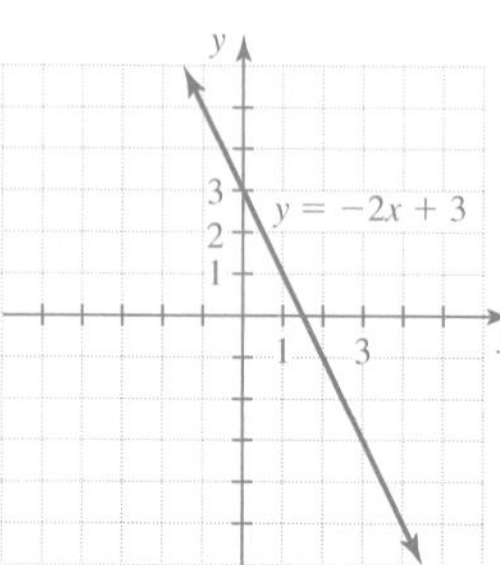

48. $y = 3x - 1$
$(-\infty, \infty), (-\infty, \infty)$

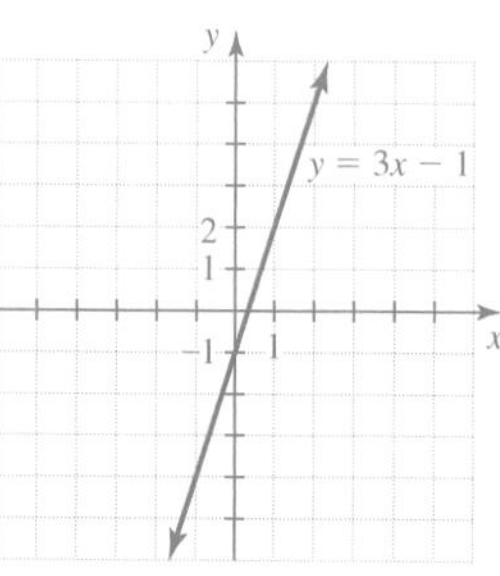

49. $y = 2(x + 3)^2 + 1$
$(-\infty, \infty), [1, \infty)$

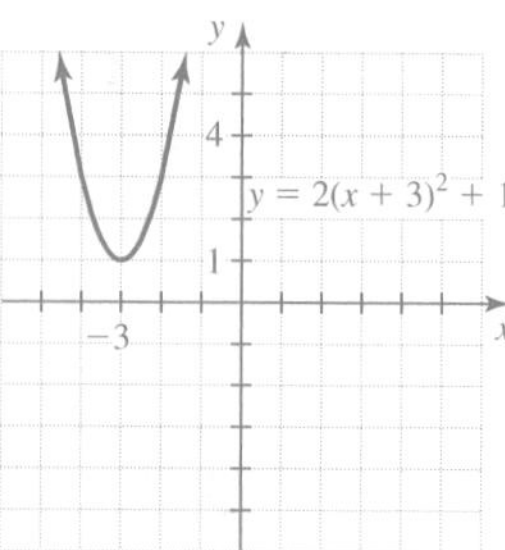

50. $y = 2(x + 1)^2 - 2$
$(-\infty, \infty), [-2, \infty)$

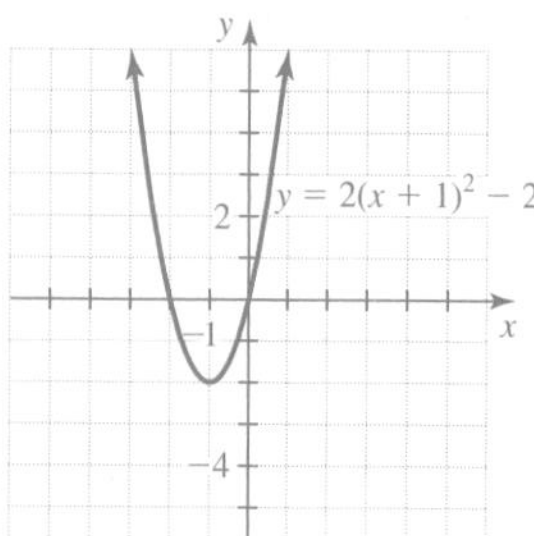

51. $y = -2(x - 4)^2 + 2$
$(-\infty, \infty), (-\infty, 2]$

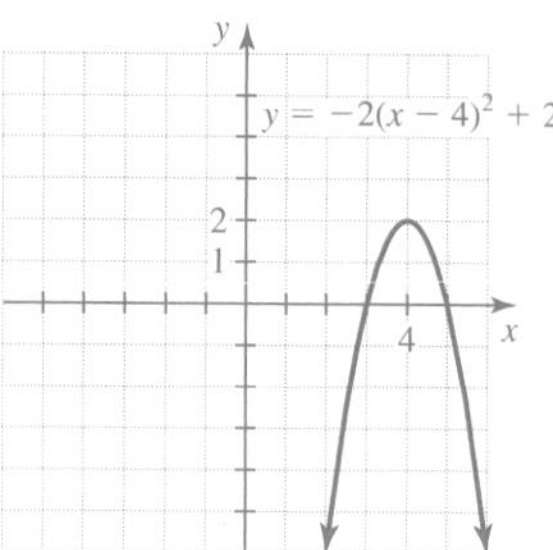

52. $y = -2(x - 1)^2 + 3$
$(-\infty, \infty), (-\infty, 3]$

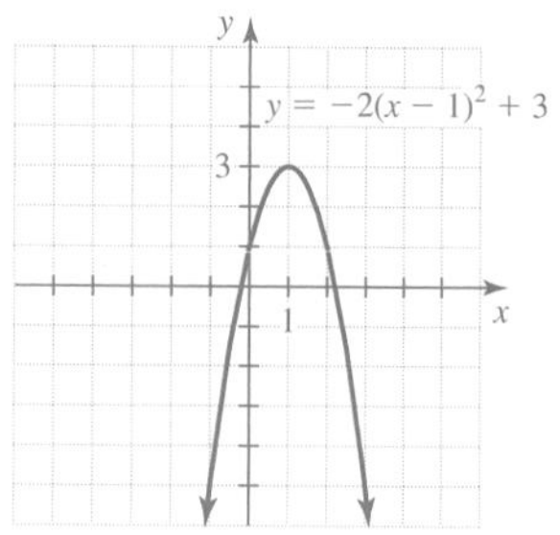

53. $y = -3(x - 1)^2 + 6$
$(-\infty, \infty), (-\infty, 6]$

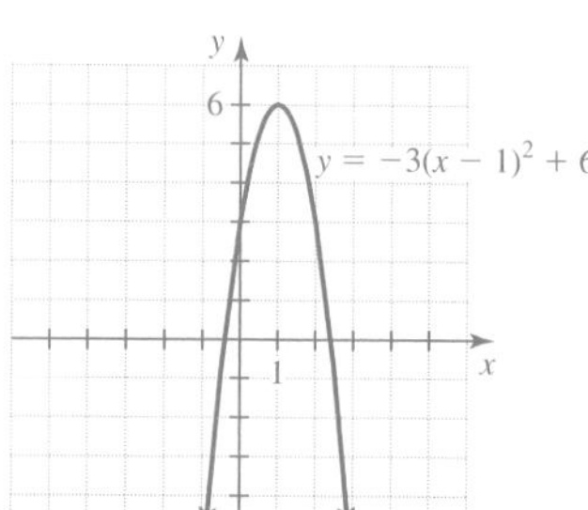

54. $y = 3(x + 2)^2 - 6$
$(-\infty, \infty), [-6, \infty)$

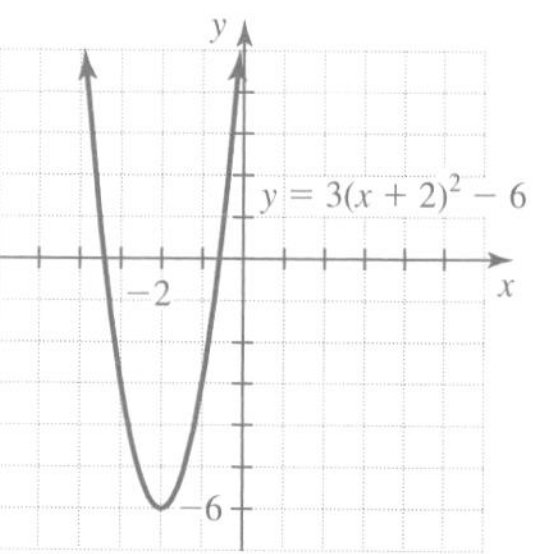

Match each function with its graph a–h.

55. $y = 2 + \sqrt{x}$ d

56. $y = \sqrt{2 + x}$ a

57. $y = 2\sqrt{x}$ e

58. $y = \sqrt{\dfrac{x}{2}}$ g

59. $y = \dfrac{1}{2}\sqrt{x}$ h

60. $y = 2 + \sqrt{x - 2}$ b

61. $y = -2\sqrt{x}$ c

62. $y = \sqrt{-x}$ f

a) **b)**

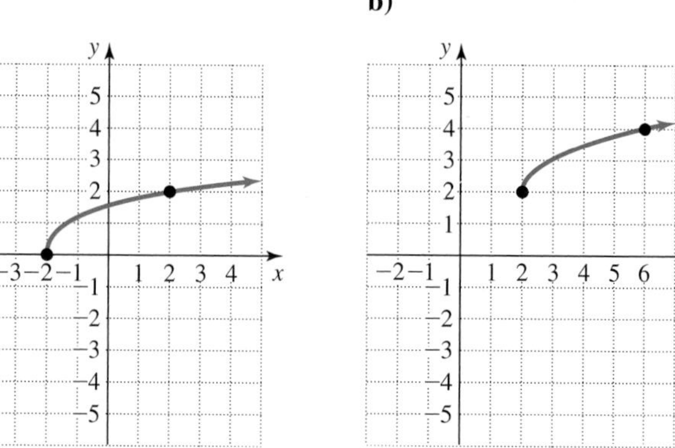

c) 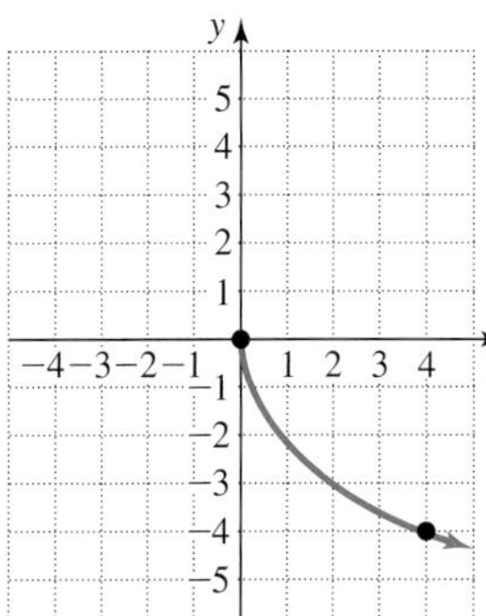

d) 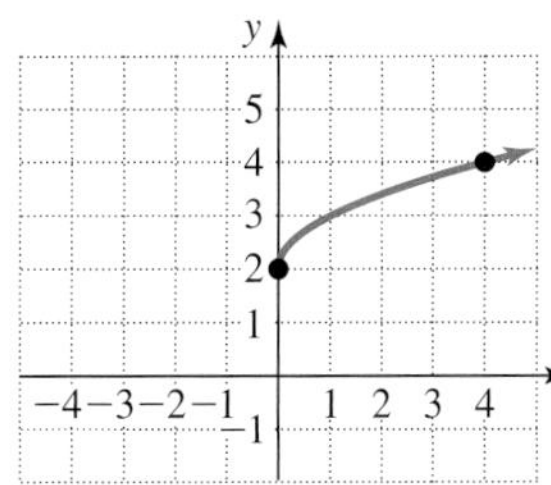

e) 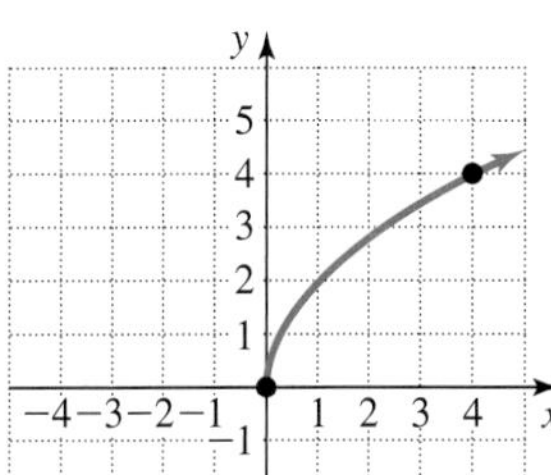

f) 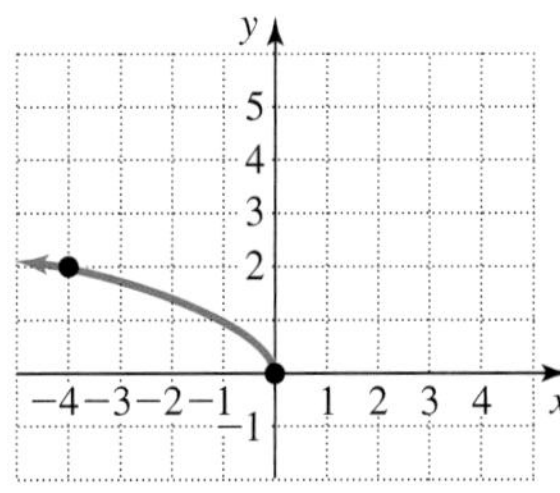

g) 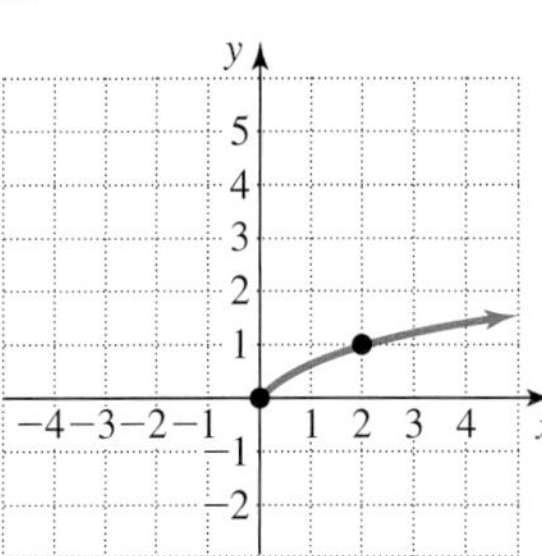

h) 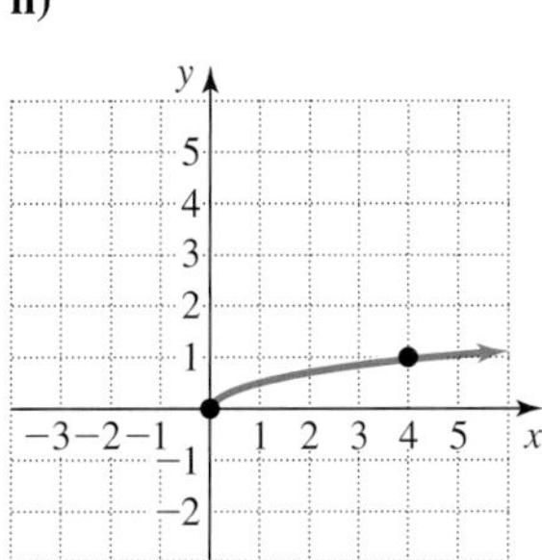

Getting More Involved

63. If the graph of $y = x^2$ is translated eight units upward, then what is the equation of the curve at that location?
$y = x^2 + 8$

64. If the graph of $y = x^2$ is translated six units to the right, then what is the equation of the curve at that location?
$y = (x - 6)^2$

65. If the graph of $y = \sqrt{x}$ is translated five units to the left, then what is the equation of the curve at that location?
$y = \sqrt{x + 5}$

66. If the graph of $y = \sqrt{x}$ is translated four units downward, then what is the equation of the curve at that location?
$y = \sqrt{x} - 4$

67. If the graph of $y = |x|$ is translated three units to the left and then five units upward, then what is the equation of the curve at that location? $y = |x + 3| + 5$

68. If the graph of $y = |x|$ is translated four units downward and then nine units to the right, then what is the equation of the curve at that location? $y = |x - 9| - 4$

Graphing Calculator Exercises

69. Graph $f(x) = |x|$ and $g(x) = |x - 20| + 30$ on the same screen of your calculator. What transformations will transform the graph of f into the graph of g?
Move f to the right 20 units and upward 30 units.

70. Graph $f(x) = (x + 3)^2$, $g(x) = x^2 + 3^2$, and $h(x) = x^2 + 6x + 9$ on the same screen of your calculator.

a) Which two of these functions has the same graph? Why are they the same?
f and h, $(x + 3)^2 = x^2 + 6x + 9$ for all x

b) Is it true that $(x + 3)^2 = x^2 + 9$ for all real numbers x?
No

c) Describe each graph in terms of a transformation of the graph of $y = x^2$. Move $y = x^2$ to the left three units to get f or h. Move $y = x^2$ upward nine units to get g.

11.4 Graphs of Polynomial Functions

We have already graphed constant functions, linear functions, and quadratic functions, which are polynomial functions of degree 0, 1, and 2, respectively. In this section we will graph some polynomial functions with degrees that are greater than 2.

Cubic Functions

A third-degree polynomial function is called a **cubic function.** The most basic third-degree polynomial function is $f(x) = x^3$, which is called the **cubing function.** We can graph it by plotting some ordered pairs that satisfy the equation $f(x) = x^3$.

EXAMPLE 1

The cubing function

Graph the function $f(x) = x^3$ and identify the intercepts.

Solution

Make a table of ordered pairs as follows:

x	-2	-1	0	1	2
$f(x) = x^3$	-8	-1	0	1	8

Plot these ordered pairs and sketch a smooth curve through them as shown in Fig. 11.27. The x-intercept and the y-intercept are both at the origin, (0, 0).

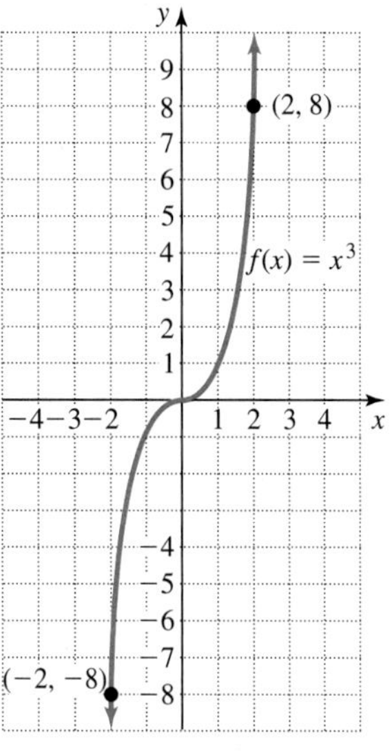

Figure 11.27

Now do Exercises 7–8

In general, the x-intercepts for a polynomial function can be difficult to find, but we will consider only polynomial functions for which the x-intercepts can be found by factoring. The next example shows a third-degree polynomial function that has three x-intercepts.

EXAMPLE 2

A cubic function with three x-intercepts

Graph the function $f(x) = x^3 - 4x$ and identify the intercepts.

Solution

The y-intercept is found by replacing x with 0. Since $f(0) = 0^3 - 4(0) = 0$, the y-intercept is (0, 0). The x-intercepts are found by replacing y or $f(x)$ with 0 and

Teaching Tip Don't be too concerned with accuracy if your students are drawing these graphs by hand.

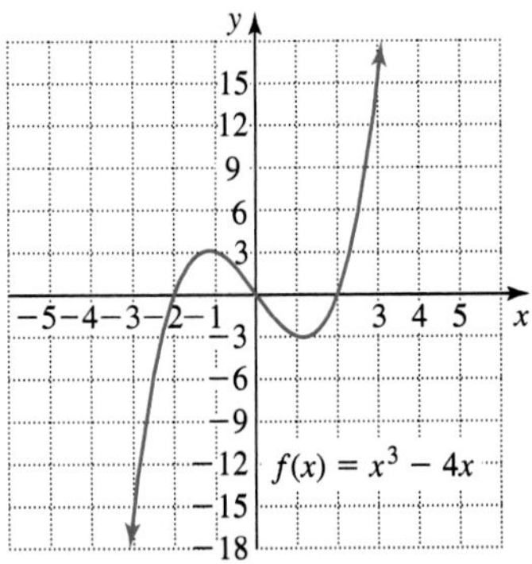

Figure 11.28

then solving for x:

$$x^3 - 4x = 0$$
$$x(x^2 - 4) = 0$$
$$x(x - 2)(x + 2) = 0 \quad \text{Factor completely.}$$
$$x = 0 \quad \text{or} \quad x - 2 = 0 \quad \text{or} \quad x + 2 = 0 \quad \text{Zero factor property}$$
$$x = 0 \quad \text{or} \quad x = 2 \quad \text{or} \quad x = -2$$

The x-intercepts are $(-2, 0)$, $(0, 0)$, and $(2, 0)$. Now make a table that includes those values for x:

x	−3	−2	−1	0	1	2	3
$f(x) = x^3 - 4x$	−15	0	3	0	−3	0	15

Plot these ordered pairs and sketch a smooth curve through them as shown in Fig. 11.28.

Now do Exercises 9–16

Quartic Functions

A fourth-degree polynomial function is called a **quartic function.** The most basic fourth-degree polynomial function is $f(x) = x^4$. We can graph it by plotting some ordered pairs that satisfy the equation $f(x) = x^4$.

EXAMPLE 3

The most basic fourth degree polynomial function

Graph $f(x) = x^4$ and identify the intercepts.

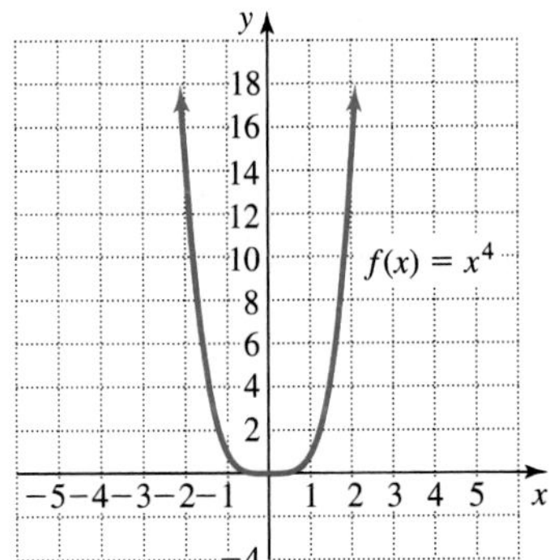

Figure 11.29

Solution

Since $f(0) = 0^4 = 0$ the y-intercept is $(0, 0)$. Since $x^4 = 0$ is satisfied only if $x = 0$, the only x-intercept is also $(0, 0)$. Make a table of ordered pairs as follows:

x	−2	−1	0	1	2
$f(x) = x^4$	16	1	0	1	16

Plot these ordered pairs and sketch a smooth curve through them as shown in Fig. 11.29. The shape of $f(x) = x^4$ is similar to a parabola, except it is "flatter" on the bottom.

Now do Exercises 17–18

The next example shows a fourth-degree polynomial function that has four x-intercepts.

EXAMPLE 4

A fourth degree polynomial function with four x-intercepts

Graph $f(x) = x^4 - 10x^2 + 9$ and identify the intercepts.

Solution

To find the y-intercept replace x with 0. Since $f(0) = 0^4 - 10(0^2) + 9 = 9$, the y-intercept is $(0, 9)$. To find the x-intercepts replace y or $f(x)$ with 0 and then solve for x:

$$x^4 - 10x^2 + 9 = 0$$

$$(x^2 - 1)(x^2 - 9) = 0$$

$$(x - 1)(x + 1)(x - 3)(x + 3) = 0 \quad \text{Factor completely.}$$

$$x - 1 = 0 \quad \text{or} \quad x + 1 = 0 \quad \text{or} \quad x - 3 = 0 \quad \text{or} \quad x + 3 = 0$$

$$x = 1 \quad \text{or} \quad x = -1 \quad \text{or} \quad x = 3 \quad \text{or} \quad x = -3$$

The four x-intercepts are $(\pm 1, 0)$ and $(\pm 3, 0)$. Now make a table that includes those values for x:

x	−4	−3	−2	−1	0	1	2	3	4
$x^4 - 10x^2 + 9$	105	0	−15	0	9	0	−15	0	105

Plot these ordered pairs and sketch a smooth curve through them as shown in Fig. 11.30.

Now do Exercises 19–26

Teaching Tip Point out how the scales on the axes must be adjusted to accommodate the large numbers in polynomial functions.

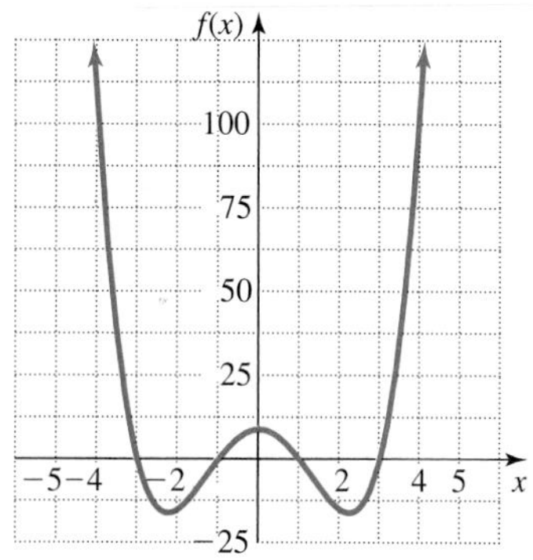

$f(x) = x^4 - 10x^2 + 9$

Figure 11.30

Behavior at the x-intercepts

The graphs of $y = x$, $y = x^2$, $y = x^3$, and $y = x^4$ all have the same x-intercept $(0, 0)$. But they have two different types of behavior at that x-intercept. The graphs of $y = x$ and $y = x^3$ cross the x-axis at $(0, 0)$, whereas the graphs of $y = x^2$ and $y = x^4$ touch but do not cross the x-axis at $(0, 0)$. The reason for this behavior is the power of the factor x. If a nonzero number is raised to an odd power, the result has the same sign as the original number. But if the power is even, the result is positive. Since $y = x$ and $y = x^3$ have odd powers, the y-coordinates are positive to the right of $(0, 0)$ and negative to the left of $(0, 0)$, and the graph crosses the x-axis at $(0, 0)$. Since the exponents in $y = x^2$ and $y = x^4$ are even, the y-coordinates are positive on either side of $(0, 0)$, and the graphs touch but do not cross the x-axis at $(0, 0)$. In general, we have the following theorem.

Behavior at the x-intercepts

Suppose that $x - c$ is a factor of a polynomial function. The graph of the function crosses the x-axis at $(c, 0)$ if $x - c$ occurs an odd number of times and touches but does not cross the x-axis if $x - c$ occurs an even number of times.

Since factoring can get difficult for higher degree polynomials, we will often discuss functions that are given in factored form as in the next example.

EXAMPLE 5

Behavior at the *x*-intercepts

Find the x-intercepts and discuss the behavior of the graph of each polynomial function at its x-intercepts.

a) $f(x) = (x - 1)^2(x - 3)$ **b)** $y = x^3 + 2x^2 - x - 2$

Teaching Tip Ask students for rough sketches of the graphs in Example 5 showing just the behavior at the x-intercepts.

Solution

a) Replace $f(x)$ with 0 to find the x-intercepts:

$$(x - 1)^2(x - 3) = 0$$

$$(x - 1)^2 = 0 \quad \text{or} \quad x - 3 = 0$$

$$x - 1 = 0 \quad \text{or} \quad x = 3$$

$$x = 1$$

The x-intercepts are $(1, 0)$ and $(3, 0)$. Since the factor corresponding to $(1, 0)$ is $x - 1$ and its power is even, the graph touches but does not cross the x-axis at $(1, 0)$. Since the factor corresponding to $(3, 0)$ is $x - 3$ and its power is odd, the graph crosses the x-axis at $(3, 0)$.

b) Replace y with 0 to find the x-intercepts:

$$x^3 + 2x^2 - x - 2 = 0$$

$$x^2(x + 2) - 1(x + 2) = 0 \quad \text{Factor by grouping.}$$

$$(x^2 - 1)(x + 2) = 0 \quad \text{Factor out } x + 2.$$

$$(x - 1)(x + 1)(x + 2) = 0 \quad \text{Factor completely.}$$

$$x - 1 = 0 \quad \text{or} \quad x + 1 = 0 \quad \text{or} \quad x + 2 = 0$$

$$x = 1 \quad \text{or} \quad x = -1 \quad \text{or} \quad x = -2$$

The x-intercepts are $(1, 0)$, $(-1, 0)$, and $(-2, 0)$. Since each factor occurs with the power of one and one is odd, the graph crosses the x-axis at each of the three x-intercepts.

Now do Exercises 27–40

Calculator Close-Up

The graphs of the functions in Example 5 support the conclusions that were made about the behavior at the x-intercepts.

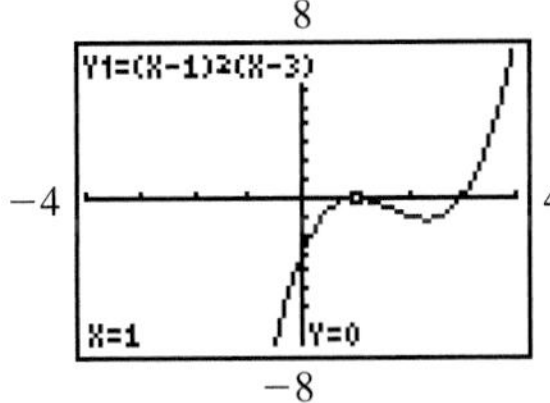

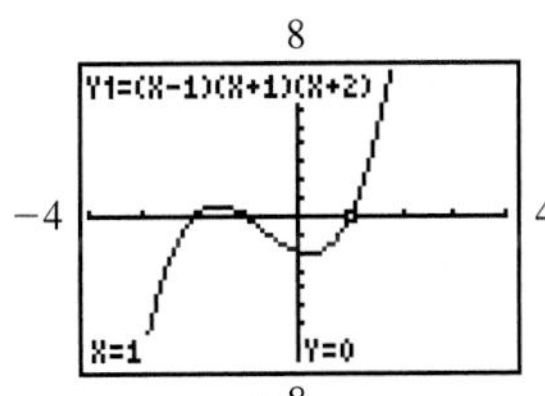

Transformations

In Section 11.3 we learned how changes in the formula defining a function can transform the graph of the function. In the next example, we perform some transformations on $f(x) = x^3$ and $f(x) = x^4$.

EXAMPLE 6

Transformations of graphs

Write the equation of each curve in its final position.

a) The graph of $f(x) = x^3$ is translated 3 units to the right and 2 units downward.

b) The graph of $f(x) = x^4$ is translated 4 units to the left and reflected in the x-axis.

Solution

a) To move the graph 3 units to the right, replace x with $x - 3$ to get $f(x) = (x - 3)^3$. To move the graph 2 units downward, subtract 2. So $f(x) = (x - 3)^3 - 2$ is the equation for the graph in its final position.

b) To move the graph 4 units to the left, replace x with $x + 4$ to get $f(x) = (x + 4)^4$. To reflect in the x-axis, multiply by -1. So $f(x) = -(x + 4)^4$ is the equation for the graph in its final position.

Now do Exercises 41–48

Calculator Close-Up

The graph of $f(x) = (x - 3)^3 - 2$ shows that it is a translation 3 units to the right and 2 units downward of $f(x) = x^3$.

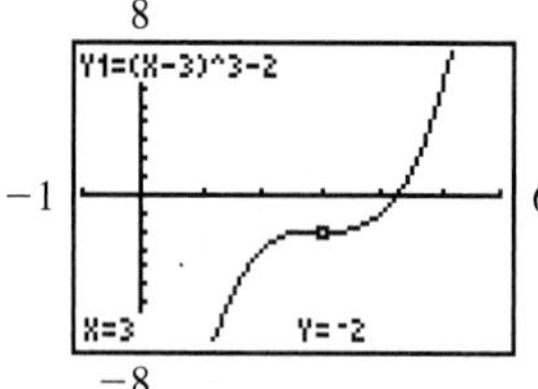

The graph of $f(x) = -(x + 4)^4$ shows that it is a translation 4 units to the left and a reflection of $f(x) = x^4$.

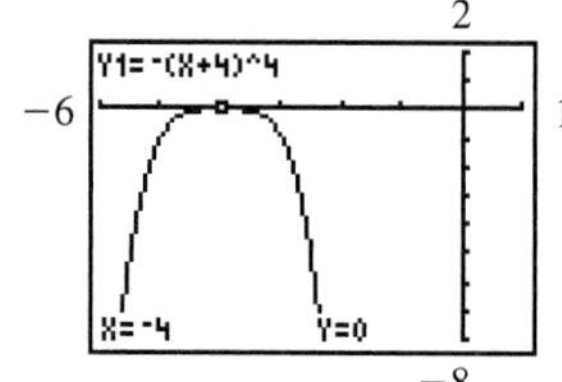

Warm-Ups ▼

True or false? Explain your answer.

1. The x-intercept for $f(x) = x^3 + 1$ is $(0, 1)$. False
2. The y-intercept for $f(x) = (x - 5)^3$ is $(0, -125)$. True
3. The graph of $y = x(x - 1)(x + 2)$ has three x-intercepts. True
4. The graph of $y = (x - 4)^4$ has four x-intercepts. False
5. The graph of $y = (x - 3)^2(x + 5)$ crosses the x-axis at $(3, 0)$ and $(-5, 0)$. False
6. The graph of $f(x) = (x - 7)^4$ touches but does not cross the x-axis at $(7, 0)$. True
7. The graph of $y = (x - 2)^3$ lies two units to the right of the graph of $y = x^3$. True
8. The graph of $y = x^4 + 3$ lies three units to the left of $y = x^4$. False
9. The graph of $y = (x + 5)^7$ lies five units to the right of the graph of $y = x^7$. False
10. The functions $y = x^3$ and $y = -x^3$ have the same graph. False

11.4 Exercises

Boost your GRADE at mathzone.com!

MathZone

- Practice Problems
- Self-Tests
- Videos
- Net Tutor
- e-Professors

Reading and Writing *After reading this section, write out the answers to these questions. Use complete sentences.*

1. What is a cubic function?
   A cubic function is a third-degree polynomial function.
2. What is a quartic function?
   A quartic function is a fourth-degree polynomial function.
3. How are x-intercepts found?
   To find x-intercepts set y equal to zero and solve the resulting equation.
4. How is the y-intercept found?
   To find the y-intercept replace x with zero and calculate the y-coordinate.
5. What is required for the graph of a polynomial function to touch but not cross the x-axis at an x-intercept?
   The factor corresponding to that intercept must occur with an even exponent.
6. What is required for the graph of a polynomial function to cross the x-axis at an x-intercept?
   The factor corresponding to that intercept must occur with an odd exponent.

Graph each function and identify the x- and y-intercepts. See Examples 1 and 2.

7. $f(x) = x^3 + 1$
   $(-1, 0), (0, 1)$

8. $f(x) = x^3 - 1$
   $(1, 0), (0, -1)$

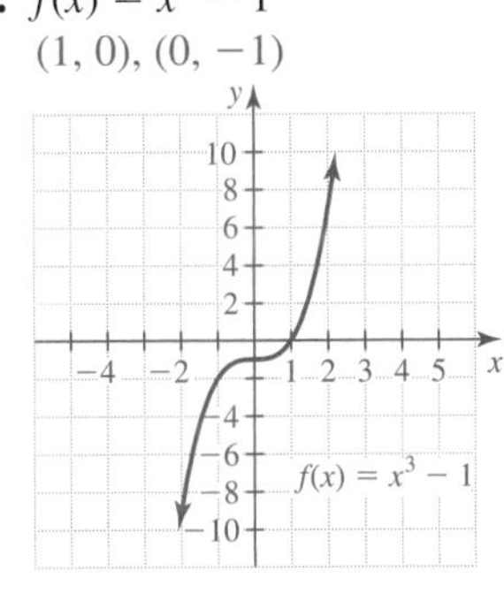

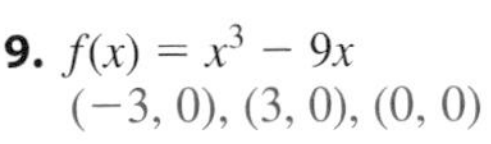

9. $f(x) = x^3 - 9x$
   $(-3, 0), (3, 0), (0, 0)$

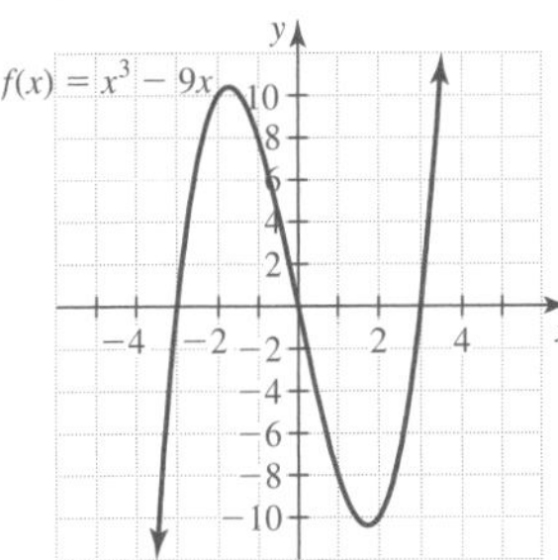

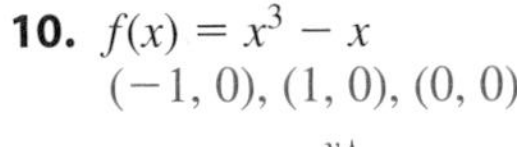

10. $f(x) = x^3 - x$
    $(-1, 0), (1, 0), (0, 0)$

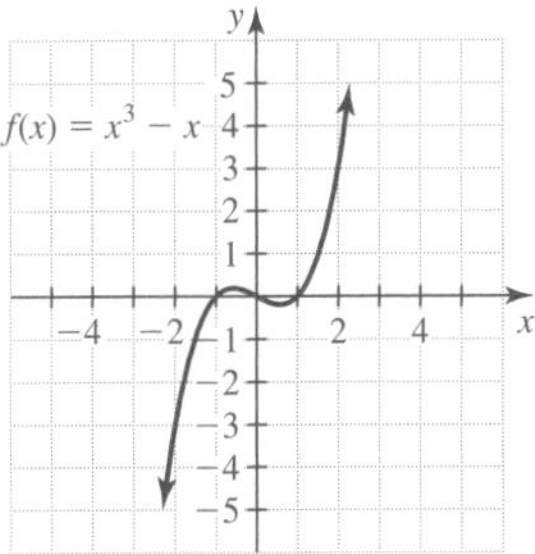

11. $f(x) = -x^3 - 4x^2$
    $(0, 0), (-4, 0)$

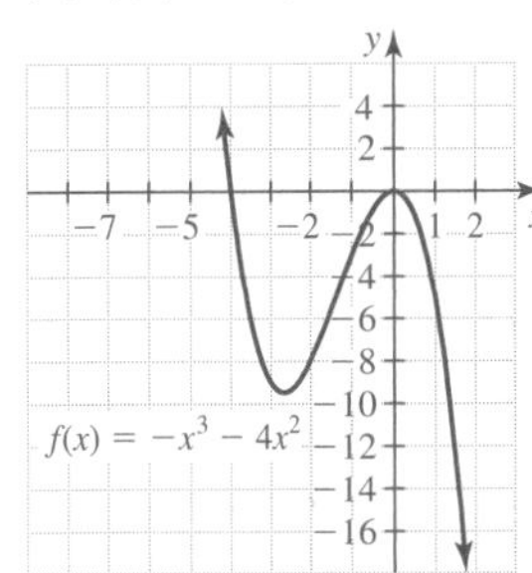

12. $f(x) = -x^3 + 3x^2$
    $(0, 0), (3, 0)$

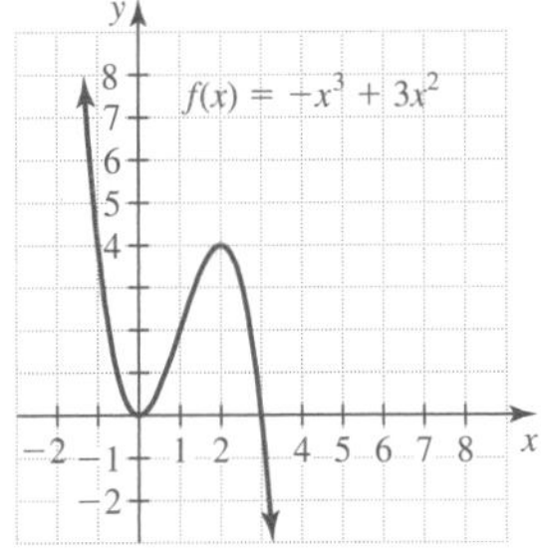

13. $f(x) = x^3 + x^2 - 4x - 4$
    $(-2, 0), (-1, 0),$
    $(2, 0), (0, -4)$

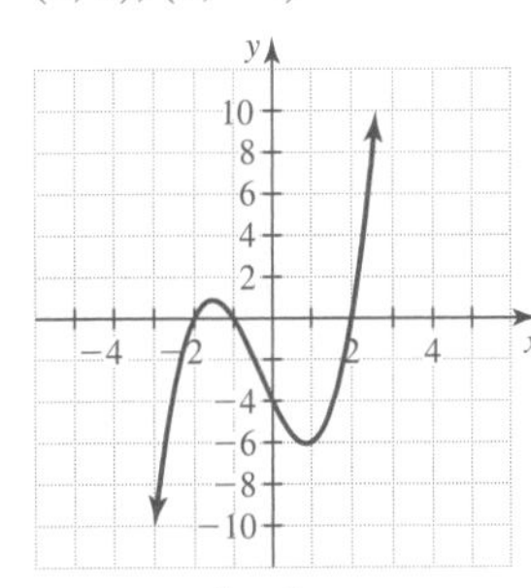

14. $f(x) = x^3 + 2x^2 - 9x - 18$
    $(-3, 0), (-2, 0),$
    $(3, 0), (0, -18)$

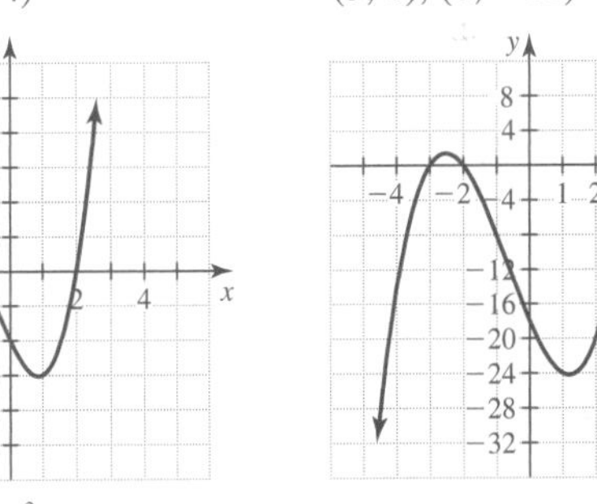

15. $f(x) = x^3 - 3x^2 - 9x + 27$
    $(-3, 0), (3, 0), (0, 27)$

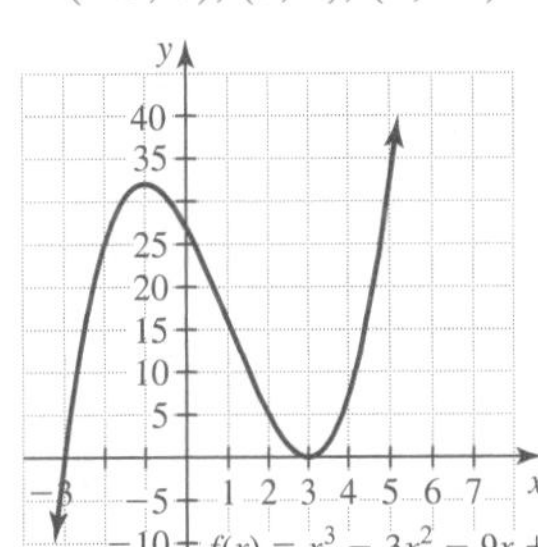

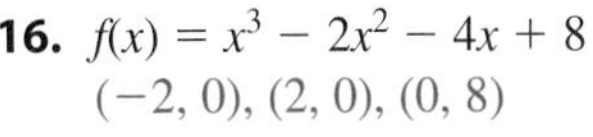

16. $f(x) = x^3 - 2x^2 - 4x + 8$
    $(-2, 0), (2, 0), (0, 8)$

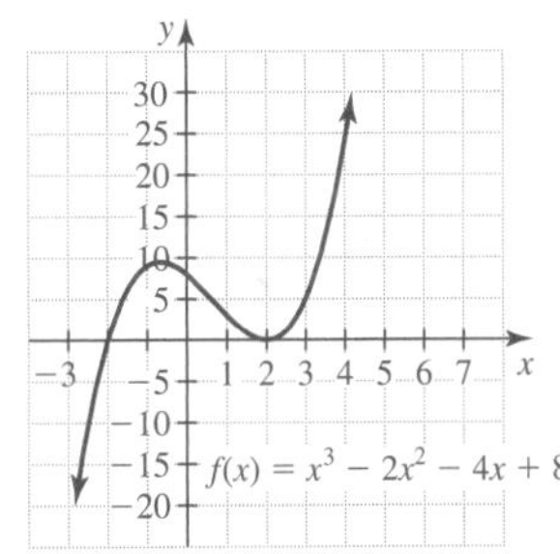

Graph each function and identify the x- and y-intercepts. See Examples 3 and 4.

17. $f(x) = x^4 - 1$
$(-1, 0), (1, 0), (0, -1)$

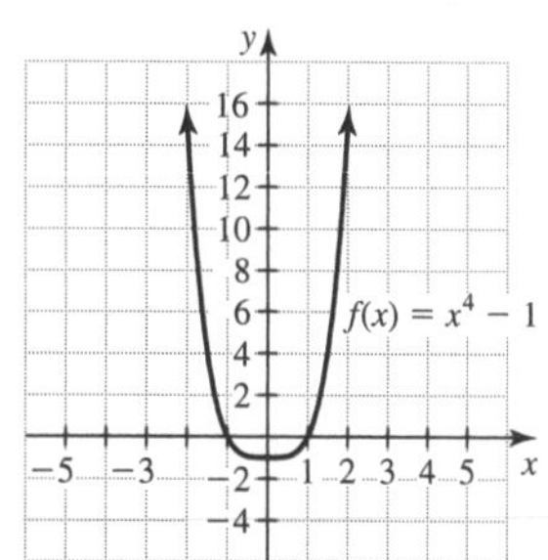

18. $f(x) = x^4 + 3$
$(0, 3)$

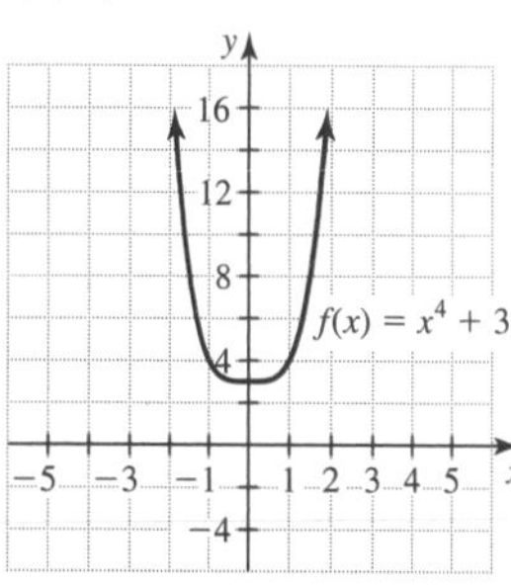

19. $f(x) = x^4 - 4x^2$
$(-2, 0), (0, 0), (2, 0)$

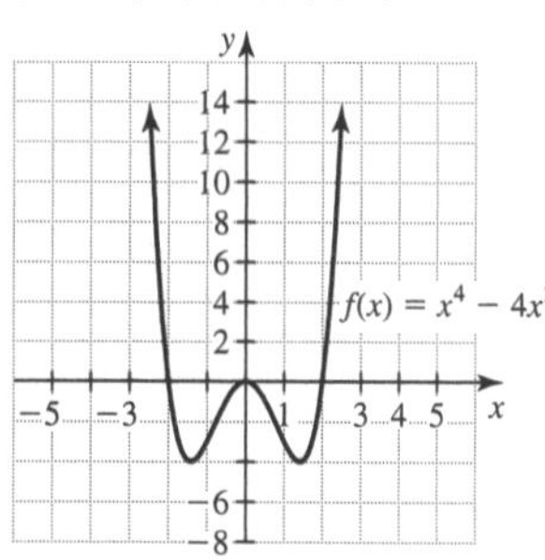

20. $f(x) = x^4 - 9x^2$
$(-3, 0), (0, 0), (3, 0)$

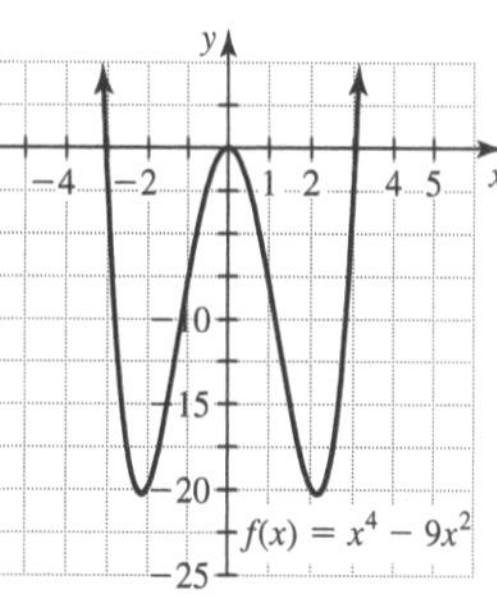

21. $f(x) = x^4 - 5x^2 + 4$
$(-2, 0), (-1, 0), (1, 0),$
$(2, 0), (0, 4)$

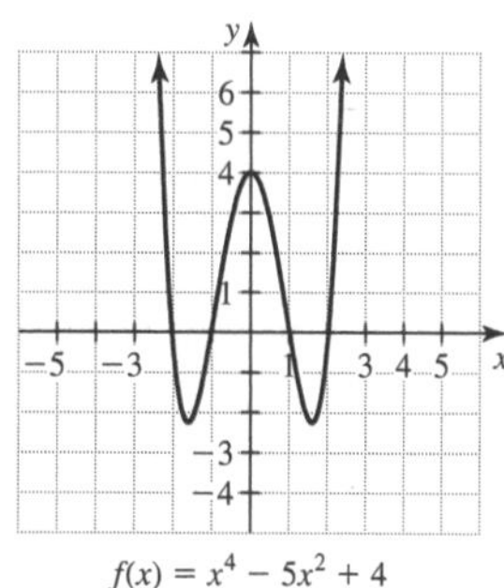

$f(x) = x^4 - 5x^2 + 4$

22. $f(x) = x^4 - 20x^2 + 64$
$(-4, 0), (-2, 0), (2, 0),$
$(4, 0), (0, 64)$

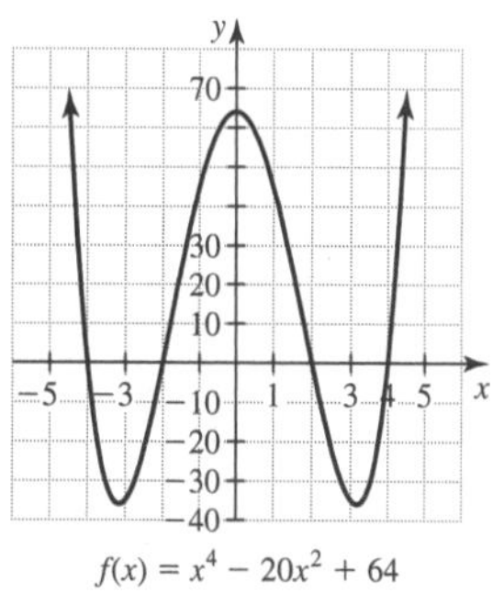

$f(x) = x^4 - 20x^2 + 64$

23. $f(x) = x^4 + x^3 - 4x^2 - 4x$
$(-2, 0), (-1, 0), (0, 0), (2, 0)$

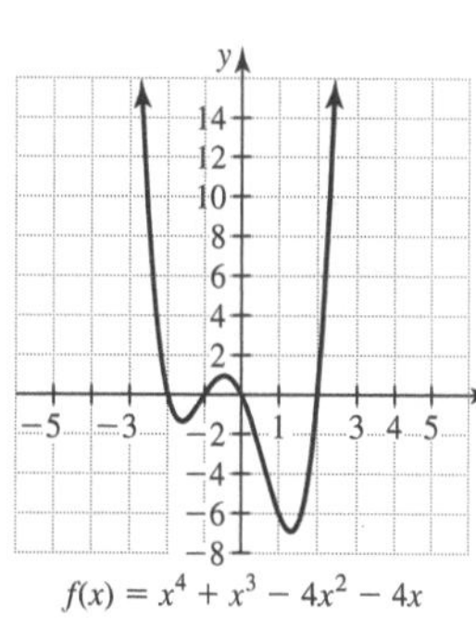

$f(x) = x^4 + x^3 - 4x^2 - 4x$

24. $f(x) = x^4 + 2x^3 - 9x^2 - 18x$
$(-3, 0), (-2, 0), (3, 0), (0, 0)$

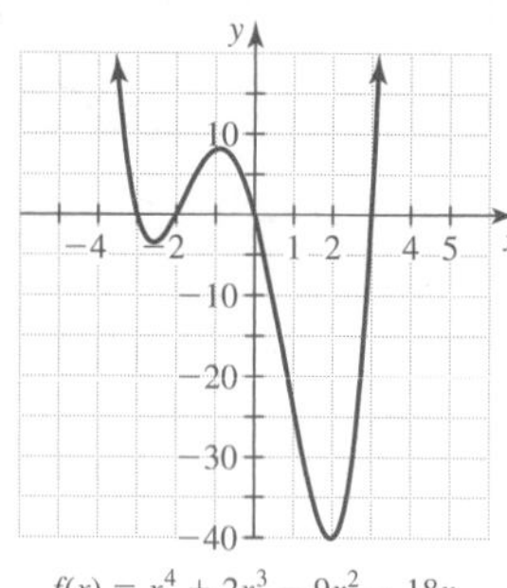

$f(x) = x^4 + 2x^3 - 9x^2 - 18x$

25. $f(x) = x^4 - 3x^3 - 9x^2 + 27x$
$(-3, 0), (0, 0), (3, 0)$

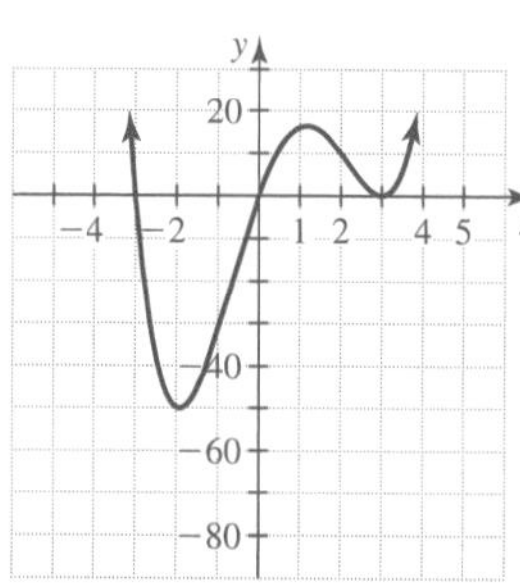

$f(x) = x^4 + 3x^3 - 9x^2 + 27x$

26. $f(x) = x^4 - 2x^3 - 4x^2 + 8x$
$(-2, 0), (0, 0), (2, 0)$

$x^3(x-2) - 4x(x-2)$

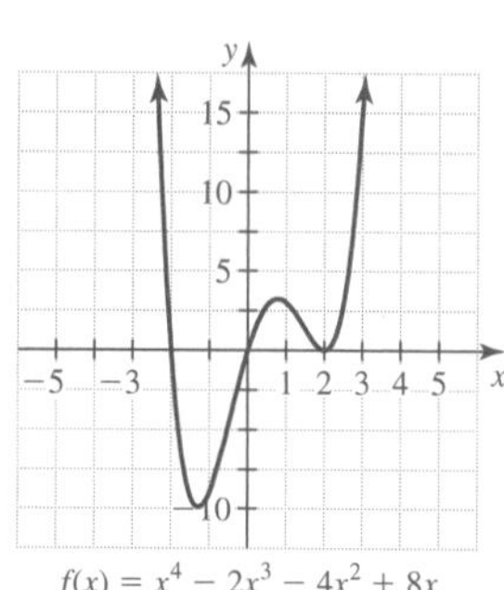

$f(x) = x^4 - 2x^3 - 4x^2 + 8x$

Find the x-intercepts and discuss the behavior of the graph of each polynomial function at its x-intercepts. Check your answers with a graphing calculator if you have one. See Example 5.

27. $f(x) = (x - 2)^2(x - 8)$
Crosses at $(8, 0)$; does not cross at $(2, 0)$.

28. $f(x) = (x + 3)^2(x - 5)$
Crosses at $(5, 0)$; does not cross at $(-3, 0)$.

29. $f(x) = (x - 1)^2(x + 4)^2$
Does not cross at $(-4, 0)$ and $(1, 0)$.

30. $f(x) = (x + 4)^2(x + 6)^2$
Does not cross at $(-6, 0)$ and $(-4, 0)$.

31. $f(x) = (x - 1)(x + 4)(x - 7)^2$
Crosses at $(-4, 0)$ and $(1, 0)$; does not cross at $(7, 0)$.

32. $f(x) = (x + 1)(x - 3)(x + 9)^2$
Crosses at $(-1, 0)$ and $(3, 0)$; does not cross at $(-9, 0)$.

33. $f(x) = x^3 + 6x^2 - x - 6$
Crosses at $(-6, 0)$, $(-1, 0)$, and $(1, 0)$.

34. $f(x) = x^3 + 5x^2 - 4x - 20$
Crosses at $(-5, 0)$, $(-2, 0)$ and $(2, 0)$.

35. $f(x) = -x^3 + 5x^2$
Crosses at (5, 0); does not cross at (0, 0).

36. $f(x) = -x^3 - 9x^2$
Crosses at (−9, 0); does not cross at (0, 0).

37. $f(x) = x^4 - 5x^3$
Crosses at (0, 0) and (5, 0).

38. $f(x) = x^4 + x^3$
Crosses at (0, 0) and (−1, 0).

39. $f(x) = x^4 + 6x^3 + 9x^2$
Does not cross at (−3, 0) and (0, 0).

40. $f(x) = x^4 - 4x^3 + 4x^2$
Does not cross at (0, 0) and (2, 0).

Write the equation of each curve in its final position. See Example 6.

41. The graph of $f(x) = x^3$ is translated 5 units to the right and 4 units downward. $f(x) = (x - 5)^3 - 4$

42. The graph of $f(x) = x^3$ is translated 2 units to the right and 1 unit upward. $f(x) = (x - 2)^3 + 1$

43. The graph of $f(x) = x^3$ is translated 6 units to the left and 3 units upward. $f(x) = (x + 6)^3 + 3$

44. The graph of $f(x) = x^3$ is translated 4 units to the left and 7 units downward. $f(x) = (x + 4)^3 - 7$

45. The graph of $f(x) = x^3$ is reflected in the x-axis. $f(x) = -x^3$

46. The graph of $f(x) = x^3$ is reflected in the x-axis and then translated 1 unit upward. $f(x) = -x^3 + 1$

47. The graph of $f(x) = x^4$ is translated 3 units to the right and then reflected in the x-axis. $f(x) = -(x - 3)^4$

48. The graph of $f(x) = x^4$ is translated 5 units to the left and then reflected in the x-axis. $f(x) = -(x + 5)^4$

Match each polynomial function with its graph a–h.

49. $f(x) = -2x + 3$ d

50. $f(x) = -2x^2 + 3$ f

51. $f(x) = -2x^3 + 3$ a

52. $f(x) = -2x^2 + 4x + 3$ g

53. $f(x) = -x^4 + 3$ c

54. $f(x) = x^3 - 3x^2$ h

55. $f(x) = x^3 + 3x^2 - x - 3$ e

56. $f(x) = \frac{1}{2}x^4 - 3$ b

a)

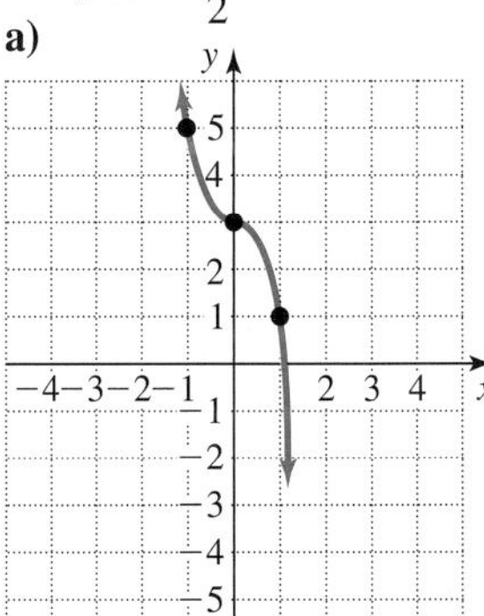

b)

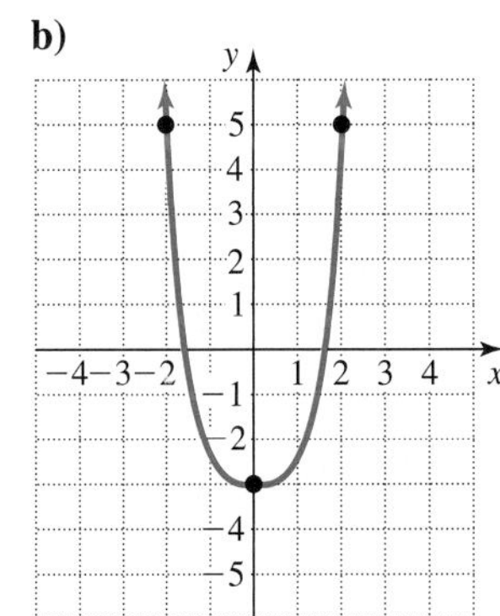

c)

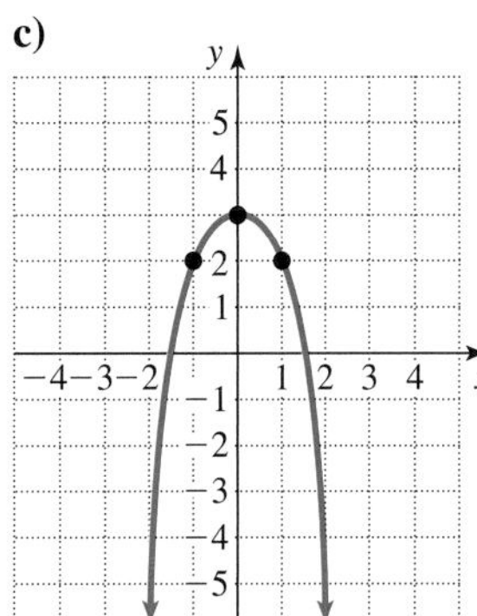

d)

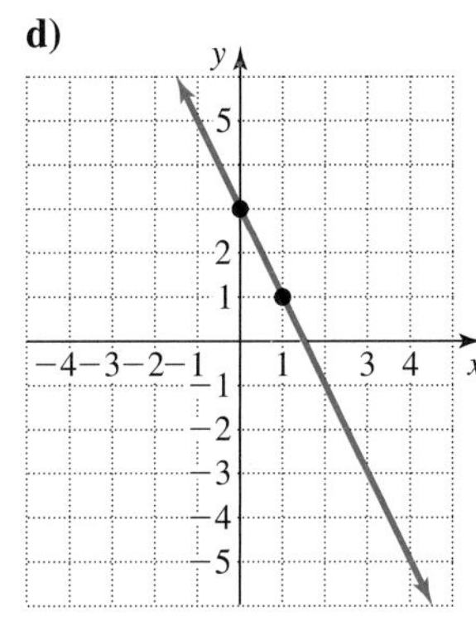

e)

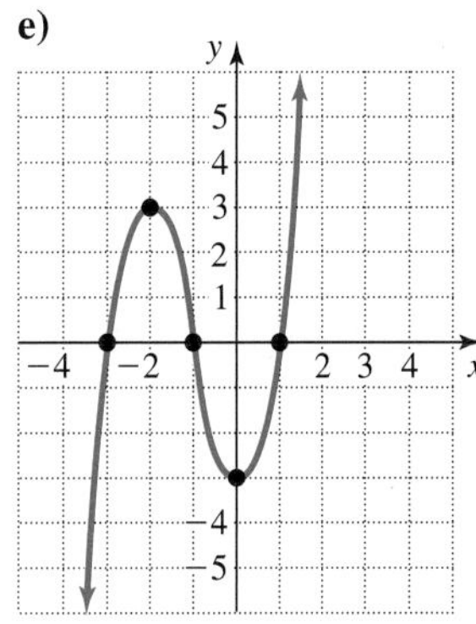

f)

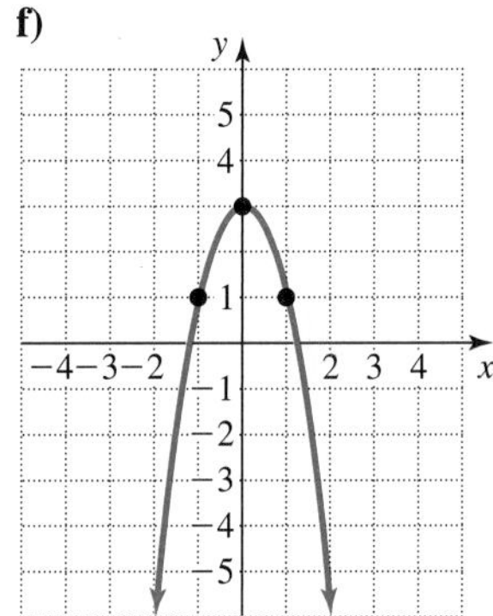

g)

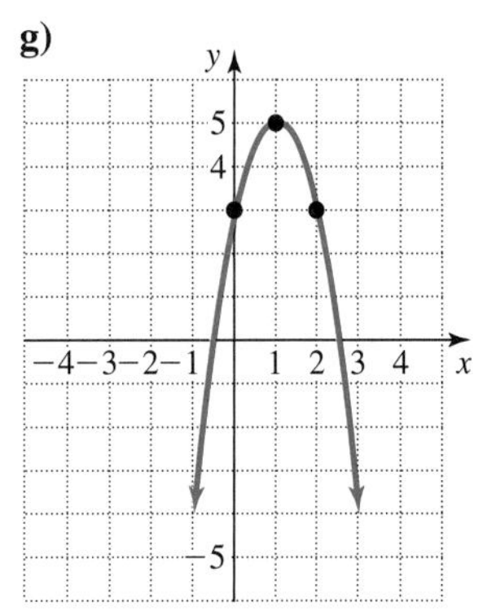

h)

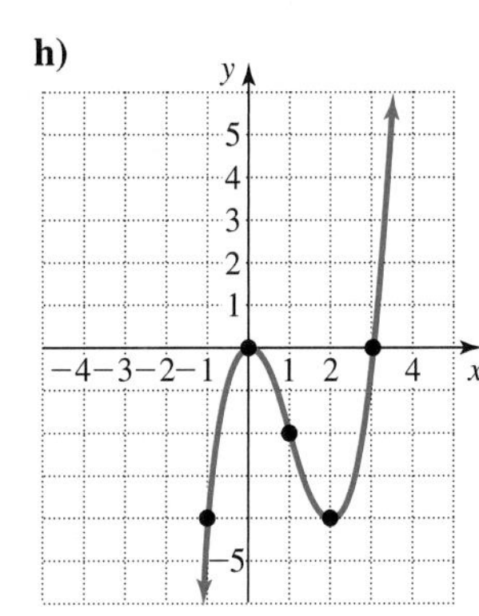

Sketch the graph of each polynomial function.

57. $f(x) = 2x - 6$

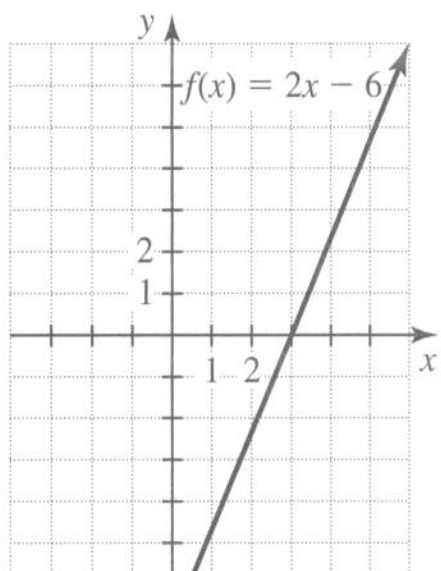

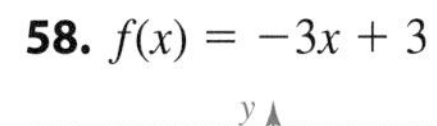

58. $f(x) = -3x + 3$

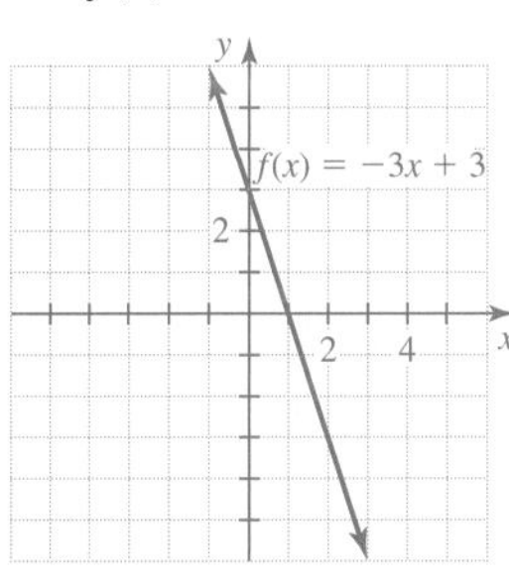

59. $f(x) = -x^2$

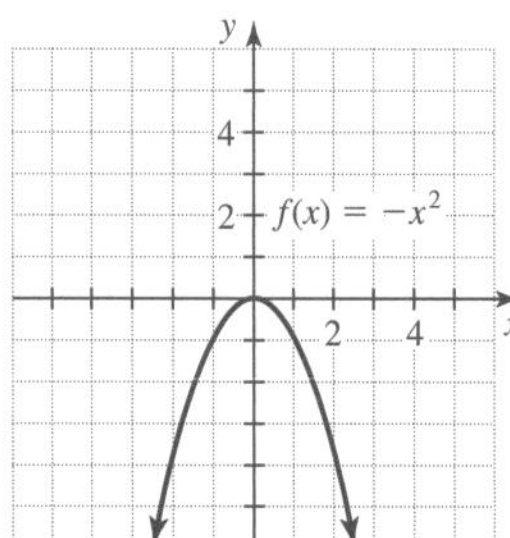

60. $f(x) = x^2 - 3$

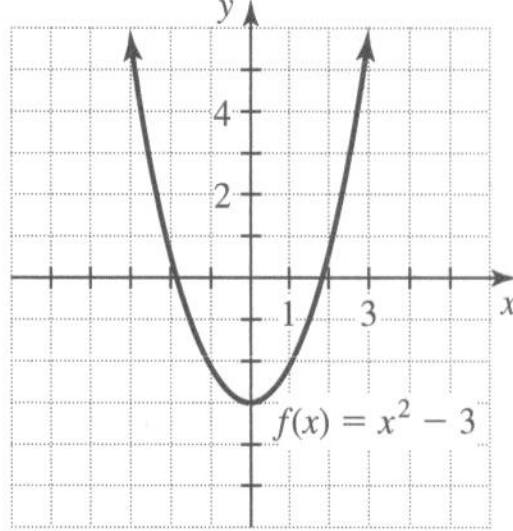

61. $f(x) = x^3 - 2x^2$

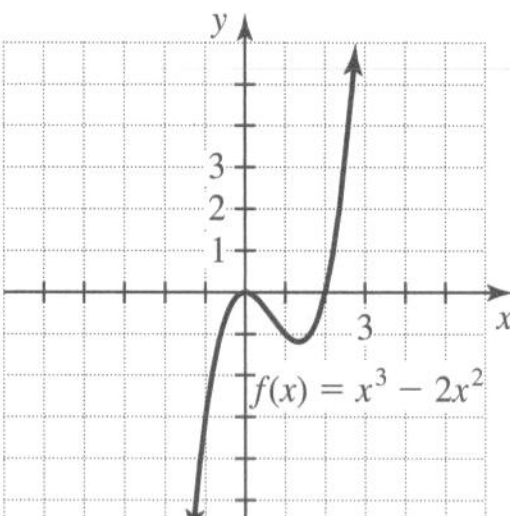

62. $f(x) = x^3 - 4x$

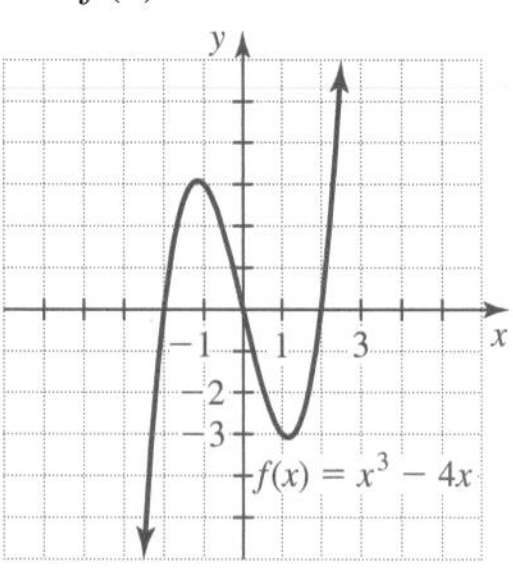

63. $f(x) = (x - 1)^2(x + 1)^2$

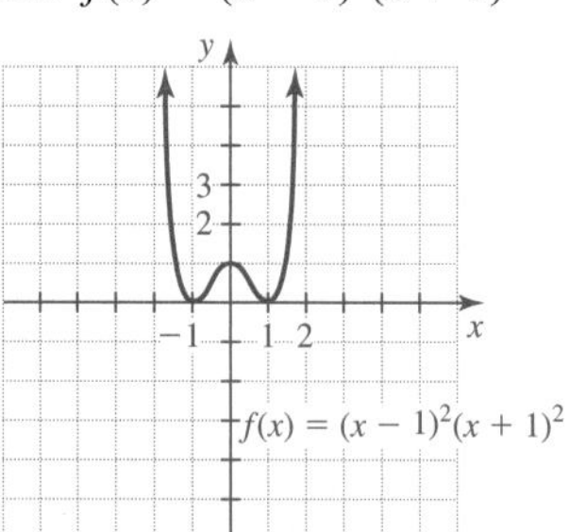

64. $f(x) = (x + 2)^2(x - 1)$

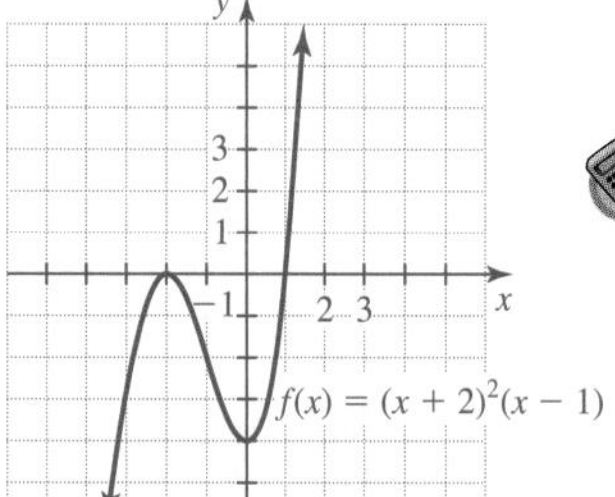

65. $f(x) = (x - 1)^2(x - 3)$

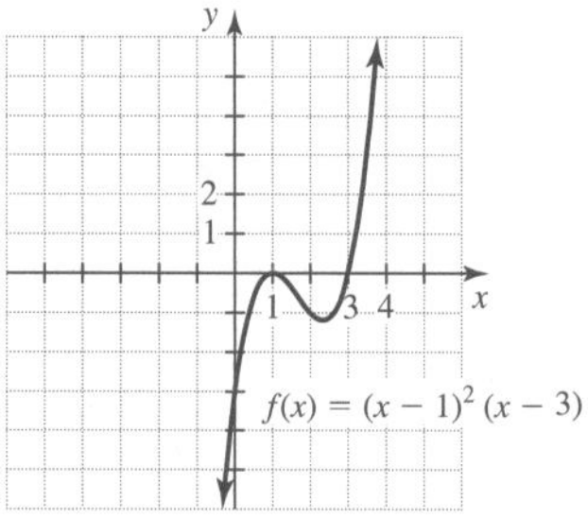

66. $f(x) = x^3 + 2x^2 - 3x$

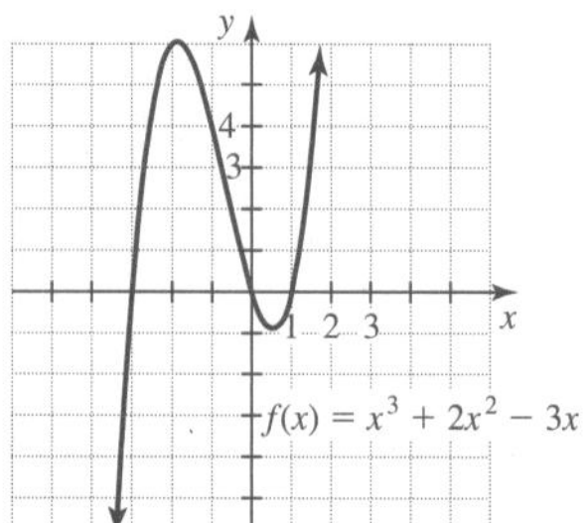

67. $f(x) = x^4 - 4x^3 + 4x^2$

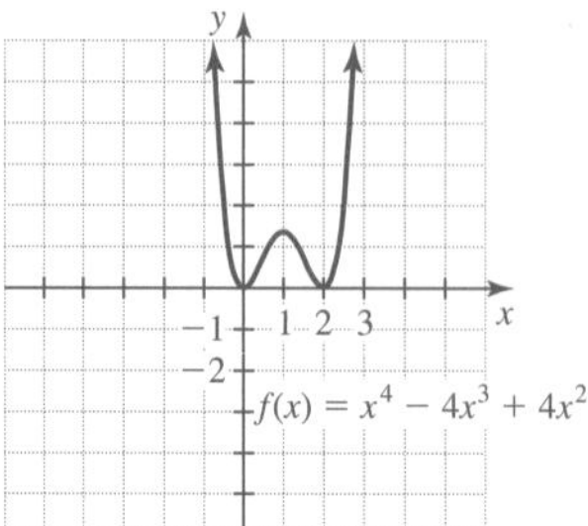

68. $f(x) = -x^4 + 6x^3 - 9x^2$

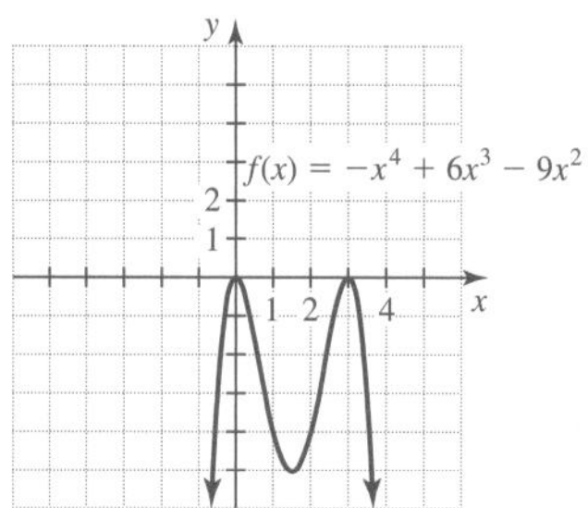

Graphing Calculator Exercises

Sketch the graph of each polynomial function. First graph the function on a calculator and use the calculator graph as a guide.

69. $f(x) = x - 20$

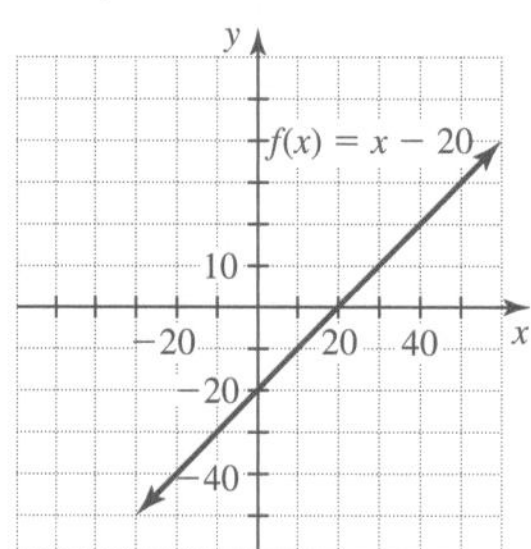

70. $f(x) = (x - 20)^2$

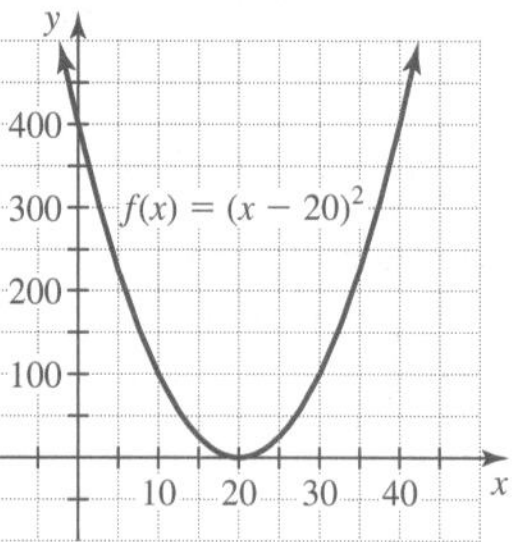

71. $f(x) = (x - 20)^2(x + 30)$

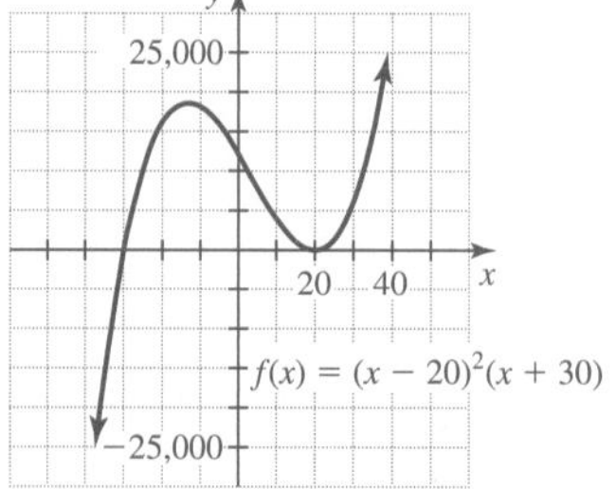

72. $f(x) = (x - 20)^2(x + 30)^2$

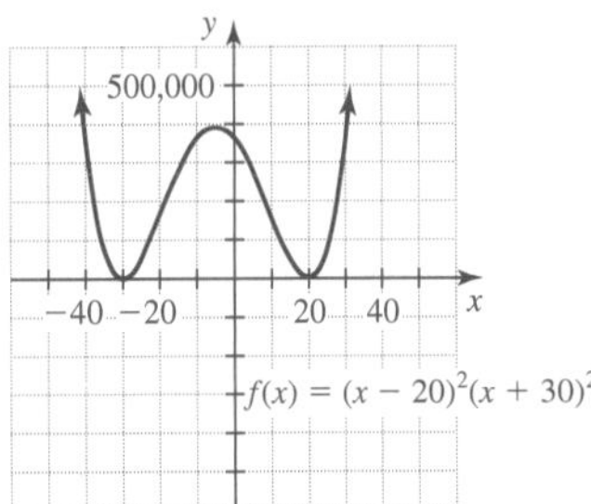

73. $f(x) = (x - 20)^2(x + 30)^2x$

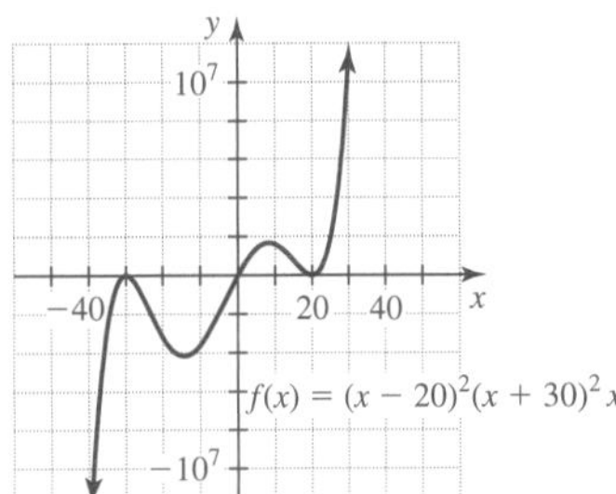

74. $f(x) = (x - 20)^2(x + 30)^2x^2$

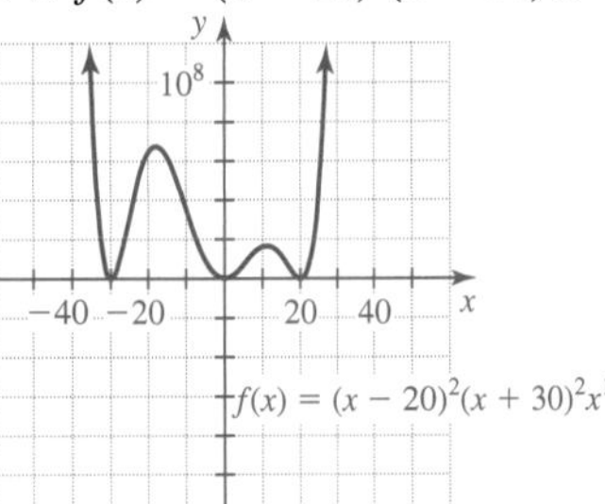

Getting More Involved

In each case, find a polynomial function whose graph behaves in the required manner. Answers may vary.

75. The graph has only one x-intercept at (3, 0) and crosses the x-axis there. $f(x) = x - 3$

76. The graph has only one x-intercept at (3, 0) but does not cross the x-axis there. $f(x) = (x - 3)^2$

77. The graph has only two x-intercepts at $(-2, 0)$ and (1, 0). It crosses the x-axis at $(-2, 0)$ but does not cross at (1, 0). $f(x) = (x + 2)(x - 1)^2$

78. The graph has only two x-intercepts at (5, 0) and $(-6, 0)$. It does not cross the x-axis at either x-intercept. $f(x) = (x - 5)^2(x + 6)^2$

11.5 Graphs of Rational Functions

In this Section

- Rational Functions
- Horizontal and Vertical Asymptotes
- Oblique Asymptotes
- Sketching the Graphs

We first studied rational expressions in Chapter 6. In this section we will study functions that are defined by rational expressions.

Rational Functions

A rational expression was defined in Chapter 6 as a ratio of two polynomials. If a ratio of two polynomials is used to define a function, then the function is called a rational function.

Rational Function

If $P(x)$ and $Q(x)$ are polynomials with no common factor and $f(x) = \frac{P(x)}{Q(x)}$ for $Q(x) \neq 0$, then $f(x)$ is called a **rational function.**

The domain of a rational function is the set of all real numbers except those that cause the denominator to have a value of 0.

EXAMPLE 1

Domain of a rational function

Find the domain of each rational function.

a) $f(x) = \dfrac{x - 3}{x - 1}$

b) $g(x) = \dfrac{2x - 3}{x^2 - 4}$

Solution

a) Since $x - 1 = 0$ only for $x = 1$, the domain of f is the set of all real numbers except 1, $(-\infty, 1) \cup (1, \infty)$.

b) Since $x^2 - 4 = 0$ for $x = \pm 2$, the domain of g is the set of all real numbers excluding 2 and -2, $(-\infty, -2) \cup (-2, 2) \cup (2, \infty)$.

Now do Exercises 7–12

Calculator Close-Up

If the viewing window is too large, a rational function will appear to touch its asymptotes.

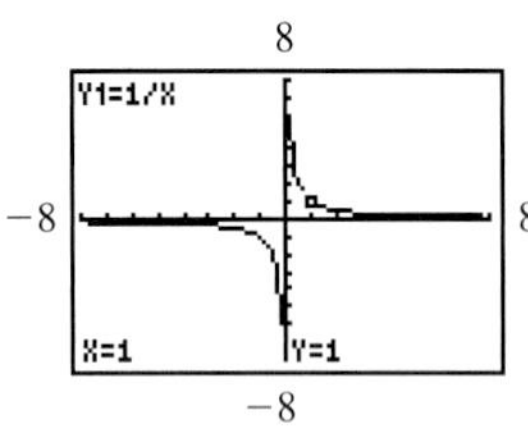

Because the asymptotes are an important feature of a rational function, we should draw it so that it approaches but does not touch its asymptotes.

Horizontal and Vertical Asymptotes

Consider the simplest rational function $f(x) = 1/x$. Its domain does not include 0, but 0 is an important number for the graph of this function. The behavior of the graph of f when x is very close to 0 is what interests us. For this function the y-coordinate is the reciprocal of the x-coordinate. When the x-coordinate is close to 0, the y-coordinate is far from 0. Consider the following tables of ordered pairs that satisfy $f(x) = 1/x$:

$x > 0$

x	y
0.1	10
0.01	100
0.001	1000
0.0001	10,000

$x < 0$

x	y
−0.1	−10
−0.01	−100
−0.001	−1000
−0.0001	−10,000

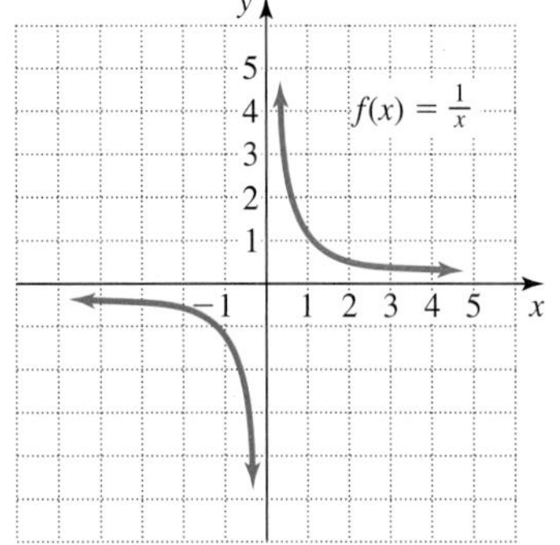

Figure 11.31

As x gets closer and closer to 0 from above 0, the value of y gets larger and larger. We say that y goes to positive infinity. As x gets closer and closer to 0 from below 0, the values of y are negative but $|y|$ gets larger and larger. We say that y goes to negative infinity. The graph of f gets closer and closer to the vertical line $x = 0$, and so $x = 0$ is called a **vertical asymptote.** On the other hand, as $|x|$ gets larger and larger, y gets closer and closer to 0. The graph approaches the x-axis as x goes to infinity, and so the x-axis is a **horizontal asymptote** for the graph of f. See Fig. 11.31 for the graph of $f(x) = 1/x$.

In general, a rational function has a vertical asymptote for every number excluded from the domain of the function. The horizontal asymptotes are determined by the behavior of the function when $|x|$ is large.

EXAMPLE 2

Horizontal and vertical asymptotes

Find the horizontal and vertical asymptotes for each rational function.

a) $f(x) = \dfrac{3}{x^2 - 1}$ **b)** $g(x) = \dfrac{x}{x^2 - 4}$ **c)** $h(x) = \dfrac{2x + 1}{x + 3}$

Calculator Close-Up

The graph for Example 2(a) should consist of three separate pieces, but in connected mode the calculator connects the separate pieces. Even though the calculator does not draw a very good graph of this function, it does support the conclusion that the horizontal asymptote is the x-axis and the vertical asymptotes are $x = -1$ and $x = 1$.

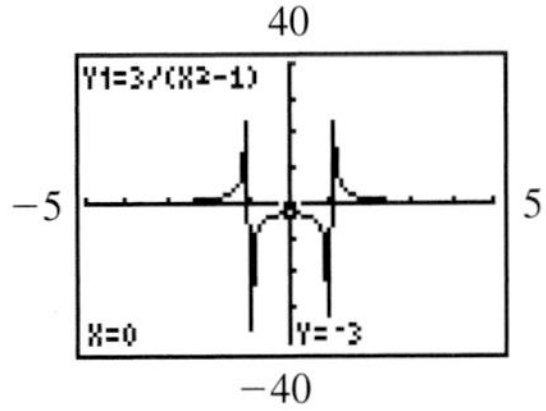

Solution

a) The denominator $x^2 - 1$ has a value of 0 if $x = \pm 1$. So the lines $x = 1$ and $x = -1$ are vertical asymptotes. If $|x|$ is very large, the value of $\frac{3}{x^2 - 1}$ is approximately 0. So the x-axis is a horizontal asymptote.

b) The denominator $x^2 - 4$ has a value of 0 if $x = \pm 2$. So the lines $x = 2$ and $x = -2$ are vertical asymptotes. If $|x|$ is very large, the value of $\frac{x}{x^2 - 4}$ is approximately 0. So the x-axis is a horizontal asymptote.

c) The denominator $x + 3$ has a value of 0 if $x = -3$. So the line $x = -3$ is a vertical asymptote. If $|x|$ is very large, the value of $h(x)$ is not approximately 0. To understand the value of $h(x)$, we change the form of the rational expression by using long division:

$$\begin{array}{r} 2 \\ x + 3 \overline{)2x + 1} \\ \underline{2x + 6} \\ -5 \end{array}$$

Writing the rational expression as quotient + $\frac{\text{remainder}}{\text{divisor}}$, we get $h(x) = \frac{2x + 1}{x + 3} = 2 + \frac{-5}{x + 3}$. If $|x|$ is very large, $\frac{-5}{x + 3}$ is approximately 0, and so the y-coordinate is approximately 2. The line $y = 2$ is a horizontal asymptote.

Now do Exercises 13–18

Example 2 illustrates two important facts about horizontal asymptotes. If the degree of the numerator is less than the degree of the denominator, then the x-axis is the horizontal asymptote. For example, $y = \frac{x - 4}{x^2 - 7}$ has the x-axis as a horizontal asymptote. If the degree of the numerator is equal to the degree of the denominator, then the ratio of the leading coefficients determines the horizontal asymptote. For example, $y = \frac{2x - 7}{3x - 5}$ has $y = \frac{2}{3}$ as its horizontal asymptote. The remaining case is when the degree of the numerator is greater than the degree of the denominator. This case is discussed next.

Oblique Asymptotes

Each rational function of Example 2 had one horizontal asymptote and a vertical asymptote for each number that caused the denominator to be 0. The horizontal asymptote $y = 0$ occurs because as $|x|$ gets larger and larger, the y-coordinate gets closer and closer to 0. Some rational functions have a nonhorizontal line for an asymptote. An asymptote that is neither horizontal nor vertical is called an **oblique asymptote** or **slant asymptote.**

EXAMPLE 3

Finding an oblique asymptote

Determine all of the asymptotes for

$$g(x) = \frac{2x^2 + 3x - 5}{x + 2}.$$

Teaching Tip Point out that curves can also be asymptotes. The graph of $y = x^2$ is an asymptote for the graph of $y = x^2 + \frac{1}{x}$.

Solution

If $x + 2 = 0$, then $x = -2$. So the line $x = -2$ is a vertical asymptote. Use long division to rewrite the function as quotient + $\frac{\text{remainder}}{\text{divisor}}$:

$$g(x) = \frac{2x^2 + 3x - 5}{x + 2} = 2x - 1 + \frac{-3}{x + 2}$$

If $|x|$ is large, the value of $\frac{-3}{x+2}$ is approximately 0. So when $|x|$ is large, the value of $g(x)$ is approximately $2x - 1$. The line $y = 2x - 1$ is an oblique asymptote for the graph of g.

Now do Exercises 19–20

We can summarize this discussion of asymptotes with the following strategy for finding asymptotes for a rational function.

Study Tip

The last couple of weeks of the semester is not the time to slack off. This is the time to double your efforts. Make a schedule and plan every hour of your time. Don't schedule anything that isn't necessary. Get an early start on studying for your final exams.

Strategy for Finding Asymptotes for a Rational Function

Suppose $f(x) = \frac{P(x)}{Q(x)}$ is a rational function with the degree of $Q(x)$ at least 1.

1. Solve the equation $Q(x) = 0$. The graph of f has a vertical asymptote corresponding to each solution to the equation.
2. If the degree of $P(x)$ is less than the degree of $Q(x)$, then the x-axis is a horizontal asymptote.
3. If the degree of $P(x)$ is equal to the degree of $Q(x)$, then find the ratio of the leading coefficients. The horizontal line through that ratio is the horizontal asymptote.
4. If the degree of $P(x)$ is one larger than the degree of $Q(x)$, then use division to rewrite the function as

$$\text{quotient} + \frac{\text{remainder}}{\text{divisor}}.$$

The equation formed by setting y equal to the quotient gives us an oblique asymptote.

Sketching the Graphs

We now use asymptotes to help us sketch the graphs of some rational functions.

EXAMPLE 4

Graphing a rational function

Sketch the graph of each rational function.

a) $f(x) = \dfrac{3}{x^2 - 1}$ **b)** $g(x) = \dfrac{x}{x^2 - 4}$

Solution

a) From Example 2(a), the lines $x = 1$ and $x = -1$ are vertical asymptotes and the x-axis is a horizontal asymptote. The vertical asymptotes are drawn with dashed lines as shown in Fig. 11.32. Next, we find some ordered pairs that satisfy $f(x) = \frac{3}{x^2 - 1}$. The graph goes through the points $(0, -3)$, $(\pm 0.9, -15.789)$, $(\pm 1.1, 14.286)$, $(\pm 2, 1)$, and $\left(\pm 3, \frac{3}{8}\right)$ as it approaches its asymptotes in Fig. 11.32.

b) From Example 2(b), the lines $x = 2$ and $x = -2$ are vertical asymptotes and the x-axis is a horizontal asymptote. The vertical asymptotes are drawn with dashed lines as shown in Fig. 11.33. Next, we find some ordered pairs that satisfy $g(x) = \frac{x}{x^2 - 4}$. The graph goes through the points $(0, 0)$, $\left(1, -\frac{1}{3}\right)$, $(1.9, -4.872)$, $(2.1, 5.122)$, $\left(3, \frac{3}{5}\right)$, and $\left(4, \frac{1}{3}\right)$ as it approaches its asymptotes in Fig. 11.33.

Calculator Close-Up

This calculator graph supports the graph drawn in Fig. 11.33. Remember that the calculator graph can be misleading. The vertical lines drawn by the calculator are not part of the graph of the function.

Y1=X/(X²-4)
X=0 Y=0
10, −10, −4, 4

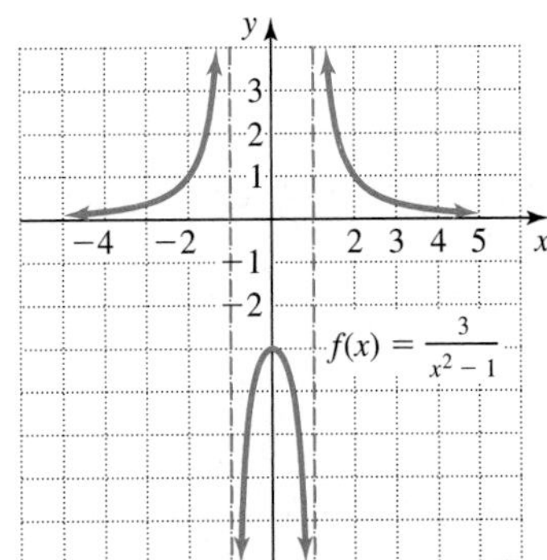

Figure 11.32

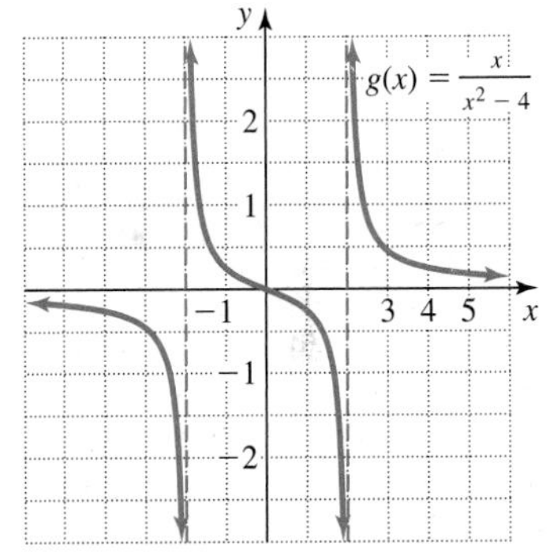

Figure 11.33

Now do Exercises 29–32

EXAMPLE 5

Graphing a rational function

Sketch the graph of each rational function.

a) $h(x) = \dfrac{2x + 1}{x + 3}$ **b)** $g(x) = \dfrac{2x^2 + 3x - 5}{x + 2}$

Solution

a) Draw the vertical asymptote $x = -3$ and the horizontal asymptote $y = 2$ from Example 2(c) as dashed lines. The points $(-2, -3)$, $\left(0, \frac{1}{3}\right)$, $\left(-\frac{1}{2}, 0\right)$, $(7, 1.5)$, $(-4, 7)$, and $(-13, 2.5)$ are on the graph shown in Fig. 11.34.

Calculator Close-Up

This calculator graph supports the graph drawn in Fig. 11.34. Note that if x is -3, there is no y-coordinate because $x = -3$ is the vertical asymptote.

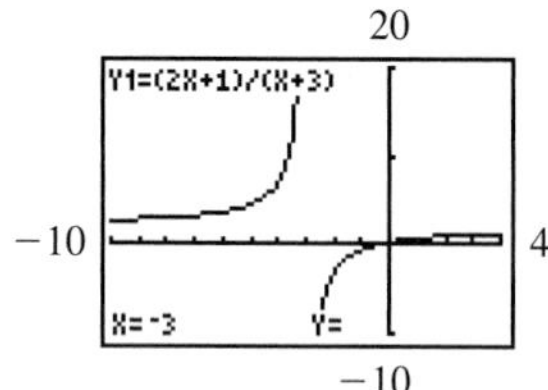

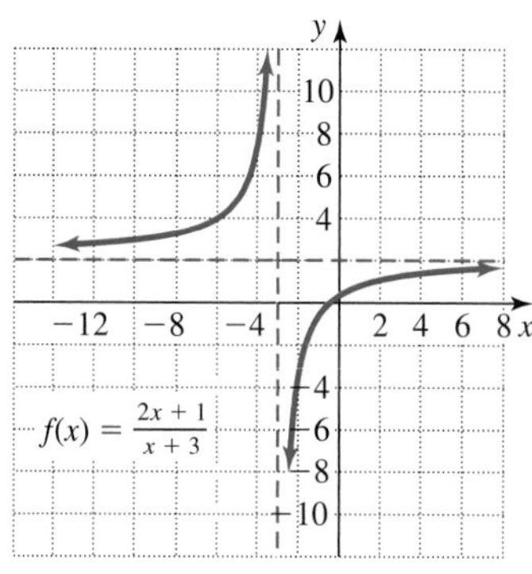

Figure 11.34

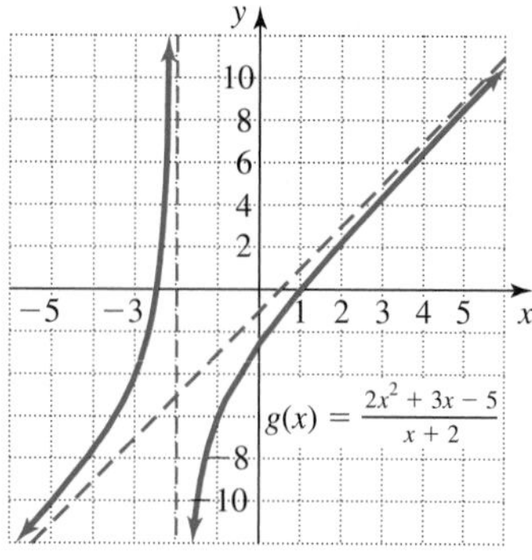

Figure 11.35

b) Draw the vertical asymptote $x = -2$ and the oblique asymptote $y = 2x - 1$ from Example 3 as dashed lines. The points $(-1, -6)$, $\left(0, -\frac{5}{2}\right)$, $(1, 0)$, $(4, 6.5)$, and $(-2.5, 0)$ are on the graph shown in Fig. 11.35.

Now do Exercises 33–38

Warm-Ups ▼

True or false? Explain your answer.

1. The domain of $f(x) = \dfrac{1}{x - 9}$ is $x = 9$. False
2. The domain of $f(x) = \dfrac{x - 1}{x + 2}$ is $(-\infty, -2) \cup (-2, 1) \cup (1, \infty)$. False
3. The domain of $f(x) = \dfrac{1}{x^2 + 1}$ is $(-\infty, -1) \cup (-1, 1) \cup (1, \infty)$. False
4. The line $x = 2$ is the only vertical asymptote for the graph of $f(x) = \dfrac{1}{x^2 - 4}$. False
5. The x-axis is a horizontal asymptote for the graph of $f(x) = \dfrac{x^2 - 3x + 5}{x^3 - 9x}$. True
6. The x-axis is a horizontal asymptote for the graph of $f(x) = \dfrac{3x - 5}{x - 2}$. False
7. The line $y = 1$ is a horizontal asymptote for $f(x) = \dfrac{x - 6}{x - 2}$. True
8. The only x-intercept for $f(x) = \dfrac{x - 6}{x - 2}$ is $(6, 0)$. True
9. The line $y = 2x - 5$ is an asymptote for the graph of $f(x) = 2x - 5 + \dfrac{1}{x}$. True
10. The line $y = 2x - 5$ is an asymptote for the graph of $f(x) = 2x - 5 + x^2$. False

11.5 Exercises

Boost your GRADE at mathzone.com!

MathZone

- Practice Problems
- Self-Tests
- Videos
- Net Tutor
- e-Professors

Reading and Writing *After reading this section, write out the answers to these questions. Use complete sentences.*

1. What is a rational function?
A rational function is of the form $f(x) = P(x)/Q(x)$, where $P(x)$ and $Q(x)$ are polynomials with no common factor and $Q(x) \neq 0$.

2. What is the domain of a rational function?
The domain of a rational function is all real numbers except those that cause the denominator to be 0.

3. What is a vertical asymptote?
A vertical asymptote is a vertical line that is approached by the graph of a rational function.

4. What is a horizontal asymptote?
A horizontal asymptote is a horizontal line that is approached by the graph of a rational function.

5. What is an oblique asymptote?
An oblique asymptote is a nonhorizontal, nonvertical line that is approached by the graph of a rational function.

6. What is a slant asymptote?
A slant asymptote is the same as an oblique asymptote.

Find the domain of each rational function. See Example 1.

7. $f(x) = \dfrac{2}{x-1}$ $(-\infty, 1) \cup (1, \infty)$

8. $f(x) = \dfrac{-2}{x+3}$ $(-\infty, -3) \cup (-3, \infty)$

9. $f(x) = \dfrac{x^2-1}{x}$ $(-\infty, 0) \cup (0, \infty)$

10. $f(x) = \dfrac{-2x+3}{x^2}$ $(-\infty, 0) \cup (0, \infty)$

11. $f(x) = \dfrac{5}{x^2-16}$ $(-\infty, -4) \cup (-4, 4) \cup (4, \infty)$

12. $f(x) = \dfrac{x+12}{x^2-x-6}$ $(-\infty, -2) \cup (-2, 3) \cup (3, \infty)$

Determine all asymptotes for the graph of each rational function. See Examples 2 and 3.

13. $f(x) = \dfrac{7}{x+4}$ Vertical: $x = -4$; horizontal: x-axis

14. $f(x) = \dfrac{-8}{x-9}$ Vertical: $x = 9$; horizontal: x-axis

15. $f(x) = \dfrac{1}{x^2-16}$ Vertical: $x = 4$, $x = -4$; horizontal: x-axis

16. $f(x) = \dfrac{-2}{x^2-5x+6}$
Vertical: $x = 2$, $x = 3$; horizontal: x-axis

17. $f(x) = \dfrac{5x}{x-7}$ Vertical: $x = 7$; horizontal: $y = 5$

18. $f(x) = \dfrac{3x+8}{x-2}$ Vertical: $x = 2$; horizontal: $y = 3$

19. $f(x) = \dfrac{2x^2}{x-3}$ Vertical: $x = 3$; oblique: $y = 2x + 6$

20. $f(x) = \dfrac{3x^2+2}{x+1}$ Vertical: $x = -1$; oblique: $y = 3x - 3$

Match each rational function with its graph a–h.

21. $f(x) = -\dfrac{2}{x}$ c

22. $f(x) = -\dfrac{1}{x-2}$ e

23. $f(x) = \dfrac{x}{x-2}$ b

24. $f(x) = \dfrac{x-2}{x}$ d

25. $f(x) = \dfrac{1}{x^2-2x}$ g

26. $f(x) = \dfrac{x^2}{x^2-4}$ h

27. $f(x) = -\dfrac{x+4}{2}$ f

28. $f(x) = \dfrac{x^2+2x+1}{x}$ a

a)

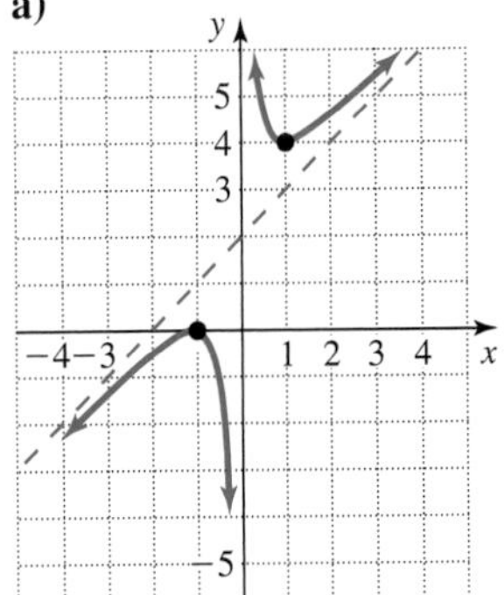

b)

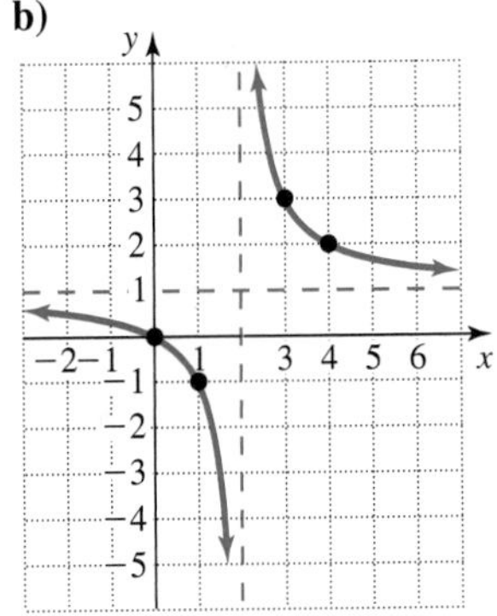

c)

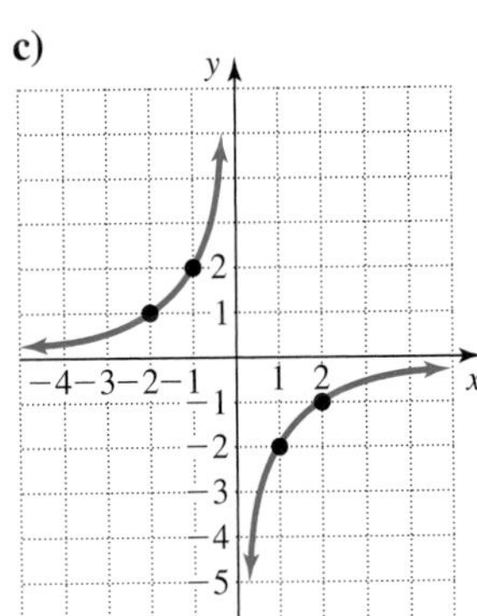

d)

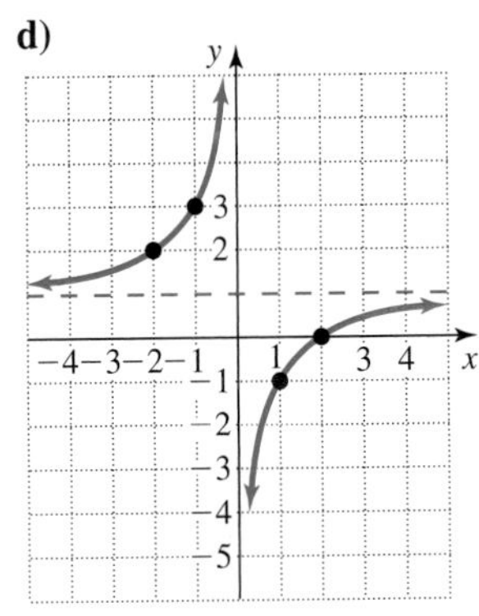

e)

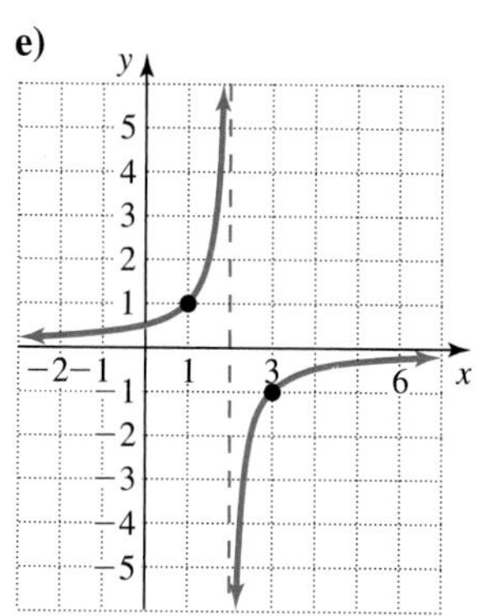

f)

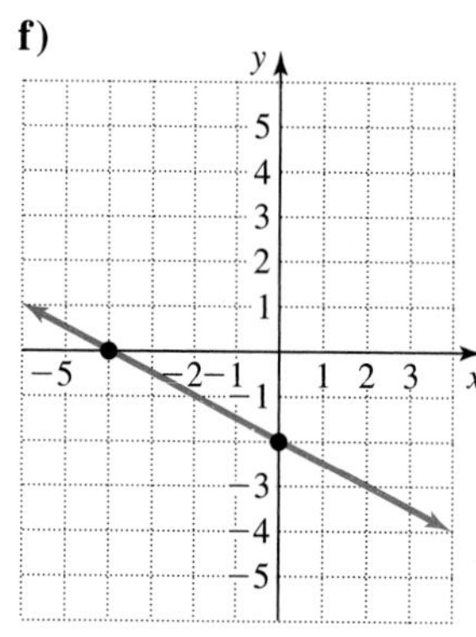

31. $f(x) = \dfrac{x}{x^2 - 9}$

$x = 3$, $x = -3$, x-axis

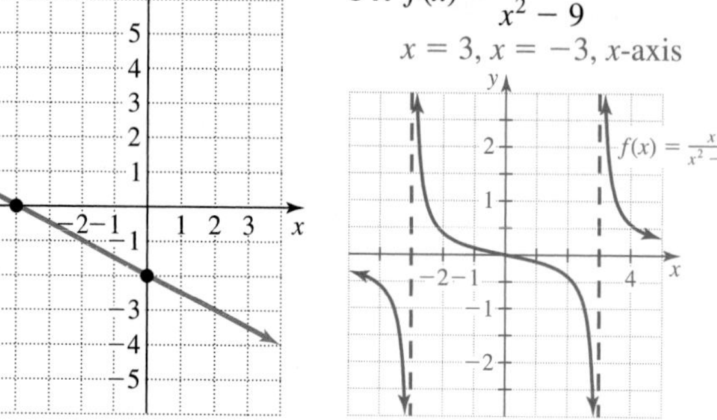

32. $f(x) = \dfrac{-2}{x^2 + x - 2}$

$x = -2$, $x = 1$, x-axis

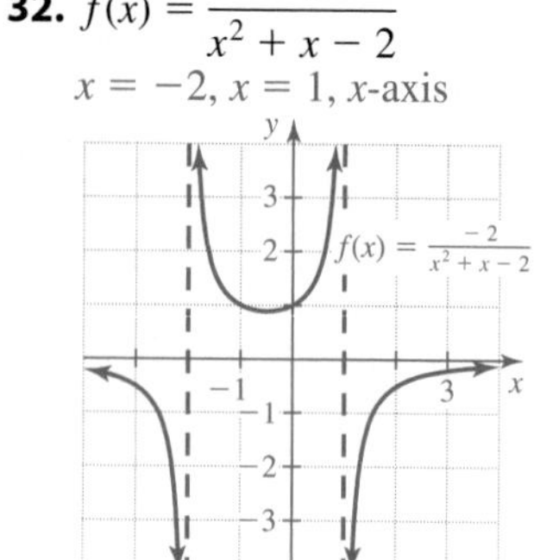

g)

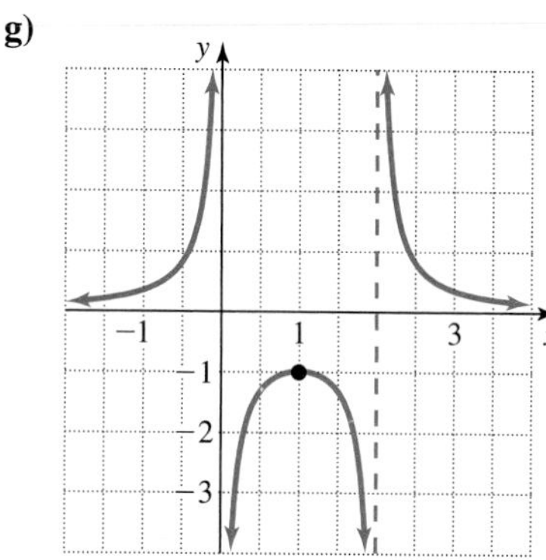

33. $f(x) = \dfrac{2x - 1}{x + 3}$

$x = -3$, $y = 2$

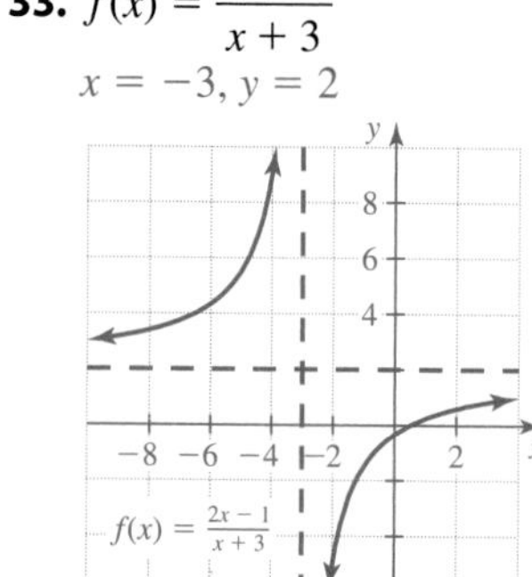

34. $f(x) = \dfrac{5 - 2x}{x - 2}$

$x = 2$, $y = -2$

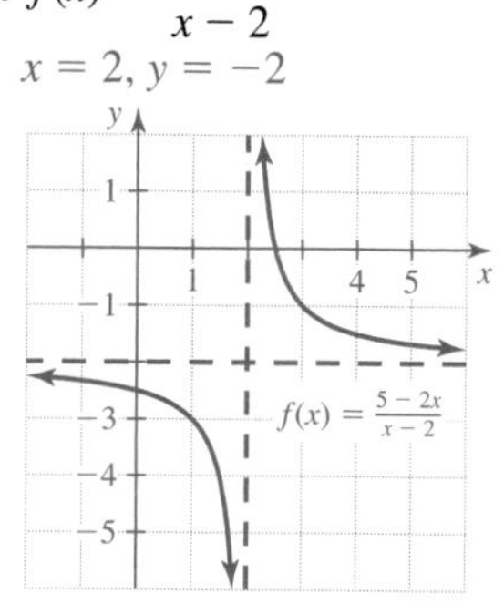

h)

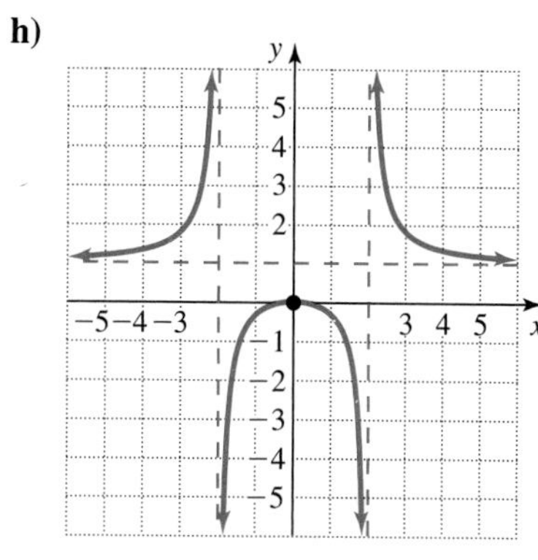

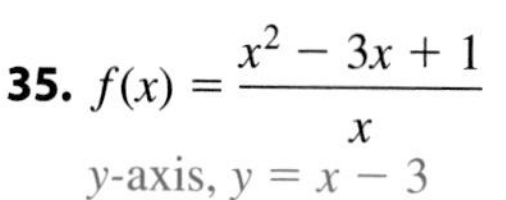

35. $f(x) = \dfrac{x^2 - 3x + 1}{x}$

y-axis, $y = x - 3$

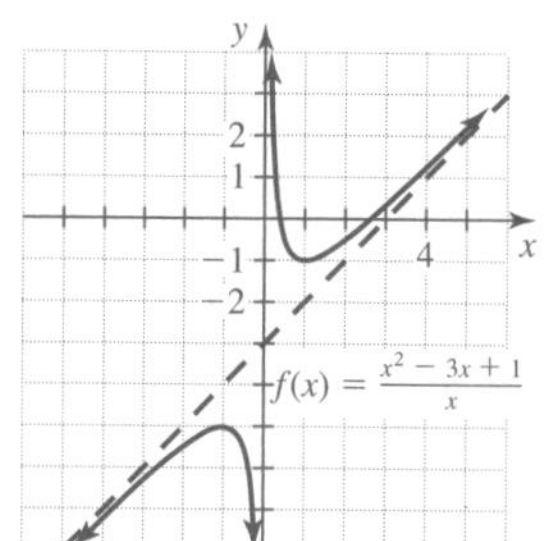

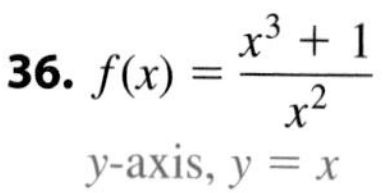

36. $f(x) = \dfrac{x^3 + 1}{x^2}$

y-axis, $y = x$

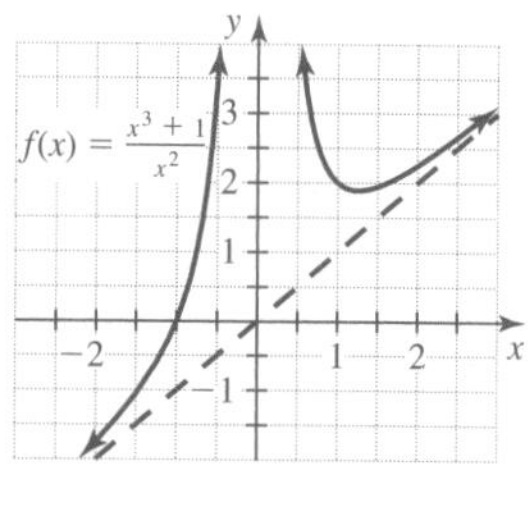

Determine all asymptotes and sketch the graph of each function. See Examples 4 and 5.

29. $f(x) = \dfrac{2}{x + 4}$

$x = -4$, x-axis

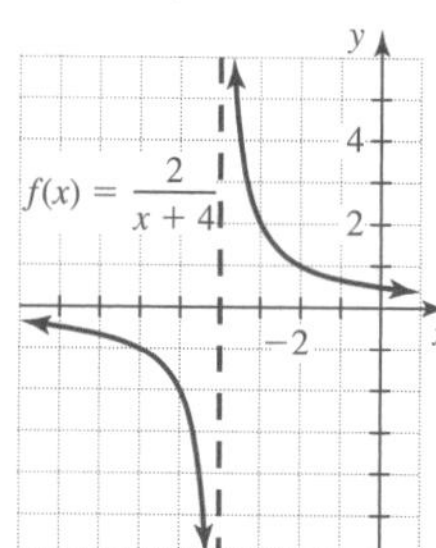

30. $f(x) = \dfrac{-3}{x - 1}$

$x = 1$, x-axis

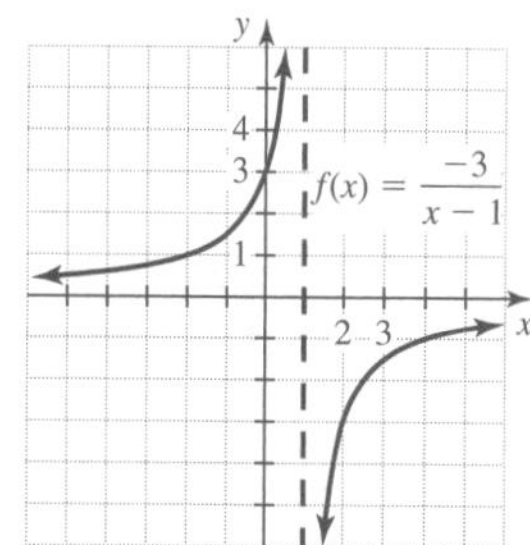

37. $f(x) = \dfrac{3x^2 - 2x}{x - 1}$

$x = 1$, $y = 3x + 1$

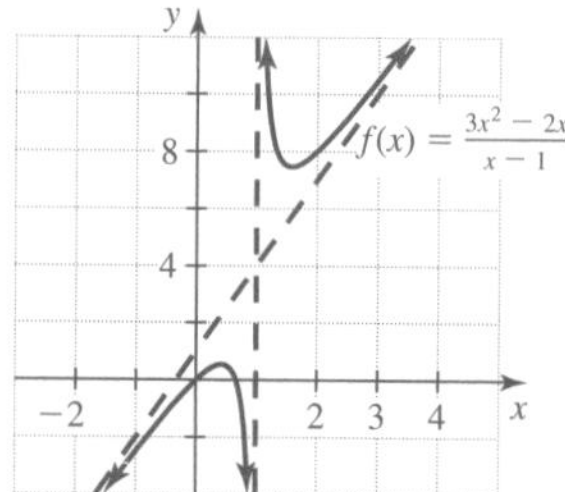

38. $f(x) = \dfrac{-x^2 + 5x - 5}{x - 3}$

$x = 3$, $y = -x + 2$

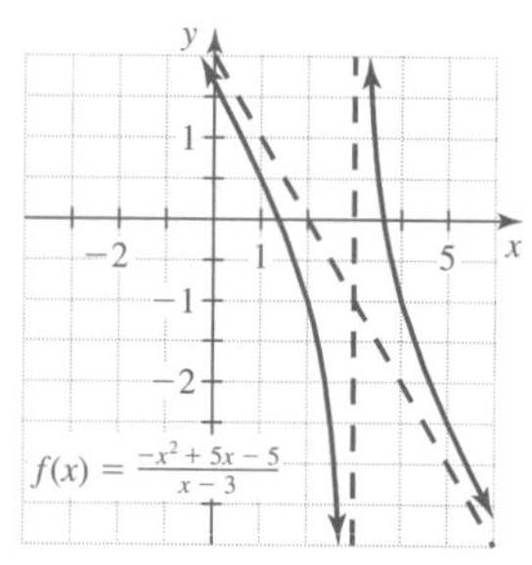

Find all asymptotes, x-intercepts, and y-intercepts for the graph of each rational function and sketch the graph of the function.

39. $f(x) = \dfrac{1}{x^2}$

$x = 0, y = 0$

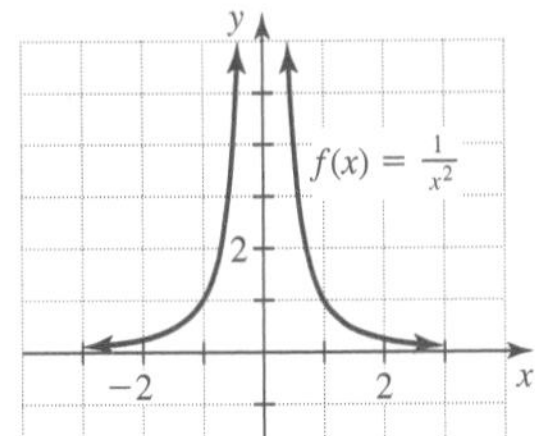

40. $f(x) = \dfrac{2}{x^2 - 4x + 4}$

$x = 2, y = 0, \left(0, \frac{1}{2}\right)$

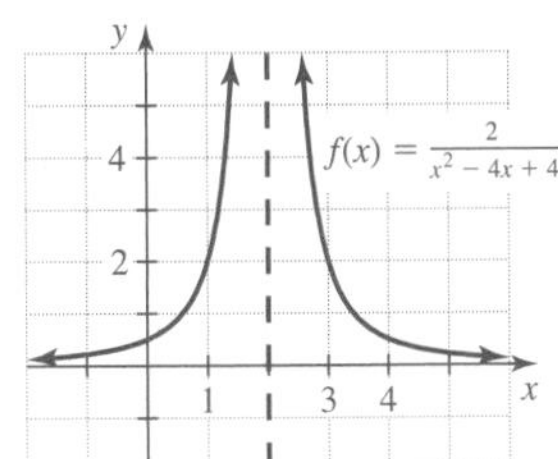

41. $f(x) = \dfrac{2x - 3}{x^2 + x - 6}$

$x = -3, x = 2, y = 0, \left(0, \frac{1}{2}\right), \left(\frac{3}{2}, 0\right)$

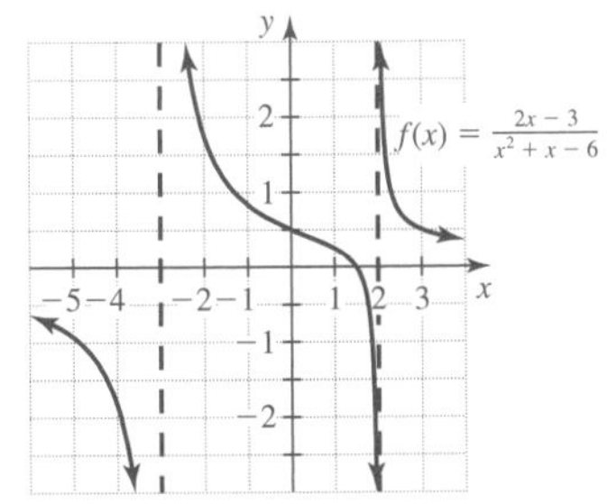

42. $f(x) = \dfrac{x}{x^2 + 4x + 4}$

$x = -2, y = 0, (0, 0)$

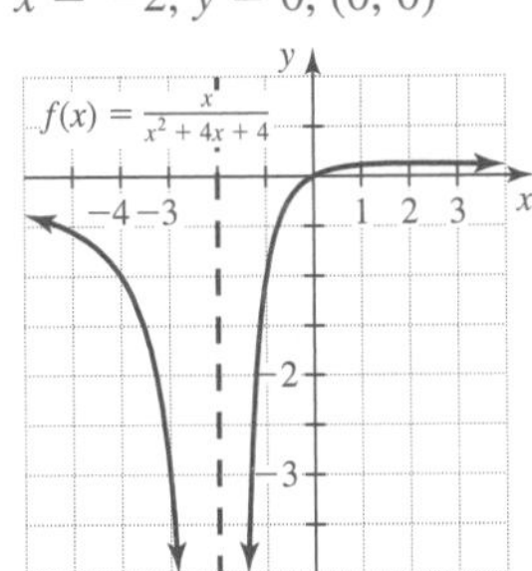

43. $f(x) = \dfrac{x + 1}{x^2}$ $x = 0, y = 0, (-1, 0)$

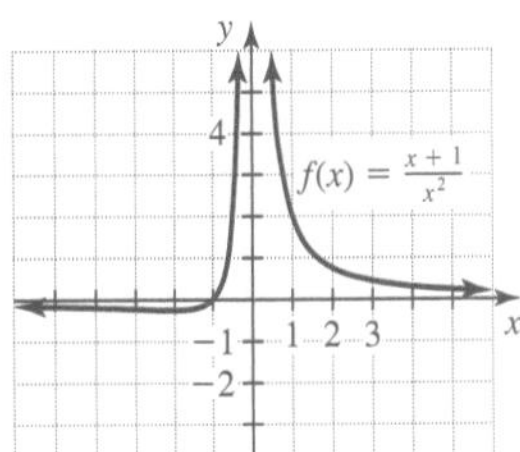

44. $f(x) = \dfrac{x - 1}{x^2}$ $x = 0, y = 0, (1, 0)$

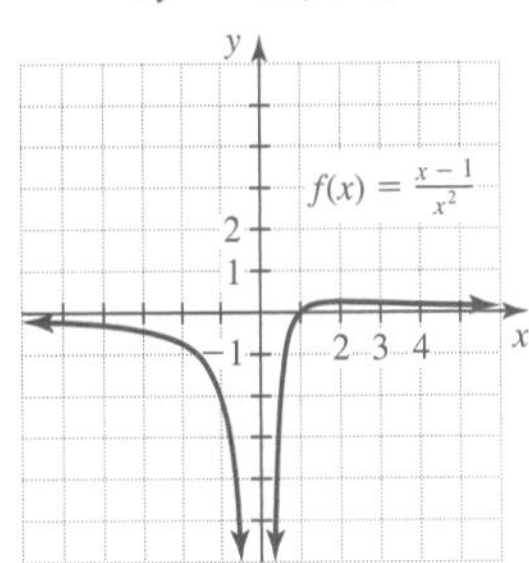

45. $f(x) = \dfrac{2x - 1}{x^3 - 9x}$ $x = 0, x = \pm 3, y = 0, \left(\frac{1}{2}, 0\right)$

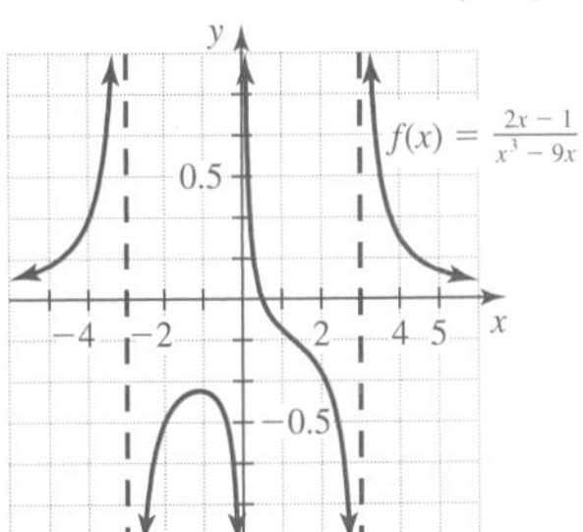

46. $f(x) = \dfrac{2x^2 + 1}{x^3 - x}$ $x = 0, x = \pm 1, y = 0$

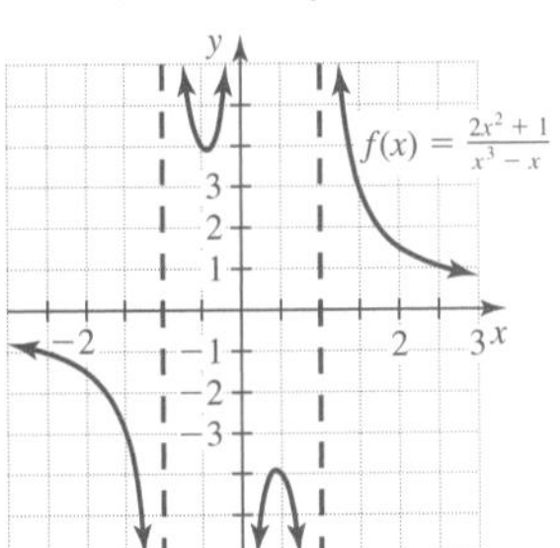

47. $f(x) = \dfrac{x}{x^2 - 1}$ $x = \pm 1, y = 0, (0, 0)$

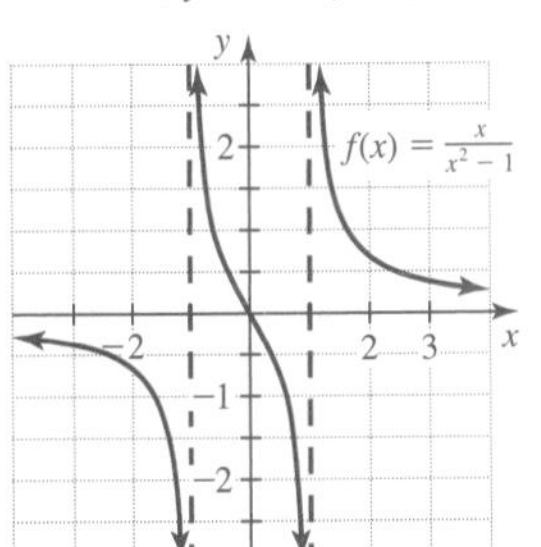

48. $f(x) = \frac{x}{x^2 + x - 2}$ $x = -2, x = 1, y = 0, (0, 0)$

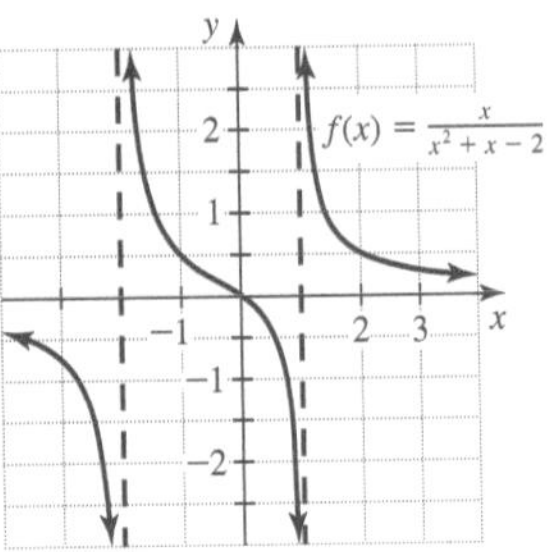

49. $f(x) = \frac{2}{x^2 + 1}$ $y = 0, (0, 2)$

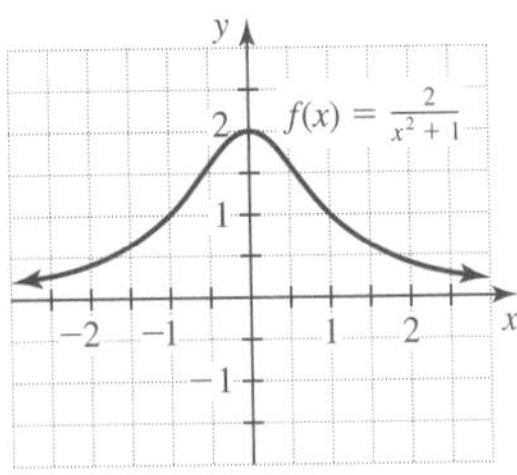

50. $f(x) = \frac{x}{x^2 + 1}$ $y = 0, (0, 0)$

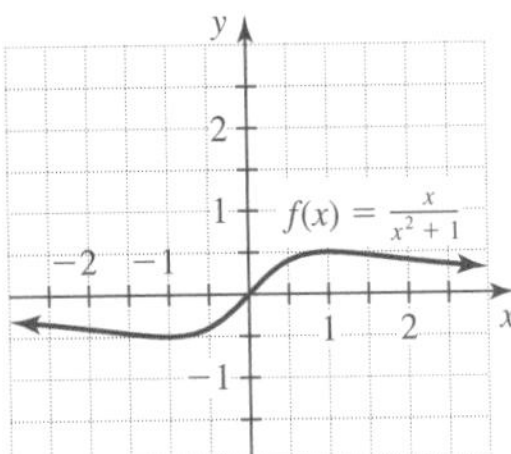

51. $f(x) = \frac{x^2}{x + 1}$ $x = -1, y = x - 1, (0, 0)$

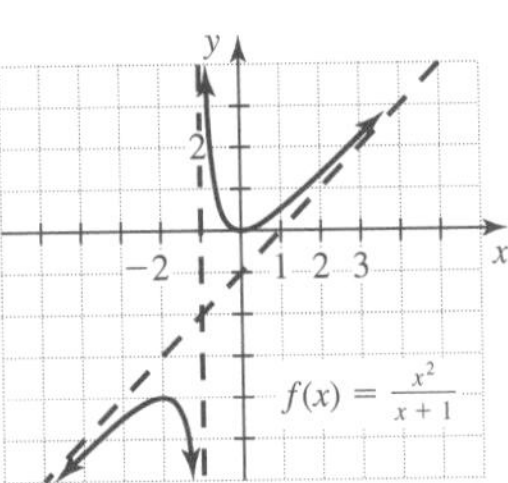

52. $f(x) = \frac{x^2}{x - 1}$ $x = 1, y = x + 1, (0, 0)$

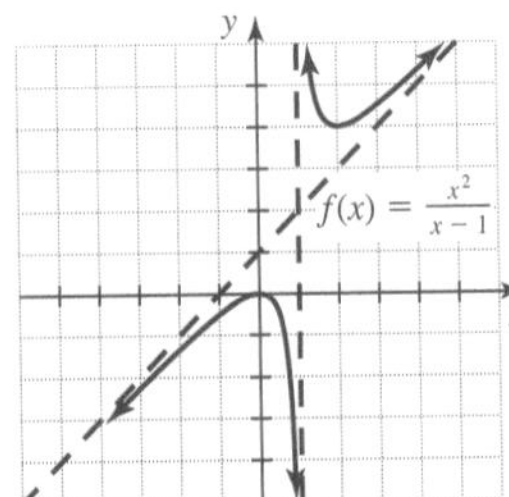

Solve each problem.

53. ***Oscillating modulators.*** The number of oscillating modulators produced by a factory in t hours is given by the polynomial function $n(t) = t^2 + 6t$ for $t \geq 1$. The cost in dollars of operating the factory for t hours is given by the function $c(t) = 36t + 500$ for $t \geq 1$. The average cost per modulator is given by the rational function $f(t) = \frac{36t + 500}{t^2 + 6t}$ for $t \geq 1$. Graph the function f. What is the average cost per modulator at time $t = 20$ and time $t = 30$? What can you conclude about the average cost per modulator after a long period of time?
$f(20) = \$2.35$, $f(30) = \$1.46$, average approaches 0

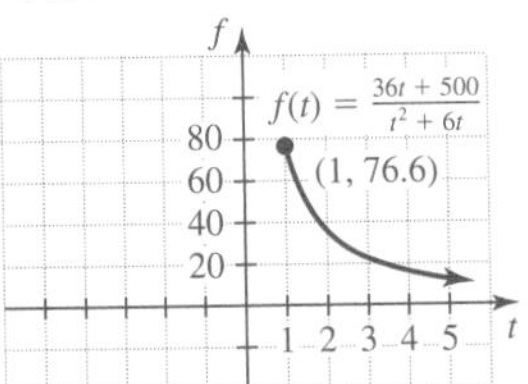

54. ***Nonoscillating modulators.*** The number of nonoscillating modulators produced by a factory in t hours is given by the polynomial function $n(t) = 16t$ for $t \geq 1$. The cost in dollars of operating the factory for t hours is given by the function $c(t) = 64t + 500$ for $t \geq 1$. The average cost per modulator is given by the rational function $f(t) = \frac{64t + 500}{16t}$ for $t \geq 1$. Graph the function f. What is the average cost per modulator at time $t = 10$ and $t = 20$? What can you conclude about the average cost per modulator after a long period of time?
$f(10) = \$7.13$, $f(20) = \$5.56$, average cost approaches \$4.00

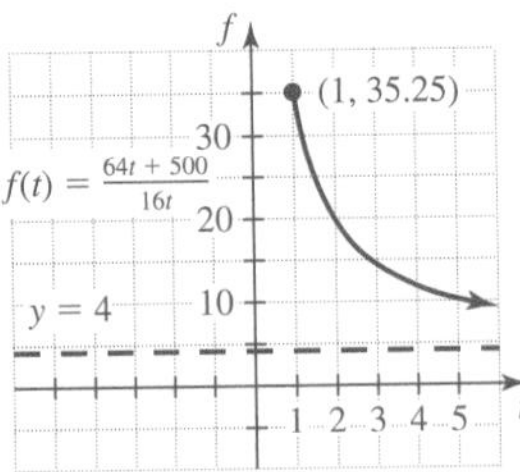

55. ***Average cost of an SUV.*** Mercedes-Benz spent \$700 million to design its new SUV (Motor Trend, www.motortrend.com). If it costs \$25,000 to manufacture each SUV, then the average cost per vehicle in dollars when x vehicles are manufactured is given by the rational function

$$A(x) = \frac{25{,}000x + 700{,}000{,}000}{x}.$$

a) What is the horizontal asymptote for the graph of this function?

b) What is the average cost per vehicle when 50,000 vehicles are made?

c) For what number of vehicles is the average cost \$30,000?

d) Graph this function for x ranging from 0 to 100,000.

a) $y = 25{,}000$ **b)** \$39,000 **c)** 140,000

d)

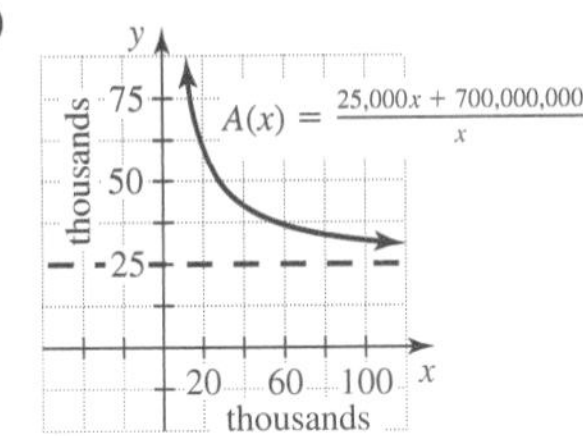

56. ***Average cost of a pill.*** Assuming Pfizer spent a typical \$350 million to develop its latest miracle drug and \$0.10 each to make the pills, then the average cost per pill in dollars when x pills are made is given by the rational function

$$A(x) = \frac{0.10x + 350{,}000{,}000}{x}.$$

a) What is the horizontal asymptote for the graph of this function?

Photo for Exercise 56

b) What is the average cost per pill when 100 million pills are made?

c) For what number of pills is the average cost per pill \$2?

d) Graph this function for x ranging from 0 to 100 million.

a) $y = 0.10$

b) \$3.60

c) 184,210,526

d)

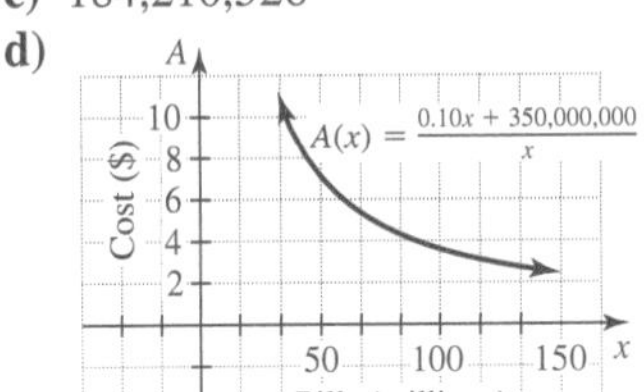

Graphing Calculator Exercises

Sketch the graph of each pair of functions in the same coordinate system. What do you observe in each case?

57. $f(x) = x^2$, $g(x) = x^2 + 1/x$

58. $f(x) = x^2$, $g(x) = x^2 + 1/x^2$

59. $f(x) = |x|$, $g(x) = |x| + 1/x$

60. $f(x) = |x|$, $g(x) = |x| + 1/x^2$

61. $f(x) = \sqrt{x}$, $g(x) = \sqrt{x} + 1/x$

62. $f(x) = x^3$, $g(x) = x^3 + 1/x^2$

For 57–62, the graph of $f(x)$ is an asymptote for the graph of $g(x)$.

Getting More Involved

In each case find a rational function whose graph has the required asymptotes. Answers may vary.

63. The graph has the x-axis as a horizontal asymptote and the y-axis as a vertical asymptote.

$f(x) = 1/x$

64. The graph has the x-axis as a horizontal asymptote and the line $x = 2$ as a vertical asymptote.

$f(x) = 1/(x - 2)$

65. The graph has the x-axis as a horizontal asymptote and lines $x = 3$ and $x = -1$ as vertical asymptotes.

$$f(x) = \frac{1}{(x - 3)(x + 1)}$$

66. The graph has the line $y = 2$ as a horizontal asymptote and the line $x = 1$ as a vertical asymptote.

$$f(x) = \frac{2x}{x - 1}$$

11.6 Combining Functions

In this Section

- **Basic Operations with Functions**
- **Composition**

In this section you will learn how to combine functions to obtain new functions.

Basic Operations with Functions

An entrepreneur plans to rent a stand at a farmers market for \$25 per day to sell strawberries. If she buys x flats of berries for \$5 per flat and sells them for \$9 per flat, then her daily cost in dollars can be written as a function of x:

$$C(x) = 5x + 25$$

Assuming she sells as many flats as she buys, her revenue in dollars is also a function of x:

$$R(x) = 9x$$

Because profit is revenue minus cost, we can find a function for the profit by subtracting the functions for cost and revenue:

$$\begin{aligned} P(x) &= R(x) - C(x) \\ &= 9x - (5x + 25) \\ &= 4x - 25 \end{aligned}$$

The function $P(x) = 4x - 25$ expresses the daily profit as a function of x. Since $P(6) = -1$ and $P(7) = 3$, the profit is negative if 6 or fewer flats are sold and positive if 7 or more flats are sold.

In the example of the entrepreneur we subtracted two functions to find a new function. In other cases we may use addition, multiplication, or division to combine two functions. For any two given functions we can define the sum, difference, product, and quotient functions as follows.

Teaching Tip Point out that the notation $(f + g)(x)$ means the only thing that it could mean: apply f to x, apply g to x, and then add the results.

Sum, Difference, Product, and Quotient Functions

Given two functions f and g, the functions $f + g$, $f - g$, $f \cdot g$, and $\frac{f}{g}$ are defined as follows:

Sum function: $(f + g)(x) = f(x) + g(x)$

Difference function: $(f - g)(x) = f(x) - g(x)$

Product function: $(f \cdot g)(x) = f(x) \cdot g(x)$

Quotient function: $\left(\frac{f}{g}\right)(x) = \frac{f(x)}{g(x)}$ provided that $g(x) \neq 0$

The domain of the function $f + g$, $f - g$, $f \cdot g$, or $\frac{f}{g}$ is the intersection of the domain of f and the domain of g. For the function $\frac{f}{g}$ we also rule out any values of x for which $g(x) = 0$.

EXAMPLE 1

Operations with functions

Let $f(x) = 4x - 12$ and $g(x) = x - 3$. Find the following.

a) $(f + g)(x)$

b) $(f - g)(x)$

c) $(f \cdot g)(x)$

d) $\left(\frac{f}{g}\right)(x)$

Helpful Hint

Note that we use $f + g$, $f - g$, $f \cdot g$, and f/g to name these functions only because there is no application in mind here. We generally use a single letter to name functions after they are combined as we did when using P for the profit function rather than $R - C$.

Solution

a) $(f + g)(x) = f(x) + g(x)$
$= 4x - 12 + x - 3$
$= 5x - 15$

b) $(f - g)(x) = f(x) - g(x)$
$= 4x - 12 - (x - 3)$
$= 3x - 9$

c) $(f \cdot g)(x) = f(x) \cdot g(x)$
$= (4x - 12)(x - 3)$
$= 4x^2 - 24x + 36$

d) $\left(\frac{f}{g}\right)(x) = \frac{f(x)}{g(x)} = \frac{4x - 12}{x - 3} = \frac{4(x - 3)}{x - 3} = 4 \quad \text{for } x \neq 3.$

Now do Exercises 5–8

EXAMPLE 2

Evaluating a sum function

Let $f(x) = 4x - 12$ and $g(x) = x - 3$. Find $(f + g)(2)$.

Solution

In Example 1(a) we found a general formula for the function $f + g$, namely, $(f + g)(x) = 5x - 15$. If we replace x by 2, we get

$$(f + g)(2) = 5(2) - 15$$
$$= -5.$$

We can also find $(f + g)(2)$ by evaluating each function separately and then adding the results. Because $f(2) = -4$ and $g(2) = -1$, we get

$$(f + g)(2) = f(2) + g(2)$$
$$= -4 + (-1)$$
$$= -5.$$

Now do Exercises 9–16

Composition

A salesperson's monthly salary is a function of the number of cars he sells: \$1000 plus \$50 for each car sold. If we let S be his salary and n be the number of cars sold, then S in dollars is a function of n:

$$S = 1000 + 50n$$

Helpful Hint

The difference between the first four operations with functions and composition is like the difference between parallel and series in electrical connections. Components connected in parallel operate simultaneously and separately. If components are connected in series, then electricity must pass through the first component to get to the second component.

Each month the dealer contributes \$100 plus 5% of his salary to a profit-sharing plan. If P represents the amount put into profit sharing, then P (in dollars) is a function of S:

$$P = 100 + 0.05S$$

Now P is a function of S, and S is a function of n. Is P a function of n? The value of n certainly determines the value of P. In fact, we can write a formula for P in terms of n by substituting one formula into the other:

$$\begin{aligned} P &= 100 + 0.05S \\ &= 100 + 0.05(1000 + 50n) \quad \text{Substitute } S = 1000 + 50n. \\ &= 100 + 50 + 2.5n \quad \text{Distributive property} \\ &= 150 + 2.5n \end{aligned}$$

Now P is written as a function of n, bypassing S. We call this idea **composition of functions.**

EXAMPLE 3

The composition of two functions

Given that $y = x^2 - 2x + 3$ and $z = 2y - 5$, write z as a function of x.

Solution

Replace y in $z = 2y - 5$ by $x^2 - 2x + 3$:

$$\begin{aligned} z &= 2y - 5 \\ &= 2(x^2 - 2x + 3) - 5 \quad \text{Replace } y \text{ by } x^2 - 2x + 3. \\ &= 2x^2 - 4x + 1 \end{aligned}$$

The equation $z = 2x^2 - 4x + 1$ expresses z as a function of x.

Now do Exercises 17–24

The composition of two functions using function notation is defined as follows.

Composition of Functions

The **composition** of f and g is denoted $f \circ g$ and is defined by the equation

$$(f \circ g)(x) = f(g(x)),$$

provided that $g(x)$ is in the domain of f.

The notation $f \circ g$ is read as "the composition of f and g" or "f compose g." The diagram in Fig. 11.36 shows a function g pairing numbers in its domain with numbers in its range. If the range of g is contained in or equal to the domain of f, then f pairs the second coordinates of g with numbers in the range of f. The composition function $f \circ g$ is a rule for pairing numbers in the domain of g directly with numbers in the range of f, bypassing the middle set. The domain of the function $f \circ g$ is the domain of g (or a subset of it) and the range of $f \circ g$ is the range of f (or a subset of it).

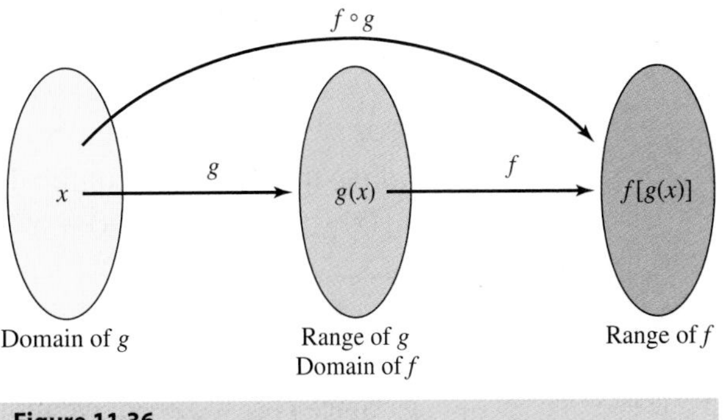

Figure 11.36

CAUTION The order in which functions are written is important in composition. For the function $f \circ g$ the function f is applied to $g(x)$. For the function $g \circ f$ the function g is applied to $f(x)$. The function closest to the variable x is applied first.

EXAMPLE 4

Calculator Close-Up

Set $y_1 = 3x - 2$ and $y_2 = x^2 + 2x$. You can find the composition for Examples 4(c) and 4(d) by evaluating $y_2(y_1(2))$ and $y_1(y_2(2))$. Note that the order in which you evaluate the functions is critical.

```
Y2(Y1(2))
                24
Y1(Y2(2))
                22
```

Evaluating compositions

Let $f(x) = 3x - 2$ and $g(x) = x^2 + 2x$. Evaluate each of the following expressions.

a) $g(f(3))$ **b)** $f(g(-4))$ **c)** $(g \circ f)(2)$ **d)** $(f \circ g)(2)$

Solution

a) Because $f(3) = 3(3) - 2 = 7$, we have

$$g(f(3)) = g(7) = 7^2 + 2 \cdot 7 = 63.$$

So $g(f(3)) = 63$.

b) Because $g(-4) = (-4)^2 + 2(-4) = 8$, we have

$$f(g(-4)) = f(8) = 3(8) - 2 = 22.$$

So $f(g(-4)) = 22$.

c) Because $(g \circ f)(2) = g(f(2))$ we first find $f(2)$:

$$f(2) = 3(2) - 2 = 4$$

Because $f(2) = 4$, we have

$$(g \circ f)(2) = g(f(2)) = g(4) = 4^2 + 2(4) = 24.$$

So $(g \circ f)(2) = 24$.

d) Because $(f \circ g)(2) = f(g(2))$, we first find $g(2)$:

$$g(2) = 2^2 + 2(2) = 8.$$

Because $g(2) = 8$, we have

$$(f \circ g)(2) = f(g(2)) = f(8) = 3(8) - 2 = 22.$$

So $(f \circ g)(2) = 22$.

Now do Exercises 25–38

In Example 4 we found specific values of compositions of two functions. In Example 5 we find a general formula for the two functions from Example 4.

EXAMPLE 5

Finding formulas for compositions

Let $f(x) = 3x - 2$ and $g(x) = x^2 + 2x$. Find the following.

a) $(g \circ f)(x)$ **b)** $(f \circ g)(x)$

Teaching Tip Note that the essence of composition is substitution. To get the new function we replace x with $3x - 2$.

Solution

a) Since $f(x) = 3x - 2$ we replace $f(x)$ with $3x - 2$:

$$\begin{aligned}(g \circ f)(x) &= g(f(x)) \\ &= g(3x - 2) && \text{Replace } f(x) \text{ with } 3x - 2. \\ &= (3x - 2)^2 + 2(3x - 2) && \text{Replace } x \text{ in } g(x) = x^2 + 2x \text{ with } 3x - 2. \\ &= 9x^2 - 12x + 4 + 6x - 4 && \text{Simplify.} \\ &= 9x^2 - 6x\end{aligned}$$

So $(g \circ f)(x) = 9x^2 - 6x$.

b) Since $g(x) = x^2 + 2x$ we replace $g(x)$ with $x^2 + 2x$:

$$\begin{aligned}(f \circ g)(x) &= f(g(x)) && \text{Definition of composition} \\ &= f(x^2 + 2x) && \text{Replace } g(x) \text{ with } x^2 + 2x. \\ &= 3(x^2 + 2x) - 2 && \text{Replace } x \text{ in } f(x) = 3x - 2 \text{ with } x^2 + 2x. \\ &= 3x^2 + 6x - 2 && \text{Simplify.}\end{aligned}$$

So $(f \circ g)(x) = 3x^2 + 6x - 2$.

Now do Exercises 39–48

Helpful Hint

A composition of functions can be viewed as two "function machines" where the output of the first is the input of the second.

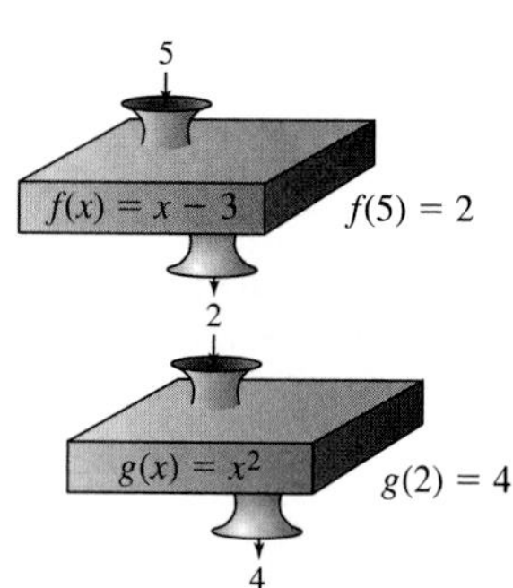

Notice that in Example 4(c) and (d), $(g \circ f)(2) \neq (f \circ g)(2)$. In Example 5(a) and (b) we see that $(g \circ f)(x)$ and $(f \circ g)(x)$ have different formulas defining them. In general, $f \circ g \neq g \circ f$. However, in Section 11.7 we will see some functions for which the composition in either order results in the same function.

It is often useful to view a complicated function as a composition of simpler functions. For example, the function $Q(x) = (x - 3)^2$ consists of two operations, subtracting 3 and squaring. So Q can be described as a composition of the functions $f(x) = x - 3$ and $g(x) = x^2$. To check this, we find $(g \circ f)(x)$:

$$\begin{aligned}(g \circ f)(x) &= g(f(x)) \\ &= g(x - 3) \\ &= (x - 3)^2\end{aligned}$$

We can express the fact that Q is the same as the composition function $g \circ f$ by writing $Q = g \circ f$ or $Q(x) = (g \circ f)(x)$.

EXAMPLE 6

Expressing a function as a composition of simpler functions

Let $f(x) = x - 2$, $g(x) = 3x$, and $h(x) = \sqrt{x}$. Write each of the following functions as a composition, using f, g, and h.

a) $F(x) = \sqrt{x - 2}$ **b)** $H(x) = x - 4$ **c)** $K(x) = 3x - 6$

Study Tip

Effective studying involves actively digging into the subject. Be sure that you are making steady progress. At the end of each week take note of the progress that you have made. What do you know on Friday that you did not know on Monday?

Solution

a) The function F consists of first subtracting 2 from x and then taking the square root of that result. So $F = h \circ f$. Check this result by finding $(h \circ f)(x)$:

$$(h \circ f)(x) = h(f(x)) = h(x - 2) = \sqrt{x - 2}$$

b) Subtracting 4 from x can be accomplished by subtracting 2 from x and then subtracting 2 from that result. So $H = f \circ f$. Check by finding $(f \circ f)(x)$:

$$(f \circ f)(x) = f(f(x)) = f(x - 2) = x - 2 - 2 = x - 4$$

c) Notice that $K(x) = 3(x - 2)$. The function K consists of subtracting 2 from x and then multiplying the result by 3. So $K = g \circ f$. Check by finding $(g \circ f)(x)$:

$$(g \circ f)(x) = g(f(x)) = g(x - 2) = 3(x - 2) = 3x - 6$$

Now do Exercises 49–58

CAUTION In Example 6(a) we have $F = h \circ f$ because in F we subtract 2 before taking the square root. If we had the function $G(x) = \sqrt{x} - 2$, we would take the square root before subtracting 2. So $G = f \circ h$. Notice how important the order of operations is here.

In Example 7 we see functions for which the composition is the identity function. Each function undoes what the other function does. We will study functions of this type further in Section 11.7.

EXAMPLE 7

Composition of functions

Show that $(f \circ g)(x) = x$ for each pair of functions.

a) $f(x) = 2x - 1$ and $g(x) = \dfrac{x + 1}{2}$

b) $f(x) = x^3 + 5$ and $g(x) = (x - 5)^{1/3}$

Solution

a)
$$\begin{aligned}(f \circ g)(x) = f(g(x)) &= f\left(\frac{x + 1}{2}\right)\\ &= 2\left(\frac{x + 1}{2}\right) - 1\\ &= x + 1 - 1\\ &= x\end{aligned}$$

b)
$$\begin{aligned}(f \circ g)(x) = f(g(x)) &= f\left((x - 5)^{1/3}\right)\\ &= \left((x - 5)^{1/3}\right)^3 + 5\\ &= x - 5 + 5\\ &= x\end{aligned}$$

Now do Exercises 59–66

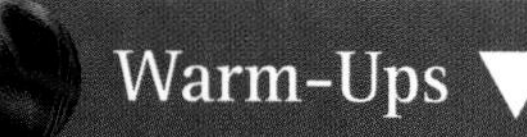

Warm-Ups

True or false? Explain your answer.

1. If $f(x) = x - 2$ and $g(x) = x + 3$, then $(f - g)(x) = -5$. True
2. If $f(x) = x + 4$ and $g(x) = 3x$, then $\left(\frac{f}{g}\right)(2) = 1$. True
3. The functions $f \circ g$ and $g \circ f$ are always the same. False
4. If $f(x) = x^2$ and $g(x) = x + 2$, then $(f \circ g)(x) = x^2 + 2$. False
5. The functions $f \circ g$ and $f \cdot g$ are always the same. False
6. If $f(x) = \sqrt{x}$ and $g(x) = x - 9$, then $g(f(x)) = f(g(x))$ for every x. False
7. If $f(x) = 3x$ and $g(x) = \frac{x}{3}$, then $(f \circ g)(x) = x$. True
8. If $a = 3b^2 - 7b$, and $c = a^2 + 3a$, then c is a function of b. True
9. The function $F(x) = \sqrt{x - 5}$ is a composition of two functions. True
10. If $F(x) = (x - 1)^2$, $h(x) = x - 1$, and $g(x) = x^2$, then $F = g \circ h$. True

11.6 Exercises

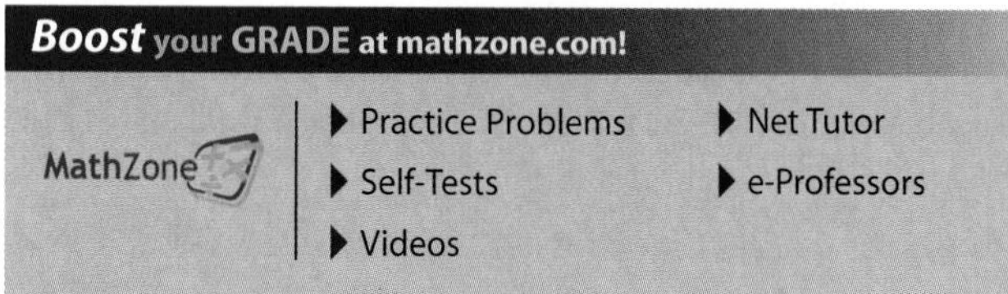

Boost your GRADE at mathzone.com!

MathZone

▸ Practice Problems ▸ Net Tutor
▸ Self-Tests ▸ e-Professors
▸ Videos

Reading and Writing *After reading this section, write out the answers to these questions. Use complete sentences.*

1. What are the basic operations with functions?
   The basic operations of functions are addition, subtraction, multiplication, and division.
2. How do we perform the basic operations with functions?
   We perform the operations with functions by adding, subtracting, multiplying, or dividing the expressions that define the functions.
3. What is the composition of two functions?
   In the composition function the second function is evaluated on the result of the first function.
4. How is the order of operations related to composition of functions?
   Since each operation is a function, the order of operations determines the order in which the functions are composed.

Let $f(x) = 4x - 3$, and $g(x) = x^2 - 2x$. Find the following. See Examples 1 and 2.

5. $(f + g)(x)$
   $x^2 + 2x - 3$
6. $(f - g)(x)$
   $-x^2 + 6x - 3$
7. $(f \cdot g)(x)$
   $4x^3 - 11x^2 + 6x$
8. $\left(\frac{f}{g}\right)(x)$
   $\frac{4x - 3}{x^2 - 2x}$
9. $(f + g)(3)$ 12
10. $(f + g)(2)$ 5
11. $(f - g)(-3)$ -30
12. $(f - g)(-2)$ -19
13. $(f \cdot g)(-1)$ -21
14. $(f \cdot g)(-2)$ -88
15. $\left(\frac{f}{g}\right)(4)$ $\frac{13}{8}$
16. $\left(\frac{f}{g}\right)(-2)$ $-\frac{11}{8}$

Use the two functions to write y as a function of x. See Example 3.

17. $y = 3a - 2$, $a = 2x - 6$ $y = 6x - 20$
18. $y = 2c + 3$, $c = -3x + 4$ $y = -6x + 11$
19. $y = 2d + 1$, $d = \frac{x + 1}{2}$ $y = x + 2$
20. $y = -3d + 2$, $d = \frac{2 - x}{3}$ $y = x$
21. $y = m^2 - 1$, $m = x + 1$ $y = x^2 + 2x$
22. $y = n^2 - 3n + 1$, $n = x + 2$ $y = x^2 + x - 1$
23. $y = \frac{a - 3}{a + 2}$, $a = \frac{2x + 3}{1 - x}$ $y = x$
24. $y = \frac{w + 2}{w - 5}$, $w = \frac{5x + 2}{x - 1}$ $y = x$

Let $f(x) = 2x - 3$, $g(x) = x^2 + 3x$, and $h(x) = \frac{x+3}{2}$. Find the following. See Examples 4 and 5.

25. $(g \circ f)(1)$ -2

26. $(f \circ g)(-2)$ -7

27. $(f \circ g)(1)$ 5

28. $(g \circ f)(-2)$ 28

29. $(f \circ f)(4)$ 7

30. $(h \circ h)(3)$ 3

31. $(h \circ f)(5)$ 5

32. $(f \circ h)(0)$ 0

33. $(f \circ h)(5)$ 5

34. $(h \circ f)(0)$ 0

35. $(g \circ h)(-1)$ 4

36. $(h \circ g)(-1)$ $\frac{1}{2}$

37. $(f \circ g)(2.36)$ 22.2992

38. $(h \circ f)(23.761)$ 23.761

39. $(g \circ f)(x)$ $4x^2 - 6x$

40. $(g \circ h)(x)$ $\frac{x^2 + 12x + 27}{4}$

41. $(f \circ g)(x)$ $2x^2 + 6x - 3$

42. $(h \circ g)(x)$ $\frac{x^2 + 3x + 3}{2}$

43. $(h \circ f)(x)$ x

44. $(f \circ h)(x)$ x

45. $(f \circ f)(x)$ $4x - 9$

46. $(g \circ g)(x)$ $x^4 + 6x^3 + 12x^2 + 9x$

47. $(h \circ h)(x)$ $\frac{x + 9}{4}$

48. $(f \circ f \circ f)(x)$ $8x - 21$

Let $f(x) = \sqrt{x}$, $g(x) = x^2$, and $h(x) = x - 3$. Write each of the following functions as a composition using f, g, or h. See Example 6.

49. $F(x) = \sqrt{x - 3}$ $F = f \circ h$

50. $N(x) = \sqrt{x} - 3$ $N = h \circ f$

51. $G(x) = x^2 - 6x + 9$ $G = g \circ h$

52. $P(x) = x$ for $x \geq 0$ $P = f \circ g$

53. $H(x) = x^2 - 3$ $H = h \circ g$

54. $M(x) = x^{1/4}$ $M = f \circ f$

55. $J(x) = x - 6$ $J = h \circ h$

56. $R(x) = \sqrt{x^2 - 3}$ $R = f \circ h \circ g$

57. $K(x) = x^4$ $K = g \circ g$

58. $Q(x) = \sqrt{x^2 - 6x + 9}$ $Q = f \circ g \circ h$

Show that $(f \circ g)(x) = x$ and $(g \circ f)(x) = x$ for each given pair of functions. See Example 7.

59. $f(x) = 3x + 5$, $g(x) = \frac{x - 5}{3}$

60. $f(x) = 3x - 7$, $g(x) = \frac{x + 7}{3}$

61. $f(x) = x^3 - 9$, $g(x) = \sqrt[3]{x + 9}$

62. $f(x) = x^3 + 1$, $g(x) = \sqrt[3]{x - 1}$

63. $f(x) = \frac{x - 1}{x + 1}$, $g(x) = \frac{x + 1}{1 - x}$

64. $f(x) = \frac{x + 1}{x - 3}$, $g(x) = \frac{3x + 1}{x - 1}$

65. $f(x) = \frac{1}{x}$, $g(x) = \frac{1}{x}$

66. $f(x) = 2x^3$, $g(x) = \left(\frac{x}{2}\right)^{1/3}$

Let $f(x) = x^2$ and $g(x) = x + 5$. Determine whether each of these statements is true or false.

67. $f(3) = 9$ True

68. $g(3) = 8$ True

69. $(f + g)(4) = 21$ False

70. $(f - g)(0) = 5$ False

71. $(f \cdot g)(3) = 72$ True

72. $(f/g)(0) = 5$ False

73. $(f \circ g)(2) = 14$ False

74. $(g \circ f)(7) = 54$ True

75. $f(g(x)) = x^2 + 25$ False

76. $(g \circ f)(x) = x^2 + 5$ True

77. If $h(x) = x^2 + 10x + 25$, then $h = f \circ g$. True

78. If $p(x) = x^2 + 5$, then $p = g \circ f$. True

Solve each problem.

79. ***Area.*** A square gate in a wood fence has a diagonal brace with a length of 10 feet.

a) Find the area of the square gate. 50 ft^2

b) Write a formula for the area of a square as a function of the length of its diagonal. $A = \frac{d^2}{2}$

80. ***Perimeter.*** Write a formula for the perimeter of a square as a function of its area. $P = 4\sqrt{A}$

81. ***Profit function.*** A plastic bag manufacturer has determined that the company can sell as many bags as it can produce each month. If it produces x thousand bags in a month, the revenue is $R(x) = x^2 - 10x + 30$ dollars, and the cost is $C(x) = 2x^2 - 30x + 200$ dollars. Use the fact that profit is revenue minus cost to write the profit as a function of x. $P(x) = -x^2 + 20x - 170$

82. ***Area of a sign.*** A sign is in the shape of a square with a semicircle of radius x adjoining one side and a semicircle of diameter x removed from the opposite side. If the sides of the square are length $2x$, then write the area of the sign as a function of x.

$A = \frac{(32 + 3\pi)x^2}{8}$

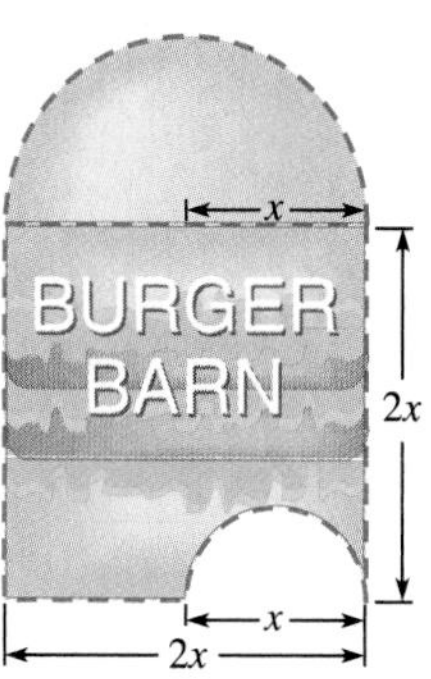

Figure for Exercise 82

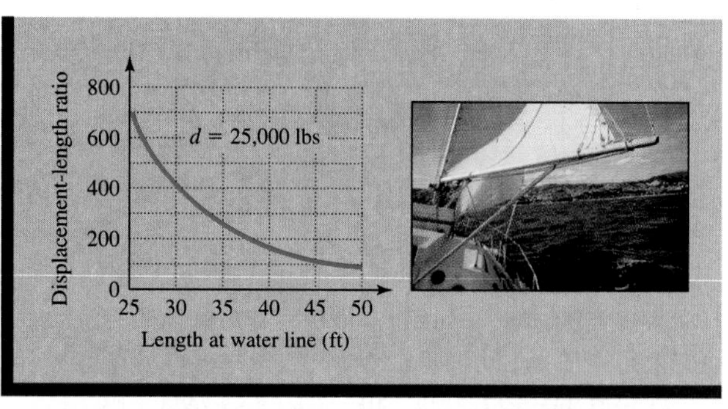

Figure for Exercise 85

83. ***Junk food expenditures.*** Suppose the average family spends 25% of its income on food, $F = 0.25I$, and 10% of each food dollar on junk food, $J = 0.10F$. Write J as a function of I.
$J = 0.025I$

84. ***Area of an inscribed circle.*** A pipe of radius r must pass through a square hole of area M as shown in the figure. Write the cross-sectional area of the pipe A as a function of M.

$A = \pi\frac{M}{4}$

Figure for Exercise 84

85. ***Displacement-length ratio.*** To find the displacement-length ratio D for a sailboat, first find x, where $x = (L/100)^3$ and L is the length at the water line in feet (www.sailing.com). Next find D, where $D = (d/2240)/x$ and d is the displacement in pounds.

a) For the Pacific Seacraft 40, $L = 30$ ft 3 in. and $d = 24{,}665$ pounds. Find D.

b) For a boat with a displacement of 25,000 pounds, write D as a function of L.

c) The graph for the function in part (b) is shown in the accompanying figure. For a fixed displacement, does the displacement-length ratio increase or decrease as the length increases?

a) 397.8 b) $D = \dfrac{1.116 \times 10^7}{L^3}$ c) decreases

86. ***Sail area-displacement ratio.*** To find the sail area-displacement ratio S, first find y, where $y = (d/64)^{2/3}$ and d is the displacement in pounds. Next find S, where $S = A/y$ and A is the sail area in square feet.

a) For the Pacific Seacraft 40, $A = 846$ square feet (ft^2) and $d = 24{,}665$ pounds. Find S.

b) For a boat with a sail area of 900 ft^2, write S as a function of d.

c) For a fixed sail area, does S increase or decrease as the displacement increases?

a) 15.97 b) $S = 14{,}400d^{-2/3}$ c) decreases

Getting More Involved

87. ***Discussion***

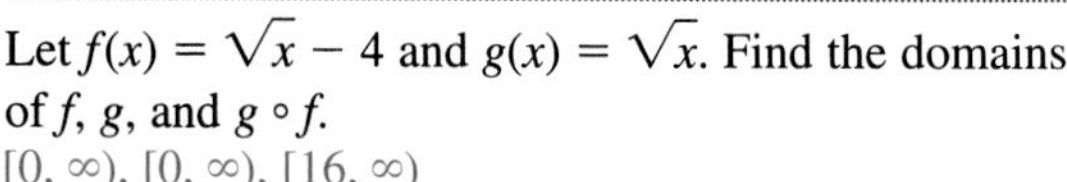
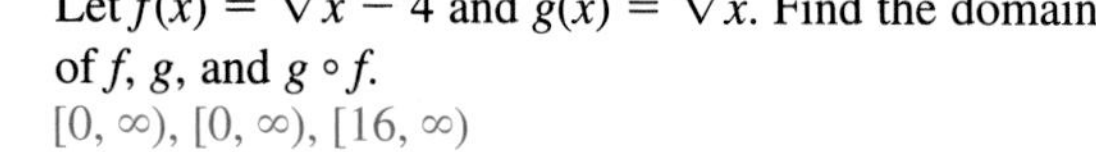

Let $f(x) = \sqrt{x} - 4$ and $g(x) = \sqrt{x}$. Find the domains of f, g, and $g \circ f$.
$[0, \infty)$, $[0, \infty)$, $[16, \infty)$

88. ***Discussion***

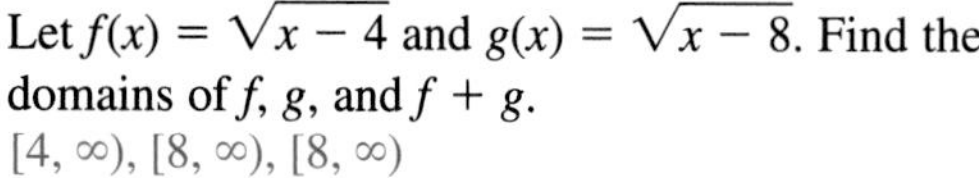

Let $f(x) = \sqrt{x - 4}$ and $g(x) = \sqrt{x - 8}$. Find the domains of f, g, and $f + g$.
$[4, \infty)$, $[8, \infty)$, $[8, \infty)$

Graphing Calculator Exercises

89. Graph $y_1 = x$, $y_2 = \sqrt{x}$, and $y_3 = x + \sqrt{x}$ in the same screen. Find the domain and range of $y_3 = x + \sqrt{x}$ by examining its graph. (On some graphing calculators you can enter y_3 as $y_3 = y_1 + y_2$.)
$[0, \infty)$, $[0, \infty)$

90. Graph $y_1 = |x|$, $y_2 = |x - 3|$, and $y_3 = |x| + |x - 3|$. Find the domain and range of $y_3 = |x| + |x - 3|$ by examining its graph.
$(-\infty, \infty)$, $[3, \infty)$

11.7 Inverse Functions

In this Section

- **Inverse of a Function**
- **Identifying Inverse Functions**
- **Switch-and-Solve Strategy**
- **Even Roots or Even Powers**
- **Graphs of f and f^{-1}**

In Section 11.6 we introduced the idea of a pair of functions such that $(f \circ g)(x) = x$ and $(g \circ f)(x) = x$. Each function reverses what the other function does. In this section we explore that idea further.

Inverse of a Function

You can buy a 6-, 7-, or 8-foot conference table in the K-LOG Catalog for \$299, \$329, or \$349, respectively. The set

$$f = \{(6, 299), (7, 329), (8, 349)\}$$

gives the price as a function of the length. We use the letter f as a name for this set or function, just as we use the letter f as a name for a function in the function notation. In the function f, lengths in the domain $\{6, 7, 8\}$ are paired with prices in the range $\{299, 329, 349\}$. The **inverse** of the function f, denoted f^{-1}, is a function whose ordered pairs are obtained from f by interchanging the x- and y-coordinates:

$$f^{-1} = \{(299, 6), (329, 7), (349, 8)\}$$

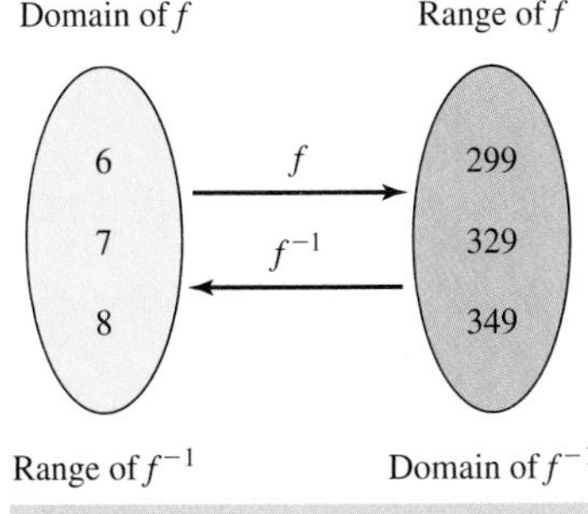

Figure 11.37

We read f^{-1} as "f inverse." The domain of f^{-1} is $\{299, 329, 349\}$, and the range of f^{-1} is $\{6, 7, 8\}$. The inverse function reverses what the function does: it pairs prices in the range of f with lengths in the domain of f. For example, to find the cost of a 7-foot table, we use the function f to get $f(7) = 329$. To find the length of a table, that costs \$349, we use the function f^{-1} to get $f^{-1}(349) = 8$. Of course, we could find the length of a \$349 table by looking at the function f, but f^{-1} is a function whose input is price and whose output is length. In general, *the domain of f^{-1} is the range of f, and the range of f^{-1} is the domain of f.* See Fig. 11.37.

Teaching Tip Ask students for examples of real-life functions and then discuss whether each function is invertible.

CAUTION The -1 in f^{-1} is not read as an exponent. It does not mean $\frac{1}{f}$.

The cost per ribbon for Apple Imagewriter ribbons is a function of the number of boxes purchased:

$$g = \{(1, 4.85), (2, 4.60), (3, 4.60), (4, 4.35)\}$$

If we interchange the first and second coordinates in the ordered pairs of this function, we get

$$\{(4.85, 1), (4.60, 2), (4.60, 3), (4.35, 4)\}.$$

This set of ordered pairs is not a function because it contains ordered pairs with the same first coordinates and different second coordinates. So g does not have an inverse function. A function is **invertible** if you obtain a function when the coordinates of all ordered pairs are reversed. So f is invertible and g is not invertible. The function g is not invertible because the definition of function allows more than one number of the domain to be paired with the same number in the range. Of course, when this pairing is reversed, the definition of function is violated.

Helpful Hint

Consider the universal product codes (UPC) and the prices for all of the items in your favorite grocery store. The price of an item is a function of the UPC because every UPC determines a price. This function is not invertible because you cannot determine the UPC from a given price.

One-to-One Function

If a function is such that no two ordered pairs have different x-coordinates and the same y-coordinate, then the function is called a **one-to-one** function.

In a one-to-one function each member of the domain corresponds to just one member of the range, and each member of the range corresponds to just one member of the domain. *Functions that are one-to-one are invertible functions.*

Inverse Function

The inverse of a one-to-one function f is the function f^{-1}, which is obtained from f by interchanging the coordinates in each ordered pair of f.

EXAMPLE 1

Identifying invertible functions

Determine whether each function is invertible. If it is invertible, then find the inverse function.

a) $f = \{(2, 4), (-2, 4), (3, 9)\}$

b) $g = \left\{\left(2, \frac{1}{2}\right), \left(5, \frac{1}{5}\right), \left(7, \frac{1}{7}\right)\right\}$

c) $h = \{(3, 5), (7, 9)\}$

Solution

a) Since (2, 4) and (−2, 4) have the same y-coordinate, this function is not one-to-one, and it is not invertible.

b) This function is one-to-one, and so it is invertible.

$$g^{-1} = \left\{\left(\frac{1}{2}, 2\right), \left(\frac{1}{5}, 5\right), \left(\frac{1}{7}, 7\right)\right\}$$

c) This function is invertible, and $h^{-1} = \{(5, 3), (9, 7)\}$.

Now do Exercises 9–16

You learned to use the vertical-line test in Section 11.1 to determine whether a graph is the graph of a function. The **horizontal-line test** is a similar visual test for determining whether a function is invertible. If a horizontal line crosses a graph two (or more) times, as in Fig. 11.38, then there are two points on the graph, say (x_1, y) and (x_2, y), that have different x-coordinates and the same y-coordinate. So the function is not one-to-one, and the function is not invertible.

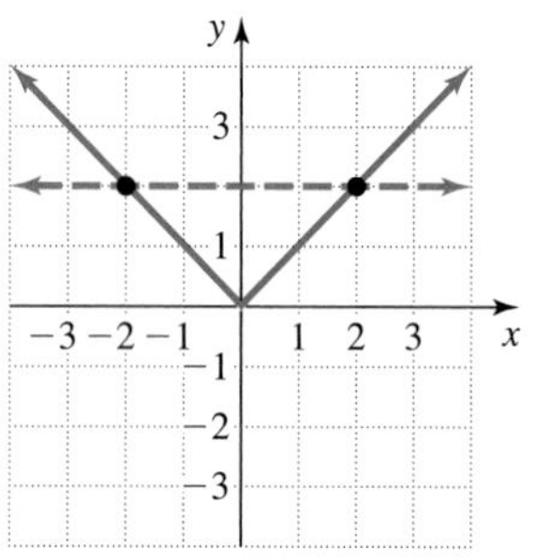

Figure 11.38

Horizontal-Line Test

A function is invertible if and only if no horizontal line crosses its graph more than once.

EXAMPLE 2

Using the horizontal-line test

Determine whether each function is invertible by examining its graph.

a) 

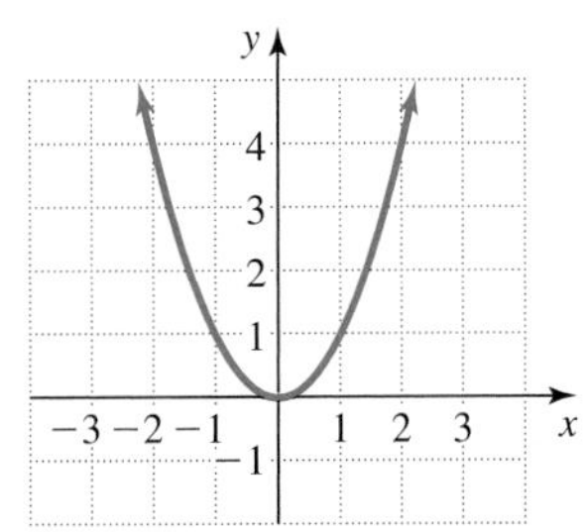

b)

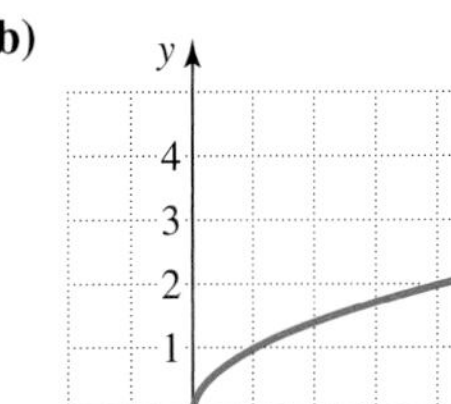

Solution

a) This function is not invertible because a horizontal line can be drawn so that it crosses the graph at $(2, 4)$ and $(-2, 4)$.

b) This function is invertible because every horizontal line that crosses the graph crosses it only once.

Now do Exercises 17–20

Helpful Hint

Tests such as the vertical-line test and the horizontal-line test are certainly not accurate in all cases. We discuss these tests to get a visual idea of what graphs of functions and invertible functions look like.

Identifying Inverse Functions

Consider the one-to-one function $f(x) = 3x$. The inverse function must reverse the ordered pairs of the function. Because division by 3 undoes multiplication by 3, we could guess that $g(x) = \frac{x}{3}$ is the inverse function. To verify our guess, we can use the following rule for determining whether two given functions are inverses of each other.

Identifying Inverse Functions

Functions f and g are inverses of each other if and only if

$(g \circ f)(x) = x$ for every number x in the domain of f and

$(f \circ g)(x) = x$ for every number x in the domain of g.

In the next example we verify that $f(x) = 3x$ and $g(x) = \frac{x}{3}$ are inverses.

EXAMPLE 3

Identifying inverse functions

Determine whether the functions f and g are inverses of each other.

a) $f(x) = 3x$ and $g(x) = \dfrac{x}{3}$ **b)** $f(x) = 2x - 1$ and $g(x) = \dfrac{1}{2}x + 1$

c) $f(x) = x^2$ and $g(x) = \sqrt{x}$

Solution

a) Find $g \circ f$ and $f \circ g$:

$$(g \circ f)(x) = g(f(x)) = g(3x) = \frac{3x}{3} = x$$

$$(f \circ g)(x) = f(g(x)) = f\left(\frac{x}{3}\right) = 3 \cdot \frac{x}{3} = x$$

Study Tip

Personal issues can have a tremendous effect on your progress in any course. So do not hesitate to deal with personal problems. If you need help, get it. Most schools have counseling centers that can help you to overcome personal issues that are affecting your studies.

Because each of these equations is true for any real number x, f and g are inverses of each other. We write $g = f^{-1}$ or $f^{-1}(x) = \frac{x}{3}$.

b) Find the composition of g and f:

$$\begin{aligned}(g \circ f)(x) &= g(f(x)) \\ &= g(2x - 1) = \frac{1}{2}(2x - 1) + 1 = x + \frac{1}{2}\end{aligned}$$

So f and g are not inverses of each other.

c) If x is any real number, we can write

$$\begin{aligned}(g \circ f)(x) &= g(f(x)) \\ &= g(x^2) = \sqrt{x^2} = |x|.\end{aligned}$$

The domain of f is $(-\infty, \infty)$, and $|x| \neq x$ if x is negative. So g and f are not inverses of each other. Note that $f(x) = x^2$ is not a one-to-one function, since both (3, 9) and (−3, 9) are ordered pairs of this function. Thus $f(x) = x^2$ does not have an inverse.

Now do Exercises 21–28

Switch-and-Solve Strategy

If an invertible function is defined by a list of ordered pairs, as in Example 1, then the inverse function is found by simply interchanging the coordinates in the ordered pairs. If an invertible function is defined by a formula, then the inverse function must reverse or undo what the function does. Because the inverse function interchanges the roles of x and y, we interchange x and y in the formula and then solve the new formula for y to undo what the original function did. This **switch-and-solve** strategy is illustrated in Examples 4 and 5.

EXAMPLE 4

The switch-and-solve strategy

Find the inverse of $h(x) = 2x + 1$.

Solution

First write the function as $y = 2x + 1$, then interchange x and y:

$$\begin{aligned} y &= 2x + 1 && \\ x &= 2y + 1 && \text{Interchange } x \text{ and } y. \\ x - 1 &= 2y && \text{Solve for } y. \\ \frac{x - 1}{2} &= y && \\ h^{-1}(x) &= \frac{x - 1}{2} && \text{Replace } y \text{ by } h^{-1}(x).\end{aligned}$$

We can verify that h and h^{-1} are inverses by using composition:

$$(h^{-1} \circ h)(x) = h^{-1}(h(x)) = h^{-1}(2x + 1) = \frac{2x + 1 - 1}{2} = \frac{2x}{2} = x$$

$$(h \circ h^{-1})(x) = h(h^{-1}(x)) = h\left(\frac{x - 1}{2}\right) = 2 \cdot \frac{x - 1}{2} + 1 = x - 1 + 1 = x$$

Now do Exercises 29–42

EXAMPLE 5

The switch-and-solve strategy

If $f(x) = \dfrac{x+1}{x-3}$, find $f^{-1}(x)$.

Solution

Replace $f(x)$ by y, interchange x and y, then solve for y:

$$
\begin{aligned}
y &= \frac{x+1}{x-3} && \text{Use } y \text{ in place of } f(x).\\
x &= \frac{y+1}{y-3} && \text{Switch } x \text{ and } y.\\
x(y-3) &= y+1 && \text{Multiply each side by } y-3.\\
xy - 3x &= y+1 && \text{Distributive property}\\
xy - y &= 3x+1 &&\\
y(x-1) &= 3x+1 && \text{Factor out } y.\\
y &= \frac{3x+1}{x-1} && \text{Divide each side by } x-1.\\
f^{-1}(x) &= \frac{3x+1}{x-1} && \text{Replace } y \text{ by } f^{-1}(x).
\end{aligned}
$$

You should check that $(f \circ f^{-1})(x) = x$ and $(f^{-1} \circ f)(x) = x$.

Now do Exercises 43–46

The strategy for finding the inverse of a function $f(x)$ is summarized as follows.

Switch-and-Solve Strategy for Finding f^{-1}

1. Replace $f(x)$ by y.
2. Interchange x and y.
3. Solve the equation for y.
4. Replace y by $f^{-1}(x)$.

Helpful Hint

You should know from memory the inverses of simple functions that involve one or two operations. For example, the inverse of $f(x) = x + 99$ is $f^{-1}(x) = x - 99$. The inverse of $f(x) = x/33 + 22$ is $f^{-1}(x) = 33(x - 22)$.

If we use the switch-and-solve strategy to find the inverse of $f(x) = x^3$, then we get $f^{-1}(x) = x^{1/3}$. For $h(x) = 6x$ we have $h^{-1}(x) = \frac{x}{6}$. The inverse of $k(x) = x - 9$ is $k^{-1}(x) = x + 9$. For each of these functions there is an appropriate operation of arithmetic that undoes what the function does.

If a function involves two operations, the inverse function undoes those operations in the opposite order from which the function does them. For example, the function $g(x) = 3x - 5$ multiplies x by 3 and then subtracts 5 from that result. To undo these operations, we add 5 and then divide the result by 3. So

$$g^{-1}(x) = \frac{x+5}{3}.$$

Note that $g^{-1}(x) \neq \frac{x}{3} + 5$.

Even Roots or Even Powers

We need to use special care in finding inverses for functions that involve even roots or even powers. We saw in Example 3(c) that $f(x) = x^2$ is not the inverse of $g(x) = \sqrt{x}$. However, because $g(x) = \sqrt{x}$ is a one-to-one function, it has an inverse. The domain of g is $[0, \infty)$, and the range is $[0, \infty)$. So the inverse of g must have domain $[0, \infty)$ and range $[0, \infty)$. See Fig. 11.39. The only reason that $f(x) = x^2$ is not the inverse of g is that it has the wrong domain. So to write the inverse function, we must use the appropriate domain:

$$g^{-1}(x) = x^2 \qquad \text{for} \quad x \geq 0$$

Note that by restricting the domain of g^{-1} to $[0, \infty)$, g^{-1} is one-to-one. With this restriction it is true that $(g \circ g^{-1})(x) = x$ and $(g^{-1} \circ g)(x) = x$ for every nonnegative number x.

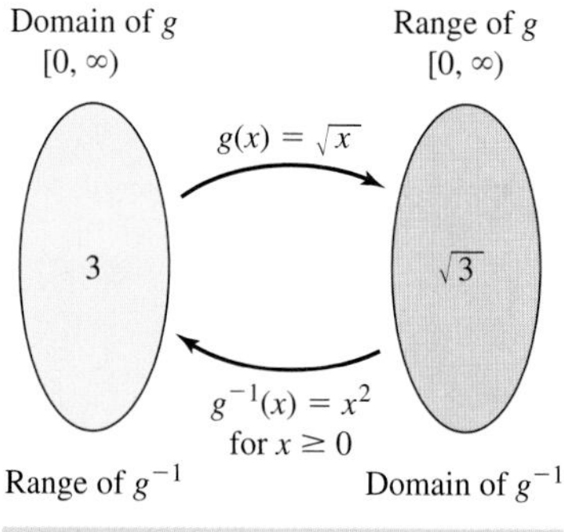

Figure 11.39

EXAMPLE 6

Inverse of a function with an even exponent

Find the inverse of the function $f(x) = (x - 3)^2$ for $x \geq 3$.

Solution

Because of the restriction $x \geq 3$, f is a one-to-one function with domain $[3, \infty)$ and range $[0, \infty)$. The domain of the inverse function is $[0, \infty)$, and its range is $[3, \infty)$. Use the switch-and-solve strategy to find the formula for the inverse:

$$\begin{aligned} y &= (x - 3)^2 \\ x &= (y - 3)^2 \\ y - 3 &= \pm\sqrt{x} \\ y &= 3 \pm \sqrt{x} \end{aligned}$$

Because the inverse function must have range $[3, \infty)$, we use the formula $f^{-1}(x) = 3 + \sqrt{x}$. Because the domain of f^{-1} is assumed to be $[0, \infty)$, no restriction is required on x.

Now do Exercises 47–54

Graphs of f and f^{-1}

Consider $f(x) = x^2$ for $x \geq 0$ and $f^{-1}(x) = \sqrt{x}$. Their graphs are shown in Fig. 11.40. Notice the symmetry. If we folded the paper along the line $y = x$, the two graphs would coincide.

Teaching Tip Have students plot points such as (2, 4) and (4, 2) and then fold the graph along the line $y = x$ to see them coincide.

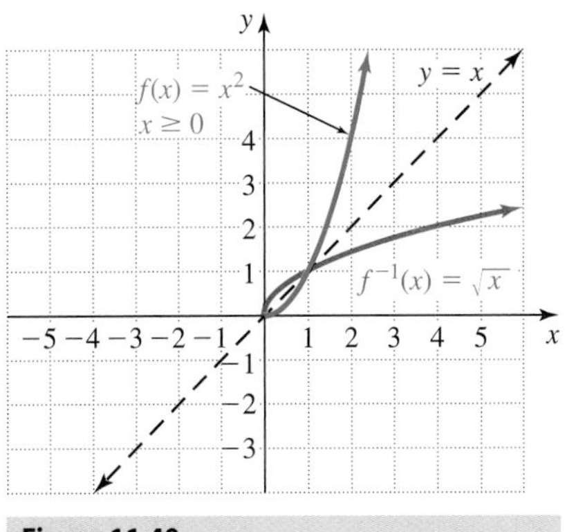

Figure 11.40

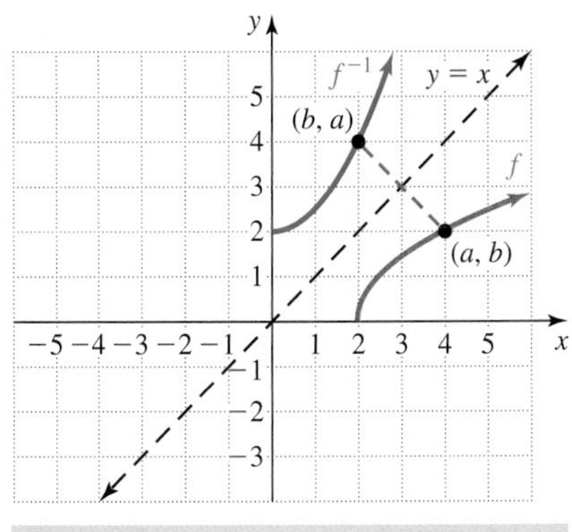

Figure 11.41

If a point (a, b) is on the graph of the function f, then (b, a) must be on the graph of $f^{-1}(x)$. See Fig. 11.41. The points (a, b) and (b, a) lie on opposite sides of the diagonal line $y = x$ and are the same distance from it. For this reason the graphs of f and f^{-1} are symmetric with respect to the line $y = x$.

EXAMPLE 7

Inverses and their graphs

Find the inverse of the function $f(x) = \sqrt{x - 1}$ and graph f and f^{-1} on the same pair of axes.

Solution

To find f^{-1}, first switch x and y in the formula $y = \sqrt{x - 1}$:

$$x = \sqrt{y - 1}$$

$$x^2 = y - 1 \quad \text{Square both sides.}$$

$$x^2 + 1 = y$$

Because the range of f is the set of nonnegative real numbers $[0, \infty)$, we must restrict the domain of f^{-1} to be $[0, \infty)$. Thus $f^{-1}(x) = x^2 + 1$ for $x \geq 0$. The two graphs are shown in Fig. 11.42.

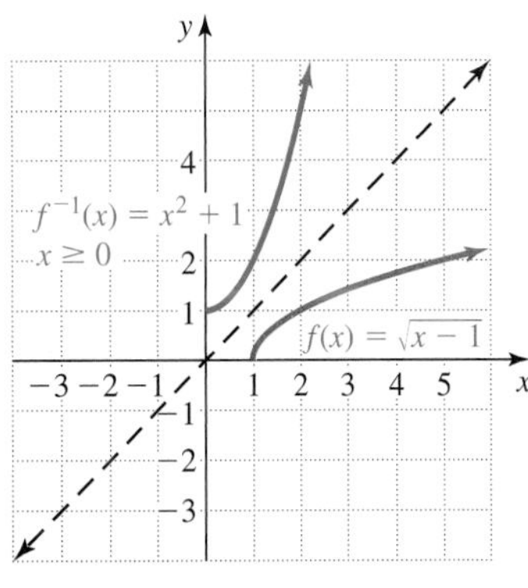

Figure 11.42

Now do Exercises 55–64

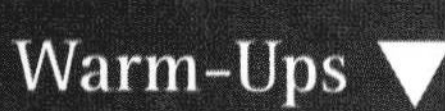

Warm-Ups

True or false? Explain your answer.

1. The inverse of $\{(1, 3), (2, 5)\}$ is $\{(3, 1), (2, 5)\}$. False
2. The function $f(x) = 3$ is a one-to-one function. False
3. If $g(x) = 2x$, then $g^{-1}(x) = \frac{1}{2x}$. False
4. Only one-to-one functions are invertible. True
5. The domain of g is the same as the range of g^{-1}. True
6. The function $f(x) = x^4$ is invertible. False
7. If $f(x) = -x$, then $f^{-1}(x) = -x$. True
8. If h is invertible and $h(7) = -95$, then $h^{-1}(-95) = 7$. True
9. If $k(x) = 3x - 6$, then $k^{-1}(x) = \frac{1}{3}x + 2$. True
10. If $f(x) = 3x - 4$, then $f^{-1}(x) = x + 4$. False

11.7 Exercises

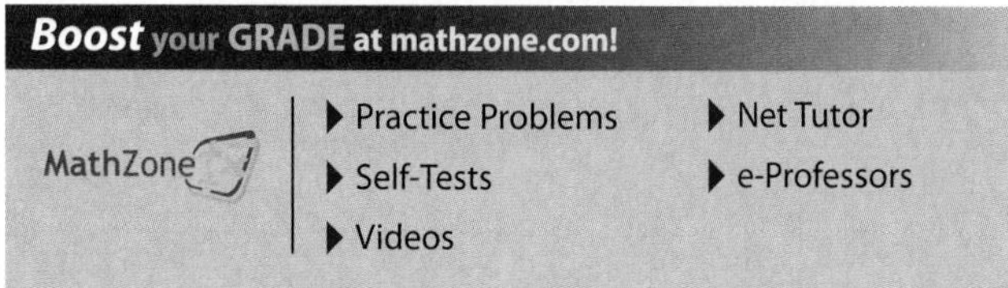

Reading and Writing *After reading this section, write out the answers to these questions. Use complete sentences.*

1. What is the inverse of a function?
The inverse of a function is a function with the same ordered pairs except that the coordinates are reversed.
2. What is the domain of f^{-1}?
The domain of f^{-1} is the range of f.
3. What is the range of f^{-1}?
The range of f^{-1} is the domain of f.
4. What does the -1 in f^{-1} mean?
The -1 in f^{-1} is not treated as an exponent. It is simply a notation for the inverse of the function f.
5. What is a one-to-one function?
A function is one-to-one if no two ordered pairs have the same second coordinate with different first coordinates.
6. What is the horizontal-line test?
The horizontal-line test says that if a horizontal line can be drawn to cross the graph of a function more than once, then the function is not one-to-one.
7. What is the switch-and-solve strategy?
The switch-and-solve strategy is used for finding a formula for an inverse function.
8. How are the graphs of f and f^{-1} related?
The graphs of f and f^{-1} are symmetric with respect to the line $y = x$.

Determine whether each function is invertible. If it is invertible, then find the inverse. See Example 1.

9. $\{(-3, 3), (-2, 2), (0, 0), (2, 2)\}$ No
10. $\{(1, 1), (2, 8), (3, 27)\}$ Yes, $\{(1, 1), (8, 2), (27, 3)\}$
11. $\{(16, 4), (9, 3), (0, 0)\}$ Yes, $\{(4, 16), (3, 9), (0, 0)\}$
12. $\{(-1, 1), (-3, 81), (3, 81)\}$ No
13. $\{(0, 5), (5, 0), (6, 0)\}$ No
14. $\{(3, -3), (-2, 2), (1, -1)\}$ Yes, $\{(-3, 3), (2, -2), (-1, 1)\}$
15. $\{(0, 0), (2, 2), (9, 9)\}$ Yes, $\{(0, 0), (2, 2), (9, 9)\}$
16. $\{(9, 1), (2, 1), (7, 1), (0, 1)\}$ No

Determine whether each function is invertible by examining the graph of the function. See Example 2.

17.

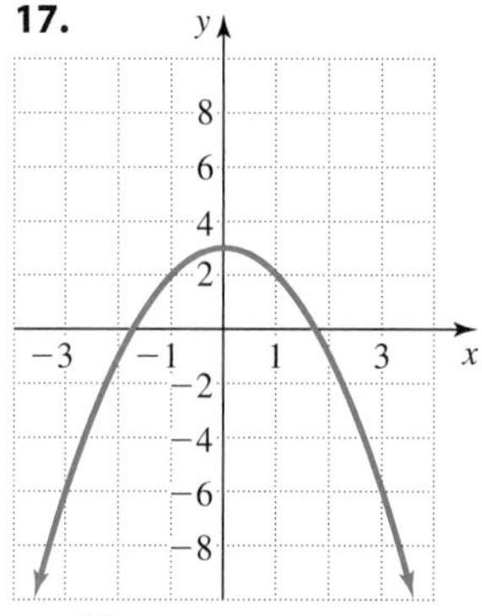

No

18.

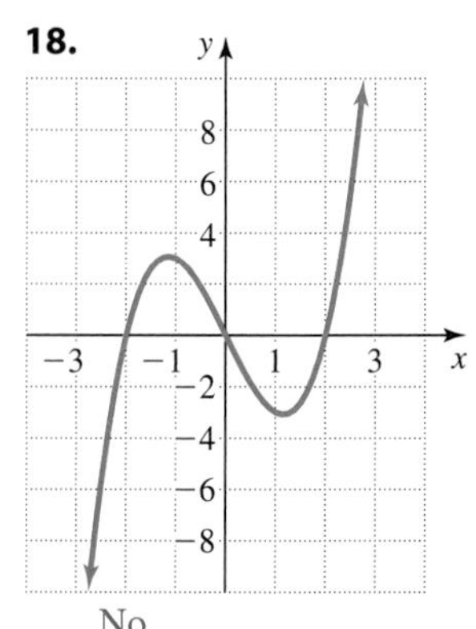

No

19.

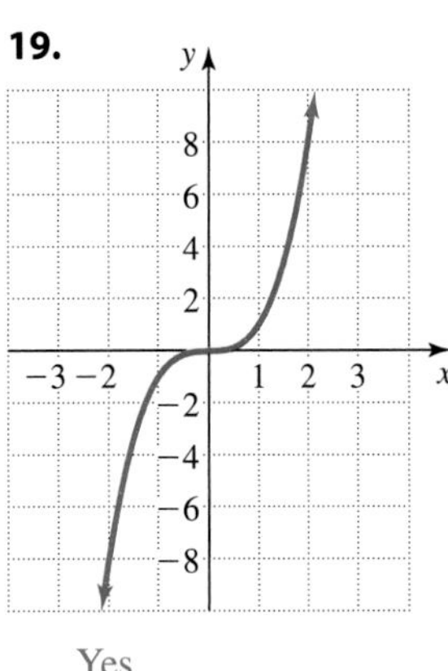

Yes

20.

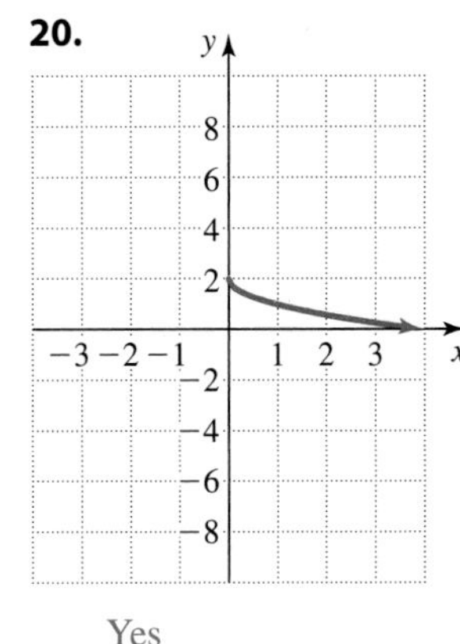

Yes

Determine whether each pair of functions f and g are inverses of each other. See Example 3.

21. $f(x) = 2x$ and $g(x) = 0.5x$ Yes

22. $f(x) = 3x$ and $g(x) = 0.33x$ No

23. $f(x) = 2x - 10$ and $g(x) = \frac{1}{2}x + 5$ Yes

24. $f(x) = 3x + 7$ and $g(x) = \frac{x - 7}{3}$ Yes

25. $f(x) = -x$ and $g(x) = -x$ Yes

26. $f(x) = \frac{1}{x}$ and $g(x) = \frac{1}{x}$ Yes

27. $f(x) = x^4$ and $g(x) = x^{1/4}$ No

28. $f(x) = |2x|$ and $g(x) = \left|\frac{x}{2}\right|$ No

Determine f^{-1} for each function by using the switch-and-solve strategy. Check that $(f \circ f^{-1})(x) = x$ and $(f^{-1} \circ f)(x) = x$. See Examples 4 and 5.

29. $f(x) = 5x$

$f^{-1}(x) = \frac{x}{5}$

30. $h(x) = -3x$

$h^{-1}(x) = -\frac{1}{3}x$

31. $g(x) = x - 9$

$g^{-1}(x) = x + 9$

32. $j(x) = x + 7$

$j^{-1}(x) = x - 7$

33. $k(x) = 5x - 9$

$k^{-1}(x) = \frac{x + 9}{5}$

34. $r(x) = 2x - 8$

$r^{-1}(x) = \frac{x + 8}{2}$

35. $m(x) = \frac{2}{x}$

$m^{-1}(x) = \frac{2}{x}$

36. $s(x) = \frac{-1}{x}$

$s^{-1}(x) = -\frac{1}{x}$

37. $f(x) = \sqrt[3]{x - 4}$

$f^{-1}(x) = x^3 + 4$

38. $f(x) = \sqrt[3]{x + 2}$

$f^{-1}(x) = x^3 - 2$

39. $f(x) = \frac{3}{x - 4}$

$f^{-1}(x) = \frac{3}{x} + 4$

40. $f(x) = \frac{2}{x + 1}$

$f^{-1}(x) = \frac{2}{x} - 1$

41. $f(x) = \sqrt[3]{3x + 7}$

$f^{-1}(x) = \frac{x^3 - 7}{3}$

42. $f(x) = \sqrt[3]{7 - 5x}$

$f^{-1}(x) = \frac{-x^3 + 7}{5}$

43. $f(x) = \frac{x + 1}{x - 2}$

$f^{-1}(x) = \frac{2x + 1}{x - 1}$

44. $f(x) = \frac{1 - x}{x + 3}$

$f^{-1}(x) = \frac{1 - 3x}{x + 1}$

45. $f(x) = \frac{x + 1}{3x - 4}$

$f^{-1}(x) = \frac{1 + 4x}{3x - 1}$

46. $g(x) = \frac{3x + 5}{2x - 3}$

$g^{-1}(x) = \frac{3x + 5}{2x - 3}$

Find the inverse of each function. See Example 6.

47. $p(x) = \sqrt[4]{x}$ $p^{-1}(x) = x^4$ for $x \ge 0$

48. $v(x) = \sqrt[6]{x}$ $v^{-1}(x) = x^6$ for $x \ge 0$

49. $f(x) = (x - 2)^2$ for $x \ge 2$ $f^{-1}(x) = 2 + \sqrt{x}$

50. $g(x) = (x + 5)^2$ for $x \ge -5$ $g^{-1}(x) = -5 + \sqrt{x}$

51. $f(x) = x^2 + 3$ for $x \ge 0$ $f^{-1}(x) = \sqrt{x - 3}$

52. $f(x) = x^2 - 5$ for $x \ge 0$ $f^{-1}(x) = \sqrt{x + 5}$

53. $f(x) = \sqrt{x + 2}$ $f^{-1}(x) = x^2 - 2$ for $x \ge 0$

54. $f(x) = \sqrt{x - 4}$ $f^{-1}(x) = x^2 + 4$ for $x \ge 0$

Find the inverse of each function and graph f and f^{-1} on the same pair of axes. See Example 7.

55. $f(x) = 2x + 3$ $f^{-1}(x) = \frac{1}{2}x - \frac{3}{2}$

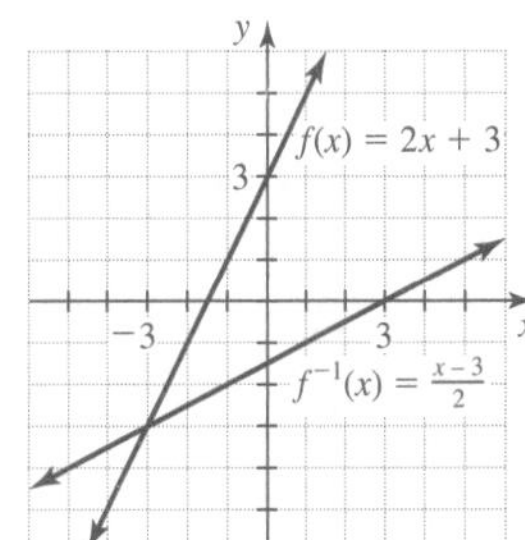

56. $f(x) = -3x + 2$ $f^{-1}(x) = -\frac{1}{3}x + \frac{2}{3}$

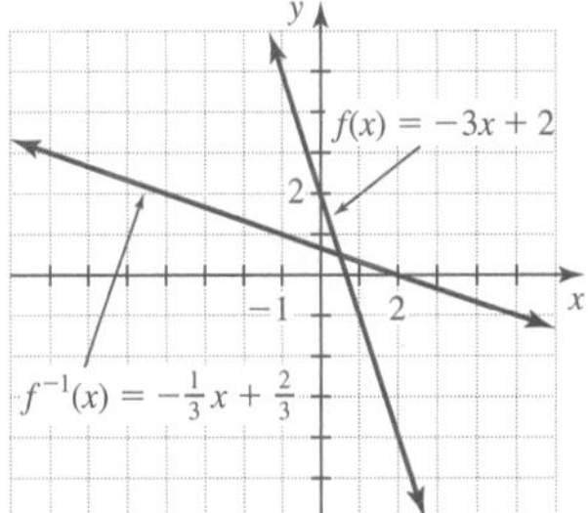

57. $f(x) = x^2 - 1$ for $x \geq 0$ $\quad f^{-1}(x) = \sqrt{x + 1}$

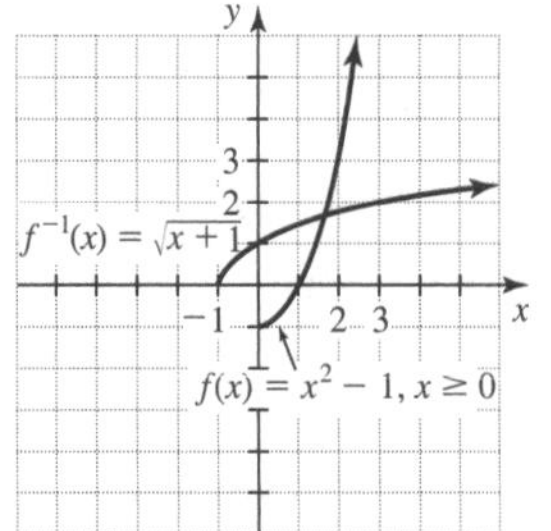

58. $f(x) = x^2 + 3$ for $x \geq 0$ $\quad f^{-1}(x) = \sqrt{x - 3}$

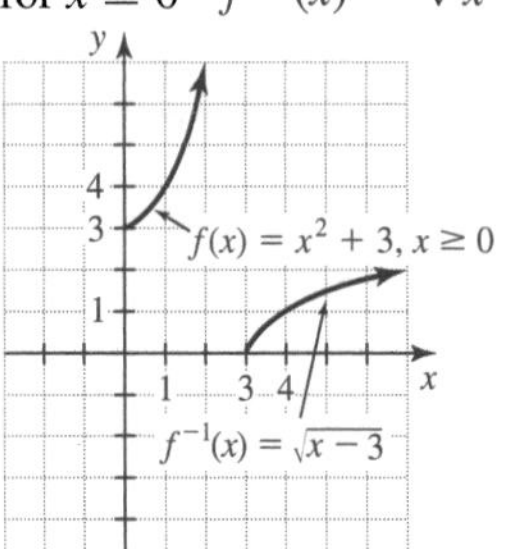

59. $f(x) = 5x$ $\quad f^{-1}(x) = \dfrac{x}{5}$

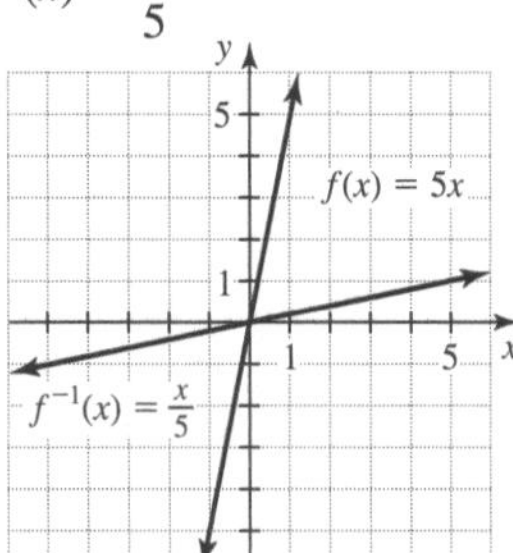

60. $f(x) = \dfrac{x}{4}$ $\quad f^{-1}(x) = 4x$

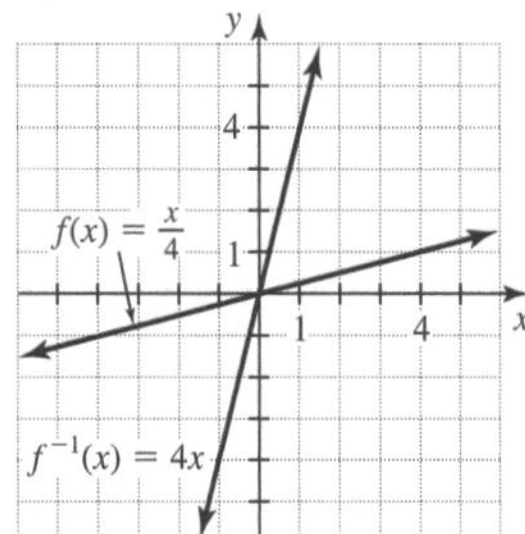

61. $f(x) = x^3$ $\quad f^{-1}(x) = \sqrt[3]{x}$

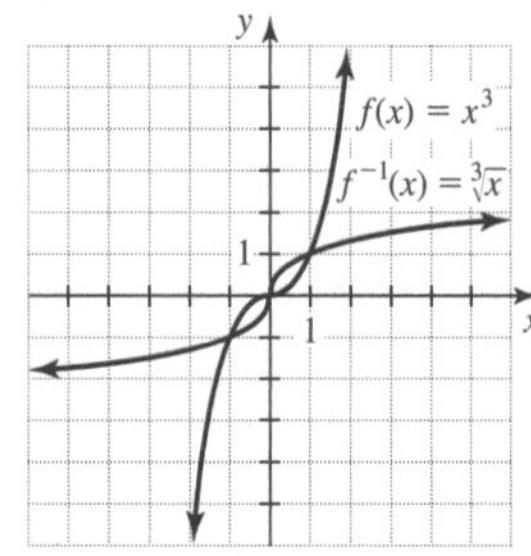

62. $f(x) = 2x^3$ $\quad f^{-1}(x) = \sqrt[3]{\dfrac{x}{2}}$

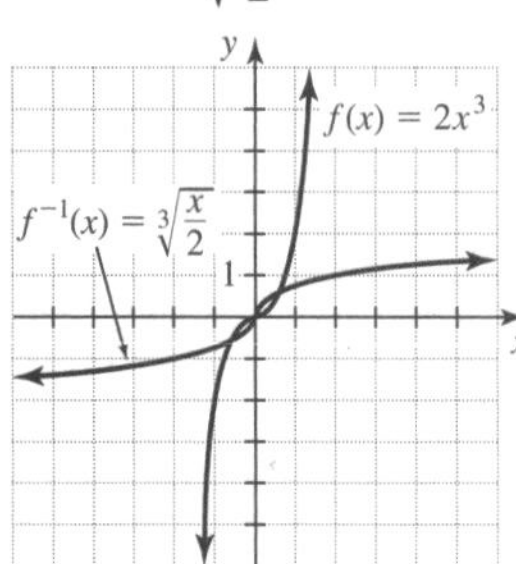

63. $f(x) = \sqrt{x - 2}$ $\quad f^{-1}(x) = x^2 + 2$ for $x \geq 0$

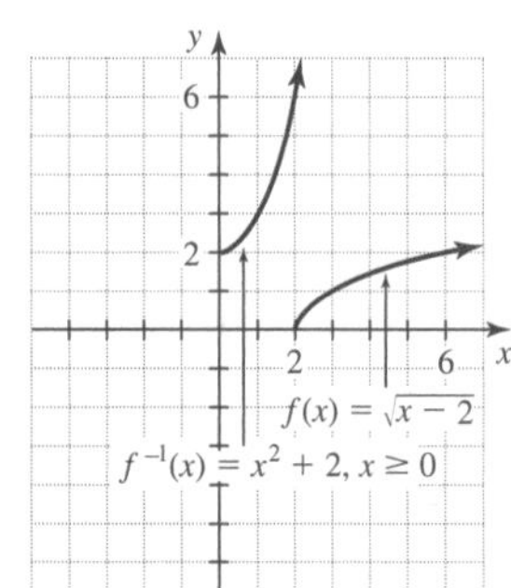

64. $f(x) = \sqrt{x + 3}$ $\quad f^{-1}(x) = x^2 - 3$ for $x \geq 0$

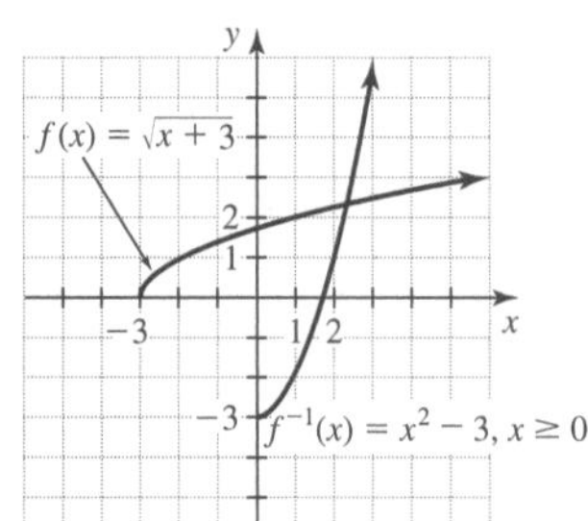

Match each function with its inverse function given in (a)–(j).

65. $f(x) = 2x$ d

66. $f(x) = x - 2$ h

67. $f(x) = 2x - 1$ i

68. $f(x) = 1 - x$ e

69. $f(x) = \sqrt{x}$ f

70. $f(x) = \sqrt[3]{x}$ b

71. $f(x) = \sqrt[3]{x - 2}$ a

72. $f(x) = \sqrt[3]{x} - 2$ j

73. $f(x) = x^4$ for $x \geq 0$ g

74. $f(x) = 1/x$ c

a) $f^{-1}(x) = x^3 + 2$

b) $f^{-1}(x) = x^3$

c) $f^{-1}(x) = 1/x$

d) $f^{-1}(x) = x/2$

e) $f^{-1}(x) = 1 - x$

f) $f^{-1}(x) = x^2$ for $x \geq 0$

g) $f^{-1}(x) = \sqrt[4]{x}$

h) $f^{-1}(x) = x + 2$

i) $f^{-1}(x) = \dfrac{x + 1}{2}$

j) $f^{-1}(x) = (x + 2)^3$

For each pair of functions, find $(f^{-1} \circ f)(x)$

75. $f(x) = x^3 - 1$ and $f^{-1}(x) = \sqrt[3]{x + 1}$

76. $f(x) = 2x^3 + 1$ and $f^{-1}(x) = \sqrt[3]{\dfrac{x - 1}{2}}$

77. $f(x) = \frac{1}{2}x - 3$ and $f^{-1}(x) = 2x + 6$

78. $f(x) = 3x - 9$ and $f^{-1}(x) = \frac{1}{3}x + 3$

79. $f(x) = \frac{1}{x} + 2$ and $f^{-1}(x) = \frac{1}{x - 2}$

80. $f(x) = 4 - \frac{1}{x}$ and $f^{-1}(x) = \frac{1}{4 - x}$

81. $f(x) = \frac{x + 1}{x - 2}$ and $f^{-1}(x) = \frac{2x + 1}{x - 1}$

82. $f(x) = \frac{3x - 2}{x + 2}$ and $f^{-1}(x) = \frac{2x + 2}{3 - x}$

For 75–82 $(f^{-1} \circ f)(x) = x$

Solve each problem.

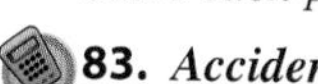

83. ***Accident reconstruction.*** The distance that it takes a car to stop is a function of the speed and the drag factor. The drag factor is a measure of the resistance between the tire and the road surface. The formula $S = \sqrt{30LD}$ is used to determine the minimum speed S [in miles per hour (mph)] for a car that has left skid marks of length L feet (ft) on a surface with drag factor D.

a) Find the minimum speed for a car that has left skid marks of length 50 ft where the drag factor is 0.75.
33.5 mph

b) Does the drag factor increase or decrease for a road surface when it gets wet?
Decreases

c) Write L as a function of S for a road surface with drag factor 1 and graph the function.
$L = \frac{S^2}{30}$

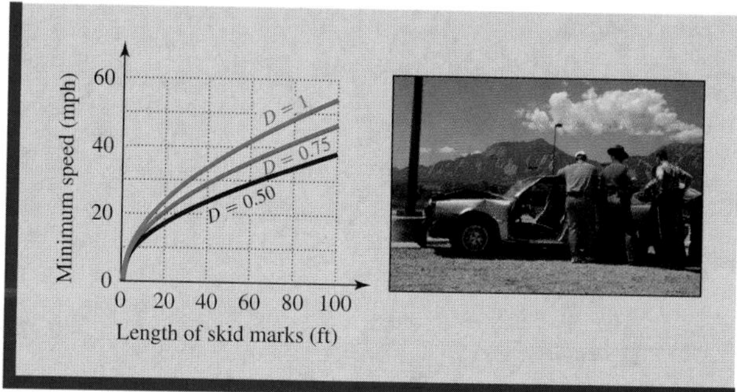

Figure for Exercise 83

84. ***Area of a circle.*** Let x be the radius of a circle and $h(x)$ be the area of the circle. Write a formula for $h(x)$ in terms of x. What does x represent in the notation $h^{-1}(x)$? Write a formula for $h^{-1}(x)$.
$h(x) = \pi x^2$, the area of the circle, $h^{-1}(x) = \sqrt{\frac{x}{\pi}}$

85. ***Vehicle cost.*** At Bill Hood Ford in Hammond a sales tax of 9% of the selling price x and a \$125 title and license fee are added to the selling price to get the total cost of a vehicle. Find the function $T(x)$ that the dealer uses to get the total cost as a function of the selling price x. Citizens National Bank will not include sales tax or fees in a loan. Find the function $T^{-1}(x)$ that the bank can use to get the selling price as a function of the total cost x.
$T(x) = 1.09x + 125$, $T^{-1}(x) = \frac{x - 125}{1.09}$

86. ***Carpeting cost.*** At the Windrush Trace apartment complex all living rooms are square, but the length of x feet may vary. The cost of carpeting a living room is \$18 per square yard plus a \$50 installation fee. Find the function $C(x)$ that gives the total cost of carpeting a living room of length x. The manager has an invoice for the total cost of a living room carpeting job but does not know in which apartment it was done. Find the function $C^{-1}(x)$ that gives the length of a living room as a function of the total cost of the carpeting job x.
$C(x) = 2x^2 + 50$, $C^{-1}(x) = \sqrt{\frac{x - 50}{2}}$

Getting More Involved

87. ***Discussion***

Let $f(x) = x^n$ for n a positive integer. For which values of n is f an invertible function? Explain.
An odd positive integer

88. ***Discussion***

Suppose f is a function with range $(-\infty, \infty)$ and g is a function with domain $(0, \infty)$. Is it possible that g and f are inverse functions? Explain. No

Graphing Calculator Exercises

89. Most graphing calculators can form compositions of functions. Let $f(x) = x^2$ and $g(x) = \sqrt{x}$. To graph the composition $g \circ f$, let $y_1 = x^2$ and $y_2 = \sqrt{y_1}$. The graph of y_2 is the graph of $g \circ f$. Use the graph of y_2 to determine whether f and g are inverse functions. Not inverses

90. Let $y_1 = x^3 - 4$, $y_2 = \sqrt[3]{x + 4}$, and $y_3 = \sqrt[3]{y_1 + 4}$. The function y_3 is the composition of the first two functions. Graph all three functions on the same screen. What do the graphs indicate about the relationship between y_1 and y_2?
They are inverse functions.

Collaborative Activities

Grouping: Three students per group

Topic: Functions, dependence, domain, and range

Life's a Function of What?

Suppose that alertness is a function of the number of cups of coffee consumed. Let x (the independent variable) represent the number of cups of coffee consumed in a morning and y (the dependent variable) represent alertness (as a percent). Suppose an average coffee drinker drinks between 0 and 5 cups in a morning. Let's say that a person is 20% alert for 0 cups and 100% alert for 5 cups. Then the domain is the interval [0, 5] and the range is [0, 1].

If our function is linear, we need only two points to draw its graph. Plot the pairs (0, 0.2) and (5, 1), and draw a line through them.

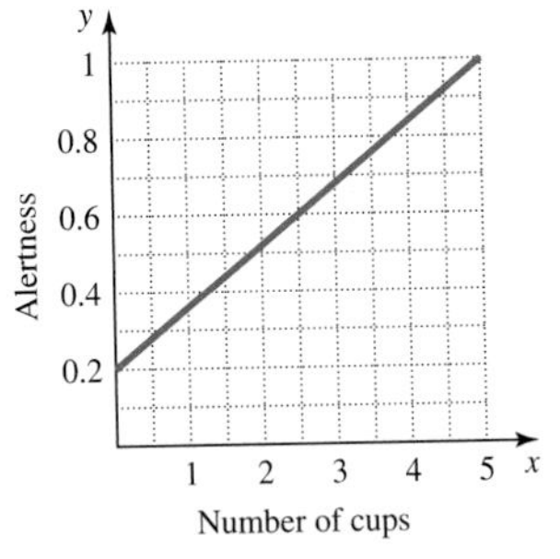

Find the slope of the line through (5, 1) and (0, 0.2):

$$m = \frac{1 - 0.2}{5 - 0} = \frac{0.8}{5} = 0.16$$

Using slope-intercept form the equation is $y = 0.16x + 0.2$. So the linear function that gives alertness in terms of cups of coffee is $f(x) = 0.16x + 0.2$.

In your groups do the following:

1. Decide on something in your life that could be modeled by a function of one variable.
2. Determine the domain and range of your function using interval notation.
3. Find two points that would make sense in your function. Graph a line through these points.
4. Find a linear equation for your graph. Write it in function notation.
5. Trade with a group near you and add, subtract, multiply, divide, and compose your functions. Discuss in your groups if these operations make sense for your functions. What would need to be true for composition to make sense? Write down the things your group discovers about operations on functions.
6. Assuming that your function is nonlinear, plot at least four points that you think would be in your function. Use the different regression programs on a graphing calculator to find the function that fits your data points the best.

Chapter 11 Wrap-Up

Summary

Relations and Functions		Examples
Relation	Any set of ordered pairs of real numbers	$\{(1, 2), (1, 3)\}$
Function	A relation in which no two ordered pairs have the same first coordinate and different second coordinates. If y is a function of x, then y is uniquely determined by x. A function may be defined by a table, a listing of ordered pairs, or an equation.	$\{(1, 2), (3, 5), (4, 5)\}$
Domain	The set of first coordinates of the ordered pairs	Function: $y = x^2$, Domain: $(-\infty, \infty)$
Range	The set of second coordinates of the ordered pairs.	Function: $y = x^2$, Range: $[0, \infty)$
Function notation	If y is a function of x, the expression $f(x)$ is used in place of y.	$y = 2x + 3$ $f(x) = 2x + 3$
Vertical-line test	If a graph can be crossed more than once by a vertical line, then it is not the graph of a function.	
Linear function	A function of the form $f(x) = mx + b$ with $m \neq 0$	$f(x) = 3x - 7$ $f(x) = -2x + 5$
Constant function	A function of the form $f(x) = b$, where b is a real number	$f(x) = 2$

Types of Functions		Examples
Linear function	$y = mx + b$ or $f(x) = mx + b$ for $m \neq 0$ Domain $(-\infty, \infty)$, range $(-\infty, \infty)$ If $m = 0$, $y = b$ is a constant function. Domain $(-\infty, \infty)$, range $\{b\}$	$f(x) = 2x - 3$
Absolute value function	$y = \lvert x\rvert$ or $f(x) = \lvert x\rvert$ Domain $(-\infty, \infty)$, range $[0, \infty)$	$f(x) = \lvert x + 5\rvert$
Quadratic function	$f(x) = ax^2 + bx + c$ for $a \neq 0$	$f(x) = x^2 - 4x + 3$
Square-root function	$f(x) = \sqrt{x}$ Domain $[0, \infty)$, range $[0, \infty)$	$f(x) = \sqrt{x - 4}$

Transformations of Graphs		
Reflecting	The graph of $y = -f(x)$ is a reflection in the x-axis of the graph of $y = f(x)$.	The graph of $y = -x^2$ is a reflection of the graph of $y = x^2$.
Translating	The graph of $y = f(x) + k$ is k units above $y = f(x)$ if $k > 0$ or $\|k\|$ units below $y = f(x)$ if $k < 0$. The graph of $y = f(x - h)$ is h units to the right of $y = f(x)$ if $h > 0$ or $\|h\|$ units to the left of $y = f(x)$ if $h < 0$.	The graph of $y = x^2 + 3$ is three units above $y = x^2$, and $y = x^2 - 3$ is three units below $y = x^2$. The graph of $y = (x - 3)^2$ is three units to the right of $y = x^2$, and $y = (x + 3)^2$ is three units to the left.
Stretching and shrinking	The graph of $y = af(x)$ is obtained by stretching (if $a > 1$) or shrinking (if $0 < a < 1$) the graph of $y = f(x)$.	The graph of $y = 5x^2$ is obtained by stretching $y = x^2$, and $y = 0.1x^2$ is obtained by shrinking $y = x^2$.
Polynomial Functions		**Examples**
Polynomial function	A function defined by a polynomial	$P(x) = x^3 - x^2 - 12x + 5$
Behavior at the x-intercepts	The graph a polynomial function crosses the x-axis at $(c, 0)$ if $(x - c)$ has an odd exponent. The graph touches but does not cross the x-axis if $(x - c)$ has an even exponent.	Graph of $f(x) = (x - 3)^2(x + 5)$ touches but does not cross x-axis at $(3, 0)$ and crosses x-axis at $(-5, 0)$.
Rational Functions		**Examples**
Rational function	If $P(x)$ and $Q(x)$ are polynomials with no common factor and $f(x) = \dfrac{P(x)}{Q(x)}$ for $Q(x) \neq 0$, then $f(x)$ is a rational function.	$f(x) = \dfrac{x^2 - 1}{3x - 2}$, $f(x) = \dfrac{1}{x - 3}$
Finding asymptotes for a rational function $f(x) = \dfrac{P(x)}{Q(x)}$	1. The graph of f has a vertical asymptote for each solution to the equation $Q(x) = 0$. 2. If the degree of $P(x)$ is less than the degree of $Q(x)$, then the x-axis is a horizontal asymptote. 3. If the degree of $P(x)$ is equal to the degree of $Q(x)$, then the horizontal asymptote is determined by the ratio of the leading coefficients. 4. If the degree of $P(x)$ is one larger than the degree of $Q(x)$, then use long division to find the quotient of $P(x)$ and $Q(x)$.	$f(x) = \dfrac{1}{x - 2}$ Vertical: $x = 2$ Horizontal: x-axis $f(x) = \dfrac{x}{x - 2}$ Vertical: $x = 2$ Horizontal: $y = 1$ $f(x) = \dfrac{2x^2 + 3x - 5}{x + 2} = 2x - 1 + \dfrac{-3}{x + 2}$ Vertical: $x = -2$ Oblique: $y = 2x - 1$

Combining Functions		**Examples**
Sum	$(f + g)(x) = f(x) + g(x)$	For $f(x) = x^2$ and $g(x) = x + 1$ $(f + g)(x) = x^2 + x + 1$
Difference	$(f - g)(x) = f(x) - g(x)$	$(f - g)(x) = x^2 - x - 1$
Product	$(f \cdot g)(x) = f(x) \cdot g(x)$	$(f \cdot g)(x) = x^3 + x^2$
Quotient	$\left(\frac{f}{g}\right)(x) = \frac{f(x)}{g(x)}$	$\left(\frac{f}{g}\right)(x) = \frac{x^2}{x + 1}$
Composition of functions	$(g \circ f)(x) = g(f(x))$ $(f \circ g)(x) = f(g(x))$	$(g \circ f)(x) = g(x^2) = x^2 + 1$ $(f \circ g)(x) = f(x + 1)$ $= x^2 + 2x + 1$

Inverse Functions		**Examples**
One-to-one function	A function in which no two ordered pairs have different x-coordinates and the same y-coordinate.	$f = \{(2, 20), (3, 30)\}$
Inverse function	The inverse of a one-to-one function f is the function f^{-1}, which is obtained from f by interchanging the coordinates in each ordered pair of f. The domain of f^{-1} is the range of f, and the range of f^{-1} is the domain of f.	$f^{-1} = \{(20, 2), (30, 3)\}$
Horizontal-line test	If there is a horizontal line that crosses the graph of a function more than once, then the function is not invertible.	
Function notation for inverse	Two functions f and g are inverses of each other if and only if both of the following conditions are met. 1. $(g \circ f)(x) = x$ for every number x in the domain of f. 2. $(f \circ g)(x) = x$ for every number x in the domain of g.	$f(x) = x^3 + 1$ $f^{-1}(x) = \sqrt[3]{x - 1}$
Switch-and-solve strategy for finding f^{-1}	1. Replace $f(x)$ by y. 2. Interchange x and y. 3. Solve for y. 4. Replace y by $f^{-1}(x)$.	$y = x^3 + 1$ $x = y^3 + 1$ $x - 1 = y^3$ $y = \sqrt[3]{x - 1}$ $f^{-1}(x) = \sqrt[3]{x - 1}$
Graphs of f and f^{-1}	Graphs of inverse functions are symmetric with respect to the line $y = x$.	

Enriching Your Mathematical Word Power

For each mathematical term, choose the correct meaning.

1. function
a. a set of ordered pairs of real numbers
b. a set of ordered pairs of real numbers in which no two have the same first coordinates and different second coordinates
c. a set of ordered pairs of real numbers in which no two have the same second coordinates and different first coordinates
d. an equation b

2. relation
a. a set of ordered pairs of real numbers
b. a set of ordered pairs of real numbers in which no two have the same first coordinates and different second coordinates
c. cousins and second cousins
d. a fraction a

3. domain
a. the range
b. the set of second coordinates of a relation
c. the independent variable
d. the set of first coordinates of a relation d

4. function notation
a. a notation where $f(x)$ is used as the independent variable
b. a notation where $f(x)$ is used as the dependent variable
c. the notation of algebra
d. the notation of exponents b

5. polynomial function
a. a function with many numbers
b. a function with many names
c. a function defined by a polynomial
d. a function that is symmetric to a polynomial c

6. rational function
a. a ratio of two polynomial functions
b. a function that has only rational roots
c. a polynomial function with rational coefficients
d. a commonsense function a

7. asymptote
a. the graph of a rational function
b. a line that is approached by a curve
c. the graph of an asymmetrical function
d. a line of symmetry b

8. oblique asymptote
a. an asymptote that is neither horizontal nor vertical
b. an asymptote of an odd function
c. a really large asymptote
d. a dashed line a

9. composition of f and g
a. the function $f \circ g$ where $(f \circ g)(x) = f(g(x))$
b. the function $f \circ g$ where $(f \circ g)(x) = g(f(x))$
c. the function $f \cdot g$ where $(f \cdot g)(x) = f(x) \cdot g(x)$
d. a diagram showing f and g a

10. sum of f and g
a. the function $f \cdot g$ where $(f \cdot g)(x) = f(x) \cdot g(x)$
b. the function $f + g$ where $(f + g)(x) = f(x) + g(x)$
c. the function $f \circ g$ where $(f \circ g)(x) = g(f(x))$
d. the function obtained by adding the domains of f and g b

11. inverse of the function f
a. a function with the same ordered pairs as f
b. the opposite of the function f
c. the function $1/f$
d. a function in which the ordered pairs of f are reversed d

12. one-to-one function
a. a constant function
b. a function that pairs 1 with 1
c. a function in which no two ordered pairs have the same first coordinate and different second coordinates
d. a function in which no two ordered pairs have the same second coordinate and different first coordinates d

13. vertical-line test
a. a visual method for determining whether a graph is a graph of a function
b. a visual method for determining whether a function is one-to-one
c. using a vertical line to check a graph
d. a test on vertical lines a

14. horizontal-line test
a. a test that horizontal lines must pass
b. a visual method for determining whether a function is one-to-one
c. a graph that does not cross the x-axis
d. a visual method for determining whether a graph is a graph of a function b

15. reflection in the x-axis
a. the graph of $y = f(-x)$
b. the graph of $y = -f(x)$
c. the graph of $y = -f(-x)$
d. the line of symmetry b

16. upward translation
a. the graph of $y = f(x) + c$ for $c > 0$
b. the graph of $y = f(x + c)$ for $c < 0$
c. the graph of $y = f(x - c)$ for $c > 0$
d. the graph of $y = f(x) + c$ for $c < 0$ a

17. translation to the left
a. the graph of $y = f(x) - c$ for $c > 0$
b. the graph of $y = f(x) + c$ for $c > 0$
c. the graph of $y = f(x - c)$ for $c > 0$
d. the graph of $y = f(x + c)$ for $c > 0$ d

Review Exercises

11.1 *Determine whether each relation is a function.*

1. $\{(5, 7), (5, 10), (5, 3)\}$ No

2. $\{(1, 3), (4, 7), (1, 6)\}$ No

3. $\{(1, 1), (2, 1), (3, 3)\}$ Yes

4. $\{(2, 4), (4, 6), (6, 8)\}$ Yes

5. $y = x^2$ Yes

6. $x^2 = 1 + y^2$ No

7. $x = y^4$ No

8. $y = \sqrt{x - 1}$ Yes

Determine the domain and range of each relation.

9. $\{(3, 5), (4, 9), (5, 1)\}$ $\{3, 4, 5\}, \{1, 5, 9\}$

10. $\{(2, 6), (6, 7), (8, 9)\}$ $\{2, 6, 8\}, \{6, 7, 9\}$

11. $y = x + 1$ $(-\infty, \infty), (-\infty, \infty)$

12. $y = 2x - 3$ $(-\infty, \infty), (-\infty, \infty)$

13. $y = \sqrt{x + 5}$ $[-5, \infty), [0, \infty)$

14. $y = \sqrt{x - 1}$ $[1, \infty), [0, \infty)$

Let $f(x) = 2x - 5$ and $g(x) = x^2 + x - 6$. Evaluate each expression.

15. $f(0)$ -5

16. $f(-3)$ -11

17. $g(0)$ -6

18. $g(-2)$ -4

19. $g\left(\frac{1}{2}\right)$ $-\frac{21}{4}$

20. $g\left(-\frac{1}{2}\right)$ $-\frac{25}{4}$

11.2 *Graph each function and state the domain and range.*

21. $f(x) = 3x - 4$ $(-\infty, \infty), (-\infty, \infty)$

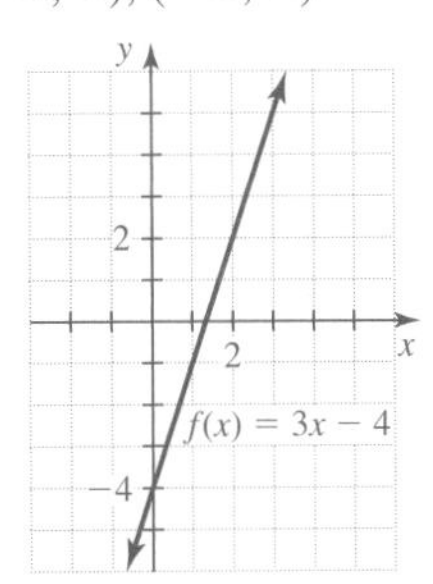

22. $y = 0.3x$ $(-\infty, \infty), (-\infty, \infty)$

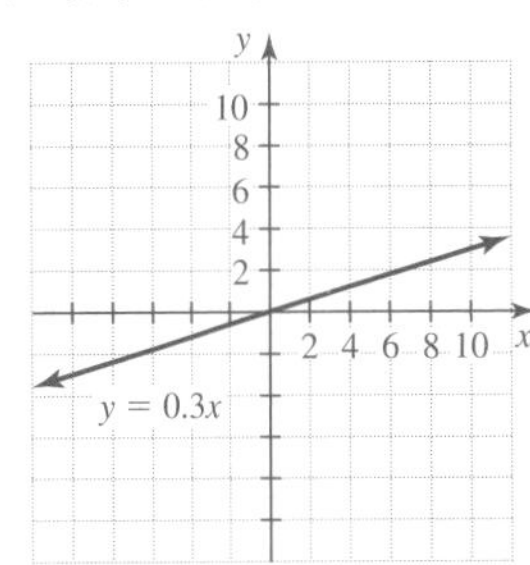

23. $h(x) = |x| - 2$ $(-\infty, \infty), [-2, \infty)$

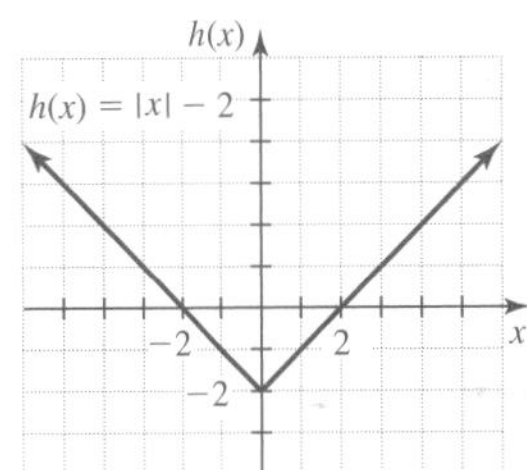

24. $y = |x - 2|$ $(-\infty, \infty), [0, \infty)$

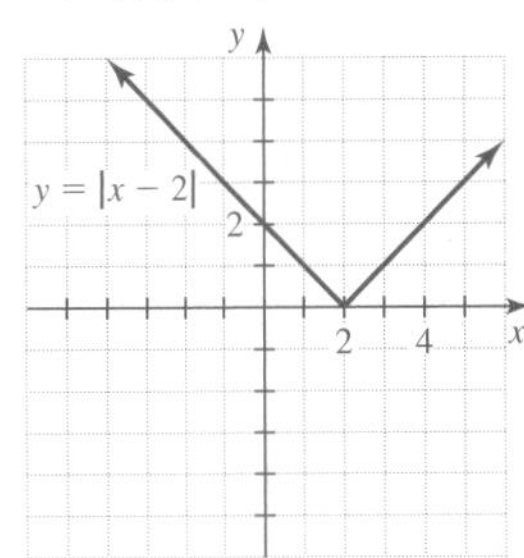

25. $y = x^2 - 2x + 1$ $(-\infty, \infty), [0, \infty)$

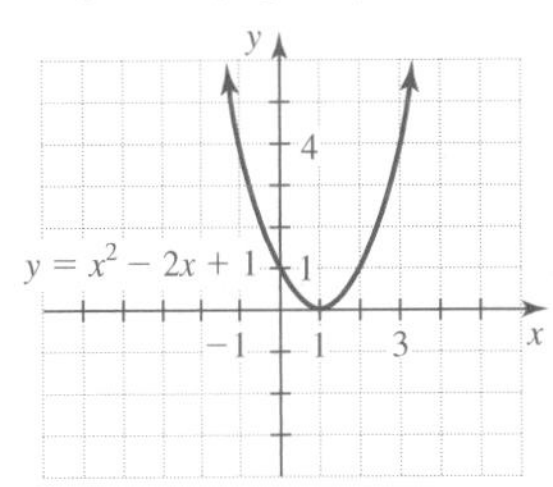

26. $g(x) = x^2 - 2x - 15$ $(-\infty, \infty), [-16, \infty)$

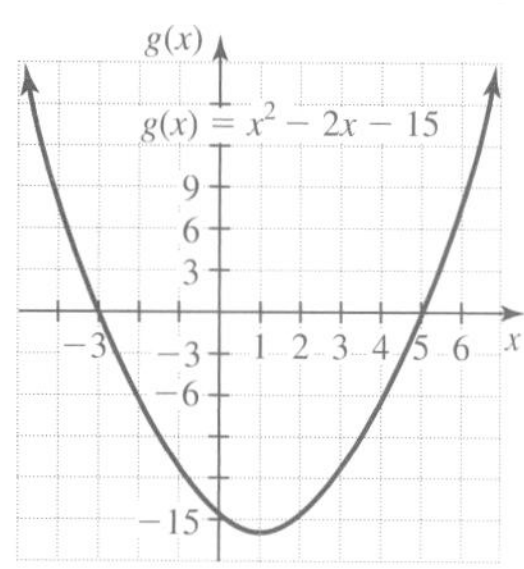

27. $k(x) = \sqrt{x} + 2$ $[0, \infty), [2, \infty)$

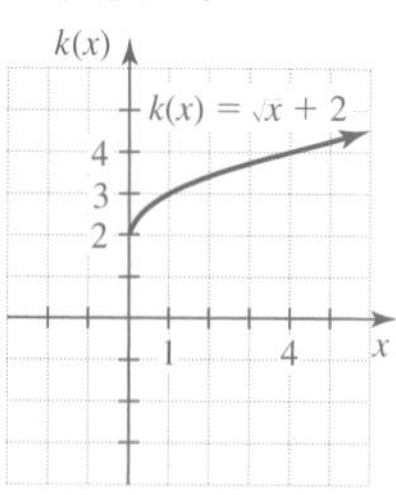

28. $y = \sqrt{x - 2}$ $[2, \infty), [0, \infty)$

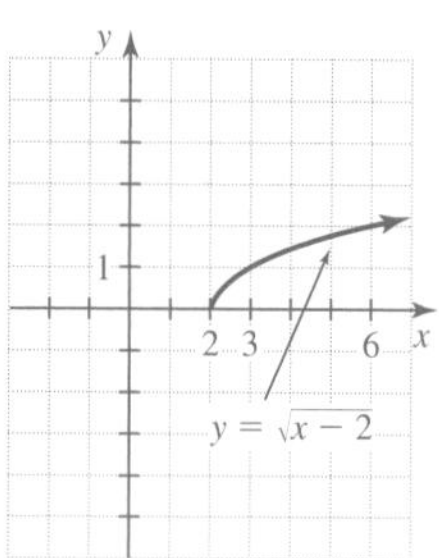

29. $y = 30 - x^2$ $(-\infty, \infty), (-\infty, 30]$

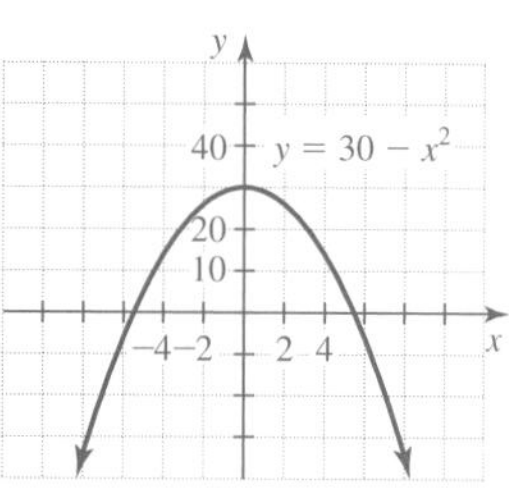

30. $y = 4 - x^2$ $(-\infty, \infty), (-\infty, 4]$

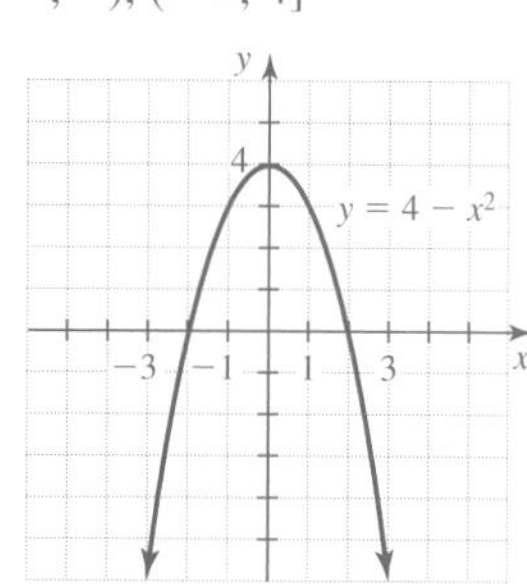

Graph each relation and state its domain and range.

31. $x = 2$ $\{2\}, (-\infty, \infty)$

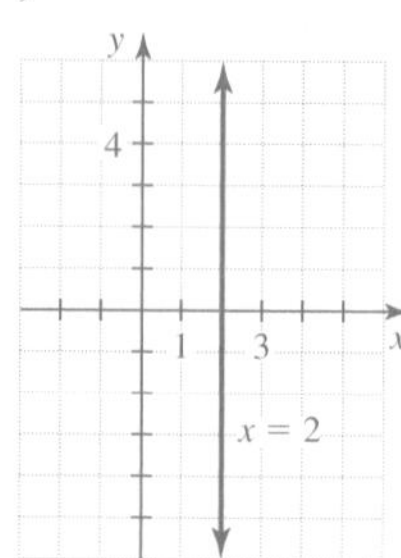

32. $x = y^2 - 1$ $[-1, \infty), (-\infty, \infty)$

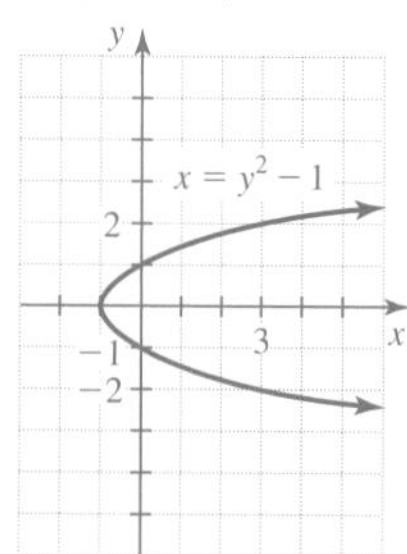

33. $x = |y| + 1$ $[1, \infty), (-\infty, \infty)$

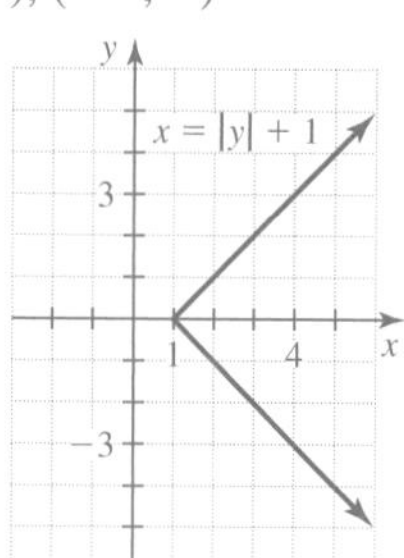

34. $x = \sqrt{y - 1}$ $[0, \infty), [1, \infty)$

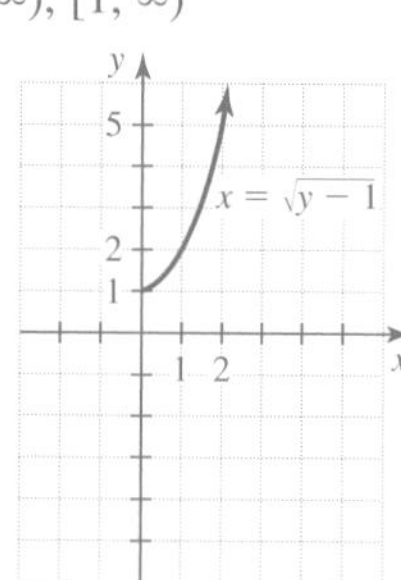

11.3 *Sketch the graph of each function and state the domain and range.*

35. $y = \sqrt{x}$ $[0, \infty), [0, \infty)$

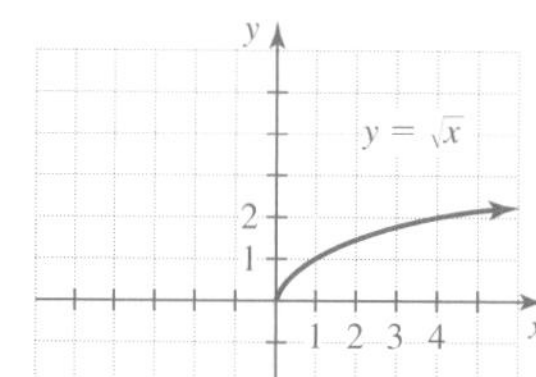

36. $y = -\sqrt{x}$ $[0, \infty), (-\infty, 0]$

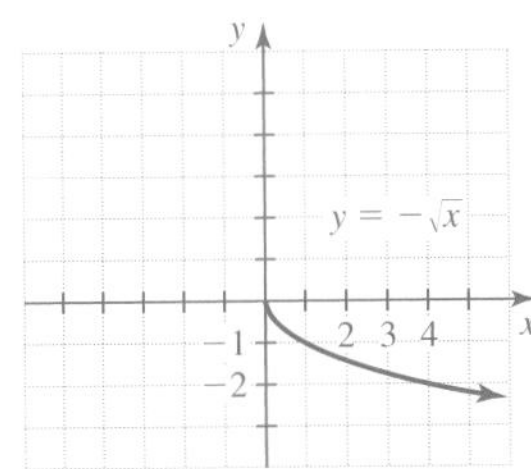

37. $y = -2\sqrt{x}$ $[0, \infty), (-\infty, 0]$

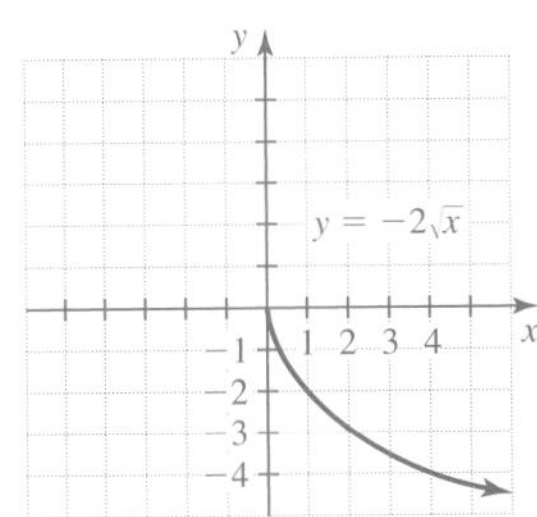

38. $y = 2\sqrt{x}$ $[0, \infty), [0, \infty)$

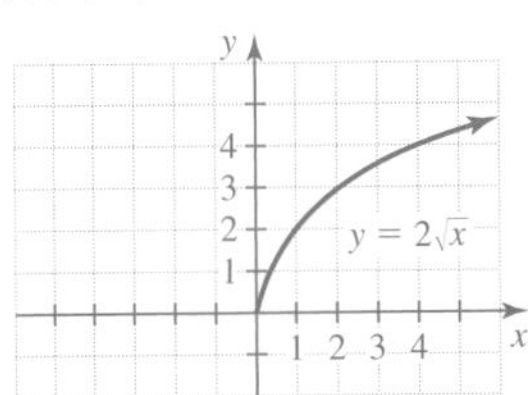

39. $y = \sqrt{x - 2}$ $[2, \infty), [0, \infty)$

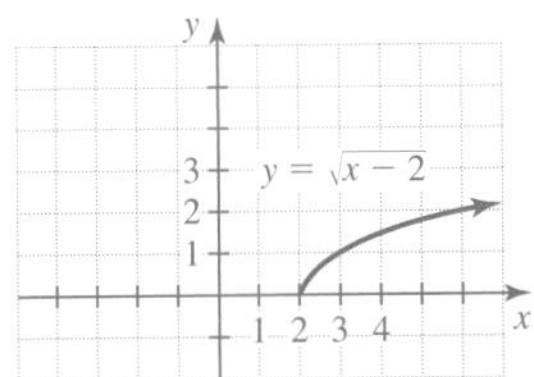

40. $y = \sqrt{x + 2}$ $[-2, \infty), [0, \infty)$

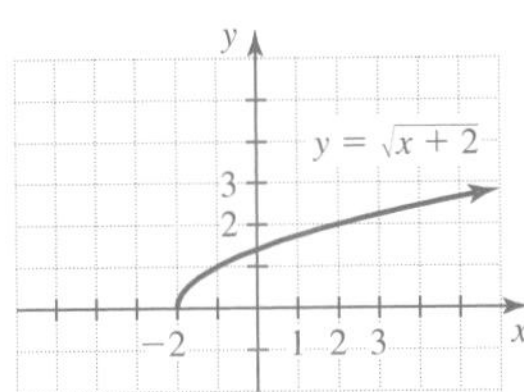

41. $y = \frac{1}{2}\sqrt{x}$ $[0, \infty), [0, \infty)$

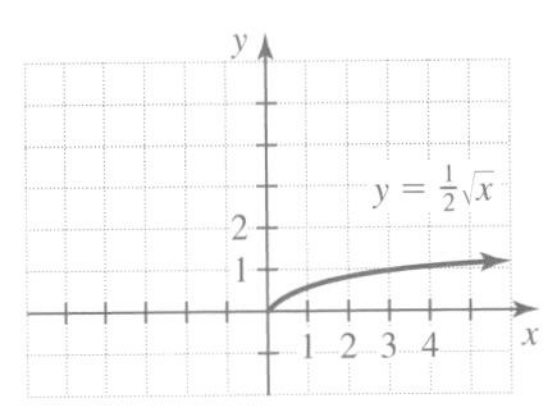

42. $y = \sqrt{x - 1} + 2$ $[1, \infty), [2, \infty)$

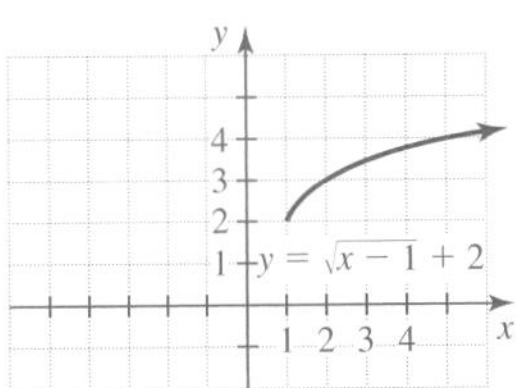

43. $y = -\sqrt{x + 1} + 3$ $[-1, \infty), (-\infty, 3]$

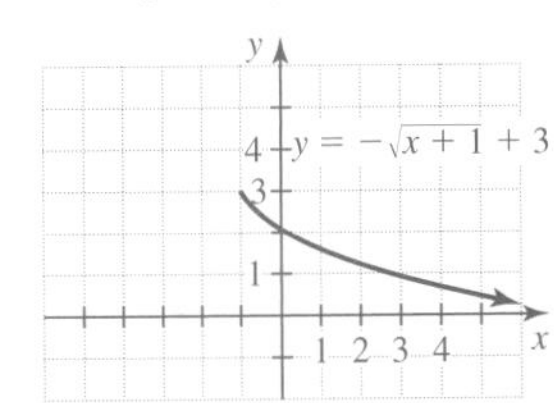

44. $y = 3\sqrt{x + 4} - 5$ $[-4, \infty), [-5, \infty)$

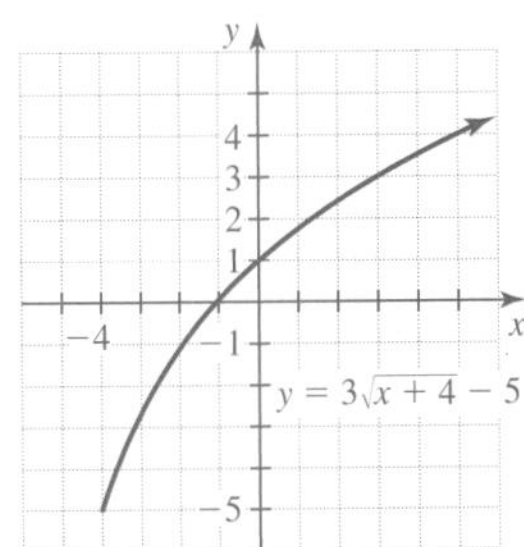

11.4 *Graph each function and identify the x- and y-intercepts.*

45. $f(x) = x^3 - 25x$ $(-5, 0), (5, 0), (0, 0)$

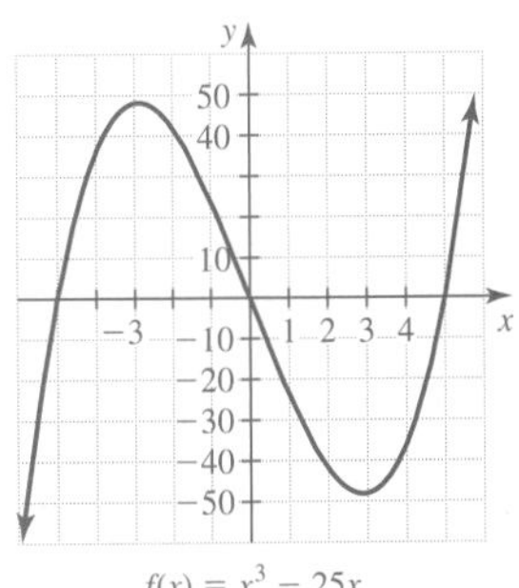

$f(x) = x^3 - 25x$

46. $f(x) = x^3 + 2x^2 - 4x - 8$ $(-2, 0), (2, 0), (0, -8)$

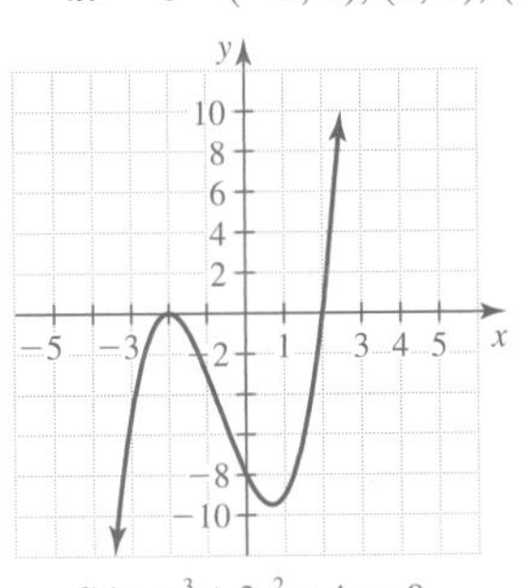

$f(x) = x^3 + 2x^2 - 4x - 8$

47. $f(x) = (x^2 - 4)(x - 1)$ $(-2, 0), (1, 0), (2, 0), (0, 4)$

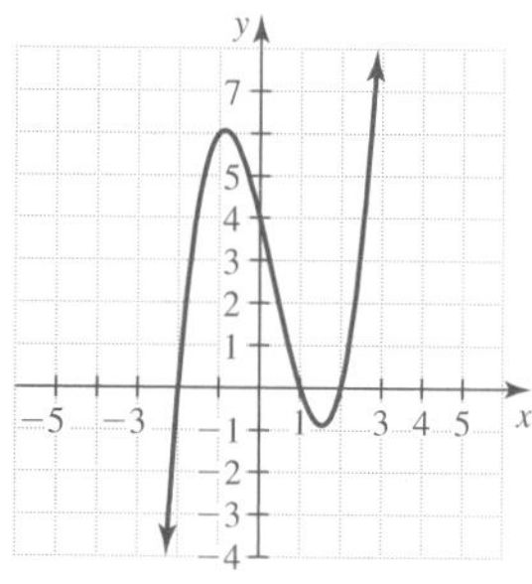

$f(x) = (x^2 - 4)(x - 1)$

48. $f(x) = (x^2 - 3x - 4)(x + 3)$
$(-3, 0), (-1, 0),$
$(4, 0), (0, -12)$

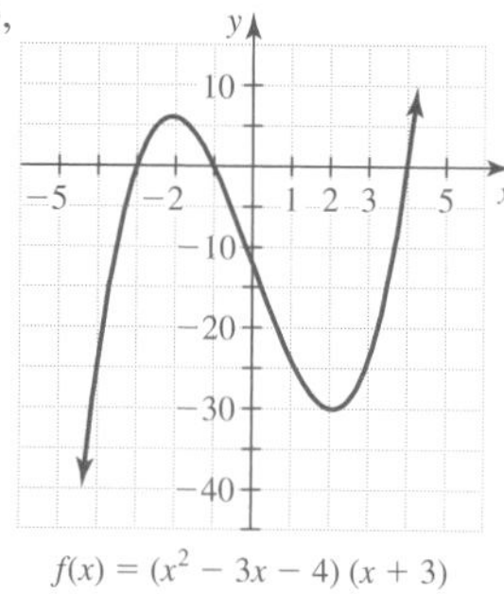

$f(x) = (x^2 - 3x - 4)(x + 3)$

49. $f(x) = x^4 - 10x^2 + 9$ $(-3, 0), (-1, 0), (1, 0), (3, 0), (0, 9)$

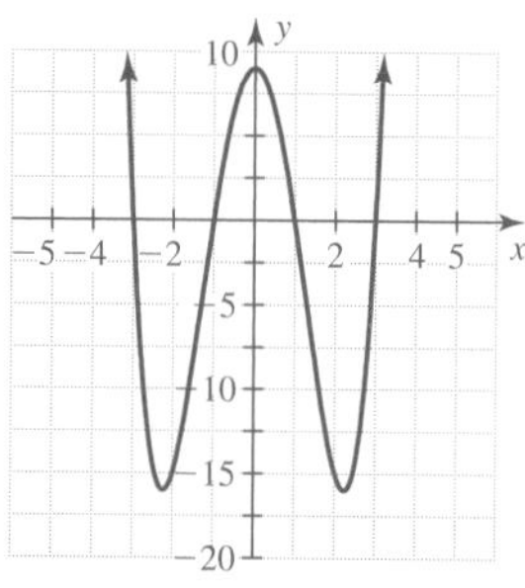

$f(x) = x^4 - 10x^2 + 9$

50. $f(x) = x^4 - 4x^3$ $(4, 0), (0, 0)$

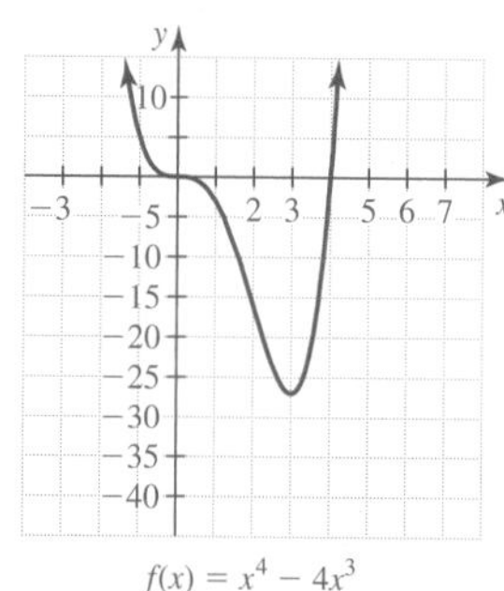

$f(x) = x^4 - 4x^3$

Find the x-intercepts and discuss the behavior of the graph of each polynomial function at its x-intercepts.

51. $f(x) = x^2 - 6x + 9$
The graph touches but does not cross the x-axis at $(3, 0)$.

52. $f(x) = x^2 - 3x - 18$
The graph crosses the x-axis at $(-3, 0)$ and $(6, 0)$.

53. $f(x) = (x - 3)(x + 5)(x - 4)^2$
The graph crosses the x-axis at $(3, 0)$ and $(-5, 0)$, and touches but does not cross at $(4, 0)$.

54. $f(x) = (x - 1)^2(x + 7)$
The graph crosses the x-axis at $(-7, 0)$ and touches but does not cross at $(1, 0)$.

55. $f(x) = x^3 - 8x^2 - 9x + 72$
The graph crosses the x-axis at $(-3, 0)$, $(3, 0)$, and $(8, 0)$.

56. $f(x) = x^4 - 29x^2 + 100$
The graph crosses the x-axis at $(-5, 0)$, $(-2, 0)$, $(2, 0)$, and $(5, 0)$.

11.5 *Find the domain of each rational function.*

57. $f(x) = \dfrac{x^2 - 1}{2x + 3}$ $\left(-\infty, -\dfrac{3}{2}\right) \cup \left(-\dfrac{3}{2}, \infty\right)$

58. $f(x) = \dfrac{3x + 2}{x^2 - x - 12}$ $(-\infty, -3) \cup (-3, 4) \cup (4, \infty)$

59. $f(x) = \dfrac{1}{x^2 + 9}$ $(-\infty, \infty)$

60. $f(x) = \dfrac{x - 4}{x^2 - 9}$ $(-\infty, -3) \cup (-3, 3) \cup (3, \infty)$

Find all asymptotes for each rational function and sketch the graph of the function.

61. $f(x) = \dfrac{2}{x - 3}$

$x = 3$, x-axis

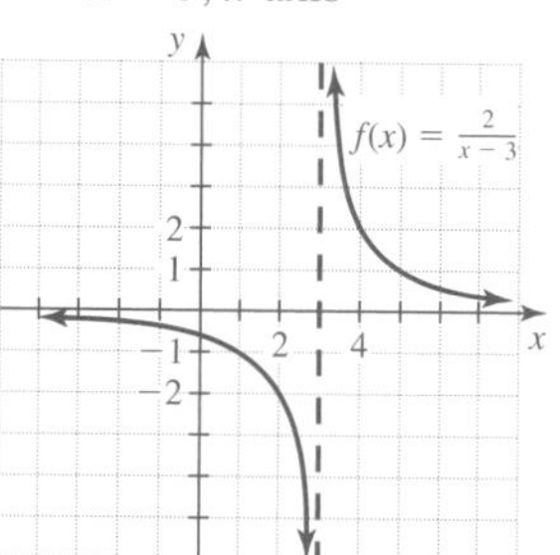

62. $f(x) = \dfrac{-1}{x + 1}$

$x = -1$, x-axis

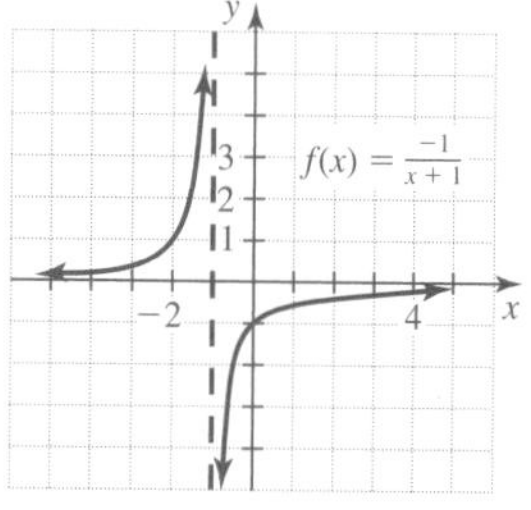

63. $f(x) = \dfrac{x}{x^2 - 4}$

$x = 2$, $x = -2$, x-axis

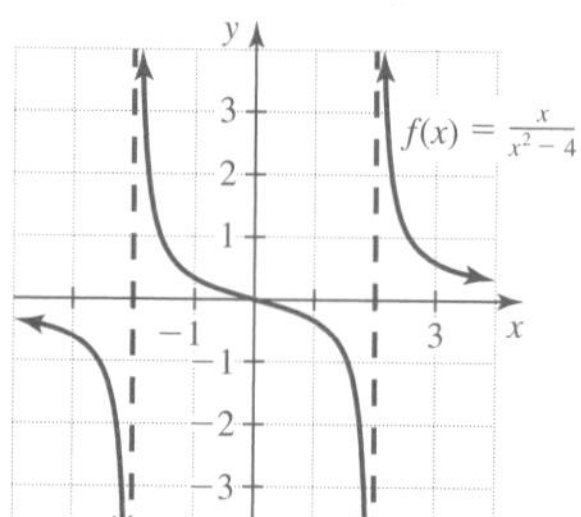

64. $f(x) = \dfrac{x^2}{x^2 - 4}$

$x = 2$, $x = -2$, $y = 1$

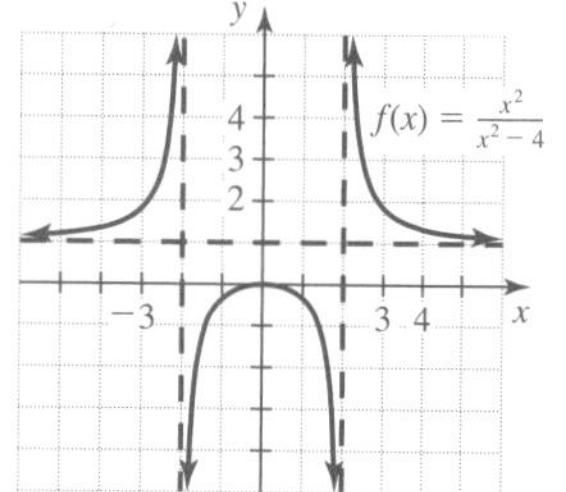

65. $f(x) = \frac{2x - 1}{x - 1}$
$x = 1, y = 2$

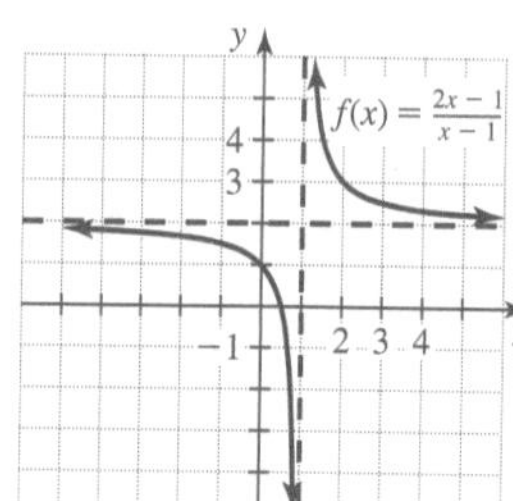

66. $f(x) = \frac{-x - 1}{x}$
y-axis, $y = -1$

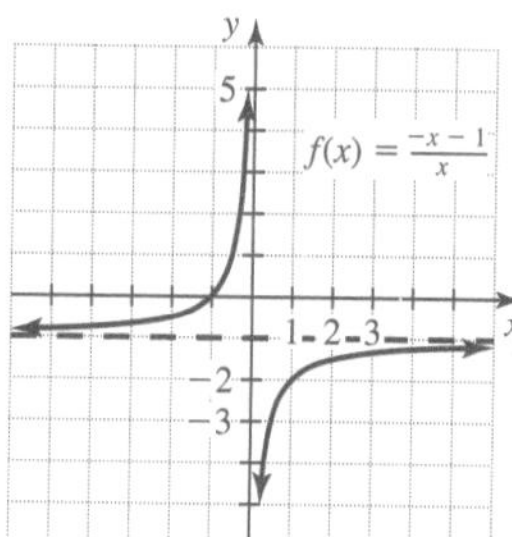

67. $f(x) = \frac{x^2 - 2x + 1}{x - 2}$
$x = 2, y = x$

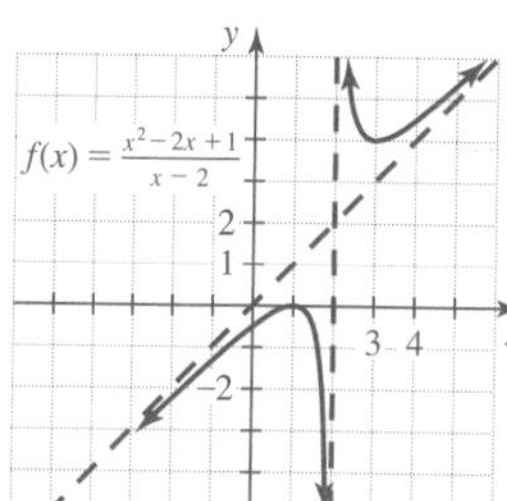

68. $f(x) = \frac{-x^2 + x + 2}{x - 1}$
$x = 1, y = -x$

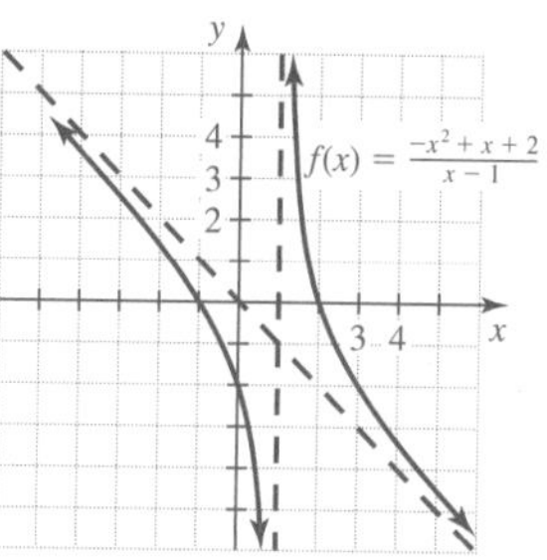

11.6 *Let* $f(x) = 3x + 5$, $g(x) = x^2 - 2x$, *and* $h(x) = \frac{x - 5}{3}$. *Find the following.*

69. $f(-3)$ -4

70. $h(-4)$ -3

71. $(h \circ f)(\sqrt{2})$ $\sqrt{2}$

72. $(f \circ h)(\pi)$ π

73. $(g \circ f)(2)$ 99

74. $(g \circ f)(x)$ $9x^2 + 24x + 15$

75. $(f + g)(3)$ 17

76. $(f - g)(x)$ $-x^2 + 5x + 5$

77. $(f \cdot g)(x)$ $3x^3 - x^2 - 10x$

78. $\left(\frac{f}{g}\right)(1)$ -8

79. $(f \circ f)(0)$ 20

80. $(f \circ f)(x)$ $9x + 20$

Let $f(x) = |x|$, $g(x) = x + 2$, *and* $h(x) = x^2$. *Write each of the following functions as a composition of functions, using f, g, or h.*

81. $F(x) = |x + 2|$
$F = f \circ g$

82. $G(x) = |x| + 2$
$G = g \circ f$

83. $H(x) = x^2 + 2$
$H = g \circ h$

84. $K(x) = x^2 + 4x + 4$
$K = h \circ g$

85. $I(x) = x + 4$
$I = g \circ g$

86. $J(x) = x^4 + 2$
$J = g \circ h \circ h$

11.7 *Determine whether each function is invertible. If it is invertible, find the inverse.*

87. $\{(-2, 4), (2, 4)\}$
No

88. $\{(1, 1), (3, 3)\}$
Yes, $\{(1, 1), (3, 3)\}$

89. $f(x) = 8x$
Yes, $f^{-1}(x) = x/8$

90. $i(x) = -\frac{x}{3}$
Yes, $i^{-1}(x) = -3x$

91. $g(x) = 13x - 6$
Yes, $g^{-1}(x) = \frac{x + 6}{13}$

92. $h(x) = \sqrt[3]{x - 6}$
Yes, $h^{-1}(x) = x^3 + 6$

93. $j(x) = \frac{x + 1}{x - 1}$
Yes, $j^{-1}(x) = \frac{x + 1}{x - 1}$

94. $k(x) = |x| + 7$
No

95. $m(x) = (x - 1)^2$
No

96. $n(x) = \frac{3}{x}$
Yes, $n^{-1}(x) = \frac{3}{x}$

Find the inverse of each function, and graph f and f^{-1} *on the same pair of axes.*

97. $f(x) = 3x - 1$
$f^{-1}(x) = \frac{1}{3}x + \frac{1}{3}$

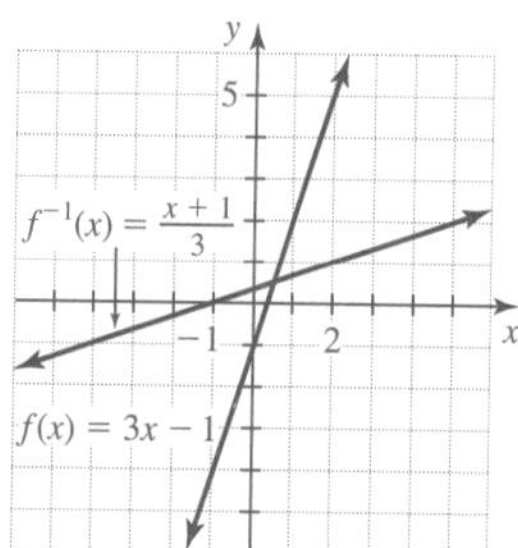

98. $f(x) = 2 - x^2$ for $x \geq 0$
$f^{-1}(x) = \sqrt{2 - x}$

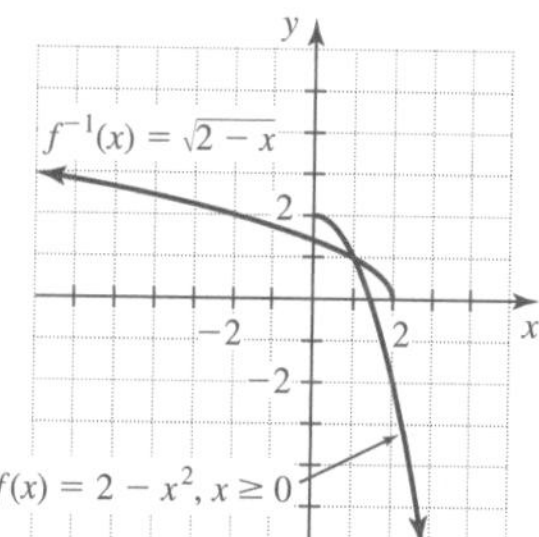

99. $f(x) = \frac{x^3}{2}$
$f^{-1}(x) = \sqrt[3]{2x}$

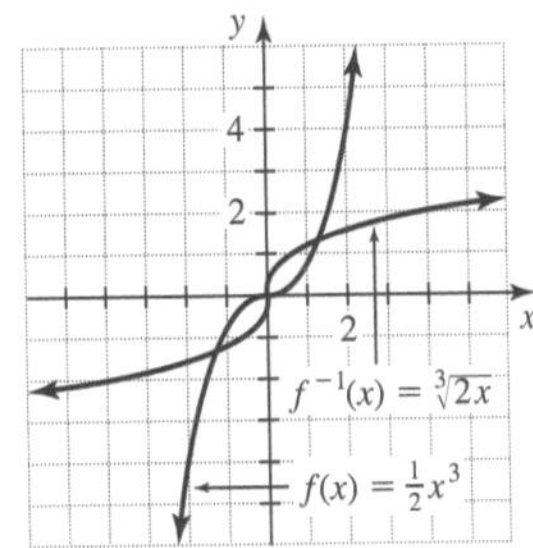

100. $f(x) = -\frac{1}{4}x$
$f^{-1}(x) = -4x$

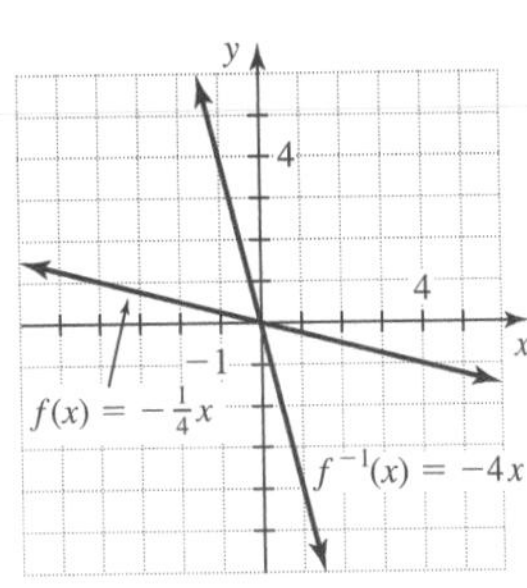

Miscellaneous

Sketch the graph of each function.

101. $f(x) = 3$

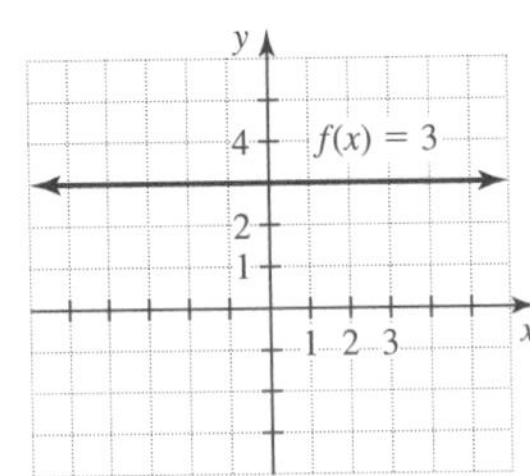

102. $f(x) = 2x - 3$

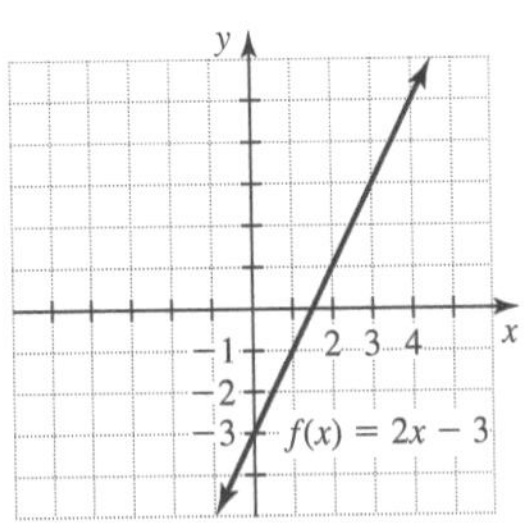

103. $f(x) = x^2 - 3$

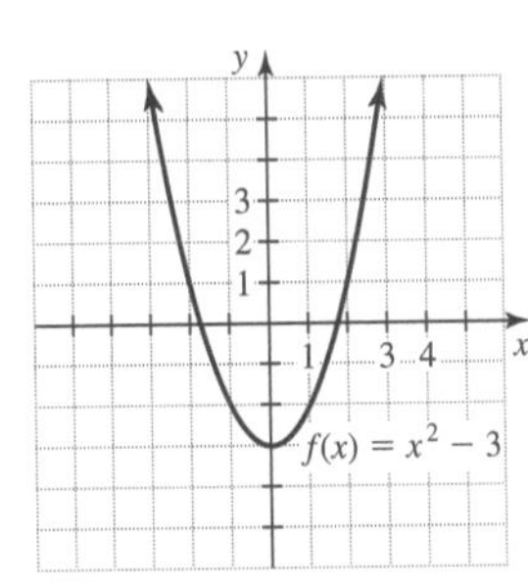

104. $f(x) = 3 - x^2$

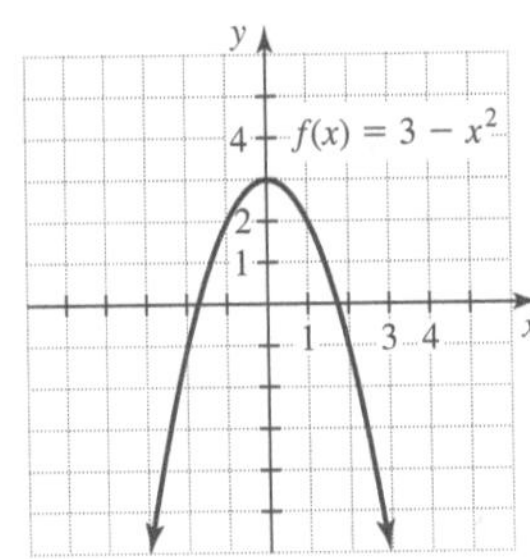

105. $f(x) = \frac{1}{x^2 - 3}$

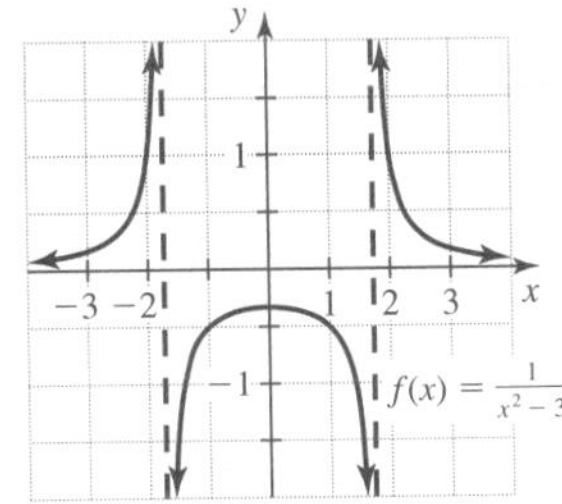

106. $f(x) = \frac{x}{(x - 1)(x + 2)}$

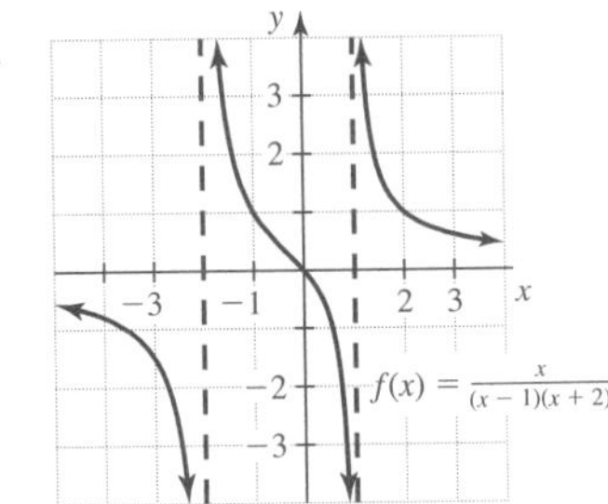

107. $f(x) = x(x - 1)(x + 2)$

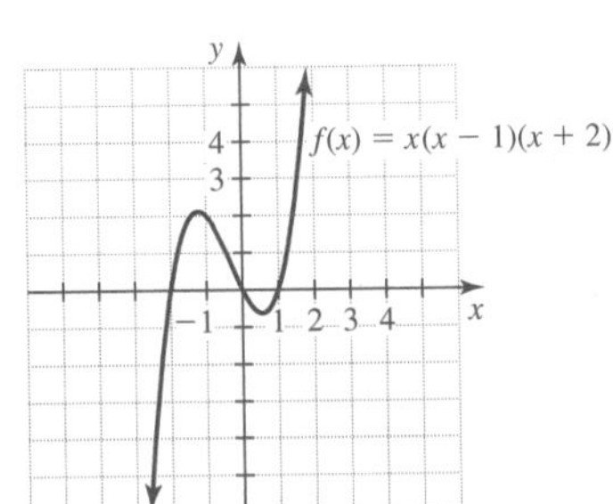

108. $f(x) = x^3 - 4x^2 + 4x$

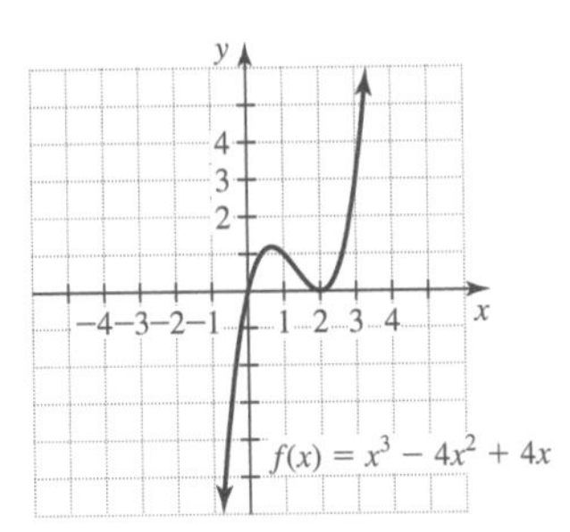

Solve each problem.

109. ***Inscribed square.*** Given that B is the area of a square inscribed in a circle of radius r and area A, write B as a function of A.
$B = \frac{2A}{\pi}$

110. ***Area of a window.*** A window is in the shape of a square of side s, with a semicircle of diameter s above it. Write a function that expresses the total area of the window as a function of s.
$A = \frac{(8 + \pi)s^2}{8}$

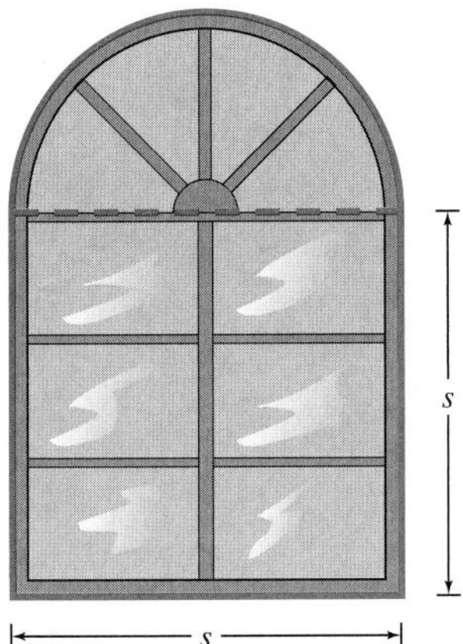

Figure for Exercise 110

111. ***Composition of functions.*** Given that $a = 3k + 2$ and $k = 5w - 6$, write a as a function of w.
$a = 15w - 16$

112. ***Volume of a cylinder.*** The volume of a cylinder with a fixed height of 10 centimeters (cm) is given by $V = 10\pi r^2$, where r is the radius of the circular base. Write the volume as a function of the area of the base, A.
$V = 10A$

113. ***Square formulas.*** Write the area of a square A as a function of the length of a side of the square s. Write the length of a side of a square as a function of the area.
$A = s^2$, $s = \sqrt{A}$

114. ***Circle formulas.*** Write the area of a circle A as a function of the radius of the circle r. Write the radius of a circle as a function of the area of the circle. Write the area as a function of the diameter d.
$A = \pi r^2$, $r = \sqrt{\frac{A}{\pi}}$, $A = \frac{\pi d^2}{4}$

Chapter 11 Test

Solve each problem.

1. Determine whether $\{(0, 5), (9, 5), (4, 5)\}$ is a function.
Yes

2. Let $f(x) = -2x + 5$. Find $f(-3)$. 11

3. Find the domain and range of the function $y = \sqrt{x - 7}$.
$[7, \infty)$, $[0, \infty)$

4. A mail-order firm charges its customers a shipping and handling fee of \$3.00 plus \$0.50 per pound for each order shipped. Express the shipping and handling fee S as a function of the weight of the order n.
$S = 0.50n + 3$

5. If a ball is tossed into the air from a height of 6 feet with a velocity of 32 feet per second, then its altitude at time t (in seconds) can be described by the function

$$A(t) = -16t^2 + 32t + 6.$$

Find the altitude of the ball at 2 seconds. 6 ft

Sketch the graph of each function or relation and state the domain and range.

6. $f(x) = -\frac{2}{3}x + 1$ $(-\infty, \infty)$, $(-\infty, \infty)$

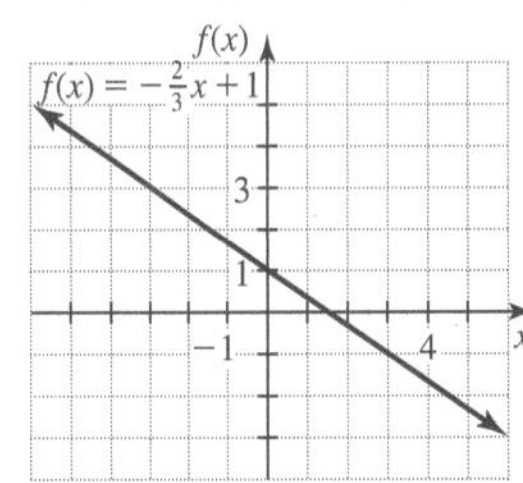

7. $y = |x| - 4$ $(-\infty, \infty)$, $[-4, \infty)$

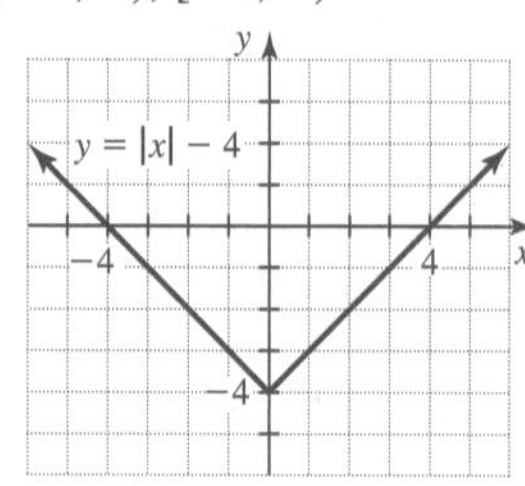

8. $g(x) = x^2 + 2x - 8$ $(-\infty, \infty)$, $[-9, \infty)$

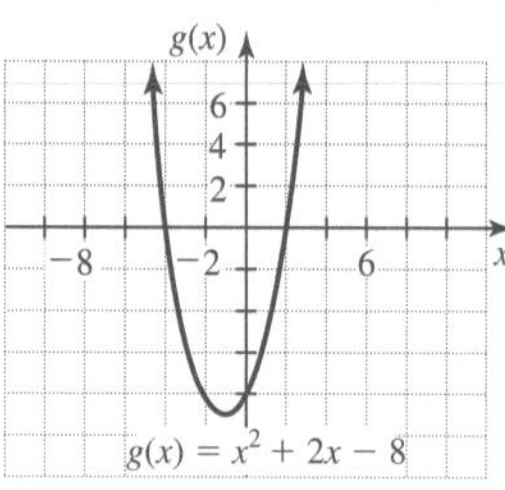

9. $x = y^2$ $[0, \infty)$, $(-\infty, \infty)$

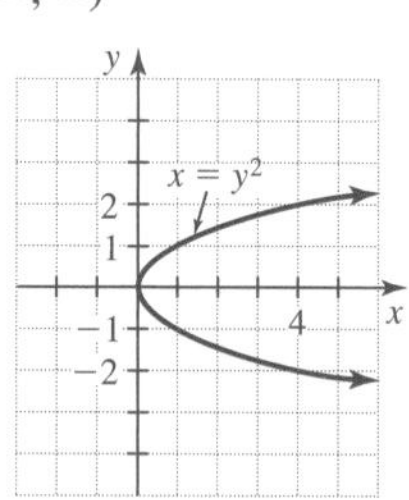

10. $y = -|x - 2|$ $(-\infty, \infty)$, $(-\infty, 0]$

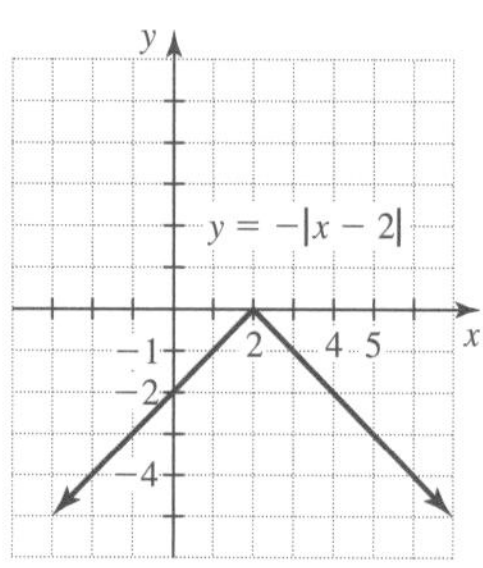

11. $y = \sqrt{x + 5} - 2$ $[-5, \infty)$, $[-2, \infty)$

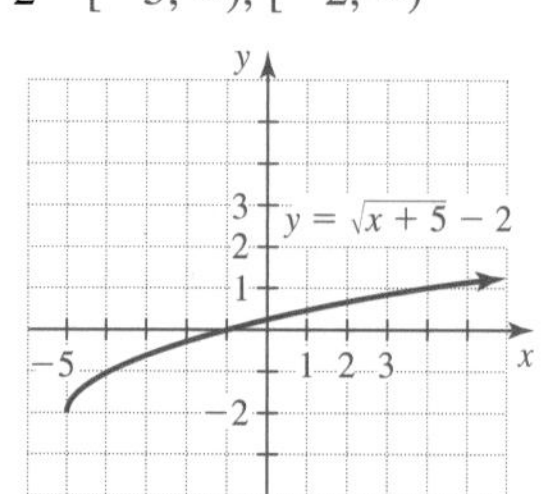

Graph each function. Identify all intercepts.

12. $f(x) = (x + 2)(x - 2)^2$
$(-2, 0)$, $(2, 0)$, $(0, 8)$

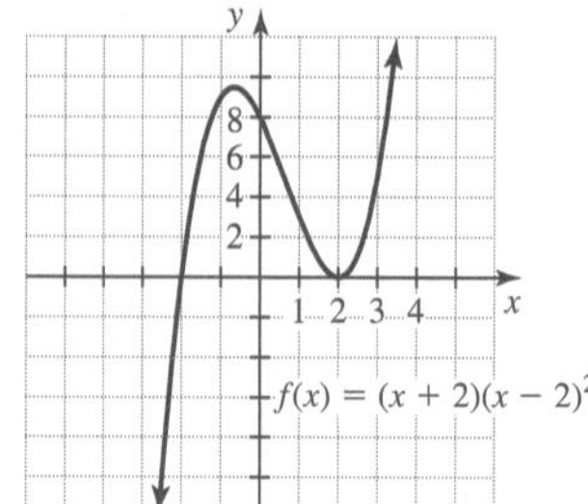

13. $f(x) = \dfrac{1}{x^2 - 4x + 4}$
$\left(0, \dfrac{1}{4}\right)$

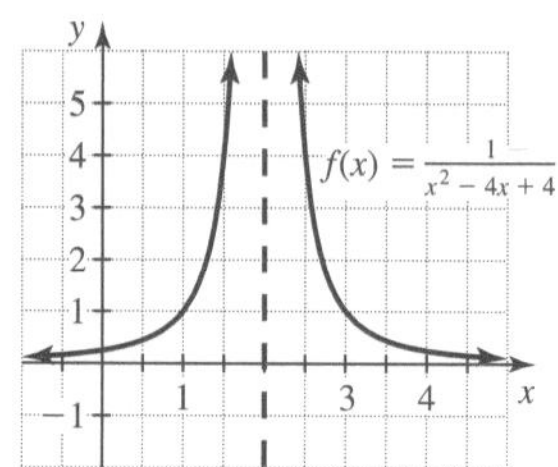

14. $f(x) = \dfrac{2x - 3}{x - 2}$
$\left(\dfrac{3}{2}, 0\right)$, $\left(0, \dfrac{3}{2}\right)$

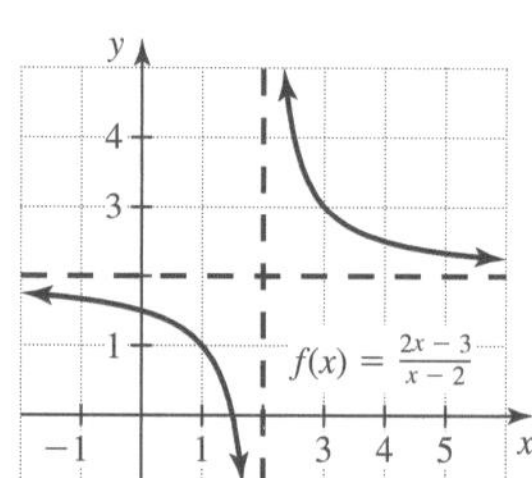

15. $f(x) = x^3 - x^2 - 4x + 4$
$(-2, 0)$, $(1, 0)$,
$(2, 0)$, $(0, 4)$

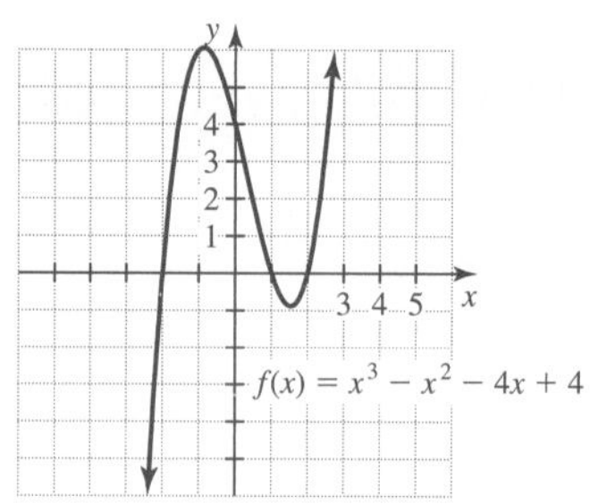

Let $f(x) = -2x + 5$ and $g(x) = x^2 + 4$. Find the following.

16. $f(-3)$
11

17. $(g \circ f)(-3)$
125

18. $f^{-1}(11)$
-3

19. $f^{-1}(x)$
$\frac{x-5}{-2}$

20. $(g + f)(x)$
$x^2 - 2x + 9$

21. $(f \cdot g)(1)$
15

22. $(f^{-1} \circ f)(1776)$
1776

23. $(f/g)(2)$
$\frac{1}{8}$

24. $(f \circ g)(x)$
$-2x^2 - 3$

25. $(g \circ f)(x)$
$4x^2 - 20x + 29$

Let $f(x) = x - 7$ and $g(x) = x^2$. Write each of the following functions as a composition of functions using f and g.

26. $H(x) = x^2 - 7$ $H = f \circ g$

27. $W(x) = x^2 - 14x + 49$ $W = g \circ f$

Determine whether each function is invertible. If it is invertible, find the inverse.

28. $\{(2, 3), (4, 3), (1, 5)\}$ Not invertible

29. $\{(2, 3), (3, 4), (4, 5)\}$ $\{(3, 2), (4, 3), (5, 4)\}$

Find the inverse of each function.

30. $f(x) = x - 5$ $f^{-1}(x) = x + 5$

31. $f(x) = 3x - 5$ $f^{-1}(x) = \frac{x+5}{3}$

32. $f(x) = \sqrt[3]{x} + 9$ $f^{-1}(x) = (x - 9)^3$

33. $f(x) = \frac{2x+1}{x-1}$ $f^{-1}(x) = \frac{x+1}{x-2}$

*Making*Connections | A Review of Chapters 1–11

Simplify each expression.

1. $125^{-2/3}$ $\frac{1}{25}$

2. $\left(\frac{8}{27}\right)^{-1/3}$ $\frac{3}{2}$

3. $\sqrt{18} - \sqrt{8}$ $\sqrt{2}$

4. $x^5 \cdot x^3$ x^8

5. $16^{1/4}$ 2

6. $\frac{x^{12}}{x^3}$ x^9

Find the real solution set to each equation.

7. $x^2 = 9$ $\{\pm 3\}$

8. $x^2 = 8$ $\{\pm 2\sqrt{2}\}$

9. $x^2 = x$ $\{0, 1\}$

10. $x^2 - 4x - 6 = 0$ $\{2 \pm \sqrt{10}\}$

11. $x^{1/4} = 3$ $\{81\}$

12. $x^{1/6} = -2$ $\varnothing$

13. $|x| = 8$ $\{\pm 8\}$

14. $|5x - 4| = 21$ $\left\{-\frac{17}{5}, 5\right\}$

15. $x^3 = 8$ $\{2\}$

16. $(3x - 2)^3 = 27$ $\left\{\frac{5}{3}\right\}$

17. $\sqrt{2x - 3} = 9$ $\{42\}$

18. $\sqrt{x - 2} = x - 8$ $\{11\}$

Sketch the graph of each set.

19. $\{(x, y) \mid y = 5\}$

20. $\{(x, y) \mid y = 2x - 5\}$

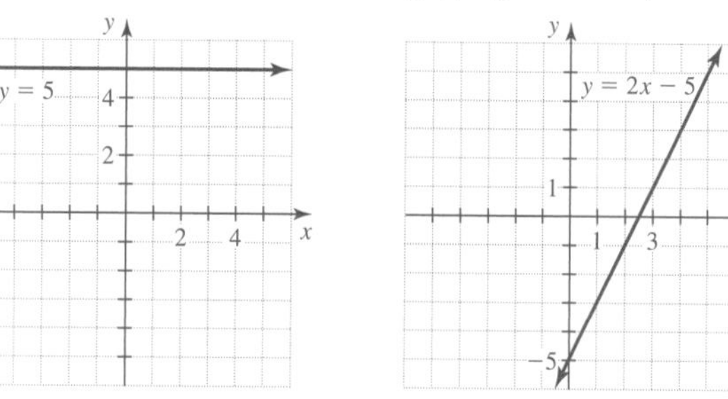

21. $\{(x, y) \mid x = 5\}$

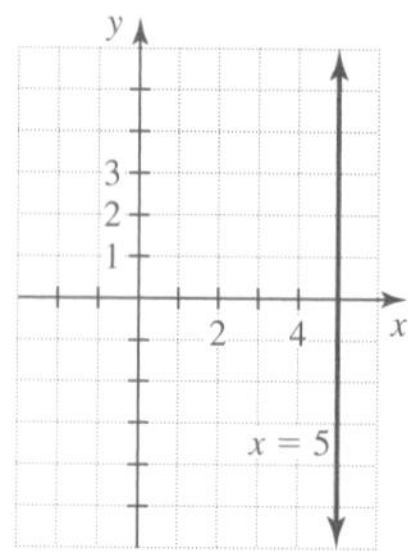

22. $\{(x, y) \mid 3y = x\}$

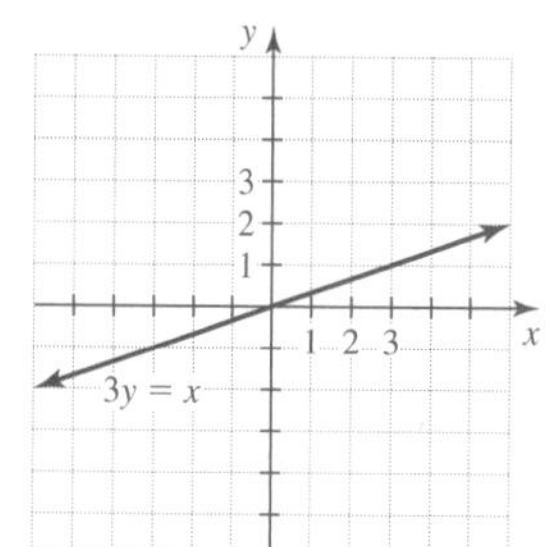

23. $\{(x, y) \mid y = 5x^2\}$

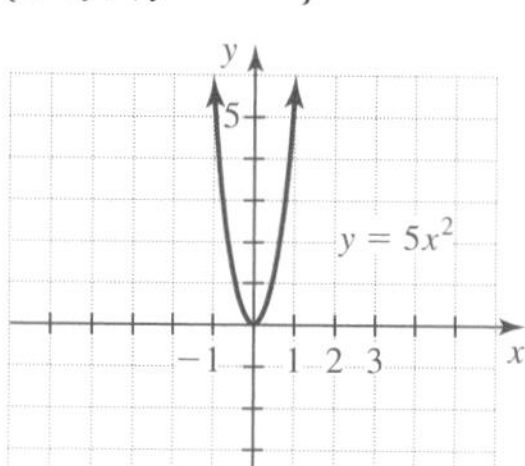

24. $\{(x, y) \mid y = -2x^2\}$

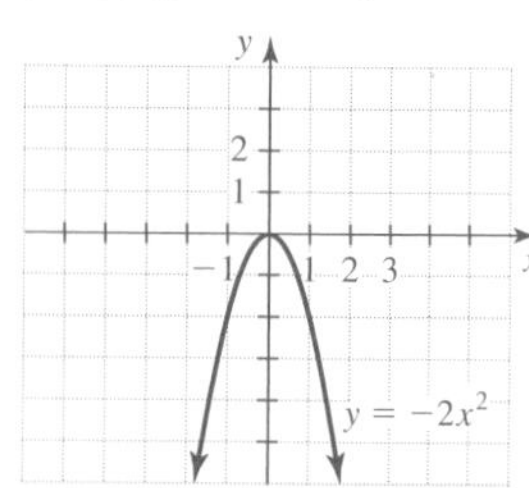

Find the missing coordinates in each ordered pair so that the ordered pair satisfies the given equation.

25. (2,), (3,), (, 2), (, 16), $2^x = y$
(2, 4), (3, 8), (1, 2), (4, 16)

26. $\left(\frac{1}{2}, \right)$, (−1,), (, 16), (, 1), $4^x = y$
$\left(\frac{1}{2}, 2\right)$, $\left(-1, \frac{1}{4}\right)$, (2, 16), (0, 1)

Find the domain of each expression.

27. $\sqrt{x}$ $[0, \infty)$

28. $\sqrt{6 - 2x}$ $(-\infty, 3]$

29. $\frac{5x - 3}{x^2 + 1}$ $(-\infty, \infty)$

30. $\frac{x - 3}{x^2 - 10x + 9}$ $(-\infty, 1) \cup (1, 9) \cup (9, \infty)$

Solve each problem.

31. ***Capital cost and operating cost.*** To decide when to replace company cars, an accountant looks at two cost components: capital cost and operating cost. The capital cost C (the difference between the original cost and the salvage value) for a certain car is \$3000 plus \$0.12 for each mile that the car is driven.

a) Write the capital cost C as a linear function of x, the number of miles that the car is driven. $C = 0.12x + 3000$

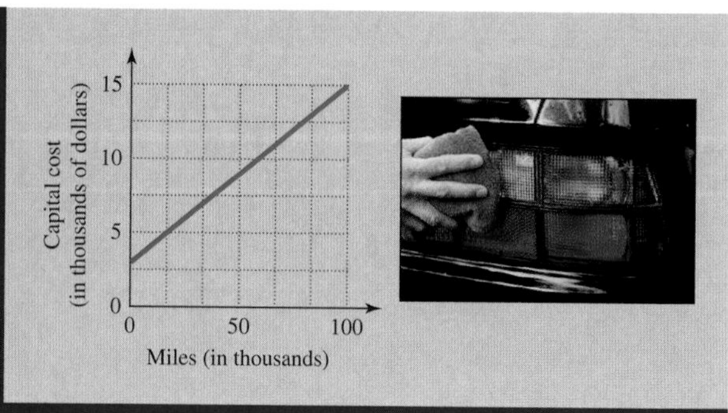

Figure for Exercise 31(a)

b) The operating cost P is \$0.15 per mile initially and increases linearly to \$0.25 per mile when the car reaches 100,000 miles. Write P as a function of x, the number of miles that the car is driven. $P = 1 \times 10^{-6}x + 0.15$

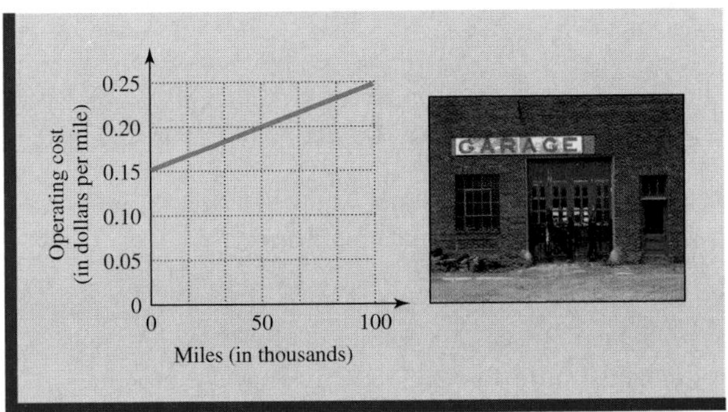

Figure for Exercise 31(b)

32. ***Total cost.*** The accountant in the previous exercise uses the function $T = \frac{C}{x} + P$ to find the total cost per mile.

a) Find T for $x = 20{,}000$, 30,000, and 90,000.
\$0.44, \$0.40, \$0.39

b) Sketch a graph of the total cost function.

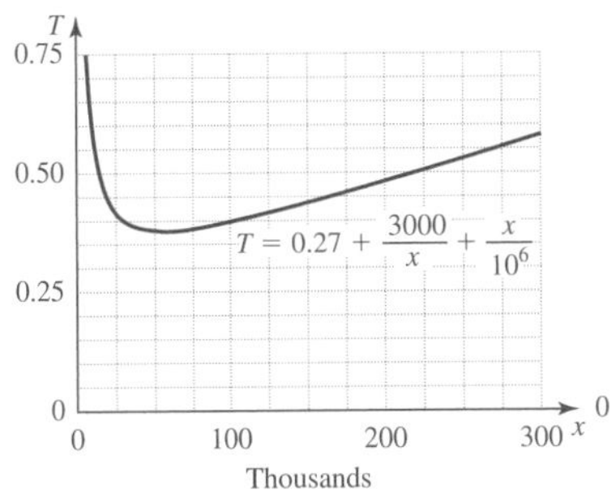

c) The accountant has decided to replace the car when T reaches \$0.38 for the second time. At what mileage will the car be replaced?
60,000 miles

d) For what values of x is T less than or equal to \$0.38?
[50,000, 60,000]

Critical **Thinking** | For Individual or Group Work | Chapter 11

These exercises can be solved by a variety of techniques, which may or may not require algebra. So be creative and think critically. Explain all answers. Answers are in the Instructor's Edition of this text.

1. ***Knight moves.*** Draw a 3 by 3 chess board on paper and place two pennies (P) and two nickels (N) in the corners as shown in (a) of the figure. Move the Ns to the positions of the Ps and the Ps to the position of the Ns using the moves that a knight can make in chess (one space vertically followed by two spaces horizontally or one space horizontally followed by two spaces vertically). If you allow a P or an N to make more than one move on a given turn, then it takes six turns. Try it. Find the minimum number of turns required to interchange the coins starting with the arrangement in (b).

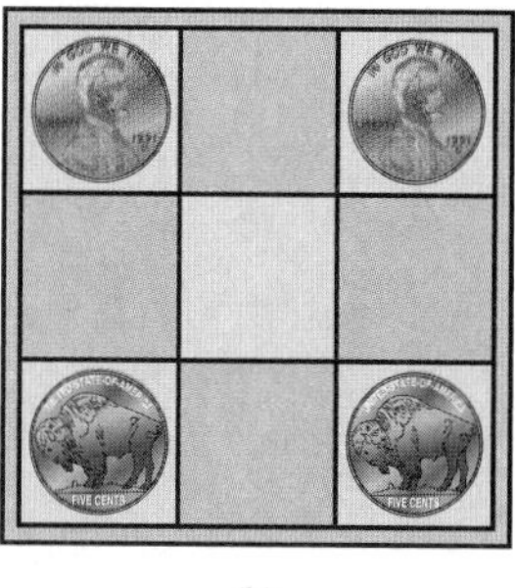

(a) (b)

Figure for Exercise 1

2. ***Friedman numbers.*** A Friedman number is a positive integer that can be written in some nontrivial way using its own digits together with the elementary operations ($+, -, \cdot, \div$, exponents, and grouping symbols). For example, $25 = 5^2$, and $126 = 21 \cdot 6$. The only two-digit Friedman number is 25. Show that 121 and 125 are Friedman numbers. There are 13 three-digit Friedman numbers. Find the other 10 three-digit Friedman numbers.

3. ***Large Friedman numbers.*** Show that 123,456,789 and 987,654,321 are Friedman numbers.

4. ***Year numbers.*** Using all four of the digits in the current year and only those digits, write expressions for the integers from 1 through 100. You may use grouping symbols, and the operations of addition, subtraction, multiplication, division, powers, roots, and factorial, but no two-digit numbers or decimal points. For example if the year is 2005, then $5^0 + 0 \cdot 2 = 1$, $5^0 + 2^0 = 2$, and so on. See how far you can go. Vary the problem by trying another year (say 1776), or allowing decimal points, or two-digit numbers.

5. ***Real numbers.*** Two real numbers have a sum of 200 and a product of 50. What is the sum of their reciprocals?

6. ***Telling time.*** Find the first time after 11 A.M. for which the minute hand and hour hand of a clock form a perfect right angle. Find the time to the nearest tenth of a second. The answer is not 11:10.

7. ***Identity crisis.*** Determine the value of a that will make this equation an identity.

$$\frac{1}{x-1} + \frac{2}{1-x} + \frac{3}{x-1} + \frac{4}{1-x} + \frac{5}{x-1} + \frac{6}{1-x} + \frac{7}{x-1} + \frac{8}{1-x} + \frac{9}{x-1} + \frac{10}{1-x} = \frac{a}{x-1}$$

8. ***Difference of two squares.*** Let $a = 7^{6006} + 7^{-6006}$ and $b = 7^{6006} - 7^{-6006}$. Find $a^2 - b^2$.

1. a)

P		N		P						P				P				P		N		P		N		P
				N				N				N		N		N		N		N						
N		P		N		P		N		P				P		P				P				P		N

b)

P	P					P		P				P				P		N		P		N				N		N		N
						P				P				P				P												
N	N			N		N		N		N		N	N				N				N	P		P	N	P		P		P

2. $121 = 11^2$, $125 = 5^{1+2}$, $126 = 6 \cdot 21$, $127 = 2^7 - 1$, $128 = 2^{8-1}$, $153 = 3 \cdot 51$, $216 = 6^{2+1}$, $289 = (8 + 9)^2$, $343 = (3 + 4)^3$, $347 = 7^3 + 4$, $625 = 5^{6-2}$, $688 = 8 \cdot 86$, $736 = 7 + 3^6$ **3.** $123{,}456{,}789 = [(86 + 2 \cdot 7)^5 - 91]/3^4$, $987{,}654{,}321 = [8 \cdot (97 + 6/2)^5 + 1]/3^4$ **4.** Answers will vary. **5.** 4 **6.** 11:10:54.5 or 10 minutes and 54.5 seconds past 11 A.M. **7.** -5 **8.** 4

12

Exponential and Logarithmic Functions

Water is one of the essentials of life, yet it is something that most of us take for granted. Among other things, the U.S. Geological Survey (U.S.G.S.) studies freshwater. For over 50 years the Water Resources Division of the U.S.G.S. has been gathering basic data about the flow of both freshwater and saltwater from streams and groundwater surfaces. This division collects, compiles, analyzes, verifies, organizes, and publishes data gathered from groundwater data collection networks in each of the 50 states, Puerto Rico, and the Trust Territories. Records of stream flow, groundwater levels, and water quality provide hydrological information needed by local, state, and federal agencies as well as the private sector.

There are many instances of the importance of the data collected by the U.S.G.S. For example, before 1987 the Tangipahoa River in Louisiana was used extensively for swimming and boating. In 1987 data gathered by the U.S.G.S. showed that fecal coliform levels in the river exceeded safe levels. Consequently, Louisiana banned recreational use of the river. Other studies by the Water Resources Division include the results of pollutants on salt marsh environments and the effect that salting highways in winter has on our drinking water supply.

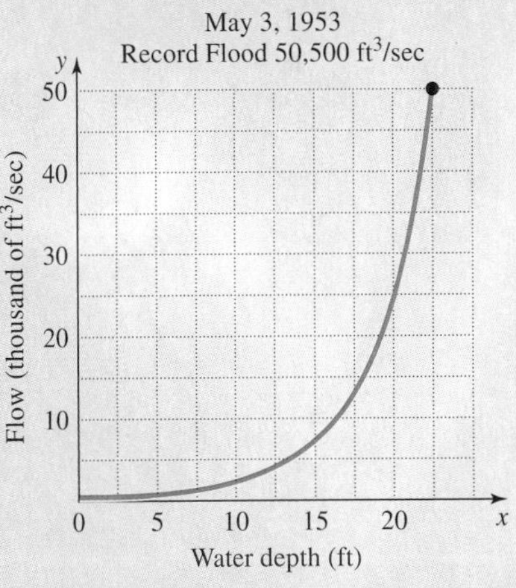

In Exercises 93 and 94 of Section 12.2 you will see how data from the U.S.G.S. is used in a logarithmic function to measure water quality.

12.1 Exponential Functions and Their Applications

In this Section

- Definition
- Domain
- Graphing Exponential Functions
- Exponential Equations
- Applications

We have studied functions such as

$$f(x) = x^2, \quad g(x) = x^3, \quad \text{and} \quad h(x) = x^{1/2}.$$

For these functions the variable is the base. In this section we discuss functions that have a variable as an exponent. These functions are called *exponential functions.*

Definition

Some examples of exponential functions are

$$f(x) = 2^x, \quad f(x) = \left(\frac{1}{2}\right)^x, \quad \text{and} \quad f(x) = 3^x.$$

Teaching Tip Have students make some tables containing positive and negative powers of 2, 3, 4, and so on.

Exponential Function

An **exponential function** is a function of the form

$$f(x) = a^x,$$

where $a > 0$ and $a \neq 1$.

We rule out the base 1 in the definition because $f(x) = 1^x$ is the same as the constant function $f(x) = 1$. Zero is not used as a base because $0^x = 0$ for any positive x and nonpositive powers of 0 are undefined. Negative numbers are not used as bases because an expression such as $(-4)^x$ is not a real number if $x = \frac{1}{2}$.

EXAMPLE 1

Evaluating exponential functions

Let $f(x) = 2^x$, $g(x) = \left(\frac{1}{4}\right)^{1-x}$, and $h(x) = -3^x$. Find the following:

a) $f\left(\frac{3}{2}\right)$ **b)** $f(-3)$ **c)** $g(3)$ **d)** $h(2)$

Solution

a) $f\left(\frac{3}{2}\right) = 2^{3/2} = \sqrt{2^3} = \sqrt{8} = 2\sqrt{2}$

b) $f(-3) = 2^{-3} = \frac{1}{2^3} = \frac{1}{8}$

c) $g(3) = \left(\frac{1}{4}\right)^{1-3} = \left(\frac{1}{4}\right)^{-2} = 4^2 = 16$

d) $h(2) = -3^2 = -9$ Note that $-3^2 \neq (-3)^2$.

Now do Exercises 7–18

For many applications of exponential functions we use base 10 or another base called e. The number e is an irrational number that is approximately 2.718. We will see how e is used in compound interest in Example 10 of this section. Base 10 will be used in the next section. Base 10 is called the **common base,** and base e is called the **natural base.**

EXAMPLE 2

Base 10 and base e

Let $f(x) = 10^x$ and $g(x) = e^x$. Find the following and round approximate answers to four decimal places:

a) $f(3)$ **b)** $f(1.51)$ **c)** $g(0)$ **d)** $g(2)$

Calculator Close-Up

Most graphing calculators have keys for the functions 10^x and e^x.

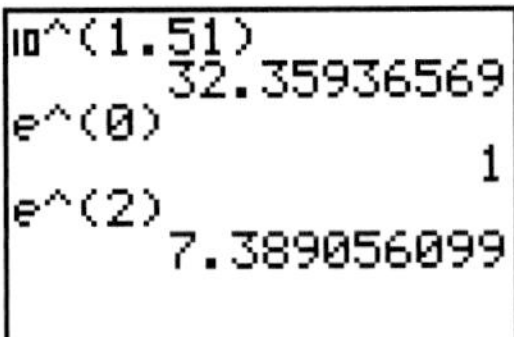

Solution

a) $f(3) = 10^3 = 1000$

b) $f(1.51) = 10^{1.51} \approx 32.3594$ Use the 10^x key on a calculator.

c) $g(0) = e^0 = 1$

d) $g(2) = e^2 \approx 7.3891$ Use the e^x key on a calculator.

Now do Exercises 19–26

Domain

In the definition of an exponential function no restrictions were placed on the exponent x because the domain of an exponential function is the set of all real numbers. So both rational and irrational numbers can be used as the exponent. We have been using rational numbers for exponents since Chapter 8, but we have not yet seen an irrational number as an exponent. Even though we do not formally define irrational exponents in this text, an irrational number such as π can be used as an exponent, and you can evaluate an expression such as 2^π by using a calculator. Try it:

$$2^\pi \approx 8.824977827$$

Graphing Exponential Functions

Even though the domain of an exponential function is the set of all real numbers, we can graph an exponential function by evaluating it for just a few integers.

EXAMPLE 3

Exponential functions with base greater than 1

Sketch the graph of each function.

a) $f(x) = 2^x$ **b)** $g(x) = 3^x$

Solution

a) We first make a table of ordered pairs that satisfy $f(x) = 2^x$:

x	-2	-1	0	1	2	3
$f(x) = 2^x$	$\frac{1}{4}$	$\frac{1}{2}$	1	2	4	8

As x increases, 2^x increases and 2^x is always positive. Because the domain of the function is $(-\infty, \infty)$, we draw the graph in Fig. 12.1 on the next page as a smooth curve through these points. From the graph we can see that the range is $(0, \infty)$.

Calculator Close-Up

The graph of $f(x) = 2^x$ on a calculator appears to touch the x-axis. When drawing this graph by hand, make sure that it does not touch the x-axis. Use zoom to see that the curve is always above the x-axis.

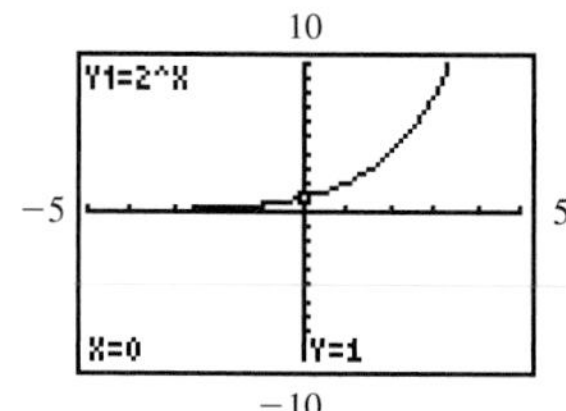

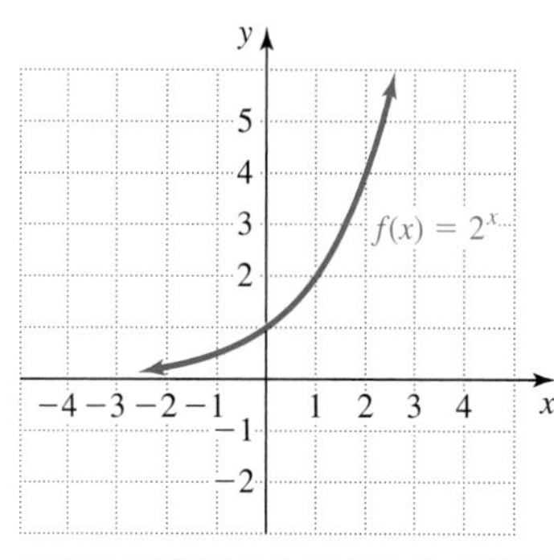

Figure 12.1

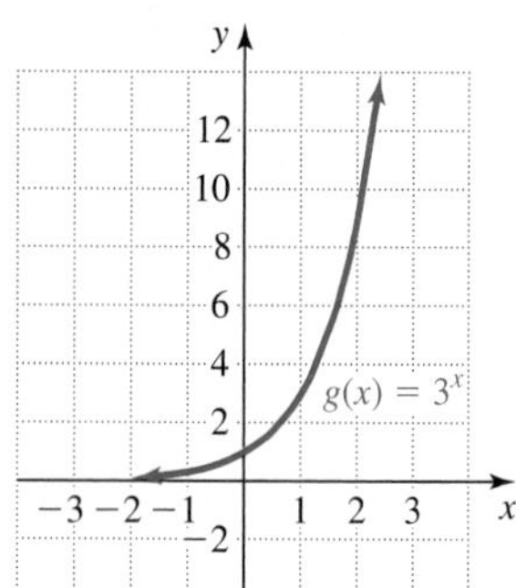

Figure 12.2

b) Make a table of ordered pairs that satisfy $g(x) = 3^x$:

x	-2	-1	0	1	2	3
$g(x) = 3^x$	$\frac{1}{9}$	$\frac{1}{3}$	1	3	9	27

As x increases, 3^x increases and 3^x is always positive. The graph is shown in Fig. 12.2. From the graph we see that the range is $(0, \infty)$.

Now do Exercises 31–32

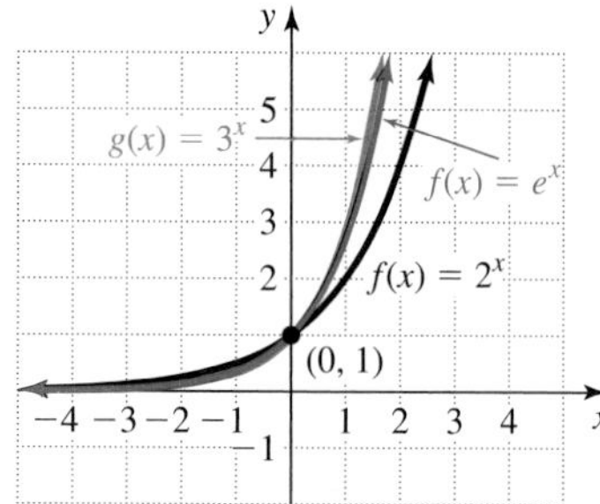

Figure 12.3

Because $e \approx 2.718$, the graph of $f(x) = e^x$ lies between the graphs of $f(x) = 2^x$ and $g(x) = 3^x$, as shown in Fig. 12.3. Note that all three functions have the same domain and range and the same y-intercept. In general, the function $f(x) = a^x$ for $a > 1$ has the following characteristics:

1. The y-intercept of the curve is $(0, 1)$.
2. The domain is $(-\infty, \infty)$, and the range is $(0, \infty)$.
3. The curve approaches the negative x-axis but does not touch it.
4. The y-values are increasing as we go from left to right along the curve.

EXAMPLE 4

Exponential functions with base between 0 and 1

Graph each function.

a) $f(x) = \left(\frac{1}{2}\right)^x$

b) $f(x) = 4^{-x}$

Solution

a) First make a table of ordered pairs that satisfy $f(x) = \left(\frac{1}{2}\right)^x$:

x	-2	-1	0	1	2	3
$f(x) = \left(\frac{1}{2}\right)^x$	4	2	1	$\frac{1}{2}$	$\frac{1}{4}$	$\frac{1}{8}$

Calculator Close-Up

The graph of $y = (1/2)^x$ is a reflection of the graph of $y = 2^x$.

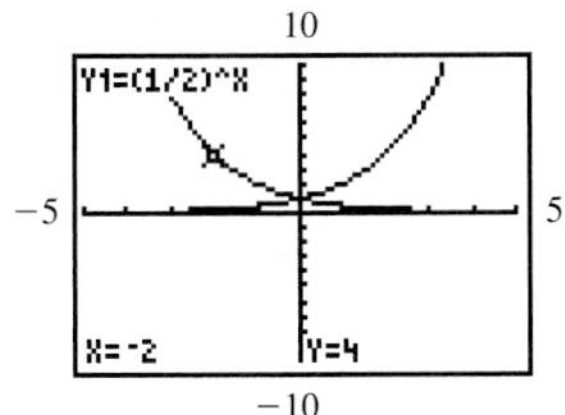

As x increases, $\left(\frac{1}{2}\right)^x$ decreases, getting closer and closer to 0. Draw a smooth curve through these points as shown in Fig. 12.4.

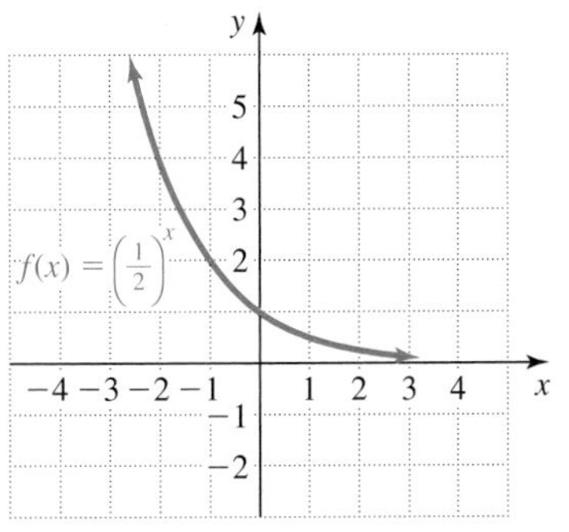

Figure 12.4

y
4
3
$f(x) = 4^{-x}$
1
−4 −3 −2 −1
1 2 3 4
x
−1

Figure 12.5

b) Because $4^{-x} = \left(\frac{1}{4}\right)^x$, we make a table for $f(x) = \left(\frac{1}{4}\right)^x$:

x	-2	-1	0	1	2	3
$f(x) = \left(\frac{1}{4}\right)^x$	16	4	1	$\frac{1}{4}$	$\frac{1}{16}$	$\frac{1}{64}$

As x increases, $\left(\frac{1}{4}\right)^x$, or 4^{-x}, decreases, getting closer and closer to 0. Draw a smooth curve through these points as shown in Fig. 12.5.

Now do Exercises 33–36

Notice the similarities and differences between the exponential function with $a > 1$ and with $0 < a < 1$. The function $f(x) = a^x$ for $0 < a < 1$ has the following characteristics:

1. The y-intercept of the curve is $(0, 1)$.
2. The domain is $(-\infty, \infty)$, and the range is $(0, \infty)$.
3. The curve approaches the positive x-axis but does not touch it.
4. The y-values are decreasing as we go from left to right along the curve.

CAUTION An exponential function can be written in more than one form. For example, $f(x) = \left(\frac{1}{2}\right)^x$ is the same as $f(x) = \frac{1}{2^x}$, or $f(x) = 2^{-x}$.

Although exponential functions have the form $f(x) = a^x$, other functions that have similar forms are also called exponential functions. Notice how changing the form of $f(x) = a^x$ in Examples 5 and 6 changes the shape and location of the graph.

EXAMPLE 5

Changing the shape and location

Sketch the graph of $f(x) = 3^{2x-1}$.

Solution

Make a table of ordered pairs:

x	-1	0	$\frac{1}{2}$	1	2
$f(x) = 3^{2x-1}$	$\frac{1}{27}$	$\frac{1}{3}$	1	3	27

The graph through these points is shown in Fig. 12.6.

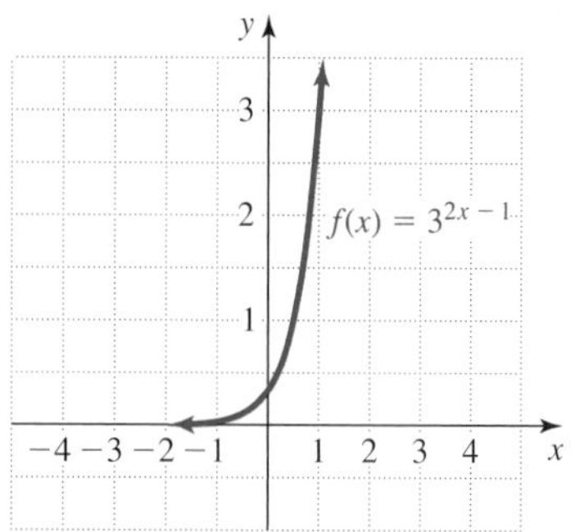

Figure 12.6

Now do Exercises 41–42

EXAMPLE 6

Changing the shape and location

Sketch the graph of $y = -2^{-x}$.

Solution

Because $-2^{-x} = -(2^{-x})$, all y-coordinates are negative. Make a table of ordered pairs:

x	-2	-1	0	1	2
$f(x) = -2^{-x}$	-4	-2	-1	$-\frac{1}{2}$	$-\frac{1}{4}$

The graph through these points is shown in Fig. 12.7.

Now do Exercises 43–52

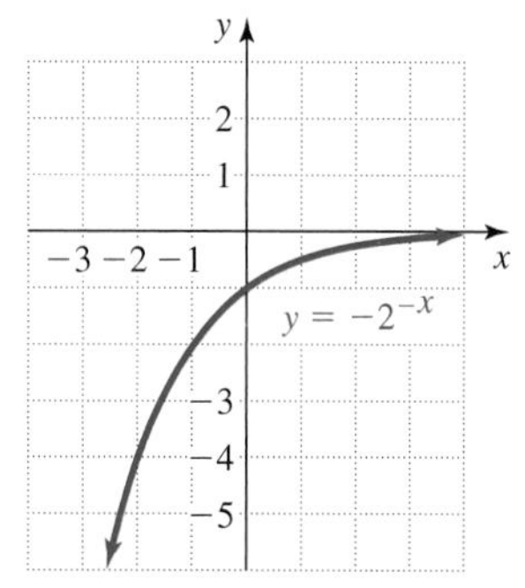

Figure 12.7

Exponential Equations

In Chapter 11 we used the horizontal-line test to determine whether a function is one-to-one. Because no horizontal line can cross the graph of an exponential function more than once, exponential functions are one-to-one functions. For an exponential function one-to-one means that *if two exponential expressions with the same base are equal, then the exponents are equal.* If $2^x = 2^y$, then $x = y$.

One-to-One Property of Exponential Functions

For $a > 0$ and $a \neq 1$,

$$\text{if} \quad a^m = a^n, \quad \text{then} \quad m = n.$$

In Example 7 we use the one-to-one property to solve equations involving exponential functions.

EXAMPLE 7

Using the one-to-one property

Solve each equation.

a) $2^{2x-1} = 8$ **b)** $9^{|x|} = 3$

c) $\frac{1}{8} = 4^x$

Calculator Close-Up

You can see the solution to $2^{2x-1} = 8$ by graphing $y_1 = 2^{2x-1}$ and $y_2 = 8$. The x-coordinate of the point of intersection is the solution to the equation.

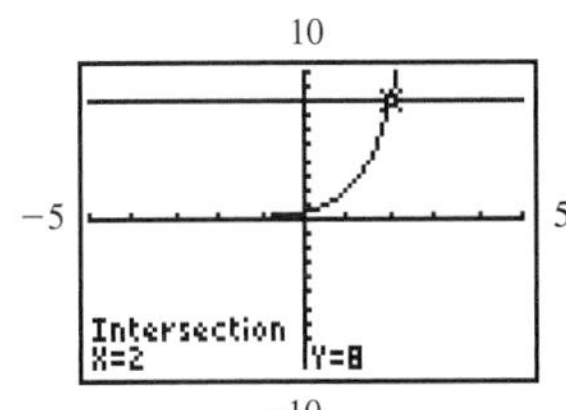

Solution

a) Because 8 is 2^3, we can write each side as a power of the same base, 2:

$$2^{2x-1} = 8 \quad \text{Original equation}$$
$$2^{2x-1} = 2^3 \quad \text{Write each side as a power of the same base.}$$
$$2x - 1 = 3 \quad \text{One-to-one property}$$
$$2x = 4$$
$$x = 2$$

Check: $2^{2 \cdot 2-1} = 2^3 = 8$. The solution set is $\{2\}$.

b) Because $9 = 3^2$, we can write each side as a power of 3:

$$9^{|x|} = 3 \quad \text{Original equation}$$
$$(3^2)^{|x|} = 3^1$$
$$3^{2|x|} = 3^1 \quad \text{Power of a power rule}$$
$$2|x| = 1 \quad \text{One-to-one property}$$
$$|x| = \frac{1}{2}$$
$$x = \pm\frac{1}{2} \quad \text{Since } \left|-\tfrac{1}{2}\right| = \left|\tfrac{1}{2}\right| = \tfrac{1}{2} \text{ there are two solutions to } |x| = \tfrac{1}{2}.$$

Check $x = \pm\frac{1}{2}$ in the original equation. The solution set is $\left\{-\frac{1}{2}, \frac{1}{2}\right\}$.

Calculator Close-Up

The equation $9^{|x|} = 3$ has two solutions because the graphs of $y_1 = 9^{|x|}$ and $y_2 = 3$ intersect twice.

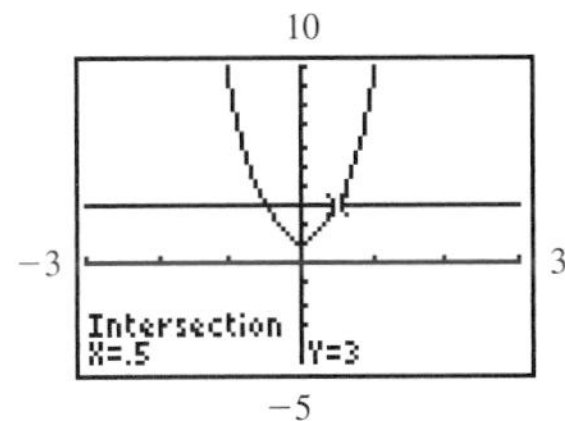

c) Because $\frac{1}{8} = 2^{-3}$ and $4 = 2^2$, we can write each side as a power of 2:

$$\frac{1}{8} = 4^x \quad \text{Original equation}$$
$$2^{-3} = (2^2)^x \quad \text{Write each side as a power of 2.}$$
$$2^{-3} = 2^{2x} \quad \text{Power of a power rule}$$
$$2x = -3 \quad \text{One-to-one property}$$
$$x = -\frac{3}{2}$$

Check $x = -\frac{3}{2}$ in the original equation. The solution set is $\left\{-\frac{3}{2}\right\}$.

Now do Exercises 53–66

The one-to-one property is also used to find the first coordinate when given the second coordinate of an exponential function.

EXAMPLE 8

Finding the x-coordinate in an exponential function

Let $f(x) = 2^x$ and $g(x) = \left(\frac{1}{2}\right)^{1-x}$. Find x if:

a) $f(x) = 32$ **b)** $g(x) = 8$

Solution

a) Because $f(x) = 2^x$ and $f(x) = 32$, we can find x by solving $2^x = 32$:

$$2^x = 32$$

$$2^x = 2^5 \quad \text{Write both sides as a power of the same base.}$$

$$x = 5 \quad \text{One-to-one property}$$

b) Because $g(x) = \left(\frac{1}{2}\right)^{1-x}$ and $g(x) = 8$, we can find x by solving $\left(\frac{1}{2}\right)^{1-x} = 8$:

$$\left(\frac{1}{2}\right)^{1-x} = 8$$

$$(2^{-1})^{1-x} = 2^3 \quad \text{Because } \tfrac{1}{2} = 2^{-1} \text{ and } 8 = 2^3$$

$$2^{x-1} = 2^3 \quad \text{Power of a power rule}$$

$$x - 1 = 3 \quad \text{One-to-one property}$$

$$x = 4$$

Now do Exercises 67–78

Teaching Tip Solving equations of this type will prepare students for logarithms.

Study Tip

Although you should avoid cramming, there are times when you have no other choice. In this case concentrate on what is in your class notes and the homework assignments. Try to work one or two problems of each type. Instructors often ask some relatively easy questions on a test to see if you have understood the major ideas.

Applications

The simple interest formula $A = P + Prt$ gives the amount A after t years for a principal P invested at simple interest rate r. If an investment is earning **compound interest,** then interest is periodically paid into the account and the interest that is paid also earns interest. To compute the amount of an account earning compound interest, the simple interest formula is used repeatedly. For example, if an account earns 6% compounded quarterly and the amount at the beginning of the first quarter is \$5000, we apply the simple interest formula with $P = \$5000$, $r = 0.06$, and $t = \frac{1}{4}$ to find the amount in the account at the end of the first quarter:

$$A = P + Prt$$

$$= P(1 + rt) \quad \text{Factor.}$$

$$= 5000\left(1 + 0.06 \cdot \frac{1}{4}\right) \quad \text{Substitute.}$$

$$= 5000(1.015)$$

$$= \$5075$$

To repeat this computation for another quarter, we multiply \$5075 by 1.015. If A represents the amount in the account at the end of n quarters, we can write A as an exponential function of n:

$$A = \$5000(1.015)^n$$

In general, the amount A is given by the following formula.

Compound Interest Formula

If P represents the principal, i the interest rate per period, n the number of periods, and A the amount at the end of n periods, then

$$A = P(1 + i)^n.$$

EXAMPLE 9

Compound interest formula

If \$350 is deposited in an account paying 12% compounded monthly, then how much is in the account at the end of 6 years and 6 months?

Calculator Close-Up

Graph $y = 350(1.01)^x$ to see the growth of the \$350 deposit in Example 9 over time. After 360 months it is worth \$12,582.37.

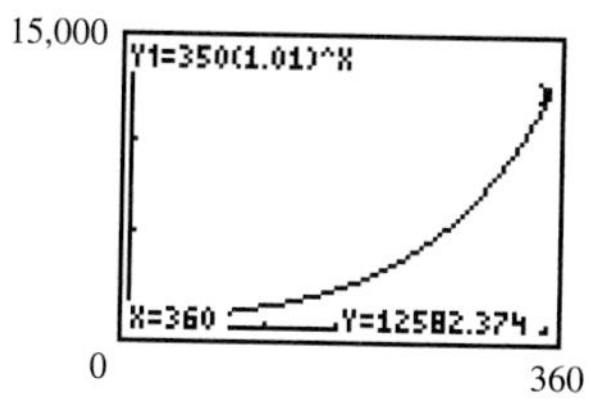

Solution

Interest is paid 12 times per year, so the account earns $\frac{1}{12}$ of 12%, or 1% each month, for 78 months. So $i = 0.01$, $n = 78$, and $P = \$350$:

$$A = P(1 + i)^n$$
$$A = \$350(1.01)^{78}$$
$$\approx \$760.56$$

Now do Exercises 83–88

If we shorten the length of the time period (yearly, quarterly, monthly, daily, hourly, etc.), the number of periods n increases while the interest rate for the period decreases. As n increases, the amount A also increases but will not exceed a certain amount. That certain amount is the amount obtained from *continuous compounding* of the interest. It is shown in more advanced courses that the following formula gives the amount when interest is compounded continuously.

Helpful Hint

Compare Examples 9 and 10 to see the difference between compounded monthly and compounded continuously. Although there is not much difference to an individual investor, there could be a large difference to the bank. Rework Examples 9 and 10 using \$50 million as the deposit.

Continuous-Compounding Formula

If P is the principal or beginning balance, r is the annual percentage rate compounded continuously, t is the time in years, and A is the amount or ending balance, then

$$A = Pe^{rt}.$$

CAUTION The value of t in the continuous-compounding formula must be in years. For example, if the time is 1 year and 3 months, then $t = 1.25$ years. If the time is 3 years and 145 days, then

$$t = 3 + \frac{145}{365}$$
$$\approx 3.3973 \text{ years.}$$

EXAMPLE 10

Continuous-compounding formula

If \$350 is deposited in an account paying 12% compounded continuously, then how much is in the account after 6 years and 6 months?

Calculator Close-Up

Graph $y = 350e^{0.12x}$ to see the growth of the \$350 deposit in Example 10 over time. After 30 years it is worth \$12,809.38.

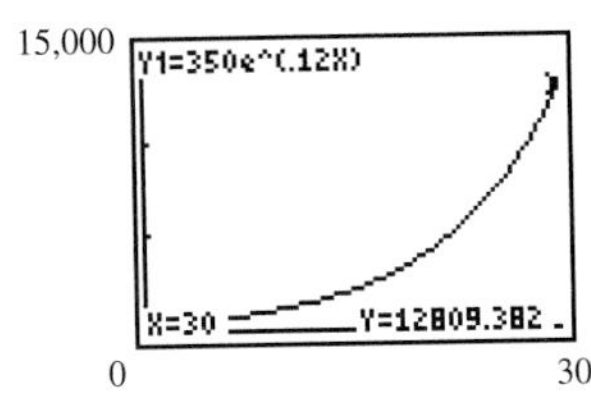

Solution

Use $r = 12\%$, $t = 6.5$ years, and $P = \$350$ in the formula for compounding interest continuously:

$$A = Pe^{rt}$$
$$= 350e^{(0.12)(6.5)}$$
$$= 350e^{0.78}$$
$$\approx \$763.52 \quad \text{Use the } e^x \text{ key on a scientific calculator.}$$

Note that compounding continuously amounts to a few dollars more than compounding monthly did in Example 9.

Now do Exercises 89–94

Warm-Ups ▼

True or false? Explain your answer.

1. If $f(x) = 4^x$, then $f\left(-\frac{1}{2}\right) = -2$. False
2. If $f(x) = \left(\frac{1}{3}\right)^x$, then $f(-1) = 3$. True
3. The function $f(x) = x^4$ is an exponential function. False
4. The functions $f(x) = \left(\frac{1}{2}\right)^x$ and $g(x) = 2^{-x}$ have the same graph. True
5. The function $f(x) = 2^x$ is invertible. True
6. The graph of $y = \left(\frac{1}{3}\right)^x$ has an x-intercept. False
7. The y-intercept for $f(x) = e^x$ is (0, 1). True
8. The expression $2^{\sqrt{2}}$ is undefined. False
9. The functions $f(x) = 2^{-x}$ and $g(x) = \frac{1}{2^x}$ have the same graph. True
10. If \$500 earns 6% compounded monthly, then at the end of 3 years the investment is worth $500(1.005)^3$ dollars. False

12.1 Exercises

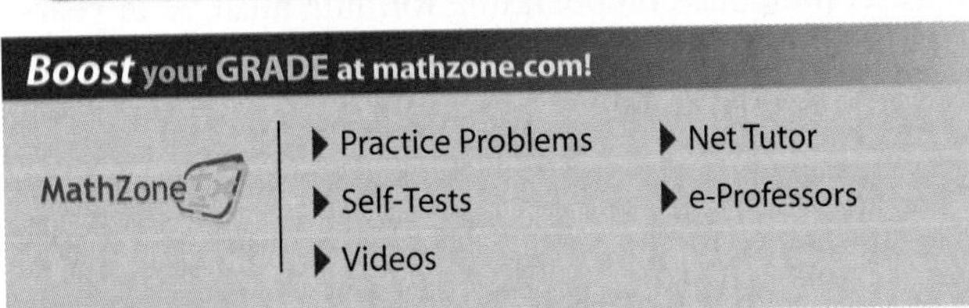

Reading and Writing *After reading this section, write out the answers to these questions. Use complete sentences.*

1. What is an exponential function?
   An exponential function has the form $f(x) = a^x$ where $a > 0$ and $a \neq 1$.
2. What is the domain of every exponential function?
   The domain of an exponential function is the set of all real numbers.
3. What are the two most popular bases?
   The two most popular bases are e and 10.
4. What is the one-to-one property of exponential functions?
   The one-to-one property states that if $a^m = a^n$, then $m = n$.
5. What is the compound interest formula?
   The compound interest formula is $A = P(1 + i)^n$.
6. What does compounded continuously mean?
   When money is compounded continuously, we use the formula $A = Pe^{rt}$.

Let $f(x) = 4^x$, $g(x) = \left(\frac{1}{3}\right)^{x+1}$, *and* $h(x) = -2^x$. *Find the following. See Example 1.*

7. $f(2)$ 16

8. $f(-1)$ $\frac{1}{4}$

9. $f\left(\frac{1}{2}\right)$ 2

10. $f\left(-\frac{3}{2}\right)$ $\frac{1}{8}$

11. $g(-2)$ 3

12. $g(1)$ $\frac{1}{9}$

13. $g(0)$ $\frac{1}{3}$

14. $g(-3)$ 9

15. $h(0)$ -1

16. $h(3)$ -8

17. $h(-2)$ $-\frac{1}{4}$

18. $h(-4)$ $-\frac{1}{16}$

Let $h(x) = 10^x$ *and* $j(x) = e^x$. *Find the following. Use a calculator as necessary and round approximate answers to three decimal places. See Example 2.*

19. $h(0)$ 1

20. $h(-1)$ 0.1

21. $h(2)$ 100

22. $h(3.4)$ 2511.886

23. $j(1)$ 2.718

24. $j(3.5)$ 33.115

25. $j(-2)$ 0.135

26. $j(0)$ 1

Fill in the missing entries in each table.

27.

x	-2	-1	0	1	2
4^x	$\frac{1}{16}$	$\frac{1}{4}$	1	4	16

28.

x	-2	-1	0	1	2
5^x	$\frac{1}{25}$	$\frac{1}{5}$	1	5	25

29.

x	-2	-1	0	1	2
$\left(\frac{1}{3}\right)^x$	9	3	1	$\frac{1}{3}$	$\frac{1}{9}$

30.

x	-2	-1	0	1	2
$\left(\frac{1}{5}\right)^x$	25	5	1	$\frac{1}{5}$	$\frac{1}{25}$

Sketch the graph of each function. See Examples 3 and 4.

31. $f(x) = 4^x$

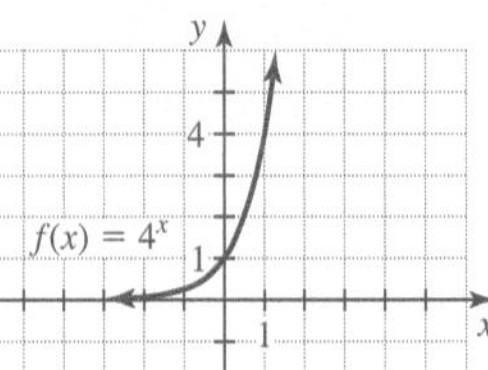

32. $g(x) = 5^x$

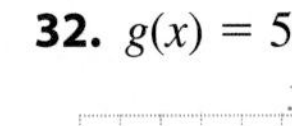

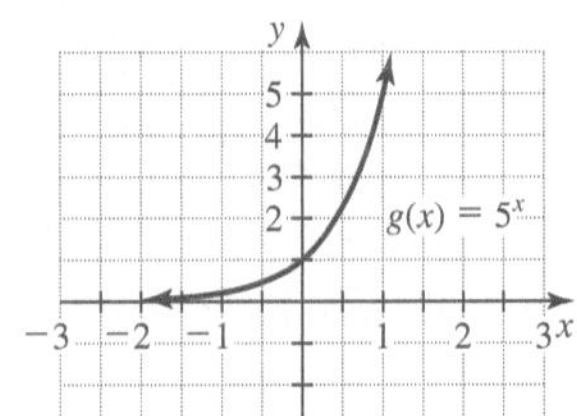

33. $h(x) = \left(\frac{1}{3}\right)^x$

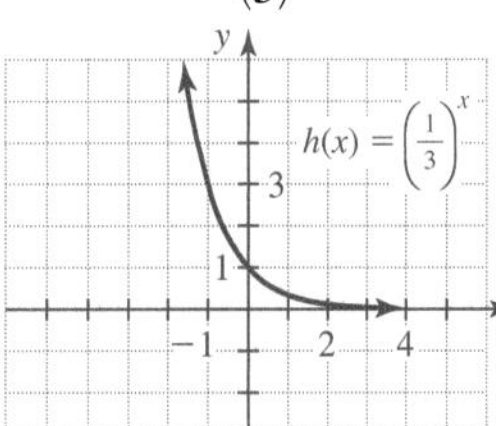

34. $i(x) = \left(\frac{1}{5}\right)^x$

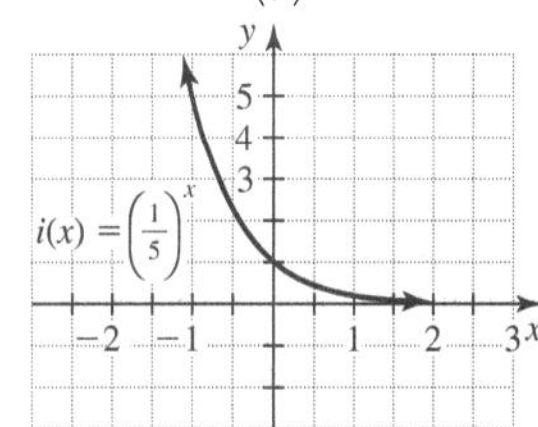

35. $y = 10^x$

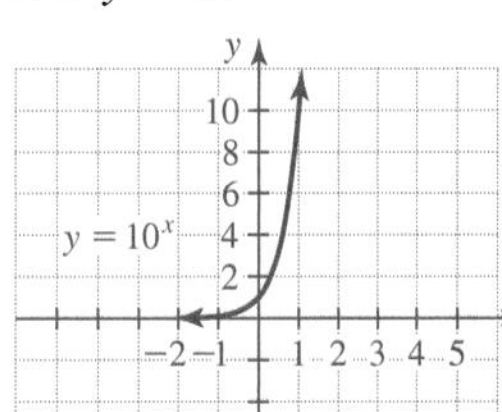

36. $y = (0.1)^x$

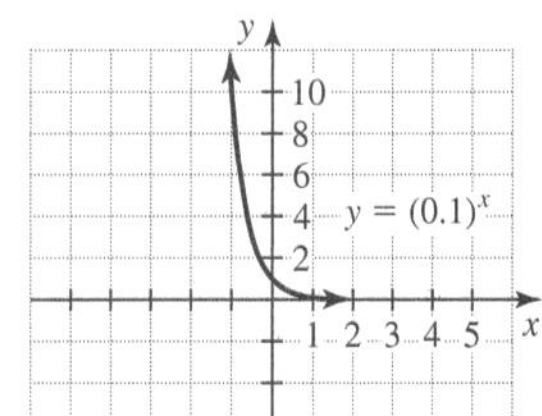

Fill in the missing entries in each table.

37.

x	-4	-3	-2	-1	0
10^{x+2}	$\frac{1}{100}$	$\frac{1}{10}$	1	10	100

38.

x	-2	-1	$-\frac{1}{2}$	0	1
3^{2x+1}	$\frac{1}{27}$	$\frac{1}{3}$	1	3	27

39.

x	-2	-1	0	1	2
-2^x	$-\frac{1}{4}$	$-\frac{1}{2}$	-1	-2	-4

40.

x	0	1	2	3	4
-2^{x-2}	$-\frac{1}{4}$	$-\frac{1}{2}$	-1	-2	-4

Sketch the graph of each function. See Examples 5 and 6.

41. $y = 10^{x+2}$

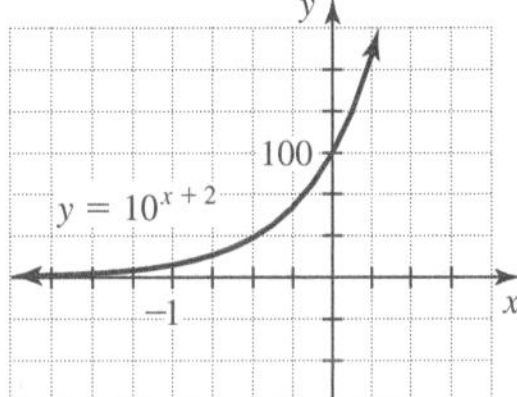

42. $y = 3^{2x+1}$

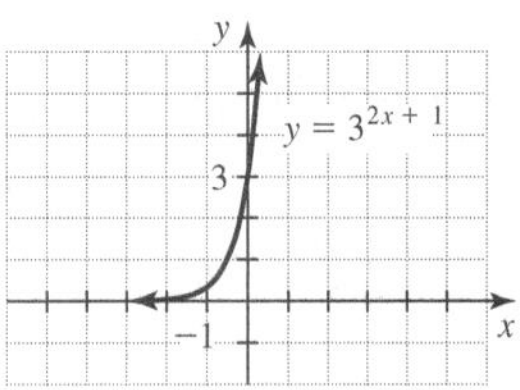

43. $f(x) = -2^x$

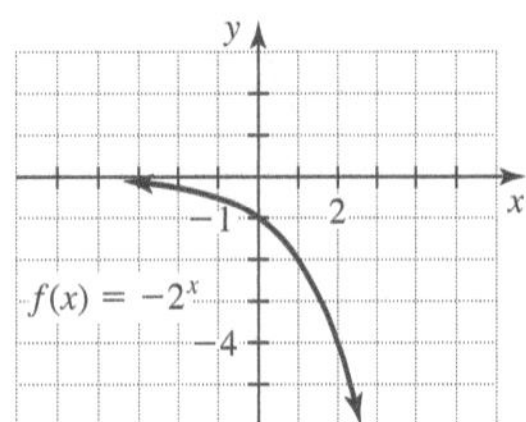

44. $k(x) = -2^{x-2}$

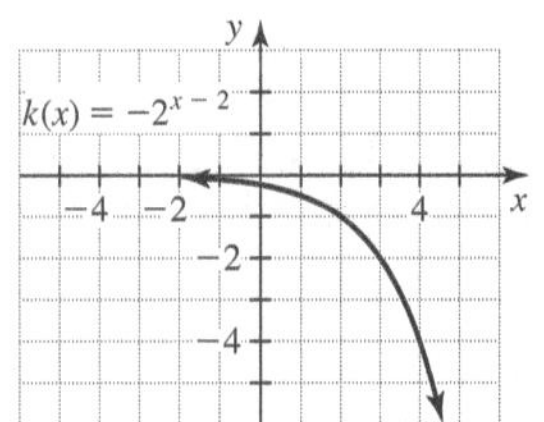

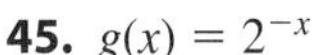

45. $g(x) = 2^{-x}$

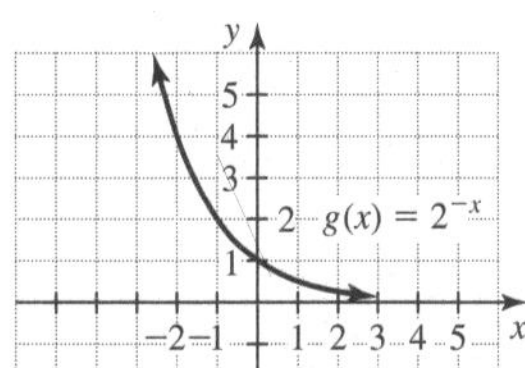

46. $A(x) = 10^{1-x}$

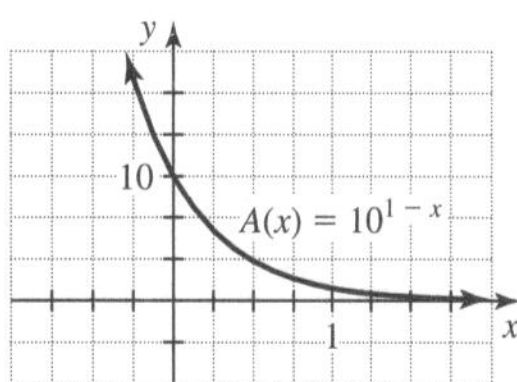

47. $f(x) = -e^x$

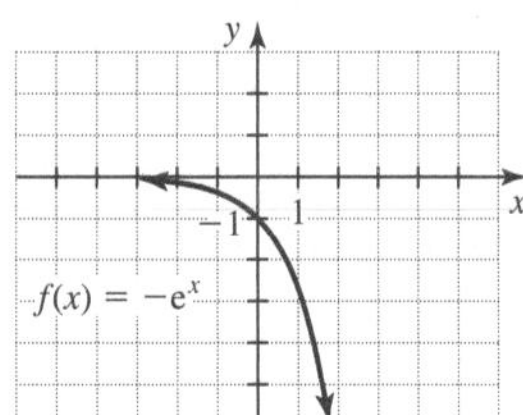

48. $g(x) = e^{-x}$

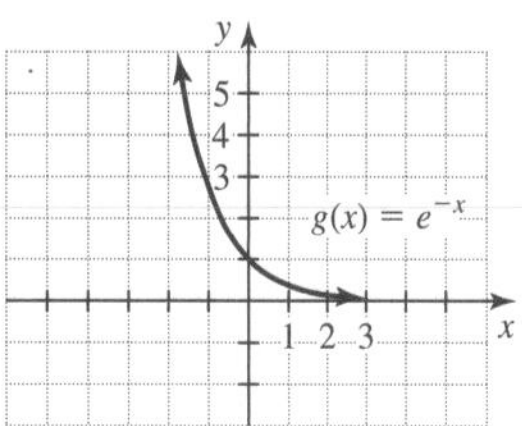

49. $H(x) = 10^{|x|}$

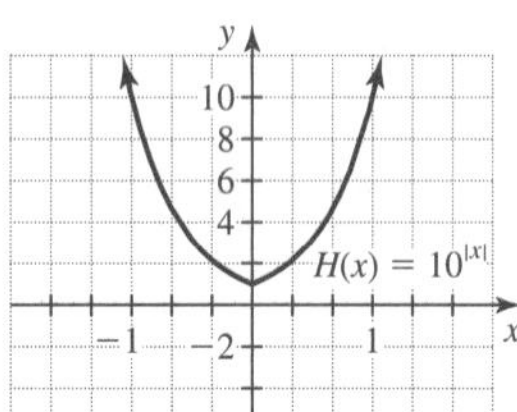

50. $s(x) = 2^{(x^2)}$

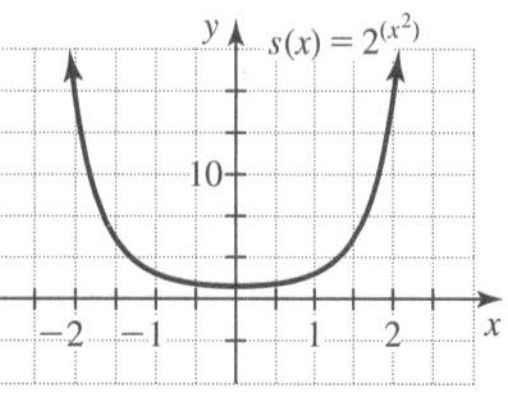

51. $P = 5000(1.05)^t$

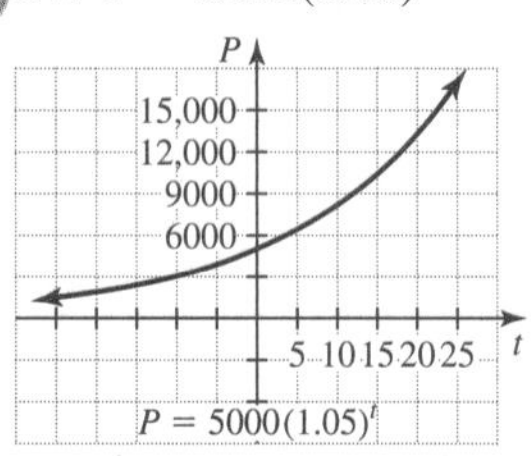

52. $d = 800 \cdot 10^{-4t}$

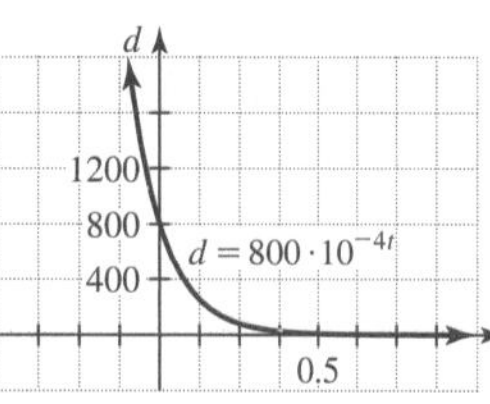

Solve each equation. See Example 7.

53. $2^x = 64$ $\{6\}$

54. $3^x = 9$ $\{2\}$

55. $10^x = 0.001$ $\{-3\}$

56. $10^{2x} = 0.1$ $\left\{-\frac{1}{2}\right\}$

57. $2^x = \frac{1}{4}$ $\{-2\}$

58. $3^x = \frac{1}{9}$ $\{-2\}$

59. $\left(\frac{2}{3}\right)^{x-1} = \frac{9}{4}$ $\{-1\}$

60. $\left(\frac{1}{4}\right)^{3x} = 16$ $\left\{-\frac{2}{3}\right\}$

61. $5^{-x} = 25$ $\{-2\}$

62. $10^{-x} = 0.01$ $\{2\}$

63. $-2^{1-x} = -8$ $\{-2\}$

64. $-3^{2-x} = -81$ $\{-2\}$

65. $10^{|x|} = 1000$ $\{-3, 3\}$

66. $3^{|2x-5|} = 81$ $\left\{\frac{1}{2}, \frac{9}{2}\right\}$

Let $f(x) = 2^x$, $g(x) = \left(\frac{1}{3}\right)^x$, *and* $h(x) = 4^{2x-1}$. *Find x in each case. See Example 8.*

67. $f(x) = 4$ 2

68. $f(x) = \frac{1}{4}$ -2

69. $f(x) = 4^{2/3}$ $\frac{4}{3}$

70. $f(x) = 1$ 0

71. $g(x) = 9$ -2

72. $g(x) = \frac{1}{9}$ 2

73. $g(x) = 1$ 0

74. $g(x) = \sqrt{3}$ $-\frac{1}{2}$

75. $h(x) = 16$ $\frac{3}{2}$

76. $h(x) = \frac{1}{2}$ $\frac{1}{4}$

77. $h(x) = 1$ $\frac{1}{2}$

78. $h(x) = \sqrt{2}$ $\frac{5}{8}$

Fill in the missing entries in each table.

79.

x	-5	-3	0	1	4
2^x	$\frac{1}{32}$	$\frac{1}{8}$	1	2	16

80.

x	-4	-2	0	1	3
3^x	$\frac{1}{81}$	$\frac{1}{9}$	1	3	27

81.

x	-3	-2	0	1	5
$\left(\frac{1}{2}\right)^x$	8	4	1	$\frac{1}{2}$	$\frac{1}{32}$

82.

x	-2	-1	0	2	3
$\left(\frac{1}{10}\right)^x$	100	10	1	$\frac{1}{100}$	$\frac{1}{1000}$

Solve each problem. See Example 9.

83. ***Compounding quarterly.*** If \$6000 is deposited in an account paying 5% compounded quarterly, then what amount will be in the account after 10 years? \$9861.72

84. ***Compounding quarterly.*** If \$400 is deposited in an account paying 10% compounded quarterly, then what amount will be in the account after 7 years? \$798.60

85. ***Outstanding performance.*** The top growth fund at Fidelity Investments from 1992 to 2002 was the Low-Priced Stock Fund (www.fidelity.com), which returned an average of 18.21% annually for those 10 years.

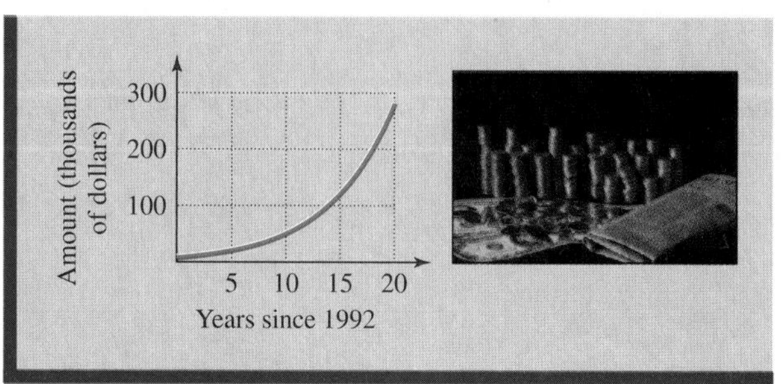

Figure for Exercise 85

a) How much was an investment of \$10,000 in this fund in 1992 worth in 2002 at 18.21% compounded annually? \$53,277.30

b) Use the accompanying graph to estimate the year in which the \$10,000 investment would be worth \$200,000 if it continued to grow at 18.21% annually. 2010

86. ***Second place.*** The second best growth fund at Fidelity Investments from 1992 to 2002 was the Contrafund Fund, which returned an average of 13.47% annually for those 10 years. How much was an investment of \$10,000 in this fund in 1992 worth in 2002?
\$35,384.30

87. ***Depreciating knowledge.*** The value of a certain textbook seems to decrease according to the formula $V = 45 \cdot 2^{-0.9t}$, where V is the value in dollars and t is the age of the book in years. What is the book worth when it is new? What is it worth when it is 2 years old?
\$45, \$12.92

88. ***Mosquito abatement.*** In a Minnesota swamp in the springtime the number of mosquitoes per acre appears to grow according to the formula $N = 10^{0.1t+2}$, where t is the number of days since the last frost. What is the size of the mosquito population at times $t = 10$, $t = 20$, and $t = 30$?
1000, 10,000, 100,000

Solve each problem. See Example 10.

89. ***Compounding continuously.*** If \$500 is deposited in an account paying 7% compounded continuously, then how much will be in the account after 3 years?
\$616.84

90. ***Compounding continuously.*** If \$7000 is deposited in an account paying 8% compounded continuously, then what will it amount to after 4 years?
\$9639.89

91. ***One year's interest.*** How much interest will be earned the first year on \$80,000 on deposit in an account paying 7.5% compounded continuously?
\$6230.73

92. ***Partial year.*** If \$7500 is deposited in an account paying 6.75% compounded continuously, then how much will be in the account after 5 years and 215 days?
\$10,937.13

93. ***Radioactive decay.*** The number of grams of a certain radioactive substance present at time t is given by the formula $A = 300 \cdot e^{-0.06t}$, where t is the number of years. Find the amount present at time $t = 0$. Find the amount present after 20 years. Use the accompanying graph to estimate the number of years that it takes for one-half of the substance to decay. Will the substance ever decay completely? 300 grams, 90.4 grams, 12 years, no

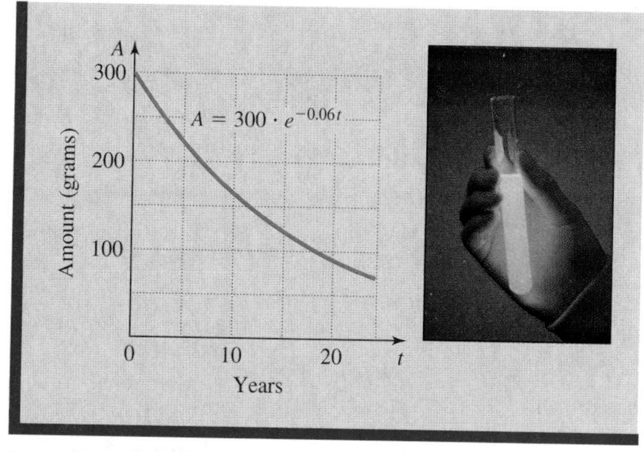

Figure for Exercise 93

94. ***Population growth.*** The population of a certain country appears to be growing according to the formula $P = 20 \cdot e^{0.1t}$, where P is the population in millions and t is the number of years since 1990. What was the population in 1990? What will the population be in the year 2010? 20 million, 147.8 million

Getting More Involved

95. ***Exploration***

An approximate value for e can be found by adding the terms in the following infinite sum:

$$1 + \frac{1}{1} + \frac{1}{2 \cdot 1} + \frac{1}{3 \cdot 2 \cdot 1} + \frac{1}{4 \cdot 3 \cdot 2 \cdot 1} + \cdots$$

Use a calculator to find the sum of the first four terms. Find the difference between the sum of the first four terms and e. (For e, use all of the digits that your calculator gives for e^1.) What is the difference between e and the sum of the first eight terms? 2.66666667, 0.0516, 2.8×10^{-5}

Graphing Calculator Exercises

96. Graph $y_1 = 2^x$, $y_2 = e^x$, and $y_3 = 3^x$ on the same coordinate system. Which point do all three graphs have in common?
(0, 1)

97. Graph $y_1 = 3^x$, $y_2 = 3^{x-1}$, and $y_3 = 3^{x-2}$ on the same coordinate system. What can you say about the graph of $y = 3^{x-h}$ for any real number h?
The graph of $y = 3^{x-h}$ lies h units to the right of $y = 3^x$ when $h > 0$ and $|h|$ units to the left of $y = 3^x$ when $h < 0$.

12.2 Logarithmic Functions and Their Applications

In this Section

- Definition
- Domain and Range
- Graphing Logarithmic Functions
- Logarithmic Equations
- Applications

In Section 12.1 you learned that exponential functions are one-to-one functions. Because they are one-to-one functions, they have inverse functions. In this section we study the inverses of the exponential functions.

Definition

We define $\log_a(x)$ as *the exponent that is used on the base a to obtain the result x.* Read the expression $\log_a(x)$ as "the base a logarithm of x." The expression $\log_a(x)$ is called a **logarithm.** If the *exponent* 3 is used on the *base* 2 then the *result* is 8 ($2^3 = 8$). So

$$\log_2(8) = 3.$$

Base Result Exponent

Because $5^2 = 25$, the exponent used to obtain 25 with base 5 is 2 and $\log_5(25) = 2$. Because $2^{-5} = \frac{1}{32}$, the exponent used to obtain $\frac{1}{32}$ with base 2 is -5 and $\log_2\left(\frac{1}{32}\right) = -5$. From these examples, we see that the definition of $\log_a(x)$ can also be stated as follows:

Definition of $\log_a(x)$

For any $a > 0$ and $a \neq 1$,

$$y = \log_a(x) \quad \text{if and only if} \quad a^y = x.$$

Note that the base of a logarithm must be a positive number and it cannot be 1.

EXAMPLE 1

Using the definition of logarithm

Write each logarithmic equation as an exponential equation and each exponential equation as a logarithmic equation.

a) $\log_5(125) = 3$ **b)** $6 = \log_{1/4}(x)$

c) $\left(\frac{1}{2}\right)^m = 8$ **d)** $7 = 3^z$

Solution

a) "The base-5 logarithm of 125 equals 3" means that 3 is the exponent on 5 that produces 125. So $5^3 = 125$.

b) The equation $6 = \log_{1/4}(x)$ is equivalent to $\left(\frac{1}{4}\right)^6 = x$ by the definition of logarithm.

c) The equation $\left(\frac{1}{2}\right)^m = 8$ is equivalent to $\log_{1/2}(8) = m$.

d) The equation $7 = 3^z$ is equivalent to $\log_3(7) = z$.

Now do Exercises 7–18

Teaching Tip To get students ready for finding logarithms drill them on solving simple equations like $2^x = 8$, $3^x = 9$, and $4^x = \frac{1}{4}$.

The inverse of the base-a exponential function $f(x) = a^x$ is the **base-*a* logarithmic function** $f^{-1}(x) = \log_a(x)$. For example, $f(x) = 2^x$ and $f^{-1}(x) = \log_2(x)$ are inverse functions as shown in Fig. 12.8. Each function undoes the other.

$$f(5) = 2^5 = 32 \quad \text{and} \quad g(32) = \log_2(32) = 5.$$

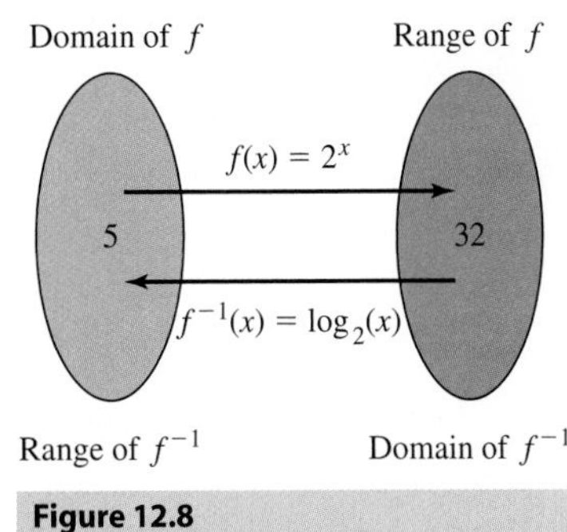

Figure 12.8

To evaluate logarithmic functions remember that a logarithm is an exponent: $\log_a(x)$ is the exponent that is used on the base a to obtain x.

EXAMPLE 2

Finding logarithms

Evaluate each logarithm.

a) $\log_5(25)$ **b)** $\log_2\left(\frac{1}{8}\right)$ **c)** $\log_{1/2}(4)$

d) $\log_{10}(0.001)$ **e)** $\log_9(3)$

Solution

a) The number $\log_5(25)$ is the exponent that is used on the base 5 to obtain 25. Because $25 = 5^2$, we have $\log_5(25) = 2$.

b) The number $\log_2\left(\frac{1}{8}\right)$ is the power of 2 that gives us $\frac{1}{8}$. Because $\frac{1}{8} = 2^{-3}$, we have $\log_2\left(\frac{1}{8}\right) = -3$.

c) The number $\log_{1/2}(4)$ is the power of $\frac{1}{2}$ that produces 4. Because $4 = \left(\frac{1}{2}\right)^{-2}$, we have $\log_{1/2}(4) = -2$.

d) Because $0.001 = 10^{-3}$, we have $\log_{10}(0.001) = -3$.

e) Because $9^{1/2} = 3$, we have $\log_9(3) = \frac{1}{2}$.

Now do Exercises 19-28

Helpful Hint

When we write $C(x) = 12x$, we may think of C as a variable and write $C = 12x$, or we may think of C as the name of a function, the cost function. In $y = \log_a(x)$ we are thinking of $\log_a$ only as the name of the function that pairs an x-value with a y-value.

There are two bases for logarithms that are used more frequently than the others: They are 10 and e. The base-10 logarithm is called the **common logarithm** and is usually written as $\log(x)$. The base-e logarithm is called the **natural logarithm** and is usually written as $\ln(x)$. Most scientific calculators have function keys for $\log(x)$ and $\ln(x)$. The simplest way to obtain a common or natural logarithm is to use a scientific calculator.

In Example 3 we find natural and common logarithms of certain numbers without a calculator.

Math *at Work* Drug Administration

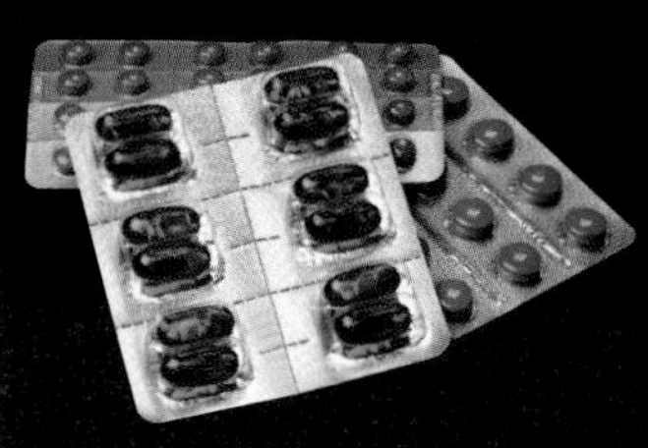

When a drug is taken continuously or intermittently, plasma concentrations of the drug increase. Over time, the rate of increase slows and eventually reaches a plateau. As concentration increases, the rate of elimination increases until a point is reached at which the amount of drug being eliminated from the body equals the amount being administered (steady state).

The time to reach steady state depends on the half-life of the drug. The half-life of a drug is the time it takes for the plasma concentration to be reduced by one-half. See the accompanying figure. The basic rule is that after administering a drug for a period equal to the half-life of the drug, plasma concentration will be halfway between the starting concentration and steady state. This rule holds for any starting concentration. Mathematically, steady state is a limit and it is never reached. It is usually assumed that when a drug reaches 90% or more of steady state it is at steady state. It takes 3.3 half-lives of drug administration to reach 90% of steady state.

The half-life $t_{1/2}$ of a drug depends on the patient and is calculated from two plasma levels separated by a time interval. The first plasma level or peak (P) is measured after the drug has been fully distributed. The second plasma lever or trough (T) is measured at some interval later (t). From P, T, and t, the elimination constant k is found by $k = \frac{\ln(P) - \ln(T)}{t}$. The half-life is then found using $t_{1/2} = \frac{\ln(2)}{k}$. When the dosing interval is much longer than the half-life, there is more time for elimination between doses and accumulation is small. When the dosing interval is much shorter than the half-life, there is little time for elimination and more accumulation of the drug.

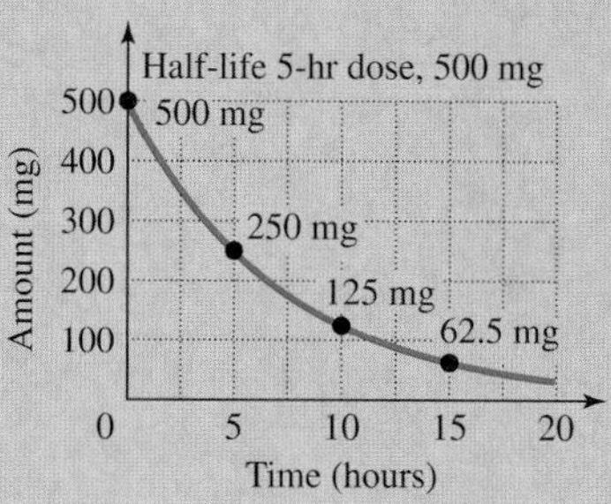

EXAMPLE 3

Calculator Close-Up

A graphing calculator has keys for the common logarithm (LOG) and the natural logarithm (LN).

```
log(1000)
                3
ln(e)
                1
log(1/10)
               -1
```

Finding common and natural logarithms

Evaluate each logarithm.

a) $\log(1000)$ **b)** $\ln(e)$

c) $\log\left(\frac{1}{10}\right)$

Solution

a) Because $10^3 = 1000$, we have $\log(1000) = 3$.

b) Because $e^1 = e$, we have $\ln(e) = 1$.

c) Because $10^{-1} = \frac{1}{10}$, we have $\log\left(\frac{1}{10}\right) = -1$.

Now do Exercises 29–40

Domain and Range

The domain of the exponential function $y = 2^x$ is $(-\infty, \infty)$, and its range is $(0, \infty)$. Because the logarithmic function $y = \log_2(x)$ is the inverse of $y = 2^x$, the domain of $y = \log_2(x)$ is $(0, \infty)$, and its range is $(-\infty, \infty)$.

CAUTION The domain of $y = \log_a(x)$ for $a > 0$ and $a \neq 1$ is $(0, \infty)$. So expressions such as $\log_2(-4)$, $\log_{1/3}(0)$, and $\ln(-1)$ are undefined, because -4, 0, and -1 are not in the domain $(0, \infty)$.

Graphing Logarithmic Functions

In Chapter 11 we saw that the graphs of a function and its inverse function are symmetric about the line $y = x$. Because the logarithm functions are inverses of exponential functions, their graphs are also symmetric about $y = x$.

EXAMPLE 4

A logarithmic function with base greater than 1

Sketch the graph of $g(x) = \log_2(x)$ and compare it to the graph of $y = 2^x$.

Solution

Make a table of ordered pairs for $g(x) = \log_2(x)$ using positive numbers for x:

x	$\frac{1}{4}$	$\frac{1}{2}$	1	2	4	8
$g(x) = \log_2(x)$	-2	-1	0	1	2	3

Draw a curve through these points as shown in Fig. 12.9. The graph of the inverse function $y = 2^x$ is also shown in Fig. 12.9 for comparison. Note the symmetry of the two curves about the line $y = x$.

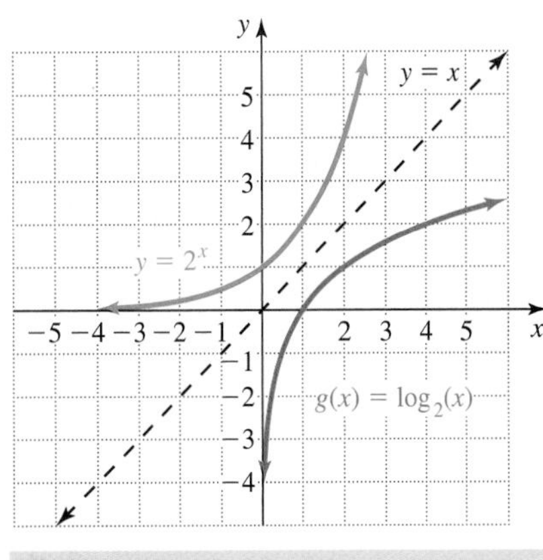

Figure 12.9

Now do Exercises 49–52

Calculator Close-Up

The graphs of $y = \ln(x)$ and $y = e^x$ are symmetric with respect to the line $y = x$. Logarithmic functions with bases other than e and 10 will be graphed on a calculator in Section 10.4.

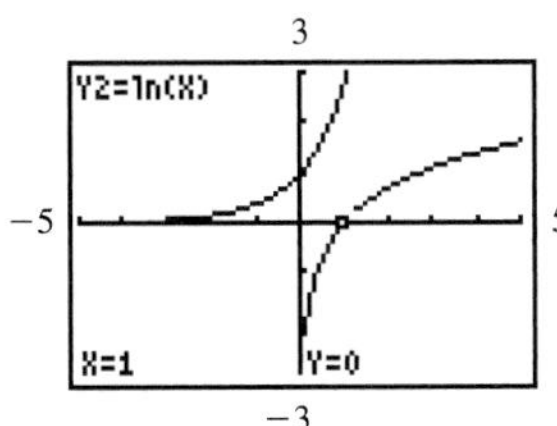

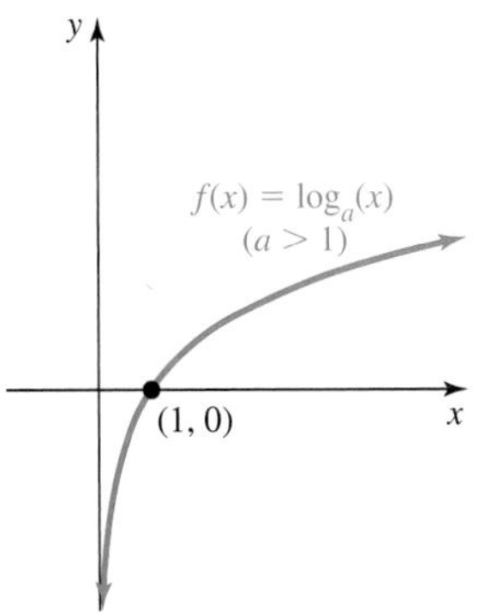

Figure 12.10

All logarithmic functions with the base greater than 1 have graphs that are similar to the one in Fig. 12.9. In general, the graph of $f(x) = \log_a(x)$ for $a > 1$ has the following characteristics (see Fig. 12.10):

1. The x-intercept of the curve is $(1, 0)$.
2. The domain is $(0, \infty)$, and the range is $(-\infty, \infty)$.

3. The curve approaches the negative y-axis but does not touch it.
4. The y-values are increasing as we go from left to right along the curve.

EXAMPLE 5

A logarithmic function with base less than 1

Sketch the graph of $f(x) = \log_{1/2}(x)$ and compare it to the graph of $y = \left(\frac{1}{2}\right)^x$.

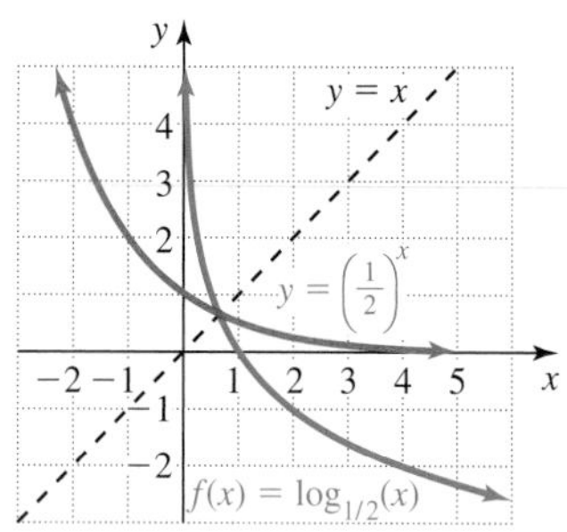

Figure 12.11

Solution

Make a table of ordered pairs for $f(x) = \log_{1/2}(x)$ using positive numbers for x:

x	$\frac{1}{4}$	$\frac{1}{2}$	1	2	4	8
$f(x) = \log_{1/2}(x)$	2	1	0	-1	-2	-3

The curve through these points is shown in Fig. 12.11. The graph of the inverse function $y = \left(\frac{1}{2}\right)^x$ is also shown in Fig. 12.11 for comparison. Note the symmetry with respect to the line $y = x$.

Now do Exercises 53–56

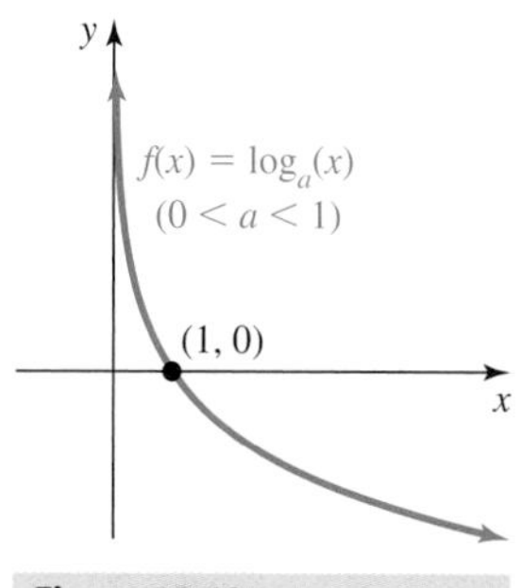

Figure 12.12

All logarithmic functions with the base between 0 and 1 have graphs that are similar to the one in Fig. 12.11. In general, the graph of $f(x) = \log_a(x)$ for $0 < a < 1$ has the following characteristics (see Fig. 12.12):

1. The x-intercept of the curve is $(1, 0)$.
2. The domain is $(0, \infty)$, and the range is $(-\infty, \infty)$.
3. The curve approaches the positive y-axis but does not touch it.
4. The y-values are decreasing as we go from left to right along the curve.

Figures 12.9 and 12.11 illustrate the fact that $y = \log_a(x)$ and $y = a^x$ are inverse functions for any base a. For any given exponential or logarithmic function the inverse function can be easily obtained from the definition of logarithm.

EXAMPLE 6

Inverses of logarithmic and exponential functions

Find the inverse of each function.

a) $f(x) = 10^x$ **b)** $g(x) = \log_3(x)$

Solution

a) To find any inverse function we switch the roles of x and y. So $y = 10^x$ becomes $x = 10^y$. Now $x = 10^y$ is equivalent to $y = \log_{10}(x)$. So the inverse of $f(x) = 10^x$ is $y = \log(x)$ or $f^{-1}(x) = \log(x)$.

b) In $g(x) = \log_3(x)$ or $y = \log_3(x)$ we switch x and y to get $x = \log_3(y)$. Now $x = \log_3(y)$ is equivalent to $y = 3^x$. So the inverse of $g(x) = \log_3(x)$ is $y = 3^x$ or $g^{-1}(x) = 3^x$.

Now do Exercises 57–62

Logarithmic Equations

In Section 12.1 we learned that the exponential functions are one-to-one functions. Because logarithmic functions are inverses of exponential functions, they are one-to-one functions also. For a base-a logarithmic function *one-to-one means that if the base-a logarithms of two numbers are equal, then the numbers are equal.*

One-to-One Property of Logarithms

For $a > 0$ and $a \neq 1$,

$$\text{if} \quad \log_a(m) = \log_a(n), \quad \text{then} \quad m = n.$$

The one-to-one property of logarithms and the definition of logarithms are the two basic tools that we use to solve equations involving logarithms. We use these tools in Example 7.

EXAMPLE 7

Logarithmic equations

Solve each equation.

a) $\log_3(x) = -2$

b) $\log_x(8) = -3$

c) $\log(x^2) = \log(4)$

Study Tip

Establish a regular routine of eating, sleeping, and exercise. The ability to concentrate depends on adequate sleep, decent nutrition, and the physical well-being that comes with exercise.

Teaching Tip Students need a lot of practice solving simple exponential and logarithmic equations.

Solution

a) Use the definition of logarithms to rewrite the logarithmic equation as an equivalent exponential equation:

$$\log_3(x) = -2$$
$$3^{-2} = x \quad \text{Definition of logarithm}$$
$$\frac{1}{9} = x$$

Because $3^{-2} = \frac{1}{9}$ or $\log_3\left(\frac{1}{9}\right) = -2$, the solution set is $\left\{\frac{1}{9}\right\}$.

b) Use the definition of logarithms to rewrite the logarithmic equation as an equivalent exponential equation:

$$\log_x(8) = -3$$
$$x^{-3} = 8 \quad \text{Definition of logarithm}$$
$$(x^{-3})^{-1} = 8^{-1} \quad \text{Raise each side to the } -1 \text{ power.}$$
$$x^3 = \frac{1}{8}$$
$$x = \sqrt[3]{\frac{1}{8}} = \frac{1}{2} \quad \text{Odd-root property}$$

Because $\left(\frac{1}{2}\right)^{-3} = 2^3 = 8$ or $\log_{1/2}(8) = -3$ the solution set is $\left\{\frac{1}{2}\right\}$.

c) To write an equation equivalent to $\log(x^2) = \log(4)$, we use the one-to-one property of logarithms:

$$\log(x^2) = \log(4)$$

$$x^2 = 4 \quad \text{One-to-one property of logarithms}$$

$$x = \pm 2 \quad \text{Even-root property}$$

If $x = \pm 2$, then $x^2 = 4$ and $\log(4) = \log(4)$. The solution set is $\{-2, 2\}$.

Now do Exercises 63–74

CAUTION If we have equality of two logarithms with the same base, we use the one-to-one property to eliminate the logarithms. If we have an equation with only one logarithm, such as $\log_a(x) = y$, we use the definition of logarithm to write $a^y = x$ and to eliminate the logarithm.

Applications

The definition of logarithm indicates that $y = \log_a(x)$ if and only if $a^y = x$. If the base is e, then the definition indicates that

$$y = \ln(x) \quad \text{if and only if} \quad e^y = x.$$

In Example 8, we use the definition of logarithm to solve a problem involving the continuous-compounding formula

$$A = Pe^{rt},$$

where A is the amount after t years of an investment of P dollars at annual percentage rate r compounded continuously.

EXAMPLE 8

Finding the time with continuous compounding

How long does it take for \$80 to grow to \$240 at 12% annual percentage rate compounded continuously?

Teaching Tip Instead of applying the definition, you can take the natural logarithm of each side of the equation.

Solution

Use $r = 0.12$, $P = \$80$, and $A = \$240$ in the formula $A = Pe^{rt}$ to get $240 = 80e^{0.12t}$. Now use the definition of logarithm to solve for t:

$$240 = 80e^{0.12t}$$

$$3 = e^{0.12t} \quad \text{Divide each side by 80.}$$

$$0.12t = \ln(3) \quad \text{Definition of logarithm: } y = e^x \text{ means } x = \ln(y)$$

$$t = \frac{\ln(3)}{0.12} \quad \text{Divide each side by 0.12.}$$

$$t \approx 9.155$$

The time is approximately 9.155 years. Multiply 365 by 0.155 to get approximately 57 days. So the time is 9 years and 57 days to the nearest day.

Now do Exercises 85–96

Note that we can also use the technique of Example 8 to solve a continuous-compounding problem in which the rate is the only unknown quantity.

Warm-Ups

True or false? Explain your answer.

1. The equation $a^3 = 2$ is equivalent to $\log_a(2) = 3$. True
2. If (a, b) satisfies $y = 8^x$, then (a, b) satisfies $y = \log_8(x)$. False
3. If $f(x) = a^x$ for $a > 0$ and $a \neq 1$, then $f^{-1}(x) = \log_a(x)$. True
4. If $f(x) = \ln(x)$, then $f^{-1}(x) = e^x$. True
5. The domain of $f(x) = \log_6(x)$ is $(-\infty, \infty)$. False
6. $\log_{25}(5) = 2$ False
7. $\log(-10) = 1$ False
8. $\log(0) = 0$ False
9. $5^{\log_5(125)} = 125$ True
10. $\log_{1/2}(32) = -5$ True

12.2 Exercises

Boost your GRADE at mathzone.com!

MathZone
- Practice Problems
- Self-Tests
- Videos
- Net Tutor
- e-Professors

Reading and Writing *After reading this section, write out the answers to these questions. Use complete sentences.*

1. What is the inverse function for the function $f(x) = 2^x$?
   If $f(x) = 2^x$, then $f^{-1}(x) = \log_2(x)$.
2. What is $\log_a(x)$?
   The expression $\log_a(x)$ is the exponent of a that produces x. So $a^{\log_a(x)} = x$.
3. What is the difference between the common logarithm and the natural logarithm?
   The common logarithm uses the base 10 and the natural logarithm uses base e.
4. What is the domain of $f(x) = \log_a(x)$?
   The domain of $f(x) = \log_a(x)$ is $(0, \infty)$.
5. What is the one-to-one property of logarithmic functions?
   The one-to-one property for logarithmic functions states that if $\log_a(m) = \log_a(n)$, then $m = n$.
6. What is the relationship between the graphs of $f(x) = a^x$ and $f^{-1}(x) = \log_a(x)$ for $a > 0$ and $a \neq 1$?
   The graphs of $f(x) = a^x$ and $f^{-1}(x) = \log_a(x)$ are symmetric about the line $y = x$.

Write each exponential equation as a logarithmic equation and each logarithmic equation as an exponential equation. See Example 1.

7. $\log_2(8) = 3$ $2^3 = 8$
8. $\log_{10}(10) = 1$ $10^1 = 10$
9. $10^2 = 100$ $\log(100) = 2$
10. $5^3 = 125$ $\log_5(125) = 3$
11. $y = \log_5(x)$ $5^y = x$
12. $m = \log_b(N)$ $b^m = N$
13. $2^a = b$ $\log_2(b) = a$
14. $a^3 = c$ $\log_a(c) = 3$
15. $\log_3(x) = 10$ $3^{10} = x$
16. $\log_c(t) = 4$ $c^4 = t$
17. $e^3 = x$ $\ln(x) = 3$
18. $m = e^x$ $\ln(m) = x$

Evaluate each logarithm. See Examples 2 and 3.

19. $\log_2(4)$ 2
20. $\log_2(1)$ 0
21. $\log_2(16)$ 4
22. $\log_4(16)$ 2
23. $\log_2(64)$ 6
24. $\log_8(64)$ 2
25. $\log_4(64)$ 3
26. $\log_{64}(64)$ 1
27. $\log_2\left(\frac{1}{4}\right)$ -2
28. $\log_2\left(\frac{1}{8}\right)$ -3
29. $\log(100)$ 2
30. $\log(1)$ 0
31. $\log(0.01)$ -2
32. $\log(10{,}000)$ 4
33. $\log_{1/3}\left(\frac{1}{3}\right)$ 1
34. $\log_{1/3}\left(\frac{1}{9}\right)$ 2
35. $\log_{1/3}(27)$ -3
36. $\log_{1/3}(1)$ 0
37. $\log_{25}(5)$ $\frac{1}{2}$
38. $\log_{16}(4)$ $\frac{1}{2}$
39. $\ln(e^2)$ 2
40. $\ln\left(\frac{1}{e}\right)$ -1

Use a calculator to evaluate each logarithm. Round answers to four decimal places.

41. $\log(5)$ 0.6990

42. $\log(0.03)$ −1.5229

43. $\ln(6.238)$ 1.8307

44. $\ln(0.23)$ −1.4697

Fill in the missing entries in each table.

45.

x	$\frac{1}{9}$	$\frac{1}{3}$	1	3	9
$\log_3(x)$	−2	−1	0	1	2

46.

x	$\frac{1}{100}$	$\frac{1}{10}$	1	10	100
$\log_{10}(x)$	−2	−1	0	1	2

47.

x	16	4	1	$\frac{1}{4}$	$\frac{1}{16}$
$\log_{1/4}(x)$	−2	−1	0	1	2

48.

x	9	3	1	$\frac{1}{3}$	$\frac{1}{9}$
$\log_{1/3}(x)$	−2	−1	0	1	2

Sketch the graph of each function. See Examples 4 and 5.

49. $f(x) = \log_3(x)$

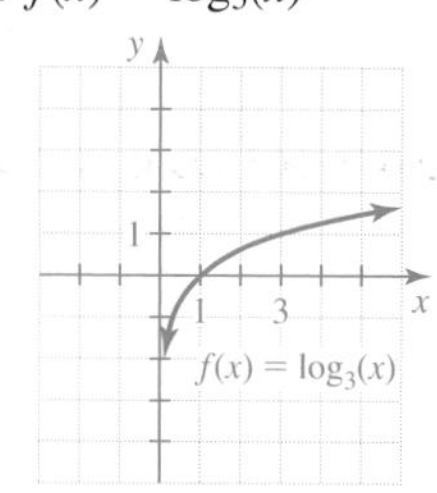

50. $g(x) = \log_{10}(x)$

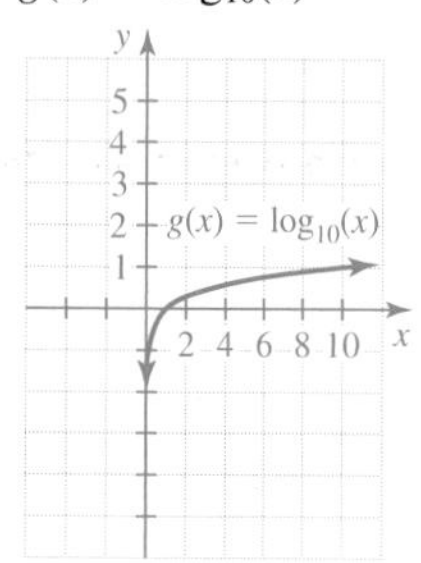

51. $y = \log_4(x)$

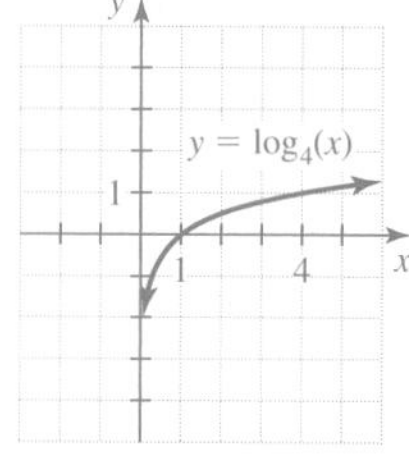

52. $y = \log_5(x)$

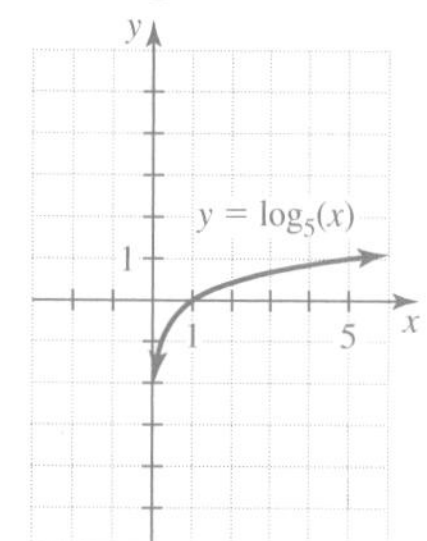

53. $h(x) = \log_{1/4}(x)$

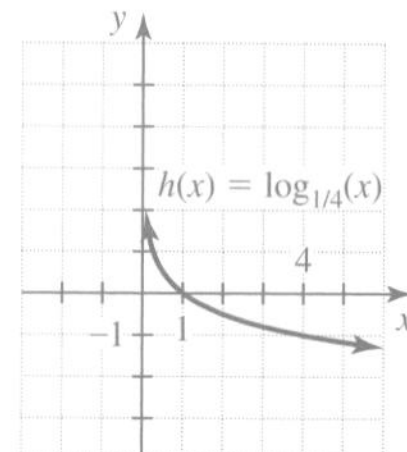

54. $y = \log_{1/3}(x)$

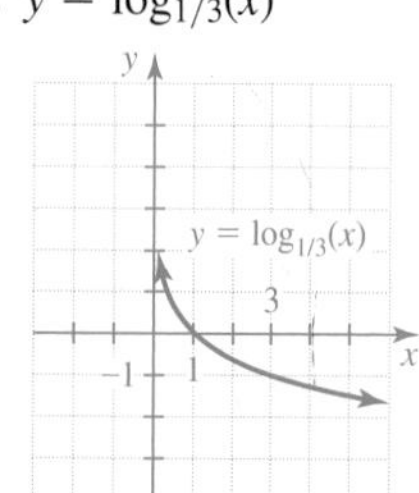

55. $y = \log_{1/5}(x)$

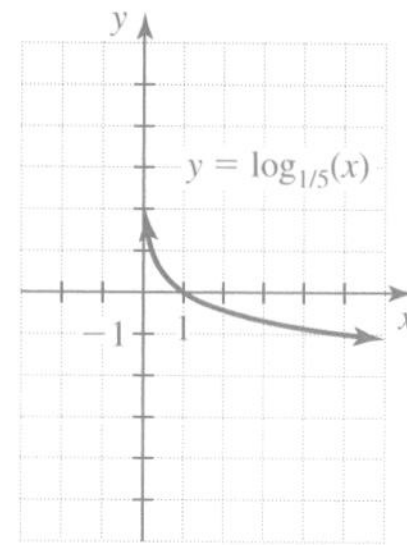

56. $y = \log_{1/6}(x)$

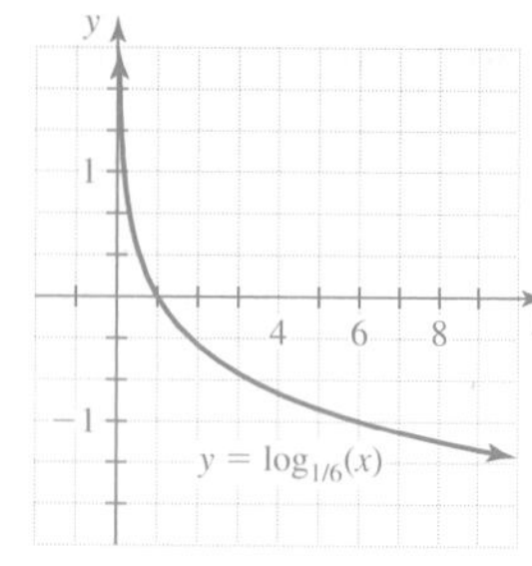

Find the inverse of each function. See Example 6.

57. $f(x) = 6^x$
$f^{-1}(x) = \log_6(x)$

58. $f(x) = 4^x$
$f^{-1}(x) = \log_4(x)$

59. $f(x) = \ln(x)$
$f^{-1}(x) = e^x$

60. $f(x) = \log(x)$
$f^{-1}(x) = 10^x$

61. $f(x) = \log_{1/2}(x)$
$f^{-1}(x) = \left(\frac{1}{2}\right)^x$

62. $f(x) = \log_{1/4}(x)$
$f^{-1}(x) = \left(\frac{1}{4}\right)^x$

Solve each equation. See Example 7.

63. $x = \left(\frac{1}{2}\right)^{-2}$ $\{4\}$

64. $x = 16^{-1/2}$ $\left\{\frac{1}{4}\right\}$

65. $5 = 25^x$ $\left\{\frac{1}{2}\right\}$

66. $0.1 = 10^x$ $\{-1\}$

67. $\log(x) = -3$ $\{0.001\}$

68. $\log(x) = 5$ $\{100{,}000\}$

69. $\log_x(36) = 2$ $\{6\}$

70. $\log_x(100) = 2$ $\{10\}$

71. $\log_x(5) = -1$ $\left\{\frac{1}{5}\right\}$

72. $\log_x(16) = -2$ $\left\{\frac{1}{4}\right\}$

73. $\log(x^2) = \log(9)$
$\{\pm 3\}$

74. $\ln(2x - 3) = \ln(x + 1)$
$\{4\}$

Use a calculator to solve each equation. Round answers to four decimal places.

75. $3 = 10^x$
$\{0.4771\}$

76. $10^x = 0.03$
$\{-1.5229\}$

77. $10^x = \frac{1}{2}$
$\{-0.3010\}$

78. $75 = 10^x$
$\{1.8751\}$

79. $e^x = 7.2$
$\{1.9741\}$

80. $e^{3x} = 0.4$
$\{-0.3054\}$

Fill in the missing entries in each table.

81.

x	$\frac{1}{4}$	$\frac{1}{2}$	1	4	16
$\log_2(x)$	−2	−1	0	2	4

82.

x	$\frac{1}{125}$	$\frac{1}{25}$	1	5	625
$\log_5(x)$	−3	−2	0	1	4

83.

x	16	4	1	$\frac{1}{2}$	$\frac{1}{4}$
$\log_{1/2}(x)$	−4	−2	0	1	2

84.

x	36	6	1	$\frac{1}{36}$	$\frac{1}{216}$
$\log_{1/6}(x)$	−2	−1	0	2	3

Solve each problem. See Example 8. Use a calculator as necessary.

85. ***Double your money.*** How long does it take \$5000 to grow to \$10,000 at 12% compounded continuously? 5.776 years

86. ***Half the rate.*** How long does it take \$5000 to grow to \$10,000 at 6% compounded continuously? 11.552 years

87. ***Earning interest.*** How long does it take to earn \$1000 in interest on a deposit of \$6000 at 8% compounded continuously? 1.927 years

88. ***Lottery winnings.*** How long does it take to earn \$1000 interest on a deposit of one million dollars at 9% compounded continuously? 4.054 days

89. ***Investing.*** An investment of \$10,000 in Bonavista Petroleum in 1997 grew to \$20,733 in 2002.

a) Assuming that the investment grew continuously, what was the annual growth rate? 14.58%

b) If Bonavista Petroleum continued to grow continuously at the rate from part a), then what would the investment be worth in 2010? \$66,576.60

90. ***Investing.*** An investment of \$10,000 in Baytex Energy in 1997 was worth \$19,568 in 2002.

a) Assuming that the investment grew continuously, what was the annual rate? 13.43%

b) If Baytex Energy continued to grow continuously at the rate from part a), then what would the investment be worth in 2012? \$74,927.17

In chemistry the pH of a solution is defined by

$$\text{pH} = -\log_{10}[H+],$$

where H+ is the hydrogen ion concentration of the solution in moles per liter. Distilled water has a pH of approximately 7. A solution with a pH under 7 is called an acid, and one with a pH over 7 is called a base.

91. ***Tomato juice.*** Tomato juice has a hydrogen ion concentration of $10^{-4.1}$ mole per liter (mol/L). Find the pH of tomato juice. 4.1

92. ***Stomach acid.*** The gastric juices in your stomach have a hydrogen ion concentration of 10^{-1} mol/L. Find the pH of your gastric juices. 1

93. ***Neuse River* pH.** The pH of a water sample is one of the many measurements of water quality done by the U.S. Geological Survey. The hydrogen ion concentration of the water in the Neuse River at New Bern, North Carolina, was 1.58×10^{-7} mol/L on April 8, 2002 (Water Resources for North Carolina, wwwnc.usgs.gov). What was the pH of the water at that time? 6.8

94. ***Roanoke River* pH.** On April 8, 2002, the hydrogen ion concentration of the water in the Roanoke River at Janesville, North Carolina, was 1.995×10^{-7} mol/L (Water Resources for North Carolina, wwwnc.usgs.gov). What was the pH of the water at that time? 6.7

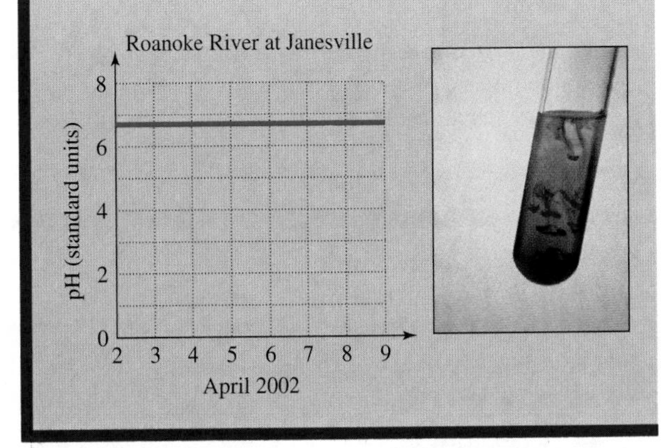

Figure for Exercise 94

Solve each problem.

95. ***Sound level.*** The level of sound in decibels (dB) is given by the formula

$$L = 10 \cdot \log(I \times 10^{12}),$$

where I is the intensity of the sound in watts per square meter. If the intensity of the sound at a rock concert is 0.001 watt per square meter at a distance of 75 meters from the stage, then what is the level of the sound at this point in the audience? 90 dB

96. ***Logistic growth.*** If a rancher has one cow with a contagious disease in a herd of 1000, then the time in days t for n of the cows to become infected is modeled by

$$t = -5 \cdot \ln\left(\frac{1000 - n}{999n}\right).$$

Find the number of days that it takes for the disease to spread to 100, 200, 998, and 999 cows. This model, called a *logistic growth model,* describes how a disease can spread very rapidly at first and then very slowly as nearly all of the population has become infected. See the figure on the next page. 23.5, 27.6, 65.6, 69.1 days

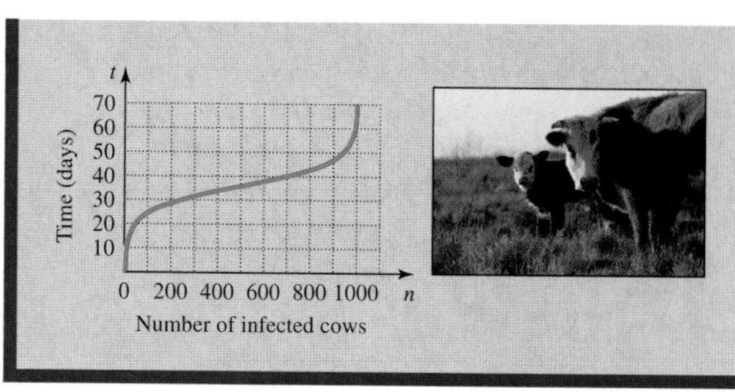

Figure for Exercise 96

Getting More Involved

97. ***Discussion***

Use the switch-and-solve method from Chapter 9 to find the inverse of the function $f(x) = 5 + \log_2(x - 3)$. State the domain and range of the inverse function.
$f^{-1}(x) = 2^{x-5} + 3, (-\infty, \infty), (3, \infty)$

98. ***Discussion***

Find the inverse of the function $f(x) = 2 + e^{x+4}$.

State the domain and range of the inverse function.
$f^{-1}(x) = \ln(x - 2) - 4, (2, \infty), (-\infty, \infty)$

Graphing Calculator Exercises

99. ***Composition of inverses.*** Graph the functions $y = \ln(e^x)$ and $y = e^{\ln(x)}$. Explain the similarities and differences between the graphs.
$y = \ln(e^x) = x$ for $-\infty < x < \infty$, $y = e^{\ln(x)} = x$ for $0 < x < \infty$

100. ***The population bomb.*** The population of the earth is growing continuously with an annual rate of about 1.6%. If the present population is 6 billion, then the function $y = 6e^{0.016x}$ gives the population in billions x years from now. Graph this function for $0 \le x \le 200$. What will the population be in 100 years and in 200 years?
29.7 billion, 147.2 billion

12.3 Properties of Logarithms

In this Section

- **Product Rule for Logarithms**
- **Quotient Rule for Logarithms**
- **Power Rule for Logarithms**
- **Inverse Properties**
- **Using the Properties**

The properties of logarithms are very similar to the properties of exponents because *logarithms are exponents.* In this section we use the properties of exponents to write some properties of logarithms. The properties will be used in solving logarithmic equations in Section 12.4.

Product Rule for Logarithms

If $M = a^x$ and $N = a^y$, we can use the product rule for exponents to write

$$MN = a^x \cdot a^y = a^{x+y}.$$

The equation $MN = a^{x+y}$ is equivalent to

$$\log_a(MN) = x + y.$$

Because $M = a^x$ and $N = a^y$ are equivalent to $x = \log_a(M)$ and $y = \log_a(N)$, we can replace x and y in $\log_a(MN) = x + y$ to get

$$\log_a(MN) = \log_a(M) + \log_a(N).$$

So *the logarithm of a product is the sum of the logarithms,* provided that all of the logarithms are defined. This rule is called the **product rule for logarithms.**

Product Rule for Logarithms

$$\log_a(MN) = \log_a(M) + \log_a(N)$$

Calculator Close-Up

You can illustrate the product rule for logarithms with a graphing calculator.

```
log(7)+log(8)
     1.748188027
log(56)
     1.748188027
```

EXAMPLE 1

Using the product rule for logarithms

Write each expression as a single logarithm.

a) $\log_2(7) + \log_2(5)$ **b)** $\ln(\sqrt{2}) + \ln(\sqrt{3})$

Solution

a) $\log_2(7) + \log_2(5) = \log_2(35)$ Product rule for logarithms

b) $\ln(\sqrt{2}) + \ln(\sqrt{3}) = \ln(\sqrt{6})$ Product rule for logarithms

Now do Exercises 7–18

Calculator Close-Up

You can illustrate the quotient rule for logarithms with a graphing calculator.

```
ln(99/2)
           3.90197267
ln(99)-ln(2)
           3.90197267
```

Quotient Rule for Logarithms

If $M = a^x$ and $N = a^y$, we can use the quotient rule for exponents to write

$$\frac{M}{N} = \frac{a^x}{a^y} = a^{x-y}.$$

By the definition of logarithm, $\frac{M}{N} = a^{x-y}$ is equivalent to

$$\log_a\left(\frac{M}{N}\right) = x - y.$$

Because $x = \log_a(M)$ and $y = \log_a(N)$, we have

$$\log_a\left(\frac{M}{N}\right) = \log_a(M) - \log_a(N).$$

So *the logarithm of a quotient is equal to the difference of the logarithms,* provided that all logarithms are defined. This rule is called the **quotient rule for logarithms.**

Quotient Rule for Logarithms

$$\log_a\left(\frac{M}{N}\right) = \log_a(M) - \log_a(N)$$

EXAMPLE 2

Using the quotient rule for logarithms

Write each expression as a single logarithm.

a) $\log_2(3) - \log_2(7)$ **b)** $\ln(w^8) - \ln(w^2)$

Solution

a) $\log_2(3) - \log_2(7) = \log_2\left(\frac{3}{7}\right)$ Quotient rule for logarithms

b) $\ln(w^8) - \ln(w^2) = \ln\left(\frac{w^8}{w^2}\right)$ Quotient rule for logarithms

$= \ln(w^6)$ Quotient rule for exponents

Now do Exercises 19–30

Calculator Close-Up

You can illustrate the power rule for logarithms with a graphing calculator.

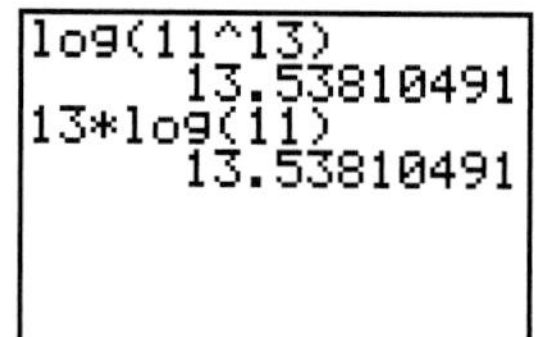

Power Rule for Logarithms

If $M = a^x$, we can use the power rule for exponents to write

$$M^N = (a^x)^N = a^{Nx}.$$

By the definition of logarithms, $M^N = a^{Nx}$ is equivalent to

$$\log_a(M^N) = Nx.$$

Because $x = \log_a(M)$, we have

$$\log_a(M^N) = N \cdot \log_a(M).$$

So *the logarithm of a power of a number is the power times the logarithm of the number,* provided that all logarithms are defined. This rule is called the **power rule for logarithms.**

Power Rule for Logarithms

$$\log_a(M^N) = N \cdot \log_a(M)$$

EXAMPLE 3

Using the power rule for logarithms

Rewrite each logarithm in terms of log(2).

a) $\log(2^{10})$ **b)** $\log(\sqrt{2})$ **c)** $\log\left(\frac{1}{2}\right)$

Solution

a) $\log(2^{10}) = 10 \cdot \log(2)$ Power rule for logarithms

b) $\log(\sqrt{2}) = \log(2^{1/2})$ Write $\sqrt{2}$ as a power of 2.

$= \frac{1}{2}\log(2)$ Power rule for logarithms

c) $\log\left(\frac{1}{2}\right) = \log(2^{-1})$ Write $\frac{1}{2}$ as a power of 2.

$= -1 \cdot \log(2)$ Power rule for logarithms

$= -\log(2)$

Now do Exercises 31–36

Inverse Properties

An exponential function and logarithmic function with the same base are inverses of each other. For example, the logarithm of 32 base 2 is 5 and the fifth power of 2 is 32. In symbols, we have

$$2^{\log_2(32)} = 2^5 = 32.$$

If we raise 3 to the fourth power, we get 81; and if we find the base-3 logarithm of 81, we get 4. In symbols, we have

$$\log_3(3^4) = \log_3(81) = 4.$$

We can state the inverse relationship between exponential and logarithm functions in general with the following inverse properties:

Inverse Properties

1. $\log_a(a^M) = M$ **2.** $a^{\log_a(M)} = M$

EXAMPLE 4

Using the inverse properties

Simplify each expression.

a) $\ln(e^5)$ **b)** $2^{\log_2(8)}$

Solution

a) Using the first inverse property, we get $\ln(e^5) = 5$.

b) Using the second inverse property, we get $2^{\log_2(8)} = 8$.

Now do Exercises 37–44

Note that there is more than one way to simplify the expressions in Example 4. Using the power rule for logarithms and the fact that $\ln(e) = 1$, we have $\ln(e^5) = 5 \cdot \ln(e) = 5$. Using $\log_2(8) = 3$, we have $2^{\log_2(8)} = 2^3 = 8$.

Study Tip

Keep track of your time for one entire week. Account for how you spend every half hour. Add up your totals for sleep, study, work, and recreation. You should be sleeping 50 to 60 hours per week and studying 1 to 2 hours for every hour you spend in the classroom.

Using the Properties

We have already seen many properties of logarithms. There are three properties that we have not yet formally stated. Because $a^1 = a$ and $a^0 = 1$, we have $\log_a(a) = 1$ and $\log_a(1) = 0$ for any positive number a. If we apply the quotient rule to $\log_a(1/N)$, we get

$$\log_a\left(\frac{1}{N}\right) = \log_a(1) - \log_a(N) = 0 - \log_a(N) = -\log_a(N).$$

So $\log_a\left(\frac{1}{N}\right) = -\log_a(N)$. These three new properties along with all of the other properties of logarithms are summarized as follows.

Properties of Logarithms

If M, N, and a are positive numbers, $a \neq 1$, then

1. $\log_a(a) = 1$ **2.** $\log_a(1) = 0$

3. $\log_a(a^M) = M$ **4.** $a^{\log_a(M)} = M$ Inverse properties

5. $\log_a(MN) = \log_a(M) + \log_a(N)$ Product rule

6. $\log_a\left(\frac{M}{N}\right) = \log_a(M) - \log_a(N)$ Quotient rule

7. $\log_a\left(\frac{1}{N}\right) = -\log_a(N)$ **8.** $\log_a(M^N) = N \cdot \log_a(M)$ Power rule

We have already seen several ways in which to use the properties of logarithms. In Examples 5, 6, and 7 we see more uses of the properties. First we use the rules of logarithms to write the logarithm of a complicated expression in terms of logarithms of simpler expressions.

EXAMPLE 5

Using the properties of logarithms

Rewrite each expression in terms of log(2) and/or log(3).

a) $\log(6)$ **b)** $\log(16)$ **c)** $\log\left(\frac{9}{2}\right)$ **d)** $\log\left(\frac{1}{3}\right)$

Calculator Close-Up

Examine the values of log(9/2), log(9) − log(2), and log(9)/log(2).

```
log(9/2)
          .6532125138
log(9)-log(2)
          .6532125138
log(9)/log(2)
          3.169925001
```

Solution

a) $\log(6) = \log(2 \cdot 3)$

$= \log(2) + \log(3)$ Product rule

b) $\log(16) = \log(2^4)$

$= 4 \cdot \log(2)$ Power rule

c) $\log\left(\frac{9}{2}\right) = \log(9) - \log(2)$ Quotient rule

$= \log(3^2) - \log(2)$

$= 2 \cdot \log(3) - \log(2)$ Power rule

d) $\log\left(\frac{1}{3}\right) = -\log(3)$ Property 7

Now do Exercises 45–56

CAUTION Do not confuse $\frac{\log(9)}{\log(2)}$ with $\log\left(\frac{9}{2}\right)$. We can use the quotient rule to write $\log\left(\frac{9}{2}\right) = \log(9) - \log(2)$, but $\frac{\log(9)}{\log(2)} \neq \log(9) - \log(2)$. The expression $\frac{\log(9)}{\log(2)}$ means $\log(9) \div \log(2)$. Use your calculator to verify these two statements.

The properties of logarithms can be used to combine several logarithms into a single logarithm (as in Examples 1 and 2) or to write a logarithm of a complicated expression in terms of logarithms of simpler expressions.

EXAMPLE 6

Using the properties of logarithms

Rewrite each expression as a sum or difference of multiples of logarithms.

a) $\log\left(\frac{xz}{y}\right)$ **b)** $\log_3\left(\frac{(x-3)^{2/3}}{\sqrt{x}}\right)$

Solution

a) $\log\left(\frac{xz}{y}\right) = \log(xz) - \log(y)$ Quotient rule

$= \log(x) + \log(z) - \log(y)$ Product rule

b) $\log_3\left(\frac{(x-3)^{2/3}}{\sqrt{x}}\right) = \log_3\left((x-3)^{2/3}\right) - \log_3\left(x^{1/2}\right)$ Quotient rule

$= \frac{2}{3}\log_3(x-3) - \frac{1}{2}\log_3(x)$ Power rule

Now do Exercises 57–68

In Example 7 we use the properties of logarithms to convert expressions involving several logarithms into a single logarithm. The skills we are learning here will be used to solve logarithmic equations in Section 12.4.

EXAMPLE 7

Combining logarithms

Rewrite each expression as a single logarithm.

a) $\frac{1}{2}\log(x) - 2 \cdot \log(x + 1)$ **b)** $3 \cdot \log(y) + \frac{1}{2}\log(z) - \log(x)$

Solution

a) $\frac{1}{2}\log(x) - 2 \cdot \log(x + 1) = \log(x^{1/2}) - \log((x + 1)^2)$ Power rule

$= \log\left(\frac{\sqrt{x}}{(x + 1)^2}\right)$ Quotient rule

b) $3 \cdot \log(y) + \frac{1}{2}\log(z) - \log(x) = \log(y^3) + \log(\sqrt{z}) - \log(x)$ Power rule

$= \log(y^3 \cdot \sqrt{z}) - \log(x)$ Product rule

$= \log\left(\frac{y^3\sqrt{z}}{x}\right)$ Quotient rule

Now do Exercises 69–80

Warm-Ups

True or false? Explain your answer.

1. $\log_2\left(\frac{x^2}{8}\right) = \log_2(x^2) - 3$ True
2. $\frac{\log(100)}{\log(10)} = \log(100) - \log(10)$ False
3. $\ln(\sqrt{2}) = \frac{\ln(2)}{2}$ True
4. $3^{\log_3(17)} = 17$ True
5. $\log_2\left(\frac{1}{8}\right) = \frac{1}{\log_2(8)}$ False
6. $\ln(8) = 3 \cdot \ln(2)$ True
7. $\ln(1) = e$ False
8. $\frac{\log(100)}{10} = \log(10)$ False
9. $\frac{\log_2(8)}{\log_2(2)} = \log_2(4)$ False
10. $\ln(2) + \ln(3) - \ln(7) = \ln\left(\frac{6}{7}\right)$ True

12.3 Exercises

Boost your GRADE at mathzone.com!

MathZone
- Practice Problems
- Self-Tests
- Videos
- Net Tutor
- e-Professors

Reading and Writing *After reading this section, write out the answers to these questions. Use complete sentences.*

1. What is the product rule for logarithms?
   The product rule for logarithms states that $\log_a(MN) = \log_a(M) + \log_a(N)$.
2. What is the quotient rule for logarithms?
   The quotient rule for logarithms states that $\log_a(M/N) = \log_a(M) - \log_a(N)$.
3. What is the power rule for logarithms?
   The power rule for logarithms states that $\log_a(M^N) = N \cdot \log_a(M)$.
4. Why is it true that $\log_a(a^M) = M$?
   Since $\log_a(a^M)$ is the exponent used on a to obtain a^M, we have $\log_a(a^M) = M$.
5. Why is it true that $a^{\log_a(M)} = M$?
   Since $\log_a(M)$ is the exponent you would use on a to obtain M, using $\log_a(M)$ as the exponent produces M: $a^{\log_a(M)} = M$.
6. Why is it true that $\log_a(1) = 0$ for $a > 0$ and $a \neq 1$?
   We have $\log_a(1) = 0$ because $a^0 = 1$.

Assume all variables involved in logarithms represent numbers for which the logarithms are defined.

Write each expression as a single logarithm and simplify. See Example 1.

7. $\log(3) + \log(7)$ $\log(21)$
8. $\ln(5) + \ln(4)$ $\ln(20)$
9. $\log_3(\sqrt{5}) + \log_3(\sqrt{x})$ $\log_3(\sqrt{5x})$
10. $\ln(\sqrt{x}) + \ln(\sqrt{y})$ $\ln(\sqrt{xy})$
11. $\log(x^2) + \log(x^3)$ $\log(x^5)$
12. $\ln(a^3) + \ln(a^5)$ $\ln(a^8)$
13. $\ln(2) + \ln(3) + \ln(5)$ $\ln(30)$
14. $\log_2(x) + \log_2(y) + \log_2(z)$ $\log_2(xyz)$
15. $\log(x) + \log(x + 3)$ $\log(x^2 + 3x)$
16. $\ln(x - 1) + \ln(x + 1)$ $\ln(x^2 - 1)$
17. $\log_2(x - 3) + \log_2(x + 2)$ $\log_2(x^2 - x - 6)$
18. $\log_3(x - 5) + \log_3(x - 4)$ $\log_3(x^2 - 9x + 20)$

Write each expression as a single logarithm. See Example 2.

19. $\log(8) - \log(2)$ $\log(4)$
20. $\ln(3) - \ln(6)$ $\ln\left(\frac{1}{2}\right)$
21. $\log_2(x^6) - \log_2(x^2)$ $\log_2(x^4)$
22. $\ln(w^9) - \ln(w^3)$ $\ln(w^6)$
23. $\log(\sqrt{10}) - \log(\sqrt{2})$ $\log(\sqrt{5})$
24. $\log_3(\sqrt{6}) - \log_3(\sqrt{3})$ $\log_3(\sqrt{2})$
25. $\ln(4h - 8) - \ln(4)$ $\ln(h - 2)$
26. $\log(3x - 6) - \log(3)$ $\log(x - 2)$
27. $\log_2(w^2 - 4) - \log_2(w + 2)$ $\log_2(w - 2)$
28. $\log_3(k^2 - 9) - \log_3(k - 3)$ $\log_3(k + 3)$
29. $\ln(x^2 + x - 6) - \ln(x + 3)$ $\ln(x - 2)$
30. $\ln(t^2 - t - 12) - \ln(t - 4)$ $\ln(t + 3)$

Write each expression in terms of $\log(3)$. *See Example 3.*

31. $\log(27)$ $3\log(3)$
32. $\log\left(\frac{1}{9}\right)$ $-2\log(3)$
33. $\log(\sqrt{3})$ $\frac{1}{2}\log(3)$
34. $\log(\sqrt[4]{3})$ $\frac{1}{4}\log(3)$
35. $\log(3^x)$ $x\log(3)$
36. $\log(3^{-99})$ $-99\log(3)$

Simplify each expression. See Example 4.

37. $\log_2(2^{10})$ 10
38. $\ln(e^9)$ 9
39. $5^{\log_5(19)}$ 19
40. $10^{\log(2.3)}$ 2.3
41. $\log(10^8)$ 8
42. $\log_4(4^5)$ 5
43. $e^{\ln(4.3)}$ 4.3
44. $3^{\log_3(5.5)}$ 5.5

Rewrite each expression in terms of $\log(3)$ *and/or* $\log(5)$. *See Example 5.*

45. $\log(15)$
    $\log(3) + \log(5)$
46. $\log(9)$
    $2\log(3)$
47. $\log\left(\frac{5}{3}\right)$
    $\log(5) - \log(3)$
48. $\log\left(\frac{3}{5}\right)$
    $\log(3) - \log(5)$
49. $\log(25)$
    $2\log(5)$
50. $\log\left(\frac{1}{27}\right)$
    $-3\log(3)$
51. $\log(75)$
    $2\log(5) + \log(3)$
52. $\log(0.6)$
    $\log(3) - \log(5)$
53. $\log\left(\frac{1}{3}\right)$
    $-\log(3)$
54. $\log(45)$
    $2\log(3) + \log(5)$
55. $\log(0.2)$
    $-\log(5)$
56. $\log\left(\frac{9}{25}\right)$
    $2\log(3) - 2\log(5)$

Rewrite each expression as a sum or a difference of multiples of logarithms. See Example 6.

57. $\log(xyz)$ $\log(x) + \log(y) + \log(z)$

58. $\log(3y)$ $\log(3) + \log(y)$

59. $\log_2(8x)$ $3 + \log_2(x)$

60. $\log_2(16y)$ $4 + \log_2(y)$

61. $\ln\left(\frac{x}{y}\right)$ $\ln(x) - \ln(y)$

62. $\ln\left(\frac{z}{3}\right)$ $\ln(z) - \ln(3)$

63. $\log(10x^2)$ $1 + 2\log(x)$

64. $\log(100\sqrt{x})$ $2 + \frac{1}{2}\log(x)$

65. $\log_5\left(\frac{(x-3)^2}{\sqrt{w}}\right)$ $2\log_5(x-3) - \frac{1}{2}\log_5(w)$

66. $\log_3\left(\frac{(y+6)^3}{y-5}\right)$ $3\log_3(y+6) - \log_3(y-5)$

67. $\ln\left(\frac{yz\sqrt{x}}{w}\right)$ $\ln(y) + \ln(z) + \frac{1}{2}\ln(x) - \ln(w)$

68. $\ln\left(\frac{(x-1)\sqrt{w}}{x^3}\right)$ $\ln(x-1) + \frac{1}{2}\ln(w) - 3\ln(x)$

Rewrite each expression as a single logarithm. See Example 7.

69. $\log(x) + \log(x-1)$ $\log(x^2 - x)$

70. $\log_2(x-2) + \log_2(5)$ $\log_2(5x - 10)$

71. $\ln(3x-6) - \ln(x-2)$ $\ln(3)$

72. $\log_3(x^2-1) - \log_3(x-1)$ $\log_3(x+1)$

73. $\ln(x) - \ln(w) + \ln(z)$ $\ln\left(\frac{xz}{w}\right)$

74. $\ln(x) - \ln(3) - \ln(7)$ $\ln\left(\frac{x}{21}\right)$

75. $3 \cdot \ln(y) + 2 \cdot \ln(x) - \ln(w)$ $\ln\left(\frac{x^2y^3}{w}\right)$

76. $5 \cdot \ln(r) + 3 \cdot \ln(t) - 4 \cdot \ln(s)$ $\ln\left(\frac{r^5t^3}{s^4}\right)$

77. $\frac{1}{2}\log(x-3) - \frac{2}{3}\log(x+1)$ $\log\left(\frac{(x-3)^{1/2}}{(x+1)^{2/3}}\right)$

78. $\frac{1}{2}\log(y-4) + \frac{1}{2}\log(y+4)$ $\log(\sqrt{y^2-16})$

79. $\frac{2}{3}\log_2(x-1) - \frac{1}{4}\log_2(x+2)$ $\log_2\left(\frac{(x-1)^{2/3}}{(x+2)^{1/4}}\right)$

80. $\frac{1}{2}\log_3(y+3) + 6 \cdot \log_3(y)$ $\log_3(y^6\sqrt{y+3})$

Determine whether each equation is true or false.

81. $\log(56) = \log(7) \cdot \log(8)$
False

82. $\log\left(\frac{5}{9}\right) = \frac{\log(5)}{\log(9)}$
False

83. $\log_2(4^2) = (\log_2(4))^2$
True

84. $\ln(4^2) = (\ln(4))^2$
False

85. $\ln(25) = 2 \cdot \ln(5)$
True

86. $\ln(3e) = 1 + \ln(3)$
True

87. $\frac{\log_2(64)}{\log_2(8)} = \log_2(8)$
False

88. $\frac{\log_2(16)}{\log_2(4)} = \log_2(4)$
True

89. $\log\left(\frac{1}{3}\right) = -\log(3)$
True

90. $\log_2(8 \cdot 2^{59}) = 62$
True

91. $\log_2(16^5) = 20$
True

92. $\log_2\left(\frac{5}{2}\right) = \log_2(5) - 1$
True

93. $\log(10^3) = 3$
True

94. $\log_3(3^7) = 7$
True

95. $\log(100 + 3) = 2 + \log(3)$
False

96. $\frac{\log_7(32)}{\log_7(8)} = \frac{5}{3}$
True

Solve each problem.

97. ***Richter scale.*** The Richter scale rating of an earthquake is given by the formula $r = \log(I) - \log(I_0)$, where I is the *intensity* of the earthquake and I_0 is the intensity of a small "benchmark" earthquake. Use the appropriate property of logarithms to rewrite this formula using a single logarithm. Find r if $I = 100 \cdot I_0$.
$r = \log(I/I_0)$, $r = 2$

98. ***Diversity index.*** The U.S.G.S. measures the quality of a water sample by using the diversity index d, given by

$$d = -[p_1 \cdot \log_2(p_1) + p_2 \cdot \log_2(p_2) + \cdots + p_n \cdot \log_2(p_n)],$$

where n is the number of different taxons (biological classifications) represented in the sample and p_1 through p_n are the percentages of organisms in each of the n taxons. The value of d ranges from 0 when all organisms in the water sample are the same to some positive number when all organisms in the sample are different. If two-thirds of the organisms in a water sample are in one taxon and one-third of the organisms are in a second taxon, then $n = 2$ and

$$d = -\left[\frac{2}{3}\log_2\left(\frac{2}{3}\right) + \frac{1}{3}\log_2\left(\frac{1}{3}\right)\right].$$

Use the properties of logarithms to write the expression on the right-hand side as $\log_2\left(\frac{3\sqrt[3]{2}}{2}\right)$. (In Section 12.4 you will learn how to evaluate a base-2 logarithm using a calculator.)

Getting More Involved

99. *Discussion*

Which of the following equations is an identity? Explain.

a) $\ln(3x) = \ln(3) \cdot \ln(x)$
b) $\ln(3x) = \ln(3) + \ln(x)$
c) $\ln(3x) = 3 \cdot \ln(x)$
d) $\ln(3x) = \ln(x^3)$ b

100. *Discussion*

Which of the following expressions is not equal to $\log(5^{2/3})$? Explain.

a) $\frac{2}{3}\log(5)$ **b)** $\frac{\log(5) + \log(5)}{3}$
c) $(\log(5))^{2/3}$ **d)** $\frac{1}{3}\log(25)$ c

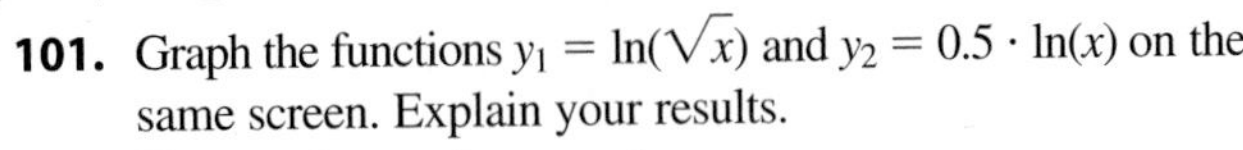

Graphing Calculator Exercises

101. Graph the functions $y_1 = \ln(\sqrt{x})$ and $y_2 = 0.5 \cdot \ln(x)$ on the same screen. Explain your results.
The graphs are the same because

$$\ln(\sqrt{x}) = \ln(x^{1/2}) = \frac{1}{2}\ln(x).$$

102. Graph the functions $y_1 = \log(x)$, $y_2 = \log(10x)$, $y_3 = \log(100x)$, and $y_4 = \log(1000x)$ using the viewing window $-2 \le x \le 5$ and $-2 \le y \le 5$. Why do these curves appear as they do?
Because $\log(10x) = 1 + \log(x)$, $\log(100x) = 2 + \log(x)$, and $\log(1000x) = 3 + \log(x)$; the graphs lie 1, 2, and 3 units above $y = \log(x)$.

103. Graph the function $y = \log(e^x)$. Explain why the graph is a straight line. What is its slope?
The graph is a straight line because $\log(e^x) = x\log(e) \approx 0.434x$. The slope is $\log(e)$ or approximately 0.434.

12.4 Solving Equations and Applications

In this Section

- **Logarithmic Equations**
- **Exponential Equations**
- **Changing the Base**
- **Strategy for Solving Equations**
- **Applications**

We solved some equations involving exponents and logarithms in Sections 12.1 and 12.2. In this section we use the properties of exponents and logarithms to solve more complex equations.

Logarithmic Equations

The main tool that we have for solving logarithmic equations is the definition of logarithms: $y = \log_a(x)$ if and only if $a^y = x$. We can use the definition to rewrite any equation that has only one logarithm as an equivalent exponential equation.

EXAMPLE 1

A logarithmic equation with only one logarithm

Solve $\log(x + 3) = 2$.

Solution

Write the equivalent exponential equation:

$$\begin{aligned} \log(x+3) &= 2 && \text{Original equation} \\ 10^2 &= x + 3 && \text{Definition of logarithm} \\ 100 &= x + 3 \\ 97 &= x \end{aligned}$$

Check: $\log(97 + 3) = \log(100) = 2$. The solution set is $\{97\}$.

Now do Exercises 3–8

In Example 2 we use the product rule for logarithms to write a sum of two logarithms as a single logarithm.

EXAMPLE 2

Teaching Tip Remind students to combine logarithms whenever possible.

Using the product rule to solve an equation

Solve $\log_2(x + 3) + \log_2(x - 3) = 4$.

Solution

Rewrite the sum of the logarithms as the logarithm of a product:

$$\log_2(x + 3) + \log_2(x - 3) = 4 \quad \text{Original equation}$$
$$\log_2[(x + 3)(x - 3)] = 4 \quad \text{Product rule}$$
$$\log_2[x^2 - 9] = 4 \quad \text{Multiply the binomials.}$$
$$x^2 - 9 = 2^4 \quad \text{Definition of logarithm}$$
$$x^2 - 9 = 16$$
$$x^2 = 25$$
$$x = \pm 5 \quad \text{Even-root property}$$

To check, first let $x = -5$ in the original equation:

$$\log_2(-5 + 3) + \log_2(-5 - 3) = 4$$
$$\log_2(-2) + \log_2(-8) = 4 \quad \text{Incorrect}$$

Because the domain of any logarithm function is the set of positive real numbers, these logarithms are undefined. Now check $x = 5$ in the original equation:

$$\log_2(5 + 3) + \log_2(5 - 3) = 4$$
$$\log_2(8) + \log_2(2) = 4$$
$$3 + 1 = 4 \quad \text{Correct}$$

The solution set is $\{5\}$.

Now do Exercises 9–16

CAUTION Always check that your solutions to a logarithmic equation do not produce undefined logarithms in the original equation.

EXAMPLE 3

Calculator Close-Up

Graph

$$y_1 = \log(x) + \log(x - 1)$$

and

$$y_2 = \log(8x - 12) - \log(2)$$

to see the two solutions to the equation in Example 3.

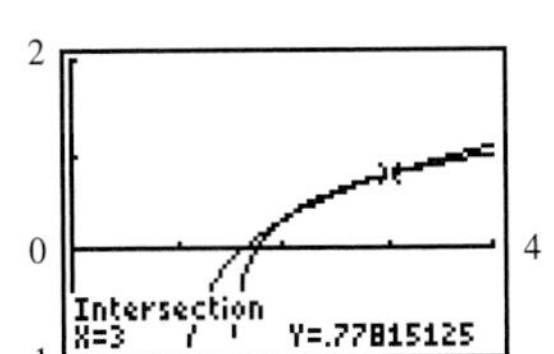

Using the one-to-one property of logarithms

Solve $\log(x) + \log(x - 1) = \log(8x - 12) - \log(2)$.

Solution

Apply the product rule to the left-hand side and the quotient rule to the right-hand side to get a single logarithm on each side:

$$\log(x) + \log(x - 1) = \log(8x - 12) - \log(2).$$
$$\log[x(x - 1)] = \log\left(\frac{8x - 12}{2}\right) \quad \text{Product rule; quotient rule}$$
$$\log(x^2 - x) = \log(4x - 6) \quad \text{Simplify.}$$
$$x^2 - x = 4x - 6 \quad \text{One-to-one property of logarithms}$$
$$x^2 - 5x + 6 = 0$$
$$(x - 2)(x - 3) = 0$$
$$x - 2 = 0 \quad \text{or} \quad x - 3 = 0$$
$$x = 2 \quad \text{or} \quad x = 3$$

Neither $x = 2$ nor $x = 3$ produces undefined terms in the original equation. Use a calculator to check that they both satisfy the original equation. The solution set is $\{2, 3\}$.

Now do Exercises 17–22

CAUTION The product rule, quotient rule, and power rule do not eliminate logarithms from equations. To do so, we use the definition to change $y = \log_a(x)$ into $a^y = x$ or the one-to-one property to change $\log_a(m) = \log_a(n)$ into $m = n$.

Exponential Equations

If an equation has a single exponential expression, we can write the equivalent logarithmic equation.

EXAMPLE 4

A single exponential expression

Find the exact solution to $2^x = 10$.

Solution

The equivalent logarithmic equation is

$$x = \log_2(10).$$

The solution set is $\{\log_2(10)\}$. The number $\log_2(10)$ is the exact solution to the equation. Later in this section you will learn how to use the base-change formula to find an approximate value for an expression of this type.

Now do Exercises 23–26

In Section 12.1 we solved some exponential equations by writing each side as a power of the same base and then applying the one-to-one property of exponential functions. We review that method in Example 5.

EXAMPLE 5

Powers of the same base

Solve $2^{(x^2)} = 4^{3x-4}$.

Solution

We can write each side as a power of the same base:

$$2^{(x^2)} = (2^2)^{3x-4} \quad \text{Because } 4 = 2^2$$

$$2^{(x^2)} = 2^{6x-8} \quad \text{Power of a power rule}$$

$$x^2 = 6x - 8 \quad \text{One-to-one property of exponential functions}$$

$$x^2 - 6x + 8 = 0$$

$$(x - 4)(x - 2) = 0$$

$$x - 4 = 0 \quad \text{or} \quad x - 2 = 0$$

$$x = 4 \quad \text{or} \quad x = 2$$

Check $x = 2$ and $x = 4$ in the original equation. The solution set is $\{2, 4\}$.

Now do Exercises 27–30

Study Tip

Success in school depends on effective time management, which is all about goals. Write down your long-term, short-term, and daily goals. Assess them, develop methods for meeting them, and reward yourself when you do.

For some exponential equations we cannot write each side as a power of the same base as we did in Example 5. In this case we take a logarithm of each side and simplify, using the rules for logarithms.

EXAMPLE 6

Exponential equation with two different bases

Find the exact and approximate solution to $2^{x-1} = 3^x$.

Teaching Tip Another method that is tricky but simpler is to divide each side by 2^x and get $2^{-1} = (3/2)^x$. Then $x = \log_{3/2}(2^{-1})$.

Solution

We first take the base-10 logarithm of each side:

$$2^{x-1} = 3^x \quad \text{Original equation}$$

$$\log(2^{x-1}) = \log(3^x) \quad \text{Take log of each side.}$$

$$(x - 1)\log(2) = x \cdot \log(3) \quad \text{Power rule}$$

$$x \cdot \log(2) - \log(2) = x \cdot \log(3) \quad \text{Distributive property}$$

$$x \cdot \log(2) - x \cdot \log(3) = \log(2) \quad \text{Get all } x\text{-terms on one side.}$$

$$x[\log(2) - \log(3)] = \log(2) \quad \text{Factor out } x.$$

$$x = \frac{\log(2)}{\log(2) - \log(3)} \quad \text{Exact solution}$$

$$x \approx -1.7095 \quad \text{Approximate solution}$$

You can use a calculator to check -1.7095 in the original equation. As the first step of the solution, we could have taken the logarithm of each side using any base. We chose base 10 so that we could use a calculator to find an approximate solution from the exact solution.

Now do Exercises 31–36

Changing the Base

Scientific calculators have an x^y key for computing any power of any base, in addition to the function keys for computing 10^x and e^x. For logarithms we have the keys ln and log, but there are no function keys for logarithms using other bases. To solve this problem, we develop a formula for expressing a base-a logarithm in terms of base-b logarithms.

If $y = \log_a(M)$, then $a^y = M$. Now we solve $a^y = M$ for y, using base-b logarithms:

$$a^y = M$$

$$\log_b(a^y) = \log_b(M) \quad \text{Take the base-}b\text{ logarithm of each side.}$$

$$y \cdot \log_b(a) = \log_b(M) \quad \text{Power rule}$$

$$y = \frac{\log_b(M)}{\log_b(a)} \quad \text{Divide each side by } \log_b(a).$$

Because $y = \log_a(M)$, we can write $\log_a(M)$ in terms of base-b logarithms.

Calculator Close-Up

The base-change formula allows you to graph logarithmic functions with bases other than e and 10. For example, to graph $y = \log_2(x)$, graph $y = \ln(x)/\ln(2)$.

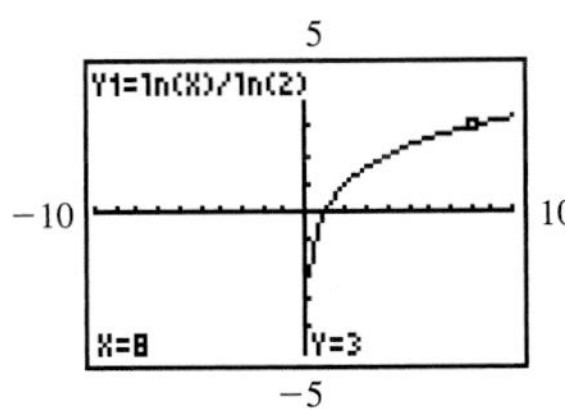

Base-Change Formula

If a and b are positive numbers not equal to 1 and M is positive, then

$$\log_a(M) = \frac{\log_b(M)}{\log_b(a)}.$$

In words, we take the logarithm with the new base and divide by the logarithm of the old base. The most important use of the base-change formula is to find base-a logarithms using a calculator. If the new base is 10 or e, then

$$\log_a(M) = \frac{\log(M)}{\log(a)} = \frac{\ln(M)}{\ln(a)}.$$

EXAMPLE 7

Using the base-change formula

Find $\log_7(99)$ to four decimal places.

Solution

Use the base-change formula with $a = 7$ and $b = 10$:

$$\log_7(99) = \frac{\log(99)}{\log(7)} \approx 2.3614$$

Check by finding $7^{2.3614}$ with your calculator. Note that we also have

$$\log_7(99) = \frac{\ln(99)}{\ln(7)} \approx 2.3614.$$

Now do Exercises 37–44

Strategy for Solving Equations

There is no formula that will solve every equation in this section. However, we have a strategy for solving exponential and logarithmic equations. The following list summarizes the ideas that we need for solving these equations.

Solving Exponential and Logarithmic Equations

1. If the equation has a single logarithm or a single exponential expression, rewrite the equation using the definition $y = \log_a(x)$ if and only if $a^y = x$.
2. Use the properties of logarithms to combine logarithms as much as possible.
3. Use the one-to-one properties:
   a) If $\log_a(m) = \log_a(n)$, then $m = n$.
   b) If $a^m = a^n$, then $m = n$.
4. To get an approximate solution of an exponential equation, take the common or natural logarithm of each side of the equation.

Applications

In compound interest problems, logarithms are used to find the time it takes for money to grow to a specified amount.

EXAMPLE 8

Finding the time

If \$500 is deposited into an account paying 8% compounded quarterly, then in how many quarters will the account have \$1000 in it?

Helpful Hint

When we get $2 = (1.02)^n$, we can use the definition of log as in Example 8 or take the natural log of each side:

$$\ln(2) = \ln(1.02^n)$$
$$\ln(2) = n \cdot \ln(1.02)$$
$$n = \frac{\ln(2)}{\ln(1.02)}$$

In either way we arrive at the same solution.

Solution

We use the compound interest formula $A = P(1 + i)^n$ with a principal of \$500, an amount of \$1000, and an interest rate of 2% each quarter:

$$A = P(1 + i)^n$$
$$1000 = 500(1.02)^n \quad \text{Substitute.}$$
$$2 = (1.02)^n \quad \text{Divide each side by 500.}$$
$$n = \log_{1.02}(2) \quad \text{Definition of logarithm}$$
$$= \frac{\ln(2)}{\ln(1.02)} \quad \text{Base-change formula}$$
$$\approx 35.0028 \quad \text{Use a calculator.}$$

It takes approximately 35 quarters, or 8 years and 9 months, for the initial investment to be worth \$1000. Note that we could also solve $2 = (1.02)^n$ by taking the common or natural logarithm of each side. Try it.

Now do Exercises 79–82

In Example 9 we find the rate in a radioactive decay problem.

EXAMPLE 9

Finding the rate in radioactive decay

The number of grams of a radioactive substance that is present in an old bone after t years is given by

$$A = 8e^{rt},$$

where r is the decay rate. How many grams of the radioactive substance were present when the bone was in a living organism at time $t = 0$? If it took 6300 years for the radioactive substance to decay from 8 grams to 4 grams, then what is the decay rate?

Solution

If $t = 0$, then $A = 8e^{r \cdot 0} = 8e^0 = 8 \cdot 1 = 8$. So the bone contained 8 grams of the substance when it was in a living organism. Now use $A = 4$ and $t = 6300$ in the formula $A = 8e^{rt}$ and solve for r:

$$4 = 8e^{6300r}$$
$$0.5 = e^{6300r} \quad \text{Divide each side by 8.}$$
$$6300r = \ln(0.5) \quad \text{Definition of logarithm}$$
$$r = \frac{\ln(0.5)}{6300} \quad \text{Divide each side by 6300.}$$
$$r \approx -1.1 \times 10^{-4} \text{ or } -0.00011$$

Note that the rate is negative because the substance is decaying.

Now do Exercises 83–94

Warm-Ups

True or false? Explain your answer.

1. If $\log(x - 2) + \log(x + 2) = 7$, then $\log(x^2 - 4) = 7$. True
2. If $\log(3x + 7) = \log(5x - 8)$, then $3x + 7 = 5x - 8$. True
3. If $e^{x-6} = e^{x^2-5x}$, then $x - 6 = x^2 - 5x$. True
4. If $2^{3x-1} = 3^{5x-4}$, then $3x - 1 = 5x - 4$. False
5. If $\log_2(x^2 - 3x + 5) = 3$, then $x^2 - 3x + 5 = 8$. True
6. If $2^{2x-1} = 3$, then $2x - 1 = \log_2(3)$. True
7. If $5^x = 23$, then $x \cdot \ln(5) = \ln(23)$. True
8. $\log_3(5) = \dfrac{\ln(3)}{\ln(5)}$ False
9. $\dfrac{\ln(2)}{\ln(6)} = \dfrac{\log(2)}{\log(6)}$ True
10. $\log(5) = \ln(5)$ False

12.4 Exercises

Boost your GRADE at mathzone.com!

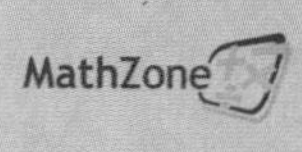

- Practice Problems
- Self-Tests
- Videos
- Net Tutor
- e-Professors

Reading and Writing *After reading this section, write out the answers to these questions. Use complete sentences.*

1. What exponential equation is equivalent to $\log_a(x) = y$?
The exponential equation $a^y = x$ is equivalent to $\log_a(x) = y$.
2. How can you find a logarithm with a base other than 10 or e using a calculator?
According to the base-change formula, $\log_a(x) = \ln(x)/\ln(a)$.

Solve each equation. See Examples 1 and 2.

3. $\log_2(x + 1) = 3$ $\{7\}$
4. $\log_3(x^2) = 4$ $\{\pm 9\}$
5. $3 \log_2(x + 1) - 2 = 13$ $\{31\}$
6. $4 \log_3(2x) - 1 = 7$ $\left\{\frac{9}{2}\right\}$
7. $12 + 2 \ln(x) = 14$ $\{e\}$
8. $23 = 3 \ln(x - 1) + 14$ $\{e^3 + 1\}$
9. $\log(x) + \log(5) = 1$ $\{2\}$
10. $\ln(x) + \ln(3) = 0$ $\left\{\frac{1}{3}\right\}$
11. $\log_2(x - 1) + \log_2(x + 1) = 3$ $\{3\}$
12. $\log_3(x - 4) + \log_3(x + 4) = 2$ $\{5\}$
13. $\log_2(x - 1) - \log_2(x + 2) = 2$ $\emptyset$
14. $\log_4(8x) - \log_4(x - 1) = 2$ $\{2\}$
15. $\log_2(x - 4) + \log_2(x + 2) = 4$ $\{6\}$
16. $\log_6(x + 6) + \log_6(x - 3) = 2$ $\{6\}$

Solve each equation. See Example 3.

17. $\ln(x) + \ln(x + 5) = \ln(x + 1) + \ln(x + 3)$ $\{3\}$
18. $\log(x) + \log(x + 5) = 2 \cdot \log(x + 2)$ $\{4\}$
19. $\log(x + 3) + \log(x + 4) = \log(x^3 + 13x^2) - \log(x)$ $\{2\}$
20. $\log(x^2 - 1) - \log(x - 1) = \log(6)$ $\{5\}$
21. $2 \cdot \log(x) = \log(20 - x)$ $\{4\}$
22. $2 \cdot \log(x) + \log(3) = \log(2 - 5x)$ $\left\{\frac{1}{3}\right\}$

Solve each equation. See Examples 4 and 5.

23. $3^x = 7$ $\{\log_3(7)\}$
24. $2^{x-1} = 5$ $\{1 + \log_2(5)\}$
25. $e^{2x} = 7$ $\left\{\frac{\ln(7)}{2}\right\}$
26. $e^{x+3} = 2$ $\{-3 + \ln(2)\}$
27. $2^{3x+4} = 4^{x-1}$ $\{-6\}$
28. $9^{2x-1} = 27^{1/2}$ $\left\{\frac{7}{8}\right\}$
29. $\left(\frac{1}{3}\right)^x = 3^{1+x}$ $\left\{-\frac{1}{2}\right\}$
30. $4^{3x} = \left(\frac{1}{2}\right)^{1-x}$ $\left\{-\frac{1}{5}\right\}$

Find the exact solution and approximate solution to each equation. Round approximate answers to three decimal places. See Example 6.

31. $2^x = 3^{x+5}$ $\frac{5\ln(3)}{\ln(2) - \ln(3)}$, -13.548

32. $e^x = 10^x$ 0

33. $5^{x+2} = 10^{x-4}$ $\frac{4 + 2\log(5)}{1 - \log(5)}$, 17.932

34. $3^{2x} = 6^{x+1}$ $\frac{\ln(6)}{\ln(9) - \ln(6)}$, 4.419

35. $8^x = 9^{x-1}$ $\frac{\ln(9)}{\ln(9) - \ln(8)}$, 18.655

36. $5^{x+1} = 8^{x-1}$ $\frac{\ln(5) + \ln(8)}{\ln(8) - \ln(5)}$, 7.849

Use the base-change formula to find each logarithm to four decimal places. See Example 7.

37. $\log_2(3)$ 1.5850

38. $\log_3(5)$ 1.4650

39. $\log_3\left(\frac{1}{2}\right)$ -0.6309

40. $\log_5(2.56)$ 0.5841

41. $\log_{1/2}(4.6)$ -2.2016

42. $\log_{1/3}(3.5)$ -1.1403

43. $\log_{0.1}(0.03)$ 1.5229

44. $\log_{0.2}(1.06)$ -0.0362

For each equation, find the exact solution and an approximate solution when appropriate. Round approximate answers to three decimal places.

45. $x \cdot \ln(2) = \ln(7)$ $\frac{\ln(7)}{\ln(2)}$, 2.807

46. $x \cdot \log(3) = \log(5)$ $\frac{\log(5)}{\log(3)}$, 1.465

47. $3x - x \cdot \ln(2) = 1$ $\frac{1}{3 - \ln(2)}$, 0.433

48. $2x + x \cdot \log(5) = \log(7)$ $\frac{\log(7)}{2 + \log(5)}$, 0.313

49. $3^x = 5$ $\frac{\ln(5)}{\ln(3)}$, 1.465

50. $2^x = \frac{1}{3}$ $-\frac{\ln(3)}{\ln(2)}$, -1.585

51. $2^{x-1} = 9$ $1 + \frac{\ln(9)}{\ln(2)}$, 4.170

52. $10^{x-2} = 6$ $2 + \log(6)$, 2.778

53. $3^x = 20$ $\log_3(20)$, 2.727

54. $2^x = 128$ 7

55. $\log_3(x) + \log_3(5) = 1$ $\frac{3}{5}$

56. $\log(x) - \log(3) = \log(6)$ 18

57. $8^x = 2^{x+1}$ $\frac{1}{2}$

58. $2^x = 5^{x+1}$ $\frac{\ln(5)}{\ln(2) - \ln(5)}$, -1.756

Solve each equation.

59. $\log_2(1 - x) = 2$ $\{-3\}$

60. $\log_5(-x) = 3$ $\{-125\}$

61. $\log_3(1 - x) + \log_3(2x + 13) = 3$ $\left\{-\frac{7}{2}, -2\right\}$

62. $\log_2(3 - x) + \log_2(x + 9) = 5$ $\{-5, -1\}$

63. $\ln(2x - 1) - \ln(x + 1) = \ln(5)$ $\varnothing$

64. $\log(x - 4) - \log(x + 5) = 1$ $\varnothing$

65. $\log_3(x - 14) - \log_3(x - 6) = 2$ $\varnothing$

66. $\log_3(7 - x^2) - \log_3(1 - x) = 1$ $\{-1\}$

67. $\log(x + 1) + \log(x - 2) = 1$ $\{4\}$

68. $\log_2(x^2 - 8) - \log_2(x^2 - 5) = 2$ $\varnothing$

69. $2 \cdot \ln(x) = \ln(2) + \ln(5x - 12)$ $\{4, 6\}$

70. $\ln(8 - x^3) - \ln(2 - x) = \ln(2x + 5)$ $\{-1, 1\}$

71. $\log_3(x^3 + 16x^2) - \log_3(x) = \log_3(36)$ $\{2\}$

72. $\ln(x) + \ln(x - 2) = \ln(x + 2) + \ln(x - 3)$ $\{6\}$

73. $\log(x) + \log(x + 5) = 2 \cdot \log(x + 2)$ $\{4\}$

74. $\log_2(x^2 - 9) - \log_2(x + 3) = \log_2(12)$ $\{15\}$

75. $\log_7(x^2 + 6x + 8) - \log_7(x + 2) = \log_7(3)$ $\{-1\}$

76. $3 \cdot \log_5(x) = 2 \cdot \log_5(x)$ $\{1\}$

77. $\ln(6) + 2 \cdot \ln(x) = \ln(38x - 30) - \ln(2)$ $\left\{\frac{3}{2}, \frac{5}{3}\right\}$

78. $3 \cdot \ln(x + 1) = \ln(x + 1) + \ln(x^2 - x + 1)$ $\{0\}$

Solve each problem. See Examples 8 and 9.

79. ***Finding the time.*** How many months does it take for \$1000 to grow to \$1500 in an account paying 12% compounded monthly? 41 months

80. ***Finding the time.*** How many years does it take for \$25 to grow to \$100 in an account paying 8% compounded annually? 18 years

81. ***Finding days.*** How many days does it take for a deposit of \$100 to grow to \$105 at 3% annual percentage rate compounded daily? Round to the nearest day. 594 days

82. ***Finding quarters.*** How many quarters does it take for a deposit of \$500 to grow to \$600 at 2% annual percentage rate compounded quarterly? Round to the nearest quarter. 37 quarters

83. ***Radioactive decay.*** The number of grams of a radioactive substance that is present in an old piece of cloth after t years is given by

$$A = 10e^{-0.0001t}.$$

How many grams of the radioactive substance did the cloth contain when it was made at time $t = 0$? If the cloth now contains only 4 grams of the substance then when was the cloth made? 10 g, 9163 years ago

84. ***Finding the decay rate.*** The number of grams of a radioactive substance that is present in an old log after t years is given by

$$A = 5e^{rt},$$

where r is the decay rate. How many grams of the radioactive substance were present when the log was alive at time $t = 0$? If it took 5000 years for the substance to decay from 5 grams to 2 grams, then what is the decay rate? 5 g, $r = -1.83 \times 10^{-4}$ or -0.000183

85. ***Going with the flow.*** The flow y [in cubic feet per second (ft^3/sec)] of the Tangipahoa River at Robert, Louisiana, is modeled by the exponential function $y = 114.308e^{0.265x}$, where x is the depth in feet. Find the flow when the depth is 15.8 feet. 7524 ft^3/sec

Figure for Exercises 85 and 86

86. ***Record flood.*** Use the formula of the previous exercise to find the depth of the Tangipahoa River at Robert, Louisiana, on May 3, 1953, when the flow reached an all-time record of 50,500 ft^3/sec (U.S.G.S., waterdata.usgs.gov). 22.98 ft

87. ***Above the poverty level.*** In a certain country the number of people above the poverty level is currently 28 million and growing 5% annually. Assuming the population is growing continuously, the population P (in millions), t years from now, is determined by the formula $P = 28e^{0.05t}$. In how many years will there be 40 million people above the poverty level? 7.1 years

88. ***Below the poverty level.*** In the same country as in Exercise 87, the number of people below the poverty level is currently 20 million and growing 7% annually. This population (in millions), t years from now, is determined by the formula $P = 20e^{0.07t}$. In how many years will there be 40 million people below the poverty level? 9.9 years

89. ***Fifty-fifty.*** For this exercise, use the information given in Exercises 87 and 88. In how many years will the number of people above the poverty level equal the number of people below the poverty level? 16.8 years

90. ***Golden years.*** In a certain country there are currently 100 million workers and 40 million retired people. The population of workers is decreasing according to the formula $W = 100e^{-0.01t}$, where t is in years and W is in millions. The population of retired people is increasing according to the formula $R = 40e^{0.09t}$, where t is in years and R is in millions. In how many years will the number of workers equal the number of retired people? 9.2 years

91. ***Ions for breakfast.*** Orange juice has a pH of 3.7. What is the hydrogen ion concentration of orange juice? (See Exercises 91–94 of Section 12.2.) 2.0×10^{-4}

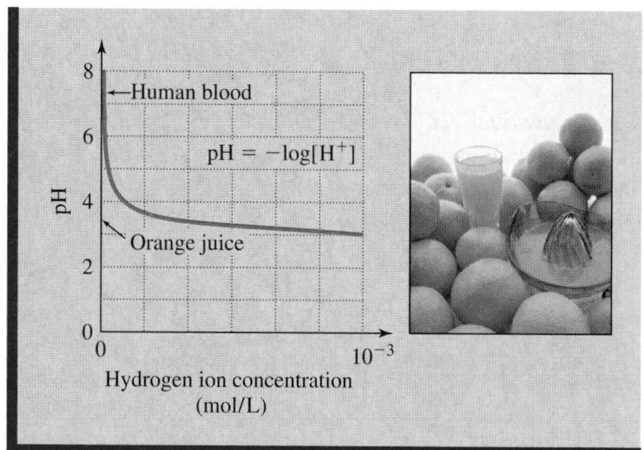

Figure for Exercises 91 and 92

92. ***Ions in your veins.*** Normal human blood has a pH of 7.4. What is the hydrogen ion concentration of normal human blood? 4.0×10^{-8}

93. ***Diversity index.*** In Exercise 98 of Section 12.3 we expressed the diversity index d for a certain water sample as

$$d = \log_2\left(\frac{3\sqrt[3]{2}}{2}\right).$$

Use the base-change formula and a calculator to calculate the value of d. Round the answer to four decimal places. 0.9183

94. ***Quality water.*** In a certain water sample, 5% of the organisms are in one taxon, 10% are in a second taxon, 20% are in a third taxon, 15% are in a fourth taxon, 23% are in a fifth taxon, and the rest are in a sixth taxon. Use the formula given in Exercise 98 of Section 12.3 with $n = 6$ to find the diversity index of the water sample.
2.42

Getting More Involved

95. ***Exploration***

Logarithms were designed to solve equations that have variables in the exponents, but logarithms can be used to solve certain polynomial equations. Consider the following example:

$$x^5 = 88$$
$$5 \cdot \ln(x) = \ln(88)$$
$$\ln(x) = \frac{\ln(88)}{5} \approx 0.895467$$
$$x = e^{0.895467} \approx 2.4485$$

Solve $x^3 = 12$ by taking the natural logarithm of each side. Round the approximate solution to four decimal places. Solve $x^3 = 12$ without using logarithms and compare with your previous answer.
$\sqrt[3]{12}$ or 2.2894

96. ***Discussion***

Determine whether each logarithm is positive or negative without using a calculator. Explain your answers.

a) $\log_2(0.45)$ Negative
b) $\ln(1.01)$ Positive
c) $\log_{1/2}(4.3)$ Negative
d) $\log_{1/3}(0.44)$ Positive

Graphing Calculator Exercises

97. Graph $y_1 = 2^x$ and $y_2 = 3^{x-1}$ on the same coordinate system. Use the intersect feature of your calculator to find the point of intersection of the two curves. Round to two decimal places. (2.71, 6.54)

98. Bob invested \$1000 at 6% compounded continuously. At the same time Paula invested \$1200 at 5% compounded monthly. Write two functions that give the amounts of Bob's and Paula's investments after x years. Graph these functions on a graphing calculator. Use the intersect feature of your graphing calculator to find the approximate value of x for which the investments are equal in value.
$y = 1000e^{0.06x}$, $y = 1200(1 + 0.05/12)^{12x}$, 18.0 years

99. Graph the functions $y_1 = \log_2(x)$ and $y_2 = 3^{x-4}$ on the same coordinate system and use the intersect feature to find the points of intersection of the curves. Round to two decimal places. [*Hint:* To graph $y = \log_2(x)$, use the base-change formula to write the function as $y = \ln(x)/\ln(2)$.]
(1.03, 0.04), (4.74, 2.24)

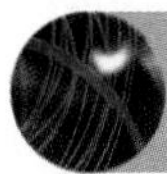

Collaborative Activities

Grouping: 2 students per group
Topic: Exponential and logarithmic functions

In How Much Space Could We Live?

The formula for population growth is $P(t) = P_0e^{kt}$, where $P(t)$ is the population after t years, P_0 is the initial population, k is the growth rate per year, and t is the number of years. In the following exercises you will find out how long it would take to cover the habitable part of the earth if the human population grows exponentially.

1. The population of the earth in 2000 was 6.06×10^9 people. If the population was 2.75×10^9 in 1964, then what is the current growth rate to the nearest tenth of a percent?

2. The earth has a total surface area of 5.1×10^{14} square meters. Seventy percent of this surface area is rock, ice, sand, and ocean. Another 8% is tundra, lakes and streams, continental shelves, algal beds and reefs, and estuaries. Assuming that the remaining area is suitable for growing food and living space find that area.

3. If 100 square meters of the earth's surface is needed for each person to grow food and live, in how many years after 2000 will all of the available surface of the earth be used?

4. Does 100 square meters per person for living space and growing food seem reasonable? Remember that tall apartment buildings use less surface area than single family dwellings.

5. Think about the land use issues for different types of foods. Would it take more surface area to grow animals for food? Would food grow better on some parts of the earth's surface than on others? Would there be any space left for wild animals or natural plant life? Would there be any space left for shopping malls, movie theaters, concert halls, factories, office buildings, or parking lots?

Chapter 12 Wrap-Up

Summary

Exponential and Logarithmic Functions		**Examples**
Exponential function	A function of the form $f(x) = a^x$ for $a > 0$ and $a \neq 1$	$f(x) = 3^x$
Logarithm function	A function of the form $f(x) = \log_a(x)$ for $a > 0$ and $a \neq 1$ $y = \log_a(x)$ if and only if $a^y = x$.	$f(x) = \log_2(x)$ $\log_3(8) = x \leftrightarrow 3^x = 8$
Common logarithm	Base-10: $f(x) = \log(x)$	$\log(100) = 2$ because $100 = 10^2$.
Natural logarithm	Base-e: $f(x) = \ln(x)$ $e \approx 2.718$	$\ln(e) = 1$ because $e^1 = e$.
Inverse functions	$f(x) = a^x$ and $g(x) = \log_a(x)$ are inverse functions.	If $f(x) = e^x$, then $f^{-1}(x) = \ln(x)$.

Properties		**Examples**
M, N, and a are positive numbers with $a \neq 1$.	$\log_a(a) = 1 \quad \log_a(1) = 0$	$\log_5(5) = 1$, $\log_5(1) = 0$
Inverse properties	$\log_a(a^M) = M \quad a^{\log_a(M)} = M$	$\log(10^7) = 7$, $e^{\ln(3.4)} = 3.4$
Product rule	$\log_a(MN) = \log_a(M) + \log_a(N)$	$\ln(3x) = \ln(3) + \ln(x)$
Quotient rule	$\log_a\left(\frac{M}{N}\right) = \log_a(M) - \log_a(N)$ $\log_a\left(\frac{1}{N}\right) = -\log_a(N)$	$\ln\left(\frac{2}{3}\right) = \ln(2) - \ln(3)$ $\ln\left(\frac{1}{3}\right) = -\ln(3)$
Power rule	$\log_a(M^N) = N \cdot \log_a(M)$	$\log(x^3) = 3 \cdot \log(x)$
Base-change formula	$\log_a(M) = \frac{\log_b(M)}{\log_b(a)}$	$\log_3(5) = \frac{\ln(5)}{\ln(3)}$

Equations Involving Logarithms and Exponents		**Examples**
Strategy	1. If there is a single logarithm or a single exponential expression, rewrite the equation using the definition of logarithms: $y = \log_a(x)$ if and only if $a^y = x$.	$2^x = 3$ and $x = \log_2(3)$ are equivalent.

2. Use the properties of logarithms to combine logarithms as much as possible.	$\log(x) + \log(x - 3) = 1$ $\log(x^2 - 3x) = 1$
3. Use the one-to-one properties:	
a) If $\log_a(m) = \log_a(n)$, then $m = n$.	$\ln(x) = \ln(5 - x)$, $x = 5 - x$
b) If $a^m = a^n$, then $m = n$.	$2^{3x} = 2^{5x-7}$, $3x = 5x - 7$
4. To get an approximate solution, take the common or natural logarithm of each side of an exponential equation.	$2^x = 3$, $\ln(2^x) = \ln(3)$ $x \cdot \ln(2) = \ln(3)$ $x = \dfrac{\ln(3)}{\ln(2)}$

Enriching Your Mathematical Word Power

For each mathematical term, choose the correct meaning.

1. exponential function
a. $f(x) = a^x$ where $a > 0$ and $a \neq 1$
b. $f(x) = ax^2$ where $a \neq 0$
c. $f(x) = ax + b$ where $a \neq 0$
d. $f(x) = x^n$ where n is an integer a

2. common base
a. base 2
b. base e
c. base π
d. base 10 d

3. natural base
a. base 2
b. base e
c. base π
d. base 10 b

4. domain
a. the range
b. the set of second coordinates of a relation
c. the independent variable
d. the set of first coordinates of a relation d

5. compound interest
a. simple interest
b. $A = Prt$
c. an irrational interest rate
d. interest is periodically paid into the account and the interest earns interest d

6. continuous compounding
a. compound interest
b. using $A = Pe^{rt}$ to compute the amount
c. frequent compounding
d. using $A = P(1 + i)^n$ to compute the amount b

7. base-*a* logarithm of *x*
a. the exponent that is used on the base a to obtain x
b. the exponent that is used on x to obtain a
c. the power of 10 that produces x
d. the power of e that produces a a

8. base-*a* logarithm function
a. $f(x) = a^x$ where $a > 0$ and $a \neq 1$
b. $f(x) = \log_a(x)$ where $a > 0$ and $a \neq 1$
c. $f(x) = \log_x(a)$ where $a > 0$ and $a \neq 1$
d. $f(x) = \log(x)$ where $x > 0$ b

9. common logarithm
a. $\log_2(x)$
b. $\log(x)$
c. $\ln(x)$
d. $\log_3(x)$ b

10. natural logarithm
a. $\log_2(x)$
b. $\log(x)$
c. $\ln(x)$
d. $\log_3(x)$ c

Review Exercises

12.1 *Use $f(x) = 5^x$, $g(x) = 10^{x-1}$, and $h(x) = \left(\frac{1}{4}\right)^x$ for Exercises 1–28. Find the following.*

1. $f(-2)$ $\frac{1}{25}$

2. $f(0)$ 1

3. $f(3)$ 125

4. $f(4)$ 625

5. $g(1)$ 1

6. $g(-1)$ $\frac{1}{100}$

7. $g(0)$ $\frac{1}{10}$

8. $g(3)$ 100

9. $h(-1)$ 4

10. $h(2)$ $\frac{1}{16}$

11. $h\left(\frac{1}{2}\right)$ $\frac{1}{2}$

12. $h\left(-\frac{1}{2}\right)$ 2

Find x in each case.

13. $f(x) = 25$ 2

14. $f(x) = -\frac{1}{125}$ No solution

15. $g(x) = 1000$ 4

16. $g(x) = 0.001$ -2

17. $h(x) = 32$ $-\frac{5}{2}$

18. $h(x) = 8$ $-\frac{3}{2}$

19. $h(x) = \frac{1}{16}$ 2

20. $h(x) = 1$ 0

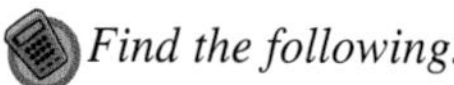

Find the following.

21. $f(1.34)$ 8.6421

22. $f(-3.6)$ 0.00305

23. $g(3.25)$ 177.828

24. $g(4.87)$ 7413.102

25. $h(2.82)$ 0.02005

26. $h(\pi)$ 0.01284

27. $h(\sqrt{2})$ 0.1408

28. $h\left(\frac{1}{3}\right)$ 0.6300

Sketch the graph of each function.

29. $f(x) = 5^x$

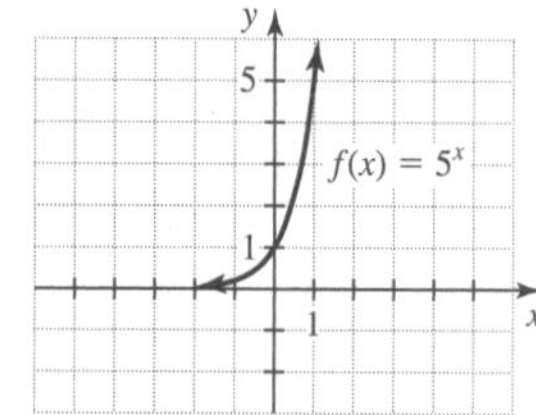

30. $g(x) = e^x$

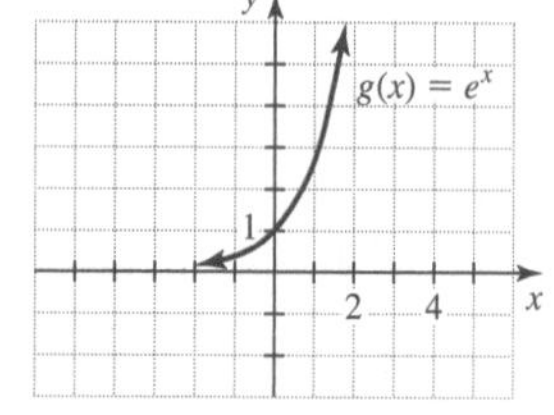

31. $y = \left(\frac{1}{5}\right)^x$

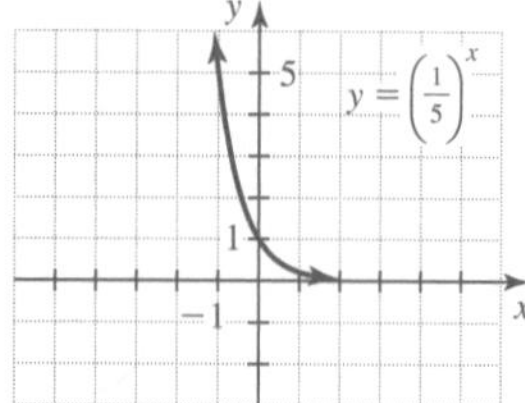

32. $y = e^{-x}$

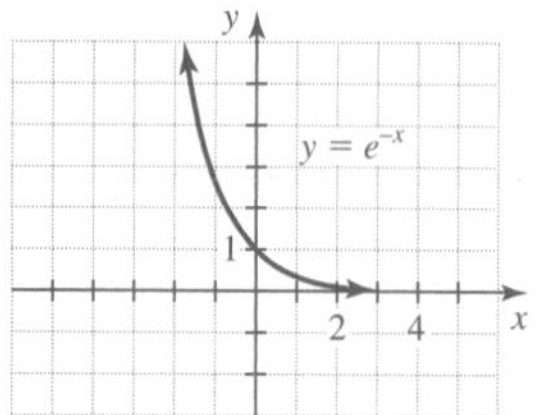

33. $f(x) = 3^{-x}$

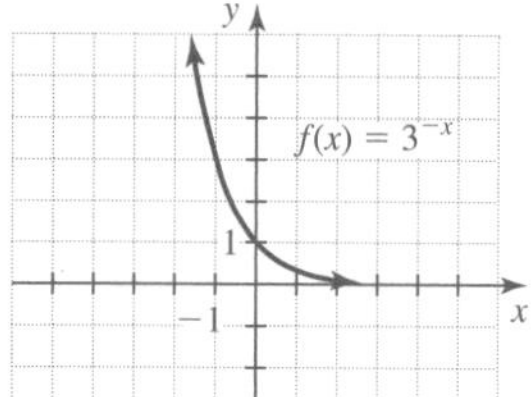

34. $f(x) = -3^{x-1}$

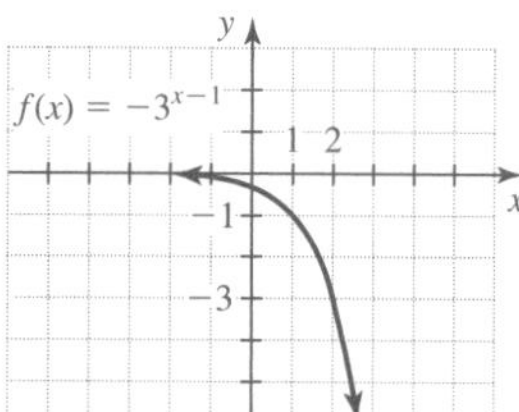

35. $y = 1 + 2^x$

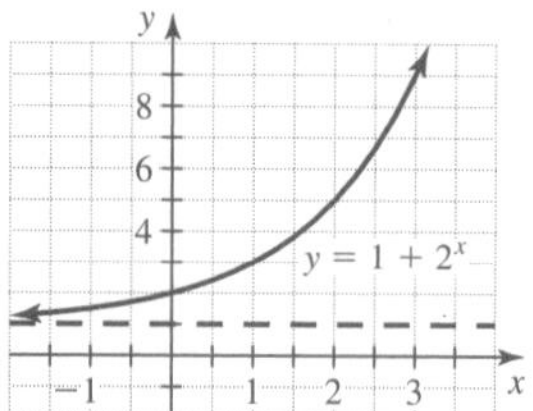

36. $y = 1 - 2^x$

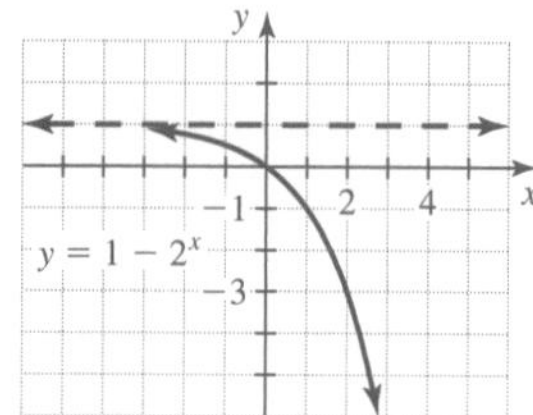

12.2 *Write each exponential equation as a logarithmic equation and each logarithmic equation as an exponential equation.*

37. $10^m = n$ $\log(n) = m$

38. $b = a^5$ $\log_a(b) = 5$

39. $h = \log_k(t)$ $k^h = t$

40. $\log_v(5) = u$ $v^u = 5$

Let $f(x) = \log_2(x)$, $g(x) = \log(x)$, *and* $h(x) = \log_{1/2}(x)$. *Find the following.*

41. $f\left(\frac{1}{8}\right)$ -3

42. $f(64)$ 6

43. $g(0.1)$ -1

44. $g(1)$ 0

45. $g(100)$ 2

46. $h\left(\frac{1}{8}\right)$ 3

47. $h(1)$ 0

48. $h(4)$ -2

49. x, if $f(x) = 8$
256

50. x, if $g(x) = 3$
1000

51. $f(77)$
6.267

52. $g(88.4)$
1.946

53. $h(33.9)$
-5.083

54. $h(0.05)$
4.322

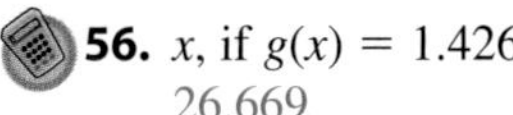

55. x, if $f(x) = 2.475$
5.560

56. x, if $g(x) = 1.426$
26.669

For each function f, find f^{-1} *and sketch the graphs of f and* f^{-1} *on the same set of axes.*

57. $f(x) = 10^x$ $f^{-1}(x) = \log(x)$

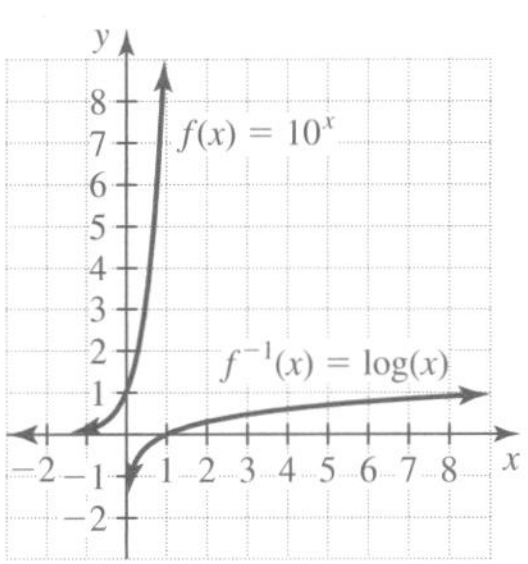

58. $f(x) = \log_8(x)$ $f^{-1}(x) = 8^x$

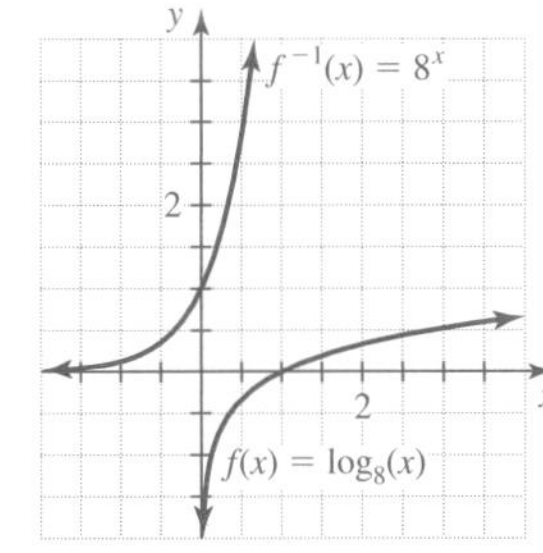

59. $f(x) = e^x$ $f^{-1}(x) = \ln(x)$

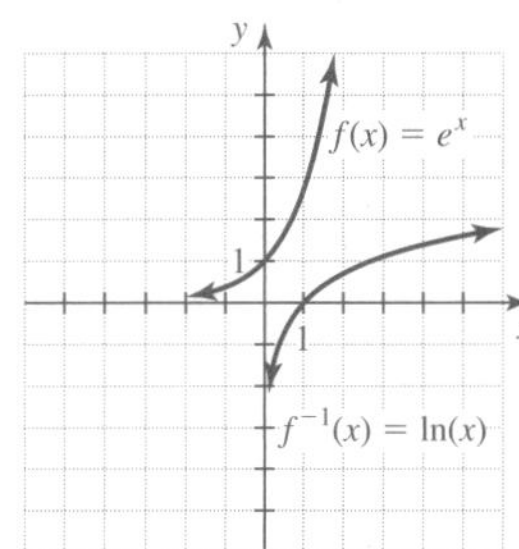

60. $f(x) = \log_3(x)$ $f^{-1}(x) = 3^x$

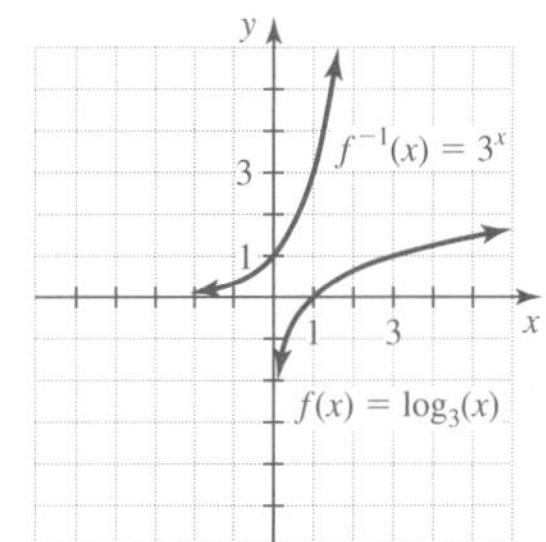

12.3 *Rewrite each expression as a sum or a difference of multiples of logarithms.*

61. $\log(x^2y)$ $2\log(x) + \log(y)$

62. $\log_3(x^2 + 2x)$ $\log_3(x) + \log_3(x + 2)$

63. $\ln(16)$ $4\ln(2)$

64. $\log\left(\frac{y}{\sqrt{x}}\right)$ $\log(y) - \frac{1}{2}\log(x)$

65. $\log_5\left(\frac{1}{x}\right)$ $-\log_5(x)$

66. $\ln\left(\frac{xy}{z}\right)$ $\ln(x) + \ln(y) - \ln(z)$

Rewrite each expression as a single logarithm.

67. $\frac{1}{2}\log(x + 2) - 2 \cdot \log(x - 1)$ $\log\left(\frac{\sqrt{x + 2}}{(x - 1)^2}\right)$

68. $3 \cdot \ln(x) + 2 \cdot \ln(y) - \frac{1}{3}\ln(z)$ $\ln\left(\frac{x^3y^2}{\sqrt[3]{z}}\right)$

12.4 *Find the exact solution to each equation.*

69. $\log_2(x) = 8$ $\{256\}$

70. $\log_3(x) = 0.5$ $\{\sqrt{3}\}$

71. $\log_2(8) = x$ $\{3\}$

72. $3^x = 8$ $\{\log_3(8)\}$

73. $x^3 = 8$ $\{2\}$

74. $3^2 = x$ $\{9\}$

75. $\log_x(27) = 3$ $\{3\}$

76. $\log_x(9) = -\frac{1}{3}$ $\left\{\frac{1}{729}\right\}$

77. $x \cdot \ln(3) - x = \ln(7)$ $\left\{\frac{\ln(7)}{\ln(3) - 1}\right\}$

78. $x \cdot \log(8) = x \cdot \log(4) + \log(9)$ $\left\{\frac{\log(9)}{\log(2)}\right\}$

79. $3^x = 5^{x-1}$ $\left\{\frac{\ln(5)}{\ln(5) - \ln(3)}\right\}$

80. $5^{(2x^2)} = 5^{3-5x}$ $\left\{-3, \frac{1}{2}\right\}$

81. $4^{2x} = 2^{x+1}$ $\left\{\frac{1}{3}\right\}$

82. $\log(12) = \log(x) + \log(7 - x)$ $\{3, 4\}$

83. $\ln(x + 2) - \ln(x - 10) = \ln(2)$ $\{22\}$

84. $2 \cdot \ln(x + 3) = 3 \cdot \ln(4)$ $\{5\}$

85. $\log(x) - \log(x - 2) = 2$ $\left\{\frac{200}{99}\right\}$

86. $\log_2(x) = \log_2(x + 16) - 1$ $\{16\}$

Use a calculator to find an approximate solution to each of the following. Round your answers to four decimal places.

87. $6^x = 12$ $\{1.3869\}$

88. $5^x = 8^{3x+2}$ $\{-0.8985\}$

89. $3^{x+1} = 5$ $\{0.4650\}$

90. $\log_3(x) = 2.634$ $\{18.0608\}$

Miscellaneous

Solve each problem.

91. ***Compounding annually.*** What does \$10,000 invested at 11.5% compounded annually amount to after 15 years? \$51,182.68

92. ***Doubling time.*** How many years does it take for an investment to double at 6.5% compounded annually? 11.007 years

93. ***Decaying substance.*** The amount, A, of a certain radioactive substance remaining after t years, is given by the formula $A = A_0e^{-0.0003t}$, where A_0 is the initial amount. If we have 218 grams of this substance today, then how much of it will be left 1000 years from now? 161.5 grams

94. ***Wildlife management.*** The number of white-tailed deer in the Hiawatha National Forest is believed to be growing according to the function

$$P = 517 + 10 \cdot \ln(8t + 1),$$

where t is the time in years from the year 2000.

a) What is the size of the population in 2000?
b) In what year will the population reach 600?
c) Does the population as shown on the accompanying graph appear to be growing faster during the period 2000 to 2005 or during the period 2005 to 2010?
d) What is the average rate of change of the population for each period in part (c)?

a) 517 **b)** 2503 **c)** faster for 2000 to 2005
d) 7.4 deer per year, 1.4 deer per year

Figure for Exercise 94

95. ***Comparing investments.*** Melissa deposited \$1000 into an account paying 5% annually; on the same day Frank deposited \$900 into an account paying 7% compounded continuously. Find the number of years that it will take for the amounts in the accounts to be equal. 5 years

96. ***Imports and exports.*** The value of imports for a small Central American country is believed to be growing according to the function

$$I = 15 \cdot \log(16t + 33),$$

and the value of exports appears to be growing according to the function

$$E = 30 \cdot \log(t + 3),$$

where I and E are in millions of dollars and t is the number of years after 2000.

a) What are the values of imports and exports in 2000? \$22.8 million, \$14.3 million
b) Use the accompanying graph to estimate the year in which imports will equal exports. 2010
c) Algebraically find the year in which imports will equal exports. 2012

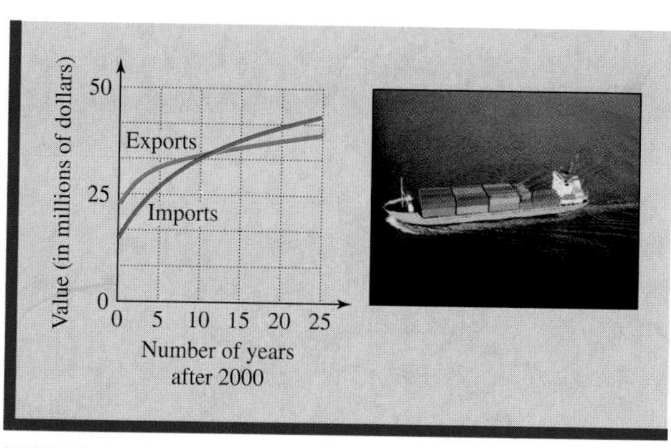

Figure for Exercise 96

97. ***Finding river flow.*** The U.S.G.S. measures the water height h (in feet above sea level) for the Tangipahoa River at Robert, Louisiana, and then finds the flow y [in cubic feet per second (ft³/sec)], using the formula

$$y = 114.308e^{0.265(h-6.87)}.$$

Find the flow when the river at Robert is 20.6 ft above sea level. 4347.5 ft³/sec

98. ***Finding the height.*** Rewrite the formula in Exercise 97 to express h as a function of y. Use the new formula to find the water height above sea level when the flow is 10,000 ft³/sec.

$h = \dfrac{\ln(y/114.308)}{0.265} + 6.87$, 23.74 ft

Chapter 12 Test

Let $f(x) = 5^x$ *and* $g(x) = \log_5(x)$. *Find the following.*

1. $f(2)$ 25

2. $f(-1)$ $\frac{1}{5}$

3. $f(0)$ 1

4. $g(125)$ 3

5. $g(1)$ 0

6. $g\left(\frac{1}{5}\right)$ -1

Sketch the graph of each function.

7. $y = 2^x$

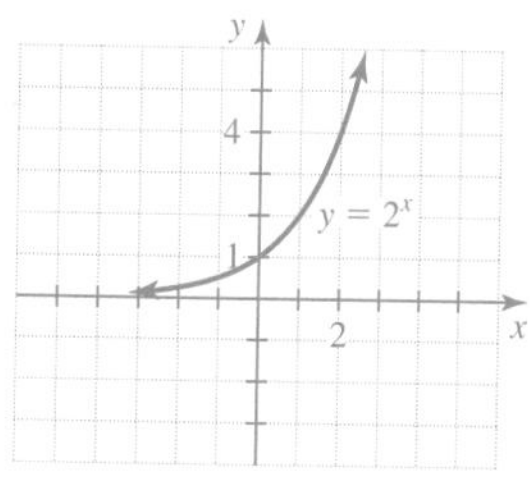

8. $f(x) = \log_2(x)$

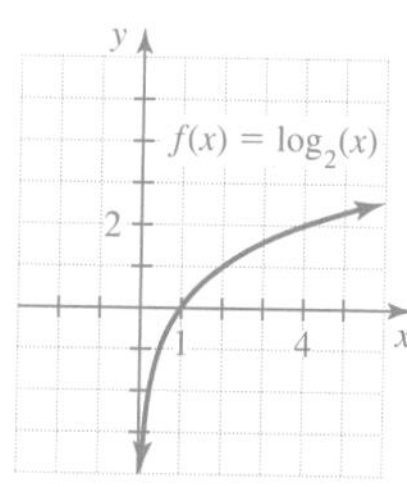

9. $y = \left(\frac{1}{3}\right)^x$

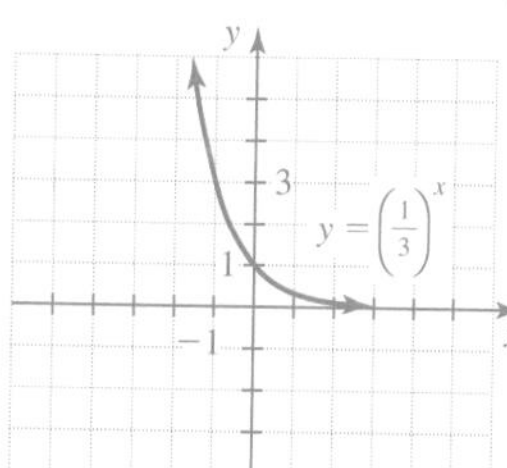

10. $g(x) = \log_{1/3}(x)$

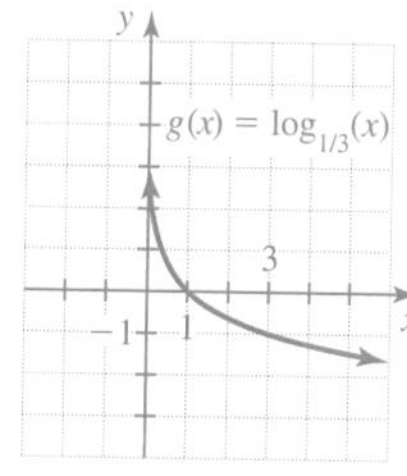

Suppose $\log_a(M) = 6$ *and* $\log_a(N) = 4$. *Find the following.*

11. $\log_a(MN)$ 10

12. $\log_a\left(\frac{M^2}{N}\right)$ 8

13. $\dfrac{\log_a(M)}{\log_a(N)}$ $\frac{3}{2}$

14. $\log_a(a^3M^2)$ 15

15. $\log_a\left(\frac{1}{N}\right)$ -4

Find the exact solution to each equation.

16. $3^x = 12$ $\{\log_3(12)\}$ or $\{\ln(12)/\ln(3)\}$

17. $\log_3(x) = \frac{1}{2}$ $\{\sqrt{3}\}$

18. $5^x = 8^{x-1}$ $\left\{\dfrac{\ln(8)}{\ln(8) - \ln(5)}\right\}$

19. $\log(x) + \log(x + 15) = 2$ $\{5\}$

20. $2 \cdot \ln(x) = \ln(3) + \ln(6 - x)$ $\{3\}$

Use a scientific calculator to find an approximate solution to each of the following. Round your answers to four decimal places.

21. Solve $20^x = 5$. $\{0.5372\}$

22. Solve $\log_3(x) = 2.75$. $\{20.5156\}$

23. The number of bacteria present in a culture at time t is given by the formula $N = 10e^{0.4t}$, where t is in hours. How many bacteria are present initially? How many are present after 24 hours? 10; 147,648

24. How many hours does it take for the bacteria population of Problem 23 to double? 1.733 hours

*Making*Connections | A Review of Chapters 1–12

Find the exact solution to each equation.

1. $(x-3)^2 = 8$ $\{3 \pm 2\sqrt{2}\}$

2. $\log_2(x-3) = 8$ $\{259\}$

3. $2^{x-3} = 8$ $\{6\}$

4. $2x - 3 = 8$ $\left\{\frac{11}{2}\right\}$

5. $|x-3| = 8$ $\{-5, 11\}$

6. $\sqrt{x-3} = 8$ $\{67\}$

7. $\log_2(x-3) + \log_2(x) = \log_2(18)$ $\{6\}$

8. $2 \cdot \log_2(x-3) = \log_2(5-x)$ $\{4\}$

9. $\frac{1}{2}x - \frac{2}{3} = \frac{3}{4}x + \frac{1}{5}$ $\left\{-\frac{52}{15}\right\}$

10. $3x^2 - 6x + 2 = 0$ $\left\{\frac{3 \pm \sqrt{3}}{3}\right\}$

Find the inverse of each function.

11. $f(x) = \frac{1}{3}x$ $f^{-1}(x) = 3x$

12. $g(x) = \log_3(x)$ $g^{-1}(x) = 3^x$

13. $f(x) = 2x - 4$ $f^{-1}(x) = \frac{x+4}{2}$

14. $h(x) = \sqrt{x}$ $h^{-1}(x) = x^2$ for $x \geq 0$

15. $j(x) = \frac{1}{x}$ $j^{-1}(x) = \frac{1}{x}$

16. $k(x) = 5^x$ $k^{-1}(x) = \log_5(x)$

17. $m(x) = e^{x-1}$ $m^{-1}(x) = 1 + \ln(x)$

18. $n(x) = \ln(x)$ $n^{-1}(x) = e^x$

Sketch the graph of each equation.

19. $y = 2x$

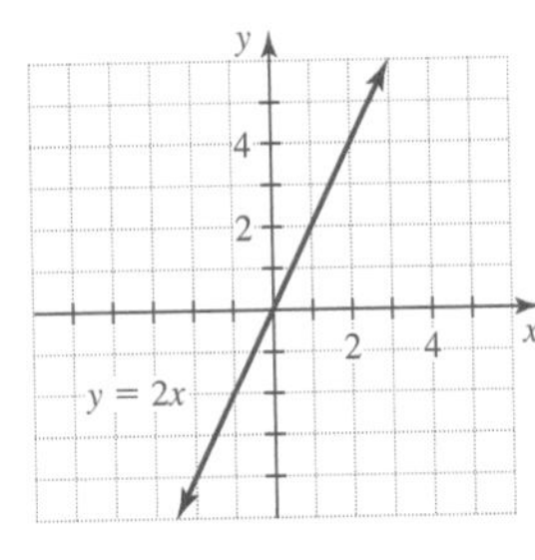

20. $y = 2^x$

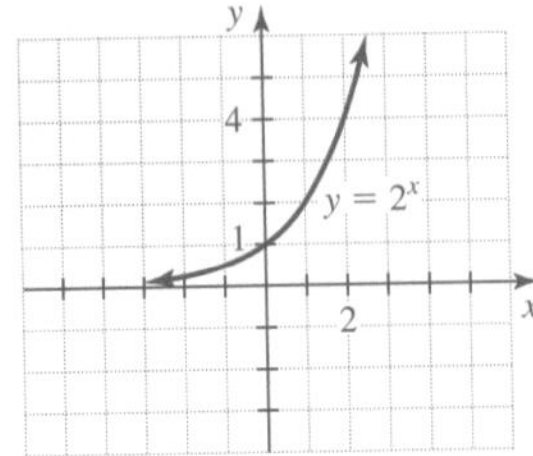

21. $y = x^2$

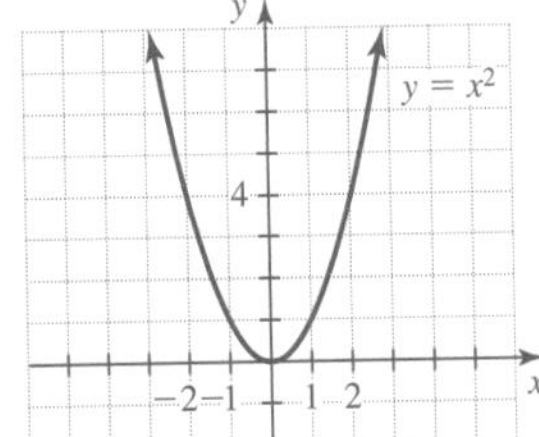

22. $y = \log_2(x)$

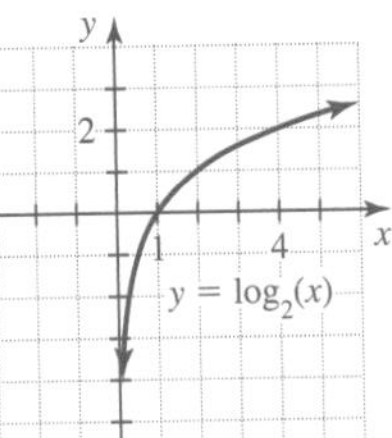

23. $y = \frac{1}{2}x - 4$

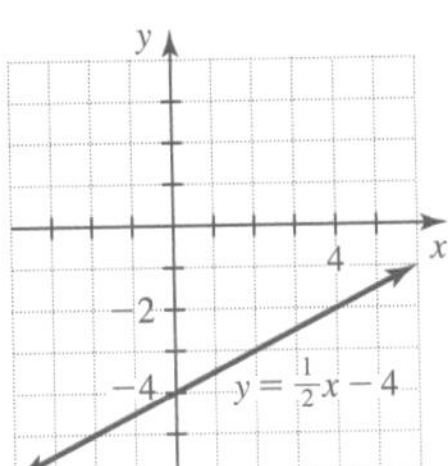

24. $y = |2 - x|$

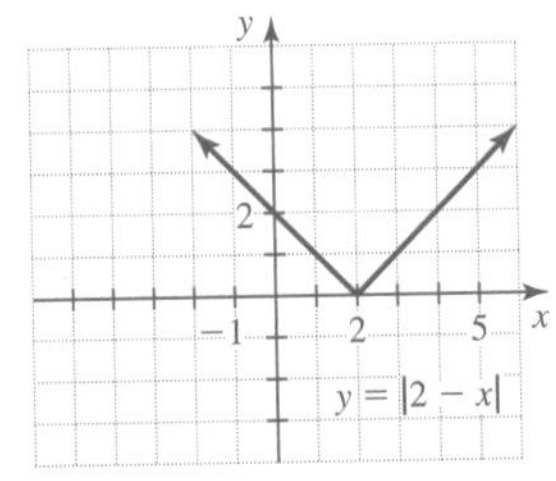

25. $y = 2 - x^2$

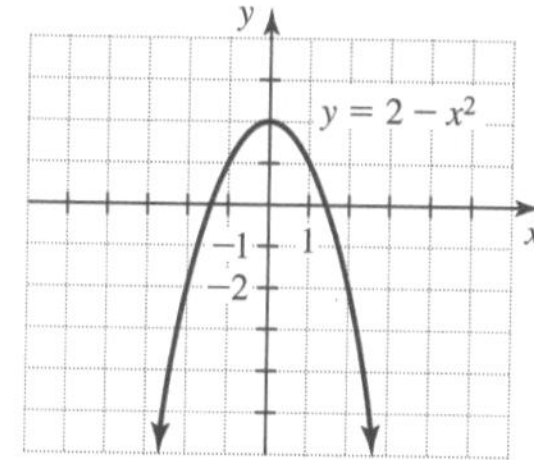

26. $y = e^2$

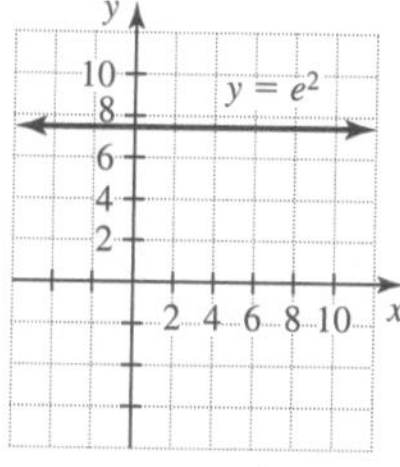

Solve each problem.

27. *Civilian labor force.* The number of workers in the civilian labor force can be modeled by the linear function

$$n(t) = 1.51t + 125.5$$

or by the exponential function

$$n(t) = 125.6e^{0.011t},$$

where t is the number of years since 1990 and $n(t)$ is in millions of workers (Bureau of Labor Statistics, www.bls.gov).

a) Graph both functions on the same coordinate system for $0 \le t \le 30$.

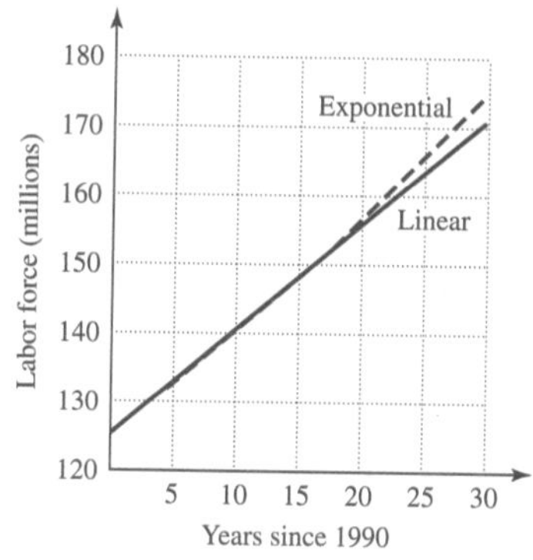

b) What does each model predict for the value of n in 2010?
Linear 155.7 million, exponential 156.5 million

c) What does each model predict for the value of n in the present year? Which model's prediction is closest to the actual size of the present civilian labor force?

28. *Measuring ocean depths.* In this exercise you will see how a geophysicist uses sound reflection to measure the depth of the ocean. Let v be the speed of sound through the water and d_1 be the depth of the ocean below the ship, as shown in the accompanying figure.

a) The time it takes for sound to travel from the ship at point S straight down to the ocean floor at point B_1 and back to point S is 0.270 second. Write d_1 as a function of v.
$d_1 = 0.135v$

b) It takes 0.432 second for sound to travel from point S to point B_2 and then to a receiver at R, which is towed 500 meters behind the ship. Assuming $d_2 = d_3$, write d_2 as a function of v.
$d_2 = 0.216v$

c) Use the Pythagorean theorem to find v. Then find the ocean depth d_1.
$v = 1482.67$ m/sec, $d_1 = 200.2$ meters

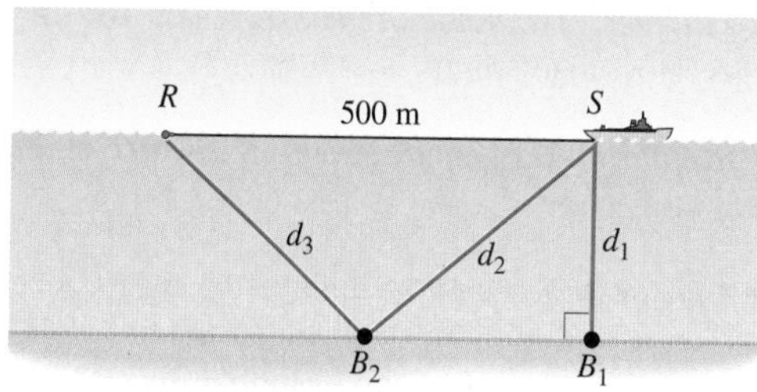

Figure for Exercise 28

Critical **Thinking** | For Individual or Group Work | Chapter 12

These exercises can be solved by a variety of techniques, which may or may not require algebra. So be creative and think critically. Explain all answers. Answers are in the Instructor's Edition of this text.

1. ***Shady crescents.*** Start with any right triangle and draw three semicircles so that each semicircle has one side of the triangle as its diameter as shown in the accompanying figure. Show that total area of the two smaller crescents is equal to the area of the largest crescent.

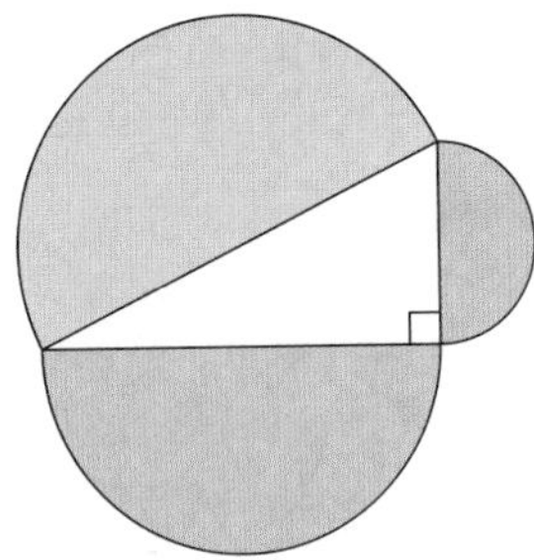

Figure for Exercise 1

2. ***Huge integer.*** The value of the expression $16^9 \cdot 5^{25}$ is an integer. How many digits does it have?

3. ***Sevens galore.*** How many seven-digit whole numbers contain the number seven at least once?

4. ***Ten-digit surprise.*** Use the digits 0 through 9 once each to construct a 10-digit number such that the first n digits (counting from the left) form a number divisible by n, for each n from 1 through 10. For example, for 3428, 3 is divisible by 1, 34 is divisible by 2, 342 is divisible by 3, and 3428 is divisible by 4, but 3428 is not a 10-digit number.

5. ***Cattle drive.*** A group of cowboys is driving a herd of cattle across the plains at a constant rate. The cowboys always keep the herd in the shape of a square that is 1 kilometer on each side. One of the cowboys starts at the left rear of the square/herd and rides his four-wheeler around the perimeter of the square at a constant rate in the same time that the herd advances 1 kilometer. How far does this cowboy travel?

Photo for Exercise 5

6. ***Counting game.*** A teacher plays a counting game with his students. The first student says 1. The second student says 2 and 3. The third student says 4, 5, and 6. The fourth says 7, 8, 9, and 10. This pattern continues with the fifth student saying the next five counting numbers, and so on. Find a formula for the sum of the numbers said by the kth student. $\left[\textit{Hint:} \text{ The sum of the first } n \text{ counting numbers is } \frac{n(n+1)}{2}.\right]$

7. ***Numerical palindrome.*** A numerical palindrome is a positive integer with at least two digits that reads the same forward or backward. For example, 55 and 343 are numerical palindromes. How many numerical palindromes are there less than 1000?

8. ***Fractional chickens.*** If 1.5 chickens lay 1.5 eggs in 1.5 days, then how many eggs do 3.5 chickens lay in 3 days?

1. Find the areas of the semicircles and use the Pythagorean theorem. **2.** 32 **3.** $9{,}000{,}000 - 8 \cdot 9^6$ or 4,748,472 **4.** 3,816,547,290 **5.** 4.18 km (obtained with an equation solver) **6.** $S_k = \frac{k(k^2+1)}{2}$ **7.** 99 **8.** 7 eggs

Nonlinear Systems and the Conic Sections

13.1 **Nonlinear Systems of Equations**

13.2 **The Parabola**

13.3 **The Circle**

13.4 **The Ellipse and Hyperbola**

13.5 **Second-Degree Inequalities**

With a cruising speed of 1540 miles per hour, the Concorde was the fastest commercial aircraft ever built. First flown in 1969, the Concorde could fly from London to New York in about 3 hours. However, the Concordes never made a profit and were all taken out of service in 2003, which ended the age of supersonic commercial air travel.

Perhaps the biggest problem for the Concorde was that it was generally prohibited from flying over land areas because of the noise. Any jet flying faster than the speed of sound creates a cone-shaped wave in the air on which there is a momentary change in air pressure. This change in air pressure causes a thunderlike sonic boom. When the jet is traveling parallel to the ground, the cone-shaped wave intersects the ground along one branch of a hyperbola. People on the ground hear the boom as the hyperbola passes them.

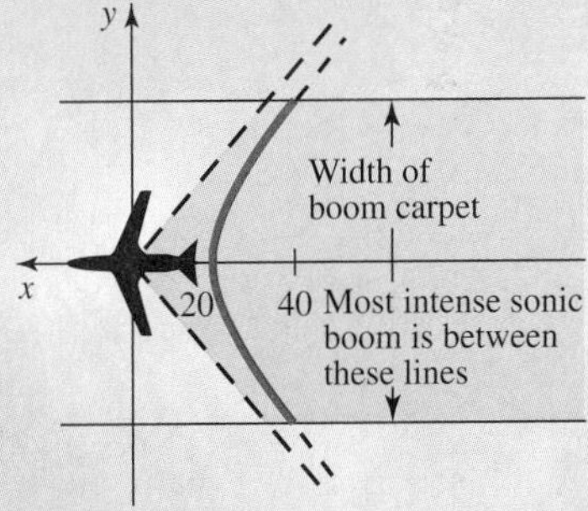

In this chapter we will discuss curves, including the hyperbola, that occur when a geometric plane intersects a cone.

In Exercise 68 of Section 13.4 you will see how the altitude of the aircraft is related to the width of the area where the sonic boom is heard.

13.1 Nonlinear Systems of Equations

In this Section

- Solving by Elimination
- Applications

We studied systems of linear equations in Chapter 7. In this section we turn our attention to nonlinear systems of equations.

Solving by Elimination

An equation whose graph is not a straight line is a **nonlinear equation.** For example,

$$y = x^2, \quad y = \sqrt{x}, \quad y = |x|, \quad y = 2^x, \quad \text{and} \quad y = \log_2(x)$$

are nonlinear equations. A **nonlinear system** is a system of equations in which there is at least one nonlinear equation. We use the same techniques for solving nonlinear systems that we use for linear systems. Graphing the equations is used to explain the number of solutions to the system, but is generally not an accurate method for solving systems of equations. Eliminating a variable by either substitution or addition is used for solving linear or nonlinear systems.

EXAMPLE 1

A parabola and a line

Solve the system of equations and draw the graph of each equation on the same coordinate system:

$$y = x^2 - 1$$
$$x + y = 1$$

Solution

We can eliminate y by substituting $y = x^2 - 1$ into $x + y = 1$:

$$x + y = 1$$
$$x + (x^2 - 1) = 1 \quad \text{Substitute } x^2 - 1 \text{ for } y.$$
$$x^2 + x - 2 = 0$$
$$(x - 1)(x + 2) = 0$$
$$x - 1 = 0 \quad \text{or} \quad x + 2 = 0$$
$$x = 1 \quad \text{or} \quad x = -2$$

Replace x by 1 and -2 in $y = x^2 - 1$ to find the corresponding values of y:

$$y = (1)^2 - 1 \qquad y = (-2)^2 - 1$$
$$y = 0 \qquad y = 3$$

Check that each of the points $(1, 0)$ and $(-2, 3)$ satisfies both of the original equations. The solution set is $\{(1, 0), (-2, 3)\}$. If we solve $x + y = 1$ for y, we get $y = -x + 1$. The line $y = -x + 1$ has y-intercept $(0, 1)$ and slope -1. The graph of $y = x^2 - 1$ is a parabola with vertex $(0, -1)$. Of course, $(1, 0)$ and $(-2, 3)$ are on both graphs. The two graphs are shown in Fig. 13.1.

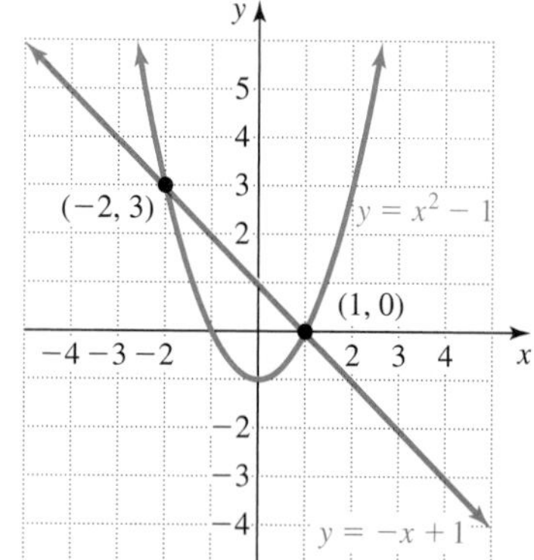

Figure 13.1

Now do Exercises 5–14

Nonlinear systems often have more than one solution and drawing the graphs helps us to understand why. However, it is not necessary to draw the graphs to solve the system, as shown in Example 2.

EXAMPLE 2

Solving a system algebraically with substitution

Solve the system:

$$x^2 + y^2 + 2y = 3$$
$$x^2 - y = 5$$

Teaching Tip Nonlinear systems are presented prior to the conic sections so that systems can be solved with each conic as it is presented.

Solution

If we substitute $y = x^2 - 5$ into the first equation to eliminate y, we will get a fourth-degree equation to solve. Instead, we can eliminate the variable x by writing $x^2 - y = 5$ as $x^2 = y + 5$. Now replace x^2 by $y + 5$ in the first equation:

$$\begin{aligned} x^2 + y^2 + 2y &= 3 \\ (y + 5) + y^2 + 2y &= 3 \\ y^2 + 3y + 5 &= 3 \\ y^2 + 3y + 2 &= 0 \\ (y + 2)(y + 1) &= 0 \quad \text{Solve by factoring.} \end{aligned}$$

$$y + 2 = 0 \quad \text{or} \quad y + 1 = 0$$
$$y = -2 \quad \text{or} \quad y = -1$$

Let $y = -2$ in the equation $x^2 = y + 5$ to find the corresponding x:

$$\begin{aligned} x^2 &= -2 + 5 \\ x^2 &= 3 \\ x &= \pm\sqrt{3} \end{aligned}$$

Now let $y = -1$ in the equation $x^2 = y + 5$ to find the corresponding x:

$$\begin{aligned} x^2 &= -1 + 5 \\ x^2 &= 4 \\ x &= \pm 2 \end{aligned}$$

Check these values in the original equations. The solution set is

$$\{(\sqrt{3}, -2), (-\sqrt{3}, -2), (2, -1), (-2, -1)\}.$$

The graphs of these two equations intersect at four points.

Now do Exercises 15–22

EXAMPLE 3

Solving a system with the addition method

Solve each system:

a) $x^2 - y^2 = 5$
$x^2 + y^2 = 7$

b) $\dfrac{2}{x} + \dfrac{1}{y} = \dfrac{1}{5}$
$\dfrac{1}{x} - \dfrac{3}{y} = \dfrac{1}{3}$

Study Tip

When you take notes leave space. Go back later and fill in more details, make corrections, or work another problem of the same type.

Solution

a) We can eliminate y by adding the equations:

$$\begin{aligned} x^2 - y^2 &= 5 \\ x^2 + y^2 &= 7 \\ \hline 2x^2 \quad &= 12 \\ x^2 &= 6 \\ x &= \pm\sqrt{6} \end{aligned}$$

Since $x^2 = 6$, the second equation yields $6 + y^2 = 7$, $y^2 = 1$, and $y = \pm 1$. If $x^2 = 6$ and $y^2 = 1$, then both of the original equations are satisfied. The solution set is

$$\{(\sqrt{6}, 1)(\sqrt{6}, -1), (-\sqrt{6}, 1), (-\sqrt{6}, -1)\}$$

b) Usually with equations involving rational expressions we first multiply by the least common denominator (LCD), but this would make the given system more complicated. So we will just use the addition method to eliminate y:

$$\frac{6}{x} + \frac{3}{y} = \frac{3}{5} \quad \text{Eq. (1) multiplied by 3}$$

$$\frac{1}{x} - \frac{3}{y} = \frac{1}{3} \quad \text{Eq. (2)}$$

$$\frac{7}{x} \quad = \frac{14}{15} \quad \frac{3}{5} + \frac{1}{3} = \frac{14}{15}$$

$$14x = 7 \cdot 15$$

$$x = \frac{7 \cdot 15}{14} = \frac{15}{2}$$

To find y, substitute $x = \frac{15}{2}$ into Eq. (1):

$$\frac{2}{\frac{15}{2}} + \frac{1}{y} = \frac{1}{5}$$

$$\frac{4}{15} + \frac{1}{y} = \frac{1}{5} \quad \frac{2}{\frac{15}{2}} = 2 \cdot \frac{2}{15} = \frac{4}{15}$$

$$15y \cdot \frac{4}{15} + 15y \cdot \frac{1}{y} = 15y \cdot \frac{1}{5} \quad \text{Multiply each side by the LCD, } 15y.$$

$$4y + 15 = 3y$$

$$y = -15$$

Check that $x = \frac{15}{2}$ and $y = -15$ satisfy both original equations. The solution set is $\left\{\left(\frac{15}{2}, -15\right)\right\}$.

Now do Exercises 23–38

A system of nonlinear equations might involve exponential or logarithmic functions. To solve such systems, you will need to recall some facts about exponents and logarithms.

EXAMPLE 4

A system involving logarithms

Solve the system

$$y = \log_2(x + 28)$$
$$y = 3 + \log_2(x)$$

Solution

Eliminate y by substituting $\log_2(x + 28)$ for y in the second equation:

$$\log_2(x + 28) = 3 + \log_2(x) \quad \text{Eliminate } y.$$
$$\log_2(x + 28) - \log_2(x) = 3 \quad \text{Subtract } \log_2(x) \text{ from each side.}$$
$$\log_2\left(\frac{x + 28}{x}\right) = 3 \quad \text{Quotient rule for logarithms}$$
$$\frac{x + 28}{x} = 8 \quad \text{Definition of logarithm}$$
$$x + 28 = 8x \quad \text{Multiply each side by } x.$$
$$28 = 7x \quad \text{Subtract } x \text{ from each side.}$$
$$4 = x \quad \text{Divide each side by 7.}$$

If $x = 4$, then $y = \log_2(4 + 28) = \log_2(32) = 5$. Check (4, 5) in both equations. The solution to the system is $\{(4, 5)\}$.

Now do Exercises 39–44

Applications

Example 5 shows a geometric problem that can be solved with a system of nonlinear equations.

EXAMPLE 5

Nonlinear equations in applications

A 15-foot ladder is leaning against a wall so that the distance from the bottom of the ladder to the wall is one-half of the distance from the top of the ladder to the ground. Find the distance from the top of the ladder to the ground.

Calculator Close-Up

To see the solutions, graph

$y_1 = \sqrt{15^2 - x^2}$,

$y_2 = -\sqrt{15^2 - x^2}$, and

$y_3 = 2x$.

The line intersects the circle twice.

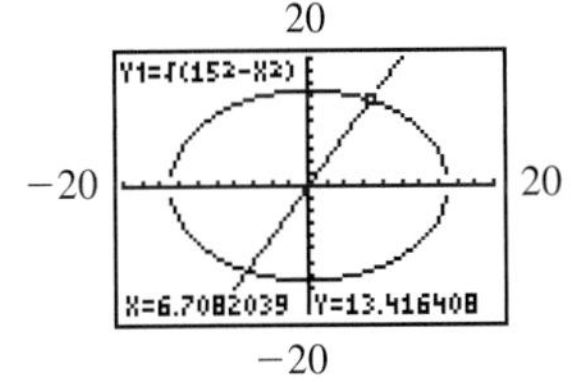

Solution

Let x be the number of feet from the bottom of the ladder to the wall and y be the number of feet from the top of the ladder to the ground (see Fig. 13.2 on the next page). We can write two equations involving x and y:

$$x^2 + y^2 = 15^2 \quad \text{Pythagorean theorem}$$
$$y = 2x$$

Solve by substitution:

$$x^2 + (2x)^2 = 225 \quad \text{Replace } y \text{ by } 2x.$$
$$x^2 + 4x^2 = 225$$
$$5x^2 = 225$$
$$x^2 = 45$$
$$x = \pm\sqrt{45} = \pm 3\sqrt{5}$$

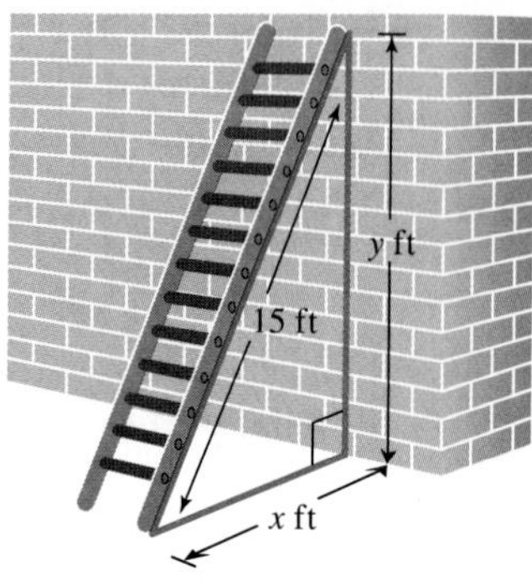

Figure 13.2

Because x represents distance, x must be positive. So $x = 3\sqrt{5}$. Because $y = 2x$, we get $y = 6\sqrt{5}$. The distance from the top of the ladder to the ground is $6\sqrt{5}$ feet.

Now do Exercises 45–48

Example 6 shows how a nonlinear system can be used to solve a problem involving work.

EXAMPLE 6

Nonlinear equations in applications

A large fish tank at the Gulf Aquarium can usually be filled in 10 minutes using pumps A and B. However, pump B can pump water in or out at the same rate. If pump B is inadvertently run in reverse, then the tank will be filled in 30 minutes. How long would it take each pump to fill the tank by itself?

Helpful Hint

Note that we could write equations about the rates. Pump A's rate is $\frac{1}{a}$ tank per minute, B's rate is $\frac{1}{b}$ tank per minute, and together their rate is $\frac{1}{10}$ tank per minute or $\frac{1}{30}$ tank per minute.

$$\frac{1}{a} + \frac{1}{b} = \frac{1}{10}$$

$$\frac{1}{a} - \frac{1}{b} = \frac{1}{30}$$

Solution

Let a represent the number of minutes that it takes pump A to fill the tank alone and b represent the number of minutes it takes pump B to fill the tank alone. The rate at which pump A fills the tank is $\frac{1}{a}$ of the tank per minute, and the rate at which pump B fills the tank is $\frac{1}{b}$ of the tank per minute. Because the work completed is the product of the rate and time, we can make the following table when the pumps work together to fill the tank:

	Rate	Time	Work
Pump A	$\frac{1}{a}\frac{\text{tank}}{\text{min}}$	10 min	$\frac{10}{a}$ tank
Pump B	$\frac{1}{b}\frac{\text{tank}}{\text{min}}$	10 min	$\frac{10}{b}$ tank

Note that each pump fills a fraction of the tank and those fractions have a sum of 1:

$$(1) \quad \frac{10}{a} + \frac{10}{b} = 1$$

Teaching Tip Note that this work problem is the same type that has been seen throughout this text, except that here the equations form a nonlinear system.

In the 30 minutes in which pump B is working in reverse, A puts in $\frac{30}{a}$ of the tank whereas B takes out $\frac{30}{b}$ of the tank. Since the tank still gets filled, we can write the following equation:

$$(2) \qquad \frac{30}{a} - \frac{30}{b} = 1$$

Multiply Eq. (1) by 3 and add the result to Eq. (2) to eliminate b:

$$\frac{30}{a} + \frac{30}{b} = 3 \quad \text{Eq. (1) multiplied by 3}$$

$$\frac{30}{a} - \frac{30}{b} = 1 \quad \text{Eq. (2)}$$

$$\frac{60}{a} = 4$$

$$4a = 60$$

$$a = 15$$

Use $a = 15$ in Eq. (1) to find b:

$$\frac{10}{15} + \frac{10}{b} = 1$$

$$\frac{10}{b} = \frac{1}{3} \quad \text{Subtract } \frac{10}{15} \text{ from each side.}$$

$$b = 30$$

So pump A fills the tank in 15 minutes working alone, and pump B fills the tank in 30 minutes working alone.

Now do Exercises 49–58

Warm-Ups ▼

True or false? Explain your answer.

1. The graph of $y = x^2$ is a parabola. True
2. The graph of $y = |x|$ is a straight line. False
3. The point $(3, -4)$ satisfies both $x^2 + y^2 = 25$ and $y = \sqrt{5x + 1}$. False
4. The graphs of $y = \sqrt{x}$ and $y = -x - 2$ do not intersect. True
5. Substitution is the only method for eliminating a variable when solving a nonlinear system. False
6. If Bob paints a fence in x hours, then he paints $\frac{1}{x}$ of the fence per hour. True
7. In a triangle whose angles are 30°, 60°, and 90°, the length of the side opposite the 30° angle is one-half the length of the hypotenuse. True
8. The formula $V = LWH$ gives the volume of a rectangular box in which the sides have lengths L, W, and H. True
9. The surface area of a rectangular box is $2LW + 2WH + 2LH$. True
10. The area of a right triangle is one-half the product of the lengths of its legs. True

13.1 Exercises

Boost your GRADE at mathzone.com!

MathZone

- Practice Problems
- Self-Tests
- Videos
- Net Tutor
- e-Professors

Reading and Writing *After reading this section, write out the answers to these questions. Use complete sentences.*

1. Why are some equations called nonlinear?
If the graph of an equation is not a straight line, then it is called nonlinear.
2. Why do we graph the equations in a nonlinear system?
With a graph we can see the approximate value of the solutions and the number of solutions.
3. Why don't we solve systems by graphing?
Graphing is not an accurate method for solving a system and the graphs might be difficult to draw.
4. What techniques do we use to solve nonlinear systems?
We generally use substitution and addition to solve nonlinear systems.

Solve each system and graph both equations on the same set of axes. See Example 1.

5. $y = x^2$
$x + y = 6$
$\{(2, 4), (-3, 9)\}$

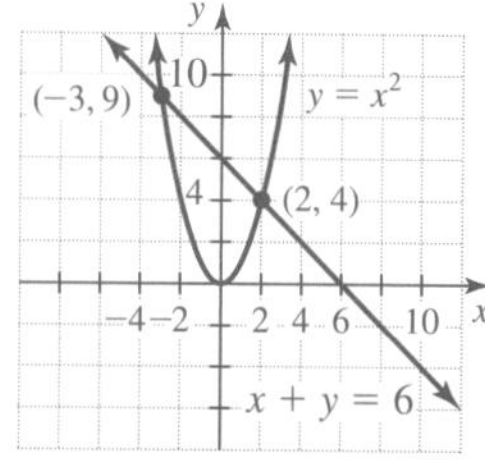

6. $y = x^2 - 1$
$x + y = 11$
$\{(-4, 15), (3, 8)\}$

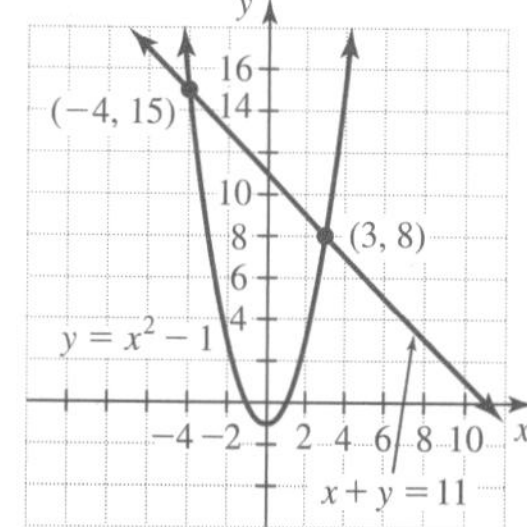

7. $y = |x|$
$2y - x = 6$
$\{(-2, 2), (6, 6)\}$

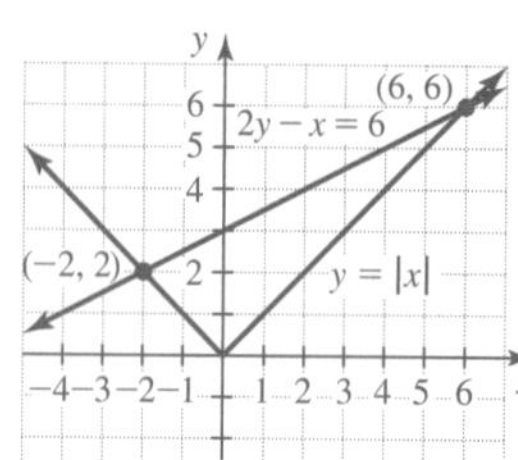

8. $y = |x|$
$3y = x + 6$
$\left\{\left(-\frac{3}{2}, \frac{3}{2}\right), (3, 3)\right\}$

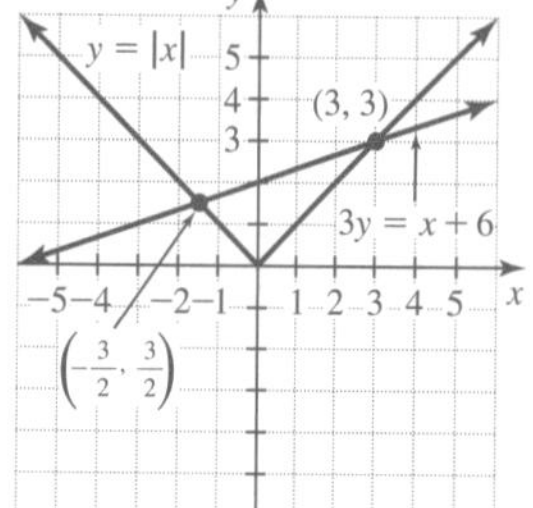

9. $y = \sqrt{2x}$
$x - y = 4$
$\{(8, 4)\}$

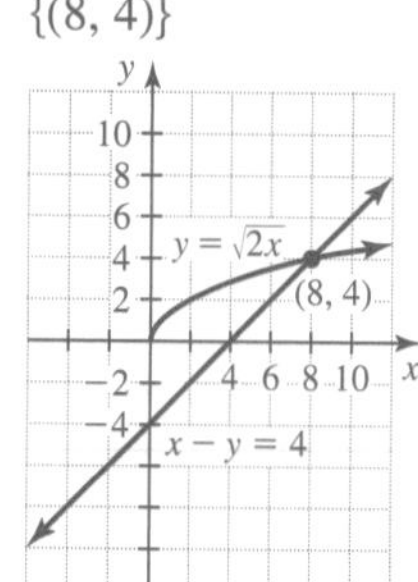

10. $y = \sqrt{x}$
$x - y = 6$
$\{(9, 3)\}$

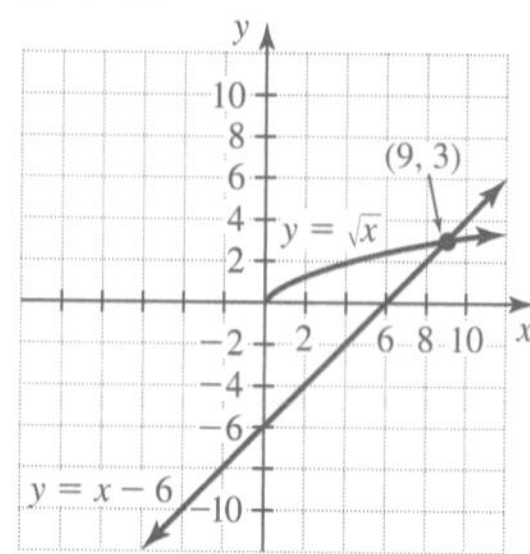

11. $4x - 9y = 9$
$xy = 1$

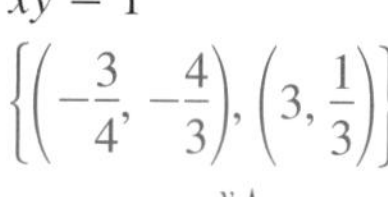

$\left\{\left(-\frac{3}{4}, -\frac{4}{3}\right), \left(3, \frac{1}{3}\right)\right\}$

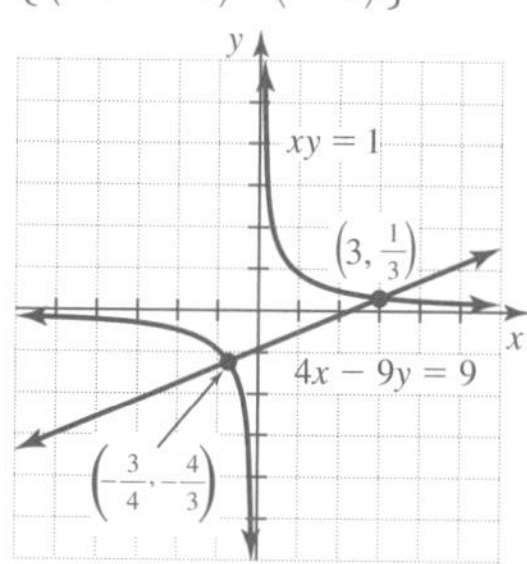

12. $2x + 2y = 3$
$xy = -1$

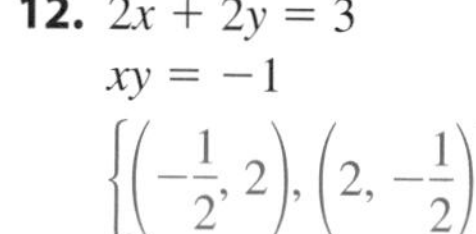

$\left\{\left(-\frac{1}{2}, 2\right), \left(2, -\frac{1}{2}\right)\right\}$

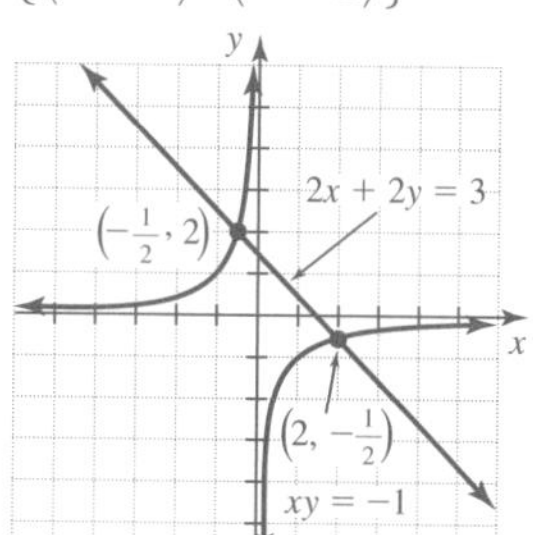

13. $y = -x^2 + 1$
$y = x^2$

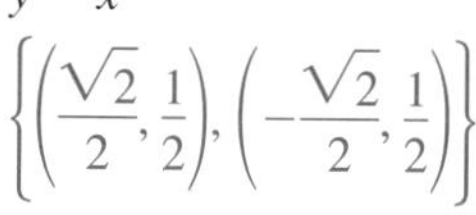

$\left\{\left(\frac{\sqrt{2}}{2}, \frac{1}{2}\right), \left(-\frac{\sqrt{2}}{2}, \frac{1}{2}\right)\right\}$

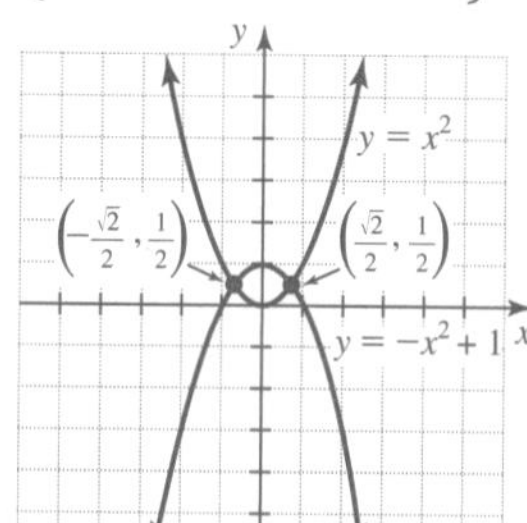

14. $y = x^2$
$y = \sqrt{x}$

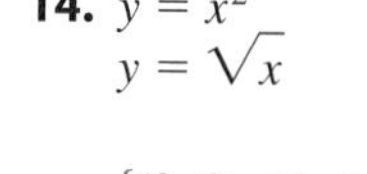

$\{(0, 0), (1, 1)\}$

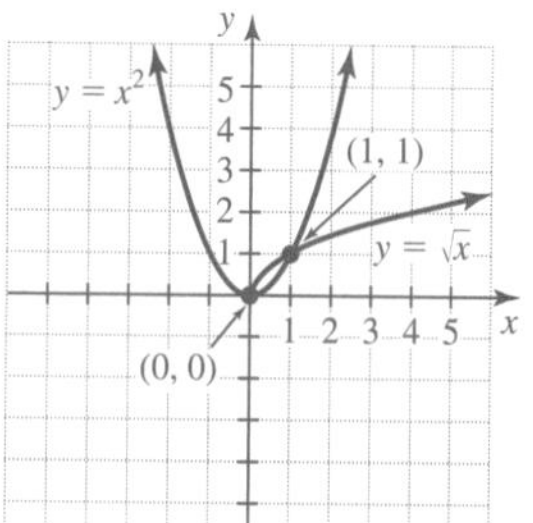

Solve each system. See Examples 2 and 3.

15. $xy = 1$
$y = x$
$\{(-1, -1), (1, 1)\}$

16. $y = x^2$
$y = x$
$\{(0, 0), (1, 1)\}$

17. $y = x^2$
$y = 2$
$\{(-\sqrt{2}, 2), (\sqrt{2}, 2)\}$

18. $xy = 3$
$y = x$
$\{(-\sqrt{3}, -\sqrt{3}), (\sqrt{3}, \sqrt{3})\}$

19. $x^2 + y^2 = 25$
$y = x^2 - 5$
$\{(0, -5), (3, 4), (-3, 4)\}$

20. $x^2 + y^2 = 25$
$y = x + 1$
$\{(-4, -3), (3, 4)\}$

21. $xy - 3x = 8$
$y = x + 1$
$\{(4, 5), (-2, -1)\}$

22. $xy + 2x = 9$
$x - y = 2$
$\{(3, 1), (-3, -5)\}$

23. $xy - x = 8$
$xy + 3x = -4$
$\left\{\left(-3, -\frac{5}{3}\right)\right\}$

24. $2xy - 3x = -1$
$xy + 5x = -7$
$\{(-1, 2)\}$

25. $x^2 + y^2 = 8$
$x^2 - y^2 = 2$
$\{(\sqrt{5}, \sqrt{3}), (\sqrt{5}, -\sqrt{3}), (-\sqrt{5}, \sqrt{3}), (-\sqrt{5}, -\sqrt{3})\}$

26. $y^2 - 2x^2 = 1$
$y^2 + 2x^2 = 5$
$\{(1, \sqrt{3}), (1, -\sqrt{3}), (-1, \sqrt{3}), (-1, -\sqrt{3})\}$

27. $x^2 + 2y^2 = 8$
$2x^2 - y^2 = 1$
$\{(\sqrt{2}, \sqrt{3}), (\sqrt{2}, -\sqrt{3}), (-\sqrt{2}, \sqrt{3}), (-\sqrt{2}, -\sqrt{3})\}$

28. $2x^2 + 3y^2 = 8$
$3x^2 + 2y^2 = 7$
$\{(1, \sqrt{2}), (1, -\sqrt{2}), (-1, \sqrt{2}), (-1, -\sqrt{2})\}$

29. $\frac{1}{x} - \frac{1}{y} = 5$
$\frac{2}{x} + \frac{1}{y} = -3$
$\left\{\left(\frac{3}{2}, -\frac{3}{13}\right)\right\}$

30. $\frac{2}{x} - \frac{3}{y} = \frac{1}{2}$
$\frac{3}{x} + \frac{1}{y} = \frac{1}{2}$
$\left\{\left(\frac{11}{2}, -22\right)\right\}$

31. $\frac{2}{x} - \frac{1}{y} = \frac{5}{12}$
$\frac{1}{x} - \frac{3}{y} = -\frac{5}{12}$
$\{(3, 4)\}$

32. $\frac{3}{x} - \frac{2}{y} = 5$
$\frac{4}{x} + \frac{3}{y} = 18$
$\left\{\left(\frac{1}{3}, \frac{1}{2}\right)\right\}$

33. $x^2y = 20$
$xy + 2 = 6x$
$\left\{\left(-\frac{5}{3}, \frac{36}{5}\right), (2, 5)\right\}$

34. $y^2x = 3$
$xy + 1 = 6x$
$\left\{\left(\frac{1}{12}, -6\right), \left(\frac{1}{3}, 3\right)\right\}$

35. $x^2 + xy - y^2 = -11$
$x + y = 7$
$\{(2, 5), (19, -12)\}$

36. $x^2 + xy + y^2 = 3$
$y = 2x - 5$
$\left\{\left(\frac{11}{7}, -\frac{13}{7}\right), (2, -1)\right\}$

37. $3y - 2 = x^4$
$y = x^2$
$\{(\sqrt{2}, 2), (-\sqrt{2}, 2), (1, 1), (-1, 1)\}$

38. $y - 3 = 2x^4$
$y = 7x^2$
$\left\{\left(\frac{\sqrt{2}}{2}, \frac{7}{2}\right), \left(-\frac{\sqrt{2}}{2}, \frac{7}{2}\right), (\sqrt{3}, 21), (-\sqrt{3}, 21)\right\}$

Solve the following systems involving logarithmic and exponential functions. See Example 4.

39. $y = \log_2(x - 1)$
$y = 3 - \log_2(x + 1)$
$\{(3, 1)\}$

40. $y = \log_3(x - 4)$
$y = 2 - \log_3(x + 4)$
$\{(5, 0)\}$

41. $y = \log_2(x - 1)$
$y = 2 + \log_2(x + 2)$
$\varnothing$

42. $y = \log_4(8x)$
$y = 2 + \log_4(x - 1)$
$\{(2, 2)\}$

43. $y = 2^{3x+4}$
$y = 4^{x-1}$
$\{(-6, 4^{-7})\}$

44. $y = 4^{3x}$
$y = \left(\frac{1}{2}\right)^{1-x}$
$\left\{\left(-\frac{1}{5}, 4^{-3/5}\right)\right\}$

Solve each problem by using a system of two equations in two unknowns. See Examples 5 and 6.

45. ***Known hypotenuse.*** Find the lengths of the legs of a right triangle whose hypotenuse is $\sqrt{15}$ feet and whose area is 3 square feet. $\sqrt{3}$ ft and $2\sqrt{3}$ ft

46. ***Known diagonal.*** A small television is advertised to have a picture with a diagonal measure of 5 inches and a viewing area of 12 square inches (in.^{2}). What are the length and width of the screen? 3 inches by 4 inches

Figure for Exercise 46

47. ***House of seven gables.*** Vincent has plans to build a house with seven gables. The plans call for an attic vent in the shape of an isosceles triangle in each gable. Because of the slope of the roof, the ratio of the height to the base of each triangle must be 1 to 4. If the vents are to provide a total ventilating area of 3500 in.^{2}, then what should be the height and base of each triangle?
Height $5\sqrt{10}$ inches, base $20\sqrt{10}$ inches

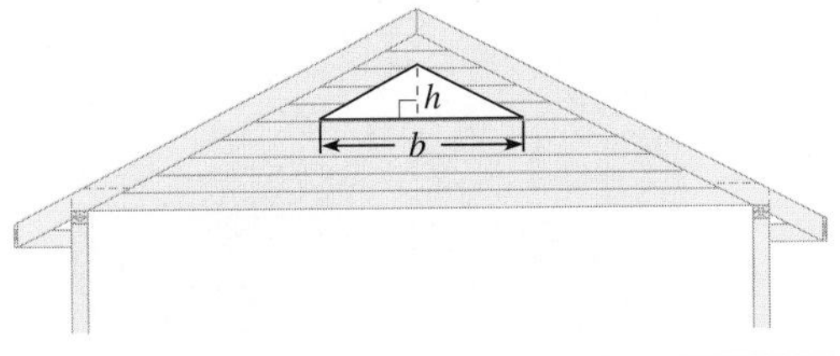

Figure for Exercise 47

48. ***Known perimeter.*** Find the lengths of the sides of a triangle whose perimeter is 6 feet (ft) and whose angles are 30°, 60°, and 90° (see Appendix A).
$3 - \sqrt{3}$ ft, $6 - 2\sqrt{3}$ ft, $-3 + 3\sqrt{3}$ ft

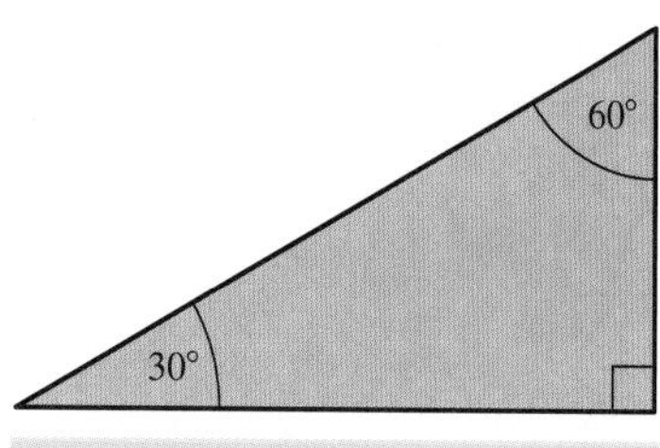

Figure for Exercise 48

49. ***Filling a tank.*** Pump A can either fill a tank or empty it in the same amount of time. If pump A and pump B are working together, the tank can be filled in 6 hours. When pump A was inadvertently left in the drain position while pump B was trying to fill the tank, it took 12 hours to fill the tank. How long would it take either pump working alone to fill the tank? Pump A 24 hours, pump B 8 hours

50. ***Cleaning a house.*** Roxanne either cleans the house or messes it up at the same rate. When Roxanne is cleaning with her mother, they can clean up a completely messed up house in 6 hours. If Roxanne is not cooperating, it takes her mother 9 hours to clean the house, with Roxanne continually messing it up. How long would it take her mother to clean the entire house if Roxanne were sent to her grandmother's house?
$\frac{36}{5}$ hours

51. ***Cleaning fish.*** Jan and Beth work in a seafood market that processes 200 pounds of catfish every morning. On Monday, Jan started cleaning catfish at 8:00 A.M. and finished cleaning 100 pounds just as Beth arrived. Beth then took over and finished the job at 8:50 A.M. On Tuesday they both started at 8 A.M. and worked together to finish the job at 8:24 A.M. On Wednesday, Beth was sick. If Jan is the faster worker, then how long did it take Jan to complete all of the catfish by herself?
40 minutes

Photo for Exercise 51

52. ***Building a patio.*** Richard has already formed a rectangular area for a flagstone patio, but his wife Susan is unsure of the size of the patio they want. If the width is increased by 2 ft, then the area is increased by 30 square feet (ft^2). If the width is increased by 1 ft and the length by 3 ft, then the area is increased by 54 ft^2. What are the dimensions of the rectangle that Richard has already formed? 12 ft by 15 ft

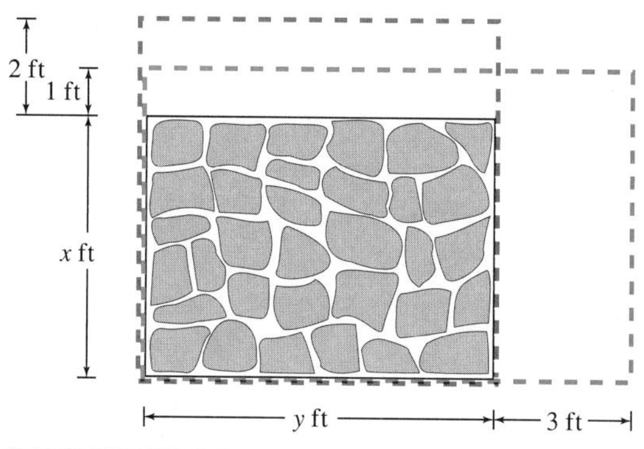

Figure for Exercise 52

53. ***Fencing a rectangle.*** If 34 ft of fencing are used to enclose a rectangular area of 72 ft^2, then what are the dimensions of the area? 8 ft by 9 ft

54. ***Real numbers.*** Find two numbers that have a sum of 8 and a product of 10. $4 - \sqrt{6}$ and $4 + \sqrt{6}$

55. ***Imaginary numbers.*** Find two complex numbers whose sum is 8 and whose product is 20. $4 - 2i$ and $4 + 2i$

56. ***Imaginary numbers.*** Find two complex numbers whose sum is -6 and whose product is 10. $-3 + i$ and $-3 - i$

57. ***Making a sign.*** Rico's Sign Shop has a contract to make a sign in the shape of a square with an isosceles triangle on top of it, as shown in the figure. The contract calls for a total height of 10 ft with an area of 72 ft^2. How long should Rico make the side of the square and what should be the height of the triangle?
Side 8 ft, height of triangle 2 ft

58. ***Designing a box.*** Angelina is designing a rectangular box of 120 cubic inches that is to contain new Eaties breakfast cereal. The box must be 2 inches thick so that it is easy to hold. It must have 184 square inches of surface area to provide enough space for all of the special offers and coupons. What should be the dimensions of the box?
6 inches by 10 inches by 2 inches

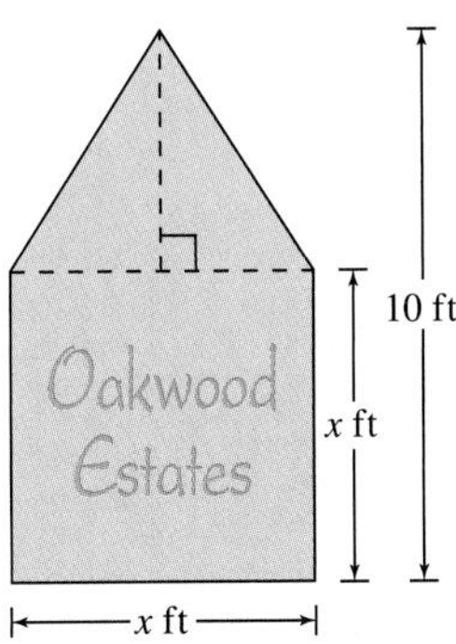

Figure for Exercise 57

Graphing Calculator Exercises

59. Solve each system by graphing each pair of equations on a graphing calculator and using the intersect feature to estimate the point of intersection. Find the coordinates of each intersection to the nearest hundredth.

a) $y = e^x - 4$
$y = \ln(x + 3)$

b) $3^{y-1} = x$
$y = x^2$

c) $x^2 + y^2 = 4$
$y = x^3$

a) (1.71, 1.55), (−2.98, −3.95)
b) (1, 1), (0.40, 0.16)
c) (1.17, 1.62), (−1.17, −1.62)

13.2 The Parabola

In this Section

- The Distance Formula
- The Geometric Definition of Parabola
- Developing the Equation
- Parabolas in the Form $y = a(x - h)^2 + k$
- Finding the Vertex, Focus, and Directrix
- Axis of Symmetry
- Changing Forms
- Parabolas Opening to the Right or Left

The **conic sections** are the four curves that are obtained by intersecting a cone and a plane as in Fig. 13.3. The figure explains why the parabola, ellipse, circle, and hyperbola are called conic sections, but it does not help us find equations for the curves. To develop equations for these curves we will redefine them more precisely using distance between points. So we will first learn the distance formula.

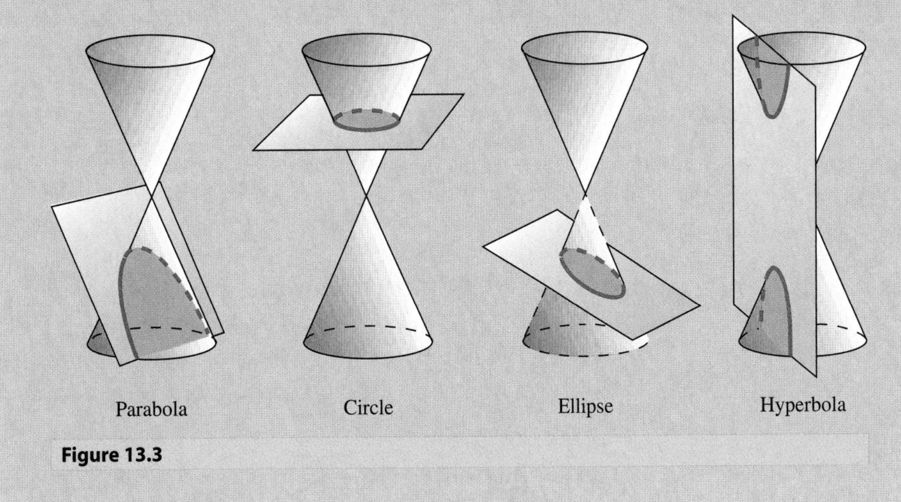

Figure 13.3

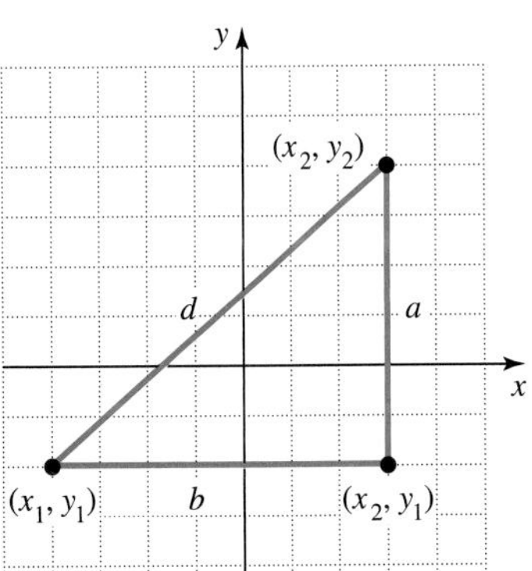

Figure 13.4

The Distance Formula

Consider the points (x_1, y_1) and (x_2, y_2), as shown in Fig. 13.4. The distance between these points is the length of the hypotenuse of a right triangle as shown in the figure. The length of side a is $y_2 - y_1$ and the length of side b is $x_2 - x_1$. Using the Pythagorean theorem, we can write

$$d^2 = (x_2 - x_1)^2 + (y_2 - y_1)^2.$$

If we apply the even-root property and omit the negative square root (because the distance is positive), we can express this formula as follows.

Distance Formula

The distance d between (x_1, y_1) and (x_2, y_2) is given by the formula

$$d = \sqrt{(x_2 - x_1)^2 + (y_2 - y_1)^2}.$$

EXAMPLE 1

Using the distance formula

Find the length of the line segment with endpoints $(-8, -10)$ and $(6, -4)$.

Solution

Let $(x_1, y_1) = (-8, -10)$ and $(x_2, y_2) = (6, -4)$. Now substitute the appropriate values into the distance formula:

$$\begin{aligned} d &= \sqrt{[6 - (-8)]^2 + [-4 - (-10)]^2} \\ &= \sqrt{(14)^2 + (6)^2} \\ &= \sqrt{196 + 36} \\ &= \sqrt{232} \\ &= \sqrt{4 \cdot 58} \\ &= 2\sqrt{58} \quad \text{Simplified form} \end{aligned}$$

The exact length of the segment is $2\sqrt{58}$.

Now do Exercises 7–14

The Geometric Definition of Parabola

In Section 9.3 we called the graph of $y = ax^2 + bx + c$ a parabola. This equation is the **standard equation** of a parabola. In this section you will see that the following geometric definition describes the same curve as the equation.

Parabola

Given a line (the **directrix**) and a point not on the line (the **focus**), the set of all points in the plane that are equidistant from the point and the line is called a **parabola.**

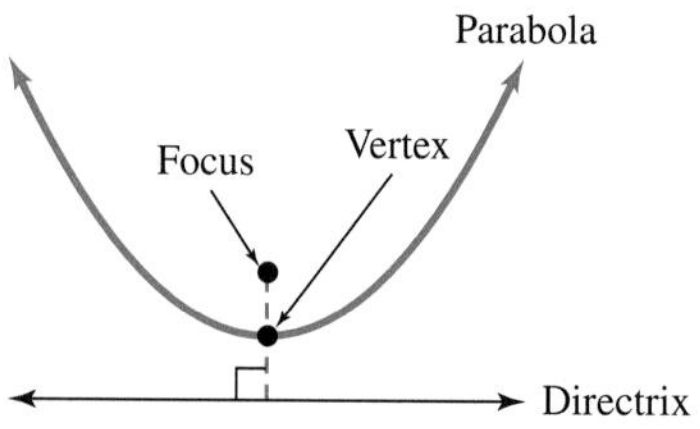

Figure 13.5

In Section 9.3 we defined the vertex as the highest point on a parabola that opens downward or the lowest point on a parabola that opens upward. We learned that $x = -b/(2a)$ gives the x-coordinate of the vertex. We can also describe the vertex of a parabola as the midpoint of the line segment that joins the focus and directrix, perpendicular to the directrix. See Fig. 13.5.

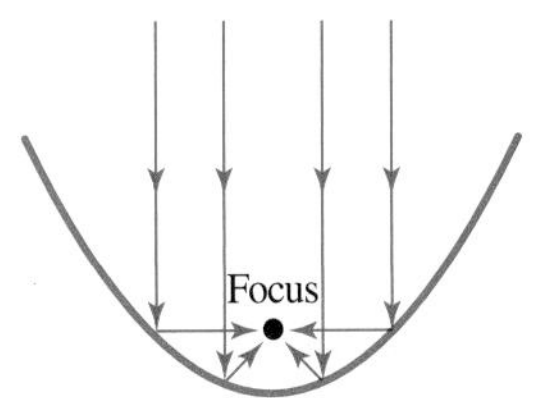

Figure 13.6

The focus of a parabola is important in applications. When parallel rays of light travel into a parabolic reflector, they are reflected toward the focus, as in Fig. 13.6. This property is used in telescopes to see the light from distant stars. If the light source is at the focus, as in a searchlight, the light is reflected off the parabola and projected outward in a narrow beam. This reflecting property is also used in camera lenses, satellite dishes, and eavesdropping devices.

Developing the Equation

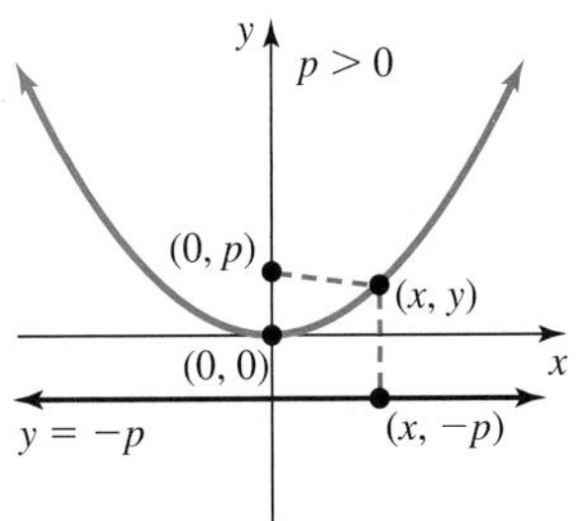

Figure 13.7

To develop an equation for a parabola, given the focus and directrix, choose the point $(0, p)$, where $p > 0$, as the focus and the line $y = -p$ as the directrix, as shown in Fig. 13.7. The vertex of this parabola is $(0, 0)$. For an arbitrary point (x, y) on the parabola the distance to the directrix is the distance from (x, y) to $(x, -p)$. The distance to the focus is the distance between (x, y) and $(0, p)$. We use the fact that these distances are equal to write the equation of the parabola:

$$\sqrt{(x-0)^2 + (y-p)^2} = \sqrt{(x-x)^2 + (y-(-p))^2}$$

To simplify the equation, first remove the parentheses inside the radicals:

$$\sqrt{x^2 + y^2 - 2py + p^2} = \sqrt{y^2 + 2py + p^2}$$

$$x^2 + y^2 - 2py + p^2 = y^2 + 2py + p^2 \quad \text{Square each side.}$$

$$x^2 = 4py \quad \text{Subtract } y^2 \text{ and } p^2 \text{ from each side.}$$

$$y = \frac{1}{4p}x^2$$

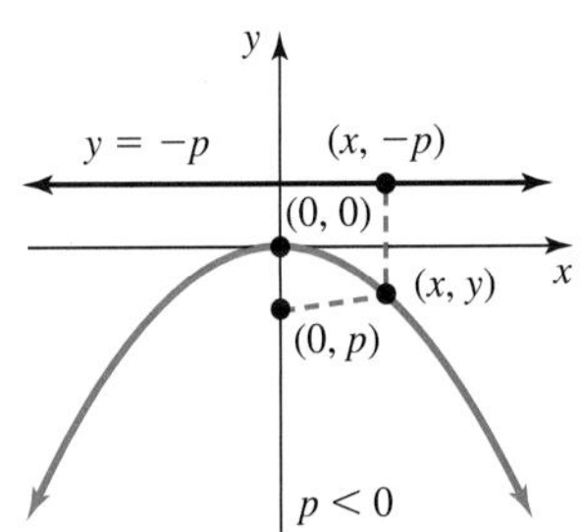

Figure 13.8

So the parabola with focus $(0, p)$ and directrix $y = -p$ for $p > 0$ has equation $y = \frac{1}{4p}x^2$. This equation has the form $y = ax^2 + bx + c$, where $a = \frac{1}{4p}$, $b = 0$, and $c = 0$.

If the focus is $(0, p)$ with $p < 0$ and the directrix is $y = -p$, then the parabola opens downward, as shown in Fig. 13.8. Deriving the equation using the distance formula again yields $y = \frac{1}{4p}x^2$.

Parabolas in the Form $y = a(x - h)^2 + k$

The simplest parabola, $y = x^2$, has vertex $(0, 0)$. The transformation $y = a(x - h)^2 + k$ is also a parabola and its vertex is (h, k). The focus and directrix of the transformation are found as follows:

Parabolas in the Form $y = a(x - h)^2 + k$

The graph of the equation $y = a(x - h)^2 + k$ $(a \neq 0)$ is a parabola with vertex (h, k), focus $(h, k + p)$, and directrix $y = k - p$, where $a = \frac{1}{4p}$. If $a > 0$, the parabola opens upward; if $a < 0$, the parabola opens downward.

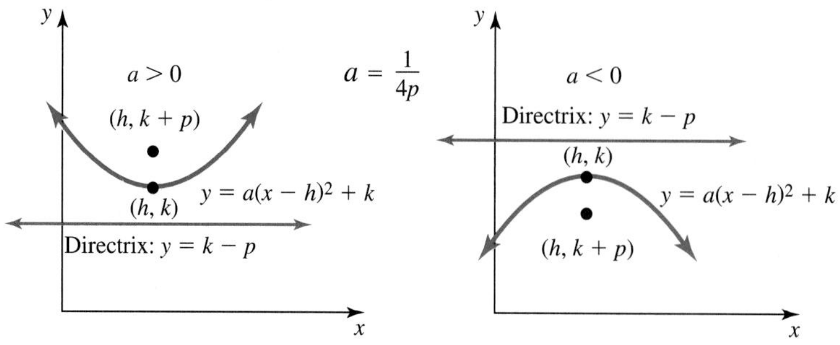

Figure 13.9

Figure 13.9 shows the location of the focus and directrix for parabolas with vertex (h, k) and opening either upward or downward. Note that the location of the focus and directrix determine the value of a and the shape and opening of the parabola.

CAUTION For a parabola that opens upward, $p > 0$, and the focus $(h, k + p)$ is above the vertex (h, k). For a parabola that opens downward, $p < 0$, and the focus $(h, k + p)$ is below the vertex (h, k). In either case, the distance from the vertex to the focus and the vertex to the directrix is $|p|$.

Finding the Vertex, Focus, and Directrix

In Example 2 we find the vertex, focus, and directrix from an equation of a parabola. In Example 3 we find the equation given the focus and directrix.

EXAMPLE 2

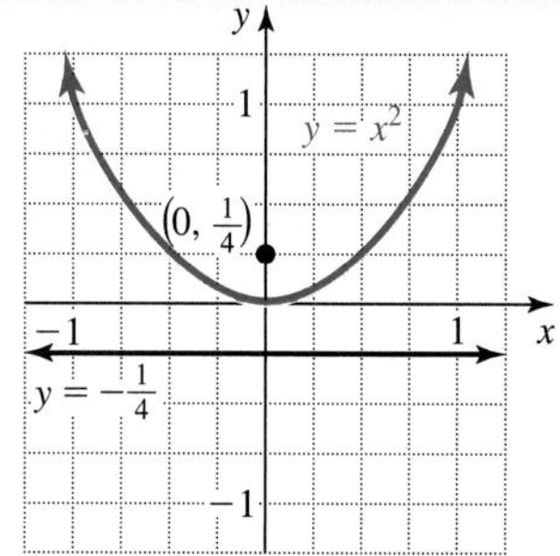

Figure 13.10

Finding the vertex, focus, and directrix, given an equation

Find the vertex, focus, and directrix for the parabola $y = x^2$.

Solution

Compare $y = x^2$ to the general formula $y = a(x - h)^2 + k$. We see that $h = 0$, $k = 0$, and $a = 1$. So the vertex is $(0, 0)$. Because $a = 1$, we can use $a = \frac{1}{4p}$ to get

$$1 = \frac{1}{4p},$$

or $p = \frac{1}{4}$. Use $(h, k + p)$ to get the focus $\left(0, \frac{1}{4}\right)$. Use the equation $y = k - p$ to get $y = -\frac{1}{4}$ as the equation of the directrix. See Fig. 13.10.

Now do Exercises 15–22

EXAMPLE 3

Finding an equation, given a focus and directrix

Find the equation of the parabola with focus $(-1, 4)$ and directrix $y = 3$.

Solution

Because the vertex is halfway between the focus and directrix, the vertex is $\left(-1, \frac{7}{2}\right)$. See Fig. 13.11 on the next page. The distance from the vertex to the focus

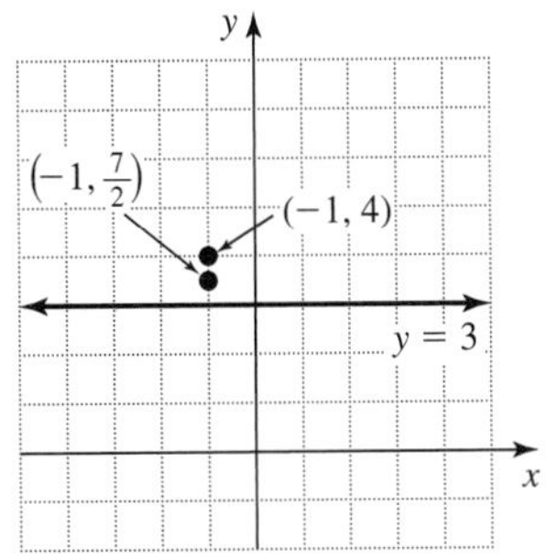

Figure 13.11

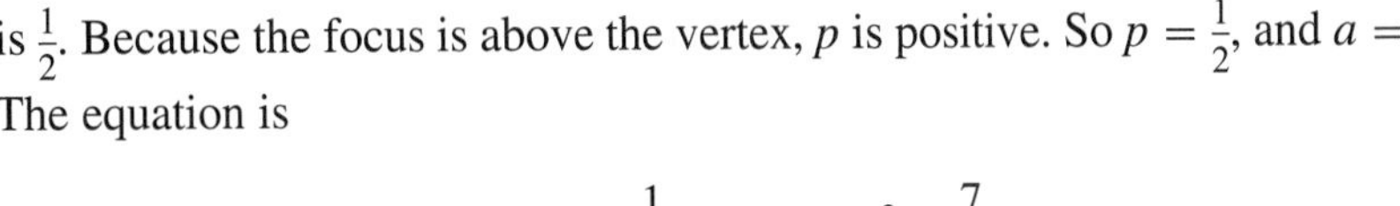

is $\frac{1}{2}$. Because the focus is above the vertex, p is positive. So $p = \frac{1}{2}$, and $a = \frac{1}{4p} = \frac{1}{2}$. The equation is

$$y = \frac{1}{2}(x - (-1))^2 + \frac{7}{2}.$$

Convert to $y = ax^2 + bx + c$ form as follows:

$$y = \frac{1}{2}(x + 1)^2 + \frac{7}{2}$$

$$y = \frac{1}{2}(x^2 + 2x + 1) + \frac{7}{2}$$

$$y = \frac{1}{2}x^2 + x + 4$$

Now do Exercises 23–32

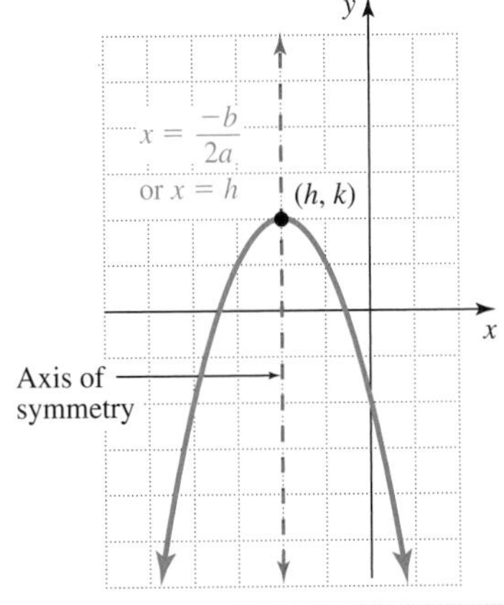

Figure 13.12

Axis of Symmetry

The graph of $y = x^2$ shown in Fig. 13.10 is **symmetric about the y-axis** because the two halves of the parabola would coincide if the paper were folded on the y-axis. In general, the vertical line through the vertex is the **axis of symmetry** for the parabola. See Fig. 13.12. In the form $y = ax^2 + bx + c$ the x-coordinate of the vertex is $-b/(2a)$ and the equation of the axis of symmetry is $x = -b/(2a)$. In the form $y = a(x - h)^2 + k$ the vertex is (h, k) and the equation for the axis of symmetry is $x = h$.

Changing Forms

Since there are two forms for the equation of a parabola, it is sometimes useful to change from one form to the other. To change from $y = a(x - h)^2 + k$ to the form $y = ax^2 + bx + c$, we square the binomial and combine like terms, as in Example 3. To change from $y = ax^2 + bx + c$ to the form $y = a(x - h)^2 + k$, we complete the square, as in Example 4.

EXAMPLE 4

Converting $y = ax^2 + bx + c$ to $y = a(x - h)^2 + k$

Write $y = 2x^2 - 4x + 5$ in the form $y = a(x - h)^2 + k$ and identify the vertex, focus, directrix, and axis of symmetry of the parabola.

Teaching Tip Students have trouble with completing the square inside the parentheses here. Go over the details carefully.

Solution

Use completing the square to rewrite the equation:

$$y = 2(x^2 - 2x) + 5$$

$$y = 2(x^2 - 2x + 1 - 1) + 5 \quad \text{Complete the square.}$$

$$y = 2(x^2 - 2x + 1) - 2 + 5 \quad \text{Move } 2(-1) \text{ outside the parentheses.}$$

$$y = 2(x - 1)^2 + 3$$

Calculator Close-Up

The graphs of

$$y_1 = 2x^2 - 4x + 5$$

and

$$y_2 = 2(x - 1)^2 + 3$$

appear to be identical. This supports the conclusion that the equations are equivalent.

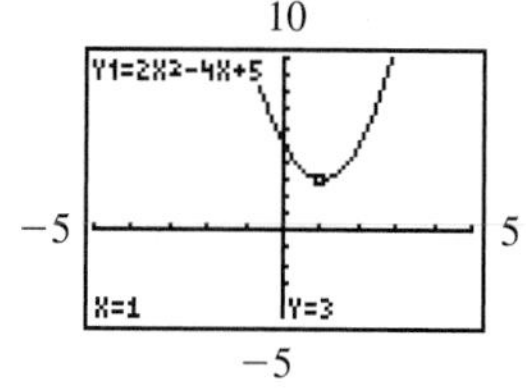

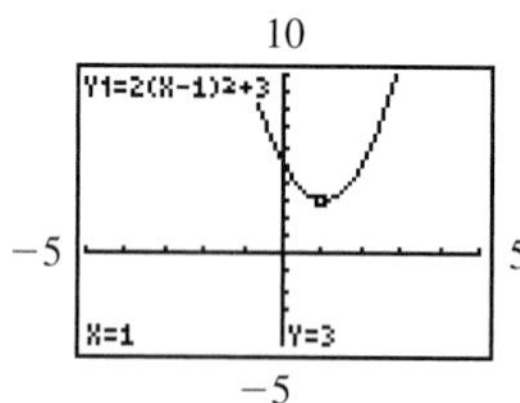

The vertex is (1, 3). Because $a = \frac{1}{4p}$, we have

$$\frac{1}{4p} = 2,$$

and $p = \frac{1}{8}$. Because the parabola opens upward, the focus is $\frac{1}{8}$ unit above the vertex at $\left(1, 3\frac{1}{8}\right)$, or $\left(1, \frac{25}{8}\right)$, and the directrix is the horizontal line $\frac{1}{8}$ unit below the vertex, $y = 2\frac{7}{8}$ or $y = \frac{23}{8}$. The axis of symmetry is $x = 1$.

Now do Exercises 33–40

CAUTION Be careful when you complete a square within parentheses as in Example 4. For another example, consider the equivalent equations

$$y = -3(x^2 + 4x),$$

$$y = -3(x^2 + 4x + 4 - 4),$$

and

$$y = -3(x + 2)^2 + 12.$$

EXAMPLE 5

Finding the features of a parabola from standard form

Find the vertex, focus, directrix, and axis of symmetry of the parabola $y = -3x^2 + 9x - 5$, and determine whether the parabola opens upward or downward.

Calculator Close-Up

A calculator graph can be used to check the vertex and opening of a parabola.

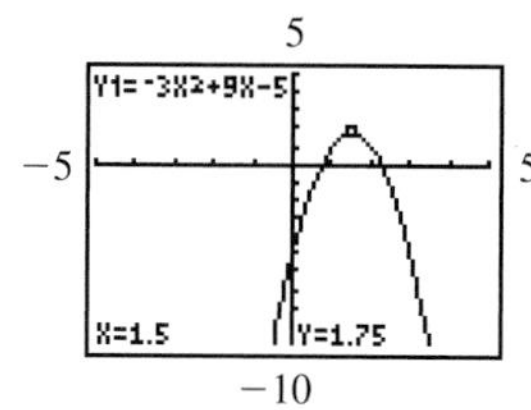

Solution

The x-coordinate of the vertex is

$$x = \frac{-b}{2a} = \frac{-9}{2(-3)} = \frac{-9}{-6} = \frac{3}{2}.$$

To find the y-coordinate of the vertex, let $x = \frac{3}{2}$ in $y = -3x^2 + 9x - 5$:

$$y = -3\left(\frac{3}{2}\right)^2 + 9\left(\frac{3}{2}\right) - 5 = -\frac{27}{4} + \frac{27}{2} - 5 = \frac{7}{4}$$

The vertex is $\left(\frac{3}{2}, \frac{7}{4}\right)$. Because $a = -3$, the parabola opens downward. To find the focus, use $-3 = \frac{1}{4p}$ to get $p = -\frac{1}{12}$. The focus is $\frac{1}{12}$ of a unit below the vertex at $\left(\frac{3}{2}, \frac{7}{4} - \frac{1}{12}\right)$ or $\left(\frac{3}{2}, \frac{5}{3}\right)$. The directrix is the horizontal line $\frac{1}{12}$ of a unit above the vertex, $y = \frac{7}{4} + \frac{1}{12}$ or $y = \frac{11}{6}$. The equation of the axis of symmetry is $x = \frac{3}{2}$.

Now do Exercises 41–50

Parabolas Opening to the Right or Left

If we interchange x and y in the equation $y = a(x - h)^2 + k$ we get the equation $x = a(y - k)^2 + h$, which is a parabola opening to the right or left.

Parabolas in the Form $x = a(y - k)^2 + h$

The graph of $x = a(y - k)^2 + h$ $(a \neq 0)$ is a parabola with vertex (h, k), focus $(h + p, k)$, and directrix $x = h - p$, where $a = \frac{1}{4p}$. If $a > 0$, the parabola opens to the right; if $a < 0$, the parabola opens to the left.

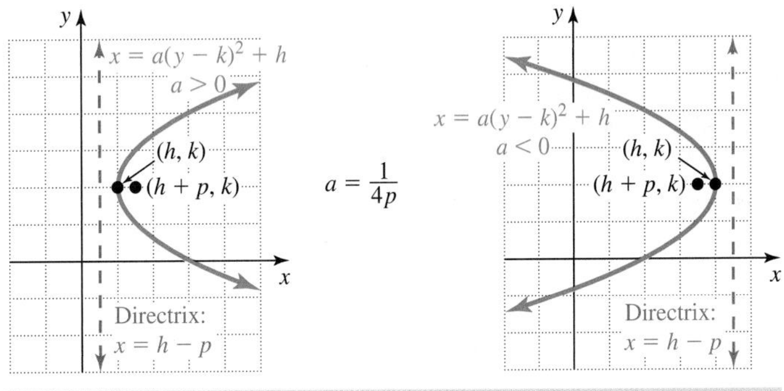

Figure 13.13

Figure 13.13 shows the location of the focus and directrix for parabolas with vertex (h, k) and opening either right or left. The location of the focus and directrix determine the value of a and the shape and opening of the parabola. Note that a and p have the same sign because $a = \frac{1}{4p}$.

The equation $x = ay^2 + by + c$ could be converted to the form $x = a(y - k)^2 + h$ from which the vertex, focus, and directrix could be determined. Without converting we can determine that the graph of $x = ay^2 + by + c$ opens to the right for $a > 0$ and to the left for $a < 0$. The y-coordinate of the vertex is $\frac{-b}{2a}$. The x-coordinate of the vertex can be determined by substituting $\frac{-b}{2a}$ for y in $x = ay^2 + by + c$.

EXAMPLE 6

Graphing a parabola opening to the right

Find the vertex, focus, and directrix for the parabola $x = \frac{1}{2}(y - 2)^2 + 1$ and sketch the graph.

Solution

In the form $x = a(y - k)^2 + h$, the vertex is (h, k). So the vertex for $x = \frac{1}{2}(y - 2)^2 + 1$ is $(1, 2)$. Since $a = \frac{1}{4p}$ and $a = \frac{1}{2}$, we have $p = \frac{1}{2}$ and the focus is

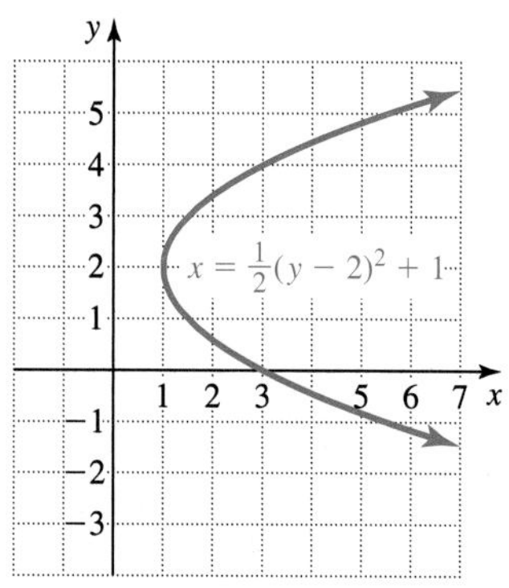

Figure 13.14

$\left(\frac{3}{2}, 2\right)$. The directrix is the vertical line $x = \frac{1}{2}$. Find a few points that satisfy $x = \frac{1}{2}(y-2)^2 + 1$ as follows:

$x = \frac{1}{2}(y-2)^2 + 1$	3	$\frac{3}{2}$	1	$\frac{3}{2}$	3
y	0	1	2	3	4

Sketch the graph through these points, as shown in Fig. 13.14.

Now do Exercises 51–56

Warm-Ups ▼

True or false? Explain your answer.

1. There is a parabola with focus (2, 3), directrix $y = 1$, and vertex (0, 0). False
2. The focus for the parabola $y = \frac{1}{4}x^2 + 1$ is (0, 2). True
3. The graph of $y - 3 = 5(x - 4)^2$ is a parabola with vertex (4, 3). True
4. The graph of $y = 6x + 3x + 2$ is a parabola. False
5. The graph of $y = 2x - x^2 + 9$ is a parabola opening upward. False
6. For $y = x^2$ the vertex and y-intercept are the same point. True
7. A parabola with vertex (2, 3) and focus (2, 4) has no x-intercepts. True
8. The parabola with focus (0, 2) and directrix $y = 1$ opens upward. True
9. The axis of symmetry for $y = a(x - 2)^2 + k$ is $x = 2$. True
10. If $a = \frac{1}{4p}$ and $a = 1$, then $p = \frac{1}{4}$. True

13.2 Exercises

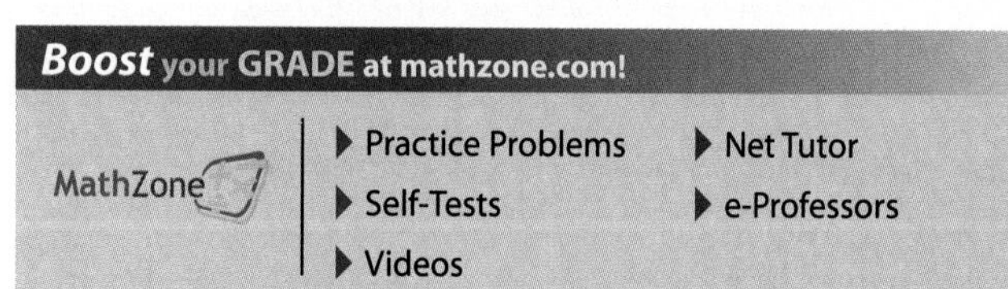

Reading and Writing *After reading this section, write out the answers to these questions. Use complete sentences.*

1. What is the definition of a parabola given in this section?
   A parabola is the set of all points in a plane that are equidistant from a given line and a fixed point not on the line.
2. What is the location of the vertex?
   The vertex is the midpoint of the line segment joining the focus and directrix, perpendicular to the directrix.
3. What are the two forms of the equation of a parabola?
   A parabola can be written in the forms $y = ax^2 + bx + c$ or $y = a(x - h)^2 + k$.
4. What is the distance from the focus to the vertex in any parabola of the form $y = ax^2 + bx + c$?
   The distance from the focus to the vertex is $|p|$, where $a = \frac{1}{4p}$.

5. How do we convert an equation of the form $y = ax^2 + bx + c$ into the form $y = a(x - h)^2 + k$?
We use completing the square to convert $y = ax^2 + bx + c$ into $y = a(x - h)^2 + k$.

6. How do we convert an equation of the form $y = a(x - h)^2 + k$ into the form $y = ax^2 + bx + c$?
To convert $y = a(x - h)^2 + k$ into the form $y = ax^2 + bx + c$, square the binomial, multiply by a, then add like terms.

Find the distance between each given pair of points. See Example 1.

7. (4, −3), (5, −2) $\sqrt{2}$
8. (−1, 5), (−2, 6) $\sqrt{2}$
9. (6, 5), (4, 2) $\sqrt{13}$
10. (7, 3), (5, 1) $2\sqrt{2}$
11. (3, 5), (1, −3) $2\sqrt{17}$
12. (6, 2), (3, −5) $\sqrt{58}$
13. (4, −2), (−3, −6) $\sqrt{65}$
14. (−2, 3), (1, −4) $\sqrt{58}$

Find the vertex, focus, and directrix for each parabola. See Example 2.

15. $y = 2x^2$ Vertex (0, 0), focus $\left(0, \frac{1}{8}\right)$, directrix $y = -\frac{1}{8}$

16. $y = \frac{1}{2}x^2$ Vertex (0, 0), focus $\left(0, \frac{1}{2}\right)$, directrix $y = -\frac{1}{2}$

17. $y = -\frac{1}{4}x^2$ Vertex (0, 0), focus (0, −1), directrix $y = 1$

18. $y = -\frac{1}{12}x^2$ Vertex (0, 0), focus (0, −3), directrix $y = 3$

19. $y = \frac{1}{2}(x - 3)^2 + 2$
Vertex (3, 2), focus (3, 2.5), directrix $y = 1.5$

20. $y = \frac{1}{4}(x + 2)^2 - 5$
Vertex (−2, −5), focus (−2, −4), directrix $y = -6$

21. $y = -(x + 1)^2 + 6$
Vertex (−1, 6), focus (−1, 5.75), directrix $y = 6.25$

22. $y = -3(x - 4)^2 + 1$
Vertex (4, 1), focus $\left(4, \frac{11}{12}\right)$, directrix $y = \frac{13}{12}$

Find the equation of the parabola with the given focus and directrix. See Example 3.

23. Focus (0, 2), directrix $y = -2$ $y = \frac{1}{8}x^2$

24. Focus (0, −3), directrix $y = 3$ $y = -\frac{1}{12}x^2$

25. Focus $\left(0, -\frac{1}{2}\right)$, directrix $y = \frac{1}{2}$ $y = -\frac{1}{2}x^2$

26. Focus $\left(0, \frac{1}{8}\right)$, directrix $y = -\frac{1}{8}$ $y = 2x^2$

27. Focus (3, 2), directrix $y = 1$ $y = \frac{1}{2}x^2 - 3x + 6$

28. Focus (−4, 5), directrix $y = 4$ $y = \frac{1}{2}x^2 + 4x + \frac{25}{2}$

29. Focus (1, −2), directrix $y = 2$ $y = -\frac{1}{8}x^2 + \frac{1}{4}x - \frac{1}{8}$

30. Focus (2, −3), directrix $y = 1$ $y = -\frac{1}{8}x^2 + \frac{1}{2}x - \frac{3}{2}$

31. Focus (−3, 1.25), directrix $y = 0.75$ $y = x^2 + 6x + 10$

32. Focus $\left(5, \frac{17}{8}\right)$, directrix $y = \frac{15}{8}$ $y = 2x^2 - 20x + 52$

Write each equation in the form $y = a(x - h)^2 + k$. Identify the vertex, focus, directrix, and axis of symmetry of each parabola. See Example 4.

33. $y = x^2 - 6x + 1$
$y = (x - 3)^2 - 8$, vertex (3, −8), focus (3, −7.75), directrix $y = -8.25$, axis $x = 3$

34. $y = x^2 + 4x - 7$
$y = (x + 2)^2 - 11$, vertex (−2, −11), focus (−2, −10.75), directrix $y = -11.25$, axis $x = -2$

35. $y = 2x^2 + 12x + 5$
$y = 2(x + 3)^2 - 13$, vertex (−3, −13), focus (−3, −12.875), directrix $y = -13.125$, axis $x = -3$

36. $y = 3x^2 + 6x - 7$
$y = 3(x + 1)^2 - 10$, vertex (−1, −10), focus $\left(-1, -9\frac{11}{12}\right)$, directrix $y = -10\frac{1}{12}$, axis $x = -1$

37. $y = -2x^2 + 16x + 1$
$y = -2(x - 4)^2 + 33$, vertex (4, 33), focus $\left(4, 32\frac{7}{8}\right)$, directrix $y = 33\frac{1}{8}$, axis $x = 4$

38. $y = -3x^2 - 6x + 7$
$y = -3(x + 1)^2 + 10$, vertex (−1, 10), focus $\left(-1, 9\frac{11}{12}\right)$, directrix $y = 10\frac{1}{12}$, axis $x = -1$

39. $y = 5x^2 + 40x$
$y = 5(x + 4)^2 - 80$, vertex (−4, −80), focus $\left(-4, -79\frac{19}{20}\right)$, directrix $y = -80\frac{1}{20}$, axis $x = -4$

40. $y = -2x^2 + 10x$
$y = -2\left(x - \frac{5}{2}\right)^2 + \frac{25}{2}$, vertex $\left(\frac{5}{2}, \frac{25}{2}\right)$, focus $\left(\frac{5}{2}, \frac{99}{8}\right)$, directrix $y = \frac{101}{8}$, axis $x = \frac{5}{2}$

Find the vertex, focus, directrix, and axis of symmetry of each parabola (without completing the square), and determine whether the parabola opens upward or downward. See Example 5.

41. $y = x^2 - 4x + 1$
Vertex (2, −3), focus $\left(2, -2\frac{3}{4}\right)$, directrix $y = -3\frac{1}{4}$, $x = 2$, upward

42. $y = x^2 - 6x - 7$
Vertex (3, −16), focus $\left(3, -15\frac{3}{4}\right)$, directrix $y = -16\frac{1}{4}$, $x = 3$, upward

43. $y = -x^2 + 2x - 3$
Vertex $(1, -2)$, focus $\left(1, -2\frac{1}{4}\right)$, directrix $y = -1\frac{3}{4}$, $x = 1$, downward

44. $y = -x^2 + 4x + 9$
Vertex $(2, 13)$, focus $\left(2, 12\frac{3}{4}\right)$, directrix $y = 13\frac{1}{4}$, $x = 2$, downward

45. $y = 3x^2 - 6x + 1$
Vertex $(1, -2)$, focus $\left(1, -1\frac{11}{12}\right)$, directrix $y = -2\frac{1}{12}$, $x = 1$, upward

46. $y = 2x^2 + 4x - 3$
Vertex $(-1, -5)$, focus $\left(-1, -4\frac{7}{8}\right)$, directrix $y = -5\frac{1}{8}$, $x = -1$, upward

47. $y = -x^2 - 3x + 2$
Vertex $\left(-\frac{3}{2}, \frac{17}{4}\right)$, focus $\left(-\frac{3}{2}, 4\right)$, directrix $y = \frac{9}{2}$, $x = -\frac{3}{2}$, downward

48. $y = -x^2 + 3x - 1$
Vertex $\left(\frac{3}{2}, \frac{5}{4}\right)$, focus $\left(\frac{3}{2}, 1\right)$, directrix $y = \frac{3}{2}$, $x = \frac{3}{2}$, downward

49. $y = 3x^2 + 5$
Vertex $(0, 5)$, focus $\left(0, 5\frac{1}{12}\right)$, directrix $y = 4\frac{11}{12}$, $x = 0$, upward

50. $y = -2x^2 - 6$
Vertex $(0, -6)$, focus $\left(0, -6\frac{1}{8}\right)$, directrix $y = -5\frac{7}{8}$, $x = 0$, downward

Find the vertex, focus, and directrix for each parabola. See Example 6.

51. $x = (y - 2)^2 + 3$ $(3, 2)$, $\left(\frac{13}{4}, 2\right)$, $x = \frac{11}{4}$

52. $x = (y + 3)^2 - 1$ $(-1, -3)$, $\left(-\frac{3}{4}, -3\right)$, $x = -\frac{5}{4}$

53. $x = \frac{1}{4}(y - 1)^2 - 2$ $(-2, 1)$, $(-1, 1)$, $x = -3$

54. $x = \frac{1}{4}(y + 1)^2 + 2$ $(2, -1)$, $(3, -1)$, $x = 1$

55. $x = -\frac{1}{2}(y - 2)^2 + 4$ $(4, 2)$, $\left(\frac{7}{2}, 2\right)$, $x = \frac{9}{2}$

56. $x = -\frac{1}{2}(y + 1)^2 - 1$ $(-1, -1)$, $\left(-\frac{3}{2}, -1\right)$, $x = -\frac{1}{2}$

Sketch the graph of each parabola.

57. $y = (x - 2)^2 + 3$

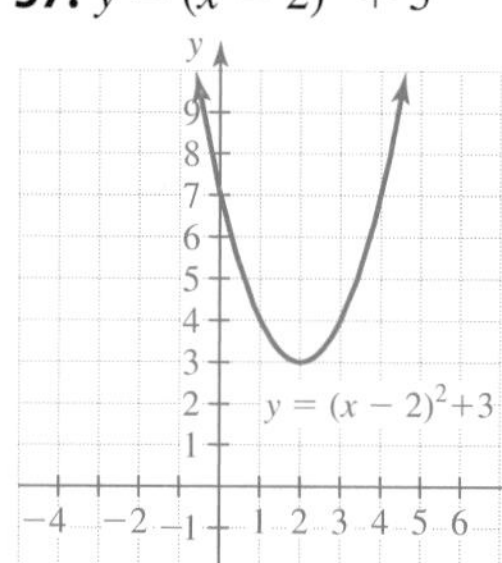

58. $y = (x + 3)^2 - 1$

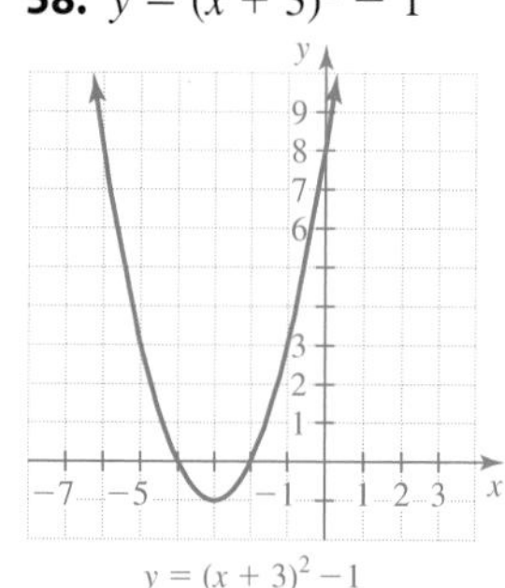

59. $y = -2(x - 1)^2 + 3$

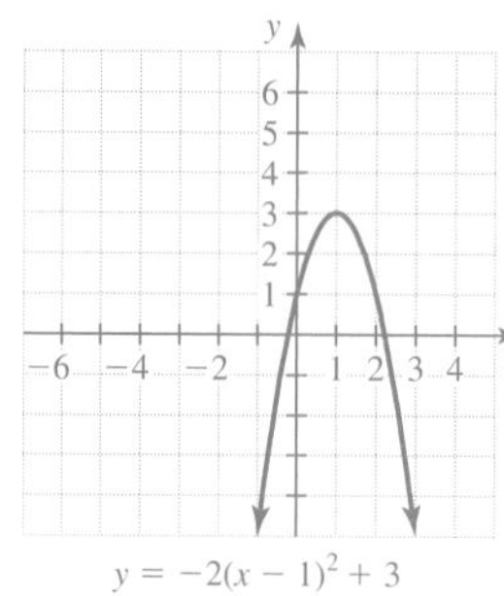

60. $y = -\frac{1}{2}(x + 1)^2 + 5$

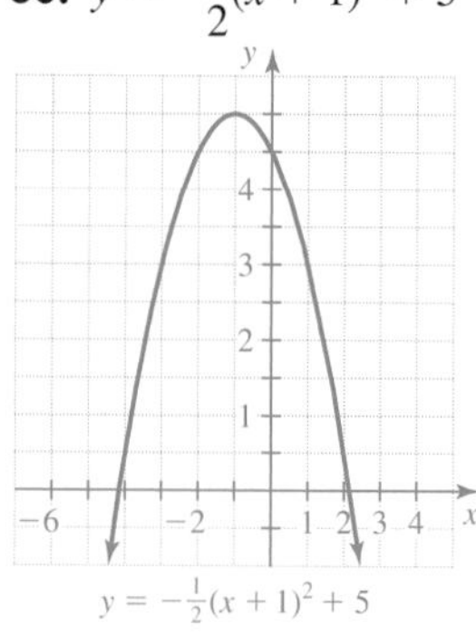

61. $x = (y - 2)^2 + 3$

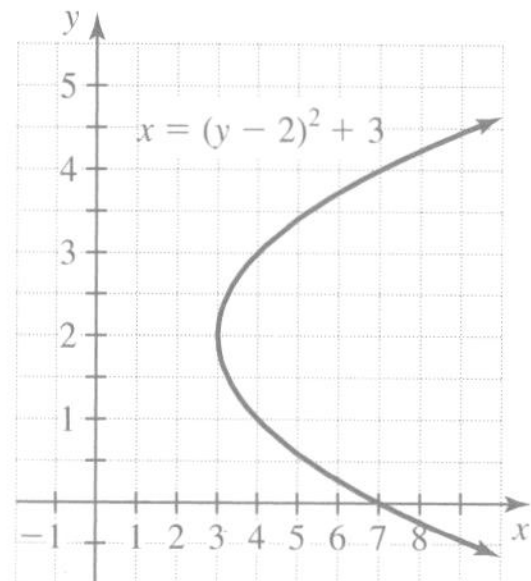

62. $x = (y + 3)^2 - 1$

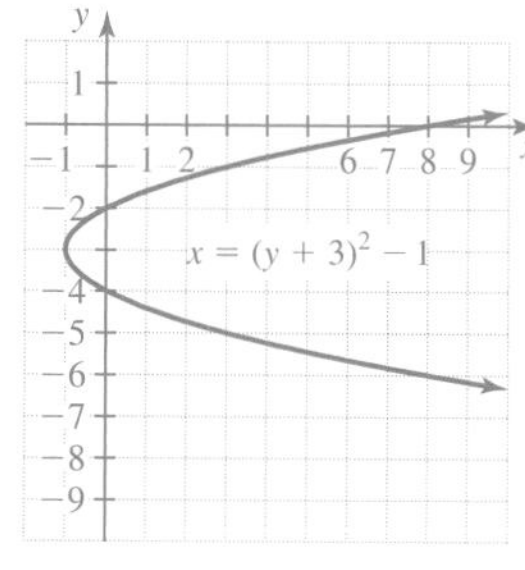

63. $x = -2(y - 1)^2 + 3$

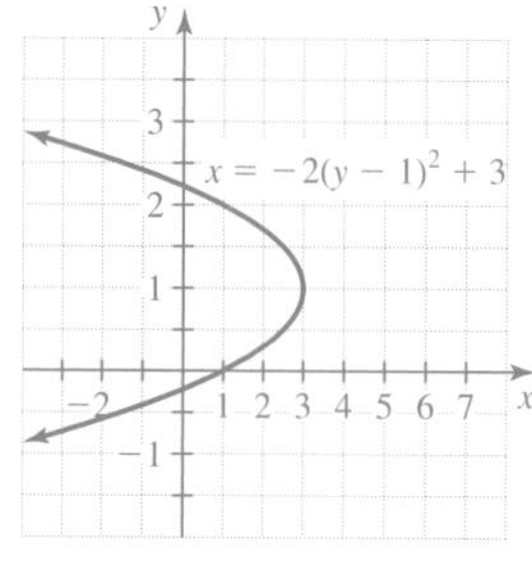

64. $x = -\frac{1}{2}(y + 1)^2 + 5$

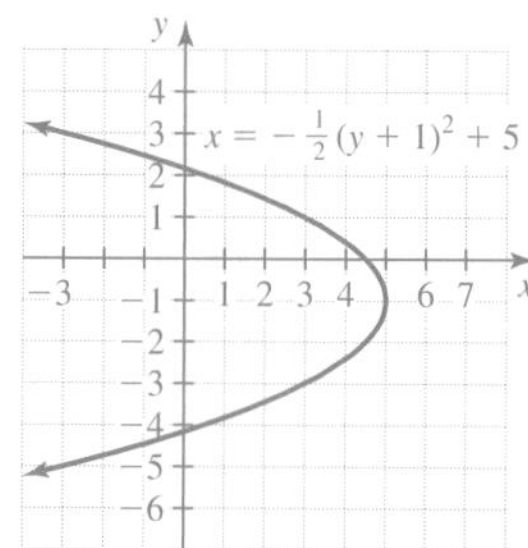

Solve each problem.

65. ***World's largest telescope.*** The largest reflecting telescope in the world is the 6-meter (m) reflector on Mount Pastukhov in Russia. The accompanying figure shows a

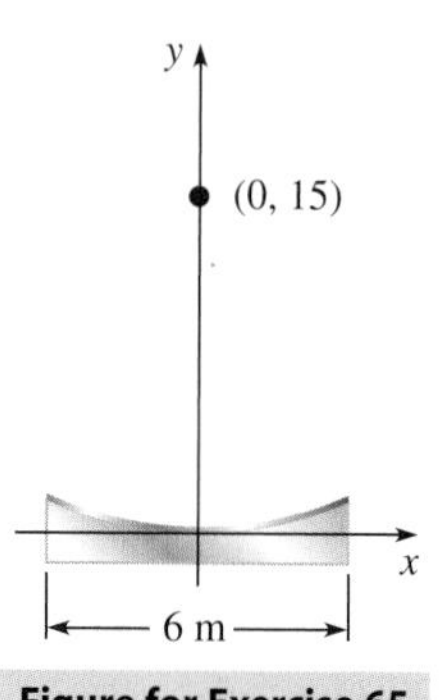

Figure for Exercise 65

cross section of a parabolic mirror 6 m in diameter with the vertex at the origin and the focus at (0, 15). Find the equation of the parabola.
$y = \dfrac{1}{60}x^2$

66. ***Arecibo Observatory.*** The largest radio telescope in the world uses a 1000-ft parabolic dish, suspended in a valley in Arecibo, Puerto Rico. The antenna hangs above the vertex of the dish on cables stretching from two towers. The accompanying figure shows a cross section of the parabolic dish and the towers. Assuming the vertex is at (0, 0), find the equation for the parabola. Find the distance from the vertex to the antenna located at the focus. $y = 0.0008x^2$, 312.5 ft

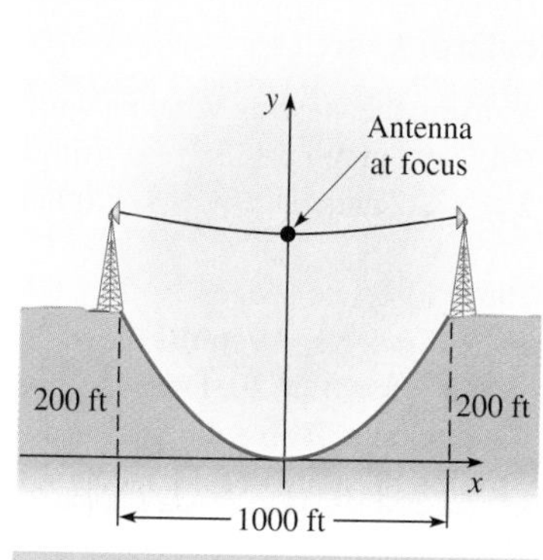

Figure for Exercise 66

Graph both equations of each system on the same coordinate axes. Use elimination of variables to find all points of intersection.

67. $y = -x^2 + 3$
$y = x^2 + 1$
$\{(-1, 2), (1, 2)\}$

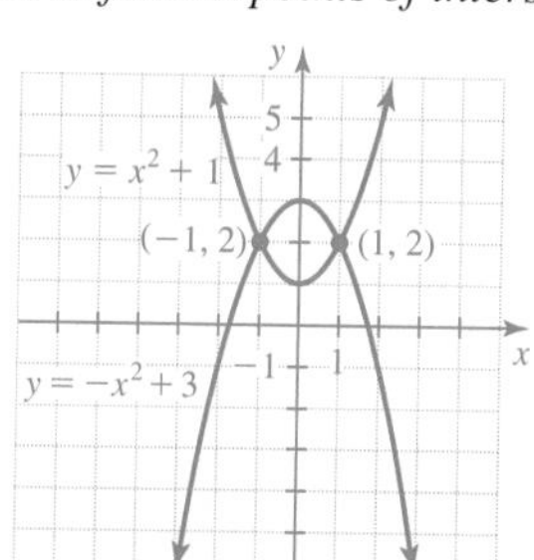

68. $y = x^2 - 3$
$y = -x^2 + 5$
$\{(2, 1), (-2, 1)\}$

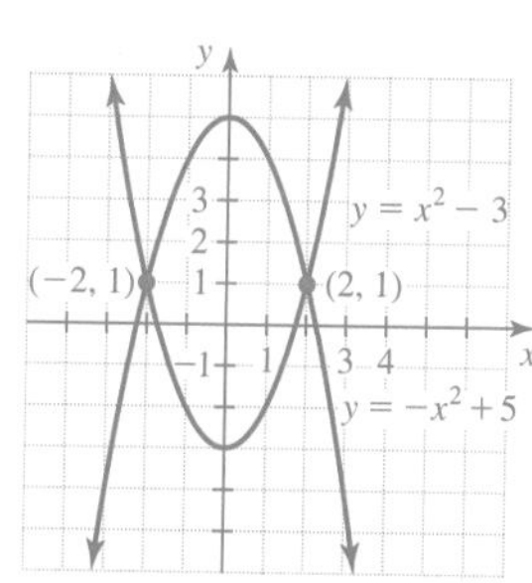

69. $y = x^2 - 2$
$y = 2x - 3$
$\{(1, -1)\}$

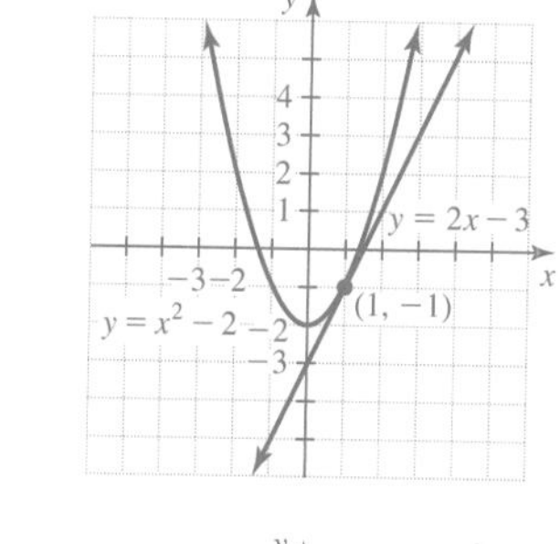

70. $y = x^2 + x - 6$
$y = 7x - 15$
$\{(3, 6)\}$

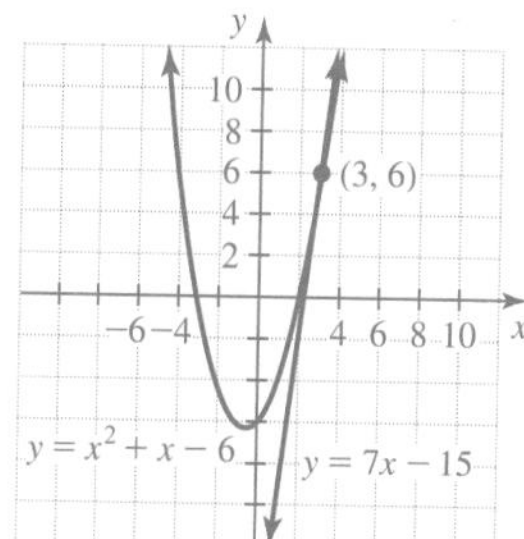

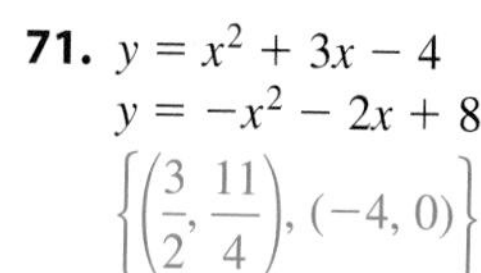
71. $y = x^2 + 3x - 4$
$y = -x^2 - 2x + 8$
$\left\{\left(\dfrac{3}{2}, \dfrac{11}{4}\right), (-4, 0)\right\}$

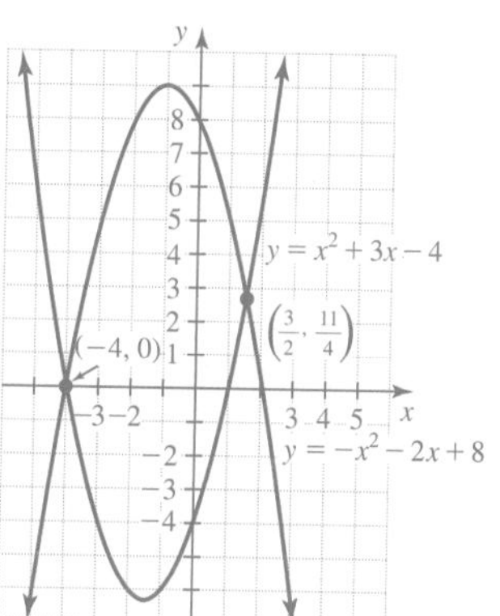

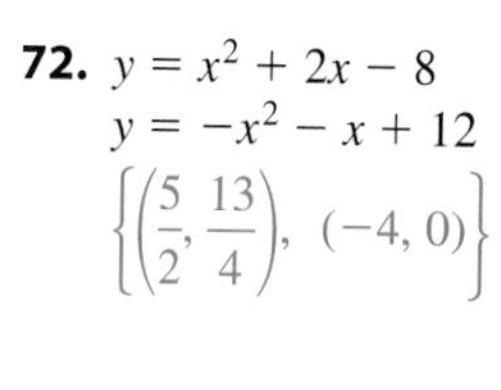
72. $y = x^2 + 2x - 8$
$y = -x^2 - x + 12$
$\left\{\left(\dfrac{5}{2}, \dfrac{13}{4}\right), (-4, 0)\right\}$

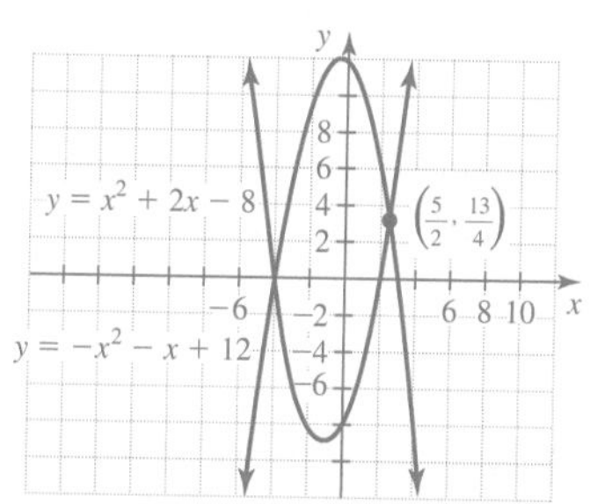

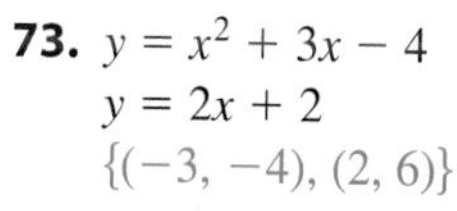
73. $y = x^2 + 3x - 4$
$y = 2x + 2$
$\{(-3, -4), (2, 6)\}$

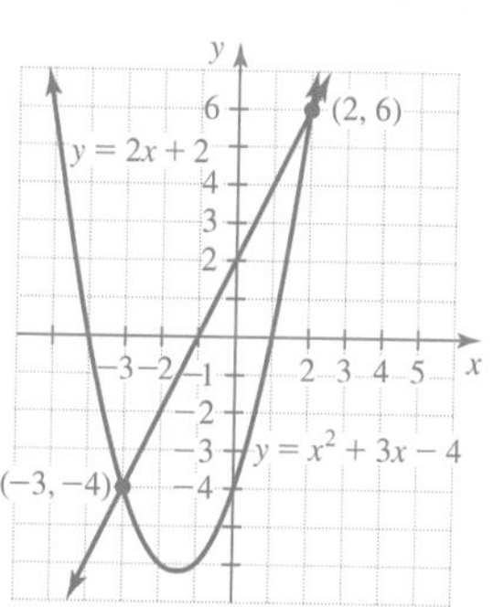

74. $y = x^2 + 5x + 6$
$y = x + 11$
$\{(-5, 6), (1, 12)\}$

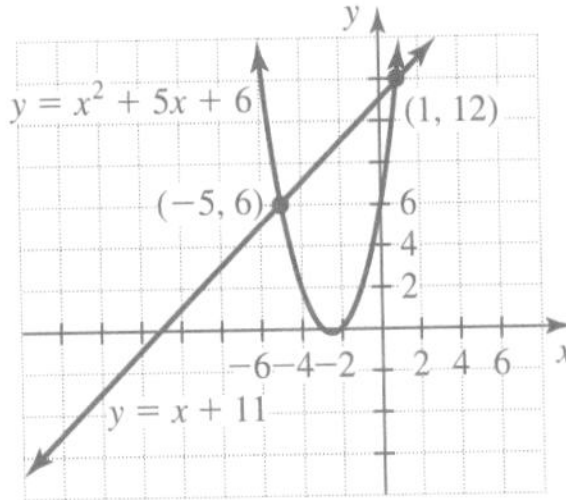

Solve each problem.

75. Find all points of intersection of the parabola $y = x^2 - 2x - 3$ and the x-axis.
$(3, 0), (-1, 0)$

76. Find all points of intersection of the parabola $y = 80x^2 - 33x + 255$ and the y-axis.
$(0, 255)$

77. Find all points of intersection of the parabola $y = 0.01x^2$ and the line $y = 4$.
$(20, 4), (-20, 4)$

78. Find all points of intersection of the parabola $y = 0.02x^2$ and the line $y = x$.
$(0, 0), (50, 50)$

79. Find all points of intersection of the parabolas $y = x^2$ and $x = y^2$. $(0, 0), (1, 1)$

80. Find all points of intersection of the parabolas $y = x^2$ and $y = (x - 3)^2$. $\left(\frac{3}{2}, \frac{9}{4}\right)$

Getting More Involved

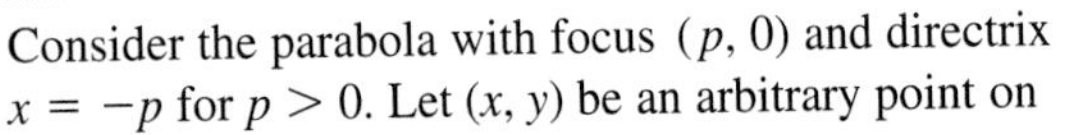

81. ***Exploration***

Consider the parabola with focus $(p, 0)$ and directrix $x = -p$ for $p > 0$. Let (x, y) be an arbitrary point on the parabola. Write an equation expressing the fact that the distance from (x, y) to the focus is equal to the distance from (x, y) to the directrix. Rewrite the equation in the form $x = ay^2$, where $a = \frac{1}{4p}$.

82. ***Exploration***

In general, the graph of $x = a(y - k)^2 + h$ for $a \neq 0$ is a parabola opening left or right with vertex at (h, k).

a) For which values of a does the parabola open to the right, and for which values of a does it open to the left?

b) What is the equation of its axis of symmetry?

c) Sketch the graphs $x = 2(y - 3)^2 + 1$ and $x = -(y + 1)^2 + 2$.

a) Right for $a > 0$ and left for $a < 0$
b) $y = k$

Graphing Calculator Exercises

83. Graph $y = x^2$ using the viewing window with $-1 \leq x \leq 1$ and $0 \leq y \leq 1$. Next graph $y = 2x^2 - 1$ using the viewing window $-2 \leq x \leq 2$ and $-1 \leq y \leq 7$. Explain what you see.
The graphs have identical shapes.

84. Graph $y = x^2$ and $y = 6x - 9$ in the viewing window $-5 \leq x \leq 5$ and $-5 \leq y \leq 20$. Does the line appear to be tangent to the parabola? Solve the system $y = x^2$ and $y = 6x - 9$ to find all points of intersection for the parabola and the line.
Intersection $(3, 9)$

13.3 The Circle

In this Section

- Developing the Equation
- Equations Not in Standard Form
- Systems of Equations

In this section we continue the study of the conic sections with a discussion of the circle.

Developing the Equation

A circle is obtained by cutting a cone, as was shown in Fig. 13.3. We can also define a circle using points and distance, as we did for the parabola.

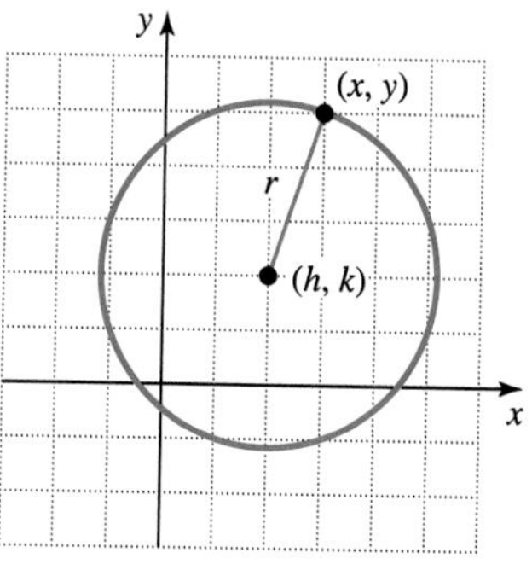

Figure 13.15

Circle

A **circle** is the set of all points in a plane that lie a fixed distance from a given point in the plane. The fixed distance is called the **radius,** and the given point is called the **center.**

We can use the distance formula of Section 13.2 to write an equation for the circle with center (h, k) and radius r, shown in Fig. 13.15. If (x, y) is a point on the circle, its distance from the center is r. So

$$\sqrt{(x - h)^2 + (y - k)^2} = r.$$

We square both sides of this equation to get the **standard form** for the equation of a circle.

Standard Equation for a Circle

The graph of the equation

$$(x - h)^2 + (y - k)^2 = r^2$$

with $r > 0$, is a circle with center (h, k) and radius r.

Note that a circle centered at the origin with radius r $(r > 0)$ has the standard equation

$$x^2 + y^2 = r^2.$$

EXAMPLE 1

Finding the equation, given the center and radius

Write the standard equation for the circle with the given center and radius.

a) Center (0, 0), radius 2 **b)** Center (−1, 2), radius 4

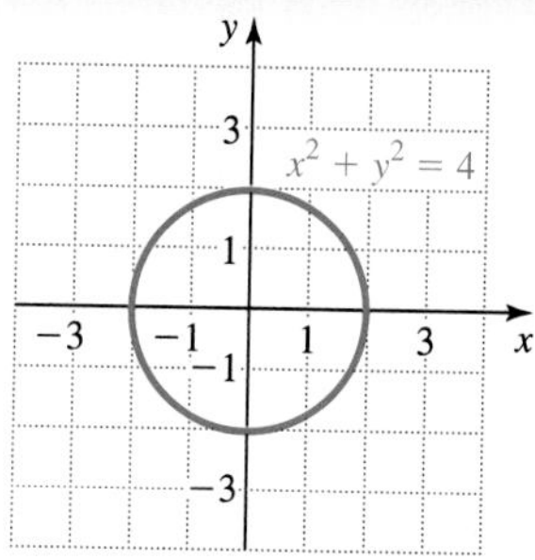

Figure 13.16

Teaching Tip When sketching a circle by hand, use the radius and center to locate points above, below, left, and right of the center. Then sketch a circle through these four points.

Solution

a) The center at (0, 0) means that $h = 0$ and $k = 0$ in the standard equation. So the equation is $(x - 0)^2 + (y - 0)^2 = 2^2$, or $x^2 + y^2 = 4$. The circle with radius 2 centered at the origin is shown in Fig. 13.16.

b) The center at $(-1, 2)$ means that $h = -1$ and $k = 2$. So

$$[x - (-1)]^2 + [y - 2]^2 = 4^2.$$

Simplify this equation to get

$$(x + 1)^2 + (y - 2)^2 = 16.$$

The circle with center $(-1, 2)$ and radius 4 is shown in Fig. 13.17.

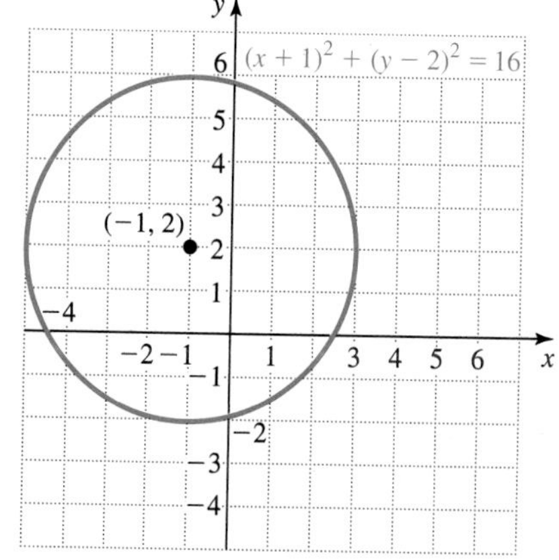

Figure 13.17

Now do Exercises 3–14

CAUTION The equations $(x - 1)^2 + (y + 3)^2 = -9$ and $(x - 1)^2 + (y + 3)^2 = 0$ might look like equations of circles, but they are not. The first equation is not satisfied by any ordered pair of real numbers because the left-hand side is nonnegative for any x and y. The second equation is satisfied only by the point $(1, -3)$.

EXAMPLE 2

Finding the center and radius, given the equation

Determine the center and radius of the circle $x^2 + (y + 5)^2 = 2$.

Solution

We can write this equation as

$$(x - 0)^2 + [y - (-5)]^2 = (\sqrt{2})^2.$$

In this form we see that the center is $(0, -5)$ and the radius is $\sqrt{2}$.

Now do Exercises 15–22

EXAMPLE 3

Graphing a circle

Find the center and radius of $(x - 1)^2 + (y + 2)^2 = 9$, and sketch the graph.

Solution

The graph of this equation is a circle with center $(1, -2)$ and radius 3. See Fig. 13.18 for the graph.

Now do Exercises 23–32

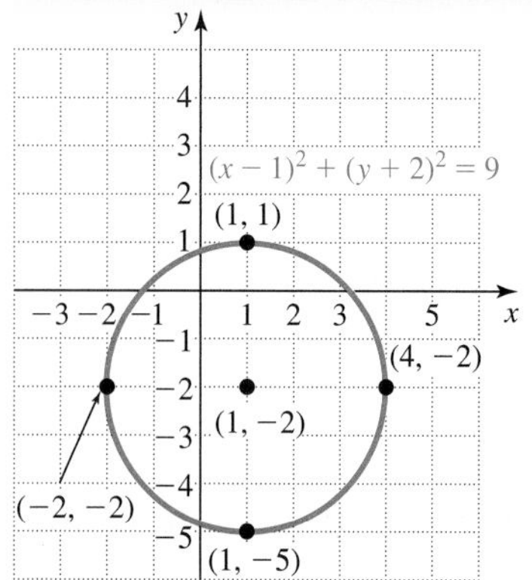

Figure 13.18

Calculator Close-Up

To graph the circle in Example 3, graph

$$y_1 = -2 + \sqrt{9 - (x - 1)^2}$$

and

$$y_2 = -2 - \sqrt{9 - (x - 1)^2}.$$

To get the circle to look round, you must use the same unit length on each axis. Most calculators have a *square* feature that automatically adjusts the window to use the same unit length on each axis.

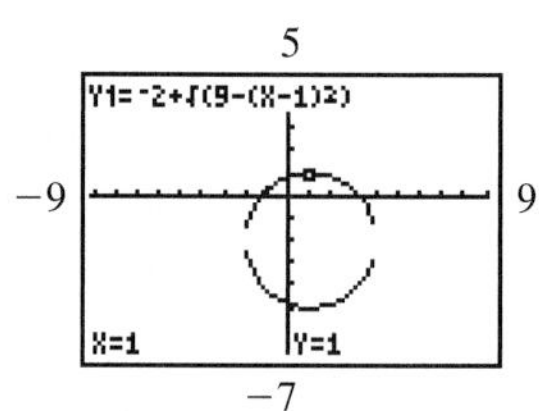

Equations Not in Standard Form

It is not easy to recognize that $x^2 - 6x + y^2 + 10y = -30$ is the equation of a circle, but it is. In Example 4 we convert this equation into the standard form for a circle by completing the squares for the variables x and y.

EXAMPLE 4

Converting to standard form

Find the center and radius of the circle given by the equation

$$x^2 - 6x + y^2 + 10y = -30.$$

Helpful Hint

What do circles and lines have in common? They are the two simplest graphs to draw. We have compasses to make our circles look good and rulers to make our lines look good.

Solution

To complete the square for $x^2 - 6x$, we add 9, and for $y^2 + 10y$, we add 25. To get an equivalent equation, we must add on both sides:

$$x^2 - 6x + \quad y^2 + 10y \quad = -30$$

$$x^2 - 6x + 9 + y^2 + 10y + 25 = -30 + 9 + 25 \quad \text{Add 9 and 25 to both sides.}$$

$$(x - 3)^2 + (y + 5)^2 = 4 \quad \text{Factor the trinomials on the left-hand side.}$$

From the standard form we see that the center is $(3, -5)$ and the radius is 2.

Now do Exercises 33–44

Systems of Equations

We first solved systems of nonlinear equations in two variables in Section 13.1. We found the points of intersection of two graphs without drawing the graphs. Here we will solve systems involving circles, parabolas, and lines. In the next example we find the points of intersection of a line and a circle.

EXAMPLE 5

Intersection of a line and a circle

Graph both equations of the system

$$(x - 3)^2 + (y + 1)^2 = 9$$

$$y = x - 1$$

on the same coordinate axes, and solve the system by elimination of variables.

Solution

The graph of the first equation is a circle with center $(3, -1)$ and radius 3. The graph of the second equation is a straight line with slope 1 and y-intercept $(0, -1)$. Both graphs are shown in Fig. 13.19. To solve the system by elimination, we substitute $y = x - 1$ into the equation of the circle:

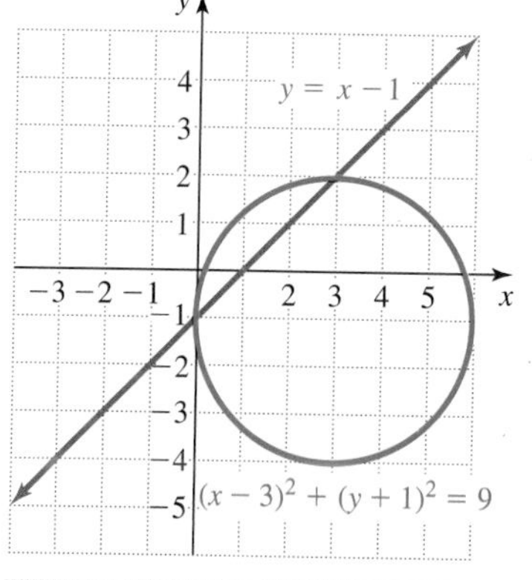

Figure 13.19

$$(x - 3)^2 + (x - 1 + 1)^2 = 9$$

$$(x - 3)^2 + x^2 = 9$$

$$x^2 - 6x + 9 + x^2 = 9$$

$$2x^2 - 6x = 0$$

$$x^2 - 3x = 0$$

$$x(x - 3) = 0$$

$$x = 0 \quad \text{or} \quad x = 3$$

$$y = -1 \qquad\quad y = 2 \quad \text{Because } y = x - 1$$

Check $(0, -1)$ and $(3, 2)$ in the original system and with the graphs in Fig. 13.19. The solution set is $\{(0, -1), (3, 2)\}$.

Now do Exercises 45–50

Warm-Ups ▼

True or false? Explain your answer.

1. The radius of a circle can be any nonzero real number. False
2. The coordinates of the center must satisfy the equation of the circle. False
3. The circle $x^2 + y^2 = 4$ has its center at the origin. True
4. The graph of $x^2 + y^2 = 9$ is a circle centered at (0, 0) with radius 9. False
5. The graph of $(x - 2)^2 + (y - 3)^2 + 4 = 0$ is a circle of radius 2. False
6. The graph of $(x - 3) + (y + 5) = 9$ is a circle of radius 3. False
7. There is only one circle centered at $(-3, -1)$ passing through the origin. True
8. The center of the circle $(x - 3)^2 + (y - 4)^2 = 10$ is $(-3, -4)$. False
9. The center of the circle $x^2 + y^2 + 6y - 4 = 0$ is on the y-axis. True
10. The radius of the circle $x^2 - 3x + y^2 = 4$ is 2. False

13.3 Exercises

Boost your GRADE at mathzone.com!

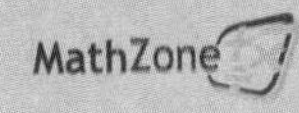

- Practice Problems
- Self-Tests
- Videos
- Net Tutor
- e-Professors

Reading and Writing *After reading this section, write out the answers to these questions. Use complete sentences.*

1. What is the definition of a circle?
   A circle is the set of all points in a plane that lie at a fixed distance from a fixed point.
2. What is the standard equation of a circle?
   The equation $(x - h)^2 + (y - k)^2 = r^2$ is the standard equation of a circle with center (h, k) and radius r (for $r > 0$).

Write the standard equation for each circle with the given center and radius. See Example 1.

3. Center (0, 0), radius 4 $x^2 + y^2 = 16$
4. Center (0, 0), radius 3 $x^2 + y^2 = 9$
5. Center (0, 3), radius 5 $x^2 + (y - 3)^2 = 25$
6. Center (2, 0), radius 3 $(x - 2)^2 + y^2 = 9$
7. Center $(1, -2)$, radius 9 $(x - 1)^2 + (y + 2)^2 = 81$
8. Center $(-3, 5)$, radius 4 $(x + 3)^2 + (y - 5)^2 = 16$
9. Center (0, 0), radius $\sqrt{3}$ $x^2 + y^2 = 3$
10. Center (0, 0), radius $\sqrt{2}$ $x^2 + y^2 = 2$
11. Center $(-6, -3)$, radius $\frac{1}{2}$ $(x + 6)^2 + (y + 3)^2 = \frac{1}{4}$
12. Center $(-3, -5)$, radius $\frac{1}{4}$ $(x + 3)^2 + (y + 5)^2 = \frac{1}{16}$
13. Center $\left(\frac{1}{2}, \frac{1}{3}\right)$, radius 0.1 $\left(x - \frac{1}{2}\right)^2 + \left(y - \frac{1}{3}\right)^2 = 0.01$
14. Center $\left(-\frac{1}{2}, 3\right)$, radius 0.2 $\left(x + \frac{1}{2}\right)^2 + (y - 3)^2 = 0.04$

Find the center and radius for each circle. See Example 2.

15. $(x - 3)^2 + (y - 5)^2 = 2$ $(3, 5), \sqrt{2}$
16. $(x + 3)^2 + (y - 7)^2 = 6$ $(-3, 7), \sqrt{6}$
17. $x^2 + \left(y - \frac{1}{2}\right)^2 = \frac{1}{2}$ $\left(0, \frac{1}{2}\right), \frac{\sqrt{2}}{2}$
18. $5x^2 + 5y^2 = 5$ $(0, 0), 1$
19. $4x^2 + 4y^2 = 9$ $(0, 0), \frac{3}{2}$
20. $9x^2 + 9y^2 = 49$ $(0, 0), \frac{7}{3}$
21. $3 - y^2 = (x - 2)^2$ $(2, 0), \sqrt{3}$
22. $9 - x^2 = (y + 1)^2$ $(0, -1), 3$

Sketch the graph of each equation. See Example 3.

23. $x^2 + y^2 = 9$

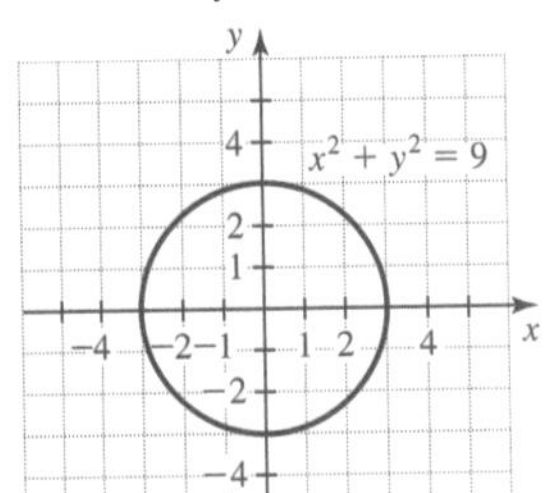

24. $x^2 + y^2 = 16$

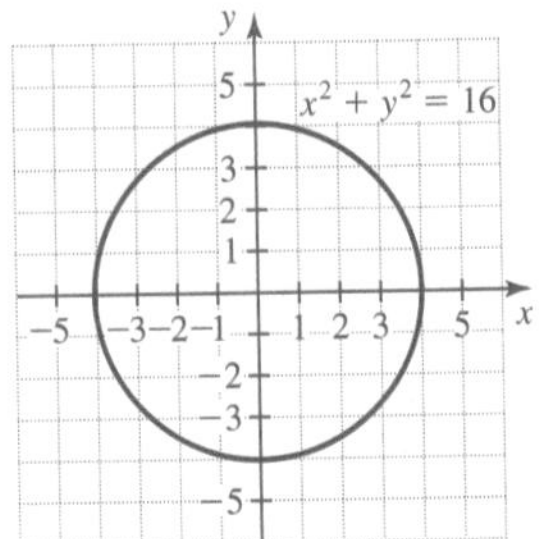

25. $x^2 + (y - 3)^2 = 9$

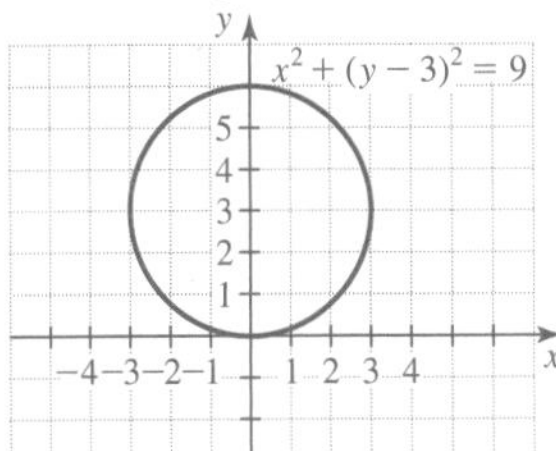

26. $(x - 4)^2 + y^2 = 16$

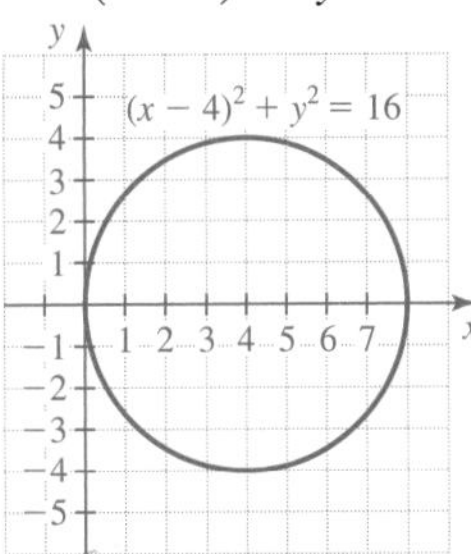

27. $(x + 1)^2 + (y - 1)^2 = 2$

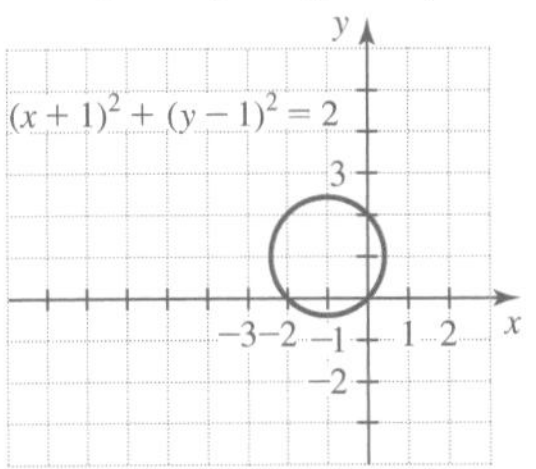

28. $(x - 2)^2 + (y + 2)^2 = 8$

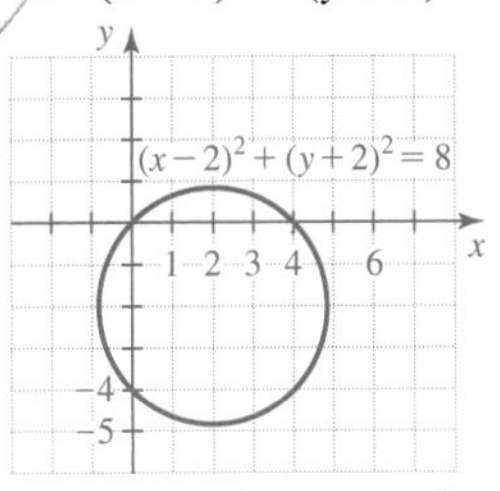

29. $(x - 4)^2 + (y + 3)^2 = 16$

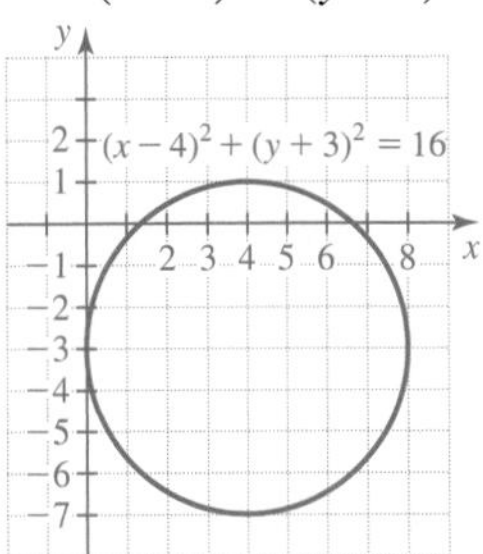

30. $(x - 3)^2 + (y - 7)^2 = 25$

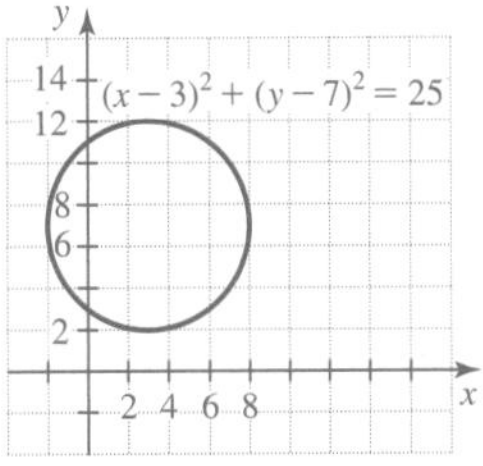

31. $\left(x - \frac{1}{2}\right)^2 + \left(y + \frac{1}{2}\right)^2 = \frac{1}{4}$

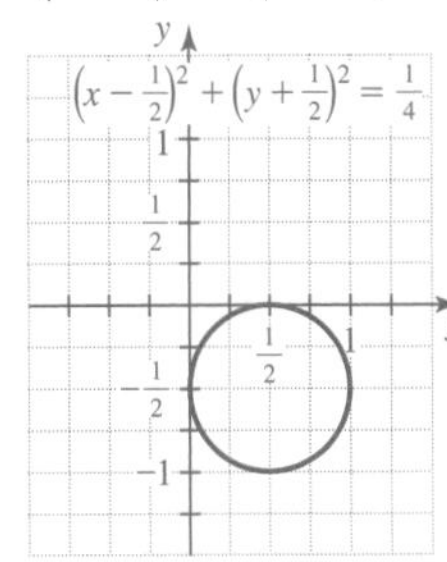

32. $\left(x + \frac{1}{3}\right)^2 + y^2 = \frac{1}{9}$

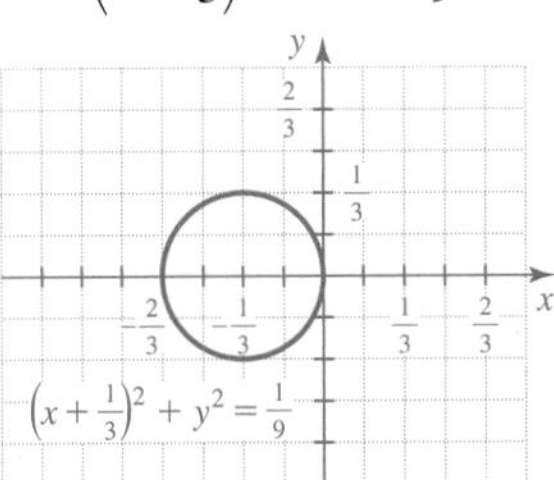

Rewrite each equation in the standard form for the equation of a circle, and identify its center and radius. See Example 4.

33. $x^2 + 4x + y^2 + 6y = 0$
$(x + 2)^2 + (y + 3)^2 = 13, (-2, -3), \sqrt{13}$

34. $x^2 - 10x + y^2 + 8y = 0$
$(x - 5)^2 + (y + 4)^2 = 41, (5, -4), \sqrt{41}$

35. $x^2 - 2x + y^2 - 4y - 3 = 0$
$(x - 1)^2 + (y - 2)^2 = 8, (1, 2), 2\sqrt{2}$

36. $x^2 - 6x + y^2 - 2y + 9 = 0$
$(x - 3)^2 + (y - 1)^2 = 1, (3, 1), 1$

37. $x^2 + y^2 = 8y + 10x - 32$
$(x - 5)^2 + (y - 4)^2 = 9, (5, 4), 3$

38. $x^2 + y^2 = 8x - 10y$
$(x - 4)^2 + (y + 5)^2 = 41, (4, -5), \sqrt{41}$

39. $x^2 - x + y^2 + y = 0$
$\left(x - \frac{1}{2}\right)^2 + \left(y + \frac{1}{2}\right)^2 = \frac{1}{2}, \left(\frac{1}{2}, -\frac{1}{2}\right), \frac{\sqrt{2}}{2}$

40. $x^2 - 3x + y^2 = 0$
$\left(x - \frac{3}{2}\right)^2 + y^2 = \frac{9}{4}, \left(\frac{3}{2}, 0\right), \frac{3}{2}$

41. $x^2 - 3x + y^2 - y = 1$
$\left(x - \frac{3}{2}\right)^2 + \left(y - \frac{1}{2}\right)^2 = \frac{7}{2}, \left(\frac{3}{2}, \frac{1}{2}\right), \frac{\sqrt{14}}{2}$

42. $x^2 - 5x + y^2 + 3y = 2$
$\left(x - \frac{5}{2}\right)^2 + \left(y + \frac{3}{2}\right)^2 = \frac{21}{2}, \left(\frac{5}{2}, -\frac{3}{2}\right), \frac{\sqrt{42}}{2}$

43. $x^2 - \frac{2}{3}x + y^2 + \frac{3}{2}y = 0$
$\left(x - \frac{1}{3}\right)^2 + \left(y + \frac{3}{4}\right)^2 = \frac{97}{144}, \left(\frac{1}{3}, -\frac{3}{4}\right), \frac{\sqrt{97}}{12}$

44. $x^2 + \frac{1}{3}x + y^2 - \frac{2}{3}y = \frac{1}{9}$
$\left(x + \frac{1}{6}\right)^2 + \left(y - \frac{1}{3}\right)^2 = \frac{1}{4}, \left(-\frac{1}{6}, \frac{1}{3}\right), \frac{1}{2}$

Graph both equations of each system on the same coordinate axes. Solve the system by elimination of variables to find all points of intersection of the graphs. See Example 5.

45. $x^2 + y^2 = 10$
$y = 3x$
$\{(1, 3), (-1, -3)\}$

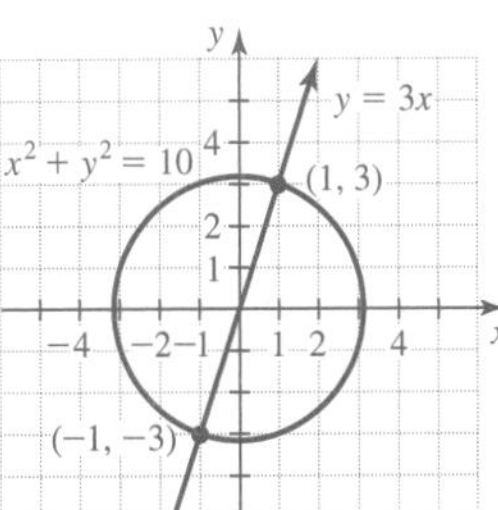

46. $x^2 + y^2 = 4$
$y = x - 2$

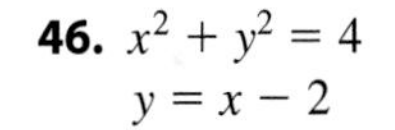
$\{(0, -2), (2, 0)\}$

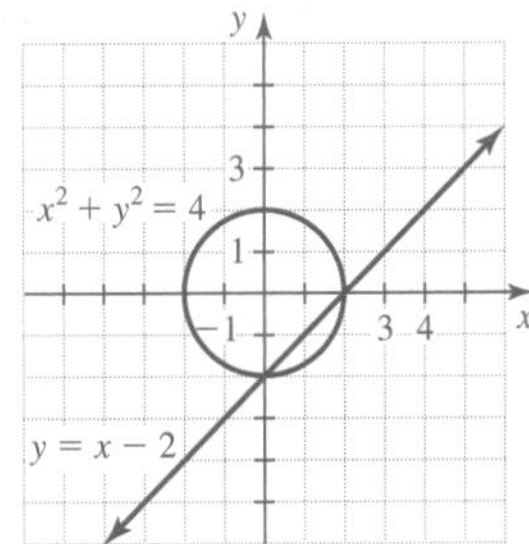

47. $x^2 + y^2 = 9$
$y = x^2 - 3$
$\{(0, -3), (\sqrt{5}, 2), (-\sqrt{5}, 2)\}$

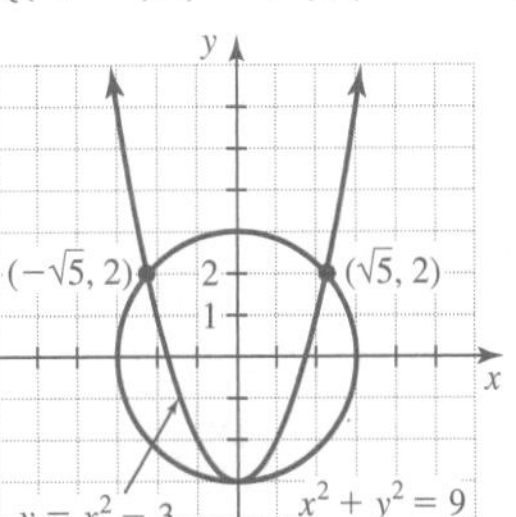

48. $x^2 + y^2 = 4$
$y = x^2 - 2$
$\{(0, -2), (-\sqrt{3}, 1), (\sqrt{3}, 1)\}$

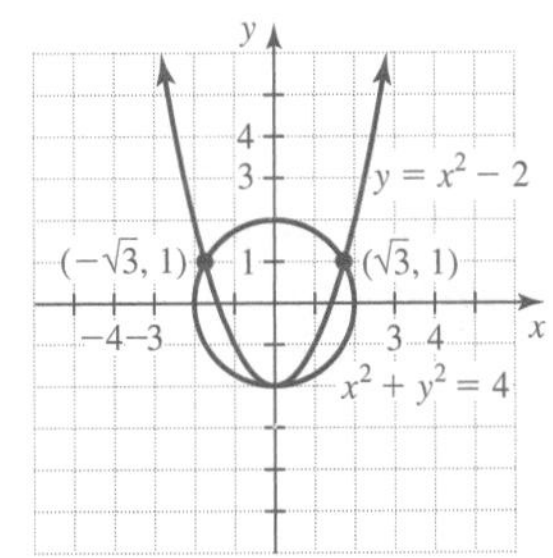

49. $(x-2)^2+(y+3)^2=4$
$y = x - 3$
$\{(0, -3), (2, -1)\}$

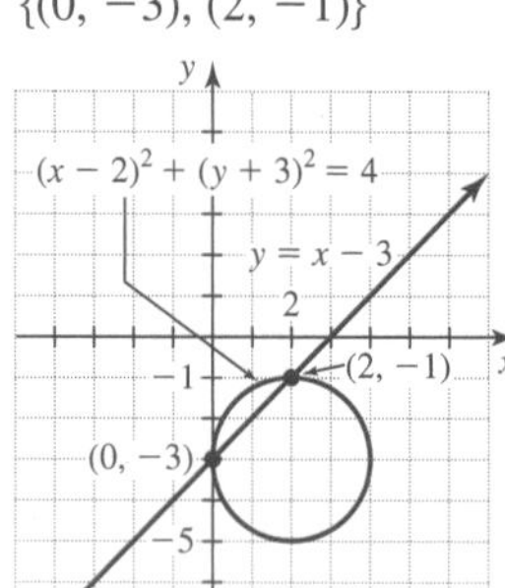

50. $(x+1)^2+(y-4)^2=17$
$y = x + 2$
$\{(3, 5), (-2, 0)\}$

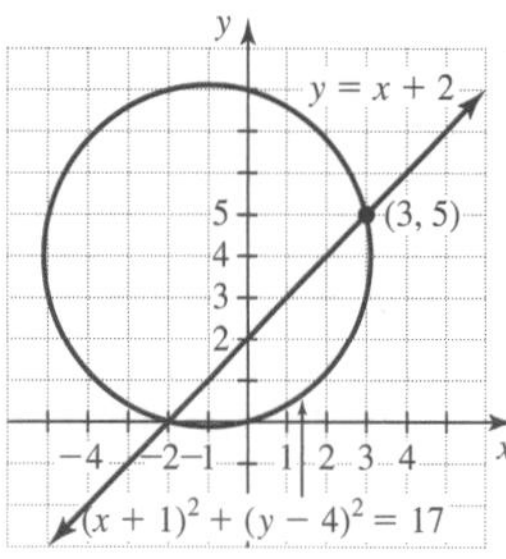

Solve each problem.

51. Determine all points of intersection of the circle $(x-1)^2 + (y-2)^2 = 4$ with the y-axis.
$(0, 2+\sqrt{3})$ and $(0, 2-\sqrt{3})$

52. Determine the points of intersection of the circle $x^2 + (y-3)^2 = 25$ with the x-axis.
$(-4, 0)$ and $(4, 0)$

53. Find the radius of the circle that has center $(2, -5)$ and passes through the origin. $\sqrt{29}$

54. Find the radius of the circle that has center $(-2, 3)$ and passes through $(3, -1)$. $\sqrt{41}$

55. Determine the equation of the circle that is centered at $(2, 3)$ and passes through $(-2, -1)$.
$(x-2)^2 + (y-3)^2 = 32$

56. Determine the equation of the circle that is centered at $(3, 4)$ and passes through the origin.
$(x-3)^2 + (y-4)^2 = 25$

57. Find all points of intersection of the circles $x^2 + y^2 = 9$ and $(x-5)^2 + y^2 = 9$.
$\left(\frac{5}{2}, -\frac{\sqrt{11}}{2}\right)$ and $\left(\frac{5}{2}, \frac{\sqrt{11}}{2}\right)$

58. A donkey is tied at the point $(2, -3)$ on a rope of length 12. Turnips are growing at the point $(6, 7)$. Can the donkey reach them? Yes

59. ***Volume of a flute.*** The volume of air in a flute is a critical factor in determining its pitch. A cross section of a Renaissance flute in C is shown in the accompanying figure. If the length of the flute is 2874 millimeters, then what is the volume of air in the flute [to the nearest cubic millimeter (mm^3)]? (*Hint:* Use the formula for the volume of a cylinder.) 755,903 mm^3

60. ***Flute reproduction.*** To make the smaller C# flute, Friedrich von Huene multiplies the length and cross-sectional area of the flute of Exercise 59 by 0.943. Find the equation for the bore hole (centered at the origin) and the volume of air in the C# flute.
$x^2 + y^2 = 78.95$, 672,186 mm^3

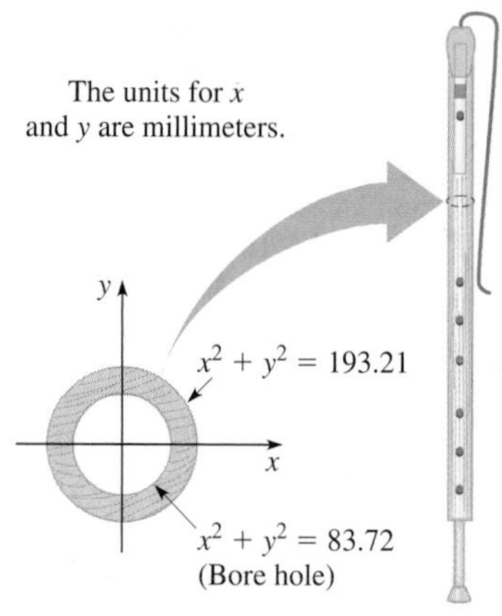

Figure for Exercises 59 and 60

Graph each equation.

61. $x^2 + y^2 = 0$ (0, 0) only

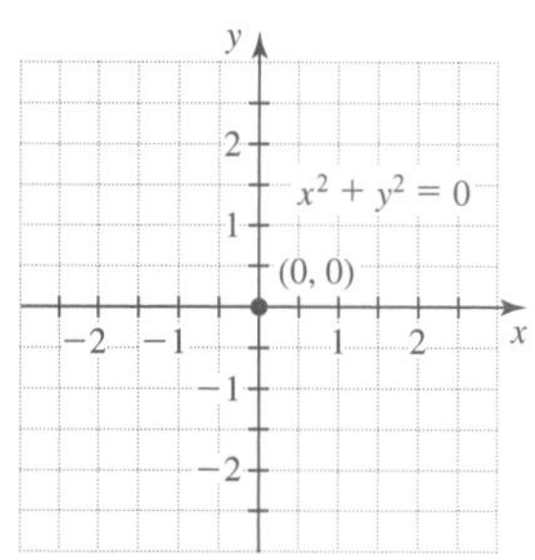

62. $x^2 - y^2 = 0$

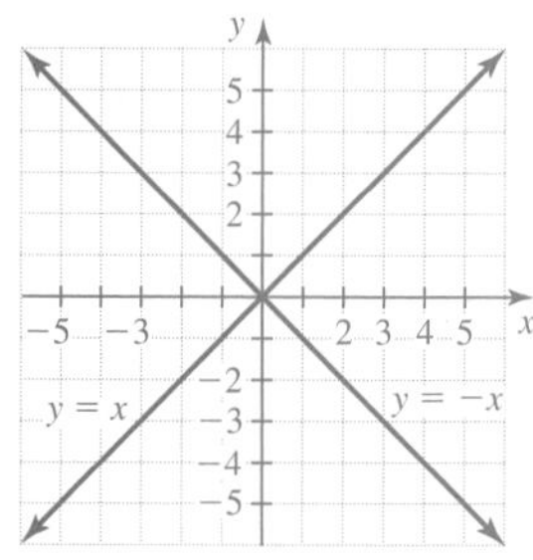

63. $y = \sqrt{1-x^2}$

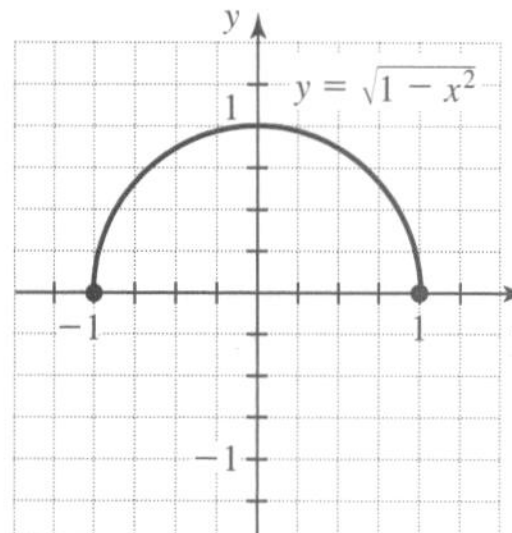

64. $y = -\sqrt{1-x^2}$

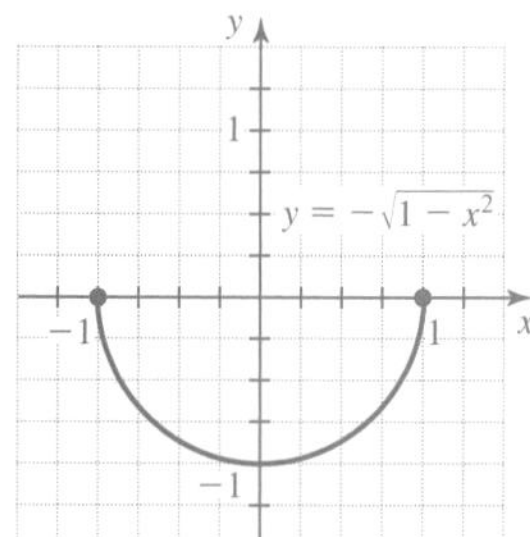

Getting More Involved

65. ***Cooperative learning***

The equation of a circle is a special case of the general equation $Ax^2 + Bx + Cy^2 + Dy = E$, where A, B, C, D, and E are real numbers. Working in small groups, find restrictions that must be placed on A, B, C, D, and E so that the graph of this equation is a circle. What does the graph of $x^2 + y^2 = -9$ look like?
B and D can be any real numbers, but A must equal C, and $4AE + B^2 + D^2 > 0$. No ordered pairs satisfy $x^2 + y^2 = -9$.

66. *Discussion*

Suppose lighthouse A is located at the origin and lighthouse B is located at coordinates (0, 6). The captain of a ship has determined that the ship's distance from lighthouse A is 2 and its distance from lighthouse B is 5. What are the possible coordinates for the location of the ship?

$\left(-\frac{\sqrt{39}}{4}, \frac{5}{4}\right)$ and $\left(\frac{\sqrt{39}}{4}, \frac{5}{4}\right)$

Graphing Calculator Exercises

Graph each relation on a graphing calculator by solving for y and graphing two functions.

67. $x^2 + y^2 = 4$
$y = \pm\sqrt{4 - x^2}$

68. $(x - 1)^2 + (y + 2)^2 = 1$
$y = -2 \pm \sqrt{1 - (x - 1)^2}$

69. $x = y^2$
$y = \pm\sqrt{x}$

70. $x = (y + 2)^2 - 1$
$y = -2 \pm \sqrt{x + 1}$

71. $x = y^2 + 2y + 1$
$y = -1 \pm \sqrt{x}$

72. $x = 4y^2 + 4y + 1$
$y = \frac{-1 \pm \sqrt{x}}{2}$

13.4 The Ellipse and Hyperbola

In this Section

- The Ellipse
- The Hyperbola

In this section we study the remaining two conic sections: the ellipse and the hyperbola.

The Ellipse

An ellipse can be obtained by intersecting a plane and a cone, as was shown in Fig. 13.3. We can also give a definition of an ellipse in terms of points and distance.

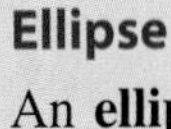

Ellipse

An **ellipse** is the set of all points in a plane such that the sum of their distances from two fixed points is a constant. Each fixed point is called a **focus** (plural: foci).

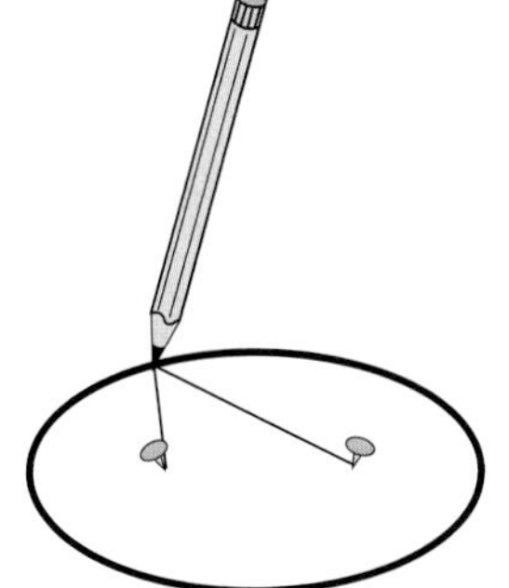

Figure 13.20

An easy way to draw an ellipse is illustrated in Fig. 13.20. A string is attached at two fixed points, and a pencil is used to take up the slack. As the pencil is moved around the paper, the sum of the distances of the pencil point from the two fixed points remains constant. Of course, the length of the string is that constant. You may wish to try this.

Like the parabola, the ellipse also has interesting reflecting properties. All light or sound waves emitted from one focus are reflected off the ellipse to concentrate at the other focus (see Fig. 13.21). This property is used in light fixtures where a concentration of light at a point is desired or in a whispering gallery such as Statuary Hall in the U.S. Capitol Building.

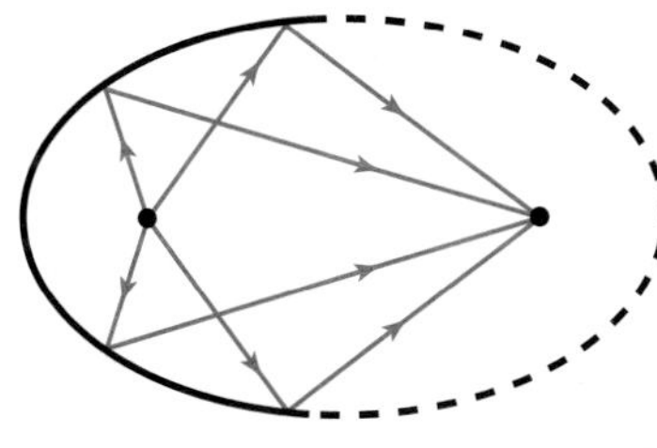

Figure 13.21

The orbits of the planets around the sun and satellites around the earth are elliptical. For the orbit of the earth around the sun, the sun is at one focus. For the elliptical path of an earth satellite, the earth is at one focus and a point in space is the other focus.

Figure 13.22 on the next page shows an ellipse with foci $(c, 0)$ and $(-c, 0)$. The origin is the center of this ellipse. In general, the **center** of an ellipse is a point midway between the foci. The ellipse in Fig. 13.22 has x-intercepts at $(a, 0)$ and $(-a, 0)$ and y-intercepts at $(0, b)$ and $(0, -b)$. The distance formula can be used to write the following equation for this ellipse. (See Exercise 55.)

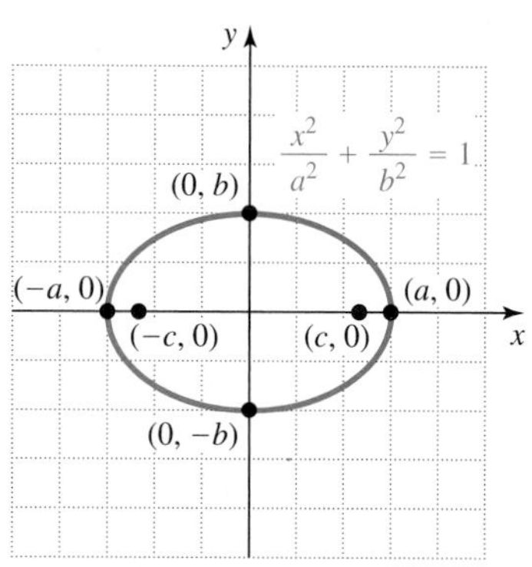

Figure 13.22

Equation of an Ellipse Centered at the Origin

An ellipse centered at (0, 0) with foci at $(\pm c, 0)$ and constant sum $2a$ has equation

$$\frac{x^2}{a^2} + \frac{y^2}{b^2} = 1,$$

where a, b, and c are positive real numbers with $c^2 = a^2 - b^2$.

To draw a "nice-looking" ellipse, we would locate the foci and use string as shown in Fig. 13.20. We can get a rough sketch of an ellipse centered at the origin by using the x- and y-intercepts only.

EXAMPLE 1

Graphing an ellipse

Find the x- and y-intercepts for the ellipse and sketch its graph.

$$\frac{x^2}{9} + \frac{y^2}{4} = 1$$

Solution

To find the y-intercepts, let $x = 0$ in the equation:

$$\frac{0}{9} + \frac{y^2}{4} = 1$$

$$\frac{y^2}{4} = 1$$

$$y^2 = 4$$

$$y = \pm 2$$

To find the x-intercepts, let $y = 0$. We get $x = \pm 3$. The four intercepts are (0, 2), (0, −2), (3, 0), and (−3, 0). Plot the intercepts and draw an ellipse through them as in Fig. 13.23.

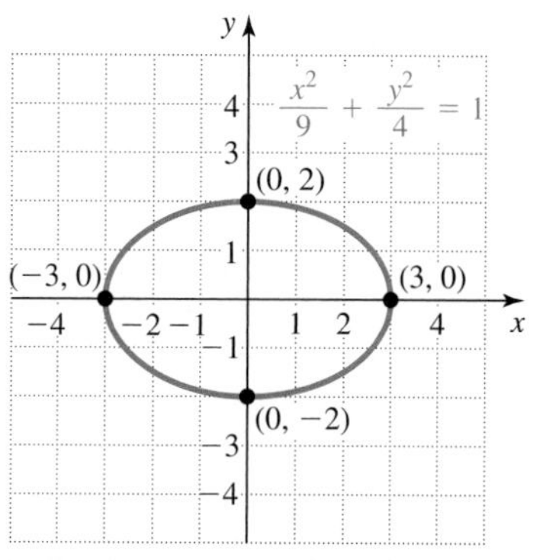

Figure 13.23

Now do Exercises 9–22

Calculator Close-Up

To graph the ellipse in Example 1, graph

$$y_1 = \sqrt{4 - 4x^2/9}$$

and

$$y_2 = -y_1$$

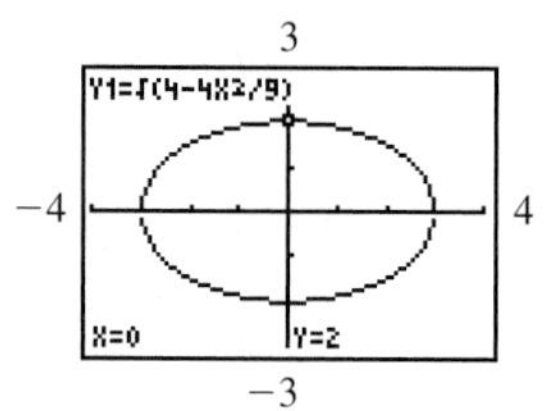

Helpful Hint

When sketching ellipses or circles by hand, use your hand like a compass and rotate your paper as you draw the curve.

Math *at Work* Kepler's Laws

With great patience, Danish astronomer Tycho Brahe (1546–1601) made very careful observations of the motion of the planets in the sky. Brahe tried to explain the orbits of the planets using circles. His assistant, Johannes Kepler (1571–1630), studied Tycho's tables and came up with three laws that better explained the motion of the planets. Kepler's first law went contrary to Brahe's theory and states that each planet moves around the sun in an elliptical orbit with the sun at one focus of the ellipse.

The second law states that the line joining a planet with the sun sweeps out equal areas in equal times. A planet moves faster when it is closer to the sun and slower when it is far from the sun. So the planet illustrated in the accompanying figure moves from A to B in the same time that it moves from C to D, even though the distance from A to B is greater. According to Kepler's law, the shaded areas in the figure are equal.

The third law states that the square of the period of a planet orbiting the sun is equal to the cube of the mean distance from the planet to the sun. In symbols, $P^2 = a^3$, where P is the number of earth years that it takes for the planet to orbit the sun, and a is the mean distance from the planet to the sun in astronomical units (AU). (One AU is the mean distance from the earth to the sun.) $P^2 = a^3$ can be written as $P = a^{3/2}$ or $a = P^{2/3}$ and used to find the period or the distance. For example, the period of Mars is observed to be 1.88 years. So the mean distance from Mars to the sun is $1.88^{2/3}$ or 1.53 AU. The mean distance from Pluto to the sun is observed to be 39.44 AU, So Pluto takes $39.44^{3/2}$ or 247.69 years to complete one orbit of the sun.

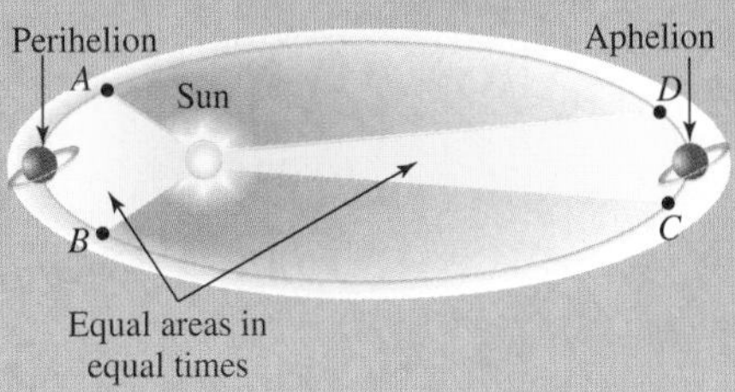

Ellipses, like circles, may be centered at any point in the plane. To get the equation of an ellipse centered at (h, k), we replace x by $x - h$ and y by $y - k$ in the equation of the ellipse centered at the origin.

Equation of an Ellipse Centered at (h, k)

An ellipse centered at (h, k) has equation

$$\frac{(x-h)^2}{a^2} + \frac{(y-k)^2}{b^2} = 1,$$

where a and b are positive real numbers.

EXAMPLE 2

An ellipse with center (h, k)

Sketch the graph of the ellipse:

$$\frac{(x-1)^2}{9} + \frac{(y+2)^2}{4} = 1$$

Teaching Tip To move $y = x^2$ with vertex (0, 0) to vertex (h, k) we could write $y - k = (x - h)^2$. This is the same idea used in moving the ellipse.

Solution

The graph of this ellipse is exactly the same size and shape as the ellipse

$$\frac{x^2}{9} + \frac{y^2}{4} = 1,$$

which was graphed in Example 1. However, the center for

$$\frac{(x-1)^2}{9} + \frac{(y+2)^2}{4} = 1$$

is $(1, -2)$. The denominator 9 is used to determine that the ellipse passes through points that are three units to the right and three units to the left of the center: $(4, -2)$ and $(-2, -2)$. See Fig. 13.24. The denominator 4 is used to determine that the ellipse passes through points that are two units above and two units below the center: $(1, 0)$ and $(1, -4)$. We draw an ellipse using these four points, just as we did for an ellipse centered at the origin.

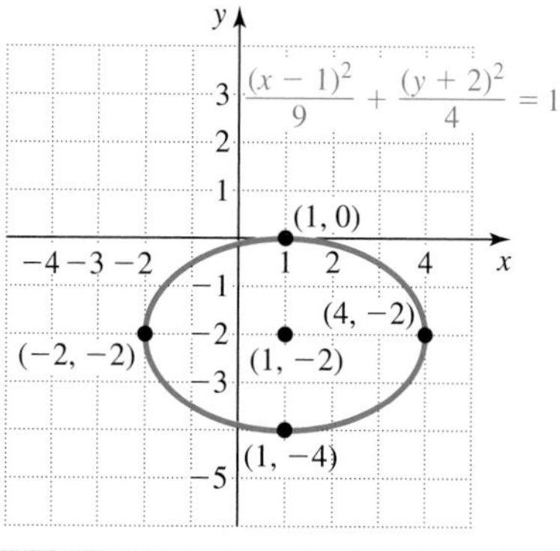

Figure 13.24

Now do Exercises 23–28

The Hyperbola

A hyperbola is the curve that occurs at the intersection of a cone and a plane, as was shown in Fig. 13.3 in Section 13.2. A hyperbola can also be defined in terms of points and distance.

> **Hyperbola**
>
> A **hyperbola** is the set of all points in the plane such that the difference of their distances from two fixed points (foci) is constant.

Like the parabola and the ellipse, the hyperbola also has reflecting properties. If a light ray is aimed at one focus, it is reflected off the hyperbola and goes to the other focus, as shown in Fig. 13.25. Hyperbolic mirrors are used in conjunction with parabolic mirrors in telescopes.

The definitions of a hyperbola and an ellipse are similar, and so are their equations. However, their graphs are very different. Figure 13.26 shows a hyperbola

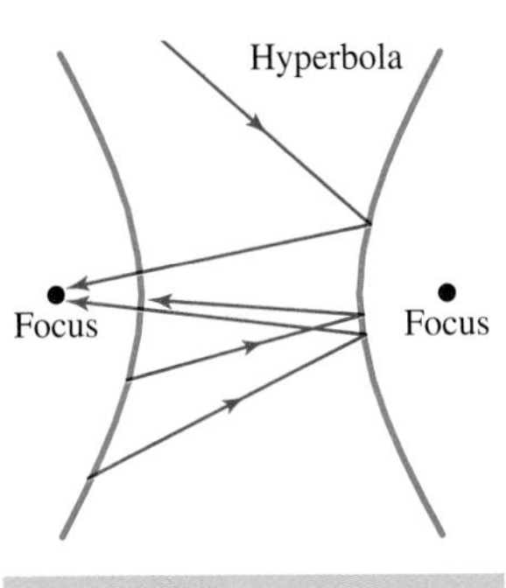

Figure 13.25

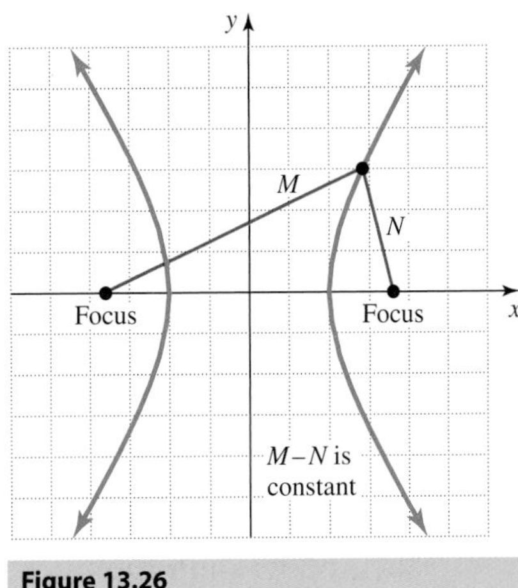

Figure 13.26

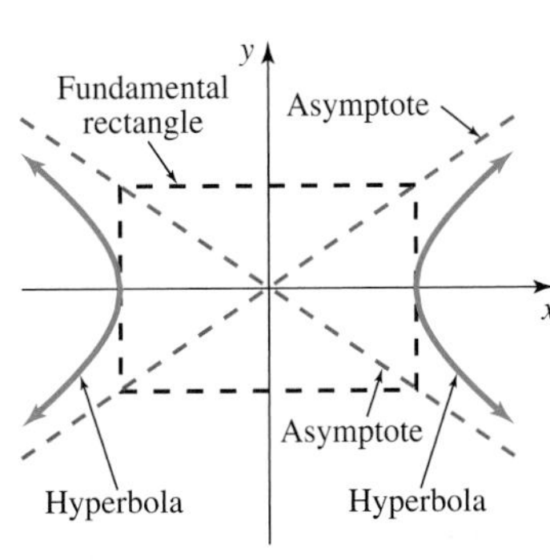

Figure 13.27

in which the distance from a point on the hyperbola to the closer focus is N and the distance to the farther focus is M. The value $M - N$ is the same for every point on the hyperbola.

A hyperbola has two parts called **branches.** These branches look like parabolas, but they are not parabolas. The branches of the hyperbola shown in Fig. 13.27 get closer and closer to the dashed lines, called **asymptotes,** but they never intersect them. The asymptotes are used as guidelines in sketching a hyperbola. The asymptotes are found by extending the diagonals of the **fundamental rectangle,** shown in Fig. 13.27. The key to drawing a hyperbola is getting the fundamental rectangle and extending its diagonals to get the asymptotes. You will learn how to find the fundamental rectangle from the equation of a hyperbola. The hyperbola in Fig. 13.27 opens to the left and right.

If we start with foci at $(\pm c, 0)$ and a positive number a, then we can use the definition of a hyperbola to derive the following equation of a hyperbola in which the constant difference between the distances to the foci is $2a$.

Equation of a Hyperbola Centered at (0, 0) Opening Left and Right

A hyperbola centered at $(0, 0)$ with foci $(c, 0)$ and $(-c, 0)$ and constant difference $2a$ has equation

$$\frac{x^2}{a^2} - \frac{y^2}{b^2} = 1,$$

where a, b, and c are positive real numbers such that $c^2 = a^2 + b^2$.

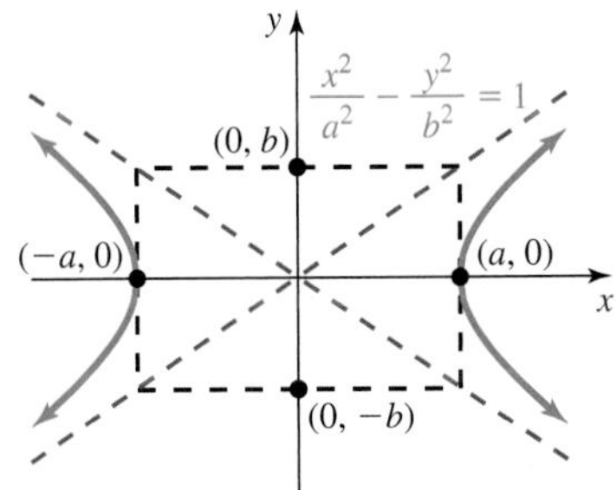

Figure 13.28

The graph of a general equation for a hyperbola is shown in Fig. 13.28. Notice that the fundamental rectangle extends to the x-intercepts along the x-axis and extends b units above and below the origin along the y-axis. Use the following procedure for graphing a hyperbola centered at the origin and opening to the left and to the right.

Graphing a Hyperbola Centered at the Origin, Opening Left and Right

To graph the hyperbola $\frac{x^2}{a^2} - \frac{y^2}{b^2} = 1$:

1. Locate the x-intercepts at $(a, 0)$ and $(-a, 0)$.
2. Draw the fundamental rectangle through $(\pm a, 0)$ and $(0, \pm b)$.
3. Draw the extended diagonals of the rectangle to use as asymptotes.
4. Draw the hyperbola to the left and right approaching the asymptotes.

EXAMPLE 3

A hyperbola opening left and right

Sketch the graph of $\frac{x^2}{36} - \frac{y^2}{9} = 1$, and find the equations of its asymptotes.

Solution

The x-intercepts are $(6, 0)$ and $(-6, 0)$. Draw the fundamental rectangle through these x-intercepts and the points $(0, 3)$ and $(0, -3)$. Extend the diagonals of the fundamental rectangle to get the asymptotes. Now draw a hyperbola passing through the x-intercepts and approaching the asymptotes as shown in Fig. 13.29. From the graph in Fig. 13.29 we see that the slopes of the asymptotes are $\frac{1}{2}$ and $-\frac{1}{2}$. Because the y-intercept for both asymptotes is the origin, their equations are $y = \frac{1}{2}x$ and $y = -\frac{1}{2}x$.

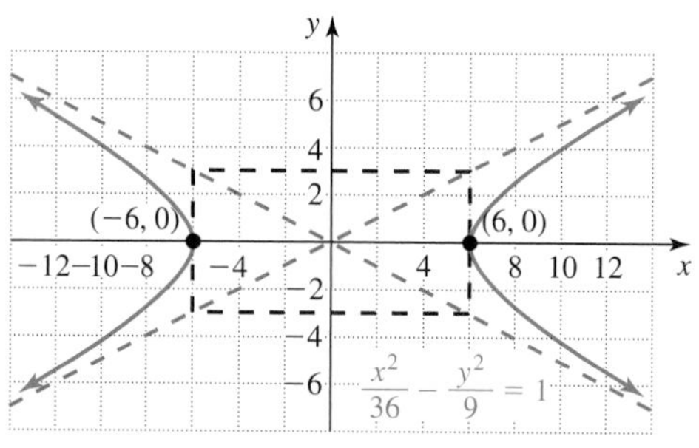

Figure 13.29

Now do Exercises 29–30

Calculator Close-Up

To graph the hyperbola and its asymptotes from Example 3, graph

$y_1 = \sqrt{x^2/4 - 9}, y_2 = -y_1,$

$y_3 = 0.5x,$ and $y_4 = -y_3.$

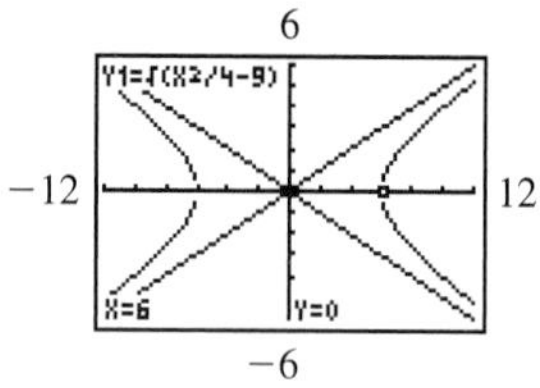

If the variables x and y are interchanged in the equation of the hyperbola, then the hyperbola opens up and down.

Equation of a Hyperbola Centered at (0, 0) Opening Up and Down

A hyperbola centered at $(0, 0)$ with foci $(0, c)$ and $(0, -c)$ and constant difference $2b$ has equation

$$\frac{y^2}{b^2} - \frac{x^2}{a^2} = 1,$$

where a, b, and c are positive real numbers such that $c^2 = a^2 + b^2$.

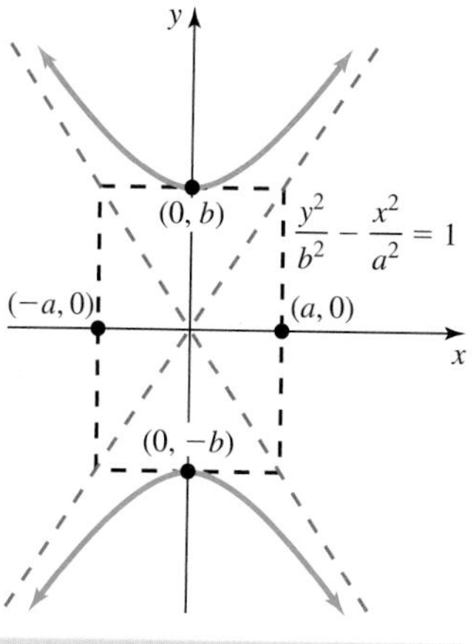

Figure 13.30

The graph of the general equation for a hyperbola opening up and down is shown in Fig. 13.30. Notice that the fundamental rectangle extends to the y-intercepts along the y-axis and extends a units to the left and right of the origin along the x-axis. The procedure for graphing a hyperbola opening up and down follows.

Graphing a Hyperbola Centered at the Origin, Opening Up and Down

To graph the hyperbola $\frac{y^2}{b^2} - \frac{x^2}{a^2} = 1$:

1. Locate the y-intercepts at $(0, b)$ and $(0, -b)$.
2. Draw the fundamental rectangle through $(0, \pm b)$ and $(\pm a, 0)$.
3. Draw the extended diagonals of the rectangle to use as asymptotes.
4. Draw the hyperbola opening up and down approaching the asymptotes.

EXAMPLE 4

A hyperbola opening up and down

Graph the hyperbola $\frac{y^2}{9} - \frac{x^2}{4} = 1$ and find the equations of its asymptotes.

Helpful Hint

We could include here general formulas for the equations of the asymptotes, but that is not necessary. It is easier first to draw the asymptotes as suggested and then to figure out their equations by looking at the graph.

Solution

If $y = 0$, we get

$$-\frac{x^2}{4} = 1$$

$$x^2 = -4.$$

Because this equation has no real solution, the graph has no x-intercepts. Let $x = 0$ to find the y-intercepts:

$$\frac{y^2}{9} = 1$$

$$y^2 = 9$$

$$y = \pm 3$$

The y-intercepts are $(0, 3)$ and $(0, -3)$, and the hyperbola opens up and down. From $a^2 = 4$ we get $a = 2$. So the fundamental rectangle extends to the intercepts $(0, 3)$ and $(0, -3)$ on the y-axis and to the points $(2, 0)$ and $(-2, 0)$ along the x-axis. We extend the diagonals of the rectangle and draw the graph of the hyperbola as shown in Fig. 13.31. From the graph in Fig. 13.31 we see that the asymptotes have slopes $\frac{3}{2}$ and $-\frac{3}{2}$. Because the y-intercept for both asymptotes is the origin, their equations are $y = \frac{3}{2}x$ and $y = -\frac{3}{2}x$.

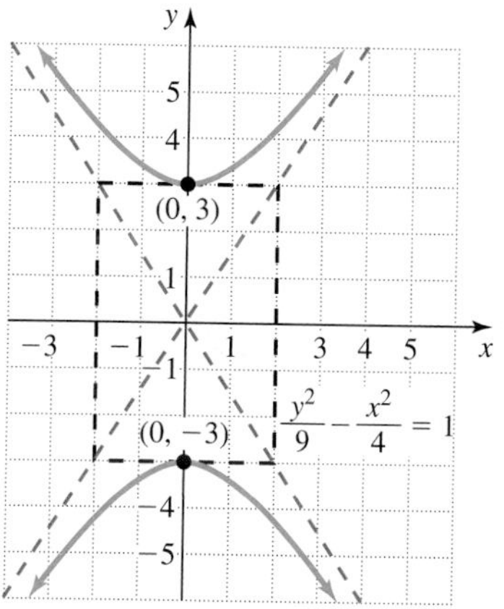

Figure 13.31

Now do Exercises 31–36

EXAMPLE 5

A hyperbola not in standard form

Sketch the graph of the hyperbola $4x^2 - y^2 = 4$.

Solution

First write the equation in standard form. Divide each side by 4 to get

$$x^2 - \frac{y^2}{4} = 1.$$

There are no y-intercepts. If $y = 0$, then $x = \pm 1$. The hyperbola opens left and right with x-intercepts at $(1, 0)$ and $(-1, 0)$. The fundamental rectangle extends to the intercepts along the x-axis and to the points $(0, 2)$ and $(0, -2)$ along the y-axis. We extend the diagonals of the rectangle for the asymptotes and draw the graph as shown in Fig. 13.32.

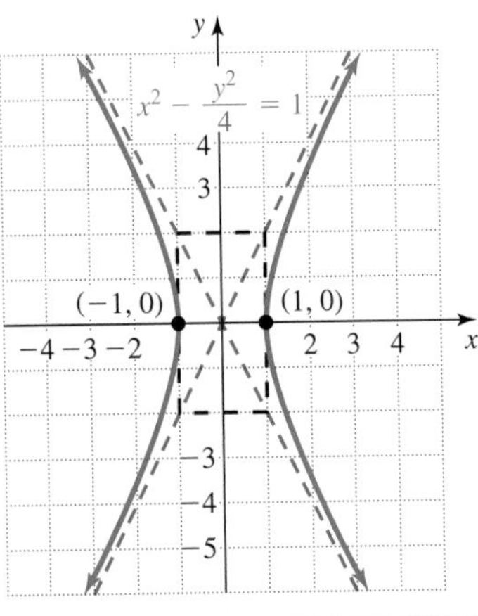

Figure 13.32

Now do Exercises 37–40

Like circles and ellipses, hyperbolas may be centered at any point in the plane. To get the equation of a hyperbola centered at (h, k), we replace x by $x - h$ and y by $y - k$ in the equation of the hyperbola centered at the origin.

Equation of a Hyperbola Centered at (h, k)

A hyperbola centered at (h, k) has one of the following equations depending on which way it opens.

Opening left and right:

$$\frac{(x - h)^2}{a^2} - \frac{(y - k)^2}{b^2} = 1$$

Opening up and down:

$$\frac{(y - k)^2}{b^2} - \frac{(x - h)^2}{a^2} = 1$$

EXAMPLE 6

Graphing a hyperbola centered at (h, k)

Graph the hyperbola $\frac{(x-3)^2}{16} - \frac{(y+1)^2}{4} = 1$.

Solution

This hyperbola is centered at $(3, -1)$ and opens left and right. It is a transformation of the graph of $\frac{x^2}{16} - \frac{y^2}{4} = 1$. The fundamental rectangle for $\frac{x^2}{16} - \frac{y^2}{4} = 1$ is centered at the origin and goes through $(\pm 4, 0)$ and $(0, \pm 2)$. So draw a fundamental rectangle centered at $(3, -1)$ that extends four units to the right and left and two units up and down as shown in Fig. 13.33. Draw the asymptotes through the vertices of the fundamental rectangle and the hyperbola opening to the left and right.

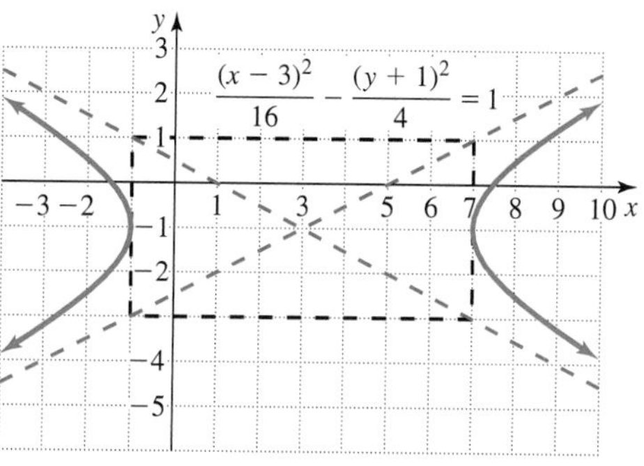

Figure 13.33

Now do Exercises 41–46

Warm-Ups

True or false? Explain your answer.

1. The x-intercepts of the ellipse $\frac{x^2}{36} + \frac{y^2}{25} = 1$ are $(5, 0)$ and $(-5, 0)$. False
2. The graph of $\frac{x^2}{9} + \frac{y}{4} = 1$ is an ellipse. False
3. If the foci of an ellipse coincide, then the ellipse is a circle. True
4. The graph of $2x^2 + y^2 = 2$ is an ellipse centered at the origin. True
5. The y-intercepts of $x^2 + \frac{y^2}{3} = 1$ are $(0, \sqrt{3})$ and $(0, -\sqrt{3})$. True
6. The graph of $\frac{x^2}{9} + \frac{y}{4} = 1$ is a hyperbola. False
7. The graph of $\frac{x^2}{25} - \frac{y^2}{16} = 1$ has y-intercepts at $(0, 4)$ and $(0, -4)$. False
8. The hyperbola $\frac{y^2}{9} - x^2 = 1$ opens up and down. True
9. The graph of $4x^2 - y^2 = 4$ is a hyperbola. True
10. The asymptotes of a hyperbola are the extended diagonals of a rectangle. True

13.4 Exercises

Boost your GRADE at mathzone.com!

MathZone

- Practice Problems
- Self-Tests
- Videos
- Net Tutor
- e-Professors

Reading and Writing *After reading this section, write out the answers to these questions. Use complete sentences.*

1. What is the definition of an ellipse?
An ellipse is the set of all points in a plane such that the sum of their distances from two fixed points is constant.

2. How can you draw an ellipse with a pencil and string?
Attach a string to two thumbtacks and use a pencil to take up the slack as shown in the text.

3. Where is the center of an ellipse?
The center of an ellipse is the point that is midway between the foci.

4. What is the equation of an ellipse centered at the origin?
The equation of an ellipse centered at the origin is $\frac{x^2}{a^2} + \frac{y^2}{b^2} = 1$.

5. What is the equation of an ellipse centered at (h, k)?
The equation of an ellipse centered at (h, k) is $\frac{(x - h)^2}{a^2} + \frac{(y - k)^2}{b^2} = 1$.

6. What is the definition of a hyperbola?
A hyperbola is the set of all points in a plane such that the difference of their distances from two fixed points is constant.

7. How do you find the asymptotes of a hyperbola?
The asymptotes of a hyperbola are the extended diagonals of the fundamental rectangle.

8. What is the equation of a hyperbola centered at the origin and opening left and right?
The equation of a hyperbola centered at the origin and opening left and right is $\frac{x^2}{a^2} - \frac{y^2}{b^2} = 1$.

Sketch the graph of each ellipse. See Example 1.

9. $\frac{x^2}{9} + \frac{y^2}{4} = 1$

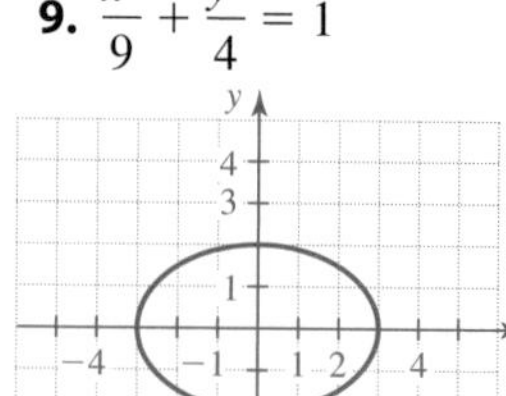

10. $\frac{x^2}{9} + \frac{y^2}{16} = 1$

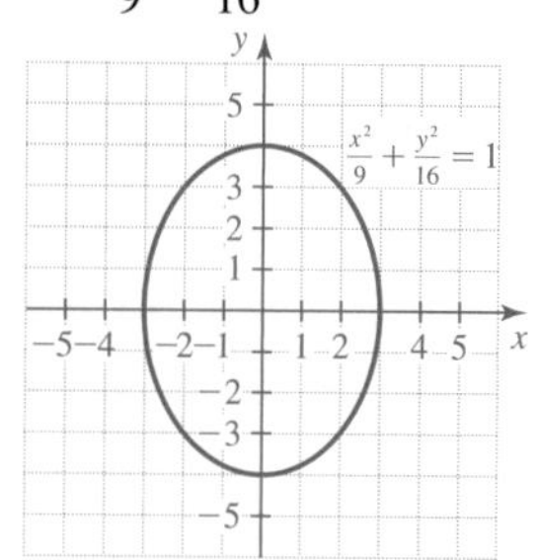

11. $\frac{x^2}{9} + y^2 = 1$

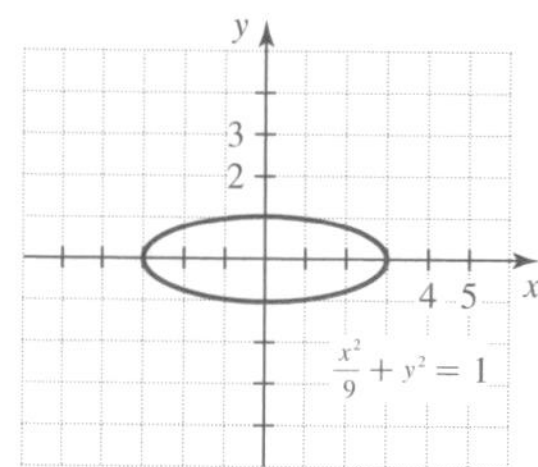

12. $x^2 + \frac{y^2}{4} = 1$

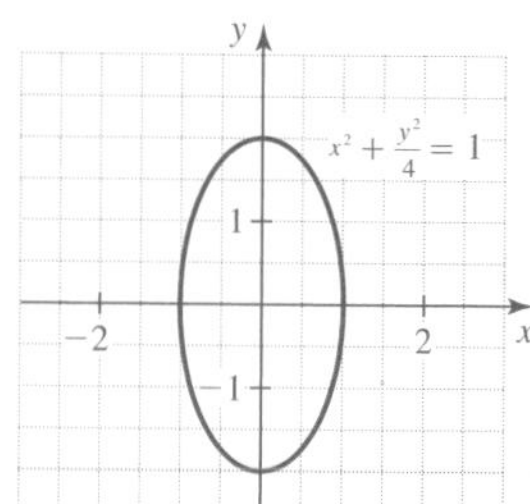

13. $\frac{x^2}{36} + \frac{y^2}{25} = 1$

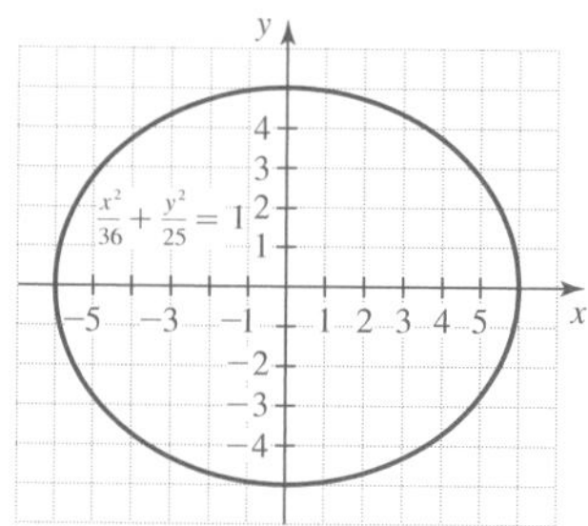

14. $\frac{x^2}{25} + \frac{y^2}{49} = 1$

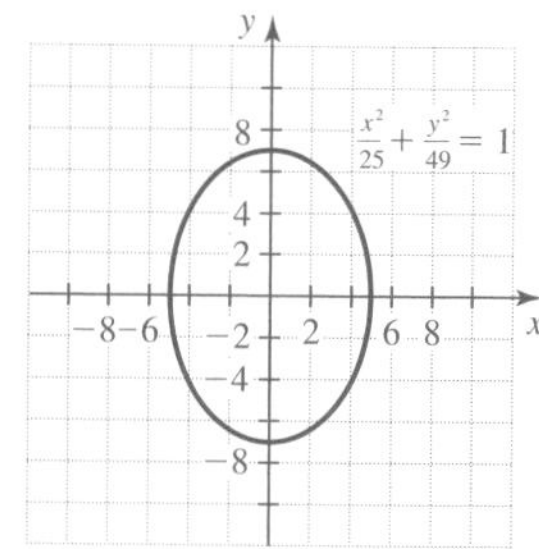

15. $\frac{x^2}{24} + \frac{y^2}{5} = 1$

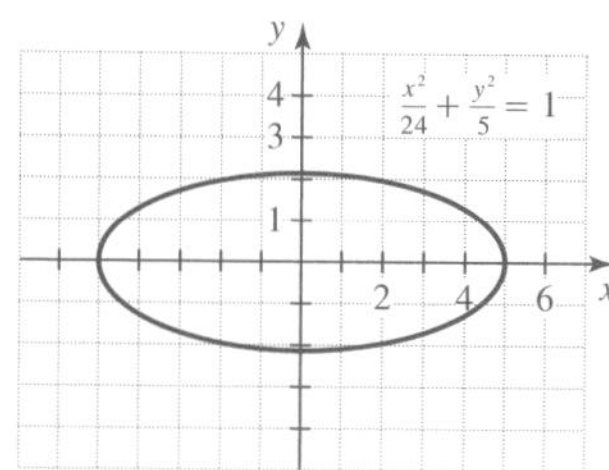

16. $\frac{x^2}{6} + \frac{y^2}{17} = 1$

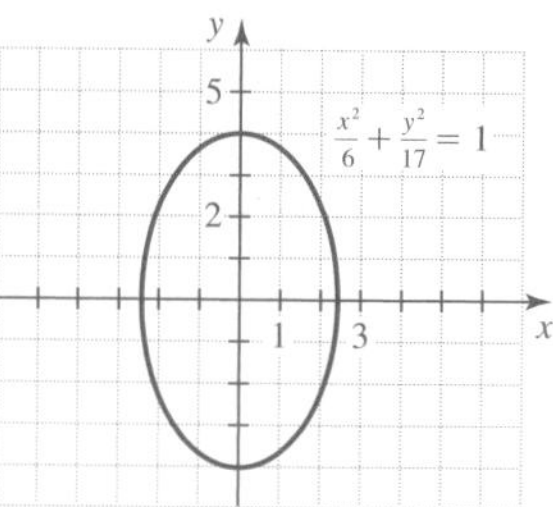

17. $9x^2 + 16y^2 = 144$

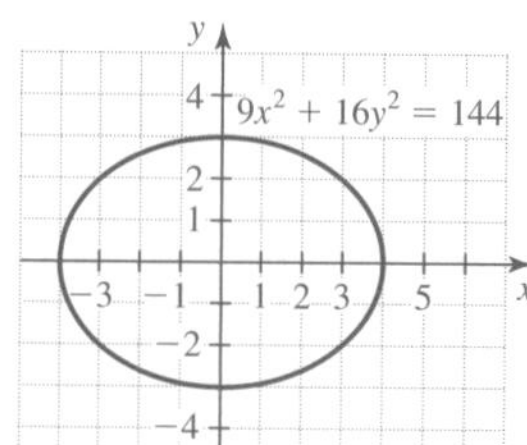

18. $9x^2 + 25y^2 = 225$

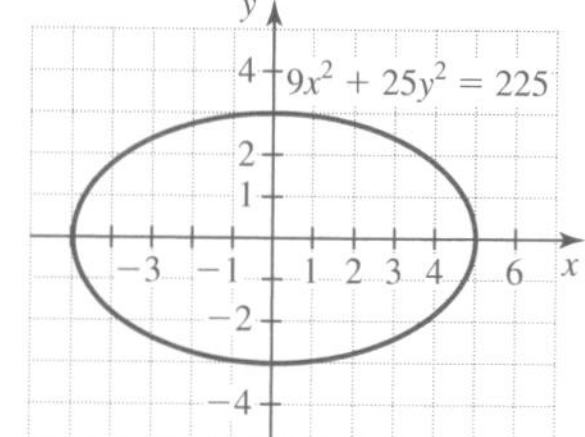

19. $25x^2 + y^2 = 25$

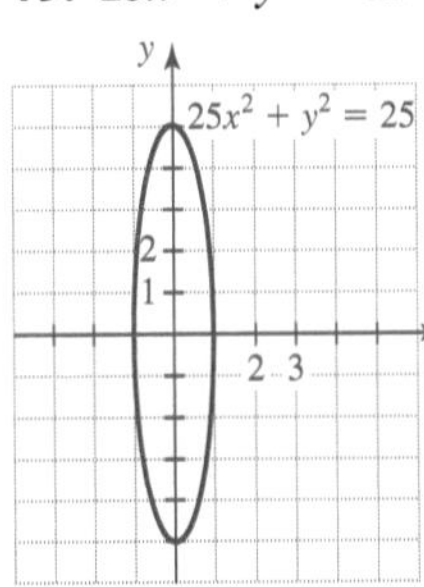

20. $x^2 + 16y^2 = 16$

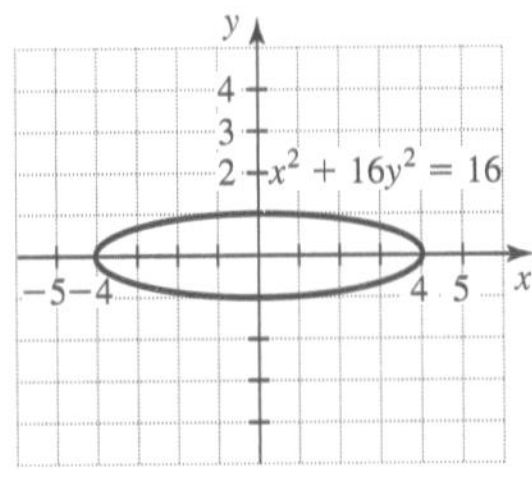

21. $4x^2 + 9y^2 = 1$

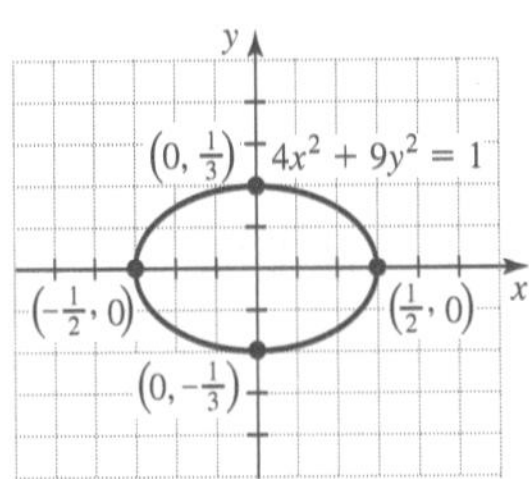

22. $25x^2 + 16y^2 = 1$

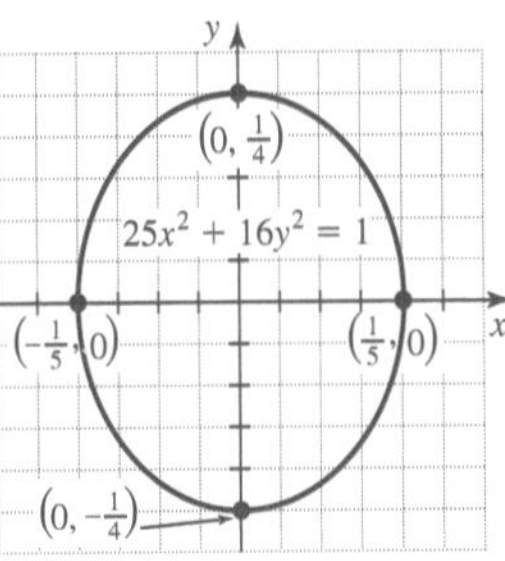

Sketch the graph of each ellipse. See Example 2.

23. $\dfrac{(x-3)^2}{4} + \dfrac{(y-1)^2}{9} = 1$

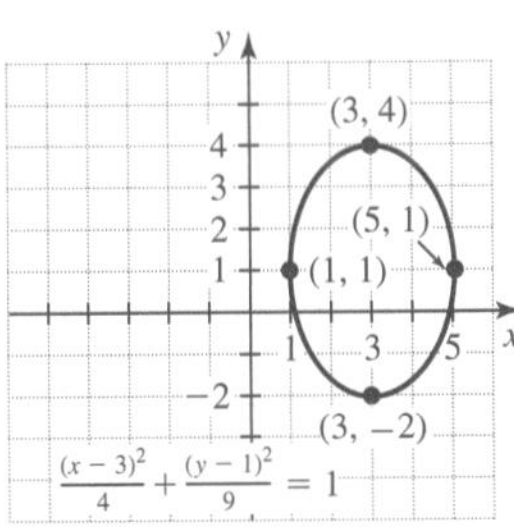

24. $\dfrac{(x+5)^2}{49} + \dfrac{(y-2)^2}{25} = 1$

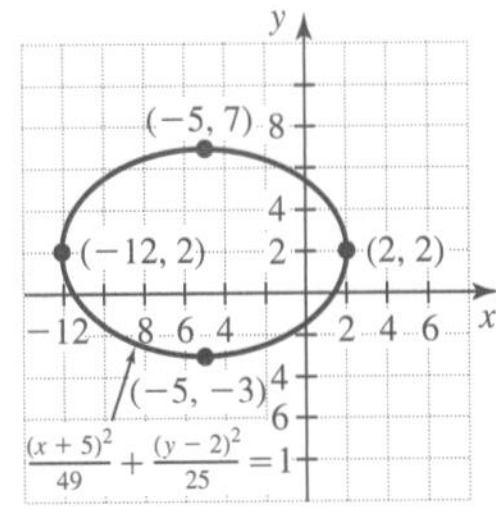

25. $\dfrac{(x+1)^2}{16} + \dfrac{(y-2)^2}{25} = 1$

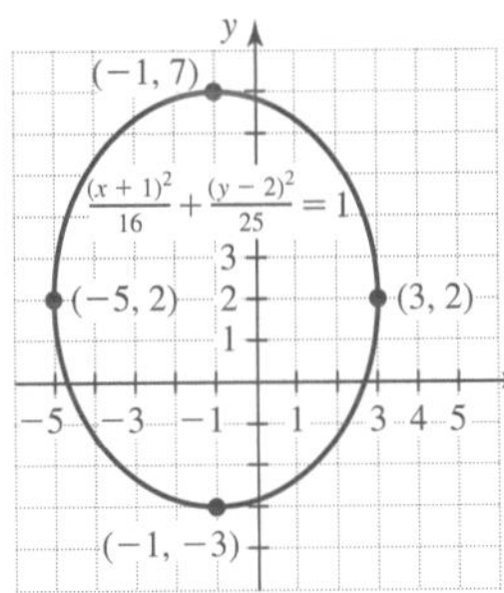

26. $\dfrac{(x-3)^2}{36} + \dfrac{(y+4)^2}{64} = 1$

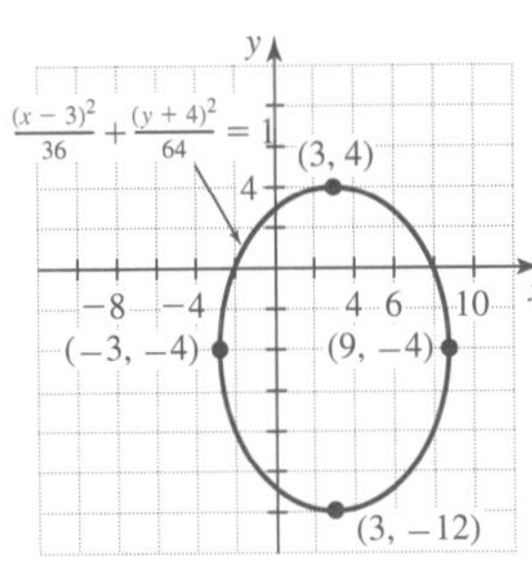

27. $(x-2)^2 + \dfrac{(y+1)^2}{36} = 1$

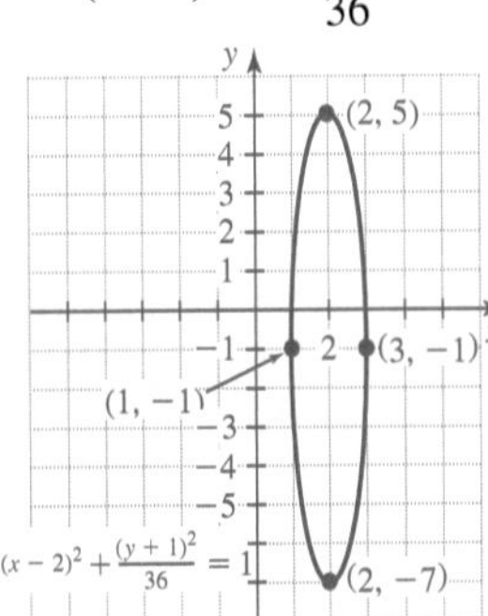

28. $\dfrac{(x+3)^2}{9} + (y+1)^2 = 1$

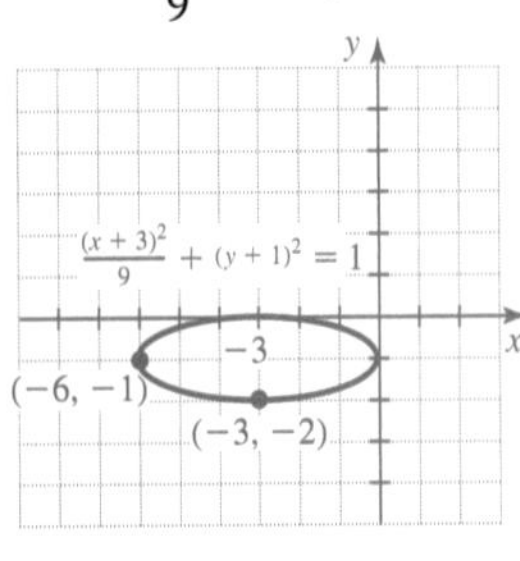

Sketch the graph of each hyperbola and write the equations of its asymptotes. See Examples 3–5.

29. $\dfrac{x^2}{4} - \dfrac{y^2}{9} = 1$

$y = \pm\dfrac{3}{2}x$

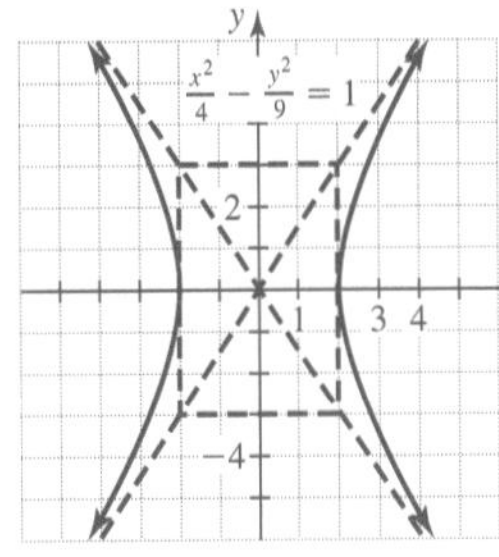

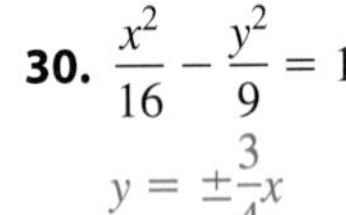

30. $\dfrac{x^2}{16} - \dfrac{y^2}{9} = 1$

$y = \pm\dfrac{3}{4}x$

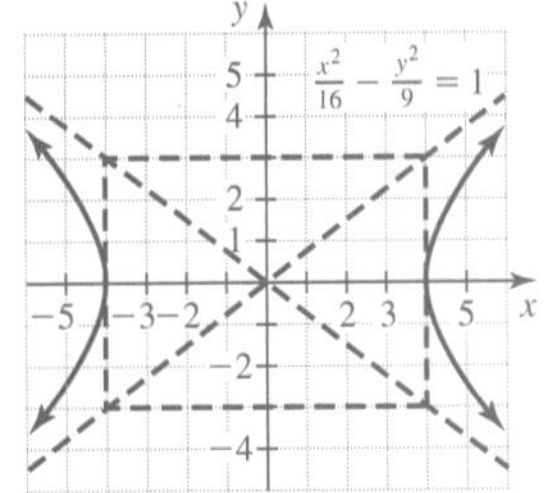

31. $\dfrac{y^2}{4} - \dfrac{x^2}{25} = 1$ $\quad y = \pm\dfrac{2}{5}x$

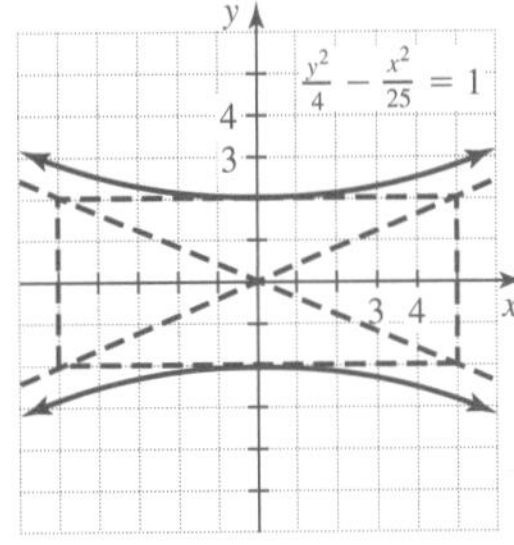

32. $\dfrac{y^2}{9} - \dfrac{x^2}{16} = 1$ $\quad y = \pm\dfrac{3}{4}x$

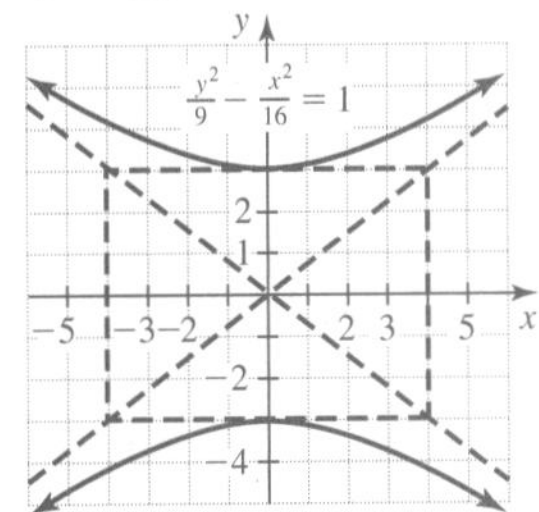

33. $\dfrac{x^2}{25} - y^2 = 1$ $\quad y = \pm\dfrac{1}{5}x$

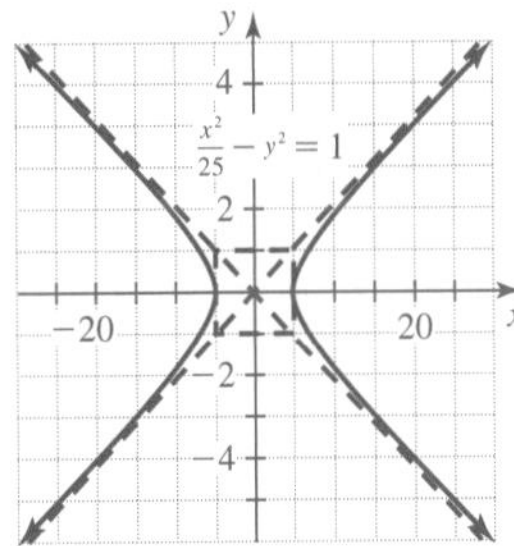

34. $x^2 - \dfrac{y^2}{9} = 1$ $\quad y = \pm 3x$

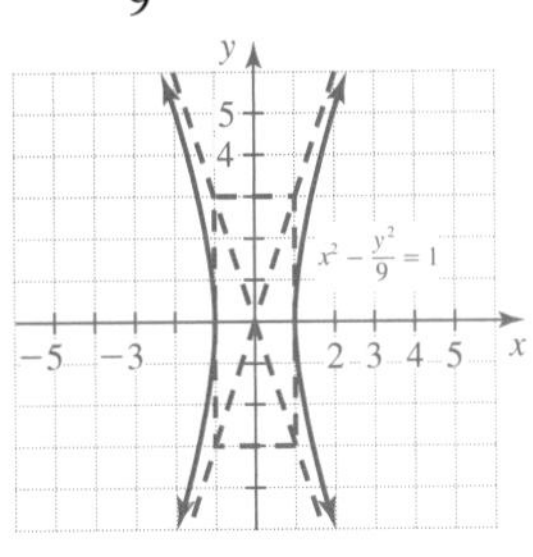

35. $x^2 - \frac{y^2}{25} = 1$

$y = \pm 5x$

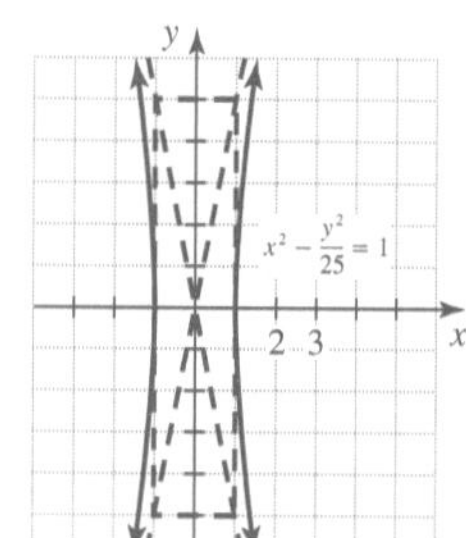

36. $\frac{x^2}{9} - y^2 = 1$

$y = \pm\frac{1}{3}x$

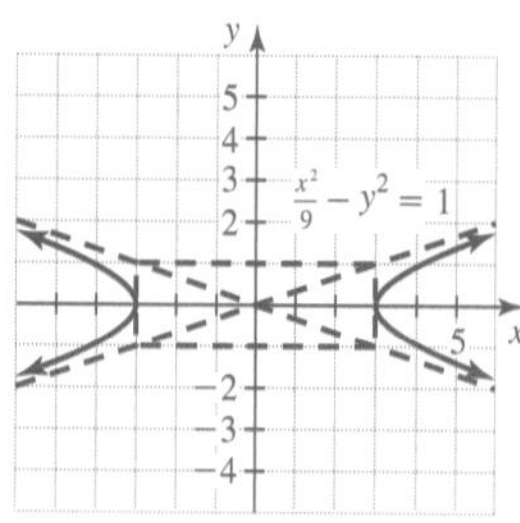

37. $9x^2 - 16y^2 = 144$

$y = \pm\frac{3}{4}x$

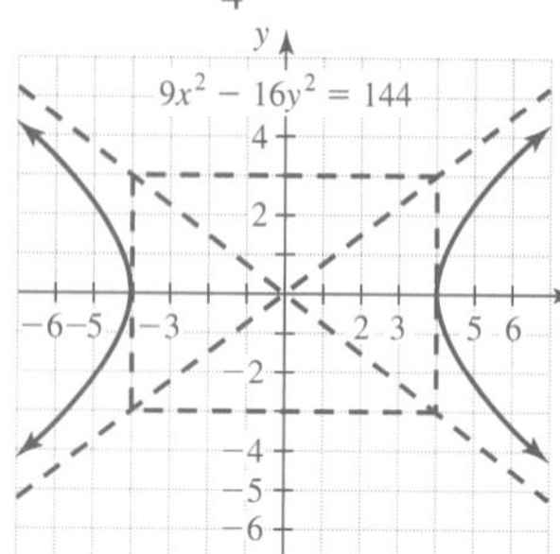

38. $9x^2 - 25y^2 = 225$

$y = \pm\frac{3}{5}x$

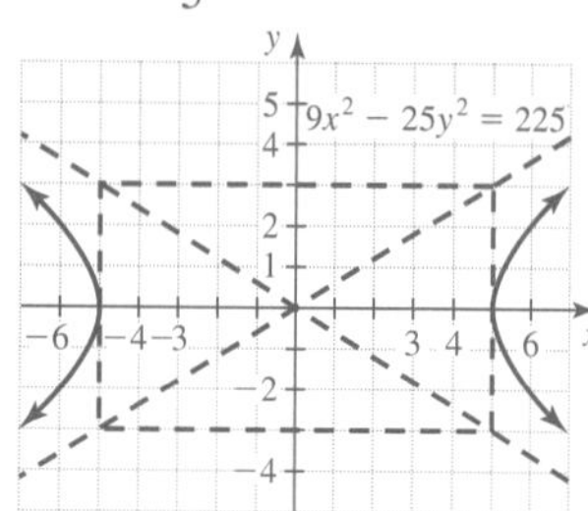

39. $x^2 - y^2 = 1$

$y = \pm x$

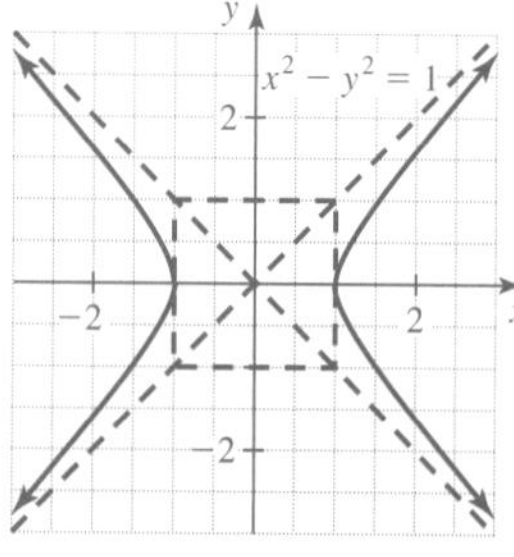

40. $y^2 - x^2 = 1$

$y = \pm x$

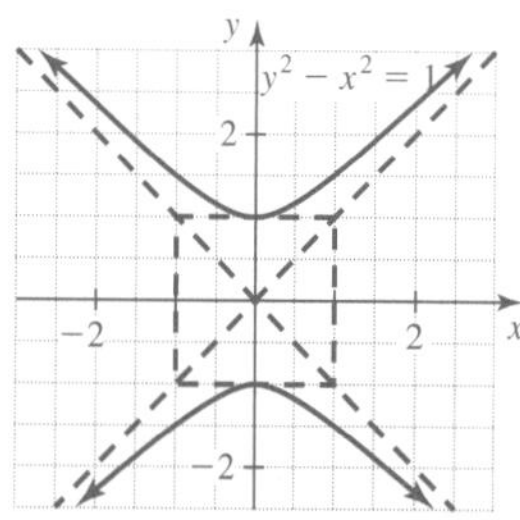

Sketch the graph of each hyperbola. See Example 6.

41. $\frac{(x-2)^2}{4} - (y+1)^2 = 1$

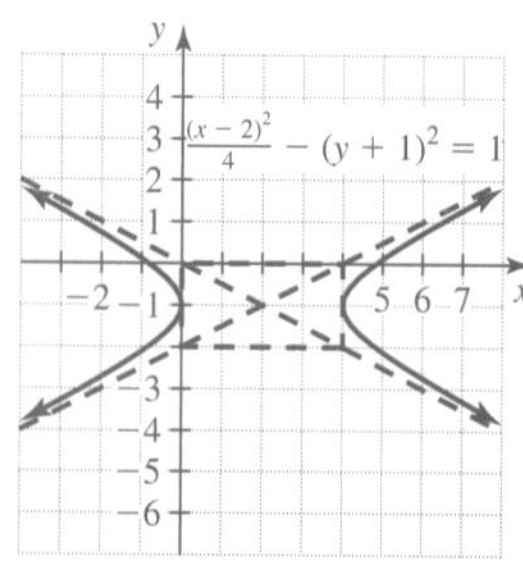

42. $(x+3)^2 - \frac{(y-1)^2}{4} = 1$

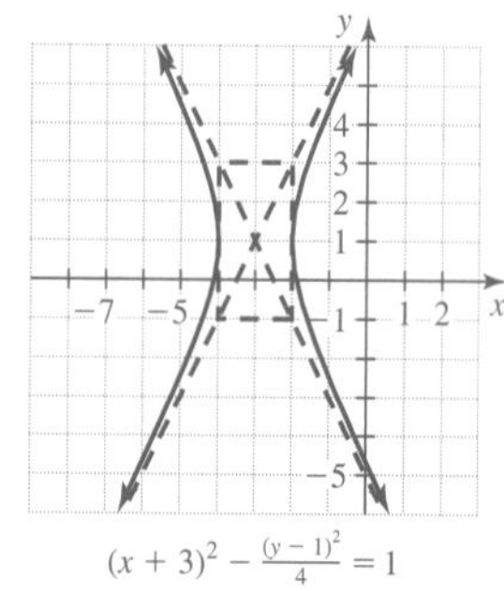

43. $\frac{(x+1)^2}{16} - \frac{(y-1)^2}{9} = 1$

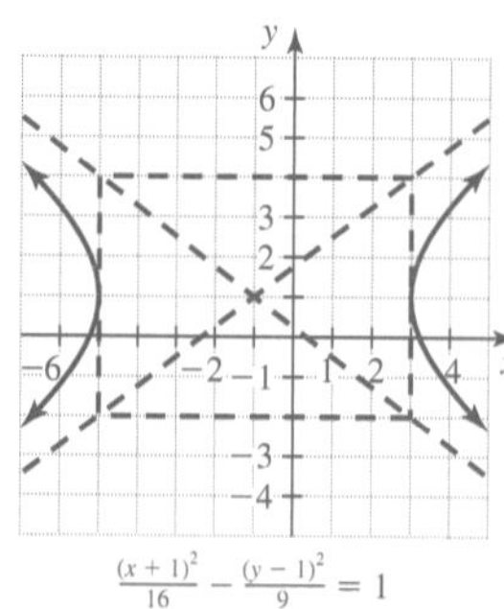

44. $\frac{(x-2)^2}{9} - \frac{(y+2)^2}{16} = 1$

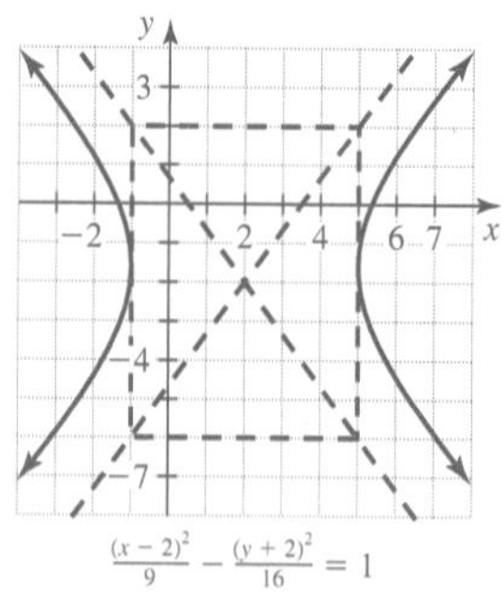

45. $\frac{(y-2)^2}{9} - \frac{(x-4)^2}{4} = 1$

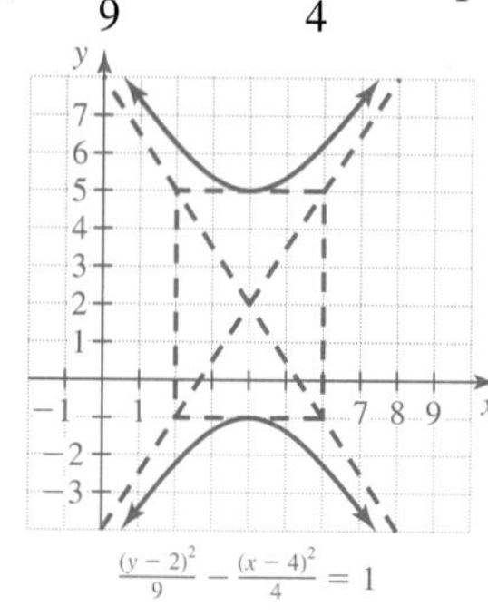

46. $\frac{(y+3)^2}{16} - \frac{(x+1)^2}{9} = 1$

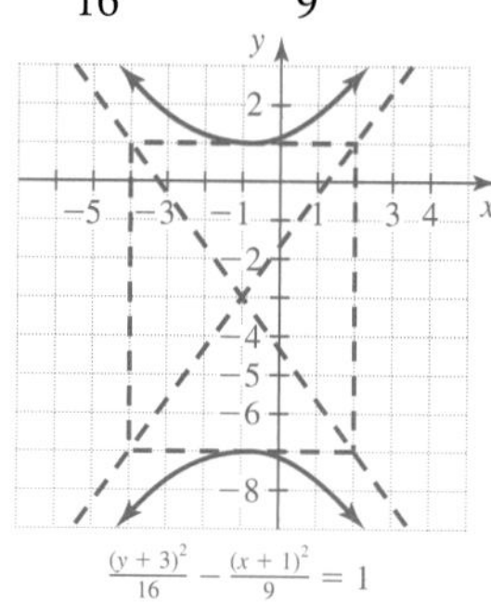

Determine whether the graph of each equation is a circle, parabola, ellipse, or hyperbola.

47. $y = x^2 + 1$ Parabola

48. $x^2 + y^2 = 1$ Circle

49. $x^2 - y^2 = 1$ Hyperbola

50. $4x^2 + y^2 = 1$ Ellipse

51. $\frac{x^2}{2} + y^2 = 1$ Ellipse

52. $x^2 - \frac{y^2}{9} = 1$ Hyperbola

53. $(x-2)^2 + (y-4)^2 = 9$ Circle

54. $(x-2)^2 + y = 9$ Parabola

Graph both equations of each system on the same coordinate axes. Use elimination of variables to find all points of intersection.

55. $\frac{x^2}{4} + \frac{y^2}{9} = 1$

$x^2 - \frac{y^2}{9} = 1$

$\left(\frac{2\sqrt{10}}{5}, \frac{3\sqrt{15}}{5}\right)$, $\left(\frac{2\sqrt{10}}{5}, -\frac{3\sqrt{15}}{5}\right)$, $\left(-\frac{2\sqrt{10}}{5}, \frac{3\sqrt{15}}{5}\right)$, $\left(-\frac{2\sqrt{10}}{5}, -\frac{3\sqrt{15}}{5}\right)$

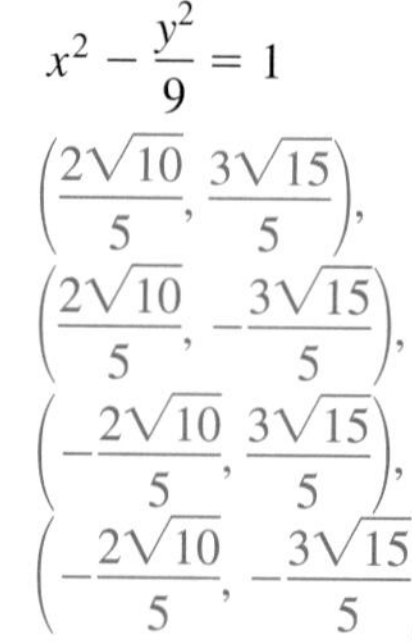

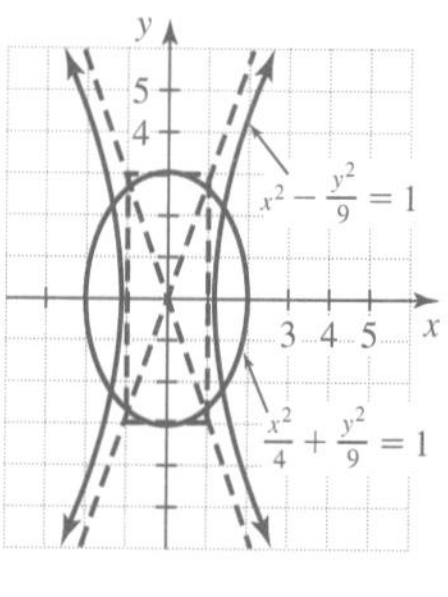

56. $x^2 - \dfrac{y^2}{4} = 1$

$\dfrac{x^2}{9} + \dfrac{y^2}{4} = 1$

$\left(\dfrac{3\sqrt{5}}{5}, \dfrac{4\sqrt{5}}{5}\right)$, $\left(\dfrac{3\sqrt{5}}{5}, -\dfrac{4\sqrt{5}}{5}\right)$, $\left(-\dfrac{3\sqrt{5}}{5}, \dfrac{4\sqrt{5}}{5}\right)$, $\left(-\dfrac{3\sqrt{5}}{5}, -\dfrac{4\sqrt{5}}{5}\right)$.

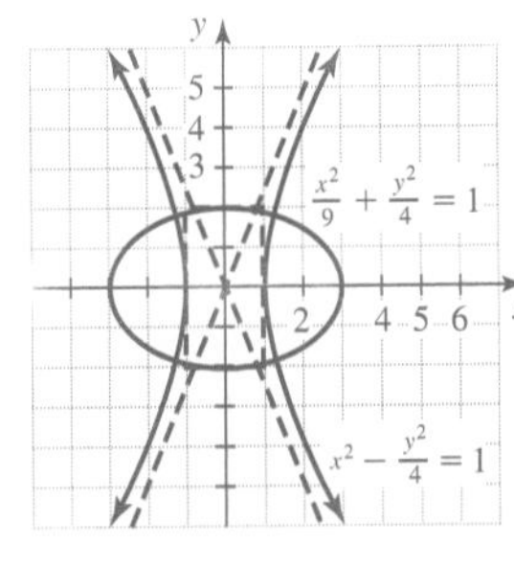

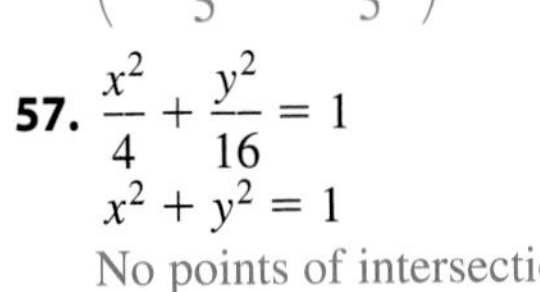

57. $\dfrac{x^2}{4} + \dfrac{y^2}{16} = 1$

$x^2 + y^2 = 1$

No points of intersection

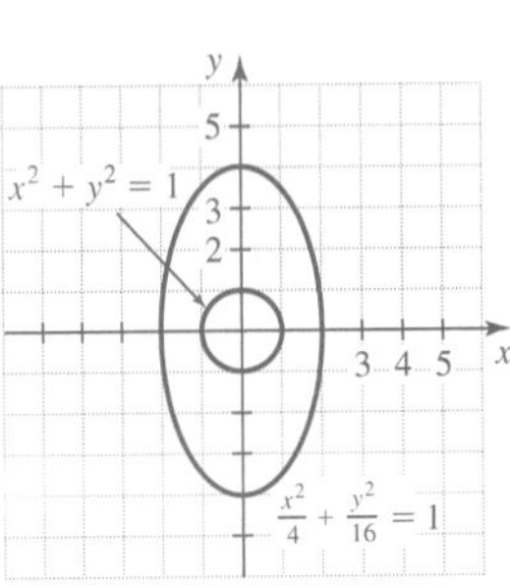

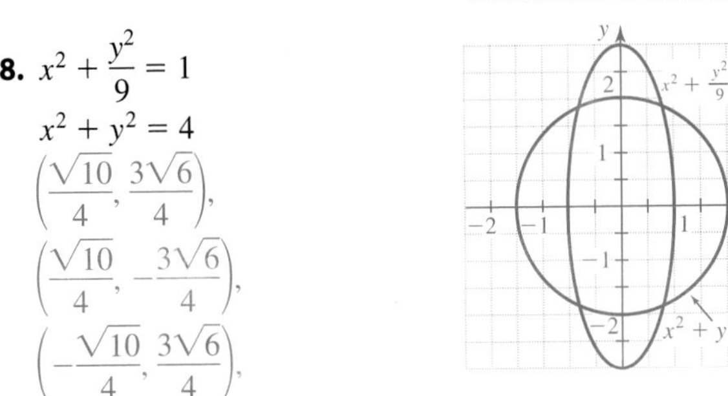

58. $x^2 + \dfrac{y^2}{9} = 1$

$x^2 + y^2 = 4$

$\left(\dfrac{\sqrt{10}}{4}, \dfrac{3\sqrt{6}}{4}\right)$, $\left(\dfrac{\sqrt{10}}{4}, -\dfrac{3\sqrt{6}}{4}\right)$, $\left(-\dfrac{\sqrt{10}}{4}, \dfrac{3\sqrt{6}}{4}\right)$, $\left(-\dfrac{\sqrt{10}}{4}, -\dfrac{3\sqrt{6}}{4}\right)$

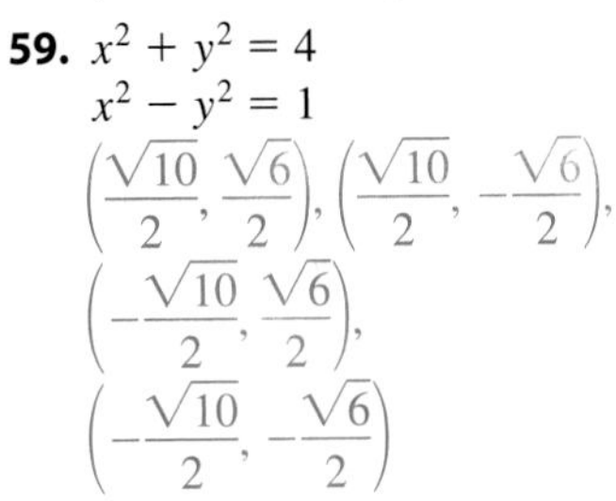

59. $x^2 + y^2 = 4$

$x^2 - y^2 = 1$

$\left(\dfrac{\sqrt{10}}{2}, \dfrac{\sqrt{6}}{2}\right)$, $\left(\dfrac{\sqrt{10}}{2}, -\dfrac{\sqrt{6}}{2}\right)$, $\left(-\dfrac{\sqrt{10}}{2}, \dfrac{\sqrt{6}}{2}\right)$, $\left(-\dfrac{\sqrt{10}}{2}, -\dfrac{\sqrt{6}}{2}\right)$

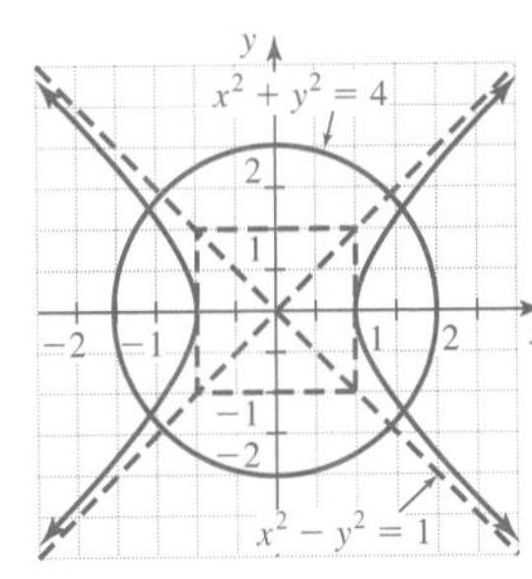

60. $x^2 + y^2 = 16$

$x^2 - y^2 = 4$

$(\sqrt{10}, \sqrt{6})$, $(\sqrt{10}, -\sqrt{6})$, $(-\sqrt{10}, \sqrt{6})$, $(-\sqrt{10}, -\sqrt{6})$

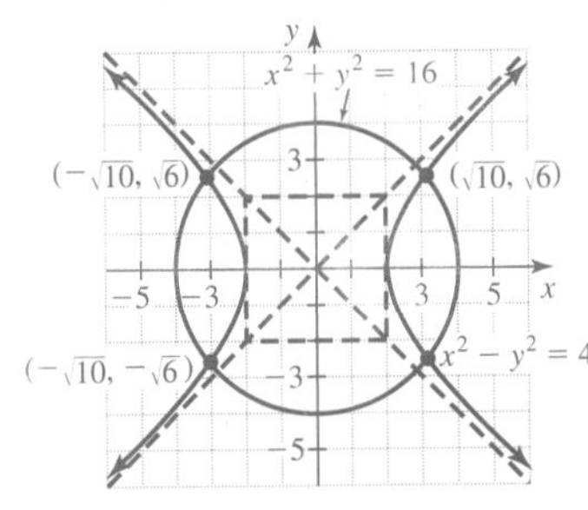

61. $x^2 + 9y^2 = 9$

$x^2 + y^2 = 4$

$\left(\dfrac{3\sqrt{6}}{4}, \dfrac{\sqrt{10}}{4}\right)$, $\left(\dfrac{3\sqrt{6}}{4}, -\dfrac{\sqrt{10}}{4}\right)$, $\left(-\dfrac{3\sqrt{6}}{4}, \dfrac{\sqrt{10}}{4}\right)$, $\left(-\dfrac{3\sqrt{6}}{4}, -\dfrac{\sqrt{10}}{4}\right)$

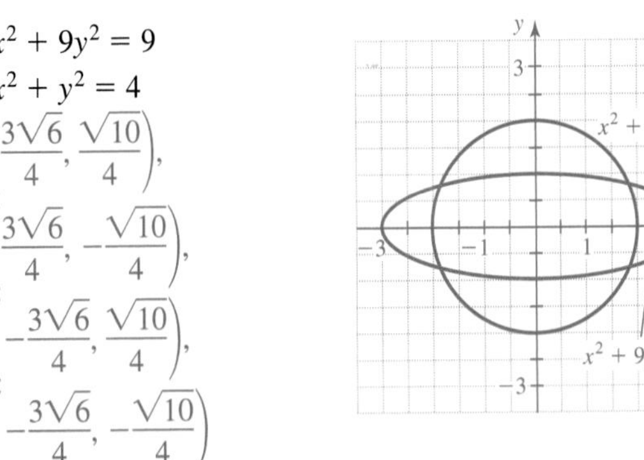

62. $x^2 + y^2 = 25$

$x^2 + 25y^2 = 25$

$(5, 0)$, $(-5, 0)$

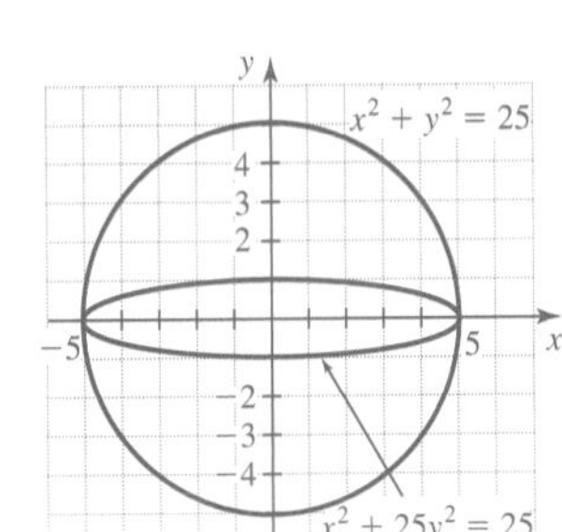

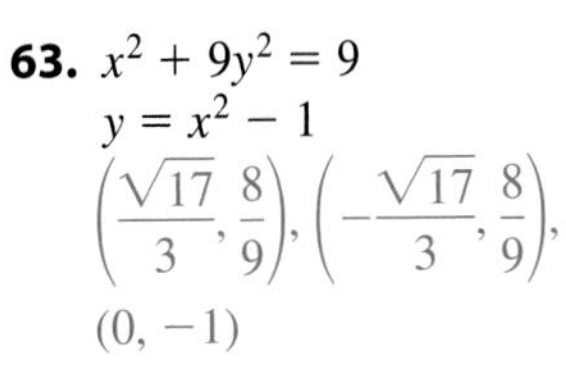

63. $x^2 + 9y^2 = 9$

$y = x^2 - 1$

$\left(\dfrac{\sqrt{17}}{3}, \dfrac{8}{9}\right)$, $\left(-\dfrac{\sqrt{17}}{3}, \dfrac{8}{9}\right)$, $(0, -1)$

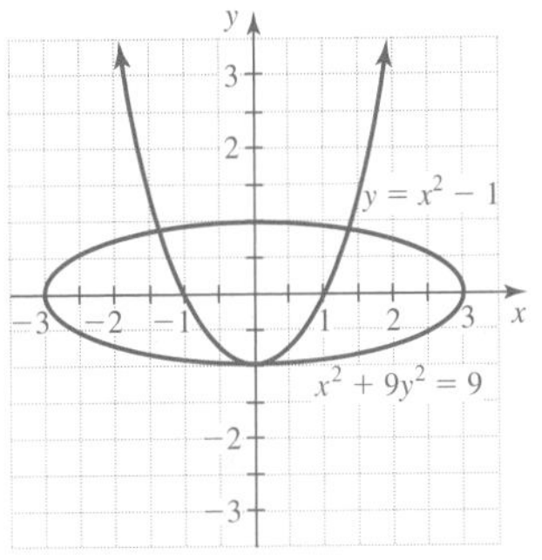

64. $4x^2 + y^2 = 4$

$y = 2x^2 - 2$

$(-1, 0)$, $(1, 0)$, $(0, -2)$

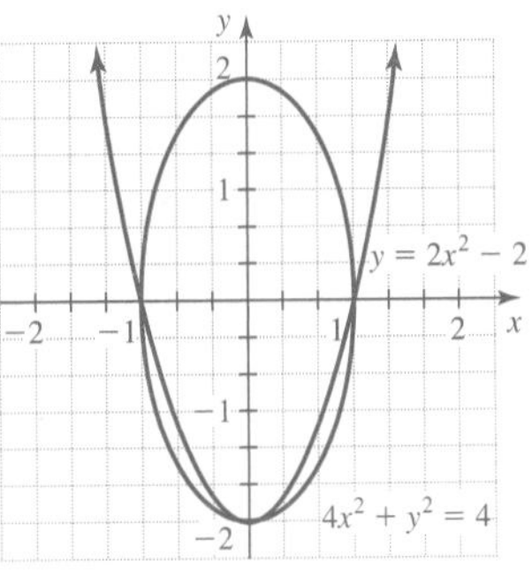

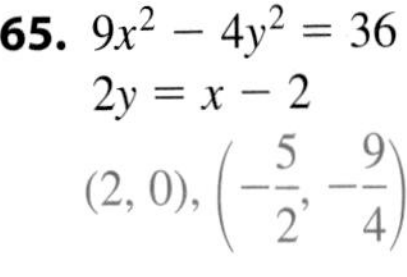

65. $9x^2 - 4y^2 = 36$

$2y = x - 2$

$(2, 0)$, $\left(-\dfrac{5}{2}, -\dfrac{9}{4}\right)$

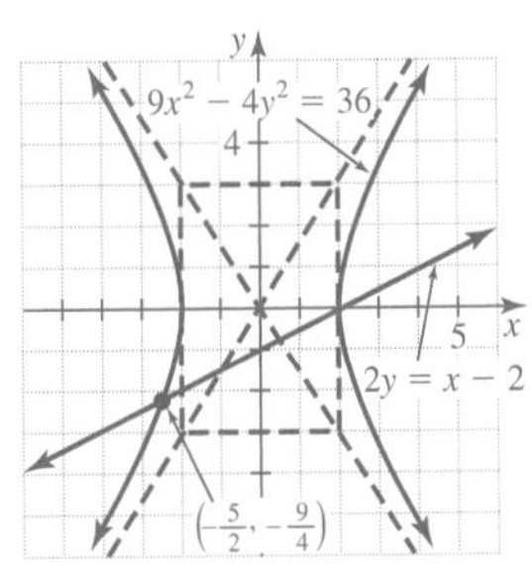

66. $25y^2 - 9x^2 = 225$
$y = 3x + 3$
$(0, 3), \left(-\frac{25}{12}, -\frac{13}{4}\right)$

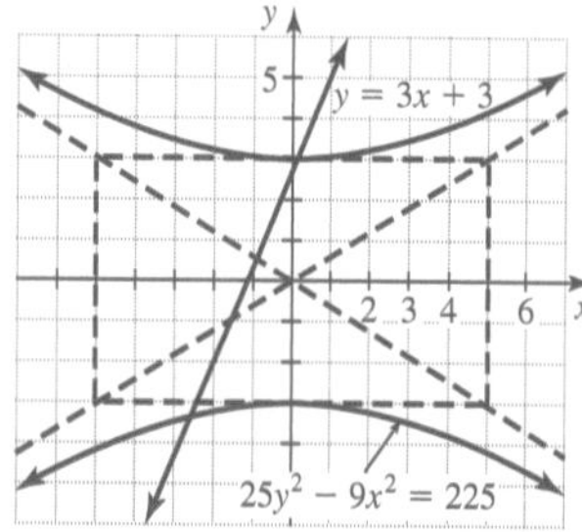

Solve each problem.

67. ***Marine navigation.*** The loran (long-range navigation) system is used by boaters to determine their location at sea. The loran unit on a boat measures the difference in time that it takes for radio signals from pairs of fixed points to reach the boat. The unit then finds the equations of two hyperbolas that pass through the location of the boat. Suppose a boat is located in the first quadrant at the intersection of $x^2 - 3y^2 = 1$ and $4y^2 - x^2 = 1$.

a) Use the accompanying graph to approximate the location of the boat.
b) Algebraically find the exact location of the boat.
a) (2.5, 1.5) b) $(\sqrt{7}, \sqrt{2})$

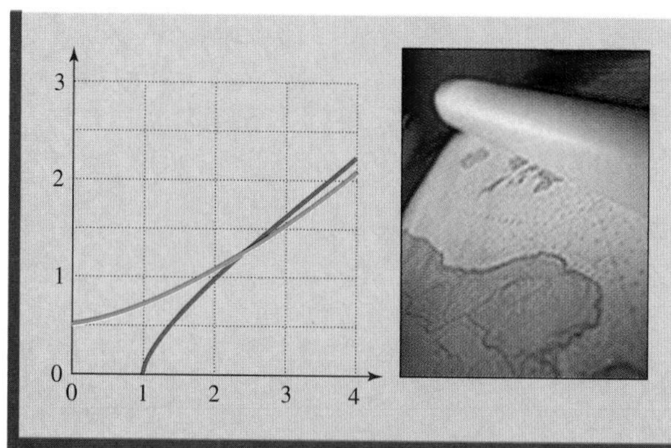

Figure for Exercise 67

68. ***Sonic boom.*** An aircraft traveling at supersonic speed creates a cone-shaped wave that intersects the ground along a hyperbola, as shown in the accompanying figure. A thunderlike sound is heard at any point on the hyperbola. This sonic boom travels along the ground, following the aircraft. The area where the sonic boom is most noticeable is called the *boom carpet.* The width of the boom carpet is roughly five times the altitude of the aircraft. Suppose the equation of the hyperbola in the figure is

$$\frac{x^2}{400} - \frac{y^2}{100} = 1,$$

where the units are miles and the width of the boom carpet is measured 40 miles behind the aircraft. Find the altitude of the aircraft.
$4\sqrt{3}$ or 6.9 miles

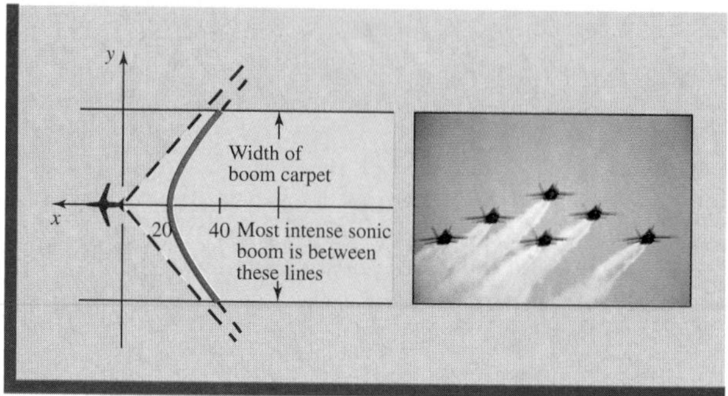

Figure for Exercise 68

Getting More Involved

69. ***Cooperative learning***

Let (x, y) be an arbitrary point on an ellipse with foci $(c, 0)$ and $(-c, 0)$ for $c > 0$. The following equation expresses the fact that the distance from (x, y) to $(c, 0)$ plus the distance from (x, y) to $(-c, 0)$ is the constant value $2a$ (for $a > 0$):

$$\sqrt{(x-c)^2 + (y-0)^2} + \sqrt{(x-(-c))^2 + (y-0)^2} = 2a$$

Working in groups, simplify this equation. First get the radicals on opposite sides of the equation, then square both sides twice to eliminate the square roots. Finally, let $b^2 = a^2 - c^2$ to get the equation

$$\frac{x^2}{a^2} + \frac{y^2}{b^2} = 1.$$

70. ***Cooperative learning***

Let (x, y) be an arbitrary point on a hyperbola with foci $(c, 0)$ and $(-c, 0)$ for $c > 0$. The following equation expresses the fact that the distance from (x, y) to $(c, 0)$ minus the distance from (x, y) to $(-c, 0)$ is the constant value $2a$ (for $a > 0$):

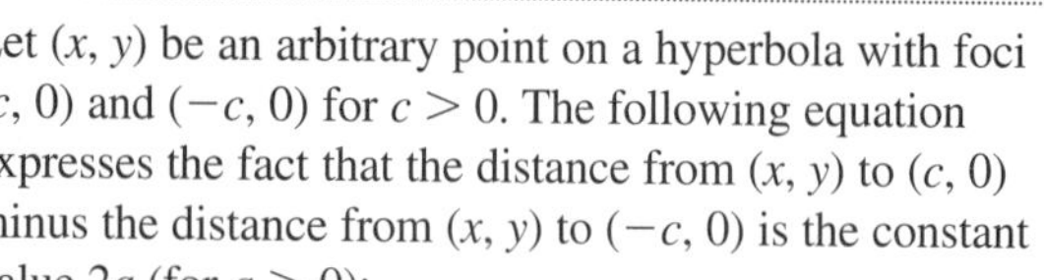

$$\sqrt{(x-c)^2 + (y-0)^2} - \sqrt{(x-(-c))^2 + (y-0)^2} = 2a$$

Working in groups, simplify the equation. You will need to square both sides twice to eliminate the square roots. Finally, let $b^2 = c^2 - a^2$ to get the equation

$$\frac{x^2}{a^2} - \frac{y^2}{b^2} = 1.$$

Graphing Calculator Exercises

71. Graph $y_1 = \sqrt{x^2 - 1}$, $y_2 = -\sqrt{x^2 - 1}$, $y_3 = x$, and $y_4 = -x$ to get the graph of the hyperbola $x^2 - y^2 = 1$ along with its asymptotes. Use the viewing window $-3 \le x \le 3$ and $-3 \le y \le 3$. Notice how the branches of the hyperbola approach the asymptotes.

72. Graph the same four functions in Exercise 71, but use $-30 \le x \le 30$ and $-30 \le y \le 30$ as the viewing window. What happened to the hyperbola?

13.5 Second-Degree Inequalities

In this Section

- **Graphing a Second-Degree Inequality**
- **Systems of Inequalities**

In this section we graph second-degree inequalities and systems of inequalities involving second-degree inequalities.

Graphing a Second-Degree Inequality

A second-degree inequality is an inequality involving squares of at least one of the variables. Changing the equal sign to an inequality symbol for any of the equations of the conic sections gives us a second-degree inequality. Second-degree inequalities are graphed in the same manner as linear inequalities.

EXAMPLE 1

A second-degree inequality

Graph the inequality $y < x^2 + 2x - 3$.

Solution

We first graph $y = x^2 + 2x - 3$. This parabola has x-intercepts at (1, 0) and (−3, 0), y-intercept at (0, −3), and vertex at (−1, −4). The graph of the parabola is drawn with a dashed line, as shown in Fig. 13.34. The graph of the parabola divides the plane into two regions. Every point on one side of the parabola satisfies the inequality $y < x^2 + 2x - 3$, and every point on the other side satisfies the inequality $y > x^2 + 2x - 3$. To determine which side is which, we test a point that is not on the parabola, say (0, 0). Because

$$0 < 0^2 + 2 \cdot 0 - 3$$

is false, the region not containing the origin is shaded, as in Fig. 13.34.

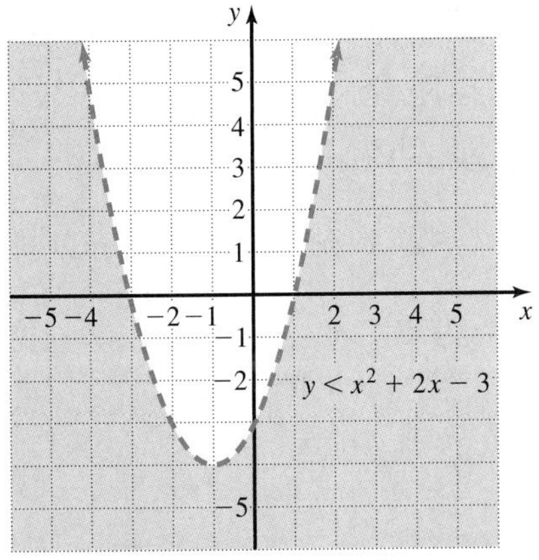

Figure 13.34

Now do Exercises 1–6

EXAMPLE 2

A second-degree inequality

Graph the inequality $x^2 + y^2 < 9$.

Solution

The graph of $x^2 + y^2 = 9$ is a circle of radius 3 centered at the origin. The circle divides the plane into two regions. Every point in one region satisfies $x^2 + y^2 < 9$, and every point in the other region satisfies $x^2 + y^2 > 9$. To identify the regions, we pick a point and test it. Select (0, 0). The inequality

$$0^2 + 0^2 < 9$$

is true. Because (0, 0) is inside the circle, all points inside the circle satisfy the inequality $x^2 + y^2 < 9$, as shown in Fig. 13.35. The points outside the circle satisfy the inequality $x^2 + y^2 > 9$.

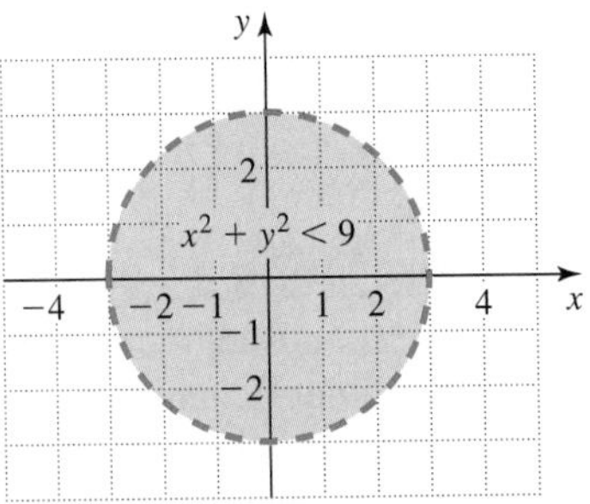

Figure 13.35

Now do Exercises 7–10

EXAMPLE 3

A second-degree inequality

Graph the inequality $\frac{x^2}{4} - \frac{y^2}{9} > 1$.

Solution

First graph the hyperbola $\frac{x^2}{4} - \frac{y^2}{9} = 1$. Because the hyperbola shown in Fig. 13.36 divides the plane into three regions, we select a test point in each region and check to see whether it satisfies the inequality. Testing the points $(-3, 0)$, $(0, 0)$, and $(3, 0)$ gives us the inequalities

$$\frac{(-3)^2}{4} - \frac{0^2}{9} > 1, \quad \frac{0^2}{4} - \frac{0^2}{9} > 1, \quad \text{and} \quad \frac{3^2}{4} - \frac{0^2}{9} > 1.$$

Because only the first and third inequalities are correct, we shade only the regions containing $(3, 0)$ and $(-3, 0)$, as shown in Fig. 13.36.

Now do Exercises 11–22

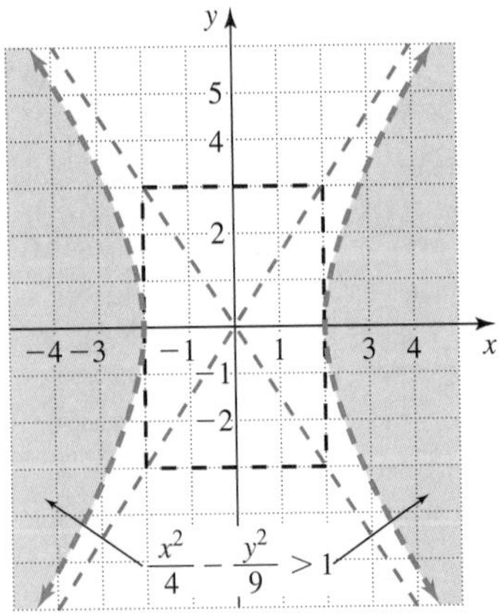

Figure 13.36

Systems of Inequalities

A point is in the solution set to a system of inequalities if it satisfies all inequalities of the system. We graph a system of inequalities by first determining the graph of each inequality and then finding the intersection of the graphs.

EXAMPLE 4

Systems of second-degree inequalities

Graph the system of inequalities:

$$\frac{y^2}{4} - \frac{x^2}{9} > 1$$

$$\frac{x^2}{9} + \frac{y^2}{16} < 1$$

Teaching Tip As with any system we seek points that satisfy both inequalities, the intersection of the individual solution sets.

Solution

Figure 13.37(a) shows the graph of the first inequality. Figure 13.37(b) shows the graphs of both inequalities on the same coordinate system. Points that are shaded for both inequalities in Fig. 13.37(b) satisfy the system. Figure 13.37(c) shows the graph of the system.

Now do Exercises 27–46

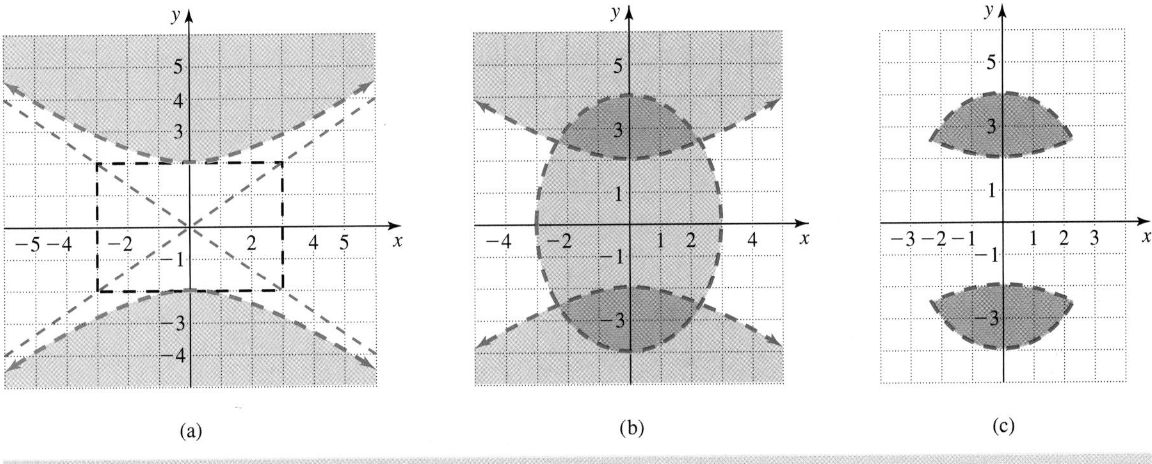

Figure 13.37

Warm-Ups ▼

True or false? Explain your answer.

1. The graph of $x^2 + y = 4$ is a circle of radius 2. False
2. The graph of $x^2 + 9y^2 = 9$ is an ellipse. True
3. The graph of $y^2 = x^2 + 1$ is a hyperbola. True
4. The point (0, 0) satisfies the inequality $2x^2 - y < 3$. True
5. The graph of the inequality $y > x^2 - 3x + 2$ contains the origin. False
6. The origin should be used as a test point for graphing $x^2 > y$. False
7. The solution set to $x^2 + 3x + y^2 + 8y + 3 < 0$ includes the origin. False
8. The graph of $x^2 + y^2 < 4$ is the region inside a circle of radius 2. True
9. The point (0, 4) satisfies $x^2 - y^2 < 1$ and $y > x^2 - 2x + 3$. True
10. The point (0, 0) satisfies $x^2 + y^2 < 1$ and $y < x^2 + 1$. True

13.5 Exercises

Boost your GRADE at mathzone.com!

MathZone: Practice Problems, Self-Tests, Videos, Net Tutor, e-Professors

Graph each inequality. See Examples 1–3.

1. $y > x^2$

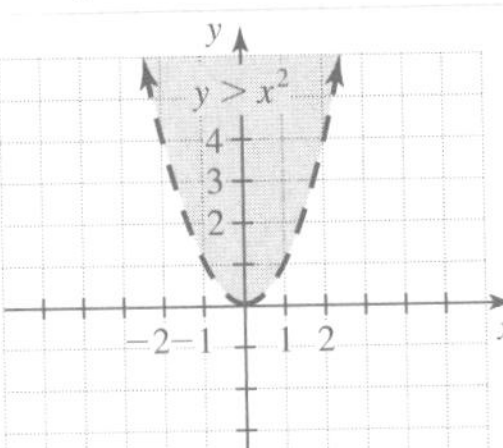

2. $y \le x^2 + 1$

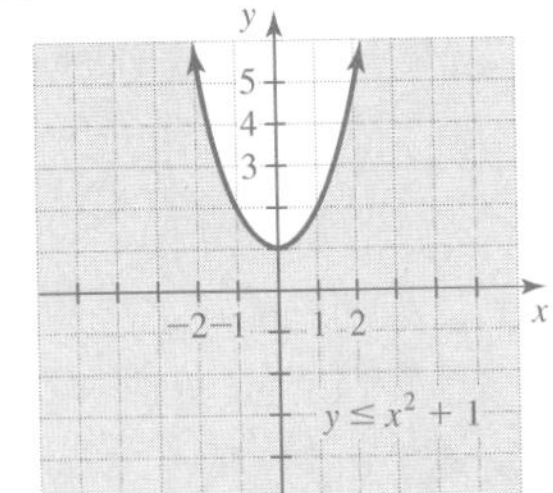

3. $y < x^2 - x$

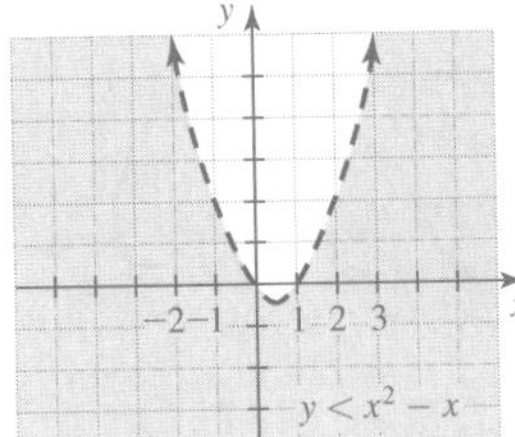

4. $y > x^2 + x$

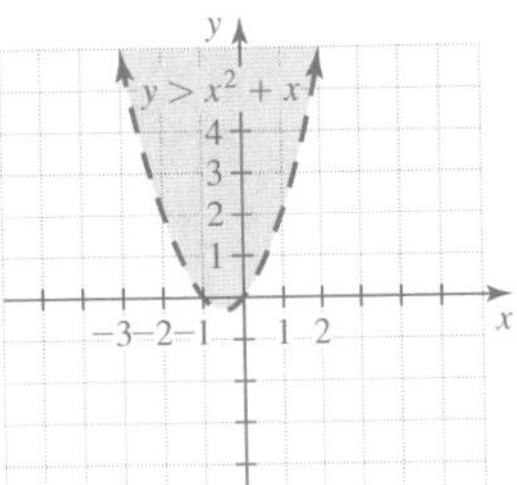

5. $y > x^2 - x - 2$

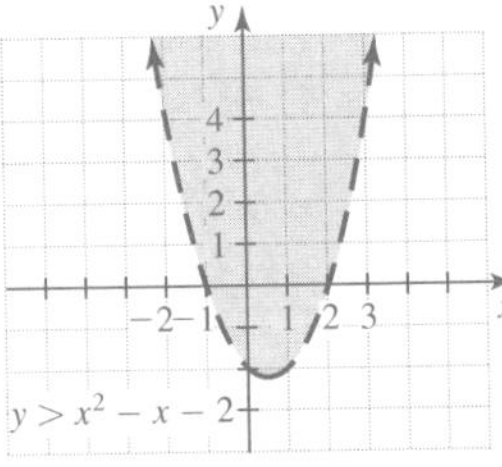

6. $y < x^2 + x - 6$

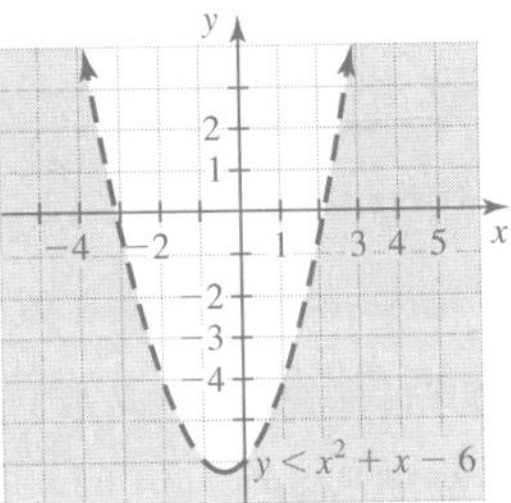

7. $x^2 + y^2 \le 9$

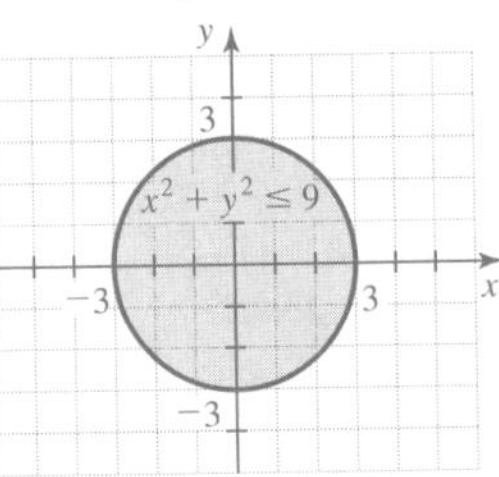

8. $x^2 + y^2 > 16$

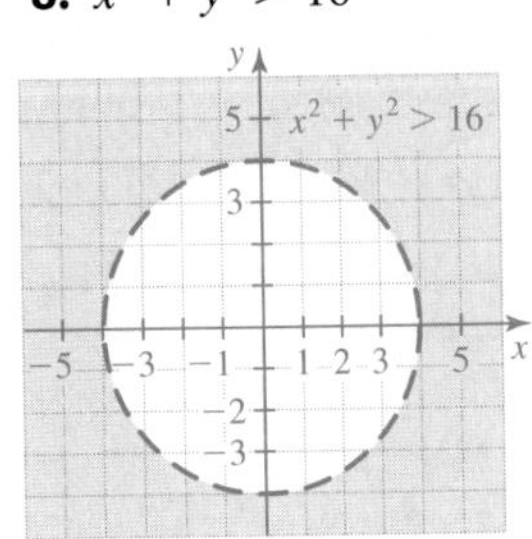

9. $x^2 + 4y^2 > 4$

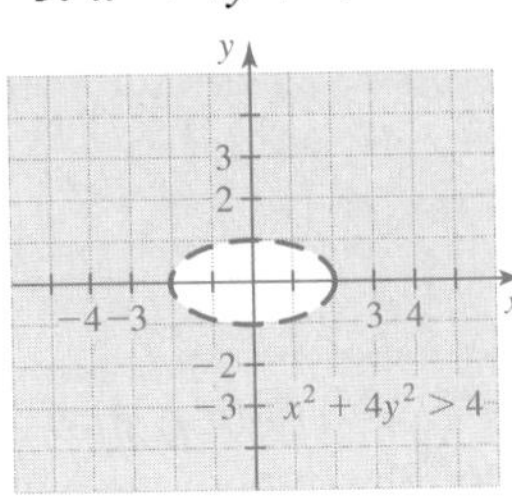

10. $4x^2 + y^2 \le 4$

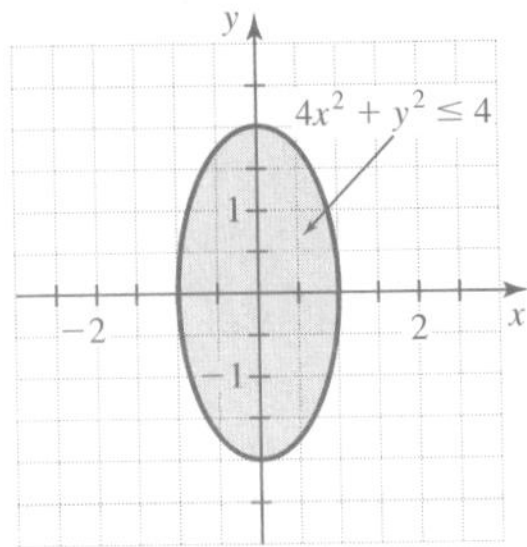

11. $4x^2 - 9y^2 < 36$

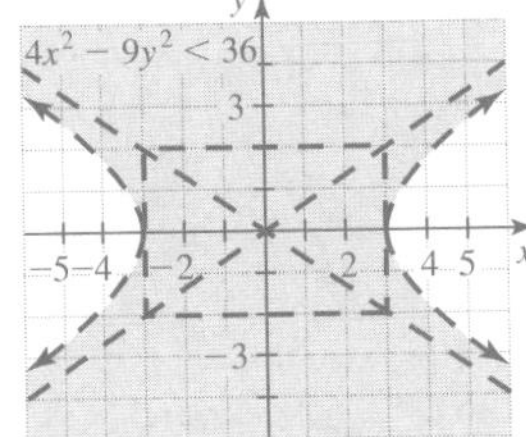

12. $25x^2 - 4y^2 > 100$

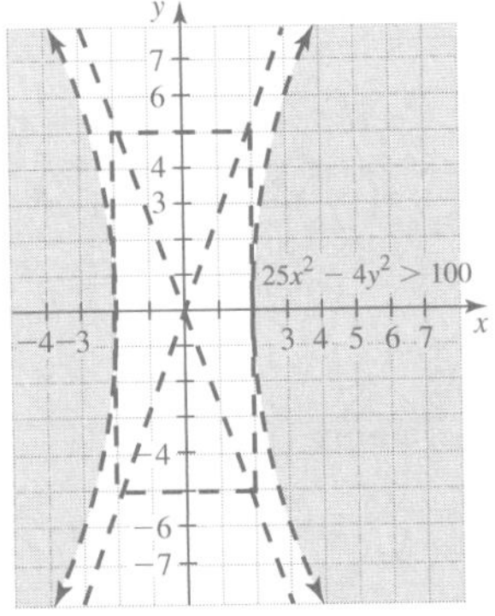

13. $(x - 2)^2 + (y - 3)^2 < 4$

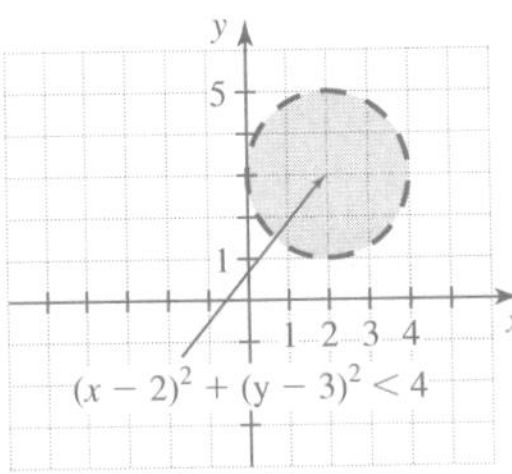

14. $(x + 1)^2 + (y - 2)^2 > 1$

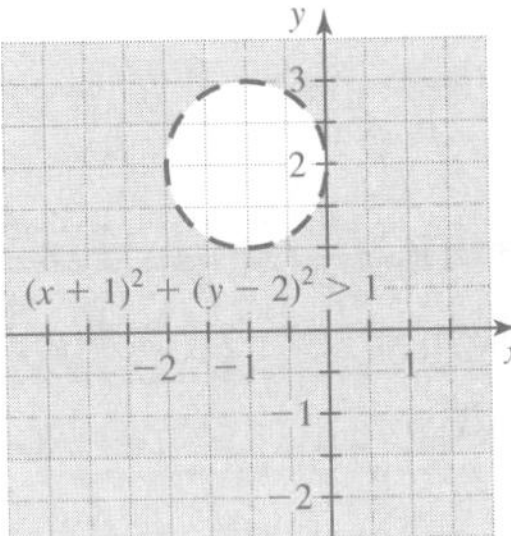

15. $x^2 + y^2 > 1$

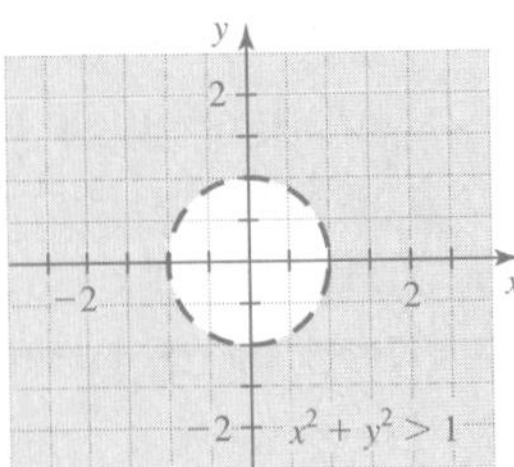

16. $x^2 + y^2 < 25$

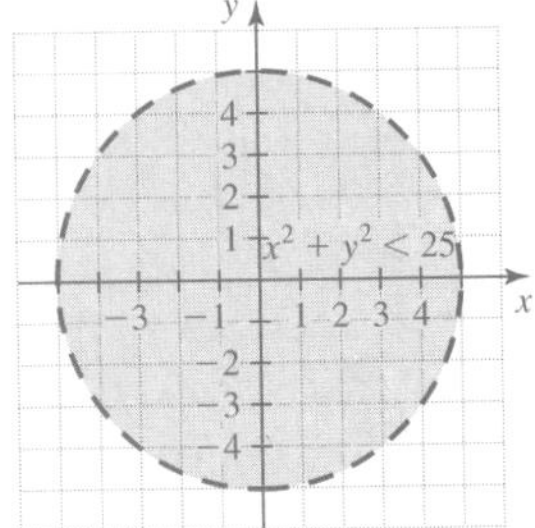

17. $4x^2 - y^2 > 4$

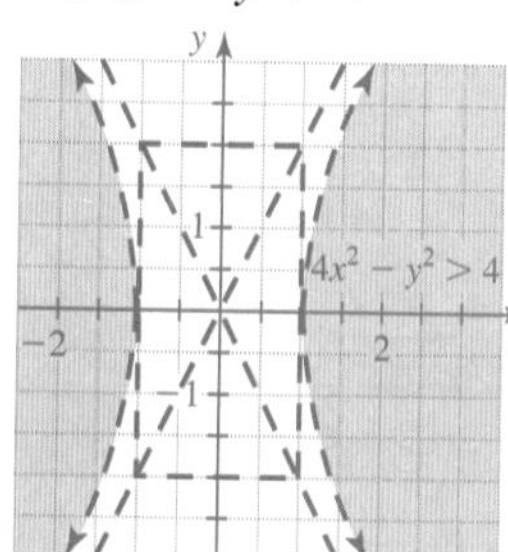

18. $x^2 - 9y^2 \leq 9$

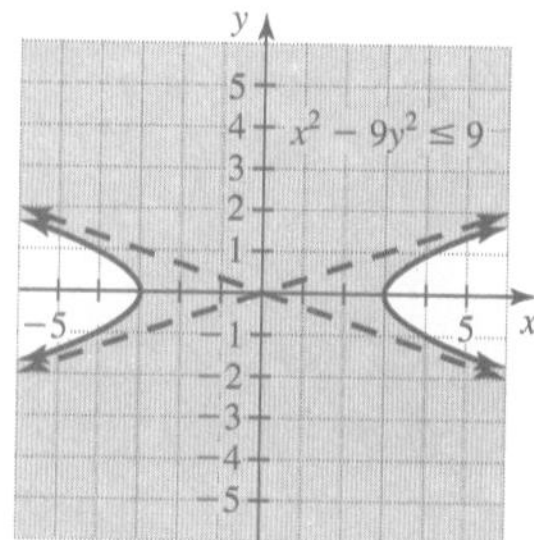

19. $y^2 - x^2 \leq 1$

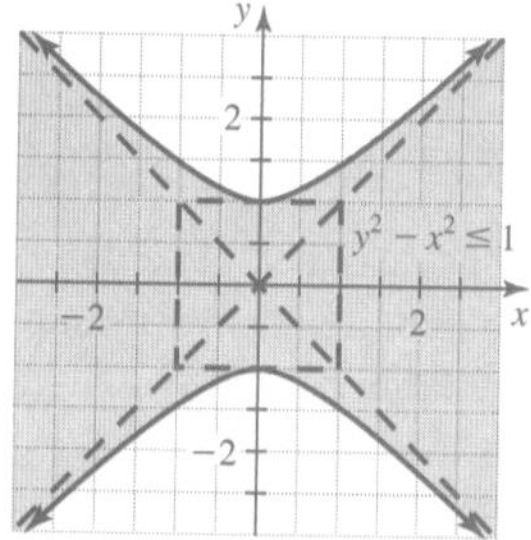

20. $x^2 - y^2 > 1$

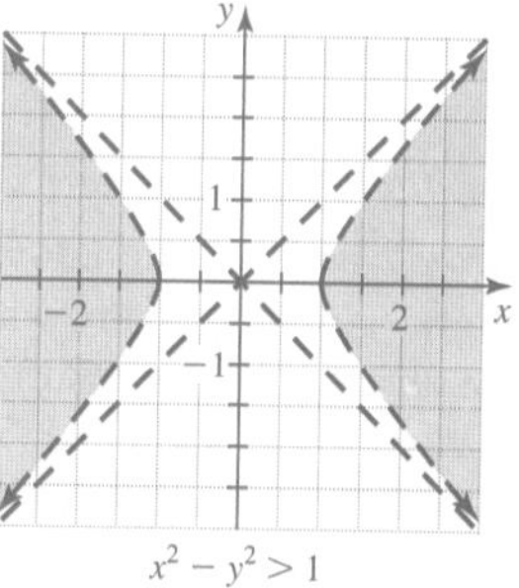
$x^2 - y^2 > 1$

21. $x > y$

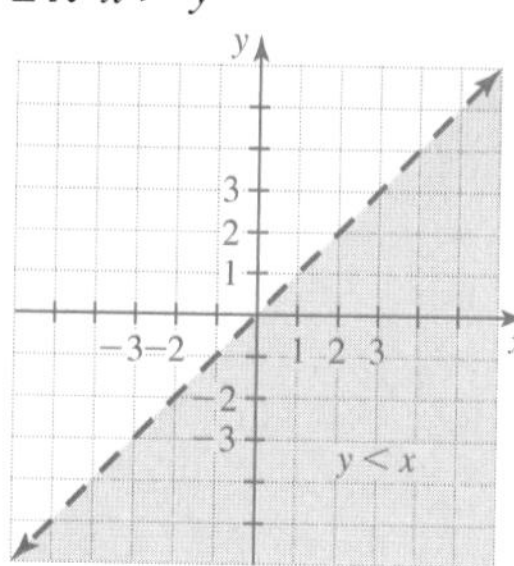

22. $x < 2y - 1$

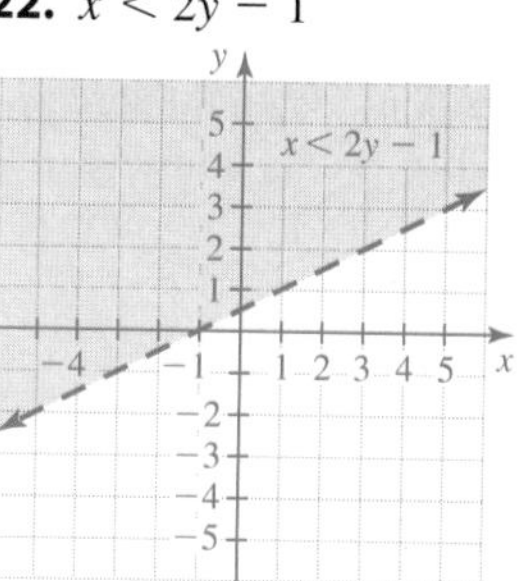

Determine whether the ordered pair (3, −4) satisfies each system of inequalities.

23. $x^2 + y^2 \leq 25$
$y \leq x^2$ Yes

24. $x^2 - y^2 < 1$
$y < x - 5$ Yes

25. $x - y > 1$
$y > (x - 2)^2 + 3$ No

26. $4x^2 + y^2 \leq 36$
$x^2 + y^2 \geq 25$ No

Graph the solution set to each system of inequalities. See Example 4.

27. $x^2 + y^2 < 9$
$y > x$

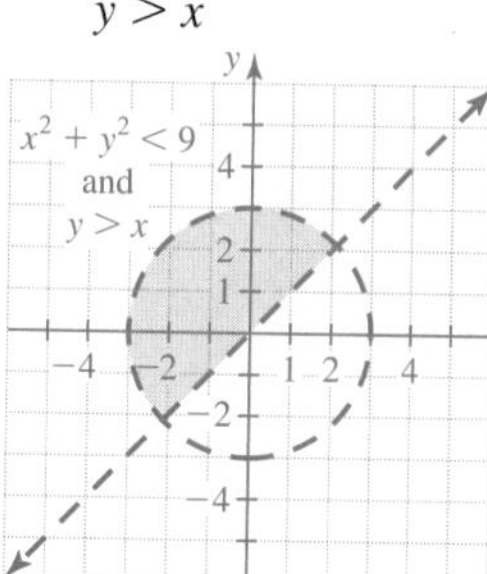

28. $x^2 + y^2 > 1$
$x > y$

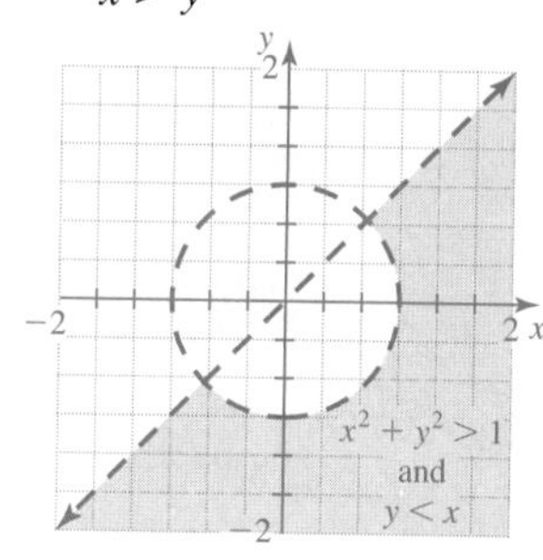

29. $x^2 - y^2 > 1$
$x^2 + y^2 < 4$

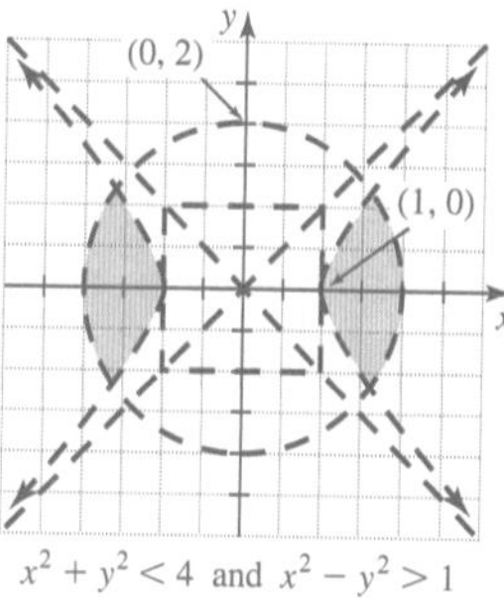

$x^2 + y^2 < 4$ and $x^2 - y^2 > 1$

30. $y^2 - x^2 < 1$
$x^2 + y^2 > 9$

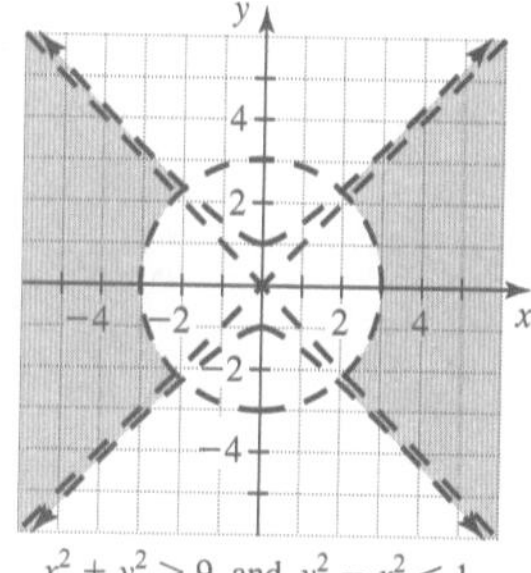
$x^2 + y^2 > 9$ and $y^2 - x^2 < 1$

31. $y > x^2 + x$
$y < 5$

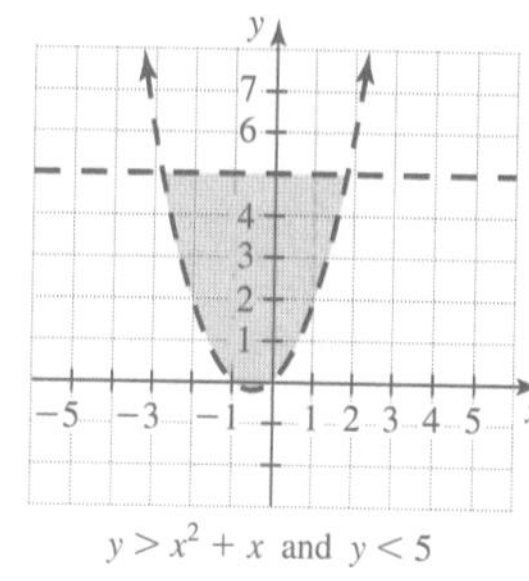
$y > x^2 + x$ and $y < 5$

32. $y > x^2 + x - 6$
$y < x + 3$

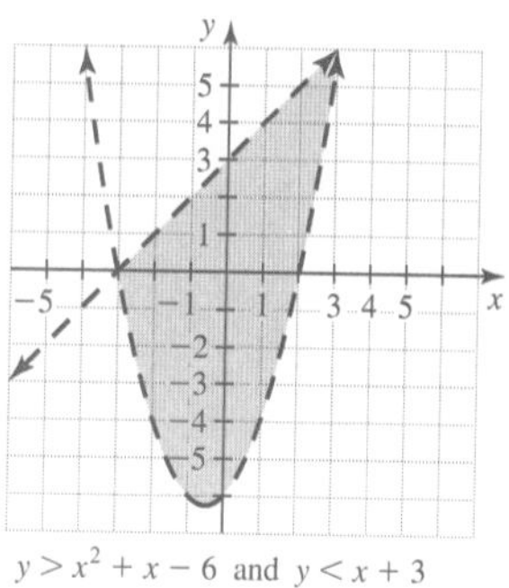
$y > x^2 + x - 6$ and $y < x + 3$

33. $y \geq x + 2$
$y \leq 2 - x$

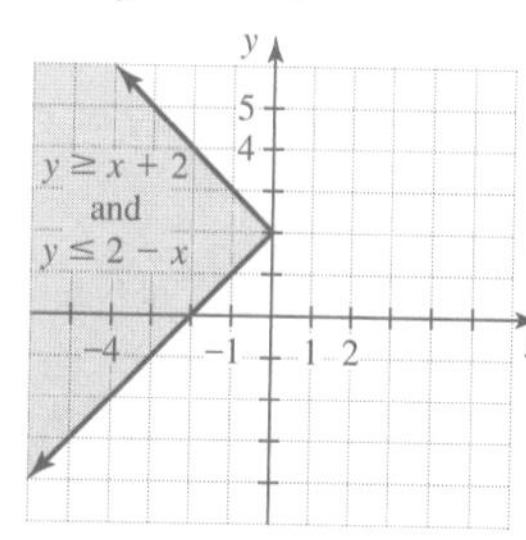

34. $y \geq 2x - 3$
$y \leq 3 - 2x$

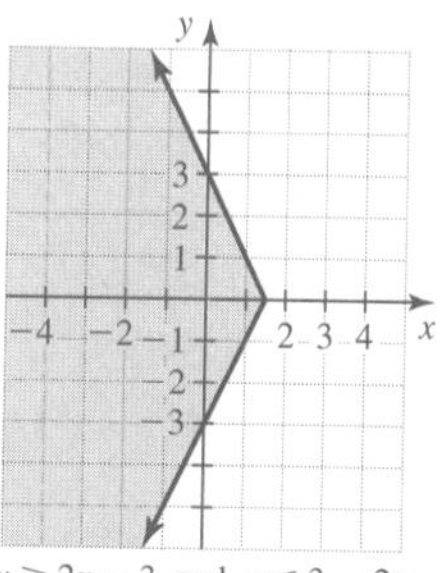
$y \geq 2x - 3$ and $y \leq 3 - 2x$

35. $4x^2 - y^2 < 4$
$x^2 + 4y^2 > 4$

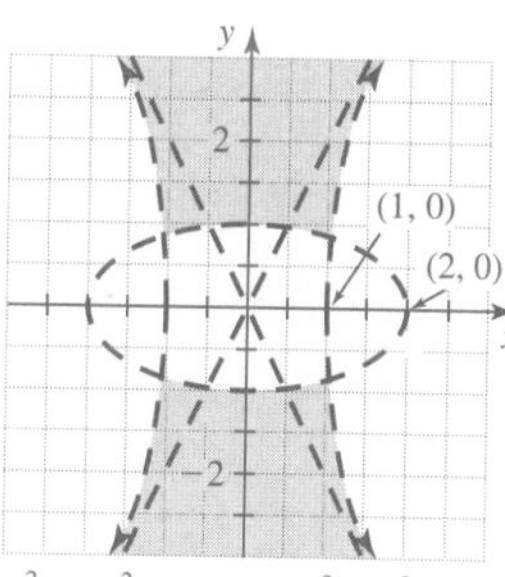

$x^2 + 4y^2 > 4$ and $4x^2 - y^2 < 4$

36. $x^2 - 4y^2 < 4$
$x^2 + 4y^2 > 4$

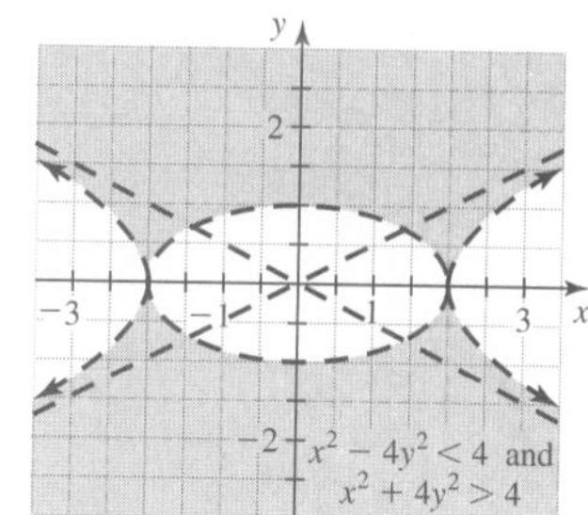

37. $x - y < 0$
$y + x^2 < 1$

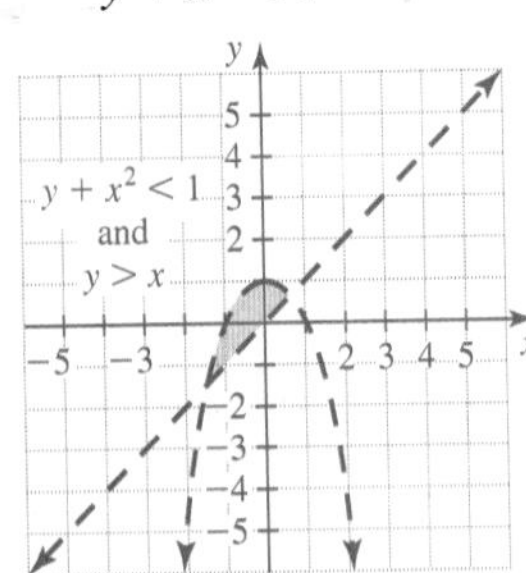

38. $y + 1 > x^2$
$x + y < 2$

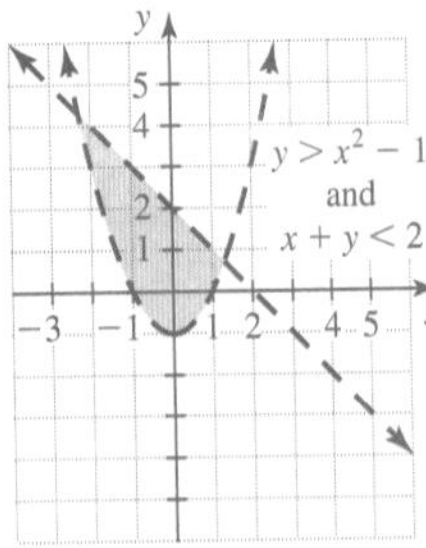

45. $y < x^2$
$x^2 + y^2 < 1$

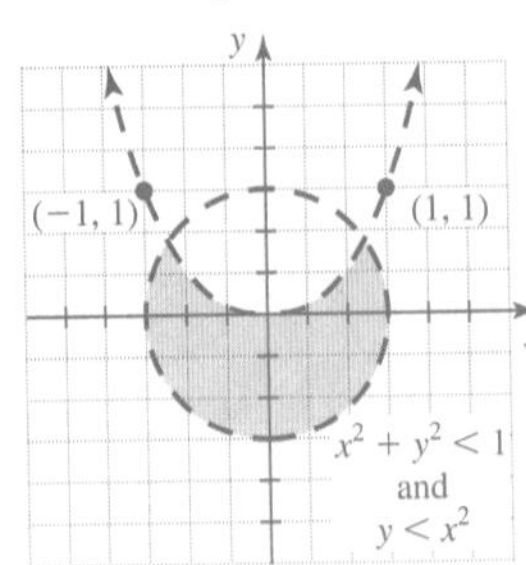

46. $y > x^2$
$4x^2 + y^2 < 4$

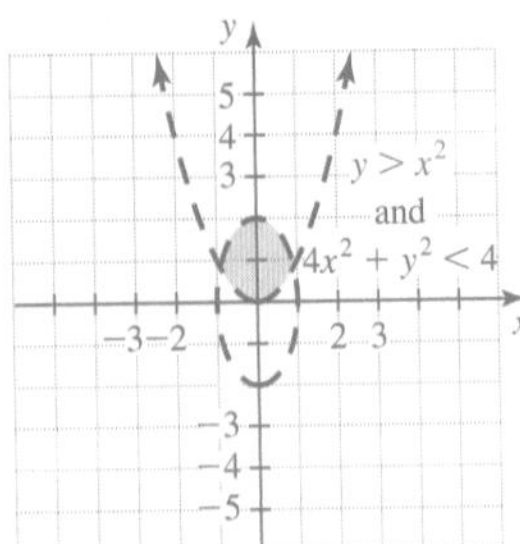

39. $y < 5x - x^2$
$x^2 + y^2 < 9$

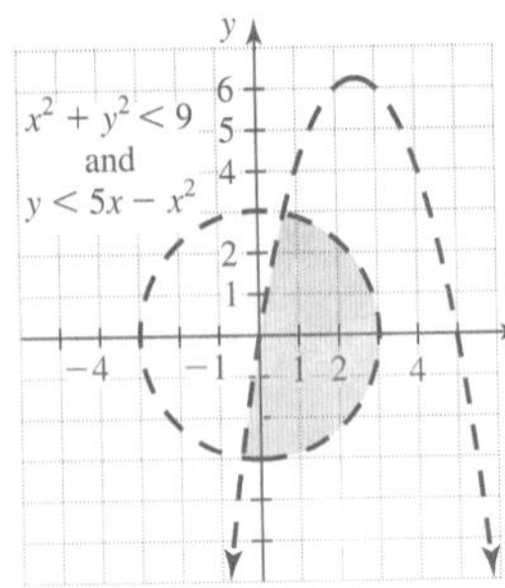

40. $y < x^2 + 5x$
$x^2 + y^2 < 16$

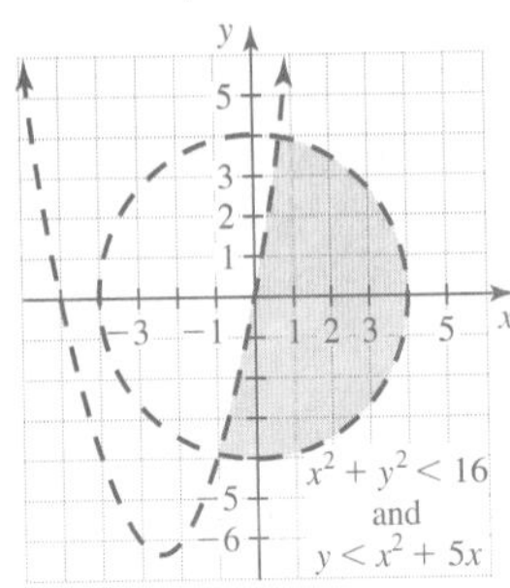

Solve the problem.

47. ***Buried treasure.*** An old pirate on his deathbed gave the following description of where he had buried some treasure on a deserted island: "Starting at the large palm tree, I walked to the north and then to the east, and there I buried the treasure. I walked at least 50 paces to get to that spot, but I was not more than 50 paces, as the crow flies, from the large palm tree. I am sure that I walked farther in the northerly direction than in the easterly direction." With the large palm tree at the origin and the positive y-axis pointing to the north, graph the possible locations of the treasure.

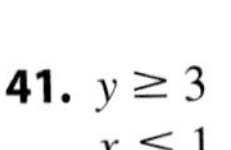

41. $y \geq 3$
$x \leq 1$

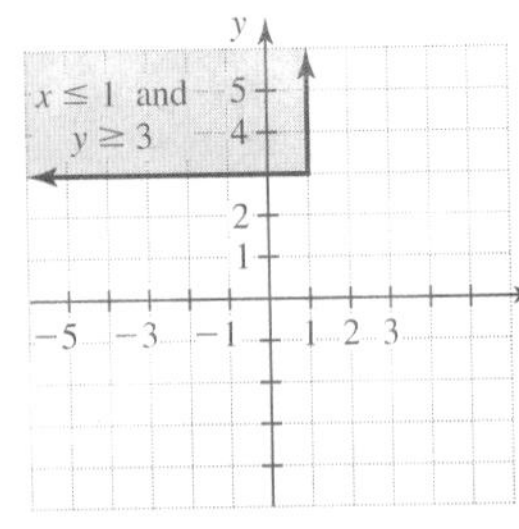

42. $x > -3$
$y < 2$

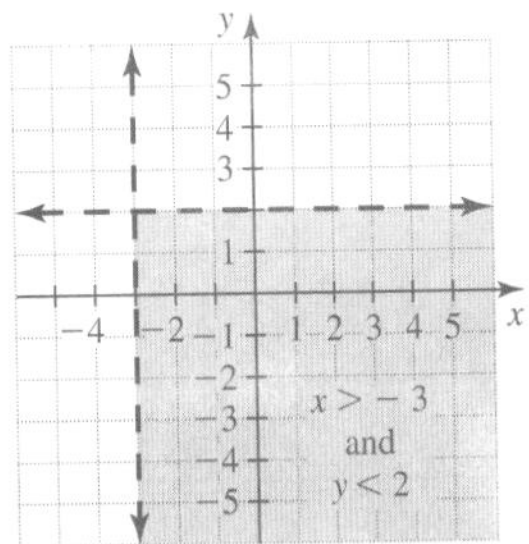

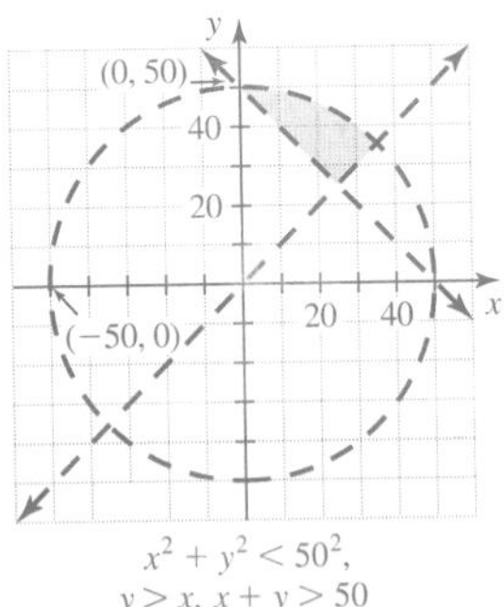

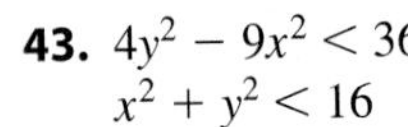

43. $4y^2 - 9x^2 < 36$
$x^2 + y^2 < 16$

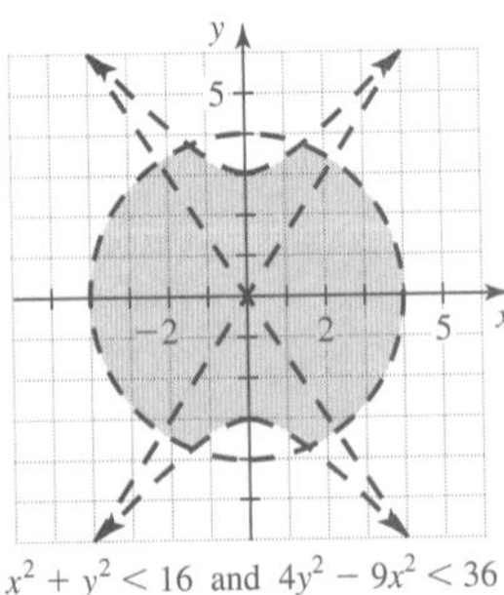

44. $25y^2 - 16x^2 < 400$
$x^2 + y^2 > 4$

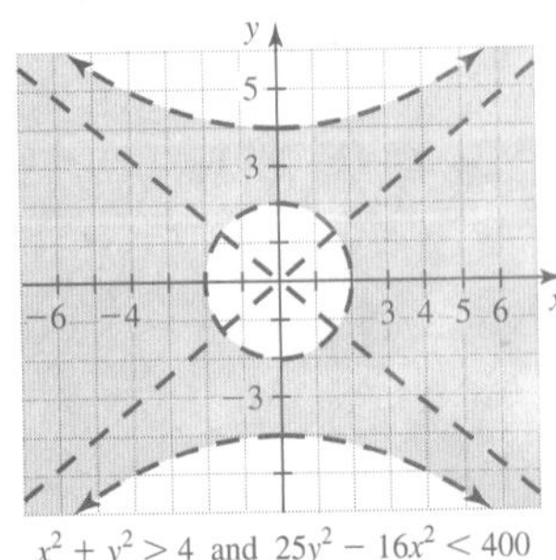

Photo for Exercise 47

Graphing Calculator Exercises

48. Use graphs to find an ordered pair that is in the solution set to the system of inequalities:

$$y > x^2 - 2x + 1$$
$$y < -1.1(x - 4)^2 + 5$$

Verify that your answer satisfies both inequalities.

49. Use graphs to find the solution set to the system of inequalities:

$$y > 2x^2 - 3x + 1$$
$$y < -2x^2 - 8x - 1$$

No solution

Collaborative Activities

Grouping: 2 students per group

Topic: Conic sections

Focus on Comets

Conic sections are used to model many different things in the natural world. Astronomers use mirrors in the shape of parabolas in telescopes. They have learned that planets can have elliptical as well as circular orbits around the sun and that comets may travel along paths that resemble hyperbolas, parabolas, or ellipses. In this activity we will consider comets with these three types of paths.

The path that a comet will take as it approaches the sun depends on its velocity (as well as other factors). If it has enough velocity to escape from the pull of the sun, it may take either a parabolic path or a hyperbolic path. If it doesn't have enough velocity, then it will take an elliptical orbit. Of course, a comet that has a parabolic or hyperbolic path will not come back again around our sun. Only comets with elliptical orbits do we see again.

For these problems round all your answers to two decimal places.

1. Halley's comet is in an elliptical orbit about the sun with the sun at one of the foci. In this problem we will make a scale model of the orbit of Halley's comet about the sun. We will choose our coordinate system so that the ellipse is centered at (0, 0). Halley's comet comes within 0.6 astronomical unit[1] from the sun at its closest point and 35 astronomical units at its farthest point. The position of the comet at these points will correspond to the horizontal vertices. Find the equation for the ellipse. Determine where the foci should be. On a piece of cardboard, put thumbtacks at the foci. Determine the length of string you will need to draw the ellipse using the scale 1 centimeter = 1 astronomical unit (AU). Draw the comet's orbit, indicating which focus is the sun.
2. If the velocity of a comet equals the escape velocity (it is going just fast enough to get away), then its path will be parabolic. The sun will be at the focus of the parabola. We will place the vertex at the point (0, 0); in this case the vertex will be where the comet is the closest to the sun. Suppose we have a comet that is 0.75 AU from the sun at its closest point. Find the equation for the parabola. Graph the parabola.
3. If the velocity of a comet is greater than the escape velocity (it can easily escape from the sun's gravitational pull), its path will resemble one-half of a hyperbola with the sun as one focus. Assuming we have a left- and a right-opening hyperbola, we can model the path of such a comet along one of its branches. We will center the hyperbola at (0, 0), and place the sun at the left focus and draw the path of the comet as it approaches from the left. Suppose that the comet will be 1.5 AUs from the sun at its closest point. Assume the sun is at the point $(-3, 0)$. Draw a sketch of this scenario. What is the equation for the hyperbola? Graph the hyperbola.

Extension: Graph all three equations on a graphing calculator or computer.

[1] An astronomical unit is the distance of the earth from the sun. The earth's orbit is almost circular and so the earth is about the same distance from the sun at any point in its orbit.

Chapter 13 Wrap-Up

Summary

Nonlinear Systems		Examples
Nonlinear systems in two variables	Use substitution or addition to eliminate variables. Nonlinear systems may have several points in the solution set.	$y = x^2$ $x^2 + y^2 = 4$ Substitution: $y + y^2 = 4$

The Distance Formula		Examples
Distance formula	The distance between (x_1, y_1) and (x_2, y_2) is $\sqrt{(x_2 - x_1)^2 + (y_2 - y_1)^2}$.	Distance between $(1, -2)$ and $(3, -4)$ is $\sqrt{2^2 + (-2)^2}$ or $2\sqrt{2}$.

Parabola		Examples
$y = a(x - h)^2 + k$	Opens upward for $a > 0$, downward for $a < 0$ Vertex at (h, k) To find focus and directrix, use $a = \frac{1}{4p}$. Distance from vertex to focus or directrix is $\lvert p \rvert$.	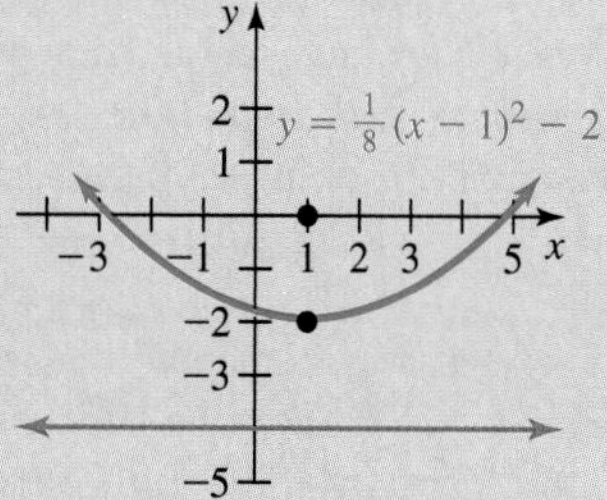
$x = a(y - k)^2 + h$	Opens right for $a > 0$, left for $a < 0$ Vertex at (h, k) To find focus and directrix use $a = \frac{1}{4p}$. Distance from vertex to focus or directrix is $\lvert p \rvert$.	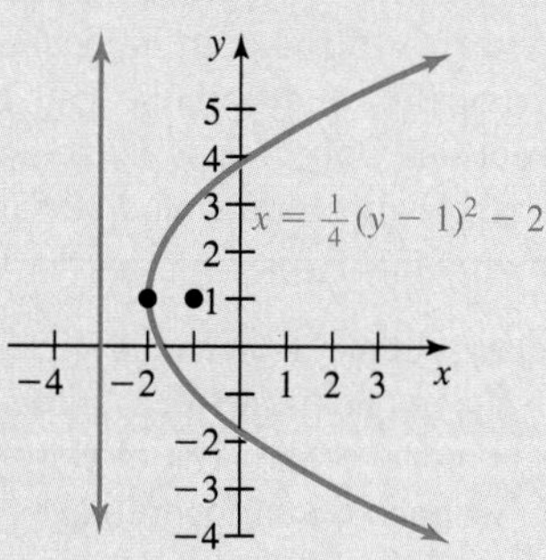
$y = ax^2 + bx + c$	Opens upward for $a > 0$, downward for $a < 0$ The x-coordinate of the vertex is $\frac{-b}{2a}$. Find the y-coordinate of the vertex by evaluating $y = ax^2 + bx + c$ for $x = \frac{-b}{2a}$.	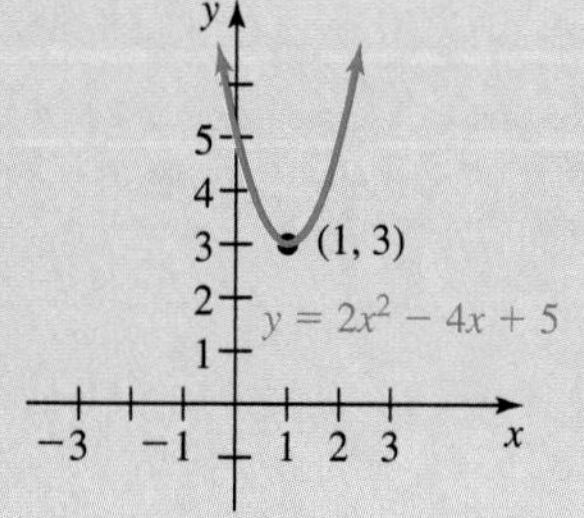

$x = ay^2 + by + c$	Opens right for $a > 0$, left for $a < 0$ The y-coordinate of the vertex is $\frac{-b}{2a}$. Find the x-coordinate of the vertex by evaluating $x = ay^2 + by + c$ for $y = \frac{-b}{2a}$.	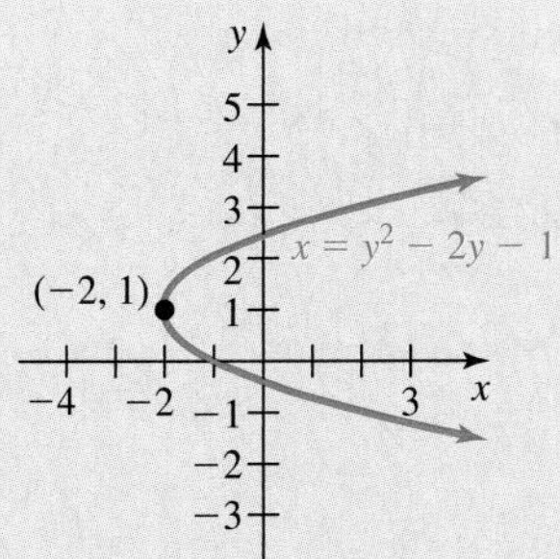

Circle | **Examples**

Centered at origin $x^2 + y^2 = r^2$	Center (0, 0) Radius r (for $r > 0$)	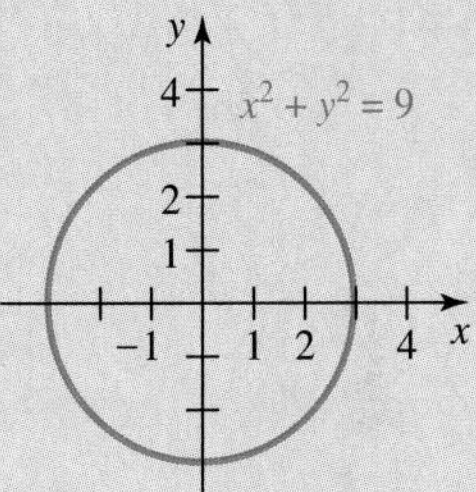
Arbitrary center $(x - h)^2 + (y - k)^2 = r^2$	Center (h, k) Radius r (for $r > 0$)	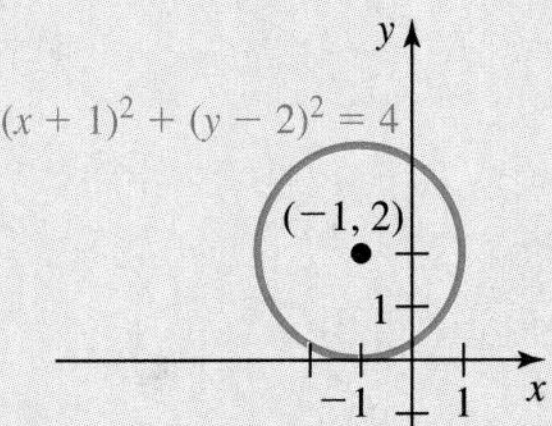

Ellipse | **Examples**

Centered at origin $\frac{x^2}{a^2} + \frac{y^2}{b^2} = 1$	Center: (0, 0) x-intercepts: $(a, 0)$ and $(-a, 0)$ y-intercepts: $(0, b)$ and $(0, -b)$ Foci: $(\pm c, 0)$ if $a^2 > b^2$ and $c^2 = a^2 - b^2$ $(0, \pm c)$ if $b^2 > a^2$ and $c^2 = b^2 - a^2$	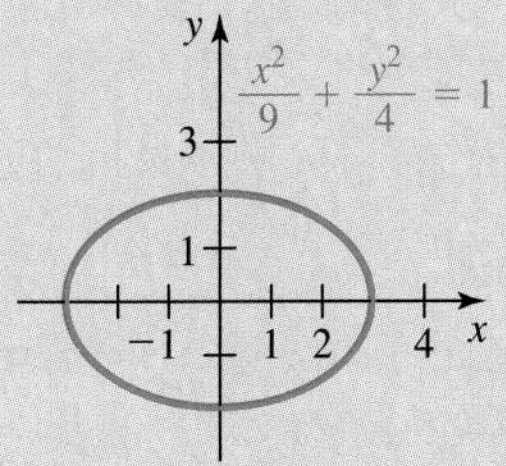
Arbitrary center $\frac{(x - h)^2}{a^2} + \frac{(y - k)^2}{b^2} = 1$	Center: (h, k)	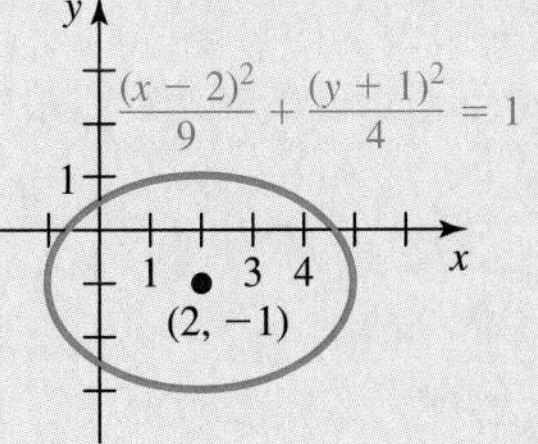

Hyperbola

Examples

Opening left and right

Centered at origin: $\dfrac{x^2}{a^2} - \dfrac{y^2}{b^2} = 1$

Center: (0, 0)

x-intercepts: $(a, 0)$ and $(-a, 0)$

y-intercepts: none

Centered at (h, k): $\dfrac{(x-h)^2}{a^2} - \dfrac{(y-k)^2}{b^2} = 1$

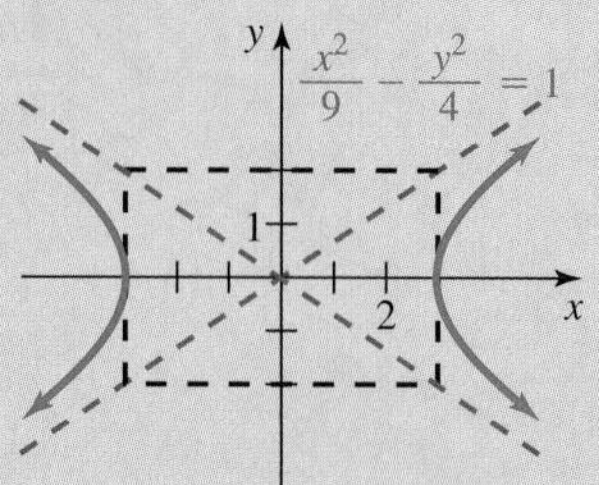

Opening up and down

Centered at origin: $\dfrac{y^2}{b^2} - \dfrac{x^2}{a^2} = 1$

Center: (0, 0)

x-intercepts: none

y-intercepts: $(0, b)$ and $(0, -b)$

Centered at (h, k): $\dfrac{(y-k)^2}{b^2} - \dfrac{(x-h)^2}{a^2} = 1$

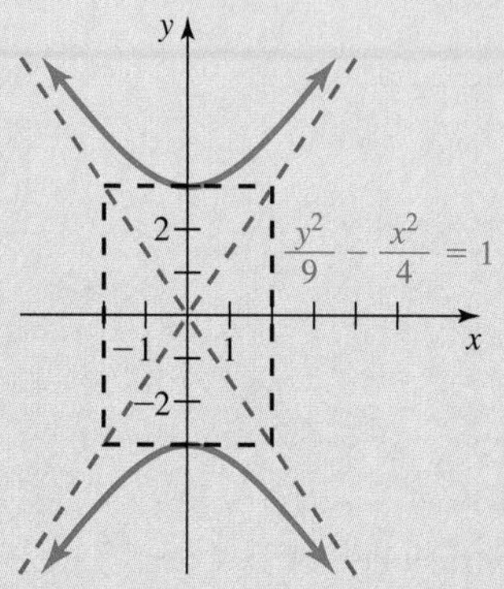

Second-Degree Inequalities

Examples

Solution set for a single inequality

Graph the boundary curve obtained by replacing the inequality symbol by the equal sign.
Use test points to determine which regions satisfy the inequality.

$x^2 + y^2 < 16$

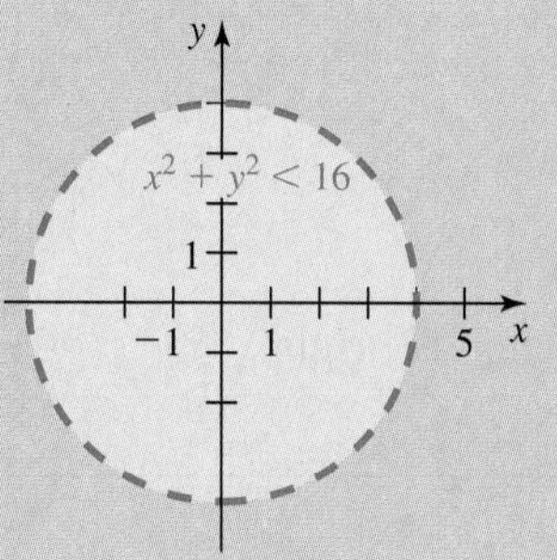

Solution set for a system of inequalities

Graph the boundary curves. Then select a test point in each region. Shade only the regions for which the test point satisfies all inequalities of the system.

$x^2 + y^2 < 16$
$y > x^2 - 1$

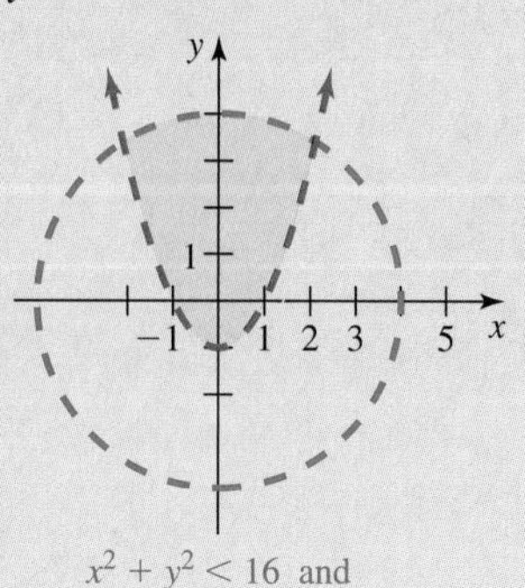

$x^2 + y^2 < 16$ and
$y > x^2 - 1$

Enriching Your Mathematical Word Power

For each mathematical term, choose the correct meaning.

1. **nonlinear equation**
   a. an equation that is not lined up
   b. an equation whose graph is a straight line
   c. an equation whose graph is not a straight line
   d. an exponential equation c
2. **parabola**
   a. the points in a plane that are equidistant from a point and a line
   b. the points in a plane that are a fixed distance from a fixed point
   c. the points in a plane that are equidistant from two fixed points
   d. the points in a plane the sum of whose distances from two fixed points is a constant a
3. **directrix**
   a. the line $y = x$
   b. the line of symmetry of a parabola
   c. the x-axis
   d. the fixed line in the definition of parabola d
4. **vertex of a parabola**
   a. the midpoint of the line segment joining the focus and directrix perpendicular to the directrix
   b. the focus
   c. the x-intercept
   d. the endpoint a
5. **conic sections**
   a. the two halves of a cone
   b. the vertex and focus
   c. the curves obtained at the intersection of a cone and a plane
   d. the asymptotes c
6. **axis of symmetry**
   a. the x-axis
   b. the y-axis
   c. the directrix
   d. the line of symmetry of a parabola d
7. **circle**
   a. the points in a plane that are equidistant from a point and a line
   b. the points in a plane that are a fixed distance from a fixed point
   c. the points in a plane that are equidistant from two fixed points
   d. the points in a plane the sum of whose distances from two fixed points is a constant b
8. **ellipse**
   a. the points in a plane that are equidistant from a point and a line
   b. the points in a plane that are a fixed distance from a fixed point
   c. the points in a plane that are equidistant from two fixed points
   d. the points in a plane such that the sum of their distances from two fixed points is constant d
9. **hyperbola**
   a. the points in a plane that are equidistant from a point and a line
   b. the points in a plane that are a fixed distance from a fixed point
   c. the points in a plane such that the difference of their distances from two fixed points is constant
   d. the points in a plane such that the sum of their distances from two fixed points is a constant c
10. **asymptotes**
    a. lines approached by a hyperbola
    b. lines approached by parabolas
    c. tangent lines to a circle
    d. lines that pass through the vertices of an ellipse a

Review Exercises

13.1 *Graph both equations on the same set of axes, then determine the points of intersection of the graphs by solving the system.*

1. $y = x^2$
$y = -2x + 15$
$\{(3, 9), (-5, 25)\}$

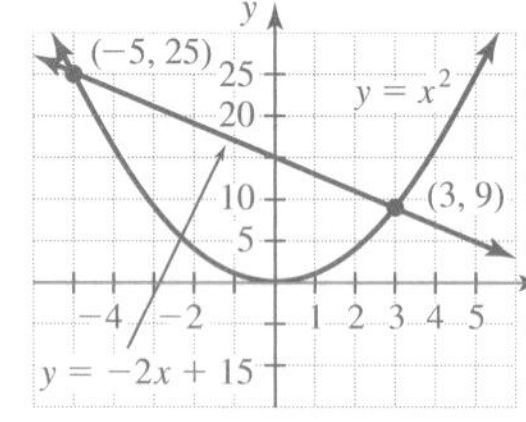

2. $y = \sqrt{x}$
$y = \dfrac{1}{3}x$ $\{(0, 0), (9, 3)\}$

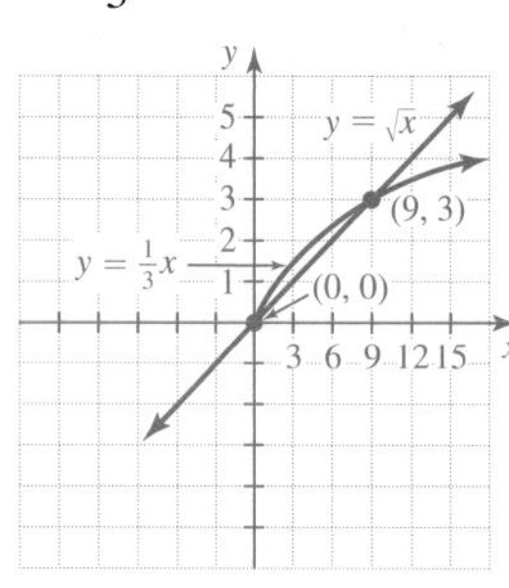

3. $y = 3x$
$y = \dfrac{1}{x}$
$\left\{\left(\dfrac{\sqrt{3}}{3}, \sqrt{3}\right), \left(-\dfrac{\sqrt{3}}{3}, -\sqrt{3}\right)\right\}$

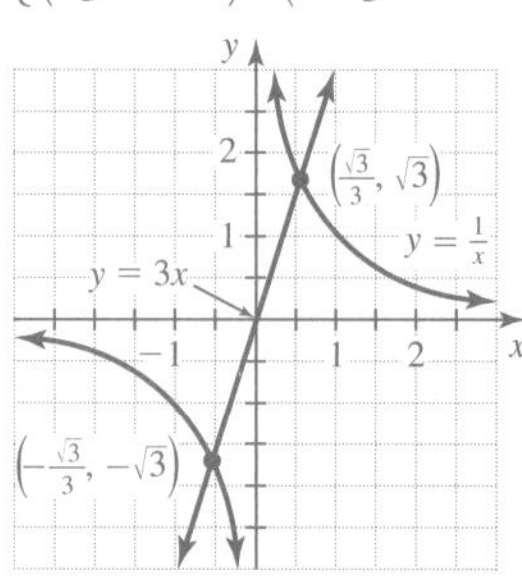

4. $y = |x|$
$y = -3x + 5$
$\left\{\left(\dfrac{5}{4}, \dfrac{5}{4}\right)\right\}$

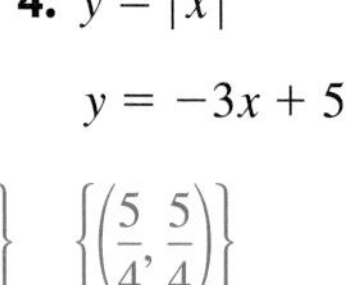

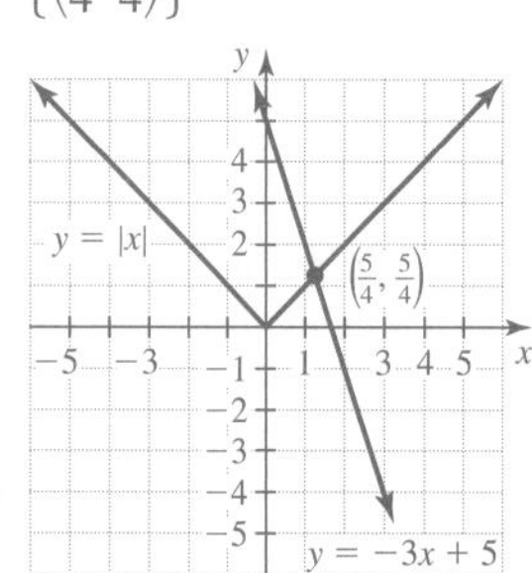

Solve each system.

5. $x^2 + y^2 = 4$
$y = \dfrac{1}{3}x^2$
$\{(\sqrt{3}, 1), (-\sqrt{3}, 1)\}$

6. $12y^2 - 4x^2 = 9$
$x = y^2$
$\left\{\left(\dfrac{3}{2}, -\dfrac{\sqrt{6}}{2}\right), \left(\dfrac{3}{2}, \dfrac{\sqrt{6}}{2}\right)\right\}$

7. $x^2 + y^2 = 34$
$y = x + 2$
$\{(-5, -3), (3, 5)\}$

8. $y = 2x + 1$
$xy - y = 5$
$\left\{\left(-\dfrac{3}{2}, -2\right), (2, 5)\right\}$

9. $y = \log(x - 3)$
$y = 1 - \log(x)$
$\{(5, \log(2))\}$

10. $y = \left(\dfrac{1}{2}\right)^x$
$y = 2^{x-1}$
$\left\{\left(\dfrac{1}{2}, \dfrac{\sqrt{2}}{2}\right)\right\}$

11. $x^4 = 2(12 - y)$
$y = x^2$
$\{(2, 4), (-2, 4)\}$

12. $x^2 + 2y^2 = 7$
$x^2 - 2y^2 = -5$
$\{(1, \sqrt{3}), (-1, \sqrt{3}), (1, -\sqrt{3}), (-1, -\sqrt{3})\}$

13.2 *Find the distance between each pair of points.*

13. $(1, 1), (3, 3)$ $2\sqrt{2}$

14. $(1, 2), (4, 5)$ $3\sqrt{2}$

15. $(-4, 6), (2, -8)$ $2\sqrt{58}$

16. $(-3, -5), (5, -7)$ $2\sqrt{17}$

Determine the vertex, axis of symmetry, focus, and directrix for each parabola.

17. $y = x^2 + 3x - 18$
Vertex $\left(-\frac{3}{2}, -\frac{81}{4}\right)$, axis of symmetry $x = -\frac{3}{2}$, focus $\left(-\frac{3}{2}, -20\right)$, directrix $y = -\frac{41}{2}$

18. $y = x - x^2$
Vertex $\left(\frac{1}{2}, \frac{1}{4}\right)$, axis of symmetry $x = \frac{1}{2}$, focus $\left(\frac{1}{2}, 0\right)$, directrix $y = \frac{1}{2}$

19. $y = x^2 + 3x + 2$
Vertex $\left(-\frac{3}{2}, -\frac{1}{4}\right)$, axis of symmetry $x = -\frac{3}{2}$, focus $\left(-\frac{3}{2}, 0\right)$, directrix $y = -\frac{1}{2}$

20. $y = -x^2 - 3x + 4$
Vertex $\left(-\frac{3}{2}, \frac{25}{4}\right)$, axis of symmetry $x = -\frac{3}{2}$, focus $\left(-\frac{3}{2}, 6\right)$, directrix $y = \frac{13}{2}$

21. $y = -\dfrac{1}{2}(x - 2)^2 + 3$
Vertex $(2, 3)$, axis of symmetry $x = 2$, focus $\left(2, \frac{5}{2}\right)$, directrix $y = \frac{7}{2}$

22. $y = \dfrac{1}{4}(x + 1)^2 - 2$
Vertex $(-1, -2)$, axis of symmetry $x = -1$, focus $(-1, -1)$, directrix $y = -3$

Write each equation in the form $y = a(x - h)^2 + k$, and identify the vertex of the parabola.

23. $y = 2x^2 - 8x + 1$ $y = 2(x - 2)^2 - 7, (2, -7)$

24. $y = -2x^2 - 6x - 1$ $y = -2\left(x + \frac{3}{2}\right)^2 + \frac{7}{2}, \left(-\frac{3}{2}, \frac{7}{2}\right)$

25. $y = -\frac{1}{2}x^2 - x + \frac{1}{2}$ $\quad y = -\frac{1}{2}(x + 1)^2 + 1, (-1, 1)$

26. $y = \frac{1}{4}x^2 + x - 9$ $\quad y = \frac{1}{4}(x + 2)^2 - 10, (-2, -10)$

13.3 *Determine the center and radius of each circle, and sketch its graph.*

27. $x^2 + y^2 = 100$
$(0, 0), 10$

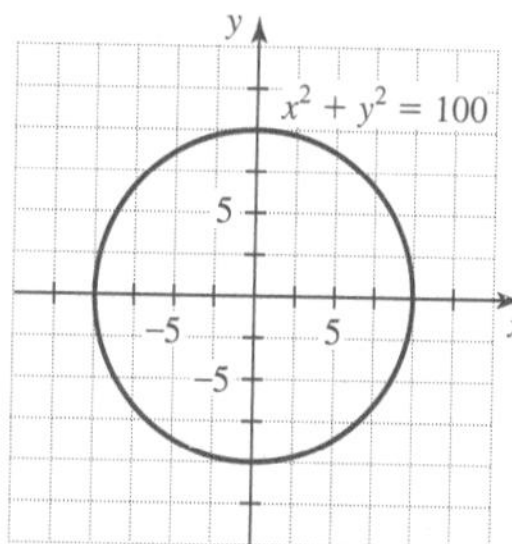

28. $x^2 + y^2 = 20$
$(0, 0), 2\sqrt{5}$

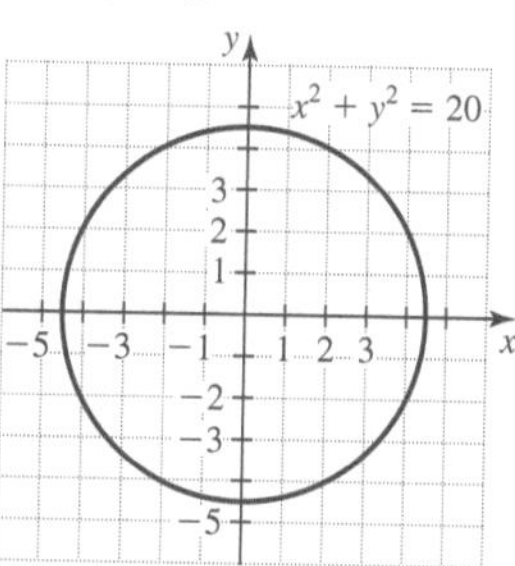

29. $(x - 2)^2 + (y + 3)^2 = 81$
$(2, -3), 9$

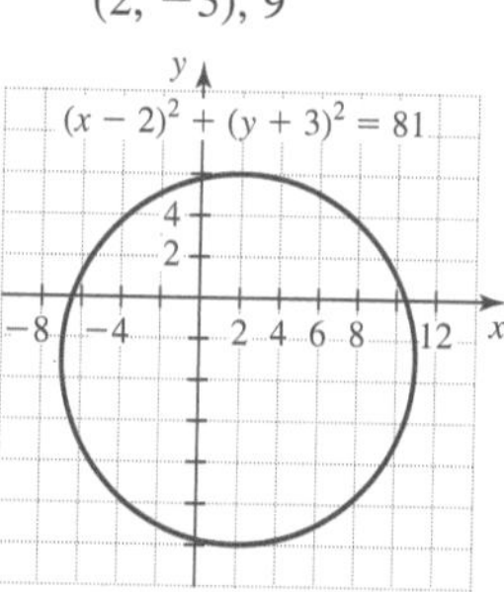

30. $x^2 + 2x + y^2 = 8$
$(-1, 0), 3$

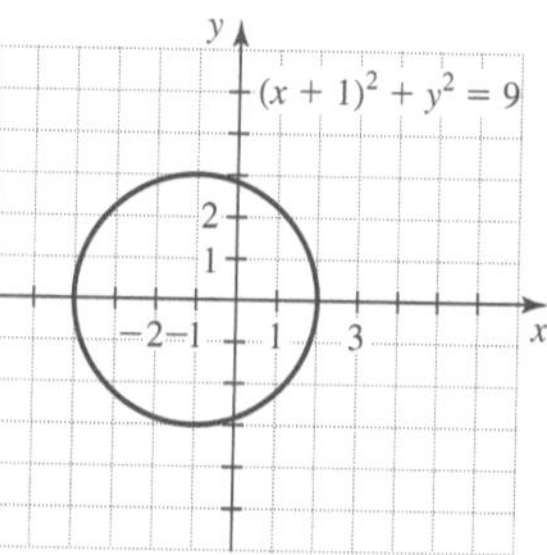

31. $9y^2 + 9x^2 = 4$ $\quad (0, 0), \frac{2}{3}$

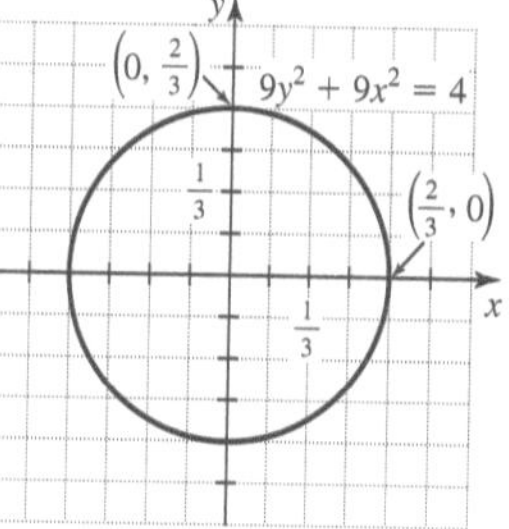

32. $x^2 + 4x + y^2 - 6y - 3 = 0$ $\quad (-2, 3), 4$

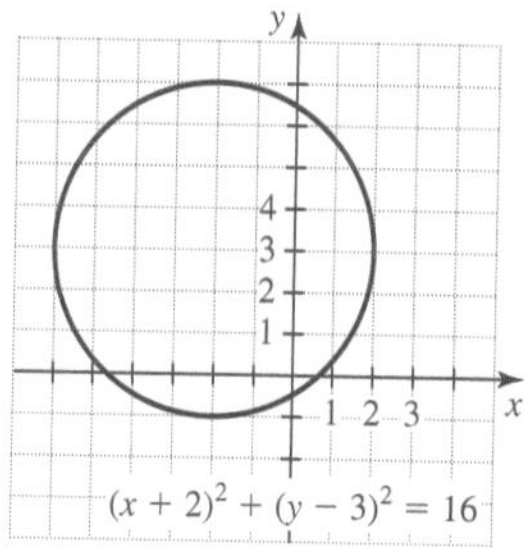

Write the standard equation for each circle with the given center and radius.

33. Center (0, 3), radius 6 $\quad x^2 + (y - 3)^2 = 36$

34. Center (0, 0), radius $\sqrt{6}$ $\quad x^2 + y^2 = 6$

35. Center (2, −7), radius 5 $\quad (x - 2)^2 + (y + 7)^2 = 25$

36. Center $\left(\frac{1}{2}, -3\right)$, radius $\frac{1}{2}$ $\quad \left(x - \frac{1}{2}\right)^2 + (y + 3)^2 = \frac{1}{4}$

13.4 *Sketch the graph of each ellipse.*

37. $\frac{x^2}{36} + \frac{y^2}{49} = 1$

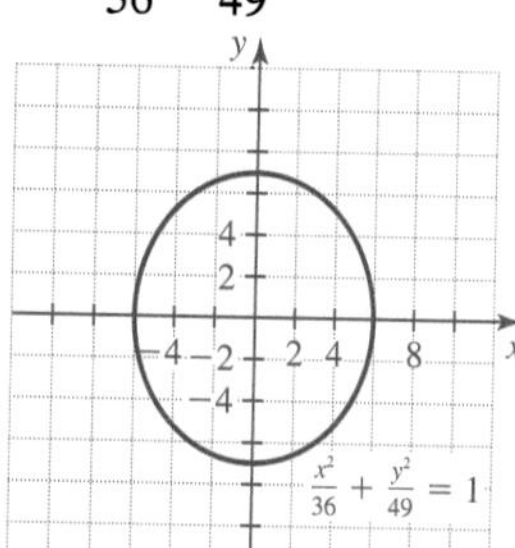

38. $\frac{x^2}{25} + y^2 = 1$

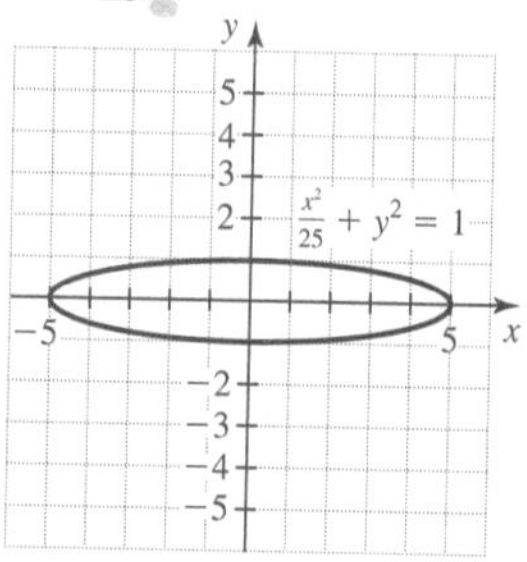

39. $25x^2 + 4y^2 = 100$

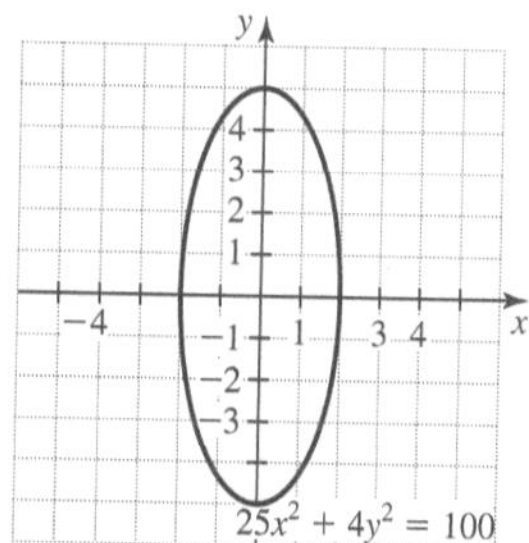

40. $6x^2 + 4y^2 = 24$

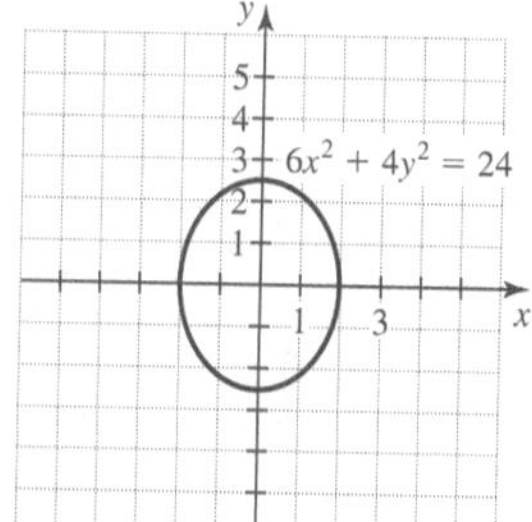

Sketch the graph of each hyperbola.

41. $\frac{x^2}{49} - \frac{y^2}{36} = 1$

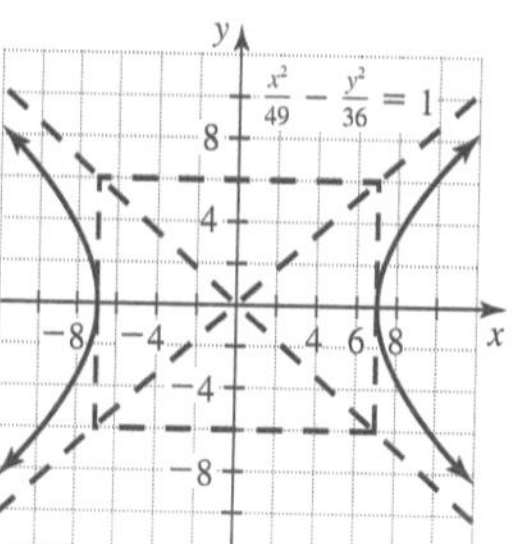

42. $\frac{y^2}{25} - \frac{x^2}{49} = 1$

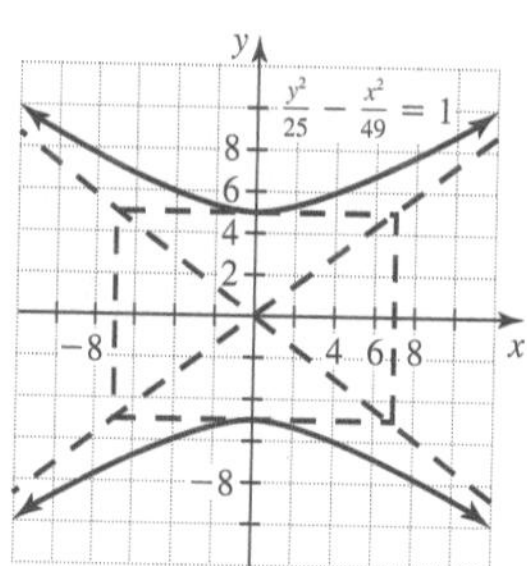

43. $4x^2 - 25y^2 = 100$

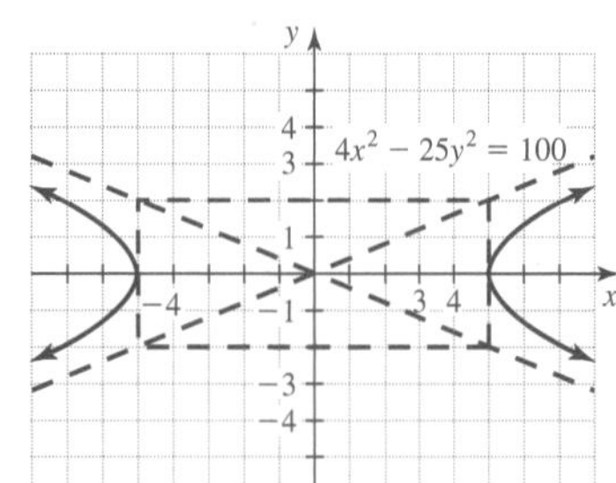

44. $6y^2 - 16x^2 = 96$

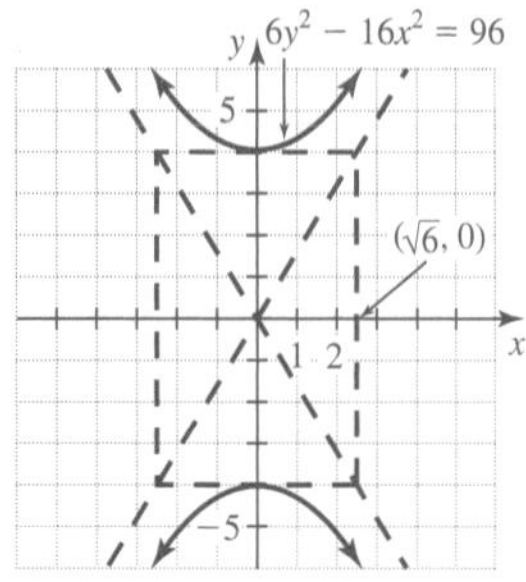

13.5 *Graph each inequality.*

45. $4x - 2y > 3$

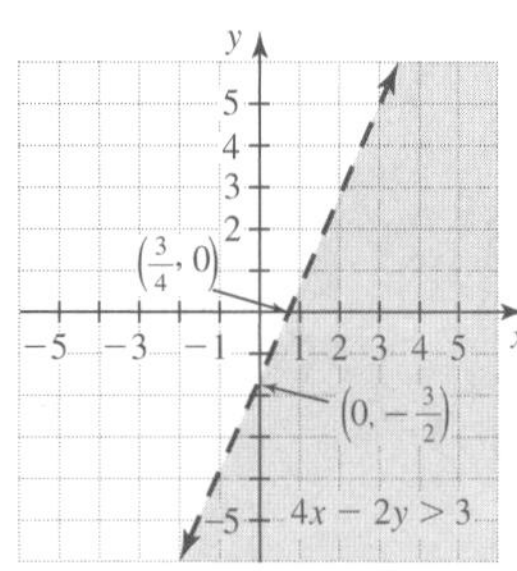

46. $y < x^2 - 3x$

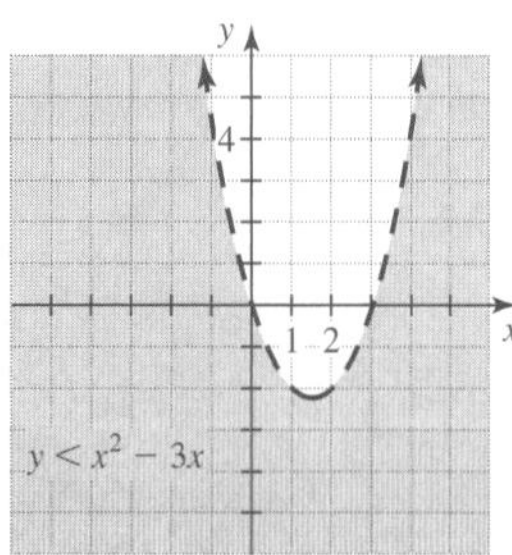

47. $y^2 < x^2 - 1$

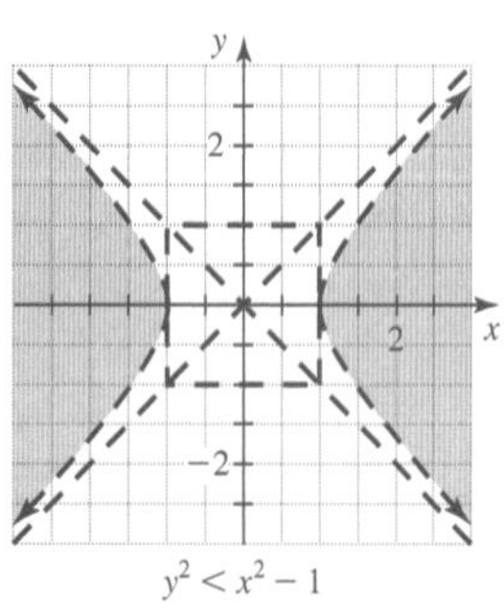

48. $y^2 < 1 - x^2$

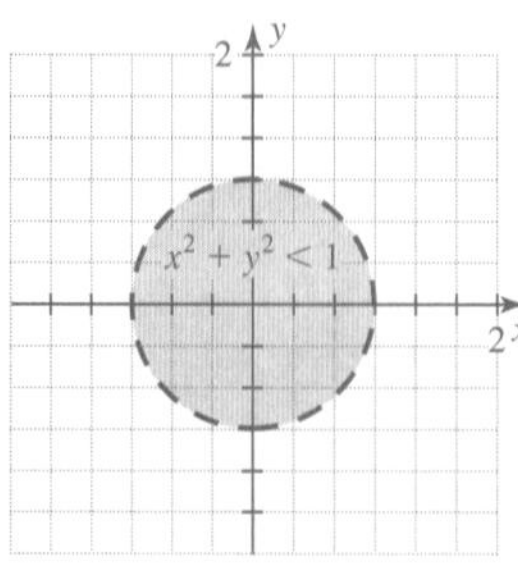

49. $4x^2 + 9y^2 > 36$

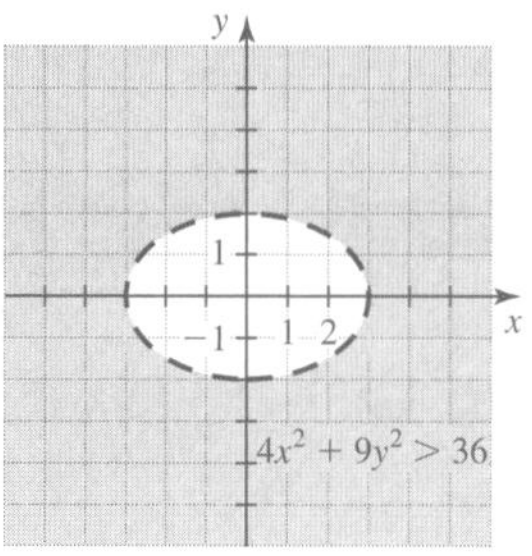

50. $x^2 + y > 2x - 1$

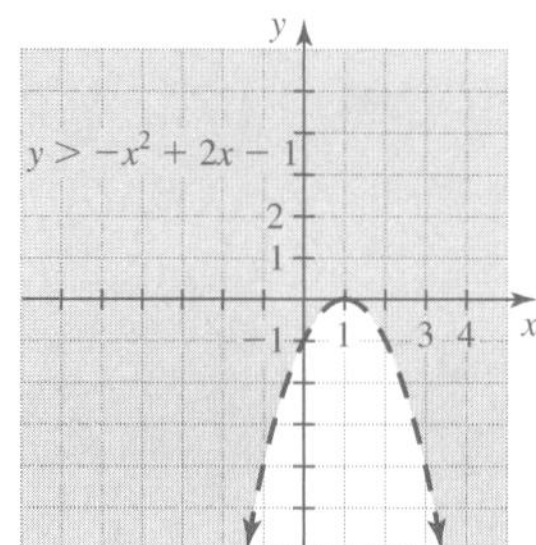

Graph the solution set to each system of inequalities.

51. $y < 3x - x^2$
$x^2 + y^2 < 9$

52. $x^2 - y^2 < 1$
$y < 1$

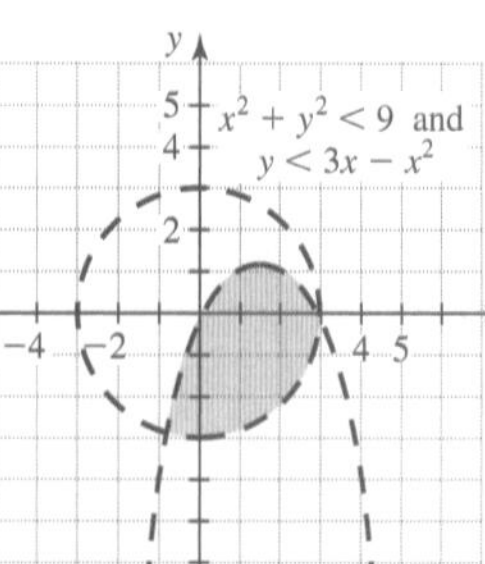

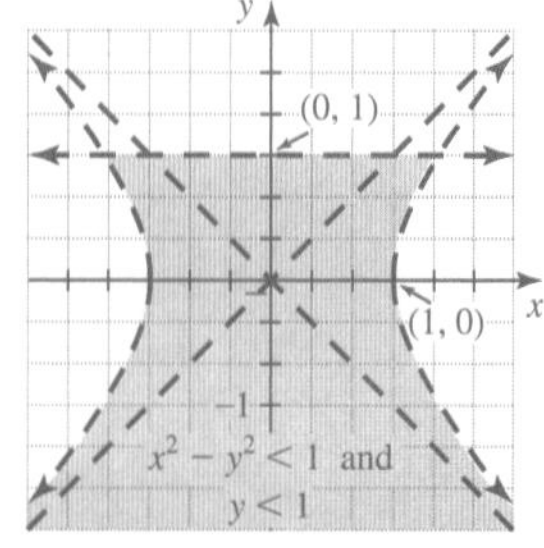

53. $4x^2 + 9y^2 > 36$
$x^2 + y^2 < 9$

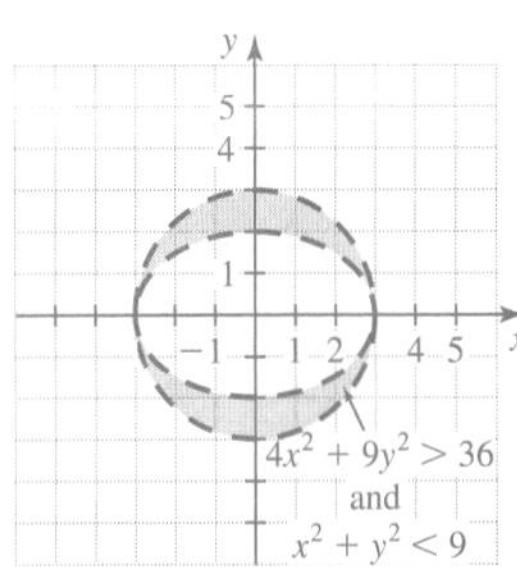

54. $y^2 - x^2 > 4$
$y^2 + 16x^2 < 16$

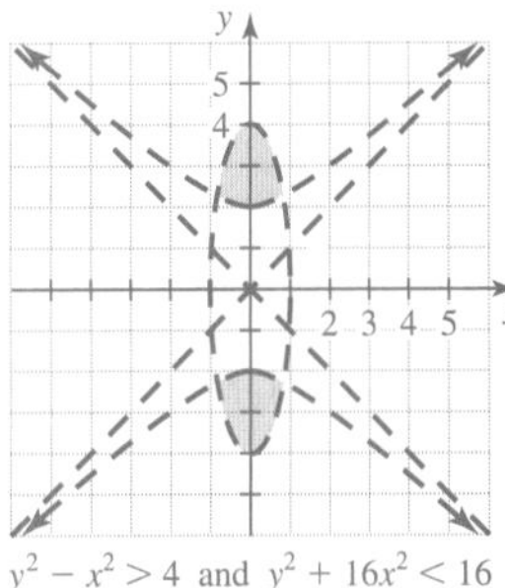

Miscellaneous

Identify each equation as the equation of a straight line, parabola, circle, hyperbola, or ellipse. Try to do these without rewriting the equations.

55. $x^2 = y^2 + 1$
Hyperbola

56. $x = y + 1$
Line

57. $x^2 = 1 - y^2$
Circle

58. $x^2 = y + 1$
Parabola

59. $x^2 + x = 1 - y^2$
Circle

60. $(x - 3)^2 + (y + 2)^2 = 7$
Circle

61. $x^2 + 4x = 6y - y^2$
Circle

62. $4x + 6y = 1$
Line

63. $\dfrac{x^2}{3} - \dfrac{y^2}{5} = 1$
Hyperbola

64. $x^2 + \dfrac{y^2}{3} = 1$
Ellipse

65. $4y^2 - x^2 = 8$
Hyperbola

66. $9x^2 + y = 9$
Parabola

Sketch the graph of each equation.

67. $x^2 = 4 - y^2$

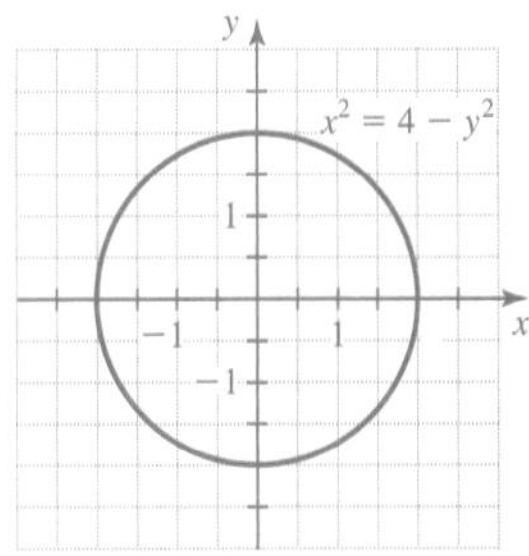

68. $x^2 = 4y^2 + 4$

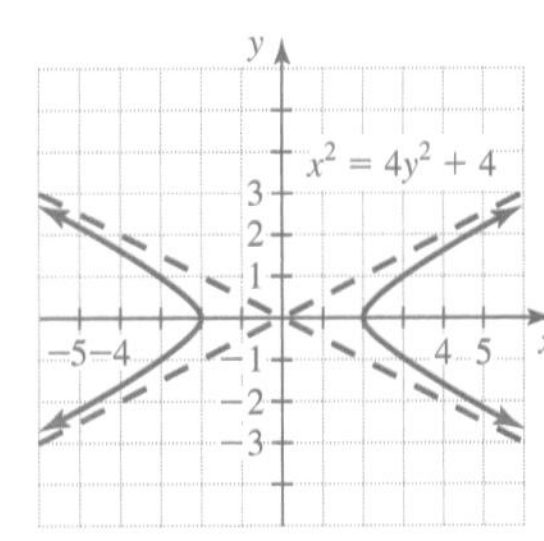

69. $x^2 = 4y + 4$

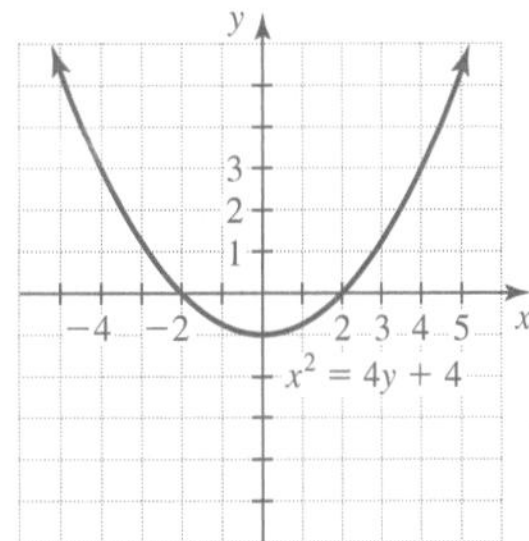

70. $x = 4y + 4$

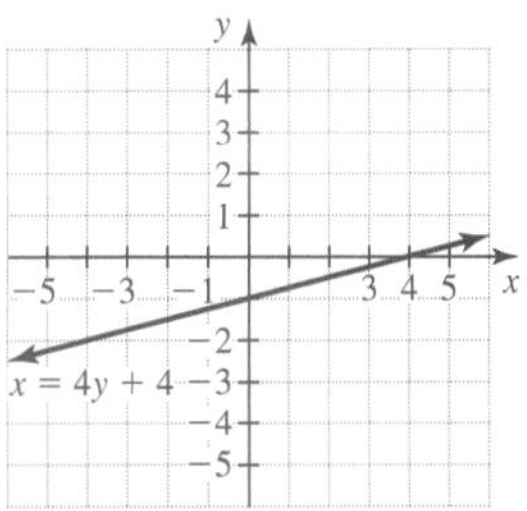

71. $x^2 = 4 - 4y^2$

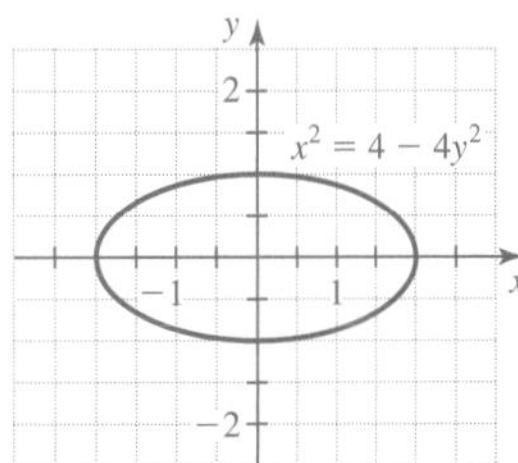

72. $x^2 = 4y - y^2$

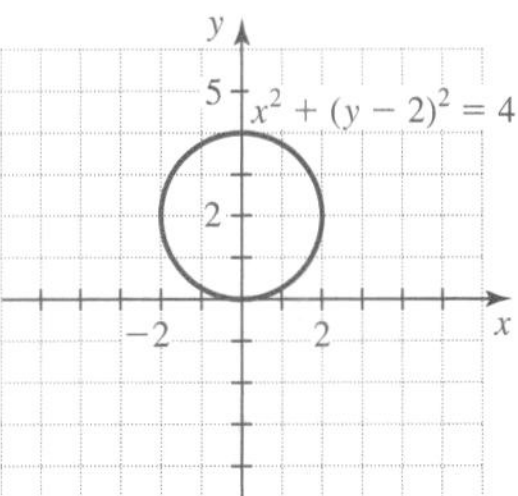

73. $x^2 = 4 - (y - 4)^2$

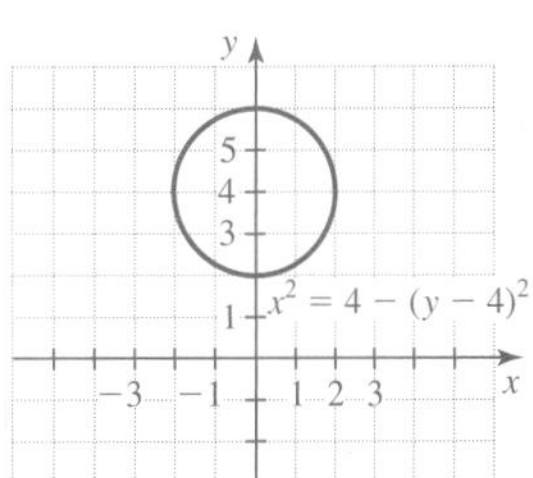

74. $(x - 2)^2 + (y - 4)^2 = 4$

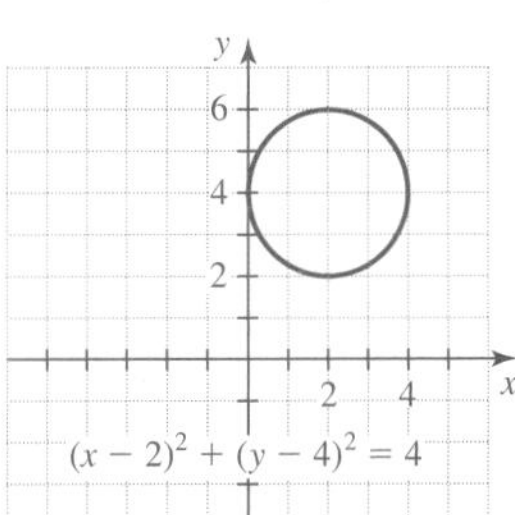

Write the equation of the circle with the given features.

75. Centered at the origin and passing through (3, 4)
$x^2 + y^2 = 25$

76. Centered at $(2, -3)$ and passing through $(-1, 4)$
$(x - 2)^2 + (y + 3)^2 = 58$

77. Centered at $(-1, 5)$ with radius 6
$(x + 1)^2 + (y - 5)^2 = 36$

78. Centered at $(0, -3)$ and passing through the origin
$x^2 + (y + 3)^2 = 9$

Write the equation of the parabola with the given features.

79. Focus (1, 4) and directrix $y = 2$
$y = \frac{1}{4}(x - 1)^2 + 3$

80. Focus $(-2, 1)$ and directrix $y = 5$
$y = -\frac{1}{8}(x + 2)^2 + 3$

81. Vertex $(0, 0)$ and focus $\left(0, \frac{1}{4}\right)$
$y = x^2$

82. Vertex $(1, 2)$ and focus $\left(1, \frac{3}{2}\right)$
$y = -\frac{1}{2}(x - 1)^2 + 2$

83. Vertex $(0, 0)$, passing through $(3, 2)$, and opening upward
$y = \frac{2}{9}x^2$

84. Vertex $(1, 3)$, passing through $(0, 0)$, and opening downward
$y = -3(x - 1)^2 + 3$

Solve each system of equations.

85. $x^2 + y^2 = 25$
$y = -x + 1$ $\{(4, -3), (-3, 4)\}$

86. $x^2 - y^2 = 1$
$x^2 + y^2 = 7$ $\{(2, \sqrt{3}), (2, -\sqrt{3}), (-2, \sqrt{3}), (-2, -\sqrt{3})\}$

87. $4x^2 + y^2 = 4$
$x^2 - y^2 = 21$ $\varnothing$

88. $y = x^2 + x$
$y = -x^2 + 3x + 12$ $\{(3, 12), (-2, 2)\}$

Solve each problem.

89. ***Perimeter of a rectangle.*** A rectangle has a perimeter of 16 feet and an area of 12 square feet. Find its length and width. 6 ft, 2 ft

90. ***Tale of two circles.*** Find the radii of two circles such that the difference in areas of the two is 10π square inches and the difference in radii of the two is 2 inches.
$\frac{7}{2}$ in., $\frac{3}{2}$ in.

Chapter 13 Test

Sketch the graph of each equation.

1. $x^2 + y^2 = 25$

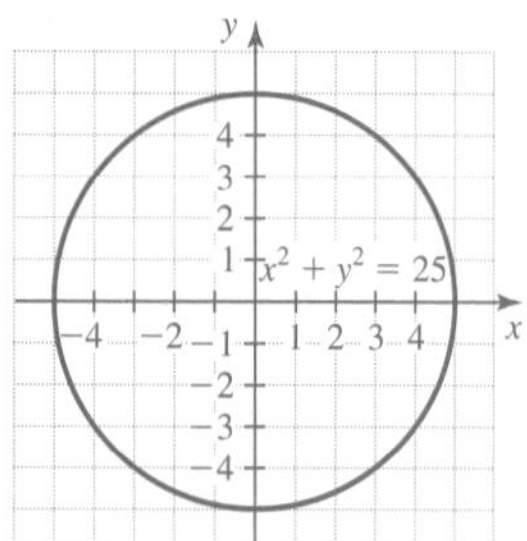

2. $\frac{x^2}{16} - \frac{y^2}{25} = 1$

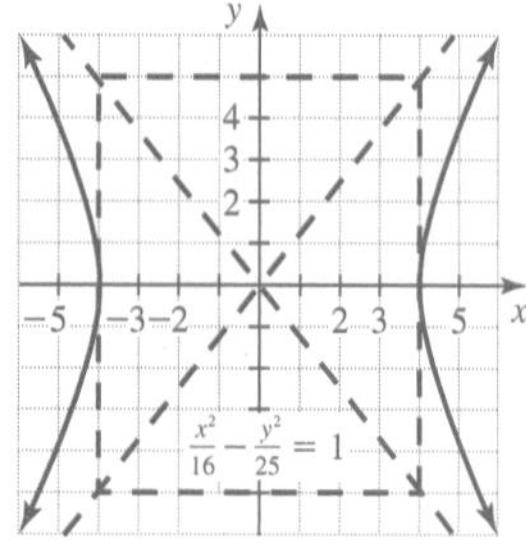

3. $y^2 + 4x^2 = 4$

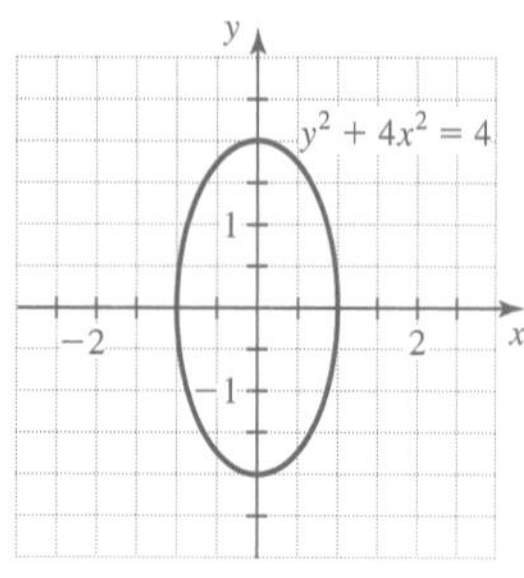

4. $y = x^2 + 4x + 4$

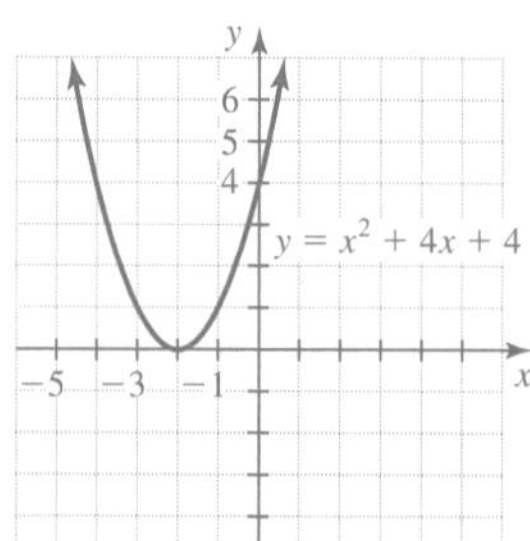

5. $y^2 - 4x^2 = 4$

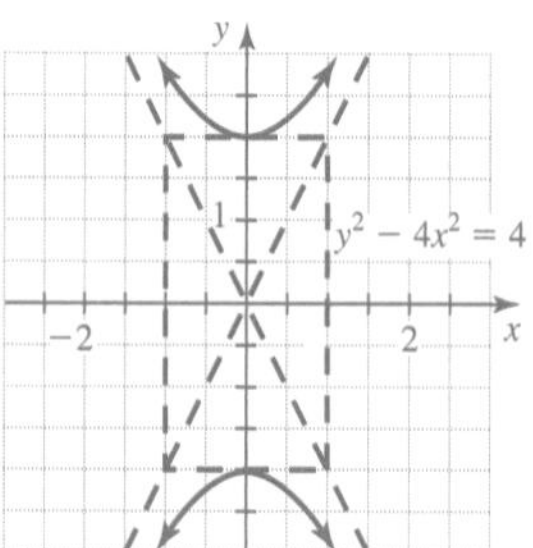

6. $y = -x^2 - 2x + 3$

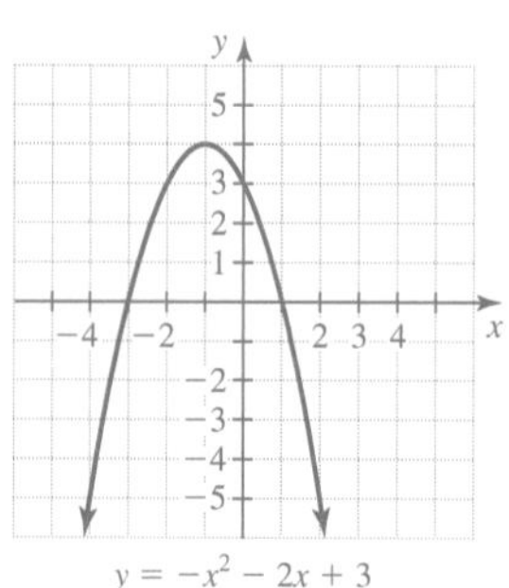

Sketch the graph of each inequality.

7. $x^2 - y^2 < 9$

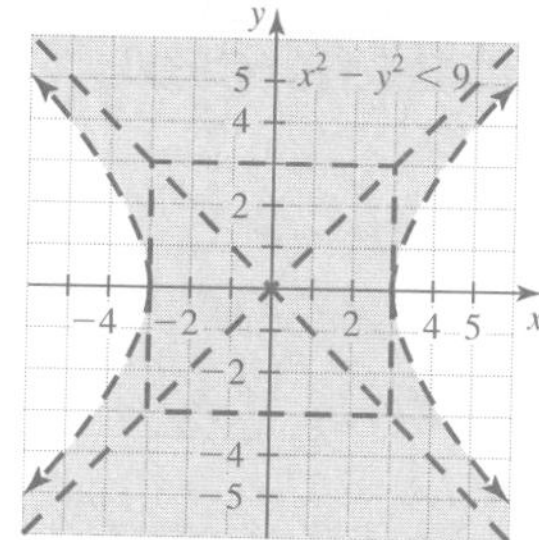

8. $x^2 + y^2 > 9$

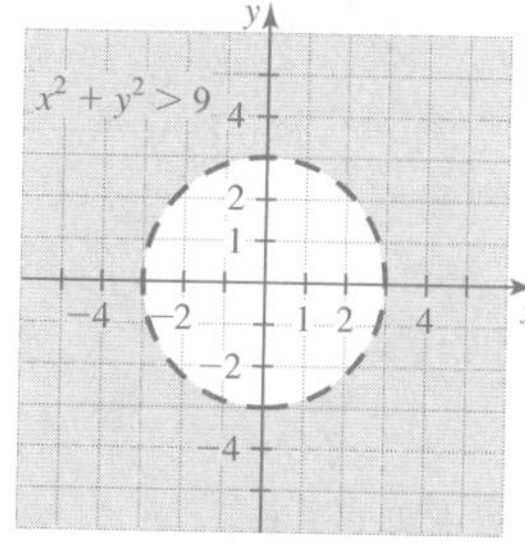

9. $y > x^2 - 9$

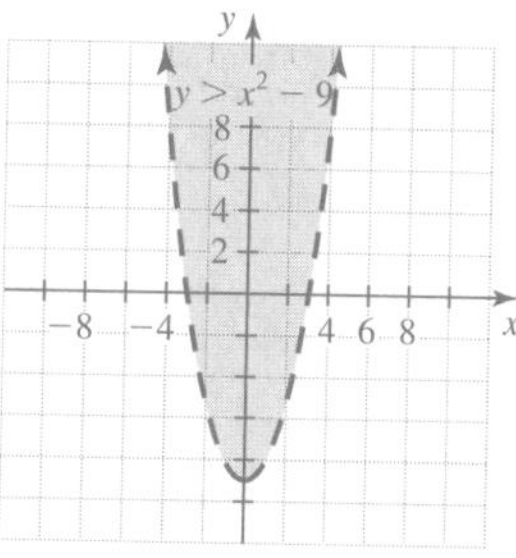

Graph the solution set to each system of inequalities.

10. $x^2 + y^2 < 9$
$x^2 - y^2 > 1$

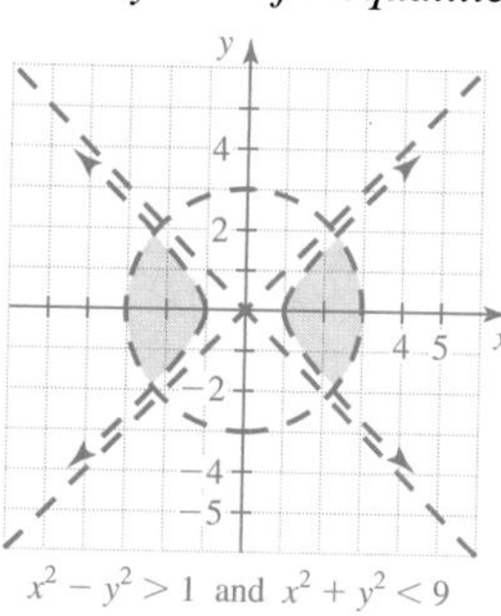

$x^2 - y^2 > 1$ and $x^2 + y^2 < 9$

11. $y < -x^2 + x$
$y < x - 4$

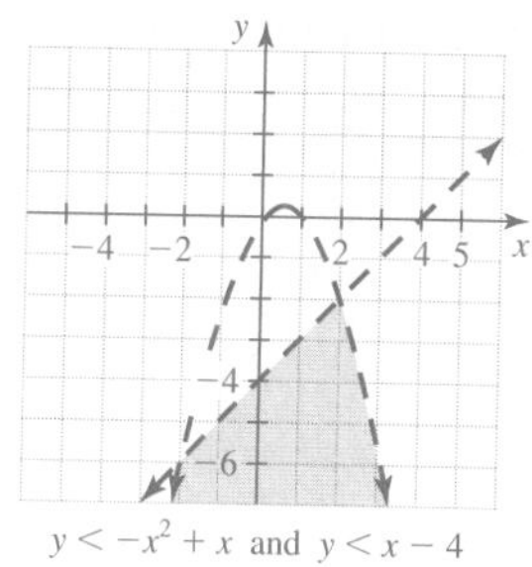

$y < -x^2 + x$ and $y < x - 4$

Solve each system of equations.

12. $y = x^2 - 2x - 8$
$y = 7 - 4x$
$\{(-5, 27), (3, -5)\}$

13. $x^2 + y^2 = 12$
$y = x^2$
$\{(\sqrt{3}, 3), (-\sqrt{3}, 3)\}$

Solve each problem.

14. Find the distance between $(-1, 4)$ and $(1, 6)$. $2\sqrt{2}$

15. Find the center and radius of the circle $x^2 + 2x + y^2 + 10y = 10$. $(-1, -5)$, 6

16. Find the vertex, focus, and directrix of the parabola $y = x^2 + x + 3$. State the axis of symmetry and whether the parabola opens up or down.
Vertex $\left(-\frac{1}{2}, \frac{11}{4}\right)$, focus $\left(-\frac{1}{2}, 3\right)$, directrix $y = \frac{5}{2}$, axis of symmetry $x = -\frac{1}{2}$, upward

17. Write the equation $y = \frac{1}{2}x^2 - 3x - \frac{1}{2}$ in the form $y = a(x - h)^2 + k$.
$y = \frac{1}{2}(x - 3)^2 - 5$

18. Write the equation of a circle with center $(-1, 3)$ that passes through $(2, 5)$.
$(x + 1)^2 + (y - 3)^2 = 13$

19. Find the length and width of a rectangular room that has an area of 108 square feet and a perimeter of 42 ft.
12 ft, 9 ft

*Making*Connections | A Review of Chapters 1–13

Sketch the graph of each equation.

1. $y = 9x - x^2$

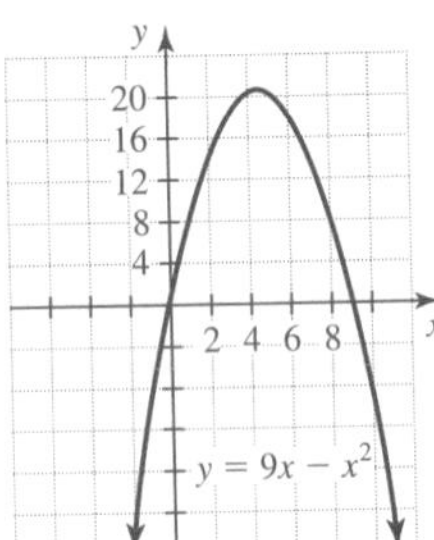

2. $y = 9x$

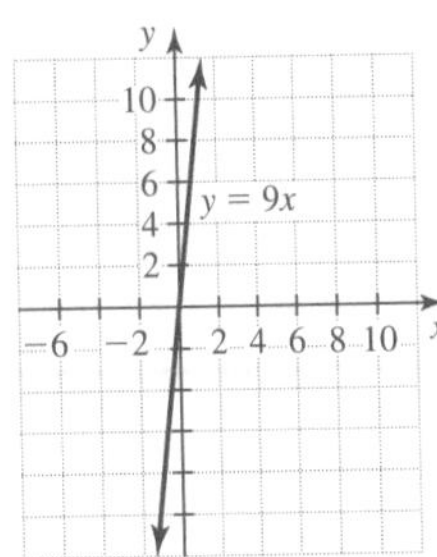

3. $y = (x - 9)^2$

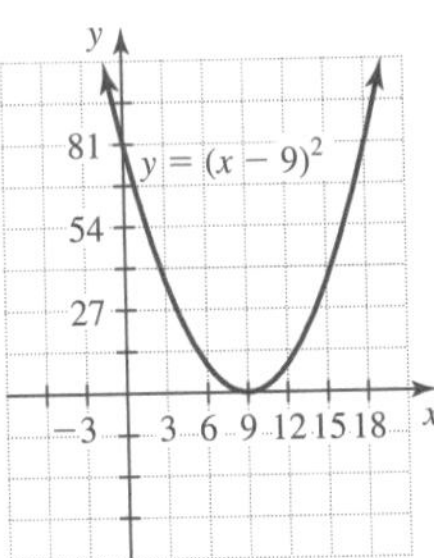

4. $y^2 = 9 - x^2$

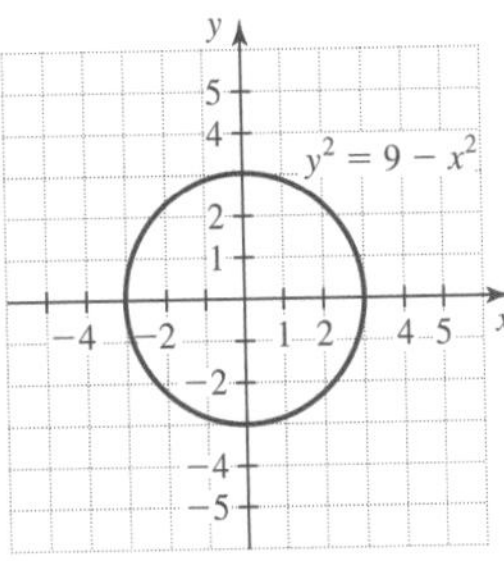

5. $y = 9x^2$

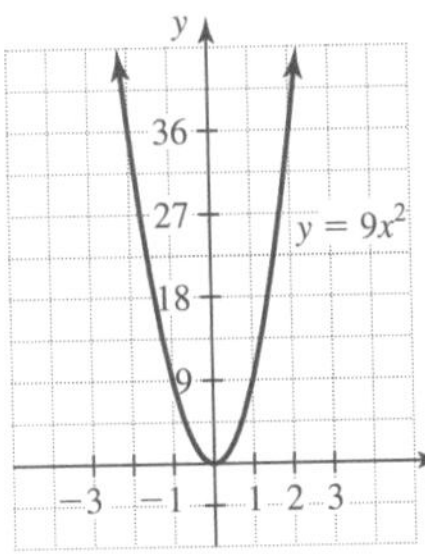

6. $y = |9x|$

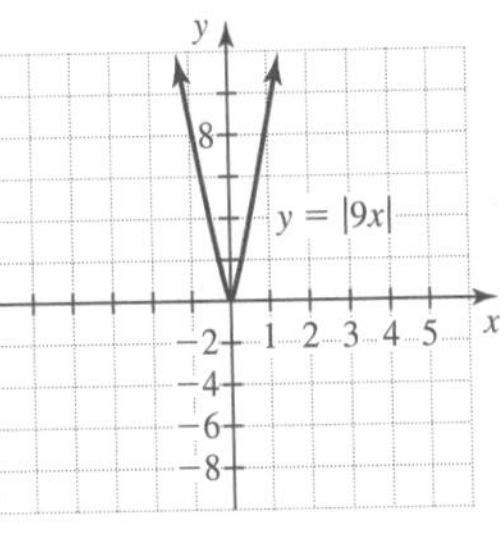

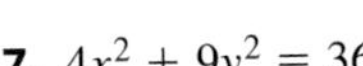

7. $4x^2 + 9y^2 = 36$

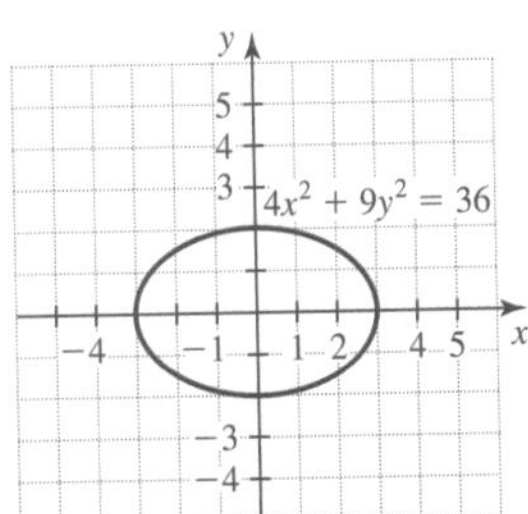

8. $4x^2 - 9y^2 = 36$

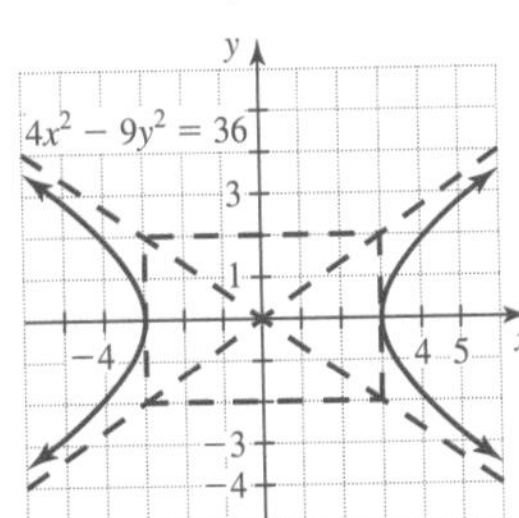

9. $y = 9 - x$

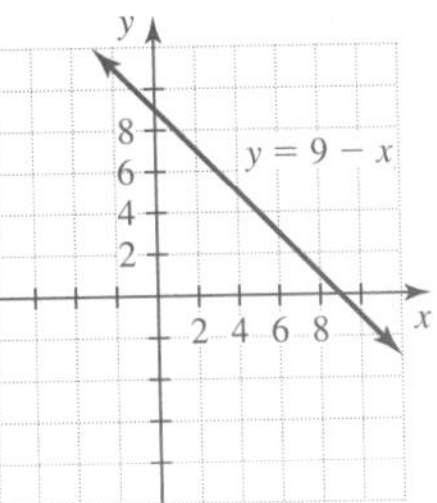

10. $y = 9^x$

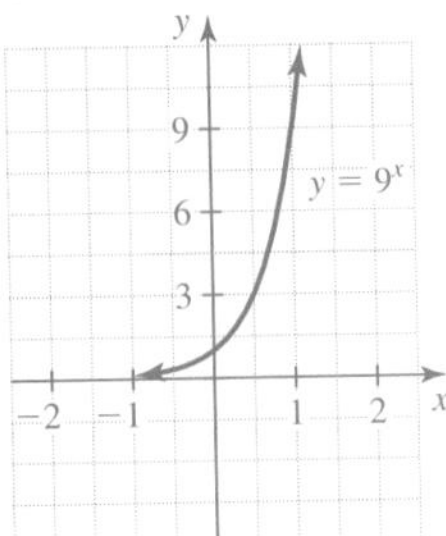

Find the following products.

11. $(x + 2y)^2$ $x^2 + 4xy + 4y^2$

12. $(x + y)(x^2 + 2xy + y^2)$ $x^3 + 3x^2y + 3xy^2 + y^3$

13. $(a + b)^3$ $a^3 + 3a^2b + 3ab^2 + b^3$

14. $(a - 3b)^2$ $a^2 - 6ab + 9b^2$

15. $(2a + 1)(3a - 5)$ $6a^2 - 7a - 5$

16. $(x - y)(x^2 + xy + y^2)$ $x^3 - y^3$

Solve each system of equations.

17. $2x - 3y = -4$
$x + 2y = 5$
$\{(1, 2)\}$

18. $x^2 + y^2 = 25$
$x + y = 7$
$\{(3, 4), (4, 3)\}$

19. $2x - y + z = 7$
$x - 2y - z = 2$
$x + y + z = 2$
$\{(1, -2, 3)\}$

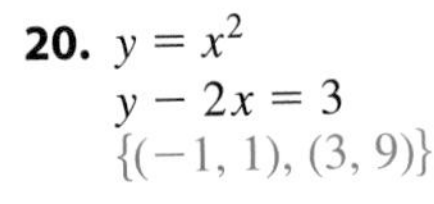

20. $y = x^2$
$y - 2x = 3$
$\{(-1, 1), (3, 9)\}$

Solve each formula for the specified variable.

21. $ax + b = 0$, for x $x = -\dfrac{b}{a}$

22. $wx^2 + dx + m = 0$, for x $x = \dfrac{-d \pm \sqrt{d^2 - 4wm}}{2w}$

23. $A = \dfrac{1}{2}h(B + b)$, for B $B = \dfrac{2A - bh}{h}$

24. $\dfrac{1}{x} + \dfrac{1}{y} = \dfrac{1}{2}$, for x $x = \dfrac{2y}{y - 2}$

25. $L = m + mxt$, for m $m = \dfrac{L}{1 + xt}$

26. $y = 3a\sqrt{t}$, for t $t = \dfrac{y^2}{9a^2}$

Solve each problem.

27. Write the equation of the line in slope-intercept form that goes through the points $(2, -3)$ and $(-4, 1)$. $y = -\frac{2}{3}x - \frac{5}{3}$

28. Write the equation of the line in slope-intercept form that contains the origin and is perpendicular to the line $2x - 4y = 5$. $y = -2x$

29. Write the equation of the circle that has center $(2, 5)$ and passes through the point $(-1, -1)$. $(x - 2)^2 + (y - 5)^2 = 45$

30. Find the center and radius of the circle $x^2 + 3x + y^2 - 6y = 0$. $\left(-\frac{3}{2}, 3\right), \frac{3\sqrt{5}}{2}$

Perform the computations with complex numbers.

31. $2i(3 + 5i)$ $-10 + 6i$

32. i^6 -1

33. $(2i - 3) + (6 - 7i)$ $3 - 5i$

34. $(3 + i\sqrt{2})^2$ $7 + 6i\sqrt{2}$

35. $(2 - 3i)(5 - 6i)$ $-8 - 27i$

36. $(3 - i) + (-6 + 4i)$ $-3 + 3i$

37. $(5 - 2i)(5 + 2i)$ 29

38. $(2 - 3i) \div (2i)$ $-\frac{3}{2} - i$

39. $(4 + 5i) \div (1 - i)$ $-\frac{1}{2} + \frac{9}{2}i$

40. $\frac{4 - \sqrt{-8}}{2}$ $2 - i\sqrt{2}$

Solve.

41. ***Going bananas.*** Salvadore has observed that when bananas are \$0.30 per pound (lb), he sells 250 lb per day, and when bananas are \$0.40 per lb, he sells only 200 lb per day.

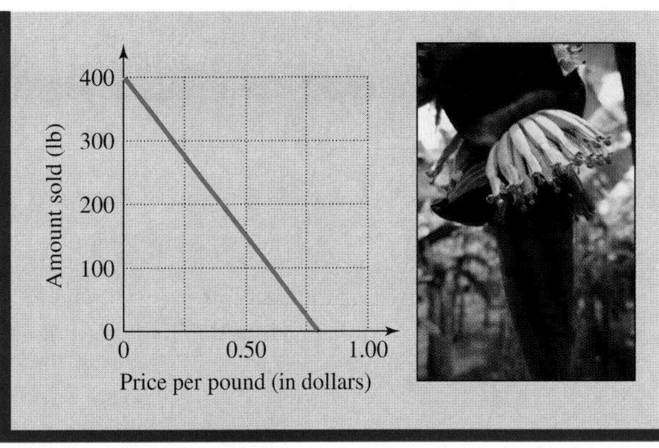

Figure for Exercise 41

a) Assume the number of pounds sold, q, is a linear function of the price per pound, x, and find that function.

b) Salvadore's daily revenue in dollars is the product of the number of pounds sold and the price per pound. Write the revenue as a function of x.

c) Graph the revenue function.

d) What price per pound maximizes his revenue?

e) What is his maximum possible revenue?

a) $q = -500x + 400$
b) $R = -500x^2 + 400x$
c)

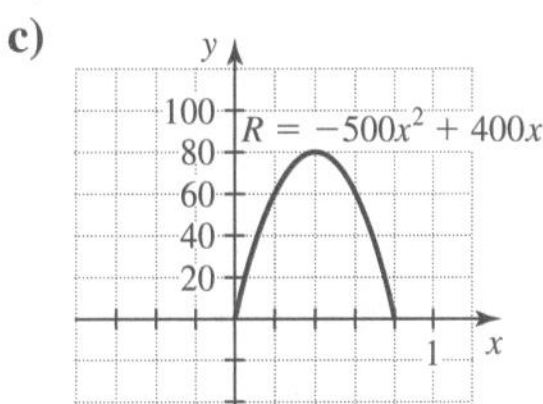

d) \$0.40 per pound
e) \$80

Critical **Thinking** | For Individual or Group Work | Chapter 13

These exercises can be solved by a variety of techniques, which may or may not require algebra. So be creative and think critically. Explain all answers. Answers are in the Instructor's Edition of this text.

1. ***Tiling a floor.*** Red and white floor tiles are used to make the arrangements shown in the accompanying figure. How many red tiles would appear in the 20th figure in this sequence?

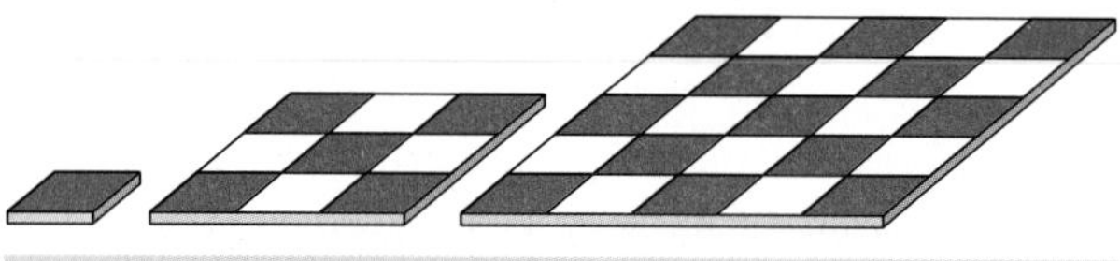

Figure for Exercise 1

2. ***Rolling dice.*** A pair of dice is rolled. What is the most likely difference between the number of dots showing on the top faces?

Photo for Exercise 2

3. ***Jocks, nerds, and turkeys.*** At Ridgemont High there are 30 jocks, 20 nerds, and some turkeys. Every nerd is a turkey. One-half of the jocks are turkeys. One-half of the turkeys are nerds. No jock is a nerd. How many turkeys are there? How many turkeys are neither nerds nor jocks?

4. ***Mind reading.*** A man and a woman are on an airplane chatting about their families. The woman says that she has three children, the age of each child is a counting number, the product of their ages is 72, and the sum of their ages is the same as the flight number. The man checks his ticket for the flight number, does a bit of figuring, and says that he needs more information to determine the ages. The woman then points to the peanuts that they are munching on and says that the oldest is allergic to peanuts. The man then tells the woman the correct ages of her children. What are the ages? Explain your answer.

5. ***Five-letter takeout.*** Take out five letters from the list

   AFLIVGEELEBTRTEARS.

   The remaining letters will form a common English word. What is it?

6. ***Heads and tails.*** A bag contains three coins. One coin has heads on both sides, one has tails on both sides, and one has heads on one side and tails on the other. A single coin accidentally falls onto the floor and you observe heads on that coin, but you cannot see the other side or the other two coins in the bag. What is the probability that the other side of the coin on the floor is heads?

7. ***Adjoining ones.*** Find a positive integer such that adjoining a 1 at both ends of it increases its value by 14,789. (Adjoining a 1 at both ends of 5 would produce 151 and increase its value by 146.)

8. ***Ending digits.*** What are the last two digits (tens and ones) of 3^{1234}?

1. 761 **2.** 1 **3.** 40, 5 **4.** 3, 3, 8 **5.** ALGEBRA **6.** 2/3 **7.** 532 **8.** 6 and 9

Chapter 14

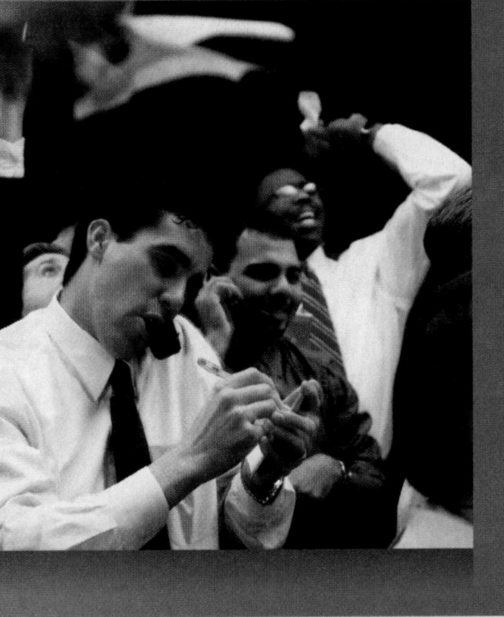

Sequences and Series

Everyone realizes the importance of investing for the future. Some people go to great pains to study the markets and to make wise investment decisions. Some stay away from investing because they do not want to take chances. However, the most important factor in investing is making regular investments (*Money,* www.money.com). According to *Money,* if you had invested \$5000 in the stock market every year at the market high for that year (the worst time to invest) for the last 40 years, your investment would be worth \$2.8 million today.

A sequence of periodic investments earning a fixed rate of interest can be thought of as a geometric sequence. In this chapter you will learn how to find the sum of a geometric sequence and to calculate the future value of a sequence of periodic investments.

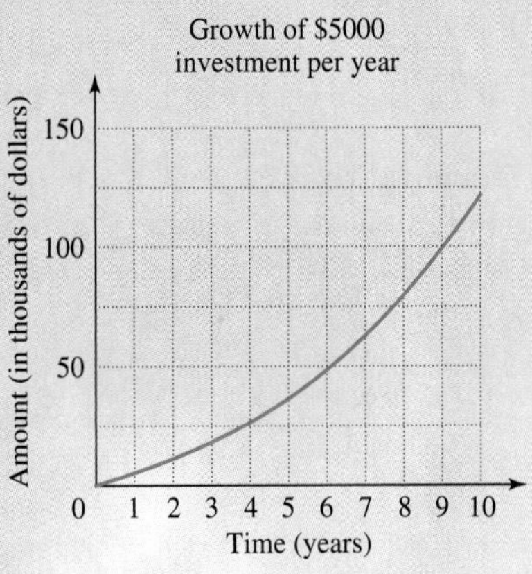

In Exercise 60 of Section 14.4 you will calculate the value of \$5000 invested each year for 10 years in Fidelity's Magellan Fund.

14.1 Sequences

In this Section

- **Definition**
- **Finding a Formula for the *n*th Term**

The word "sequence" is a familiar word. We may speak of a sequence of events or say that something is out of sequence. In this section we give the mathematical definition of a sequence.

Definition

In mathematics we think of a sequence as a list of numbers. Each number in the sequence is called a **term** of the sequence. There is a first term, a second term, a third term, and so on. For example, the daily high temperature readings in Minot, North Dakota, for the first 10 days in January can be thought of as a finite sequence with 10 terms:

$$-9, -2, 8, -11, 0, 6, 14, 1, -5, -11$$

The set of all positive even integers,

$$2, 4, 6, 8, 10, 12, 14, \ldots,$$

can be thought of as an infinite sequence.

To give a precise definition of sequence, we use the terminology of functions. The list of numbers is the range of the function.

Teaching Tip Ask students for any function of one variable and then list the terms of the corresponding sequence.

Sequence

A **finite sequence** is a function whose domain is the set of positive integers less than or equal to some fixed positive integer. An **infinite sequence** is a function whose domain is the set of all positive integers.

When the domain is apparent, we will refer to either a finite sequence or an infinite sequence simply as a sequence. For the independent variable of the function we will usually use n (for natural number) rather than x. For the dependent variable we write a_n (read "a sub n") rather than y. We call a_n the ***n*th term,** or the **general term** of the sequence. Rather than use the $f(x)$ notation for functions, we will define sequences with formulas. When n is used as a variable, we will assume it represents natural numbers only.

EXAMPLE 1

Listing terms of a finite sequence

List all of the terms of each finite sequence.

a) $a_n = n^2$ for $1 \le n \le 5$ **b)** $a_n = \dfrac{1}{n+2}$ for $1 \le n \le 4$

Calculator Close-Up

We can define the sequence with the Y= key and make a list of the terms.

X	Y1	
1	1	
2	4	
3	9	
4	16	
5	25	
6	36	
7	49	

Y1■X²

Solution

a) Using the natural numbers from 1 through 5 in $a_n = n^2$, we get

$$a_1 = 1^2 = 1,$$
$$a_2 = 2^2 = 4,$$
$$a_3 = 3^2 = 9,$$
$$a_4 = 4^2 = 16,$$

and

$$a_5 = 5^2 = 25.$$

The five terms of this sequence are 1, 4, 9, 16, and 25. We often refer to the listing of the terms of the sequence as the sequence.

b) Using the natural numbers from 1 through 4 in $a_n = \frac{1}{n + 2}$, we get the terms

$$a_1 = \frac{1}{1 + 2} = \frac{1}{3},$$

$$a_2 = \frac{1}{2 + 2} = \frac{1}{4},$$

$$a_3 = \frac{1}{5},$$

and

$$a_4 = \frac{1}{6}.$$

The four terms of the sequence are $\frac{1}{3}, \frac{1}{4}, \frac{1}{5}$, and $\frac{1}{6}$.

Now do Exercises 5–18

EXAMPLE 2

Listing terms of an infinite sequence

List the first three terms of the infinite sequence whose nth term is

$$a_n = \frac{(-1)^n}{2^{n+1}}.$$

Solution

Using the natural numbers 1, 2, and 3 in the formula for the nth term yields

$$a_1 = \frac{(-1)^1}{2^{1+1}} = -\frac{1}{4}, \quad a_2 = \frac{(-1)^2}{2^{2+1}} = \frac{1}{8}, \quad \text{and} \quad a_3 = \frac{(-1)^3}{2^{3+1}} = -\frac{1}{16}.$$

We write the sequence as follows:

$$-\frac{1}{4}, \frac{1}{8}, -\frac{1}{16}, \ldots$$

Now do Exercises 19–26

Calculator Close-Up

Some calculators have a sequence feature that allows you to specify the formula and which terms to evaluate. We can even get the terms as fractions.

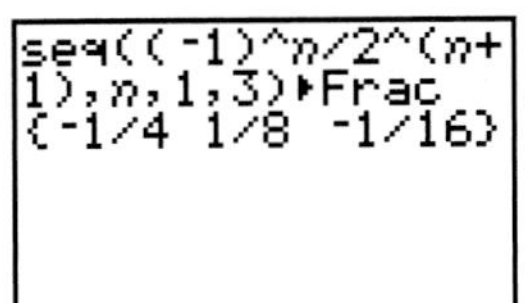

Finding a Formula for the *n*th Term

We often know the terms of a sequence and want to write a formula that will produce those terms. To write a formula for the nth term of a sequence, examine the terms and look for a pattern. Each term is a function of the term number. The first term corresponds to $n = 1$, the second term corresponds to $n = 2$, and so on.

EXAMPLE 3

A familiar sequence

Write the general term for the infinite sequence

$$3, 5, 7, 9, 11, \ldots.$$

Helpful Hint

Finding a formula for a sequence could be extremely difficult. For example, there is no known formula that will produce the sequence of prime numbers:

$$2, 3, 5, 7, 11, 13, 17, 19, \ldots$$

Solution

The even numbers are all multiples of 2 and can be represented as $2n$. Because each odd number is 1 more than an even number, a formula for the nth term might be

$$a_n = 2n + 1.$$

To be sure, we write out a few terms using the formula:

$$a_1 = 2(1) + 1 = 3$$
$$a_2 = 2(2) + 1 = 5$$
$$a_3 = 2(3) + 1 = 7$$

So the general term is $a_n = 2n + 1$.

Now do Exercises 27–28

CAUTION There can be more than one formula that produces the given terms of a sequence. For example, the sequence

$$1, 2, 4, \ldots$$

could have nth term $a_n = 2^{n-1}$ or $a_n = \frac{1}{2}n^2 - \frac{1}{2}n + 1$. The first three terms for both of these sequences are identical, but their fourth terms are different.

EXAMPLE 4

A sequence with alternating signs

Write the general term for the infinite sequence

$$1, -\frac{1}{4}, \frac{1}{9}, -\frac{1}{16}, \ldots.$$

Solution

To obtain the alternating signs, we use powers of -1. Because any even power of -1 is positive and any odd power of -1 is negative, we use $(-1)^{n+1}$. The denominators are the squares of the positive integers. So the nth term of this infinite sequence is given by the formula

$$a_n = \frac{(-1)^{n+1}}{n^2}.$$

Check this sequence by using this formula to find the first four terms.

Now do Exercises 29–40

Math *at Work* Piano Tuning

If middle C on a piano has a frequency of 261 cycles per second or 261 hertz (Hz), then the C note one octave higher is 522 Hz. But what should be the frequencies of the 11 notes in between? On a violin, the frequencies of the notes are selected by the musician as the instrument is played, but with a piano the frequency is selected by the piano tuner.

One method, the Just scale, uses the naturally occurring overtone series for systems such as vibrating strings or air columns. All the notes are related by rational numbers. Because the ratio of the frequencies of successive notes is not constant, the tuning depends on the scale you are using. For example, the tunings for C major and for D major are different.

The equal-tempered scale was developed as a compromise scale for keyboard instruments played in many keys. The equal tempered system uses a constant ratio of $2^{1/12}$. So playing in any key sounds equally good or equally bad, depending on your point of view. The accompanying table shows the ratio of the frequency of each note in the C major scale to middle C and the frequencies of the notes for Just and equal temperament. For this chart middle C was chosen as 261.63 so that A would be 440 Hz in the equal tempered scale. For example, D is $\frac{9}{8} \cdot 261.63$ for the Just scale or $2^{2/12} \cdot 261.63$ for equal temperament. Note that the frequencies of the notes differ by as much as 4 Hz in the two scales. Since a human ear can hear a difference of less than 1 Hz, it is easy to hear the difference between these two scales.

Note	Just Scale Ratio	Equal Temperament Ratio	Just Scale (Hz)	Equal Temperament (Hz)
C	1	1	261.63	261.63
C♯	25/24	$2^{1/12}$	272.54	277.18
D	9/8	$2^{2/12}$	294.33	293.66
E♭	6/5	$2^{3/12}$	313.96	311.13
E	5/4	$2^{4/12}$	327.03	329.63
F	4/3	$2^{5/12}$	348.83	349.23
F♯	45/32	$2^{6/12}$	367.92	369.99
G	3/2	$2^{7/12}$	392.44	392.00
A♭	8/5	$2^{8/12}$	418.60	415.30
A	5/3	$2^{9/12}$	436.05	440.00
B♭	9/5	$2^{10/12}$	470.93	466.16
B	15/8	$2^{11/12}$	490.55	493.88
C	2	2	523.25	523.25

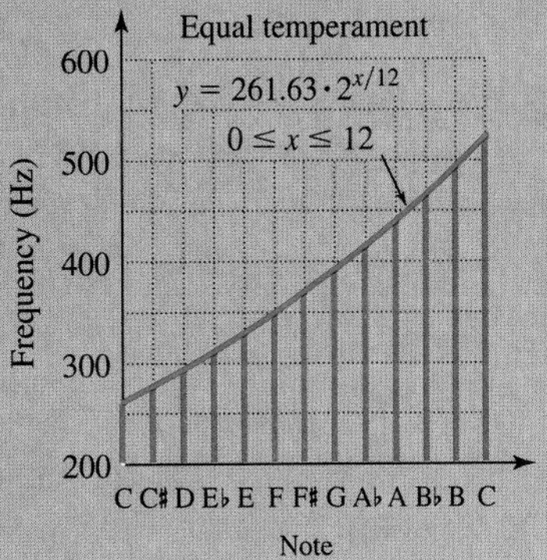

In Example 5 we use a sequence to model a physical situation.

EXAMPLE 5

The bouncing ball

Suppose a ball always rebounds $\frac{2}{3}$ of the height from which it falls and the ball is dropped from a height of 6 feet. Write a sequence whose terms are the heights from which the ball falls. What is a formula for the nth term of this sequence?

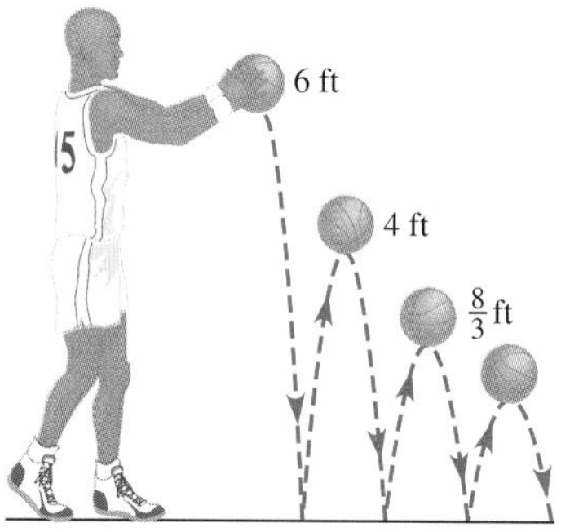

Figure 14.1

Solution

On the first fall the ball travels 6 feet (ft), as shown in Fig. 14.1. On the second fall it travels $\frac{2}{3}$ of 6, or 4 ft. On the third fall it travels $\frac{2}{3}$ of 4, or $\frac{8}{3}$ ft, and so on. We write the sequence as follows:

$$6, 4, \frac{8}{3}, \frac{16}{9}, \frac{32}{27}, \ldots$$

The nth term can be written by using powers of $\frac{2}{3}$:

$$a_n = 6\left(\frac{2}{3}\right)^{n-1}$$

Now do Exercises 41–48

Warm-Ups ▼

True or false? Explain your answer.

1. The nth term of the sequence 2, 4, 6, 8, 10, . . . is $a_n = 2n$. True
2. The nth term of the sequence 1, 3, 5, 7, 9, . . . is $a_n = 2n - 1$. True
3. A sequence is a function. True
4. The domain of a finite sequence is the set of positive integers. False
5. The nth term of $-1, 4, -9, 16, -25, \ldots$ is $a_n = (-1)^{n+1}n^2$. False
6. For the infinite sequence $b_n = \frac{1}{n}$, the independent variable is $\frac{1}{n}$. False
7. For the sequence $c_n = n^3$, the dependent variable is c_n. True
8. The sixth term of the sequence $a_n = (-1)^{n+1}2^n$ is 64. False
9. The symbol a_n is used for the dependent variable of a sequence. True
10. The tenth term of the sequence 2, 4, 8, 16, 32, 64, 128, . . . is 1024. True

14.1 Exercises

Boost your GRADE at mathzone.com!

MathZone

▶ Practice Problems ▶ Net Tutor
▶ Self-Tests ▶ e-Professors
▶ Videos

Reading and Writing *After reading this section, write out the answers to these questions. Use complete sentences.*

1. What is a sequence?
   A sequence is a list of numbers.
2. What is a term of a sequence?
   Each number in the sequence is called a "term" of the sequence.

3. What is a finite sequence?
A finite sequence is a function whose domain is the set of positive integers less than or equal to some fixed positive integer.

4. What is an infinite sequence?
An infinite sequence is a function whose domain is the set of all positive integers.

List all terms of each finite sequence. See Example 1.

5. $a_n = 2n$ for $1 \le n \le 5$ $2, 4, 6, 8, 10$

6. $a_n = 2n - 1$ for $1 \le n \le 4$ $1, 3, 5, 7$

7. $a_n = n^2$ for $1 \le n \le 8$ $1, 4, 9, 16, 25, 36, 49, 64$

8. $a_n = -n^2$ for $1 \le n \le 4$ $-1, -4, -9, -16$

9. $b_n = \frac{(-1)^n}{n}$ for $1 \le n \le 10$
$-1, \frac{1}{2}, -\frac{1}{3}, \frac{1}{4}, -\frac{1}{5}, \frac{1}{6}, -\frac{1}{7}, \frac{1}{8}, -\frac{1}{9}, \frac{1}{10}$

10. $b_n = \frac{(-1)^{n+1}}{n}$ for $1 \le n \le 6$ $1, -\frac{1}{2}, \frac{1}{3}, -\frac{1}{4}, \frac{1}{5}, -\frac{1}{6}$

11. $c_n = (-2)^{n-1}$ for $1 \le n \le 5$ $1, -2, 4, -8, 16$

12. $c_n = (-3)^{n-2}$ for $1 \le n \le 5$ $-\frac{1}{3}, 1, -3, 9, -27$

13. $a_n = 2^{-n}$ for $1 \le n \le 6$ $\frac{1}{2}, \frac{1}{4}, \frac{1}{8}, \frac{1}{16}, \frac{1}{32}, \frac{1}{64}$

14. $a_n = 2^{-n+2}$ for $1 \le n \le 5$ $2, 1, \frac{1}{2}, \frac{1}{4}, \frac{1}{8}$

15. $b_n = 2n - 3$ for $1 \le n \le 7$ $-1, 1, 3, 5, 7, 9, 11$

16. $b_n = 2n + 6$ for $1 \le n \le 7$ $8, 10, 12, 14, 16, 18, 20$

17. $c_n = n^{-1/2}$ for $1 \le n \le 5$ $1, \frac{\sqrt{2}}{2}, \frac{\sqrt{3}}{3}, \frac{1}{2}, \frac{\sqrt{5}}{5}$

18. $c_n = n^{1/2}2^{-n}$ for $1 \le n \le 4$ $\frac{1}{2}, \frac{\sqrt{2}}{4}, \frac{\sqrt{3}}{8}, \frac{1}{8}$

Write the first four terms of the infinite sequence whose nth term is given. See Example 2.

19. $a_n = \frac{1}{n^2 + n}$
$\frac{1}{2}, \frac{1}{6}, \frac{1}{12}, \frac{1}{20}$

20. $b_n = \frac{1}{(n + 1)(n + 2)}$
$\frac{1}{6}, \frac{1}{12}, \frac{1}{20}, \frac{1}{30}$

21. $b_n = \frac{1}{2n - 5}$
$-\frac{1}{3}, -1, 1, \frac{1}{3}$

22. $a_n = \frac{4}{2n + 5}$
$\frac{4}{7}, \frac{4}{9}, \frac{4}{11}, \frac{4}{13}$

23. $c_n = (-1)^n(n - 2)^2$
$-1, 0, -1, 4$

24. $c_n = (-1)^n(2n - 1)^2$
$-1, 9, -25, 49$

25. $a_n = \frac{(-1)^{2n}}{n^2}$
$1, \frac{1}{4}, \frac{1}{9}, \frac{1}{16}$

26. $a_n = (-1)^{2n+1}2^{n-1}$
$-1, -2, -4, -8$

Write a formula for the general term of each infinite sequence. See Examples 3 and 4.

27. $1, 3, 5, 7, 9, \ldots$ $a_n = 2n - 1$

28. $5, 7, 9, 11, 13, \ldots$ $a_n = 2n + 3$

29. $1, -1, 1, -1, \ldots$ $a_n = (-1)^{n+1}$

30. $-1, 1, -1, 1, \ldots$ $a_n = (-1)^n$

31. $0, 2, 4, 6, 8, \ldots$ $a_n = 2n - 2$

32. $4, 6, 8, 10, 12, \ldots$ $a_n = 2n + 2$

33. $3, 6, 9, 12, \ldots$ $a_n = 3n$

34. $4, 8, 12, 16, \ldots$ $a_n = 4n$

35. $4, 7, 10, 13, \ldots$ $a_n = 3n + 1$

36. $3, 7, 11, 15, \ldots$ $a_n = 4n - 1$

37. $-1, 2, -4, 8, -16, \ldots$ $a_n = (-1)^n 2^{n-1}$

38. $1, -3, 9, -27, \ldots$ $a_n = (-3)^{n-1}$

39. $0, 1, 4, 9, 16, \ldots$ $a_n = (n - 1)^2$

40. $0, 1, 8, 27, 64, \ldots$ $a_n = (n - 1)^3$

Solve each problem. See Example 5.

41. ***Football penalties.*** A football is on the 8-yard line, and five penalties in a row are given that move the ball half the distance to the (closest) goal. Write a sequence of five terms that specify the location of the ball after each penalty.
$4, 2, 1, \frac{1}{2}, \frac{1}{4}$ yard line

42. ***Infestation.*** Leona planted 9 acres of soybeans, but by the end of each week, insects had destroyed one-third of the acreage that was healthy at the beginning of the week. How many acres does she have left after 6 weeks?
$\frac{64}{81}$ acre

43. ***Constant rate of increase.*** The MSRP for the 2004 Ford F-250 Lariat 4WD Super Duty Super Cab was \$35,960 (Edmund's New Car Prices, www.edmunds.com). Suppose the price of this truck increases by 5% each year. Find the prices to the nearest dollar for the 2005 through 2010 models.
\$37,758, \$39,646, \$41,628, \$43,710, \$45,895, \$48,190

Figure for Exercise 43

44. ***Constant increase.*** The MSRP for a new 2004 Dodge Viper was \$84,795 (Edmund's New Car Prices, www.edmunds.com). Suppose the price of this car

increases by $1000 each year. Find the prices of the 2005 through 2010 models.
$85,795, $86,795, $87,795, $88,795, $89,795, $90,795

45. ***Economic impact.*** To assess the economic impact of a factory on a community, economists consider the annual amount the factory spends in the community, then the portion of the money that is respent in the community, then the portion of the respent money that is respent in the community, and so on. Suppose a garment manufacturer spends $1 million annually in its community and 80% of all money received in the community is respent in the community. Find the first four terms of the economic impact sequence.
$1,000,000, $800,000, $640,000, $512,000

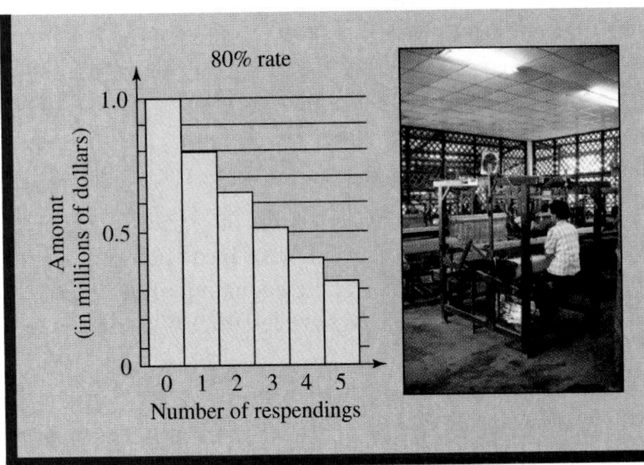

Figure for Exercise 45

46. ***Less impact.*** The rate at which money is respent in a community varies from community to community. Find the first four terms of the economic impact sequence for the manufacturer in Exercise 45, assuming only 50% of money received in the community is respent in the community.
$1,000,000, $500,000, $250,000, $125,000

47. ***Fabric design.*** A fabric designer must take into account the capability of textile machines to produce material with vertical repeats. A textile machine can be set up for a vertical repeat every $\frac{27}{n}$ inches (in.), where n is a natural number. Write the first five terms of the sequence $a_n = \frac{27}{n}$, which gives the possible vertical repeats for a textile machine.
27 in., 13.5 in., 9 in., 6.75 in., 5.4 in.

48. ***Musical tones.*** The note middle C on a piano is tuned so that the string vibrates at 262 cycles per second, or 262 hertz (Hz). The C note one octave higher is tuned to 524 Hz. The tuning for the 11 notes in between using the method called *equal temperament* is determined by the sequence $a_n = 262 \cdot 2^{n/12}$. Find the tuning for the 11 notes in between.
278, 294, 312, 330, 350, 371, 393, 416, 441, 467, 495 Hz.

Getting More Involved

49. ***Discussion***

Everyone has two (biological) parents, four grandparents, eight great-grandparents, 16 great-great-grandparents, and so on. If we put the word "great" in front of the word "grandparents" 35 times, then how many of this type of relative do you have? Is this more or less than the present population of the earth? Give reasons for your answers.
137,438,953,472, larger

50. ***Discussion***

If you deposit 1 cent into your piggy bank on September 1 and each day thereafter deposit twice as much as on the previous day, then how much will you be depositing on September 30? The total amount deposited for the month can be found without adding up all 30 deposits. Look at how the amount on deposit is increasing each day and see whether you can find the total for the month. Give reasons for your answers.
$5,368,709.12, $10,737,418.23

51. ***Cooperative learning***

Working in groups, have someone in each group make up a formula for a_n, the nth term of a sequence, but do not show it to the other group members. Write the terms of the sequence on a piece of paper one at a time. After each term is given, ask whether anyone knows the next term. When the group can correctly give the next term, ask for a formula for the nth term.

52. ***Exploration***

Find a real-life sequence in which all of the terms are the same. Find one in which each term after the first is one larger than the previous term. Find out what the sequence of fines is on your campus for your first, second, third, and fourth parking ticket.

53. ***Exploration***

Consider the sequence whose nth term is $a_n = (0.999)^n$.

a) Calculate a_{100}, a_{1000}, and $a_{10,000}$.
0.9048, 0.3677, 0.00004517

b) What happens to a_n as n gets larger and larger?
a_n goes to zero

14.2 Series

In this Section

- Summation Notation
- Series
- Changing the Index

If you make a sequence of bank deposits, then you might be interested in the total value of the terms of the sequence. Of course, if the sequence has only a few terms, you can simply add them. In Sections 14.3 and 14.4 we will develop formulas that give the sum of the terms for certain finite and infinite sequences. In this section you will first learn a notation for expressing the sum of the terms of a sequence.

Summation Notation

To describe the sum of the terms of a sequence, we use **summation notation.** The Greek letter Σ (sigma) is used to indicate sums. For example, the sum of the first five terms of the sequence $a_n = n^2$ is written as

$$\sum_{n=1}^{5} n^2.$$

You can read this notation as "the sum of n^2 for n between 1 and 5, inclusive." To find the sum, we let n take the values 1 through 5 in the expression n^2:

$$\begin{aligned}\sum_{n=1}^{5} n^2 &= 1^2 + 2^2 + 3^2 + 4^2 + 5^2\\ &= 1 + 4 + 9 + 16 + 25\\ &= 55\end{aligned}$$

In this context the letter n is the **index of summation.** Other letters may also be used. For example, the expressions

$$\sum_{n=1}^{5} n^2, \quad \sum_{j=1}^{5} j^2, \quad \text{and} \quad \sum_{i=1}^{5} i^2$$

all have the same value. Note that i is used as a variable here and not as an imaginary number.

EXAMPLE 1

Evaluating a sum in summation notation

Find the value of the expression

$$\sum_{i=1}^{3} (-1)^i(2i + 1).$$

Teaching Tip Students will confuse sequences and series. They might need to see many examples in class.

Solution

Replace i by 1, 2, and 3, and then add the results:

$$\begin{aligned}\sum_{i=1}^{3} (-1)^i(2i + 1) &= (-1)^1[2(1) + 1] + (-1)^2[2(2) + 1] + (-1)^3[2(3) + 1]\\ &= -3 + 5 - 7\\ &= -5\end{aligned}$$

Now do Exercises 5–18

Series

The sum of the terms of the sequence 1, 4, 9, 16, 25 is written as

$$1 + 4 + 9 + 16 + 25.$$

This expression is called a *series*. It indicates that we are to add the terms of the given sequence. The sum, 55, is the sum of the series.

Series

The indicated sum of the terms of a sequence is called a **series.**

Just as a sequence may be finite or infinite, a series may be finite or infinite. In this section we discuss finite series only. In Section 14.4 we will discuss one type of infinite series.

Summation notation is a convenient notation for writing a series.

EXAMPLE 2

Converting to summation notation

Write the series in summation notation:

$$2 + 4 + 6 + 8 + 10 + 12 + 14$$

Solution

The general term for the sequence of positive even integers is $2n$. If we let n take the values from 1 through 7, then $2n$ ranges from 2 through 14. So

$$2 + 4 + 6 + 8 + 10 + 12 + 14 = \sum_{n=1}^{7} 2n.$$

Now do Exercises 19–20

EXAMPLE 3

Converting to summation notation

Write the series

$$\frac{1}{2} - \frac{1}{3} + \frac{1}{4} - \frac{1}{5} + \frac{1}{6} - \frac{1}{7} + \cdots + \frac{1}{50}$$

in summation notation.

Solution

For this series we let n be 2 through 50. The expression $(-1)^n$ produces alternating signs. The series is written as

$$\sum_{n=2}^{50} \frac{(-1)^n}{n}.$$

Now do Exercises 21–34

Helpful Hint

A series is called an *indicated sum* because the addition is indicated but not actually being performed. The sum of a series is the real number obtained by actually performing the indicated addition.

Changing the Index

In Example 3 we saw the index go from 2 through 50, but this is arbitrary. A series can be written with the index starting at any given number.

EXAMPLE 4

Changing the index

Rewrite the series

$$\sum_{i=1}^{6} \frac{(-1)^i}{i^2}$$

with an index j, where j starts at 0.

Solution

Because i starts at 1 and j starts at 0, we have $i = j + 1$. Because i ranges from 1 through 6 and $i = j + 1$, j must range from 0 through 5. Now replace i by $j + 1$ in the summation notation:

$$\sum_{j=0}^{5} \frac{(-1)^{j+1}}{(j+1)^2}$$

Check that these two series have exactly the same six terms.

Now do Exercises 35–44

Warm-Ups ▼

True or false? Explain your answer.

1. A series is the indicated sum of the terms of a sequence. True
2. The sum of a series can never be negative. False
3. There are eight terms in the series $\sum_{i=2}^{10} i^3$. False
4. The series $\sum_{i=1}^{9} (-1)^i i^2$ and $\sum_{j=0}^{8} (-1)^j (j+1)^2$ have the same sum. False
5. The ninth term of the series $\sum_{i=1}^{100} \frac{(-1)^i}{(i+1)(i+2)}$ is $\frac{1}{110}$. False
6. $\sum_{i=1}^{2} (-1)^i 2^i = 2$ True
7. $\sum_{i=1}^{5} 3i = 3\left(\sum_{i=1}^{5} i\right)$ True
8. $\sum_{i=1}^{5} 4 = 20$ True
9. $\sum_{i=1}^{5} 2i + \sum_{i=1}^{5} 7i = \sum_{i=1}^{5} 9i$ True
10. $\sum_{i=1}^{3} (2i + 1) = \left(\sum_{i=1}^{3} 2i\right) + 1$ False

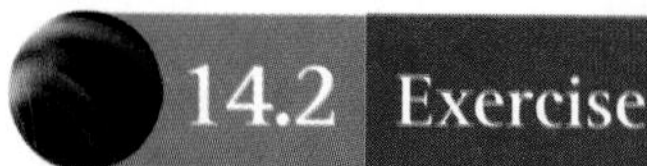

14.2 Exercises

Boost your GRADE at mathzone.com!

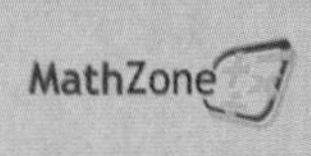

- Practice Problems
- Self-Tests
- Videos
- Net Tutor
- e-Professors

Reading and Writing *After reading this section, write out the answers to these questions. Use complete sentences.*

1. What is summation notation?
Summation notation provides a way to write a sum without writing out all of the terms.

2. What is the index of summation?
The index of summation is the variable used in summation notation.

3. What is a series?
A series is the indicated sum of the terms of a sequence.

4. What is a finite series?
A finite series is the indicated sum of the terms of a finite sequence.

Find the sum of each series. See Example 1.

5. $\sum_{i=1}^{5} i$ 15

6. $\sum_{i=1}^{6} 2i$ 42

7. $\sum_{i=1}^{4} i^2$ 30

8. $\sum_{j=0}^{3} (j+1)^2$ 30

9. $\sum_{j=0}^{5} (2j-1)$ 24

10. $\sum_{i=1}^{6} (2i-3)$ 24

11. $\sum_{i=1}^{5} 2^{-i}$ $\frac{31}{32}$

12. $\sum_{i=1}^{5} (-2)^{-i}$ $-\frac{11}{32}$

13. $\sum_{i=1}^{10} 5i^0$ 50

14. $\sum_{j=1}^{20} 3$ 60

15. $\sum_{i=1}^{3} (i-3)(i+1)$ -7

16. $\sum_{i=0}^{5} i(i-1)(i-2)(i-3)$ 144

17. $\sum_{j=1}^{10} (-1)^j$ 0

18. $\sum_{j=1}^{11} (-1)^j$ -1

Write each series in summation notation. Use the index i, and let i begin at 1 in each summation. See Examples 2 and 3.

19. $1 + 2 + 3 + 4 + 5 + 6$ $\sum_{i=1}^{6} i$

20. $2 + 4 + 6 + 8 + 10$ $\sum_{i=1}^{5} 2i$

21. $-1 + 3 - 5 + 7 - 9 + 11$ $\sum_{i=1}^{6} (-1)^i(2i-1)$

22. $1 - 3 + 5 - 7 + 9$ $\sum_{i=1}^{5} (-1)^{i+1}(2i-1)$

23. $1 + 4 + 9 + 16 + 25 + 36$ $\sum_{i=1}^{6} i^2$

24. $1 + 8 + 27 + 64 + 125$ $\sum_{i=1}^{5} i^3$

25. $\frac{1}{3} + \frac{1}{4} + \frac{1}{5} + \frac{1}{6}$ $\sum_{i=1}^{4} \frac{1}{2+i}$

26. $1 - \frac{1}{2} + \frac{1}{3} - \frac{1}{4} + \frac{1}{5} - \frac{1}{6}$ $\sum_{i=1}^{6} \frac{(-1)^{i+1}}{i}$

27. $\ln(2) + \ln(3) + \ln(4)$ $\sum_{i=1}^{3} \ln(i+1)$

28. $e^1 + e^2 + e^3 + e^4$ $\sum_{i=1}^{4} e^i$

29. $a_1 + a_2 + a_3 + a_4$ $\sum_{i=1}^{4} a_i$

30. $a^2 + a^3 + a^4 + a^5$ $\sum_{i=1}^{4} a^{i+1}$

31. $x_3 + x_4 + x_5 + \cdots + x_{50}$ $\sum_{i=1}^{48} x_{i+2}$

32. $y_1 + y_2 + y_3 + \cdots + y_{30}$ $\sum_{i=1}^{30} y_i$

33. $w_1 + w_2 + w_3 + \cdots + w_n$ $\sum_{i=1}^{n} w_i$

34. $m_1 + m_2 + m_3 + \cdots + m_k$ $\sum_{i=1}^{k} m_i$

Complete the rewriting of each series using the new index as indicated. See Example 4.

35. $\sum_{i=1}^{5} i^2 = \sum_{j=0}$
$\sum_{j=0}^{4} (j+1)^2$

36. $\sum_{i=1}^{6} i^3 = \sum_{j=0}$
$\sum_{j=0}^{5} (j+1)^3$

37. $\sum_{i=0}^{12} (2i-1) = \sum_{j=1}$
$\sum_{j=1}^{13} (2j-3)$

38. $\sum_{i=1}^{3} (3i+2) = \sum_{j=0}$
$\sum_{j=0}^{2} (3j+5)$

39. $\sum_{i=4}^{8} \frac{1}{i} = \sum_{j=1}$
$\sum_{j=1}^{5} \frac{1}{j+3}$

40. $\sum_{i=5}^{10} 2^{-i} = \sum_{j=1}$
$\sum_{j=1}^{6} 2^{-j-4}$

41. $\sum_{i=1}^{4} x^{2i+3} = \sum_{j=0}$
$\sum_{j=0}^{3} x^{2j+5}$

42. $\sum_{i=0}^{2} x^{3-2i} = \sum_{j=1}$
$\sum_{j=1}^{3} x^{5-2j}$

43. $\sum_{i=1}^{n} x^{i} = \sum_{j=0}$
$\sum_{j=0}^{n-1} x^{j+1}$

44. $\sum_{i=0}^{n} x^{-i} = \sum_{j=1}$
$\sum_{j=1}^{n+1} x^{-j+1}$

Write out the terms of each series.

45. $\sum_{i=1}^{6} x^{i}$ $x + x^2 + x^3 + x^4 + x^5 + x^6$

46. $\sum_{i=1}^{5} (-1)^{i} x^{i-1}$ $-1 + x - x^2 + x^3 - x^4$

47. $\sum_{j=0}^{3} (-1)^{j} x_j$ $x_0 - x_1 + x_2 - x_3$

48. $\sum_{j=1}^{5} \frac{1}{x_j}$ $\frac{1}{x_1} + \frac{1}{x_2} + \frac{1}{x_3} + \frac{1}{x_4} + \frac{1}{x_5}$

49. $\sum_{i=1}^{3} ix^{i}$ $x + 2x^2 + 3x^3$

50. $\sum_{i=1}^{5} \frac{x}{i}$ $x + \frac{x}{2} + \frac{x}{3} + \frac{x}{4} + \frac{x}{5}$

A series can be used to model the situation in each of the following problems.

51. ***Leap frog.*** A frog with a vision problem is 1 yard away from a dead cricket. He spots the cricket and jumps halfway to the cricket. After the frog realizes that he has not reached the cricket, he again jumps halfway to the cricket. Write a series in summation notation to describe how far the frog has moved after nine such jumps.
$\sum_{i=1}^{9} 2^{-i}$

52. ***Compound interest.*** Cleo deposited \$1000 at the beginning of each year for 5 years into an account paying 10% interest compounded annually. Write a series using summation notation to describe how much she has in the account at the end of the fifth year. Note that the first \$1000 will receive interest for 5 years, the second \$1000 will receive interest for 4 years, and so on.
$\sum_{i=1}^{5} 1000(1.1)^{i}$

53. ***Total economic impact.*** In Exercise 45 of Section 14.1 we described a factory that spends \$1 million annually in a community in which 80% of all money received in the community is respent in the community. Use summation notation to write the sum of the first four terms of the economic impact sequence for the factory.
$\sum_{i=1}^{4} 1{,}000{,}000(0.8)^{i-1}$

54. ***Total earnings.*** Suppose you earn \$1 on January 1, \$2 on January 2, \$3 on January 3, and so on. Use summation notation to write the sum of your earnings for the entire month of January.
$\sum_{i=1}^{31} i$

Getting More Involved

55. ***Discussion***

What is the difference between a sequence and a series?
A sequence is basically a list of numbers. A series is the indicated sum of the terms of a sequence.

56. ***Discussion***

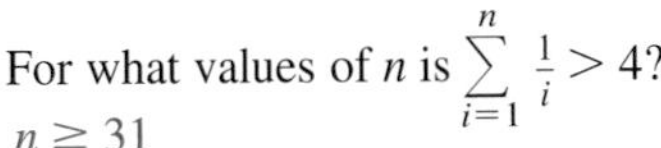

For what values of n is $\sum_{i=1}^{n} \frac{1}{i} > 4$?
$n \geq 31$

14.3 Arithmetic Sequences and Series

In this Section

- Arithmetic Sequences
- Arithmetic Series

We defined sequences and series in Sections 14.1 and 14.2. In this section you will study a special type of sequence known as an arithmetic sequence. You will also study the series corresponding to this sequence.

Arithmetic Sequences

Consider the following sequence:

$$5, 9, 13, 17, 21, \ldots$$

Helpful Hint

Arithmetic used as an adjective (ar-ith-met'-ic) is pronounced differently from arithmetic used as a noun (a-rith'-me-tic). Arithmetic (the adjective) is accented similarly to geometric.

This sequence is called an arithmetic sequence because of the pattern for the terms. Each term is 4 larger than the previous term.

Arithmetic Sequence

A sequence in which each term after the first is obtained by adding a fixed amount to the previous term is called an **arithmetic sequence.**

The fixed amount is called the **common difference** and is denoted by the letter d. If a_1 is the first term, then the second term is $a_1 + d$. The third term is $a_1 + 2d$, the fourth term is $a_1 + 3d$, and so on.

Formula for the *n*th Term of an Arithmetic Sequence

The nth term, a_n, of an arithmetic sequence with first term a_1 and common difference d is

$$a_n = a_1 + (n - 1)d.$$

EXAMPLE 1

The *n*th term of an arithmetic sequence

Write a formula for the nth term of the arithmetic sequence

$$5, 9, 13, 17, 21, \ldots.$$

Solution

Each term of the sequence after the first is 4 more than the previous term. Because the common difference is 4 and the first term is 5, the nth term is given by

$$a_n = 5 + (n - 1)4.$$

We can simplify this expression to get

$$a_n = 4n + 1.$$

Check a few terms: $a_1 = 4(1) + 1 = 5$, $a_2 = 4(2) + 1 = 9$, and $a_3 = 4(3) + 1 = 13$.

Now do Exercises 5–12

Teaching Tip Point out that the formula for an arithmetic sequence is simply a linear function. The constant difference is the slope.

In the next example the common difference is negative.

EXAMPLE 2

An arithmetic sequence of decreasing terms

Write a formula for the nth term of the arithmetic sequence

$$4, 1, -2, -5, -8, \ldots.$$

Solution

Each term is 3 less than the previous term, so $d = -3$. Because $a_1 = 4$, we can write the nth term as

$$a_n = 4 + (n - 1)(-3),$$

or

$$a_n = -3n + 7.$$

Check a few terms: $a_1 = -3(1) + 7 = 4$, $a_2 = -3(2) + 7 = 1$, and $a_3 = -3(3) + 7 = -2$.

Now do Exercises 13–20

In Example 3 we find some terms of an arithmetic sequence using a given formula for the nth term.

EXAMPLE 3

Writing terms of an arithmetic sequence

Write the first five terms of the sequence in which $a_n = 3 + (n - 1)6$.

Solution

Let n take the values from 1 through 5, and find a_n:

$$a_1 = 3 + (1 - 1)6 = 3$$
$$a_2 = 3 + (2 - 1)6 = 9$$
$$a_3 = 3 + (3 - 1)6 = 15$$
$$a_4 = 3 + (4 - 1)6 = 21$$
$$a_5 = 3 + (5 - 1)6 = 27$$

Notice that $a_n = 3 + (n - 1)6$ gives the general term for an arithmetic sequence with first term 3 and common difference 6. Because each term after the first is 6 more than the previous term, the first five terms that we found are correct.

Now do Exercises 21–34

The formula $a_n = a_1 + (n - 1)d$ involves four variables: a_1, a_n, n, and d. If we know the values of any three of these variables, we can find the fourth.

EXAMPLE 4

Finding a missing term of an arithmetic sequence

Find the twelfth term of the arithmetic sequence whose first term is 2 and whose fifth term is 14.

Solution

Before finding the twelfth term, we use the given information to find the missing common difference. Let $n = 5$, $a_1 = 2$, and $a_5 = 14$ in the formula $a_n = a_1 + (n - 1)d$ to find d:

$$14 = 2 + (5 - 1)d$$
$$14 = 2 + 4d$$
$$12 = 4d$$
$$3 = d$$

Now use $a_1 = 2$, $d = 3$ and $n = 12$ in $a_n = a_1 + (n - 1)d$ to find a_{12}:

$$a_{12} = 2 + (12 - 1)3$$
$$a_{12} = 35$$

Now do Exercises 35–42

Study Tip

Stay alert for the entire class period. The first 20 minutes are the easiest and the last 20 minutes are the hardest. Some students put down their pencils, fold up their notebooks, and daydream for those last 20 minutes. Don't give in. Recognize when you are losing it and force yourself to stay alert. Think of how much time you will have to spend outside of class figuring out what happened during those last 20 minutes.

Arithmetic Series

The indicated sum of an arithmetic sequence is called an **arithmetic series.** For example, the series

$$2 + 4 + 6 + 8 + 10 + \cdots + 54$$

is an arithmetic series because there is a common difference of 2 between the terms.

We can find the actual sum of this arithmetic series without adding all of the terms. Write the series in increasing order, and below that write the series in decreasing order. We then add the corresponding terms:

$$\begin{aligned} S &= 2 + 4 + 6 + 8 + \cdots + 52 + 54 \\ S &= 54 + 52 + 50 + 48 + \cdots + 4 + 2 \\ \hline 2S &= 56 + 56 + 56 + 56 + \cdots + 56 + 56 \end{aligned}$$

Now, how many times does 56 appear in the sum on the right? Because

$$2 + 4 + 6 + \cdots + 54 = 2 \cdot 1 + 2 \cdot 2 + 2 \cdot 3 + \cdots + 2 \cdot 27,$$

there are 27 terms in this sum. Because 56 appears 27 times on the right, we have $2S = 27 \cdot 56$, or

$$S = \frac{27 \cdot 56}{2} = 27 \cdot 28 = 756.$$

If $S_n = a_1 + a_2 + a_3 + \cdots + a_n$ is any arithmetic series, then we can find its sum using the same technique. Rewrite S_n as follows:

$$\begin{aligned} S_n &= a_1 + (a_1 + d) + (a_1 + 2d) + \cdots + a_n \\ S_n &= a_n + (a_n - d) + (a_n - 2d) + \cdots + a_1 \\ \hline 2S_n &= (a_1 + a_n) + (a_1 + a_n) + (a_1 + a_n) + \cdots + (a_1 + a_n) \quad \text{Add.} \end{aligned}$$

Because $(a_1 + a_n)$ appears n times on the right, we have $2S_n = n(a_1 + a_n)$. Divide each side by 2 to get the following formula.

Sum of an Arithmetic Series

The sum, S_n, of the first n terms of an arithmetic series with first term a_1 and nth term a_n, is given by

$$S_n = \frac{n}{2}(a_1 + a_n).$$

EXAMPLE 5

The sum of an arithmetic series

Find the sum of the positive integers from 1 to 100 inclusive.

Solution

The described series, $1 + 2 + 3 + \cdots + 100$, has 100 terms. So we can use $n = 100$, $a_1 = 1$, and $a_n = 100$ in the formula for the sum of an arithmetic series:

$$\begin{aligned} S_n &= \frac{n}{2}(a_1 + a_n) \\ S_{100} &= \frac{100}{2}(1 + 100) \\ &= 50(101) = 5050 \end{aligned}$$

Now do Exercises 43–44

Helpful Hint

Legend has it that Carl F. Gauss knew this formula when he was in grade school. Gauss's teacher told him to add up the numbers from 1 through 100 for busy work. He immediately answered 5050.

EXAMPLE 6

The sum of an arithmetic series

Find the sum of the series

$$12 + 16 + 20 + \cdots + 84.$$

Solution

This series is an arithmetic series with $a_n = 84$, $a_1 = 12$, and $d = 4$. To get the number of terms, n, we use $a_n = a_1 + (n - 1)d$:

$$84 = 12 + (n - 1)4$$
$$84 = 8 + 4n$$
$$76 = 4n$$
$$19 = n$$

Now find the sum of these 19 terms:

$$S_{19} = \frac{19}{2}(12 + 84) = 912$$

Now do Exercises 45–56

Warm-Ups ▼

True or false? Explain your answer.

1. The arithmetic sequence $3, 1, -1, -3, -5, \ldots$ has common difference 2. False
2. The sequence $2, 5, 9, 14, 20, 27, \ldots$ is an arithmetic sequence. False
3. The sequence $2, 4, 2, 0, 2, 4, 2, 0, \ldots$ is an arithmetic sequence. False
4. The nth term of an arithmetic sequence with first term a_1 and common difference d is given by the formula $a_n = a_1 + nd$. False
5. If $a_1 = 5$ and $a_3 = 10$ in an arithmetic sequence, then $a_4 = 15$. False
6. If $a_1 = 6$ and $a_3 = 2$ in an arithmetic sequence, then $a_2 = 10$. False
7. An arithmetic series is the indicated sum of an arithmetic sequence. True
8. The series $\sum_{i=1}^{5}(3 + 2i)$ is an arithmetic series. True
9. The sum of the first n counting numbers is $\frac{n(n + 1)}{2}$. True
10. The sum of the even integers from 8 through 28 inclusive is $5(8 + 28)$. False

14.3 Exercises

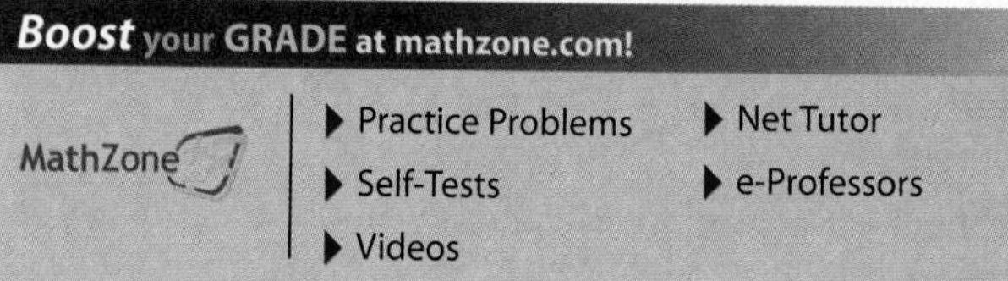

Reading and Writing *After reading this section, write out the answers to these questions. Use complete sentences.*

1. What is an arithmetic sequence?
An arithmetic sequence is one in which each term after the first is obtained by adding a fixed amount to the previous term.

2. What is the nth term of an arithmetic sequence?
The nth term of an arithmetic sequence is $a_1 + (n - 1)d$, where a_1 is the first term.

3. What is an arithmetic series?
An arithmetic series is an indicated sum of an arithmetic sequence.

4. What is the formula for the sum of the first n terms of an arithmetic series?
The formula for the sum of the first n terms of an arithmetic series is $\frac{n}{2}(a_1 + a_n)$.

Write a formula for the nth term of each arithmetic sequence. See Examples 1 and 2.

5. $2, 4, 6, 8, 10, \ldots$ $a_n = 2n$
6. $1, 3, 5, 7, 9, \ldots$ $a_n = 2n - 1$
7. $0, 6, 12, 18, 24, \ldots$ $a_n = 6n - 6$
8. $0, 5, 10, 15, 20, \ldots$ $a_n = 5n - 5$
9. $7, 12, 17, 22, 27, \ldots$ $a_n = 5n + 2$
10. $4, 15, 26, 37, 48, \ldots$ $a_n = 11n - 7$
11. $-4, -2, 0, 2, 4, \ldots$ $a_n = 2n - 6$
12. $-3, 0, 3, 6, 9, \ldots$ $a_n = 3n - 6$
13. $5, 1, -3, -7, -11, \ldots$ $a_n = -4n + 9$
14. $8, 5, 2, -1, -4, \ldots$ $a_n = -3n + 11$
15. $-2, -9, -16, -23, \ldots$ $a_n = -7n + 5$
16. $-5, -7, -9, -11, -13, \ldots$ $a_n = -2n - 3$
17. $-3, -2.5, -2, -1.5, -1, \ldots$ $a_n = 0.5n - 3.5$
18. $-2, -1.25, -0.5, 0.25, \ldots$ $a_n = 0.75n - 2.75$
19. $-6, -6.5, -7, -7.5, -8, \ldots$ $a_n = -0.5n - 5.5$
20. $1, 0.5, 0, -0.5, -1, \ldots$ $a_n = -0.5n + 1.5$

Write the first five terms of the arithmetic sequence whose nth term is given. See Example 3.

21. $a_n = 9 + (n - 1)4$ 9, 13, 17, 21, 25
22. $a_n = 13 + (n - 1)6$ 13, 19, 25, 31, 37
23. $a_n = 7 + (n - 1)(-2)$ 7, 5, 3, 1, −1
24. $a_n = 6 + (n - 1)(-3)$ 6, 3, 0, −3, −6
25. $a_n = -4 + (n - 1)3$ −4, −1, 2, 5, 8
26. $a_n = -19 + (n - 1)12$ −19, −7, 5, 17, 29
27. $a_n = -2 + (n - 1)(-3)$ −2, −5, −8, −11, −14
28. $a_n = -1 + (n - 1)(-2)$ −1, −3, −5, −7, −9
29. $a_n = -4n - 3$ −7, −11, −15, −19, −23
30. $a_n = -3n + 1$ −2, −5, −8, −11, −14
31. $a_n = 0.5n + 4$ 4.5, 5, 5.5, 6, 6.5
32. $a_n = 0.3n + 1$ 1.3, 1.6, 1.9, 2.2, 2.5
33. $a_n = 20n + 1000$ 1020, 1040, 1060, 1080, 1100
34. $a_n = -600n + 4000$ 3400, 2800, 2200, 1600, 1000

Find the indicated part of each arithmetic sequence. See Example 4.

35. Find the eighth term of the sequence that has a first term of 9 and a common difference of 6. 51

36. Find the twelfth term of the sequence that has a first term of −2 and a common difference of −3. −35

37. Find the common difference if the first term is 6 and the twentieth term is 82. 4

38. Find the common difference if the first term is −8 and the ninth term is −64. −7

39. If the common difference is −2 and the seventh term is 14, then what is the first term? 26

40. If the common difference is 5 and the twelfth term is −7, then what is the first term? −62

41. Find the sixth term of the sequence that has a fifth term of 13 and a first term of −3. 17

42. Find the eighth term of the sequence that has a sixth term of −42 and a first term of 3. −60

Find the sum of each given series. See Examples 5 and 6.

43. $1 + 2 + 3 + \cdots + 48$ 1176
44. $1 + 2 + 3 + \cdots + 12$ 78
45. $8 + 10 + 12 + \cdots + 36$ 330
46. $9 + 12 + 15 + \cdots + 72$ 891
47. $-1 + (-7) + (-13) + \cdots + (-73)$ −481
48. $-7 + (-12) + (-17) + \cdots + (-72)$ −553
49. $-6 + (-1) + 4 + 9 + \cdots + 64$ 435
50. $-9 + (-1) + 7 + \cdots + 103$ 705
51. $20 + 12 + 4 + (-4) + \cdots + (-92)$ −540
52. $19 + 1 + (-17) + \cdots + (-125)$ −477

53. $\sum_{i=1}^{12} (3i - 7)$ 150
54. $\sum_{i=1}^{7} (-4i + 6)$ −70
55. $\sum_{i=1}^{11} (-5i + 2)$ −308
56. $\sum_{i=1}^{19} (3i - 5)$ 475

Solve each problem using the ideas of arithmetic sequences and series.

57. ***Increasing salary.*** If a lab technician has a salary of \$22,000 her first year and is due to get a \$500 raise each year, then what will her salary be in her seventh year? \$25,000

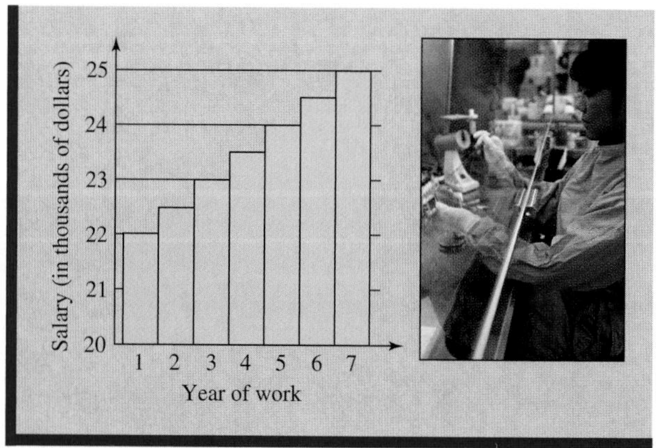

Figure for Exercise 57

58. ***Seven years of salary.*** What is the total salary for 7 years of work for the lab technician of Exercise 57? $164,500

59. ***Light reading.*** On the first day of October an English teacher suggests to his students that they read five pages of a novel and every day thereafter increase their daily reading by two pages. If his students follow this suggestion, then how many pages will they read during October? 1085

60. ***Heavy penalties.*** If an air-conditioning system is not completed by the agreed upon date, the contractor pays a penalty of $500 for the first day that it is overdue, $600 for the second day, $700 for the third day, and so on. If the system is completed 10 days late, then what is the total amount of the penalties that the contractor must pay? $9500

Getting More Involved

61. ***Discussion***

Which of the following sequences is not an arithmetic sequence? Explain your answer. b

a) $\frac{1}{2}, 1, \frac{3}{2}, \ldots$

b) $\frac{1}{2}, \frac{1}{3}, \frac{1}{4}, \ldots$

c) $5, 0, -5, \ldots$

d) $2, 3, 4, \ldots$

62. ***Discussion***

What is the smallest value of n for which $\sum_{i=1}^{n} \frac{i}{2} > 50$? 14

14.4 Geometric Sequences and Series

In this Section

- **Geometric Sequences**
- **Finite Geometric Series**
- **Infinite Geometric Series**
- **Annuities**

In Section 14.3 you studied the arithmetic sequences and series. In this section you will study sequences in which each term is a *multiple* of the term preceding it. You will also learn how to find the sum of the corresponding series.

Geometric Sequences

In an arithmetic sequence such as 2, 4, 6, 8, 10, . . . there is a common difference between consecutive terms. In a geometric sequence there is a common ratio between consecutive terms. The following table contains several geometric sequences and the common ratios between consecutive terms.

Geometric Sequence	Common Ratio
$3, 6, 12, 24, 48, \ldots$	2
$27, 9, 3, 1, \frac{1}{3}, \ldots$	$\frac{1}{3}$
$1, -10, 100, -1000, \ldots$	-10

Note that every term after the first term of each geometric sequence can be obtained by multiplying the previous term by the common ratio.

Geometric Sequence

A sequence in which each term after the first is obtained by multiplying the preceding term by a constant is called a **geometric sequence.**

The constant is denoted by the letter r and is called the **common ratio.** If a_1 is the first term, then the second term is a_1r. The third term is a_1r^2, the fourth term is a_1r^3, and so on. We can write a formula for the nth term of a geometric sequence by following this pattern.

Teaching Tip Point out that the formula for a geometric sequence is an exponential function, but in a sequence the base can be negative.

Formula for the *n*th Term of a Geometric Sequence

The nth term, a_n, of a geometric sequence with first term a_1 and common ratio r is

$$a_n = a_1 r^{n-1}.$$

The first term and the common ratio determine all of the terms of a geometric sequence.

EXAMPLE 1

Finding the *n*th term

Write a formula for the nth term of the geometric sequence

$$6, 2, \frac{2}{3}, \frac{2}{9}, \ldots.$$

Solution

We can obtain the common ratio by dividing any term after the first by the term preceding it. So

$$r = 2 \div 6 = \frac{1}{3}.$$

Because each term after the first is $\frac{1}{3}$ of the term preceding it, the nth term is given by

$$a_n = 6\left(\frac{1}{3}\right)^{n-1}.$$

Check a few terms: $a_1 = 6\left(\frac{1}{3}\right)^{1-1} = 6$, $a_2 = 6\left(\frac{1}{3}\right)^{2-1} = 2$, and $a_3 = 6\left(\frac{1}{3}\right)^{3-1} = \frac{2}{3}$.

Now do Exercises 7–12

EXAMPLE 2

Finding the *n*th term

Find a formula for the nth term of the geometric sequence

$$2, -1, \frac{1}{2}, -\frac{1}{4}, \ldots.$$

Solution

We obtain the ratio by dividing a term by the term preceding it:

$$r = -1 \div 2 = -\frac{1}{2}$$

Each term after the first is obtained by multiplying the preceding term by $-\frac{1}{2}$. The formula for the nth term is

$$a_n = 2\left(-\frac{1}{2}\right)^{n-1}.$$

Check a few terms: $a_1 = 2\left(-\frac{1}{2}\right)^{1-1} = 2$, $a_2 = 2\left(-\frac{1}{2}\right)^{2-1} = -1$, and $a_3 = 2\left(-\frac{1}{2}\right)^{3-1} = \frac{1}{2}$.

Now do Exercises 13–18

In Example 3 we use the formula for the nth term to write some terms of a geometric sequence.

EXAMPLE 3

Writing the terms

Write the first five terms of the geometric sequence whose nth term is

$$a_n = 3(-2)^{n-1}.$$

Solution

Let n take the values 1 through 5 in the formula for the nth term:

$$a_1 = 3(-2)^{1-1} = 3$$
$$a_2 = 3(-2)^{2-1} = -6$$
$$a_3 = 3(-2)^{3-1} = 12$$
$$a_4 = 3(-2)^{4-1} = -24$$
$$a_5 = 3(-2)^{5-1} = 48$$

Notice that $a_n = 3(-2)^{n-1}$ gives the general term for a geometric sequence with first term 3 and common ratio -2. Because every term after the first can be obtained by multiplying the previous term by -2, the terms 3, -6, 12, -24, and 48 are correct.

Now do Exercises 19–26

The formula for the nth term involves four variables: a_n, a_1, r, and n. If we know the value of any three of them, we can find the value of the fourth.

EXAMPLE 4

Finding a missing term

Find the first term of a geometric sequence whose fourth term is 8 and whose common ratio is $\frac{1}{2}$.

Solution

Let $a_4 = 8$, $r = \frac{1}{2}$, and $n = 4$ in the formula $a_n = a_1r^{n-1}$:

$$8 = a_1\left(\frac{1}{2}\right)^{4-1}$$
$$8 = a_1 \cdot \frac{1}{8}$$
$$64 = a_1$$

So the first term is 64.

Now do Exercises 27–32

Study Tip

Many schools have study skills centers that offer courses, workshops, and individual help on how to study. A search for "study skills" on the World Wide Web will turn up more information than you could possibly read. If you are not having the success in school that you would like, do something about it. What you do now will affect you the rest of your life.

Finite Geometric Series

Consider the following series:

$$1 + 2 + 4 + 8 + 16 + \cdots + 512$$

The terms of this series are the terms of a finite geometric sequence. The indicated sum of a geometric sequence is called a **geometric series.**

We can find the actual sum of this finite geometric series by using a technique similar to the one used for the sum of an arithmetic series. Let

$$S = 1 + 2 + 4 + 8 + \cdots + 256 + 512.$$

Because the common ratio is 2, multiply each side by -2:

$$-2S = -2 - 4 - 8 - \cdots - 512 - 1024$$

Adding the last two equations eliminates all but two of the terms on the right:

$$\begin{aligned} S &= 1 + 2 + 4 + 8 + \cdots + 256 + 512 \\ -2S &= \quad -2 - 4 - 8 - \cdots \qquad - 512 - 1024 \\ \hline -S &= 1 \qquad\qquad\qquad\qquad\qquad - 1024 && \text{Add.} \\ -S &= -1023 \\ S &= 1023 \end{aligned}$$

If $S_n = a_1 + a_1r + a_1r^2 + \cdots + a_1r^{n-1}$ is any geometric series, we can find the sum in the same manner. Multiplying each side of this equation by $-r$ yields

$$-rS_n = -a_1r - a_1r^2 - a_1r^3 - \cdots - a_1r^n.$$

If we add S_n and $-rS_n$, all but two of the terms on the right are eliminated:

Teaching Tip Note the similarities between the proofs for the sum of a geometric series and the sum of an arithmetic series.

$$\begin{aligned} S_n &= a_1 + a_1r + a_1r^2 + \cdots \qquad + a_1r^{n-1} \\ -rS_n &= \quad - a_1r - a_1r^2 - a_1r^3 - \cdots \qquad - a_1r^n \\ \hline S_n - rS_n &= a_1 \qquad\qquad\qquad\qquad - a_1r^n && \text{Add.} \\ (1 - r)S_n &= a_1(1 - r^n) && \text{Factor out common factors.} \end{aligned}$$

Now divide each side of this equation by $1 - r$ to get the formula for S_n.

Sum of *n* Terms of a Geometric Series

If S_n represents the sum of the first n terms of a geometric series with first term a_1 and common ratio r $(r \neq 1)$, then

$$S_n = \frac{a_1(1 - r^n)}{1 - r}.$$

EXAMPLE 5

The sum of a finite geometric series

Find the sum of the series

$$\frac{1}{3} + \frac{1}{9} + \frac{1}{27} + \cdots + \frac{1}{729}.$$

Solution

The first term is $\frac{1}{3}$, and the common ratio is $\frac{1}{3}$. So the nth term can be written as

$$a_n = \frac{1}{3}\left(\frac{1}{3}\right)^{n-1}.$$

We can use this formula to find the number of terms in the series:

$$\frac{1}{729} = \frac{1}{3}\left(\frac{1}{3}\right)^{n-1}$$

$$\frac{1}{729} = \left(\frac{1}{3}\right)^{n}$$

Because $3^6 = 729$, we have $n = 6$. (Of course, you could use logarithms to solve for n.) Now use the formula for the sum of six terms of this geometric series:

$$S_6 = \frac{\frac{1}{3}\left[1 - \left(\frac{1}{3}\right)^6\right]}{1 - \frac{1}{3}} = \frac{\frac{1}{3}\left[1 - \frac{1}{729}\right]}{\frac{2}{3}}$$

$$= \frac{1}{3} \cdot \frac{728}{729} \cdot \frac{3}{2}$$

$$= \frac{364}{729}$$

Now do Exercises 33–38

EXAMPLE 6

The sum of a finite geometric series

Find the sum of the series

$$\sum_{i=1}^{12} 3(-2)^{i-1}.$$

Solution

This series is geometric with first term 3, ratio -2, and $n = 12$. We use the formula for the sum of the first 12 terms of a geometric series:

$$S_{12} = \frac{3[1 - (-2)^{12}]}{1 - (-2)} = \frac{3[-4095]}{3} = -4095$$

Now do Exercises 39–44

Infinite Geometric Series

Consider how a very large value of n affects the formula for the sum of a finite geometric series,

$$S_n = \frac{a_1(1 - r^n)}{1 - r}.$$

If $|r| < 1$, then the value of r^n gets closer and closer to 0 as n gets larger and larger. For example, if $r = \frac{2}{3}$ and $n = 10$, 20, and 100, then

$$\left(\frac{2}{3}\right)^{10} \approx 0.0173415, \quad \left(\frac{2}{3}\right)^{20} \approx 0.0003007, \quad \text{and} \quad \left(\frac{2}{3}\right)^{100} \approx 2.460 \times 10^{-18}.$$

Calculator Close-Up

Experiment with your calculator to see what happens to r^n as n gets larger and larger.

```
.99^100
             .3660323413
.99^1000
         4.317124741E-5
.99^10000
         2.24877485E-44
```

Because r^n is approximately 0 for large values of n, $1 - r^n$ is approximately 1. If we replace $1 - r^n$ by 1 in the expression for S_n, we get

$$S_n \approx \frac{a_1}{1 - r}.$$

So as n gets larger and larger, the sum of the first n terms of the infinite geometric series

$$a_1 + a_1 r + a_1 r^2 + \cdots$$

gets closer and closer to $\frac{a_1}{1 - r}$, provided that $|r| < 1$. Therefore we say that $\frac{a_1}{1 - r}$ is the sum of *all* of the terms of the infinite geometric series.

Sum of an Infinite Geometric Series

If $a_1 + a_1 r + a_1 r^2 + \cdots$ is an infinite geometric series, with $|r| < 1$, then the sum S of all of the terms of this series is given by

$$S = \frac{a_1}{1 - r}.$$

EXAMPLE 7

Sum of an infinite geometric series

Find the sum

$$\frac{1}{2} + \frac{1}{4} + \frac{1}{8} + \frac{1}{16} + \cdots.$$

Solution

This series is an infinite geometric series with $a_1 = \frac{1}{2}$ and $r = \frac{1}{2}$. Because $r < 1$, we have

$$S = \frac{\frac{1}{2}}{1 - \frac{1}{2}} = 1.$$

Now do Exercises 45–50

Helpful Hint

You can imagine this series in a football game. The Bears have the ball on the Lions' 1-yard line. The Lions continually get penalties that move the ball one-half of the distance to the goal. Theoretically, the ball will never reach the goal, but the total distance it moves will get closer and closer to 1 yard.

For an infinite series the index of summation i takes the values 1, 2, 3, and so on, without end. To indicate that the values for i keep increasing without bound, we say that *i takes the values from 1 through ∞* (infinity). Note that the symbol "∞" does not represent a number. Using the ∞ symbol, we can write the indicated sum of an infinite geometric series (with $|r| < 1$) by using summation notation as follows:

$$a_1 + a_1 r + a_1 r^2 + \cdots = \sum_{i=1}^{\infty} a_1 r^{i-1}$$

EXAMPLE 8

Sum of an infinite geometric series

Find the value of the sum

$$\sum_{i=1}^{\infty} 8\left(\frac{3}{4}\right)^{i-1}.$$

Solution

This series is an infinite geometric series with first term 8 and ratio $\frac{3}{4}$. So

$$S = \frac{8}{1 - \frac{3}{4}} = 8 \cdot \frac{4}{1} = 32.$$

Now do Exercises 51–58

EXAMPLE 9

Follow the bouncing ball

Suppose a ball always rebounds $\frac{2}{3}$ of the height from which it falls and the ball is dropped from a height of 6 feet. Find the total distance that the ball travels.

Solution

The ball falls 6 feet (ft) and rebounds 4 ft, then falls 4 ft and rebounds $\frac{8}{3}$ ft. The following series gives the total distance that the ball falls:

$$F = 6 + 4 + \frac{8}{3} + \frac{16}{9} + \cdots$$

The distance that the ball rebounds is given by the following series:

$$R = 4 + \frac{8}{3} + \frac{16}{9} + \cdots$$

Each of these series is an infinite geometric series with ratio $\frac{2}{3}$. Use the formula for an infinite geometric series to find each sum:

$$F = \frac{6}{1 - \frac{2}{3}} = 6 \cdot \frac{3}{1} = 18 \text{ ft}, \qquad R = \frac{4}{1 - \frac{2}{3}} = 4 \cdot \frac{3}{1} = 12 \text{ ft}$$

The total distance traveled by the ball is the sum of F and R, 30 ft.

Now do Exercises 59–60

Annuities

One of the most important applications of geometric series is in calculating the value of an annuity. An **annuity** is a sequence of periodic payments. The payments might be loan payments or investments.

EXAMPLE 10

Teaching Tip Point out that \$1000 per year is probably less than the cost of smoking for 1 year. Do this same example with some different interest rates.

Value of an annuity

A deposit of \$1000 is made at the beginning of each year for 30 years and earns 6% interest compounded annually. What is the value of this annuity at the end of the thirtieth year?

Solution

The last deposit earns interest for only 1 year. So at the end of the thirtieth year it amounts to \$1000(1.06). The next to last deposit earns interest for 2 years and amounts to $\$1000(1.06)^2$. The first deposit earns interest for 30 years and amounts to $\$1000(1.06)^{30}$. So the value of the annuity at the end of the thirtieth year is the sum of the finite geometric series

$$1000(1.06) + 1000(1.06)^2 + 1000(1.06)^3 + \cdots + 1000(1.06)^{30}.$$

Use the formula for the sum of 30 terms of a finite geometric series with $a_1 = 1000(1.06)$ and $r = 1.06$:

$$S_{30} = \frac{1000(1.06)(1 - (1.06)^{30})}{1 - 1.06} \approx \$83{,}801.68$$

So 30 annual deposits of \$1000 each amount to \$83,801.68.

Now do Exercises 61–64

Warm-Ups ▼

True or false? Explain your answer.

1. The sequence 2, 6, 24, 120, . . . is a geometric sequence. False
2. For $a_n = 2^n$ there is a common difference between adjacent terms. False
3. The common ratio for the geometric sequence $a_n = 3(0.5)^{n-1}$ is 0.5. True
4. If $a_n = 3(2)^{-n+3}$, then $a_1 = 12$. True
5. In the geometric sequence $a_n = 3(2)^{-n+3}$ we have $r = \frac{1}{2}$. True
6. The terms of a geometric series are the terms of a geometric sequence. True
7. To evaluate $\sum_{i=1}^{10} 2^i$, we must list all of the terms. False
8. $\sum_{i=1}^{5} 6\left(\frac{3}{4}\right)^{i-1} = \dfrac{9\left[1 - \left(\frac{3}{4}\right)^5\right]}{1 - \frac{3}{4}}$ False
9. $10 + 5 + \frac{5}{2} + \cdots = \dfrac{10}{1 - \frac{1}{2}}$ True
10. $2 + 4 + 8 + 16 + \cdots = \dfrac{2}{1 - 2}$ False

14.4 Exercises

Boost your GRADE at mathzone.com!

MathZone

- Practice Problems
- Self-Tests
- Videos
- Net Tutor
- e-Professors

Reading and Writing *After reading this section, write out the answers to these questions. Use complete sentences.*

1. What is a geometric sequence?
   A geometric sequence is one in which each term after the first is obtained by multiplying the preceding term by a constant.

2. What is the nth term of a geometric sequence?
The nth term of a geometric sequence is $a_1 r^{n-1}$, where a_1 is the first term and r is the common ratio.

3. What is a geometric series?
A geometric series is an indicated sum of a geometric sequence.

4. What is the formula for the sum of the first n terms of a geometric series?
The sum of the first n terms of a geometric series is given by $S_n = \frac{a_1(1 - r^n)}{1 - r}$.

5. What is the approximate value of r^n when n is large and $|r| < 1$?
The approximate value of r^n when n is large and $|r| < 1$ is 0.

6. What is the formula for the sum of an infinite geometric series?
The sum of an infinite geometric series is given by $S = \frac{a_1}{1 - r}$, provided $|r| < 1$.

Write a formula for the nth term of each geometric sequence. See Examples 1 and 2.

7. 1, 2, 4, 8, . . . $a_n = 2^{n-1}$

8. 1, 3, 9, 27, . . . $a_n = 3^{n-1}$

9. $\frac{1}{3}$, 1, 3, 9, . . . $a_n = \frac{1}{3}(3)^{n-1}$

10. $\frac{1}{4}$, 2, 16, . . . $a_n = \frac{1}{4}(8)^{n-1}$

11. 64, 8, 1, . . . $a_n = 64\left(\frac{1}{8}\right)^{n-1}$

12. 100, 10, 1, . . . $a_n = 100\left(\frac{1}{10}\right)^{n-1}$

13. 8, −4, 2, −1, . . . $a_n = 8\left(-\frac{1}{2}\right)^{n-1}$

14. −9, 3, −1, . . . $a_n = -9\left(-\frac{1}{3}\right)^{n-1}$

15. 2, −4, 8, −16, . . . $a_n = 2(-2)^{n-1}$

16. $-\frac{1}{2}$, 2, −8, 32, . . . $a_n = -\frac{1}{2}(-4)^{n-1}$

17. $-\frac{1}{3}, -\frac{1}{4}, -\frac{3}{16}, \ldots$ $a_n = -\frac{1}{3}\left(\frac{3}{4}\right)^{n-1}$

18. $-\frac{1}{4}, -\frac{1}{5}, -\frac{4}{25}, \ldots$ $a_n = -\frac{1}{4}\left(\frac{4}{5}\right)^{n-1}$

Write the first five terms of the geometric sequence with the given nth term. See Example 3.

19. $a_n = 2\left(\frac{1}{3}\right)^{n-1}$
$2, \frac{2}{3}, \frac{2}{9}, \frac{2}{27}, \frac{2}{81}$

20. $a_n = -5\left(\frac{1}{2}\right)^{n-1}$
$-5, -\frac{5}{2}, -\frac{5}{4}, -\frac{5}{8}, -\frac{5}{16}$

21. $a_n = (-2)^{n-1}$
1, −2, 4, −8, 16

22. $a_n = \left(-\frac{1}{3}\right)^{n-1}$
$1, -\frac{1}{3}, \frac{1}{9}, -\frac{1}{27}, \frac{1}{81}$

23. $a_n = 2^{-n}$
$\frac{1}{2}, \frac{1}{4}, \frac{1}{8}, \frac{1}{16}, \frac{1}{32}$

24. $a_n = 3^{-n}$
$\frac{1}{3}, \frac{1}{9}, \frac{1}{27}, \frac{1}{81}, \frac{1}{243}$

25. $a_n = (0.78)^n$
0.78, 0.6084, 0.4746, 0.3702, 0.2887

26. $a_n = (-0.23)^n$
−0.23, 0.0529, −0.0122, 0.0028, −0.0006

Find the required part of each geometric sequence. See Example 4.

27. Find the first term of the geometric sequence that has fourth term 40 and common ratio 2. 5

28. Find the first term of the geometric sequence that has fifth term 4 and common ratio $\frac{1}{2}$. 64

29. Find r for the geometric sequence that has $a_1 = 6$ and $a_4 = \frac{2}{9}$. $\frac{1}{3}$

30. Find r for the geometric sequence that has $a_1 = 1$ and $a_4 = -27$. −3

31. Find a_4 for the geometric sequence that has $a_1 = -3$ and $r = \frac{1}{3}$. $-\frac{1}{9}$

32. Find a_5 for the geometric sequence that has $a_1 = -\frac{2}{3}$ and $r = -\frac{2}{3}$. $-\frac{32}{243}$

Find the sum of each geometric series. See Examples 5 and 6.

33. $\frac{1}{2} + \frac{1}{4} + \frac{1}{8} + \cdots + \frac{1}{512}$ $\frac{511}{512}$

34. $1 + \frac{1}{3} + \frac{1}{9} + \cdots + \frac{1}{81}$ $\frac{121}{81}$

35. $\frac{1}{2} - \frac{1}{4} + \frac{1}{8} - \frac{1}{16} + \frac{1}{32}$ $\frac{11}{32}$

36. $3 - 1 + \frac{1}{3} - \frac{1}{9} + \frac{1}{27} - \frac{1}{81}$ $\frac{182}{81}$

37. $30 + 20 + \frac{40}{3} + \cdots + \frac{1280}{729}$ $\frac{63{,}050}{729}$

38. $9 - 6 + 4 - \cdots - \frac{128}{243}$ $\frac{1261}{243}$

39. $\sum_{i=1}^{10} 5(2)^{i-1}$ 5115

40. $\sum_{i=1}^{7} (10{,}000)(0.1)^{i-1}$ 11,111.11

41. $\sum_{i=1}^{6} (0.1)^i$ 0.111111

42. $\sum_{i=1}^{5} (0.2)^i$ 0.24992

43. $\sum_{i=1}^{6} 100(0.3)^i$ 42.8259

44. $\sum_{i=1}^{7} 36(0.5)^i$ 35.71875

Find the sum of each infinite geometric series. See Examples 7 and 8.

45. $\frac{1}{8}+\frac{1}{16}+\frac{1}{32}+\cdots$ $\frac{1}{4}$

46. $\frac{1}{9}+\frac{1}{27}+\frac{1}{81}+\cdots$ $\frac{1}{6}$

47. $3+2+\frac{4}{3}+\cdots$ 9

48. $2+1+\frac{1}{2}+\cdots$ 4

49. $4-2+1-\frac{1}{2}+\cdots$ $\frac{8}{3}$

50. $16-12+9-\frac{27}{4}+\cdots$ $\frac{64}{7}$

51. $\sum_{i=1}^{\infty}(0.3)^i$ $\frac{3}{7}$

52. $\sum_{i=1}^{\infty}(0.2)^i$ $\frac{1}{4}$

53. $\sum_{i=1}^{\infty}3(0.5)^{i-1}$ 6

54. $\sum_{i=1}^{\infty}7(0.4)^{i-1}$ $\frac{35}{3}$

55. $\sum_{i=1}^{\infty}3(0.1)^i$ $\frac{1}{3}$

56. $\sum_{i=1}^{\infty}6(0.1)^i$ $\frac{2}{3}$

57. $\sum_{i=1}^{\infty}12(0.01)^i$ $\frac{4}{33}$

58. $\sum_{i=1}^{\infty}72(0.01)^i$ $\frac{8}{11}$

Use the ideas of geometric series to solve each problem. See Examples 9 and 10.

59. ***Retirement fund.*** Suppose a deposit of \$2000 is made at the beginning of each year for 45 years into an account paying 12% compounded annually. What is the amount of this annuity at the end of the forty-fifth year?
\$3,042,435.27

60. ***World's largest mutual fund.*** If you had invested \$5000 at the beginning of each year for the past 10 years in the Fidelity's Magellan Fund you would have averaged 12.46% compounded annually (www.fidelity.com). Find the amount of this annuity at the end of the tenth year.
\$100,897.81

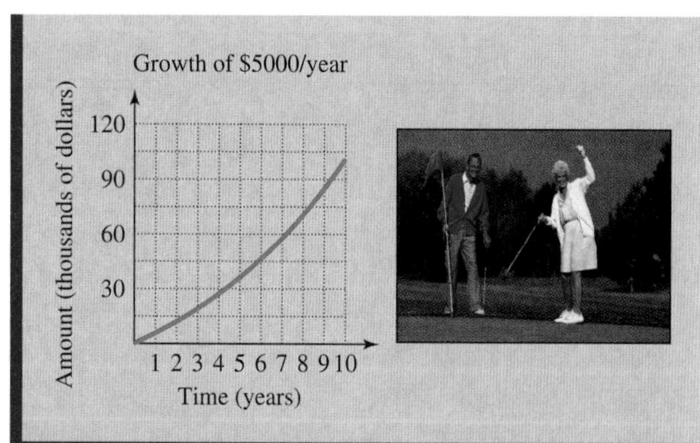

Figure for Exercise 60

61. ***Big saver.*** Suppose you deposit one cent into your piggy bank on the first day of December and, on each day of December after that, you deposit twice as much as on the previous day. How much will you have in the bank after the last deposit? \$21,474,836.47

62. ***Big family.*** Consider yourself, your parents, your grandparents, your great-grandparents, your great-great-grandparents, and so on, back to your grandparents with the word "great" used in front 40 times. What is the total number of people you are considering?
8.796×10^{12}

63. ***Total economic impact.*** In Exercise 45 of Section 14.1 we described a factory that spends \$1 million annually in a community in which 80% of the money received is respent in the community. Economists assume the money is respent again and again at the 80% rate. The total economic impact of the factory is the total of all of this spending. Find an approximation for the total by using the formula for the sum of an infinite geometric series with a rate of 80%.
\$5,000,000

64. ***Less impact.*** Repeat Exercise 63, assuming money is respent again and again at the 50% rate.
\$2,000,000

Getting More Involved

65. ***Discussion***

Which of the following sequences is not a geometric sequence? Explain your answer.

a) 1, 2, 4, . . .
b) 0.1, 0.01, 0.001, . . .
c) −1, 2, −4, . . .
d) 2, 4, 6, . . .

d

66. ***Discussion***

The repeating decimal number 0.44444 . . . can be written as

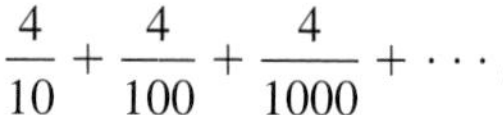

$$\frac{4}{10}+\frac{4}{100}+\frac{4}{1000}+\cdots,$$

an infinite geometric series. Find the sum of this geometric series.
$\frac{4}{9}$

67. ***Discussion***

Write the repeating decimal number 0.24242424 . . . as an infinite geometric series. Find the sum of the geometric series.
$\frac{8}{33}$

14.5 Binomial Expansions

In this Section

- **Some Examples**
- **Obtaining the Coefficients**
- **The Binomial Theorem**

In Chapter 4 you learned how to square a binomial. In this section you will study higher powers of binomials.

Some Examples

We know that $(x + y)^2 = x^2 + 2xy + y^2$. To find $(x + y)^3$, we multiply $(x + y)^2$ by $x + y$:

$$\begin{aligned}(x + y)^3 &= (x^2 + 2xy + y^2)(x + y)\\ &= (x^2 + 2xy + y^2)x + (x^2 + 2xy + y^2)y\\ &= x^3 + 2x^2y + xy^2 + x^2y + 2xy^2 + y^3\\ &= x^3 + 3x^2y + 3xy^2 + y^3\end{aligned}$$

The sum $x^3 + 3x^2y + 3xy^2 + y^3$ is called the **binomial expansion** of $(x + y)^3$. If we again multiply by $x + y$, we will get the binomial expansion of $(x + y)^4$. This method is rather tedious. However, if we examine these expansions, we can find a pattern and learn how to find binomial expansions without multiplying.

Consider the following binomial expansions:

$$\begin{aligned}&(x + y)^0 = 1\\ &(x + y)^1 = x + y\\ &(x + y)^2 = x^2 + 2xy + y^2\\ &(x + y)^3 = x^3 + 3x^2y + 3xy^2 + y^3\\ &(x + y)^4 = x^4 + 4x^3y + 6x^2y^2 + 4xy^3 + y^4\\ &(x + y)^5 = x^5 + 5x^4y + 10x^3y^2 + 10x^2y^3 + 5xy^4 + y^5\end{aligned}$$

Observe that the exponents on the variable x are decreasing, whereas the exponents on the variable y are increasing, as we read from left to right. Also notice that the sum of the exponents in each term is the same for that entire line. For instance, in the fourth expansion the terms x^4, x^3y, x^2y^2, xy^3, and y^4 all have exponents with a sum of 4. If we continue the pattern, the expansion of $(x + y)^6$ will have seven terms containing x^6, x^5y, x^4y^2, x^3y^3, x^2y^4, xy^5, and y^6. Now we must find the pattern for the coefficients of these terms.

Obtaining the Coefficients

If we write out only the coefficients of the expansions that we already have, we can easily see a pattern. This triangular array of coefficients for the binomial expansions is called **Pascal's triangle.**

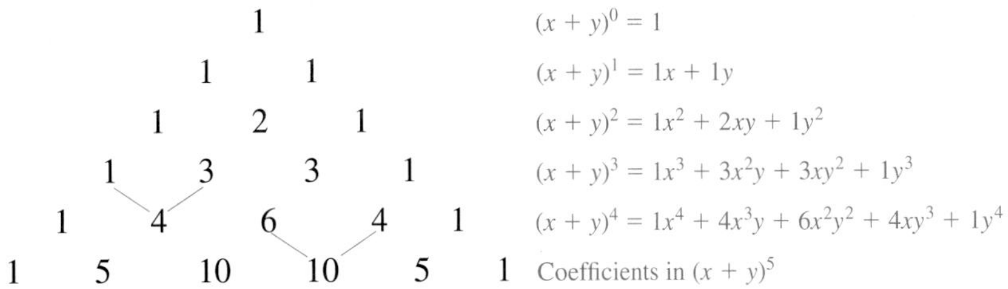

Notice that each line starts and ends with a 1 and that each entry of a line is the sum of the two entries above it in the previous line. For instance, $4 = 3 + 1$, and $10 = 6 + 4$. Following this pattern, the sixth and seventh lines of coefficients are

$$\begin{array}{ccccccccccccccc} & 1 & & 6 & & 15 & & 20 & & 15 & & 6 & & 1 & \\ 1 & & 7 & & 21 & & 35 & & 35 & & 21 & & 7 & & 1. \end{array}$$

Pascal's triangle gives us an easy way to get the coefficients for the binomial expansion with small powers, but it is impractical for larger powers. For larger powers we use a formula involving **factorial notation.**

> ***n*! (*n* factorial)**
>
> If n is a positive integer, $n!$ (read "n factorial") is defined to be the product of all of the positive integers from 1 through n. We also define $0!$ to be 1.

Calculator Close-Up

You can evaluate the coefficients using either the factorial notation or $_nC_r$. The factorial symbol and $_nC_r$ are found in the MATH menu under PRB.

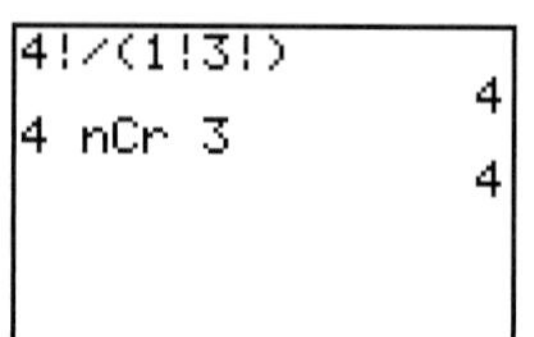

For example, $3! = 3 \cdot 2 \cdot 1 = 6$, and $5! = 5 \cdot 4 \cdot 3 \cdot 2 \cdot 1 = 120$.

Before we state a general formula, consider how the coefficients for $(x + y)^4$ are found by using factorials:

$$\frac{4!}{4!0!} = \frac{4 \cdot 3 \cdot 2 \cdot 1}{4 \cdot 3 \cdot 2 \cdot 1 \cdot 1} = 1 \quad \text{Coefficient of } x^4 \text{ (or } x^4y^0\text{)}$$

$$\frac{4!}{3!1!} = \frac{4 \cdot 3 \cdot 2 \cdot 1}{3 \cdot 2 \cdot 1 \cdot 1} = 4 \quad \text{Coefficient of } x^3y$$

$$\frac{4!}{2!2!} = \frac{4 \cdot 3 \cdot 2 \cdot 1}{2 \cdot 1 \cdot 2 \cdot 1} = 6 \quad \text{Coefficient of } x^2y^2$$

$$\frac{4!}{1!3!} = \frac{4 \cdot 3 \cdot 2 \cdot 1}{1 \cdot 3 \cdot 2 \cdot 1} = 4 \quad \text{Coefficient of } xy^3$$

$$\frac{4!}{0!4!} = \frac{4 \cdot 3 \cdot 2 \cdot 1}{1 \cdot 4 \cdot 3 \cdot 2 \cdot 1} = 1 \quad \text{Coefficient of } y^4 \text{ (or } x^0y^4\text{)}$$

Note that each expression has $4!$ in the numerator, with factorials in the denominator corresponding to the exponents on x and y.

The Binomial Theorem

We now summarize these ideas in the **binomial theorem.**

> **The Binomial Theorem**
>
> In the expansion of $(x + y)^n$ for a positive integer n, there are $n + 1$ terms, given by the following formula:
>
> $$(x + y)^n = \frac{n!}{n!0!}x^n + \frac{n!}{(n-1)!1!}x^{n-1}y + \frac{n!}{(n-2)!2!}x^{n-2}y^2 + \cdots + \frac{n!}{0!n!}y^n$$

The notation $\binom{n}{r}$ is often used in place of $\frac{n!}{(n-r)!r!}$ in the binomial expansion. Using this notation, we write the expansion as

$$(x + y)^n = \binom{n}{0}x^n + \binom{n}{1}x^{n-1}y + \binom{n}{2}x^{n-2}y^2 + \cdots + \binom{n}{n}y^n.$$

Another notation for $\frac{n!}{(n-r)!r!}$ is ${}_nC_r$. Using this notation, we have

$$(x + y)^n = {}_nC_0x^n + {}_nC_1x^{n-1}y + {}_nC_2x^{n-2}y^2 + \cdots + {}_nC_ny^n.$$

EXAMPLE 1

Calculating the binomial coefficients

Evaluate each expression.

a) $\frac{7!}{4!\,3!}$ **b)** $\frac{10!}{8!\,2!}$

Solution

a) $\frac{7!}{4!\,3!} = \frac{7 \cdot 6 \cdot 5 \cdot \not{4} \cdot \not{3} \cdot \not{2} \cdot \not{1}}{\not{4} \cdot \not{3} \cdot \not{2} \cdot \not{1} \cdot 3 \cdot 2 \cdot 1} = \frac{7 \cdot 6 \cdot 5}{3 \cdot 2 \cdot 1} = 35$

b) $\frac{10!}{8!\,2!} = \frac{10 \cdot 9 \cdot \not{8} \cdot \not{7} \cdot \not{6} \cdot \not{5} \cdot \not{4} \cdot \not{3} \cdot \not{2} \cdot \not{1}}{\not{8} \cdot \not{7} \cdot \not{6} \cdot \not{5} \cdot \not{4} \cdot \not{3} \cdot \not{2} \cdot \not{1} \cdot 2 \cdot 1} = \frac{10 \cdot 9}{2 \cdot 1} = 45$

Now do Exercises 5–10

EXAMPLE 2

Using the binomial theorem

Write out the first three terms of $(x + y)^9$.

Solution

$$(x + y)^9 = \frac{9!}{9!0!}x^9 + \frac{9!}{8!\,1!}x^8y + \frac{9!}{7!2!}x^7y^2 + \cdots = x^9 + 9x^8y + 36x^7y^2 + \cdots$$

Now do Exercises 11–16

EXAMPLE 3

Using the binomial theorem

Write the binomial expansion for $(x^2 - 2a)^5$.

Solution

We expand a difference by writing it as a sum and using the binomial theorem:

$$\begin{aligned}(x^2 - 2a)^5 &= (x^2 + (-2a))^5 \\ &= \frac{5!}{5!0!}(x^2)^5 + \frac{5!}{4!\,1!}(x^2)^4(-2a)^1 + \frac{5!}{3!2!}(x^2)^3(-2a)^2 + \frac{5!}{2!3!}(x^2)^2(-2a)^3 \\ &\quad + \frac{5!}{1!\,4!}(x^2)^1(-2a)^4 + \frac{5!}{0!\,5!}(-2a)^5 \\ &= x^{10} - 10x^8a + 40x^6a^2 - 80x^4a^3 + 80x^2a^4 - 32a^5\end{aligned}$$

Now do Exercises 17–32

EXAMPLE 4

Finding a specific term

Find the fourth term of the expansion of $(a + b)^{12}$.

Solution

The variables in the first term are $a^{12}b^0$, those in the second term are $a^{11}b^1$, those in the third term are $a^{10}b^2$, and those in the fourth term are a^9b^3. So

$$\frac{12!}{9!\,3!}a^9b^3 = 220a^9b^3.$$

The fourth term is $220a^9b^3$.

Now do Exercises 33–36

Calculator Close-Up

Because ${}_nC_r = \frac{n!}{(n-r)!\,r!}$, we have

$${}_{12}C_9 = \frac{12!}{3!\,9!} \text{ and } {}_{12}C_3 = \frac{12!}{9!\,3!}.$$

So there is more than one way to compute 12!/(9! 3!):

```
12!/(9!3!)
                220
12 nCr 9
                220
12 nCr 3
                220
```

Using the ideas of Example 4, we can write a formula for any term of a binomial expansion.

Formula for the *k*th Term of $(x + y)^n$

For k ranging from 1 to $n + 1$, the kth term of the expansion of $(x + y)^n$ is given by the formula

$$\frac{n!}{(n - k + 1)!(k - 1)!}x^{n-k+1}y^{k-1}.$$

EXAMPLE 5

Finding a specific term

Find the sixth term of the expansion of $(a^2 - 2b)^7$.

Solution

Use the formula for the kth term with $k = 6$ and $n = 7$:

$$\frac{7!}{(7 - 6 + 1)!(6 - 1)!}(a^2)^2(-2b)^5 = 21a^4(-32b^5) = -672a^4b^5$$

Now do Exercises 37–40

We can think of the binomial expansion as a finite series. Using summation notation, we can write the binomial theorem as follows.

The Binomial Theorem (Using Summation Notation)

For any positive integer n,

$$(x + y)^n = \sum_{i=0}^{n} \frac{n!}{(n - i)!\,i!}x^{n-i}y^i \quad \text{or} \quad (x + y)^n = \sum_{i=0}^{n} \binom{n}{i} x^{n-i}y^i.$$

EXAMPLE 6

Using summation notation

Write $(a + b)^5$ using summation notation.

Solution

Use $n = 5$ in the binomial theorem:

$$(a + b)^5 = \sum_{i=0}^{5} \frac{5!}{(5 - i)!\,i!} a^{5-i} b^i$$

Now do Exercises 41–44

Warm-Ups ▼

True or false? Explain your answer.

1. There are 12 terms in the expansion of $(a + b)^{12}$. False
2. The seventh term of $(a + b)^{12}$ is a multiple of a^5b^7. False
3. For all values of x, $(x + 2)^5 = x^5 + 32$. False
4. In the expansion of $(x - 5)^8$ the signs of the terms alternate. True
5. The eighth line of Pascal's triangle is

   1 8 28 56 70 56 28 8 1. True
6. The sum of the coefficients in the expansion of $(a + b)^4$ is 2^4. True
7. $(a + b)^3 = \sum_{i=0}^{3} \frac{3!}{(3 - i)!\,i!} a^{3-i} b^i$ True
8. The sum of the coefficients in the expansion of $(a + b)^n$ is 2^n. True
9. $0! = 1!$ True
10. $\frac{7!}{5!2!} = 21$ True

14.5 Exercises

Boost your GRADE at mathzone.com!

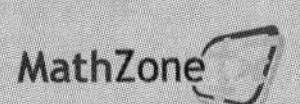

- Practice Problems
- Self-Tests
- Videos
- Net Tutor
- e-Professors

Reading and Writing *After reading this section, write out the answers to these questions. Use complete sentences.*

1. What is a binomial expansion?

   The sum obtained for a power of a binomial is called a binomial expansion.

2. What is Pascal's triangle and how do you make it?
Pascal's triangle gives the coefficients for $(a + b)^n$ for $n = 1, 2, 3$, and so on. Each row starts and ends with a 1. The other terms are obtained by adding the closest two terms in the preceding row.

3. What does $n!$ mean?
The expression $n!$ is the product of the positive integers from 1 through n.

4. What is the binomial theorem?
The binomial theorem gives the expansion of $(a + b)^n$.

Evaluate each expression. See Example 1.

5. $\dfrac{4!}{4!\,0!}$ 1

6. $\dfrac{5!}{5!\,0!}$ 1

7. $\dfrac{5!}{2!\,3!}$ 10

8. $\dfrac{6!}{5!\,1!}$ 6

9. $\dfrac{8!}{5!\,3!}$ 56

10. $\dfrac{9!}{2!\,7!}$ 36

Use the binomial theorem to expand each binomial. See Examples 2 and 3.

11. $(x + 1)^3$ $x^3 + 3x^2 + 3x + 1$

12. $(y + 1)^4$ $y^4 + 4y^3 + 6y^2 + 4y + 1$

13. $(a + 2)^3$ $a^3 + 6a^2 + 12a + 8$

14. $(b + 3)^3$ $b^3 + 9b^2 + 27b + 27$

15. $(r + t)^5$ $r^5 + 5r^4t + 10r^3t^2 + 10r^2t^3 + 5rt^4 + t^5$

16. $(r + t)^6$ $r^6 + 6r^5t + 15r^4t^2 + 20r^3t^3 + 15r^2t^4 + 6rt^5 + t^6$

17. $(m - n)^3$ $m^3 - 3m^2n + 3mn^2 - n^3$

18. $(m - n)^4$ $m^4 - 4m^3n + 6m^2n^2 - 4mn^3 + n^4$

19. $(x + 2a)^3$ $x^3 + 6ax^2 + 12a^2x + 8a^3$

20. $(a + 3b)^4$ $a^4 + 12a^3b + 54a^2b^2 + 108ab^3 + 81b^4$

21. $(x^2 - 2)^4$ $x^8 - 8x^6 + 24x^4 - 32x^2 + 16$

22. $(x^2 - a^2)^5$ $x^{10} - 5a^2x^8 + 10a^4x^6 - 10a^6x^4 + 5a^8x^2 - a^{10}$

23. $(x - 1)^7$ $x^7 - 7x^6 + 21x^5 - 35x^4 + 35x^3 - 21x^2 + 7x - 1$

24. $(x + 1)^6$ $x^6 + 6x^5 + 15x^4 + 20x^3 + 15x^2 + 6x + 1$

Write out the first four terms in the expansion of each binomial. See Examples 2 and 3.

25. $(a - 3b)^{12}$ $a^{12} - 36a^{11}b + 594a^{10}b^2 - 5940a^9b^3$

26. $(x - 2y)^{10}$ $x^{10} - 20x^9y + 180x^8y^2 - 960x^7y^3$

27. $(x^2 + 5)^9$ $x^{18} + 45x^{16} + 900x^{14} + 10{,}500x^{12}$

28. $(x^2 + 1)^{20}$ $x^{40} + 20x^{38} + 190x^{36} + 1140x^{34}$

29. $(x - 1)^{22}$ $x^{22} - 22x^{21} + 231x^{20} - 1540x^{19}$

30. $(2x - 1)^8$ $256x^8 - 1024x^7 + 1792x^6 - 1792x^5$

31. $\left(\dfrac{x}{2} + \dfrac{y}{3}\right)^{10}$ $\dfrac{x^{10}}{1024} + \dfrac{5x^9y}{768} + \dfrac{5x^8y^2}{256} + \dfrac{5x^7y^3}{144}$

32. $\left(\dfrac{a}{2} + \dfrac{b}{5}\right)^{8}$ $\dfrac{a^8}{256} + \dfrac{a^7b}{80} + \dfrac{7a^6b^2}{400} + \dfrac{7a^5b^3}{500}$

Find the indicated term of the binomial expansion. See Examples 4 and 5.

33. $(a + w)^{13}$, 6th term $1287a^8w^5$

34. $(m + n)^{12}$, 7th term $924m^6n^6$

35. $(m - n)^{16}$, 8th term $-11{,}440m^9n^7$

36. $(a - b)^{14}$, 6th term $-2002a^9b^5$

37. $(x + 2y)^8$, 4th term $448x^5y^3$

38. $(3a + b)^7$, 4th term $2835a^4b^3$

39. $(2a^2 - b)^{20}$, 7th term $635{,}043{,}840a^{28}b^6$

40. $(a^2 - w^2)^{12}$, 5th term $495a^{16}w^8$

Write each expansion using summation notation. See Example 6.

41. $(a + m)^8$ $\displaystyle\sum_{i=0}^{8} \frac{8!}{(8 - i)!\,i!}a^{8-i}m^i$

42. $(z + w)^{13}$ $\displaystyle\sum_{i=0}^{13} \frac{13!}{(13 - i)!\,i!}z^{13-i}w^i$

43. $(a - 2x)^5$ $\displaystyle\sum_{i=0}^{5} \frac{5!(-2)^i}{(5 - i)!\,i!}a^{5-i}x^i$

44. $(w - 3m)^7$ $\displaystyle\sum_{i=0}^{7} \frac{7!(-3)^i}{(7 - i)!i!}w^{7-i}m^i$

Getting More Involved

45. ***Discussion***

Find the trinomial expansion for $(a + b + c)^3$ by using $x = a$ and $y = b + c$ in the binomial theorem.
$a^3 + b^3 + c^3 + 3a^2b + 3a^2c + 3ab^2 + 3ac^2 + 3b^2c + 3bc^2 + 6abc$

46. ***Discussion***

What problem do you encounter when trying to find the fourth term in the binomial expansion for $(x + y)^{120}$? How can you overcome this problem? Find the fifth term in the binomial expansion for $(x - 2y)^{100}$.
$280{,}840x^{117}y^3$, $62{,}739{,}600x^{96}y^4$

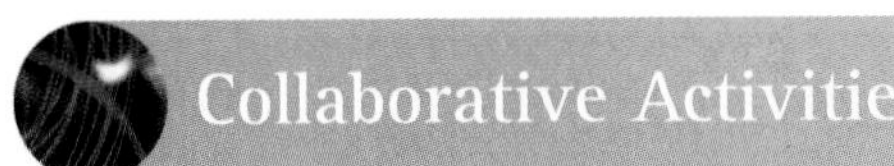

Collaborative Activities

Grouping: 2 to 4 students per group

Topic: Sequences and series

A Sequence of Investments Can Be Series(ous)

Roberto, his brother Horatio, and his sister Genevieve each have a three-year-old child. Each would like to save money for his or her child's college expenses and decide to set aside \$5 each week to the cause. Horatio plans to use his \$5 to buy lottery tickets each week for the next 15 years, hoping to win and use the money for his child's college expenses. Genevieve plans to invest her \$5 in a mutual fund and Roberto plans to invest in an education Individual Retirement Account (IRA).

1. Write the first 10 terms of the sequence in which the nth term is the total amount that Horatio has spent after n weeks. What type of sequence is this? How much money will Horatio spend on lottery tickets after 15 years? Assume that there are 52 weeks per year.
2. For every \$5.00 Horatio spends each week on lottery tickets, his average winnings are \$3.00 per week. He decides to buy a new certificate of deposit (CD) with his winnings at the end of each year. How much money will he put into a CD each year? At the end of the 15th year he has purchased 15 CDs. Assume his CDs pay 3.75% annual interest compounded annually. Write a sequence of 15 terms that gives the amounts of each of the 15 CDs at the end of the 15th year. What type of sequence is this? Find the sum of the 15 terms.
3. Roberto sets aside \$5 per week and pays into his IRA at the end of each quarter. The education IRA pays 4.5% annual interest compounded quarterly. Assume that there are 13 weeks per quarter. Determine the amount Roberto will have at the end of the 15 years.
4. Genevieve sets aside \$5 per week and pays into her mutual fund at the end of each year. If her mutual fund pays 7.375% annual interest compounded annually, then what amount will Genevieve have at the end of the 15 years?
5. Discuss in your groups the amount of risk in each of the investment strategies. Do Horatio's chances increase the longer he buys lottery tickets? What should he do if he "wins big"? Are Genevieve's and Roberto's investment strategies sure things?

Chapter 14 Wrap-Up

Summary

Sequences and Series

		Examples
Sequence	Finite—A function whose domain is the set of positive integers less than or equal to a fixed positive integer	3, 5, 7, 9, 11 $a_n = 2n + 1$ $1 \le n \le 5$
	Infinite—A function whose domain is the set of positive integers	2, 4, 6, 8, . . . $a_n = 2n$
Series	The indicated sum of a sequence	$2 + 4 + 6 + \cdots + 50$
Summation notation	$\sum_{i=1}^{n} a_i = a_1 + a_2 + a_3 + \cdots + a_n$	$\sum_{i=1}^{25} 2i = 2 + 4 + \cdots + 50$

Arithmetic Sequences and Series

		Examples
Arithmetic sequence	Each term after the first is obtained by adding a fixed amount to the previous term.	6, 11, 16, 21, . . . Fixed amount, d, is 5.
nth term	The nth term of an arithmetic sequence is $a_n = a_1 + (n - 1)d$.	If $a_1 = 6$ and $d = 5$, then $a_n = 6 + (n - 1)5$.
Arithmetic series	The sum of an arithmetic sequence	$6 + 11 + 16 + 21$
Sum of first n terms	$S_n = \frac{n}{2}(a_1 + a_n)$	$S_4 = \frac{4}{2}(6 + 21) = 54$

Geometric Sequences and Series

		Examples
Geometric sequence	Each term after the first is obtained by multiplying the preceding term by a constant.	2, 6, 18, 54, . . . Constant, r, is 3.
nth term	The nth term of a geometric sequence is $a_n = a_1r^{n-1}$.	$a_1 = 2, r = 3$ $a_n = 2 \cdot 3^{n-1}$
Geometric series (finite)	The indicated sum of a finite geometric sequence. $a_1 + a_1r + a_1r^2 + \cdots + a_1r^{n-1}$	$2 + 6 + 18 + 54 + 162$
Sum of first n terms	$S_n = \frac{a_1(1 - r^n)}{1 - r}$	$a_1 = 2, r = 3, n = 5$ $S_5 = \frac{2(1 - 3^5)}{1 - 3} = 242$

Geometric series (infinite)	$a_1 + a_1r + a_1r^2 + a_1r^3 + \cdots$	$8 + 4 + 2 + 1 + \frac{1}{2} + \cdots$
Sum of an infinite geometric series	$S = \frac{a_1}{1 - r}$, provided that $\lvert r \rvert < 1$	$a_1 = 8,\ r = \frac{1}{2}$ $S = \frac{8}{1 - \frac{1}{2}} = 16$
Factorial notation	The notation $n!$ represents the product of the positive integers from 1 through n.	$5! = 5 \cdot 4 \cdot 3 \cdot 2 \cdot 1 = 120$
Binomial theorem	$(x + y)^n = \frac{n!}{n!\,0!}x^n + \frac{n!}{(n-1)!\,1!}x^{n-1}y + \frac{n!}{(n-2)!\,2!}x^{n-2}y^2 + \cdots + \frac{n!}{0!\,n!}y^n$ Using summation notation: $(x + y)^n = \sum_{i=0}^{n} \frac{n!}{(n-i)!\,i!}x^{n-i}y^i = \sum_{i=0}^{n} \binom{n}{i} x^{n-i}y^i$	$(x + y)^3 = x^3 + 3x^2y + 3xy^2 + y^3$
kth term of $(x + y)^n$	$\frac{n!}{(n - k + 1)!(k - 1)!}x^{n-k+1}y^{k-1}$	Third term of $(a + b)^{10}$ is $\frac{10!}{8!\,2!}a^8b^2 = 45a^8b^2$.

Enriching Your Mathematical Word Power

For each mathematical term, choose the correct meaning.

1. **sequence**
   a. a list of numbers
   b. a procedure for getting the answer
   c. events that happen in order
   d. a linear function a

2. **finite sequence**
   a. a short sequence
   b. a sequence of whole numbers
   c. a function whose domain is the set of positive integers
   d. a function whose domain is the set of positive integers less than or equal to a fixed positive integer d

3. **infinite sequence**
   a. a short sequence
   b. a sequence of whole numbers
   c. a function whose domain is the set of positive integers
   d. a function whose domain is the set of positive integers less than or equal to a fixed positive integer c

4. **series**
   a. a special sequence
   b. the indicated sum of the terms of a sequence
   c. a sequence of positive numbers
   d. a show with many episodes b

5. **arithmetic sequence**
   a. a sequence in which each term after the first is obtained by adding a fixed amount to the previous term
   b. a sequence of fractions
   c. a sequence found in arithmetic
   d. a finite sequence a

6. geometric sequence
a. a sequence of rectangles
b. a sequence of geometric formulas
c. a sequence in which each term after the first is obtained by multiplying the preceding term by a constant
d. a sequence in which the terms are geometric c

7. geometric series
a. a series of geometric shapes
b. the indicated sum of an arithmetic sequence
c. a series of ratios
d. the indicated sum of a geometric sequence d

8. binomial expansion
a. the trinomial obtained when a binomial is stretched
b. the expression obtained from raising a binomial to a whole number power
c. the coefficients of a binomial
d. the various powers of a binomial b

9. Pascal's triangle
a. an equilateral triangle
b. a triangle formed by the graphs of three linear equations
c. the right triangle in the Pythagorean theorem
d. a triangular array of coefficients for binomial expansions d

10. $n!$
a. the product of the positive integers from 1 through n
b. the binomial coefficients
c. the n vertices of Pascal's triangle
d. 3.141592654 a

Review Exercises

14.1 *List all terms of each finite sequence.*

1. $a_n = n^3$ for $1 \le n \le 5$ 1, 8, 27, 64, 125

2. $b_n = (n-1)^4$ for $1 \le n \le 4$ 0, 1, 16, 81

3. $c_n = (-1)^n(2n-3)$ for $1 \le n \le 6$
1, 1, −3, 5, −7, 9

4. $d_n = (-1)^{n-1}(3-n)$ for $1 \le n \le 7$
2, −1, 0, 1, −2, 3, −4

Write the first three terms of the infinite sequence whose nth term is given.

5. $a_n = -\frac{1}{n}$ $-1, -\frac{1}{2}, -\frac{1}{3}$

6. $b_n = \frac{(-1)^n}{n^2}$ $-1, \frac{1}{4}, -\frac{1}{9}$

7. $b_n = \frac{(-1)^{2n}}{2n+1}$ $\frac{1}{3}, \frac{1}{5}, \frac{1}{7}$

8. $a_n = \frac{-1}{2n-3}$ $1, -1, -\frac{1}{3}$

9. $c_n = \log_2(2^{n+3})$ 4, 5, 6

10. $c_n = \ln(e^{2n})$ 2, 4, 6

14.2 *Find the sum of each series.*

11. $\sum_{i=1}^{3} i^3$ 36

12. $\sum_{i=0}^{4} 6$ 30

13. $\sum_{n=1}^{5} n(n-1)$ 40

14. $\sum_{j=0}^{3} (-2)^j$ −5

Write each series in summation notation. Use the index i, and let i begin at 1.

15. $\frac{1}{4} + \frac{1}{6} + \frac{1}{8} + \cdots$ $\sum_{i=1}^{\infty} \frac{1}{2(i+1)}$

16. $\frac{1}{3} + \frac{1}{4} + \frac{1}{5} + \cdots$ $\sum_{i=1}^{\infty} \frac{1}{i+2}$

17. $0 + 1 + 4 + 9 + 16 + \cdots$ $\sum_{i=1}^{\infty} (i-1)^2$

18. $-1 + 2 - 3 + 4 - 5 + 6 - \cdots$ $\sum_{i=1}^{\infty} i(-1)^i$

19. $x_1 - x_2 + x_3 - x_4 + \cdots$ $\sum_{i=1}^{\infty} (-1)^{i+1}x_i$

20. $-x^2 + x^3 - x^4 + x^5 - \cdots$ $\sum_{i=1}^{\infty} (-1)^i x^{i+1}$

14.3 *Write the first four terms of the arithmetic sequence with the given nth term.*

21. $a_n = 6 + (n-1)5$ 6, 11, 16, 21

22. $a_n = -7 + (n-1)4$ −7, −3, 1, 5

23. $a_n = -20 + (n-1)(-2)$ −20, −22, −24, −26

24. $a_n = 10 + (n-1)(-2.5)$ 10, 7.5, 5, 2.5

25. $a_n = 1000n + 2000$ 3000, 4000, 5000, 6000

26. $a_n = -500n + 5000$ 4500, 4000, 3500, 3000

Write a formula for the nth term of each arithmetic sequence.

27. $\frac{1}{3}, \frac{2}{3}, 1, \frac{4}{3}, \ldots$ $a_n = \frac{n}{3}$

28. $10, 6, 2, -2, \ldots$ $a_n = -4n + 14$

29. $2, 4, 6, 8, \ldots$ $a_n = 2n$

30. $20, 10, 0, -10, \ldots$ $a_n = -10n + 30$

Find the sum of each arithmetic series.

31. $1 + 2 + 3 + \cdots + 24$ 300

32. $-5 + (-2) + 1 + 4 + \cdots + 34$ 203

33. $\frac{1}{6} + \frac{1}{2} + \frac{5}{6} + \frac{7}{6} + \cdots + \frac{11}{2}$ $\frac{289}{6}$

34. $-3 - 6 - 9 - 12 - \cdots - 36$ -234

35. $\sum_{i=1}^{7} (2i - 3)$ 35

36. $\sum_{i=1}^{6} [12 + (i - 1)5]$ 147

14.4 *Write the first four terms of the geometric sequence with the given nth term.*

37. $a_n = 3\left(\frac{1}{2}\right)^{n-1}$ $3, \frac{3}{2}, \frac{3}{4}, \frac{3}{8}$

38. $a_n = 6\left(-\frac{1}{3}\right)^n$ $-2, \frac{2}{3}, -\frac{2}{9}, \frac{2}{27}$

39. $a_n = 2^{1-n}$ $1, \frac{1}{2}, \frac{1}{4}, \frac{1}{8}$

40. $a_n = 5(10)^{n-1}$ 5, 50, 500, 5000

41. $a_n = 23(10)^{-2n}$ 0.23, 0.0023, 0.000023, 0.00000023

42. $a_n = 4(10)^{-n}$ 0.4, 0.04, 0.004, 0.0004

Write a formula for the nth term of each geometric sequence.

43. $\frac{1}{2}, 3, 18, \ldots$ $a_n = \frac{1}{2}(6)^{n-1}$

44. $-6, 2, -\frac{2}{3}, \frac{2}{9}, \ldots$ $a_n = -6\left(-\frac{1}{3}\right)^{n-1}$

45. $\frac{7}{10}, \frac{7}{100}, \frac{7}{1000}, \ldots$ $a_n = 0.7(0.1)^{n-1}$

46. $2, 2x, 2x^2, 2x^3, \ldots$ $a_n = 2x^{n-1}$

Find the sum of each geometric series.

47. $\frac{1}{3} + \frac{1}{9} + \frac{1}{27} + \frac{1}{81}$ $\frac{40}{81}$

48. $2 + 4 + 8 + 16 + \cdots + 512$ 1022

49. $\sum_{i=1}^{10} 3(10)^{-i}$ 0.3333333333

50. $\sum_{i=1}^{5} (0.1)^i$ 0.11111

51. $\frac{1}{4} + \frac{1}{12} + \frac{1}{36} + \frac{1}{108} + \cdots$ $\frac{3}{8}$

52. $12 + (-6) + 3 + \left(-\frac{3}{2}\right) + \cdots$ 8

53. $\sum_{i=1}^{\infty} 18\left(\frac{2}{3}\right)^{i-1}$ 54

54. $\sum_{i=1}^{\infty} 9(0.1)^i$ 1

14.5 *Use the binomial theorem to expand each binomial.*

55. $(m + n)^5$ $m^5 + 5m^4n + 10m^3n^2 + 10m^2n^3 + 5mn^4 + n^5$

56. $(2m - y)^4$ $16m^4 - 32m^3y + 24m^2y^2 - 8my^3 + y^4$

57. $(a^2 - 3b)^3$ $a^6 - 9a^4b + 27a^2b^2 - 27b^3$

58. $\left(\frac{x}{2} + 2a\right)^5$ $\frac{x^5}{32} + \frac{5x^4a}{8} + 5x^3a^2 + 20x^2a^3 + 40xa^4 + 32a^5$

Find the indicated term of the binomial expansion.

59. $(x + y)^{12}$, 5th term $495x^8y^4$

60. $(x - 2y)^9$, 5th term $2016x^5y^4$

61. $(2a - b)^{14}$, 3rd term $372{,}736a^{12}b^2$

62. $(a + b)^{10}$, 4th term $120a^7b^3$

Write each expression in summation notation.

63. $(a + w)^7$ $\sum_{i=0}^{7} \frac{7!}{(7 - i)!\,i!} a^{7-i}w^i$

64. $(m - 3y)^9$ $\sum_{i=0}^{9} \frac{9!(-3)^i}{(9 - i)!\,i!} m^{9-i}y^i$

Miscellaneous

Identify each sequence as an arithmetic sequence, a geometric sequence, or neither.

65. 1, 3, 6, 10, 15, . . . Neither

66. 9, 12, 16, $\frac{64}{3}$, . . . Geometric

67. 9, 12, 15, 18, . . . Arithmetic

68. 2, 4, 8, 16, . . . Geometric

69. 0, 2, 4, 6, 8, . . . Arithmetic

70. 0, 3, 9, 27, 81, . . . Neither

Solve each problem.

71. Find the common ratio for the geometric sequence with first term 6 and fourth term $\frac{1}{30}$.
$\frac{1}{\sqrt[3]{180}}$ or $\frac{\sqrt[3]{150}}{30}$

72. Find the common difference for an arithmetic sequence with first term 6 and fourth term 36. 10

73. Write out all of the terms of the series

$$\sum_{i=1}^{5} \frac{(-1)^i}{i!}.$$

$-1 + \frac{1}{2} - \frac{1}{6} + \frac{1}{24} - \frac{1}{120}$

74. Write out the first eight rows of Pascal's triangle.

75. Write out all of the terms of the series

$$\sum_{i=0}^{5} \frac{5!}{(5-i)!\,i!} a^{5-i}b^i.$$

$a^5 + 5a^4b + 10a^3b^2 + 10a^2b^3 + 5ab^4 + b^5$

76. Write out all of the terms of the series

$$\sum_{i=0}^{8} \frac{8!}{(8-i)!\,i!} x^{8-i}y^i.$$

$x^8 + 8x^7y + 28x^6y^2 + 56x^5y^3 + 70x^4y^4 + 56x^3y^5$
$+ 28x^2y^6 + 8xy^7 + y^8$

77. How many terms are there in the expansion of $(a + b)^{25}$? 26

78. Calculate $\frac{12!}{8!4!}$. 495

79. If \$3000 is deposited at the beginning of each year for 16 years into an account paying 10% compounded annually, then what is the value of the annuity at the end of the 16th year? \$118,634.11

80. If \$3000 is deposited at the beginning of each year for 8 years into an account paying 10% compounded annually, then what is the value of the annuity at the end of the eighth year? How does the value of the annuity in this exercise compare to that of Exercise 79?
\$37,738.43. The time is half as much, and the amount is less than one-third as much.

81. If one deposit of \$3000 is made into an account paying 10% compounded annually, then how much will be in the account at the end of 16 years? Note that a single deposit is not an annuity.
\$13,784.92

Chapter 14 Test

List the first four terms of the sequence whose nth term is given.

1. $a_n = -10 + (n - 1)6$ $\quad -10, -4, 2, 8$

2. $a_n = 5(0.1)^{n-1}$ $\quad 5, 0.5, 0.05, 0.005$

3. $a_n = \frac{(-1)^n}{n!}$ $\quad -1, \frac{1}{2}, -\frac{1}{6}, \frac{1}{24}$

4. $a_n = \frac{2n - 1}{n^2}$ $\quad 1, \frac{3}{4}, \frac{5}{9}, \frac{7}{16}$

Write a formula for the nth term of each sequence.

5. $7, 4, 1, -2, \ldots$ $\quad a_n = 10 - 3n$

6. $-25, 5, -1, \frac{1}{5}, \ldots$ $\quad a_n = -25\left(-\frac{1}{5}\right)^{n-1}$

7. $2, -4, 6, -8, 10, -12, \ldots$ $\quad a_n = (-1)^{n-1}2n$

8. $1, 4, 9, 16, 25, \ldots$ $\quad a_n = n^2$

Write out all of the terms of each series.

9. $\sum_{i=1}^{5} (2i + 3)$ $\quad 5 + 7 + 9 + 11 + 13$

10. $\sum_{i=1}^{6} 5(2)^{i-1}$ $\quad 5 + 10 + 20 + 40 + 80 + 160$

11. $\sum_{i=0}^{4} \frac{4!}{(4 - i)!i!} m^{4-i}q^i$ $\quad m^4 + 4m^3q + 6m^2q^2 + 4mq^3 + q^4$

Find the sum of each series.

12. $\sum_{i=1}^{20} (6 + 3i)$ $\quad 750$

13. $\sum_{i=1}^{5} 10\left(\frac{1}{2}\right)^{i-1}$ $\quad \frac{155}{8}$

14. $\sum_{i=1}^{\infty} 0.35(0.93)^{i-1}$ $\quad 5$

15. $2 + 4 + 6 + \cdots + 200$ $\quad 10{,}100$

16. $\frac{1}{4} + \frac{1}{8} + \frac{1}{16} + \cdots$ $\quad \frac{1}{2}$

17. $2 + 1 + \frac{1}{2} + \frac{1}{4} + \cdots + \frac{1}{128}$ $\quad \frac{511}{128}$

Solve each problem.

18. Find the common ratio for the geometric sequence that has first term 3 and fifth term 48. ± 2

19. Find the common difference for the arithmetic sequence that has first term 1 and twelfth term 122. 11

20. Find the fifth term in the expansion of $(r - t)^{15}$. $1365r^{11}t^4$

21. Find the fourth term in the expansion of $(a^2 - 2b)^8$. $-448a^{10}b^3$

22. If \$800 is deposited at the beginning of each year for 25 years into an account earning 10% compounded annually, then what is the value of this annuity at the end of the 25th year? \$86,545.41

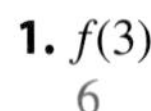

*Making*Connections | A Review of Chapters 1–14

Let $f(x) = x^2 - 3$, $g(x) = 2x - 1$, $h(x) = 2^x$, and $m(x) = \log_2(x)$. Find the following.

1. $f(3)$
6

2. $f(n)$
$n^2 - 3$

3. $f(x + h)$
$x^2 + 2xh + h^2 - 3$

4. $f(x) - g(x)$
$x^2 - 2x - 2$

5. $g(f(3))$
11

6. $(f \circ g)(2)$
6

7. $m(16)$
4

8. $(h \circ m)(32)$
32

9. $h(-1)$
$\frac{1}{2}$

10. $h^{-1}(8)$
3

11. $m^{-1}(0)$
1

12. $(m \circ h)(x)$
x

Solve each variation problem.

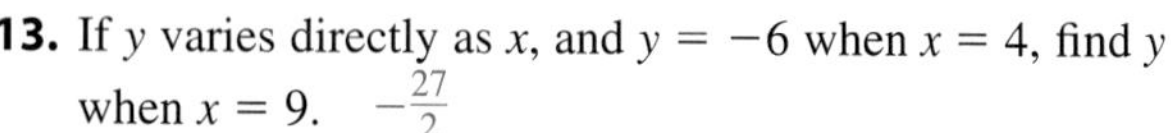

13. If y varies directly as x, and $y = -6$ when $x = 4$, find y when $x = 9$. $-\frac{27}{2}$

14. If a varies inversely as b, and $a = 2$ when $b = -4$, find a when $b = 3$. $-\frac{8}{3}$

15. If y varies directly as w and inversely as t, and $y = 16$ when $w = 3$ and $t = -4$, find y when $w = 2$ and $t = 3$. $-\frac{128}{9}$

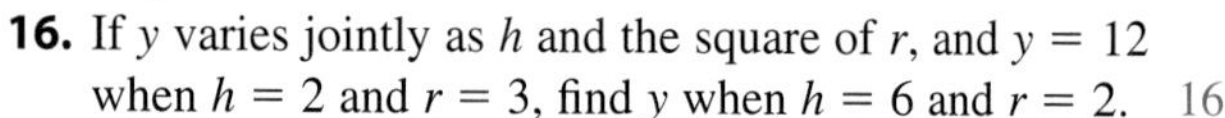

16. If y varies jointly as h and the square of r, and $y = 12$ when $h = 2$ and $r = 3$, find y when $h = 6$ and $r = 2$. 16

Sketch the graph of each inequality or system of inequalities.

17. $x > 3$ and $x + y < 0$

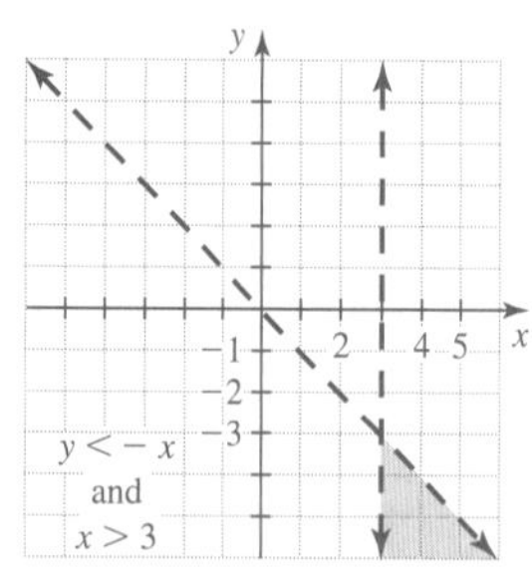

18. $|x - y| \geq 2$

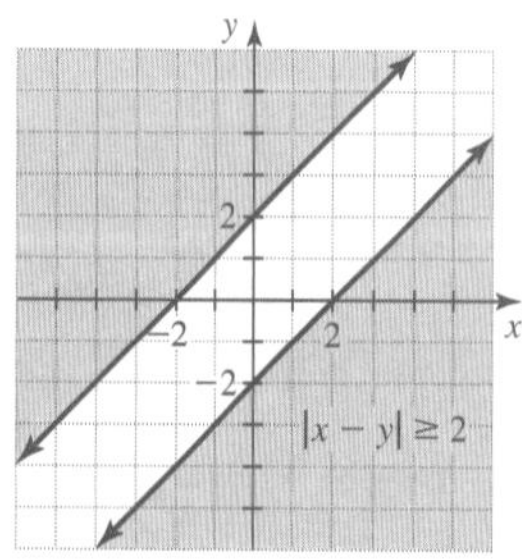

19. $y < -2x + 3$ and $y > 2^x$

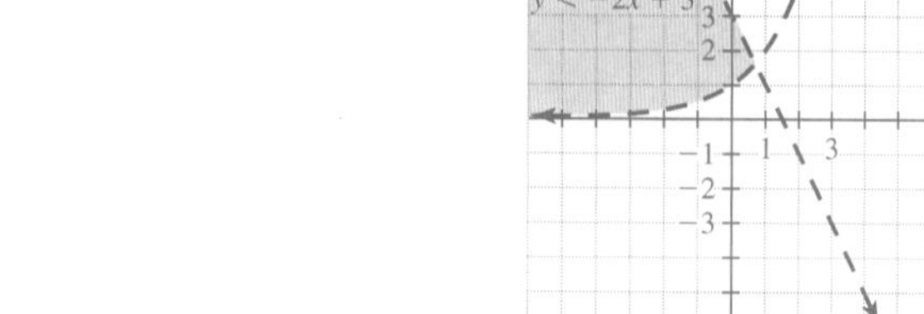

20. $|y + 2x| < 1$

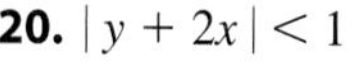

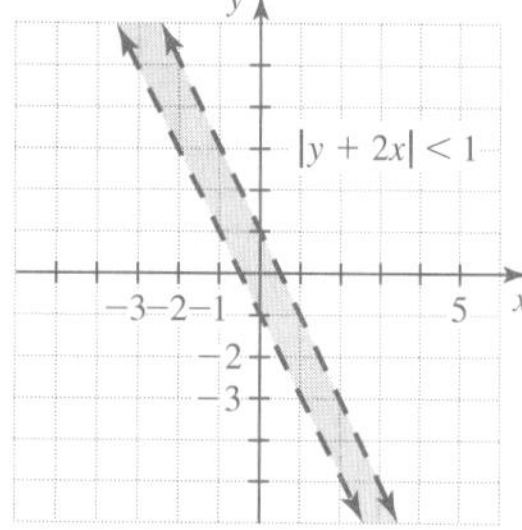

21. $x^2 + y^2 < 4$

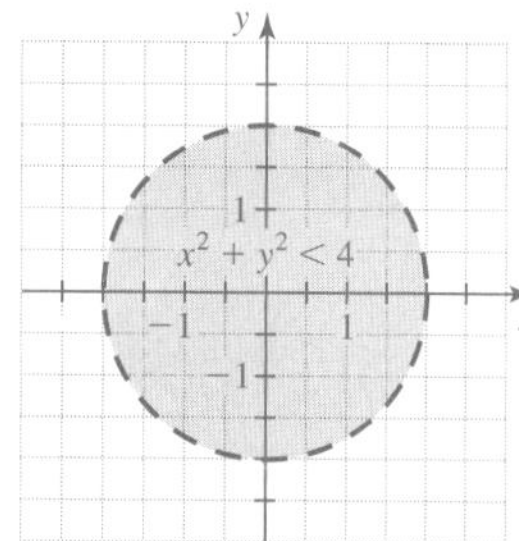

22. $x^2 - y^2 < 1$

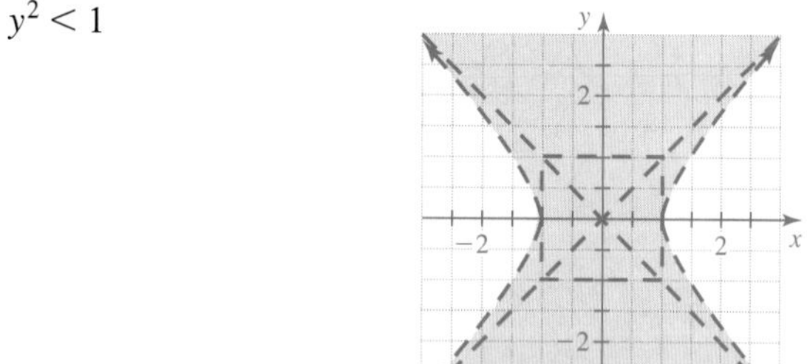

23. $y < \log_2(x)$

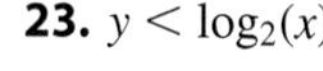

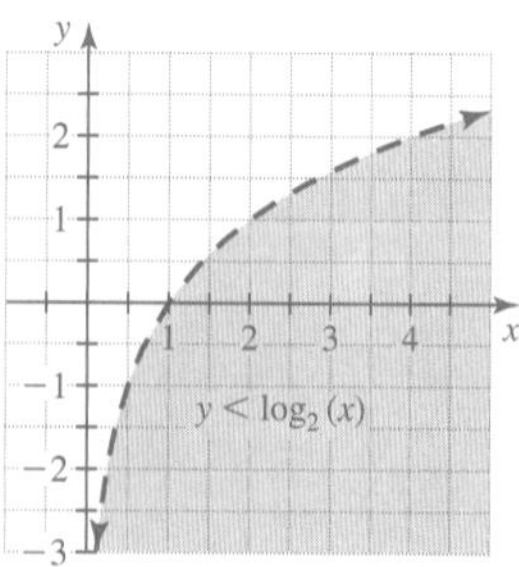

24. $x^2 + 2y < 4$

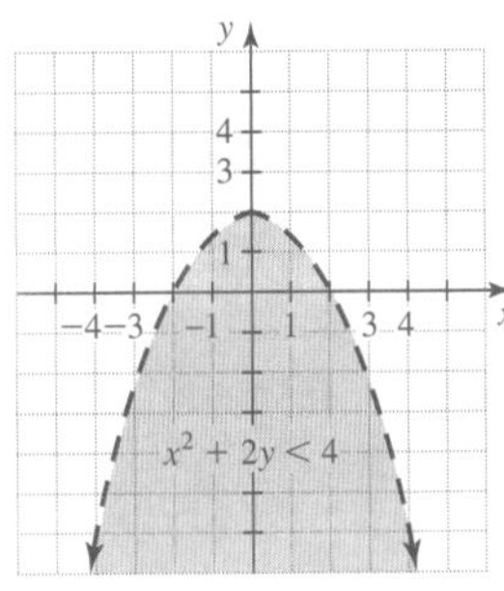

25. $\frac{x^2}{4} + \frac{y^2}{9} < 1$ and $y > x^2$

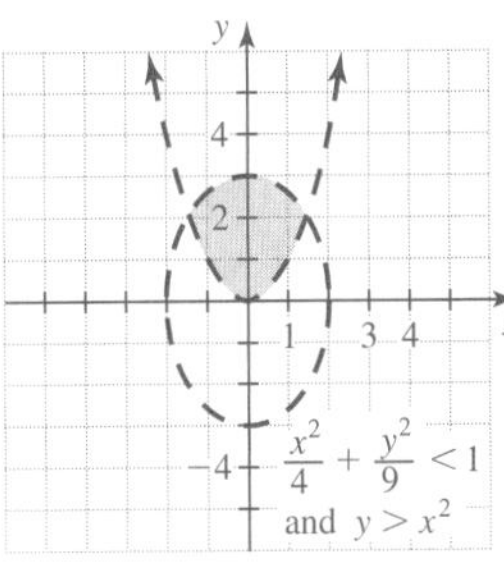

Perform the indicated operation and simplify. Write answers with positive exponents.

26. $\frac{a}{b} + \frac{b}{a}$ $\frac{a^2 + b^2}{ab}$

27. $1 - \frac{3}{y}$ $\frac{y - 3}{y}$

28. $\frac{x - 2}{x^2 - 9} - \frac{x - 4}{x^2 - 2x - 3}$ $\frac{10}{(x - 3)(x + 3)(x + 1)}$

29. $\frac{x^2 - 16}{2x + 8} \cdot \frac{4x^2 + 16x + 64}{x^3 - 16}$ $\frac{2(x^3 - 64)}{x^3 - 16}$

30. $\frac{(a^2b)^3}{(ab^2)^4} \cdot \frac{ab^3}{a^{-4}b^2}$ $\frac{a^7}{b^4}$

31. $\frac{x^2y}{(xy)^3} \div \frac{xy^2}{x^2y^4}$ 1

Simplify.

32. $8^{2/3}$ 4

33. $16^{-5/4}$ $\frac{1}{32}$

34. $-4^{1/2}$ -2

35. $27^{-2/3}$ $\frac{1}{9}$

36. -2^{-3} $-\frac{1}{8}$

37. $2^{-3/5} \cdot 2^{-7/5}$ $\frac{1}{4}$

38. $5^{-2/3} \div 5^{1/3}$ $\frac{1}{5}$

39. $(9^{1/2} + 4^{1/2})^2$ 25

Solve.

40. ***Predicting heights of preschoolers.*** A popular model in pediatrics for predicting the height of preschoolers is the JENNS model. According to this model, if $h(x)$ is the height [in centimeters (cm)] at age x (in years) for $0.25 \le x \le 6$, then

$$h(x) = 79.041 + 6.39x - e^{(3.261 - 0.993x)}.$$

a) Find the predicted height in inches for a child of age 4 years, 3 months.

b) If you have a graphing calculator, graph the function as shown in the accompanying figure.

c) Use your graphing calculator to find the age to the nearest tenth of a year for a child who has a height of 80 cm.

a) 105.8 cm or 41.7 in. **c)** 1.3 years

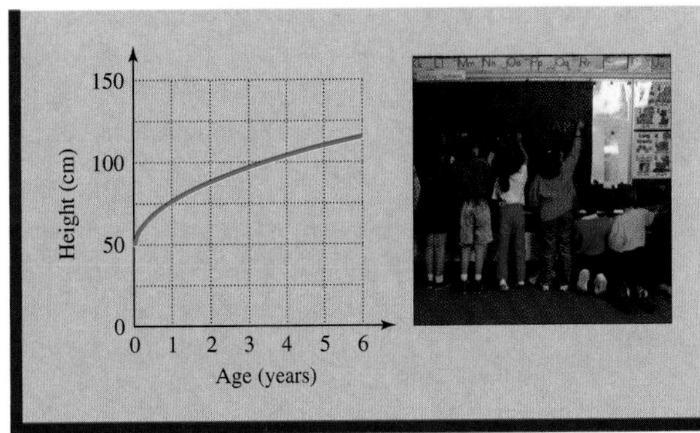

Figure for Exercise 40

Critical **Thinking** | For Individual or Group Work | Chapter 14

These exercises can be solved by a variety of techniques, which may or may not require algebra. So be creative and think critically. Explain all answers. Answers are in the Instructor's Edition of this text.

1. ***Table game.*** Place one of the integers from 1 through 9 in each cell of table (a) of the accompanying figure. Do not use an integer more than once. Integers in cells that touch must differ by more than 1. Repeat this process with table (b).

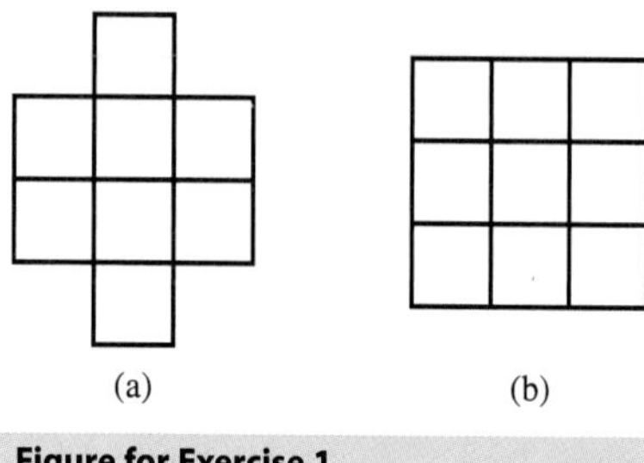

Figure for Exercise 1

2. ***Let's Make a Deal.*** Monte Hall shows you three boxes. He tells you that one of the boxes contains a diamond ring and the other two are empty. Monte knows which one contains the ring. He lets you choose a box but not open it. He then opens one of the unchosen boxes and shows you that it is empty. He then gives you the opportunity to trade the originally chosen box for the other unopened box. What should you do?

3. ***Going to class.*** Al, Bob, and Coddy must all get to an 8 A.M. class that is 6 miles from their house. They average 3 mph walking or 30 mph riding Al's motorcycle. Of course the motorcycle holds only 2 people.

a) What the is minimum amount of time needed to get all of them to class?

b) What if there is a fourth person and only one motorcycle?

c) If we keep increasing the number of people, what happens to the minimum time?

4. ***Factorial fever.*** The number 53! is the product of the positive integers from 1 through 53. This number is huge. With what digit does 53! end? How many times does that digit appear consecutively at the end of the number?

5. ***Angle bisectors.*** The angle bisectors of any triangle meet at a single point. If the hypotenuse of a 30-60-90 triangle is 4 units, then what is the exact distance from the vertex of the right angle to the point where the angle bisectors meet?

6. ***Powers of i.*** Evaluate

$$i^{0!} + i^{1!} + i^{2!} + \dots + i^{100!}.$$

7. ***Summing integers.*** Find the exact sum of all positive 10-digit integers.

8. ***Open and shut case.*** At Brentwood High the lockers are numbered 1 through 500 in order down a long hallway. All lockers are closed and the students are standing by their lockers. A student "changes the status of a locker" by opening a closed locker or closing an open locker. The first student changes the status of every locker starting with his. Then the second student changes the status of every other locker starting with hers. Then the third student changes the status of every third locker starting with his. Then the fourth student changes the status of every fourth locker starting with hers. This exercise continues through the five-hundredth student. Which lockers will be open when this exercise is finished?

Photo for Exercise 8

1. Table (a):

	3	
7	1	6
5	9	4
	2	

Table (b): impossible. **2.** Trade, because you have $\frac{1}{3}$ chance that the ring is in the original box and $\frac{2}{3}$ chance that it is not. So the probability is $\frac{2}{3}$ that it is in the box that Monte did not open. **3. a)** 29/55 hr **b)** 499/605 hr **c)** Minimum time approaches 2 hours **4.** 0, 10 **5.** $\sqrt{6} - \sqrt{2}$ **6.** $95 + 2i$ **7.** 4,949,999,995,450,000,000 **8.** The perfect square lockers: 1, 4, 9, 16, 25, . . . , 484

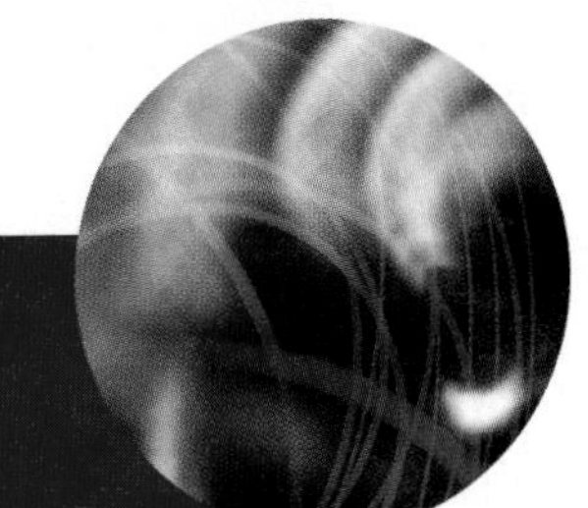

Appendix A

Geometry Review Exercises

(Answers are at the end of the answer section in this text.)

1. Find the perimeter of a triangle whose sides are 3 in., 4 in., and 5 in. 12 in.
2. Find the area of a triangle whose base is 4 ft and height is 12 ft. 24 ft^2
3. If two angles of a triangle are 30° and 90°, then what is the third angle? 60°
4. If the area of a triangle is 36 ft^2 and the base is 12 ft, then what is the height? 6 ft
5. If the side opposite 30° in a 30-60-90 right triangle is 10 cm, then what is the length of the hypotenuse? 20 cm
6. Find the area of a trapezoid whose height is 12 cm and whose parallel sides are 4 cm and 20 cm. 144 cm^2
7. Find the area of the right triangle that has sides of 6 ft, 8 ft, and 10 ft. 24 ft^2
8. If a right triangle has sides of 5 ft, 12 ft, and 13 ft, then what is the length of the hypotenuse? 13 ft
9. If the hypotenuse of a right triangle is 50 cm and the length of one leg is 40 cm, then what is the length of the other leg? 30 cm
10. Is a triangle with sides of 5 ft, 10 ft, and 11 ft a right triangle? No
11. What is the area of a triangle with sides of 7 yd, 24 yd, and 25 yd? 84 yd^2
12. Find the perimeter of a parallelogram in which one side is 9 in. and another side is 6 in. 30 in.
13. Find the area of a parallelogram which has a base of 8 ft and a height of 4 ft. 32 ft^2
14. If one side of a rhombus is 5 km, then what is its perimeter. 20 km
15. Find the perimeter and area of a rectangle whose width is 18 in. and length is 2 ft. 7 ft, 3 ft^2
16. If the width of a rectangle is 8 yd and its perimeter is 60 yd, then what is its length? 22 yd
17. The radius of a circle is 4 ft. Find its area to the nearest tenth of a square foot. 50.3 ft^2
18. The diameter of a circle is 12 ft. Find its circumference to the nearest tenth of a foot. 37.7 ft
19. A right circular cone has radius 4 cm and height 9 cm. Find its volume to the nearest hundredth of a cubic centimeter. 150.80 cm^3
20. A right circular cone has a radius 12 ft and a height of 20 ft. Find its lateral surface area to the nearest hundredth of a square foot. 879.29 ft^2
21. A shoe box has a length of 12 in., a width of 6 in., and a height of 4 in. Find its volume and surface area. 288 in.^{3}, 288 in.^{2}
22. The volume of a rectangular solid is 120 cm^3. If the area of its bottom is 30 cm^2, then what is its height? 4 cm
23. What is the area and perimeter of a square in which one of the sides is 10 mi long? 100 mi^2, 40 mi
24. Find the perimeter of a square whose area is 25 km^2. 20 km
25. Find the area of a square whose perimeter is 26 cm. 42.25 cm^2
26. A sphere has a radius of 2 ft. Find its volume to the nearest thousandth of a cubic foot and its surface area to the nearest thousandth of a square foot. 33.510 ft^3, 50.265 ft^2
27. A can of soup (right circular cylinder) has a radius of 2 in. and a height of 6 in. Find its volume to the nearest tenth of a cubic inch and total surface area to the nearest tenth of a square inch. 75.4 in.^{3}, 100.5 in.^{2}
28. If one of two complementary angles is 34°, then what is the other angle? 56°
29. If the perimeter of an isosceles triangle is 29 cm and one of the equal sides is 12 cm, then what is the length of the shortest side of the triangle? 5 cm
30. A right triangle with sides of 6 in., 8 in., and 10 in., is similar to another right triangle that has a hypotenuse of 25 in. What are the lengths of the other two sides in the second triangle? 15 in. and 20 in.
31. If one of two supplementary angles is 31°, then what is the other angle? 149°
32. Find the perimeter of an equilateral triangle in which one of the sides is 4 km. 12 km
33. Find the length of a side of an equilateral triangle that has a perimeter of 30 yd. 10 yd

Appendix B

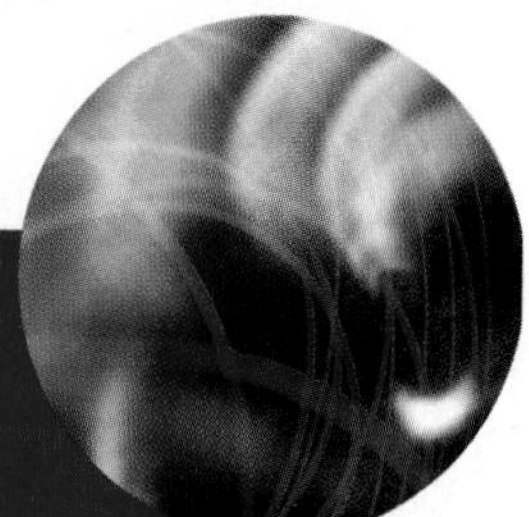

Sets

Every subject has its own terminology, and **algebra** is no different. In this section we will learn the basic terms and facts about sets.

Set Notation

A **set** is a collection of objects. At home you may have a set of dishes and a set of steak knives. In algebra we generally discuss sets of numbers. For example, we refer to the numbers 1, 2, 3, 4, 5, and so on as the set of **counting numbers** or **natural numbers.** Of course, these are the numbers that we use for counting.

The objects or numbers in a set are called the **elements** or **members** of the set. To describe sets with a convenient notation, we use braces, { }, and name the sets with capital letters. For example,

$$A = \{1, 2, 3\}$$

means that set A is the set whose members are the natural numbers 1, 2, and 3. The letter N is used to represent the entire set of natural numbers.

A set that has a fixed number of elements such as {1, 2, 3} is a **finite** set, whereas a set without a fixed number of elements such as the natural numbers is an **infinite** set. When listing the elements of a set, we use a series of three dots to indicate a continuing pattern. For example, the set of natural numbers is written as

$$N = \{1, 2, 3, \ldots\}.$$

The set of natural numbers *between* 4 and 40 can be written

$$\{5, 6, 7, 8, \ldots, 39\}.$$

Note that since the members of this set are *between* 4 and 40, it does not include 4 or 40.

Set-builder notation is another method of describing sets. In this notation we use a variable to represent the numbers in the set. A **variable** is a letter that is used to stand for some numbers. The set is then built from the variable and a description of the numbers that the variable represents. For example, the set

$$B = \{1, 2, 3, \ldots, 49\}$$

is written in set-builder notation as

$$B = \{x \mid x \text{ is a natural number less than } 50\}.$$

↑ The set of numbers ↑ such that ↑ condition for membership

This notation is read as "B is the set of numbers x such that x is a natural number less than 50." Notice that the number 50 is not a member of set B.

The symbol $\in$ is used to indicate that a specific number is a member of a set, and $\notin$ indicates that a specific number is not a member of a set. For example, the statement $1 \in B$ is read as "1 is a member of B," "1 belongs to B," "1 is in B," or "1 is an element of B." The statement $0 \notin B$ is read as "0 is not a member of B," "0 does not belong to B," "0 is not in B," or "0 is not an element of B."

Two sets are **equal** if they contain exactly the same members. Otherwise, they are said to be not equal. To indicate equal sets, we use the symbol $=$. For sets that are not equal we use the symbol $\neq$. The elements in two equal sets do not need to be written in the same order. For example, $\{3, 4, 7\} = \{3, 4, 7\}$ and $\{2, 4, 1\} = \{1, 2, 4\}$, but $\{3, 5, 6\} \neq \{3, 5, 7\}$.

EXAMPLE 1

Set notation

Let $A = \{1, 2, 3, 5\}$ and $B = \{x \mid x \text{ is an even natural number less than } 10\}$. Determine whether each statement is true or false.

a) $3 \in A$ **b)** $5 \in B$ **c)** $4 \notin A$ **d)** $A = N$

e) $A = \{x \mid x \text{ is a natural number less than } 6\}$ **f)** $B = \{2, 4, 6, 8\}$

Solution

a) True, because 3 is a member of set A.

b) False, because 5 is not an even natural number.

c) True, because 4 is not a member of set A.

d) False, because A does not contain all of the natural numbers.

e) False, because 4 is a natural number less than 6, and $4 \notin A$.

f) True, because the even counting numbers less than 10 are 2, 4, 6, and 8.

Union of Sets

Any two sets A and B can be combined to form a new set called their union that consists of all elements of A together with all elements of B.

Union of Sets

If A and B are sets, the **union** of A and B, denoted $A \cup B$, is the set of all elements that are either in A, in B, or in both. In symbols,

$$A \cup B = \{x \mid x \in A \text{ or } x \in B\}.$$

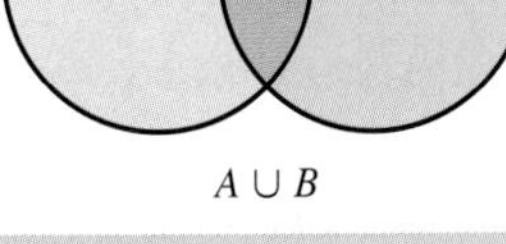

Figure B.1

In mathematics the word "or" is always used in an inclusive manner (allowing the possibility of both alternatives). The diagram in Fig. B.1 can be used to illustrate $A \cup B$. Any point that lies within circle A, circle B, or both is in $A \cup B$. Diagrams (like Fig. B.1) that are used to illustrate sets are called **Venn diagrams.**

EXAMPLE 2

Union of sets

Let $A = \{0, 2, 3\}$, $B = \{2, 3, 7\}$, and $C = \{7, 8\}$. List the elements in each of these sets.

a) $A \cup B$ **b)** $A \cup C$

Solution

a) $A \cup B$ is the set of numbers that are in A, in B, or in both A and B.

$$A \cup B = \{0, 2, 3, 7\}$$

b) $A \cup C = \{0, 2, 3, 7, 8\}$

Helpful Hint

To remember what "union" means think of a labor union, which is a group formed by joining together many individuals.

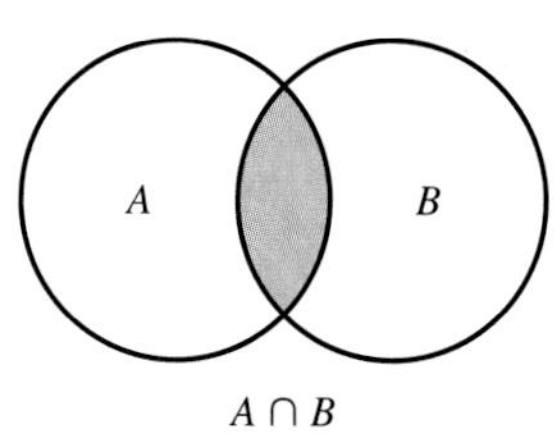

Figure B.2

Intersection of Sets

Another way to form a new set from two known sets is by considering only those elements that the two sets have in common. The diagram shown in Fig. B.2 illustrates the intersection of two sets A and B.

Intersection of Sets

If A and B are sets, the **intersection** of A and B, denoted $A \cap B$, is the set of all elements that are in both A and B. In symbols,

$$A \cap B = \{x \mid x \in A \text{ and } x \in B\}.$$

Helpful Hint

To remember the meaning of "intersection," think of the intersection of two roads. At the intersection you are on both roads.

It is possible for two sets to have no elements in common. A set with no members is called the **empty set** and is denoted by the symbol $\varnothing$. Note that $A \cup \varnothing = A$ and $A \cap \varnothing = \varnothing$ for any set A.

CAUTION The set $\{0\}$ is not the empty set. The set $\{0\}$ has one member, the number 0. Do not use the number 0 to represent the empty set.

EXAMPLE 3

Intersection of sets

Let $A = \{0, 2, 3\}$, $B = \{2, 3, 7\}$, and $C = \{7, 8\}$. List the elements in each of these sets.

a) $A \cap B$ **b)** $B \cap C$ **c)** $A \cap C$

Solution

a) $A \cap B$ is the set of all numbers that are in both A and B. So $A \cap B = \{2, 3\}$.

b) $B \cap C = \{7\}$ **c)** $A \cap C = \varnothing$

EXAMPLE 4

Membership and equality

Let $A = \{1, 2, 3, 5\}$, $B = \{2, 3, 7, 8\}$, and $C = \{6, 7, 8, 9\}$. Place one of the symbols $=$, $\neq$, $\in$, or $\notin$ in the blank to make each statement correct.

a) 5 _____ $A \cup B$ **b)** 5 _____ $A \cap B$

c) $A \cup B$ _____ $\{1, 2, 3, 5, 7, 8\}$ **d)** $A \cap B$ _____ $\{2\}$

Solution

a) $5 \in A \cup B$ because 5 is a member of A.

b) $5 \notin A \cap B$ because 5 must belong to *both* A and B to be a member of $A \cap B$.

c) $A \cup B = \{1, 2, 3, 5, 7, 8\}$ because the elements of A together with those of B are listed. Note that 2 and 3 are members of both sets but are listed only once.

d) $A \cap B \neq \{2\}$ because $A \cap B = \{2, 3\}$.

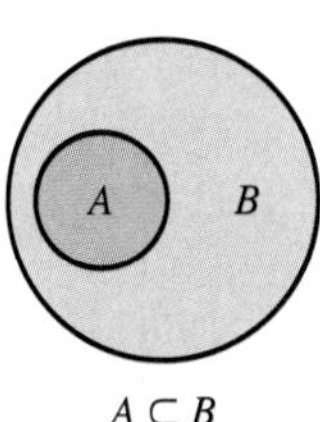

$A \subseteq B$

Figure B.3

Subsets

If every member of set A is also a member of set B, then we write $A \subseteq B$ and say that A is a **subset** of B. See Fig. B.3. For example,

$$\{2, 3\} \subseteq \{2, 3, 4\}$$

because $2 \in \{2, 3, 4\}$ and $3 \in \{2, 3, 4\}$. Note that the symbol for membership ($\in$) is used between a single element and a set, whereas the symbol for subset ($\subseteq$) is used between two sets. If A is not a subset of B, we write $A \not\subseteq B$.

CAUTION To claim that $A \not\subseteq B$, there *must* be an element of A that does *not* belong to B. For example,

$$\{1, 2\} \not\subseteq \{2, 3, 4\}$$

because 1 is a member of the first set but not of the second.

Is the empty set $\varnothing$ a subset of $\{2, 3, 4\}$? If we say that $\varnothing$ is *not* a subset of $\{2, 3, 4\}$, then there must be an element of $\varnothing$ that does not belong to $\{2, 3, 4\}$. But that cannot happen because $\varnothing$ is empty. So $\varnothing$ is a subset of $\{2, 3, 4\}$. In fact, by the same reasoning, *the empty set is a subset of every set.*

EXAMPLE 5

Subsets

Determine whether each statement is true or false.

a) $\{1, 2, 3\}$ is a subset of the set of natural numbers.

b) The set of natural numbers is not a subset of $\{1, 2, 3\}$.

c) $\{1, 2, 3\} \not\subseteq \{2, 4, 6, 8\}$

d) $\{2, 6\} \subseteq \{1, 2, 3, 4, 5\}$

e) $\varnothing \subseteq \{2, 4, 6\}$

Solution

a) True, because 1, 2, and 3 are natural numbers.

b) True, because 5, for example, is a natural number and $5 \notin \{1, 2, 3\}$.

c) True, because 1 is in the first set but not in the second.

d) False, because 6 is in the first set but not in the second.

e) True, because we cannot find anything in $\varnothing$ that fails to be in $\{2, 4, 6\}$.

Helpful Hint

The symbols $\subseteq$ and $\subset$ are often used interchangeably. The symbol $\subseteq$ combines the subset symbol $\subset$ and the equal symbol $=$. We use it when sets are equal, $\{1, 2\} \subseteq \{1, 2\}$, and when they are not, $\{1\} \subseteq \{1, 2\}$. When sets are not equal, we could simply use $\subset$, as in $\{1\} \subset \{1, 2\}$.

Combining Three or More Sets

We know how to find the union and intersection of two sets. For three or more sets we use parentheses to indicate which pair of sets to combine first. In Example 6, notice that different results are obtained from different placements of the parentheses.

EXAMPLE 6

Operations with three sets

Let $A = \{1, 2, 3, 4\}$, $B = \{2, 5, 6, 8\}$, and $C = \{4, 5, 7\}$. List the elements of each of these sets.

a) $(A \cup B) \cap C$

b) $A \cup (B \cap C)$

Solution

a) The parentheses indicate that the union of A and B is to be found first and then the result, $A \cup B$, is to be intersected with C.

$$A \cup B = \{1, 2, 3, 4, 5, 6, 8\}$$

Now examine $A \cup B$ and C to find the elements that belong to both sets:

$$A \cup B = \{1, 2, 3, 4, 5, 6, 8\}$$
$$C = \{4, 5, 7\}$$

The only numbers that are members of $A \cup B$ and C are 4 and 5. Thus

$$(A \cup B) \cap C = \{4, 5\}.$$

b) In $A \cup (B \cap C)$, first find $B \cap C$:

$$B \cap C = \{5\}$$

Now $A \cup (B \cap C)$ consist of all members of A together with 5 from $B \cap C$:

$$A \cup (B \cap C) = \{1, 2, 3, 4, 5\}$$

Exercises

Boost your GRADE at mathzone.com!

MathZone

- Practice Problems
- Self-Tests
- Videos
- Net Tutor
- e-Professors

Reading and Writing *After reading this section, write out the answers to these questions. Use complete sentences.*

1. What is a set? A set is a collection of objects.

2. What is the difference between a finite set and an infinite set? A finite set has a fixed number of elements and an infinite set does not.

3. What is a Venn diagram used for? A Venn diagram is used to illustrate relationships between sets.

4. What is the difference between the intersection and the union of two sets? The intersection of two sets consists of elements that are in both sets, whereas the union of two sets consists of elements that are in one, in the other, or in both sets.

5. What does it mean to say that set A is a subset of set B? Every member of set A is also a member of set B.

6. Which set is a subset of every set? The empty set is a subset of every set.

Using the sets A, B, C, and N, determine whether each statement is true or false. Explain. See Example 1.

$A = \{1, 3, 5, 7, 9\}$ $B = \{2, 4, 6, 8\}$
$C = \{1, 2, 3, 4, 5\}$ $N = \{1, 2, 3, \ldots\}$

7. $6 \in A$ False

8. $8 \in A$ False

9. $A \neq B$ True

10. $A = \{1, 3, 5, 7, \ldots\}$ False

11. $3 \in C$ True

12. $4 \notin B$ False

13. $A = \{1, 3, 7, 9\}$ False

14. $B \neq C$ True

15. $0 \in N$ False

16. $2.5 \in N$ False

17. $C = N$ False

18. $N = A$ False

Using the sets A, B, C, and N, list the elements in each set. If the set is empty write ∅. See Examples 2 and 3.

$A = \{1, 3, 5, 7, 9\}$ $B = \{2, 4, 6, 8\}$
$C = \{1, 2, 3, 4, 5\}$ $N = \{1, 2, 3, \ldots\}$

19. $A \cap B$ $\varnothing$

20. $A \cup B$ $\{1, 2, 3, 4, 5, 6, 7, 8, 9\}$

21. $A \cap C$ $\{1, 3, 5\}$

22. $A \cup C$ $\{1, 2, 3, 4, 5, 7, 9\}$

23. $B \cup C$ $\{1, 2, 3, 4, 5, 6, 8\}$

24. $B \cap C$ $\{2, 4\}$

25. $A \cup \varnothing$ A

26. $B \cup \varnothing$ B

27. $A \cap \varnothing$ $\varnothing$

28. $B \cap \varnothing$ $\varnothing$

29. $A \cap N$ A

30. $A \cup N$ N

Use one of the symbols ∈, ∉, =, ≠, ∪, or ∩ in each blank to make a true statement. See Example 4.

$A = \{1, 3, 5, 7, 9\}$ $B = \{2, 4, 6, 8\}$
$C = \{1, 2, 3, 4, 5\}$ $N = \{1, 2, 3, \ldots\}$

31. $A \cap B$ _=_ $\varnothing$

32. $A \cap C$ _≠_ $\varnothing$

33. A _∪_ $B = \{1, 2, 3, 4, 5, 6, 7, 8, 9\}$

34. A _∩_ $B = \varnothing$

35. B _∩_ $C = \{2, 4\}$

36. B _∪_ $C = \{1, 2, 3, 4, 5, 6, 8\}$

37. 3 _∉_ $A \cap B$ **38.** 3 _∈_ $A \cap C$

39. 4 _∈_ $B \cap C$ **40.** 8 _∈_ $B \cup C$

Determine whether each statement is true or false. Explain your answer. See Example 5.

$A = \{1, 3, 5, 7, 9\}$ $B = \{2, 4, 6, 8\}$
$C = \{1, 2, 3, 4, 5\}$ $N = \{1, 2, 3, \ldots\}$

41. $A \subseteq N$ True **42.** $B \subseteq N$ True

43. $\{2, 3\} \subseteq C$ True **44.** $C \subseteq A$ False

45. $B \not\subseteq C$ True **46.** $C \not\subseteq A$ True

47. $\varnothing \subseteq B$ True **48.** $\varnothing \subseteq C$ True

49. $A \subseteq \varnothing$ False **50.** $B \subseteq \varnothing$ False

51. $A \cap B \subseteq C$ True **52.** $B \cap C \subseteq \{2, 4, 6, 8\}$ True

Using the sets D, E, and F, list the elements in each set. If the set is empty write ∅. See Example 6.

$D = \{3, 5, 7\}$ $E = \{2, 4, 6, 8\}$ $F = \{1, 2, 3, 4, 5\}$

53. $D \cup E$
$\{2, 3, 4, 5, 6, 7, 8\}$

54. $D \cap E$
$\varnothing$

55. $D \cap F$
$\{3, 5\}$

56. $D \cup F$
$\{1, 2, 3, 4, 5, 7\}$

57. $E \cup F$
$\{1, 2, 3, 4, 5, 6, 8\}$

58. $E \cap F$
$\{2, 4\}$

59. $(D \cup E) \cap F$
$\{2, 3, 4, 5\}$

60. $(D \cup F) \cap E$
$\{2, 4\}$

61. $D \cup (E \cap F)$
$\{2, 3, 4, 5, 7\}$

62. $D \cup (F \cap E)$
$\{2, 3, 4, 5, 7\}$

63. $(D \cap F) \cup (E \cap F)$
$\{2, 3, 4, 5\}$

64. $(D \cap E) \cup (F \cap E)$
$\{2, 4\}$

65. $(D \cup E) \cap (D \cup F)$
$\{2, 3, 4, 5, 7\}$

66. $(D \cup F) \cap (D \cup E)$
$\{2, 3, 4, 5, 7\}$

Use one of the symbols ∈, ⊆, =, ∪, or ∩ in each blank to make a true statement.

$D = \{3, 5, 7\}$ $E = \{2, 4, 6, 8\}$ $F = \{1, 2, 3, 4, 5\}$

67. D _⊆_ $\{x \mid x$ is an odd natural number$\}$

68. E _=_ $\{x \mid x$ is an even natural number smaller than $9\}$

69. 3 _∈_ D **70.** $\{3\}$ _⊆_ D

71. D _∩_ $E = \varnothing$ **72.** $D \cap E$ _⊆_ D

73. $D \cap F$ _⊆_ F **74.** $3 \notin E$ _∩_ F

75. $E \not\subseteq E$ _∩_ F **76.** $E \subseteq E$ _∪_ F

77. D _∪_ $F = F \cup D$ **78.** E _∩_ $F = F \cap E$

List the elements in each set.

79. $\{x \mid x$ is an even natural number less than $20\}$
$\{2, 4, 6, \ldots, 18\}$

80. $\{x \mid x$ is a natural number greater than $6\}$
$\{7, 8, 9, \ldots\}$

81. $\{x \mid x$ is an odd natural number greater than $11\}$
$\{13, 15, 17, \ldots\}$

82. $\{x \mid x$ is an odd natural number less than $14\}$
$\{1, 3, 5, \ldots, 13\}$

83. $\{x \mid x$ is an even natural number between 4 and $79\}$
$\{6, 8, 10, \ldots, 78\}$

84. $\{x \mid x$ is an odd natural number between 12 and $57\}$
$\{13, 15, 17, \ldots, 55\}$

Write each set using set-builder notation. Answers may vary.

85. $\{3, 4, 5, 6\}$
$\{x \mid x$ is a natural number between 2 and $7\}$

86. $\{1, 3, 5, 7\}$
$\{x \mid x$ is an odd natural number less than $8\}$

87. $\{5, 7, 9, 11, \ldots\}$
$\{x \mid x$ is an odd natural number greater than $4\}$

88. $\{4, 5, 6, 7, \ldots\}$
$\{x \mid x$ is a natural number greater than $3\}$

89. $\{6, 8, 10, 12, \ldots, 82\}$
$\{x \mid x$ is an even natural number between 5 and $83\}$

90. $\{9, 11, 13, 15, \ldots, 51\}$
$\{x \mid x$ is an odd natural number between 8 and $52\}$

Determine whether each statement is true or false.

$A = \{1, 2, 3, 4\}$ $B = \{3, 4, 5\}$ $C = \{3, 4\}$

91. $A = \{x \mid x$ is a counting number$\}$ False

92. The set B has an infinite number of elements. False

93. The set of counting numbers less than 50 million is an infinite set. False

94. $1 \in A \cap B$ False **95.** $3 \in A \cup B$ True

96. $A \cap B = C$ True **97.** $C \subseteq B$ True

98. $A \subseteq B$ False **99.** $\varnothing \subseteq C$ True

100. $A \not\subseteq C$ True

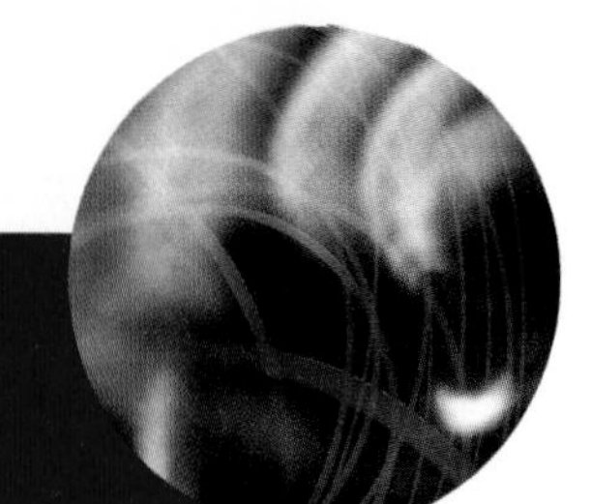

Appendix C

Chapters 1–6 Diagnostic Test

Use this test to check your knowledge of Chapters 1–6. The test is arranged by chapters so that you can determine the chapters that you need to review. There is a review section for each of Chapters 1–6 in Appendix D, immediately following this test. Answers to this test and the review sections can be found at the end of the Answer Section of this text.

Chapter 1

Write each interval of real numbers in interval notation and graph it on the number line.

1. The set of real numbers greater than 2
   $(2, \infty)$

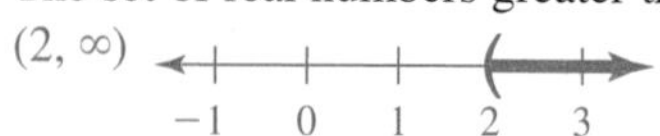

2. The set of real numbers less than or equal to -1
   $(-\infty, -1]$ 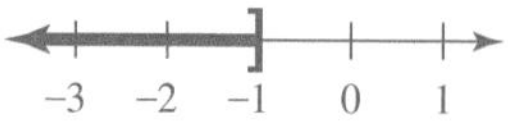
3. The set of real numbers between 0 and 1
   $(0, 1)$ 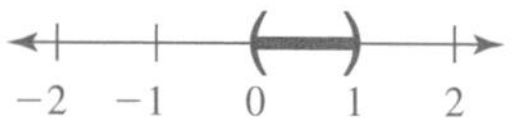
4. The set of real numbers greater than -4 and less than or equal to -2 $(-4, -2]$

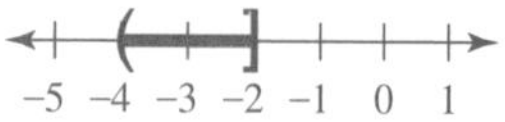

Evaluate each expression.

5. $\frac{3}{4} \cdot \frac{7}{9}$ $\frac{7}{12}$
6. $\frac{1}{4} + \frac{5}{6}$ $\frac{13}{12}$
7. $\frac{8}{9} \div 4$ $\frac{2}{9}$
8. $-4^2 - 3^3$ -43
9. $|3 - 2^2| - |7 - 19|$ -11
10. $\frac{-3 - 5}{-2 - (-1)}$ 8

Name the property that justifies each equation.

11. $3(x + 4) = 3x + 12$ Distributive property
12. $x \cdot 7 = 7x$ Commutative property of multiplication
13. $4 + (9 + y) = (4 + 9) + y$
    Associative property of addition
14. $0 + 3 = 3$ Additive identity

Simplify each expression.

15. $5x - (3 - 8x)$ $13x - 3$
16. $x + 3 - 0.2(5x - 30)$ 9
17. $(-3x)(-5x)$ $15x^2$
18. $\frac{3x + 12}{-3}$ $-x - 4$

Chapter 2

Solve each equation and check your answer.

19. $11x - 2 = 3$
    $\left\{\frac{5}{11}\right\}$
20. $4x - 5 = 12x + 11$
    $\{-2\}$
21. $3(x - 6) = 3x - 6$
    No solution, $\emptyset$
22. $x - 0.1x = 0.9x$
    All real numbers

Solve each equation for y.

23. $5x - 3y = 9$
    $y = \frac{5}{3}x - 3$
24. $ay + b = 0$
    $y = -\frac{b}{a}$
25. $a = t - by$
    $y = \frac{t - a}{b}$
26. $\frac{a}{2} + \frac{y}{3} = \frac{3a}{4}$
    $y = \frac{3}{4}a$

Solve each problem. Show all details.

27. The sum of three consecutive integers is 102. What are the integers? 33, 34, 35
28. The perimeter of a rectangular painting is 100 inches. If the width is 4 inches less than the length, then what is the width? 23 in.
29. The area of a triangular piece of property is 44,000 square feet. If the base of the triangle is 400 feet, then what is the height? 220 ft
30. Ivan has 400 pounds of mixed nuts that contain no peanuts. How many pounds of peanuts should he put into the mixed nuts so that 20% of the mixture is peanuts? 100 pounds

Solve each inequality. State the solution set using interval notation and graph the solution set.

31. $3x - 4 \le 11$ $(-\infty, 5]$ 
32. $5 - 7w > 26$ $(-\infty, -3)$

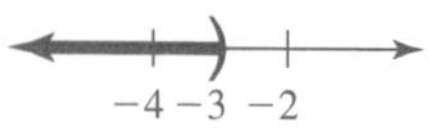

33. $-1 < 2a - 9 \le 7$ $(4, 8]$

0 2 4 6 8 10

34. $5 < 6 - x < 6$ $(0, 1)$

−2 −1 0 1 2

Chapter 3

Graph each equation in the coordinate plane and identify all intercepts.

35. $y = \frac{2}{3}x - 2$
$(0, -2), (3, 0)$

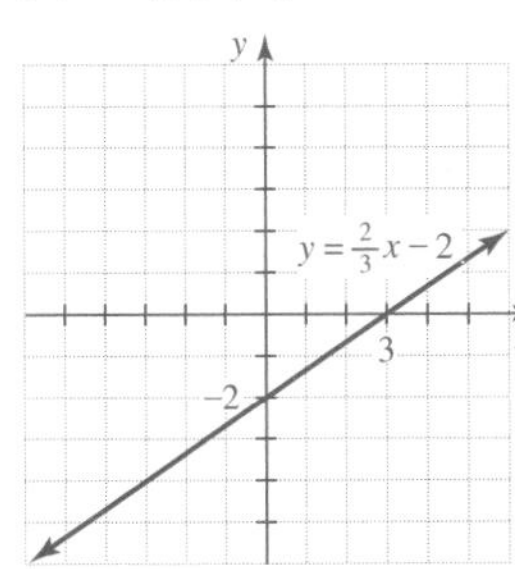

36. $3x - 5y = 150$
$(0, -30), (50, 0)$

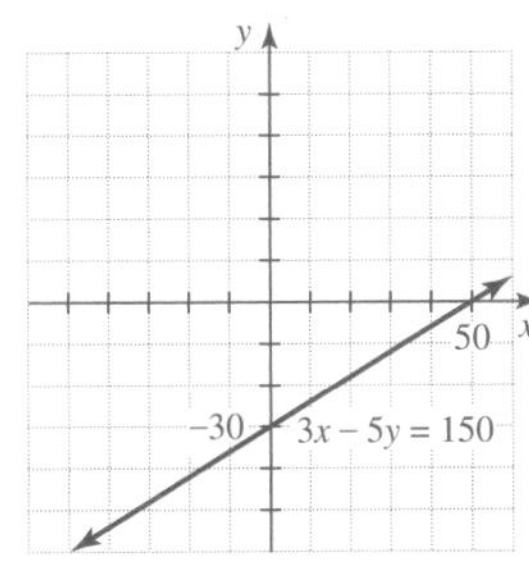

37. $y = 2$ $(0, 2)$

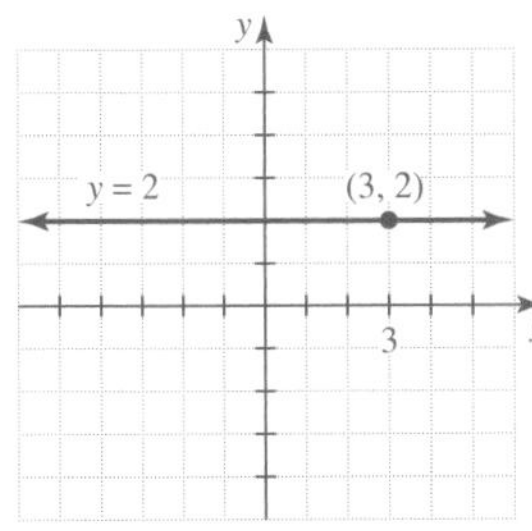

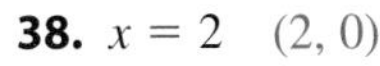

38. $x = 2$ $(2, 0)$

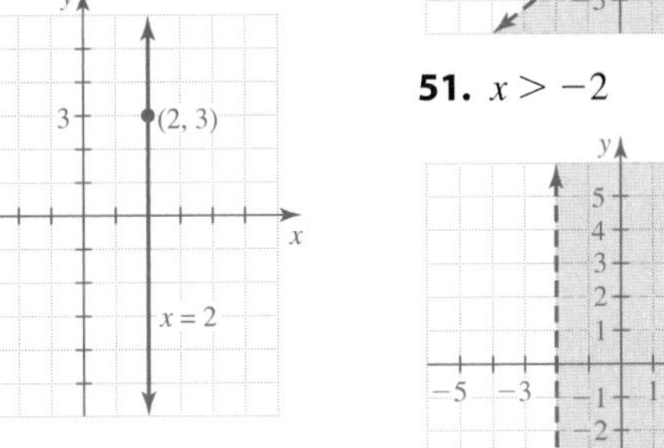

Find the slope of each line.

39. The line passing through the points (1, 2) and (3, 6) 2

40. The line $y = \frac{1}{2}x - 4$ $\frac{1}{2}$

41. The line parallel to $2x + 3y = 9$ $-\frac{2}{3}$

42. The line perpendicular to $y = -3x + 5$ $\frac{1}{3}$

Find the equation of each line in slope-intercept form when possible.

43. The line passing through the points (0, 3) and (2, 11)
$y = 4x + 3$

44. The line passing through the points (−2, 4) and (1, −2)
$y = -2x$

45. The line through (3, 5) that is parallel to $x = 4$ $x = 3$

46. The line through (0, 8) that is perpendicular to $y = \frac{1}{2}x$
$y = -2x + 8$

Solve each variation problem.

47. The time that it takes to mow a large lawn varies inversely with the number of mowers working on the job. If it takes 30 hours with three mowers, then how long would it take with five mowers? 14 hours

48. The cost of installing ceramic floor tile in a rectangular room varies jointly with the length and the width of the room. If the cost is \$810 for a 9 ft by 12 ft room, then what is the cost for a 14 ft by 18 ft room? \$1890

Graph the solution set to each inequality in the coordinate plane.

49. $3x - 4y > 12$

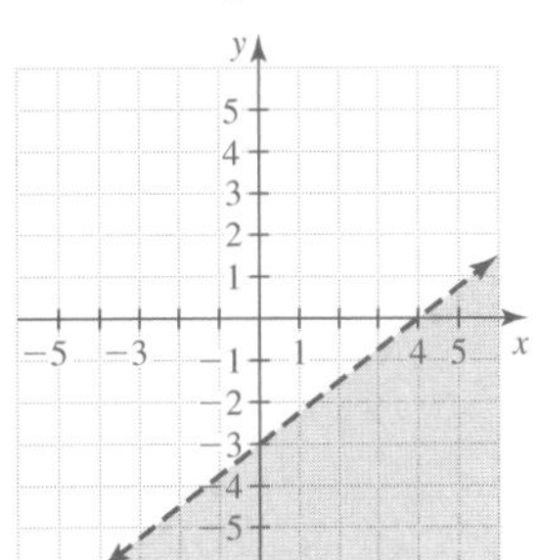

50. $y \le 3x + 2$

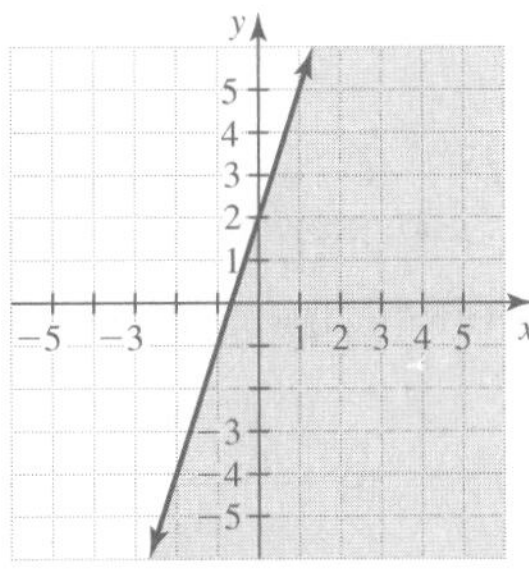

51. $x > -2$

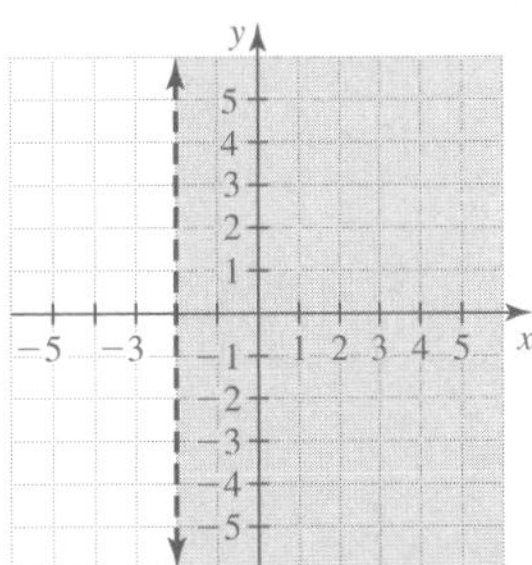

52. $y \le 4$

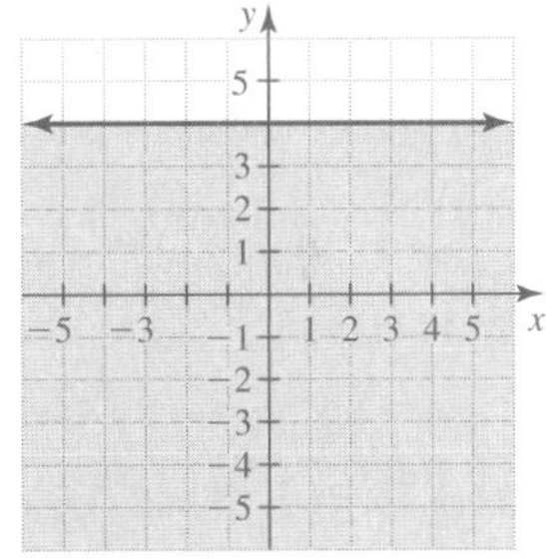

Chapter 4

Perform the indicated operations.

53. $(x^2 - 3x + 2) - (3x^2 + 9x - 4)$ $-2x^2 - 12x + 6$

54. $-3x^2(-2x^2 - 3)$ $6x^4 + 9x^3$

55. $(x + 7)(x - 9)$ $x^2 - 2x - 63$

56. $(x + 2)(x^2 - 2x + 4)$ $x^3 + 8$

57. $(4w^2 - 3)^2$ $16w^4 - 24w^2 + 9$

58. $(-8m^7) \div (2m^2)$ $-4m^5$

59. $(-9y^3 - 6y^2 + 3y) \div (3y)$ $-3y^2 - 2y + 1$

60. $(x^3 - 2x^2 - x - 6) \div (x - 3)$ $x^2 + x + 2$

Use the rules of exponents to simplify each expression. Write the answers without negative exponents.

61. $-8x^4 \cdot 4x^3$ $-32x^7$

62. $3x(5x^2)^3$ $375x^7$

63. $\dfrac{-6x^2y^3}{-2x^{-3}y^4}$ $\dfrac{3x^5}{y}$

64. $\left(\dfrac{2a^2}{a^{-3}}\right)^3$ $8a^{15}$

Perform each operation without a calculator. Write the answer in scientific notation.

65. $400{,}000 \cdot 600$
2.4×10^8

66. $(9 \times 10^3)(2 \times 10^6)$
1.8×10^{10}

67. $(2 \times 10^{-3})^4$
1.6×10^{-11}

68. $\dfrac{2 \times 10^9}{2000}$
1×10^{-12}

Chapter 5

Factor each polynomial completely.

69. $24x^2y^3 + 18xy^5$ $6xy^3(4x + 3y^2)$

70. $x^2 + 2x + ax + 2a$ $(x + a)(x + 2)$

71. $4m^2 - 49$ $(2m - 7)(2m + 7)$

72. $x^2 - 3x - 54$ $(x - 9)(x + 6)$

73. $6t^2 - 11t - 10$ $(2t - 5)(3t + 2)$

74. $4w^2 - 36w + 81$ $(2w - 9)^2$

75. $2a^3 - 6a^2 - 108a$ $2a(a - 9)(a + 6)$

76. $w^3 - 27$ $(w - 3)(w^2 + 3w + 9)$

Solve each equation.

77. $x^2 = x$ $\{0, 1\}$

78. $2x^3 - 8x = 0$ $\{-2, 0, 2\}$

79. $a^2 + a - 6 = 0$ $\{-3, 2\}$

80. $(b - 2)(b + 3) = 24$ $\{-6, 5\}$

Write a complete solution to each problem.

81. The sum of two numbers is 10 and their product is 21. Find the numbers. 3 and 7

82. The length of a new television screen is 14 inches larger than the width and the diagonal is 26 inches. What are the length and width? Length 24 in., width 10 in.

Chapter 6

Perform the indicated operation. Write each answer in lowest terms.

83. $\dfrac{5x}{2} + \dfrac{3x}{4}$ $\dfrac{13x}{4}$

84. $\dfrac{5}{x - 2} - \dfrac{3}{2 - x}$ $\dfrac{8}{x - 2}$

85. $\dfrac{9}{x^2 - 9} + \dfrac{2x}{x - 3}$ $\dfrac{2x^2 + 6x + 9}{(x + 3)(x - 3)}$

86. $\dfrac{2}{a - 5} + \dfrac{3}{a + 4}$ $\dfrac{5a - 7}{(a - 5)(a + 4)}$

87. $\dfrac{w^3}{2w - 4} \cdot \dfrac{w^2 - 4}{w}$ $\dfrac{w^3 + 2w^2}{2}$

88. $\dfrac{5ab^2}{6a^2b^3} \div \dfrac{10a}{21b^6}$ $\dfrac{7b^5}{4a^2}$

Solve each equation.

89. $\dfrac{2}{x} = \dfrac{3}{4}$ $\left\{\dfrac{8}{3}\right\}$

90. $\dfrac{1}{w - 3} = \dfrac{2}{w + 5}$ $\{11\}$

91. $\dfrac{1}{x} + \dfrac{3}{7} = \dfrac{1}{3x}$ $\left\{-\dfrac{14}{9}\right\}$

92. $\dfrac{3}{a - 1} + \dfrac{1}{a + 2} = \dfrac{17}{10}$ $\left\{-\dfrac{23}{13}\right\}$

Solve each formula for y.

93. $\dfrac{3}{y} = \dfrac{5}{x}$ $y = \dfrac{3}{5}x$

94. $a = \dfrac{1}{2}y(w - c)$ $y = \dfrac{2a}{w - c}$

95. $\dfrac{y - 3}{x + 5} = -3$ $y = -3x - 12$

96. $\dfrac{3}{y} + \dfrac{1}{2} = \dfrac{1}{t}$ $y = \dfrac{6t}{2 - t}$

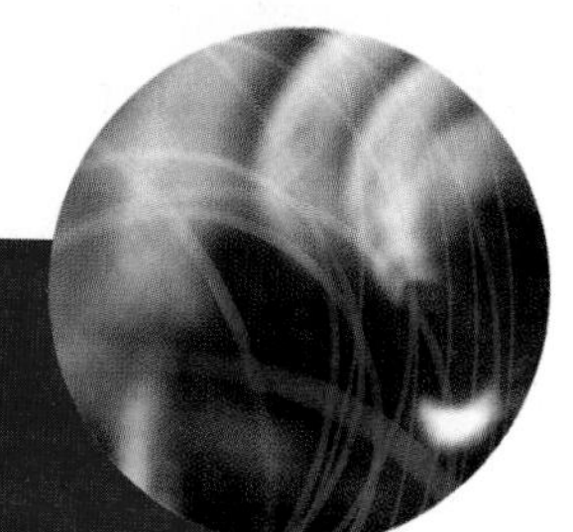

Appendix D

Chapters 1–6 Review

R.1 Real Numbers and Their Properties

This section is a review of Chapter 1 of this text. All topics in this review section are explained in greater detail in Chapter 1.

The Real Numbers

The numbers that we use in algebra are called the **real numbers.** There is a one-to-one correspondence between the set of real numbers and the points on the number line. Certain subsets of the set of real numbers are given special names.

Subsets of the Set of Real Numbers

Natural numbers	$\{1, 2, 3, \ldots\}$
Whole numbers	$\{0, 1, 2, 3, \ldots\}$
Integers	$\{\ldots, -3, -2, -1, 0, 1, 2, 3, \ldots\}$
Rational numbers	$\left\{\frac{a}{b} \,\middle|\, a \text{ and } b \text{ are integers, with } b \neq 0\right\}$
Irrational numbers	Real numbers that cannot be expressed as a ratio of integers

An **interval** of real numbers is the set of real numbers that are between two real numbers, which are called the **endpoints** of the interval. If a is less than b, then the set of real numbers between a and b, not including a or b, is written in interval notation as (a, b). If the endpoints are to be included, then we write $[a, b]$. An interval of real numbers may extend infinitely far to the right or left on the number line. In this case the infinity symbol ∞ is used as an endpoint.

EXAMPLE 1

Interval notation

Write each interval of real numbers in interval notation and graph it on a number line.

a) The set of real numbers greater than 2 and less than or equal to 4

b) The set of real numbers between -1 and 3 inclusive

c) The set of real numbers greater than or equal to 0

d) The set of real numbers less than 10

Solution

a) The set of real numbers greater than 2 and less than or equal to 4 does not include 2, but does include 4. So the interval is written as $(2, 4]$ and graphed in Fig. R.1.

0 1 2 3 4 5

Figure R.1

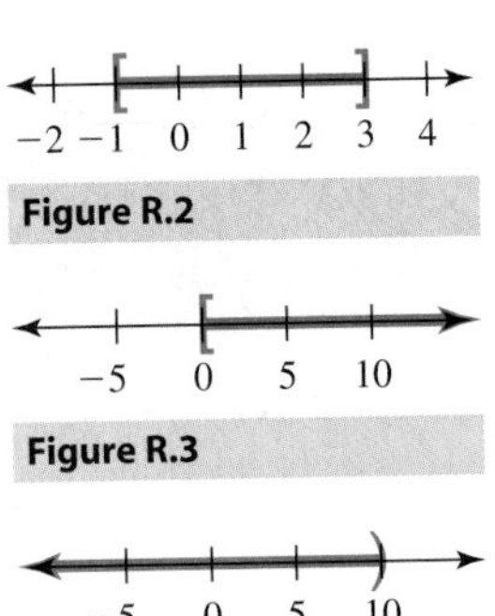

Figure R.2

Figure R.3

Figure R.4

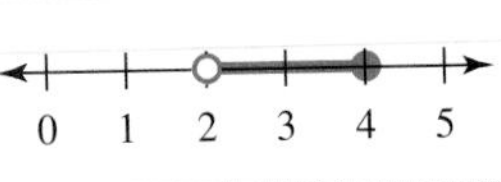

Figure R.5

b) The set of real numbers between -1 and 3 inclusive includes both endpoints. So the interval is written as $[-1, 3]$ and graphed in Fig. R.2.

c) The set of real numbers greater than or equal to 0 extends infinitely far to the right on the number line. So the interval is written as $[0, \infty)$ and graphed in Fig. R.3.

d) The set of real numbers less than 10 extends infinitely far to the left on the number line. So the interval is written as $(-\infty, 10)$ and graphed in Fig. R.4.

It is also common to draw the graph of an interval of real numbers using an open circle for an endpoint that does not belong to the interval and a closed circle for an endpoint that belongs to the interval. For example, the graph of $(2, 4]$ can be drawn as shown in Fig. R.5. In this text, parentheses and brackets are used so that the graphs agree with interval notation.

The **absolute value** of a real number is the number's distance from 0 on the number line. A number and its opposite have the same absolute value. For example, $|5| = 5$ and $|-5| = 5$. So the absolute value of a nonnegative number is the number and the absolute value of a negative number is the opposite of the number. In symbols,

$$|a| = a \text{ if } a \text{ is nonnegative} \quad \text{and} \quad |a| = -a \text{ if } a \text{ is negative.}$$

EXAMPLE 2

Absolute value

Find each absolute value.

a) $|4|$ **b)** $|-4|$ **c)** $|0|$ **d)** $|-3.9|$

Solution

a) Since 4 is 4 units from 0 on the number line $|4| = 4$.

b) Since -4 is 4 units from 0 on the number line $|-4| = 4$.

c) Since 0 is 0 units from 0 on the number line $|0| = 0$.

d) Since -3.9 is negative, $|-3.9| = -(-3.9) = 3.9$.

Fractions

Every fraction can be written in infinitely many equivalent forms. Consider the following equivalent forms of $\frac{2}{3}$:

$$\frac{2}{3} = \frac{4}{6} = \frac{6}{9} = \frac{8}{12} = \frac{10}{15} = \dots$$

Note that each equivalent form of $\frac{2}{3}$ can be obtained by multiplying the numerator and denominator of $\frac{2}{3}$ by a natural number. Converting a fraction into an equivalent form with a larger denominator is called **building up** the fraction. Converting a fraction into an equivalent form with a smaller denominator is called **reducing the fraction.** A fraction that cannot be reduced is in **lowest terms.**

EXAMPLE 3

Building up or reducing fractions

Complete each equation to make the fractions equivalent.

a) $\frac{3}{4} = \frac{?}{20}$ **b)** $\frac{12}{30} = \frac{?}{5}$

Solution

a) Since $20 = 4 \cdot 5$ we can multiply the numerator and denominator of $\frac{3}{4}$ by 5 to obtain an equivalent fraction with a denominator of 20:

$$\frac{3}{4} = \frac{3 \cdot 5}{4 \cdot 5} = \frac{15}{20}$$

Note that multiplying the numerator and denominator by 5 can also be accomplished by multiplying the fraction by the number 1 in its equivalent form $\frac{5}{5}$:

$$\frac{3}{4} = \frac{3}{4} \cdot 1 = \frac{3}{4} \cdot \frac{5}{5} = \frac{15}{20}$$

b) Since $30 = 6 \cdot 5$ and $12 = 6 \cdot 2$ we can factor the numerator and denominator. Then we divide out or cancel the common factor:

$$\frac{12}{30} = \frac{\cancel{6} \cdot 2}{\cancel{6} \cdot 5} = \frac{2}{5}$$

In Example 4, we illustrate the four basic operations with fractions. Fractions are multiplied by multiplying their numerators and denominators. Fractions are divided by inverting the divisor and multiplying. To add or subtract fractions the fractions must have identical denominators.

EXAMPLE 4

Operations with fractions

Perform the indicated operations with fractions. Express answers in lowest terms.

a) $\frac{5}{6} \cdot \frac{3}{20}$ **b)** $\frac{2}{3} \div \frac{2}{5}$ **c)** $\frac{1}{3} + \frac{2}{7}$ **d)** $\frac{5}{6} - \frac{4}{15}$

Solution

a) $\frac{5}{6} \cdot \frac{3}{20} = \frac{15}{120} = \frac{\cancel{15} \cdot 1}{\cancel{15} \cdot 8} = \frac{1}{8}$

b) $\frac{2}{3} \div \frac{2}{5} = \frac{2}{3} \cdot \frac{5}{2} = \frac{5}{3}$

c) $\frac{1}{3} + \frac{2}{7} = \frac{1 \cdot 7}{3 \cdot 7} + \frac{2 \cdot 3}{7 \cdot 3} = \frac{7}{21} + \frac{6}{21} = \frac{13}{21}$

d) $\frac{5}{6} - \frac{4}{15} = \frac{5 \cdot 5}{6 \cdot 5} - \frac{4 \cdot 2}{15 \cdot 2} = \frac{25}{30} - \frac{8}{30} = \frac{17}{30}$

Operations with Real Numbers

To find the sum of two numbers with the same sign, add their absolute values. The sum has the same sign as the original numbers. To find the sum of two numbers with unlike signs subtract their absolute values. The answer is positive if the number with the larger absolute value is positive. The answer is negative if the number with the larger absolute value is negative. The answer is zero if the original numbers have equal absolute values. All subtraction of signed numbers can be written in terms of addition according to the rule $a - b = a + (-b)$.

EXAMPLE 5

Adding and subtracting signed numbers

Perform the indicated operations.

a) $-4 + (-5)$ **b)** $-5 + 8$ **c)** $6 + (-30)$

d) $-9 + 9$ **e)** $15 - 18$ **f)** $-3 - (-9)$

Solution

a) Since -4 and -5 have the same sign we add their absolute values $(4 + 5 = 9)$ and then give that result a negative sign. So $-4 + (-5) = -9$.

b) Since -5 and 8 have opposite signs, we subtract their absolute values $(8 - 5 = 3)$. We give the result a positive sign because 8 has the larger absolute value. So $-5 + 8 = 3$.

c) Since 6 and -30 have opposite signs we subtract their absolute values $(30 - 6 = 24)$. We give the result a negative sign because -30 has the larger absolute value. So $6 + (-30) = -24$.

d) Since -9 and 9 have opposite signs and the same absolute value, their sum is 0. So $-9 + 9 = 0$.

e) Write all subtraction of signed numbers in terms of addition and follow the rules for addition. So $15 - 18 = 15 + (-18) = -3$.

f) Write subtraction in terms of addition and then follow the rules for addition of signed numbers. So $-3 - (-9) = -3 + 9 = 6$.

The result of multiplying two numbers is called the **product** of the numbers. To find the product of two nonzero real numbers, multiply their absolute values. The product is positive if the numbers have like signs. The product is negative if the numbers have unlike signs. If one or more of the numbers multiplied is zero, then the product is zero.

The result of dividing two numbers is called the **quotient** of the numbers. To find the quotient of two nonzero real numbers, divide their absolute values. The quotient is positive if the numbers have like signs. The quotient is negative if the numbers have unlike signs. Zero divided by any nonzero real number is zero. Division of any real number by zero is an undefined operation.

EXAMPLE 6

Multiplying and dividing signed numbers

Perform the indicated operations.

a) $(-4)(-5)$ **b)** $-8 \cdot 5$ **c)** $-6(0)$

d) $(-9) \div (3)$ **e)** $-15 \div (-3)$ **f)** $0 \div (-9.34)$

g) $-\frac{1}{2} \div 0$

Solution

a) Multiply the absolute values of -4 and -5 to get $4 \cdot 5 = 20$. Since -4 and -5 have the same sign the product is positive. So $(-4)(-5) = 20$.

b) Multiply the absolute values of -8 and 5 to get $8 \cdot 5 = 40$. Since -8 and 5 have opposite signs the product is negative. So $-8 \cdot 5 = -40$.

c) Since the product of zero and any real number is zero, we have $-6(0) = 0$.

d) Divide the absolute values of -9 and 3 to get $9 \div 3 = 3$. Since -9 and 3 have unlike signs, the quotient is negative. So $(-9) \div (3) = -3$.

e) Divide the absolute values of -15 and -3 to get $15 \div 3 = 5$. Since -15 and -3 have like signs, the quotient is positive. So $-15 \div (-3) = 5$.

f) Zero divided by any nonzero real number is zero. So $0 \div (-9.34) = 0$.

g) Since division by zero is undefined, there is no quotient for $-\frac{1}{2} \div 0$.

Exponential Expressions and the Order of Operations

The result of writing numbers in a meaningful combination with the ordinary operations of arithmetic is called an **arithmetic expression** or simply an **expression.** To simplify the writing of repeated factors in multiplication we use exponents to indicate the number of factors that are multiplied. For example, $3 \cdot 3 \cdot 3 \cdot 3 = 3^4$. Note that in an expression such as -9^2 the exponent applies only to the 9. So $-9^2 = -(9 \cdot 9) = -81$, whereas $(-9)^2 = (-9)(-9) = 81$.

When we evaluate expressions, operations within grouping symbols are always performed first. For example, $3(2 + 5) = 3(7) = 21$. To make expressions look simpler, we often omit some or all parentheses. In this case, we follow the accepted **order of operations:** evaluate exponential expressions first, then multiplication and division, and finally addition and subtraction.

EXAMPLE 7

Evaluating arithmetic expressions

Evaluate.

a) $-4^2 + 5^3$ **b)** $(-3 + 2)(8 - 9)$ **c)** $5 \cdot 2 + 3^2$

d) $3|7 - 9| + 4$ **e)** $\dfrac{-1 - 5}{4 - (-6)}$

Solution

a) $-4^2 + 5^3 = -16 + 125 = 125 - 16$
$= 109$

b) $(-3 + 2)(8 - 9) = (-1)(-1)$
$= 1$

c) $5 \cdot 2 + 3^2 = 10 + 9$
$= 19$

d) $3|7 - 9| + 4 = 3|-2| + 4 = 3 \cdot 2 + 4 = 6 + 4$
$= 10$

e) $\dfrac{-1 - 5}{4 - (-6)} = \dfrac{-6}{10} = \dfrac{-3 \cdot 2}{5 \cdot 2}$
$= -\dfrac{3}{5}$

Algebraic Expressions

The result of combining numbers and variables with the ordinary operations of arithmetic in some meaningful way is called an **algebraic expression** or simply an **expression.** Expressions are named by the last operation to be performed in the expression. So $2a + b$ is a sum, $ab - xy$ is a difference, $a(x + 3)$ is a product, $\frac{a-3}{b-2}$ is a quotient, and $(a + b)^2$ is a square. An algebraic expression has a value only if a value is known for every variable in the expression.

EXAMPLE 8

Writing and evaluating algebraic expressions

Write the algebraic expression that is described and evaluate it for the given value(s) of the variable(s).

a) The sum of $5x$ and 3; $x = -8$

b) The product of $a + b$ and $a - b$; $a = -7$ and $b = 9$

c) The difference of x^2 and y^2; $x = -2$ and $y = -5$

d) The quotient of $x - y$ and $y - x$; $x = -2$ and $y = -5$

e) The square of the sum $-3x + 1$; $x = -2$

Solution

a) The sum of $5x$ and 3 is written as $5x + 3$. If $x = -8$, then

$$5x + 3 = 5(-8) + 3 = -40 + 3 = -37.$$

b) The product of $a + b$ and $a - b$ is written as $(a + b)(a - b)$. If $a = -7$ and $b = 9$, then

$$(a + b)(a - b) = (-7 + 9)(-7 - 9) = (2)(-16) = -32.$$

c) The difference of x^2 and y^2 is written as $x^2 - y^2$. If $x = -2$ and $y = -5$, then

$$x^2 - y^2 = (-2)^2 - (-5)^2 = 4 - 25 = -21.$$

d) The quotient of $x - y$ and $y - x$ is written as $\frac{x-y}{y-x}$. If $x = -2$ and $y = -5$, then

$$\frac{x - y}{y - x} = \frac{-2 - (-5)}{-5 - (-2)} = \frac{3}{-3} = -1.$$

e) The square of the sum $-3x + 1$ is written as $(-3x + 1)^2$. If $x = -2$, then

$$(-3x + 1)^2 = (-3(-2) + 1)^2 = 7^2 = 49.$$

Properties of the Real Numbers

The properties of the real numbers are useful in algebra. The properties are listed as follows.

Properties of the Real Numbers

For any real numbers a, b, and c the following properties are true.

Commutative property	of addition	$a + b = b + a$
	of multiplication	$ab = ba$
Associative property	of addition	$(a + b) + c = a + (b + c)$
	of multiplication	$(ab)c = a(bc)$
Distributive property	for addition	$a(b + c) = ab + ac$
	for subtraction	$a(b - c) = ab - ac$
Identity property	for addition	$a + 0 = 0 + a = a$
	for multiplication	$a \cdot 1 = 1 \cdot a = a$
Inverse property	for addition	$a + (-a) = 0$
	for multiplication	$a \cdot \frac{1}{a} = 1 \ (a \neq 0)$
Multiplication property of zero		$0 \cdot a = a \cdot 0 = 0$

EXAMPLE 9

Properties of the real numbers

Name the property that justifies each equation.

a) $11 \cdot 19 = 19 \cdot 11$

b) $(x + 2) + 3 = x + (2 + 3)$ for any real number x

c) $\pi a^2 + \pi b^2 = \pi(a^2 + b^2)$ for any real numbers a and b

d) $5 \cdot \frac{1}{5} = 1$

e) $0(499 - 365 \cdot 288) = 0$

f) $3x^2 + 0 = 3x^2$ for any real number x

Solution

a) Commutative property of multiplication

b) Associative property of addition

c) Distributive property for addition

d) Inverse property for multiplication

e) Multiplication property of zero

f) Identity property for addition

An expression containing a number or the product of a number and one or more variables raised to powers is called a **term.** The number preceding the variables in a term is called the **coefficient.** If two terms contain the same variables with the same exponents, they are called **like terms.** Using the distributive property on a sum or difference of like terms allows us to combine the like terms and simplify the expression:

$$3x + 5x = (3 + 5)x \quad \text{Distributive property}$$
$$= 8x \quad \text{Add the coefficients.}$$

In Example 10, we use the idea of combining like terms and other properties of the real numbers to simplify expressions.

EXAMPLE 10

Using the properties of the real numbers to simplify expressions

Simplify each expression.

a) $(4x - 3) + (5x - 7)$

b) $-3a + 6 - 5(4 - 5a)$

c) $(-4b)(-7a) - (-3)(4a)$

d) $\frac{10y + 5}{5}$

Solution

a) $(4x - 3) + (5x - 7) = 4x + 5x - 3 - 7$ Commutative and associative properties. Combine like terms.
$= 9x - 10$

b) $-3a + 6 - 5(4 - 5a) = -3a + 6 - 20 + 25a$ Distributive property
$= 22a - 14$ Combine like terms.

c) $(4b)(7a) - (-3)(4a) = (4)(7)ab - (-3 \cdot 4)a$ Commutative and associative properties. Simplify.
$= 28ab + 12a$

d) $\frac{10y + 5}{5} = (10y + 5) \cdot \frac{1}{5}$ Invert 5 and multiply.
$= 2y + 1$ Distributive property

Note that in Example 10(b) the distributive property allows us to divide 5 into both terms in the numerator of the fraction. We cannot divide the denominator into just one term of the numerator. So we cannot simplify $\frac{6a+b}{3}$ to get $2a + b$. We could write $\frac{6a+b}{3} = 2a + \frac{1}{3}b$.

R.1 Exercises

Boost your GRADE at mathzone.com!

MathZone ▶ Practice Problems ▶ Net Tutor ▶ Self-Tests ▶ e-Professors ▶ Videos

Write each interval of real numbers in interval notation and graph it on a number line. See Example 1.

1. The set of real numbers between 0 and 3 inclusive
[0, 3]

2. The set of real numbers between −2 and 5
(−2, 5)

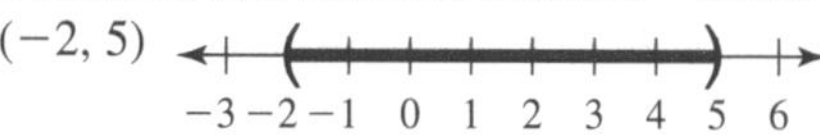

3. The set of real numbers greater than or equal to −4 and less than 0 [−4, 0)

−6 −4 −2 0 2 4

4. The set of real numbers greater than 3 and less than or equal to 8 (3, 8]

0 1 2 3 4 5 6 7 8 9

5. The set of real numbers less than −1
(−∞, −1)

−3 −2 −1 0 1 2

6. The set of real numbers less than or equal to 6
(−∞, 6]

−6 −3 0 3 6 9

7. The set of real numbers greater than or equal to 50
[50, ∞)

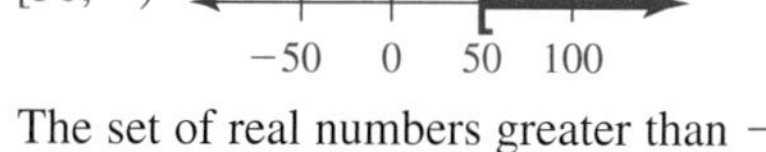

8. The set of real numbers greater than −10
(−10, ∞)

−20 −10 0 10

Give a verbal description of each interval.

9. (−2, 9) The set of real numbers between −2 and 9

10. [−4, −3]
The set of real numbers between −4 and −3 inclusive

11. [11, 13)
The set of real numbers greater than or equal to 11 and less than 13

12. (22, 26]
The set of real numbers greater than 22 and less than or equal to 26

13. (0, ∞) The set of real numbers greater than 0

14. [99, ∞) The set of real numbers greater than or equal to 99

15. (−∞, −6] The set of real numbers less than or equal to −6

16. (−∞, 18) The set of real numbers less than 18

Find each absolute value. See Example 2.

17. $|-1|$ 1

18. $|-9.35|$ 9.35

19. $|0|$ 0

20. $|5-5|$ 0

21. $|50|$ 50

22. $|6.87|$ 6.87

Complete each equation to make the fractions equivalent. See Example 3.

23. $\frac{1}{2} = \frac{?}{20}$ $\frac{10}{20}$

24. $\frac{2}{3} = \frac{?}{18}$ $\frac{12}{18}$

25. $\frac{3}{4} = \frac{?}{24}$ $\frac{18}{24}$

26. $\frac{7}{8} = \frac{?}{56}$ $\frac{49}{56}$

27. $\frac{12}{20} = \frac{?}{5}$ $\frac{3}{5}$

28. $\frac{16}{24} = \frac{?}{3}$ $\frac{2}{3}$

29. $\frac{14}{48} = \frac{?}{24}$ $\frac{7}{24}$

30. $\frac{24}{84} = \frac{?}{7}$ $\frac{2}{7}$

Reduce each fraction to lowest terms.

31. $\frac{6}{10}$ $\frac{3}{5}$

32. $\frac{7}{14}$ $\frac{1}{2}$

33. $\frac{28}{49}$ $\frac{4}{7}$

34. $\frac{48}{72}$ $\frac{2}{3}$

35. $\frac{36}{108}$ $\frac{1}{3}$

36. $\frac{51}{68}$ $\frac{3}{4}$

37. $\frac{30}{100}$ $\frac{3}{10}$

38. $\frac{400}{1000}$ $\frac{2}{5}$

Perform the indicated operations. Express answers in lowest terms. See Example 4.

39. $\frac{3}{8} \cdot \frac{2}{3}$ $\frac{1}{4}$

40. $\frac{2}{5} \cdot \frac{15}{26}$ $\frac{3}{13}$

41. $\frac{1}{4} \div \frac{5}{2}$ $\frac{1}{10}$

42. $\frac{3}{7} \div \frac{9}{14}$ $\frac{2}{3}$

43. $\frac{2}{5} \cdot 25$ 10

44. $\frac{5}{8} \cdot 40$ 25

45. $\frac{2}{3} \div 5$ $\frac{2}{15}$

46. $6 \div \frac{1}{7}$ 42

47. $\frac{1}{8} + \frac{2}{3}$ $\frac{19}{24}$

48. $\frac{1}{5} + \frac{3}{4}$ $\frac{19}{20}$

49. $\frac{5}{12} - \frac{5}{18}$ $\frac{5}{36}$

50. $\frac{5}{16} - \frac{1}{12}$ $\frac{11}{48}$

51. $\frac{5}{8} + 2$ $\frac{21}{8}$

52. $\frac{3}{7} + 1$ $\frac{10}{7}$

Perform the indicated operations. See Examples 5 and 6.

53. $-20 + (-6)$ -26

54. $-19 + (-8)$ -27

55. $-30 + 7$ -23

56. $18 + (-9)$ 9

57. $6 + (-5)$ 1

58. $-7 + 12$ 5

59. $-30 - 6$ -36

60. $-15 - 12$ -27

61. $20 - (-4)$ 24

62. $88 - (-12)$ 100

63. $-3 - (-5)$ 2

64. $-9 - (-6)$ -3

65. $(-3)(-60)$ 180

66. $(-8)(-12)$ 96

67. $(-7)(12)$ -84

68. $(13)(-3)$ -39

69. $(-30) \div (-2)$ 15

70. $(-90) \div (-15)$ 6

71. $-40 \div 5$ -8

72. $100 \div (-20)$ -5

73. $0 \div (-7)$ 0

74. $0 \div (-2000)$ 0

Evaluate each arithmetic expression. See Example 7.

75. $-3^2 - 9^2$ -90

76. $(-4)^3 - 5^2$ -89

77. $(4 + 2^3)(1 - 4)$ -36

78. $(4 - 5)^3(3 - 6^2)$ 33

79. $3 + 5 \cdot 7$ 38

80. $10 - 6 \cdot 2$ -2

81. $2^4 - 3 \cdot 7$ -5

82. $3 \cdot 2^5 - 5 \cdot 2^4$ 16

83. $|3 - 9| - |5 - 8|$ 3

84. $2|3 - 5 \cdot 4|$ 34

85. $|-6| - 3|2 - 2^3|$ -12

86. $|5 \cdot 4 - 10| - |-3 \cdot 2|$ 4

87. $\frac{-4 - 2}{1 - 3}$ 3

88. $\frac{-2^2 - 3^3}{1 - (-30)}$ -1

89. $\frac{-3 \cdot 5 - 2}{1 - 3 \cdot 6}$ 1

90. $\frac{4 - 2 \cdot 7}{2 - 3 \cdot 2^2}$ 1

Write the algebraic expression that is described and evaluate it for the given value(s) of the variable(s). See Example 8.

91. The sum of $5x$ and $-3y$; $x = -2$ and $y = 5$
$5x + (-3y)$, -25

92. The difference of a^3 and b^3; $a = -2$ and $b = 4$
$a^3 - b^3$, -72

93. The product of $a + b$ and $a^2 - ab + b^2$; $a = -1$ and $b = -3$ $(a + b)(a^2 - ab + b^2)$, -28

94. The quotient of $x - 7$ and $7 - x$; $x = 9$ $\frac{x-7}{7-x}$, -1

95. The square of $2x - 3$; $x = 5$ $(2x - 3)^2$, 49

96. The cube of $a - b$; $a = 3$ and $b = -1$ $(a - b)^3$, 64

Determine whether each expression is a sum, difference, product, quotient, square, or cube.

97. $a^3 - b^3$ Difference

98. $a^2 + b^2$ Sum

99. $5a - b$ Difference

100. $5(a - b)$ Product

101. $\frac{6 - a}{6a}$ Quotient

102. $(5a - b)^2$ Square

103. $(3a)^3$ Cube

104. $3 + a^3$ Sum

Name the property that justifies each equation. See Example 9.

105. $a(3) = 3a$ Commutative property of multiplication

106. $3 + a = a + 3$ Commutative property of addition

107. $5(x + 1) = 5x + 5$ Distributive property

108. $(w^2 + 8) + 7 = w^2 + (8 + 7)$
Associative property of addition

109. $5 \cdot 1 = 5$ Multiplicative identity

110. $3 + 0 = 3$ Additive identity

111. $m^2 \cdot 0 = 0$ Multiplication property of zero

112. $6 \cdot \frac{1}{6} = 1$ Multiplicative inverse property

113. $3(5x) = (3 \cdot 5)x$ Associative property of multiplication

114. $a + (-a) = 0$ Additive inverse property

Simplify each expression. See Example 10.

115. $(2x - 9) + (7 - 3x)$ $-x - 2$

116. $(-3x - y) + (9y - 8x)$ $-11x + 8y$

117. $5 + 3(4 + x)$ $3x + 17$

118. $x + 7(x + y)$ $8x + 7y$

119. $6 + 7xy - 4(3 - 6xy)$ $31xy - 6$

120. $4 + 3a - 5(4 - 7a)$ $38a - 16$

121. $(-2a)(5b) - 5(4ab)$ $-30ab$

122. $(-x)(-y) - 5(-4xy)$ $21xy$

123. $\frac{3(4 - 2x)}{6}$ $2 - x$

124. $\frac{2(3x - 3y)}{6}$ $x - y$

125. $\frac{44 - 2x}{-2}$ $-22 + x$

126. $\frac{20 + 8x}{-4}$ $-5 - 2x$

R.2 Linear Equations and Inequalities in One Variable

This section is a review of Chapter 2 of this text. All topics in this review section are explained in greater detail in Chapter 2.

Solving Linear Equations

An **equation** is a statement that two expressions are equal. The equations that we study in this section will contain only one variable. If the equation is correct when a number is used in place of the variable, then that number is a **solution** to the equation. The set containing all solutions to an equation is the **solution set** to the equation. Equations that have the same solution set are **equivalent equations.** To **solve** an equation means to find all solutions to the equation or to find the solution set to the equation.

A **linear equation in one variable** x is an equation of the form $ax + b = 0$, where a and b are real numbers with $a \neq 0$. Other equations that are equivalent to $ax + b = 0$ may also be called linear equations. To solve linear equations we use the properties of equality. The **addition property of equality** indicates that adding the same number to both sides of an equation does not change the solution set to the equation. The **multiplication property of equality** indicates that multiplying both sides of an equation by the same nonzero number does not change the solution set to the equation. Since subtraction and division are defined in terms of addition and multiplication, respectively, we can also subtract the same number from both sides or divide both sides by the same nonzero number.

EXAMPLE 1

Using the properties of equality to solve linear equations

Solve each equation and check.

a) $x - 5 = -13$ **b)** $\frac{2}{3}a = -4$

Solution

a) We can isolate the variable x by adding 5 to each side of the equation:

$$x - 5 = -13 \quad \text{Original equation}$$
$$x - 5 + 5 = -13 + 5 \quad \text{Add 5 to each side.}$$
$$x = -8 \quad \text{Simplify.}$$

All of the equations are equivalent and only -8 satisfies the last equation. So -8 should be the only solution to the original equation. To check, replace x with -8:

$$x - 5 = -13$$
$$-8 - 5 = -13 \quad \text{Correct}$$

By checking, we are sure that the solution set is $\{-8\}$.

b) We can isolate a by multiplying each side of the equation by $\frac{3}{2}$:

$$\frac{2}{3}a = -4 \quad \text{Original equation}$$
$$\frac{3}{2} \cdot \frac{2}{3}a = \frac{3}{2}(-4) \quad \text{Multiply each side by } \tfrac{3}{2}.$$
$$a = -6 \quad \text{Simplify.}$$

Since $\frac{2}{3}(-6) = -4$ is correct, the solution set is $\{-6\}$.

In Example 2 we will solve equations that require several steps and more than one property of equality.

EXAMPLE 2

Using the addition and multiplication properties of equality

Solve each equation and check.

a) $3x + 5 = 9$ **b)** $2b - 3 = 3 + 4(b - 1)$

Solution

a) We can isolate the variable x by subtracting 5 from each side of the equation and then dividing each side by 3:

$$3x + 5 = 9 \quad \text{Original equation}$$

$$3x + 5 - 5 = 9 - 5 \quad \text{Subtract 5 from each side.}$$

$$3x = 4 \quad \text{Simplify.}$$

$$\frac{3x}{3} = \frac{4}{3} \quad \text{Divide each side by 3.}$$

$$x = \frac{4}{3} \quad \text{Simplify.}$$

To check, replace x with $\frac{4}{3}$:

$$3x + 5 = 9$$

$$3\left(\frac{4}{3}\right) + 5 = 9 \quad \text{Correct}$$

By checking, we are sure that the solution set is $\left\{\frac{4}{3}\right\}$.

b) Before we can apply the properties of equality we simplify the right side:

$$2b - 3 = 3 + 4(b - 1) \quad \text{Original equation}$$

$$2b - 3 = 4b - 1 \quad \text{Simplify.}$$

$$2b = 4b + 2 \quad \text{Add 3 to each side.}$$

$$-2b = 2 \quad \text{Subtract } 4b \text{ from each side.}$$

$$b = -1 \quad \text{Divide each side by } -2.$$

Check -1 in the original equation $2b - 3 = 3 + 4(b - 1)$:

$$2(-1) - 3 = 3 + 4(-1 - 1) \quad \text{Replace } b \text{ with } -1.$$

$$-5 = -5 \quad \text{Correct}$$

Since -1 satisfies the original equation, we can be sure that the solution set is $\{-1\}$.

An **identity** is an equation that is satisfied for every real number for which both sides are defined. Equations such as $x + 1 = 1 + x$, $\frac{1}{x} = \frac{1}{x}$, and $2(3x) = 6x$ are identities. A **conditional equation** has at least one solution, but is not an identity. The equations that we solved in Examples 1 and 2 are conditional equations. (They are satisfied on the condition that the appropriate number is chosen to replace the variable.) An equation that has no solution is called an **inconsistent equation.** The equation $x + 1 = x + 2$ is inconsistent.

If an equation involves fractions it is usually a good idea to multiply each side by the least common denominator to eliminate all of the fractions. If an equation involves decimals, then it is usually a good idea to multiply both sides of the equation by a power of 10 that eliminates all of the decimals. We illustrate these techniques in Example 3.

EXAMPLE 3

Equations with fractions or decimals

Solve each equation. Identify each equation as a conditional equation, an inconsistent equation, or an identity.

a) $\frac{1}{2}y - \frac{1}{3}y = y - \frac{5}{6}y$ **b)** $0.1b - 0.03 = 0.03b + 0.05$

c) $\frac{w}{4} - \frac{w}{5} = \frac{w}{20} + \frac{1}{10}$

Solution

a) Multiply each side by 6, the least common denominator:

$$\frac{1}{2}y - \frac{1}{3}y = y - \frac{5}{6}y \quad \text{Original equation}$$

$$6\left(\frac{1}{2}y - \frac{1}{3}y\right) = 6\left(y - \frac{5}{6}y\right) \quad \text{Multiply each side by 6.}$$

$$3y - 2y = 6y - 5y \quad \text{Distributive property}$$

$$y = y \quad \text{Simplify.}$$

The equation $y = y$ is satisfied by every real number. So the solution set to the original equation is the set of all real numbers, which is written symbolically as R or $(-\infty, \infty)$. The equation is an identity.

b) First multiply each side by 100 to eliminate the decimals:

$$0.1b - 0.03 = 0.03b + 0.05 \quad \text{Original equation}$$

$$100(0.1b - 0.03) = 100(0.03b + 0.05) \quad \text{Multiply by 100.}$$

$$10b - 3 = 3b + 5 \quad \text{Distributive property}$$

$$10b = 3b + 8 \quad \text{Add 3 to each side.}$$

$$7b = 8 \quad \text{Subtract } 3b \text{ from each side.}$$

$$b = \frac{8}{7} \quad \text{Divide each side by 7.}$$

Check in the original equation. The solution set is $\left\{\frac{8}{7}\right\}$ and the equation is a conditional equation.

c) Multiply each side by 20, the least common denominator:

$$\frac{w}{4} - \frac{w}{5} = \frac{w}{20} + \frac{1}{10} \quad \text{Original equation}$$

$$20\left(\frac{w}{4} - \frac{w}{5}\right) = 20\left(\frac{w}{20} + \frac{1}{10}\right) \quad \text{Multiply by 20.}$$

$$5w - 4w = w + 2 \quad \text{Distributive property}$$

$$w = w + 2 \quad \text{Simplify.}$$

$$0 = 2 \quad \text{Subtract } w \text{ from each side.}$$

The equation $0 = 2$ is not satisfied by any real number. So the original equation has no solution and is an inconsistent equation. The solution set is the empty set, $\varnothing$.

Formulas

A **formula** or **literal equation** is an equation involving two or more variables. The process of rewriting a formula for one variable in terms of the others is called **solving for a certain variable.** To solve a formula for a certain variable, we use the same techniques that we use in solving equations containing only one variable.

EXAMPLE 4

Solving for a certain variable

Solve $P = 2L + 2W$ for W.

Solution

To solve for W we can start with $2L + 2W = P$:

$$2L + 2W = P \quad \text{Original equation}$$

$$2W = P - 2L \quad \text{Subtract } 2L \text{ from each side.}$$

$$W = \frac{P - 2L}{2} \quad \text{Divide each side by 2.}$$

The equation solved for W is $W = \frac{P - 2L}{2}$.

Translating Verbal Expressions into Algebraic Expressions

The mathematical operation of addition can be indicated verbally by words such as sum, added to, more than, and increased by. Subtraction can be indicated by words such as subtracted from, less than, difference, and decreased by. Multiplication can be indicated by words such as product, twice, and a fraction or percent of. Division is indicated by ratio, quotient, and divided by.

EXAMPLE 5

Writing algebraic expressions

Translate each verbal expression into an algebraic expression.

a) The sum of a and b

b) Twelve percent of x

c) The quotient of w and 4

d) The number x decreased by 6

Solution

a) Because sum means addition, the sum of a and b is expressed as $a + b$.

b) A percent of a number is the product of the percent and the number. So twelve percent of x is expressed as $0.12x$.

c) Because quotient indicates division, the quotient of w and 4 is $\frac{w}{4}$.

d) Because decreased by indicates subtraction, the number x decreased by 6 is expressed as $x - 6$.

Problem Solving

In Examples 6 and 7 we apply the ideas of Example 5 to solve problems by first writing an equation that **models** or describes the problem and then solving the equation. In Example 6, we use the formula for the perimeter of a rectangle.

EXAMPLE 6

A geometric problem

The length of a rectangular patio is 1 foot larger than twice the width. If the perimeter is 92 feet, then what are the length and width?

Figure R.6

Solution

Let W represent the width and $2W + 1$ represent the length of the patio as shown in Fig. R.6. Since the perimeter of a rectangle is twice the width plus twice the length ($P = 2W + 2L$), we can write the following equation:

$$2W + 2(2W + 1) = 92 \quad 2W + 2L = P$$
$$2W + 4W + 2 = 92 \quad \text{Distributive property}$$
$$6W = 90 \quad \text{Simplify.}$$
$$W = 15 \quad \text{Divide each side by 6.}$$
$$2W + 1 = 31 \quad \text{Evaluate } 2W + 1 \text{ with } W = 15.$$

So the width is 15 feet and the length is 31 feet. Since $2(15) + 2(31) = 92$ we can be sure that the answer is correct.

In Example 7 we will use the formula $D = RT$, which is the formula for uniform motion (motion at a constant rate).

EXAMPLE 7

A uniform motion problem

A 44-foot-wide highway has concrete lanes and asphalt shoulders of equal width, as shown in Fig. R.7. A turtle crossing the highway travels his usual speed on the shoulders and 2 feet per hour faster on the concrete lanes. If it takes him 3 hours to cross one shoulder and 4 hours to cross the concrete lanes, then what is his usual speed and what is his speed on the concrete?

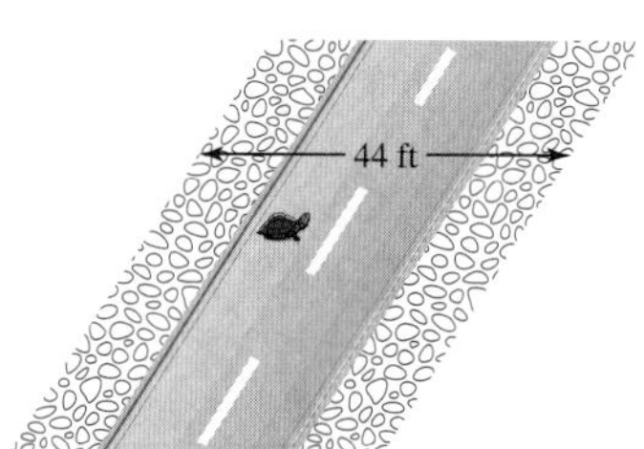

Figure R.7

Solution

Let x represent the turtles usual speed in feet per hour and $x + 2$ represent his speed on the concrete lanes. Make a table showing rate, time, and distance for the asphalt shoulders and the concrete, using the formula $D = RT$. Note that it takes him 6 hr to cross both asphalt shoulders.

	Rate	Time	Distance
Asphalt shoulders	x ft/hr	6 hr	$6x$ ft
Concrete lanes	$x + 2$ ft/hr	4 hr	$4(x + 2)$ ft

Since the total distance is 44 feet, we can write the following equation:

$$6x + 4(x + 2) = 44 \quad \text{Total distance is 44 feet.}$$
$$6x + 4x + 8 = 44 \quad \text{Distributive property}$$
$$10x + 8 = 44 \quad \text{Simplify.}$$
$$10x = 36 \quad \text{Subtract 8 from each side.}$$
$$x = 3.6 \quad \text{Divide each side by 10.}$$
$$x + 2 = 5.6 \quad \text{Evaluate } x + 2 \text{ with } x = 3.6.$$

So his usual speed is 3.6 ft/hr and his speed on the concrete is 5.6 ft/hr. At 3.6 ft/hr for 6 hr, his distance is 21.6 ft and at 5.6 ft/hr for 4 hr his distance is 22.4 ft. Since 21.6 ft plus 22.4 ft is 44 ft, we can be sure that the answer is correct.

In mixture problems the solutions might contain fat, alcohol, salt, or some other substance. We always assume that the substance in the solution neither appears nor disappears in the process. For example, if there are 3 grams of salt in one glass of water and 5 grams in another, then there are exactly 8 grams in a mixture of the two glasses of water.

EXAMPLE 8

A mixture problem

A 40-pound bag of potting soil contains 10% sand. How many pounds of sand must be added to get a mixture that is 20% sand?

Solution

Let x represent the number of pounds of sand to be added to the 40-pound bag. We can make a table as follows:

	Amount	**% sand**	**Amount of sand**
Original bag	40 lb	10%	0.10(40) lb
Sand added	x lb	100%	x lb
Mixture	$x + 40$ lb	20%	$0.20(x + 40)$ lb

Since the amount of sand in the final mixture is the sum of the sand in the original bag and the amount added, we can write the following equation:

$$0.10(40) + x = 0.20(x + 40) \quad \text{Total amounts of sand.}$$
$$4 + x = 0.20x + 8 \quad \text{Distributive property}$$
$$40 + 10x = 2x + 80 \quad \text{Multiply each side by 10.}$$
$$8x = 40 \quad \text{Subtract } 2x\text{; subtract 40.}$$
$$x = 5 \quad \text{Divide each side by 8.}$$

So to get 20% sand, 5 pounds of sand should be added. Note that the original bag contains 4 pounds of sand and that adding 5 more gives 9 pounds of sand out of 45 pounds which is 20% sand.

Inequalities

The inequality symbols that we use are $<$ (less than), $\leq$ (less than or equal to), $>$ (greater than), and $\geq$ (greater than or equal to). To indicate that x is between a and b, where $a < b$, we often use the compound inequality $a < x < b$. Inequalities are solved in the same manner that we solve equations. However, to obtain an equivalent inequality when each side is multiplied or divided by a negative number the inequality symbol must be reversed.

EXAMPLE 9

Solving inequalities

Solve each inequality. State the solution set in interval notation and graph the solution set.

a) $5x - 4 \geq 6$

b) $-3x + 5 < x - 15$

c) $-3 \leq 4x + 1 < 13$

Solution

a) To isolate x add 4 to each side and then divide each side by 5:

$5x - 4 \geq 6$	Original inequality
$5x \geq 10$	Add 4 to each side.
$\frac{5x}{5} \geq \frac{10}{5}$	Divide each side by 5.
$x \geq 2$	Simplify.

Figure R.8

The solution set is the interval of real numbers $[2, \infty)$. The graph of the solution set is shown in Fig. R.8.

b) First subtract x from each side and them subtract 5 from each side:

$-3x + 5 < x - 15$	Original inequality
$-4x + 5 < -15$	Subtract x from each side.
$-4x < -20$	Subtract 5 from each side.
$\frac{-4x}{-4} > \frac{-20}{-4}$	Divide each side by -4 and reverse the inequality.
$x > 5$	Simplify.

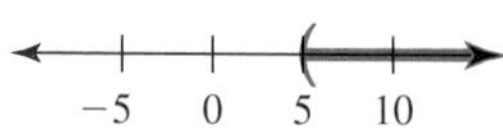

Figure R.9

The solution set is the interval of real numbers $(5, \infty)$. The graph is shown in Fig. R.9.

c) To isolate x in the middle, subtract 1 from all three parts of the inequality and then divide all three parts by 4:

$-3 \leq 4x + 1 < 13$	Original inequality
$-4 \leq 4x < 12$	Subtract 1 from all three parts.
$-1 \leq x < 3$	Divide all three parts by 4.

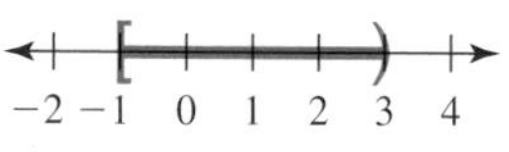

Figure R.10

The solution set is the interval $[-1, 3)$, which includes -1 but does not include 3. The graph is shown in Fig. R.10.

R.2 Exercises

Boost your GRADE at mathzone.com!

MathZone

- Practice Problems
- Self-Tests
- Videos
- Net Tutor
- e-Professors

Solve each equation and check your answer. See Examples 1 and 2.

1. $x - 9 = -2$ $\{7\}$

2. $w - 8 = 7$ $\{15\}$

3. $n + 5 = -3$ $\{-8\}$

4. $z + 4 = 21$ $\{17\}$

5. $3a = 51$ $\{17\}$

6. $-5b = 45$ $\{-9\}$

7. $\frac{3}{4}x = -6$ $\{-8\}$

8. $-\frac{5}{3}m = 15$ $\{-9\}$

9. $4a - 1 = 49$ $\left\{\frac{25}{2}\right\}$

10. $3b + 2 = 0$ $\left\{-\frac{2}{3}\right\}$

11. $14 - 2x = 6 - x$ $\{8\}$

12. $-7 - 5x = 12 - 4x$ $\{-19\}$

13. $2x - 3 = 4x + 9$ $\{-6\}$

14. $5 - 4x = 3 - 2x$ $\{1\}$

15. $x - 3 = 2 + 3(x + 1)$ $\{-4\}$

16. $-3(x - 4) = 2x + 7$ $\{1\}$

Solve each equation. Identify each equation as a conditional equation, an inconsistent equation, or an identity. See Example 3

17. $\frac{13}{15}x - \frac{4}{5}x = \frac{1}{5}x - \frac{2}{15}x$ $(-\infty, \infty)$, identity

18. $x + \frac{2}{3} = \frac{1}{3}(3x + 1) + \frac{1}{3}$ $(-\infty, \infty)$, identity

19. $\frac{w}{12} - \frac{w}{4} = \frac{w}{3} - 12$ $\{24\}$, conditional equation

20. $\frac{a}{6} - 5 = \frac{a}{15} - 2$ $\{30\}$, conditional equation

21. $0.05a - 0.7 = 0.12a + 0.7$ $\{-20\}$, conditional equation

22. $0.03(z - 4) = 0.05z + 0.8$ $\{-46\}$, conditional equation

23. $\frac{1}{8}y - \frac{1}{9}y = \frac{1}{72}y + \frac{1}{2}$ $\varnothing$, inconsistent equation

24. $\frac{1}{6}m + \frac{1}{7}m = \frac{13}{42}m - \frac{1}{21}$ $\varnothing$, inconsistent equation

25. $\frac{5}{3}t - 2\left(\frac{2}{3}t + 1\right) = 3\left(\frac{t}{3} - \frac{1}{9}\right) - \frac{7}{3}t$
$\{1\}$, conditional equation

26. $\frac{3}{2}v - 4\left(\frac{v}{2} + \frac{5}{2}\right) = \frac{v}{2} - (v + 10)$ $(-\infty, \infty)$, identity

27. $0.001x + 0.02 = 0.2(0.1x - 0.03)$
$\left\{\frac{26}{19}\right\}$, conditional equation

28. $0.2(0.3q + 0.04) = 0.005q - 0.087$
$\left\{-\frac{19}{11}\right\}$, conditional equation

Solve each formula for the indicated variable. See Example 4.

29. $D = RT$ for R $R = \frac{D}{T}$

30. $E = mc^2$ for m $m = \frac{E}{c^2}$

31. $K = \frac{1}{2}mv^2$ for m $m = \frac{2K}{v^2}$

32. $A = \frac{1}{2}bh$ for b $b = \frac{2A}{h}$

33. $P = 2L + 2W$ for L $L = \frac{P - 2W}{2}$

34. $A = \frac{1}{2}h(b_1 + b_2)$ for b_2 $b_2 = \frac{2A - hb_1}{h}$

35. $A = P + Prt$ for r $r = \frac{A - P}{Pt}$

36. $2x - 3y = 6$ for y $y = \frac{2x - 6}{3}$

Solve each problem.

37. ***Traveling by bus.*** A bus averaged 40 miles per hour while traveling from New Orleans to Memphis. If the distance is 400 miles, then how long did the bus take for the trip? 10 hr

38. ***Right triangle.*** In a right triangle the perpendicular sides are called legs. If the area of a right triangle is 10 square meters and one leg is 4 meters, then what is the length of the other leg? 5 m

39. ***Rectangular field.*** If the length of a rectangular field is 45 meters and the perimeter is 150 meters, then what is the width? 30 m

40. ***CD case.*** If the length of a rectangular plastic CD case is 14 centimeters and the perimeter is 53 centimeters, then what is the width? 12.5 cm

41. ***Kinetic energy.*** The kinetic energy K in Joules for an object of mass m kilograms with velocity v meters per second is given by $K = \frac{1}{2}mv^2$. If the kinetic energy for an object with velocity 30 meters per second is 1800 Joules, then what is the mass of the object? 4 kg

42. ***Upper base.*** The height of a trapezoid is 4 centimeters and its area is 40 square centimeters. If the lower base is 12 centimeters then what is the length of the upper base? 8 cm

Translate each verbal expression into an algebraic expression. See Example 5.

43. The sum of a^2 and b^2 $a^2 + b^2$

44. The number x increased by 5 $x + 5$

45. The number y decreased by 6 $y - 6$

46. The difference between a and b $a - b$

47. The product of a and b^2 ab^2

48. Ten percent of x $0.10x$

49. The quotient of x and y $\frac{x}{y}$

50. The number 14 divided by x $\frac{14}{x}$

51. One-half of x $\frac{1}{2}x$

52. Two-thirds of y $\frac{2}{3}y$

53. Twice the sum of a and b $2(a + b)$

54. The square of the sum of a and b $(a + b)^2$

Solve each problem. See Examples 6–8.

55. ***Rectangular planter.*** The width of a rectangular planter is 6 inches less than its length. If the perimeter of the planter is 84 inches, then what are the length and width? Length 24 in., width 18 in.

56. ***Rectangular reflecting pool.*** The length of a rectangular reflecting pool is 5 meters less than twice the width. If the perimeter of the pool is 170 meters, then what are the length and width? Length 55 m, width 30 m

57. ***El Paso to L.A.*** On Monday, Chip drove from El Paso to Phoenix in 8 hours. On Tuesday he drove from Phoenix to Los Angeles in 10 hours. If he averaged 15 miles per hour more on the first day and the total trip was 840 miles, then what was his average speed on the first day? 55 mph

58. ***L.A. to Portland.*** On Wednesday, Chip averaged 50 miles per hour driving from Los Angeles to San Francisco. On Thursday, he continued on to Portland, averaging 64 mph. If his travel time on Wednesday was 2 hours less than his travel time on Thursday and the total trip from L.A. to Portland was 1040 miles, then what was his traveling time on Wednesday? 8 hr

59. ***Mixing concrete.*** Concrete is a mixture of aggregate, cement, and water. A concrete truck contains 10,000 pounds of concrete that is 17% cement. How much cement must be added to the mixture to get the mixture up to 18% cement? Approximately 121.95 lb

60. ***Diluting a solution.*** How many ounces of pure water must be added to 100 ounces of a saline solution that is 12% salt to get a solution that is 8% salt? 50 oz

61. ***Mixing alcohol.*** How many liters of a 50% alcohol solution must be added to 10 liters of a 20% alcohol solution to obtain a solution that is 30% alcohol? 5 L

62. ***Mixing punch.*** One hundred liters of fruit punch that is 30% fruit juice is mixed with 200 liters of another fruit punch. The result is a mixture that is 20% juice. What is the percentage of fruit juice in the 200 liters of punch? 15%

63. ***Catching a speeder.*** A police officer was parked on the shoulder of a highway when he was passed by a speeder. It took the officer 2 minutes to get his car started. He then averaged 100 miles per hour for 12 minutes to catch the speeder. How fast was the speeder traveling? Approximately 85.71 mph

64. ***Catching up.*** At 7 A.M. the Garcia's left the campground and headed east at 80 kilometers per. At 7:20 the Anderson's left the same campground and headed east on the same road at 100 kilometers per hour. At what time will the Anderson's catch up with the Garcia's? 8:40 A.M.

Solve each inequality. State the solution set using interval notation and graph the solution set. See Example 9.

65. $3x - 1 \geq 14$ $[5, \infty)$

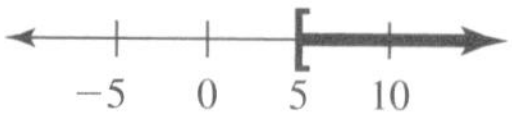

−5 0 5 10

66. $2x + 5 \leq 17$ $(-\infty, 6]$

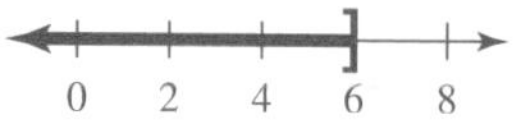

0 2 4 6 8

67. $4 - 3y < 0$ $\left(\frac{4}{3}, \infty\right)$

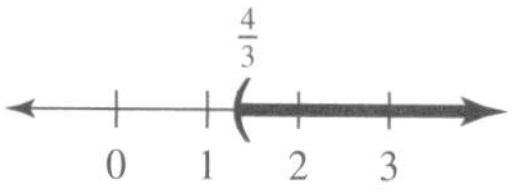

$\frac{4}{3}$

0 1 2 3

68. $5 - t > 0$ $(-\infty, 5)$

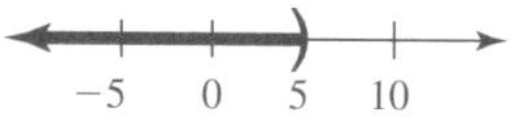

−5 0 5 10

69. $-\frac{1}{2}n + 6 < 7$ $(-2, \infty)$

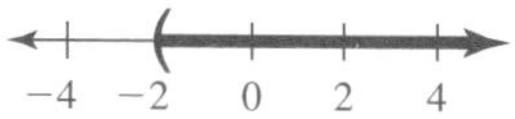

−4 −2 0 2 4

70. $-\frac{3}{4}m - 1 > 5$ $(-\infty, -8)$

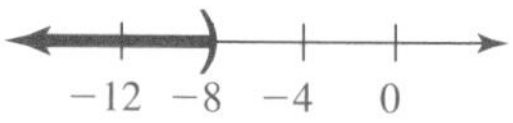

−12 −8 −4 0

71. $5x + 7 < 2x - 8$ $(-\infty, -5)$

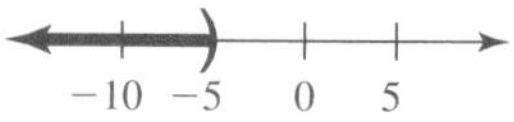

−10 −5 0 5

72. $6w - 9 > w + 31$ $(8, \infty)$

0 4 8 12 16

73. $-2z + 3 < z - 6$ $(3, \infty)$

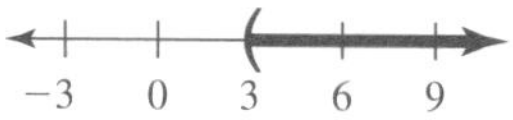

−3 0 3 6 9

74. $-5x - 8 < 2x + 13$ $(-3, \infty)$

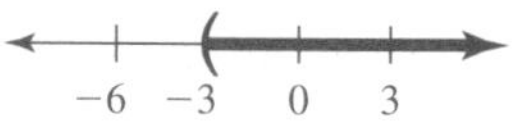

−6 −3 0 3

75. $-1 \leq 2b + 3 < 19$ $[-2, 8)$

−4 −2 0 2 4 6 8 10

76. $1 < 5a - 4 \leq 21$ $(1, 5]$

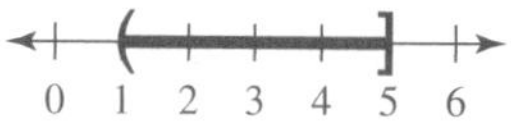

0 1 2 3 4 5 6

77. $-5 < 3 - 2w < 31$ $(-14, 4)$

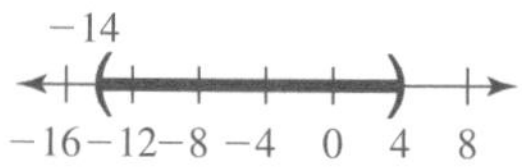

−14

−16 −12 −8 −4 0 4 8

78. $4 \leq 1 - x \leq 5$ $[-4, -3]$

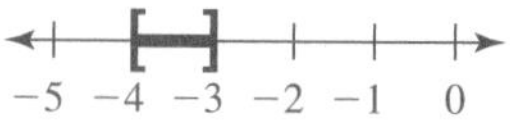

−5 −4 −3 −2 −1 0

R.3 Linear Equations and Inequalities in Two Variables

This section is a review of Chapter 3 of this text. All topics in this review section are explained in greater detail in Chapter 3.

Graphing Lines in the Coordinate Plane

A **linear equation in two variables** is an equation of the form $Ax + By = C$, where A, B, and C are real numbers, with A and B not both equal to zero. The graph of a linear equation in two variables is a straight line in the rectangular coordinate system. The graph is a picture of the set of all ordered pairs that satisfy the equation. If $A = 0$ and $B \neq 0$, then the graph is a horizontal line. If $B = 0$ and $A \neq 0$, then the graph is a vertical line. A point at which a line crosses the x-axis is called the ***x*-intercept.** A point at which a line crosses the y-axis is called the ***y*-intercept.**

EXAMPLE 1

Graphing linear equations using the intercepts

Graph each equation and identify all intercepts.

a) $3x - 5y = 15$ **b)** $y = 4$ **c)** $x = 3$

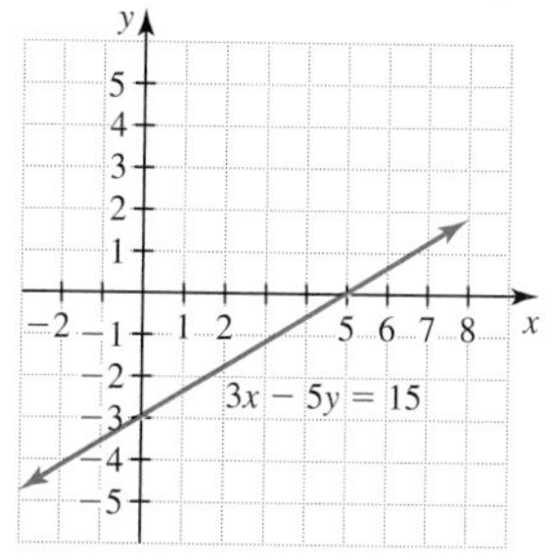

Figure R.11

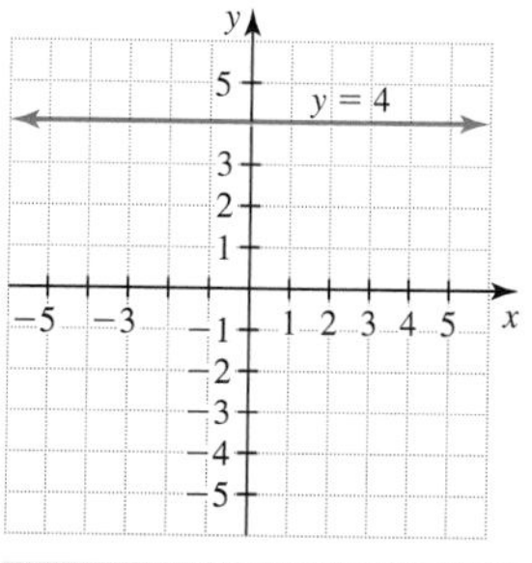

Figure R.12

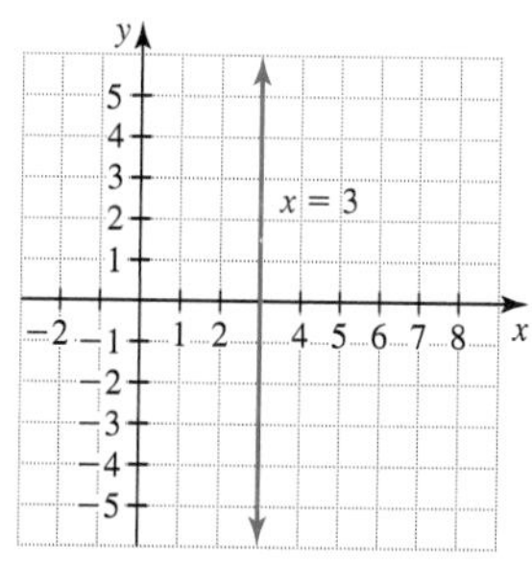

Figure R.13

Solution

a) To find the y-intercept let $x = 0$ in $3x - 5y = 15$:

$$3(0) - 5y = 15$$
$$y = -3$$

The y-intercept is $(0, -3)$. To find the x-intercept let $y = 0$ in $3x - 5y = 15$:

$$3x - 5(0) = 15$$
$$x = 5$$

The x-intercept is $(5, 0)$. Now let $x = 10$ in $3x - 5y = 15$:

$$3(10) - 5y = 15$$
$$-5y = -15$$
$$y = 3$$

So the line goes through the intercepts and $(10, 3)$. Plot these three points and draw a line through them as shown in Fig. R.11.

b) Since the coefficient of x is zero, the graph is a horizontal line with y-intercept $(0, 4)$. Note that any number can be used for x as long as we choose $y = 4$. So the ordered pairs $(-1, 4)$, $(1, 4)$, and $(2, 4)$ also satisfy the equation. Plot these points and draw a line through them as shown in Fig. R.12.

c) Since the coefficient of y is zero, the graph is a vertical line with x-intercept $(3, 0)$. The graph also goes through $(3, -1)$ and $(3, 2)$. Plot these points and draw a line through them as shown in Fig. R.13.

Slope

The **slope** of a line is the number obtained by dividing the change in y-coordinate by the change in x-coordinate for any two points on a line. The change in y-coordinate and the change in x-coordinate are also called the **rise** and the **run,** respectively. The slope of the line containing the points (x_1, y_1) and (x_2, y_2) is given by

$$m = \frac{\text{change in } y\text{-coordinate}}{\text{change in } x\text{-coordinate}} = \frac{\text{rise}}{\text{run}} = \frac{y_2 - y_1}{x_2 - x_1},$$

provided that $x_2 - x_1 \neq 0$. If $x_2 - x_1 = 0$, then the line is a vertical line and the slope of the line is not defined. Parallel lines have the same slope. If m_1 and m_2 are the slopes of two perpendicular lines, then $m_1 = -\frac{1}{m_2}$.

EXAMPLE 2

Finding slopes

Find the slope of each line.

a) The line through $(-3, 5)$ and $(-1, -2)$

b) The line through $(0, 2)$ and $(5, 2)$

c) The line through $(3, 0)$ and $(3, 6)$

d) A line parallel to the line through $(-1, 2)$ and $(3, 4)$

e) A line perpendicular to the line through $(0, 6)$ and $(2, 0)$

Solution

a) Use $(-3, 5)$ and $(-1, -2)$ in the formula $m = \frac{y_2 - y_1}{x_2 - x_1}$:

$$m = \frac{-2 - 5}{-1 - (-3)} = \frac{-7}{2} = -\frac{7}{2}$$

b) Use $(0, 2)$ and $(5, 2)$ in the formula $m = \frac{y_2 - y_1}{x_2 - x_1}$:

$$m = \frac{2 - 2}{5 - 0} = 0$$

c) The line through $(3, 0)$ and $(3, 6)$ is a vertical line and does not have slope.

d) Use $(-1, 2)$ and $(3, 4)$ in the formula $m = \frac{y_2 - y_1}{x_2 - x_1}$:

$$m = \frac{4 - 2}{3 - (-1)} = \frac{2}{4} = \frac{1}{2}$$

Any line parallel to the line through $(-1, 2)$ and $(3, 4)$ also has slope $\frac{1}{2}$.

e) Use $(0, 6)$ and $(2, 0)$ in the formula $m = \frac{y_2 - y_1}{x_2 - x_1}$:

$$m = \frac{0 - 6}{2 - 0} = -3$$

Any line perpendicular to the line through $(0, 6)$ and $(2, 0)$ has slope $\frac{1}{3}$.

Equations of Lines in Slope-Intercept Form

The equation of the line with y-intercept $(0, b)$ and slope m is

$$y = mx + b.$$

The form $y = mx + b$ is called **slope-intercept form.** Of course, lines that do not have slope (vertical lines) cannot be written in this form. Every line has an equation in **standard form,** $Ax + By = C$, where A and B are not both zero. We can use the y-intercept and the slope to graph a line.

EXAMPLE 3

Using y-intercept and slope to graph a line

Identify the slope and y-intercept for each line and then graph the line.

a) $y = \frac{1}{2}x - 2$ **b)** $2x + 3y = 6$ **c)** $y = 6$

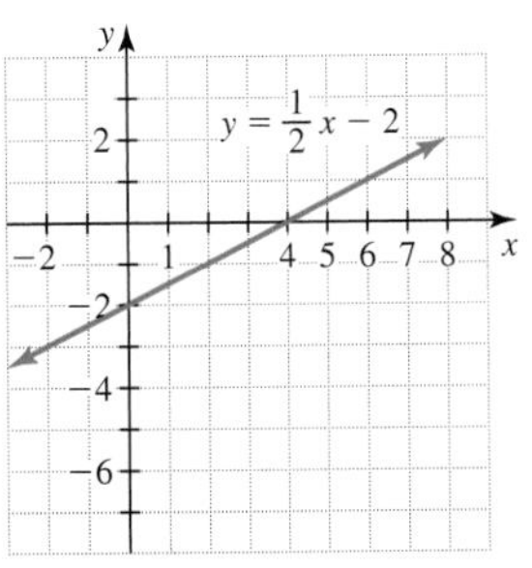

Figure R.14

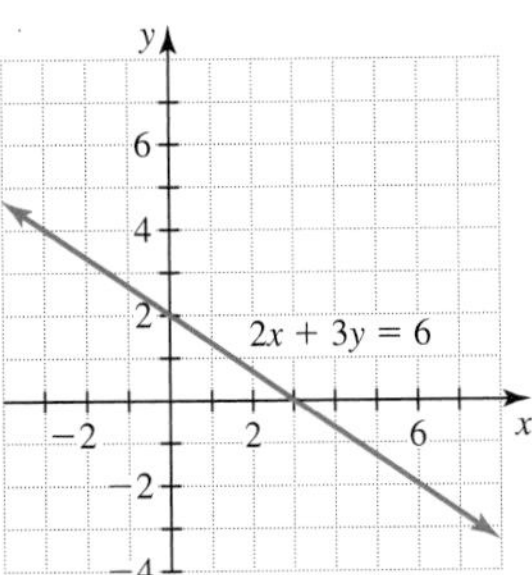

Figure R.15

Solution

a) The slope is $\frac{1}{2}$ and the y-intercept is $(0, -2)$. Since $\frac{1}{2} = \frac{\text{rise}}{\text{run}}$, start at $(0, -2)$ and move 1 unit upward and 2 units to the right to obtain a second point on the line, $(2, -1)$. Again rise 1 and run 2 to obtain a third point on the line, $(4, 0)$. Draw a line through these points as shown in Fig. R.14.

b) First solve $2x + 3y = 6$ for y:

$$\begin{aligned} 2x + 3y &= 6 \\ 3y &= -2x + 6 \\ y &= -\frac{2}{3}x + 2 \end{aligned}$$

The slope is $-\frac{2}{3}$ and the y-intercept is $(0, 2)$. Start at $(0, 2)$ and move 2 units downward and 3 units to the right to obtain a second point on the line, $(3, 0)$. From $(3, 0)$ again move 2 units down and 3 units to the right to obtain a third point on the line, $(6, -2)$. Draw a line through these points as shown in Fig. R.15.

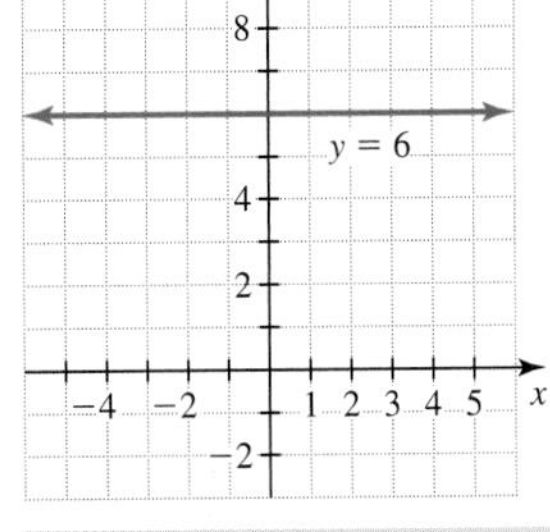

Figure R.16

c) For $y = 6$ the slope is 0 and the y-intercept is $(0, 6)$. So the graph is a horizontal line through $(0, 6)$ as shown in Fig. R.16.

If we can determine the y-intercept and the slope from a description of a line, then we can write its equation using the slope-intercept form.

EXAMPLE 4

Writing the equation for a line using slope-intercept form

Write the equation in slope-intercept form for each line.

a) The line through $(0, 3)$ and $(4, 0)$

b) The line through $(0, -4)$ that is parallel to $y = \frac{3}{4}x - 5$

c) The line through $(0, -2)$ that is perpendicular to $2x - 5y = 3$

Solution

a) The line through $(0, 3)$ and $(4, 0)$ has slope $-\frac{3}{4}$ and y-intercept $(0, 3)$. So the equation is $y = -\frac{3}{4}x + 3$.

b) The line $y = \frac{3}{4}x - 5$ has slope $\frac{3}{4}$ and so does any line parallel to it. So the equation of the line through $(0, -4)$ that is parallel to $y = \frac{3}{4}x - 5$ is $y = \frac{3}{4}x - 4$.

c) Solve $2x - 5y = 2$ for y to determine its slope:

$$\begin{aligned} 2x - 5y &= 3 \\ -5y &= -2x + 3 \\ y &= \frac{2}{5}x - \frac{3}{5} \end{aligned}$$

The slope of $2x - 5y = 3$ is $\frac{2}{5}$ and any line perpendicular to it has slope $-\frac{5}{2}$. The equation of the line through $(0, -2)$ with slope $-\frac{5}{2}$ is $y = -\frac{5}{2}x - 2$.

The Point-Slope Form

The equation of the line through the point (x_1, y_1) with slope m is

$$y - y_1 = m(x - x_1).$$

This form is called the **point-slope form** for the equation of a line. To write the equation of a line with slope-intercept form you must know the slope and the y-intercept. Using the point-slope form, the point can be any point on the line.

EXAMPLE 5

Writing the equation for a line using point-slope form

Find the equation for each line. Write the answer in standard form $Ax + By = C$, where A, B, and C are integers.

a) The line through (1, 5) and (4, 2)

b) The line through $(2, -3)$ that is parallel to $y = \frac{1}{2}x - 2$

c) The line through $(1, -4)$ that is perpendicular to $3x - y = 1$

Solution

a) The line through (1, 5) and (4, 2) has slope $\frac{2-5}{4-1}$ or -1. Now use one of the points, say, (1, 5), and slope -1 in the point-slope form:

$$\begin{aligned} y - 5 &= -1(x - 1) \\ y - 5 &= -x + 1 \\ x + y &= 6 \end{aligned}$$

The equation of the line in standard form is $x + y = 6$. Note that this answer is not unique. Multiplying each side of $x + y = 6$ by any nonzero integer will give an equivalent equation.

b) The line $y = \frac{1}{2}x - 2$ has slope $\frac{1}{2}$ and so does any line parallel to it. So use the point $(2, -3)$ and slope $\frac{1}{2}$ in the point-slope form:

$$\begin{aligned} y - (-3) &= \frac{1}{2}(x - 2) && \text{Point-slope form} \\ y + 3 &= \frac{1}{2}x - 1 \\ -\frac{1}{2}x + y &= -4 \\ x - 2y &= 8 && \text{Multiply each side by } -2. \end{aligned}$$

The equation of the line in standard form is $x - 2y = 8$.

c) Solve $3x - y = 1$ for y to get $y = 3x - 1$. This line has slope 3 and any line perpendicular to it has slope $-\frac{1}{3}$. Use the point $(1, -4)$ and slope $-\frac{1}{3}$ in the point-slope form:

$$\begin{aligned} y - (-4) &= -\frac{1}{3}(x - 1) && \text{Point-slope form} \\ y + 4 &= -\frac{1}{3}x + \frac{1}{3} \\ 3y + 12 &= -x + 1 && \text{Multiply each side by 3.} \\ x + 3y &= -11 && \text{Standard form} \end{aligned}$$

The equation of the line in standard form is $x + 3y = -11$.

Variation

Some basic relationships between variables are expressed in terms of variation. The statement **"y varies directly as x"** or **"y is directly proportional to x"** means that $y = kx$. The statement **"y varies inversely as x"** or **"y is inversely proportional to x"** means that $y = \frac{k}{x}$. The statement **"y varies jointly as x and z"** or **"y is jointly proportional to x and z"** means that $y = kxz$. In each case, k is a nonzero constant and is called the **variation constant.**

EXAMPLE 6

Using variation terms

Solve each problem.

a) Distance varies directly with the average speed. Willy drove 200 miles with an average speed of 40 mph. Find the constant of variation.

b) The time that it takes to harvest a field of beans varies inversely with the number of pickers. If 10 pickers can harvest the field in 3 hours, then how long would it take 15 pickers?

c) The cost of waterproofing a rectangular roof varies jointly with the length and the width. If a 30-ft by 40-ft roof costs \$3072, then what is the cost for a 25-ft by 50-ft roof?

Solution

a) Since distance D varies directly with the average speed R, we have $D = kR$ for some constant k. Since $D = 200$ when $R = 40$, we have $200 = k(40)$. Since 200 miles divided by 40 mph is 5 hours, the constant is 5 hours.

b) Since the time t varies inversely with the number of pickers n, we have $t = \frac{k}{n}$ for some constant k. Since $t = 3$ hr when $n = 10$ pickers, we have $3 = \frac{k}{10}$ or $k = 30$. Since 30 is obtained by multiplying hours and pickers the units for the constant are picker-hours. It takes 30 picker-hours to harvest the field. So 1 picker can do it in 30 hours, 2 pickers in 15 hours, 3 pickers in 10 hours, and so on.

c) Since the cost C varies jointly as the length L and width W, we have $C = kLW$ for some constant k. Since $C = \$3072$ when $W = 30$ ft and $L = 40$ ft, we have $3072 = k(30)(40)$, or $k = 2.56$. Since k is obtained by dividing dollars by square feet, k is \$2.56 per square foot. The cost for a 25-ft by 50-ft roof is 2.56(25)(50) or \$3200.

Graphing Linear Inequalities in Two Variables

Linear inequalities in two variables have the same form as linear equations in two variables. If A, B, and C are real numbers with A and B not both zero, then $Ax + By < C$ is a **linear inequality in two variables.** In place of $<$ we can also use $\leq$, $>$, or $\geq$. The solution set to a linear inequality in two variables consists of infinitely many ordered pairs that lie in a region of the coordinate plane. So to graph a linear inequality, we first graph the boundary line $Ax + By = C$ and then use a test point to determine which side of the line satisfies the inequality. All points on one side of the line satisfy $Ax + By > C$ and all points on the other side satisfy $Ax + By < C$.

EXAMPLE 7

Graphing linear inequalities in two variables

Graph the solution set to each inequality in the coordinate plane.

a) $3x - 5y > 30$ **b)** $y \le -2x + 3$ **c)** $x < 3$

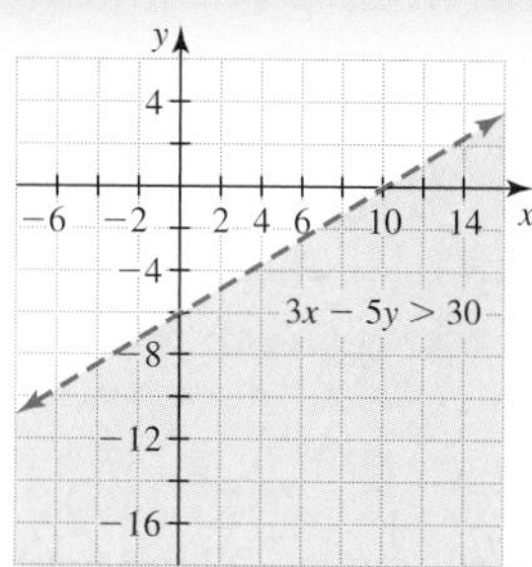

Figure R.17

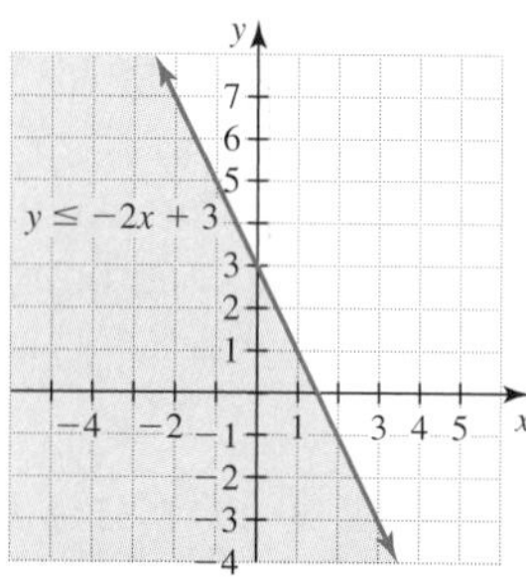

Figure R.18

Solution

a) First graph the boundary line $3x - 5y = 30$ by using its x-intercept (10, 0) and its y-intercept $(0, -6)$. Draw the line dashed because it is not included in the solution set to the inequality. Next select a test point on one side of the line, say (1, 1). Since $3(1) - 5(1) > 30$ is incorrect, all points on the other side of the line must satisfy the inequality. Shade that region as shown in Fig. R.17.

b) First graph the boundary line $y = -2x + 3$ using its slope -2 and y-intercept (0, 3). The line is drawn solid because it is included in the solution set to $y \le -2x + 3$. Next select a test point on one side of the line, say $(-1, 0)$. Because $0 \le -2(-1) + 3$ is correct, all points on that side of the line satisfy the inequality. Shade that region as shown in Fig. R.18

c) First graph the vertical boundary line $x = 3$ as a dashed line. Select a test point, say (0, 0). Since $0 < 3$ is correct, shade the region to the left of the line $x = 3$ as shown in Fig. R.19

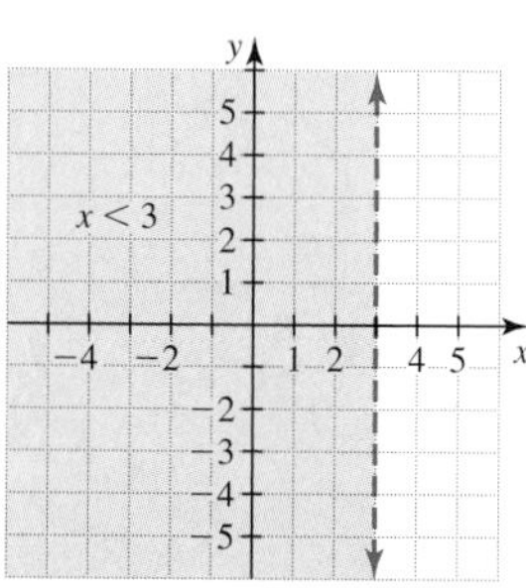

Figure R.19

R.3 Exercises

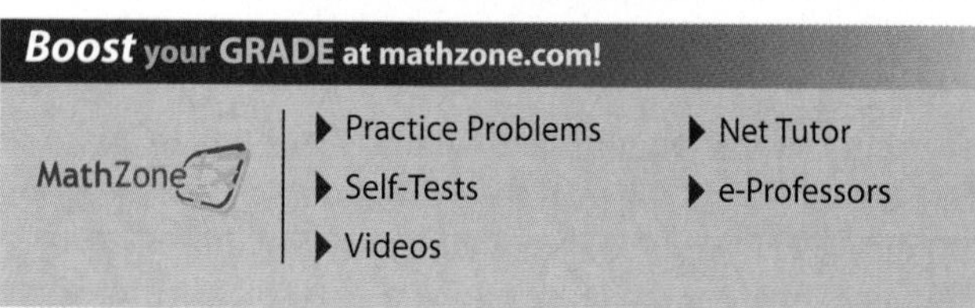

Graph each equation and identify all intercepts. See Example 1.

1. $3x - 4y = 12$
(4, 0), (0, −3)

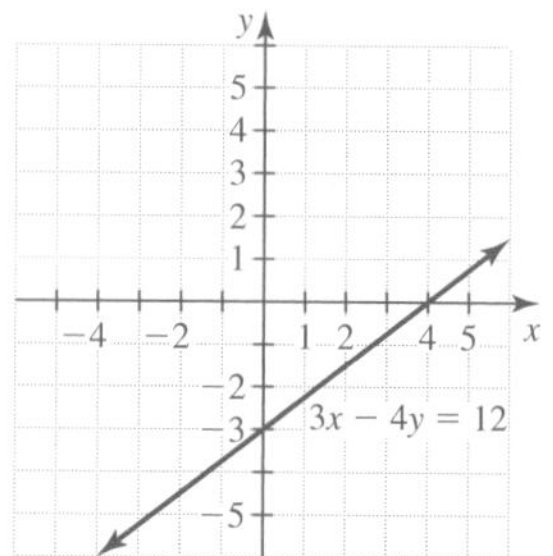

2. $x - 2y = 10$ (10, 0), (0, −5)

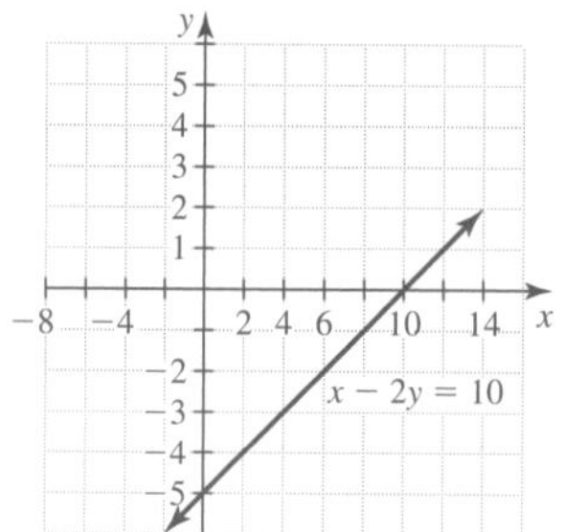

3. $2x + y = 6$ (3, 0), (0, 6)

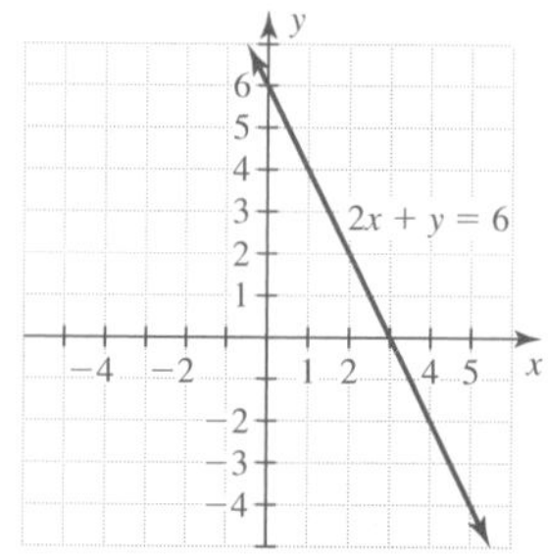

4. $3x + 7y = 21$ (7, 0), (0, 3)

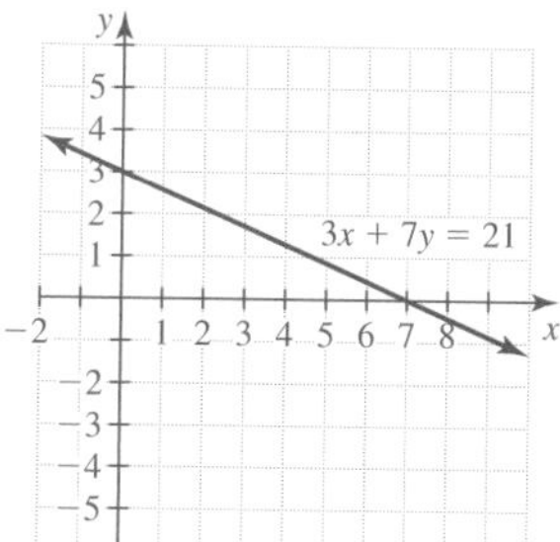

5. $x = -3$ (−3, 0)

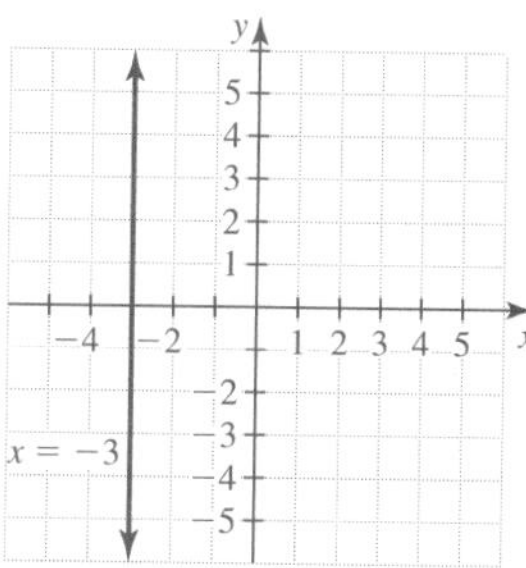

6. $x = 5$ (5, 0)

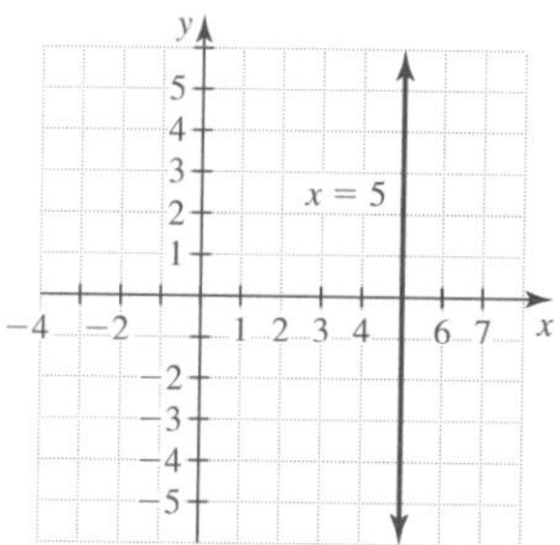

7. $y = 2$ (0, 2)

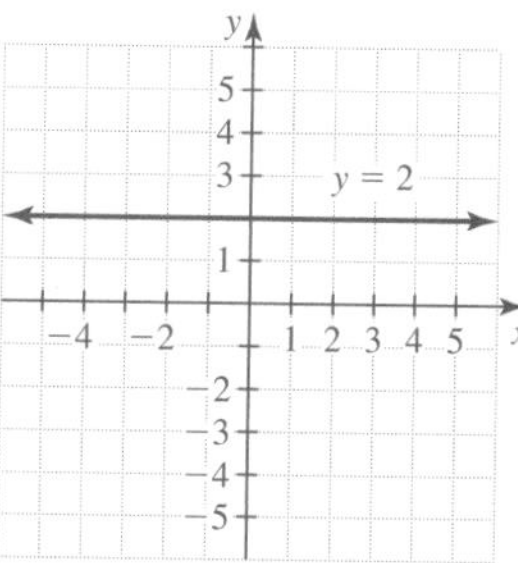

8. $y = -4$ (0, −4)

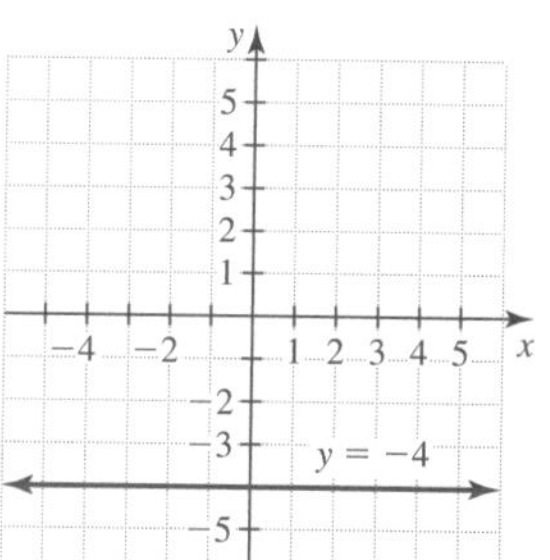

9. $y = \frac{1}{2}x - 30$

(60, 0), (0, −30)

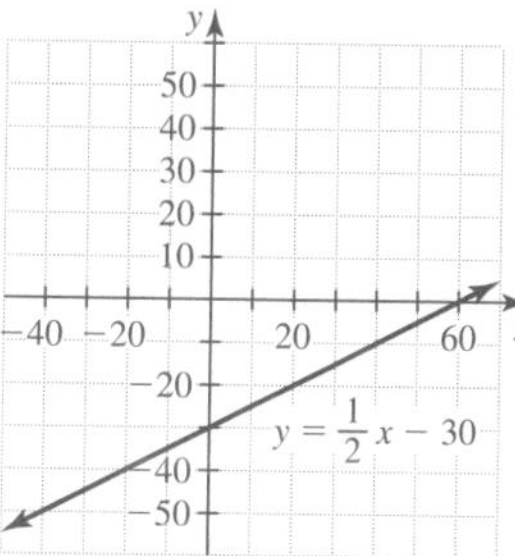

10. $y = -\frac{2}{3}x + 20$

(30, 0), (0, 20)

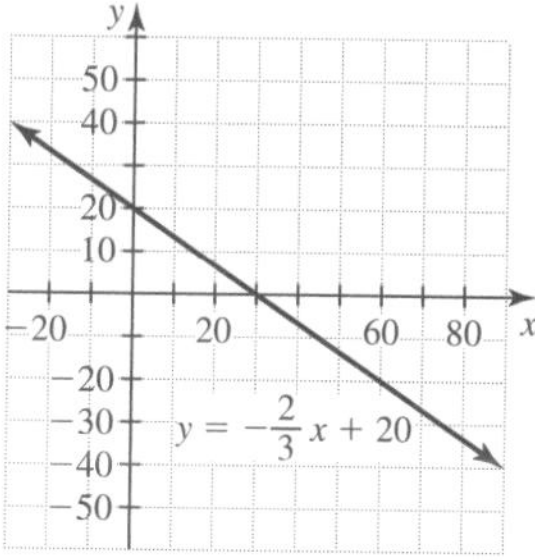

Find the slope of each line. See Example 2.

11. The line through (−2, 1) and (3, 6) 1

12. The line through (−1, −3) and (5, 5) $\frac{4}{3}$

13. The line through (−3, 3) and (1, −1) −1

14. The line through (0, 0) and (−5, −5) 1

15. The line through (2, 1) and (2, 7) No slope

16. The line through (−3, −1) and (−3, 4) No slope

17. The line through (4, 1) and (−2, 1) 0

18. The line through (−3, 5) and (3, 5) 0

19. A line parallel to the line through (1, 4) and (4, 16) 4

20. A line parallel to the line through (3, 2) and (−6, 2) 0

21. A line perpendicular to the line through (−1, −1) and (2, 3) $-\frac{3}{4}$

22. A line perpendicular to the line through (−5, 8) and (5, −8) $\frac{5}{8}$

23. A line perpendicular to the line $x = 3$ 0

24. A line parallel to the line $y = -5$ 0

Identify the slope and y-intercept for each line and then graph the line. See Example 3.

25. $y = \frac{1}{3}x + 1$ $\frac{1}{3}$, (0, 1)

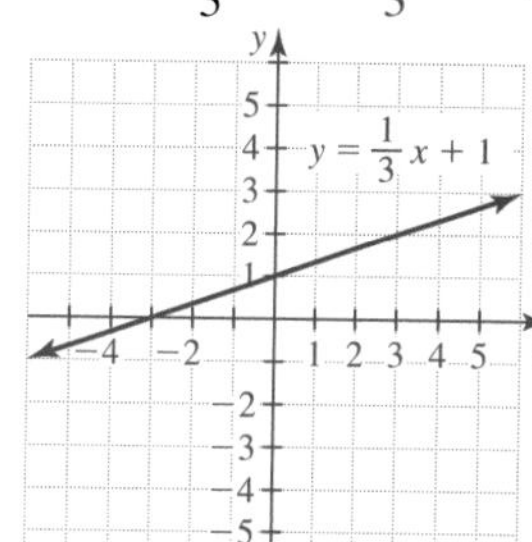

26. $y = \frac{2}{3}x - 2$ $\frac{2}{3}$, (0, −2)

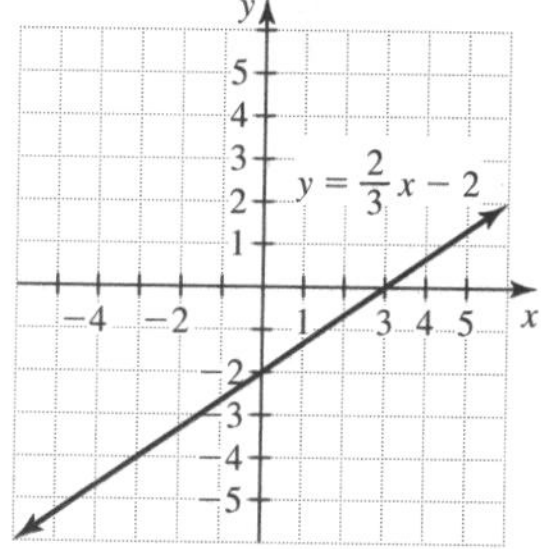

27. $y = -3x + 4$

−3, (0, 4)

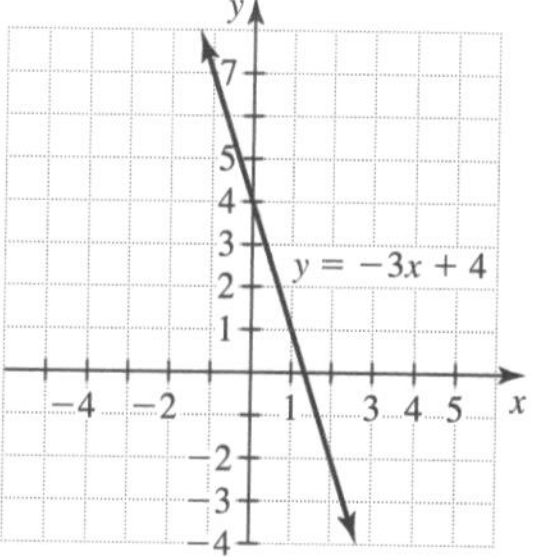

28. $y = 2x - 5$

2, (0, −5)

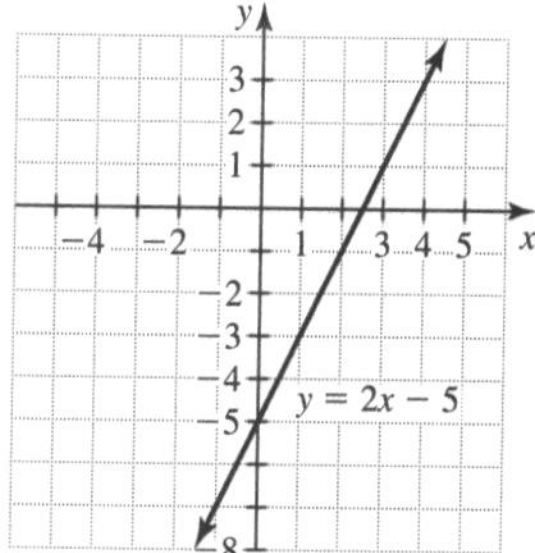

29. $x - y = 5$ 1, (0, −5)

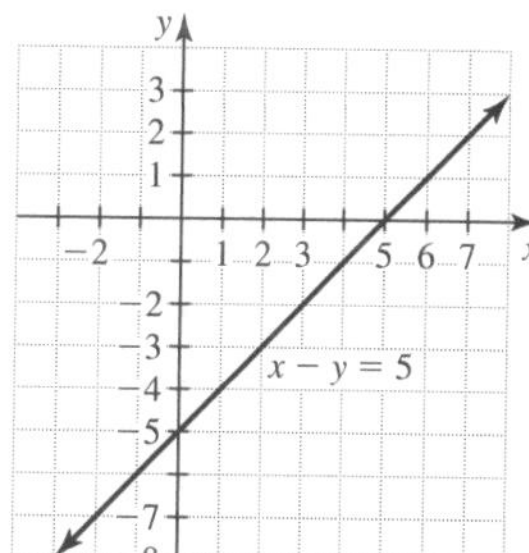

30. $x + 2y = 4$ $-\frac{1}{2}$, (0, 2)

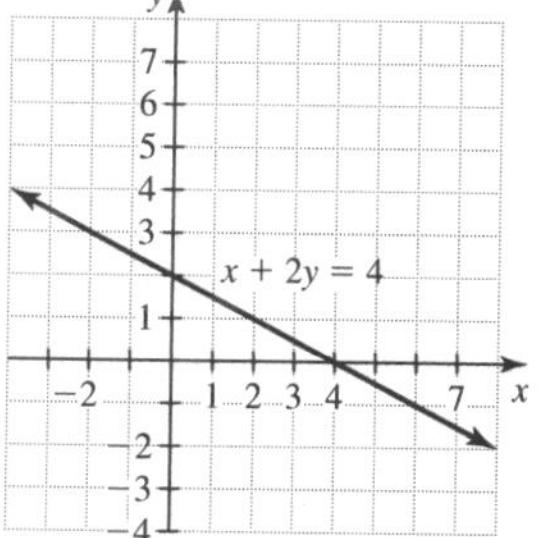

31. $3x - 5y = 10$
$\frac{3}{5}$, $(0, -2)$

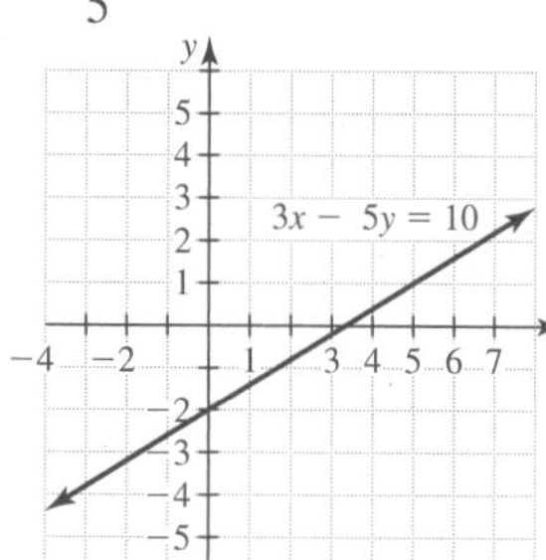

32. $-2x + 3y = 9$
$\frac{2}{3}$, $(0, 3)$

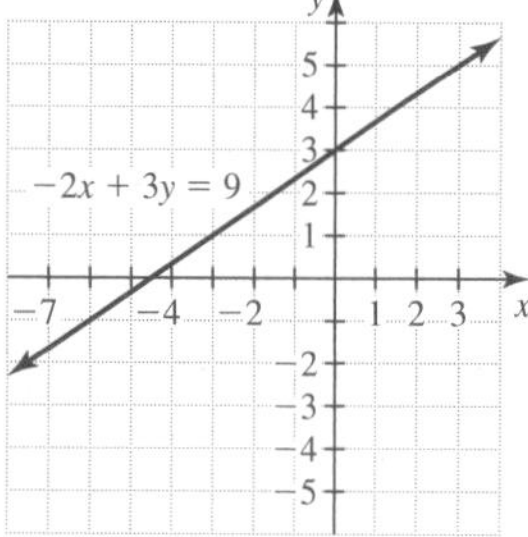

33. $y = 4$ 0, $(0, 4)$

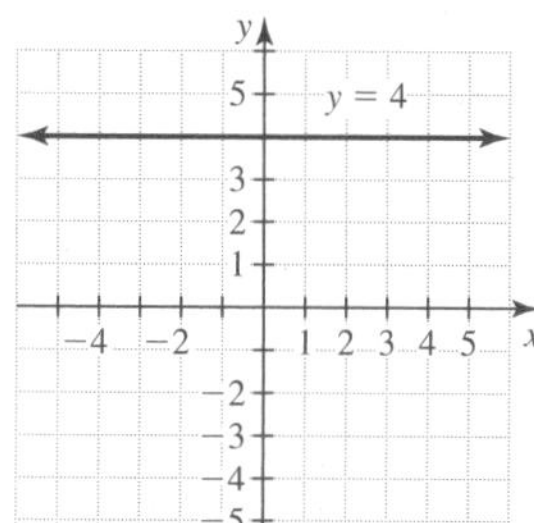

34. $y = -5$ 0, $(0, -5)$

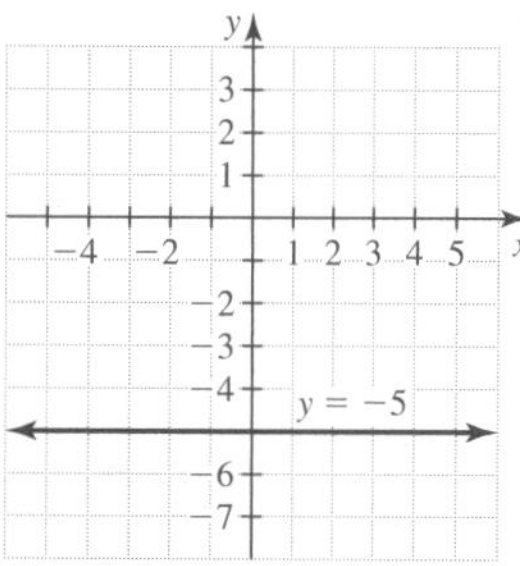

Write the equation in slope-intercept form for each line. See Example 4.

35. The line through $(0, -2)$ and $(5, 0)$ $y = \frac{2}{5}x - 2$

36. The line through $(0, 5)$ and $(-3, -4)$ $y = 3x + 5$

37. The line through $(0, 6)$ that is parallel to $y = \frac{2}{7}x + 3$
$y = \frac{2}{7}x + 6$

38. The line through $(0, -2)$ that is parallel to $y = -5x - 4$
$y = -5x - 2$

39. The line through $(0, 12)$ that is perpendicular to $x - 4y = 1$
$y = -4x + 12$

40. The line through $(0, -14)$ that is perpendicular to $3x - y = 2$ $y = -\frac{1}{3}x - 14$

41. The line through $(0, 3)$ that is parallel to $y = -1$ $y = 3$

42. The line through $(0, 5)$ that is perpendicular to $x = 3$
$y = 5$

Find the equation for each line. Write the answer in standard form $Ax + By = C$, where A, B, and C are integers. See Example 5

43. The line through $(-2, 4)$ and $(3, 7)$ $3x - 5y = -26$

44. The line through $(2, -5)$ and $(3, 9)$ $14x - y = 33$

45. The line through $(-1, 3)$ and $(5, 0)$ $x + 2y = 5$

46. The line through $(2, 0)$ and $(-6, 8)$ $x + y = 2$

47. The line through $(1, -4)$ that is parallel to $y = \frac{2}{3}x + 6$
$2x - 3y = 14$

48. The line through $(3, -5)$ that is parallel to $y = -\frac{1}{4}x - 9$
$x + 4y = -17$

49. The line through $(2, -5)$ that is perpendicular to $2x + y = 5$ $x - 2y = 12$

50. The line through $(3, -6)$ that is perpendicular to $4x - y = 2$ $x + 4y = -21$

Solve each variation problem. See Example 6.

51. ***Average speed.*** Distance varies directly with the time. Billy drove 200 miles in 4 hours. Find the constant of variation. 50 mph

52. ***Hiking time.*** Distance varies directly with the average speed. Cortez hiked 15 miles at 3 miles per hour. Find the constant of variation. 5 hr

53. ***Picking oranges.*** The time that it takes to pick the entire orange grove varies inversely with the number of pickers. If 30 pickers can pick the entire grove in 14 hours, then how long would it take 40 pickers? 10.5 hr

54. ***Sharing cookies.*** A box of cookies is divided among the cub scouts at the meeting. The number of cookies each scout receives varies inversely as the number of scouts in attendance. When 4 scouts are in attendance each scout receives 12 cookies. How many cookies will each scout receive when 16 scouts are in attendance? 3 cookies

55. ***Area of a rectangle.*** The cost of wood laminate flooring for a rectangular room varies jointly as the length and width of the room. If the cost is \$1148.16 for a 12-ft by 16-ft room, then what is the cost for a room that is 10 ft by 14 ft? \$837.20

56. ***Building bookcases.*** The cost for a custom oak bookcase varies jointly with the width and height. If a bookcase that is 7 ft high and 30 in. wide costs \$441, then what is the cost for a bookcase that is 32 in. wide and 6 ft high? \$403.20

Graph the solution set to each inequality in the coordinate plane. See Example 7.

57. $3x - 2y > 6$

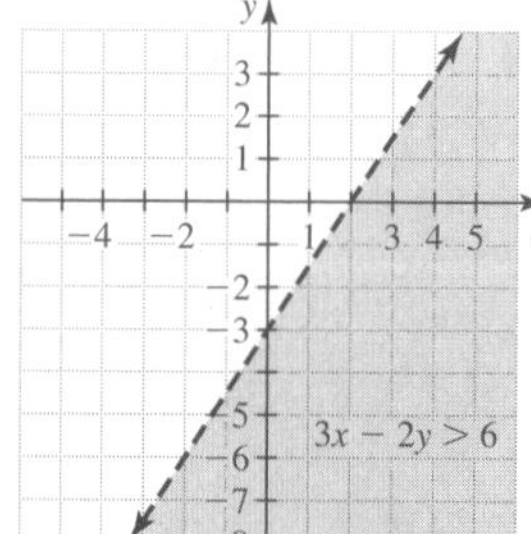

58. $x - y < 5$

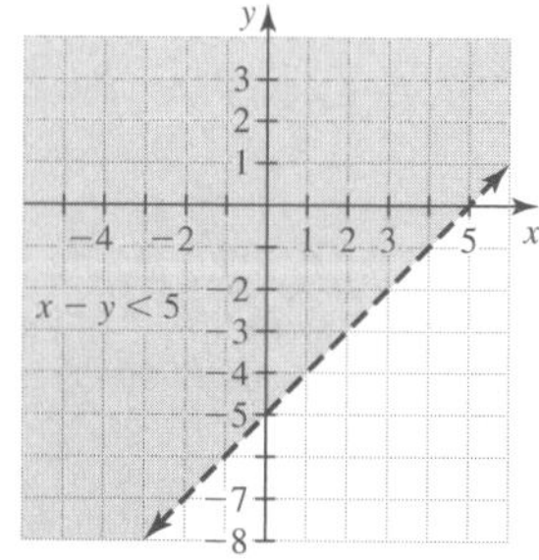

59. $x + 3y \leq 9$

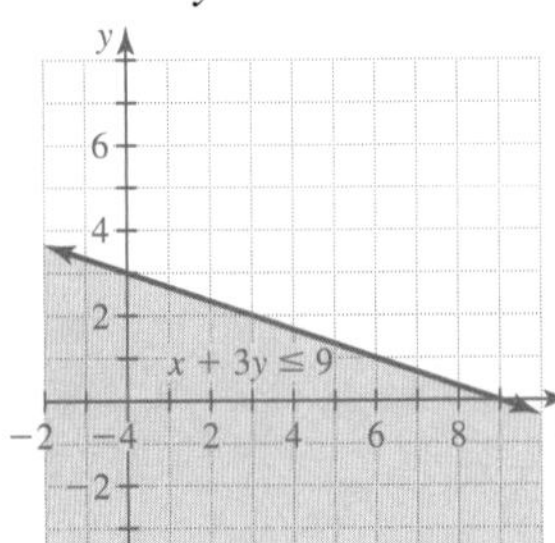

60. $6x + y \geq 12$

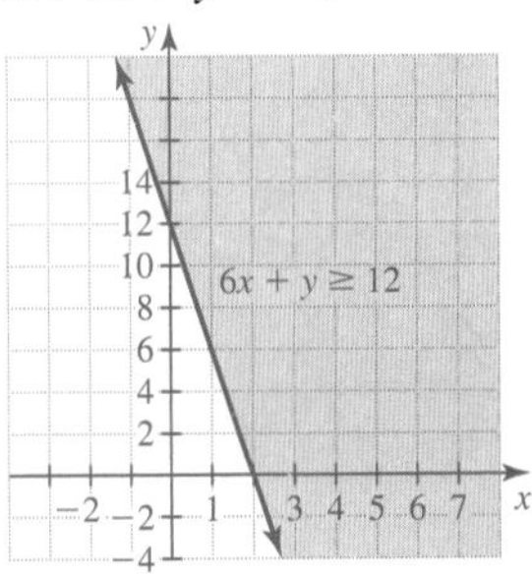

61. $y \leq -x + 3$

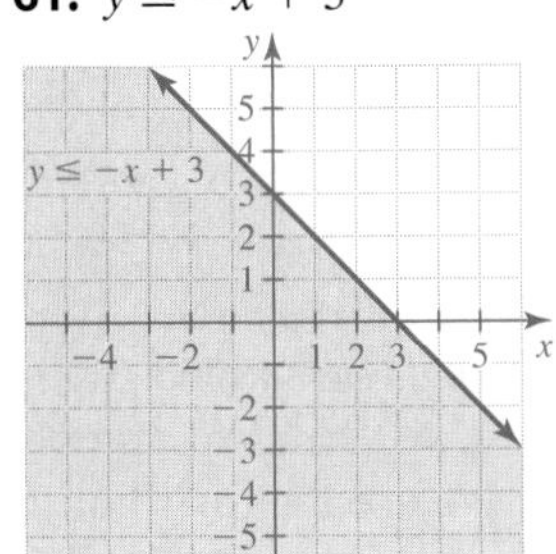

62. $y \geq 2x + 1$

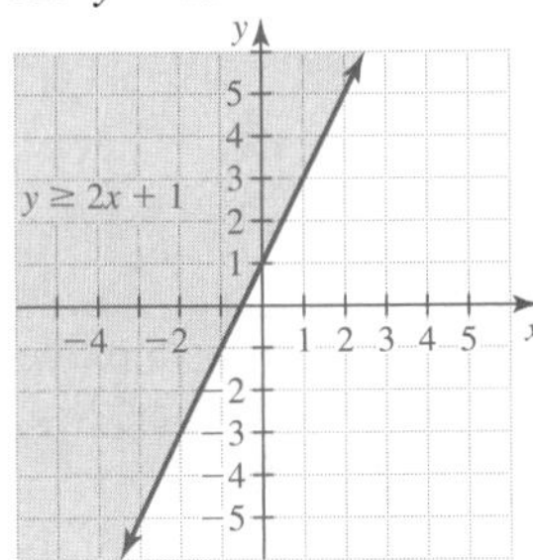

63. $y > 3x - 4$

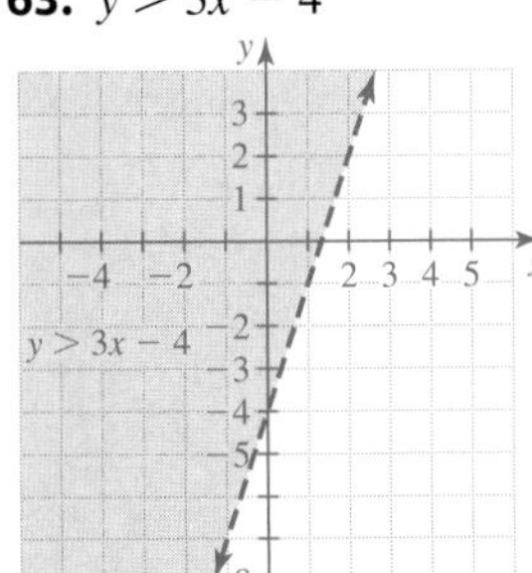

64. $y < -2x + 2$

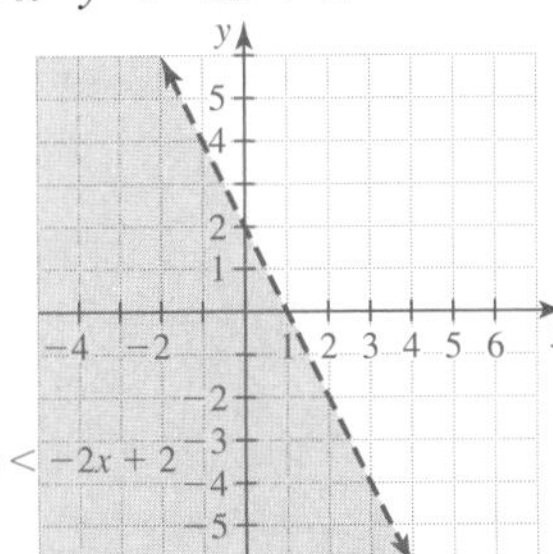

65. $x < 2$

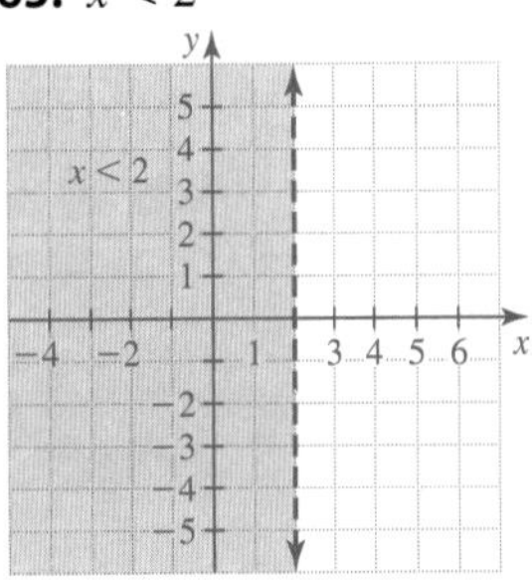

66. $x > -3$

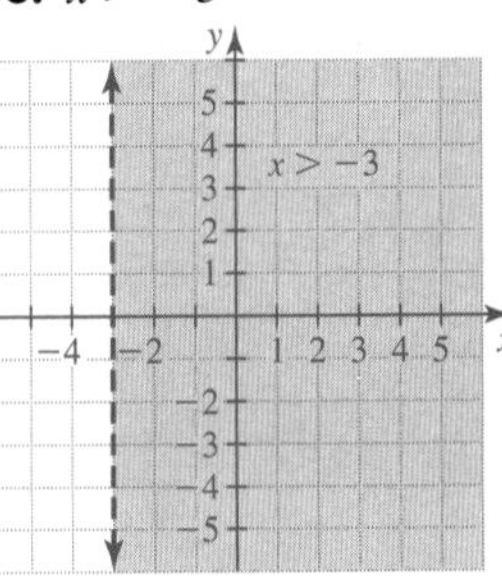

67. $x \geq -1$

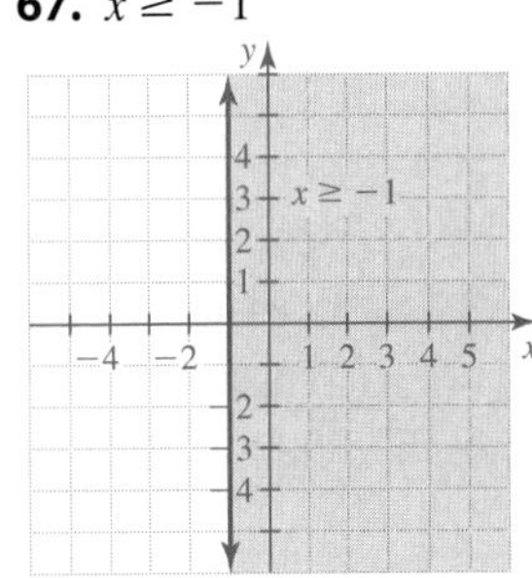

68. $x \leq 5$

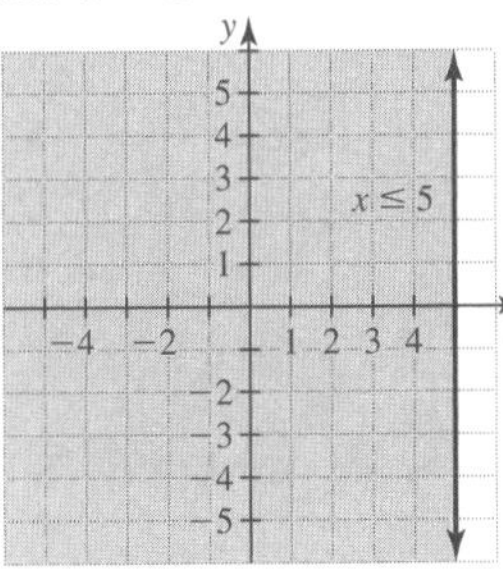

69. $y < 4$

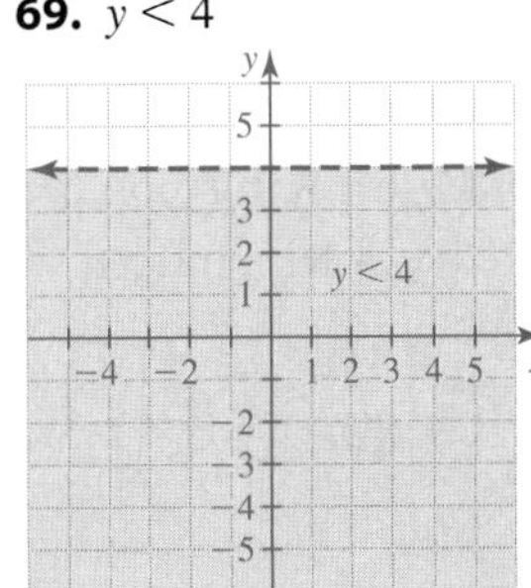

70. $y > -2$

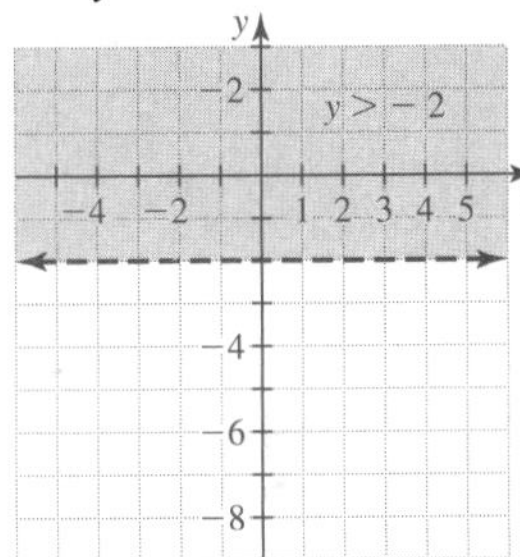

R.4 Polynomials and Exponents

This section is a review of Chapter 4 of this text. All topics in this review section are explained in greater detail in Chapter 4.

Polynomials

A **polynomial** is a single term or a finite sum of terms. The **degree of a polynomial** in one variable is the highest power of the variable in the polynomial. The number preceding the variable in each term is called the **coefficient** of that variable or the coefficient of that term. A **monomial** has one term, a **binomial** has two terms, and a **trinomial** has three terms. For example, the polynomial $5x^2 - 2x + 3$ is a trinomial with degree two and the coefficient of x^2 is 5. We can also write

$$P = 5x^2 - 2x + 3 \quad \text{or} \quad P(x) = 5x^2 - 2x + 3.$$

If $x = 1$, then we can evaluate $5(1)^2 - 2(1) + 3$ to get 6. We say that the value of the polynomial is 6 when $x = 1$, or $P = 6$ when $x = 1$, or $P(1) = 6$ (read "P of 1 equals 6"). Polynomials can be added or subtracted by adding or subtracting like terms.

EXAMPLE 1

Adding and subtracting polynomials

Perform the indicated operations.

a) $(x^2 - 6x + 3) + (-3x^2 - 5x - 4)$

b) $(-3x^3 - 4x + 2) - (-x^3 + 4x^2 - 5)$

Solution

a) $(x^2 - 6x + 3) + (-3x^2 - 5x - 4) = x^2 - 3x^2 - 6x - 5x + 3 - 4$

$= -2x^2 - 11x - 1$

b) $(-3x^3 - 4x + 2) - (-x^3 + 4x^2 - 5) = -3x^3 - 4x + 2 + x^3 - 4x^2 + 5$

$= -2x^3 - 4x^2 - 4x + 7$

Multiplication of Polynomials

The **product rule for exponents** indicates that the exponents are added when multiplying powers of the same base. In symbols, $a^m \cdot a^n = a^{m+n}$ for any real number a and positive integers m and n. For example, $2x^3 \cdot 4x^2 = 8x^5$. We use the distributive property and the product rule for exponents to multiply polynomials.

EXAMPLE 2

Multiplying polynomials

Find each product.

a) $3x(x^2 - 6x + 3)$

b) $(w + 3)(w + 5)$

c) $(y - 1)(y^2 + 4y - 6)$

Solution

a) $3x(x^2 - 6x + 3) = 3x(x^2) + 3x(-6x) + 3x(3)$ Distributive property

$= 3x^3 - 18x^2 + 9x$ Multiply the monomials.

b) $(w + 3)(w + 5) = (w + 3)w + (w + 3)5$ Distributive property

$= w^2 + 3w + 5w + 15$ Distributive property

$= w^2 + 8w + 15$ Combine like terms.

c) $(y - 1)(y^2 + 4y - 6) = (y - 1)y^2 + (y - 1)4y + (y - 1)(-6)$

$= y^3 - y^2 + 4y^2 - 4y - 6y + 6$

$= y^3 + 3y^2 - 10y + 6$

Multiplication of Binomials

We can use the distributive property to multiply binomials as was done in Example 2(c). Because multiplication of binomials is done so frequently, we usually use the **FOIL method** instead. With FOIL we find the product of the first terms of each binomial, the product of the outer terms, the product of the inner terms, and finally the product of the last terms. In many cases, the product of the inner terms and the product of the outer terms are like terms and they can be combined.

EXAMPLE 3

Multiplying binomials using FOIL

Use the FOIL method to find each product.

a) $(a + b)(c + d)$ **b)** $(2x + 3)(x - 5)$

c) $(3a^2 - 5)(7a^2 + 2)$

Solution

a) For $(a + b)(c + d)$ the product of the first terms is ac, the product of the outer terms is ad, the product of the inner terms is bc, and the product of the last terms is bd:

$$(a + b)(c + d) = ac + ad + bc + bd$$

In this case, there are no like terms to combine.

b) $(2x + 3)(x - 5) = 2x \cdot x + (2x)(-5) + 3x + (3)(-5)$ FOIL

$= 2x^2 - 10x + 3x - 15$ Simplify.

$= 2x^2 - 7x - 15$ Combine like terms.

c) $(3a^2 - 5)(7a^2 + 2) = 12a^4 - 13a^2 + 6a^2 - 10$ FOIL

$= 12a^4 - 7a^2 - 10$ Combine like terms.

The idea of the FOIL method is to get the product of two binomials quickly. In Example 3 we showed more steps than are necessary. When you use the FOIL method you should write only the steps that are necessary for you to get the correct product.

Special Products

The square of a sum, the square of a difference, and the product of a sum and a difference are called the **special products.** You can use FOIL to find these products, but it is better to learn the following rules for these products:

The Special Products

The square of a sum:	$(a + b)^2 = a^2 + 2ab + b^2$
The square of a difference:	$(a - b)^2 = a^2 - 2ab + b^2$
The product of a sum and a difference:	$(a + b)(a - b) = a^2 - b^2$

EXAMPLE 4

Using the special product rules

Find each product.

a) $(x + 5)^2$ **b)** $(2x - 3)^2$ **c)** $(3w + 5)(3w - 5)$

Solution

a) Use $(a + b)^2 = a^2 + 2ab + b^2$ with $a = x$ and $b = 5$:

$$(x + 5)^2 = x^2 + 2(x)(5) + 5^2$$

$$= x^2 + 10x + 25$$

b) Use $(a - b)^2 = a^2 - 2ab + b^2$ with $a = 2x$ and $b = 3$:

$$(2x - 3)^2 = (2x)^2 - 2(2x)(3) + 3^2$$
$$= 4x^2 - 12x + 9$$

c) Use $(a + b)(a - b) = a^2 - b^2$ with $a = 3w$ and $b = 5$:

$$(3w + 5)(3w - 5) = (3w)^2 - 5^2$$
$$= 9w^2 - 25$$

Division of Polynomials

The **quotient rule for exponents** indicates that the exponents are subtracted when dividing powers of the same base. In symbols, $\frac{a^m}{a^n} = a^{m-n}$ for any nonzero real number a and positive integers m and n, where $m \geq n$. If $m < n$, then $\frac{a^m}{a^n} = \frac{1}{a^{n-m}}$. For example, $\frac{x^3}{x^9} = \frac{1}{x^6}$. If $a \div b = c$, then a is the **dividend,** b is the **divisor,** and c (or $a \div b$) is the **quotient.** We can use the quotient rule to divide a monomial by a monomial, but to divide polynomials with higher degrees we use a process similar to the long division process that is used to divide whole numbers.

EXAMPLE 5

Dividing polynomials

Find each quotient.

a) $(9x^6) \div (3x^4)$

b) $(12a^3 - 8a^2 + 4a) \div (2a)$

c) $(x^3 - 4x^2 + 9) \div (x - 3)$

Solution

a) $(9x^6) \div (3x^4) = \dfrac{9x^6}{3x^4} = \dfrac{9}{3}x^{6-4} = 3x^2$

b)
$$(12a^3 - 8a^2 + 4a) \div (2a) = \frac{12a^3 - 8a^2 + 4a}{2a}$$
$$= \frac{12a^3}{2a} + \frac{-8a^2}{2a} + \frac{4a}{2a}$$
$$= 6a^2 - 4a + 2$$

c) When dividing by a binomial use the long division process:

$$\begin{array}{r l}
x^2 - x - 3 & \\
x - 3 \overline{) x^3 - 4x^2 + 0 \cdot x + 9} & \\
\underline{x^3 - 3x^2} \qquad\qquad & x^2(x - 3) = x^3 - 3x^2 \\
-x^2 + 0 \cdot x \qquad & -4x^2 - (-3x^2) = -x^2 \\
\underline{-x^2 + 3x} \qquad & -x(x - 3) = -x^2 + 3x \\
-3x + 9 & \text{Subtract: } 0 \cdot x - 3x = -9x \\
\underline{-3x + 9} & -3(x - 3) = -3x + 9 \\
0 & \text{Subtract: } 9 - 9 = 0
\end{array}$$

The quotient is $x^2 - x - 3$.

If the remainder in long division is not zero, then the product of the quotient and divisor, plus the remainder, is equal to the dividend:

$$\text{dividend} = (\text{quotient})(\text{divisor}) + (\text{remainder})$$

or

$$\frac{\text{dividend}}{\text{divisor}} = \text{quotient} + \frac{\text{remainder}}{\text{divisor}}.$$

Nonnegative Integral Exponents

We have just seen the product rules and the quotient rule for exponents. These rules along with several other rules for exponents are stated in the following box.

Rules for Nonnegative Integral Exponents

The following rules hold for nonzero real numbers a and b and nonnegative integers m and n.

1. $a^0 = 1$ — Definition of zero exponent
2. $a^m \cdot a^n = a^{m+n}$ — Product rule
3. $\frac{a^m}{a^n} = a^{m-n}$ for $m \geq n$, $\frac{a^m}{a^n} = \frac{1}{a^{n-m}}$ for $n > m$ — Quotient rule
4. $(a^m)^n = a^{mn}$ — Power rule
5. $(ab)^n = a^n \cdot b^n$ — Power of a product rule
6. $\left(\frac{a}{b}\right)^n = \frac{a^n}{b^n}$ — Power of a quotient rule

These rules are used to simplify expressions in Example 6.

EXAMPLE 6 Using the rules of exponents

Simplify each expression.

a) $\frac{2x^3 \cdot 3x^4}{12x^7}$ **b)** $(-2d^2)^3(3d^3)^4$ **c)** $\left(\frac{2a^3}{4b^2}\right)^2$

Solution

a)
$$\frac{2x^3 \cdot 3x^4}{12x^7} = \frac{6x^7}{12x^7} \quad \text{Product rule}$$
$$= \frac{6x^0}{12} \quad \text{Quotient rule}$$
$$= \frac{6 \cdot 1}{12} \quad \text{Definition of zero exponent}$$
$$= \frac{1}{2} \quad \text{Reduce.}$$

b)
$$(-2d^2)^3(3d^3)^4 = (-2)^3(d^2)^3 \cdot 3^4(d^3)^4 \quad \text{Power of a product rule}$$
$$= (-2)^3\, d^6 \cdot 3^4 d^{12} \quad \text{Power rule}$$
$$= (-2)^3 3^4 d^{18} \quad \text{Product rule}$$
$$= -648d^{18} \quad (-2)^3\,3^4 = -8 \cdot 81 = -648$$

c) $\left(\frac{2a^3}{4b^2}\right)^2 = \frac{(2a^3)^2}{(4b^2)^2}$ Power of a quotient rule

$= \frac{2^2(a^3)^2}{4^2(b^2)^2}$ Power of a product rule

$= \frac{2^2a^6}{4^2b^4}$ Power rule

$= \frac{a^6}{4b^4}$ Simplify: $\frac{2^2}{4^2} = \frac{4}{16} = \frac{1}{4}$

Negative Exponents and Scientific Notation

A negative exponent is defined as a reciprocal. If a is a nonzero real number and n is a positive integer, then $a^{-n} = \frac{1}{a^n}$. So $2^{-3} = \frac{1}{2^3}$. All of the rules for positive exponents that we stated previously also hold for negative exponents. So we will not restate them here. In addition, there are few new rules for negative exponents.

Rules for Negative Exponents

If a and b are nonzero real numbers and n is a positive integer, then

$$a^{-n} = \left(\frac{1}{a}\right)^n,\ a^{-1} = \frac{1}{a},\ \frac{1}{a^{-n}} = a^n,\ \left(\frac{a}{b}\right)^{-n} = \left(\frac{b}{a}\right)^n.$$

Using the rules for negative exponents we have $3^{-2} = \left(\frac{1}{3}\right)^2$, $3^{-1} = \frac{1}{3}$, $\frac{1}{3^{-2}} = 3^2$, and $\left(\frac{2}{3}\right)^{-3} = \left(\frac{3}{2}\right)^3$.

EXAMPLE 7

Using the rules for integral exponents

Simplify each expression. Write the answer with positive exponents only.

a) $\frac{-2x^{-3} \cdot 5x^4}{20x^{-6}}$ **b)** $(-2a^{-2})^{-3}(3a^3)^{-4}$ **c)** $\left(\frac{a^{-3}}{b^2}\right)^{-2}$

Solution

a) $\frac{-2x^{-3} \cdot 5x^4}{20x^{-6}} = \frac{-10x^1}{20x^{-6}}$ Product rule

$= \frac{-10x^{-1-(-6)}}{20}$ Quotient rule

$= -\frac{1}{2}x^5$ Simplify.

b) $(-2a^{-2})^{-3}(3a^3)^{-4} = (-2)^{-3}(a^{-2})^{-3} \cdot 3^{-4}(a^3)^{-4}$ Power of a product rule

$= -\frac{1}{8}a^6 \cdot \frac{1}{81}a^{-12}$ Power rule

$= -\frac{1}{648}a^{-6}$ Product rule

$= -\frac{1}{648a^6}$ Definition of negative exponent

c) $\left(\frac{a^{-3}}{b^2}\right)^{-2} = \frac{(a^{-3})^{-2}}{(b^2)^{-2}}$ Power of a quotient rule

$= \frac{a^6}{b^{-4}}$ Power rule

$= a^6b^4$ Definition of negative exponent

A number in scientific notation is written as a product of a number between 1 and 10 and a power of 10. In scientific notation there is one digit to the left of the decimal point. For example 3.5×10^3 and 2.36×10^{-4} are numbers in scientific notation. To convert these numbers to standard notation the decimal point is moved to the right for a positive power of 10 or to the left for a negative power of 10. So $3.5 \times 10^3 = 3500$ and $2.36 \times 10^{-4} = 0.000236$. To convert from standard notation to scientific notation, the process is reversed. When computing with numbers in scientific notation, we use the rules of exponents.

EXAMPLE 8

Computing with scientific notation

Evaluate each expression by first writing each number in scientific notation.

a) $2{,}000{,}000 \cdot (50{,}000)^3$ **b)** $\frac{80{,}000{,}000}{0.0004}$

Solution

a) $2{,}000{,}000 \cdot (50{,}000)^3 = 2 \times 10^6 \cdot (5 \times 10^4)^3$ Scientific notation

$= 2 \times 10^6 \cdot 125 \times 10^{12}$ Power rule

$= 250 \times 10^{18}$ Product rule

$= 2.5 \times 10^2 \times 10^{18}$ Scientific notation

$= 2.5 \times 10^{20}$ Product rule

b) $\frac{80{,}000{,}000}{0.0004} = \frac{8 \times 10^7}{4 \times 10^{-4}}$ Scientific notation

$= 2 \times 10^{11}$ Quotient rule

R.4 Exercises

Boost your GRADE at mathzone.com!

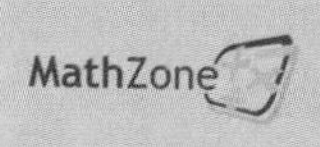

- Practice Problems
- Self-Tests
- Videos
- Net Tutor
- e-Professors

Perform the indicated operation. See Example 1.

1. $(x^2 + 2x) + (x^3 - 5x)$ $x^3 + x^2 - 3x$

2. $(x^2 - 3x) + (-2x^3 - 9x)$ $-2x^3 + x^2 - 12x$

3. $(-w^2 + 5w - 1) + (2w^2 - w - 5)$ $w^2 + 4w - 6$

4. $(-2a^2 + 6a - 9) + (5a^2 - 3a + 8)$ $3a^2 + 3a - 1$

5. $(-2y^2 + 6y) - (y^2 + 5y)$ $-3y^2 + y$

6. $(-5z + 7) - (-6z - 8)$ $z + 15$

7. $(-3t^2 + 5t + 1) - (-t^2 + 4t - 2)$ $-2t^2 + t + 3$

8. $(-n^2 - 3n + 9) - (-4n^2 - 2n + 1)$ $3n^2 - n + 8$

Find each product. See Example 2.

9. $2x(4x - 3)$ $8x^2 - 6x$

10. $5x(-6x + 2)$ $-30x^2 + 10x$

11. $-2a(a^2 - 4a + 9)$ $-2a^3 + 8a^2 - 18a$

12. $-3b(2b^2 - 5b - 1)$ $-6b^3 + 15b^2 + 3b$
13. $6w^2(w^3 - w^2 + w + 3)$ $6w^5 - 6w^4 + 6w^3 + 18w^2$
14. $5t^3(2t^3 + t^2 - 8t - 3)$ $10t^6 + 5t^5 - 40t^4 - 15t^3$
15. $(x + 2)(x + 4)$ $x^2 + 6x + 8$
16. $(a + 5)(a + 7)$ $a^2 + 12a + 35$
17. $(2s - 3)(3s + 1)$ $6s^2 - 7s - 3$
18. $(4t - 1)(t - 2)$ $4t^2 - 9t + 2$
19. $(-2x^2 + 1)(-3x^2 - 5)$ $6x^4 + 7x^2 - 5$
20. $(-x^3 + 5x)(2x^3 - 3x)$ $-2x^6 + 13x^4 - 15x^2$
21. $(x - 3)(x^2 + 3x - 9)$ $x^3 - 18x + 27$
22. $(a - 2)(a^2 + 5a - 8)$ $a^3 + 3a^2 - 18a + 16$
23. $(w + 3)(3w^2 + 5w - 2)$ $3w^3 + 14w^2 + 13w - 6$
24. $(m + 7)(-2m^2 + 4m - 9)$ $-2m^3 - 10m^2 + 19m - 63$

Use the FOIL method to find each product. See Example 3.

25. $(a + m)(b + n)$ $ab + an + mb + mn$
26. $(x + t)(y + s)$ $xy + sx + yt + st$
27. $(x + 2)(x - 6)$ $x^2 - 4x - 12$
28. $(x - 5)(x + 3)$ $x^2 - 2x - 15$
29. $(2a + 1)(3a - 4)$ $6a^2 - 5a - 4$
30. $(3b - 7)(5b - 9)$ $15b^2 - 62b + 63$
31. $(-2x + 1)(-5x + 7)$ $10x^2 - 19x + 7$
32. $(-3x - 2)(-x - 6)$ $3x^2 + 20x + 12$
33. $(2a^3 - 6)(5a^3 + 3)$ $10a^6 - 24a^3 - 18$
34. $(4w^3 - 5)(3w^3 - 7)$ $12w^6 - 43w^3 + 35$
35. $(4x^4 - x)(4x^4 + x)$ $16x^8 - x^2$
36. $(5a^4 + x^3)(5a^4 - x^3)$ $25a^8 - x^6$

Find each product using the special product rules. See Example 4.

37. $(x + 5)^2$ $x^2 + 10x + 25$
38. $(y + 3)^2$ $y^2 + 6y + 9$
39. $(2t + 7)^2$ $4t^2 + 28t + 49$
40. $(3w + 4)^2$ $9w^2 + 24w + 16$
41. $(s - 2)^2$ $s^2 - 4s + 4$
42. $(h - 3)^2$ $h^2 - 6h + 9$
43. $(3y - 5)^2$ $9y^2 - 30y + 25$
44. $(6x - 1)^2$ $36x^2 - 12x + 1$
45. $(3q + 4)(3q - 4)$ $9q^2 - 16$
46. $(5m + 6)(5m - 6)$ $25m^2 - 36$
47. $(2x^2 - 3n)(2x^2 + 3n)$ $4x^4 - 9n^2$
48. $(5t^2 - 3m)(5t^2 + 3m)$ $25t^4 - 9m^2$

Find each quotient. See Example 5.

49. $(6x^8) \div (3x^2)$ $2x^6$
50. $(-12a^{14}) \div (-3a^2)$ $4a^{12}$
51. $(-4w^5) \div (2w^4)$ $-2w$
52. $(20b^{12}) \div (-5b^{10})$ $-4b^2$
53. $(3x^{22}) \div (6x^{20})$ $\frac{1}{2}x^2$
54. $(-4t^{16}) \div (8t^8)$ $-\frac{1}{2}t^8$
55. $(30x^3 - 20x^2 + 10x) \div (10x)$ $3x^2 - 2x + 1$
56. $(25a^3 + 20a^2 + 5a) \div (-5a)$ $-5a^2 - 4a - 1$
57. $(-3x^5 - 9x^4 + 3x^3 - 6x^2) \div (-3x^2)$ $x^3 + 3x^2 - x + 2$
58. $(-8w^4 - 6w^3 + 4w^2) \div (-2w^2)$ $4w^2 + 3w - 2$
59. $(x^3 - 4x^2 + 3) \div (x - 1)$ $x^2 - 3x - 3$
60. $(2x^3 + 3x + 5) \div (x + 1)$ $2x^2 - 2x + 5$
61. $(x^3 - 4x^2 + x + 6) \div (x - 2)$ $x^2 - 2x - 3$
62. $(2x^3 + 3x^2 - 5x + 12) \div (x + 3)$ $2x^2 - 3x + 4$
63. $(2x^3 - x^2 + 3x + 2) \div (2x + 1)$ $x^2 - x + 2$
64. $(2x^3 - x^2 - 9x + 9) \div (2x - 3)$ $x^2 + x - 3$

Use the rules of exponents to simplify each expression. See Example 6.

65. $\frac{3x^5 \cdot 5x^9}{45x^{14}}$ 3
66. $\frac{-2y^3 \cdot 4y^6}{-24y^9}$ $\frac{1}{3}$
67. $\frac{2a^2 \cdot 6a^4}{(-2a^2)^3}$ $-\frac{3}{2}$
68. $\frac{(-2w^3)(8w^{15})}{(-2w^3)^6}$ $-\frac{1}{4}$
69. $(-3a^2)^3(2a^4)^5$ $-864a^{26}$
70. $(-2b)^4(2b^3)^2$ $64b^{10}$
71. $(-5x^3)^2(-2x^2)^3$ $-200x^{12}$
72. $(-5y^5)^2(-3y^3)^2$ $225y^{16}$
73. $\left(\frac{3x^4}{6y^2}\right)^3$ $\frac{x^{12}}{8y^6}$
74. $\left(\frac{-2q^3}{4p^2}\right)^3$ $-\frac{q^9}{8p^6}$
75. $\left(\frac{2ab \cdot 3a^2b}{-4b^2}\right)^2$ $\frac{9a^6}{4}$
76. $\left(\frac{3ab^2 \cdot 6a^2b^3}{(2ab)^3}\right)^2$ $\frac{81b^4}{16}$

Simplify each expression. Write the answer with positive exponents only. See Example 7.

77. $\frac{-3a^{-2} \cdot 4a^3}{2a^{-5}}$ $-6a^6$
78. $\frac{-5b^{-6} \cdot 6b^{-5}}{2b^{-20}}$ $-15b^9$
79. $\frac{3w^{-7} \cdot 5w^4}{30w^{-9}}$ $\frac{w^6}{2}$
80. $\frac{4t^{-5} \cdot 8t^9}{16t^{18}}$ $\frac{2}{t^{14}}$
81. $(-3x^{-1})^{-4}$ $\frac{x^4}{81}$
82. $(-5y^{-6})^{-2}$ $\frac{y^{12}}{25}$
83. $(-2a^2)^{-5}(a^{-3})^6$ $-\frac{1}{32a^{28}}$
84. $(2b^{-1})^{-2}(-3b^{-2})^{-3}$ $-\frac{b^8}{108}$
85. $\left(\frac{x^{-2}}{y^3}\right)^{-3}$ x^6y^9
86. $\left(\frac{a^3}{b^{-5}}\right)^{-4}$ $\frac{1}{a^{12}b^{20}}$
87. $\left(\frac{2x^{-2} \cdot 3x^5}{15x^{-8}}\right)^{-2}$ $\frac{25}{4x^{22}}$
88. $\left(\frac{2y^{-1} \cdot 5y^7}{20y^2}\right)^{-2}$ $\frac{4}{y^8}$

Evaluate each expression by first writing each number in scientific notation. See Example 8.

89. $5{,}000 \cdot (20{,}000)^4$
8×10^{20}

90. $30{,}000 \cdot (20{,}000)^5$
9.6×10^{25}

91. $(0.00005)^2(2000)^3$
2×10^1

92. $(0.0006)^2(1000)^6$
3.6×10^{11}

93. $\dfrac{(10{,}000)^2}{0.000002}$ 5×10^{13}

94. $\dfrac{(8000)^2}{(0.00001)^3}$ 6.4×10^{22}

95. $\dfrac{(0.002)^3(40{,}000{,}000)^3}{(10{,}000)^5}$
5.12×10^{-6}

96. $\dfrac{(0.0005)^2(10{,}000)}{(500)^4}$
4×10^{-14}

R.5 Factoring

This section is a review of Chapter 5 of this text. All topics in this review section are explained in greater detail in Chapter 5.

Factoring Out Common Factors

To **factor** an expression means to write the expression as a product. For example, we factor 6 by writing 6 as $2 \cdot 3$. The largest integer that is a factor of two or more integers is the **greatest common factor (GCF)** of the integers. For example, the GCF for 12 and 18 is 6. The greatest common factor for a group of monomials includes the GCF for the coefficients of the monomials and each variable that is common to all of the monomials, where the exponent on each variable is the smallest power of that variable in any of the monomials. So the GCF or $12x^2y^3$ and $18x^4y$ is $6x^2y$. The distributive property is used to factor out the greatest common factor from a polynomial.

EXAMPLE 1 **Factoring out the greatest common factor**

Factor each polynomial by factoring out the greatest common factor.

a) $20x + 30$ **b)** $12x^2y^3 - 18x^4y$ **c)** $9a^3 - 12a^2 + 6a$

Solution

a) The GCF for $20x$ and 30 is 10:

$$20x + 30 = 10(2x + 3)$$

b) The GCF for $12x^2y^3$ and $18x^4y$ is $6x^2y$:

$$12x^2y^3 - 18x^4y = 6x^2y(2y^2 - 3x^2)$$

c) The GCF for $9a^3$, $12a^2$, and $6a$ is $3a$:

$$9a^3 - 12a^2 + 6a = 3a(3a^2 - 4a + 2)$$

Factoring the Special Products

We learned the rules for finding the special products in Section R.5. The same rules are used to factor the special products. The trinomials $a^2 + 2ab + b^2$ and $a^2 - 2ab + b^2$ are called perfect square trinomials because they are the squares of binomials.

Factoring the Special Products

Perfect square trinomials: $a^2 + 2ab + b^2 = (a + b)^2$
$a^2 - 2ab + b^2 = (a - b)^2$

Difference of two squares: $a^2 - b^2 = (a + b)(a - b)$

EXAMPLE 2

Factoring the special products

Factor each polynomial.

a) $x^2 + 6x + 9$ **b)** $4s^2 - 12st + 9t^2$ **c)** $25y^2 - 16$

Solution

a) The trinomial $x^2 + 6x + 9$ is a perfect square trinomial. To factor it, let $a = x$ and $b = 3$ in the formula $a^2 + 2ab + b^2 = (a + b)^2$:

$$\begin{aligned} x^2 + 6x + 9 &= x^2 + 2 \cdot x \cdot 3 + 3^2 \\ &= (x + 3)^2 \end{aligned}$$

b) The trinomial $4s^2 - 12st + 9t^2$ is a perfect square trinomial. To factor it let $a = 2s$ and $b = 3t$ in the formula $a^2 - 2ab + b^2 = (a - b)^2$:

$$\begin{aligned} 4s^2 - 12st + 9t^2 &= (2s)^2 - 2(2s)(3t) + (3t)^2 \\ &= (2s - 3t)^2 \end{aligned}$$

c) The binomial $25y^2 - 16$ is a difference of two squares. To factor it let $a = 5y$ and $b = 4$ in the formula $a^2 - b^2 = (a + b)(a - b)$:

$$\begin{aligned} 25y^2 - 16 &= (5y)^2 - 4^2 \\ &= (5y + 4)(5y - 4) \end{aligned}$$

Factoring by Grouping

The product of two binomials can be a polynomial with four terms. For example,

$$\begin{aligned} (x + b)(x + 2) &= (x + b)x + (x + b)2 \\ &= x^2 + bx + 2x + 2b. \end{aligned}$$

We can factor certain polynomials with four terms by reversing this process.

EXAMPLE 3

Factoring four-term polynomials by grouping

Factor each polynomial by grouping.

a) $x^2 + 3x + cx + 3c$ **b)** $2x^3 - x^2 + 2x - 1$ **c)** $a^2 - 3a + 3b - ab$

Solution

a) First factor out a common factor from the first two terms and from the last two terms:

$$\begin{aligned} x^2 + 3x + cx + 3c &= x(x + 3) + c(x + 3) \\ &= (x + c)(x + 3) \end{aligned}$$

Of course, the final answer could also be $(x + 3)(x + c)$.

b) First factor out a common factor from the first two terms and from the last two terms:

$$\begin{aligned} 2x^3 - x^2 + 2x - 1 &= x^2(2x - 1) + 1(2x - 1) \\ &= (x^2 + 1)(2x - 1) \end{aligned}$$

Note that $x^2 + 1$ is a sum of two squares and cannot be factored. It is a prime polynomial.

c) Factor a out of the first two terms and $-b$ out of the last two terms:

$$\begin{aligned} a^2 - 3a + 3b - ab &= a(a - 3) - b(a - 3) \\ &= (a - b)(a - 3) \end{aligned}$$

Factoring $ax^2 + bx + c$ with $a = 1$

To factor $ax^2 + bx + c$ with $a = 1$, find two integers with a product of c and a sum of b.

EXAMPLE 4

Factoring $ax^2 + bx + c$ with $a = 1$

Factor each polynomial.

a) $x^2 + 6x + 8$ **b)** $b^2 - b - 20$ **c)** $a^2 - 10a + 24$

Solution

a) Two integers with a product of 8 and a sum of 6 are 4 and 2. So we replace $6x$ with $4x + 2x$ and factor by grouping:

$$\begin{aligned} x^2 + 6x + 8 &= x^2 + 4x + 2x + 8 \\ &= x(x + 4) + 2(x + 4) \\ &= (x + 2)(x + 4) \end{aligned}$$

Check that $(x + 2)(x + 4) = x^2 + 6x + 8$ to be sure that the factorization is correct.

b) Two integers with a product of -20 and a sum of -1 are -5 and 4. It is not necessary to write all of the steps shown in part (a). We can simply write

$$b^2 - b - 20 = (b - 5)(b + 4).$$

Use the FOIL method to check.

c) Two integers with a product of 24 and a sum of -10 are -6 and -4. So,

$$a^2 - 10a + 24 = (a - 6)(a - 4).$$

Use the FOIL method to check.

Factoring $ax^2 + bx + c$ with $a \neq 1$

To factor $ax^2 + bx + c$ with $a \neq 1$ by the ***ac* method,** find two integers with a product of ac and a sum of b. Then factor by grouping, as done in Example 4(a).

EXAMPLE 5

Factoring $ax^2 + bx + c$ with $a \neq 1$

Factor each polynomial.

a) $6x^2 + 13x + 6$ **b)** $2w^2 + 7w - 4$ **c)** $12t^2 - 17t + 6$

Solution

a) In this case $ac = 36$ and $b = 13$. Two integers with a product of 36 and a sum of 13 are 9 and 4. So replace $13x$ with $9x + 4x$ and factor by grouping:

$$\begin{aligned} 6x^2 + 13x + 6 &= 6x^2 + 9x + 4x + 6 \\ &= 3x(2x + 3) + 2(2x + 3) \\ &= (3x + 2)(2x + 3) \end{aligned}$$

Check that $(3x + 2)(2x + 3) = 6x^2 + 13x + 6$ to be sure that the factorization is correct.

b) Two integers with a product of -8 and a sum of 7 are -1 and 8. So replace $7w$ with $-1w + 8w$ and factor by grouping:

$$\begin{aligned} 2w^2 + 7w - 4 &= 2w^2 - 1w + 8w - 4 \\ &= w(2w - 1) + 4(2w - 1) \\ &= (w + 4)(2w - 1) \end{aligned}$$

Use the FOIL method to check.

c) Two integers with a product of 72 and a sum of -17 are -9 and -8. So replace $-17t$ with $-9t - 8t$ and factor by grouping:

$$\begin{aligned} 12t^2 - 17t + 6 &= 12t^2 - 9t - 8t + 6 \\ &= 3t(4t - 3) - 2(4t - 3) \\ &= (3t - 2)(4t - 3) \end{aligned}$$

Use the FOIL method to check.

Another method that is commonly used to factor $ax^2 + bx + c$ with $a \neq 1$ is called **trial and error.** This method is not systematic like the *ac* method. For trial and error factoring simply try a pair of possible factors and check by FOIL. If it does not check then try again. For example, to factor $6x^2 + 13x + 6$ we might try $(6x + 1)(x + 6)$. However,

$$(6x + 1)(x + 6) = 6x^2 + 37x + 6$$

and the middle term is wrong. With trial and error we try factors that give the correct first and last terms and then use FOIL to see if the middle term is correct.

Factoring a Difference or Sum of Two Cubes

A difference or sum of two cubes can be factored using the following rules.

Factoring a Difference or Sum of Two Cubes

$a^3 - b^3 = (a - b)(a^2 + ab + b^2)$

$a^3 + b^3 = (a + b)(a^2 - ab + b^2)$

EXAMPLE 6

Factoring a difference or sum of two cubes

Factor each polynomial.

a) $x^3 - 125$ **b)** $8y^3 - 1$ **c)** $64w^3 + 27z^3$

Solution

a) Use $a = x$ and $b = 5$ in the formula $a^3 - b^3 = (a - b)(a^2 + ab + b^2)$:

$$\begin{aligned} x^3 - 125 &= x^3 - 5^3 \\ &= (x - 5)(x^2 + 5x + 25) \end{aligned}$$

b) Use $a = 2y$ and $b = 1$ in the formula $a^3 - b^3 = (a - b)(a^2 + ab + b^2)$:

$$\begin{aligned} 8y^3 - 1 &= (2y)^3 - 1^3 \\ &= (2y - 1)(4y^2 + 2y + 1) \end{aligned}$$

c) Use $a = 4w$ and $b = 3z$ in the formula $a^3 + b^3 = (a + b)(a^2 - ab + b^2)$:

$$\begin{aligned} 64w^3 + 27z^3 &= (4w)^3 + (3z)^3 \\ &= (4w + 3z)(16w^2 - 12wz + 9z^2) \end{aligned}$$

Factoring Completely

A polynomial that cannot be factored is a **prime polynomial.** A polynomial is factored completely when all of the factors are prime polynomials.

EXAMPLE 7

Factoring a polynomial completely

Factor $8x^5 - 8xy^4$ completely.

Solution

First factor out the GCF $8x$, then factor the difference of two squares:

$$\begin{aligned} 8x^5 - 8xy^4 &= 8x(x^4 - y^4) && \text{Factor out the GCF.} \\ &= 8x(x^2 - y^2)(x^2 + y^2) && \text{Factor the difference of two squares.} \\ &= 8x(x - y)(x + y)(x^2 + y^2) && \text{Factor the difference of two squares.} \end{aligned}$$

Even though 8 could be factored, we do not usually factor any common integers when factoring polynomials. Note that $x^2 + y^2$ is a sum of two squares and it is a prime polynomial.

Solving Quadratic Equations by Factoring

An equation of the form $ax^2 + bx + c = 0$ with $a \neq 0$ is called a **quadratic equation.** To solve a quadratic equation by factoring we use the **zero factor property:** if $ab = 0$, then either $a = 0$ or $b = 0$.

EXAMPLE 8

Solving a quadratic equation by factoring

Solve $2x^2 + 5x - 12 = 0$ by factoring.

Solution

First factor $2x^2 + 5x - 12$ by the *ac* method or trial and error, then set each factor equal to zero.

$$2x^2 + 5x - 12 = 0$$

$$(2x - 3)(x + 4) = 0 \quad \text{Factor the polynomial.}$$

$$2x - 3 = 0 \quad \text{or} \quad x + 4 = 0 \quad \text{Zero factor property}$$

$$2x = 3 \quad \text{or} \quad x = -4 \quad \text{Solve each linear equation.}$$

$$x = \frac{3}{2}$$

Check $\frac{3}{2}$ and -4 in the original equation:

$$2\left(\frac{3}{2}\right)^2 + 5\left(\frac{3}{2}\right) - 12 = 0 \qquad 2(-4)^2 + 5(-4) - 12 = 0$$

$$\frac{9}{2} + \frac{15}{2} - \frac{24}{2} = 0 \qquad 32 - 20 - 12 = 0$$

The solution set is $\left\{-4, \frac{3}{2}\right\}$.

R.5 Exercises

Boost your GRADE at mathzone.com!

MathZone

- Practice Problems
- Self-Tests
- Videos
- Net Tutor
- e-Professors

Factor each polynomial by factoring out the greatest common factor. See Example 1.

1. $12x + 8$ $\quad 4(3x + 2)$

2. $18a + 30$ $\quad 6(3a + 5)$

3. $15y^3 - 6y^2$ $\quad 3y^2(5y - 2)$

4. $48z^4 - 32z^3$ $\quad 16z^3(3z - 2)$

5. $8a^3b^2 + 20a^4b$ $\quad 4a^3b(2b + 5a)$

6. $24y^4z^3 + 36y^3z^4$ $\quad 12y^3z^3(2y + 3z)$

7. $12x^4 - 20x^3 - 24x^2$ $\quad 4x^2(3x^2 - 5x - 6)$

8. $14y^3 - 21y^2 - 28y$ $\quad 7y(2y^2 - 3y - 4)$

9. $2a^3b - 6a^2b + 6ab$ $\quad 2ab(a^2 - 3a + 3)$

10. $3w^3z - 12w^2z - 9wz$ $\quad 3wz(w^2 - 4w - 3)$

Complete the factoring of each polynomial.

11. $4x^3 - 6x^2 = (2x)(2x^2 - 3x)$

12. $5y^4 - 10y^2 = (5y^2)(y^2 - 2)$

13. $-2x^2 - 6x = (-2x)(x + 3)$

14. $-3y^3 - 9y = (-3y)(y^2 + 3)$

15. $-5a^5 + 10a^2 = (-5a^2)(a^3 - 2)$

16. $-4b^4 - 12b^2 = (-4b^2)(b^2 + 3)$

17. $-w^3x - w^2x = (-w^2x)(w + 1)$

18. $-zy^3 + zy^2 = (-zy^2)(y - 1)$

Factor each special product. See Example 2.

19. $x^2 + 8x + 16$ $\quad (x + 4)^2$

20. $x^2 + 4x + 4$ $\quad (x + 2)^2$

21. $a^2 - 2a + 1$ $\quad (a - 1)^2$

22. $b^2 - 10b + 25$ $\quad (b - 5)^2$

23. $y^2 - 9$ $\quad (y + 3)(y - 3)$

24. $n^2 - 4$ $\quad (n + 2)(n - 2)$

25. $9x^2 + 6x + 1$ $\quad (3x + 1)^2$

26. $25y^2 + 20y + 4$ $(5y + 2)^2$
27. $16m^2 - 40mt + 25t^2$ $(4m - 5t)^2$
28. $9s^2 - 24st + 16t^2$ $(3s - 4t)^2$
29. $9x^2 - 16$ $(3x + 4)(3x - 4)$
30. $81a^2 - 25$ $(9a + 5)(9a - 5)$
31. $64n^2 + 48n + 9$ $(8n + 3)^2$
32. $81s^2 - 18s + 1$ $(9s - 1)^2$
33. $25x^2 - 49y^2$ $(5x + 7y)(5x - 7y)$
34. $a^2b^2 - y^2$ $(ab + y)(ab - y)$

Factor each polynomial by grouping. See Example 3.

35. $a^2 + 6a + ab + 6b$ $(a + b)(a + 6)$
36. $w^2 - 3w + wx - 3x$ $(w + x)(w - 3)$
37. $6x^2 - 10x + 3ax - 5a$ $(2x + a)(3x - 5)$
38. $10ax + 5a + 2x + 1$ $(5a + 1)(2x + 1)$
39. $3y^3 - 4y^2 + 3y - 4$ $(y^2 + 1)(3y - 4)$
40. $6x^3 - 3x^2 + 10x - 5$ $(3x^2 + 5)(2x - 1)$
41. $8a^3 - 4a^2 + 14a - 7$ $(4a^2 + 7)(2a - 1)$
42. $5t^3 - 10t^2 + 6t - 12$ $(5t^2 + 6)(t - 2)$
43. $ab - 2b - 3a + 6$ $(b - 3)(a - 2)$
44. $x^2 - xy - 7x + 7y$ $(x - 7)(x - y)$
45. $x^3 - x^2 + 3 - 3x$ $(x^2 - 3)(x - 1)$
46. $ax^2 - 4x^2 + 20 - 5a$ $(x^2 - 5)(a - 4)$

Factor each polynomial. See Example 4.

47. $x^2 + 5x + 6$ $(x + 2)(x + 3)$
48. $x^2 + 11x + 30$ $(x + 5)(x + 6)$
49. $w^2 + 8w + 15$ $(w + 3)(w + 5)$
50. $u^2 + 19u + 18$ $(u + 18)(u + 1)$
51. $v^2 - 2v - 12$ $(v - 6)(v + 4)$
52. $m^2 - 9m - 22$ $(m - 11)(m + 2)$
53. $t^2 - 12t - 28$ $(t - 14)(t + 2)$
54. $q^2 - 4q - 32$ $(q - 8)(q + 4)$
55. $b^2 - 15b + 26$ $(b - 13)(b - 2)$
56. $p^2 - 26p + 25$ $(p - 25)(p - 1)$
57. $c^2 - 11c + 24$ $(c - 8)(c - 3)$
58. $n^2 - 10n + 21$ $(n - 3)(n - 7)$

Factor each polynomial. See Example 5.

59. $2x^2 + 7x + 6$ $(2x + 3)(x + 2)$
60. $3w^2 + 16w + 5$ $(3w + 1)(w + 5)$
61. $15t^2 + 17t + 4$ $(3t + 1)(5t + 4)$
62. $6m^2 + 29m + 20$ $(6m + 5)(m + 4)$
63. $3n^2 + 16n - 12$ $(3n - 2)(n + 6)$
64. $4y^2 + 17y - 15$ $(4y - 3)(y + 5)$
65. $8m^2 + 6m - 27$ $(2m - 3)(4m + 9)$
66. $18p^2 + 9p - 5$ $(3p - 1)(6p + 5)$
67. $8q^2 - 14q + 3$ $(4q - 1)(2q - 3)$
68. $6t^2 - 11t + 4$ $(3t - 4)(2t - 1)$
69. $15z^2 - 19z + 6$ $(5z - 3)(3z - 2)$
70. $10k^2 - 41k + 4$ $(k - 4)(10k - 1)$

Factor each polynomial. See Example 6.

71. $x^3 - 1$ $(x - 1)(x^2 + x + 1)$
72. $y^3 - 27$ $(y - 3)(y^2 + 3y + 9)$
73. $a^3 - 8$ $(a - 2)(a^2 + 2a + 4)$
74. $b^3 - 1000$ $(b - 10)(b^2 + 10b + 100)$
75. $125x^3 - 1$ $(5x - 1)(25x^2 + 5x + 1)$
76. $8a^3 - 125$ $(2a - 5)(4a^2 + 10a + 25)$
77. $125q^3 - 27$ $(5q - 3)(25q^2 + 15q + 9)$
78. $1000b^3 - 343$ $(10b - 7)(100b^2 + 70b + 49)$
79. $27x^3 + 64y^3$ $(3x + 4y)(9x^2 - 12xy + 16y^2)$
80. $8h^3 + 125k^3$ $(2h + 5k)(4h^2 - 10hk + 25k^2)$
81. $343m^3 + 8n^3$ $(7m + 2n)(49m^2 - 14mn + 4n^2)$
82. $a^3b^3 + x^3y^3$ $(ab + xy)(a^2b^2 - abxy + x^2y^2)$

Factor each polynomial completely. See Example 7.

83. $2x^2 + 8x + 6$ $2(x + 1)(x + 3)$
84. $3x^2 + 6x - 45$ $3(x + 5)(x - 3)$
85. $-2x^2 - 12x - 18x$ $-2x(x + 3)^2$
86. $-4x^4 + 40x^3 - 100x^2$ $-4x^2(x - 5)^2$
87. $3a^4 - 3b^4$ $3(a - b)(a + b)(a^2 + b^2)$
88. $w^5 - wq^4$ $w(w - q)(w + q)(w^2 + q^2)$
89. $-a^3b - 8b^4$ $-b(a + 2b)(a^2 + 2ab + 4b^2)$
90. $-24x^3 + 81$ $-3(2x - 3)(4x^2 + 6x + 9)$
91. $a^3 + 3a^2 - 4a - 12$ $(a - 2)(a + 2)(a + 3)$
92. $x^3 - 5x^2 - 9x + 45$ $(x - 3)(x + 3)(x - 5)$

Solve each quadratic equation. See Example 8.

93. $x^2 - 2x - 12 = 0$ $\{-4, 6\}$
94. $y^2 + y - 20 = 0$ $\{-5, 4\}$
95. $2t^2 + 5t - 3 = 0$ $\left\{-3, \frac{1}{2}\right\}$
96. $3p^2 - 14p + 8 = 0$ $\left\{\frac{2}{3}, 4\right\}$
97. $4m^2 - 12m + 5 = 0$ $\left\{\frac{1}{2}, \frac{5}{2}\right\}$
98. $15w^2 - 8w + 1 = 0$ $\left\{\frac{1}{5}, \frac{1}{3}\right\}$
99. $r^3 + 5r^2 + 6r = 0$ $\{-3, -2, 0\}$
100. $2c^3 - 2c^2 - 4c = 0$ $\{-1, 0, 2\}$

R.6 Rational Expressions

This section is a review of Chapter 6 of this text. All topics in this review section are explained in greater detail in Chapter 6.

Reducing Rational Expressions

A **rational expression** is the ratio of two polynomials with the denominator not equal to 0. Like rational numbers, rational expressions have infinitely many equivalent forms. If a rational expression has no factors common to the numerator and denominator, then the rational expression is in **lowest terms.** A rational expression is reduced to lowest terms by dividing out or canceling the greatest common factor for the numerator and denominator.

EXAMPLE 1

Reducing rational expressions to lowest terms

Reduce each rational expression to lowest terms. Express answers with positive exponents only.

a) $\dfrac{a^2 - 25}{a^2 + 10a + 25}$ **b)** $\dfrac{12s^2t^3}{18s^3t}$ **c)** $\dfrac{-6a + 6b}{a^2b - 2ab^2 + b^3}$

Solution

a) Factor the numerator and denominator completely and then divide out the GCF.

$$\frac{a^2 - 25}{a^2 + 10a + 25} = \frac{(a + 5)(a - 5)}{(a + 5)^2} = \frac{a - 5}{a + 5}$$

b) The GCF is $6s^2t$:

$$\frac{12s^2t^3}{18s^3t} = \frac{6s^2t(2t^2)}{6s^2t(3s)} = \frac{2t^2}{3s}$$

c) We can factor -6 or positive 6 from the numerator. In this case -6 is the better choice:

$$\frac{-6a + 6b}{a^2b - 2ab^2 + b^3} = \frac{-6(a - b)}{b(a - b)^2} = \frac{-6}{b(a - b)}$$

Multiplication and Division

Rational expressions are multiplied in the same manner that rational numbers are multiplied. As with rational numbers, we can factor, reduce, and then multiply. To divide rational expressions we invert the divisor and multiply.

EXAMPLE 2

Multiplying and dividing rational expressions

Perform the indicated operations. Express the answer in lowest terms.

a) $\dfrac{9x}{10y} \cdot \dfrac{5y^2}{6x^3}$ **b)** $\dfrac{a}{a^2 + 2ab + b^2} \cdot \dfrac{a^2 - b^2}{2a}$ **c)** $\dfrac{20x^2y^3}{y^2 - xy} \div \dfrac{12x^4y}{x - y}$

Solution

a) Factor the numerators and denominators completely and then divide out the common factors:

$$\frac{9x}{10y} \cdot \frac{5y^2}{6x^3} = \frac{3 \cdot 3x}{2 \cdot 5y} \cdot \frac{5y^2}{2 \cdot 3x^3}$$
$$= \frac{3y}{4x^2}$$

b)
$$\frac{a}{a^2 + 2ab + b^2} \cdot \frac{a^2 - b^2}{2a} = \frac{a}{(a + b)^2} \cdot \frac{(a + b)(a - b)}{2a}$$
$$= \frac{a - b}{2(a + b)}$$

c)
$$\frac{20x^2y^3}{y^2 - xy} \div \frac{12x^4y}{x - y} = \frac{20x^2y^3}{y^2 - xy} \cdot \frac{x - y}{12x^4y}$$
$$= \frac{4 \cdot 5x^2y^3(x - y)}{4 \cdot 3x^4y(-1)(x - y)}$$
$$= -\frac{5y^2}{3x^2}$$

Addition and Subtraction

We can add or subtract rational expressions only if they have identical denominators. If the denominators are not identical, then we must build up each rational expression to get identical denominators. Any common denominator will work for addition or subtraction, but the least common denominator (LCD) is the most efficient.

EXAMPLE 3

Adding and subtracting rational expressions

Perform the indicated operations. Express the answer in lowest terms.

a) $\frac{3}{10y} + \frac{5}{10y}$ **b)** $\frac{a}{a + 2} - \frac{a - 3}{a^2 - 4}$ **c)** $\frac{y}{y^2 - y} + \frac{y}{y + 2}$

Solution

a) Since the denominators are identical, the rational expressions can be added without building them up:

$$\frac{3}{10y} + \frac{5}{10y} = \frac{8}{10y} = \frac{4}{5y}$$

b) Since $a^2 - 4 = (a + 2)(a - 2)$, the LCD for these denominators is $(a + 2)(a - 2)$. To get identical denominators multiply the numerator and denominator of the first rational expression by $a - 2$:

$$\frac{a}{a + 2} - \frac{a - 3}{a^2 - 4} = \frac{a(a - 2)}{(a + 2)(a - 2)} - \frac{a - 3}{(a + 2)(a - 2)}$$
$$= \frac{a^2 - 2a - (a - 3)}{(a + 2)(a - 2)}$$
$$= \frac{a^2 - 3a + 3}{(a + 2)(a - 2)}$$

c) Since $y^2 - y = y(y - 1)$ the LCD is $y(y - 1)(y + 2)$.

$$\frac{3}{y^2 - y} + \frac{y}{y + 2} = \frac{3}{y(y - 1)} + \frac{y}{y + 2}$$

$$= \frac{3(y + 2)}{y(y - 1)(y + 2)} + \frac{y \cdot y(y - 1)}{(y + 2) \cdot y(y - 1)}$$

$$= \frac{y^3 - y^2 + 3y + 6}{y(y - 1)(y + 2)}$$

Complex Fractions

A **complex fraction** is a fraction that has rational expressions in its numerator, denominator, or both. The easiest way to simplify a complex fraction is to multiply its numerator and denominator by the LCD of all of the fractions.

EXAMPLE 4

Simplifying complex fractions

Simplify. Express the answer in lowest terms.

a) $\dfrac{\frac{1}{3} + \frac{1}{4}}{\frac{5}{6} - \frac{1}{2}}$ **b)** $\dfrac{\frac{1}{5x^2} - \frac{2}{3x}}{\frac{3}{10x} - \frac{4}{x}}$

Solution

a) The LCD for the denominators 3, 4, 6, and 2 is 12. So multiply the numerator and denominator by 12:

$$\frac{\frac{1}{3} + \frac{1}{4}}{\frac{5}{6} - \frac{1}{2}} = \frac{12\left(\frac{1}{3} + \frac{1}{4}\right)}{12\left(\frac{5}{6} - \frac{1}{2}\right)} = \frac{4 + 3}{10 - 6} = \frac{7}{4}$$

b) The LCD for $5x^2$, $3x$, $10x$, and x is $30x^2$. So multiply the numerator and denominator by $30x^2$.

$$\frac{\frac{1}{5x^2} - \frac{2}{3x}}{\frac{3}{10x} - \frac{4}{x}} = \frac{30x^2\left(\frac{1}{5x^2} - \frac{2}{3x}\right)}{30x^2\left(\frac{3}{10x} - \frac{4}{x}\right)} = \frac{6 - 20x}{9x - 120x}$$

$$= \frac{6 - 20x}{-111x}$$

$$= \frac{20x - 6}{111x}$$

Solving Equations with Rational Expressions

If an equation contains rational expressions, it is usually best to eliminate the rational expressions by multiplying both sides of the equation by the LCD.

EXAMPLE 5

Solving equations containing rational expressions

Solve the equation $\frac{15}{2x} + \frac{1}{4x} = \frac{1}{x} + \frac{11}{4}$.

Solution

The LCD for $2x$, $4x$, x, and 4 is $4x$. Multiply each side of the equation by $4x$:

$$\frac{15}{2x} + \frac{1}{4x} = \frac{1}{x} + \frac{11}{4}$$

$$4x\left(\frac{15}{2x} + \frac{1}{4x}\right) = 4x\left(\frac{1}{x} + \frac{11}{4}\right) \quad \text{Multiply each side by } 4x.$$

$$30 + 1 = 4 + 11x \quad \text{Distributive property}$$

$$27 = 11x \quad \text{Subtract 4 from each side.}$$

$$\frac{27}{11} = x \quad \text{Divide each side by 11.}$$

Check $\frac{27}{11}$ in the original equation. The solution set is $\left\{\frac{27}{11}\right\}$.

Applications of Ratios and Proportions

If a and b are real numbers, with $b \neq 0$, then $\frac{a}{b}$ is called the **ratio of a and b** or the **ratio of a to b.** Ratios are treated just like fractions. We can reduce ratios and build them up. When possible we usually convert ratios to ratios of integers in lowest terms. A **proportion** is a statement expressing the equality of two ratios. The equation

$$\frac{a}{b} = \frac{c}{d} \quad \text{or} \quad a : b = c : d$$

is a proportion. The numbers in the positions of a and d are called the **extremes.** The numbers in the positions of b and c are called the **means.** The **extremes-means property** indicates that *the product of the means is equal to the product of the extremes.*

EXAMPLE 6

Solving a proportion problem

The ratio of male employees to female employees at ABC Insurance is 3 to 2. If there are 20 more men than women, then how many men and how many women work at ABC?

Solution

Let x represent the number of men and $x - 20$ represent the number of women. Since the ratio of men to women is 3 to 2 we have the following proportion:

$$\frac{3}{2} = \frac{x}{x-20} \quad \text{The ratio of men to women is 3 to 2.}$$
$$3(x-20) = 2x \quad \text{Extremes-means property}$$
$$3x - 60 = 2x \quad \text{Distributive property}$$
$$3x = 2x + 60 \quad \text{Add 60 to each side.}$$
$$x = 60 \quad \text{Subtract } 2x \text{ from each side.}$$

So there are 60 males and 40 females at ABC Insurance.

Applications of Rational Expressions

Many applied problems can be solved using equations that involve rational expressions.

EXAMPLE 7

Solving a uniform motion problem

Kaiser drove 600 miles from his home to Memphis. On the way back home he averaged 10 miles per hour less and the drive back took him 2 hours longer. Find Kaiser's average speed on the way to Memphis.

Solution

Let x represent his average speed on the way to Memphis and $x - 10$ represent his average speed on the way back. Use the formula $T = \frac{D}{R}$ to make the following table:

	D	R	T
To Memphis	600 mi	x mi/hr	$\frac{600}{x}$ hr
Returning	600 mi	$x - 10$ mi/hr	$\frac{600}{x-10}$ hr

Since the time for the return trip was 2 hours more, we have the following equation:

$$\frac{600}{x} = \frac{600}{x-10} - 2$$
$$x(x-10)\left(\frac{600}{x}\right) = x(x-10)\left(\frac{600}{x-10} - 2\right) \quad \text{Multiply each side by the LCD.}$$
$$600x - 6000 = 600x - 2(x)(x-10)$$
$$600x - 6000 = -2x^2 + 620x$$
$$2x^2 - 20x - 6000 = 0$$
$$x^2 - 10x - 3000 = 0$$
$$(x-60)(x+50) = 0$$
$$x - 60 = 0 \quad \text{or} \quad x + 50 = 0$$
$$x = 60 \quad \text{or} \quad x = -50$$

Since $x = -50$ is meaningless, the solution is $x = 60$. If he averaged 60 mph going to Memphis and 50 mph returning, then the time going was $600/60$ or 10 hours and the time returning was $600/50$ or 12 hours, which is 2 hours longer. So his average speed on the way to Memphis was 60 mph.

R.6 Exercises

Boost your GRADE at mathzone.com!

MathZone

- Practice Problems
- Self-Tests
- Videos
- Net Tutor
- e-Professors

Reduce each rational expression to lowest terms. Express answers with positive exponents only. See Example 1.

1. $\dfrac{b^2-16}{b^2+4b+16}$ $\quad \dfrac{b-4}{b+4}$

2. $\dfrac{2x^2-2y^2}{2x^2-4xy+2y^2}$ $\quad \dfrac{x+y}{x-y}$

3. $\dfrac{4x^2+4x-24}{2x^2-18}$ $\quad \dfrac{2x-4}{x-3}$

4. $\dfrac{2a^3+2a^2-40a}{a^3+4a^2-5a}$ $\quad \dfrac{2a-8}{a-1}$

5. $\dfrac{6x^3y^6}{8x^3y}$ $\quad \dfrac{3y^5}{4}$

6. $\dfrac{10a^3b^2}{15ab^4}$ $\quad \dfrac{2a^2}{3b^2}$

7. $\dfrac{-20wz^9}{25w^3z^2}$ $\quad -\dfrac{4z^7}{5w^2}$

8. $\dfrac{21r^2t}{-28r^5t^3}$ $\quad -\dfrac{3}{4r^3t^2}$

9. $\dfrac{-2a-2y}{-4a^2+4y^2}$ $\quad \dfrac{1}{2(a-y)}$

10. $\dfrac{-4a^2-12a+40}{-2a+4}$ $\quad 2a+10$

11. $\dfrac{-3x^3+3y^3}{-3x^2+3y^2}$ $\quad \dfrac{x^2+xy+y^2}{x+y}$

12. $\dfrac{2x^2+10x+12}{2x^3+16}$ $\quad \dfrac{x+3}{x^2-2x+4}$

Perform the indicated operations. Express the answer in lowest terms. See Example 2.

13. $\dfrac{4b^2}{21a}\cdot\dfrac{35a^2}{8b^4}$ $\quad \dfrac{5a}{6b^2}$

14. $\dfrac{9w^3}{5t^2}\cdot\dfrac{10t^5}{27w^8}$ $\quad \dfrac{2t^3}{3w^5}$

15. $\dfrac{6ab^3}{40}\cdot\dfrac{25}{18a^7b}$ $\quad \dfrac{5b^2}{24a^6}$

16. $\dfrac{3xy^3}{15xy}\cdot\dfrac{45xy^2}{18xy^9}$ $\quad \dfrac{a}{2y^5}$

17. $\dfrac{15x^3}{x^2-2xy+y^2}\cdot\dfrac{x^2-y^2}{5x^7}$ $\quad \dfrac{3x+3y}{x^4(x-y)}$

18. $\dfrac{20a^6}{9a^2+12ab+4b^2}\cdot\dfrac{9a^2-4b^2}{4a^3}$ $\quad \dfrac{15a^4-10a^3b}{3a+2b}$

19. $\dfrac{5x+10}{x^2+5x+6}\cdot\dfrac{x^2+6x+9}{10x+30}$ $\quad \dfrac{1}{2}$

20. $\dfrac{x^2-x-12}{x^2+x-12}\cdot\dfrac{x^2+4x}{x^2-4x}$ $\quad \dfrac{x+3}{x-3}$

21. $\dfrac{4a^5b^4}{a^2-ab}\div\dfrac{24a^8b}{a^2-b^2}$ $\quad \dfrac{ab^3+b^4}{6a^4}$

22. $\dfrac{17x^5y^6}{x^2-y^2}\div\dfrac{51x^5y}{x^2+2xy+y^2}$ $\quad \dfrac{xy^5+y^6}{3(x-y)}$

23. $\dfrac{a^2-a-2}{a^2+a}\div\dfrac{a^2-2a}{a^3+3a^2}$ $\quad a+3$

24. $\dfrac{3w^2-3w-18}{6w^2-18w}\div\dfrac{w+2}{2w^2+2w}$ $\quad w+1$

Perform the indicated operations. Express the answer in lowest terms. See Example 3.

25. $\dfrac{8}{3x}+\dfrac{4}{3x}$ $\quad \dfrac{4}{x}$

26. $\dfrac{3}{5x^2y}+\dfrac{2}{5x^2y}$ $\quad \dfrac{1}{x^2y}$

27. $\dfrac{14b}{7b+1}+\dfrac{2}{7b+1}$ $\quad 2$

28. $\dfrac{2w^2+1}{w^2+4}+\dfrac{w^2+11}{w^2+4}$ $\quad 3$

29. $\dfrac{1}{x-y}-\dfrac{2x}{x^2-y^2}$ $\quad \dfrac{-1}{x+y}$

30. $\dfrac{1}{x^2-x-2}-\dfrac{1}{x-2}$ $\quad \dfrac{-x}{(x-2)(x+1)}$

31. $\dfrac{4-3w}{2w^2-5w-3}-\dfrac{w}{2w+1}$ $\quad \dfrac{4-w^2}{(2w+1)(w-3)}$

32. $\frac{t}{3t^2 - t - 2} - \frac{t}{3t + 2}$ $\frac{2t - t^2}{(3t + 2)(t - 1)}$

33. $\frac{m}{m^2 + m} + \frac{5}{m^2 + 3m}$ $\frac{m^2 + 8m + 5}{m(m + 1)(m + 3)}$

34. $\frac{n}{n^2 - 9} + \frac{2}{n^2 + 3n}$ $\frac{n^2 + 2n - 6}{n(n - 3)(n + 3)}$

Simplify. Express the answer in lowest terms. See Example 4.

35. $\frac{\frac{1}{2} - \frac{1}{3}}{\frac{5}{4} - \frac{1}{6}}$ $\frac{2}{13}$

36. $\frac{\frac{3}{8} + \frac{2}{3}}{\frac{1}{2} - \frac{1}{4}}$ $\frac{25}{6}$

37. $\frac{\frac{1}{a} + \frac{2}{b}}{\frac{3}{ab} - \frac{1}{ab}}$ $\frac{b + 2a}{2}$

38. $\frac{\frac{4}{xy} - \frac{3}{xy}}{\frac{2}{x} - \frac{5}{y}}$ $\frac{1}{2y - 5x}$

39. $\frac{\frac{1}{3t^3} - \frac{5}{6t}}{\frac{4}{9t} - \frac{5}{2t^2}}$ $\frac{6 - 15t^2}{8t^2 - 45t}$

40. $\frac{\frac{2}{5m^2} + 3}{\frac{1}{10m} - 2}$ $\frac{4 + 30m^2}{m - 20m^2}$

Solve each equation. See Example 5.

41. $\frac{3}{x} + \frac{1}{2x} = \frac{1}{6x} + \frac{10}{3}$ $\{1\}$

42. $\frac{1}{t} + \frac{2}{3t} = \frac{3}{4t} + \frac{1}{6}$ $\left\{\frac{11}{2}\right\}$

43. $\frac{3}{x - 2} - \frac{2}{x + 2} = \frac{1}{x^2 - 4}$ $\{-9\}$

44. $\frac{4}{y - 3} + \frac{6}{y + 1} = \frac{3y}{y^2 - 2y - 3}$ $\{2\}$

45. $\frac{5}{a + 5} + \frac{7}{2a - 3} = \frac{4a}{2a^2 + 7a - 15}$ $\left\{-\frac{20}{13}\right\}$

46. $\frac{3}{3m + 4} + \frac{2}{2m - 1} = \frac{m}{6m^2 + 5m - 4}$ $\left\{-\frac{5}{11}\right\}$

Solve each problem. See Example 6.

47. ***Students and teachers.*** The student-teacher ratio at Bellmont High is 22.4 to 1. If there are 1904 students, then how many teachers are there? 85 teachers

48. ***Water and oatmeal.*** The recipe for hot oatmeal calls for a ratio of water to cereal of 2 to 1. If 12 cups of water are used, then how many cups of cereal should be used? 6 cups of cereal

49. ***Just Paws.*** The ratio of dogs to cats boarded at Just Paws Kennel is 4 to 3. If there are 12 more dogs than cats, then how many dogs and how many cats are boarded at Just Paws? 48 dogs and 36 cats

50. ***Cars and trucks.*** At noon the ratio of trucks to cars at a rest stop in Texas was 3 to 7. If there were 12 fewer trucks than cars, then how many cars and how many trucks were at the rest stop? 21 cars and 9 trucks

Solve each problem. See Example 7.

51. ***Driving to Dallas.*** Ken drove 1400 miles from his home to Dallas. On the way back home he averaged 6 miles per hour more and the drive back took him 3 hours less. Find Ken's average speed on the way to Dallas. 50 mph

52. ***Driving to San Francisco.*** Amelia drove 600 miles on the first day and 400 miles on the second day of her trip to San Francisco. On the second day she averaged 10 miles per hour less and drove for 2 fewer hours. Find her average speed for each day.
First day 60 mph and second day 50 mph or first day 50 and second day 40.

53. ***Sharing expenses.*** A group of students can rent a motorhome and drive it to Florida for \$2100. If they can get four more students to share the cost with them, then the cost per person will decrease by \$400. How many students are in the original group? 3 students

54. ***Sharing expenses.*** A group of students can rent a small limousine for \$250. If they can get 2 more couples they can get a large limousine for \$340 and pay \$20 less per person. How many students are in the original group? 4 students

Answers to Selected Exercises

Chapter 1

Section 1.1 Warm-Ups T T F F T F T T F F

1. The integers are the numbers in the set $\{\ldots, -3, -2, -1, 0, 1, 2, 3, \ldots\}$.
3. A rational number is a ratio of integers and an irrational number is not.
5. The number a is larger than b if a lies to the right of b on the number line.

7. 6 **9.** 0 **11.** -2 **13.** -12 **15.** -2.1

17. 1, 2, 3, 4, 5

19. 0, 1, 2, 3, 4

21. 0, 1, 2, 3, 4

23. 1, 2, 3, 4, 5, . . .

25. 1, 2, 3, 4, 5, . . .

27. True **29.** False **31.** True **33.** True
35. True **37.** False

39. (0, 1)

41. [−2, 2]

43. (0, 5]

45. $(4, \infty)$

47. $(-\infty, -1]$

49. $[0, \infty)$

51. 6 **53.** 0 **55.** 7 **57.** 9 **59.** 45 **61.** $\frac{3}{4}$ **63.** 5.09

65. -16 **67.** $-\frac{5}{2}$ **69.** 2 **71.** 3 **73.** -9 **75.** 16

77. -4 **79.** -1.99 **81.** 74 **83.** 5.25 **85.** 40 **87.** $\frac{1}{2}$

89. -3 and 3 **91.** $-4, -3, 3, 4$ **93.** $-1, 0, 1$

95. [3, 8] **97.** $(-30, -20]$ **99.** $[30, \infty)$ **101.** True

103. True **105.** True

107. What is the probability that a tossed coin turns up heads?

109. If a is negative, then $-a$ and $|-a|$ are positive. The rest are negative.

Section 1.2 Warm-Ups T T F T T T T T F T

1. If two fractions are identical when reduced to lowest terms, then they are equivalent fractions.
3. To reduce a fraction to lowest terms means to find an equivalent fraction that has no factor common to the numerator and denominator.
5. Convert a fraction to a decimal by dividing the denominator into the numerator.

7. $\frac{6}{8}$ **9.** $\frac{32}{12}$ **11.** $\frac{10}{2}$ **13.** $\frac{75}{100}$ **15.** $\frac{30}{100}$ **17.** $\frac{70}{42}$ **19.** $\frac{1}{2}$

21. $\frac{2}{3}$ **23.** 3 **25.** $\frac{1}{2}$ **27.** 2 **29.** $\frac{3}{8}$ **31.** $\frac{13}{21}$ **33.** $\frac{12}{13}$

35. $\frac{10}{27}$ **37.** 5 **39.** $\frac{7}{10}$ **41.** $\frac{7}{13}$ **43.** $\frac{3}{5}$ **45.** $\frac{1}{6}$ **47.** 3

49. $\frac{1}{15}$ **51.** 4 **53.** $\frac{4}{5}$ **55.** $\frac{3}{40}$ **57.** $\frac{1}{2}$ **59.** $\frac{1}{3}$ **61.** $\frac{1}{4}$

63. $\frac{7}{12}$ **65.** $\frac{1}{12}$ **67.** $\frac{19}{24}$ **69.** $\frac{11}{72}$ **71.** $\frac{199}{48}$ **73.** 60%, 0.6

75. $\frac{9}{100}$, 0.09 **77.** 8%, $\frac{2}{25}$ **79.** 0.75, 75% **81.** $\frac{1}{50}$, 0.02

83. $\frac{1}{100}$, 1% **85.** 3 **87.** 1 **89.** $\frac{71}{96}$ **91.** $\frac{17}{120}$

93. $\frac{65}{16}$ **95.** $\frac{69}{4}$ **97.** $\frac{13}{12}$ **99.** $\frac{1}{8}$ **101.** $\frac{3}{8}$ **103.** $\frac{3}{16}$

105. $\frac{2}{3}$ **107.** $\frac{1}{2}$ **109.** $\frac{19}{96}$

111. a) 1.3 yd^3 b) $36\frac{11}{24}$ ft^3 or $1\frac{227}{648}$ yd^3

115. Each daughter gets 3 $km^2 \div 4$ or a $\frac{3}{4}$ km^2 piece of the farm. Divide the farm into 12 equal squares. Give each daughter an L-shaped piece consisting of 3 of those 12 squares.

Section 1.3 Warm-Ups T T T F F F T F T F

1. We studied addition and subtraction of signed numbers.
3. Two numbers are additive inverses of each other if their sum is zero.
5. To find the sum of two numbers with unlike signs, subtract their absolute values. The answer is given the sign of the number with the larger absolute value.

7. 13 **9.** -13 **11.** -1.15 **13.** $-\frac{1}{2}$ **15.** 0 **17.** 0

19. 2 **21.** -6 **23.** 5.6 **25.** -2.9 **27.** $-\frac{1}{4}$ **29.** $8 + (-2)$

31. $4 + (-12)$ **33.** $-3 + 8$ **35.** $8.3 + (1.5)$ **37.** -4

39. -10 **41.** 11 **43.** -11 **45.** $-\frac{1}{4}$ **47.** $\frac{3}{4}$ **49.** 7

51. 0.93 **53.** 9.3 **55.** -5.03 **57.** 3 **59.** -9 **61.** -120

63. 78 **65.** -27 **67.** -7 **69.** -201 **71.** -322

73. -15.97 **75.** -2.92 **77.** -3.73 **79.** 3.7 **81.** $\frac{3}{20}$ **83.** $\frac{7}{24}$

85. 13 **87.** -10 **89.** 14 **91.** -4 **93.** -3 **95.** -3.49

97. -0.3422 **99.** -48.84 **101.** -8.85 **103.** $-\$8.85$

105. $-7°$C

107. When adding signed numbers, we add or subtract only positive numbers which are the absolute values of the original numbers. We then determine the appropriate sign for the answer.

109. The distance between x and y is given by either $|x - y|$ or $|y - x|$.

Section 1.4 Warm-Ups T F T F T T T F T F

1. We learned to multiply and divide signed numbers.

3. To find the product of signed numbers, multiply their absolute values and then affix a negative sign if the two original numbers have opposite signs.

5. To find the quotient of nonzero numbers divide their absolute values and then affix a negative sign if the two original numbers have opposite signs.

7. -27 **9.** 132 **11.** $-\frac{1}{3}$ **13.** -0.3 **15.** 144 **17.** 0

19. -1 **21.** 3 **23.** $-\frac{2}{3}$ **25.** $\frac{5}{6}$ **27.** Undefined **29.** 0

31. -80 **33.** 0.25 **35.** -100 **37.** 27 **39.** -3 **41.** -4

43. -30 **45.** 19 **47.** -0.18 **49.** 0.3 **51.** -6

53. 1.5 **55.** 22 **57.** $-\frac{1}{3}$ **59.** -164.25 **61.** 1529.41

63. -12 **65.** -8 **67.** -6 **69.** -1 **71.** 5 **73.** 16

75. -8 **77.** 0 **79.** 0 **81.** -3.9 **83.** -40 **85.** 0.4

87. 0.4 **89.** -0.2 **91.** -7.5 **93.** $-\frac{1}{30}$ **95.** $-\frac{1}{10}$

97. 7.562 **99.** 19.35 **101.** 0 **103.** Undefined

Section 1.5 Warm-Ups F F T F F F F T F T

1. An arithmetic expression is the result of writing numbers in a meaningful combination with the ordinary operations of arithmetic.

3. An exponential expression is an expression of the form a^n.

5. The order of operations tells us the order in which to perform operations when grouping symbols are omitted.

7. -4 **9.** 1 **11.** -8 **13.** -7 **15.** -16 **17.** -4

19. 4^4 **21.** $(-5)^4$ **23.** $(-y)^3$ **25.** $\left(\frac{3}{7}\right)^5$ **27.** $5 \cdot 5 \cdot 5$

29. $b \cdot b$ **31.** $\left(-\frac{1}{2}\right)\left(-\frac{1}{2}\right)\left(-\frac{1}{2}\right)\left(-\frac{1}{2}\right)\left(-\frac{1}{2}\right)$

33. (0.22)(0.22)(0.22)(0.22) **35.** 81 **37.** 0 **39.** 625

41. -216 **43.** 100,000 **45.** -0.001 **47.** $\frac{1}{8}$ **49.** $\frac{1}{4}$

51. -64 **53.** -4096 **55.** 27 **57.** -13 **59.** 36 **61.** 18

63. -19 **65.** -17 **67.** -44 **69.** 18 **71.** -78 **73.** 0

75. 27 **77.** 1 **79.** 8 **81.** 7 **83.** 11 **85.** 111 **87.** 21

89. -1 **91.** -11 **93.** 9 **95.** 16 **97.** 28 **99.** 121

101. -73 **103.** 25 **105.** 0 **107.** -2 **109.** 12 **111.** 82

113. -54 **115.** -79 **117.** -24 **119.** 41.92

121. 184.643547 **123.** 8.0548

125. **a)** 330.2 million **b)** 2022

127. $(-5)^3 = -(5^3) = -5^3 = -1 \cdot 5^3$ and $-(-5)^3 = 5^3$

Section 1.6 Warm-Ups T F T F T F F F T F

1. An algebraic expression is the result of combining numbers and variables with the operations of arithmetic in some meaningful way.

3. An algebraic expression is named according to the last operation to be performed.

5. An equation is a sentence that expresses equality between two algebraic expressions.

7. Difference **9.** Cube **11.** Sum **13.** Difference

15. Product **17.** Square **19.** The difference of x^2 and a^2

21. The square of $x - a$ **23.** The quotient of $x - 4$ and 2

25. The difference of $\frac{x}{2}$ and 4 **27.** The cube of ab

29. $8 + y$ **31.** $5xz$ **33.** $8 - 7x$ **35.** $\frac{6}{x + 4}$

37. $(a + b)^2$ **39.** $x^3 + y^2$ **41.** $5m^2$ **43.** $(s + t)^2$

45. 3 **47.** 3 **49.** 16 **51.** -9 **53.** -3 **55.** -8

57. $-\frac{2}{3}$ **59.** 4 **61.** -1 **63.** 1 **65.** -4 **67.** 0

69. Yes **71.** No **73.** Yes **75.** Yes **77.** Yes **79.** Yes

81. No **83.** No **85.** $5x + 3x = 8x$ **87.** $3(x + 2) = 12$

89. $\frac{x}{3} = 5x$ **91.** $(a + b)^2 = 9$

93. $-7, -5, -3, -1, 1$

95. 4, 8, 16; $\frac{1}{4}, \frac{1}{8}, \frac{1}{16}$; 100, 1000, 10,000; 0.01, 0.001, 0.0001

97. 14.65 **99.** 37.12 **101.** 169.3 cm, 41 cm

103. 6, 15, 30, 38 **105.** 920 feet

107. For the square of the sum consider $(2 + 3)^2 = 5^2 = 25$. For the sum of the squares consider $2^2 + 3^2 = 4 + 9 = 13$. So $(2 + 3)^2 \neq 2^2 + 3^2$.

Section 1.7 Warm-Ups F F T F T T T T T T

1. The commutative property says that $a + b = b + a$ and the associative property says that $(a + b) + c = a + (b + c)$.

3. Factoring is the process of writing an expression or number as a product.

5. The properties help us to understand the operations and how they are related to each other.

7. $r + 9$ **9.** $3(x + 2)$ **11.** $-5x + 4$ **13.** $6x$

15. $-2(x - 4)$ **17.** $4 - 8y$ **19.** $4w^2$ **21.** $3a^2b$ **23.** $9x^3z$

25. -3 **27.** -10 **29.** -21 **31.** 0.6 **33.** -22.4

35. $3x - 15$ **37.** $2a + at$ **39.** $-3w + 18$ **41.** $-20 + 4y$

43. $-a + 7$ **45.** $-t - 4$ **47.** $2(m + 6)$ **49.** $4(x - 1)$

51. $4(y - 4)$ **53.** $4(a + 2)$ **55.** $x(1 + y)$ **57.** $2(3a - b)$

59. 2 **61.** $-\frac{1}{5}$ **63.** $\frac{1}{7}$ **65.** 1 **67.** -4 **69.** $\frac{2}{5}$

71. Commutative property of multiplication

73. Distributive property

75. Associative property of multiplication

77. Additive inverse property

79. Commutative property of multiplication

81. Multiplicative identity property

83. Distributive property

85. Additive inverse property

87. Multiplication property of 0

89. Distributive property

91. $y + a$ **93.** $(5a)w$ **95.** $\frac{1}{2}(x + 1)$ **97.** $3(2x + 5)$

99. 1 **101.** 0 **103.** $\frac{100}{33}$ **105.** **a)** 45 bricks/hour **b)** Bricklayer

107. **a)** 2.3213 people/second **b)** 1,403,900 people/week

109. The perimeter is twice the sum of the length and width.
111. a) Commutative **b)** Not commutative

Section 1.8 Warm-Ups T F T T F F F F F T

1. Like terms are terms with the same variables and exponents.
3. We can add or subtract like terms.
5. If a negative sign precedes a set of parentheses, then signs for all terms in the parentheses are changed when the parentheses are removed.
7. 7000 **9.** 1 **11.** 356 **13.** 350 **15.** 36 **17.** 36,000
19. 0 **21.** 98 **23.** $11w$ **25.** $3x$ **27.** $5x$ **29.** $-a$
31. $-2a$ **33.** $10 - 6t$ **35.** $8x^2$ **37.** $-4x + 2x^2$
39. $-7mw^2$ **41.** $\frac{5}{6}a$ **43.** $12h$ **45.** $-18b$ **47.** $-9m^2$
49. $12d^2$ **51.** y^2 **53.** $-15ab$ **55.** $-6a - 3ab$
57. $-k + k^2$ **59.** y **61.** $-3y$ **63.** y **65.** $2y^2$ **67.** $2a - 1$
69. $3x - 2$ **71.** $-2x + 1$ **73.** $8 - y$ **75.** $m - 6$
77. $w - 5$ **79.** $8x + 15$ **81.** $5x - 1$ **83.** $-2a - 1$
85. $5a - 2$ **87.** $6x^2 + x - 15$ **89.** $-2b^2 - 7b + 4$
91. $3m - 18$ **93.** $-3x - 7$ **95.** $0.95x - 0.5$
97. $4x - 4$ **99.** $2y + 4$ **101.** $2y + m - 1$ **103.** 3
105. $\frac{7}{6}a + \frac{13}{6}$ **107.** $0.15x - 0.4$ **109.** $-14k + 23$
111. 45 **113. a)** $0.25x - 6380$ **b)** \$13,620 **c)** \$48,000 **d)** \$300,000 **115.** $4x + 80$, 200 feet
117. If $x = 5$, then $1/2 \cdot 5 = \frac{1}{2} \cdot 5 = 2.5$ because we do division and multiplication from left to right.

Enriching Your Mathematical Word Power

1. c **2.** b **3.** a **4.** d **5.** b **6.** d **7.** a **8.** d
9. c **10.** a

Review Exercises

1. 0, 1, 2, 10 **3.** −2, 0, 1, 2, 10 **5.** $-\sqrt{5}, \pi$
7. True **9.** False **11.** False **13.** True
15. **17.**

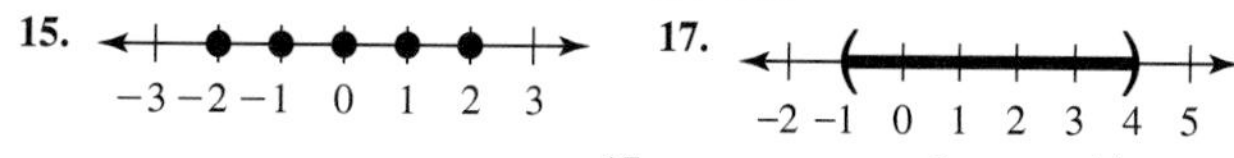

19. [4, 6] **21.** $[-30, \infty)$ **23.** $\frac{17}{24}$ **25.** 6 **27.** $\frac{3}{7}$ **29.** $\frac{14}{3}$
31. $\frac{13}{12}$ **33.** 2 **35.** −13 **37.** −7 **39.** −7 **41.** 11.95
43. −0.05 **45.** $-\frac{1}{6}$ **47.** $-\frac{11}{15}$ **49.** −15 **51.** 4 **53.** 5
55. $\frac{1}{6}$ **57.** −0.3 **59.** −0.24 **61.** 1 **63.** 66 **65.** 49
67. 41 **69.** 1 **71.** 50 **73.** −135 **75.** −2 **77.** −16
79. 16 **81.** 5 **83.** 9 **85.** 7 **87.** $-\frac{1}{3}$ **89.** 1 **91.** −9
93. Yes **95.** No **97.** Yes **99.** No **101.** Distributive property
103. Multiplicative inverse property **105.** Additive identity property
107. Associative property of addition
109. Commutative property of multiplication
111. Additive inverse property **113.** Multiplicative identity property
115. $-a + 12$ **117.** $6a^2 - 6a$ **119.** $-12t + 39$
121. $-0.9a - 0.57$ **123.** $-0.05x - 4$ **125.** $27x^2 + 6x + 5$
127. $-2a$ **129.** $x^2 + 4x - 3$ **131.** 0 **133.** 8 **135.** −21
137. $\frac{1}{2}$ **139.** −0.5 **141.** −1 **143.** $x + 2$ **145.** $4 + 2x$
147. $2x$ **149.** $-4x + 8$ **151.** $6x$ **153.** x **155.** $8x$
157. $-x^2 + 6x - 8$ **159.** $\frac{1}{4}x - \frac{3}{2}$ **161.** 3, 2, 1, 0, −1
163. 25, 125, 625; 16, −64, 256 **165.** 18 memberships per hour

Chapter 1 Test

1. 0, 8 **2.** −3, 0, 8 **3.** $-3, -\frac{1}{4}, 0, 8$ **4.** $-\sqrt{3}, \sqrt{5}, \pi$
5. −21 **6.** −4 **7.** 9 **8.** −7 **9.** −0.95 **10.** −56
11. 978 **12.** 13 **13.** −1 **14.** 0 **15.** 9740 **16.** $-\frac{7}{24}$
17. −20 **18.** $-\frac{1}{6}$ **19.** −39
20. −1 0 1 2 3 4 5 **21.** −1 0 1 2 3 4 5
22. $(2, \infty)$ **23.** [3, 9) **24.** Distributive property
25. Commutative property of multiplication
26. Associative property of addition
27. Additive inverse property **28.** Multiplicative identity property
29. Multiplication property of 0 **30.** $3(x + 10)$ **31.** $7(w - 1)$
32. $6x + 6$ **33.** $4x - 2$ **34.** $7x - 3$ **35.** $0.9x + 7.5$
36. $14a^2 + 5a$ **37.** $x + 2$ **38.** $4t$ **39.** $54x^2y^2$
40. $\frac{3}{4}x + \frac{3}{2}$ **41.** 41 **42.** 5 **43.** −12 **44.** No **45.** Yes
46. Yes **47.** 9 deliveries per hour
48. $3.66R - 0.06A + 82.205$, 168.905 cm

Chapter 2

Section 2.1 Warm-Ups T T F T F T T T T T

1. The addition property of equality says that adding the same number to each side of an equation does not change the solution to the equation.
3. The multiplication property of equality says that multiplying both sides of an equation by the same nonzero number does not change the solution to the equation.
5. Replace the variable in the equation with your solution. If the resulting statement is correct, then the solution is correct.
7. {1} **9.** {9} **11.** {1} **13.** $\left\{\frac{2}{3}\right\}$ **15.** {0.12} **17.** {−9}
19. {−19} **21.** $\left\{\frac{1}{4}\right\}$ **23.** {0} **25.** {5.95} **27.** {−5} **29.** {−4}
31. {3} **33.** $\left\{\frac{1}{4}\right\}$ **35.** {−8} **37.** {1.8} **39.** $\left\{\frac{2}{3}\right\}$ **41.** $\left\{\frac{1}{2}\right\}$
43. {−5} **45.** {5} **47.** {1.25} **49.** $\left\{\frac{1}{4}\right\}$ **51.** $\left\{\frac{3}{20}\right\}$ **53.** {−2}
55. {120} **57.** $\left\{\frac{5}{9}\right\}$ **59.** $\left\{-\frac{1}{2}\right\}$ **61.** {−8} **63.** $\left\{\frac{1}{3}\right\}$ **65.** {−3.4}
67. {99} **69.** {−7} **71.** {9} **73.** {8} **75.** {5} **77.** {−5}
79. {−8} **81.** {2} **83.** $\left\{\frac{1}{6}\right\}$ **85.** $\left\{-\frac{1}{3}\right\}$ **87.** {44} **89.** $\left\{\frac{3}{4}\right\}$
91. {7} **93.** {−14} **95.** $\left\{\frac{3}{8}\right\}$
97. a) $\frac{4}{5}x = 48.5$, 60.6 births per 1000 females **b)** 54 births per 1000 females
99. 2877 stocks

Section 2.2 Warm-Ups T T T F T F T T T T

1. We can solve $ax + b = 0$ with the addition property and the multiplication property of equality.
3. Use the multiplication property of equality to solve $-x = 8$.
5. {2} **7.** {−2} **9.** $\left\{\frac{2}{3}\right\}$ **11.** $\left\{-\frac{5}{2}\right\}$ **13.** {6} **15.** {12}
17. $\left\{\frac{1}{2}\right\}$ **19.** $\left\{-\frac{1}{6}\right\}$ **21.** {4} **23.** $\left\{\frac{5}{6}\right\}$ **25.** {4} **27.** {−5}

29. {34} **31.** {9} **33.** {1.2} **35.** {3} **37.** {4} **39.** {−3}
41. $\left\{\frac{1}{2}\right\}$ **43.** {30} **45.** {6} **47.** {−2} **49.** {18} **51.** {0}
53. $\left\{\frac{1}{6}\right\}$ **55.** {−2} **57.** $\left\{\frac{7}{3}\right\}$ **59.** {1} **61.** {−6} **63.** {−12}
65. {−4} **67.** {−13} **69.** {1.7} **71.** {2} **73.** {4.6}
75. {8} **77.** {34} **79.** {6} **81.** {0} **83.** {−10} **85.** {18}
87. {−20} **89.** {−3} **91.** {−4.3} **93.** 17 hr **95.** 20°C
97. 9 ft **99.** $14,550

Section 2.3 Warm-Ups T T F F F T T F T T
1. If an equation involves fractions we usually multiply each side by the LCD of all of the fractions.
3. An identity is an equation that is satisfied by all numbers for which both sides are defined.
5. An inconsistent equation has no solutions.
7. $\left\{\frac{6}{5}\right\}$ **9.** $\left\{\frac{2}{9}\right\}$ **11.** {7} **13.** {24} **15.** {16} **17.** {−12}
19. {60} **21.** {24} **23.** {90} **25.** {6} **27.** {−2}
29. {80} **31.** {60} **33.** {200} **35.** {800} **37.** $\left\{\frac{9}{2}\right\}$ **39.** {3}
41. {25} **43.** {−2} **45.** {−3} **47.** {5} **49.** {−10} **51.** {2}
53. All real numbers, identity **55.** ∅, inconsistent
57. {0}, conditional **59.** ∅, inconsistent **61.** ∅, inconsistent
63. {1}, conditional **65.** ∅, inconsistent
67. All real numbers, identity **69.** All nonzero real numbers, identity
71. All real numbers, identity **73.** {−4} **75.** R **77.** R **79.** {100}
81. $\left\{-\frac{3}{2}\right\}$ **83.** {30} **85.** {6} **87.** {0.5} **89.** {19,608}
91. $128,000 **93. a)** $240,000 **b)** $239,653

Section 2.4 Warm-Ups F F F F F T T T F T
1. A formula is an equation with two or more variables.
3. To solve for a variable means to find an equivalent equation in which the variable is isolated.
5. To find the value of a variable in a formula, we can solve for the variable and then insert values for the other variables, or insert values for the other variables and then solve for the variable.
7. $R = \frac{D}{T}$ **9.** $D = \frac{C}{\pi}$ **11.** $P = \frac{I}{rt}$ **13.** $C = \frac{5}{9}(F - 32)$
15. $h = \frac{2A}{b}$ **17.** $L = \frac{P - 2W}{2}$ **19.** $a = 2A - b$
21. $r = \frac{S - P}{Pt}$ **23.** $a = \frac{2A - bh}{h}$ **25.** $x = \frac{b - a}{2}$ **27.** $x = -7a$
29. $x = 12 - a$ **31.** $x = 7ab$ **33.** $y = -x - 9$ **35.** $y = -x + 6$
37. $y = 2x - 2$ **39.** $y = 3x + 4$ **41.** $y = -\frac{1}{2}x + 2$ **43.** $y = x - \frac{1}{2}$
45. $y = 3x - 14$ **47.** $y = \frac{1}{2}x$ **49.** $y = \frac{3}{2}x + 6$ **51.** $y = \frac{3}{2}x + \frac{13}{2}$
53. $y = -\frac{1}{4}x + \frac{5}{8}$ **55.** 60, 30, 0, −30, −60 **57.** 14, 23, 32, 104, 212
59. 40, 20, 10, 5, 4 **61.** 1, 3, 6, 10, 15 **63.** 2 **65.** 7 **67.** $-\frac{9}{5}$
69. 1 **71.** 1.33 **73.** 4% **75.** 4 years **77.** 7 yards
79. 225 feet **81.** $60,500 **83.** $300 **85.** 20% **87.** 160 feet
89. 24 cubic feet **91.** 4 inches **93.** 8 feet **95.** 12 inches
97. 640 milligrams, age 13 **99.** 3.75 milliliters
101. $L = F\sqrt{S} - 2D + 5.688$

Section 2.5 Warm-Ups T T T F T F F F T F
1. To express addition we use words such as plus, sum, increased by, and more than.
3. Complementary angles have degree measures with a sum of 90°.
5. Distance is the product of rate and time.
7. $x + 3$ **9.** $x - 3$ **11.** $5x$ **13.** $0.1x$ **15.** $\frac{x}{3}$ **17.** $\frac{1}{3}x$
19. x and $x + 15$ **21.** x and $6 - x$ **23.** x and $-4 - x$
25. x and $x + 3$ **27.** x and $0.05x$ **29.** x and $1.30x$
31. x and $90 - x$ **33.** x and $120 - x$
35. n and $n + 2$, where n is an even integer
37. x and $x + 1$, where x is an integer
39. x, $x + 2$, and $x + 4$, where x is an odd integer
41. x, $x + 2$, $x + 4$, and $x + 6$, where x is an even integer
43. $3x$ miles **45.** $0.25q$ dollars **47.** $\frac{x}{20}$ hour
49. $\frac{x - 100}{12}$ meters per second **51.** $5x$ square meters
53. $2w + 2(w + 3)$ inches **55.** $150 - x$ feet **57.** $2x + 1$ feet
59. $x(x + 5)$ square meters **61.** $0.18(x + 1000)$
63. $\frac{16.50}{x}$ dollars per pound **65.** $90 - x$ degrees
67. x is the smaller number, $x(x + 5) = 8$
69. x is the selling price, $x - 0.07x = 84{,}532$
71. x is the percent, $500x = 100$
73. x is the number of nickels, $0.05x + 0.10(x + 2) = 3.80$
75. x is the number, $x + 5 = 13$
77. x is the smallest integer, $x + (x + 1) + (x + 2) = 42$
79. x is the smaller integer, $x(x + 1) = 182$
81. x is Harriet's income, $0.12x = 3000$
83. x is the number, $0.05x = 13$
85. x is the width, $x(x + 5) = 126$
87. n is the number of nickels, $5n + 10(n - 1) = 95$
89. x is the measure of the larger angle, $x + x - 38 = 180$
91. a) $r + 0.6(220 - (30 + r)) = 144$, where r is the resting heart rate
b) Target heart rate increases as resting heart rate increases.
93. $6 + x$ **95.** $m + 9$ **97.** $11t$ **99.** $5(x - 2)$ **101.** $m - 3m$
103. $\frac{h + 8}{h}$ **105.** $\frac{5}{y - 9}$ **107.** $\frac{w - 8}{2w}$ **109.** $-3v - 9$
111. $x - \frac{x}{7}$ **113.** $m^2 - (m + 7)$ **115.** $x + (9x - 8)$ **117.** $13n - 9$
119. $6 + \frac{1}{3}(x + 2)$ **121.** $\frac{x}{2} + x$ **123.** $x(x + 3) = 24$
125. $w(w - 4) = 24$

Section 2.6 Warm-Ups F T T F F T T T F T
1. In this section we studied number, geometric, and uniform motion problems.
3. Uniform motion is motion at a constant rate of speed.
5. Complementary angles are angles whose degree measures have a sum of 90°.
7. 46, 47, 48 **9.** 75, 77 **11.** 47, 48, 49, 50
13. Length 50 meters, width 25 meters
15. Width 42 inches, length 46 inches
17. 13 inches **19.** 35° **21.** 1152 in. **23.** 22.88 km **25.** 5.31 in.
27. 402.57 g **29.** 58.67 ft/sec **31.** 548.53 km/hr
33. 65 miles per hour **35.** 55 miles per hour **37.** 4 hours, 2048 miles
39. Length 20 inches, width 12 inches **41.** 5 ft, 5 ft, 3 ft
43. 20°, 40°, 120° **45.** 20°, 80°, 80° **47.** Raiders 32, Vikings 14
49. 3 hours, 106 miles **51.** Crawford 1906, Wayne 1907, Stewart 1908
53. 7 ft, 7 ft, 16 ft

Section 2.7 Warm-Ups T F T F T T F T F T

1. We studied discount, investment, and mixture problems in this section.
3. The product of the rate and the original price gives the amount of discount. The original price minus the discount is the sale price.
5. A table helps us to organize the information given in a problem.
7. \$320 **9.** \$400 **11.** \$125,000 **13.** \$30.24
15. 100 Fund \$10,000, 101 Fund \$13,000
17. Fidelity \$14,000, Price \$11,000
19. 30 gallons **21.** 20 liters of 5% alcohol, 10 liters of 20% alcohol
23. 55,700 **25.** \$15,000 **27.** 75% **29.** 600
31. 42 private rooms, 30 semiprivate rooms **33.** 12 pounds
35. 4 nickels, 6 dimes **37.** 800 gallons **39.** $\frac{2}{3}$ gal
41. Shorts \$12, tops \$6

Section 2.8 Warm-Ups T T F T F T F F T F

1. The inequality symbols are $<$, $\le$, $>$, and $\ge$.
3. For $\le$ and $\ge$ use a bracket and for $<$ and $>$ use a parenthesis.
5. The compound inequality $a < b < c$ means $b > a$ and $b < c$, or b is between a and c.
7. True **9.** True **11.** False **13.** True **15.** True **17.** True
19. True

21. $(-\infty, 3]$
−1 0 1 2 3 4 5

23. $(-2, \infty)$
−4 −3 −2 −1 0 1 2

25. $(-\infty, -1)$
−5 −4 −3 −2 −1 0 1

27. $[-2, \infty)$
−4 −3 −2 −1 0 1 2

29. $\left[\frac{1}{2}, \infty\right)$
$\frac{1}{2}$
−1 0 1 2 3

31. $(-\infty, 5.3]$
5.3
1 2 3 4 5 6 7

33. $(-3, 1)$
−4 −3 −2 −1 0 1 2

35. $[3, 7]$
2 3 4 5 6 7 8

37. $[-5, 0)$
−5 −4 −3 −2 −1 0 1

39. $(40, 100]$
20 40 60 80 100 120

41. $x > 3$, $(3, \infty)$ **43.** $x \le 2$, $(-\infty, 2]$ **45.** $0 < x < 2$, $(0, 2)$
47. $-5 < x \le 7$, $(-5, 7]$ **49.** $x > -4$, $(-4, \infty)$
51. Yes **53.** No **55.** No **57.** Yes **59.** Yes **61.** Yes
63. No **65.** Yes **67.** No **69.** 0, 5.1 **71.** 5.1 **73.** 5.1
75. −5.1, 0, 5.1 **77.** $0.08p > 1500$ **79.** $p + 2p + p + 0.25 < 2.00$
81. $\frac{44 + 72 + s}{3} \ge 60$ **83.** $396 < 8R < 453$ **85.** $60 < 90 - x < 70$
87. a) $45 + 2(30) + 2h \le 130$ **b)** Approximately 12 in.
89. 79, moderate effort on level ground

Section 2.9 Warm-Ups T F F T F T F T T F

1. Equivalent inequalities are inequalities that have the same solutions.
3. According to the multiplication property of inequality, the inequality symbol is reversed when multiplying (or dividing) by a negative number and not reversed when multiplying (or dividing) by a positive number.
5. We solve compound inequalities using the properties of inequality as we do for simple inequalities.
7. $>$ **9.** $\ge$ **11.** $>$ **13.** $\le$

15. $(-3, \infty)$
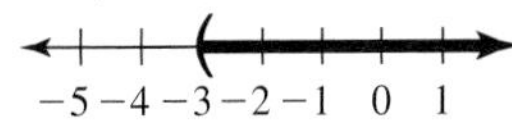

17. $(-2, \infty)$
−2 −1 0 1 2 3

19. $(-\infty, 4)$
−1 0 1 2 3 4 5

21. $\left[-\frac{1}{2}, \infty\right)$
$-\frac{1}{2}$
−2 −1 0 1 2

23. $(-\infty, 3)$
−1 0 1 2 3 4 5

25. $\left[-\frac{1}{3}, \infty\right)$
$-\frac{1}{3}$
−2 −1 0 1 2

27. $(-3, \infty)$
−4 −3 −2 −1 0 1

29. $(-\infty, 13)$
9 10 11 12 13 14 15

31. $(-\infty, 24]$
20 22 24 26

33. $\left(-\infty, \frac{7}{2}\right]$
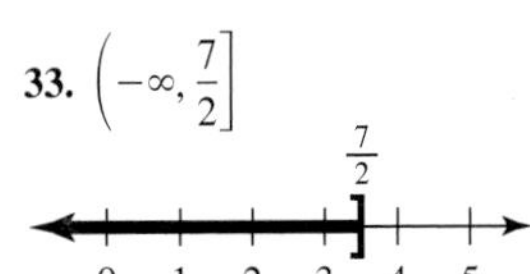

35. $(-1.5, \infty)$
−1.5
−2 −1 0 1 2

37. $(-\infty, -11)$
−15 −14 −13 −12 −11 −10 −9

39. $(-10, \infty)$
−12 −11 −10 −9 −8 −7 −6

41. $(-\infty, 614.3)$
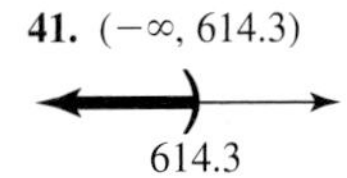

43. $(8, 10)$
6 7 8 9 10 11 12

45. $\left(1, \frac{9}{2}\right)$
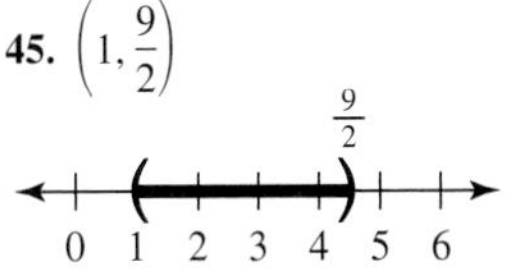

47. $[-2, 9]$
9
−2 0 2 4 6 8 10

49. $[-5, 3)$
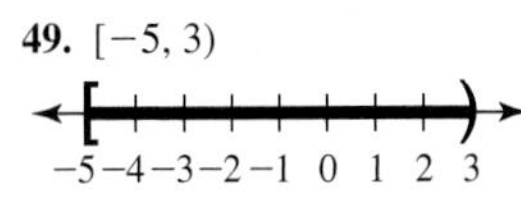

51. $(12, 30)$
12 18 24 30

53. $\left(-\frac{1}{2}, \frac{3}{2}\right]$
$-\frac{1}{2}$ $\frac{3}{2}$
−2 −1 0 1 2 3

55. $(102.1, 108.3)$

102.1 108.3

57. $(-\infty, 6]$

1 2 3 4 5 6 7

59. $(-\infty, 0)$

−2 −1 0 1 2 3

61. $(2, 3)$

1 2 3 4

63. At least 28 meters **65.** Less than \$9358 **67.** At most \$550 **69.** At least 64 **71.** Between 81 and 94.5 inclusive **73.** Between 49.5 and 56.625 miles per hour **75.** Between 55° and 85° **77. a)** Between 27 and 35 teeth inclusive **b)** Between 23.02 in. and 24.79 in. **c)** At least 14 teeth

Enriching Your Mathematical Word Power

1. b **2.** d **3.** c **4.** c **5.** d **6.** d **7.** a **8.** b **9.** c **10.** d

Review Exercises

1. {35} **3.** {−6} **5.** {−7} **7.** {13} **9.** {7} **11.** {2} **13.** {7} **15.** {0} **17.** {−8} **19.** ∅, inconsistent **21.** All real numbers, identity **23.** All nonzero real numbers, identity **25.** {24}, conditional **27.** {80}, conditional **29.** {1000}, conditional **31.** $\left\{\frac{1}{4}\right\}$ **33.** $\left\{\frac{21}{8}\right\}$ **35.** $\left\{-\frac{4}{5}\right\}$ **37.** {4} **39.** {24} **41.** {−100} **43.** $x = -\frac{b}{a}$ **45.** $x = \frac{b+2}{a}$ **47.** $x = \frac{V}{LW}$ **49.** $x = -\frac{b}{3}$ **51.** $y = -\frac{5}{2}x + 3$ **53.** $y = -\frac{1}{2}x + 4$ **55.** $y = -2x + 16$ **57.** −13 **59.** $-\frac{2}{5}$ **61.** 17 **63.** 15, 10, 5, 0, −5 **65.** −3, −1, 1, 3 **67.** $x + 9$, where x is the number **69.** x and $x + 8$, where x is the smaller number **71.** $0.65x$, where x is the number **73.** $x(x + 5) = 98$, where x is the width **75.** $2x = 3(x - 10)$, where x is Jim's rate **77.** $x + x + 2 + x + 4 = 90$, where x is the smallest of the three even integers **79.** $t + 2t + t - 10 = 180$, where t is the degree measure of an angle **81.** 77, 79, 81 **83.** Betty 45 mph, Lawanda 60 mph **85.** Wanda \$36,000, husband \$30,000 **87.** No **89.** No **91.** $x > 1$, $(1, \infty)$ **93.** $x \ge 2$, $[2, \infty)$ **95.** $-3 \le x < 3$, $[-3, 3)$ **97.** $x < -1$, $(-\infty, -1)$

99. $(-1, \infty)$

−3 −2 −1 0 1 2 3

101. $(-\infty, 3)$

−1 0 1 2 3 4

103. $(-\infty, -4]$

−8 −7 −6 −5 −4 −3 −2

105. $(-4, \infty)$

−6 −5 −4 −3 −2 −1 0

107. $(-1, 5)$

−1 0 1 2 3 4 5

109. $\left(-2, \frac{1}{2}\right]$

$\frac{1}{2}$

−3 −2 −1 0 1 2 3

111. $[0, 3]$

−1 0 1 2 3 4

113. $(0, 1)$

−1 0 1 2

115. \$537.50 **117.** 400 **119.** 31° **121.** Less than 6 feet

Chapter 2 Test

1. {−7} **2.** {2} **3.** {−9} **4.** {700} **5.** {1} **6.** $\left\{\frac{7}{6}\right\}$ **7.** {2} **8.** ∅ **9.** All real numbers **10.** $y = \frac{2}{3}x - 3$ **11.** $a = \frac{m + w}{P}$ **12.** $-3 < x \le 2$, $(-3, 2]$ **13.** $x > 1$, $(1, \infty)$

14. $(19, \infty)$

17 18 19 20 21 22 23

15. $(-7, -1)$

−7 −6 −5 −4 −3 −2 −1

16. $(1, 3)$

−1 0 1 2 3 4 5

17. $(-6, \infty)$

−8 −7 −6 −5 −4 −3 −2

18. 14 meters **19.** 9 in. **20.** 150 liters **21.** At most \$2000 **22.** 30°, 60°, 90°

Making Connections Chapters 1–2

1. $8x$ **2.** $15x^2$ **3.** $2x + 1$ **4.** $4x - 7$ **5.** $-2x + 13$ **6.** 60 **7.** 72 **8.** −10 **9.** $-2x^3$ **10.** −1 **11.** $\frac{2}{3}$ **12.** $\frac{1}{6}$ **13.** $\frac{1}{9}$ **14.** $\frac{5}{9}$ **15.** 13 **16.** 8 **17.** $2x + 1$ **18.** $10x - 9$ **19.** $\left\{\frac{2}{3}\right\}$ **20.** $\left\{\frac{1}{6}\right\}$ **21.** $\left(\frac{2}{3}, \infty\right)$ **22.** $\left(-\infty, \frac{1}{6}\right]$ **23.** $\left\{\frac{1}{9}\right\}$ **24.** $\left\{\frac{5}{9}\right\}$ **25.** $\left[-\frac{1}{9}, \infty\right)$ **26.** $\left(-\infty, -\frac{5}{9}\right)$ **27.** $\left\{\frac{3}{10}\right\}$ **28.** $\left\{\frac{16}{5}\right\}$ **29.** $\left\{\frac{1}{2}\right\}$ **30.** $\left\{\frac{7}{5}\right\}$ **31.** {1} **32.** All real numbers **33.** {0} **34.** {1} **35.** $(0, \infty)$ **36.** ∅ **37.** {2} **38.** {2} **39.** $\left\{\frac{13}{2}\right\}$ **40.** {200} **41. a)** \$13,600 **b)** \$10,000 **c)** \$12,000

Chapter 3

Section 3.1 Warm-Ups F F F F T T T F F T

1. An ordered pair is a pair of numbers in which there is a first number and a second number, usually written as (a, b).
3. The origin is the point of intersection of the x-axis and y-axis.
5. A linear equation in two variables is an equation of the form $Ax + By = C$, where A and B are not both zero.
7. (0, 9), (5, 24), (2, 15) **9.** $(0, -7)$, $\left(\frac{1}{3}, -8\right)$, $\left(-\frac{2}{3}, -5\right)$
11. (0, 54.3), (10, 66.3), (0.5, 54.9) **13.** (3, 0), (0, −2), (12, 6)
15. (5, −3), (5, 5), (5, 0)
17–31 odd

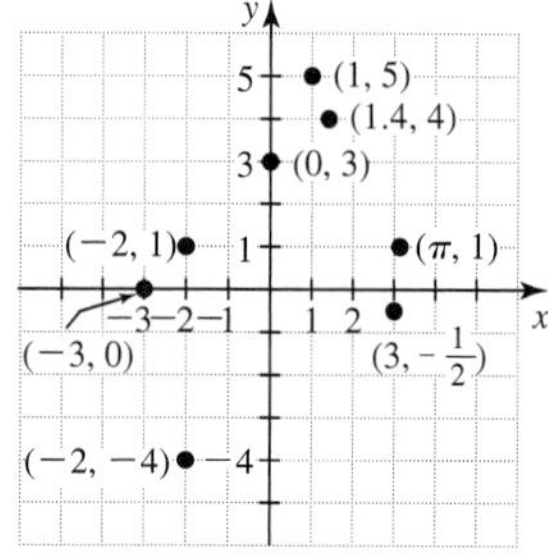

33. (−2, 9), (0, 5), (2, 1), (4, −3), (6, −7)
35. (−6, 0), (−3, 1), (0, 2), (3, 3)

37. $(-30, -200), (-20, 0), (-10, 200), (0, 400), (10, 600)$

39. $y = x + 1$

41. $y = 2x + 1$

43.

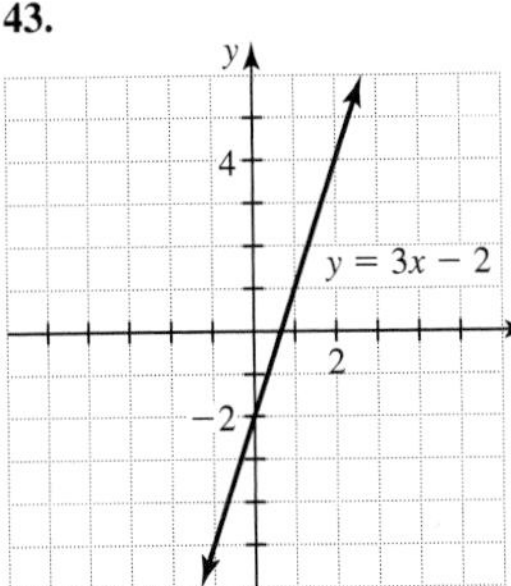

45.

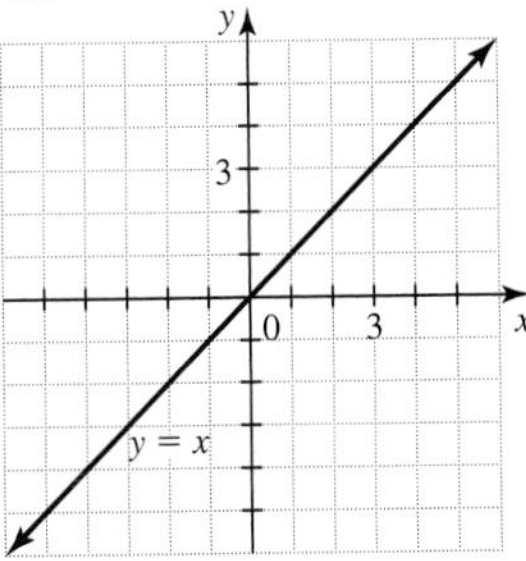

47.

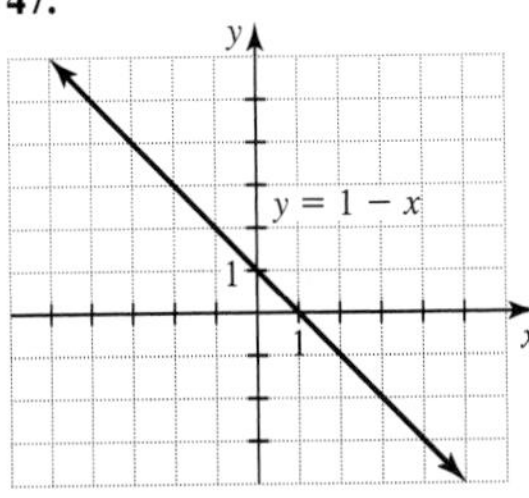

49.

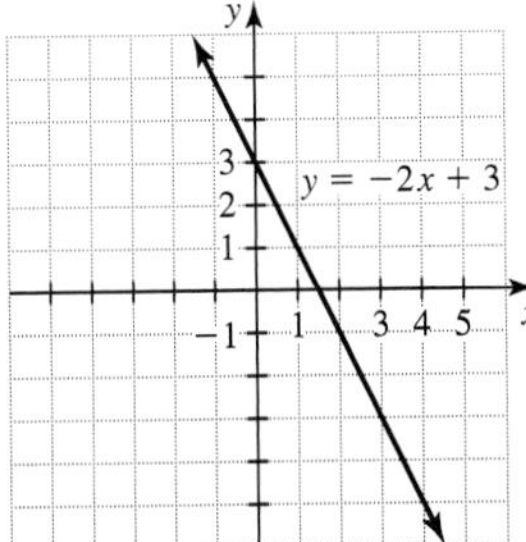

51.

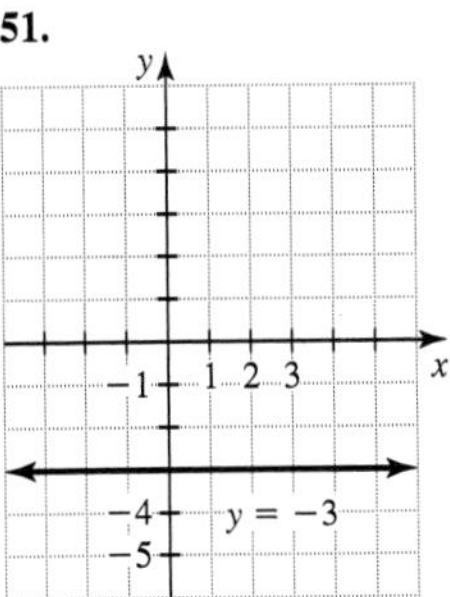

53.

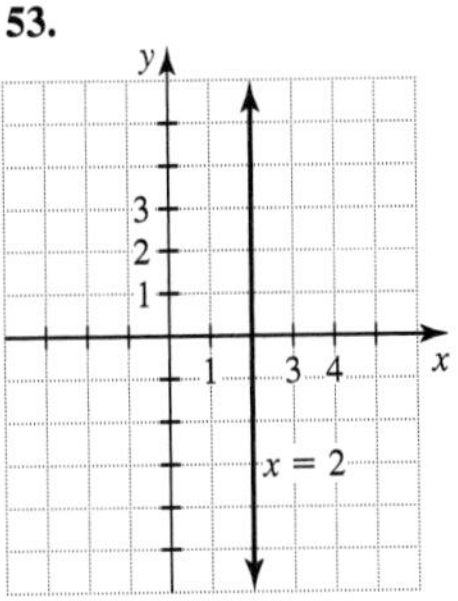

55.

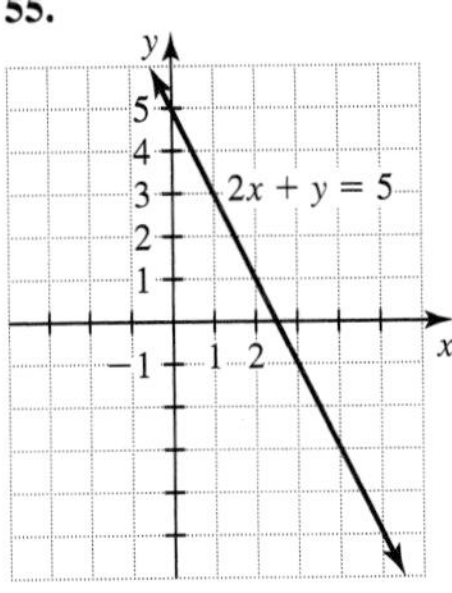

57.

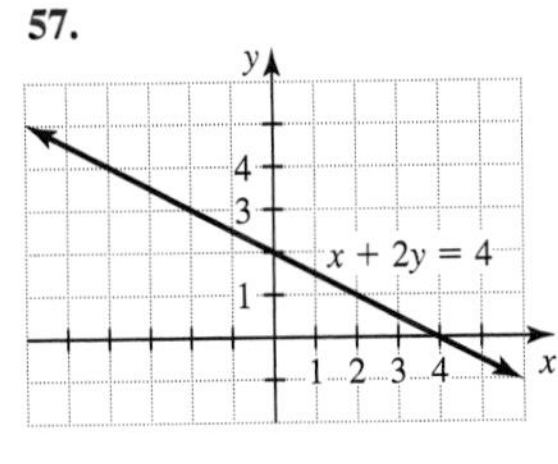

59.

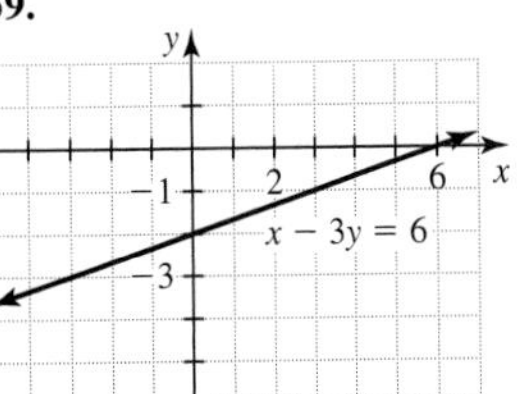

61.

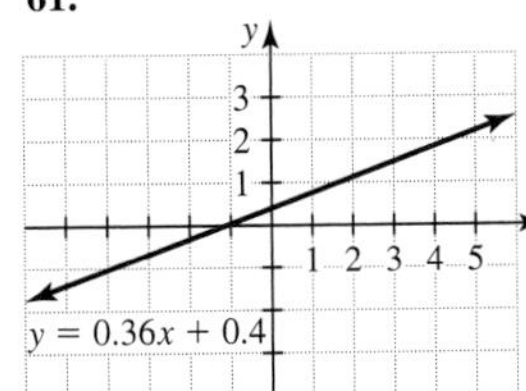

63. Quadrant II **65.** x-axis **67.** Quadrant III **69.** Quadrant I **71.** Quadrant II **73.** y-axis

75.

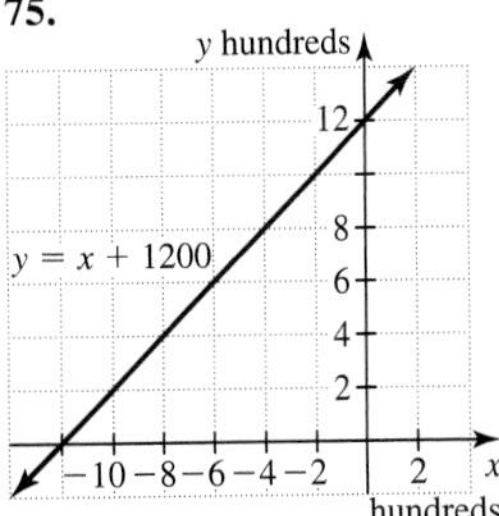

77.

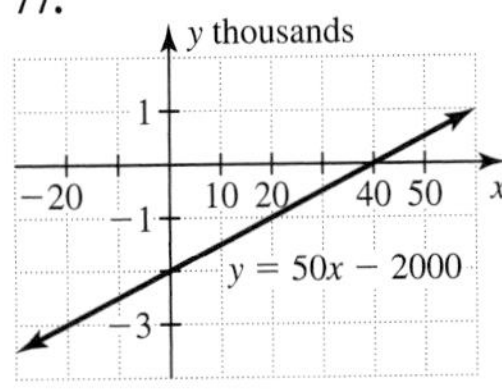

79.

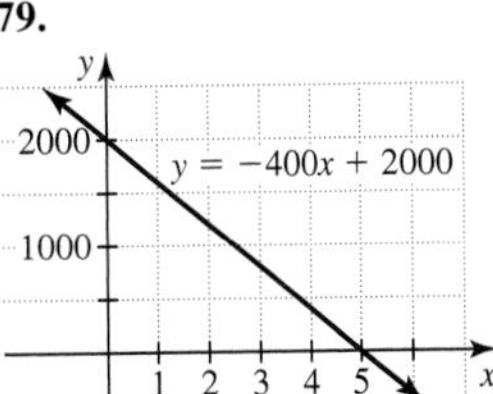

81. $(2, 0), (0, 3)$

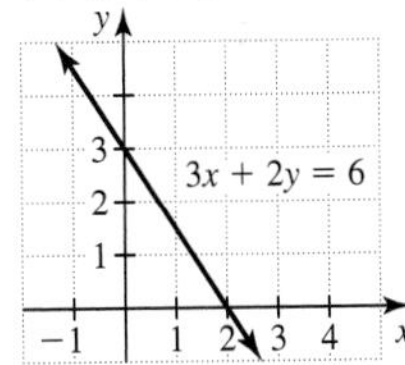

83. $(4, 0), (0, -1)$

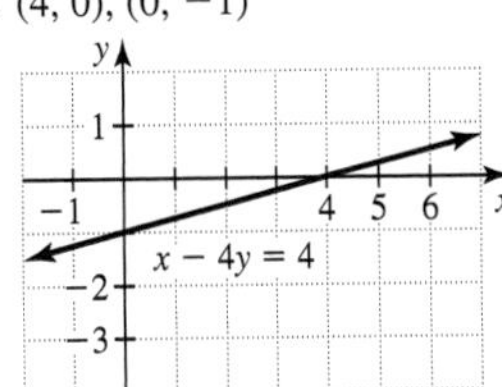

85. $(12, 0), (0, -9)$

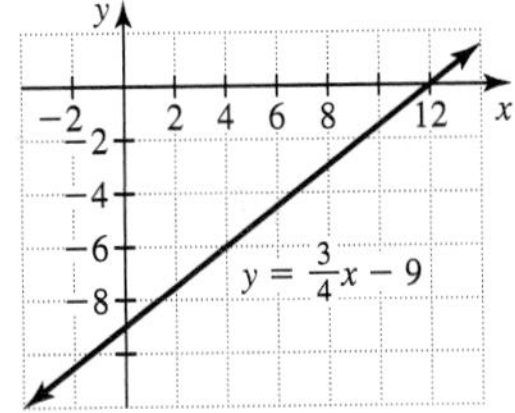

87. $(2, 0), (0, 4)$

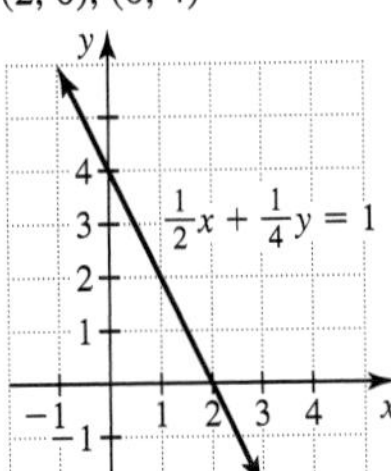

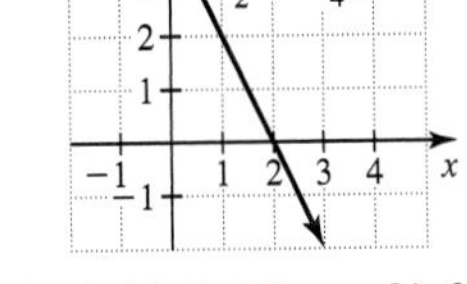

89. 75%, 67, 68 and up

91. a) \$97.3 billion **b)** 2016
c)

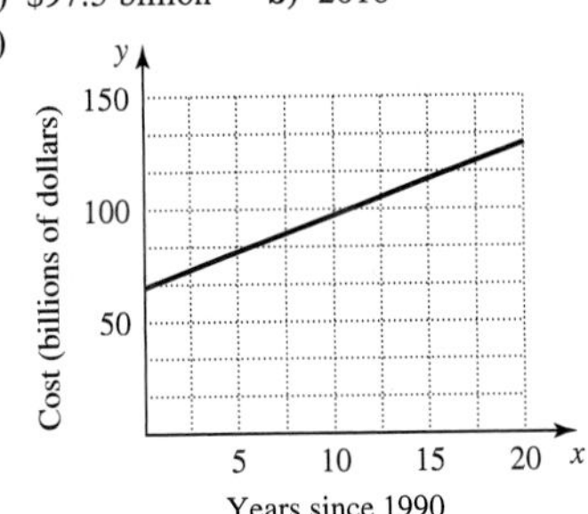

93. **a)** 4 atm **b)** 130 ft
c)

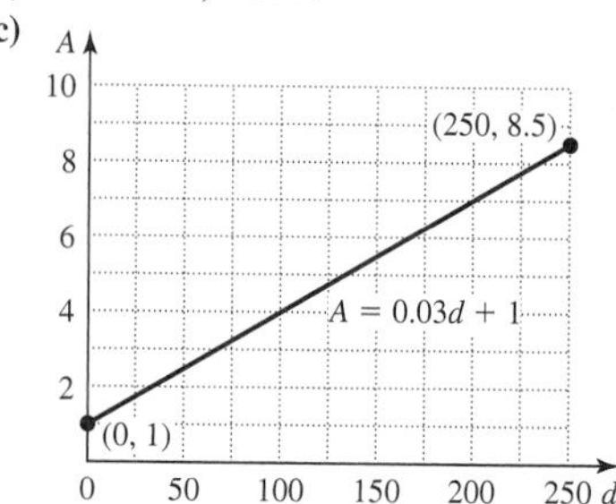

95. $x =$ the number of radio ads,
$y =$ the number of TV ads, 21 solutions

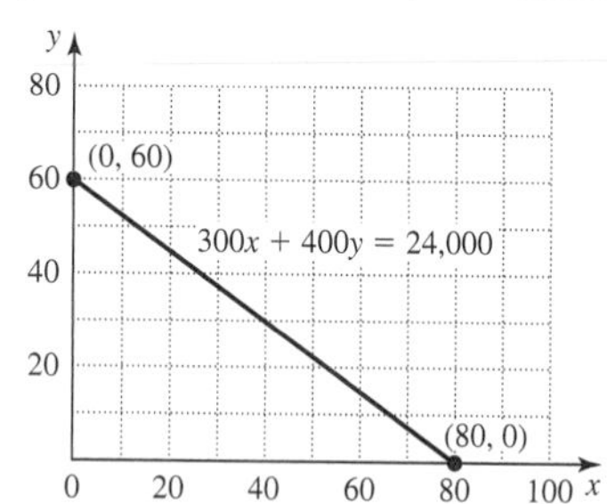

97.

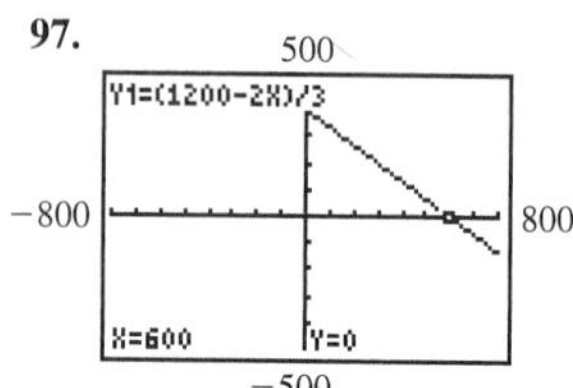

99.

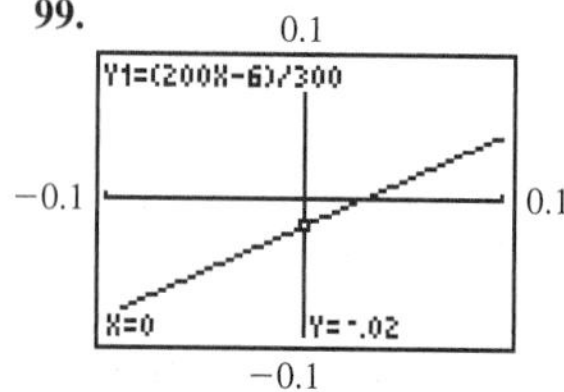

101.

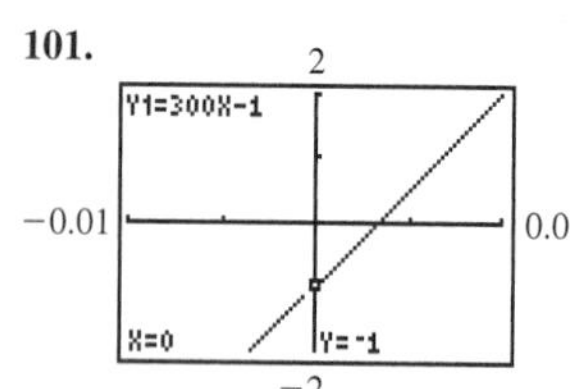

Section 3.2 Warm-Ups T T F T F F F F T T

1. The slope of a line is the ratio of its rise and run.
3. Slope is undefined for vertical lines.
5. Lines with positive slope are rising as you go from left to right, while lines with negative slope are falling as you go from left to right.

7. $-\frac{2}{3}$ **9.** $\frac{2}{3}$ **11.** $\frac{3}{2}$ **13.** 0 **15.** $\frac{2}{5}$ **17.** Undefined **19.** 2
21. $-\frac{5}{3}$ **23.** $\frac{5}{7}$ **25.** $-\frac{4}{3}$ **27.** -1 **29.** 1 **31.** Undefined
33. 0 **35.** 3

37.

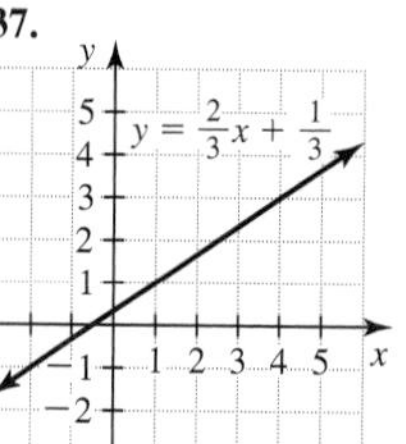

39.

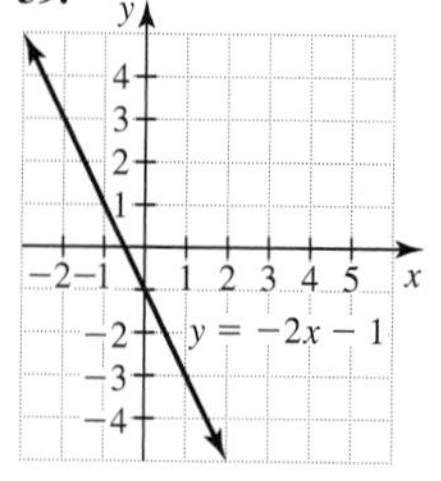

41.

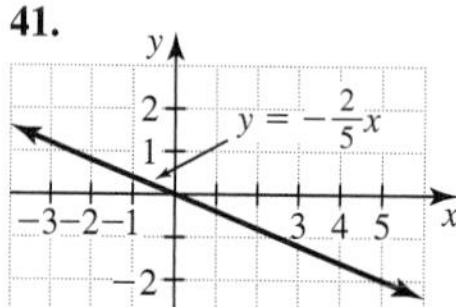

43.

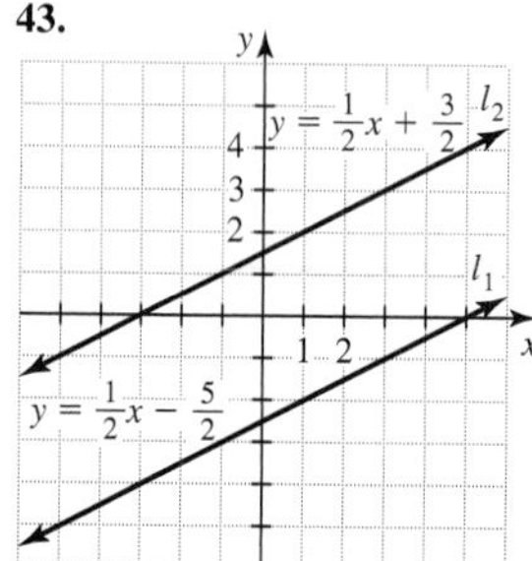

45.

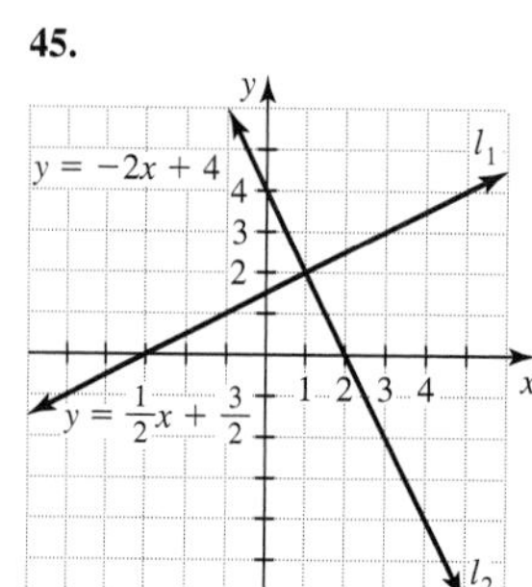

47. $-\frac{4}{3}$

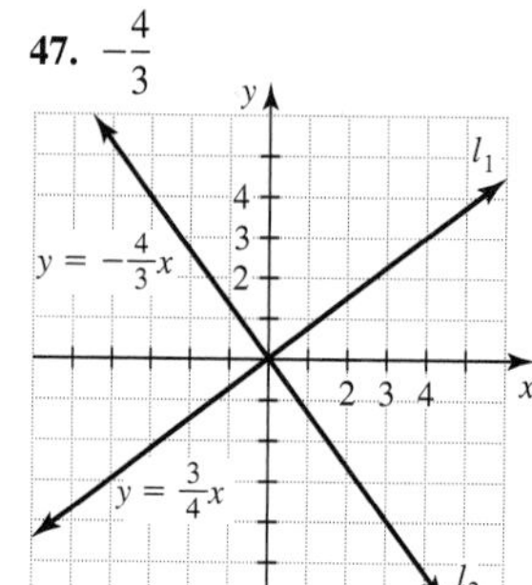

49. $\frac{1}{2}$

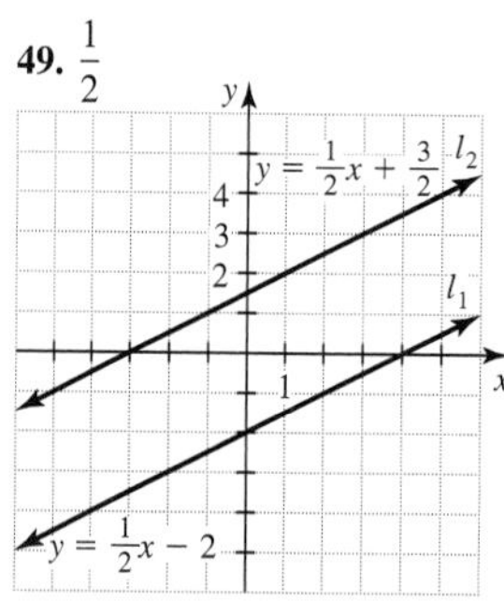

51. 1

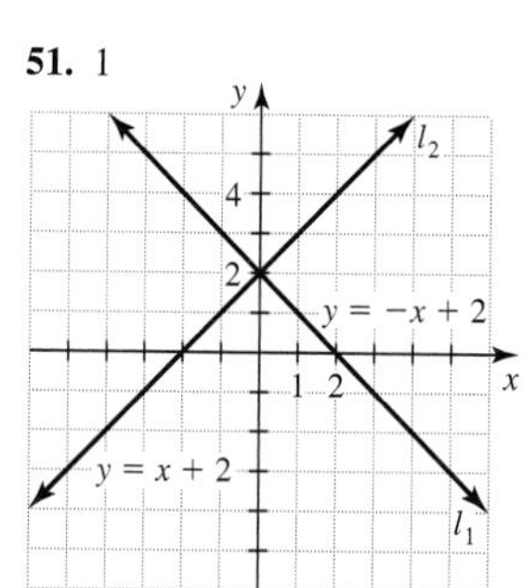

53. Parallel **55.** Neither **57.** Parallel **59.** Perpendicular
61. **a)** Approximately 0.183 slope; Cost is increasing about \$183,000 per year. **b)** \$2.03 million; yes **c)** \$3.13 million
63. 1 slope; The percentage increases 1% per year.
65. (2000, 28,100), (2003, 29,300), (2012, 32,900), (2015, 34,100)
67. Yes **69.** No

Section 3.3 Warm-Ups T F T T T F F T T F

1. Slope-intercept form is $y = mx + b$.
3. The standard form is $Ax + By = C$.
5. The slope-intercept form allows us to write the equation from the y-intercept and the slope.

7. $y = \frac{3}{2}x + 1$ **9.** $y = -2x + 2$ **11.** $y = x - 2$ **13.** $y = -x$
15. $y = -1$ **17.** $x = -2$ **19.** 3, $(0, -9)$ **21.** $-\frac{1}{2}$, $(0, 3)$

23. 0, (0, 4) **25.** −3, (0, 0) **27.** −1, (0, 5) **29.** $\frac{1}{2}$, (0, −2)
31. $\frac{2}{5}$, (0, −2) **33.** 2, (0, 3) **35.** Undefined slope, no y-intercept
37. $x + y = 2$ **39.** $x - 2y = -6$ **41.** $9x - 6y = 2$
43. $6x + 10y = 7$ **45.** $x = -10$ **47.** $3y = 10$ **49.** $5x - 6y = 0$
51. $x - 50y = -25$

53.

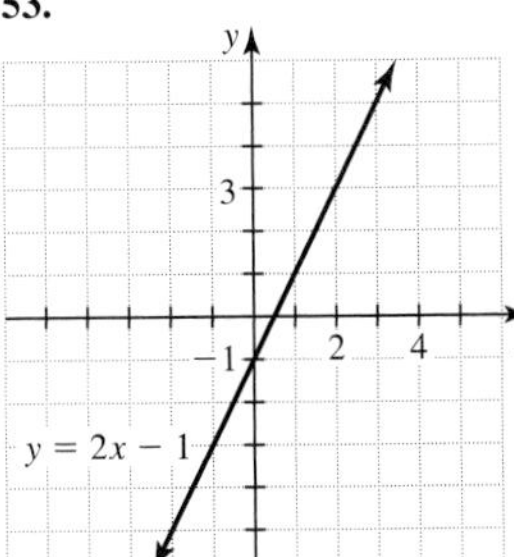

55.

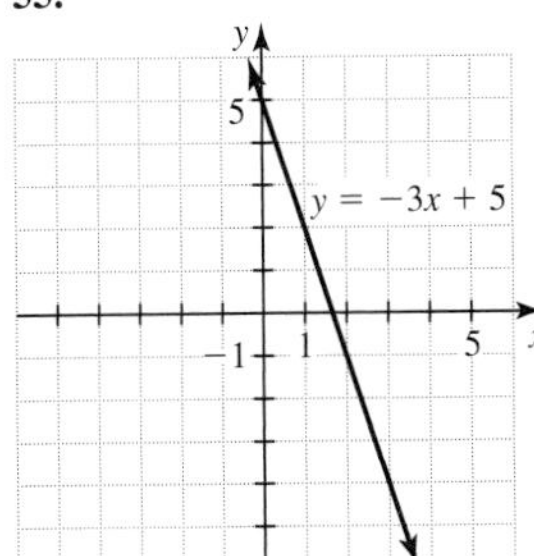

57.

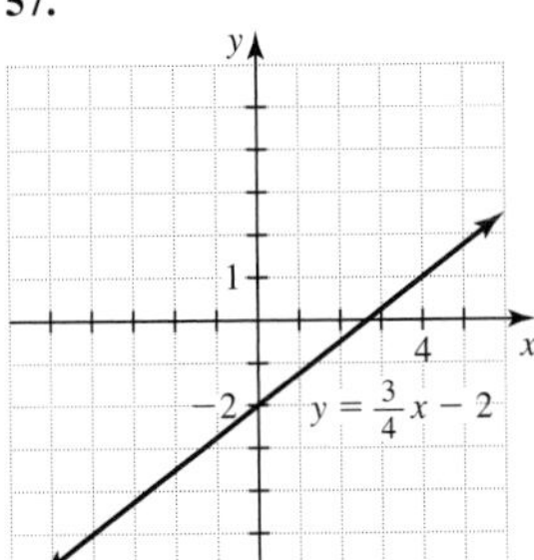

59.

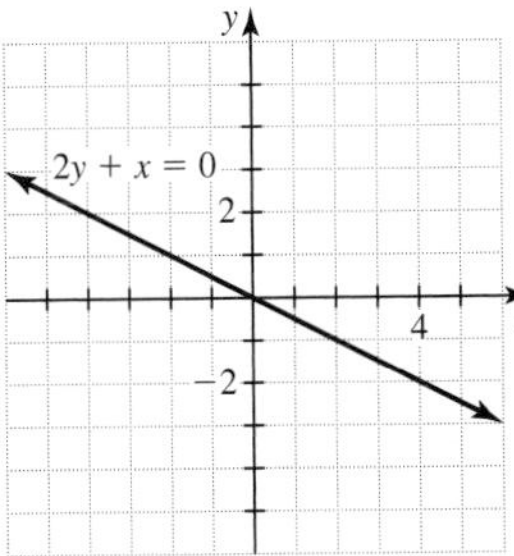

61.

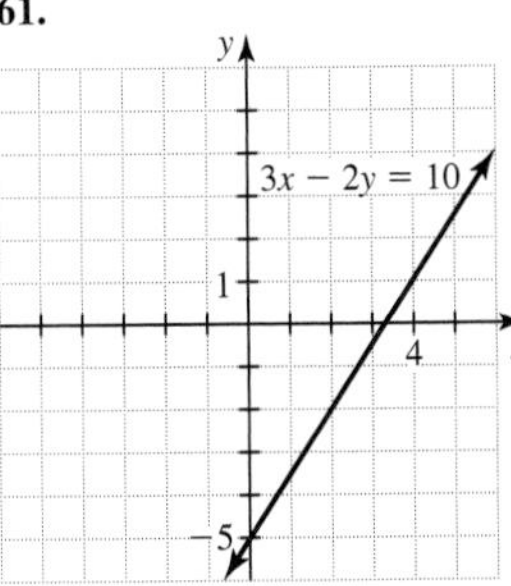

63.

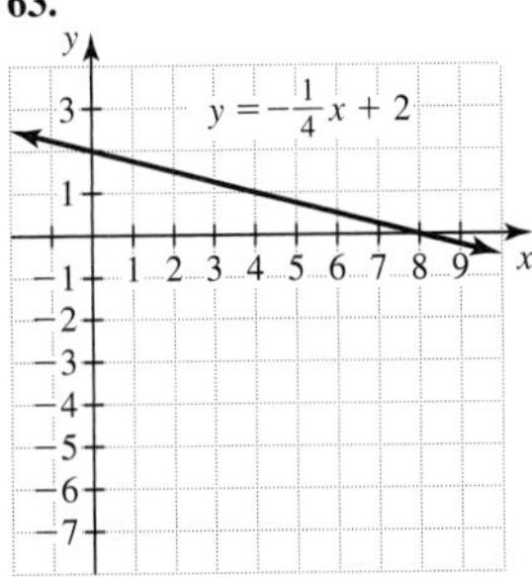

65.

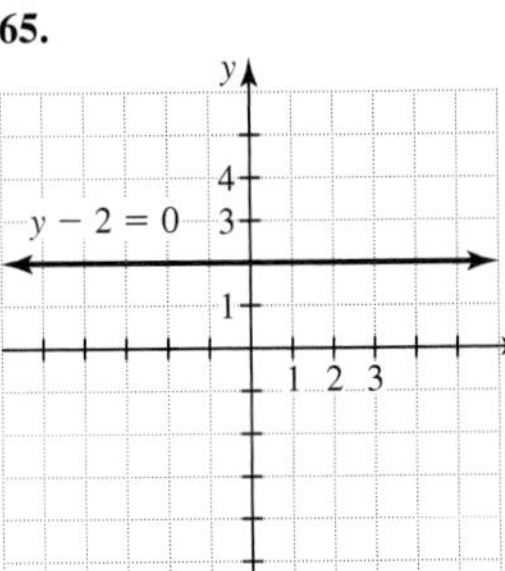

67. Parallel **69.** Neither
71. Parallel **73.** Perpendicular
75. $y = \frac{1}{2}x - 4$ **77.** $y = 2x + 3$
79. $y = -\frac{1}{3}x + 6$
81. $y = -2x + 3$ **83.** $y = 3$
85. $y = -\frac{3}{2}x + 4$
87. $y = -\frac{4}{5}x + 4$
89. \$1,150,000, \$1,150,200, \$200

91. a) A slope of 1 means that the percentage of workers receiving training is going up 1% per year.
b) $y = x + 5$ where x is the number of years since 1982
c) The y-intercept (0, 5) means that 5% of the workers received training in 1982.
d) 33%

93. a) x = the number of packs of pansies, y = the number of packs of snapdragons

b)

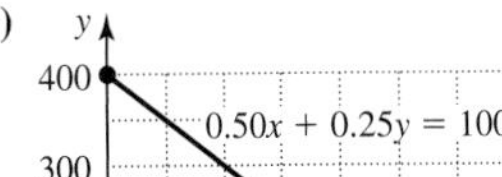

c) $y = -2x + 400$
d) −2
e) If the number of packs of pansies goes up by 1, then the number of packs of snapdragons goes down by 2.

95.

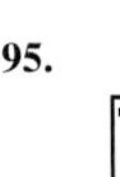

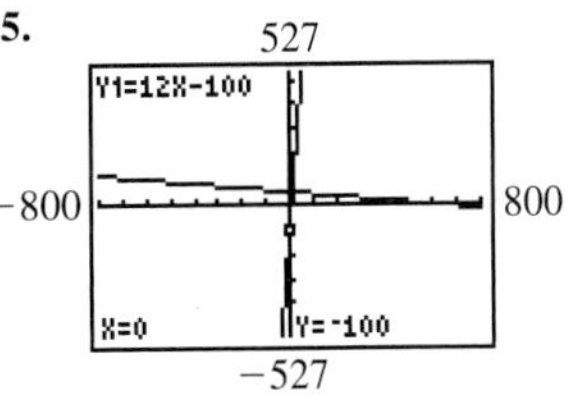

Section 3.4 Warm-Ups F F T T F T T T T T

1. Point-slope form is $y - y_1 = m(x - x_1)$.
3. If you know two points on a line, find the slope. Then use it along with a point in point-slope form to write the equation of the line.
5. Nonvertical parallel lines have equal slopes.
7. $y = 5x + 11$ **9.** $y = \frac{3}{4}x - 20$ **11.** $y = \frac{2}{3}x + \frac{1}{3}$ **13.** $y = 3x - 1$
15. $y = \frac{1}{2}x + 3$ **17.** $y = \frac{1}{3}x + \frac{7}{3}$ **19.** $y = -\frac{1}{2}x + 4$
21. $y = -6x - 13$ **23.** $2x - y = 7$ **25.** $x - 2y = 6$
27. $2x - 3y = 2$ **29.** $2x - y = -1$ **31.** $x - y = 0$
33. $3x - 2y = -1$ **35.** $3x + 5y = -11$ **37.** $x - y = -2$
39. $x = 2$ **41.** $y = 9$ **43.** $y = -x + 4$ **45.** $y = \frac{5}{3}x - 1$
47. $y = -\frac{1}{3}x + 5$ **49.** $y = x + 3$ **51.** $y = -\frac{2}{3}x + \frac{5}{3}$
53. $y = -2x - 5$ **55.** $y = \frac{1}{3}x + \frac{7}{3}$ **57.** $y = 2x - 1$ **59.** $y = 2$
61. $y = \frac{2}{3}x$ **63.** $y = -x$ **65.** $y = 50$ **67.** $y = -\frac{3}{5}x - 4$
69. e **71.** f **73.** h **75.** g
77. a) Slope 0.9 means that the number of ATM transactions is increasing by 0.9 billion per year. **b)** $y = 0.9x + 10.6$ **c)** 23.2 billion
79. a) $y = 1.5x + 53.8$ **b)** x = years since 1990, y = GDP in thousands of dollars **c)** \$83,800
d)

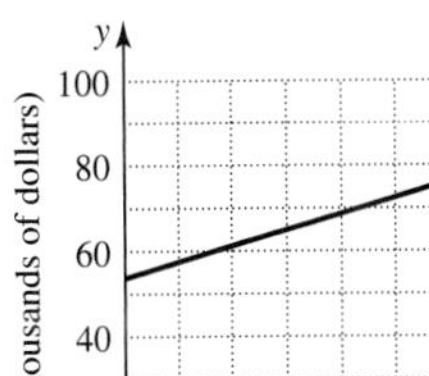

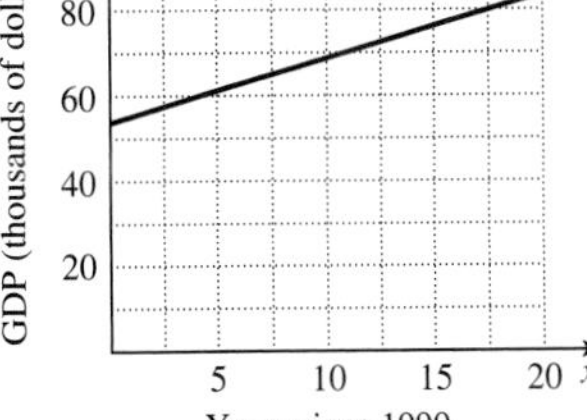

81. $C = 20n + 30$, \$170 **83.** $S = 3L - \frac{41}{4}$, 8.5
85. $v = 32t + 10$, 122 ft/sec
87. a) $w = -\frac{1}{120}t + \frac{3}{2}$ **b)** $\frac{5}{6}$ inch **c)** 60°F

89. $A = 0.6w$, 3.6 in. **91. a)** $a = 0.08c$ **b)** 0.24 **c)** 6.25 mg/ml

93. $2, 3, -\frac{2}{3}; 4, -5, \frac{4}{5}; \frac{1}{2}, 3, -\frac{1}{6}; 2, -\frac{1}{3}, 6$

95. a)

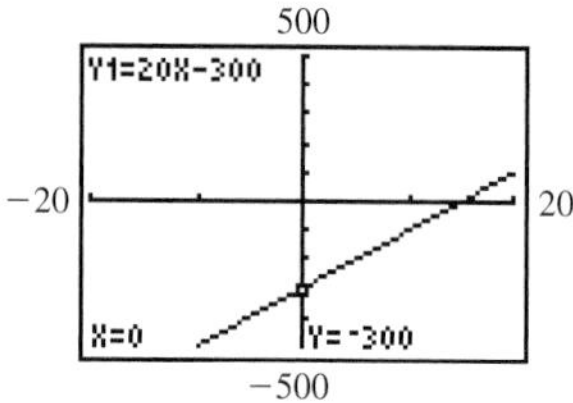

b)

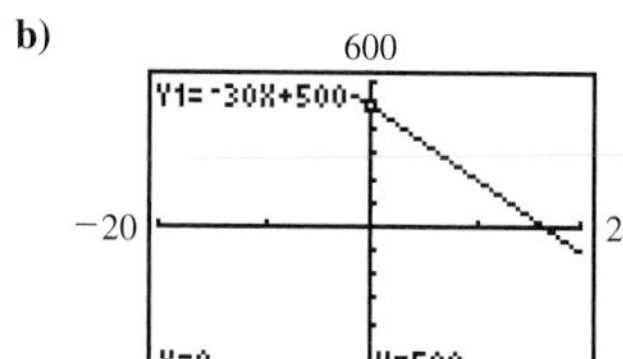

c)

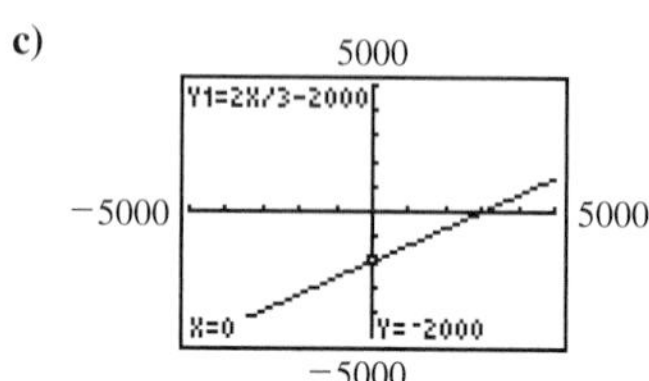

97. $-1 \le x \le 1, -1 \le y \le 1$

Section 3.5 Warm-Ups T F T F F T T T F F

1. If y varies directly as x, then there is a constant k such that $y = kx$.

3. If y is inversely proportional to x, then there is a constant k such that $y = \frac{k}{x}$.

5. $T = kh$ **7.** $y = \frac{k}{r}$ **9.** $R = kts$ **11.** $i = kb$ **13.** $A = kym$

15. $y = \frac{5}{3}x$ **17.** $A = \frac{6}{B}$ **19.** $m = \frac{198}{p}$ **21.** $A = 2tu$ **23.** $T = \frac{9}{2}u$

25. 25 **27.** 1 **29.** 105

31. $\left(\frac{1}{2}, 600\right)$, (1, 300), (30, 10), $\left(900, \frac{1}{3}\right)$, Inversely

33. $\left(\frac{1}{3}, \frac{1}{4}\right)$, (8, 6), (12, 9), (20, 15), Directly **35.** Directly, $y = 3.5x$

37. Inversely, $y = \frac{20}{x}$ **39.** (1, 65), (2, 130), (3, 195), (4, 260)

41. (20, 20), (40, 10), (50, 8), (200, 2) **43.** 1600, 12, 12

45. 100.3 pounds **47.** 50 minutes **49.** \$17.40 **51.** 80 mph

53. 3 days **55.** k, (0, 0), no, $y = kx$

Section 3.6 Warm-Ups T T T F F F T F T F

1. A linear inequality has the same form as a linear equation except that an inequality symbol is used.

3. If the inequality symbol includes equality, then the boundary line is solid; otherwise it is dashed.

5. In the test point method we test a point to see which side of the boundary line satisfies the inequality.

7. (−3, −9) **9.** (3, 0), (1, 3) **11.** (2, 3), (0, 5)

13.

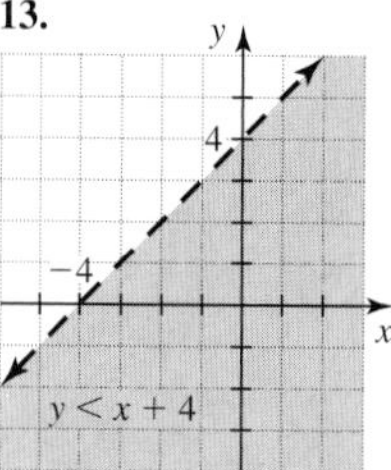

15.

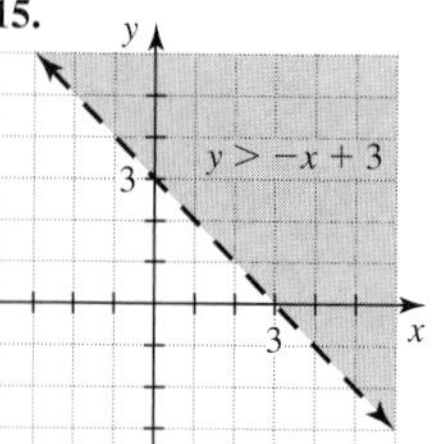

17.

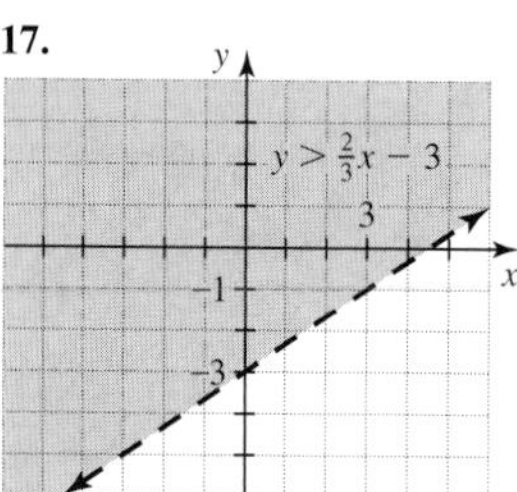

19.

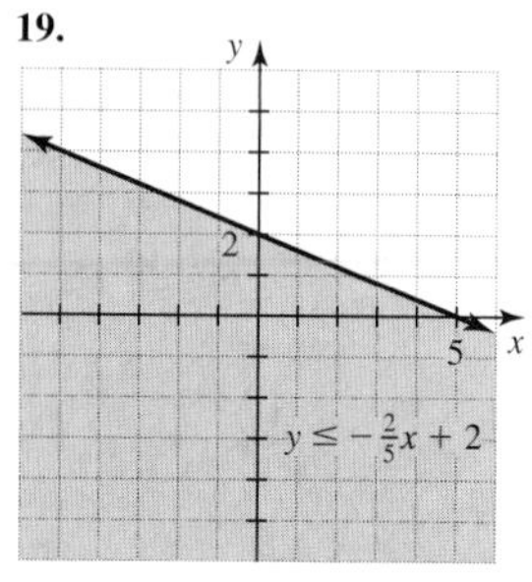

21.

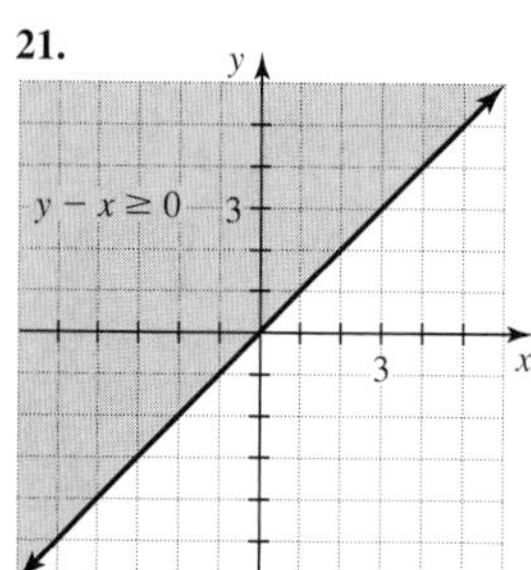

23.

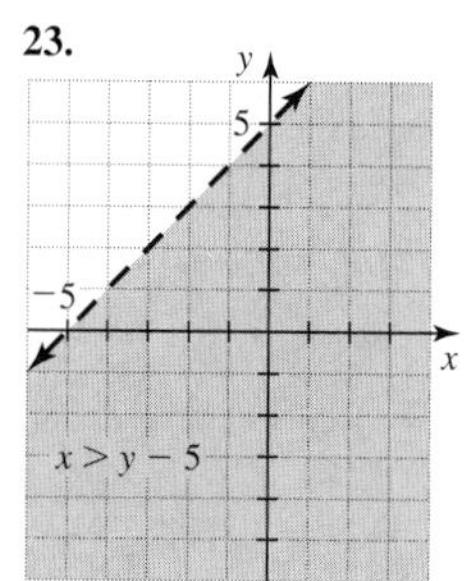

25.

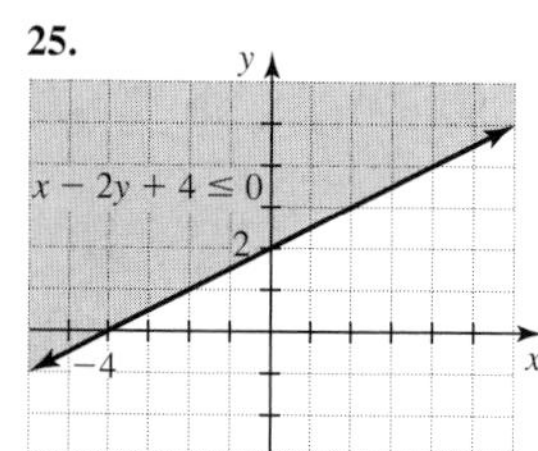

27.

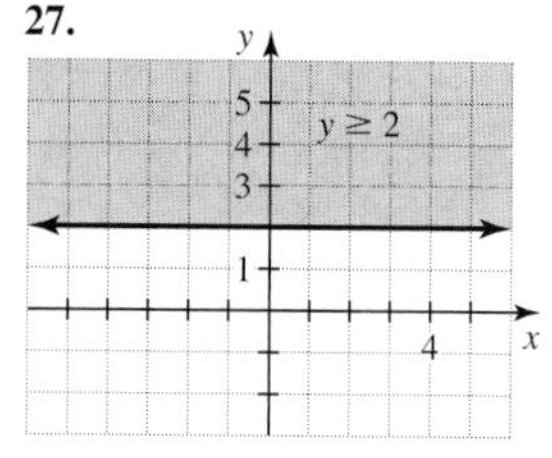

29.

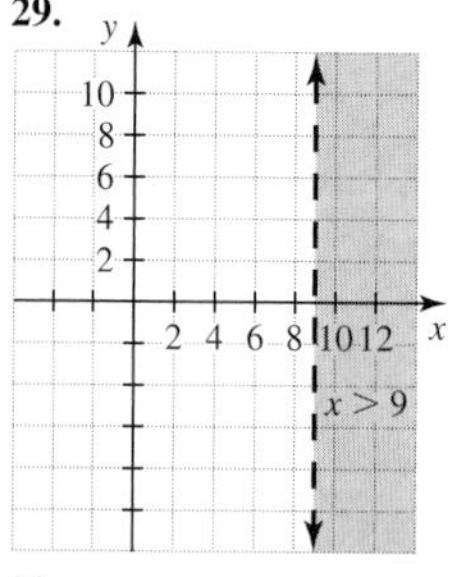

31.

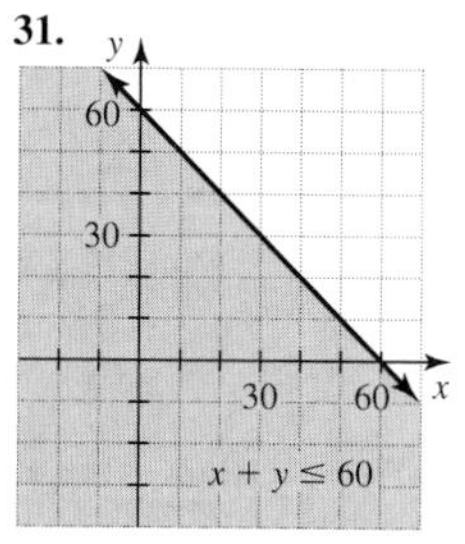

33.

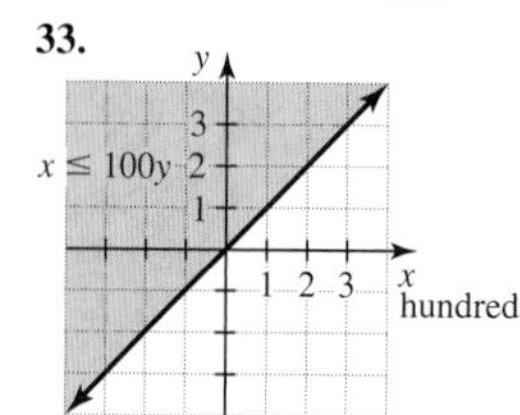

35.

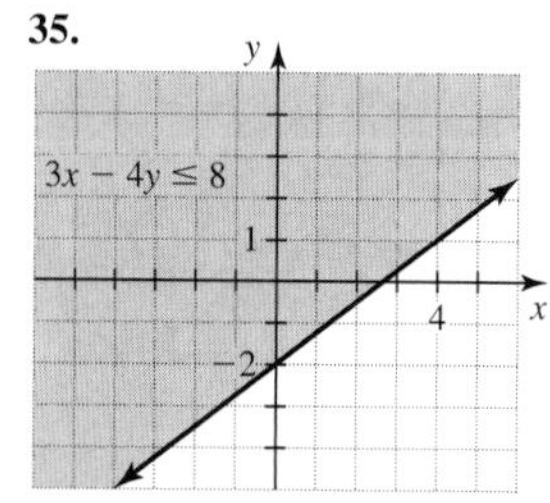

37.

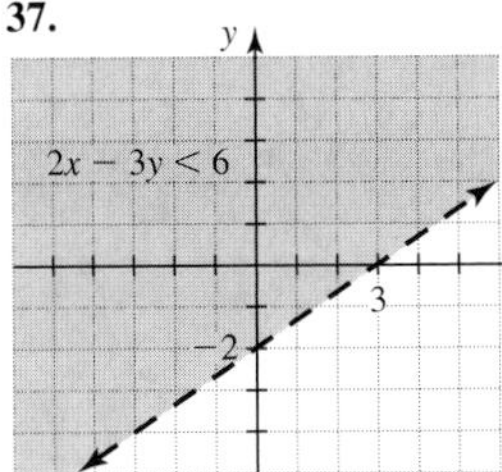

39.

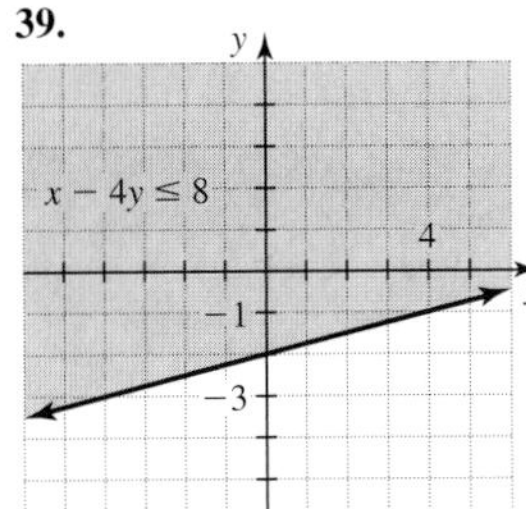

41.

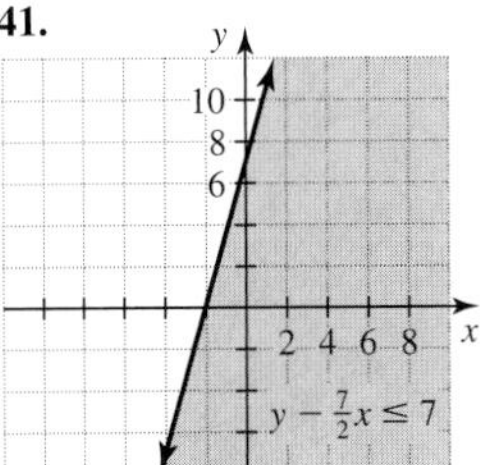

43.

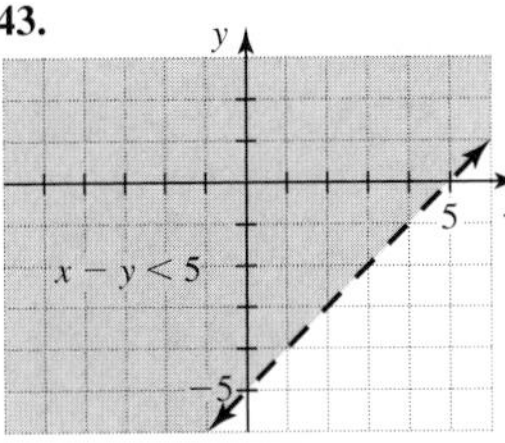

45.

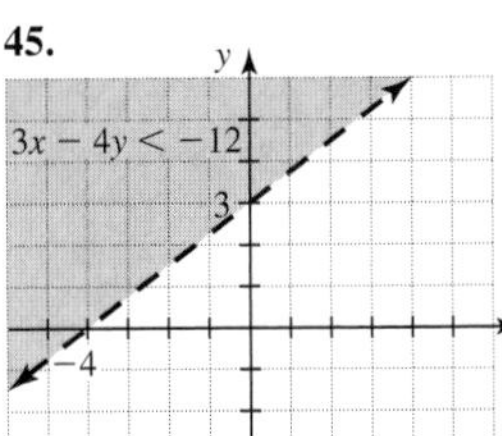

47.

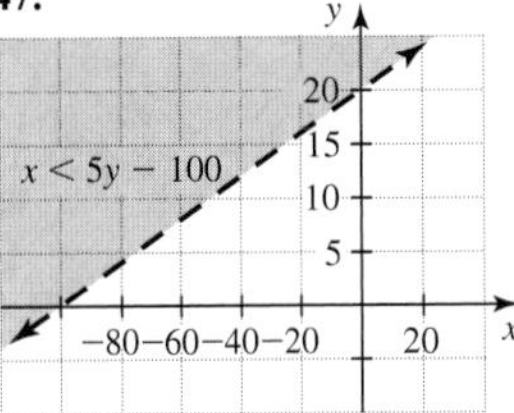

49. $5x + 7y \le 770$

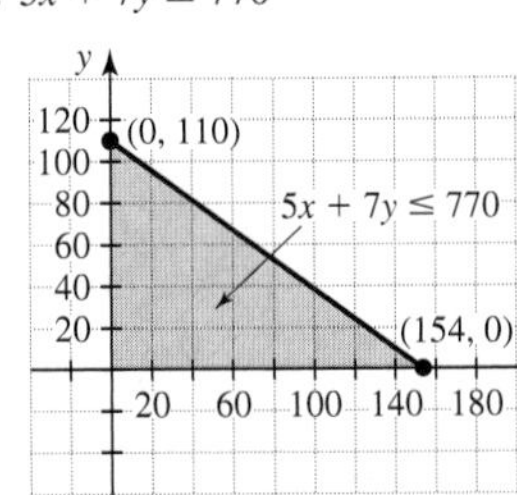

51. $5x + 8y \le 80$

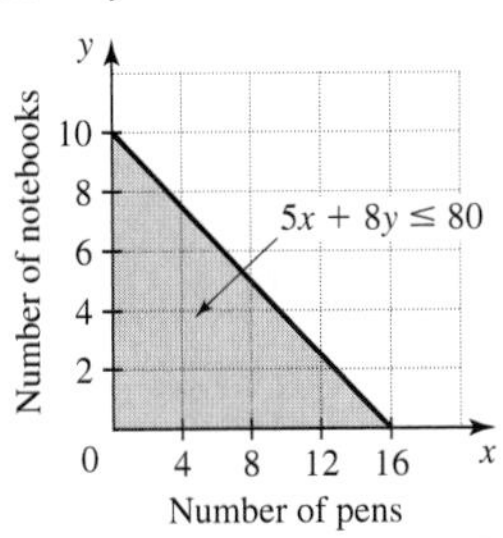

Enriching Your Mathematical Word Power

1. d **2.** a **3.** b **4.** c **5.** b **6.** a **7.** c **8.** c **9.** d
10. b **11.** c **12.** d **13.** c

Review Exercises

1. Quadrant II **3.** x-axis **5.** y-axis **7.** Quadrant IV
9. $(0, -5), (-3, -14), (4, 7)$
11. $\left(0, -\frac{8}{3}\right), \left(3, -\frac{2}{3}\right), \left(-6, -\frac{20}{3}\right)$

13.

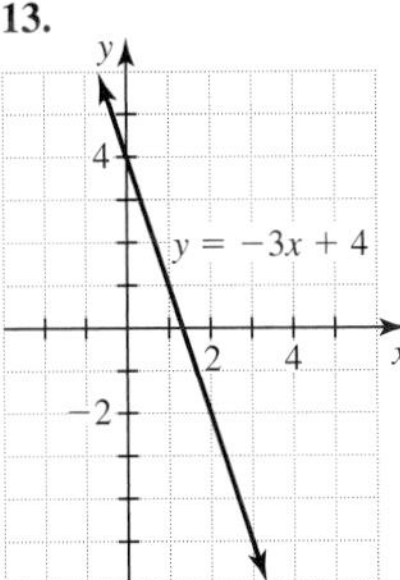

15.

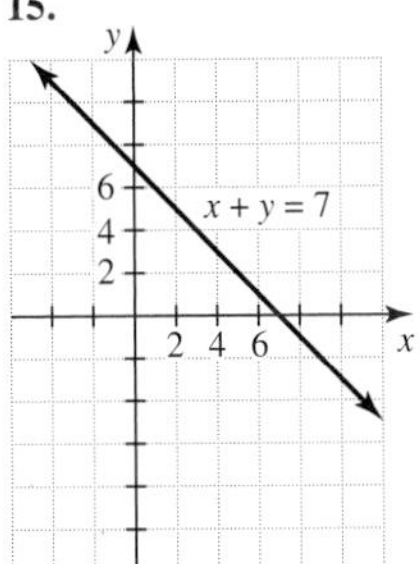

17. 1 **19.** $\frac{3}{2}$ **21.** $\frac{3}{7}$ **23.** 3, $(0, -18)$ **25.** 2, $(0, -3)$
27. 2, $(0, -4)$

29.

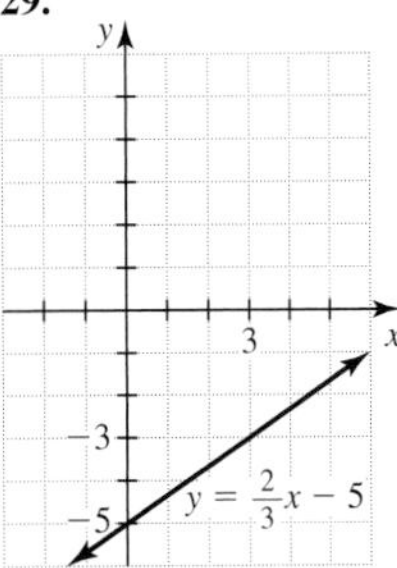

31.

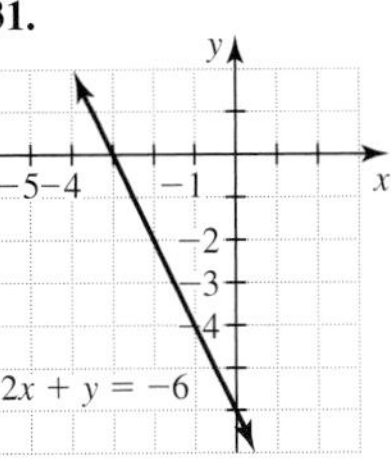

33.

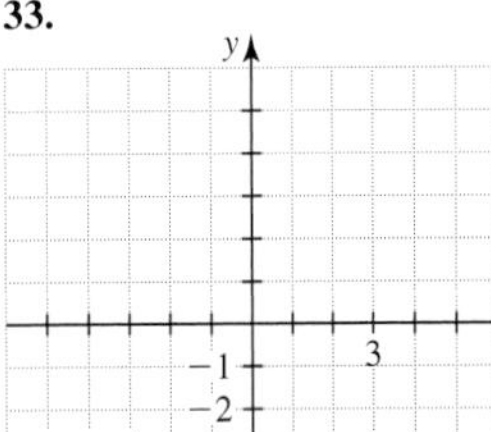

35. $x - 3y = -12$
37. $x + 2y = 0$
39. $y = 5$
41. $y = \frac{2}{3}x + 7$
43. $y = \frac{3}{7}x - 2$
45. $y = -\frac{3}{4}x + \frac{17}{4}$

47. $y = -2x - 1$ **49.** $y = \frac{6}{5}x + \frac{17}{5}$
51. $y = 3x - 14$ **53.** $C = 32n + 49$, \$177
55. a) $q = 1 - p$ **b)** 1 **57.** $y = 0.1x + 0.6$ **59.** 132 **61.** 2
63. 60 **65. a)** $C = 0.75T$ **b)** \$15 **c)** Increasing

67.

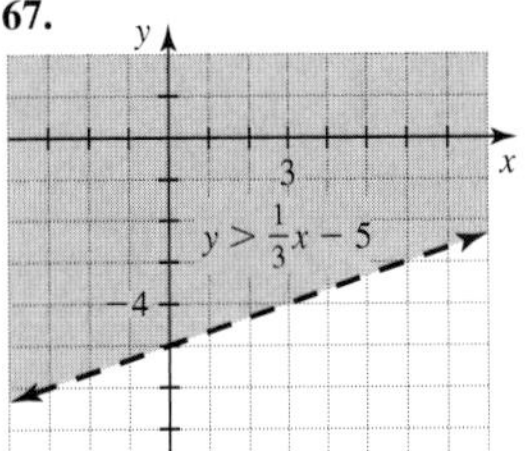

69.

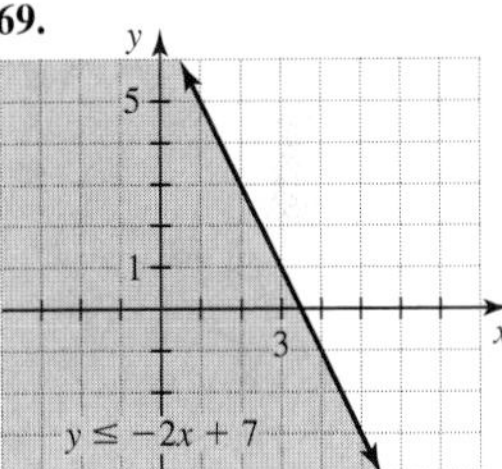

71.

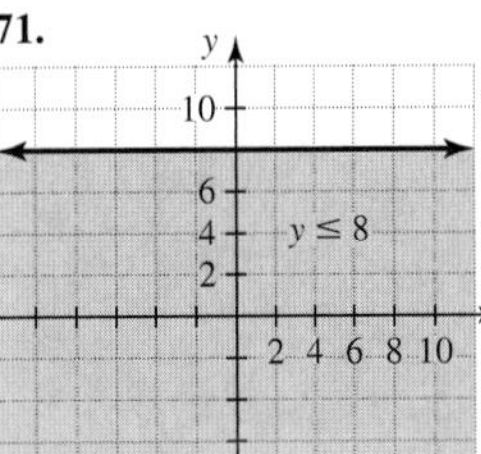

73.

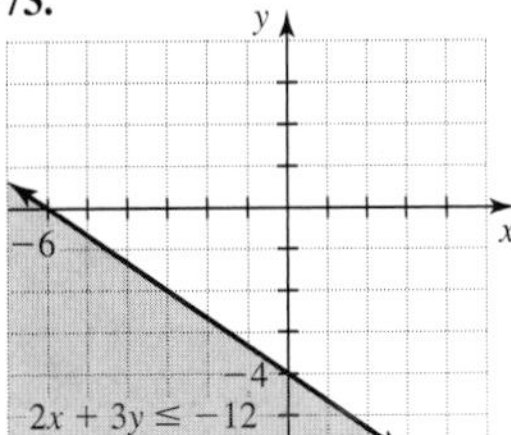

Chapter 3 Test

1. Quadrant II **2.** x-axis **3.** Quadrant IV **4.** y-axis **5.** 1
6. $-\frac{5}{6}$ **7.** 3 **8.** 0 **9.** Undefined **10.** $\frac{2}{3}$
11. $y = -\frac{1}{2}x + 3$ **12.** $y = \frac{3}{7}x - \frac{11}{7}$ **13.** $x - 3y = 11$
14. $5x + 3y = 27$

15.

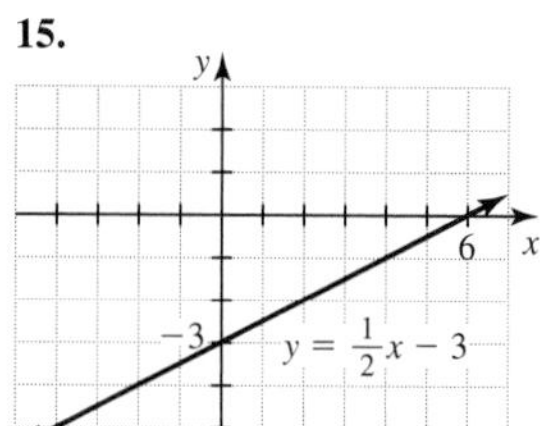

16.

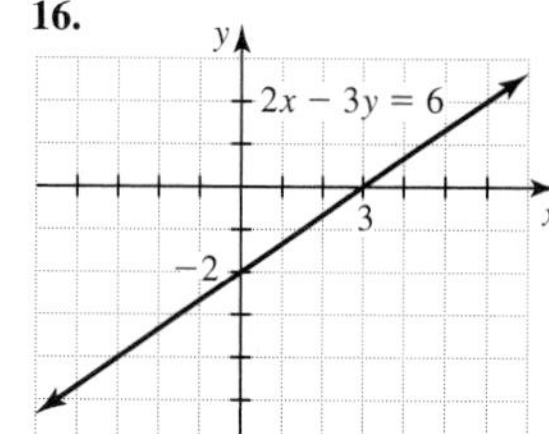

17.

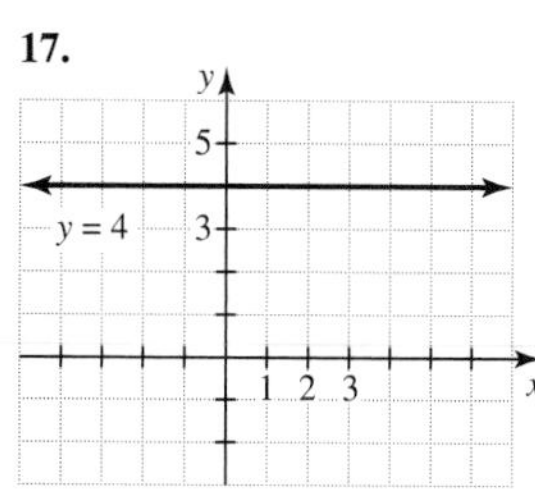

18.

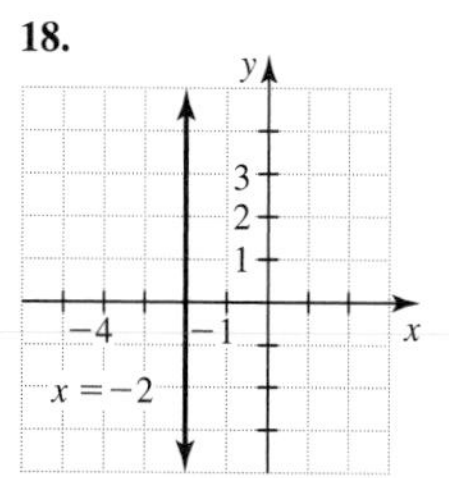

19.

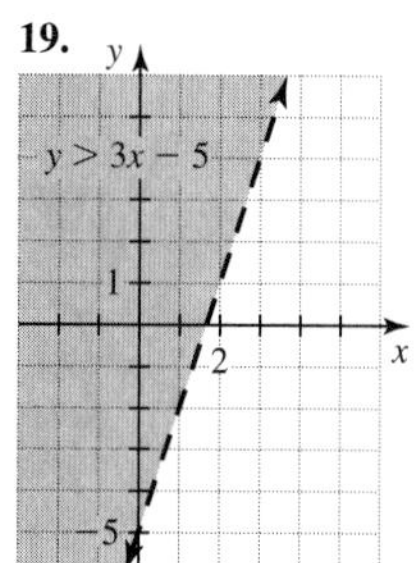

20.

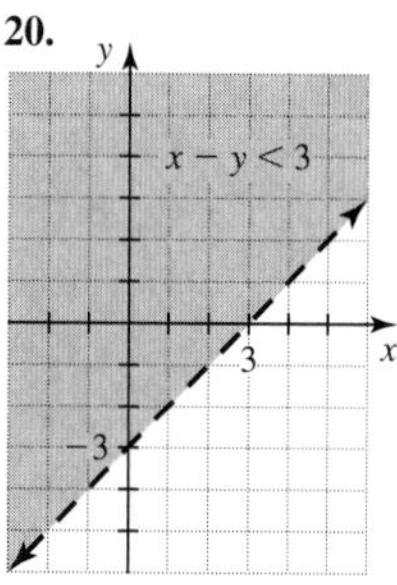

21.

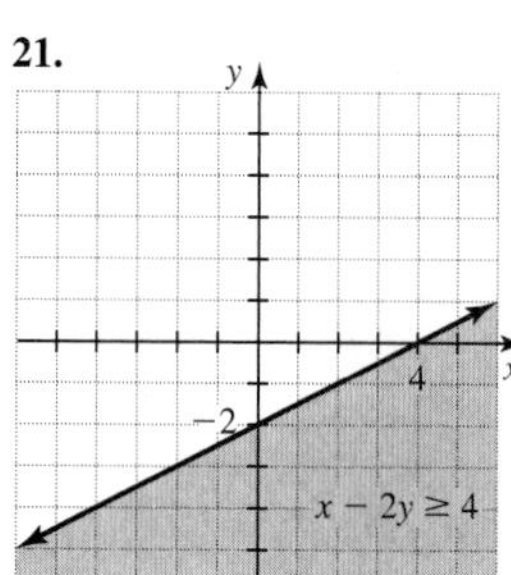

22. $S = 0.75n + 2.50$
23. $P = 3v + 20$, 80 cents
24. \$2.80
25. 18.75 days, decreases
26. \$770

Making Connections Chapters 1–3

1. -1 **2.** -34 **3.** 1 **4.** 72 **5.** -4
6. -28 **7.** $-\frac{7}{2}$ **8.** 0.4 **9.** $\frac{1}{10}$ **10.** 15 **11.** $13x$
12. $3x - 36$ **13.** $\left\{\frac{5}{2}\right\}$ **14.** $\left\{\frac{7}{3}\right\}$ **15.** $\frac{1}{6}$ **16.** $\frac{5}{12}$
17. $\{2\}$ **18.** $\{-4\}$ **19.** $2x - 4$ **20.** $x + 2$
21. $\{5\}$ **22.** $\{3\}$ **23.** $\varnothing$ **24.** All real numbers
25. $(4.5, \infty)$ **26.** $\left(-\frac{2}{3}, \infty\right)$ **27.** $[10, \infty)$ **28.** $[20, \infty)$
29. $\left[-\frac{1}{2}, \frac{5}{2}\right)$ **30.** $\left[0, \frac{2}{3}\right)$ **31.** $y = \frac{t - 2}{3\pi}$
32. $y = mx + b$ **33.** $y = x - 4$ **34.** $y = 6$
35. $y = \frac{4}{5}$ **36.** $y = 200$
37. a) $\frac{2}{15}$ **b)** $\frac{1}{5}$ **c)** About 13% per year
d) \$276,000 saved, \$12,000 per year

Chapter 4

Section 4.1 Warm-Ups F F T T F T F T T F

1. A term is a single number or the product of a number and one or more variables raised to powers.
3. The degree of a polynomial in one variable is the highest power of the variable in the polynomial.
5. Polynomials are added by adding the like terms.
7. $-3, 7$ **9.** $0, 6$ **11.** $\frac{1}{3}, \frac{7}{2}$ **13.** Monomial, 0
15. Monomial, 3 **17.** Binomial, 1 **19.** Trinomial, 10
21. Binomial, 6 **23.** Trinomial, 3 **25.** 6 **27.** $\frac{5}{8}$ **29.** -85
31. 5 **33.** 71 **35.** -4.97665 **37.** $4x - 8$ **39.** $2q$
41. $x^2 + 3x - 2$ **43.** $x^3 + 9x - 7$ **45.** $3a^2 - 7a - 4$
47. $-3w^2 - 8w + 5$ **49.** $9.66x^2 - 1.93x - 1.49$
51. $-4x + 6$ **53.** -5 **55.** $-z^2 + 2z$ **57.** $w^5 + w^4 - w^3 - w^2$
59. $2t + 13$ **61.** $-8y + 7$ **63.** $-22.85x - 423.2$
65. $4a + 2$ **67.** $-2x + 4$ **69.** $2a$ **71.** $-5m + 7$
73. $4x^2 + 1$ **75.** $a^3 - 9a^2 + 2a + 7$ **77.** $-3x + 9$
79. $2y^3 + 7y^2 - 4y - 14$ **81.** $-3m + 3$ **83.** $-11y - 3$
85. $2x^2 - 6x + 12$ **87.** $-5z^4 - 8z^3 + 3z^2 + 7$
89. $P(x) = 100x + 500$ dollars, \$5500
91. $P(x) = 6x + 3$, $P(4) = 27$ meters
93. $5x + 40$ miles, 140 miles
95. 800 feet, 800 feet
97. $0.17x + 74.47$ dollars, \$244.47
99. 1321.39 calories
101. Yes, yes, yes
103. The highest power of x is 3.

Section 4.2 Warm-Ups F F T F T T T T T F

1. The product rule for exponents says that $a^m \cdot a^n = a^{m+n}$.
3. To multiply a monomial and a polynomial we use the distributive property.
5. To multiply any two polynomials we multiply each term of the first polynomial by every term of the second polynomial.
7. $27x^5$ **9.** $14a^{11}$ **11.** $-30x^4$ **13.** $27x^{17}$ **15.** $-54s^2t^2$
17. $24t^7w^8$ **19.** $25y^2$ **21.** $4x^6$ **23.** $x^2 + xy^2$ **25.** $4y^7 - 8y^3$
27. $-18y^2 + 12y$ **29.** $-3y^3 + 15y^2 - 18y$ **31.** $-xy^2 + x^3$
33. $15a^4b^3 - 5a^5b^2 - 10a^6b$ **35.** $-2t^5v^3 + 3t^3v^2 + 2t^2v^2$
37. $x^2 + 3x + 2$ **39.** $x^2 + 2x - 15$ **41.** $t^2 - 13t + 36$
43. $x^3 + 3x^2 + 4x + 2$ **45.** $6y^3 + y^2 + 7y + 6$
47. $2y^8 - 3y^6z - 5y^4z^2 + 3y^2z^3$ **49.** $2a^2 + 7a - 15$
51. $14x^2 + 95x + 150$ **53.** $20x^2 - 7x - 6$
55. $2am - 6an + bm - 3bn$ **57.** $x^3 + 9x^2 + 16x - 12$
59. $-4a^4 + 9a^2 - 8a - 12$ **61.** $x^2 - y^2$ **63.** $x^3 + y^3$
65. $u - 3t$ **67.** $-3x - y$ **69.** $3a^2 + a - 6$ **71.** $-3v^2 - v + 6$
73. $-6x^2 + 27x$ **75.** $-6x^2 + 27x + 2$ **77.** $-x - 7$ **79.** $36x^{12}$
81. $-6a^3b^{10}$ **83.** $25x^2 + 60x + 36$ **85.** $25x^2 - 36$
87. $6x^7 - 8x^4$ **89.** $m^3 - 1$ **91.** $3x^3 - 5x^2 - 25x + 18$
93. $x^2 + 4x$ square feet, 140 square feet
95. $A(x) = x^2 + \frac{1}{2}x$, $A(5) = 27.5$ square feet
97. $x^2 + 5x$ **99.** $8.05x^2 + 15.93x + 6.12$ square meters
101. 30,000, \$300,000, $40{,}000p - 1000p^2$
103. $10x^5 + 10x^4 + 10x^3 + 10x^2 + 10x$, \$67.16

Section 4.3 Warm-Ups F T T T T F T F F F

1. We use the distributive property to find the product of two binomials.
3. The purpose of FOIL is to provide a faster method for finding the product of two binomials.

5. $x^2 + 6x + 8$ **7.** $a^2 + 5a + 4$ **9.** $x^2 + 19x + 90$
11. $2x^2 + 7x + 3$ **13.** $a^2 - a - 6$ **15.** $2x^2 - 5x + 2$
17. $2a^2 - a - 3$ **19.** $w^2 - 60w + 500$ **21.** $y^2 + 5y - ay - 5a$
23. $5w + 5m - w^2 - mw$ **25.** $10m^2 - 9mt - 9t^2$
27. $45a^2 + 53ab + 14b^2$ **29.** $x^4 - 3x^2 - 10$ **31.** $h^6 + 10h^3 + 25$
33. $3b^6 + 14b^3 + 8$ **35.** $y^3 - 2y^2 - 3y + 6$ **37.** $6m^6 + 7m^3n^2 - 3n^4$
39. $12u^4v^2 + 10u^2v - 12$ **41.** $b^2 + 9b + 20$ **43.** $x^2 + 6x - 27$
45. $a^2 + 10a + 25$ **47.** $4x^2 - 4x + 1$ **49.** $z^2 - 100$
51. $a^2 + 2ab + b^2$ **53.** $a^2 - 3a + 2$ **55.** $2x^2 + 5x - 3$
57. $5t^2 - 7t + 2$ **59.** $h^2 - 16h + 63$ **61.** $h^2 + 14hw + 49w^2$
63. $4h^4 - 4h^2 + 1$ **65.** $a^3 + 4a^2 - 7a - 10$
67. $h^3 + 9h^2 + 26h + 24$ **69.** $x^3 - 2x^2 - 64x + 128$
71. $x^3 + 8x^2 - \frac{1}{4}x - 2$ **73.** $x^2 + 15x + 50$ **75.** $x^2 + x + \frac{1}{4}$
77. $8x^2 + 2x + \frac{1}{8}$ **79.** $8a^2 + a - \frac{1}{4}$ **81.** $\frac{1}{8}x^2 + \frac{1}{6}x - \frac{1}{6}$
83. $a^3 + 7a^2 + 12a$ **85.** $x^5 + 13x^4 + 42x^3$
87. $-12x^6 - 26x^5 + 10x^4$ **89.** $x^3 + 3x^2 - x - 3$
91. $9x^3 + 45x^2 - 4x - 20$ **93.** $2x + 10$
95. $2x^2 + 5x - 3$ square feet
97. $5.2555x^2 + 0.41095x - 1.995$ square meters
99. 12 ft², $3h$ ft², $4h$ ft², h^2 ft², $h^2 + 7h + 12$ ft², $(h + 3)(h + 4) = h^2 + 7h + 12$

Section 4.4 Warm-Ups F T T T F T T T F F
1. The special products are $(a + b)^2$, $(a - b)^2$, and $(a + b)(a - b)$.
3. It is faster to do by the new rule than with FOIL.
5. $(a + b)(a - b) = a^2 - b^2$ **7.** $x^2 + 2x + 1$ **9.** $y^2 + 8y + 16$
11. $m^2 + 12m + 36$ **13.** $9x^2 + 48x + 64$ **15.** $s^2 + 2st + t^2$
17. $4x^2 + 4xy + y^2$ **19.** $4t^2 + 12ht + 9h^2$ **21.** $p^2 - 4p + 4$
23. $a^2 - 6a + 9$ **25.** $t^2 - 2t + 1$ **27.** $9t^2 - 12t + 4$
29. $s^2 - 2st + t^2$ **31.** $9a^2 - 6ab + b^2$ **33.** $9z^2 - 30yz + 25y^2$
35. $a^2 - 25$ **37.** $y^2 - 1$ **39.** $9x^2 - 64$ **41.** $r^2 - s^2$
43. $64y^2 - 9a^2$ **45.** $25x^4 - 4$
47. $x^3 + 3x^2 + 3x + 1$ **49.** $8a^3 - 36a^2 + 54a - 27$
51. $a^4 - 12a^3 + 54a^2 - 108a + 81$ **53.** $a^4 + 4a^3b + 6a^2b^2 + 4ab^3 + b^4$
55. $a^2 - 400$ **57.** $x^2 + 15x + 56$ **59.** $16x^2 - 1$
61. $81y^2 - 18y + 1$ **63.** $6t^2 - 7t - 20$ **65.** $4t^2 - 20t + 25$
67. $4t^2 - 25$ **69.** $x^4 - 1$ **71.** $4y^6 - 36y^3 + 81$
73. $4x^6 + 12x^3y^2 + 9y^4$ **75.** $\frac{1}{4}x^2 + \frac{1}{3}x + \frac{1}{9}$
77. $0.04x^2 - 0.04x + 0.01$ **79.** $a^3 + 3a^2b + 3ab^2 + b^3$
81. $2.25x^2 + 11.4x + 14.44$ **83.** $12.25t^2 - 6.25$
85. $x^2 - 25$ square feet, 25 square feet smaller
87. $3.14b^2 + 6.28b + 3.14$ square meters
89. $v = k(R^2 - r^2)$ **91.** $P + 2Pr + Pr^2$, \$242 **93.** \$20,230.06
95. The first is an identity and the second is a conditional equation.

Section 4.5 Warm-Ups F F T F T F T T T T
1. The quotient rule is used for dividing monomials.
3. When dividing a polynomial by a monomial the quotient should have the same number of terms as the polynomial.
5. The long division process stops when the degree of the remainder is less than the degree of the divisor.
7. 1 **9.** 1 **11.** 1 **13.** 1 **15.** x^6 **17.** $\frac{1}{a^9}$ **19.** $\frac{3}{a^5}$ **21.** a^6
23. $\frac{-4}{x^4}$ **25.** $-y$ **27.** $-3x$ **29.** $\frac{-3}{x^3}$ **31.** $x - 2$
33. $x^3 + 3x^2 - x$ **35.** $4xy - 2x + y$ **37.** $y^2 - 3xy$ **39.** 2, -1
41. $x + 5$, 16 **43.** $x + 2$, 7 **45.** 2, -10 **47.** $a^2 + 2a + 8$, 13
49. $x - 4$, 4 **51.** $h^2 + 3h + 9$, 0 **53.** $2x - 3$, 1 **55.** $x^2 + 1$, -1
57. $3 + \frac{15}{x - 5}$ **59.** $-1 + \frac{3}{x + 3}$ **61.** $1 - \frac{1}{x}$ **63.** $3 + \frac{1}{x}$
65. $x - 1 + \frac{1}{x + 1}$ **67.** $x - 2 + \frac{8}{x + 2}$ **69.** $x^2 + 2x + 4 + \frac{8}{x - 2}$
71. $x^2 + \frac{3}{x}$ **73.** $-3a$ **75.** $\frac{4t^4}{w^5}$ **77.** $-a + 4$ **79.** $x - 3$
81. $-6x^2 + 2x - 3$ **83.** $t + 4$ **85.** $2w + 1$ **87.** $4x^2 - 6x + 9$
89. $t^2 - t + 3$ **91.** $v^2 - 2v + 1$ **93.** $x - 5$ meters
95. $x^8 + x^7 + x^6 + x^5 + x^4 + x^3 + x^2 + x + 1$
97. $10x \div 5x$ is not equivalent to the other two.

Section 4.6 Warm-Ups F F F F F F T F F T
1. The product rule says that $a^m a^n = a^{m+n}$.
3. These rules do not make sense without identical bases.
5. The power of a product rule says that $(ab)^n = a^n b^n$.
7. 128 **9.** $6u^{10}$ **11.** a^4b^{10} **13.** $\frac{-1}{2a^4}$ **15.** $\frac{2a^6}{5b^4}$ **17.** 200
19. x^6 **21.** $2x^{12}$ **23.** $\frac{1}{t^2}$ **25.** $\frac{1}{2}$ **27.** x^3y^6 **29.** $-8t^{15}$
31. $-8x^6y^{15}$ **33.** $a^9b^2c^{14}$ **35.** $\frac{x^{12}}{64}$ **37.** $\frac{16a^8}{b^{12}}$ **39.** $-\frac{x^6}{8y^3}$
41. $\frac{4z^{12}}{x^8}$ **43.** 45 **45.** 81 **47.** -19 **49.** -1 **51.** $\frac{8}{125}$
53. 200 **55.** 128 **57.** $\frac{1}{16}$ **59.** x^7 **61.** a^{32} **63.** $a^{12}b^6$
65. $\frac{1}{x^3}$ **67.** a^4 **69.** $\frac{a^9}{b^{12}}$ **71.** $\frac{1}{x^5}$ **73.** $15x^{11}$ **75.** $-125x^{12}$
77. $-27y^6z^{19}$ **79.** $\frac{3v}{u}$ **81.** $-16x^9t^6$ **83.** $\frac{8}{x^6}$ **85.** $\frac{-32a^{15}b^{20}}{c^{25}}$
87. $\frac{y^5}{32x^5}$ **89.** Product rule, $P(1 + r)^{15}$

Section 4.7 Warm-Ups T F F T F T T T T F
1. A negative exponent means "reciprocal," as in $a^{-n} = \frac{1}{a^n}$.
3. The new quotient rule is $a^m/a^n = a^{m-n}$ for any integers m and n.
5. Convert from standard notation by counting the number of places the decimal must move so that there is one nonzero digit to the left of the decimal point.
7. $\frac{1}{3}$ **9.** $\frac{1}{16}$ **11.** $-\frac{1}{16}$ **13.** 4 **15.** $\frac{8}{125}$ **17.** $\frac{1}{3}$ **19.** 1250
21. 82 **23.** x **25.** $-\frac{16}{x^4}$ **27.** $\frac{6}{a^5}$ **29.** $\frac{1}{u^8}$ **31.** $-4t^2$
33. $2x^{11}$ **35.** $\frac{1}{x^{10}}$ **37.** a^9 **39.** $\frac{x^{12}}{16}$ **41.** $\frac{y^6}{16x^4}$ **43.** $\frac{x^2}{4y^6}$
45. $\frac{a^{16}}{16c^8}$ **47.** $\frac{6}{w^5}$ **49.** $\frac{1}{8h^3}$ **51.** $\frac{1}{x^{18}}$ **53.** b^{13} **55.** v^{23}
57. $\frac{1}{c^9}$ **59.** $\frac{1}{6}$ **61.** $\frac{3}{2}$ **63.** $-14x^6$ **65.** $\frac{2a^4}{b^2}$
67. 9,860,000,000 **69.** 0.00137 **71.** 0.000001 **73.** 600,000
75. 9×10^3 **77.** 7.8×10^{-4} **79.** 8.5×10^{-6} **81.** 5.25×10^{11}
83. 6×10^{-10} **85.** 2×10^{-38} **87.** 5×10^{27} **89.** 9×10^{24}
91. 1.25×10^{14} **93.** 2.5×10^{-33} **95.** 8.6×10^9
97. 2.1×10^2 **99.** 2.7×10^{-23} **101.** 3×10^{15}
103. 9.135×10^2 **105.** 5.715×10^{-4} **107.** 4.426×10^7
109. 1.577×10^{182} **111.** 4.910×10^{11} feet
113. 4.65×10^{-28} hours **115.** 9.040×10^8 feet **117.** \$10,727.41
119. **a)** $w < 0$ **b)** m is odd **c)** $w < 0$ and m odd

Enriching Your Mathematical Word Power
1. a **2.** d **3.** b **4.** c **5.** d **6.** b **7.** a **8.** b
9. c **10.** a **11.** a **12.** c

Review Exercises

1. $5w - 2$ **3.** $-6x + 4$ **5.** $2w^2 - 7w - 4$ **7.** $-2m^2 + 3m - 1$ **9.** $-50x^{11}$ **11.** $121a^{14}$ **13.** $-4x + 15$ **15.** $3x^2 - 10x + 12$ **17.** $15m^5 - 3m^3 + 6m^2$ **19.** $x^3 - 7x^2 + 20x - 50$ **21.** $3x^3 - 8x^2 + 16x - 8$ **23.** $q^2 + 2q - 48$ **25.** $2t^2 - 21t + 27$ **27.** $20y^2 - 7y - 6$ **29.** $6x^4 + 13x^2 + 5$ **31.** $z^2 - 49$ **33.** $y^2 + 14y + 49$ **35.** $w^2 - 6w + 9$ **37.** $x^4 - 9$ **39.** $9a^2 + 6a + 1$ **41.** $16 - 8y + y^2$ **43.** $-5x^2$ **45.** $\frac{-2a^2}{b^2}$ **47.** $-x + 3$ **49.** $-3x^2 + 2x - 1$ **51.** -1 **53.** $m^3 + 2m^2 + 4m + 8$ **55.** $m^2 - 3m + 6, 0$ **57.** $b - 5, 15$ **59.** $2x - 1, -8$ **61.** $x^2 + 2x - 9, 1$ **63.** $2 + \frac{6}{x - 3}$ **65.** $-2 + \frac{2}{1 - x}$ **67.** $x - 1 - \frac{2}{x + 1}$ **69.** $x - 1 + \frac{1}{x + 1}$ **71.** $6y^{30}$ **73.** $\frac{-5}{c^6}$ **75.** b^{30} **77.** $-8x^9y^6$ **79.** $\frac{8a^3}{b^3}$ **81.** $\frac{8x^6y^{15}}{z^{18}}$ **83.** $\frac{1}{32}$ **85.** $\frac{1}{1000}$ **87.** $\frac{1}{x^3}$ **89.** a^4 **91.** a^{10} **93.** $\frac{1}{x^{12}}$ **95.** $\frac{x^9}{8}$ **97.** $\frac{9}{a^2b^6}$ **99.** 5×10^3 **101.** 340,000 **103.** 4.61×10^{-5} **105.** 0.00000569 **107.** 7×10^{-4} **109.** 1.6×10^{-15} **111.** 8×10^1 **113.** 3.2×10^{-34} **115.** $x^2 + 10x + 21$ **117.** $t^2 - 7ty + 12y^2$ **119.** 2 **121.** $-27h^3t^{18}$ **123.** $2w^2 - 9w - 18$ **125.** $9u^2 - 25v^2$ **127.** $9h^2 + 30h + 25$ **129.** $x^3 + 9x^2 + 27x + 27$ **131.** $14s^5t^6$ **133.** $\frac{k^8}{16}$ **135.** $x^2 - 9x - 5$ **137.** $5x^2 - x - 12$ **139.** $x^3 - x^2 - 19x + 4$ **141.** $x + 6$ **143.** $P(w) = 4w + 88$, $A(w) = w^2 + 44w$, $P(50) = 288$ ft, $A(50) = 4700$ ft^2 **145.** $R = -15p^2 + 600p$, \$5040, \$20

Chapter 4 Test

1. $7x^3 + 4x^2 + 2x - 11$ **2.** $-x^2 - 9x + 2$ **3.** $-2y^2 + 3y$ **4.** -1 **5.** $x^2 + x - 1$ **6.** $15x^5 - 21x^4 + 12x^3 - 3x^2$ **7.** $x^2 + 3x - 10$ **8.** $6a^2 + a - 35$ **9.** $a^2 - 14a + 49$ **10.** $16x^2 + 24xy + 9y^2$ **11.** $b^2 - 9$ **12.** $9t^4 - 49$ **13.** $4x^4 + 5x^2 - 6$ **14.** $x^3 - 3x^2 - 10x + 24$ **15.** $2 + \frac{6}{x - 3}$ **16.** $x - 5 + \frac{15}{x + 2}$ **17.** $-35x^8$ **18.** $12x^5y^9$ **19.** $-2ab^4$ **20.** $15x^5$ **21.** $\frac{-32a^5}{b^{10}}$ **22.** $\frac{3a^4}{b^2}$ **23.** $\frac{3}{t^{16}}$ **24.** $\frac{1}{w^2}$ **25.** $\frac{s^6}{9t^4}$ **26.** $\frac{-8y^3}{x^{18}}$ **27.** 5.433×10^6 **28.** 6.5×10^{-6} **29.** 4.8×10^{-1} **30.** 8.1×10^{-27} **31.** $x - 2, 3$ **32.** $-2x^2 + x + 15$ **33.** $A(x) = x^2 + 4x$, $P(x) = 4x + 8$, $A(4) = 32$ ft^2, $P(4) = 24$ ft **34.** $R = -150q^2 + 3000q$, \$14,400

Making Connections A Review of Chapters 1–4

1. 8 **2.** 32 **3.** 41 **4.** -2 **5.** 32 **6.** 32 **7.** -144 **8.** 144 **9.** $\frac{5}{8}$ **10.** $\frac{1}{9}$ **11.** 64 **12.** 34 **13.** $\frac{5}{6}$ **14.** $\frac{5}{36}$ **15.** 899 **16.** -1 **17.** $x^2 + 8x + 15$ **18.** $4x + 15$ **19.** $-15t^5v^7$ **20.** $5tv$ **21.** $x^2 + 9x + 20$ **22.** $x^2 + 7x + 10$ **23.** $x + 3$ **24.** $x^3 + 13x^2 + 55x + 75$ **25.** $3y - 4$ **26.** $6y^2 - 4y + 1$ **27.** $\left\{-\frac{1}{2}\right\}$ **28.** $\{7\}$ **29.** $\left\{\frac{14}{3}\right\}$ **30.** $\left\{\frac{7}{4}\right\}$ **31.** $\{0\}$ **32.** All real numbers **33.** $\left(-\frac{1}{2}, 0\right)$ **34.** $(0, -7)$ **35.** 2 **36.** $\frac{2}{3}$ **37.** $\frac{14}{3}$ **38.** $-\frac{1}{2}$ **39.** $\frac{2.25n + 100{,}000}{n}$, \$102.25, \$3.25, \$2.35, It averages out to 10 cents per disk.

Chapter 5

Section 5.1 Warm-Ups F F F T T T T F F T

1. To factor means to write as a product.
3. You can find the prime factorization by dividing by prime factors until the result is prime.
5. The GCF for two monomials consists of the GCF of their coefficients and every variable that they have in common raised to the lowest power that appears on the variable.
7. $2 \cdot 3^2$ **9.** $2^2 \cdot 13$ **11.** $2 \cdot 7^2$ **13.** $2^2 \cdot 5 \cdot 23$ **15.** $2^2 \cdot 3 \cdot 7 \cdot 11$ **17.** 4 **19.** 12 **21.** 8 **23.** 4 **25.** 1 **27.** $2x$ **29.** $2x$ **31.** xy **33.** $12ab$ **35.** 1 **37.** $6ab$ **39.** $3x$ **41.** $3t$ **43.** $9y^3$ **45.** u^3v^2 **47.** $-7n^3$ **49.** $11xy^2z$ **51.** $2(w + 2t)$ **53.** $6(2x - 3y)$ **55.** $x(x^2 - 6)$ **57.** $5a(x + y)$ **59.** $h^3(h^2 + 1)$ **61.** $2k^3m^4(-k^4 + 2m^2)$ **63.** $2x(x^2 - 3x + 4)$ **65.** $6x^2t(2x^2 + 5x - 4t)$ **67.** $(x - 3)(a + b)$ **69.** $(x - 5)(x - 1)$ **71.** $(m + 1)(m + 9)$ **73.** $(a + b)(y + 1)^2$ **75.** $8(x - y), -8(-x + y)$ **77.** $4x(-1 + 2x), -4x(1 - 2x)$ **79.** $1(x - 5), -1(-x + 5)$ **81.** $1(4 - 7a), -1(-4 + 7a)$ **83.** $8a^2(-3a + 2), -8a^2(3a - 2)$ **85.** $6x(-2x - 3), -6x(2x + 3)$ **87.** $2x(-x^2 - 3x + 7), -2x(x^2 + 3x - 7)$ **89.** $2ab(2a^2 - 3ab - 2b^2), -2ab(-2a^2 + 3ab + 2b^2)$ **91.** $x + 2$ hours **93.** **a)** $S = 2\pi r(r + h)$ **b)** $S = 2\pi r^2 + 10\pi r$ **c)** 3 in. **95.** The GCF is an algebraic expression.

Section 5.2 Warm-Ups F T F F T T F F T T

1. A perfect square is a square of an integer or an algebraic expression.
3. A perfect square trinomial is of the form $a^2 + 2ab + b^2$ or $a^2 - 2ab + b^2$.
5. A polynomial is factored completely when it is a product of prime polynomials.
7. $(a - 2)(a + 2)$ **9.** $(x - 7)(x + 7)$ **11.** $(y + 3x)(y - 3x)$ **13.** $(5a + 7b)(5a - 7b)$ **15.** $(11m + 1)(11m - 1)$ **17.** $(3w - 5c)(3w + 5c)$ **19.** Perfect square trinomial **21.** Neither **23.** Perfect square trinomial **25.** Neither **27.** Difference of two squares **29.** Perfect square trinomial **31.** $(x + 1)^2$ **33.** $(a + 3)^2$ **35.** $(x + 6)^2$ **37.** $(a - 2)^2$ **39.** $(2w + 1)^2$ **41.** $(4x - 1)^2$ **43.** $(2t + 5)^2$ **45.** $(3w + 7)^2$ **47.** $(n + t)^2$ **49.** $5(x - 5)(x + 5)$ **51.** $-2(x - 3)(x + 3)$ **53.** $a(a - b)(a + b)$ **55.** $3(x + 1)^2$ **57.** $-5(y - 5)^2$ **59.** $x(x - y)^2$ **61.** $-3(x - y)(x + y)$ **63.** $2a(x - 7)(x + 7)$ **65.** $3a(b - 3)^2$ **67.** $-4m(m - 3n)^2$ **69.** $(b + c)(x + y)$ **71.** $(x - 2)(x + 2)(x + 1)$ **73.** $(3 - x)(a - b)$ **75.** $(a^2 + 1)(a + 3)$ **77.** $(a + 3)(x + y)$ **79.** $(c - 3)(ab + 1)$ **81.** $(a + b)(x - 1)(x + 1)$ **83.** $(y + b)(y + 1)$ **85.** $6ay(a + 2y)^2$ **87.** $6ay(2a - y)(2a + y)$ **89.** $2a^2y(ay - 3)$ **91.** $(b - 4w)(a + 2w)$ **93.** $h = -16(t - 20)(t + 20)$, 6336 feet **95.** $y - 3$ inches

Section 5.3 Warm-Ups T T F F T F T F F F

1. We factored $ax^2 + bx + c$ with $a = 1$.
3. If there are no two integers that have a product of c and a sum of b, then $x^2 + bx + c$ is prime.
5. A polynomial is factored completely when all of the factors are prime polynomials.
7. $(x + 3)(x + 1)$ **9.** $(x + 3)(x + 6)$ **11.** $(a + 2)(a + 5)$

13. $(a-3)(a-4)$ **15.** $(b-6)(b+1)$ **17.** $(x-2)(x+5)$
19. $(y+2)(y+5)$ **21.** $(a-2)(a-4)$ **23.** $(m-8)(m-2)$
25. $(w+10)(w-1)$ **27.** $(w-4)(w+2)$ **29.** Prime
31. $(m+16)(m-1)$ **33.** Prime **35.** $(z-5)(z+5)$ **37.** Prime
39. $(m+2)(m+10)$ **41.** Prime **43.** $(m-18)(m+1)$ **45.** Prime
47. $(t+8)(t-3)$ **49.** $(t-6)(t+4)$ **51.** $(t-20)(t+10)$
53. $(x-15)(x+10)$ **55.** $(y+3)(y+10)$ **57.** $(x+3a)(x+2a)$
59. $(x-6y)(x+2y)$ **61.** $(x-12y)(x-y)$ **63.** Prime
65. $5x(x^2+1)$ **67.** $w(w-8)$ **69.** $2(w-9)(w+9)$
71. $-2(b^2+49)$ **73.** $(x+3)(x-3)(x-2)$ **75.** Prime
77. $x^2(w^2+9)$ **79.** $(w-9)^2$ **81.** $6(w-3)(w+1)$
83. $3(y^2+25)$ **85.** $(a+c)(x+y)$ **87.** $-2(x+2)(x+3)$
89. $2x^2(4-x)(4+x)$ **91.** $3(w+3)(w+6)$ **93.** $w(w^2+18w+36)$
95. $(3y+1)^2$ **97.** $8v(w+2)^2$ **99.** $6xy(x+3y)(x+2y)$
101. $(3w+5)(w+1)$ **103.** $-3y(y-1)^2$ **105.** $(a+3)(a^2+b)$
107. $x+4$ feet **109.** 3 feet and 5 feet **111.** d

Section 5.4 Warm-Ups T F T F T F F F F T
1. We factored ax^2+bx+c with $a \neq 1$.
3. If there are no two integers whose product is ac and whose sum is b, then ax^2+bx+c is prime.
5. 2 and 10 **7.** -6 and 2 **9.** 3 and 4 **11.** -2 and -9
13. -3 and 4 **15.** $(2x+1)(x+1)$ **17.** $(2x+1)(x+4)$
19. $(3t+1)(t+2)$ **21.** $(2x-1)(x+3)$ **23.** $(3x-1)(2x+3)$
25. Prime **27.** $(2x-3)(x-2)$ **29.** $(5b-3)(b-2)$
31. $(4y+1)(y-3)$ **33.** Prime **35.** $(4x+1)(2x-1)$
37. $(3t-1)(3t-2)$ **39.** $(5x+1)(3x+2)$ **41.** $(2a+3b)(2a+5b)$
43. $(3m-5n)(2m+n)$ **45.** $(x-y)(3x-5y)$ **47.** $(5a+1)(a+1)$
49. $(2x+1)(3x+1)$ **51.** $(5a+1)(a+2)$ **53.** $(2w+3)(2w+1)$
55. $(5x-2)(3x+1)$ **57.** $(4x-1)(2x-1)$ **59.** $(15x-1)(x-2)$
61. Prime **63.** $2(x^2+9x-45)$ **65.** $(3x-5)(x+2)$
67. $(5x+y)(2x-y)$ **69.** $(6a-b)(7a-b)$ **71.** $3x+1$
73. $x+2$ **75.** $2a-5$ **77.** $w(9w-1)(9w+1)$
79. $2(2w-5)(w+3)$ **81.** $3(2x+3)^2$ **83.** $(3w+5)(2w-7)$
85. $3z(x-3)(x+2)$ **87.** $3x(3x^2-7x+6)$ **89.** $(a+5b)(a-3b)$
91. $y^2(2x^2+x+3)$ **93.** $-t(3t+2)(2t-1)$ **95.** $2t^2(3t-2)(2t+1)$
97. $y(2x-y)(2x-3y)$ **99.** $-1(w-1)(4w-3)$
101. $-2a(2a-3b)(3a-b)$ **103.** $h=-8(2t+1)(t-3)$, 0 feet
105. a) ± 4 b) $\pm 8, \pm 16$ c) $\pm 1, \pm 7, \pm 13, \pm 29$

Section 5.5 Warm-Ups F F T T F T F T T F
1. If there is no remainder, then the dividend factors as the divisor times the quotient.
3. If you divide a^3+b^3 by $a+b$ there will be no remainder.
5. $a^3+b^3=(a+b)(a^2-ab+b^2)$
7. $(x+4)(x-3)(x+2)$ **9.** $(x-1)(x+3)(x+2)$
11. $(x-2)(x^2+2x+4)$ **13.** $(x+5)(x^2-x+2)$
15. $(x+1)(x^2+x+1)$ **17.** $(m-1)(m^2+m+1)$
19. $(x+2)(x^2-2x+4)$ **21.** $(a+5)(a^2-5a+25)$
23. $(c-7)(c^2+7c+49)$ **25.** $(2w+1)(4w^2-2w+1)$
27. $(2t-3)(4t^2+6t+9)$ **29.** $(x-y)(x^2+xy+y^2)$
31. $(2t+y)(4t^2-2ty+y^2)$ **33.** $(x-y)(x+y)(x^2+y^2)$
35. $(x-1)(x+1)(x^2+1)$ **37.** $(2b-1)(2b+1)(4b^2+1)$
39. $(a-3b)(a+3b)(a^2+9b^2)$ **41.** $2(x-3)(x+3)$
43. Prime **45.** $4(x+5)(x-3)$ **47.** $x(x+2)^2$
49. $5am(x^2+4)$ **51.** Prime **53.** $(3x+1)^2$ **55.** Prime
57. $(w-z)(w+z)(w^2+z^2)$ **59.** $y(3x+2)(2x-1)$
61. Prime **63.** $3(4a-1)^2$ **65.** $2(4m+1)(2m-1)$
67. $(s-2t)(s+2t)(s^2+4t^2)$ **69.** $(3a+4)^2$ **71.** $2(3x-1)(4x-3)$
73. $3(m^2+9)$ **75.** $3a(a-9)$ **77.** $2(2-x)(2+x)$ **79.** Prime
81. $x(6x^2-5x+12)$ **83.** $ab(a-2)(a+2)$ **85.** $(x-2)(x+2)^2$
87. $-7mn(m^2+4n^2)$ **89.** $2(x+2)(x^2-2x+4)$
91. $2w(w-2)(w^2+2w+4)$ **93.** $3w(a-3)^2$
95. $5(x-10)(x+10)$ **97.** $(2-w)(m+n)$
99. $3x(x+1)(x^2-x+1)$ **101.** $4(w^2+w-1)$
103. $a^2(a+10)(a-3)$ **105.** $aw(2w-3)^2$ **107.** $(t+3)^2$
109. Length $x+5$ cm, width $x+3$ cm
111. $(-1+1)^3=(-1)^3+1^3$, $(1+2)^3 \neq 1^3+2^3$

Section 5.6 Warm-Ups F F T T T F T T T F
1. A quadratic equation has the form $ax^2+bx+c=0$ with $a \neq 0$.
3. The zero factor property says that if $ab=0$ then $a=0$ or $b=0$.
5. Dividing each side by a variable is not usually done because the variable might have a value of zero.
7. $-4, -5$ **9.** $-\frac{5}{2}, \frac{4}{3}$ **11.** $-2, -1$ **13.** 2, 7 **15.** $-4, 6$
17. $-1, \frac{1}{2}$ **19.** 0, 1 **21.** $0, -7$ **23.** $-5, 4$ **25.** $\frac{1}{2}, -3$
27. $0, -8$ **29.** $-\frac{9}{2}, 2$ **31.** $\frac{2}{3}, -4$ **33.** 5 **35.** $\frac{3}{2}$ **37.** $0, -3, 3$
39. $-4, -2, 2$ **41.** $-1, 1, 3$ **43.** 0, 4, 5 **45.** $-4, 4$ **47.** $-3, 3$
49. $0, -1, 1$ **51.** $-3, -2$ **53.** $-\frac{3}{2}, -4$ **55.** $-6, 4$ **57.** $-1, 3$
59. $-4, 2$ **61.** $-5, -3, 5$ **63.** Length 12 ft, width 5 ft
65. Width 5 ft, length 12 ft **67.** 2 and 3, or -3 and -2 **69.** 5 and 6
71. $-8, -6, -4$, or 4, 6, 8 **73.** -2 and -1, or 3 and 4
75. -7 and -2, or 2 and 7 **77.** Length 12 feet, width 6 feet
79. 9 meters and 12 meters
81. a) 25 sec b) last 5 sec c) increasing **83.** 6 sec
85. Base 6 in., height 13 in. **87.** 20 ft by 20 ft **89.** 80 ft
91. 3 yd by 3 yd, 6 yd by 6 yd **93.** 12 mi **95.** 25%

Enriching Your Mathematical Word Power
1. a **2.** d **3.** c **4.** a **5.** c **6.** b **7.** c **8.** a
9. d **10.** c

Review Exercises
1. $2^4 \cdot 3^2$ **3.** $2 \cdot 29$ **5.** $2 \cdot 3 \cdot 5^2$ **7.** 18 **9.** $4x$ **11.** $x+2$
13. $-a+10$ **15.** $a(2-a)$ **17.** $3x^2y(2y-3x^3)$
19. $3y(x^2-4x-3y)$ **21.** $(y-20)(y+20)$ **23.** $(w-4)^2$
25. $(2y+5)^2$ **27.** $(r-2)^2$ **29.** $2t(2t-3)^2$ **31.** $(x+6y)^2$
33. $(x-y)(x+5)$ **35.** $(b+8)(b-3)$ **37.** $(r-10)(r+6)$
39. $(y-11)(y+5)$ **41.** $(u+20)(u+6)$ **43.** $3t^2(t+4)$
45. $5w(w^2+5w+5)$ **47.** $ab(2a+b)(a+b)$
49. $x(3x-y)(3x+y)$ **51.** $(7t-3)(2t+1)$ **53.** $(3x+1)(2x-7)$
55. $(3p+4)(2p-1)$ **57.** $-2p(5p+2)(3p-2)$
59. $(6x+y)(x-5y)$ **61.** $2(4x+y)^2$ **63.** $5x(x^2+8)$
65. $(3x-1)(3x+2)$ **67.** Prime **69.** $(x+2)(x-1)(x+1)$
71. $xy(x-16y)$ **73.** Prime **75.** $(a+1)^2$ **77.** $(x^2+1)(x-1)$
79. $(a+2)(a+b)$ **81.** $-2(x-6)(x-2)$
83. $(m-10)(m^2+10m+100)$ **85.** $(p-q)(p+q)(p^2+q^2)$
87. $(x+2)(x^2-2x+5)$ **89.** $(x+4)(x+5)(x-3)$
91. 0, 5 **93.** 0, 5 **95.** $-\frac{1}{2}, 5$ **97.** $-4, -3, 3$ **99.** $-2, -1$
101. $-\frac{1}{2}, \frac{1}{4}$ **103.** 5, 11 **105.** 6 in. by 8 in.
107. $v=k(R-r)(R+r)$ **109.** 6 ft

Chapter 5 Test
1. $2 \cdot 3 \cdot 11$ **2.** $2^4 \cdot 3 \cdot 7$ **3.** 16 **4.** 6 **5.** $3y^2$ **6.** $6ab$
7. $5x(x-2)$ **8.** $6y^2(x^2+2x+2)$ **9.** $3ab(a-b)(a+b)$
10. $(a+6)(a-4)$ **11.** $(2b-7)^2$ **12.** $3m(m^2+9)$

13. $(a+b)(x-y)$ **14.** $(a-5)(x-2)$ **15.** $(3b-5)(2b+1)$
16. $(m+2n)^2$ **17.** $(2a-3)(a-5)$ **18.** $z(z+3)(z+6)$
19. $(x+5)(x^2-5x+25)$ **20.** $a(a-b)(a^2+ab+b^2)$
21. $(x-1)(x-2)(x-3)$ **22.** -3 **23.** $\frac{3}{2}, -4$ **24.** $0, -2, 2$
25. $-2, \frac{5}{6}$ **26.** Length 12 ft, width 9 ft **27.** -4 and 8

Making Connections A Review of Chapters 1–5

1. -1 **2.** 2 **3.** -3 **4.** 57 **5.** 16 **6.** 7 **7.** $2x^2$ **8.** $3x$
9. $3+x$ **10.** $6x$ **11.** $24yz$ **12.** $6y+8z$ **13.** $4z-1$ **14.** t^6
15. t^{10} **16.** $4t^6$
17. $(-\infty, -9)$

−13 −12 −11 −10 −9 −8 −7

18. $[3, \infty)$

1 2 3 4 5 6 7

19. $(12, \infty)$

10 11 12 13 14 15 16

20. $(-\infty, 600)$

0 200 400 600 800

21. $\left\{\frac{3}{2}\right\}$ **22.** $\left\{-\frac{1}{2}\right\}$ **23.** $\{3, -5\}$ **24.** $\left\{\frac{3}{2}, -\frac{1}{2}\right\}$ **25.** $\{0, 3\}$
26. $\{0, 1\}$ **27.** R **28.** No solution or $\emptyset$ **29.** $\{10\}$
30. $\{40\}$ **31.** $\{-3, 3\}$ **32.** $\left\{-5, \frac{3}{2}\right\}$
33. Length 21 ft, width 13.5 ft

Chapter 6

Section 6.1 Warm-Ups F T T F F T T F F T

1. A rational number is a ratio of two integers with the denominator not 0.
3. A rational number is reduced to lowest terms by dividing the numerator and denominator by the GCF.
5. The quotient rule is used in reducing ratios of monomials.
7. -3 **9.** 5 **11.** $-0.6, 9, 401, -199$ **13.** -1
15. $\frac{5}{3}$ **17.** $4, -4$ **19.** Any number can be used. **21.** $\frac{2}{9}$
23. $\frac{7}{15}$ **25.** $\frac{2a}{5}$ **27.** $\frac{13}{5w}$ **29.** $\frac{3x+1}{3}$ **31.** $\frac{2}{3}$ **33.** $w-7$
35. $\frac{a-1}{a+1}$ **37.** $\frac{x+1}{2(x-1)}$ **39.** $\frac{x+3}{7}$ **41.** x^3 **43.** $\frac{1}{z^5}$
45. $-2x^2$ **47.** $\frac{-3m^3n^2}{2}$ **49.** $\frac{-3}{4c^3}$ **51.** $\frac{5c}{3a^4b^{16}}$ **53.** $\frac{35}{44}$
55. $\frac{11}{8}$ **57.** $\frac{21}{10x^4}$ **59.** $\frac{33a^4}{16}$ **61.** -1 **63.** $-h-t$
65. $\frac{-2}{3h+g}$ **67.** $\frac{-x-2}{x+3}$ **69.** -1 **71.** $\frac{-2y}{3}$ **73.** $\frac{x+2}{2-x}$
75. $\frac{-6}{a+3}$ **77.** $\frac{x^4}{2}$ **79.** $\frac{x+2}{2x}$ **81.** -1 **83.** $\frac{-2}{c+2}$
85. $\frac{x+2}{x-2}$ **87.** $\frac{-2}{x+3}$ **89.** q^2 **91.** $\frac{u+2}{u-8}$
93. $\frac{a^2+2a+4}{2}$ **95.** $y+2$ **97.** $\frac{300}{x+10}$ hr
99. $\frac{4.50}{x+4}$ dollars/lb **101.** $\frac{1}{x}$ pool/hr
103. a) \$0.75 **b)** \$0.75, \$0.63, \$0.615 **c)** Approaches \$0.60

Section 6.2 Warm-Ups T T T F T F F T T T

1. Rational numbers are multiplied by multiplying their numerators and their denominators.
3. Reducing can be done before multiplying rational numbers or expressions.
5. $\frac{5}{9}$ **7.** $\frac{7}{9}$ **9.** $\frac{18}{5}$ **11.** $\frac{42}{5}$ **13.** $\frac{5}{6}$ **15.** $\frac{a}{44}$ **17.** $\frac{-x^5}{a^3}$
19. $\frac{18t^8y^7}{w^4}$ **21.** $\frac{5}{7}$ **23.** $\frac{2a}{a-b}$ **25.** $3x-9$ **27.** $\frac{8a+8}{5(a^2+1)}$
29. $\frac{1}{2}$ **31.** 30 **33.** $\frac{2}{3}$ **35.** $\frac{10}{9}$ **37.** $\frac{x}{2}$ **39.** $\frac{7x}{2}$ **41.** $\frac{2m^2}{3n^6}$
43. -3 **45.** $\frac{2}{x+2}$ **47.** $\frac{1}{4(t-5)}$ **49.** x^2-1 **51.** $2x-4y$
53. $\frac{x+2}{2}$ **55.** $\frac{x^2+9}{15}$ **57.** $9x+9y$ **59.** -3 **61.** $\frac{a+b}{a}$
63. $\frac{2b}{a}$ **65.** $\frac{y}{x}$ **67.** $\frac{-a^6b^8}{2}$ **69.** $\frac{1}{9m^3n}$ **71.** $\frac{x^2+5x}{3x-1}$
73. $\frac{a^3+8}{2(a-2)}$ **75.** 1 **77.** $\frac{m^2+6m+9}{(m-3)(m+k)}$ **79.** $\frac{13.1}{x}$ mi
81. 5 square meters **83. a)** $\frac{1}{8}$ **b)** $\frac{4}{3}$ **c)** $\frac{2x}{3}$ **d)** $\frac{3x}{4}$

Section 6.3 Warm-Ups F F T T F F F F T T

1. We can build up a denominator by multiplying the numerator and denominator of a fraction by the same nonzero number.
3. For fractions, the LCD is the smallest number that is a multiple of all of the denominators.
5. $\frac{9}{27}$ **7.** $\frac{12}{16}$ **9.** $\frac{12}{6}$ **11.** $\frac{5a}{ax}$ **13.** $\frac{14x}{2x}$ **15.** $\frac{15t}{3bt}$
17. $\frac{-36z^2}{8awz}$ **19.** $\frac{10a^2}{15a^3}$ **21.** $\frac{8xy^3}{10x^2y^5}$ **23.** $\frac{10}{2x+6}$ **25.** $\frac{-20}{-8x-8}$
27. $\frac{-32ab}{20b^2-20b^3}$ **29.** $\frac{3x-6}{x^2-4}$ **31.** $\frac{3x^2+3x}{x^2+2x+1}$ **33.** $\frac{y^2-y-30}{y^2+y-20}$
35. 48 **37.** 180 **39.** $30a^2$ **41.** $12a^4b^6$
43. $(x-4)(x+4)^2$ **45.** $x(x+2)(x-2)$ **47.** $2x(x-4)(x+4)$
49. $\frac{4}{24}, \frac{9}{24}$ **51.** $\frac{3}{6x}, \frac{5}{6x}$ **53.** $\frac{4b}{6ab}, \frac{3a}{6ab}$ **55.** $\frac{9b}{252ab}, \frac{20a}{252ab}$
57. $\frac{2x^3}{6x^5}, \frac{9}{6x^5}$ **59.** $\frac{4x^4}{36x^3y^5z}, \frac{3y^6z}{36x^3y^5z}, \frac{6xy^4z}{36x^3y^5z}$
61. $\frac{2x^2+4x}{(x-3)(x+2)}, \frac{5x^2-15x}{(x-3)(x+2)}$ **63.** $\frac{4}{a-6}, \frac{-5}{a-6}$
65. $\frac{x^2-3x}{(x-3)^2(x+3)}, \frac{5x^2+15x}{(x-3)^2(x+3)}$
67. $\frac{w^2+3w+2}{(w-5)(w+3)(w+1)}, \frac{-2w^2-6w}{(w-5)(w+3)(w+1)}$
69. $\frac{-5x-10}{6(x-2)(x+2)}, \frac{6x}{6(x-2)(x+2)}, \frac{9x-18}{6(x-2)(x+2)}$
71. $\frac{2q+8}{(2q+1)(q-3)(q+4)}, \frac{3q-9}{(2q+1)(q-3)(q+4)}, \frac{8q+4}{(2q+1)(q-3)(q+4)}$
73. Identical denominators are needed for addition and subtraction.

Section 6.4 Warm-Ups F T T T T F T F T F

1. We can add rational numbers with identical denominators as follows: $\frac{a}{c} + \frac{b}{c} = \frac{a+b}{c}$.
3. The LCD is the smallest number that is a multiple of all denominators.
5. $\frac{1}{5}$ **7.** $\frac{3}{4}$ **9.** $-\frac{2}{3}$ **11.** $-\frac{3}{4}$ **13.** $\frac{5}{9}$ **15.** $\frac{103}{144}$ **17.** $-\frac{31}{40}$
19. $\frac{5}{24}$ **21.** $\frac{1}{x}$ **23.** $\frac{5}{w}$ **25.** 3 **27.** -2 **29.** $\frac{3}{h}$

31. $\frac{x-4}{x+2}$ **33.** $\frac{3}{2a}$ **35.** $\frac{5x}{6}$ **37.** $\frac{6m}{5}$ **39.** $\frac{2x+y}{xy}$
41. $\frac{17}{10a}$ **43.** $\frac{w}{36}$ **45.** $\frac{b^2-4ac}{4a}$ **47.** $\frac{2w+3z}{w^2z^2}$
49. $\frac{2x+2}{x(x+2)}$ **51.** $\frac{-x-3}{x(x+1)}$ **53.** $\frac{3a+b}{(a-b)(a+b)}$
55. $\frac{15-4x}{5x(x+1)}$ **57.** $\frac{a^2+5a}{(a-3)(a+3)}$ **59.** 0 **61.** $\frac{7}{2(a-1)}$
63. $\frac{-2x+1}{(x-5)(x+2)(x-2)}$ **65.** $\frac{7x+17}{(x+2)(x-1)(x+3)}$
67. $\frac{bc+ac+ab}{abc}$ **69.** $\frac{2x^2-x-4}{x(x-1)(x+2)}$ **71.** $\frac{a+51}{6a(a-3)}$
73. a) F b) A c) E d) B e) D f) C **75.** $\frac{p+6}{p(p+4)}$
77. $\frac{6}{(a+1)(a+3)}$ **79.** $\frac{1}{(b+1)(b+2)}$ **81.** $\frac{-1}{2(t+2)}$
83. $\frac{11}{x}$ feet **85.** $\frac{315x+600}{x(x+5)}$ hours, 5 hours **87.** $\frac{4x+6}{x(x+3)}$ job, $\frac{5}{9}$ job

Section 6.5 Warm-Ups F T F F F F F T T T
1. A complex fraction is a fraction that has fractions in its numerator, denominator, or both.
3. $\frac{3}{5}$ **5.** $-\frac{10}{3}$ **7.** $\frac{22}{7}$ **9.** $\frac{2}{3}$ **11.** $\frac{14}{17}$ **13.** $\frac{45}{23}$ **15.** $\frac{1}{2}$
17. $\frac{3a+b}{a-3b}$ **19.** $\frac{5a-3}{3a+1}$ **21.** $\frac{x^2-4x}{2(3x^2-1)}$ **23.** $\frac{10b}{3b^2-4}$ **25.** $\frac{1}{3}$
27. $\frac{y-2}{3y+4}$ **29.** $\frac{x^2-2x+4}{x^2-3x-1}$ **31.** $\frac{5x-14}{2x-7}$ **33.** $\frac{a-6}{3a-1}$
35. $\frac{-3m+12}{4m-3}$ **37.** $\frac{-w+5}{9w+1}$ **39.** −1 **41.** $\frac{a+2}{a+4}$ **43.** $\frac{3}{2x-1}$
45. $\frac{x-2}{x+3}$ **47.** $\frac{6x-27}{2(2x-3)}$ **49.** $\frac{2x^2}{3y}$ **51.** $\frac{a^2+7a+6}{a+3}$ **53.** $1-x$
55. $\frac{32}{95}, \frac{11}{35}$ **57.** a) Neither b) $\frac{8}{13}, \frac{13}{21}$ c) Converging to 0.61803

Section 6.6 Warm-Ups F F F F F T T T T T
1. The first step is usually to multiply each side by the LCD.
3. An extraneous solution is a number that appears to be a solution when we solve an equation, but it does not check in the original equation.
5. −4 **7.** 12 **9.** 30 **11.** 5 **13.** 4 **15.** $\frac{2}{5}$ **17.** $\frac{3}{7}$
19. 4 **21.** 4 **23.** 3 **25.** 2 **27.** −5, 2 **29.** −3, 2 **31.** 2, 3
33. −3, 3 **35.** 2 **37.** No solution **39.** No solution **41.** 3
43. 10 **45.** 0 **47.** −5, 5 **49.** 3, 5 **51.** 1 **53.** 3
55. 0 **57.** 4 **59.** −20 **61.** 3 **63.** 3 **65.** $54\frac{6}{11}$ mm

Section 6.7 Warm-Ups T F F T T T F F F T
1. A ratio is a comparison of two numbers.
3. Equivalent ratios are ratios that are equivalent as fractions.
5. In the proportion $\frac{a}{b} = \frac{c}{d}$ the means are b and c and the extremes are a and d.
7. $\frac{2}{3}$ **9.** $\frac{4}{3}$ **11.** $\frac{5}{7}$ **13.** $\frac{8}{15}$ **15.** $\frac{7}{2}$ **17.** $\frac{9}{14}$ **19.** $\frac{5}{2}$
21. $\frac{15}{1}$ **23.** 3 to 2 **25.** 9 to 16 **27.** 31 to 1 **29.** 2 to 3 **31.** 6
33. $-\frac{2}{5}$ **35.** $-\frac{27}{5}$ **37.** 5 **39.** $-\frac{3}{4}$ **41.** $\frac{5}{4}$ **43.** 108
45. 176,000 **47.** Lions 85, Tigers 51
49. 40 luxury cars, 60 sports cars **51.** 84 in. **53.** 15 min
55. $\frac{1610}{3}$ or 536.7 mi **57.** 3920 lbs, 2000 lbs **59.** 6000
61. a) 3 to 17 b) $\frac{201}{14}$ or 14.4 lbs **63.** 4074

Section 6.8 Warm-Ups T T F T T F F T F T
1. $y = 2x - 5$ **3.** $y = -\frac{1}{2}x - 2$ **5.** $y = mx - mb - a$
7. $y = -\frac{1}{3}x - \frac{1}{3}$ **9.** $C = \frac{B}{A}$ **11.** $p = \frac{a}{1+am}$ **13.** $m_1 = \frac{r^2F}{km_2}$
15. $a = \frac{bf}{b-f}$ **17.** $r = \frac{S-a}{S}$ **19.** $P_2 = \frac{P_1V_1T_2}{T_1V_2}$ **21.** $h = \frac{3V}{4\pi r^2}$
23. $\frac{5}{12}$ **25.** $-\frac{6}{23}$ **27.** $\frac{128}{3}$ **29.** −6 **31.** $\frac{6}{5}$
33. Marcie 4 mph, Frank 3 mph **35.** Bob 25 mph, Pat 20 mph
37. 5 mph **39.** 6 hours **41.** 40 minutes **43.** 1 hour 36 minutes
45. Bananas 8 pounds, apples 10 pounds **47.** 80 gallons
49. 140 mph **51.** 10 mph **53.** Ben 15 mph, Jerry 7.5 mph
55. 1800 miles **57.** 4 hours **59.** 1.2 hours or 1 hour 12 minutes
61. 24 minutes

Enriching Your Mathematical Word Power
1. b **2.** a **3.** a **4.** d **5.** a **6.** b **7.** d **8.** a
9. c **10.** d

Review Exercises
1. $\frac{6}{7}$ **3.** $\frac{c^2}{4a^2}$ **5.** $\frac{2w-3}{3w-4}$ **7.** $-\frac{x+1}{3}$ **9.** $\frac{1}{2}k$ **11.** $\frac{2x}{3y}$
13. $a^2 - a - 6$ **15.** $\frac{1}{2}$ **17.** 108 **19.** $24a^7b^3$ **21.** $12x(x-1)$
23. $(x+1)(x-2)(x+2)$ **25.** $\frac{15}{36}$ **27.** $\frac{10x}{15x^2y}$ **29.** $\frac{-10}{12-2y}$
31. $\frac{x^2+x}{x^2-1}$ **33.** $\frac{29}{63}$ **35.** $\frac{3x-4}{x}$ **37.** $\frac{2a-b}{a^2b^2}$
39. $\frac{27a^2-8a-15}{(2a-3)(3a-2)}$ **41.** $\frac{3}{a-8}$ **43.** $\frac{3x+8}{2(x+2)(x-2)}$
45. $-\frac{3}{14}$ **47.** $\frac{6b+4a}{3(a-6b)}$ **49.** $\frac{-2x+9}{3x-1}$ **51.** $\frac{x^2+x-2}{-4x+13}$
53. $-\frac{15}{2}$ **55.** 9 **57.** −3 **59.** $\frac{21}{2}$ **61.** 5
63. 8 **65.** 56 cups water, 28 cups rice **67.** $y = mx + b$
69. $m = \frac{1}{F-v}$ **71.** $y = 4x - 13$ **73.** 200 hours
75. Bert 60 cars, Ernie 50 cars **77.** 27.83 million tons
79. $\frac{10}{2x}$ **81.** $\frac{-2}{5-a}$ **83.** $\frac{3x}{x}$ **85.** $2m$ **87.** $\frac{1}{6}$ **89.** $\frac{1}{a+1}$
91. $\frac{5-a}{5a}$ **93.** $\frac{a-2}{2}$ **95.** $b-a$ **97.** $\frac{1}{10a}$ **99.** $\frac{3}{2x}$
101. $\frac{4+y}{6xy}$ **103.** $\frac{8}{a-5}$ **105.** −1, 2 **107.** $-\frac{5}{3}$ **109.** 6 **111.** $\frac{1}{2}$
113. $\frac{3x+7}{(x-5)(x+5)(x+1)}$ **115.** $\frac{-5a}{(a-3)(a+3)(a+2)}$ **117.** $\frac{2}{5}$

Chapter 6 Test
1. −1, 1 **2.** $\frac{2}{3}$ **3.** 0 **4.** $-\frac{14}{45}$ **5.** $\frac{1+3y}{y}$ **6.** $\frac{4}{a-2}$
7. $\frac{-x+4}{(x+2)(x-2)(x-1)}$ **8.** $\frac{2}{3}$ **9.** $\frac{-2}{a+b}$ **10.** $\frac{a^3}{18b^4}$

11. $-\frac{4}{3}$ **12.** $\frac{-3x+4}{2(x-3)}$ **13.** $\frac{15}{7}$ **14.** 2, 3 **15.** 12
16. $y = -\frac{1}{5}x + \frac{13}{5}$ **17.** $c = \frac{3M - bd}{b}$ **18.** 29 **19.** 7.2 minutes
20. Brenda 15 mph and Randy 20 mph, or Brenda 10 mph and Randy 15 mph
21. \$72 billion

Making Connections A Review of Chapters 1–6

1. $\frac{7}{3}$ **2.** $-\frac{10}{3}$ **3.** -2 **4.** No solution **5.** 0 **6.** $-4, -2$
7. $-1, 0, 1$ **8.** $-\frac{15}{2}$ **9.** $-6, 6$ **10.** $-2, 4$ **11.** 5 **12.** 3
13. $y = \frac{c-2x}{3}$ **14.** $y = \frac{1}{2}x + \frac{1}{2}$ **15.** $y = \frac{c}{2-a}$ **16.** $y = \frac{AB}{C}$
17. $y = 3B - 3A$ **18.** $y = \frac{6A}{5}$ **19.** $y = \frac{8}{3-5a}$
20. $y = 0$ or $y = B$ **21.** $y = \frac{2A - hb}{h}$ **22.** $y = -\frac{b}{2}$
23. 64 **24.** 16 **25.** 49 **26.** 121 **27.** $-2x - 2$
28. $2a^2 - 11a + 15$ **29.** x^4 **30.** $\frac{2x+1}{5}$ **31.** $\frac{1}{2x}$ **32.** $\frac{x+2}{2x}$
33. $\frac{x}{2}$ **34.** $\frac{x-2}{2x}$ **35.** $-\frac{7}{5}$ **36.** $\frac{3a}{4}$ **37.** $x^2 - 64$
38. $3x^3 - 21x$ **39.** $10a^{14}$ **40.** x^{10} **41.** $k^2 - 12k + 36$
42. $j^2 + 10j + 25$ **43.** -1 **44.** $3x^2 - 4x$
45. $P = \frac{r+2}{(1+r)^2}$, \$1.81, \$7.72

Chapter 7

Section 7.1 Warm-Ups T F F T T T T T T T
1. The intersection point of the graphs is the solution to an independent system.
3. The graphing method can be very inaccurate.
5. If the equation you get after substituting turns out to be incorrect, such as $0 = 9$, then the system has no solution.
7. $\{(1, 2)\}$ **9.** $\{(0, -1)\}$ **11.** $\{(2, -1)\}$ **13.** $\varnothing$
15. $\{(x, y) \mid x + 2y = 8\}$ **17.** $\{(-1, 2)\}$ **19.** $\varnothing$ **21.** c **23.** b
25. $\{(8, 3)\}$, independent **27.** $\{(-3, 2)\}$, independent
29. $\{(20, 10)\}$, independent **31.** $\varnothing$, inconsistent
33. $\{(x, y) \mid y = 2x - 5\}$, dependent **35.** $\{(5, -1)\}$, independent
37. $\{(7, 7)\}$, independent **39.** $\{(15, 25)\}$, independent
41. $\{(0, 0)\}$, independent **43.** $\{(x, y) \mid 3y - 2x = -3\}$, dependent
45. $\varnothing$, inconsistent
47. $\left\{\left(\frac{6}{17}, \frac{15}{17}\right)\right\}$ **49.** $\left\{\left(\frac{9}{2}, -\frac{1}{2}\right)\right\}$ **51.** $\left\{\left(\frac{1}{2}, \frac{1}{4}\right)\right\}$ **53.** $\left\{\left(\frac{3}{2}, -\frac{5}{2}\right)\right\}$
55. $\left\{\left(-\frac{2}{9}, \frac{1}{6}\right)\right\}$ **57.** $\left\{\left(-\frac{1}{7}, \frac{2}{7}\right)\right\}$ **59.** $\left\{\left(-\frac{1}{14}, \frac{5}{28}\right)\right\}$
61. $\{(0.8, 0.7)\}$ **63.** Length 27 ft, width 15 ft
65. Length 10 ft, width 4 ft **67.** 3.5 and 6.5 **69.** -9.5 and 10.5
71. 120 tickets for \$200, 80 tickets for \$250
73. 55 tickets for \$6, 110 tickets for \$11
75. \$30,000 at 5%, \$10,000 at 8% **77.** \$14,000 at 5%, \$16,000 at 10%
79. -12 and 14 **81.** 94 toasters, 6 vacation coupons
83. State tax \$3553, federal tax \$28,934 **85.** \$20,000
87. **a)** \$500,000 **b)** \$300,000 **c)** 20,000 **d)** \$400,000 **89.** a
91. **a)** (2.8, 2.6) **b)** (1.0, −0.2)

Section 7.2 Warm-Ups T F T T F T T F T T
1. In this section we learned the addition method.
3. In some cases we multiply one or both of the equations on each side to change the coefficients of the variable that we are trying to eliminate.
5. If an identity, such as $0 = 0$, results from addition of the equations, then the equations are dependent.
7. $\{(8, -1)\}$ **9.** $\{(5, -7)\}$
11. $\left\{\left(\frac{3}{8}, -\frac{31}{8}\right)\right\}$ **13.** $\{(-1, 3)\}$ **15.** $\left\{\left(\frac{7}{9}, \frac{2}{3}\right)\right\}$ **17.** $\{(-1, -3)\}$
19. $\{(-2, -5)\}$ **21.** $\{(22, 26)\}$ **23.** $\varnothing$, inconsistent
25. $\{(x, y) \mid 5x - y = 1\}$, dependent **27.** $\left\{\left(\frac{5}{2}, 0\right)\right\}$, independent
29. $\{(12, 6)\}$ **31.** $\{(-8, 6)\}$ **33.** $\{(16, 12)\}$ **35.** $\left\{\left(\frac{1}{2}, \frac{1}{3}\right)\right\}$
37. $\{(12, 7)\}$ **39.** $\{(400, 800)\}$ **41.** $\{(1.5, 1.25)\}$ **43.** $\left\{\left(\frac{3}{4}, \frac{2}{3}\right)\right\}$
45. $\{(5, 6)\}$ **47.** $\{(2, -17)\}$ **49.** $\{(0, 1)\}$ **51.** $\{(3, 4)\}$
53. $\left\{\left(\frac{1}{2}, \frac{1}{3}\right)\right\}$ **55.** $\varnothing$ **57.** $\{(x, y) \mid y = x\}$ **59.** $a = -1$
61. $a = 2$, $b = -1$ **63.** \$1.40 **65.** 1380 students
67. 31 dimes, 4 nickels
69. **a)** 20 pounds chocolate, 30 pounds peanut butter
b) 20 pounds chocolate, 30 pounds peanut butter
71. 4 hours **73.** 80% **75.** Width 150 meters, length 200 meters

Section 7.3 Warm-Ups F F T F F T T F F F
1. A linear equation in three variables is an equation of the form $Ax + By + Cz = D$ where A, B, and C cannot all be zero.
3. A solution to a system of linear equations in three variables is an ordered triple that satisfies all of the equations in the system.
5. The graph of a linear equation in three variables is a plane in a three-dimensional coordinate system.
7. $\{(2, 3, 4)\}$ **9.** $\{(2, 3, 5)\}$ **11.** $\{(1, 2, 3)\}$ **13.** $\{(1, 2, -1)\}$
15. $\{(1, 3, 2)\}$ **17.** $\{(1, -5, 3)\}$ **19.** $\{(-1, 2, -1)\}$
21. $\{(-1, -2, 4)\}$ **23.** $\{(1, 3, 5)\}$ **25.** $\{(3, 4, 5)\}$ **27.** $\varnothing$
29. $\{(x, y, z) \mid x + y - z = 2\}$ **31.** $\varnothing$
33. $\{(x, y, z) \mid -x + 2y - 3z = -6\}$ **35.** $\varnothing$
37. $\{(x, y, z) \mid 5x + 4y - 2z = 150\}$ **39.** $\{(0.1, 0.3, 2)\}$
41. Chevrolet \$20,000, Ford \$22,000, Toyota \$24,000
43. First 10 hr, second 12 hr, third 14 hr
45. \$1500 stocks, \$4500 bonds, \$6000 mutual fund
47. Anna 108 pounds, Bob 118 pounds, Chris 92 pounds
49. 3 nickels, 6 dimes, 4 quarters
51. \$24,000 teaching, \$18,000 painting, \$6000 royalties
53. Edwin 24, father 51, grandfather 84

Section 7.4 Warm-Ups T T T F T F F F T F
1. A matrix is a rectangular array of numbers.
3. The size of a matrix is the number of rows and columns.
5. An augmented matrix is a matrix where the entries in the first column are the coefficients of x, the entries in the second column are the coefficients of y, and the entries in the third column are the constants from a system of two linear equations in two unknowns.
7. 2×2 **9.** 3×2 **11.** 3×1
13. $\left[\begin{array}{rr|r} 2 & -3 & 9 \\ -3 & 1 & -1 \end{array}\right]$ **15.** $\left[\begin{array}{rrr|r} 1 & -1 & 1 & 1 \\ 1 & 1 & -2 & 3 \\ 0 & 1 & -3 & 4 \end{array}\right]$
17. $5x + y = -1$
$2x - 3y = 0$

19. $\begin{aligned} x \quad &= 6 \\ -x + z &= -3 \\ x + y &= 1 \end{aligned}$

21. $\left[\begin{array}{cc|c} 1 & 0 & 6 \\ 0 & 2 & 4 \end{array}\right]$ **23.** $\left[\begin{array}{cc|c} 1 & 3 & 4 \\ 2 & -4 & 3 \end{array}\right]$

25. $\left[\begin{array}{cc|c} 1 & 0 & -3 \\ 0 & 2 & 1 \end{array}\right]$ **27.** $\left[\begin{array}{cc|c} 1 & 2 & 3 \\ 0 & 7 & 11 \end{array}\right]$

29. $R_1 \leftrightarrow R_2$

31. $\frac{1}{5}R_2 \to R_2$ **33.** $\{(1, 4)\}$

35. $\{(-8, 2)\}$ **37.** $\{(5, -2)\}$ **39.** $\{(1, 2)\}$

41. $\{(4, 5)\}$ **43.** $\{(1, -1)\}$ **45.** $\{(7, 6)\}$ **47.** $\varnothing$

49. $\{(x, y) \mid x + 2y = 1\}$ **51.** $\{(2, 4, 2)\}$ **53.** $\{(1, 2, 3)\}$

55. $\{(1, 1, 1)\}$ **57.** $\{(1, 2, 0)\}$ **59.** $\{(1, 0, 1)\}$

61. $\{(x, y, z) \mid x - y + z = 1\}$ **63.** $\varnothing$ **65.** 5 and 7

67. Length 11 in., width 8.5 in.

69. Buys for \$14, sells for \$16

71. 45 four-wheel cars, 2 three-wheel cars, and 3 two-wheel motorcycles

Section 7.5 Warm-Ups T F F T T T T T T T

1. A determinant is a real number associated with a square matrix.

3. Cramer's rule works on systems that have exactly one solution.

5. A minor for an element is obtained by deleting the row and column of the element and finding the determinant of the 2 × 2 matrix that remains.

7. -1 **9.** -3 **11.** -14 **13.** 0.4 **15.** $\{(2, 6)\}$ **17.** $\{(-8, 8)\}$

19. $\{(1, -3)\}$ **21.** $\{(1, 1)\}$ **23.** $\left\{\left(\frac{23}{13}, \frac{9}{13}\right)\right\}$ **25.** $\{(10, 15)\}$

27. $\left\{\left(\frac{27}{4}, \frac{13}{2}\right)\right\}$ **29.** 11 **31.** 4 **33.** 3 **35.** 1 **37.** -7

39. -1 **41.** 9 **43.** 5 **45.** 22 **47.** 6 **49.** 70

51. 25 **53.** $\{(1, 2, 3)\}$ **55.** $\{(-1, 1, 2)\}$ **57.** $\{(-3, 2, 1)\}$

59. $\left\{\left(\frac{3}{2}, \frac{1}{2}, 2\right)\right\}$ **61.** $\{(0, 1, -1)\}$

63. **a)** 9 servings peas, 11 servings beets
b) 9 servings peas, 11 servings beets

65. Milk \$2.40, magazine \$2.25 **67.** 12 singles, 10 doubles

69. Gary 39, Harry 34 **71.** Square 10 feet, triangle $\frac{40}{3}$ feet

73. 10 gallons of 10% solution, 20 gallons of 25% solution

75. Mimi 36 pounds, Mitzi 32 pounds, Cassandra 107 pounds

77. 39°, 51°, 90° **79.** Use another method.

81. No. These are nonlinear equations.

Enriching Your Mathematical Word Power

1. c **2.** a **3.** a **4.** d **5.** b **6.** c **7.** a **8.** c **9.** d
10. b **11.** a **12.** d

Review Exercises

1. $\{(1, 1)\}$, independent **3.** $\{(x, y) \mid x + 2y = 4\}$, dependent

5. $\varnothing$, inconsistent **7.** $\{(-3, 2)\}$, independent **9.** $\varnothing$, inconsistent

11. $\{(x, y) \mid 2x - y = 3\}$, dependent **13.** $\{(30, 12)\}$, independent

15. $\left\{\left(\frac{1}{5}, \frac{2}{5}\right)\right\}$, independent **17.** $\{(-1, 5)\}$, independent

19. $\{(x, y) \mid 3x - 2y = 12\}$, dependent **21.** $\varnothing$, inconsistent

23. $\left\{\left(2, -\frac{1}{3}\right)\right\}$, independent **25.** $\{(20, 60)\}$, independent

27. $\{(2, 4, 6)\}$ **29.** $\{(1, -3, 2)\}$ **31.** $\varnothing$

33. $\{(x, y, z) \mid x - 2y + z = 8\}$ **35.** $\{(3, 4)\}$ **37.** $\{(2, -4)\}$

39. $\{(1, 1, 2)\}$ **41.** 2 **43.** -0.2 **45.** $\{(-1, -2)\}$

47. $\{(2, 1)\}$ **49.** 58 **51.** -30 **53.** $\{(1, 2, -3)\}$

55. Width 13 feet, length 28 feet **57.** 78 **59.** 36 minutes

61. 4 liters of A, 8 liters of B, 8 liters of C **63.** Three servings of each

Chapter 7 Test

1. $\{(1, 3)\}$ **2.** $\left\{\left(\frac{5}{2}, -3\right)\right\}$ **3.** $\{(x, y) \mid y = x - 5\}$

4. $\{(-1, 3)\}$ **5.** $\varnothing$ **6.** Inconsistent **7.** Dependent

8. Independent **9.** $\{(1, -2, -3)\}$ **10.** $\{(2, 5)\}$

11. $\{(3, 1, 1)\}$ **12.** -18 **13.** -2 **14.** $\{(-1, 2)\}$

15. $\{(2, -2, 1)\}$ **16.** Singles \$18, doubles \$25

17. Jill 17 hours, Karen 14 hours, Betsy 62 hours

Making Connections A Review of Chapters 1–7

1. -81 **2.** 7 **3.** 73 **4.** 5.94 **5.** $-t - 3$ **6.** $-0.9x + 0.9$

7. $3x^2 + 2x - 1$ **8.** y **9.** $y = \frac{3}{5}x - \frac{7}{5}$ **10.** $y = \frac{C}{D}x - \frac{W}{D}$

11. $y = \frac{K}{W - C}$ **12.** $y = \frac{bw - 2A}{b}$ **13.** $\{(4, -1)\}$

14. $\{(500, 700)\}$ **15.** $\{(x, y) \mid x + 17 = 5y\}$ **16.** $\varnothing$

17. $y = \frac{5}{9}x + 55$ **18.** $y = -\frac{11}{6}x + \frac{2}{3}$ **19.** $y = 5x + 26$

20. $y = \frac{1}{2}x + 5$ **21.** $y = 5$ **22.** $x = -7$

23. **a)** Machine A
b) Machine B \$0.04 per copy, machine A \$0.03 per copy
c) The slopes 0.04 and 0.03 are the per copy cost for each machine.
d) B : $y = 0.04x + 2000$, A : $y = 0.03x + 4000$
e) 200,000

Chapter 8

Section 8.1 Warm-Ups T T F T T T F T F T

1. A compound inequality consists of two inequalities joined with the words "and" or "or."

3. A compound inequality using "or" is true when either one or the other or both inequalities is true.

5. The inequality $a < b < c$ means that $a < b$ and $b < c$.

7. No **9.** Yes **11.** No **13.** No **15.** Yes **17.** Yes

19. −1 0 1 2 3 4 **21.** −4 −3 −2 −1 0 1 2

23. **25.**

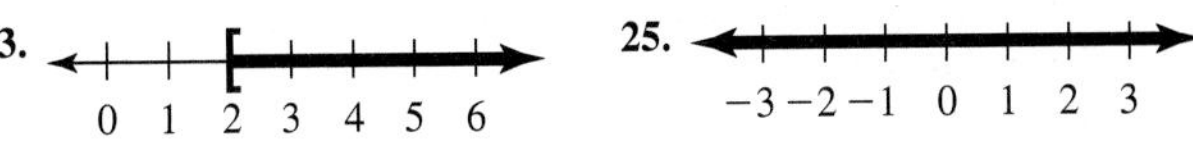

27. $\varnothing$ **29.**

31. $\varnothing$

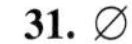

33. $(-\infty, 1) \cup (10, \infty)$ **35.** $(9, \infty)$

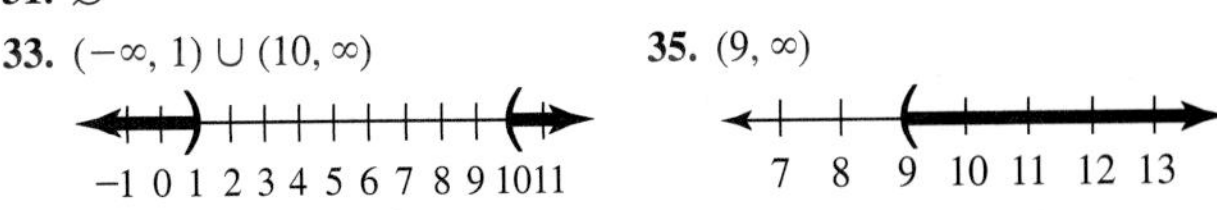

37. $(-6, \infty)$ **39.** $(1, 4]$

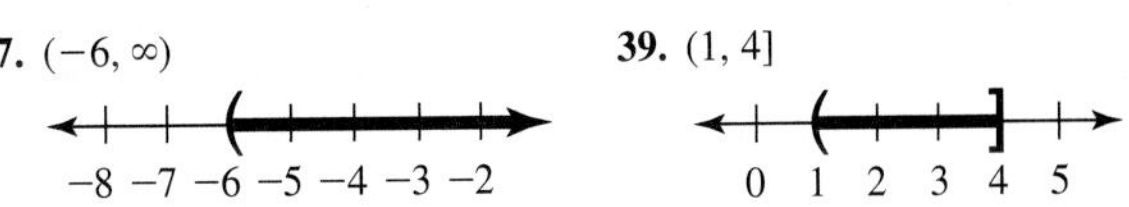

41. $(-\infty, \infty)$ **43.** $\varnothing$

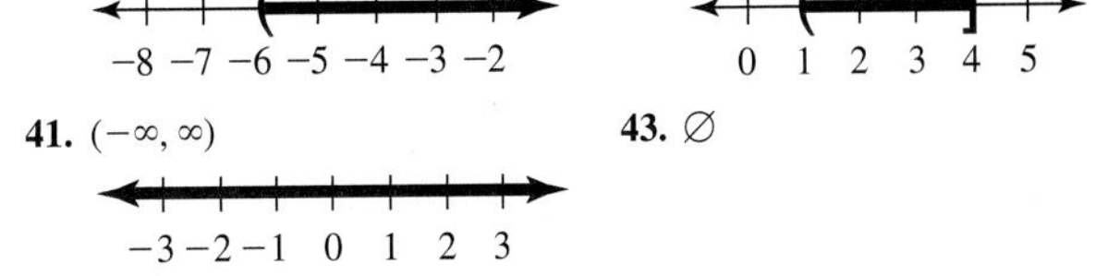

45. $(-4, 2)$

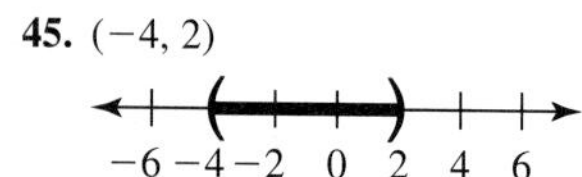

47. $(4, 7)$

49. $[-3, 2)$

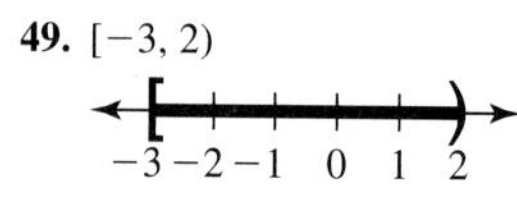

51. $\left(-\frac{7}{3}, 3\right]$

53. $(-1, 5)$

55. $[2, 3]$

57. $(2, \infty)$ **59.** $(-\infty, 5)$ **61.** $[2, 4]$ **63.** $(-\infty, \infty)$ **65.** $\emptyset$
67. $[4, 5)$ **69.** $[1, 6]$ **71.** $x > 2$ **73.** $x < 3$ **75.** $x > 2$ or $x \le -1$
77. $-2 \le x < 3$ **79.** $x \ge -3$ **81.** $(50{,}000, \infty)$
83. $(-\infty, 20) \cup (30, \infty)$ **85.** x = final exam score, $73 \le x \le 86.5$
87. x = price of truck, $\$11{,}033 \le x \le \$13{,}811$
89. x = number of cigarettes on the run, $4 \le x \le 18$
91. **a)** 1,226,950 **b)** 2011 **c)** 2019 **d)** 2011
93. $-b < x < -a$ provided $a < b$
95. **a)** $(12, 32)$ **b)** $(-20, 10]$ **c)** $(0, 9)$ **d)** $[-3, -1]$

Section 8.2 Warm-Ups T F F T F T F F T F

1. Absolute value of a number is the number's distance from 0 on the number line.
3. Since both 4 and -4 are four units from 0, $|x| = 4$ has two solutions.
5. Since the distance from 0 for every number on the number line is greater than or equal to 0, $|x| \ge 0$.
7. $\{-5, 5\}$ **9.** $\{2, 4\}$ **11.** $\{-3, 9\}$ **13.** $\left\{-\frac{8}{3}, \frac{16}{3}\right\}$ **15.** $\{12\}$
17. $\{-20, 80\}$ **19.** $\emptyset$ **21.** $\{0, 5\}$ **23.** $\{0.143, 1.298\}$
25. $\{-2, 2\}$ **27.** $\{-11, 5\}$ **29.** $\{0, 3\}$ **31.** $\left\{-6, \frac{4}{3}\right\}$ **33.** $\{1, 3\}$
35. $(-\infty, \infty)$ **37.** $|x| < 2$ **39.** $|x| > 3$ **41.** $|x| \le 1$
43. $|x| \ge 2$ **45.** No **47.** Yes **49.** No **51.** Yes

53. $(-\infty, -6) \cup (6, \infty)$

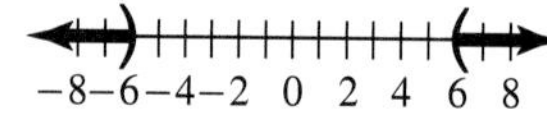

55. $[-2, 2]$

57. $(-3, 3)$

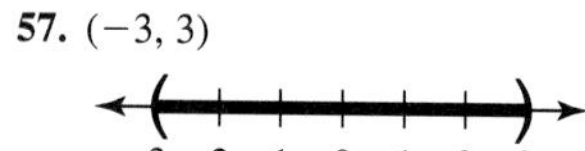

59. $(-\infty, -1] \cup [5, \infty)$

61. $\left(-\frac{1}{2}, \frac{9}{2}\right)$

63. $[-2, 12]$

65. $\left(-\infty, -\frac{9}{2}\right] \cup \left[\frac{15}{2}, \infty\right)$

67. $(-\infty, 0) \cup (0, \infty)$

69. $\{0\}$

71. $(-\infty, \infty)$

73. $\emptyset$ 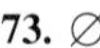

75. $(-\infty, \infty)$

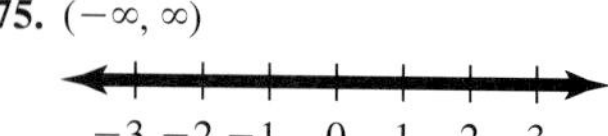

77. $(-\infty, -3) \cup (-1, \infty)$
79. $(-4, 4)$ **81.** $(-1, 1)$ **83.** $(0.255, 0.847)$ **85.** 1401 or 1429
87. Between 121 and 133 pounds
89. **a)** 1 second **b)** 1 second **c)** $0.5 < t < 1.5$
91. **a)** $(-\infty, \infty)$ **b)** $(-\infty, \infty)$ **c)** all reals except $n = 0$

Section 8.3 Warm-Ups T F T F T T F T F T

1. A compound inequality in two variables is formed by connecting two simple inequalities with "and" or "or."
3. A point satisfies an "and" inequality only if it satisfies both inequalities.
5. A test point is used to check whether all points in the region of the test point satisfy the compound inequality.
7. $(-6, -4)$ **9.** $(1, 3), (-2, 5), (-6, -4)$ **11.** $(7, -8)$

13.

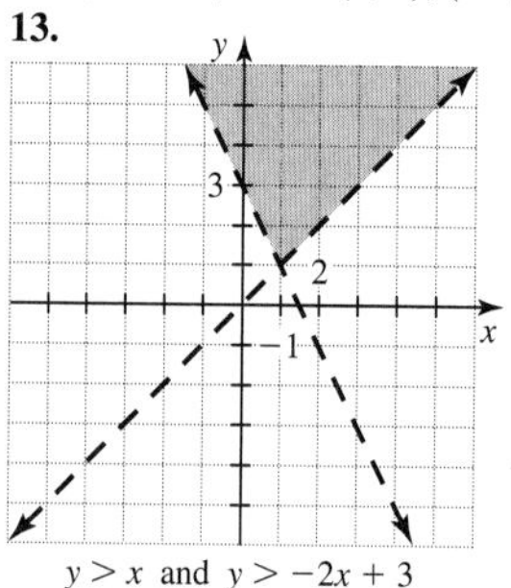

15.

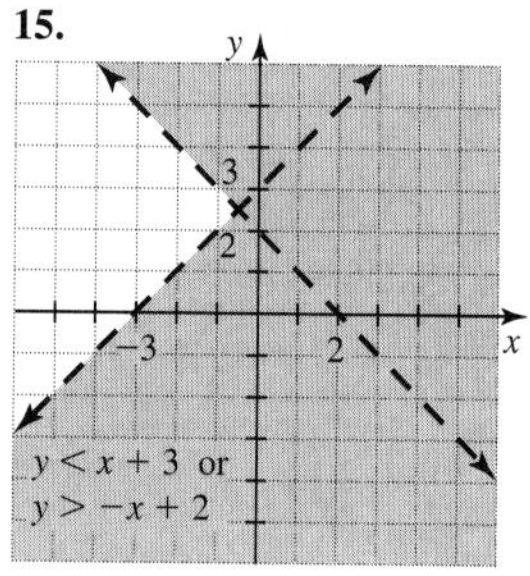

17.

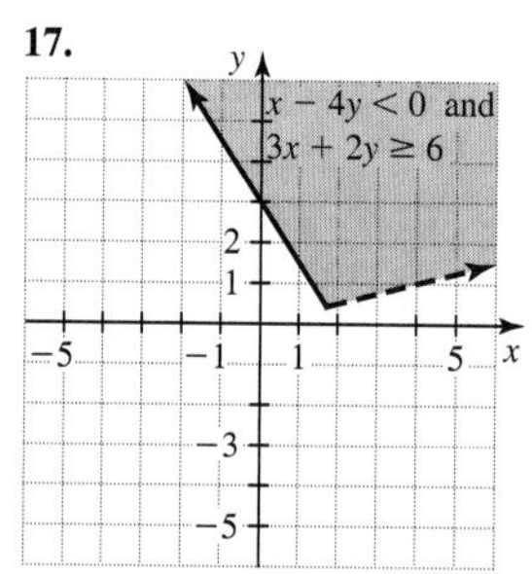

19.

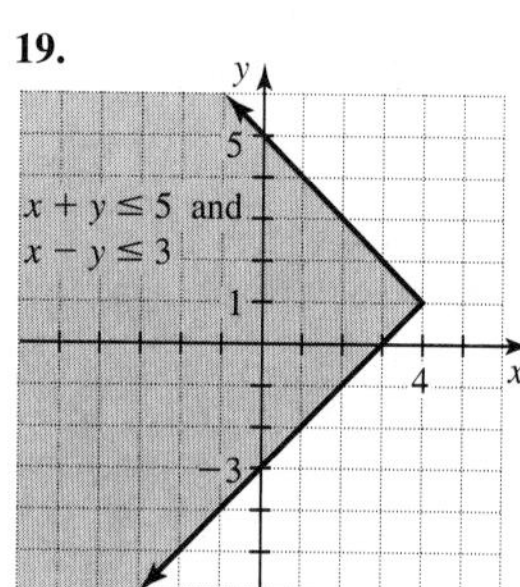

21.

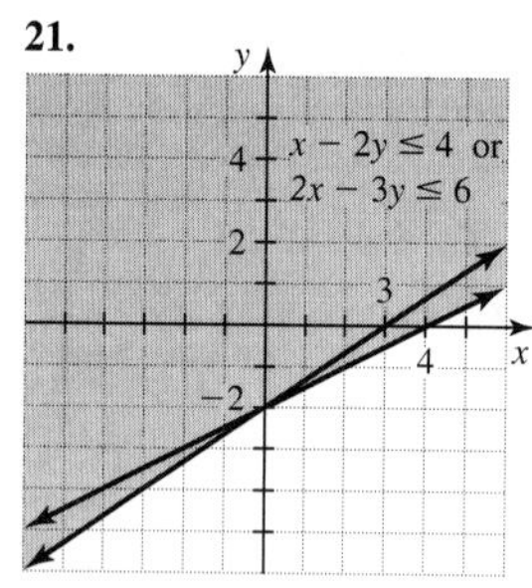

23.

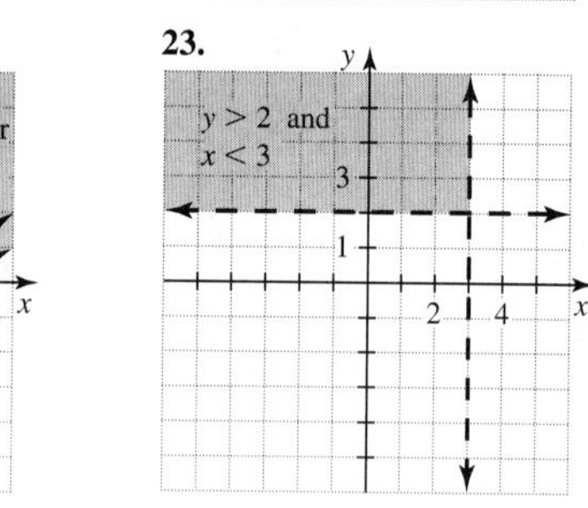

25.

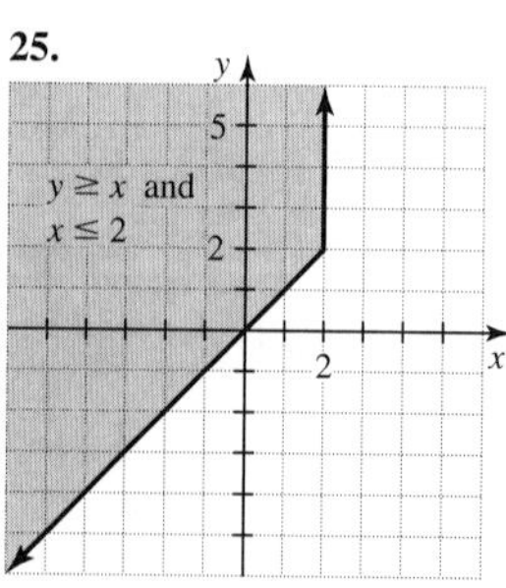

27.

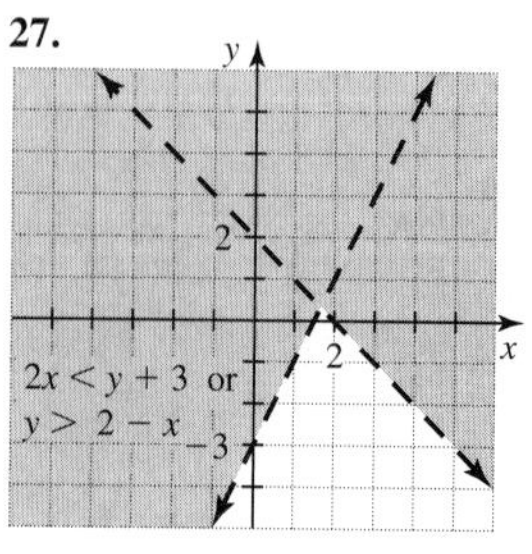

29.

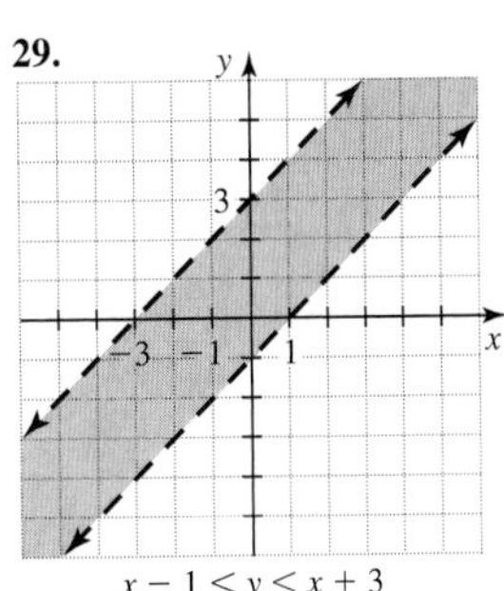

$x - 1 < y < x + 3$

31.

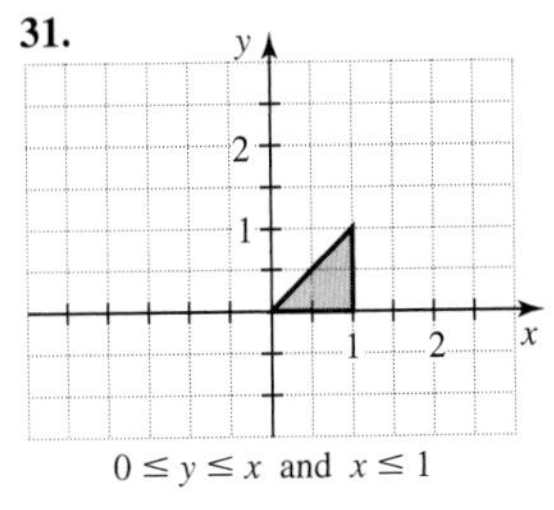

$0 \le y \le x$ and $x \le 1$

33.

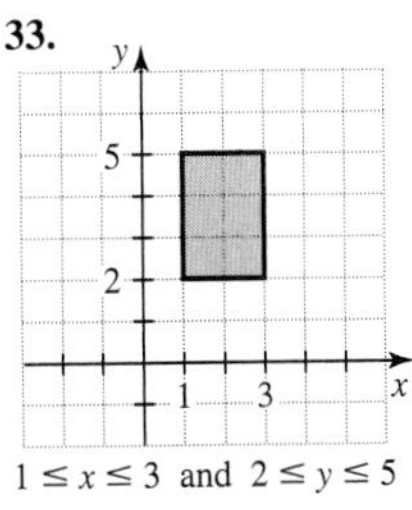

$1 \le x \le 3$ and $2 \le y \le 5$

35.

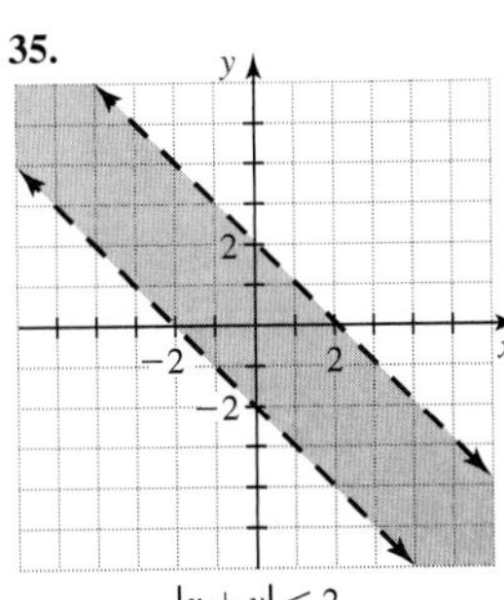

$|x + y| < 2$

37.

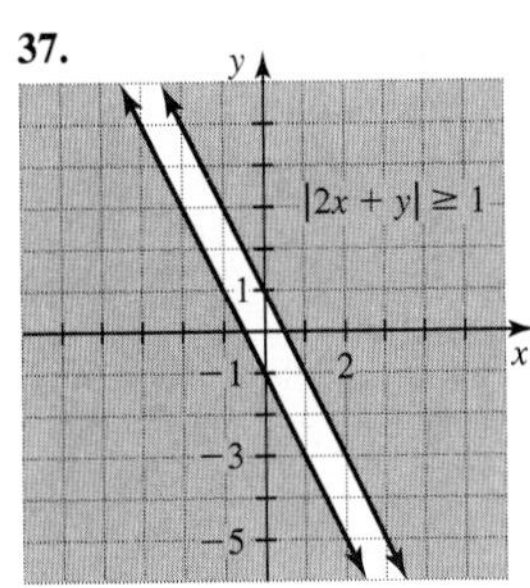

39.

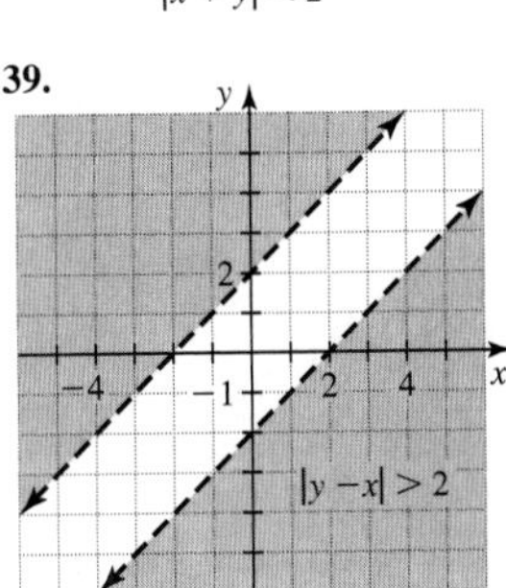

41.

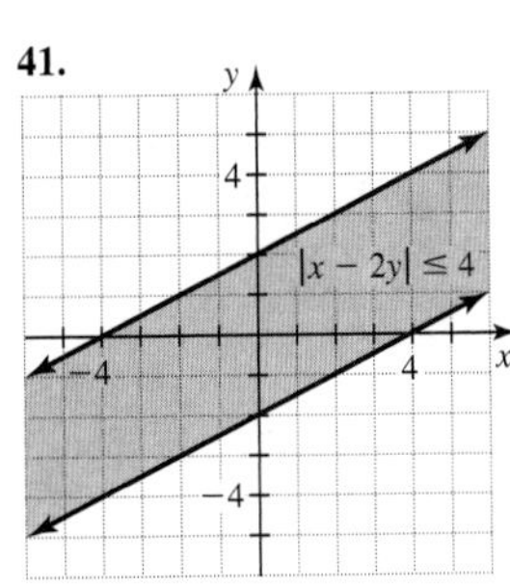

43.

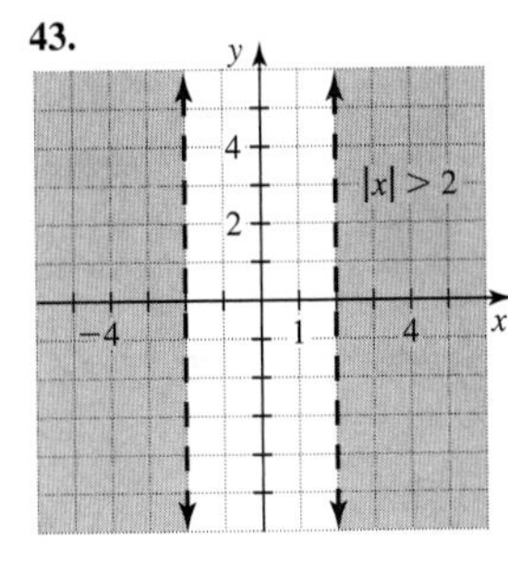

45.

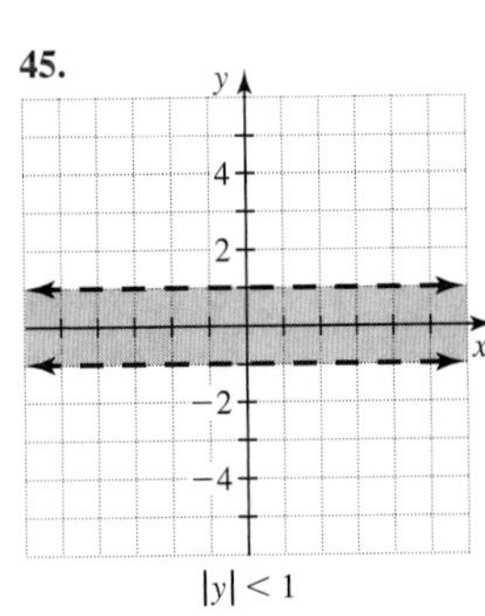

$|y| < 1$

47.

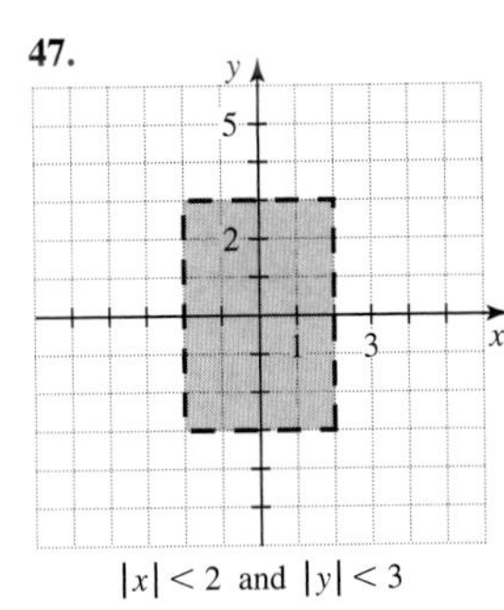

$|x| < 2$ and $|y| < 3$

49.

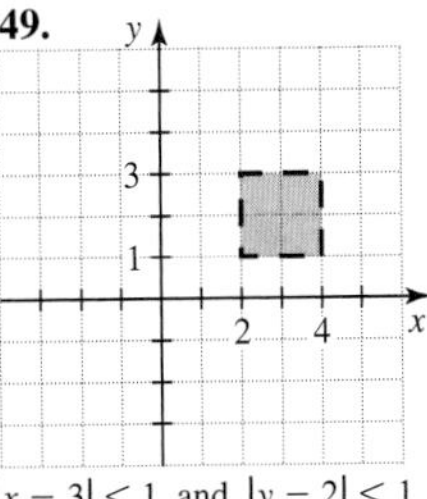

$|x - 3| < 1$ and $|y - 2| < 1$

51. Not the empty set
53. $\varnothing$
55. Not the empty set
57. Not the empty set
59. $\varnothing$
61. $\varnothing$
63. $\varnothing$
65. Not the empty set

67.

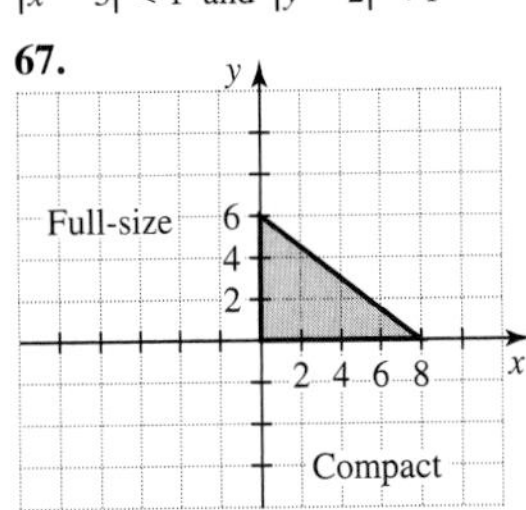

$x \ge 0,\ y \ge 0,\ 3x + 4y \le 24$

69.

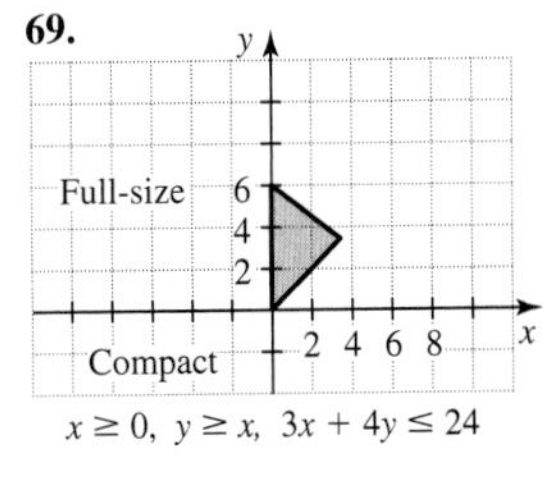

$x \ge 0,\ y \ge x,\ 3x + 4y \le 24$

71.

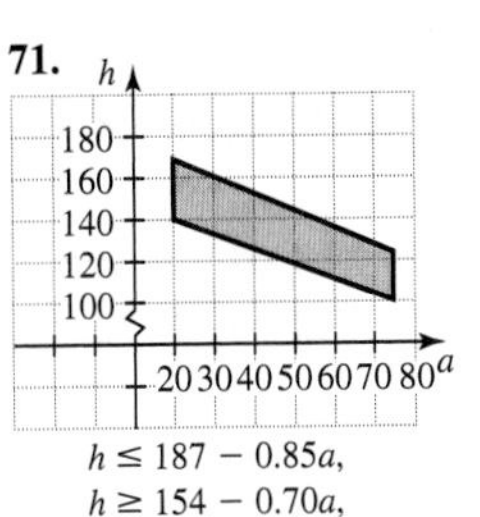

$h \le 187 - 0.85a,$
$h \ge 154 - 0.70a,$
$a \ge 20,\ a \le 75$

73.

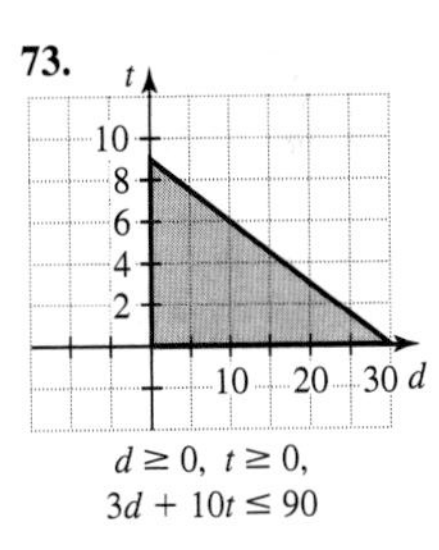

$d \ge 0,\ t \ge 0,$
$3d + 10t \le 90$

Section 8.4 Warm-Ups F F F F F T F T F T

1. A constraint is an inequality that restricts the values of the variables.
3. Constraints may be limitations on the amount of available supplies, money, or other resources.
5. The maximum or minimum of a linear function subject to linear constraints occurs at a vertex of the region determined by the constraints.

7.

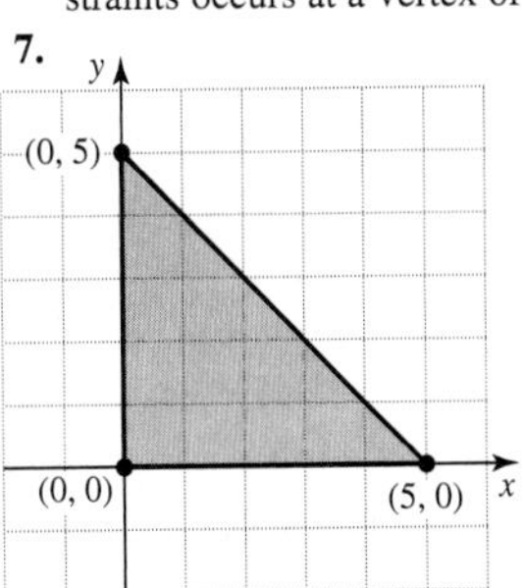

9.

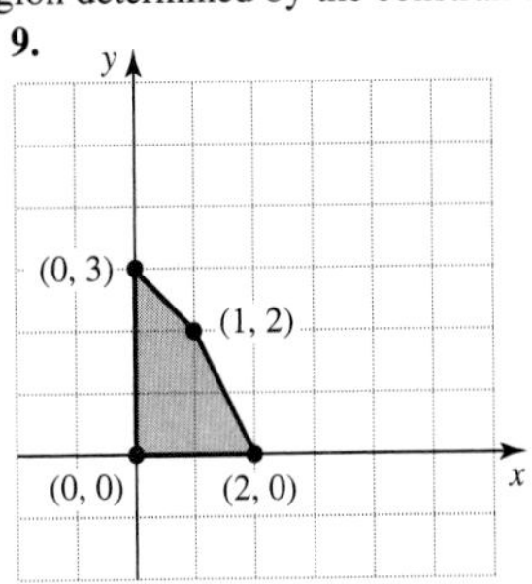

11.

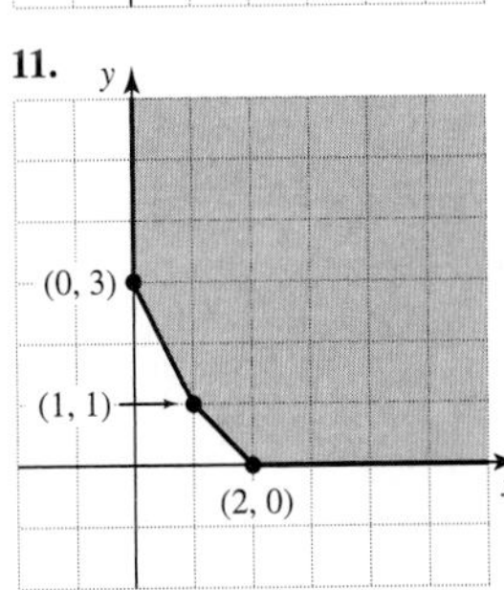

13.

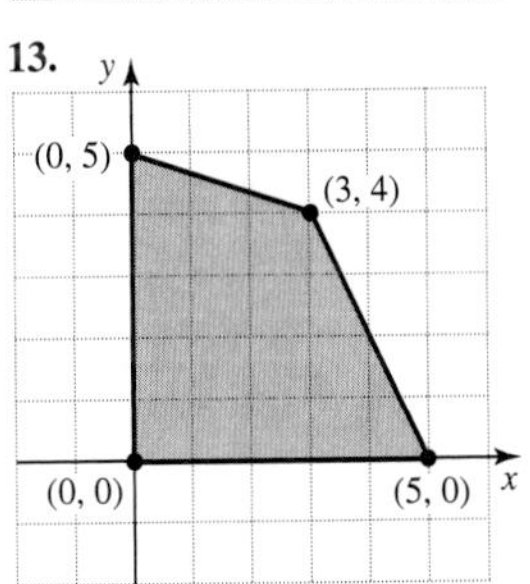

15.

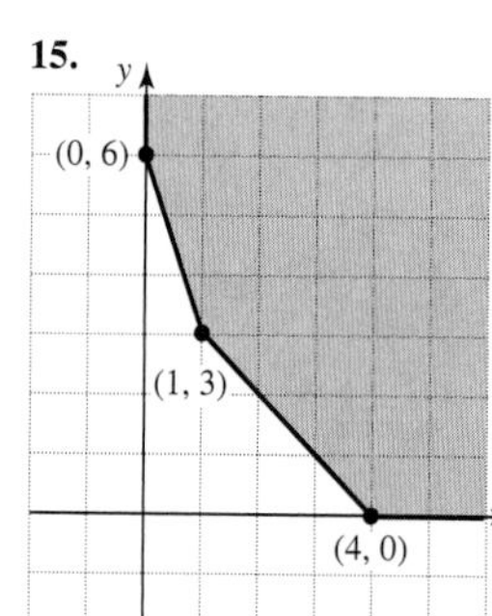

17. 46
19. 88
21. 128
23. **a)** 0, 320,000, 510,000, 450,000
b) 30 TV ads and 60 radio ads
25. 6 doubles, 4 triples
27. 0 doubles, 8 triples
29. 1.75 cups Doggie Dinner, 5.5 cups Puppy Power
31. 10 cups Doggie Dinner, 0 cups Puppy Power

33. Laundromat \$8000, car wash \$16,000

Enriching Your Mathematical Word Power

1. c **2.** d **3.** a **4.** b **5.** a **6.** d **7.** c **8.** a **9.** c
10. a **11.** b

Review Exercises

1. $(-\infty, -4) \cup (1, \infty)$

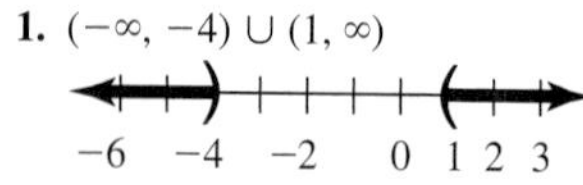

3. $(0, 9)$

5. $(0, \infty)$

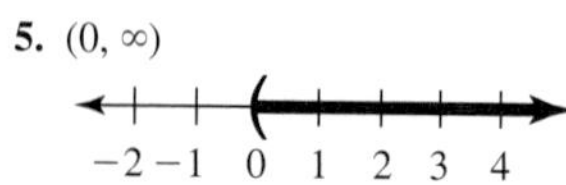

7. $(-\infty, 4)$

9. $\varnothing$ **11.** $(-\infty, \infty)$

13. $\left[-\frac{17}{2}, \frac{13}{2}\right]$

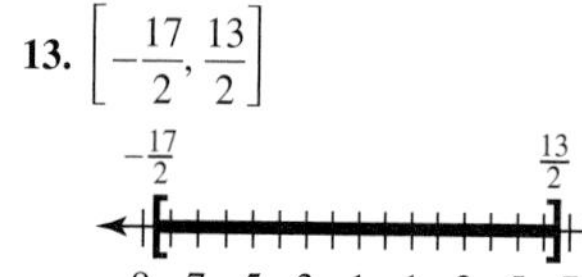

15. $[1, \infty)$ **17.** $(3, 6)$ **19.** $(-\infty, \infty)$ **21.** $[-2, -1]$

23. $\{-14, 14\}$

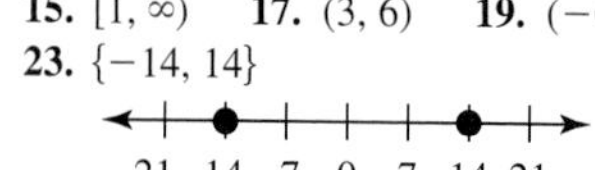

25. $\{3\}$

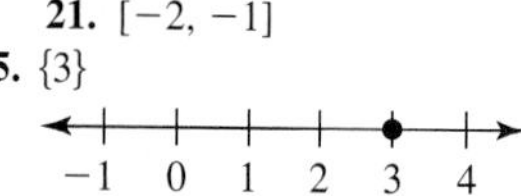

27. $\varnothing$

29. $\{-1, 2\}$

31. $(-\infty, -4] \cup [4, \infty)$

33. $(-\infty, -4) \cup (14, \infty)$

35. $\varnothing$

37. $(-\infty, \infty)$

39. $(-\infty, 1) \cup (3, \infty)$

41.

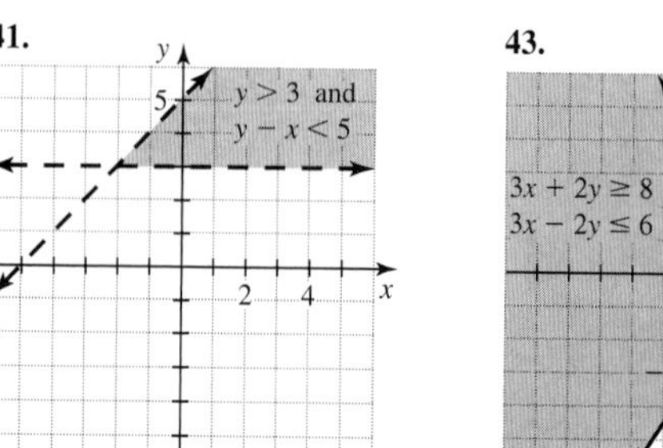

43.

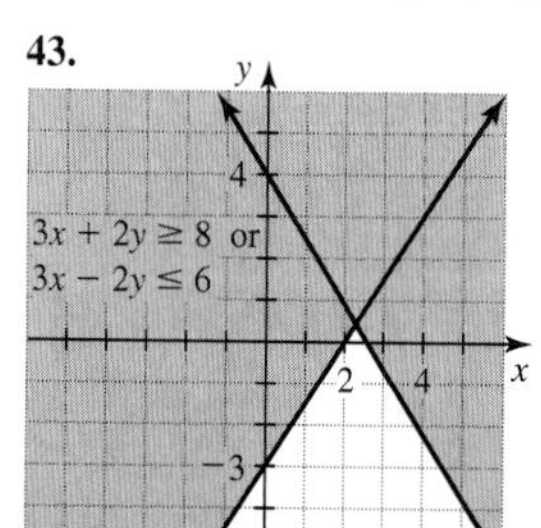

45.

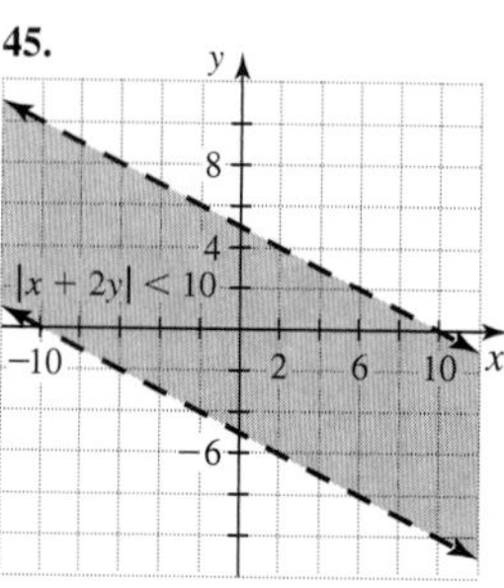

47.

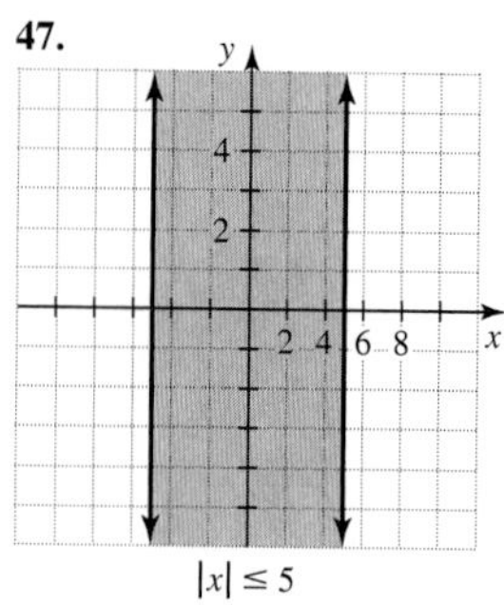

49.

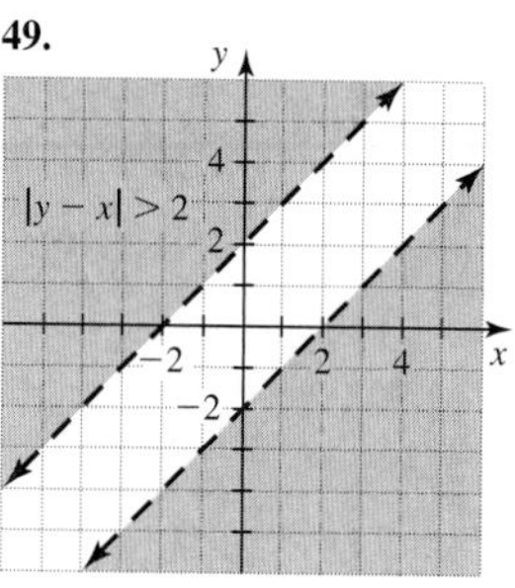

51.

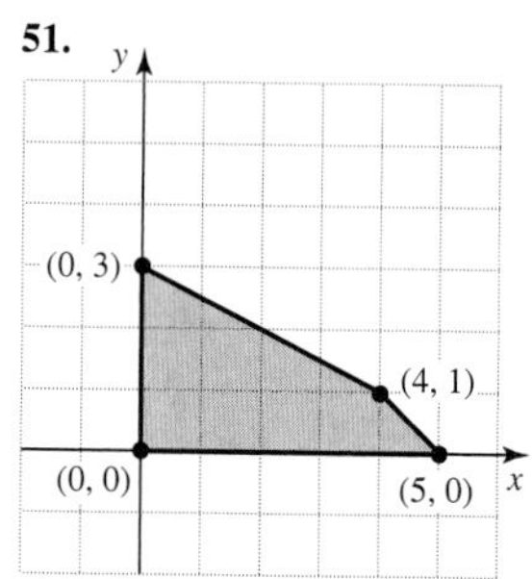

53. 30 **55.** x = rental price, $\$3 \le x \le \$5$ **57.** (40.2, 53.6)
59. 81 or 91 **61.** $x > 1$ **63.** $|x - 2| = 0$ **65.** $|x| = 3$
67. $x \le -1$ **69.** $|x| \le 2$ **71.** $x \le 2$ or $x \ge 7$ **73.** $|x| > 3$
75. $5 < x < 7$ or $|x - 6| < 1$ **77.** $|x| > 0$

Chapter 8 Test

1. $-3 < x \le 2$ **2.** $x > 1$ **3.** $[3, \infty)$ **4.** $(1, 6]$
5. $(-\infty, 5) \cup (9, \infty)$ **6.** $(-3, 3)$ **7.** $(-\infty, -2) \cup (2, \infty)$

8. $(-1, \infty)$

9. $[4, 8]$

10. $(-\infty, -7) \cup (13, \infty)$

11. $(5, \infty)$

12. $[-5, 3)$

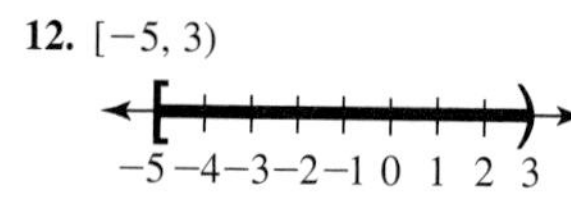

13. $(-\infty, 15)$

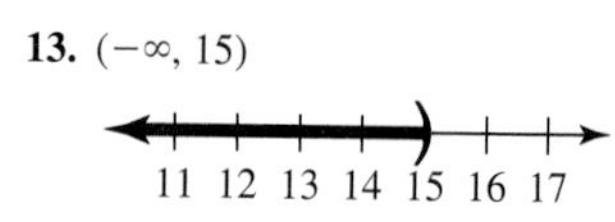

14. $\varnothing$
15. $(-\infty, \infty)$
16. $\varnothing$
17. $\{2.5\}$
18. $\varnothing$
19. $(-\infty, \infty)$

20.

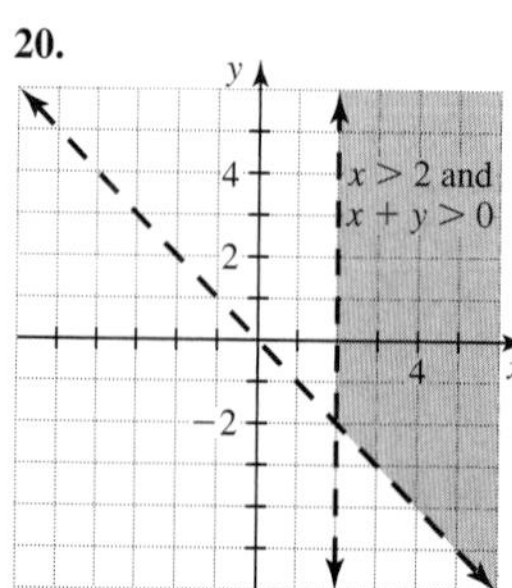

21.

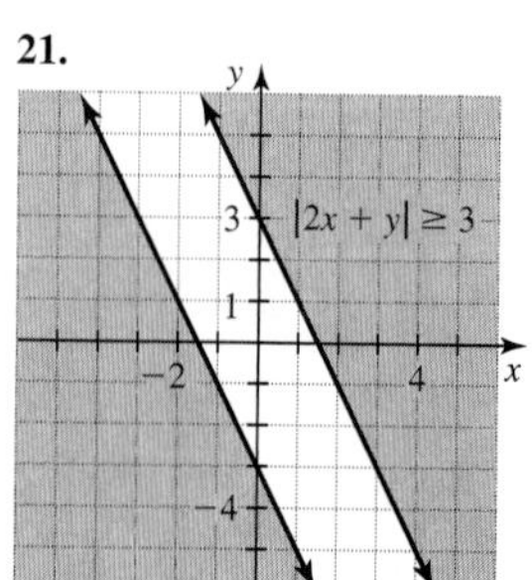

22.

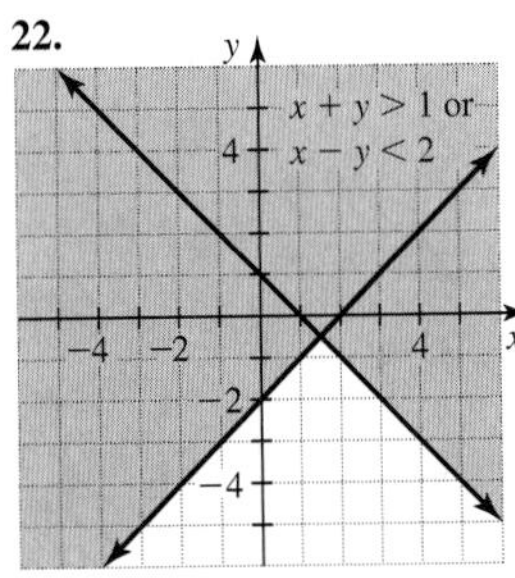

23. $|x - 28{,}000| > 3{,}000$ where x is Brenda's salary, Brenda makes more than \$31,000 or less than \$25,000.
24. 44

Making Connections A Review of Chapters 1–8

1. $11x$ **2.** $30x^2$ **3.** $3x + 1$ **4.** $4x - 3$ **5.** 899 **6.** 961 **7.** 841 **8.** 25 **9.** 13 **10.** -25 **11.** 5 **12.** -4 **13.** $-2x + 13$ **14.** 60 **15.** 72 **16.** -9 **17.** $\{0\}$ **18.** R or $(-\infty, \infty)$ **19.** $\{0\}$ **20.** $\{1\}$ **21.** $\left\{-\frac{1}{3}\right\}$ **22.** $\{1\}$ **23.** $\{1000\}$ **24.** $\left\{-\frac{17}{5}, 1\right\}$ **25.** $\{(4, -3)\}$ **26.** $\varnothing$ **27.** $\{(-2, 4)\}$ **28.** $\{(8, 15)\}$ **29.** E **30.** F **31.** G **32.** D **33.** H **34.** C **35.** B **36.** I **37.** A **38.** J **39. a)** 87,500 **b)** $C_r = 4500 + 0.06x$, $C_b = 8000 + 0.02x$ **c)** 87,500 **d)** Buying is \$1300 cheaper **e)** (75,000, 100,000)

Chapter 9

Section 9.1 Warm-Ups T F T F T F F F T T

1. If $b^n = a$, then b is an nth root of a.
3. If $b^n = a$, then b is an even root of a provided n is even or an odd root of a provided n is odd.
5. The product rule for radicals says that $\sqrt[n]{a} \cdot \sqrt[n]{b} = \sqrt[n]{ab}$ provided all of these roots are real.
7. 6 **9.** 10 **11.** -3 **13.** 2 **15.** -2 **17.** 2 **19.** 10 **21.** Not a real number **23.** -2 **25.** m **27.** x^8 **29.** y^3 **31.** y^5 **33.** m **35.** w^3 **37.** $3\sqrt{y}$ **39.** $2a$ **41.** x^2y **43.** $m^6\sqrt{5}$ **45.** $2\sqrt[3]{y}$ **47.** $a^2\sqrt[3]{3}$ **49.** $2\sqrt{5}$ **51.** $5\sqrt{2}$ **53.** $6\sqrt{2}$ **55.** $2\sqrt[3]{5}$ **57.** $3\sqrt[3]{3}$ **59.** $2\sqrt[4]{3}$ **61.** $2\sqrt[5]{3}$ **63.** $a\sqrt{a}$ **65.** $3a^3\sqrt{2}$ **67.** $2x^2\sqrt{5xy}$ **69.** $2m\sqrt[3]{3m}$ **71.** $2a\sqrt[4]{2a}$ **73.** $2x\sqrt[5]{2x}$ **75.** $4xy^4z^3\sqrt{3xz}$ **77.** $\frac{\sqrt{t}}{2}$ **79.** $\frac{25}{4}$ **81.** $\sqrt{10}$ **83.** $\frac{\sqrt[3]{t}}{2}$ **85.** $\frac{-2x^2}{y}$ **87.** $\frac{2a^3}{3}$ **89.** $\frac{2\sqrt{3}}{5}$ **91.** $\frac{3\sqrt{3}}{4}$ **93.** $\frac{a\sqrt[3]{a}}{5}$ **95.** $\frac{3\sqrt[3]{3}}{2b}$ **97.** $\frac{x\sqrt[4]{x^3}}{y^2}$ **99.** $\frac{a\sqrt[4]{a}}{2b^3}$ **101.** $[2, \infty)$ **103.** $(-\infty, \infty)$ **105.** $(-\infty, 3]$ **107.** $\left[-\frac{1}{2}, \infty\right)$ **109.** -4°F, -10°F **111. a)** $t = \frac{\sqrt{h}}{4}$ **b)** $\frac{\sqrt{10}}{2}$ sec **c)** 100 ft **113.** 5.8 knots **115.** 114.1 ft/sec, 77.8 mph **117. a)** Yes **b)** No **c)** Yes **d)** Yes **119.** Arithmetic mean

Section 9.2 Warm-Ups T F F T T T T F T T

1. The nth root of a is $a^{1/n}$.
3. The expression $a^{-m/n}$ means $\frac{1}{a^{m/n}}$.
5. The operations can be performed in any order, but the easiest is usually root, power, and then reciprocal.
7. $7^{1/4}$ **9.** $(5x)^{1/2}$ **11.** $\sqrt[5]{9}$ **13.** $\sqrt{a}$ **15.** 5 **17.** -5 **19.** 2 **21.** Not a real number **23.** $w^{7/3}$ **25.** $2^{-10/3}$ **27.** $\sqrt[4]{\frac{1}{w^3}}$ **29.** $\sqrt{(ab)^3}$ **31.** 25 **33.** 125 **35.** $\frac{1}{81}$ **37.** $\frac{1}{64}$ **39.** $-\frac{1}{3}$ **41.** Not a real number **43.** $3^{7/12}$ **45.** 1 **47.** $\frac{1}{2}$ **49.** 2 **51.** 6 **53.** 4 **55.** 81 **57.** $\frac{1}{4}$ **59.** $\frac{9}{8}$ **61.** $|x|$ **63.** a^4 **65.** y **67.** $|3x^3y|$ **69.** $\left|\frac{3x^3}{y^5}\right|$ **71.** $x^{3/4}$ **73.** $\frac{y^{3/2}}{x^{1/4}}$ **75.** $\frac{1}{w^{8/3}}$ **77.** $12x^8$ **79.** $\frac{a^2}{b}$ **81.** $8w^{13/4}$ **83.** $\frac{h^{1/6}}{3k^{1/2}}$ **85.** 9 **87.** $-\frac{1}{8}$ **89.** $\frac{1}{625}$ **91.** $2^{1/4}$ **93.** 3 **95.** 3 **97.** $\frac{4}{9}$ **99.** Not a real number **101.** $\frac{4}{3}$ **103.** $-\frac{216}{125}$ **105.** $3x^{9/2}$ **107.** $\frac{a^2}{27}$ **109.** $a^{5/4}b$ **111.** $k^{9/2}m^4$ **113.** 1.2599 **115.** -1.4142 **117.** 2 **119.** 2.5 **121.** $a^{3m/4}$ **123.** $a^{2m/15}$ **125.** a^nb^m **127.** $a^{4m}b^{2n}$ **129.** 13 inches **131.** 274.96 m² **133.** 26.26% **135.** 6.12% **137.** Second is incorrect.

Section 9.3 Warm-Ups F T F F T F T F F T

1. Like radicals are radicals with the same index and the same radicand.
3. In the product rule the radicals must have the same index but do not have to have the same radicand.
5. $-\sqrt{3}$ **7.** $9\sqrt{7x}$ **9.** $5\sqrt[3]{2}$ **11.** $4\sqrt{3} - 2\sqrt{5}$ **13.** $5\sqrt[3]{x}$ **15.** $2\sqrt[3]{x} - \sqrt{2x}$ **17.** $2\sqrt{2} + 2\sqrt{7}$ **19.** $5\sqrt{2}$ **21.** 0 **23.** $-\sqrt{2}$ **25.** $x\sqrt{5x} + 2x\sqrt{2}$ **27.** $7\sqrt[3]{3}$ **29.** $-4\sqrt[4]{3}$ **31.** $ty\sqrt[3]{2t}$ **33.** $\sqrt{15}$ **35.** $30\sqrt{2}$ **37.** $6a\sqrt{14}$ **39.** $3\sqrt[4]{3}$ **41.** 12 **43.** $6\sqrt{2} + 18$ **45.** $5\sqrt{2} - 2\sqrt{5}$ **47.** $3\sqrt[3]{t^2} - t\sqrt[3]{3}$ **49.** $-7 - 3\sqrt{3}$ **51.** 2 **53.** $-8 - 6\sqrt{5}$ **55.** $-6 + 9\sqrt{2}$ **57.** $\sqrt[6]{3^5}$ **59.** $\sqrt[12]{5^7}$ **61.** $\sqrt[6]{500}$ **63.** $\sqrt[12]{432}$ **65.** -1 **67.** 3 **69.** 19 **71.** 13 **73.** $25 - 9x$ **75.** $11\sqrt{3}$ **77.** $10\sqrt{30}$ **79.** $8 - \sqrt{7}$ **81.** $16w$ **83.** $3x^2\sqrt{2x}$ **85.** $28 + \sqrt{10}$ **87.** $\frac{8\sqrt{2}}{15}$ **89.** 17 **91.** $9 + 6\sqrt{x} + x$ **93.** $25x - 30\sqrt{x} + 9$ **95.** $x + 3 + 2\sqrt{x + 2}$ **97.** $-\sqrt{w}$ **99.** $a\sqrt{a}$ **101.** $3x^2\sqrt{x}$ **103.** $13x\sqrt[3]{2x}$ **105.** $\sqrt[6]{32x^5}$ **107.** $3\sqrt{2}$ square feet (ft²) **109.** $\frac{9\sqrt{2}}{2}$ ft² **111.** No **113. a)** $(y - \sqrt{3})(y + \sqrt{3})$, $(\sqrt{2}a - \sqrt{7})(\sqrt{2}a + \sqrt{7})$ **b)** $\{\pm 2\sqrt{2}\}$ **c)** $\{\pm\sqrt{a}\}$

Section 9.4 Warm-Ups T T F T F T F T T T

1. $\frac{2\sqrt{5}}{5}$ **3.** $\frac{\sqrt{21}}{7}$ **5.** $\frac{\sqrt[3]{2}}{2}$ **7.** $\frac{\sqrt[3]{150}}{5}$ **9.** $\frac{\sqrt{15}}{6}$ **11.** $\frac{1}{2}$ **13.** $\frac{\sqrt{2}}{2}$ **15.** $\frac{\sqrt[3]{18}}{3}$ **17.** $\frac{\sqrt[3]{14}}{2}$ **19.** $\frac{\sqrt{xy}}{y}$ **21.** $\frac{a\sqrt{ab}}{b^4}$ **23.** $\frac{\sqrt{3ab}}{3b}$ **25.** $\frac{\sqrt[3]{ab^2}}{b}$ **27.** $\frac{\sqrt[3]{20b}}{2b}$ **29.** $\sqrt{3}$ **31.** $\frac{\sqrt{15}}{5}$ **33.** $\frac{3\sqrt{2}}{10}$ **35.** $\frac{\sqrt{2}}{3}$ **37.** $\frac{\sqrt{3a}}{3}$ **39.** $\sqrt[3]{10}$ **41.** 2 **43.** $\frac{2}{w}$ **45.** $2 + \sqrt{5}$ **47.** $1 - \sqrt{3}$ **49.** $2\sqrt{2} - 2$ **51.** $\frac{\sqrt{11} + \sqrt{5}}{2}$ **53.** $\frac{1 + \sqrt{6} + \sqrt{2} + \sqrt{3}}{2}$ **55.** $\frac{2\sqrt{3} - \sqrt{6}}{3}$ **57.** $\frac{6\sqrt{6} + 2\sqrt{15}}{13}$ **59.** $128\sqrt{2}$ **61.** $x^2\sqrt{x}$ **63.** $-27x^4\sqrt{x}$ **65.** $8x^5$ **67.** $4\sqrt[3]{25}$

69. x^4 **71.** $\frac{\sqrt{6}+2\sqrt{2}}{2}$ **73.** $2\sqrt{6}$ **75.** $\frac{\sqrt{2}}{2}$ **77.** $\frac{2}{3}$
79. $\frac{2-\sqrt{2}}{5}$ **81.** $\frac{1+\sqrt{3}}{2}$ **83.** $a-3\sqrt{a}$ **85.** $4a\sqrt{a}+4a$
87. $12m$ **89.** $4xy^2z$ **91.** $m-m^2$ **93.** $5x\sqrt[3]{x}$ **95.** $8m^4\sqrt[4]{8m^2}$
97. $\sqrt{x}+3$ **99.** $\frac{3k-3\sqrt{7k}}{k-7}$ **101.** $2+8\sqrt{2}$ **103.** $\frac{3\sqrt{2}+2\sqrt{3}}{6}$
105. $7\sqrt{2}-1$ **107.** $\frac{4x+4\sqrt{x}}{x-4}$ **109.** $\frac{x+\sqrt{x}}{x(1-x)}$
111. a) x^3-2 **b)** $(x+\sqrt[3]{5})(x^2-\sqrt[3]{5}x+\sqrt[3]{25})$ **c)** 3
d) $(\sqrt[3]{a}+\sqrt[3]{b})(\sqrt[3]{a^2}-\sqrt[3]{ab}+\sqrt[3]{b^2})$, $(\sqrt[3]{a}-\sqrt[3]{b})(\sqrt[3]{a^2}+\sqrt[3]{ab}+\sqrt[3]{b^2})$

Section 9.5 Warm-Ups F T F F T F F T T T

1. The odd-root property says that if n is an odd positive integer, then $x^n = k$ is equivalent to $x = \sqrt[n]{k}$ for any real number k.
3. An extraneous solution is a solution that appears when solving an equation but does not satisfy the original equation.
5. $\{-10\}$ **7.** $\left\{\frac{1}{2}\right\}$ **9.** $\{1\}$ **11.** $\{-2\}$ **13.** $\{-5, 5\}$
15. $\{-2\sqrt{5}, 2\sqrt{5}\}$ **17.** No real solution **19.** $\{-1, 7\}$
21. $\{-1-2\sqrt{2}, -1+2\sqrt{2}\}$ **23.** $\{-\sqrt{10}, \sqrt{10}\}$ **25.** $\{3\}$
27. $\{-2, 2\}$ **29.** $\{52\}$ **31.** $\left\{\frac{9}{4}\right\}$ **33.** $\{9\}$ **35.** $\{3\}$ **37.** $\{3\}$
39. $\{-5, 3\}$ **41.** $\{1\}$ **43.** $\varnothing$ **45.** $\{4\}$ **47.** $\{2\}$ **49.** $\{6\}$
51. $\{7\}$ **53.** $\{-5\}$ **55.** $\varnothing$ **57.** $\{0\}$ **59.** $\{-3\sqrt{3}, 3\sqrt{3}\}$
61. $\left\{-\frac{1}{27}, \frac{1}{27}\right\}$ **63.** $\{512\}$ **65.** $\left\{\frac{1}{81}\right\}$ **67.** $\left\{0, \frac{2}{3}\right\}$
69. $\left\{\frac{4-\sqrt{2}}{4}, \frac{4+\sqrt{2}}{4}\right\}$ **71.** No real solution **73.** $\{-\sqrt{2}, \sqrt{2}\}$
75. $\{-5\}$ **77.** No real solution **79.** $\{-9\}$ **81.** $\left\{\frac{5}{4}\right\}$ **83.** $\varnothing$
85. $\left\{-\frac{2}{3}, 2\right\}$ **87.** $\{-2-2\sqrt[4]{2}, -2+2\sqrt[4]{2}\}$ **89.** $\{0\}$ **91.** $\left\{\frac{1}{2}\right\}$
93. $4\sqrt{2}$ feet **95.** $5\sqrt{2}$ feet **97.** 50 feet
99. a) 1.89 **b)** $d = \frac{64b^3}{C^3}$ **c)** $d > 19{,}683$ pounds
101. $\sqrt[6]{32}$ meters **103.** $\sqrt{73}$ kilometers (km)
105. $S = P(1+r)^n$, $P = S(1+r)^{-n}$ **107.** 9.5 AU **109.** $\{-1.8, 1.8\}$
111. $\{4.993\}$ **113.** $\{-26.372, 26.372\}$

Section 9.6 Warm-Ups T F F T T T T F T F

1. A complex number is a number of the form $a + bi$, where a and b are real numbers.
3. The union of the real numbers and the imaginary numbers is the set of complex numbers.
5. The conjugate of $a + bi$ is $a - bi$.
7. $-2+8i$ **9.** $-4+4i$ **11.** -2 **13.** $-8-2i$ **15.** $6+15i$
17. $-2-10i$ **19.** $-4-12i$ **21.** $-10+24i$ **23.** $-1+3i$
25. $-5i$ **27.** 29 **29.** 2 **31.** 20 **33.** -9 **35.** -25 **37.** 16
39. i **41.** 34 **43.** 5 **45.** 5 **47.** 7 **49.** $\frac{12}{17}-\frac{3}{17}i$
51. $\frac{4}{13}+\frac{7}{13}i$ **53.** $3-4i$ **55.** $1+3i$ **57.** $\frac{1}{13}-\frac{5}{13}i$ **59.** $-2i$
61. $2+2i$ **63.** $5+6i$ **65.** $7-i\sqrt{6}$ **67.** $5i\sqrt{2}$ **69.** $1+i\sqrt{3}$
71. $-1-\frac{1}{2}i\sqrt{6}$ **73.** $-2\sqrt{3}$ **75.** -9 **77.** $-i\sqrt{2}$ **79.** $\{\pm 6i\}$
81. $\{\pm 2i\sqrt{3}\}$ **83.** $\left\{\pm\frac{i\sqrt{10}}{2}\right\}$ **85.** $\{\pm i\sqrt{2}\}$ **87.** $18-i$
89. $5+i$ **91.** $-\frac{6}{25}-\frac{17}{25}i$ **93.** $3+2i$ **95.** -9 **97.** $3i\sqrt{3}$
99. $-5-12i$ **101.** $-2+2i\sqrt{2}$

Enriching Your Mathematical Word Power

1. d **2.** b **3.** b **4.** b **5.** d **6.** b **7.** c **8.** a **9.** a
10. d **11.** c **12.** a **13.** c **14.** d **15.** b

Review Exercises

1. 2 **3.** 10 **5.** $6\sqrt{2}$ **7.** x^6 **9.** x^2 **11.** $x^4\sqrt{2x}$
13. $2w^2\sqrt{2w}$ **15.** $2x\sqrt[3]{2x}$ **17.** $a^2b\sqrt[4]{ab}$ **19.** $\frac{x\sqrt{x}}{4}$ **21.** $[2.5, \infty)$
23. $(-\infty, \infty)$ **25.** $\left(-\infty, \frac{1}{3}\right]$ **27.** $[-2, \infty)$ **29.** $\frac{1}{9}$ **31.** 4
33. $\frac{1}{1000}$ **35.** $27x^{1/2}$ **37.** $a^{7/2}b^{7/2}$ **39.** $x^{3/4}y^{5/4}$ **41.** 13
43. $3\sqrt{5}-2\sqrt{3}$ **45.** $30-21\sqrt{6}$ **47.** $6-3\sqrt{3}+2\sqrt{2}-\sqrt{6}$
49. $\frac{5\sqrt{2}}{2}$ **51.** $\frac{\sqrt{10}}{5}$ **53.** $\frac{\sqrt[3]{18}}{3}$ **55.** $\frac{2\sqrt{3x}}{3x}$ **57.** $\frac{y\sqrt{15y}}{3}$
59. $\frac{3\sqrt[3]{4a^2}}{2a}$ **61.** $\frac{5\sqrt[4]{27x^2}}{3x}$ **63.** 9 **65.** $1-\sqrt{2}$ **67.** $\frac{-\sqrt{6}-3\sqrt{2}}{2}$
69. $\frac{3\sqrt{2}+2}{7}$ **71.** $256w^{10}$ **73.** $\{-4, 4\}$ **75.** $\{3, 7\}$
77. $\{-1-\sqrt{5}, -1+\sqrt{5}\}$ **79.** No real solution **81.** $\{10\}$
83. $\{9\}$ **85.** $\{-8, 8\}$ **87.** $\{124\}$ **89.** $\{7\}$ **91.** $\{2, 3\}$ **93.** $\{9\}$
95. $\{4\}$ **97.** $5+25i$ **99.** $7-3i$ **101.** $-1+2i$ **103.** $2+i$
105. $2-i\sqrt{3}$ **107.** $\frac{5}{17}-\frac{14}{17}i$ **109.** $\{\pm 10i\}$ **111.** $\left\{\pm\frac{3i\sqrt{2}}{2}\right\}$
113. False **115.** True **117.** True **119.** False **121.** False
123. False **125.** False **127.** True **129.** False **131.** True
133. False **135.** False **137.** True **139.** True
141. $5\sqrt{30}$ seconds **143.** $10\sqrt{7}$ feet **145.** $200\sqrt{2}$ feet
147. $26.4\sqrt[3]{25}$ ft^2 **149. a)** 5.7% **b)** Approximately \$2300 billion
151. $V = \frac{29\sqrt{LCS}}{CS}$

Chapter 9 Test

1. 4 **2.** $\frac{1}{8}$ **3.** $\sqrt{3}$ **4.** 30 **5.** $3\sqrt{5}$ **6.** $\frac{6\sqrt{5}}{5}$ **7.** 2
8. $6\sqrt{2}$ **9.** $\frac{\sqrt{15}}{6}$ **10.** $\frac{2+\sqrt{2}}{2}$ **11.** $4-3\sqrt{3}$ **12.** $2ay^2\sqrt[4]{2a}$
13. $\frac{\sqrt[3]{4x}}{2x}$ **14.** $\frac{2a^4\sqrt{2ab}}{b^2}$ **15.** $-3x^3$ **16.** $2m\sqrt{5m}$ **17.** $x^{3/4}$
18. $3y^2x^{1/4}$ **19.** $2x^2\sqrt[3]{5x}$ **20.** $19+8\sqrt{3}$ **21.** $(-\infty, 4]$
22. $(-\infty, \infty)$ **23.** $\frac{5+\sqrt{3}}{11}$ **24.** $\frac{6\sqrt{2}-\sqrt{3}}{23}$ **25.** $22+7i$
26. $1-i$ **27.** $\frac{1}{5}-\frac{7}{5}i$ **28.** $-\frac{3}{4}+\frac{1}{4}i\sqrt{3}$ **29.** $\{-5, 9\}$ **30.** $\left\{-\frac{7}{4}\right\}$
31. $\{-8, 8\}$ **32.** $\left\{\pm\frac{4}{3}i\right\}$ **33.** $\{3\}$ **34.** $\{5\}$ **35.** $\frac{3\sqrt{2}}{2}$ feet
36. 25 and 36 **37.** Length 6 ft, width 4 ft **38.** 39.53 AU, 164.97 years

Making Connections A Review of Chapters 1–9

1. $\left\{-\frac{4}{7}\right\}$ **2.** $\left\{\frac{3}{2}\right\}$ **3.** $(-\infty, -3) \cup (-2, \infty)$
−5 −4 −3 −2 −1 0
4. $\left\{\frac{3}{2}\right\}$ **5.** $(-\infty, 1)$
−3 −2 −1 0 1 2 3
6. $\varnothing$ **7.** $\{9\}$

8. $\varnothing$ **9.** $\{-12, -2\}$ **10.** $\left\{\frac{1}{16}\right\}$

11. $(-6, \infty)$

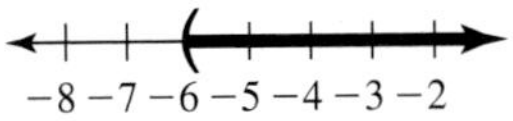

12. $\left\{-\frac{1}{64}, \frac{1}{64}\right\}$

13. $\left\{-\frac{\sqrt{3}}{3}, \frac{\sqrt{3}}{3}\right\}$ **14.** R **15.** $\left(-\frac{1}{3}, 3\right)$

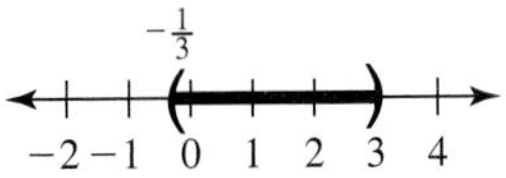

16. $\left\{\frac{1}{3}\right\}$ **17.** $\{82\}$ **18.** $\left\{\frac{6}{5}, \frac{12}{5}\right\}$ **19.** $\{100\}$ **20.** R **21.** $\{4\sqrt{30}\}$

22. $\{400\}$ **23.** $\left\{\frac{13 + 9\sqrt{2}}{3}\right\}$ **24.** $\{-3\sqrt{2}, 3\sqrt{2}\}$ **25.** $\{5\}$

26. $\{7 + 3\sqrt{6}\}$ **27.** $\{-2, 3\}$ **28.** $\{-5, 2\}$ **29.** $\{-2, 3\}$ **30.** $\left\{\frac{1}{2}, 3\right\}$

31. 3 **32.** -2 **33.** $\frac{1}{2}$ **34.** $\frac{1}{3}$

35. **a)** 48.5 cm^3 **b)** 14% **c)** 56 cm^3

Chapter 10

Section 10.1 Warm-Ups F F F F T F F T F F

1. In this section quadratic equations are solved by factoring, the even-root property, and completing the square.

3. The last term is the square of one-half the coefficient of the middle term.

5. $\{-2, 3\}$ **7.** $\{-5, 3\}$ **9.** $\left\{-1, \frac{3}{2}\right\}$ **11.** $\{-7\}$ **13.** $\{-4, 4\}$

15. $\{-9, 9\}$ **17.** $\left\{-\frac{4}{3}, \frac{4}{3}\right\}$ **19.** $\{-1, 7\}$

21. $\{-1 - \sqrt{5}, -1 + \sqrt{5}\}$ **23.** $\left\{\frac{3 - \sqrt{7}}{2}, \frac{3 + \sqrt{7}}{2}\right\}$

25. $x^2 + 2x + 1$ **27.** $x^2 - 3x + \frac{9}{4}$ **29.** $y^2 + \frac{1}{4}y + \frac{1}{64}$

31. $x^2 + \frac{2}{3}x + \frac{1}{9}$ **33.** $(x + 4)^2$ **35.** $\left(y - \frac{5}{2}\right)^2$ **37.** $\left(z - \frac{2}{7}\right)^2$

39. $\left(t + \frac{3}{10}\right)^2$ **41.** $\{-3, 5\}$ **43.** $\{-5, 7\}$ **45.** $\{-4, 5\}$

47. $\{-7, 2\}$ **49.** $\left\{-1, \frac{3}{2}\right\}$ **51.** $\{-2 - \sqrt{10}, -2 + \sqrt{10}\}$

53. $\{-4 - 2\sqrt{5}, -4 + 2\sqrt{5}\}$ **55.** $\left\{\frac{1 - \sqrt{2}}{2}, \frac{1 + \sqrt{2}}{2}\right\}$

57. $\left\{\frac{-3 - \sqrt{41}}{4}, \frac{-3 + \sqrt{41}}{4}\right\}$ **59.** $\{4\}$ **61.** $\left\{\frac{1 + \sqrt{17}}{8}\right\}$

63. $\{1, 6\}$ **65.** $\{-2 - \sqrt{2}, -2 + \sqrt{2}\}$ **67.** $\{-1 - 2i, -1 + 2i\}$

69. $\{3 + i\sqrt{2}, 3 - i\sqrt{2}\}$ **71.** $\left\{\pm\frac{i\sqrt{2}}{2}\right\}$ **73.** $\{-2i\sqrt{3}, 2i\sqrt{3}\}$

75. $\left\{\frac{2 \pm i}{5}\right\}$ **77.** $\{\pm 11i\}$ **79.** $\left\{-\frac{5}{2}i, \frac{5}{2}i\right\}$ **81.** $\{-2, 1\}$

83. $\left\{\frac{-2 - \sqrt{19}}{5}, \frac{-2 + \sqrt{19}}{5}\right\}$ **85.** $\{-6, 4\}$ **87.** $\{2 \pm 3i\}$

89. $\{-2, 3\}$ **91.** $\{3 - i, 3 + i\}$ **93.** $\{6\}$

95. $\left\{\frac{9 - \sqrt{65}}{2}, \frac{9 + \sqrt{65}}{2}\right\}$ **101.** 136.9 ft/sec **103.** 12

105. c **109.** $\{4.56, 2.74\}$ **111.** $\{3.53\}$

Section 10.2 Warm-Ups T F T F T T T T F F

1. The quadratic formula can be used to solve any quadratic equation.

3. Factoring is used when the quadratic polynomial is simple enough to factor.

5. The discriminant is $b^2 - 4ac$.

7. $\{-3, -2\}$ **9.** $\{-3, 2\}$ **11.** $\left\{-\frac{1}{3}, \frac{3}{2}\right\}$ **13.** $\left\{\frac{1}{2}\right\}$ **15.** $\left\{\frac{1}{3}\right\}$

17. $\left\{-\frac{3}{4}\right\}$ **19.** $\{-4 \pm \sqrt{10}\}$ **21.** $\left\{\frac{-5 \pm \sqrt{29}}{2}\right\}$

23. $\left\{\frac{3 \pm \sqrt{7}}{2}\right\}$ **25.** $\left\{\frac{3 \pm i}{2}\right\}$ **27.** $\left\{\frac{3 \pm i\sqrt{39}}{4}\right\}$ **29.** $\{5 \pm i\}$

31. 28, 2 **33.** -23, 0 **35.** 0, 1 **37.** $-\frac{3}{4}$, 0 **39.** 97, 2

41. 0, 1 **43.** 140, 2 **45.** 1, 2 **47.** $\{-2 \pm 2\sqrt{2}\}$ **49.** $\left\{-2, \frac{1}{2}\right\}$

51. $\left\{\frac{-1 \pm \sqrt{13}}{3}\right\}$ **53.** $\{0\}$ **55.** $\left\{\frac{13}{9}, \frac{17}{9}\right\}$ **57.** $\{\pm 5\sqrt{3}\}$

59. $\{4 \pm 2i\}$ **61.** $\{2 \pm i\sqrt{6}\}$ **63.** $\left\{-\frac{3}{4}, \frac{5}{2}\right\}$ **65.** $\{-4.474, 1.274\}$

67. $\{3.7\}$ **69.** $\{-2.979, -0.653\}$ **71.** $\{-4792.983, -0.017\}$

73. $\{-0.079, 0.078\}$ **75.** $\frac{1 + \sqrt{65}}{2}$ and $\frac{-1 + \sqrt{65}}{2}$, or 4.5 and 3.5

77. $3 + \sqrt{5}$ and $3 - \sqrt{5}$, or 5.2 and 0.8

79. $W = \frac{-1 + \sqrt{5}}{2} \approx 0.6$ ft, $L = \frac{1 + \sqrt{5}}{2} \approx 1.6$ ft

81. $W = -2 + \sqrt{14} \approx 1.7$ ft, $L = 2 + \sqrt{14} \approx 5.7$ ft

83. 3 sec **85.** $\frac{5 + \sqrt{105}}{16}$ or 1.0 sec

87. 7.0 sec **89.** 4 in.

91. 4 **93.** 250 melons

99. 2 **101.** 0 **103.** 0

Section 10.3 Warm-Ups T F T T F T T T T F

1. The graph of $y = ax^2 + bx + c$ with $a \neq 0$ is a parabola.

3. To find the x-intercepts solve $ax^2 + bx + c = 0$?

5. The x-coordinate of the vertex is $-b/(2a)$.

7. $(3, -6)$, $(4, 0)$, $(-3, 0)$

9. $(4, -128)$, $(0, 0)$, $(2, 0)$

11. Upward

13. Downward

15. Upward

17.

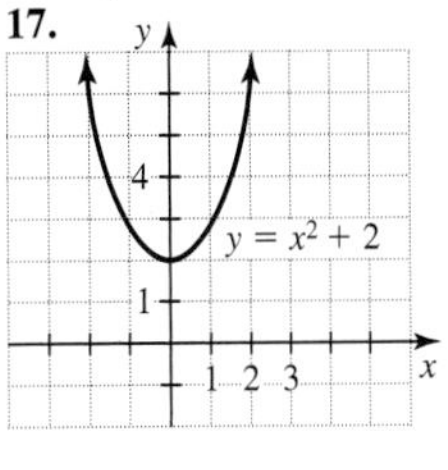

19.

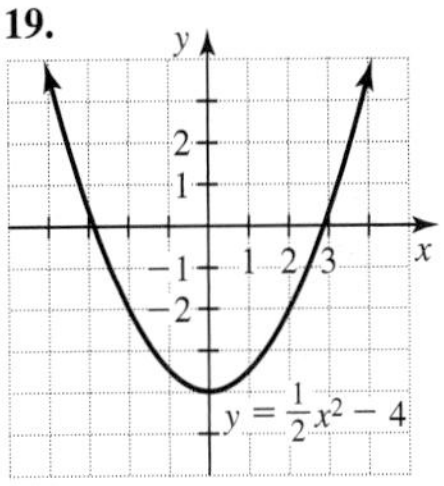

21.

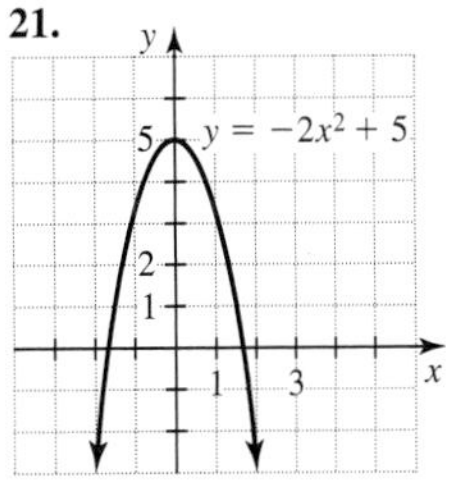

23.

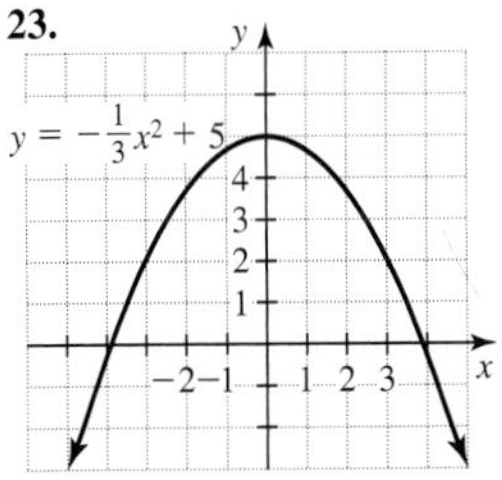

25.

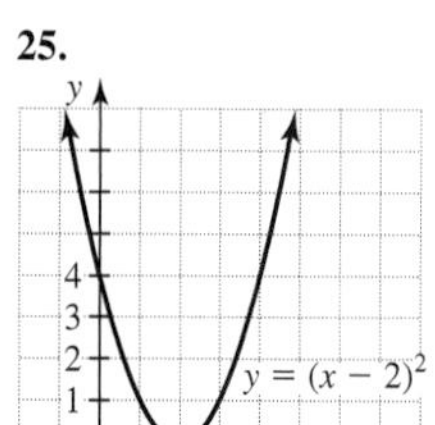

27. $(0, -9)$ **29.** $(2, -3)$

31. $(5, 51)$ **33.** $\left(\frac{1}{2}, \frac{3}{4}\right)$

35. $(0, 16), (-4, 0), (4, 0)$

37. $(0, -8), (-2, 0), (4, 0)$

39. $(0, -9), \left(\frac{3}{2}, 0\right)$

41. Vertex $\left(\frac{1}{2}, -\frac{9}{4}\right)$, intercepts $(0, -2), (-1, 0), (2, 0)$

$f(x) = x^2 - x - 2$

43. Vertex $(-1, -9)$, intercepts $(0, -8), (-4, 0), (2, 0)$

$g(x) = x^2 + 2x - 8$

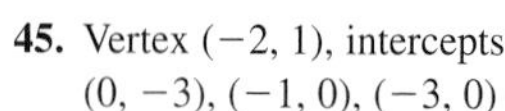

45. Vertex $(-2, 1)$, intercepts $(0, -3), (-1, 0), (-3, 0)$

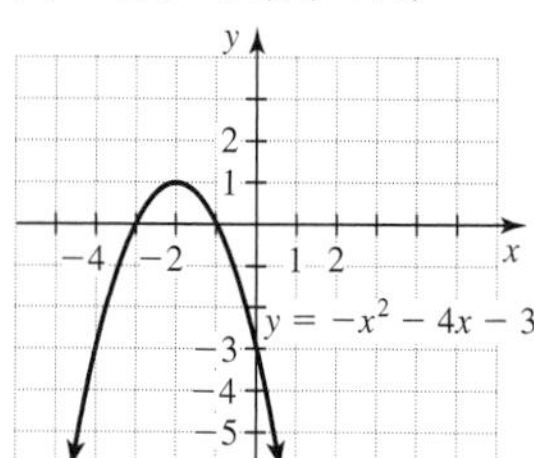

47. Vertex $\left(\frac{3}{2}, \frac{25}{4}\right)$, intercepts $(0, 4), (4, 0), (-1, 0)$

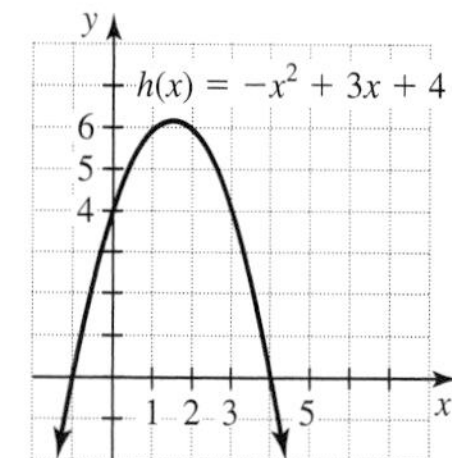

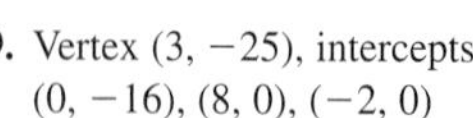

49. Vertex $(3, -25)$, intercepts $(0, -16), (8, 0), (-2, 0)$

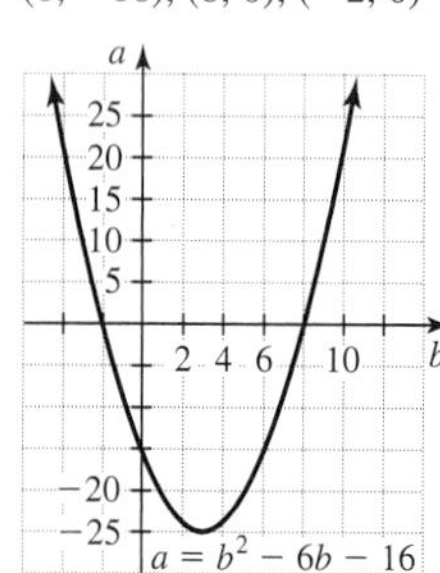

51. Minimum -8

53. Maximum 14

55. Minimum 2

57. Maximum 2

59. Maximum 64 feet

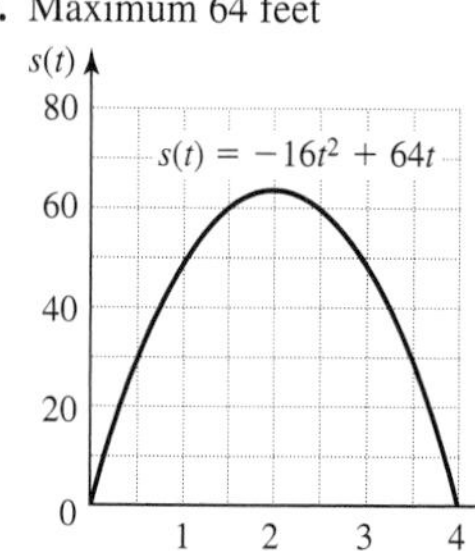

61. 100 **63.** 625 square meters **65.** 2 P.M. **67.** 15 meters, 25 meters

69. The graph of $y = ax^2$ gets narrower as a gets larger.

71. The graph of $y = x^2$ has the same shape as $x = y^2$.

73. a) Vertex $(0.84, -0.68)$, x-intercepts $(1.30, 0)$, $(0.38, 0)$
b) Vertex $(5.96, 46.26)$, x-intercepts $(12.48, 0)$, $(-0.55, 0)$

Section 10.4 Warm-Ups T F F T F F F T F F

1. If the coefficients are integers and the discriminant is a perfect square, then the quadratic polynomial can be factored.

3. If the solutions are a and b, then the quadratic equation $(x - a)(x - b) = 0$ has those solutions.

5. $x^2 + 4x - 21 = 0$ **7.** $x^2 - 5x + 4 = 0$ **9.** $x^2 - 5 = 0$
11. $x^2 + 16 = 0$ **13.** $x^2 + 2 = 0$ **15.** $6x^2 - 5x + 1 = 0$
17. Prime **19.** Prime **21.** $(3x - 4)(2x + 9)$ **23.** Prime
25. $(4x - 15)(2x + 3)$ **27.** $\{-1, 5\}$ **29.** $\left\{-\frac{3}{2}, \frac{3}{2}\right\}$
31. $\left\{\frac{-3 \pm \sqrt{5}}{2}\right\}$ **33.** $\{\pm 2, \pm 3\}$ **35.** $\{1, 3\}$ **37.** $\{\pm\sqrt{5}, \pm 3\}$
39. $\{-2, 1\}$ **41.** $\{0, \pm 3\}$ **43.** $\{-1 \pm \sqrt{5}, -3, 1\}$
45. $\{-3, -2, 1, 2\}$ **47.** $\{1, 4\}$ **49.** $\{-27, -1\}$ **51.** $\{16, 81\}$
53. $\{9\}$ **55.** $\left\{-\frac{1}{3}, \frac{1}{2}\right\}$ **57.** $\{64\}$ **59.** $\left\{\frac{2}{3}, \frac{3}{2}\right\}$
61. $\left\{\pm\frac{\sqrt{14}}{2}, \pm\frac{\sqrt{38}}{2}\right\}$ **63.** $\{-1 + \sqrt{2}, -1 - \sqrt{2}\}$ **65.** $\{\pm 2i\}$
67. $\{\pm i\sqrt{2}, \pm 2i\}$ **69.** $\{\pm 2, \pm 2i\}$ **71.** $\left\{\pm\frac{1}{2}, \pm\frac{i}{2}\right\}$
73. $\left\{\frac{1 \pm i\sqrt{3}}{2}, -1\right\}$ **75.** $\{1 \pm i\sqrt{3}, -2\}$ **77.** $\left\{\frac{1 \pm 2i}{5}\right\}$
79. $\{1 \pm i\}$ **81.** 2:00 P.M.
83. Before $-5 + \sqrt{265}$ or 11.3 mph, after $-9 + \sqrt{265}$ or 7.3 mph
85. Andrew $\frac{13 + \sqrt{265}}{2}$ or 14.6 hours, John $\frac{19 + \sqrt{265}}{2}$ or 17.6 hours
87. Length $5 + 5\sqrt{41}$ or 37.02 ft, width $-5 + 5\sqrt{41}$ or 27.02 ft
89. $14 + 2\sqrt{58}$ or 29.2 hours **91.** $-5 + 5\sqrt{5}$ or 6.2 meters
95. $\{1, 2\}$ **97.** $\{-4.25, -3.49, 0.49, 1.25\}$

Section 10.5 Warm-Ups F F F F T T T T T F

1. A quadratic inequality has the form $ax^2 + bx + c > 0$. In place of $>$ we can also use $<$, $\leq$, or $\geq$.

3. A rational inequality is an inequality involving a rational expression.

5. $(-3, 2)$

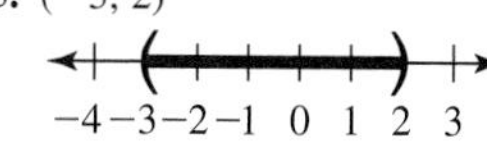

7. $(-\infty, -1] \cup [4, \infty)$

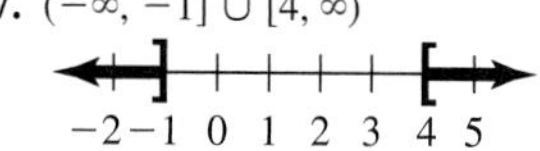

9. $[-2, 4]$

11. $(-\infty, -4] \cup \left[\frac{3}{2}, \infty\right)$

13. $(-\infty, 0] \cup [2, \infty)$

15. $(-\infty, 0) \cup \left(\frac{1}{2}, \infty\right)$

17. $(-\infty, \infty)$

19. $\varnothing$

21. $\left\{\frac{5}{2}\right\}$

23. $\left(-\infty, -\frac{1}{5}\right) \cup \left(-\frac{1}{5}, \infty\right)$

25. $(0, \infty)$

27. $(-\infty, 0) \cup (3, \infty)$

29. $[-2, 0)$

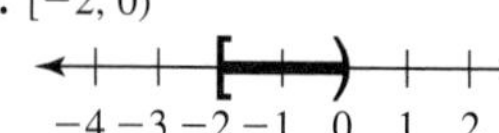

31. $(-\infty, -6) \cup (3, \infty)$

33. $(-\infty, -2) \cup (-1, \infty)$

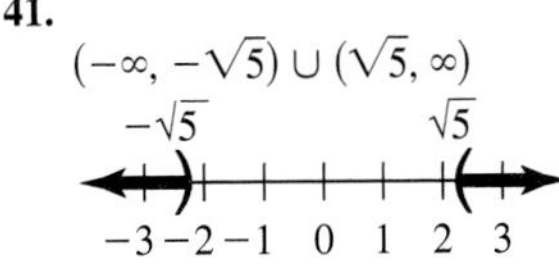

35. $(-13, -4) \cup (5, \infty)$

−4

−13 −9 −5 −1 1 3 5 7

37. $(-\infty, -5) \cup (1, 3) \cup (5, \infty)$

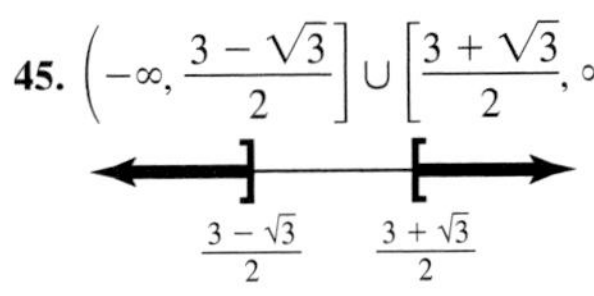

39. $[-6, 3) \cup [4, 6)$

−6 −4 −2 0 2 4 6

41. $(-\infty, -\sqrt{5}) \cup (\sqrt{5}, \infty)$

$-\sqrt{5}$ $\sqrt{5}$

−3 −2 −1 0 1 2 3

43. $[1 - \sqrt{6}, 1 + \sqrt{6}]$

$1 - \sqrt{6}$ $1 + \sqrt{6}$

45. $\left(-\infty, \frac{3 - \sqrt{3}}{2}\right] \cup \left[\frac{3 + \sqrt{3}}{2}, \infty\right)$

$\frac{3-\sqrt{3}}{2}$ $\frac{3+\sqrt{3}}{2}$

47. $\left[\frac{3 - 3\sqrt{5}}{2}, \frac{3 + 3\sqrt{5}}{2}\right]$

$\frac{3-3\sqrt{5}}{2}$ $\frac{3+3\sqrt{5}}{2}$

49. $(-\infty, \infty)$ **51.** $\varnothing$ **53.** $(-\infty, \infty)$ **55.** $(-\infty, 0) \cup (0, \infty)$
57. $(-\infty, \infty)$ **59.** $(-\infty, 0)$ **61.** $[-3, 3]$ **63.** $(-4, 4)$
65. $(-\infty, 0] \cup [4, \infty)$ **67.** $\left(-\frac{3}{2}, \frac{5}{3}\right)$ **69.** $(-\infty, -2] \cup [6, \infty)$
71. $(-\infty, -3) \cup (5, \infty)$ **73.** $(-\infty, -4] \cup [2, \infty)$ **75.** $(-3, 4]$
77. $[-1, 2] \cup [5, \infty)$ **79.** $(-\infty, -3) \cup (-1, 1)$ **81.** $(-27.58, -0.68)$
83. $(-\infty, -2 - \sqrt{6}) \cup (-3, -2 + \sqrt{6}) \cup (2, \infty)$
85. Greater than 5, or 6, 7, 8, . . . **87.** 4 seconds
89. a) 900 ft **b)** 3 seconds **c)** 3 seconds
91. a) (h, k) **b)** $(-\infty, h) \cup (k, \infty)$ **c)** $(-k, -h)$
d) $(-\infty, -k] \cup [-h, \infty)$ **e)** $(-\infty, h] \cup (k, \infty)$ **f)** $(-k, -h]$
93. c **95.** b

Enriching Your Mathematical Word Power

1. b **2.** a **3.** d **4.** c **5.** b **6.** b **7.** c **8.** a **9.** c
10. a **11.** c

Review Exercises

1. $\{-3, 5\}$ **3.** $\left\{-3, \frac{5}{2}\right\}$ **5.** $\{-5, 5\}$ **7.** $\left\{\frac{3}{2}\right\}$ **9.** $\{\pm 2\sqrt{3}\}$

11. $\{-2, 4\}$ **13.** $\left\{\frac{4 \pm \sqrt{3}}{2}\right\}$ **15.** $\left\{\pm\frac{3}{2}\right\}$ **17.** $\{2, 4\}$ **19.** $\{2, 3\}$

21. $\left\{\frac{1}{2}, 3\right\}$ **23.** $\{-2 \pm \sqrt{3}\}$ **25.** $\{-2, 5\}$ **27.** $\left\{-\frac{1}{3}, \frac{3}{2}\right\}$

29. $\{-2 \pm \sqrt{2}\}$ **31.** $\left\{\frac{5 \pm \sqrt{13}}{6}\right\}$ **33.** 0, 1 **35.** −19, 0

37. 17, 2 **39.** $\left\{\frac{2 \pm i\sqrt{2}}{2}\right\}$ **41.** $\left\{\frac{3 \pm i\sqrt{15}}{4}\right\}$

43. $\left\{\frac{-1 \pm i\sqrt{5}}{3}\right\}$ **45.** $\{-3 \pm i\sqrt{7}\}$

47. Vertex $(3, -9)$, intercepts $(0, 0)$, $(6, 0)$

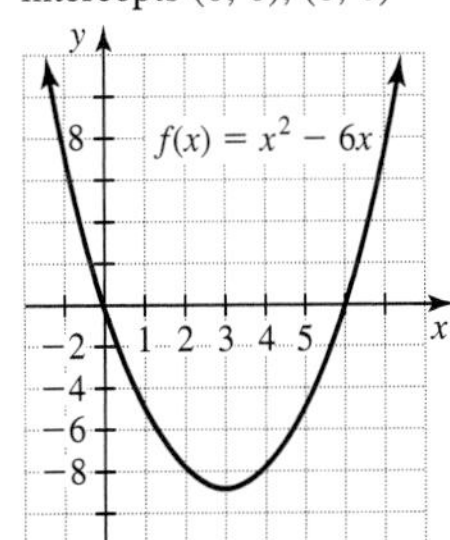

49. Vertex $(2, -16)$, intercepts $(0, -12)$, $(-2, 0)$, and $(6, 0)$

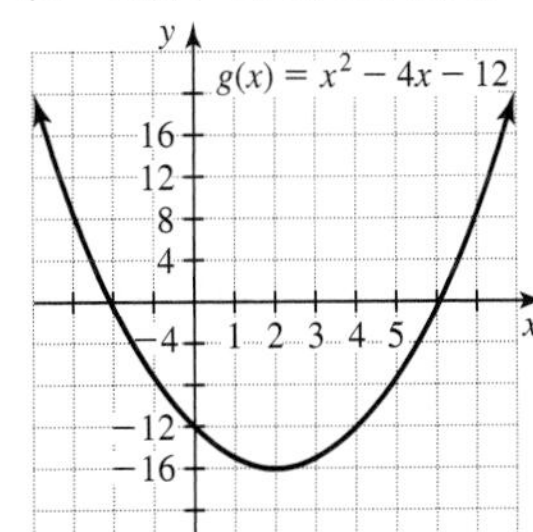

51. Vertex $(2, 8)$, intercepts $(0, 0)$, $(4, 0)$

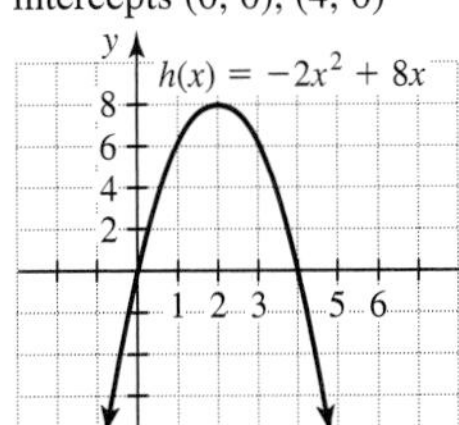

53. Vertex $(1, 4)$, intercepts $(0, 3)$, $(-1, 0)$, $(3, 0)$

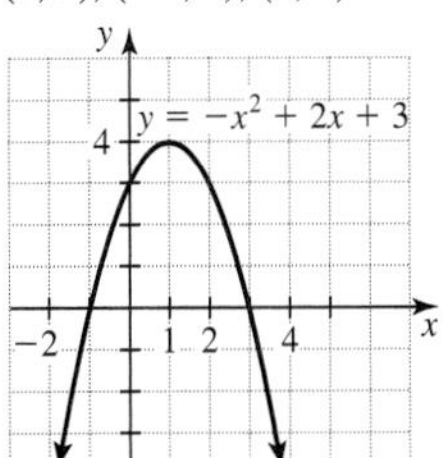

55. Minimum, −3
57. Maximum, 4.125 **59.** $(4x + 1)(2x - 3)$
61. Prime **63.** $(4y - 5)(2y + 5)$ **65.** $x^2 + 9x + 18 = 0$
67. $x^2 - 50 = 0$ **69.** $\{-2, 1\}$ **71.** $\{\pm 2, \pm 3\}$ **73.** $\{-6, -5, 2, 3\}$
75. $\{-2, 8\}$ **77.** $\left\{-\frac{1}{9}, \frac{1}{4}\right\}$ **79.** $\{16, 81\}$

81. $(-\infty, -3) \cup (2, \infty)$

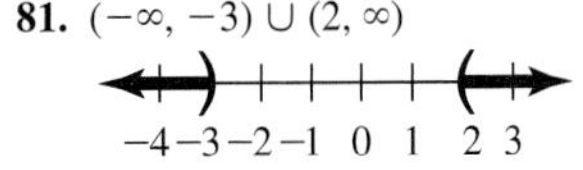

83. $[-4, 5]$

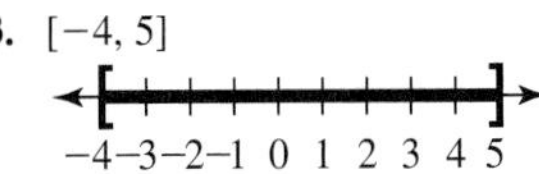

85. $(0, 1)$

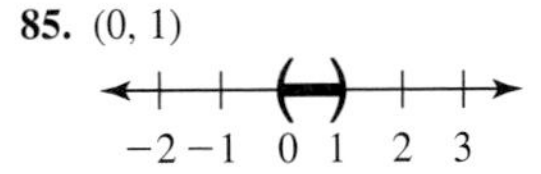

87. $(-\infty, -2) \cup [4, \infty)$

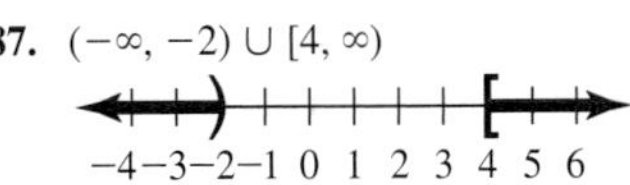

89. $(-3, \infty)$

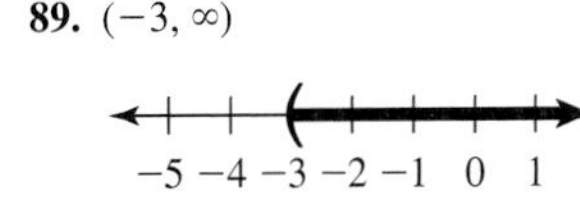

91. $(-2, -1) \cup \left(-\frac{1}{2}, \infty\right)$

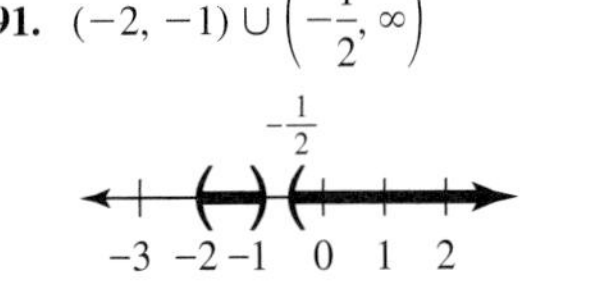

93. $\left\{\frac{5}{12}\right\}$ **95.** $\left\{\frac{-3 \pm \sqrt{5}}{2}\right\}$ **97.** $\left\{\frac{4 \pm 2i}{3}\right\}$ **99.** $\left\{\frac{5}{2}\right\}$

101. $\left\{-2, -\frac{1}{4}\right\}$ **103.** $\{625, 10{,}000\}$

105. $-2 + 2\sqrt{2}$ and $2 + 2\sqrt{2}$, or 0.83 and 4.83

107. Width $\frac{4 + \sqrt{706}}{2}$ or 15.3 inches, height $\frac{-4 + \sqrt{706}}{2}$ or 11.3 inches

109. 2 inches **111.** Width 5 ft, length 9 ft **113.** $20.40, 400
115. 0.5 second and 1.5 seconds

Chapter 10 Test

1. −7, 0 **2.** 13, 2 **3.** 0, 1 **4.** $\left\{-3, \frac{1}{2}\right\}$ **5.** $\{-3 \pm \sqrt{3}\}$

6. $\{-5\}$ **7.** $\left\{-2, \frac{3}{2}\right\}$ **8.** $\{-4, 3\}$ **9.** $\{\pm 1, \pm 2\}$ **10.** $\{11, 27\}$

11. $\{\pm 6i\}$ **12.** $\{-3 \pm i\}$ **13.** $\left\{\frac{1 \pm i\sqrt{11}}{6}\right\}$

14. Vertex $(0, 16)$, intercepts $(0, 16)$, $(-4, 0)$, $(4, 0)$, maximum y-value 16

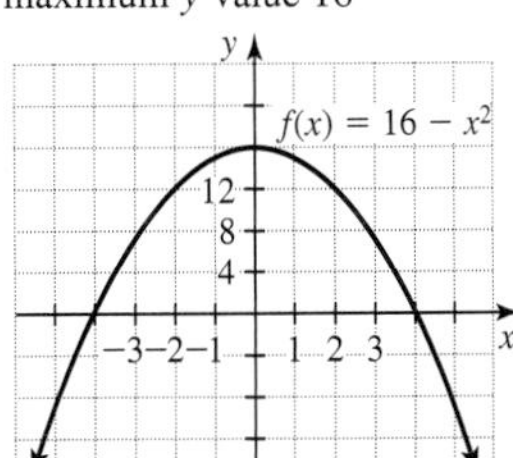

15. Vertex $(1.5, -2.25)$, intercepts $(0, 0)$, $(3, 0)$, minimum y-value −2.25

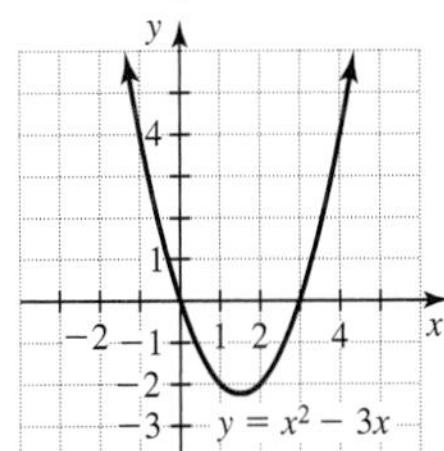

16. $x^2 - 2x - 24 = 0$ **17.** $x^2 + 25 = 0$

18. $(-6, 3)$ **19.** $(-1, 2) \cup (8, \infty)$

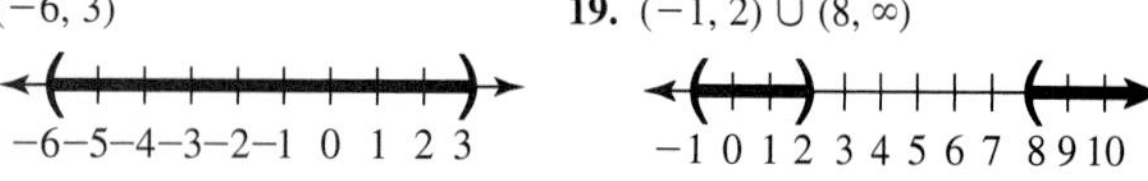

20. Width $-1 + \sqrt{17}$ ft, length $1 + \sqrt{17}$ ft **21.** $\dfrac{5 + \sqrt{37}}{2}$ or 5.5 hours

22. 36 feet

Making Connections A Review of Chapters 1–10

1. $\left\{\dfrac{15}{2}\right\}$ **2.** $\left\{\pm\dfrac{\sqrt{30}}{2}\right\}$ **3.** $\left\{-3, \dfrac{5}{2}\right\}$ **4.** $\left\{\dfrac{-2 \pm \sqrt{34}}{2}\right\}$

5. $\left\{-\dfrac{7}{2}, -2\right\}$ **6.** $\left\{-3, \dfrac{1}{4}, \dfrac{-11 \pm \sqrt{73}}{8}\right\}$ **7.** $\{9\}$ **8.** $\left\{-\dfrac{3}{2}, \dfrac{13}{2}\right\}$

9. $(-4, \infty)$ **10.** $\left[\dfrac{1}{2}, 5\right]$ **11.** $\left[\dfrac{1}{2}, 5\right)$ **12.** $(2, 8)$ **13.** $[-3, 2)$

14. $(-\infty, \infty)$ **15.** $y = \dfrac{2}{3}x - 3$ **16.** $y = -\dfrac{1}{2}x + 2$

17. $y = \dfrac{-c \pm \sqrt{c^2 - 12d}}{6}$ **18.** $y = \dfrac{n \pm \sqrt{n^2 + 4mw}}{2m}$

19. $y = \dfrac{5}{6}x - \dfrac{25}{12}$ **20.** $y = -\dfrac{2}{3}x + \dfrac{17}{3}$ **21.** $\dfrac{4}{3}$ **22.** $-\dfrac{11}{7}$

23. -2 **24.** $\dfrac{58}{5}$ **25.** 40,000, 38,000, \$32.50

26. \$800,000, \$950,000, \$40 or \$80, \$60

Chapter 11

Section 11.1 Warm-Ups F T T F T F T F T T

1. It means that b is uniquely determined by a.
3. A relation is any set of ordered pairs.
5. The range of a relation is the set of all second coordinates.
7. Yes **9.** No **11.** Yes **13.** No **15.** $C = 0.50t + 5$
17. $T = 1.09S$ **19.** $C = 2\pi r$ **21.** $P = 4s$ **23.** $A = 5h$
25. Yes **27.** Yes **29.** No **31.** Yes **33.** Yes **35.** No
37. No **39.** Yes **41.** (2, 1), (2, −1) **43.** (8, 4), (8, −4)
45. (0, 1), (0, −1) **47.** (16, 2), (16, −2) **49.** (3, 1), (3, −1)
51. Yes **53.** No **55.** Yes **57.** No **59.** Yes **61.** No
63. No **65.** Yes **67.** No **69.** No **71.** Yes **73.** No
75. {4, 7}, {1} **77.** {2}, {3, 5, 7} **79.** $(-\infty, \infty), (-\infty, \infty)$
81. $(-\infty, \infty), (-\infty, \infty)$ **83.** $[2, \infty), [0, \infty)$ **85.** $[0, \infty), [0, \infty)$
87. −2 **89.** 10 **91.** −12 **93.** 1 **95.** 2.236
97. 2 **99.** 0 **101.** −10 **103.** a) 192 ft b) 0 ft
105. $A = s^2$ or $A(s) = s^2$ **107.** $C(x) = 3.98x$, \$11.94
109. $C(n) = 14.95 + 0.50n$, \$17.95

Section 11.2 Warm-Ups T T T T T F T T F T

1. A linear function is a function of the form $f(x) = mx + b$, where m and b are real numbers with $m \neq 0$.
3. The graph of a constant function is a horizontal line.
5. The graph of a quadratic function is a parabola.

7. $(-\infty, \infty), \{-2\}$

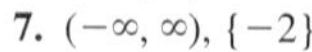

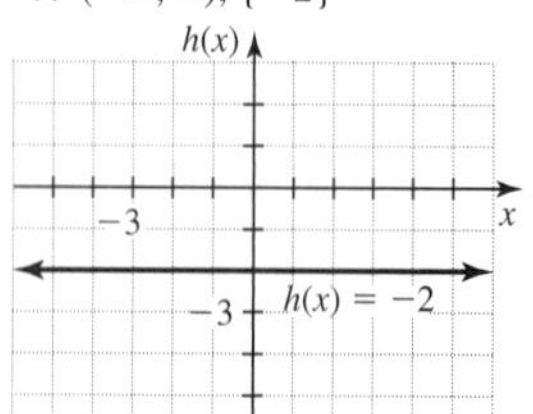

9. $(-\infty, \infty), (-\infty, \infty)$

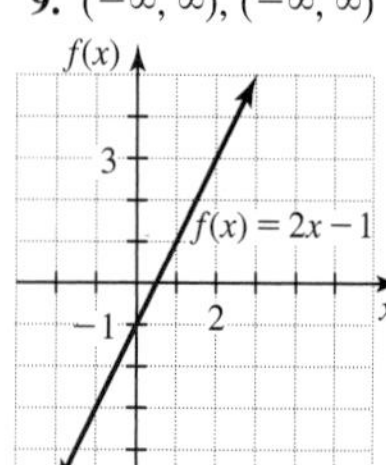

11. $(-\infty, \infty), (-\infty, \infty)$

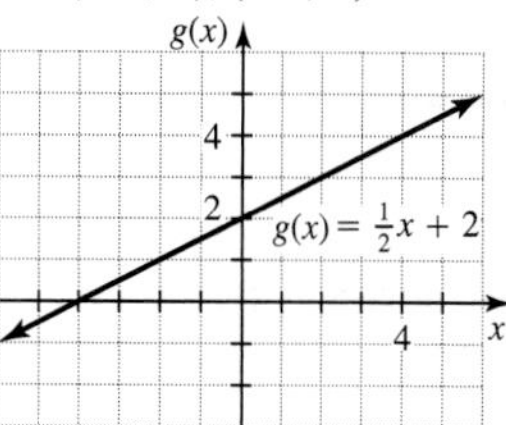

13. $(-\infty, \infty), (-\infty, \infty)$

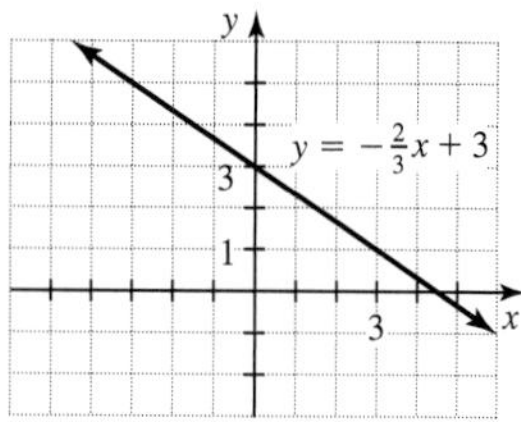

15. $(-\infty, \infty), (-\infty, \infty)$

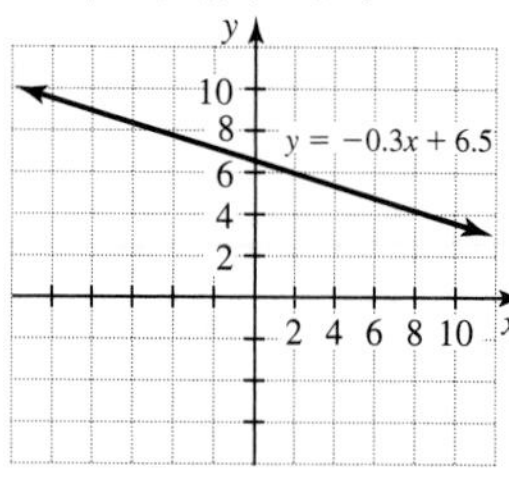

17. $(-\infty, \infty), [1, \infty)$

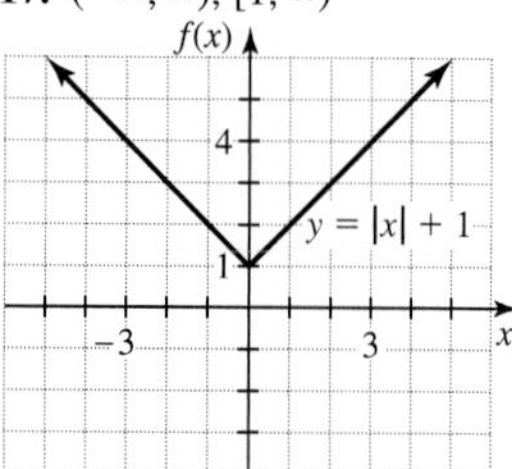

19. $(-\infty, \infty), [0, \infty)$

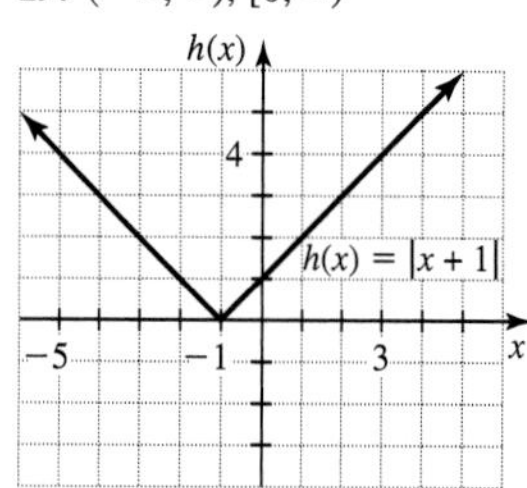

21. $(-\infty, \infty), [0, \infty)$

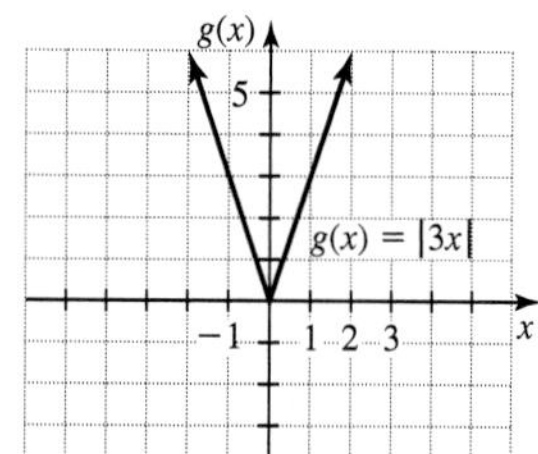

23. $(-\infty, \infty), [0, \infty)$

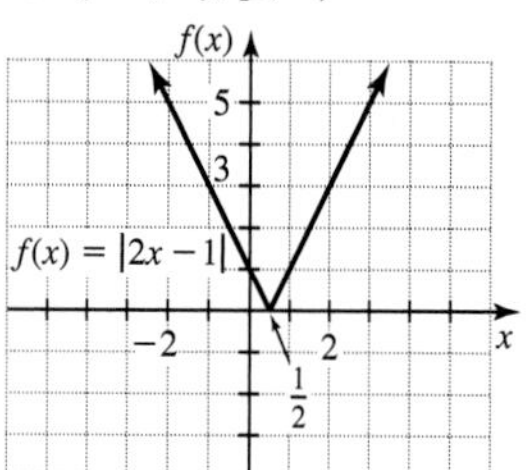

25. $(-\infty, \infty), [1, \infty)$

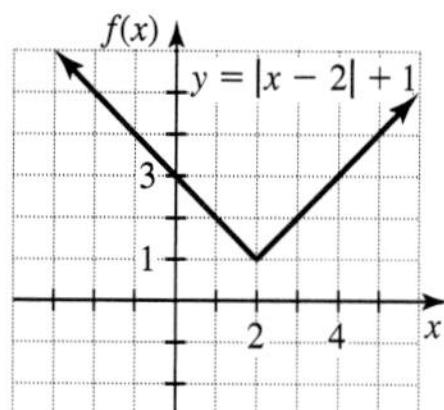

27. $(-\infty, \infty), [0, \infty)$

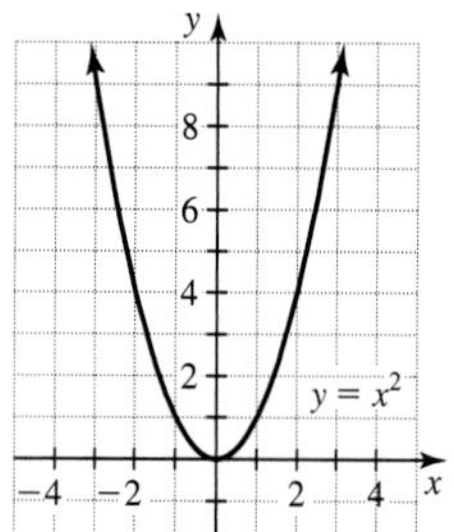

29. $(-\infty, \infty), [2, \infty)$

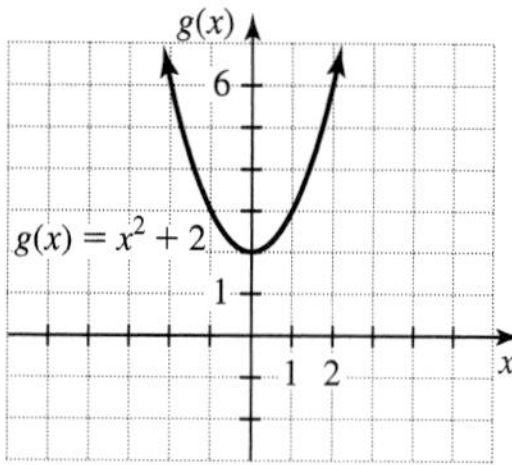

31. $(-\infty, \infty), [0, \infty)$

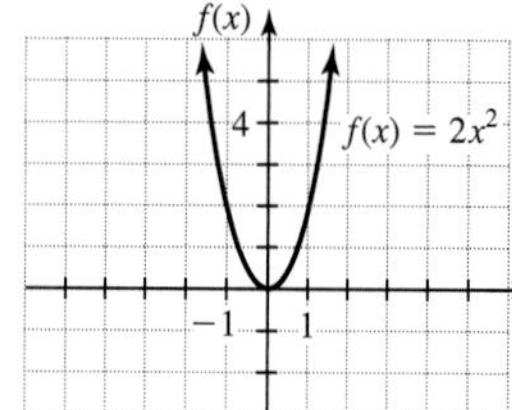

33. $(-\infty, \infty), (-\infty, 6]$

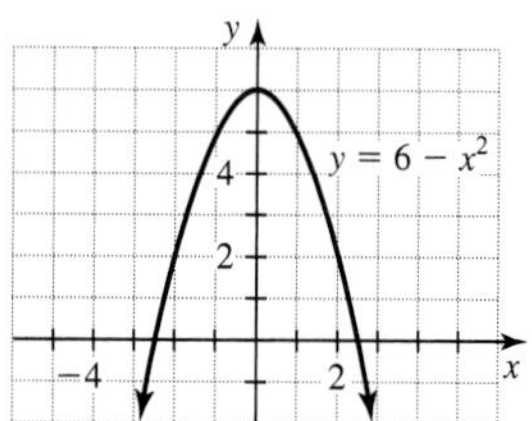

35. $[0, \infty), [0, \infty)$

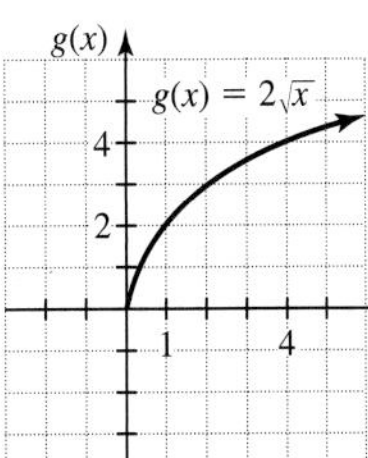

37. $[1, \infty), [0, \infty)$

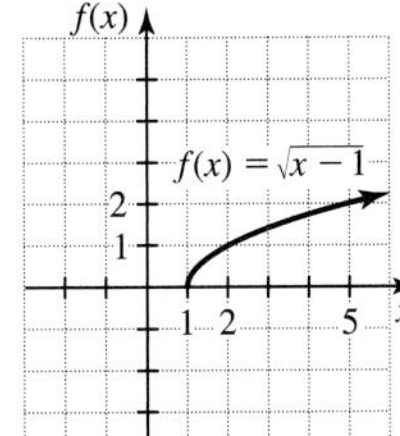

39. $[0, \infty), (-\infty, 0]$

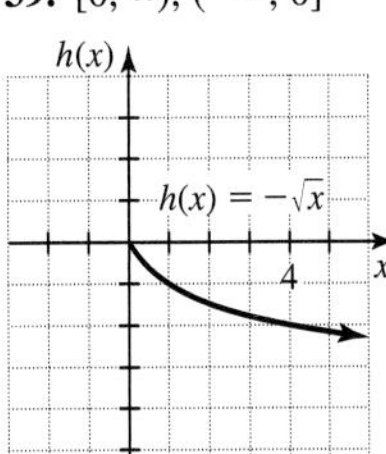

41. $[0, \infty), [2, \infty)$

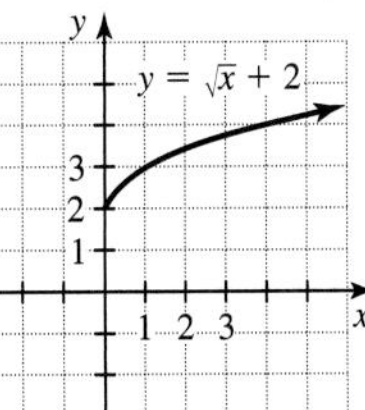

43. $[0, \infty), (-\infty, \infty)$

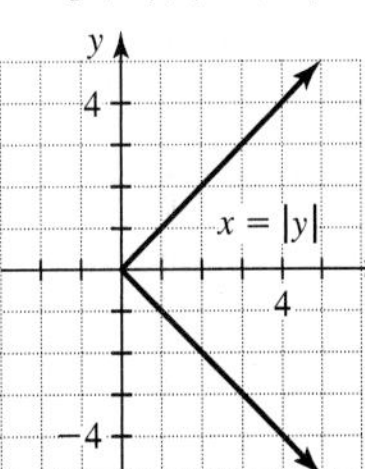

45. $(-\infty, 0], (-\infty, \infty)$

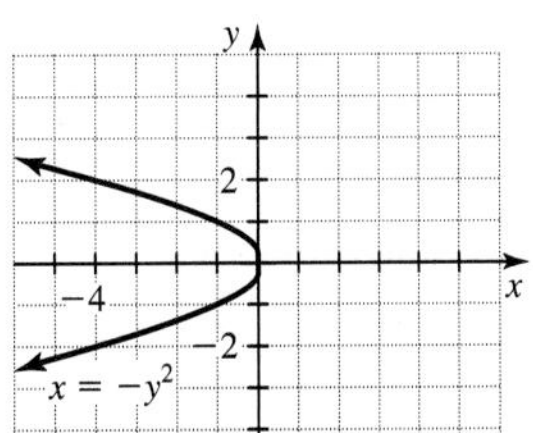

47. $\{5\}, (-\infty, \infty)$

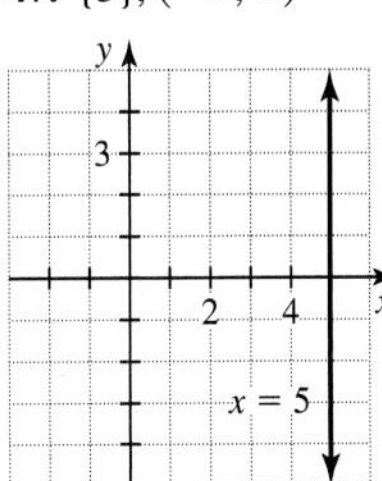

49. $[-9, \infty), (-\infty, \infty)$

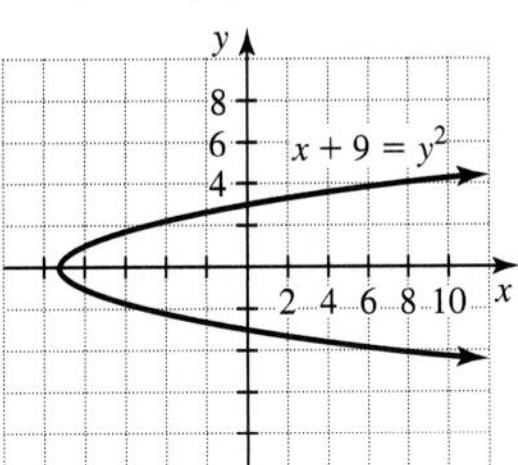

51. $[0, \infty), [0, \infty)$

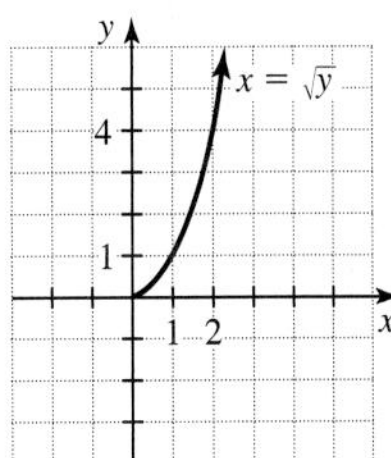

53. $[0, \infty), (-\infty, \infty)$

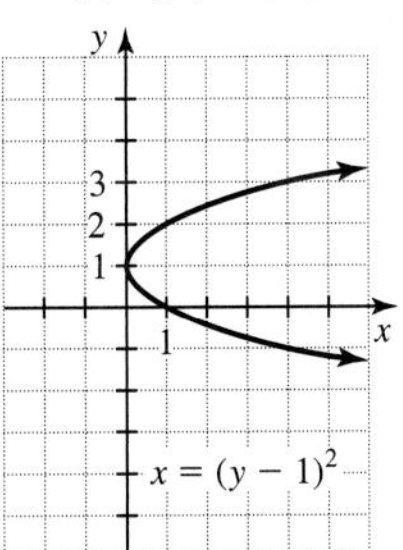

55. $(-\infty, \infty), (-\infty, 1]$

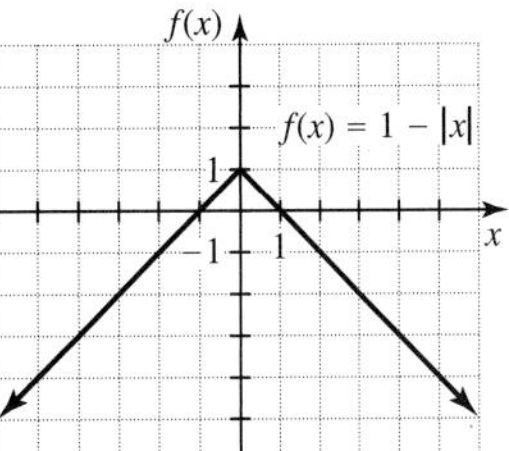

57. $(-\infty, \infty), [-1, \infty)$

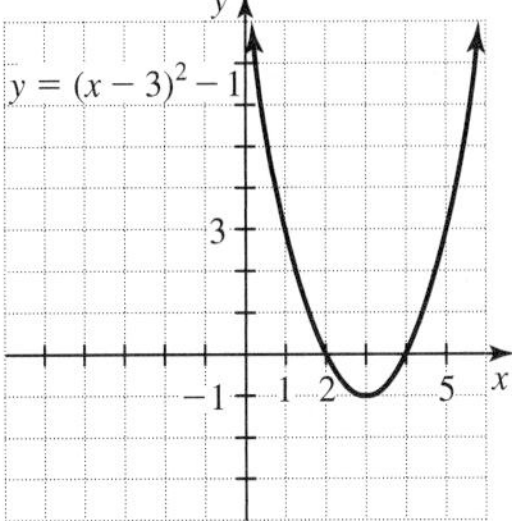

59. $(-\infty, \infty), [1, \infty)$

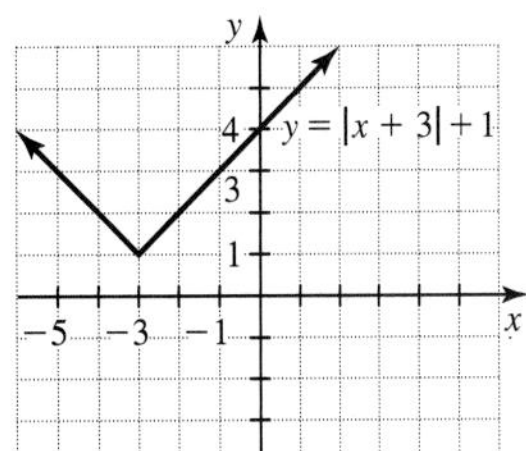

61. $[0, \infty), [-3, \infty)$

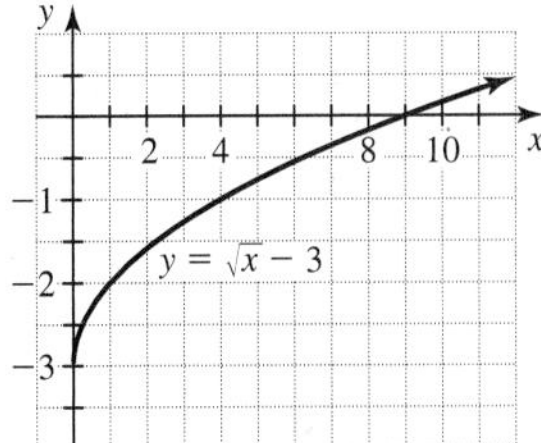

63. $(-\infty, \infty), (-\infty, \infty)$

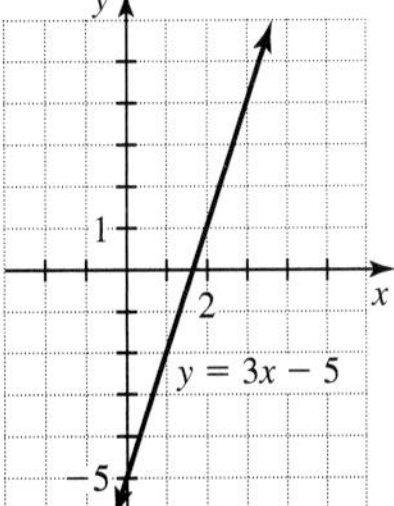

65. $(-\infty, \infty), (-\infty, 0]$

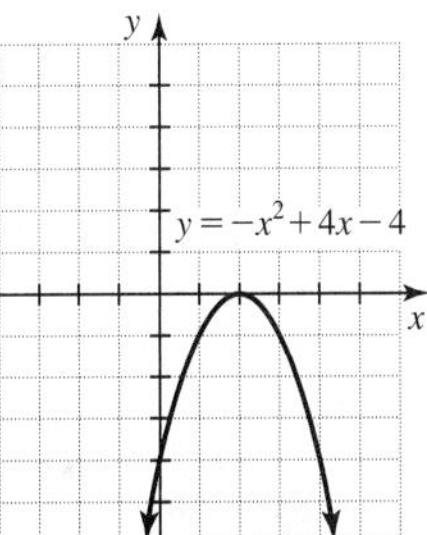

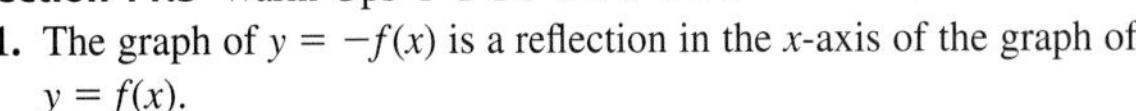

67. The graph of $f(x) = \sqrt{x^2}$ is the same as the graph of $f(x) = |x|$.

69. For large values of a the graph gets narrower and for smaller values of a the graph gets broader.

71. The graph of $y = (x - h)^2$ moves to the right for $h > 0$ and to the left for $h < 0$.

73. The graph of $y = f(x - h)$ lies to the right of the graph of $y = f(x)$ when $h > 0$.

Section 11.3 Warm-Ups F T T F T T F T T F

1. The graph of $y = -f(x)$ is a reflection in the x-axis of the graph of $y = f(x)$.

3. The graph of $y = f(x) + k$ for $k < 0$ is a downward translation of $y = f(x)$.

5. The graph of $y = f(x - h)$ for $h < 0$ is a translation to the left of $y = f(x)$.

7.

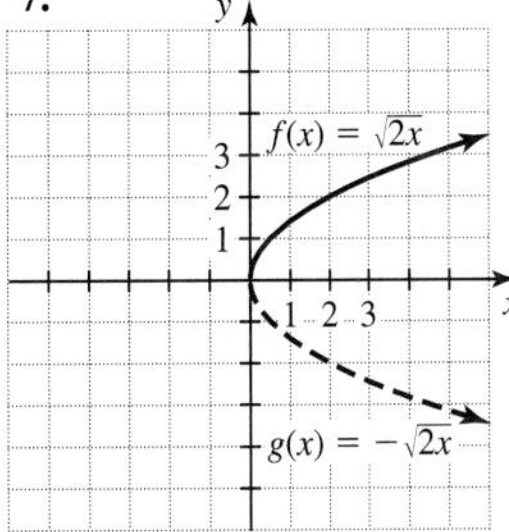

9.

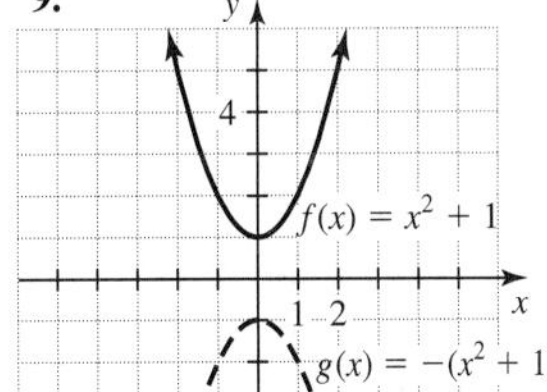

11.

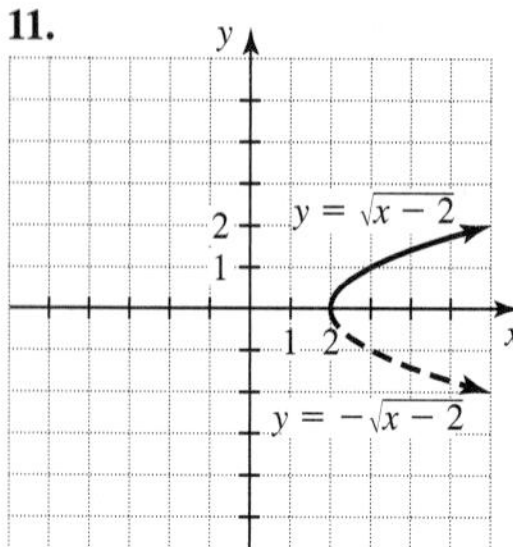

13.

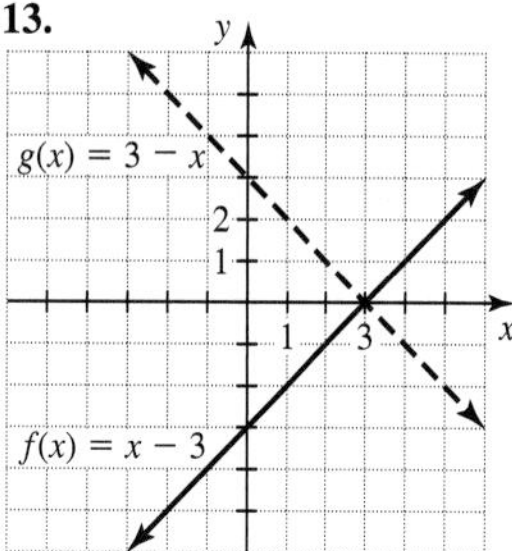

15. $(-\infty, \infty)$, $[-4, \infty)$

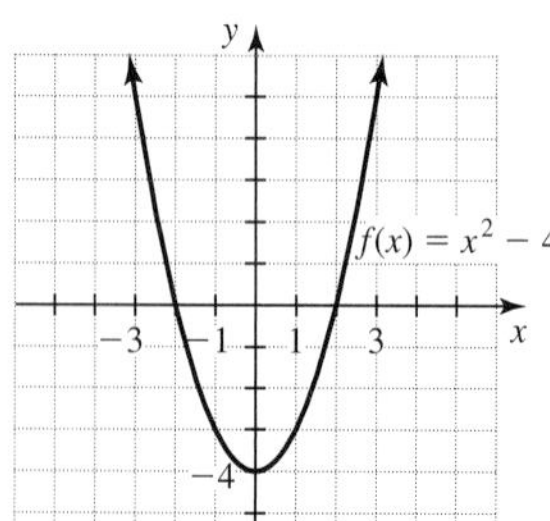

17. $(-\infty, \infty)$, $(-\infty, \infty)$

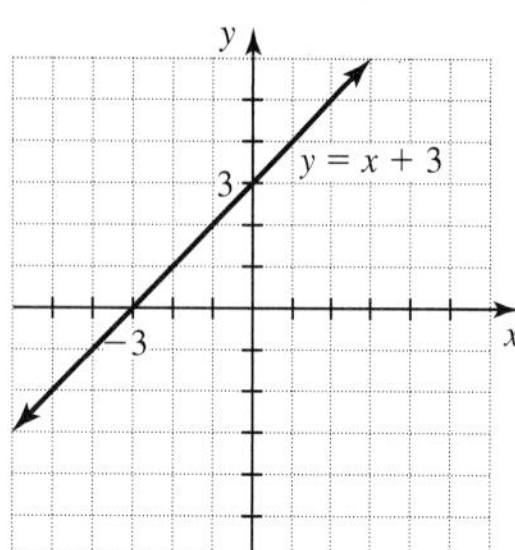

19. $(-\infty, \infty)$, $[0, \infty)$

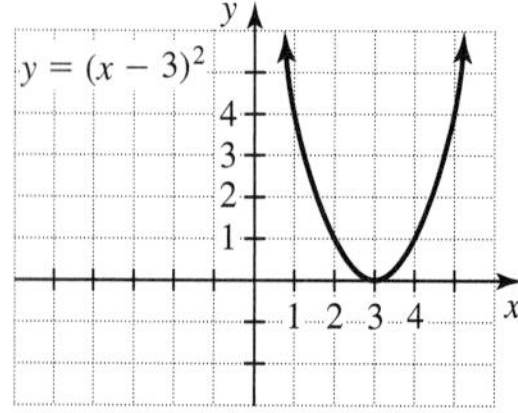

21. $[0, \infty)$, $[1, \infty)$

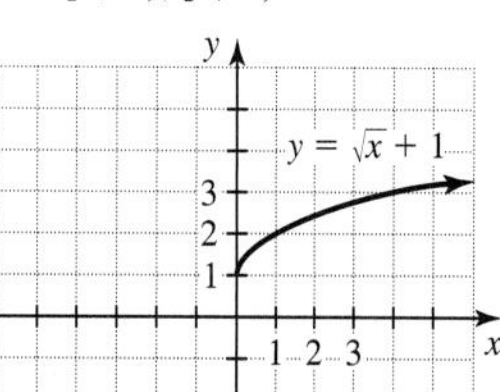

23. $(-\infty, \infty)$, $[0, \infty)$

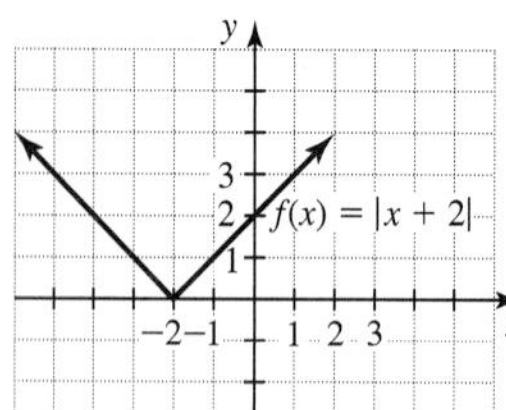

25. $(-\infty, \infty)$, $[2, \infty)$

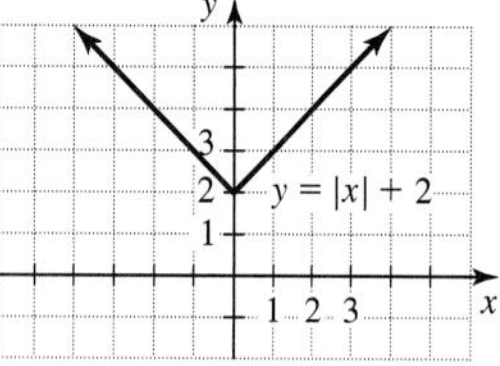

27. $[1, \infty)$, $[0, \infty)$

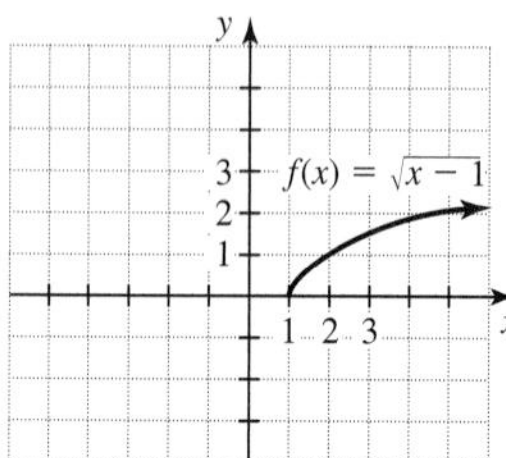

29. $(-\infty, \infty)$, $[0, \infty)$

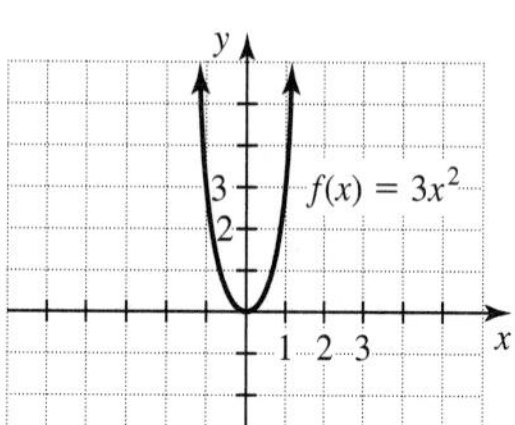

31. $(-\infty, \infty)$, $(-\infty, \infty)$

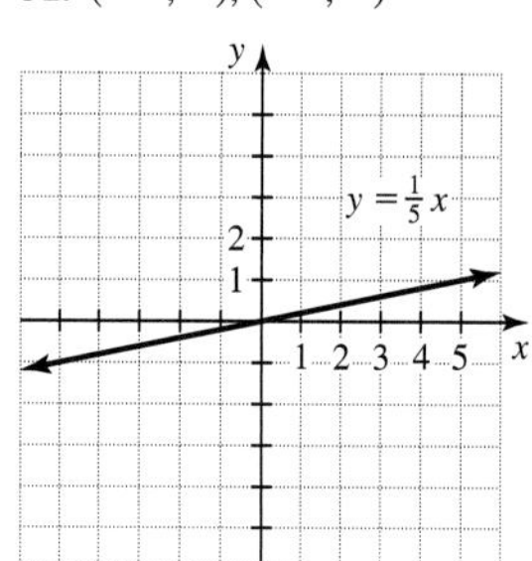

33. $[0, \infty)$, $[0, \infty)$

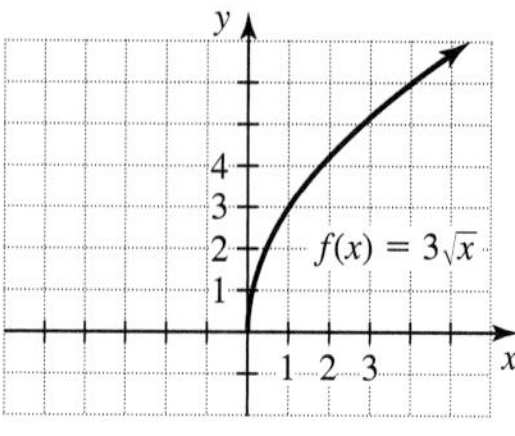

35. $(-\infty, \infty)$, $[0, \infty)$

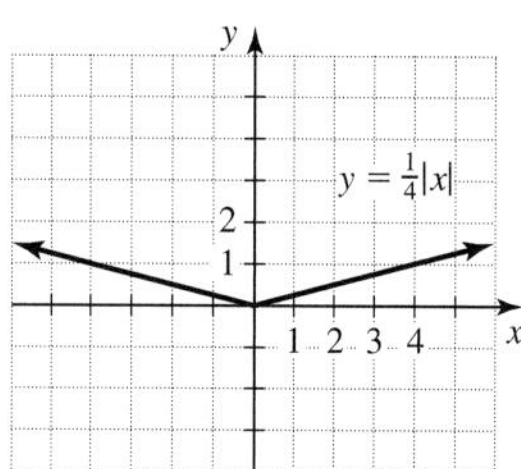

37. $[2, \infty)$, $[1, \infty)$

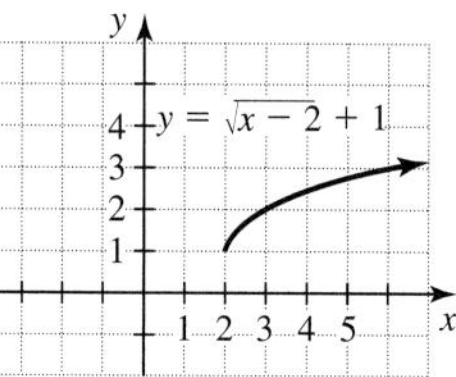

39. $(-\infty, \infty)$, $[-5, \infty)$

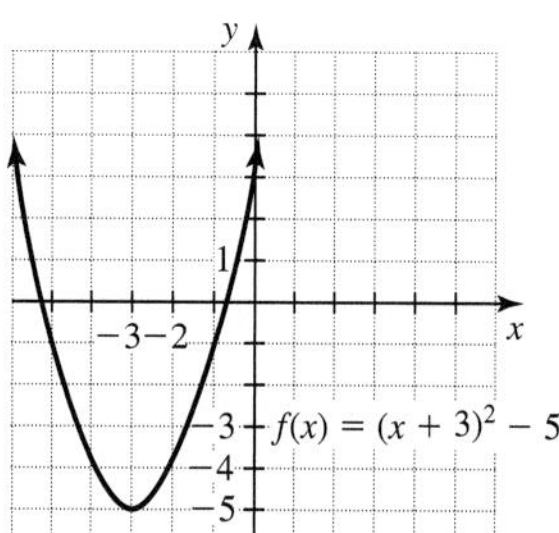

41. $(-\infty, \infty)$, $(-\infty, 0]$

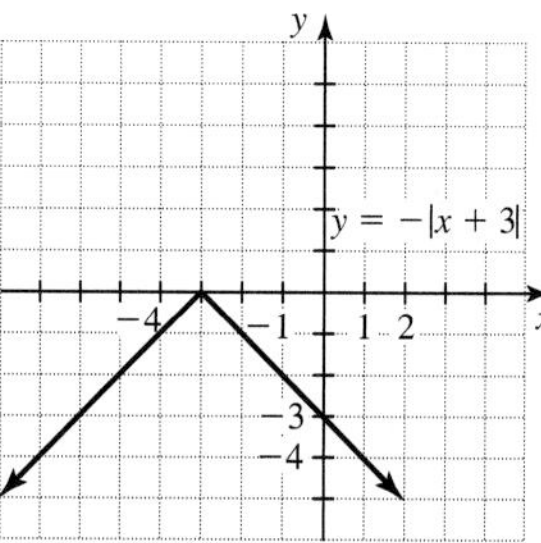

43. $[-1, \infty)$, $(-\infty, -2]$

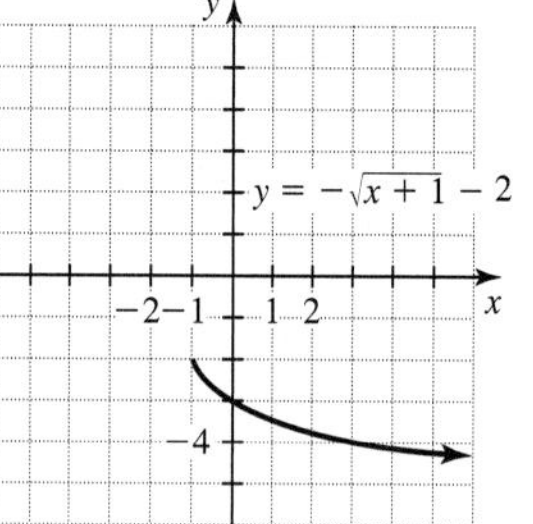

45. $(-\infty, \infty)$, $(-\infty, 4]$

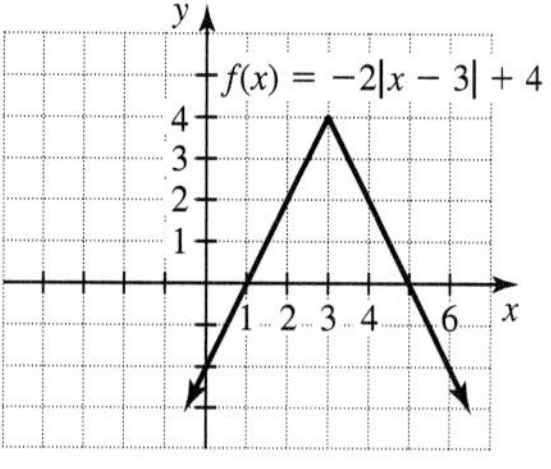

47. $(-\infty, \infty)$, $(-\infty, \infty)$

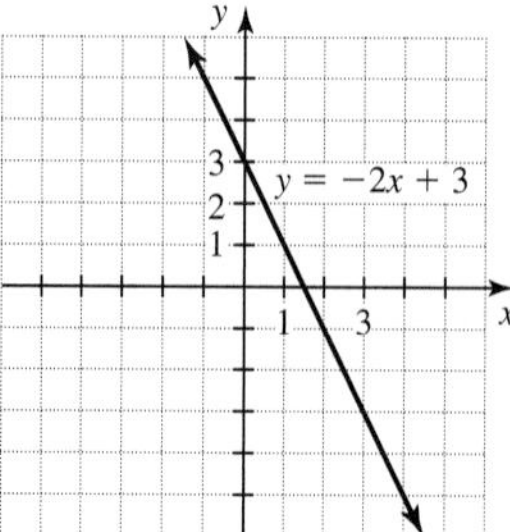

49. $(-\infty, \infty)$, $[1, \infty)$

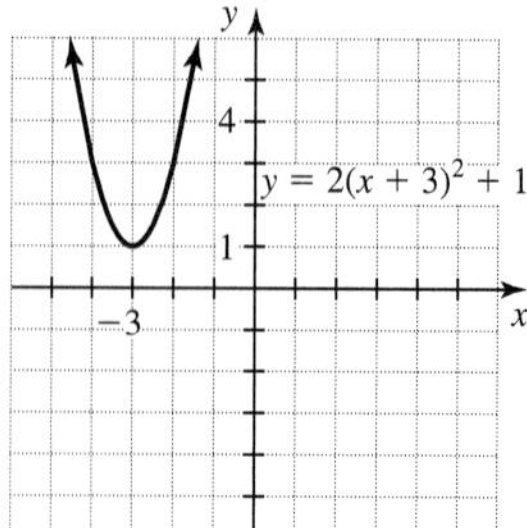

51. $(-\infty, \infty)$, $(-\infty, 2]$

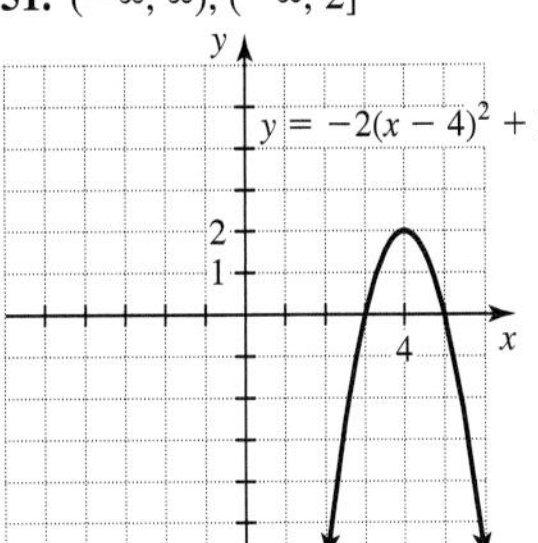

53. $(-\infty, \infty)$, $(-\infty, 6]$

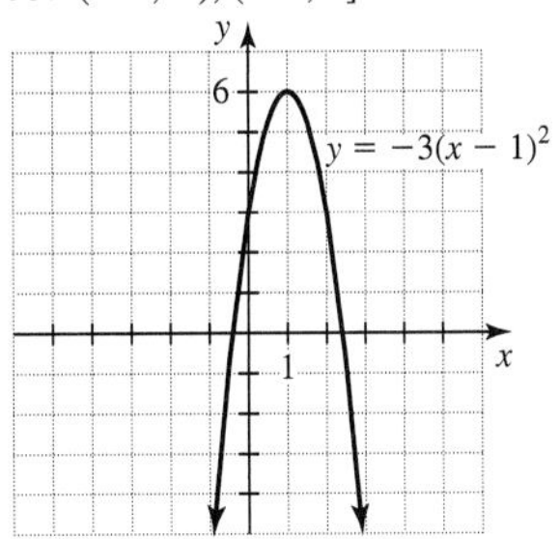

55. d **57.** e **59.** h **61.** c **63.** $y = x^2 + 8$
65. $y = \sqrt{x + 5}$ **67.** $y = |x + 3| + 5$
69. Move f to the right 20 units and upward 30 units.

Section 11.4 Warm-Ups F T T F F T T F F F

1. A cubic function is a third-degree polynomial function.
3. To find x-intercepts set y equal to zero and solve the resulting equation.
5. The factor corresponding to that intercept must occur with an even exponent.

7. $(-1, 0)$, $(0, 1)$

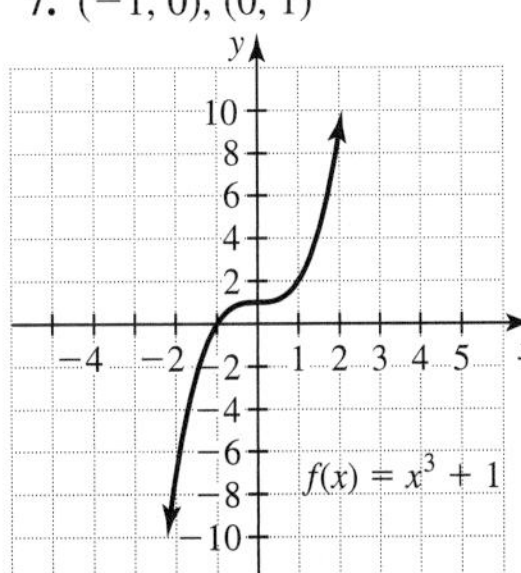

9. $(-3, 0)$, $(3, 0)$, $(0, 0)$

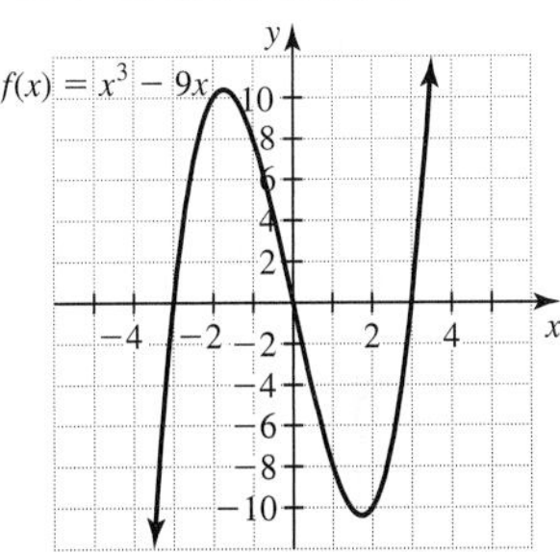

11. $(0, 0)$, $(-4, 0)$

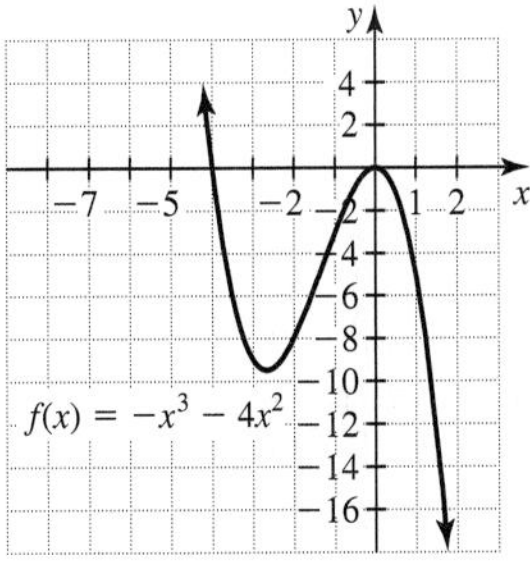

13. $(-2, 0)$, $(-1, 0)$, $(2, 0)$, $(0, -4)$

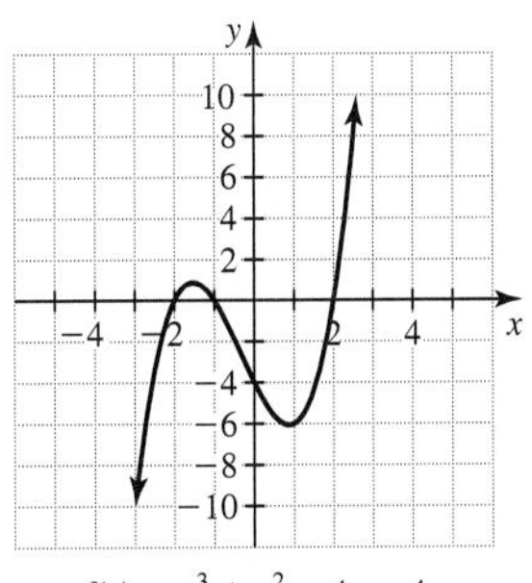

$f(x) = x^3 + x^2 - 4x - 4$

15. $(-3, 0)$, $(3, 0)$, $(0, 27)$

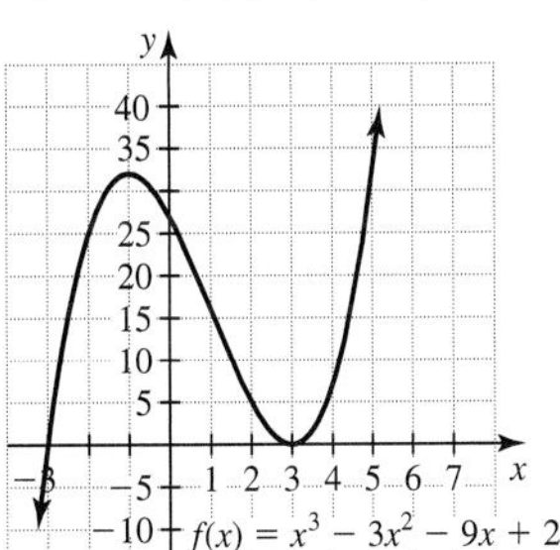

17. $(-1, 0)$, $(1, 0)$, $(0, -1)$

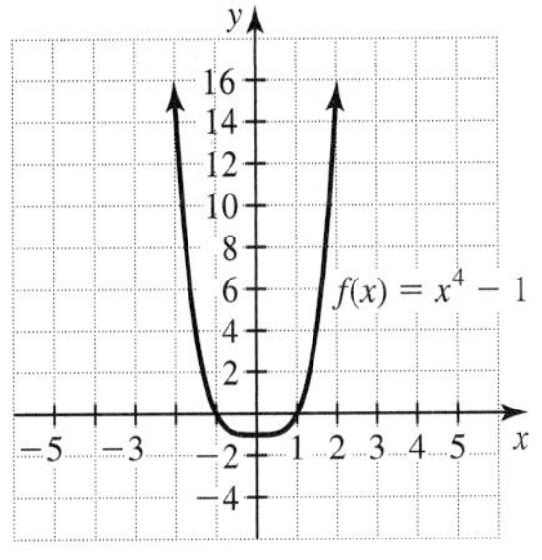

19. $(-2, 0)$, $(0, 0)$, $(2, 0)$

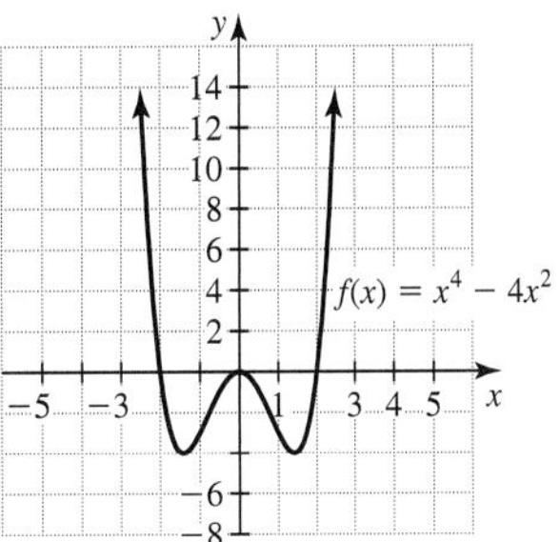

21. $(-2, 0)$, $(-1, 0)$, $(1, 0)$, $(2, 0)$, $(0, 4)$

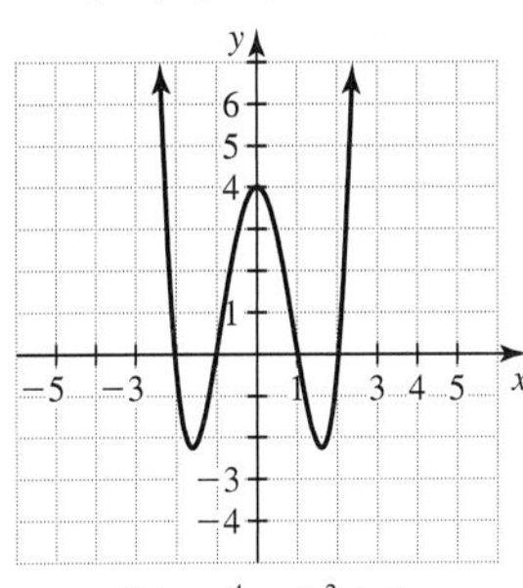

$f(x) = x^4 - 5x^2 + 4$

23. $(-2, 0)$, $(-1, 0)$, $(0, 0)$, $(2, 0)$

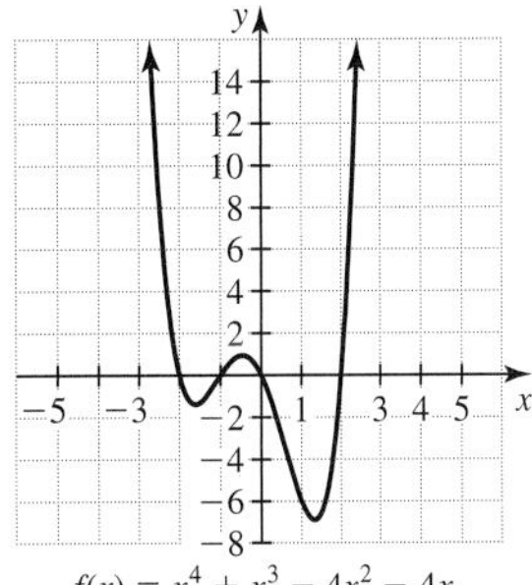

$f(x) = x^4 + x^3 - 4x^2 - 4x$

25. $(-3, 0)$, $(0, 0)$, $(3, 0)$

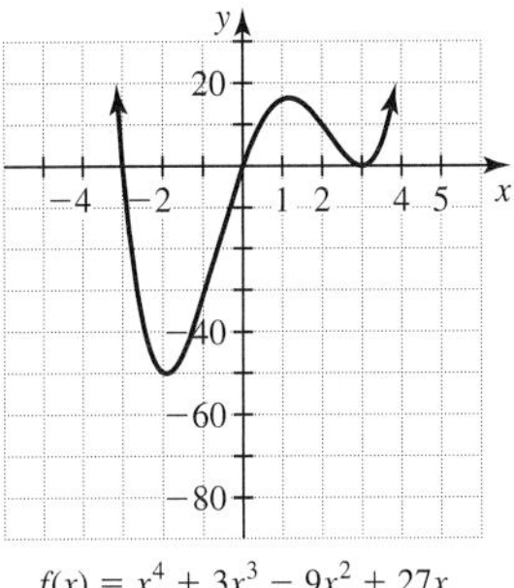

$f(x) = x^4 + 3x^3 - 9x^2 + 27x$

27. Crosses at $(8, 0)$; does not cross at $(2, 0)$.
29. Does not cross at $(-4, 0)$ and $(1, 0)$.
31. Crosses at $(-4, 0)$ and $(1, 0)$; does not cross at $(7, 0)$.
33. Crosses at $(-6, 0)$, $(-1, 0)$, and $(1, 0)$.
35. Crosses at $(5, 0)$; does not cross at $(0, 0)$.
37. Crosses at $(0, 0)$ and $(5, 0)$.
39. Does not cross at $(-3, 0)$ and $(0, 0)$.
41. $f(x) = (x - 5)^3 - 4$ **43.** $f(x) = (x + 6)^3 + 3$ **45.** $f(x) = -x^3$
47. $f(x) = -(x - 3)^4$ **49.** d **51.** a **53.** c **55.** e

57.

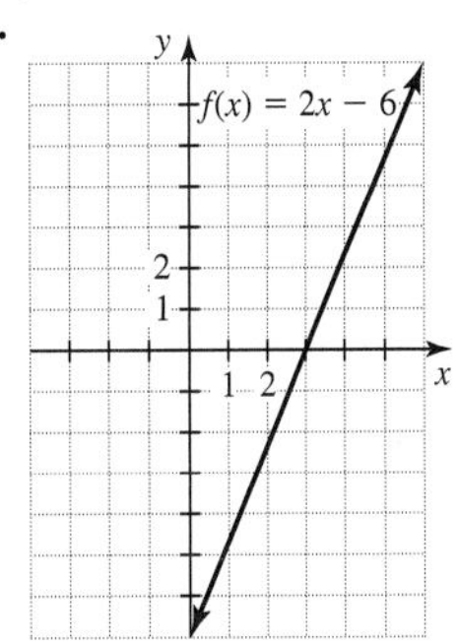

59.

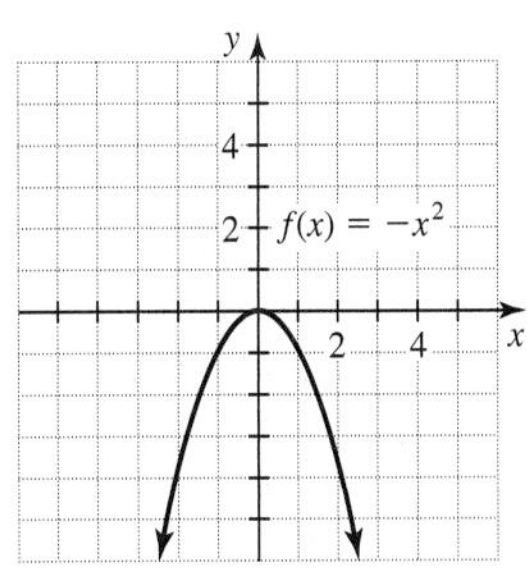

61.

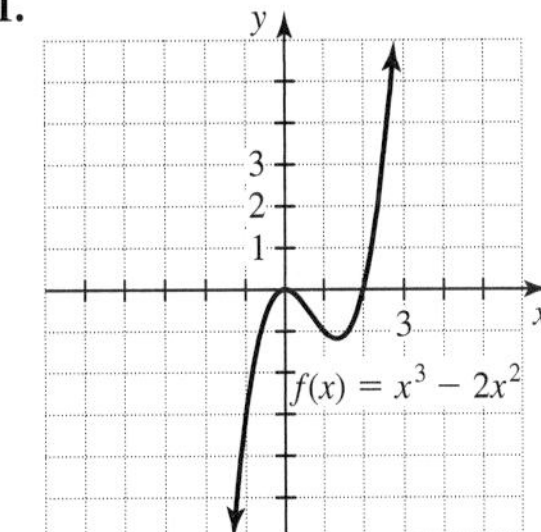

63.

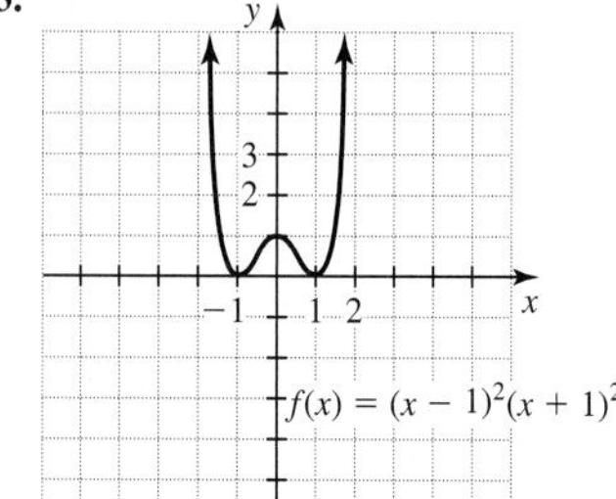

65.

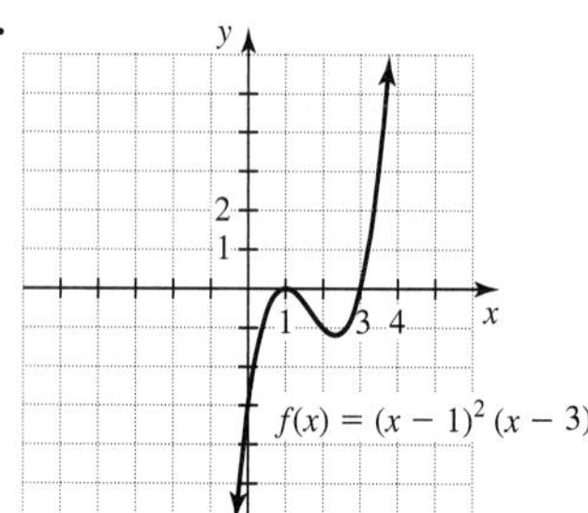

67.

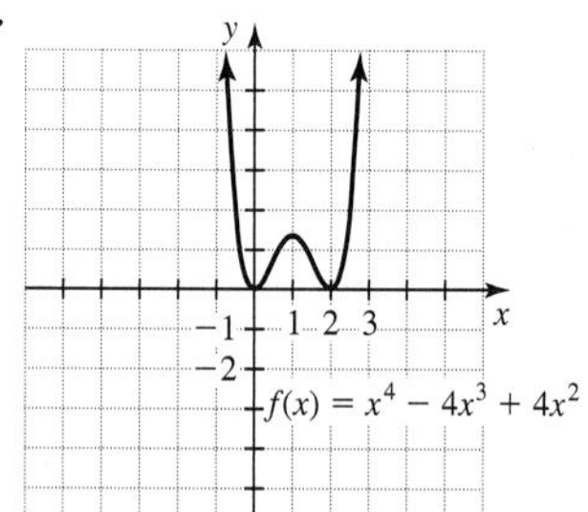

69.

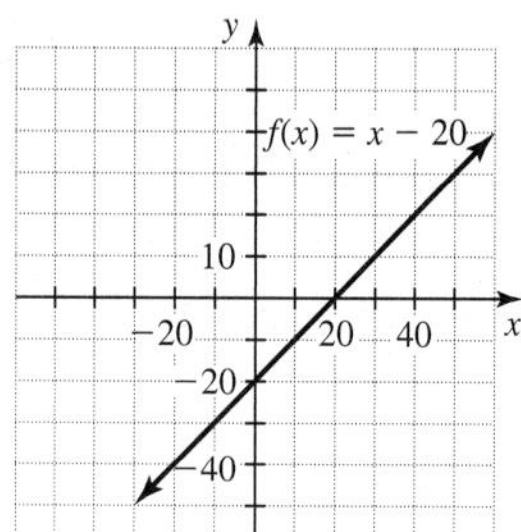

71.

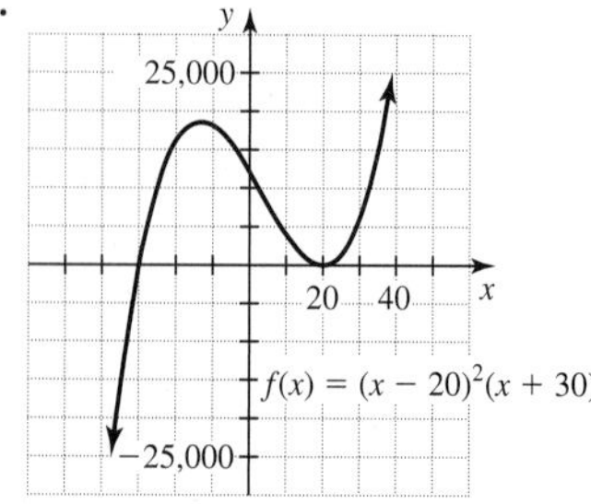

73.

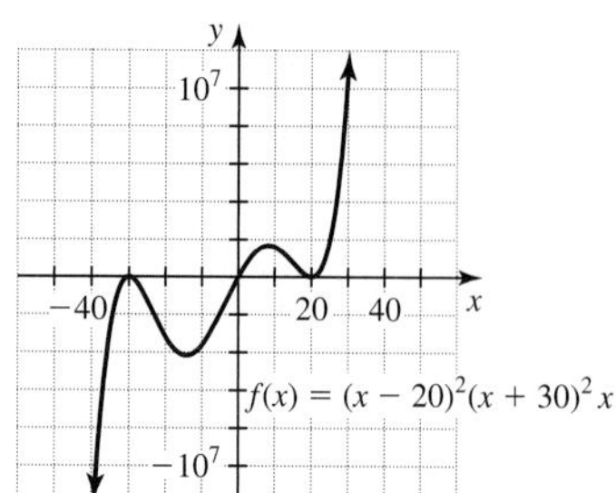

75. $f(x) = x - 3$ **77.** $f(x) = (x + 2)(x - 1)^2$

Section 11.5 Warm-Ups F F F F T F T T T F

1. A rational function is of the form $f(x) = P(x)/Q(x)$, where $P(x)$ and $Q(x)$ are polynomials with no common factor and $Q(x) \neq 0$.
3. A vertical asymptote is a vertical line that is approached by the graph of a rational function.
5. An oblique asymptote is a nonhorizontal, nonvertical line that is approached by the graph of a rational function.
7. $(-\infty, 1) \cup (1, \infty)$ **9.** $(-\infty, 0) \cup (0, \infty)$
11. $(-\infty, -4) \cup (-4, 4) \cup (4, \infty)$
13. Vertical: $x = -4$; horizontal: x-axis
15. Vertical: $x = 4$, $x = -4$; horizontal: x-axis
17. Vertical: $x = 7$; horizontal: $y = 5$
19. Vertical: $x = 3$; oblique: $y = 2x + 6$ **21.** c **23.** b **25.** g **27.** f
29. $x = -4$, x-axis **31.** $x = 3$, $x = -3$, x-axis

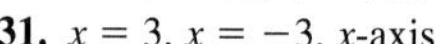

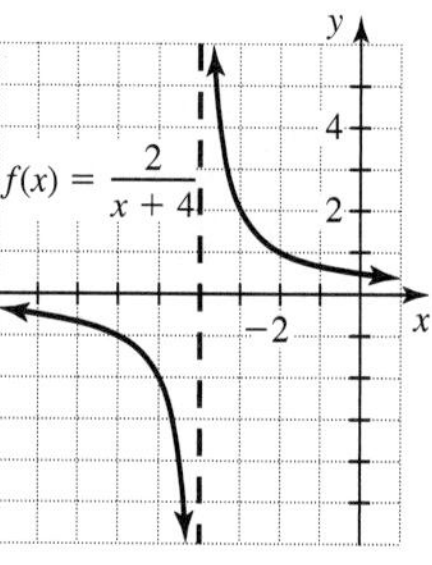

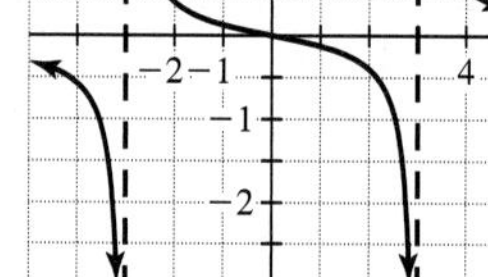

33. $x = -3$, $y = 2$ **35.** y-axis, $y = x - 3$

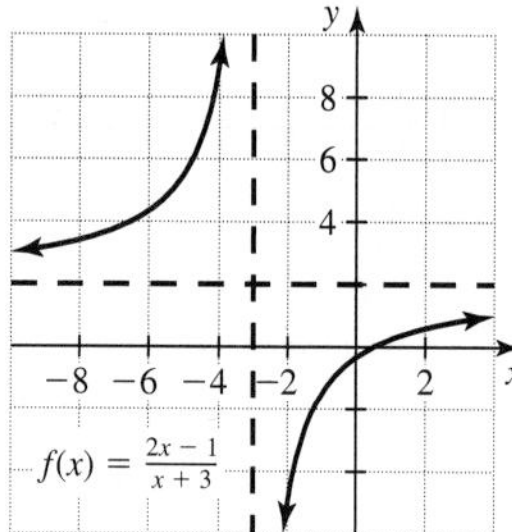

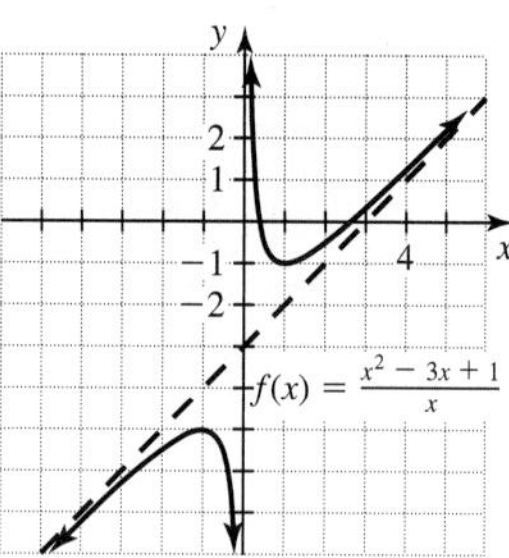

37. $x = 1$, $y = 3x + 1$ **39.** $x = 0$, $y = 0$

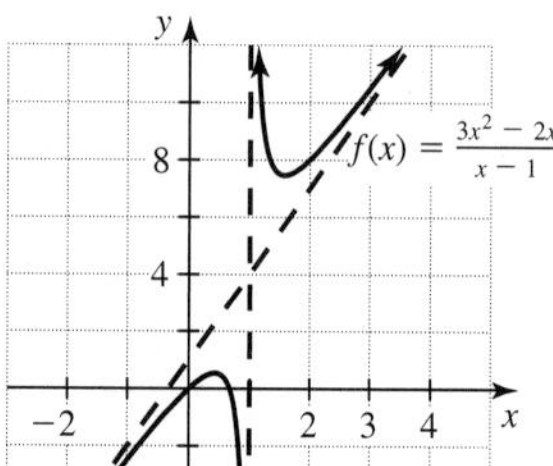

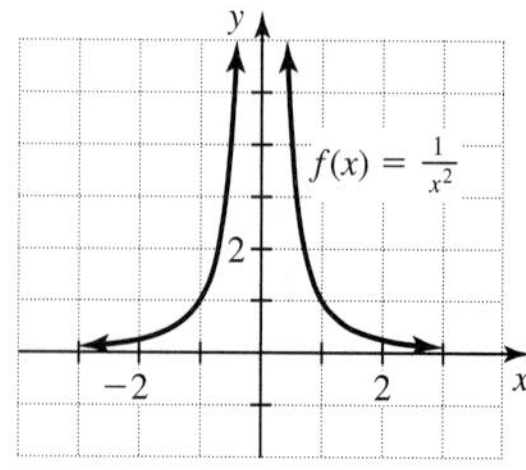

41. $x = -3, x = 2, y = 0, \left(0, \frac{1}{2}\right), \left(\frac{3}{2}, 0\right)$

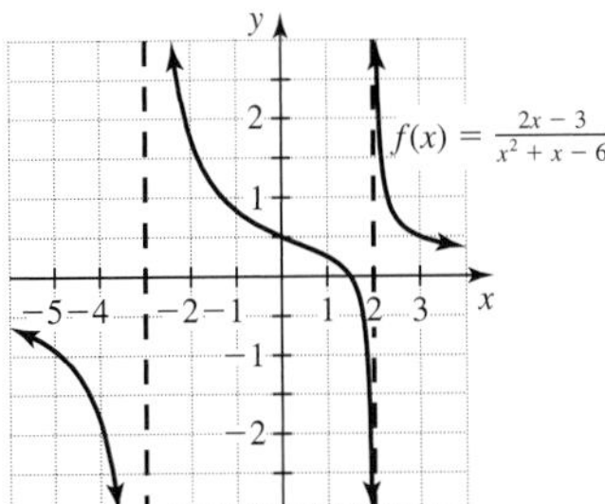

43. $x = 0, y = 0, (-1, 0)$

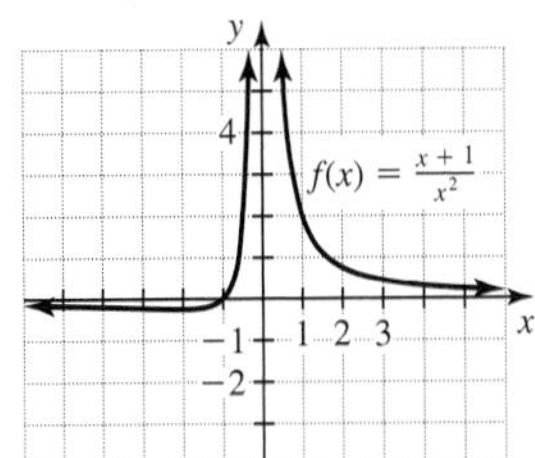

45. $x = 0, x = \pm 3, y = 0, \left(\frac{1}{2}, 0\right)$

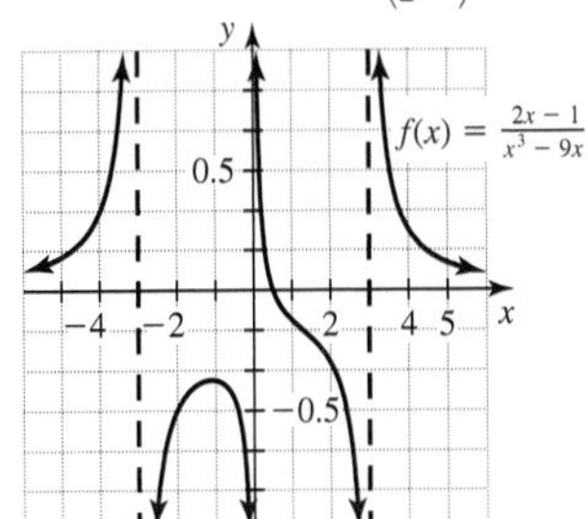

47. $x = \pm 1, y = 0, (0, 0)$

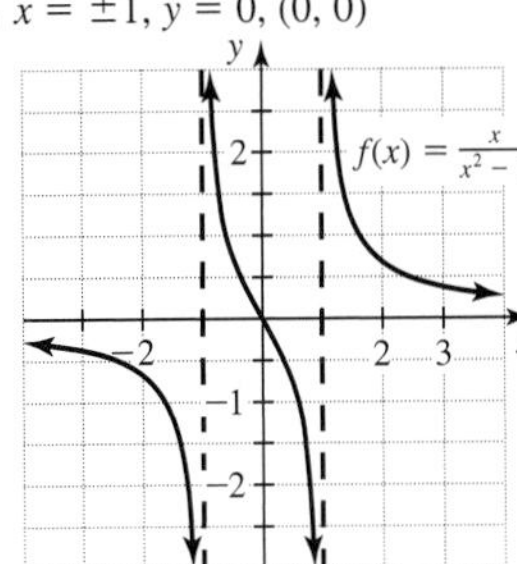

49. $y = 0, (0, 2)$

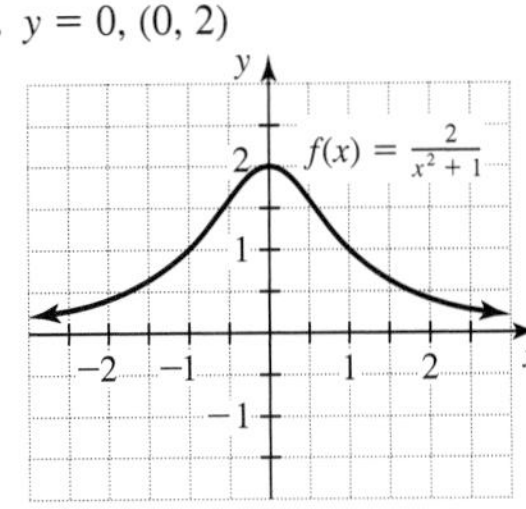

51. $x = -1, y = x - 1, (0, 0)$

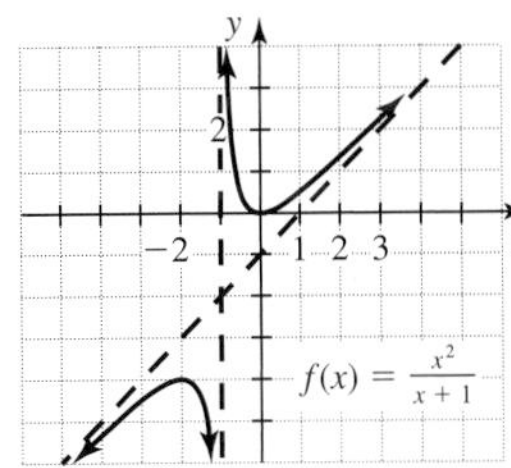

53. $f(20) = \$2.35$, $f(30) = \$1.46$, average approaches 0

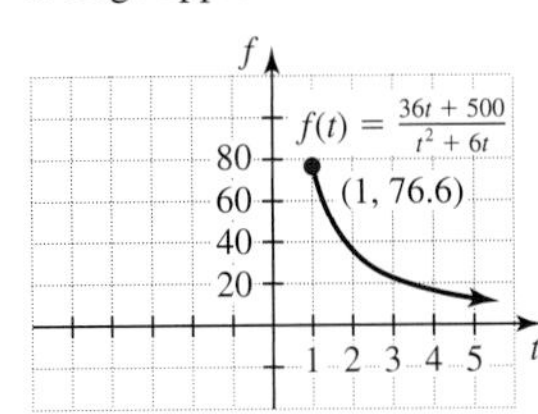

55. a) $y = 25{,}000$ **b)** \$39,000 **c)** 140,000
d)

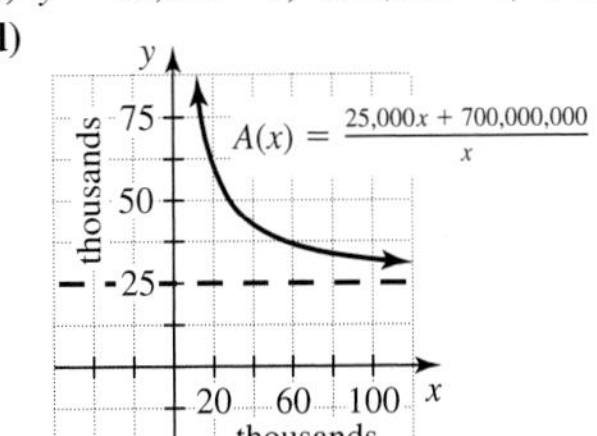

57, 59, and 61. The graph of $f(x)$ is an asymptote for the graph of $g(x)$.
63. $f(x) = 1/x$
65. $f(x) = \dfrac{1}{(x-3)(x+1)}$

Section 11.6 Warm-Ups T T F F F F T T T T

1. The basic operations of functions are addition, subtraction, multiplication, and division.
3. In the composition function the second function is evaluated on the result of the first function.

5. $x^2 + 2x - 3$ **7.** $4x^3 - 11x^2 + 6x$ **9.** 12 **11.** -30
13. -21 **15.** $\frac{13}{8}$ **17.** $y = 6x - 20$ **19.** $y = x + 2$
21. $y = x^2 + 2x$ **23.** $y = x$ **25.** -2 **27.** 5 **29.** 7
31. 5 **33.** 5 **35.** 4 **37.** 22.2992 **39.** $4x^2 - 6x$
41. $2x^2 + 6x - 3$ **43.** x **45.** $4x - 9$ **47.** $\frac{x+9}{4}$
49. $F = f \circ h$ **51.** $G = g \circ h$ **53.** $H = h \circ g$ **55.** $J = h \circ h$
57. $K = g \circ g$ **67.** True **69.** False **71.** True **73.** False
75. False **77.** True **79. a)** 50 ft^2 **b)** $A = \frac{d^2}{2}$
81. $P(x) = -x^2 + 20x - 170$ **83.** $J = 0.025I$
85. a) 397.8 **b)** $D = \frac{1.116 \times 10^7}{L^3}$ **c)** decreases
87. $[0, \infty), [0, \infty), [16, \infty)$ **89.** $[0, \infty), [0, \infty)$

Section 11.7 Warm-Ups F F F T T F T T T F

1. The inverse of a function is a function with the same ordered pairs except that the coordinates are reversed.
3. The range of f^{-1} is the domain of f.
5. A function is one-to-one if no two ordered pairs have the same second coordinate with different first coordinates.
7. The switch-and-solve strategy is used for finding a formula for an inverse function.

9. No **11.** Yes, $\{(4, 16), (3, 9), (0, 0)\}$ **13.** No
15. Yes, $\{(0, 0), (2, 2), (9, 9)\}$ **17.** No **19.** Yes **21.** Yes
23. Yes **25.** Yes **27.** No **29.** $f^{-1}(x) = \frac{x}{5}$
31. $g^{-1}(x) = x + 9$ **33.** $k^{-1}(x) = \frac{x+9}{5}$ **35.** $m^{-1}(x) = \frac{2}{x}$
37. $f^{-1}(x) = x^3 + 4$ **39.** $f^{-1}(x) = \frac{3}{x} + 4$ **41.** $f^{-1}(x) = \frac{x^3 - 7}{3}$
43. $f^{-1}(x) = \frac{2x+1}{x-1}$ **45.** $f^{-1}(x) = \frac{1+4x}{3x-1}$
47. $p^{-1}(x) = x^4$ for $x \ge 0$ **49.** $f^{-1}(x) = 2 + \sqrt{x}$
51. $f^{-1}(x) = \sqrt{x-3}$ **53.** $f^{-1}(x) = x^2 - 2$ for $x \ge 0$

55. $f^{-1}(x) = \frac{1}{2}x - \frac{3}{2}$

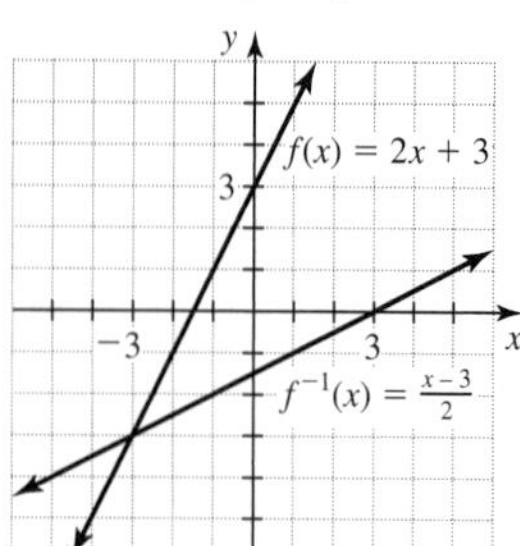

57. $f^{-1}(x) = \sqrt{x+1}$

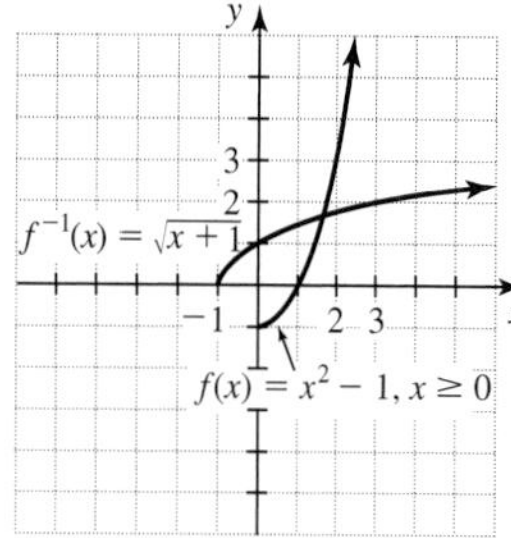

59. $f^{-1}(x) = \frac{x}{5}$

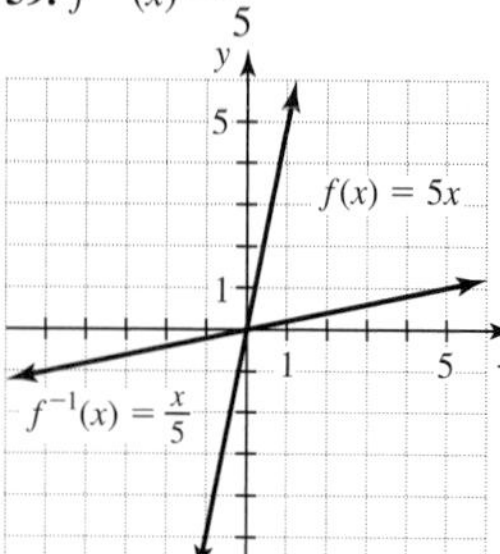

61. $f^{-1}(x) = \sqrt[3]{x}$

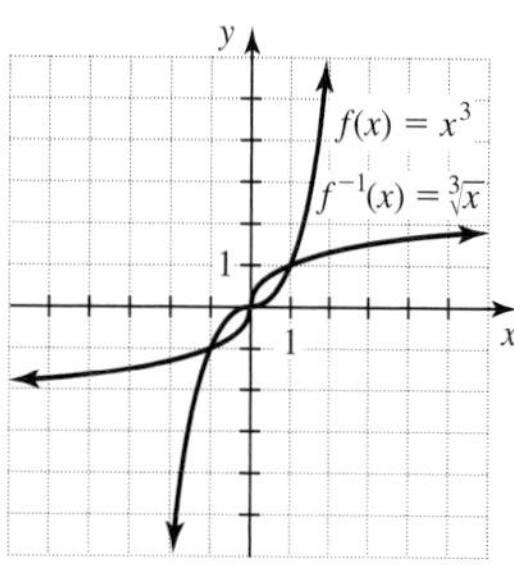

63. $f^{-1}(x) = x^2 + 2$ for $x \geq 0$

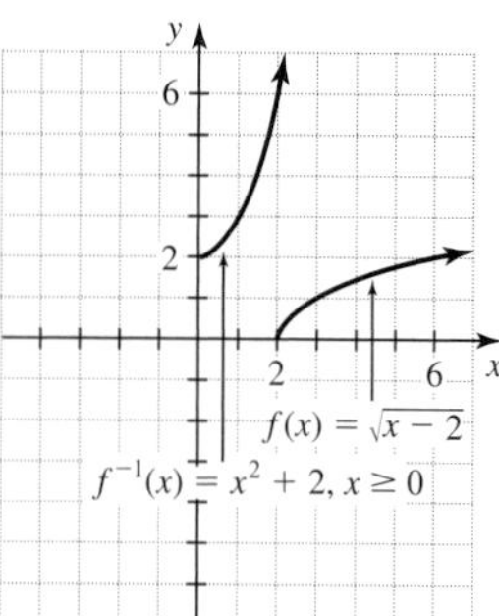

65. d **67.** i **69.** f **71.** a
73. g **75–82.** $(f^{-1} \circ f)(x) = x$

83. a) 33.5 mph

b) Decreases **c)** $L = \frac{S^2}{30}$

85. $T(x) = 1.09x + 125$,
$T^{-1}(x) = \frac{x - 125}{1.09}$

87. An odd positive integer
89. Not inverses

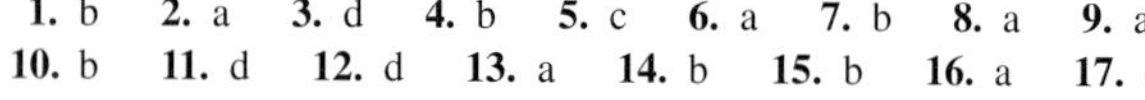

Enriching Your Mathematical Word Power

1. b **2.** a **3.** d **4.** b **5.** c **6.** a **7.** b **8.** a **9.** a
10. b **11.** d **12.** d **13.** a **14.** b **15.** b **16.** a **17.** d

Review Exercises

1. No **3.** Yes **5.** Yes **7.** No **9.** {3, 4, 5}, {1, 5, 9}
11. $(-\infty, \infty)$, $(-\infty, \infty)$ **13.** $[-5, \infty)$, $[0, \infty)$
15. −5 **17.** −6 **19.** $-\frac{21}{4}$

21. $(-\infty, \infty)$, $(-\infty, \infty)$

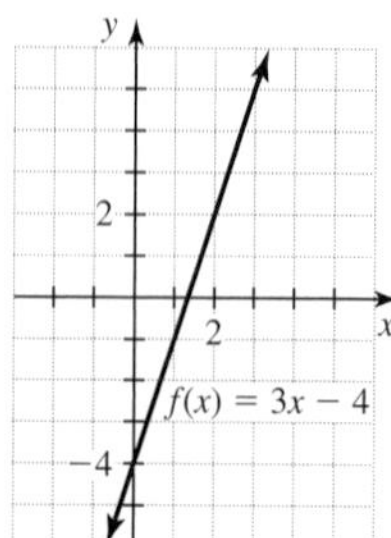

23. $(-\infty, \infty)$, $[-2, \infty)$

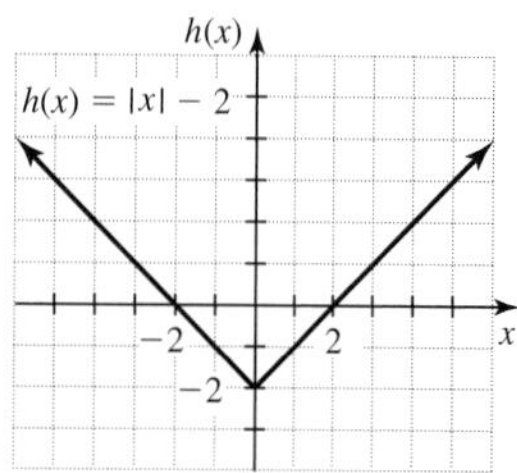

25. $(-\infty, \infty)$, $[0, \infty)$

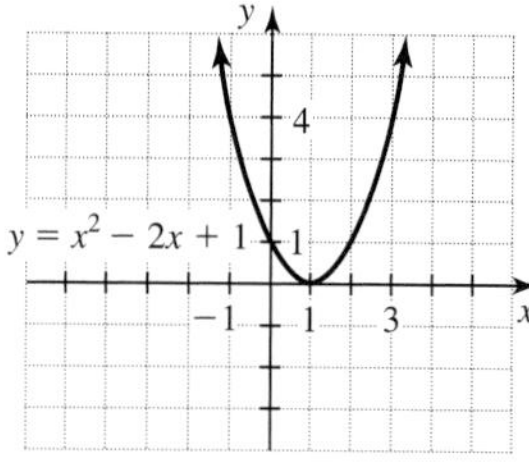

27. $[0, \infty)$, $[2, \infty)$

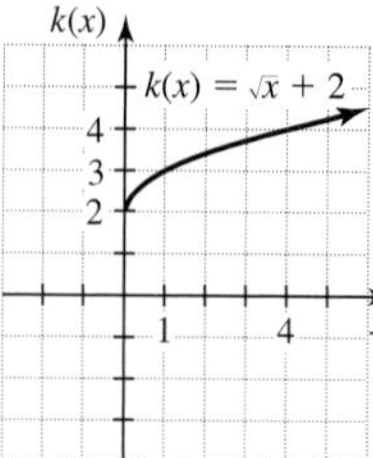

29. $(-\infty, \infty)$, $(-\infty, 30]$

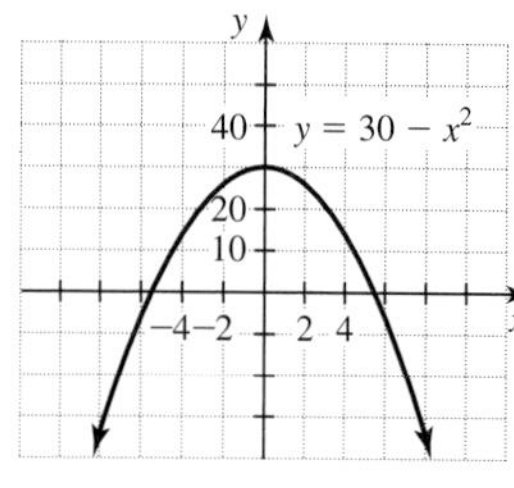

31. {2}, $(-\infty, \infty)$

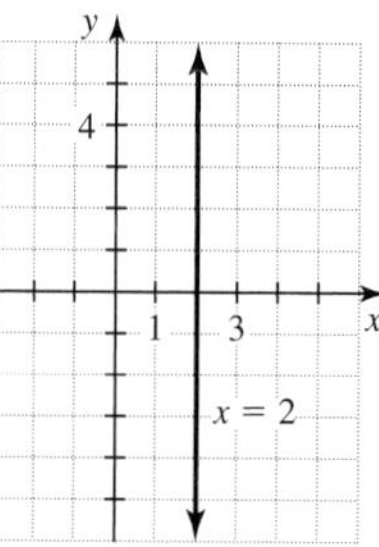

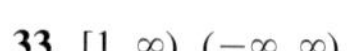

33. $[1, \infty)$, $(-\infty, \infty)$

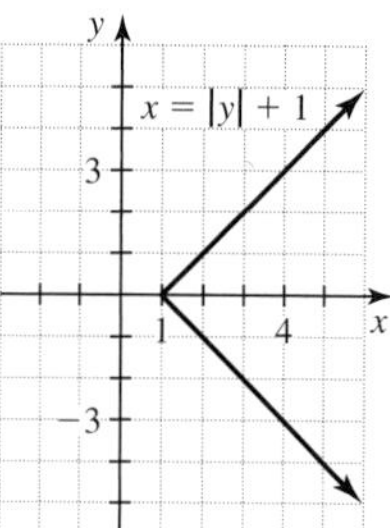

35. $[0, \infty)$, $[0, \infty)$

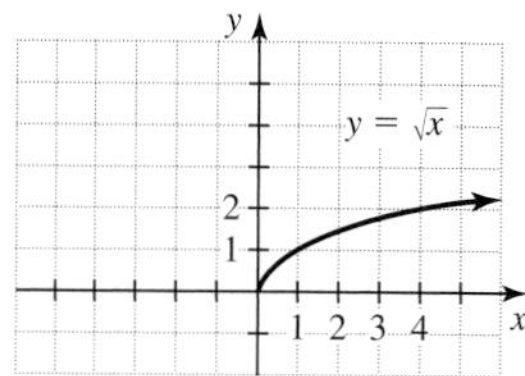

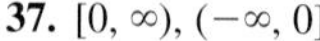

37. $[0, \infty)$, $(-\infty, 0]$

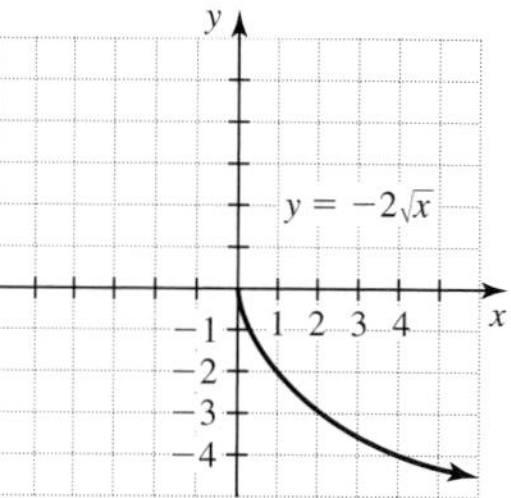

39. $[2, \infty)$, $[0, \infty)$

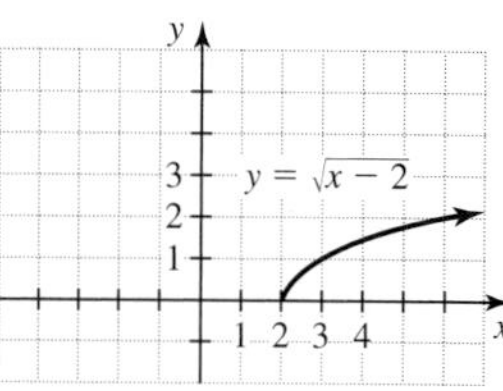

41. $[0, \infty)$, $[0, \infty)$

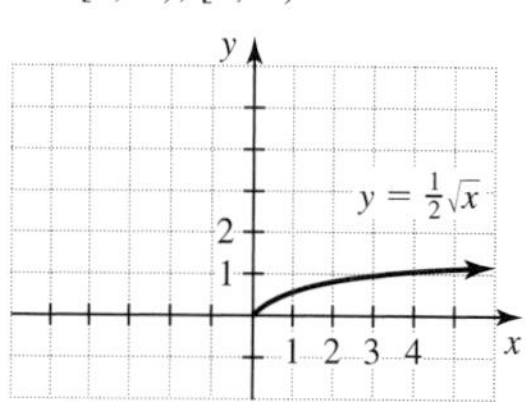

43. $[-1, \infty)$, $(-\infty, 3]$

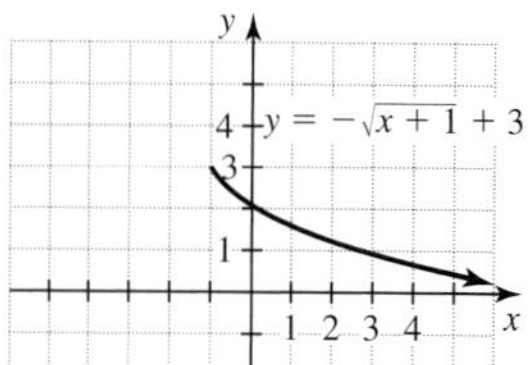

45. $(-5, 0), (5, 0), (0, 0)$

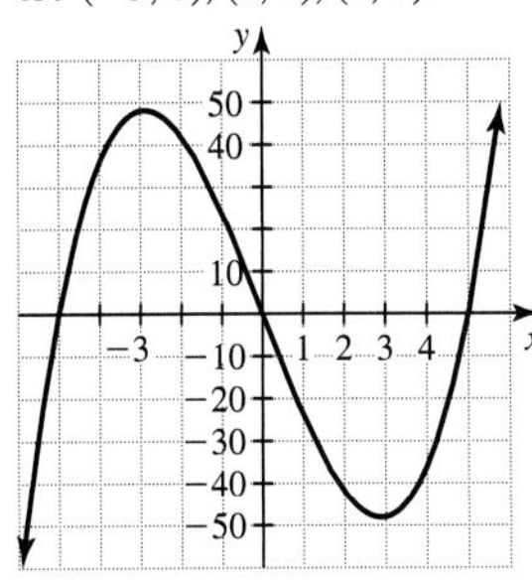

$f(x) = x^3 - 25x$

47. $(-2, 0), (1, 0), (2, 0), (0, 4)$

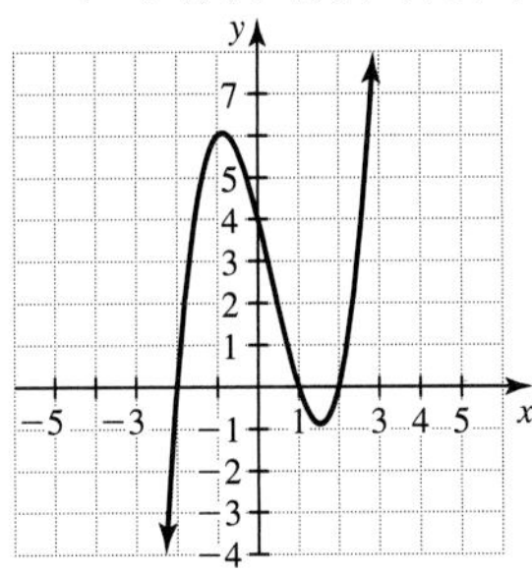

$f(x) = (x^2 - 4)(x - 1)$

49. $(-3, 0), (-1, 0), (1, 0), (3, 0), (0, 9)$

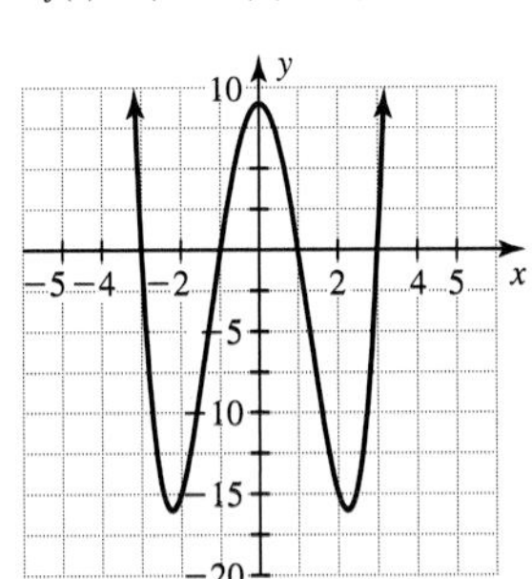

$f(x) = x^4 - 10x^2 + 9$

51. The graph touches but does not cross the x-axis at $(3, 0)$.

53. The graph crosses the x-axis at $(3, 0)$ and $(-5, 0)$, and touches but does not cross at $(4, 0)$.

55. The graph crosses the x-axis at $(-3, 0)$, $(3, 0)$, and $(8, 0)$.

57. $\left(-\infty, -\frac{3}{2}\right) \cup \left(-\frac{3}{2}, \infty\right)$ **59.** $(-\infty, \infty)$

61. $x = 3$, x-axis **63.** $x = 2$, $x = -2$, x-axis

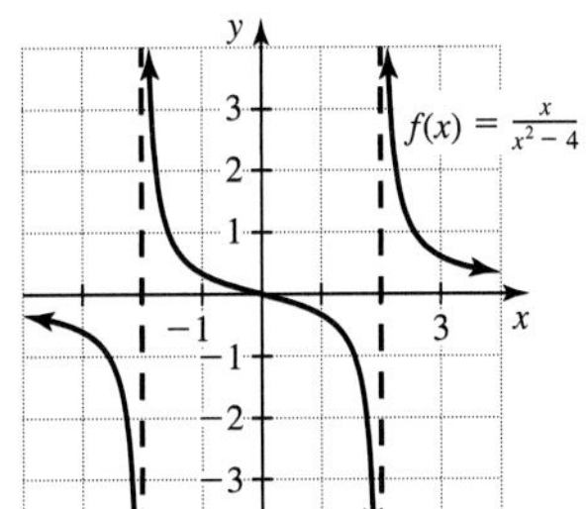

65. $x = 1, y = 2$ **67.** 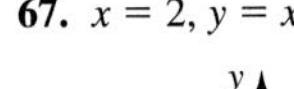 $x = 2, y = x$

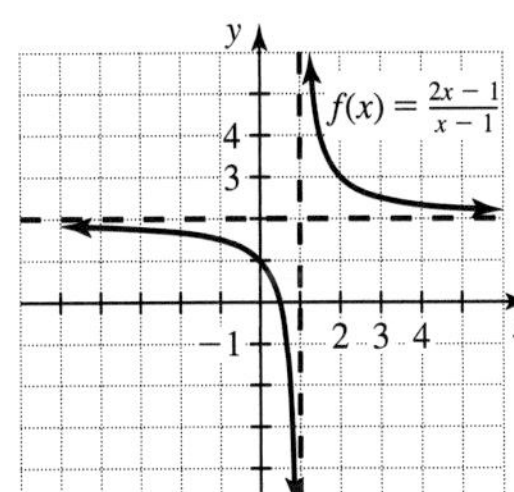

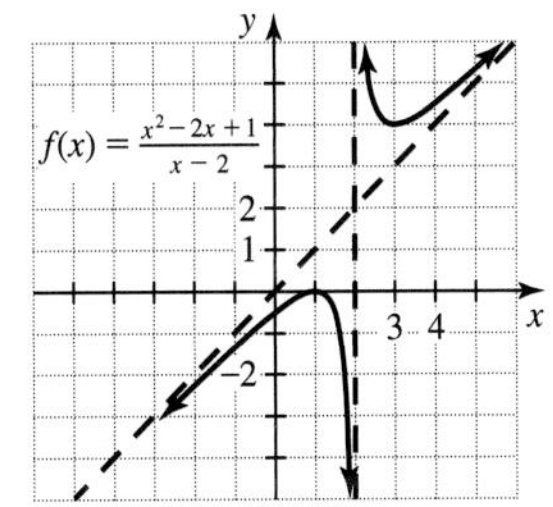

69. -4 **71.** $\sqrt{2}$ **73.** 99 **75.** 17 **77.** $3x^3 - x^2 - 10x$

79. 20 **81.** $F = f \circ g$ **83.** $H = g \circ h$ **85.** $I = g \circ g$

87. No **89.** Yes, $f^{-1}(x) = x/8$ **91.** Yes, $g^{-1}(x) = \dfrac{x + 6}{13}$

93. Yes, $j^{-1}(x) = \dfrac{x + 1}{x - 1}$ **95.** No

97. $f^{-1}(x) = \frac{1}{3}x + \frac{1}{3}$

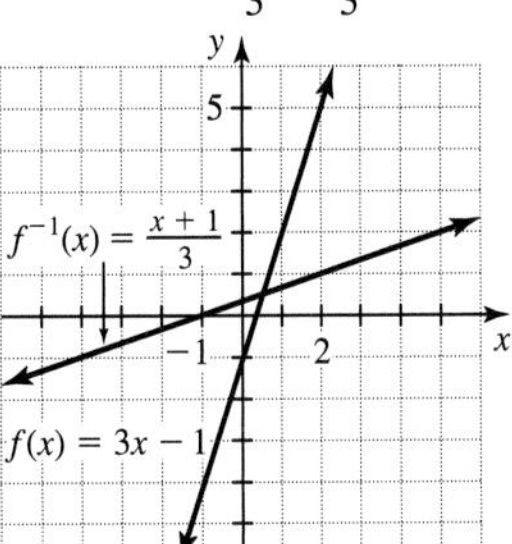

99. 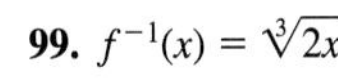 $f^{-1}(x) = \sqrt[3]{2x}$

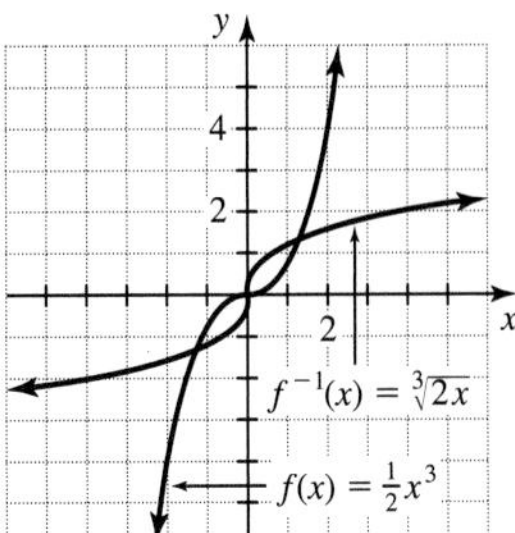

101.

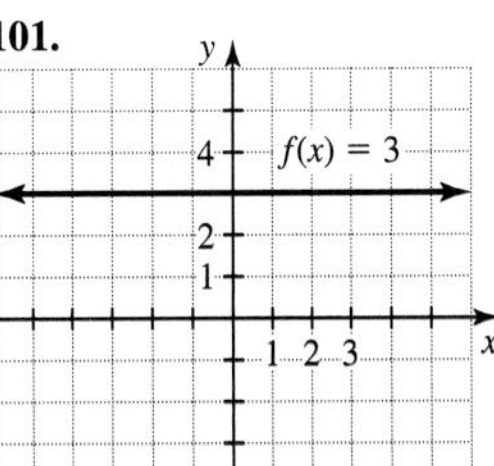

103.

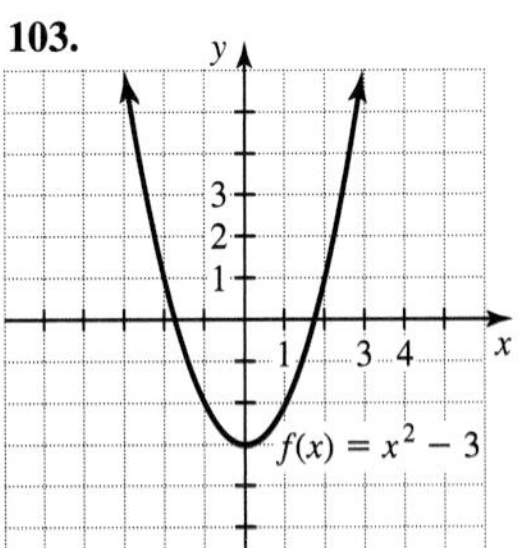

105.

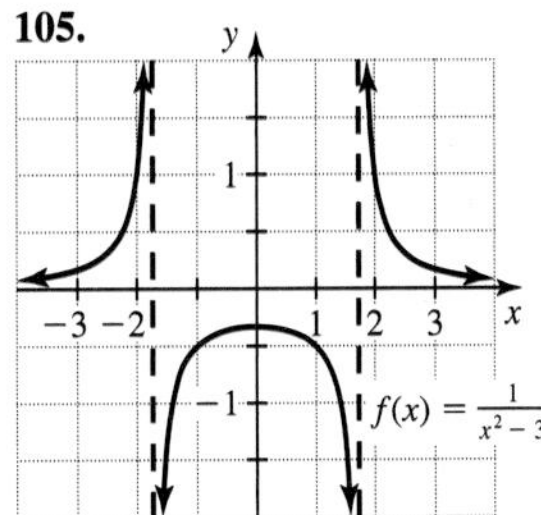

107.

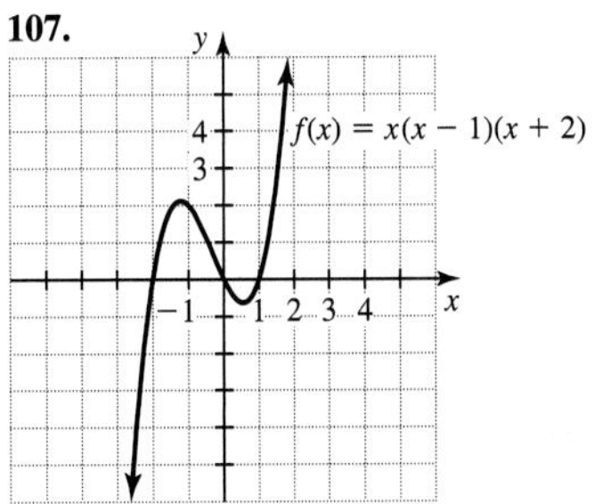

109. $B = \dfrac{2A}{\pi}$ **111.** $a = 15w - 16$

113. $A = s^2, s = \sqrt{A}$

Chapter 11 Test

1. Yes **2.** 11 **3.** $[7, \infty), [0, \infty)$ **4.** $S = 0.50n + 3$ **5.** 6 ft

6. $(-\infty, \infty), (-\infty, \infty)$ **7.** $(-\infty, \infty), [-4, \infty)$

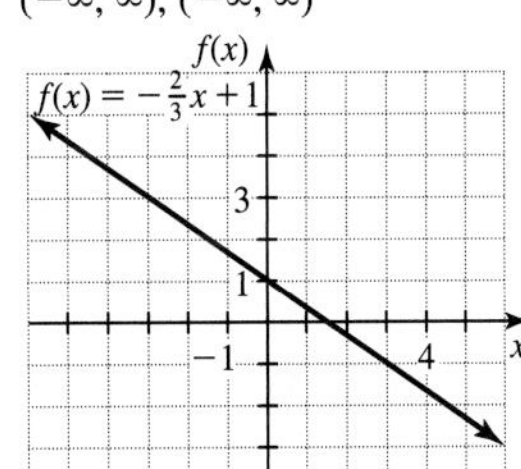

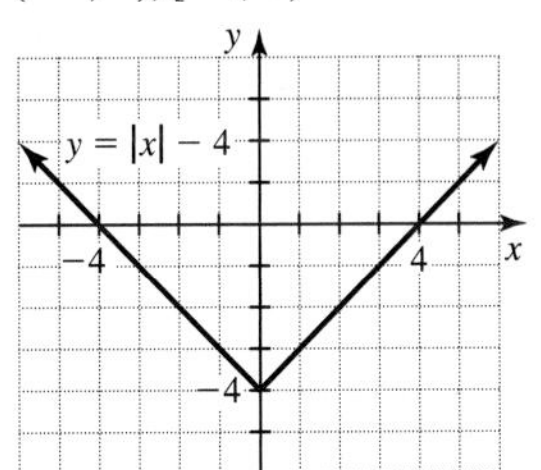

8. $(-\infty, \infty)$, $[-9, \infty)$

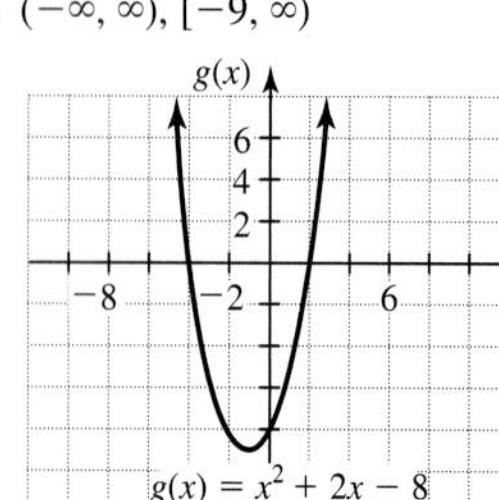

9. $[0, \infty)$, $(-\infty, \infty)$

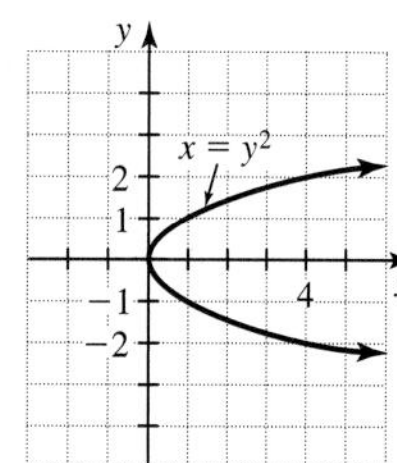

10. $(-\infty, \infty)$, $(-\infty, 0]$

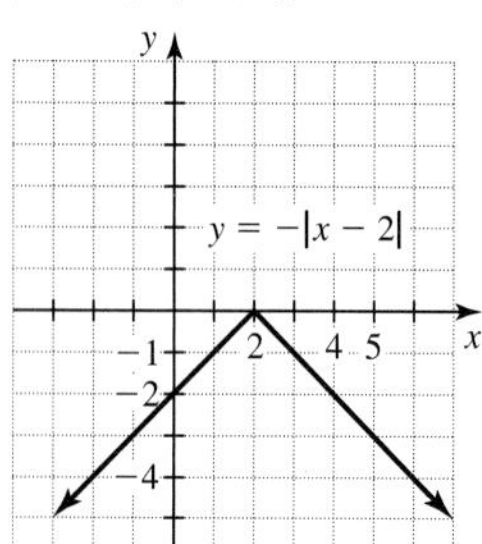

11. $[-5, \infty)$, $[-2, \infty)$

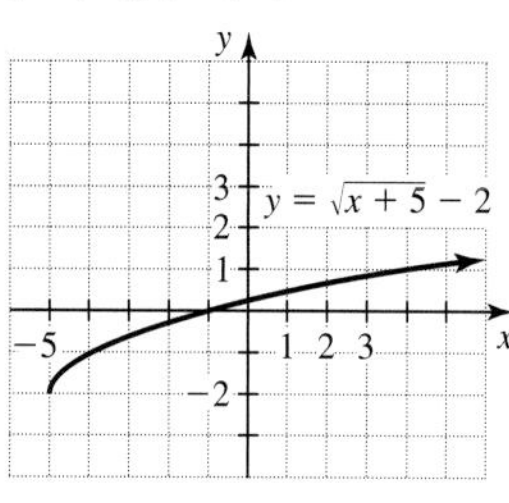

12. $(-2, 0)$, $(2, 0)$, $(0, 8)$

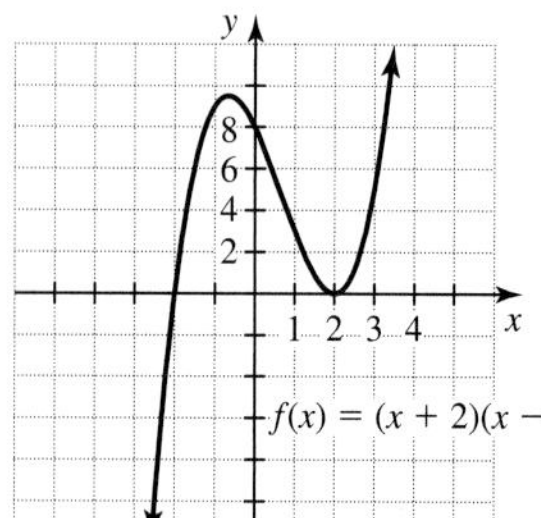

13. $\left(0, \frac{1}{4}\right)$

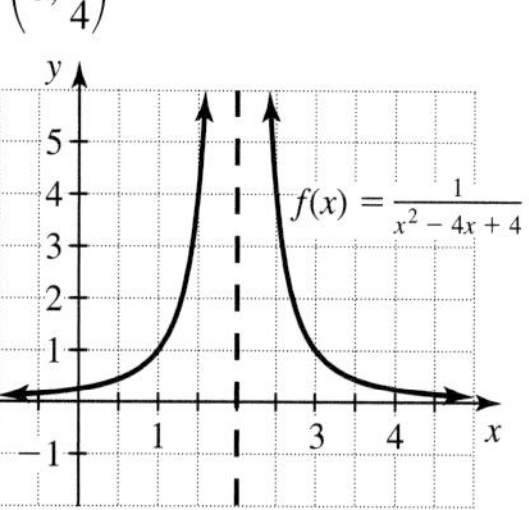

14. $\left(\frac{3}{2}, 0\right)$, $\left(0, \frac{3}{2}\right)$

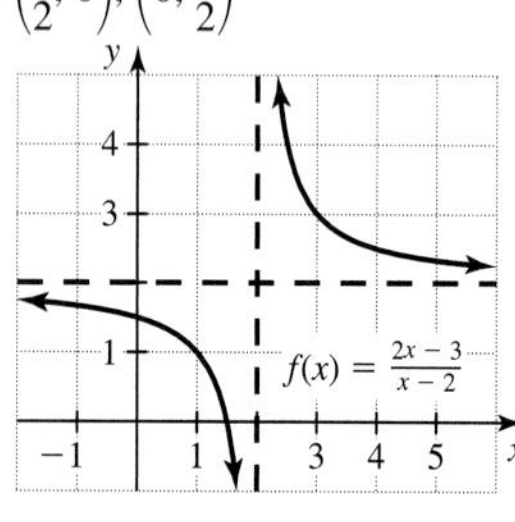

15. $(-2, 0)$, $(1, 0)$, $(2, 0)$, $(0, 4)$

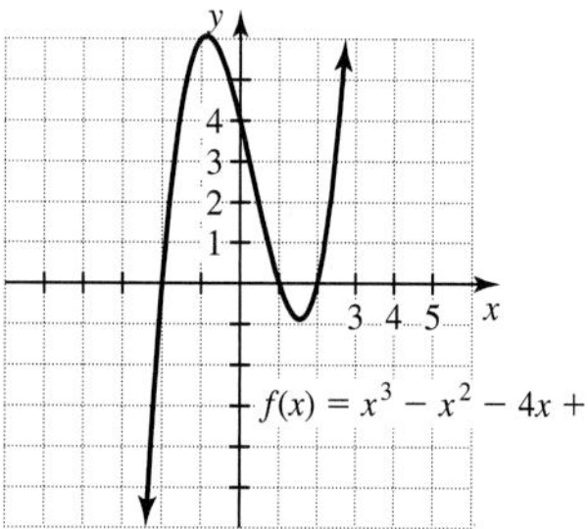

16. 11 **17.** 125 **18.** -3 **19.** $\frac{x - 5}{-2}$ **20.** $x^2 - 2x + 9$

21. 15 **22.** 1776 **23.** $\frac{1}{8}$ **24.** $-2x^2 - 3$ **25.** $4x^2 - 20x + 29$

26. $H = f \circ g$ **27.** $W = g \circ f$ **28.** Not invertible

29. $\{(3, 2), (4, 3), (5, 4)\}$ **30.** $f^{-1}(x) = x + 5$ **31.** $f^{-1}(x) = \frac{x + 5}{3}$

32. $f^{-1}(x) = (x - 9)^3$ **33.** $f^{-1}(x) = \frac{x + 1}{x - 2}$

Making Connections A Review of Chapters 1–11

1. $\frac{1}{25}$ **2.** $\frac{3}{2}$ **3.** $\sqrt{2}$ **4.** x^8 **5.** 2 **6.** x^9 **7.** $\{\pm 3\}$

8. $\{\pm 2\sqrt{2}\}$ **9.** $\{0, 1\}$ **10.** $\{2 \pm \sqrt{10}\}$ **11.** $\{81\}$ **12.** $\varnothing$

13. $\{\pm 8\}$ **14.** $\left\{-\frac{17}{5}, 5\right\}$ **15.** $\{2\}$ **16.** $\left\{\frac{5}{3}\right\}$ **17.** $\{42\}$ **18.** $\{11\}$

19.

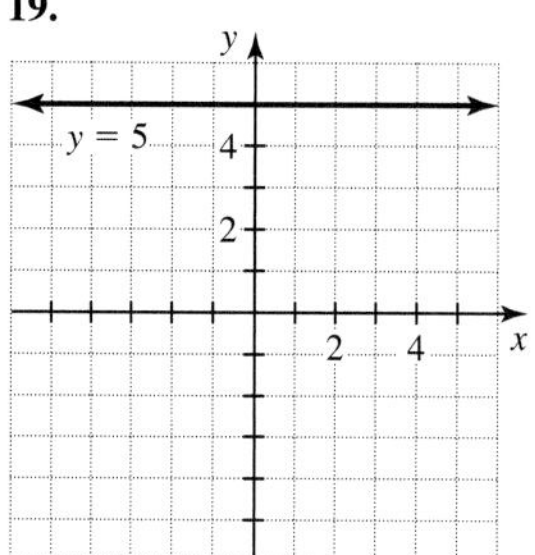

20.

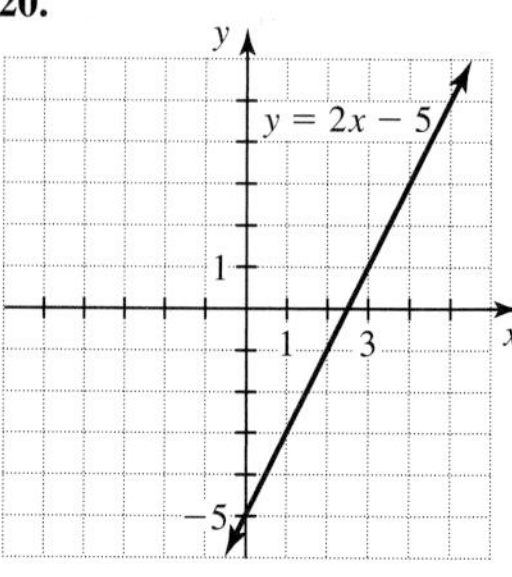

21.

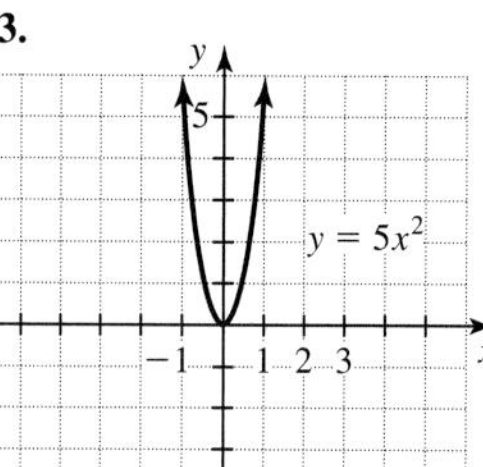

22.

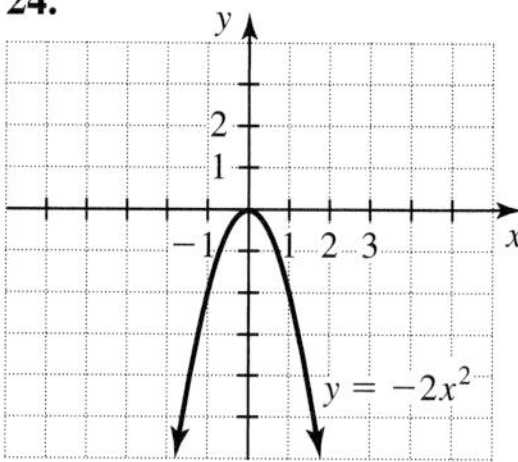

23.

$y = 5x^2$

24.

$y = -2x^2$

25. $(2, 4)$, $(3, 8)$, $(1, 2)$, $(4, 16)$

26. $\left(\frac{1}{2}, 2\right)$, $\left(-1, \frac{1}{4}\right)$, $(2, 16)$, $(0, 1)$

27. $[0, \infty)$ **28.** $(-\infty, 3]$ **29.** $(-\infty, \infty)$

30. $(-\infty, 1) \cup (1, 9) \cup (9, \infty)$

31. a) $C = 0.12x + 3000$ **b)** $P = 1 \times 10^{-6}x + 0.15$

32. a) \$0.44, \$0.40, \$0.39

b)

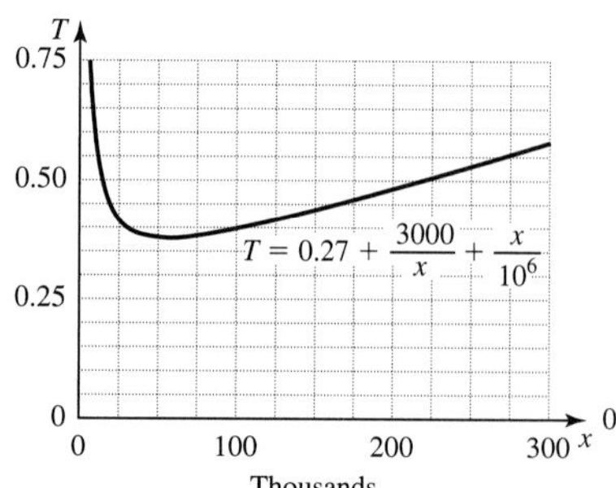

c) 60,000 miles

d) [50,000, 60,000]

Chapter 12

Section 12.1 Warm-Ups F T F T T F T F T F

1. An exponential function has the form $f(x) = a^x$ where $a > 0$ and $a \neq 1$.
3. The two most popular bases are e and 10.
5. The compound interest formula is $A = P(1 + i)^n$.

7. 16 **9.** 2 **11.** 3 **13.** $\frac{1}{3}$ **15.** -1 **17.** $-\frac{1}{4}$ **19.** 1

21. 100 **23.** 2.718 **25.** 0.135 **27.** $\frac{1}{16}, \frac{1}{4}, 1, 4, 16$

29. $9, 3, 1, \frac{1}{3}, \frac{1}{9}$

31.

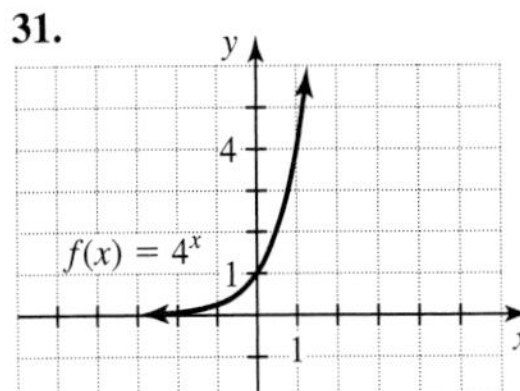

33.

$h(x) = \left(\frac{1}{3}\right)^x$

35.

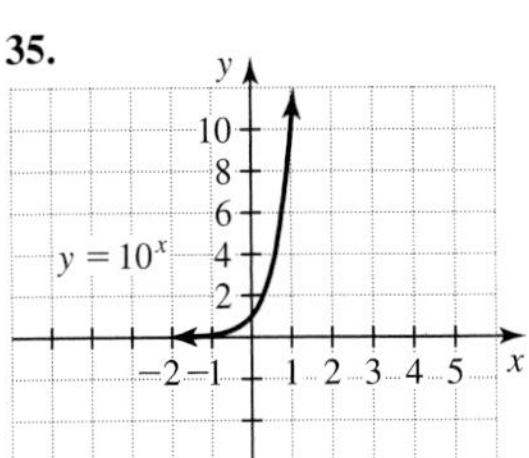

37. $\frac{1}{100}, \frac{1}{10}, 1, 10, 100$

39. $-\frac{1}{4}, -\frac{1}{2}, -1, -2, -4$

41.

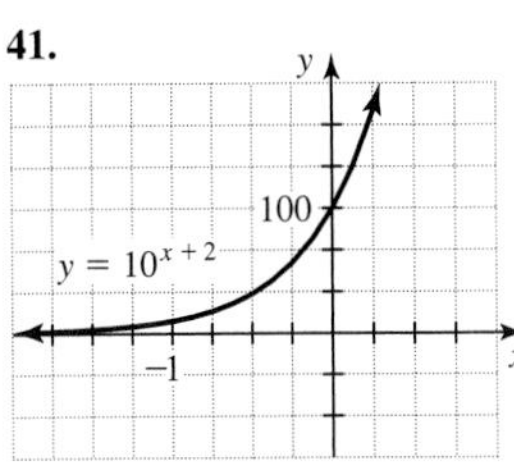

43.

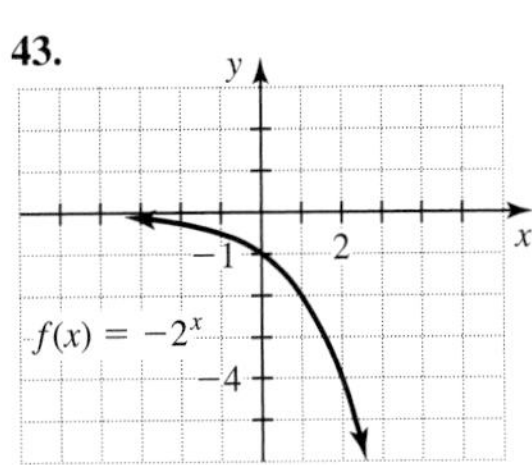

45.

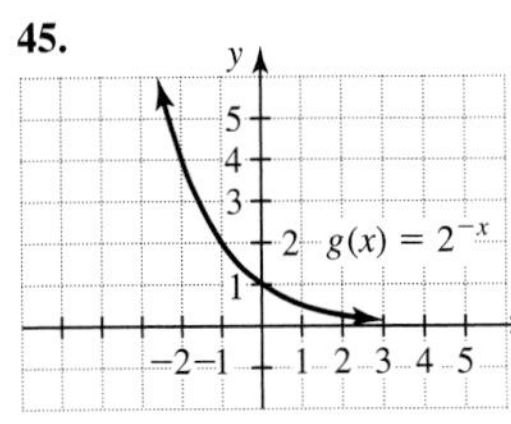

47.

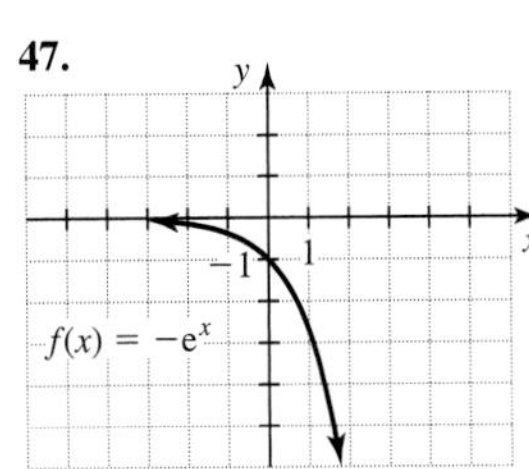

49.

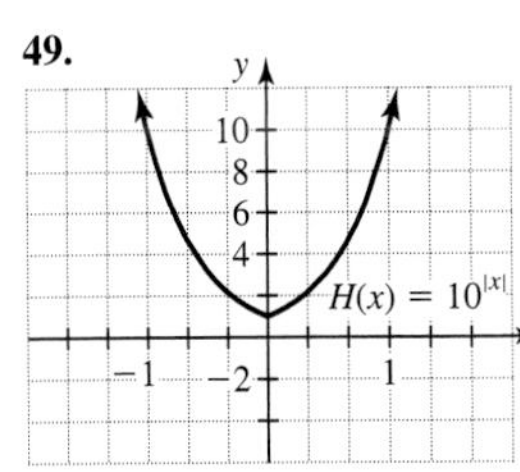

51.

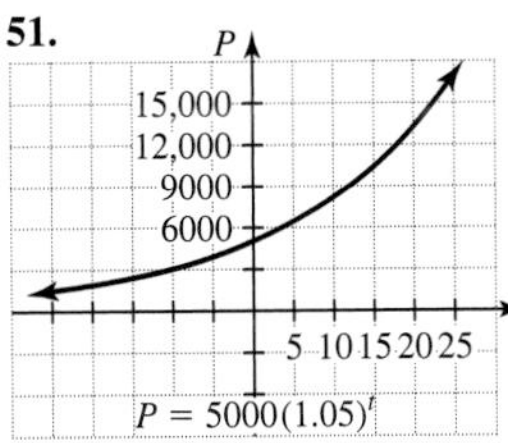

53. $\{6\}$ **55.** $\{-3\}$ **57.** $\{-2\}$ **59.** $\{-1\}$ **61.** $\{-2\}$ **63.** $\{-2\}$

65. $\{-3, 3\}$ **67.** 2 **69.** $\frac{4}{3}$ **71.** -2 **73.** 0 **75.** $\frac{3}{2}$ **77.** $\frac{1}{2}$

79. $\frac{1}{32}, -3, 1, 1, 16$ **81.** $-3, 4, 0, \frac{1}{2}, 5$ **83.** $9861.72

85. a) $53,277.30 **b)** 2010 **87.** $45, $12.92 **89.** $616.84

91. $6230.73 **93.** 300 grams, 90.4 grams, 12 years, no

95. 2.66666667, 0.0516, 2.8×10^{-5}

97. The graph of $y = 3^{x-h}$ lies h units to the right of $y = 3^x$ when $h > 0$ and $|h|$ units to the left of $y = 3^x$ when $h < 0$.

Section 12.2 Warm-Ups T F T T F F F F T T

1. If $f(x) = 2^x$, then $f^{-1}(x) = \log_2(x)$.
3. The common logarithm uses the base 10 and the natural logarithm uses base e.
5. The one-to-one property for logarithmic functions states that if $\log_a(m) = \log_a(n)$, then $m = n$.

7. $2^3 = 8$ **9.** $\log(100) = 2$ **11.** $5^y = x$ **13.** $\log_2(b) = a$

15. $3^{10} = x$ **17.** $\ln(x) = 3$ **19.** 2 **21.** 4 **23.** 6 **25.** 3

27. -2 **29.** 2 **31.** -2 **33.** 1 **35.** -3 **37.** $\frac{1}{2}$ **39.** 2

41. 0.6990 **43.** 1.8307 **45.** $-2, -1, 0, 1, 2$

47. $-2, -1, 0, 1, 2$

49.

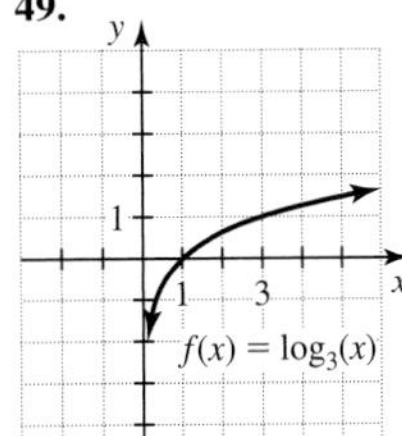

51.

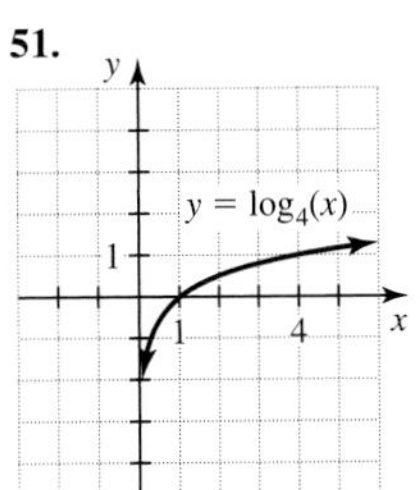

53.

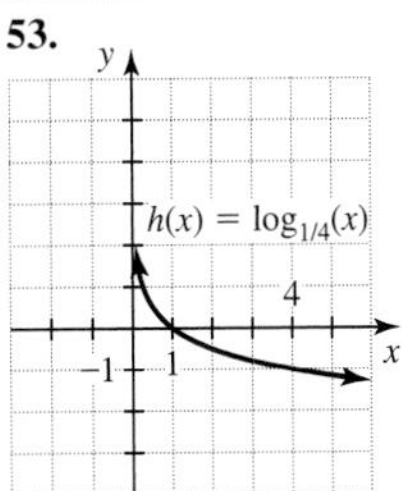

55.

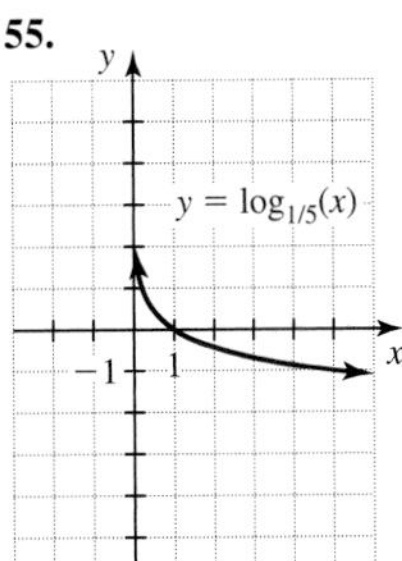

57. $f^{-1}(x) = \log_6(x)$ **59.** $f^{-1}(x) = e^x$ **61.** $f^{-1}(x) = \left(\frac{1}{2}\right)^x$

63. $\{4\}$ **65.** $\left\{\frac{1}{2}\right\}$ **67.** $\{0.001\}$ **69.** $\{6\}$ **71.** $\left\{\frac{1}{5}\right\}$ **73.** $\{\pm 3\}$

75. $\{0.4771\}$ **77.** $\{-0.3010\}$ **79.** $\{1.9741\}$

81. $-2, \frac{1}{2}, 0, 4, 4$ **83.** $16, -2, 1, 1, \frac{1}{4}$

85. 5.776 years **87.** 1.927 years

89. a) 14.58% **b)** $66,576.60 **91.** 4.1 **93.** 6.8 **95.** 90 dB

97. $f^{-1}(x) = 2^{x-5} + 3$, $(-\infty, \infty)$, $(3, \infty)$

99. $y = \ln(e^x) = x$ for $-\infty < x < \infty$, $y = e^{\ln(x)} = x$ for $0 < x < \infty$

Section 12.3 Warm-Ups T F T T F T F F F T

1. The product rule for logarithms states that $\log_a(MN) = \log_a(M) + \log_a(N)$.
3. The power rule for logarithms states that $\log_a(M^N) = N \cdot \log_a(M)$.
5. Since $\log_a(M)$ is the exponent you would use on a to obtain M, using $\log_a(M)$ as the exponent produces M: $a^{\log_a(M)} = M$.

7. $\log(21)$ **9.** $\log_3(\sqrt{5x})$ **11.** $\log(x^5)$ **13.** $\ln(30)$

15. $\log(x^2 + 3x)$ **17.** $\log_2(x^2 - x - 6)$ **19.** $\log(4)$

21. $\log_2(x^4)$ **23.** $\log(\sqrt{5})$ **25.** $\ln(h - 2)$ **27.** $\log_2(w - 2)$
29. $\ln(x - 2)$ **31.** $3\log(3)$ **33.** $\frac{1}{2}\log(3)$ **35.** $x\log(3)$ **37.** 10
39. 19 **41.** 8 **43.** 4.3 **45.** $\log(3) + \log(5)$
47. $\log(5) - \log(3)$ **49.** $2\log(5)$ **51.** $2\log(5) + \log(3)$
53. $-\log(3)$ **55.** $-\log(5)$ **57.** $\log(x) + \log(y) + \log(z)$
59. $3 + \log_2(x)$ **61.** $\ln(x) - \ln(y)$ **63.** $1 + 2\log(x)$
65. $2\log_5(x - 3) - \frac{1}{2}\log_5(w)$ **67.** $\ln(y) + \ln(z) + \frac{1}{2}\ln(x) - \ln(w)$
69. $\log(x^2 - x)$ **71.** $\ln(3)$ **73.** $\ln\left(\frac{xz}{w}\right)$ **75.** $\ln\left(\frac{x^2y^3}{w}\right)$
77. $\log\left(\frac{(x-3)^{1/2}}{(x+1)^{2/3}}\right)$ **79.** $\log_2\left(\frac{(x-1)^{2/3}}{(x+2)^{1/4}}\right)$ **81.** False
83. True **85.** True **87.** False **89.** True **91.** True
93. True **95.** False **97.** $r = \log(I/I_0)$, $r = 2$ **99.** b
101. The graphs are the same because $\ln(\sqrt{x}) = \ln(x^{1/2}) = \frac{1}{2}\ln(x)$.
103. The graph is a straight line because $\log(e^x) = x\log(e) \approx 0.434x$. The slope is $\log(e)$ or approximately 0.434.

Section 12.4 Warm-Ups T T T F T T T F T F
1. The exponential equation $a^y = x$ is equivalent to $\log_a(x) = y$.
3. {7} **5.** {31} **7.** {e} **9.** {2} **11.** {3} **13.** ∅ **15.** {6}
17. {3} **19.** {2} **21.** {4} **23.** $\{\log_3(7)\}$ **25.** $\left\{\frac{\ln(7)}{2}\right\}$ **27.** {−6}
29. $\left\{-\frac{1}{2}\right\}$ **31.** $\frac{5\ln(3)}{\ln(2) - \ln(3)}$, −13.548 **33.** $\frac{4 + 2\log(5)}{1 - \log(5)}$, 17.932
35. $\frac{\ln(9)}{\ln(9) - \ln(8)}$, 18.655 **37.** 1.5850 **39.** −0.6309 **41.** −2.2016
43. 1.5229 **45.** $\frac{\ln(7)}{\ln(2)}$, 2.807 **47.** $\frac{1}{3 - \ln(2)}$, 0.433 **49.** $\frac{\ln(5)}{\ln(3)}$, 1.465
51. $1 + \frac{\ln(9)}{\ln(2)}$, 4.170 **53.** $\log_3(20)$, 2.727 **55.** $\frac{3}{5}$ **57.** $\frac{1}{2}$
59. {−3} **61.** $\left\{-\frac{7}{2}, -2\right\}$ **63.** ∅ **65.** ∅ **67.** {4} **69.** {4, 6}
71. {2} **73.** {4} **75.** {−1} **77.** $\left\{\frac{3}{2}, \frac{5}{3}\right\}$ **79.** 41 months
81. 594 days **83.** 10 g, 9163 years ago **85.** 7524 ft³/sec
87. 7.1 years **89.** 16.8 years **91.** 2.0×10^{-4} **93.** 0.9183
95. $\sqrt[3]{12}$ or 2.2894 **97.** (2.71, 6.54) **99.** (1.03, 0.04), (4.74, 2.24)

Enriching Your Mathematical Word Power
1. a **2.** d **3.** b **4.** d **5.** d **6.** b **7.** a **8.** b
9. b **10.** c

Review Exercises
1. $\frac{1}{25}$ **3.** 125 **5.** 1 **7.** $\frac{1}{10}$ **9.** 4 **11.** $\frac{1}{2}$ **13.** 2 **15.** 4
17. $-\frac{5}{2}$ **19.** 2 **21.** 8.6421 **23.** 177.828 **25.** 0.02005
27. 0.1408
29.

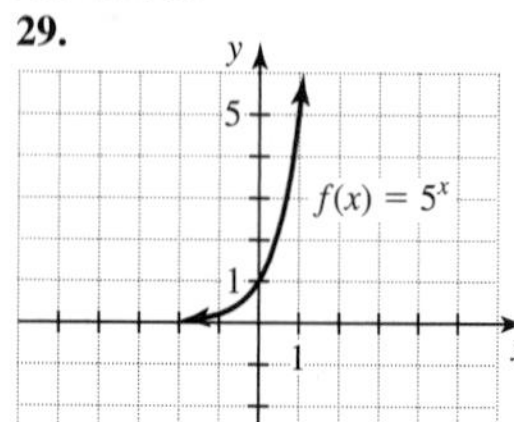

31.

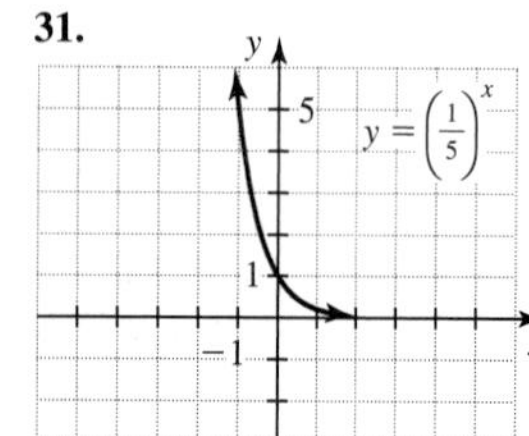

33.

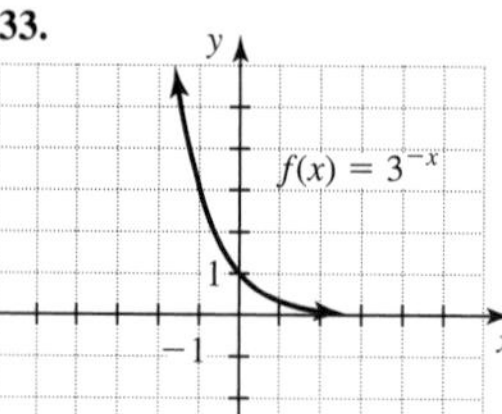

35.

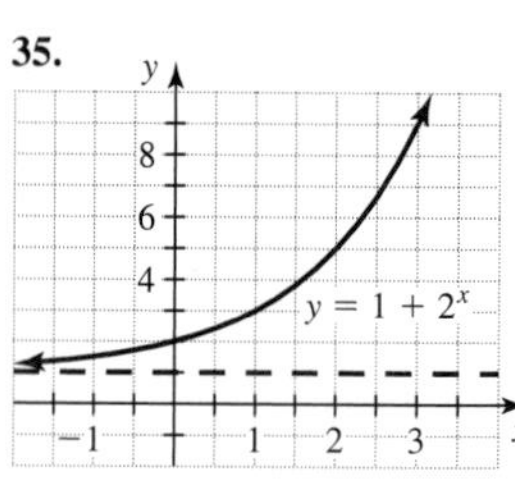

37. $\log(n) = m$ **39.** $k^h = t$ **41.** −3 **43.** −1 **45.** 2
47. 0 **49.** 256 **51.** 6.267 **53.** −5.083 **55.** 5.560
57. $f^{-1}(x) = \log(x)$ **59.** $f^{-1}(x) = \ln(x)$

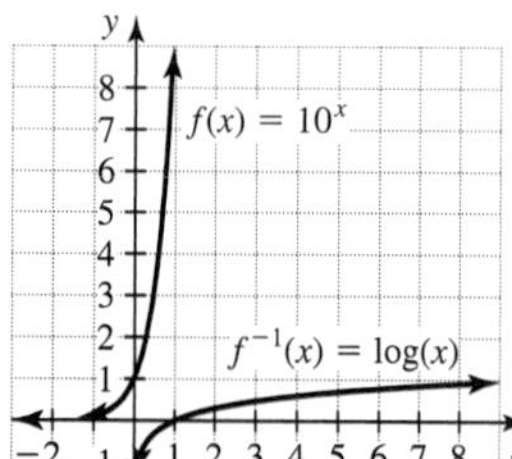

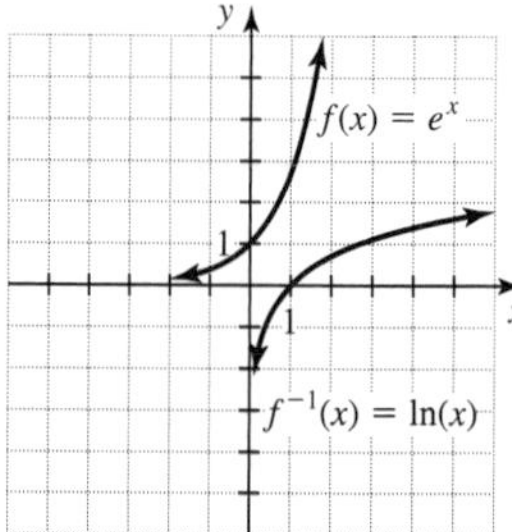

61. $2\log(x) + \log(y)$ **63.** $4\ln(2)$ **65.** $-\log_5(x)$ **67.** $\log\left(\frac{\sqrt{x+2}}{(x-1)^2}\right)$
69. {256} **71.** {3} **73.** {2} **75.** {3} **77.** $\left\{\frac{\ln(7)}{\ln(3) - 1}\right\}$
79. $\left\{\frac{\ln(5)}{\ln(5) - \ln(3)}\right\}$ **81.** $\left\{\frac{1}{3}\right\}$ **83.** {22} **85.** $\left\{\frac{200}{99}\right\}$ **87.** {1.3869}
89. {0.4650} **91.** \$51,182.68 **93.** 161.5 grams **95.** 5 years
97. 4347.5 ft³/sec

Chapter 12 Test
1. 25 **2.** $\frac{1}{5}$ **3.** 1 **4.** 3 **5.** 0 **6.** −1
7.

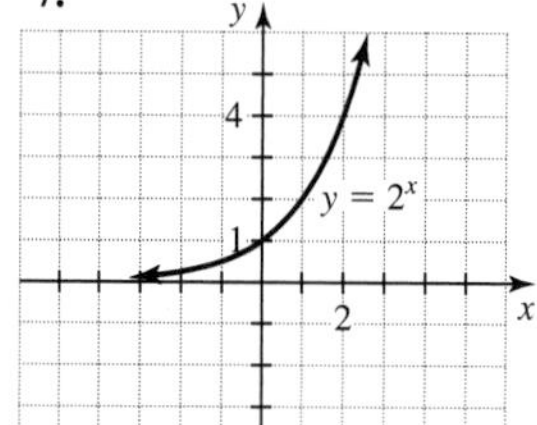

8.

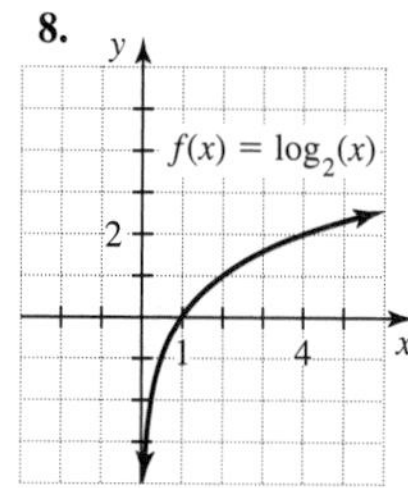

9.

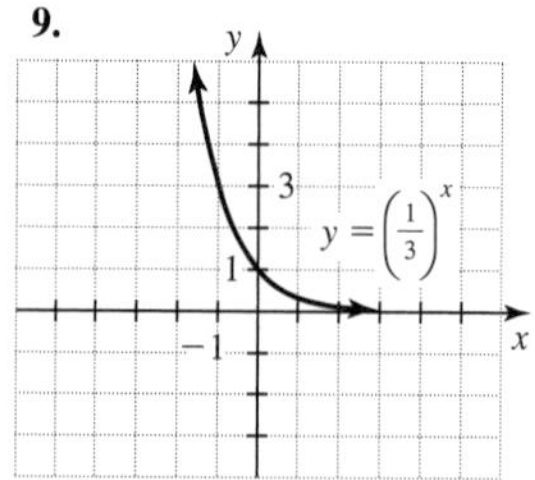

10.

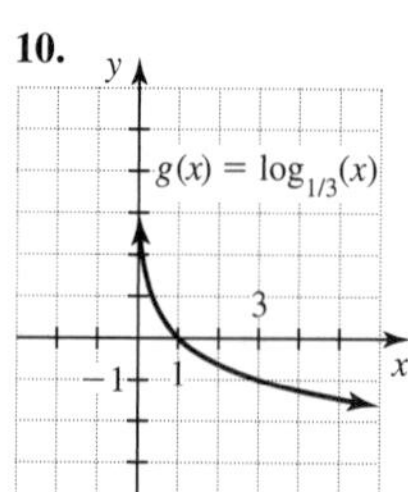

11. 10 **12.** 8 **13.** $\frac{3}{2}$ **14.** 15 **15.** −4
16. $\{\log_3(12)\}$ or $\{\ln(12)/\ln(3)\}$ **17.** $\{\sqrt{3}\}$ **18.** $\left\{\frac{\ln(8)}{\ln(8) - \ln(5)}\right\}$
19. {5} **20.** {3} **21.** {0.5372} **22.** {20.5156}
23. 10; 147,648 **24.** 1.733 hours

Making Connections A Review of Chapters 1–12

1. $\{3 \pm 2\sqrt{2}\}$ **2.** $\{259\}$ **3.** $\{6\}$ **4.** $\left\{\frac{11}{2}\right\}$ **5.** $\{-5, 11\}$

6. $\{67\}$ **7.** $\{6\}$ **8.** $\{4\}$ **9.** $\left\{-\frac{52}{15}\right\}$ **10.** $\left\{\frac{3 \pm \sqrt{3}}{3}\right\}$

11. $f^{-1}(x) = 3x$ **12.** $g^{-1}(x) = 3^x$ **13.** $f^{-1}(x) = \frac{x+4}{2}$

14. $h^{-1}(x) = x^2$ for $x \geq 0$ **15.** $j^{-1}(x) = \frac{1}{x}$ **16.** $k^{-1}(x) = \log_5(x)$

17. $m^{-1}(x) = 1 + \ln(x)$ **18.** $n^{-1}(x) = e^x$

19.

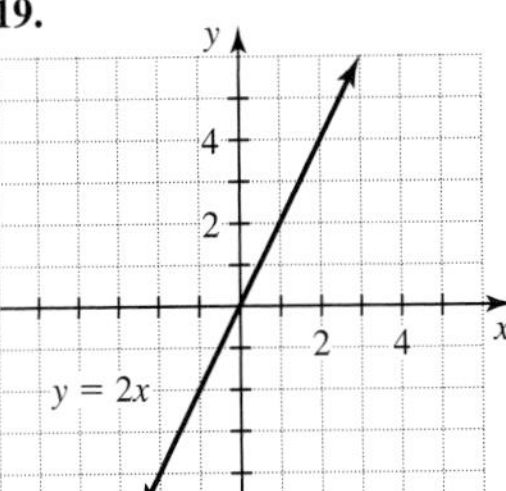

20.

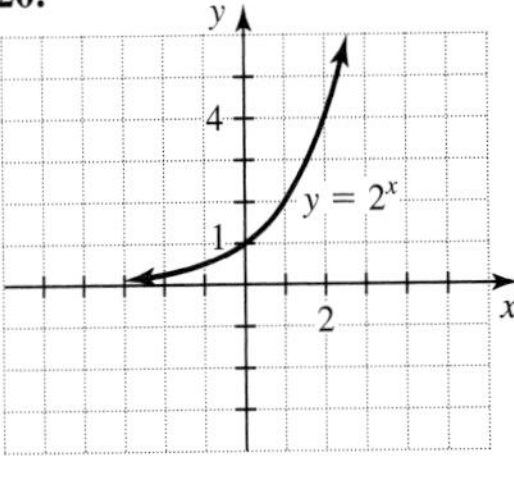

21.

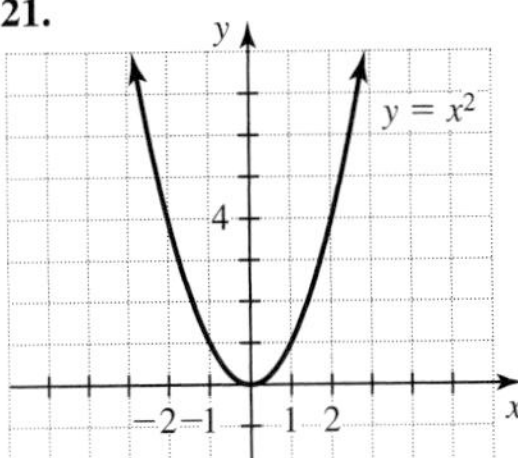

22.

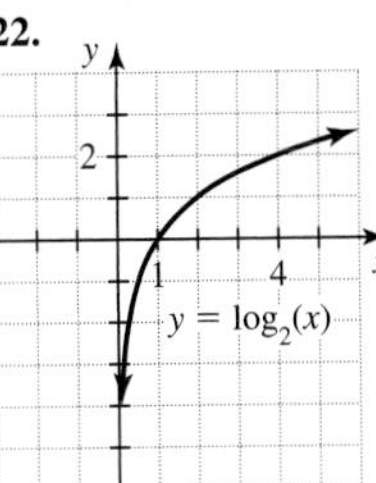

23.

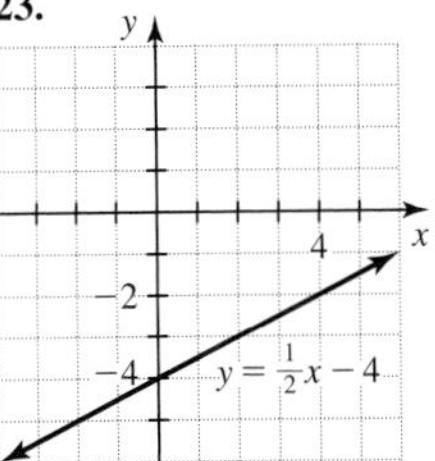

24.

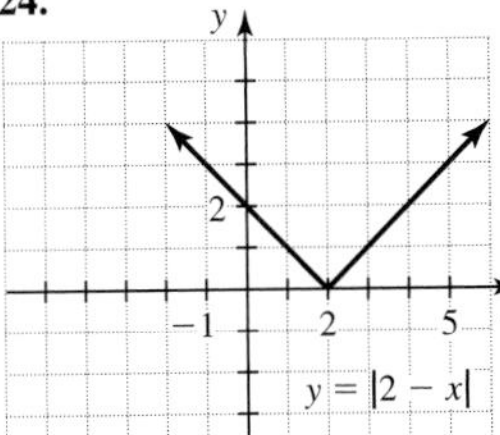

25.

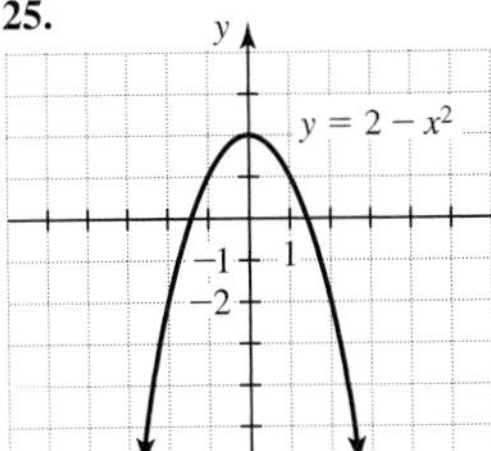

26.

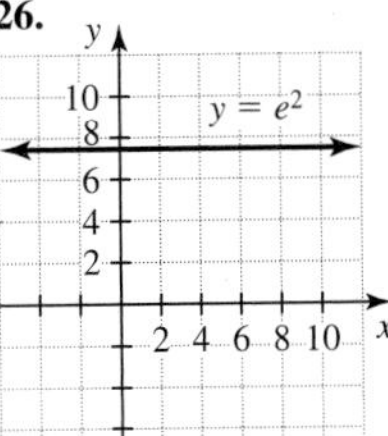

27. a)

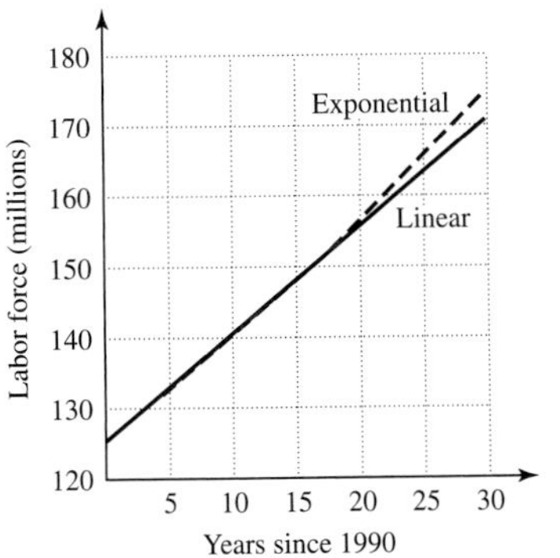

b) Linear 155.7 million, exponential 156.5 million

28. a) $d_1 = 0.135v$ **b)** $d_2 = 0.216v$
c) $v = 1482.67$ m/sec, $d_1 = 200.2$ meters

Chapter 13

Section 13.1 Warm-Ups T F F T F T T T T T

1. If the graph of an equation is not a straight line, then it is called nonlinear.

3. Graphing is not an accurate method for solving a system and the graphs might be difficult to draw.

5. $\{(2, 4), (-3, 9)\}$

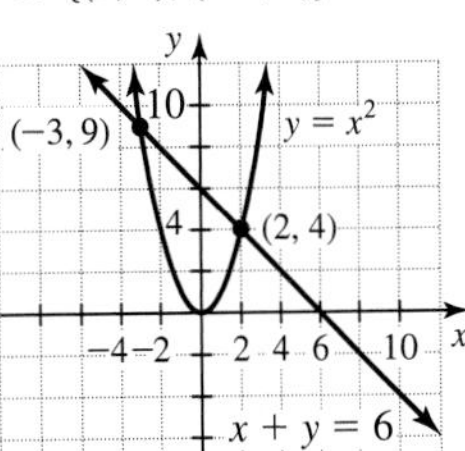

7. $\{(-2, 2), (6, 6)\}$

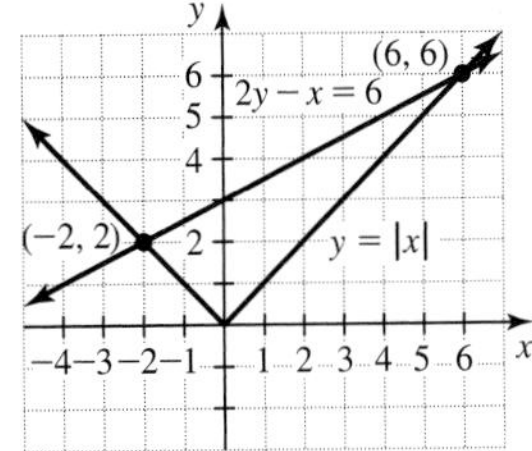

9. $\{(8, 4)\}$

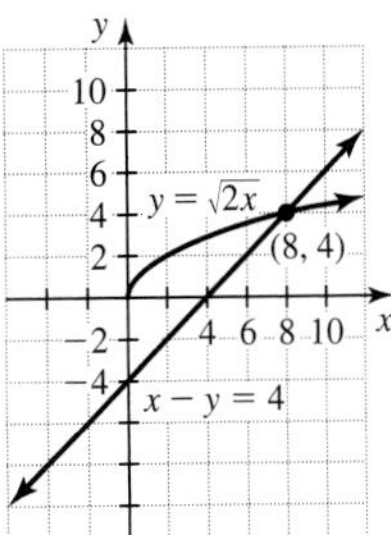

11. $\left\{\left(-\frac{3}{4}, -\frac{4}{3}\right), \left(3, \frac{1}{3}\right)\right\}$

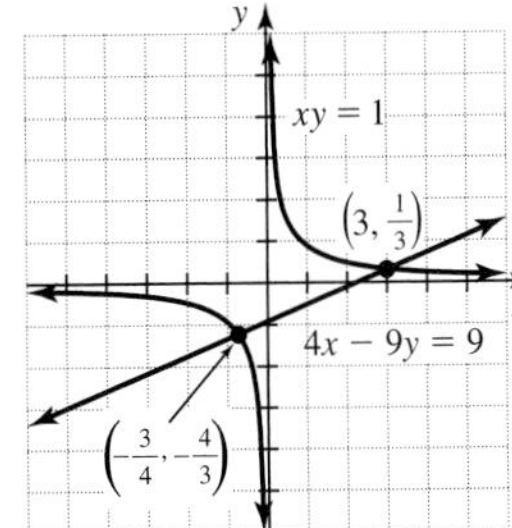

13. $\left\{\left(\frac{\sqrt{2}}{2}, \frac{1}{2}\right), \left(-\frac{\sqrt{2}}{2}, \frac{1}{2}\right)\right\}$

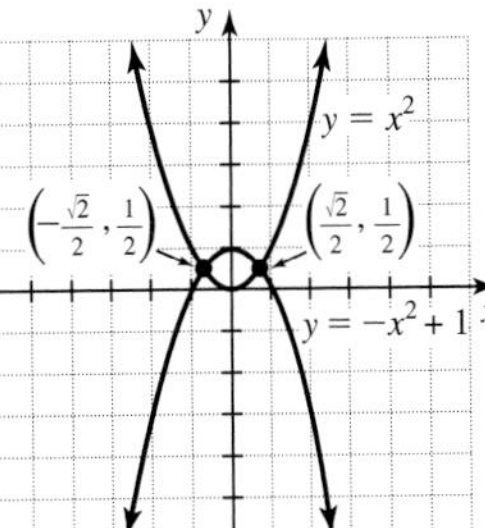

15. $\{(-1, -1), (1, 1)\}$
17. $\{(-\sqrt{2}, 2), (\sqrt{2}, 2)\}$
19. $\{(0, -5), (3, 4), (-3, 4)\}$
21. $\{(4, 5), (-2, -1)\}$
23. $\left\{\left(-3, -\frac{5}{3}\right)\right\}$

25. $\{(\sqrt{5}, \sqrt{3}), (\sqrt{5}, -\sqrt{3}), (-\sqrt{5}, \sqrt{3}), (-\sqrt{5}, -\sqrt{3})\}$
27. $\{(\sqrt{2}, \sqrt{3}), (\sqrt{2}, -\sqrt{3}), (-\sqrt{2}, \sqrt{3}), (-\sqrt{2}, -\sqrt{3})\}$
29. $\left\{\left(\frac{3}{2}, -\frac{3}{13}\right)\right\}$ **31.** $\{(3, 4)\}$ **33.** $\left\{\left(-\frac{5}{3}, \frac{36}{5}\right), (2, 5)\right\}$
35. $\{(2, 5), (19, -12)\}$ **37.** $\{(\sqrt{2}, 2), (-\sqrt{2}, 2), (1, 1), (-1, 1)\}$
39. $\{(3, 1)\}$ **41.** $\varnothing$ **43.** $\{(-6, 4^{-7})\}$ **45.** $\sqrt{3}$ ft and $2\sqrt{3}$ ft
47. Height $5\sqrt{10}$ in., base $20\sqrt{10}$ in.
49. Pump A 24 hours, pump B 8 hours **51.** 40 minutes
53. 8 ft by 9 ft **55.** $4 - 2i$ and $4 + 2i$
57. Side 8 ft, height of triangle 2 ft
59. a) (1.71, 1.55), (−2.98, −3.95) **b)** (1, 1), (0.40, 0.16)
c) (1.17, 1.62), (−1.17, −1.62)

Section 13.2 Warm-Ups F T T F F T T T T T

1. A parabola is the set of all points in a plane that are equidistant from a given line and a fixed point not on the line.
3. A parabola can be written in the forms $y = ax^2 + bx + c$ or $y = a(x - h)^2 + k$.
5. We use completing the square to convert $y = ax^2 + bx + c$ into $y = a(x - h)^2 + k$.
7. $\sqrt{2}$ **9.** $\sqrt{13}$ **11.** $2\sqrt{17}$ **13.** $\sqrt{65}$
15. Vertex (0, 0), focus $\left(0, \frac{1}{8}\right)$, directrix $y = -\frac{1}{8}$
17. Vertex (0, 0), focus (0, −1), directrix $y = 1$
19. Vertex (3, 2), focus (3, 2.5), directrix $y = 1.5$
21. Vertex (−1, 6), focus (−1, 5.75), directrix $y = 6.25$
23. $y = \frac{1}{8}x^2$ **25.** $y = -\frac{1}{2}x^2$ **27.** $y = \frac{1}{2}x^2 - 3x + 6$
29. $y = -\frac{1}{8}x^2 + \frac{1}{4}x - \frac{1}{8}$ **31.** $y = x^2 + 6x + 10$
33. $y = (x - 3)^2 - 8$, vertex (3, −8), focus (3, −7.75), directrix $y = -8.25$, axis $x = 3$
35. $y = 2(x + 3)^2 - 13$, vertex (−3, −13), focus (−3, −12.875), directrix $y = -13.125$, axis $x = -3$
37. $y = -2(x - 4)^2 + 33$, vertex (4, 33), focus $\left(4, 32\frac{7}{8}\right)$, directrix $y = 33\frac{1}{8}$, axis $x = 4$
39. $y = 5(x + 4)^2 - 80$, vertex (−4, −80), focus $\left(-4, -79\frac{19}{20}\right)$, directrix $y = -80\frac{1}{20}$, axis $x = -4$
41. Vertex (2, −3), focus $\left(2, -2\frac{3}{4}\right)$, directrix $y = -3\frac{1}{4}$, $x = 2$, upward
43. Vertex (1, −2), focus $\left(1, -2\frac{1}{4}\right)$, directrix $y = -1\frac{3}{4}$, $x = 1$, downward
45. Vertex (1, −2), focus $\left(1, -1\frac{11}{12}\right)$, directrix $y = -2\frac{1}{12}$, $x = 1$, upward
47. Vertex $\left(-\frac{3}{2}, \frac{17}{4}\right)$, focus $\left(-\frac{3}{2}, 4\right)$, directrix $y = \frac{9}{2}$, $x = -\frac{3}{2}$, downward
49. Vertex (0, 5), focus $\left(0, 5\frac{1}{12}\right)$, directrix $y = 4\frac{11}{12}$, $x = 0$, upward
51. (3, 2), $\left(\frac{13}{4}, 2\right)$, $x = \frac{11}{4}$ **53.** (−2, 1), (−1, 1), $x = -3$
55. (4, 2), $\left(\frac{7}{2}, 2\right)$, $x = \frac{9}{2}$

57\.

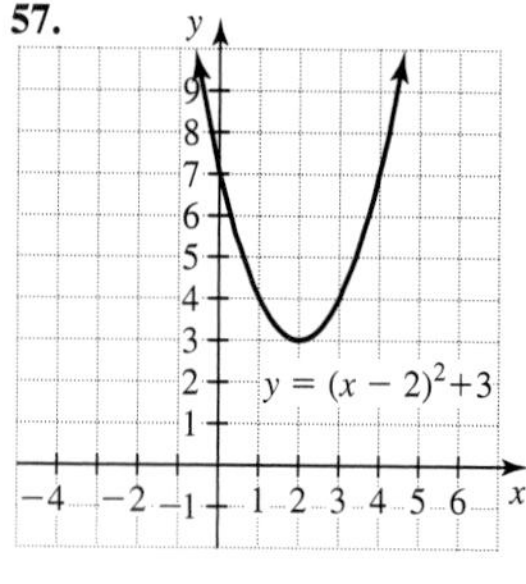

59\.

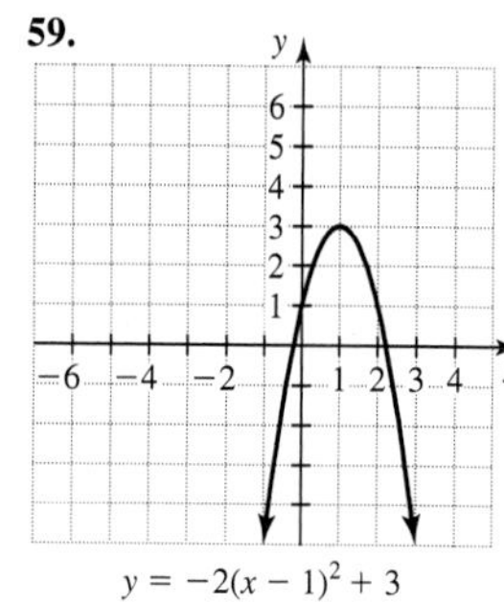

61\.

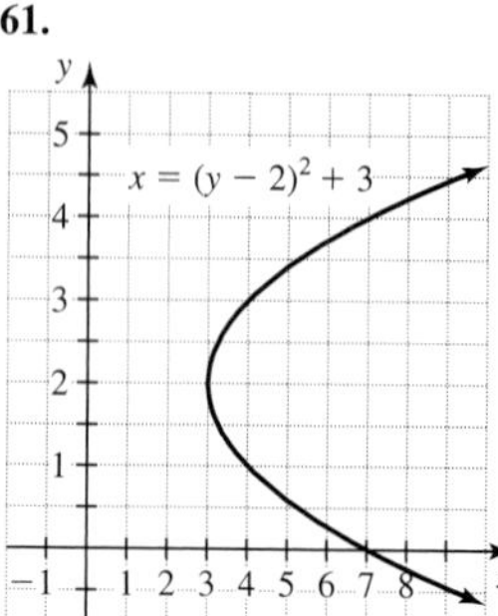

63\.

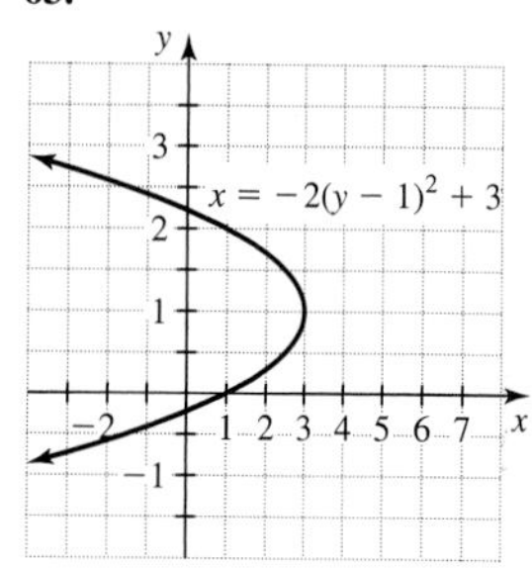

65. $y = \frac{1}{60}x^2$

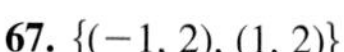

67. {(−1, 2), (1, 2)}

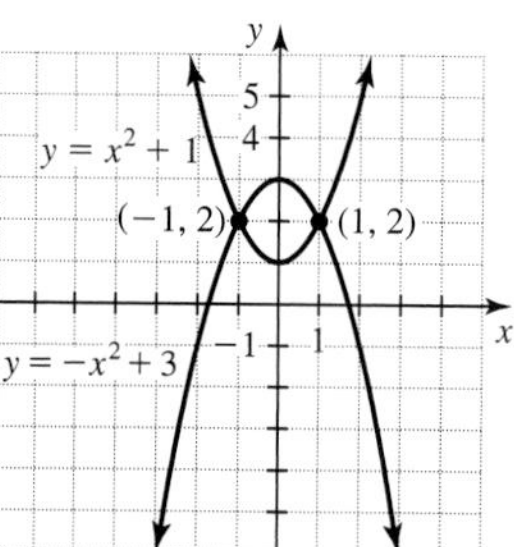

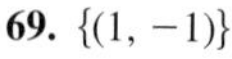

69. {(1, −1)}

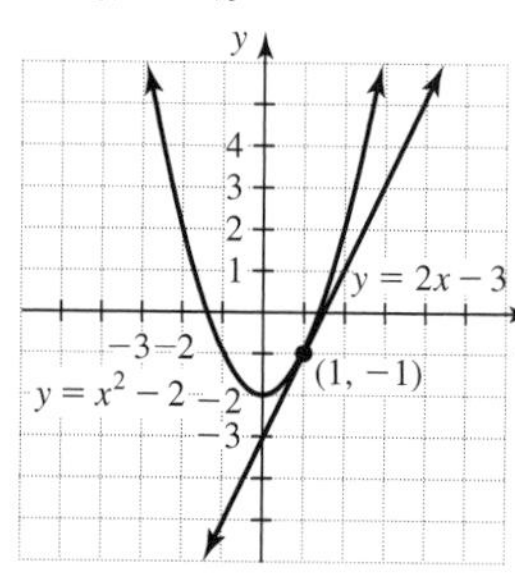

71. $\left\{\left(\frac{3}{2}, \frac{11}{4}\right), (-4, 0)\right\}$

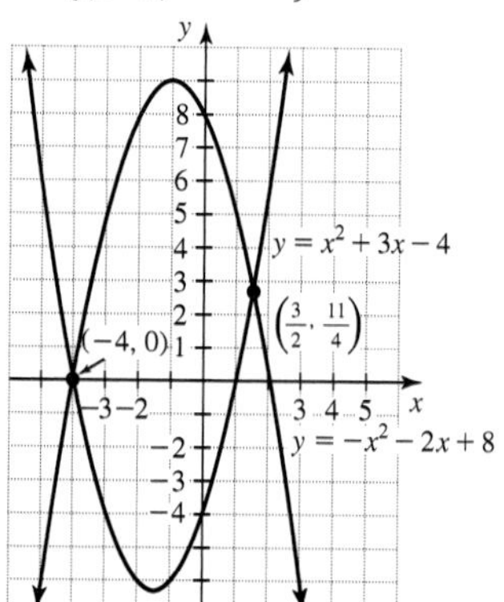

73. {(−3, −4), (2, 6)}

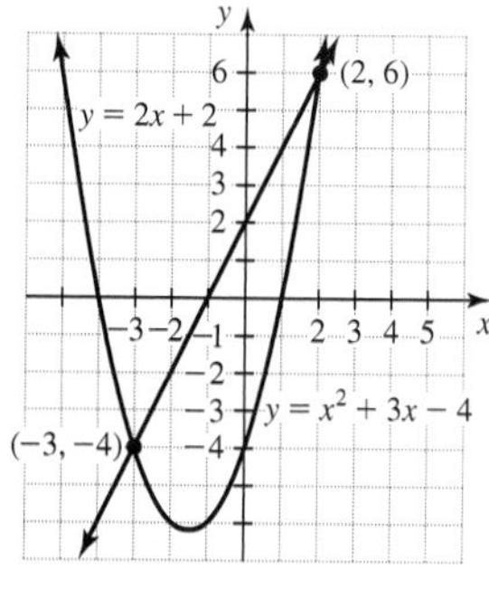

75. (3, 0), (−1, 0) **77.** (20, 4), (−20, 4)
79. (0, 0), (1, 1)
83. The graphs have identical shapes.

Section 13.3 Warm-Ups F F T F F F T F T F

1. A circle is the set of all points in a plane that lie at a fixed distance from a fixed point.
3. $x^2 + y^2 = 16$ **5.** $x^2 + (y - 3)^2 = 25$
7. $(x - 1)^2 + (y + 2)^2 = 81$
9. $x^2 + y^2 = 3$ **11.** $(x + 6)^2 + (y + 3)^2 = \frac{1}{4}$
13. $\left(x - \frac{1}{2}\right)^2 + \left(y - \frac{1}{3}\right)^2 = 0.01$ **15.** (3, 5), $\sqrt{2}$
17. $\left(0, \frac{1}{2}\right)$, $\frac{\sqrt{2}}{2}$ **19.** (0, 0), $\frac{3}{2}$ **21.** (2, 0), $\sqrt{3}$

23\.

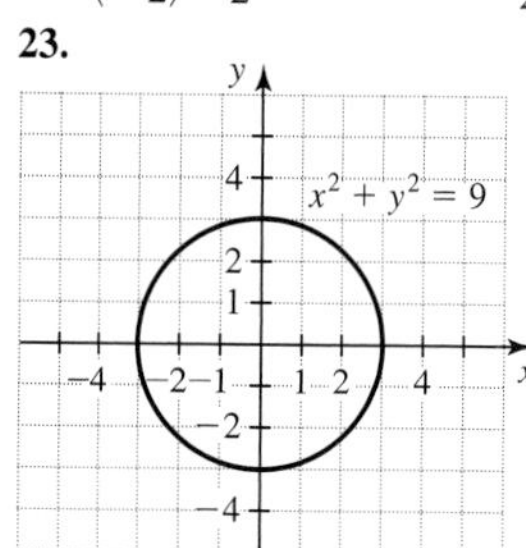

25\.

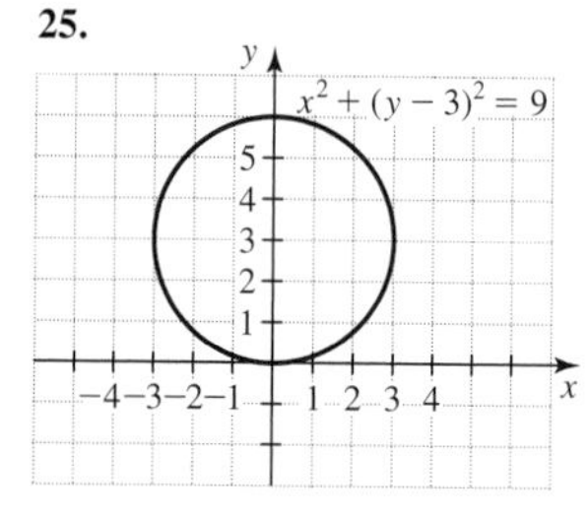

27.

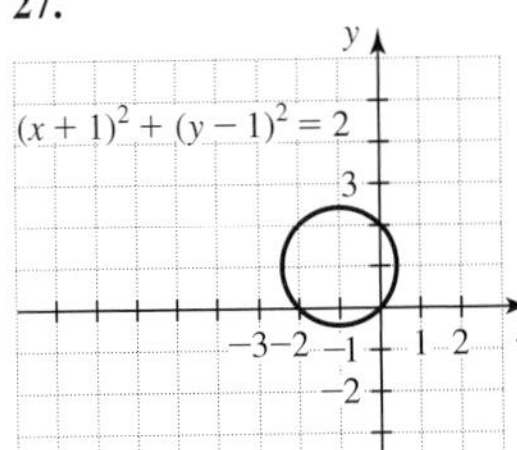

29.

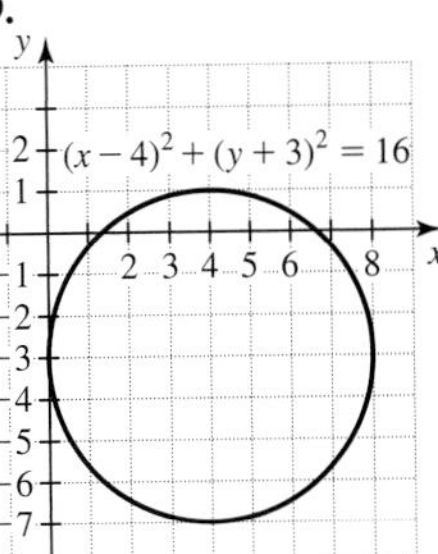

31.

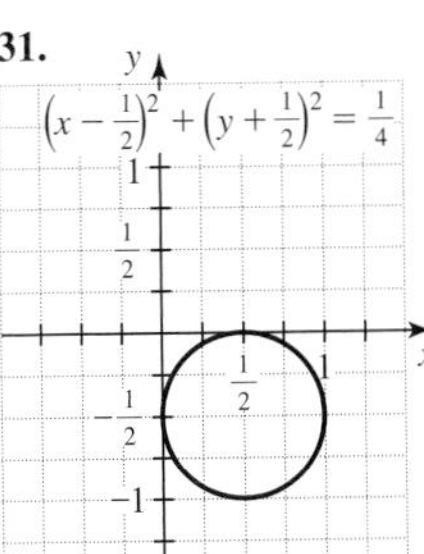

33. $(x + 2)^2 + (y + 3)^2 = 13, (-2, -3), \sqrt{13}$

35. $(x - 1)^2 + (y - 2)^2 = 8, (1, 2), 2\sqrt{2}$

37. $(x - 5)^2 + (y - 4)^2 = 9, (5, 4), 3$

39. $\left(x - \frac{1}{2}\right)^2 + \left(y + \frac{1}{2}\right)^2 = \frac{1}{2}, \left(\frac{1}{2}, -\frac{1}{2}\right), \frac{\sqrt{2}}{2}$

41. $\left(x - \frac{3}{2}\right)^2 + \left(y - \frac{1}{2}\right)^2 = \frac{7}{2}, \left(\frac{3}{2}, \frac{1}{2}\right), \frac{\sqrt{14}}{2}$

43. $\left(x - \frac{1}{3}\right)^2 + \left(y + \frac{3}{4}\right)^2 = \frac{97}{144}, \left(\frac{1}{3}, -\frac{3}{4}\right), \frac{\sqrt{97}}{12}$

45. $\{(1, 3), (-1, -3)\}$

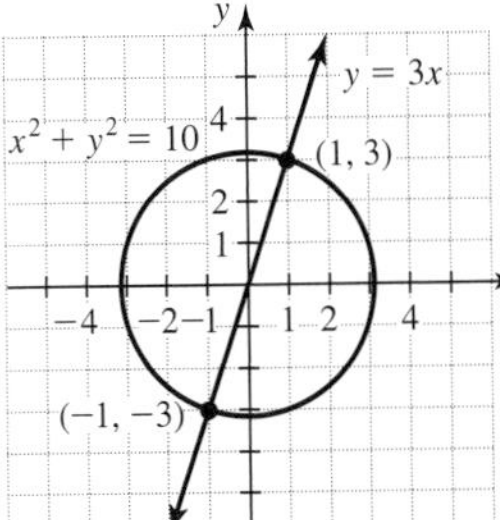

47. $\{(0, -3), (\sqrt{5}, 2), (-\sqrt{5}, 2)\}$

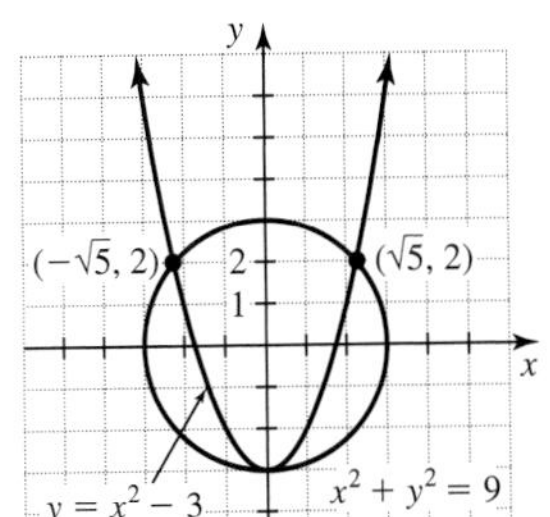

49. $\{(0, -3), (2, -1)\}$

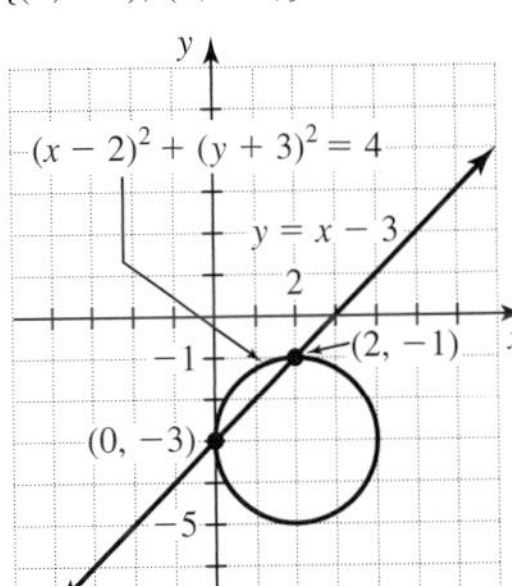

51. $(0, 2 + \sqrt{3})$ and $(0, 2 - \sqrt{3})$

53. $\sqrt{29}$ **55.** $(x - 2)^2 + (y - 3)^2 = 32$

57. $\left(\frac{5}{2}, -\frac{\sqrt{11}}{2}\right)$ and $\left(\frac{5}{2}, \frac{\sqrt{11}}{2}\right)$

59. 755,903 mm^3

61. (0, 0) only

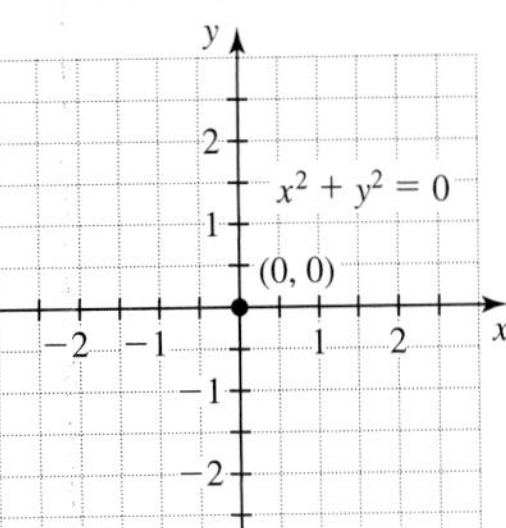

63.

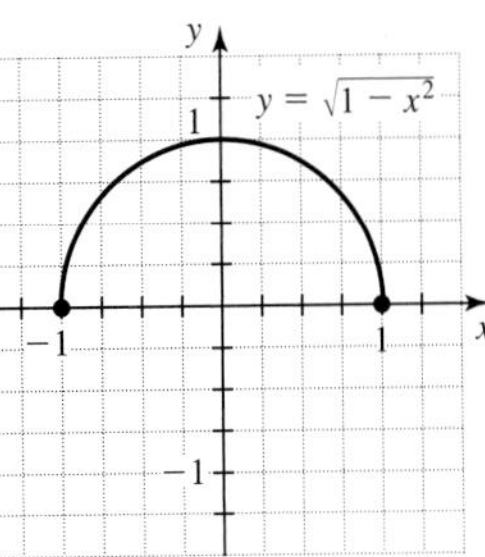

65. B and D can be any real numbers, but A must equal C, and $4AE + B^2 + D^2 > 0$. No ordered pairs satisfy $x^2 + y^2 = -9$.

67. $y = \pm\sqrt{4 - x^2}$ **69.** $y = \pm\sqrt{x}$

71. $y = -1 \pm \sqrt{x}$

Section 13.4 Warm-Ups F F T T T F F T T T

1. An ellipse is the set of all points in a plane such that the sum of their distances from two fixed points is constant.
3. The center of an ellipse is the point that is midway between the foci.
5. The equation of an ellipse centered at (h, k) is $\frac{(x - h)^2}{a^2} + \frac{(y - k)^2}{b^2} = 1$.
7. The asymptotes of a hyperbola are the extended diagonals of the fundamental rectangle.

9.

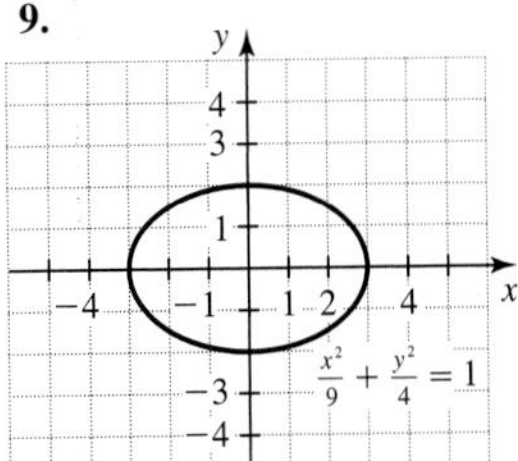

11.

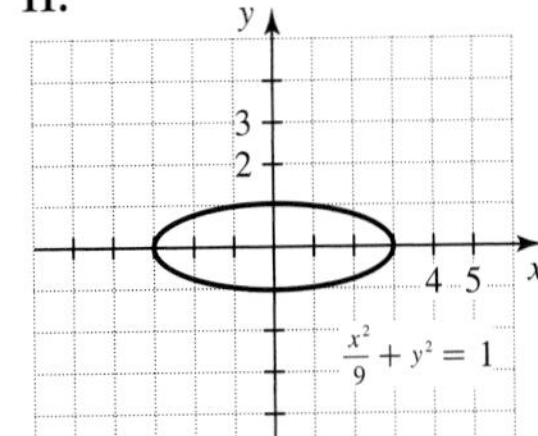

13.

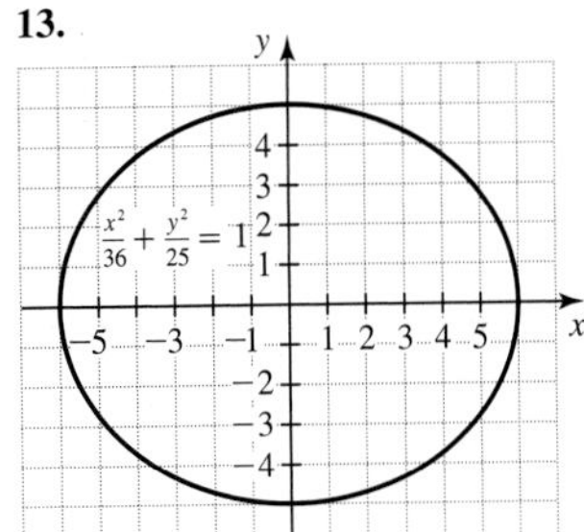

15.

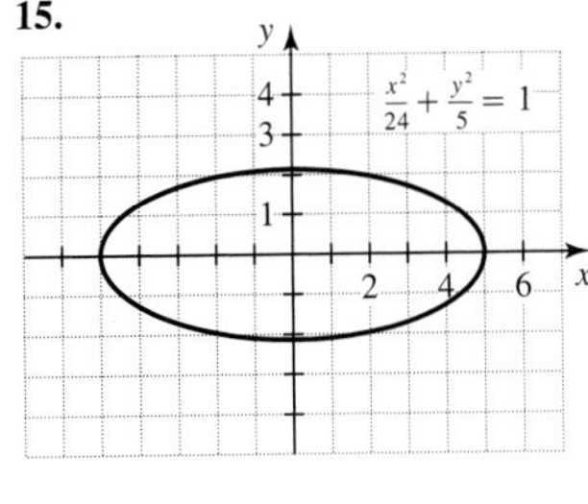

17.

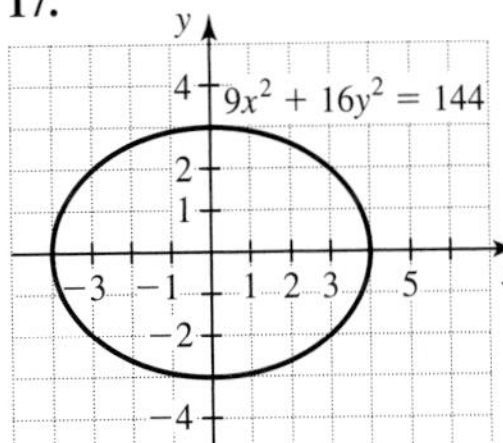

19.

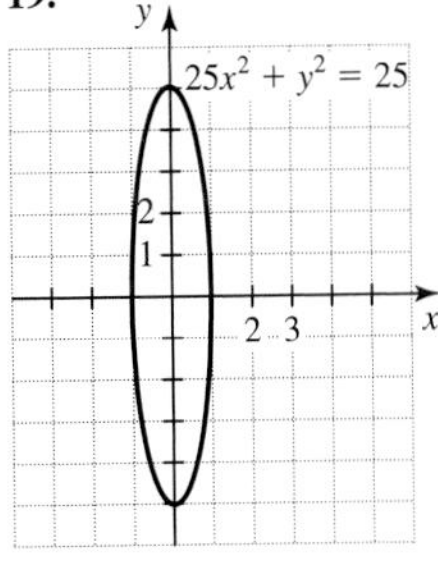

21.

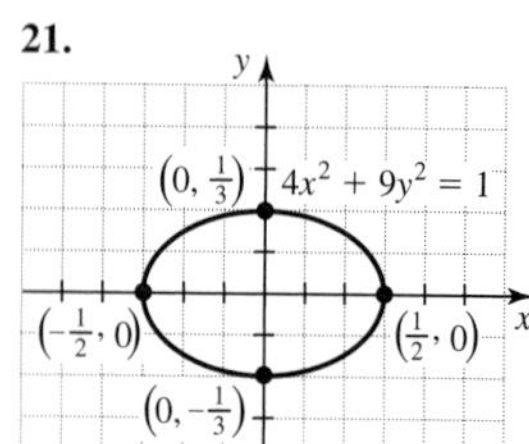

23.

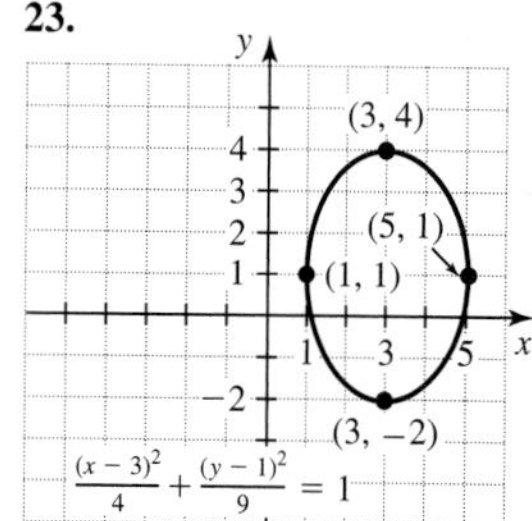

25.

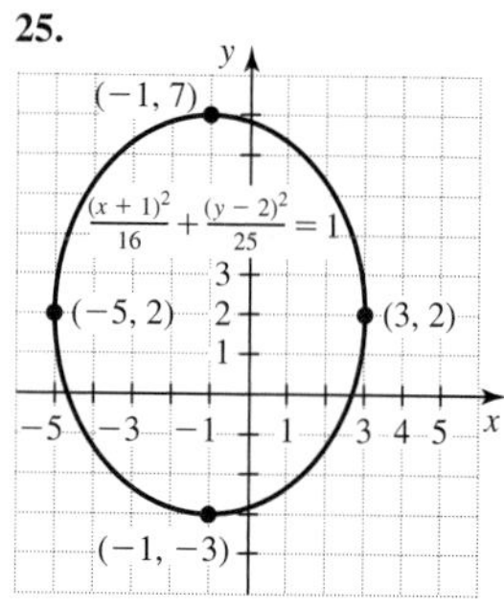

27.

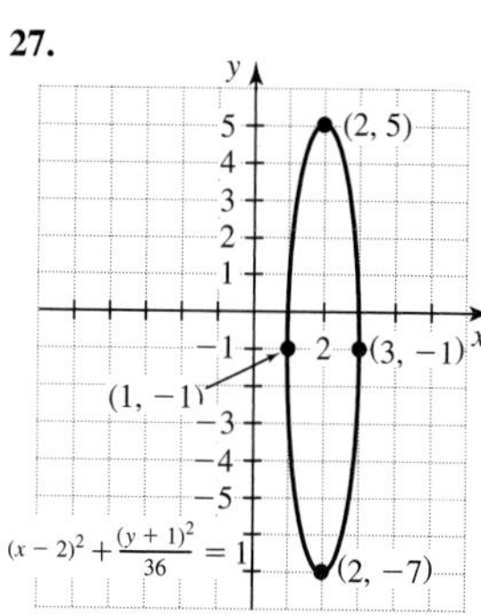

29. $y = \pm\frac{3}{2}x$

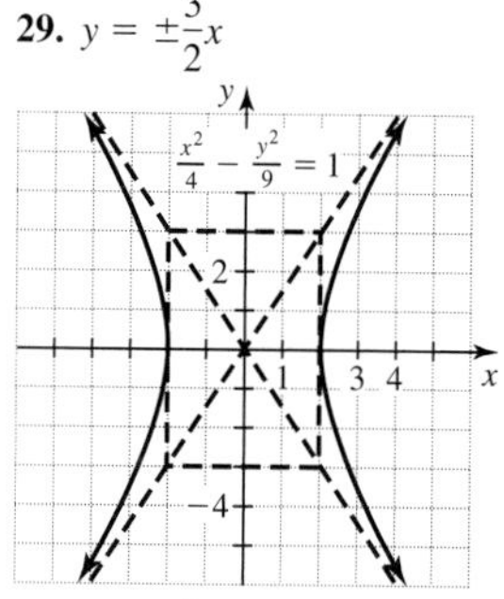

31. $y = \pm\frac{2}{5}x$

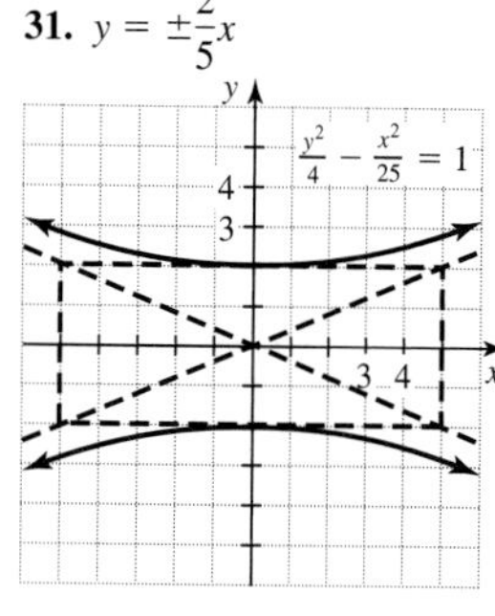

33. $y = \pm\frac{1}{5}x$

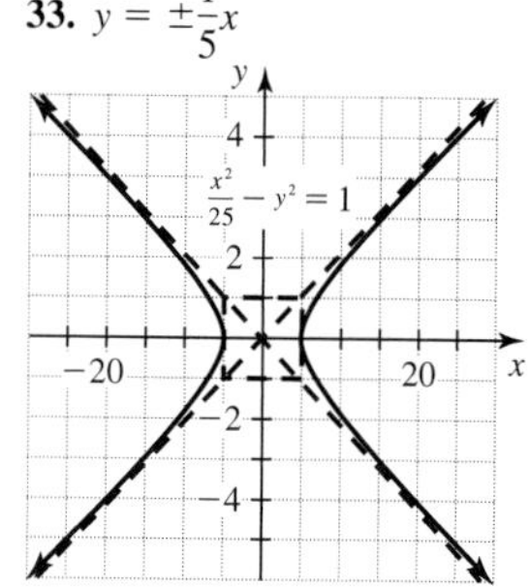

35. $y = \pm 5x$

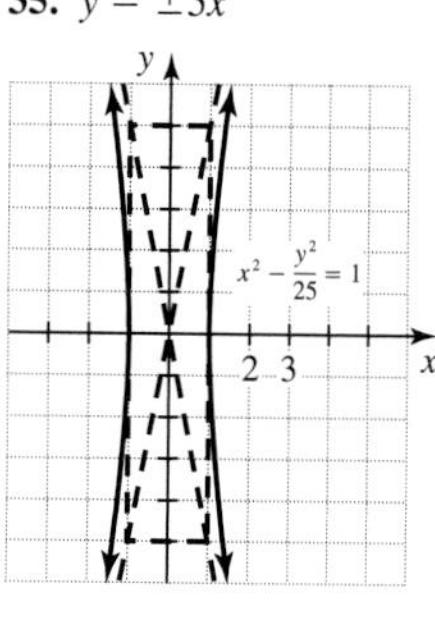

37. $y = \pm\frac{3}{4}x$

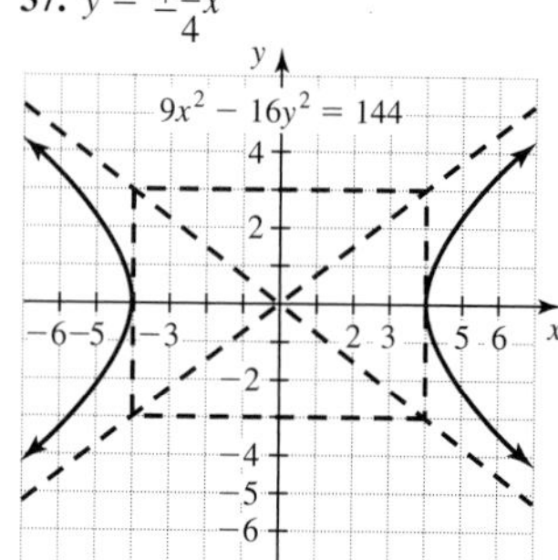

39. $y = \pm x$

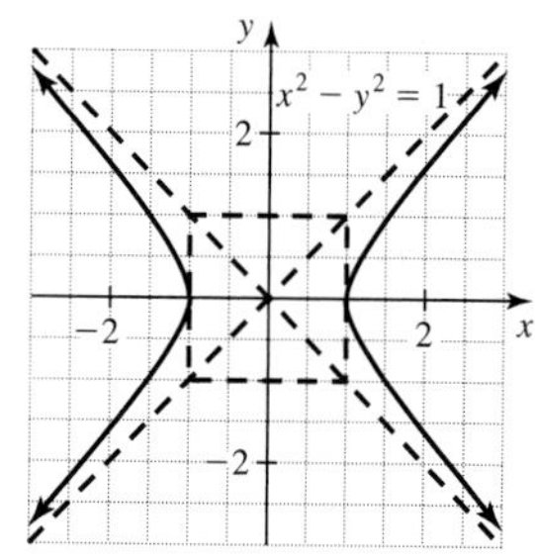

41.

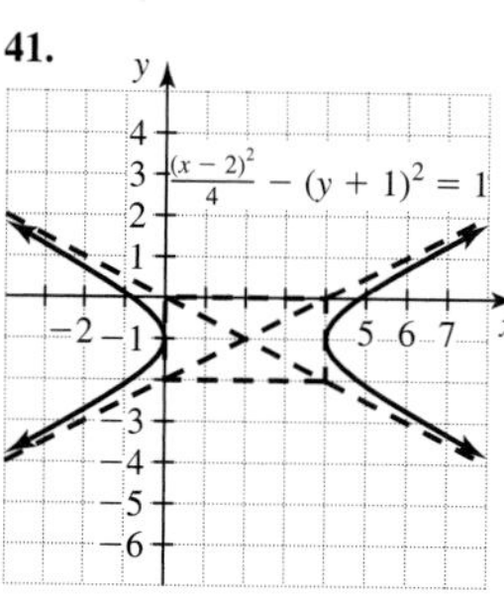

43.

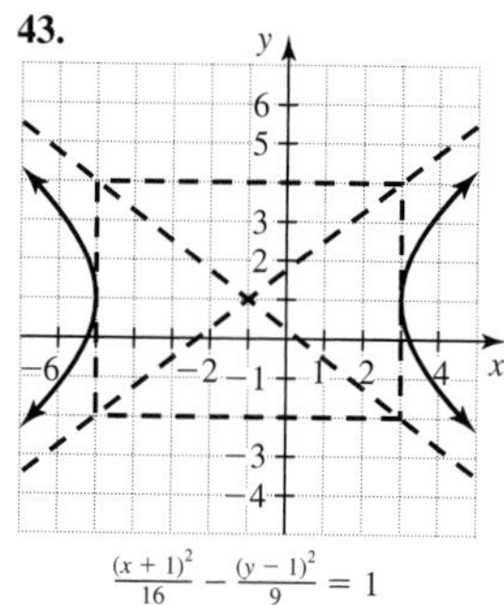

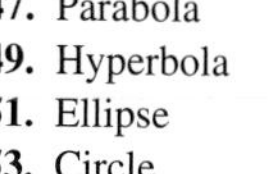

45.

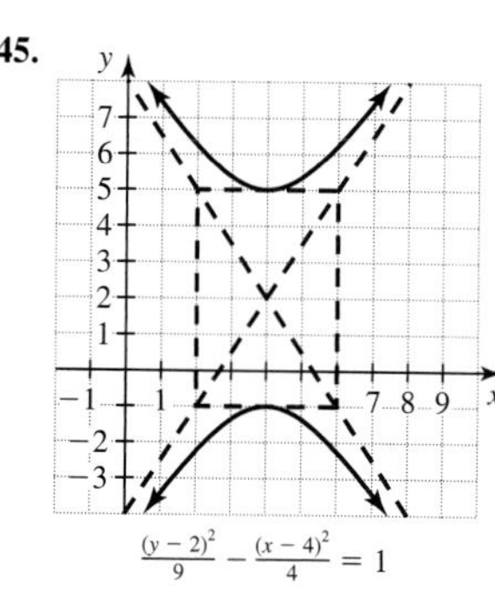

47. Parabola
49. Hyperbola
51. Ellipse
53. Circle

55. $\left(\frac{2\sqrt{10}}{5}, \frac{3\sqrt{15}}{5}\right)$, $\left(\frac{2\sqrt{10}}{5}, -\frac{3\sqrt{15}}{5}\right)$, $\left(-\frac{2\sqrt{10}}{5}, \frac{3\sqrt{15}}{5}\right)$, $\left(-\frac{2\sqrt{10}}{5}, -\frac{3\sqrt{15}}{5}\right)$

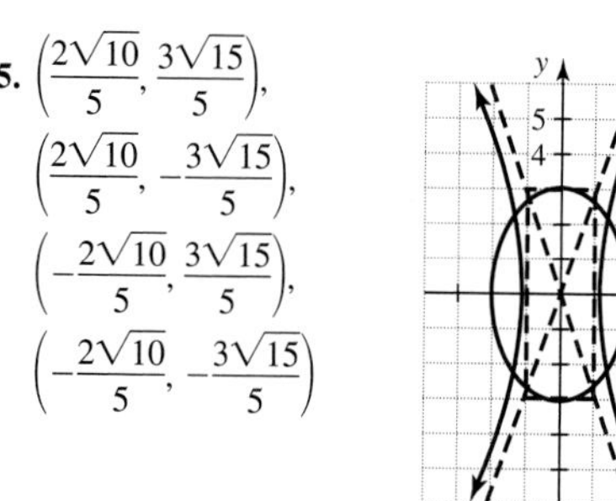

57. No points of intersection

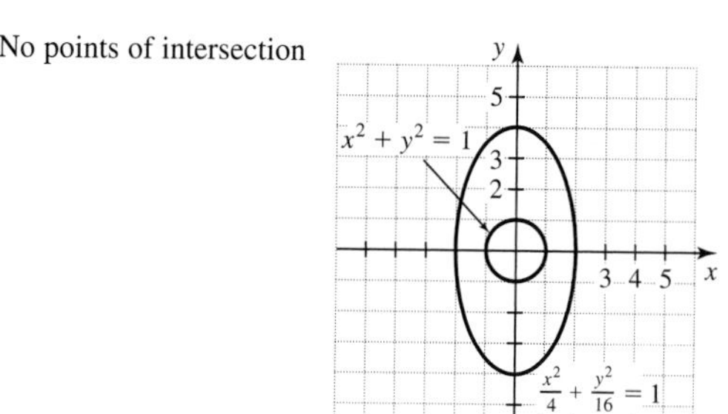

59. $\left(\frac{\sqrt{10}}{2}, \frac{\sqrt{6}}{2}\right)$, $\left(\frac{\sqrt{10}}{2}, -\frac{\sqrt{6}}{2}\right)$, $\left(-\frac{\sqrt{10}}{2}, \frac{\sqrt{6}}{2}\right)$, $\left(-\frac{\sqrt{10}}{2}, -\frac{\sqrt{6}}{2}\right)$

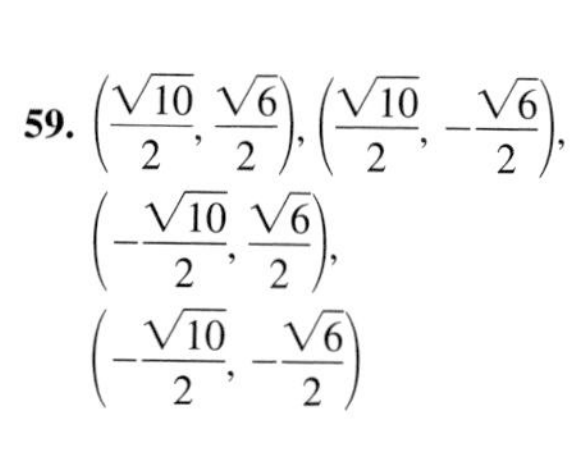

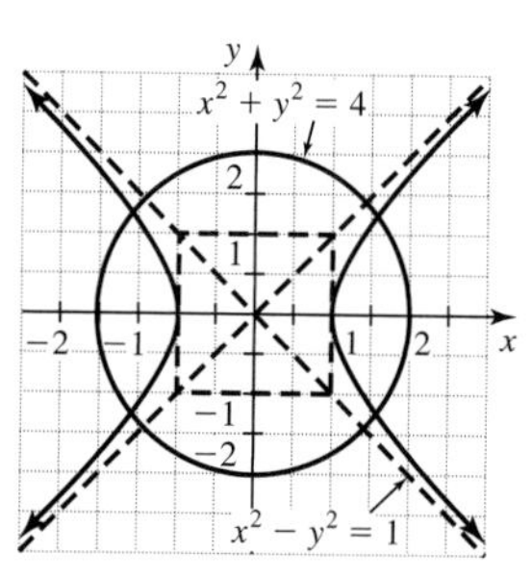

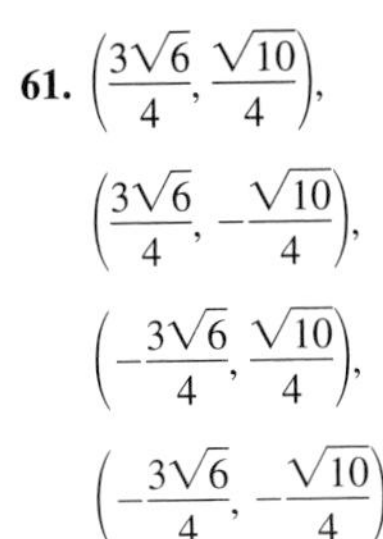

61. $\left(\frac{3\sqrt{6}}{4}, \frac{\sqrt{10}}{4}\right)$, $\left(\frac{3\sqrt{6}}{4}, -\frac{\sqrt{10}}{4}\right)$, $\left(-\frac{3\sqrt{6}}{4}, \frac{\sqrt{10}}{4}\right)$, $\left(-\frac{3\sqrt{6}}{4}, -\frac{\sqrt{10}}{4}\right)$

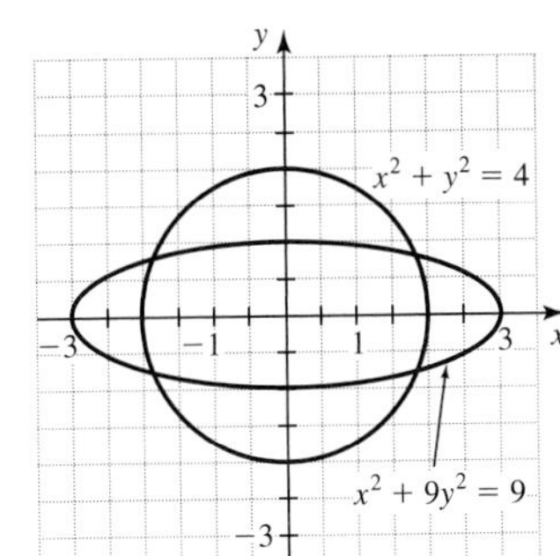

63. $\left(\frac{\sqrt{17}}{3}, \frac{8}{9}\right)$, $\left(-\frac{\sqrt{17}}{3}, \frac{8}{9}\right)$, $(0, -1)$

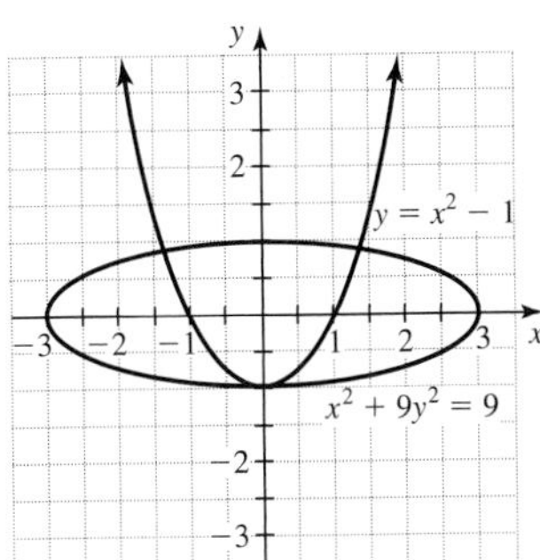

65. $(2, 0)$, $\left(-\frac{5}{2}, -\frac{9}{4}\right)$

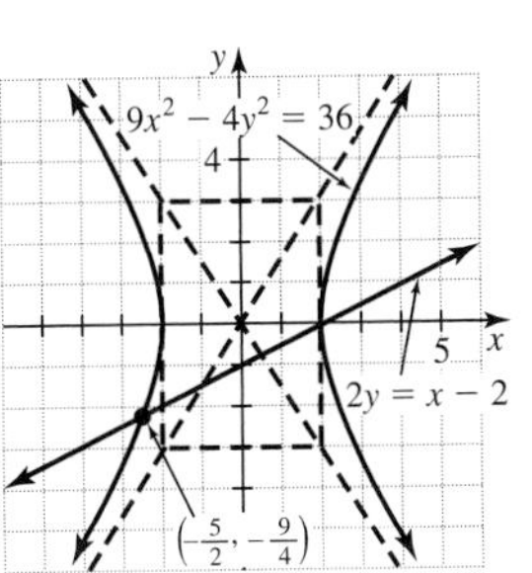

67. a) $(2.5, 1.5)$ **b)** $(\sqrt{7}, \sqrt{2})$

Section 13.5 Warm-Ups F T T T F F F T T T

1.

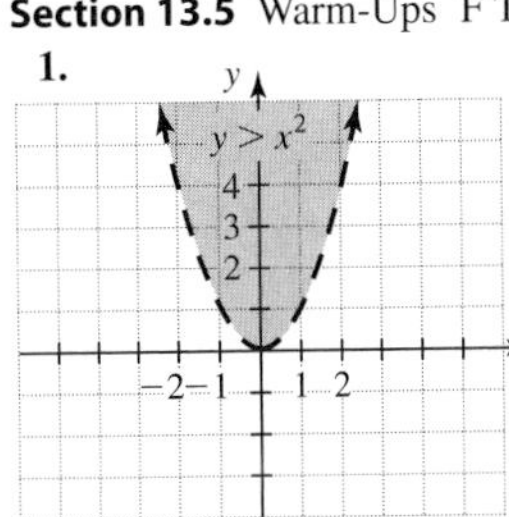

3.

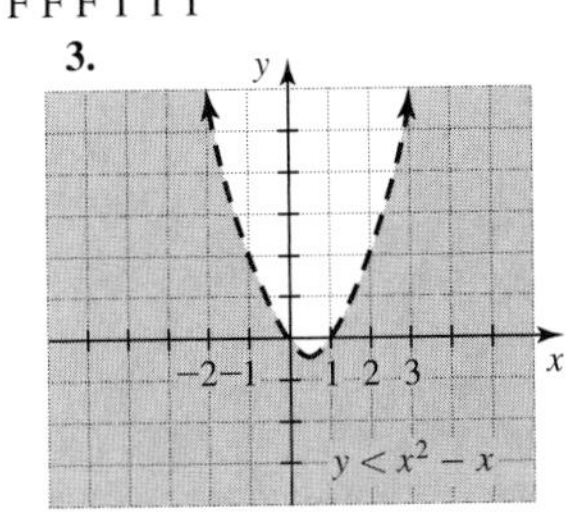

5.

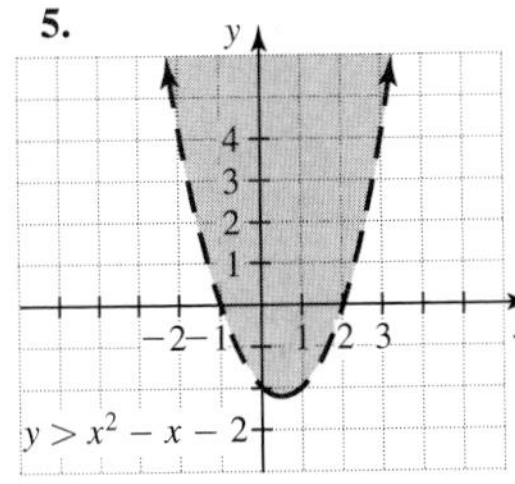

7.

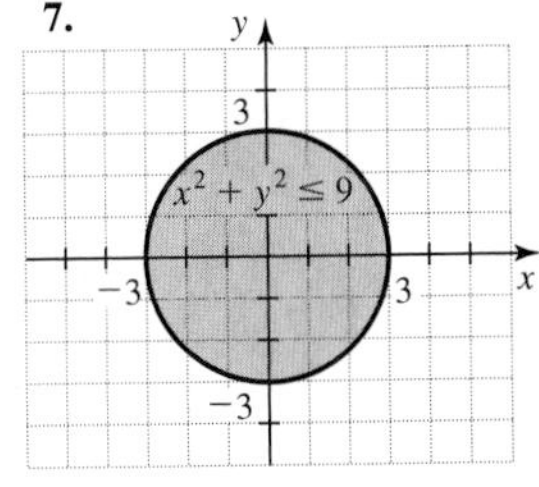

9.

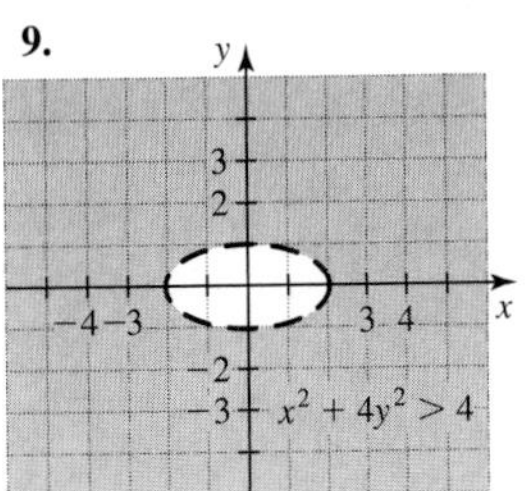

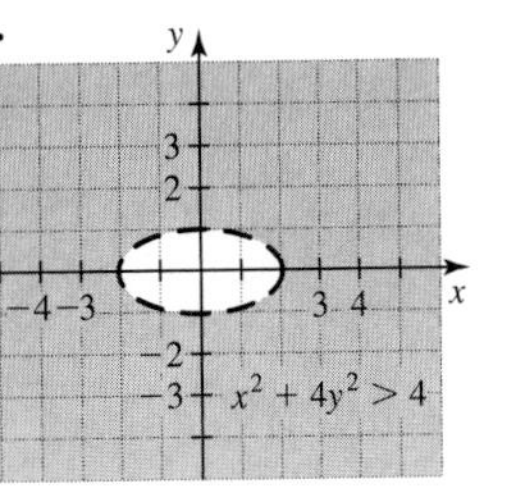

11.

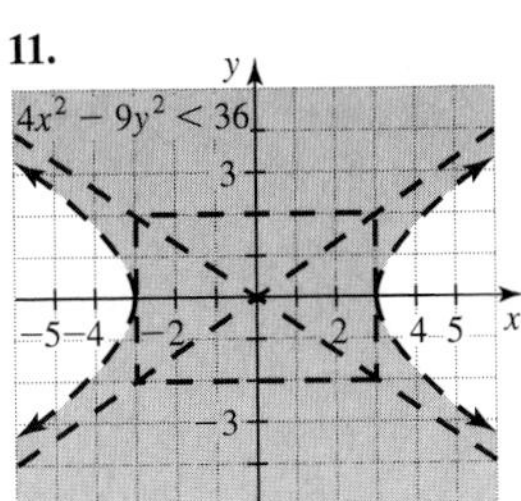

13.

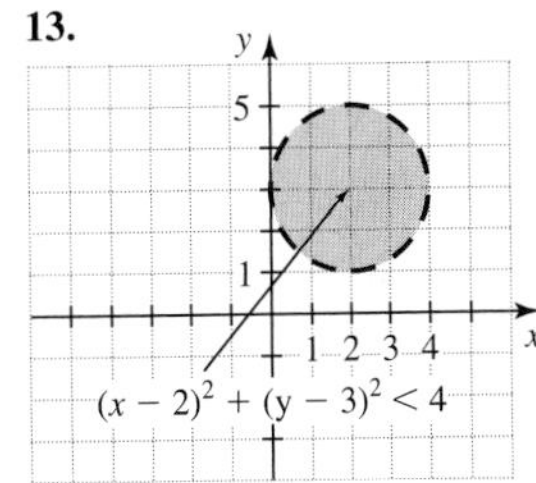

15.

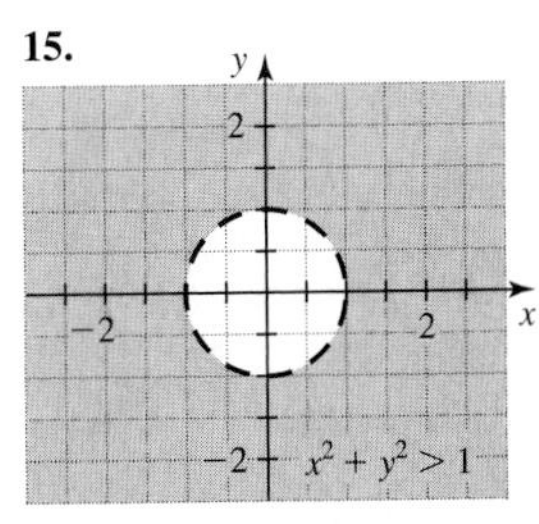

17.

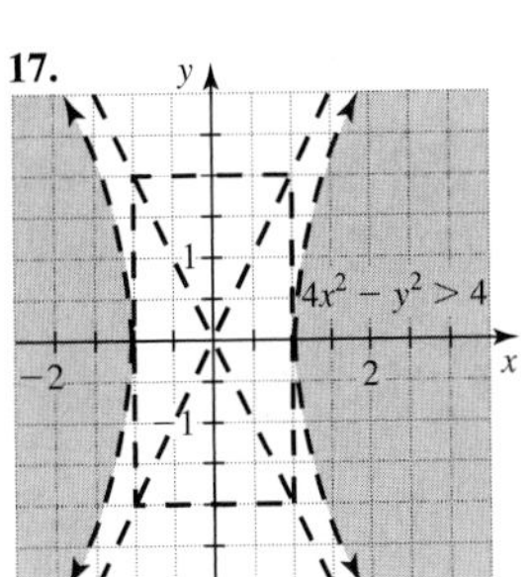

19.

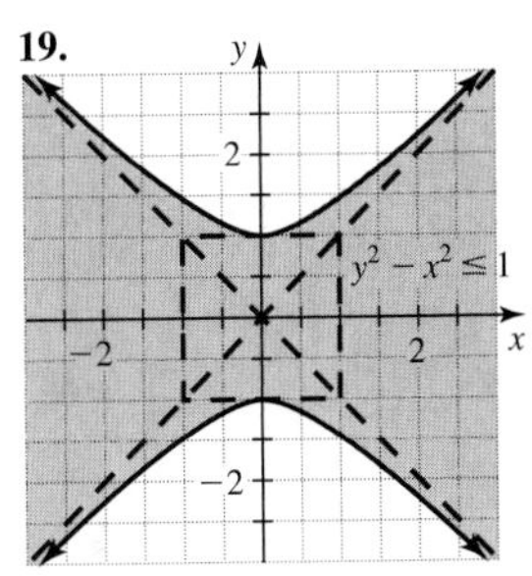

21. $x > y$

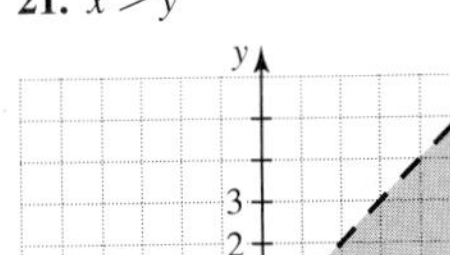

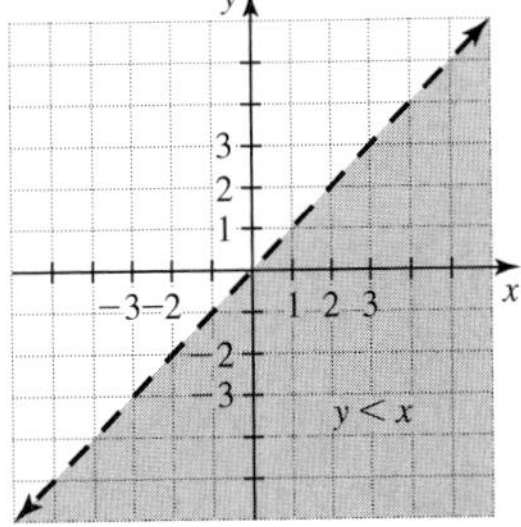

23. Yes **25.** No

27.

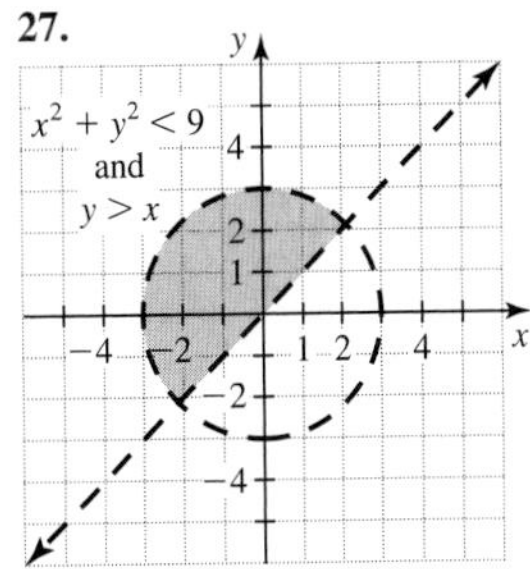

29.

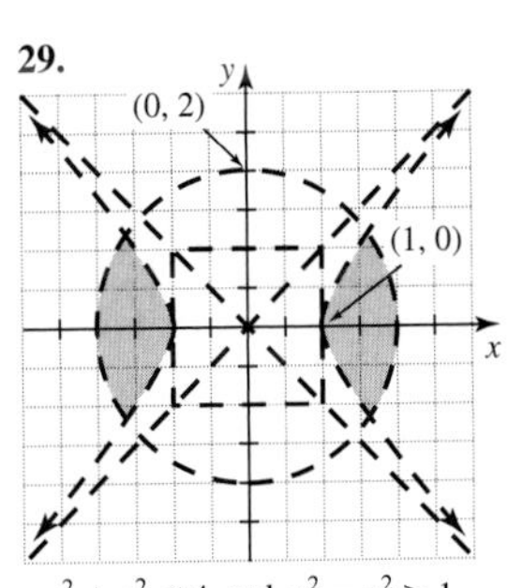

$x^2 + y^2 < 4$ and $x^2 - y^2 > 1$

31.

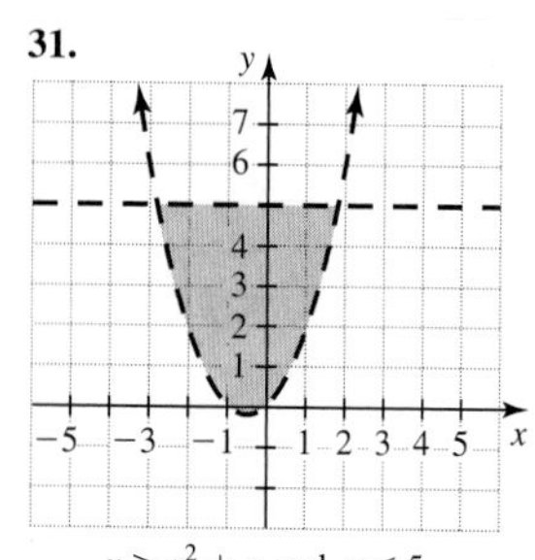

$y > x^2 + x$ and $y < 5$

33.

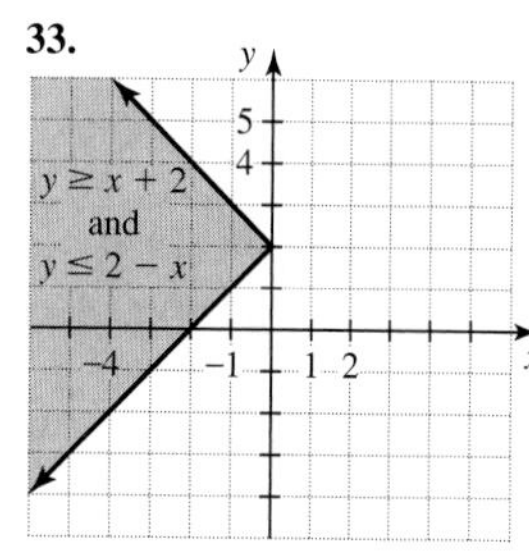

35.

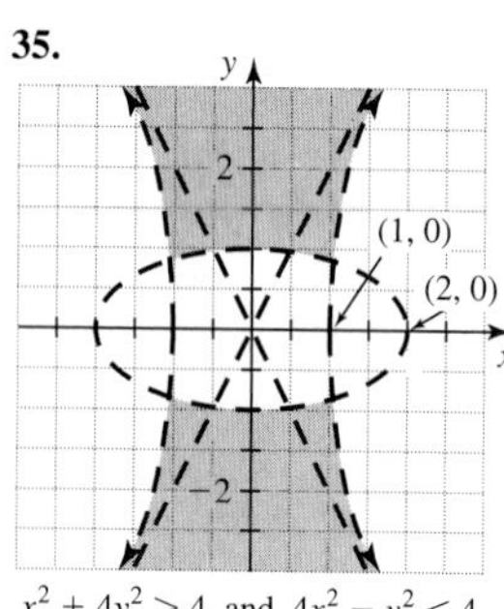

$x^2 + 4y^2 > 4$ and $4x^2 - y^2 < 4$

37.

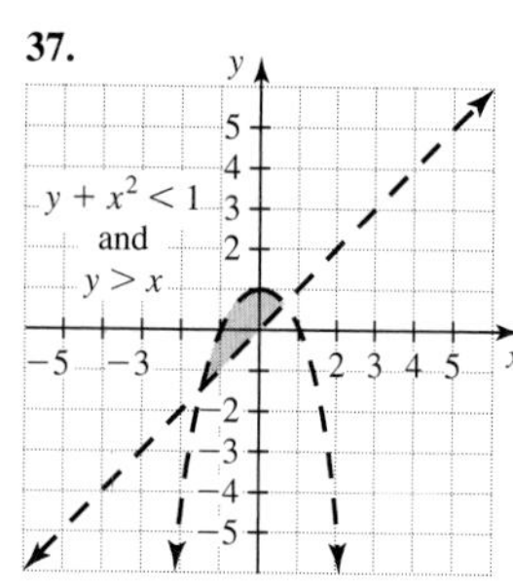

39.

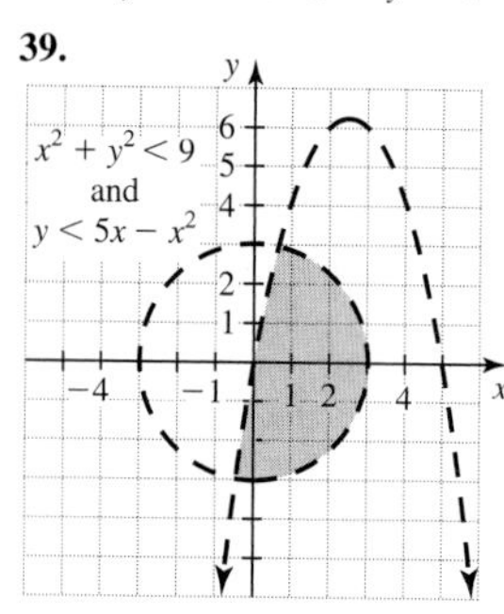

41.

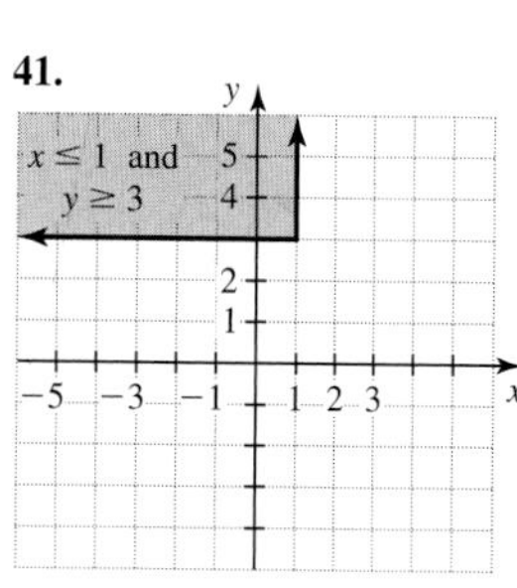

43.

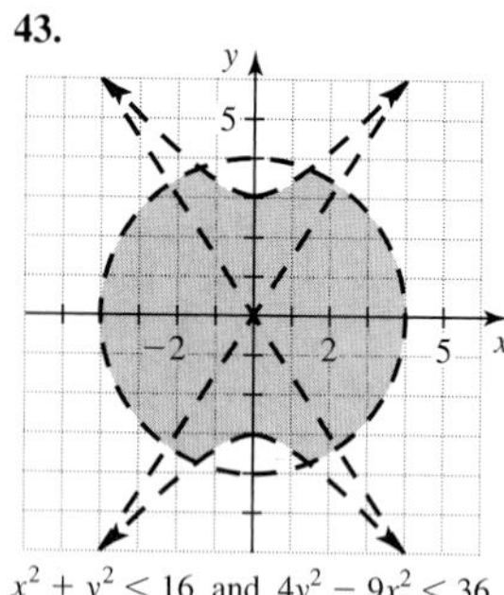

$x^2 + y^2 < 16$ and $4y^2 - 9x^2 < 36$

45.

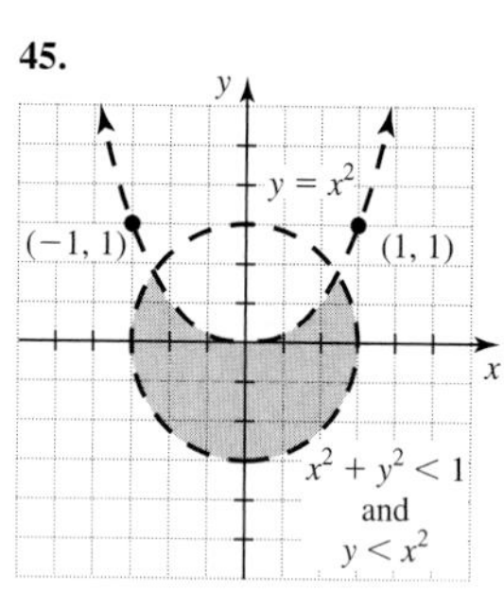

47.

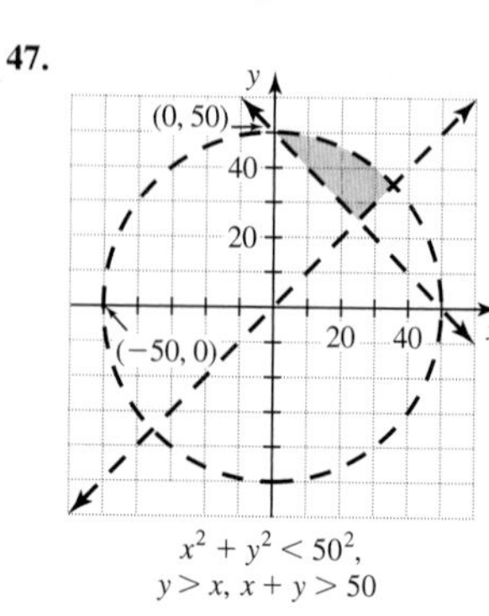

$x^2 + y^2 < 50^2$,
$y > x$, $x + y > 50$

49. No solution

Enriching Your Mathematical Word Power

1. c **2.** a **3.** d **4.** a **5.** c **6.** d **7.** b **8.** d **9.** c **10.** a

Review Exercises

1. $\{(3, 9), (-5, 25)\}$

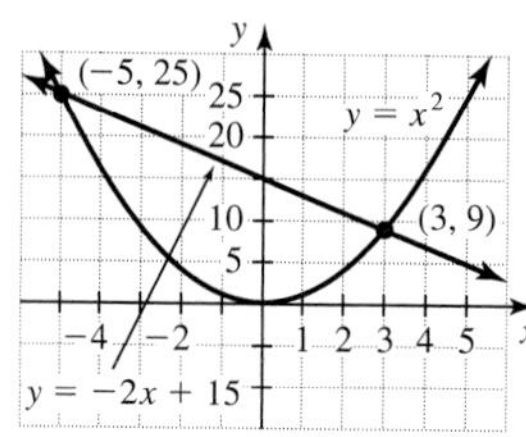

3. $\left\{\left(\frac{\sqrt{3}}{3}, \sqrt{3}\right), \left(-\frac{\sqrt{3}}{3}, -\sqrt{3}\right)\right\}$

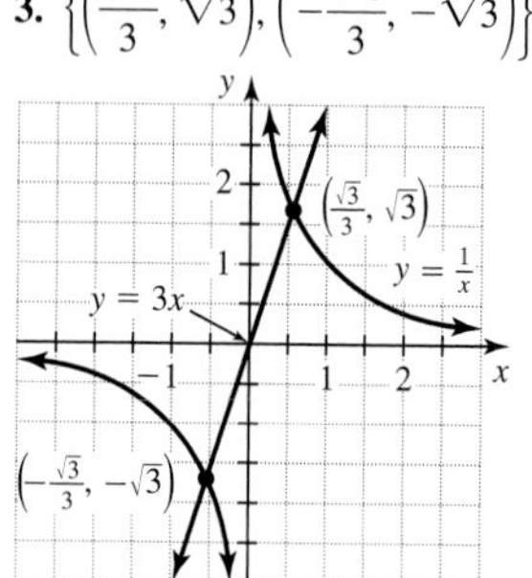

5. $\{(\sqrt{3}, 1), (-\sqrt{3}, 1)\}$ **7.** $\{(-5, -3), (3, 5)\}$
9. $\{(5, \log(2))\}$ **11.** $\{(2, 4), (-2, 4)\}$
13. $2\sqrt{2}$ **15.** $2\sqrt{58}$

17. Vertex $\left(-\frac{3}{2}, -\frac{81}{4}\right)$, axis of symmetry $x = -\frac{3}{2}$, focus $\left(-\frac{3}{2}, -20\right)$, directrix $y = -\frac{41}{2}$

19. Vertex $\left(-\frac{3}{2}, -\frac{1}{4}\right)$, axis of symmetry $x = -\frac{3}{2}$, focus $\left(-\frac{3}{2}, 0\right)$, directrix $y = -\frac{1}{2}$

21. Vertex (2, 3), axis of symmetry $x = 2$, focus $\left(2, \frac{5}{2}\right)$, directrix $y = \frac{7}{2}$

23. $y = 2(x - 2)^2 - 7$, $(2, -7)$ **25.** $y = -\frac{1}{2}(x + 1)^2 + 1$, $(-1, 1)$

27. (0, 0), 10

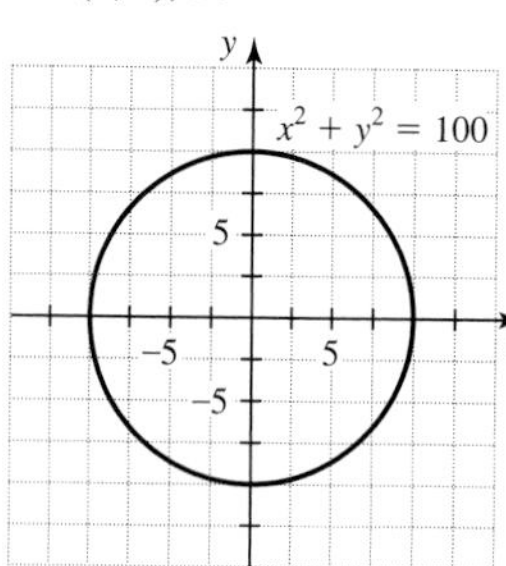

29. (2, −3), 9

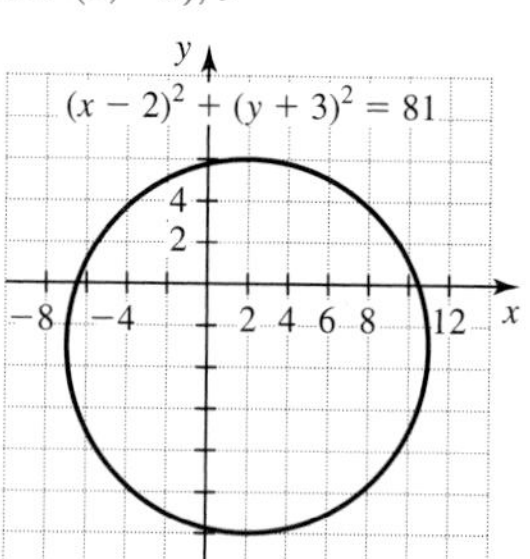

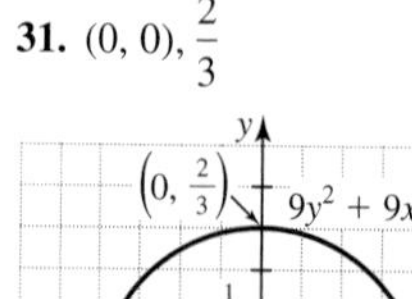

31. (0, 0), $\frac{2}{3}$

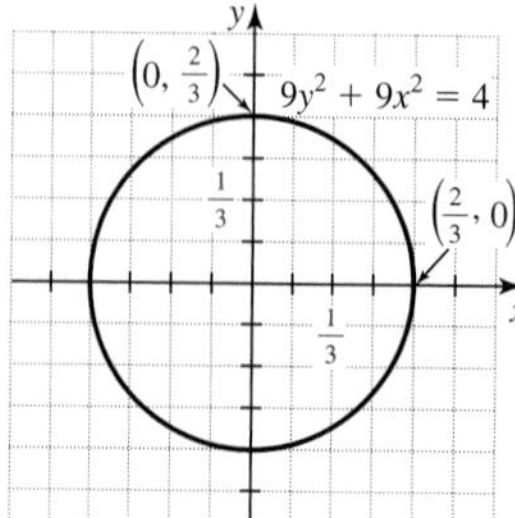

33. $x^2 + (y - 3)^2 = 36$
35. $(x - 2)^2 + (y + 7)^2 = 25$

37.

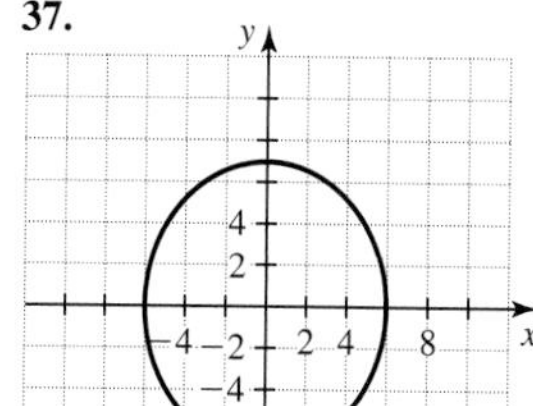

39.

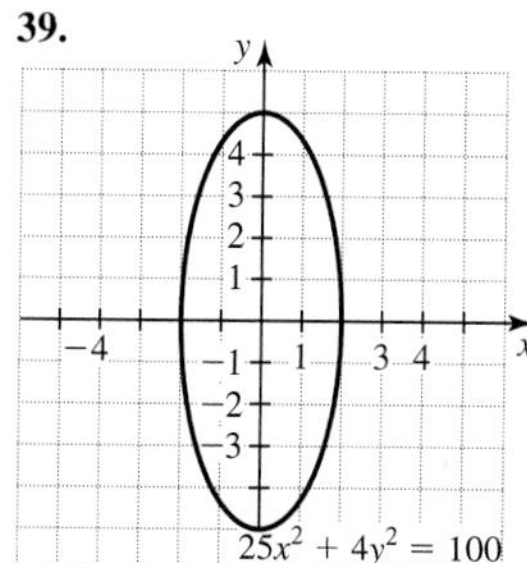

41.

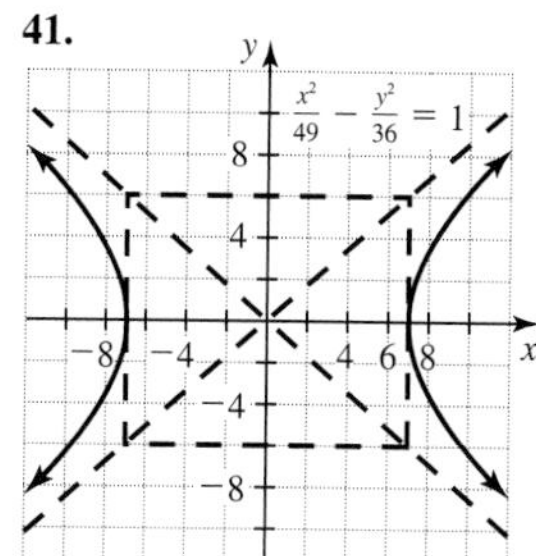

43.

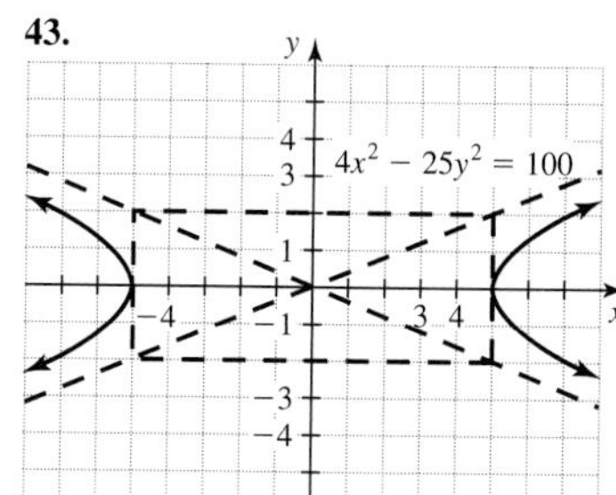

45.

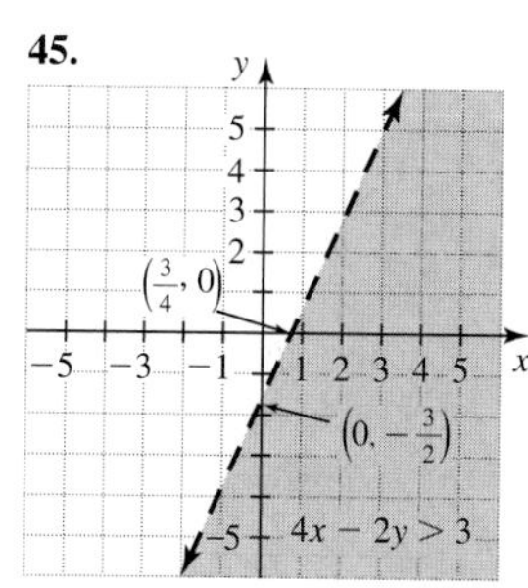

47.

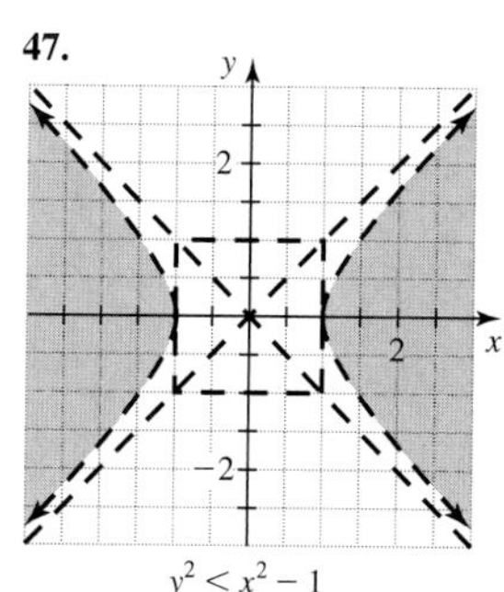

49.

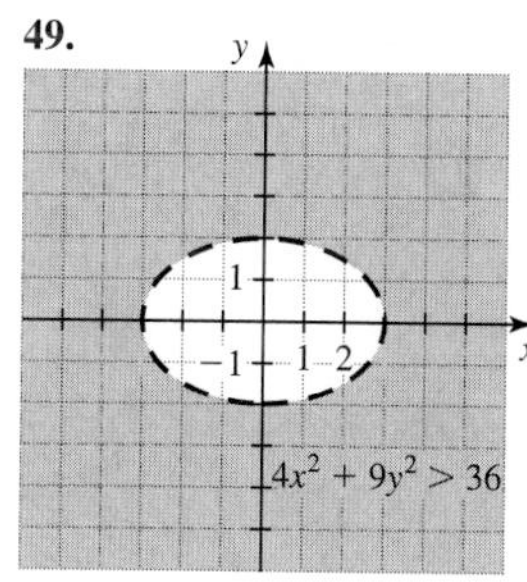

51.

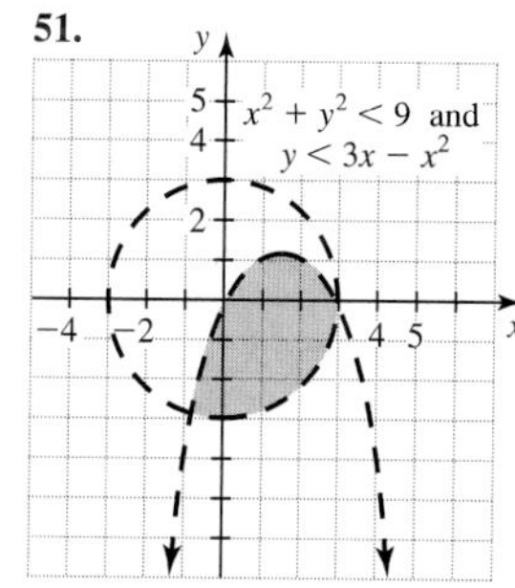

53.

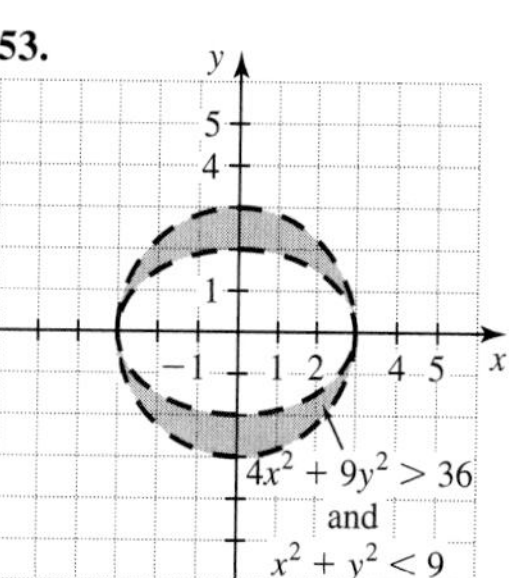
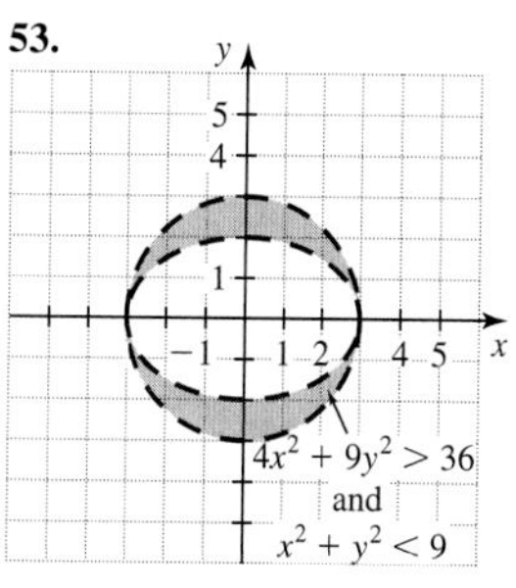
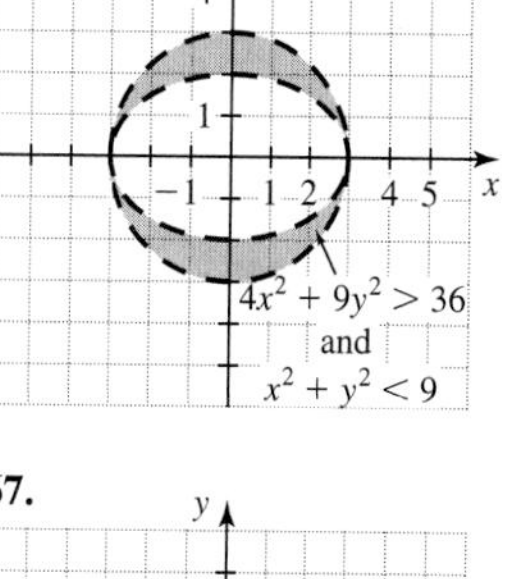

55. Hyperbola
57. Circle
59. Circle
61. Circle
63. Hyperbola
65. Hyperbola

67.

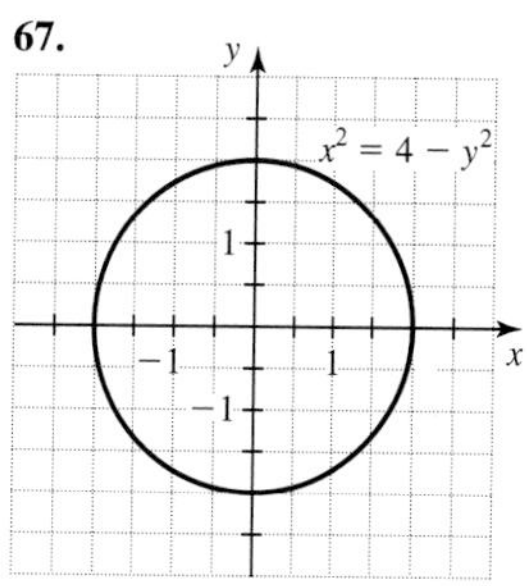

69.

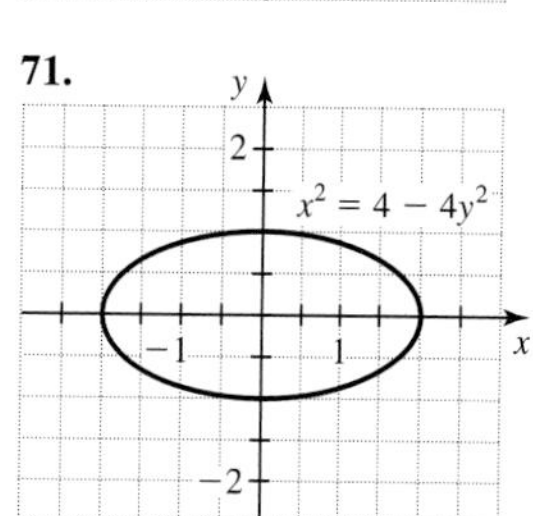

71.

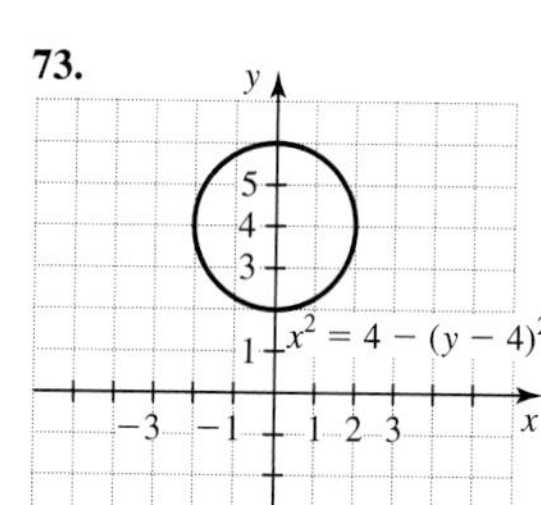

73.

75. $x^2 + y^2 = 25$ **77.** $(x + 1)^2 + (y - 5)^2 = 36$

79. $y = \frac{1}{4}(x - 1)^2 + 3$ **81.** $y = x^2$ **83.** $y = \frac{2}{9}x^2$

85. $\{(4, -3), (-3, 4)\}$ **87.** $\varnothing$ **89.** 6 ft, 2 ft

Chapter 13 Test

1.

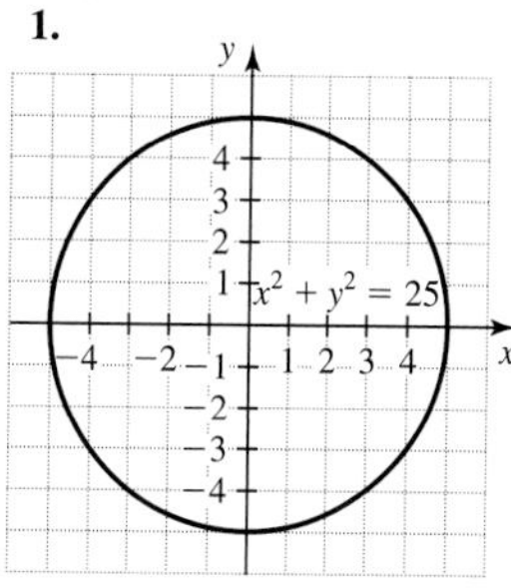

2.

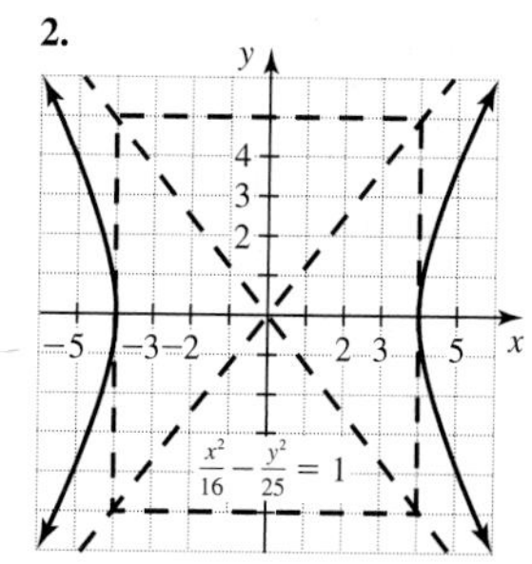

3.

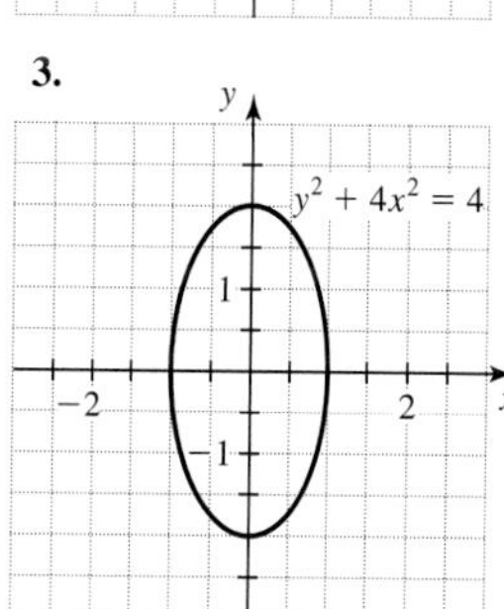

4.

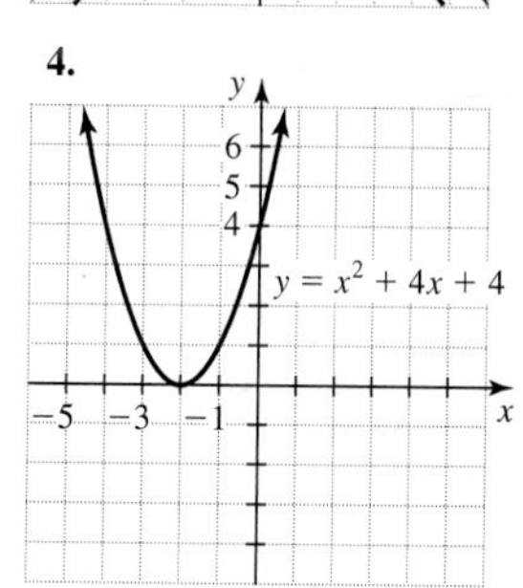

5.

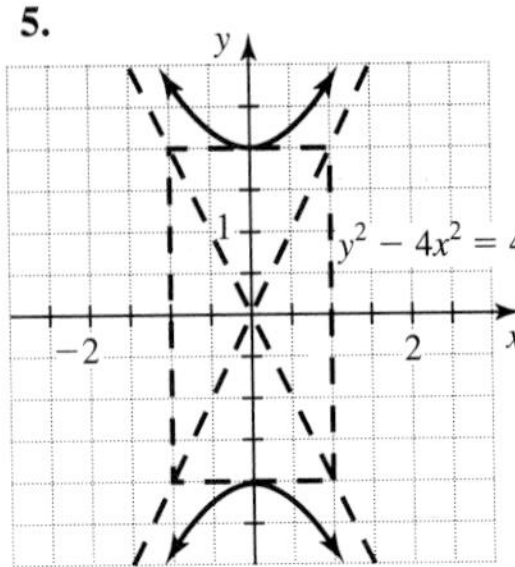

6.

$y = -x^2 - 2x + 3$

7.

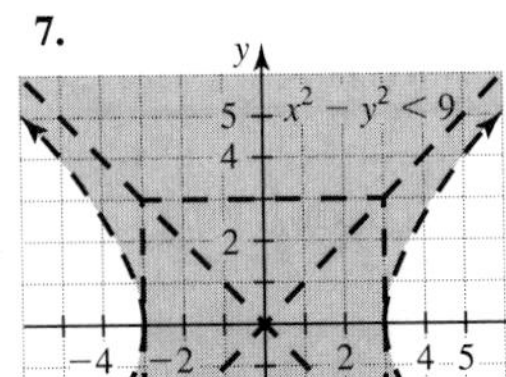

8.

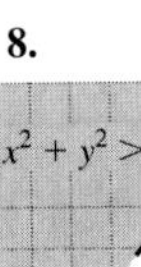

9.

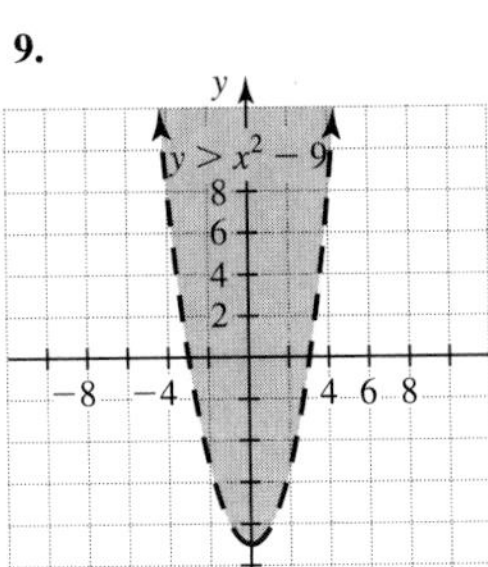

10.

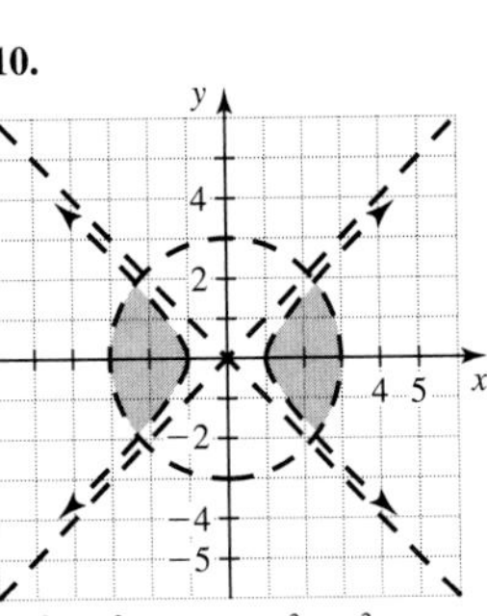

$x^2 - y^2 > 1$ and $x^2 + y^2 < 9$

11.

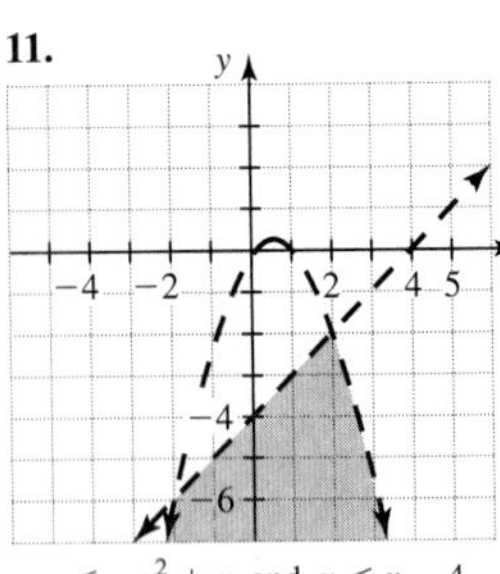

$y < -x^2 + x$ and $y < x - 4$

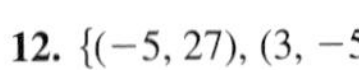

12. $\{(-5, 27), (3, -5)\}$
13. $\{(\sqrt{3}, 3), (-\sqrt{3}, 3)\}$
14. $2\sqrt{2}$
15. $(-1, -5)$, 6
16. Vertex $\left(-\frac{1}{2}, \frac{11}{4}\right)$, focus $\left(-\frac{1}{2}, 3\right)$, directrix $y = \frac{5}{2}$, axis of symmetry $x = -\frac{1}{2}$, upward
17. $y = \frac{1}{2}(x - 3)^2 - 5$ **18.** $(x + 1)^2 + (y - 3)^2 = 13$
19. 12 ft, 9 ft

Making Connections A Review of Chapters 1–13

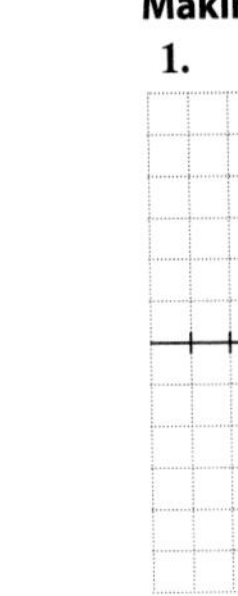

1.

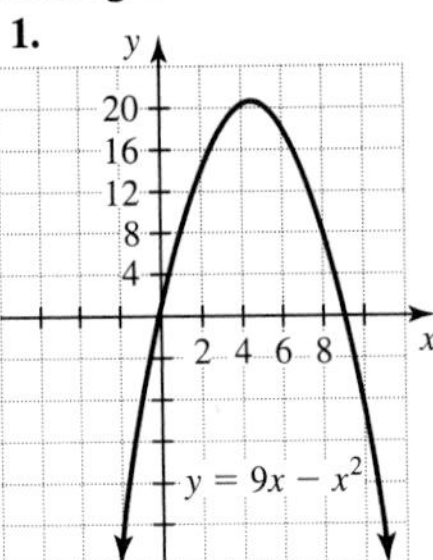

2.

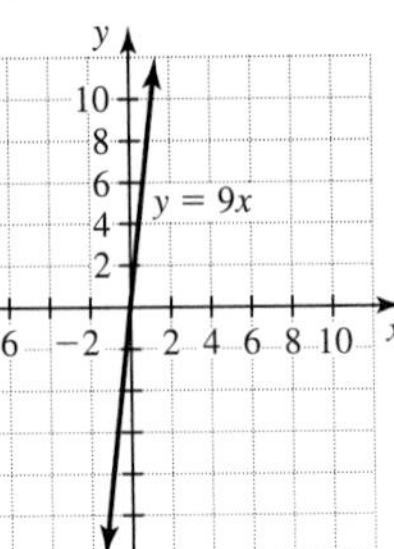

3.

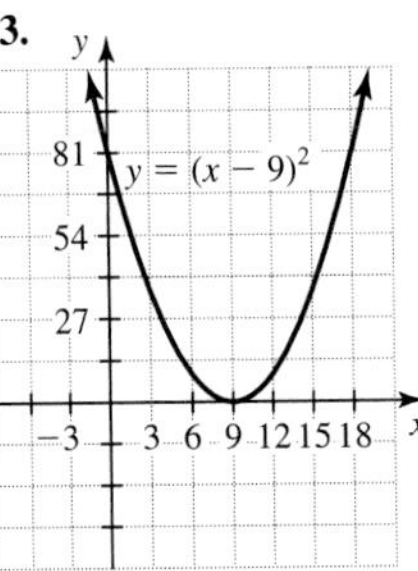

4.

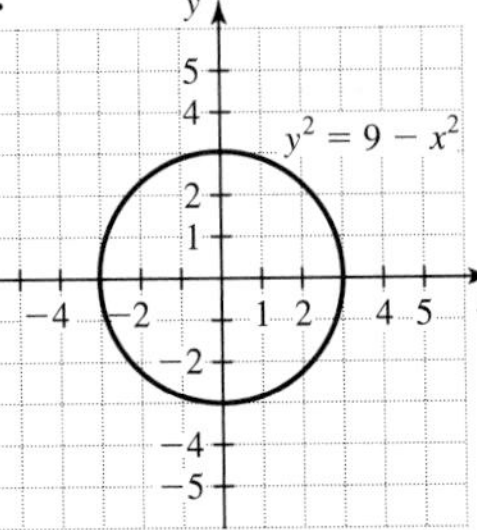

5.

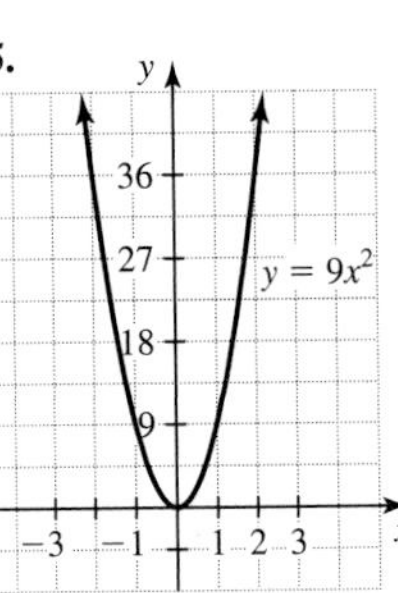

6.

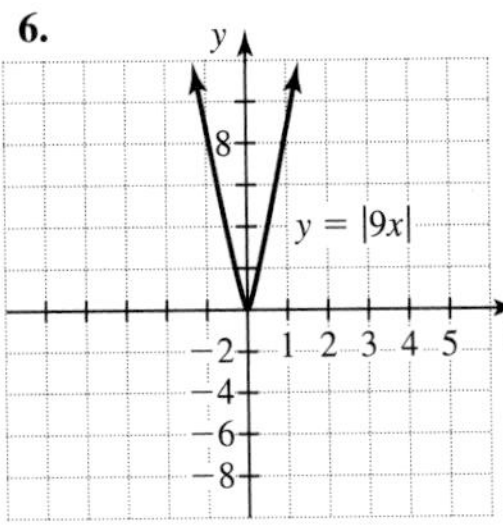

7.

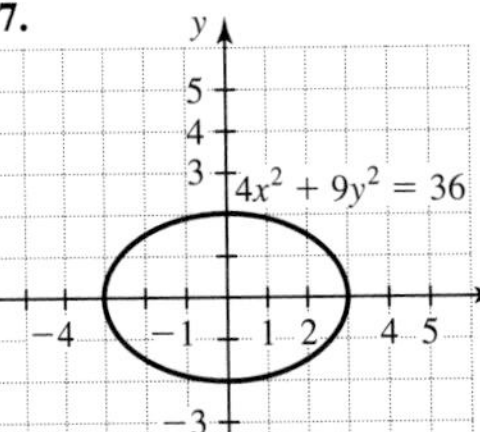

8.

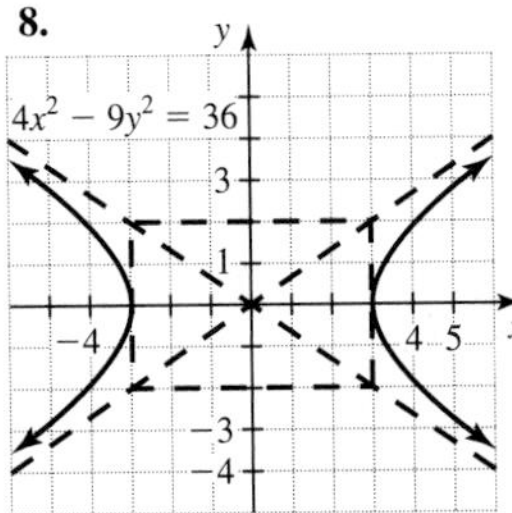

9.

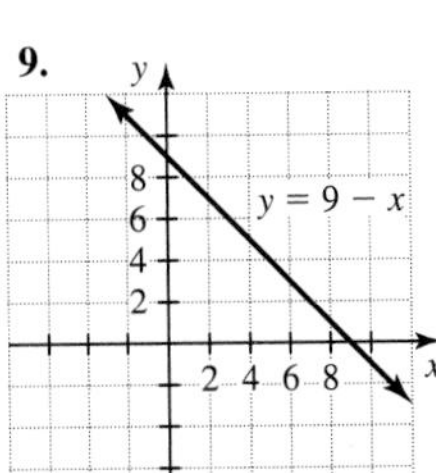

10.

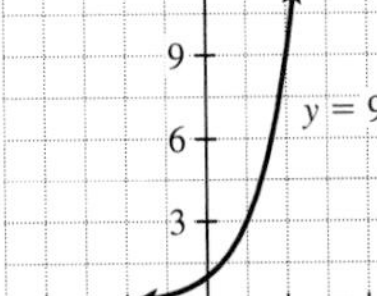

11. $x^2 + 4xy + 4y^2$ **12.** $x^3 + 3x^2y + 3xy^2 + y^3$
13. $a^3 + 3a^2b + 3ab^2 + b^3$ **14.** $a^2 - 6ab + 9b^2$ **15.** $6a^2 - 7a - 5$
16. $x^3 - y^3$ **17.** $\{(1, 2)\}$ **18.** $\{(3, 4), (4, 3)\}$ **19.** $\{(1, -2, 3)\}$

20. $\{(-1, 1), (3, 9)\}$ **21.** $x = -\frac{b}{a}$ **22.** $x = \frac{-d \pm \sqrt{d^2 - 4wm}}{2w}$

23. $B = \frac{2A - bh}{h}$ **24.** $x = \frac{2y}{y - 2}$ **25.** $m = \frac{L}{1 + xt}$

26. $t = \frac{y^2}{9a^2}$ **27.** $y = -\frac{2}{3}x - \frac{5}{3}$ **28.** $y = -2x$

29. $(x - 2)^2 + (y - 5)^2 = 45$ **30.** $\left(-\frac{3}{2}, 3\right), \frac{3\sqrt{5}}{2}$

31. $-10 + 6i$ **32.** -1 **33.** $3 - 5i$ **34.** $7 + 6i\sqrt{2}$ **35.** $-8 - 27i$

36. $-3 + 3i$ **37.** 29 **38.** $-\frac{3}{2} - i$ **39.** $-\frac{1}{2} + \frac{9}{2}i$ **40.** $2 - i\sqrt{2}$

41. a) $q = -500x + 400$
b) $R = -500x^2 + 400x$
c)

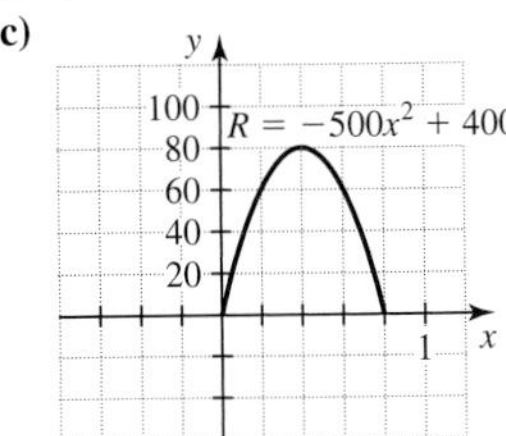

d) \$0.40 per pound **e)** \$80

Chapter 14

Section 14.1 Warm-Ups T T T F F F T F T T

1. A sequence is a list of numbers.
3. A finite sequence is a function whose domain is the set of positive integers less than or equal to some fixed positive integer.
5. 2, 4, 6, 8, 10 **7.** 1, 4, 9, 16, 25, 36, 49, 64
9. $-1, \frac{1}{2}, -\frac{1}{3}, \frac{1}{4}, -\frac{1}{5}, \frac{1}{6}, -\frac{1}{7}, \frac{1}{8}, -\frac{1}{9}, \frac{1}{10}$ **11.** $1, -2, 4, -8, 16$
13. $\frac{1}{2}, \frac{1}{4}, \frac{1}{8}, \frac{1}{16}, \frac{1}{32}, \frac{1}{64}$ **15.** $-1, 1, 3, 5, 7, 9, 11$
17. $1, \frac{\sqrt{2}}{2}, \frac{\sqrt{3}}{3}, \frac{1}{2}, \frac{\sqrt{5}}{5}$ **19.** $\frac{1}{2}, \frac{1}{6}, \frac{1}{12}, \frac{1}{20}$ **21.** $-\frac{1}{3}, -1, 1, \frac{1}{3}$
23. $-1, 0, -1, 4$ **25.** $1, \frac{1}{4}, \frac{1}{9}, \frac{1}{16}$ **27.** $a_n = 2n - 1$
29. $a_n = (-1)^{n+1}$ **31.** $a_n = 2n - 2$ **33.** $a_n = 3n$ **35.** $a_n = 3n + 1$
37. $a_n = (-1)^n 2^{n-1}$ **39.** $a_n = (n - 1)^2$ **41.** $4, 2, 1, \frac{1}{2}, \frac{1}{4}$ yard line
43. \$37,758, \$39,646, \$41,628, \$43,710, \$45,895, \$48,190
45. \$1,000,000, \$800,000, \$640,000, \$512,000
47. 27 in., 13.5 in., 9 in., 6.75 in., 5.4 in.
49. 137,438,953,472, larger
53. a) 0.9048, 0.3677, 0.00004517 **b)** a_n goes to zero

Section 14.2 Warm-Ups T F F F F F T T T T F

1. Summation notation provides a way to write a sum without writing out all of the terms.
3. A series is the indicated sum of the terms of a sequence.
5. 15 **7.** 30 **9.** 24 **11.** $\frac{31}{32}$ **13.** 50 **15.** -7 **17.** 0
19. $\sum_{i=1}^{6} i$ **21.** $\sum_{i=1}^{6} (-1)^i(2i - 1)$ **23.** $\sum_{i=1}^{6} i^2$ **25.** $\sum_{i=1}^{4} \frac{1}{2 + i}$
27. $\sum_{i=1}^{3} \ln(i + 1)$ **29.** $\sum_{i=1}^{4} a_i$ **31.** $\sum_{i=1}^{48} x_{i+2}$ **33.** $\sum_{i=1}^{n} w_i$
35. $\sum_{j=0}^{4} (j + 1)^2$ **37.** $\sum_{j=1}^{13} (2j - 3)$ **39.** $\sum_{j=1}^{5} \frac{1}{j + 3}$ **41.** $\sum_{j=0}^{3} x^{2j+5}$
43. $\sum_{j=0}^{n-1} x^{j+1}$ **45.** $x + x^2 + x^3 + x^4 + x^5 + x^6$
47. $x_0 - x_1 + x_2 - x_3$ **49.** $x + 2x^2 + 3x^3$ **51.** $\sum_{i=1}^{9} 2^{-i}$
53. $\sum_{i=1}^{4} 1{,}000{,}000(0.8)^{i-1}$
55. A sequence is basically a list of numbers. A series is the indicated sum of the terms of a sequence.

Section 14.3 Warm-Ups F F F F F F T T T F

1. An arithmetic sequence is one in which each term after the first is obtained by adding a fixed amount to the previous term.
3. An arithmetic series is an indicated sum of an arithmetic sequence.
5. $a_n = 2n$ **7.** $a_n = 6n - 6$ **9.** $a_n = 5n + 2$ **11.** $a_n = 2n - 6$
13. $a_n = -4n + 9$ **15.** $a_n = -7n + 5$ **17.** $a_n = 0.5n - 3.5$
19. $a_n = -0.5n - 5.5$ **21.** 9, 13, 17, 21, 25 **23.** 7, 5, 3, 1, -1
25. $-4, -1, 2, 5, 8$ **27.** $-2, -5, -8, -11, -14$
29. $-7, -11, -15, -19, -23$ **31.** 4.5, 5, 5.5, 6, 6.5
33. 1020, 1040, 1060, 1080, 1100 **35.** 51 **37.** 4 **39.** 26
41. 17 **43.** 1176 **45.** 330 **47.** -481 **49.** 435 **51.** -540
53. 150 **55.** -308 **57.** \$25,000 **59.** 1085 **61.** b

Section 14.4 Warm-Ups F F T T T T F F T F

1. A geometric sequence is one in which each term after the first is obtained by multiplying the preceding term by a constant.
3. A geometric series is an indicated sum of a geometric sequence.
5. The approximate value of r^n when n is large and $|r| < 1$ is 0.
7. $a_n = 2^{n-1}$ **9.** $a_n = \frac{1}{3}(3)^{n-1}$ **11.** $a_n = 64\left(\frac{1}{8}\right)^{n-1}$
13. $a_n = 8\left(-\frac{1}{2}\right)^{n-1}$ **15.** $a_n = 2(-2)^{n-1}$ **17.** $a_n = -\frac{1}{3}\left(\frac{3}{4}\right)^{n-1}$
19. $2, \frac{2}{3}, \frac{2}{9}, \frac{2}{27}, \frac{2}{81}$ **21.** $1, -2, 4, -8, 16$ **23.** $\frac{1}{2}, \frac{1}{4}, \frac{1}{8}, \frac{1}{16}, \frac{1}{32}$
25. 0.78, 0.6084, 0.4746, 0.3702, 0.2887 **27.** 5 **29.** $\frac{1}{3}$
31. $-\frac{1}{9}$ **33.** $\frac{511}{512}$ **35.** $\frac{11}{32}$ **37.** $\frac{63{,}050}{729}$ **39.** 5115
41. 0.111111 **43.** 42.8259 **45.** $\frac{1}{4}$ **47.** 9 **49.** $\frac{8}{3}$ **51.** $\frac{3}{7}$
53. 6 **55.** $\frac{1}{3}$ **57.** $\frac{4}{33}$ **59.** \$3,042,435.27 **61.** \$21,474,836.47
63. \$5,000,000 **65.** d **67.** $\frac{8}{33}$

Section 14.5 Warm-Ups F F F T T T T T T T

1. The sum obtained for a power of a binomial is called a binomial expansion.
3. The expression $n!$ is the product of the positive integers from 1 through n.
5. 1 **7.** 10 **9.** 56 **11.** $x^3 + 3x^2 + 3x + 1$
13. $a^3 + 6a^2 + 12a + 8$ **15.** $r^5 + 5r^4t + 10r^3t^2 + 10r^2t^3 + 5rt^4 + t^5$
17. $m^3 - 3m^2n + 3mn^2 - n^3$ **19.** $x^3 + 6ax^2 + 12a^2x + 8a^3$
21. $x^8 - 8x^6 + 24x^4 - 32x^2 + 16$
23. $x^7 - 7x^6 + 21x^5 - 35x^4 + 35x^3 - 21x^2 + 7x - 1$
25. $a^{12} - 36a^{11}b + 594a^{10}b^2 - 5940a^9b^3$
27. $x^{18} + 45x^{16} + 900x^{14} + 10{,}500x^{12}$
29. $x^{22} - 22x^{21} + 231x^{20} - 1540x^{19}$
31. $\frac{x^{10}}{1024} + \frac{5x^9y}{768} + \frac{5x^8y^2}{256} + \frac{5x^7y^3}{144}$ **33.** $1287a^8w^5$ **35.** $-11{,}440m^9n^7$
37. $448x^5y^3$ **39.** $635{,}043{,}840a^{28}b^6$ **41.** $\sum_{i=0}^{8} \frac{8!}{(8 - i)!\,i!} a^{8-i}m^i$
43. $\sum_{i=0}^{5} \frac{5!(-2)^i}{(5 - i)!\,i!} a^{5-i}x^i$
45. $a^3 + b^3 + c^3 + 3a^2b + 3a^2c + 3ab^2 + 3ac^2 + 3b^2c + 3bc^2 + 6abc$

Enriching Your Mathematical Word Power

1. a **2.** d **3.** c **4.** b **5.** a **6.** c **7.** d **8.** b **9.** d **10.** a

Review Exercises

1. 1, 8, 27, 64, 125 **3.** 1, 1, −3, 5, −7, 9 **5.** $-1, -\frac{1}{2}, -\frac{1}{3}$ **7.** $\frac{1}{3}, \frac{1}{5}, \frac{1}{7}$ **9.** 4, 5, 6 **11.** 36 **13.** 40 **15.** $\sum_{i=1}^{\infty} \frac{1}{2(i+1)}$ **17.** $\sum_{i=1}^{\infty} (i-1)^2$ **19.** $\sum_{i=1}^{\infty} (-1)^{i+1}x_i$ **21.** 6, 11, 16, 21 **23.** −20, −22, −24, −26 **25.** 3000, 4000, 5000, 6000 **27.** $a_n = \frac{n}{3}$ **29.** $a_n = 2n$ **31.** 300 **33.** $\frac{289}{6}$ **35.** 35 **37.** $3, \frac{3}{2}, \frac{3}{4}, \frac{3}{8}$ **39.** $1, \frac{1}{2}, \frac{1}{4}, \frac{1}{8}$ **41.** 0.23, 0.0023, 0.000023, 0.00000023 **43.** $a_n = \frac{1}{2}(6)^{n-1}$ **45.** $a_n = 0.7(0.1)^{n-1}$ **47.** $\frac{40}{81}$ **49.** 0.3333333333 **51.** $\frac{3}{8}$ **53.** 54 **55.** $m^5 + 5m^4n + 10m^3n^2 + 10m^2n^3 + 5mn^4 + n^5$ **57.** $a^6 - 9a^4b + 27a^2b^2 - 27b^3$ **59.** $495x^8y^4$ **61.** $372{,}736a^{12}b^2$ **63.** $\sum_{i=0}^{7} \frac{7!}{(7-i)!\,i!} a^{7-i}w^i$ **65.** Neither **67.** Arithmetic **69.** Arithmetic **71.** $\frac{1}{\sqrt[3]{180}}$ or $\frac{\sqrt[3]{150}}{30}$ **73.** $-1 + \frac{1}{2} - \frac{1}{6} + \frac{1}{24} - \frac{1}{120}$ **75.** $a^5 + 5a^4b + 10a^3b^2 + 10a^2b^3 + 5ab^4 + b^5$ **77.** 26 **79.** \$118,634.11 **81.** \$13,784.92

Chapter 14 Test

1. −10, −4, 2, 8 **2.** 5, 0.5, 0.05, 0.005 **3.** $-1, \frac{1}{2}, -\frac{1}{6}, \frac{1}{24}$ **4.** $1, \frac{3}{4}, \frac{5}{9}, \frac{7}{16}$ **5.** $a_n = 10 - 3n$ **6.** $a_n = -25\left(-\frac{1}{5}\right)^{n-1}$ **7.** $a_n = (-1)^{n-1}2n$ **8.** $a_n = n^2$ **9.** 5 + 7 + 9 + 11 + 13 **10.** 5 + 10 + 20 + 40 + 80 + 160 **11.** $m^4 + 4m^3q + 6m^2q^2 + 4mq^3 + q^4$ **12.** 750 **13.** $\frac{155}{8}$ **14.** 5 **15.** 10,100 **16.** $\frac{1}{2}$ **17.** $\frac{511}{128}$ **18.** ±2 **19.** 11 **20.** $1365r^{11}t^4$ **21.** $-448a^{10}b^3$ **22.** \$86,545.41

Making Connections A Review of Chapters 1–14

1. 6 **2.** $n^2 - 3$ **3.** $x^2 + 2xh + h^2 - 3$ **4.** $x^2 - 2x - 2$ **5.** 11 **6.** 6 **7.** 4 **8.** 32 **9.** $\frac{1}{2}$ **10.** 3 **11.** 1 **12.** x **13.** $-\frac{27}{2}$ **14.** $-\frac{8}{3}$ **15.** $-\frac{128}{9}$ **16.** 16

17.

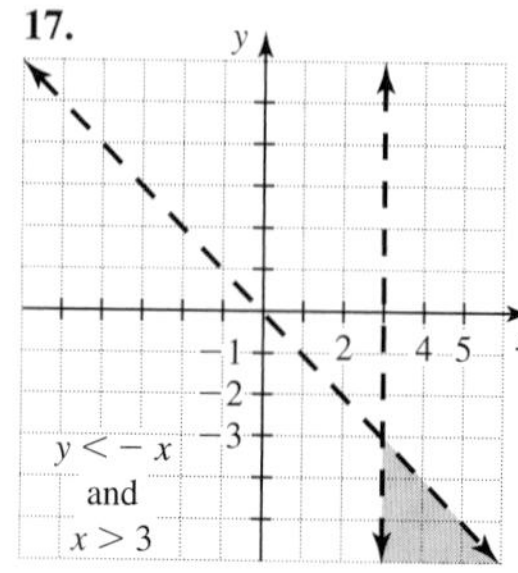

18.

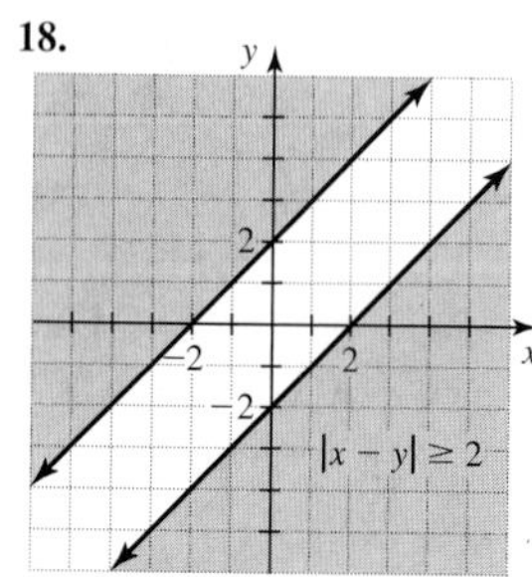

19.

20.

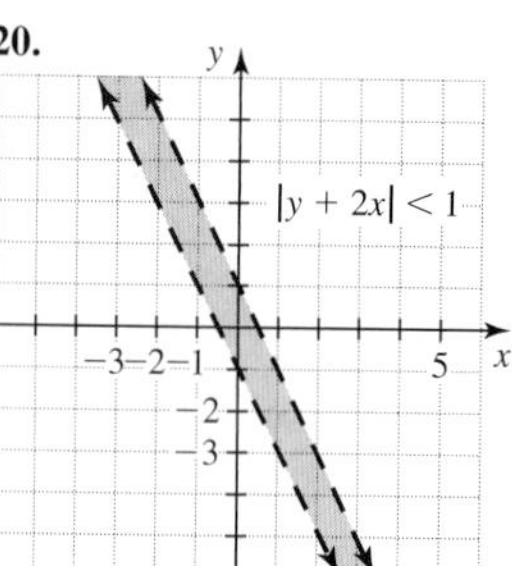

21.

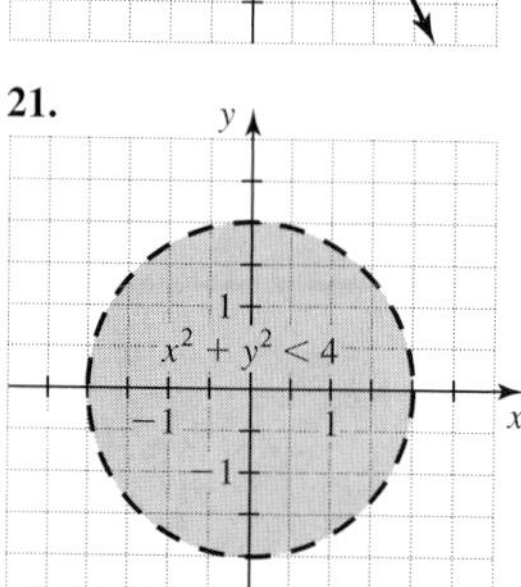

22.

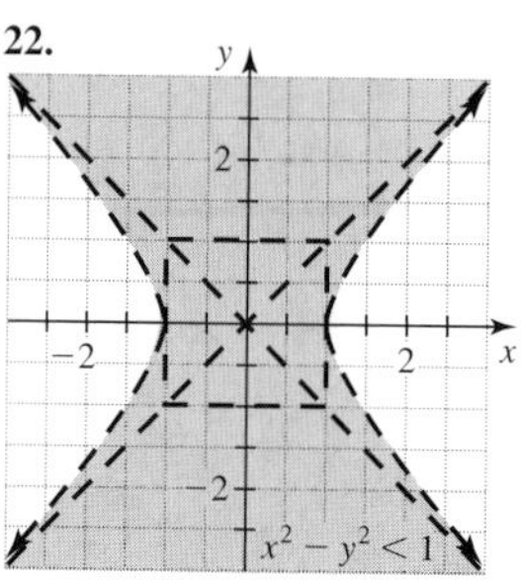

23.

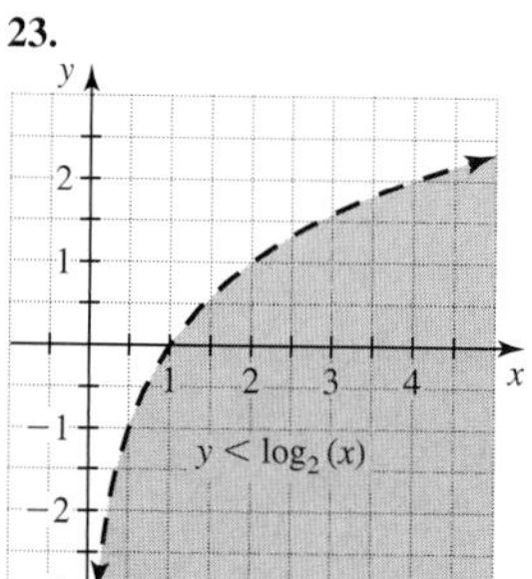

24.

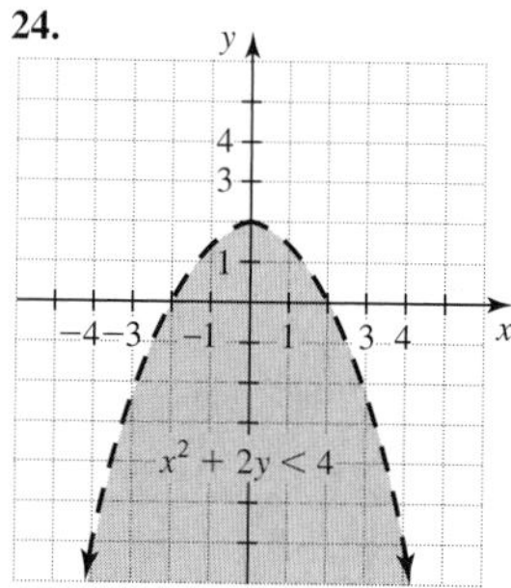

25.

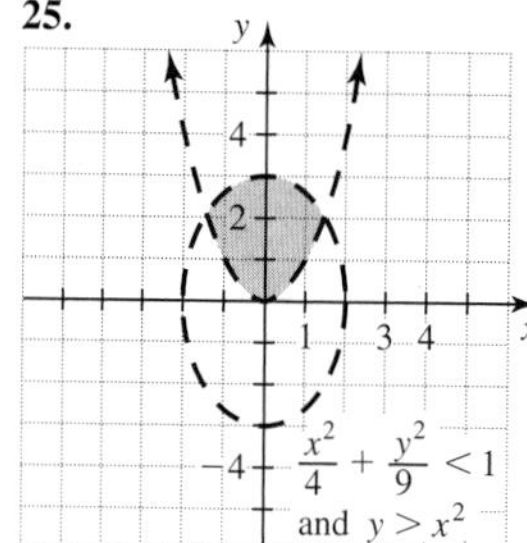

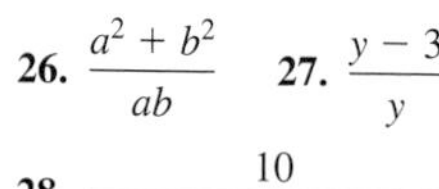

26. $\frac{a^2 + b^2}{ab}$ **27.** $\frac{y-3}{y}$ **28.** $\frac{10}{(x-3)(x+3)(x+1)}$ **29.** $\frac{2(x^3 - 64)}{x^3 - 16}$ **30.** $\frac{a^7}{b^4}$ **31.** 1 **32.** 4 **33.** $\frac{1}{32}$ **34.** −2 **35.** $\frac{1}{9}$ **36.** $-\frac{1}{8}$ **37.** $\frac{1}{4}$ **38.** $\frac{1}{5}$ **39.** 25 **40. a)** 105.8 cm or 41.7 in. **c)** 1.3 years

Appendix A

Geometry Review Exercises

1. 12 in. **2.** 24 ft^2 **3.** 60° **4.** 6 ft **5.** 20 cm **6.** 144 cm^2 **7.** 24 ft^2 **8.** 13 ft **9.** 30 cm **10.** No **11.** 84 yd^2 **12.** 30 in. **13.** 32 ft^2 **14.** 20 km **15.** 7 ft, 3 ft^2 **16.** 22 yd **17.** 50.3 ft^2 **18.** 37.7 ft **19.** 150.80 cm^3 **20.** 879.29 ft^2 **21.** 288 in.^{3}, 288 in.^{2} **22.** 4 cm **23.** 100 mi^2, 40 mi **24.** 20 km **25.** 42.25 cm^2 **26.** 33.510 ft^3, 50.265 ft^2 **27.** 75.4 in.^{3}, 100.5 in.^{2} **28.** 56° **29.** 5 cm **30.** 15 in. and 20 in. **31.** 149° **32.** 12 km **33.** 10 yd

Appendix B

Sets

1. A set is a collection of objects.
2. A finite set has a fixed number of elements and an infinite set does not.
3. A Venn diagram is used to illustrate relationships between sets.
4. The intersection of two sets consists of elements that are in both sets, whereas the union of two sets consists of elements that are in one, in the other, or in both sets.
5. Every member of set A is also a member of set B.
6. The empty set is a subset of every set.

7. False **8.** False **9.** True **10.** False **11.** True **12.** False **13.** False **14.** True **15.** False **16.** False **17.** False **18.** False **19.** $\varnothing$ **20.** $\{1, 2, 3, 4, 5, 6, 7, 8, 9\}$ **21.** $\{1, 3, 5\}$ **22.** $\{1, 2, 3, 4, 5, 7, 9\}$ **23.** $\{1, 2, 3, 4, 5, 6, 8\}$ **24.** $\{2, 4\}$ **25.** A **26.** B **27.** $\varnothing$ **28.** $\varnothing$ **29.** A **30.** N **31.** $=$ **32.** $\neq$ **33.** $\cup$ **34.** $\cap$ **35.** $\cap$ **36.** $\cup$ **37.** $\notin$ **38.** $\in$ **39.** $\in$ **40.** $\in$ **41.** True **42.** True **43.** True **44.** False **45.** True **46.** True **47.** True **48.** True **49.** False **50.** False **51.** True **52.** True **53.** $\{2, 3, 4, 5, 6, 7, 8\}$ **54.** $\varnothing$ **55.** $\{3, 5\}$ **56.** $\{1, 2, 3, 4, 5, 7\}$ **57.** $\{1, 2, 3, 4, 5, 6, 8\}$ **58.** $\{2, 4\}$ **59.** $\{2, 3, 4, 5\}$ **60.** $\{2, 4\}$ **61.** $\{2, 3, 4, 5, 7\}$ **62.** $\{2, 3, 4, 5, 7\}$ **63.** $\{2, 3, 4, 5\}$ **64.** $\{2, 4\}$ **65.** $\{2, 3, 4, 5, 7\}$ **66.** $\{2, 3, 4, 5, 7\}$ **67.** $\subseteq$ **68.** $=$ **69.** $\in$ **70.** $\subseteq$ **71.** $\cap$ **72.** $\subseteq$ **73.** $\subseteq$ **74.** $\cap$ **75.** $\cap$ **76.** $\cup$ **77.** $\cup$ **78.** $\cap$ **79.** $\{2, 4, 6, \ldots, 18\}$ **80.** $\{7, 8, 9, \ldots\}$ **81.** $\{13, 15, 17, \ldots\}$ **82.** $\{1, 3, 5, \ldots, 13\}$ **83.** $\{6, 8, 10, \ldots, 78\}$ **84.** $\{13, 15, 17, \ldots, 55\}$

85. $\{x \mid x$ is a natural number between 2 and 7$\}$
86. $\{x \mid x$ is an odd natural number less than 8$\}$
87. $\{x \mid x$ is an odd natural number greater than 4$\}$
88. $\{x \mid x$ is a natural number greater than 3$\}$
89. $\{x \mid x$ is an even natural number between 5 and 83$\}$
90. $\{x \mid x$ is an odd natural number between 8 and 52$\}$

91. False **92.** False **93.** False **94.** False **95.** True **96.** True **97.** True **98.** False **99.** True **100.** True

Appendix C

Chapters 1–6 Diagnostic Test

1. $(2, \infty)$

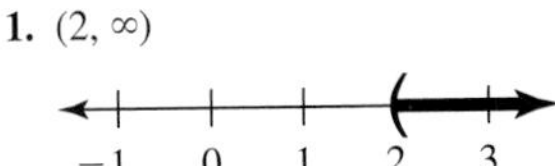

2. $(-\infty, -1]$

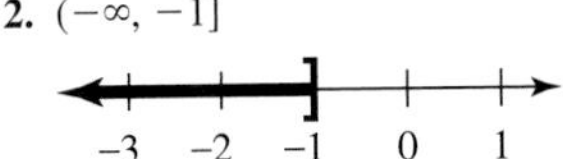

3. $(0, 1)$

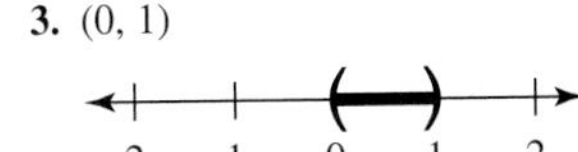

4. $(-4, -2]$

−5 −4 −3 −2 −1 0 1

5. $\frac{7}{12}$ **6.** $\frac{13}{12}$ **7.** $\frac{2}{9}$ **8.** -43 **9.** -11 **10.** 8 **11.** Distributive property **12.** Commutative property of multiplication **13.** Associative property of addition **14.** Additive identity **15.** $13x - 3$ **16.** 9 **17.** $15x^2$ **18.** $-x - 4$ **19.** $\left\{\frac{5}{11}\right\}$ **20.** $\{-2\}$ **21.** No solution, $\varnothing$ **22.** All real numbers **23.** $y = \frac{5}{3}x - 3$ **24.** $y = -\frac{b}{a}$ **25.** $y = \frac{t-a}{b}$ **26.** $y = \frac{3}{4}a$ **27.** 33, 34, 35 **28.** 23 in. **29.** 220 ft **30.** 100 pounds

31. $(-\infty, 5]$

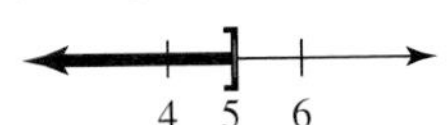

32. $(-\infty, -3)$

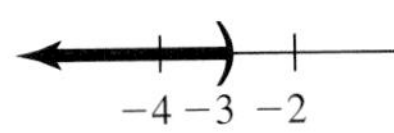

33. $(4, 8]$

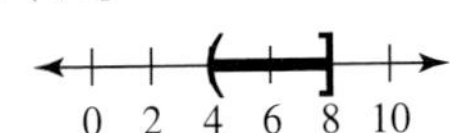

34. $(0, 1)$

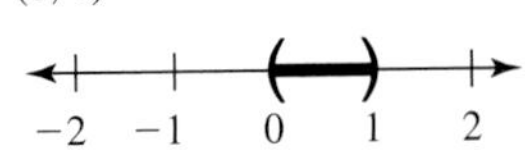

35. $(0, -2), (3, 0)$

$y = \frac{2}{3}x - 2$

36. $(0, -30), (50, 0)$

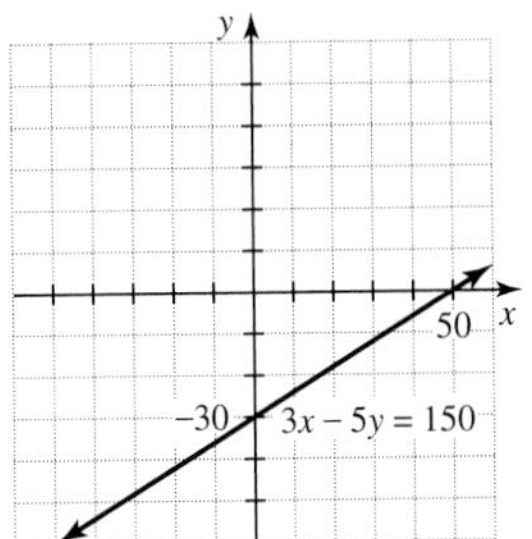

37. $(0, 2)$

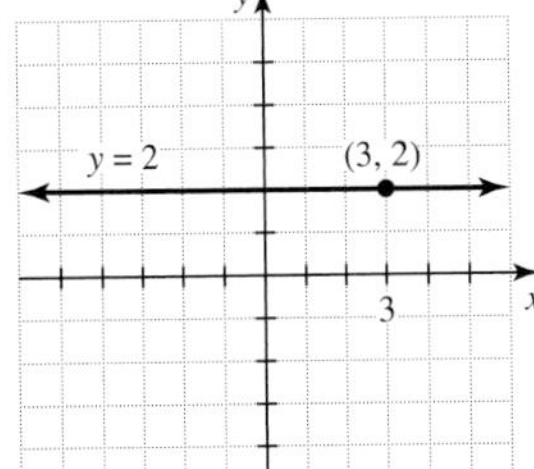

38. $(2, 0)$

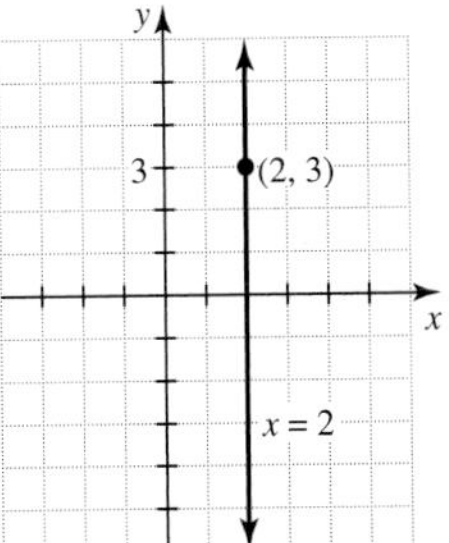

39. 2 **40.** $\frac{1}{2}$ **41.** $-\frac{2}{3}$ **42.** $\frac{1}{3}$ **43.** $y = 4x + 3$ **44.** $y = -2x$ **45.** $x = 3$ **46.** $y = -2x + 8$ **47.** 14 hours **48.** \$1890

49.

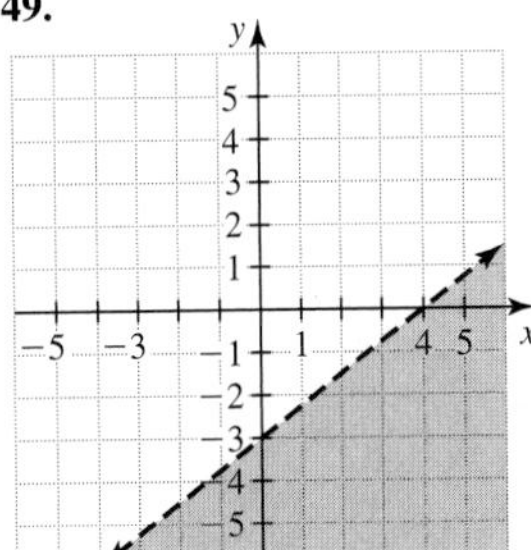

50.

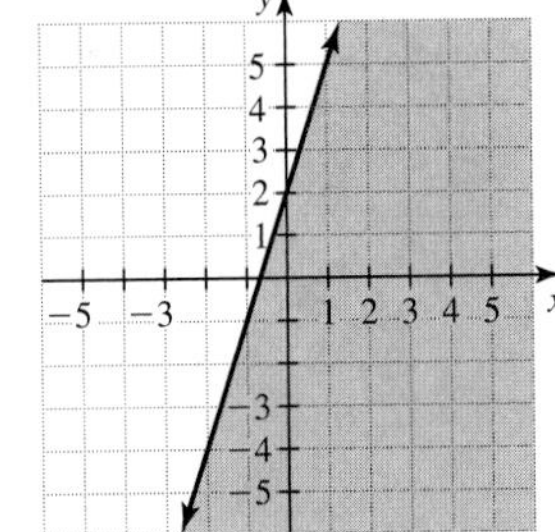

51.

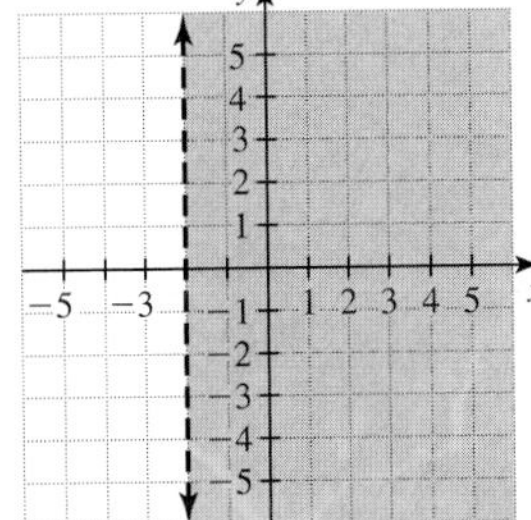

52.

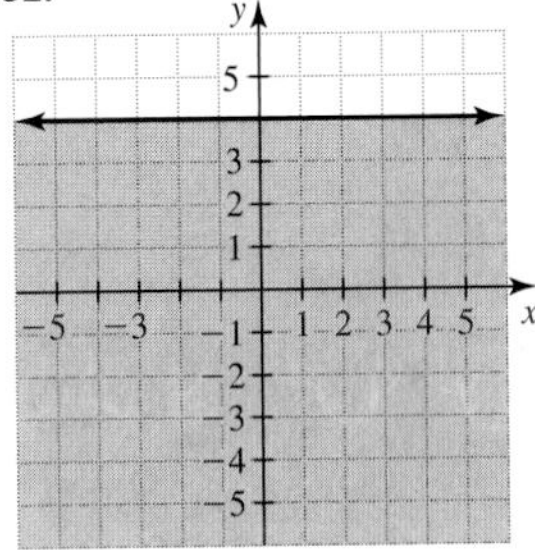

53. $-2x^2 - 12x + 6$ **54.** $6x^4 + 9x^3$ **55.** $x^2 - 2x - 63$ **56.** $x^3 + 8$ **57.** $16w^4 - 24w^2 + 9$ **58.** $-4m^5$ **59.** $-3y^2 - 2y + 1$ **60.** $x^2 + x + 2$ **61.** $-32x^7$ **62.** $375x^7$ **63.** $\frac{3x^5}{y}$ **64.** $8a^{15}$ **65.** 2.4×10^8 **66.** 1.8×10^{10}

67. 1.6×10^{-11} **68.** 1×10^{-12} **69.** $6xy^3(4x + 3y^2)$
70. $(x + a)(x + 2)$ **71.** $(2m - 7)(2m + 7)$ **72.** $(x - 9)(x + 6)$
73. $(2t - 5)(3t + 2)$ **74.** $(2w - 9)^2$ **75.** $2a(a - 9)(a + 6)$
76. $(w - 3)(w^2 + 3w + 9)$ **77.** $\{0, 1\}$ **78.** $\{-2, 0, 2\}$
79. $\{-3, 2\}$ **80.** $\{-6, 5\}$ **81.** 3 and 7
82. Length 24 in., width 10 in. **83.** $\frac{13x}{4}$ **84.** $\frac{8}{x - 2}$
85. $\frac{2x^2 + 6x + 9}{(x + 3)(x - 3)}$ **86.** $\frac{5a - 7}{(a - 5)(a + 4)}$ **87.** $\frac{w^3 + 2w^2}{2}$ **88.** $\frac{7b^5}{4a^2}$
89. $\left\{\frac{8}{3}\right\}$ **90.** $\{11\}$ **91.** $\left\{-\frac{14}{9}\right\}$ **92.** $\left\{-\frac{23}{13}\right\}$ **93.** $y = \frac{3}{5}x$
94. $y = \frac{2a}{w - c}$ **95.** $y = -3x - 12$ **96.** $y = \frac{6t}{2 - t}$

Appendix D

Chapters 1–6 Review

R.1 Exercises

1. $[0, 3]$
-1 0 1 2 3 4

2. $(-2, 5)$
-3 -2 -1 0 1 2 3 4 5 6

3. $[-4, 0)$
-6 -4 -2 0 2 4

4. $(3, 8]$
0 1 2 3 4 5 6 7 8 9

5. $(-\infty, -1)$
-3 -2 -1 0 1 2

6. $(-\infty, 6]$
-6 -3 0 3 6 9

7. $[50, \infty)$
-50 0 50 100

8. $(-10, \infty)$
-20 -10 0 10

9. The set of real numbers between -2 and 9
10. The set of real numbers between -4 and -3 inclusive
11. The set of real numbers greater than or equal to 11 and less than 13
12. The set of real numbers greater than 22 and less than or equal to 26
13. The set of real numbers greater than 0
14. The set of real numbers greater than or equal to 99
15. The set of real numbers less than or equal to -6
16. The set of real numbers less than 18

17. 1 **18.** 9.35 **19.** 0 **20.** 0 **21.** 50 **22.** 6.87 **23.** $\frac{10}{20}$
24. $\frac{12}{18}$ **25.** $\frac{18}{24}$ **26.** $\frac{49}{56}$ **27.** $\frac{3}{5}$ **28.** $\frac{2}{3}$ **29.** $\frac{7}{24}$ **30.** $\frac{2}{7}$ **31.** $\frac{3}{5}$
32. $\frac{1}{2}$ **33.** $\frac{4}{7}$ **34.** $\frac{2}{3}$ **35.** $\frac{1}{3}$ **36.** $\frac{3}{4}$ **37.** $\frac{3}{10}$ **38.** $\frac{2}{5}$ **39.** $\frac{1}{4}$
40. $\frac{3}{13}$ **41.** $\frac{1}{10}$ **42.** $\frac{2}{3}$ **43.** 10 **44.** 25 **45.** $\frac{2}{15}$ **46.** 42
47. $\frac{19}{24}$ **48.** $\frac{19}{20}$ **49.** $\frac{5}{36}$ **50.** $\frac{11}{48}$ **51.** $\frac{21}{8}$ **52.** $\frac{10}{7}$ **53.** -26
54. -27 **55.** -23 **56.** 9 **57.** 1 **58.** 5 **59.** -36 **60.** -27
61. 24 **62.** 100 **63.** 2 **64.** -3 **65.** 180 **66.** 96 **67.** -84
68. -39 **69.** 15 **70.** 6 **71.** -8 **72.** -5 **73.** 0 **74.** 0
75. -90 **76.** -89 **77.** -36 **78.** 33 **79.** 38 **80.** -2
81. -5 **82.** 16 **83.** 3 **84.** 34 **85.** -12 **86.** 4 **87.** 3
88. -1 **89.** 1 **90.** 1 **91.** $5x + (-3y), -25$ **92.** $a^3 - b^3, -72$
93. $(a + b)(a^2 - ab + b^2), -28$ **94.** $\frac{x - 7}{7 - x}, -1$ **95.** $(2x - 3)^2, 49$
96. $(a - b)^3, 64$ **97.** Difference **98.** Sum **99.** Difference
100. Product **101.** Quotient **102.** Square **103.** Cube **104.** Sum
105. Commutative property of multiplication
106. Commutative property of addition **107.** Distributive property
108. Associative property of addition **109.** Multiplicative identity
110. Additive identity **111.** Multiplication property of zero
112. Multiplicative inverse property
113. Associative property of multiplication
114. Additive inverse property
115. $-x - 2$ **116.** $-11x + 8y$ **117.** $3x + 17$ **118.** $8x + 7y$
119. $31xy - 6$ **120.** $38a - 16$ **121.** $-30ab$ **122.** $21xy$
123. $2 - x$ **124.** $x - y$ **125.** $-22 + x$ **126.** $-5 - 2x$

R.2 Exercises

1. $\{7\}$ **2.** $\{15\}$ **3.** $\{-8\}$ **4.** $\{17\}$ **5.** $\{17\}$ **6.** $\{-9\}$
7. $\{-8\}$ **8.** $\{-9\}$ **9.** $\left\{\frac{25}{2}\right\}$ **10.** $\left\{-\frac{2}{3}\right\}$ **11.** $\{8\}$ **12.** $\{-19\}$
13. $\{-6\}$ **14.** $\{1\}$ **15.** $\{-4\}$ **16.** $\{1\}$ **17.** $(-\infty, \infty)$, identity
18. $(-\infty, \infty)$, identity **19.** $\{24\}$, conditional equation
20. $\{30\}$, conditional equation **21.** $\{-20\}$, conditional equation
22. $\{-46\}$, conditional equation **23.** $\varnothing$, inconsistent equation
24. $\varnothing$, inconsistent equation **25.** $\{1\}$, conditional equation
26. $(-\infty, \infty)$, identity **27.** $\left\{\frac{26}{19}\right\}$, conditional equation
28. $\left\{-\frac{19}{11}\right\}$, conditional equation **29.** $R = \frac{D}{T}$ **30.** $m = \frac{E}{c^2}$
31. $m = \frac{2K}{v^2}$ **32.** $b = \frac{2A}{h}$ **33.** $L = \frac{P - 2W}{2}$ **34.** $b_2 = \frac{2A - hb_1}{h}$
35. $r = \frac{A - P}{Pt}$ **36.** $y = \frac{2x - 6}{3}$ **37.** 10 hr **38.** 5 m **39.** 30 m
40. 12.5 cm **41.** 4 kg **42.** 8 cm **43.** $a^2 + b^2$ **44.** $x + 5$
45. $y - 6$ **46.** $a - b$ **47.** ab^2 **48.** $0.10x$ **49.** $\frac{x}{y}$ **50.** $\frac{14}{x}$
51. $\frac{1}{2}x$ **52.** $\frac{2}{3}y$ **53.** $2(a + b)$ **54.** $(a + b)^2$
55. Length 24 in., width 18 in. **56.** Length 55 m, width 30 m
57. 55 mph **58.** 8 hr **59.** Approximately 121.95 lb **60.** 50 oz
61. 5 L **62.** 15% **63.** Approximately 85.71 mph **64.** 8:40 A.M.

65. $[5, \infty)$
-5 0 5 10

66. $(-\infty, 6]$
0 2 4 6 8

67. $\left(\frac{4}{3}, \infty\right)$
$\frac{4}{3}$
0 1 2 3

68. $(-\infty, 5)$
-5 0 5 10

69. $(-2, \infty)$
-4 -2 0 2 4

70. $(-\infty, -8)$
-12 -8 -4 0

71. $(-\infty, -5)$
-10 -5 0 5

72. $(8, \infty)$
0 4 8 12 16

73. $(3, \infty)$
-3 0 3 6 9

74. $(-3, \infty)$
-6 -3 0 3

75. $[-2, 8)$
-4 -2 0 2 4 6 8 10

76. $(1, 5]$
0 1 2 3 4 5 6

77. $(-14, 4)$
-14
-16 -12 -8 -4 0 4 8

78. $[-4, -3]$
-5 -4 -3 -2 -1 0

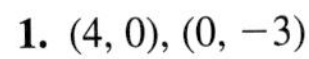

R.3 Exercises

1. (4, 0), (0, −3)

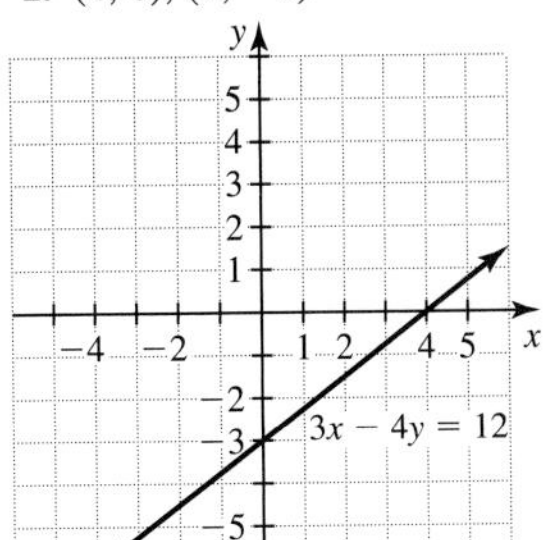

2. (10, 0), (0, −5)

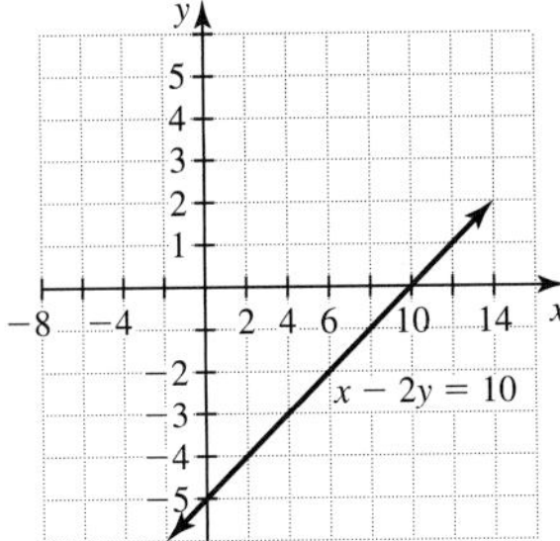

3. (3, 0), (0, 6)

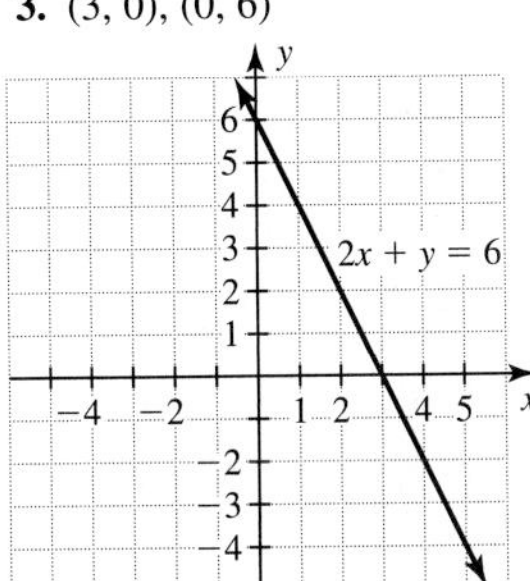

4. (7, 0), (0, 3)

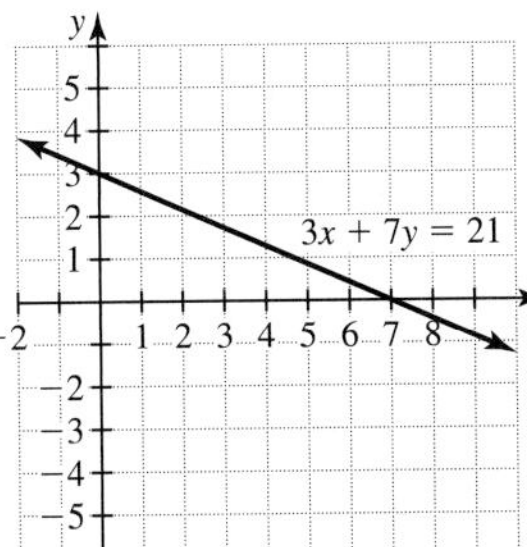

5. (−3, 0)

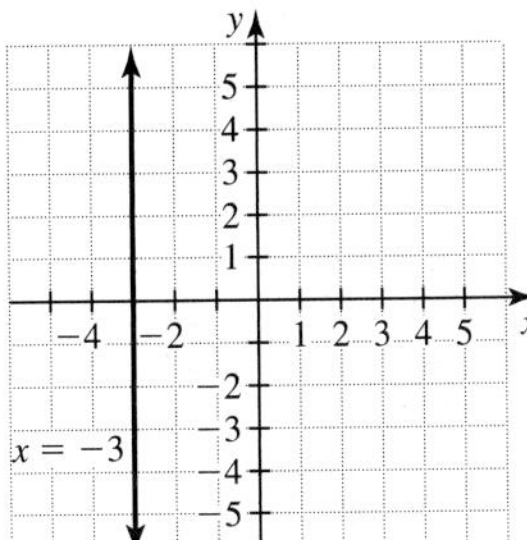

6. (5, 0)

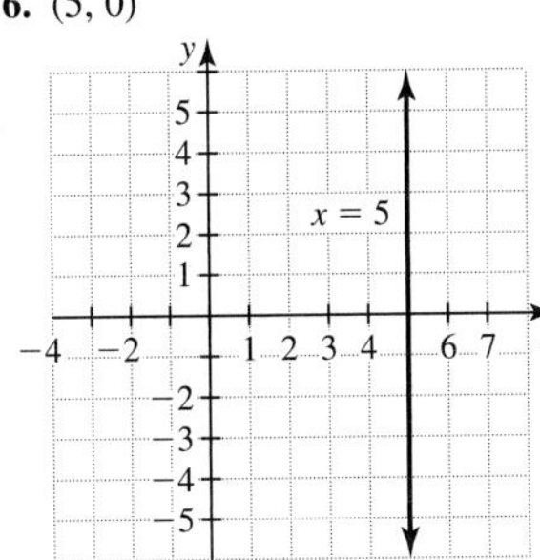

7. (0, 2)

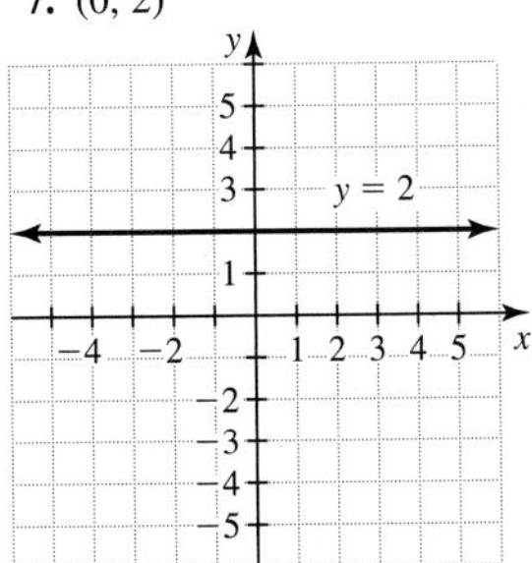

8. (0, −4)

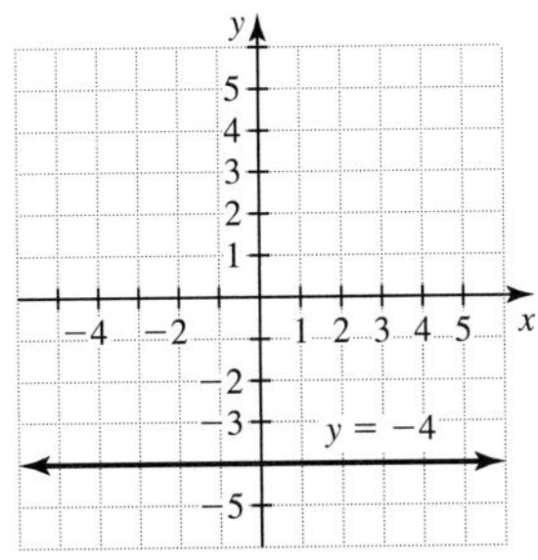

9. (60, 0), (0, −30)

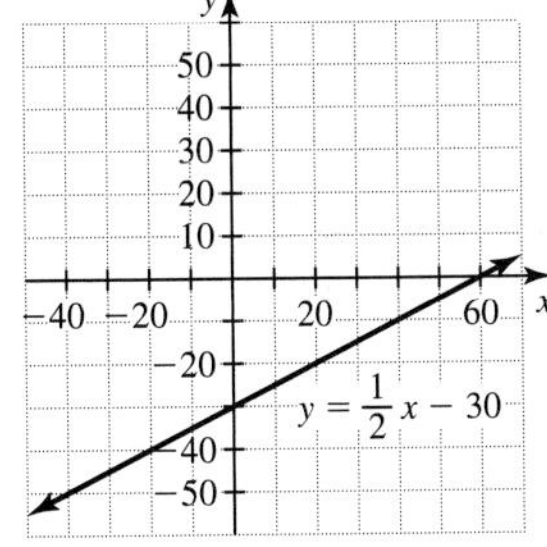

10. (30, 0), (0, 20)

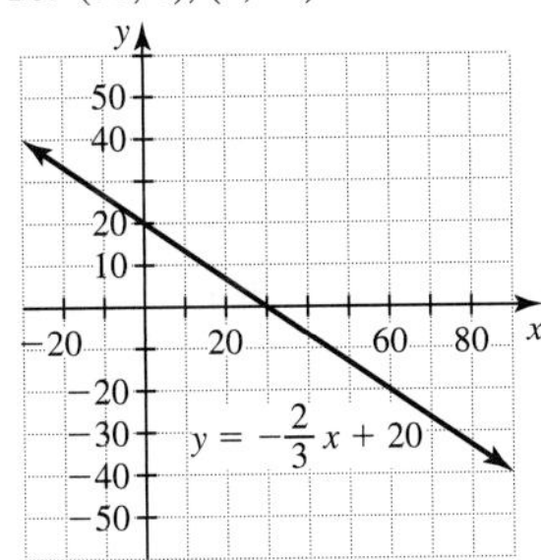

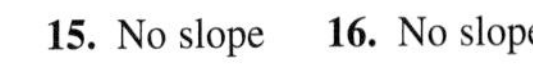

11. 1 **12.** $\frac{4}{3}$ **13.** −1 **14.** 1 **15.** No slope **16.** No slope **17.** 0 **18.** 0 **19.** 4 **20.** 0 **21.** $-\frac{3}{4}$ **22.** $\frac{5}{8}$ **23.** 0 **24.** 0

25. $\frac{1}{3}$, (0, 1)

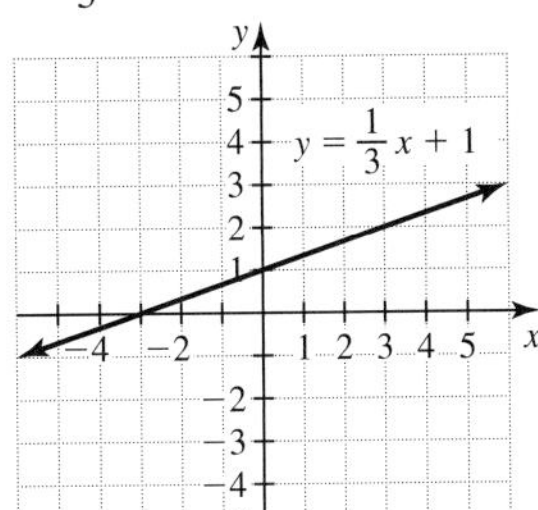

26. $\frac{2}{3}$, (0, −2)

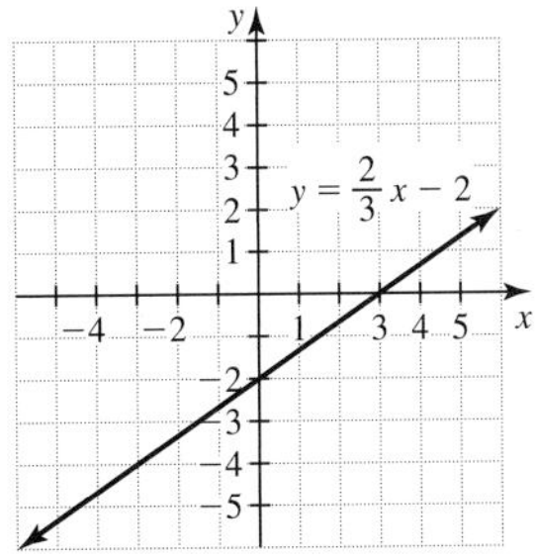

27. −3, (0, 4)

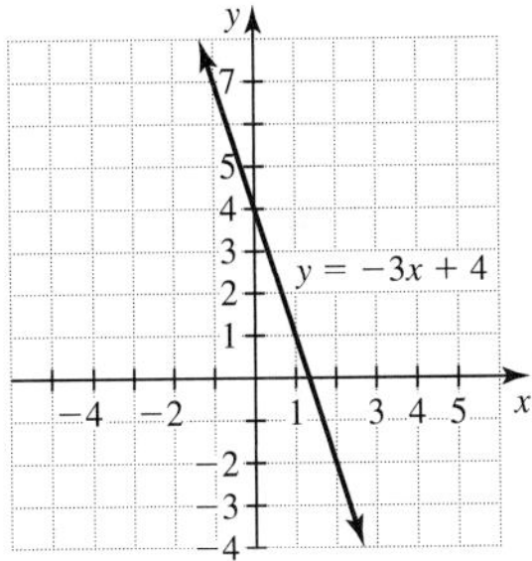

28. 2, (0, −5)

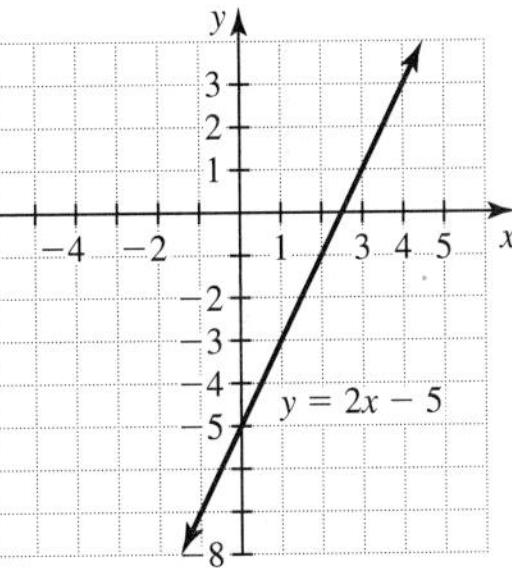

29. 1, (0, −5)

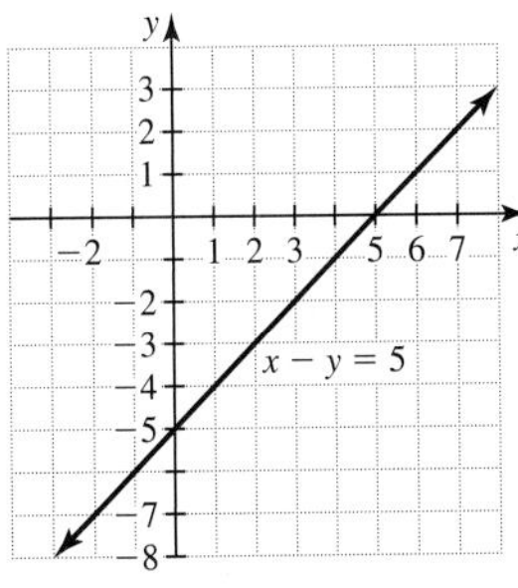

30. $-\frac{1}{2}$, (0, 2)

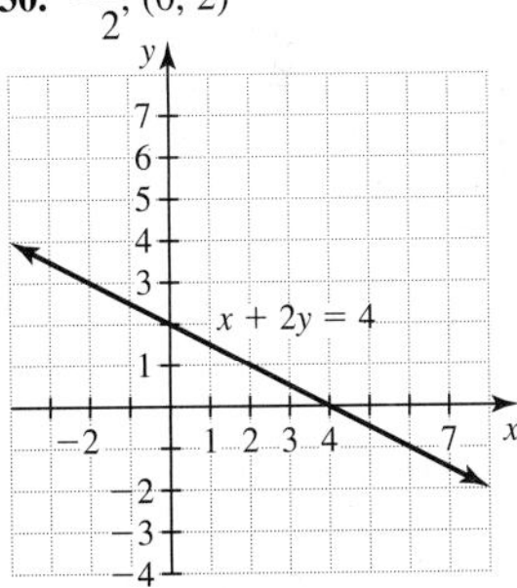

31. $\frac{3}{5}$, (0, −2)

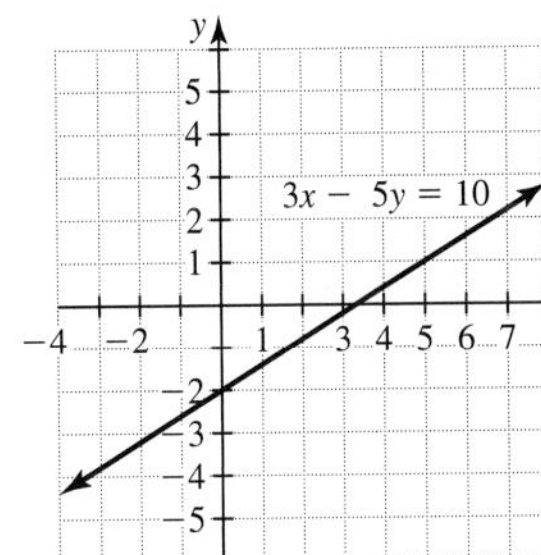

32. $\frac{2}{3}$, (0, 3)

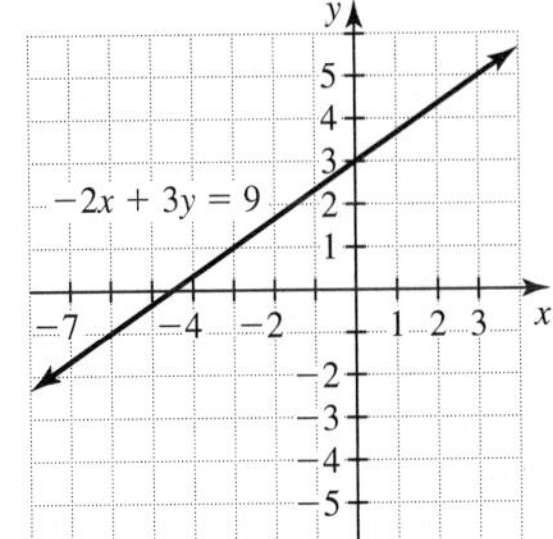

33. 0, (0, 4)

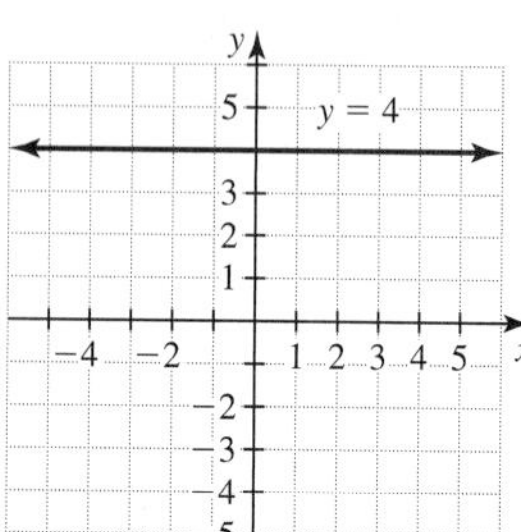

34. 0, (0, −5)

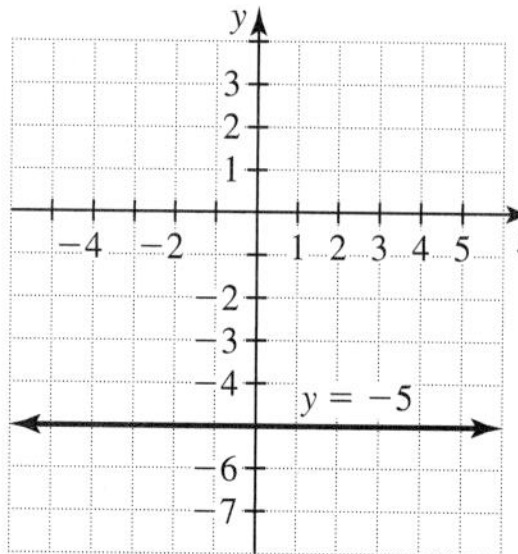

35. $y = \frac{2}{5}x - 2$ **36.** $y = 3x + 5$ **37.** $y = \frac{2}{7}x + 6$

38. $y = -5x - 2$ **39.** $y = -4x + 12$ **40.** $y = -\frac{1}{3}x - 14$

41. $y = 3$ **42.** $y = 5$ **43.** $3x - 5y = -26$ **44.** $14x - y = 33$
45. $x + 2y = 5$ **46.** $x + y = 2$ **47.** $2x - 3y = 14$
48. $x + 4y = -17$ **49.** $x - 2y = 12$ **50.** $x + 4y = -21$
51. 50 mph **52.** 5 hr **53.** 10.5 hr **54.** 3 cookies **55.** \$837.20
56. \$403.20

57.

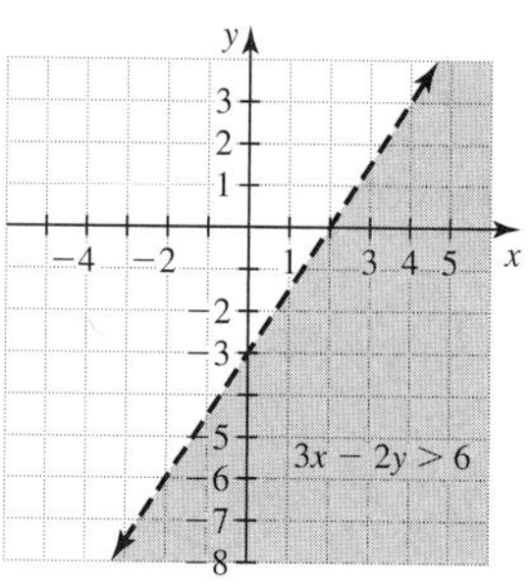

58.

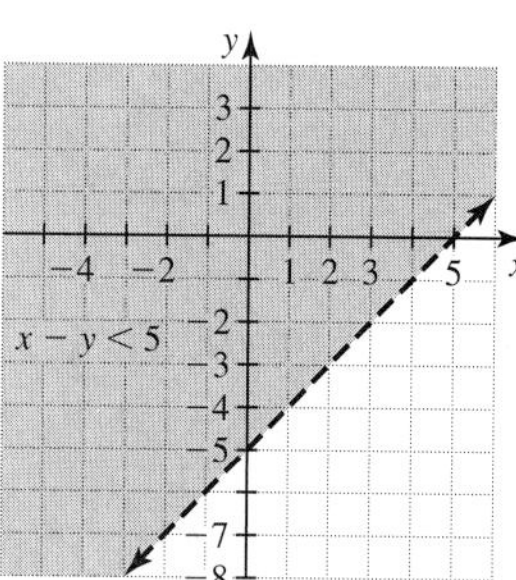

59.

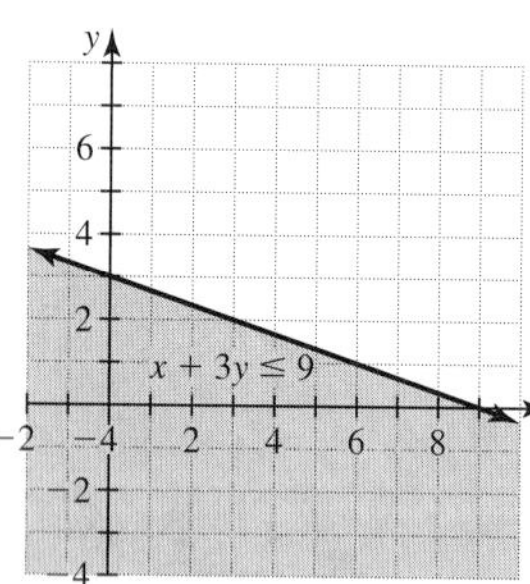

60.

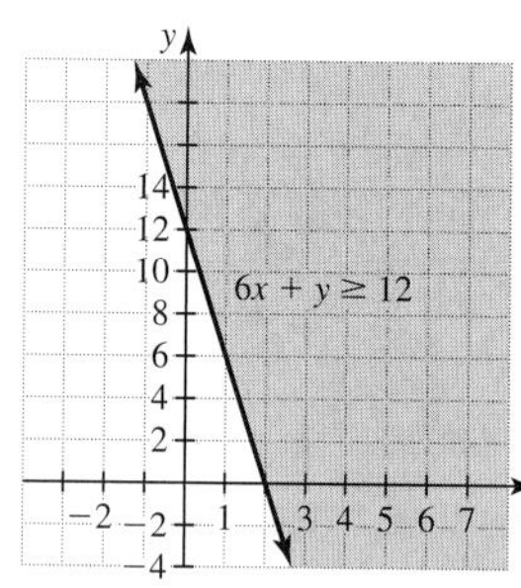

61.

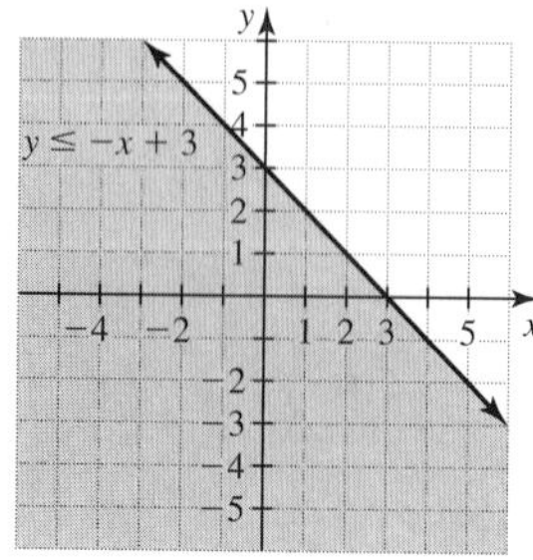

62.

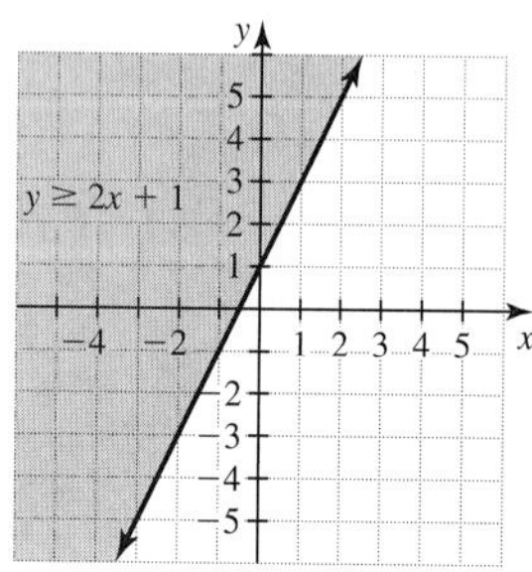

63.

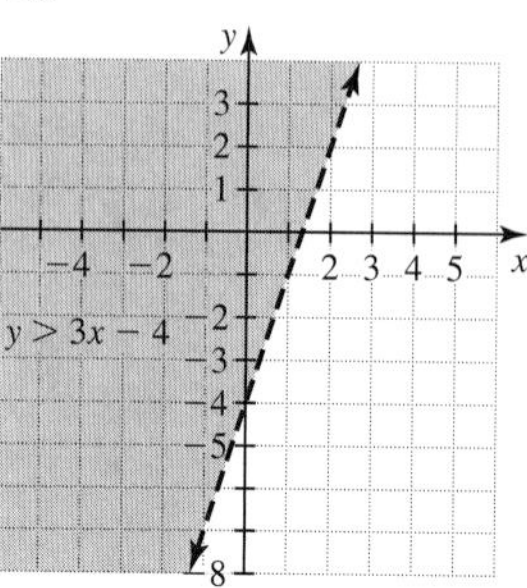

64.

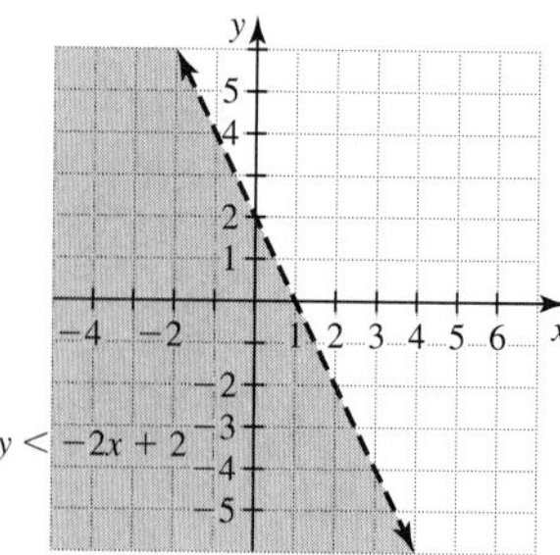

65.

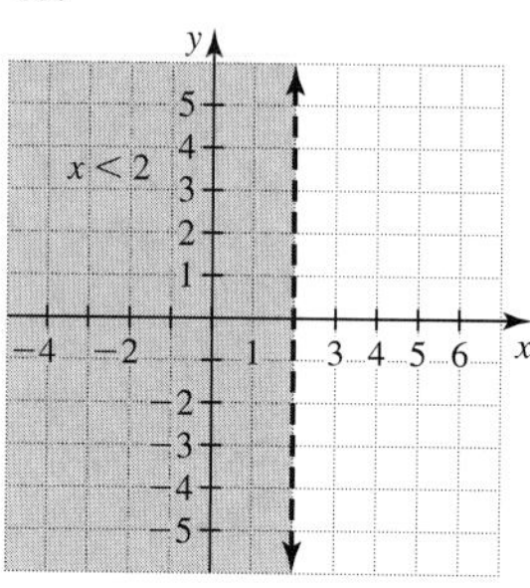

66.

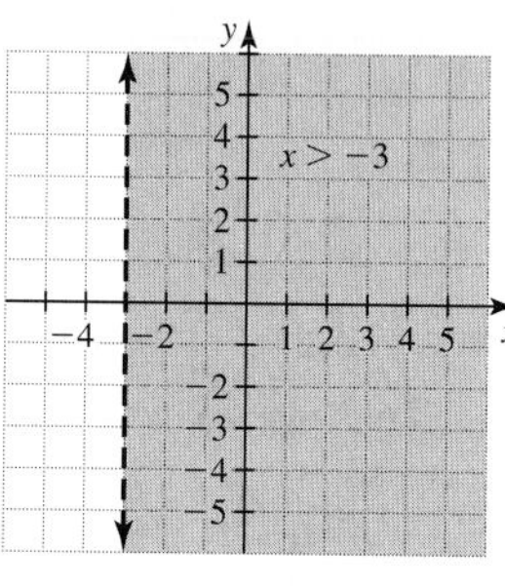

67.

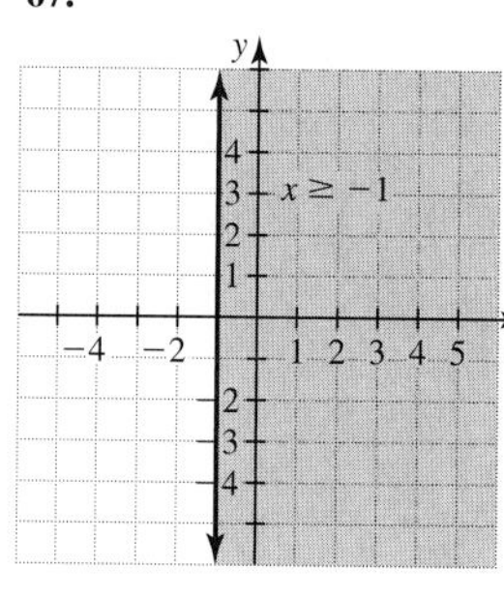

68.

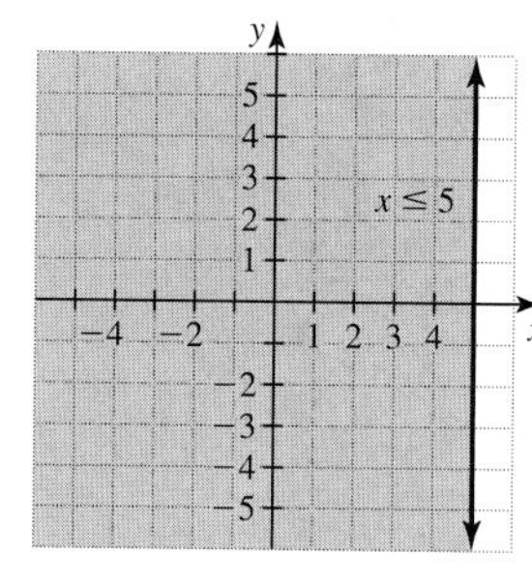

69.

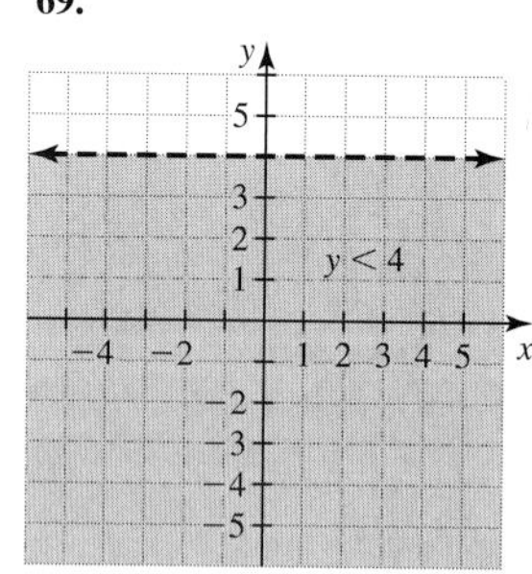

70.

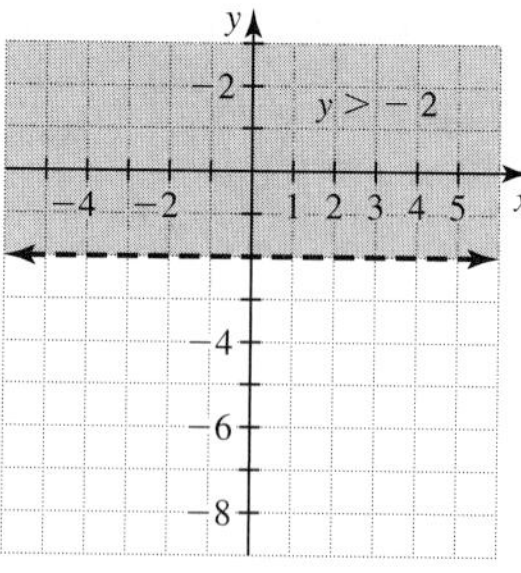

R.4 Exercises

1. $x^3 + x^2 - 3x$ **2.** $-2x^3 + x^2 - 12x$ **3.** $w^2 + 4w - 6$
4. $3a^2 + 3a - 1$ **5.** $-3y^2 + y$ **6.** $z + 15$
7. $-2t^2 + t + 3$ **8.** $3n^2 - n + 8$ **9.** $8x^2 - 6x$
10. $-30x^2 + 10x$ **11.** $-2a^3 + 8a^2 - 18a$
12. $-6b^3 + 15b^2 + 3b$ **13.** $6w^5 - 6w^4 + 6w^3 + 18w^2$
14. $10t^6 + 5t^5 - 40t^4 - 15t^3$ **15.** $x^2 + 6x + 8$
16. $a^2 + 12a + 35$ **17.** $6s^2 - 7s - 3$ **18.** $4t^2 - 9t + 2$
19. $6x^4 + 7x^2 - 5$ **20.** $-2x^6 + 13x^4 - 15x^2$
21. $x^3 - 18x + 27$ **22.** $a^3 + 3a^2 - 18a + 16$

23. $3w^3 + 14w^2 + 13w - 6$ **24.** $-2m^3 - 10m^2 + 19m - 63$
25. $ab + an + mb + mn$ **26.** $xy + sx + yt + st$
27. $x^2 - 4x - 12$ **28.** $x^2 - 2x - 15$ **29.** $6a^2 - 5a - 4$
30. $15b^2 - 62b + 63$ **31.** $10x^2 - 19x + 7$ **32.** $3x^2 + 20x + 12$
33. $10a^6 - 24a^3 - 18$ **34.** $12w^6 - 43w^3 + 35$ **35.** $16x^8 - x^2$
36. $25a^8 - x^6$ **37.** $x^2 + 10x + 25$ **38.** $y^2 + 6y + 9$
39. $4t^2 + 28t + 49$ **40.** $9w^2 + 24w + 16$ **41.** $s^2 - 4s + 4$
42. $h^2 - 6h + 9$ **43.** $9y^2 - 30y + 25$ **44.** $36x^2 - 12x + 1$
45. $9q^2 - 16$ **46.** $25m^2 - 36$ **47.** $4x^4 - 9n^2$ **48.** $25t^4 - 9m^2$
49. $2x^6$ **50.** $4a^{12}$ **51.** $-2w$ **52.** $-4b^2$ **53.** $\frac{1}{2}x^2$ **54.** $-\frac{1}{2}t^8$
55. $3x^2 - 2x + 1$ **56.** $-5a^2 - 4a - 1$ **57.** $x^3 + 3x^2 - x + 2$
58. $4w^2 + 3w - 2$ **59.** $x^2 - 3x - 3$ **60.** $2x^2 - 2x + 5$
61. $x^2 - 2x - 3$ **62.** $2x^2 - 3x + 4$ **63.** $x^2 - x + 2$ **64.** $x^2 + x - 3$
65. 3 **66.** $\frac{1}{3}$ **67.** $-\frac{3}{2}$ **68.** $-\frac{1}{4}$ **69.** $-864a^{26}$ **70.** $64b^{10}$
71. $-200x^{12}$ **72.** $225y^{16}$ **73.** $\frac{x^{12}}{8y^6}$ **74.** $-\frac{q^9}{8p^6}$ **75.** $\frac{9a^6}{4}$ **76.** $\frac{81b^4}{16}$
77. $-6a^6$ **78.** $-15b^9$ **79.** $\frac{w^6}{2}$ **80.** $\frac{2}{t^{14}}$ **81.** $\frac{x^4}{81}$ **82.** $\frac{y^{12}}{25}$
83. $-\frac{1}{32a^{28}}$ **84.** $-\frac{b^8}{108}$ **85.** x^6y^9 **86.** $\frac{1}{a^{12}b^{20}}$ **87.** $\frac{25}{4x^{22}}$ **88.** $\frac{4}{y^8}$
89. 8×10^{20} **90.** 9.6×10^{25} **91.** 2×10^1 **92.** 3.6×10^{11}
93. 5×10^{13} **94.** 6.4×10^{22} **95.** 5.12×10^{-6} **96.** 4×10^{-14}

R.5 Exercises

1. $4(3x + 2)$ **2.** $6(3a + 5)$ **3.** $3y^2(5y - 2)$ **4.** $16z^3(3z - 2)$
5. $4a^3b(2b + 5a)$ **6.** $12y^3z^3(2y + 3z)$ **7.** $4x^2(3x^2 - 5x - 6)$
8. $7y(2y^2 - 3y - 4)$ **9.** $2ab(a^2 - 3a + 3)$ **10.** $3wz(w^2 - 4w - 3)$
11. $2x$ **12.** $5y^2$ **13.** $x + 3$ **14.** $y^2 + 3$ **15.** $-5a^2$ **16.** $-4b^2$
17. $w + 1$ **18.** $y - 1$ **19.** $(x + 4)^2$ **20.** $(x + 2)^2$ **21.** $(a - 1)^2$
22. $(b - 5)^2$ **23.** $(y + 3)(y - 3)$ **24.** $(n + 2)(n - 2)$ **25.** $(3x + 1)^2$
26. $(5y + 2)^2$ **27.** $(4m - 5t)^2$ **28.** $(3s - 4t)^2$ **29.** $(3x + 4)(3x - 4)$
30. $(9a + 5)(9a - 5)$ **31.** $(8n + 3)^2$ **32.** $(9s - 1)^2$
33. $(5x + 7y)(5x - 7y)$ **34.** $(ab + y)(ab - y)$ **35.** $(a + b)(a + 6)$
36. $(w + x)(w - 3)$ **37.** $(2x + a)(3x - 5)$ **38.** $(5a + 1)(2x + 1)$
39. $(y^2 + 1)(3y - 4)$ **40.** $(3x^2 + 5)(2x - 1)$ **41.** $(4a^2 + 7)(2a - 1)$
42. $(5t^2 + 6)(t - 2)$ **43.** $(b - 3)(a - 2)$ **44.** $(x - 7)(x - y)$
45. $(x^2 - 3)(x - 1)$ **46.** $(x^2 - 5)(a - 4)$ **47.** $(x + 2)(x + 3)$
48. $(x + 5)(x + 6)$ **49.** $(w + 3)(w + 5)$ **50.** $(u + 18)(u + 1)$
51. $(v - 6)(v + 4)$ **52.** $(m - 11)(m + 2)$ **53.** $(t - 14)(t + 2)$
54. $(q - 8)(q + 4)$ **55.** $(b - 13)(b - 2)$ **56.** $(p - 25)(p - 1)$
57. $(c - 8)(c - 3)$ **58.** $(n - 3)(n - 7)$ **59.** $(2x + 3)(x + 2)$
60. $(3w + 1)(w + 5)$ **61.** $(3t + 1)(5t + 4)$ **62.** $(6m + 5)((m + 4)$
63. $(3n - 2)(n + 6)$ **64.** $(4y - 3)(y + 5)$ **65.** $(2m - 3)(4m + 9)$
66. $(3p - 1)(6p + 5)$ **67.** $(4q - 1)(2q - 3)$ **68.** $(3t - 4)(2t - 1)$
69. $(5z - 3)(3z - 2)$ **70.** $(k - 4)(10k - 1)$ **71.** $(x - 1)(x^2 + x + 1)$
72. $(y - 3)(y^2 + 3y + 9)$ **73.** $(a - 2)(a^2 + 2a + 4)$
74. $(b - 10)(b^2 + 10b + 100)$ **75.** $(5x - 1)(25x^2 + 5x + 1)$
76. $(2a - 5)(4a^2 + 10a + 25)$ **77.** $(5q - 3)(25q^2 + 15q + 9)$
78. $(10b - 7)(100b^2 + 70b + 49)$ **79.** $(3x + 4y)(9x^2 - 12xy + 16y^2)$
80. $(2h + 5k)(4h^2 - 10hk + 25k^2)$ **81.** $(7m + 2n)(49m^2 - 14mn + 4n^2)$
82. $(ab + xy)(a^2b^2 - abxy + x^2y^2)$ **83.** $2(x + 1)(x + 3)$
84. $3(x + 5)(x - 3)$ **85.** $-2x(x + 3)^2$ **86.** $-4x^2(x - 5)^2$
87. $3(a - b)(a + b)(a^2 + b^2)$ **88.** $w(w - q)(w + q)(w^2 + q^2)$
89. $-b(a + 2b)(a^2 + 2ab + 4b^2)$ **90.** $-3(2x - 3)(4x^2 + 6x + 9)$
91. $(a - 2)(a + 2)(a + 3)$ **92.** $(x - 3)(x + 3)(x - 5)$
93. $\{-4, 6\}$ **94.** $\{-5, 4\}$ **95.** $\left\{-3, \frac{1}{2}\right\}$ **96.** $\left\{\frac{2}{3}, 4\right\}$ **97.** $\left\{\frac{1}{2}, \frac{5}{2}\right\}$
98. $\left\{\frac{1}{5}, \frac{1}{3}\right\}$ **99.** $\{-3, -2, 0\}$ **100.** $\{-1, 0, 2\}$

R.6 Exercises

1. $\frac{b-4}{b+4}$ **2.** $\frac{x+y}{x-y}$ **3.** $\frac{2x-4}{x-3}$ **4.** $\frac{2a-8}{a-1}$ **5.** $\frac{3y^5}{4}$
6. $\frac{2a^2}{3b^2}$ **7.** $-\frac{4z^7}{5w^2}$ **8.** $-\frac{3}{4r^3t^2}$ **9.** $\frac{1}{2(a-y)}$ **10.** $2a + 10$
11. $\frac{x^2 + xy + y^2}{x + y}$ **12.** $\frac{x+3}{x^2 - 2x + 4}$ **13.** $\frac{5a}{6b^2}$ **14.** $\frac{2t^3}{3w^5}$
15. $\frac{5b^2}{24a^6}$ **16.** $\frac{a}{2y^5}$ **17.** $\frac{3x + 3y}{x^4(x - y)}$ **18.** $\frac{15a^4 - 10a^3b}{3a + 2b}$
19. $\frac{1}{2}$ **20.** $\frac{x+3}{x-3}$ **21.** $\frac{ab^3 + b^4}{6a^4}$ **22.** $\frac{xy^5 + y^6}{3(x - y)}$ **23.** $a + 3$
24. $w + 1$ **25.** $\frac{4}{x}$ **26.** $\frac{1}{x^2y}$ **27.** 2 **28.** 3 **29.** $\frac{-1}{x+y}$
30. $\frac{-x}{(x-2)(x+1)}$ **31.** $\frac{4 - w^2}{(2w + 1)(w - 3)}$ **32.** $\frac{2t - t^2}{(3t + 2)(t - 1)}$
33. $\frac{m^2 + 8m + 5}{m(m + 1)(m + 3)}$ **34.** $\frac{n^2 + 2n - 6}{n(n - 3)(n + 3)}$ **35.** $\frac{2}{13}$ **36.** $\frac{25}{6}$
37. $\frac{b + 2a}{2}$ **38.** $\frac{1}{2y - 5x}$ **39.** $\frac{6 - 15t^2}{8t^2 - 45t}$ **40.** $\frac{4 + 30m^2}{m - 20m^2}$
41. $\{1\}$ **42.** $\left\{\frac{11}{2}\right\}$ **43.** $\{-9\}$ **44.** $\{2\}$ **45.** $\left\{-\frac{20}{13}\right\}$ **46.** $\left\{-\frac{5}{11}\right\}$
47. 85 teachers **48.** 6 cups of cereal **49.** 48 dogs and 36 cats
50. 21 cars and 9 trucks **51.** 50 mph
52. First day 60 mph and second day 50 mph or first day 50 and second day 40.
53. 3 students **54.** 4 students

Subject Index

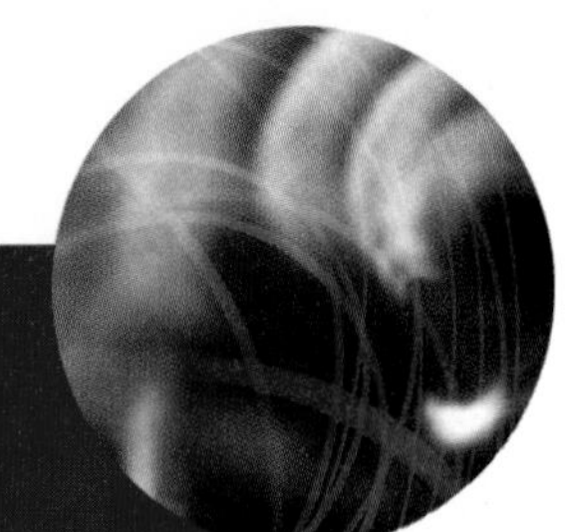

D

E

F

J

K

L

M

Q

R

S

T

DEFINITIONS, RULES, AND FORMULAS

Subsets of the Real Numbers

Natural Numbers = $\{1, 2, 3, \ldots\}$

Whole Numbers = $\{0, 1, 2, 3, \ldots\}$

Integers = $\{\ldots -3, -2, -1, 0, 1, 2, 3, \ldots\}$

Rational = $\left\{\frac{a}{b} \middle| a \text{ and } b \text{ are integers with } b \neq 0\right\}$

Irrational = $\{x \mid x \text{ is not rational}\}$

Properties of the Real Numbers

For all real numbers a, b, and c

$a + b = b + a$; $a \cdot b = b \cdot a$ Commutative

$(a + b) + c = a + (b + c)$; $(ab)c = a(bc)$ Associative

$a(b + c) = ab + ac$; $a(b - c) = ab - ac$ Distributive

$a + 0 = a$; $1 \cdot a = a$ Identity

$a + (-a) = 0$; $a \cdot \frac{1}{a} = 1$ $(a \neq 0)$ Inverse

$a \cdot 0 = 0$ Multiplication property of 0

Absolute Value

$$|a| = \begin{cases} a & \text{for } a \geq 0 \\ -a & \text{for } a < 0 \end{cases}$$

Order of Operations

No parentheses or absolute value present:

1. Exponential expressions
2. Multiplication and division
3. Addition and subtraction

With parentheses or absolute value:

First evaluate within each set of parentheses or absolute value, using the order of operations.

Exponents

$a^0 = 1$ $\qquad$ $a^{-1} = \frac{1}{a}$

$a^{-r} = \frac{1}{a^r} = \left(\frac{1}{a}\right)^r$ $\qquad$ $\frac{1}{a^{-r}} = a^r$

$a^r a^s = a^{r+s}$ $\qquad$ $\frac{a^r}{a^s} = a^{r-s}$

$(a^r)^s = a^{rs}$ $\qquad$ $(ab)^r = a^r b^r$

$\left(\frac{a}{b}\right)^r = \frac{a^r}{b^r}$ $\qquad$ $\left(\frac{a}{b}\right)^{-r} = \left(\frac{b}{a}\right)^r$

Roots and Radicals

$a^{1/n} = \sqrt[n]{a}$ $\qquad$ $a^{m/n} = \left(\sqrt[n]{a}\right)^m = \sqrt[n]{a^m}$

$\sqrt[n]{ab} = \sqrt[n]{a} \cdot \sqrt[n]{b}$ $\qquad$ $\sqrt[n]{\frac{a}{b}} = \frac{\sqrt[n]{a}}{\sqrt[n]{b}}$

Factoring

$a^2 + 2ab + b^2 = (a + b)^2$

$a^2 - 2ab + b^2 = (a - b)^2$

$a^2 - b^2 = (a + b)(a - b)$

$a^3 - b^3 = (a - b)(a^2 + ab + b^2)$

$a^3 + b^3 = (a + b)(a^2 - ab + b^2)$

Rational Expressions

$\frac{a}{b} + \frac{c}{b} = \frac{a + c}{b}$ $\qquad$ $\frac{a}{b} - \frac{c}{b} = \frac{a - c}{b}$

$\frac{ac}{bc} = \frac{a}{b}$ $\qquad$ $\frac{a}{b} + \frac{c}{d} = \frac{ad + bc}{bd}$

$\frac{a}{b} \cdot \frac{c}{d} = \frac{ac}{bd}$ $\qquad$ $\frac{a}{b} \div \frac{c}{d} = \frac{a}{b} \cdot \frac{d}{c}$

If $\frac{a}{b} = \frac{c}{d}$, then $ad = bc$.